Freedom in the World 2019
The Annual Survey of
Political Rights & Civil Liberties

Arch Puddington
General Editor

Shannon O'Toole
Managing Editor

Christopher Brandt, Isabel Linzer, Sarah Repucci, Tyler Roylance, Mai Truong, Amy Slipowitz, Caitlin Watson
Associate Editors

Freedom House • New York, NY, and Washington, DC

ROWMAN & LITTLEFIELD PUBLISHERS, INC.
Lanham • Boulder • New York • Toronto • Oxford

Published by Rowman & Littlefield
An imprint of The Rowman & Littlefield Publishing Group, Inc.
4501 Forbes Boulevard, Suite 200, Lanham, Maryland 20706
www.rowman.com

6 Tinworth Street, London SE11 5AL, United Kingdom

British Library Cataloguing in Publication Information Available

Library of Congress Cataloging-in-Publication Data

978-1-5381-3456-6 (paperback)
978-1-5381-3457-3 (electronic)

♾™ The paper used in this publication meets the minimum requirements of
American National Standard for Information Sciences—Permanence of Paper for
Printed Library Materials, ANSI/NISO Z39.48-1992.

Contents

Acknowledgments

Freedom in the World 2019 could not have been completed without the contributions of numerous Freedom House staff members and consultants. The section titled "Survey Team" contains a detailed list of the writers and advisers without whose efforts this project would not have been possible.

Sarah Repucci served as the project director for this year's survey and Mai Truong served as the research director for management and strategy. Christopher Brandt, Sonya Guimet, Isabel Linzer, Shannon O'Toole, Tyler Roylance, Nate Schenkkan, Adrian Shabhaz, Amy Slipowitz, and Caitlin Watson provided extensive research, analytical, editorial, and administrative assistance. John Cunningham, Jacqueline Laks Gorman, Christine Homan, Anne Kosseff-Jones, M. L. Liu, Janet Olson, Richard Palladry, and Peter Schmidtke served as fact-checkers on country reports. Caroline Hall, Joy Hammer, Dillan Jacobson, Krister Lansing, SaraJane Renfroe, and Grace Vedock provided additional support. Overall guidance for the project was provided by Michael J. Abramowitz, president of Freedom House, Arch Puddington, distinguished fellow for democracy studies, and Vanessa Tucker, vice president for research and analysis. A number of Freedom House staff offered valuable additional input on the country reports and/or ratings process.

Freedom House would like to acknowledge the generous financial support for *Freedom in the World* by the Achelis & Bodman Foundation, the Jyllands-Posten Foundation, the William and Flora Hewlett Foundation, the William & Sheila Konar Foundation, the Lilly Endowment, and the Fritt Ord Foundation. Freedom House is solely responsible for the report's content.

Freedom in the World 2019
Democracy in Retreat

In 2018, *Freedom in the World* recorded the 13th consecutive year of decline in global freedom. The reversal has spanned a variety of countries in every region, from long-standing democracies like the United States to consolidated authoritarian regimes like China and Russia. The overall losses are still shallow compared with the gains of the late 20th century, but the pattern is consistent and ominous. Democracy is in retreat.

In states that were already authoritarian, earning Not Free designations from Freedom House, governments have increasingly shed the thin façade of democratic practice that they established in previous decades, when international incentives and pressure for reform were stronger. More authoritarian powers are now banning opposition groups or jailing their leaders, dispensing with term limits, and tightening the screws on any independent media that remain. Meanwhile, many countries that democratized after the end of the Cold War have regressed in the face of rampant corruption, antiliberal populist movements, and breakdowns in the rule of law. Most troublingly, even long-standing democracies have been shaken by populist political forces that reject basic principles like the separation of powers and target minorities for discriminatory treatment.

Some light shined through these gathering clouds in 2018. Surprising improvements in individual countries—including Malaysia, Armenia, Ethiopia, Angola, and Ecuador—show that democracy has enduring appeal as a means of holding leaders accountable and creating the conditions for a better life. Even in the countries of Europe and North America where democratic institutions are under pressure, dynamic civic movements for justice and inclusion continue to build on the achievements of their predecessors, expanding the scope of what citizens can and should expect from democracy. The promise of democracy remains real and powerful. Not only defending it but broadening its reach is one of the great causes of our time.

THE WAVE OF DEMOCRATIZATION ROLLS BACK

The end of the Cold War accelerated a dramatic wave of democratization that began as early as the 1970s. The fall of the Berlin Wall in 1989 and the Soviet Union's collapse in 1991 cleared the way for the formation or restoration of liberal democratic institutions not only in Eastern Europe, but also in the Americas, sub-Saharan Africa, and Asia. Between 1988 and 2005, the percentage of countries ranked Not Free in *Freedom in the World* dropped by almost 14 points (from 37 to 23 percent), while the share of Free countries grew (from 36 to 46 percent). This surge of progress has now begun to roll back. Between 2005 and 2018, the share of Not Free countries rose to 26 percent, while the share of Free countries declined to 44 percent.

The reversals may be a result of the euphoric expansion of the 1990s and early 2000s. As that momentum has worn off, many countries have struggled to accommodate the political swings and contentious debates intrinsic to democracy. Rapidly erected democratic institutions have come under sustained attack in nations that remain economically fragile or are still riven by deep-seated class or ethnic conflicts. Of the 23 countries that suffered a negative status change over the past 13 years (moving from Free to Partly Free, or Partly Free to Not Free), almost two-thirds (61 percent) had earned a positive status change after

1988. For example, Hungary, which became Free in 1990, fell back to Partly Free this year after five consecutive years of decline and 13 years without improvement.

AN EBB TIDE IN ESTABLISHED DEMOCRACIES

With the post–Cold War transition period now over, another shift in the global order is challenging long-standing democracies, from within and without. A crisis of confidence in these societies has intensified, with many citizens expressing doubts that democracy still serves their interests. Of the 41 countries that were consistently ranked Free from 1985 to 2005, 22 have registered net score declines in the last five years.

The crisis is linked to a changing balance of power at the global level. The share of international power held by highly industrialized democracies is dwindling as the clout of China, India, and other newly industrialized economies increases. China's rise is the most stunning, with GDP per capita increasing by 16 times from 1990 to 2017. The shift has been driven by a new phase of globalization that unlocked enormous wealth around the world. The distribution of benefits has been highly uneven, however, with most accruing to either the wealthiest on a global scale or to workers in industrializing countries. Low- and medium-skilled workers in long-industrialized democracies have gained relatively little from the expansion, as stable, well-paying jobs have been lost to a combination of foreign competition and technological change.

These developments have contributed to increasing anger and anxiety in Europe and the United States over economic inequality and loss of personal status. The center of the political spectrum, which dominated politics in the established democracies as the changes unfolded, failed to adequately address the disruption and dislocation they caused. This created political opportunities for new competitors on the left and right, who were able to cast existing elites as complicit in or benefiting from the erosion of citizens' living standards and national traditions.

So far it has been antiliberal populist movements of the far right—those that emphasize national sovereignty, are hostile to immigration, and reject constitutional checks on the will of the majority—that have been most effective at seizing the open political space. In countries from Italy to Sweden, antiliberal politicians have shifted the terms of debate and won elections by promoting an exclusionary national identity as a means for frustrated majorities to gird themselves against a changing global and domestic order. By building alliances with or outright capturing mainstream parties on the right, antiliberals have been able to launch attacks on the institutions designed to protect minorities against abuses and prevent monopolization of power. Victories for antiliberal movements in Europe and the United States in recent years have emboldened their counterparts around the world, as seen most recently in the election of Jair Bolsonaro as president of Brazil.

These movements damage democracies internally through their dismissive attitude toward core civil and political rights, and they weaken the cause of democracy around the world with their unilateralist reflexes. For example, antiliberal leaders' attacks on the media have contributed to increasing polarization of the press, including political control over state broadcasters, and to growing physical threats against journalists in their countries. At the same time, such attacks have provided cover for authoritarian leaders abroad, who now commonly cry "fake news" when squelching critical coverage.

Similarly, punitive approaches to immigration are resulting in human rights abuses by democracies—such as Australia's indefinite confinement of seaborne migrants in squalid camps on the remote island of Nauru, the separation of migrant children from their detained parents by the United States, or the detention of migrants by Libyan militias at the behest of Italy—that in turn offer excuses for more aggressive policies towards migrants and refugees elsewhere in the world. Populist politicians' appeals to "unique" or "traditional" national values in democracies threaten the protection of individual rights as a universal value, which allows authoritarian states to justify much more egregious human rights violations. And by unilaterally assailing international institutions like the United Nations or the International Criminal Court without putting forward serious alternatives, antiliberal governments weaken the capacity of the international system to constrain the behavior of China and other authoritarian powers.

The gravity of the threat to global freedom requires the United States to shore up and expand its alliances with fellow democracies and deepen its own commitment to the values they share. Only a united front among the world's democratic nations—and a defense of democracy as a universal right rather than the historical inheritance of a few Western societies—can roll back the world's current authoritarian and antiliberal trends. By contrast, a withdrawal of the United States from global engagement on behalf of democracy, and a shift to transactional or mercenary relations with allies and rivals alike, will only accelerate the decline of democratic norms.

THE COSTS OF FALTERING LEADERSHIP

There should be no illusions about what the deterioration of established democracies could mean for the cause of freedom globally. Neither America nor its most powerful allies have ever been perfect models—the United States ranks behind 51 of the 87 other Free countries in *Freedom in the World*—and their commitment to democratic governance overseas has always competed with other priorities. But the post-Soviet wave of democratization did produce lasting gains and came in no small part because of support and encouragement from the United States and other leading democratic nations. Despite the regression in many newly democratized countries described above, two-thirds of the countries whose freedom status improved between 1988 and 2005 have maintained their new status to date.

That major democracies are now flagging in their efforts, or even working in the opposite direction, is cause for real alarm. The truth is that democracy needs defending, and as traditional champions like the United States stumble, core democratic norms meant to ensure peace, prosperity, and freedom for all people are under serious threat around the world.

For example, elections are being hollowed out as autocracies find ways to control their results while sustaining a veneer of competitive balloting. Polls in which the outcome is shaped by coercion, fraud, gerrymandering, or other manipulation are increasingly common. Freedom House's indicators for elections have declined at twice the rate of overall score totals globally during the last three years.

In a related phenomenon, the principle of term limits for executives, which have a long provenance in democracies but spread around the world after the end of the Cold War, is weakening. According to Freedom House's data, leaders in 34 countries have tried to revise term limits—and have been successful 31 times—since the 13-year global decline began. Attacks on term limits have been especially prominent in Africa, Latin America, and the former Soviet Union.

Freedom of expression has come under sustained attack, through both assaults on the press and encroachments on the speech rights of ordinary citizens. *Freedom in the World* data show freedom of expression declining each year over the last 13 years, with sharper drops since 2012. This year, press freedom scores fell in four out of six regions in the world. Flagrant violations, like the imprisonment of journalists Wa Lone and Kyaw Soe Oo for their investigative reporting in Myanmar, have become more widespread. Even more stark have been the declines in personal expression, as governments have cracked down on critical discussion among citizens, especially online. The explosion of criminal cases for "insulting the president" in Turkey—more than 20,000 investigations and 6,000 prosecutions in 2017 alone—is one of the most glaring examples of this global trend.

The offensive against freedom of expression is being supercharged by a new and more effective form of digital authoritarianism. As documented in Freedom House's most recent *Freedom on the Net* report, China is now exporting its model of comprehensive internet censorship and surveillance around the world, offering trainings, seminars, and study trips as well as advanced equipment that takes advantage of artificial intelligence and facial recognition technologies. As the internet takes on the role of a virtual public sphere, and as the cost of sophisticated surveillance declines, Beijing's desire and capacity to spread totalitarian models of digitally enabled social control pose a major risk to democracy worldwide.

Another norm under siege is protection of the rights of migrants and refugees, including the rights to due process, to freedom from discrimination, and to seek asylum. All countries have the legitimate authority to regulate migration, but they must do so in line with international human rights standards and without violating the fundamental principles of justice provided by their own laws and constitutions. Antiliberal populist leaders have increasingly demonized immigrants and asylum seekers and targeted them for discriminatory treatment, often using them as scapegoats to marginalize any political opponents who come to their defense. In *Freedom in the World*, eight democracies have suffered score declines in the past four years alone due to their treatment of migrants. With some 257 million people estimated to be in migration around the world, the persistent assault on the rights of migrants is a significant threat to human rights and a potential catalyst for other attacks on democratic safeguards.

In addition to mistreating those who arrive in their territory in search of work or protection, a growing number of governments are reaching beyond their borders to target expatriates, exiles, and diasporas. Freedom House found 24 countries around the world—including heavyweights like Russia, China, Turkey, Iran, and Saudi Arabia—that have recently targeted political dissidents abroad with practices such as harassment, extradition requests, kidnapping, and even assassination. Saudi Arabia's murder of journalist Jamal Khashoggi in Turkey put a spotlight on authoritarian regimes' aggressive pursuit of prominent critics. Turkey itself, which has sought to keep Khashoggi's murder on the front pages, has by its own account captured 104 of its citizens from 21 countries over the last two years in a global crackdown on perceived enemies of the state. Beijing's growing apparatus for policing opinions and enforcing its views among Chinese citizens and communities overseas has led to outcomes including the forced repatriation of Uighurs from countries where they sought safety and the surveillance of Chinese students at foreign universities. Interpol's notification system has become a tool for authoritarian governments to detain and harass citizens in exile. The normalization of such transnational violence and harassment would not just shut down the last refuges for organized opposition to many repressive regimes. It would also contribute to a broader breakdown in international law and order, a world of borderless persecution in which any country could be a hunting ground for spies and assassins dispatched by tyrants looking to crush dissent.

Most disturbingly, Freedom House's global survey shows that ethnic cleansing is a growing trend. In 2005, *Freedom in the World* reduced the scores of just three countries for ethnic cleansing or other egregious efforts to alter the ethnic composition of their territory; this number has since grown to 11, and in some cases the scale or intensity of such activities has increased over time as well. In Syria and Myanmar, hundreds of thousands of civilians from certain ethnic and religious groups have been killed or displaced as world powers either fail to respond adequately or facilitate the violence. Russia's occupation of Crimea has included targeted repression of Crimean Tatars and those who insist on maintaining their Ukrainian identity. China's mass internment of Uighurs and other Muslims—with some 800,000 to 2 million people held arbitrarily in "reeducation" camps—can only be interpreted as a superpower's attempt to annihilate the distinct identities of minority groups.

BREAKTHROUGHS AND MOVEMENTS FOR JUSTICE

Despite this grim global environment, positive breakthroughs in countries scattered all over the world during 2018 showed that the universal promise of democracy still holds power.

- In **Angola**, new president João Lourenço took notable actions against corruption and impunity, reducing the outsized influence of his long-ruling predecessor's family and granting the courts greater independence.
- In **Armenia**, massive nonviolent demonstrations forced the resignation of Serzh Sargsyan, the country's leader since 2008, who had tried to evade term limits by moving from the presidency to the prime minister's office. After snap elections in December, a new reformist majority in the parliament has pledged to promote transparency and accountability for corruption and abuse of office.
- In **Ecuador**, President Lenín Moreno has defied expectations by breaking with the antidemocratic practices of former president Rafael Correa, including by adopting a more relaxed stance toward media criticism, barring those convicted of corruption from holding office, and passing a constitutional referendum that restored presidential term limits.
- In **Ethiopia**, the monopolistic ruling party began to loosen its grip in response to three years of protests, installing a reform-minded prime minister who oversaw the lifting of a state of emergency, the release of political prisoners, and the creation of space for more public discussion of political issues.
- In **Malaysia**, voters threw out disgraced prime minister Najib Razak and a political coalition that had governed since independence, clearing the way for a new government that quickly took steps to hold Najib and his family to account for a massive corruption scandal.

In all of these cases, politicians responded or were forced to respond to public demands for democratic change, unexpectedly disrupting long patterns of repression. Such openings serve as a reminder that people continue to strive for freedom, accountability, and dignity, including in countries where the odds seem insurmountable.</indent>

While some progress has come in the form of sudden breakthroughs at the leadership level, more incremental societal change offers another reason for hope.

Even in a time of new threats to democracy, social movements around the world are expanding the scope of democratic inclusion. They are part of a multigenerational transformation in how the rights of women, of ethnic, sexual, and religious minorities, of migrants, and of people with disabilities are recognized and upheld in practice—not least in places where they were already constitutionally enshrined. Authoritarian and antiliberal actors fear these movements for justice and participation because they challenge unfair concentrations of status and power. The transformation may still be fragile and incomplete, but its underlying drive—to make good on the 20th century's promise of universal human rights and democratic institutions—is profound.

In this sense, the current moment contains not only danger, but also opportunity for democracy. Those committed to human rights and democratic governance should not limit themselves to a wary defense of the status quo. Instead we should throw ourselves into projects intended to renew national and international orders, to make protections for human dignity even more just and more comprehensive, including for workers whose lives are disrupted by technological and economic change. Democracy requires continuous effort to thrive, and a constant willingness to broaden and deepen the application of its principles. The future of democracy depends on our ability to show that it is more than a set of bare-minimum defenses against the worst abuses of tyrants—it is a guarantee of the freedom to choose and live out one's own destiny. We must demonstrate that the full promise of democracy can be realized, and recognize that no one else will do it for us.

REGIONAL TRENDS

Americas: Crises Spur Migration, Populist Leaders Win Key Elections

Latin America in 2018 was embroiled in a migration crisis driven in part by government repression in Venezuela and Nicaragua. Elections brought new populist leaders to power in Mexico and in Brazil, where the tense campaign period was marred by political violence.

In Venezuela, President Nicolás Maduro extended his authoritarian rule with a profoundly flawed presidential election characterized by bans on prominent opposition candidates and voter intimidation. Maduro has presided over an economic collapse and accompanying humanitarian crisis that has left millions struggling to meet their basic needs. In Nicaragua, President Daniel Ortega pursued a ferocious crackdown on a nationwide antigovernment protest movement, with violence by state forces and allied armed groups resulting in hundreds of deaths. The harsh conditions in Nicaragua and Venezuela have added to the region's already substantial migration crisis.

Right-wing populist candidate Jair Bolsonaro captured Brazil's presidency after a contentious preelection period that featured disinformation campaigns and political violence. Bolsonaro's rhetoric was steeped in disdain for democratic principles and aggressive pledges to wipe out corruption and violent crime, which resonated with a deeply frustrated electorate. In Mexico, promises to end corruption and confront violent drug gangs also propelled left-wing populist Andrés Manuel López Obrador to the presidency, though he has yet to explain how he will accomplish his goals.

Democratic gains continued in Ecuador, where space for civil society and the media has opened. Yet it too grapples with serious challenges. An Ecuadoran journalist and two of his colleagues were killed along the Colombian border by leftist guerrillas, and anti-immigrant sentiment is on the rise.

Asia-Pacific: Military Influence and Persecution of Minorities

The military and other security forces played an influential role in key Asian elections and perpetrated gross rights abuses against minorities during 2018. However, a dramatic political shift in Malaysia raised hopes for democratic reform.

Cambodian prime minister Hun Sen cemented his grip on power with lopsided general elections that came after authorities dissolved the main opposition party and shuttered independent media outlets. The military and police openly campaigned for the ruling party, which won all the seats in the legislature. While Pakistan's elections were more competitive, the military's influence over the courts and the media was widely thought to have tilted the contest in favor of Imran Khan, who took office as prime minister.

Myanmar's military was accused by UN investigators of committing genocide against the Rohingya people, over 700,000 of whom have fled to Bangladesh since the start of a violent crackdown in 2017. In China, it is estimated that over a million ethnic Uighurs, Kazakhs, and Hui have been forced into "reeducation" centers, from which grisly reports of torture and custodial deaths are emerging. Meanwhile, Communist Party leader Xi Jinping secured a potential life tenure in March, when the National People's Congress rubber-stamped a decision to remove the constitution's two-term limit on the presidency.

In a positive development, outrage over a massive corruption scandal helped an opposition alliance defeat incumbent prime minister Najib Razak's Barisan Nasional coalition, which had ruled Malaysia for decades; Najib was arrested and charged soon after. The new government pledged to roll back restrictive laws.

In Bangladesh, security forces cracked down on the opposition ahead of parliamentary elections, intimidating and arresting prominent figures. The polls themselves were marked by widespread irregularities and interparty violence that resulted in more than a dozen deaths.

In Sri Lanka, President Maithripala Sirisena's unilateral dismissal of the prime minister threatened recent democratic gains. Sirisena attempted to disband the parliament when legislators rejected the move, but in a decision reflecting the judiciary's independence, the Supreme Court declared the dissolution unconstitutional, and the prime minister was restored to office.

Eurasia: A Breakthrough in Armenia as other Regimes Harden Authoritarian Rule

Entrenched elites in many Eurasian countries continued exploiting the advantages of incumbency to maintain their grip on power. However, Armenia broke that pattern with the ouster of an unpopular leader and the election of a new, reform-minded government.

In the spring of 2018, Armenians took to the streets in protest of an attempt by Serzh Sargsyan to extend his rule by shifting from the presidency to the prime minister's office. To widespread surprise, the protests culminated in Sargsyan's resignation and the rise of opposition leader Nikol Pashinyan to the premiership. Pashinyan's My Step alliance decisively won snap parliamentary elections in December, clearing the way for systemic reforms.

Uzbekistan experienced another year of incremental improvement, as the government continued to release political prisoners and ease restrictions on NGOs. However, reports of torture persisted, as did the long-standing practice of forced labor in the cotton fields.

Russia's Vladimir Putin and Azerbaijan's Ilham Aliyev each secured new presidential terms, benefiting from strong-arm tactics including the repression of independent media and civil society, the abuse of state resources, and the persecution of genuine political opponents—as well as outright fraud.

Journalists and activists in Russia and other countries continued to operate under perilous conditions, risking arrest, violence, and even death for their independent reporting in 2018. Several Russian journalists died under suspicious circumstances, while in Ukraine, reporters endured harassment and assaults. In Kazakhstan and Belarus, strict new media laws further limited journalists who were already operating under severe constraints.

Some governments stepped up internet censorship in order to stamp out dissent. In Kyrgyzstan, the government used laws against extremism to block websites, video-sharing platforms, and even the music-streaming service SoundCloud, while Tajikistan blocked independent media websites and social networks.

Europe: Antidemocratic Leaders Undermine Critical Institutions

Antidemocratic leaders in Central Europe and the Balkans—including some who have brazenly consolidated power beyond constitutional limits—continued undermining institutions that protect freedoms of expression and association and the rule of law.

In Hungary, Prime Minister Viktor Orbán has presided over one of the most dramatic declines ever charted by Freedom House within the European Union. Having worked methodically to deny critical voices a platform in the media or civil society, Orbán and his right-wing nationalist Fidesz party easily defended their parliamentary supermajority in 2018 elections. Soon after, the government forced the closure of Central European University, evicting its vibrant academic community. However, the year ended with vigorous dissent from thousands of protesters who took to the streets to denounce Orbán's abuses.

In Poland, the conservative Law and Justice party led by Jarosław Kaczyński—who plays a dominant political role despite holding no formal executive position—laid waste to the country's legal framework in its drive to assert political control over the entire judiciary. The year included attempts to force the retirement of Supreme Court judges and gain partisan influence over the selection of election commission members.

Meanwhile, attacks on media independence spread to other European democracies. Austria's new right-wing government put pressure on the public broadcaster, while Czech prime minister Andrej Babiš drew on closely allied media outlets to combat unflattering scandals. In Slovakia, investigative reporter Ján Kuciak was shot to death in his home after uncovering corrupt links between government officials and organized crime.

In the Balkans, President Aleksandar Vučić of Serbia and President Milo Đukanović of Montenegro continued to consolidate state power around themselves and their cliques, subverting basic standards of good governance and exceeding their assigned constitutional roles.

In Turkey, simultaneous parliamentary and presidential elections took place in June despite a two-year state of emergency that included the imprisonment of the leaders of a key opposition party and extreme curbs on freedoms of association, assembly, and expression. Although the state of emergency was lifted following the election, the authorities continued to engage in purges of state institutions and arrests of journalists, civil society members, and academics.

Middle East and North Africa: Repression Grows as Democracies Stumble

Authoritarian states across the Middle East and North Africa continued to suppress dissent during 2018, and even the few democracies in the region suffered from self-inflicted wounds. However, elections held in Iraq and Lebanon could stabilize those countries and open the way for modest progress.

Political repression worsened in Egypt, where President Abdel Fattah al-Sisi was reelected with 97 percent of the vote after security forces arbitrarily detained potential challengers. In Saudi Arabia, after the government drew praise for easing its draconian ban on women driving, authorities arrested high-profile women's rights activists and clamped down on even mild forms of dissent. Evidence also mounted that Crown Prince Mohammed bin Salman had personally ordered the assassination of self-exiled critic and *Washington Post* columnist Jamal Khashoggi in Istanbul, dashing any remaining hopes that the young prince might emerge as a reformer.

The consolidation of democracy in Tunisia continued to sputter, as freedoms of assembly and association were imperiled by legislative changes and the leadership's failure to set up a Constitutional Court undermined judicial independence and the rule of law.

Nationalism escalated in Israel—the only other country in the region designated as Free—placing strain on its democracy. A new law allowed the interior minister to revoke the residency of Jerusalem-based Palestinians for, among other things, a "breach of loyalty" to Israel. Moreover, an addition to the country's Basic Law downgraded the status of the Arabic language and introduced the principle that only the Jewish people have the right to exercise self-determination in the country.

National elections in Iraq and Lebanon held some promise of further gains. Despite allegations of fraud and a controversial recount, Iraqis witnessed a peaceful transfer of power following competitive parliamentary polls. However, antigovernment protests in the southern city of Basra at year's end were met with a disproportionately violent response by security forces. In Lebanon, parliamentary elections took place for the first time since 2009, restoring a degree of legitimacy to the government after repeated postponements of the balloting.

Sub-Saharan Africa: Historic Openings Offset by Creeping Restrictions Elsewhere

The year brought notable democratic progress in a number of pivotal African countries and increasing threats to freedom in others.

Angola and Ethiopia—both historically closed countries ruled by autocratic leaders—experienced dramatic openings in 2018. While their new leaders, President João Lourenço and Prime Minister Ahmed Abiy, respectively, each emerged from the countries' dominant political cliques, both have expressed a commitment to important reforms. If the new administrations are able to dismantle the repressive legal and political frameworks they inherited, they may serve as important models for their neighbors and significantly improve the democratic trajectory of the continent as a whole.

The Gambia made rapid democratic gains for a second year, following the dramatic exit of strongman Yahya Jammeh in early 2017. The political opening under President Adama Barrow was reinforced by 2018 legislative elections, in which seven parties and several independent candidates won seats.

Yet many countries in the region still struggled to deliver basic freedoms and protect human rights. Zimbabwe's political system returned in some ways to its precoup status quo, as the ruling ZANU-PF party won deeply flawed general elections following the military's ouster of longtime president Robert Mugabe in 2017. Despite President Emmerson Mnangagwa's pledges to respect political institutions and govern in the interest of all Zimbabweans, his new administration has shown few signs that it is committed to fostering genuine political competition, and it has continued to enforce laws that limit expression.

Space for political activity continued to close in several countries, notably Tanzania, where the government arrested prominent opposition leaders, stifled antigovernment protests, and pushed for legislation that further strengthens the ruling party's stranglehold on domestic politics. In Uganda, long-ruling president Yoweri Museveni's administration sought to constrain dissent by implementing new surveillance systems and instituting a regressive tax on social media use. Senegal's reputation as one of the most stable democracies in West Africa was threatened by new regulatory barriers that could limit the opposition's participation in upcoming elections. The arbitrary detention and prosecution of a potential opposition presidential candidate cast doubt on the independence of the judiciary and the government's commitment to the rule of law.

Several of the continent's aging authoritarian leaders continued to cling to power. In Cameroon, President Paul Biya, now in office for 36 years, presided over deeply flawed elections in which he secured a seventh term, while in Uganda, Museveni—in office for 32 years—oversaw the removal of a presidential age cap from the constitution, allowing him to run for a sixth term in 2021. In Togo, one of only two countries in West Africa without term limits, President Faure Gnassingbé (whose family has been in power since 1967) resisted popular efforts to impose such a barrier.

UNPACKING 13 YEARS OF DECLINE

Freedom in the World has recorded global declines in political rights and civil liberties for an alarming 13 consecutive years, from 2005 to 2018. The global average score has declined each year, and countries with net score declines have consistently outnumbered those with net improvements.

- **A widespread problem:** The 13 years of decline have touched all parts of the world and affected Free, Partly Free, and Not Free countries alike. Every region except Asia-Pacific has a lower average score for 2018 than it did in 2005, and even Asia declined when countries with less than 1 million people—mostly small Pacific

Island states—are excluded. Not Free countries as a group suffered a more significant score drop than Free or Partly Free countries, which also declined.

- **Faltering post–Cold War democratization:** The end of the Cold War facilitated a wave of democratization in the late 20th century, but a large share of countries that made progress during that time were unable to maintain it. On average, countries that earned a status upgrade—from Not Free to Partly Free, or Partly Free to Free—between 1988 and 2005 have faced an 11 percent drop in their numerical score during the 13 years of decline. The backsliding in these countries outpaces the decline of all global scores on average, demonstrating the particular vulnerability of countries whose democratic institutions have shallow roots. The group faced its most acute losses in the Rule of Law subcategory (15 percent), closely followed by Functioning of Government (14 percent).

- **Consolidated democracies slip:** Social and economic changes related to globalization have contributed to a crisis of confidence in the political systems of long-standing democracies. The democratic erosion seen among Free countries is concentrated in consolidated democracies—those that were rated Free from 1985 through 2005, the 20-year period before the 13-year decline. The average freedom score for consolidated democracies has declined every year for the last 11 years.

- **Evolution of the decline:** Globally, scores in the Rule of Law subcategory suffered the most during the past 13 years. However, the scores driving the decline have shifted more recently. In the last six years, Freedom of Expression and Belief, and especially the indicator focused on people's freedom to express their personal views without surveillance or retribution, suffered the most. In the last three years, Electoral Process declined more than any other subcategory.

FREEDOM IN THE WORLD 2019 STATUS CHANGES

Hungary

Hungary's status declined from Free to Partly Free due to sustained attacks on the country's democratic institutions by Prime Minister Viktor Orbán's Fidesz party, which has used its parliamentary supermajority to impose restrictions on or assert control over the opposition, the media, religious groups, academia, NGOs, the courts, asylum seekers, and the private sector since 2010.

Nicaragua

Nicaragua's status declined from Partly Free to Not Free due to authorities' brutal repression of an antigovernment protest movement, which has included the arrest and imprisonment of opposition figures, intimidation and attacks against religious leaders, and violence by state forces and allied armed groups that resulted in hundreds of deaths.

Serbia

Serbia's status declined from Free to Partly Free due to deterioration in the conduct of elections, continued attempts by the government and allied media outlets to undermine the independent journalists through legal harassment and smear campaigns, and President Aleksandar Vučić's de facto accumulation of executive powers that conflict with his constitutional role.

Uganda

Uganda's status declined from Partly Free to Not Free due to attempts by long-ruling president Yoweri Museveni's government to restrict free expression, including through surveillance of electronic communications and a regressive tax on social media use.

Zimbabwe

Zimbabwe's status improved from Not Free to Partly Free because the 2018 presidential election, though deeply flawed, granted a degree of legitimacy to the rule of President Emmerson Mnangagwa, who had taken power after the military forced his predecessor's resignation in 2017.

COUNTRIES IN THE SPOTLIGHT

The following countries saw important developments during the survey period that affected their democratic trajectory, and deserve special scrutiny in 2019.

- In a region dominated by entrenched elites, **Armenia** made a breakthrough with the victory of reform-minded leader Nikol Pashinyan in snap elections that were called after unpopular incumbent Serzh Sargsyan attempted to evade term limits and extend his rule.
- Right-wing candidate Jair Bolsonaro captured **Brazil**'s presidency after expressing disdain for democratic principles and promising extreme measures to wipe out corruption and violent crime.
- **Cambodia**'s prime minister, Hun Sen, fortified his near-total grip on power in lopsided general elections that came after authorities dissolved the main opposition party and shuttered independent media outlets.
- President Paul Biya of **Cameroon**—who has been in office for over three decades—extended his rule through deeply flawed elections, while violence accompanying an ongoing crisis in the Anglophone region threatened to erupt into civil war.
- In **China**, over a million ethnic Uighurs, Kazakhs, and Hui were forced into brutal "reeducation" centers, and a rubber-stamp decision by the National People's Congress cleared the way for President Xi Jinping to remain in office indefinitely.
- Following sustained protests in **Ethiopia**, the ruling party installed a reformist prime minister who lifted a state of emergency, released political prisoners, and permitted more open political debate.
- Despite allegations of fraud and a controversial recount, **Iraq** underwent a peaceful transfer of power following competitive parliamentary elections.
- In **Poland**, the conservative Law and Justice party has laid waste to the country's legal framework—and the underpinnings of its democracy—in its drive to assert control over the judiciary.
- In **Sri Lanka**, President Maithripala Sirisena's attempt to unilaterally dismiss the prime minister threatened recent democratic gains, though the Supreme Court exhibited its independence by declaring the move unconstitutional.
- In **Tanzania**, the government arrested prominent opposition leaders, stifled antigovernment protests, and pushed for legislation that further strengthens the ruling party's stranglehold on politics.

THE UNITED STATES IN DECLINE

Freedom House has tracked a slow overall decline in political rights and civil liberties in the United States for the past eight years, punctuated by an unusual three-point drop for developments in 2017. Prominent concerns have included Russian interference in US elections, domestic attempts to manipulate the electoral system, executive and legislative dysfunction, conflicts of interest and lack of transparency, and pressure on judicial independence and the rule of law.

This year, the United States' total score on the 100-point scale used by *Freedom in the World* remains the same as in the report covering 2017, with two indicators changing in opposite directions:

- The score for freedom of assembly improved, as there was no repetition of the protest-related violence that had led to a lower score for the previous two years. In fact, there was an upsurge of civic action and demonstrations on issues ranging from women's rights and immigration policy to the problem of mass shootings in schools.
- The score for equal treatment before the law declined due to government policies and actions that improperly restricted the legal rights of asylum seekers, signs of discrimination in the acceptance of refugees for resettlement, and excessively harsh or haphazard immigration enforcement policies that resulted in the separation of children from adult family members, among other problematic outcomes.

The United States currently receives a score of 86 out of 100 points. While this places it below other major democracies such as France, Germany, and the United Kingdom, it is still firmly in the Free category. Nevertheless, its decline of eight points in as many years is significant. The United States' closest peers with respect to total *Freedom in the World* scores are Belize, Croatia, Greece, Latvia, and Mongolia.

RECOMMENDATIONS FOR DEMOCRACIES

Democracies face threats at home and abroad. A crisis of confidence in open societies is sapping faith in democracy as a system. Domestic attacks on key institutions—the judiciary, the media, and electoral mechanisms—are undermining the foundations of democracy. At the same time, a global assault on the norms of democracy, led by an increasingly assertive China, challenges their spread around the world.

Only by strengthening democracy at home, and standing together in its defense around the world, can democracies protect their values and preserve their ability to expand freedom globally. The following recommendations are intended to provide a framework for democratic countries as they pursue these twin goals.

Strengthening and Protecting Core Values in Established Democracies

- **Respect human rights at home.** Attacks by elected leaders on democratic institutions—including the press, an independent judiciary, and due process of law—undermine faith in democracy around the world. Democratic leaders should demonstrate respect for fundamental norms at home, including by welcoming media scrutiny and fact-based reporting as an aid to good governance, enforcing robust protections against corruption and conflicts of interest, easing rather than obstructing citizens' participation in elections, and dedicating the time and resources necessary to ensure that all migrants, refugees, and asylum seekers receive fair and proper treatment under the law.
- **Invest in civic education.** To protect freedom domestically and build support for an informed foreign policy, it is essential to foster a stronger public understanding of democratic principles—especially among young people. In the United States, new legislation could require each state to develop basic content and benchmarks of achievement for civic education, including instruction on the fundamental tenets of democracy. In the absence of new legislation, the US Department of Education

should, to the extent possible, make funding available to states for civic education that focuses on democratic principles.

• **Strengthen laws that guard against foreign influence over government officials.** Legislative proposals requiring greater transparency about officials' personal finances and campaign donations, more rigorous standards for the disclosure of conflicts of interest, and the establishment of a clear code of conduct for engagement with foreign officials can help insulate governments from foreign attempts to subvert democratic institutions. In the United States, this could include passing legislation to enforce the principles of the constitution's foreign emoluments clause, closing loopholes in rules on reporting foreign influence, and modernizing financial disclosure requirements for elected officials.

• **Invest in elections infrastructure to guard against foreign interference in balloting.** In the United States, funding should focus on replacing outdated voting machines, strengthening cybersecurity for existing systems, and improving the technological expertise of state elections staff.

• **Require social media companies to report foreign efforts to spread online disinformation and propaganda.** Social media companies that operate in the United States should be required to report regularly on efforts by foreign governments and nonstate actors to manipulate American public opinion and undercut democracy by spreading disinformation and propaganda on their platforms. The US government should assess which entities would be the most appropriate to receive these reports, since this information is of interest across jurisdictions, including to intelligence agencies, Congress, the US State Department's Global Engagement Center, the Securities and Exchange Commission, and the Department of Justice. The US government should carefully decide on the types and sizes of social media companies required to comply, the data they must submit, and appropriate penalties for noncompliance. The entity receiving the information should report findings regularly to the public and should make the data publicly available to researchers, while ensuring the protection of users' privacy.

Defending and Expanding Democracy around the World

• **Invest in alliances with other democracies, and in multilateral institutions.** Confronting authoritarian and antiliberal trends globally requires a united front among democratic nations. Democracies are a beacon of freedom that others emulate, and their policies help to shape international standards. By vocally emphasizing their shared values and coordinating their aid and public diplomacy efforts, democratic countries can offer a consistent, attainable alternative to repression and coercion. They can reinforce this collective effort and constrain the behavior of autocratic powers by investing in multilateral institutions. Starting from the assumption that a country's individual sovereignty is threatened by deep cooperation with allies will only isolate democracies from one another, leaving them weaker and less capable of meeting the challenge of resurgent authoritarianism.

• **Confront abuses of international institutions.** Illiberal leaders have grown more brazen in their attempts to manipulate international institutions for their own ends. Among other tactics, they have exploited Interpol to pursue political dissidents in exile, blocked civil society participation in multilateral bodies, and engineered the insertion or deletion of key phrasing in documents that affect international law and governance. (For example, China's use of the phrase "mutually beneficial cooperation" in a resolution adopted by the Human Rights Council could be interpreted to mean refraining from criticizing another state's human rights record.) Democratic states should firmly oppose such efforts, ensuring that dissidents are not wrongly handed over to their persecutors, and forming alliances within international bodies to prevent authoritarian regimes from warping the original missions of these institutions and undermining the fundamental rights they were created to uphold.

• **Encourage and protect journalists and freedom of the press.** A free and vibrant media sector is a foundational element of a healthy democratic system. Citizens should have access to fact-based information—both in traditional news sources and on social media—in order to understand how their governments function and to hold their leaders accountable for their words and actions. Democratic governments can help protect media freedom by reaffirming the critical role of the press in furthering good governance, transparency, and the rule of law, pushing back against anti-media rhetoric that aims to strip journalists of legitimacy, supporting programs to strengthen the technical capacity of journalists around the world, and ensuring that attacks on journalists are prosecuted.

• **Be prepared to promptly challenge preelection rights abuses.** Crackdowns on the political opposition and other perceived opponents of the government often occur before elections. The international community should be especially vigilant when monitoring preelection periods in countries where internet blocking, media restrictions, suppression of protests, or arrests of opposition candidates are likely. If such misconduct occurs, international leaders should immediately and publicly condemn the action, press the government to reverse course, and work to assist the victims. Specific responses could include publicly calling for the release of those wrongly imprisoned, sending embassy officials to monitor court proceedings, and—in extreme cases—issuing emergency humanitarian visas for those under attack.

• **Impose targeted sanctions on individuals and entities involved in human rights abuses and acts of corruption.** In the United States, a law known as the Global Magnitsky Act allows authorities to block visas for and freeze the assets of any person or entity—including private companies—that has engaged in or supported corruption or human rights abuses, providing a measure of accountability for the perpetrators without harming the general population. Countries with similar laws should robustly enforce them, and legislatures in countries without such laws should seek to pass them.

• **Emphasize democracy-strengthening programs in foreign assistance.** Democratic governance is a key component of economic development and a basic necessity for long-term success, requiring active public participation. In addition to critical institution-building efforts—such as strengthening the rule of law, bolstering judicial independence, and ensuring free, fair, transparent, and inclusive elections—democracy programs should prioritize engaging and empowering local citizens so that institutional investments are effective and sustainable. A recent poll in the United States conducted by Freedom House, the George W. Bush Institute, and the Penn Biden Center found that 71 percent of respondents are in favor of the US government taking steps to support democracy and human rights in other countries.

• **Focus on countries at critical junctures.** These include countries that have experienced recent expansions in freedom, such as Angola, Ethiopia, Armenia, and Ecuador, as well as countries in which democratic progress is threatened, such as Senegal, Tanzania, and Tunisia. Foreign assistance for these countries should prioritize and incentivize democratic reforms designed to consolidate gains, address threats, and prevent backsliding. Policymakers should engage in high-level public diplomacy to signal international commitment to democratic progress, and assist democratically inclined leaders in delivering the tangible expansion of political rights and civil liberties. Consistency and predictability of both funding and diplomatic engagement are critical to long-term success for states at tipping points.

Recommendations for the Private Sector

The internet and other digital technologies have become ubiquitous as a means of accessing information, communicating, and participating in public debates. Consequently, technology and social media companies play an increasingly important role in sustaining—or weakening—democracy. They have a special responsibility to be mindful of the impact their business activities may have on democracy and human rights. Private companies should:

- **Adhere to the UN Guiding Principles on Business and Human Rights.** This includes avoiding commercial relationships with authoritarian governments that force them to violate fundamental rights. Instead, companies should commit to respecting the human rights of their customers and workers. As part of this effort, they should conduct periodic assessments to help them fully understand the effects of their products and activities. Upon completion of these assessments, companies should develop actionable plans to remedy any evident or potential harm. Given its unique position in authoritarian settings, the technology sector in particular should refuse business arrangements that require either active complicity in or passive acceptance of political censorship and information controls.
- **Use internal expertise to help counter Chinese state censorship and protect the public.** The technology sector should assist users in China by developing accessible tools that keep pace with innovations by the Chinese government and complicit Chinese firms. For example, leading international companies could develop mobile phone applications that enhance digital security, enable the sharing of images in a way that evades artificial intelligence–driven censorship, and incorporate circumvention capabilities into apps focused on other services.

The Struggle Comes Home
Attacks on Democracy in the United States

By Mike Abramowitz
President, Freedom House

Freedom House has advocated for democracy around the world since its founding in 1941, and since the early 1970s it has monitored the global status of political rights and civil liberties in the annual *Freedom in the World* report. During the report's first three decades, as the Cold War gave way to a general advance of liberal democratic values, we urged on reformist movements and denounced the remaining dictators for foot-dragging and active resistance. We raised the alarm when progress stagnated in the 2000s, and called on major democracies to maintain their support for free institutions.

Today, after 13 consecutive years of decline in global freedom, backsliding among new democracies has been compounded by the erosion of political rights and civil liberties among the established democracies we have traditionally looked to for leadership and support. Indeed, the pillars of freedom have come under attack here in the United States. And just as we have called out foreign leaders for undermining democratic norms in their countries, we must draw attention to the same sorts of warning signs in our own country. It is in keeping with our mission, and given the irreplaceable role of the United States as a champion of global freedom, it is a priority we cannot afford to ignore.

US FREEDOM IN DECLINE

The great challenges facing US democracy did not commence with the inauguration of President Donald Trump. Intensifying political polarization, declining economic mobility, the outsized influence of special interests, and the diminished influence of fact-based reporting in favor of bellicose partisan media were all problems afflicting the health of American democracy well before 2017. Previous presidents have contributed to the pressure on our system by infringing on the rights of American citizens. Surveillance programs such as the bulk collection of communications metadata, initially undertaken by the George W. Bush administration, and the Obama administration's overzealous crackdown on press leaks are two cases in point.

At the midpoint of his term, however, there remains little question that President Trump exerts an influence on American politics that is straining our core values and testing the stability of our constitutional system. No president in living memory has shown less respect for its tenets, norms, and principles. Trump has assailed essential institutions and traditions including the separation of powers, a free press, an independent judiciary, the impartial delivery of justice, safeguards against corruption, and most disturbingly, the legitimacy of elections. Congress, a coequal branch of government, has too frequently failed to push back against these attacks with meaningful oversight and other defenses.

We recognize the right of freely elected presidents and lawmakers to set immigration policy, adopt different levels of regulation and taxation, and pursue other legitimate aims related to national security. But they must do so according to rules designed to protect individual rights and ensure the long-term survival of the democratic system. There are no ends that justify nondemocratic means.

Freedom House is not alone in its concern for US democracy. Republicans, Democrats, and independents expressed deep reservations about its performance in a national poll conducted last year by Freedom House, the George W. Bush Institute, and the Penn Biden Center. A substantial majority of respondents said it is "absolutely important" to live in a democracy, but 55 percent agreed that American democracy is weak, and 68 percent said it is getting weaker. Big money in politics, racism and discrimination, and the inability of government to get things done—all long-standing problems—were the top concerns of those surveyed.

And yet Republicans and Democrats alike expressed strong attachments to individual liberty. A solid majority, 54 percent, believes it is more important for the rights of the minority to be protected than for the will of the majority to prevail.

So far, America's institutions have largely honored this deeply democratic sentiment. The resilience of the judiciary, the press corps, an energetic civil society, the political opposition, and other guardrails of the constitutional system—as well as some conscientious lawmakers and officeholders from the president's own party—have checked the chief executive's worst impulses and mitigated the effects of his administration's approach. While the United States suffered an unusual three-point drop on *Freedom in the World*'s 100-point scale for 2017, there was no additional net decline for 2018, and the total score of 86 still places the country firmly in the report's Free category.

But the fact that the system has proven durable so far is no guarantee that it will continue to do so. Elsewhere in the world, in places like Hungary, Venezuela, or Turkey, Freedom House has watched as democratic institutions gradually succumbed to sustained pressure from an antidemocratic leadership, often after a halting start. Irresponsible rhetoric can be a first step toward real restrictions on freedom. The United States has already been weakened by declines in the rule of law, the conduct of elections, and safeguards against corruption, among other important indicators measured by *Freedom in the World*. The current overall US score puts American democracy closer to struggling counterparts like Croatia than to traditional peers such as Germany or the United Kingdom.

The stakes in this struggle are high. For all the claims that the United States has lost global influence over the past decade, the reality is that other countries pay close attention to the conduct of the world's oldest functioning democracy. The continuing deterioration of US democracy will hasten the ongoing decline in global democracy. Indeed, it has already done so.

Ronald Reagan declared in his first inaugural address, "As we renew ourselves here in our own land, we will be seen as having greater strength throughout the world. We will again be the exemplar of freedom and a beacon of hope for those who do not now have freedom." Nearly four decades later, the idea that the United States is such an exemplar is being steadily discredited.

ASSAILING THE RULE OF LAW

In any democracy, it is the role of independent judges and prosecutors to defend the supremacy and continuity of constitutional law against excesses by elected officials, to ensure that individual rights are not abused by hostile majorities or other powerful interests, and to prevent the politicization of justice so that competing parties can alternate in office without fear of unfair retribution. While not without problems, the United States has enjoyed a strong tradition of respect for the rule of law.

President Trump has repeatedly shown disdain for this tradition. Late in 2018, after a federal judge blocked the administration's plan to consider asylum claims only from those who cross the border at official ports of entry, the president said, "This was an Obama judge. And I'll tell you what, it's not going to happen like this anymore."

The remark drew a rare rebuke from Chief Justice John Roberts, who declared "we don't have Obama judges or Trump judges, Bush judges or Clinton judges," and defended an independent judiciary as "something we should all be thankful for." But Trump shrugged off Roberts's intervention of behalf of the judicial branch, insisting that the US Court of Appeals for the Ninth Circuit was "a complete and total disaster" and that if his asylum policy was obstructed, "there will be only bedlam, chaos, injury and death."

Nor was this the first sign of hostility to the rule of law from the president. As a candidate in 2016, he questioned the impartiality of an American-born judge with a Hispanic surname who presided over a fraud suit filed against "Trump University." Soon after taking office, he disparaged a federal judge who ruled against his travel ban on several Muslim-majority countries as "this so-called judge."

The president has since urged the Department of Justice to prosecute his political opponents and critics. He has used his pardon power to reward political and ideological allies and encourage targets of criminal investigations to refuse cooperation with the government. He has expressed contempt for witnesses who are cooperating with law enforcement in cases that could harm his interests and praised those who remain silent. His administration's harsh policies on immigrants and asylum seekers have restricted their rights, belittled our nation's core ideals, and seriously compromised equal treatment under the law. In October 2018, the president went so far as to claim that he could unilaterally overturn the constitutional guarantee of birthright citizenship.

The president's attacks on the judiciary and law enforcement, echoed by media allies, are eroding the public's trust in the third branch of government and the rule of law. Without that trust, the outright politicization of justice could well ensue, threatening the very stability of our democracy. Any American is free to contest the wisdom of a judge's ruling, but no one—least of all the president—should challenge the authority of the courts themselves or use threats and incentives to pervert the legal process.

DEMONIZING THE PRESS

Legal protections for reporters are enshrined in America's founding documents, and press freedom remains strong in practice. An array of independent media organizations have continued to produce vigorous coverage of the administration. But the constant vilification of such outlets by President Trump, in an already polarized media environment, is accelerating the breakdown of public confidence in journalism as a legitimate, fact-based check on government power. We have seen in other countries how such practices paved the way to more tangible erosions of press freedom and, in extreme cases, put journalists in physical danger. It would be foolish to assume it could never happen here.

In a tweet posted two days after a mass shooting at a Pittsburgh synagogue last October, and not long after a series of pipe bombs had been sent by a Trump supporter to targets including CNN, the president blamed the media for inciting public rage: "There is great anger in our Country caused in part by inaccurate, and even fraudulent, reporting of the news," Trump wrote. "The Fake News Media, the true Enemy of the People, must stop the open & obvious hostility & report the news accurately & fairly. That will do much to put out the flame . . . of Anger and Outrage and we will then be able to bring all sides together in Peace and Harmony. Fake News Must End!"

Previous presidents have criticized the press, sometimes bitterly, but none with such relentless hostility for the institution itself. Trump alone has deployed slurs like "enemy of the people," flirted with the idea that the media are responsible for and perhaps deserving of violence, and defended his own routine falsehoods while accusing journalists of lying with malicious, even treasonous intent.

These practices have added to negative trends that were already apparent by 2017, including the emergence of more polarized media outlets on the right and left, the decline of independent reporting at the state and municipal level, the consolidation of ownership in certain sectors, and the rise of social media platforms that reward extreme views and fraudulent content. In this environment, more Americans are likely to seek refuge in media echo chambers, heeding only "reporting" that affirms their opinions rather than obtaining the factual information necessary to self-governance.

An independent, pluralistic, and vigilant press corps often antagonizes the subjects it covers. That is an acceptable consequence of the essential service it provides—keeping our democratic system honest, transparent, and accountable to the people. The press exposes private and public-sector corruption, abuses of power, invasions of privacy, and threats to public health and safety. Attempts by our leaders to disrupt this process through smears and intimidation could leave all Americans, the president's supporters and detractors alike, more vulnerable to exploitation, perfidy, and physical hazard.

SELF-DEALING AND CONFLICTS OF INTEREST

Corruption and transparency are crucial factors in Freedom House's assessments of democracy around the world. When officials use their positions to enrich themselves, or even tolerate conflicts of interest that sow public doubts about their motivations, citizens lose faith in the system and begin to avoid their own responsibilities, including paying taxes, participating in elections, and obeying the law in general. To avoid such decay, it is imperative that government and citizens alike uphold ethical rules and norms against corruption.

The United States benefits from a number of strong antigraft protections, including independent courts, congressional oversight mechanisms, and active monitoring by the media and civil society. But as on other topics, President Trump has broken with his modern predecessors in flouting the ethical standards of public service.

From the outset of his administration, the president has been willing to ignore obvious conflicts of interest, most prominently with his decision not to divest ownership of his businesses or place them in a blind trust. Instead, he moved them into a revocable trust, managed by his sons, of which he is the sole beneficiary. During his presidency, his businesses have accepted money from foreign lenders, including banks controlled by the Chinese government. Trump has swept aside the norm against nepotism by having his daughter and son-in-law, both seemingly saddled with their own conflicts of interest, serve as senior White House advisers. He also rejected the tradition obliging presidents to release their income tax records.

Trump properties have hosted foreign delegations, business dinners, trade association conferences, and Republican Party fund-raising events, complete with Trump-branded wines and other products, likely arranged in the hope of earning the president's gratitude. The *Washington Post* revealed that a month after President Trump's election, lobbyists representing Saudi Arabia booked hundreds of rooms at Trump International Hotel in the capital. Indeed, a number of foreign and domestic interests allegedly sought to influence the new administration by arranging donations to Trump's inauguration festivities, which are now under investigation.

The unusual nature of President Trump's approach to conflicts of interest has been underscored by the emergence of first-of-their-kind lawsuits accusing him of violating the constitution's prohibition on public officials accepting gifts or "emoluments" from foreign states. The nation's founders understood the corrosive threat of such corruption, and so have most presidents.

ATTACKING THE LEGITIMACY OF ELECTIONS

The importance of credible elections to the health of a democracy should be self-evident. If citizens believe that the polls are rigged, they will neither take part in the exercise nor accept the legitimacy of those elected.

Nevertheless, unsubstantiated accusations of voter fraud have been a staple of the president's assault on political norms. During the 2018 midterm elections, he suggested without evidence that Democrats were stealing a Senate seat in Arizona and committing fraud in Florida's senatorial and gubernatorial balloting. He complained that undocumented asylum seekers were invading the country so they could vote for Democrats. He suggested that Democratic voters were returning to the polls in disguise to vote more than once.

Months before his own election in 2016, candidate Trump began alleging voter fraud and warned that he might not accept the results if he lost. Even after winning, he insisted that millions of fraudulent votes had been cast against him. To substantiate his claims, he created a special commission to investigate the problem. It was quietly disbanded in early 2018 without producing any evidence.

At the same time, the administration has shown little interest in addressing genuine and documented threats to the integrity of US elections, including chronic problems like partisan gerrymandering and the fact that balloting is overseen by partisan officials in the states.

But the most glaring lapse is the president's refusal to clearly acknowledge and comprehensively combat Russian and other foreign attempts to meddle in American elections since 2016. The Homeland Security Department provided some assistance to states in protecting their voting and counting systems from outside meddling in 2018, but recent reports commissioned by the Senate Intelligence Committee indicate that foreign influence operations are ongoing across multiple online platforms, and that such campaigns are likely to expand and multiply in the future.

THE THREAT TO AMERICAN IDEALS ABROAD

Our poll found that a strong majority of Americans, 71 percent, believe the US government should actively support democracy and human rights in other countries. But America's commitment to the global progress of democracy has been seriously compromised by the president's rhetoric and actions. His attacks on the judiciary and the press, his resistance to anticorruption safeguards, and his unfounded claims of voting fraud by the opposition are all familiar tactics to foreign autocrats and populist demagogues who seek to subvert checks on their power.

Such leaders can take heart from Trump's bitter feuding with America's traditional democratic allies and his reluctance to uphold the nation's collective defense treaties, which have helped guarantee international security for decades. As former US defense secretary James Mattis put it in his resignation letter, "While the US remains the indispensable nation in the free world, we cannot protect our interests or serve that role effectively without maintaining strong alliances and showing respect to those allies."

Trump has refused to advocate for America's democratic values, and he seems to encourage the forces that oppose them. His frequent, fulsome praise for some of the world's worst dictators reinforces this perception. Particularly striking was his apparent willingness, at a summit in Helsinki, to accept the word of Vladimir Putin over his own intelligence agencies in assessing Russia's actions in the 2016 elections.

The president's rhetoric is echoed in countries with weaker defenses against attacks on their democratic institutions, where the violation of norms is often followed by systemic changes that intensify repression and entrench authoritarian governance.

For example, Cambodian strongman Hun Sen consolidated one-party rule in sham elections last summer after banning the main opposition party and shutting down independent media. He acknowledged that he and President Trump shared a point of view about journalists, saying, "Donald Trump understands that they are an anarchic group." Poland's president, whose party has sought to annihilate judicial independence and assert control over the press, similarly thanked Trump for fighting "fake news." Saudi Arabia's crown prince almost certainly ordered the assassination of a leading journalistic critic, apparently believing that the action would not rupture relations with the president of the United States. It seems he was correct.

As the United States ceases its global advocacy of freedom and justice, and the president casts doubt on the importance of basic democratic values for our own society, more nations may turn to China, a rising alternative to US leadership. The Chinese Communist Party has welcomed this trend, offering its authoritarian system as a model for developing nations. The resulting damage to the liberal international order—a system of alliances, norms, and institutions built up under Trump's predecessors to ensure peace and prosperity after World War II—will not be easily repaired after he leaves office.

NEITHER DESPAIR NOR COMPLACENCY

Ours is a well-established and resilient democracy, and we can see the effect of its antibodies on the viruses infecting it. The judiciary has repeatedly checked the power of the president, and the press has exposed his actions to public scrutiny. Protests and other forms of civic mobilization against administration policies are large and robust. More people turned out for the midterm elections than in previous years, and there is a growing awareness of the threat that authoritarian practices pose to Americans.

Yet the pressure on our system is as serious as any experienced in living memory. We cannot take for granted that institutional bulwarks against abuse of power will retain their strength, or that our democracy will endure perpetually. Rarely has the need to defend its rules and norms been more urgent. Congress must perform more scrupulous oversight of the administration than it has to date. The courts must continue to resist pressures on their independence. The media must maintain their vigorous reporting even as they defend their constitutional prerogatives. And citizens, including Americans who are typically reluctant to engage in the public square, must be alert to new infringements on their rights and the rule of law, and demand that their elected representatives protect democratic values at home and abroad.

Freedom House will also be watching and speaking out in defense of US democracy. When leaders like Mohammed bin Salman or Victor Orbán take actions that threaten human liberty, it is our mission to document their abuses and condemn them. We must do no less when the threats come from closer to home.

Introduction

The *Freedom in the World 2019* survey contains reports on 195 countries and 14 territories. Each country report begins with a section containing the following information: **population, capital, political rights rating** (numerical rating), **civil liberties rating** (numerical rating), **freedom rating** (the average of the political rights and civil liberties ratings), **freedom status** (Free, Partly Free, or Not Free), and **"electoral democracy" designation**.. Each territory report begins with a section containing the same information, except for the capital and the electoral democracy designation. The population figures are drawn primarily from the *2018 World Population Data Sheet* of the Population Reference Bureau.

The **political rights** and **civil liberties** ratings range from 1 to 7, with 1 representing the most free and 7 the least free. The **status** designation of Free, Partly Free, or Not Free, which is determined by the average of the political rights and civil liberties ratings, indicates the general state of freedom in a country or territory. A brief explanation of status changes is provided for each country or territory as required. Any improvements or declines in the ratings since the previous survey are noted next to the relevant number in each report. For a full description of the methods used to determine the survey's ratings, please see the chapter on the survey's methodology.

Following the section described above, each country and territory report is composed of three parts: an **overview**, bullets on **key developments**, and an analysis of **political rights and civil liberties**. The overview provides a succinct, general description that explains the country or territory's place on the 0–7 rating scale; bullets on key developments summarize key events that took place in 2018; and the section on political rights and civil liberties analyzes the degree of respect for the rights and liberties that Freedom House uses to evaluate freedom in the world. This section is composed of seven parts that correspond to the seven main subcategories in the methodology and justify a country or territory's score for each indicator. The scores for each indicator, subcategory, and category, along with any changes from the previous year, are noted next to the relevant subheading.

Country Reports

Afghanistan

Population: 36,500,000
Capital: Kabul
Political Rights Rating: 5
Civil Liberties Rating: 6
Freedom Rating: 5.5
Freedom Status: Not Free
Electoral Democracy: No

Overview: Afghanistan's constitution provides for a unitary state, headed by a directly elected president, with significant checks from the parliament and a wide range of rights guaranteed to citizens. However, an insurgency waged by Islamist militants has undermined the writ of the state in much of the rural hinterland. Political rights and civil liberties are curtailed in practice by violence, corruption, patronage, and flawed electoral processes.

KEY DEVELOPMENTS IN 2018:

- The Taliban rebel movement further escalated its military campaign; meanwhile, fighters loyal to the Islamic State (IS) militant group attacked Shiite targets. American air strikes against both groups continued throughout the year. The conflict continued to cause mass internal displacement, and civilian casualties increased compared to the previous year.
- After a four-year delay, more than four million people voted in the October parliamentary elections, despite severe security threats from the Taliban and long lines at polling stations caused by poor organization. Due to the chaos surrounding the elections, official results had not yet been published at year's end.
- In October, newly appointed US Special Envoy Zalmay Khalilzad met with Taliban representatives in Qatar to discuss a resolution to the long-standing Afghan conflict. The meeting reportedly occurred without the knowledge of the Afghan government, with which the Taliban refuses to negotiate.
- Attacks by IS and the Taliban threatened journalists throughout the year; in April, nine journalists were killed when a bomb detonated at the site of an earlier suicide bombing in Kabul. IS claimed responsibility for both attacks.

POLITICAL RIGHTS: 13 / 40 (+1)

A. ELECTORAL PROCESS: 3 / 12 (+1)

A1. Was the current head of government or other chief national authority elected through free and fair elections? 1 / 4

Afghanistan's president is directly elected for up to two five-year terms and has the power to appoint ministers, subject to parliamentary approval. In the 2014 presidential election, the two first-round winners—Abdullah Abdullah, a former foreign minister, who received 45 percent of the vote, and Ashraf Ghani, a former finance minister, who took 32 percent—faced off in a final round held that June, with a high reported turnout. After the Independent Election Commission (IEC) published preliminary results showing Ghani leading by more than 10 percentage points, the Abdullah camp alleged voter fraud, claimed victory, and threatened to overthrow the government. The United States brokered an agreement calling for an internationally supervised audit and the formation of a National Unity Government (NUG). Ghani became president, and Abdullah became chief executive, a new post resembling that of a prime minister, which was not supported by the constitution. The final vote tallies for the two candidates were not officially announced, and the NUG's stated goals of overhauling the electoral system and convening a *loya jirga* on constitutional reforms have yet to be accomplished.

A2. Were the current national legislative representatives elected through free and fair elections? 1 / 4 (+1)

In the directly elected lower house of the National Assembly, the 249-seat Wolesi Jirga (House of the People), members stand for five-year terms. In the 102-seat Meshrano Jirga (House of Elders), the upper house, the provincial councils elect two-thirds of the members for three- or four-year terms, and the president appoints the remaining third for five-year terms. The constitution envisages the election of district councils, which would also send members to the Meshrano Jirga, though these have not been established. Ten Wolesi Jirga seats are reserved for the nomadic Kuchi community, including at least three women, and 65 of the chamber's general seats are reserved for women.

Parliamentary elections, originally scheduled for 2014, were postponed amid security concerns, and the president extended the legislature's mandate with an apparently unconstitutional decree until elections were finally held in October 2018. Despite security threats from the Taliban, which threatened to punish people for voting, and poor organization by the IEC, more than four million people voted (approximately half of registered voters). Some poll workers were absent on election day due to fears of violence, and difficulties with the untested biometric identification system contributed to delays in opening polling stations, and long lines. Many people reportedly waited hours to vote, and some left before casting their ballots. The Taliban followed through on threats to carry out attacks across the country, which, according to the United Nations, killed 56 people and injured 379. The technical challenges and insecurity forced the IEC to add a second day of voting in some regions. In December, the Electoral Complaints Commission (ECC) ruled that all votes cast in Kabul Province were invalid due to widespread fraud, but the IEC subsequently overruled the decision. As a result of the chaos surrounding the election, official results had not been declared by the end of the year.

Score Change: The score improved from 0 to 1 because overdue parliamentary elections were held in October.

A3. Are the electoral laws and framework fair, and are they implemented impartially by the relevant election management bodies? 1 / 4

Elections are administered by the IEC, and disputes are adjudicated by the ECC. The dispute between the IEC and the ECC surrounding the latter body's decision to cancel all votes in Kabul during the 2018 parliamentary elections was the latest development reflecting longstanding dysfunction and weak management of the electoral process, which has often led to delays in holding elections and low turnout. In addition to fraud, the ECC had cited mismanagement by the IEC as among the reasons for its decision. The IEC in turn called the ECC's decision politically motivated before revoking it. Civil society groups complained that the ECC had acted hastily in annulling all votes in the populous region, a decision which, if enforced, would have disenfranchised approximately one million voters. The chaos and delays that surrounded the Kabul voting controversy prompted speculation that the 2019 presidential vote could also be delayed.

In 2016, after delays, a new electoral law was adopted. However, among other shortcomings, it retained the provincial boundaries as parliamentary constituencies, resulting in some excessively large constituencies—such as Kabul—as well as several ethnically polarized constituencies.

B. POLITICAL PLURALISM AND PARTICIPATION: 7 / 16

B1. Do the people have the right to organize in different political parties or other competitive political groupings of their choice, and is the system free of undue obstacles to the rise and fall of these competing parties or groupings? 2 / 4

Most candidates for elected office run as independents and participate in fluid alliances linked to local and regional patronage networks. Political parties have been free to seek registration since 2005, though they are typically centered on particular ethnic groups or personalities rather than coherent policy platforms.

B2. Is there a realistic opportunity for the opposition to increase its support or gain power through elections? 2 / 4

Multiple opposition leaders and parties seek power through elections, but the recurrent problem of fraud and the lack of a stable party system mean they cannot be certain that their popular support will translate into victory at the polls.

Opposition figures have accused the government of undermining them and promoting rivals. In 2018, President Ghani continued his efforts to remove Atta Mohammed Noor, a prominent member of the opposition Coalition for the Salvation of Afghanistan and leader of the Jamiat-e Islami party, from his position as provincial governor of Balkh Province. Noor accused Ghani of trying to force the removal in order to neutralize him as a potential candidate for the 2019 presidential election. Noor finally agreed to step down in March in exchange for a number of concessions from Ghani.

In July, the Coalition for the Salvation of Afghanistan announced that it was forming the new Grand National Coalition of Afghanistan, which brought together almost all significant opposition parties representing a broad cross section of ethnic groups. Analysts believe the new coalition, which has the support of former president Hamid Karzai, could field a strong competitor in the 2019 presidential election.

B3. Are the people's political choices free from domination by the military, foreign powers, religious hierarchies, economic oligarchies, or any other powerful group that is not democratically accountable? 1 / 4

The insurgency waged by the Taliban movement across the country is the main constraint on Afghans' political choices. The Taliban threatened and intimidated voters ahead of the 2018 parliamentary elections to discourage their participation, and carried out a number of attacks, both during the campaign period and on election day, which forced residents to choose between exercising their democratic rights or ensuring their personal safety.

Normal political activity is also hampered by the presence of IS and various militias with links to the government, local power brokers, or foreign states. Government officials and politicians at all levels are regularly targeted for assassination, including Abdul Jabar Qahraman, a member of parliament from Helmand, who was killed in October 2018 when a bomb exploded in his campaign office; the Taliban claimed responsibility for the attack.

B4. Do various segments of the population (including ethnic, religious, gender, LGBT, and other relevant groups) have full political rights and electoral opportunities? 2 / 4

The constitution recognizes multiple ethnic and linguistic minorities and provides more guarantees of equal status to minorities than historically have been available in Afghanistan. Since 2001, the traditionally marginalized Shiite Muslim minority, which includes most ethnic Hazaras, has enjoyed increased levels of political representation and participation in national institutions. Nevertheless, participation is curtailed for all segments of the population by insecurity, flawed elections, and the dominance of powerful patronage networks. Members of minority groups have limited practical opportunities to organize independently, outside the networks of established leaders.

Women's political participation has been constrained by threats, harassment, and social restrictions on traveling alone and appearing in public. The proportion of women registered as voters declined from 41 percent in 2010 to 34 percent in 2018. In 2018, over 400 women competed for the 68 parliamentary seats allocated to female representatives.

C. FUNCTIONING OF GOVERNMENT: 3 / 12

C1. Do the freely elected head of government and national legislative representatives determine the policies of the government? 1 / 4

The ability of the president and his cabinet, acting in concert with the legislature, to set and implement state policies is limited by a number of factors. The government remains heavily dependent on military and economic support from the United States and its allies, and it is unable to enforce its laws and decisions in parts of the country controlled by the Taliban and other insurgents.

An October 2018 meeting between newly appointed US Special Envoy Zalmay Khalilzad and Taliban representatives, which reportedly occurred in Qatar without President Ghani's knowledge, raised concerns about the marginalization of the NUG. Ghani had repeatedly asserted that any peace process must be "Afghan-led and Afghan-owned," but the Taliban has refused to negotiate directly with the Afghan government. Ghani expressed concerns that his exclusion from negotiations could further weaken his coalition, already under strain due to insecurity and political opposition, and hinder his ability to govern.

C2. Are safeguards against official corruption strong and effective? 1 / 4

There have been periodic arrests, prosecutions, and dismissals of civilian and military officials accused of corruption, and an Anti-Corruption Justice Centre (ACJC) was established in 2016, bringing together specialized police, prosecutors, and courts to focus on high-level malfeasance. Nevertheless, corruption remains an endemic problem, law enforcement agencies and the judiciary are themselves compromised by graft and political pressure, and the most powerful officials and politicians effectively enjoy impunity. An October 2018 report from the US Special Inspector General for Afghanistan Reconstruction (SIGAR) confirmed that the ACJC was failing to prosecute senior officials accused of corruption.

Afghan commentators report that many senior positions in government can only be obtained through corrupt payments to figures in the relevant ministry and presidential office. Ethnic background and personal or political ties also play an influential role in appointments.

C3. Does the government operate with openness and transparency? 1 / 4

The government has made some progress on fiscal probity and oversight of state spending. For example, the National Procurement Commission, established in 2014 and chaired by the president to guide the National Procurement Authority (NPA), has taken the lead in reforming procurement procedures and attempting to maintain transparency throughout the government. The NPA has centralized supervision of state contracts and claims to have saved hundreds of millions of dollars in 4,780 approved contracts through the end of 2018, though its lack of independence from the president has raised concerns about impartiality.

The beneficial ownership of mining companies that receive government contracts is often unknown, allowing individuals and entities legally prohibited from winning contracts, such as members of parliament, to participate.

CIVIL LIBERTIES: 14 / 60
D. FREEDOM OF EXPRESSION AND BELIEF: 6 / 16
D1. Are there free and independent media? 2 / 4

Afghanistan is home to a vibrant media sector, with multiple outlets in print, radio, and television that collectively carry a wide range of views and are generally uncensored. Media providers include independent and commercial firms, as well as a state broadcaster and outlets tied to specific political interests.

However, journalists face the threat of harassment and attack by IS, the Taliban, and government-related figures attempting to influence how they are covered in the news. The media advocacy organization Nai recorded dozens of incidents of violence and harassment against media workers and journalists in 2018, and the Committee to Protect Journalists (CPJ) said 13 journalists were killed in connection with their work during the year. These included nine journalist killed in April 2018, when a bomb detonated at the site of an earlier suicide bombing in Kabul. IS claimed responsibility for both attacks.

A rapid expansion in the availability of mobile phones, the internet, and social media has granted many Afghans greater access to diverse views and information. The NUG has publicly supported media freedom and cooperated with initiatives to counter security threats to the media. Despite these stated commitments to a free press, high-level officials, including President Ghani, frequently question the validity of stories critical of the government and attempt to discredit journalists, undermining trust and confidence in the media.

D2. Are individuals free to practice and express their religious faith or nonbelief in public and private? 1 / 4

While religious freedom has improved since 2001, it is still hampered by violence and discrimination aimed at religious minorities and reformist Muslims. The constitution established Islam as the official religion and guaranteed freedom of worship to other religions. Blasphemy and apostasy by Muslims are considered capital crimes, and non-Muslim proselytizing is strongly discouraged. Conservative social attitudes, intolerance, and the inability or unwillingness of law enforcement officials to defend individual freedoms mean that those perceived as violating religious and social norms are highly vulnerable to abuse.

During 2016 and 2017, the UN documented 51 attacks against places of worship and religious leaders. IS militants continued their campaign of deadly attacks on Shiite mosques and cultural centers in 2018. In August, IS claimed responsibility for a suicide attack on a Shiite mosque in Gardez that killed at least 48 people. In July, an IS suicide bomber attacked a delegation of Sikh and Hindu leaders in Jalalabad to meet with President Ghani, killing 19, including a Sikh parliamentary candidate.

D3. Is there academic freedom, and is the educational system free from extensive political indoctrination? 1 / 4

Academic freedom is largely tolerated in government-controlled areas. In addition to public schooling, there has been a growth in private education, with new universities enjoying full autonomy from the government, though there are serious shortages of qualified instructors and up-to-date teaching materials. Government security forces and the Taliban have both taken over schools to use as military posts. The expansion of Taliban control in rural areas has left an increasing number of public schools outside of government control.

The Taliban operate an education commission in parallel to the official Ministry of Education. Although their practices vary between areas, some schools under Taliban control reportedly allow teachers to continue teaching, but ban certain subjects and replace them with Islamic studies.

D4. Are individuals free to express their personal views on political or other sensitive topics without fear of surveillance or retribution? 2 / 4

Although private discussion in government-held areas is largely free and unrestrained, discussion of a political nature is more dangerous for Afghans living in contested or Taliban-controlled areas. Government security agencies have increased their ability to monitor the internet, including social media platforms. However, this monitoring has not yet had a perceptible impact on social media use.

E. ASSOCIATIONAL AND ORGANIZATIONAL RIGHTS: 4 / 12

E1. Is there freedom of assembly? 2 / 4

The constitution guarantees the right to peaceful assembly, subject to some restrictions, but it is upheld erratically from region to region. The police sometimes fire live ammunition when attempting to break up demonstrations. Protests are also vulnerable to attacks by IS and the Taliban. In September 2018, a suicide bomber killed 68 demonstrators in Nangarhar Province who were protesting the alleged abuses of a high-ranking security official. No group claimed responsibility for the attack, but IS has an active presence in the region.

In January, the Wolesi Jirga voted to reject a presidential decree that would have given the police broad authority to prevent demonstrations.

E2. Is there freedom for nongovernmental organizations, particularly those that are engaged in human rights- and governance-related work? 1 / 4

The constitution guarantees the right to form nongovernmental organizations (NGOs), and both the legal framework and the national authorities are relatively supportive of civil society groups. NGOs play an important role in the country, particularly in urban areas, where thousands of cultural, welfare, and sports associations operate with little interference from authorities. However, NGOs are sometimes hampered by official corruption and bureaucratic reporting requirements, and the threat of violence by armed groups is a major obstacle to their activities. In January 2018, the international NGO Save the Children temporarily suspended its activities after an attack on its office in Jalalabad by a suicide bomber killed four of its staff.

E3. Is there freedom for trade unions and similar professional or labor organizations? 1 / 4

Despite broad constitutional protections for workers, labor rights are not well defined in law, and no effective enforcement or dispute-resolution mechanisms are currently in place. Unions are largely absent from the informal and agricultural sectors, which account for most Afghan workers.

F. RULE OF LAW: 2 / 16

F1. Is there an independent judiciary? 1 / 4

The judicial system operates haphazardly, and justice in many places is administered on the basis of a mixture of legal codes by inadequately trained judges. Corruption in the judiciary is extensive, with judges and lawyers often subject to threats and bribes from local leaders or armed groups. Informal justice systems, employing variants of both customary law and Sharia (Islamic law), are widely used to arbitrate disputes, especially in rural areas.

The Taliban have installed their own judiciary in areas they control, but many Taliban commanders impose arbitrary punishments without reference to this system.

F2. Does due process prevail in civil and criminal matters? 0 / 4

Prosecutions and trials suffer from a number of weaknesses, including lack of proper representation, excessive reliance on uncorroborated witness testimony, lack of reliable forensic evidence, arbitrary decision-making, and failure to publish court decisions. The police force is heavily militarized and primarily focused on its role as a first line of defense against insurgents in administrative centers. There are high levels of corruption and complicity in organized crime among police, particularly near key smuggling routes.

There is an entrenched culture of impunity for the country's political and military power brokers. In 2016, the former governor of Jowzjan Province, Ahmad Ishchi, accused First Vice President Abdul Rashid Dostum of ordering his arbitrary detention and sexual assault. During the subsequent investigation, Dostum was reportedly placed under house arrest but later left the country and remained abroad until July 2018. Upon his return, the charges against Dostum reportedly remained active, but authorities had not moved to prosecute him at year's end, and he was allowed to remain in office. Dostum had previously clashed with President Ghani, raising suspicions that the government was using the case to marginalize him politically, even if it lacked the will or power to uphold the law.

F3. Is there protection from the illegitimate use of physical force and freedom from war and insurgencies? 0 / 4

Despite peace talks between the US government and the Taliban, the militant group steadfastly refused to negotiate with the Afghan government through the end of 2018. The civil conflict continued to take a heavy toll on civilian life and safety in 2018, as the Taliban and IS carried out high-profile suicide attacks. The United Nations documented 3,804 civilian deaths and 7,189 injuries in 2018, a marked increase in casualties from 2017. Afghan security forces have also endured significant losses in the conflict; according to the government, as of November, more than 28,000 security personnel had been killed since 2015. The US further escalated its combat activities during the year, increasing air strikes, but President Donald Trump announced in December that the US military would withdraw 7,000 troops from Afghanistan in 2019.

The torture of detainees by Afghan police, military, and intelligence services reportedly remains common. Government-aligned strongmen and powerful figures within the security forces operate illegal detention centers. In 2018, President Ghani claimed to be cracking down on militia commanders who have perpetrated widespread abuses. In July, however, videos emerged of security personnel, deployed to arrest a Faryab military commander accused of rights violations, apparently abusing the commander's bodyguards, stoking outrage and leading to condemnation by human rights groups. At the end of the year, no charges had been filed against any of the perpetrators.

F4. Do laws, policies, and practices guarantee equal treatment of various segments of the population? 1 / 4

Despite some legal protections, religious and ethnic minorities remain subject to harassment and discrimination, including in employment and education. Ethnic-based patronage practices affect different groups' access to jobs depending on the local context. The population of non-Muslim minorities such as Hindus and Sikhs has shrunk to a tiny fraction of its former size due to emigration in recent decades. Women face severe disadvantages in the justice system, access to employment, and other matters, with harmful societal norms often overriding legal guarantees.

There is no legal protection for LGBT (lesbian, gay, bisexual, and transgender) people, who face societal disapproval and abuse by police. Same-sex sexual activity is considered illegal under the penal code and Sharia.

G. PERSONAL AUTONOMY AND INDIVIDUAL RIGHTS: 2 / 16

G1. Do individuals enjoy freedom of movement, including the ability to change their place of residence, employment, or education? 0 / 4

The constitution grants Afghans freedom of movement, residence, and travel abroad. These freedoms are severely circumscribed in practice by the ongoing civil conflict, which continued to cause mass displacement and render travel unsafe in much of the country in 2018. According to the Office of the UN High Commissioner for Refugees (UNHCR), more than 343,000 people were displaced by conflict in 2018. Opportunities for Afghans to seek refuge abroad have been curtailed in recent years, as the European Union (EU) has attempted to reinforce its external border and member states have increased deportations of failed asylum seekers, while Iran and Pakistan have compelled hundreds of thousands of refugees to return home.

G2. Are individuals able to exercise the right to own property and establish private businesses without undue interference from state or non-state actors? 1 / 4

Citizens are formally free to own property, buy and sell land, and establish businesses. However, economic freedoms are constrained by patronage, corruption, and the dominant economic role of a narrow, politically connected elite. Over the past decade the most profitable activities available to Afghans have been government and defense contracting, narcotics trafficking, and property and minerals development. Investors in all of these sectors have depended on connections to those in power, and land theft backed by the threat of force is a serious problem. A combination of harassment, extortion, and arbitrary taxation make for a highly unfavorable business climate for any investor hoping to operate within the law.

G3. Do individuals enjoy personal social freedoms, including choice of marriage partner and size of family, protection from domestic violence, and control over appearance? 0 / 4

Domestic violence against women remains pervasive. In 2017, the Ministry of Public Health estimated that 51 percent of women experience domestic violence in their lifetimes. However, women's rights activists maintain that only a small proportion of actual incidents are reported. According to a May 2018 report published by the United Nations, many cases of violence against women are dealt with by traditional mediation, rather than through the criminal justice system; this largely enables impunity for perpetrators.

Women's choices regarding marriage and divorce remain restricted by custom and discriminatory laws. The forced marriage of young girls to older men or widows to their husbands' male relations is a problem, and many girls continue to be married before the legal age of 16. The courts and the detention system have been used to enforce social control of women, for example by jailing those who defy their families' wishes regarding marriage.

G4. Do individuals enjoy equality of opportunity and freedom from economic exploitation? 1 / 4

The constitution bans forced labor and gives all citizens the right to work. However, debt bondage remains a problem, as does child labor, which is particularly prevalent in the carpet industry. Most human trafficking victims in Afghanistan are children trafficked internally to work in various industries, become domestic servants, settle debts, or be subjected to sexual exploitation. Children are also vulnerable to recruitment by armed militant groups, and to a lesser extent by government security forces.

Albania

Population: 2,900,000
Capital: Tirana
Political Rights Rating: 3
Civil Liberties Rating: 3
Freedom Rating: 3.0
Freedom Status: Partly Free
Electoral Democracy: Yes

Overview: Albania has a record of competitive elections, though political parties are highly polarized and often organized around leading personalities. Religious freedom and freedom of assembly are generally respected. Corruption and organized crime remain serious problems despite recent government efforts to address them, and the intermingling of powerful business, political, and media interests inhibits the development of truly independent news outlets.

KEY DEVELOPMENTS IN 2018:

- A number of antigovernment protests underscored public discontent with the government. These included massive demonstrations by university students against tuition hikes, and separate protests against a new toll road, a major development plan in Tirana, and a taxation scheme opposed by many small business owners.
- In response to the student protests, Prime Minister Edi Rama reshuffled half his cabinet in late December, and promised dialogue with students and fulfilment of their demands.
- An ongoing vetting process for members of the judiciary led to the dismissal or resignation of numerous judges over unexplained assets.
- A number of members of the ruling Socialist Party (PS) were charged with involvement in drug trafficking schemes.

POLITICAL RIGHTS: 28 / 40

A. ELECTORAL PROCESS: 8 / 12

A1. Was the current head of government or other chief national authority elected through free and fair elections? 3 / 4

The president is the head of state and is chosen by the parliament for a maximum of two five-year terms; the office does not hold executive power, though the president heads the military and plays a key role in selecting senior judges. The prime minister is the head of government, and is designated by the majority party or coalition. Because both the president and prime minister are selected by lawmakers, their legitimacy is generally dependent on the conduct of parliamentary elections.

In April 2017, Ilir Meta, the head of the Socialist Movement for Integration (LSI), was selected as president. PS leader Edi Rama retained his position as prime minister of Albania following the 2017 parliamentary elections.

A2. Were the current national legislative representatives elected through free and fair elections? 3 / 4

Albania is a parliamentary republic. The unicameral, 140-member Kuvendi (Assembly) is elected through proportional representation in 12 regional districts of varying size. All members serve four-year terms.

Events preceding the 2017 elections reflected ongoing distrust between the Democratic Party (PD)—the main opposition grouping—and the ruling PS. In December 2016, the president called parliamentary election for the following June. The PD began boycotting the parliament the following February, claiming that the PS would commit massive electoral fraud. A standoff ensued, with tensions escalating in May 2017, when the PD held a large opposition protest in Tirana. However, international mediators from the US and European Union (EU) facilitated an agreement between the two parties later that month, under which the PD was guaranteed several positions in the government, including one deputy prime minister, six ministers, the chairperson of the Central Election Commission (CEC), and directors of several public agencies.

Elections were held in June 2017, a week later than initially scheduled. The PS won 74 of the 140 seats, enough to govern without the support of other parties. Voter turnout was 46.8 percent. Election monitors from the Organization for Security and Co-operation in Europe (OSCE) praised the polls' conduct, but noted that the mediated agreement that facilitated the elections resulted in the "selective and inconsistent application" of electoral laws. The mission also noted allegations of vote-buying and voter intimidation.

A3. Are the electoral laws and framework fair, and are they implemented impartially by the relevant election management bodies? 2 / 4

The OSCE, in its report on the 2017 polls, expressed concern that the CEC had not always operated with transparency, and at times had failed to sanction parties that committed electoral violations, such as failing to adhere to gender quotas in certain districts. The OSCE additionally noted that the CEC faced a number of logistical challenges in administering elections due to the provisions of the political agreement that facilitated the polls, and that the agreement had subverted parts of the electoral framework. For example, as part of the deal a new CEC chairperson was installed weeks before the elections, outside of the standard legal procedure.

B. POLITICAL PLURALISM AND PARTICIPATION: 13 / 16

B1. Do the people have the right to organize in different political parties or other competitive political groupings of their choice, and is the system free of undue obstacles to the rise and fall of these competing parties or groupings? 3 / 4

Albanian citizens generally have the right to organize in political parties. The two main parties, the PS and the PD, are sharply polarized and given to personality-driven rivalry.

Candidates for legislative elections who do not belong to a party currently seated in the parliament must collect a set number of signatures in order to run. The OSCE noted that in 2017, the CEC refused requests by the opposition for additional scrutiny of signatures supporting candidates for certain parties, which reduced transparency and could potentially contribute to an unequal playing field among political parties.

B2. Is there a realistic opportunity for the opposition to increase its support or gain power through elections? 4 / 4

Albania's multiparty system provides ample opportunity for opposition parties to participate in the political process, and elections have resulted in the rotation of power among parties.

B3. Are the people's political choices free from domination by the military, foreign powers, religious hierarchies, economic oligarchies, or any other powerful group that is not democratically accountable? 3 / 4

People are generally free to make their own political choices, but powerful economic actors have some ability to shape the political sphere through their media holdings and influence on electoral campaigns.

B4. Do various segments of the population (including ethnic, religious, gender, LGBT, and other relevant groups) have full political rights and electoral opportunities? 3 / 4

Election officials provided voter education materials in minority languages for the 2017 polls.

Members of the Roma minority and other marginalized groups remain vulnerable to political exploitation and vote-buying schemes, such as ones involving the distribution of fuel vouchers or cash. Women are underrepresented both in politics and election administration roles.

C. FUNCTIONING OF GOVERNMENT: 7 / 12

C1. Do the freely elected head of government and national legislative representatives determine the policies of the government? 3 / 4

In 2017, elections, and thus the timely formation of a new government, were threatened by an impasse between the PD and PS that persisted until international mediators facilitated a political agreement. Once installed, Albanian governments are generally able to formulate and implement policy.

C2. Are safeguards against official corruption strong and effective? 2 / 4

Corruption is pervasive, and the EU has repeatedly called for rigorous implementation of antigraft measures. The Special Prosecutor Service was established as part of 2016 reforms, and is tasked with prosecuting high-level corruption; it is functional but has yet to achieve full operational capacity.

A number of high-profile PS figures have been recently accused with involvement in drug-trafficking schemes. PS lawmaker and former interior minister Saimir Tahiri was charged with corruption and drug trafficking in May 2018 and temporarily placed under house arrest. He resigned from the Assembly after being charged, and proceedings against him were ongoing at year's end. In October, two former Socialist lawmakers were arrested on charges of corruption and involvement in organized crime related to drug trafficking. They were released and placed under house arrest in November.

Fatmir Xhafaj, who had succeeded Tahiri as interior minister, resigned in October amid protests by the opposition that it was inappropriate for him to lead the ministry, given his half-brother's past drug-trafficking conviction. He was not charged with any crime.

C3. Does the government operate with openness and transparency? 2 / 4

A robust law on access to information is not well implemented. Public procurement processes and public finances are frequently opaque, though parliamentary procedures are more open and accessible.

CIVIL LIBERTIES: 40 / 60

D. FREEDOM OF EXPRESSION AND BELIEF: 13 / 16

D1. Are there free and independent media? 2 / 4

While the constitution guarantees freedom of expression, the intermingling of powerful business, political, and media interests inhibits the development of independent news outlets; most are seen as biased toward either the PS or the PD. Reporters have little job security and remain subject to lawsuits, intimidation, and occasional physical attacks by those facing media scrutiny. Print media has continued to experience declining revenue, which has driven down journalists' salaries.

The OSCE and international media organizations criticized an October 2018 announcement by Rama that news websites must register with the tax authority, as well as the Communications Authority's subsequent publication of a list of noncompliant sites, which it threatened with closure. Many of the outlets claimed they were already registered as businesses or nongovernmental organizations (NGOs). Rama claimed that registration requirement was part of antidefamation campaign.

D2. Are individuals free to practice and express their religious faith or nonbelief in public and private? 4 / 4

The constitution provides for freedom of religion, which is generally upheld in practice.

D3. Is there academic freedom, and is the educational system free from extensive political indoctrination? 3 / 4

The government typically does not limit academic freedom, though teachers in several districts have faced pressure ahead of elections to participate in political rallies. Access to higher education is affected by corruption.

D4. Are individuals free to express their personal views on political or other sensitive topics without fear of surveillance or retribution? 4 / 4

There are no significant restrictions on free and open private discussion, including for online blogs and social media.

E. ASSOCIATIONAL AND ORGANIZATIONAL RIGHTS: 9 / 12

E1. Is there freedom of assembly? 4 / 4

Freedom of assembly is generally respected. Demonstrations by opposition parties and civic groups are common, and they have generally been peaceful. A number of demonstrations took place in 2018. Civil society organizations demonstrated in July against a proposal to demolish the National Theatre in Tirana in order to build a new theatre and several skyscrapers. Following massive student protests against a university fee increase, which later grew to include demands for major changes in the university system, the prime minister reshuffled half his cabinet in late December, promising dialogue with students and fulfilment of their demands. Other protests during 2018, including those by small business owners over matters related to taxation, and local residents against a new toll road on a national highway, underscored public discontent with the government.

E2. Is there freedom for nongovernmental organizations, particularly those that are engaged in human rights- and governance-related work? 3 / 4

NGOs generally function without restriction, but have limited funding and policy influence.

E3. Is there freedom for trade unions and similar professional or labor organizations? 2 / 4

The constitution guarantees workers the rights to organize and bargain collectively, and most have the right to strike. However, effective collective bargaining remains limited, and union members have little protection against discrimination by employers.

F. RULE OF LAW: 9 / 16

F1. Is there an independent judiciary? 2 / 4

The constitution provides for an independent judiciary, but the underfunded courts are subject to political pressure and influence, and public trust in judicial institutions is low. Corruption in the judiciary remains a serious problem, and convictions of high-ranking judges for corruption and abuse of power are rare.

In 2016, parliament approved a variety of reforms designed to boost the independence and capacity of the judiciary, including the evaluation of current and prospective judges and prosecutors based on their professionalism, moral integrity, and independence. Vetting processes are ongoing, and in 2018 again led to the dismissal or resignation of many judges over unexplained assets.

F2. Does due process prevail in civil and criminal matters? 2 / 4

Constitutional guarantees of due process are upheld inconsistently. Trial procedures can be affected by corruption within the judicial system, and are sometimes closed to the public. Legal counsel is not always provided to those that cannot afford their own.

F3. Is there protection from the illegitimate use of physical force and freedom from war and insurgencies? 2 / 4

Reports of police abuse of detainees continues. Prison inmates suffer from poor living conditions and a lack of adequate medical treatment.

Drug-related crime remains a problem, as Albania is a transit country for heroin smugglers and a key site for European cannabis production.

Traditional tribal law is practiced in parts of northern Albania, and sometimes involves revenge killings.

F4. Do laws, policies, and practices guarantee equal treatment of various segments of the population? 3 / 4

Roma face significant discrimination in education, health care, employment, and housing. A 2010 law bars discrimination based on race and several other categories, including sexual orientation and gender identity, and a 2013 reform of the criminal code introduced protections against hate crimes and hate speech based on sexual orientation and gender identity. However, bias against LGBT (lesbian, gay, bisexual, and transgender) people remains strong in practice. Women are underrepresented in the workforce. Women living in rural areas, in particular, have fewer opportunities for employment and education than do men.

G. PERSONAL AUTONOMY AND INDIVIDUAL RIGHTS: 9 / 16

G1. Do individuals enjoy freedom of movement, including the ability to change their place of residence, employment, or education? 3 / 4

Albanians generally enjoy freedom of movement, though criminal activity and practices related to traditional honor codes limit these rights in some areas. People are generally free to change their place of residence or employment.

G2. Are individuals able to exercise the right to own property and establish private businesses without undue interference from state or nonstate actors? 2 / 4

Numerous property-restitution cases related to confiscations during the communist era remain unresolved. Illegal construction is a major problem, as is bribery linked to government approval of development projects.

G3. Do individuals enjoy personal social freedoms, including choice of marriage partner and size of family, protection from domestic violence, and control over appearance? 2 / 4

The government generally does not place explicit restrictions on social freedoms. Authorities in the past have indicating a willingness to recognize same-sex marriages, but no policy developments have followed.

Domestic violence is widespread, and while the parliament has adopted some measures to combat the problem in recent years, few cases are prosecuted. Police are poorly equipped to handle cases of domestic violence or spousal rape, which is often not understood to be a crime. A UN Women study found that 38 percent of women had been sexually harassed, or felt as risk of it, in public spaces in Albania, and many had not reported it to the police.

G4. Do individuals enjoy equality of opportunity and freedom from economic exploitation? 2 / 4

Albania has relatively robust labor laws, but lacks the capacity to enforce workplace safety and other protections. Conditions in the manufacturing, construction, and mining sectors are often substandard and put workers at risk.

Albania continues to struggle with human trafficking. However, authorities are becoming more proactive in addressing the issue, according to the US State Department's 2018 *Trafficking in Persons Report*, which noted an increased in funding for trafficking victims.

Algeria

Population: 42,700,000
Capital: Algiers
Political Rights Rating: 6
Civil Liberties Rating: 5
Freedom Rating: 5.5
Freedom Status: Not Free
Electoral Democracy: No

Overview: Political affairs in Algeria are dominated by a closed elite based in the military and the ruling party, the National Liberation Front (FLN). While there are multiple opposition parties in the parliament, elections are distorted by fraud, and electoral processes are not transparent. Other concerns include the suppression of street protests, legal restrictions on media freedom, and rampant corruption.

KEY DEVELOPMENTS IN 2018:
- In January, police violently broke up a sit-in protest by striking doctors, injuring dozens of participants and arresting others. Similar incidents were reported in March and April as the labor protests continued.
- Authorities pursued an ongoing series of prosecutions against adherents of Ahmadiyya, a heterodox Muslim group, during the year. In May, 27 Ahmadis received suspended prison sentences ranging from three to six months.
- Several journalists and bloggers faced criminal penalties for their work, including Marzoug Touati, who was sentenced to seven years in prison by an appeals court in June, in part for an interview with an Israeli government spokesperson that he disseminated online.

- In August and September, police cracked down on attempted gatherings by the reformist opposition movement Mouwatana, carrying out arrests and confiscating activists' mobile phones.

POLITICAL RIGHTS: 10 / 40

A. ELECTORAL PROCESS: 3 / 12

A1. Was the current head of government or other chief national authority elected through free and fair elections? 1 / 4

The president is directly elected to a five-year term. Constitutional revisions approved in 2016 reintroduced a two-term limit for the presidency, though President Abdelaziz Bouteflika, who had been in power since 1999 and was serving his fourth term as of 2018, was nevertheless eligible to seek reelection in 2019. The 2014 presidential vote was marred by ballot stuffing, multiple voting, inflated electoral rolls, and the misuse of state resources to benefit the incumbent. Moreover, the authorities were unable to give election observers access to the national electoral roll. Bouteflika was officially credited with 81.5 percent of the vote, easily defeating independent former prime minister Ali Benflis.

A2. Were the current national legislative representatives elected through free and fair elections? 1 / 4

The 462 members of the People's National Assembly, the lower house of Parliament, are directly elected to five-year terms. In the May 2017 elections, the ruling FLN and Democratic National Rally (RND) won a combined 261 seats. Several other parties each won a far smaller share of seats. An unpublished European Union (EU) assessment of the polls, acquired by the Algerian newspaper *Liberté*, noted serious deficiencies in the electoral process, including a general lack of access to voter lists and opaque vote-counting procedures. Opposition parties and other observers alleged widespread fraud, and media outlets carried videos recorded by voters that appeared to show ballot-box stuffing and other irregularities. Vote buying was also reported. Turnout was just under 36 percent.

The president appoints one-third of the members of the upper legislative house, the Council of the Nation, which has 144 members serving six-year terms. The other two-thirds are indirectly elected by local and provincial assemblies. Half of the chamber's mandates come up for renewal every three years. The ruling FLN secured 29 of the 48 indirectly elected seats at stake in December 2018, with the RND and smaller factions or independents taking the remainder.

A3. Are the electoral laws and framework fair, and are they implemented impartially by the relevant election management bodies? 1 / 4

Electoral management bodies are subject to government influence. In 2016, the government created the High Independent Commission for Election Oversight (HIISE) to supervise elections and respond to complaints. However, the body's head and all of its members are appointed by the president, and the Interior Ministry continues to play an important role in electoral administration. In 2017, the opposition and other observers questioned the independence of the HIISE and criticized the generally opaque management of the year's elections.

B. POLITICAL PLURALISM AND PARTICIPATION: 4 / 16

B1. Do the people have the right to organize in different political parties or other competitive political groupings of their choice, and is the system free of undue obstacles to the rise and fall of these competing parties or groupings? 1 / 4

The Interior Ministry must approve political parties before they can operate legally. Parties cannot form along explicitly ethnic lines. The Islamic Salvation Front (FIS), which swept the 1990 and 1991 elections that preceded Algeria's decade-long civil war, remains banned.

B2. Is there a realistic opportunity for the opposition to increase its support or gain power through elections? 1 / 4

Opposition parties play a marginal role in the national legislature. Election boycotts by opposition groups are not uncommon. Indecision among the opposition on whether to boycott the 2017 polls contributed to depressed turnout that harmed the competitiveness of the parties that chose to participate.

In August and September 2018, police cracked down on attempted gatherings by the new opposition movement Mouwatana, in some cases carrying out arrests and confiscating activists' mobile phones. Mouwatana, which formed earlier in 2018, opposed a fifth term for Bouteflika and called for democratic reforms.

B3. Are the people's political choices free from domination by the military, foreign powers, religious hierarchies, economic oligarchies, or any other powerful group that is not democratically accountable? 1 / 4

In recent years, there have been allegations of corruption and financial influence in the selection of political candidates, and of vote buying during elections. In 2017, gendarmes caught the son of FLN secretary general Djamel Ould Abbes with several candidate lists and around €200,000 ($230,000) in cash. He was detained but released shortly afterward, apparently without being charged.

B4. Do various segments of the population (including ethnic, religious, gender, LGBT, and other relevant groups) have full political rights and electoral opportunities? 1 / 4

Parties dominated by the ethnic Amazigh (Berber) community, like the Rally for Culture and Democracy (RCD) and the Socialist Forces Front (FFS), are allowed to operate, although they sometimes boycott elections. Such parties control a handful of municipalities, mainly concentrated in the Kabylie region.

Women hold 26 percent of the seats in the lower house. While women's participation in politics is increasing, many women are reportedly reluctant to run for office and have difficulty securing meaningful influence in the legislature and in intraparty debates. In 2017, some parties obscured the faces of women candidates on their campaign posters.

LGBT (lesbian, gay, bisexual, and transgender) people are politically marginalized and have little practical ability to fight for relevant antidiscrimination laws or the repeal of laws criminalizing same-sex sexual relations.

C. FUNCTIONING OF GOVERNMENT: 3 / 12

C1. Do the freely elected head of government and national legislative representatives determine the policies of the government? 1 / 4

The executive is extremely powerful, and Parliament plays only a marginal role in policymaking. Bouteflika, aging and in poor health, has increasingly withdrawn from political life and public appearances; several other figures exert strong influence over executive decisions, including the president's brother, Saïd Bouteflika; wealthy government-aligned businessmen; and senior military officials.

C2. Are safeguards against official corruption strong and effective? 1 / 4

Anticorruption laws, a lack of government transparency, low levels of judicial independence, and bloated bureaucracies contribute to widespread corruption. While lower-level officials have been held accountable for corrupt behavior, few corruption cases are filed against senior officials. In May 2018, the seizure of 701 kilograms of cocaine in the port of Oran led to an investigation that uncovered links between organized crime, security officers, public officials, and the children of prominent politicians. The head of the national police was dismissed in the wake of the scandal.

C3. Does the government operate with openness and transparency? 1 / 4

The country lacks legislation that guarantees citizens' access to official information. There is considerable opacity surrounding official decision-making procedures, the publication of official acts is rarely timely, and rules on asset disclosure by government officials are weak and poorly enforced.

CIVIL LIBERTIES: 24 / 60 (–1)
D. FREEDOM OF EXPRESSION AND BELIEF: 7 / 16
D1. Are there free and independent media? 1 / 4

Although some newspapers are privately owned and some journalists remain aggressive in their coverage of government affairs, most papers rely on government agencies for printing and advertising, encouraging self-censorship. Authorities sometimes block distribution of independent news outlets that are based abroad or online. A cybercrime law gives authorities the right to block websites that are "contrary to the public order or decency." Viewers can access unlicensed private television channels located in Algeria but legally based outside the country, though these are subject to government crackdowns, including office raids and confiscation of equipment. In September 2018, a group of 16 filmmakers denounced government attempts to censor their work or block its release in the country.

Authorities use legal mechanisms to harass the media and censor or punish controversial reporting. Several journalists and bloggers faced brief detentions, short jail terms, suspended sentences, or fines during 2018 for offenses including defamation and "undermining national unity." In one of the harsher verdicts, an appeals court sentenced blogger Merzoug Touati to seven years in prison in June; he had been arrested in January 2017 after conducting an interview with an Israeli Foreign Ministry spokesperson and publishing it online.

D2. Are individuals free to practice and express their religious faith or nonbelief in public and private? 1 / 4

Algeria's population is overwhelmingly Sunni Muslim. Religious communities may only gather to worship at state-approved locations. Proselytizing by non-Muslims is illegal. Religious minorities sometimes face repression. Authorities have cracked down on the small Ahmadi minority, claiming that its members denigrate Islam, threaten national security, and violate laws on associations. Among other cases in recent years, in June 2018 a group of 27 Ahmadis received suspended prison sentences ranging from three to six months each. Christians also occasionally suffer from state persecution. Several Protestant churches were ordered closed for legal violations during 2018, a Christian was fined for illegal proselytism in May, and a group of five Christians were charged with the same offense in October.

D3. Is there academic freedom, and is the educational system free from extensive political indoctrination? 2 / 4

Authorities generally do not interfere directly with the operations of universities, though due to restrictive laws that apply more generally, debate is somewhat circumscribed in practice. Academic work is also affected by state censorship of domestically published and imported books.

D4. Are individuals free to express their personal views on political or other sensitive topics without fear of surveillance or retribution? 3 / 4

Private discussion can take place relatively freely when it does not focus on certain sensitive topics. The government monitors internet activity in the name of national security and does not disclose information about the program's targets or range, which is thought to be extensive. Social media users and bloggers, particularly those with higher profiles, are subject to prosecution for critical comments. For example, activist blogger Abdullah Benaoum was sentenced to two years in prison in April 2018 over Facebook posts in which he accused the authorities of human rights abuses.

E. ASSOCIATIONAL AND ORGANIZATIONAL RIGHTS: 4 / 12 (−1)

E1. Is there freedom of assembly? 2 / 4

While protests are fairly common, engaging in unauthorized demonstrations can draw up to a year in prison, and the government regularly uses force to disrupt public assemblies. A long-standing ban on demonstrations in Algiers remained in place during 2018. Police intervened to preempt or disperse protests on political, economic, and labor issues throughout the year.

E2. Is there freedom for nongovernmental organizations, particularly those that are engaged in human rights- and governance-related work? 1 / 4

The 2012 law on associations effectively restricts the formation, funding, and activities of nongovernmental organizations (NGOs). Permits and receipts of application submission are required to establish and operate NGOs, but organizations often face considerable delays and bureaucratic obstacles when attempting to obtain such documents, leaving them in a legally precarious position. Two women's rights organizations were temporarily closed by the authorities in February 2018 on the grounds that they lacked registration receipts, which were eventually issued to them in September under a court order. NGOs must notify the government of staffing changes and submit detailed reports on their funding; those that accept foreign funding without government approval risk fines or imprisonment. In October 2018, a group of NGOs demanded the repeal of the law on associations.

E3. Is there freedom for trade unions and similar professional or labor organizations? 1 / 4 (−1)

The main labor federation, the General Union of Algerian Workers, has been criticized for being too close to the government and failing to advocate for workers' interests. Workers require government approval to establish new unions, and this is difficult to obtain in practice, leaving many unions without legal status. Authorities have increasingly clamped down on efforts to form independent unions and to stage strikes. In January 2018, security forces broke up a rally by workers affiliated with the Autonomous National Union of Electricity and Gas Workers (SNATEGS), which is not recognized by the authorities, and arrested more than 1,000 people. Also that month, police violently dispersed a sit-in protest by striking doctors in Algiers, reportedly injuring dozens of the protesters and arresting others. The doctors' labor protests continued over the subsequent months, and similar police actions occurred in March and April.

Score Change: The score declined from 2 to 1 due to the government's ongoing refusal to recognize many independent trade unions and its violent suppression of labor-related protests during the year.

F. RULE OF LAW: 6 / 16

F1. Is there an independent judiciary? 1 / 4

The judiciary is susceptible to government pressure, for instance regarding cases against people close to the presidency. Judges are appointed by the High Council of the Judiciary, which is led by the president and the justice minister. Individuals with financial resources or political connections can also influence judicial decisions. In July 2018, several judges were dismissed or placed under scrutiny after being implicated in the drug-trafficking case that was uncovered in May; the businessman at the center of the case had reportedly recorded his corrupt interactions with magistrates and other officials.

F2. Does due process prevail in civil and criminal matters? 1 / 4

The lack of independence on the part of judges and prosecutors often erodes the due process rights of defendants, particularly in politically fraught trials. Lengthy delays in bringing cases to trial are common. Prosecutors' requests to extend pretrial detention periods are typically granted. Security forces frequently conduct warrantless searches and engage in arbitrary arrests and short-term detentions.

F3. Is there protection from the illegitimate use of physical force and freedom from war and insurgencies? 2 / 4

A 2006 reconciliation law gave immunity to perpetrators of serious crimes during the civil war. Allegations of torture have decreased since the end of the war, but human rights activists still accuse the police of using excessive force and abusing detainees.

Terrorist groups continue to operate in Algeria, and in July 2018, a clash between security forces and an alleged jihadist cell led to the deaths of seven soldiers. However, attacks have grown less frequent in recent years, and no terrorist bombings were reported during 2018.

F4. Do laws, policies, and practices guarantee equal treatment of various segments of the population? 2 / 4

Officials have made modest efforts to address the Amazigh community's cultural demands. Tamazight, the Berber language, is now a national language.

Sub-Saharan African migrants, including refugees and asylum seekers, are often arbitrarily arrested and deported from the country—or simply abandoned at the desert border—without being given the opportunity to challenge the actions in court. In May 2018, the United Nations criticized the government for engaging in mass deportations of migrants.

LGBT people face severe discrimination and the risk of violence for expressing their sexual orientation, and many LGBT activists have fled the country. Same-sex sexual relations are punishable with two months to two years in prison; arrests have been reported in recent years, though prosecutions are less common.

The constitution guarantees gender equality, but women continue to face both legal and societal discrimination. Many women make lower wages than men in similar positions, and there are few women in company leadership positions. Sexual harassment, while punishable with fines and jail time, is nevertheless common in workplaces.

G. PERSONAL AUTONOMY AND INDIVIDUAL RIGHTS: 7 / 16

G1. Do individuals enjoy freedom of movement, including the ability to change their place of residence, employment, or education? 2 / 4

While most citizens are relatively free to travel domestically and abroad, the authorities closely monitor and limit access to visas for non-Algerians. Men of military draft age are not allowed to leave the country without official consent. The land border between Algeria and Morocco has been closed for years, separating families that live in the border areas and forcing many to resort to illegal smuggling networks for routine travel. Police reportedly limit the movement of sub-Saharan African migrants attempting to reach the Mediterranean coast. Married women younger than 18 must obtain the permission of their husbands to travel abroad.

G2. Are individuals able to exercise the right to own property and establish private businesses without undue interference from state or nonstate actors? 2 / 4

The government plays a dominant role in the economy, leaving little room for private competitors. Cronyism is also a major obstacle to private enterprise, with businesspeople not aligned with the regime often facing harassment by the authorities. Numerous regulations and their flawed implementation make Algeria one of the most difficult environments in the world in which to establish and operate a business. Inheritance rules favor men over women.

G3. Do individuals enjoy personal social freedoms, including choice of marriage partner and size of family, protection from domestic violence, and control over appearance? 2 / 4

Women do not enjoy equal rights in marriage and divorce. Domestic violence is common, and the laws against it are weak; for example, cases can be dropped if the victim forgives the alleged abuser. Women's rights groups report that between 100 and 200 women are killed in domestic abuse incidents each year. No law addresses spousal rape.

G4. Do individuals enjoy equality of opportunity and freedom from economic exploitation? 1 / 4

The weak rule of law, government involvement in the economy, and bureaucratic obstacles pose barriers to social mobility.

A 2009 law criminalized all forms of trafficking in persons, and Algeria reported its first conviction under the law in 2015. In recent years, the government has made an effort to enforce the ban through prosecutions and has provided protection for victims, though not systematically. Undocumented sub-Saharan African migrants are particularly susceptible to labor or sexual exploitation, including through debt bondage.

Andorra

Population: 80,000
Capital: Andorra la Vella
Political Rights Rating: 1
Civil Liberties Rating: 1
Freedom Rating: 1.0
Freedom Status: Free
Electoral Democracy: Yes

Overview: Andorra has a parliamentary system of government and regularly holds free and fair elections. However, the country has strict naturalization criteria, and more than 50 percent of the population consists of noncitizens who do not have the right to vote. Political rights and civil liberties are generally respected and safeguarded. However, domestic violence is a problem, the country is not fully compliant with international standards on accessibility for disabled people, and there is a notable wage gap between men and women. The small Muslim and Jewish communities lack dedicated cemeteries, and the country has no recognized mosque.

KEY DEVELOPMENTS IN 2018:

- In July, a well-publicized labor abuse scandal unfolded, involving an Andorran company that hired three Colombian employees without residence and work permits, and reportedly failed to pay their wages. The Department of Immigration legalized the employees' immigration status after the case came to light, and an investigation was initiated against the employer.
- In March, Andorra saw its first major strike in 85 years, when civil servants walked out on the job in protest of contract reforms proposed by the administration of Antoni Martí.
- In September, a protest against Andorra's strict antiabortion laws took place.
- Authorities continued working to address longstanding concerns about abuse of the country's banking system. A new law discouraging banking secrecy took effect at the start of the year.

POLITICAL RIGHTS: 39 / 40
A. ELECTORAL PROCESS: 12 / 12
A1. Was the current head of government or other chief national authority elected through free and fair elections? 4 / 4

Andorra has a parliamentary system, with a prime minister elected by and accountable to the parliament. The prime minister is usually the head of the largest party in the parliament, and their legitimacy rests largely on the conduct of parliamentary elections, which have historically been competitive and credible. Martí, head of the Democrats for Andorra (DA), was reelected as prime minister following that party's victory in the 2015 legislative elections.

Two unelected "co-princes," the French president and the bishop of La Seu d'Urgell, Spain, serve jointly as ceremonial heads of state.

A2. Were the current national legislative representatives elected through free and fair elections? 4 / 4

Members of the unicameral, 28-member Consell General are directly elected every four years through a mixed voting system. The most recent elections occurred in March 2015. The DA won 15 seats, followed by the Liberal Party of Andorra (PLA) with 8, an independent coalition with 3, and the Social Democracy and Progress party (SDP) with 2. International observers deemed the polls competitive, credible, and generally well administered. The next parliamentary elections are scheduled for April 2019.

A3. Are the electoral laws and framework fair, and are they implemented impartially by the relevant election management bodies? 4 / 4

The Electoral Law, which was last changed in 2014 to introduce regulations on campaign finance, provides a sound framework for free and fair elections. The Electoral Board supervises elections impartially.

B. POLITICAL PLURALISM AND PARTICIPATION: 15 / 16

B1. Do the people have the right to organize in different political parties or other competitive political groupings of their choice, and is the system free of undue obstacles to the rise and fall of these competing parties or groupings? 4 / 4

Political parties may form and operate freely, and there are a number of active parties in Andorra.

B2. Is there a realistic opportunity for the opposition to increase its support or gain power through elections? 4 / 4

There are no restrictions preventing the opposition from increasing its support through elections. Multiple opposition parties are currently represented in the Consell General.

B3. Are the people's political choices free from domination by the military, foreign powers, religious hierarchies, economic oligarchies, or any other powerful group that is not democratically accountable? 4 / 4

There are no powerful groups without democratic legitimacy that influence or limit the people's political choices.

B4. Do various segments of the population (including ethnic, religious, gender, LGBT, and other relevant groups) have full political rights and electoral opportunities? 3 / 4

More than 50 percent of the population consists of noncitizens who do not have the right to vote in national elections or run for elected office. Under Andorra's restrictive naturalization criteria, one must marry a resident Andorran or live in the country for more than 20 years to qualify for citizenship. Prospective citizens are also required to learn Catalan, the national language.

There are no specific policies to encourage the political participation of women, but women are active in politics, and hold 36 percent of seats in the legislature.

C. FUNCTIONING OF GOVERNMENT: 12 / 12

C1. Do the freely elected head of government and national legislative representatives determine the policies of the government? 4 / 4

The elected government and parliament exercise their powers without undue restraints from nonelected or nonstate actors, and freely determine the policies of the government.

C2. Are safeguards against official corruption strong and effective? 4 / 4

Government corruption is not viewed as a pressing issue in Andorra.

Significant progress was made to address concerns raised in a 2011 report by the Council of Europe's Group of States against Corruption (GRECO) about Andorra's laws concerning bribery and campaign finance. In a 2017 progress report, GRECO notes that eighteen of the twenty recommendations have now been satisfactorily implemented.

Authorities have continued making efforts to address longstanding concerns about abuse of the country's banking system. A law renouncing banking secrecy entered into force at the start of 2018. The bill was passed in 2016 and brings Andorra into line with European standards by mandating certain disclosures of information about accounts held by nonresidents.

C3. Does the government operate with openness and transparency? 4 / 4

No law exists to provide public access to government information. However, the government weekly publishes its main actions in a bulletin, which is accessible online.

CIVIL LIBERTIES: 55 / 60 (–2)
D. FREEDOM OF EXPRESSION AND BELIEF: 14 / 16 (–1)
D1. Are there free and independent media? 3 / 4

There are a number of daily and weekly newspapers, and one Andorran television station, operated by the public broadcaster Ràdio i Televisió d'Andorra. Business, political, and religious interests heavily influence media coverage. Reporting on the activities of Andorra's banks is particularly difficult.

D2. Are individuals free to practice and express their religious faith or nonbelief in public and private? 3 / 4 (–1)

Freedom of religion is generally respected, but the Catholic Church enjoys a privileged position that allows it to draw on some state support, and to bypass some bureaucratic processes that other faiths must adhere to.

Despite years of negotiations between the Muslim community and the government, there is no recognized mosque for the country's roughly 2,000 Muslims. The government has organized meetings with Jewish and Muslim communities to talk about the possible construction of a special cemetery where these groups may conduct burials according to their customs and beliefs, but progress toward establishing one has stalled.

Score Change: The score declined from 4 to 3 because the government continued to block the construction of a mosque, and because Jews and Muslims do not have their own cemeteries at which they may conduct burials according to their customs.

D3. Is there academic freedom, and is the educational system free from extensive political indoctrination? 4 / 4

There are no restrictions on academic freedom, and the educational system is free from indoctrination.

D4. Are individuals free to express their personal views on political or other sensitive topics without fear of surveillance or retribution? 4 / 4

Individuals are free to express views on sensitive subjects without fear of surveillance or retribution. Authorities are not known to illegally monitor private online communications.

E. ASSOCIATIONAL AND ORGANIZATIONAL RIGHTS: 11 / 12
E1. Is there freedom of assembly? 4 / 4

Andorran law provides for freedom of assembly, and the government respects this right in practice. Demonstrations against government policy and in response to other social and political topics take place on occasion. In September 2018, a protest against Andorra's strict antiabortion laws took place.

E2. Is there freedom for nongovernmental organizations, particularly those that are engaged in human rights- and governance-related work? 4 / 4

Various nongovernmental organizations (NGOs) are active in the country, and function without restriction. Human rights groups freely publish their findings, and sometimes cooperate with the government.

E3. Is there freedom for trade unions and similar professional or labor organizations? 3 / 4

The right to unionize is protected by the law and the constitution, but the right to strike is not legally guaranteed. There are also no laws in place to penalize antiunion discrimination or regulate collective bargaining. Fear of retribution prevents many employees from openly admitting their union membership.

However, in March 2018, Andorra saw its first major strike in 85 years, when civil servants walked out on the job in protest of reforms to their contracts proposed by the Martí administration.

F. RULE OF LAW: 15 / 16

F1. Is there an independent judiciary? 4 / 4

The judiciary is impartial and independent, and is generally free from pressure from the government.

F2. Does due process prevail in civil and criminal matters? 4 / 4

Defendants enjoy the presumption of innocence and the right to a fair trial, and due process is generally upheld in the criminal justice system. The constitution prohibits arbitrary arrest and imprisonment, but police can detain suspects for up to 48 hours without charge.

F3. Is there protection from the illegitimate use of physical force and freedom from war and insurgencies? 4 / 4

Andorra is free from war and insurgencies, and law enforcement agents are not known to use excessive force against civilians. Prison conditions are adequate.

F4. Do laws, policies, and practices guarantee equal treatment of various segments of the population? 3 / 4

Discrimination against women is illegal. However, the law does not require equal pay for equal work, and the Department of Statistics has estimated that women earned 22 percent less than men for comparable work, with the discrepancy rising for work in the financial sector. The government has sought to implement pay equality for public jobs.

In 2017, the government approved a law to protect the rights of people with disabilities and provide assistance to victims of racism or discrimination. However, the country is not fully compliant with international standards on accessibility for disabled people and ensuring their entry into the workforce.

G. PERSONAL AUTONOMY AND INDIVIDUAL RIGHTS: 15 / 16 (−1)

G1. Do individuals enjoy freedom of movement, including the ability to change their place of residence, employment, or education? 4 / 4

There are no restrictions on the freedom of movement, and people are generally free to change their place of employment, residence, and education.

G2. Are individuals able to exercise the right to own property and establish private businesses without undue interference from state or nonstate actors? 4 / 4

Citizens enjoy the right to own property and establish businesses.

G3. Do individuals enjoy personal social freedoms, including choice of marriage partner and size of family, protection from domestic violence, and control over appearance? 3 / 4 (−1)

Domestic violence is prohibited by law and punishable with prison sentences. The government pursues domestic violence cases and provides resources for victims. Nevertheless, domestic violence remains a serious problem, and sometimes involves violence against children.

Andorra remains one of the few countries in Europe where abortion is illegal, and women can serve jail time for undergoing the procedure. However, abortion remains relatively accessible in neighboring France and Spain.

A bill providing for civil unions between same-sex couples was ratified in 2014, but same-sex marriage is banned.

Score Change: The score declined from 4 to 3 due the persistence of restrictions on personal social freedoms, including a ban on same-sex marriage.

G4. Do individuals enjoy equality of opportunity and freedom from economic exploitation? 4 / 4

Andorran laws provide protections for most workers, including migrant workers. However, temporary workers are in a precarious position, as they must leave the country when their employment contract expires, leaving those with expired contracts vulnerable to potential abuse by employers. The Labor Inspections Office is proactive in addressing cases of violations of workers' rights.

In July 2018 a well-publicized labor abuse scandal unfolded, involving an Andorran company that had hired three Colombian employees without residence and work permits. The employees, who said their wages went unpaid and that labor conditions were inadequate, were initially ordered to leave Andorra. However, the Department of Immigration later legalized their immigration status, and an investigation was initiated against the employer.

There were no confirmed reports of human trafficking in Andorra in the past year.

Angola

Population: 30,400,000
Capital: Luanda
Political Rights Rating: 6
Civil Liberties Rating: 5 ↑
Freedom Rating: 5.5
Freedom Status: Not Free
Electoral Democracy: No

Overview: Angola has been ruled by the same party since independence, and authorities have systematically repressed political dissent. Corruption, due process violations, and abuses by security forces all remain common. Since President João Lourenço's election in 2017, the government has taken steps to crack down on endemic corruption and eased restrictions on the press and civil society, but serious governance and human rights challenges persist.

KEY DEVELOPMENTS IN 2018:
- In July, a Luanda court acquitted prominent journalist Rafael Marques de Morais and Mariano Bras, editor of the weekly newspaper *O Crime*, of defamation charges stemming from a 2016 story by Marques that implicated the attorney general in a corruption scheme.

- In September, former president José Eduardo dos Santos stepped down as chair of the ruling Popular Movement for the Liberation of Angola (MPLA) and was replaced by President Lourenço, a move that consolidated the president's control of the government.
- Also in September, authorities arrested José Filomeno dos Santos, former president dos Santos's son and former head of Angola's sovereign wealth fund, for alleged fraud, embezzlement of public funds, and money laundering. Filomeno is the most high-profile figure arrested since Lourenço initiated an anticorruption campaign following his 2017 election.

POLITICAL RIGHTS: 11 / 40 (+1)

A. ELECTORAL PROCESS: 3 / 12

A1. Was the current head of government or other chief national authority elected through free and fair elections? 0 / 4

The 2010 constitution abolished direct presidential elections. Instead, the head of the national list of the political party receiving the most votes in general elections becomes president, without any confirmation process by the elected legislature. The constitution permits the president to serve a maximum of two five-year terms, and to directly appoint the vice president, cabinet, and provincial governors.

In December 2016, the MPLA announced that Defense Minister João Lourenço, who was also the MPLA vice president, would be its presidential candidate in 2017. The decision was made by the MPLA's political bureau, without public consultation. The MPLA retained power in the 2017 legislative elections, and Lourenço succeeded dos Santos, who had been in power for 38 years.

A2. Were the current national legislative representatives elected through free and fair elections? 2 / 4

Angola's 220-seat, unicameral National Assembly, whose members are elected to five-year terms by proportional representation, has little power, and most legislation originates in the executive branch.

In the 2017 legislative polls, the MPLA won 61 percent of the vote and 150 seats, while the opposition National Union for the Total Independence of Angola (UNITA) took 27 percent and 51 seats, and the Broad Convergence for the Salvation of Angola–Electoral Coalition (CASA–CE) won 9 percent and 16 seats. Two smaller parties won the remainder. An African Union (AU) monitoring mission praised the elections' conduct, noting that they were peaceful and that there was a broad consensus that polling preparations and processes were better organized than in past elections. However, the prevalence of biased progovernment media, deficiencies in voter registration processes, and the MPLA's use of public resources in its campaign hampered the opposition. There were also reports of postelection violence in some locations.

Alleging grave irregularities at the National Election Commission (CNE), including manipulation of the vote count, opposition leaders called the polls fraudulent and jointly disputed the results. The Constitutional Court dismissed their claim, citing a lack of evidence. Opposition figures elected to the National Assembly ultimately took their seats—a move that prompted intense criticism from their political base.

A3. Are the electoral laws and framework fair, and are they implemented impartially by the relevant election management bodies? 1 / 4

The law states that the makeup of the CNE should reflect the disposition of power in the National Assembly, which gives an advantage to the MPLA. The political opposition, in its challenge of the 2017 election results, cited serious misconduct and a lack of transparency on the part of the CNE.

B. POLITICAL PLURALISM AND PARTICIPATION: 6 / 16

B1. Do the people have the right to organize in different political parties or other competitive political groupings of their choice, and is the system free of undue obstacles to the rise and fall of these competing parties or groupings? 2 / 4

There is a multiparty system in place, but competition is limited. The process for creating new political parties is fraught with bureaucratic obstacles and attempts at co-optation, factors that severely hinder public confidence in new parties.

B2. Is there a realistic opportunity for the opposition to increase its support or gain power through elections? 1 / 4

There is little space for the opposition to increase its parliamentary representation, much less gain power through elections. Angola has never experienced a transfer of power between rival parties. Nevertheless, opposition parties are building public support, particularly in Luanda.

B3. Are the people's political choices free from domination by the military, foreign powers, religious hierarchies, economic oligarchies, or any other powerful group that is not democratically accountable? 1 / 4

MPLA-aligned economic oligarchies nurture a system of dependency and patronage that can subvert candidates' and voters' ability to freely express their political choices.

B4. Do various segments of the population (including ethnic, religious, gender, LGBT, and other relevant groups) have full political rights and electoral opportunities? 2 / 4

While societal pressures can discourage women from active political participation, women's rights advocates have an increasingly vocal presence in political life. In September 2018, Luísa Damião became the deputy president of the MPLA, making her the highest-ranking woman in the party leadership, which has long been dominated by men.

Discussion of issues affecting LGBT (lesbian, gay, bisexual, and transgender) people are taboo, and such topics remain absent from political debate.

C. FUNCTIONING OF GOVERNMENT: 2 / 12 (+1)

C1. Do the freely elected head of government and national legislative representatives determine the policies of the government? 1 / 4

The country has been ruled by the MPLA since independence, and the president is expected to consult routinely with the party's political bureau. Former president dos Santos retained his position as head of the MPLA for a year after President Lourenço's election, allowing him to maintain considerable power and influence over governance. In September 2018, dos Santos was finally replaced by Lourenço as party leader, enabling the new president to consolidate his authority.

Executive powers are broad and varied, leaving the parliament to act largely as a rubber stamp in approving the president's policies. Like his predecessor, President Lourenço frequently adopts legislation by presidential decree, including a major law enacted in May to regulate the natural-gas sector.

C2. Are safeguards against official corruption strong and effective? 1 / 4 (+1)

After decades of MPLA rule, corruption and patronage have become entrenched in nearly all segments of public and private life.

President Lourenço has stressed his willingness to fight endemic corruption since his 2017 election campaign, and a number of high-profile former officials from the dos Santos administration have been arrested. In September 2018, José Filomeno dos Santos, the former president's son and former head of Angola's sovereign wealth fund, was arrested for alleged fraud, embezzlement of public funds, and money laundering. Filomeno allegedly transferred $500 million in state funds to a bank account in the United Kingdom. He remained in detention at year's end. Isabel dos Santos, the daughter of the former president, had been fired in 2017 from her position as head of the state oil company, Sonangol, whose revenues largely funded the patronage system that helped keep her father in power for nearly four decades.

Score Change: The score improved from 0 to 1 because an anticorruption drive under President João Lourenço has led to the arrests of some powerful political figures.

C3. Does the government operate with openness and transparency? 0 / 4

Government operations are generally opaque. However, Lourenço's administration has moved to improve transparency in the notoriously corrupt oil sector. In August 2018, the oil minister announced that a new independent regulator would be established to oversee the industry beginning in 2019, curtailing the power of Sonangol. Most importantly, the regulator will manage concessions, which were still controlled by Sonangol as of 2018.

CIVIL LIBERTIES: 20 / 60 (+4)

D. FREEDOM OF EXPRESSION AND BELIEF: 7 / 16

D1. Are there free and independent media? 1 / 4

The Angolan state owns most media in the country. Many ostensibly private outlets are owned by senior officials of the MPLA and act as mouthpieces of the regime. However, in 2017, Lourenço replaced the heads of several major state-owned media outlets and called for the outlets to serve the public. In 2018, more voices gained access to the media, including civil society groups and opposition figures, and news outlets showed a greater willingness to carry criticism of the government.

In July 2018, a Luanda court acquitted prominent journalist Rafael Marques de Morais and Mariano Bras, editor of the weekly newspaper *O Crime*, on charges of "outrage to a body of sovereignty and injury against public authority." The case stemmed from a 2016 story by Marques that implicated the attorney general in a corruption scheme. Observers viewed the acquittal as a step forward for press freedom, given Angola's history of repression and intimidation of critical journalists.

Despite these improvements, the legal and regulatory environment for journalists remained restrictive at year's end. Defamation was still considered a criminal offense, and press freedom advocates had yet to convince the government to reform the repressive legal framework.

D2. Are individuals free to practice and express their religious faith or nonbelief in public and private? 2 / 4

The constitution guarantees religious freedom, but the government imposes onerous criteria on religious groups for official recognition, which is required for the legal construction of houses of worship. Notably, many Pentecostal churches—which have had a profound social impact in Angola—remain unregistered. In October 2018, the government passed a decree giving unregistered churches 30 days to collect 100,000 membership signatures. Once the deadline passed, authorities began closing down the 4,000 unregistered churches across the country that failed to gather the required signatures, leading to an outcry among religious leaders. The decree also barred all meetings by unregistered religious groups, even in private homes.

There are no registered Muslim groups, and Muslim communities have been more vocal in their demands for recognition and the right to worship freely.

D3. Is there academic freedom, and is the educational system free from extensive political indoctrination? 2 / 4

Academics must maintain a façade of agreement with the MPLA's preferred narratives and refrain from open criticism of the party, or risk losing their positions. Those who voice dissent are often monitored by security services.

D4. Are individuals free to express their personal views on political or other sensitive topics without fear of surveillance or retribution? 2 / 4

In recent years, there has been somewhat less fear of retribution for expressing criticism of the government or controversial opinions in private conversations. However, self-censorship persists, fueled by concerns that a perceived intent to organize against the government could result in reprisals.

While internet access is increasing in Angola, the government actively monitors online activity. Known surveillance of civil society groups, journalists, and academics can leave people reluctant to speak out.

E. ASSOCIATIONAL AND ORGANIZATIONAL RIGHTS: 6 / 12 (+3)

E1. Is there freedom of assembly? 2 / 4 (+1)

Although constitutional guarantees of freedom of assembly have been poorly upheld, President Lourenço's government showed greater tolerance for public demonstrations during 2018, as reflected by a dramatic increase in protests and a corresponding decline in police crackdowns and arrests of demonstrators throughout the year.

Despite these advances, the authorities did arrest and detain some peaceful demonstrators. In August, for example, security forces arrested 13 separatists in the Cabinda region who were organizing a public debate on independence for the oil-rich exclave. A week after their arrest, a court dismissed the charges against them.

Score Change: The score improved from 1 to 2 due to a decrease in crackdowns on protests and public demonstrations, which encouraged people to exercise assembly rights more robustly.

E2. Is there freedom for nongovernmental organizations, particularly those that are engaged in human rights- and governance-related work? 2 / 4 (+1)

Nongovernmental organizations (NGOs) working on human rights and governance are closely monitored. The MPLA traditionally made vocal attempts to discredit their work and sometimes threatened such groups with lawsuits and outright closure, prompting many to curtail their activities.

In 2018, however, the environment for NGOs improved significantly, with a reduction in official interference. The government showed a greater willingness to engage in constructive dialogue with civil society groups. In December, Lourenço met with a number of prominent NGO leaders, including several who have been highly critical of the government.

Score Change: The score improved from 1 to 2 because NGOs, including those that were critical of the government, were able to operate with less interference from authorities, and the government showed greater receptiveness to the views of civil society.

E3. Is there freedom for trade unions and similar professional or labor organizations? 2 / 4 (+1)

Certain employees who provide services considered essential—including prison guards and firefighters, but also workers in the oil sector—may not legally strike. Unions not associated with the MPLA have faced interference and harassment. However, the government allowed more strikes to proceed without interference or repression in 2018. Notably, the National Teachers' Union (SINPROF) organized a strike in April that resulted in a deal with the government for improved pay and working conditions. Additional strikes by nurses and workers in the justice sector also went ahead without incident during the year.

Score Change: The score improved from 1 to 2 because authorities allowed more strikes to occur without intervening.

F. RULE OF LAW: 4 / 16 (+1)

F1. Is there an independent judiciary? 1 / 4

The president appoints Supreme Court judges to life terms without legislative input. Corruption and political pressure from the MPLA contribute to the judiciary's general inefficacy and undermine its independence. In 2018, political interference in the courts appeared to subside somewhat, as demonstrated by the acquittals of Marques and Bras, who had exposed alleged corruption among political elites, as well as the dismissal of some charges against peaceful demonstrators.

In 2017, the Constitutional Court also displayed independence by striking down a presidential decree signed by dos Santos in 2015 that imposed tighter restrictions on NGOs. However, another controversial ruling that year by the same court dismissed an opposition challenge of the 2017 election results and further concluded that claimants had forged documents they submitted to the court.

F2. Does due process prevail in civil and criminal matters? 1 / 4

Constitutional guarantees of due process are poorly upheld. Many defendants are unable to afford legal counsel, and the state largely fails to provide qualified legal aid to those who need it. Arbitrary arrest and lengthy pretrial detention remain problems.

F3. Is there protection from the illegitimate use of physical force and freedom from war and insurgencies? 1 / 4 (+1)

Security forces enjoy impunity for violent acts, including torture and extrajudicial killings committed against detainees, activists, and others, although the frequency of politicized abuses has apparently decreased in recent years. Angolan prisons are reported to be overcrowded, unhygienic, lacking in necessities, and plagued by sexual abuse.

According to government statistics, violent crime, including robberies, assaults, and homicides, has increased in Luanda in recent years.

A low-level separatist insurgency in the isolated Cabinda region continues to pose a security threat, though no major attacks were reported in 2018.

Score Change: The score improved from 0 to 1 because the frequency of politicized abuses carried out by state security agents has apparently decreased somewhat in recent years, and most residents are free from war and insurgencies.

F4. Do laws, policies, and practices guarantee equal treatment of various segments of the population? 1 / 4

Security forces allegedly harass and abuse immigrant communities, and the government has failed to adequately protect refugees and asylum seekers. In October 2018, authorities expelled more than 400,000 primarily Congolese migrants from Angola. Security forces allegedly killed dozens of people and set fire to scores of homes during the operation, which the government justified with a baseless claim that irregular migrants were responsible for illegal mining and diamond smuggling.

National law criminalizes "acts against nature," though there have been no recent cases of this provision being applied to same-sex sexual activity. LGBT people sometimes suffer harassment, and few formal LGBT rights or support organizations exist.

Women face discrimination in the workplace that makes it difficult for them to rise to senior positions. There have been reports of abuse of women and children accused of practicing witchcraft.

G. PERSONAL AUTONOMY AND INDIVIDUAL RIGHTS: 3 / 16

G1. Do individuals enjoy freedom of movement, including the ability to change their place of residence, employment, or education? 1 / 4

Several organizations have been working to remove land mines that were placed during Angola's decades-long civil war. Land mines inhibit agriculture, construction, and freedom of movement, particularly in rural areas.

The process for securing entry and exit visas remains difficult and mired in corruption. Individuals who are critical of the government have faced problems when attempting to leave or enter the country. Bribes are frequently required in order to obtain employment and residence.

G2. Are individuals able to exercise the right to own property and establish private businesses without undue interference from state or nonstate actors? 1 / 4

Predatory Angolan elites tend to either disrupt or co-opt emerging new businesses. Authorities at times have expropriated land and demolished homes without providing any compensation. Customary law practices can leave women with unequal inheritance rights.

G3. Do individuals enjoy personal social freedoms, including choice of marriage partner and size of family, protection from domestic violence, and control over appearance? 1 / 4

Domestic violence is widespread in Angola, and perpetrators are rarely prosecuted. Child marriage remains common, particularly in rural areas. According to 2017 UNICEF statistics, 8 percent of girls are married by the age of 15, and 30 percent are married by 18.

G4. Do individuals enjoy equality of opportunity and freedom from economic exploitation? 0 / 4

Public oil revenues are not equitably distributed or used to benefit the entire population. Rural regions in particular have inadequate infrastructure and access to services, leading to inequities in economic opportunity.

Child labor is a major problem, and foreign workers are vulnerable to sex trafficking and forced labor in the construction and mining industries. The authorities have failed to effectively investigate human trafficking or prosecute offenders.

Antigua and Barbuda

Capital: St. John's
Population: 100,000
Political Rights Rating: 2
Civil Liberties Rating: 2
Freedom Rating: 2.0
Freedom Status: Free
Electoral Democracy: Yes

Overview: Antigua and Barbuda is a democracy that holds regular elections. Corruption in government is a concern, and women and LGBT (lesbian, gay, bisexual, and transgender) people are underrepresented in politics and suffer some discrimination. In 2017, Hurricane Irma devastated Barbuda: the entire island was evacuated, and many residents lost their livelihoods and have yet to return home. The government has since sought to weaken the island's longstanding system of communal land rights.

KEY DEVELOPMENTS IN 2018:
- In March, the Antigua and Barbuda Labour Party (ABLP), led by Prime Minister Gaston Browne, won a general election with almost 60 per cent of the vote, amounting to 15 seats in the 17-seat House of Representatives.
- The government continued its efforts to weaken the longstanding system of communal land rights in Barbuda. In January, lawmakers amended the Barbuda Land Act to permit Barbudans to hold private ownership of land on Barbuda.
- Minister of Investment and Trade Asot Michael resigned in May over allegations he had engaged in illegal campaign financing and bribe-taking while serving as the energy minister. An investigation was launched, but no charges appear to have been filed.
- A number of employees of the Social Security Board briefly walked out on the job in support of an employee who claimed that a supervisor had touched her inappropriately, and had not been disciplined following her report of the incident.

POLITICAL RIGHTS: 33 / 40

A. ELECTORAL PROCESS: 12 / 12

A1. Was the current head of government or other chief national authority elected through free and fair elections? 4 / 4

The 1981 constitution establishes a parliamentary system, with a governor-general representing the British monarch as ceremonial head of state. Antigua and Barbuda's prime minister is the head of government, and is typically the leader of the majority party that emerges from legislative elections. ABLP leader Gaston Browne once again became prime minister after his party won a majority in parliament in snap 2018 elections.

A2. Were the current national legislative representatives elected through free and fair elections? 4 / 4

The bicameral Parliament is composed of a 17-seat Senate, whose members are appointed by the governor-general, and the House of Representatives, whose 17 members are directly elected in single-seat constituencies by simple majority; representatives serve five-year terms.

In February 2018, citing a need to demonstrate state stability to investors, Browne called snap elections. The move came after the High Court of Justice denied his government's attempt to block a case in which plaintiffs were disputing state-backed development plans for Barbuda.

The elections were held in March, a yeah ahead of schedule. The campaign period was at times rancorous, with the Commonwealth Observer Group noting a "surge of vitriolic and personal attacks exchanged between political parties and candidates." The governing ABLP took 59 percent of the total vote and won 15 constituencies, translating to 15 seats, up from 14 previously. The main opposition United Progressive Party (UPP) took 37 percent of the vote, but only one constituency, and thus 1 seat, down from 3 previously. The Barbuda People's Movement (BPM) won the Barbuda constituency, which had previously been held by the ABLP. Observers deemed the polls generally competitive and credible. Turnout was high, at about 76 percent.

A3. Are the electoral laws and framework fair, and are they implemented impartially by the relevant election management bodies? 4 / 4

Electoral laws are generally fair, and are implemented impartially by the relevant election management bodies. However, in 2018, polling for all Barbudans on took place on Antigua, requiring that many people travel between the islands to vote. The government provided services to those needing to travel, however, and 87 percent of eligible Barbudans participated.

Separately, since 1984, the electoral boundaries of Antigua and Barbuda have shifted only slightly. As a consequence there is now a significant disparity in constituency size, from 1,138 (St. Phillip South) to 4,878 (St. George).

B. POLITICAL PLURALISM AND PARTICIPATION: 13 / 16

B1. Do the people have the right to organize in different political parties or other competitive political groupings of their choice, and is the system free of undue obstacles to the rise and fall of these competing parties or groupings? 3 / 4

Political parties can organize and operate freely. While there are a number of small political parties in the country, elections have been won by either the ABLP or the UPP since 1994. In 2018, the ABLP fielded a full slate of 17 candidates; the UPP fielded 16, the DNA 13, and a number of smaller parties put up 1 or 2. The BPM was among them, and won entry to the House of Representatives, which in its previous incarnation had included only the ABLP and UPP.

Inadequate campaign finance regulations allow candidates and parties to accept donations without disclosing donors' identities.

B2. Is there a realistic opportunity for the opposition to increase its support or gain power through elections? 4 / 4

There are realistic opportunities for opposition parties to increase their support or gain power through elections. Power has rotated frequently between the ABLP and UPP.

B3. Are the people's political choices free from domination by the military, foreign powers, religious hierarchies, economic oligarchies, or any other powerful group that is not democratically accountable? 3 / 4

People's political choices are generally free from the influence of nondemocratic actors. However, a lack of transparency for party and campaign financing has given rise to concerns about the potential influence of unknown domestic and foreign interests over political candidates.

B4. Do various segments of the population (including ethnic, religious, gender, LGBT, and other relevant groups) have full political rights and electoral opportunities? 3 / 4

Women are underrepresented in politics, and only two women were elected to the House of Representatives in 2018.

The LGBT community is marginalized, and this impacts its ability to engage fully in political processes.

C. FUNCTIONING OF GOVERNMENT: 8 / 12

C1. Do the freely elected head of government and national legislative representatives determine the policies of the government? 3 / 4

The elected prime minister, cabinet, and national legislative representatives determine the policies of the government. There are some concerns about the influence of businesses on policymaking.

C2. Are safeguards against official corruption strong and effective? 2 / 4

Government corruption remains a concern, and anticorruption laws are enforced unevenly. In May 2018, Minister of Investment and Trade Asot Michael resigned over allegations he had engaged in illegal campaign financing and bribe-taking while serving as the energy minister. Michael denied the allegations. The Antiguan Integrity Commission indicated it would open an investigation into the allegations, but no charges appeared to have been filed at year's end.

Antigua's Citizenship by Investment Program (CIP) and Permanent Residence Certificate (PRC), in which individuals can be granted citizenship or residency in exchange for a sizable business investment or contribution, have come under sustained scrutiny in recent years. In 2018, the US Department of State noted that the CIP left the country "susceptible to money laundering and other financial crimes," and raised questions about the program's autonomy from politicians who might seek to misuse it. The Organisation for Economic Co-operation and Development (OECD) has also raised concerns about the programs.

C3. Does the government operate with openness and transparency? 3 / 4

Antigua and Barbuda has seen gradual improvement in accountability structures since 2004, when the government enacted a Freedom of Information Act. The Public Accounts Committee can also expose governmental improprieties and wrongdoings, but historically it has not functioned effectively, and there have been lengthy delays in submission of the Auditor General's report.

CIVIL LIBERTIES: 51 / 60 (+1)

D. FREEDOM OF EXPRESSION AND BELIEF: 15 / 16

D1. Are there free and independent media? 3 / 4

Press freedom is generally respected in Antigua and Barbuda. Criminal defamation was abolished in 2015. However, under the Sedition and Undesirable Publications Act, seditious libel is a criminal offence punishable by a maximum of two years in prison and a maximum fine of $5,000. The prime minister has threatened critical journalists with libel suits and threats to withdraw advertising, and has characterized the frequently critical Observer outlet as "fake news" and a threat to the country.

The majority of media outlets are concentrated among a small number of firms affiliated with either the current ABLP government or the UPP.

D2. Are individuals free to practice and express their religious faith or nonbelief in public and private? 4 / 4

The constitution provides for freedom of worship as well as the right to practice and change religion, and these freedoms are generally respected. A law that outlaws blasphemous language is not enforced.

D3. Is there academic freedom, and is the educational system free from extensive political indoctrination? 4 / 4

Academic freedom is generally respected.

D4. Are individuals free to express their personal views on political or other sensitive topics without fear of surveillance or retribution? 4 / 4

Individuals are generally free to express their personal views on political or other sensitive topics.

E. ASSOCIATIONAL AND ORGANIZATIONAL RIGHTS: 9 / 12
E1. Is there freedom of assembly? 3 / 4

Freedom of assembly is guaranteed under the constitution, and the government generally respects these rights in practice. A number of demonstrations took place in 2018, including a UPP-led march against corruption and other alleged government failures, and a protest against a government plan to repeal the Barbuda Land Act of 2007, which protects the longstanding communal land ownership system in Barbuda. Demonstrators are occasionally subject to police harassment.

E2. Is there freedom for nongovernmental organizations, particularly those that are engaged in human rights-and governance-related work? 3 / 4

The country's few nongovernmental organizations (NGOs) are active, though inadequately funded and often influenced by the government.

E3. Is there freedom for trade unions and similar professional or labor organizations? 3 / 4

Labor unions can organize freely and bargain collectively. Workers providing essential services must give notice two weeks before intent to strike, and the International Labor Organization (ILO) has described the list of essential services as excessively broad. Strikes are fairly rare. However, a labor walkout took place in September 2018, when a number of employees of the Social Security Board briefly halted work in support of an employee who claimed that a supervisor had touched her inappropriately, and had not been disciplined following her report of the incident.

F. RULE OF LAW: 14 / 16 (+1)
F1. Is there an independent judiciary? 4 / 4 (+1)

The constitution provides for an independent judiciary, which is generally respected by the government. In November 2018, voters rejected in a referendum the chance to adopt the Caribbean Court of Justice as their highest appellate court. Thus, the Judicial Committee of the Privy Council based in London retains that role.

Past ABLP governments man ipulated the judicial system, but in recent years the courts have increasingly asserted independence, with the support of the Eastern Caribbean Supreme Court. The High Court of Justice issued several rulings in 2018 that slowed government-backed development plans for Barbuda, which sustained serious damage during 2017's Hurricane Irma. In August, the court halted construction of an airport on Barbuda, while a separate lawsuit over the legality of its construction played out. In February, the High Court ruled against the government in its attempt to block a case disputing a 2015 law that facilitated development in Barbuda; that ruling prompted the year's snap elections. (Earlier in the year, the High Court refused petitions that it halt parliamentary discussion of another land law that would facilitate development in Barbuda.)

Score Change: The score improved from 3 to 4 due to a reduction in political interference in the courts, and record of court decisions that reflect judicial independence.

F2. Does due process prevail in civil and criminal matters? 3 / 4

Constitutional guarantees of due process are mostly upheld. However, prisoners on remand often remain in jail for an average of three to four years before their cases are heard.

F3. Is there protection from the illegitimate use of physical force and freedom from war and insurgencies? 4 / 4

Residents of Antigua and Barbuda do not face any significant security threats. However, prisons are severely overcrowded, and conditions within them are poor.

F4. Do laws, policies, and practices guarantee equal treatment of various segments of the population? 3 / 4

The 2005 Equal Opportunity Act bars discrimination on the basis of race, gender, class, political affinity, or place of origin. There are no specific laws prohibiting discrimination against people with disabilities, or LGBT individuals. Same-sex sexual activity remains criminalized under a 1995 law; however, it is not strictly enforced. Societal norms discourage participation of women in some employment sectors, and few women hold leadership positions.

G. PERSONAL AUTONOMY AND INDIVIDUAL RIGHTS: 13 / 16

G1. Do individuals enjoy freedom of movement, including the ability to change their place of residence, employment, or education? 4 / 4

Individuals enjoy freedom of movement, including the ability to change their place of residence, employment, or education.

G2. Are individuals able to exercise the right to own property and establish private businesses without undue interference from state or non-state actors? 3 / 4

While the government has historically encouraged both national and foreign investors to operate businesses in the country, taxation procedures remain cumbersome.

Many Barbudans forced to evacuate the island due to Hurricane Irma have opposed moves by lawmakers in Antigua to eliminate the communal land ownership system that has governed the island for almost two centuries, and instead establish private land ownership. The government argues that the change is necessary to assist Barbuda's recovery in the aftermath of the hurricane; opponents claim authorities are seeking to take advantage of the devastation to develop rural Barbuda for mass tourism. In early 2018, lawmakers amended the Barbuda Land Act to permit Barbudans private ownership of land on Barbuda.

G3. Do individuals enjoy personal social freedoms, including choice of marriage partner and size of family, protection from domestic violence, and control over appearance? 3 / 4

The Domestic Violence Act of 2015 strengthened the measures that can be taken against the perpetrators of domestic violence, and laid out a process for victims to obtain an order of protection. However, domestic violence remains a serious problem. Same-sex marriage and civil partnerships are not recognized.

G4. Do individuals enjoy equality of opportunity and freedom from economic exploitation? 3 / 4

Antigua and Barbuda is a destination and transit country for the trafficking of men, women, and children for the purposes of forced labor and sexual exploitation. Government efforts to address the problem are inadequate, but progress is being made, according to the US State Department *Trafficking in Persons* report for 2018. In particular, the report noted that the government had supervised more investigations and improved victim identification; conducted its first trafficking raid; established a new trafficking unit to coordinate and expedite efforts across the government; tripled its budget for combating trafficking; created new agreements with government agencies to improve coordination and victim protection; and developed a new database to better track cases.

Argentina

Population: 44,500,000
Capital: Buenos Aires
Political Rights Rating: 2
Civil Liberties Rating: 2
Freedom Rating: 2.0
Freedom Status: Free
Electoral Democracy: Yes

Overview: Argentina is a vibrant representative democracy with competitive elections, lively media and civil society sectors, and unfettered public debate. Corruption in the government and judiciary and drug-related violence are among the country's most serious challenges.

KEY DEVELOPMENTS IN 2018:
- The detailed revelations of a former government driver brought to light the "notebooks" scandal, in which former public officials and prominent business figures were implicated in a multimillion dollar bribery scheme. Former president and current senator Cristina Fernández de Kirchner is among those charged in connection with the scandal.
- A sharp recession, high inflation, and cuts to public spending exacerbated social polarization and prompted antigovernment demonstrations. The economic difficulties led the government of Mauricio Macri to turn to the International Monetary Fund (IMF) for an assistance package, which was settled in September.
- In November, a court closed an investigation into the 2017 disappearance and death of indigenous rights activist Santiago Maldonado, without clarifying the circumstances of either.

POLITICAL RIGHTS: 34 / 40 (+1)

A. ELECTORAL PROCESS: 11 / 12

A1. Was the current head of government or other chief national authority elected through free and fair elections? 4 / 4

The constitution provides for a president to be elected for a four-year term, with the option of reelection for one additional term. Presidential candidates must win 45 percent of the vote to avoid a runoff. Macri was elected president in 2015 in a poll deemed competitive and credible by international observers. Macri has announced his intention of running for a second term in the next election, set for October 2019.

A2. Were the current national legislative representatives elected through free and fair elections? 4 / 4

Legislative elections, including the most recent ones held in October 2017, are generally free and fair. The National Congress consists of a 257-member Chamber of Deputies, whose representatives are directly elected for four-year terms with half of the seats up for election every two years; and the 72-member Senate, whose representatives are directly elected for six-year terms, with one third of the seats up for election every two years. Legislators are elected through a proportional representation system with a closed party list.

A3. Are the electoral laws and framework fair, and are they implemented impartially by the relevant election management bodies? 3 / 4

Argentina has a clear, detailed, and fair legislative framework for conducting elections. There is universal suffrage, and voting is compulsory. However, the system suffers from some shortcomings, including inconsistent enforcement of electoral laws and campaign finance regulations. Further, aspects of election management fall under the purview of the executive branch, as Argentina's National Electoral Chamber (CNE) works in conjunction with the National Electoral Directorate, a department of the Ministry of the Interior.

B. POLITICAL PLURALISM AND PARTICIPATION: 15 / 16 (+1)

B1. Do the people have the right to organize in different political parties or other competitive political groupings of their choice, and is the system free of undue obstacles to the rise and fall of these competing parties or groupings? 4 / 4

Argentina has competitive political parties that operate without encountering undue obstacles.

B2. Is there a realistic opportunity for the opposition to increase its support or gain power through elections? 4 / 4 (+1)

Argentina's multiparty political system affords opposition candidates the realistic opportunity to compete for political power, and opposition parties command significant popular support and hold positions in national and subnational government.

While Macri defeated the Peronist candidate in the 2015 presidential election, the Peronist party (in its various ideological forms) has dominated the political scene since 1946. Non-Peronist presidents, once elected, have struggled to win reelection in the post-dictatorship period. Amid a sharp recession and economic crisis, support for President Macri has waned in the run-up to the 2019 presidential election.

Score Change: The score improved from 3 to 4 because opposition parties command significant popular support, hold positions in national and subnational government, and face no significant legal or administrative restrictions.

B3. Are the people's political choices free from domination by the military, foreign powers, religious hierarchies, economic oligarchies, or any other powerful group that is not democratically accountable? 4 / 4

Argentines' political choices are generally free from domination by groups that are not democratically accountable.

B4. Do various segments of the population (including ethnic, religious, gender, LGBT, and other relevant groups) have full political rights and electoral opportunities? 3 / 4

Ethnic and religious minorities have full political rights in Argentina. However, in practice, the government frequently ignores legal obligations to consult with indigenous communities about legislation and government actions that affect them.

Since 1991, the country has had a law requiring that at least 30 percent of a party's legislative candidates be women, and around 40 percent of seats in both houses of Congress are currently held by women. In 2017, Congress passed a new law stipulating that future party lists must have full gender parity, with men and women alternating.

C. FUNCTIONING OF GOVERNMENT: 8 / 12

C1. Do the freely elected head of government and national legislative representatives determine the policies of the government? 3 / 4

Argentina's elected officials are duly installed in office without interference. However, the political system is characterized by a powerful executive, with the president having authority to implement some policies by decree, thereby bypassing the legislative branch. Provincial governors are also powerful and tend to influence lawmakers representing their provinces.

In 2018, the Macri government continued its efforts to restore macroeconomic credibility to the country through a $57 billion IMF-endorsed adjustment program finalized in September, which has led to an erosion of real wages and a reduction in public spending.

C2. Are safeguards against official corruption strong and effective? 2 / 4

Corruption scandals are common, and several members of the political class—including former presidents—have been charged with or found guilty of malfeasance in recent years. However, weak anticorruption bodies and the politicization of the judicial system hamper institutional safeguards against corruption. Many politicians hold immunity in connection with their posts, and are thus shielded from legal consequences for corrupt behavior.

Former president Cristina Fernández de Kirchner faces several investigations for alleged corruption during her time in office and has been indicted on numerous occasions, though she is protected from arrest through legislative immunity as a current member of the Senate. The most recent, notable case is the 2018 "notebooks" scandal, based on the detailed records kept by a former government driver who allegedly delivered bags of cash to the offices of government officials and to the private home of Cristina Fernández de Kirchner and her husband, Néstor Kirchner, who held the presidency before her (and died in 2010). Fernández, for her part, is accused of having received millions of dollars in cash from public construction companies in exchange for government contracts. She was indicted in September, and in December a federal appeals court upheld the decision that she be tried for bribery in connection with the case. A number of prominent businessmen were also named in the driver's records.

Powerful members of Fernández's administration, including former planning minister Julio de Vido and former economy minister and vice president Amado Boudou, are serving jail sentences in connection with corruption charges, and many other former officials await trial. However, it remains to be seen if ongoing corruption investigations and legal proceedings are enough to break Argentina's historic culture of impunity.

C3. Does the government operate with openness and transparency? 3 / 4

In recent years, the government has taken some steps to improve transparency, including by enacting an access to information law that established the autonomous Public Information Agency, through which citizens may request information from state agencies. The government has also taken steps to digitize state records and procedures and to publish information online, including on public procurement and contracting bids.

Macri's government has revamped the country's statistics agency, which under the Kirchner administration had been censured by the IMF\ for misrepresenting data. The government now publishes timely data that offers an accurate picture of the economy. Government officials hold press conferences and make other efforts to communicate policy objectives to voters.

Adherence to and enforcement of public asset disclosure regulations is inconsistent. Members of the Macri administration, as well as Macri himself, have ties to companies registered in tax havens.

CIVIL LIBERTIES: 50 / 60

D. FREEDOM OF EXPRESSION AND BELIEF: 15 / 16

D1. Are there free and independent media? 3 / 4

Argentine law guarantees freedom of expression, and Congress decriminalized libel and slander in 2009. Macri's government holds regular press conferences and has a much more open relationship with the press than the previous administrations of Cristina Fernández de Kirchner and her late husband, Néstor Kirchner.

Macri has also reduced the state's role in advertising compared to the previous Kirchner administrations, which funded a number of friendly print and broadcasting outlets and denied advertising contracts to critical media. However, the reduction in spending, combined with the country's difficult economic situation, affected media businesses' financial sustainability, and resulted in the closure of a number of largely left-leaning outlets, in effect narrowing the scope of opposition voices. While media ownership is concentrated among large conglomerates—which tend to side with the government—Argentineans nevertheless enjoy a robust and lively media environment, and there is no official censorship.

Journalists face occasional harassment and violence. Those covering discrimination against LGBT (lesbian, gay, bisexual, and transgender) people report frequent threats on social media. Separately, in May, police raided the Buenos Aires home of a photographer with the community news website *La Garganta Poderosa*, and confiscated equipment. The raid took place after he had photographed what *La Garganta Poderosa* said was an illegal police operation aimed at intimidating witnesses in a police brutality investigation.

D2. Are individuals free to practice and express their religious faith or nonbelief in public and private? 4 / 4

Argentina's constitution guarantees freedom of religion. While the population is largely Roman Catholic, public education is secular, and religions minorities express their faiths freely. The government has formally acknowledged more than 5,300 non-Catholic organizations, granting them tax-exempt status and other benefits.

D3. Is there academic freedom, and is the educational system free from extensive political indoctrination? 4 / 4

Academic freedom is guaranteed by law and largely observed in practice.

D4. Are individuals free to express their personal views on political or other sensitive topics without fear of surveillance or retribution? 4 / 4

Private discussion is vibrant and unrestricted. However, activists and opposition leaders report online harassment and intimidation by progovernment trolls, especially on Twitter, and some have accused authorities of financially sponsoring trolling efforts. The government denies any involvement.

E. ASSOCIATIONAL AND ORGANIZATIONAL RIGHTS: 11 / 12

E1. Is there freedom of assembly? 4 / 4

Freedom of assembly is generally respected, and citizens frequently organize protests to make their voices heard. In mid-2018, hundreds of thousands took to the streets across Argentina to express their views regarding the legalization of abortion, as it was being debated in Congress. An October demonstration at the National Congress against austerity measures in Macri's proposed 2019 budget saw clashes between a small contingent of rock-throwing protesters, and police, who responded to them with tear gas, water cannons, and rubber bullets.

E2. Is there freedom for nongovernmental organizations, particularly those that are engaged in human rights- and governance-related work? 4 / 4

NGOs generally operate without restrictions. Civic organizations, especially those focused on human rights and abuses committed under the 1976–83 dictatorship, are robust and play a major role in society, although some fall victim to Argentina's pervasive corruption.

E3. Is there freedom for trade unions and similar professional or labor organizations? 3 / 4

Organized labor remains dominated by Peronist unions, and union influence has decreased in recent years. Most labor unions have been controlled by the same individuals or groups since the 1980s, and internal opposition to union leadership has been limited by fraud and intimidation. Labor groups continued to call nationwide strikes in 2018, largely in protest of the government's austerity measures and real wage losses caused by high inflation.

F. RULE OF LAW: 10 / 16

F1. Is there an independent judiciary? 2 / 4

Inefficiencies and delays plague the judicial system, which is susceptible to political manipulation, particularly at lower levels. Some federal judges are known to maintain close ties with political actors, and to engage in corrupt practices. A former federal judge has been charged with corruption in the "notebooks" case, accused of having been part of the bribery scheme benefiting members of the administrations of Cristina Fernández de Kirchner and Néstor Kirchner.

The Supreme Court, however, has maintained relative independence, and has pushed back against executive overreach during both the Kirchner and Macri administrations.

F2. Does due process prevail in civil and criminal matters? 3 / 4

Due process rights are protected by the constitution and are generally upheld. However, the justice system and security forces, especially at the provincial level, have been accused of having ties with drug-trafficking operations and engaging in other corruption.

Court cases dating from the mid-2000s have allowed the prosecution of crimes against humanity committed during the 1976–83 dictatorship. Dozens of military and police officers have been convicted of torture, murder, and forced disappearance, and sentenced to life in prison, helping to combat a culture of impunity.

In November 2018, a court closed an investigation into the 2017 disappearance and death of indigenous rights activist Santiago Maldonado without clarifying the circumstances of either. Maldonado disappeared after being arrested by border guards, who took him into custody following his participation in a demonstration in support of land claims by the indigenous Mapuche people. His body was recovered later in 2017, with an autopsy determining that he had drown.

F3. Is there protection from the illegitimate use of physical force and freedom from war and insurgencies? 2 / 4

Drug-related violence remained a serious issue in 2018 as international criminal organizations used the country as both an operational base and a transit route; the northern and central regions are particularly affected. Rosario—the country's third largest city and an important port—has been at the center of a spike in drug-related violence and unrest that has featured armed attacks against courts and intimidation of public officials.

Police misconduct, including torture and brutality against suspects in custody, is endemic. Prisons are overcrowded, and conditions remain substandard throughout the country. Arbitrary arrests and abuse by police are rarely punished in the courts, and police collusion with drug traffickers is common. In July 2018, President Macri controversially announced the lifting of a ban on involvement of the armed forces in internal security operations. The government claims that soldiers will only provide logistical support for antidrug operations in border areas.

F4. Do laws, policies, and practices guarantee equal treatment of various segments of the population? 3 / 4

Argentina's indigenous peoples, who comprise approximately 2.4 percent of the population, are largely neglected by the government and suffer disproportionately from extreme poverty and illness. Only 11 of Argentina's 23 provinces have constitutions recognizing the rights of indigenous peoples.

Women enjoy legal equality, but continue to face economic discrimination and gender-based wage gaps.

Argentina's LGBT population enjoys full legal rights, including marriage, adoption, and the right to serve in the military. However, LGBT people face some degree of societal discrimination, and occasionally, serious violence.

G. PERSONAL AUTONOMY AND INDIVIDUAL RIGHTS: 14 / 16

G1. Do individuals enjoy freedom of movement, including the ability to change their place of residence, employment, or education? 4 / 4

The government respects citizens' constitutional right to free travel both inside and outside of Argentina. The Macri government's 2015 move to lift Kirchner-era currency controls increased access to foreign currency, making travel abroad more accessible. The government has also liberalized commercial air travel, with new companies offering new routes connecting Argentine cities with each other and with international destinations.

People are free to change their place of education or employment.

G2. Are individuals able to exercise the right to own property and establish private businesses without undue interference from state or nonstate actors? 3 / 4

Citizens generally enjoy the right to own property and establish private businesses, and the Macri administration has made some effort to reduce bureaucracy as a means of encouraging entrepreneurship.

Approximately 70 percent of the country's rural indigenous communities lack titles to their lands, and forced evictions, while technically illegal, still occur. Indigenous communities continue to struggle to defend their land rights against oil and gas prospectors, and to reclaim traditional lands.

G3. Do individuals enjoy personal social freedoms, including choice of marriage partner and size of family, protection from domestic violence, and control over appearance? 4 / 4

Argentineans enjoy broad freedom regarding marriage and divorce. Same-sex marriage has been legal nationwide since 2010. A 2012 gender identity law allows people to legally change their gender.

Violence against women remains a serious problem. Activists continue to hold highly visible protests and events aimed at drawing attention to the issue.

Access to abortion is legal only in cases where the mother's life or health are in danger, or if the pregnancy is the result of rape; women in more remote parts of the country report difficulty in accessing an abortion even when these conditions are met. In June 2018, the Chamber of Deputies approved a bill that would have legalized abortion, but it was rejected by the Senate in August. The Catholic Church and evangelical churches played a key role in the bill's narrow defeat.

G4. Do individuals enjoy equality of opportunity and freedom from economic exploitation? 3 / 4

Some sectors of the charcoal and brick-producing industries profit from the forced labor of men, women, and children from Argentina as well as from neighboring countries; forced labor is also present in the agriculture sector and among domestic workers and street vendors. Exploitation is made easier by the prevalence of informal work: more than a third of Argentines work in the informal sector, without proper benefits.

Men, women, and children are subject to sex trafficking. The government has taken steps to identify more victims, deliver antitrafficking trainings, and prosecute officials involved in trafficking, according to the US State Department's 2018 *Trafficking in Persons Report*.

Armenia

Population: 3,000,000
Capital: Yerevan
Political Rights Rating: 4 ↑
Civil Liberties Rating: 4
Freedom Rating: 4.0
Freedom Status: Partly Free
Electoral Democracy: No

Note: The numerical ratings and status listed above do not reflect conditions in Nagorno-Karabakh, which is examined in a separate report.

Overview: Armenia is in the midst of a significant transition following mass antigovernment protests and elections in 2018 that forced out an entrenched political elite. The new government has pledged to deal with long-standing problems including systemic corruption, opaque policymaking, a flawed electoral system, and weak rule of law.

KEY DEVELOPMENTS IN 2018:

- Serzh Sargsyan, the country's president since 2008, attempted to extend his rule in April by becoming prime minister under a new parliamentary system, prompting mass demonstrations across the country that led to his swift resignation and the parliament's election of protest leader Nikol Pashinyan to replace him in May.
- Ruling with an interim cabinet of deputies from his Yelq Alliance even as Sargsyan's Republican Party of Armenia (HHK) continued to dominate the parliament, Pashinyan attempted to enact electoral reforms, combat corruption, and improve socioeconomic conditions.
- Although the interim government was unable to pass electoral reforms, Pashinyan's new My Step Alliance swept snap parliamentary elections in December, taking 70 percent of the vote. The new parliament was set to convene in early 2019.

POLITICAL RIGHTS: 20 / 40 (+5)
A. ELECTORAL PROCESS: 6 / 12 (+2)
A1. Was the current head of government or other chief national authority elected through free and fair elections? 2 / 4 (+1)

In late 2015, voters approved constitutional changes that, among other things, transformed the country from a semipresidential to a parliamentary republic. The president, who had been directly elected for up to two five-year terms, would henceforth be chosen by the parliament for a single seven-year term, and most executive power would shift to the prime minister, who would also be chosen by a parliamentary majority. The new system took full effect in April 2018, when Sargsyan completed his second consecutive presidential term. The parliament elected diplomat Armen Sarkissian as president, and although Sargsyan had pledged to refrain from extending his rule by seeking the premiership, the HHK nevertheless nominated him and ushered him into the post. The move prompted mass antigovernment protests and led to Sargsyan's resignation after less than a week in office. Pashinyan, a deputy with the opposition Yelq Alliance who emerged as the leader of the demonstrations, sought and gained appointment as interim prime minister in May.

The executive elections held prior to 2018 had been dominated by the HHK, with incumbent elites benefiting from the abuse of administrative resources and severe limitations imposed on opposition candidates. However, Pashinyan and his new My Step Alliance swept the December parliamentary elections, which were markedly freer and fairer than elections in previous years, meaning the next chief executive—now the prime minister rather than the president—would be seated in early 2019 through a much improved democratic process.

Even before the December elections, there were signs of improvement at the subnational level. For example, municipal elections were held in Yerevan in September after the incumbent HHK mayor resigned amid corruption allegations, and very few irregularities were reported compared with previous balloting. Hayk Marutyan of My Step was chosen as mayor by the newly elected city council.

Score Change: The score improved from 1 to 2 because the resignation of Serzh Sargsyan as president and prime minister cleared the way for more free and fair executive elections at both the municipal and national levels in the subsequent months.

A2. Were the current national legislative representatives elected through free and fair elections? 2 / 4 (+1)

The National Assembly consists of a minimum of 101 members elected for five-year terms through a combination of national and district-based proportional representation. Up to four additional seats are reserved for ethnic minority representatives, and further seats can be added to ensure that opposition parties hold at least 30 percent of the seats.

Pashinyan announced his resignation as prime minister in October 2018 in order to trigger snap parliamentary elections in December. Preliminary reports by local and international observers noted that the elections were credible. The Organization for Security and Co-operation in Europe (OSCE) found that "the general absence of electoral malfeasance, including of vote-buying and pressure on voters, allowed for genuine competition." The My Step Alliance won 70 percent of the vote and was allotted 88 seats, including the four ethnic minority mandates. Prosperous Armenia, headed by wealthy businessman Gagik Tsarukyan, took 8 percent and 26 seats, while Bright Armenia, a small liberal party that had been part of the Yelq Alliance, took 6 percent and 18 seats. The HHK failed to cross the 5 percent threshold for representation.

Score Change: The score improved from 1 to 2 because the December 2018 parliamentary balloting featured fewer abuses and irregularities than past national legislative elections.

A3. Are the electoral laws and framework fair, and are they implemented impartially by the relevant election management bodies? 2 / 4

Members of Central Election Commission (CEC) are recommended and then confirmed by the National Assembly for six-year terms. The CEC has generally been subservient to the HHK and shown reluctance to investigate alleged electoral violations by the party. This has resulted in a low level of public trust in the election process and the CEC. However, the commission reportedly exhibited more professional conduct for the December 2018 snap elections, making preparations on a shortened timeline, conducting voter education campaigns, and handling voter rolls, candidate registration, and publication of results in a transparent manner.

Pashinyan and other critics of the electoral code put in place by the former government have argued that its complex system for voting and seat allocation gave an undue advantage to the HHK and affiliated business magnates. Pashinyan's interim government was unable to pass electoral reforms during 2018 due to resistance from HHK and other incumbent lawmakers.

B. POLITICAL PLURALISM AND PARTICIPATION: 10 / 16 (+3)

B1. Do the people have the right to organize in different political parties or other competitive political groupings of their choice, and is the system free of undue obstacles to the rise and fall of these competing parties or groupings? 3 / 4 (+1)

The HHK's political dominance and control of administrative resources has historically prevented a level playing field among the country's many competing parties. However, the 2018 protest movement that forced Sargsyan from office also increased pressure on the HHK to refrain from interfering in party activities, giving opposition groups significantly more freedom to operate ahead of the December national elections.

Score Change: The score improved from 2 to 3 due to a decrease in government and ruling party interference in the peaceful political activities of rival parties and movements, including preelection campaigning.

B2. Is there a realistic opportunity for the opposition to increase its support or gain power through elections? 3 / 4 (+1)

The HHK had been the main ruling party since 1999, and opposition groups had little chance of winning power in the flawed elections before 2018. However, the December parliamentary elections transformed the political landscape, leaving the HHK with no representation and paving the way for the opposition My Step Alliance to select the new prime minister in early 2019. Opposition parties also defeated the HHK in elections for key municipal councils that it had long dominated, including in the capital, Yerevan. The size of the new parliamentary majority raised some concerns at year's end that the two minor parties set to serve as the opposition would not be able to provide a sufficient check on the incoming government.

Score Change: The score improved from 2 to 3 because the My Step Alliance, comprising several opposition parties, was able to gain power through elections for the national parliament and a number of municipal councils.

B3. Are the people's political choices free from domination by the military, foreign powers, religious hierarchies, economic oligarchies, or any other powerful group that is not democratically accountable? 2 / 4 (+1)

Local and national elections in 2018 featured a decrease in practices like vote buying, voter intimidation, and abuse of administrative resources, which the HHK and allied economic elites have historically used to distort citizens' political choices. In September, the parliament adopted legislation that criminalized various acts related to vote buying.

Score Change: The score improved from 1 to 2 due to a reduction in the use of bribery and intimidation to influence the choices of voters and candidates.

B4. Do various segments of the population (including ethnic, religious, gender, LGBT, and other relevant groups) have full political rights and electoral opportunities? 2 / 4

A system introduced as part of the 2015 constitutional reforms mandates the inclusion of up to four members of parliament representing ethnic minorities. However, the four representatives are required to be elected on a party list. In the December 2018 voting, My Step won all four minority seats, representing ethnic Russians, Yazidis, Assyrians, and Kurds.

No openly LGBT (lesbian, gay, bisexual, and transgender) people have ever run in elections or been appointed to a public office in Armenia. Women remain underrepresented in politics and government, and most parties do little to address women's interests aside from meeting the 25 percent gender quota on candidate lists. Despite his praise of women's role in the spring protests and promises for equality, Pashinyan named just two female ministers to his 17-member cabinet after taking office as prime minister in May. In October, the city of Ejmiatsin elected the country's first female mayor.

C. FUNCTIONING OF GOVERNMENT: 4 / 12

C1. Do the freely elected head of government and national legislative representatives determine the policies of the government? 1 / 4

The HHK dominated parliamentary decision-making throughout the year, although Pashinyan's appointment as prime minister in May created some balance between the executive and legislative branches.

So-called oligarchs, or wealthy businessmen who have close relationships with the government, can exert undue influence over policymaking. Russia has significant influence in Armenia, and its strategic priorities have prompted some significant policy changes in the past. However, Moscow refrained from interfering with the 2018 antigovernment demonstrations or the subsequent power transfer, and Pashinyan pledged to maintain close ties with Russia.

C2. Are safeguards against official corruption strong and effective? 1 / 4

Armenia does not have effective safeguards against corruption. The parliament in power through 2018 included some of the country's wealthiest business leaders, who continued their private entrepreneurial activities despite conflicts of interest. Relationships between politicians and other oligarchs have also historically influenced policy and contributed to selective application of the law.

After Pashinyan took office as prime minister in May, law enforcement agencies initiated a number of high-profile corruption investigations, with targets including Yerevan mayor Taron Margaryan; parliament member Manvel Grigoryan and his son, Ejmiatsin mayor Karen Grigoryan; and Sargsyan's brother and nephew. While most observers agreed that there was abundant evidence of wrongdoing, some warned that there was a thin line separating sound legal cases from politically motivated ones. HHK-allied elites showed significant resistance to these probes and seemed likely to complicate the new government's anticorruption drive.

C3. Does the government operate with openness and transparency? 2 / 4

The government's level of openness and transparency has historically been limited, and enforcement of asset-declaration rules for public officials has been weak, though some legal improvements have been enacted in recent years. In 2018, Pashinyan and his allies made efforts to give citizens greater access to their representatives, speaking more frequently to the press and the general population, including through live video streaming on social media.

CIVIL LIBERTIES: 31 / 60 (+1)

D. FREEDOM OF EXPRESSION AND BELIEF: 9 / 16

D1. Are there free and independent media? 2 / 4

Independent and investigative journalists operate in Armenia, but their work is generally found online. Most print and broadcast outlets are affiliated with political or larger commercial interests. Many journalists practice self-censorship to avoid harassment by government or business figures. Small independent outlets provided robust coverage of the 2018 protests, challenging the narratives of state broadcasters and other establishment media. A number of reporters were physically assaulted by police during the protest period. There were no major restrictions on press freedom during the 2018 parliamentary election campaign, though politically aligned outlets continued to favor their affiliated parties and candidates.

D2. Are individuals free to practice and express their religious faith or nonbelief in public and private? 2 / 4

Article 18 of the constitution recognizes the Armenian Apostolic Church as a "national church" responsible for the preservation of Armenian national identity. Religious minorities have reported discrimination in the past, and some have faced difficulty obtaining permits to build houses of worship.

D3. Is there academic freedom, and is the educational system free from extensive political indoctrination? 2 / 4

Although the constitution protects academic freedom, government officials hold several board positions at state universities, leaving administrative and accreditation processes open to political influence. There is some self-censorship among academics on politically sensitive subjects.

D4. Are individuals free to express their personal views on political or other sensitive topics without fear of surveillance or retribution? 3 / 4

Private discussion is relatively free and vibrant. The law prohibits wiretapping or other electronic surveillance without judicial approval, though the judiciary lacks independence and has been accused of excessive deference to law enforcement agencies requesting consent.

E. ASSOCIATIONAL AND ORGANIZATIONAL RIGHTS: 7 / 12 (+1)
E1. Is there freedom of assembly? 3 / 4 (+1)

The right to free assembly is legally guaranteed but inconsistently upheld in practice. From March to May 2018, mass antigovernment demonstrations were organized across the country under the slogan Reject Serzh, aiming to stop the outgoing president from governing as prime minister. Despite some violent interference by police and the temporary detention of hundreds of protesters—including Pashinyan, the movement's leader, in April—the demonstrations encountered fewer obstacles than those in past years.

Score Change: The score improved from 2 to 3 because antigovernment demonstrations were able to proceed with less police interference and other obstruction from authorities than in previous years.

E2. Is there freedom for nongovernmental organizations, particularly those that are engaged in human rights- and governance-related work? 2 / 4

Nongovernmental organizations (NGOs) lack local funding and largely rely on foreign donors. There are a few outspoken human rights organizations and watchdog groups, mostly in Yerevan and in northern Armenia. Civil society was very active in the 2018 protests, subsequent consultations with the government on policy matters, and monitoring activities associated with the December elections.

E3. Is there freedom for trade unions and similar professional or labor organizations? 2 / 4

The law protects the rights of workers to form and join independent unions, strike, and engage in collective bargaining. However, these protections are not well enforced, and employers are generally able to block union activity in practice.

F. RULE OF LAW: 6 / 16
F1. Is there an independent judiciary? 1 / 4

The courts face systemic political influence, and judicial institutions are undermined by corruption. Judges reportedly feel pressure to work with prosecutors to convict defendants, and acquittal rates are extremely low.

F2. Does due process prevail in civil and criminal matters? 1 / 4

Authorities apply the law selectively, and due process is not guaranteed in civil or criminal cases. Lengthy pretrial detention remains a problem, and judges are generally reluctant to challenge arbitrary arrests. Pashinyan was among those who were subjected to arbitrary detention during the antigovernment protests in early 2018.

A number of jailed hard-line opposition figures were granted release following campaigns by Yelq lawmakers during the year. Some observers criticized an amnesty law passed in October for having political motives; it included amnesty for members of Sasna Tsrer, an armed opposition group that seized a police building in 2016 and caused the deaths of three officers, with the stipulation that victims could block the militants' release if they objected.

The raft of corruption investigations aimed at HHK elites after the change in government prompted concerns about the ability of the country's judicial and investigative mechanisms to ensure fair application of the law.

F3. Is there protection from the illegitimate use of physical force and freedom from war and insurgencies? 2 / 4

Reports of police abuse of detainees and poor conditions in prisons persist. After the change in government in May 2018, law enforcement agencies renewed dormant investigations into past cases of physical violence by police. Most controversially, former president Robert Kocharyan was investigated and later charged in July with attempting to overthrow the constitutional order for his alleged role in fatal clashes between police and protesters during the 2008 presidential election period.

Areas adjacent to Azerbaijan and Nagorno-Karabakh, an Armenian-majority territory that gained de facto independence from Azerbaijan following the breakup of the Soviet Union, remained tense in 2018, with a lingering risk of shelling and skirmishes across the line of contact.

F4. Do laws, policies, and practices guarantee equal treatment of various segments of the population? 2 / 4

Rights watchdogs have criticized the government for discriminating against asylum seekers who are not of ethnic Armenian origin. Although same-sex sexual activity was decriminalized in 2003, LGBT people continue to face violence and mistreatment at the hands of police and civilians. Women are reportedly subject to de facto discrimination in employment and education, despite legal protections.

G. PERSONAL AUTONOMY AND INDIVIDUAL RIGHTS: 9 / 16

G1. Do individuals enjoy freedom of movement, including the ability to change their place of residence, employment, or education? 3 / 4

The law protects freedom of movement and the rights of individuals to change their place of residence, employment, and education. In practice, access to higher education is somewhat hampered by a culture of bribery. Exit visas for foreign travel are required but simple to obtain; international travel is constrained by the country's closed borders with Turkey and Azerbaijan.

G2. Are individuals able to exercise the right to own property and establish private businesses without undue interference from state or nonstate actors? 2 / 4

Economic diversification and simpler regulations have increased the ease of doing business in recent years, but a lack of transparency and persistent cronyism continue to create unfair advantages for those with ties to public officials. Armenian law adequately protects property rights, though officials do not always uphold them.

G3. Do individuals enjoy personal social freedoms, including choice of marriage partner and size of family, protection from domestic violence, and control over appearance? 2 / 4

The constitution defines marriage as a union between a man and a woman. Domestic violence is common and not adequately prosecuted, and services for victims are inadequate. A new law on domestic violence that took effect in January 2018 placed an emphasis on "restoring family harmony," raising concerns that it would deter victims from leaving dangerous situations.

G4. Do individuals enjoy equality of opportunity and freedom from economic exploitation? 2 / 4

Legal protections against exploitative or dangerous working conditions are poorly enforced, and about half of workers are employed in the informal sector, where they may be more exposed to such conditions. Armenians are subjected to sex and labor trafficking abroad, and some children in the country work in agriculture and other sectors. According to the US State Department, the government has made efforts to address trafficking in persons in recent years, in part by raising awareness of the problem and training law enforcement authorities, but it has done little to identify victims proactively, and the number of successful prosecutions remains small.

Australia

Population: 24,100,000
Capital: Canberra
Political Rights Rating: 1
Civil Liberties Rating: 1
Freedom Rating: 1.0
Freedom Status: Free
Electoral Democracy: Yes

Overview: Australia has a strong record of advancing and protecting political rights and civil liberties. Challenges to these freedoms include the threat of foreign political influence, harsh policies toward asylum seekers, and ongoing difficulties ensuring the equal rights of indigenous Australians.

KEY DEVELOPMENTS IN 2018:

- In August, Scott Morrison became prime minister after successfully challenging Malcolm Turnbull for leadership of the Liberal Party, continuing a pattern in which prime ministers fail to serve their full terms due to "leadership coups."
- In December, Parliament passed the Assistance and Access Act, which requires technology companies to provide law enforcement agencies with access to encrypted communications. Rights groups criticized the new law's broad reach and relative lack of oversight.
- Parliament passed a number of laws designed to limit foreign influence in politics during the year, including a law passed in June requiring lobbying groups that represent foreign interests to register publicly, as well as a law passed in November prohibiting foreign donations to political parties, independent candidates, and other political campaign groups.

POLITICAL RIGHTS: 40 / 40

A. ELECTORAL PROCESS: 12 / 12

A1. Was the current head of government or other chief national authority elected through free and fair elections? 4 / 4

The Australian government is a parliamentary democracy under a constitutional monarchy. The leader of the popularly elected majority party or coalition is designated as prime minister, and serves as head of government. Scott Morrison, now head of the Liberal Party, became prime minister in August 2018, when he successfully challenged Malcolm Turnbull for leadership of the party. Morrison's ascension continued a pattern in which prime ministers fail to serve their full terms due to "leadership coups," which have drawn criticism for failing to reflect the will of the voters. After becoming party leader, Morrison took steps in December to limit leadership coups in the Liberal Party by introducing rules requiring a two-thirds majority vote in order to change the prime minister.

A governor general, appointed on the recommendation of the prime minister, represents the British monarch as head of state. The powers of the monarchy are extremely limited.

A2. Were the current national legislative representatives elected through free and fair elections? 4 / 4

The bicameral legislative branch consists of a 150-member House of Representatives and 76-member Senate. The Liberal Party–National Party coalition won a slim majority in the House of Representatives in 2016 elections, which were free and fair. The Liberal–National coalition lost its parliamentary majority after former prime minister Turnbull resigned from Parliament in August 2018, leading to a by-election in October in which an independent candidate won his seat.

A3. Are the electoral laws and framework fair, and are they implemented impartially by the relevant election management bodies? 4 / 4

Australian electoral laws and procedures are generally fair and impartial. The Australian Electoral Commission (AEC)—an independent federal agency—coordinates all federal elections and referendums, draws seat boundaries, and keeps the electoral rolls. Voting is compulsory, and a registered voter's failure to vote may result in a small fine, which if unpaid can increase, and ultimately lead to a criminal conviction.

B. POLITICAL PLURALISM AND PARTICIPATION: 16 / 16

B1. Do the people have the right to organize in different political parties or other competitive political groupings of their choice, and is the system free of undue obstacles to the rise and fall of these competing parties or groupings? 4 / 4

Australians may organize political parties without restrictions. Registration and recognition as a political party requires a party constitution and either one member in Parliament, or at least 500 members on the electoral roll.

B2. Is there a realistic opportunity for the opposition to increase its support or gain power through elections? 4 / 4

Power rotates between parties frequently, traditionally alternating between the Labor Party and the Liberal–National coalition. The Australian Greens and smaller left-leaning parties tend to ally with Labor, while rural-oriented and conservative parties often ally with Liberals.

B3. Are the people's political choices free from domination by the military, foreign powers, religious hierarchies, economic oligarchies, or any other powerful group that is not democratically accountable? 4 / 4

Political participation in Australia is free from undue influence of the military, religious organizations, or other powerful groups. The British monarch remains the Australian head of state, but the monarchy's power is strictly limited by the Australian constitution and legal precedent.

Concerns about foreign interference in politics, particularly from China, persisted during 2018. Chinese actors had allegedly funded particular candidates and parties, and a senator resigned in 2017 due to his financial ties with companies linked to the Chinese government. Responding to these concerns, the government passed a law in November banning foreign donations to political parties, independent candidates, and other political campaign groups. Additionally, the Foreign Influence Transparency Scheme, which was passed in June and came into force in December, requires persons who engage in political activities, such as lobbying, on behalf of a foreign government or other entity, to register publicly.

B4. Do various segments of the population (including ethnic, religious, gender, LGBT, and other relevant groups) have full political rights and electoral opportunities? 4 / 4

Political rights and electoral opportunities are granted to all Australians. However, the interests of some groups, including women and indigenous Australians, are inadequately represented, and women members of Parliament have reported being bullied, intimidated, and harassed. Some voting restrictions—including requirements that voters hold a fixed address and a ban on voting by prisoners serving long sentences—disproportionately affect indigenous Australians.

In the 2016 legislative elections, the first indigenous woman was elected to the House of Representatives.

C. FUNCTIONING OF GOVERNMENT: 12 / 12

C1. Do the freely elected head of government and national legislative representatives determine the policies of the government? 4 / 4

The freely elected government is generally able to develop and implement policy.

C2. Are safeguards against official corruption strong and effective? 4 / 4

Laws against official corruption are generally well enforced. In December 2018, Prime Minister Morrison announced the formation of a new anticorruption commission, although Labor politicians criticized the commission for lacking transparency and holding limited power.

C3. Does the government operate with openness and transparency? 4 / 4

Government operations are characterized by a high degree of transparency, and political affairs are openly discussed in Parliament and in the media. Parliamentary records and commissioned reports are readily available. The Freedom of Information Act allows people to access a wide range of government documents.

CIVIL LIBERTIES: 58 / 60

D. FREEDOM OF EXPRESSION AND BELIEF: 16 / 16

D1. Are there free and independent media? 4 / 4

The constitution does not explicitly protect press freedom. However, journalists scrutinize lawmakers and the government and cover controversial topics, generally without encountering serious obstacles or risking harassment or violence.

Suppression orders can sometimes inhibit journalism. For example, a judge in Victoria issued a suppression order that largely prevented reporting on the trial of Cardinal George Pell, an Australian Vatican official convicted of sexual assault in December 2018. While the order aimed to prevent jeopardizing potential future trials involving the cardinal, it was criticized for stifling reporting on a story of great public interest.

D2. Are individuals free to practice and express their religious faith or nonbelief in public and private? 4 / 4

The constitution explicitly prohibits laws that would either impose or restrict religious expression, and individuals are generally able to express religious beliefs or nonbelief.

D3. Is there academic freedom, and is the educational system free from extensive political indoctrination? 4 / 4

Academic freedom is generally respected. However, in 2017, federal officials warned of Chinese attempts to monitor Chinese students in Australia, and to question academics whose views differed with those of the Chinese government.

D4. Are individuals free to express their personal views on political or other sensitive topics without fear of surveillance or retribution? 4 / 4

Generally, people in Australia may freely discuss personal views on sensitive topics. The government passed a number of laws in recent years increasing its surveillance powers. In December 2018, the government passed the Assistance and Access Act, which requires technology companies to provide law enforcement agencies with access to encrypted communications on grounds that include preventing terrorism and crime. Rights groups criticized the new law's broad reach, relative lack of oversight, and steep fines for companies that do not comply.

A data retention law that came into effect in 2017 requires telecommunications companies to store users' metadata for two years. The law sparked concerns about the government's ability to track mobile and online communications. Some experts have warned of the potential for data breaches, and have argued that the law undermines civil liberties.

E. ASSOCIATIONAL AND ORGANIZATIONAL RIGHTS: 12 / 12

E1. Is there freedom of assembly? 4 / 4

Freedom of assembly is not explicitly codified in law, but the government generally respects the right to peaceful assembly in practice. There are some limited restrictions meant to ensure public safety.

There has been some concern in recent years about measures designed to discourage protests at certain kinds of workplaces. In 2016, the New South Wales state government passed laws apparently meant to curb a protest movement targeting mining operations.

E2. Is there freedom for nongovernmental organizations, particularly those that are engaged in human rights- and governance-related work? 4 / 4

NGOs are generally free to form, function, and receive funding. Earlier versions of the bill passed in November 2018 banning foreign donations to political parties also sought to limit donations to certain charities from foreign entities, which raised concerns that it would severely impact the ability of NGOs to function. However, after pressure from Labor and the Greens, the bill was amended to specify that it does not apply to charities and advocacy groups.

E3. Is there freedom for trade unions and similar professional or labor organizations? 4 / 4

Workers can freely organize and bargain collectively, and trade unions actively engage in political debates and campaigns. However, strikes are only allowed when negotiating new union agreements, and may only pertain to issues under negotiation. In 2017, a High

Court ruling prohibited organizations that had previously violated orders from the Fair Work Commission from holding strikes during negotiations. The court described the right to strike as a "privilege."

F. RULE OF LAW: 15 / 16

F1. Is there an independent judiciary? 4 / 4

The Australian judiciary is generally independent.

F2. Does due process prevail in civil and criminal matters? 4 / 4

The right to due process is generally respected. Defendants and detainees are presumed innocent until proven guilty and can only be held for 24 hours without being charged for a crime, with exceptions for terrorism cases.

F3. Is there protection from the illegitimate use of physical force and freedom from war and insurgencies? 4 / 4

Australia provides protection from the illegitimate use of force, and Australians have means to seek redress for harm. Prison conditions mostly meet international standards. However, conditions at numerous juvenile detention centers are substandard, and children have been held at adult prisons.

F4. Do laws, policies, and practices guarantee equal treatment of various segments of the population? 3 / 4

Indigenous Australians continue to lag behind other groups in key social and economic indicators, suffer higher rates of incarceration, and report routine mistreatment by police and prison officials. Indigenous children are placed in detention at a rate 25 times higher than that of nonindigenous children. Additionally, people with disabilities make up over half the prison population, and face harassment and violence in prisons.

Men and women have the same legal rights, and discrimination based on sexual orientation or gender identity is prohibited. In practice, women and the lesbian, gay, bisexual, and transgender (LGBT) population experience employment discrimination and occasional harassment.

Religious exemptions within the Sex Discrimination Act of 1984 allow for the expulsion of students and dismissal of teachers on the basis of their sexual orientation. While it appears that this power is rarely exercised, some recent examples of discrimination have come to light. In October 2018, parts of a religious freedom report commissioned by the government in late 2017 were published, which contained recommendations that schools retain the right to discriminate based on sexual orientation. Prime Minister Morrison has faced pressure from rights groups to remove the exemptions and from religious groups to retain and even bolster them. Responding to the controversy, Morrison unveiled a bill in December aimed at protecting LGBT students from discrimination.

Domestic and international condemnation of Australia's harsh asylum and immigration policies persisted in 2018. Rights groups and other observers continued to condemn the country's policy of transporting many refugees and asylum seekers to offshore facilities that are characterized by poor living conditions, inadequate safety for women and children, delays in processing applications, and a lack of sufficient healthcare and education services. The offshore processing center on Manus Island in Papua New Guinea was closed in 2017, and asylum seekers in offshore detention centers in Nauru have been increasingly transferred to Australia. However, over 1,000 people remained in detention on Manus Island and Nauru at the end of 2018.

A section of the 2015 Border Force Act threatens a prison sentence of up to two years for service providers who disclose unauthorized information about the facilities. In 2017, the government amended the law to narrow the scope of information that would qualify as protected information, thus lessening the danger of criminal charges for service workers who disclose such information.

G. PERSONAL AUTONOMY AND INDIVIDUAL RIGHTS: 15 / 16

G1. Do individuals enjoy freedom of movement, including the ability to change their place of residence, employment, or education? 4 / 4

The government respects the freedom of movement, and neither state nor nonstate actors interfere with the choice of residence, employment, or institution of higher education.

G2. Are individuals able to exercise the right to own property and establish private businesses without undue interference from state or nonstate actors? 4 / 4

With an open and free market economy, businesses and individuals enjoy a high level of economic freedom and strong protections for property rights.

G3. Do individuals enjoy personal social freedoms, including choice of marriage partner and size of family, protection from domestic violence, and control over appearance? 4 / 4

The government generally does not restrict social freedoms. In 2017, Parliament legalized same-sex marriage following a nationwide, nonbinding postal survey in which more than 60 percent of participants favored legalization.

Violence against women remains a national concern, particularly for indigenous women. Abortion law is decided by state and territory governments, and abortion is illegal in some regions.

G4. Do individuals enjoy equality of opportunity and freedom from economic exploitation? 3 / 4

Australians generally enjoy robust economic opportunities and freedom from exploitation. However, indigenous people continue to face economic hardships. Census data from 2016 revealed that the indigenous employment rates in remote areas have declined since 2006, impeding their upward social mobility.

In November 2018, Parliament passed the Modern Slavery Act, requiring large businesses to be more transparent about potential slavery in their supply chains and to make efforts to address the problem. While the law, which takes effect in early 2019, has been largely viewed favorably, some critics have noted that it fails to impose penalties for noncompliance.

Austria

Population: 8,800,000
Capital: Vienna
Political Rights Rating: 1
Civil Liberties Rating: 1
Freedom Rating: 1.0
Freedom Status: Free
Electoral Democracy: Yes

Overview: Austria has a democratic system of government that guarantees political rights and civil liberties. It has frequently been governed by a grand coalition of the center-left Social Democratic Party of Austria (SPÖ), and the center-right Austrian People's Party (ÖVP). However, in recent years, the political system has faced pressure from the Freedom Party of Austria (FPÖ), a right-wing, populist party that openly entertains nationalist and xenophobic sentiments. The FPÖ entered the Austrian government in coalition with the ÖVP in 2017.

KEY DEVELOPMENTS IN 2018:

- Threats to press freedom grew in 2018, including harsh verbal attacks on journalists by FPÖ officials throughout the year; draft guidelines issued by the Austrian Broadcasting Corporation (ORF) in June, directing journalists to refrain from criticizing or endorsing government policies and politicians on social media platforms; and efforts by government entities to limit the amount of information provided to media outlets perceived as overly critical.
- In February, the police, at the behest of the FPÖ-controlled Interior Ministry, raided the Office for the Protection of the Constitution and Counterterrorism (BVT), a domestic intelligence agency, and seized documents with information about ongoing investigations into far-right groups with ties to the FPÖ. Several BVT employees were also fired. The raid and firings raised suspicions that the FPÖ was politicizing the agency and attempting to replace its leadership.
- The government continued to pursue policies that aim to crack down on migrants and asylum seekers, including draft legislation announced in November that would reduce welfare benefits for people with poor German skills.

POLITICAL RIGHTS: 37 / 40
A. ELECTORAL PROCESS: 12 / 12
A1. Was the current head of government or other chief national authority elected through free and fair elections? 4 / 4

Executive elections in Austria are generally free and fair. The president is elected for a six-year term and has predominantly ceremonial duties. The president does, however, appoint the chancellor, who also needs the support of the legislature to govern. Austria's current president is the former head of the Green Party, Alexander Van der Bellen, who was elected in 2017 after a close and controversial poll that featured a repeat of the run-off between Van der Bellen and FPÖ candidate Norbert Hofer. The run-off was repeated after the Constitutional Court established that there had been problems with the handling of postal ballots.

Following the 2017 elections to the National Council (Nationalrat), the lower house of parliament, ÖVP head Sebastian Kurz became chancellor with support of the right-wing, populist FPÖ.

A2. Were the current national legislative representatives elected through free and fair elections? 4 / 4

Legislative elections in Austria are generally considered credible. The National Council has 183 members chosen through proportional representation at the district, state, and federal levels. Members serve five-year terms. The 62 members of the upper house, the Federal Council (Bundesrat), are chosen by state legislatures for five- or six-year terms.

Snap elections to the National Council took place in 2017, one year early, following the collapse of the coalition between the SPÖ and the ÖVP. Animosities between the two former coalition partners were reflected in an antagonistic, heavily-fought election campaign. Migration and asylum issues were particularly prominent. ÖVP leader Kurz became a proponent of some of the restrictive policies supported by the right-wing, populist FPÖ, reflecting a rightward shift in Austrian politics.

The ÖVP took 62 mandates—the most of any party but not enough for a governing majority. The SPÖ received 52 mandates, and the FPÖ took 51; the remaining votes were split between smaller parties. Voter turnout was around 80 percent.

The ÖVP formed a coalition government with the FPÖ in late 2017 under the leadership of Sebastian Kurz. The new coalition made Austria the only western European country to have a far-right party included in the government.

A3. Are the electoral laws and framework fair, and are they implemented impartially by the relevant election management bodies? 4 / 4

Austria's electoral laws and framework are fair and generally implemented impartially by the relevant bodies.

B. POLITICAL PLURALISM AND PARTICIPATION: 15 / 16

B1. Do the people have the right to organize in different political parties or other competitive political groupings of their choice, and is the system free of undue obstacles to the rise and fall of these competing parties or groupings? 4 / 4

Austria has competitive political parties that form and operate without encountering undue obstacles. Recent years have seen the rise and fall of various competing parties and coalitions through democratic processes. The Green Party lost its seats in the National Council after failing to meet the 4 percent voting threshold in the 2017 elections, while the recently formed Pilz List entered the chamber for the first time.

B2. Is there a realistic opportunity for the opposition to increase its support or gain power through elections? 4 / 4

Opposition parties have a realistic opportunity to gain representation. Austria has frequently been governed by grand coalitions, a trend that has fostered some public disillusionment with the political process. The SPÖ had formed a grand coalition with the ÖVP in 2013 after winning a plurality of seats in that year's elections. However, following the 2017 polls, the SPÖ was pushed into the opposition after the best-performing ÖVP entered a coalition with the FPÖ.

B3. Are the people's political choices free from domination by the military, foreign powers, religious hierarchies, economic oligarchies, or any other powerful group that is not democratically accountable? 4 / 4

Austrians are generally free to make their own political choices without pressure from the military, business leaders, or other groups that are not democratically accountable.

B4. Do various segments of the population (including ethnic, religious, gender, LGBT, and other relevant groups) have full political rights and electoral opportunities? 3 / 4

The participation of Slovene, Hungarian, and Roma minorities in local government remains limited. There is little minority representation in the legislature. The number of people who have been naturalized (thus gaining certain political rights) has fallen dramatically since the establishment of a more restrictive national integration policy in 2009.

A number of political parties include support for gender equality in their platforms. In the 2017 elections, 34 percent of the members elected to the parliament were women.

C. FUNCTIONING OF GOVERNMENT: 10 / 12
C1. Do the freely elected head of government and national legislative representatives determine the policies of the government? 4 / 4

The freely elected president and legislative representatives work with the chancellor, vice-chancellor, and cabinet ministers to determine the policies of the government.

C2. Are safeguards against official corruption strong and effective? 3 / 4

Austria has some problems with public-sector corruption, and the political class is perceived by many as corrupt. The trial against former finance minister Karl-Heinz Grasser, which commenced in late 2017, was still ongoing at the end of 2018; he is charged with bribery and embezzlement in connection with the sale of state housing in 2004. The Council of Europe's Group of States against Corruption (GRECO) has criticized Austria for weak party finance legislation, and for failing to adequately regulate lobbying and prevent corruption amongst parliamentarians.

C3. Does the government operate with openness and transparency? 3 / 4

Austria's government has frequently been criticized for inadequate transparency. Official secrecy remains enshrined in the constitution. For over five years, a draft freedom of information law has been mired in parliamentary procedures, and it remained stalled in the parliament at year's end. Austria's overall legal framework on access to information, containing vague criteria for compliance and lacking a strong appeals mechanism, is weak.

CIVIL LIBERTIES: 56 / 60 (–1)
D. FREEDOM OF EXPRESSION AND BELIEF: 14 / 16 (–1)
D1. Are there free and independent media? 3 / 4 (–1)

The federal constitution and the Media Law of 1981 provide the basis for free media in Austria, and the government generally respects these provisions in practice. However, libel and slander laws protect politicians and government officials, many of whom—particularly members of the FPÖ—have filed defamation suits in recent years. Media ownership remains highly concentrated, particularly in the provinces.

The government exerts some influence on the state broadcaster, the ORF. The FPÖ-ÖVP government was criticized throughout 2018 for increasing pressure on independent journalists. In a February Facebook post, Heinz-Christian Strache, the head of the FPÖ and vice-chancellor, directly attacked Armin Wolf, a prominent ORF journalist, and accused the broadcaster of spreading lies and propaganda. In May, former FPÖ lawmaker Norbert Steger was appointed head of the ORF's board of trustees. In an April interview, Steger had sharply criticized the ORF and threatened "to cut a third of foreign correspondents, should they not report correctly." In June, the ORF released draft social media guidelines for journalists, which directed them to refrain from criticizing or endorsing government policies and politicians, including on their private accounts. Reporters Without Borders (RSF) condemned the guidelines for "violating not only their [journalists'] freedom of expression but also their right to inform."

The government has increasingly shown favoritism for its preferred media outlets and taken steps to limit access for journalists and entities it views as oppositional. In September, an email written by Interior Minister Herbert Kickl's spokesperson was leaked, which called on the ministry and the police to reduce the amount of information provided to media outlets critical of the government.

While there is no official censorship, Austrian law prohibits any form of neo-Nazism or anti-Semitism, as well as the public denial, approval, or justification of Nazi crimes, including the Holocaust.

Score Change: The score declined from 4 to 3 due to increased pressure and verbal attacks against journalists by government officials, the release of draft guidelines by the Austrian Broadcasting Corporation directing journalists to refrain from expressing political opinions on social media, and efforts by the government to limit access for critical journalists.

D2. Are individuals free to practice and express their religious faith or nonbelief in public and private? 3 / 4

Religious freedom is constitutionally guaranteed. Austrian law divides religious organizations into three legal categories: officially recognized religious societies, religious confessional communities, and associations. Many religious minority groups allege that the law impedes their legitimate claims for recognition, and demotes them to second- or third-class status.

Foreign funding for Muslim houses of worship and imams is prohibited by a 2015 law; Orthodox Christian and Jewish groups with similarly strong links to communities abroad face no such restrictions. The FPÖ has been criticized for stoking anti-Muslim sentiment through controversial advertising campaigns. Some Muslims in Austria have told journalists that they feel the need to keep a low profile since the formation of the ÖVP-FPÖ government. In June 2018, the government announced that it would expel up to 60 imams and close seven mosques for promoting political Islam, which is prohibited under Austrian law. The imams allegedly received illegal funding from Turkey. The move was criticized as a further encroachment on the right to practice Islam in Austria. However, supporters of the decision defended it on national-security grounds, citing the fact that some of the mosques closed were associated with militant and far-right groups.

Full-face coverings were banned in 2017, which was generally interpreted as targeting women who wear burqas and niqabs (facial veils), even though very few women in Austria wear those garments.

D3. Is there academic freedom, and is the educational system free from extensive political indoctrination? 4 / 4

Academic freedom is generally upheld, and the educational system is free from extensive political indoctrination.

D4. Are individuals free to express their personal views on political or other sensitive topics without fear of surveillance or retribution? 4 / 4

Private discussion in Austria is generally free and unrestricted. However, there have been some difficulties related to the balance between ensuring freedom of speech, and enforcing legal prohibitions on hate speech. In June 2018, a Croatian national received a 15-month suspended sentence for performing a Nazi salute at a festival.

E. ASSOCIATIONAL AND ORGANIZATIONAL RIGHTS: 12 / 12
E1. Is there freedom of assembly? 4 / 4

Freedom of assembly is protected in the constitution and in practice.

E2. Is there freedom for nongovernmental organizations, particularly those that are engaged in human rights- and governance-related work? 4 / 4

Nongovernmental organizations (NGOs) operate without restrictions. In 2017, then foreign minister Sebastian Kurz strongly attacked international and other NGOs that aid migrants attempting to cross the Mediterranean, accusing them of supporting human trafficking.

E3. Is there freedom for trade unions and similar professional or labor organizations? 4 / 4

Trade unions are free to organize and to strike, and they are considered an essential partner in national policymaking. Around 27 percent of Austrian employees are unionized, according to 2016 figures.

F. RULE OF LAW: 15 / 16

F1. Is there an independent judiciary? 4 / 4

The judiciary is independent, and the Constitutional Court examines the compatibility of legislation with the constitution without political influence or interference.

F2. Does due process prevail in civil and criminal matters? 4 / 4

Due process generally prevails in civil and criminal matters. However, a scandal that unfolded throughout the year, involving Austria's intelligence apparatus, raised concerns about the potential politicization of the justice system, as well as respect for due process. In February 2018, police raided the offices of the BVT, Austria's domestic intelligence agency, at the behest of FPÖ members in control of the Interior Ministry. The pretext for the raids was the alleged abuse of office by the agency's head, Peter Gridling, who was later suspended, and several other BVT employees. However, critics assailed the raids as politically motivated. Sensitive documents were seized during the raid on the BVT's offices, including information about ongoing investigations into far-right groups with ties to the FPÖ, and several top BVT officials were fired, leading to accusations that the Interior Ministry was attempting to change the leadership of the agency.

In May, a court reversed the suspension of Gridling. In August, a regional court in Vienna ruled that a lower court's approval for the raid on the BVT offices, as well as raids on the homes of three BVT staff members, was illegal, because the information seized could have been collected by simply requesting it from the BVT. As outrage over the raids continued, a parliamentary investigation into the scandal commenced in September.

F3. Is there protection from the illegitimate use of physical force and freedom from war and insurgencies? 4 / 4

People in Austria are generally free from the illegitimate use of physical force, war, and insurgencies. However, terrorist threats are a concern.

Conditions in prisons generally meet high European standards.

F4. Do laws, policies, and practices guarantee equal treatment of various segments of the population? 3 / 4

Some marginalized groups face difficulty exercising their human rights before the law. Strong rhetoric has been directed against refugees and migrants in recent years. Some asylum seekers can be deported while appeals are pending. During the year, the government continued to pursue policies aimed at cracking down on asylum seekers and migrants. In November 2018, the government announced proposed legislation that would reduce welfare benefits for people with poor German skills, which drew condemnation from rights groups.

LGBT (lesbian, gay, transgender, and bisexual) people face some societal discrimination. Hate crime legislation prohibits incitement based on sexual orientation. However, no law prohibits service providers from denying services on that basis. In August, reports emerged that the asylum application of a gay man from Afghanistan was denied because he did not "walk, act, or dress" like a gay man, and thus should not fear persecution in his home country. On the other hand, a gay Iraqi man's asylum application was rejected because the authorities claimed he acted "too girlish," making his sexuality "not believable."

Rights groups denounced the decisions and the stereotypical language used to justify them, and claimed that the asylum process is discriminatory against both LGBT people and other vulnerable groups.

G. PERSONAL AUTONOMY AND INDIVIDUAL RIGHTS: 15 / 16

G1. Do individuals enjoy freedom of movement, including the ability to change their place of residence, employment, or education? 4 / 4

Austrian citizens enjoy freedom of movement and choice of residence. Roma and other ethnic minorities face discrimination in the labor and housing markets. The Labor Ministry has sought to promote integration of younger immigrants by providing German-language instruction and job training.

G2. Are individuals able to exercise the right to own property and establish private businesses without undue interference from state or nonstate actors? 4 / 4

Austrians may freely exercise the right to own property and establish businesses.

G3. Do individuals enjoy personal social freedoms, including choice of marriage partner and size of family, protection from domestic violence, and control over appearance? 4 / 4

. In 2017, Austria's Constitutional Court ruled that same-sex marriage will be legal starting in 2019, overturning the 2009 law that permitted civil partnerships for same-sex couples. Since 2016, there are no longer restrictions on same-sex couples adopting children.

The 2009 Second Protection against Violence Act increased penalties for perpetrators of domestic violence, and authorized further punitive measures against chronic offenders.

G4. Do individuals enjoy equality of opportunity and freedom from economic exploitation? 3 / 4

A 1979 law guarantees women's freedom from discrimination in various areas, including the workplace. However, the income gap between men and women remains significant. According to the US State Department's 2018 *Trafficking in Persons Report*, Austria remains "a destination and transit country for men, women, and children subjected to sex trafficking and forced labor," but the government is making efforts to fight human trafficking; convictions and prosecutions for trafficking-related offenses have increased, and the government makes efforts at identifying victims among refugee and migrant populations.

Azerbaijan

Population: 9,900,000
Capital: Baku
Political Rights Rating: 7
Civil Liberties Rating: 6
Freedom Rating: 6.5
Freedom Status: Not Free
Electoral Democracy: No

Note: The numerical ratings and status listed above do not reflect conditions in Nagorno-Karabakh, which is examined in a separate report.

Overview: In Azerbaijan's authoritarian government, power remains heavily concentrated in the hands of Ilham Aliyev, who has served as president since 2003. Corruption is rampant, and following years of persecution, formal political opposition is weak. The regime has overseen an extensive crackdown on civil liberties in recent years, leaving little room for independent expression or activism.

KEY DEVELOPMENTS IN 2018:

- In April, President Aliyev was elected to a fourth term in a process that lacked genuine competition, amid evidence of electoral fraud and tight restrictions on the media and opposition.
- In August, opposition leader Ilgar Mammadov was released by an appeals court after five years in prison on politically motivated charges. However, other opposition figures faced arrest and imprisonment during the year.
- The government continued to crack down on the media throughout the year, blocking independent news sites and detaining and prosecuting critical journalists.

POLITICAL RIGHTS: 2 / 40 (–1)
A. ELECTORAL PROCESS: 0 / 12 (–1)
A1. Was the current head of government or other chief national authority elected through free and fair elections? 0 / 4

The president is head of state and is directly elected to seven-year terms. There are no term limits. Since the early 1990s, elections have not been considered credible or competitive by international observers. A February 2018 presidential decree moved the presidential election, originally planned for October, up to April. President Aliyev—who succeeded his father, Heydar, in 2003—won a fourth term in a predictable landslide victory amid evidence of electoral fraud. An observer mission from the Organization for Security and Co-operation in Europe (OSCE) found that the election lacked genuine competition due to a restrictive political environment in which opposition candidates did not openly confront or criticize the president.

In 2017, President Aliyev appointed his wife, Mehriban Aliyeva, as vice president. The post had been created via constitutional changes that were pushed through in 2016 without meaningful parliamentary debate or public consultation.

A2. Were the current national legislative representatives elected through free and fair elections? 0 / 4

Elections to the 125 seats in Azerbaijan's unicameral Milli Mejlis, or National Assembly, were held in 2015 amid a government campaign against criticism and dissent. The main opposition parties boycotted the vote. According to official results, Aliyev's ruling Yeni Azerbaijan Party (YAP) won 71 seats, with 41 going to independent candidates who tend to support the ruling party, and the remaining 12 split among small progovernment parties. The international election monitoring mission from the OSCE declined to send observers, saying restrictions placed by the government on the number of observers permitted would make effective and credible observation impossible.

A3. Are the electoral laws and framework fair, and are they implemented impartially by the relevant election management bodies? 0 / 4 (–1)

The electoral laws and framework do not ensure free and fair elections. The nomination process for members of electoral commissions places the bodies under the influence of the ruling party. The performance of the Central Election Commission (CEC) during the 2018 presidential election demonstrated its lack of independence, as commissioners expressed no dissenting opinions at public sessions and decisions were made unanimously with little or no deliberation. The CEC also failed to prevent instances of ballot box stuffing and other forms of fraud reported at some polling stations, and disregarded many mandatory procedures meant to safeguard the integrity of the vote.

Commission members have been known to unlawfully interfere with the election process and obstruct the activities of observers. Complaints of electoral violations do not receive adequate or impartial treatment.

In 2016, voters approved a package of constitutional changes that were pushed through without meaningful debate or consultation; among other changes, the legislation further concentrated power within the president's office.

Score Change: The score declined from 1 to 0 because the conduct of the 2018 presidential election demonstrated the electoral commission's lack of independence, its widespread disregard for procedural safeguards against fraud and other abuses, and the biased nature of the electoral framework, which favors the ruling party.

B. POLITICAL PLURALISM AND PARTICIPATION: 2 / 16

B1. Do the people have the right to organize in different political parties or other competitive political groupings of their choice, and is the system free of undue obstacles to the rise and fall of these competing parties or groupings? 1 / 4

The political environment in Azerbaijan is neither pluralistic nor competitive, and mechanisms for public participation are limited by the dominance of the president's YAP party. A number of laws passed over the past decade limit candidates' ability to organize and hold rallies. The political opposition has virtually no access to coverage on television, which remains the most popular news source in Azerbaijan.

B2. Is there a realistic opportunity for the opposition to increase its support or gain power through elections? 0 / 4

The biased electoral framework and repressive media and political environment make it nearly impossible for opposition parties to gain power through elections. The main opposition parties boycotted the 2015 parliamentary elections and the 2018 presidential election rather than take part in a flawed vote. Opposition figures complained that moving the 2018 election forward from October to April further disadvantaged them by allowing inadequate time to prepare their campaigns.

Opposition politicians and party officials are subject to arbitrary arrest on dubious charges, as well as physical violence and other forms of intimidation. In January 2018, Gozel Bayramli, the deputy chairperson of the opposition Azerbaijan Popular Front Party (APFP), was sentenced to three years in prison on charges of carrying undeclared funds into the country; she maintains that her arrest and prosecution was politically motivated. The nongovernmental organization (NGO) Working Group on a Unified List of Political Prisoners estimated that there were 128 political prisoners in the country as of September.

In August, Ilgar Mammadov, a leader of the Republican Alternative movement, was released following a ruling by the Shaki Court of Appeals. After more than five years of imprisonment on politically motivated charges, the remaining two years of Mammadov's seven-year sentence was commuted to a suspended sentence, during which he cannot leave the country.

B3. Are the people's political choices free from domination by the military, foreign powers, religious hierarchies, economic oligarchies, or any other powerful group that is not democratically accountable? 1 / 4

The authoritarian one-party system in Azerbaijan largely excludes the public from any genuine and autonomous political participation.

B4. Do various segments of the population (including ethnic, religious, gender, LGBT, and other relevant groups) have full political rights and electoral opportunities? 0 / 4

The dominance of the ruling party limits political parties' freedom to represent a diversity of interests and views. There are no meaningful mechanisms to promote representation of minorities.

C. FUNCTIONING OF GOVERNMENT: 0 / 12

C1. Do the freely elected head of government and national legislative representatives determine the policies of the government? 0 / 4

The head of government and national legislative representatives are not elected in a free or fair manner. Aliyev and the YAP determine and implement the policies of the government with little opposition.

C2. Are safeguards against official corruption strong and effective? 0 / 4

Corruption is pervasive. In the absence of a free press and independent judiciary, officials are rarely held accountable for corrupt behavior.

In 2017, a network of international media outlets exposed a $2.9 billion slush fund, held within United Kingdom–registered shell companies and linked to the Azerbaijani ruling elite, including the Aliyev family. Leaked banking records from 2012–14 have revealed payments to, among others, former members of the Parliamentary Assembly of the Council of Europe (PACE), London- and US-based lobbyists, and senior officials in the Azerbaijani government.

Britain's *Guardian* newspaper, one of the outlets that exposed the scheme, credited lobbying operations associated with the fund for a move by PACE to vote down a 2013 report critical of Azerbaijan's rights record. In April, an independent investigation body, tasked by PACE to investigate the allegations, stated that Azerbaijan's government exerted "undue influence" on various political processes within PACE in order to minimize criticism of its elections and alleged rights abuses.

C3. Does the government operate with openness and transparency? 0 / 4

Government operations are opaque. Although public officials are nominally required to submit financial disclosure reports, procedures and compliance remain unclear, and the reports are not publicly accessible. There are legal guarantees for citizens' access to information, but also broad exceptions to the right, and authorities at all levels systematically refuse to respond to information requests.

In 2017, Azerbaijan withdrew from the Extractive Industries Transparency Initiative (EITI), an international platform that promotes good governance and transparency in resource-rich countries, having been suspended due to ongoing noncompliance with EITI human rights standards.

CIVIL LIBERTIES: 9 / 60
D. FREEDOM OF EXPRESSION AND BELIEF: 2 / 16
D1. Are there free and independent media? 0 / 4

Constitutional guarantees for press freedom are routinely and systematically violated, as the government works to maintain a tight grip on the information landscape. Defamation remains a criminal offense. Journalists—and their relatives—faced harassment, threats, violence, and intimidation by authorities. Many have been detained or imprisoned on fabricated charges, while others face travel bans. In January 2018, for example, investigative journalist Afgan Mukhtarli, who was abducted from Tbilisi, Georgia in 2017, was sentenced to six years in prison on smuggling charges, a sentence observers considered politically motivated. According to the Committee to Protect Journalists (CPJ), there were 10 journalists imprisoned in Azerbaijan as of December.

Legal amendments passed in 2017 extended government control over online media, allowing blocking of websites without a court order if deemed to contain content posing a danger to the state or society. Many prominent independent news sites have since been blocked, including four sites that were blocked in August for allegedly defaming government officials. Also in August, progovernment news agency APA and its three affiliate outlets were shut down for apparently misquoting the president on Armenian-Azerbaijani relations and the Nagorno-Karabakh conflict. However, observers suspect that financial issues might have behind the move.

D2. Are individuals free to practice and express their religious faith or nonbelief in public and private? 0 / 4

The government restricts the practice of minority and "nontraditional" religions and denominations, largely through burdensome registration requirements and interference with the importation and distribution of printed religious materials. In February 2018, the State Committee for Work with Religious Organizations prohibited the publication of a book on Islam by a theologian due to a disagreement over its religious content.

A number of mosques have been closed in recent years, ostensibly for registration or safety violations. Jehovah's Witnesses face continued harassment; in July, a conscientious objector was convicted of evading military service, even though he had suggested alternative public service. No sentence was ultimately imposed.

In May, the government pardoned 7 of the 17 members of the Muslim Unity Movement (MUM), a conservative Shiite group, who were sentenced to up to 20 years in prison in 2017 on charges that included conspiracy to overthrow the government. Some members of the group have been tortured in prison. Despite the pardons, the group's members continued to face harassment and arrest in 2018. In March, MUM coordinator Ahsan Nuruzade was sentenced to seven years in prison after being convicted on drug charges.

D3. Is there academic freedom, and is the educational system free from extensive political indoctrination? 1 / 4

The authorities have long curtailed academic freedom. Some educators have reported being dismissed for links to opposition groups, and students have faced expulsion and other punishments for similar reasons.

D4. Are individuals free to express their personal views on political or other sensitive topics without fear of surveillance or retribution? 1 / 4

Law enforcement bodies are suspected of monitoring private telephone and online communications—particularly of activists, political figures, and foreign nationals—without judicial oversight. The escalation of government persecution of critics and their families has undermined the assumption of privacy and eroded the openness of private discussion.

In recent years, activists have reported being targeted by spear-phishing campaigns designed to install malware on their computers or steal personal information.

E. ASSOCIATIONAL AND ORGANIZATIONAL RIGHTS: 1 / 12
E1. Is there freedom of assembly? 0 / 4

National law imposes tight restrictions on freedom of assembly, and under 2016 amendments, the right to free assembly is contingent on not violating "public order and morals." Unsanctioned gatherings can draw a harsh police response and fines for participants.

In March 2018, in advance of a rally in Baku organized by several opposition parties to protest the early presidential election, six party members from the APFP were arrested and detained for between 15 and 20 days, and dozens of other activists were summoned for questioning. The APFP claimed that the pressure placed on party activists by the authorities was meant to discourage the event and intimidate its organizers.

After the attempted assassination in July of Elmar Valiyev, the mayor of Ganja, protesters gathered in support of the detained suspect and demanded an investigation into the mayor himself, who had been accused of corruption. The demonstration turned violent and two police officers were killed. Around 40 people were arrested at the protest, and mobile data service in the area was shut down to restrict the spread of information.

E2. Is there freedom for nongovernmental organizations, particularly those that are engaged in human rights- and governance-related work? 0 / 4

Repressive laws on NGOs have been used to pressure both local and foreign organizations, many of which suspended operations when their bank accounts were frozen or their offices raided. In June 2018, human rights lawyer Emin Aslan, who has worked on behalf of a number of NGOs, was arrested, held incommunicado, and sentenced to 30 days in jail for allegedly disobeying the police. However, observers asserted that Aslan's detention was connected to his work as a human rights defender.

E3. Is there freedom for trade unions and similar professional or labor organizations? 1 / 4

Although the law permits the formation of trade unions and the right to strike, the majority of unions remain closely affiliated with the government, and most major industries are dominated by state-owned enterprises.

F. RULE OF LAW: 1 / 16
F1. Is there an independent judiciary? 0 / 4

The judiciary is corrupt, inefficient, and subservient to the executive. Although nominally independent, the Bar Association acts on the orders of the Ministry of Justice, and is complicit in the harassment of human rights lawyers.

F2. Does due process prevail in civil and criminal matters? 1 / 4

Constitutional guarantees of due process are not upheld. Arbitrary arrest and detention are common, and detainees are often held for long periods before trial. Opposition figures, journalists, and activists arrested or sentenced in recent years have reported restricted access to legal counsel, fabrication and withholding of evidence, and physical abuse. In July 2018, police arrested a suspect, Yunis Safarov, for the assassination attempt on Valiyev. The government said, without providing evidence, that Safarov is a militant motivated by a desire to impose Islamic rule on Azerbaijan. Critics claimed that the authorities were linking the suspect to extremism in order to deflect anger about corruption and poor governance in

Ganja and across the country, which opposition activists argued could be the motive for the attack. Safarov awaited trial at year's end.

A bill passed in 2017 restricts court representation by lawyers who are not members of the bar, giving the politicized Bar Association full control over the legal profession and seriously limiting access to representation.

F3. Is there protection from the illegitimate use of physical force and freedom from war and insurgencies? 0 / 4

Reports of the use of torture to extract confessions continue. Prison conditions are substandard; medical care is generally inadequate, and overcrowding is common.

F4. Do laws, policies, and practices guarantee equal treatment of various segments of the population? 0 / 4

Members of ethnic minority groups have complained of discrimination in areas including education, employment, and housing. Although same-sex sexual activity is legal, LGBT (lesbian, gay, bisexual, and transgender) people experience societal discrimination and risk harassment by the police. In 2017, police fined or detained dozens of people for weeks in a coordinated crackdown on LGBT residents, which led many to flee the country.

G. PERSONAL AUTONOMY AND INDIVIDUAL RIGHTS: 5 / 16

G1. Do individuals enjoy freedom of movement, including the ability to change their place of residence, employment, or education? 1 / 4

The government restricts freedom of movement, particularly foreign travel, for opposition politicians, journalists, and civil society activists.

People with disabilities and psychiatric patients are routinely institutionalized; there is no clear procedure to review their confinement.

G2. Are individuals able to exercise the right to own property and establish private businesses without undue interference from state or nonstate actors? 1 / 4

Property rights and free choice of residence are affected by government-backed development projects that often entail forced evictions, unlawful expropriations, and demolitions with little or no notice.

G3. Do individuals enjoy personal social freedoms, including choice of marriage partner and size of family, protection from domestic violence, and control over appearance? 2 / 4

Domestic violence committed against women, men, and children is a problem. Conservative social norms contribute to the widespread view that gender-based violence is a private matter, which discourages victims from reporting perpetrators to the police. Child marriage remains common throughout the country.

G4. Do individuals enjoy equality of opportunity and freedom from economic exploitation? 1 / 4

Azerbaijan is a source, transit point, and destination for forced labor and sex trafficking. Romany children are particularly susceptible to forced labor, often working in restaurants or as roadside vendors, while some are victims of forced begging. The government has taken some efforts to combat trafficking, including by prosecuting traffickers and providing services to victims.

Bahamas

Capital: Nassau
Population: 400,000
Political Rights Rating: 1
Civil Liberties Rating: 1
Freedom Rating: 1.0
Freedom Status: Free
Electoral Democracy: Yes

Overview: The Bahamas are a stable democracy where political rights and civil liberties are generally respected. However, the islands have a relatively high homicide rate. Harsh immigration policies, which mainly affect Haitian-Bahamians and Haitian migrants, are often executed in the absence of due process. Government corruption is a serious problem that is thought to have had significant economic consequences.

KEY DEVELOPMENTS IN 2018:

- In January, the Bahamian Supreme Court ruled that Jean-Rony Jean Charles, a Bahamian-born man of Haitian descent who was deported to Haiti in 2017, must be permitted to return to the Bahamas and granted legal status. A government appeal of the decision was thrown out in November.
- In August, the Supreme Court ordered that the government and utility providers halt service disconnections and evictions in shantytowns, which the government had been ordering as part of its immigration crackdown. The stay order was in effect at year's end pending a review of the government's efforts to dismantle such settlements.
- In June, the government allocated $1 million to defray the costs of bringing a dormant Freedom of Information law into effect.
- A Fiscal Responsibility Law that aims to improve transparency of public-sector spending, and mandates the establishment of an independent oversight and enforcement body, took effect in October.

POLITICAL RIGHTS: 38 / 40

A. ELECTORAL PROCESS 12 / 12

A1. Was the current head of government or other chief national authority elected through free and fair elections? 4 / 4

The Bahamas are governed under a parliamentary system, and a mostly ceremonial governor-general is appointed by the British monarch as head of state. The prime minister is head of government, and is appointed by the governor-general; the office is usually held by the leader of the largest party in parliament or head of a parliamentary coalition. Hubert Minnis became prime minister following the victory of his party, the Free National Movement (FNM), in the May 2017 legislative elections.

A2. Were the current national legislative representatives elected through free and fair elections? 4 / 4

Members of the lower chamber of the bicameral Parliament, the 39-member House of Assembly, are directly elected to five-year terms. The 16 members of the Senate are appointed for five-year terms by the governor-general based on recommendations made by the prime minister and the opposition leader.

In May 2017 general elections, the ruling Progressive Liberal Party (PLP) was defeated by the FNM, which won 35 out of 39 seats in the House of Assembly; Minnis, the FNM leader, was then appointed prime minister. International monitors praised the electoral process, but expressed concern about an outdated voter registration system, and the replacement of the parliamentary commissioner—a key administrative official—and the redrawing of electoral districts just before the polls.

A3. Are the electoral laws and framework fair, and are they implemented impartially by the relevant election management bodies? 4 / 4

The electoral process is regulated by the Parliamentary Elections Act and managed by the Parliamentary Registration Department. The parliamentary commissioner heads the department, and is appointed by the governor-general acting on the recommendation of the prime minister after consultation with the opposition leader.

B. POLITICAL PLURALISM AND PARTICIPATION 16 / 16

B1. Do the people have the right to organize in different political parties or other competitive political groupings of their choice, and is the system free of undue obstacles to the rise and fall of these competing parties or groupings? 4 / 4

Political parties may organize freely, and operate unhindered. However, electoral financing is not regulated, there is no legal obligation to disclose funding sources, and there are no limits on campaign spending. Observers noted that a Fiscal Responsibility Law that took effect in October 2018 lacked provisions on campaign finance and spending.

B2. Is there a realistic opportunity for the opposition to increase its support or gain power through elections? 4 / 4

Opposition parties operate without undue interference. Political power has alternated between the PLP and the FNM since the country achieved independence from the United Kingdom in 1973.

B3. Are the people's political choices free from domination by the military, foreign powers, religious hierarchies, economic oligarchies, or any other powerful group that is not democratically accountable? 4 / 4

Voters and candidates are generally able to exercise their political choices freely. However, a lack of campaign finance regulations leaves open avenues for the outsized role of money in politics.

B4. Do various segments of the population (including ethnic, religious, gender, LGBT, and other relevant groups) have full political rights and electoral opportunities? 4 / 4

Only citizens may vote, and protracted and obscure citizenship and naturalization proceedings make achieving citizenship difficult for those born in the Bahamas to foreign parents. Though women remain underrepresented in politics, 7 out of 16 Senators are women, including both the president and vice president of the Senate.

C. FUNCTIONING OF GOVERNMENT 10 / 12

C1. Do the freely elected head of government and national legislative representatives determine the policies of the government? 4 / 4

Freely elected officials are generally able to determine national policies in a free and unhindered manner.

C2. Are safeguards against official corruption strong and effective? 3 / 4

The country's anticorruption mechanisms are relatively weak, and there is no agency specifically empowered to handle allegations of government corruption. Rates of reporting corruption are low, as whistleblowers fear retaliation. Domestic transparency advocates have alleged that widespread government corruption has been a significant contributor to a recent economic downturn and increased tax rates.

Bribery cases against former labor minister Shane Gibson and former housing and environment minister Kenred Dorsett were ongoing at year's end.

C3. Does the government operate with openness and transparency? 3 / 4

Government procurement processes have lacked transparency, and political parties and campaigns are not required to disclose their finances. A long-awaited Freedom of Information Act was passed in February 2017 but lacked key provisions, including whistleblower protection. In June 2018, the government allocated $1 million to defray the costs of bringing the law into effect.

Legislators and other high-ranking public officials are required to disclose their income and assets under the Public Disclosure Act of 1976, but in 2018, the government did not follow through on its promise to prosecute three parliamentarians—who have become known in the media as the "disclosure three"—who failed to submit the required information. Infighting at the Bahamas Power and Light (BPL) that led to the dissolution of its board, and Oban Energies' securing of a long-term government contract without an environmental impact statement, furthered concerns about a lack of government transparency in 2018.

A Fiscal Responsibility Law that took effect in October aims to improve transparency of public-sector spending and mandates the establishment of an independent oversight and enforcement body, among other provisions. Observers noted that the law's efficacy will depend on authorities' willingness to enforce it.

CIVIL LIBERTIES: 53 / 60

D. FREEDOM OF EXPRESSION AND BELIEF 15 / 16

D1. Are there free and independent media? 3 / 4

Press freedom in the Bahamas is constitutionally guaranteed and generally respected in practice. Libel is a criminal offense punishable by up to two years in prison, but it is rarely invoked.

The country's privately owned newspapers and radio broadcasters freely express a variety of views, although partisanship is common in many media outlets.

D2. Are individuals free to practice and express their religious faith or nonbelief in public and private? 4 / 4

Religious freedom is generally respected.

D3. Is there academic freedom, and is the educational system free from extensive political indoctrination? 4 / 4

Academic institutions are generally free from political pressure and other interference.

D4. Are individuals free to express their personal views on political or other sensitive topics without fear of surveillance or retribution? 4 / 4

People can freely express personal views in private and in public without fear of retribution or surveillance.

E. ASSOCIATIONAL AND ORGANIZATIONAL RIGHTS 12 / 12

E1. Is there freedom of assembly? 4 / 4

Freedom of assembly is protected by the constitution, and the government respects this right in practice.

E2. Is there freedom for nongovernmental organizations, particularly those that are engaged in human rights- and governance-related work? 4 / 4

Freedom of association is generally protected, and there is no specific legislation governing registration procedures for nongovernmental organizations (NGOs). A variety of NGOs operate in the country.

E3. Is there freedom for trade unions and similar professional or labor organizations? 4 / 4

Labor, business, and professional organizations are generally free from government interference. Unions have the right to strike, and collective bargaining is prevalent.

F. RULE OF LAW 13 / 16

F1. Is there an independent judiciary? 4 / 4

The judicial system is headed by the Supreme Court and a court of appeals, with the additional right of appeal to the Privy Council in London under certain circumstances. The Bahamian judiciary is predominantly independent, and there have been no major reports in recent years of attempts by powerful figures to use political or other influence to secure favorable rulings.

F2. Does due process prevail in civil and criminal matters? 3 / 4

Due process in civil and criminal matters generally prevails. However, the government only appoints counsel to defendants in capital cases, leaving some people without legal representation. While there were some examples of migrants given hearings before a magistrate ahead of the execution of a deportation order, generally migrants do not enjoy due process before detention or deportation. In 2018, the government announced it intended to amend immigration laws to make it easier to deport migrants without due process.

F3. Is there protection from the illegitimate use of physical force and freedom from war and insurgencies? 4 / 4

Homicide and violent crime rates in the Bahamas remain among the highest in the Caribbean. However, state security agents generally do not engage in the illegal use of force against civilians, and the population is not threatened by large-scale violence or insurgencies.

Prison conditions are poor, and reports of violence against prisoners by guards continue.

F4. Do laws, policies, and practices guarantee equal treatment of various segments of the population? 2 / 4

The Constitution does not grant equal rights between men and women in the transmission of nationality to their children and spouses, effectively denying many Bahaman-born people the rights and access to services associated with citizenship.

Despite a change in government, harsh immigration policies enacted in 2014 are still in effect, and have exacerbated stigma and discrimination against the targeted populations, mainly Haitians and Haitian-Bahamians. Police actions against migrants surged after Prime Minister Minnis announced in 2017 that all irregular migrants had until the end of that year to secure legal status, or be "aggressively pursued and deported." Individuals born in the Bahamas to foreign parents who have a constitutional right to citizenship have been removed as part of the crackdown, with at least one such case, that of Jean-Rony Jean Charles, prompting court proceedings. In January 2018, the Bahamian Supreme Court ruled that Jean Charles, a Bahamian-born man of Haitian descent who was deported to Haiti in 2017, must be permitted to return to the Bahamas and granted legal status. A government appeal of the decision was thrown out in November.

Allegations of inhumane conditions at migrant detention centers have persisted. Civil society groups have reported that individuals held at Carmichael Road Immigration Detention Center are often unable to receive family visits, and guards have forced them to pay to receive food or other supplies brought by family members. In 2018, the government acknowledged substandard conditions at the Carmichael Road Center and said regulations for detainees' welfare had been drafted. These had not been released at year's end.

Discrimination based on sexual orientation or gender identity is not prohibited by law, and LGBT (lesbian, gay, bisexual, and transgender) people report discrimination in employment and housing. The government has rejected proposals to address this discrimination, citing the country's adherence to Christian values.

G. PERSONAL AUTONOMY AND INDIVIDUAL RIGHTS 13 / 16

G1. Do individuals enjoy freedom of movement, including the ability to change their place of residence, employment, or education? 3 / 4

The freedom of movement is protected. However, the immigration policies adopted by the previous government are still enforced and have had an impact on people of Haitian descent in the exercise of their individual rights, including their ability to move freely and choose their places of employment and education.

Roadblocks have been erected as part of immigration enforcement actions.

G2. Are individuals able to exercise the right to own property and establish private businesses without undue interference from state or non-state actors? 4 / 4

The country has a strong private sector and the economy relies mostly on tourism and financial services. Individuals are free to establish businesses subject to legal requirements.

The ongoing immigration crackdown has seen operations to tear down shantytowns that mainly house migrants, though the Supreme Court in August 2018 ordered that the government and utility providers halt any planned service disconnections or evictions there. The stay order was in effect at year's end, pending a review of the government's efforts to dismantle such settlements.

G3. Do individuals enjoy personal social freedoms, including choice of marriage partner and size of family, protection from domestic violence, and control over appearance? 3 / 4

The government does not place explicit restrictions on social freedoms. Violence against women, including domestic violence and marital rape, constitutes a serious issue in the country. No law permits same-sex marriage.

G4. Do individuals enjoy equality of opportunity and freedom from economic exploitation? 3 / 4

The Bahamas is a source, destination, and transit country for men, women, and children for forced labor and sexual exploitation. The government fully complies with minimum international standards to address the problem and has made significant efforts to prosecute traffickers. Migrant workers, many of whom arrive in the Bahamas to work in the agricultural sector and in domestic services, are particularly vulnerable to exploitation.

Bahrain

Population: 1,500,000
Capital: Manama
Political Rights Rating: 7
Civil Liberties Rating: 6
Freedom Rating: 6.5
Freedom Status: Not Free
Electoral Democracy: No

Overview: Bahrain was once viewed as a promising model for political reform and democratic transition, but it has become one of the Middle East's most repressive states. Since violently crushing a popular prodemocracy protest movement in 2011, the Sunni-led monarchy has systematically eliminated a broad range of political rights and civil liberties, dismantled the political opposition, and cracked down harshly on persistent dissent in the Shiite population.

KEY DEVELOPMENTS IN 2018:

- In November, elections were held for the lower chamber of parliament, but the country's main opposition groups had been banned, and most opposition leaders were in prison or exile. Ahead of the polls, the leader of the largest opposition group, Ali Salman of Al-Wefaq, was sentenced to life in prison on charges of espionage.
- In May, the parliament approved legislation that barred the electoral candidacies of anyone who belonged to the dissolved political groups, had boycotted or been expelled from the parliament in the past, or had ever received a prison sentence of at least six months.
- Also that month, a court revoked the citizenship of 115 Bahrainis who had been convicted on terrorism-related charges after a flawed mass trial. The London-based Bahrain Institute for Rights and Democracy said that more than 800 Bahrainis had been stripped of their nationality since 2012, including 304 in 2018 alone.

POLITICAL RIGHTS: 2 / 40

A. ELECTORAL PROCESS: 2 / 12

A1. Was the current head of government or other chief national authority elected through free and fair elections? 0 / 4

The 2002 constitution gives the king power over the executive, legislative, and judicial authorities. The monarch appoints and dismisses the prime minister and cabinet members, who are responsible to him rather than the legislature. However, since independence from Britain in 1971, the country has had only one prime minister, Khalifa bin Salman al-Khalifa, the uncle of the current king, Hamad bin Isa al-Khalifa.

A2. Were the current national legislative representatives elected through free and fair elections? 1 / 4

The king appoints the 40-member Consultative Council, the upper house of the National Assembly. The lower house, or Council of Representatives, consists of 40 elected members serving four-year terms. Formal political parties are not permitted, but members of "political societies" have participated in elections in practice.

Lower house elections were held in November 2018, with a runoff round in December, but with bans on the country's main opposition groups in place, the exercise featured little meaningful competition. In May the parliament had passed a law prohibiting the candidacy of anyone who belonged to the dissolved political societies, had boycotted or been expelled from the parliament, or had received a prison sentence of at least six months.

Most seats went to independents, though small Sunni Islamist groups won several seats and a leftist group won two. As in previous years, turnout figures were disputed amid a lack of independent election monitoring. Al-Wefaq had called for a boycott, and one of its former lawmakers, Ali al-Sheehri, was arrested and threatened with criminal charges for saying on social media that he planned to boycott the elections. A stamp was placed in each voter's passport to indicate that they had participated, meaning those who boycotted could face repercussions when attempting to travel.

A3. Are the electoral laws and framework fair, and are they implemented impartially by the relevant election management bodies? 1 / 4

Bahrain's electoral framework is unfair, with electoral districts deliberately designed to underrepresent Shiites, who form a majority of the citizen population. The government has also allegedly drawn district borders to put certain political societies, including leftist and Sunni Islamist groups, at a disadvantage. The government directorate responsible for administering elections is headed by the justice minister, a member of the royal family, and is not an independent body.

B. POLITICAL PLURALISM AND PARTICIPATION: 0 / 16

B1. Do the people have the right to organize in different political parties or other competitive political groupings of their choice, and is the system free of undue obstacles to the rise and fall of these competing parties or groupings? 0 / 4

Formal political parties are illegal, and a 2005 law makes it illegal to form political associations based on class, profession, or religion. A 2016 amendment bans serving religious clerics from engaging in political activity. The law permits "political societies," with some of the functions of a political party, to operate after registering with the government, but the authorities have recently shuttered the country's main opposition societies. The Shiite Islamist society Al-Wefaq was forcibly disbanded in 2016 for allegedly encouraging violence. Bahrain's second-largest opposition group, the secularist National Democratic Action Society (Wa'ad), was banned in 2017 after it criticized the execution of three men on terrorism charges and expressed solidarity with Al-Wefaq following its dissolution.

The regime has also cracked down on opposition leaders, forcing many into prison or exile. Al-Wefaq's general secretary, Ali Salman, was arrested on various incitement charges in 2014 and fought a series of legal battles, finally receiving a four-year prison sentence from the Court of Cassation in 2017. In November 2018, an appellate court sentenced Salman to life in prison for alleged espionage on behalf of Qatar. Also during 2018, opposition figures such as Hasan al-Marzooq, the general secretary of the small but still legal opposition group Al-Wahdawi, and Ibrahim Sharif, the former general secretary of Wa'ad, were summoned for questioning over their social media comments.

B2. Is there a realistic opportunity for the opposition to increase its support or gain power through elections? 0 / 4

The ruling family maintains a monopoly on political power, and the system's structure excludes the possibility of a change in government through elections. Shiite opposition forces chose to boycott the 2014 legislative elections rather than participate in an unfair process, and former members of the now-disbanded main opposition groups were barred from running in the 2018 elections. The polls did feature a high rate of turnover, with just three incumbent lawmakers returning to the new parliament; many senior incumbents chose not to run or were blocked from doing so by the government.

B3. Are the people's political choices free from domination by the military, foreign powers, religious hierarchies, economic oligarchies, or any other powerful group that is not democratically accountable? 0 / 4

The monarchy generally excludes the public from any meaningful political participation. Since 2011 it has used the security forces to isolate the country's Shiite population and suppress political dissent.

B4. Do various segments of the population (including ethnic, religious, gender, LGBT, and other relevant groups) have full political rights and electoral opportunities? 0 / 4

Although Shiites make up a majority of the country's citizens, they have tended to be underrepresented in both chambers of the National Assembly and the cabinet. The regime, which is dominated by a Sunni ruling family, is committed to preventing the Shiite community from organizing independently to advance their political interests, though it is also keen to ensure that at least some progovernment Shiites and members of religious minorities are present in the legislature and cabinet.

Women formally enjoy full political rights, but they are typically marginalized in practice. Six women were elected to the lower house in 2018, up from three, and a woman was chosen as speaker for the first time; nine women were named to the upper house.

Noncitizens make up just over half of the total population, and most have no political rights, but expatriates who own property in the kingdom are allowed to vote in municipal elections. Citizenship generally must be inherited from a Bahraini father, and foreign men married to Bahraini women do not have access to naturalization.

C. FUNCTIONING OF GOVERNMENT: 3 / 12

C1. Do the freely elected head of government and national legislative representatives determine the policies of the government? 1 / 4

The king and other unelected officials, particularly those from the ruling family, hold most authority over the development and implementation of laws and policies. The National Assembly may propose legislation to the government, but it is the government that drafts and submits the bills for consideration by the legislature. With the main opposition groups no longer participating in the National Assembly, the body has become increasingly silent on politically sensitive topics, but it does feature debate about economic reforms and austerity measures.

C2. Are safeguards against official corruption strong and effective? 2 / 4

There are some laws in place to combat corruption, but enforcement is weak, and high-ranking officials suspected of corruption are rarely punished. The media are not sufficiently free to independently air allegations of corruption against officials. Civil society anticorruption efforts are also restricted; the current and former chairs of the Bahrain Transparency Society have periodically been banned from travel.

C3. Does the government operate with openness and transparency? 0 / 4

Parliamentary proceedings are public, and the parliament is entitled to scrutinize the government budget, but the executive issues orders and laws without providing insight or allowing meaningful public consultation on their development. There is no law guaranteeing public access to government information, and officials are not obliged to disclose their assets or income.

ADDITIONAL DISCRETIONARY POLITICAL RIGHTS QUESTION

Is the government or occupying power deliberately changing the ethnic composition of a country or territory so as to destroy a culture or tip the political balance in favor of another group? −3 / 0

The government has made concerted efforts to erode the Shiite citizen majority and tip the country's demographic balance in favor of the Sunni minority, mostly by recruiting foreign-born Sunnis to serve in the security forces and become citizens. Meanwhile, hundreds of Bahrainis have had their citizenship revoked in recent years, including a number of Shiite leaders and activists. In May 2018, a court revoked the citizenship of 115 Bahrainis who had been convicted on terrorism-related charges after a flawed mass trial. According to the London-based Bahrain Institute for Rights and Democracy, more than 800 Bahrainis have been stripped of their nationality since 2012, including 304 in 2018 alone. Since 2011, the government has maintained a heavy security presence in primarily Shiite villages. Security personnel restrict the movements of Shiite citizens and periodically destroy their property.

CIVIL LIBERTIES: 10 / 60

D. FREEDOM OF EXPRESSION AND BELIEF: 2 / 16

D1. Are there free and independent media? 0 / 4

The government owns all broadcast media outlets, and the private owners of Bahrain's main newspapers have close ties to the state. The only independent newspaper, *Al-Wasat*, was shuttered by the authorities in 2017. Self-censorship is encouraged by the vaguely worded Press Law, which allows the state to imprison journalists for criticizing the king or Islam or for threatening national security. Insulting the king is punishable by up to seven years in prison. A 2016 edict regulates newspapers' use of the internet and social media to disseminate content, and requires the outlets to apply for a one-year renewable license. The government selectively blocks online content, including opposition websites and content that criticizes religion or highlights human rights abuses. Authorities have also blocked online access to Qatari news outlets since diplomatic relations with Qatar broke down during 2017.

Journalists continue to face legal and bureaucratic obstacles to their work in practice. Bahraini authorities have refused to renew the credentials of several Bahraini journalists working with foreign media outlets. Six journalists remained behind bars as of December 2018, according to the Committee to Protect Journalists, and seven were stripped of their nationality between the uprising in February 2011 and February 2018, according to Reporters Without Borders.

D2. Are individuals free to practice and express their religious faith or nonbelief in public and private? 1 / 4

Islam is the state religion, and the penal code criminalizes blasphemy-related offenses. Some media material and websites are censored on religious grounds. However, non-Muslim minorities are generally free to practice their faiths. Muslim and non-Muslim religious groups are required to register with government ministries, though the government has not actively punished groups that operate without permits. Muslim religious groups register with the Ministry of Justice and Islamic Affairs through the Sunni or Shiite awqaf (endowments). The awqaf oversee mosques and prayer houses, and their directors are appointed by royal decree and paid by the government.

Although Shiite communities are free to carry out religious observances, such as the annual Ashura processions, Shiite clerics and community leaders often face harassment, interrogation, prosecution, and imprisonment, typically due to allegations that they have incited sectarian hatred or violence. Some Sunnis have also been charged with such offenses. An estimated 45 Shiite religious sites were demolished or vandalized in 2011 in apparent reprisal for the role of Shiite opposition groups in that year's protests. The Islamic Ulema Council, a group of Shiite clerics, was banned in 2014. The government revoked the citizenship of senior Shiite cleric Isa Qassim in 2016, and he was given a suspended one-year prison sentence for money laundering in 2017. Other Shiite clergy were among those detained or questioned in 2017 for allegedly participating in a sustained sit-in protest around Qassim's home that led to clashes with security forces. Protests and police restrictions periodically obstruct access to mosques.

D3. Is there academic freedom, and is the educational system free from extensive political indoctrination? 0 / 4

Academic freedom is not formally restricted, but scholars who criticize the government are subject to dismissal. In 2011, a number of faculty members and administrators were fired for supporting the call for democracy, and hundreds of students were expelled. Those who remained were forced to sign loyalty pledges.

D4. Are individuals free to express their personal views on political or other sensitive topics without fear of surveillance or retribution? 1 / 4

The penal code includes a variety of punishments for offenses such as insulting the king or state institutions and spreading false news. Many Bahrainis have been convicted and jailed for political speech, including on social media, particularly since the 2011 uprising. In 2017, when Bahrain joined a regional boycott of Qatar, the Interior Ministry said expressions of sympathy or support for that country were prohibited, with a penalty of up to five years in prison. A prominent Bahraini activist has been jailed for criticizing the Saudi-led military campaign in Yemen on social media.

The security forces are believed to use networks of informers, and the government monitors the personal communications of activists, critics, and opposition members. In 2018, several exiled Bahraini opposition activists brought a court case against a British spyware company that they accused of helping the Bahraini authorities to hack and surveil their computers.

E. ASSOCIATIONAL AND ORGANIZATIONAL RIGHTS: 1 / 12
E1. Is there freedom of assembly? 0 / 4

Citizens must obtain a permit to hold demonstrations, and a variety of onerous restrictions make it difficult to organize a legal gathering in practice. Police regularly use force to break up political protests, most of which occur in Shiite villages. Participants can face long jail terms, particularly if the demonstrations involve clashes with security personnel.

E2. Is there freedom for nongovernmental organizations, particularly those that are engaged in human rights- and governance-related work? 0 / 4

Nongovernmental organizations (NGOs) are prohibited from operating without a permit, and authorities have broad discretion to deny or revoke permits. The government also reserves the right to replace the boards of NGOs. Bahraini human rights defenders and their family members are subject to harassment, intimidation, and prosecution. Many of them were either in prison or in exile as of 2018. In December, the Court of Cassation upheld a five-year prison sentence against Nabeel Rajab, head of the Bahrain Center for Human Rights, for social media posts that criticized the torture of prisoners in Bahrain as well as the conduct of the Saudi-led military campaign in Yemen (in which Bahrain takes part).

E3. Is there freedom for trade unions and similar professional or labor organizations? 1 / 4

Bahrainis have the right to establish independent labor unions, but workers must give two weeks' notice before a strike, and strikes are banned in a variety of economic sectors. Trade unions cannot operate in the public sector, and collective-bargaining rights are limited even in the private sector. Harassment and firing of unionist workers occurs in practice. Household servants, agricultural workers, and temporary workers do not have the right to join or form unions.

F. RULE OF LAW: 1 / 16

F1. Is there an independent judiciary? 0 / 4

The king appoints all judges and heads the Supreme Judicial Council, which administers the courts and proposes judicial nominees. The courts are subject to government pressure in practice. The country's judicial system is seen as corrupt and biased in favor of the royal family and its allies, particularly in politically sensitive cases. Once made, judicial decisions are generally enforced.

F2. Does due process prevail in civil and criminal matters? 1 / 4

Law enforcement officers reportedly violate due process during arrests and detention, in part by obstructing detainees' access to attorneys. Detainees are sometimes held incommunicado in practice. Judicial proceedings often put defendants at a disadvantage, with judges denying bail requests or restricting defense attorneys' attendance or arguments without explanation. The government claims it does not hold political prisoners, but scores of opposition figures, human rights and democracy advocates, and ordinary citizens have been jailed for their political views and activities.

In 2017, the government restored the National Security Agency's power to make arrests. This reversed one of the key reforms undertaken in 2011 after an inquiry into human rights abuses. The agency has been accused of torture and other abuses. Also in 2017, the constitution was amended to permit military trials for civilians in security-related cases, further threatening due process rights. In December of that year, a military court sentenced a Shiite soldier and five Shiite civilians to death for alleged terrorism offenses, though the sentences were commuted to imprisonment by the king in 2018.

F3. Is there protection from the illegitimate use of physical force and freedom from war and insurgencies? 0 / 4

Torture is criminalized, but detainees frequently report mistreatment by security forces and prison officials, who are rarely held accountable for abuse. The Interior Ministry ombudsman's office has failed to provide a meaningful check on such impunity. In 2017, the authorities executed three Shiite men for allegedly killing police officers in 2014. The men received an unfair trial and were reportedly subjected to torture. The executions were the first in the kingdom since 2010.

Police have been targeted in small bombings and armed attacks in recent years. Four officers were killed during 2017, and multiple injuries were reported in 2018.

F4. Do laws, policies, and practices guarantee equal treatment of various segments of the population? 0 / 4

Women enjoy legal equality on some issues, and gender-based discrimination in employment is prohibited. Nevertheless, discrimination is common in practice, and women are generally at a disadvantage in matters of family law.

Shiites of both Arab and Persian ethnicity face de facto discrimination in matters including public and private employment. They are largely excluded from the security forces, except when serving as unarmed community police officers. There is a general perception that Shiite public employees are relegated to nonsecurity ministries, like those focused on health and education, which may put Sunni applicants at a disadvantage in such sectors. The government does not publish socioeconomic or population data that are broken down by religious sect.

Discrimination based on sexual orientation is common. The law does not provide protections against such bias, though same-sex sexual activity is not criminalized for those aged 21 and older. Public displays of same-sex affection could fall afoul of public decency laws.

Bahrain is not a signatory to the 1951 refugee convention and does not recognize refugee status.

G. PERSONAL AUTONOMY AND INDIVIDUAL RIGHTS: 6 / 16

G1. Do individuals enjoy freedom of movement, including the ability to change their place of residence, employment, or education? 1 / 4

Authorities restrict movement inside the country for residents of largely Shiite villages outside Manama, where the government maintains a heavy security presence. The government also obstructs foreign travel by numerous opposition figures and activists.

Bahrain established a new "flexible" permit for foreign workers in 2017, aiming to ease the workers' ability to change jobs; the traditional sponsorship system ties migrant workers to a specific employer. However, participation in the new scheme has so far been very limited, in part because of the high cost of the flexible permit relative to the low salaries typically paid to noncitizen workers.

G2. Are individuals able to exercise the right to own property and establish private businesses without undue interference from state or nonstate actors? 2 / 4

Although registered businesses are largely free to operate, obtaining approval can be difficult in practice. Legal reforms in recent years have sought to lower the capital requirements and other obstacles to registering and operating businesses. For the wealthy elites who dominate the business sector, property rights are generally respected, and expropriation is rare. However, Shiite citizens encounter difficulties obtaining affordable housing and in some cases face bans on purchasing land. Much of the country's scarce land is occupied by royal properties and military facilities. Noncitizens can only own property in designated areas. Women may inherit property, but their rights are not equal to those of men.

G3. Do individuals enjoy personal social freedoms, including choice of marriage partner and size of family, protection from domestic violence, and control over appearance? 2 / 4

Personal status issues such as marriage, divorce, and child custody are governed by a 2017 unified family law. Previously only a Sunni family code was in place, with Shiite personal status matters adjudicated by Shiite religious courts according to their interpretation of Islamic jurisprudence. Some Shiite leaders objected to the new law. The law's provisions are still based on Sharia (Islamic law) principles that put women at a disadvantage on many issues.

Accused rapists can avoid punishment by marrying their victims, and spousal rape is not specifically outlawed. Adultery is illegal, and those who kill a spouse caught in the act of adultery are eligible for lenience in sentencing.

G4. Do individuals enjoy equality of opportunity and freedom from economic exploitation? 1 / 4

Some employers subject migrant workers to forced labor and withhold their salaries, and there are reports that abusers illegally withhold workers' documentation in order to prevent them from leaving or reporting abuse to the authorities. Bahrain's new "flexible" work permit is prohibitively expensive for the household workers and laborers who have historically been exploited. The government has taken steps to combat human trafficking in recent years, but efforts to investigate and prosecute perpetrators remain weak.

Revenues from oil and gas exports, the main source of income for the government, are used to fund public-sector jobs and services. All citizens thus receive some benefit from the state-owned energy industry, but not to an equal degree. In particular there is discrimination in the allocation of public-sector jobs and promotion opportunities, depending on one's social and sectarian background and personal connections.

Bangladesh

Capital: Dhaka
Population: 166,400,000
Political Rights Rating: 5 ↓
Civil Liberties Rating: 5 ↓
Freedom Rating: 5.0
Freedom Status: Partly Free
Electoral Democracy: No

Overview: The ruling Awami League (AL) has consolidated political power through sustained harassment of the opposition and those perceived to be allied with it, as well as of critical media and voices in civil society. Corruption is a serious problem, and anticorruption efforts have been weakened by politicized enforcement. Due process guarantees are poorly upheld and security forces carry out a range of human right abuses with near impunity. The threat posed by Islamist extremists has receded since 2016, when the government enacted a harsh crackdown that saw the arrest of some 15,000 people.

KEY DEVELOPMENTS IN 2018:

- The ruling Awami League (AL) overwhelmingly won parliamentary elections in December, which were marked by violence, the intimidation of opposition candidates and supporters, allegations of fraud benefiting the ruling party, and the exclusion of respected election monitors.
- In February, in advance of the polls, former prime minister and Bangladesh Nationalist Party (BNP) leader Khaleda Zia was convicted on corruption charges and jailed. In December, the attorney general announced that, per a recent Supreme Court ruling, she could not contest the elections due to a ban on political candidacy by anyone sentenced more than two years in prison.
- A number of large student protests held on campuses and in the streets were met with attacks by AL supporters and were violently dispersed by police, and many participants were arrested.
- Approximately 700,000 Rohingya refugees who had fled Myanmar since 2017 remained in Bangladesh, where most live in precarious camps that lack basic services.

POLITICAL RIGHTS: 17 / 40 (−2)

A. ELECTORAL PROCESS: 5 / 12 (−2)

A1. Was the current head of government or other chief national authority elected through free and fair elections? 2 / 4

A largely ceremonial president, who serves for five years, is elected by the legislature. President Abdul Hamid was elected to his second term in 2018.

The leader of the party that wins the most seats in the unicameral National Parliament assumes the position of prime minister and wields effective power. Hasina was expected to be sworn in for her third term as prime minister in early 2019 following the AL's victory in the 2018 elections, which were marked by violence, intimidation of opposition candidates and supporters, and allegations of fraud benefiting the ruling party.

A2. Were the current national legislative representatives elected through free and fair elections? 1 / 4 (−1)

The National Parliament is composed of 350 members, 300 of whom are directly elected. Political parties elect a total of 50 female members based on their share of elected seats.

Hasina's AL overwhelmingly won the December 2018 polls, taking 288 of the 300 directly elected seats. Election day and the campaign that preceded it were marked by political violence in which at least 17 people were killed, as well as legal and extralegal harassment of government opponents. The opposition BNP claimed that 6,000 of its supporters and 10 of its candidates had been arrested ahead of the elections, and that its candidates were subject to intimidation and violence. Zia, the BNP's leader, was convicted on corruption charges and jailed ahead of the polls and later banned from participating in them as a candidate, significantly harming the BNP's competitiveness.

In the election's wake, the BNP issued allegations that the AL had benefit from widespread electoral fraud carried out by AL supporters with the complicity of law enforcement agents. The government also faced criticism for long delays in approving the accreditation of the Asian Network for Free Elections (ANFREL), which ultimately cancelled its election monitoring mission. A number of domestic missions, including one run by the highly regarded human rights organization Odhikar, were also unable to observe the elections due to similar delays, or authorities' outright denial of accreditation.

The previous general election in 2014 was boycotted by the main opposition party and was disrupted by significant violence.

Score Change: The score declined from 2 to 1 because the year's parliamentary elections were marred by violence, intimidation against the opposition, allegations of fraud, and the obstruction of election monitoring missions.

A3. Are the electoral laws and framework fair, and are they implemented impartially by the relevant election management bodies? 2 / 4 (−1)

The independence of the Election Commission (EC) and its ability to investigate complaints has long been questioned by opposition parties and outside observers, including by foreign governments and international organizations that have withdrawn financial assistance to the commission over such concerns. The EC's stewardship of the 2018 elections gave further credence to complaints that it favors the ruling party. In the run-up to the 2018 polls, the commission disqualified 141 BNP candidates for various violations, but only 3 from the AL. (Anticipating such disqualifications, the BNP designated multiple nominees for a number of posts to minimize disruptions to its campaign.) Moreover, the EC failed to order additional security measures following outbreaks of political violence that preceded the vote, or to meaningfully address many complaints filed by opposition figures about election-related violence and other electoral irregularities.

Score Change: The score declined from 3 to 2 because rulings by the Electoral Commission favored the ruling Awami League, and because it failed to address complaints about election-related violence and other electoral irregularities.

B. POLITICAL PLURALISM AND PARTICIPATION: 7 / 16

B1. Do the people have the right to organize in different political parties or other competitive political groupings of their choice, and is the system free of undue obstacles to the rise and fall of these competing parties or groupings? 2 / 4

Bangladesh has a two-party system in which power has historically alternated between political coalitions led by the AL and BNP; third parties have traditionally had difficulty achieving traction. Both parties are nondemocratic in terms of internal structure, and are led by families that have competed to lead Bangladesh since independence, along with a small coterie of advisers. A crackdown on the BNP ahead of the 2018 elections significantly disrupted its operations. There were also reports that the party's campaign materials were suppressed.

The constitution bans religiously based political parties, and the Jamaat-i-Islami (JI) party was prohibited from taking part in the 2014 and 2018 elections because of its overtly Islamist charter, though some JI members ran as independents. Bangladesh's International Crimes Tribunal—named as such despite lacking international oversight—was created in 2010 by Hasina to try people suspected of committing war crimes during Bangladesh's 1971 war of independence from Pakistan. Critics of the tribunal claim it was established to persecute Hasina's political opponents, notably those in JI.

B2. Is there a realistic opportunity for the opposition to increase its support or gain power through elections? 1 / 4

The main opposition BNP has been weakened by regular harassment and arrests of key members that have significantly harmed its ability to challenge the AL in elections. The 2018 election campaign was characterized by a crackdown on dissent that saw thousands of people and several political candidates arrested. There were also a number of acts of violence committed against opposition figures.

In the run-up to the polls, former prime minister and BNP leader Khaleda Zia was sentenced to five years' imprisonment for corruption, and the term was doubled in October, and the same month she was also sentenced to seven years in another case. In December, the attorney general announced that, per a recent Supreme Court ruling, she could not contest the elections due to a ban on political candidacy by anyone sentenced more than two years in prison. Zia's imprisonment severely hampered the competiveness of the BNP.

A JI spokesman said more than 1,850 party members were arrested ahead of the 2018 elections, and some party members claimed they had been subject to torture while in custody.

B3. Are the people's political choices free from domination by the military, foreign powers, religious hierarchies, economic oligarchies, or any other powerful group that is not democratically accountable? 2 / 4

The rival AL and BNP parties dominate politics and limit political choices for those who question internal party structures or hierarchy, or who would create alternative parties or political groupings.

Animosity between Hasina and Zia, as well as between lower-level cadres, has contributed to continued political violence. The human rights group Odhikar registered 79 deaths and 3,826 people injured as a result of inter- or intraparty clashes from January through November 2018.

B4. Do various segments of the population (including ethnic, religious, gender, LGBT, and other relevant groups) have full political rights and electoral opportunities? 2 / 4

In the National Parliament, 50 seats are allotted to women, who are elected by political parties based on their overall share of elected seats, and women lead both main political parties. Nevertheless, societal discrimination against women, as well as against as well against LGBT (lesbian, gay, bisexual, and transgender) communities, limits their participation in politics. Religious minorities remain underrepresented in politics and state agencies, though the AL government has appointed several members of such groups to leadership positions.

C. FUNCTIONING OF GOVERNMENT: 5 / 12

C1. Do the freely elected head of government and national legislative representatives determine the policies of the government? 2 / 4

Policy is set by the ruling AL, and weaknesses in the country's institutions have reduced checks on its processes and decision-making. Low representation of opposition lawmakers in the National Parliament significantly reduces its ability to provide thorough scrutiny of or debate on government policies, budgets, and proposed legislation.

C2. Are safeguards against official corruption strong and effective? 1 / 4

Under the AL government, anticorruption efforts have been weakened by politicized enforcement and subversion of the judicial process. In particular, the Anti-Corruption Commission (ACC) has become ineffective and subject to overt political interference. The government continues to bring or pursue politicized corruption cases against BNP party leaders.

C3. Does the government operate with openness and transparency? 2 / 4

Endemic corruption and criminality, weak rule of law, limited bureaucratic transparency, and political polarization have long undermined government accountability. The 2009 Right to Information Act mandates public access to all information held by public bodies and overrides secrecy legislation. Although it has been unevenly implemented, journalists and civil society activists have had some success in using it to obtain information from local governing authorities.

CIVIL LIBERTIES: 24 / 60 (−2)

D. FREEDOM OF EXPRESSION AND BELIEF: 6 / 16 (−1)

D1. Are there free and independent media? 1 / 4

Journalists and media outlets face many forms of pressure, including frequent lawsuits, harassment, and serious or deadly physical attacks. The threat of physical reprisals against bloggers and publishers in connection with their work remained high in 2018. In June, secular blogger Shahjahan Bachchu was murdered after receiving death threats from Sunni extremists. A climate of impunity remains the norm, with little progress made on ensuring justice for the series of blogger murders since 2015. Dozens of bloggers remain in hiding or exile.

Separately, in August 2018, photographer Shahidul Alam was arrested under the Information and Communication Technology (ICT) Act for posting a video of student protests on Facebook. The Digital Security Act, which became law in October 2018 and replaced the

ICT Act, allows the government to conduct searches or arrest individuals without a warrant and criminalizes various forms of speech, and was vehemently opposed by journalists.

Forms of artistic expression contained in books, films, and other materials are occasionally banned or censored.

D2. Are individuals free to practice and express their religious faith or nonbelief in public and private? 2 / 4

Bangladesh is a secular state, but Islam is designated as the official religion. Although religious minorities have the right to worship freely, they occasionally face legal repercussions for proselytizing. Members of minority groups—including Hindus, Christians, Buddhists, and Shiite and Ahmadiyya Muslims—face harassment and violence, including mob violence against their houses of worship. Those with secular or nonconformist views can face societal opprobrium and attacks from hardline Islamist groups.

D3. Is there academic freedom, and is the educational system free from extensive political indoctrination? 1 / 4 (–1)

In recent years, Bangladesh's academic institutions have increasingly faced threats from a variety of actors, resulting in reduced autonomy and rising self-censorship. Faculty hiring and promotion are often linked to support for the AL, and campus debate is stifled by the AL's student wing. In 2018, several campus demonstrations by students and professors who objected to a quota scheme for government jobs were set upon by assailants and violently dispersed by police, and many participants were arrested. The police dispersal of one protest at Dhaka University involved the use of rubber bullets and tear gas.

Changes made to the Bengali-language textbooks used widely throughout the educational system and distributed in 2017—at the behest of Islamist groups, who demanded the removal of content they claimed was "atheistic"—raised concerns among intellectuals regarding the influence of these groups over government policy and standards. Separately, Islamic extremists have attacked secular professors.

Score Change: The score declined from 2 to 1 due to an increase in political pressure, intimidation, and self-censorship affecting university students, faculty, and administrators in recent years.

D4. Are individuals free to express their personal views on political or other sensitive topics without fear of surveillance or retribution? 2 / 4

Open private discussion of sensitive religious and political issues is restrained by fears of harassment. Advocacy group Human Rights Watch (HRW) said the crackdown preceding the 2018 elections created "a climate of fear extending from prominent voices in society to ordinary citizens." Censorship of digital content and surveillance of telecommunications and social media have become increasingly common.

E. ASSOCIATIONAL AND ORGANIZATIONAL RIGHTS: 5 / 12

E1. Is there freedom of assembly? 2 / 4

The constitution provides for the rights of assembly and association, but the government regularly bans gatherings of more than five people. Many demonstrations took place in 2018, though authorities sometimes try to prevent rallies by arresting party activists, and protesters are frequently injured and occasionally killed during clashes in which police have used excessive force. In 2018, large street protests regarding economic and social issues, comprised mostly of students, were attacked by allies of the ruling party and prompted violent police responses and arrests.

E2. Is there freedom for nongovernmental organizations, particularly those that are engaged in human rights- and governance-related work? 2 / 4

Many nongovernmental organizations (NGOs) operate in Bangladesh and are able to function without onerous restrictions, but the use of foreign funds must be cleared by the NGO Affairs Bureau, which can also approve or reject individual projects. The 2016 Foreign Donations (Voluntary Activities) Regulation Act made it more difficult for NGOs to obtain foreign funds and gave officials broad authority to deregister NGOs. Democracy, governance, and human rights NGOs are regularly denied permission for proposed projects and are subject to harassment and surveillance.

E3. Is there freedom for trade unions and similar professional or labor organizations? 1 / 4

Legal reforms in 2015 eased restrictions on the formation of unions. However, union leaders who attempt to organize or unionize workers continue to face dismissal or physical intimidation, and organizations that advocate for labor rights have faced increased harassment. Worker grievances fuel unrest at factories, particularly in the garment industry, where protests against low wages and unsafe working conditions are common. Protesting workers often face violence, arrest, and dismissal.

F. RULE OF LAW: 4 / 16 (−1)
F1. Is there an independent judiciary? 1 / 4 (−1)

Politicization of and pressure against the judiciary is persists. In 2017, the Chief Justice of the Supreme Court retired; he left the country and said, in an autobiography published in September 2018 that he had been forced to retire after threats from Bangladeshi military intelligence because of rulings he had made against the government. In 2018, other allegations of political pressure on judges continued to emerge, as did allegations that unqualified AL loyalists were being appointed to court positions.

Separately, the opposition alleged that the slew of corruption cases lodged against Zia, and the sentences handed down in 2018 in connection with her convictions, had been designed to prevent her from running for a seat in the year's elections. The justice system is racked by delays, and Zia noted that her cases were adjudicated far more rapidly than other prominent criminal cases.

Score Change: The score declined from 2 to 1 due to continued political pressure against members of the judiciary, including the former chief justice's allegation that the government had forced him to resign in 2017.

F2. Does due process prevail in civil and criminal matters? 1 / 4

Individuals' ability to access justice is compromised by endemic corruption within the court system and severe backlogs. Pretrial detention is often lengthy, and many defendants lack counsel. Suspects are routinely subject to arbitrary arrest and detention, demands for bribes, and physical abuse by police. Criminal cases against ruling party activists are regularly withdrawn on the grounds of "political consideration," undermining the judicial process and entrenching a culture of impunity.

The 1974 Special Powers Act permits arbitrary detention without charge, and the criminal procedure code allows detention without a warrant. A 2009 counterterrorism law includes a broad definition of terrorism and generally does not meet international standards.

Concerns have repeatedly been raised that the International Crimes Tribunal's procedures and verdicts do not meet international standards on issues such as victim and witness protection, the presumption of innocence, defendant access to counsel, and the right to bail. The tribunal continued to hand down sentences, including death sentences, in 2018.

F3. Is there protection from the illegitimate use of physical force and freedom from war and insurgencies? 1 / 4

Terrorist attacks by Islamist militant groups continued to decline in 2018 following a crackdown on these groups in the latter half of 2016, during which more than 15,000 people were arrested. The South Asia Terrorism Portal documented only three civilian fatalities related to Islamist extremism in 2018, down from 9 in 2017 and 43 in 2016.

However, a range of human rights abuses by law enforcement agencies—including enforced disappearances, custodial deaths, arbitrary arrests, and torture—have continued unabated. A 2017 Human Rights Watch report documented the use of detention and enforced disappearance against members of the political opposition, despite the government's promise to address the issue. In May 2018, the government initiated a "war on drugs;" by the end of the month, thousands had been arrested and over 100 were killed.

The incidence of custodial deaths has remained high. Odhikar reported a total of 456 extrajudicial killings perpetrated by law enforcement agencies between January and November 2018, in addition to 83 enforced disappearances. Prison conditions are extremely poor; severe overcrowding is common, and juveniles are often incarcerated with adults.

F4. Do laws, policies, and practices guarantee equal treatment of various segments of the population? 1 / 4

Members of ethnic and religious minority groups face some discrimination under law as well as harassment and violations of their rights in practice. Indigenous people in the Chittagong Hill Tracts (CHT) remain subject to physical attacks, property destruction, land grabs by Bengali settlers, and occasional abuses by security forces.

Bangladesh has hosted roughly 270,000 ethnic Rohingyas who fled from Myanmar beginning in the 1990s. The vast majority do not have official refugee status; suffer from a complete lack of access to health care, employment, and education; and are subject to substantial harassment. In response to a sharp escalation in violence directed against Rohingyas in Myanmar's Rakhine State in 2017, some 700,000 refugees poured across the border into Bangladesh, creating a humanitarian crisis. Most live in precarious camps that lack basic services. Authorities reached a repatriation agreement with Myanmar in October, but the UN refugee agency said conditions in Myanmar were not fit for the refugees' return and that safeguards for them were "absent." At year's end the repatriation plan had not been implemented.

A criminal ban on same-sex sexual acts is rarely enforced, but societal discrimination remains the norm, and dozens of attacks on LGBT individuals are reported every year. A number of LGBT individuals remain in exile following the 2016 murder of Xulhaz Mannan, a prominent LGBT activist, by Islamist militants. Despite legal recognition for transgender people as an optional "third gender," they face persecution.

G. PERSONAL AUTONOMY AND INDIVIDUAL RIGHTS: 9 / 16

G1. DO INDIVIDUALS ENJOY FREEDOM OF MOVEMENT, INCLUDING THE ABILITY TO CHANGE THEIR PLACE OF RESIDENCE, EMPLOYMENT, OR EDUCATION? 3 / 4

The ability to move within the country is relatively unrestricted, as is foreign travel, though there are some rules on travel into and around the CHT districts by foreigners as well as into Rohingya refugee camps. There are few legal restrictions regarding choice of education or employment.

G2. Are individuals able to exercise the right to own property and establish private businesses without undue interference from state or nonstate actors? 2 / 4

Property rights are unevenly enforced, and the ability to engage freely in private economic activity is somewhat constrained. Corruption and bribery, inadequate infrastructure, and official bureaucratic and regulatory hurdles hinder business activities throughout the country. State involvement and interference in the economy is considerable. The 2011 Vested Properties Return Act allows Hindus to reclaim land that the government or other individuals seized, but it has been unevenly implemented. Tribal minorities have little control over land decisions affecting them, and Bengali-speaking settlers continue to illegally encroach on tribal lands in the CHT. A commission set up in 2009 to allocate land to indigenous tribes has suffered from delays.

G3. Do individuals enjoy personal social freedoms, including choice of marriage partner and size of family, protection from domestic violence, and control over appearance? 2 / 4

Under personal status laws affecting all religions, women have fewer marriage, divorce, and inheritance rights than men, and face discrimination in social services and employment. Rape, acid throwing, and other forms of violence against women occur regularly despite laws offering some level of protection. A law requiring rape victims to file police reports and obtain medical certificates within 24 hours of the crime in order to press charges prevents most cases from reaching the courts. Giving or receiving dowry is a criminal offense, but coercive requests remain a problem; Odhikar reported 142 cases of dowry-related violence against women in 2018. A high rate of early marriage persists, with 59 percent of girls married by age 18, according to statistics from the United Nations Children's Fund (UNICEF) for 2017. Despite a stated government commitment in 2014 to abolish the practice by 2041, in 2017 parliament approved a law that would permit girls under the age of 18 to marry under certain circumstances, reversing a previous legal ban on the practice.

G4. Do individuals enjoy equality of opportunity and freedom from economic exploitation? 2 / 4

Socioeconomic inequality is widespread. Working conditions in the garment industry remain extremely unsafe in most factories despite the renewal of a legally binding accord between unions and clothing brands to improve safety practices. Comprehensive reforms of the industry are hampered by the fact that a growing number of factory owners are also legislators or influential businesspeople.

Bangladesh remains both a major supplier of and transit point for trafficking victims, with tens of thousands of people trafficked each year. Women and children are trafficked both overseas and within the country for the purposes of domestic servitude and sexual exploitation, while men are trafficked primarily for labor abroad. A comprehensive 2013 antitrafficking law provides protection to victims and increased penalties for traffickers, but enforcement remains inadequate.

Barbados

Population: 300,000
Capital: Bridgetown
Political Rights Rating: 1
Civil Liberties Rating: 1
Freedom Rating: 1.0
Freedom Status: Free
Electoral Democracy: Yes

Overview: Barbados is a democracy that regularly holds competitive elections and upholds civil liberties. Challenges include official corruption and a lack of government transparency, discrimination against the LGBT (lesbian, gay, bisexual, and transgender) population, violent crime, and poverty.

KEY DEVELOPMENTS IN 2018:
- The Barbados Labour Party (BLP), led by Mia Mottley, defeated the ruling Democratic Labour Party (DLP) in the May general elections, taking all 30 seats in the House of Assembly. Mottley was subsequently appointed the country's first female prime minister.
- In June, LGBT activists filed a petition at the Inter-American Commission on Human Rights to challenge laws that criminalize same-sex sexual relations.
- To address a deepening fiscal crisis, in October, the International Monetary Fund (IMF) approved a $290 million loan package to Barbados. The deal followed Prime Minister Mottley's disclosure in June that the extent of the country's debt burden was more severe than previously thought.

POLITICAL RIGHTS: 38 / 40
A. ELECTORAL PROCESS: 12 / 12
A1. Was the current head of government or other chief national authority elected through free and fair elections? 4 / 4

The prime minister, usually the leader of the largest party in Parliament, is head of government. The British monarch is head of state, and is represented by a governor general.

Mia Mottley of the BLP was appointed prime minister after her party decisively won the May 2018 general elections, unseating the incumbent, Freundel Stuart of the DLP. The polls were regarded as competitive and credible, despite some allegations of vote buying. Dame Sandra Mason was sworn in as governor general in January.

A2. Were the current national legislative representatives elected through free and fair elections? 4 / 4

Members of the 30-member House of Assembly, the lower house of the bicameral Parliament, are directly elected for five-year terms. The governor general appoints the 21 members of the upper house, the Senate: 12 on the advice of the prime minister, 2 on the advice of the leader of the opposition, and the remaining 7 at their own discretion. Senators serve five-year terms.

The parliamentary elections held in May 2018 were peaceful and stakeholders accepted their results. The opposition BLP took all 30 seats in the House of Assembly, in a stunning rebuke of the DLP and Stuart.

A3. Are the electoral laws and framework fair, and are they implemented impartially by the relevant election management bodies? 4 / 4

The independent Electoral and Boundaries Commission oversees elections in Barbados in a professional manner. Its five commissioners, chosen on the basis of expertise, are selected by the prime minister and the opposition for a maximum term of five years.

B. POLITICAL PLURALISM AND PARTICIPATION: 16 / 16

B1. Do the people have the right to organize in different political parties or other competitive political groupings of their choice, and is the system free of undue obstacles to the rise and fall of these competing parties or groupings? 4 / 4

Political parties form and operate freely. As the 2018 general elections approached, new parties emerged to challenge the traditionally dominant BLP and DLP. These include the United Progressive Party, the Barbados Integrity Movement, and Solutions Barbados. However, the new parties failed to win any seats in the 2018 polls.

B2. Is there a realistic opportunity for the opposition to increase its support or gain power through elections? 4 / 4

Opposition parties have a realistic chance of gaining power through elections, and power has historically rotated between the BLP and DLP. The opposition BLP's landslide victory over the incumbent DLP in the 2018 elections highlighted the competitiveness of the political system.

B3. Are the people's political choices free from domination by the military, foreign powers, religious hierarchies, economic oligarchies, or any other powerful group that is not democratically accountable? 4 / 4

Voters and candidates are generally able to express their political choices without interference from actors that are not democratically accountable.

B4. Do various segments of the population (including ethnic, religious, gender, LGBT, and other relevant groups) have full political rights and electoral opportunities? 4 / 4

Barbados's population is fully enfranchised, with adult citizens, Commonwealth citizens, and foreigners with seven years' residency able to vote. Laws protect the political rights of women, but commonly held societal attitudes can discourage women from running for office, and women actively participating in politics face marginalization. Women compose only 20 percent of the House of Assembly.

Mia Mottley became the country's first female prime minister in 2018. During the campaign, Mottley endured a number of discriminatory attacks from some political opponents who insinuated that she is gay. Mottley's success, despite the DLP's appeals to anti-LGBT sentiment, was considered by some observers to be a turning point for LGBT people's political representation; the BLP has called for greater tolerance toward LGBT people in its platform.

C. FUNCTIONING OF GOVERNMENT: 10 / 12

C1. Do the freely elected head of government and national legislative representatives determine the policies of the government? 4 / 4

The prime minister and members of Parliament are largely unimpeded in their ability to craft and implement policy, notwithstanding the powerful role played by labor unions.

C2. Are safeguards against official corruption strong and effective? 3 / 4

Barbados's government has failed to implement key anticorruption measures, despite evidence of official corruption. The Integrity in Public Life Bill, which would strengthen protections for whistleblowers, require members of Parliament to declare their personal wealth, create a new anticorruption investigative unit, and make penalties for those convicted of corruption more severe, was unveiled in June 2018, but had not yet been passed at year's end. Barbados has yet to sign or ratify the Inter-American Convention on Mutual Assistance in Criminal Matters, or ratify the UN Convention on Corruption. However, in January Barbados ratified the Inter-American Convention against Corruption, having signed the treaty in 2001.

Civil society groups and some individuals in the business community have continued to voice concerns about corruption in Barbados. The attorney general claimed that he discovered "startling" evidence of official corruption during his first months on the job, but no major figures in the government had been arrested or charged with corruption by the end of the year. Direct allegations of corruption are rare because potential whistleblowers are unwilling to risk costly defamation suits.

C3. Does the government operate with openness and transparency? 3 / 4

The government largely operates with openness and transparency. However, Barbados lacks key laws that would help ensure transparency—notably a long-promised Freedom of Information Act, and a measure that would require public officials to disclose income and assets. Information on the budget is difficult to obtain.

The newly elected BLP government has shown an inclination towards greater transparency. Some members of the press have praised the Mottley government for being far more communicative than the Stuart administration during its first months. The Barbados Government Information Service has dramatically improved the functionality and accuracy of its web portal, which contains information about government policies and initiatives. In June 2018, the government revealed the extent of the country's debt burden and financial liabilities, much of which had not been disclosed by the previous government.

CIVIL LIBERTIES: 58 / 60

D. FREEDOM OF EXPRESSION AND BELIEF: 16 / 16

D1. Are there free and independent media? 4 / 4

The media are free from censorship and government control. Newspapers, including the two major dailies, are privately owned. Four private and two government-run radio stations operate in the country. The government-owned Caribbean Broadcasting Corporation (CBC) presents a wide range of political viewpoints.

D2. Are individuals free to practice and express their religious faith or nonbelief in public and private? 4 / 4

The constitution guarantees freedom of religion, which is widely respected for mainstream religious groups. However, members of Barbados's small Rastafarian and Muslim communities have reported some discrimination.

D3. Is there academic freedom, and is the educational system free from extensive political indoctrination? 4 / 4

Academic freedom is respected, though members of the government occasionally disparage academics who criticize government policy.

D4. Are individuals free to express their personal views on political or other sensitive topics without fear of surveillance or retribution? 4 / 4

Freedom of speech is largely respected in Barbados, with commentators and members of the public free to express their views on most topics without encountering negative consequences.

E. ASSOCIATIONAL AND ORGANIZATIONAL RIGHTS: 12 / 12

E1. Is there freedom of assembly? 4 / 4

Barbados's legal framework guarantees freedom of assembly, which is upheld in practice. A number of protests and marches took place peacefully in 2018, including the island's first pride parade, which was held in Bridgetown in July.

E2. Is there freedom for nongovernmental organizations, particularly those that are engaged in human rights- and governance-related work? 4 / 4

Nongovernmental organizations (NGOs) operate without restriction or surveillance. There are a number of NGOs active in the country, which primarily focus on cultural, homelessness, environmental, and women's issues.

E3. Is there freedom for trade unions and similar professional or labor organizations? 4 / 4

The right to form labor unions is respected, and unions are active and politically influential. In January 2018, the National Union of Public Workers went on strike to demand pay increases for public-sector workers.

F. RULE OF LAW: 15 / 16

F1. Is there an independent judiciary? 4 / 4

The judiciary generally operates with independence. The Supreme Court includes a high court and a court of appeals. The Caribbean Court of Justice is the highest appellate court for Barbados.

F2. Does due process prevail in civil and criminal matters? 4 / 4

Constitutional guarantees of due process are generally upheld. The court system continued to face excessive delays and a large case backlog in 2018, although the government took some action during the year to address the problem. In 2017, the judiciary adopted a protocol to prevent gender discrimination in the administration of justice. The protocol, drafted with UN support, is the first of its kind in the Caribbean Community (CARICOM).

F3. Is there protection from the illegitimate use of physical force and freedom from war and insurgencies? 4 / 4

Barbados is free from war and insurgencies. However, there are occasional complaints of excessive force by the Royal Barbados Police Force. There is also growing concern about gun violence, and the ability of police to address it.

The government has taken some positive steps to address prison overcrowding and abuse. In June 2018, the Caribbean Court of Justice ruled that the mandatory death penalty for those convicted of murder in Barbados was unconstitutional. However, the Senate failed to pass legislation to comply with the decision in November. The last execution in Barbados occurred in 1984.

F4. Do laws, policies, and practices guarantee equal treatment of various segments of the population? 3 / 4

Women compose roughly half of the country's workforce, although they tend to earn less than men for comparable work. In 2017, legislation requiring workplaces to articulate a policy against sexual harassment was proclaimed. LGBT people face discrimination in housing, employment, and access to health care. In June 2018, LGBT activists filed a petition at the Inter-American Commission on Human Rights to challenge laws that criminalize same-sex sexual relations. The laws are largely unenforced.

G. PERSONAL AUTONOMY AND INDIVIDUAL RIGHTS: 15 / 16

G1. Do individuals enjoy freedom of movement, including the ability to change their place of residence, employment, or education? 4 / 4

Individuals in Barbados are generally free to move, live, and work across the territory as they see fit.

G2. Are individuals able to exercise the right to own property and establish private businesses without undue interference from state or nonstate actors? 4 / 4

The legal framework generally supports property rights and private businesses activity. The government has worked to ensure a healthy environment for business and to attract domestic and foreign investment, particularly in the tourism industry.

G3. Do individuals enjoy personal social freedoms, including choice of marriage partner and size of family, protection from domestic violence, and control over appearance? 3 / 4

Violence against women remains widespread, and laws addressing domestic violence are not well enforced. Reports of child abuse have increased in recent years, according to the US State Department.

Same-sex marriage remains illegal.

G4. Do individuals enjoy equality of opportunity and freedom from economic exploitation? 4 / 4

Residents generally have access to economic opportunity, and the law provides some protections against exploitative labor practices. However, nearly 18 percent of the population lives in poverty.

The government has recently enacted harsher penalties for offenses related to human trafficking, and has conducted awareness trainings with government officials and NGO workers. However, there have been no prosecutions for trafficking since 2013, and government agencies that work on trafficking-related issues are poorly funded.

Belarus

Population: 9,500,000
Capital: Minsk
Political Rights Rating: 7 ↓
Civil Liberties Rating: 6
Freedom Rating: 6.5
Freedom Status: Not Free
Electoral Democracy: No

Overview: Belarus is an authoritarian state in which elections are openly orchestrated and civil liberties are tightly restricted. After permitting limited displays of dissent as part of a drive to pursue better relations with the European Union (EU) and the United States, the government has more recently sought to increase control of the public sphere through restrictions on journalists, online media, and demonstrations. In an apparent attempt to mute criticism of the country's rights record, penalties for dissent have increasingly taken the form of fines, or have been handed down after delays in order to avoid media coverage.

KEY DEVELOPMENTS IN 2018:

- In June, the parliament passed legislation allowing the prosecution of anyone deemed to be spreading false information online, while amendments to the media law that took effect in December mandated bureaucratic registration requirements for online media outlets.
- The offices of two news outlets were raided in August, and three journalists were temporarily detained, as part of an investigation into whether the outlets had accessed news releases of the state-run information agency without a paid subscription. Authorities also attempted to recruit at least one journalist as an informant against his colleagues by threatening consequences for him and his family.
- In May, scores of activists were detained, put under administrative arrest, or fined in connection with protests against the opening of a restaurant near Kurapaty, the site of mass killings during the Stalinist repressions of the 1930s.
- In August, a court sentenced two leaders of the Radioelectronic Industry Union to four years of restricted freedom for tax evasion. The prosecution heavily relied on an informant recruited by the KGB who worked in the union as a secretary. Other witnesses said their initial statements were obtained through coercion.

POLITICAL RIGHTS: 5 / 40 (−1)

A. ELECTORAL PROCESS: 0 / 12

A1. Was the current head of government or other chief national authority elected through free and fair elections? 0 / 4

The president is elected for five-year terms without limits. Alyaksandr Lukashenka was first elected in 1994, in the country's only democratic election. He has since extended his rule in a series of unfair contests, and secured his fifth consecutive term in a noncompetitive presidential race in 2015. Organization for Security and Co-operation in Europe (OSCE) monitors noted that longstanding deficiencies in Belarusian elections had not been addressed, including a restrictive legal framework, media coverage that fails to help voters make informed choices, irregularities in vote counting, and restrictions on free expression and assembly during the campaign period. The group concluded that the elections fell considerably short of democratic standards.

A2. Were the current national legislative representatives elected through free and fair elections? 0 / 4

The 110 members of the Chamber of Representatives, the lower house of the rubber-stamp National Assembly, are popularly elected to four-year terms from single-mandate constituencies. The upper chamber, the Council of the Republic, consists of 64 members serving four-year terms: 56 are elected by regional councils, and 8 are appointed by the president.

An OSCE observation mission assessing the 2016 parliamentary elections concluded that the polls took place in a restrictive environment, and that electoral procedures lacked transparency. Local elections held in February 2018 took place in a similarly controlled environment.

A3. Are the electoral laws and framework fair, and are they implemented impartially by the relevant election management bodies? 0 / 4

The legal framework for elections fails to meet democratic standards. Among other problems, electoral commission members of all levels are politically aligned with and dependent on the government, and independent observers have no access to ballot-counting processes.

Early in 2018, the chairperson of the Central Election Commission indicated that electoral reforms could be a component of Lukashenka's previously stated intention to "modernize" the Constitution. However, in an April address, Lukashenka indicated that no constitutional referendum was forthcoming.

B. POLITICAL PLURALISM AND PARTICIPATION: 3 / 16 (−1)

B1. Do the people have the right to organize in different political parties or other competitive political groupings of their choice, and is the system free of undue obstacles to the rise and fall of these competing parties or groupings? 1 / 4

There is no official progovernment political party, and very few lawmakers are affiliated with any party. Political parties face formidable challenges when seeking official registration. While the Tell the Truth movement was finally registered in 2017 after six failed attempts, authorities have repeatedly blocked registration of the Belarusian Christian Democracy party, which has now been seeking official status for almost a decade. Most recently, the Justice Ministry said in March 2018 that its latest attempt to register had been suspended, without offering any justification. Such futile attempts to gain official status serve to discourage other politically active Belarusians from organizing and attempting to gain formal party recognition.

Involvement in political activism is considered risky in Belarus, and can result in a loss of employment, expulsion from educational institutions, smear campaigns in the media, fines, and the confiscation of property.

B2. Is there a realistic opportunity for the opposition to increase its support or gain power through elections? 0 / 4 (−1)

Belarus has never experienced a democratic transfer of power, and there is effectively no opportunity for genuine opposition candidates to gain power through elections. While two candidates not aligned with Lukashenka became members of parliament in 2016, many analysts have dismissed their election as immaterial and designed to placate the opposition, or democratic European countries with which the government seeks to better relations.

Registered opposition candidates made up about 2 percent of all candidates in 2018 local elections. And, in some 18,000 races, just two opposition candidates won seats—one of whom was an independent, and another of whom belonged to an unregistered party.

Score Change: The score declined from 1 to 0 because of repression conditions that allowed the victory of just two opposition candidates in the roughly 18,000 races in 2018 local elections.

B3. Are the people's political choices free from domination by the military, foreign powers, religious hierarchies, economic oligarchies, or any other powerful group that is not democratically accountable? 1 / 4

While private citizens and political candidates have some limited opportunities to express their views and make political choices, Lukashenka's regime is unaccountable to voters, and meaningful participation in politics is generally not possible.

B4. Do various segments of the population (including ethnic, religious, gender, LGBT, and other relevant groups) have full political rights and electoral opportunities? 1 / 4

No registered party represents the specific interests of ethnic or religious minority groups. Women formally enjoy equal political rights but are underrepresented in political leadership positions. Women's advocacy groups have diverging positions on promoting the political rights of women, with some such groups taking the position that there is no need for gender equality initiatives in Belarus. There has been some visible activism by women's groups seeking to raise awareness of violence against women.

C. FUNCTIONING OF GOVERNMENT: 2 / 12

C1. Do the freely elected head of government and national legislative representatives determine the policies of the government? 0 / 4

The Constitution vests power in the president, stating that presidential decrees have higher legal force than legislation. Lukashenka, who was not freely elected, considers himself the head of all branches of government.

C2. Are safeguards against official corruption strong and effective? 1 / 4

The state controls an estimated 70 percent of the economy, and graft is encouraged by a lack of transparency and accountability in government. There are no independent bodies to investigate corruption cases, and graft trials are typically closed. Presidential clemency is issued frequently to free convicted corrupt officials, some of whom Lukashenka puts back into positions of authority.

C3. Does the government operate with openness and transparency? 1 / 4

Governmental institutions for the most part fail to adhere to legal requirements providing for access to information. However, in recent years, authorities have moved to make some basic information about government operations available online. Additionally, in 2017, authorities announced that all websites will publish information in both Belarusian and Russian, and other languages as necessary, beginning in 2019.

CIVIL LIBERTIES: 14 / 60 (−1)
D. FREEDOM OF EXPRESSION AND BELIEF: 2 / 16 (−1)
D1. Are there free and independent media? 0 / 4 (−1)

The government exercises unrestricted control over mainstream media. The 2008 media law secures a state monopoly over information about political, social, and economic affairs. Libel is both a civil and criminal offense, and the criminal code contains provisions protecting the "honor and dignity" of high-ranking officials. The government owns the only internet service provider and controls the internet through legal and technical means. The official definition of mass media includes websites and blogs, placing them under Information Ministry's supervision. Most independent journalists operate under the assumption that they are under surveillance by the Committee for State Security (KGB).

In 2018, the state enacted measures that effectively impose restrictions on independent online media. In June, the parliament passed legislation allowing the prosecution of anyone deemed to be spreading false information online, while amendments to the media law that took effect in December mandated highly bureaucratic registration requirements for online media outlets.

In another development, authorities launched a criminal investigation into the so-called BelTA case, in which journalists from the online portal TUT.by, the information agency BelaPAN, and other outlets were accused of receiving access to news releases of the state-run

BelTA information agency without a paid subscription. The offices of TUT.by and BelaPAN were raided in August, and three journalists were temporarily detained as part of the investigation. Authorities also attempted to recruit at least one journalist as an informant against his colleagues by threatening consequences for him and members of his family.

Authorities also continued to impose disproportionately heavy fines on journalists for trumped-up or minor violations, including working for foreign media outlets that had been denied official accreditation. In 2018, journalists were fined 106 times for "illegal production and distribution of media products." Numerous journalists were detained and fined for live streaming demonstrations at Kurapaty, where protests broke out against the opening of a restaurant near a site where thousands of people had been executed as part of Soviet leader Joseph Stalin's purges.

Score Change: The score declined from 1 to 0 due to a crackdown on journalists that included new restrictions on online media, a criminal case against journalists accused of illegally obtaining content from the state news agency, and the frequent detention and issuing of fines against reporters in connection with their work.

D2. Are individuals free to practice and express their religious faith or nonbelief in public and private? 1 / 4

Despite constitutional guarantees of religious equality, government decrees and registration requirements maintained some restrictions on religious activity. Legal amendments in 2002 provided for government censorship of religious publications and barred foreigners from leading religious groups. The amendments also placed strict limitations on religious groups active in Belarus for less than 20 years. In 2003, the government signed a concordat with the Belarusian Orthodox Church, which is controlled by the Russian Orthodox Church, giving it a privileged position.

D3. Is there academic freedom, and is the educational system free from extensive political indoctrination? 0 / 4

Academic freedom remains subject to intense state ideological pressures, and academic personnel face harassment and dismissal if they use liberal curriculum or are suspected of disloyalty. Students and professors who join opposition protests face threat of dismissal and revocation of degrees.

D4. Are individuals free to express their personal views on political or other sensitive topics without fear of surveillance or retribution? 1 / 4

The use of wiretapping and other surveillance by state security agencies limits the right to free private discussion. Private citizens often avoid discussing sensitive issues over the phone or via internet communication platforms, for fear that state security agents are monitoring conversations.

E. ASSOCIATIONAL AND ORGANIZATIONAL RIGHTS: 3 / 12

E1. Is there freedom of assembly? 1 / 4

The government restricts freedom of assembly. Protests require permission from local authorities, who often arbitrarily deny it. In the past, police routinely broke up public demonstrations and arrested participants. The pursuit of better relations with democracies in the region has more recently prompted authorities to rely on fines as a means of punishing demonstrators. However, arrests and the use of force to disperse protests still sometimes occur.

In May 2018, activists peacefully protested against the opening of a restaurant near Kurapaty, the site of mass executions during the Stalinist repressions of the 1930s. Authorities, often represented by law enforcement officials in plain clothes, placed themselves on the side of restaurant owners, and scores of activists were detained, put under administrative arrest, or fined. Punitive measures were often implemented long after protests, when the attention of media was diverted.

E2. Is there freedom for nongovernmental organizations, particularly those that are engaged in human rights and governance-related work? 1 / 4

Freedom of association is severely restricted. Registration of groups remains selective, and regulations ban foreign assistance to entities and individuals deemed to promote foreign meddling in internal affairs. A few human rights groups continue to operate, but staff and supporters risk prosecution and fines for their activism.

Participation in unregistered or liquidated organizations, which had been criminalized in 2005, was decriminalized in 2018. Instead, the Criminal Code introduced the prospect of large fines which, like recent efforts to fine rather than detain protesters, make civil liberties infringement less visible to rights watchdogs and democratic governments.

E3. Is there freedom for trade unions and similar professional or labor organizations? 1 / 4

Independent labor unions face harassment, and their leaders are frequently fired and prosecuted for engaging in peaceful protests. No independent unions have been registered since 1999, when Lukashenka issued a decree setting extremely restrictive registration requirements.

In August 2018, a court sentenced two leaders of the Radioelectronic Industry Union for allegedly evading taxes to four years of restricted freedom. Notably, the prosecution heavily relied on an informant recruited by the KGB who worked in the union as an office secretary.

F. RULE OF LAW: 2 / 16

F1. Is there an independent judiciary? 0 / 4

Courts are subservient to the president, who appoints Supreme Court justices with the approval of the rubber-stamp parliament.

F2. Does due process prevail in civil and criminal matters? 1 / 4

The right to a fair trial is not respected in cases with political overtones. In a departure from international norms, the power to extend pretrial detention lies with a prosecutor rather than a judge. The absence of independent oversight allows police to routinely and massively violate legal procedures. The vast majority of people convicted of administrative offenses in connection with their participation in protests in Kurapaty were convicted in summary trials.

The government regularly attacks attorneys, who often remain the only connection between imprisoned activists and their families and society. A number of witnesses in the 2018 trial of the Radioelectronic Industry Union leaders said their initial statements had been obtained through coercion.

F3. Is there protection from the illegitimate use of physical force and freedom from war and insurgencies? 0 / 4

Law enforcement agencies have broad powers to employ physical force against suspects, who have little opportunity for recourse if they are abused. Human rights groups continue to document instances of beatings, torture, and pressure during detention.

F4. Do laws, policies, and practices guarantee equal treatment of various segments of the population? 1 / 4

Authorities have sought to increase the dominance of the Russian language, and the UN Educational, Scientific, and Cultural Organization (UNESCO) recognizes Belarusian as "vulnerable." The regime in recent years has been less wary of issues involving Belarusian national identity, though official usage of Belarusian remains rare. Ethnic Poles and Roma often face undue pressure from authorities.

Widely accepted societal values hold that women should be mothers, and while this has helped maintain social benefits including generous maternity leave, the prevalence of these views in practice restrict the opportunities of women.

LGBT (lesbian, gay, bisexual, and transgender) people face widespread societal discrimination, and law enforcement authorities are reluctant to investigate and prosecute attacks against them. In May 2018, the Ministry of Internal Affairs accused the British Embassy in Belarus of "causing problems" after it flew an LGBT flag on the International Day against Homophobia, adding that same-sex relationships were "fake" and not supported by a majority of Belarusians.

G. PERSONAL AUTONOMY AND INDIVIDUAL RIGHTS: 7 / 16

G1. Do individuals enjoy freedom of movement, including the ability to change their place of residence, employment, or education? 2 / 4

Opposition activists are occasionally detained at the border for lengthy searches. Passports are used as a primary identity document in Belarus, and authorities are known to harass people living in a different location than indicated by domestic stamps in their passport.

G2. Are individuals able to exercise the right to own property and establish private businesses without undue interference from state or non-state actors? 2 / 4

Limits on economic freedom have eased in recent years, allowing for greater property ownership and small business operations. However, state interference in the economy still affects larger businesses, and large business owners are never secure from arbitrary government pressure and harassment.

G3. Do individuals enjoy personal social freedoms, including choice of marriage partner and size of family, protection from domestic violence, and control over appearance? 2 / 4

The constitution explicitly bans same-sex marriage. The Belarusian government led an effort in 2016 to block LGBT rights from being part of a UN international initiative focused on urban areas.

Domestic violence is a pervasive problem in Belarus. Some ostensibly protective mechanisms can make finding help more difficult for victims, who are usually women. For example, families with minor children can be deemed to be in a "socially precarious" situation if a parent reports domestic violence, a designation that can allow social services to take any children into custody.

In October 2018, Lukashenka blocked a draft law on the prevention of domestic violence jointly developed by the law enforcement agencies and civil society representatives. Specifically, he called attitudes against the corporal punishment of children "nonsense from the West" and insisted that "good" punishment of children could be useful to them.

G4. Do individuals enjoy equality of opportunity and freedom from economic exploitation? 1 / 4

Mandatory unpaid national work days, postgraduate employment allocation, compulsory labor for inmates in state rehabilitation facilities, and restrictions on leaving employment in specific industries have led labor activists to conclude that all Belarusian citizens experience forced labor at some stage of their life. The lack of economic opportunities led many women to become victims of the international sex trade.

In 2018, based on a presidential decree, the government effectively revived a plan to tax the unemployed (the so-called social parasite tax) by mandating full payment for housing and utility services starting in 2019. An attempt to impose the tax in 2017 was met with mass protests that were brutally suppressed.

Belgium

Population: 11,400,000
Capital: Brussels
Political Rights Rating: 1
Civil Liberties Rating: 1
Freedom Rating: 1.0
Freedom Status: Free
Electoral Democracy: Yes

Overview: Belgium is an electoral democracy with a long record of peaceful transfers of power. Political rights and civil liberties are legally guaranteed and largely respected in practice. Major concerns in recent years have included the threat of terrorism as well as corruption scandals that have unsettled the country's complex governing coalitions.

KEY DEVELOPMENTS IN 2018:

- In January, the authorities lowered the country's terrorism threat level from three to two, with four representing the highest threat level. The last major attacks occurred in 2016.
- Local elections were held in October, yielding gains for leftist and Green parties as well as the separatist New Flemish Alliance (N-VA). Center-left and center-right parties generally lost ground.
- In December, the N-VA quit the governing coalition, citing its objection to a UN migration agreement backed by the government. Prime Minister Charles Michel, left with a minority in Parliament, resigned, but he remained in place as a caretaker pending federal elections in May 2019.

POLITICAL RIGHTS: 39 / 40

A. ELECTORAL PROCESS: 12 / 12

A1. Was the current head of government or other chief national authority elected through free and fair elections? 4 / 4

The Belgian monarchy is largely ceremonial, although the king retains constitutional authority to mediate during the process of government formation. The prime minister, who is the leader of the majority party or coalition, is appointed by the monarch and approved by the legislature. After the 2014 parliamentary elections, Charles Michel of the Movement for Reform (MR), a center-right Francophone party, became prime minister in a government that also included the N-VA, the Christian Democratic and Flemish (CD&V) party, and the Open Flemish Liberals and Democrats (VLD). In December 2018 the N-VA quit the Michel government over a disagreement on the approval of a UN migration pact. Michel submitted his resignation, but the king asked him to remain in place at the head of a caretaker government until federal elections scheduled for May 2019.

Belgium's multilayered subnational administrative units have their own governments with varying degrees of autonomy. In addition to the three main geographic divisions of French-speaking Wallonia in the south, Flemish-speaking Flanders in the north, and the bilingual Brussels capital region, there are overlapping governments for the French Community, the Flemish Community, and the German-speaking community. Beneath these are provincial and various local governments.

A2. Were the current national legislative representatives elected through free and fair elections? 4 / 4

Belgium's Federal Parliament consists of two houses: the Chamber of Representatives and the Senate. The 150 members of the lower house are elected directly by proportional representation. The Senate is composed of 50 members selected by community and regional parliaments, and an additional 10 members chosen by the first 50 based on the results of the Chamber of Representatives elections. Members serve five-year terms in both houses, and elections are generally free and fair.

In the 2014 elections, the N-VA took 33 seats in the Chamber of Representatives, while outgoing prime minister Elio Di Rupo's Francophone Socialist Party (PS) won 23 seats. The MR captured 20 seats, the CD&V took 18, the VLD won 14, and the Flemish Socialist Party secured 13. Several smaller parties, including the Humanist Democratic Centre (CDH) with 9, accounted for the remainder.

Municipal and provincial elections held in October 2018 resulted in victories for the N-VA in the north of the country, setbacks for the PS and MR, and related gains for the Green party and the left-wing Workers' Party of Belgium (PTB-PVDA).

A3. Are the electoral laws and framework fair, and are they implemented impartially by the relevant election management bodies? 4 / 4

Despite the complexity of the political system, the electoral laws and framework are generally fair and impartially implemented.

B. POLITICAL PLURALISM AND PARTICIPATION: 16 / 16

B1. Do the people have the right to organize in different political parties or other competitive political groupings of their choice, and is the system free of undue obstacles to the rise and fall of these competing parties or groupings? 4 / 4

The party system is robust but highly fragmented, with separate Flemish and Walloon political parties representing various positions on the left-right spectrum.

B2. Is there a realistic opportunity for the opposition to increase its support or gain power through elections? 4 / 4

Belgium's coalition-based politics allow individual parties to move easily in and out of government, and there is a long record of peaceful transfers of power between rival parties at the federal level. The most recent such transfer occurred after the 2014 elections, when the center-right MR captured the premiership from the left-leaning PS. The 2018 local elections showed a weakening of the federal governing parties, aside from the N-VA, whose departure from the government in December was seen as part of its preparation for the May 2019 federal elections.

B3. Are the people's political choices free from domination by the military, foreign powers, religious hierarchies, economic oligarchies, or any other powerful group that is not democratically accountable? 4 / 4

The political choices of voters and candidates are generally free from undue interference.

B4. Do various segments of the population (including ethnic, religious, gender, LGBT, and other relevant groups) have full political rights and electoral opportunities? 4 / 4

Members of minority groups are free to participate in national and subnational politics, and women also enjoy full political rights. In the 2014 elections, women won approximately 39 percent of the seats in the Chamber of Representatives and 50 percent of the seats in the Senate, which must have a minimum of 20 women senators.

C. FUNCTIONING OF GOVERNMENT: 11 / 12

C1. Do the freely elected head of government and national legislative representatives determine the policies of the government? 4 / 4

Elected officials generally adopt and implement laws and policies without improper interference from unelected entities, though the difficulty of forming majority coalitions has sometimes disrupted governance over the past decade. The country went roughly 19 months without a government in 2010–11 due to protracted coalition talks.

C2. Are safeguards against official corruption strong and effective? 3 / 4

Public officials can face heavy fines and up to 10 years' imprisonment for corruption-related offenses, and enforcement of anticorruption legislation is generally adequate. However, recent scandals have drawn attention to abuses involving politicians who hold multiple positions on the boards of public and private entities, with some officials holding more than a dozen paid positions. Among other corruption and ethics cases during 2018, in June a court found that Alain Mathot, a PS member of Parliament and the mayor of Seraing, had received €700,000 in corrupt proceeds from the award of a contract for an incinerator facility. He was not immediately prosecuted due to his parliamentary immunity, but he did not run in the October local elections.

C3. Does the government operate with openness and transparency? 4 / 4

The law provides mechanisms for the public to access government information, and these procedures generally function in practice. Legislators and other high-ranking elected officials are required by law to regularly disclose their assets as well as paid or unpaid mandates, executive functions, and occupations to the Court of Audit. Information about asset declarations is not publicly accessible, but declarations of interests are published in the official government gazette.

CIVIL LIBERTIES: 57 / 60 (+1)

D. FREEDOM OF EXPRESSION AND BELIEF: 15 / 16

D1. Are there free and independent media? 4 / 4

Freedom of the press is guaranteed by the constitution and generally respected by the government, though some law enforcement actions affecting journalists have raised concerns in recent years. Belgians have access to numerous public and private media outlets that present a range of views. Internet access is unrestricted.

In June 2018, members of a television crew were arrested and temporarily detained while covering a protest against a new detention center for migrant families. At least two other journalists were reportedly detained briefly during antigovernment protests in November.

D2. Are individuals free to practice and express their religious faith or nonbelief in public and private? 3 / 4

More than half of the country's population identifies as Roman Catholic. Freedom of religion is generally protected, but members of minority religious groups have complained of discrimination and harassment. A ban on the partial or total covering of the face in public locations, which is understood to target ultraconservative Muslims, has been in effect since 2011. Offenders can face a fine or up to a week in jail.

D3. Is there academic freedom, and is the educational system free from extensive political indoctrination? 4 / 4

The government does not restrict academic freedom. Schools are free from political indoctrination, and there are no significant impediments to scholarly research or discussion.

D4. Are individuals free to express their personal views on political or other sensitive topics without fear of surveillance or retribution? 4 / 4

Private discussion is open and vibrant, and freedom of expression is guaranteed by the constitution, though there are laws banning incitement to hatred and other such offenses.

E. ASSOCIATIONAL AND ORGANIZATIONAL RIGHTS: 12 / 12

E1. Is there freedom of assembly? 4 / 4

Freedom of assembly is protected by law and generally respected in practice. While most protests proceed without incident, demonstrations inspired by France's "yellow vest" movement—which aired grievances related to unfair tax burdens, high living expenses, and perceived government neglect—descended into violence in November and December, as some protesters damaged property and threw objects at police, who responded with water cannons, tear gas, and hundreds of arrests. A December protest by far-right groups against the UN migration pact featured similar clashes with police.

E2. Is there freedom for nongovernmental organizations, particularly those that are engaged in human rights- and governance-related work? 4 / 4

Freedom of association is guaranteed by the constitution, and nongovernmental organizations operate without undue restrictions.

E3. Is there freedom for trade unions and similar professional or labor organizations? 4 / 4

Workers at companies that employ more than 50 people have the right to organize and join unions and to bargain collectively. Employers found guilty of firing workers because of union activities are required to reinstate the workers or pay an indemnity. During 2018, labor unions led a number of strikes and demonstrations against the economic policies of the Michel government, especially its plans to reform the pension system.

F. RULE OF LAW: 15 / 16 (+1)

F1. Is there an independent judiciary? 4 / 4

The judiciary is independent by law and in practice, and court rulings are duly enforced by other state entities.

F2. Does due process prevail in civil and criminal matters? 4 / 4

The judicial process generally guarantees a fair trial, and the authorities typically observe safeguards against arbitrary arrest and detention. Extraordinary security measures adopted in the period surrounding terrorist attacks in 2015 and 2016 have eased significantly in the years since, though a 2017 legal change increased the maximum length of detention in police custody without a judicial order from 24 to 48 hours.

F3. Is there protection from the illegitimate use of physical force and freedom from war and insurgencies? 4 / 4 (+1)

Although conditions in prisons and detention centers meet most international standards, the facilities continue to suffer from overcrowding and other problematic living conditions.

There have been no major terrorist attacks in Belgium since 2016, and in January 2018 the government lowered its terrorism threat level from three to two on a four-point scale, except in undisclosed high-risk areas.

Score Change: The score improved from 3 to 4 because the threat of imminent terrorist violence apparently receded.

F4. Do laws, policies, and practices guarantee equal treatment of various segments of the population? 3 / 4

Antidiscrimination legislation prohibits bias and acts of hatred and incitement based on categories including gender, race, ethnicity, nationality, and sexual orientation. Nevertheless, some groups, including immigrants and Romany residents, continue to face a degree of discrimination in practice.

Legislation adopted in 2017 tightened Belgium's asylum policies, in part by reducing the time and scope for appeals of negative asylum decisions and expanding the grounds for detention of asylum seekers. Advocacy organizations said that the changes often reduced the country's standards to the minimum allowed by the European Union.

G. PERSONAL AUTONOMY AND INDIVIDUAL RIGHTS: 15 / 16

G1. Do individuals enjoy freedom of movement, including the ability to change their place of residence, employment, or education? 4 / 4

The law provides for freedom of domestic movement and foreign travel, and the government upholds these rights in practice. There are no restrictions on the right to change one's place of residence, employment, or education.

G2. Are individuals able to exercise the right to own property and establish private businesses without undue interference from state or nonstate actors? 4 / 4

The legal framework supports property rights, and commercial activity is regulated without arbitrary interference.

G3. Do individuals enjoy personal social freedoms, including choice of marriage partner and size of family, protection from domestic violence, and control over appearance? 4 / 4

There are few significant restrictions on personal social freedoms. Belgium legalized same-sex marriage in 2003, and in 2006 same-sex couples gained the right to adopt children.

G4. Do individuals enjoy equality of opportunity and freedom from economic exploitation? 3 / 4

Immigration has increased in recent years, but labor-market integration of non-EU immigrants and their native-born children is comparatively low. Despite government efforts to combat the problem, Belgium remains a destination country for human trafficking, particularly for sexual exploitation and domestic labor; victims generally originate in Eastern Europe, Asia, and Africa.

Belize

Population: 400,000
Capital: Belmopan
Political Rights Rating: 1
Civil Liberties Rating: 2
Freedom Rating: 1.5
Freedom Status: Free
Electoral Democracy: Yes

Overview: Belize is a democracy that has experienced regular rotations of power through competitive elections. Civil liberties are mostly respected. Government corruption is a concern, as is the high rate of violent crime. Authorities have been slow to address persistent problems of police brutality and human trafficking within the country's borders.

KEY DEVELOPMENTS IN 2018:

- In March, the Roman Catholic Church withdrew its appeal of a 2016 court ruling that decriminalized same-sex sexual activity. A government appeal that accepted decriminalization but challenged an antidiscrimination component of the ruling was still pending at year's end.
- In September, responding to a spike in gun violence, the government introduced a 30-day state of emergency in two gang-plagued areas of Belize City, granting police enhanced powers to arrest and detain suspects.

POLITICAL RIGHTS: 36 / 40

A. ELECTORAL PROCESS: 12 / 12

A1. Was the current head of government or other chief national authority elected through free and fair elections? 4 / 4

The prime minister, usually the leader of the largest party in the parliament, is head of government. Formally, the prime minister is appointed by the governor general, who represents the British monarch as head of state. The legitimacy of the prime minister is largely dependent on the conduct of legislative elections, which are typically credible and well administered. Dean Barrow, the prime minister since 2008, returned for another term following the victory of his United Democratic Party (UDP) in the 2015 elections.

A2. Were the current national legislative representatives elected through free and fair elections? 4 / 4

The 31 members of the House of Representatives are directly elected for five-year terms. The Senate has 12 seats. The ruling party, the opposition, and several civil associations select the senators, who are then appointed by the governor general.

In the 2015 legislative polls, the incumbent UDP increased its representation to 19 seats in the House of Representatives and entered an unprecedented third consecutive term in government. The opposition People's United Party (PUP) took the remaining 12 seats. Observers from the Organization of American States (OAS) said the polls were conducted in a fair and professional manner.

A3. Are the electoral laws and framework fair, and are they implemented impartially by the relevant election management bodies? 4 / 4

Electoral laws are generally fair, although ahead of the 2015 polls it was reported that the chief elections officer and her family were threatened by masked men. In response, police provided added security at her home. Separately, the OAS has suggested that the role of the Elections and Boundaries Commission and the Elections and Boundaries Department be strengthened, and that authorities work to reduce partisanship associated with the confirmation of their appointees. It further noted that voter lists should be reviewed.

B. POLITICAL PLURALISM AND PARTICIPATION: 14 / 16

B1. Do the people have the right to organize in different political parties or other competitive political groupings of their choice, and is the system free of undue obstacles to the rise and fall of these competing parties or groupings? 4 / 4

Political parties can organize freely. The effects of the country's "first-past-the-post" electoral system have entrenched the two largest parties. While a number of smaller parties have competed, only the PUP and UDP have won seats in the parliament.

B2. Is there a realistic opportunity for the opposition to increase its support or gain power through elections? 4 / 4

The political system allows for opposition parties to increase their support or gain power through elections. Since 1984 there have been fairly regular transfers of power between the two main parties.

B3. Are the people's political choices free from domination by the military, foreign powers, religious hierarchies, economic oligarchies, or any other powerful group that is not democratically accountable? 4 / 4

Recent elections, including those in 2015, have been viewed as generally free of undue interference from entities outside the democratic political sphere. However, the OAS has raised concerns about the potential impact of unregulated campaign financing on the transparency of the political process.

B4. Do various segments of the population (including ethnic, religious, gender, LGBT, and other relevant groups) have full political rights and electoral opportunities? 2 / 4

Women hold only two seats in the current House of Representatives and three seats in the Senate. There were 11 women candidates out of a total of 88 in the 2015 elections. However, women play a significant role in the political system more generally.

Indigenous people, particularly those of Mayan descent, are not well represented in politics. The LGBT (lesbian, gay, bisexual, and transgender) community faces discrimination, and this affects the ability of LGBT people to engage fully in political and electoral processes. A collection of religious denominations nominate one member of the Senate, but non-Christian groups are not included in the process.

C. FUNCTIONING OF GOVERNMENT: 10 / 12

C1. Do the freely elected head of government and national legislative representatives determine the policies of the government? 4 / 4

The elected prime minister, cabinet, and national legislative representatives are duly seated following elections and are able to freely determine the policies of the government.

C2. Are safeguards against official corruption strong and effective? 2 / 4

Belize continues to struggle with corruption, and there is little political will to address the problem. Anticorruption laws are poorly enforced; for example, no one has ever been prosecuted under the Prevention of Corruption in Public Life Act, which has been on the books for over 20 years. Among other scandals in recent years, the Lands and Surveys Department of the Ministry of Natural Resources has been accused of illegally distributing land to UDP supporters.

C3. Does the government operate with openness and transparency? 4 / 4

The government generally operates with openness and transparency. However, while the law requires public officials to submit annual financial disclosure statements for review by the Integrity Commission, the body had been defunct for years until members were finally appointed by the ruling party and the opposition in 2017. There is little opportunity for the public to challenge the disclosures. Members of the country's business community allege that favoritism influences the government's awarding of licenses and public contracts.

CIVIL LIBERTIES: 50 / 60
D. FREEDOM OF EXPRESSION AND BELIEF: 15 / 16
D1. Are there free and independent media? 3 / 4

The constitution guarantees freedom of the press, though it includes exceptions for interests such as national security, public order, and morality. While reporting generally covers a wide range of viewpoints in practice, journalists sometimes face threats, physical harassment, or assault in the course of their work. In May 2018, a state-owned telecommunications firm reportedly stopped advertising with a media group that had links to the opposition PUP.

D2. Are individuals free to practice and express their religious faith or nonbelief in public and private? 4 / 4

Freedom of religion is constitutionally protected and largely respected in practice. Religious groups must register with the authorities, and foreign missionaries are required to obtain a visa and permit, but the procedures are not onerous.

D3. Is there academic freedom, and is the educational system free from extensive political indoctrination? 4 / 4

Academic freedom is generally respected.

D4. Are individuals free to express their personal views on political or other sensitive topics without fear of surveillance or retribution? 4 / 4

There are no significant constraints on individual expression regarding politics or other such matters, whether in private discussion or on social media.

E. ASSOCIATIONAL AND ORGANIZATIONAL RIGHTS: 10 / 12
E1. Is there freedom of assembly? 3 / 4

Freedom of assembly is constitutionally protected, and the government generally respects this right. Protests occasionally lead to clashes with police, though no major incidents were reported during 2018.

E2. Is there freedom for nongovernmental organizations, particularly those that are engaged in human rights-and governance-related work? 4 / 4

Nongovernmental organizations are generally free from government interference.

E3. Is there freedom for trade unions and similar professional or labor organizations? 3 / 4

Unions are free to form and operate, and employers have been penalized for violating union rights under the labor code. However, while labor unions are active and politically influential, their ability to protect workers' rights is limited in practice. There are some restrictions on the right to strike, including an official definition of "essential" workers that is broader than the International Labour Organization's standard.

F. RULE OF LAW: 12 / 16

F1. Is there an independent judiciary? 3 / 4

The judiciary, though lacking in resources, is generally independent. There have been attempts by political and business interests to interfere with the composition of the judiciary. In a long-running dispute, a group of companies controlled by businessman Michael Ashcroft has attempted to have Samuel Awich removed as a judge on the Court of Appeal, Belize's highest judicial body. In July 2018, the Caribbean Court of Justice ordered Belize's Judicial and Legal Services Commission to review Ashroft's complaint, reversing an earlier decision by the Court of Appeal.

F2. Does due process prevail in civil and criminal matters? 3 / 4

Detainees and defendants are guaranteed a range of legal rights, which are mostly respected in practice. However, police have reportedly detained suspects without charge for longer than is permitted by the law, and have used the threat of extended detention to intimidate suspects. Judicial delays and a large backlog of cases contribute to the length of trials and other procedures, with many defendants spending years in pretrial detention.

F3. Is there protection from the illegitimate use of physical force and freedom from war and insurgencies? 3 / 4

Belize is free from major threats to physical security, such as war and insurgencies. The homicide rate remains high, with 143 murders recorded in 2018, for a rate of about 36 murders per 100,000 people. The problem stems from gang violence focused largely on the south side of Belize City, though some violent crime has spread to other parts of the country. In September 2018, the government declared a 30-day state of emergency in two areas of Belize City's south side in response to an uptick in gang violence, granting police enhanced powers to arrest and detain suspects.

Cases of police brutality continue to be reported. The Police Amendment Act, promulgated in April 2018, was designed to improve disciplinary procedures and increase penalties for police misconduct.

F4. Do laws, policies, and practices guarantee equal treatment of various segments of the population? 3 / 4

The constitution and laws protect against many forms of discrimination, but there are no specific provisions addressing sexual orientation or gender identity.

Discrimination against LGBT people persists. In 2016 the country's Supreme Court struck down a portion of the criminal code that outlawed same-sex sexual activity. The government accepted the decriminalization, but in September 2017 it appealed a portion of the judgement finding that unconstitutional discrimination based on sex includes sexual orientation. Although the Roman Catholic Church appealed the entire ruling, it withdrew from the case in March 2018. The Court of Appeal had yet to rule on the government's petition at the end of 2018.

Women face employment discrimination and are less likely than men to hold managerial positions. However, the government has actively pursued programs aimed at encouraging gender equality and protecting women's rights.

G. PERSONAL AUTONOMY AND INDIVIDUAL RIGHTS: 13 / 16

G1. Do individuals enjoy freedom of movement, including the ability to change their place of residence, employment, or education? 4 / 4

The government generally respects freedom of internal movement and foreign travel.

G2. Are individuals able to exercise the right to own property and establish private businesses without undue interference from state or non-state actors? 3 / 4

Individuals have the right to own property and establish private businesses. However, legal regulations are at times poorly enforced. Leaders of the indigenous Maya community have alleged that their ancestral land rights are not protected, particularly with regard to oil exploration and logging activities.

G3. Do individuals enjoy personal social freedoms, including choice of marriage partner and size of family, protection from domestic violence, and control over appearance? 3 / 4

Personal social freedoms are generally respected, though domestic violence remains a serious problem despite government measures to combat it. Rape, including spousal rape under some circumstances, is illegal, but reporting and conviction rates are low, and sentences are sometimes light.

G4. Do individuals enjoy equality of opportunity and freedom from economic exploitation? 3 / 4

Some legal protections against exploitative working conditions are respected and enforced. However, Belizean and foreign women and girls are vulnerable to sex trafficking, and migrant workers are sometimes subjected to forced labor in agriculture, fisheries, and retail businesses. In 2018, the US State Department's *Trafficking in Persons Report* continued to rank Belize in its lowest tier. The report noted that the government identified some possible victims and investigated cases, but it was critical of the fact that no traffickers were prosecuted or convicted during the coverage period. The government did not target public officials involved in trafficking "despite allegations of a significant level of official complicity," the report said.

Benin

Population: 11,500,000
Capital: Porto-Novo
Political Rights Rating: 2
Civil Liberties Rating: 2
Freedom Rating: 2.0
Freedom Status: Free
Electoral Democracy: Yes

Overview: Benin remains among the most stable democracies in sub-Saharan Africa, having witnessed multiple free and fair elections and peaceful transfers of power since its transition to democracy in 1991. Freedom of expression is generally respected, although critical media outlets are occasionally suspended. Under President Patrice Talon, opposition politicians have increasingly been targeted for prosecution, while judicial independence has been undermined by the appointment of the president's personal attorney as president of the Constitutional Court and the creation of a new anticorruption court, which has been accused of targeting Talon's political rivals.

KEY DEVELOPMENTS IN 2018:

- In February, President Patrice Talon appointed his personal lawyer as president of the Constitutional Court (he was confirmed in June), raising concerns about a potential erosion in judicial independence.
- In June, the Constitutional Court reversed its January decision that struck down a law passed in 2017 banning strikes by many public-sector workers; while in September, the legislature passed a new law that limited strikes by private-sector workers and eligible public employees to 10 days per year.
- In July, the parliament rejected constitutional amendments which would have required presidential, parliamentary, and local elections to be held concurrently, among other provisions.
- In October, a newly formed anticorruption court, the Court of Punishment of Economic Crimes and Terrorism (CRIET), sentenced Sébastien Ajavon, one of President Talon's most prominent rivals, to 20 years in prison for drug trafficking. Critics have accused the court of being politicized and used as a tool to pursue the president's political opponents.

POLITICAL RIGHTS: 32 / 40 (−1)

A. ELECTORAL PROCESS: 9 / 12

A1. Was the current head of government or other chief national authority elected through free and fair elections? 3 / 4

The president is elected by popular vote for up to two five-year terms and serves as both the chief of state and head of government. Former president Thomas Boni Yayi respected the constitutionally mandated term limits and did not seek reelection in 2016. None of the 33 candidates who ran in the 2016 presidential election won a majority of votes in the first round, leading to a second round in which Patrice Talon defeated former prime minister Lionel Zinsou with 65 percent of the vote. Talon, Benin's richest businessman, ran as an independent, supported by the business sector and a number of small political parties. Zinsou represented the incumbent party, the Cowry Forces for an Emerging Benin (FCBE). The election was generally held in accordance with international standards, although some delays in voting were reported due to voter card shortages and the late delivery of materials to polling stations.

A2. Were the current national legislative representatives elected through free and fair elections? 3 / 4

Delegates to the 83-member, unicameral National Assembly serve four-year terms and are elected by proportional representation. International observers deemed the last legislative elections held in 2015 to be credible, noting only minor logistical issues, including delays in poll openings and shortages of voting materials.

A3. Are the electoral laws and framework fair, and are they implemented impartially by the relevant election management bodies? 3 / 4

Elections are conducted by the Autonomous National Electoral Commission (CENA), which includes representatives from both the ruling party and the opposition. The CENA generally administers elections fairly and transparently. However, concerns about the accuracy of the computerized voter roll introduced in 2013 have persisted; due to resource constraints and organizational shortcomings, the voter roll has not been updated frequently enough.

In July 2018, the parliament voted against a constitutional reform which would have required presidential, parliamentary, and local elections to be held concurrently, among other provisions. The amendment had enough support to be put to a vote in a referendum, but President Talon decided to abandon the reform effort in late July.

B. POLITICAL PLURALISM AND PARTICIPATION: 15 / 16 (-1)

B1. Do the people have the right to organize in different political parties or other competitive political groupings of their choice, and is the system free of undue obstacles to the rise and fall of these competing parties or groupings? 4 / 4

Dozens of political parties operate openly regardless of ethnic or regional affiliation, and there are no unreasonable constraints on the formation of new parties. Five major parties and several minor parties are represented in the legislature. However, the parliament passed amendments to the electoral code in September 2018 that could impact the viability of many parties. One of the provisions in the law imposes an unusually high 10 percent threshold for party lists to win representation in the parliament. Additionally, the new code drastically increased candidate registration fees; fees for presidential candidates increased from $27,000 to $445,000, while candidate-list fees for parliamentary elections rose from $15,000 to $443,000.

B2. Is there a realistic opportunity for the opposition to increase its support or gain power through elections? 3 / 4 (-1)

The opposition has historically had a realistic opportunity to gain power through elections. Talon's defeat of Zinsou, the incumbent president's chosen successor in the 2016 election, marked Benin's fourth electoral turnover at the presidential level since multiparty elections were restored in 1991.

In recent years, however, the government has introduced obstacles that could reduce the competitiveness of opposition parties. Notably, opposition parties have accused the government of targeting potential presidential candidates and other opposition figures with criminal investigations. Sébastien Ajavon, a business magnate who finished third in the 2016 presidential election, was sentenced in absentia (Ajavon is living in exile in France) in October 2018 to 20 years in prison for drug trafficking by a newly established anticorruption court, the CRIET. Critics condemned the decision as politically motivated and part of a pattern of intimidation against opposition figures. The charges, which date to the seizure of cocaine at one of Ajavon's businesses in 2016, had previously been dismissed by a Cotonou court. In December, the African Court on Human and People's Rights ordered that the sentence not be imposed on Ajavon, which the government had not complied with at year's end. Additionally, in July, the National Assembly voted to lift the parliamentary immunity of three opposition deputies so they could face corruption charges.

Score Change: The score declined from 4 to 3 because the targeting of prominent opposition figures for investigation and prosecution reduced the competitiveness of opposition parties.

B3. Are the people's political choices free from domination by the military, foreign powers, religious hierarchies, economic oligarchies, or any other powerful group that is not democratically accountable? 4 / 4

Politics are generally free from interference by the military or other powerful groups.

B4. Do various segments of the population (including ethnic, religious, gender, LGBT, and other relevant groups) have full political rights and electoral opportunities? 4 / 4

Women and minority groups are not legally constrained from participation in the political process, but cultural factors do limit women's political engagement. Women won just 7 percent of the seats in the 2015 parliamentary elections.

Benin has historically been divided between northern and southern ethnic groups, but presidential candidates from both the north and the south have won the presidency.

C. FUNCTIONING OF GOVERNMENT: 8 / 12

C1. Do the freely elected head of government and national legislative representatives determine the policies of the government? 3 / 4

The president and the National Assembly generally determine government policies. In many rural areas, the government struggles to deliver basic services and citizens rely on local customary and religious leaders to fulfill those functions.

C2. Are safeguards against official corruption strong and effective? 2 / 4

Corruption remains a widespread problem in Benin. The government's main anti-corruption body, the National Anti-Corruption Authority (ANLC), has the ability to hear complaints, recommend measures, and pass cases to the courts, but it has no enforcement authority. Corrupt officials have rarely faced prosecution, contributing to a culture of impunity. Parliamentary immunity is often used to avoid corruption charges.

The CRIET was established in August 2018 to focus on the prosecution of corruption, drug trafficking, and terrorism cases. However, critics have complained that the new court has targeted the government's political opponents, including Ajavon.

In June, authorities issued two international arrest warrants for former Cotonou mayor Léhady Soglo, who was removed from office in 2017 over corruption allegations and is living in exile in France. Opposition parties claimed that this and other anticorruption cases pursued by the government in 2018 were thinly veiled attempts to neutralize the president's opponents.

C3. Does the government operate with openness and transparency? 3 / 4

The 2015 Information and Communication Code provides for access to government information. However, information deemed sensitive, including national security, trade, and judicial documents, remains restricted.

CIVIL LIBERTIES: 47 / 60 (–2)

D. FREEDOM OF EXPRESSION AND BELIEF: 15 / 16

D1. Are there free and independent media? 3 / 4

Constitutional guarantees of freedom of expression are largely respected in practice. Print media exhibit pluralism of opinion and viewpoints. However, most media outlets receive direct financial support from politicians and few are considered genuinely independent.

Defamation remains a crime punishable by fine, and media outlets critical of the government have increasingly risked suspension in recent years. In May 2018, the High Authority for Audiovisual Media and Communication (HAAC) suspended one of the country's most popular newspapers, *La Nouvelle Tribune,* for publishing articles critical of the president. The suspension remained in place at year's end, although the publication was still accessible to readers online.

D2. Are individuals free to practice and express their religious faith or nonbelief in public and private? 4 / 4

Religious freedom is constitutionally guaranteed and generally respected in practice.

D3. Is there academic freedom, and is the educational system free from extensive political indoctrination? 4 / 4

Academic freedom is largely respected. However, in February 2018, police arrested nine students at the University of Abomey-Calavi in Cotonou for protesting increased enrollment fees. The students were released after three days, following a strike by three student unions.

D4. Are individuals free to express their personal views on political or other sensitive topics without fear of surveillance or retribution? 4 / 4

Individuals are generally free to express their views on politics without fear of surveillance. A controversial social media tax on platforms such as Facebook, Twitter, and WhatsApp, as well as a tax on text messages and mobile phone calls, went into effect in September 2018. However, in response to a public outcry against the measures, the government repealed the taxes after just three days.

E. ASSOCIATIONAL AND ORGANIZATIONAL RIGHTS: 11 / 12 (–1)
E1. Is there freedom of assembly? 4 / 4

Freedom of assembly is generally respected; permit and registration requirements for demonstrations are not always enforced. In February 2018, security forces prevented a women's march in Cotonou from traveling along the organizers' planned route, even though the demonstration was approved by the authorities. The event was ultimately cancelled.

E2. Is there freedom for nongovernmental organizations, particularly those that are engaged in human rights- and governance-related work? 4 / 4

Nongovernmental organizations (NGOs), including human rights groups, generally operate freely.

E3. Is there freedom for trade unions and similar professional or labor organizations? 3 / 4 (–1)

The right to form unions is respected. However, employees in the public sector are restricted in their ability to bargain collectively.

During the year, union rights were threatened by two new laws limiting strikes. In January 2018, the Constitutional Court ruled against a controversial law that prohibited public-sector workers in the defense, health, justice, and security sectors from striking. In June, newly appointed justices on the court reversed the earlier decision and ruled in favor of the ban. In September, the legislature passed a law limiting strikes to a maximum of 10 days per year for private-sector workers and public employees not covered by the aforementioned ban.

Score Change: The score declined from 4 to 3 because newly appointed members of the Constitutional Court upheld a ban strikes by many public-sector workers, and a new law was passed limiting strikes by private-sector workers and eligible public employees to 10 days per year.

F. RULE OF LAW: 11 / 16 (-1)

F1. Is there an independent judiciary? 2 / 4 (-1)

Although the judiciary has demonstrated some independence, the courts are inefficient and susceptible to corruption. The process of nominating and promoting judges lacks transparency.

Judicial independence was further threatened by the February 2018 appointment of President Talon's personal lawyer, Joseph Djogbénou, as president of the Constitutional Court, followed by his confirmation in June. Prior to Djogbénou's appointment, the court had served as a strong check on executive power, ruling in 2017 that a government ban on student associations was illegal, among other displays of independence. The decision by the Djogbénou-led court to reverse the earlier ruling on public-sector strikes intensified concerns about a potential erosion in the court's independence.

Furthermore, critics claim that the newly formed CRIET lacks independence. In addition to allegations that the court has been instrumentalized to prosecute the president's political opponents, judges on the court were appointed in July by government decree, in lieu of a confirmation process.

Score Change: The score declined from 3 to 2 because judicial independence has been threatened by the appointment of the president's personal lawyer as president of the Constitutional Court, as well as the apparent politicization of the Court of Punishment of Economic Crimes and Terrorism, which has prosecuted the president's political opponents.

F2. Does due process prevail in civil and criminal matters? 3 / 4

Due process usually prevails in criminal and civil matters. However, judicial inefficiency, corruption, and a shortage of attorneys in the north inhibit the right to a fair trial. Lack of resources contributes to often lengthy pretrial detentions. Arbitrary arrest and detention occasionally occurs.

F3. Is there protection from the illegitimate use of physical force and freedom from war and insurgencies? 3 / 4

Benin is free from war and insurgencies. Prison conditions are often harsh, and prisoners face overcrowding, lack of access to food and water, and occasional physical abuse, despite a ban on torture. Police brutality remained a problem in 2018, including beatings and torture of suspects. Perpetrators are frequently shielded from prosecution by their superiors.

F4. Do laws, policies, and practices guarantee equal treatment of various segments of the population? 3 / 4

Relations among Benin's ethnic groups are generally amicable. Minority ethnic groups are represented in government agencies, the civil service, and the armed forces. The constitution prohibits discrimination based on race, gender, and disability, but not sexual orientation. The only legislation directly restricting the rights of LGBT (lesbian, gay, bisexual, and transgender) people is the penal code of 1996, which imposes a higher age of consent for same-sex sexual activity (21) than for heterosexual activity (13). LGBT people face social stigma and discrimination in practice.

Women experience discrimination in employment and access to credit, healthcare, and education.

G. PERSONAL AUTONOMY AND INDIVIDUAL RIGHTS: 10 / 16

G1. Do individuals enjoy freedom of movement, including the ability to change their place of residence, employment, or education? 3 / 4

Individuals can generally move freely throughout the country. However, in some rural areas, cultural traditions force women to remain indoors for extended periods. Roadblocks set up by the police can make travel difficult, and police officers occasionally demand bribes for travelers to pass through.

G2. Are individuals able to exercise the right to own property and establish private businesses without undue interference from state or nonstate actors? 3 / 4

Improvements to the business registration process, anticorruption efforts, and regulatory reform since 2010 have improved Benin's commercial environment.

It is difficult to register property in Benin, and the enforcement of contracts is uneven. Despite laws guaranteeing equal rights to inheritance for women, many women are denied the right to inherit property in practice.

G3. Do individuals enjoy personal social freedoms, including choice of marriage partner and size of family, protection from domestic violence, and control over appearance? 2 / 4

Domestic violence remains a serious problem, and women are often reluctant to report instances of domestic abuse. A 2003 law that prohibits female genital mutilation (FGM) reduced the incidence of the practice, but it still persists, particularly in the northeast. Although the law prohibits marriage for those under 18 years old, the government allows exceptions for 14- to 17-year-olds if there is parental consent. Child marriage and forced marriage remain common in rural areas.

G4. Do individuals enjoy equality of opportunity and freedom from economic exploitation? 2 / 4

Human trafficking is widespread in Benin, despite a recent uptick in prosecutions for the crime. Trafficking of children is illegal; legislation that specifically addresses adult trafficking remains under review. The practice of sending young girls to wealthy families to work as domestic servants has led to cases of exploitation and sexual slavery. Children from low-income families are less likely to attend school, hindering social mobility.

Bhutan

Population: 800,000
Capital: Thimphu
Political Rights Rating: 3
Civil Liberties Rating: 4
Freedom Rating: 3.5
Freedom Status: Partly Free
Electoral Democracy: Yes

Overview: Bhutan is a constitutional monarchy that has made significant strides toward becoming a consolidated democracy over the past decade. It has held credible elections and undergone transfers of power to opposition parties. Ongoing problems include discrimination against Nepali-speaking and non-Buddhist minorities, media self-censorship, and, increasingly, the use of libel and defamation cases to silence journalists.

KEY DEVELOPMENTS IN 2018:
- National Assembly elections held in September and October resulted in a sizable victory for the opposition Bhutan United Party (DNT). After the DNT's victory, the king appointed Lotay Tshering as prime minister.
- Turnout was high for National Council elections held in April, which some observers ascribed to reforms designed to encourage voting and make casting ballots easier for residents, such as a new system of voting by post.

POLITICAL RIGHTS: 29 / 40 (+1)

A. ELECTORAL PROCESS: 10 / 12

A1. Was the current head of government or other chief national authority elected through free and fair elections? 3 / 4

King Jigme Khesar Namgyel Wangchuck formally succeeded his father in 2008. The monarch is head of state, appoints a number of high officials in consultation with other bodies, and retains a waning degree of influence over ministerial positions. The king nominates the leader of the majority party in the elected National Assembly to serve as prime minister. The 2018 elections for the National Assembly, held in September and October, were free and fair, and resulted in a sizable victory for the opposition DNT. After the DNT's victory, the king appointed Lotay Tshering as prime minister.

A2. Were the current national legislative representatives elected through free and fair elections? 4 / 4

The constitution provides for a bicameral Parliament, with a 25-seat upper house, the National Council, and a 47-seat lower house, the National Assembly. Members of both houses serve five-year terms. The king appoints five members of the nonpartisan National Council, and the remaining 20 are popularly elected as independents; the National Assembly is entirely elected. Elections for the upper house in April 2018 saw record turnout; some observers ascribed the higher turnout to reforms designed to encourage voting and make casting ballots easier for residents, such as a new system of voting by post. The National Assembly elections were held in two rounds in September and October, with the two parties that won the most support in the first round advancing to the second. The DNT, which launched in 2013, won 30 out of 47 seats, followed by the Bhutan Peace and Prosperity Party (DPT), which won 17 seats. The ruling People's Democratic Party (PDP) did not advance to the runoff.

A3. Are the electoral laws and framework fair, and are they implemented impartially by the relevant election management bodies? 3 / 4

Elections are administered by the Election Commission of Bhutan (ECB). The commission is thought to act impartially, although some of its regulations regarding which parties can compete in elections are controversial.

B. POLITICAL PLURALISM AND PARTICIPATION: 11 / 16 (+1)

B1. Do the people have the right to organize in different political parties or other competitive political groupings of their choice, and is the system free of undue obstacles to the rise and fall of these competing parties or groupings? 3 / 4

Citizens must receive government approval to form political parties. Obtaining approval is difficult, and the government has denied registration to several newly formed parties. In March 2018, for example, the ECB rejected the registration application of the newly formed Bhutan Happiness Party, claiming there were irregularities in its membership list.

B2. Is there a realistic opportunity for the opposition to increase its support or gain power through elections? 4 / 4

The opposition has a realistic chance to increase its support through elections. In 2018, the DNT won control of Parliament for the first time, and another opposition party, the DPT, finished second, despite having won no seats in 2013.

B3. Are the people's political choices free from domination by the military, foreign powers, religious hierarchies, economic oligarchies, or any other powerful group that is not democratically accountable? 2 / 4

India still has a strong influence over the choices of Bhutanese voters and politicians. In 2013, just before the parliamentary elections, India withdrew subsidies for oil and kerosene. Many observers viewed the decision as retaliation for the DPT government's move toward closer ties with China and an attempt to swing the elections toward the PDP. China does not have an official diplomatic relationship with Bhutan but has assiduously courted Bhutanese leaders in recent years, especially since a 2017 standoff between China and India over territory claimed by both Bhutan and China.

The royal family also retains significant influence. Most members of the political elite, including members of Parliament, steadfastly support the king and are hesitant to take any positions in direct opposition to the royal family.

B4. Do various segments of the population (including ethnic, religious, gender, LGBT, and other relevant groups) have full political rights and electoral opportunities? 2 / 4 (+1)

Electoral rules stipulate that political parties must not be limited to members of any regional, ethnic, or religious group. There is no party that represents Nepali speakers. Citizenship rules are strict, and many Nepali-speaking people have not attained citizenship, effectively disenfranchising them. International election monitors have noted that Nepali speakers have been turned away from voting.

Women are underrepresented in public office, but the proportion of women in the National Assembly increased from 8 percent to 15 percent following the 2018 elections. Although no women were elected to the National Council in the 2013 elections, in 2018 two women won seats; men won eighteen. Traditional customs inhibit women's political participation. The electoral reforms introduced for the year's polling also boosted turnout, including among women. The government has supported several programs to empower women and increase their engagement in politics.

Score Change: The score improved from 1 to 2 because recent procedural reforms resulted in somewhat greater turnout among women in the 2018 elections, and more women were elected to Parliament.

C. FUNCTIONING OF GOVERNMENT: 9 / 12

C1. Do the freely elected head of government and national legislative representatives determine the policies of the government? 3 / 4

Bhutan has made a successful transition from a system in which the monarch and his advisers dominated governance to one in which policies and legislation are mostly determined by elected officials.

India still has an influence on policymaking in Bhutan, and China has also become an important player in recent years. India provides significant foreign aid to Bhutan. As a result, the Bhutanese government is hesitant to make policies that will upset the relationship with India. In a 2017 incident that highlighted the impact of Bhutan's powerful neighbors, India sent troops to confront Chinese military personnel attempting to build a road on the Doklam plateau, on territory claimed by both Bhutan and China. Indian and Chinese troops withdrew after a tense three-month standoff.

C2. Are safeguards against official corruption strong and effective? 3 / 4

The government generally enforced anticorruption laws effectively. The 2006 Anti-Corruption Act established whistle-blower protections. The Anti-Corruption Commission (ACC), which had its role strengthened and expanded in 2011, is tasked with investigating and preventing graft, and has successfully prosecuted several high-profile cases.

Nepotism and favoritism in public procurement and government employment remained a problem in 2018.

C3. Does the government operate with openness and transparency? 3 / 4

Although Bhutan lacks comprehensive freedom of information legislation, the government has strengthened transparency by making the salaries of officials public and making the central and local budgets more open to review. A right to information law passed by the National Assembly in 2014 was designed to put the onus on government officials and agencies to release information. However, the National Council did not approve the bill, and by the end of 2018 it had yet to win final passage.

ADDITIONAL DISCRETIONARY POLITICAL RIGHTS QUESTION

Is the government or occupying power deliberately changing the ethnic composition of a country or territory so as to destroy a culture or tip the political balance in favor of another group? −1 / 0

The government has for decades attempted to diminish and repress the rights of ethnic Nepalis, forcing many of them to leave Bhutan. The government expelled a large percentage of Nepali speakers in the early 1990s; in 1992, well over 100,000 refugees living in Nepal were denied reentry to Bhutan. A resettlement effort aimed at transferring the refugees to other countries began in 2007, resulting in the resettlement of the majority of refugees, but over 6,500 people remained in camps in Nepal at the end of 2018.

CIVIL LIBERTIES: 30 / 60 (+3)
D. FREEDOM OF EXPRESSION AND BELIEF: 9 / 16
D1. Are there free and independent media? 2 / 4

While there are multiple private media outlets, many depend on advertising from state bodies, and Bhutan's media environment remained subject to a high degree of self-censorship, especially regarding criticism of the royal family. Powerful individuals can use defamation laws to retaliate against critics. In August 2018, a journalist was sentenced to three months in prison for libel, after she posted on Facebook about a woman who allegedly mistreated her stepdaughter.

In 2017, the Bhutan Information Communications and Media Act was passed, replacing a 2006 law. The government said it would strengthen the independence of the media and promote a free and vibrant media industry. The legislation mandated the establishment of an independent body called the Media Council, which was formed in August. The council monitors the media to determine which content is harmful or offensive. Press freedom advocates fear that the new body will further erode press freedom and contribute to greater self-censorship.

D2. Are individuals free to practice and express their religious faith or nonbelief in public and private? 2 / 4

The constitution protects freedom of religion, but local authorities are known to harass non-Buddhists. While Bhutanese of all faiths can worship freely in private, people experience pressure to participate in Buddhist ceremonies and practices.

Christian churches have often been unable to obtain registration from the government, which means that they cannot raise funds or buy property, placing constraints on their activities. Christian children are sometimes not allowed into schools based on their religion.

D3. Is there academic freedom, and is the educational system free from extensive political indoctrination? 2 / 4

Few restrictions on academic freedom have been reported. However, Bhutanese university students are often hesitant to speak out on controversial political issues and practice self-censorship. Students, in conducting research, tend to receive negative feedback for posing questions that could be considered offensive or too blunt.

D4. Are individuals free to express their personal views on political or other sensitive topics without fear of surveillance or retribution? 3 / 4

Freedom of expression is constitutionally guaranteed and generally respected. However, under the National Security Act, speech that creates or attempts to create "hatred and disaffection among the people" or "misunderstanding or hostility between the government and people," among other offenses, can be punished with imprisonment. The broad language of the law makes it vulnerable to misuse.

E. ASSOCIATIONAL AND ORGANIZATIONAL RIGHTS: 5 / 12 (+1)

E1. Is there freedom of assembly? 2 / 4

The constitution guarantees freedom of assembly, but this right is limited by government-imposed restrictions. Public gatherings require government permission, which is sometimes denied. Curfews and restrictions on the location of demonstrations also serve to curtail assembly rights.

E2. Is there freedom for nongovernmental organizations, particularly those that are engaged in human rights- and governance-related work? 2 / 4 (+1)

Nongovernmental organizations (NGOs) that work on issues related to ethnic Nepalis are not allowed to operate, but other local and international NGOs work with increasing freedom on a wide range of issues. Under the 2007 Civil Society Organization Act, all new NGOs must register with the government. Registration is granted to NGOs that are determined by the government to be "not harmful to the peace and unity of the country."

Score Change: The score improved from 1 to 2 because nongovernmental organizations have been able to work with relative freedom in recent years.

E3. Is there freedom for trade unions and similar professional or labor organizations? 1 / 4

The constitution nominally guarantees the right of workers to form unions, but the right to strike is not legally protected. Workers may bargain collectively, and antiunion discrimination is prohibited. Most of the country's workforce is engaged in small-scale agriculture and is therefore not unionized.

F. RULE OF LAW: 8 / 16 (+2)

F1. Is there an independent judiciary? 3 / 4

The independence of the judiciary is largely respected. Senior judges are appointed by the king on the recommendation of the National Judicial Commission. However, the rulings of judges often lack consistency, and many people view the judiciary as corrupt.

F2. Does due process prevail in civil and criminal matters? 2 / 4 (+1)

Although the right to a fair trial is largely guaranteed and arbitrary arrest is not a widespread problem, plaintiffs and defendants in civil disputes often represent themselves. Many people who are unable to repay debts are held in detention, which is considered arbitrary under international law. Overall, however, the rule of law and due process has improved substantially in civil and criminal matters. In recent years, Bhutan's courts have functioned with a relatively high degree of effectiveness.

Score Change: The score improved from 1 to 2 due to gradual gains in the quality of civil and criminal legal proceedings.

F3. Is there protection from the illegitimate use of physical force and freedom from war and insurgencies? 2 / 4 (+1)

The civilian police force generally operates within the law, and incidents of excessive force are rare. In recent years, the crime rates have generally been low. However, insurgents from the Indian state of Assam sometimes enter Bhutan and undermine security. Occasional instances of kidnapping and robbery occur along the border with India.

Score Change: The score improved from 1 to 2 due to low crime rates and a lack of other significant threats to physical security in recent years.

F4. Do laws, policies, and practices guarantee equal treatment of various segments of the population? 1 / 4

The constitution protects against discrimination based on sex, race, disability, language, religion, or societal status. However, Nepali-speaking people reportedly face employment discrimination and other forms of bias.

LGBT (lesbian, gay, bisexual, and transgender) people experience societal discrimination and social stigma, and there are no specific legal protections for transgender people. Same-sex sexual activity remains a criminal offense and can be punished with up to a year in prison, although the law is not generally enforced. Despite recent gains, discrimination in employment and education persists for women in Bhutan.

G. PERSONAL AUTONOMY AND INDIVIDUAL RIGHTS: 8 / 16

G1. Do individuals enjoy freedom of movement, including the ability to change their place of residence, employment, or education? 2 / 4

Bhutanese citizens generally have the freedom to travel domestically and internationally. However, the government has established different categories of citizenship, which restricts foreign travel for some. These restrictions reportedly have the greatest effect on Nepali speakers. Bhutanese security forces sometimes arrest Nepali people seeking to enter the country.

G2. Are individuals able to exercise the right to own property and establish private businesses without undue interference from state or nonstate actors? 2 / 4

Individuals generally have rights to own property and establish businesses, but the process of registering a new business can be cumbersome and hinder business development. Some ethnic Nepalis who lack a security clearance certificate face difficulties in starting a business. The property registration process can also be lengthy.

G3. Do individuals enjoy personal social freedoms, including choice of marriage partner and size of family, protection from domestic violence, and control over appearance? 2 / 4

Reports of domestic violence have increased in recent years. Societal taboos lead many incidents of rape and domestic violence to go unreported. Child marriage still occurs with some frequency; according to UNICEF data from 2017, 26 percent of women are married before age 18.

G4. Do individuals enjoy equality of opportunity and freedom from economic exploitation? 2 / 4

Female household workers, who often come from rural areas or India, are vulnerable to forced labor and other abuse, as are foreign workers in the construction and hydropower sectors. Child labor continued to be a problem in 2018, mostly in the agriculture and construction sectors. Girls often served as household workers and were vulnerable to abuse.

Sex trafficking remained a problem in 2018, and the government's enforcement efforts were inadequate to address it effectively; no prosecutions for trafficking were reported during the year. However, the government has provided funds for an NGO that helps shelter victims of trafficking.

Bolivia

Population: 11,300,000
Capital: La Paz (administrative), Sucre (judicial)
Political Rights Rating: 3
Civil Liberties Rating: 3
Freedom Rating: 3.0
Freedom Status: Partly Free
Electoral Democracy: Yes

Overview: Bolivia is a democracy where credible elections are held regularly. However, child labor and violence against women are persistent problems, independent and investigative journalists face harassment, and demonstrations and political movements are at times marred by violence. A 2017 ruling by the Constitutional Tribunal cleared the way for President Evo Morales, head of the ruling Movement toward Socialism (MAS) to run for a fourth term in 2019. The decision overturned the result of a 2016 referendum in which a majority of voters had indicated a desire to retain presidential term limits.

KEY DEVELOPMENTS IN 2018:

- In December, the Supreme Electoral Tribunal (TSE) confirmed the 2017 ruling of the Constitutional Tribunal, which struck down presidential limits, allowing President Morales to seek a fourth term in 2019. Demonstrations by both Morales supporters and opponents followed, including an anti-Morales protest in Santa Cruz at which the regional TSE building was burned down.
- Earlier, in September, the MAS-dominated legislature passed a law on political organizations, which aims to promote internal party democracy and transparency, but which the opposition said disadvantaged them by effectively mandating that opposition coalitions be formalized long before presidential elections.
- Confrontations between coca farmers and Bolivian authorities regarding regional limits on coca production continued during the year, resulting in the death of a police officer and two coca producers in separate incidents in August.
- In February, the Constitutional Tribunal ruled that a section of a 2014 law that allowed children as young as 10 to work was unconstitutional. However, child labor remained a serious problem that drew international scrutiny during the year.

POLITICAL RIGHTS: 28 / 40

A. ELECTORAL PROCESS: 10 / 12

A1. Was the current head of government or other chief national authority elected through free and fair elections? 4 / 4

Bolivia's president is both chief of state and head of government, and is directly elected to a five-year term. In the 2014 general elections, Evo Morales of MAS was reelected president with 61 percent of the vote. An Organization of American States (OAS) electoral observation mission stated that the election reflected the will of the people. A 2017 Constitutional Tribunal ruling, confirmed by the TSE in December 2018, permits Morales to run for a fourth term; the controversial rulings followed the failure of a 2016 referendum on extending term limits.

In 2015 subnational elections, the MAS won control of more departments and municipalities across the country than any other party. However, the opposition won key mayoralties and governorships—including those of La Paz, El Alto, Cochabamba and Santa Cruz,

Bolivia's four largest cities. An OAS electoral observation mission reported overwhelming citizen participation in the elections, but expressed concern about last-minute disqualifications and substitutions of candidates, which occurred after the ballots had been printed.

A2. Were the current national legislative representatives elected through free and fair elections? 4 / 4

The Plurinational Legislative Assembly (ALP) consists of a 130-member Chamber of Deputies and a 36-member Senate. Legislative terms are five years. All senators and 53 deputies are elected by proportional representation; 70 deputies are elected in individual districts through a majoritarian system. Seven seats in the Chamber of Deputies are reserved for indigenous representatives. In the 2014 legislative elections, Morales's MAS maintained a two-thirds majority in the legislature, the share necessary to select the members of the TSE, preselect upper-level judiciary candidates, and pass constitutional reforms.

A3. Are the electoral laws and framework fair, and are they implemented impartially by the relevant election management bodies? 2 / 4

For some years, Bolivian politics have been characterized by efforts by Morales and the MAS to abolish presidential term limits. In 2015, the ALP voted to amend the constitution in order to allow presidents to run for three consecutive terms instead of two, but voters rejected the change in a 2016 referendum. However, in 2017, MAS lawmakers filed a suit asking the Constitutional Tribunal to declare that certain legal provisions and articles in the constitution that ban reelection were unconstitutional and "inapplicable." (While Constitutional Tribunal justices are elected by voters, judicial candidates are preselected by the MAS-dominated legislature, and the Tribunal tends to favor the MAS.) In 2017, the court assented, effectively overturning the results of the previous year's referendum and clearing the way for Morales to run for a fourth term in 2019. In December 2018, the TSE confirmed the 2017 Constitutional Tribunal ruling when it approved President Morales's candidacy for the 2019 election.

B. POLITICAL PLURALISM AND PARTICIPATION: 11 / 16

B1. Do the people have the right to organize in different political parties or other competitive political groupings of their choice, and is the system free of undue obstacles to the rise and fall of these competing parties or groupings? 3 / 4

Citizens have the right to organize political parties. Since Morales's election to the presidency in 2005, the formerly dominant parties have all but collapsed, giving way to a series of new political groupings and short-lived opposition coalitions. The MAS draws support from a diverse range of social movements, unions, and civil society actors. Opposition politicians have claimed that the Morales administration persecutes them through the judiciary.

In September 2018, the MAS-dominated ALP passed the Political Organizations Law, which aims to promote internal party democracy and transparency by increasing party financing regulations and establishing primary elections through which party groupings will decide their presidential and vice presidential candidates. However, opposition leaders claimed that the provision requiring intraparty primaries hampers the ability of opposition parties to form coalitions to challenge the MAS, by effectively mandating that coalitions be formalized long before presidential elections take place. Under the law, coalitions must be formally declared 75 days before the intraparty primaries are held.

B2. Is there a realistic opportunity for the opposition to increase its support or gain power through elections? 2 / 4

There are no formal institutional barriers impeding opposition parties from participating in elections. However, the overwhelming dominance of the MAS makes it difficult for opposition parties to gain power through elections.

B3. Are the people's political choices free from domination by the military, foreign powers, religious hierarchies, economic oligarchies, or any other powerful group that is not democratically accountable? 3 / 4

People are generally free to make political decisions without undue influence from the military, foreign powers, or other influential groups. However, opposition members claimed that November 2017 rallies held in favor of Morales's reelection were filled with public employees coerced by their employers to attend.

B4. Do various segments of the population (including ethnic, religious, gender, LGBT, and other relevant groups) have full political rights and electoral opportunities? 3 / 4

The constitution recognizes 36 indigenous nationalities, declares Bolivia a plurinational state, and formalizes political autonomy within indigenous territories. Adult citizens enjoy universal and equal suffrage. Although they are well represented in government, the interests of indigenous groups are often overlooked by politicians.

Formally, Bolivia has progressive legislation that guarantees equal political representation for women and seeks to protect women from political violence. Moreover, the 2018 Political Organizations Law requires the equal participation of women and men in political party organization and decision-making. However, despite being well-represented in politics, sexism and patriarchal attitudes undermine the work of women politicians, and cases of violence and harassment against them continue, particularly at local levels.

Judicial elections originally scheduled for 2017 were postponed for several weeks due to concerns that not enough women and indigenous candidates were registered in some regions of the country.

C. FUNCTIONING OF GOVERNMENT: 7 / 12

C1. Do the freely elected head of government and national legislative representatives determine the policies of the government? 3 / 4

Elected officials are free to set and implement government policy without undue interference from nonstate actors. However, opposition members charge that the MAS majority in the legislature, in conjunction with the country's powerful presidency, allows for strong executive influence on legislative processes.

C2. Are safeguards against official corruption strong and effective? 2 / 4

Anticorruption laws are poorly enforced, and corruption affects a range of government entities and economic sectors, including law enforcement bodies and extractive industries. Public procurement processes are frequently compromised by bribery.

Reports that surfaced in April 2018 implicated three Bolivian officials in a corruption scheme involving bribes paid by a Brazilian company, Camargo Corrêa, that had been contracted for road construction projects. Morales announced a special commission to investigate the claims, but opposition lawmakers refused to participate in it, objecting to its limited scope: the probe looked only at a limited number of contracts awarded before Morales took office.

C3. Does the government operate with openness and transparency? 2 / 4

Bolivia has no law guaranteeing access to public information. Elected officials by law must make asset declarations, but these are unavailable to the public.

CIVIL LIBERTIES: 39 / 60
D. FREEDOM OF EXPRESSION AND BELIEF: 14 / 16
D1. Are there free and independent media? 2 / 4

While the constitution guarantees freedom of expression, in practice, journalists frequently encounter harassment in connection with critical or investigative reporting. Such harassment at times comes from government officials, who have characterized journalists as liars and participants in an international conspiracy against Morales. In October 2018, security guards blocked a number of journalists from attending an event marking the opening of the country's new presidential residence, and beat two women journalists who protested. In a separate incident, a journalist was detained in a courtroom and intimidated by a judge and courtroom staff, who attempted to coerce her to delete photographs from her mobile phone.

In January, Bolivian journalists condemned sections of the new penal code they said could allow criminal defamation proceedings. In August, President Morales floated the idea of passing a law against lies, applicable to media outlets (as well as public authorities). Separately, in November, the National Press Association of Bolivia (ANP) expressed concern about reports of police surveillance of journalists' online activity.

Media outlets with editorial positions perceived as hostile by the Morales administration are denied access to public advertising contracts.

D2. Are individuals free to practice and express their religious faith or nonbelief in public and private? 4 / 4

Freedom of religion is guaranteed by the constitution and generally upheld in practice. The 2009 constitution ended the Roman Catholic Church's official status, and created a secular state.

D3. Is there academic freedom, and is the educational system free from extensive political indoctrination? 4 / 4

Academic freedom is legally guaranteed and upheld in practice.

D4. Are individuals free to express their personal views on political or other sensitive topics without fear of surveillance or retribution? 4 / 4

Private discussion is robust and generally free from interference or surveillance. However, since the 2016 referendum on term limits, some MAS legislators have discussed introducing regulations for social media outlets that would prohibit anonymous users, and allow for sanctions against those who insult public officials. In September 2018, two legislators praised Morales's call for a law against lies, and proposed that the legislation include speech on social media.

E. ASSOCIATIONAL AND ORGANIZATIONAL RIGHTS: 9 / 12

E1. Is there freedom of assembly? 3 / 4

Bolivian law protects the right to peaceful assembly. However, protests are sometimes marred by clashes between demonstrators and police, or other violence. In December 2018, the TSE building in Santa Cruz was burned down during an antigovernment demonstration that erupted after the TSE confirmed Morales's candidacy in the upcoming presidential election. Instances of violence have accompanied an ongoing protest movement led by coca producers who say regional ceilings on coca cultivation have harmed their livelihoods.

E2. Is there freedom for nongovernmental organizations, particularly those that are engaged in human rights– and governance-related work? 3 / 4

Many nongovernmental organizations (NGOs) operate, but they are subject to some legal restrictions. In 2016, the Constitutional Court dismissed a petition arguing that two statutes in the country's NGO law gave the government license to improperly dissolve such groups. Government officials have at times smeared rights groups as antigovernment conspirators.

In August 2018, a delegation from the International Rights of Nature Tribunal was denied permission to enter the Indigenous Territory and National Park of Isiboro Sécure (TIPNIS), where they were to have met local leaders to discuss a controversial, government-backed highway construction project.

E3. Is there freedom for trade unions and similar professional or labor organizations? 3 / 4

Labor and peasant unions are an active force in society and wield significant political influence.

The country's official labor code is inconsistent with Bolivian law; for example, it prohibits public sector unions, yet many public workers are able to legally unionize. A National

Labor Court hears cases of antiunion discrimination, but tends to hand down verdicts slowly, and penalties for antiunion discrimination are not consistently applied.

F. RULE OF LAW: 6 / 16
F1. Is there an independent judiciary? 1 / 4

Bolivia stands as the sole country that appoints justices via popular elections. Judges on the Supreme Court, the Constitutional Tribunal, and other entities are nominated through a two-thirds vote in the legislature, which allows the MAS to dominate the candidate selection process and has produced a judiciary that favors the party. In addition to its politicization, the judiciary remains overburdened and beset by corruption.

In 2017, shortly after the Constitutional Tribunal ruled that Morales could run for another term in 2019, elections were held to fill positions for 26 judges on four high courts. A majority of participating voters heeded the opposition's calls to spoil their ballots. Prior to the polls, opposition figures argued that MAS legislators had coordinated their votes on judicial candidates improperly, and that the candidates were selected through opaque processes. There were also complaints brought to electoral authorities that some candidates had violated the prohibition on campaigning.

F2. Does due process prevail in civil and criminal matters? 1 / 4

Many people have difficulty accessing the justice system due to a lack of the relevant offices in the areas where they live, and also because services, where provided, are often insufficient. Police are poorly paid and receive inadequate training, and corruption within the police force remains a problem. Police officers who attempted to expose corruption often face repercussions.

While the constitution and jurisdictional law recognize indigenous customary law on conflict resolution, reform efforts have not fully resolved questions regarding the territorial, personal, and material reach of its jurisdiction and proper application.

F3. Is there protection from the illegitimate use of physical force and freedom from war and insurgencies? 2 / 4

Several pardon programs enacted in recent years, as well as fast-track trial procedures, have eased severe prison overcrowding, though some critics contend that fast-track trials push innocent people to plead guilty in exchange for reduced sentences and less time spent in court. Assaults in prisons continue to pose a significant problem.

Impunity for crimes has prompted some to engage in vigilante justice against alleged criminals, including lynchings.

Confrontations between coca farmers and Bolivian authorities regarding regional limits on coca production continued during the year, resulting in the death of a police officer and two coca producers in separate incidents in August.

F4. Do laws, policies, and practices guarantee equal treatment of various segments of the population? 2 / 4

The 2010 antiracism law contains measures to combat discrimination and impose criminal penalties for discriminatory acts. However, racism and associated discrimination is rife in the country, especially against indigenous groups.

Bolivia has laws in place that prohibit discrimination against LGBT (lesbian, gay, bisexual, and transgender) people. However, these laws are rarely enforced, and LGBT people experience widespread societal discrimination. Many transgender people have resorted to sex work in dangerous conditions due to employment discrimination and groundless rejection of their credentials.

G. PERSONAL AUTONOMY AND INDIVIDUAL RIGHTS: 10 / 16

G1. Do individuals enjoy freedom of movement, including the ability to change their place of residence, employment, or education? 3 / 4

There are no formal limits on people's ability to change their place of residence, employment, or education, but choices can be limited by socioeconomic difficulties. Roads are occasionally blockaded as part of protest actions, impeding free movement.

G2. Are individuals able to exercise the right to own property and establish private businesses without undue interference from state or nonstate actors? 2 / 4

Women enjoy the same formal rights to property ownership as men but discrimination is common, leading to disparities in property ownership and access to resources.

The rights of indigenous people to prior consultation in cases of natural resource extraction and land development are not fully upheld by law or in practice. Some groups argue that a highway development project in TIPNIS Morales formally revived in 2017 is moving forward in violation of this right.

G3. Do individuals enjoy personal social freedoms, including choice of marriage partner and size of family, protection from domestic violence, and control over appearance? 3 / 4

The constitution reserves marriage as a bond between a man and a woman, and makes no provision for same-sex civil unions. In 2017, the TSE determined that transgender people who have legally changed their gender on their identification documents may marry.

Domestic violence, which mainly affects women, is a serious problem, and laws criminalizing violence against women are not well enforced. Many women lack access to birth control and reproductive health care.

G4. Do individuals enjoy equality of opportunity and freedom from economic exploitation? 2 / 4

Bolivia is a source country for the trafficking of men, women, and children for forced labor and prostitution, and the country faced increased international criticism over child labor in 2018. In February 2018, the Constitutional Tribunal voided a section of a 2014 law that allowed children as young as 10 to work certain jobs. However, hundreds of thousands of children are still working in Bolivia's mines, and ranches, and in other sectors. In July, the United States downgraded Bolivia to its lowest "Tier 3" category in its annual *Trafficking in Persons* report, and announced cuts in aid over the issue in December.

Bosnia and Herzegovina

Population: 3,500,000
Capital: Sarajevo
Political Rights Rating: 4
Civil Liberties Rating: 4
Freedom Rating: 4.0
Freedom Status: Partly Free
Electoral Democracy: No

Overview: Bosnia and Herzegovina (BiH) is a highly decentralized parliamentary republic whose complex constitutional regime is embedded in the Dayton Peace Agreement, which ended the 1992–95 Bosnian War. Political affairs are characterized by severe partisan gridlock among nationalist leaders from the country's Bosniak, Serb, and Croat communities. Corruption remains a serious problem.

KEY DEVELOPMENTS IN 2018:

- In January, the government of BiH's Serb-majority Republika Srpska (RS) entity was revealed to be recruiting the services of Russian-trained paramilitaries from Serbia. It emerged in February that the RS government was acquiring significant quantities of arms in an effort to militarize the entity's police forces.
- Protests began in late March and continued throughout the year following the unexplained death—and presumed murder—of David Dragičević, a 21-year-old Banja Luka man. Demonstrators accused RS authorities of involvement in the death or a subsequent cover-up amid broader concerns about policing and the rule of law in the entity.
- In October, BiH held its eighth general elections since the conclusion of the war. The balloting was marked by irregularities and mostly confirmed the positions of the entrenched nationalist blocs, though negotiations on a new government were ongoing at year's end.

POLITICAL RIGHTS: 19 / 40 (−2)
A. ELECTORAL PROCESS: 6 / 12 (−1)

A1. Was the current head of government or other chief national authority elected through free and fair elections? 2 / 4 (−1)

The 1995 Dayton Accords that ended the civil war in BiH created a loosely knit state composed of two entities—the Federation, whose citizens are mainly Bosniak and Croat, and the Serb-dominated RS—that operate under a weak central government. The position of head of state is held by a three-member presidency comprising one Bosniak, one Serb, and one Croat; they are each elected to a four-year term, which they serve concurrently.

The chair of the Council of Ministers, or prime minister, is nominated by the presidency and approved by the House of Representatives. The chair in turn nominates other ministers for approval by the House.

The October 2018 elections were once again led by the country's three entrenched nationalist blocs: the Bosniak nationalist Party of Democratic Action (SDA), the Croat nationalist Croatian Democratic Union (HDZ-BiH), and the Serb nationalist Alliance of Independent Social Democrats (SNSD). Milorad Dodik of the SNSD, the longtime president of the RS entity, won the Serb seat in BiH's state presidency, and Šefik Džaferović of the SDA won the Bosniak seat. However, Željko Komšić of the center-left Democratic Front party decisively defeated the HDZ-BiH incumbent for the Croat seat of the presidency. At year's end, the exact shape of the ruling coalitions at the state level and at most other levels of government remained unclear, as negotiations were ongoing. In December, however, five parties from across the political spectrum formed a coalition without the SDA in the Sarajevo Canton, and the SNSD formed another government in the RS, with Radovan Višković replacing Željka Cvijanović, now the entity president, as prime minister.

Serious concerns were raised about the integrity of the elections, with the Organization for Security and Co-operation in Europe (OSCE) noting a "lack of confidence in the impartiality of all levels of the election administration, largely due to suspected commissioners' political and ethnic bias." Prior to the elections, independent media revealed a fraudulent absentee voter registration scheme—allegedly supported by Moscow—that implicated the HDZ of Croatia and its Bosnian sister party, the HDZ-BiH. Over 450,000 ballots, about 7 percent of those cast, were disqualified by the Central Electoral Commission (CIK), raising suspicions of potential voter fraud. The postelection period was marked by growing concerns about the extent of the alleged fraud, with the Social Democratic Party (SDP), whose candidate finished a close second in the race for the state presidency's Bosniak seat, demanding a formal recount.

Score Change: The score declined from 3 to 2 due to credible reports of large-scale fraud in the 2018 presidential elections.

A2. Were the current national legislative representatives elected through free and fair elections? 2 / 4

The Parliamentary Assembly, a state-level body, has two chambers. The 15-seat upper house, the House of Peoples, consists of five members from each of the three main ethnic groups, elected by the Federation and RS legislatures for four-year terms. The lower house, the House of Representatives, has 42 popularly elected members serving four-year terms, with 28 seats assigned to representatives from the Federation and 14 to representatives from the RS.

The SDA, HDZ-BiH, and SNSD dominated the 2018 general elections, capturing nine, five, and six seats in the highly fragmented House of Representatives and many other posts at the entity, canton, and municipal levels. However, they faced stiff competition from other parties, particularly the SDP, which took five House of Representatives seats, and the left-wing Democratic Front–Civic Alliance, which won three. Nine smaller parties also won representation at the state level. Election monitors noted significant irregularities and a decline in overall quality as compared with prior polls.

A3. Are the electoral laws and framework fair, and are they implemented impartially by the relevant election management bodies? 2 / 4

Under BiH's constitutional regime, the CIK administers elections with the help of municipal election commissions. Both are subject to significant political party interference. The CIK is a largely ineffectual body, unable to act decisively without political support. The election of its president in September 2018 was criticized as illegal by the winner's opponent, who argued that the law did not allow a commissioner to serve as president twice in the same seven-year mandate.

Conflicts over fair ethnic representation continue to surround aspects of the constitution. For example, BiH citizens who do not identify as members of the country's Bosniak, Serb, or Croat "constitutive peoples" remain barred from the presidency and membership in the House of Peoples, despite 2009 and 2016 rulings by the European Court of Human Rights that the exclusion of members of other ethnic groups violated the European Convention on Human Rights.

The Federation's upper house, also known as the House of Peoples, had yet to be formed at the end of 2018 due to an unresolved legal dispute over its system of ethnic seat allocations. A 2017 Constitutional Court ruling had struck down the existing legal provisions, and after Federation lawmakers failed to enact new rules, the CIK attempted to resolve the problem in December. However, the SDA and other Bosniak-led parties appealed the decision to the Constitutional Court. The dispute also held up the formation of the state-level House of Peoples, whose members are appointed by the entity legislatures.

Separately, the city of Mostar has not held municipal elections since 2008 due to an unresolved legal dispute over the allocation of city council seats between Croats and Bosniaks.

B. POLITICAL PLURALISM AND PARTICIPATION: 9 / 16 (−1)

B1. Do the people have the right to organize in different political parties or other competitive political groupings of their choice, and is the system free of undue obstacles to the rise and fall of these competing parties or groupings? 3 / 4

Political parties typically organize and operate freely, though the political arena in the Federation is generally limited to Bosniaks and Croats, while Serbs dominate politics in the RS. While coalitions at all levels of government shift frequently, incumbent parties maintain their positions with the help of vast patronage networks, making it difficult for smaller reform-oriented forces to achieve meaningful breakthroughs.

B2. Is there a realistic opportunity for the opposition to increase its support or gain power through elections? 2 / 4 (−1)

There are no explicit legal barriers preventing opposition parties from entering government, but expansive veto powers granted to the constitutive peoples and their representatives have helped the dominant nationalist parties to manipulate the system and shut out reformist and multiethnic challengers. This pattern was largely reinforced in the 2018 elections, despite the HDZ-BiH's defeat in the contest for the Croat seat of the state presidency.

Score Change: The score declined from 3 to 2 because a series of elections in recent years have demonstrated that the political system created by the Dayton Accords favors establishment parties.

B3. Are the people's political choices free from domination by the military, foreign powers, religious hierarchies, economic oligarchies, or any other powerful group that is not democratically accountable? 2 / 4

The Office of the High Representative (OHR), which was created by the Dayton Accords, operates under the auspices of the United Nations and has the authority to remove elected officials if they are deemed to be obstructing the peace process. In recent years, the OHR has been reluctant to intervene in the country's politics.

Both Serbia and Croatia wield outsized influence in the Bosnian political sphere through their respective local allies, the SNSD and the HDZ-BiH. Two other foreign states, Russia and Turkey, have offered support to preferred parties and candidates.

B4. Do various segments of the population (including ethnic, religious, gender, LGBT, and other relevant groups) have full political rights and electoral opportunities? 2 / 4

Political rights in BiH are in large part contingent on one's ethnic background and place of residence. Ethnic minorities including Jews and Roma are constitutionally barred from the presidency and from membership in the House of Peoples, despite the European Court of Human Rights rulings against those provisions. Serbs who live in the Federation and Croats and Bosniaks who live in the RS are also excluded from the presidency. Some Croats argue that their rights to representation are violated by electoral laws allowing non-Croats a significant voice in the selection of the Croat member of the presidency and Croat members of the House of Peoples, contributing to the ongoing legal dispute over the Federation's House of Peoples. Women are underrepresented in politics and government. Nine women won seats in the House of Representatives in 2018.

C. FUNCTIONING OF GOVERNMENT: 4 / 12

C1. Do the freely elected head of government and national legislative representatives determine the policies of the government? 2 / 4

Government formation and policy implementation are seriously impeded by the country's complex system of ethnic representation. Under the Dayton Accords, representatives from each of the three major ethnic groups, at both the state and entity levels, may exercise a veto on legislation deemed harmful to their interests.

The state government is undercut by movements within each of BiH's entities for greater autonomy. In the RS, the hard-line SNSD government has deepened its security ties with Russia. In January 2018, evidence emerged that Dodik had hosted Russian-trained paramilitaries from Serbia—who were said to be establishing a paramilitary unit within the RS—in the entity's presidential palace. In February, follow-up reports found a sharp increase in the RS government's procurement of arms, which the OHR characterized as a push to militarize the entity's police force.

In May 2018, canton police units controlled by the HDZ-BiH obstructed a migrant convoy accompanied by state police from Sarajevo. The ensuing hours-long standoff raised fears of a possible shooting incident.

C2. Are safeguards against official corruption strong and effective? 1 / 4

Corruption remains widespread and systemic, and legislation designed to combat the problem is poorly enforced. When corruption probes are actually opened, they rarely result in convictions. In June 2017, Transparency International BiH said it had noted a significant decline in the efficiency of corruption adjudication in the country over the last eight years, and particularly in 2015 and 2016. In September 2018, the US State Department imposed sanctions on a state-level lawmaker and high-ranking member of the SNSD, Nikola Špirić, on the grounds that he had "engaged in and benefited from public corruption."

C3. Does the government operate with openness and transparency? 1 / 4

Government operations remain largely inaccessible to the public. Procurement awards are often made in secret and, according to a 2017 report published by Mediacentar Sarajevo, a local nongovernmental organization (NGO), most public institutions do not comply with BiH's legal requirements related to freedom of information. Candidates for major offices are required to make financial disclosures, but the relevant laws do not meet international standards, and the resulting disclosures are considered unreliable. Debate and decisions on matters of great public interest, including legislation and subjects pertaining to EU accession, routinely occur during interparty negotiations that take place behind closed doors, outside of government institutions.

CIVIL LIBERTIES: 34 / 60

D. FREEDOM OF EXPRESSION AND BELIEF: 10 / 16

D1. Are there free and independent media? 2 / 4

Freedom of expression is legally guaranteed but limited in practice. Journalists face harassment and threats as well as political pressure. In 2017, the Institution of the Human Rights Ombudsman of BiH issued a report recommending that the country build a stronger legal infrastructure for punishing attacks on journalists. In August 2018, a reporter covering ongoing protests over the RS government's response to the presumed murder of David Dragičević in Banja Luka was attacked and beaten with rods by two unknown assailants. Several other assaults and threats against journalists were reported during the year.

D2. Are individuals free to practice and express their religious faith or nonbelief in public and private? 3 / 4

Religious freedom is not subject to formal restrictions, but in practice religious communities face some discrimination in areas where they constitute a minority. Acts of vandalism against religious sites continue to be reported.

D3. Is there academic freedom, and is the educational system free from extensive political indoctrination? 2 / 4

The education system is racked by corruption and clientelism, and the curriculum is politicized at all levels of education. At some schools in the Federation, Bosniak and Croat students are divided into separate classes on the basis of their ethnicity. Some Bosniak returnees in the RS have sent their children to temporary alternative schools to avoid curriculums they call discriminatory, and some Serb families have described discriminatory educational environments in the Federation.

D4. Are individuals free to express their personal views on political or other sensitive topics without fear of surveillance or retribution? 3 / 4

Freedom of expression for individuals in BiH is generally protected from overt government interference. However, peer pressure and the risk of an adverse public reaction remain significant curbs on the discussion of sensitive topics. The news media often report on "controversial" social media posts by members of the public.

E. ASSOCIATIONAL AND ORGANIZATIONAL RIGHTS: 7 / 12
E1. Is there freedom of assembly? 3 / 4

Freedom of assembly is generally respected in BiH, and peaceful protests are common. However, demonstrators sometimes encounter administrative obstacles or police violence. In 2018, persistent and often large-scale protests followed the unexplained death—and presumed murder—in March of David Dragičević, a 21-year-old Banja Luka resident whose case touched on broader concerns about policing and the rule of law in the RS. Dragičević's father and opposition leaders have accused the RS police, prosecutor's office, and political leadership of either playing a role in or covering up his son's death. In an attempt to clamp down on the movement, police on Christmas Day closed off a Banja Luka square utilized by protesters and arrested some 20 people, allegedly using excessive force in the process.

E2. Is there freedom for nongovernmental organizations, particularly those that are engaged in human rights- and governance-related work? 2 / 4

The NGO sector in BiH remains robust but is sometimes exposed to government pressure and interference. There have been reports of prolonged tax investigations of NGOs by the RS government. Many organizations rely on government funding, posing a potential conflict if they seek to criticize the authorities. In 2018, a proposed RS law that would have placed restrictions on foreign donations to NGOs was withdrawn in the face of organized objections from civil society.

E3. Is there freedom for trade unions and similar professional or labor organizations? 2 / 4

Labor unions operate freely in the whole of BiH, although workers often have limited bargaining power in practice. The right to strike is legally protected, but labor law in the Federation erects significant barriers to the exercise of this right. Legal protections against antiunion action by employers are weakly enforced. The leading political blocs in the country have significant sway over unions in their respective strongholds.

F. RULE OF LAW: 7 / 16

F1. Is there an independent judiciary? 1 / 4

The judiciary is formally independent, but weak in practice, and the Constitutional Court continues to face challenges from the SNSD and HDZ-BiH in particular. Dozens of Constitutional Court decisions have been disregarded by political leaders. In August 2017, after the Constitutional Court ruled that all military installations in the RS were BiH state property, RS government figures indicated that they would ignore it. In January of that year, the president of the HDZ-BiH joined Dodik in questioning the inclusion of foreign judges on the Constitutional Court.

The existence of four separate court systems—for the central state, the RS, the Federation, and the self-governing Brčko district—contributes to overall inefficiency.

F2. Does due process prevail in civil and criminal matters? 2 / 4

Guarantees of due process are inconsistently upheld. Access to adequate legal counsel can be contingent on one's financial standing. Police corruption is a problem and sometimes stems from links to organized crime. Public prosecutors are widely reputed to be corrupt and under political control.

The process of prosecuting war crimes in domestic courts has been slow, with political interference and courts' lack of resources and capacity contributing to a large backlog of cases. A push to reinvigorate the process was ongoing at year's end, but impunity for war crimes including killings and sexual violence has persisted.

F3. Is there protection from the illegitimate use of physical force and freedom from war and insurgencies? 2 / 4

Harassment by police remains routine for vulnerable groups, which now includes a significant population of migrants. Many prisons are overcrowded or feature other substandard conditions, and detainees are subject to physical abuse by prison authorities.

Active land mines still in place following the war continue to pose a threat to civilians. The reports of paramilitary activity and rearmament by politically controlled police units during 2018 raised concerns about the possibility of renewed conflict in the country.

F4. Do laws, policies, and practices guarantee equal treatment of various segments of the population? 2 / 4

Discrimination against minorities is illegal but nevertheless widespread, particularly against members of the Romany minority. Bosniaks and Croats in the RS experience difficulties accessing social services. Members of the LGBT (lesbian, gay, bisexual, and transgender) community face discrimination, harassment, and occasional physical attacks, and authorities often fail to investigate and prosecute crimes against LGBT individuals adequately. People who returned to their homes after being displaced during the war face discrimination in employment and housing in regions where their ethnic group constitutes a minority. Women are legally entitled to full equality with men but face discrimination in the workplace in practice.

More than 20,000 migrants and asylum seekers arrived in the country during 2018, marking a sharp increase from previous years. Most lacked accommodation and basic services, as the authorities' limited capacity to provide for them was overwhelmed. The influx resulted in political disputes among different levels of government over responsibility for the newcomers.

G. PERSONAL AUTONOMY AND INDIVIDUAL RIGHTS: 10 / 16

G1. Do individuals enjoy freedom of movement, including the ability to change their place of residence, employment, or education? 3 / 4

The law protects freedom of movement, and this right is generally upheld in practice. Land mines limit movement in some areas. Corruption and bureaucratic obstacles can hamper people's ability to change their formal residency or place of employment.

G2. Are individuals able to exercise the right to own property and establish private businesses without undue interference from state or nonstate actors? 2 / 4

Although the legal framework broadly supports property rights and private business activity, widespread corruption and patronage remain major barriers to free enterprise. There is no comprehensive legislation on restitution of property seized during and after World War II, and individuals who returned to their homes after being displaced by the 1992–95 war have faced attacks on their property. The European Commission has called for further progress on compensating people for property that cannot be returned.

G3. Do individuals enjoy personal social freedoms, including choice of marriage partner and size of family, protection from domestic violence, and control over appearance? 3 / 4

Individual freedom on personal status matters such as marriage and divorce is generally protected. Same-sex marriage is not recognized, though the Federation government agreed in October 2018 to consider legalizing such marriages.

Domestic violence remains a serious concern despite some government efforts to combat it. Incidents of abuse are believed to be considerably underreported, and civic groups have found that law enforcement authorities are often reluctant to intervene or impose strong penalties.

G4. Do individuals enjoy equality of opportunity and freedom from economic exploitation? 2 / 4

Legal protections against exploitative working conditions are poorly enforced, and workers in some industries face hazardous conditions. In January 2018, factory workers in Zenica engaged in hunger strikes and protests over unpaid salaries and pension contributions. Patronage and clientelism continue to adversely affect hiring practices and contribute to de facto restrictions on economic opportunity.

According to the US State Department's 2018 *Trafficking in Persons Report*, men, women, and children are subject to trafficking for the purposes of sexual exploitation and forced labor, with Romany children particularly vulnerable to forced begging and forced marriages that amount to domestic servitude. According to the report, the government was making efforts toward prosecuting perpetrators, protecting victims, and preventing trafficking, though its efforts in the first two areas decreased somewhat during the coverage period.

Botswana

Population: 2,200,000
Capital: Gaborone
Political Rights Rating: 3
Civil Liberties Rating: 2
Freedom Rating: 2.5
Freedom Status: Free
Electoral Democracy: Yes

Overview: While it is considered one of the most stable democracies in Africa, Botswana has been dominated by a single party since independence. Media freedom remains under threat. The indigenous San people, as well as migrants, refugees, and LGBT (lesbian, gay, bisexual, and transgender) people, face discrimination.

KEY DEVELOPMENTS IN 2018:

- Mokgweetsi Masisi became caretaker president of Botswana in April, upon the end of the constitutional term of President Ian Khama. Masisi will serve in that capacity until lawmakers elect a new president after the 2019 general elections.
- In May, Masisi fired the chief of the Directorate of Intelligence and Security Services, (DISS), Colonel Isaac Seabelo Kgosi. The spy agency was accused of corruption and human rights abuses under Kgosi's leadership.
- Masisi transferred the DISS and the Financial Intelligence Agency (FIA), to the president's office, prompting concerns about the improper centralization of power. The DISS had previously been part of the Justice Ministry, and the FIA part of the Finance Ministry.
- In April, security personnel physically prevented journalists from covering the return of elite national athletes to Sir Seretse Khama International Airport, near Gaborone.
- In September, the government withdrew sedition charges against *Sunday Standard* editor Outsa Mokone. The charges were filed in 2014, after he reported that Khama had been involved in a traffic accident.

POLITICAL RIGHTS: 28 / 40

A. ELECTORAL PROCESS: 10 / 12

A1. Was the current head of government or other chief national authority elected through free and fair elections? 3 / 4

The president is indirectly elected by the National Assembly for a five-year term and is eligible for reelection. The vice president is appointed by the president and confirmed by the National Assembly. The president holds significant power, including the authority to prolong or dismiss the National Assembly.

President Khama's constitutional term expired at the end of March 2018, and Vice President Mokgweetsi Masisi was sworn in as interim president according to legal procedure the next day. He will serve in that capacity until a new presidential election is held following general elections set for 2019. This scripted succession seemingly gives new leaders of the incumbent party—in this case the Botswana Democratic Party (BDP), which has been in power for over five decades—the opportunity to consolidate the advantages of incumbency ahead of presidential elections.

A2. Were the current national legislative representatives elected through free and fair elections? 4 / 4

Botswana has a unicameral, 65-seat National Assembly. Voters directly elect 57 members to five-year terms, 6 members are nominated by the president and approved by the National Assembly, and the other 2 members are the president and the speaker. The 2014 parliamentary elections, in which the ruling party won 37 out of 57 seats, were declared credible by regional and international monitoring bodies.

A3. Are the electoral laws and framework fair, and are they implemented impartially by the relevant election management bodies? 3 / 4

The Independent Electoral Commission (IEC) administers elections, and is generally considered independent and capable. However, its voter registration drive ahead of the 2019 general elections saw the theft of two voter registration books, containing a few dozen complete and incomplete registration forms, from an electoral officer's house.

The Electoral Amendment Act of 2016, which introduced electronic voting for the 2019 general elections, continued to cause controversy in 2018. The opposition Botswana Congress Party (BCP) had claimed that electronic voting was susceptible to manipulation in favor of the BDP, and had threatened to boycott 2019 general elections if the new voting technology was implemented. Plans for the system's deployment remained unclear throughout most of 2018; it was only in September that the government unexpectedly withdrew several sections of the 2016 electoral law, among them the one that had mandated electronic voting. Masisi said the decision was made in order to avoid election-related violence.

B. POLITICAL PLURALISM AND PARTICIPATION: 10 / 16

B1. Do the people have the right to organize in different political parties or other competitive political groupings of their choice, and is the system free of undue obstacles to the rise and fall of these competing parties or groupings? 3 / 4

The right of political parties to form and operate is largely respected. However, the opposition alleges that the BDP abuses state resources, including the influential state media, to its own benefit, and that a lack of public financing for political parties gives the long-ruling party an unfair advantage. The withdrawal in 2018 of a section of the Electoral Amendment Act of 2016 that had increased fees for candidates contesting elections brought some relief to opposition parties.

B2. Is there a realistic opportunity for the opposition to increase its support or gain power through elections? 2 / 4

The BDP, drawing on the advantages of its long incumbency, has dominated the political landscape since 1966; no opposition party has ever won power. However, in 2014 the BDP took less than 50 percent of the vote for the first time in its history.

In 2012, several of the largest opposition parties formed a coalition, the Umbrella for Democratic Change (UDC), to contest elections, and there is some hope among its members and supporters that it might unseat the ruling party in 2019 elections. However, persistent political fights within the coalition—including the expulsion in October 2018 of the Botswana Movement for Democracy (BMD), and resulting jockeying for the constituencies its members vacated—threaten the coalition's competitiveness ahead of 2019 polls.

B3. Are the people's political choices free from domination by the military, foreign powers, religious hierarchies, economic oligarchies, or any other powerful group that is not democratically accountable? 3 / 4

People's political choices are largely free from domination by unelected outside groups. The House of Chiefs, a 35-member body composed mostly of traditional leaders, representatives they elect, and representatives appointed by the president, acts as an advisory body to legislators on tribal and customary matters, but generally does not exercise decisive influence on them. There have been some past reports of vote buying during elections.

B4. Do all segments of the population (including ethnic, religious, gender, LGBT, and other relevant groups) have full political rights and electoral opportunities? 2 / 4

Women have full political rights, but cultural factors limit their participation, and their interests are not necessarily addressed by elected leaders. Only five women sit in the National Assembly and only two women serve in the House of Chiefs.

Smaller ethnic and tribal groups tend to be left out of the political process. People with disabilities participated at low levels in the 2014 parliamentary elections. Political parties generally do not represent the interests of LGBT people.

C. FUNCTIONING OF GOVERNMENT: 8 / 12

C1. Do the freely elected head of government and national legislative representatives determine the policies of the government? 3 / 4

Elected executive and legislative officials determine government's policies. However, opposition parties have criticized the executive branch for dominating the National Assembly and rushing bills through the legislative process without adequate deliberation. In 2016, lawmakers approved an amendment that increased the number of National Assembly members appointed by the president from four to six. Opposition leaders argued that the change would further strengthen executive power at the expense of the National Assembly's independence.

After taking office in 2018, Masisi transferred the DISS and the Financial Intelligence Agency (FIA), to the president's office, prompting concerns about the improper centralization of power. The DISS had previously been part of the Justice Ministry, and the FIA part of the Finance Ministry.

C2. Are safeguards against official corruption strong and effective? 3 / 4

Although corruption laws are generally enforced, the main anticorruption agency, the Directorate on Corruption and Economic Crime (DCEC), stands accused of being ineffective in pursuing cases of high-level corruption, and its independence has been questioned after it was transferred from the Justice Ministry to the Office of the President in 2012. However, at the end of 2018, the DCEC issued several charges in connection with an ongoing corruption scandal involving the National Petroleum Fund.

An amendment to the Financial Intelligence Act approved in June transferred the FIA from the Finance Ministry to the president's office, raising similar concerns about the independence of that body.

C3. Does the government operate with openness and transparency? 2 / 4

Botswana lacks a freedom of information law, which limits government's transparency. Budget processes are opaque, and Section 44 of the Corruption and Economic Crime Act prohibits publishing information on investigations by the DCEC. Public contracts are often awarded through patronage networks.

Masisi has held several press conferences since taking power in April 2018—in contrast to Khama, who held none.

CIVIL LIBERTIES: 44 / 60
D. FREEDOM OF EXPRESSION AND BELIEF: 12 / 16
D1. Are there free and independent media? 2 / 4

Freedom of expression is constitutionally guaranteed. However, journalists endured harassment and intimidation under Khama's government, and concerning incidents have been reported under the new administration. For example, in April, security personnel physically prevented journalists from covering the return of national athletes to Sir Seretse Khama International Airport near Gaborone.

State-run media dominate the broadcasting sector, and continue to exhibit bias in favor of the ruling party. A government ban on advertising in private media remains in place, and harms the competitiveness and economic viability of many outlets. The 2008 Media Practitioners Act established a statutory media regulatory body and mandated the registration of all media workers and media outlets—including websites and blogs—with violations being punishable by either a fine or prison time.

In a positive development, in September 2018, Masisi's administration withdraw sedition charges against *Sunday Standard* editor Outsa Mokone. The charges were filed in 2014, after he reported that Khama had been involved in a traffic accident.

D2. Are individuals free to practice and express their religious faith or nonbelief in public and private? 4 / 4

Religious freedom is generally respected in practice, though all religious organizations must register with the government.

D3. Is there academic freedom, and is the educational system free from extensive political indoctrination? 3 / 4

Although academic freedom is generally respected, professors often practice self-censorship when addressing sensitive topics. In the past, foreign academics have been deported for publishing work that was critical of the government, contributing to cautiousness among many scholars.

D4. Are individuals free to express their personal views on political or other sensitive topics without fear of surveillance or retribution? 3 / 4

Although freedom of expression is constitutionally protected, there are numerous restrictions on it in practice, prompting self-censorship among many ordinary people. Insulting the president, a lawmaker, or public official is punishable by a fine. The 2008 Public Service Act restricts the ability of public-sector workers to air their political views, and a 2017 judgment by the Court of Appeal affirmed this. In October 2018, President Masisi reminded a teacher of this restriction at a kgotla (public meeting) in Serowe during which the teacher questioned Masisi about his work during the Khama administration, and about perceived disputes between the two.

In recent years, the DISS has developed technology to monitor private online communications.

E. ASSOCIATIONAL AND ORGANIZATIONAL RIGHTS: 10 / 12
E1. Is there freedom of assembly? 4 / 4
Freedom of assembly is guaranteed by the constitution and largely upheld in practice. However, the Public Order Act requires citizens to

seek permission from the police to exercise this right. The constitutionality of this clause has been questioned in the past, and permission at times has been denied on unclear grounds by the police.

E2. Is there freedom for nongovernmental organizations, particularly those that are engaged in human rights- and governance-related work? 4 / 4

Nongovernmental organizations (NGOs), including human rights groups, generally operate without restrictions. However, in late May 2018, President Masisi banned a well-known South African human rights lawyer, Joao Carlos Salbany, from entering Botswana. He reversed the decision after coming under criticism from the Media Institute of Southern Africa (MISA) and other rights advocates.

E3. Is there freedom for trade unions and similar professional or labor organizations? 2 / 4

The right to form a union is respected, but the Trade Dispute Act places restrictions on who can strike. As a result, the government declares many strikes to be illegal, putting employees' jobs at risk. The law does not always protect workers from antiunion discrimination by employers.

In October 2018, the government moved ahead with plans to derecognize public service unions for allegedly not complying with provisions of the Public Service Act of 2008. Labor leaders condemned authorities' demands as sudden and arbitrary and challenged them in a trade court, which temporarily blocked the government's action.

F. RULE OF LAW: 11 / 16

F1. Is there an independent judiciary? 3 / 4

The judiciary is generally independent and free from interference. In 2017, a judicial crisis involving then-President Khama's attempts to reappoint justices after their fixed terms raised concerns about interference in the judiciary, but there were no controversies of that scale in 2018. However, there are calls to reform the selection and appointment processes for judges and acting judges in a way that ensures transparency, impartiality, and public oversight.

F2. Does due process prevail in civil and criminal matters? 3 / 4

The right to a fair trial is protected by the constitution and generally upheld in practice. However, the judiciary lacks human and financial resources, which has led to case backlogs, which in turn results in lengthy pretrial detentions and postponement of cases. Attorneys are provided to all defendants in capital cases, but defendants in noncapital cases must pay for their own counsel. The DISS has the power to arrest suspects without a warrant if agents believe they have committed or will commit a crime.

After taking office in April, Masisi moved the DISS to the purview of the president's office, prompting concerns about the centralization of power. It had been a part of the Justice Department previously.

F3. Is there protection from the illegitimate use of physical force and freedom from war and insurgencies? 3 / 4

Although citizens are largely protected from the illegitimate use of force, corporal punishment is imposed in some cases. Instances of police brutality have been reported, and perpetrators are rarely held accountable. Botswana still lacks an independent body to investigate police abuses.

The DISS is besieged by corruption allegations and has been accused of unlawful arrests and extrajudicial killings, among other abuses. Masisi fired its feared director, Isaac

Kgosi, in May 2018, effectively canceling the five-year extension Khama had granted Kgosi before leaving office. Peter Magosi, a former head of the military intelligence service, was named the new DISS director.

Masisi in May also halted Botswana's unwritten shoot-to-kill policy adopted by at least 2013, and possibly earlier, to deter wildlife poachers. Over the past two decades, anti-poaching operations had killed at least 30 Namibians and 22 Zimbabweans.

F4. Do laws, policies, and practices guarantee equal treatment of various segments of the population? 2 / 4

Customary law, commonly applied in rural areas, often discriminates against women. The indigenous San people tend to be economically marginalized and lack access to education and other public services including use of their language in schools, government meetings, and state media. There have been reports of beatings, abuse, and arbitrary arrests of San by police and park rangers. Botswana also has no human rights body to investigate violations.

Same-sex sexual relations remain criminalized, although law is not actively enforced and faces court challenge. LGBT people continue to experience discrimination, especially in accessing health care. However, following a High Court ruling the previous year, a transgender man in January 2018 was issued a new identity document that listed his stated gender identity.

Refugees in Botswana are detained in encampments where they are denied the ability to work and integrate into local communities. In June, police returned back to Botswana's Dukwi Refugee Camp refugees from Namibia who were protesting outside Southern African Development Community (SADC) headquarters against repatriation plans they said would subject them to continued persecution in Namibia.

In January 2018, a number of refugees and asylum seekers at Francistown Centre for Illegal Immigrants alleged ill-treatment and regular assaults by prison officials, whom they further accused of failing to investigate cases of sexual assault.

G. PERSONAL AUTONOMY AND INDIVIDUAL RIGHTS: 11 / 16

G1. Do individuals enjoy freedom of movement, including the ability to change their place of residence, employment, or education? 3 / 4

Most citizens can move freely throughout the country and travel internationally. However, in addition to the movement restrictions on refugees and asylum seekers, San have limited access to their traditional lands in the Central Kalahari Game Reserve. The government's long-standing policy has been to relocate San out of the reserve, and those who still have relatives living there must apply for a permit to visit them.

G2. Are individuals able to exercise the right to own property and establish private businesses without undue interference from state or nonstate actors? 3 / 4

Botswana has generally sound legal protections for property rights, and they are enforced in practice. However, customary law discriminates against women in property and inheritance matters; for example, a woman has no right to her husband's property upon his death.

The country's regulatory framework is considered conducive to establishing and operating private businesses.

G3. Do individuals enjoy personal social freedoms, including choice of marriage partner and size of family, protection from domestic violence, and control over appearance? 2 / 4

Domestic violence and rape are pervasive problems. The law does not recognize spousal rape as a crime. Customary law restricts women's rights within a marriage. When husbands and wives separate, custody is traditionally granted to the father. Child and forced marriages still occur under customary law. However, in April 2018, Parliament passed the Penal Code Amendment Bill, which introduced stronger penalties for rape, and raised the age of consent from 16 to 18.

Women can experience harassment for not dressing conservatively.

G4. Do individuals enjoy equality of opportunity and freedom from economic exploitation? 3 / 4

Workers enjoy a number of protections against exploitative labor practices. However, employer abuses in retail stores, the tourism industry, and private security sector are an ongoing problem. Botswana lacks a strong regulatory framework for labor brokers that dispatch workers to clients on short-term contracts, in which exploitation is common. Human trafficking remains a challenge. However, the four-year-old Anti-Human Trafficking Act was amended in 2018 to include stiffer financial penalties.

Brazil

Population: 209,400,000
Capital: Brasília
Political Rights Rating: 2
Civil Liberties Rating: 2
Freedom Rating: 2.0
Freedom Status: Free
Electoral Democracy: Yes

Overview: Brazil is a democracy that holds competitive elections and is characterized by vibrant public debate. However, independent journalists and civil society activists risk harassment and violent attack, and the government has proven unable to curb a rising homicide rate or address disproportionate violence against and economic exclusion of minorities. Corruption is endemic at top levels, contributing to disillusionment with traditional political parties.

KEY DEVELOPMENTS IN 2018:

- Far-right candidate Jair Bolsonaro of the Social Liberal Party (PSL) secured the presidency in October after a runoff in which he defeated the Workers' Party (PT) candidate, Fernando Haddad. Bolsonaro's campaign was characterized by aggressive pledges to wipe out corruption and violent crime, as well as by attacks on critical media. The new president's history of abusive language against women and minorities alarmed many observers, who questioned the incoming administration's commitment to upholding equal rights.
- The campaign period was marred by political violence and the spread of election-related disinformation and hate speech on social media and messaging platforms.
- The country faced a worsening security environment, with an increasing murder rate driven in large part by the prevalence of highly organized drug-trafficking groups. In February, then president Michel Temer authorized military police to take charge of security in Rio de Janeiro State.
- Violence related to land and resource disputes has been intensifying, and two activists were murdered during the year.

POLITICAL RIGHTS: 30 / 40 (-1)

A. ELECTORAL PROCESS: 10 / 12 (-1)

A1. Was the current head of government or other chief national authority elected through free and fair elections? 3 / 4 (-1)

Brazil is a federal republic governed under a presidential system. The president is elected by popular vote for a four-year term and is eligible for reelection to a second term. In 2016, Michel Temer of the Brazilian Democratic Movement Party (PMDB) was confirmed president. His predecessor, Dilma Rousseff of the PT, was impeached by the Senate on charges that she had manipulated the federal budget in an effort to hide Brazil's economic problems. Temer served as president for the remainder of Rousseff's term.

In the 2018 race, candidates made their cases to voters disillusioned by persistent corruption scandals, and increasingly concerned by a difficult economic environment and a rise in violent crime. Jair Bolsonaro of the PSL won the election, taking 55.1 percent of the vote in a runoff against Fernando Haddad of PT. Bolsonaro's campaign was characterized by a disdain for democratic principles and aggressive pledges to wipe out corruption and violent crime. An Organization of American States (OAS) election observation mission generally praised the poll's administration, and stakeholders quickly accepted its result. However, the highly polarized campaign was marred by the spread of fake news, conspiracy theories, and aggressive rhetoric on social networks and online messaging services (notably WhatsApp). There was also a high rate of preelection threats and violence targeting candidates, political supporters, journalists, and members of the judiciary. Investigative journalism group Agência Pública reported more than 70 physical attacks linked to the race between September 30 and October 10. While most of the reported incidents appeared to involve attacks by Bolsonaro supporters, his backers were also targeted. Among these attacks, PT campaign buses were shot at in March, and Bolsonaro was stabbed at a rally in early September, forcing him to cut back on public appearances a month before the election.

In October 2018, the electoral court and federal police announced investigations amid reports of the existence of organized disinformation campaigns on social media.

Score Change: The score declined from 4 to 3 due to a high rate of political violence during the campaign period, as well as the spread of election-related disinformation and hate speech on social media and messaging platforms, which contributed to a threatening campaign environment.

A2. Were the current national legislative representatives elected through free and fair elections? 3 / 4

Legislative elections are generally free and fair. The bicameral National Congress is composed of an 81-member Senate and a 513-member Chamber of Deputies. Senators serve staggered eight-year terms, with one- to two-thirds coming up for election every four years. Members of the Chamber of Deputies serve four-year terms.

In October 2018 elections, the PT lost seats but remained the largest party in the lower house, with 56 deputies. Bolsonaro's PSL captured 52 seats, up from just a single seat previously. In the Senate, which will begin its new session in 2019, the Brazilian Democratic Movement (MDB, previously PMDB) maintained its lead with a total of 12 seats, while the Brazilian Social Democratic Party (PSDB) will have 9, followed by the Social Democratic Party (PSD), Democrats (DEM), and PT, which will each hold 4 seats. Bolsonaro's PSL entered the chamber after capturing 4 seats.

The 2018 legislative elections were held concurrently with the first round of the presidential election, thus campaigning took place in the same highly polarized environment, marked by aggressive rhetoric and instances of political violence. In one instance, a gay candidate contesting a spot in the São Paulo legislature was surrounded by a group of men and slapped while campaigning.

A3. Are the electoral laws and framework fair, and are they implemented impartially by the relevant election management bodies? 4 / 4

Brazilian election laws are generally well enforced. A Supreme Electoral Court presides over cases related to violations of electoral law.

In a 6-1 ruling in August 2018, the Supreme Electoral Court declared that former president Luiz Inácio "Lula" da Silva was ineligible to run as a presidential candidate based on a "clean slate" law that prohibits candidates with criminal sentences confirmed on appeal from running for office. Lula withdrew in favor of replacement Haddad shortly before the deadline for candidate registration. The UN Human Rights Committee had urged authorities to guarantee his rights to political participation and allow him to run "until his appeals before the courts have been completed in fair judicial proceedings."

B. POLITICAL PLURALISM AND PARTICIPATION: 14 / 16

B1. Do the people have the right to organize in different political parties or other competitive political groupings of their choice, and is the system free of undue obstacles to the rise and fall of these competing parties or groupings? 4 / 4

Brazil has an unfettered multiparty system marked by vigorous competition between rival parties. The electoral framework encourages the proliferation of parties, a number of which are based in a single state. Some parties display little ideological consistency. Party switching is common by members of Congress, rendering electoral coalitions fragile. The sheer number of parties means that the executive branch must piece together diverse and ideologically incoherent coalitions to pass legislation, which may encourage corruption.

Ahead of the 2018 elections, 35 parties were registered, 30 of which won seats in the lower chamber—the largest number of parties seated there since the redemocratization of Brazil in 1985.

B2. Is there a realistic opportunity for the opposition to increase its support or gain power through elections? 4 / 4

Opposition parties are able to compete freely and gain power through elections. Ahead of the 2018 polls, Bolsonaro's small, far-right PSL succeeded in attracting widespread support in a short amount of time.

B3. Are the people's political choices free from domination by the military, foreign powers, religious hierarchies, economic oligarchies, or any other powerful group that is not democratically accountable? 3 / 4

Recent investigations into corruption have exposed how wealthy business interests undermine democratic accountability by facilitating or encouraging corruption among elected officials. Criminal groups have carried out attacks against political candidates.

B4. Do various segments of the population (including ethnic, religious, gender, LGBT, and other relevant groups) have full political rights and electoral opportunities? 3 / 4

The constitution guarantees equal rights without prejudice, but some groups have greater political representation than others. Afro-Brazilians and women remain underrepresented in electoral politics and in government. As a result of the 2018 elections, women will hold 15 percent of seats in the Chamber of Deputies, and 16 percent in the Senate. However, by December, Bolsonaro had awarded only two cabinet posts to women. Separately, he also announced that month that the National Indian Foundation (FUNAI), the government office that manages the affairs of indigenous people, would be moved from the Justice Ministry to a new ministry of Women, Family, and Human Rights. The development came after Bolsonaro had indicated that his administration would permit greater development of indigenous lands and deny more land claims by indigenous peoples.

Increasing societal discrimination and violence against LGBT (lesbian, gay, bisexual, and transgender) people can discourage their political participation. In March 2018, Rio de Janeiro councilwoman Marielle Franco, a black lesbian politician who was an outspoken advocate for minorities, was murdered.

C. FUNCTIONING OF GOVERNMENT: 6 / 12
C1. Do the freely elected head of government and national legislative representatives determine the policies of the government? 2 / 4

Widespread corruption undermines the government's ability to make and implement policy without undue influence from private or criminal interests. Corruption was a chief concern for voters in 2018, as political crises linked with the numerous ongoing corruption investigations against senior officials dominated the political sphere.

C2. Are safeguards against official corruption strong and effective? 2 / 4

Corruption and graft are endemic in Brazil, especially among elected officials. Beginning in 2014, an ongoing investigation known as Operation Car Wash has focused on bribery, money laundering, and bid rigging involving state oil company Petrobrás and private construction companies. In addition to former Petrobrás executives and heads of major construction firms, its findings have also implicated elected officials from across the political spectrum. A number of prominent figures associated with Temer have been convicted on charges related to the investigation.

Former president Lula, who was convicted of corruption and money laundering in 2017, lost an appeal in January 2018 and began serving a 12-year sentence in April; additional appeals of his conviction are pending. In October, a police report recommended that Temer face new corruption charges, and that authorities confiscate his and several associates' assets, in connection with a decree on port management Temer had approved in 2017. Related charges were filed in December against Temer and five others. Although the lower house voted twice in 2017 to shield Temer from trial on corruption charges, his presidential immunity will be revoked when he formally leaves office in 2019.

C3. Does the government operate with openness and transparency? 2 / 4

Brazil enacted an Access to Information Law in 2012, but in practice, the government does not always release requested information.

Temer's 2016 decision to convert the National Controller's Office into a new Ministry of Transparency, Monitoring, and Oversight was considered to be detrimental to the independence of the agency.

CIVIL LIBERTIES: 45 / 60 (-2)
D. FREEDOM OF EXPRESSION AND BELIEF 15 / 16
D1. Are there free and independent media? 3 / 4

The constitution guarantees freedom of expression, and the media scene is vibrant. However, in 2018 politicians and influential businesspersons continued to make use of existing laws, including criminal defamation laws, to curtail critical reporting. Investigative journalists, particularly those who cover corruption and crime, face threats, harassment, obstruction, and violence, which in some cases has been deadly.

In January 2018, radio presenter Jefferson Pureza Lopes, who was known for his scrutiny of local politicians in Goiás State, was shot dead at his home after repeated threats. In April, a police investigation concluded that a local politician had ordered the murder for political and personal reasons; he and two others were awaiting trial as of September. Another radio journalist, Jairo de Sousa, was killed in June while arriving at his station's offices in the northern state of Pará; prior to his death de Sousa, known for his denunciations of local corruption, reportedly occasionally wore a bulletproof vest due to persistent threats.

As of October, the Brazilian Association of Investigative Journalism (Abraji) had registered more than 150 physical or online attacks perpetrated against journalists covering the 2018 elections. Throughout 2018, Bolsonaro denounced investigative outlets as peddlers of "fake news," singling out the daily *Folha de São Paulo* in particular; among other reports, the newspaper published an article in October indicating that digital marketing companies had used WhatsApp to circulate attacks on Haddad, which apparently prompted the subsequent investigations by the electoral court and federal police into the existence of organized disinformation campaigns on social media. Individual journalists who wrote critical stories about Bolsonaro faced threats and harassment offline and online, including hacking and other technical attacks.

D2. Are individuals free to practice and express their religious faith or nonbelief in public and private? 4 / 4

The constitution guarantees freedom of religion, and the government generally respects this right in practice.

D3. Is there academic freedom, and is the educational system free from extensive political indoctrination? 4 / 4

Academic debate is vibrant and freedom is generally unrestricted in schools and universities.

D4. Are individuals free to express their personal views on political or other sensitive topics without fear of surveillance or retribution? 4 / 4

People are generally able to express political or controversial views in public without fear of surveillance or retaliation. However, in the tense 2018 campaign atmosphere, some political speech was met with acts of violence. In October, a 63-year-old capoeira master died after being stabbed by a Bolsonaro fan at a bar in Salvador; the man had attacked him after he expressed his support for Haddad. A prevalence of violent homophobic rhetoric in 2018 contributed to a sense of fear among many that open discussion of LGBT rights and issues could be met with harassment or attack.

E. ASSOCIATIONAL AND ORGANIZATIONAL RIGHTS: 9 / 12 (−1)
E1. Is there freedom of assembly? 3 / 4

While freedom of assembly is generally respected, police or other security agents sometimes use excessive force against demonstrations.

In late May, Temer issued a controversial decree order giving the military several days' authorization to clear a disruptive demonstration by truckers who were protesting rising fuel prices by blockading key sections of highways nationwide. While the order did not lead to violence, Amnesty International and other observers criticized it as a disproportionate response.

E2. Is there freedom for nongovernmental organizations, particularly those that are engaged in human rights- and governance-related work? 3 / 4 (-1)

Nongovernmental organizations (NGOs) are able to operate freely in a variety of fields. However, activists working on land rights and environmental protection issues have faced increasing harassment, threats, and violence in recent years. In March, the indigenous leader Paulo Sergio Almeida Nascimento was murdered; he had vocally criticized a Norwegian-owned refinery for polluting rivers in Pará State. Nazildo dos Santos Brito, the leader of an agricultural community association in Pará State and an anti–palm oil campaigner, was killed in April 2018 after receiving death threats.

Score Change: The score declined from 4 to 3 due to increasing intimidation and violence against land rights activists.

E3. Is there freedom for trade unions and similar professional or labor organizations? 3 / 4

Industrial labor unions are well organized, and although they are politically connected, Brazilian unions tend to be freer from political party control than their counterparts in other Latin American countries. However, controversial labor reforms enacted in 2017 diminished the strength and role of unions in collective bargaining with businesses.

F. RULE OF LAW: 8 / 16 (-1)
F1. Is there an independent judiciary? 3 / 4

The judiciary, though largely independent, is overburdened, inefficient, and often subject to intimidation and other external influences, especially in rural areas. Access to justice also varies greatly due to Brazil's high level of income inequality. Despite these shortcomings, the country's progressive constitution has resulted in an active judiciary that often rules in favor of citizens over the state.

F2. Does due process prevail in civil and criminal matters? 2 / 4

The judiciary generally upholds the right to a fair trial. However, federal, state, and appellate courts are severely backlogged. The state struggles to provide legal counsel for defendants and prisoners who are unable to afford an attorney.

Under a 2017 law, members of the armed forces and military police accused of certain serious crimes against civilians can be tried in military, rather than civilian, courts.

F3. Is there protection from the illegitimate use of physical force and freedom from war and insurgencies? 1 / 4 (-1)

Brazil has a relatively high homicide rate; in August 2018, the Brazilian Forum of Public Security reported a rate of 30.8 homicides per 100,000 residents in 2017, a 3 percent increase over the previous year. Many of the victims are bystanders caught in crossfire between highly organized and well-armed drug-trafficking outfits, as well as between those outfits and security forces.

Brazil's police force remains mired in corruption, and serious police abuses, including extrajudicial killings, continued in 2018. Police officers are rarely prosecuted for abuses, and those charged are almost never convicted. A 2018 Brazilian Forum of Public Security report found that, on average, 14 people died per day in 2017 due to the actions of police officers, a 20 percent increase from the previous year. In response to ongoing violence in the state of Rio de Janeiro, in February 2018 Temer ordered emergency measures authorizing the military to take charge of security there.

Conditions in Brazil's severely overcrowded prisons are life-threatening, characterized by disease, a lack of adequate food, and deadly gang-related violence. Violence is more likely to affect poor, black prisoners. Wealthy inmates often enjoy better conditions than poorer prisoners.

Score Change: The score declined from 2 to 1 due to increasing violence, much of which is among drug-trafficking gangs or between these gangs and security forces, and the government's inability to curb it.

F4. Do laws, policies, and practices guarantee equal treatment of various segments of the population? 2 / 4

Some populations are not able to fully exercise their human rights in practice. Many indigenous communities—who comprise about 1 percent of the population—suffer from poverty and lack adequate sanitation and education services.

Just over half of Brazil's population identifies as black or of mixed race. Afro-Brazilians suffer from high rates of poverty and illiteracy, and almost 80 percent of Brazilians living in extreme poverty are black or mixed race. Victims of violence in Brazil are predominantly young, black, and poor.

Although Brazil has a largely tolerant society, it reportedly has one of the world's highest levels of violence against LGBT people. According to Grupo Gay da Bahia, an LGBT advocacy organization, 445 LGBT people were killed in 2017 as a result of homophobic violence, marking a 30 percent increase from the group's figures for the previous year.

Bolsonaro has a history of making aggressively misogynistic and homophobic statements. LGBT activists reported numerous acts of intimidation and outright attacks against LGBT people by Bolsonaro supporters during the 2018 campaign.

G. PERSONAL AUTONOMY AND INDIVIDUAL RIGHTS: 13 / 16

G1. Do individuals enjoy freedom of movement, including the ability to change their place of residence, employment, or education? 4 / 4

Brazilians enjoy freedom to travel within and outside of the country, and to make decisions about their places of residence and employment, though access to high-quality education across all levels remains a challenge. Gang violence in favelas (low-income urban areas) at times has impeded free movement, and has prompted schools to shut down temporarily.

G2. Are individuals able to exercise the right to own property and establish private businesses without undue interference from state or nonstate actors? 3 / 4

While property rights are generally enforced, laws granting indigenous populations exclusive use of certain lands are not always upheld, sometimes leading to violent conflicts. According to figures released by the Pastoral Land Commission in April 2018, at least 70 people were murdered over land and resource disputes in 2017. Requirements for starting new businesses are often onerous, and corruption and organized crime sometimes pose obstacles to private business activity.

G3. Do individuals enjoy personal social freedoms, including choice of marriage partner and size of family, protection from domestic violence, and control over appearance? 3 / 4

The government generally does not restrict social freedoms. Same-sex marriage became legal in 2013. However, while a 2006 law sought to address Brazil's high rates of impunity for domestic violence, violence against women and girls remains widespread. Abortion is legal only in the case of rape, a threat to the mother's life, or a rare and usually fatal brain deformity in the fetus. These restrictions limit women's reproductive choices and impinge on family planning.

G4. Do individuals enjoy equality of opportunity and freedom from economic exploitation? 3 / 4

Slavery-like working conditions pose a significant problem in rural and, increasingly, in urban zones. A 2012 constitutional amendment allows the government to confiscate all property of landholders found to be using slave labor.

The government has sought to address the problem of child labor by cooperating with various NGOs, increasing inspections, and offering cash incentives to keep children in school. Legislation enacted in 2014 classifies the sexual exploitation of minors as "a heinous crime," with penalties of four to 10 years in prison without eligibility for bail or amnesty.

Brunei

Population: 400,000
Capital: Bandar Seri Begawan
Political Rights Rating: 6
Civil Liberties Rating: 5
Freedom Rating: 5.5
Freedom Status: Not Free
Electoral Democracy: No

Overview: Brunei is an absolute monarchy in which the sultan exercises executive power. There are no elected representatives at the national level. Freedoms of the press and assembly are significantly restricted. Online speech is monitored by authorities, but lively nevertheless.

KEY DEVELOPMENTS IN 2018:

- In March, the sultan approved a draft bill that could lead to the implementation of the second phase of a controversial Sharia (Islamic law) penal code, which would potentially impose harsh penalties for violations, such as amputations and death by stoning.
- The government continued to prosecute officials accused of corruption in 2018. In July, two former judges were indicted for allegedly embezzling over $7 million from a court's bankruptcy office. At year's end, the defendants awaited trial.

POLITICAL RIGHTS: 7 / 40 (+1)

A. ELECTORAL PROCESS: 0 / 12

A1. Was the current head of government or other chief national authority elected through free and fair elections? 0 / 4

The hereditary sultan, Hassanal Bolkiah Mu'izzaddin Waddaulah, is the head of state and prime minister, and continues to wield broad powers under a long-standing state of emergency imposed in 1984.

In recent years, Brunei has appeared to be paving the way for Hassanal's son, Prince Al-Muhtadee Billah, to eventually take power. There are no indications that any transition would also involve moving away from a traditional monarchy.

A2. Were the current national legislative representatives elected through free and fair elections? 0 / 4

The unicameral Legislative Council has no political standing independent of the sultan, who appoints most members. Brunei has not held direct legislative elections since 1962.

Elections are held for village-level councils that play a consultative role, though candidates are vetted by the government.

A3. Are the electoral laws and framework fair, and are they implemented impartially by the relevant election management bodies? 0 / 4

There are no national-level electoral laws, since there have not been any national, direct legislative elections in over five decades.

B. POLITICAL PLURALISM AND PARTICIPATION: 3 / 16

B1. Do the people have the right to organize in different political parties or other competitive political groupings of their choice, and is the system free of undue obstacles to the rise and fall of these competing parties or groupings? 1 / 4

Genuine political activity by opposition groups remains extremely limited. The National Development Party (NDP) was permitted to register in 2005 after pledging to work as a partner with the government and swearing loyalty to the sultan; it is the only registered party.

B2. Is there a realistic opportunity for the opposition to increase its support or gain power through elections? 0 / 4

There are no national-level elections in which opposition forces could gain power. Since the National Solidarity Party was deregistered without explanation in 2008, the NDP has been Brunei's sole legal political party. It has no formal political role, few activities in practice, and a small membership, and is unable to challenge the sultan's power in any meaningful way.

B3. Are the people's political choices free from domination by the military, foreign powers, religious hierarchies, economic oligarchies, or any other powerful group that is not democratically accountable? 1 / 4

With the dominance of the sultan and lack of elections, residents have few avenues for genuine and autonomous political participation. However, people have some very limited ability to challenge unpopular policies through the organization of social movements.

B4. Do various segments of the population (including ethnic, religious, gender, LGBT, and other relevant groups) have full political rights and electoral opportunities? 1 / 4

Ethnic and religious minorities have few opportunities for political participation, even on a local level. Village council candidates must be Muslim, and ministers and deputy ministers must be Muslim and Malay unless the sultan grants an exception.

C. FUNCTIONING OF GOVERNMENT: 4 / 12 (+1)

C1. Do the freely elected head of government and national legislative representatives determine the policies of the government? 0 / 4

None of Brunei's national-level policymakers are chosen through elections. The sultan wields broad powers, and is counseled by appointed advisory bodies and the appointed legislature.

C2. Are safeguards against official corruption strong and effective? 3 / 4 (+1)

In 2015, the government enacted amendments to the Prevention of Corruption Act, which strengthened the anticorruption framework by establishing new conflict of interest rules for public officials, among other provisions. The government claims to have a zero-tolerance policy on corruption, and its Anti-Corruption Bureau has successfully prosecuted a number of lower-level officials in recent years. In July 2018, two former judges were indicted for allegedly embezzling over $7 million from a court's bankruptcy office. At year's end, the defendants awaited trial.

Score Change: The score improved from 2 to 3 due to the authorities' efforts to prosecute official corruption since 2015 reforms strengthened the legal framework for combating graft.

C3. Does the government operate with openness and transparency? 1 / 4

Although the appointed Legislative Council has no independent power, it formally passes the state budget and engages in question-and-answer sessions with government officials. The council meets once each year for a session lasting approximately two weeks. However, in general there is little transparency in the operations of the Brunei government, and this lack of transparency is exacerbated by the country's lack of press freedom.

CIVIL LIBERTIES: 22 / 60
D. FREEDOM OF EXPRESSION AND BELIEF: 6 / 16
D1. Are there free and independent media? 1 / 4

Officials may close newspapers without cause and fine and imprison journalists for up to three years for reporting deemed "false and malicious." Brunei's only television station is state-run. The country's main English-language daily newspaper, the *Borneo Bulletin*, is controlled by the sultan's family and its journalists often practice self-censorship. Another former English-language newspaper, the *Brunei Times*, closed abruptly in 2016, allegedly after complaints from the Saudi embassy in Brunei over critical coverage of Saudi hajj policies. A new online outlet, the *Scoop*, which launched in late 2017, contains somewhat independent coverage of Brunei society and politics.

D2. Are individuals free to practice and express their religious faith or nonbelief in public and private? 1 / 4

The state religion is the Shafi'i school of Sunni Islam, but the constitution allows for the practice of other religions. Non-Shafi'i forms of Islam are actively discouraged, and marriage between Muslims and non-Muslims is not allowed. Muslims require permission from the Ministry of Religious Affairs to convert to other faiths. Christians are allowed to hold low-key Christmas celebrations inside churches or at homes, but not outdoors or at shopping malls.

In 2014, Brunei implemented new criminal regulations based on Sharia, which include limits on the use of certain words and expressions deemed to be sacred to Islam in reference to other religions. The new code also includes a ban on proselytizing of a religion other than Islam to Muslims or atheists, and requires Muslims to participate in fasts and other religious observances.

D3. Is there academic freedom, and is the educational system free from extensive political indoctrination? 2 / 4

Academic freedom is respected to some extent, although institutions must seek approval from authorities to host visiting scholars, public lectures, and conferences. Scholars reportedly practice self-censorship or release their work under pseudonyms in overseas publications to avoid repercussions in Brunei.

D4. Are individuals free to express their personal views on political or other sensitive topics without fear of surveillance or retribution? 2 / 4

The government utilizes an informant system to monitor suspected dissidents, and online communications are monitored for subversive content. In November 2018, a government employee, on trial for sedition over a 2017 Facebook post complaining about new government halal certification regulations, fled to Canada before a verdict was handed down. The defendant faced up to two years in prison. Nevertheless, Brunei has an active online discussion community, although there are reports of self-censorship online regarding issues related to the monarchy.

E. ASSOCIATIONAL AND ORGANIZATIONAL RIGHTS: 3 / 12

E1. Is there freedom of assembly? 1 / 4

Long-standing state-of-emergency laws continue to restrict freedom of assembly. No more than 10 people can assemble for any purpose without a permit, and these laws are frequently enforced.

E2. Is there freedom for nongovernmental organizations, particularly those that are engaged in human rights- and governance-related work? 1 / 4

Most nongovernmental organizations (NGOs) are professional or business groups, although a few work on issues related to social welfare. All groups must register, registration can be refused for any reason, and registered groups can be suspended.

E3. Is there freedom for trade unions and similar professional or labor organizations? 1 / 4

The law guarantees the right to form and join a union, but the agreement that had permitted Brunei's only active union, the Brunei Oilfield Workers Union, is now expired. Strikes are illegal, and collective bargaining is not recognized.

F. RULE OF LAW: 6 /16

F1. Is there an independent judiciary? 1 / 4

Brunei has a dual judicial system of secular and Sharia courts; all senior judges are appointed by the sultan. The courts appear to act independently when handling civil matters, and have yet to be tested in political cases.

F2. Does due process prevail in civil and criminal matters? 2 / 4

Civil and criminal law is based on English common law and is enforced in secular courts, while Sharia is enforced in Sharia courts. People detained under the Internal Security Act (ISA) lack due process rights including the presumption of innocence.

The country's controversial new penal code, based on Sharia, continued to be delayed; Brunei implemented the first phase of the new code in 2014 but has held off implementing phases two and three, which contain more severe penalties for violations, including amputations and death by stoning. However, a draft bill that could pave the way for implementation of the second phase was approved by the sultan in March 2018. The Sharia penal code includes rules that apply to non-Muslims as well as Muslims. Many of the new Sharia rules overlap with existing provisions of the civil and criminal laws, but under the new Sharia code there are different sentences and burdens of proof.

The government only provides an attorney to indigent defendants in death penalty cases. To address this gap in access to justice, the Law Society of Brunei launched a pilot program for the country's first legal aid fund in August 2018, but attorneys are only provided to defendants who plead guilty.

F3. Is there protection from the illegitimate use of physical force and freedom from war and insurgencies? 2 / 4

Phased amendments to the new Sharia code permit the death penalty for drug-related offenses and other, more serious offenses, but these amendments have not yet been enacted. Brunei retained the death penalty for crimes including drug trafficking before the new Sharia code was launched. However, only one person was known to be on death row in 2018, and no individual has been executed since 1957. Secular law allows for dozens of offenses to be punished by caning. Prison conditions generally meet international standards.

F4. Do laws, policies, and practices guarantee equal treatment of various segments of the population? 1 / 4

Brunei citizenship is inherited automatically from citizen fathers. Citizen mothers must complete an application to pass citizenship on to children born to a noncitizen father.

Thousands of stateless residents of Brunei, including longtime ethnic Chinese residents, are denied the full rights and benefits granted to citizens. Same-sex sexual activity is a crime, and the government does not offer lesbian, gay, bisexual, and transgender (LGBT) individuals protections against discrimination. The results of a study released in 2017 by the Women Graduates Association of Brunei Darussalam (PSW) found that more than half of the female respondents had faced sexual harassment at work.

G. PERSONAL AUTONOMY AND INDIVIDUAL RIGHTS 7 / 16

G1. Do individuals enjoy freedom of movement, including the ability to change their place of residence, employment, or education? 2 / 4

Freedom of movement is respected. All government employees, domestic and foreign, must apply for permission to travel abroad, but permission is easily obtained. Stateless children do not have free access to education and instead must apply to enroll in schools; if accepted they sometimes have to pay tuition not required of citizens.

G2. Are individuals able to exercise the right to own property and establish private businesses without undue interference from state or nonstate actors? 2 / 4

Brunei citizens are able to own property and can establish businesses with relative ease, but protections for private property are not strong. State-linked firms dominate many sectors of the economy and the government heavily subsidizes a number of industries. Islamic law generally disadvantages women in cases of inheritance.

G3. Do individuals enjoy personal social freedoms, including choice of marriage partner and size of family, protection from domestic violence, and control over appearance? 1 / 4

Islamic law generally disadvantages women in matters involving divorce and child custody. The new Sharia penal code criminalizes "indecent behavior" and enjoins women to dress "modestly." There is no specific law against domestic violence, and although rape is a crime, spousal rape is not criminalized.

G4. Do individuals enjoy equality of opportunity and freedom from economic exploitation? 2 / 4

There is no private-sector minimum wage in Brunei. Labor inspections are frequent, but are often aimed at identifying undocumented migrant workers.

Migrants who come to Brunei to serve as household workers are often coerced into involuntary servitude or debt bondage, and can be subject to varying forms of abuse. Workers who overstay visas are regularly imprisoned and, in some cases, caned. In 2018, the government took steps to crack down on employers who abuse their domestic workers. In July, a woman was found guilty of abusing an Indonesian domestic worker she employed, and sentenced to six years in prison.

According to the US State Department's 2018 *Trafficking in Persons Report*, Brunei has made gains in combating trafficking, including by expanding protections for migrant workers and boosting the number of people served at its shelter. Despite this progress, the report noted that the government did not pursue any trafficking prosecutions between April 2017 and March 2018. In July, however, a court sentenced a Malaysian man to four years in prison for trafficking.

Bulgaria

Population: 7,000,000
Capital: Sofia
Political Rights Rating: 2
Civil Liberties Rating: 2
Freedom Rating: 2.0
Freedom Status: Free
Electoral Democracy: Yes

Overview: Multiple parties compete in Bulgaria's democratic system, and there have been several transfers of power between rival parties in recent decades. The country continues to struggle with political corruption and organized crime. While the media sector remains pluralistic, ownership concentration is a growing problem. Journalists encounter threats or violence in the course of their work. Ethnic minorities, particularly Roma, face discrimination. Despite funding shortages and other obstacles, civil society groups have been active and influential.

KEY DEVELOPMENTS IN 2018:
- In January, the parliament overrode a presidential veto and adopted legislation that would establish a new commission tasked with combating official corruption.
- In July, the Constitutional Court found that the Council of Europe's Istanbul Convention on gender-based violence was unconstitutional. The government had introduced the convention for ratification by the parliament, but it drew significant opposition.

POLITICAL RIGHTS: 33 / 40
A. ELECTORAL PROCESS: 11 / 12
A1. Was the current head of government or other chief national authority elected through free and fair elections? 4 / 4

The president, who is directly elected for up to two five-year terms, is the head of state but has limited powers. In 2016, former air force commander Rumen Radev—an independent supported by the opposition Bulgarian Socialist Party (BSP)—defeated parliament speaker Tsetska Tsacheva of the ruling Citizens for European Development of Bulgaria (GERB) party, taking more than 59 percent of the vote. The election was generally well administered, and stakeholders accepted the results.

The legislature chooses the prime minister, who serves as head of government. Prime Minister Boyko Borisov of the center-right GERB was returned to office after his party's victory in the 2017 parliamentary elections.

A2. Were the current national legislative representatives elected through free and fair elections? 4 / 4

The unicameral National Assembly, composed of 240 members, is elected every four years in 31 multimember constituencies. The 2017 elections were deemed free and fair by international observers. GERB led with 95 seats, followed by the BSP with 80, the nationalist United Patriots alliance with 27, the Movement for Rights and Freedoms (DPS) with 26, and the right-wing populist Volya with 12. Following the elections, a coalition government consisting of GERB and the United Patriots took office.

A3. Are the electoral laws and framework fair, and are they implemented impartially by the relevant election management bodies? 3 / 4

The Central Election Commission administers Bulgarian elections and generally works professionally and impartially, though some flaws have been reported in past elections. The parliament passed controversial reforms to the electoral laws in 2016, including the introduction of compulsory voting and new rules on voting abroad that limited the number of polling places and led to protests throughout the diaspora. In 2017, the Constitutional Court struck down the law on compulsory voting.

Further proposed changes to the electoral system in a 2016 referendum, such as the introduction of a majoritarian system for parliamentary elections, were supported by a majority of voters but failed to reach the turnout threshold for the votes to be binding.

B. POLITICAL PLURALISM AND PARTICIPATION: 14 / 16

B1. Do the people have the right to organize in different political parties or other competitive political groupings of their choice, and is the system free of undue obstacles to the rise and fall of these competing parties or groupings? 4 / 4

The Bulgarian party system is competitive and dynamic, featuring long-term players like the BSP and DPS as well as cycles in which new parties emerge while others decline or disappear. GERB first won seats in the parliament only in 2009, and the 2017 elections featured the emergence of the United Patriots alliance with 27 seats.

B2. Is there a realistic opportunity for the opposition to increase its support or gain power through elections? 4 / 4

There have been multiple peaceful transfers of power between rival parties through elections since the end of communist rule in 1990. In the 2017 parliamentary elections, the BSP, currently the main opposition party, gained 41 seats compared with the previous balloting.

B3. Are the people's political choices free from domination by the military, foreign powers, religious hierarchies, economic oligarchies, or any other powerful group that is not democratically accountable? 3 / 4

Bulgarians are generally free to make independent political choices. However, economic oligarchs dominate the major political parties and influence their platforms, a problem that is exacerbated by a lack of transparency in campaign finance law.

B4. Do various segments of the population (including ethnic, religious, gender, LGBT, and other relevant groups) have full political rights and electoral opportunities? 3 / 4

While women and minorities generally have full political rights, the law dictates that electoral campaigns must be conducted in the Bulgarian language, which hinders outreach to non-Bulgarian-speaking minority groups. The ethnic Turkish minority is represented by the DPS, but the Romany minority is more marginalized. Small Romany parties are active, and many Roma reportedly vote for the DPS, though none hold seats in the parliament. Members of far-right nationalist parties, including the United Patriots, engage in hate speech against ethnic Turks, Roma, Jews, Muslims, migrants, and refugees, among other groups, particularly during election periods, raising concerns about the normalization of xenophobia and discrimination.

C. FUNCTIONING OF GOVERNMENT: 8 / 12

C1. Do the freely elected head of government and national legislative representatives determine the policies of the government? 4 / 4

Elected executive and legislative officials are generally able to set and implement policies without undue interference from external or unelected entities. However, oligarch politicians dominate the government and greatly influence policymaking.

C2. Are safeguards against official corruption strong and effective? 2 / 4

Bulgaria, which joined the European Union (EU) in 2007, has struggled to meet the bloc's anticorruption requirements amid resistance from much of the political class. Anticorruption laws are not adequately enforced, including in high-profile cases, contributing to a culture of impunity. The country remains subject to long-term monitoring by the EU's cooperation and verification mechanism (CVM), whose annual reports have called for new legislative efforts to combat corruption.

In January 2018, the parliament overrode a presidential veto and adopted legislation that would create a centralized anticorruption commission to replace multiple existing bodies. The new commission would assess officials' asset declarations and flag conflicts of interest, and it would have the authority to initiate the seizure of illegally obtained assets. Some analysts remained concerned about the effectiveness and possible politicization of the new agency.

C3. Does the government operate with openness and transparency? 2 / 4

Although Bulgaria has laws meant to ensure that the government operates with transparency, they are not well enforced. Public access to information about the budgets and spending of various government agencies is often lacking in practice.

CIVIL LIBERTIES: 47 / 60
D. FREEDOM OF EXPRESSION AND BELIEF: 14 / 16
D1. Are there free and independent media? 3 / 4

The constitution protects freedom of expression, including for the press, but journalists face threats and occasional violence. In May 2018, investigative journalist Hristo Geshov was assaulted outside his home by an unidentified attacker. Two other reporters were arrested and briefly detained while investigating alleged fraud involving EU funds in September. In October, Viktoria Marinova, a television journalist who had recently interviewed the two fraud investigators, was raped and killed in the town of Ruse. However, a suspect was quickly arrested with the help of German authorities, and despite ongoing doubts, there was apparently no evidence linking the crime to Marinova's work.

The media sector is pluralistic, but many outlets are dependent on financial contributions from the state, often in the form of advertising, which can lead to demands for favorable coverage of the government. Domestic ownership of media has become more concentrated in the hands of wealthy Bulgarian businessmen, leaving the sector vulnerable to political and economic pressures and limiting the diversity of perspectives available to the public. News outlets often tailor coverage to suit the interests of their owners. In July 2018, newspapers in a conglomerate owned by lawmaker Delyan Peevski called on a television station to dismiss a presenter who had inquired about Peevski's businesses on air.

D2. Are individuals free to practice and express their religious faith or nonbelief in public and private? 3 / 4

Religious freedom is generally respected, but members of minority faiths in the mostly Orthodox Christian country have reported instances of harassment and discrimination, and some local authorities have prohibited proselytizing and other religious activities by such groups. A 2016 law that imposed fines for the wearing of face-covering garments in public locations was widely understood to be directed against Muslims.

D3. Is there academic freedom, and is the educational system free from extensive political indoctrination? 4 / 4

Academic freedom is generally upheld in practice.

D4. Are individuals free to express their personal views on political or other sensitive topics without fear of surveillance or retribution? 4 / 4

Freedom of expression is guaranteed by the constitution, and there are no significant impediments to free and open private discussion.

E. ASSOCIATIONAL AND ORGANIZATIONAL RIGHTS: 11 / 12
E1. Is there freedom of assembly? 4 / 4

The authorities generally respect constitutional guarantees of freedom of assembly. A number of mass demonstrations proceeded without incident during 2018, with participants airing grievances on issues including construction projects in national parks, a controversial annual march by far-right groups, and the cost of living.

E2. Is there freedom for nongovernmental organizations, particularly those that are engaged in human rights– and governance-related work? 4 / 4

Nongovernmental organizations (NGOs) operate freely and have a degree of influence, though they suffer from funding shortages, often rely on foreign donors, and sometimes face hostility from politicians and interest groups.

E3. Is there freedom for trade unions and similar professional or labor organizations? 3 / 4

Workers have the right to join trade unions, which are generally able to operate, but some public employees cannot legally strike, and none are permitted to bargain collectively. Private employers often discriminate against union members, including by terminating them, without facing serious repercussions. In May 2018, trade union federations organized protests calling for salaries to match those of other EU countries.

F. RULE OF LAW: 10 / 16

F1. Is there an independent judiciary? 3 / 4

Bulgaria's judiciary has benefited from legal and institutional reforms associated with EU membership, but it is still prone to politicization. A new Supreme Judicial Council, which is responsible for judicial appointments and management, was installed under revised rules in 2017, with half the members elected by fellow magistrates and half by a two-thirds parliamentary majority. The parliamentary portion of the process was criticized for political bargaining and a lack of transparency, though the CVM report released in November 2018 generally praised the initial performance of the new council. Other recent reforms strengthened the inspectorate responsible for investigating conflicts of interest among judges, verifying their asset declarations, and contributing to disciplinary proceedings.

F2. Does due process prevail in civil and criminal matters? 2 / 4

Constitutional rights to due process are not always upheld. Police have been accused of misconduct including arbitrary arrests and failure to inform suspects of their rights. Public trust in the justice system is low due to its reputed vulnerability to political and other outside pressure.

F3. Is there protection from the illegitimate use of physical force and freedom from war and insurgencies? 3 / 4

Although the population faces few acute threats to physical security, police brutality, including abuse of suspects in custody, remains a problem. Overcrowding and violence plague many of Bulgaria's prisons. Organized crime is still a major issue, and scores of suspected contract killings since the 1990s are unsolved.

F4. Do laws, policies, and practices guarantee equal treatment of various segments of the population? 2 / 4

Ethnic minorities, particularly Roma, face discrimination in employment, health care, education, and housing, though the government and NGOs operate a number of programs meant to improve their social integration. Authorities periodically demolish illegally constructed or irregular housing—mostly in areas occupied by Roma—without providing alternative shelter.

Migrants and asylum seekers have reportedly faced various forms of mistreatment by Bulgarian authorities, including beatings and extortion. According to a July 2018 report by the Bulgaria-based Foundation for Access to Rights, the rate of detention for asylum seekers has remained high despite a decline in new arrivals in recent years.

Discrimination based on sexual orientation or gender identity is illegal, but societal bias against LGBT (lesbian, gay, bisexual, and transgender) people reportedly persists. In July 2018, the Constitutional Court ruled that the Council of Europe's Istanbul Convention on preventing gender-based violence was unconstitutional, finding fault with its conceptualization of gender. Conservative critics argued that the convention, which the government had signed in 2016 and introduced in the parliament for possible ratification in January, would create a basis for expanded rights for LGBT people.

A gender equality law passed in 2016 was designed to foster equal opportunity for women, but they still face discrimination in employment, with higher levels of unemployment and lower pay than their male counterparts.

G. PERSONAL AUTONOMY AND INDIVIDUAL RIGHTS: 12 / 16

G1. Do individuals enjoy freedom of movement, including the ability to change their place of residence, employment, or education? 4 / 4

For the most part, Bulgarians face no major restrictions on their freedom of movement. Corruption and bias can sometimes hamper efforts to change one's place of employment. In 2017, the government issued a rule that restricted the ability of asylum seekers to move outside of the district where they are housed.

G2. Are individuals able to exercise the right to own property and establish private businesses without undue interference from state or nonstate actors? 3 / 4

The legal and regulatory framework is generally supportive of property rights and private business, though property rights are not always respected in practice, and corruption continues to hamper business and investment. The so-called grey economy of undeclared business activity is estimated at nearly 30 percent of the gross domestic product.

G3. Do individuals enjoy personal social freedoms, including choice of marriage partner and size of family, protection from domestic violence, and control over appearance? 3 / 4

The law generally grants equal rights to men and women regarding personal status matters such as marriage and divorce. Domestic violence remains a problem. Victims and NGOs have complained that state authorities are often ineffective in providing protection and pursuing criminal charges when abuse is reported.

Same-sex marriage is illegal in Bulgaria, and same-sex couples are barred from adopting children.

G4. Do individuals enjoy equality of opportunity and freedom from economic exploitation? 2 / 4

Labor laws provide basic protections against exploitative working conditions, but they do not extend in practice to informal or grey-market employment. Roma and other ethnic minorities are particularly vulnerable to trafficking for sexual and labor exploitation. Although the government has continued to step up efforts to combat trafficking, shelter victims, and punish perpetrators, these measures have not matched the scale of the problem, and punishments remain light in practice.

Burkina Faso

Population: 20,300,000
Capital: Ouagadougou
Political Rights Rating: 4
Civil Liberties Rating: 3
Freedom Rating: 3.5
Freedom Status: Partly Free
Electoral Democracy: Yes

Overview: Multiparty presidential and legislative elections held in late 2015 ushered in a new government and laid a foundation for the continued development of democratic institutions. Despite extreme poverty, terrorism, and corruption, civil society and the media remain strong forces for democracy and for the respect of civil liberties.

KEY DEVELOPMENTS IN 2018:
- In February, a highly anticipated military trial of 84 people accused of involvement in a failed 2015 coup commenced. After a number of delays, the trial was ongoing at the end of the year.
- In March, attacks by armed militants in downtown Ouagadougou targeted the military's headquarters and the French embassy, claiming at least 30 lives. The security situation also continued to deteriorate in the north and east as Islamic militants carried out regular attacks. In response to the growing crisis, President Kaboré declared a state of emergency in December.
- In July, the parliament passed a new electoral code that drew criticism from opposition parties for making it more difficult for people living abroad to register and vote.

POLITICAL RIGHTS: 23 / 40

A. ELECTORAL PROCESS: 7 / 12

A1. Was the current head of government or other chief national authority elected through free and fair elections? 2 / 4

The president is head of state and is directly elected to no more than two five-year terms. Roch Marc Christian Kaboré, of the People's Movement for Progress (MPP), won the 2015 presidential election with just over 53 percent of the vote. Observers described the election as the most competitive ever to be held in the country. However, a number of politicians who had supported an ultimately unsuccessful attempt by former president Blaise Compaoré to amend the constitution to allow himself a third presidential term were barred from contesting the election. (Compaoré's 2014 move to amend the constitution had prompted profound political instability and violent protests; Compaoré subsequently stepped down from office. Following 16 days of provisional military control, a transitional government was established in late 2014, and administered presidential and parliamentary elections in 2015.)

The prime minister is head of government and is appointed by the president with the approval of the National Assembly, and is responsible for recommending a cabinet that is formally appointed by the president. Kaboré appointed economist Paul Kaba Thieba to the post in early 2016.

A2. Were the current national legislative representatives elected through free and fair elections? 2 / 4

The 127 members of the National Assembly are directly elected to five-year terms under a proportional representation system. The 2015 legislative elections were held concurrently with the presidential election and were viewed as generally credible, despite the exclusion of a number of candidates who had supported Compaoré's term-limit changes. The MPP won a plurality, but not a majority, in the National Assembly, with 55 of the 127 seats.

Municipal elections held in 2016 reflected continuing erosion of support for the Congress for Democracy and Progress (CDP), the former ruling party, and increasing support for the MPP. Election observers from local civil society groups and international missions noted only minor irregularities in the polls. However, election-related violence prevented polling in a number of districts, which, according to some observers, contributed to relatively low turnout. Makeup elections for several constituencies were held peacefully in 2017, though once again some candidates were reportedly excluded.

A3. Are the electoral laws and framework fair, and are they implemented impartially by the relevant election management bodies? 3 / 4

The Independent National Electoral Commission (CENI) is responsible for organizing elections, and the 2015 and 2016 polls were generally well administered.

A new electoral code adopted in July 2018 was criticized by opposition parties for imposing new restrictions on voters living abroad. The 2018 code requires either the national identity card or a Burkinabè passport for those living abroad to register to vote, whereas a consular card was considered an acceptable document in the previous code. Opposition critics claimed that many Burkinabès abroad, particularly those in Côte d'Ivoire, would not possess the required documents and would therefore be disenfranchised.

B. POLITICAL PLURALISM AND PARTICIPATION: 10 / 16

B1. Do the people have the right to organize in different political parties or other competitive political groupings of their choice, and is the system free of undue obstacles to the rise and fall of these competing parties or groupings? 2 / 4

The constitution guarantees the right to form political parties. Following the 2015 legislative elections, 14 parties held seats in the National Assembly, though 99 parties had participated in the elections. The 2015 Election Code prohibited some former ruling party members from participating in the 2015 presidential election.

The MPP and the CDP both have extensive patronage networks and disproportionate access to media coverage, making it difficult for other political parties to build their support bases.

B2. Is there a realistic opportunity for the opposition to increase its support or gain power through elections? 3 / 4

The end of former president Compaoré's 27-year regime in 2014 has given way to a freer environment, in which opposition parties were able to consolidate popular support and gain power through recent elections. However, a history of rotation of power between parties has yet to be firmly established.

B3. Are the people's political choices free from domination by the military, foreign powers, religious hierarchies, economic oligarchies, or any other powerful group that is not democratically accountable? 2 / 4

Burkina Faso's military maintains a significant presence in the political sphere. In 2015, the presidential guard, which was loyal to former president Compaoré, attempted to stage a military coup. The maneuver sparked widespread protests, and failed after the national military's chief of staff moved to support the transitional government. The history of military intervention poses a persistent threat to democratic stability in Burkina Faso.

B4. Do various segments of the population (including ethnic, religious, gender, LGBT, and other relevant groups) have full political rights and electoral opportunities? 3 / 4

The constitution enshrines full political rights and electoral opportunities for all segments of the population. However, a small educated elite, the military, and labor unions have historically dominated political life.

Women are underrepresented in political leadership positions, and within parties are frequently relegated to women's secretariats that have little influence. However, there have been some initiatives aimed at establishing greater legal protections for women and encouraging women's political participation, including proposed revisions to an unevenly enforced quota law.

C. FUNCTIONING OF GOVERNMENT: 6 / 12

C1. Do the freely elected head of government and national legislative representatives determine the policies of the government? 2 / 4

Laws are promulgated and debated by the elected National Assembly members. While democratic institutions continue to develop, they are not yet strong enough to withstand the influence of the military and other elite groups. Attacks by Islamic militants, which have increased in frequency in recent years, severely impede the government's ability to implement its policies in the insecure north and east.

C2. Are safeguards against official corruption strong and effective? 2 / 4

Corruption is widespread, and particularly affects the police force. Anticorruption laws and bodies are generally ineffective, though local nongovernmental organizations (NGOs) provide some accountability by publicizing official corruption and its effects.

C3. Does the government operate with openness and transparency? 2 / 4

The successful 2015 elections and installation of a civilian government signified a marked improvement in government representation, accountability, and transparency. However, government procurement processes are opaque, and procedures meant to increase transparency are often not followed. Government officials are required to make financial disclosures, but the information is rarely made public, and the penalties for noncompliance do not appear to be enforced.

CIVIL LIBERTIES: 37 / 60
D. FREEDOM OF EXPRESSION AND BELIEF: 13 / 16
D1. Are there free and independent media? 3 / 4

The environment for media has improved since the end of Compaoré's rule. Since then, defamation has been decriminalized, reporters at the public broadcaster have experienced less political interference, self-censorship among journalists has eased, and journalists are generally able to report freely and critically on the government and its activities. There are several private television stations and dozens of private radio stations and newspapers.

Nevertheless, libel convictions still carry onerous financial penalties, journalists at times have experienced pressure from government officials, and media workers face a challenging economic environment. In July 2018, activist Naïm Touré was sentenced to two months in jail after being convicted of "incitement to revolt" for a Facebook post that criticized a military counterterrorism operation.

D2. Are individuals free to practice and express their religious faith or nonbelief in public and private? 4 / 4

Burkina Faso is a secular state, and freedom of religion is generally respected. The population is predominately Muslim with a large Christian minority. Followers of both religions often engage in syncretic practices. Recent actions by Islamic militant groups, which have attacked and intimidated civilians in the north and east, contributed to increased tensions between Muslims and Christians, although religious tolerance remains the norm.

D3. Is there academic freedom, and is the educational system free from extensive political indoctrination? 3 / 4

Academic freedom is unrestricted, though due to the former regime's repressive tactics against student-led protests, a legacy of tension between the government and academic organizations persists. Islamic militant groups in the north have threatened teachers in an effort to force them to adopt Islamic teachings, resulting in the closure of schools.

D4. Are individuals free to express their personal views on political or other sensitive topics without fear of surveillance or retribution? 3 / 4

Private discussion is unrestricted in much of the country. However, attacks and intimidation by militant Islamic groups in the north and east, and an increased security presence in response to their activities, have dissuaded people from speaking about local news and politics and other sensitive topics.

E. ASSOCIATIONAL AND ORGANIZATIONAL RIGHTS: 9 / 12
E1. Is there freedom of assembly? 3 / 4

The constitution guarantees freedom of assembly, which is largely upheld in practice. Under the new government, space for demonstrations and protests has opened. Several peaceful protests took place in 2018. However, past government repression of peaceful demonstrations can still discourage such events, and the ability to demonstrate is restricted in areas affected by militant activity.

E2. Is there freedom for nongovernmental organizations, particularly those that are engaged in human rights– and governance-related work? 3 / 4

While many NGOs operate openly and freely, human rights groups have reported abuses by security forces in the past. NGOs still face harassment in carrying out their work, and NGO leaders argue that some legal provisions, including vaguely worded terrorism laws, are vulnerable to being misused to silence human rights defenders.

E3. Is there freedom for trade unions and similar professional or labor organizations? 3 / 4

The constitution guarantees the right to strike, and unions frequently and freely engage in strikes and collective bargaining, although a minority of workers are unionized. Labor organizers can face fines or prison time if a labor action results in property damage.

F. RULE OF LAW: 7 / 16
F1. Is there an independent judiciary? 2 / 4

The judiciary is formally independent but has historically been subject to executive influence and corruption. In February 2018, a highly anticipated military trial of 84 people accused of involvement in the failed 2015 coup commenced. Some analysts have questioned whether the accused could receive a fair trial, since the members of the military tribunal ruling on the case are appointed by the Defense Ministry and the president, and the government body tasked with ensuring judicial independence does not have control over military courts. The trial was suspended several times throughout the year, and was ongoing at year's end.

F2. Does due process prevail in civil and criminal matters? 2 / 4

Constitutional guarantees of due process are undermined by corruption and inefficacy of the judiciary and police force. A 2017 report by the Anticorruption National Network (REN-LAC) identified the municipal police as the government office perceived to be the most corrupt. Police often disregard pretrial detention limits.

The military has been accused of arbitrarily detaining large groups of men in the vicinity of attacks by Islamic militants. While most detainees are released in a matter of days, some have been held for months.

F3. Is there protection from the illegitimate use of physical force and freedom from war and insurgencies? 1 / 4

The security environment has declined in recent years due to activity by Islamic militant groups and bandits. In March 2018, attacks by armed militants in downtown Ouagadougou targeted the military's headquarters and the French embassy, claiming at least 30 lives. Dozens have been killed in attacks by militant groups and bandits in the north, mainly along the borders with Mali and Niger. Insecurity also grew in the east in 2018, with regular attacks against civilians and the military. In December, President Kaboré declared a state of emergency in 14 provinces in response to the growing crisis.

In some cases, security forces have reportedly responded to the insecurity with extrajudicial killings and torture. In September, for example, at least 29 individuals were summarily executed by security forces in the northern province of Soum. Authorities claimed that those executed were militants. Victims have complained that the authorities have largely failed to investigate human rights abuses perpetrated by security forces.

Allegations of torture and abuse of suspects in custody by the police are common, and prisons are often overcrowded.

F4. Do laws, policies, and practices guarantee equal treatment of various segments of the population? 2 / 4

Discrimination against ethnic minorities occurs, but is not widespread. LGBT (lesbian, gay, bisexual, and transgender) people, as well as those infected with HIV, routinely experience discrimination. While illegal, gender discrimination remains common in employment and education.

Reports of growing racial, ethnic, and religious stigmatization within historically tolerant Burkinabè society emerged in the wake of continuing terrorist activities in the north. This increased prejudice has most affected people appearing to be of Tuareg, Fulani, or Arab descent.

G. PERSONAL AUTONOMY AND INDIVIDUAL RIGHTS: 8 / 16

G1. Do individuals enjoy freedom of movement, including the ability to change their place of residence, employment, or education? 2 / 4

Due to increasing insecurity, the government has established a number of heavily guarded checkpoints on roads near the northern border and the capital, and has instituted curfews in some places. The deteriorating security situation in the east has also impinged on freedom of movement there. Since 2017, schools have been targeted by armed groups in the north, and the number of people that have fled their homes has increased.

G2. Are individuals able to exercise the right to own property and establish private businesses without undue interference from state or nonstate actors? 2 / 4

In recent years, the government has implemented reforms in the business sector by reducing the amount of capital necessary to start a business, facilitating the ability to obtain credit information, and improving the insolvency resolution process. However, the business environment is hampered by corruption. Laws and practices involving inheritance discriminate against women.

G3. Do individuals enjoy personal social freedoms, including choice of marriage partner and size of family, protection from domestic violence, and control over appearance? 2 / 4

Women face discrimination in cases involving family rights. Early marriage remains an issue, especially in the north. The practice of female genital mutilation is less common than in the past, but still takes place. Domestic violence remains a problem despite government efforts to combat it.

G4. Do individuals enjoy equality of opportunity and freedom from economic exploitation? 2 / 4

Burkina Faso is a source, transit, and destination country for trafficking in women and children. Child labor is present in the agricultural and mining sectors, among other industries. Women from neighboring countries are recruited by traffickers and transported to Burkina Faso, where they are forced into prostitution. In the US Department of State's 2018 *Trafficking in Persons Report*, Burkina Faso was upgraded to a Tier 2 country by accelerating efforts to combat human trafficking through increased convictions and improved efforts to protect victims of trafficking.

Burundi

Population: 11,800,000
Capital: Bujumbura
Political Rights Rating: 7
Civil Liberties Rating: 6
Freedom Rating: 6.5
Freedom Status: Not Free
Electoral Democracy: No

Overview: Democratic gains made after the 12-year civil war ended in 2005 are being undone by a shift toward authoritarian politics, and ongoing repression of and violence against the opposition and those perceived to support it.

KEY DEVELOPMENTS IN 2018:

- In May, a constitutional referendum to extend presidential term limits passed after a campaign of violence and intimidation against all perceived opponents to the change.
- In September, the government announced that it was suspending nearly all international NGOs. The suspension was lifted in late November.
- in September, UN Human Rights Council (UNHRC) Commission of Inquiry on Burundi released a report finding that widespread human rights violations perpetrated by state and state-aligned actors against opponents of the regime persisted throughout the year.

POLITICAL RIGHTS: 3 / 40 (-1)
A. ELECTORAL PROCESS: 0 / 12 (-1)
A1. Was the current head of government or other chief national authority elected through free and fair elections? 0 / 4

Burundi adopted a new constitution in 2005 after a series of agreements ended the country's 12-year civil war. According to the charter, the president appoints two vice presidents, one Tutsi and one Hutu, who must be approved separately by a two-thirds majority in both the lower and upper houses of Parliament.

In April 2015, the ruling National Council for the Defense of Democracy–Forces for the Defense of Democracy (CNDD–FDD) announced that President Pierre Nkurunziza would seek a third presidential term. Critics charged that the move contravened the constitution and would jeopardize the country's fragile peace. Nkurunziza and his supporters argued that he was eligible to run again because he had been elected by Parliament rather than through a popular vote for his first term in office. Despite widespread public protests and international condemnation of the move, the Constitutional Court in May 2015 ruled in favor of Nkurunziza, even as one of the court's justices fled abroad. Days later, a group of military leaders led a coup attempt against Nkurunziza. Government forces quickly reasserted control and began a crackdown on those suspected of involvement in the plot or opposition to the president. Due to ongoing unrest in the country, the Independent National Electoral Commission (CENI) postponed the presidential poll until that July.

In the election, Nkurunziza defeated National Forces of Liberation (FNL) leader Agathon Rwasa, 69 percent to 19 percent, although the latter boycotted the poll. International observers from some organizations, including the EU and African Union (AU), refused to monitor the election, saying it could not be free or fair given the violence and climate of intimidation. A UN mission observing the poll stated that the environment was not conducive to a free and fair electoral process, and that violence had "remained an unfortunate feature of the entire process."

Nkurunziza's move to pursue a third term sparked violence including assassinations, arrests, and torture of government critics. The unrest has continued in 2018, though at a lower rate than at its outset.

In May 2018, Nkurunziza further consolidated his rule through the passage of a constitutional referendum, which, among other provisions, lengthens presidential terms from five to seven years. In June, however, Nkurunziza vowed to step down in 2020, despite the fact that the new constitution allows him to stay in power through 2034.

A2. Were the current national legislative representatives elected through free and fair elections? 0 / 4

The 100 members of the lower house, the National Assembly, are directly elected by proportional representation for five-year terms. The upper house, the Senate, consists of 36 members chosen by locally elected officials for five-year terms.

Due to the unrest in 2015, the CENI postponed the year's National Assembly elections by several weeks, and they eventually took place in late June 2015. Indirect senatorial elections were held that July. The volatile environment surrounding the legislative vote prevented it from being free or fair. The opposition boycotted the polls, and the CNDD–FDD took significant majorities in both the National Assembly and the Senate.

A3. Are the electoral laws and framework fair, and are they implemented impartially by the relevant election management bodies? 0 / 4 (–1)

The CENI is comprised of five members. In 2015, two CENI members who fled the country amid the year's unrest were replaced with pro-Nkurunziza appointments approved by a CNDD-FDD–controlled Parliament.

The CNDD-FDD conducted a violent intimidation campaign ahead of the May 2018 referendum, with authorities arresting perceived opponents and threatening to assassinate those who did not vote in favor of the changes. According to Human Rights Watch (HRW), at least 15 people died in violence connected to the referendum campaign. The referendum passed with 73 percent of the vote. In addition to extending presidential term limits, the revisions further consolidate power in the executive, allow for future revision of Burundi's ethnic power-sharing system, and create new obstacles for opposition parties.

Score Change: The score declined from 1 to 0 because a constitutional referendum that extended presidential term limits was marred by intimidation and harassment of the political opposition.

B. POLITICAL PLURALISM AND PARTICIPATION: 3 / 16

B1. Do the people have the right to organize in different political parties or other competitive political groupings of their choice, and is the system free of undue obstacles to the rise and fall of these competing parties or groupings? 1 / 4

Legally, political party formation is not difficult. In practice, the activities of parties and political leaders perceived as opposing Nkurunziza are severely discouraged by the threat of retaliatory violence, repression, or arrest. Many political parties include youth branches that intimidate and attack opponents, the most prominent of which is the ruling party's Imbonerakure.

A network of independent journalists reported that more than 50 members of the opposition coalition Hope for Burundi, who were campaigning against the passage of the referendum, were arrested in a single week in April 2018.

B2. Is there a realistic opportunity for the opposition to increase its support or gain power through elections? 0 / 4

The opposition has little realistic opportunity to increase its popular support through elections. Opposition parties, politicians, and their supporters have faced harassment, intimidation, and assassination since 2015, which severely undercuts their electoral competitiveness. Many opposition politicians and groups continue to operate in exile, and face arrest if they return home.

B3. Are the people's political choices free from domination by the military, foreign powers, religious hierarchies, economic oligarchies, or any other powerful group that is not democratically accountable? 0 / 4

The Imbonerakure, the National Intelligence Services (SNR), and the Burundian police are strong allies of the ruling coalition, and use violence and intimidation to influence people's political choices. During the 2018 referendum campaign, for example, members of the Imbonerakure reportedly assaulted and arrested people who were not registered to vote or who stated that they would vote against passing the referendum.

B4. Do various segments of the population (including ethnic, religious, gender, LGBT, and other relevant groups) have full political rights and electoral opportunities? 2 / 4

The 2005 constitution requires power-sharing between Hutus and Tutsis in the National Assembly and Senate, and additionally stipulates that women and members of the Twa minority be seated in both houses. However, the constitutional revisions approved in May 2018 stipulate that these ethnic quotas, which were originally negotiated to prevent a resumption of conflict between Hutus and Tutsis, be reviewed over the next five years, opening the door for their elimination and the potential political exclusion of the Tutsi minority.

Women face social pressure that can deter active political participation, and few women hold political office at senior levels.

The current political environment is characterized by the dominance of the CNDD–FDD and repression of its opponents, reducing meaningful openings for effective political representation of ethnic and religious minorities and other distinct groups.

C. FUNCTIONING OF GOVERNMENT: 0 / 12

C1. Do the freely elected head of government and national legislative representatives determine the policies of the government? 0 / 4

The ruling CNDD–FDD, which took power in 2015 elections that fell far short of international standards, controls policy development and implementation.

C2. Are safeguards against official corruption strong and effective? 0 / 4

Corruption is a significant problem in Burundi, and there is little political will to address it. Corrupt officials generally enjoy impunity, even when wrongdoing is exposed by nongovernmental organizations (NGOs) and other actors. Anticorruption organizations are underresourced and ineffective.

C3. Does the government operate with openness and transparency? 0 / 4

Government operations are opaque, and government officials are generally unaccountable to voters. There are few opportunities for civil society actors and others to participate in policymaking. Due to recurrent assassinations and assassination attempts, politicians are wary of organizing town hall–style meetings or making other public appearances before voters.

CIVIL LIBERTIES: 11 / 60 (–3)

D. FREEDOM OF EXPRESSION AND BELIEF: 5 / 16 (–1)

D1. Are there free and independent media? 0 / 4

Freedom of expression is constitutionally guaranteed, but severely restricted in practice by draconian press laws and a dangerous operating environment for media workers, who risk threats, harassment, and arrest in response to their coverage. A 2013 media law limits the protection of journalistic sources, requires journalists to meet certain educational and professional standards, and bans content related to national defense, security, public safety, and the state currency. The law empowers the media regulatory body to issue press cards to journalists, suspend or withdraw cards as a result of defamation cases, and impose financial penalties for media offenses. The government dominates the media through its ownership of the public television broadcaster, radio stations, and *Le Renouveau*, the only daily newspaper. Key independent news outlets destroyed in the political violence of 2015 have yet to be reestablished. Since 2015, many journalists have been forced to flee the country.

In 2018, the government continued to harass and intimidate outlets and journalists that questioned or criticized its policies. In May, the government announced a six-month ban on local radio broadcasting by the British Broadcasting Corporation (BBC) and Voice of America (VOA), both of which the National Council for Communication (CNC) accused of "breaching professional ethics." The government also issued warnings against two local radio stations that allegedly did not follow guidelines on sourcing for their reports.

D2. Are individuals free to practice and express their religious faith or nonbelief in public and private? 3 / 4

Freedom of religion is generally observed in Burundi, though relations between the government and the Roman Catholic Church, of which a majority of Burundians are members, has been strained at times; senior government officials have engaged in strongly worded verbal attacks against the church that could discourage open worship. In 2017, the government set up a commission to monitor religious groups and guard against political subversion within them.

D3. Is there academic freedom, and is the educational system free from extensive political indoctrination? 2 / 4

For many years, civil strife and Tutsi social and institutional dominance impeded academic freedom by limiting educational opportunities for the Hutu, but this situation has improved since 2005. However, there have been allegations that both university students and staff who support the CNDD–FDD receive preferential treatment at academic institutions. Continued intimidation of opposition supporters has created an atmosphere of fear and limited free speech on university campuses.

D4. Are individuals free to express their personal views on political or other sensitive topics without fear of surveillance or retribution? 0 / 4 (–1)

The SNR and the Imbonerakure actively conduct surveillance activities on private citizens. There is a reluctance to engage in speech which could be perceived as critical of the ruling party due to fears of harassment, threats of violence, and other reprisals. Ahead of the 2018 referendum, the SNR and Imbonerakure expanded their surveillance and harassment to include those perceived as apolitical. For example, the Imbonerakure checked citizens to ensure that they registered to vote and paid election taxes, and frequently harassed and attacked those who had not. Members of the Imbonerakure also reportedly assaulted individuals they overheard expressing opposition to the referendum in private conversations at bars and restaurants.

Score Change: The score declined from 1 to 0 due to increased repression and surveillance around the 2018 referendum, which affected not only opposition voices but also those deemed too apolitical, including people who were not registered to vote or had not paid election taxes.

E. ASSOCIATIONAL AND ORGANIZATIONAL RIGHTS: 1 / 12 (–1)

E1. Is there freedom of assembly? 0 / 4

Opposition or antigovernment meetings and rallies are usually prevented or dispersed, and participants in gatherings seen as antigovernment face harassment or arrest. Many people who participated in 2015 protests against Nkurunziza fled Burundi amid the subsequent crackdown.

E2. Is there freedom for nongovernmental organizations, particularly those that are engaged in human rights– and governance-related work? 0 / 4 (–1)

NGOs in Burundi face increasingly restrictive registration laws and persecution for activity seen as hostile to the government. A number of human rights and other groups perceived as antigovernment have been banned, and many of their members have chosen to flee the country rather than face surveillance, intimidation, threats, and arrest in Burundi.

The environment for NGOs deteriorated even further in 2018. In September, the government announced that it was suspending nearly all international NGOs for three months, which authorities claimed was for violating a 2017 law requiring NGOs to adhere to ethnic quotas in hiring national staff. The only international NGOs not included in the suspension were those that manage schools and hospitals. The suspension was lifted in late November. In April, the government expelled a team of experts from the UNHRC's Commission of Inquiry on Burundi, which has been highly critical of Burundi's human rights record, and in December, it formally requested the UNHRC close its office and leave the country.

Score Change: The score declined from 1 to 0 because the environment for NGOs deteriorated further with the government's sweeping suspension of international NGOs and the continued repression of domestic civil society groups.

E3. Is there freedom for trade unions and similar professional or labor organizations? 1 / 4

The constitution provides protections for organized labor, and the labor code guarantees the right to strike. However, it is unlikely that union members would feel free to exercise the collective bargaining rights guaranteed by the law in the current political climate.

F. RULE OF LAW: 1 / 16

F1. Is there an independent judiciary? 0 / 4

Burundi's judiciary is hindered by corruption and a lack of resources and training, and is generally subservient to the executive. In 2015, justices on the Constitutional Court were reportedly intimidated into ruling in favor of Nkurunziza's decision to stand for a third term. The executive regularly interferes in the criminal justice system to protect ruling party and Imbonerakure members, as well as persecute the political opposition.

F2. Does due process prevail in civil and criminal matters? 0 / 4

Constitutional guarantees of due process are poorly enforced. Arbitrary arrest and lengthy pretrial detention are common. There have been reports that detainees' families were able to secure their release only upon making large payments to the SNR or Imbonerakure.

Defendants must provide their own legal representation, making trial rights dependent on the ability to afford a lawyer. Some detainees accused of participating in the 2015 protests or subsequent antigovernment violence did not have access to lawyers and were forced to make false confessions under threat of death. Because the courts, police, and security forces do not operate independently or professionally, critics argue the country is not capable of handling cases involving human rights violations.

In 2017 the International Criminal Court (ICC) opened an investigation into alleged crimes against humanity committed by government actors. Two days after the investigation's launch, Burundi left the ICC, becoming the first country ever to do so.

F3. Is there protection from the illegitimate use of physical force and freedom from war and insurgencies? 0 / 4

The security situation in Burundi is poor. A September 2018 report issued by the UNHRC's Commission of Inquiry on Burundi found that widespread human rights violations persisted during the year, including instances of "summary execution, disappearance (including enforced disappearance), arbitrary arrest and detention, torture and other cruel, inhumane, or degrading treatment, sexual violence, and violations of civil liberties such as the freedoms of expression, association, assembly, and movement." The report identified the police and the SNR as the principal perpetrators, but noted the increasing role of the Imbonerakure. More than 430,000 refugees had fled Burundi in response to the ongoing crisis as of March 2018.

A December investigative report by the BBC found that the government operates at least 22 secret facilities where political dissidents have reportedly been tortured and killed. The government responded to the report by calling it "fake" and threatening to sue the BBC.

F4. Do laws, policies, and practices guarantee equal treatment of various segments of the population? 1 / 4

Albinos face systematic discrimination and violence in Burundi. LGBT (lesbian, gay, bisexual, and transgender) people also experience official and societal discrimination. The 2009 penal code criminalizes same-sex sexual activity, and punishments include up to two years in prison.

Discrimination against women is common in access to education, healthcare, and employment.

G. PERSONAL AUTONOMY AND INDIVIDUAL RIGHTS: 4 / 16 (–1)

G1. Do individuals enjoy freedom of movement, including the ability to change their place of residence, employment, or education? 1 / 4

Since 2015, concerns for personal safety have restricted free movement, particularly in neighborhoods regarded as opposition strongholds, where security forces frequently conduct search operations. In 2017 and 2018, refugees reported an increase in police and Imbonerakure checkpoints, which further restricted freedom of movement, as well as attacks against those attempting to flee.

G2. Are individuals able to exercise the right to own property and establish private businesses without undue interference from state or nonstate actors? 1 / 4 (–1)

Land conflict has been an explosive issue in Burundi for decades, which was exacerbated by the return of displaced populations after the civil war ended in 2005. Many of the returnees found new owners occupying their land, and the courts have often failed to fairly adjudicate land disputes. There are additional reports that some refugees who fled in 2015 are returning to find their land occupied.

Due to customary law, women typically are unable to inherit property. The deteriorating security situation hampers private business activity in the country, as does rampant corruption.

Score Change: The score declined from 2 to1 because many people who have returned to their land after fleeing from conflict have found their properties occupied, and the poor security situation and rampant corruption have hindered business activity.

G3. Do individuals enjoy personal social freedoms, including choice of marriage partner and size of family, protection from domestic violence, and control over appearance? 1 / 4

Sexual and domestic violence are serious problems but are rarely reported to law enforcement agencies. Rights monitors continue to report sexual violence carried out by security forces and Imbonerakure, and perpetrators act with impunity. Women are often targeted for rape if they or their spouses refuse to join the CNDD-FDD, and men sometimes experience sexual abuse while in government custody.

According to the Citizenship Code, a Burundian woman married to a foreign national cannot pass on her citizenship to her husband or children.

G4. Do individuals enjoy equality of opportunity and freedom from economic exploitation? 1 / 4

Women have limited opportunities for advancement in the workplace. Much of the population is impoverished. In 2017, "vagrancy" and begging by able-bodied persons became formal offenses under the penal code. The ongoing political and humanitarian crisis has contributed to an economic decline, less access to basic services, and deteriorating living conditions.

The government has conducted some trainings for government officials on handling cases of human trafficking. However, the government has largely failed to prevent domestic human trafficking, to protect victims, and to prosecute perpetrators.

Cambodia

Population: 16,000,000
Capital: Phnom Penh
Political Rights Rating: 6
Civil Liberties Rating: 5
Freedom Rating: 5.5
Freedom Status: Not Free
Electoral Democracy: No

Overview: Cambodia's political system has been dominated by Prime Minister Hun Sen and his Cambodian People's Party (CPP) for more than three decades. The country has conducted semicompetitive elections in the past, but the 2018 polls were held in a severely repressive environment that offered voters no meaningful choice. The main opposition party was banned, opposition leaders were in jail or exiled, and independent media and civil society outlets were curtailed. The CPP won every seat in the lower house for the first time since the end of the Cambodian Civil War, as well as every elected seat in the upper house in indirect elections held earlier in the year.

KEY DEVELOPMENTS IN 2018:

- The CPP won every seat in the lower house, the National Assembly, in July elections. The polls were held amid a period of repression that began in earnest in 2017, and saw the banning of the main opposition party, opposition leaders jailed or forced into exile, and remaining major independent media outlets reined in or closed. The CPP also dominated elections for the upper house, or Senate, held in February, taking every elected seat.
- The *Phnom Penh Post*, regarded by many observers as the last remaining independent media outlet in Cambodia, was taken over by a Malaysian businessman with links to Hun Sen.
- A Cambodian court sentenced an Australian filmmaker to six years in jail on charges of espionage. He had been arrested after denouncing rights abuses and filming political rallies.
- In November, the UN-assisted court known as the Khmer Rouge Tribunal found Nuon Chea and Khieu Samphan, two surviving leaders of the Khmer Rouge, guilty of genocide and crimes against humanity. The verdict for the first time legally defined the Khmer Rouge's crimes as genocide.

POLITICAL RIGHTS: 6 / 40 (–4)

A. ELECTORAL PROCESS: 1 / 12 (–3)

A1. Was the current head of government or other chief national authority elected through free and fair elections? 0 / 4 (–1)

King Norodom Sihamoni is chief of state, but has little political power. The prime minister is head of government, and is appointed by the monarch from among the majority coalition or party in parliament following legislative elections. Hun Sen first became prime minister in 1985. He was nominated most recently after 2018 National Assembly polls, which offered voters no meaningful choice. Most international observation groups were not present due to the highly restrictive nature of the contest.

Score Change: The score declined from 1 to 0 because the incumbent prime minister was unanimously confirmed for another term after parliamentary elections that offered voters no meaningful choice.

A2. Were the current national legislative representatives elected through free and fair elections? 0 / 4 (–1)

The bicameral parliament consists of the 62-seat Senate and the 125-seat National Assembly. Members of parliament and local councilors indirectly elect 58 senators, and the king and National Assembly each appoint 2. Senators serve six-year terms, while National Assembly members are directly elected to five-year terms.

In 2018, the CPP won every seat in both chambers in elections that were considered neither free nor fair by established international observers, which declined to monitor them. In the months before the polls, the Supreme Court had banned the main opposition Cambodia National Rescue Party (CNRP) and jailed many of its members, and closed media outlets and intimidated journalists to the extent that there was almost no independent reporting on the campaign or the polls. Several small, obscure new "opposition parties" ran candidates in the lower house elections, though many of the parties were widely believed to have been manufactured to suggest multiparty competition. Following calls for an election boycott by former CNRP leaders, Hun Sen repeatedly warned that people who did not vote in the election could be punished. The election was condemned by many democracies. The United States responded by imposing targeted sanctions on Cambodian leaders, while the EU threatened to roll back a preferential trade agreement.

Score Change: The score declined from 1 to 0 because the parliamentary elections took place in a highly repressive environment that offered voters no meaningful choice, and produced a one-party legislature.

A3. Are the electoral laws and framework fair, and are they implemented impartially by the relevant election management bodies? 1 / 4 (–1)

In 2015, Cambodia passed two new election laws that permit security forces to take part in campaigns, punish parties that boycott parliament, and mandate a shorter campaign period of 21 days. The laws have been broadly enforced.

Voting is tied to a citizen's permanent resident status in a village, township, or urban district, and this status cannot be changed easily. In 2017, an amendment to the electoral law banned political parties from association with anyone convicted of a criminal offense.

The National Election Committee (NEC) was reformed in 2013, but the CPP has since asserted complete control over its nine seats. Criminal charges were brought against the body's one independent member in 2016, who was then jailed and removed from the body. The four NEC members affiliated with the CNRP resigned following the party's 2017 dissolution. In 2018, the NEC sought to aid the CPP's campaign by threatening to prosecute any figures that urged an election boycott, and informing voters via text message that criticism of the CPP was prohibited.

Score Change: The score declined from 2 to 1 because the election commission, controlled by the ruling party since the ouster of independent and opposition members, participated in the government's efforts to control the outcome of the parliamentary elections.

B. POLITICAL PLURALISM AND PARTICIPATION: 2 / 16 (-1)

B1. Do the people have the right to organize in different political parties or other competitive political groupings of their choice, and is the system free of undue obstacles to the rise and fall of these competing parties or groupings? 0 / 4 (-1)

Following the 2018 elections, Cambodia is a de facto one-party state. The main opposition CNRP was banned and its leaders have been charged with crimes, while other prominent party figures have fled the country. Although several small opposition parties contested the 2018 July lower house elections, none won seats. All of the smaller parties were permitted to run by the CPP-controlled National Election Committee, and both domestic and international observers widely questioned their authenticity.

Score Change: The score declined from 1 to 0 because the only significant opposition party remained banned and persecuted even as multiple parties of dubious authenticity were allowed to register for parliamentary elections, creating an illusion of competition.

B2. Is there a realistic opportunity for the opposition to increase its support or gain power through elections? 0 / 4

The political opposition has been quashed, with the CNRP banned and its leaders facing criminal charges. The high rate of spoiled ballots in the 2018 lower house election—8.6 percent of all votes, according to the NEC—suggested strong popular discontent with the lack of choice, especially given that Hun Sen had repeatedly warned Cambodians not to spoil ballots. Elections for the upper house earlier in the year were similarly structured so that the CPP had no real opposition. There were widespread reports of voters being bullied and intimidated before the July lower house elections into casting a vote for the CPP.

After the elections, amid increasing international scrutiny, Hun Sen and the CPP modestly eased pressure on the opposition. In August, the king pardoned 14 CNRP members who had been jailed for "insurrection." CNRP co-leader Kem Sokha was released on bail in September after spending a year in solitary confinement on treason charges, though he still faced significant restrictions on his movement. Late in 2018, the government initiated legislation that could allow bans on political activity for some opposition figures to be lifted.

CNRP co-leader Sam Rainsy has remained abroad; he was convicted of defamation in 2017 and faces a number of other legal cases in Cambodia, and risks imprisonment if he returns. Many other prominent CNRP figures remain in exile. At year's end, the opposition appeared ready to split, with supporters of Rainsy and Kem Sokha seemingly parting ways.

B3. Are the people's political choices free from domination by the military, foreign powers, religious hierarchies, economic oligarchies, or any other powerful group that is not democratically accountable? 1 / 4

The ruling party is not democratically accountable, and top leaders, especially Hun Sen, use the police and armed forces as a tool of repression. The military has stood firmly behind Hun Sen and his violent threats, and his crackdown on opposition. Hun Sen has built a personal bodyguard unit in the armed forces that he reportedly uses to harass and abuse CPP opponents.

Before the 2018 lower house elections, Human Rights Watch reported that the security forces were illegally campaigning for the CPP. Additionally, several top military commanders won seats in the lower house as CPP legislators. One, General Pol Saroeun, then vacated his seat to become a senior minister in the new government.

B4. Do various segments of the population (including ethnic, religious, gender, LGBT, and other relevant groups) have full political rights and electoral opportunities? 1 / 4

Ethnic Vietnamese are regularly excluded from the political process and scapegoated by both parties. Women make up 15 percent of the National Assembly, but their interests, like those of all citizens, are not well represented.

C. FUNCTIONING OF GOVERNMENT: 3 / 12

C1. Do the freely elected head of government and national legislative representatives determine the policies of the government? 1 / 4

Hun Sen has increasingly centralized power, and figures outside of his close circle have little impact on policymaking. Some reports suggest he is preparing to eventually hand power to his son, Hun Manet, who has deep ties throughout the armed forces. In September, Hun Manet was promoted to commander of the armed forces.

C2. Are safeguards against official corruption strong and effective? 1 / 4

Anticorruption laws are poorly enforced, and corruption remains a serious challenge in Cambodia. A 2016 Global Witness report suggested that Hun Sen's family had amassed wealth totaling between $500 million and $1 billion, claims that the prime minister and his family deny. Corruption is rampant in public procurement, tax administration, customs administration, and other state processes, and bribes are frequently required in dealings with various government departments.

C3. Does the government operate with openness and transparency? 1 / 4

Nepotism and patronage undermine the functioning of a transparent bureaucratic system. A draft access to information law was made public in January 2018, though domestic observers expressed concern that upon implementation it would be ignored or misused. The law was pending at year's end.

CIVIL LIBERTIES: 20 / 60
D. FREEDOM OF EXPRESSION AND BELIEF: 8 / 16
D1. Are there free and independent media? 1 / 4

The government uses lawsuits, criminal prosecutions, massive tax bills, and occasionally violent attacks as means of intimidation against the media. There are private print and broadcast outlets, but many are owned and operated by the CPP.

Starting in 2017 the government engaged in an intense crackdown on independent media, and these efforts continued throughout 2018. In 2017, the independent *Cambodia Daily* closed under pressure from the government regarding its tax bills. In 2018, the *Phnom Penh Post*, known for its independent and investigative reporting, was sold to a Malaysian investor with links to Hun Sen, and many of its editors and reporters quit or were fired following the sale. In addition, many other local media outlets were intimidated into closing or, in the run-up to the July lower house elections, becoming government mouthpieces. Before the lower house elections, the election commission released a code of conduct for journalists that mandated fines of as much as $7,500 for using "their own ideas to make conclusions" or publishing news deemed to "affect political and social stability" or cause "confusion and loss of confidence" regarding the election.

Two Radio Free Asia journalists arrested in 2017 on charges of espionage still face trial in Cambodia. In August 2018, an Australian filmmaker was sentenced to six years in jail for espionage, after creating footage about rights abuses and public rallies. Late in 2018, Hun Sen publicly promised to ease pressure on independent media, as well as on civil society more generally and on the political opposition; his government offered to allow the *Cambodia Daily* and Radio Free Asia to reopen in Cambodia, although it remained unclear whether they would do so.

D2. Are individuals free to practice and express their religious faith or nonbelief in public and private? 3 / 4

The majority of Cambodians are Theravada Buddhists and can practice their faith freely, but societal discrimination against religious and ethnic minorities persists.

D3. Is there academic freedom, and is the educational system free from extensive political indoctrination? 2 / 4

Teachers and students practice self-censorship regarding discussions about Cambodian politics and history. Criticism of the prime minister and his family is often punished.

D4. Are individuals free to express their personal views on political or other sensitive topics without fear of surveillance or retribution? 2 / 4

The state generally does not intervene in people's private discussions, though open criticism of the prime minister can result in reprisals. In 2018, however, Hun Sen and other government leaders warned ahead of the lower house election that criticism of the government would be punished severely. Additionally, an order issued before the election required internet service providers (ISPs) to install software necessary to monitor, filter, and block "illegal" online content, including social media accounts.

Earlier, in February, an amendment to the criminal code introduced a new *lèse-majesté* offense that made it illegal to defame, insult, or threaten the king. The law carries a sentence of between one and five years in jail, and a fine of 2 to 10 million riel (about $500 to $2,500).

E. ASSOCIATIONAL AND ORGANIZATIONAL RIGHTS: 3 / 12
E1. Is there freedom of assembly? 1 / 4

Authorities are openly hostile to free assembly. The shooting deaths of five postelection protesters by security forces in 2014 discouraged opposition demonstrations, as have continued government assertions that dissent will not be tolerated. The few small opposition parties that did contest the lower house elections had few or no events. In March, a land dispute in Kratie over the activities of a rubber plantation resulted in police firing on protestors and possibly killing eight people, although reports of the incident vary.

E2. Is there freedom for nongovernmental organizations, particularly those that are engaged in human rights- and governance-related work? 1 / 4

Activists and civil society groups dedicated to justice and human rights face increasing state harassment. Prominent activist Kem Ley was murdered in broad daylight in 2016. In January 2018, three activists involved with planning his funeral were charged with embezzlement, though charges against one of them were later dropped. A number of other activists faced legal harassment during the year, including some with the Cambodian Human Rights and Development Association (ADHOC). The National Democratic Institute, a US-based nongovernmental organization (NGO), was forced to shut its Cambodia operations in 2017.

A variety of less overtly political groups are able to operate.

E3. Is there freedom for trade unions and similar professional or labor organizations? 1 / 4

Cambodia has a small number of independent trade unions, and workers have the right to strike, but many face retribution for doing so. A 2016 law on trade unions imposed restrictions such as excessive requirements for union formation.

F. RULE OF LAW: 3 / 16
F1. Is there an independent judiciary? 0 / 4

The judiciary is marred by corruption and a lack of independence. Judges have facilitated the government's ability to pursue charges against a broad range of opposition politicians, and played a central role in keeping Kem Sokha in a remote jail, without bail, despite significant health problems, for nearly a year. He was finally freed on bail in September 2018, but with severe restrictions on his movement.

F2. Does due process prevail in civil and criminal matters? 1 / 4

Due process rights are poorly upheld in Cambodia. Abuse by law enforcement officers and judges, including illegal detention, remains extremely common. Sham trials are frequent, while elites generally enjoy impunity. When lawyers or others criticize judges, they often face retribution.

F3. Is there protection from the illegitimate use of physical force and freedom from war and insurgencies? 1 / 4

Cambodians live in an environment of tight repression and fear. The torture of suspects and prisoners is frequent. The security forces are regularly accused of using excessive force against detained suspects.

The ongoing work of the Extraordinary Chambers in the Courts of Cambodia (ECCC), established to try the leaders of the former Khmer Rouge regime, has brought convictions for crimes against humanity, homicide, torture, and religious persecution. In November 2018, the tribunal found Nuon Chea and Khieu Samphan, two surviving leaders of the Khmer Rouge, guilty of genocide and crimes against humanity. They both received life sentences; both had already been sentenced to life in prison for past convictions of crimes against humanity. The 2018 convictions marked the first time the Khmer Rouge crimes were legally defined as genocide.

While others closer to the regime have faced allegations of involvement in these crimes, there is little indication the Hun Sen government will support additional prosecutions. It appears likely that there will be no further cases brought to the ECCC.

F4. Do laws, policies, and practices guarantee equal treatment of various segments of the population? 1 / 4

Minorities, especially those of Vietnamese descent, often face legal and societal discrimination. Officials and opposition leaders, including Sam Rainsy, have demonized minorities publicly.

The Cambodian government frequently refuses to grant refugee protections to Montagnards fleeing Vietnam, where they face persecution by the Vietnamese government.

While same-sex relationships are not criminalized, LGBT individuals have no legal protections from discrimination.

G. PERSONAL AUTONOMY AND INDIVIDUAL RIGHTS: 6 / 16
G1. Do individuals enjoy freedom of movement, including the ability to change their place of residence, employment, or education? 2 / 4

The constitution guarantees the rights to freedom of travel and movement, and the government generally respects these rights in practice. However, restrictions do occur, notably when the government tries to prevent activists from traveling around the country.

G2. Are individuals able to exercise the right to own property and establish private businesses without undue interference from state or nonstate actors? 1 / 4

Land and property rights are regularly abused for the sake of private development projects. Over the past several years, hundreds of thousands of people have been forcibly removed from their homes, with little or no compensation, to make room for commercial plantations, mine operations, factories, and high-end residential developments.

G3. Do individuals enjoy personal social freedoms, including choice of marriage partner and size of family, protection from domestic violence, and control over appearance? 2 / 4

The government does not frequently repress personal social freedoms, but women suffer widespread social discrimination. Rape and violence against women are common.

G4. Do individuals enjoy equality of opportunity and freedom from economic exploitation? 1 / 4

Equality of opportunity is severely limited in Cambodia, where a small elite controls most of the economy. Labor conditions can be harsh, sometimes sparking protests. Sex and labor trafficking remains a significant problem, and while the government's program to combat it is inadequate, the US State Department has said the Cambodian government has increased its antitrafficking efforts.

Cameroon

Population: 25,600,000
Capital: Yaoundé
Political Rights Rating: 6
Civil Liberties Rating: 6
Freedom Rating: 6.0
Freedom Status: Not Free
Electoral Democracy: No

Overview: President Paul Biya has ruled Cameroon since 1982. His Cameroon People's Democratic Movement (CPDM) has maintained power by rigging elections, using state resources for political patronage, and limiting the activities of opposition parties. Security forces use violence to disperse antigovernment protests. The Boko Haram insurgent group continues to attack civilians in northern Cameroon, and security forces responding to the insurgency have been accused of committing human rights violations against civilians. The conflict between security forces and separatists in the Anglophone Northwest and Southwest Regions has intensified, resulting in widespread civilian deaths and displacements.

KEY DEVELOPMENTS IN 2018:
- President Paul Biya won a seventh term in October's presidential election, which was marked by low turnout and a lack of genuine democratic competition. Threats of violence and intimidation in the Anglophone Northwest and Southwest Regions

made voting nearly impossible in some areas. Senatorial elections in March 2018 resulted in the ruling CPDM winning 63 of 70 contested seats.

- In July, the government announced that local and legislative elections scheduled for October 2018 would be postponed until October 2019, citing the logistical difficulty of managing presidential, legislative, and municipal elections concurrently.
- The conflict in the Anglophone regions worsened throughout the year, with increased civilian deaths and displacements. Intense fighting between separatists and security forces threatened to escalate into civil war.
- The government continued to crack down on journalists and civil society leaders who criticized policies in the Anglophone regions. In May, radio journalist and Anglophone advocate Mancho Bibixy was sentenced to prison along with six other Anglophone activists after being convicted on terrorism charges.

POLITICAL RIGHTS: 7 / 40 (-2)

A. ELECTORAL PROCESS: 1 / 12 (-2)

A1. Was the current head of government or other chief national authority elected through free and fair elections? 0 / 4 (-1)

The president, who holds most executive power, is directly elected to a seven-year term in a single voting round and may serve an unlimited number of terms. The president appoints the prime minister, who lacks power but formally serves as head of government. President Paul Biya won a seventh term in the October 2018 presidential election, taking 71 percent of the vote in a process marked by low turnout and a lack of genuine democratic competition. Maurice Kamto of the Cameroon Renaissance Movement (CRM) came in second with 14 percent of the vote. The election was tainted by irregularities such as unsigned results sheets, and intimidation and fear in the Anglophone regions kept many from casting their votes. A television report in the aftermath of the election that included supposed Transparency International observers praising the electoral process caused confusion and controversy; Transparency International issued a statement after the report aired asserting that they had no election observers in Cameroon.

In the Anglophone Northwest and Southwest Regions, separatists called for an election boycott, and armed militants used threats and intimidation to keep voters away from the polls. Out of 2,300 polling stations in the Northwest Region, only 74 opened on election day. Approximately 15 percent of registered voters cast ballots in the Southwest Region, while turnout was only 5 percent in the Northwest Region.

Score Change: The score declined from 1 to 0 due to the creation of a new Constitutional Council with power to certify election results and adjudicate election disputes that is comprised mostly of individuals with links to the ruling party.

A2. Were the current national legislative representatives elected through free and fair elections? 1 / 4

The upper chamber of Cameroon's bicameral Parliament is the 100-member Senate. Senators serve five-year terms; 70 are elected through indirect suffrage by regional councils, while the remaining 30 are appointed by the president. The 180 members of the National Assembly, the lower chamber, are directly elected in single-member and multimember constituencies to five-year terms.

Senatorial elections in March 2018 resulted in the ruling CPDM winning 63 of 70 contested seats. The main opposition party, the Anglophone-led Social Democratic Front (SDF) won the remaining 7 seats, all based in the Northwest Region, even as separatist groups warned that they would not permit voting. The 30 remaining senators, appointed by the president at his prerogative, all belong to the CPDM. The SDF alleged fraud and intimidation in the Northwest and Southwest Regions, and petitioned the Constitutional Council to cancel election results in the Southwest Region, but the council rejected the petition.

In July, the government announced that local and legislative elections scheduled for October 2018 would be postponed until October 2019, citing the logistical difficulty of managing presidential, legislative, and municipal elections concurrently.

The last National Assembly elections were held in 2013, in which the CPDM took 148 out of 180 seats. Although some observers claimed the poll was credible, the CPDM enjoyed significant structural advantages over the weak and fragmented opposition parties, reducing the competitiveness of the process.

A3. Are the electoral laws and framework fair, and are they implemented impartially by the relevant election management bodies? 0 / 4 (–1)

The independence and integrity of Cameroon's electoral framework was compromised by the creation of the Constitutional Council in February 2018, just eight months before the presidential election. The new council has the power to validate election results and adjudicate election disputes, and the majority of its 11 members have ties to the ruling party. The council rejected all 18 petitions to cancel the presidential election results filed by opposition parties in October, despite credible allegations of fraud and intimidation.

The other electoral body, Elections Cameroon (ELECAM), is responsible for organizing the polls. ELECAM was created in 2006 to address concerns about the fair management of previous elections. However, President Biya chooses its members, and CPDM partisans have historically dominated the body.

Score Change: The score declined from 1 to 0 due to the creation of a new Constitutional Council that has the power to certify election results and adjudicate election disputes, and which is comprised mostly of individuals with links to the ruling party.

B. POLITICAL PLURALISM AND PARTICIPATION: 3 / 16

B1. Do the people have the right to organize in different political parties or other competitive political groupings of their choice, and is the system free of undue obstacles to the rise and fall of these competing parties or groupings? 1 / 4

The ability to organize political groups, and their freedom to operate, is subject to the whims of the central government, and opposition leaders risk arrest and imprisonment. In 2018, several opposition figures were investigated, harassed, or arrested by authorities. On election day in October, CRM official Thierry Okala Ebode was arrested and held in a Yaoundé jail for eight days after protesting alleged fraud at a local polling station. During the immediate postelection period, the police and security forces raided the home of democracy activist Yondo Black hours before a planned press conference with CRM candidate Maurice Kamto. The police, without a warrant, later interrupted the press conference, which had been relocated to another CRM supporter's home.

Opposition rallies are also frequently prohibited. In October, police disrupted an unauthorized rally organized by the SDF in Douala to protest the election by encircling the home of the protest's leader before it was to begin. Some 30 people were additionally arrested along the planned protest route. On election day in October, opposition party representatives were expelled from some polling stations by supporters of the CPDM.

B2. Is there a realistic opportunity for the opposition to increase its support or gain power through elections? 0 / 4

Despite the existence of hundreds of registered political parties, Cameroon remains essentially a one-party state. The organizational advantages of the ruling party's long incumbency, its dominance over electoral bodies, and its superior access to media and resources disadvantages opposition candidates. Opposition parties are highly fragmented, preventing any one of them from becoming a viable alternative to the ruling CPDM. An opposition coalition formed ahead of the October 2018 presidential election, when Akere Muna of the People's Development Front (FDP) withdrew his candidacy to support Kamto, was unable to mobilize enough support to mount a strong challenge Biya.

Frequent harassment, intimidation, and arrests of opposition figures further reduces the ability of opposition parties to gain power through elections.

B3. Are the people's political choices free from domination by the military, foreign powers, religious hierarchies, economic oligarchies, or any other powerful group that is not democratically accountable? 1 / 4

State patronage and President Biya's control of high-level appointments help the CPDM retain power. Insecurity in the Anglophone regions caused by violence between armed militants and the military made voting nearly impossible in the October 2018 presidential election, effectively denying voters a political choice.

B4. Do various segments of the population (including ethnic, religious, gender, LGBT, and other relevant groups) have full political rights and electoral opportunities? 1 / 4

Groups advocating for greater self-determination in the Anglophone regions remain marginalized and excluded from political debate, as reflected by, among other things, the 2017 banning of the Southern Cameroons National Council (SCNC), an Anglophone political group. LGBT (lesbian, gay, bisexual, and transgender) people, and some ethnic minorities, such as the Bamiléké, are generally excluded from political processes, and their interests are poorly represented by elected officials.

In practice, women are able to advocate for their interests only through representation in the CPDM. The government has expressed a commitment to increasing women's representation in Parliament. In the National Assembly, 31 percent of deputies are women, while 26 percent of senators are women. However, only 30 percent of registered voters in 2018 were women.

C. FUNCTIONING OF GOVERNMENT: 3 / 12

C1. Do the freely elected head of government and national legislative representatives determine the policies of the government? 1 / 4

In principle, laws and policies in Cameroon are created and approved by Parliament and the president. In practice, many policies are adopted by presidential decree. Otherwise, Parliament shows little independence and largely acts as a rubber stamp for the president's policy initiatives. President Biya has extensive executive authority, including wide-ranging appointment powers and strong control over state institutions.

C2. Are safeguards against official corruption strong and effective? 1 / 4

Corruption is systemic and bribery is commonplace in all sectors. Corrupt officials often act with impunity. Initiatives to fight corruption, including the creation of the National Anticorruption Commission (CONAC), have been insufficient. Although a number of former high-level government officials have been successfully prosecuted and imprisoned for corruption, analysts suspect that many such cases were politically motivated and do not reflect a commitment to tackling the systemic nature of the problem.

C3. Does the government operate with openness and transparency? 1 / 4

Decisions, especially those made by presidential decree, are often adopted with little or no public consultation. Cameroon lacks an access to information law, and it is difficult to gain access to government documents or statistics in practice. Despite the launch of an e-governance initiative in 2006, which was tasked with making government data more available online, the websites of most ministries do not provide substantial information.

CIVIL LIBERTIES: 12 / 60 (-1)
D. FREEDOM OF EXPRESSION AND BELIEF: 5 / 16 (-1)
D1. Are there free and independent media? 0 / 4 (-1)

Independent and critical journalists face pressure and the risk of detention or arrest in connection with their work. Defamation remains a criminal offense, and the National Communications Council (CNC), a media regulatory body, has a history of harassing journalists and outlets.

In 2018, the government continued to clamp down on media coverage of the Anglophone protest movement. Radio journalist Mancho Bibixy, who was arrested in 2017 on terrorism charges after he advocated for Anglophone rights and criticized government policies, was sentenced to 15 years' imprisonment in May. In October, journalist Michel Biem Tong, who reported on the crisis in the Anglophone regions, was arrested and charged with "glorifying terrorism." He was later among the 289 people pardoned by President Biya who had been arrested in connection with the Anglophone conflict. However, other journalists remained imprisoned or jailed for their reporting at year's end.

A series of internet shutdowns in the Northwest and Southwest Regions that began in early 2017 continued into 2018. Between January 2017 and March 2018, the internet was shut down for a total of 230 days in the Anglophone regions, curtailing free expression and the exchange of information among those impacted.

The national television channel, CRTV, has been criticized for favoring the CPDM in its political coverage. CRTV aired the segment in October that featured fake election observers from Transparency International approving of the conduct of the presidential poll. At year's end, the debunked story remained on CRTV's website.

Score Change: The score declined from 1 to 0 due to an internet shutdown that continued for nearly a year in the Anglophone regions, and the persistent harassment and arrests of journalists, particularly those covering the Anglophone crisis.

D2. Are individuals free to practice and express their religious faith or nonbelief in public and private? 2 / 4

Religious freedom is somewhat restricted in northern areas affected by the presence of the Boko Haram militant group, which has carried out violent attacks against places of worship. In 2015, the government banned full-face veils in the Far North Region following suicide bombings that were attributed to veiled women associated with Boko Haram.

There were violent attacks against Roman Catholic clergy, believers, and facilities in 2018 in connection with the conflict in the Anglophone regions. These included the murders and detentions of priests, and the burning of a Catholic primary school in Bamessing.

Separately, the government has at times closed churches in order to encourage resolutions to leadership disputes.

D3. Is there academic freedom, and is the educational system free from extensive political indoctrination? 2 / 4

There are no legal restrictions on academic freedom, but state security informants operate on university campuses and academics can face negative repercussions for criticizing the government. In late 2017, Patrice Nganang, a literature professor at Stony Brook University (State University of New York), was arrested by authorities while attempting to leave Cameroon, following the publication of an article he wrote that was critical of the government. Nganang was released at the end of 2017 and barred from returning to Cameroon.

D4. Are individuals free to express their personal views on political or other sensitive topics without fear of surveillance or retribution? 1 / 4

Public criticism of the government and membership in opposition political parties can have a negative impact on professional opportunities and advancement. Cameroonians tend to avoid discussing sensitive political issues for fear of reprisals, notably the potential for a return to a federal system that would grant the Anglophone regions more autonomy, or the regions' outright secession.

Authorities have also periodically blocked or slowed access to social networking sites to quash dissent and prevent opposition forces from mobilizing. In October 2018, as the government prepared to announce the election results, access to social media platforms including Facebook, Twitter, and WhatsApp was slowed by internet service providers.

E. ASSOCIATIONAL AND ORGANIZATIONAL RIGHTS: 2 / 12

E1. Is there freedom of assembly? 0 / 4

Freedom of assembly is subject to significant restrictions. Authorities continued to repress protests in the Anglophone regions in 2018. In March, more than 100 women in the Cameroon People's Party (CPP) were arrested and detained for several days for staging a demonstration to protest the humanitarian crisis in the Anglophone regions. Ahead of October 1, which Anglophone separatists consider their symbolic "independence day," a 48-hour curfew was imposed in the Anglophone regions, and gatherings of more than four people were prohibited. Assembly rights were also curtailed after the election. In November, authorities arrested 20 protesters in Yaoundé who claimed that Maurice Kamto had won the election.

E2. Is there freedom for nongovernmental organizations, particularly those that are engaged in human rights– and governance-related work? 1 / 4

The influence of civil society has gradually weakened over the years, with many nongovernmental organizations (NGOs) relying entirely on foreign assistance, and others coopted by the regime.

Anglophone activists have faced harassment, violence, and arrest for their work. In May 2018, six other Anglophone activists received prison sentences after being convicted on terrorism charges. In 2017, the SCNC, an Anglophone political group, was banned for supporting secession.

LGBT organizations have also been targeted by law enforcement. In April, four members of AJO, an NGO that works on behalf of sex workers and LGBT people, were arrested for homosexuality and jailed for a week before the charges were dropped.

E3. Is there freedom for trade unions and similar professional or labor organizations? 1 / 4

Trade unions, strikes, and collective bargaining are legally permitted, although unions are still subject to numerous restrictions in the exercise of their rights.

F. RULE OF LAW: 1 / 16

F1. Is there an independent judiciary? 0 / 4

The judiciary is subordinate to the Ministry of Justice, and political influence and corruption weaken courts. Judges are appointed by the president, who may also dismiss them at will. Executive interference can influence judicial proceedings: prosecutors have been pressured to stop pursuing corruption cases against some high-profile officials, while critics allege that corruption charges have been used to punish officials who have fallen out of favor with the regime.

F2. Does due process prevail in civil and criminal matters? 1 / 4

Due process rights are generally not respected. Lengthy pretrial detentions are commonplace. State security forces have carried out arbitrary detentions in connection with the Anglophone crisis, and in the Far North Region in response to Boko Haram activity. Defendants are frequently not afforded the right to a fair trial, particularly in terrorism cases. French legal norms are regularly imposed upon Cameroonians in Anglophone regions.

F3. Is there protection from the illegitimate use of physical force and freedom from war and insurgencies? 0 / 4

Active conflicts involving both Boko Haram and Anglophone separatists threaten the security of millions of people in Cameroon. Clashes between state security forces and separatists intensified in the Anglophone regions in 2018. As of December, homes and buildings in more than 100 villages had been burned by security forces. Both separatists and soldiers have killed scores of civilians in the escalating violence that has brought the country to the brink of civil war.

Although the conflict with Boko Haram deescalated in 2018, insurgents continue to conduct attacks in the Far North Region, and state security forces there have been accused of torturing alleged Boko Haram collaborators, many of whom are held without charge. In July, a video circulated online that showed the extrajudicial executions of two women and two children by soldiers who accused them of involvement with Boko Haram. The video sparked international outrage, and in September, after initially denying that the military was responsible for the crimes, the government announced that seven soldiers had been arrested and would be tried for murder.

In December, President Biya established a National Disarmament, Demobilization, and Reintegration Committee (NDDRC) for ex-fighters of Boko Haram and armed Anglophone separatist groups. Analysts are skeptical about whether the committee will be able to effectively address the conflict in the Anglophone regions, given government policies and practices that have exacerbated the crisis there.

F4. Do laws, policies, and practices guarantee equal treatment of various segments of the population? 0 / 4

Discrimination against Anglophone Cameroonians and individuals from certain ethnic groups including the Bamiléké is common. The government imposes the French language in Anglophone regions, and Anglophone Cameroonians are frequently denied senior jobs in the civil service. Discrimination against the LGBT community is rife, and violence against LGBT people is not uncommon. The penal code forbids "sexual relations with a person of the same sex" and includes prison sentences of up to five years for the crime. In practice, people are frequently prosecuted with no evidence of sexual activity, but rather on suspicions that they are gay.

The Boko Haram conflict in the Far North Region and the Anglophone crisis has led thousands to flee their homes. As of December 2018, there were approximately 437,500 internally displaced persons (IDPs) in the Northwest and Southwest Regions. IDPs struggle to access food, education, and other basic needs, and displaced women commonly face gender-based violence.

G. PERSONAL AUTONOMY AND INDIVIDUAL RIGHTS: 4 / 16

G1. Do individuals enjoy freedom of movement, including the ability to change their place of residence, employment, or education? 1 / 4

Free movement is difficult in parts of the Far North Region due to Boko Haram activity. Movement in the two Anglophone regions has been impeded by the ongoing crisis there, as well. In September 2018, the governor of the Northwest Region imposed a dusk-to-dawn curfew in response to separatist attacks. The curfew was temporarily suspended at the end of the year. A 48-hour curfew was also imposed in the Anglophone regions leading up to "independence day" on October 1.

G2. Are individuals able to exercise the right to own property and establish private businesses without undue interference from state or nonstate actors? 1 / 4

Harassment of small business owners by state agents is common. Agribusinesses and logging operations are often carried out without consulting local inhabitants. Customary law makes it difficult for women to own property. In many regions, women are still dispossessed of their inheritance rights.

G3. Do individuals enjoy personal social freedoms, including choice of marriage partner and size of family, protection from domestic violence, and control over appearance? 1 / 4

The constitution guarantees equal rights to men and women, but traditional legal values and practices often take precedence and do not always provide women with full rights. The Boko Haram conflict has exacerbated the already prevalent practice of child marriage and sexual abuse of minors in the Far North Region. Customary law can allow rapists to escape punishment if the victim consents to marriage. Despite laws guaranteeing equal rights to men and women to file for divorce, in practice courts often disadvantage women by making proceedings prohibitively expensive or lengthy. Domestic violence and rape are widespread, and perpetrators are rarely prosecuted.

G4. Do individuals enjoy equality of opportunity and freedom from economic exploitation? 1 / 4

Despite a 2011 law against human trafficking, Cameroon remains a source, transit, and destination country for forced labor and sex trafficking of children, as well as a source country for women who are subject to forced labor and prostitution in Europe. Child labor remains common, and child workers are frequently exposed to hazardous working conditions, particularly when collecting scrap metal for sale.

Canada

Population: 37,200,000
Capital: Ottawa
Political Rights Rating: 1
Civil Liberties Rating: 1
Freedom Rating: 1.0
Freedom Status: Free
Electoral Democracy: Yes

Overview: Canada has a strong history of respect for political rights and civil liberties, though recent years have seen concerns about the scope of government surveillance laws, as well as about court rulings compelling journalists to reveal their sources. While indigenous peoples and other vulnerable populations still face discrimination and other economic, social, and political challenges, the federal government has acknowledged and made some moves to address these issues.

KEY DEVELOPMENTS IN 2018:

- In December, the government passed a law that relaxed stringent voter identification requirements contained in the 2014 Fair Elections Act, which had drawn criticism for disadvantaging indigenous voters.
- The new law, which will be in effect for the next scheduled federal elections, additionally granted voting rights to all Canadians living abroad, improved privacy protections for voters, banned foreign donations to partisan campaigns, and required major online platforms to create a registry of digital political advertisements.
- Three bills working their way through Parliament were criticized for, respectively, making it harder to request information from government; giving excessive powers to spy agencies; and failing to effectively curb the use of solitary confinement in prisons. All were pending at year's end.
- In November, the Supreme Court upheld a police order that *Vice News* hand over correspondence between its reporter and a Canadian-Somali citizen facing terrorism charges.

POLITICAL RIGHTS: 40 / 40

A. ELECTORAL PROCESS: 12 / 12

A1. Was the current head of government or other chief national authority elected through free and fair elections? 4 / 4

The British monarch is head of state, represented by a ceremonial governor general who is appointed on the advice of the prime minister. The prime minister is the head of government and is designated by the general governor after elections; the office is usually held by the leader of the majority party or coalition in parliament.

A2. Were the current national legislative representatives elected through free and fair elections? 4 / 4

The parliament consists of an elected 338-member House of Commons, and an appointed 105-member Senate. Lower-house elections are held every four years on fixed dates;

early elections may be called by the governor general if the government loses a parliamentary no-confidence vote, or on the advice of the prime minister.

The most recent elections were held in 2015. The Organization for Security and Co-operation in Europe (OSCE) conducted a needs assessment mission before the election, as well as a mission during the vote. The group concluded that the elections were competitive and credible, but called for greater minority participation.

A3. Are the electoral laws and framework fair, and are they implemented impartially by the relevant election management bodies? 4 / 4

Electoral laws are generally fair and are well enforced by the relevant bodies. However, some observers have expressed concern about the 2014 Fair Elections Act, arguing that its stringent voter identification requirements place indigenous peoples at a disadvantage. In December 2018, the Liberal government passed a bill relaxing some of the criticized provisions. The new law also restricts spending by political parties and other actors during elections, gives voting rights to all Canadians living abroad, improves the privacy of voters' information within political parties' databases, and increases the power of the Commissioner of Elections to investigate violations of election laws. It also bans using foreign donations to run partisan campaigns and requires major online platforms, such as Facebook and Google, to create a registry of digital political advertisements.

B. POLITICAL PLURALISM AND PARTICIPATION: 16 / 16

B1. Do the people have the right to organize in different political parties or other competitive political groupings of their choice, and is the system free of undue obstacles to the rise and fall of these competing parties or groupings? 4 / 4

Canadians are free to organize in different political parties, and the system is open to the rise and fall of competing parties. While two parties have traditionally dominated the political system—the Conservative Party, espousing a center-right to right-wing political position, and the Liberal Party, espousing a center to center-left position—recent years have seen the rise of new groups. A total of 23 political parties were registered in the 2015 election.

B2. Is there a realistic opportunity for the opposition to increase its support or gain power through elections? 4 / 4

Opposition parties have a realistic chance of gaining power through elections. In 2015, the center-left New Democratic Party (NDP) lost its status as the official opposition party in the House of Commons after the vote, and the Conservatives became the dominant opposition to the Liberal government.

B3. Are the people's political choices free from domination by the military, foreign powers, religious hierarchies, economic oligarchies, or any other powerful group that is not democratically accountable? 4 / 4

People's political choices are generally free from domination by actors that are not democratically accountable.

B4. Do various segments of the population (including ethnic, religious, gender, LGBT, and other relevant groups) have full political rights and electoral opportunities? 4 / 4

Members of religious minorities and indigenous people are seated in the parliament, as are many women. However, their political interests are not always well represented. For example, critical issues facing Canada's indigenous peoples, including high rates of suicide, violent victimization, and murder, received little attention in the 2015 electoral campaign.

The rights and interests of LGBT (lesbian, gay, bisexual, and transgender) people are protected. A 2017 law explicitly prohibits discrimination based on gender identity or gender expression, affording transgender individuals among others more protection against hate crimes.

C. FUNCTIONING OF GOVERNMENT: 12 / 12

C1. Do the freely elected head of government and national legislative representatives determine the policies of the government? 4 / 4

Canada's freely elected government determines policy.

C2. Are safeguards against official corruption strong and effective? 4 / 4

Canada has a reputation for clean government and a record of vigorous prosecution of corruption cases.

C3. Does the government operate with openness and transparency? 4 / 4

Canadians may request public information under the provisions of the Access to Information Act, but may face delays or excessive costs. In 2017, the Liberal government proposed a number of reforms to the act, but the measures have been criticized as inadequate; the Information Commissioner of Canada argued that the proposal would actually "result in a regression of existing rights" by creating new hurdles for requesters and giving agencies additional grounds for refusing requests. This bill passed in the House of Commons in late 2017 with no substantial amendments, and remained before the Senate in 2018.

CIVIL LIBERTIES: 59 / 60

D. FREEDOM OF EXPRESSION AND BELIEF: 16 / 16

D1. Are there free and independent media? 4 / 4

Canada's media are generally free; journalists are mostly protected from violence and harassment in their work and are able to express diverse viewpoints. A law permitting journalists greater ability to protect their sources took effect in 2017. It stipulates that journalists cannot be required to disclose confidential sources unless a Superior Court judge is persuaded that the information cannot be obtained through other means, and that it is in the public interest for the source to be revealed. Nevertheless, there were two notable rulings against journalists in 2018. In March, a court in Quebec ruled that an investigative journalist with the public broadcaster must disclose the identity of her sources as part of an ongoing corruption case involving members of the Liberal Party. And in November, the Supreme Court upheld a police order that *Vice News* hand over correspondence between its reporter and a former Calgary resident and Somali-Canadian citizen facing terrorism charges over alleged links to the Islamic State (IS) militant group.

D2. Are individuals free to practice and express their religious faith or nonbelief in public and private? 4 / 4

The constitution and other legislation protect religious freedom. However, controversy erupted in October 2018 when it was reported that the new provincial government in Quebec intended to prohibit the wearing of religious symbols such as yarmulkes or hijabs by public employees at work.

There are occasional instances of vandalism of Jewish and Muslim places of worship and cultural centers.

D3. Is there academic freedom, and is the educational system free from extensive political indoctrination? 4 / 4

Academic freedom is generally respected.

D4. Are individuals free to express their personal views on political or other sensitive topics without fear of surveillance or retribution? 4 / 4

Private discussion in Canada is generally free and unrestrained. However, in 2015, the former Conservative government passed a controversial antiterrorism law granting the Canadian Security Intelligence Service (CSIS) wider authority to conduct surveillance and share information about individuals with other agencies. Its passage elicited considerable condemnation from Canadian intellectuals as well as both domestic and foreign civil liberties watchdogs, who warned that it undermined the concept of privacy and could harm freedom of expression.

In 2017, the Liberal government introduced a bill that would reverse some of the law's provisions and establish an independent review and complaints body and a parliamentary committee to monitor Canada's intelligence-gathering agencies. However, it has also been criticized for giving Canada's spy agencies excessive powers to perform surveillance on Canadians without their knowledge, and for failing to explicitly prohibit the use of intelligence gathered by foreign entities through torture. The bill passed in the House of Commons in June 2018, and remained before the Senate at the end of the year.

E. ASSOCIATIONAL AND ORGANIZATIONAL RIGHTS: 12 / 12
E1. Is there freedom of assembly? 4 / 4

Freedom of assembly is constitutionally protected and upheld in practice.

E2. Is there freedom for nongovernmental organizations, particularly those that are engaged in human rights– and governance-related work? 4 / 4

Nongovernmental organizations (NGOs) operate freely and frequently inform policy discussions.

E3. Is there freedom for trade unions and similar professional or labor organizations? 4 / 4

Trade unions and business associations enjoy high levels of membership and are well organized.

F. RULE OF LAW: 15 / 16
F1. Is there an independent judiciary? 4 / 4

Canada's judiciary is generally independent.

F2. Does due process prevail in civil and criminal matters? 4 / 4

Constitutionally protected due process rights are generally upheld in practice. Canada's criminal law is based on legislation enacted by Parliament; its tort and contract law is based on English common law, with the exception of Quebec, where it is based on the French civil code.

F3. Is there protection from the illegitimate use of physical force and freedom from war and insurgencies? 4 / 4

The use of solitary confinement for extended periods of time in Canada's prisons has been controversial, with many critics charging that the time that inmates are excluded from the general population of prisoners is becoming excessive, and that prisoners with mental health issues are frequently placed in solitary confinement, resulting in harm. Provincial courts have ruled that parts of the federal law governing solitary confinement violated the rights of prisoners guaranteed by the Canadian Charter of Rights and Freedoms. The federal government in 2017 introduced a bill mandating that federal inmates may not stay in solitary confinement for longer than 21 consecutive days—with the cap lowered to 15 days 18 months after the legislation comes into force—unless the prison warden specifically orders otherwise. Legal advocates for prisoners claim the bill would have little practical effect other than to force wardens to review solitary confinement orders slightly earlier than they do presently. In response to criticism of the bill, the government introduced a second piece of legislation in October 2018. However, critics have charged that this new bill does no more than "rebrand" solitary confinement in a way that still allows Canadian prisons to keep people in isolation with few limitations.

F4. Do laws, policies, and practices guarantee equal treatment of various segments of the population? 3 / 4

The government had made increasing efforts to enforce equal rights and opportunities for minority groups, although some problems persist, particularly for Canada's indigenous peoples, who remain subject to discrimination and have unequal access to education, health care, and employment.

In May 2018, the House of Commons approved a bill that would mandate the development and implementation of a national action plan to achieve the objectives of the United Nations Declaration on the Rights of Indigenous Peoples. At the end of the year the bill remained before the Senate.

G. PERSONAL AUTONOMY AND INDIVIDUAL RIGHTS: 16 / 16

G1. Do individuals enjoy freedom of movement, including the ability to change their place of residence, employment, or education? 4 / 4

Freedom of movement is constitutionally protected and upheld in practice.

G2. Are individuals able to exercise the right to own property and establish private businesses without undue interference from state or nonstate actors? 4 / 4

Property rights are not constitutionally guaranteed, but in practice they are generally well protected by laws and through the enforcement of contracts.

G3. Do individuals enjoy personal social freedoms, including choice of marriage partner and size of family, protection from domestic violence, and control over appearance? 4 / 4

Canada legalized same-sex marriage in 2005.

Domestic violence is a problem that disproportionately affects women, particularly indigenous women, and is underreported. There have been initiatives in recent years to train police in handling of domestic violence cases.

G4. Do individuals enjoy equality of opportunity and freedom from economic exploitation? 4 / 4

There have been some reports of forced labor in the agricultural, food processing, construction, and other sectors, as well as among domestic workers. However the government, aided by NGOs that work to reveal forced labor and sex trafficking, works to hold perpetrators accountable and to provide aid to victims.

There is no national minimum wage, though provinces have set their own. Occupational safety standards are robust and generally well enforced. However, young workers, migrants, and new immigrants remain vulnerable to abuses in the workplace.

Cape Verde

Population: 600,000
Capital: Praia
Political Rights Rating: 1
Civil Liberties Rating: 1
Freedom Rating: 1.0
Freedom Status: Free
Electoral Democracy: Yes

Overview: Cape Verde is a stable democracy with competitive elections and periodic transfers of power between rival parties. Civil liberties are generally protected, but access to justice is impaired by an overburdened court system, and crime remains a concern. Other outstanding problems include persistent inequities for women and migrant workers.

KEY DEVELOPMENTS IN 2018:

- José Barbosa, the president of the national police union, remained suspended from his position throughout the year. He was initially suspended in late 2017, after the union staged a three-day walkout over benefits and pay.
- As part of a drive to reduce crime, a system of surveillance cameras was established in Praia, and began operation in July. Authorities pledged that the system would respect citizens' fundamental rights.
- In October, the National Assembly passed a resolution supporting gender parity, and authorizing the establishment of a commission to encourage gender parity in public policy.
- In March, the country joined the Equal Rights Coalition, an intergovernmental grouping dedicated to the protection of LGBT (lesbian, gay, bisexual, and transgender) rights, and participated in its annual conference later in the year. However, same-sex marriage is still unrecognized.

POLITICAL RIGHTS: 37 / 40

A. ELECTORAL PROCESS: 12 / 12

A1. Was the current head of government or other chief national authority elected through free and fair elections? 4 / 4

The president is directly elected for up to two consecutive five-year terms. The prime minister, who holds most executive authority, is nominated by and accountable to the National Assembly, and is formally appointed by the president.

Incumbent president Jorge Carlos Fonseca of the Movement for Democracy (MpD) was reelected in October 2016 with 74 percent of the vote. His main challenger was independent candidate Albertino Graça, who took about 23 percent. The voting was generally considered free and fair. Ulisses Correia e Silva, also of the MpD, was appointed as prime minister in 2016, a month after legislative elections.

A2. Were the current national legislative representatives elected through free and fair elections? 4 / 4

Members of the 72-seat National Assembly are directly elected in multimember constituencies to serve five-year terms. In the 2016 elections, the MpD, then in opposition, won

40 seats. The governing African Party for the Independence of Cape Verde (PAICV) was reduced to 29 seats, and the Democratic and Independent Cape Verdean Union (UCID) took 3. International observers assessed the elections as largely free and fair.

A3. Are the electoral laws and framework fair, and are they implemented impartially by the relevant election management bodies? 4 / 4

The legal framework provides for fair and competitive elections. The National Elections Commission, whose members are elected by a two-thirds majority in the National Assembly, is generally considered impartial.

B. POLITICAL PLURALISM AND PARTICIPATION: 15 / 16

B1. Do the people have the right to organize in different political parties or other competitive political groupings of their choice, and is the system free of undue obstacles to the rise and fall of these competing parties or groupings? 4 / 4

There are no significant impediments to the formation and competition of political parties. A number of different parties are active, though only the PAICV and the MpD have held power at the national level.

B2. Is there a realistic opportunity for the opposition to increase its support or gain power through elections? 4 / 4

The opposition has a realistic opportunity to gain power through elections. There have been three democratic transfers of power between the PAICV and the MpD since independence in 1975, the most recent in 2016.

B3. Are the people's political choices free from domination by the military, foreign powers, religious hierarchies, economic oligarchies, or any other powerful group that is not democratically accountable? 4 / 4

The political choices of voters and candidates are free from undue external influence. However, there were some reports of vote buying and of voters being pressured near polling stations during the 2016 elections.

B4. Do various segments of the population (including ethnic, religious, gender, LGBT, and other relevant groups) have full political rights and electoral opportunities? 3 / 4

Women have full and equal political rights, but traditional social constraints have impaired their participation somewhat in practice. Women won 17 seats in the 2016 National Assembly elections.

C. FUNCTIONING OF GOVERNMENT: 10 / 12

C1. Do the freely elected head of government and national legislative representatives determine the policies of the government? 4 / 4

The prime minister and cabinet determine the policies of the government, under the supervision of the National Assembly and the president. The government is able to implement laws and policies without undue interference from unelected entities.

C2. Are safeguards against official corruption strong and effective? 3 / 4

Cape Verde has relatively low levels of corruption overall, but bribery and nepotism are problems at the municipal level in particular. Allegations of graft have surrounded costly infrastructure projects and other spending measures in recent years.

C3. Does the government operate with openness and transparency? 3 / 4

The current government has taken a number of steps to improve transparency, including the publication of more information about state operations and finances online. The government generally adheres to legal guarantees of public access to information. However, many officeholders fail to comply with rules requiring them to declare their personal assets and income.

CIVIL LIBERTIES: 53 / 60
D. FREEDOM OF EXPRESSION AND BELIEF: 15 / 16
D1. Are there free and independent media? 3 / 4

Freedom of the press is guaranteed by law and generally respected in practice, although Article 105 of the electoral code prohibits media organizations from disseminating opinions on or criticism of parties and candidates after a certain date in the campaign period. Both public and privately owned media are for the most part free and independent from government control. However, public remarks by the culture minister about hiring and programming at state-owned media in 2017 raised concerns about improper government meddling, and drew objections from the journalists' union.

The main constraints affecting the media are economic. Precarious finances at many outlets undermine journalists' job security and their ability to undertake investigative reporting projects. In recent years, the government has been reducing its advertising in private print outlets, compounding an already difficult situation. A lack of funding has contributed to the closure of a number of privately owned newspapers, decreasing the diversity of information in the print sector.

D2. Are individuals free to practice and express their religious faith or nonbelief in public and private? 4 / 4

The constitution establishes the separation of church and state, though the Roman Catholic Church receives some privileges, such as the recognition of Catholic marriages under civil law. While all religious groups are required to register with the Justice Ministry to obtain tax and other benefits, the process is not restrictive, and there are no limitations on freedom of worship.

D3. Is there academic freedom, and is the educational system free from extensive political indoctrination? 4 / 4

Academic freedom is respected, and the educational system is not affected by political indoctrination.

D4. Are individuals free to express their personal views on political or other sensitive topics without fear of surveillance or retribution? 4 / 4

There are no significant constraints on individuals' freedom of expression. The government is not known to engage in online surveillance or improper monitoring of personal communications.

E. ASSOCIATIONAL AND ORGANIZATIONAL RIGHTS: 11 / 12
E1. Is there freedom of assembly? 4 / 4

Freedom of assembly is legally guaranteed and observed in practice. A number of demonstrations took place in 2018, including ones against unemployment and other economic difficulties, as well as in support of the national police chief, Elias Silva, who was suspended in April after calling for fewer restrictions on gun ownership.

E2. Is there freedom for nongovernmental organizations, particularly those that are engaged in human rights and governance-related work? 4 / 4

Numerous nongovernmental organizations operate freely in the country, focusing on a variety of social, economic, environmental, and cultural issues. International human rights institutions, local organizations, and journalists are able to monitor prison conditions and other human rights indicators without government interference.

E3. Is there freedom for trade unions and similar professional or labor organizations? 3 / 4

The constitution protects the right to unionize, and workers may form and join unions in practice. However, the government restricts the right to strike in broadly defined essential industries, and formal collective bargaining is reportedly uncommon in the private sector.

In December 2017, the national police staged a three-day strike over benefits and pay. José Barbosa, the president of the national police union, was suspended after the strike, and remained so at the end of 2018.

F. RULE OF LAW: 14 / 16

F1. Is there an independent judiciary? 4 / 4

The judiciary is independent, though the courts are overburdened and understaffed.

F2. Does due process prevail in civil and criminal matters? 3 / 4

Police and prosecutors generally observe legal safeguards against arbitrary arrest and detention. Defense attorneys are provided to indigent defendants. However, due to the limited capacity of the court system, there are often delays in detainees' first hearing before a judge, and many cases are dropped because defendants in detention are denied a timely trial.

F3. Is there protection from the illegitimate use of physical force and freedom from war and insurgencies? 4 / 4

Law enforcement officials are sometimes accused of excessive force, but perpetrators are often investigated and punished by oversight bodies. The country is generally free from major violence or unrest. The murder rate in 2018 decreased by 18.5 percent compared to the previous year, according to police statistics, dropping for the third year in a row. And in December, the government announced a 20 percent decrease in the overall crime rate. Nevertheless, there is a widespread perception that street crime and smuggling are growing problems. A system of video cameras for surveillance began operation in July in Praia to prevent urban crime. Authorities pledged that the system would respect citizens' fundamental rights, including the right to privacy.

Prison conditions are poor and often overcrowded, but the government is implementing a program to improve conditions for prisoners, which includes the constructions of more cells and bathrooms.

F4. Do laws, policies, and practices guarantee equal treatment of various segments of the population? 3 / 4

Gender discrimination is prohibited by law, but wage discrimination and unequal access to education persist for women. In October, the National Assembly passed a resolution supporting gender parity, and authorizing the establishment of a commission to encourage gender parity in public policy. Immigrants often face discriminatory treatment by employers.

Same-sex sexual activity is not criminalized, and the law provides protections against job discrimination based on sexual orientation. In 2017, the LGBT community in Cape Verde announced that it would organize a petition to request the legalization of same-sex marriage, though there was no significant progress on the initiative in 2018. However, in March 2018 the country joined the Equal Rights Coalition, an intergovernmental coalition dedicated to the protection of LGBT rights, and participated in its annual conference later in the year.

G. PERSONAL AUTONOMY AND INDIVIDUAL RIGHTS: 13 / 16

G1. Do individuals enjoy freedom of movement, including the ability to change their place of residence, employment, or education? 4 / 4

Individual freedom of movement is recognized by law, and there are no significant restrictions in practice. People may freely change their place of employment or education.

G2. Are individuals able to exercise the right to own property and establish private businesses without undue interference from state or nonstate actors? 3 / 4

Property rights are generally respected. The legal framework and government policies are supportive of private business activity, though obstacles such as corruption and legal and bureaucratic inefficiency remain a concern. Small and medium-size businesses are one of the main sources of income for families whose members are not directly employed in the public services.

G3. Do individuals enjoy personal social freedoms, including choice of marriage partner and size of family, protection from domestic violence, and control over appearance? 3 / 4

Personal social freedoms are generally protected, including in matters of marriage and family law. Authorities enforce laws against rape and domestic abuse, but such violence remains a serious problem, and insufficient public resources are dedicated to supporting and protecting victims.

Same-sex marriages are not recognized.

G4. Do individuals enjoy equality of opportunity and freedom from economic exploitation? 3 / 4

The law prohibits forced labor and other exploitative practices, and the government actively enforces such safeguards in the formal sector. However, migrant workers who lack employment contracts remain vulnerable to abuses, and children are reportedly exposed to sex trafficking and illegal work in agriculture or domestic service.

Central African Republic

Population: 4,700,000
Capital: Bangui
Political Rights Rating: 7
Civil Liberties Rating: 7
Freedom Rating: 7.0
Freedom Status: Not Free
Electoral Democracy: No

Overview: The Central African Republic suffers from pervasive insecurity and an absence of state authority in much of the country. Efforts to reach a negotiated settlement between the government and various armed groups have not yet produced major agreements. The country faces a humanitarian crisis, and violent attacks against civilians, including sexual violence, are an acute risk in many areas.

KEY DEVELOPMENTS IN 2018:

- The African Union (AU) continued efforts to help broker a settlement between armed groups and the government—as did Russia and Sudan, in a parallel effort. However, these initiatives failed to produce major developments, and the government remained unable to restore the authority of the state beyond the capital city.
- Russia increased its military presence in the country, deploying military advisors and civilian instructors in Bangui, and delivering several shipments of arms and ammunition.
- In July, three Russian journalists were ambushed and killed near the northern city of Sibut. The journalists had been investigating the activities of a Russian security group operating in the country for a news outlet owned by an opponent of Russian president Vladimir Putin.
- Citing corruption allegations, the National Assembly in October voted to dismiss its president, Abdou Karim Meckassoua, a moderate politician who represented the district in Bangui home to most of the city's Muslims. Meckassoua's supporters claimed his firing represented an attempt by President Faustin-Archange Touadéra to consolidate control over opposition in the parliament.

POLITICAL RIGHTS: 4 / 40

A. ELECTORAL PROCESS: 3 / 12

A1. Was the current head of government or other chief national authority elected through free and fair elections? 1 / 4

The president is chief of state and is directly elected to up to two five-year terms. President Touadéra was elected in February 2016. The elections were monitored by the African Union Election Observation Mission (AUEOM), and were regarded as generally successful and a step towards peace and stabilization. Fears of widespread electoral violence were not realized, but there were many reports of serious irregularities at the polls. Moreover, many voters were unable to participate because insecurity prevented voter registration, or because they had fled to other countries as refugees and the state was unable to set up effective absentee voting procedures.

A2. Were the current national legislative representatives elected through free and fair elections? 1 / 4

Members of parliament are directly elected to five-year terms. The current parliament was elected in February 2016, followed by a second round of by-elections that March. The polls were generally regarded as successful, but like the presidential polls, were plagued by irregularities and the disenfranchisement of voters unable to access the polls due to security concerns or refugee status. Moreover, a first round had to be nullified following a slew of allegations of fraud and other misconduct, by actors ranging from armed groups to political candidates to the National Electoral Authority.

A new constitution adopted in 2015 stipulated the creation of a Senate, but it has not been established.

A3. Are the electoral laws and framework fair, and are they implemented impartially by the relevant election management bodies? 1 / 4

The electoral laws of the Central African Republic permit multiparty competition, and adult citizens enjoy universal and equal suffrage. However, the broader electoral framework of the country remains challenged by a weak judicial system, inadequate funding and training for election officials, and a lack of transparency in the composition of national election authorities.

B. POLITICAL PLURALISM AND PARTICIPATION: 2 / 16

B1. Do the people have the right to organize in different political parties or other competitive political groupings of their choice, and is the system free of undue obstacles to the rise and fall of these competing parties or groupings? 1 / 4

While political parties are legally able to form and operate, party members conducting political activities are at risk of intimidation and violence in areas controlled by irregular armed groups.

B2. Is there a realistic opportunity for the opposition to increase its support or gain power through elections? 1 / 4

Several opposition parties exist in the parliament. However, politicians are at risk of intimidation, harassment, or violence in areas controlled by armed groups, and opposition parties are limited in their ability to garner support in those areas.

B3. Are the people's political choices free from domination by the military, foreign powers, religious hierarchies, economic oligarchies, or any other powerful group that is not democratically accountable? 0 / 4

Citizens are vulnerable to pressure and intimidation from nonstate armed groups. Due to enduring insecurity, voters outside the capital are largely unable to participate in political processes.

In 2018, a Russian military presence in Central African Republic became increasingly visible. Early in the year, after the UN Security Council, the United States, and France assented, Russia deployed military advisors and civilian instructors in Bangui, and made several deliveries of arms and ammunition. Wagner Group, a Russian security company with links to Russian President Vladimir Putin, also began providing personal security for President Touadéra. Members of the same group were reportedly providing security at gold mines in the country.

B4. Do various segments of the population (including ethnic, religious, gender, LGBT, and other relevant groups) have full political rights and electoral opportunities? 0 / 4

Enduring insecurity and an accompanying lack of access to political processes precludes many minority groups from achieving political representation. Sectarian violence affecting Muslims has decreased their ability to participate in politics. Women are underrepresented in politics, and just 11 sit in the 140-seat parliament. Societal and legal discrimination against LGBT (lesbian, gay, bisexual, and transgender) people prevent them from working to see their interests represented in the political sphere.

C. FUNCTIONING OF GOVERNMENT: 0 / 12

C1. Do the freely elected head of government and national legislative representatives determine the policies of the government? 0 / 4

Presidential and parliamentary elections held in early 2016 led to a peaceful transfer of power from the National Transitional Council to an elected government. However, while the elected representatives can determine the policies of the government, the weak authority of the state in many areas severely limits the government's ability to implement policy decisions.

Citing corruption allegations, the National Assembly in October 2018 voted to dismiss its president, Abdou Karim Meckassoua, a moderate politician who represented the district in Bangui home to most of the city's Muslims. Meckassoua's supporters claimed his firing represented an attempt by Touadéra to consolidate control over opposition in the parliament.

C2. Are safeguards against official corruption strong and effective? 0 / 4

Corruption and nepotism have long been pervasive in all branches of government, and addressing public-sector corruption is difficult given capacity limitations. The UN Panel of Experts on Central African Republic noted in December 2017 abuses by local officials who had partnered with international investors in the mining sector.

C3. Does the government operate with openness and transparency? 0 / 4

Government operations are largely nontransparent, and civil society groups and others have limited opportunity to comment upon or influence impending policy decisions. Citizens outside of the capital have limited access to their elected representatives in the national legislature.

ADDITIONAL DISCRETIONARY POLITICAL RIGHTS QUESTION
Is the government or occupying power deliberately changing the ethnic composition of a country or territory so as to destroy a culture or tip the political balance in favor of another group? −1 / 0

Targeted violence against civilians by armed groups such as the Muslim-dominated Popular Front for the Renaissance of Central Africa (FPRC) as well as Christian anti-Balaka militias, continued in 2018 in northwestern, central, and eastern regions of the country. Hundreds of thousands of civilians remain internally displaced or confined to ethnic and sectarian enclaves.

CIVIL LIBERTIES: 5 / 60
D. FREEDOM OF EXPRESSION AND BELIEF: 4 / 16
D1. Are there free and independent media? 1 / 4

Reporters face restricted access to many areas of the country due to insecurity. Few residents outside Bangui enjoy access to national or international media sources or the internet. Since the onset of conflict in 2013, many community radio stations have been shuttered. However, some independently run stations continue to operate and host robust debates, with active participation from callers-in.

In July 2018, three Russian journalists were ambushed and killed near the northern city of Sibut. The journalists had been investigating the activities of the Wagner Group for the Investigation Control Centre, an online news outlet owned by prominent Putin critic Mikhail Khodorkovsky.

D2. Are individuals free to practice and express their religious faith or nonbelief in public and private? 0 / 4

Officially Central African Republic is a secular state, but religious and sectarian cleavages often overlap with the country's political divisions. In 2018, sectarian clashes between Christian and Muslim populations continued to threaten the free practice of religion. Muslims and Christian residents in Bangui remain segregated in separate enclaves, and fears of identity-based violence by armed actors impede free religious expression.

D3. Is there academic freedom, and is the educational system free from extensive political indoctrination? 2 / 4

While the educational system is generally free of extensive political indoctrination, many schools and universities remain closed, or operate without adequate resources.

D4. Are individuals free to express their personal views on political or other sensitive topics without fear of surveillance or retribution? 1 / 4

Public discussion and political debates are generally free from surveillance by state authorities. However, political instability and the risk of violent retaliation for challenging the presence of armed groups or expressing opinions on other sensitive topics inhibits free expression.

E. ASSOCIATIONAL AND ORGANIZATIONAL RIGHTS: 1 / 12

E1. Is there freedom of assembly? 0 / 4

Although freedom of assembly and the right to political protest is guaranteed under the constitution, in practice these liberties continued to be curtailed in 2018 due to widespread insecurity.

In April, demonstrators placed outside the United Nations office in Bangui the bodies of over a dozen people they said were civilians killed in clashes between UN forces and armed groups. A UN spokesperson condemned the action as propaganda, and said the dead were criminals who had attacked UN forces.

E2. Is there freedom for nongovernmental organizations, particularly those that are engaged in human rights- and governance-related work? 0 / 4

While the government does not restrict nongovernmental organizations (NGOs), and frequently cooperates with them, their operations in practice are severely restricted by poor security conditions. More than 270 recorded security incidents involved relief workers between January and September 2018, causing 6 deaths and at least 15 NGOs to suspend humanitarian activities.

E3. Is there freedom for trade unions and similar professional or labor organizations? 1 / 4

Trade unions and collective bargaining are permitted, although union organizers are sometimes subject to arbitrary detention or arrest. Small-scale agricultural organizations and cooperatives exist throughout the country, including organizations for women farmers.

F. RULE OF LAW: 0 / 16

F1. Is there an independent judiciary? 0 / 4

Courts are inefficient and politicized. Judicial salaries have often gone unpaid, and there is a shortage of judges. The government has limited authority to enforce judicial decisions in the many areas of the country controlled by armed groups.

F2. Does due process prevail in civil and criminal matters? 0 / 4

Arbitrary detention and lengthy pretrial detention are commonplace in Central African Republic, and the state justice system has limited presence beyond Bangui. Impunity for violence, economic crimes, and human rights violations remained widespread in 2018.

In October 2018, the Special Criminal Court (SCC) in Bangui opened. The SCC has 13 Central African judges and 12 foreign judges, and is tasked with ending impunity by perpetrators of human rights abuses since 2003. The opening of the SCC is regarded by victims and members of the legal community as a significant step towards improving accountability and prosecuting individuals responsible for child recruitment, sexual abuse, and other crimes. However, the Court has not yet proven its ability to successfully prosecute alleged perpetrators and end impunity.

In November 2018, authorities transferred Alfred Yekatom to the International Criminal Court (ICC) in The Hague, the Netherlands; he stands accused of war crimes and crimes against humanity in connection with his leadership of anti-Balaka militia groups that terrorized the country's Muslim population after predominantly Muslim Séléka rebels seized power in 2013. Separately, in December 2018, French authorities arrested a former anti-Balaka militia leader, Patrice-Edouard Ngaïssona, in France on an ICC arrest warrant alleging war crimes and crimes against humanity.

F3. Is there protection from the illegitimate use of physical force and freedom from war and insurgencies? 0 / 4

Armed nonstate actors—many of which are successors to the Muslim Séléka rebels and Christian anti-Balaka militias involved in violent atrocities since the onset of the country's current crisis in 2013—continue to operate with impunity in the eastern, northern, and northwestern regions of the country. These groups were responsible for violent attacks against civilians, often on the basis of ethnic and religious identity, as well as attacks against international peacekeeping forces and humanitarian aid workers.

In August and September 2018, fighting between armed groups for control of diamond mining territory near Bria resulted in the deaths of at least 30 people. Violent competition among insurgent groups for control of territory and natural resources keeps over 600,000 Central Africans internally displaced. Conflict between farmers and nomadic pastoralists in the border areas near Chad, Cameroon, Sudan, and South Sudan further destabilized the country in 2018.

In addition to mediation efforts between armed militia groups and the government led by the African Union (AU), Russia and Sudan organized a parallel negotiating track in 2018. In August, at a meeting in Khartoum, four factions signed an initial declaration of intent to negotiate in connection with the Russian-Sudanese effort, but key signatories withdrew in October. Mediation efforts by the AU similarly failed to produce major developments.

F4. Do laws, policies, and practices guarantee equal treatment of various segments of the population? 0 / 4

Same-sex sexual acts are illegal, and punishable by fines and imprisonment. While enforcement of these laws is uncommon, societal discrimination against LGBT people remains acute. Discrimination continues against the nomadic pastoralist Mbororo minority, as well as the forest-dwelling Ba'aka.

The independent High Authority for Good Governance is tasked with protecting the rights of minorities and the handicapped, though its reach is limited.

G. PERSONAL AUTONOMY AND INDIVIDUAL RIGHTS: 0 / 16

G1. Do individuals enjoy freedom of movement, including the ability to change their place of residence, employment, or education? 0 / 4

Free movement by citizens is inhibited by the lack of security and targeted violence. Transportation routes are threatened by banditry and theft in many areas.

G2. Are individuals able to exercise the right to own property and establish private businesses without undue interference from state or nonstate actors? 0 / 4

Businesses and homes are regularly looted or extorted by armed militants, with little prospect for compensation or legal recourse for victims. The agricultural economy—the livelihood of the majority of the population—remains restricted by ongoing violence and insecurity.

G3. Do individuals enjoy personal social freedoms, including choice of marriage partner and size of family, protection from domestic violence, and control over appearance? 0 / 4

Abuse, rape, and sexual slavery against women by armed groups threaten the security of women and girls. Sexual violence is used as a deliberate tool of warfare, and attackers enjoy broad impunity. Constitutional guarantees for women's rights are rarely enforced, especially in rural areas. Sexual abuses by UN peacekeeping forces have been documented, but many instances have not been investigated or prosecuted.

G4. Do individuals enjoy equality of opportunity and freedom from economic exploitation? 0 / 4

Economic opportunity is heavily restricted by the presence of armed groups in many areas of the country. Approximately one in two Central Africans depend on access to humanitarian assistance for survival. Many armed groups exploit gold and diamond mines, and forced labor and child recruitment for soldiering are common practices.

Chad

Population: 15,400,000
Capital: N'Djamena
Political Rights Rating: 7
Civil Liberties Rating: 6
Freedom Rating: 6.5
Freedom Status: Not Free
Electoral Democracy: No

Overview: Chad has held regular presidential elections since 1996, but no election has ever produced a change in power. Legislative elections are routinely delayed, and have not been held since 2011. Opposition activists risk arrest and severe mistreatment while in detention. The state faces multiple insurgencies led by militants in the north and around Lake Chad.

KEY DEVELOPMENTS IN 2018:
- The National Assembly approved a new constitution in an April vote boycotted by the opposition, and President Idriss Déby Itno signed it into law in May. The opposition and civil society had called for more inclusive and expansive consultation processes, and for the draft constitution to be put to a national referendum.
- The new constitution significantly increased the powers of the president, redrew legislative districts, and introduced term limits that would come into force after the 2021 elections. The new charter allows President Déby, who has held power since 1990, the opportunity to run for sixth and seventh terms that would keep him in power until 2033.
- Boko Haram in the Lake Chad region and insurgent groups in the northern Tibesti region bordering Libya launched destabilizing attacks targeting security authorities and civilians.

- Public sector workers continued to face unpaid or late compensation, and unions representing the education, health, and justice sectors held periodic strikes in protest.

POLITICAL RIGHTS: 3 / 40 (−1)

A. ELECTORAL PROCESS: 1 / 12 (−1)

A1. Was the current head of government or other chief national authority elected through free and fair elections? 1 / 4

The president is directly elected to a five-year term. President Idriss Déby Itno took power in 1990 during a rebellion, and then overwhelmingly won elections in 1996, 2001, 2006, and 2011. In the 2016 poll, he received just under 60 percent of the vote, defeating opposition leader Saleh Kebzabo, who took 13 percent. The opposition rejected the result, citing a variety of electoral irregularities.

A new constitution promulgated in May 2018 eliminated the office of prime minister and gave the president exclusive and sweeping powers to appoint state officials. It also reinstalled term limits: under its provisions, the president serves a six-year term that is renewable once. However, the term limit mandate is not retroactive and does not take effect until after the 2021 presidential election, thus permitting Déby the opportunity to run for sixth and seventh terms that could keep him in power until 2033.

A2. Were the current national legislative representatives elected through free and fair elections? 0 / 4

The unicameral National Assembly consists of 188 members elected to four-year terms. However, elections have not been organized since 2011, with the 2015 parliamentary elections having been repeatedly postponed. The ruling political party, Déby's Patriotic Salvation Movement (MPS), and allied parties control 117 seats, more than a two-thirds majority.

A3. Are the electoral laws and framework fair, and are they implemented impartially by the relevant election management bodies? 0 / 4 (−1)

An Independent National Electoral Commission (CENI) is established prior to elections. However, its leadership is appointed by the country's entrenched political class through the National Framework for Political Dialogue (CNDP), and civil society is excluded from the process.

In April 2018, the MPS-controlled National Assembly—whose mandate had long since expired—adopted a new constitution that significantly increased the powers of the president and redrew legislative districts, among other changes, and Déby promulgated it in May. The government rejected calls from the opposition, civil society groups, and the Catholic Church in Chad to put the new charter to a referendum. Authorities organized a national forum to debate constitutional reforms, but opposition parties and civil society organizations boycotted it, calling for a more inclusive dialog that addressed a broader range of issues.

The CNDP in 2018 failed to fulfill its mandates. Despite the promulgation of the new constitution and Déby's calls to hold legislative elections, it has not established a new electoral code, nor has it appointed a CENI.

Score Change: The score declined from 1 to 0 because the electoral commission has failed to organize legislative elections originally scheduled for 2015, and because a new constitution was approved by lawmakers with expired mandates and in the absence of consultations with the opposition and civil society.

B. POLITICAL PLURALISM AND PARTICIPATION: 1 / 16

B1. Do the people have the right to organize in different political parties or other competitive political groupings of their choice, and is the system free of undue obstacles to the rise and fall of these competing parties or groupings? 1 / 4

There are more than 130 registered political parties in Chad, though most of them are aligned with the ruling party. The MPS enjoys significant influence, and has held a majority in the National Assembly since legislative elections in 1997.

B2. Is there a realistic opportunity for the opposition to increase its support or gain power through elections? 0 / 4

The mandate of the current legislature expired in 2015 and new elections have been repeatedly postponed, leaving the opposition no avenue to increase support or gain power through elections. The political opposition is given legal recognition, but opposition leaders who publicly criticize the government risk severe harassment and arrest. Opposition leaders have disappeared after entering state custody. In 2018, the state continued to forbid the organization of opposition activities including rallies, marches, and other public demonstrations, as well as meetings between opposition officials.

B3. Are the people's political choices free from domination by the military, foreign powers, religious hierarchies, economic oligarchies, or any other powerful group that is not democratically accountable? 0 / 4

The extensive and complicated kinship networks tied to the president and his family have resulted in a concentration of political and economic power. The government is not accountable to voters in practice, and voters have few effective means of influencing or participating in political affairs.

B4. Do various segments of the population (including ethnic, religious, gender, LGBT, and other relevant groups) have full political rights and electoral opportunities? 0 / 4

Members of the Zaghawa ethnic group, and other northern ethnic groups, control Chad's political and economic systems, causing resentment among the country's 200 other ethnic groups. Although they comprise roughly 44 percent of the population, Christians in the south have largely been excluded from political power for roughly 40 years. While some Christians hold positions in the current government, their representation and voice are limited to a few token ministerial positions. The new constitution requires cabinet members and some other officials to be sworn in on either a Bible or a Quran, and to invoke Allah, the Arabic-language name of God. Following cabinet shuffles, some officials were fired after they refused to take the oath on grounds that it violated secularism or provisions of their Christian faith. One official was reportedly permitted by Déby to invoke the name of God in French, rather than Arabic.

Despite some government efforts to encourage their political participation, women hold few senior positions in government and political parties. Women living in rural areas are largely excluded from local governance bodies. The LGBT (lesbian, gay, bisexual, and transgender) community is severely marginalized, and this impacts the ability of LGBT people to engage in political processes and advocate for their interests.

C. FUNCTIONING OF GOVERNMENT: 1 / 12

C1. Do the freely elected head of government and national legislative representatives determine the policies of the government? 1 / 4

Déby enjoys unlimited discretionary power over the composition of the government and routinely reshuffles the cabinet, including in 2018. The elimination of the prime minister's office further concentrated the executive powers of government in the presidency. The significant influence of the presidential office impedes the National Assembly from steering national policies.

C2. Are safeguards against official corruption strong and effective? 0 / 4

Corruption, bribery, and nepotism are endemic and pervasive in Chad. High-profile journalists, labor leaders, and religious figures have faced harsh reprisals for speaking out about corruption, including arrest, prosecution, and expulsion from the country. Corruption charges against high-level officials that do go forward are widely viewed as selective prosecutions meant to discredit those who pose a threat to Déby or his allies.

C3. Does the government operate with openness and transparency? 0 / 4

Chad has no law establishing the right to access official information. Déby, his family, and his associates dominate government and have little incentive to share even basic information about government operations with journalists, transparency advocates, or ordinary citizens.

CIVIL LIBERTIES: 14 / 60

D. FREEDOM OF EXPRESSION AND BELIEF: 6 / 12

D1. Are there free and independent media? 1 / 4

The constitution formally provides for freedom of the press, but press freedom is restricted in practice. Although criticism of the government is generally permitted within certain boundaries, reporters and editors practice self-censorship to avoid reprisals, including arbitrary detention and other harassment and abuse. Many of Chad's most prominent news outlets are either state-owned or controlled by those with close ties to the government, and have limited editorial independence.

The internet and social media are heavily regulated and restricted. Beginning in March 2018, shortly after protests against proposed constitutional changes took place, state authorities pressured internet providers in Chad to block access to social media platforms and messaging apps, and they remained inaccessible at the end of the year. The courts in October upheld the state's authority to regulate internet access.

D2. Are individuals free to practice and express their religious faith or nonbelief in public and private? 1 / 4

The state imposes a number of religious restrictions, primarily against certain Muslim sects. Several sects deemed to promote violence are banned, despite limited evidence of such activity. Imams are subject to governance by the semi-state run High Council for Islamic Affairs (HCIA), which is led by a group of imams belonging to the Tijanyya Sufi order. Terrorist attacks are considered an acute threat against Muslim and Christian places of worship, and the state has provided security to some houses of worship in response to such concerns. The government has engaged in a highly visible campaign to ban burqas, and has detained women who choose to wear them in public.

D3. Is there academic freedom, and is the educational system free from extensive political indoctrination? 2 / 4

The government does not restrict academic freedom, but funds meant for the education system, as well as government-funded stipends, are regularly in arrears. In May 2018, university lecturers, students, and staff at the University of N'Djamena and its satellite campuses went on strike, citing months of unpaid salary and other benefits. The primary and secondary education systems also experienced strikes, disrupting their academic calendars.

D4. Are individuals free to express their personal views on political or other sensitive topics without fear of surveillance or retribution? 2 / 4

Space for open and free private discussion exists, but tends to be heavily self-censored due to fears of reprisal from the state's repressive apparatus.

E. ASSOCIATIONAL AND ORGANIZATIONAL RIGHTS: 4 / 12
E1. Is there freedom of assembly? 1 / 4

Constitutional guarantees of free assembly are not upheld by authorities, who routinely ban gatherings and persecute organizers. A number of demonstrations were banned in 2018, and in January, security forces dispersed crowds with tear gas and arrested around sixty student protesters who organized to support the strike of civil servants in the education sector. Several other demonstrations of protest were met with police repression throughout the year.

E2. Is there freedom for nongovernmental organizations, particularly those that are engaged in human rights- and governance-related work? 1 / 4

Nongovernmental organizations (NGOs) must receive government approval to operate legally, and few such applications are approved. Most legal NGOs operate in the humanitarian and development sectors. Intelligence agents target and intimidate local activists who attempt to address issues related to governance or human rights.

E3. Is there freedom for trade unions and similar professional or labor organizations? 2 / 4

The constitution guarantees the rights to strike and unionize, but a 2007 law imposed limits on public sector workers' right to strike. In 2017, trade unions and the government reached an agreement to form a new tripartite arbitration committee composed of state officials, employers, and union representatives. However, the committee failed to reach a consensus in 2018. Several strikes took place during the year in response to reductions to or unpaid salaries and benefits, particularly in the public sector.

F. RULE OF LAW: 1 / 16
F1. Is there an independent judiciary? 0 / 4

The rule of law and judicial system remain weak because the political leadership, especially the executive, heavily influences the courts.

F2. Does due process prevail in civil and criminal matters? 1 / 4

Security forces routinely ignore constitutional protections regarding search, seizure, and detention. Detained persons may be denied access to lawyers, notably those detained in connection with their involvement in antigovernment protests or activities. Many people suspected of committing crimes are held for lengthy periods without charge.

F3. Is there protection from the illegitimate use of physical force and freedom from war and insurgencies? 0 / 4

Civilian leaders do not maintain control of the security forces, who stand accused of killing and torturing with impunity. The militant group Boko Haram operates near Lake Chad, and in 2018 it continued to carry out abductions and killings of civilians, and burned dozens of homes, leading to increased internal displacement. Rebel groups formed an alliance in southern Libya and led attacks on security forces in northern Chad in August. This represents a new front and insurgency facing the Chadian state in 2018. Increased insecurity from insurgent activities in Libya led Chad to move the command center of the G5 Sahel, a regional military partnership comprised primarily of Chadian forces, from N'Djamena to northern Chad.

Cleavages between different ethno-regional groups have at times sparked violent conflict between communities.

Conditions in prisons are dangerous.

F4. Do laws, policies, and practices guarantee equal treatment of various segments of the population? 0 / 4

Due to cultural stigmatization, LGBT citizens are forced to conceal their sexual orientation and gender identity. The current penal code criminalizes same-sex sexual activity. Women face pervasive discrimination. Girls have limited access to education.

The government struggles to provide services to internationally displaced persons (IDPs) and the more than 450,000 refugees in Chad at the end of 2018 who fled conflicts in neighboring Central African Republic, Sudan, Nigeria, and the Democratic Republic of the Congo.

G. PERSONAL AUTONOMY AND INDIVIDUAL RIGHTS: 3 / 16

G1. Do individuals enjoy freedom of movement, including the ability to change their place of residence, employment, or education? 1 / 4

Although constitutional guarantees for the freedom of movement exist, in practice militant activity and consequent security responses limit movement, particularly in the Lake Chad region.

Significant structural constraints on the resources available to everyday citizens restrict the ability of individuals to pursue employment or educational opportunities outside of their local areas.

A report by the Centre for Studies and Training for Development (CEFOD) released in 2017 cited early marriage as a key cause of girls dropping out of school.

G2. Are individuals able to exercise the right to own property and establish private businesses without undue interference from state or nonstate actors? 1 / 4

Laws establishing land and property rights are nominally in force, but they are functionally irrelevant to the majority of the country's population owing to the state's minimal presence in rural areas; customary law governs land ownership and use rights in practice. Laws protecting the right of women to inherit land are not enforced.

Due to high levels of corruption, establishing and operating a business in Chad is extremely difficult.

G3. Do individuals enjoy personal social freedoms, including choice of marriage partner and size of family, protection from domestic violence, and control over appearance? 0 / 4

Violence against women is common. Female genital mutilation is illegal but widely practiced.

The penal code bans child marriage, setting the legal age of marriage at 18, but the courts rarely hold those who practice it accountable. This issue received some attention in a recent case in which a girl accused a man of rape; she had married him when she was 13 and said he had kidnapped her. The courts acquitted the accused in 2017 but the verdict was appealed, and he was retried in October 2018. He was found guilty in November and sentenced to a year in prison, but had not been taken into custody at year's end.

G4. Do individuals enjoy equality of opportunity and freedom from economic exploitation? 1 / 4

Chad has adopted minimum wage and occupational health and safety laws, but authorities do not enforce them well, and many workers are unaware of or lack access to formal channels through which they may seek redress for mistreatment by employers; corruption also impedes workers from obtaining redress. Unpaid wages are a serious problem in many sectors.

Chad is a source, transit, and destination country for child trafficking, and the government has made minimal efforts to eliminate the problem. Children can be found engaged in forced begging and forced labor. Young girls who travel to look for work often end up either forced into prostitution or abusive domestic servitude.

Chile

Population: 18,600,000
Capital: Santiago
Political Rights Rating: 1
Civil Liberties Rating: 1
Freedom Rating: 1.0
Freedom Status: Free
Electoral Democracy: Yes

Overview: Chile is a stable democracy that has experienced a significant expansion of political rights and civil liberties since the return of civilian rule in 1990. Ongoing concerns include corruption and unrest linked to land disputes with the indigenous Mapuche population.

KEY DEVELOPMENTS IN 2018:

- Conservative politician and former president Sebastián Piñera took office in March for a second, nonconsecutive four-year term, replacing President Michelle Bachelet. The new legislature elected in 2017 held its first session the same month.
- In December, President Piñera asked for the resignation of the director of the *carabineros* (militarized police), Hermes Soto, due to the irregular handling of the murder of an indigenous Mapuche man by police officers.
- In September, lawmakers narrowly defeated an opposition-led initiative to remove three Supreme Court justices for "abandonment of duties" after they had granted parole to seven prisoners convicted of human rights violations committed during the 1973-1990 dictatorship of Augusto Pinochet. Numerous jurists accused the Chamber of Deputies of attempting to curb judicial independence.
- A number of arson attacks led by Mapuche activists took place during the year. Meanwhile, authorities continued to draw criticism for prosecuting violent actions of Mapuche activists under antiterrorism laws.

POLITICAL RIGHTS: 37 / 40

A. ELECTORAL PROCESS: 12 / 12

A1. Was the current head of government or other chief national authority elected through free and fair elections? 4 / 4

Presidential elections in Chile are widely regarded as free and fair. The president is elected to a four-year term, and consecutive terms are not permitted. Piñera was elected in December 2017 to serve his second term; he had served as president previously, from 2010 to 2014.

A2. Were the current national legislative representatives elected through free and fair elections? 4 / 4

The 2017 legislative polls were the first to take place under new rules that established more proportional districts, and increased the number of seats in both houses. The Chamber of Deputies now has 155 seats, up from 120 previously. The number of Senate seats was increased from 38 to 50, but the new seats will be introduced gradually, with the Senate reaching its new 50-seat capacity in 2022.

Senators serve eight-year terms, with half up for election every four years, and members of the Chamber of Deputies are elected to four-year terms. Since 1990, congressional elections have been widely regarded as free and fair.

A3. Are the electoral laws and framework fair, and are they implemented impartially by the relevant election management bodies? 4 / 4

Chile's electoral framework is robust and generally well implemented.

B. POLITICAL PLURALISM AND PARTICIPATION: 15 / 16

B1. Do the people have the right to organize in different political parties or other competitive political groupings of their choice, and is the system free of undue obstacles to the rise and fall of these competing parties or groupings? 4 / 4

Chile has a multiparty political system. The new Congress, which held its first session in March 2018, includes representatives from more than a dozen political parties, as well as several independent candidates. Additionally, the number of important legislative coalitions has increased from two to three, with the leftist Frente Amplio, or Broad Front, joining the existing major blocs: the center-left Nueva Mayoría, or New Majority, and center-right Vamos Chile, or Let's Go Chile. Parties operate freely, and new parties have emerged in recent years.

B2. Is there a realistic opportunity for the opposition to increase its support or gain power through elections? 4 / 4

Power alternation between parties occurs regularly, both in Congress and for the presidency. In 2014, center-left President Bachelet succeeded conservative President Piñera, who in turn succeeded Bachelet in 2018.

B3. Are the people's political choices free from domination by the military, foreign powers, religious hierarchies, economic oligarchies, or any other powerful group that is not democratically accountable? 4 / 4

People are generally free to exercise their political choices without undue influence from actors that are not democratically accountable.

B4. Do various segments of the population (including ethnic, religious, gender, LGBT, and other relevant groups) have full political rights and electoral opportunities? 3 / 4

Women are represented in government, and the new electoral system includes a quota for women in the legislature. However, the presence of women in Congress and in other government positions does not guarantee that their interests are represented, and women report difficulty gaining influence in intraparty debates.

The interests of the Mapuche minority, which represents about 9 percent of the population, are present in political life, with Mapuche activists regularly making their voices heard in street demonstrations. However, this activism has yet to translate into significant legislative power. In 2017, two Mapuche candidates were elected; one to the Senate and one to the Chamber of Deputies.

C. FUNCTIONING OF GOVERNMENT: 10 / 12

C1. Do the freely elected head of government and national legislative representatives determine the policies of the government? 4 / 4

While lobbying and interest groups exist and work to shape policy, there is little significant intervention by actors who are not democratically accountable in the policymaking process.

C2. Are safeguards against official corruption strong and effective? 3 / 4

Anticorruption laws are generally enforced, though high-level corruption scandals crop up with some regularity. In November 2018, Piñera dismissed 21 army generals amid multiple corruption scandals in the military, making the biggest change of the army's high command since 1990. The reputation of the army was further affected when it was revealed the same month that the commander-in-chief, General Ricardo Martínez, had disclosed during a military event that army officials had sold weapons to criminal groups. The government claimed that the general was referring to past incidents that had already been adjudicated, but requested details from the general regarding his statements.

Corruption scandals dented former president Bachelet's popularity during her presidency, as well as that of her coalition.

C3. Does the government operate with openness and transparency? 3 / 4

The government operates with relative transparency. In 2009 the Transparency and Access to Public Information Law came into force; it increases public access to information and created a Council on Transparency. Agencies have generally been responsive to information requests, and failures to comply with the law or other measures designed to encourage transparent operations have been punished with fines.

However, the legislature has limited ability under the constitution to supervise or alter the executive budget. Moreover, a legal provision reserves 10 percent of copper export revenues for the military, with little independent oversight.

CIVIL LIBERTIES: 57 / 60

D. FREEDOM OF EXPRESSION AND BELIEF: 16 / 16

D1. Are there free and independent media? 4 / 4

Guarantees of free speech are generally respected, though some laws barring defamation of state institutions remain on the books. In 2018, journalist Javier Ignacio Rebolledo Escobar faced charges of "damaging the honor" of a former military officer who had been convicted of crimes against humanity for acts committed during the Pinochet dictatorship. The charges, which carried a prison sentence of up to three years, were related to material in a book Rebolledo had released in 2017. In October, a judge dismissed them without ruling on their merit, citing instead a procedural irregularity.

Media ownership is highly concentrated.

D2. Are individuals free to practice and express their religious faith or nonbelief in public and private? 4 / 4

The constitution provides for religious freedom, and the government generally upholds this right in practice.

D3. Is there academic freedom, and is the educational system free from extensive political indoctrination? 4 / 4

Academic freedom is unrestricted.

D4. Are individuals free to express their personal views on political or other sensitive topics without fear of surveillance or retribution? 4 / 4

Chileans enjoy open and free private discussion.

E. ASSOCIATIONAL AND ORGANIZATIONAL RIGHTS: 12 / 12

E1. Is there freedom of assembly? 4 / 4

The right to assemble peacefully is widely respected, though protests are sometimes marred by violence. In July 2018, an altercation erupted between demonstrators marching in support of free and safe abortion, and counterprotesters. Three women suffered stab injuries, and several people were arrested. Separately, protests against police brutality gained momentum throughout the country following the police shooting of a young Mapuche man in November.

E2. Is there freedom for nongovernmental organizations, particularly those that are engaged in human rights– and governance-related work? 4 / 4

Nongovernmental organizations (NGOs) form and operate without interference.

E3. Is there freedom for trade unions and similar professional or labor organizations? 4 / 4

There are strong laws protecting worker and union rights, but some limited antiunion practices by private-sector employers continue to be reported.

F. RULE OF LAW: 14 / 16

F1. Is there an independent judiciary? 4 / 4

The constitution provides for an independent judiciary, and the courts are generally free from political interference. However, judicial independence was tested in September 2018, when opposition deputies tried to remove three Supreme Court justices for "abandonment of duties" after they granted parole to seven prisoners convicted of human rights violations committed during the Pinochet dictatorship. Although the Chamber of Deputies narrowly rejected the impeachment, the voting strained relations between the legislative and judicial branches, and numerous jurists accused the Chamber of Deputies of trying to curb judicial independence.

F2. Does due process prevail in civil and criminal matters? 4 / 4

The right to legal counsel is constitutionally guaranteed and due process generally prevails in civil and criminal matters. However, indigent defendants do not always receive effective legal representation.

Rights groups and the United Nations have criticized the government's use of antiterrorism laws, which do not guarantee due process, to prosecute acts of violence by Mapuche activists. In May 2018, three Mapuche land-rights activists were convicted under antiterrorism laws of arson in connection with the deaths of two prominent landowners, and of them two received life sentences. Their case had been dismissed previously, in 2017, due to a lack of evidence, but that trial was later annulled.

F3. Is there protection from the illegitimate use of physical force and freedom from war and insurgencies? 3 /4

While the government has developed mechanisms to investigate and punish police abuses, excessive force and human rights abuses committed by the carabineros (militarized police) still occur. In a high-profile scandal, in November 2018 carabineros personnel killed 24-year-old Camilo Catrillanca, grandson of a prominent Mapuche indigenous leader, in Araucanía Region. Initially, the carabineros claimed that the killing was part of a confrontation, but in December the Chilean media released videos that supported the description of a witness who claimed that Catrillanca had been shot in the back. Piñera consequently removed carabineros director Hermes Soto, and a number of other officials including some high ranking ones were removed or stepped down, as did the governor of Araucanía. Four agents involved face murder and other charges.

The slow and delayed repatriation of the ancestral land of the Mapuche indigenous group has been a cause of years of violent protests, and a number of arson attacks led by Mapuche activists took place in 2018. Targets included trucks and equipment belonging to logging operations.

F4. Do laws, policies, and practices guarantee equal treatment of various segments of the population? 3 / 4

While indigenous people still experience societal discrimination and police brutality, their poverty levels have declined somewhat, aided by government scholarships, land transfers, and social spending.

LGBT people continue to face societal bias, despite a 2012 antidiscrimination law that covers sexual orientation and gender identity. In September 2018, Congress approved a gender identity law allowing for gender identity to be changed on the civil registry, and the president signed it into law in November.

In 2018, massive protests against practices, specifically in the education system, that perpetuate gender inequality, abuses, and discrimination helped bring visibility to gender disparities in Chilean society. In response, in May the government announced a number of legal initiatives intended to reduce gender inequality.

G. PERSONAL AUTONOMY AND INDIVIDUAL RIGHTS: 15 / 16

G1. Do individuals enjoy freedom of movement, including the ability to change their place of residence, employment, or education? 4 / 4

The constitution protects the freedom of movement, and the government respects this right in practice.

G2. Are individuals able to exercise the right to own property and establish private businesses without undue interference from state or nonstate actors? 4 / 4

Individuals generally have the right to own property and establish and operate private businesses, and are able to do so without interference from the government or other actors. However, Mapuche activists continue to demand territorial rights to land, ancestral waters, and natural resources.

G3. Do individuals enjoy personal social freedoms, including choice of marriage partner and size of family, protection from domestic violence, and control over appearance? 4 / 4

The government generally does not restrict personal social freedoms. However, violence against children and women remains a problem.

A law against femicide went into force in 2010, but gender violence remains. A total of 42 femicides and 118 attempted femicides were reported in 2018. Gender abuses and discrimination prompted massive feminist protests during the year.

In 2017, a law introduced by then-president Bachelet that decriminalized abortion in the events of rape, an inviable fetus, or danger to the life of the mother, took effect.

A 2015 law recognizes civil unions for same-sex and opposite-sex couples.

G4. Do individuals enjoy equality of opportunity and freedom from economic exploitation? 3 / 4

While compulsory labor is illegal, forced labor, particularly among foreign citizens, continues to occur in the agriculture, mining, and domestic service sectors.

Although there have been improvements in fighting child labor, minors still suffer commercial sexual exploitation and work unprotected in the agricultural sector. Moreover, there is limited public information about forced child labor.

China

Population: 1,393,800,000
Capital: Beijing
Political Rights Rating: 7
Civil Liberties Rating: 6
Freedom Rating: 6.5
Freedom Status: Not Free
Electoral Democracy: No

Note: The numerical ratings and status listed above do not reflect conditions in Hong Kong or Tibet, which are examined in separate reports.

Overview: China's authoritarian regime has become increasingly repressive in recent years. The ruling Chinese Communist Party (CCP) is tightening its control over the state bureaucracy, the media, online speech, religious groups, universities, businesses, and civil society associations, and it has undermined its own already modest rule-of-law reforms. The CCP leader and state president, Xi Jinping, has consolidated personal power to a degree not seen in China for decades, but his actions have also triggered rising discontent among elites within and outside the party. The country's budding human rights movements continue to seek avenues for protecting basic rights despite a multiyear crackdown.

KEY DEVELOPMENTS IN 2018:

- President Xi strengthened his hold on power in March, when the National People's Congress amended the country's constitution to enshrine "Xi Jinping Thought" and remove the two-term limit on the presidency. Observers warned that Xi's personalization of power and departure from previous norms—including his failure to appoint a potential successor to the CCP's Politburo Standing Committee—could have negative consequences for China's future political stability.

- Also in March, as part of a larger set of changes that increased the CCP's role in the government and society, a powerful new National Supervisory Commission was established to lead anticorruption efforts. The commission's structure and mandate further blurred the line between party and state mechanisms while expanding its predecessors' jurisdiction to encompass a broader swath of public employees.
- Internet censorship and surveillance reached new heights as implementation of the 2017 Cybersecurity Law continued to be rolled out, various new measures restricting online and mobile communications came into effect, and advancements in artificial intelligence and facial recognition technologies were incorporated into the regime's information control and public surveillance apparatus.
- The government's persecution of predominantly Muslim ethnic minorities in Xinjiang intensified dramatically, with an estimated one million or more individuals subjected to extralegal detention in "political reeducation" centers. Reports of torture and other abuse at the camps emerged during the year. Authorities also increased repression of Christians and Muslims elsewhere in China following new regulations on religious affairs that took effect nationwide in February, and persecution of the banned spiritual movement Falun Gong continued unabated.
- The authorities continued a years-long crackdown on independent civil society, carrying out arrests and criminal prosecutions of bloggers, activists, and human rights lawyers. Government and CCP influence over foreign and domestic nongovernmental organizations (NGOs) increased via funding and registration rules as full-scale implementation of a 2017 law on foreign NGOs took effect.

POLITICAL RIGHTS: −1 / 40 (−1)
A. ELECTORAL PROCESS: 0 / 12
A1. Was the current head of government or other chief national authority elected through free and fair elections? 0 / 4

There are no direct or competitive elections for national executive leaders. The National People's Congress (NPC) formally elects the state president for five-year terms and confirms the premier after he is nominated by the president, but both positions are decided in advance at the relevant CCP congress. The CCP's seven-member Politburo Standing Committee (PSC), headed by Xi Jinping in his role as the party's general secretary, sets government and party policy in practice. Xi also holds the position of state president and serves as chairman of the state and party military commissions.

Xi was awarded a second five-year term as general secretary at the 19th Party Congress in October 2017, and at the NPC session in March 2018 he was confirmed for a second five-year term as state president. Also at that session, the NPC approved amendments to China's constitution that abolished the two-term limit for the state presidency and vice presidency. Combined with the absence of another PSC member young enough to serve as Xi's successor in 2022, the move reinforced predictions that he planned to break with precedent and remain China's paramount leader for the foreseeable future.

A2. Were the current national legislative representatives elected through free and fair elections? 0 / 4

The 3,000 NPC members are formally elected for five-year terms by subnational congresses, but in practice all candidates are vetted by the CCP. Only the NPC's standing committee meets regularly, with the full congress convening for just two weeks a year to approve proposed legislation; party organs and the State Council, or cabinet, effectively control lawmaking. The current NPC was seated in March 2018.

A3. Are the electoral laws and framework fair, and are they implemented impartially by the relevant election management bodies? 0 / 4

Political positions are directly elected only at the lowest administrative levels. Independent candidates who obtain the signatures of 10 supporters are by law allowed to run for seats in the county-level people's congresses, and elections for village committees are also supposed to give residents the chance to choose their representatives. In practice, however, independent candidates for these posts are often kept off the ballot or out of office through intimidation, harassment, fraud, and in some cases detention. Only a very small number of independent candidates have gained office in elections, though some attempt to do so in each election cycle.

Elections are not administered by an independent body. The indirect elections that populate people's congresses at various levels are conducted by those congresses' standing committees, while village-level elections are conducted by a village electoral committee.

B. POLITICAL PLURALISM AND PARTICIPATION: 0 / 16

B1. Do the people have the right to organize in different political parties or other competitive political groupings of their choice, and is the system free of undue obstacles to the rise and fall of these competing parties or groupings? 0 / 4

The CCP seeks to monopolize all forms of political organization and does not permit any meaningful political competition. Eight small noncommunist parties are allowed to play a minor role in China's political system, and are represented on the Chinese People's Political Consultative Conference (CPPCC), an official advisory body. However, their activities are tightly circumscribed, and they must accept the CCP's leadership as a condition for their existence.

Citizens seeking to establish genuinely independent political parties and other democracy campaigners are harshly punished. China's most prominent political dissident, Nobel Peace Prize winner Liu Xiaobo, died from cancer in 2017 while serving an 11-year prison sentence for organizing a prodemocracy manifesto. His widow, Liu Xia, had been kept under strict house arrest, but following an international campaign on her behalf, she was released and permitted to leave the country for Germany in July 2018. Also in July, 64-year-old democracy advocate Qin Yongmin, who had already spent a total of 22 years behind bars since the 1980s, was sentenced to 13 years in prison for having led a prodemocracy group that circulated online statements criticizing government policies.

B2. Is there a realistic opportunity for the opposition to increase its support or gain power through elections? 0 / 4

China's one-party system rigorously suppresses the development of any organized political opposition, and the CCP has ruled without interruption since winning a civil war against the Nationalist Party (Kuomintang) in 1949. Even within the CCP, Xi Jinping has steadily increased his own power and authority since 2012, pursuing a selective anticorruption campaign that has eliminated potential rivals. He personally heads an unusually large number of "leading groups" that give him direct supervision over a variety of policy areas. Xi's official contributions to party ideology were formally added to the CCP and national constitutions in October 2017 and March 2018, respectively, elevating his status above that of his immediate predecessors.

B3. Are the people's political choices free from domination by the military, foreign powers, religious hierarchies, economic oligarchies, or any other powerful group that is not democratically accountable? 0 / 4

The authoritarian CCP is not accountable to voters and denies the public any meaningful influence or participation in political affairs.

B4. Do various segments of the population (including ethnic, religious, gender, LGBT, and other relevant groups) have full political rights and electoral opportunities? 0 / 4

Societal groups such as women, ethnic and religious minorities, and LGBT (lesbian, gay, bisexual, and transgender) people have no opportunity to gain meaningful political representation and are barred from advancing their interests outside the formal structures of the CCP. Nominal representatives of ethnic minority groups—such as Tibetans, Uighurs, and Mongolians—participate in party and state bodies like the NPC, but their role is largely symbolic. Women are severely underrepresented in top CCP and government positions, and the situation has grown slightly worse in recent years. Just one woman was named to the 25-member Politburo at the 19th Party Congress in 2017, down from the previous two. No woman has ever sat on the PSC.

C. FUNCTIONING OF GOVERNMENT: 2 / 12

C1. Do the freely elected head of government and national legislative representatives determine the policies of the government? 0 / 4

None of China's national leaders are freely elected, and the legislature plays no significant role in policymaking or the development of new laws. The continuing concentration of power in Xi Jinping's hands, an emerging cult of personality, and Xi's calls for greater ideological conformity and party supremacy have further reduced the limited space for policy debate even within the CCP.

C2. Are safeguards against official corruption strong and effective? 1 / 4

Since becoming CCP leader in 2012, Xi has pursued an extensive anticorruption campaign. Well over a million officials have been investigated and punished, according to official figures, including senior state and party officials from the security apparatus, the military, the Foreign Ministry, state-owned enterprises, and state media. In October 2018, for example, Lu Wei, the former head of China's powerful internet regulator, pleaded guilty to charges of bribery; Lu was expelled from the party in February, having risen to the rank of deputy director of the CCP's Central Committee. Sun Zhengcai, a former Politburo member and potential candidate for its Standing Committee, was purged in 2017 and sentenced to life in prison in May on corruption and bribery charges. The anticorruption effort has generated a chilling effect among officials and reduced ostentatious displays of wealth, but corruption is believed to remain extensive at all levels of government. Moreover, the initiative has been heavily politicized, as many of the elites targeted were seen as Xi's former or potential rivals, and a 2017 change to party regulations shifted the focus of disciplinary inspections to enforcing party ideology and loyalty.

The authorities have failed to adopt basic reforms that would address corruption more comprehensively, such as requiring officials to publicly disclose their assets, creating genuinely independent oversight bodies, and allowing independent media, courts, and civic activists to function as watchdogs. Instead, in March 2018, the NPC established the National Supervisory Commission (NSC), a powerful new agency that merges the anticorruption functions of various state and party entities, while expanding its jurisdiction to include a broader swath of public-sector employees. The new commission is headed by a Politburo member and shares personnel and a website with the CCP's internal disciplinary agency, further blurring the lines between party rules and institutions and the state legal system. In late September, Meng Hongwei, the president of Interpol and China's vice minister of public security, disappeared into custody during a visit to China, with news later emerging that he had been placed under investigation by the NSC for "alleged violations of laws."

C3. Does the government operate with openness and transparency? 1 / 4

The Chinese government and CCP are notoriously opaque. Since open-government regulations took effect in 2008, more official documents and information have been made available to the public. However, resistance on the part of government organs to providing specific information requested by citizens has dampened initial optimism, and budgetary information available to the public is minimal.

The scope for public input and consultation on laws and policies narrowed further over the past two years as policy advocacy NGOs and intellectuals came under intensified pressure, including those working in areas that were previously not considered sensitive, such as the environment, public health, and women's rights.

ADDITIONAL DISCRETIONARY POLITICAL RIGHTS QUESTION
Is the government or occupying power deliberately changing the ethnic composition of a country or territory so as to destroy a culture or tip the political balance in favor of another group? −3 / 0 (−1)

The government has intensified policies—including large-scale resettlement, work-transfer programs, and mass internment—that are altering the demography of ethnic minority regions, especially Xinjiang, Tibet, and Inner Mongolia, contributing to a steady increase of Han Chinese as a proportion of the regional populations. Conditions in Xinjiang deteriorated sharply during the past two years as human rights groups estimated that more than one million ethnic Uighurs, Kazakhs, and Hui were detained in an expanded network of "political reeducation" centers to undergo political and religious indoctrination. The number and size of orphanages and boarding schools have also been expanded to absorb the growing number of minority children who have been sent away for immersive Chinese-language education or whose parents are being held indefinitely in the camps. Cases of torture and deaths in custody at the political reeducation camps were reported throughout 2018, as was evidence that Uighurs were being transferred in large numbers to detention facilities in other provinces. [Note: Tibet is examined in a separate report.]

Score Change: The score declined from −2 to −3 due to intensified government efforts to break down the ethnic and religious identities and control the overall numbers of Muslim minorities in Xinjiang.

CIVIL LIBERTIES: 12 / 60 (−2)
D. FREEDOM OF EXPRESSION AND BELIEF: 2 / 16 (−1)
D1. Are there free and independent media? 0 / 4 (−1)

China is home to one of the world's most restrictive media environments and its most sophisticated system of censorship, particularly online. The CCP maintains control over news reporting via direct ownership, accreditation of journalists, harsh penalties for public criticism, and daily directives to media outlets and websites that guide coverage of breaking news stories. State management of the telecommunications infrastructure enables the blocking of websites, removal of mobile-phone applications from the domestic market, and mass deletion of microblog posts, instant messages, and user accounts that touch on banned political, social, economic, and religious topics. Thousands of websites have been blocked, many for years, including major news and social media hubs like the *New York Times*, *Le Monde*, YouTube, Twitter, and Facebook.

The already limited space for media freedom shrank further during 2018, as internet restrictions increased and investigative journalism struggled. Online controls were particularly evident surrounding the announcement in late February of the planned constitutional amendment to abolish presidential term limits. The news triggered massive censorship of critical and humorous commentary, including large-scale deletions of both posts and accounts on the microblogging platform Sina Weibo, the blocking of dozens of keywords, the suspension of at least one mobile phone application, and the interrogation of users of the popular instant-messaging tool WeChat.

Continued implementation of the 2017 Cybersecurity Law, along with other regulations and increased pressure on private technology companies, resulted in greater and more sophisticated internet censorship, including on video-streaming platforms and WeChat, which began employing artificial intelligence to scan and delete images deemed to include banned content. In April, several extremely popular applications that provided news or enabled the sharing of humorous content to tens of millions of users were abruptly suspended or shut down for failing to "rectify" their content sufficiently.

The increased media controls also affected the entertainment industry, which received orders in July to ensure that multimedia productions brim with "positive energy" and "illustrate core socialist values." Meanwhile, authorities sought to improve their monitoring and management of influential online commentators, mysteriously detained movie star Fan Bingbing for alleged tax evasion, and blocked the website of US television network HBO after British comedian John Oliver critiqued Xi Jinping on his satirical news program.

According to the Committee to Protect Journalists (CPJ), 47 journalists were jailed in China as of December 2018, although the actual number of people held for uncovering or sharing newsworthy information is much greater. Foreign journalists continued to face various forms of harassment during the year, including physical abuse, short-term detention to prevent meetings with certain individuals, intimidation of Chinese sources and staff, the withholding of or threats to withhold visas, and surveillance.

Despite heavy restrictions on media freedom, Chinese journalists, grassroots activists, and internet users continue to seek out and exploit new ways to expose official misconduct, access uncensored information, and share incisive political commentary, although they risked reprisals when doing so. Tens of millions of people used circumvention tools like virtual private networks (VPNs) to reach the uncensored global internet or accessed blocked overseas broadcasts via satellite, but a number of activists were sentenced to prison for selling VPN services or helping people to install satellite dishes for viewing overseas Chinese stations.

Score Change: The score declined from 1 to 0 because the already limited space for media freedom shrank further during 2018, as the government worked more vigorously to eliminate the remaining avenues for circumventing censorship.

D2. Are individuals free to practice and express their religious faith or nonbelief in public and private? 0 / 4

The CCP regime has established a multifaceted apparatus to control all aspects of religious activity, including by vetting religious leaders for political reliability, placing limits on the number of new monastics or priests, and manipulating religious doctrine according to party priorities. The ability of China's religious believers to practice their faith varies dramatically based on religious affiliation, location, and registration status. Many do not necessarily feel constrained, particularly if they are Chinese Buddhists or Taoists. However, a 2017 Freedom House report found that at least 100 million believers belong to groups facing high or very high levels of religious persecution, namely Protestant Christians, Tibetan Buddhists, Uighur Muslims, and Falun Gong practitioners.

During 2018, the government increased restrictions on a range of religious communities, including state-sanctioned Christian congregations and Hui Muslims. New regulations on religious affairs that took effect in February strengthened controls on places of worship, travel for religious purposes, and children's religious education. In May, online retailers were barred from selling copies of the Bible. The Vatican and the Chinese government reached a provisional agreement in September on the appointment of Catholic bishops. While the deal was not made public, it would reportedly allow the government to nominate bishops and the Vatican to exercise a veto. The Vatican also recognized seven government-approved bishops who had previously been excommunicated; the status of dozens of existing bishops recognized by the Vatican but not by the government remained unclear. Persecution of unofficial Protestant groups continued during the year. In January, authorities in Shanxi Province demolished the Golden Lampstand Church, where an unregistered congregation of more than 50,000 people had worshipped, and placed some church members under house arrest.

The especially intense and intrusive curbs on the practice of Islam in Xinjiang, which are apparently aimed at breaking down the religious identify of Muslims in the region, have affected the wearing of religious attire, attendance at mosques, fasting during Ramadan, choice of baby names, and other basic forms of religious expression. In 2018, the Chinese authorities increased the punishment of peaceful religious practices under charges of "religious extremism," resulting in detention and indoctrination for many Uighur, Kazakh, and Hui Muslims. Among other cases during the year, a prominent scholar of Islam, 82-year-old Muhammad Salih Hajim, died in custody at a reeducation camp in January, about 40 days after he was detained. In September, Radio Free Asia reported that most of his family members were in detention or missing, including his young grandchildren.

The regime's campaign against the Falun Gong spiritual group continued in 2018. Hundreds of Falun Gong practitioners have received long prison terms in recent years, and many others are arbitrarily detained in various "legal education" facilities. Detainees typically face torture aimed at forcing them to abandon their beliefs, sometimes resulting in deaths in custody. Although repression of the group appears to have declined in some locales, a leaked document from Liaoning Province called for an intensified effort to crack down on Falun Gong and the Church of Almighty God—a banned quasi-Christian group—in the province from October to December, with a particular emphasis on suppressing means of communication that are used to disseminate reports of abuse outside China.

D3. Is there academic freedom, and is the educational system free from extensive political indoctrination? 1 / 4

Academic freedom is restricted with respect to politically sensitive issues, and the room for academic discussion dwindled further in 2018, even on what were previously less sensitive topics like labor rights, the rule of law, or economics. Efforts to police day-to-day classroom discussions have increased at all levels of education, including via installation of surveillance cameras in some classrooms and the creation of special departments to supervise the political thinking of teaching staff. The CCP controls the appointment of top university officials. Many scholars practice self-censorship to protect their careers, and several professors faced reprisals during the year for expressing views that were deemed critical of the CCP's governance, whether in class, online, or in interviews with overseas media. Political indoctrination—including the study of "Xi Jinping Thought"—is a required component of the curriculum at all levels of education. In October, Cornell University in the United States ended its joint program with Renmin University in Beijing due to concerns about restrictions on academic freedom and reprisals against left-wing Chinese student activists who campaigned for the rights of low-income workers.

D4. Are individuals free to express their personal views on political or other sensitive topics without fear of surveillance or retribution? 1 / 4

The government's ability to monitor citizens' lives and communications has increased dramatically in recent years, inhibiting online and offline conversations. Social media applications like WeChat, used by hundreds of millions of people, are known to closely monitor user discussions so as to conform with government content restrictions. Surveillance cameras, increasingly augmented with facial recognition software, cover many urban areas and public transportation, and are expanding into rural regions. Pilot programs for a Social Credit System—expected to become mandatory and nationally operational in 2020—rate citizens' trustworthiness based not only on financial responsibility or debt records, but also on purchasing behavior, video gaming habits, social acquaintances, and adherence to rules in public spaces. Devices used by police to quickly extract and scan data from smartphones, initially deployed in Xinjiang, have spread nationwide. The 2017 Cybersecurity Law requires companies to store Chinese users' data in China and submit to potentially intrusive security reviews. Apple was one of several international companies to comply with the provisions in 2018, transferring its iCloud data to servers run by a company owned by the Guizhou provincial government.

Electronic surveillance is supplemented with offline monitoring by neighborhood party committees, "public security volunteers" who are visible during large events, students who report on classmates and teachers, and an especially heavy police presence in places like Xinjiang.

Court verdicts have cited private social media communications, public surveillance video, and personal meetings as evidence in cases where citizens were punished for expressing their views on political or religious topics.

E. ASSOCIATIONAL AND ORGANIZATIONAL RIGHTS: 2 / 12 (−1)
E1. Is there freedom of assembly? 1 / 4

China's constitution protects the right of citizens to demonstrate, but in practice protesters rarely obtain approval and risk punishment for assembling without permission. Spontaneous demonstrations have thus become a common form of protest. Some are met with police violence, and organizers often face reprisals, even in cases where local officials ultimately concede to protesters' demands. Armed police have been accused of opening fire during past protests in Xinjiang.

E2. Is there freedom for nongovernmental organizations, particularly those that are engaged in human rights- and governance-related work? 0 / 4 (−1)

The ability of civil society organizations to engage in work related to human rights and governance is extremely constrained and has decreased over the past two years. Implementation of a 2017 law on foreign NGOs and 2016 legislation governing philanthropy has significantly reduced civic groups' access to funding from foreign sources and has increased supervision and funding from the government. NGOs that attempt to retain a greater degree of independence, including those working on human rights and the rule of law, are increasingly marginalized. The space for organizations to operate without formal registration, a previously common practice, has also shrunk, although some continue to do so. Several prominent NGOs that focused on policy advocacy, including in less politically sensitive areas like public health or women's rights, have been shuttered in recent years under government pressure. Hundreds of thousands of NGOs are formally registered, but many operate more as government-sponsored entities and focus on service delivery.

The foreign NGO law that took effect in 2017 prohibits the groups from engaging in activities that the government deems to "endanger China's national unity, security, or ethnic unity" or "harm China's national interests and the public interest." Foreign NGOs operating in China are required to register with the Ministry of Public Security instead of the Ministry of Civil Affairs, which has managed civil society organizations in the past, and to find a "professional supervisory unit"—a Chinese entity willing to act as sponsor. The changes give the police the authority search NGOs' premises without a warrant, seize property, detain personnel, and initiate criminal procedures. The law's implementation impeded the activities of foreign and domestic NGOs during 2018. Hundreds of foreign NGOs had registered offices or temporary activities, though the vast majority were trade and agricultural associations, or groups involved in issues such as cultural exchange, public health, or disability rights. A list of sponsoring Chinese entities documented by the China-File NGO Project indicated a heavy presence of state and CCP-affiliated organizations. In December, Chinese officials attempted to justify the arrest of former Canadian diplomat Michael Kovrig for "endangering national security"—in apparent retribution for Canada's detention of Chinese telecommunications executive Meng Wanzhou, who was accused of fraud related to US sanctions against Iran—by noting that the International Crisis Group, for which he worked as a senior adviser, was not registered.

Score Change: The score declined from 1 to 0 because implementation of a 2017 law on foreign NGOs and 2016 legislation regulating philanthropy has significantly reduced NGOs' ability to operate legally and independently, and several prominent groups have been forced to close in recent years.

E3. Is there freedom for trade unions and similar professional or labor organizations? 1 / 4

The only legal labor union organization is the government-controlled All-China Federation of Trade Unions (ACFTU), which has long been criticized for failing to properly defend workers' rights, but has reportedly become even less of an ally to workers in recent years. The authorities continued a multiyear crackdown on labor activists and NGOs during 2018. Beginning in July, police and managers engaged in reprisals against workers at Shenzhen Jasic Technology in Guangdong Province who had tried to establish a union and elect their own leaders, despite the fact that the group initially had approval from a local unit of the ACFTU. The crackdown extended to student activists and representatives of labor NGOs who sought to support the workers; they were variously harassed, detained, interrogated, and threatened.

Despite the constraints on legal union activity, strikes and labor protests continued to be reported across the country. About 1,700 such incidents were documented by the China Labour Bulletin in 2018.

F. RULE OF LAW: 2 / 16
F1. Is there an independent judiciary? 1 / 4

The CCP dominates the judicial system, with courts at all levels supervised by party political-legal committees that have influence over the appointment of judges, court operations, and verdicts and sentences. CCP oversight is especially evident in politically sensitive cases, and most judges are CCP members. In March 2018, Supreme People's Court president Zhou Qiang stated that the judiciary's first priority during the year would be to defend "the party's centralized and unified leadership, with Xi Jinping as the core leader." He advocated ideological conformity and absolute obedience to the CCP for the country's judges.

Incremental reforms aimed at improving judicial performance, while maintaining party supremacy, have been introduced since 2014. The changes focused on increasing transparency, professionalism, and autonomy from local authorities. Many judges complain about local officials interfering in cases to protect powerful litigants, support important industries, or avoid their own potential liability.

F2. Does due process prevail in civil and criminal matters? 1 / 4

Broader judicial reforms introduced in recent decades have sought to guarantee better access to lawyers, allow witnesses to be cross-examined, and establish other safeguards to prevent wrongful convictions and miscarriages of justice. However, limitations on due process—including excessive use of pretrial detention—remain rampant, and a multiyear crackdown on human rights lawyers has weakened defendants' access to independent legal counsel. Rights attorney Wang Quanzhang was put on trial in late December after 3.5 years of incommunicado detention; police harassed and mistreated his wife during the year when she sought information on his whereabouts and physical condition, and she was barred from attending the trial.

Criminal trials are frequently closed to the public, and the conviction rate is estimated at 98 percent or more. Adjudication of minor civil and administrative disputes is relatively fair, but cases that touch on politically sensitive issues or the interests of powerful groups are subject to decisive "guidance" from political-legal committees.

In recent years, a series of human rights lawyers, activists, and other high-profile detainees have been presented in the media giving what are widely assumed to be forced confessions, undermining their right to due process. A report published in April 2018 by the rights group Safeguard Defenders documented the details surrounding 45 such confessions recorded between 2013 and 2018, noting in particular the collaboration of state broadcaster China Central Television in the repressive practice.

Despite the abolition of "reeducation through labor" camps at the end of 2013, large numbers of people—particularly petitioners, grassroots rights activists, Falun Gong adherents, and Uighur Muslims—are still held in other forms of arbitrary detention, including the growing network of extralegal political indoctrination centers in Xinjiang. A new form of extrajudicial detention for targets of anticorruption and official misconduct investigations, known as *liuzhi*, was introduced in 2018, in tandem with the establishment of the NSC. Individuals can be held in *liuzhi* for up to six months without access to legal counsel.

F3. Is there protection from the illegitimate use of physical force and freedom from war and insurgencies? 0 / 4

Conditions in places of detention are harsh, with reports of inadequate food, regular beatings, and deprivation of medical care. Recent legal amendments encourage judges to exclude evidence obtained through torture, but in practice, torture and other forms of coercion are widely used to extract confessions or force political and religious dissidents to recant their beliefs. During 2018, human rights lawyers detained for their work reportedly experienced severe abuse in custody, including forced medication, while other activists were denied medical parole or treatment despite serious health concerns. Security agents routinely flout legal protections, and impunity is the norm for police brutality and suspicious deaths in custody. Citizens who seek redress for abuse in custody often meet with reprisals and even imprisonment. In May 2018, the first known death of a *liuzhi* detainee was reported. The man, whose body showed signs of abuse, was the 45-year-old driver of a Fujian Province official being investigated for corruption.

The government has gradually reduced the number of crimes that carry the death penalty, which totaled 46 as of 2018, but it is estimated that thousands of inmates are executed each year; the true figure is considered a state secret. The government claims it has ended the transplantation of organs from executed prisoners. However, the scale of the transplantation industry and the speed with which some organs are procured far exceed what is feasible via the country's nascent voluntary donation system. Rights activists, journalists, and medical professionals continued to express concerns in 2018 regarding unethical and illicit organ sourcing from prisoners, including religious and ethnic minorities such as Falun Gong adherents and Uighurs.

F4. Do laws, policies, and practices guarantee equal treatment of various segments of the population? 0 / 4

Chinese laws formally prohibit discrimination based on nationality, ethnicity, race, gender, religion, or health condition, but these protections are often violated in practice. Several laws bar gender discrimination in the workplace, and gender equality has reportedly improved over the past decade. Nevertheless, bias remains widespread, including in job recruitment and college admissions. The #MeToo movement against sexual harassment, which began in the United States and has spread to China, helped to raise awareness of the problem during 2018. A section on workplace sexual harassment was included in a draft of the new civil code published in August and set to be adopted in 2020; it imposes new requirements on employers to prevent abuses and address complaints. New stories of sexual harassment or assault went viral online on a regular basis, even as the hashtag itself and a prominent feminist Weibo account were censored during the year.

Ethnic and religious minorities, LGBT people, the disabled, and people with HIV/AIDS, hepatitis B, or other illnesses also face widespread discrimination in employment and access to education. Religious and ethnic minorities—especially Falun Gong adherents, Uighurs, and Tibetans—are disproportionately targeted and abused by security forces and the criminal justice system. For example, official figures published during 2018 showed that the number of criminal arrests in Xinjiang in 2017 made up over 21 percent of the national total, even though the region's population amounts to less than 2 percent of China's total.

Despite China's international obligation to protect the rights of asylum seekers and refugees, Chinese law enforcement agencies continue to repatriate North Korean defectors, who face imprisonment or execution upon return. During 2018, the authorities introduced new security measures to limit the flow of refugees at the border and increased rewards for informants who identify those hiding in China.

G. PERSONAL AUTONOMY AND INDIVIDUAL RIGHTS: 6 / 16

G1. Do individuals enjoy freedom of movement, including the ability to change their place of residence, employment, or education? 1 / 4

China's *hukou* (household registration) system prevents roughly 290 million internal migrants from enjoying full legal status as residents in cities where they work. The government has announced plans to gradually reform the system, expanding the benefits of urban residency to 100 million migrants based on their education, employment record, and housing status, with the most stringent requirements in major cities like Shanghai and Beijing and much looser standards applied in smaller municipalities. The plan would still leave a large majority of migrants without equal rights or full access to social services such as education for their children in local schools. During 2018, authorities in Beijing continued implementing forced evictions and demolitions that began in November 2017 in neighborhoods where migrants lived or worked; officials cited safety violations, but observers linked the clearances to government plans to cap Beijing's population.

Many other Chinese citizens also face obstacles to freedom of movement within the country. Police checkpoints throughout Xinjiang limit residents' ability to travel or even leave their hometown. Elsewhere in China, as initial stages of a Social Credit System were introduced during 2018, millions of citizens reportedly encountered restrictions on air and train travel due to their low scores. While China's constitution gives individuals the right to petition the government concerning a grievance or injustice, in practice petitioners are routinely intercepted in their efforts to reach Beijing, forcefully returned to their hometowns, or extralegally detained in "black jails," psychiatric institutions, and other sites, where they are at risk of abuse.

Millions of people are affected by government restrictions on their access to foreign travel and passports, many of them Uighurs and Tibetans. Overseas Chinese nationals who engage in politically sensitive activities are at risk of being prevented by the authorities from returning to China, or choose not to return for fear of being arrested.

G2. Are individuals able to exercise the right to own property and establish private businesses without undue interference from state or nonstate actors? 1 / 4

The authorities dominate the economy through state-owned enterprises in key sectors such as banking and energy, and through state ownership of land. Chinese citizens are legally permitted to establish and operate private businesses. However, those without strong informal ties to powerful officials often find themselves at a disadvantage in legal disputes with competitors, in dealings with regulators, or in the context of politicized anticorruption campaigns. Foreign companies and executives can face arbitrary regulatory obstacles, debilitating censorship, demands for bribes, travel restrictions, or negative media campaigns. In June 2018, regulators pressured private firms listed on the country's stock exchanges to "strengthen party-building" within their ranks; official sources reported in 2017 that 70 percent of private companies in China had internal party organizations.

Property rights protection remains weak. Urban land is owned by the state, with only the buildings themselves in private hands. Rural land is collectively owned by villages. Farmers enjoy long-term lease rights to the land they work, but they have been restricted in their ability to transfer, sell, or develop it. Low compensation and weak legal protections have facilitated land seizures by local officials, who often evict residents and transfer the land rights to developers. Corruption is endemic in such projects, and local governments rely on land development as a key source of revenue.

G3. Do individuals enjoy personal social freedoms, including choice of marriage partner and size of family, protection from domestic violence, and control over appearance? 2 / 4

A legal amendment allowing all families to have two children—effectively abolishing the one-child policy that had long applied to most citizens—took effect in 2016. While the authorities continue to regulate reproduction, the change means that fewer families are likely to encounter the punitive aspects of the system, such as high fines, job dismissal, reduced government benefits, and occasionally detention. Abuses such as forced abortions and sterilizations are less common than in the past but continue to occur. Ethnic minorities are still permitted to have up to three children.

Muslims in Xinjiang face restrictions and penalties related to aspects of their appearance with religious connotations, such as face-covering veils on women or long beards on men.

The country's first law designed to combat domestic violence came into effect in 2016, but domestic violence continues to be a serious problem, affecting one-quarter of Chinese women, according to official figures. Activists have complained that the new law fails to provide support for victims, and that it is extremely difficult for victims to win court cases against their abusers.

G4. Do individuals enjoy equality of opportunity and freedom from economic exploitation? 2 / 4

While workers in China are afforded important protections under existing laws, violations of labor and employment regulations are widespread. Local CCP officials have long been incentivized to focus on economic growth rather than the enforcement of labor laws. Exploitative employment practices such as wage theft, excessive overtime, student labor, and unsafe working conditions are pervasive in many industries. Forced labor and trafficking are also common, frequently affecting rural migrants, and Chinese nationals are similarly trafficked abroad. Forced labor is the norm in prisons and other forms of administrative detention for criminal, political, and religious detainees. In 2018, authorities in Xinjiang reportedly began using detainees in the region's new network of detention camps for forced or low-paid labor at factories built inside or near the facilities.

Colombia

Population: 49,800,000
Capital: Bogotá
Political Rights Rating: 3
Civil Liberties Rating: 3
Freedom Rating: 3.0
Freedom Status: Partly Free
Electoral Democracy: Yes

Overview: Colombia is among the longest-standing democracies in Latin America, but one with a history of widespread violence and serious human rights abuses. The incidence of violence has declined in recent years, and public institutions have demonstrated the capacity to check executive power and enforce the rule of law. The government and the country's main left-wing guerrilla group signed a peace accord in 2016, but as of 2018 Colombia still faced enormous challenges in consolidating peace and guaranteeing political rights and civil liberties throughout its territory.

KEY DEVELOPMENTS IN 2018:

- Right-wing candidate Iván Duque was elected president in June, defeating leftist Gustavo Petro in a second-round runoff to replace outgoing two-term president Juan Manuel Santos.
- The peace accord signed in 2016 between the government and the left-wing Revolutionary Armed Forces of Colombia (FARC) rebel group remained intact during the year, but implementation delays prompted concern about the pact's durability.
- A wave of lethal attacks against human rights defenders and other social activists continued throughout the year. Scores of activists were murdered, and the perpetrators of such crimes generally enjoyed impunity.

POLITICAL RIGHTS: 29 / 40
A. ELECTORAL PROCESS: 10 / 12

A1. Was the current head of government or other chief national authority elected through free and fair elections? 4 / 4

The president is directly elected to a four-year term. As part of a series of 2015 constitutional amendments, immediate presidential reelection was eliminated, making incumbent president Santos, reelected in 2014, the last to serve two consecutive terms.

The peace accord was a significant issue in the 2018 election. Duque of the Democratic Center (CD) party, a protégé of former president and chief peace accord critic Álvaro Uribe, pledged throughout the campaign to alter the pact's terms, which he characterized as overly magnanimous toward the guerrillas. However, corruption, crime, and social services were also prominent themes during the campaign, as was the ongoing political and economic crisis in neighboring Venezuela.

Duque easily led the first round in May with 39 percent of the vote, followed by left-wing candidate and former Bogotá mayor Gustavo Petro, whose 25 percent share narrowly held off centrist candidate and former Antioquia governor Sergio Fajardo. The tone of the second round in June was highly polarized: Petro and his supporters tarred Duque as Uribe's puppet, while the CD and its allies described Petro as liable to lead Colombia toward a Venezuela-style implosion. Duque won with 54 percent of the vote, leaving Petro with 42 percent. The balloting was considered competitive and credible, though election observers logged sporadic reports of vote buying and other violations in both the first and second rounds.

A2. Were the current national legislative representatives elected through free and fair elections? 3 / 4

Congress is composed of the Senate and the Chamber of Representatives, with all seats up for election every four years. The nation at large selects 100 Senate members using a proportional representation system; two additional members are chosen by indigenous communities, one seat is awarded to the runner-up in the presidential election, and another five seats were reserved in 2018 and 2022 for the FARC under the peace accord. The Chamber of Representatives consists of 172 members, with 161 elected by proportional representation in multimember districts, two chosen by Afro-Colombian communities, one each by indigenous and expatriate voters, one seat reserved for the runner-up vice presidential candidate, and five seats reserved for the FARC, as in the Senate.

The March 2018 legislative elections were relatively peaceful, though observers noted accusations of fraud, vote buying, and connections between candidates and organized crime figures. Threats and attacks against FARC candidates prompted the party to suspend campaign activity in February. Senate seats were dispersed, with six parties winning 10 or more seats, led by Duque's CD with 19. In the Chamber of Representatives, five parties won 21 or more seats, led by the Liberal Party with 35; the CD garnered 32 seats. In its first balloting as a legal party, the FARC managed a meager 0.3 percent of the vote in the Senate and 0.2 percent in the House of Representatives, meaning it took no seats aside from the five guaranteed to it in each chamber.

A3. Are the electoral laws and framework fair, and are they implemented impartially by the relevant election management bodies? 3 / 4

The legal framework generally allows for competitive balloting in practice, though the National Electoral Council (CNE)—which oversees the conduct of the country's elections, including the financing of political campaigns and the counting of votes—has faced criticism for ineffective enforcement of electoral laws, blamed in part on the partisan selection system for its members. The nine members of the CNE are elected by Congress for four-year terms based on party nominations. In August 2018, congressional leaders again used the party-quota system to elect a new slate of councillors, despite new laws that could have produced a more meritocratic process.

B. POLITICAL PLURALISM AND PARTICIPATION: 11 / 16

B1. Do the people have the right to organize in different political parties or other competitive political groupings of their choice, and is the system free of undue obstacles to the rise and fall of these competing parties or groupings? 3 / 4

Colombia's historically rigid two-party system has undergone a protracted process of realignment and diversification in recent years. The 2018 elections brought into the legislature a relatively balanced mix of parties—some of which remain focused on leading personalities—from the left, right, and center. Nonetheless, this balance, coupled with intraparty splits, left Duque without a stable majority in either legislative chamber.

The FARC, whose acronym now stands for Common Alternative Revolutionary Force, officially reorganized as a political party in 2017 and was allowed to participate in the 2018 elections. While its candidates faced threats and attacks, the congressional seats it received under the peace accord gave it far more representation than it would have earned through normal voting.

B2. Is there a realistic opportunity for the opposition to increase its support or gain power through elections? 3 / 4

Democratic transfers of power between rival parties is routine at both the national level and in the regions, though some areas remain under the long-term control of machine-style political clans with ties to organized crime. Petro's performance in the 2018 presidential election marked the strongest showing for the political left in a modern presidential campaign, demonstrating the viability of a broader range of candidates for high-level office.

B3. Are the people's political choices free from domination by the military, foreign powers, religious hierarchies, economic oligarchies, or any other powerful group that is not democratically accountable? 2 / 4

Despite the peace accord with the FARC, activity by the smaller National Liberation Army (ELN) leftist guerrilla group, the successors of previously disbanded right-wing paramilitary groups, and criminal gangs has continued to impair the ability of citizens in some areas to participate freely in the political process.

B4. Do various segments of the population (including ethnic, religious, gender, LGBT, and other relevant groups) have full political rights and electoral opportunities? 3 / 4

While progress remains slow, the government has undertaken a series of steps to incorporate indigenous and Afro-Colombian voices into national political debates in recent years. The 2016 peace accord included provisions for improving consultation mechanisms for marginalized groups.

Women enjoy equal political rights, and at least 30 percent of the candidates on party lists must be women. About 20 percent of the seats in each congressional chamber are currently held by women.

C. FUNCTIONING OF GOVERNMENT: 8 / 12

C1. Do the freely elected head of government and national legislative representatives determine the policies of the government? 3 / 4

Elected officials generally determine government policy without interference. However, the Colombian state has long struggled to establish a secure presence in all parts of its territory, meaning threats from guerrilla groups and criminal gangs can disrupt policymaking and implementation in certain regions and localities.

C2. Are safeguards against official corruption strong and effective? 2 / 4

Corruption occurs at multiple levels of public administration. Graft scandals have emerged in recent years within an array of federal agencies, but investigations do result in convictions, including against senior officials. Numerous members of the two Uribe administrations (2002–10) were convicted of corruption, trading favors, and spying on political opponents.

A multicountry bribery scandal centered on the Brazilian construction firm Odebrecht led to charges in 2017 against two senators and multiple former legislators and bureaucrats. The November 2018 death of Jorge Enrique Pizano, a key witness in the Odebrecht investigation, followed three days later by the mysterious poisoning death of his son, returned the scandal to the headlines. In 2015, Pizano had passed along information regarding financial irregularities at Odebrecht to Néstor Humberto Martínez, at that time a lawyer for one of Colombia's largest conglomerates and now Colombia's attorney general. In December 2018, a special prosecutor was selected to continue the investigation. Separately, the former head of the anticorruption unit within the attorney general's office, Luis Gustavo Moreno, was extradited to the United States in May to face charges that he took bribes from the target of a corruption probe.

C3. Does the government operate with openness and transparency? 3 / 4

Government information is generally available to the public, though information related to military and security affairs can be difficult to access. Congress maintains an online platform on which legislators can voluntarily publish financial disclosures.

A proposal that was put to a referendum in August 2018 would have committed lawmakers to passing a set of reforms meant to increase government transparency and combat corruption. The changes included more public and competitive state contracting procedures, citizen participation in budget making, mandatory public financial disclosures for officials, and congressional disclosures on lobbying activity. Although support for the measures was nearly unanimous, turnout narrowly failed to reach the one-third of registered voters necessary for the outcome to be binding. Many of the referendum proposals were introduced to Congress in September with President Duque's support, but they failed to gain legislative traction.

CIVIL LIBERTIES: 37 / 60 (+1)

D. FREEDOM OF EXPRESSION AND BELIEF: 12 / 16

D1. Are there free and independent media? 2 / 4

The constitution guarantees freedom of expression, and opposition views are commonly aired in the media. However, journalists face intimidation, kidnapping, and violence both in the course of reporting and as retaliation for their work. Dozens of journalists have been murdered since the mid-1990s, many of them targeted for reporting on drug trafficking and corruption. The government has prosecuted several notorious cases of murdered journalists in recent years, but convictions are rare, and the statute of limitations has expired for many cases. According to local press group Foundation for Press Freedom, threats against journalists rose significantly in the first half of 2018. Two Ecuadorian journalists were killed in Colombia by FARC dissidents in April, and multiple prominent Colombian reporters received death threats from the Black Eagles paramilitary successor group in July.

Self-censorship is common, and slander and defamation remain criminal offenses. The government does not restrict access to the internet, nor does it censor websites. Twitter and other social media platforms have become important arenas for political discourse.

D2. Are individuals free to practice and express their religious faith or nonbelief in public and private? 4 / 4

The constitution provides for freedom of religion, and the government generally respects this right in practice.

D3. Is there academic freedom, and is the educational system free from extensive political indoctrination? 3 / 4

Academic freedom is generally respected. University debates are often vigorous, though armed groups maintain a presence on some campuses to generate political support and intimidate opponents. Starting in October 2018, tens of thousands of university students initiated the first major protests of the Duque administration, demanding increased funding for higher education. An agreement on greater education investment was reached in December.

D4. Are individuals free to express their personal views on political or other sensitive topics without fear of surveillance or retribution? 3 / 4

Individual expression is generally protected in major urban centers, but it remains inhibited in more remote areas where the state, insurgents, and criminals vie for control.

E. ASSOCIATIONAL AND ORGANIZATIONAL RIGHTS: 6 / 12 (+1)

E1. Is there freedom of assembly? 2 / 4

Although provided for in the constitution, freedom of assembly is restricted in practice by violence. The riot police are known for moving aggressively to break up protests, sometimes using deadly force.

E2. Is there freedom for nongovernmental organizations, particularly those that are engaged in human rights- and governance-related work? 2 / 4

The legal framework generally supports nongovernmental organizations, and civil society is diverse and active, but the threat of violent reprisal poses a major obstacle to freedom of association. While the government provides protection to hundreds of threatened human rights workers, trust in the service varies widely. Hundreds of activists have been murdered in recent years, mostly by the criminal organizations that succeeded right-wing paramilitary groups following a government-backed demobilization process in 2005. Although the Duque administration has reiterated its respect for civil society groups and in August 2018 signed an agreement committing the government to developing more effective protection policies, violations against activists have continued to rise. The Ombudsman's Office registered 172 killings during the year. We Are Defenders, a coalition of local and international rights groups, noted in a September report that the country suffered from a 91 percent impunity rate for the 563 activists killed between 2009 and 2017. Land rights and victims' rights campaigners in particular are threatened by former paramilitaries and other local actors seeking to deflect attention from assets acquired during the conflict and to halt the implementation of rural development programs.

E3. Is there freedom for trade unions and similar professional or labor organizations? 2 / 4 (+1)

Workers may form and join trade unions, bargain collectively, and strike, and antiunion discrimination is prohibited. Over the past two decades, Colombia's illegal armed groups have killed more than 2,600 labor union activists and leaders. Killings have declined substantially from their peak in the early 2000s, though 28 unionists were murdered between January and November 2018. A special prosecutorial unit has substantially increased prosecutions for such assassinations since 2007, but few investigations have targeted those who ordered the killings.

Score Change: The score improved from 1 to 2 because while attacks against labor leaders and activists persist, their frequency has decreased over the last decade.

F. RULE OF LAW: 9 / 16

F1. Is there an independent judiciary? 3 / 4

The justice system remains compromised by corruption and extortion. The Constitutional Court and the Supreme Court have consistently exhibited independence from the executive, though corruption allegations involving Supreme Court justices that emerged in 2017 and remained under investigation in 2018 damaged the high court's credibility.

The Constitutional Court has repeatedly been asked to mediate polarizing political disputes, especially with respect to the Special Jurisdiction for Peace (JEP), a parallel court structure or tribunal that lies at the heart of the 2016 peace accord's transitional justice system. In August 2018 the court upheld most of the 2017 statutory law governing the JEP; it must still consider the implementing regulations passed in June 2018. The August ruling struck down several provisions that would have restricted the JEP's power, but key questions, including the incarceration regime for convicted war criminals and the extent of criminal culpability for military officers whose subordinates committed grave rights abuses, remained hotly disputed throughout the year. Tensions regarding the relative authority of the attorney general's office and the JEP were recurrent in 2018. In October, representatives from the attorney general's office attempted to seize documents from the JEP before backing down, and the entities clashed on other occasions over the handling of a US extradition request for FARC leader Jesús Santrich, who was arrested in April on accusations of cocaine trafficking.

F2. Does due process prevail in civil and criminal matters? 2 / 4

Due process protections remain weak, and trial processes move very slowly. However, in recent years the government has been able to assert state control over more territory, bringing basic due process rights to more people. The prosecutorial service is relatively professional, and long-delayed changes to the criminal procedure code that were intended to ameliorate extended pretrial detention took effect in 2017. Separately, the two key transitional justice bodies, the JEP and the Truth Commission, began operations in January and November 2018, respectively, amid anticipation and uncertainty about the extent to which the bodies would be able to render a comprehensive historical and judicial accounting of Colombia's conflict.

F3. Is there protection from the illegitimate use of physical force and freedom from war and insurgencies? 2 / 4

Many soldiers operate with limited civilian oversight, though the government has in recent years increased human rights training and investigated a greater number of violations by security forces personnel. Collaboration between security forces and illegal armed groups has declined, but rights groups report official toleration of paramilitary successor groups in some regions. The police are more professional than many in neighboring countries but lack necessary resources, are sometimes accused of colluding with criminals, and are largely absent from many rural areas where the most dangerous groups are active.

Civil-military relations have been a source of significant tension in recent years. A portion of the armed forces opposed the peace process, and public uncertainty regarding the ability of accused human rights violators within the military to receive benefits under the transitional justice system is one of the most controversial elements of the process. The systematic killing of civilians to fraudulently inflate guerrilla death tolls resulted in as many as 3,000 murders by the military between 2002 and 2008. As of November 2018, at least nine generals were among the thousands of soldiers seeking benefits under the transitional justice process after being convicted or investigated for these and other abuses.

Some parts of the country, particularly resource-rich zones and drug-trafficking corridors, remain highly insecure. Remnant guerrilla forces—including both the ELN and dissident factions of the FARC—and paramilitary successor groups regularly abuse the civilian population, especially in coca-growing areas. Cultivation of the plant has increased dramatically since the peace process took hold. Impunity for crime in general is rampant, and most massacres that took place during the conflict have gone unpunished. In July 2018 the Supreme Court opened a formal case against Uribe for bribery and witness tampering, and multiple other cases against him, including for massacres, are in the investigation phase. The September announcement prompted Uribe to declare later that month that he was resigning from the Senate, but he subsequently rescinded his resignation.

During 2018 a steady stream of former FARC combatants—including former second-in-command Iván Márquez—returned to clandestine life, in some cases joining the estimated 1,200 to 2,800 "dissidents" who had shunned the peace process in favor of criminal or insurgent activity. In December, Colombian troops killed one of the most aggressive dissidents, Walter Arizala, who had contributed to a wave of violence in the southwest department of Nariño. Meanwhile, peace talks between the government and the ELN stalled after the latter broke a cease-fire in January, then resumed in May. After Duque assumed the presidency, he suspended the talks again in September, and they remained suspended for the rest of the year.

Despite these problems, violence overall has significantly subsided since the early 2000s. In 2017, the homicide rate declined to its lowest point in four decades—roughly 24 per 100,000 people—and the number of conflict-related victims plummeted as a result of the peace process. Nonetheless, according to a September 2018 report from the think tank Ideas for Peace Foundation, violence and forced displacement rose in the first seven months of 2018 in 170 areas designated as priority development zones. The national homicide rate rose slightly to 25 per 100,000 people for the year.

F4. Do laws, policies, and practices guarantee equal treatment of various segments of the population? 2 / 4

The legal framework provides protections against various forms of discrimination based on gender, race and ethnicity, sexual orientation and gender identity, and other categories, and the government takes some measures to enforce these protections. Nevertheless, several vulnerable groups suffer serious disadvantages in practice.

Afro-Colombians, who account for as much as 25 percent of the population, make up the largest segment of the more than 7 million people who have been displaced by violence, and some 80 percent of Afro-Colombians live below the poverty line. Areas with concentrated Afro-Colombian populations continue to suffer from abuses by leftist guerrillas, security forces, and paramilitary successors.

Most of Colombia's indigenous inhabitants, who make up more than 3 percent of the population, live on approximately 34 million hectares granted to them by the government, often in resource-rich, strategic regions that are highly contested by armed groups. Indigenous people have been targeted by all sides in the country's various conflicts. In 2018, indigenous communities in the departments of Cauca and Nariño suffered violence and displacement perpetrated by the ELN, former FARC members, and paramilitary successors.

Women face employment discrimination and sexual harassment in the workplace, as well as gender-based violence. LGBT (lesbian, gay, bisexual, and transgender) people suffer societal discrimination and abuse, and there are also high levels of impunity for crimes committed against them.

More than a million Venezuelan migrants have entered Colombia since 2017, and the government has offered work permits and access to services to those who register, including Venezuelans who crossed the border irregularly.

G. PERSONAL AUTONOMY AND INDIVIDUAL RIGHTS: 10 / 16

G1. Do individuals enjoy freedom of movement, including the ability to change their place of residence, employment, or education? 3 / 4

Freedom of movement has improved substantially in tandem with the peace process, but it remains restricted by ongoing violence in certain regions, particularly for vulnerable minority groups. Travel in some remote areas is further limited by illegal checkpoints operated by criminal and guerrilla groups.

G2. Are individuals able to exercise the right to own property and establish private businesses without undue interference from state or nonstate actors? 2 / 4

Violence and instability in some areas threaten property rights and the ability to establish businesses. Guerrillas, paramilitary successor groups, and common criminals regularly extort payments from business owners. Corruption as well as undue pressure exerted on prosecutors and members of the judiciary can disrupt legitimate business activity.

Progress remains slow on the implementation of the landmark 2011 Victims and Land Law, which recognized the legitimacy of claims by victims of conflict-related abuses, including those committed by government forces. While affected citizens continue receiving compensation, the legal process for land restitution is heavily backlogged, and the resettlement of those who were displaced during the conflict continues to move slowly.

G3. Do individuals enjoy personal social freedoms, including choice of marriage partner and size of family, protection from domestic violence, and control over appearance? 3 / 4

Personal social freedoms, such as those related to marriage and divorce, are largely respected. In 2016, after several years of contradictory judicial and administrative decisions regarding same-sex unions, the Constitutional Court voted to legalize them. The court had legalized adoptions by same-sex couples in 2015. The country still has restrictive abortion laws, though in October 2018 the Constitutional Court reaffirmed a 2006 ruling that allowed abortion in cases of rape or incest, severe fetal malformation, or a threat to the life of the mother. Gender-based violence in Colombia has included thousands of rapes associated with the civil conflict, with perpetrators generally enjoying impunity.

G4. Do individuals enjoy equality of opportunity and freedom from economic exploitation? 2 / 4

Child labor, the recruitment of children by illegal armed groups, and related sexual abuse are serious problems in Colombia; recruitment has declined but not ended since the peace accord. A 2011 free trade agreement with the United States and a subsequent Labor Action Plan called for enhanced investigation of abusive labor practices and rights violations, but progress remains deficient in several areas. In coca-growing zones, armed groups exert coercive pressure on farmers to engage in coca cultivation and shun crop-substitution programs.

Comoros

Population: 800,000
Capital: Moroni
Political Rights Rating: 4↓
Civil Liberties Rating: 4
Freedom Rating: 4.0
Freedom Status: Partly Free
Electoral Democracy: No

Overview: Comoros's volatile political history includes a number of coups and attempted coups, though recent presidential and legislative elections have been reasonably well administered. In 2018, a controversial referendum ushered in a number of major systemic changes, and opponents of the referendum and its main proponent, President Azali Assoumani, were severely persecuted. Systemic corruption and poverty remain problems.

KEY DEVELOPMENTS IN 2018:
- Electoral authorities said a July constitutional referendum introducing major systemic changes was approved by 93 percent of voters. However, the referendum was boycotted by the opposition, who denounced it as an unconstitutional power grab by President Azali, and it was marred by allegations of intimidation and fraud. Many figures who spoke out against the referendum faced persecution.
- The referendum extended presidential term limits, abolished the previous system under which the presidency rotated among the country's three main islands, and enshrined Sunni Islam as the national religion. It additionally abolished the Constitutional Court, the country's highest, and transferred its competencies to a new chamber of the Supreme Court.
- Azali banned protests in May, ahead of the referendum, but antigovernment demonstrations took place throughout the year and were often met with violence by security forces. In October, three people were killed in chaotic protests that took place on Anjouan Island, where demonstrators alleged that the new constitution would lock the island's representatives out of government permanently.
- The year saw a wide-ranging crackdown on opposition figures that publicly criticized the referendum, including key figures who were convicted of plotting against the state. Separately, former president Ahmed Abdallah Mohamed Sambi—an opponent of Azali's who had been seen as a contender to win the presidency under the previous, rotating system—was arrested and jailed in August on corruption charges connected to an illicit passport-sale scheme.

POLITICAL RIGHTS: 21 / 40 (−3)
A. ELECTORAL PROCESS: 8 / 12 (−1)
A1. Was the current head of government or other chief national authority elected through free and fair elections? 3 / 4

Under the 2001 constitution, the president is directly elected for a single five-year term, with eligibility rotating among the main islands of Grande Comore (Ngazidja), Anjouan, and Mohéli. However, a new constitution, approved in a controversial July 2018 referendum boycotted by the opposition, allows the president to run for two consecutive five-year terms, and abolished the system of rotating power among the islands. Under the new constitution, President Azali of the Convention for the Renewal of the Comoros (CRC) will be able to run for two more terms. Early elections were set for 2019 by a December 2018 presidential decree.

Comoros held relatively free and fair presidential elections in 2016. The presidency rotated from Mohéli to Grande Comore. The cycle skipped the island of Mayotte, which Comoros claims but which remains under French administration. Azali won the election with 41 percent of the vote. International election observers noted some flaws during the first round in administration by the Independent National Electoral Commission (CENI), and disputes, in the second round, over alleged electoral fraud on Anjouan Island that sparked violence in several constituencies. The Constitutional Court ordered that polling at 13 stations be rerun due to these irregularities; the results of the rerun were roughly the same as in the annulled round.

A2. Were the current national legislative representatives elected through free and fair elections? 3 / 4

The unicameral Assembly of the Union consists of 33 members, 9 selected by the assemblies of the three islands and 24 by direct popular vote, who serve five-year terms. In 2015 elections, the Union for the Development of Comoros (UPDC) won 11 seats, the Juwa 10, the Democratic Rally of the Comoros (RDC) 4, and the CRC 2; the remaining seats were split between smaller parties and independent candidates. Although international observers said it was a calm and transparent election, the polls were marred by accusations of fraud, and of misuse of state resources by then president Ikililou Dhoinine's UPDC.

A3. Are the electoral laws and framework fair, and are they implemented impartially by the relevant election management bodies? 2 / 4 (−1)

The CENI, while generally able to run credible elections, has faced accusations of bias and corruption among its members. In 2016, CENI president Ahmed Djaza and three others members were detained for embezzlement. However, Djaza was reelected as its president in 2017.

The disputed constitutional referendum held in July 2018, which the CENI said passed with 93 percent of the vote, was marred by a boycott by the opposition, which denounced it as an unconstitutional power grab by Azali and said Azali's dismissal of the Constitutional Court ahead of the vote rendered it illegal. There were also allegations of voter intimidation and fraud. Later, upon facing growing dissent in the parliament, Azali fired the top opposition representative in the CENI.

The new constitution contains a number of new and significant provisions, including allowing the president to run for two consecutive five-year terms, abolishing the system of rotating power among the islands as well as the three vice-presidential posts (one representing each island), and declaring Sunni Islam as the national religion. It further transfers the competencies of the Constitutional Court, which was seen as having the capability to impartially decide electoral matters, to a new chamber of the Supreme Court.

Score Change: The score declined from 3 to 2 because a constitutional referendum that extended presidential term limits, among other changes, was marred by an opposition boycott, as well as allegations of intimidation and fraud, and because the top opposition representative in the electoral commission was dismissed by the president.

B. POLITICAL PLURALISM AND PARTICIPATION: 9 / 16 (−2)

B1. Do the people have the right to organize in different political parties or other competitive political groupings of their choice, and is the system free of undue obstacles to the rise and fall of these competing parties or groupings? 2 / 4 (−1)

Political parties are mainly formed around specific leaders and draw on island or ethnic bases of support. In the past, parties have generally been able to operate freely, though the government occasionally disrupted opposition parties' activities by denying them meeting and assembly space. However, 2018 was marked by a wide-ranging crackdown on opposition figures that publicly criticized the constitutional referendum, both before and after it took place. In June, Juwa secretary general Ahmed el-Barwane was arrested for his involvement in demonstrations against President Azali. In December, he was sentenced to seven years in prison after being convicted of directing an attack against a soldier during the protests.

El-Barwane was one of among some two dozen opposition figures to receive harsh sentences in December in connection with their public opposition to the referendum. Four key figures, including former vice president Djaffar Said Ahmed Hassane and former army head Ibrahim Salim, received life sentences with hard labor after being convicted of plotting against the state. At year's end, Juwa claimed that 100 of its members including Barwane had been arrested.

The string of arrests, prosecutions, and convictions prompted some Azali opponents to go into hiding. Hassane, for his part, was in exile in Tanzania at year's end. The crackdown on demonstrations also hampers the ability of opposition parties to gain support.

Score Change: The score declined from 3 to 2 because the arbitrary detentions, prosecutions, and convictions of key opposition leaders for protest activities has hindered the ability of opposition parties to freely operate.

B2. Is there a realistic opportunity for the opposition to increase its support or gain power through elections? 2 / 4 (−1)

In the past, Comoros's numerous opposition parties have seen a realistic chance of gaining power through elections, though they were impeded by occasional government interference in their operations, and allegations of misuse of state resources by incumbents were not uncommon. However, the arrests, convictions, and harsh sentences against opposition leaders who spoke out against the constitutional referendum and the president in 2018 hamper the ability of opposition parties to compete in elections, including in the upcoming 2019 presidential election.

Score Change: The score declined from 3 to 2 because the convictions and heavy sentences levied against opposition leaders after they spoke out against the president hampers the ability of opposition to compete in elections.

B3. Are the people's political choices free from domination by the military, foreign powers, religious hierarchies, economic oligarchies, or any other powerful group that is not democratically accountable? 3 / 4

People are generally free to exercise their political choices. However, the influence of Comoros's powerful army—which has cracked down on dissent—as well as of religious authorities can place pressure on voters and candidates.

B4. Do various segments of the population (including ethnic, religious, gender, LGBT, and other relevant groups) have full political rights and electoral opportunities? 2 / 4

There are no laws preventing various segments of the population from having full political rights and electoral opportunities. However, traditional attitudes discourage women from participating in politics, and women won just two seats in the legislature in 2015 elections. Legal and societal discrimination against LGBT (lesbian, gay, bisexual, and transgender) people makes political advocacy for LGBT rights difficult.

C. FUNCTIONING OF GOVERNMENT: 4 / 12

C1. Do the freely elected head of government and national legislative representatives determine the policies of the government? 2 / 4

According to the constitution, the president decides on the policies of the state, which are executed by the government. However, irregular activity in the legislature has hampered representative policymaking in recent years. In 2015, the newly installed Assembly of the Union chose its president in an irregular election that sparked accusations of an "institutional coup" from the opposition. During the vote, opposition members were prevented from accessing the chamber, at times through the intervention of security forces. The opposition parties, deeming the election illegitimate, unsuccessfully brought a case calling for the dismissal of the assembly president to the Constitutional Court.

C2. Are safeguards against official corruption strong and effective? 1 / 4

There are reports of corruption at all levels, including within the judiciary, civil service, and security forces. The Azali administration dissolved the National Commission for Preventing and Fighting Corruption (CNPLC) in 2016.

In August 2018, former president Ahmed Abdallah Mohamed Sambi was arrested for corruption, embezzlement of public funds, and forgery in connection with a large-scale passport sales scheme. A parliamentary report revealed that the plan had cost the country up to \$971 million. Sambi, who was from Anjouan, was considered to have been a likely contender to succeed Azali in the presidential race had the system of rotation of power between islands been preserved.

C3. Does the government operate with openness and transparency? 1 / 4

Government operations are characterized by a lack of transparency. Various reform initiatives have so far not successfully addressed the problem. Financial asset disclosures by public officials are not released to the public. Comoros provides the public with no opportunities to engage in the budget process.

CIVIL LIBERTIES: 29 / 60 (−2)
D. FREEDOM OF EXPRESSION AND BELIEF: 10 / 16
D1. Are there free and independent media? 2 / 4

The constitution and laws provide for freedom of speech and of the press. However, the use of censorship laws to prosecute legitimate journalistic work, and other pressure, has prompted widespread self-censorship. A series of press freedom infractions took place in 2018, including the closing of some private radio stations as criticism of Azali and the constitutional referendum gained traction. In July, the interior minister threatened to prosecute journalist Faïza Soulé Youssouf over her reporting on the referendum. In October, she was arrested while covering opposition protests.

D2. Are individuals free to practice and express their religious faith or nonbelief in public and private? 2 / 4

Islam is the state religion, and 98 percent of the population is Sunni Muslim. The July 2018 referendum officially made Sunni Islam the state religion, and resulted in some wariness of the government among adherents of minority religions. Previously, the state religion had been "Islam;" some observers suggested the change reflected efforts by Azali to bring the country closer to Saudi Arabia, and to counter the influence of a rival, former president Sambi, who is seen as close to Iran.

Anti-Shia sentiments have been publicly expressed by some government figures, while many Christians keep their faith private in order to avoid harassment. Proselytizing and public religious ceremonies are prohibited for all religions except Sunni Islam.

D3. Is there academic freedom, and is the educational system free from extensive political indoctrination? 3 / 4

Comoros has two types of schools: madrassas, where the Quran is integral, and state-run schools with French instruction. Academic freedom is generally respected, though the education system is sometimes affected by unrest from student protests and teacher strikes.

D4. Are individuals free to express their personal views on political or other sensitive topics without fear of surveillance or retribution? 3 / 4

Private discussion is generally free. However, the legacies of the country's volatile political history, which involves a number of coups and attempted coups, as well as the crackdown on the opposition that surrounded the 2018 referendum, can discourage people from openly discussing politics in some situations.

E. ASSOCIATIONAL AND ORGANIZATIONAL RIGHTS: 6 / 12 (−1)
E1. Is there freedom of assembly? 1 / 4 (−1)

Freedoms of assembly and association are protected by the constitution, but these freedoms have been inconsistently upheld, and deteriorated significantly in 2018. Azali outlawed demonstrations in May, ahead of the referendum, though antigovernment protests nevertheless took place throughout the year and were often met with violence by security forces. In October, violence erupted in Anjouan over the dissolution of the rotating presidency, as the island had been set to hold it next; protesters moreover claimed the new constitution would effectively lock representatives of Anjouan out of power for good. Sporadic gunfire, explosions, water and power cuts, and roadblocks took place during several days of protests, and three people were killed, at least two of whom were shot dead by members of the security forces.

Score Change: The score declined from 2 to 1 because protests against the constitutional referendum were met with violence by security forces, and the president banned demonstrations ahead of the vote.

E2. Is there freedom for nongovernmental organizations, particularly those that are engaged in human rights- and governance-related work? 2 / 4

Nongovernmental organizations (NGOs) at times face bureaucratic interference, including requirements to secure permits from high-level officials in order to visit prisons. Some NGO representatives spoke out against the referendum and atmosphere of repression in 2018, but did so at some risk in light of the broad crackdown on dissent.

E3. Is there freedom for trade unions and similar professional or labor organizations? 3 / 4

Workers have the right to form unions, bargain collectively, and strike. In cases of national interest, the government may require essential personnel to return to work. No law prohibits antiunion discrimination or protects workers from retribution for striking. There are some laws that impose mandatory arbitration processes for labor disputes.

F. RULE OF LAW: 7 / 16 (−1)

F1. Is there an independent judiciary? 1 / 4 (−1)

The judicial system is based on both Sharia (Islamic law) and the French legal code. Though the law establishes mechanisms for the selection of judges and attorneys, the executive branch often disregards these and simply appoints people to their positions. Court decisions are not always upheld.

In April, Azali abruptly suspended the Constitutional Court, the country's highest, saying it was dysfunctional; the court had not been operating since 2017 because its bench was not full and new judges had not been appointed. (Opposition parties alleged that the 2018 referendum was illegal because it was held after the court's suspension.) The 2018 referendum abolished the Constitutional Court and established a new constitutional chamber of the Supreme Court.

Score Change: The score declined from 2 to 1 because the president suspended the Constitutional Court, the country's highest, in the run-up to the year's controversial referendum, the results of which ultimately transferred the Constitutional Court's competencies to a new chamber.

F2. Does due process prevail in civil and criminal matters? 2 / 4

All defendants have the right to a fair public trial, but they often face lengthy delays. Corruption can prevent guarantees of due process. A number of politicized prosecutions against figures who opposed the year's referendum took place in 2018.

F3. Is there protection from the illegitimate use of physical force and freedom from war and insurgencies? 2 / 4

The law prohibits the illegitimate use of physical force, but security agents have engaged in excessive force, and are generally not held accountable for such behavior. There are questions about the will or capacity of the army to identify and punish abuses within its ranks.

F4. Do laws, policies, and practices guarantee equal treatment of various segments of the population? 2 / 4

The law provides for equality of persons. However, same-sex sexual activity is illegal, with punishments of a fine and up to five years in prison. Few women hold positions of responsibility in business, outside of elite families. Laws requiring that services be provided for people with disabilities are not well enforced.

G. PERSONAL AUTONOMY AND INDIVIDUAL RIGHTS: 6 / 16

G1. Do individuals enjoy freedom of movement, including the ability to change their place of residence, employment, or education? 2 / 4

The constitution and law provide for freedom of movement, both internally and externally. While these rights are generally respected by the government, in practice, poverty frequently prevents travel between the islands as well as access to higher education.

G2. Are individuals able to exercise the right to own property and establish private businesses without undue interference from state or nonstate actors? 2 / 4

In accordance with civil and some customary laws, women have equal rights in inheritance matters. Local cultures on Grande Comore and Mohéli are matrilineal, with women legally possessing all inheritable property. However, this is complicated by the concurrent application of Sharia, interpretations of which can limit gender equality. In addition, a poor system of land registration and women's difficulties in securing loans hampers women's right to own land.

Endemic corruption and a lack of a culture of transparency hampers normal business activity.

G3. Do individuals enjoy personal social freedoms, including choice of marriage partner and size of family, protection from domestic violence, and control over appearance? 1 / 4

Early and forced marriages have been reported in Comoros. The law prohibits domestic violence, but courts rarely fined or ordered the imprisonment of convicted perpetrators, and women and children rarely filed official complaints. Sexual violence and workplace harassment are believed to be widespread, but are rarely reported to authorities.

G4. Do individuals enjoy equality of opportunity and freedom from economic exploitation? 1 / 4

The Comorian economy, which is primarily agricultural, relies heavily on remittances from Comorian citizens in France. Many young people struggle to find sustainable opportunities for employment. Poverty has driven many people to attempt the dangerous trip to Mayotte, a French territory, in flimsy boats known as kwassa-kwassa.

Government efforts to identify and prosecute human trafficking are minimal, and trafficking cases, if addressed, are often done so through informal mediation processes. At times, these mechanisms have facilitated the return of trafficking victims to traffickers.

Congo, Republic of (Brazzaville)

Population: 5,400,000
Capital: Brazzaville
Political Rights Rating: 7
Civil Liberties Rating: 5
Freedom Rating: 6.0
Freedom Status: Not Free
Electoral Democracy: No

Overview: President Denis Sassou Nguesso has maintained power for more than three decades by severely repressing the opposition. Corruption and decades of political instability have contributed to poor economic performance and high levels of poverty. Abuses by security forces are frequently reported and rarely investigated. While a variety of media operate, independent coverage is limited by widespread self-censorship and the influence of owners. Human rights and governance-related nongovernmental organizations (NGOs) scrutinize state abuses, but also self-censor to avoid reprisals. Religious freedom is generally respected.

KEY DEVELOPMENTS IN 2018:

- In May, retired general Jean-Marie Michel Mokoko, a former presidential candidate and key opposition leader, was sentenced to 20 years in prison on charges of violating state security and illegal possession of weapons. Prosecutors had argued that he was plotting to overthrow the government.
- In September, opposition leader Paulin Makaya was released from prison after serving a two-year sentence for inciting disorder, handed down in connection with his participation in antigovernment protests. However, authorities have since blocked him from leaving the country.
- Authorities announced some anticorruption efforts during the year, but they appeared to be more related to efforts to secure a loan from the International Monetary Fund (IMF) than an attempt to address systemic problems. Members of the Sassou Nguesso family continued to face allegations of corruption in connection with stewardship of the national oil company during the year.
- In July, 13 young men were killed after being detained at a Brazzaville police station. Police initially claimed the victims were criminals, but as human rights groups investigated, they admitted that the victims were killed at the station, and offered their families money to cover burial costs. A number of police officers were charged with manslaughter and criminal negligence, and their trial opened in October.

POLITICAL RIGHTS: 2 / 40

A. ELECTORAL PROCESS: 0 / 12

A1. Was the current head of government or other chief national authority elected through free and fair elections? 0 / 4

The president is directly elected to five-year terms. The 2002 constitution restricted the president to two terms and set an age limit of 70. However, an October 2015 constitutional referendum proposed by the president removed age and term-limit restrictions on the presidency so that President Denis Sassou Nguesso could run again. The referendum passed, amidst widespread protests and claims of fraud.

Sassou Nguesso has held power since 1979, with the exception of a five-year period in the 1990s. In March 2016, he secured a third presidential term since reclaiming power in 1997, winning 60 percent of the vote in an election marked by fraud, intimidation, and an internet shutdown.

A2. Were the current national legislative representatives elected through free and fair elections? 0 / 4

Congo's parliament consists of a 72-seat Senate and a 151-seat National Assembly. Councilors from every department each elect senators to six-year terms. National Assembly members are directly elected to five-year terms.

The July 2017 legislative elections were boycotted by several opposition parties amid credible allegations that the vote would be rigged. Sassou Nguesso's Congolese Labor Party (PCT) claimed 96 of 151 seats, and its allies won 12, in a process tainted by widespread fraud and low voter turnout. Elections were indefinitely postponed in nine districts in the Pool Region, where the military had been engaged in a campaign against a rebel group accused of launching attacks on the capital.

A3. Are the electoral laws and framework fair, and are they implemented impartially by the relevant election management bodies? 0 / 4

The 2015 constitutional referendum to increase presidential term limits consolidated the PCT's dominance of the political system by allowing Sassou Nguesso to run for a third term. Elections are administered by the Independent National Election Commission (CENI), which was established in 2016 after a nontransparent planning process. Analysts assert that the CENI lacks independence from Sassou Nguesso and his administration.

B. POLITICAL PLURALISM AND PARTICIPATION: 2 / 16

B1. Do the people have the right to organize in different political parties or other competitive political groupings of their choice, and is the system free of undue obstacles to the rise and fall of these competing parties or groupings? 1 / 4

The government routinely intimidates and represses opposition parties. In July 2016, opposition leader Paulin Makaya of the United for Congo (UPC) party was sentenced to two years in prison following his arrest on charges of inciting disorder over his participation in protests against the 2015 constitutional referendum. Makaya was released in September 2018 but police have blocked him from boarding international flights at least twice since. Earlier, in March, rights group Amnesty International called on authorities to release political prisoners, including opposition figures and activists accused of inciting public unrest and other crimes related to their participation in 2015–16 protests of Sassou Nguesso's bid for a third term.

Political parties are sometimes denied registration without cause. During the 2017 legislative campaign, the Yuki party was denied official party status, forcing its candidates to run independently.

The government banned private campaign contributions in 2016, leaving opposition parties and candidates dependent on limited public financing.

B2. Is there a realistic opportunity for the opposition to increase its support or gain power through elections? 0 / 4

There is little opportunity for the opposition to gain power through elections, and opposition leaders frequently experience harassment, intimidation, and arrest. Two of Sassou Nguesso's rivals in the 2016 presidential race—Mokoko, and André Okombi Salissa, president of an opposition coalition called the Initiative for Democracy in Congo (IDC)—were repeatedly harassed during the election campaign, and Mokoko was incarcerated in June 2016 and Okombi Salissa in January 2017. In May 2018, Mokoko was sentenced to 20 years in prison on charges of violating state security and illegal possession of weapons; prosecutors had argued that he was plotting to overthrow the government. Salissa remains in prison, awaiting trial on the same charges.

B3. Are the people's political choices free from domination by the military, foreign powers, religious hierarchies, economic oligarchies, or any other powerful group that is not democratically accountable? 0 / 4

The Sassou Nguesso government routinely uses military and police forces to intimidate citizens. Employers engage in widespread labor-market discrimination based on political beliefs.

B4. Do various segments of the population (including ethnic, religious, gender, LGBT, and other relevant groups) have full political rights and electoral opportunities? 1 / 4

Members of Sassou Nguesso's northern Mbochi ethnic group control key government posts. Insofar as the government includes representatives from other regional and ethnic groups, their ability to shape policy is very limited. The government also routinely suppresses political parties that draw support from Congo's southern regions, which have long opposed Sassou Nguesso. Although there are no legal restrictions on political participation by religion, gender, sexual identity, or ethnic group, indigenous populations face many barriers to political participation, including isolation in rural areas and low levels of civic literacy.

Women are underrepresented in government, holding just 15 of 151 seats in the National Assembly and 14 of 72 seats in the Senate. In 2017, a new 35-member cabinet was selected, of which 8 members are women. Societal constraints limit women's political participation in practice.

C. FUNCTIONING OF GOVERNMENT 0 / 12

C1. Do the freely elected head of government and national legislative representatives determine the policies of the government? 0 / 4

Government policy is set by President Sassou Nguesso, who was reelected in a deeply flawed process in 2016. There is little oversight from the parliament, which is dominated by the ruling PCT and protects the executive from accountability.

C2. Are safeguards against official corruption strong and effective? 0 / 4

Corruption is endemic, and domestic prosecutions for corruption are often politically motivated. The president's family and advisers effectively control the state oil company without meaningful oversight, and offshore companies are allegedly used to embezzle funds from the company. Reports of serious corruption at the state oil company continued to emerge in 2018, including on bribes paid to Sassou Nguesso and his family in exchange for oil contracts.

In response to pressure from the International Monetary Fund (IMF) authorities in early 2018 arrested the official in charge of public procurement at the Treasury, while Sassou Nguesso in September dissolved two existing anticorruption bodies and approved the establishment of a new one, the High Authority for the Fight against Corruption. However, these efforts appeared to be more a drive to secure an IMF bailout than an effort to address systemic corruption or establish more effective anticorruption institutions.

C3. Does the government operate with openness and transparency? 0 / 4

Government operations are opaque. Although the constitution guarantees access to information, there is no implementing legislation, nor is there a specific law mandating public access to official information. Public procurement procedures are nontransparent. Authorities generally do not publish draft legislation or regulations.

Although Congo became fully compliant with the Extractive Industries Transparency Initiative (EITI) in 2013, the government has developed techniques to circumvent relevant transparency standards. In August 2017, the IMF accused the government of concealing debt. In March of that year, the IMF estimated that government debt was 77 percent of gross domestic product (GDP). By August, taking into account the hidden debt, the figure was revised to 117 percent of GDP.

CIVIL LIBERTIES: 19 / 60

D. FREEDOM OF EXPRESSION AND BELIEF 7 / 16

D1. Are there free and independent media? 1 / 4

While the constitution provides for freedom of speech and press, the government routinely pressures, threatens, and incarcerates journalists. In 2017, Ghys Fortuné Dombé Bemba, editor of *Talassa*, an independent newspaper, was arrested after publishing a statement by a former Pool rebel leader. He was provisionally released in July 2018 after 18 months' imprisonment, reportedly due to his deteriorating health, but still faces charges of "complicity in threats to state security." In June 2018, the government detained journalist Fortunat Ngolali after a member of the ruling PCT accused him of leaking a recording of a meeting between a PCT leader and Congolese youths. He was released without charge after 48 hours.

While there are numerous media outlets, many are owned by government allies who influence their coverage. Widespread self-censorship among journalists also discourages independent reporting in practice.

Internet and text messaging were blocked during the 2016 election in what observers described as a means to prevent reports of suspected electoral fraud from being disseminated. While generally aimed at media, the effort also prevented communications among ordinary citizens.

D2. Are individuals free to practice and express their religious faith or nonbelief in public and private? 3 / 4

Although religious freedom is generally respected, pastors are reticent to make statements that could be construed as hostile to the Sassou Nguesso government. In 2015, the government banned the wearing of the niqab, the full face veil, in public, citing concerns about security and terrorism.

D3. Is there academic freedom, and is the educational system free from extensive political indoctrination? 1 / 4

Academic freedom is tenuous. Most university professors avoid discussions of or research on politically sensitive topics. In October 2018, the government announced that it would ban a book, published in Paris, about widespread human rights abuses perpetrated by the military in the Pool Region between 2016 and 2017. Separately, in February 2018, there were reports of the arrest of a student union leader, after the union called on the government to pay overdue stipends.

D4. Are individuals free to express their personal views on political or other sensitive topics without fear of surveillance or retribution? 2 / 4

The government reportedly surveils electronic communications of private individuals, and those who speak out against the government are occasionally arrested.

E. ASSOCIATIONAL AND ORGANIZATIONAL RIGHTS 5 / 12
E1. Is there freedom of assembly? 1 / 4

The government restricts freedom of assembly. Groups must receive official authorization from local and federal authorities to hold public assemblies, and permission is routinely denied. Government forces sometimes employ violence against protesters or disperse assemblies. In 2017, authorities denied a coalition of NGOs permission to hold a demonstration in the capital drawing attention to human rights abuses in prisons and elsewhere.

E2. Is there freedom for nongovernmental organizations, particularly those that are engaged in human rights- and governance-related work? 2 / 4

Although the constitution guarantees freedom of association, NGOs must register with the Ministry of Interior. Those critical of the government often encounter a more burdensome registration process. Groups commonly curtail reporting on human rights abuses, or word criticism of authorities carefully, in order to avoid reprisals or harassment. NGOs have also encountered restrictions on access to certain areas, including the Pool Region. In February 2018, reports emerged of the arbitrary arrests of several civil society activists, as well as a raid by authorities on a human rights group.

E3. Is there freedom for trade unions and similar professional or labor organizations? 2 / 4

Although union rights are nominally protected, laws protecting union members are not always enforced. The government has intervened in labor disputes by harassing and arresting laborers and pressuring union leaders, particularly against the country's largest labor union, the Congolese Trade Union Confederation (CSC).

F. RULE OF LAW 1 / 16

F1. Is there an independent judiciary? 0 / 4

Congo's judiciary is dominated by Sassou Nguesso's allies, crippled by lack of resources, and vulnerable to corruption and political influence. In 2015, the Constitutional Court's confirmation of the constitutional referendum results was viewed as a rubber-stamp approval of Sassou Nguesso's efforts to remain in power.

F2. Does due process prevail in civil and criminal matters? 1 / 4

Defendants, including the government's political opponents, are routinely denied due process. Arbitrary arrests and detentions are common, despite being prohibited by the constitution. Other fair trial rights guaranteed by law, including the right to legal assistance for those who cannot afford it, are not always honored in practice.

F3. Is there protection from the illegitimate use of physical force and freedom from war and insurgencies? 0 / 4

Citizens in some neighborhoods are at risk of intimidation and violent crime by young men known as *bébés noirs*, who often form gangs. There have also been reports of arbitrary arrests and physical abuses by police attempting to curb the activities of such groups.

In July 2018, 13 young men were killed after being detained at a Brazzaville police station. The Congolese Observatory of Human Rights (OCDH) said the youths were "tortured and executed," and condemned the ensuing police investigation as grossly inadequate. Authorities initially responded to reports of the deaths by claiming the victims were *bébés noirs*, but later admitted that they were killed at the station and provided 2 million CFA francs ($3,600) to each of their families for burial costs. A number of police officers were charged with manslaughter and criminal negligence, and their trial opened in October. OCDH said its own investigation found that the victims were unlikely to be *bébés noirs*.

Reports of human rights violations by security forces are generally not investigated by the government. In 2016, Sassou Nguesso launched a military assault in the Pool Region after blaming a former rebel group for a series of attacks in Brazzaville. In reality, the rebel group largely disbanded a decade earlier, and responsibility for the attacks remains unclear. The ensuing military campaign displaced more than 80,000 citizens. To conceal the death toll, the government denied human rights organizations access to Pool, including Amnesty International, which denounced the government for "deliberately and unlawfully" attacking civilians. The United Nations Population Fund (UNPF) documented 110 cases of rape by "men in uniform" in Pool between April and September of 2017.

F4. Do laws, policies, and practices guarantee equal treatment of various segments of the population? 0 / 4

Employment discrimination against women persists. Refugees and other foreign workers are prevented by the government from holding certain jobs, and refugees sometimes face harassment and arrest by authorities.

While no law specifically prohibits same-sex sexual relations between adults, LGBT (lesbian, gay, bisexual, and transgender) people experience occasional harassment from the police.

The indigenous population experiences severe discrimination in employment, housing, and education. Indigenous communities often live in substandard housing on the outskirts of villages, and beatings and murders of indigenous people by members of the majority Bantu population sometimes occur.

The government exhibits widespread discrimination against residents of Congo's southern regions. They are routinely denied high-paying jobs in the public sector, as well as admission to the public university.

G. PERSONAL AUTONOMY AND INDIVIDUAL RIGHTS: 6 / 16

G1. Do individuals enjoy freedom of movement, including the ability to change their place of residence, employment, or education? 2 / 4

Although private citizens generally enjoy freedom of movement, activists and opposition leaders can face restrictions and confiscation of their passports.

The 2016–17 conflict in Pool led to the displacement of many of its residents. An estimated 81,000 people left their homes, and many remain displaced.

G2. Are individuals able to exercise the right to own property and establish private businesses without undue interference from state or nonstate actors? 2 / 4

Legal protections for business and property rights can be undermined by bureaucracy, poor judicial safeguards, and corruption. The government directly or indirectly controls property in key industries such as oil, minerals, and aviation.

G3. Do individuals enjoy personal social freedoms, including choice of marriage partner and size of family, protection from domestic violence, and control over appearance? 1 / 4

Violence against women, including domestic violence and rape, is widespread, but rarely reported. There are no specific laws forbidding domestic violence other than general assault statutes.

Men are legally considered the head of the household, and divorce settlements are thus skewed against women. Adultery is illegal for both men and women, but women convicted of the crime face a potential prison sentence, while the penalty for men is a fine.

G4. Do individuals enjoy equality of opportunity and freedom from economic exploitation? 1 / 4

Congo is a source and destination country for human trafficking, and allegations of complicity in trafficking by government officials did not lead to prosecutions in 2018. According to local NGOs, indigenous people are often conscripted into forced farm labor by members of the Bantu ethnic majority. Child labor laws are reportedly not effectively enforced.

Congo, Democratic Republic of (Kinshasa)

Population: 84,300,000
Capital: Kinshasa
Political Rights Rating: 7
Civil Liberties Rating: 6
Freedom Rating: 6.5
Freedom Status: Not Free
Electoral Democracy: No

Overview: The political system in the Democratic Republic of Congo (DRC) has been paralyzed in recent years by the repeated postponement of elections, though highly problematic balloting was finally held at the end of 2018. Citizens are unable to freely exercise basic civil liberties, and corruption is endemic throughout the government. Physical security is tenuous due to violence and human rights abuses committed by government forces as well as armed rebel groups and militias that are active in many areas of the country.

KEY DEVELOPMENTS IN 2018:

- President Joseph Kabila, whose last term officially expired in late 2016, remained in power throughout the year due to the repeated postponement of elections.
- Demonstrators across the country protested the electoral delays and flawed preparations for the planned voting. In several incidents, security forces used live ammunition, tear gas, arbitrary arrests, and detentions to quell demonstrations. Authorities also detained and harassed journalists who covered the protests and restricted the movement of some opposition leaders.
- General elections were finally held at the end of December, but major flaws were reported, and voting in three opposition strongholds was postponed on the grounds that ethnic violence, rebel attacks, and the spread of the Ebola virus made it impossible to proceed with the balloting in those areas. The results of the elections had yet to be announced at year's end.

POLITICAL RIGHTS: 3 / 40 (−1)

A. ELECTORAL PROCESS: 0 / 12

A1. Was the current head of government or other chief national authority elected through free and fair elections? 0 / 4

According to the constitution, the president is elected for a maximum of two five-year terms. Incumbent Joseph Kabila was declared the winner of his second term in office in 2011 amid widespread criticism of the election by international observers; he defeated longtime opposition leader Étienne Tshisekedi, 49 percent to 32 percent, according to the Independent National Electoral Commission (CENI).

Kabila's constitutional mandate expired in December 2016, but a contentious Constitutional Court ruling allowed him to remain in office until a successor was in place. Under the mediation of the Roman Catholic Church's National Episcopal Conference of Congo (CENCO), representatives of the government and an opposition bloc reached an agreement to hold elections in December 2017. However, in November 2017, CENI announced that elections would take place in December 2018, effectively violating the agreement and provoking a series of protests across the country.

Elections were eventually held on December 30, 2018, pitting Emmanuel Ramazani Shadary—backed by Kabila's People's Party for Reconstruction and Democracy (PPRD)—against Félix Tshisekedi of the opposition Union for Democracy and Social Progress (UDPS) and Martin Fayulu, the candidate of a broader opposition alliance. Several other opposition candidates were barred from competing. Major international monitoring organizations were not permitted to observe, though regional groups were given some access. CENI announced its satisfaction with the vote, but CENCO reported a number of serious problems, including widespread violations of ballot-validation procedures, large vote-counting discrepancies, and confusion over the locations of vote-counting centers. Many polling stations opened late, and results were not publicly posted at some sites, in violation of electoral law. Election observers were denied access to polling stations in some cases. Voting in three areas that were known as opposition strongholds—Beni and Butembo in North Kivu Province and Yumbi in Mai-Ndombe Province—was postponed until March 2019, ostensibly due to an Ebola outbreak and attacks by armed groups, meaning the national results would be announced before residents of those areas could vote. The outcome of the presidential race had yet to be announced at year's end.

A2. Were the current national legislative representatives elected through free and fair elections? 0 / 4

The 500-seat National Assembly is directly elected for five-year terms, and the 108-seat Senate is elected by provincial assemblies. The 2011 elections for the National Assembly, held concurrently with the presidential vote, were also criticized as deeply flawed. The PPRD itself won 62 seats, but its parliamentary coalition took a total of 260 seats. The UDPS took 41, and smaller parties captured the remainder.

The electoral mandate of the incumbent National Assembly expired in 2016, and overdue elections for the legislature and provincial assemblies were held alongside the presidential vote in December 2018, with all the associated problems. Provincial assembly elections had last been held in 2006, and Senate elections were last held in 2007, meaning the incumbents' five-year mandates had long since expired; as of 2018 the indirect Senate voting was scheduled for early 2019. Results of the 2018 legislative elections had yet to be announced at year's end.

A3. Are the electoral laws and framework fair, and are they implemented impartially by the relevant election management bodies? 0 / 4

The country's electoral framework does not ensure transparent elections. Opposition parties and civil society frequently criticize CENI and the Constitutional Court for lacking independence and for bias in favor of Kabila and the PPRD. In 2018, CENI failed to meet a legal obligation to publish the voter lists at least 90 days before elections to allow verification. Opposition parties alleged that there were some 10 million "ghost" voters on the rolls. An independent inquiry found discrepancies that could affect millions of voters, including the fact that 500,000 blank electoral cards and voter registration kits were missing. The political opposition repeatedly protested that the electoral process was unfair and alleged government tampering with voting machines. Separately, internally displaced people throughout the country faced practical obstacles to participating in the elections.

B. POLITICAL PLURALISM AND PARTICIPATION: 2 / 16 (−1)

B1. Do the people have the right to organize in different political parties or other competitive political groupings of their choice, and is the system free of undue obstacles to the rise and fall of these competing parties or groupings? 1 / 4

People have the right to organize political parties. Hundreds of parties exist, with many configured along ethnic, communal, or regional lines. However, most lack national reach, and their ability to function is limited in practice. Opposition leaders and their supporters are often intimidated and face restrictions on their movement and right to organize public events.

In June 2018, Kabila and his party, the PPRD, formed the Common Front for Congo (FCC) coalition, which included parliamentary leaders, governors, and some civil society members and journalists. Key opposition groupings include the UDPS, headed by Félix Tshisekedi, and the Lamuka (Wake Up) coalition, which chose Martin Fayulu as its presidential candidate.

B2. Is there a realistic opportunity for the opposition to increase its support or gain power through elections? 0 / 4

Although opposition groups enjoy significant public support, the repeated postpone-ment of elections and various forms of interference and obstruction by the government and its allies have prevented the opposition from taking power to date. As of 2018, the DRC had never experienced a peaceful transfer of power between rival parties.

In the run-up to the 2018 elections, CENI rejected the candidacy of six opposition politicians, including former rebel leader Jean-Pierre Bemba and former Katanga governor Moïse Katumbi. Government authorities regularly blocked or delayed the campaign activ-ities of opposition candidates. Congolese officials notably prevented Katumbi from reen-tering the country, and the head of his foundation was briefly kidnapped and interrogated in Kinshasa in October. Nonstate armed groups also obstructed candidate movements and looted opposition offices. However, Congolese authorities facilitated the movements and campaign activities of Shadary, Kabila's preferred successor.

B3. Are the people's political choices free from domination by the military, foreign powers, reli-gious hierarchies, economic oligarchies, or any other powerful group that is not democratically accountable? 0 / 4 (−1)

The military, security services, and armed rebel or militia groups interfere with citizens' political choices. Throughout 2018, government security personnel used excessive force against opposition supporters, including tear gas and live ammunition, and allegedly paid supporters to provoke violence during opposition rallies. Systematic repression in major cities across the country intensified in the lead-up to elections. In some areas, soldiers and armed groups at polling stations reportedly coerced voters to cast ballots for Shadary and the FCC. The activities of nonstate armed groups in parts of the country also hindered citizens' ability to participate in the political process. Ethnic violence and militia attacks, along with an Ebola outbreak, were cited as justification for postponing the elections in Beni, Butembo, and Yumbi until March 2019.

Score Change: The score declined from 1 to 0 because armed groups, including state and nonstate actors, used violence or the threat of violence to intimidate voters and disrupt election-related activities.

B4. Do various segments of the population (including ethnic, religious, gender, LGBT, and other relevant groups) have full political rights and electoral opportunities? 1 / 4

Ethnic discrimination and lack of access to public services and state institutions in rural areas hinder political participation; certain segments of the population, such as indigenous groups, are particularly marginalized. Women are severely underrepresented in government, making up only 9 percent of the incumbent National Assembly and 6 percent of the Senate. Of the 21 registered candidates for president in December 2018, only one was a woman.

C. FUNCTIONING OF GOVERNMENT: 1 / 12

C1. Do the freely elected head of government and national legislative representatives deter-mine the policies of the government? 0 / 4

The incumbent president, national legislature, and provincial assemblies as of 2018 had exceeded their electoral mandates by two years or more, undermining the legitimacy of their decisions on state policy and other matters. Moreover, the government lacks effective con-trol over some parts of the country, particularly in the provinces of North and South Kivu.

C2. Are safeguards against official corruption strong and effective? 0 / 4

Extensive corruption in the government, security forces, and mineral extraction industries have corroded basic public services and development efforts. Appointments to high-level positions in government are often determined by nepotism and other malfeasance. Accountability mechanisms are weak, and impunity prevails. In 2018, a civil society group, the Congolese Association for Access to Justice, reported finding evidence that the president's political platform, the FCC, had illegally used public funds to finance its activities.

C3. Does the government operate with openness and transparency? 1 / 4

Despite previous incremental improvements in revenue reporting, there is little transparency in the state's financial affairs. The law does not provide for public access to government information, and citizens often lack the practical ability to obtain records on public expenditures and state operations. Required financial disclosures from top officials have not typically been made public.

CIVIL LIBERTIES: 12 / 60 (−1)
D. FREEDOM OF EXPRESSION AND BELIEF: 7 / 16
D1. Are there free and independent media? 1 / 4

Although constitutionally guaranteed, freedom of the press is restricted in practice. Radio is the dominant medium, and newspapers are found in large cities. An estimated 80 percent of the country's media outlets are controlled by politicians. While the media frequently criticized Kabila and his government, political harassment of reporters is common, and outlets encounter pressure to carry progovernment content. Journalists often face criminal defamation suits, threats, detentions, arbitrary arrests, and physical attacks in the course of their work.

Throughout 2018, there were numerous reported cases of intelligence and security services interfering with the media. Several journalists covering demonstrations or politics were detained, arrested, and beaten. Journalists in Danger and its partner organization, Reporters Without Borders, identified 121 attacks on journalists between November 2017 and November 2018, including 54 arrests, 37 cases of censorship, and threats against another 30 journalists. In July 2018, journalists who had worked on a documentary film examining land grabs by Kabila and his family were forced into hiding. A journalist was detained in Kinshasa in November for allegedly defaming the prime minister's family.

In recent years, the government has closed media outlets linked to the political opposition, and such pressure affected election coverage in 2018. Five opposition outletsremained closed during the year while public stations aired pro-Shadary content. In September, journalist Hassan Murhabazi was abducted and held for nearly three days after he received threats for hosting a political program about Shadary. In late December, the government revoked the accreditation of a Radio France Internationale journalist who was reporting on the elections and subsequently cut the service's FM broadcast signal.

D2. Are individuals free to practice and express their religious faith or nonbelief in public and private? 3 / 4

The constitution guarantees freedom of religion, and authorities generally respect this right in practice. Although religious groups must register with the government to be recognized, unregistered groups operate unhindered. Some church facilities, personnel, and services have been affected by violence in conflict areas. In 2017 and 2018, as the Catholic Church and some Protestant groups pressed for credible elections, the authorities' aggressive response to their protest activities often entailed violence in and around places of worship, arrests of church leaders and parishioners, and disruption of religious services.

D3. Is there academic freedom, and is the educational system free from extensive political indoctrination? 2 / 4

There are no formal restrictions on academic freedom. Primary and secondary school curriculums are regulated but not strongly politicized. However, political events and protests at universities and schools are subject to violent repression. In October 2018, for example, police used force and tear gas to disperse an assembly at a school in Lubumbashi, injuring and arresting protesters. In November, two students were killed when police fired live ammunition to disperse a campus protest against a teachers' strike at the University of Kinshasa.

D4. Are individuals free to express their personal views on political or other sensitive topics without fear of surveillance or retribution? 1 / 4

Private discussion of politically sensitive topics can be open, but civilians sometimes face reprisal for voicing critical views in public, and conditions have grown worse during the political crisis surrounding Kabila's tenure and the delayed elections. Internet and telecommunications services were temporarily shut down on at least two occasions in early 2018, and on December 31 the government imposed another shutdown, preventing citizens from sharing information and election observers from reporting findings.

E. ASSOCIATIONAL AND ORGANIZATIONAL RIGHTS: 1 / 12 (−1)

E1. Is there freedom of assembly? 0 / 4

The constitution guarantees freedom of assembly, and demonstrations are held regularly, but those who participate risk arrests, beatings, and lethal violence in practice. The government repeatedly banned opposition demonstrations and used force against protesters during 2018. Among numerous other incidents over the course of the year, in January security forces arrested church-led protesters calling for elections across the country. In July, police arrested peaceful protesters from two youth organizations who were demanding the release of fellow activists detained in Kinshasa. In August, government forces used tear gas and live ammunition to disperse opposition protests. Protest-related violence continued as the December elections approached, and more than a dozen people were reportedly killed at various demonstrations in the final weeks before the balloting.

E2. Is there freedom for nongovernmental organizations, particularly those engaged in human rights- and governance-related work? 0 / 4 (−1)

Thousands of nongovernmental organizations (NGOs) are active in the country, but many face violence and other obstacles to their work. Domestic human rights advocates in particular are subject to harassment, arbitrary arrest, and detention. In September 2018, four democracy activists affiliated with the citizens' movement Filimbi who had been arrested in December 2017 for mobilizing against Kabila's extended tenure in office were sentenced to a year in prison. Also that month, more than 30 activists from the Struggle for Change (LUCHA) democracy organization were arrested for demanding an audit of voter lists. A leading LUCHA activist died in mysterious circumstances in a house fire in June; state authorities found that the fire was accidental, but the victim's colleagues alleged that the government was responsible. Another member of the organization was kidnapped and held for three days by unidentified assailants in November.

Score Change: The score declined from 1 to 0 due to increased disruption of NGO activity related to human rights and governance, including arrests, detentions, and extralegal violence affecting members of prominent organizations.

E3. Is there freedom for trade unions and similar professional or labor organizations? 1 / 4

A number of national labor unions and professional associations, covering parts of the public and private sectors, operate legally in the DRC, but the overwhelming majority of workers are informally employed. Congolese and foreigners who meet a residency requirement of 20 years can hold union posts. Some civil servants and members of state security forces are not permitted to unionize and bargain collectively. Violations of the procedures for a legal strike can result in prison terms. Although it is against the law for employers to retaliate against workers for union activities, such legal protections are poorly enforced, particularly in the private sector.

F. RULE OF LAW: 0 / 16

F1. Is there an independent judiciary? 0 / 4

The president appoints all members of the judiciary, which is seen as corrupt and subject to political manipulation. The judiciary often shows bias against the opposition and civil society, while the government and its allies typically enjoy impunity for abuses.

F2. Does due process prevail in civil and criminal matters? 0 / 4

Courts are concentrated in urban areas; the majority of the country relies on customary courts or informal justice mechanisms that lack due process. Civilian cases are often tried in military courts, which have weak safeguards for defendants' rights and are subject to interference from high-ranking military personnel. Arbitrary arrests and detentions are common, as is prolonged pretrial detention. Most of the prison population reportedly consists of pretrial detainees.

F3. Is there protection from the illegitimate use of physical force and freedom from war and insurgencies? 0 / 4

Prison conditions are life threatening, and torture of detainees is common. Civilian authorities do not effectively control security forces. The military is notoriously undisciplined. Incidents of soldiers exchanging intelligence and weapons with rebel or militia groups continued during 2018. Soldiers and police regularly commit serious human rights abuses, including rape and other physical attacks. In July, Kabila promoted Generals Gabriel Amisi and John Numbi, both of whom had been subjected to sanctions by the United States and the European Union for alleged involvement in human rights violations.

Rebel groups have also contributed to years of armed conflicts and communal violence that have had a catastrophic impact on civilians, with over five million conflict-related deaths since 1998. Ongoing insecurity in the eastern provinces during 2018 obstructed efforts to contain an Ebola virus outbreak. Separately, violence between rival ethnic groups in Mai-Ndombe Province killed hundreds of people in December.

Government officials have been implicated in the 2017 murder of two UN experts who were investigating human rights violations associated with a civil conflict in the Kasaï region; four Congolese traveling with the experts also went missing. A trial of suspects accused of involvement in the crime was ongoing at the end of 2018.

F4. Do laws, policies, and practices guarantee equal treatment of various segments of the population? 0 / 4

Ethnic discrimination is common, contributing to many of the country's local armed conflicts. While the constitution prohibits discrimination against people with disabilities, they often encounter obstacles when attempting to find employment, attend school, or access government services. Discrimination based on HIV status is also prohibited, but people with HIV similarly face difficulties accessing health care and education. LGBT (lesbian, gay, bisexual, and transgender) people can be prosecuted for same-sex sexual activity under public decency laws.

Although the constitution prohibits discrimination against women, in practice they face discrimination in nearly every aspect of their lives, especially in rural areas. The family code assigns women a subordinate role in the household. Young women are increasingly seeking professional work outside the home, particularly in urban centers, though they continue to face disparities in wages and promotions.

G. PERSONAL AUTONOMY AND INDIVIDUAL RIGHTS: 4 / 16

G1. Do individuals enjoy freedom of movement, including the ability to change their place of residence, employment, or education? 1 / 4

Freedom of movement is protected by law but seriously curtailed in practice, in large part due to armed conflicts and other security problems. An estimated 4.5 million people are displaced within the country. In 2018, Angola expelled 360,000 Congolese who had sought work and refuge there, and they were forced to return to the Kasaï region, where they face ongoing insecurity. In Ituri Province, the government ordered tens of thousands of internally displaced people to return home, despite concerns about further violence, which had forced others to flee to neighboring Uganda. Various armed groups, including government forces, impose illegal tolls on travelers passing through territory under their control.

G2. Are individuals able to exercise the right to own property and establish private businesses without undue interference from state or nonstate actors? 1 / 4

Individuals have the right to own property and establish private businesses. In conflict zones, however, armed groups and government soldiers have seized private property and destroyed homes. Property ownership and business activity are also hampered by pervasive corruption and a complicated system of taxation and regulation that further encourages bribery.

Although the constitution prohibits discrimination against women, some laws and customary practices put women at a disadvantage with respect to inheritance and land ownership.

G3. Do individuals enjoy personal social freedoms, including choice of marriage partner and size of family, protection from domestic violence, and control over appearance? 1 / 4

Sexual and gender-based violence is common, especially in conflict zones; sex crimes affect women, girls, men, and boys. Rebel fighters and government soldiers have regularly been implicated in rape and sexual abuse. Convictions for these offenses remain rare. Abortion is prohibited except to save the life of a pregnant woman, and illegal abortions can draw lengthy prison sentences.

The family code obliges wives to obey their husbands, who are designated as the heads of their households. Married women are under the legal guardianship of their husbands. Although the legal minimum age for marriage is 18, an estimated 37 percent of women aged 20 to 24 were married before reaching 18.

G4. Do individuals enjoy equality of opportunity and freedom from economic exploitation? 1 / 4

Formal protections against economic exploitation are poorly enforced, and most Congolese are informally employed. Although the law prohibits all forced or compulsory labor, such practices are common and include forced child labor in mining, street vending, domestic service, and agriculture. Some government forces and other armed groups force civilians to work for them, and the recruitment and use of child soldiers remains widespread.

Costa Rica

Population: 5,000,000
Capital: San José
Political Rights Rating: 1
Civil Liberties Rating: 1
Freedom Rating: 1.0
Freedom Status: Free
Electoral Democracy: Yes

Overview: Costa Rica has a long history of democratic stability, with a multiparty political system and regular rotations of power through credible elections. Freedoms of expression and association are robust. The rule of law is generally strong, though presidents have often been implicated in corruption scandals, and prisons remain overcrowded. Among other ongoing concerns, the LGBT (lesbian, gay, bisexual, and transgender) community and indigenous people face discrimination, and land disputes involving indigenous communities persist.

KEY DEVELOPMENTS IN 2018:
- In April, Carlos Alvarado Quesada of the governing Citizen Action Party (PAC) was elected president in the second round of voting. International observers deemed the election credible.
- In January, the Inter-American Court of Human Rights issued an advisory opinion stating that member states of the American Convention on Human Rights, including Costa Rica, are obligated to legally recognize same-sex marriage. The Supreme Court then ruled in August that the prohibition of same-sex marriage was unconstitutional. However, the court allowed the legislature up to 18 months to pass legislation to legalize same-sex marriage.
- The Cementazo corruption scandal over Chinese cement exports to Costa Rica, which in 2017 implicated a number of high-level government officials, continued to roil the country's politics during the year. In April, the Public Ethics Office of the Attorney General, which investigated former president Luis Guillermo Solís for his alleged role in the scandal, cleared him of wrongdoing, although some members of the Legislative Assembly claimed that the office mishandled the case.

POLITICAL RIGHTS: 38 / 40

A. ELECTORAL PROCESS: 12 / 12

A1. Was the current head of government or other chief national authority elected through free and fair elections? 4 / 4

The president is directly elected for a four-year term and can seek a nonconsecutive second term. Presidential candidates must win 40 percent of the vote to avoid a runoff. In April 2018, Carlos Alvarado Quesada of the governing PAC was elected president in the second round of voting. Alvarado faced Fabricio Alvarado Muñoz of the evangelical National Restoration Party (PRN) in the runoff and won decisively, with over 60 percent of the vote. Both rounds of voting were deemed credible by international observers.

A2. Were the current national legislative representatives elected through free and fair elections? 4 / 4

Elections for the 57-seat unicameral Legislative Assembly occur every four years, and deputies are elected by proportional representation. Deputies may not run for two consecutive terms, but may run again after skipping a term. In the February 2018 legislative elections, which were held concurrently with the first round of the presidential poll, no party came close to winning a majority. The PAC took 10 seats, the PRN won 14, and the National Liberation Party (PLN), historically one of the most powerful parties in Costa Rican politics, won 17 seats. As with the presidential election, the legislative elections were deemed credible by international observers.

A3. Are the electoral laws and framework fair, and are they implemented impartially by the relevant election management bodies? 4 / 4

A special chamber of the Supreme Court appoints the independent national election commission, the Supreme Electoral Tribunal (TSE), which is responsible for administering elections. The TSE carries out its functions impartially and the electoral framework is fair.

B. POLITICAL PLURALISM AND PARTICIPATION: 15 / 16

B1. Do the people have the right to organize in different political parties or other competitive political groupings of their choice, and is the system free of undue obstacles to the rise and fall of these competing parties or groupings? 4 / 4

People have the right to organize in different political parties without undue obstacles. The historical dominance of the PLN and the Social Christian Unity Party (PUSC) has waned in recent years, as newly formed parties have gained traction, leading to the collapse of the traditional two-party system. (Seven parties won seats in the 2018 legislative elections). The PRN, which was founded in 2005, emerged as a major force in politics in 2018, as evidenced by Alvarado Muñoz's second-place finish in the presidential election and relatively strong showing in the legislative elections.

B2. Is there a realistic opportunity for the opposition to increase its support or gain power through elections? 4 / 4

Power regularly alternates in Costa Rica and opposition parties compete fiercely in presidential and legislative elections. Luis Guillermo Solís won the 2014 presidential election as the candidate of PAC, an opposition party at the time. Parties along a wide spectrum of the political order freely competed in the 2018 elections, and the PRN made major gains, winning 14 seats in the legislature after capturing just 1 seat in the 2014 contest.

B3. Are the people's political choices free from domination by the military, foreign powers, religious hierarchies, economic oligarchies, or any other powerful group that is not democratically accountable? 4 / 4

Citizens' political choices are free from domination by unelected elites and foreign powers.

B4. Do various segments of the population (including ethnic, religious, gender, LGBT, and other relevant groups) have full political rights and electoral opportunities? 3 / 4

In 2015, the legislature passed a constitutional amendment declaring Costa Rica to be "multiethnic and plurinational." However, indigenous rights have not historically been prioritized by politicians, and there are no indigenous representatives in the legislature.

Women are represented in government—46 percent of seats in the Legislative Assembly are held by women following the 2018 elections. Five of the six key leadership roles in the Legislative Assembly, including the presidency of the legislature, are held by women. Epsy Campbell Barr became the first Afro-Costa Rican woman to serve as vice president in

2018. The government has introduced initiatives to increase women's political participation, such as the institution of gender quotas in order to ensure gender parity in political parties.

C. FUNCTIONING OF GOVERNMENT: 11 / 12

C1. Do the freely elected head of government and national legislative representatives determine the policies of the government? 4 / 4

Costa Rica's freely elected government and lawmakers set and implement state policy without interference. However, legislative gridlock has been a major issue in recent years. After failing for years to pass legislation to address the country's growing national debt, in December 2018 the Legislative Assembly passed a controversial law that raised taxes and imposed limits on public spending.

C2. Are safeguards against official corruption strong and effective? 3 / 4

Costa Rica has effective laws against corruption, which are generally well enforced. Despite its functioning anticorruption mechanisms, nearly every president since 1990 has been accused of corruption after leaving office. In 2017, former president Luis Guillermo Solís was implicated in the Cementazo scandal, involving influence peddling related to Chinese cement exports to Costa Rica. A legislative commission found that close to 30 people, including prominent officials from all three branches of government, were involved in the scandal. In April 2018, the Public Ethics Office of the Attorney General, which investigated Solís based on the commission's findings, cleared him of wrongdoing, although some members of the Legislative Assembly claimed that the office mishandled the case. In July, the president of the Supreme Court resigned over his role in the scandal.

C3. Does the government operate with openness and transparency? 4 / 4

Citizens generally have access to government information. However, there are some deficiencies in the reporting of budgets to the public, including a lack of transparency in communicating the objectives of the annual budget. Senior government officials are required to make financial disclosures, but that information is not available to the public.

CIVIL LIBERTIES: 53 / 60

D. FREEDOM OF EXPRESSION AND BELIEF: 16 / 16

D1. Are there free and independent media? 4 / 4

Freedom of the press is largely respected in Costa Rica. Defamation laws are on the books, but imprisonment was removed as a punishment for defamation in 2010.

There are six privately owned daily newspapers. Both public and commercial broadcast outlets are available, including at least 6 private television stations and more than 100 private radio stations.

D2. Are individuals free to practice and express their religious faith or nonbelief in public and private? 4 / 4

Roman Catholicism is the official religion, but the constitution guarantees the freedom of religion, which is generally respected in practice.

D3. Is there academic freedom, and is the educational system free from extensive political indoctrination? 4 / 4

Academic freedom is constitutionally protected and generally upheld.

D4. Are individuals free to express their personal views on political or other sensitive topics without fear of surveillance or retribution? 4 / 4

Private discussion is free and the government is not known to surveil the electronic communications of Costa Ricans.

E. ASSOCIATIONAL AND ORGANIZATIONAL RIGHTS: 11 / 12

E1. Is there freedom of assembly? 4 / 4

Freedom of assembly is constitutionally protected, and this right is largely upheld in practice. A diverse range of groups, including LGBT and environmental organizations, hold regular rallies and protests without government interference.

E2. Is there freedom for nongovernmental organizations, particularly those that are engaged in human rights- and governance-related work? 4 / 4

Nongovernmental organizations, including those engaged in human rights work, are active and do not encounter undue obstacles.

E3. Is there freedom for trade unions and similar professional or labor organizations? 3 / 4

Although labor unions are free to organize and mount frequent protests and strikes with minimal governmental interference, the law requires a minimum of 12 employees to form a union, which may negatively impact union rights at small enterprises. Rates of union membership in the private sector are low, due in part to discrimination by employers against union members. Employers have been known to occasionally fire workers who attempt to form unions.

F. RULE OF LAW: 13 / 16

F1. Is there an independent judiciary? 4 / 4

The judicial branch is generally independent and impartial. Supreme Court judges are elected by a supermajority of the legislature.

F2. Does due process prevail in civil and criminal matters? 3 / 4

Due process rights are enshrined in the constitution, and they are protected for the most part. However, there are often substantial delays in the judicial process, resulting in lengthy pretrial detentions.

F3. Is there protection from the illegitimate use of physical force and freedom from war and insurgencies? 3 / 4

Violent crime in Costa Rica has increased in recent years. In 2018, the country documented 586 murders, a rate of 11.7 murders per 100,000 people. The Pacific coast serves as a drug transshipment route, and the government has reported that many homicides are related to organized crime and drug trafficking. There are reports of occasional police abuse, including violence and degrading treatment; confirmed cases are generally investigated and prosecuted.

Overcrowding, poor sanitation, insufficient access to healthcare, and violence remain serious problems in Costa Rica's prisons. Recurrent abuse by prison police has not been thoroughly investigated due to victims' reluctance to file formal complaints.

F4. Do laws, policies, and practices guarantee equal treatment of various segments of the population? 3 / 4

The constitution outlines general equal rights for all people, but those rights are not always respected. Indigenous people, who compose 3 percent of the population, continue to face discrimination, particularly in regard to land rights and access to basic services. Costa Ricans of African descent have also faced discrimination in health care, education, and employment.

Women experience discrimination due to entrenched gender stereotypes, which can limit their equal access to employment, health services, and the justice system. Executive orders prohibit discrimination on the basis of sexual orientation and gender identity, and the government has expressed commitment to the protection of the LGBT community. However, law enforcement officials have discriminated against LGBT people, including attacks on transgender sex workers. In 2016, a new law provided disabled people greater personal autonomy. Prior to the law's passage, family members often had legal guardianship over some disabled people.

The number of asylum seekers from Nicaragua increased sharply in 2018. More than 23,000 Nicaraguans filed asylum claims in Costa Rica during the year, compared to 2,700 registered Nicaraguan asylum seekers globally in 2017. Thousands more had not yet filed their official claims at year's end due to backlogs in the overburdened registration system. Although the law entitles asylum seekers to access public services, discrimination sometimes prevented them from taking advantage of those benefits, and legal restrictions limit employment opportunities for asylum seekers.

G. PERSONAL AUTONOMY AND INDIVIDUAL RIGHTS: 13 / 16

G1. Do individuals enjoy freedom of movement, including the ability to change their place of residence, employment, or education? 4 / 4

Freedom of movement is constitutionally guaranteed and Costa Ricans enjoy relative freedom in their choice of residence and employment.

G2. Are individuals able to exercise the right to own property and establish private businesses without undue interference from state or nonstate actors? 3 / 4

Property rights are generally protected. However, laws protecting intellectual property are not always adequately enforced in practice.

Individuals are free to establish businesses, and the business and investment climate is relatively open, although the complicated bureaucracy can deter entrepreneurs seeking to establish a business.

G3. Do individuals enjoy personal social freedoms, including choice of marriage partner and size of family, protection from domestic violence, and control over appearance? 3 / 4

Despite the existence of domestic violence legislation, violence against women and children remains a problem. In 2017, the National Women's Institute, a government agency committed to advancing women's rights, revealed a plan to combat violence against women and address the social and cultural factors that contribute to it.

In January 2018, the Inter-American Court of Human Rights issued an advisory opinion stating that member states of the American Convention on Human Rights, including Costa Rica, have an obligation to legally recognize same-sex marriage. The issue became central to the presidential election, with Alvarado Muñoz expressing strong opposition to same-sex marriage in his campaign, which, according to some analysts, contributed to his strong showing in the first round. In August, the Supreme Court ruled that the prohibition of same-sex marriage was unconstitutional. However, the court allowed the legislature up to 18 months to pass legislation to legalize same-sex marriage, leaving the current ban in place (although same-sex couples can obtain common-law marital status). President Alvarado also signed decrees in December requiring residency cards to recognize transgender people's preferred identity, and compelling insurers to cover hormone treatments for transgender people.

Abortions are illegal in Costa Rica except when the health of the mother is in danger. Health professionals' lack of knowledge of the law and fear of repercussions make it difficult for women to secure even a legal abortion.

G4. Do individuals enjoy equality of opportunity and freedom from economic exploitation? 3 / 4

Despite legal protections, domestic workers, particularly migrant workers, are subject to exploitation and forced labor. Employers often ignore minimum wage and social security laws, and the resulting fines for violations are insignificant. Child labor is a problem in the informal economy.

Sex trafficking and child sex tourism are also serious problems. A law that took effect in 2013 established penalties for human trafficking and organ trafficking, as well as a fund for victims and prevention efforts. The US State Department's 2018 *Trafficking in Persons Report* found that government antitrafficking efforts were improving, noting the increased number of trafficking convictions and trafficking victims identified. However, there were issues with the disbursement of antitrafficking funds and the government did not provide adequate victim care services.

Côte d'Ivoire

Population: 24,900,000
Capital: Yamoussoukro (official), Abidjan (de facto)
Political Rights Rating: 4
Civil Liberties Rating: 4
Freedom Rating: 4.0
Freedom Status: Partly Free
Electoral Democracy: No

Overview: Côte d'Ivoire continues to recover from an armed conflict that ended in 2011. While security concerns and interference by security forces can constrain freedoms of expression and association, these are generally upheld; freedom of movement has improved, and the economy has seen steady growth. However, unrest within the armed forces and growing tensions within the ruling coalition threaten stability, and several root causes of the country's violent conflict remain, including ethnic and regional tensions, land disputes, corruption, and impunity. Women are significantly underrepresented in politics.

KEY DEVELOPMENTS IN 2018:

- A split between the two main parties in the ruling Rally of Houphouëtists for Democracy and Peace (RHDP) coalition—president Alassane Ouattara's Rally of the Republicans (RDR) and former president Henri Konan Bédié's Democratic Party of Côte d'Ivoire (PDCI)—preceded October's municipal elections.
- After municipal election results showed a robust performance by the RHDP, PDCI supporters staged protests and accused the government of electoral fraud. Some protests erupted into violence, resulting in the deaths of at least three people.

- Elections to the country's new Senate were held in March 2018, but the body was not fully functional at year's end due to a lack of resources and unresolved political disputes.
- In a move he said was meant to foster reconciliation, Ouattara pardoned some 800 people accused or convicted of committing acts of violence during the 2010–11 crisis, including former first lady Simone Gbagbo. She remained wanted by the International Criminal Court (ICC).
- The ICC case against former president Laurent Gbagbo, who faces charges of crimes against humanity, was ongoing at year's end.

POLITICAL RIGHTS: 19 / 40
A. ELECTORAL PROCESS: 7 / 12
A1. Was the current head of government or other chief national authority elected through free and fair elections? 3 / 4

The president is directly elected to a five-year term, and will be subject to a two-term limit after the 2020 election. Ouattara won the 2015 presidential election in the first round. Despite tensions and some government crackdowns on opposition rallies in the lead-up, the election itself was deemed credible by international and domestic observers, and was the first peaceful presidential election in Côte d'Ivoire in more than two decades. Ouattara, who is currently serving his second term, has claimed that the 2016 constitution permits him to run for a third in 2020.

The prime minister is head of government, and is appointed by the president and responsible for designating a cabinet, which is also approved by the president. Amadou Gon Coulibaly was appointed prime minister in early 2017, after the victory of the RHDP in the December 2016 legislative elections.

RHDP candidates posted the strongest performance in October 2018 mayoral elections, held concurrently with elections to local councils. PDCI supporters staged protests and accused the government of electoral fraud after the announcement of election results; some protests erupted into violence, resulting in deaths of at least three people.

A2. Were the current national legislative representatives elected through free and fair elections? 2 / 4

The bicameral parliament consists of a 255-seat lower house, the National Assembly, and a 99-seat Senate, which was envisaged by the 2016 constitution and seated in March 2018. National Assembly members are directly elected to five-year terms. Of the Senate's 99 seats, 66 are indirectly elected by the National Assembly and members of various local councils, and 33 members are appointed by the president; all members serve five-year terms.

The members of the current National Assembly were directly elected in credible, largely peaceful polls held in December 2016. The ruling RHDP won a solid majority, taking 167 of 255 seats. Independent candidates took the majority of remaining seats. In the March 2018 Senate elections, RHDP candidates won 50 of the 66 elected seats, and independent candidates took the remaining 16; the opposition boycotted the vote over allegations of bias by the Côte d'Ivoire's Independent Electoral Commission (CEI), as well as over claims that the body's establishment would help Ouattara consolidate power. (The opposition had also boycotted the referendum on the draft constitution that established the new body.)

While the new Senate members were seated, the new legislative body has yet to become fully functional, due mainly to a lack of funding and unresolved disputes among political factions.

RHDP candidates posted strong results in the October 2018 elections to regional councils, held concurrently with mayoral elections. The postelection environment saw allegations of fraud against the RHDP by members of the PDCI, and was marred by some instances of violence.

A3. Are the electoral laws and framework fair, and are they implemented impartially by the relevant election management bodies? 2 / 4

In 2016, the African Court on Human and People's Rights ruled that the CEI is imbalanced in favor of the government, undermining independence and impartiality, and ordered that the electoral law be amended. In August 2018, President Ouattara conceded to the reorganization of the CEI, but these reforms have yet to take effect. Opposition parties boycotted the March 2018 Senate elections in part due to concerns about the independence of the CEI.

Some of the violence that followed the October 2018 municipal elections arose from disputes that came in the wake of delayed results. Activists affiliated with the PDCI who staged protests after the elections accused the CEI of fraud and progovernment bias.

B. POLITICAL PLURALISM AND PARTICIPATION: 8 / 16

B1. Do the people have the right to organize in different political parties or other competitive political groupings of their choice, and is the system free of undue obstacles to the rise and fall of these competing parties or groupings? 2 / 4

The constitution of Côte d'Ivoire permits multiparty competition, and recent presidential and legislative elections have been contested by a large number of parties and independent candidates. In recent years, the ruling RHDP coalition—dominated by Ouattara's RDR and former President Henri Konan Bédié's PDCI—has held a virtual lock on national political power. However, after months of growing tensions between President Ouattara and Bédié over the question of who the RHDP's nominee should be for the 2020 presidential election, a significant faction of PDCI candidates defected and ran against the RHDP in the October 2018 municipal elections.

B2. Is there a realistic opportunity for the opposition to increase its support or gain power through elections? 2 / 4

Former president Laurent Gbagbo's Ivorian Popular Front (FPI) holds seats in parliament but remains relatively weak and disorganized, with members split between two main factions. The first is hardliners who insist on boycotting elections until Gbagbo's release from the custody of the ICC, where he faces charges of crimes against humanity; the second is comprised of moderates who support Pascal Affi N'Guessan, who served as prime minister during Gbagbo's presidency.

While the RHDP posted the strongest performance in the 2018 municipal elections, the PDCI won control of a handful of key municipalities, including the business district of Abidjan.

B3. Are the people's political choices free from domination by the military, foreign powers, religious hierarchies, economic oligarchies, or any other powerful group that is not democratically accountable? 2 / 4

Recent elections have been generally free from extensive voter intimidation or harassment. However, leaders within the military, especially former rebel commanders, are viewed as having significant political influence in the country.

Tensions ahead of the 2018 municipal polls contributes to some unease among voters, with the split between the RHDP and PDCI prompting some concern that the polls could be accompanied by violence. Roughly 30,000 police, gendarmes, and soldiers were deployed across the country to maintain security for the vote. Separately, there were some reports of candidates handing out cash to voters.

B4. Do various segments of the population (including ethnic, religious, gender, LGBT, and other relevant groups) have full political rights and electoral opportunities? 2 / 4

Citizenship has been a source of tension since the 1990s, when Ivorian nationalists adopted former president Bédié's concept of "Ivoirité" to exclude perceived foreigners (including Ouattara) from the political process. A law relaxing some conditions for citizenship went into effect in 2014 but its application remains uneven, and hundreds of thousands of individuals, mostly northerners, lack documentation.

Women are poorly represented in in the parliament, holding just 11 percent of seats in the National Assembly and 12 percent in the Senate. A 2017 cabinet reshuffle left 6 women in a 28-member cabinet.

A north-south, Muslim-Christian schism has been a salient feature of Ivorian life for decades, and was exacerbated by the 2002–11 crisis. However, the schism has since receded, and the current coalition government includes Muslims and Christians.

C. FUNCTIONING OF GOVERNMENT: 4 / 12

C1. Do the freely elected head of government and national legislative representatives determine the policies of the government? 2 / 4

Though defense and security forces are nominally under civilian control, problems of parallel command and control systems within the armed forces, known as the Republican Forces of Côte d'Ivoire (FRCI), remain a significant challenge. Additionally, after several years of relative calm, military mutinies in 2017 exposed the fragility of the civilian government's control over the state armed forces.

Especially in northern and western areas of the country, non-state armed actors and former rebels enjoy significant influence relative to elected representatives.

C2. Are safeguards against official corruption strong and effective? 1 / 4

Corruption and bribery remain endemic, and particularly affect the judiciary, police, and government contracting operations. Petty bribery also hampers citizens' access to quotidian services ranging from obtaining a birth certificate to clearing goods through customs. Perpetrators at all levels seldom face prosecution.

C3. Does the government operate with openness and transparency? 1 / 4

The government generally awards contracts in a nontransparent manner. Access to up-to-date information from government ministries is difficult for ordinary citizens to acquire, although some ministries do publish information online. In 2013, the National Assembly passed an access to information law, but enforcement has been inconsistent. The High Authority for Good Governance, an anticorruption body, requires public officials to submit asset declarations, but this is not well enforced.

CIVIL LIBERTIES: 32 / 60
D. FREEDOM OF EXPRESSION AND BELIEF: 11 / 16
D1. Are there free and independent media? 2 / 4

Conditions for the press have improved since the end of the 2010–11 conflict, and incidents of serious violence against journalists are rare. However, journalists face intimidation and occasional violence by security forces in connection with their work. In March 2018, a blogger was assaulted by police while attempting to cover an opposition protest, and was not permitted to file a formal complaint about the incident.

Most national media sources, especially newspapers, exhibit partisanship in their news coverage, consistently favoring either the government or the opposition.

D2. Are individuals free to practice and express their religious faith or nonbelief in public and private? 3 / 4

Legal guarantees of religious freedom are typically upheld. Relations between Muslims and Christians were exacerbated by the 2002–11 crisis, but tensions have since receded. In 2016, local authorities closed a mosque in Man in order to resolve leadership dispute that had prompted violent incidents.

D3. Is there academic freedom, and is the educational system free from extensive political indoctrination? 3 / 4

Public universities were closed and used as military bases during the 2010–11 conflict, and now suffer from a lack of adequate resources and facilities. However, academic freedom is usually upheld. In 2018, labor strikes by university employees claiming back wages disrupted classes for thousands of students, but took place peacefully and without interference.

D4. Are individuals free to express their personal views on political or other sensitive topics without fear of surveillance or retribution? 3 / 4

People are generally free to engage in political discussion and debate without fear of harassment or detention. However, the legacy of violent conflict can chill public debate of some topics.

E. ASSOCIATIONAL AND ORGANIZATIONAL RIGHTS: 8 / 12
E1. Is there freedom of assembly? 2 / 4

The constitution protects the right to free assembly, but in practice the government has attempted to restrict or forcibly disperse peaceful gatherings, and sometimes violence between demonstrators and police has erupted. Despite risks and restrictions, public protests and demonstrations are common. In 2018, protests by PDCI activists after the October municipal elections turned violent in a number of areas, resulting in property destruction and at least three deaths.

E2. Is there freedom for nongovernmental organizations, particularly those that are engaged in human rights- and governance-related work? 3 / 4

Domestic and international nongovernmental organizations (NGOs) are generally free to operate. However, poor security conditions—especially in northern and western areas of the country—are a constraint for some organizations.

E3. Is there freedom for trade unions and similar professional or labor organizations? 3 / 4

The right to organize and join labor unions is constitutionally guaranteed. Workers have the right to bargain collectively. Côte d'Ivoire typically has various professional strikes every year, though sometimes strikes have become violent. In 2018, teachers, university professors, police, and civil servants all organized labor strikes in demand of back pay from the government, with some such actions apparently inspired by the military mutinies the previous year.

F. RULE OF LAW: 6 / 16

F1. Is there an independent judiciary? 1 / 4

The judiciary is not independent, and judges are highly susceptible to external interference and bribes. Processes governing the assignment of cases to judges are opaque.

F2. Does due process prevail in civil and criminal matters? 1 / 4

The constitution guarantees equal access to justice and due process for all citizens, but these guarantees are poorly upheld in practice. Prolonged pretrial detention is a serious problem for both adults and minors, with some detainees spending years in prison without trial. The state struggles to provide attorneys to defendants who cannot afford legal counsel.

Security officials are susceptible to bribery and are rarely held accountable for misconduct.

F3. Is there protection from the illegitimate use of physical force and freedom from war and insurgencies? 2 / 4

Overall levels of violence in the country are lower than during the height of the political-military crisis in 2010–11. However, physical violence against civilians in the form of extortion, banditry, and sexual violence, sometime perpetrated by members of the state armed forces, remain common. In many areas of the country, and particularly in the west, disputes over land use and ownership between migrants, and those who claim customary land rights, sometimes turn violent.

The country's prisons are severely overcrowded, and incarcerated adults and minors are not always separated.

Concerns about impunity, victor's justice, and reconciliation have persisted after the close of the 2010–11 crisis. To date, only a handful of individuals have been put on trial for crimes committed during that period, and most prosecutions have focused on figures associated with Gbagbo. In an August 2018 move he said was meant to foster reconciliation, Ouattara pardoned some 800 people accused or convicted of committing acts of violence during the 2010–11 crisis, including former first lady Simone Gbagbo, who remains wanted by the ICC. A number of those released had been held without trial for extended periods.

Meanwhile, the ICC continued its trial of former president Gbagbo in 2018 on charges of crimes against humanity committed during the 2010–11 crisis. The ICC has said it is investigating pro-Ouattara actors for crimes committed by former rebels, but it has filed charges only against pro-Gbagbo defendants so far.

F4. Do laws, policies, and practices guarantee equal treatment of various segments of the population? 2 / 4

Same-sex sexual conduct is not specifically criminalized in Côte d'Ivoire, but LGBT (lesbian, gay, bisexual, and transgender) people can face prosecution under measures criminalizing acts of "public indecency." No law prohibits discrimination on the basis of sexual orientation. LGBT people face societal prejudice as well as violence and harassment by state security forces.

Intercommunal tensions over land rights frequently involve migrants from neighboring countries, who sometimes experience violent intimidation.

G. PERSONAL AUTONOMY AND INDIVIDUAL RIGHTS: 7 / 16

G1. Do individuals enjoy freedom of movement, including the ability to change their place of residence, employment, or education? 2 / 4

Freedom of movement has improved since the end of the civil war in 2011, with fewer illegal roadblocks along major roads and within Abidjan. However, irregular checkpoints and acts of extortion continue in some areas of the country, particularly in the west and north, and near gold and diamond-producing regions. The government's efforts to combat these practices have been undermined by inconsistent financial support and a failure to investigate and prosecute perpetrators. Women are generally afforded equal freedom of movement, though risks of insecurity and sexual violence hinder this in practice.

G2. Are individuals able to exercise the right to own property and establish private businesses without undue interference from state or nonstate actors? 2 / 4

Citizens have the right to own and establish private businesses, and private industry has grown since the end of the crisis in 2011. The country has also attracted significant investment. However, property and land rights remain weak and poorly regulated, especially in the west, where conflict over land tenure between migrants and those who claim customary land rights remains a significant source of tension.

G3. Do individuals enjoy personal social freedoms, including choice of marriage partner and size of family, protection from domestic violence, and control over appearance? 1 / 4

Women suffer significant legal and economic discrimination, and sexual and gender-based violence are widespread. Impunity for perpetrators also remains a problem, and when it is prosecuted, rape is routinely reclassified as indecent assault. Costly medical certificates are often essential for convictions, yet are beyond the means of victims who are impoverished.

G4. Do individuals enjoy equality of opportunity and freedom from economic exploitation? 2 / 4

Despite efforts by the government and international industries in recent years to counter the phenomenon, child labor is a frequent problem, particularly in the cocoa industry. Human trafficking is prohibited by the new constitution, but government programs for victims of trafficking—often children—are inadequate.

Croatia

Capital: Zagreb
Population: 4,100,000
Political Rights Rating: 1
Civil Liberties Rating: 2
Freedom Rating: 1.5
Freedom Status: Free
Electoral Democracy: Yes

Overview: Croatia is a parliamentary republic that regularly holds free elections. Civil and political rights are generally respected, though corruption in the public sector is a serious issue. The Roma and Serb minorities face discrimination, as do LGBT (lesbian, gay, bisexual, and transgender) people. Recent years have seen increasing concern about the presence in public life of far-right groups and figures that espouse discriminatory values.

KEY DEVELOPMENTS IN 2018:
- Zagreb mayor Milan Bandić and twelve associates went on trial in October on charges including abuse of power, influence peddling, tax evasion, and customs fraud.

- Economy Minister Martina Dalić resigned in May, in the wake of media reports suggesting that she and a group of well-connected figures had crafted the so-called *lex agrok*or—the 2017 law that allowed the government to take over management of the troubled agricultural giant Agrokor—behind closed doors and in a manner that suggested a variety of conflicts of interest.
- Ivica Todorović, the former owner of Agrokor being investigated for fraud, was extradited from the United Kingdom in November. He was arrested upon arrival in Croatia, but released days later after posting €1 million bail, and had not been indicted at year's end.
- Croatia's second-place finish at the World Cup in July was marred by the appearance of a far-right, nationalist singer at the homecoming celebrations in Zagreb, which prompted criticism domestically and from some foreign journalists and rights activists.
- In April, lawmakers ratified the Istanbul Convention, a treaty on preventing and combating domestic violence. The treaty was unpopular among conservative and far-right groups, who viewed its definition of gender as having the potential to prompt the legal introduction of same-sex marriage or a third gender category, or to affect curriculum taught in schools.

POLITICAL RIGHTS: 36 / 40 (−1)

A. ELECTORAL PROCESS: 12 / 12

A1. Was the current head of government or other chief national authority elected through free and fair elections? 4 / 4

The president, who is head of state, is elected by popular vote for a maximum of two five-year terms. The prime minister is head of government, and is appointed by the president with parliamentary approval.

Croatia held the runoff to its December 2014 presidential election in January 2015. Outgoing president Ivo Josipović of the Social Democratic Party (SDP) lost to Kolinda Grabar-Kitarović of the conservative Croatian Democratic Union (HDZ) by a margin of less than one percent. Election monitors and stakeholders broadly accepted the poll's result.

HDZ chairman Andrej Plenković became prime minister following the 2016 legislative elections, in which HDZ won a plurality of seats.

A2. Were the current national legislative representatives elected through free and fair elections? 4 / 4

Members of the 151-member unicameral Croatian Parliament (Hrvatski Sabor) are elected to four-year terms.

Snap parliamentary elections in 2016—which were held after the previous prime minister lost a no-confidence vote, and were the second legislative polls in less than a year—were considered free and fair, but were marked by low turnout. The HDZ and its allies won 61 seats, and the party has since led a coalition government, the composition of which has changed occasionally.

The HDZ posted strong results in municipal elections held in 2017.

A3. Are the electoral laws and framework fair, and are they implemented impartially by the relevant election management bodies? 4 / 4

While some concerns about the use of public funds for political campaigns persist, in general, the State Election Commission implements robust electoral laws effectively.

B. POLITICAL PLURALISM AND PARTICIPATION: 14 / 16 (−1)

B1. Do the people have the right to organize in different political parties or other competitive political groupings of their choice, and is the system free of undue obstacles to the rise and fall of these competing parties or groupings? 4 / 4

Citizens may freely organize and participate in the activities of a wide variety of political parties. Small far-left and far-right parties made gains in the 2017 local elections.

The composition of the government changed in 2017, after the reformist Bridge of Independent Lists (Most) withdrew from the HDZ-led coalition after refusing to back Finance Minister Zdravko Marić, who had been implicated in a conflict-of-interest controversy related to his time working at Agrokor. The HDZ then allied with the liberal Croatian People's Party (HNS), which had been part of the SDP-led opposition coalition.

The HNS's decision to join the HDZ's government prompted the party's own fragmentation. Anka Mrak-Taritaš, who had been an HNS candidate for the 2017 municipal elections, formed her own party—the Civic Liberal Alliance (GLAS)—with three other HNS lawmakers.

B2. Is there a realistic opportunity for the opposition to increase its support or gain power through elections? 4 / 4

The SDP-led opposition coalition holds a significant bloc of seats in the legislature, and is generally able to operate without facing restrictions or election-related intimidation. But in general, the HDZ has dominated politics, and draws support from the Roman Catholic Church, veterans, and a growing number of conservative nongovernmental organizations (NGOs). The main, SDP-led opposition bloc has won the most seats in only two parliamentary elections since 1991, although the country was headed by an SDP president from 2010 to 2015.

B3. Are the people's political choices free from domination by the military, foreign powers, religious hierarchies, economic oligarchies, or any other powerful group that is not democratically accountable? 3 / 4 (−1)

While voters and candidates are generally able to freely express their political choices, many public servants obtained their positions through patronage networks, and thus risk becoming beholden to a party or special interest as a result. Patronage networks are particularly influential in Zagreb, which has been under the stewardship of Mayor Milan Bandić—who is affiliated with the HDZ and considered one of the country's most powerful politicians—close to continuously for the past 20 years. Bandić's tenure has been marked by corruption allegations, including conflict-of-interest cases, and credible allegations regarding improper hiring practices and public procurement deals.

Score Change: The score declined from 4 to 3 due to the persistent, influential role of patronage networks in the country's politics.

B4. Do various segments of the population (including ethnic, religious, gender, LGBT, and other relevant groups) have full political rights and electoral opportunities? 3 / 4

Eight parliamentary seats are set aside for ethnic minorities, including three for ethnic Serbs. However, the political interests of minority groups, notably Roma and Serbs, are underrepresented.

Women are represented across political parties, and a woman currently holds Croatia's presidency. However, the number of women in parliament decreased in 2016 after the Constitutional Court struck down a law requiring that 40 percent of a party's candidates be women. A 2016 Organization for Security and Co-operation in Europe (OSCE) election monitoring mission called for political parties to run more women candidates, and to promote more women to senior party leadership positions.

In September 2018, sitting lawmaker and Independent Democratic Serb Party (SDS) leader Milorad Pupovac was pelted with food items by a protester in Zagreb. Pupovac characterized the incident as reflective of growing hostility toward the Serb minority population by ascendant right-wing and nationalist movements in the country, many of which appear to enjoy the tacit support of the ruling HDZ.

Societal discrimination against LGBT people can discourage their participation in politics, and elements of the political establishment have espoused such discriminatory attitudes in their activism.

C. FUNCTIONING OF GOVERNMENT: 10 / 12

C1. Do the freely elected head of government and national legislative representatives determine the policies of the government? 4 / 4

Democratically elected representatives are duly installed into office, and are generally able to make public policy without undue external influence or pressure.

C2. Are safeguards against official corruption strong and effective? 3 / 4

A criminal code in effect since 2013 enforces stiffer penalties for various forms of corruption, and while some progress has been made, official corruption—including nepotism, bribery, fraud, and patronage—remains serious problems. Numerous high-level corruption cases have been filed in recent years, but many have yet to see a verdict. International bodies including the European Commission have called for greater efforts to eliminate malfeasance in public procurement processes.

In October, Bandić was acquitted of charges that he had cost the city of Zagreb some €41,500 euros ($47,700) by allowing a church-affiliated group to collect campaign signatures without paying appropriate fees. Bandić and a number of associates went on trial in October on charges including abuse of power, influence peddling, tax evasion, and customs fraud. The actions alleged are said to have cost the city and state budgets some 3.3 million euros ($3.8 million).

Several government figures have been implicated in mismanagement or wrongdoing in connection with the collapse of the food and retail group Agrokor, the region's largest employer, which the government took management of in 2017.

C3. Does the government operate with openness and transparency? 3 / 4

In 2013, Croatia adopted the Law on the Right of Access to Information. The legislation includes a proportionality and public-interest test designed to determine a balance between reasons for disclosing information and reasons for restricting it, and establishes an independent information commissioner to monitor compliance. However, government bodies do not always release requested information in a timely manner.

Media reports that emerged in 2018 suggested that Economy Minister Martina Dalić and a group of well-connected businesspeople and lawyers crafted the so-called *lex agrok*or—the 2017 law that allowed the government to take over management of the troubled agricultural company—outside of legislative bodies and out of view of the public. Facing related conflict-of-interest allegations, she resigned in May.

CIVIL LIBERTIES: 49 / 60
D. FREEDOM OF EXPRESSION AND BELIEF: 13 / 16

D1. Are there free and independent media? 3 / 4

Media in Croatia is highly polarized, but generally free from overt political interference or manipulation. However, journalists continue to face threats, harassment, and occasional attacks. In June 2018, reporter Hrvoje Bajlo was attacked and severely beaten in the city of Zadar, by a man Bajlo said threatened him with further harm if he did not discontinue reporting on the HDZ and a former minister of sea, traffic and infrastructure, and an under-secretary in the ministry, both of whom had been charged with embezzling from state-run companies. Earlier, Veterans' Minister Tomo Medved had allegedly threatened to beat jour-nalist Vojislav Mazzocco over a story detailing allegations of nepotism benefiting Medved's son. The Croatian Journalists Association characterized the attack on Bajlo as a consequence of authorities' failure to condemn the earlier threat against Mazzocco, and other attacks and harassment against journalists.

D2. Are individuals free to practice and express their religious faith or nonbelief in public and private? 3 / 4

The Croatian constitution guarantees freedom of religion, and this is generally upheld in practice. However, the small Serb Orthodox community remains vulnerable to harassment, and members have reported vandalism of their churches. Jewish and other groups have ex-pressed increasing concern about Holocaust denial and displays by right-wing nationalists of symbols and slogans associated with the fascist Ustaša regime that governed Croatia during World War II. Revisionist accounts of the Ustaša period continued to be promoted by far-right groups and newspapers in 2018.

D3. Is there academic freedom, and is the educational system free from extensive political indoctrination? 3 / 4

While there are generally not overt restrictions on speech in schools and universities, critics continue to allege inappropriate political interference at all levels of education. While aspects of a long-planned modernization of school curriculum were approved in the parlia-ment in July 2018, the HDZ has long sought to delay the popular modernization plan, and has moved to install its own members into the group tasked with developing the policies—including extremely conservative members opposed to sex education.

Also in July, a far-right movement sought the firing of three academics at the University of Zagreb for a paper they had published on the surging far-right in the country. While the academics were not fired, the allegations prompted an initial investigation by the university, and reflected the increasing presence and influence of such groups.

D4. Are individuals free to express their personal views on political or other sensitive topics without fear of surveillance or retribution? 4 / 4

People are generally free to engage in discussions of a sensitive nature without fearing surveillance or retribution.

E. ASSOCIATIONAL AND ORGANIZATIONAL RIGHTS: 12 / 12
E1. Is there freedom of assembly? 4 / 4

Freedom of assembly is protected and respected in Croatia.

E2. Is there freedom for nongovernmental organizations, particularly those that are engaged in human rights- and governance-related work? 4 / 4

The NGO sector in Croatia remains robust, active, and free from restrictions.

E3. Is there freedom for trade unions and similar professional or labor organizations? 4 / 4

The constitution allows workers to form and join trade unions, and this right is generally respected in practice.

F. RULE OF LAW: 11 / 16
F1. Is there an independent judiciary? 3 / 4

While judicial independence is generally respected, there have been recent concerns about the influence of far-right–wing groups on the judiciary. For example, in 2017, a court reversed a 1945 conviction of an academic who was found to be complicit in atrocities committed by the fascist Ustaša regime. Critics allege the courts have been ruling in line with the views of right-wing NGOs and the ruling HDZ, while the courts maintain in response that they are redressing partisan rulings of the Yugoslav communist courts.

F2. Does due process prevail in civil and criminal matters? 3 / 4

Due process rights are generally upheld, but the system tends to work more efficiently for individuals with abundant resources or high social standing.

In November 2018, Ivica Todorović, the former owner of Agrokor under investigation for fraud in relation to the company's collapse, was extradited from the United Kingdom. He was arrested upon arrival in Croatia, but released days later after posting €1 million bail, and had not been indicted at year's end.

The International Commission on Missing Persons has criticized Croatia for its slow progress in identifying human remains of victims of the 1991–95 conflicts, and in making reparations to survivors and their families.

F3. Is there protection from the illegitimate use of physical force and freedom from war and insurgencies? 3 / 4

Violence by state and nonstate actors is uncommon. Prison conditions do not meet international standards due to overcrowding and inadequate medical care.

F4. Do laws, policies, and practices guarantee equal treatment of various segments of the population? 2 / 4

Ethnic and religious minorities and LGBT people in Croatia face discrimination, and there are concerns about the increasing visibility of far-right, nationalist groups that spread discriminatory rhetoric. In perhaps the year's most visible reflection of increasing right-wing sentiment in public life, Croatia's second-place finish at the World Cup in July 2018 was marred by the presence of a far-right, nationalist singer at the homecoming celebrations in Zagreb; the appearance prompted criticism domestically and from some foreign journalists and rights activists. Occasional moves by the government suggest endorsement of far-right groups, and observers have expressed concern that such statements amount to tacit approval of discriminatory behavior. A group of NGOs in December 2018 criticized the government for lacking a comprehensive human rights policy, and warned of continuing deterioration of the protection of human rights in the country, especially for minorities and woman.

The constitution prohibits gender discrimination, but women earn less than men for comparable work and hold fewer leadership positions.

Reports of police violence against migrants, refugees, and asylum-seekers continued in 2018. Most such incidents took place along the border with Bosnia and Herzegovina, rather than Serbia, as in the past.

G. PERSONAL AUTONOMY AND INDIVIDUAL RIGHTS: 13 / 16

G1. Do individuals enjoy freedom of movement, including the ability to change their place of residence, employment, or education? 4 / 4

Freedom of movement is protected by the constitution and upheld in practice. People may freely change their place of residence, employment, or education.

G2. Are individuals able to exercise the right to own property and establish private businesses without undue interference from state or nonstate actors? 3 / 4

Property rights are generally well protected. However, corruption can inhibit normal business operations.

G3. Do individuals enjoy personal social freedoms, including choice of marriage partner and size of family, protection from domestic violence, and control over appearance? 3 / 4

In 2014, following a 2013 referendum that banned same-sex marriage, the parliament passed a law allowing same-sex civil unions. The law affords same-sex couples equal rights in inheritance, social benefits, and taxation, but same-sex couples may not adopt children.

Domestic violence remains a concern. Convictions for rape and domestic violence can bring lengthy prisons terms. However, police sometimes fail to adhere to recommended procedures for handling reports of domestic violence.

In April 2018, lawmakers ratified the Istanbul Convention, a treaty on preventing and combating violence against women and domestic violence. The treaty was unpopular among conservative and far-right groups, who viewed its definition of gender as having the potential to prompt the legal introduction of same-sex marriage or a third gender category, or to affect curriculum taught in schools, and there were protests against it. In response to protests, the government adopted a statement saying the treaty's adoption would not change the legal definition of marriage.

G4. Do individuals enjoy equality of opportunity and freedom from economic exploitation? 3 / 4

Worker protection laws are robust, and the Office of the Labor Inspectorate actively investigates work sites. However, labor violation remain a problem within the hospitality sector. Workers in the informal sector have less access to legal protections.

Human trafficking remains a problem, sentences for those convicted of it can be light, and witness statements are not always given the appropriate consideration in court cases.

Cuba

Population: 11,100,000
Capital: Havana
Political Rights Rating: 7
Civil Liberties Rating: 6
Freedom Rating: 6.5
Freedom Status: Not Free
Electoral Democracy: No

Overview: Cuba is a one-party communist state that outlaws political pluralism, suppresses dissent, and severely restricts basic civil liberties. The government continues to dominate the economy despite recent reforms that permit some private-sector activity. The regime's undemocratic character has not changed despite new leadership in 2018 and a process of diplomatic "normalization" with Washington, which has stalled in recent years.

KEY DEVELOPMENTS IN 2018:

- Systematic repression of independent activists, journalists, and civil society groups continued during the year.
- A new National Assembly was chosen through noncompetitive elections in March, and in April it met to install Miguel Díaz-Canel as president of the Council of State. Raúl Castro left the presidency after two five-year terms, but he remained first secretary of the Communist Party of Cuba (PCC).
- Strict new regulations were announced for the private sector in July, but after sustained criticism, some elements were revised before they took effect in December.
- Also in December, third-generation (3G) mobile data service became available to Cubans for the first time, and the National Assembly unanimously approved a new constitution that was set for ratification in a national referendum in early 2019. Despite some changes, the constitution would largely preserve the country's one-party system.

POLITICAL RIGHTS: 1 / 40

A. ELECTORAL PROCESS: 0 / 12

A1. Was the current head of government or other chief national authority elected through free and fair elections? 0 / 4

Every five years, the National Assembly designates the members of the Council of State through a noncompetitive process. This body in turn appoints the Council of Ministers in consultation with its president, who serves as both chief of state and head of government. The draft constitution approved by lawmakers in December 2018 would separate those roles, creating the post of prime minister to serve as head of government and stipulating that members of the Council of Ministers could not also be members of the Council of State.

Raúl Castro, having served as president since he succeeded his brother Fidel in 2008, stepped down in April 2018, and the National Assembly named Díaz-Canel to replace him. The draft constitution set a limit of two consecutive five-year terms for the presidency, as well as an age limit of 60 years for the start of a president's first term. Raúl Castro, who turned 87 in June 2018, remained first secretary of the PCC. Díaz-Canel, who turned 59 in April, pledged that Castro would continue to "lead the most important decisions for the present and the future of the nation." A similar process of generational transition and partial decoupling of top party and government posts was unfolding across the executive. Only 9 members of the PCC's Political Bureau also sat on the Council of State chosen in April; following the 2013 elections, the overlap had been 13.

A2. Were the current national legislative representatives elected through free and fair elections? 0 / 4

In the 2018 National Assembly elections, held in March, voters were asked to either support or reject a single PCC-approved candidate for each of the unicameral body's 605 seats. All candidates were elected.

A3. Are the electoral laws and framework fair, and are they implemented impartially by the relevant election management bodies? 0 / 4

The only Cuban elections that offer a choice of more than one candidate per office are those for municipal assemblies, but no campaigning is allowed. This is not expected to change under the new electoral law that will follow ratification of the new constitution in 2019.

Ahead of the municipal voting held in late 2017, the government worked to intimidate voters, manipulate nomination meetings, detain or jail opposition figures, and otherwise thwart the candidacies of a group of 175 opposition activists associated with the Otro18 coalition, none of whom were ultimately able to secure a place on the ballot. Activists also faced detentions and intimidation while attempting to monitor polling places and vote counting.

B. POLITICAL PLURALISM AND PARTICIPATION: 0 / 16

B1. Do the people have the right to organize in different political parties or other competitive political groupings of their choice, and is the system free of undue obstacles to the rise and fall of these competing parties or groupings? 0 / 4

Political parties other than the PCC are illegal. Political dissent is a punishable offense, and dissidents are systematically harassed, detained, physically assaulted, and frequently imprisoned for minor infractions. Supposedly spontaneous mob attacks, known as "acts of repudiation," are often used to silence political dissidents. The Cuban Commission for Human Rights and National Reconciliation (CCDHRN), a nongovernmental organization, reported 2,873 arbitrary arrests of peaceful opponents during 2018, a significant decrease from the 5,155 detained in 2017 and the 9,940 held in 2016. Such brief politically motivated detentions were a key repressive tactic under the government of Raúl Castro, but the 2018 total was the lowest in eight years.

B2. Is there a realistic opportunity for the opposition to increase its support or gain power through elections? 0 / 4

The PCC and the Castro brothers in particular have dominated government and politics in Cuba since 1959, allowing no transfer or rotation of power between rival groups. While the unprecedented attempt by dissident groups to field independent candidates in the 2017 municipal elections was aimed at challenging the PCC's monopoly, the authorities' successful campaign to block opposition candidacies ensured that those elections and the subsequent provincial and national elections in 2018 would again feature no independent candidates.

B3. Are the people's political choices free from domination by the military, foreign powers, religious hierarchies, economic oligarchies, or any other powerful group that is not democratically accountable? 0 / 4

The authoritarian one-party system in Cuba largely excludes the public from any genuine and autonomous political participation. The military and intelligence agencies play an important role in suppressing dissent. Several members of the extended Castro family hold important government positions, though none (apart from PCC first secretary Raúl Castro) were granted seats on the PCC's Central Committee during the Seventh Party Congress in 2016, and none currently serve on either the Council of Ministers or the Council of State.

B4. Do various segments of the population (including ethnic, religious, gender, LGBT, and other relevant groups) have full political rights and electoral opportunities? 0 / 4

Since political rights are denied to all Cuban citizens, women and members of minority groups are unable to choose their representatives or organize independently to assert their interests in the political sphere. The PCC leadership does exhibit a growing gender and racial diversity. At the 2016 party congress, the proportion of women on the PCC Central Committee rose to 44.4 percent, from 41.7 percent in 2011. Afro-Cubans accounted for 35.9 percent, up from 31.3 percent in 2011. Women also now hold more than half of the 605 National Assembly seats and make up almost half of the 31-member Council of State; Cubans of African and mixed-race descent make up about half of each body. Half of Cuba's six vice presidents are black, including First Vice President Salvador Valdés Mesa, and three are women.

C. FUNCTIONING OF GOVERNMENT: 1 / 12

C1. Do the freely elected head of government and national legislative representatives determine the policies of the government? 0 / 4

None of Cuba's nominally elected officials are chosen through free and fair contests, and major policy decisions are reserved for the PCC leadership in practice. The National Assembly, which the constitution describes as the "supreme organ of state power," has little independent influence and meets for brief sessions only twice a year.

C2. Are safeguards against official corruption strong and effective? 1 / 4

Corruption remains a serious problem in Cuba, with widespread illegality permeating everyday life. The state enjoys a monopoly on most large business transactions, and there are no independent mechanisms to hold officials accountable for wrongdoing. During his 10 years as president, Raúl Castro prioritized the fight against corruption; a new comptroller general was installed, and long prison sentences were imposed on high-level Cuban officials and foreign businessmen found guilty of corruption-related charges. However, the government has not enacted internal reforms that would make the system more transparent and less prone to abuse, nor does it allow civil society groups, journalists, or courts to serve as external checks on its authority.

C3. Does the government operate with openness and transparency? 0 / 4

Cuba lacks effective laws that provide for freedom of information and access to official records. Recent demands by journalists for a new media law that would grant citizens the right to information and offer legal protection for the emerging nonstate media sector have made little headway with the government.

CIVIL LIBERTIES: 13 / 60
D. FREEDOM OF EXPRESSION AND BELIEF: 5 / 16
D1. Are there free and independent media? 1 / 4

The news media are owned and controlled by the state. The tiny independent press corps is illegal, its publications are considered "enemy propaganda," and its journalists are frequently harassed, detained, and prohibited from traveling abroad. Government agents routinely accuse independent journalists of being mercenaries, and many face charges of "usurpation of legal capacity" or other trumped-up offenses. Despite these obstacles, independent digital media outlets have continued to emerge in recent years.

President Díaz-Canel has publicly rejected the need for any fundamental change in the state-run media model. In April 2018, he signed into law Decree 349, which aimed to extend state control over the thriving independent artistic community by requiring prior Ministry of Culture approval for both public and private cultural activities. It also banned audiovisual material with ill-defined unpatriotic symbols, pornography, violence, or "sexist, vulgar, or obscene language," as well as books with content that is harmful to "ethical and cultural values."

Only a small percentage of the population has access to the global internet, as opposed to a government-controlled national intranet. Critical blogs and websites are often blocked. Under a program that began in 2015, the state telecommunications monopoly Etecsa continued to deploy Wi-Fi hotspots in public spaces such as parks, with the number reaching

800 by the end of 2018. It also extended its rollout of home-based internet access, which reached 67,000 homes by December. The first-ever 3G mobile internet access for Cuban citizens was launched that month, but high prices put the service out of reach for most, and the connections were reported to be slow and riddled with technical problems.

D2. Are individuals free to practice and express their religious faith or nonbelief in public and private? 3 / 4

Religious freedom has gradually improved over the past decade, but official obstacles still make it difficult for churches to operate without interference and conduct ordinary educational activities. Given its positive role in US-Cuban diplomatic talks, the Roman Catholic Church has enjoyed an expansion of its pastoral rights, including periodic access to state media and public spaces and the ability to build new churches and distribute its own publications. Protestant and evangelical groups tend to face greater restrictions, though they too have experienced improved conditions in recent years. In 2018, the government allowed various churches to mount a public campaign against a proposed constitutional reform that would have supported the legalization of same-sex marriage.

D3. Is there academic freedom, and is the educational system free from extensive political indoctrination? 0 / 4

Academic freedom is restricted in Cuba, and private schools and universities have been banned since the early 1960s. New self-employment regulations issued in July 2018 explicitly outlawed using freelancer licenses to set up private schools or academies, and while private day-care centers can continue operating, they must do so under strict regulatory oversight. Teaching materials often contain ideological content, and educators commonly require PCC affiliation to advance in their careers. University students have been expelled for dissident behavior. Despite the elimination of exit visas in 2013, university faculty must still obtain permission from their superiors to travel to academic conferences abroad. Cuban officials often prevent dissident intellectuals from traveling abroad and deny entry to prominent exiled intellectuals who have been critical of the regime.

D4. Are individuals free to express their personal views on political or other sensitive topics without fear of surveillance or retribution? 1 / 4

Neighborhood-level "Committees for the Defense of the Revolution" assist security agencies by monitoring, reporting, and suppressing dissent. Cubans often engage in robust private discussions regarding everyday issues like the economy, food prices, foreign travel, and difficulties gaining internet access, but they tend to avoid discussing more sensitive political issues such as human rights and civil liberties. The second half of 2018 featured public and online debate over the draft constitution, though the changes made for the final draft did not always reflect public concerns.

E. ASSOCIATIONAL AND ORGANIZATIONAL RIGHTS: 0 / 12
E1. Is there freedom of assembly? 0 / 4

Restrictions on freedom of assembly remain a key form of political control. Security forces and government-backed thugs routinely break up peaceful gatherings or protests by political dissidents and civic activists. The existing constitution limits the rights of assembly and association to prevent their exercise "against the existence and objectives of the Socialist State." While some of the harsher language banning independent or opposition gatherings was eliminated in the draft of the new constitution, it still qualifies the right to assembly by requiring that it be exercised "with respect to public order and in compliance with the precepts established by the law."

E2. Is there freedom for nongovernmental organizations, particularly those that are engaged in human rights- and governance-related work? 0 / 4

Based on the 1985 Law on Associations, the government refuses to register any new organization that is not state supervised. Nearly all politically motivated short-term detentions in recent years have targeted members of independent associations, think tanks, human rights groups, political parties, or trade unions.

A number of independent civil society organizations suffered repression during 2018, with some activists detained on arbitrary charges, prevented from traveling abroad, or forced into exile. The dissident groups most commonly persecuted by the government include the Ladies in White, the Patriotic Union of Cuba (UNPACU), Cuba Decide, the Christian Liberation Movement (MCL), Somos Más, and the independent think tank Convivencia Cuba Studies Center.

E3. Is there freedom for trade unions and similar professional or labor organizations? 0 / 4

Cuban workers do not have the right to strike or bargain collectively, and independent labor unions are illegal.

F. RULE OF LAW: 2 / 16

F1. Is there an independent judiciary? 0 / 4

The Council of State has full control over the courts, whose rulings typically conform to the interests of the PCC. Judges are tasked with enforcing laws on vaguely defined offenses such as "public disorder," "contempt," "disrespect for authority," "pre-criminal dangerousness," and "aggression," which are used to prosecute the regime's political opponents.

F2. Does due process prevail in civil and criminal matters? 0 / 4

Multiple legal cases against dissidents during 2018 illustrated the systematic violation of due process. These included the prosecution of scientist and environmental activist Ariel Ruiz Urquiola, who was arrested in May and quickly sentenced to a year in jail for the crime of *desacato* (disrespect) after his farm was raided by state forest rangers. Thought to be a pretext to end his independent environmental activism and seize his farm, the charges were criticized by Amnesty International, which declared Urquiola a prisoner of conscience in June, and by Bishop Jorge Serpa of Pinar del Río, who that month called on the government to review the case. As a result of such pressure and Urquiola's own hunger strike, he was granted a conditional release for health reasons in July, though the verdict and sentence remained in effect. The CCDHRN reported that as of the end of May there were 120 cases of political prisoners, down from 140 a year earlier.

F3. Is there protection from the illegitimate use of physical force and freedom from war and insurgencies? 1 / 4

Opposition activists, human rights defenders, and other perceived enemies of the regime are routinely subjected to public assaults as well as abuse in custody. For example, during the month of October 2018, the CCDHRN documented 6 cases of physical aggression and 14 acts of harassment against dissidents that were organized or encouraged by state security forces.

The government has refused to allow international monitoring of its prisons. Prison conditions are poor, featuring overcrowding, forced labor, inadequate sanitation and medical care, and physical abuse. In one high-profile case, MCL activist Eduardo Cardet, who was sentenced to three years in prison in 2017, has been physically attacked in custody and denied medical attention and family visits.

F4. Do laws, policies, and practices guarantee equal treatment of various segments of the population? 1 / 4

Women enjoy legal equality and are well represented in most professions, though their labor force participation rate stands at about 40 percent, suggesting persistent economic disparities and cultural double standards.

While racial discrimination has long been outlawed, Cubans of African descent have reported widespread discrimination and profiling by police. Many lack access to the dollar economy. A recent survey found that 78 percent of hard currency remittances sent to the island from abroad go to white Cubans, leaving Afro-Cubans at an even greater disadvantage.

Discrimination based on sexual orientation is illegal in areas such as employment and housing, and Mariela Castro Espín, Raúl Castro's daughter and the director of the National Center for Sexual Education (CENESEX), has advocated on behalf of the LGBT (lesbian, gay, bisexual, and transgender) community. However, the advocacy efforts of independent LGBT groups are either ignored or actively suppressed.

Article 42 of the draft constitution extends protection from discrimination to a wider array of vulnerable groups, explicitly adding categories such as ethnic origin, gender identity, sexual orientation, age, and disability to the existing safeguards regarding race, sex, national origin, and religion.

G. PERSONAL AUTONOMY AND INDIVIDUAL RIGHTS: 6 / 16

G1. Do individuals enjoy freedom of movement, including the ability to change their place of residence, employment, or education? 1 / 4

Freedom of movement and the right to choose one's residence and place of employment are restricted. Cubans who move to Havana without authorization are subject to removal. Some dissidents are barred from foreign travel, despite a 2013 migration law that rescinded Cuba's exit visa requirement. Cubans still face extremely high passport fees relative to their very low incomes, and Cuban doctors, diplomats, and athletes who "defect" are barred from visiting for eight years. Former political prisoners are often encouraged to go into exile or forced to live with severely restricted freedoms, including limits on foreign travel.

G2. Are individuals able to exercise the right to own property and establish private businesses without undue interference from state or nonstate actors? 1 / 4

While the number of Cubans licensed as "self-employed" reached 591,456 by the end of May 2018, in July the government issued a 129-page compendium of new regulations designed to rein in the nonstate sector, curbing "illegalities" and preventing the private concentration of wealth and property. The regulations, which took effect in December, aimed to limit entrepreneurs to a single license, ban doing business with foreign entities, and prohibit the use of stand-ins as business owners and the operation of private schools, academies, and real-estate agencies. Following a broad-based pushback from private operators, the government announced changes to some of the most consistently criticized regulations before they came into force. For example, entrepreneurs would still be able to hold more than one license under certain conditions, and the size of Cuba's popular private *paladar* restaurants would only be limited by the size of the dining area, not by an arbitrary "50-chair" rule.

Nevertheless, private employment opportunities remain restricted, with most professions excluded. The new regulations failed to provide Cuba's true small- and medium-sized enterprises with legal recognition, stunting their growth and placing them in legal jeopardy. While the draft constitution recognizes the existence of private property and the market, it also emphasizes that state-owned enterprises and the central planning system will remain dominant.

G3. Do individuals enjoy personal social freedoms, including choice of marriage partner and size of family, protection from domestic violence, and control over appearance? 3 / 4

Individuals enjoy broad freedom in their interpersonal, romantic, and sexual relationships. While divorce is common, men and women enjoy equal rights to marital goods and child custody. The draft constitution does not contain language in the existing charter that defines marriage as a union between a man and a woman, raising the possibility that same-sex marriage could be legalized in the future, though a change that would have more explicitly supported legalization was ultimately rejected.

Violent crime, including rape and domestic abuse, is believed to be relatively uncommon, though official statistics on crime are rarely published, and domestic violence is not treated as a separate legal category.

G4. Do individuals enjoy equality of opportunity and freedom from economic exploitation? 1 / 4

Average official salaries remain extremely low at about $30 per month, and the national currency is very weak, encouraging an exodus of trained personnel into the private and tourism sectors, where the convertible peso—pegged to the US dollar—is used. Cubans employed by foreign firms are often much better remunerated than their fellow citizens, even though most are contracted through a state employment agency that siphons off the bulk of their wages and uses political criteria in screening applicants.

State employees who express political dissent or disagreement with the authorities often face harassment or dismissal. Professionals dismissed from their jobs in the state sector have difficulty continuing their careers, as licenses for professions are not available in the private sector.

Cyprus

Population: 1,200,000
Capital: Nicosia
Political Rights Rating: 1
Civil Liberties Rating: 1
Freedom Rating: 1.0
Freedom Status: Free
Electoral Democracy: Yes

Note: The numerical rankings and status listed above do not reflect conditions in Northern Cyprus, which is examined in a separate report.

Overview: The Republic of Cyprus is a democracy that has de jure sovereignty over the entire island. In practice, however, the government controls only the southern, largely Greek-speaking part of the island, as the northern area is ruled by the self-declared Turkish

Republic of Northern Cyprus (TRNC), recognized only by Turkey. Political rights and civil liberties are generally respected in the Republic of Cyprus. Ongoing concerns include societal discrimination against minority groups and weaknesses in the asylum system.

KEY DEVELOPMENTS IN 2018:

- In February, President Nicos Anastasiades was elected for another five-year term, taking 56 percent of the second-round vote.
- In a sign of the economy's ongoing recovery from a banking crisis five years earlier, the European Central Bank resumed buying Cypriot bonds in September.
- The country experienced an influx of irregular migrants and asylum seekers during the year, putting additional strain on the government's ability to house them and process their cases in a fair and timely manner.
- Two new crossing points along the UN buffer zone between the TRNC and the Republic of Cyprus opened in November as a confidence-building measure ahead of the anticipated renewal of UN-sponsored reunification talks.

POLITICAL RIGHTS: 38 / 40

A. ELECTORAL PROCESS: 12 / 12 (+1)

A1. Was the current head of government or other chief national authority elected through free and fair elections? 4 / 4

The president is elected by popular vote for five-year terms. The current president, Nicos Anastasiades of the center-right Democratic Rally (DISY), won a second term with 56 percent of the vote in a February 2018 runoff against Stavros Malas, who was backed by the left-wing Progressive Party of the Working People (AKEL). The two had outpolled seven other candidates in the first round in January. Analysts attributed the incumbent's victory to the recovery of the Cypriot economy since a 2013 banking crisis; the European Central Bank resumed purchases of Cypriot bonds following an improvement in the country's credit rating in September. International observers found that the overall election process adhered to democratic principles.

A2. Were the current national legislative representatives elected through free and fair elections? 4 / 4

The unicameral House of Representatives has 80 seats filled through proportional representation for five-year terms. The Turkish Cypriot community has 24 reserved seats, which have been unfilled since Turkish Cypriot representatives withdrew from the chamber in 1964.

In the 2016 legislative elections, which were held in accordance with international standards, DISY led the voting with 18 seats, down slightly from 2011, followed by AKEL with 16, also a decline. The Democratic Party (DIKO) received 9 seats, the Movement for Social Democracy (EDEK) took 3, and the Green Party secured 2. Three new parties won seats for the first time: the far-right National Popular Front (ELAM) took 2, while 3 each went to the center-left Citizens' Alliance (SYPOL) and the right-wing Solidarity, an offshoot of DISY.

A3. Are the electoral laws and framework fair, and are they implemented impartially by the relevant election management bodies? 4 / 4 (+1)

Electoral laws are generally fair. In their report on the 2018 presidential vote, election monitors from the Organization for Security and Co-operation in Europe (OSCE) noted some improvements since the 2013 contest, including 2017 legal changes that abolished most mandatory-voting provisions and established a ceiling of €1 million ($1.1 million) for candidates' campaign spending. The report found that the election was administered in a "highly professional, efficient, and transparent manner."

Score Change: The score improved from 3 to 4 because robust electoral laws and their fair application by the Central Electoral Office ensured the credibility of the 2018 presidential poll.

B. POLITICAL PLURALISM AND PARTICIPATION: 15 / 16 (−1)

B1. Do the people have the right to organize in different political parties or other competitive political groupings of their choice, and is the system free of undue obstacles to the rise and fall of these competing parties or groupings? 4 / 4

A wide array of parties compete in the political system. Cyprus's two main parties, DISY on the right and AKEL on the left, usually split the largest share of the vote, but neither has dominated politics, and other parties are often able to play significant roles. Both DISY and AKEL lost seats in the 2016 parliamentary elections, and despite an increase in the vote threshold for representation, from 1.8 percent to 3.6 percent, three new parties were able to enter the parliament.

B2. Is there a realistic opportunity for the opposition to increase its support or gain power through elections? 4 / 4

Cyprus has experienced regular democratic transfers of power between rival parties in recent decades, and multiple opposition parties are able to gain representation in the legislature.

B3. Are the people's political choices free from domination by the military, foreign powers, religious hierarchies, economic oligarchies, or any other powerful group that is not democratically accountable? 4 / 4

People are generally able to express their political choices without undue interference from outside actors.

B4. Do various segments of the population (including ethnic, religious, gender, LGBT, and other relevant groups) have full political rights and electoral opportunities? 3 / 4 (−1)

Three recognized Christian minorities—the Armenians, the Latins, and the Maronites—each have one nonvoting representative in the parliament. Members of these minority groups vote in special elections for their representatives, as well as in the general elections. The Turkish Cypriot community's 24 seats remain unfilled.

Women in Cyprus have equal political rights, but they are underrepresented in political parties. No parliamentary party is led by a woman, and parties have failed to meet internal quotas mandating that 30 to 35 percent of their candidates be women. Women hold about 18 percent of the seats in the House of Representatives. No women ran for president in 2018. Sexism and patriarchal attitudes discourage women from playing a more active role in politics.

The interests of the LGBT (lesbian, gay, bisexual, and transgender) community, which still faces significant discrimination from some sectors of society, are not always well represented in the political system.

Score Change: The score declined from 4 to 3 because the political system has failed over time to ensure adequate representation for women and their interests.

C. FUNCTIONING OF GOVERNMENT: 11 / 12

C1. Do the freely elected head of government and national legislative representatives determine the policies of the government? 4 / 4

The freely elected government is able to make and implement policy without improper interference from unelected entities.

C2. Are safeguards against official corruption strong and effective? 3 / 4

Cyprus has strong anticorruption laws that are, for the most part, adequately enforced. However, there have been a number of high-profile corruption scandals in recent years, and critics of the government's record have raised concerns about early releases and pardons of individuals convicted on corruption charges. For example, in 2017, former deputy attorney general Rikkos Erotokritou was sentenced to three and a half years in prison for accepting bribes while in office in 2015, but he was granted release on parole in August 2018 under a law adopted in May that allows such releases for convicts who meet certain requirements. Opposition lawmakers said the measure seemed designed to benefit convicts with political connections.

C3. Does the government operate with openness and transparency? 4 / 4

In general, the government operates with openness and transparency. However, Cyprus lacks a freedom of information law; a draft bill that was presented for public comment in 2015 has yet to advance in the parliament, and civil society groups have criticized many of its provisions.

CIVIL LIBERTIES: 56 / 60
D. FREEDOM OF EXPRESSION AND BELIEF: 15 / 16
D1. Are there free and independent media? 4 / 4

Freedom of speech is constitutionally guaranteed, and media freedom is generally respected. A vibrant independent press frequently criticizes the authorities. Numerous private outlets compete with public media, and there are no restrictions on access to online news sources.

D2. Are individuals free to practice and express their religious faith or nonbelief in public and private? 4 / 4

Freedom of religion is guaranteed by the constitution and generally protected in practice. Nearly 90 percent of those living in government-controlled Cyprus are Orthodox Christians, and the Orthodox Church enjoys certain privileges, including religious instruction and some religious services in public schools. Non-Orthodox students may opt out of such activities. The government recognizes Muslim religious institutions and facilitates crossings at the UN buffer zone between north and south for the purpose of worship at religious sites. Muslim groups have occasionally faced obstacles in the operation of their religious sites. Other religious minorities sometimes encounter discrimination.

D3. Is there academic freedom, and is the educational system free from extensive political indoctrination? 3 / 4

Academic freedom is respected in Cyprus. However, state schools use textbooks containing negative language about Turkish Cypriots and Turkey, and there is some political pressure regarding schools' treatment of sensitive historical and unification-related issues.

D4. Are individuals free to express their personal views on political or other sensitive topics without fear of surveillance or retribution? 4 / 4

People are generally free to engage in political and other sensitive discussions without fear of retribution or surveillance.

E. ASSOCIATIONAL AND ORGANIZATIONAL RIGHTS: 12 / 12

E1. Is there freedom of assembly? 4 / 4

Freedom of assembly is constitutionally guaranteed and generally respected.

E2. Is there freedom for nongovernmental organizations, particularly those that are engaged in human rights- and governance-related work? 4 / 4

Nongovernmental organizations (NGOs) usually operate without government interference. A memorandum of cooperation was signed in 2017 between the police and 12 NGOs to improve relations and prevent misunderstandings.

E3. Is there freedom for trade unions and similar professional or labor organizations? 4 / 4

Workers have the right to strike, form independent trade unions, and engage in collective bargaining. The law provides remedies for antiunion discrimination, though enforcement is uneven.

F. RULE OF LAW: 15 / 16

F1. Is there an independent judiciary? 4 / 4

The judiciary, which operates principally according to the British tradition, is independent in practice. Since the country joined the EU in 2004, the legal system has been gradually brought into harmony with EU law.

F2. Does due process prevail in civil and criminal matters? 4 / 4

The justice system generally upholds due process standards. Law enforcement agencies largely observe safeguards against arbitrary arrest and detention, and criminal defendants have access to counsel and fair trial procedures.

F3. Is there protection from the illegitimate use of physical force and freedom from war and insurgencies? 4 / 4

Residents of Cyprus are free from major threats to physical security, though human rights monitors have noted cases of police brutality. Overcrowding and other problematic conditions have been reported at prisons and migrant detention centers.

In an attempt to block Cyprus's efforts to explore for offshore oil and gas, Turkey has threatened to use force against drilling vessels. Ankara argues that the maritime areas in question are under the jurisdiction of either Turkey or the TRNC.

F4. Do laws, policies, and practices guarantee equal treatment of various segments of the population? 3 / 4

Despite government efforts to combat prejudice and inequality, non-Greek Cypriot minorities, including migrants and asylum seekers, face discrimination and occasional violence. The country experienced an influx of new migrants and asylum seekers during 2018, and while many were quickly released from overburdened reception centers, they often lacked access to other housing. Asylum claims take up to five years to process amid a growing backlog of cases.

Gender discrimination in the workplace remains a problem, including with respect to hiring practices, salaries, and sexual harassment; laws against it have not been adequately enforced.

Antidiscrimination laws generally prohibit bias based on sexual orientation, and there are legal protections for transgender people on some issues as well. For example, laws barring incitement to hatred apply to both sexual orientation and gender identity. However, the LGBT community continues to face societal discrimination in practice.

G. PERSONAL AUTONOMY AND INDIVIDUAL RIGHTS: 14 / 16

G1. Do individuals enjoy freedom of movement, including the ability to change their place of residence, employment, or education? 3 / 4

There are few impediments to freedom of movement within the government-controlled area of the Republic of Cyprus. The UN buffer zone dividing the island remains in place, though travel between north and south has improved since 2004 due to an increase in the number of border crossings. In November 2018, two new crossing points opened at Deryneia and Lefka-Aplici.

G2. Are individuals able to exercise the right to own property and establish private businesses without undue interference from state or nonstate actors? 4 / 4

Property rights are generally respected in Cyprus. A 1991 law stipulates that property left by Turkish Cypriots after 1974, when a Turkish invasion divided the island, belongs to the state. Under the law in the north, Greek Cypriots can appeal to the Immovable Property Commission (IMP), which in 2010 was recognized by the European Court of Human Rights as a responsible authority for the resolution of property disputes. However, its work has been seriously impaired in recent years by a lack of funding from the TRNC and Ankara.

G3. Do individuals enjoy personal social freedoms, including choice of marriage partner and size of family, protection from domestic violence, and control over appearance? 4 / 4

Personal social freedoms are largely unrestricted. Same-sex civil unions are allowed under a 2015 law, but it did not include adoption rights for same-sex couples. In 2018, the government was considering legislation that would establish a procedure to correct one's registered gender. Domestic violence is a growing problem despite official efforts to prevent and punish it. Two government-funded shelters are open to survivors of domestic abuse.

G4. Do individuals enjoy equality of opportunity and freedom from economic exploitation? 3 / 4

The legal framework generally protects workers against exploitative conditions of employment, and the government has made genuine progress in combating human trafficking. However, persistent problems include a lack of resources for labor inspectors and illegally low pay for undocumented migrant workers. Migrant workers and asylum seekers remain vulnerable to sexual exploitation and forced labor.

Czech Republic

Capital: Prague
Population: 10,600,000
Political Rights Rating: 1
Civil Liberties Rating: 1
Freedom Rating: 1.0
Freedom Status: Free
Electoral Democracy: Yes

Overview: The Czech Republic is a parliamentary democracy in which political rights and civil liberties are generally respected. However, in recent years, the country has experienced a number of corruption scandals and political disputes that hampered normal legislative activity. Illiberal rhetoric and the influence of powerful business entities in the political arena are increasingly visible.

KEY DEVELOPMENTS IN 2018:

- President Miloš Zeman won reelection in January, defeating Jiří Drahoš in the second round of voting. An online disinformation campaign, which analysts believe emanated from Russia, led to the circulation of rumors on social media that Drahoš had worked with the secret police during the Communist era, among other smears.
- After nearly nine months of negotiations, in July, Prime Minister Andrej Babiš formed a coalition government consisting of his ANO 2011 party, the Czech Social Democratic Party (ČSSD), and the Communist Party of Bohemia and Moravia (KSČM).
- Corruption allegations against Babiš continued to roil Czech politics throughout the year. Media reports in November revealed that Babiš reportedly arranged for his son to be sent to Crimea against his will, in order to prevent him from being interrogated in the investigation of his father. The revelation led to a vote of no confidence in November, which the prime minister survived.

POLITICAL RIGHTS: 36 / 40 (–1)

A. ELECTORAL PROCESS: 12 / 12

A1. Was the current head of government or other chief national authority elected through free and fair elections? 4 / 4

The president is the head of state but holds limited powers, and is directly elected to up to two five-year terms. The January 2018 presidential election was considered credible. President Miloš Zeman of the Party of Civic Rights was reelected, defeating his opponent, Jiří Drahoš, in the second of voting. Zeman won 51.4 percent of the vote while Drahoš took 48.6 percent. An online disinformation campaign, which analysts believe emanated from Russia, led to the circulation of rumors on social media that Drahoš had worked with the secret police during the communist era, among other smears.

The prime minister is the head of government and holds most executive power. In December 2017, controversial billionaire Andrej Babiš of the ANO was sworn in as prime minister, following elections that were held in accordance with international standards.

A2. Were the current national legislative representatives elected through free and fair elections? 4 / 4

The 200 members of the Chamber of Deputies, the lower house of Parliament, are elected to four-year terms by proportional representation. The Senate, the upper chamber, which holds limited legislative power, has 81 members elected for six-year terms, with one-third up for election every two years.

The ANO, led by Babiš, won 78 seats in the Chamber of Deputies in the October 2017 legislative elections, followed by the Civic Democratic Party (ODS) with 25, and the populist, anti-immigration Freedom and Direct Democracy (SPD) party with 22. The polls were generally well administered, and the results broadly accepted by stakeholders.

Babiš was sworn in as prime minister in late 2017, but the mainstream parties refused to cooperate with him, and he struggled to assemble a coalition. Facing corruption allegations, Babiš lost a vote of no confidence in January 2018, raising doubts about his ability to form a government. In July, after nearly nine months of negotiations, the ANO, the ČSSD, and the KSČM successfully formed a coalition government.

The most recent Senate elections were held in October 2018, with 27 seats contested. The opposition ODS won the most seats, with 10.

A3. Are the electoral laws and framework fair, and are they implemented impartially by the relevant election management bodies? 4 / 4

The electoral framework is robust and generally well implemented by the State Election Commission. However, the body does not always operate with transparency, and a 2017 Organization for Co-operation in Europe (OSCE) needs assessment mission expressed concern that its meetings were typically closed to the public and opposition representatives. The OSCE mission also criticized the decentralized procedures surrounding the maintenance of voter lists, which made the lists difficult to verify. However, the state of voter lists was not a major concern to any party during the 2017 and 2018 polls.

B. POLITICAL PLURALISM AND PARTICIPATION: 15 / 16

B1. Do the people have the right to organize in different political parties or other competitive political groupings of their choice, and is the system free of undue obstacles to the rise and fall of these competing parties or groupings? 4 / 4

Political parties are free to form and operate. Since the 2013 elections, the political scene has seen somewhat of a shake-up, with the establishment ODS and the ČSSD losing support, and space opening up for the populist ANO, anti-immigration and nationalist SPD, and liberal Czech Pirate Party.

B2. Is there a realistic opportunity for the opposition to increase its support or gain power through elections? 4 / 4

Power rotates between parties regularly. The opposition holds a significant bloc of seats in Parliament.

B3. Are the people's political choices free from domination by the military, foreign powers, religious hierarchies, economic oligarchies, or any other powerful group that is not democratically accountable? 4 / 4

The influence of politically connected media outlets has been a growing concern in recent years, notably after a controversy arose in 2017 involving the daily newspaper *MF Dnes*, which is among the assets Babiš placed in a trust to comply with 2016 conflict-of-interest legislation. In a leaked recording, Babiš could apparently be heard directing one of the paper's journalists to publish stories damaging to his political rivals. Babiš condemned the leaked recording, but did not deny its authenticity. Critics have accused Babiš of using *MF*

Dnes and another newspaper his trust owns, *Lidove noviny,* as tools to advance his political and business interests.

The disinformation campaign on social media against Drahoš during the 2018 presidential race highlighted Russia's influence on the political choices of Czech voters.

B4. Do various segments of the population (including ethnic, religious, gender, LGBT, and other relevant groups) have full political rights and electoral opportunities? 3 / 4

By law, all citizens have full political rights and electoral opportunities. However, the Romany minority lacks meaningful political representation. Women increased their representation in Parliament in the 2017 elections, but remain underrepresented in politics and public bodies generally, and there are few initiatives aimed at boosting their political participation.

C. FUNCTIONING OF GOVERNMENT: 9 / 12 (-1)

C1. Do the freely elected head of government and national legislative representatives determine the policies of the government? 4 / 4

Elected officials are duly installed and generally able to craft and implement policy. Political polarization and the controversy surrounding Babiš contributed to the drawn-out negotiations that left the country without a governing coalition through the first half of 2018.

C2. Are safeguards against official corruption strong and effective? 2 / 4 (-1)

Corruption remains a problem in Czech politics, but institutions have generally been responsive to corruption allegations and scandals. An investigation into Babiš by Czech police and the European Anti-Fraud Office, which commenced in 2017 following allegations of improprieties regarding the disbursement of European Union (EU) subsidy funds to one of his firms, continued through the year. It was alleged that Babiš's large conglomerate, Agrofert, had wrongfully accepted some 50 million crowns ($2 million) through its anonymous ownership of a farm and hotel complex. Fraud charges were filed against him in late 2017, and in January 2018, the Chamber of Deputies lifted Babiš's immunity for the second time. In response, the prime minister claimed that the investigation was a politically motivated attack orchestrated by his rivals. Media reports that Babiš arranged for his son to be sent to Crimea against his will, in order to prevent him from being interrogated about the fraud allegations, led to another vote of no confidence in November. Babiš survived the vote because ČSSD deputies abstained and KSČM members supported the prime minister.

In November, a leaked European Commission legal opinion concluded that despite Babiš's formal transfer of Agrofert to two trusts, he still essentially retained ownership of the company, creating a conflict of interest due to the fact that the prime minister stands to benefit from the disbursement of EU funds that he has control over. Agrofert received €82 million ($96 million) in EU funds in 2018.

Score Change: The score declined from 3 to 2 due to conflicts of interest arising from Prime Minister Andrej Babiš's failure to substantively divest himself from his sprawling agribusiness conglomerate, Agrofert.

C3. Does the government operate with openness and transparency? 3 / 4

Although the government generally operates with transparency, there is no law regulating lobbying. The government often fails to proactively publish information about procurement processes, public officials' salaries, and public spending, and requires that members of the public request a time-sensitive password to view asset declarations online. In January

2018, new legislation came into force requiring that the "ultimate beneficial owners" of companies and trust funds be disclosed in a register. Although the register is not available to the public, law enforcement agencies, the courts, and several other entities can access it. Analysts viewed the register as a step forward for transparency and a tool for identifying conflicts of interest.

CIVIL LIBERTIES: 55 / 60 (-1)

D. FREEDOM OF EXPRESSION AND BELIEF: 14 / 16 (-1)

D1. Are there free and independent media? 3 / 4 (-1)

The media operate relatively freely, and the government does not place undue restrictions on content. Legislation protects private ownership of media outlets, but concerns remain about the extent to which the media is controlled by wealthy business figures and its potential impact on journalists' ability to investigate commercial interests.

Although Babiš placed his significant media holdings in a trust, the trust is controlled in part by Babiš's close associates. Critics have accused both of his newspapers of biased coverage, claiming that they are being used as tools to advance the prime minister's political interests. In September 2018, seasoned war reporter Petra Procházková resigned from *Lidove noviny,* citing political interference from the prime minister's office in the paper's editorial line.

Verbal and physical attacks, harassment, and intimidation of journalists were problems in 2018. Both Zeman and Babiš have made inflammatory remarks about the press, contributing to a hostile environment for journalists. In April, three investigative journalists released a statement asserting that they had been summoned for questioning several times regarding their reporting on the corruption allegations against the prime minister. In January, videos posted on social media showed reporters at President Zeman's campaign headquarters being shoved and harassed on election night by supporters of the president.

Score Change: The score declined from 4 to 3 due to the continued intimidation and harassment of journalists by public officials, and the prime minister's ability to exert influence through media outlets he retains control over.

D2. Are individuals free to practice and express their religious faith or nonbelief in public and private? 3 / 4

The government generally upholds freedom of religion. Tax benefits and financial support are provided to registered religious groups. The state has initiated a process to return land confiscated from churches by the former communist regime, which will take place over the next 30 years.

However, anti-Islamic attitudes have increased in the wake of the refugee crisis confronting European states, and the country's legal battle with the EU about accepting refugee quotas. The populist and anti-immigration SPD relied heavily on Islamophobic rhetoric during the 2017 election campaign, calling Islam "incompatible with freedom and democracy" and purchasing billboards that read "No to Islam."

D3. Is there academic freedom, and is the educational system free from extensive political indoctrination? 4 / 4

Academic freedom is respected. Ceremonial presidential approval is required for academic positions.

D4. Are individuals free to express their personal views on political or other sensitive topics without fear of surveillance or retribution? 4 / 4

People are generally able to express controversial or political opinions without fear of surveillance or retribution.

E. ASSOCIATIONAL AND ORGANIZATIONAL RIGHTS: 12 / 12

E1. Is there freedom of assembly? 4 / 4

Freedom of assembly is upheld in practice, and demonstrations take place frequently and without incident. Thousands of protesters assembled in Prague in November 2018 to demand Prime Minister Babiš's resignation over corruption allegations.

E2. Is there freedom for nongovernmental organizations, particularly those that are engaged in human rights– and governance-related work? 4 / 4

Tens of thousands of registered nongovernmental organizations (NGOs) operate in the country, generally without interference from the government or security forces. However, the environment for civil society has grown increasingly antagonistic as the government and its allies have harshly criticized some critical NGOs. In January 2018, the SPD issued a statement accusing financier George Soros of imposing "supranational governance" on the country, and said it would support measures to curtail the impact of Soros's Open Society Foundations on Czech society. In August, the ANO proposed sweeping cuts of $135 million (approximately 20 percent) to funding for Czech NGOs, which civil society leaders suspected would be aimed at organizations that focus on politics and governance.

E3. Is there freedom for trade unions and similar professional or labor organizations? 4 / 4

Trade unions and professional associations function freely, though they are weak in practice. Workers have the right to strike, though this right is limited for essential public employees, such as hospital workers and air traffic controllers.

F. RULE OF LAW: 14 / 16

F1. Is there an independent judiciary? 3 / 4

The judiciary is largely independent, though its complexity and multilayered composition have led to slow delivery of judgments.

F2. Does due process prevail in civil and criminal matters? 4 / 4

The rule of law generally prevails in civil and criminal matters. While corruption and political pressure remain within law enforcement agencies, the office of the public prosecutor has become more independent in recent years.

F3. Is there protection from the illegitimate use of physical force and freedom from war and insurgencies? 4 / 4

The Czech Republic is free from war in insurgencies. However, prisons are overcrowded and at times unsanitary.

F4. Do laws, policies, and practices guarantee equal treatment of various segments of the population? 3 / 4

The 2009 Antidiscrimination Act provides for equal treatment regardless of sex, race, age, disability, belief, or sexual orientation. The Romany minority faces discrimination in the job market and significantly poorer housing conditions than non-Roma, as well as occasional threats and violence from right-wing groups. Many Roma children attend ethnically segregated schools.

Women are underrepresented at the highest levels of business. According to data from the European Commission, the gender pay gap in the Czech Republic is one of the largest in the EU.

Asylum seekers are routinely detained, and conditions in detention centers are generally poor. Xenophobic, antirefugee rhetoric has been voiced by Prime Minister Babiš and President Zeman. In 2017, after accepting just 12 asylum seekers of its EU-mandated quota of around 2,700, authorities announced the country would no longer comply with the program. According to Eurostat, the Czech Republic was the least likely country in the EU to grant asylum in 2018, offering protection to just 1 in 10 applicants. No refugees were resettled in the country during the year.

G. PERSONAL AUTONOMY AND INDIVIDUAL RIGHTS: 15 / 16

G1. Do individuals enjoy freedom of movement, including the ability to change their place of residence, employment, or education? 4 / 4

Individuals enjoy freedom of movement, including the ability to change their place of residence, employment, or education.

G2. Are individuals able to exercise the right to own property and establish private businesses without undue interference from state or nonstate actors? 4 / 4

The rights to own property and operate private businesses are established in the law and upheld in practice.

G3. Do individuals enjoy personal social freedoms, including choice of marriage partner and size of family, protection from domestic violence, and control over appearance? 4 / 4

Authorities generally do not restrict social freedoms, though same-sex marriages are not legally recognized. While gender discrimination is legally prohibited, sexual harassment in the workplace appears to be fairly common.

G4. Do individuals enjoy equality of opportunity and freedom from economic exploitation? 3 / 4

Human trafficking remains a problem as organized criminal groups use the country as a source, transit, and destination point; women and children are particularly vulnerable to being trafficked for the purpose of sexual exploitation. The government has made increasing efforts in recent years to fund protective services and other resources for victims, and to prosecute perpetrators.

Denmark

Population: 5,700,000
Capital: Copenhagen
Political Rights Rating: 1
Civil Liberties Rating: 1
Freedom Rating: 1.0
Freedom Status: Free
Electoral Democracy: Yes

Overview: Denmark is a robust democracy with regular free and fair elections. Citizens enjoy full political rights, the government protects free expression and association, and the judiciary functions independently. However, Denmark has struggled to uphold fundamental freedoms for immigrants and other newcomers.

KEY DEVELOPMENTS IN 2018:

- In August, a vaguely worded ban on the public wearing of face coverings took effect. The measure was widely interpreted as a "burqa ban" aimed at Muslim women, and at least two women have since been fined under its provisions for wearing a niqab or burqa.
- In October, the government reaffirmed Denmark's nonparticipation in the UN refugee quota system.
- In December, lawmakers controversially approved the establishment of a housing facility for refused asylum seekers who have completed jail sentences following criminal convictions, but who cannot be deported due to the likelihood that they would face persecution in their home countries. The planned facility will be located on an isolated island previously used to study contagious diseases in animals.
- In the wake of a series of financial scandals, the Group of States against Corruption (GRECO) deemed Denmark noncompliant with its standards, citing deficient accountability mechanisms for the judiciary and for members of Parliament.

POLITICAL RIGHTS: 40 / 40
A. ELECTORAL PROCESS: 12 / 12
A1. Was the current head of government or other chief national authority elected through free and fair elections? 4 / 4

The constitution retains a monarch, currently Queen Margrethe II, with mostly ceremonial duties. The monarch chooses the prime minister, usually the leader of the majority party or government coalition. Prime Minister Lars Løkke Rasmussen, representing the Liberal Party, was appointed by Queen Margrethe following competitive and free 2015 general elections.

A2. Were the current national legislative representatives elected through free and fair elections? 4 / 4

The 179 members of Denmark's unicameral parliament are elected to four-year terms through a system of modified proportional representation.

The most recent parliamentary elections were held in 2015. Rasmussen's Liberal Party won 47 seats, and Rasmussen formed a minority government. The populist, anti-immigration, Euro-sceptic Danish People's Party (DPP) had a successful showing, winning 37 seats to become the second-largest party in the parliament. The elections were considered credible and free, and their results were accepted by stakeholders and the public.

A3. Are the electoral laws and framework fair, and are they implemented impartially by the relevant election management bodies? 4 / 4

Robust electoral laws are upheld impartially by the various bodies tasked with implementation. A 2015 Organization for Co-operation in Europe (OSCE) preelection assessment mission reported a high level of public confidence in the country's election laws and administration.

B. POLITICAL PLURALISM AND PARTICIPATION: 16 / 16

B1. Do the people have the right to organize in different political parties or other competitive political groupings of their choice, and is the system free of undue obstacles to the rise and fall of these competing parties or groupings? 4 / 4

Numerous political parties compete freely.

B2. Is there a realistic opportunity for the opposition to increase its support or gain power through elections? 4 / 4

The Danish political system is open to the rise of opposition parties through elections. In recent years, the most significant political ascent has been that of the DPP; while it has never formally been in government, it lends support to the current coalition, led by the Liberal Party.

The new Nye Borgerlige (New Right) party was established in 2015 by former DPP members, and has been gaining support outside Parliament on the basis of its anti-immigrant, anti-European Union (EU) libertarian-leaning agenda. While polls suggest it has secured the support of only about 4 percent of the electorate, it has gained the requisite signatures to participate in the 2019 parliamentary elections, and is expected to attract previous DPP voters.

B3. Are the people's political choices free from domination by the military, foreign powers, religious hierarchies, economic oligarchies, or any other powerful group that is not democratically accountable? 4 / 4

Voters and political figures are generally free from undue influences by actors who are not democratically accountable.

B4. Do various segments of the population (including ethnic, religious, gender, LGBT, and other relevant groups) have full political rights and electoral opportunities? 4 / 4

The electoral laws guarantee universal suffrage for citizens, as well as representation in regional and municipal elections for permanent residents. Refugees and other immigrants may vote in municipal and regional elections after having obtained permanent residence at least three years before an election date. Women, LGBT (lesbian, gay, bisexual, and transgender) people, and members of ethnic and religious minorities are active in political life.

The territories of Greenland and the Faroe Islands each have two representatives in the parliament. They also have their own elected institutions, which have power over almost all areas of governance, except foreign and financial policy.

C. FUNCTIONING OF GOVERNMENT: 12 / 12

C1. Do the freely elected head of government and national legislative representatives determine the policies of the government? 4 / 4

Denmark's freely elected government is able to craft and implement policy. Danish governments most often control a minority of seats in the parliament, ruling with the aid of one or more supporting parties. Since 1909, no single party has held a majority of seats, helping to create a tradition of compromise.

C2. Are safeguards against official corruption strong and effective? 4 / 4

Anticorruption laws and bodies are generally effective, and corruption is not considered an urgent problem in Denmark. However, in September 2018, the Council of Europe's anticorruption body, GRECO, deemed Denmark noncompliant with its standards, citing deficient accountability mechanisms for the judiciary and for members of Parliament. The move came in the wake of a number of financial scandals involving public officials, as well as auditor reports suggesting misuse of EU subsidies.

C3. Does the government operate with openness and transparency? 4 / 4

Government operations are generally transparent. However, the government has come under pressure to amend the Public Information Act to remove restrictions on certain information, including documents that are shared between ministers and their advisers.

CIVIL LIBERTIES: 57 / 60

D. FREEDOM OF EXPRESSION AND BELIEF: 16 / 16

D1. Are there free and independent media? 4 / 4

Domestic media reflect a wide variety of political opinions and are frequently critical of the government.

D2. Are individuals free to practice and express their religious faith or nonbelief in public and private? 4 / 4

Freedom of worship is legally protected. However, the Evangelical Lutheran Church is subsidized by the government as the official state religion. The faith is taught in public schools, though students may withdraw from religious classes with parental consent.

In 2015, a Danish citizen of Palestinian origin launched an attack on a freedom of expression event and then on a Copenhagen synagogue, killing several people. Since the attack, the government has provided security for Jewish religious and cultural facilities considered to be at risk of attack.

In August 2018, a ban on the public wearing of face coverings—widely referred to as a "burqa ban" applicable to Muslim women—took effect, and at least two women have since been fined for wearing a niqab or burqa. Police have expressed some confusion about how to enforce the vaguely worded law, with some noting that it was unclear if it applied to people who wore masks designed to protect against air pollution. Participants in a demonstration against the ban who themselves wore burqas and niqabs were not penalized, with police reportedly saying the wearing of the garments at a protest was protected by guarantees for free speech.

In December 2018, Parliament adopted a law requiring mandatory participation in a ceremony for confirmation of newly granted Danish citizenship, with guidelines expected to include a requirement for shaking hands. The expected hand-shaking provision was viewed as a means of requiring Muslims who refuse to touch someone of a different gender on religious grounds to adopt practices seen as "Danish."

D3. Is there academic freedom, and is the educational system free from extensive political indoctrination? 4 / 4

Academic freedom is generally respected.

D4. Are individuals free to express their personal views on political or other sensitive topics without fear of surveillance or retribution? 4 / 4

Private discussion is vibrant and unrestricted.

E. ASSOCIATIONAL AND ORGANIZATIONAL RIGHTS: 12 / 12

E1. Is there freedom of assembly? 4 / 4

The constitution provides for freedom of assembly, which is upheld in practice. A number of demonstrations took place peacefully in 2018.

E2. Is there freedom for nongovernmental organizations, particularly those that are engaged in human rights– and governance-related work? 4 / 4

Nongovernmental organizations (NGOs) operate freely in Denmark, and frequently inform policy debates.

E3. Is there freedom for trade unions and similar professional or labor organizations? 4 / 4

Workers are free to organize and bargain collectively.

F. RULE OF LAW: 14 / 16

F1. Is there an independent judiciary? 4 / 4

The judiciary is independent. Judges are formally appointed by the monarch, but are recommended by the justice minister in consultation with the independent Judicial Appointments Council.

F2. Does due process prevail in civil and criminal matters? 3 / 4

Citizens enjoy full due-process rights. However, individuals who were denied asylum in Denmark, but whom the government is for various reasons unable to deport, may be subject to administrative measures parallel to those imposed on people who have been convicted of crimes. For example, many such individuals must live at isolated centers with poor facilities where they are subject to travel restrictions, and have no legal option to challenge their placement. In 2017, the Danish Helsinki Committee criticized the conditions of one detention center in particular, Kærshovedgård, for offering worse conditions than Danish prisons. In May 2018, the Danish Ombudsman stated that although the placement of refused asylum seekers at Kærshovedgård did not amount to detention without trial, conditions there remained unsatisfactory. As of October 2018, the number of individuals at the Kærshovedgård detention center was at an all-time high of 241 residents.

In December 2018, lawmakers approved funding for a controversial new facility to house about 100 refused asylum seekers who have completed jail sentences following criminal convictions, but cannot be deported because of the likelihood that they would face persecution in their home countries. The new center would be established, after decontamination procedures, on a former veterinary quarantine station where scientists had studied contagious diseases, located on an island in Danish waters and connected to the outside world by a nonpublic ferry.

F3. Is there protection from the illegitimate use of physical force and freedom from war and insurgencies? 4 / 4

People in Denmark are generally free from violent crime and physical abuse by state authorities.

F4. Do laws, policies, and practices guarantee equal treatment of various segments of the population? 3 / 4

Danish immigration laws have long been some of the harshest in Europe, and immigration laws and asylum policies were further tightened in response to the massive influx of refugees and asylum seekers entering Europe beginning in 2015; the influx has since waned. In the first 11 months of 2018, 2,600 individuals had sought asylum in Denmark, compared to some 21,000 in 2015. In October 2018, the government reaffirmed its decision the previous year to refuse to admit refugees as assigned by a UN quota; previously the country had received 500 annually since 1989.

Families of rejected asylum seekers who cannot be deported are increasingly required to reside at a facility in Sjælsmark. Following an inspection visit in December 2018, the Ombudsman expressed concern that the conditions for the close to 100 children, many of whom have stayed at the center for several years, put them at risk in terms of their healthy growth and development.

Discrimination, including based on gender identity or sexual orientation, is prohibited by law. As of 2017 identifying as transgender is no longer considered a mental disorder. However, procedures related to legally changing one's gender remain onerous.

The Greenlandic Inuit community faces social marginalization in Denmark, though the government has implemented programs to address this issue.

G. PERSONAL AUTONOMY AND INDIVIDUAL RIGHTS: 15 / 16

G1. Do individuals enjoy freedom of movement, including the ability to change their place of residence, employment, or education? 4 / 4

Freedom of movement is protected by law and generally respected by the government. However, in March 2018, the government proposed an "anti-ghetto" initiative, applicable to neighborhoods identified as having high unemployment and crime rates, and a high percentage of foreign-born residents. It aims to shift the areas' demographics, institute daycare requirements for foreign children that would integrate them into Danish society through language and culture lessons, and enact stricter punishments for crimes committed there. Legislation to demolish certain housing structures to meet demographic quotas passed in November, and the daycare provision was approved in December.

Since 2015, the government has enacted a number of measures that allow authorities to restrict the movement of people who seek to join, or have joined, extremist groups abroad—notably the Islamic State (IS) militant group. Some of the measures have been criticized for having a low evidentiary threshold or for lacking appropriate oversight mechanisms. A number of people have seen their passports revoked under the measures.

G2. Are individuals able to exercise the right to own property and establish private businesses without undue interference from state or nonstate actors? 4 / 4

Private business activity is free from undue influence by government officials or nonstate actors.

G3. Do individuals enjoy personal social freedoms, including choice of marriage partner and size of family, protection from domestic violence, and control over appearance? 3 / 4

Refugees and other newcomers face lengthy waiting times for family reunification, including in cases involving small children, and restrictions on family reunification were tightened in the wake of the 2015 refugee crisis. In 2018, an all-time high of 42 percent of applications for family reunification were denied.

In 1989, Denmark became the first country in the world to adopt same-sex civil unions, and in 2012, the parliament overwhelmingly passed same-sex marriage legislation enabling couples to wed in the Lutheran state church of their choosing. Priests are not obligated to officiate but, when requested to do so, must find a colleague who will.

G4. Do individuals enjoy equality of opportunity and freedom from economic exploitation? 4 / 4

Public- and private-sector workers are generally free from exploitation by employers. However, migrants engaged in forced labor can be found in some sectors, including the agricultural and service industries. Women and children, also primarily migrants, can be found engaged in forced sex work. The government and NGOs work, frequently in conjunction, to identify and prevent human trafficking and to provide aid to victims.

Djibouti

Population: 1,000,000
Capital: Djibouti
Political Rights Rating: 6
Civil Liberties Rating: 5
Freedom Rating: 5.5
Freedom Status: Not Free
Electoral Democracy: No

Overview: Djibouti is a republic ruled by a powerful president, Ismail Omar Guelleh, who has been in office since 1999 and is not subject to term limits. While Djibouti technically has a multiparty political system, the ruling Union for a Presidential Majority (UMP) uses authoritarian means to maintain its dominant position. The opposition's ability to operate is severely constrained, and journalists and activists who air criticism of Guelleh or the UMP are regularly harassed or arrested.

KEY DEVELOPMENTS IN 2018:

- Legislative elections were held in February, but most of the opposition boycotted due to the ruling party's refusal to implement a 2014 political agreement, and the party won 57 of 65 seats in the National Assembly.
- Security forces in May violently dispersed a demonstration in Tadjourah as jobless youth protested nepotism and discrimination in hiring, particularly at Djibouti's ports. Dozens of people were detained, and six were charged with "threatening public order."

POLITICAL RIGHTS: 7 / 40

A. ELECTORAL PROCESS: 2 / 12

A1. Was the current head of government or other chief national authority elected through free and fair elections? 0 / 4

The president, who holds most executive power in Djibouti, serves five-year terms under current rules. President Guelleh was elected to a fourth term in 2016, having been credited with 87 percent of the vote. The opposition fractured, with some groups boycotting the poll and others running competing candidates. The lead-up to the election was marked by restrictions on the media and the harassment or detention of opposition figures. Among other reported irregularities on election day, opposition parties complained that their monitors were turned away from polling sites.

A2. Were the current national legislative representatives elected through free and fair elections? 1 / 4

The 65 members of the unicameral legislature, the National Assembly, are directly elected for five-year terms. Constitutional changes in 2010 called for the creation of an upper house, the Senate, but steps to establish the new chamber have yet to be taken.

Citing the government's failure to implement electoral reforms in keeping with a 2014 political agreement, most of the opposition boycotted legislative elections held in February 2018. The process was marked by irregularities, and the UMP increased its majority to 57 of 65 seats. The opposition Union for Democracy and Justice–Djiboutian Democratic Party (UDJ-PDD) won seven seats, and the Center of Unified Democrats (CDU) took one.

A3. Are the electoral laws and framework fair, and are they implemented impartially by the relevant election management bodies? 1 / 4

A core element of the 2014 political agreement—meant to end the opposition's boycott of the legislature following deeply flawed elections in 2013—was a pledge to reform the Independent National Electoral Commission (CENI), which the opposition has accused of bias. No such reforms took place before the 2016 presidential election or the 2018 legislative elections. Other provisions of the electoral framework give an advantage to the dominant party, for example by awarding at least 80 percent of the seats in each multimember parliamentary district to the party that wins a majority in that district.

B. POLITICAL PLURALISM AND PARTICIPATION: 3 / 16

B1. Do the people have the right to organize in different political parties or other competitive political groupings of their choice, and is the system free of undue obstacles to the rise and fall of these competing parties or groupings? 1 / 4

While Djibouti technically has a multiparty political system, parties must register with the government to operate legally, and the authorities have denied recognition to some opposition parties, including the Movement for Democratic Renewal and Development (MRD). The Republican Alliance for Development (ARD) reportedly lost its recognition after a leadership shuffle in August 2018.

Opposition party activities are subject to interference by security forces. In March 2018, for example, police raided the headquarters of the unrecognized Rally for Democratic Action and Ecological Development (RADDE), confiscated equipment, and arrested one person as the party was preparing nonviolent demonstrations. Several other arrests of opposition figures were reported in October.

B2. Is there a realistic opportunity for the opposition to increase its support or gain power through elections? 0 / 4

President Guelleh has been in power since 1999, when he succeeded his uncle, the only other president since independence in 1977. The 2013 elections marked the first time that the opposition had won any seats in the National Assembly. Opposition parties have traditionally been disadvantaged by Djibouti's first-past-the-post electoral system, controls on the media, abuse of state resources to favor incumbents, and regular arrests and harassment of opposition leaders and supporters.

B3. Are the people's political choices free from domination by the military, foreign powers, religious hierarchies, economic oligarchies, or any other powerful group that is not democratically accountable? 1 / 4

The ruling party dominates the state apparatus and uses security forces and other administrative resources to marginalize, disrupt, and suppress independent political activity.

B4. Do various segments of the population (including ethnic, religious, gender, LGBT, and other relevant groups) have full political rights and electoral opportunities? 1 / 4

Minority groups, including the Afar, Yemeni Arabs, and non-Issa Somalis, are represented at all levels of the government, but the president's majority Issa group holds paramount positions in the ruling party, the civil service, and the security forces. In practice, the authoritarian political system restricts the ability of ethnic and religious minorities to organize independently and advance their interests.

Women's ability to engage in independent political activism is also constrained, and they are underrepresented in leadership positions, partly due to societal discrimination. In the 2018 elections, women won 15 seats in the National Assembly, though that still fell short of the country's new 25 percent quota for women in the legislature. The president's cabinet includes one woman.

C. FUNCTIONING OF GOVERNMENT: 2 / 12

C1. Do the freely elected head of government and national legislative representatives determine the policies of the government? 0 / 4

The president, who is not freely elected, effectively controls policymaking and governance, and the UMP-dominated parliament does not serve as a meaningful check on executive power.

C2. Are safeguards against official corruption strong and effective? 1 / 4

Corruption is a serious problem, and efforts to curb malfeasance in public agencies have met with little success. State bodies tasked with combating corruption lack the resources and independence to function effectively. Prosecutions of senior officials are rare.

C3. Does the government operate with openness and transparency? 1 / 4

The government has made legislation publicly available and created some mechanisms for citizens to request information, but there is no law establishing the right to access government information. Policymaking, public administration, and contracting remain largely nontransparent. Rules on asset disclosure by public officials are poorly enforced.

There is little transparency regarding Guelleh's personal deal-making with countries like China, through which they are authorized to provide loans, build infrastructure, or operate special economic zones. His decisions have resulted in a massive amount of public debt—China alone is owed the equivalent of more than 80 percent of Djibouti's gross domestic product—and spread discontent among local communities that were not consulted on the location or terms of foreign investment projects.

CIVIL LIBERTIES: 19 / 60

D. FREEDOM OF EXPRESSION AND BELIEF: 6 / 16

D1. Are there free and independent media? 1 / 4

Despite constitutional protections, freedom of speech is not upheld in practice, and *journalists engage in self-censorship to avoid professional or legal repercussions for critical reporting.* A 1992 communications law establishes defamation and distribution of false information as criminal offenses, while also imposing restrictive requirements on senior employees of media outlets. The government owns the dominant newspaper, television station, and radio broadcaster.

While the government typically places few restrictions on the internet, some outlets have faced interference and harassment. The websites of the *opposition radio station La Voix de Djibouti, run by exiles in Europe, and the Association for Respect for Human Rights in Djibouti (ARDHD) are sometimes blocked by the state-owned internet service provider.*

D2. Are individuals free to practice and express their religious faith or nonbelief in public and private? 1 / 4

Islam is the state religion, and 94 percent of the population is Sunni Muslim. The Ministry of Islamic Affairs oversees religious matters; a 2013 law and 2014 implementing decree gave it authority over mosques, which were converted into government property, and imams, who became civil service employees. While the government has claimed that this supervision is meant to counter foreign influence, it has also been used to curb dissent. Security services have questioned imams who give sermons on political or social justice themes, and some have been jailed.

D3. Is there academic freedom, and is the educational system free from extensive political indoctrination? 2 / 4

Academic freedom is not always respected. Teachers and other education staff have at times been dismissed for alleged affiliation with opposition groups and trade unions in recent years. The state oversees the curriculum of the secular public school system and those of the country's Islamic schools.

D4. Are individuals free to express their personal views on political or other sensitive topics without fear of surveillance or retribution? 2 / 4

Open discussion of sensitive political issues is impeded by restrictive laws on defamation and other speech-related offenses. The government reportedly monitors social media for critical content and conducts surveillance on perceived opponents.

E. ASSOCIATIONAL AND ORGANIZATIONAL RIGHTS: 3 / 12
E1. Is there freedom of assembly? 0 / 4

Freedom of assembly, while nominally protected under the constitution, is not respected in practice. Permits are required for public assemblies. In May 2018, jobless young people in Tadjourah mounted a demonstration to express frustration with discrimination and nepotism in hiring. Police used violence to disperse them, wounding several and arresting dozens; the wounded reported being afraid to seek formal medical care for fear of arrest. Six protesters were charged with "threatening public order" and placed in pretrial detention. Activists alleged that security forces employed gas grenades and live ammunition and cut telecommunications services to the protest area. A subsequent protest over aid delivery in a district of the capital was similarly broken up by police, who arrested several dozen protesters.

E2. Is there freedom for nongovernmental organizations, particularly those that are engaged in human rights- and governance-related work? 1 / 4

Local human rights groups that work on politically sensitive matters cannot operate freely and are often the target of government harassment and intimidation. In April 2018, human rights defender Kadar Abdi Ibrahim, who is also the secretary general of the unrecognized opposition Movement for Development and Liberty (MoDEL), was arbitrarily detained and had his passport confiscated and his home searched upon return from UN-related human rights activities abroad. Some organizations that focus on social and economic development, including women's rights groups, are tolerated or supported by the government.

E3. Is there freedom for trade unions and similar professional or labor organizations? 2 / 4

Though workers may legally join unions and strike, the government has been known to intimidate labor leaders and obstruct union activities. The Labor Ministry has broad discretion over union registration, allowing it to support progovernment unions and deny recognition to independent labor groups. The country's designated economic free zones

(EFZs) operate under separate rules that provide fewer rights to workers, according to the US State Department.

F. RULE OF LAW: 4 / 16

F1. Is there an independent judiciary? 0 / 4

The courts are not independent of the government and reportedly suffer from corruption. Supreme Court judges are appointed by the president, with the advice of a judicial council dominated by presidential and UMP nominees. The president and parliamentary majority also control appointments to the Constitutional Council.

F2. Does due process prevail in civil and criminal matters? 2 / 4

Security forces frequently make arrests without the required court approval, and lengthy pretrial detention is a problem, with detainees often waiting years to go to trial. Allegations of politically motivated prosecutions are common, and opposition groups consistently accuse the government of sanctioning arbitrary arrests and detentions.

F3. Is there protection from the illegitimate use of physical force and freedom from war and insurgencies? 1 / 4

Security forces regularly engage in physical abuse and torture during arrest and detention. Occasional clashes between the rebel group Front for the Restoration of Unity and Democracy (FRUD-Armé) and Djiboutian security forces occur on the country's periphery. The rebels released two hostages in February 2018. In September, Djibouti and Eritrea, which has been accused of supporting FRUD-Armé, agreed to normalize relations and ask the United Nations to mediate a border dispute.

F4. Do laws, policies, and practices guarantee equal treatment of various segments of the population? 1 / 4

Though the law provides for equal treatment of all Djiboutian citizens, minority ethnic groups and clans suffer from discrimination that contributes to their social and economic marginalization. Women have fewer employment opportunities and are paid less than men for the same work. An estimated 60 percent of girls now receive primary education following efforts to increase female enrollment in schools; the figure for boys is more than 67 percent. While the law requires at least 20 percent of upper-level public service positions to be held by women, this rule has not been enforced.

Same-sex sexual activity is not specifically banned, but such conduct has been penalized under broader morality laws, and there are no laws in place to prevent discrimination against LGBT (lesbian, gay, bisexual, and transgender) people. Matters of sexual orientation and gender identity are generally not discussed publicly.

Djibouti hosted more than 27,000 refugees in 2018, mostly from Somalia, Ethiopia, Eritrea, and Yemen. However, slow processing of asylum claims leaves many asylum seekers at risk of deportation. A law signed in 2017 provides for refugees' access to health care, employment, and education; registered refugees are able to work without a permit.

G. PERSONAL AUTONOMY AND INDIVIDUAL RIGHTS: 6 / 16

G1. Do individuals enjoy freedom of movement, including the ability to change their place of residence, employment, or education? 2 / 4

Due to counterinsurgency operations related to FRUD-Armé, civilian movement in Djibouti's militarized border areas is restricted.

G2. Are individuals able to exercise the right to own property and establish private businesses without undue interference from state or nonstate actors? 2 / 4

Private property protections are weak, according to the Heritage Foundation's Index of Economic Freedom, and court proceedings on business and property matters are "time-consuming, prone to corruption, and politically manipulated."

Customary practices and personal status rules based on Sharia (Islamic law) place women at a disadvantage regarding inheritance and property ownership.

G3. Do individuals enjoy personal social freedoms, including choice of marriage partner and size of family, protection from domestic violence, and control over appearance? 1 / 4

The law prohibits female genital mutilation, but most women and girls in the country have undergone the procedure. Domestic violence is rarely reported and prosecuted, and spousal rape is not specifically criminalized. The Sharia-based family code requires women to obtain a guardian's consent to marry, among other discriminatory provisions surrounding marriage and divorce.

G4. Do individuals enjoy equality of opportunity and freedom from economic exploitation? 1 / 4

There are limited employment prospects in the formal sector, as the president and the ruling party tightly control all large-scale economic activity, including that surrounding lucrative military bases leased by foreign powers. Efforts like the Chinese-built Djibouti International Free Trade Zone, which was launched in July 2018 and will be home to businesses from more than 20 countries, are heralded as employment opportunities, but workers in the special economic zones remain vulnerable to exploitation.

A new law on human trafficking was adopted in 2016, prescribing strong penalties for trafficking offenses and providing for victim-assistance programs. The government has made some progress in enforcing the law, according to the US State Department, but it continued to fall short in 2018 on matters such as identifying and assisting victims.

Dominica

Population: 100,000
Capital: Roseau
Political Rights Rating: 1
Civil Liberties Rating: 1
Freedom Rating: 1.0
Freedom Status: Free
Electoral Democracy: Yes

Overview: Dominica is a parliamentary democracy, and has been governed by the Dominica Labor Party (DLP) since 2000. While the country is committed to democratic governance and civil liberties are generally upheld, a number of concerns persist; these include effective management of elections, judicial efficiency, and government integrity—notably relating to the country's Citizenship by Investment Program (CIP).

KEY DEVELOPMENTS IN 2018:

- In October, Charles Savarin was sworn to the country's ceremonial presidency, and began his second term.
- Despite receiving the full support of the DLP, the opposition United Workers Party (UWP) walked out of Savarin's parliamentary confirmation session in protest of what they said was an irregular nominating process. The controversy did not appear to draw public concern from regional monitors.
- In 2018, riot police deployed tear gas against demonstrators with the Concerned Citizens Movement—a civil society group that frequently criticizes the government—who had blocked a road and refused calls to disperse.

POLITICAL RIGHTS: 37 / 40

A. ELECTORAL PROCESS: 11 / 12

A1. Was the current head of government or other chief national authority elected through free and fair elections? 4 / 4

The president, who is the ceremonial head of state, is nominated by the prime minister and opposition leader, and elected by the House of Assembly for a five-year term. The prime minister is head of government and is appointed by the president.

The leader of the governing DLP, Roosevelt Skerrit, retained his position as prime minister after his party won a majority of the parliamentary seats in the 2014 general elections, which were competitive and credible.

In October 2018, the government reelected former minister of security Charles Savarin as president. Savarin received the full support of the DLP, but the opposition UWP walked out of the parliamentary confirmation session in protest of what they said was an irregular nominating process. The controversy did not appear to draw public concern from regional monitors.

A2. Were the current national legislative representatives elected through free and fair elections? 4 / 4

Dominica's unicameral House of Assembly consists of 30 members who serve five-year terms; 21 members are directly elected, 5 senators are appointed by the prime minister, and 4 are appointed by the opposition leader. There are 2 ex-officio members: the house speaker and the clerk of the house.

The DLP won 15 seats in the 2014 general elections, and the UWP captured 6. The electoral observation mission of the Organization of American States (OAS) deemed the elections well run and credible, although it cited some irregularities; these included stringent standards for what constituted a valid mark on a ballot, which led to the rejection of some legitimately marked ballots. The next parliamentary elections are scheduled for December 2019.

A3. Are the electoral laws and framework fair, and are they implemented impartially by the relevant election management bodies? 3 / 4

The Electoral Commission manages and organizes the election process, and the electoral laws are generally fair. However, constituencies in Dominica have not changed since 1990, and after the 2014 elections the OAS raised concerns about their unbalanced sizes, with the largest constituency having over 7,000 registered voters and the smallest having just over 1,500. The OAS also expressed concern about outdated voter lists and procedures for evaluating marks on ballots.

B. POLITICAL PLURALISM AND PARTICIPATION: 16 / 16

B1. Do the people have the right to organize in different political parties or other competitive political groupings of their choice, and is the system free of undue obstacles to the rise and fall of these competing parties or groupings? 4 / 4

Political parties are free to organize and operate. The effects of the country's "first-past-the-post" electoral system has entrenched two-party politics, and while there are a number of small political parties in the country, since 2005 only the DLP and UWP have won seats in parliament.

B2. Is there a realistic opportunity for the opposition to increase its support or gain power through elections? 4 / 4

Opposition parties are unencumbered by formal restrictions and are generally free to operate. There has not been a change of party in government since 2000, but this has more to do with the weakness of the opposition than any unfairness in the electoral system.

After a series of antigovernment protests in 2017, the government denied several demonstration permits to the opposition, citing public security grounds.

B3. Are the people's political choices free from domination by the military, foreign powers, religious hierarchies, economic oligarchies, or any other powerful group that is not democratically accountable? 4 / 4

Voters and candidates are generally able to express their political choices without undue influence from actors that are not democratically accountable.

B4. Do various segments of the population (including ethnic, religious, gender, LGBT, and other relevant groups) have full political rights and electoral opportunities? 4 / 4

All adult citizens may vote. Women are underrepresented in politics generally. Out of 44 candidates in the last election, only 6 were woman, and of them, only 3 won seats. There are 3 female senators out of 9 appointees. The position of house speaker—one of two ex-officio members of the legislature—is held by a woman.

The indigenous Carib-Kalinago population participates in the political process, with members generally supporting one of the two major political parties. The LGBT (lesbian, gay, bisexual, and transgender) community is marginalized, and this impacts the ability of LGBT people to engage fully in political processes.

C. FUNCTIONING OF GOVERNMENT: 10 / 12

C1. Do the freely elected head of government and national legislative representatives determine the policies of the government? 4 / 4

The freely elected prime minister, cabinet, and national legislative representatives determine the policies of the government.

C2. Are safeguards against official corruption strong and effective? 3 / 4

While the government generally implements anticorruption laws effectively, domestic and international observers have raised concerns over Dominica's CIP, a citizenship program that allows foreigners to gain citizenship through an economic investment in the country. These have included persistent allegations that the government has sold diplomatic passports to noncitizens.

In February 2017, the prime minister announced an interim policy to tighten the issuance of diplomatic passports, following a controversy in which an Iranian national ensnared in a corruption scandal in Iran was found to hold a Dominican diplomatic passport. That year, the

US State Department described CIP as vulnerable and "susceptible to abuse by criminal actors." It again criticized the program in a March 2018 report, saying Dominica's CIP "does not maintain adequate autonomy from politicians to prevent political interference in its decisions."

C3. Does the government operate with openness and transparency? 3 / 4

The government of Dominica generally operates with openness and transparency, though there are concerns that the long-incumbent DLP had been less forthcoming in recent years with information on some programs, including the CIP. Government officials are required to submit financial accounts, but these accounts are frequently incomplete.

Access to information is not protected by law, but the government makes efforts to provide information on many topics, and makes information related to the budget available online.

CIVIL LIBERTIES: 56 / 60

D. FREEDOM OF EXPRESSION AND BELIEF: 15 / 16

D1. Are there free and independent media? 3 / 4

Freedom of expression is constitutionally guaranteed, and the press is generally free in practice. However, defamation remains a criminal offense punishable by imprisonment or fines. Defamation lawsuits and threats of lawsuits are commonly used by the Skerrit government against members of the media, resulting in some self-censorship.

D2. Are individuals free to practice and express their religious faith or nonbelief in public and private? 4 / 4

Freedom of religion is protected under the constitution and other laws, and is generally respected in practice.

D3. Is there academic freedom, and is the educational system free from extensive political indoctrination? 4 / 4

Academic freedom is generally respected.

D4. Are individuals free to express their personal views on political or other sensitive topics without fear of surveillance or retribution? 4 / 4

Individuals are generally free to express their personal views on political or other sensitive topics.

E. ASSOCIATIONAL AND ORGANIZATIONAL RIGHTS: 11 / 12

E1. Is there freedom of assembly? 3 / 4

Freedom of assembly is guaranteed under the constitution, and the government has generally respected these rights. However, protests sometimes become violent, or give way to looting or acts of vandalism. Some unrest took place at opposition protests in 2017, and the prime minister characterized the protest events as threats to state security. In December 2018, riot police deployed tear gas against demonstrators with the Concerned Citizens Movement—a civil society group that frequently criticizes the government—who blocked a road and refused calls to disperse.

E2. Is there freedom for nongovernmental organizations, particularly those that are engaged in human rights–and governance-related work? 4 / 4

Nongovernmental organizations (NGOs) and advocacy groups generally operate without interference.

E3. Is there freedom for trade unions and similar professional or labor organizations? 4 / 4

Workers have the right to organize, strike, and bargain collectively, and laws prohibit antiunion discrimination by employers. However, the country's definition of "essential" workers is broad, extending to those in the agricultural sector, and there are burdensome restrictions on the ability of these workers to strike.

F. RULE OF LAW: 15 / 16

F1. Is there an independent judiciary? 4 / 4

An independent judiciary is provided for in the constitution, and judicial independence is generally respected. Courts are subordinate to the inter-island Eastern Caribbean Supreme Court (ECSC).

F2. Does due process prevail in civil and criminal matters? 4 / 4

The constitution provides for due process rights, and these are generally observed in practice. While the judicial system generally operates efficiently, staffing shortages remain a problem and can result in prolonged pretrial detention, which can last as long as 24 months.

F3. Is there protection from the illegitimate use of physical force and freedom from war and insurgencies? 4 / 4

People in Dominica generally enjoy freedom from illegitimate force. The Dominica police force operates professionally, and there have been few complaints of violations of human rights by officers in recent years.

F4. Do laws, policies, and practices guarantee equal treatment of various segments of the population? 3 / 4

Members of Dominica's small indigenous population, the Carib-Kalinago, face discrimination and a variety of accompanying challenges, including high poverty levels and difficulties in obtaining loans from banks. Rastafarians have reported discrimination and profiling by police. Same-sex sexual relations are illegal, though the relevant provisions of the Sexual Offences Act are not enforced. Sexual harassment is not prohibited by law and remains a widespread problem.

G. PERSONAL AUTONOMY AND INDIVIDUAL RIGHTS: 15 / 16

G1. Do individuals enjoy freedom of movement, including the ability to change their place of residence, employment, or education? 4 / 4

Individuals in Dominica generally enjoy freedom of movement, though those outside the established Carib-Kalinago community must apply for special access to the Carib Reserve area, which is granted by the Carib Council. There are no restrictions on people's ability to change their place of employment or education.

G2. Are individuals able to exercise the right to own property and establish private businesses without undue interference from state or non-state actors? 4 / 4

The government of Dominica is pro-business, and supports both domestic and foreign investment. Property rights are generally safeguarded. However, women have more limited rights because property is deeded to the head of household, who is usually a man.

G3. Do individuals enjoy personal social freedoms, including choice of marriage partner and size of family, protection from domestic violence, and control over appearance? 3 / 4

Women and children have some limitations on their personal freedoms, including freedom from violence. There is little protection against domestic abuse, and both violence against women and child abuse remain widespread problems.

G4. Do individuals enjoy equality of opportunity and freedom from economic exploitation? 4 / 4

Revisions to labor laws have strengthened worker protections in recent years, though there are reports of violations of overtime laws in the tourism sector. The labor commissioner operates within the Justice Department, and is under resourced. The government has made efforts to address poverty and unemployment, including in the wake of Hurricane Maria, which devastated the island in 2017.

Trafficking in persons was not a major problem in Dominica in 2018.

Dominican Republic

Population: 10,800,000
Capital: Santo Domingo
Political Rights Rating: 3
Civil Liberties Rating: 3
Freedom Rating: 3.0
Freedom Status: Partly Free
Electoral Democracy: Yes

Overview: The Dominican Republic holds regular elections that are relatively free, though recent years have been characterized by controversies involving the electoral framework. Pervasive corruption undermines state institutions, and discrimination against Dominicans of Haitian descent and Haitian migrants, as well as against LGBT (lesbian, gay, bisexual, and transgender) people, remains a serious problem.

KEY DEVELOPMENTS IN 2018:

- A controversial new electoral law was promulgated in August after winning approval from legislators, and work began on its implementation.
- The new law quickly became the subject of legal challenges from across the political spectrum. Challenged provisions included those mandating that the electoral commission administer party primaries; requiring a minimum time candidates must be associated with parties for which they aspire to run; and placing limitations on when new parties may join existing alliances.
- Seven current and former officials were charged in June in connection with a wide-ranging corruption scandal involving the Brazilian construction firm Odebrecht. However, many more officials have been implicated, and the government has not responded to requests to establish an independent inquiry into the allegations.
- While the homicide rate in 2018 was down approximately 15 percent compared to the previous year, violent crime remained high. The Citizen Security Observatory, a governmental body that records crime statistics, reported 801 homicides between January and September.

POLITICAL RIGHTS: 26 / 40

A. ELECTORAL PROCESS: 9 / 12

A1. Was the current head of government or other chief national authority elected through free and fair elections? 3 / 4

The president is both head of state and chief of government, and is elected to a four-year term. A 2015 constitutional amendment allowed presidents to run for a second term; Danilo Medina, of the Dominican Liberation Party (PLD), won a second term in 2016.

In 2016, observers from the Organization of American States (OAS) monitored the presidential and concurrent legislative elections, and deemed them credible. However, they called for major reforms to guarantee equal access to party financing and access to media by participating political parties. The OAS also expressed concern about serious complications involving new electronic voting and vote-counting infrastructure; delays in tabulation resulted in the full final results not being made public until 13 days after the elections. Six people were killed in election-related violence the Central Election Board (JCE) head claimed had erupted due to frustration with delays created by demands for manual vote-counting.

A2. Were the current national legislative representatives elected through free and fair elections? 3 / 4

The Dominican Republic's bicameral National Congress consists of the 32-member Senate and the 190-member Chamber of Deputies, with members of both chambers directly elected to four-year terms.

In the 2016 legislative elections, held concurrently with presidential election, the ruling PLD captured 26 Senate seats and 106 seats in the Chamber of Deputies. The OAS observer mission deemed the polls credible, but called for major reforms to guarantee equal access to party financing and media coverage, questioned the efficacy of the new electronic voting and vote-counting infrastructure, and condemned the election-related violence.

A3. Are the electoral laws and framework fair, and are they implemented impartially by the relevant election management bodies? 3 / 4

The 2016 general elections exposed serious problems with electoral infrastructure and the capacities of the JCE, with some saying the delays in vote-counting precipitated the post-election violence. The polls also exposed irregularities in party financing.

Electoral reform has since been heavily debated in the legislature. In August 2018, the Law of Political Parties, Groups, and Movements was enacted by President Medina after winning approval from lawmakers. Under the new law, among other provisions, the JCE will administer the primary elections of political parties, rather than the parties themselves under their own statutes. (The law's approval was seen as a victory for Medina, who was facing some dissent from within his own party.) A number of figures, including PLD members, members of an opposition bloc, constitutional experts, and lawyers have since challenged various parts of the law as unconstitutional. Nevertheless, after holding public consultations, the JCE adopted the regulations for application of the law in December.

Despite the JCE's past shortcomings, the body operates with some transparency and cooperates with international election monitors, opposition parties, and other relevant groups.

B. POLITICAL PLURALISM AND PARTICIPATION: 10 / 16

B1. Do the people have the right to organize in different political parties or other competitive political groupings of their choice, and is the system free of undue obstacles to the rise and fall of these competing parties or groupings? 3 / 4

Political parties are generally free to form and operate. However, under current electoral laws, newer and smaller parties struggle to access to public financing and secure equal media coverage, hampering their competitiveness. Provisions of the electoral law enacted in August 2018 require a minimum time candidates must be associated with the parties for which they aspire to run, though this was being challenged at year's end.

B2. Is there a realistic opportunity for the opposition to increase its support or gain power through elections? 3 / 4

Opposition parties and candidates generally do not face selective restrictions during election periods but are disadvantaged by elements of the electoral framework. Provisions of the electoral law enacted in August 2018 prohibit parties running in an election for the first time from joining preexisting alliances, though this was being challenged at year's end.

The governing PLD has won legislative majorities in the last four elections.

B3. Are the people's political choices free from domination by the military, foreign powers, religious hierarchies, economic oligarchies, or any other powerful group that is not democratically accountable? 3 / 4

People are generally free to exercise their political choices. However, a history of violent police responses to social and political demonstrations may deter political participation by some, and economic oligarchies and organized crime groups have some influence over the political sphere. Private donations to political parties are unlimited and unregulated, allowing wealthy donors significant influence over politics.

B4. Do various segments of the population (including ethnic, religious, gender, LGBT, and other relevant groups) have full political rights and electoral opportunities? 1 / 4

A 2013 Constitutional Court decision stripped Dominican-born descendants of Haitian migrants of their citizenship, and thus their right to vote.

Parity laws have led to a higher number of women in the legislature, but the Dominican Republic is among countries with the lowest representation of women at the ministerial level, with only 17.3 percent of positions occupied by women. Woman lawmakers report that it is difficult for them to exert influence over their parties' positions and to secure funding for political candidacies.

Discriminatory attitudes and occasional acts of targeted violence against LGBT people discourages their political participation.

C. FUNCTIONING OF GOVERNMENT: 7 / 12

C1. Do the freely elected head of government and national legislative representatives determine the policies of the government? 3 / 4

Government and legislative representatives are generally able to determine national policies in a free and unhindered manner.

C2. Are safeguards against official corruption strong and effective? 2 / 4

Corruption remains a serious, systemic problem at all levels of the government, judiciary, and security forces, and in the private sector. A US Justice Department investigation into the Brazilian construction company Odebrecht, the results of which surfaced in late 2016—revealed that $92 million had been paid to public officials to obtain contracts for major infrastructure projects in the country during three consecutive governments. Numerous officials from both the previous and current administration were linked to the scandal, but only seven were formally charged, in June 2018. The government has not responded to requests to establish an independent inquiry into the Odebrecht corruption allegations.

C3. Does the government operate with openness and transparency? 2 / 4

The government does not always operate with transparency. Although state agencies generally respond to information requests, they often provide inaccurate or incomplete responses. Public officials are required to publicly disclose assets, but nongovernmental organizations (NGOs) have cast doubt upon the accuracy of these disclosures. Public contracting and purchasing processes are opaque and allow for high levels of corruption, as reflected in the Odebrecht scandal.

CIVIL LIBERTIES: 41 / 60

D. FREEDOM OF EXPRESSION AND BELIEF: 14 / 16

D1. Are there free and independent media? 2 / 4

The law guarantees freedom of speech and of the press, but journalists risk intimidation and violence when investigating sensitive issues, particularly drug trafficking and corruption. In April 2018, an appeals court sentenced Matias Avelino Castro to 20 years in prison for orchestrating the 2011 murder of journalist, magazine director, and television host, José Agustín Silvestre; Silvestre was killed after promising to publicize information linking Castro to drug trafficking operations. Prior to the verdict, a journalist received threats for covering the trial. The attorney general communicated on Twitter that his office was beginning an inquiry into the threats and would offer her protective measures.

Several national daily newspapers and a large number of local publications operate in the country. There are more than 300 privately owned radio stations and several private television networks alongside the state-owned Radio Televisión Dominicana (RTVD), though ownership of private outlets is highly concentrated.

D2. Are individuals free to practice and express their religious faith or nonbelief in public and private? 4 / 4

Religious freedom is generally upheld. However, the Catholic Church receives special privileges from the state including funding for construction, and exemptions from custom duties.

D3. Is there academic freedom, and is the educational system free from extensive political indoctrination? 4 / 4

Constitutional guarantees regarding academic freedom are generally observed.

D4. Are individuals free to express their personal views on political or other sensitive topics without fear of surveillance or retribution? 4 / 4

People are generally free to express personal views in public and privately without fear of retribution or surveillance.

E. ASSOCIATIONAL AND ORGANIZATIONAL RIGHTS: 10 / 12

E1. Is there freedom of assembly? 3 / 4

Freedom of assembly is guaranteed by the constitution, and demonstrations are common, but sometimes subject to violent dispersal by police. There was a large protest against government corruption in August 2018, and throughout the year smaller demonstrations were held at which participants called for the decriminalization of abortion, protested rising fuel prices and frequent power outages, and expressed support for the recognition of social, cultural, economic, and environmental rights.

Several people were injured in September when demonstrators protesting high fuel prices and electricity shortages clashed with police. In October, one person was reportedly killed by police gunfire in Santiago de los Caballeros as police moved against protesters, some of whom were working to block roads into their neighborhood ahead of a planned nationwide strike.

E2. Is there freedom for nongovernmental organizations, particularly those that are engaged in human rights- and governance-related work? 4 / 4

Freedom of association is constitutionally guaranteed, and the government respects the right to form civic groups.

E3. Is there freedom for trade unions and similar professional or labor organizations? 3 / 4

Workers other than military and police personnel may form and join unions, though over 50 percent of workers at a workplace must be union members in order to engage in collective bargaining. Workers must exhaust mediation measures and meet other criteria in order for a strike to be considered legal. In practice, workers are often dissuaded from joining unions, and risk dismissal for joining a union. In May 2018, the National Confederation of Trade Union Unit registered a complaint against the Dominican Republic before the International Labor Organization for a breach of international conventions on freedom of association and collective bargaining at several companies.

Several strikes took place in 2018 over high fuel prices and other economic difficulties.

F. RULE OF LAW: 8 / 16

F1. Is there an independent judiciary? 3 / 4

Justices of the Supreme Court and Constitutional Court are appointed to seven- and nine-year terms, respectively, by the appointed by the National Council of the Judiciary. That body is comprised of the president, the leaders of both chambers of congress, the Supreme Court president, and a congressional representative from an opposition party.

The judiciary is plagued by corruption and is susceptible to political pressure. Reports of selective prosecution and the improper dismissal of cases continue. The National Council of the Judiciary has taken some action to curb judicial abuses, and announced in 2018 that since 2012 it had dismissed 22 judges over questionable rulings in favor of defendants.

F2. Does due process prevail in civil and criminal matters? 2 / 4

Corruption and politicization of the justice system have significant impact on due process, and strongly limits access to justice for people without resources or political connections. Corruption within law enforcement agencies remains a serious challenge.

In late 2018, 60 percent of people being held in prisons were in pretrial detention.

F3. Is there protection from the illegitimate use of physical force and freedom from war and insurgencies? 2 / 4

Rates of murder and other violent crime are high. While the 2018 homicide rate was down approximately 15 percent compared to the previous year, the Citizen Security Observatory (a governmental body that records crime statistics) reported 801 homicides between January and September.

Prisons are severely overcrowded, though the government has indicated it plans to use money from fines resulting from the Odebrecht prosecution to construct new prisons.

The National Human Rights Commission and nongovernmental organizations (NGOs) report that security forces, including joint military and police patrols dispatched by the government to curb violence, committed extrajudicial killings in 2018.

F4. Do laws, policies, and practices guarantee equal treatment of various segments of the population? 1 / 4

Dominicans of Haitian descent and Haitian migrants face persistent discrimination, including obstacles in securing legal documents such as identification, birth certificates, and marriage licenses, and have difficulty registering their children as Dominican citizens. This lack of documentation makes it difficult for those affected to attend school and university, and obtain legal employment.

LGBT people suffer from violence and discrimination. They are still barred from working in certain public sectors, such as the police and armed forces. An antidiscrimination bill remained stalled in 2018 despite renewed calls from civil society to bring it into effect.

G. PERSONAL AUTONOMY AND INDIVIDUAL RIGHTS: 9 / 16

G1. Do individuals enjoy freedom of movement, including the ability to change their place of residence, employment, or education? 2 / 4

While citizens are generally free to move around the country, asylum seekers and refugees must pay a fee to gain travel documents. Separately, the prevalence of drive-by robberies by armed assailants has prompted some reluctance to move about freely, particularly at night.

G2. Are individuals able to exercise the right to own property and establish private businesses without undue interference from state or non-state actors? 3 / 4

Private business activity remains susceptible to undue influence by organized crime and corrupt officials, though the World Economic Forum's Global Competitive Index points to some improvement in these areas.

G3. Do individuals enjoy personal social freedoms, including choice of marriage partner and size of family, protection from domestic violence, and control over appearance? 2 / 4

Violence and discrimination against women remains pervasive. According to 2017 statistics from the UN Children's Fund (UNICEF), 36 percent of girls are married before their 18th birthday. Poor medical care has left the country with one of the highest maternal mortality rates in the region. After a 2014 law decriminalizing abortion in some situations was struck down in 2015 by the Constitutional Court, a complete ban on abortion was effectively reinstated.

In 2017, the Senate rejected proposed amendments recommended by Medina that would have decriminalized abortion when the life of the mother is endangered or in cases of incest, rape, or fetal impairment. The House shortly afterward voted against the Senate's rejection, thus setting the stage for another legislative vote on the issue. In 2018, a national survey revealed that a majority of the population supported decriminalization of abortion in each of those instances.

G4. Do individuals enjoy equality of opportunity and freedom from economic exploitation? 2 / 4

Many workers in the country are employed informally, leaving them without legal protections.

The Dominican Republic remains a source, transit, and destination country for the trafficking of men, women and children for sexual exploitation and forced labor. Haitians who lack documentation and clear legal status are particularly susceptible to forced labor.

Ecuador

Population: 17,000,000
Capital: Quito
Political Rights Rating: 3
Civil Liberties Rating: 3
Freedom Rating: 3.0
Freedom Status: Partly Free
Electoral Democracy: Yes

Overview: Elections take place regularly, though there are persistent concerns about politicization of the National Electoral Council (CNE). A leftist government has ruled the country since 2007. While former president Rafael Correa imposed restrictions on the media and civil society, the new administration of President Lenín Moreno has begun rolling back repressive Correa-era policies. The administration, which came to power in 2017, has taken concrete steps to fight corruption, bolster security, remove restrictions on civil society, encourage the free press, and strengthen democratic governance.

KEY DEVELOPMENTS IN 2018:
- In a February referendum, Ecuadorians voted to reinstate presidential term limits, which will prevent former president Correa from seeking a third term.
- In December, the legislature approved a draft law to reform the restrictive Organic Communications Law, which would, among other provisions, eliminate the notorious Superintendency of Information and Communication (SUPERCOM), a body that investigates and issues sanctions against critical journalists.
- Referendum voters also approved a measure to restructure the powerful National Council of Citizen Participation and Social Control (CPCCS), which is responsible for appointing CNE members, the attorney general, and the Judiciary Council, among other powers; Correa-era members of the CPCCS, which had been politicized, were removed, and a transitional CPCCS was appointed by Moreno.
- In August, the transitional CPCCS voted to remove all nine judges on the Constitutional Court, citing corruption and a lack of independence within the body. However, the move was controversial, as the Constitutional Court was not among the bodies the CPCCS has jurisdiction over.

POLITICAL RIGHTS: 25 / 40
A. ELECTORAL PROCESS: 7 / 12
A1. Was the current head of government or other chief national authority elected through free and fair elections? 3 / 4
The 2008 constitution provides for a directly elected president, who can serve up to two terms. The president has the authority to dissolve the legislature, which triggers new elections for both the assembly and the presidency.

In April 2017, Lenín Moreno of the Proud and Sovereign Fatherland (PAIS) alliance won the presidential runoff with 51 percent of the vote, defeating Guillermo Lasso of the Creating Opportunities–Society United for More Action (CREO-SUMA) alliance, who took 49 percent. Some observers expressed concerns about the use of state resources to produce materials favoring Moreno.

While Lasso denounced the results as fraudulent and refused to concede, international observers generally praised the election's conduct. Lasso requested a full recount of the vote, though the CNE granted only a partial one. The CNE stated that the recount failed to reveal any significant discrepancy from the previous count, and ratified the election's result.

A2. Were the current national legislative representatives elected through free and fair elections? 3 / 4

Ecuador has a 137-seat unicameral National Assembly, with 116 members directly elected, 15 elected by proportional representation, and 6 elected through multiseat constituencies for Ecuadorians living abroad; members serve four-year terms. International and domestic observers generally praised the February 2017 legislative elections, though an Organization of American States (OAS) mission urged reforms including removing the names of deceased persons from the voter rolls, and called for more training to be made available to various actors in the electoral process. The ruling PAIS alliance won 74 out of 137 seats, followed by the opposition CREO-SUMA, which took 28. The rest of the seats were captured by nine other parties.

A3. Are the electoral laws and framework fair, and are they implemented impartially by the relevant election management bodies? 1 / 4

The CNE is considered to be government-controlled. The body faced some criticism for its administration of the 2017 elections, including for slow vote counting and irregularities on the voter rolls. In response to the criticism, the transitional CPCCS dismissed all sitting CNE members in July 2018, and in November, five newly appointed members began a six-year term. It remains to be seen whether the new CNE members will improve the performance and independence of the body.

The seat allocation formula for the parliament favors larger parties, which benefits the PAIS alliance. In February 2018, voters approved a referendum that restores term limits, which had been eliminated in a 2015 constitutional amendment under former president Correa; the president can now serve up to two terms, which effectively bars Correa from reclaiming the presidency. The US State Department praised the conduct of the referendum as "peaceful and fair."

B. POLITICAL PLURALISM AND PARTICIPATION: 11 / 16

B1. Do the people have the right to organize in different political parties or other competitive political groupings of their choice, and is the system free of undue obstacles to the rise and fall of these competing parties or groupings? 3 / 4

According to the 2008 constitution, political organizations must register in order to participate in general elections, with a requirement that groupings must collect voters' signatures equivalent to 1.5 percent of the electoral rolls to win recognition. If a party or grouping fails to win 5 percent of the vote for two consecutive elections, its registration can be revoked, disadvantaging smaller parties. In September 2018, the transitional CNE announced that there were 276 political organizations registered for the 2019 elections.

B2. Is there a realistic opportunity for the opposition to increase its support or gain power through elections? 2 / 4

For decades, Ecuador's political parties have been largely personality based, clientelist, and fragile. The ruling PAIS alliance remains the largest bloc in the legislature, in spite of a split between Correa supporters and Moreno supporters that widened with the passage of the referendum reinstalling term limits. There were reports that the government abused administrative resources ahead of the 2017 polls, tilting the playing field in PAIS's favor. Restrictive campaign finance laws also reduce the competitiveness of opposition parties.

B3. Are the people's political choices free from domination by the military, foreign powers, religious hierarchies, economic oligarchies, or any other powerful group that is not democratically accountable? 3 / 4

The people's political choices are generally free from domination by powerful groups that are not democratically accountable. However, wealthy business interests can undermine democratic accountability by facilitating or encouraging corruption among elected officials.

B4. Do various segments of the population (including ethnic, religious, gender, LGBT, and other relevant groups) have full political rights and electoral opportunities? 3 / 4

Ecuador's constitution promotes nondiscrimination and provides for the adoption of affirmative action measures to guarantee equality and representation of minorities. In practice, however, indigenous groups often lack a voice in key decisions pertaining to their land and resources. Despite gender parity measures, women's interests are not well represented in politics, as reflected in a persistent lack of access to reproductive health care.

C. FUNCTIONING OF GOVERNMENT: 7 / 12

C1. Do the freely elected head of government and national legislative representatives determine the policies of the government? 3 / 4

Elected officials are generally free to set and implement government policy without undue interference from nonstate actors. However, the executive has exhibited a strong influence on other branches of the government, and political actors are susceptible to manipulation by powerful business interests.

President Moreno has taken steps to reduce the dominance of the executive. The fracturing of the PAIS alliance, with more than one-third of its members in the parliament defecting in January 2018 to a new coalition that backs Correa, has compelled Moreno to work with opposition lawmakers to advance legislation.

C2. Are safeguards against official corruption strong and effective? 2 / 4

Ecuador has long been racked by corruption, and the weak judiciary and lack of investigative capacity in government oversight agencies contribute to an environment of impunity. President Moreno campaigned on a promise to tackle high-level corruption, and in 2017, he stripped Vice President Jorge Glas of his powers amid corruption allegations regarding Glas's involvement with the Odebrecht scandal, which involved kickbacks paid to Ecuadorian officials by the Brazilian construction company. Later in 2017, Glas was convicted and sentenced to six years in prison for his role in the scandal. In December 2018, Moreno suspended Vice President María Alejandra Vicuña, who had been accused of accepting bribes from an aide during her time as a lawmaker, and at the end of the year she was under investigation by the chief prosecutor.

In the February 2018 referendum, voters approved a measure to ban anyone convicted on corruption charges from ever holding public office.

C3. Does the government operate with openness and transparency? 2 / 4

The law guarantees citizens' right to access public information, and although compliance has improved over the years, some government bodies remain reluctant to disclose public information. In 2018, the government took steps to enhance access to information, including the establishment of a transparency monitoring mechanism to ensure that public agencies provide relevant information online. Public procurement processes are frequently opaque.

CIVIL LIBERTIES: 38 / 60 (+3)
D. FREEDOM OF EXPRESSION AND BELIEF: 12 / 16
D1. Are there free and independent media? 2 / 4

Media freedom improved noticeably after President Moreno took office in 2017. Upon his election, Moreno met with the owners of private media outlets and pledged to usher in a new, more open environment for journalists. His administration has permitted more diverse coverage in the country's state-run media, which had previously shown clear bias toward Correa and the PAIS alliance.

In December 2018, the National Assembly approved a reform of the restrictive Organic Communications Law, including the elimination of the notorious SUPERCOM, which monitors media content, investigates journalists, and issues fines and other sanctions. The legislation also removes a provision that allowed the criminalization of investigative reporting.

However, challenges remain. Correa's long history of harassing the media both verbally and through lawsuits encouraged widespread self-censorship, which Ecuadorian media advocates say will take years for the country's press corps to shake off. Criminal defamation laws remain on the books, and journalists continued to report harassment, although attacks on reporters declined significantly in 2018.

D2. Are individuals free to practice and express their religious faith or nonbelief in public and private? 4 / 4

Freedom of religion is constitutionally guaranteed and generally respected in practice.

D3. Is there academic freedom, and is the educational system free from extensive political indoctrination? 3 / 4

In May 2018, the National Assembly approved reforms to the Organic Law on Higher Education, which restores public funding for research at universities that operate in Ecuador under international agreements. The legislation that removed the funding, passed in 2016, had threatened the viability of two graduate institutions, Universidad Andina Simón Bolívar and FLACSO Ecuador.

D4. Are individuals free to express their personal views on political or other sensitive topics without fear of surveillance or retribution? 3 / 4

Discussion of controversial topics among private citizens is generally free. However, crackdowns on social media have led some online outlets to disable sections for public commentary for fear of reprisals, limiting the freedom of private discussion online. In August 2018, a teacher employed by a government agency was fired, which he claims was retribution for appearing on a television show and criticizing the Moreno government.

E. ASSOCIATIONAL AND ORGANIZATIONAL RIGHTS: 9 / 12 (+2)
E1. Is there freedom of assembly? 3 / 4

Numerous protests occur throughout the country without incident, and restrictions on assembly rights have eased under President Moreno. However, national security legislation provides a broad definition of sabotage and terrorism, extending to acts against persons and property by unarmed individuals, which can be used to limit assembly rights.

E2. Is there freedom for nongovernmental organizations, particularly those that are engaged in human rights– and governance-related work? 3 / 4 (+1)

In 2017, President Moreno rescinded controversial Correa-era decrees that had introduced onerous requirements for forming a nongovernmental organization (NGO), granted officials broad authority to dissolve organizations, and obliged NGOs to register all members. However, while observers say Moreno's new regime for NGO regulation is an improvement, it has also drawn criticism for retaining excessive government regulatory power. For example, Moreno's NGO regulations allow authorities to close an NGO deemed to be performing activities different from those for which it was created, or to be participating in politics.

In 2018, President Moreno continued to engage in constructive dialogue with civil society groups, expressed willingness to hear the viewpoints of NGOs, and has pledged further reforms to open civic space. During the year, Moreno also met with international NGOs such as the Committee to Protect Journalists (CPJ) and Human Rights Watch (HRW). Additionally, threats and denunciations of NGOs by high ranking public officials, which were common in the Correa era, have subsided since Moreno took office.

Score Change: The score improved from 2 to 3 because President Moreno has taken steps to loosen constraints on NGOs and has engaged in constructive dialogue with them, and because threats and denunciations against by senior officials NGOs have subsided.

E3. Is there freedom for trade unions and similar professional or labor organizations? 3 / 4 (+1)

Private-sector labor unions have the right to strike, though the labor code limits public-sector strikes. Only a small portion of the general workforce is unionized, partly because many people work in the informal sector. In March 2018, the National Union of Educators (UNE), which had been dissolved by the government in 2016 under restrictive NGO regulations, was able to resume operations when it was registered as a union.

Score Change: The score improved from 2 to 3 because the National Union of Educators was able to resume operations after being dissolved in 2016 on dubious administrative grounds by the previous administration.

F. RULE OF LAW: 7 / 16 (+1)

F1. Is there an independent judiciary? 1 / 4

Ecuador's highest-ranking judicial bodies are the 21-member National Court of Justice and the 9-member Constitutional Court. Both courts faced attacks on their autonomy during the Correa era, but President Moreno has moved to increase judicial independence. One of the measures passed in the February 2018 referendum involved restructuring the CPCCS, a powerful body responsible for appointing the attorney general and the Judiciary Council, which in turn appoints judges. The referendum's passage led to the sacking of all CPCCS members, who were considered allies of the Correa government and had previously ensured the removal of independent judges and the appointment of judges loyal to the former president. In June, the transitional CPCCS appointed by Moreno replaced all members of the Judiciary Council with transitional members who have expressed commitment to an independent judiciary. Permanent CPCCS members will be elected by popular vote in March 2019, which should further strengthen the institution's independence.

More controversially, in August, the transitional CPCCS voted to remove all nine judges on the Constitutional Court, citing corruption and a lack of independence within the body. The referendum did not include the Constitutional Court as one of the bodies the CP-CCS has jurisdiction over, meaning the move itself could be construed as an impingement on judicial independence.

F2. Does due process prevail in civil and criminal matters? 2 / 4 (+1)

Judicial processes remain slow, and procedures designed to expedite cases have been implemented at the detriment of defendants' due process rights. Many people are held in pretrial detention for longer than is permitted by law. While the number of public defenders has increased in recent years, the state is still unable to provide adequate legal counsel for all defendants who are unable to supply their own.

During his tenure, former president Correa and his allies frequently intervened in court cases, telling judges how they should rule, and sometimes removing judges who refused to comply. Under President Moreno, such blatant interference in court proceedings has subsided, allowing defendants more fair public hearings of their cases.

Score Change: The score improved from 1 to 2 because political interference in court proceedings has decreased under the Moreno administration, allowing greater access to fair public hearings.

F3. Is there protection from the illegitimate use of physical force and freedom from war and insurgencies? 2 / 4

Allegations of police abuse of suspects and detainees continue. The prison system is overcrowded, and some facilities lack basic amenities like potable water. Prisoners risk ill-treatment and threats by guards, and violence at the hands of other prisoners.

F4. Do laws, policies, and practices guarantee equal treatment of various segments of the population? 2 / 4

Indigenous people continue to suffer widespread societal discrimination, and oil-drilling projects on indigenous lands are frequently carried out without consulting local indigenous communities, as required by the constitution.

The constitution includes the right to decide one's sexual orientation, and discrimination based on sexual orientation is prohibited by law. Nevertheless, LGBT (lesbian, gay, bisexual, and transgender) individuals continue to face discriminatory treatment.

Ecuador is the largest recipient of refugees in Latin America; as of October 2018, approximately 250,000 refugees from Colombia alone had entered Ecuador since the late 1990s. In 2017, the Law on Human Mobility, which secures the rights of refugees, took effect; the law won praise from the Inter-American Commission on Human Rights (IACHR) and the UN High Commissioner for Refugees (UNHCR) for opening new avenues for refugees to claim resident status. However, the political and economic crisis in Venezuela has led to a mass influx of Venezuelan refugees; according to the International Organization for Migration, many have reported facing discrimination and xenophobia.

G. PERSONAL AUTONOMY AND INDIVIDUAL RIGHTS: 10 / 16

G1. Do individuals enjoy freedom of movement, including the ability to change their place of residence, employment, or education? 3 / 4

Freedom of movement outside and inside the country is largely unrestricted. Workers in the palm oil industry, however, have faced restrictions on their movement imposed by employers, including curfews. Individuals may generally determine their place of employment and education.

G2. Are individuals able to exercise the right to own property and establish private businesses without undue interference from state or nonstate actors? 2 / 4

The government does not impose significant restrictions on the right to own property and establish private businesses. However, widespread corruption by both public officials and private-sector actors can obstruct normal business activity and weakens the protection of property rights.

G3. Do individuals enjoy personal social freedoms, including choice of marriage partner and size of family, protection from domestic violence, and control over appearance? 3 / 4

The government has taken steps to protect women's rights through public campaigns and legal measures. Sexual harassment is punishable by up to two years in prison. The criminal code includes femicide as a crime, with penalties reaching 34 years in prison. However, violence against women remains a serious problem, with police reporting 64 cases of femicide between January and October 2018.

The constitution does not provide for same-sex marriage, but civil unions are recognized.

G4. Do individuals enjoy equality of opportunity and freedom from economic exploitation? 2 / 4

Men, women, and children are sometimes subjected to forced labor and sex work in Ecuador; indigenous and Afro-Ecuadorian individuals, as well as migrants and refugees, remain most vulnerable. The government has taken some action to address the problem, including by increasing trafficking-related law enforcement operations. However, services for victims are inadequate, and some public officials believed to be complicit in trafficking operations have escaped punishment.

Egypt

Population: 97,000,000
Capital: Cairo
Political Rights Rating: 6
Civil Liberties Rating: 6
Freedom Rating: 6.0
Freedom Status: Not Free
Electoral Democracy: No

Overview: President Abdel Fattah al-Sisi, who first took power in a July 2013 coup, continues to govern Egypt in an increasingly authoritarian manner. Meaningful political opposition is virtually nonexistent, as both liberal and Islamist activists face criminal prosecution and imprisonment. Terrorism persists in the Sinai Peninsula and has also struck the Egyptian mainland, despite the government's use of aggressive and often abusive tactics to combat it.

KEY DEVELOPMENTS IN 2018:

- In March, President Sisi was reelected with 97 percent of the vote in an election marred by low turnout, the use of state resources and media to support Sisi's candidacy, voter intimidation, and vote buying.
- In January, Sami Anan, Sisi's most prominent challenger, was arrested and detained after he announced his candidacy, while other legitimate opposition candidates were pressured to withdraw, leaving only one progovernment candidate in the race. Many more government critics, opposition figures, and journalists were also arrested in the run-up to the election.
- In February, the military launched a major antiterrorism campaign called Operation Sinai 2018, which has resulted in the deaths of hundreds of fighters affiliated with the Islamic State (IS) militant group and dozens of military personnel in the North Sinai region. The military has also killed dozens of civilians and summarily demolished at least 3,000 businesses and homes over the course of the campaign.
- Two laws ratified in August, the Anti-Cyber and Information Technology Crimes Law and the Media Regulation Law, further threatened freedom of expression and freedom of the press by imposing prison sentences on journalists who "incite violence," giving the government wide latitude to block websites, and granting security services broad surveillance powers over internet users, among other provisions.

POLITICAL RIGHTS: 8 / 40 (–2)

A. ELECTORAL PROCESS: 2 / 12 (–1)

A1. Was the current head of government or other chief national authority elected through free and fair elections? 0 / 4 (–1)

The president is elected by popular vote for up to two terms. In 2013, President Abdel Fattah al-Sisi, then the defense minister and armed forces commander, seized power through a coup that overthrew elected president Mohamed Morsi of the Muslim Brotherhood's Freedom and Justice Party (FJP). In the March 2018 presidential election, Sisi won a second term with 97 percent of the vote, in a process that did not offer voters a genuine choice. Legitimate opposition candidates were pressured to withdraw ahead of campaigning. Ultimately, Sisi faced an approved challenger, Mousa Mostafa Mousa, head of the loyal opposition party Al-Ghad. Mousa had campaigned on Sisi's behalf before entering the race. Prior to voting, Sisi's regime obeyed "few boundaries on its untamed repression of all forms of dissent," according to Human Rights Watch (HRW), detaining and silencing vocal opposition figures. The vote was marred by low turnout, the use of state resources and media to support Sisi's candidacy, voter intimidation, and vote buying. The electoral commission threatened nonvoters with fines in an attempt to increase turnout.

Score Change: The score declined from 1 to 0 because the 2018 presidential election did not offer voters a genuine democratic choice, and polling was marred by voter intimidation and vote buying, among other irregularities.

A2. Were the current national legislative representatives elected through free and fair elections? 1 / 4

Of the 596 members of the unicameral House of Representatives, 448 are directly elected, 120 are elected by party list, and 28 are appointed by the president; members serve five-year terms. Parliamentary elections took place in two stages in 2015. The elections featured low turnout, intimidation, and abuse of state resources. The progovernment coalition For the Love of Egypt, consisting of some 10 parties, won all 120 bloc-vote seats. Independents, a number of whom were aligned with the coalition, won 351 of the 448 constituency seats, and the coalition parties' candidates generally outpolled their rivals in the remaining districts. Just three parties outside For the Love of Egypt won more than 10 seats: Protectors of the Homeland (18), the Republican People's Party (13), and Al-Nour (11), a Salafist group that was the only major Islamist party to participate in the elections. Many parties—including moderate Islamist parties and liberal and leftist factions—boycotted the elections and voiced serious reservations about their fairness, accusing security forces of harassment and intimidation. In 2016, the parties associated with For the Love of Egypt formed a parliamentary bloc, In Support of Egypt, which controlled a majority of the chamber.

As of 2018, Egypt remained without the elected local councils called for in the 2014 constitution, due to ongoing delays in holding the elections. In April, a parliamentary spokesperson announced that municipal elections would likely occur during the first half of 2019, after a draft local administration law is passed. The last councils were elected in 2008 and dissolved in 2011 after the ouster of longtime authoritarian president Hosni Mubarak. Since 2011, government-appointed officials have controlled local governance.

A3. Are the electoral laws and framework fair, and are they implemented impartially by the relevant election management bodies? 1 / 4

The current constitution, passed in 2014, was not drafted in a fair or transparent manner, and the referendum through which it was adopted was tightly controlled, with little opportunity for public debate or an opposition campaign. While the electoral laws themselves might have provided some basis for credible elections, electoral authorities largely failed in practice to ensure an open and competitive campaign environment during the most recent presidential and parliamentary elections.

In 2017, Sisi signed a law creating the National Electoral Commission (NEC), as called for in the 2014 constitution. The commission's board consists of senior judges drawn from some of Egypt's highest courts to serve six-year terms. However, the NEC legislation phases out direct judicial supervision of elections by 2024, which critics argue will damage the integrity of elections and reduce public trust in the results.

B. POLITICAL PLURALISM AND PARTICIPATION: 3 / 16 (–1)

B1. Do the people have the right to organize in different political parties or other competitive political groupings of their choice, and is the system free of undue obstacles to the rise and fall of these competing parties or groupings? 0 / 4 (–1)

Legally, political parties are allowed to form and operate if they meet membership thresholds, pay fees, and comply with other requirements established by law. However, in practice, there are no political parties that offer meaningful opposition to the ruling party. Conditions for opposition parties worsened in 2018, particularly surrounding the presidential election. While most prospective candidates withdrew from the race under government pressure, the most prominent opposition candidate, Sami Anan of the Egypt Arabism Democratic Party, was arrested and detained in January, ending his candidacy. Arrests, harsh prison terms, death sentences, extrajudicial violence, and various forms of pressure targeting activists, parties, and political movements that criticize the government were common in 2018.

Parties formed on the basis of religion are forbidden, and while some Islamist parties still operate in a precarious legal position, the Muslim Brotherhood was outlawed in 2013 as a terrorist organization and its political party, the Freedom and Justice Party, banned. Since then, authorities have systematically persecuted its members and supporters. In September,

Muslim Brotherhood leader Mohamed Badie and 65 others were sentenced to life in prison for a 2013 attack on a police station.

Score Change: The score declined from 1 to 0 because opposition leaders and candidates were intimidated, detained, and prevented from engaging in political activities, especially surrounding the 2018 presidential election.

B2. Is there a realistic opportunity for the opposition to increase its support or gain power through elections? 0 / 4

The persecution of Sisi's potential challengers in the 2018 presidential election illustrated the regime's determination to eliminate any opportunity for a peaceful change in leadership. By tightly controlling the electoral process, intimidating presidential candidates into withdrawing, and offering credible opposition parties no significant space to function effectively, the government makes it nearly impossible for the opposition to gain power through elections.

B3. Are the people's political choices free from domination by the military, foreign powers, religious hierarchies, economic oligarchies, or any other powerful group that is not democratically accountable? 1 / 4

Since the 2013 coup, the military has dominated the political system, with most power and patronage flowing from Sisi and his allies in the armed forces and security agencies. Most of Egypt's provincial governors are former military or police commanders.

B4. Do various segments of the population (including ethnic, religious, gender, LGBT, and other relevant groups) have full political rights and electoral opportunities? 2/ 4

The constitution and Egyptian laws grant political rights to all citizens regardless of religion, gender, race, ethnicity, or any other such distinction. However, women, Christians, Shiite Muslims, people of color, and LGBT (lesbian, gay, bisexual, and transgender) people face indirect forms of discrimination that limit their political participation to varying degrees.

Coptic Christians, who account for some 10 percent of the population, are allocated 24 of the parliament's 120 party-list seats. Thirty-six Christians were elected in 2015, and some were also among the lawmakers appointed by the president. Thanks in large part to quotas, women won 75 seats in the 596-seat parliament in 2015, and another 14 were appointed by the president. The party-list quotas also set aside small numbers of seats for workers and farmers, people under 35, people with disabilities, and Egyptians living abroad.

C. FUNCTIONING OF GOVERNMENT: 3 / 12

C1. Do the freely elected head of government and national legislative representatives determine the policies of the government? 1 / 4

President Sisi, who was not freely elected, ruled by decree until the new parliament was seated in 2016, as the remaining chamber of the old legislature had been dissolved at the time of the coup. Since then, the parliament has played a growing if still modest role in forming and debating laws and policies. However, it does not provide a meaningful check on executive power, which Sisi continued to consolidate in 2018.

The 2014 constitution increased the military's independence from civilian oversight, including through the selection process for the post of defense minister, who must be a military officer. Sisi continues to rule in a style that entrenches military privilege and shields the armed forces from accountability for their actions.

C2. Are safeguards against official corruption strong and effective? 1 / 4 .

Corruption is pervasive at all levels of government. Official mechanisms for investigating and punishing corrupt activity remain weak and ineffective. Under a 2015 amendment to the penal code, defendants in financial corruption cases can avoid imprisonment by paying restitution, and punishments are typically light in practice. The Administrative Control Authority (ACA), the body responsible for most anticorruption initiatives, often pursues politically motivated corruption cases and operates opaquely.

In 2018, several high-level officials were prosecuted for corruption, including the former governors of Helwan and Menoufia, who were convicted on bribery charges and received prison sentences of 5 and 10 years, respectively. It is unclear whether these cases represent a meaningful commitment to address corruption on the part of the government.

C3. Does the government operate with openness and transparency? 1 / 4

The Sisi administration has offered very little transparency regarding government spending and operations. Civil society groups and independent journalists have few opportunities to comment on or influence state policies and legislation. The military is notoriously opaque with respect to its core expenditures and its extensive business interests, including in major infrastructure and land-development projects. This leads to an almost complete lack of accountability for any malpractice.

CIVIL LIBERTIES: 14 / 60 (−2)
D. FREEDOM OF EXPRESSION AND BELIEF: 4 / 16 (−1)
D1. Are there free and independent media? 1 / 4

The Egyptian media sector is dominated by progovernment outlets; most critical or opposition-oriented outlets were shut down in the wake of the coup. Moreover, in recent years, a number of private television channels and newspapers have been launched or acquired by progovernment businessmen and individuals with ties to the military and intelligence services. Journalists who fail to align their reporting with the interests of owners or the government risk dismissal. Egyptian journalists also continued to face arrest for their work. According to Reporters without Borders (RSF), more than 20 journalists were arrested in the six months leading up to the 2018 presidential elections, and as of December, the Committee to Protect Journalists (CPJ) reported that 25 journalists were imprisoned. The disappearance of former member of parliament and journalist Mostafa al-Naggar highlighted the dangers faced by individuals who speak out against the regime. Naggar had been sentenced to three years in prison for "insulting the judiciary" before his disappearance in September. Authorities denied that Naggar was in government custody, and his whereabouts remained unknown at the end of the year.

Two new laws ratified by President Sisi in August posed additional threats to press freedom. The Media Regulation Law imposes prison sentences on journalists who "incite violence" and permits censorship that does not require judicial approval, among other provisions. The Anti-Cyber and Information Technology Crimes Law is ostensibly intended to combat extremism and terrorism, but allows authorities to block any website considered to be a threat to national security, a broad provision which is vulnerable to abuse. Nearly 500 websites, including news sites, were blocked between May 2017 and February 2018, according to the Association for Freedom of Thought and Expression (AFTE), a nongovernmental organization (NGO).

D2. Are individuals free to practice and express their religious faith or nonbelief in public and private? 1 / 4

While Article 2 of the 2014 constitution declares Islam to be the official religion of the state, Article 64 states that "freedom of belief is absolute." Most Egyptians are Sunni Muslims. Coptic Christians form a substantial minority, and there are smaller numbers of Shiite Muslims, non-Coptic Christian denominations, and other groups. Religious minorities and atheists have faced persecution and violence, with Copts in particular suffering numerous cases of forced displacement, physical assaults, bomb and arson attacks, and blocking of church construction in recent years.

D3. Is there academic freedom, and is the educational system free from extensive political indoctrination? 1 / 4

The state controls education and curriculums in public schools and to a lesser degree in some of the country's private institutions. Faculty members and departments have some autonomy in shaping the specific syllabus for their courses, though many scholars self-censor to avoid any punitive measures.

The government continued its efforts to constrain academic research on sensitive topics in 2018. In May, University of Washington graduate student Walid Salem, who was researching Egypt's judiciary, was arrested and detained for over six months on suspicion of spreading false news and membership in a terrorist organization, but he was not formally charged. Although he was released in December, Salem still faced potential criminal charges at year's end.

Despite a ban on political protests, universities have been a center of antigovernment demonstrations and the target of violent government crackdowns since the 2013 coup. A 2017 AFTE report on university students' rights documented 1,181 arrests, 1,051 disciplinary sanctions such as expulsion, 65 military trials, and 21 extrajudicial killings between 2013 and 2016. A 2015 decree allows for the dismissal of university professors who engage in on-campus political activity, and in 2016 the government reportedly began imposing more systematic requirements for academics to obtain approval from security officials for travel abroad.

D4. Are individuals free to express their personal views on political or other sensitive topics without fear of surveillance or retribution? 1 / 4 (−1)

The security services have reportedly upgraded their surveillance equipment and techniques in recent years so as to better monitor social media platforms and mobile phone applications. Progovernment media figures and state officials regularly call for national unity and suggest that only enemies of the state would criticize the authorities. The spate of arrests of government critics ahead of the 2018 presidential election sent a clear message that voicing dissent could result in arrest and imprisonment, which has led to more self-censorship and guarded discussion among ordinary Egyptians.

Both of the new laws ratified in August 2018 to regulate the media and the internet posed serious threats to online expression. The Media Regulation Law subjects any social media user with more than 5,000 followers to government monitoring and regulation. The Anti-Cyber and Information Technology Crimes Law requires telecommunications companies to store users' data for 180 days, enabling widespread government surveillance, and vaguely worded language in the law criminalizes online expression that "threatens national security," which rights activists suspect could be used to crack down on online political discourse.

Score Change: The score declined from 2 to 1 due to the string of arrests of opposition figures ahead of the 2018 presidential election, which led to greater self-censorship among ordinary Egyptians; and the passage of the Media Regulation Law and the Anti-Cyber and Information Technology Crimes Law, both of which threaten online expression.

E. ASSOCIATIONAL AND ORGANIZATIONAL RIGHTS: 1 / 12 (−1)

E1. Is there freedom of assembly? 0 / 4 (−1)

According to the constitution, freedom of assembly should not be restricted. However, a 2013 decree regulating protests severely constrained such rights, giving police great leeway to ban and forcibly disperse gatherings of 10 or more people, prohibiting all protests at places of worship, and requiring protest organizers to inform police at least three days in advance. Thousands of people have since been arrested under the law. The Interior Ministry can ban, postpone, or relocate protests with a court's approval. In July 2018, 75 protesters were sentenced to death for their role in a 2013 demonstration against the overthrow of former president Morsi. The severity of the crackdown on assembly rights has made protests extremely rare.

Score Change: The score declined from 1 to 0 because the crackdown on assembly rights, including the death sentence imposed on 75 protesters for a 2013 demonstration, has made protests extremely rare.

E2. Is there freedom for nongovernmental organizations, particularly those that are engaged in human rights- and governance-related work? 0 / 4

NGOs in Egypt have faced mass closures as well as harassment in the form of office raids, arrests of members, lengthy legal cases, and restrictions on travel in recent years. A highly restrictive law on the creation and regulation of NGOs was signed by the president in 2017. The law established a new regulatory body dominated by security agencies; banned NGOs from engaging in work deemed to harm "national security, public order, public morality, or public health"; and required the regulator's approval for any field research or polling and any type of cooperation with foreign NGOs. All NGO funding and basic management decisions are also subject to the regulator's approval. Violations of the law can lead to fines and up to five years in prison. Although 43 employees of several international and local democracy-support NGOs were acquitted in December 2018 on charges from 2013 of illegally receiving foreign funding for their operations, the climate for NGOs remained highly repressive throughout the year.

E3. Is there freedom for trade unions and similar professional or labor organizations? 1 / 4

The government only recognizes unions affiliated with the state-controlled Egyptian Trade Union Federation, which held its first elections in 12 years in May 2018, amid accusations that the government prevented independent labor leaders from running. While Article 15 of the constitution provides for the right to organize peaceful strikes, they are not tolerated in practice, and the 2013 law on protests prohibits gatherings that impede labor and production. Striking workers are regularly arrested and prosecuted, particularly since labor protests increased in 2016; workers at military-owned businesses are subject to trials by military courts.

In 2017, the parliament approved a law on trade unions that forced independent unions to dissolve and resubmit applications for recognition, effectively compelling them to join the state-controlled federation. The law also set membership threshold requirements that made unionization impossible in enterprises with fewer than 150 workers. Employers who violate the law face limited financial penalties, while workers involved with illegal unions could face imprisonment.

F. RULE OF LAW: 3 / 16

F1. Is there an independent judiciary? 1 / 4

The executive branch exerts influence over the courts, which typically protect the interests of the government and military and have often disregarded due process and other basic safeguards in cases against the government's political opponents. In 2017, the president signed an amendment to the Judicial Authority Law that gave the president the power to appoint the heads of four key judicial bodies: the State Lawsuits Authority, the Administrative Prosecution, the Court of Cassation, and the State Council. Prior to the law's passage, the heads were selected based on seniority.

Some of the government critics and opposition figures arrested before and after the 2018 presidential election have been prosecuted in the Emergency State Security Courts created when President Sisi declared a state of emergency in 2017 (which has been repeatedly renewed through 2018). President Sisi has control over these courts, whose decisions are subject to executive approval; the president can suspend any of the court's rulings or order a retrial.

F2. Does due process prevail in civil and criminal matters? 1 / 4

Although the constitution limits military trials of civilians to crimes directly involving the military, its personnel, or its property, a 2014 presidential decree placed all "public and vital facilities" under military jurisdiction, resulting in the referral of thousands of civilian defendants to military courts. Charges brought in military courts are often vague or fabricated, defendants are denied due process, and basic evidentiary standards are routinely disregarded. The Emergency State Security Courts also disregard due process protections, including the right to appeal convictions.

A series of mass trials in recent years have resulted in harsh sentences, including life imprisonment or the death penalty, based on negligible evidence and most likely related to political motivations. They have generally targeted suspected members of the Muslim Brotherhood, although journalists and non-Brotherhood activists were also convicted in mass trials in 2018. However, appeals of the initial verdicts have resulted in retrials, reduced sentences, and acquittals in a number of cases. Among other prominent examples during 2018, the Cairo Criminal Court in September ordered the retrial of Mohamed Badie and other senior Muslim Brotherhood members, who had received life sentences in 2015 for violence surrounding Morsi's 2013 removal.

F3. Is there protection from the illegitimate use of physical force and freedom from war and insurgencies? 0 / 4

Police brutality and impunity for abuses by security forces were catalysts for the 2011 uprising against Mubarak, but no reforms have since been enacted. Reports of torture, alleged extrajudicial killings, and forced disappearances continued throughout 2018, with NGOs documenting hundreds of cases. Prison conditions are very poor; inmates are subject to torture, overcrowding, and a lack of sanitation and medical care. A 2015 antiterrorism law provided a vague definition for terrorism and granted law enforcement personnel sweeping powers and immunity.

Fighting continued between security forces and IS-affiliated militants in the North Sinai region in 2018. In February, the government launched a major antiterrorism campaign called Operation Sinai 2018, which has resulted in the deaths of hundreds of militants and dozens of military personnel. According to the Egyptian Institute for Studies, the army has killed dozens of civilians while carrying out the campaign. A military lockdown has left the region's 400,000 residents without basic services.

According to the government, the number of terrorist attacks in Egypt decreased from 50 in 2017 to 8 in 2018.

F4. Do laws, policies, and practices guarantee equal treatment of various segments of the population? 1 / 4

Women enjoy legal equality on many issues, and their court testimony is equal to that of men except in cases involving personal status matters such as divorce, which are more influenced by religious law. In practice, however, women face extensive discrimination in employment, among other disadvantages. Other segments of the population that face various forms of harassment and discrimination include religious minorities, people of color from southern Egypt, migrants and refugees from sub-Saharan Africa, people with disabilities, and LGBT people.

While same-sex sexual activity is not explicitly banned, LGBT people have been charged with prostitution or "debauchery." After concert attendees waved a rainbow flag in 2017, the authorities launched a crackdown on suspected LGBT people, detaining nearly 60 people amid reports of abuse in custody and imposing prison sentences of up to six years. The persecution of LGBT Egyptians continued in 2018, with police officers using the dating app Grindr to entrap gay men, and several media outlets publishing stories meant to stoke hostility towards LGBT people.

G. PERSONAL AUTONOMY AND INDIVIDUAL RIGHTS: 6 / 16

G1. Do individuals enjoy freedom of movement, including the ability to change their place of residence, employment, or education? 1 / 4

The constitution guarantees freedom of movement, but internal travel and access are restricted tightly in North Sinai and to a lesser extent in other governorates along Egypt's borders. Sinai residents are subject to curfews, checkpoints, and other obstacles to travel.

Individuals seeking to change their place of employment or education can encounter bureaucratic barriers and scrutiny from security officials. In addition, a growing list of rights activists, journalists, political party members, bloggers, and academics have been subjected to arbitrary bans on international travel in recent years. A number of foreign researchers or activists have been expelled or denied entry to the country.

G2. Are individuals able to exercise the right to own property and establish private businesses without undue interference from state or non-state actors? 2 / 4

While a new 2017 investment law was designed to encourage private investment in underdeveloped areas, bureaucratic barriers and related corruption remain serious problems, and the growing role of military-affiliated companies has hindered and crowded out private businesses. Property rights in Sinai and other border areas are affected by the activities of security forces. In 2018, the military expanded the summary demolitions of homes and commercial buildings beyond the security buffer zone, destroying at least 3,000 structures as part of Operation Sinai 2018.

Women are at a legal disadvantage in property and inheritance matters, typically receiving half the inheritance due to a man. Societal biases also discourage women's ownership of land.

G3. Do individuals enjoy personal social freedoms, including choice of marriage partner and size of family, protection from domestic violence, and control over appearance? 2 / 4

Domestic violence, sexual harassment, and female genital mutilation (FGM) are still among the most acute problems in Egyptian society. The country has adopted laws to combat these practices in recent years, and FGM is reportedly becoming less common over time.

However, the effectiveness of such laws is hindered by societal resistance, poor enforcement, abuses by the police themselves, and lack of adequate protection for witnesses, which deter victims from reporting abuse and harassment. Spousal rape is not a crime.

Personal status rules based on religious affiliation put women at a disadvantage in marriage, divorce, and custody matters. Muslim women cannot marry non-Muslim men, for example, and the Coptic Church rarely permits divorce.

G4. Do individuals enjoy equality of opportunity and freedom from economic exploitation? 1 / 4

Egyptian women and children, migrants from sub-Saharan Africa and Asia, and Syrian refugees are vulnerable to forced labor and sex trafficking in Egypt. The Egyptian authorities routinely punish individuals for offenses that stemmed directly from their circumstances as trafficking victims. Military conscripts are exploited as cheap labor to work on military- or state-affiliated development projects.

In late 2016, Egypt removed a number of controls on currency exchange, imports, and foreign loans. Combined with government efforts to reduce budget deficits and subsidies, these moves continue to spur inflation which causes acute economic hardship for many Egyptians.

El Salvador

Population: 6,500,000
Capital: San Salvador
Political Rights Rating: 2
Civil Liberties Rating: 3
Freedom Rating: 2.5
Freedom Status: Free
Electoral Democracy: Yes

Overview: Elections in El Salvador are largely credible and free. However, corruption is a serious problem that undermines democracy and rule of law, and violence remains a grave problem. Authorities have pursued a harsh, militarized response to the country's gangs, resulting in allegations of abuse. The country has a lively press and civil society sector, though journalists risk harassment and violence in connection with work related to gang activity or corruption.

KEY DEVELOPMENTS IN 2018:

- The Nationalist Republican Alliance (ARENA) posted the strongest performance legislative elections held in March, though votes for both ARENA and El Salvador's other dominant party, the Farabundo Martí National Liberation Front (FMLN) declined compared to past elections, with smaller parties benefiting from the difference. Monitors said the polls were generally peaceful and well conducted.
- The year saw mixed results in the fight against corruption. Former president Antonio "Tony" Saca was given a 10-year prison sentence after pleading guilty to charges of embezzlement and money laundering. However, the year also saw efforts by elected officials to obstruct the work of Attorney General Douglas Meléndez, and the legislature voted against reinstating him to a second term at year's end.

- The Constitutional Chamber of the Supreme Court was left vacant for several months while lawmakers wrangled to see their preferred candidates confirmed to its benches.
- The homicide rate continued to decline, but remained high, with roughly 3,300 homicides during the year. However, the number of disappearances increased to over 3,500—about 200 more than in 2017.

POLITICAL RIGHTS: 32 / 40 (−2)

A. ELECTORAL PROCESS: 11 / 12

A1. Was the current head of government or other chief national authority elected through free and fair elections? 4 / 4

El Salvador's president is directly elected for a five-year term. Salvador Sánchez Cerén, the candidate of the FMLN, won the 2014 presidential election. The runner-up, Norman Quijano of ARENA, accused the Supreme Electoral Tribunal (TSE) of fraud, but domestic and international observers considered the elections competitive and credible.

Municipal elections in March 2018 resulted in a decisive win for ARENA candidates. A European Union (EU) observation mission said that the elections were generally well run, but noted that some incumbent mayors used office staff for campaign activities, and handed out food and other goods to voters.

A2. Were the current national legislative representatives elected through free and fair elections? 3 / 4

The 84-member, unicameral Legislative Assembly is elected for three years. In the March 2018 elections, ARENA won 37 seats, the FMLN won 23, Grand Alliance for National Unity (GANA) won 10, and the National Conciliation Party (PCN) won 9; the rest went to smaller parties and coalitions. Votes for the ARENA and FMLN parties declined compared to previous legislative elections. Turnout was roughly 46 percent.

The EU observation mission declared the elections well organized, transparent, and the calmest since the 1992 peace accords. However, the mission noted a lack of voter education, particularly regarding the issue of cross-voting, a procedure that allows voters to vote for candidates from more than one party list.

A3. Are the electoral laws and framework fair, and are they implemented impartially by the relevant election management bodies? 4 / 4

The country's electoral framework has undergone a number of changes in recent years, at times contributing to inefficiencies and confusion surrounding electoral processes. Implementation of a 2015 reform by which citizens, as opposed to partisan representatives, are called on to oversee vote counting was delayed ahead of the 2018 polls, resulting in inadequate training for the citizens drafted. Additionally, there were reports that the TSE dismissed nonpartisans in favor of partisans.

Separately, in February 2018 a list of donors (from 2006–17) to political parties was published for the first time, marking an improvement in campaign transparency.

B. POLITICAL PLURALISM AND PARTICIPATION: 13 / 16 (−1)

B1. Do the people have the right to organize in different political parties or other competitive political groupings of their choice, and is the system free of undue obstacles to the rise and fall of these competing parties or groupings? 4 / 4

Salvadorans are free to organize in different political parties or organizations. While two parties, FMLN and ARENA, have dominated the country's system for the past few decades, new parties have emerged and are able to participate and compete in political processes. In 2018, the first independent candidate was elected to the legislature.

Campaign donation records released in 2018 showed that between 2006 and 2017, ARENA received more donations than any other party, and that most of its donations had come from companies. The FMLN collected the second-most donations, with most of those funds coming from individuals.

B2. Is there a realistic opportunity for the opposition to increase its support or gain power through elections? 4 / 4

Opposition parties have the ability to increase support and gain power through elections. Historically, executive elections are closely contested between the two main parties, but in legislative elections, smaller parties stand to gain power.

B3. Are the people's political choices free from domination by the military, foreign powers, religious hierarchies, economic oligarchies, or any other powerful group that is not democratically accountable? 2 / 4 (−1)

Criminal groups hold significant influence over Salvadoran political life. Political candidates face threats from such groups, though there are also persistent reports of negotiations and transactions between political parties and criminal organizations. For example, party leaders negotiate with criminal leaders in order to secure permission to hold rallies or otherwise operate in gang-controlled areas; police have asserted that all major political parties engage in such negotiations, and some politicians upon questioning have openly admitted to it, describing the deals as a reality that accompanies political operations in parts the country. Parties have paid gangs to coerce or intimidate voters into casting ballots for particular parties or candidates. Parties also hire gangs to provide security for their events. Transactions between parties and gangs also involve deals in which gang leaders receive special access to politicians, or a party's investment in social services for the families of gang members.

Since the transition to democracy, the military has been an apolitical institution—though it has not always cooperated with civilian authorities.

Score Change: The score declined from 3 to 2 due to the ongoing, significant influence of criminal organizations on the behavior of voters, politicians, and political parties.

B4. Do various segments of the population (including ethnic, religious, gender, LGBT, and other relevant groups) have full political rights and electoral opportunities? 3 / 4

Ethnic, religious, and gender groups, and LGBT (lesbian, gay, bisexual, and transgender) people, have full political and electoral opportunities, but are underrepresented in the legislature and in high-level government positions. In 2018, the first openly transgender candidate ran for election, for a seat on the San Salvador Municipal Council. A 2013 statute requires that 30 percent of legislative and municipal candidates be women, and just over 30 percent of seats in the Legislative Assembly were held by women following the 2018 elections. However, only 10 percent of women held mayoral seats after the year's municipal elections, and the interests of women are not well represented in practice.

C. FUNCTIONING OF GOVERNMENT: 8 / 12 (−1)

C1. Do the freely elected head of government and national legislative representatives determine the policies of the government? 3 / 4

The freely elected government is generally able to determine policies. However, the government lacks authority over some areas that are controlled by criminal groups, and public officials are known to collaborate with criminal organizations. Several mayors have been accused of facilitating extortion rackets, assassinations, and buying campaign support from gangs and criminal networks.

Salvadorans continue to express concern that multinational corporations exert influence over local and national government officials. Separately, in August 2018, in the wake of a Chinese lobbying effort, the government announced that it would break ties with Taiwan and establish diplomatic relations with China. The US threatened severe sanctions over the move, but eventually backed down.

C2. Are safeguards against official corruption strong and effective? 2 / 4 (−1)

Corruption is a serious problem in El Salvador. The office of the attorney general, the Probity Section of the Supreme Court, and other institutions continued to pursue an active agenda against official corruption in 2018.

However, the year saw the continued obstruction and underresourcing of the attorney general's office and other institutions working to combat entrenched corruption. In August, President Sánchez Cerén vetoed an amendment that would have granted broad autonomy to the attorney general's financial intelligence unit, a move Attorney General Douglas Meléndez said would compromise his ability to investigate financial crimes. El Salvador was suspended from a key multinational financial intelligence group due to Sánchez Cerén's veto, and Meléndez alleged that Sánchez Cerén stood to benefit from the suspension because he would no longer be obligated to respond to a number of information requests about his personal dealings. In December, the legislature voted not to reinstate Meléndez, who during his career as attorney general had prosecuted former president Saca and attempted to extradite former president Mauricio Funes. His successor has no experience in constitutional or criminal law.

Meanwhile, major corruption cases proceeded, but with somewhat mixed results. In August, former president Saca pleaded guilty to embezzlement and money laundering of public funds exceeding $300 million. In exchange for his plea agreement, his sentence was reduced from 30 to 10 years in prison, though critics argued that the sentence was too light. Earlier, in June, an arrest warrant was issued for former president Funes, who had been convicted in absentia of illicit enrichment in 2017; related arrest warrants were also issued against 31 people involved in the same scandal, which prosecutors dubbed the "public looting" case and involved the alleged embezzlement of $351 million from the state bank, much of which was carried out in cash-filled trash bags. In a separate case, arrest warrants were issued in October for Funes, former attorney general Luis Martínez, businessman Enrique Rais, and nearly two dozen others accused of providing perks to the former attorney general's office in exchange for favoritism in corruption cases against political officials and business elites. At year's end, Funes remained in Nicaragua, where he has been granted asylum; Rais was reportedly in Switzerland.

Score Change: The score declined from 3 to 2 due to the obstruction of the attorney general's office in its pursuit of high-profile cases.

C3. Does the government operate with openness and transparency? 3 / 4

There have been advances in the implementation of the Access to Public Information Law, but challenges remain, including delays in responding to information requests and the denial of requests on dubious grounds, or for reasons not sufficiently explained. In 2017, the Constitutional Chamber added additional limits to the law's reach when ruling on a case involving the travel expenses of former president Funes. According to the ruling, the current government did not have to disclose information related to incidents that took place during previous administrations, because it would not have sufficient information regarding those events.

In 2018, media reports revealed that presidents Sánchez Cerén, Saca, and Funes had redirected tens of millions of dollars to secret discretionary funds. Auditors had reportedly noted the movement of funds, but were unable to access information about how they were spent.

CIVIL LIBERTIES: 35 / 60 (-1)

D. FREEDOM OF EXPRESSION AND BELIEF: 12 / 16

D1. Are there free and independent media? 2 / 4

The Constitution provides for freedom of the press. In practice, the media scene is robust, but reporters face significant challenges. Harassment and acts of violence following coverage of corruption and gang violence have led reporters to engage in self-censorship. Officials at times prevent journalists from taking audio or video recordings of government affairs. In 2018, recording devices were banned during former president Saca's corruption trial.

Most of the country depends on privately owned television and radio networks for news, and ownership in the broadcast sector is highly concentrated. Access to the internet is unrestricted. Online outlets like El Faro and Revista Factum are critical sources of independent reporting.

D2. Are individuals free to practice and express their religious faith or nonbelief in public and private? 4 / 4

Religious freedom is generally respected. However, religious leaders working with former gang members or who have been critical of the government have faced harassment.

D3. Is there academic freedom, and is the educational system free from extensive political indoctrination? 3 / 4

Academic freedom is respected and the educational system is generally free from extensive political indoctrination. However, intimidation and violence by gang members against teachers and students continues to present a challenge to the education system.

D4. Are individuals free to express their personal views on political or other sensitive topics without fear of surveillance or retribution? 3 / 4

While private discussion is generally free, the prevalence of gang activity requires many Salvadorans to curtail discussion of gang-related and other sensitive topics outside of their homes.

E. ASSOCIATIONAL AND ORGANIZATIONAL RIGHTS: 8 / 12

E1. Is there freedom of assembly? 3 / 4

Freedom of assembly is generally upheld, and public protests and gatherings are permitted. However, due to the prevalence of violence in El Salvador, the safety of participants is impossible to guarantee.

Protesters clashed with police forces during June 2018 demonstrations in the capital against the privatization of water services. The police used tear gas to disperse the crowd, and protestors responded by throwing rocks at the national assembly building, resulting in damage.

E2. Is there freedom for nongovernmental organizations, particularly those that are engaged in human rights- and governance-related work? 3 / 4

Nongovernmental organizations (NGOs) operate freely and play an important role in society and policymaking. However, groups involved with human rights– and governance-related topics sometimes face threats and extortion attempts from criminal groups. Impunity for such attacks, as well as occasional pressure on NGOs by police, has prompted some observers to question the government's commitment to the protection of freedom of association and human rights.

Several NGOs and associations have reported discovering microphones or other listening devices on their premises in recent years, including the National Association of Private Companies (ANEP), the Salvadoran Foundation for Economic and Social Development (FUSADES), and the National Development Foundation (FUNDE).

Land rights defender Dina Yeseni Puente was murdered in August 2018 in Mesas de Jujutla. The motive was unknown, but there was suspicion that she was killed in connection with her activism.

E3. Is there freedom for trade unions and similar professional or labor organizations? 2 / 4

Labor unions have long faced obstacles in a legal environment that has traditionally favored business interests, including by mandating only light penalties for employers who interfere with strikes. The law prohibits strikes in sectors deemed essential, but is vague about the type of work falling within this designation.

F. RULE OF LAW: 7 / 16 (−1)

F1. Is there an independent judiciary? 2 / 4 (−1)

Judicial independence is not consistently respected by the government, and the judicial system is hampered by corruption. The legislature does not always observe Supreme Court rulings. Powerful individuals can evade justice by exerting pressure on the judiciary.

While the Supreme Court's Constitutional Chamber has been relatively well-regarded, a 2018 standoff over nominees to its benches reflected the politicization of judicial appointment procedures, and prompted criticism from some analysts who said the justices eventually selected comprised a weakened court. Firstly, candidate screening processes by national bar associations and the National Council of the Judiciary (CNJ) meant to vet candidates for integrity and professionalism were criticized as inadequate. After the mandated 30 candidates were selected through the screening procedures, the chamber's seats remained vacant for several months past the deadline upon which they were have to been filled, as legislators engaged in extended interparty wrangling over which candidates could gain enough support to achieve confirmation. There were also allegations that members of the legislature facing corruption investigations by the Supreme Court's Probity Section sought to nominate judges that were unqualified, had apparent conflicts of interest, or had dubious track records with regard to corruption cases. The seats were eventually filled in November. Legislators openly admitted that the aim of the interparty negotiations was to see that each of the involved parties was able to secure a candidate they believed would rule in their party's favor.

Score Change: The score declined from 3 to 2 because a months-long standoff over nominees to Supreme Court's Constitutional Chamber reflected the politicization of judicial appointment procedures and inadequacies in related screening processes.

F2. Does due process prevail in civil and criminal matters? 2 / 4

Due process rights are guaranteed by the constitution, but upheld inconsistently. Interpreters are not always provided for defendants who do not speak Spanish. Rights advocates report that police have carried out arbitrary arrests and detentions as part of the country's crackdown on gangs. In 2018, there were concerns about the selection process for the new attorney general. Four of the seven members of congress in charge of selecting the next attorney general had been accused of various forms of corruption.

There was some progress in addressing crimes committed during El Salvador's civil war following the 2016 Supreme Court ruling that the Amnesty Law, which prevented the prosecution of civil war crimes, was unconstitutional. The trial on the massacre at El Mozote, an attack that killed almost 1,000 civilians in 1981, continued since being reopened in 2016. In October 2018, just days after Archbishop Óscar Romero was canonized, an arrest warrant was issued for his killer, a former military officer. Romero was murdered in 1980, presumably by a right-wing death squad for criticizing the government.

Despite this progress, in July the Supreme Court ruled that the government had failed to provide restorative justice to victims, and ordered the Defense Ministry to preserve its archives and make them available.

F3. Is there protection from the illegitimate use of physical force and freedom from war and insurgencies? 1 / 4

Violence, much of which is linked to criminal gangs, remains a grave problem. However, the official homicide rate continued to decline in 2018; police reported that there were roughly 3,300 homicides during the year, compared to about 3,900 in 2017, 5,300 in 2016 and 6,700 in 2015. However, the number of disappearances increased to over 3,500 in 2018—about 200 more than the previous year—raising questions about whether homicides had actually been reduced.

Police have been implicated in hundreds of extrajudicial killings as part of an ongoing militarized response to the country's criminal gangs, and in February 2018, the attorney general's office formally accused high-ranking military officials of ordering the extrajudicial killings of suspected gang members. However, concerns remain that senior-level officials are evading prosecution. Additionally, several police officers were convicted in 2018 of participating in extrajudicial killings. Gangs, in turn, continue to target members of security forces and their families.

Prisons remain extremely overcrowded, and conditions within can be lethal due to disease, lack of adequate medical care, and the risk of attack by other inmates. In August 2018, the legislature voted to make permanent the "extraordinary measures" implemented in 2016 to increase security in prisons. Human rights groups and the UN High Commissioner for Human Rights criticized the decision, with the latter saying that conditions permitted under the measures led him to the conclusion that "these are implemented for the primary purpose of dehumanizing the detainees." Nearly 30 percent of people held in prison are in pretrial detention.

F4. Do laws, policies, and practices guarantee equal treatment of various segments of the population? 2 / 4

Women are granted equal rights under the law, but are often subject to discrimination. Indigenous people face poverty, unemployment, and labor discrimination. Discrimination on the basis of sexual orientation is prevalent, and LGBT people and groups are often the targets of hate crimes and violence, including by state security agents.

Underrepresented populations, particularly internally displaced persons and LGBT people, have limited access to the justice system. However, in a development reflecting increasing attention to discrimination against LGBT people, the government in April 2018 approved an Institutional Policy for the Care of the LGBT Population. Officials signaled the government's commitment to its tenets in public statements and events, but its practical effect remains to be seen.

G. PERSONAL AUTONOMY AND INDIVIDUAL RIGHTS: 8 / 16

G1. Do individuals enjoy freedom of movement, including the ability to change their place of residence, employment, or education? 2 / 4

Freedom of travel within El Salvador is complicated by gang activity. The MS-13 and Barrio 18 gangs control certain neighborhoods, making it dangerous for residents to travel, work, and attend school. The Internal Displacement Monitoring Center (IDMC) has estimated that hundreds of thousands of people have been displaced by violence in recent years.

In July 2018, the Supreme Court ruled that the government had failed to protect victims forcibly displaced by violence, and gave the government six months to develop policies and legislation to protect and assist victims of displacement.

G2. Are individuals able to exercise the right to own property and establish private businesses without undue interference from state or nonstate actors? 2 / 4

Businesses and private citizens are regularly subject to extortion. Indigenous people face difficulties securing land rights and accessing credit.

G3. Do individuals enjoy personal social freedoms, including choice of marriage partner and size of family, protection from domestic violence, and control over appearance? 2 / 4

Abortion is punishable by imprisonment, including in cases where a woman's life is at risk due to her pregnancy, and the Constitutional Chamber affirmed in 2013 that the "rights of the mother cannot be privileged over the fetus." Some women have been jailed despite credible claims that their pregnancies ended due to miscarriage.

Domestic and sexual violence remains high. There were approximately 380 femicides in 2018, though that was down from 468 in 2017. In one prominent case, *La Prensa Gráfica* journalist Karla Turcios was murdered by her husband in April 2018.

Adolescent pregnancy is a serious problem in El Salvador. Between 2013 and 2015, adolescent pregnancies accounted for one out of every three pregnancies in El Salvador. Many are the result of sexual assault.

G4. Do individuals enjoy equality of opportunity and freedom from economic exploitation? 2 / 4

El Salvador remains a source, transit, and destination country for the trafficking of women and children, though some sex trafficking cases have been prosecuted. There are instances of forced labor in the construction and informal sectors. The U.S. Department of State's 2018 *Trafficking in Persons* report noted that El Salvador has investigated and prosecuted more trafficking cases, opened new victim services offices, and introduced a new trafficking awareness campaign.

Equatorial Guinea

Population: 1,300,000
Capital: Malabo
Political Rights Rating: 7
Civil Liberties Rating: 7
Freedom Rating: 7.0
Freedom Status: Not Free
Electoral Democracy: No

Overview: Equatorial Guinea holds regular elections, but the voting is neither free nor fair. The current president, who took power in a military coup that deposed his uncle, has led a highly repressive authoritarian regime since 1979. Oil wealth and political power are concentrated in the hands of the president's family. The government frequently detains the few opposition politicians in the country, cracks down on civil society groups, and censors journalists. The judiciary is under presidential control, and security forces engage in torture and other violence with impunity.

KEY DEVELOPMENTS IN 2018:

- In February, 21 members of the main opposition Convergence for Innovation (CI) party, including Jesús Mitogo, its only member of parliament, were sentenced to 30 years in prison on charges including sedition, attacks on authority, and causing serious bodily harm. The prosecutions were related to a late 2017 confrontation between CI demonstrators and police who had attempted to stop the rally, in which several police officers were injured.
- The same month, a court ordered the CI dissolved on grounds that it undermined state security.
- In October, the CI said 34 of its members including Mitogo had received presidential pardons. It said the detained party members had been subjected to torture, and one had died from resulting injuries.
- The political cartoonist Ramón Nsé Esono Ebalé was released in March after a police officer admitted that the state's charges of money laundering and counterfeiting had been fabricated. There has been no accountability for the fraudulent arrest.
- In January, authorities announced that security agents, in cooperation with Cameroonian forces, had prevented armed attackers from launching a coup from Cameroon, and that the alleged attackers had been recruited by "certain radical opposition parties."

POLITICAL RIGHTS: 0 / 40 (−1)

A. ELECTORAL PROCESS: 0 / 12

A1. Was the current head of government or other chief national authority elected through free and fair elections? 0 / 4

President Teodoro Obiang Nguema Mbasogo, Africa's longest-serving head of state, has held power since 1979. He was awarded a new seven-year term in the April 2016 presidential election, reportedly winning 93.5 percent of the vote. The main opposition party at the time, Convergence for Social Democracy (CPDS), boycotted the election, and other factions faced police violence, detentions, and torture. One opposition figure who had been barred from running for president, Gabriel Nsé Obiang Obono, was put under house arrest during the election, and police used live ammunition against supporters gathered at his home.

A2. Were the current national legislative representatives elected through free and fair elections? 0 / 4

The bicameral parliament consists of a 70-seat Senate and a 100-seat Chamber of Deputies, with members of both chambers serving five-year terms. Fifteen senators are appointed by the president, 55 are directly elected, and there can be several additional ex officio members. The Chamber of Deputies is directly elected.

In the November 2017 legislative elections, the ruling Democratic Party of Equatorial Guinea (PDGE) and its subordinate allied parties won 99 seats in the lower house, all 55 of the elected seats in the Senate, and control of all municipal councils. The opposition CI, led by Nsé Obiang, took a single seat in the Chamber of Deputies and a seat on the capital's city council. The preelection media environment was tightly controlled, and a wave of arrests of CI supporters began when police dispersed an opposition rally ahead of the voting. Among other irregularities on election day, a ban on private vehicles prevented many voters from reaching distant polling stations, and polls closed one hour earlier than scheduled.

A3. Are the electoral laws and framework fair, and are they implemented impartially by the relevant election management bodies? 0 / 4

Equatorial Guinea does not have an independent electoral body; the head of the National Election Commission is also the country's interior minister and a prominent figure in the ruling PDGE. Elections are not fairly managed in practice.

B. POLITICAL PLURALISM AND PARTICIPATION: 0 / 16 (−1)

B1. Do the people have the right to organize in different political parties or other competitive political groupings of their choice, and is the system free of undue obstacles to the rise and fall of these competing parties or groupings? 0 / 4 (−1)

The PDGE is the dominant party, operating in conjunction with a number of subordinate parties in its coalition.

The regime keeps the country's handful of opposition parties under strict control. In late 2017, dozens of CI members were arrested following a confrontation between police and CI members and supporters at a rally in Aconibe, which erupted when police tried to disperse the rally. In February 2018, 21 detained CI activists, including Mitogo, the party's only member of parliament, were sentenced to 30 years in prison on charges including sedition, attacks on authority, and causing serious bodily harm, in connection with the Aconibe confrontation. The CI was also banned on grounds of being a threat to security. The country's highest court upheld the sentences and dissolution ruling in May.

In July, President Obiang promised amnesty for political prisoners in advance of a "national dialogue." However, only one CI member was subsequently released. Later, in October, the CI announced that 34 of its members including Mitogo were among those who received presidential pardons from Obiang and released as part of an amnesty marking the Independence Day holiday. The party claimed that some of those detained had been tortured in prison by security agents, and that party member Juan Obama Edu, who was among those to receive a 30-year sentence, had died in July as a result.

Score Change: The score declined from 1 to 0 because the main opposition Citizens for Innovation (CI) party was banned.

B2. Is there a realistic opportunity for the opposition to increase its support or gain power through elections? 0 / 4

Equatorial Guinea has never had a peaceful transfer of power through elections. President Obiang appointed his son, Teodoro "Teodorín" Nguema Obiang Mangue, as vice president in 2016, paving the way for a dynastic succession.

Nsé Obiang, the CI leader, was disqualified from running in the 2016 presidential vote on the grounds that he did not meet residency requirements. In the wake of the 2017 legislative elections, the authorities intensified their crackdown on the CI, effectively removing it as a potential threat to the PDGE's supremacy. The CI was officially banned as a political party in 2018, and its members face imprisonment and regular threats of imprisonment by the state.

B3. Are the people's political choices free from domination by the military, foreign powers, religious hierarchies, economic oligarchies, or any other powerful group that is not democratically accountable? 0 / 4

The regime routinely uses the security forces to attack and intimidate opposition supporters, and political loyalty to the ruling party is treated as a condition for obtaining and keeping public-sector employment.

B4. Do various segments of the population (including ethnic, religious, gender, LGBT, and other relevant groups) have full political rights and electoral opportunities? 0 / 4

The ethnic Fang majority dominates political life in Equatorial Guinea, leaving minority ethnic groups with little influence; power is concentrated in the hands of the president's family and regional group in particular. Women formally enjoy equal political rights, holding a number of positions in government, 20 percent of the seats in the Chamber of Deputies, and 15 percent of the seats in the Senate. However, they have little opportunity to independently advocate for their interests or organize politically. While no law prevents LGBT (lesbian, gay, bisexual, and transgender) people from exercising their political rights, societal discrimination discourages activism for LGBT-friendly policies and protections in the political sphere.

C. FUNCTIONING OF GOVERNMENT: 0 / 12

C1. Do the freely elected head of government and national legislative representatives determine the policies of the government? 0 / 4

The executive branch—headed by the president, who is not freely elected—sets and implements government policy, leaving the legislature with no meaningful role in the policymaking process.

C2. Are safeguards against official corruption strong and effective? 0 / 4

There are no independent anticorruption mechanisms, and the government is marked by nepotism and graft. Hiring and promotions within the government, army, and civil service favor those with ties to the president and his family. One of the president's sons, Gabriel Mbega Obiang Lima, is the minister of mines and hydrocarbons, granting him sweeping control over the country's natural resources. Teodorín, the vice president, has been the focus of money-laundering investigations in other countries. In September 2018, Brazilian authorities confiscated $1.5 million in cash from Teodorín during a visit with his entourage, along with twelve watches worth an estimated $15 million.

International financial organizations and human rights groups alike have criticized the government for pouring resources into wasteful infrastructure projects while neglecting health and social spending. According to IMF data from 2011, the most recent year available, the government spent just 5 percent of its budget on education and health.

C3. Does the government operate with openness and transparency? 0 / 4

The government's budget process and procurement system are opaque, as are the finances of state-owned companies. In 2010, Equatorial Guinea failed in its bid to join the Extractive Industries Transparency Initiative (EITI), which found that it did not meet the group's standards. A significant percentage of revenue from the country's oil reserves are funneled to Obiang's allies through noncompetitive, nontransparent construction contracts, often for projects of questionable value. (The International Monetary Fund [IMF] has estimated that the country's current oil reserves will run out in 2035.)

CIVIL LIBERTIES: 6 / 60

D. FREEDOM OF EXPRESSION AND BELIEF: 3 / 16

D1. Are there free and independent media? 0 / 4

Press freedom is severely limited, despite constitutional protections. Journalists consistently exercise self-censorship, and those who do criticize the regime face dismissal and other reprisals. The government has sought to block access to the websites of opposition parties and exile groups since 2013. The handful of private newspapers and magazines in operation face intense financial and political pressure and are unable to publish regularly. Online versions of Spanish newspapers are regularly blocked. The only private television broadcaster is controlled by Teodorín.

Ramón Nsé Esono Ebalé, a political cartoonist arrested by the government on charges of money laundering and counterfeiting in 2017, was released in March after a police officer admitted that he had been ordered to fabricate the evidence.

D2. Are individuals free to practice and express their religious faith or nonbelief in public and private? 2 / 4

The constitution protects religious freedom, though in practice it is sometimes affected by the country's broader political repression and endemic corruption. The Roman Catholic Church is the dominant faith and is exempt from registration and permit requirements that apply to other groups. Government officials have reportedly been required to attend Catholic masses on ceremonial occasions, such as the president's birthday.

D3. Is there academic freedom, and is the educational system free from extensive political indoctrination? 1 / 4

Academic freedom is politically constrained, and self-censorship among faculty is common. University professors and teachers have reportedly been hired or dismissed due to their political affiliations.

D4. Are individuals free to express their personal views on political or other sensitive topics without fear of surveillance or retribution? 0 / 4

Freedom of private discussion is limited. The government uses informants and electronic surveillance to monitor members of the opposition, nongovernmental organizations (NGOs), and journalists, including the few members of the foreign press in the country. Critics of the government are subject to arbitrary arrest, physical abuse, and trumped-up charges. The government has obstructed access to the internet in times of political tension. Access to social media platforms such as Facebook and WhatsApp were blocked by the government in the aftermath of arrests of political opposition figures in December 2017 and January 2018. Earlier, in 2017, it blocked access to the internet as voting in the year' presidential election took place.

E. ASSOCIATIONAL AND ORGANIZATIONAL RIGHTS: 0 / 12

E1. Is there freedom of assembly? 0 / 4

Freedom of assembly is severely restricted. Opposition gatherings are typically blocked or dispersed, and citizens are sometimes pressured to attend progovernment events.

E2. Is there freedom for nongovernmental organizations, particularly those that are engaged in human rights- and governance-related work? 0 / 4

All associations must register with the government through an onerous process, and independent NGOs face state persecution. In October 2018, the prominent anticorruption and human rights activist Alfredo Okenve of the Center for Development Studies and Initiatives (CEID) was beaten and stabbed, allegedly by plainclothes security forces.

E3. Is there freedom for trade unions and similar professional or labor organizations? 0 / 4

The constitution provides for the right to organize unions, but there are many legal and practical barriers to union formation, collective bargaining, and strikes. The government has refused to register a number of trade unions; a farmers' organization is the only legal union.

F. RULE OF LAW: 0 / 16

F1. Is there an independent judiciary? 0 / 4

The judiciary is not independent, and judges in sensitive cases often consult with the office of the president before issuing a ruling. Under the constitution, the president is the nation's first magistrate. He also oversees the body that appoints judges. The court system's impartiality is further undermined by corruption.

F2. Does due process prevail in civil and criminal matters? 0 / 4

The security forces routinely detain people without charge or trial. Graft is endemic in the police and other law enforcement bodies. In 2018, dozens of opposition party members were detained without due process. The detention of Ebalé, the political cartoonist, was not investigated even after a police officer said he had been ordered to fabricate evidence against him.

F3. Is there protection from the illegitimate use of physical force and freedom from war and insurgencies? 0 / 4

Beatings and torture by security forces are reportedly common. Prisons are over-crowded and feature harsh conditions, including physical abuse, poor sanitation, and denial of medical care.

F4. Do laws, policies, and practices guarantee equal treatment of various segments of the population? 0 / 4

Women face discrimination in employment and other matters, particularly in rural areas. The ethnic Bubi minority suffers persistent societal discrimination. Immigrants, including irregular migrants, are subject to raids, physical abuse, and extortion by police. While LGBT people face social stigma and discrimination, same-sex sexual activity is not illegal.

G. PERSONAL AUTONOMY AND INDIVIDUAL RIGHTS: 3 / 16

G1. Do individuals enjoy freedom of movement, including the ability to change their place of residence, employment, or education? 1 / 4

Freedom of movement is protected by law but restricted in practice through measures such as police checkpoints, which often require the payment of bribes. Authorities have denied opposition members and other dissidents reentry from abroad or restricted their movements within the country. In July 2018, a government order mandated that all parliamentarians must obtain permission from the vice president before travelling abroad.

A Ministry of Education order that took effect for the 2016–17 school year requires female students to take pregnancy tests and bars pregnant girls from school.

G2. Are individuals able to exercise the right to own property and establish private businesses without undue interference from state or nonstate actors? 1 / 4

Pervasive corruption and onerous bureaucratic procedures serve as major impediments to private business activity. In September 2018 the government demanded that oil companies must increase drilling in 2019 or risk losing their permits to work in the country's oil fields. Most women face disadvantages regarding inheritance and property rights under both the civil code and customary practices, though women enjoy greater customary rights among the Bubi minority.

G3. Do individuals enjoy personal social freedoms, including choice of marriage partner and size of family, protection from domestic violence, and control over appearance? 1 / 4

The civil code and customary law put women at a disadvantage with respect to personal status matters like marriage and child custody, with some exceptions among the Bubi. Laws against rape and domestic violence are not enforced effectively. The government does little to collect data, raise awareness, or support civil society efforts to combat such problems.

G4. Do individuals enjoy equality of opportunity and freedom from economic exploitation? 0 / 4

The country's oil wealth is concentrated among the ruling elite, leaving much of the population without access to basic services. Despite national economic growth driven by natural resource exploitation, Equatorial Guinea continues to score poorly on social and economic development indicators.

Foreign workers in the oil and construction industries are subject to passport confiscation and forced labor. Equatoguineans are also vulnerable to forced labor, including in the sex trade. Corrupt officials are often complicit in human trafficking, according to the US State Department.

Eritrea

Population: 6,000,000
Capital: Asmara
Political Rights Rating: 7
Civil Liberties Rating: 7
Freedom Rating: 7.0
Freedom Status: Not Free
Electoral Democracy: No

Overview: Eritrea is a militarized authoritarian state that has not held a national election since independence from Ethiopia in 1993. The People's Front for Democracy and Justice (PFDJ), headed by President Isaias Afwerki, is the sole political party. Arbitrary detention is commonplace, and citizens are required to perform national service, often for their entire working lives. The government shut down all independent media in 2001.

KEY DEVELOPMENTS IN 2018:

- Political reforms in Ethiopia led to a thaw in relations with Eritrea, which had been frozen since the war of 1998–2000. Ethiopia's new prime minister, Abiy Ahmed, reached out to President Isaias Afwerki in April. In July, they signed a deal to officially end the war.

- The rapid improvements to Eritrea's external relations had little discernible impact on internal conditions, and authorities continued to deprive citizens of basic rights.
- Mass emigration continued, with tens of thousands of Eritreans risking their lives to seek asylum in neighboring countries or in Europe. Nearly 4,000 Eritreans claimed asylum in Ethiopia in a single week in September.
- In March, protests erupted following the death in custody of the former board chairman of an Islamic school, who had resisted government interference in its management. Hundreds of people were reportedly detained.

POLITICAL RIGHTS: 1 / 40

A. ELECTORAL PROCESS: 0 / 12

A1. Was the current head of government or other chief national authority elected through free and fair elections? 0 / 4

Following Eritrea's formal independence from Ethiopia in 1993, an unelected Transitional National Assembly chose Isaias to serve as president until elections could be held under a new constitution. He has remained in office since then, without ever obtaining a mandate from voters.

A2. Were the current national legislative representatives elected through free and fair elections? 0 / 4

A constitution ratified in 1997 calls for an elected 150-seat National Assembly, which would choose the president from among its members by a majority vote. However, national elections have been postponed indefinitely, and the transitional assembly has not met since 2002. Local and regional assembly elections have been held periodically, but they are carefully orchestrated by the PFDJ and offer no meaningful choice to voters.

A3. Are the electoral laws and framework fair, and are they implemented impartially by the relevant election management bodies? 0 / 4

The 1997 constitution calls for an electoral commission whose head is appointed by the president and confirmed by the National Assembly, but it has never been implemented, and national elections have never been conducted. Subnational elections are controlled by the ruling party.

B. POLITICAL PLURALISM AND PARTICIPATION: 0 / 16

B1. Do the people have the right to organize in different political parties or other competitive political groupings of their choice, and is the system free of undue obstacles to the rise and fall of these competing parties or groupings? 0 / 4

The PFDJ is the only legally recognized political party in Eritrea. Alternative groups must operate from abroad among the diaspora community. Many such groups were hosted by Ethiopia. However, in July 2018, following the rapprochement between the two countries, the Ethiopian government ordered all Eritrean opposition parties in the country to cease operations. In August, an adviser to President Isaias said the PFDJ was examining ways to broaden political participation, but did not offer details.

In September, former finance minister Berhane Abrehe was arrested; he had recently written a book calling for a democratic transition, and had released an audio recording challenging President Isaias to a public debate.

The government has refused to divulge information about a group of prominent dissidents held incommunicado since 2001. Reports in February 2018 suggested that one member of the group, former foreign minister Haile "Durue" Woldensae, had died in detention.

B2. Is there a realistic opportunity for the opposition to increase its support or gain power through elections? 0 / 4

President Isaias and the PFDJ have been in power without interruption since independence, and since multiparty elections have never been allowed, opposition groups have had no opportunity to compete or enter government.

B3. Are the people's political choices free from domination by the military, foreign powers, religious hierarchies, economic oligarchies, or any other powerful group that is not democratically accountable? 0 / 4

Eritrean society is dominated by the military, with most citizens required to perform open-ended military or other national service. The authorities' intolerance of dissent and the absence of elections or opposition parties leaves individuals with no political options other than loyalty to the PFDJ, imprisonment, or illegal emigration.

B4. Do various segments of the population (including ethnic, religious, gender, LGBT, and other relevant groups) have full political rights and electoral opportunities? 0 / 4

Women and various ethnic groups are nominally represented within the PFDJ, but they have no practical ability to organize independently or advocate for their interests through the political system.

C. FUNCTIONING OF GOVERNMENT: 1 / 12

C1. Do the freely elected head of government and national legislative representatives determine the policies of the government? 0 / 4

Power is concentrated in the hands of the unelected president, who reportedly determines policy with the help of an informal circle of advisers, leaving the cabinet and security officials to merely carry out his decisions. A 2016 UN Human Rights Council (UNHRC) commission of inquiry noted that military personnel are overrepresented among the president's closest associates.

C2. Are safeguards against official corruption strong and effective? 1 / 4

Petty bribery and influence peddling are thought to be endemic, and larger-scale corruption is a problem among some party officials and military leaders. The government's control over foreign exchange effectively gives it sole authority over imports, and those in favor with the regime are allowed to profit from the smuggling and sale of scarce goods such as food, building materials, and alcohol. Senior military officials have allegedly profited from smuggling Eritreans out of the country. There are no independent agencies or mechanisms in place to prevent or punish corruption. Special anticorruption courts overseen by the military nominally exist, but are mostly inactive.

C3. Does the government operate with openness and transparency? 0 / 4

The government operates without public scrutiny. Basic data about the state budget and its appropriations are not publicly disclosed, and officials are not required to disclose their assets.

CIVIL LIBERTIES: 1 / 60 (−1)

D. FREEDOM OF EXPRESSION AND BELIEF: 0 / 16

D1. Are there free and independent media? 0 / 4

The government shut down all independent media outlets in 2001, leaving only state-controlled news services in operation. Several foreign-based organizations try to provide coverage to Eritreans who can receive it, including the British Broadcasting Corporation (BBC), which launched internet news services in local languages in 2017. However, internet penetration is low.

At the end of 2018, 16 journalists were behind bars because of their work, according to the Committee to Protect Journalists (CPJ); almost all of had been imprisoned since 2001. Additionally, according to Radio Erena, an Eritrean news outlet based in France, two reporters working for newspapers put out by the Information Ministry were detained in March, without explanation. They were not included in CPJ's count and their status was unknown at year's end.

D2. Are individuals free to practice and express their religious faith or nonbelief in public and private? 0 / 4

The government places strict limits on the exercise of religion. Eritrea officially recognizes only four faiths: Islam, Orthodox Christianity, Roman Catholicism, and Lutheranism as practiced by the Evangelical Church of Eritrea. Followers of other denominations are subject to arrest. Jehovah's Witnesses face severe persecution, including denial of citizenship and travel papers. Religious practice is prohibited among members of the military. The patriarch of the Orthodox Church, Abune Antonios, has been held under house arrest since 2006, when he called for political prisoners to be released. In February 2018, five Catholic-run clinics were shuttered as part of a government process to assume direct control of all health facilities and places of education.

D3. Is there academic freedom, and is the educational system free from extensive political indoctrination? 0 / 4

Academic freedom is greatly constrained. Students in their last year of secondary school are subject to obligatory military service at the Sawa military training center, where conditions are harsh. Academics practice self-censorship, and the government interferes with their course content and limits their ability to conduct research abroad.

Government attempts to nationalize an Islamic school in Asmara as part of a broader policy to assert state control of the education system led to rare demonstrations in late 2017. The former chairman of the school board, 93 year-old Musa Mohammed Nur, was arrested for opposing the new policy, and died in custody in March 2018. His arrest and death both prompted protests, which security forces violently dispersed.

D4. Are individuals free to express their personal views on political or other sensitive topics without fear of surveillance or retribution? 0 / 4

Freedoms of expression and private discussion are severely inhibited by fear of government informants and the likelihood of arrest and arbitrary detention for any airing of dissent. While access to the internet is limited, the authorities attempt to monitor online communications. According to reports received by the UNHRC, internet cafes are required to register customers and track their activity.

E. ASSOCIATIONAL AND ORGANIZATIONAL RIGHTS: 0 / 12
E1. Is there freedom of assembly? 0 / 4

Freedom of assembly is not recognized by the authorities. Those who take to the streets to protest face the threat of deadly force at the hands of the state security forces, or arbitrary detention. In 2017 and 2018, reports emerged indicating that rare public protests were met with such repression. By one account, over two dozen people were killed by the security forces during the October 2017 demonstrations in support of Musa Mohammed Nur. His funeral in March 2018 prompted mass protests that erupted into clashes between protesters and police; news sources reported that protesters were arrested, with numbers ranging from a handful, to close to a thousand.

E2. Is there freedom for nongovernmental organizations, particularly those that are engaged in human rights- and governance-related work? 0 / 4

The law requires all nongovernmental organizations to undergo an onerous and arbitrary annual registration process, and limits their activities to providing humanitarian relief. In reality, there are no independent civil society organizations based in Eritrea. The government continues to deny permission for external human rights organizations to enter the country.

E3. Is there freedom for trade unions and similar professional or labor organizations? 0 / 4

There are no independent trade unions in Eritrea. The only union umbrella group, the National Confederation of Eritrean Workers, is affiliated with the ruling party. Relatively autonomous student and teachers' unions operated during the early years of independence but were gradually shut down in the late 1990s and early 2000s. According to reports to the UNHRC, the government has prevented new unions from being formed.

F. RULE OF LAW: 0 / 16

F1. Is there an independent judiciary? 0 / 4

The judiciary has no independence from the executive branch. The Supreme Court called for in the constitution has never been established, nor has a Judicial Commission tasked with appointing judges. Instead, the president controls the appointment and dismissal of all judges; even nominally elected judges in local community courts are controlled by the Justice Ministry, according to UN investigators. Many judges are military officers.

F2. Does due process prevail in civil and criminal matters? 0 / 4

Basic principles of due process are systematically violated. Arbitrary arrests and detentions are common; targets include those who evade military service, try to flee the country, or are suspected of practicing an unauthorized religion. Eritreans who offend high-ranking government or party officials are also reportedly subject to arbitrary arrest.

Prisoners are routinely held incommunicado for indefinite periods without charge or trial, with the authorities refusing even to inform family members whether they are still alive. There is no operational system of public defense lawyers. Thousands of political prisoners and prisoners of conscience remain behind bars.

F3. Is there protection from the illegitimate use of physical force and freedom from war and insurgencies? 0 / 4

UN investigators have described the routine and systematic use of physical and psychological torture in both civilian and military detention centers. Deaths in custody or in military service due to torture and other harsh conditions have been reported. Security forces employ lethal violence arbitrarily and with impunity. Individuals attempting to escape military service or flee the country have been fired on by soldiers.

F4. Do laws, policies, and practices guarantee equal treatment of various segments of the population? 0 / 4

There are allegations that two of Eritrea's nine recognized ethnic groups, the Kunama and Afar, face severe discrimination.

Efforts have been made to promote the rights of women, who played a critical role in Eritrea's independence struggle. Laws mandate equal educational opportunity and equal pay for equal work. However, traditional societal discrimination against women persists in the countryside, and the deeply flawed legal system does not effectively uphold their formal rights.

Same-sex sexual relations are criminalized, and LGBT (lesbian, gay, bisexual, and transgender) people enjoy no legal protections from societal discrimination.

G. PERSONAL AUTONOMY AND INDIVIDUAL RIGHTS: 1 / 16 (−1)

G1. Do individuals enjoy freedom of movement, including the ability to change their place of residence, employment, or education? 0 / 4

Freedom of movement is heavily restricted. Eritreans young enough for national service are rarely given permission to go abroad, and those who try to travel outside the country without the correct documents face imprisonment. Individuals also require permits to travel within the country. Eritrean refugees and asylum seekers who are repatriated from other countries are subject to detention under harsh conditions.

The opening of the border with Ethiopia in September 2018 raised hopes that conditions could improve in the future. However, tens of thousands of Eritreans continued to flee the county, risking their lives to seek asylum in neighboring countries, or in Europe. Nearly 4,000 Eritreans claimed asylum in Ethiopia in a single week in September.

G2. Are individuals able to exercise the right to own property and establish private businesses without undue interference from state or nonstate actors? 0 / 4

The national conscription system denies much of the working-age population the opportunity to establish and run their own businesses. Both the authorities and private actors with regime support are able to confiscate property and evict occupants without due process. Hundreds of small businesses were forced to close at the end of 2017 after the authorities accused them of breaking laws restricting foreign currency transfers. They were permitted to reopen in January 2018 after paying large fines.

G3. Do individuals enjoy personal social freedoms, including choice of marriage partner and size of family, protection from domestic violence, and control over appearance? 1 / 4 (−1)

Men and women have equal rights under laws governing marriage, nationality, and other personal status matters. However, girls in rural areas remain vulnerable to early or forced marriage. Rape of women and sexualized forms of violence against men are common in detention and in military service. Sexual assault of female conscripts is endemic and has not been thoroughly investigated by the authorities. The government has banned and attempted to reduce the practice of female genital mutilation, but it remains widespread in rural areas.

Score Change: The score declined from 2 to 1 because women performing their national service, particularly in the military, face the threat of rape and sexual assault, and because there is widespread impunity for such attacks.

G4. Do individuals enjoy equality of opportunity and freedom from economic exploitation? 0 / 4

Eritrea's conscription system ties most able-bodied men and women—including those under 18 who are completing secondary school—to obligatory military service, which can also entail compulsory labor for enterprises controlled by the political elite. National service is supposed to last 18 months but is open-ended in practice. UN human rights experts have described this system as enslavement. Following the signing of a peace deal with Ethiopia, the government said it was reviewing the national service system with a view to reducing the number of citizens in military uniform and boosting those engaged in development activities. No demobilization plan had been introduced the by year's end.

Cash withdrawal limits imposed in 2015 have hampered citizens' ability to buy food and other essential goods.

Estonia

Population: 1,300,000
Capital: Tallinn
Political Rights Rating: 1
Civil Liberties Rating: 1
Freedom Rating: 1.0
Freedom Status: Free
Electoral Democracy: Yes

Overview: Democratic institutions are strong, and political and civil rights are widely respected in Estonia. However, about 6 percent of the population remains stateless, and thus may not participate in national elections. Corruption remains a challenge, as does discrimination against ethnic Russians, members of the Romany minority, and LGBT (lesbian, gay, bisexual, and transgender) people. Women earn significantly less than men for performing similar duties.

KEY DEVELOPMENTS IN 2018:

- The governing coalition was weakened by a dispute related to the reluctance of a junior partner, the conservative Union of Pro Patria and Res Publica (IRL), to endorse the UN Global Compact for Migration, a nonbinding document intended to provide a political basis for improving migration management. The matter was ultimately resolved by the parliament (Riigikogu), which voted to endorse the compact.
- In an unusual incident in November, a European Parliament member and member of the Social Democratic Party (SDE) was kicked by supporters of the far-right Conservative People's Party (EKRE) at a protest outside the Riigikogu. The SDE member had attempted to seize a microphone from an EKRE lawmaker.
- In September, an investigation commissioned by Danske Bank revealed that roughly \$230 billion had been laundered through its Estonian branch between 2007 and 2015—raising questions about the performance of Estonia's supervisory and regulatory bodies. The government commissioned its own audit of the bank in October, and at year's end was examining a set of reforms aimed at rooting out financial-sector corruption.
- In July, Estonia introduced the free use of public buses across the country.

POLITICAL RIGHTS: 38 / 40

A. ELECTORAL PROCESS: 12 / 12

A1. Was the current head of government or other chief national authority elected through free and fair elections? 4 / 4

The prime minister is head of government, and is nominated by the president and approved by the parliament (Riigikogu). Current prime minister Jüri Ratas of the Center Party was confirmed by the Riigikogu following the formation of a coalition in 2016 between the Center Party and two smaller partners, the center-left SDE, and the conservative IRL. Ratas's selection and confirmation took place according to legal procedures.

The president is elected by parliamentary ballot to a five-year term, filling the largely ceremonial role of head of state. Current president Kersti Kaljulaid was elected as a nonpartisan consensus candidate in a sixth round of voting in 2016. Although the overall election process was free and fair, it was criticized as lengthy and not entirely transparent.

A2. Were the current national legislative representatives elected through free and fair elections? 4 / 4

The constitution establishes a 101-seat, unicameral parliament whose members are elected for four-year terms. The 2015 elections were free and fair. The Reform Party took 30 seats, the Center Party 27, SDE 15, and IRL 14. The remainder went to two new parties, the conservative, antiestablishment Free Party (EV), and the far-right EKRE, which took 8 and 7 seats, respectively.

The Center Party leads the correct governing coalition, with support from SDE and IRL. However, the coalition was weakened in 2018 by a serious dispute related to IRL's reluctance to endorse the UN Global Compact for Migration, which is intended to provide a political but not legal basis for improving migration management. SDE and the Center Party asked the Riigikogu to settle the matter, and lawmakers ultimately voted to endorse the compact. The Reform Party declined to vote, characterizing the affair as a government failure. The controversy played out just a few months ahead of the next Riigikogu elections, set for March 2019.

A3. Are the electoral laws and framework fair, and are they implemented impartially by the relevant election management bodies? 4 / 4

The legal framework for conducting elections is clear and detailed. Online voting is widespread. October 2017 municipal elections witnessed record turnout online, with 32 percent of participating voters using this method, thus demonstrating strong public confidence in the e-voting system.

Administrative reforms in 2017 merged municipalities, reduced the number of electoral seats by almost half, and abolished the county level of administration. Upon review, the Supreme Court allowed the changes to stand.

B. POLITICAL PLURALISM AND PARTICIPATION: 15 / 16

B1. Do the people have the right to organize in different political parties or other competitive political groupings of their choice, and is the system free of undue obstacles to the rise and fall of these competing parties or groupings? 4 / 4

Estonia's political parties organize and operate freely, and the system is open to the rise and fall of various parties. The 2015 election brought two new parties to the parliament: the conservative, antiestablishment EV, and the far-right EKRE.

B2. Is there a realistic opportunity for the opposition to increase its support or gain power through elections? 4 / 4

The system is open to the rotation of power. In the 2015 elections, the center-right Reform Party, which had led the previous government, captured the most seats (30), and subsequently formed a coalition with its previous coalition partner, the SDE, as well as the IRL. In 2016, however, the Center Party, which held 27 seats, formed a new ruling coalition with the SDE and the IRL. The Center Party won local elections in 2017.

B3. Are the people's political choices free from domination by the military, foreign powers, religious hierarchies, economic oligarchies, or any other powerful group that is not democratically accountable? 4 / 4

People's political choices are generally not influenced by undemocratic forces. However, concerns remain about the prevalence and influence of online disinformation ahead of the 2019 elections.

While the governing Center Party has not fully renounced its cooperation agreement with United Russia, the main political party in Russia, this has not led to foreign interference with Estonians' political rights.

B4. Do various segments of the population (including ethnic, religious, gender, LGBT, and other relevant groups) have full political rights and electoral opportunities? 3 / 4

About 6 percent of the country's population—mostly ethnic Russians—remain stateless and thus may not participate in national elections. Resident noncitizens are permitted to vote in local elections, but may not run as candidates or join political parties. The authorities have adopted policies to assist those seeking naturalization. Although women only make up 27 percent of members of parliament, women's interests are represented through a variety of programs and government initiatives.

C. FUNCTIONING OF GOVERNMENT 11 / 12

C1. Do the freely elected head of government and national legislative representatives determine the policies of the government? 4 / 4

Both the government and the parliament are freely elected and function without interference from external or nonstate actors.

C2. Are safeguards against official corruption strong and effective? 3 / 4

Recent years have seen heavily publicized allegations of corruption within the main political parties, as well as in the public sector. The trial of Edgar Savisaar, former leader of the Center Party and Tallinn city mayor, on charges of bribery, money laundering, and embezzlement, is ongoing. The Supervisory Committee on Party Financing (ERJK) in 2017 found that the Center Party had accepted illegal donations, and a Tallinn court in 2018 rejected the party's appeal against an ERJK ruling to pay the amount of the illicit donation—€220,000 ($256,000)—back to the state.

While the government has taken some action toward curbing private-sector corruption, significant progress has yet to be observed. In September, an investigation commissioned by Danske Bank revealed that roughly $230 billion had been laundered through its Estonian branch between 2007 and 2015, raising questions about the performance of Estonia's regulatory and supervisory bodies. The government commissioned its own audit of the bank in October, and ten employees of the branch were arrested in December. At year's end, the government was considering a number of reforms aimed at rooting out corruption in the financial sector.

C3. Does the government operate with openness and transparency? 4 / 4

Estonia is well-known for its transparency and developed e-governance services. Recently, however, several security flaws in e-governance services were revealed in media reports; the government in April announced actions to remedy the situation and to provide additional resources to support the maintenance and further expansion of the e-governance system.

Public access to government information and asset declarations of officials is provided for both in law and in practice.

CIVIL LIBERTIES: 56 / 60

D. FREEDOM OF EXPRESSION AND BELIEF: 16 / 16

D1. Are there free and independent media? 4 / 4

The government generally respects freedom of the press. Public and private television and radio stations operate in Estonia, and there are a number of independent newspapers. The government does not restrict access to the internet.

D2. Are individuals free to practice and express their religious faith or nonbelief in public and private? 4 / 4

Religious freedom is respected in law and in practice.

D3. Is there academic freedom, and is the educational system free from extensive political indoctrination? 4 / 4

Academic freedom is respected. However, by law, public Russian-language high schools must teach 60 percent of their curriculum in the Estonian language.

D4. Are individuals free to express their personal views on political or other sensitive topics without fear of surveillance or retribution? 4 / 4

Individuals are free to express political views without fear of surveillance or retribution.

E. ASSOCIATIONAL AND ORGANIZATIONAL RIGHTS: 12 / 12

E1. Is there freedom of assembly? 4 / 4

The constitution guarantees freedom of assembly, and the government upholds this right in practice.

In an unusual incident in November 2018, Indrek Tarand, a member of the European Parliament and an SDE member, was kicked by EKRE supporters at a protest outside the Riigikogu after he had attempted to seize a microphone from an EKRE lawmaker, Martin Helme. The EKRE had called on supporters to turn out to express their disapproval of the UN Global Compact for Migration.

E2. Is there freedom for nongovernmental organizations, particularly those that are engaged in human rights- and governance-related work? 4 / 4

The government honors the civic rights of associations and does not restrict or control the activities of nongovernmental organizations (NGOs).

E3. Is there freedom for trade unions and similar professional or labor organizations? 4 / 4

Workers may organize freely, strike, and bargain collectively, although public servants at the municipal and state levels may not strike.

F. RULE OF LAW: 14 / 16

F1. Is there an independent judiciary? 4 / 4

The judiciary is independent and generally free from government or other interference.

F2. Does due process prevail in civil and criminal matters? 4 / 4

Legal processes in civil and criminal matters are generally free and fair. Laws prohibiting arbitrary arrest and detention and ensuring the right to a fair trial are largely observed.

F3. Is there protection from the illegitimate use of physical force and freedom from war and insurgencies? 3 / 4

While Estonia is generally safe and peaceful, it had one of the highest intentional homicide rates in the European Union (EU) in 2016, according to the most recent data from Eurostat, the EU's statistical office. There have been reports of law enforcement officials using excessive force when arresting suspects. Some inmates reportedly have inadequate access to health care. Estonia has a relatively high incarceration rate, with data from the World Prison Brief, a project of the University of London, for 2018 showing that 198 per 100,000 residents are in Estonian prisons. Council of Europe statistics for 2015 showed 222 prisoners per 100,000 inhabitants; among the countries it surveyed, only Latvia and Lithuania had higher incarceration rates.

F4. Do laws, policies, and practices guarantee equal treatment of various segments of the population? 3 / 4

Russian-speakers continue to face societal discrimination, which is reinforced by laws such as the Equal Treatment Act, which does not consider Estonian linguistic requirements for public officials discriminatory. Women in Estonia earn on average 25 percent less than men according to 2016 Eurostat data. Discrimination based on sexual orientation is legally prohibited, though harassment of members of the LGBT (lesbian, gay, bisexual, and transgender) community is reportedly common. Members of the Romany minority face employment discrimination and drop out of school at high rates, suggesting that Estonian schools fail to meet their needs.

G. PERSONAL AUTONOMY AND INDIVIDUAL RIGHTS 14 / 16

G1. Do individuals enjoy freedom of movement, including the ability to change their place of residence, employment, or education? 4 / 4

Citizens and residents enjoy free movement inside Estonia and freedom to leave the country.

In July 2018, Estonia introduced the free use of public buses across the country. Transit in Tallinn on public buses, trains, trams, and trollies has been free since 2013.

G2. Are individuals able to exercise the right to own property and establish private businesses without undue interference from state or nonstate actors? 4 / 4

Estonian residents enjoy strong property rights and can freely establish private businesses.

G3. Do individuals enjoy personal social freedoms, including choice of marriage partner and size of family, protection from domestic violence, and control over appearance? 3 / 4

Violence against women, including domestic violence, remains a problem.

At the end of 2018, the Riigikogu had yet to adopt necessary amendments for the implementation of a 2014 law permitting same-sex civil unions.

G4. Do individuals enjoy equality of opportunity and freedom from economic exploitation? 3 / 4

Estonia is a source, transit point, and destination for women and girls trafficked for the purpose of prostitution. The government makes efforts to prosecute traffickers and provide services to victims, though the US State Department's 2018 *Trafficking in Persons Report* called for better training for investigators and prosecutors of trafficking crimes.

Estonia's unemployment rate is relatively low, ranging from 5.0 to 6.4 percent in 2018. However, according to Eurostat, 23.4 percent of the population was at risk of poverty or social exclusion in 2017. The current government has sought to ease economic pressures; among other measures, in December 2018 lawmakers raised the minimum monthly wage from 500 to 540 euros ($590 to 630), to take effect at the beginning of 2019.

Eswatini

Population: 1,400,000
Capital: Mbabane (administrative), Lobamba (legislative, royal)
Political Rights Rating: 7
Civil Liberties Rating: 6
Freedom Rating: 6.5
Freedom Status: Not Free
Electoral Democracy: No

Overview: Eswatini (known internationally as Swaziland until 2018) is a monarchy currently ruled by King Mswati III. The king exercises ultimate authority over all branches of the national government and effectively controls local governance through his influence over traditional chiefs. Political dissent and civic and labor activism are subject to harsh punishment under sedition and other laws. Additional human rights problems include impunity for security forces and discrimination against women and LGBT (lesbian, gay, bisexual, and transgender) people.

KEY DEVELOPMENTS IN 2018:

- In April, King Mswati III unilaterally changed the country's name from Swaziland to Eswatini.
- In July, Parliament passed the Sexual Offences and Domestic Violence Bill, which criminalizes marital rape, calls for the creation of specialized domestic violence courts, and establishes new mechanisms for reporting domestic violence, among other provisions.
- General elections were held in September in a highly restrictive environment in which political parties were banned from competing, and almost all candidates were loyal to the king.
- In October, Ambrose Dlamini was appointed prime minister, although he was not a member of Parliament at the time of his appointment, as required by the constitution.

POLITICAL RIGHTS: 1 / 40

A. ELECTORAL PROCESS: 0 / 12

A1. Was the current head of government or other chief national authority elected through free and fair elections? 0 / 4

The king, who remains the chief executive authority, is empowered to appoint and dismiss the prime minister and members of the cabinet. The prime minister is ostensibly the head of government, but has little power in practice. Ambrose Dlamini was appointed prime minister in October 2018, although he was not a member of Parliament at the time of his appointment, as required by the constitution.

Traditional chiefs govern their respective localities and typically report directly to the king. While some chiefs inherit their positions according to custom, others are appointed through royal interventions, as allowed by the constitution.

A2. Were the current national legislative representatives elected through free and fair elections? 0 / 4

The 69-member House of Assembly, the lower chamber of the bicameral Parliament, features 59 members elected by popular vote within the *tinkhundla* system, which allows local chiefs to vet candidates and influence outcomes in practice; the king appoints the other 10 members. The king appoints 20 members of the 30-seat Senate, the upper chamber, with the remainder selected by the House of Assembly. All members of Parliament serve five-year terms. After the parliamentary elections in September 2018, the king appointed six members of the royal family to the House of Assembly, and eight to the Senate. The elections, which were tightly controlled and featured a slate of candidates almost entirely loyal to the king, did not offer voters a genuine choice.

In August, a senior official at the Elections and Boundaries Commission (EBC) reported that members of the House of Assembly were accepting bribes in exchange for their votes in Senate elections. At year's end, no apparent consequences had followed.

A3. Are the electoral laws and framework fair, and are they implemented impartially by the relevant election management bodies? 0 / 4

The EBC is not considered impartial. It is financially and administratively dependent on the executive, and its members are appointed by the king on the advice of the Judicial Service Commission, whose members are also royal appointees. The EBC chairman, Gija Dlamini, is a half-brother of the king. At the end of the year, the EBC had not yet released detailed results from the September 2018 elections with a full accounting of votes received by each candidate.

Traditional chiefs also play an important role in elections, as candidates effectively need their approval to run for office.

B. POLITICAL PLURALISM AND PARTICIPATION: 1 / 16

B1. Do the people have the right to organize in different political parties or other competitive political groupings of their choice, and is the system free of undue obstacles to the rise and fall of these competing parties or groupings? 0 / 4

Election to public office is based on "individual merit," according to the constitution. There is no legal avenue for parties to register and participate in elections, though some political associations exist without legal recognition. Over the years, political parties seeking legal recognition have suffered court defeats, including a Supreme Court ruling in September 2018 rejecting a challenge by the Swazi Democratic Party (SWADEPA) to the ban on political parties competing in elections.

B2. Is there a realistic opportunity for the opposition to increase its support or gain power through elections? 0 / 4

The king has tight control over the political system in law and in practice, leaving no room for the emergence of an organized opposition with the potential to enter government. The vast majority of candidates who contested the 2018 general elections were supporters of the king.

B3. Are the people's political choices free from domination by the military, foreign powers, religious hierarchies, economic oligarchies, or any other powerful group that is not democratically accountable? 0 / 4

Traditional chiefs, as the king's representatives, wield enormous influence over their subjects. In addition to vetting prospective candidates for office, they have been accused of ordering residents to vote or not vote for certain candidates.

B4. Do various segments of the population (including ethnic, religious, gender, LGBT, and other relevant groups) have full political rights and electoral opportunities? 1 / 4

There are virtually no members of minority groups in the government, as most officials have some connection to the royal family or its broader clan. Women are politically marginalized, and the authorities have not adhered to the constitutional gender quota requiring 30 percent of representatives in Parliament to be women. The passage of the Election of Women Members to the House of Assembly Bill ahead of the 2018 elections requires the House of Assembly to elect four women if the quota is not met. In 2018, only two women were directly elected to Parliament, and with the addition of the women appointed by the king and elected to the Senate by the House of Assembly, as well as the election of four more women resulting from the new legislation, Eswatini still falls short of the quota. Customary restrictions on widows in mourning—a period that can last from one to three years—effectively bar them from participating in public affairs. Members of the LGBT community and people with disabilities also remain politically marginalized.

C. FUNCTIONING OF GOVERNMENT: 0 / 12

C1. Do the freely elected head of government and national legislative representatives determine the policies of the government? 0 / 4

The king and his government determine policy and legislation; members of Parliament hold no real power and effectively act as a rubber stamp in approving the king's legislative priorities. Parliament cannot initiate legislation and has little oversight or influence on budgetary matters. The king is also constitutionally empowered to veto any legislation. The absolute authority of the king was demonstrated by his decision to rename the country in April 2018 without any constitutional process or parliamentary approval.

C2. Are safeguards against official corruption strong and effective? 0 / 4

Corruption is a major problem, and implicated officials generally enjoy impunity. The Anti-Corruption Commission (ACC) is perceived to be ineffective, with civil society groups accusing it of pursuing politically motivated cases and serving the interests of the prime minister. The commission, which reports to the Justice Ministry, lacks adequate financial and human resources, and must consult with the minister on hiring. In March 2018, the ACC's budget was suspended by Parliament pending an investigation into corruption allegations within the body itself.

In November, a cabinet committee was established to develop a zero-tolerance policy on corruption in government, but it remains to be seen whether the committee can produce an effective anticorruption framework.

C3. Does the government operate with openness and transparency? 0 / 4

Eswatini lacks access to information laws and there is no culture of proactive disclosure of government information. Public requests for information are largely ignored in practice, and the budgeting process lacks transparency. The authorities tightly restrict access to data on spending by the royal family and the security forces. Transparency was further reduced by Parliament's passage of the Public Service Act in June 2018, which broadly prevents officials from providing public information to the media unless given express permission by the secretary of the cabinet.

CIVIL LIBERTIES: 15 / 60

D. FREEDOM OF EXPRESSION AND BELIEF: 5 / 16

D1. Are there free and independent media? 1 / 4

A variety of laws, including the Sedition and Subversive Activities Act (SSAA) and defamation laws, can be used to restrict media coverage. The state broadcaster is tightly controlled by the government, and the *Swazi Observer*, a major newspaper, is effectively owned by the king. Journalists often face harassment, assault, and intimidation, and self-censorship is reportedly common. In January 2018, Zweli Dlamini, the editor of the independent business publication *Swaziland Shopping,* fled to South Africa after receiving death threats over a 2017 article alleging the king's manipulation of the telecommunications industry to benefit a company he owns. *Swaziland Shopping* was also shut down on the king's orders in the wake of the article's publication.

D2. Are individuals free to practice and express their religious faith or nonbelief in public and private? 2 / 4

The constitution guarantees religious freedom and bars discrimination based on religion. Rules requiring registration of religious organizations are not strictly enforced. However, members of the Muslim minority allege discrimination by officials and Christian residents, and police reportedly monitor mosques. Non-Christian groups are also denied airtime on state broadcasters. Construction of religious buildings must be approved by the government or local chiefs. Christian education is compulsory in public schools, and in 2017, the government banned the teaching of other religions in the public school curriculum.

D3. Is there academic freedom, and is the educational system free from extensive political indoctrination? 1 / 4

Academic freedom is limited by restrictive laws such as the Suppression of Terrorism Act (STA) and SSAA. Student activists face potential violence, arrest, and suspension. In January 2018, police arrested 11 students protesting the administration at Swaziland Christian University and reportedly fired live ammunition into the demonstration.

D4. Are individuals free to express their personal views on political or other sensitive topics without fear of surveillance or retribution? 1 / 4

Constitutional rights to free expression are severely restricted in practice. Security agencies reportedly monitor personal communications, social media, and public gatherings, and criticism of the king or other elements of the regime can be punished under laws such as the SSAA, the STA, and the Public Order Act. Under revisions to the Public Order Act passed in 2017, any criticism of Swazi culture and traditions or defacement of national symbols —including the king's image—can draw fines and up to two years in prison.

E. ASSOCIATIONAL AND ORGANIZATIONAL RIGHTS: 2 / 12
E1. Is there freedom of assembly? 0 / 4

Freedom of assembly remained heavily restricted in 2018. Demonstrations are often violently dispersed by police, and protesters risk arrest and detention. In September, civil servants marching for pay increases were met by police who fired stun grenades into the crowd and assaulted demonstrators. Surveillance of protests is common, and the information collected is reportedly used to deny protesters access to government jobs and services.

E2. Is there freedom for nongovernmental organizations, particularly those that are engaged in human rights- and governance-related work? 1 / 4

The operation of nongovernmental organizations has been inhibited by the broadly written sedition and terrorism laws as well as police monitoring and interference. Organizations that advocate for democracy remain banned.

E3. Is there freedom for trade unions and similar professional or labor organizations? 1 / 4

Eswatini has active labor unions, but workers' rights are not upheld in practice. Although workers in most sectors, with the exception of essential services defined by the labor minister, can join unions, strikes and other labor activism routinely trigger crackdowns and arrests by the police. In June 2018, four protesters were seriously injured at a demonstration organized by the Trade Union Congress of Swaziland to protest corruption in the national pension fund and restrictions on collective bargaining, among other issues. Police fired rubber bullets and tear gas into the crowd. In September, a court banned a strike by public-sector workers, which was already underway, on the grounds that adequate notice was not provided.

F. RULE OF LAW: 4 / 16

F1. Is there an independent judiciary? 1 / 4

Although the judiciary displays a degree of independence in some cases, the king holds ultimate authority over the appointment and removal of judges, acting on advice from a Judicial Service Commission made up of royal appointees.

F2. Does due process prevail in civil and criminal matters? 1 / 4

Safeguards against arbitrary arrest and detention, such as time limits on detention without charge, are not always respected in practice. Detainees are generally granted access to lawyers, though only those facing life imprisonment or capital punishment can obtain counsel at public expense. Lengthy pretrial detention is common. In January 2018, the *Swazi Observer* reported that one murder suspect had spent nearly 10 years in jail awaiting trial. Politically sensitive cases often feature high bail levels. Fair trial rights are not respected by traditional courts, which often adjudicate minor offenses and use customary law.

F3. Is there protection from the illegitimate use of physical force and freedom from war and insurgencies? 1 / 4

Despite the June 2018 passage of the Police Service Act, which prescribes disciplinary measures for police officers who use illegitimate force, physical abuse of suspects and inmates by law enforcement officials is an ongoing problem, and investigations into such abuse lack independence and transparency. Some prisons also suffer from overcrowding and other harsh conditions.

F4. Do laws, policies, and practices guarantee equal treatment of various segments of the population? 1 / 4

Women's rights remain restricted in law and in practice. Both civil and customary law treat women as dependents of their fathers or husbands, and societal discrimination further impairs their access to education and employment. Residents who are not ethnic Swazis also face de facto discrimination. People with disabilities experience social stigma as well as discrimination in education and employment. At the end of 2018, Parliament had not yet passed the Rights of Persons with Disabilities Bill of 2015, which is intended to address many of the inequities experienced by disabled residents.

Discrimination against LGBT people is not prohibited by law and is widespread in practice. A criminal ban on same-sex sexual activity is not regularly enforced. In June 2018, the police allowed the first LGBT pride march in Eswatini's history, but the chief police spokesperson said before the march that the LGBT community would not be tolerated.

G. PERSONAL AUTONOMY AND INDIVIDUAL RIGHTS: 4 / 16

G1. Do individuals enjoy freedom of movement, including the ability to change their place of residence, employment, or education? 1 / 4

The constitution guarantees freedom of movement. However, minority ethnic groups and political activists have faced delays in obtaining passports and other citizenship documents. Traditional chiefs regulate movement and residence within their communities and generally deny access to groups advocating human rights or democracy. Individuals who violate customary rules can face eviction from their localities. Widows in mourning are barred from approaching chiefs or the king and excluded from certain public places and activities.

G2. Are individuals able to exercise the right to own property and establish private businesses without undue interference from state or nonstate actors? 1 / 4

The constitution provides legal protections for property rights, but women generally face limitations under customary rules that subordinate them to male relatives. Widows in particular face expropriation by the deceased husband's family. Chiefs have broad authority to allocate and withdraw rights to communal land.

Individuals can face expropriation due to land claims by state-owned companies and powerful private interests, and constitutional guarantees of fair compensation are not upheld. In April 2018, Amnesty International reported that 61 people were forcibly evicted from their homes on land owned by a private agriculture company in the town of Malkerns; the residents were not given adequate notice of the eviction, nor were they provided with substantial compensation.

G3. Do individuals enjoy personal social freedoms, including choice of marriage partner and size of family, protection from domestic violence, and control over appearance? 1 / 4

Women's social freedoms are restricted by both civil and customary law, which puts them at a disadvantage regarding marriage, divorce, and child custody. Customary law allows girls as young as 13 to marry. Sexual and domestic violence remains extremely common, and any penalties for perpetrators are often lenient. In July 2018, Parliament passed the Sexual Offences and Domestic Violence Act, which criminalizes marital rape, calls for the creation of specialized domestic violence courts, and establishes new mechanisms for reporting domestic violence, among other provisions.

G4. Do individuals enjoy equality of opportunity and freedom from economic exploitation? 1 / 4

Residents have some access to formal employment and economic opportunity, but the majority of the population lives in poverty. Forced labor remains a problem, with some chiefs compelling Swazis, including children, to work in their communities or the king's fields. Among other forms of child labor, girls are particularly vulnerable to domestic servitude and commercial sexual exploitation.

Ethiopia

Population: 107,500,000
Capital: Addis Ababa
Political Rights Rating: 6 ↑
Civil Liberties Rating: 6
Freedom Rating: 6.0
Freedom Status: Not Free
Electoral Democracy: No

Overview: Ethiopia is undergoing a potential transition, set off by the 2018 appointment of Prime Minister Abiy Ahmed following sustained antigovernment protests. Abiy has pledged to reform Ethiopia's authoritarian state, ruled by the Ethiopian People's Revolutionary Democratic Front (EPRDF) since 1991, and rewrite the country's repressive electoral, terrorism, and media laws. However, Ethiopia remains beset by political factionalism and intercommunal violence, abuses by security forces and violations of due process are still common, and many restrictive laws remain in force.

KEY DEVELOPMENTS IN 2018:

- In February, Prime Minister Hailemariam Desalegn resigned unexpectedly amid growing antigovernment protests. Abiy Ahmed—a 42-year-old former military officer from Ethiopia's largest ethnic group, the Oromo, and a member of the ruling EPRDF—was confirmed as the new prime minister in April, and has embarked on an ambitious reform agenda aimed at opening civic and political space.
- The environment for the media improved significantly during the year. The government released imprisoned journalists, and by December, there were no journalists in Ethiopian prisons for the first time since 2004, according to the Committee to Protect Journalists (CPJ). In June, authorities lifted bans against the diaspora-run media channels Ethiopian Satellite Television (ESAT), and the Oromo Media Network (OMN), which then opened operations in Ethiopia.
- Restrictions on opposition leader and groups eased throughout the year. In January, the government released hundreds of political prisoners, including Merera Gudina, leader of the Oromo Federalist Congress (OFC). In June, Parliament removed Ginbot 7, the Oromo Liberation Front (OLF), and the Ogaden National Liberation Front (ONLF) from its list of terrorist organizations.
- Intercommunal violence related to political, ethnic, border, and land issues continued throughout the year in locations across the country, and displaced at least a million people in 2018 alone.

POLITICAL RIGHTS: 7 / 40 (+3)

A. ELECTORAL PROCESS: 1 / 12

A1. Was the current head of government or other chief national authority elected through free and fair elections? 0 / 4

The president is the head of state and is indirectly elected to a six-year term by both chambers of Parliament. The prime minister is head of government, and is selected by the largest party in Parliament after elections, or in the case of a resignation. Prime Minister Abiy Ahmed—a 42-year-old former military officer from Ethiopia's largest ethnic group, the

Oromo, and a member of the ruling EPRDF—was sworn in as prime minister in April 2018, succeeding Hailemariam Desalegn, who resigned in February amid growing protests at which demonstrators demanded greater political rights. Abiy was reconfirmed at the EPRDF party congress in October. The last parliamentary elections, which led to the selection of Desalegn as prime minister in 2015, were not held in accordance with democratic standards.

A2. Were the current national legislative representatives elected through free and fair elections? 0 / 4

The bicameral Parliament includes the 153-seat House of Federation, whose members are elected by state assemblies to five-year terms, and the House of People's Representatives, with 547 members directly elected to five-year terms.

The 2015 parliamentary and regional elections were tightly controlled by the EPRDF, with reports of voter coercion, intimidation, and registration barriers. The opposition lost its sole parliamentary seat, as the EPRDF and its allies took all 547 seats in the House of People's Representatives.

A3. Are the electoral laws and framework fair, and are they implemented impartially by the relevant election management bodies? 1 / 4

The 2015 elections were held on time and official results were released within a month. However, opposition parties repeatedly questioned the independence of the National Electoral Board of Ethiopia (NEBE), and the Unity for Democracy and Justice (UDJ) party alleged that it blocked its leaders from registering as candidates.

Prime Minister Abiy has promised electoral reforms, and in November 2018, he met with opposition leaders to discuss how to make the electoral framework fairer. Also in November, Parliament confirmed Birtukan Mideksa, a prominent, previously exiled former opposition leader, to serve as head of the NEBE. At year's end, Parliament was considering a draft bill designed to increase the independence of the NEBE.

B. POLITICAL PLURALISM AND PARTICIPATION: 3 / 16 (+3)

B1. Do the people have the right to organize in different political parties or other competitive political groupings of their choice, and is the system free of undue obstacles to the rise and fall of these competing parties or groupings? 1 / 4 (+1)

Opponents of the EPRDF have found it nearly impossible to operate inside Ethiopia and were subject to prosecution under restrictive antiterrorism and other legislation. However, in 2018, authorities took a number of actions that gave political groupings more freedom to operate.

In January 2018, the government released hundreds of political prisoners, including Merera Gudina, leader of the OFC. Bekele Gerba, another prominent OFC figure, was freed in February. Both Merera and Bekele had been jailed on trumped-up charged of terrorism. In May, Andargachew Tsige, who had been sentenced to death for his membership in the banned opposition group Ginbot 7, was pardoned. In June, Parliament removed Ginbot 7 and two other groups—the OLF, and the ONLF—from its list of terrorist organizations as a first step toward fostering peaceful and constructive political dialogue. And in July, Parliament approved a widespread amnesty for thousands of individuals charged with treason and other crimes against the state, most of whom had been released earlier in the year. These changes have paved the way for many high-profile opposition figures to return from exile, including Birhanu Nega of Ginbot 7, who returned in September after 11 years in exile.

Abiy's administration has pledged reforms that will ease the legal and practical requirements for opposition parties to operate, though substantial changes are necessary before political parties can carry out activities freely.

Score Change: The score improved from 0 to 1 because the government took a number of steps that allowed political groupings greater freedom to operate, including releasing political prisoners, pardoning opposition leaders, and enacting an amnesty for thousands of people charged with crimes against the state.

B2. Is there a realistic opportunity for the opposition to increase its support or gain power through elections? 1 / 4 (+1)

The EPRDF still maintains numerous formal and informal advantages over opposition parties, and there are no opposition parties represented in Parliament. However, the changes Prime Minister Abiy's government began to implement in 2018 improved conditions for opposition groupings, which may now prepare more openly for the 2020 parliamentary elections. Abiy in August 2018 expressed a commitment to democratic polls, and pledged that he would not allow his reforms to delay the vote.

Score Change: The score improved from 0 to 1 because Prime Minister Abiy's reforms allow opposition groupings to operate more openly in advance of 2020 elections.

B3. Are the people's political choices free from domination by the military, foreign powers, religious hierarchies, economic oligarchies, or any other powerful group that is not democratically accountable? 0 / 4

Ethiopia's powerful military has been influential in the country's politics, and patronage networks, often based on ethnicity, often drive political decision-making. The authoritarian one-party system in Ethiopia largely excludes the public from genuine political participation, though nascent attempts by Abiy to include more diverse voices in the political system could yield positive results.

B4. Do various segments of the population (including ethnic, religious, gender, LGBT, and other relevant groups) have full political rights and electoral opportunities? 1 / 4 (+1)

Women hold nearly 39 percent of seats in the lower house and 32 percent in the upper house, but in practice, the interests of women are not well represented in politics. Prime Minister Abiy has made some effort, however, to include women in high-level decision-making processes. In 2018, women were appointed to a number of prominent positions including the presidency, head of the NEBE, head of the Supreme Court, and to half of all cabinet posts.

Political parties in Ethiopia are often based on ethnicity. The country's major ethnic parties are allied with the EPRDF, but have historically had little room to effectively advocate for their constituents. Ongoing friction inside the ruling coalition between the Tigrayan People's Liberation Front (TPLF), which previously dominated decision-making as well as resource allocation, and the other ethnically based parties, including Prime Minister Abiy's Oromo People's Democratic Organization (OPDO), continues.

Score Change: The score improved from 0 to 1 due to the appointments of women to a number of senior government posts.

C. FUNCTIONING OF GOVERNMENT: 3 / 12

C1. Do the freely elected head of government and national legislative representatives determine the policies of the government? 0 / 4

None of Ethiopia's nominally elected officials were chosen through credible elections, and the country's governance institutions remain dominated by the EPRDF.

C2. Are safeguards against official corruption strong and effective? 2 / 4

Corruption and unequal resource distribution are significant problems that have contributed to the unrest that has plagued Ethiopia in recent years. The government has taken some steps to address the issue, which remains a priority for Prime Minister Abiy's administration.

In November and December 2018, a number of high-profile military and government officials were arrested and charged with corruption. Notably, 26 high-level employees of the military-run Metals and Engineering Corporation (MeTEC), including its chief executive, were arrested on corruption charges, and were awaiting trial at the end of the year. Some critics have accused the government of selectively prosecuting officials from the Tigray ethnic group, which has dominated the military for decades. However, a number of non-Tigray officials were also arrested in the sweep.

C3. Does the government operate with openness and transparency? 1 / 4

Although EPRDF operations and decision-making processes have generally been opaque, the government has attempted to increase transparency in recent years, and in 2018 consulted with community organizations and journalists to advance reform efforts. The Legal and Justice Affairs Advisory Council was established in June 2018, and has a three-year term to study the country's restrictive terrorism, media, and nongovernmental organization (NGO) laws and recommend reforms to them. The council includes a number of legal professionals with various areas of expertise.

However, government procurement processes remain largely opaque, and some companies are still awarded government contracts without a tender. Due to widespread insecurity, in April the government postponed the census, which was originally scheduled for November 2017, by one year. (Carrying out the census is essential for planning the budget.)

CIVIL LIBERTIES: 12 / 60 (+4)

D. FREEDOM OF EXPRESSION AND BELIEF: 4 / 16 (+2)

D1. Are there free and independent media? 1 / 4 (+1)

After years of severe restrictions on press freedom, the government took initial steps to increase freedoms for independent media in 2018. A number of prominent journalists were released from prison during the year, including Eskinder Nega and Woubshet Taye, who were both freed in February after they each had served almost seven years in prison for criticizing the restrictive 2009 terrorism laws. As of December, no journalists were imprisoned in Ethiopia for the first time since 2004, according to CPJ. However, this progress was tempered somewhat by the arrests and detentions of five journalists and bloggers along with several politicians in March; they had been attending a party, which violated a state of emergency imposed the previous month that required permission for gatherings. After being detained for 12 days, the journalists were released with the others.

Ethiopia's media landscape is dominated by state-owned broadcasters and government-oriented newspapers. However, since Prime Minister Abiy took office in April, the government has eased restrictions on independent media, permitting both greater freedom for journalists and a more diverse range of news for consumers. In June, the government lifted bans on 264 websites (including news sites and blogs) and television networks. Among the outlets allowed to reopen were the US-based diaspora satellite television stations, Ethiopian Satellite Television (ESAT), and the Oromo Media Network (OMN), which had been charged with inciting terrorism and banned in 2017. They each opened offices in Ethiopia after the bans were lifted; earlier, in May, the charges against both networks were dropped.

The government has promised to revise its controversial 2008 mass media law, which gives broad powers to the government to prosecute defamation, but at the end of 2018 legislation had not yet been drafted.

Score Change: The score improved from 0 to 1 because the government eased restrictions on media, including by lifting bans on news outlets and releasing imprisoned journalists.

D2. Are individuals free to practice and express their religious faith or nonbelief in public and private? 2 / 4

The constitution guarantees religious freedom, but the government has historically discriminated against Muslims, who comprise about 34 percent of the population. In 2018, however, the relationship between the government and the Muslim community began to improve. Between February and May, more than a dozen prominent Muslim activists who had been convicted under the country's antiterrorism law in 2015 for protesting against the government's treatment of Muslims were released from prison. Additionally, Prime Minister Abiy facilitated dialogues during the year to heal schisms in both the Ethiopian Orthodox Church and among the country's Islamic leaders.

D3. Is there academic freedom, and is the educational system free from extensive political indoctrination? 0 / 4

Academic freedom is restricted in Ethiopia. The government has accused universities of being pro-opposition and prohibits political activities on campuses. There are reports of students being pressured into joining the EPRDF in order to secure employment or admission to universities; professors are similarly pressured in order to ensure favorable positions or promotions. The Ministry of Education closely monitors and regulates official curricula, and the research, speech, and assembly rights of both professors and students are frequently restricted.

D4. Are individuals free to express their personal views on political or other sensitive topics without fear of surveillance or retribution? 1 / 4 (+1)

Wide-reaching surveillance programs and the presence of the EPRDF at all levels of society have inhibited private discussion. However, broad political changes in 2018, including the release of political prisoners and lifting of bans against prominent government critics in the media and other sectors has fostered a more open atmosphere for private discussion. And unlike in some previous years, in 2018 there were no reported arrests of private citizens in connection with antigovernment remarks.

Some international organizations have expressed concerns about a proposed hate speech law that the Office of the Attorney General began drafting in November, arguing that it could curtail free speech. The draft legislation could place restrictions on social media posts, which some government officials have partially blamed for ethnic violence that wracked the country in 2018. The law had not yet been enacted as of December.

In response to violence or unrest, the government is known to shut down internet access, curtailing people's ability to communicate. In August, in response to ethnic clashes, the government shut down mobile and broadband internet access in the Somali Region for several days.

Score Change: The score improved from 0 to 1 because broad political reforms have resulted in individuals' increased willingness to express political views in private discussions.

E. ASSOCIATIONAL AND ORGANIZATIONAL RIGHTS: 2 / 12 (+2)
E1. Is there freedom of assembly? 1 / 4 (+1)

Severe restrictions on freedom of assembly imposed by the EPRDF government in the past eased somewhat in 2018, as demonstrations were more frequently allowed to occur without interference. However, protests were still sometimes violently dispersed by security forces. In August, for example, police opened fire on a group of demonstrators protesting the looting of property owned by ethnic minorities in the Somali Region, killing four people.

A government-imposed state of emergency, which was announced in February in response to the escalating ethnic violence and the resignation of former prime minister Hailemariam Desalegn, effectively banned public protests until it was lifted in June, two months earlier than planned. The internet was blocked several times in 2018 in response to mass demonstrations, hampering their organization. In September, mobile internet was blocked for three days in Addis Ababa in the wake of protests.

Score Change: The score improved from 0 to 1 because demonstrations were more frequently allowed to occur without interference.

E2. Is there freedom for nongovernmental organizations, particularly those that are engaged in human rights– and governance-related work? 1 / 4 (+1)

In 2018, the space for NGOs to operate opened significantly. NGOs can now more freely organize public events, renew registration, and make public statements that are critical of the government without facing harassment or intimidation by authorities.

The 2009 Charities and Societies Proclamation restricts the activities of foreign NGOs by prohibiting work on political and human rights issues, though Prime Minister Abiy has promised to revise the legislation, and the Legal and Justice Affairs Advisory Council sought input from an array of NGOs during its review of the law. A draft of the new proclamation, which would ease funding restrictions for human rights groups and politically oriented NGOs and limit the ability of the Charities and Societies Agency to interfere with their operations, was under consideration by the Council of Ministers at the end of 2018.

Score Change: The score improved from 0 to 1 because government interference with the work of NGOs decreased.

E3. Is there freedom for trade unions and similar professional or labor organizations? 0 / 4

Trade union rights are tightly restricted. Neither civil servants nor teachers have collective bargaining rights. All unions must be registered, and the government retains the authority to cancel registration. Two-thirds of union members belong to organizations affiliated with the Confederation of Ethiopian Trade Unions, which is under government influence. Independent unions face harassment, and trade union leaders are regularly imprisoned. There has not been a legal strike since 1993, though unsanctioned ones sometimes take place.

F. RULE OF LAW: 2 / 16
F1. Is there an independent judiciary? 1 / 4

The judiciary is officially independent, but in practice it is subject to political interference, and judgments rarely deviate from government policy. The November 2018 appointment of lawyer and civil society leader Meaza Ashenafi as chief justice of the Supreme

Court has raised hopes for judicial reform. Ashenafi has promised to build judicial independence and reduce corruption in the courts, and she claims to have the support of Prime Minister Abiy in this endeavor.

F2. Does due process prevail in civil and criminal matters? 0 / 4

Due process rights are generally not respected. However, in 2018, the Legal and Justice Affairs Advisory Council began a review of the 2009 Anti-Terrorism Proclamation, which has been used to arbitrarily arrest opposition figures, NGO leaders, journalists, and other critics of the government. In February 2018, 10,000 people who had been arbitrarily detained under a state of emergency imposed in October 2017 were released, though the government also said it intended to bring charges against thousands of others detained in the sweep.

Despite some positive developments in 2018, arbitrary arrest and detention remains common. During one weekend in September, nearly 3,000 people were arrested in a sweep purportedly meant to address rising crime in Addis Ababa, with many detained for activities that are not criminal offenses in Ethiopia, such as smoking shisha. Although many of those arrested were promptly released, some 1,200 youths detained for their alleged participation in September protests against ethnic violence were sent to a military facility for a month, for "rehabilitation." The right to a fair trial is often not respected, particularly for opponents of the government charged under the antiterrorism law.

F3. Is there protection from the illegitimate use of physical force and freedom from war and insurgencies? 0 / 4

Ethnic violence and unrest continued in numerous regions of Ethiopia in 2018, mainly between members of the Oromo community and other groups, and the violence escalated after Abiy, an ethnic Oromo, took office. In response to the crisis, in which numerous people were killed and at least a million people were displaced in 2018 alone, Parliament approved a new reconciliation commission in December to promote dialogue and encourage a peaceful resolution to the conflicts.

Earlier, in August, Prime Minister Abiy deployed the army to the eastern Somali Region amid an apparent dispute between regional and federal authorities and an outbreak of violence against ethnic minorities; federal forces subsequently arrested and imprisoned the region's president, Abdi Illey, on charges of orchestrating widespread rights abuses and stoking ethnic violence.

Security forces frequently commit human rights violations including torture and extrajudicial killings, and often act with impunity. However, the new government has shown some willingness to hold police and military personnel accountable. In November, 36 senior intelligence officials were arrested for human rights abuses including torture, and awaited trial at year's end.

F4. Do laws, policies, and practices guarantee equal treatment of various segments of the population? 1 / 4

Repression of the Oromo and ethnic Somalis, and government attempts to coopt their political parties into EPRDF allies, has fueled nationalism in the Oromia and Somali regions. The property of ethnic minorities, and of people living in areas where they are not members of the majority group, are frequently targeted in the unrest that has wracked Ethiopia.

Same-sex sexual activity is prohibited by law and punishable by up to 15 years' imprisonment. Women face discrimination in education, access to credit, and employment.

G. PERSONAL AUTONOMY AND INDIVIDUAL RIGHTS: 4 / 16

G1. Do individuals enjoy freedom of movement, including the ability to change their place of residence, employment, or education? 1 / 4

While the constitution establishes freedom of movement, violence, particularly in the Oromia and Somali regions, impedes people's ability to travel freely.

In September 2018, following a declaration of peace between Ethiopia and Eritrea in July, key border crossings between the two countries opened for the first time in 20 years.

G2. Are individuals able to exercise the right to own property and establish private businesses without undue interference from state or nonstate actors? 1 / 4

Private business opportunities are limited by rigid state control of economic life and the prevalence of state-owned enterprises. Prime Minister Abiy has promised to implement significant economic reforms, and in June 2018, the government announced that it would open state monopolies in aviation and telecommunications to private investment.

All land must be leased from the state. The government has evicted indigenous groups from various areas to make way for infrastructure projects. It has also leased large tracts of land to foreign governments and investors for agricultural development in opaque deals that have resulted in the displacement of thousands of people.

Evictions have taken place in the Lower Omo Valley, where government-run sugar plantations and hydroelectric dams have put thousands of pastoralists at risk by diverting their water supplies.

G3. Do individuals enjoy personal social freedoms, including choice of marriage partner and size of family, protection from domestic violence, and control over appearance? 1 / 4

Legislation protects women's rights, but these rights are routinely violated in practice. Enforcement of laws against rape and domestic abuse is inconsistent, and cases routinely stall in the courts. In 2018, a joint research project conducted by academics at Debre Markos University in Ethiopia and the University of Queensland in Australia concluded that almost half of Ethiopian women become victims of gender-based violence in their lifetimes.

Forced child marriage is illegal but common in Ethiopia, and prosecutions for the crime are rare. According to UN International Children's Emergency Fund (UNICEF) statistics for 2017, 40 percent of women are married before the age of 18. Female genital mutilation (FGM) is also illegal, but the law is inconsistently enforced, and the 2016 Ethiopian Demographic Health Survey found that 65 percent of women between the ages of 15 and 49 had undergone the practice. However, reports suggest that FGM rates have reduced in recent years due to efforts by both NGOs and the government to combat the practice.

G4. Do individuals enjoy equality of opportunity and freedom from economic exploitation? 1 / 4

Trafficking convictions have increased in recent years, though the US government continues to urge its Ethiopian counterparts to more aggressively pursue trafficking cases. Many children continue to work in dangerous sectors and lack access to basic education and services. Most agricultural labor in rural areas is performed by women, but these women are generally excluded from decision-making processes regarding their work.

Fiji

Population: 900,000
Capital: Suva
Political Rights Rating: 3
Civil Liberties Rating: 3
Freedom Rating: 3.0
Freedom Status: Partly Free
Electoral Democracy: Yes

Overview: The repressive climate that followed a 2006 coup has eased since democratic elections were held in 2014 and 2018. However, the ruling party frequently interferes with opposition activities, the judiciary is subject to political influence, and military and police brutality is a significant problem.

KEY DEVELOPMENTS IN 2018:

- In the November parliamentary elections, Prime Minister Frank Bainimarama's FijiFirst Party won 50 percent of the total vote and 27 seats in the 51-member Parliament; international observers deemed the poll largely credible.
- In May, three *Fiji Times* executives and a staff writer were acquitted on charges of sedition, which stemmed from the publication of a controversial letter in 2016 that the prosecution had claimed promoted feelings of "ill will" about Muslims.
- Also in May, Parliament passed the Online Safety Act, which criminalizes people who are found to cause harm to others through electronic communications. Rights groups assailed the legislation, arguing that it could be misused to punish online dissent.

POLITICAL RIGHTS: 24 / 40

A. ELECTORAL PROCESS: 8 / 12

A1. Was the current head of government or other chief national authority elected through free and fair elections? 3 / 4

The prime minister is the head of government and serves four-year terms. The party that wins the most seats in parliamentary elections selects the prime minister, who is then appointed by the president. In the November 2018 parliamentary elections, Prime Minister Frank Bainimarama's FijiFirst Party won 50 percent of the total vote and 27 seats in the 51-member Parliament. The Multinational Observer Group reported that the polling "was transparent and credible overall and the outcome broadly represented the will of Fijian voters." However, in a preelection debate with opposition leader and former prime minister Sitiveni Rabuka, Bainimarama refused to decisively rule out a coup if his party lost.

The president is elected by Parliament, which chooses between two candidates: one named by the prime minister and one by the leader of the opposition. As head of state, the president—who is elected to a three-year term and is eligible for reelection—holds a largely ceremonial role. President George Konrote was elected to a second term by Parliament in August.

A2. Were the current national legislative representatives elected through free and fair elections? 2 / 4

Parliament is Fiji's unicameral legislative body, with 51 members elected to serve four-year terms. International observers regarded the 2018 parliamentary elections, held in November, to be largely credible, although civil society participation was limited.

Municipal councils continue to be run by government-appointed administrators, having been dissolved in 2009 in the wake of the abrogation of the 1997 constitution. As a result, municipal elections have not been held since 2005.

A3. Are the electoral laws and framework fair, and are they implemented impartially by the relevant election management bodies? 3 / 4

The legal framework for Fijian elections is considered fair. However, the structure of the electoral system has raised concerns about potential political interference. FijiFirst's general secretary, Aiyaz Sayed-Khaiyum, serves as minister of elections, as well as attorney general. Opposition parties claim that this creates a bias in the Electoral Commission, which administers elections, and affects the independence of the body. In December 2018, opposition parties withdrew petitions filed with the Court of Disputed Returns, which alleged unlawful actions by some FijiFirst candidates and irregularities in the conduct of the polling, counting, and tallying processes.

B. POLITICAL PLURALISM AND PARTICIPATION: 9 / 16

B1. Do the people have the right to organize in different political parties or other competitive political groupings of their choice, and is the system free of undue obstacles to the rise and fall of these competing parties or groupings? 3 / 4

The right to form political parties is constitutionally guaranteed, but the government has eligibility requirements that discourage the formation of smaller parties: prospective parties must submit 5,000 signatures to become registered. The 5 percent nationwide threshold for representation in Parliament further disincentivizes the formation of smaller parties.

B2. Is there a realistic opportunity for the opposition to increase its support or gain power through elections? 1 / 4

The dominance of FijiFirst in Parliament and its popularity with the public has left little space for opposition forces to assert themselves politically. However, the major opposition party, the Social Democratic Liberal Party (SODELPA), won 21 seats in 2018, up from 15 in 2014. FijiFirst has used state resources to advance its political campaigns. The Multinational Observer Group noted that during the 2018 parliamentary campaign, government ministers and high-level officials engaged in a number of high-profile activities, such as opening buildings, signing commercial contracts, and disbursing government grants and funds, which could have provided an electoral advantage to FijiFirst.

Prime Minister Bainimarama has, in the past, stated that he would not allow the opposition parties to assume office. Ahead of the 2018 elections, he issued warnings of instability in the event FijiFirst was defeated.

Opposition figures have been targeted by corruption charges they claim are politically motivated. In May, the Fiji Independent Commission against Corruption (FICAC) charged Sitiveni Rabuka with making a false declaration of assets. He was acquitted in October, but FICAC appealed the decision, and the case was ultimately dismissed two days before the elections in November. Had he been convicted, Rabuka would have been barred from the contest. In the days before the elections, Rabuka was questioned by the police, reportedly over statements he made on a radio show.

B3. Are the people's political choices free from domination by the military, foreign powers, religious hierarchies, economic oligarchies, or any other powerful group that is not democratically accountable? 2 / 4

Despite constitutional guarantees that it remain apolitical, the military has a history of interference in Fijian politics. The leaders of the two major political parties are former military officials, which contributes to the perception that the military has an undue political influence. In 2017, some military officials made statements directed against opposition politicians. However, in July 2018, Viliame Naupoto, the commander of the military forces, said that "the coup days are over" and assured the public that the military would accept whatever government was selected by the people.

B4. Do various segments of the population (including ethnic, religious, gender, LGBT, and other relevant groups) have full political rights and electoral opportunities? 3 / 4

The law does not restrict the participation of minorities and women in politics. However, due to cultural traditions, the participation of indigenous women is limited. Only 10 out of the 51 members of Parliament are women.

Smaller minority groups, including Banabans, Chinese, and people from other Polynesian islands, lack significant political representation.

Historically, political affiliations have been associated with ethnicity. The Bainimarama-led interim government pushed for national unity and a national identity transcending ethnicity, race, and religion. For the 2018 general elections, all political parties were required to have English names to appeal to all ethnic groups, and to demonstrate support from all four official regions. Reserved seats and special considerations for ethnic and religious groups have been eliminated.

C. FUNCTIONING OF GOVERNMENT: 7 / 12

C1. Do the freely elected head of government and national legislative representatives determine the policies of the government? 3 / 4

The executive branch under Prime Minister Bainimarama determines the policies of government. With FijiFirst holding a strong parliamentary majority prior to the 2018 elections, the government has frequently pushed through bills and budgets with minimal scrutiny from the opposition in Parliament.

C2. Are safeguards against official corruption strong and effective? 2 / 4

Safeguards against corruption are limited in their effectiveness. The FICAC had limited success combatting institutional corruption in 2018, pursuing several high-profile cases. In October, two officials with the Fiji Revenue and Customs Service were charged with corruption for allegedly falsifying documents, which led to a substantial loss in revenue. The case was ongoing at year's end. However, corruption remains a serious problem and many officials still act with impunity. FICAC has also allegedly pursued politically motivated corruption cases.

C3. Does the government operate with openness and transparency? 2 / 4

Since the restoration of elective democracy in 2014, government transparency and openness has improved. The government now organizes an annual briefing for civil society organizations on the budget. Parliamentary sessions are broadcast live, and Hansard (an official report of parliamentary proceedings) is updated regularly. Although candidates for election are required to declare their assets, there is no law requiring public asset disclosures by members of Parliament. Fiji lacks an access to information law, and requests for information from the media and the public are sometimes denied. In recent years, FijiFirst has used its majority in Parliament to rewrite parliamentary standing orders in a manner that limits debate on legislation and parliamentary scrutiny of official statements.

CIVIL LIBERTIES: 37 / 60 (+2)
D. FREEDOM OF EXPRESSION AND BELIEF: 12 / 16
D1. Are there free and independent media? 2 / 4

Fiji has an active media sector, with several private television stations, radio stations, and newspapers. The opposition and other critics of the government have accused the government of using state power to silence critics. For example, the vaguely worded Media Industry Development Decree bans reporting that is critical of the government or harmful to "national interest public order." The restrictive press laws are sometimes enforced by the government, which leads to self-censorship. In May 2018, publisher Hank Arts, two other *Fiji Times* executives, and a staff writer were acquitted on charges of sedition, which stemmed from the publication of a controversial letter in 2016 that the prosecution had claimed promoted feelings of "ill will" about Muslims.

D2. Are individuals free to practice and express their religious faith or nonbelief in public and private? 4 / 4

Freedom of religion is generally respected. However, several Hindu temples have been vandalized in recent years, including three temples near Suva in January 2018. In 2017, 15 people were convicted of sedition in Ra province for attempting to form a Christian state.

D3. Is there academic freedom, and is the educational system free from extensive political indoctrination? 3 / 4

Academic freedom is not overtly constrained, but government control over funding has been used to exert influence over tertiary institutions. The University of the South Pacific prohibits the majority of its employees from taking on an official position with a political party or running for office.

D4. Are individuals free to express their personal views on political or other sensitive topics without fear of surveillance or retribution? 3 / 4

There were no confirmed reports of government restrictions on private discussion on political matters or other sensitive topics during the year. However, the government places constraints on free speech, such as a law banning the burning of the national flag.

In May 2018, Parliament passed the Online Safety Act. Under the law, people who are found to cause harm to others through electronic communications could be sentenced to up to five years in prison. Rights groups assailed the legislation, arguing that it could be misused to punish online dissent.

E. ASSOCIATIONAL AND ORGANIZATIONAL RIGHTS: 8 / 12 (+2)
E1. Is there freedom of assembly? 3 / 4 (+1)

Respect for assembly rights improved in 2018. The Public Order Act was amended in 2017, which ended a requirement that organizers of public demonstrations obtain a police permit seven days before the event, although some events are still subjected to the permitting requirement. During the 2018 campaign period, parties were largely able to hold rallies and campaign events without restrictions. However, the constitution gives the government wide latitude to prohibit protests, including on the basis of public safety and public morality.

Score Change: The score improved from 2 to 3 because past restrictions on public gather-ings were eased ahead of the 2018 elections.

E2. Is there freedom for nongovernmental organizations, particularly those that are engaged in human rights- and governance-related work? 3 / 4 (+1)

Fiji has an extensive nongovernmental organization (NGO) network, which largely operates without government interference. The amendments to the Public Order Act further lifted restrictions on civil society activities such as meetings and other public gatherings, and the environment for NGOs continued to improve in 2018. Despite these improvements, government officials placed some pressure on civil society during the year. In August, the attorney general accused NGOs of being "politically aligned" and lacking independence.

Strict sedition laws, which criminalize criticism of the government, place constraints on the range of initiatives that NGOs can undertake. NGOs have been critical of the proposed Parliamentary Powers and Privileges Bill, which they claim criminalizes criticism of Parlia-ment and could further erode civic space.

Score Change: The score improved from 2 to 3 because NGOs have been freer to organize meetings and events than in previous years, and they continued to speak out on controversial topics despite some pressure from authorities.

E3. Is there freedom for trade unions and similar professional or labor organizations? 2 / 4

The general environment for trade unions has improved. Since the passage of the 2016 Employment Relations (Amendment) Act, all workers have the right to form unions and strike. However, public-sector unions claim that the government has denied them the right to collective bargaining. The law restricts political activities by union members, prohibiting union members from becoming members of Parliament and impeding their ability to join political parties.

F. RULE OF LAW: 7 / 16

F1. Is there an independent judiciary? 2 / 4

While the constitution guarantees an independent judiciary, there have been credible allegations of political interference. The prime minister has substantial appointment pow-ers, with the authority to both appoint and dismiss judges on the Supreme Court and other high courts. These powers leave the judiciary vulnerable to interference and abuse by the executive.

F2. Does due process prevail in civil and criminal matters? 1 / 4

Due process rights are often not respected in practice. Corruption is a major problem in the police force. Due to resource shortages, lengthy pretrial detentions are common. The law allows suspects to be arrested without a warrant for violating the Crimes Decree. Politically motivated criminal charges are not uncommon.

In December 2018, members of the FijiFirst government sought to evade opposition efforts to serve an election petition on cabinet ministers ordered by the Court of Disputed Returns, which alleged "unlawful conduct" by 27 members of Parliament when they were candidates. The ministers slept for two nights in the attorney general's office, but the court ul-timately allowed the petitions to be considered served through their publication in the media.

F3. Is there protection from the illegitimate use of physical force and freedom from war and insurgencies? 2 / 4

Torture and beatings by police remain a serious issue. In October 2018, 26-year-old Joseua Lalauvaki died after reportedly being beaten by the police following his arrest in Suva in September. Two police officers were charged with his murder in November, and the case was ongoing at year's end. Despite these charges, police officers and military officials who commit abuses are rarely brought to justice, and those who are convicted of crimes are frequently pardoned or have their convictions overturned on appeal. Prisons are often overcrowded, lack sanitation, and provide inadequate health services.

F4. Do laws, policies, and practices guarantee equal treatment of various segments of the population? 2 / 4

Lesbian, gay, bisexual, and transgender (LGBT) people face discrimination in employment and access to healthcare. Women experience discrimination in employment as well, and a gender pay gap persists.

Relations between indigenous Fijians and Indo-Fijians remain strained. Indigenous Fijians previously enjoyed legal advantages in education and political representation. However, the interim government, after the 2006 coup, removed many of these privileges in a bid to foster a sense of national unity.

G. PERSONAL AUTONOMY AND INDIVIDUAL RIGHTS: 10 / 16

G1. Do individuals enjoy freedom of movement, including the ability to change their place of residence, employment, or education? 3 / 4

Citizens enjoy the freedom to travel, live, work, and seek education inside and outside the country. However, the law gives the government broad powers to restrict both internal and foreign travel. The government did not utilize the law to impose any new restrictions on travel in 2018.

G2. Are individuals able to exercise the right to own property and establish private businesses without undue interference from state or nonstate actors? 3 / 4

Property rights are generally respected. However, it is difficult to obtain land titles. The government amended the Land Sales Act in 2014 to require foreign nationals who fail to build a dwelling on their land within two years of acquisition to pay a fine equivalent to 10 percent of the land value every six months. Under the law, urban residential freehold land cannot be sold to foreigners.

G3. Do individuals enjoy personal social freedoms, including choice of marriage partner and size of family, protection from domestic violence, and control over appearance? 2 / 4

Domestic violence remains a problem in Fiji, and perpetrators who are convicted of the crime often receive light sentences. The Fiji Women's Crisis Center estimates that 64 percent of women who have been in a relationship have been victims of violence committed by their partner. To address the problem, the government established a toll-free helpline in 2017 to support victims of domestic violence. Rape is also a serious issue in Fiji.

G4. Do individuals enjoy equality of opportunity and freedom from economic exploitation? 2 / 4

Sex trafficking of children remained a problem in 2018, and the government was ineffective in addressing it; there were no convictions for the crime during the year. Safety standards at workplaces are not always adequately enforced. Long work hours are common in some jobs, including transportation and shipping.

Finland

Population: 5,500,000
Capital: Helsinki
Political Rights Rating: 1
Civil Liberties Rating: 1
Freedom Rating: 1.0
Freedom Status: Free
Electoral Democracy: Yes

Overview: Finland's parliamentary system features free and fair elections and robust multi-party competition. Corruption is not a significant problem, and freedoms of speech, religion, and association are respected. The judiciary is independent under the constitution and in practice. Women and ethnic minority groups enjoy equal rights, though harassment and hate speech aimed at minority groups does occur.

KEY DEVELOPMENTS IN 2018:

- In January, former finance minister and current president Sauli Niinistö of the National Coalition Party (KOK) handily won a second presidential term in elections considered free and fair.
- In October, the parliament overwhelmingly approved a constitutional amendment that provided an exception to the constitutionally guaranteed right to privacy, applicable in instances where intelligence-gathering operations are undertaken in the interest of national security. The move paved the way for the eventual implementation of an intelligence bill that if approved, would expand government surveillance powers.
- In June, Abderrahman Bouanane, the Moroccan asylum seeker who killed two women and injured eight people in a knife attack in Turku in 2017, was found guilty of two counts of murder with terrorist intent, and eight counts of attempted murder with terrorist intent, and sentenced to life imprisonment. The ruling marked the first time a crime had legally been classified as terrorism in Finland.

POLITICAL RIGHTS: 40 / 40
A. ELECTORAL PROCESS: 12 / 12
A1. Was the current head of government or other chief national authority elected through free and fair elections? 4 / 4

The president, whose role is mainly ceremonial, is directly elected for up to two six-year terms. In January 2018, former finance minister and incumbent president Sauli Niinistö of the National Coalition Party (KOK) won a second presidential term with 62.6 percent of the vote. The elections were considered broadly free and fair.

The prime minister is head of government, and is selected by Finland's freely elected parliament. Center Party (KESK) leader Juha Sipilä became prime minister in 2015, after his party took the greatest number of seats in the year's parliamentary elections and formed a coalition government.

A2. Were the current national legislative representatives elected through free and fair elections? 4 / 4

Representatives in the 200-seat, unicameral parliament, the Eduskunta, are elected to four-year terms. The Organization for Security and Co-operation in Europe (OSCE) deployed a preliminary elections assessment mission ahead of the 2015 parliamentary polls; its findings cited "a high level of confidence in all the aspects of the electoral process" and the OSCE consequently declined to monitor the polls themselves.

KESK took the greatest number of seats, with 49, and formed a government with KOK and the Finns Party; Sipilä, KESK's leader, became prime minister. The next parliamentary elections are set for April 2019.

A3. Are the electoral laws and framework fair, and are they implemented impartially by the relevant election management bodies? 4 / 4

The OSCE, ahead of the 2015 polls, expressed concern about limits on election-related appeals processes, and the timely adjudication of such complaints. However, Finland's electoral laws are robust and generally well implemented by the relevant authorities.

B. POLITICAL PLURALISM AND PARTICIPATION: 16 / 16

B1. Do the people have the right to organize in different political parties or other competitive political groupings of their choice, and is the system free of undue obstacles to the rise and fall of these competing parties or groupings? 4 / 4

Political parties are generally free to organize and operate, and rise and fall according to popular support and political developments.

In June 2017, the anti-immigrant Finns Party split into two separate parties following the controversial election of a hardline right-wing party leader. The former party leader and all of the Finns' government ministers formed a new party called New Alternative. The Finns Party was subsequently ejected from the government, after KESK and KOK formed a coalition with the New Alternative.

B2. Is there a realistic opportunity for the opposition to increase its support or gain power through elections? 4 / 4

Finland boasts a robust multiparty system with strong opposition parties, and there are no impediments to the rotation of power.

B3. Are the people's political choices free from domination by the military, foreign powers, religious hierarchies, economic oligarchies, or any other powerful group that is not democratically accountable? 4 / 4

People's political choices are generally free from domination by actors that are not democratically accountable.

B4. Do various segments of the population (including ethnic, religious, gender, LGBT, and other relevant groups) have full political rights and electoral opportunities? 4 / 4

Citizens from minority ethnic groups enjoy full political rights. The Åland Islands—an autonomous region located off the southwestern coast whose inhabitants speak Swedish—have their own 30-seat parliament, as well as one seat in the national legislature.

The indigenous Sami population of northern Finland, who constitute about 0.1 percent of the population, enjoy full civil and political rights. They have a legislature with limited powers, but they do not have guaranteed representation in the parliament. Members of the Sami community continue to call for greater inclusion in political decision-making processes.

Women and women's interests are reasonably well-represented in politics, as are LGBT (lesbian, gay bisexual, and transgender) people and their specific interests.

C. FUNCTIONING OF GOVERNMENT: 12 / 12
C1. Do the freely elected head of government and national legislative representatives determine the policies of the government? 4 / 4
Finland's freely elected government representatives are able to effectively develop and implement policy.

C2. Are safeguards against official corruption strong and effective? 4 / 4
Corruption is not a significant problem in Finland, and is generally punished under relevant laws when discovered. However, in March 2018, the Council of Europe's anticorruption agency urged Finland to bolster corruption prevention and detection policies within government and law enforcement agencies, including by increasing whistleblower protection. It further warned of possible risks of public-private sector conflicts of interest in the government's planned social and health care system reforms.

C3. Does the government operate with openness and transparency? 4 / 4
Laws permitting access to public information are generally well enforced, though there are some limits on the disclosure of information related to national security, foreign affairs, trade secrets, and criminal investigations. All citizens including government officials are required by law to make public asset declarations, though there are no penalties for noncompliance. Companies perceive corruption risks and favoritism within public procurement as low, however "old boys' networks," notably at the local level, are still believed to hold influence over procurement decisions.

CIVIL LIBERTIES: 60 / 60
D. FREEDOM OF EXPRESSION AND BELIEF: 16 / 16
D1. Are there free and independent media? 4 / 4
Freedom of expression is protected by Article 12 of the constitution and the 2003 Act on the Exercise of Freedom of Expression in Mass Media. Media outlets in Finland are typically independent and free from political pressure or censorship. Finland ranked as first in the European Union (EU) for public trust in the media, according to a Eurobarometer survey conducted in March 2018.

However, decreasing advertising spending continues to pose a challenge for the media sector, especially for print publications. Separately, in recent years the Union of Journalists in Finland (UJF) has filed formal complaints with the Finnish prosecutor's office over its reluctance to press charges in connection with the severe harassment of journalists, notably those who cover topics related to immigrants and immigration.

D2. Are individuals free to practice and express their religious faith or nonbelief in public and private? 4 / 4
Religious freedom is guaranteed in the constitution and generally respected in practice. However, Jewish communities in Finland have reported a rise in anti-Semitic hate speech online in recent years. Some actors, including municipal-level public officials, characterized a planned mosque complex in Helsinki as a security threat. (Helsinki's Urban Environment Division rejected the proposal to build it in December 2017, citing issues with sustainable funding, but the project manager has pledged to continue pursuing its construction.)

D3. Is there academic freedom, and is the educational system free from extensive political indoctrination? 4 / 4
Academic freedom is generally respected.

D4. Are individuals free to express their personal views on political or other sensitive topics without fear of surveillance or retribution? 4 / 4

There are few impediments to open and free private discussion. However, in January 2018, the parliament began debating an intelligence bill that would expand the government's surveillance powers. The bill came in response to a 2017 attack in Turku in which an assailant killed two women and injured eight other people in a knife attack considered the country's first-ever terrorist attack. The bill would permit intelligence agencies to access confidential exchanges between people deemed a potential threat to national security. Critics have raised concerns that if passed, the bill would threaten individual privacy.

In October 2018, in an apparent move to facilitate the intelligence law's eventual approval and implementation, the parliament overwhelmingly approved a constitutional amendment that provided an exception to the constitutionally guaranteed right to privacy. The exception is applicable to intelligence-gathering operations undertaken in the interest of national security.

E. ASSOCIATIONAL AND ORGANIZATIONAL RIGHTS: 12 / 12
E1. Is there freedom of assembly? 4 / 4

Freedom of assembly is protected by law and upheld in practice.

E2. Is there freedom for nongovernmental organizations, particularly those that are engaged in human rights– and governance-related work? 4 / 4

Nongovernmental organizations (NGOs) operate without restriction.

E3. Is there freedom for trade unions and similar professional or labor organizations? 4 / 4

Workers have the right to organize and bargain collectively, though public-sector workers who provide services deemed essential may not strike. Approximately 70 percent of workers belong to trade unions.

F. RULE OF LAW: 16 / 16
F1. Is there an independent judiciary? 4 / 4

The constitution provides for an independent judiciary, and the courts operate without political interference in practice.

F2. Does due process prevail in civil and criminal matters? 4 / 4

Due process is generally respected in Finland. The results of a Eurobarometer survey conducted in March 2018 showed that 83 percent of those surveyed had expressed trust in the legal system.

In April 2018, the trial of Abderrahman Bouanane, the Moroccan asylum seeker who killed two women and injured eight people in a knife attack in Turku in August 2017, commenced. In June, he was convicted of two counts of murder with terrorist intent, and eight counts of attempted murder with terrorist intent, and sentenced to life in prison. The ruling marks the first time a crime had legally been categorized as terrorism in Finland.

F3. Is there protection from the illegitimate use of physical force and freedom from war and insurgencies? 4 / 4

People in Finland generally enjoy freedom from violent attacks by state and nonstate actors.

Following the August 2017 attack in Turku, a team from the Safety Investigation Authority conducted a report on the attack, and how to prevent similar incidents from occurring. Their report was released in June 2018 and recommended, among other things, improved governmental interagency communications, implementation of measures to reduce radicalization of asylum seekers, reducing the processing time for asylum decisions, and setting up a resource agency to offer assistance to asylum seekers during the asylum process.

F4. Do laws, policies, and practices guarantee equal treatment of various segments of the population? 4 / 4

The constitution guarantees the Sami people cultural autonomy and the right to pursue their traditional livelihoods, which include fishing and reindeer herding. However, representatives of the community have said that they cannot exercise their rights in practice and face restrictions on land use. While Roma make up a very small percentage of the Finnish population, they are significantly disadvantaged and marginalized.

Women enjoy equal rights, but despite a law stipulating equal pay for equal work, women earn only about 85 percent as much as men with the same qualifications.

In 2016, Finland amended its asylum law to limit the aid available to asylum seekers. The amendments prompted concern from the UN refugee agency, which suggested that Finland abandoned good practices and sought to align its policies with the minimum required by international treaties governing the treatment of refugees.

A 2018 EU report on discrimination against people of African descent in 12 EU member state, which was released in November 2018, found that Finland had the highest rate of respondents who had experienced racist harassment in the last 5 years (63 percent). The country also had the highest rate of respondents who said they had experienced racist violence during the same period (14 percent). Finnish police received more than 1,100 complaints related to suspected hate crimes in 2017, representing an 8 percent increase from 2016.

The National Police Board has attempted to ban the Nordic Resistance Movement, a neo-Nazi organization it has called "violent and openly racist."

G. PERSONAL AUTONOMY AND INDIVIDUAL RIGHTS: 16 / 16

G1. Do individuals enjoy freedom of movement, including the ability to change their place of residence, employment, or education? 4 / 4

Individuals in Finland may move about freely. The country has one of the most expansive "freedom to roam" policies in the world, allowing people to use any public or private land for recreational purposes as long as the privacy of a private residence is not violated and no environmental damage is incurred. There are no restrictions on people's ability to change their place of education or employment.

G2. Are individuals able to exercise the right to own property and establish private businesses without undue interference from state or nonstate actors? 4 / 4

Intellectual and physical property rights are upheld in Finland. There are no major obstacles to establishing a business, and the country boasts a well-regulated, transparent, and open economy.

G3. Do individuals enjoy personal social freedoms, including choice of marriage partner and size of family, protection from domestic violence, and control over appearance? 4/ 4

People's social choices are for the most part unrestricted. Same-sex marriage has been allowed since March 2017. However, legislation requires that transgender people be sterilized and have a mental health diagnosis in order to obtain legal recognition of their gender. In 2017, the UN Human Rights Council (UNHRC) called for Finland to eliminate these impediments to legal gender recognition. The UNHRC has also recommended that Finland amend its criminal code to no longer define rape according to the degree of violence used by the perpetrator. Domestic violence is an ongoing concern.

G4. Do individuals enjoy equality of opportunity and freedom from economic exploitation? 4 / 4

Finland remains a destination and a transit country for men, women, and children who are subjected to sex trafficking and labor exploitation in various industries. According to the US State Department, the government actively prosecutes trafficking offenses, and victims have access to protection and assistance, though victim identification remains a challenge, particularly for child victims.

France

Population: 65,100,000
Capital: Paris
Political Rights Rating: 1
Civil Liberties Rating: 2
Freedom Rating: 1.5
Freedom Status: Free
Electoral Democracy: Yes

Overview: The French political system features vibrant democratic processes and generally strong protections for civil liberties and political rights. However, due to a number of deadly terrorist attacks in recent years, successive governments have been willing to curtail constitutional protections and empower law enforcement to act in ways that impinge on personal freedoms. Anti-Muslim and anti-immigrant sentiment continue to be rife.

KEY DEVELOPMENTS IN 2018:

- In November and December, the large-scale yellow vest protests against anticipated fuel tax increases broke out across the country. Although some of the protests devolved into riots, with demonstrators blocking roads and destroying property, security forces responded to the demonstrations in a manner that Amnesty International described as "extremely heavy-handed," injuring hundreds with tear gas, rubber bullets, and sting-ball grenades.
- After two years without a major terrorist incident, five people were killed in December by a gunman at the Christmas market in Strasbourg.
- The Macron administration endured sustained criticism for its handling of the Benalla affair, in which video of former deputy chief of staff Alexandre Benalla assaulting a protester during a May Day parade surfaced in July. Critics accused the government of covering up the incident, and assailed Macron's administration for initially suspending Benalla for two weeks before firing him after the public learned of the assault.

POLITICAL RIGHTS 38 / 40

A. ELECTORAL PROCESS 12 / 12

A1. Was the current head of government or other chief national authority elected through free and fair elections? 4 / 4

The French president is chief of state, and is elected to five-year terms by direct, universal suffrage in a two-round system. The prime minister is head of government, and is appointed by the president. Emmanuel Macron, a centrist newcomer to politics, won the first round of the presidential election in April 2017. In the second round, Macron bested Marine Le Pen of the far-right National Front (FN), taking 66 percent of the vote. Le Pen had campaigned on pledges to suspend immigration and hold a referendum on France's EU membership. The turnout in the first round was 77 percent, but lower in the second, with over 25 percent of voters abstaining.

The Organization for Security and Co-operation in Europe (OSCE), following a needs assessment mission, expressed confidence in the integrity of French elections and sent only a limited observer mission to assess campaign finance processes and media coverage surrounding the presidential poll. It expressed concern over legal provisions under which journalists could be compelled to reveal their sources if it were deemed in the public interest, but generally praised the media environment surrounding the election.

Documents from the Macron campaign were leaked ahead of the election, with many analysts suggesting that Russia-based hackers were responsible. The country's election commission responded swiftly, warning media outlets to respect the campaign blackout period during which the documents were released and not to report on them, and noting that some of the leaked information appeared to have been fabricated.

A2. Were the current national legislative representatives elected through free and fair elections? 4 / 4

Members of the lower house of Parliament, the 577-seat National Assembly, are elected to five-year terms in a two-round system. The upper house, the 348-seat Senate, is an indirectly elected body whose members serve six-year terms. In the June 2017 legislative elections, Macron's La République en Marche (LREM) and its centrist ally won a comfortable majority in the National Assembly, with 350 out of 577 seats. The center-right Republicans (LR) and their allies finished second, and the center-left Socialist Party (PS) and its allies finished a distant third. Despite securing 13 percent of the vote nationally, only 8 FN candidates were elected to the National Assembly; remaining seats were split among a number of other parties. The legislative election saw record low turnout, with 49.7 percent turnout in the first round and 42.6 percent in the second.

The OSCE declined to send a mission to observe the polls, having expressed general confidence in French elections and saying there was no need for a second mission following its earlier evaluation of the presidential election.

A3. Are the electoral laws and framework fair, and are they implemented impartially by the relevant election management bodies? 4 / 4

France's electoral laws and framework are fair and implemented impartially. While generally praising the electoral framework, the OSCE in its assessment of the 2017 presidential poll recommended that officials work to close loopholes that can allow actors to sidestep campaign finance regulations.

B. POLITICAL PLURALISM AND PARTICIPATION: 15 / 16

B1. Do the people have the right to organize in different political parties or other competitive political groupings of their choice, and is the system free of undue obstacles to the rise and fall of these competing parties or groupings? 4 / 4

Parties are generally able to organize and operate freely. For the first time, France held live televised debates during the first round of the 2017 presidential race, providing a platform for the top five candidates to express their views, and expanding the national exposure of less dominant parties.

B2. Is there a realistic opportunity for the opposition to increase its support or gain power through elections? 4 / 4

The 2017 legislative elections, which saw strong performances by the LREM, the FN, and the far-left France Insoumise (FI)—demonstrated that parties outside the political mainstream can gain power through elections.

B3. Are the people's political choices free from domination by the military, foreign powers, religious hierarchies, economic oligarchies, or any other powerful group that is not democratically accountable? 4 / 4

People's political choices are generally free from domination.

B4. Do various segments of the population (including ethnic, religious, gender, LGBT, and other relevant groups) have full political rights and electoral opportunities? 3 / 4

No laws restrict the political participation of women, LGBT (lesbian, gay, bisexual, and transgender) people, or ethnic, religious, and racial minorities. However, the rise of far-right parties and accompanying mainstreaming of nationalist ideas have caused certain minorities to feel excluded from the political sphere, most notably Muslim communities.

C. FUNCTIONING OF GOVERNMENT: 11 / 12

C1. Do the freely elected head of government and national legislative representatives determine the policies of the government? 4 / 4

In general, the elected head of government and national legislative representatives determine the policies of the government. However, under the administration of former president François Hollande, the government used Article 49.3 of the constitution to bypass Parliament in the passage of legislation. Since becoming president, Macron has used the *ordonnance* process to similarly bypass parliamentary debate on his overhaul of labor laws.

C2. Are safeguards against official corruption strong and effective? 3 / 4

Corruption remains an issue, as reflected by recent allegations against presidential candidates Le Pen of FN and François Fillon of the LR involving the payment of large salaries to close associates and family members who had been granted "assistant" positions. A 2017 law on "moralization" sought to reduce such conflicts of interest by banning lawmakers at national and local levels as well as civil servants from employing family members, among other provisions.

Corruption allegations have been lodged against a number of high-level government officials in recent years. In March 2018, magistrates ordered former president Nicolas Sarkozy to stand trial on charges of corruption and influence-peddling. While president, Sarkozy allegedly attempted to offer a magistrate investigating other charges against him a job in exchange for information about the case. Sarkozy appealed the decision, and a trial had not yet commenced at year's end.

C3. Does the government operate with openness and transparency? 4 / 4

The government generally operates with openness and transparency, although the use in recent years of Article 49.3 and *ordonnances* demonstrates some desire by the executive to make policy without legislative or public scrutiny.

The Benalla affair, which roiled French politics for much of 2018, raised questions about transparency in Macron's administration. In July, video circulated online of Alexandre Benalla, the former deputy chief of staff to Macron, wearing a police helmet and assaulting a protester during a May Day celebration. Critics accused the Macron administration of covering up the assault, which it learned of in May. Although Benalla was initially suspended for the incident (he was later fired after the story broke), the administration did not share this information with the judiciary in a timely manner, as protocol dictates, and the public remained unaware of the incident until July.

CIVIL LIBERTIES: 52 / 60

D. FREEDOM OF EXPRESSION AND BELIEF: 14 / 16

D1. Are there free and independent media? 4 / 4

The media operate freely and represent a wide range of political opinions. However, high concentration of media ownership remains a concern.

D2. Are individuals free to practice and express their religious faith or nonbelief in public and private? 3 / 4

The constitution protects freedom of religion. Antidefamation laws penalize religiously motivated abuse, and Holocaust denial is illegal. France maintains the policy of *laïcité* (secularism), whereby religion and state affairs are strictly separated, though the government maintains relationships with organizations representing the country's three major religions, Christianity, Islam, and Judaism.

Since 2015, France's already damaged relationship with its Muslim communities has grown increasingly fraught in the wake of terrorist attacks, some of which the Islamic State (IS) militant group claimed responsibility for. Islamophobic rhetoric from prominent politicians and public figures on both the left and right is not uncommon.

D3. Is there academic freedom, and is the educational system free from extensive political indoctrination? 4 / 4

There are no formal restrictions on academic freedom in France.

D4. Are individuals free to express their personal views on political or other sensitive topics without fear of surveillance or retribution? 3 / 4

Private discussion remains generally open and vibrant, despite new laws that permit government surveillance. In 2015, Parliament approved a law granting the government expanded powers to conduct domestic surveillance, including bulk collection of communications data as well as wider authority to use hidden cameras and microphones. The law authorizes the use of sophisticated intelligence technology to intercept all telephone conversations, text messages, and emails in targeted areas. The law only prescribes limited judicial oversight of these activities.

E. ASSOCIATIONAL AND ORGANIZATIONAL RIGHTS: 11 / 12

E1. Is there freedom of assembly? 3 / 4

Freedom of assembly is normally respected. However, rights organizations expressed concern that an antiterrorism law passed in 2017 limits the right to demonstrate.

In November 2018, the yellow vest protests against anticipated fuel tax increases broke out across the country. The protests grew into a mass movement that reflected deep-seated discontent with French political elites among working– and middle-class people. Some of the protests devolved into riots, with demonstrators blocking roads and damaging property, including the interior of the Arc de Triomphe. However, security forces responded to the demonstrations in a manner that Amnesty International described as "extremely heavy-handed," injuring hundreds with tear gas, rubber bullets, and sting-ball grenades. Ten people died during the protests, which continued through the end of the year, often from car accidents at roadblocks.

E2. Is there freedom for nongovernmental organizations, particularly those that are engaged in human rights- and governance-related work? 4 / 4

Nongovernmental organizations, including those that are engaged in human rights– and governance-related work, can generally operate freely.

E3. Is there freedom for trade unions and similar professional or labor organizations? 4 / 4

Trade unions are free to operate without any undue restrictions.

F. RULE OF LAW: 13 / 16

F1. Is there an independent judiciary? 4 / 4

France has an independent judiciary, and the rule of law generally prevails in court proceedings.

F2. Does due process prevail in civil and criminal matters? 3 / 4

Due process generally prevails in civil and criminal matters, but antiterrorism legislation passed in 2017, which replaced a state of emergency in place since the 2015 terror attacks in Paris, enshrined controversial administrative control measures into law. These measures give authorities the power, often based on secret information, and outside the purview of the traditional legal system, to restrict people's movement, require them to check in with the police (sometimes on a daily basis), and forbid contact with certain individuals. Rights activists have criticized the measures for violating the rights of suspects.

F3. Is there protection from the illegitimate use of physical force and freedom from war and insurgencies? 3 / 4

The threat of terrorism remains significant in France. In December 2018, five people were killed and eleven injured in Strasbourg when a gunman who had pledged allegiance to the Islamic State (IS) opened fire on a Christmas market.

The police sustained criticism for using excessive force during the yellow vest protests, in which many demonstrators were injured by rubber bullets and sting-ball grenades.

F4. Do laws, policies, and practices guarantee equal treatment of various segments of the population? 3 / 4

Migrants and refugees in France continue to suffer both from societal discrimination and abuse by government officials. Surging immigration and refugee flows from Muslim-majority countries have exacerbated anti-Muslim sentiment, and reports of vandalism of mosques, verbal assaults, and xenophobic graffiti continue. Anti-Semitism has been on the rise in recent years. According to the Interior Ministry, the number of reported anti-Semitic acts increased by 74 percent in 2018.

The #MeToo movement has had an impact in France, drawing attention to pervasive sexual harassment in French society, but it also faced a backlash in 2018. Some prominent critics argued that the movement was threatening the French culture of "seduction" and undermining sexual freedom. Despite the resistance, many advocates pressed forward in their efforts to raise awareness about harassment and sexism, and the public debate about the issue persisted throughout the year.

French law forbids the categorization of people according to ethnic origin, and no official statistics are collected on ethnicity. Discrimination based on sexual orientation is prohibited by law.

G. PERSONAL AUTONOMY AND INDIVIDUAL RIGHTS: 14 / 16

G1. Do individuals enjoy freedom of movement, including the ability to change their place of residence, employment, or education? 4 / 4

There are normally no restrictions on freedom of travel or choice of residence or employment in France. However, measures allowing authorities to institute restrictions on movement are permitted in the 2017 antiterrorism law.

G2. Are individuals able to exercise the right to own property and establish private businesses without undue interference from state or nonstate actors? 4 / 4

Private businesses are free to operate. In 2016, major reforms to the labor code were enacted, further shifting power over hiring, firing, and working conditions to businesses and away from labor. These shifts were reinforced by Macron's 2017 changes to the labor code.

G3. Do individuals enjoy personal social freedoms, including choice of marriage partner and size of family, protection from domestic violence, and control over appearance? 3 / 4

Individuals generally enjoy personal social freedoms, including choice of marriage partner and size of family, protection from domestic violence, and control over appearance. However, a number of laws against religious clothing have forced some women to dress against their will.

G4. Do individuals enjoy equality of opportunity and freedom from economic exploitation? 3 / 4

Employment discrimination against women, French Muslims, immigrants of North African descent, and others outside the traditional elite hinders equality of opportunity. While France's government takes action against human trafficking, the problem persists in the commercial sex trade; some victims are also forced into domestic labor.

Gabon

Population: 2,100,000
Capital: Libreville
Political Rights Rating: 7
Civil Liberties Rating: 5
Freedom Rating: 6.0
Freedom Status: Not Free
Electoral Democracy: No

Overview: Although Gabon holds multiparty elections, President Ali Bongo Ondimba maintains political dominance through a combination of patronage and repression, having succeeded his father when he died in 2009 after more than 40 years in power. The executive branch effectively controls the judiciary, and prisoners suffer from harsh conditions. Other significant problems include discrimination against African immigrants, marginalization of indigenous people, and legal and de facto inequality for women.

KEY DEVELOPMENTS IN 2018:

- In January, after receiving final approval from Parliament, the government promulgated constitutional amendments that further consolidated executive power and excluded opposition proposals to impose presidential term limits.
- Legislative elections, scheduled for 2016 but postponed twice, were held in October. Some opposition parties boycotted the voting amid credible allegations of fraud, and the ruling party retained an overwhelming majority of seats.
- President Bongo suffered a stroke that month, and a lack of public information about his health status through the end of the year fueled speculation about his ability to govern.

POLITICAL RIGHTS: 4 / 40

A. ELECTORAL PROCESS: 0 / 12

A1. Was the current head of government or other chief national authority elected through free and fair elections? 0 / 4

The president, who wields executive authority, is elected by popular vote for seven-year terms. Presidential term limits were abolished in 2003. The president nominates and can dismiss the prime minister at will.

The August 2016 presidential election pitted incumbent Ali Bongo Ondimba against Jean Ping of the opposition Union of Forces for Change (UFC). The electoral commission declared Bongo the winner with 49.8 percent of the vote, compared with 48.2 percent for Ping. In Haut-Ogooué Province, a Bongo family stronghold, the commission claimed a turnout rate of 99.9 percent, with 95 percent for Bongo, even though turnout in the rest of the country was just 54 percent. Both Ping and observers from the European Union called for a recount.

Meanwhile, violent protests erupted, and security forces stormed Ping's headquarters. Although the government claimed the death toll from the unrest was under 10, journalists and opposition leaders estimated that more than 50 people had died, and hundreds of others were arrested.

The Constitutional Court, headed by a longtime Bongo family ally, rebuffed an observation mission from the African Union during the recount. The president was credited with 50.66 percent of the vote, leaving Ping with 47.24 percent. Ping rejected the results.

A2. Were the current national legislative representatives elected through free and fair elections? 0 / 4

Gabon's Parliament consists of the National Assembly, whose members are elected by popular vote for five-year terms, and the Senate, which is indirectly elected by regional and municipal officials for six-year terms. Under the 2018 constitution, the size of the National Assembly increased from 120 to 143 seats, and the Senate was set to decrease in size from 102 to 52 members at its next elections in 2020. The most recent Senate elections were held in 2014, with Bongo's Gabonese Democratic Party (PDG) claiming 81 seats.

National Assembly elections were originally due in 2016 but were repeatedly postponed. The incumbent assembly was finally dissolved in April 2018, leaving the Senate as the only legislative body for most of the year. The PDG claimed 98 seats in the National Assembly elections in October, which were boycotted by several opposition parties due to the government's failure to create a genuinely independent electoral commission. PDG allies won roughly 10 more seats, and no single party other than the PDG took more than 11.

The elections were marked by credible allegations of fraud and repression. The president's eldest daughter was credited with more than 99 percent of the vote for the seat she won.

A3. Are the electoral laws and framework fair, and are they implemented impartially by the relevant election management bodies? 0 / 4

Gabon's electoral laws and framework do not ensure credible elections. The electoral commission, the Interior Ministry, and the Constitutional Court all play important roles in managing elections, and all are widely seen as loyal to the president.

In January 2018, Parliament gave its final approval to constitutional amendments that were developed in an opaque process without meaningful input from opposition parties or civil society. Among other changes, the amendments introduced a runoff system for presidential elections if no candidate wins a majority in the first round, granted the president authority to set state policy unilaterally rather than in concert with the prime minister and cabinet, and required ministers to pledge allegiance to the president. Lawmakers rejected opposition proposals including the imposition of presidential term limits.

B. POLITICAL PLURALISM AND PARTICIPATION: 2 / 16

B1. Do the people have the right to organize in different political parties or other competitive political groupings of their choice, and is the system free of undue obstacles to the rise and fall of these competing parties or groupings? 1 / 4

The PDG dominates the nominally multiparty system. Opposition parties remain fragmented, and the government has disrupted their activities by denying them permits for public gatherings, arresting participants in their largely peaceful protests, and incarcerating their leaders. A number of opposition figures arrested in 2016 and 2017 remained in detention during 2018.

B2. Is there a realistic opportunity for the opposition to increase its support or gain power through elections? 0 / 4

The PDG has monopolized the executive branch since the 1960s, and there is no realistic opportunity for the opposition to gain power through elections. In 2017, Ping called for a civil disobedience campaign, arguing that he had exhausted all institutional remedies for the fraudulent 2016 election. He and some other opposition leaders boycotted the 2018 National Assembly elections.

B3. Are the people's political choices free from domination by the military, foreign powers, religious hierarchies, economic oligarchies, or any other powerful group that is not democratically accountable? 0 / 4

The Bongo family and its associates have acquired enormous wealth and economic control after decades in power. These resources are allegedly used to sustain political patronage networks and vote-buying during elections. The leadership also relies on security forces to intimidate the opposition. Ahead of the 2018 National Assembly elections, there were some reports of opposition candidates and supporters being detained and threatened with violence.

B4. Do various segments of the population (including ethnic, religious, gender, LGBT, and other relevant groups) have full political rights and electoral opportunities? 1 / 4

While women and ethnic minorities formally enjoy full political rights, in practice they have little ability to organize independently and gain political influence given the dominance of the PDG structure. Key government and military posts are held by loyalists from all major ethnic groups except indigenous populations, which are poorly represented in politics and government. Women are also underrepresented, including in both chambers of Parliament.

C. FUNCTIONING OF GOVERNMENT: 2 / 12

C1. Do the freely elected head of government and national legislative representatives determine the policies of the government? 0 / 4

Government policy is set by the president, who is not freely elected, and his senior aides. President Bongo apparently remained out of the country at the end of 2018 after suffering a stroke in October, which raised questions about his ability to govern. In November, the Constitutional Court unilaterally altered the constitution to allow the vice president to assume some of the president's functions if he is "temporarily unavailable." The constitution had only provided for the president's permanent incapacitation, in which case the Senate president would serve as interim president and an election would be called within 60 days.

Parliament is dominated by the ruling party and provides little oversight of the executive branch. Moreover, due to the Constitutional Court's April 2018 dissolution of the National Assembly, whose mandate had expired, the country had only one chamber of Parliament for the remainder of the year; the new National Assembly had yet to convene at year's end.

C2. Are safeguards against official corruption strong and effective? 1 / 4

Relatively robust anticorruption laws as well as anticorruption institutions launched since Ali Bongo took office are not employed effectively, and both corruption and impunity remain major problems. Authorities have reportedly used anticorruption efforts to target regime opponents. In 2017, the government criticized an ongoing French corruption probe focused on Marie-Madeleine Mborantsuo, a Bongo family ally who serves as president of the Constitutional Court. A special criminal court for cases involving the theft of public funds was established in 2018, but critics said prosecutions remained selective.

C3. Does the government operate with openness and transparency? 1 / 4

The government operates with little transparency, particularly regarding expenditures. The presidency's budget is not subject to the same oversight as those for other institutions. High-level civil servants are required to disclose their assets, but the declarations are not made public.

CIVIL LIBERTIES: 19 / 60

D. FREEDOM OF EXPRESSION AND BELIEF: 8 / 16

D1. Are there free and independent media? 1 / 4

Press freedom is guaranteed by law and the constitution but restricted in practice, and self-censorship to avoid legal repercussions for critical reporting is common. A new communications code that went into effect in 2017 was criticized by activists for provisions that restricted media freedom, including an obligation for media to promote "the country's image and national cohesion."

A new state media regulator created in February 2018, the High Authority of Communication, imposed suspensions on three news outlets in August in response to reporting on government corruption, and another newspaper was suspended for three months in November for an article on Bongo's health. Workers at the public broadcaster went on strike for several days between April and May 2018, complaining of unpaid salaries and government meddling in their work. The strike was suspended to allow for talks with the government. Landry Amiang Washington, an activist blogger arrested in 2016, remained in prison at the end of 2018.

D2. Are individuals free to practice and express their religious faith or nonbelief in public and private? 3 / 4

Although religious freedom is enshrined in the constitution and generally respected, some heterodox religious groups reportedly have difficulty obtaining registration from the government.

D3. Is there academic freedom, and is the educational system free from extensive political indoctrination? 2 / 4

Omar Bongo University, Gabon's main center for tertiary education, is state run, and academic freedom there is tenuous. Professors are believed to self-censor to protect their positions and avoid conflicts with the authorities. Police used violence to disperse student protests regarding university tuition hikes and other grievances during 2017.

D4. Are individuals free to express their personal views on political or other sensitive topics without fear of surveillance or retribution? 2 / 4

Ordinary individuals' freedom to express criticism of the government is limited by restrictive laws and deterred by the authorities' surveillance and detention of opposition figures and activists.

E. ASSOCIATIONAL AND ORGANIZATIONAL RIGHTS: 3 / 12
E1. Is there freedom of assembly? 1 / 4

Freedom of assembly is limited. In recent years the government has repeatedly denied permits for meetings and used tear gas and arrests to disperse unauthorized demonstrations. A 2017 law further limited the freedom to assemble, in part by making organizers responsible for offenses committed during a public gathering.

E2. Is there freedom for nongovernmental organizations, particularly those that are engaged in human rights- and governance-related work? 1 / 4

Relatively few nongovernmental organizations (NGOs) are able to operate in Gabon. Freedom of association is guaranteed by the constitution, but the process for formally registering NGOs is onerous and implemented inconsistently, leaving groups vulnerable to accusations that they are not in compliance with the law.

E3. Is there freedom for trade unions and similar professional or labor organizations? 1 / 4

Workers are legally permitted to join unions, engage in collective bargaining, and strike, but the government has cracked down on union activism in recent years. In April 2018, the authorities were accused of forcibly dispersing a sit-in at the Education Ministry by teachers who were protesting the government's failure to pay salaries. Among other labor actions during the year, attempts by unions to mount strikes and protests against government austerity measures in August prompted bans from the interior minister and short-terms arrests for some participants.

F. RULE OF LAW: 3 / 16
F1. Is there an independent judiciary? 0 / 4

The judiciary is accountable to the Ministry of Justice, through which the president has the power to appoint and dismiss judges. Under the amended constitution, the country's highest judicial body, the Constitutional Court, is composed of three members appointed by the president, two by the National Assembly, one by the Senate, and three by the Superior Council of the Judiciary, which itself is headed by the president and justice minister. The

2018 constitution also created a new special court, the Court of Justice of the Republic, which alone has the authority to judge top executive and judicial officials. It consists of seven members appointed by the Superior Council of the Judiciary and six members of Parliament.

The Constitutional Court's handling of the 2016 presidential election, its approval of lengthy delays in the National Assembly elections, and its legally dubious response to Bongo's health crisis in late 2018 further demonstrated its lack of impartiality. Critics have noted that Mborantsuo, the court's president for more than 20 years, had been a mistress of late president Omar Bongo, bearing him two children and winning appointment to another high court at age 28. She has been accused of amassing illicit wealth while in office.

A magistrates' union ended a weeks-long strike in February 2018 after the justice minister, who had accused judges of corruption and allegedly interfered with a ruling, was replaced.

F2. Does due process prevail in civil and criminal matters? 1 / 4

Legal safeguards against arbitrary arrest and detention are not upheld by police, and detainees are often denied access to lawyers. Lengthy pretrial detention is common. Cases of arbitrary arrests linked to opposition activism have reportedly increased since the 2016 election crisis. Several detained opposition figures have been denied due process.

F3. Is there protection from the illegitimate use of physical force and freedom from war and insurgencies? 1 / 4

Prison conditions are harsh, and facilities are severely overcrowded, with limited access to proper medical care. Torture is outlawed by the constitution, but detainees and inmates continue to face physical abuse. Violent crime and ritual killings remain serious concerns in Gabon. Following the 2016 elections, the authorities used indiscriminate and often deadly force against political opponents and protesters, causing a number of fatalities.

F4. Do laws, policies, and practices guarantee equal treatment of various segments of the population? 1 / 4

The country's large population of noncitizen African immigrants is subject to harassment and extortion, including by police. Indigenous people reportedly experience discrimination in the workplace and often live in extreme poverty.

Women have equal legal rights on some issues but face significant de facto discrimination in employment and other economic matters. Sexual harassment in the workplace, which is not prohibited by law, is reportedly common.

Gabon has no specific statute outlawing same-sex sexual activity, but bias against LGBT (lesbian, gay, bisexual, and transgender) people remains a problem. Those who live openly risk housing and employment discrimination.

G. PERSONAL AUTONOMY AND INDIVIDUAL RIGHTS: 5 / 16

G1. Do individuals enjoy freedom of movement, including the ability to change their place of residence, employment, or education? 2 / 4

There are no laws restricting internal travel, but police often monitor travelers at checkpoints and demand bribes. Married women seeking to obtain a passport or travel abroad must have permission from their husbands. The government has imposed travel bans on opposition leaders in recent years.

G2. Are individuals able to exercise the right to own property and establish private businesses without undue interference from state or nonstate actors? 1 / 4

Bureaucratic and judicial delays can pose difficulties for businesses. Enforcement of contracts and property rights is weak, and the process for property registration is lengthy. Bongo and his associates play a dominant role in the economy, impairing fair competition and favoring those with connections to the leadership.

G3. Do individuals enjoy personal social freedoms, including choice of marriage partner and size of family, protection from domestic violence, and control over appearance? 1 / 4

Personalized forms of violence are believed to be widespread, and perpetrators generally enjoy impunity. Rape and domestic abuse are rarely reported to authorities or prosecuted. Spousal rape is not specifically prohibited. Abortion is a punishable crime under most circumstances. The minimum age for marriage is 15 for women and 18 for men. About 22 percent of women aged 20–24 were first married before age 18, according to UN data. The civil code states that a wife must obey her husband as the head of household.

G4. Do individuals enjoy equality of opportunity and freedom from economic exploitation? 1 / 4

Wage standards and laws against forced labor are weakly enforced, particularly in the informal sector and with respect to foreign workers. Both adults and children are exploited in a number of different occupations, and foreign women are trafficked to Gabon for prostitution or domestic servitude.

The Gambia

Population: 2,200,000
Capital: Banjul
Political Rights Rating: 4
Civil Liberties Rating: 5
Freedom Rating: 4.5
Freedom Status: Partly Free
Electoral Democracy: No

Overview: The Gambia was ruled for over two decades by former president Yahya Jammeh, who mounted a bloodless coup in 1994 and consistently violated political rights and civil liberties. The 2016 election resulted in a surprise victory for opposition candidate Adama Barrow. Fundamental freedoms including the rights of assembly, association, and speech improved thereafter, but the rule of law is unconsolidated, LGBT (lesbian, gay, bisexual, and transgender) people face severe discrimination, and violence against women remains a serious problem.

KEY DEVELOPMENTS IN 2018:
- Local government elections were held in April and May without major incident.
- In May, the Supreme Court upheld sections of the Criminal Code prohibiting "false publication and broadcasting." In the same ruling, however, the court struck down criminal defamation and libel laws.
- In June, three civilians in Faraba Banta were killed when police fired live ammunition into an environmental protest. Five police officers were charged with murder for their role in the deaths.

- In October, the government established the Truth, Reconciliation, and Reparations Commission to investigate human rights abuses committed during the Jammeh era.

POLITICAL RIGHTS: 20 / 40
A. ELECTORAL PROCESS: 7 / 12
A1. Was the current head of government or other chief national authority elected through free and fair elections? 2 / 4

The president is directly elected to five-year terms, and there are no term limits. International observers were not allowed into The Gambia ahead of the December 2016 presidential election, and internet and international telephone services were cut on election day. Despite these obstacles, the Independent Electoral Commission was able to conduct an impartial vote count, and declared that Barrow, the candidate of the United Democratic Party (UDP), had won. Incumbent president Jammeh initially conceded defeat, but then reversed his position, and had not stepped down by the time Barrow was inaugurated in Senegal in January 2017. The Economic Community of West African States (ECOWAS) then sent in troops under a previously approved authorization to intervene militarily if a peaceful transfer of power did not begin by the last day of Jammeh's mandate. Within days of the deployment, Jammeh conceded defeat and left the country, allowing Barrow to take office.

A2. Were the current national legislative representatives elected through free and fair elections? 3 / 4

Of the 58 members of the unicameral National Assembly, 53 are elected by popular vote, with the remainder appointed by the president; members serve five-year terms. The April 2017 parliamentary elections were transparent, peaceful, and neutrally managed, and were commended by ECOWAS, the African Union (AU), the European Union (EU), and the United Nations. Weaknesses included low turnout, incomplete updating of the voter registry, and weak organization of vote collation processes. Nevertheless, most polling stations operated on time and vote counting was transparent.

A3. Are the electoral laws and framework fair, and are they implemented impartially by the relevant election management bodies? 2 / 4

The Independent Electoral Commission adequately managed the 2017 National Assembly elections, as well as local elections held in April and May 2018, but nevertheless faces serious challenges. Election observers have called for improvements to voter registration processes, improved polling station conditions, and more standardized counting and collation processes, as well as the redrawing of election district boundaries.

In 2017, the National Assembly amended the Elections Act to dramatically reduce deposits required to run for office at various levels.

B. POLITICAL PLURALISM AND PARTICIPATION: 9 / 16
B1. Do the people have the right to organize in different political parties or other competitive political groupings of their choice, and is the system free of undue obstacles to the rise and fall of these competing parties or groupings? 2 / 4

The Gambia currently has 10 political parties, which generally have not faced undue obstacles to form and operate in recent years. To register a new party, organizers must pay a 1 million dalasi ($21,000) registration fee and garner the signatures of 10,000 registered voters, with at least 1,000 from each of the country's seven regions. Parties centered on a particular religion, ethnicity, or region are banned. Prior to the 2016 presidential election, the Alliance for Patriotic Reorientation and Construction (APRC) had long dominated politics, and the rise and fall of competing political parties has yet to be institutionalized.

B2. Is there a realistic opportunity for the opposition to increase its support or gain power through elections? 3 / 4

The UDP won 31 seats in the 2017 National Assembly elections, taking an absolute majority and displacing Jammeh's APRC, which took 5 seats, down from the 48 it held previously. A number of other opposition groups gained representation in the elections. Previously, under Jammeh, the APRC had dominated the legislature over a period of two decades. Politicized security forces had suppressed the opposition during the 2016 election period.

UDP and APRC supporters clashed several times in 2018, particularly surrrounding the April and May local elections. In January, for example, UDP supporters allegedly attacked APRC members on a number of stops during a campaign tour.

B3. Are the people's political choices free from domination by the military, foreign powers, religious hierarchies, economic oligarchies, or any other powerful group that is not democratically accountable? 2 / 4

While people's political choices are more free from the undue dominance of unelected groups since the end of Jammeh's 22-year rule, military forces and foreign powers remain influential in Gambian politics. The ECOWAS Mission in The Gambia (ECOMIG) was scheduled to end in May 2018, but its mandate was extended by one year at the request of the Barrow government to further facilitate security sector reform, and due to ongoing concerns that pro-Jammeh loyalists in the military could cause political instability.

B4. Do various segments of the population (including ethnic, religious, gender, LGBT, and other relevant groups) have full political rights and electoral opportunities? 2 / 4

While political rights and electoral opportunities have recently improved, women remain underrepresented in politics. The National Assembly elected in 2017 includes the first-ever woman speaker and a disabled person; both are presidential appointees. The Jola-dominated APRC no longer monopolizes political space.

Since ethnic tensions escalated toward the end of the Jammeh regime, both the APRC and UDP have become more ethnically polarized, with Jola people largely gravitating toward the APRC and Mandinkas supporting the UDP.

C. FUNCTIONING OF GOVERNMENT: 4 / 12

C1. Do the freely elected head of government and national legislative representatives determine the policies of the government? 2 / 4

Nonstate actors, armed forces, and foreign governments do not appear to enjoy preponderant influence over the Barrow regime. However, despite these improvements, representative rule has yet to be consolidated.

C2. Are safeguards against official corruption strong and effective? 1 / 4

The Barrow government has undertaken limited initiatives to reduce corruption, which remains a serious problem. Allegations of corruption by officials at all levels of government are frequently lodged. A Commission of Inquiry is investigating former president Jammeh's use of state funds for private gain, and froze his assets. However, challenges remain. Gambians continue to call for laws establishing an anticorruption commission and requiring public asset declarations by government officials. In his State of the Nation speech in September

2018, Barrow stated that legislation to create the commission would soon be submitted to the cabinet for approval. There is currently no law to protect whistleblowers.

C3. Does the government operate with openness and transparency? 1 / 4

Government operations are generally opaque, but limited steps were taken toward improving transparency in 2018. Government officials are now required to make asset declarations to the ombudsman, but the declarations are not open to public and media scrutiny; Barrow has defended this withholding of information, citing privacy concerns. There are widespread allegations of corruption in public procurement processes.

CIVIL LIBERTIES: 25 / 60 (+4)

D. FREEDOM OF EXPRESSION AND BELIEF: 8 / 16 (+1)

D1. Are there free and independent media? 2 / 4

Journalists have cited improvements in the media environment under Barrow's administration. These include decreased self-censorship, which journalists attribute to a lifting of the climate of fear most had operated in under Jammeh's severely restrictive administration, when coverage of sensitive topics could result in arrest or abduction. In the newly opened environment, more people are entering the profession, and exiled journalists have returned to the country.

Nevertheless, restrictive media laws remain on the books, and some have been upheld by courts. In May 2018, the Supreme Court upheld sections of the Criminal Code prohibiting "false publication and broadcasting," in a decision condemned by foreign and domestic media. In the same ruling, however, the court struck down criminal defamation and libel laws.

Despite the progress in recent years, journalists still risk arrest and assault by the police. In June, for example, security forces arrested radio station manager Pa Modou Bojang, who was covering a police crackdown on a protest in the village of Faraba Banta, and allegedly beat him in custody.

D2. Are individuals free to practice and express their religious faith or nonbelief in public and private? 2 / 4

The Barrow government has maintained that the Gambia is a secular society in which all faiths can practice freely. In practice, non-Sunni Islamic groups have experienced discrimination. Ahmadiyya Muslims have been publicly denounced as non-Muslims by the quasi-governmental Supreme Islamic Council, and a 2015 fatwa by the council denied Ahmadiyya burial rights in Muslim ceremonies.

D3. Is there academic freedom, and is the educational system free from extensive political indoctrination? 2 / 4 (+1)

Academic freedom was severely limited at the University of The Gambia under Jammeh. However, since Barrow took office, the environment for the free exchange of ideas among students and professors has improved, despite lingering challenges. In January 2018, a lecturer at the University of The Gambia was arrested and briefly detained by the police over a newspaper interview in which he criticized the Barrow government's security policies. A student protest against the lecturer's arrest was held peacefully, one of several student demonstrations that were carried out without incident during the year.

Score Change: The score improved from 1 to 2 because the climate for both students and professors to express themselves freely has improved.

D4. Are individuals free to express their personal views on political or other sensitive topics without fear of surveillance or retribution? 2 / 4

Following years of repressive rule under Jammeh, freedom for ordinary people to express views—particularly those of a political nature—without fear of retaliation has increased since Barrow's administration took power. The Supreme Court ruled in May 2018 that sedition laws in the Criminal Code were constitutional, which some analysts argued could be used to criminalize criticism of the government on social media.

E. ASSOCIATIONAL AND ORGANIZATIONAL RIGHTS: 6 / 12 (+1)

E1. Is there freedom of assembly? 2 / 4 (+1)

The constitution guarantees freedom of assembly, and while limitations to this right remain under the Barrow administration, the environment improved further in 2018, with a number of demonstrations and political rallies in the run-up to the elections held without incident.

Despite these improvements, security forces violently dispersed some protests during the year. In June 2018, for example, three civilians in Faraba Banta were killed when police fired live ammunition into an environmental protest. The Barrow administration quickly launched an inquiry into the violence and accepted the resignation of the police inspector general, who drew heavy criticism for the police's conduct, days after the incident. Five police officers were charged with murder for their role in the deaths at the end of June. In November, the inquiry commission's report was published, which ordered the prosecution of the five officers. Some analysts asserted that Barrow's response signaled a commitment to accountability for police violence against demonstrators.

The Public Order Act, which was used by Jammeh to restrict protests, was upheld by the Supreme Court in late 2017. Under the act, permits from the police inspector general are required for public assemblies. Opposition leader Mama Kandeh was denied a permit in 2017, which led to a public outcry.

Score Change: The score improved from 1 to 2 because the space for peaceful assembly has increased under the Barrow administration, and the government has taken measures to promote accountability for violence against protesters.

E2. Is there freedom for nongovernmental organizations, particularly those that are engaged in human rights- and governance-related work? 2 / 4

There are a number of nongovernmental organizations (NGOs) in the Gambia focused on human rights and governance issues. Under Jammeh, NGO workers faced a serious risk of detention and other reprisals, but there were few reports of such suppression in 2018.

E3. Is there freedom for trade unions and similar professional or labor organizations? 2 / 4

Workers—except for civil servants, household workers, and security forces—may form unions, strike, and bargain for wages, but the labor minister has the discretion to exclude other categories of workers. Domestic and international trade union activity took place peacefully during the year with the support of the government.

F. RULE OF LAW: 5 / 16 (+2)

F1. Is there an independent judiciary? 1 / 4

The judiciary is hampered by corruption and inefficiency. The executive dominates judicial appointment processes. The Barrow administration has taken steps to appoint more Gambian citizens in the judiciary, as Jammeh had frequently appointed foreign judges whose terms he could easily cancel if they issued rulings he opposed. However, the judiciary remains reliant on foreign judges.

F2. Does due process prevail in civil and criminal matters? 1 / 4 (+1)

Constitutional guarantees of due process remain poorly upheld, but the situation has improved significantly under President Barrow. Political dissidents face less risk of arrest and prosecution. There were several high-profile reports of arbitrary detention in 2018, but most of those detained were released after a short time with no explanation. The government has taken steps to arrest and prosecute security officers responsible for human rights abuses during the Jammeh regime. The trial of seven former officers in the now defunct National Intelligence Agency (NIA), who are accused of murder in the 2016 death of rights activist Ebrima Solo Sandeng, was ongoing at year's end. One of the accused, the former deputy director of the NIA, Louis Gomez, died in prison in October 2018.

Score Change: The score improved from 0 to 1 because political dissidents faced less risk of arbitrary arrest and prosecution, and the government has taken steps to hold perpetrators of abuses during the Jammeh regime accountable.

F3. Is there protection from the illegitimate use of physical force and freedom from war and insurgencies? 2 / 4 (+1)

The use of illegitimate physical force by security agents has been less frequent under the Barrow administration. In October 2018, the government established the Truth, Reconciliation, and Reparations Commission to investigate human rights abuses committed during the Jammeh era. The commission will recommend individuals for prosecution and identify victims who will be eligible for financial compensation.

However, serious challenges persist. There are few safeguards to prevent people accused of committing human rights abuses from holding positions of authority within the criminal justice and prison systems. Prison conditions are harsh and unsanitary, and there have been reports of torture in prisons.

Score Change: The score improved from 1 to 2 due to a reduction in abuses by security forces, and government efforts to pursue justice for human rights violations committed during the Jammeh era.

F4. Do laws, policies, and practices guarantee equal treatment of various segments of the population? 1 / 4

A number of groups encounter serious difficulties in exercising their human rights. Legal protections for disabled people require strengthening and enforcement. LGBT people face severe societal discrimination, and same-sex relations remain criminalized. In 2017, Vice President Ousainou Darboe called for decriminalization, but in April 2018 Barrow dismissed homosexuality as a "nonissue" in The Gambia. The constitution prohibits discrimination, but this "does not apply in respect to adoption, marriage, divorce, burial, and devolution of property upon death."

G. PERSONAL AUTONOMY AND INDIVIDUAL RIGHTS: 6 / 16

G1. Do individuals enjoy freedom of movement, including the ability to change their place of residence, employment, or education? 2 / 4

Freedom of movement is hampered by poor roads and transportation infrastructure. Security checkpoints are common, particularly at night.

G2. Are individuals able to exercise the right to own property and establish private businesses without undue interference from state or nonstate actors? 2 / 4

Gambian law provides formal protection of property rights, although Sharia (Islamic law) provisions on family law and inheritance can facilitate discrimination against women. Corruption hampers legitimate business activity.

G3. Do individuals enjoy personal social freedoms, including choice of marriage partner and size of family, protection from domestic violence, and control over appearance? 1 / 4

Rape and domestic violence are illegal, but common. There are no laws prohibiting polygamy, or levirate marriage (in which a widow is married off to the younger brother of her spouse). Female genital mutilation (FGM) was outlawed in 2015, but is still practiced by some. Activists have called on Barrow to clearly indicate that the law prohibiting it will remain on the books. There is some evidence that rates of FGM and child marriage have increased since the end of the Jammeh regime. In November 2018, the Ministry of Justice established a specialized unit to address sexual and gender-based violence.

G4. Do individuals enjoy equality of opportunity and freedom from economic exploitation? 1 / 4

Women enjoy less access to higher education, justice, and employment than men. Although child labor and forced labor are illegal, some women and children are subject to sex trafficking, domestic servitude, and forced begging. The government has recently made an increased effort to address human trafficking, including by training security officials and border guards to identify victims, and by providing better services to those identified. However, the impact of these changes has been modest.

Georgia

Population: 3,900,000
Capital: Tbilisi
Political Rights Rating: 3
Civil Liberties Rating: 3
Freedom Rating: 3.0
Freedom Status: Partly Free
Electoral Democracy: Yes

Note: The numerical scores and status listed here do not reflect conditions in the territories of South Ossetia or Abkhazia, which are examined in separate reports.

Overview: Georgia holds regular and competitive elections, and its democratic trajectory showed signs of improvement during the period surrounding a change in government in 2012–13. However, progress has stagnated in recent years. Oligarchic actors hold outsized influence over policy and political choices, and the rule of law continues to be stymied by political interests.

KEY DEVELOPMENTS IN 2018:

- Giorgi Kvirikashvili stepped down as prime minister in June and was replaced by Mamuka Bakhtadze, previously the finance minister. Kvirikashvili said his resignation resulted from disagreements over economic policy with Bidzina Ivanishvili—a former prime minister, founder of the ruling Georgian Dream party, and the richest man in the country. Ivanishvili currently holds no elected office, though he did return to his former position as chairman of Georgian Dream at a party congress in May.

- There were a series of large demonstrations in Tbilisi during the year. Protests erupted in May in response to raids on two popular nightclubs where police said illegal drugs were being sold. Far-right groups then mounted counterdemonstrations. In June, fresh protests were prompted by the partial acquittal of a defendant in a prominent 2017 murder case; protest leaders and more than a dozen participants were arrested.
- A two-round presidential election was held in October and November. Salome Zourabichvili, an independent supported by Georgian Dream, took a narrow lead in the first round and ultimately defeated the opposition United National Movement (UNM) candidate in the runoff, becoming the first elected female president of Georgia. While the election took place in a generally peaceful environment, it was marred by allegations of vote buying, voter intimidation, and ballot-box stuffing.

POLITICAL RIGHTS: 25 / 40 (−1)

A. ELECTORAL PROCESS: 8 / 12 (−1)

A1. Was the current head of government or other chief national authority elected through free and fair elections? 2 / 4 (−1)

Georgia has a dual executive, with the prime minister serving as head of government and the president as head of state. The president had been directly elected for up to two five-year terms, but under constitutional changes approved in 2017, the president elected in 2018 is to serve a six-year term, after which presidents will be chosen by a 300-member electoral college comprising national lawmakers and regional and local officials. The president formally appoints the prime minister, who is nominated by Parliament.

In the October first round of the 2018 presidential election, Zourabichvili, an independent former foreign minister supported by Georgian Dream, won 39 percent of the vote, followed by Grigol Vashadze, a former foreign minister running for the UNM, with 38 percent. Observers reported that the balloting took place in a largely peaceful environment, but there were allegations of vote buying, predominantly by the ruling party, as well as reports of illegal campaign donations from the ruling party to Zourabichvili and of voter intimidation.

Zourabichvili won about 60 percent of the vote in the second round in November. While the electoral environment was again largely peaceful, significant problems in the preelectoral period and voter intimidation on election day marred the quality of the runoff. Abuse of administrative resources and limited instances of vote buying and ballot-box stuffing were reported. Outside a significant share of voting stations, the presence of Georgian Dream party activists with lists of local voters created an intimidating atmosphere. Just days before the runoff, a charitable foundation controlled by Ivanishvili promised to write off the debts of over 600,000 Georgians, or about one in six eligible voters.

Mamuka Bakhtadze, formerly the finance minister, replaced Giorgi Kvirikashvili as prime minister in June after the latter resigned over policy disagreements with Ivanishvili. Kvirikashvili had served as prime minister since late 2015.

Score Change: The score declined from 3 to 2 due to irregularities during the 2018 presidential election, including credible allegations of vote buying, abuse of administrative resources, and voter intimidation.

A2. Were the current national legislative representatives elected through free and fair elections? 3 / 4

Georgia's unicameral Parliament is composed of 150 members, with 77 selected through nationwide proportional representation and 73 in single-member districts. Members serve four-year terms.

In the 2016 parliamentary elections, Georgian Dream won a total of 115 seats, including 71 of the majoritarian contests. The UNM garnered 27 seats through the proportional vote but did not win any majoritarian districts. Smaller parties and an independent took the remainder. An observer mission from the Organization for Security and Co-operation in Europe (OSCE) found the elections competitive and largely fair, but noted that administrative funds were used for campaign purposes and that changes to rules governing party registration were made too close to the elections. A small number of violent incidents were reported during the campaign period and the first round of polling.

Under the constitutional amendments approved in 2017, the parliament will be elected entirely by proportional representation beginning in 2024.

A3. Are the electoral laws and framework fair, and are they implemented impartially by the relevant election management bodies? 3 / 4

The country's electoral laws are generally fair, and the bodies that implement them have typically done so impartially. However, following the 2016 legislative elections, OSCE monitors noted a lack of transparency in the adjudication of election-related complaints by the courts and the electoral commission. After the 2017 mayoral and municipal polls, an OSCE monitoring mission noted that the parliament's approval of a new head of the State Audit Office two weeks before the elections had prompted concerns about the office's impartiality; it is charged with regulating and overseeing campaign financing.

The Venice Commission expressed concern that the 2017 constitutional amendments would not be fully implemented until 2024. The delay was approved over the objections of opposition parties and civil society groups, which argued that it would benefit Georgian Dream in the 2020 parliamentary elections by maintaining the current mixed voting system for another cycle.

B. POLITICAL PLURALISM AND PARTICIPATION: 10 / 16

B1. Do the people have the right to organize in different political parties or other competitive political groupings of their choice, and is the system free of undue obstacles to the rise and fall of these competing parties or groupings? 3 / 4

Georgian political life is vibrant, and people are generally able to form political parties and assert their own candidacies with little interference. However, a pattern of single-party dominance since the 2000s has inhibited the development and stability of competing groups.

In the 2017 mayoral elections, independent candidates had significantly less time to collect signatures to register for ballot placement than candidates who belonged to a party.

B2. Is there a realistic opportunity for the opposition to increase its support or gain power through elections? 3 / 4

Georgia underwent a peaceful transfer of power between rival groups in 2012–13, when Georgian Dream defeated the UNM in parliamentary and presidential elections. The UNM splintered in 2017, leaving behind two smaller parties that were less capable of mounting a credible opposition. The weakened UNM and the new offshoot, European Georgia, failed to secure extensive representation in that year's municipal elections. Georgian Dream won most mayoral and gubernatorial seats, including the Tbilisi mayoralty. In the 2018 presidential vote, European Georgia's candidate ran a distant third in the first round and endorsed the UNM's Vashadze in the runoff.

Constitutional changes approved in 2017 prohibited multiple small parties from forming electoral blocs to overcome a 5 percent voting threshold needed to enter the parliament via proportional representation beginning in 2024. The ban on party blocs could further diminish the electoral prospects of the fragmented parliamentary opposition. (The 2020 legislative elections will feature a lower threshold of 3 percent.)

B3. Are the people's political choices free from domination by the military, foreign powers, religious hierarchies, economic oligarchies, or any other powerful group that is not democratically accountable? 2 / 4

Ivanishvili, the wealthy businessman who founded Georgian Dream in 2011, resigned as prime minister and as the ruling party's chairman in 2013, but he remained its primary financial backer and continued to control it informally. His successors as prime minister and party chairman have been close confidants and former employees of institutions he controls, suggesting that he plays a large role in determining the country's leadership. Ivanishvili was reelected as chairman of Georgian Dream at a party congress in May 2018.

Recent elections have featured allegations of various forms of vote buying and intimidation, including pressure on public employees and recipients of social benefits to support the ruling party.

B4. Do various segments of the population (including ethnic, religious, gender, LGBT, and other relevant groups) have full political rights and electoral opportunities? 2 / 4

No laws prevent women or members of minority groups from participating in the political process, but in practice these groups and their interests are underrepresented at all levels of government. A woman was elected president in 2018, but women hold just 24 seats in the 150-seat Parliament.

C. FUNCTIONING OF GOVERNMENT: 7 / 12

C1. Do the freely elected head of government and national legislative representatives determine the policies of the government? 2 / 4

The ability of elected officials to determine and implement government policy is impaired by the informal role of Ivanishvili, who holds no public office but exerts significant influence over executive and legislative decision-making. His de facto authority was demonstrated in June 2018, when Prime Minister Kvirikashvili resigned due to disagreements with Ivanishvili over economic policy.

Ivanishvili's policy influence is also visible in connection with his financial and business interests, and in particular the multibillion-dollar Georgian Co-Investment Fund (GCF), which was unveiled in 2013 and is active in large real-estate development projects in Tbilisi. In 2017, observers raised suspicions that a major development project opposed by many civil society actors but backed by GCF was receiving favorable treatment from the authorities in large part due to Ivanishvili's political connections.

C2. Are safeguards against official corruption strong and effective? 2 / 4

While the country has made significant progress in combating petty corruption, corruption within the government remains a problem. In some cases it has allegedly taken the form of nepotism or cronyism in government hiring. Effective application of anticorruption laws and regulations is impaired by a lack of independence among law enforcement bodies and the judiciary, and successful cases against high-ranking officials who are on good terms with the Georgian Dream leadership remain rare.

C3. Does the government operate with openness and transparency? 3 / 4

Government operations are generally subject to scrutiny by auditing bodies, the media, civil society organizations, and the public. However, the Institute for the Development of Freedom of Information (IDFI), a Georgian advocacy group, reports that access to public information has been uneven since 2010. In 2018 the institute reiterated its calls for a stronger law on access to information and urged greater transparency regarding officials' income declarations. Civil society activists have also expressed concern about a lack of transparency regarding rezoning and land sales in Tbilisi.

CIVIL LIBERTIES: 38 / 60
D. FREEDOM OF EXPRESSION AND BELIEF: 10 / 16 (−1)
D1. Are there free and independent media? 2 / 4

Georgia's media environment is robust and competitive, but frequently partisan. In 2018, a long-running legal dispute over the ownership of the opposition-aligned television station Rustavi 2 was awaiting a final judgment from the European Court of Human Rights (ECHR). In 2017, the ECHR had ruled that a Georgian Supreme Court decision to transfer the station to its former owner—Kibar Khalvashi, who is seen as more sympathetic to Georgian Dream—should be suspended while it considered the case, and warned authorities not to interfere with the station's editorial policies. The Georgian branch of Transparency International and other nongovernmental organizations (NGOs) had expressed serious concerns about procedural shortcomings at the Georgian court, and about the court's independence.

The Georgian Public Broadcaster (GPB) has recently made personnel changes that included the hiring of numerous people who were considered Ivanishvili allies, with some taking senior positions; civil society groups issued a joint statement in 2017 to express concern about these hires and about the station's coverage, which they said had become less critical of the government. Controversy over the GPB continued in 2018, as NGOs reacted to a State Audit Office report that found problems involving spending, procurement, and conflicts of interest at the broadcaster. Separately, civil society organizations reported that two of the five members of the Georgian National Communications Commission, which regulates broadcast media and internet services, lacked the academic credentials that were legally required for their positions.

D2. Are individuals free to practice and express their religious faith or nonbelief in public and private? 2 / 4

The constitution guarantees freedom of religion but grants unique privileges to the Georgian Orthodox Church, including immunity for its patriarch. Georgia's religious minorities—among them Jehovah's Witnesses, Baptists, Pentecostals, and Muslims—have reported discrimination and hostility, including from Georgian Orthodox priests and adherents, and are insufficiently protected by the state. Some minority religious groups have faced difficulty gaining permits from local officials to construct houses of worship.

D3. Is there academic freedom, and is the educational system free from extensive political indoctrination? 3 / 4 (−1)

Academic freedom is generally respected in Georgia. However, in August 2018, Georgian authorities froze the assets of the International Black Sea University and prevented it from accepting students for the new academic year, citing tax arrears that were allegedly owed by the private institution. The asset freeze was eventually lifted in October after the debt was paid, though the university maintained that the tax claim was unlawful. The International Black Sea University is associated with the movement led by Turkish Islamic preacher Fethullah Gülen, which the Turkish government has declared a terrorist organization. In 2017, Georgian authorities had closed two schools associated with Gülen's movement, citing regulatory violations. The seemingly disproportionate and arbitrary nature of the enforcement actions raised suspicions that they were carried out under pressure from the Turkish government.

Score Change: The score declined from 4 to 3 due to the government's arbitrary regulatory pressure on the International Black Sea University and other schools associated with the Turkish Islamic preacher Fethullah Gülen.

D4. Are individuals free to express their personal views on political or other sensitive topics without fear of surveillance or retribution? 3 / 4

Georgians generally enjoy freedom of expression, including in their online communications. However, watchdog groups have expressed concerns in recent years that various security-related laws empower state agencies to conduct surveillance and data collection without adequate independent oversight. A 2017 law created a new electronic surveillance agency under the umbrella of the State Security Service that would have the authority to fine service providers for failure to cooperate with its work. Privacy advocates questioned whether the law complied with earlier Constitutional Court rulings on state surveillance practices.

E. ASSOCIATIONAL AND ORGANIZATIONAL RIGHTS: 8 / 12

E1. Is there freedom of assembly? 3 / 4

Freedom of assembly is generally respected, but police sometimes respond to demonstrations with excessive force. In 2017, a protest in Batumi against exorbitant fines for traffic violations became violent; police employed tear gas and rubber bullets, and a number of injuries were reported. Protests during 2018 proceeded more peacefully. They included demonstrations in May in response to aggressive raids on two popular nightclubs where police said illegal drugs were being sold, and counterdemonstrations mounted by far-right organizations—part of an ongoing debate over drug laws and their enforcement in the country. Separate protests erupted in June after the partial acquittal of a defendant in the Khorava Street murders, a 2017 incident in which two teenagers were killed in a street brawl; at least 19 protest leaders and participants were arrested, including Parliament member Nika Melia and Tbilisi City Council member Irakli Nadiradze, both of the UNM.

E2. Is there freedom for nongovernmental organizations, particularly those that are engaged in human rights- and governance-related work? 3 / 4

The civil society sector has grown significantly in recent years, but it remains concentrated in the capital. Some groups are included in policy discussions, while others report facing political pressure, largely in the form of public criticism by both government officials and opposition figures. In 2018, high-level officials continued to make aggressive public statements aimed at discrediting NGOs and activists including Eka Gigauri, the head of Transparency International Georgia. In October, Public Defender Nino Lomjaria, the country's ombudsperson, called on the authorities to refrain from such attacks and adhere to their international obligations regarding the protection of human rights defenders. A coalition of NGOs released a similar statement later the same day.

E3. Is there freedom for trade unions and similar professional or labor organizations? 2 / 4

Workers are legally allowed to organize, bargain collectively, and strike, though there are some restrictions on the right to strike, including a ban on strikes by certain categories of workers. Legal protections against antiunion discrimination by employers are weak and poorly enforced.

F. RULE OF LAW: 8 / 16

F1. Is there an independent judiciary? 2 / 4

Despite ongoing judicial reforms, executive and legislative interference in the courts remains a substantial problem, as does corruption and a lack of transparency and professionalism surrounding judicial proceedings. In August 2018, Nino Gvenetadze resigned as head of the Supreme Court, ostensibly for health reasons. However, many observers suggested that she was pressured to resign. Under a new constitutional framework that took effect after the 2018 presidential election, Supreme Court judges are nominated by the High Council of Justice rather than the president, then approved by Parliament. A judicial self-governing body elects a majority of the council's members. In December, the council presented a list of Supreme Court nominees, but a coalition of NGOs argued that it had used an opaque process and selected judges with tainted reputations. The coalition called on Parliament to adopt more robust qualification rules and transparent procedures for selecting Supreme Court judges before it considered any nominees from the council.

F2. Does due process prevail in civil and criminal matters? 2 / 4

The law guarantees due process, but this protection is not always respected in practice. The office of the country's public defender, or ombudsperson, has reported problems including a failure to fully implement Constitutional Court rulings, administrative delays in court proceedings, the violation of the accused's right to a presumption of innocence, and the denial of access to a lawyer upon arrest.

F3. Is there protection from the illegitimate use of physical force and freedom from war and insurgencies? 2 / 4

Human rights watchdogs and the ombudsperson continue to express concern about the physical abuse of detainees during arrest and in police custody, and have noted the lack of an independent system for supervising police conduct and addressing claims of mistreatment. In July 2018, Parliament approved legislation to establish a new state inspector's office tasked with investigating police abuses, but it would not be independent from the prosecutor's office, a shortcoming that drew criticism from human rights groups. Violence and harsh conditions in prisons remain a problem.

F4. Do laws, policies, and practices guarantee equal treatment of various segments of the population? 2 / 4

A 2014 antidiscrimination law providing protection against discrimination on the basis of various factors, including race, gender, age, sexual orientation, and gender identity, is enforced unevenly. Women and people with disabilities reportedly suffer from discrimination in employment, among other problems. LGBT (lesbian, gay, bisexual, and transgender) people face societal discrimination and are occasionally the targets of serious violence.

G. PERSONAL AUTONOMY AND INDIVIDUAL RIGHTS: 12 / 16 (+1)

G1. Do individuals enjoy freedom of movement, including the ability to change their place of residence, employment, or education? 4 / 4 (+1)

There are ongoing restrictions on travel to and from the separatist territories of Abkhazia and South Ossetia, and individuals who approach their de facto borders can face short-term detention. Nevertheless, Georgians are generally free to travel abroad and within government-controlled territory, and they can change their place of residence, employment, or education without undue interference.

Score Change: The score improved from 3 to 4 because, while some obstructions remain with respect to the de facto borders of separatist regions, people in Georgia are largely free to travel and change their places of residence, employment, and education.

G2. Are individuals able to exercise the right to own property and establish private businesses without undue interference from state or nonstate actors? 3 / 4

The legal framework and government policies are generally supportive of private business activity, and conditions for entrepreneurs have reportedly improved in recent years. However, protection for property rights remains weak, and deficiencies in judicial independence and government transparency hamper economic freedom.

G3. Do individuals enjoy personal social freedoms, including choice of marriage partner and size of family, protection from domestic violence, and control over appearance? 3 / 4

Personal social freedoms are generally respected. However, constitutional changes approved in 2017 define marriage as "a union between a man and a woman for the purpose of creating a family," and there is no law allowing civil unions for same-sex couples.

Domestic violence remains a problem in Georgia, and the response from police is often reportedly inadequate, though changing societal attitudes have contributed to more frequent reporting and some improvements in enforcement in recent years. Spousal rape is not specifically criminalized.

G4. Do individuals enjoy equality of opportunity and freedom from economic exploitation? 2 / 4

The public defender in December 2017 called workplace injuries and fatalities a "systemic problem" and has commented on the lack of government action in implementing and strengthening labor protections. Unsafe conditions continued to contribute to workplace deaths during 2018, including 11 deaths in the country's mines.

Georgia is a source, destination, and transit country for human trafficking linked to sexual exploitation and forced labor. However, according to the US State Department's 2018 *Trafficking in Persons Report*, the government continued its enforcement efforts and improved its performance on victim identification.

Germany

Population: 82,800,000
Capital: Berlin
Political Rights Rating: 1
Civil Liberties Rating: 1
Freedom Rating: 1.0
Freedom Status: Free
Electoral Democracy: Yes

Overview: Germany, a member of the European Union (EU), is a representative democracy with a vibrant political culture and civil society. Political rights and civil liberties are largely assured both in law and practice. The political system is influenced by the country's totalitarian past, with constitutional safeguards designed to prevent authoritarian rule. Although Germany has generally been stable since the mid-20th century, political tensions have grown following an influx of asylum seekers into the country and the growing popularity of a right-wing party, among other issues.

KEY DEVELOPMENTS IN 2018:

- After lengthy negotiations, Chancellor Angela Merkel formed a coalition government in March that includes her center-right Christian Democratic Union (CDU), its Bavarian sister party, the Christian Social Union (CSU), and the center-left Social Democratic Party (SPD). All three parties had suffered heavy losses in the 2017 federal election.
- After 18 years as the head of the CDU, Merkel announced in October that she would step down as chairperson at year's end, and that she would not seek another term as chancellor in the 2021 elections.
- In August and September, anti-immigration protests in Chemnitz turned violent when far-right demonstrators attacked and harassed people they perceived to be immigrants. Clashes also erupted between the right-wing protestors and counter-demonstrators, and a number of journalists reported being assaulted while trying to cover the unrest.
- In January, the controversial Network Enforcement Act, which compels social media companies to delete content deemed hate speech, came into full effect. Some rights groups claimed that thousands of posts that do not actually constitute hate speech were removed by social media platforms trying to comply with the law.

POLITICAL RIGHTS: 39 / 40
A. ELECTORAL PROCESS: 12 / 12
A1. Was the current head of government or other chief national authority elected through free and fair elections? 4 / 4

Germany's head of state is a largely ceremonial president, chosen by the Federal Convention, a body formed jointly by the Bundestag (Federal Parliament) and state representatives. The president can serve up to two five-year terms. Former foreign minister Frank-Walter Steinmeier of the SPD was elected president in early 2017.

The federal chancellor—the head of government—is elected by the Bundestag and usually serves for the duration of a legislative session. The chancellor's term can be cut short only if the Bundestag chooses a replacement in a so-called constructive vote of no confidence. Angela Merkel won a fourth term as chancellor following 2017 Bundestag elections, which were held in accordance with democratic standards. After 18 years as the head of the CDU, Merkel announced in October that she would step down as chairperson at year's end, and that she would not seek another term as chancellor in the 2021 elections.

A2. Were the current national legislative representatives elected through free and fair elections? 4 / 4

The German constitution provides for a lower house of parliament, the Bundestag, as well as an upper house, the Bundesrat (Federal Council), which represents the country's 16 federal states. The Bundestag is elected at least every four years through a mixture of proportional representation and single-member districts, which can lead the number of seats to vary from the minimum of 598. The 2017 elections saw 709 representatives elected to the Bundestag. Election monitors from the Organization for Security and Co-operation in Europe deemed the elections transparent and free from manipulation.

Merkel's CDU-CSU won 246 seats. The SPD, the CDU-CSU's coalition partner in the last government, took 153 seats. Both parties posted their worst results since 1949. The liberal Free Democratic Party (FDP) reentered the Bundestag with 80 seats, and the Greens won 67. The far-left party the Left, widely viewed as a successor to the East German communists, took 69 seats. The right-wing populist Alternative for Germany (AfD) entered the Bundestag for the first time in its history, taking 94 seats, posting particularly strong results in the former German Democratic Republic (GDR). Following negotiations of an unprecedented length, the CDU-CSU and SPD renewed their coalition government, and in March 2018, the new government under Merkel was sworn in.

In Germany's federal system, state governments have considerable authority over matters such as education, policing, taxation, and spending. State governments appoint Bundesrat members, and in this manner can influence national policies. Two state elections took place in October, in Bavaria and Hesse. In both elections, the parties that compose the governing coalition suffered heavy losses, leading to doubts about the sustainability of the coalition.

A3. Are the electoral laws and framework fair, and are they implemented impartially by the relevant election management bodies? 4 / 4

Germany's electoral laws and framework are fair and impartial. A failure to reform the problem of so-called overhang seats led to an inflated number of Bundestag members following the 2017 elections. (German voters cast two ballots—one for a candidate in their constituency and another for a party, with the latter vote determining the total number of seats a party will hold in the Bundestag. If a party wins more seats in the first vote than are permitted by results of the second, it gets to keep these "overhang" seats. The extra seats are costly, and in the past have been deemed unconstitutional for allowing a party more seats than it is formally allotted.) With 709 members, Germany now has the world's second-largest national parliament, after China.

B. POLITICAL PLURALISM AND PARTICIPATION: 15 / 16

B1. Do the people have the right to organize in different political parties or other competitive political groupings of their choice, and is the system free of undue obstacles to the rise and fall of these competing parties or groupings? 4 / 4

The dominant political parties have traditionally been the SPD and the CDU-CSU, although other parties have increased their support in recent years. Parties do not face undue restrictions on registration or operation, although under electoral laws that, for historical reasons, are intended to restrict the far left and far right, a party must receive either 5 percent of the national vote or win at least three directly elected seats to gain representation in the parliament. The constitution makes it possible to ban political parties, although a party must be judged to pose a threat to democracy for a ban to be legal, and no party has been successfully banned since 1956. More recently, in 2017 the Federal Constitutional Court found the extreme-right National Democratic Party (NPD) to be unconstitutional, but ruled that it did not pose a great enough threat to merit a ban.

Support for the AfD has risen in recent years, as the party has moved further to the right of the political spectrum. As of 2018, the party is represented in the Bundestag, as well as in all state parliaments. While the increase in popularity has shaken the German political system, most parties oppose the AfD.

B2. Is there a realistic opportunity for the opposition to increase its support or gain power through elections? 4 / 4

While German government is very much consensus oriented, opposition parties have a realistic opportunity to increase their support and gain power through elections. Merkel, during her time as chancellor, has changed her coalition partners a number of times.

B3. Are the people's political choices free from domination by the military, foreign powers, religious hierarchies, economic oligarchies, or any other powerful group that is not democratically accountable? 4 / 4

The German government is democratically accountable to the voters, who are free to throw their support behind their preferred candidates and parties without undue influence on their political choices.

B4. Do various segments of the population (including ethnic, religious, gender, LGBT, and other relevant groups) have full political rights and electoral opportunities? 3 / 4

Germany's constitution gives all citizens age 18 or older the right to vote, and this guarantee applies regardless of gender, ethnicity, religion, sexual orientation, or gender identity. However, some groups are underrepresented in politics. The 2017 federal elections saw a decrease in the representation of women in the Bundestag, down to 30.9 percent, the lowest number since 1998. In the Bundestag, 8 percent of members are from immigrant backgrounds, having at least one parent who was born without German citizenship.

Nearly eight million foreign-born residents were unable to vote in the 2017 federal elections, a high number that is partly a result of restrictive citizenship and voting laws. In order to gain German citizenship, residents must renounce the citizenship of their home countries, which contributes to low rates of naturalization and large numbers of long-term residents who cannot vote in federal elections.

C. FUNCTIONING OF GOVERNMENT: 12 / 12

C1. Do the freely elected head of government and national legislative representatives determine the policies of the government? 4 / 4

Democratically elected representatives decide and implement policy without undue interference.

C2. Are safeguards against official corruption strong and effective? 4 / 4

Germany generally has strong and effective safeguards against corruption. However, the regulatory framework on lobbying members of parliament is considered inadequate by Transparency Germany. For example, there is no central lobbying register in Germany. In a report released in February 2018, The Council of Europe's Group of States against Corruption (GRECO) criticized Germany for a lack of transparency in the financing of political parties.

Watchdogs continue to express concerns about a controversial 2015 data retention law, which they view as a threat not only to general privacy (the law requires telecommunications companies to store users' telephone and internet data for 10 weeks) but also to whistleblowers, who could be punished under a section detailing illegal data handling. In 2017, a court suspended implementation of the law, stating that it could be in violation of EU law. In April, the Administrative Court of Cologne ruled that the legislation was indeed incompatible with EU law. Whistleblowers receive few legal protections in Germany.

C3. Does the government operate with openness and transparency? 4 / 4

The government is held accountable for its performance through open parliamentary debates, which are covered widely in the media. In June 2018, the government introduced question time, in which the chancellor answers questions from the parliament three times per year.

In late 2016, Germany joined the Open Government Partnership. In 2017 the government published a National Action Plan that detailed initiatives designed to improve transparency and encourage citizen involvement in government, although the government had made little progress in implementing these measures at the end of 2018.

CIVIL LIBERTIES: 55 / 60
D. FREEDOM OF EXPRESSION AND BELIEF 14 / 16
D1. Are there free and independent media? 4 / 4

Freedom of expression is enshrined in the constitution, and the media are largely free and independent. Hate speech, such as racist agitation or anti-Semitism, is punishable by law. It is also illegal to advocate Nazism, deny the Holocaust, or glorify the ideology of Hitler.

In September 2018, Reporters Without Borders (RSF) reported an increase in attacks against journalists during the year, including at demonstrations in the city of Chemnitz in late August and early September, which broke out after two immigrants allegedly stabbed and killed a German man at the city's street festival. Several journalists were reportedly assaulted while attempting to report on the far-right demonstrations. Journalists and NGOs subsequently criticized the police for not doing enough to protect journalists at far-right protests, and called on the authorities to provide the security necessary for reporters to safely cover such events. In August, the police came under criticism for preventing a television crew from ZDF, a public television broadcaster, from filming for 45 minutes at a demonstration in Dresden by Patriotic Europeans Against the Islamization of the Occident (PEGIDA), a far-right anti-Islamic group, after an off-duty police officer claimed they were not allowed to record the event.

D2. Are individuals free to practice and express their religious faith or nonbelief in public and private? 3 / 4

Freedom of belief is legally protected. However, eight states have passed laws prohibiting schoolteachers from wearing headscarves, while Berlin and the state of Hesse have adopted legislation banning headscarves for civil servants.

Interior Minister Horst Seehofer caused controversy in March 2018 by stating that "Islam does not belong to Germany" in response to Chancellor Merkel's assertion that the religion does have a place in the country. In April, the state government of Bavaria was criticized for ordering crosses to be displayed in all government buildings beginning in June.

D3. Is there academic freedom, and is the educational system free from extensive political indoctrination? 4 / 4

Academic freedom is generally respected, though legal prohibitions on extremist speech are enforceable in school and university settings.

D4. Are individuals free to express their personal views on political or other sensitive topics without fear of surveillance or retribution? 3 / 4

Private discussion and internet access are generally unrestricted, but recent developments have prompted concern about government surveillance of private communications. In 2013, documents leaked by former US National Security Agency (NSA) contractor Edward Snowden revealed that the NSA, in collaboration with Germany's Federal Intelligence

Service (BND), had secretly collected extensive data on communications in Germany. A parliamentary inquiry into the nature of cooperation between the NSA and BND concluded in 2017 and had inconclusive results. In 2017, the Bundestag passed a law allowing state security services to use spyware to conduct surveillance of encrypted online messaging services like WhatsApp when conducting criminal investigations.

In January 2018, the controversial Network Enforcement Act came into full effect.. The law compels social media companies to delete content deemed to clearly constitute illegal hate speech within 24 hours of being reported, and content that appears to be illegal hate speech within seven days. RSF claims that, to comply with the law, social media platforms including Facebook, YouTube, and Twitter removed thousands of posts that should not be considered hate speech during the year.

E. ASSOCIATIONAL AND ORGANIZATIONAL RIGHTS: 12 / 12
E1. Is there freedom of assembly? 4 / 4
The right to peaceful assembly is enshrined in the German constitution and is generally respected in practice, except in the case of outlawed groups, such as those advocating Nazism or opposing democratic order. In August and September 2018, anti-immigration protests in Chemnitz turned violent when far-right protestors attacked and harassed people they perceived to be immigrants. Clashes also erupted between the right-wing protestors and counterdemonstrators, with both sides throwing projectiles at each other. As a result of the unrest, at least 18 people were injured.

E2. Is there freedom for nongovernmental organizations, particularly those that are engaged in human rights- and governance-related work? 4 / 4
Germany has a vibrant sphere of NGOs and associations, which operate freely.

E3. Is there freedom for trade unions and similar professional or labor organizations? 4 / 4
Trade unions, farmers' groups, and business confederations are generally free to organize, and play an important role in shaping Germany's economic model.

F. RULE OF LAW: 14 / 16
F1. Is there an independent judiciary? 4 / 4
The judiciary is independent, and generally enforces the rights provided by Germany's laws and constitution. A debate surrounding the independence of the judiciary broke out in August 2018 after a minister in the state of North Rhine-Westphalia (NRW) criticized a court decision ordering the return of a man with former ties to al-Qaeda, at taxpayer expense, who had been deported to Tunisia in July. The court stated that immigration authorities had deceived the court which had ordered the deportation of the man, who had been living illegally in Germany since 2007 and had allegedly served as Osama bin Laden's bodyguard. In response to the ruling, NRW Interior Minister Herbert Reul of the CDU stated that judges' decisions should be consistent with the public's "sense of justice," for which he later expressed regret.

F2. Does due process prevail in civil and criminal matters? 4 / 4
The rule of law prevails in Germany. Civil and criminal matters are treated according to legal provisions and with due process. However, courts can authorize "preventive detention" practices, by which a person who was convicted of certain violent crimes can be detained after serving their sentence in full if they are deemed to pose a danger to the public.

In 2018, the state governments of Bavaria and NRW passed controversial police laws that significantly increased the surveillance powers of law enforcement. The Bavarian police law, passed in May, gives the police sweeping powers to bug private apartments, restaurants, and offices; open mail; and access private data stored in the cloud. The law also allows police to take preemptive action if they believe there is an "impending danger," a vaguely defined term that critics assert could make the law vulnerable to abuse. NRW passed a similar law in December, and several other states were considering police legislation that could threaten civil liberties at year's end.

Hans-Georg Maassen, the former head of the domestic intelligence agency, the Federal Office for the Protection of the Constitution (BfV), came under scrutiny in 2018 for allegedly supporting the AfD by informing party leaders about BfV investigations into AfD officials, as well as sharing sensitive information with and advising AfD members on how to avoid surveillance. Maassen was reassigned to a senior position in the Interior Ministry in September, following these revelations and remarks he made insinuating that reports of attacks against people who appeared foreign during the Chemnitz demonstrations was fake news. He was fired from his Interior Ministry position in November.

F3. Is there protection from the illegitimate use of physical force and freedom from war and insurgencies? 3 / 4

Attacks on refugees and refugee housing continued to decline from a peak of 3,500 in 2016. In the first half of 2018, around 700 such attacks were reported. Reported attacks on Muslims and mosques also decreased from 950 in 2017 to 813 in 2018. However, the government reported that the number of documented anti-Semitic attacks increased by 10 percent during the year.

The threat posed by terrorist groups to national and regional security remained a significant concern in 2018, but no major attacks occurred during the year.

F4. Do laws, policies, and practices guarantee equal treatment of various segments of the population? 3 / 4

The constitution and other laws guarantee equality and prohibit discrimination on the basis of origin, gender, religion or belief, disability, age, or sexual orientation. However, a number of obstacles stand in the way of equal treatment of all segments of the population. Rhetoric against refugees remained prominent in the German public sphere in 2018. PEGIDA, which developed into a large protest movement in 2014, remained active in 2018 and continued to be one of the most vocal opponents of asylum and migration. The AfD used strong rhetoric against asylum seekers and migrants throughout its state election campaigns.

In July, in order to maintain her governing coalition amidst intense pressure from Interior Minister Seehofer, Chancellor Merkel agreed to restrictive new asylum and migration policies, which include building camps along Germany's international borders to hold asylum seekers, and deporting any asylum seeker who had previously applied for asylum in another EU country.

G. PERSONAL AUTONOMY AND INDIVIDUAL RIGHTS: 15 / 16

G1. Do individuals enjoy freedom of movement, including the ability to change their place of residence, employment, or education? 4 / 4

Freedom of movement is legally protected and generally respected, although the refugee crisis and security concerns related to activity by the Islamic State (IS) militant group have led to some restrictions on travel. In 2015, the government introduced legislation allowing the confiscation of identity documents from German citizens suspected of terrorism as a way to prevent them from traveling abroad, particularly to Iraq and Syria.

G2. Are individuals able to exercise the right to own property and establish private businesses without undue interference from state or nonstate actors? 4 / 4

The rights to own property and engage in commercial activity are respected.

G3. Do individuals enjoy personal social freedoms, including choice of marriage partner and size of family, protection from domestic violence, and control over appearance? 4 / 4

The government generally does not restrict social freedoms. Women's rights are protected under antidiscrimination laws. However, a considerable gender wage gap persists, with women earning approximately 22 percent less in gross wages than men. A law requiring large German companies to reserve at least 30 percent of seats on their non-executive boards for women came into effect in 2016, but affects a limited number of companies. Adoption and tax legislation passed in 2014 gave equal rights to same-sex couples in these areas. The government legalized same-sex marriage in 2017.

In 2018, a debate continued over a Nazi-era law banning doctors from providing information on or advertising abortion services. While abortion is permitted in Germany within the first trimester, a doctor was fined in 2017 for listing abortion services on her website, which led to calls to reform or repeal the law. In December, the government proposed a reform that would allow clinics and doctors to state that they offer abortions, but maintain a ban on advertising the procedure.

G4. Do individuals enjoy equality of opportunity and freedom from economic exploitation? 3 / 4

According to the US State Department's 2018 *Trafficking in Persons* report, migrants from Eastern Europe, Africa, and Asia are targeted for sex trafficking and forced labor. Asylum seekers, especially unaccompanied minors, are also particularly vulnerable to exploitation.

Ghana

Population: 29,500,000
Capital: Accra
Political Rights Rating: 1
Civil Liberties Rating: 2
Freedom Rating: 1.5
Freedom Status: Free
Electoral Democracy: Yes

Overview: Since 1992, Ghana has held competitive multiparty elections and undergone peaceful transfers of power between the two main political parties. Although the country has a relatively strong record of upholding civil liberties, discrimination against women and LGBT (lesbian, gay, bisexual, and transgender) people persists. There are some weaknesses in judicial independence and the rule of law, and political corruption presents challenges to government performance.

KEY DEVELOPMENTS IN 2018:

- In February, Martin Amidu was sworn in as the special prosecutor, a position created under a 2017 law with the aim of combating corruption. However, he complained in September that a lack of resources from the government was stymying his office's operations.

- In June, President Nana Akufo-Addo fired the chairperson of the Electoral Commission (EC), Charlotte Osei, and two senior members of the commission on the recommendation of a five-member judicial panel convened by Chief Justice Sophia Akuffo. In July, Akufo-Addo nominated Jean Mensah as the new chairperson of the EC.
- Also in June, a commission of inquiry recommended to the president that the number of regions in Ghana be increased from 10 to 16. In December, voters approved the new boundaries in a referendum.
- In October, members of Delta Force, a vigilante group aligned with the ruling party, attempted to attack a government minister during a party meeting in the Ashanti Region. The vigilantes were reportedly angry that the minister had not followed through on a promise to recruit them into the security forces. Civil society activists have expressed concern about the involvement of such groups in the country's partisan politics.

POLITICAL RIGHTS: 36 / 40 (−1)

A. ELECTORAL PROCESS: 12 / 12

A1. Was the current head of government or other chief national authority elected through free and fair elections? 4 / 4

The president, who serves as head of state and head of government, is directly elected for up to two four-year terms. International and domestic observers generally praised the 2016 presidential election, and all major political parties accepted the results. Akufo-Addo, the New Patriotic Party (NPP) candidate, won with 53.9 percent of the vote, while incumbent John Mahama of the National Democratic Congress (NDC) took 44.4 percent.

Although the election and its immediate aftermath were peaceful, the campaign period was contentious. There were several reports of clashes between NPP and NDC supporters, as well as attacks on EC officials. Moreover, civil society representatives raised concerns about what they claimed were alarming levels of hate speech used by politicians, as well as alleged abuse of state resources.

A2. Were the current national legislative representatives elected through free and fair elections? 4 / 4

Members of Ghana's unicameral, 275-seat Parliament are elected directly in single-member constituencies to serve four-year terms. International and domestic observers generally praised the 2016 parliamentary elections, which were held at the same time as the presidential election. The NPP captured 169 seats, while the NDC, which held a majority going into the vote, took the remaining 106 seats.

A3. Are the electoral laws and framework fair, and are they implemented impartially by the relevant election management bodies? 4 / 4

Despite controversy surrounding preparations for the December 2016 balloting, domestic and international observers generally commended the EC for its management of the process. The commission had disqualified 13 presidential candidates that October due to irregularities with their nomination papers or failure to pay the nomination fee. The Supreme Court rescinded the EC's decision in early November, giving the disqualified candidates an opportunity to rectify the problems. In the end, three of the originally disqualified candidates were allowed to stand for election.

In June 2018, President Akufo-Addo fired EC chairperson Charlotte Osei and two senior members of the commission based on the recommendation of a five-member judicial panel convened by the chief justice. The judicial panel found that Osei and her deputies were guilty of mismanagement concerning the awarding of contracts leading up to the 2016 general elections. In July, Akufo-Addo nominated Jean Mensah, a prominent lawyer and civil society activist and the executive director of the Institute of Economic Affairs, as the new EC chairperson; he also nominated replacements for the two other fired commissioners and for a fourth commissioner who was retiring. Although several civil society groups lauded the nomination of Mensah, the NDC argued that the choice was influenced by partisan considerations. The new commissioners were sworn into office in August.

Also in June, a commission of inquiry headed by retired Supreme Court justice Stephen Brobbey recommended to the president that the number of regions in Ghana be increased from 10 to 16. In December, voters in the proposed regions approved the new boundaries, despite a legal challenge regarding the constitutionality of the referendum by a group with ties to the political opposition.

B. POLITICAL PLURALISM AND PARTICIPATION: 14 / 16 (−1)

B1. Do the people have the right to organize in different political parties or other competitive political groupings of their choice, and is the system free of undue obstacles to the rise and fall of these competing parties or groupings? 3 / 4 (−1)

The constitution guarantees the right to form political parties, and this right is generally respected. However, a significant increase in candidate nomination fees for the 2016 elections, along with the difficulties in nomination procedures highlighted by the presidential candidate disqualifications, presented challenges to participation, especially for candidates from smaller parties. The Progressive People's Party (PPP) mounted an unsuccessful legal challenge against the nomination fees ahead of the elections.

In October 2018, members of Delta Force, a pro-NPP vigilante group, attempted to attack Anthony Akoto Osei, an NPP lawmaker and the country's minister for monitoring and evaluation, during a party meeting in Tafo Pankrono in the Ashanti Region. The Delta Force members, who were later arrested and charged, were reportedly angry that Akoto Osei had not followed through on a promise to recruit them into the security forces in exchange for their campaign-related work. In 2017, Delta Force members had attacked the Ashanti Region's new security coordinator, George Adjei, and subsequently stormed a circuit court in Kumasi, the regional capital, in a bid to release 13 suspects on trial for the initial attack. Civil society groups have expressed concern about the rising involvement of pro-NPP vigilante groups such as Delta Force, and pro-NDC vigilante groups such as the Azorka Boys in the Northern Region, in inter- and intraparty disputes.

Score Change: The score declined from 4 to 3 because partisan vigilante groups have carried out attacks on politicians and become involved in party disputes in recent years.

B2. Is there a realistic opportunity for the opposition to increase its support or gain power through elections? 4 / 4

The NPP and its chief rival, the NDC, dominate the political system, but there have been multiple peaceful transfers of power between them, and parties in opposition enjoy meaningful opportunities to increase their public support and win office. Mahama's defeat by Akufo-Addo in the 2016 presidential race marked the first time since the reintroduction of the multiparty system in 1992 that an incumbent president had stood for reelection and lost.

B3. Are the people's political choices free from domination by the military, foreign powers, religious hierarchies, economic oligarchies, or any other powerful group that is not democratically accountable? 4 / 4

Ghanaians are generally free from undue interference with their political choices by powerful groups that are not democratically accountable.

B4. Do various segments of the population (including ethnic, religious, gender, LGBT, and other relevant groups) have full political rights and electoral opportunities? 3 / 4

Ghanaian laws provide for equal participation in political life by the country's various cultural, religious, and ethnic minorities. Women formally enjoy political equality, but they hold comparatively few leadership positions in practice. In the 2016 elections, women candidates received less media coverage than men and took just 37 of the 275 parliamentary seats, though this was the largest share since the reintroduction of multiparty rule in 1992. The National House of Chiefs, Ghana's highest body of customary authority, has been under pressure to include women as members.

C. FUNCTIONING OF GOVERNMENT: 10 / 12

C1. Do the freely elected head of government and national legislative representatives determine the policies of the government? 4 / 4

Elected officials are generally free to set and implement government policy without improper influence from unelected entities.

C2. Are safeguards against official corruption strong and effective? 3 / 4

Political corruption remains a problem despite active media coverage, fairly robust laws and institutions, and government antigraft initiatives. Legislation adopted in 2017 established the Office of the Special Prosecutor to investigate political corruption. President Akufo-Addo nominated former attorney general Martin Amidu, a member of the opposition NDC, as the special prosecutor in January 2018, and he took office the following month. However, in September Amidu complained publicly about the lack of government funding for the office's operations. Several new corruption scandals emerged during the year. Critics in the media, opposition parties, and nongovernmental organizations (NGOs) have deemed the government's anticorruption efforts inadequate.

C3. Does the government operate with openness and transparency? 3 / 4

The government operates with relative transparency, though there are weaknesses in the legal framework. Despite more than a decade of consideration by Parliament and continued efforts by advocates in 2018, the Right to Information Bill had not passed by year's end.

CIVIL LIBERTIES: 47 / 60 (+1)

D. FREEDOM OF EXPRESSION AND BELIEF: 14 / 16

D1. Are there free and independent media? 3 / 4

Freedom of the press is constitutionally guaranteed and generally respected in practice. Ghana has a diverse and vibrant media landscape that includes state and privately owned television and radio stations as well as a number of independent newspapers and magazines. Online news media operate without government restrictions.

Government agencies occasionally limit press freedom through harassment and arrests of journalists, especially those reporting on politically sensitive issues. In February 2018, Christopher Kevin Asima, a radio presenter for A1 Radio, was allegedly assaulted by three police officers while reporting on a fire in Bolgatanga, the capital of the Upper East Region.

The regional police commander and his deputy apologized for the incident and promised that there would be consequences for the officers involved. In March, Latif Iddrisu, a reporter for JoyNews and JoyFM, was allegedly attacked by police officers stationed at the Criminal Investigations Department headquarters in Accra. According to Iddrisu, the beating occurred after he inquired about the arrest of a senior NDC official who had predicted an uprising against the president; the charges in that case were later dropped. In June, the Media Foundation for West Africa issued a statement expressing concern about incidents the previous month in which two journalists and a civil society activist had been threatened because of their work.

D2. Are individuals free to practice and express their religious faith or nonbelief in public and private? 3 / 4

Religious freedom is constitutionally and legally protected, and the government largely upholds these protections in practice. However, public schools feature mandatory religious education courses drawing on Christianity and Islam, and Muslims students have allegedly been required to participate in Christian prayer sessions and church services in some publicly funded Christian schools.

D3. Is there academic freedom, and is the educational system free from extensive political indoctrination? 4 / 4

Academic freedom is legally guaranteed and generally upheld in practice.

D4. Are individuals free to express their personal views on political or other sensitive topics without fear of surveillance or retribution? 4 / 4

Private discussion is both free and vibrant. The government does not restrict individual expression on social media.

E. ASSOCIATIONAL AND ORGANIZATIONAL RIGHTS: 11 / 12

E1. Is there freedom of assembly? 4 / 4

The right to peaceful assembly is constitutionally guaranteed and generally respected. Permits are not required for meetings or demonstrations.

E2. Is there freedom for nongovernmental organizations, particularly those that are engaged in human rights- and governance-related work? 4 / 4

NGOs are generally able to operate freely and play an important role in ensuring government accountability and transparency.

E3. Is there freedom for trade unions and similar professional or labor organizations? 3 / 4

Under the constitution and 2003 labor laws, workers have the right to form and join trade unions. However, the government forbids or restricts organized labor action in a number of sectors, including fuel distribution and utilities, public transportation, and ports and harbor services.

F. RULE OF LAW: 11 / 16

F1. Is there an independent judiciary? 2 / 4

Judicial independence in Ghana is constitutionally and legally enshrined. While the judiciary has demonstrated greater levels of impartiality in recent years, corruption and bribery continue to pose challenges. In May 2018, President Akufo-Addo suspended four High Court judges based on allegations of bribe taking that dated back to 2015.

F2. Does due process prevail in civil and criminal matters? 3 / 4

Constitutional protections for due process and defendants' rights are mostly upheld. However, police have been known to accept bribes, make arbitrary arrests, and hold people without charge for longer than the legally permitted limit of 48 hours. The government is not obliged to provide the accused with legal counsel, and many people unable to afford lawyers are forced to represent themselves in court.

F3. Is there protection from the illegitimate use of physical force and freedom from war and insurgencies? 3 / 4

Ghana's prisons are overcrowded, and conditions are often life-threatening, though the prison service has attempted to reduce congestion and improve the treatment of inmates in recent years. Communal and ethnic violence occasionally flare in some parts of the country. In June 2018, a clash over land in the Chereponi District, Northern Region, between members of the Konkomba and Chekosi ethnic groups led to at least two deaths and left several others wounded.

F4. Do laws, policies, and practices guarantee equal treatment of various segments of the population? 3 / 4

Despite equal rights under the law, women suffer societal discrimination, especially in rural areas, where their opportunities for education and employment are limited. However, women's enrollment in universities is increasing. People with disabilities and LGBT people also face societal discrimination. Same-sex sexual activity remains criminalized, encouraging police harassment and impunity for violence. Speaker of Parliament Aaron Mike Oquaye, an outspoken critic of LGBT rights, threatened to resign in 2018 if any laws were enacted to legalize same-sex sexual activity.

G. PERSONAL AUTONOMY AND INDIVIDUAL RIGHTS: 11 / 16 (+1)

G1. Do individuals enjoy freedom of movement, including the ability to change their place of residence, employment, or education? 3 / 4

Freedom of movement is guaranteed by the constitution and respected by the government, and Ghanaians are free to change their place of residence. However, poorly developed road networks and banditry can make travel outside the capital and touristic areas difficult. Police have been known to set up illegal checkpoints to demand bribes from travelers. Bribery is also rife in the education sector.

G2. Are individuals able to exercise the right to own property and establish private businesses without undue interference from state or nonstate actors? 3 / 4

Although the legal framework generally supports property ownership and private business activity, weaknesses in the rule of law, corruption, and an underregulated property rights system remain impediments. Bribery is a common practice when starting a business and registering property. The World Bank's 2019 Doing Business index noted improvements in the process for acquiring construction permits and the ease of international trade in Ghana.

G3. Do individuals enjoy personal social freedoms, including choice of marriage partner and size of family, protection from domestic violence, and control over appearance? 3 / 4 (+1)

Domestic violence and rape are serious problems, and harmful traditional practices including female genital mutilation or cutting and early or forced marriage persist in some regions. The government has worked to combat gender-based violence over the past decade, including by expanding the police's domestic violence and victim support units and creating special courts for gender-based violence, though such services reportedly suffer from insufficient resources.

Score Change: The score improved from 2 to 3 because government policies, including the establishment of special courts and the activities of the police's domestic violence and victim support units, have provided greater recourse to victims of domestic abuse over time.

G4. Do individuals enjoy equality of opportunity and freedom from economic exploitation? 2 / 4

The exploitation of children in the agricultural and mining sectors remains a problem. Similar abuses in the fishing industry have also been reported, especially in the region surrounding Lake Volta. While the government has taken some positive steps to address human trafficking in recent years, it has not adequately funded enforcement efforts or services for victims.

Greece

Population: 10,600,000
Capital: Athens
Political Rights Rating: 1 ↑
Civil Liberties Rating: 2
Freedom Rating: 1.5
Freedom Status: Free
Electoral Democracy: Yes

Overview: Greece's parliamentary democracy features vigorous competition between political parties and a strong if imperfect record of upholding civil liberties. Ongoing concerns include corruption, discrimination against immigrants and minorities, and poor conditions for undocumented migrants and refugees.

KEY DEVELOPMENTS IN 2018:

- Housing and welfare problems for migrants and refugees persisted during the year as officials struggled with a backlog of asylum applications.
- In January, the parliament adopted legislation that limited the jurisdiction of Sharia (Islamic law) among Muslims in Thrace to family law disputes in which all parties consent to the arrangement.
- In May, lawmakers approved a measure permitting same-sex couples to serve as foster parents.
- Long-delayed construction on an official mosque for Athens proceeded during the year, but it had yet to open at year's end.

POLITICAL RIGHTS: 36 / 40 (+1)

A. ELECTORAL PROCESS: 12 / 12

A1. Was the current head of government or other chief national authority elected through free and fair elections? 4 / 4

The largely ceremonial president is elected by a parliamentary supermajority for a five-year term. The prime minister is chosen by the president and is usually the leader of the largest party in the parliament. Current president Prokopis Pavlopoulos, a conservative former cabinet minister, was elected in February 2015. Prime Minister Alexis Tsipras of the Coalition of the Radical Left (SYRIZA) took office after January 2015 elections and won reelection in a snap vote in September of that year.

A2. Were the current national legislative representatives elected through free and fair elections? 4 / 4

The 300 members of the unicameral Hellenic Parliament are elected to serve four-year terms through a mixture of 8 single-member constituencies, 48 multimember constituencies, and a national constituency with 12 seats. Under current electoral law, the party with the most votes receives a 50-seat bonus, which is designed to make it easier to form a governing majority.

In the September 2015 elections, which were considered free and fair, SYRIZA took 145 seats and renewed its ruling coalition with the right-wing populist Independent Greeks (ANEL) party, which won 10. The center-right opposition New Democracy (ND) party took 75 seats; the ultranationalist Golden Dawn won 18; the center-left Democratic Coalition, an electoral alliance of the Panhellenic Socialist Movement (PASOK) and the Democratic Left (DIMAR), took 17; the Communist Party of Greece (KKE), 15; the new center-left To Potami (the River), 11; and the Union of Centrists (EK), 9.

A3. Are the electoral laws and framework fair, and are they implemented impartially by the relevant election management bodies? 4 / 4

The country has generally fair electoral laws, equal campaigning opportunities, and a weakly enforced system of compulsory voting. If passed with a two-thirds supermajority, changes to the electoral laws are implemented for the next elections. If passed with a simple majority, they go into effect in the following elections. An amendment that was passed in 2016 without a supermajority will abolish the 50-seat bonus that is awarded to the winning party. It will also lower the voting age from 18 to 17.

B. POLITICAL PLURALISM AND PARTICIPATION: 15 / 16

B1. Do the people have the right to organize in different political parties or other competitive political groupings of their choice, and is the system free of undue obstacles to the rise and fall of these competing parties or groupings? 4 / 4

The political system features vigorous competition among a variety of parties. Eight were represented in the parliament as of 2018. Many other parties participated in the last elections but did not reach the 3 percent vote threshold to secure representation.

B2. Is there a realistic opportunity for the opposition to increase its support or gain power through elections? 4 / 4

Greece has established a strong pattern of democratic transfers of power between rival parties, with PASOK and ND alternating in government for most of the past four decades. SYRIZA entered government for the first time in 2015.

B3. Are the people's political choices free from domination by the military, foreign powers, religious hierarchies, economic oligarchies, or any other powerful group that is not democratically accountable? 4 / 4

No group or institution from outside the political system exerts undue influence over the choices of voters and candidates.

B4. Do various segments of the population (including ethnic, religious, gender, LGBT, and other relevant groups) have full political rights and electoral opportunities? 3 / 4

Greece's largest recognized minority population, the Muslim community of Thrace, has full political rights, and four members of the community won seats in the last parliamentary elections. The authorities have rejected some ethnic groups' attempts to secure official recognition or to register associations with names referring to their ethnic identity, affecting their ability to organize and advocate for their political interests, though such associations are generally able to operate without legal recognition. Since 2010, documented immigrants have been allowed to vote in municipal elections.

There are no significant legal or practical barriers to women's political participation. Women won about 20 percent of the seats in the 2015 parliamentary elections. However, sexism and patriarchal attitudes discourage women from playing a more active role in politics.

C. FUNCTIONING OF GOVERNMENT: 9 / 12 (+1)

C1. Do the freely elected head of government and national legislative representatives determine the policies of the government? 3 / 4

Greek elected officials generally set and implement government policies. However, their fiscal policy choices in particular have been limited in recent years by the main creditor institutions that have guided the country through its public debt crisis—the European Commission, the European Central Bank, the European Stability Mechanism, and the International Monetary Fund. In August 2018, Greece exited its third and final bailout program, which began in 2015.

C2. Are safeguards against official corruption strong and effective? 3 / 4 (+1)

Official corruption remains a problem in Greece, and institutions tasked with combating it have inadequate resources. Tax officials in past years have been implicated in tax evasion schemes, which seriously complicate the government's fiscal reform efforts.

Nevertheless, there has been gradual improvement in enforcement of anticorruption laws. In October 2018, former defense minister Yiannos Papantoniou and his wife Stavroula Kourakou were placed in pretrial detention on corruption charges. Papantoniou was accused of accepting $2.8 million in kickbacks for a 2003 contract to improve six navy frigates. In November, it was reported that authorities investigating possible money laundering had moved to access bank accounts held by former prime minister Costas Simitis and his relatives, as well as two former PASOK ministers.

Score Change: The score improved from 2 to 3 because anticorruption laws have been more effectively enforced over the past several years.

C3. Does the government operate with openness and transparency? 3 / 4

A number of laws and government programs are designed to ensure the transparency of official decisions and provide public access to information. Officials are required to make public declarations of their assets and income. Corruption related to state contracts remains a concern; a number of former officials, including former cabinet members, have been prosecuted for contract-related bribery schemes.

CIVIL LIBERTIES: 51 / 60 (+1)

D. FREEDOM OF EXPRESSION AND BELIEF: 14 / 16

D1. Are there free and independent media? 3 / 4

The constitution includes provisions for freedoms of speech and the press, and these rights are generally protected. Citizens enjoy access to a broad array of privately owned print, broadcast, and online news outlets. There are some limits on hate speech and related content.

Defamation is a criminal offense, and journalists face defamation suits by political figures in practice. In September 2018, the publisher, the political editor, and the editor in chief of the newspaper *Phileleftheros* were briefly detained at the request of Defense Minister Panos Kammenos over an article that alleged the mishandling of European Union (EU) funds intended to improve conditions in high-volume migration chokepoints. The article alleged that recipients of the EU funds included businessmen connected to Kammenos, who accused the journalists of defamation.

Reporters are sometimes subject to physical assaults, particularly while covering protests. In the most serious attack during 2018, a bomb placed outside the headquarters of Skai TV in Athens in December caused extensive damage to the building, which also housed the *Kathimerini* newspaper, though no one was injured. A left-wing militant group later claimed responsibility for the bombing.

Political polarization in the media remains a problem. In July 2018, following deadly wildfires in Mati, SYRIZA and its ally ANEL decided that their members would not participate in any programs on Skai TV and Skai Radio, accusing the broadcasters of systematic antigovernment reporting surrounding the disaster. In September, the opposition ND announced that its members would not make appearances on the public television station, which it said was operating as if it belonged to SYRIZA.

D2. Are individuals free to practice and express their religious faith or nonbelief in public and private? 3 / 4

The constitution guarantees freedom of religion, and this is generally respected in practice. However, the Orthodox Church of Greece—which has a special constitutional status as the "prevailing religion" of the country—receives government subsidies, and its clergy's salaries and pensions are paid for by the state. The constitution prohibits proselytizing, but this restriction is rarely enforced. Members of some minority religions face discrimination and legal barriers, such as permit requirements to open houses of worship. Opposition to the construction of an official mosque in Athens remains substantial; the project proceeded during 2018, but it was not yet complete at year's end. To date, the city's nearly 200,000 Muslim inhabitants have worshiped in improvised mosques.

D3. Is there academic freedom, and is the educational system free from extensive political indoctrination? 4 / 4

There are no significant constraints on academic freedom in Greece, and the educational system is free of political indoctrination.

D4. Are individuals free to express their personal views on political or other sensitive topics without fear of surveillance or retribution? 4 / 4

The government does not engage in improper monitoring of personal expression. Individuals are generally free to discuss their views in practice.

E. ASSOCIATIONAL AND ORGANIZATIONAL RIGHTS: 12 / 12

E1. Is there freedom of assembly? 4 / 4

Freedom of assembly is guaranteed by the constitution, and the government generally protects this right. Austerity-related protests over the past decade have sometimes grown violent, and extremist groups like Golden Dawn have attempted to attack and intimidate assemblies in support of migrants' rights or other causes they oppose. However, such instances have become less frequent since a crackdown on Golden Dawn's leadership began in 2013, and police have improved their handling of security surrounding demonstrations.

Largely peaceful protests were held during 2018 in opposition to a bilateral deal signed in June that would allow the former Yugoslav republic of Macedonia to be called "North Macedonia"; Athens had previously objected to the neighboring country's use of the name "Macedonia," arguing that it was part of Greece's ancient heritage and could imply territorial claims over a Greek region of the same name.

E2. Is there freedom for nongovernmental organizations, particularly those that are engaged in human rights– and governance-related work? 4 / 4

Nongovernmental organizations (NGOs) generally operate without interference from the authorities.

E3. Is there freedom for trade unions and similar professional or labor organizations? 4 / 4

Most workers have the right to form and join unions, bargain collectively, and strike. The law provides protections against antiunion discrimination, and the government generally upholds union rights.

F. RULE OF LAW: 11 / 16

F1. Is there an independent judiciary? 3 / 4

The judiciary is largely independent, though its autonomy is undermined somewhat by corruption. Judges are appointed by the president on the advice of the Supreme Judicial Council, which is mostly composed of other judges. They serve until retirement age and cannot be removed arbitrarily.

F2. Does due process prevail in civil and criminal matters? 3 / 4

The law provides safeguards against arbitrary arrest and detention, ensures access to defense counsel, and provides for fair trial conditions. Persistent problems include court backlogs that lead to prolonged pretrial detention as well as improper detention of asylum seekers.

F3. Is there protection from the illegitimate use of physical force and freedom from war and insurgencies? 3 / 4

While overall rates of violent crime are low, there are occasional acts of politically motivated violence and vandalism by left- or right-wing extremist groups. For example, in recent years the anarchist group Rouvikonas (Rubicon) has damaged the property or ransacked the premises of NGOs, corporations, universities, churches, government buildings, embassies and consulates, and other targets. In May 2018, far-right attackers assaulted the 75-year-old liberal mayor of Thessaloniki, Yiannis Boutaris, who had to be treated in a hospital.

Some prisons and detention centers suffer from substandard conditions, and law enforcement personnel have at times been accused of physical abuse, particularly against vulnerable groups such as migrants and asylum seekers.

F4. Do laws, policies, and practices guarantee equal treatment of various segments of the population? 2 / 4

Women generally enjoy equality before the law, though they continue to face workplace discrimination in practice.

Violence targeting immigrants, refugees, and LGBT (lesbian, gay, bisexual, and transgender) people remains a problem. The Romany minority is also subject to discrimination despite legal protections. According to the Racist Violence Recording Network (RVRN), the number of attacks has declined overall in the past several years, though slight annual increases have been reported since 2016. The declines were due in large part to a law enforcement crackdown on Golden Dawn; a trial against dozens of the group's members and leaders was ongoing during 2018.

Since 2016, when the EU reached an agreement with Turkey to curb the westward flow of migrants and refugees, the number entering Greece has been significantly reduced. However, there were more than 71,000 in the country as of December 2018, according to the Office of the UN High Commissioner for Refugees (UNHCR), with many living in Reception and Identification Centers on the Aegean islands or in camps on the mainland as Greek officials struggled to process asylum claims in a timely manner. Some of these sites feature harsh living conditions, violence, the harassment of women, and endangerment of children; under pressure from NGOs, officials have attempted to close the worst facilities and increase the use of urban accommodation. There have been some reports of summary pushbacks along the land border with Turkey, and observers have questioned whether individuals who are formally deported to Turkey under the EU agreement are being returned to a safe third country.

G. PERSONAL AUTONOMY AND INDIVIDUAL RIGHTS: 14 / 16 (+1)

G1. Do individuals enjoy freedom of movement, including the ability to change their place of residence, employment, or education? 4 / 4

Freedom of movement is generally unrestricted for most residents.

G2. Are individuals able to exercise the right to own property and establish private businesses without undue interference from state or nonstate actors? 3 / 4

The government and legal framework are generally supportive of property rights and entrepreneurship, but bureaucratic obstacles can inhibit business activity. Those who have political connections or are willing to pay bribes can sometimes expedite official procedures.

G3. Do individuals enjoy personal social freedoms, including choice of marriage partner and size of family, protection from domestic violence, and control over appearance? 4 / 4 (+1)

There are no major constraints on personal social freedoms, though domestic violence remains a problem.

In January 2018, the parliament adopted legislation that curbed the jurisdiction of muftis applying Sharia to family law disputes among Muslims in Thrace. Official recognition of the Sharia system stemmed from treaties that followed World War I. The new law stipulated that civil courts have priority, and that Sharia courts could only adjudicate cases in which all parties agree to the arrangement. The European Court of Human Rights ruled in December 2018 that the system in place before the legal change was discriminatory.

A 2017 law allowed unmarried transgender people over age 15 to change their legal gender on identity documents without undergoing gender reassignment surgery or other such procedures, subject to validation by a judge. In May 2018, the parliament approved legislation that permitted same-sex couples to serve as foster parents.

Score Change: The score improved from 3 to 4 due to the implementation of laws that voided a rule compelling Greek Muslims in Thrace to settle family disputes under Sharia law and permitted same-sex couples to care for foster children.

G4. Do individuals enjoy equality of opportunity and freedom from economic exploitation? 3 / 4

Most residents enjoy legal protections against exploitative working conditions, but labor laws are not always adequately enforced. Migrants and asylum seekers are especially vulnerable to trafficking for forced labor or sexual exploitation, and government efforts to combat the problem, while increasing, remain insufficient, according to the US State Department.

Grenada

Population: 100,000
Capital: St. George's
Political Rights Rating: 1
Civil Liberties Rating: 2
Freedom Rating: 1.5
Freedom Status: Free
Electoral Democracy: Yes

Overview: Grenada is a parliamentary democracy that regularly holds credible elections. Ongoing concerns include corruption, discrimination against the LGBT (lesbian, gay, bisexual, and transgender) community, and violence against women and children.

KEY DEVELOPMENTS IN 2018:
- In March, the incumbent New National Party (NNP), led by Prime Minister Keith Mitchell, won the general elections, once again capturing all 15 seats in the House of Representatives with 59 percent of the vote.
- Press freedom advocates expressed concerns about censorship at the country's largest broadcaster, the Grenada Broadcasting Network (GBN), which reportedly prohibited the network's reporters from covering a protest held by GBN staff members against their general manager in September.
- In November, a referendum that would have eliminated the Judicial Committee of the Privy Council in London as Grenada's final court of appeal failed to pass for the second time.

POLITICAL RIGHTS: 37 / 40

A. ELECTORAL PROCESS: 11 / 12

A1. Was the current head of government or other chief national authority elected through free and fair elections? 4 / 4

The prime minister, usually the leader of the largest party in Parliament, is head of government. The prime minister is appointed by the governor general, who represents the British monarch as head of state.

Following the March 2018 elections, NNP leader Keith Mitchell was sworn in for a second consecutive term as prime minister.

Cécile La Grenade was sworn in as Grenada's first female governor general in 2013.

A2. Were the current national legislative representatives elected through free and fair elections? 4 / 4

The bicameral Parliament consists of the directly elected, 15-seat House of Representatives, whose members serve five-year terms, and the 13-seat Senate, which is appointed by the governor general. Ten Senate seats are appointed on the advice of the prime minister, and the remaining three on the advice of the opposition leader; senators also serve five-year terms.

The NNP won the elections held in March 2018, capturing all 15 seats in the House of Representatives with 59 percent of the vote. The National Democratic Congress (NDC) received 41 percent of the vote. The electoral observation mission of the Organization of American States (OAS) expressed concern over a lack of campaign finance regulations and other issues, but deemed the polls credible.

A3. Are the electoral laws and framework fair, and are they implemented impartially by the relevant election management bodies? 3 / 4

Electoral laws are generally fair, and they are usually implemented impartially by the supervisor of elections, who heads the Parliamentary Elections Office.

In Grenada's 2016 constitutional referendum, all of the proposals—including setting a three-term limit for the prime minister, establishing fixed dates for elections, and reforming the electoral authority and the body that sets constituent boundaries—failed. Turnout was low, at just 32 percent.

The unbalanced size of constituencies has resulted in unequal voting power among citizens. For example, in a country of 100,000 people, the largest of Grenada's 15 constituencies has around 6,000 more registered voters than the smallest. This long-standing discrepancy has not been addressed.

B. POLITICAL PLURALISM AND PARTICIPATION: 16 / 16

B1. Do the people have the right to organize in different political parties or other competitive political groupings of their choice, and is the system free of undue obstacles to the rise and fall of these competing parties or groupings? 4 / 4

Political parties can organize freely. While a number of small political parties have competed in elections, the first-past-the-post system encourages two-party politics, and since 1999 only the NNP and NDC have won seats in Parliament. Additionally, weak campaign finance laws potentially create an unfair advantage for certain parties.

B2. Is there a realistic opportunity for the opposition to increase its support or gain power through elections? 4 / 4

There are realistic opportunities for opposition parties to increase their support or gain power through elections, and power has rotated on several occasions since the first election in 1984, after democracy was restored to Grenada. However, the NNP has won a majority of the elections since then, and some analysts have raised concerns about the NDC's failure to win any seats in the House of Representatives in both the 2013 and 2018 elections.

B3. Are the people's political choices free from domination by the military, foreign powers, religious hierarchies, economic oligarchies, or any other powerful group that is not democratically accountable? 4 / 4

People are generally able to express their political choices without encountering pressure from outside actors. However, the OAS has expressed concern about a lack of transparency and general regulation of campaign finance procedures, which could create avenues for undue influence over candidates and voters by business or other special interest groups.

B4. Do various segments of the population (including ethnic, religious, gender, LGBT, and other relevant groups) have full political rights and electoral opportunities? 4 / 4

Grenada's constitution guarantees universal suffrage for adult citizens. Women remain underrepresented in politics, but 7 out of 15 seats in the House of Representatives were won by women in 2018. Women's advocacy groups have influence in the general political sphere. The marginalization of the LGBT community impacts its ability to engage fully in political and electoral processes.

C. FUNCTIONING OF GOVERNMENT: 10 / 12

C1. Do the freely elected head of government and national legislative representatives determine the policies of the government? 4 / 4

The appointed prime minister, cabinet, and freely elected Parliament representatives are able to determine the policies of the government. However, because of concerns over the lack of an opposition in the House of Representatives, three NDC members were appointed to the Senate after the 2013 and 2018 elections.

C2. Are safeguards against official corruption strong and effective? 3 / 4

Corruption remains a prominent issue in Grenada, despite safeguards enshrined in the Prevention of Corruption Act and the Integrity in Public Life Act. In August 2018, the Integrity Commission began an investigation into allegations that the Marketing and National Importing Board had misappropriated public funds over a five-year period. The investigation was ongoing at year's end.

A number of suggested amendments in the 2016 constitutional reform package would have strengthened anticorruption safeguards, but all were voted down by significant margins.

Grenada's Citizenship by Investment Program (CBI), which allows foreigners to gain citizenship through an economic investment in the country, continued to trouble some analysts in 2018 due to the potential for fraud and abuse, despite the tightening of rules governing it in 2017.

C3. Does the government operate with openness and transparency? 3 / 4

The government of Grenada generally operates with transparency. A decree passed in 2013 under the authority of the Integrity in Public Life Act requires all public officials to declare their personal assets. In 2017, Parliament passed an amendment to the Mutual Exchange of Information on Tax Matters Bill, which allows Grenadian authorities to request financial information about its citizens residing abroad in an effort to prevent tax avoidance.

However, there is no law to ensure public access to information, even though the government pledged to introduce such an act in 2008.

CIVIL LIBERTIES: 52 / 60 (+1)
D. FREEDOM OF EXPRESSION AND BELIEF: 15 / 16
D1. Are there free and independent media? 3 / 4

In 2012, Grenada became the first Caribbean country to decriminalize defamation, but seditious libel remains a criminal offense. Politicians have initiated defamation lawsuits against the media, contributing to self-censorship among journalists who may not be able to afford legal costs or resulting fines. Press freedom advocates criticized censorship at the country's largest broadcaster, the GBN, which reportedly prohibited the network's reporters from covering a protest held by GBN staff members against their general manager in September 2018.

D2. Are individuals free to practice and express their religious faith or nonbelief in public and private? 4 / 4

Freedom of religion is protected under the constitution and this right is generally respected in practice.

D3. Is there academic freedom, and is the educational system free from extensive political indoctrination? 4 / 4

The government generally respects academic freedom.

D4. Are individuals free to express their personal views on political or other sensitive topics without fear of surveillance or retribution? 4 / 4

Individuals are free to express their personal views on political or other sensitive topics.

E. ASSOCIATIONAL AND ORGANIZATIONAL RIGHTS: 11 / 12
E1. Is there freedom of assembly? 4 / 4

Freedom of assembly is constitutionally guaranteed, and that right is generally respected in practice.

E2. Is there freedom for nongovernmental organizations, particularly those that are engaged in human rights–and governance-related work? 4 / 4

Nongovernmental organizations (NGOs) are generally free to operate.

E3. Is there freedom for trade unions and similar professional or labor organizations? 3 / 4

The right of workers to form and join labor unions is constitutionally protected, though unions and labor activists face some obstacles. Workers have the right to strike, organize, and bargain collectively, though employers are not legally bound to recognize a union if a majority of workers do not join. Essential services workers may strike, but compulsory arbitration can be used to resolve disputes. The list of essential services is extensive, and includes services that should not be considered as such according to International Labor Organization (ILO) standards.

F. RULE OF LAW: 13 / 16 (+1)
F1. Is there an independent judiciary? 4 / 4 (+1)

An independent judiciary is constitutionally guaranteed. Courts have demonstrated independence in recent years, as evidenced by a 2017 Supreme Court decision that prevented the government from expropriating property owned by the company Rex Resorts. There has not been tangible evidence of political interference in the judiciary in the last several years.

Grenada is a member of the Organization of Eastern Caribbean States court system, and is a charter member of the Caribbean Court of Justice, but relies on the Judicial Committee of the Privy Council in London as its final court of appeal. In 2016, Parliament approved legislation to eliminate the Privy Council as the final court, but the measure was defeated in the year's constitutional referendum. A second referendum on the matter again failed in November 2018.

Score Change: The score improved from 3 to 4 as a result of further consolidation of an independent judiciary and a consistent lack of tangible political interference for several consecutive years.

F2. Does due process prevail in civil and criminal matters? 3 / 4

Detainees and defendants are guaranteed a range of legal rights, including the presumption of innocence and the right to trial without delay, which are mostly respected in practice. However, due to case backlogs, in practice trial delays are common. Additionally, due to staffing shortages, not all indigent defendants could be provided legal counsel.

F3. Is there protection from the illegitimate use of physical force and freedom from war and insurgencies? 3 / 4

Grenada is free from war and insurgencies. Flogging remains a punishment for petty crimes, and the prison system is overcrowded. Although considered one of the safer Caribbean islands, there has been a rise in reports of sexual assault in recent years.

F4. Do laws, policies, and practices guarantee equal treatment of various segments of the population? 3 / 4

Same-sex sexual activity is a criminal offense in Grenada, and LGBT people face significant societal discrimination. The 2016 constitutional referendum included an amendment to protect the equal treatment of people in Grenada, but that amendment was overwhelmingly rejected due to concerns that language in the amendment might lead to the legalization of same-sex marriage.

The constitution bars gender discrimination, as do the 1999 Employment and Education Acts. However, cultural norms perpetuate discrimination in practice, and sexual harassment is common.

G. PERSONAL AUTONOMY AND INDIVIDUAL RIGHTS: 13 / 16

G1. Do individuals enjoy freedom of movement, including the ability to change their place of residence, employment, or education? 4 / 4

Freedom of movement is constitutionally guaranteed, and this right is generally respected in practice.

G2. Are individuals able to exercise the right to own property and establish private businesses without undue interference from state or non-state actors? 3 / 4

The government of Grenada has actively encouraged both national and foreign investors to operate businesses in the country, but procedures involved in establishing a new business can be onerous. Following court rulings in 2017 that prevented the government from expropriating the Grenadian hotel from its owners, the government continued its attempts to acquire the property through the courts in 2018.

G3. Do individuals enjoy personal social freedoms, including choice of marriage partner and size of family, protection from domestic violence, and control over appearance? 3 / 4

Violence against women and children is a widespread issue in Grenada. Domestic violence legislation came into effect in 2011, but enforcement has been limited. In 2017, the cabinet appointed a committee to address child sexual abuse. In September 2018, the Royal Grenada Police Force launched the Special Victims Unit to handle cases of sexual assault, domestic violence, and child abuse, as well as a new hotline for reporting sexual abuse.

G4. Do individuals enjoy equality of opportunity and freedom from economic exploitation? 3 / 4

Poverty and unemployment are pervasive, and hamper the social mobility of many Grenadians.

A 2015 law punishes human trafficking with up to 25 years in jail and large fines. However, reports of human trafficking are rare.

Guatemala

Population: 17,200,000
Capital: Guatemala City
Political Rights Rating: 4
Civil Liberties Rating: 4
Freedom Rating: 4.0
Freedom Status: Partly Free
Electoral Democracy: Yes

Overview: While Guatemala holds regular elections that are generally free, organized crime and corruption severely impact the functioning of government. Violence and criminal extortion schemes are serious problems, and victims have little recourse to justice. Journalists, activists, and public officials who confront crime, corruption, and other sensitive issues risk attack.

KEY DEVELOPMENTS IN 2018:

- In August, the attorney general and the UN-backed International Commission against Impunity in Guatemala (CICIG) made a third request to lift President Jimmy Morales's immunity, after collecting further evidence suggesting that the president and his party, the National Convergence Front (FCN), had received illegal contributions during the 2015 campaign period. However, Congress subsequently voted to retain Morales's immunity in October.
- Responding to the increased pressure from the CICIG, President Morales declared in late August that he would not renew its mandate and in September barred Iván Velásquez, the commission's head, from reentering the country. The Constitutional Court subsequently ruled that the government must allow Velásquez's return. However, Morales still refused to permit his reentry at year's end, in defiance of the court's ruling.
- In December, the solicitor general accused three Constitutional Court judges who had ruled in favor of the CICIG of malfeasance and violating the constitution, and petitioned the Supreme Court to allow a vote in Congress to lift the judges' immunity, which would clear the way for their potential impeachment.
- A report published by the newspaper *Nuestro Diario* in August uncovered widespread monitoring and illegal surveillance of diplomats, politicians, journalists, civil society activists, and other critics of the government.

POLITICAL RIGHTS: 22 / 40 (−1)

A. ELECTORAL PROCESS: 8 / 12

A1. Was the current head of government or other chief national authority elected through free and fair elections? 3 / 4

The constitution stipulates a four-year presidential term, and prohibits reelection. In a runoff election in 2015, President Morales won a plurality of the vote, with 67 percent. The election was judged as generally credible, although electoral observers reported some irregularities, including intimidation and vote buying. An estimated 20 election-related murders occurred during the campaign period, mostly involving mayoral candidates and their relatives.

In August 2018, the attorney general and the CICIG indicated that they had gathered further evidence suggesting that the president and his party, the FCN, had received illegal contributions during the 2015 campaign period. They subsequently filed a third request to lift the president's immunity, after two attempts in 2017 failed. However, Congress voted to retain Morales's immunity in October.

A2. Were the current national legislative representatives elected through free and fair elections? 3 / 4

Members of the 158-seat, unicameral Congress are elected to four-year terms. Like the presidential election, the 2015 polls were deemed credible, but observers noted irregularities, and 11 municipal contests had to be repeated. A CICIG report released that year stated that 25 percent of campaign contributions to political parties had come from business interests, and another 25 percent originated with organized crime groups.

A3. Are the electoral laws and framework fair, and are they implemented impartially by the relevant election management bodies? 2 / 4

Authorities and lawmakers in recent years have taken some steps to address a serious lack of transparency in party financing, and to prevent illegal party financing—both of which were serious problems in the 2015 polls. In 2016, the legislature approved electoral reforms that included stronger oversight of parties' financial disclosures, and in 2017, the Supreme Electoral Tribunal (TSE) implemented mechanisms to monitor financing procedures and penalize illegal electoral financing. In June 2018, the TSE announced that it would dissolve the ruling FCN due to party finance violations. Five other parties were also targeted for dissolution by the TSE for financial irregularities during the year. However, it was unclear at year's end whether the TSE's decisions would be enforced, and a court halted the dissolution process for the FCN in October.

In October, Congress passed legislation to reform the penal code, which weakened the legal framework by reducing penalties related to party finance violations from four to twelve years in prison to one to five years, and allowing such sentences to be commuted.

B. POLITICAL PLURALISM AND PARTICIPATION: 10 / 16

B1. Do the people have the right to organize in different political parties or other competitive political groupings of their choice, and is the system free of undue obstacles to the rise and fall of these competing parties or groupings? 3 / 4

Political groups and organizations generally operate without encountering legal restrictions. However, new groups sometimes face bureaucratic delays from the TSE when attempting to register.

Elections take place within an inchoate multiparty system in which new parties are frequently created. New parties that lack resources and infrastructure face disadvantages in gaining broad support. A lack of party finance regulations allows some candidates and parties access to vast resources.

B2. Is there a realistic opportunity for the opposition to increase its support or gain power through elections? 3 / 4

Elections at the national and local levels are competitive, and new parties routinely gain significant quotas of power. Guatemalan politics are unstable and power rotates between parties frequently, which can discourage a traditional opposition from coalescing. Political candidates risk attack during campaign periods.

B3. Are the people's political choices free from domination by the military, foreign powers, religious hierarchies, economic oligarchies, or any other powerful group that is not democratically accountable? 2 / 4

Verbal harassment and physical violence against voters is common during elections, and can deter political participation. Weak campaign finance regulations permit lopsided financing of candidates, as well as financing of candidates by special interests and organized criminal groups, distorting the political choices of citizens. In April 2018, the attorney general and CICIG revealed that President Morales and his party may have received over $2 million in illegal campaign contributions from Guatemalan businesses. Direct vote buying is also common.

B4. Do various segments of the population (including ethnic, religious, gender, LGBT, and other relevant groups) have full political rights and electoral opportunities? 2 / 4

Minorities struggle to fully exercise their political rights. Members of indigenous communities hold just 20 seats in the 158-seat legislature, although they comprise over 40 percent of the population, and there are few initiatives aimed at promoting their participation. Women are underrepresented in politics, though small women's rights groups, mainly those working to draw attention to violence against women, have some visibility in the political sphere. At the end of 2018, the Minister of Foreign Relations was the only woman in the president's cabinet. A representative in the current legislature is the first to self-identify as a member of the LGBT (lesbian, gay, bisexual and transgender) community.

C. FUNCTIONING OF GOVERNMENT: 4 / 12 (−1)

C1. Do the freely elected head of government and national legislative representatives determine the policies of the government? 2 / 4

The elected government and legislature determine government policies, but they are frequently subject to influence by outside interests. The president's party, the FCN, was established by former military officials, and Morales's association with them has raised questions about military influence in his administration. The media outlet *Nómada* revealed in 2017 that the president and the military's high-ranking officers were receiving a monthly bonus from the Ministry of Defense. Former defense minister Williams Mansilla resigned over the controversy, and he was arrested in January 2018 on corruption charges in connection with Morales's bonus. Mansilla awaited trial at year's end.

Recent investigations of electoral and party finance corruption have shed light on the influence of nonelected and illicit groups over the government.

C2. Are safeguards against official corruption strong and effective? 1 / 4 (−1)

Corruption, which is often related to organized crime, remains a serious problem. The CICIG and the attorney general have pressed forward with investigations of high-level officials in current and past administrations, but authorities and lawmakers have repeatedly attempted to undermine their work.

After the CICIG and attorney general petitioned to lift Morales's immunity, the president announced in August 2018 that he would not renew the commission's mandate, which is due to expire in September 2019. On the day of his announcement, a convoy of military vehicles repeatedly drove around the CICIG's offices, the US embassy, and other embassies that support the CICIG, a move viewed by observers as an act of intimidation. In September, Morales declared the CICIG's head, Iván Velásquez, a threat to public security and banned his reentry into the country. Two weeks later, the Constitutional Court ordered the government to allow Velásquez's return, but Morales defied the ruling and had not allowed him to reenter Guatemala at year's end. Also in December, the government revoked the diplomatic credentials of 11 foreign nationals working for CICIG, forcing them to leave the country.

Score Change: The score declined from 2 to 1 because the government made consistent efforts during the year to undermine anticorruption work, including attempts to dismantle the UN-backed anticorruption body, the International Commission against Impunity in Guatemala.

C3. Does the government operate with openness and transparency? 1 / 4

Public information offices frequently fail to publish data about public expenditures as required. The Law on Access to Information is poorly enforced, and dedicated nongovernmental organizations (NGOs) continue to file grievances over its nonapplication and, together with the Office of the Human Rights Ombudsman (PDH), work to encourage the government to adhere to its provisions.

The government's contracting and budgeting processes are opaque and racked with corruption. The CICIG has continued to investigate violations and to call for reforms to address these problems, though there is little political will to implement its recommendations.

CIVIL LIBERTIES: 31 / 60 (−2)
D. FREEDOM OF EXPRESSION AND BELIEF: 11 / 16 (−1)
D1. Are there free and independent media? 2 / 4

While the constitution protects freedom of speech, journalists often face threats and practice self-censorship when covering sensitive topics such as drug trafficking, corruption, organized crime, and human rights violations. Threats come from public officials, illicit actors, the police, and individuals aligned with companies operating on indigenous lands. Physical attacks against journalists occur each year. In February 2018, a newspaper journalist and radio station publicist were found murdered near Santo Domingo. It was not clear whether the murders were connected to the journalist's reporting. Media workers have reiterated demands that the government implement a journalists' protection program that was agreed to in 2012, but despite Morales' verbal commitment, no progress has been made.

In January, Congressman Julio Juárez Ramírez was arrested and charged with plotting the murder of two journalists in 2015. One of the murdered reporters had been investigating corruption in a municipality where Ramírez was mayor. He awaited trial at year's end.

Despite threats facing journalists, independent media outfits including *el Periódico, Nómada,* and *Plaza Pública* continue to provide critical information.

D2. Are individuals free to practice and express their religious faith or nonbelief in public and private? 4 / 4

The constitution guarantees religious freedom, and individuals are free to practice and express their religious faith or nonbelief in practice.

D3. Is there academic freedom, and is the educational system free from extensive political indoctrination? 3 / 4

Although the government does not interfere with academic freedom, scholars have received death threats for questioning past human rights abuses or continuing injustices.

D4. Are individuals free to express their personal views on political or other sensitive topics without fear of surveillance or retribution? 2 / 4 (−1)

Many Guatemalans take precautions when speaking about social and political issues outside of their homes due to a high level of insecurity in the country.

A report published by the newspaper *Nuestro Diario* in August 2018 uncovered widespread monitoring and illegal surveillance of diplomats, politicians, journalists, civil society activists, and other critics of the government by authorities between 2012 and 2015. Journalists and human rights defenders also reported being surveilled throughout 2018. The stepped-up surveillance, along with increased intimidation and harassment of perceived opponents of the government, has encouraged greater self-censorship among ordinary citizens.

Score Change: The score declined from 3 to 2 because reports of widespread surveillance of politicians, journalists, civil society activists, and other government critics, along with increased intimidation and harassment of perceived opponents of the government, has encouraged greater self-censorship among ordinary citizens.

E. ASSOCIATIONAL AND ORGANIZATIONAL RIGHTS: 6 / 12
E1. Is there freedom of assembly? 2 / 4

The constitution guarantees freedom of assembly, but this right is not always protected. Police frequently threaten force, and at times use violence against protesters. Protests related to environmental or indigenous rights issues were met with harsh resistance from the police and other armed groups during the year.

In September 2018, Guatemalans took to the streets in a march to condemn corruption and demand the continuation of the CICIG. The government deployed thousands of military and police personnel to prevent the marchers from approaching Congress.

E2. Is there freedom for nongovernmental organizations, particularly those that are engaged in human rights- and governance-related work? 2 / 4

The constitution guarantees freedom of association, and a variety of NGOs operate. However, groups associated with human rights, indigenous rights, and environmental rights face violence and intimidation. According to the Ireland-based rights group Front Line Defenders, 26 human rights defenders were killed in Guatemala in 2018; many of those killed advocated for indigenous rights. In September 2018, the Unit for the Protection of Human Rights Defenders in Guatemala (UDEFEGUA), an NGO, reported intimidation and surveillance of several human rights leaders following the government's August announcement that it would not renew the CICIG's mandate.

E3. Is there freedom for trade unions and similar professional or labor organizations? 2 / 4

Guatemala is home to a vigorous labor movement, but workers are frequently denied the right to organize and face mass firings and blacklisting. Trade-union members are also subject to intimidation, violence, and murder, particularly in rural areas.

F. RULE OF LAW: 6 / 16 (−1)
F1. Is there an independent judiciary? 2 / 4

The judiciary is hobbled by corruption, inefficiency, capacity shortages, and the intimidation of judges, prosecutors, and witnesses, both by outside actors and influential figures within the judiciary. However, the Constitutional Court demonstrated independence in several notable rulings in 2018, including those that blocked legal maneuvers by the government aimed at dismantling the CICIG and undermining its investigations. Nonetheless, the president's refusal to comply with the court's ruling that ordered the CICIG head's reentry to Guatemala raised serious concerns about attacks on the judiciary's independence.

Additionally, in December 2018, the solicitor general accused three Constitutional Court judges who had ruled in favor of the CICIG of malfeasance and violating the constitution, and petitioned the Supreme Court to allow a vote in Congress to lift the judges' immunity, which would clear the way for their potential impeachment.

F2. Does due process prevail in civil and criminal matters? 1 / 4 (−1)

Due process rights are guaranteed in the constitution, but those rights are inconsistently upheld, due in part to corruption in the judiciary and an ineffective police force in which many police officers routinely violate the law, and the rights of citizens. Access to justice remains a problem, especially for the indigenous community. In 2017, CICIG Commissioner Velásquez claimed that 97 percent of crimes committed in Guatemala go unpunished, and placed the blame for such impunity on criminal networks that had infiltrated state institutions.

In 2018, the new minister of the interior implemented several measures that weakened the independence and professionalism of the police force, including the removal of senior officials and detectives without due process or justification, such as the head of the police and his top advisers, as well as 11 investigators who were working with the CICIG. Promotions in the police force were also granted to personnel who, according to some experts, did not meet the required qualifications.

Disciplinary action was taken against a number of independent judges during the year, in apparent retaliation for their rulings on sensitive cases related to corruption and human rights abuses. According to the Human Rights Unit of the Public Prosecutor's Office, 62 reports of harassment and threats against judges and prosecutors were filed between January and July 2018.

Score Change: The score declined from 2 to 1 because the interior minister took measures to undermine the independence and professionalization of the police force, including the removal of police leadership and senior officers without justification, and due to pressure on prosecutors and judges in corruption and human rights cases.

F3. Is there protection from the illegitimate use of physical force and freedom from war and insurgencies? 2 / 4

High levels of violence, kidnappings, and extortions at the hands of the police, drug traffickers, and street gangs continue, with related fears and risks routinely affecting the lives of ordinary people. The link between the state, politicians, the military, and illicit actors complicates a cohesive response to the country's security challenges. Despite these challenges, the homicide rate dropped for the ninth straight year in 2018. At the end of the year, police reported 3,881 homicides, compared to 4,409 homicides in 2017, and 4,550 in 2016.

Prison facilities are grossly overcrowded and rife with gang and drug-related violence and corruption. Prison riots are common, and are frequently deadly.

Some perpetrators of past human rights abuses were held accountable in 2018, including three former military officers who were sentenced to 58 years in prison in May for a rape and forced disappearance dating to 1981. Former military dictator Efraín Ríos Montt, who was convicted of genocide in 2013 before the Constitutional Court overturned his verdict and rolled back his trial, died in April with his case still pending. In September, a national court ruled that the Guatemalan army committed genocide during Montt's rule in 1982 and 1983, but found José Mauricio Rodríguez Sánchez, Montt's director of military intelligence, not guilty of crimes against humanity.

F4. Do laws, policies, and practices guarantee equal treatment of various segments of the population? 1 / 4

Equal rights are guaranteed in the constitution, but minorities continue to face unequal treatment. Indigenous communities suffer from high rates of poverty, illiteracy, and infant mortality. Indigenous women are particularly marginalized. Discrimination against the Mayan community is a major concern.

LGBT people are not covered under antidiscrimination laws. They face discrimination, violence, and police abuse. The PDH has stated that people suffering from HIV/AIDS also face discrimination.

The constitution prohibits discrimination based on gender, but women continue to face gender-based inequality, and sexual harassment in the workplace is not penalized.

G. PERSONAL AUTONOMY AND INDIVIDUAL RIGHTS: 8 / 16

G1. Do individuals enjoy freedom of movement, including the ability to change their place of residence, employment, or education? 3 / 4

While there are no explicit restrictions on free movement, violence and the threat of violence by gangs and organized criminal groups inhibits this right in practice, and has prompted the displacement of thousands of people.

G2. Are individuals able to exercise the right to own property and establish private businesses without undue interference from state or nonstate actors? 2 / 4

Protections for property rights and economic freedom rarely extend beyond Guatemalans with wealth and political connections. Access to land is especially limited for the indigenous community and for women in particular. Business activity is hampered by criminal activity including extortion and fraud. An inefficient state bureaucracy, rife with unclear and complicated regulations, also contributes to difficulties in establishing and operating a business.

G3. Do individuals enjoy personal social freedoms, including choice of marriage partner and size of family, protection from domestic violence, and control over appearance? 2 / 4

Physical and sexual violence against women and children remains high, with perpetrators rarely prosecuted. The National Institute of Forensic Sciences (INACIF) reported 671 femicides between January and the end of November 2018. The law permits abortion only when a pregnancy threatens the life of the woman. In 2017, a decree banned marriages for children under the age of 18, though some observers expressed skepticism that it would be enforced.

G4. Do individuals enjoy equality of opportunity and freedom from economic exploitation? 1 / 4

The indigenous community's access to economic opportunities and socioeconomic mobility remain limited, with more than 70 percent of the indigenous population living in poverty. Guatemala has one of the highest rates of child labor in the Americas, with over 800,000 children working in the country. Criminal gangs often force children and young men to join their organizations or perform work for them.

Guinea

Population: 11,900,000
Capital: Conakry
Political Rights Rating: 5
Civil Liberties Rating: 4 ↑
Freedom Rating: 4.5
Freedom Status: Partly Free
Electoral Democracy: No

Overview: Since Guinea returned to civilian rule in 2010 following a 2008 military coup and decades of authoritarian governance, elections have been plagued by violence, delays, and other flaws. The government uses restrictive criminal laws to discourage dissent, and ethnic divisions and pervasive corruption often exacerbate political disputes. Regular abuse of civilians by military and police forces reflects a deep-seated culture of impunity.

KEY DEVELOPMENTS IN 2018:

- Long-delayed local elections were held in February, but the opposition claimed that polling was marred by fraud and disputed the results, which delayed the seating of elected officials and led to widespread protests in which dozens were injured by security forces; at least 7 people were shot dead in Conakry during the unrest.
- In August, the ruling party and opposition leaders reached an agreement to end the impasse, which included the resolution of several contested mayoral races. However, some opposition politicians were dissatisfied with the agreement, and further protests erupted in October, leading to another violent crackdown by security forces.
- Kéléfa Sall, the head of the Constitutional Court and an outspoken critic of President Condé, was dismissed in September, in a move condemned by the opposition as politically motivated.

POLITICAL RIGHTS: 17 / 40

A. ELECTORAL PROCESS: 6 / 12

A1. Was the current head of government or other chief national authority elected through free and fair elections? 3 / 4

Guinea's president is elected by popular vote for up to two five-year terms. In the 2015 election, incumbent Alpha Condé of the Rally of the Guinean People (RPG) defeated former prime minister Cellou Dalein Diallo of the Union of Democratic Forces of Guinea (UFDG), taking 57.8 percent of the vote to secure a second and final term. The months preceding the election were characterized by ethnic tensions, violence between RPG and UFDG members, and clashes between opposition supporters and security forces that left several people dead. Election day itself was peaceful, but opposition candidates filed unsuccessful legal challenges of the results, claiming fraud and vote rigging. Despite a number of logistical problems, international observers deemed the vote valid.

A2. Were the current national legislative representatives elected through free and fair elections? 1 / 4

Of the unicameral National Assembly's 114 seats, 38 are awarded through single-member constituency races and 76 are filled through nationwide proportional representation, all for five-year terms. Political and protest-related violence in the period before the 2013 parliamentary elections was severe, with dozens of people killed and hundreds injured. Ethnic tensions and disputes over the rules governing the polls contributed to the unrest. The RPG won 53 seats, the UFDG won 37, and a dozen smaller parties divided the remainder.

After a lengthy delay, local government elections were finally held in February 2018, the first since 2005. The opposition claimed that the polling was marred by widespread fraud, and violence broke out after the elections between opposition supporters and security forces. Opposition leaders disputed many of the results, which delayed the seating of numerous local officials. In August, the RPF and the UFDG reached an agreement to end the impasse, which included the resolution of several contested mayoral races. However, some opposition politicians were dissatisfied with the agreement, and in October, Diallo and several other opposition leaders called for mass protests, accusing authorities of violating the agreement by allegedly bribing officials in order to retain control of local governments.

A3. Are the electoral laws and framework fair, and are they implemented impartially by the relevant election management bodies? 2 / 4

While the electoral framework has allowed credible elections to proceed in some cases, it has consistently been subject to political dispute, with rival factions claiming a lack of fair representation on electoral commissions. Elections at the local level were not held between 2005 and 2018 due to the 2008 military coup, the outbreak of the Ebola virus that lasted from 2013 to 2016, and political gridlock. The elections were finally carried out in February 2018.

In July, the National Assembly passed a new law reforming the Independent National Electoral Commission (CENI). The legislation reduces the number of commissioners from 25 to 17, and mandates that 7 commissioners be from the opposition, 7 from the ruling party, 2 from civil society, and 1 from the executive branch. The law also requires political parties to hold two seats in the National Assembly and to have contested the last presidential election to gain representation in the CENI.

B. POLITICAL PLURALISM AND PARTICIPATION: 8 / 16

B1. Do the people have the right to organize in different political parties or other competitive political groupings of their choice, and is the system free of undue obstacles to the rise and fall of these competing parties or groupings? 2 / 4

The main political parties are the ruling RPG and the opposition UFDG. More than 130 parties are registered, most of which have clear ethnic or regional bases. Relations between the RPG and opposition parties are strained, and violent election-related clashes between RPG and UFDG supporters often bring about tensions.

Violence was widespread in the aftermath of the long-delayed 2018 local government elections. According to Human Rights Watch (HRW), at least 89 people were wounded in February and March during a police crackdown on opposition protests, and 7 protesters were killed in Conakry. The authorities violently dispersed further opposition protests in October, after Diallo claimed security forces opened fired on his car during a rally in protest of the local elections.

B2. Is there a realistic opportunity for the opposition to increase its support or gain power through elections? 2 / 4

Although multiparty elections have been held since the 1990s, Guinea has not established a pattern of peaceful democratic power transfers between rival parties. Before becoming president in 2010, Condé was an opposition leader under longtime president Lansana Conté. However, rather than defeating an incumbent leader, Condé won the first election after a period of military rule that followed Conté's death in 2008.

Security forces frequently attack rallies and protests organized by the opposition, making it more difficult for opposition parties to mobilize their supporters. The government also banned a number of demonstrations by opposition parties in 2018, including the October protest in which Diallo alleges that security forces shot at his car.

B3. Are the people's political choices free from domination by the military, foreign powers, religious hierarchies, economic oligarchies, or any other powerful group that is not democratically accountable? 2 / 4

While the military's role in politics has waned since the return to civilian rule, ethnic loyalty continues to play an outsized role in the political choices of voters and party leaders. Rather than organizing around policy platforms or political ideologies and trying to attract new supporters, each party tacitly pledges allegiance to its respective ethnic group, contributing to the threat of mutual hostility and violence.

B4. Do various segments of the population (including ethnic, religious, gender, LGBT, and other relevant groups) have full political rights and electoral opportunities? 2 / 4

Women and minority groups have full political rights, but ethnic divisions and gender bias limit their participation in practice. Parties do not always observe a legal obligation to grant women at least 30 percent of the places on their proportional representation lists for the National Assembly. Women hold nearly 22 percent of the seats in the assembly.

C. FUNCTIONING OF GOVERNMENT: 3 / 12

C1. Do the freely elected head of government and national legislative representatives determine the policies of the government? 1 / 4

The flawed electoral process undermines the legitimacy of executive and legislative officials. In addition, their ability to determine and implement laws and policies without undue interference is impeded by factors including impunity among security forces and rampant corruption.

C2. Are safeguards against official corruption strong and effective? 1 / 4

The National Anti-Corruption Agency (ANLC) reports directly to the presidency, and is considered to be underfunded and understaffed. A government audit whose findings were released in 2016 uncovered thousands of civil service positions held by absent or deceased workers. Some lower-level officials have been prosecuted on corruption charges in recent years, but major cases involving senior politicians and the lucrative mining industry have mainly been pursued in foreign courts.

In 2017, the National Assembly adopted an anticorruption law that restructures the ANLC and establishes new procedures for receiving corruption complaints and protecting whistle-blowers. The law had not been applied by the end of 2018, but in October the government held a workshop that brought together stakeholders to work towards its implementation.

C3. Does the government operate with openness and transparency? 1 / 4

While Guinea was declared in full compliance with the Extractive Industries Transparency Initiative in 2014, allegations of high-level corruption in the mining sector have continued. An access to information law adopted in 2010 has never been enacted.

CIVIL LIBERTIES: 26 / 60 (+2)

D. FREEDOM OF EXPRESSION AND BELIEF: 11 / 16 (+1)

D1. Are there free and independent media? 2 / 4 (+1)

The 2010 constitution guarantees media freedom, but Guinea has struggled to uphold freedom of expression in practice. A new criminal code adopted in 2016 retained penalties of up to five years in prison for defamation or insult of public figures, contributing to self-censorship among journalists. A cybersecurity law passed the same year criminalized similar offenses online, as well as the dissemination of information that is false, protected on national security grounds, or "likely to disturb law and order or public security or jeopardize human dignity."

Several dozen newspapers publish regularly in Guinea, though most have small circulations. More than 30 private radio stations and a few private television stations compete with the public broadcaster, Radio Télévision Guinéenne (RTG). Due to the high illiteracy rate, most of the population accesses information through radio.

The climate for journalists has improved somewhat in recent years, with fewer violent attacks and prosecutions for defamation. One online journalist, however, was sentenced to probation in July 2018 for defamation, over an article accusing the attorney general of corruption.

Score Change: The score improved from 1 to 2 because the climate for journalists has improved in recent years.

D2. Are individuals free to practice and express their religious faith or nonbelief in public and private? 3 / 4

Religious rights are generally respected in practice. Some non-Muslim government workers have reported occasional discrimination. People who convert from Islam to Christianity sometimes encounter pressure from their community.

D3. Is there academic freedom, and is the educational system free from extensive political indoctrination? 3 / 4

Academic freedom has historically faced political restrictions under authoritarian regimes. The problem has eased in recent years, particularly since the return to civilian rule in 2010, though self-censorship still tends to reduce the vibrancy of academic discourse.

D4. Are individuals free to express their personal views on political or other sensitive topics without fear of surveillance or retribution? 3 / 4

There are few practical limits on private discussion, though ethnic tensions and laws restricting freedom of expression may deter open debate in some circumstances.

E. ASSOCIATIONAL AND ORGANIZATIONAL RIGHTS: 5 / 12

E1. Is there freedom of assembly? 1 / 4

Freedom of assembly is enshrined in the constitution, but this right is often restricted. Assemblies held without notification, a requirement under Guinean law, are considered unauthorized and are often violently dispersed, leading to deaths, injuries, and arrests. Several such incidents occurred during 2018, including at the opposition protests against the local election results that occurred throughout the year. According to Amnesty International, at least 18 people were killed in violence related to demonstrations by the end of October.

E2. Is there freedom for nongovernmental organizations, particularly those that are engaged in human rights– and governance-related work? 2 / 4

Regulatory restrictions on nongovernmental organizations (NGOs) are not severe. However, Guinean civil society remains weak, ethnically divided, and subject to periodic harassment and intimidation.

E3. Is there freedom for trade unions and similar professional or labor organizations? 2 / 4

Although workers are allowed to form trade unions, strike, and bargain collectively, they must provide 10 days' notice before striking, and strikes are banned in broadly defined essential services. In February 2018, a nationwide teachers' strike commenced over low salaries and high commodity prices. Protests in support of the strike led to clashes with security forces. In March, the government reached an agreement with the teachers' union to raise salaries, ending the strike after one month.

F. RULE OF LAW: 4 / 16

F1. Is there an independent judiciary? 1 / 4

The judicial system has demonstrated some degree of independence since 2010, though it remains subject to political influence and corruption. In September 2018, Kéléfa Sall, the head of the Constitutional Court and an outspoken critic of President Condé, was dismissed. Opposition leaders condemned the move as an attack on judicial independence, claiming that Sall's dismissal was intended to enable Condé to potentially introduce a referendum that would allow him to run for a third term.

F2. Does due process prevail in civil and criminal matters? 1 / 4

Security forces engage in arbitrary arrests, often disregarding legal safeguards. Most prison inmates are being held in prolonged pretrial detention, though justice reforms in recent years have reduced the number of such detainees. Due process rights pertaining to trials are frequently denied, and many disputes are settled informally through traditional justice systems.

F3. Is there protection from the illegitimate use of physical force and freedom from war and insurgencies? 1 / 4

The new criminal code adopted in 2016 eliminated the death penalty and explicitly outlawed torture for the first time. However, human rights watchdogs noted that the criminal code categorized a number of acts that fall within the international definition of torture as merely "inhuman and cruel," a category that does not carry any explicit penalties in the code. In practice, security forces continued to engage in torture and other forms of physical violence with apparent impunity.

The justice system has largely failed to hold perpetrators accountable for past atrocities under military rule. In April 2018, however, the Ministry of Justice formed a steering committee to prepare for the trial of 13 suspects indicted in late 2017 for the 2009 Conakry stadium massacre, in which over 150 opposition protesters were killed by security forces. The trial had not yet commenced at year's end.

F4. Do laws, policies, and practices guarantee equal treatment of various segments of the population? 1 / 4

Women face pervasive societal discrimination and disadvantages in both the formal and traditional justice systems. Various ethnic groups engage in mutual discrimination with respect to hiring and other matters. Antidiscrimination laws do not protect LGBT (lesbian, gay, bisexual, and transgender) people. Same-sex sexual activity is a criminal offense that can be punished with up to three years in prison; although this law is rarely enforced, LGBT people have been arrested on lesser charges.

G. PERSONAL AUTONOMY AND INDIVIDUAL RIGHTS: 6 / 16 (+1)

G1. Do individuals enjoy freedom of movement, including the ability to change their place of residence, employment, or education? 2 / 4 (+1)

Guineans generally enjoyed freedom of movement for both domestic and international travel in 2018. However, rampant crime in some neighborhoods can impede movement.

Score Change: The score improved from 1 to 2 because Guineans were largely able to travel both internally and internationally without restriction in 2018.

G2. Are individuals able to exercise the right to own property and establish private businesses without undue interference from state or nonstate actors? 2 / 4

Private business activity is hampered by corruption and political instability, among other factors. A centralized Agency for the Promotion of Private Investments aims to ease the business registration process. Following recent reforms, property registration processes have become faster and less expensive.

Women face gender-based disadvantages in laws and practices governing inheritance and property rights.

G3. Do individuals enjoy personal social freedoms, including choice of marriage partner and size of family, protection from domestic violence, and control over appearance? 1 / 4

Rape and domestic violence are common but underreported due to fears of stigmatization, and there is no specific legislation meant to address domestic abuse. Female genital mutilation is nearly ubiquitous despite a legal ban, affecting up to 97 percent of girls and women in the country, the second-highest rate in the world. The new criminal code adopted in 2016 set the legal age for marriage at 18, but early and forced marriages remained common.

A revised civil code, which includes a controversial provision that effectively legalizes polygamy, was adopted by the parliament in December 2018. However, the draft law does provide women with parental authority equal to men and increases the rights of women in seeking a divorce. President Condé criticized the draft law for legalizing polygamy and indicated that he would not sign it.

G4. Do individuals enjoy equality of opportunity and freedom from economic exploitation? 1 / 4

The 2016 criminal code specifically criminalized trafficking in persons and debt bondage, but reduced the minimum penalties for such crimes, and enforcement has been weak. Guinean boys have been forced to work in mines in Guinea and in neighboring countries, while women and children have been trafficked for sexual exploitation to other parts of West Africa as well as Europe and the Middle East.

Guinea-Bissau

Population: 1,900,000
Capital: Bissau
Political Rights Rating: 5
Civil Liberties Rating: 4 ↑
Freedom Rating: 4.5
Freedom Status: Partly Free
Electoral Democracy: No

Overview: Guinea-Bissau's 2014 elections moved the country back toward democratic governance after a 2012 military coup. Since then, however, the political system has been paralyzed by divisions between the president and the parliament, and within the ruling party. A consensus transitional government was formed in 2018, but elections due that year were postponed to 2019. Restrictions on the media and freedom of association have eased somewhat, though police continued to disrupt some demonstrations. Corruption is a major problem that has been exacerbated by organized criminal activity, including drug trafficking.

KEY DEVELOPMENTS IN 2018:
- In January, President José Mário Vaz appointed a member of the African Party for the Independence of Guinea-Bissau and Cabo Verde (PAIGC), which controlled a parliamentary majority, as prime minister in a bid to end an impasse that began when the president dismissed a PAIGC leader from the premiership in 2015. However, the nominee failed to garner enough support to form a government. In April, Vaz appointed Aristides Gomes as part of a consensus between the PAIGC and the Party of Social Renewal (PRS), the second-largest party.
- Parliamentary elections were originally due in November, but they were postponed due to delays in the voter registration process amid claims of irregularities. In December, a presidential decree set the elections for March 2019.
- Demonstrators protesting the political crisis and a lack of public services assembled several times during the year, in some cases triggering clashes with the police. In November, a student demonstration over delays in classes due to a teachers' strike was violently repressed, leaving several people injured.

POLITICAL RIGHTS: 15 / 40 (−1)
A. ELECTORAL PROCESS: 6 / 12 (−1)
A1. Was the current head of government or other chief national authority elected through free and fair elections? 2 / 4

The president is elected through a two-round voting system for a term of five years. The prime minister is appointed by the president "in accordance with the election results" after consulting with the parliamentary parties, and the government must be dissolved if the parliament rejects its proposed budget.

In the 2014 presidential election, José Mário Vaz of the PAIGC took 61.9 percent of the second-round vote, defeating independent Nuno Gomes Nabiam, who took 38.08 percent. The election was considered largely free and fair. However, Vaz's 2015 dismissal of PAIGC leader Domingos Simões Pereira as prime minister touched off a political crisis. A series of subsequent governments appointed by Vaz failed to secure parliamentary approval. In

2017, the UN Security Council urged Vaz and other leaders to implement the internationally brokered Conakry Agreement of 2016, which called for an inclusive government led by a consensus prime minister.

In January 2018, Prime Minister Umaro Sissoco Embaló resigned, and President Vaz appointed a PAIGC member—Artur Silva—as prime minister, but without the party's agreement. Silva could not form a government with parliamentary support, as both the PAIGC and the PRS denounced his unilateral appointment. In February, the Economic Community of West African States (ECOWAS) imposed sanctions on some of Vaz's supporters and family members for allegedly sabotaging the political process and the implementation of the Conakry Agreement. Vaz finally nominated a consensus prime minister, Aristides Gomes, in April, and he remained in office through the end of 2018.

A2. Were the current national legislative representatives elected through free and fair elections? 2 / 4 (−1)

Members of the 102-seat National People's Assembly are elected by popular vote for four-year terms. In the 2014 elections, the PAIGC took 55 seats and was allocated two additional seats for diaspora representation, bringing its total to 57. The PRS secured 41 seats, the Party for Democratic Convergence (PDC) took two seats, and the Party for a New Democracy (PND) and the Union for Change (UM) won one seat each.

Monitoring groups and local human rights organizations reported some instances of intimidation or beatings of election officials and candidates during the election period. One PRS candidate for the legislature was reportedly kidnapped by unknown armed assailants. Voting was otherwise relatively peaceful and transparent, and the legislative elections were considered largely free and fair by international observers.

The incumbent assembly's four-year mandate, which was set to expire in April 2018, was extended to allow elections scheduled for November, but the voting was then postponed again due to delays in the voter registration process. Both the PAIGC and the PRS agreed to the extension of the mandate even as some politicians and civil society organizations argued that the measure was unconstitutional. In December, a presidential decree set the legislative elections for March 2019.

Score Change: The score declined from 3 to 2 because legislative elections scheduled for 2018 were postponed and the original mandate of the incumbent legislature expired.

A3. Are the electoral laws and framework fair, and are they implemented impartially by the relevant election management bodies? 2 / 4

There are some problems with the country's electoral laws and framework, including weak controls on campaign spending and vote buying and a lack of legal provisions for domestic poll observers. The 2014 elections were delayed in part due to a lack of funding, and the postponement of the legislative elections due in 2018 was accompanied by allegations from some parties of irregularities in the stalled voter registration process.

B. POLITICAL PLURALISM AND PARTICIPATION: 8 / 16

B1. Do the people have the right to organize in different political parties or other competitive political groupings of their choice, and is the system free of undue obstacles to the rise and fall of these competing parties or groupings? 3 / 4

Dozens of political parties are active in Guinea-Bissau, and 15 of them competed in the 2014 legislative elections. The political crisis since 2015 has led to some instances of violence and intimidation among partisan groups.

B2. Is there a realistic opportunity for the opposition to increase its support or gain power through elections? 2 / 4

Guinea-Bissau has a limited record of democratic power transfers between rival political parties, as the PAIGC or military rulers have governed for most of the period since independence. In 2014, Vaz succeeded an independent serving as acting president in the wake of the 2012 coup. Nevertheless, despite the repeated delays and tensions with the president, opposition forces were expected to have an opportunity to increase their representation in the 2019 legislative elections.

B3. Are the people's political choices free from domination by the military, foreign powers, religious hierarchies, economic oligarchies, or any other powerful group that is not democratically accountable? 1 / 4

The military has apparently refrained from interfering in politics since 2014, but the choices of voters and politicians continue to be influenced by corruption and patronage networks. Organized crime linked to drug trafficking and money laundering has contributed to the country's political instability in recent decades.

B4. Do various segments of the population (including ethnic, religious, gender, LGBT, and other relevant groups) have full political rights and electoral opportunities? 2 / 4

Women enjoy equal political rights, but their participation is limited in practice by cultural obstacles, and they are underrepresented in leadership positions. Just 14 women won seats in the last parliamentary elections. During 2018, women advocated for more equal political representation, and in November the assembly passed legislation requiring 36 percent of candidates on party lists to be women, though it did not require gender alternation on the lists. The president signed the bill into law in December.

Ethnicity plays a role in politics. For example, one of the larger groups, the Balanta, have traditionally dominated the military and cast votes for the PRS.

C. FUNCTIONING OF GOVERNMENT: 1 / 12

C1. Do the freely elected head of government and national legislative representatives determine the policies of the government? 1 / 4

Governance has been impaired by the political crisis that began in 2015. The constitutional legitimacy of the prime minister and cabinet remained in doubt until the appointment of a consensus prime minister in April 2018, and the expiration of the legislature's original mandate that month raised questions about its authority as well. Until it met in April, the full legislature had not convened for over two years. Aristides Gomes was the seventh prime minister to be appointed since President Vaz took office in 2014.

C2. Are safeguards against official corruption strong and effective? 0 / 4

Corruption is pervasive, including among senior government figures. Both military and civilian officials have been accused of involvement in the illegal drug trade. Critics of past corruption investigations targeting former high-ranking officials have argued that they were politically motivated.

C3. Does the government operate with openness and transparency? 0 / 4

There are no effective legal provisions to facilitate public access to government information, and government officials do not disclose their personal financial information as required by law. The political impasse and related parliamentary dysfunction have further obstructed oversight of government spending in recent years.

In May 2018, civil society organizations and members of the public criticized the government's gift—requested from and sponsored by Morocco—of 90 new cars to parliamentary deputies. Opponents of the donation noted that the health care and education systems were in dire need of funding.

CIVIL LIBERTIES: 27 / 60 (+2)

D. FREEDOM OF EXPRESSION AND BELIEF: 11 / 16 (+1)

D1. Are there free and independent media? 2 / 4 (+1)

The constitution provides for freedom of the press, and there is some media diversity. Journalists regularly face harassment and intimidation, including pressure regarding their coverage from political figures and government officials. However, reports of threats and censorship diminished in 2018 compared with previous years, and in April the president stated that freedom of expression and the press should be protected.

Score Change: The score improved from 1 to 2 because threats to journalists and efforts to control the media appeared to decrease in comparison with previous years.

D2. Are individuals free to practice and express their religious faith or nonbelief in public and private? 3 / 4

Religious freedom is legally protected and usually respected in practice. Government licensing requirements are not onerous and often disregarded. Some Muslims have reportedly raised concerns about the influence of foreign imams who preach a more rigorous or austere form of Islam.

D3. Is there academic freedom, and is the educational system free from extensive political indoctrination? 3 / 4

Academic freedom is guaranteed and generally upheld, though the education system is poor in terms of access, quality, and basic resources. Public schools were closed for much of 2018 due to ongoing teachers' strikes, and in November police used force to remove students who attempted to assemble in schools as part of their protests against the prolonged closures.

D4. Are individuals free to express their personal views on political or other sensitive topics without fear of surveillance or retribution? 3 / 4

Individuals are relatively free to express their views on political topics in the private and social sphere, though some more public figures have faced the threat of arrest or charges in retaliation for their remarks in recent years.

E. ASSOCIATIONAL AND ORGANIZATIONAL RIGHTS: 7 / 12 (+1)

E1. Is there freedom of assembly? 1 / 4

Freedom of assembly is frequently restricted. The authorities have repeatedly interfered with demonstrations linked to the political tensions between the president and the legislature. In August 2018 the police blocked a march against an agreement with Senegal to explore for oil in Guinea-Bissau's waters, which would give the majority of proceeds to Senegal. Police violently suppressed a student march in November that was meant to protest delays in classes stemming from the teachers' strike, leaving at least eight people injured. A subsequent student demonstration outside government headquarters was reportedly allowed to proceed.

E2. Is there freedom for nongovernmental organizations, particularly those that are engaged in human rights– and governance-related work? 3 / 4 (+1)

Nongovernmental organizations (NGOs) are generally able to operate. Some groups have faced intimidation and other obstacles, particularly those that are associated with street demonstrations, but no major cases of repressive measures against NGOs were reported during 2018.

Score Change: The score improved from 2 to 3 because there were no reports of serious threats or repressive measures against NGOs during the year.

E3. Is there freedom for trade unions and similar professional or labor organizations? 3 / 4

Workers are allowed to form and join independent trade unions, but few work in the wage-earning formal sector. Private employers sometimes engage in improper interference with union organizing and other activities. The right to strike is protected, and government workers frequently exercise this right. Several strikes took place during 2018, including actions by civil servants, teachers, and state media employees.

F. RULE OF LAW: 4 / 16

F1. Is there an independent judiciary? 1 / 4

Judges are highly susceptible to corruption and political pressure, and the court system as a whole lacks the resources and capacity to function effectively.

F2. Does due process prevail in civil and criminal matters? 0 / 4

Corruption is common among police, and officers often fail to observe legal safeguards against arbitrary arrest and detention. Very few criminal cases are brought to trial or successfully prosecuted, partly due to the limited material and human resources available to investigators. Most of the population lacks access to the justice system in practice.

F3. Is there protection from the illegitimate use of physical force and freedom from war and insurgencies? 1 / 4

Conditions in prisons and detention centers are often extremely poor, and law enforcement personnel generally enjoy impunity for abuses. A number of cases of torture and beatings by police have been reported in recent years, including in 2018.

Because of its weak institutions and porous borders, Guinea-Bissau has become a transit point for criminal organizations trafficking various types of contraband. The armed forces and some other state entities have been linked to drug trafficking. Criminal violence, including homicides, continues to threaten residents' physical security.

F4. Do laws, policies, and practices guarantee equal treatment of various segments of the population? 2 / 4

Women face significant societal discrimination and traditional biases, despite some legal protections. They generally do not receive equal pay for similar work and have fewer opportunities for education and employment.

There are virtually no effective legal protections against discrimination on other grounds, including ethnicity, sexual orientation, and gender identity, though same-sex sexual activity is not specifically criminalized.

G. PERSONAL AUTONOMY AND INDIVIDUAL RIGHTS: 5 / 16

G1. Do individuals enjoy freedom of movement, including the ability to change their place of residence, employment, or education? 2 / 4

There are few formal restrictions on freedom of movement, but widespread corruption among police and other public officials can limit this right in practice, as can criminal activity.

G2. Are individuals able to exercise the right to own property and establish private businesses without undue interference from state or nonstate actors? 1 / 4

Illegal economic activity, including logging, by organized groups remains a problem. The quality of enforcement of property rights is generally poor, and the formal procedures for establishing a business are relatively onerous.

Women, particularly those from certain ethnic groups in rural areas, face restrictions on their ability to own and inherit property.

G3. Do individuals enjoy personal social freedoms, including choice of marriage partner and size of family, protection from domestic violence, and control over appearance? 1 / 4

Domestic violence is not specifically addressed by law, and it is reportedly common. Victims of rape and domestic abuse rarely report the crimes to authorities. The government, international organizations, and community leaders have worked to eliminate female genital mutilation, though nearly half of the country's women have undergone such traditional practices. Early and forced marriages remain common.

G4. Do individuals enjoy equality of opportunity and freedom from economic exploitation? 1 / 4

Guinea-Bissau is one of the world's poorest countries, with most families relying on unstable employment in the informal economy or remittances from migrant workers abroad. Public services have deteriorated in recent years amid irregular payment of public-sector workers.

Boys are vulnerable to organized exploitation as beggars and to forced labor in sectors including mining and agriculture. Girls are frequently victims of sexual exploitation or domestic servitude. Government officials have been accused of complicity in trafficking activity, including sex tourism schemes in the Bijagós islands.

Guyana

Population: 800,000
Capital: Georgetown
Political Rights Rating: 2
Civil Liberties Rating: 3
Freedom Rating: 2.5
Freedom Status: Free
Electoral Democracy: Yes

Overview: Guyana is a parliamentary democracy that features regular elections, a lively press, and a robust civil society. However, discrimination against indigenous and LGBT (lesbian, gay, bisexual, and transgender) people and violent crime remain significant problems. The recent discovery of rich oil and natural gas reserves beneath Guyana's coastal waters has prompted calls for continued progress on anticorruption reforms. The prospect of increased revenues also appears to be exacerbating traditional ethnopolitical divisions.

KEY DEVELOPMENTS IN 2018:

- Several board members at the state-owned newspaper *Guyana Chronicle* resigned in March amid allegations of political interference, and in July lawmakers passed a cybercrime bill that opponents said could harm freedom of expression despite last-minute amendments meant to address such concerns.
- Ethnopolitical tensions surfaced between the predominantly Afro-Guyanese government and the mainly Indo-Guyanese opposition during the year, especially in connection with a disputed appointment to the elections commission. The governing coalition, consisting of A Partnership for National Unity (APNU) and the Alliance for Change (AFC), lost ground in local elections in November.
- The coalition narrowly lost a parliamentary confidence vote in late December. While some in the government initially appeared to accept that new elections would have to be held within 90 days, at year's end the coalition was preparing to challenge the vote in court.

POLITICAL RIGHTS: 32 / 40

A. ELECTORAL PROCESS: 11 / 12

A1. Was the current head of government or other chief national authority elected through free and fair elections? 4 / 4

The president, who serves as both chief of state and head of government, appoints the cabinet, though ministers are collectively responsible to the National Assembly. Parties designate a presidential candidate ahead of National Assembly elections, with the winning party's candidate assuming the presidency. The president serves five-year terms.

David Granger, head of the APNU-AFC coalition, became president after the bloc won the 2015 National Assembly elections. However, the government narrowly lost a confidence vote in late December 2018, meaning elections originally due in 2020 would have to be held in 2019. A court challenge of the vote's validity was pending at year's end.

A2. Were the current national legislative representatives elected through free and fair elections? 4 / 4

Members of the unicameral, 65-seat National Assembly are elected to five-year terms; 25 representatives are elected in 10 geographical constituencies, while 40 are elected by proportional representation in one nationwide constituency. Up to seven unelected cabinet ministers and parliamentary officials may also hold ex-officio seats.

In the 2015 elections, the APNU-AFC coalition won 50.3 percent of the vote and 33 seats, ending 23 years of rule by the People's Progressive Party/Civic (PPP/C), which won 32 seats. While the APNU-AFC won the elections by a very tight margin, the transfer of power was smooth and peaceful. Observers reported a tense atmosphere on election day and recommended numerous electoral reforms, but they generally praised the conduct of the vote.

In November 2018, local elections were held for the second time since 1994. Turnout was low, at 36 percent, down from 47 percent in 2016. While the PPP/C made important gains, the APNU retained control in the capital and some other municipalities.

A3. Are the electoral laws and framework fair, and are they implemented impartially by the relevant election management bodies? 3 / 4

The Carter Center, after monitoring the 2015 polls, made multiple recommendations on how to improve the fairness and efficiency of electoral laws. It expressed some concern over the independence and capacity of the Guyana Elections Commission (GECOM).

GECOM was the subject of renewed concern in 2017 and 2018 after President Granger rejected multiple lists of candidates for the position of chairman that were put forward by the opposition and instead appointed James Patterson to the role unilaterally in October 2017, prompting protests from the opposition. The PPP/C filed appeals contesting the selection, but the Guyanese courts ultimately upheld the appointment in October 2018. A appeal to the Caribbean Court of Justice (CCJ) was pending at year's end.

In June 2018, the CCJ ruled that a 2000 constitutional amendment barring presidents from serving more than two terms in office was valid, reversing decisions by Guyanese courts in 2015 and 2017 that struck down the term limit. The ruling would prevent opposition leader Bharrat Jagdeo, who had already served two terms from 1999 to 2011, from seeking the presidency in the next elections.

B. POLITICAL PLURALISM AND PARTICIPATION: 13 / 16

B1. Do the people have the right to organize in different political parties or other competitive political groupings of their choice, and is the system free of undue obstacles to the rise and fall of these competing parties or groupings? 4 / 4

Political parties may form freely, and they generally operate without interference. A long-standing deadlock between two major parties organized on ethnic lines had softened somewhat in recent years, with the multiethnic AFC emerging to join the predominantly Afro-Guyanese APNU and the mainly Indo-Guyanese PPP/C on the political stage. However, observers warned that ethnopolitical divisions could be revived after an Indo-Guyanese AFC member switched sides to oppose the government in the 2018 confidence vote.

The 2015 Carter Center election monitoring mission noted that Guyana lacked legislation on the formation of political parties and recommended a new law whose requirements would promote the establishment and free operation of multiethnic parties. The mission also recommended allowing individual or independent candidates to stand for the presidency, which is currently not permitted.

B2. Is there a realistic opportunity for the opposition to increase its support or gain power through elections? 4 / 4

The PPP/C ruled from 1992 to 2015, and the APNU-AFC victory in that year's elections marked only the second democratic rotation of power in the country's modern history. Nevertheless, the orderly handover demonstrated the ability of opposition parties to win elections and enter government.

B3. Are the people's political choices free from domination by the military, foreign powers, religious hierarchies, economic oligarchies, or any other powerful group that is not democratically accountable? 3 / 4

Voters are largely free to make their own political choices. However, there is concern that political affairs could be improperly influenced by the largely Indo-Guyanese economic elite.

B4. Do various segments of the population (including ethnic, religious, gender, LGBT, and other relevant groups) have full political rights and electoral opportunities? 2 / 4

Women and ethnic minorities have equal political rights under the law, though ethnic divisions have long played a powerful role in politics, with the two largest parties drawing most of their support from either the Indo-Guyanese or the Afro-Guyanese community. The indigenous minority, which represents about 10 percent of the population, generally remains politically marginalized. The interests of women are also not well represented in the political sphere. However, at least a third of each party's candidate list must consist of women, and of 69 members of the National Assembly, 22 (32 percent) are women.

In 2017, the government initiated public consultations on planned constitutional reforms with representatives of religious minorities and indigenous communities, but little progress was reported in 2018.

C. FUNCTIONING OF GOVERNMENT: 8 / 12

C1. Do the freely elected head of government and national legislative representatives determine the policies of the government? 4 / 4

The president and the legislative majority are generally able to create and implement policy without improper interference.

C2. Are safeguards against official corruption strong and effective? 2 / 4

In recent years, the government has made progress in introducing durable safeguards against corruption, notably by strengthening controls on money laundering and empowering a new agency to audit state-owned companies. However, official corruption remains a serious problem, and the discovery of rich oil and natural gas reserves beneath the country's coastal waters has added urgency to antigraft efforts. Discussion continued in 2018 over the best mechanisms for administering this new energy wealth.

C3. Does the government operate with openness and transparency? 2 / 4

Laws designed to ensure government transparency are inconsistently upheld. Guyana's Access to Information Act came into force in 2013, but its provisions are weak, allowing the government to refuse requests with little or no justification.

In February 2018, a long-dormant integrity commission tasked with reviewing officials' asset disclosures was finally reestablished, though it was not expected to be fully operational until early 2019. By the end of 2018, over 400 financial declarations had been submitted to the commission by government officials.

Guyana's application for membership in the Extractive Industries Transparency Initiative (EITI), which asks countries to submit reports detailing the proceeds they have gained from the extraction of their natural resources, was accepted in 2017.

CIVIL LIBERTIES: 43 / 60 (+1)

D. FREEDOM OF EXPRESSION AND BELIEF: 15 / 16

D1. Are there free and independent media? 3 / 4

Although freedom of the press is generally respected, government officials have initiated libel lawsuits and have occasionally made outright threats against journalists in response to negative coverage.

Amendments to the Broadcasting Act adopted in 2017 prompted concerns due to a lack of prior consultation with broadcasters and the possibility that the act could be used to suppress unfavorable political coverage. In 2018, the Guyana National Broadcasting Authority (GNBA) began more strictly enforcing licensing regulations, launching initial proceedings against some outlets for content violations related primarily to obscenity.

In March 2018, four directors resigned from the board of the state-owned *Guyana Chronicle* after the newspaper's editor in chief fired two columnists who were regularly critical of the government. The editor and the government insisted that the paper was free from political interference.

D2. Are individuals free to practice and express their religious faith or nonbelief in public and private? 4 / 4

Religious freedom is constitutionally guaranteed and generally respected in practice. Rules limiting visas for foreign missionaries and barring blasphemous libel are not actively enforced. Religious groups can register places of worship and receive associated benefits without difficulty.

D3. Is there academic freedom, and is the educational system free from extensive political indoctrination? 4 / 4

Academic freedom is largely upheld.

D4. Are individuals free to express their personal views on political or other sensitive topics without fear of surveillance or retribution? 4 / 4

People are generally free to express their views without fear of retaliation or other repercussions. In July 2018, lawmakers approved a controversial cybercrime bill with last-minute amendments designed to address concerns about freedom of expression. However, opponents argued that the final legislation still contained problematic provisions on sedition, secrecy, and offenses against the state that could be used to stifle dissent.

E. ASSOCIATIONAL AND ORGANIZATIONAL RIGHTS: 11 / 12 (+1)
E1. Is there freedom of assembly? 4 / 4 (+1)

While police violence toward protesters has been an issue in the past, the authorities have more recently upheld the right to peaceful assembly, including in 2018. For example, Guyana's first gay pride parade proceeded in June without incident.

Score Change: The score improved from 3 to 4 because authorities have generally upheld the right to peaceful assembly in recent years.

E2. Is there freedom for nongovernmental organizations, particularly those that are engaged in human rights- and governance-related work? 4 / 4

Nongovernmental organizations (NGOs) operate freely. The government has consulted with NGOs on various policy initiatives, including measures designed to combat human trafficking.

E3. Is there freedom for trade unions and similar professional or labor organizations? 3 / 4

The rights to form labor unions, bargain collectively, and strike are generally upheld, and unions are well organized. However, laws against antiunion discrimination are poorly enforced.

F. RULE OF LAW: 8 / 16
F1. Is there an independent judiciary? 2 / 4

The functioning of the courts is impaired by political disputes. The Granger government has publicly emphasized the importance of an independent judiciary, but it has struggled to appoint senior jurists due to disagreements with the opposition. According to the constitution, the president must obtain the agreement of the leader of the opposition to appoint the chancellor of the judiciary and the chief justice; both positions remained vacant in 2018, with officials serving in an acting capacity. Other judges are appointed by the president on the advice of a Judicial Service Commission, most of whose members are also chosen with input from the opposition. Staff shortages and lack of resources hamper the judiciary's effectiveness.

F2. Does due process prevail in civil and criminal matters? 2 / 4

Observance of due process safeguards is uneven. Defendants are often held in pretrial detention for periods longer than their maximum possible sentence if convicted. The police do not always operate with professionalism, and some officers have reportedly accepted bribes. Recent years have featured efforts to prosecute police officers engaged in a variety of crimes. A new police commissioner took office in August 2018 with a mandate to make reforms and improve police conduct.

F3. Is there protection from the illegitimate use of physical force and freedom from war and insurgencies? 2 / 4

Reports of police violence, abuse of detainees, and harsh, overcrowded prison conditions persist in Guyana. The rate of violent crime has fallen somewhat in recent years but remains among the highest in the region.

The limited threat of territorial conflict with Venezuela lingered in 2018 following the collapse of a UN-sponsored mediation process. In January, the United Nations recommended that the dispute be resolved by the International Court of Justice (ICJ), and Guyana submitted an application against Venezuela with the ICJ in March. In late December, the Venezuelan navy drove off an ExxonMobil ship in Guyanese waters, claiming the ship was in Venezuelan territory.

F4. Do laws, policies, and practices guarantee equal treatment of various segments of the population? 2 / 4

Laws barring discrimination based on race, gender, and other categories are not effectively enforced. Women continue to suffer from workplace bias and significantly lower pay compared with men. Despite some recent advances, Guyana's nine principal indigenous groups face disparities in the provision of health care, education, and justice. Same-sex sexual activity is punishable with harsh jail terms, and the LGBT community is subject to police harassment and discrimination.

G. PERSONAL AUTONOMY AND INDIVIDUAL RIGHTS: 9 / 16

G1. Do individuals enjoy freedom of movement, including the ability to change their place of residence, employment, or education? 3 / 4

There are no undue legal restrictions on freedom of movement, including with respect to residency, employment, and education. However, factors including bribery, racial polarization, and neglected infrastructure in some regions limit this right in practice.

G2. Are individuals able to exercise the right to own property and establish private businesses without undue interference from state or nonstate actors? 2 / 4

The legal framework generally supports the rights to own property and operate private businesses, but corruption and organized crime sometimes inhibit business activity. The land rights of indigenous communities are impaired by flawed consultation and demarcation procedures, as well as by unauthorized exploitation of titled indigenous lands.

G3. Do individuals enjoy personal social freedoms, including choice of marriage partner and size of family, protection from domestic violence, and control over appearance? 2 / 4

Individual freedom on personal status matters such as marriage and divorce is generally respected, though same-sex marriage and civil unions are prohibited. Legal exceptions allow marriage before age 18 with judicial or parental permission, and such marriages are reportedly common.

Domestic abuse is widespread, and conviction rates for such abuse and for sexual offenses are low. A string of murders and an apparent spike in domestic abuse cases in 2017–18 prompted concerns about the adequacy of the government's response.

G4. Do individuals enjoy equality of opportunity and freedom from economic exploitation? 2 / 4

Legal protections against exploitative working conditions are not enforced consistently. Those working in the informal sector and extractive industries in the country's interior are particularly vulnerable to abuses.

The US State Department detailed Guyana's continued efforts to address human trafficking in 2018, citing increased funding of victim-support programs and expanded identification of victims. However, there were few successful prosecutions, and support for child or male victims was limited. Trafficking of Venezuelan nationals has reportedly increased in connection with that country's economic and humanitarian crisis.

Haiti

Population: 10,800,000
Capital: Port-au-Prince
Political Rights Rating: 5
Civil Liberties Rating: 5
Freedom Rating: 5.0
Freedom Status: Partly Free
Electoral Democracy: No

Overview: Haiti's elections are regularly subject to delays, fraud, and violence, and the political system as a whole is undermined by corruption. The criminal justice system lacks the resources, independence, and integrity to uphold due process and ensure physical security for the population. Antigovernment protests often result in excessive use of force by police.

KEY DEVELOPMENTS IN 2018:

- Prime Minister Jack Guy Lafontant resigned in July after an attempt to cut fuel subsidies, in keeping with an International Monetary Fund (IMF) agreement, prompted violent protests. Parliament confirmed Jean-Henry Céant as his replacement in September.
- A series of protests calling for President Jovenel Moïse's resignation over the alleged misuse of some $3.8 billion in aid from Venezuela began in September and gained momentum through the end of the year.
- Violence by armed gangs increased insecurity in parts of Port-au-Prince, with human rights investigators citing evidence that gangs involved in a massacre of civilians in November received support from police.

POLITICAL RIGHTS: 17 / 40

A. ELECTORAL PROCESS: 5 / 12

A1. Was the current head of government or other chief national authority elected through free and fair elections? 2 / 4

In Haiti's semipresidential system, the president is directly elected for a five-year term. The prime minister is appointed by the president and confirmed by Parliament.

Jovenel Moïse of the Haitian Tet Kale Party (PHTK), the handpicked successor of incumbent Michel Martelly, won the 2015 presidential election, but the contest was nullified due to extensive fraud. Moïse went on to win the repeat election in November 2016, taking 55.6 percent of the vote. He was inaugurated in early 2017 after an electoral tribunal verified the election result, stating that there had been irregularities but no evidence of widespread fraud. While they acknowledged improvements over the 2015 election, civil society groups claimed that fraud in the vote tally, inconsistent voter registration lists, voter disenfranchisement, and a low voter turnout of just 21 percent undermined the mandate of the new president.

Prime Minister Jack Guy Lafontant, in office since March 2017, resigned in July 2018 after his government's attempt to cut fuel subsidies in keeping with an IMF agreement triggered violent protests. In September, after several weeks of negotiation, Parliament confirmed a new cabinet with Jean-Henry Céant as prime minister.

A2. Were the current national legislative representatives elected through free and fair elections? 1 / 4

The directly elected, bicameral Parliament is composed of a Senate, with 30 members who serve six-year terms, and a Chamber of Deputies, with 119 members who serve four-year terms. The 2015 legislative elections were plagued by disorder, fraud, and violence. Despite concerns about the elections' credibility, 92 lawmakers took office in early 2016. Elections for a portion of the Senate and the runoff elections for the remaining seats in the Chamber of Deputies were held in 2016 along with the repeat presidential election, and the contests were marred by low voter turnout and fraud. The PHTK emerged as the largest single party in both chambers, followed by Truth (Vérité), though most of the seats were divided among a large number of smaller parties.

A3. Are the electoral laws and framework fair, and are they implemented impartially by the relevant election management bodies? 2 / 4

The Provisional Electoral Council (CEP) was established in the late 1980s as a temporary body, but it continues to be responsible for managing the electoral process. Although the constitution has provisions to prevent executive dominance of the CEP, the executive branch asserts significant control over it in practice. Legislative elections were not held from 2011 until 2015 because a number of electoral councils appointed by former president Martelly did not meet constitutional requirements or receive parliamentary approval; critics claimed that CEP members would have been beholden to Martelly. New council members were appointed in 2015 in a manner closer to the constitutional provisions. Despite discussions about establishing a permanent electoral council, the CEP in 2018 started planning the 2019 legislative elections.

B. POLITICAL PLURALISM AND PARTICIPATION: 7 / 16

B1. Do the people have the right to organize in different political parties or other competitive political groupings of their choice, and is the system free of undue obstacles to the rise and fall of these competing parties or groupings? 2 / 4

Legal and administrative barriers that had prevented some parties from registering or running in past elections have largely been eliminated. The number of members required to form a political party was reduced from 500 to 20 in 2014, leading to the creation of dozens of new parties. However, the risk of violence continues to impair normal political activity.

Opposition party leaders are sometimes threatened, and protests organized by opposition parties are regularly met with repressive force by the government.

B2. Is there a realistic opportunity for the opposition to increase its support or gain power through elections? 1 / 4

Haiti does not have a strong record of peaceful democratic transfers of power, and it remains difficult for the opposition to increase its support or gain power through elections, which have repeatedly been postponed, disrupted by violence, or marred by fraud and disputed results in recent years. The PHTK has consolidated power in the legislature and at the local level, in part through alliances with smaller parties.

B3. Are the people's political choices free from domination by the military, foreign powers, religious hierarchies, economic oligarchies, or any other powerful group that is not democratically accountable? 2 / 4

Haitians' political choices are free from explicit domination by the military and other forces outside the political system. However, many politicians rely on money linked to drug trafficking and other illegal sources of funding to finance their campaigns, which has a considerable influence over political outcomes in the country.

B4. Do various segments of the population (including ethnic, religious, gender, LGBT, and other relevant groups) have full political rights and electoral opportunities? 2 / 4

Haitian women are underrepresented in political life, with only four out of 149 parliamentary seats held by women in 2018. The constitution mandates that 30 percent of public officials should be women, but the government lacks penalties for noncompliance. Election-related violence, along with social and cultural constraints, discourages women from participating in politics. Due to societal discrimination, the interests of LGBT (lesbian, gay, bisexual, and transgender) people are not represented in the political system.

C. FUNCTIONING OF GOVERNMENT: 5 / 12

C1. Do the freely elected head of government and national legislative representatives determine the policies of the government? 2 / 4

The legitimacy of Haiti's executive and legislative officials is undermined by the many problems surrounding their election. Moreover, due to corruption, instability, and security threats, the government struggles to carry out its own policies and provide basic services across the country.

C2. Are safeguards against official corruption strong and effective? 1 / 4

Corruption is widespread in Haiti, as are allegations of impunity for government officials. A 2017 law reduced the independence and powers of the Central Financial Intelligence Unit (UCREF), which was responsible for investigating money-laundering cases. Also that year, Moïse replaced the heads of the Anticorruption Unit (ULCC) and the UCREF with political allies and former members of the Martelly administration; both units had been investigating Moïse for potential money laundering.

Officials from the Martelly administration have been accused of misappropriating an estimated $3.8 billion in low-interest loans from Venezuela. Although Senate commissions documented a number of these abuses in 2017, Haitian human rights groups have criticized the Senate majority for obstructing further action on the scandal. The lack of accountability for the aid funds fueled a series of large antigovernment protests from September 2018 through the end of the year.

C3. Does the government operate with openness and transparency? 2 / 4

Haitians' general distrust of the government stems in large part from the absence of transparency and accountability measures that are needed to reduce corruption. There are no laws providing the public with access to state information, and it is reportedly very difficult to obtain government documents and data in practice. All government officials must file financial disclosure forms within 90 days of taking office and within 90 days of leaving office, though these requirements are not well enforced, and the reports are not made public.

CIVIL LIBERTIES: 24 / 60

D. FREEDOM OF EXPRESSION AND BELIEF: 10 / 16

D1. Are there free and independent media? 2 / 4

The constitution includes protections for press freedom, and the media sector is pluralistic, but the work of journalists is constrained by threats and violence as well as government interference. The March 2018 disappearance of journalist Vladjimir Legagneur while on assignment in Port-au-Prince remained unsolved at year's end, with police reporting some arrests in the case but otherwise releasing little information.

D2. Are individuals free to practice and express their religious faith or nonbelief in public and private? 3 / 4

Freedom of religion is constitutionally guaranteed, and religious groups generally practice freely. However, the traditionally dominant Roman Catholic Church receives certain privileges from the state, practitioners of the Vodou religion face social stigma, and the government has denied registration to the small Muslim community.

D3. Is there academic freedom, and is the educational system free from extensive political indoctrination? 2 / 4

Educational institutions and academics choose their curriculum freely, but university associations and student groups that protest government actions are often met with police violence. Three people were shot in November 2018 during a protest for better conditions by high school students in a poor neighborhood of Port-au-Prince. Earlier in the year, students and professors condemned the deployment of riot police in January to two schools at the state university, which have been the sites of public criticism of the government in the past.

D4. Are individuals free to express their personal views on political or other sensitive topics without fear of surveillance or retribution? 3 / 4

There are few significant constraints on freedom of private discussion. The government does not engage in widespread surveillance, nor is it known to illegally monitor private online communications. However, the penal code includes defamation-related offenses, and the risk of violent reprisals may also serve as a deterrent to unfettered discussion of sensitive issues such as gangs and organized crime.

E. ASSOCIATIONAL AND ORGANIZATIONAL RIGHTS: 4 / 12

E1. Is there freedom of assembly? 2 / 4

The constitution guarantees freedom of assembly, but this right is often violated in practice. Antigovernment street protests, which intensified during 2018, drew a violent police response. At one large anticorruption march in October, eight people were shot dead, 61 were injured, and 42 were arrested by police, according to human rights activists.

E2. Is there freedom for nongovernmental organizations, particularly those that are engaged in human rights- and governance-related work? 1 / 4

Human rights defenders and activists with nongovernmental organizations (NGOs) that address sensitive topics are subject to threats and violence, which creates a climate of fear. Violence against activists is rarely investigated or prosecuted.

E3. Is there freedom for trade unions and similar professional or labor organizations? 1 / 4

Workers' right to unionize is protected under the law, and strikes are not uncommon, though the union movement in Haiti is weak and lacks collective bargaining power in practice. Most citizens are informally employed. Workers who engage in union activity frequently face harassment, suspension, termination, and other repercussions from employers.

F. RULE OF LAW: 4 / 16

F1. Is there an independent judiciary? 1 / 4

Despite constitutional guarantees of independence, the judiciary is susceptible to pressure from the executive and legislative branches. A lack of resources has contributed to bribery throughout the judicial system, and weak oversight means that most corrupt officials are not held accountable. When President Moïse's government took power, all 18 chief prosecutors in the judicial jurisdictions were replaced; this opened new avenues for executive interference in the judiciary, since prosecutors can determine which cases end up before a judge. Moïse complained in 2017 that he felt forced to nominate corrupt judges based on lists submitted by the judicial council, which is tasked with vetting judges.

F2. Does due process prevail in civil and criminal matters? 1 / 4

Constitutionally protected due process rights are regularly violated in practice. Arbitrary arrest is common, as are extortion attempts by police. Most suspects do not have legal representation, and those who do suffer from long delays and case mismanagement. Three-quarters of the inmate population is in pretrial detention due to a large backlog of cases and resource constraints, with even higher figures in the capital. Many have never appeared before a judge despite the legal requirement of a court hearing within 48 hours of arrest.

F3. Is there protection from the illegitimate use of physical force and freedom from war and insurgencies? 1 / 4

A culture of impunity in law enforcement, in addition to widespread criminal violence, leaves civilians in Haiti with little protection from the illegitimate use of force. More than 750 homicides were reported in 2018, down from nearly 900 in 2017, but crime statistics are difficult to authenticate, and crimes are underreported. Police are regularly accused of abusing suspects and detainees. Conditions in Haiti's prisons, which are among the world's most overcrowded, are extremely poor.

In November 2018, at least 59 people were killed, seven were sexually assaulted, and 150 houses were burned during an outbreak of violence in the La Saline neighborhood of Port-au-Prince. Some accounts characterized the episode as part of a conflict between rival gangs, but human rights researchers cited allegations of police involvement, and critics accused the government of organizing the massacre to suppress anticorruption protests.

In March, Moïse appointed commanders for the new national army, which was expected to expand to 5,000 soldiers after being unveiled in 2017. Haiti's military had been disbanded in 1995 following a series of political interventions and human rights abuses, and its revival has led to fears about potential future violations.

F4. Do laws, policies, and practices guarantee equal treatment of various segments of the population? 1 / 4

Discrimination against women, the LGBT community, and people with disabilities is pervasive. Among other problems, women face bias in employment and disparities in access to financial services.

Harassment and discrimination on the basis of sexual orientation occur regularly, and neither is prohibited by law. In 2017, a bill that would limit LGBT people's access to employment and education was passed by the Senate. The Chamber of Deputies had not voted on the bill as of 2018.

G. PERSONAL AUTONOMY AND INDIVIDUAL RIGHTS: 6 / 16

G1. Do individuals enjoy freedom of movement, including the ability to change their place of residence, employment, or education? 2 / 4

The government generally does not restrict travel or place limits on the ability to change one's place of employment or education. However, corruption and insecurity remain obstacles to free movement, and the government's flawed response to natural disasters has prevented many displaced residents from returning to their homes, forcing them to live in poor conditions for extended periods. As of 2018, more than 30,000 people resided in camps built for those displaced by the 2010 earthquake. In October 2018, an earthquake killed 17 people, injured 427, and destroyed 7,430 houses in Haiti's rural north.

G2. Are individuals able to exercise the right to own property and establish private businesses without undue interference from state or nonstate actors? 2 / 4

Although the legal framework protects property rights and private business activity, it is difficult in practice to register property, enforce contracts, and obtain credit. Poor record keeping and corruption contribute to inconsistent enforcement of property rights.

In July 2018, the authorities moved to demolish about 35 homes near President Moïse's residence, reportedly acting without warning and stating that the homes presented a security threat. Several homes were destroyed, but the demolitions were stalled after residents protested and civil society organizations denounced the action.

G3. Do individuals enjoy personal social freedoms, including choice of marriage partner and size of family, protection from domestic violence, and control over appearance? 2 / 4

Basic freedoms related to marriage, divorce, and custody are generally respected. However, there are no laws addressing domestic violence, which is a widespread problem. Both domestic violence and rape are underreported and rarely result in successful prosecutions, with justice officials often favoring reconciliation or other forms of settlement.

G4. Do individuals enjoy equality of opportunity and freedom from economic exploitation? 0 / 4

Socioeconomic mobility is obstructed by entrenched poverty, with low national literacy rates and nearly 60 percent of Haitians living on two dollars a day or less. Legal protections against exploitative working conditions in formal employment are weakly enforced, and most workers are informally employed. As many as 300,000 children work as domestic servants, often without pay or access to education, and they are especially vulnerable to physical or sexual abuse. Other forms of child labor are common.

Honduras

Population: 9,000,000
Capital: Tegucigalpa
Political Rights Rating: 4
Civil Liberties Rating: 4
Freedom Rating: 4.0
Freedom Status: Partly Free
Electoral Democracy: No

Overview: Institutional weakness, corruption, violence, and impunity undermine the overall stability of Honduras. Journalists, political activists, and women are often the victims of violence, and perpetrators are rarely brought to justice. While Honduras holds regular elections, irregularities surrounding the 2017 presidential poll prompted election monitors to call the result into question.

KEY DEVELOPMENTS IN 2018:

- In February, the head of the Mission to Support the Fight against Corruption and Impunity in Honduras (MACCIH) resigned, citing hostility from the government and a lack of support from the Organization for American States (OAS), which backs the panel.
- Despite government efforts to undermine the work of the MACCIH, in June the body announced charges against 38 government officials and politicians, who are accused of misusing public funds for the president's 2013 campaign, as well as opposition campaigns. Among those implicated are high-ranking members of the ruling National Party (PN) and opposition Liberal Party (PL), a number of former government ministers, and members of Congress.
- In November, a court found seven of the eight suspects in the 2016 killing of indigenous rights activist Berta Cáceres guilty of murder. However, rights activists expressed concern that the masterminds of the crime had not been identified.

POLITICAL RIGHTS: 20 / 40

A. ELECTORAL PROCESS: 7 / 12

A1. Was the current head of government or other chief national authority elected through free and fair elections? 2 / 4

The president is both chief of state and head of government, and is elected by popular vote to four-year terms. The leading candidate is only required to win a plurality; there is no runoff system.

In a controversial 2015 decision, the Honduran Supreme Court voided Article 239 of the constitution, which had limited presidents to one term. President Juan Orlando Hernández was subsequently reelected in 2017, with the Supreme Electoral Council (TSE) announcing in December—three weeks after the actual poll—that he had taken 42.95 percent of the vote, to opposition candidate Salvador Nasralla's 41.42 percent. The OAS noted numerous issues with the electoral process, which it said "was characterized by irregularities and deficiencies, with very low technical quality and lacking integrity," and appealed for new elections to be held. The government dismissed the OAS petition, and by year's end the United States, the European Union (EU), and Canada had recognized Hernández as the winner of the election.

Post-election protests led to clashes between civilians and security forces, resulting in the deaths of 23 protesters.

A2. Were the current national legislative representatives elected through free and fair elections? 3 / 4

Members of the 128-seat, unicameral National Congress are elected for four-year terms using proportional representation by department. In the 2017 polls, the governing PN acquired an additional 13 seats, but still fell short of holding a legislative majority. The opposition Liberty and Refoundation (LIBRE) party and PL lost seven seats, and one seat, respectively. While the 2017 presidential and parliamentary votes were held concurrently, stakeholders accepted the results of the legislative elections; only the presidential poll was disputed.

A3. Are the electoral laws and framework fair, and are they implemented impartially by the relevant election management bodies? 2 / 4

The TSE came under heavy criticism for its administration of the 2017 presidential poll, notably after a preliminary vote count had showed Nasralla with a significant lead, but later announcements and ultimately the final result—which was released three weeks after the elections—showed a victory by Hernández. The delay prompted protests and widespread allegations of TSE incompetence and bias toward the ruling party. As the vote-counting process dragged on, OAS and EU election monitors expressed concerns regarding the lack of transparency and irregularities surrounding the presidential vote, and voiced support for Nasralla's demand for a recount. The OAS eventually called for the poll to be rerun, but authorities dismissed the recommendation.

B. POLITICAL PLURALISM AND PARTICIPATION: 8 / 16

B1. Do the people have the right to organize in different political parties or other competitive political groupings of their choice, and is the system free of undue obstacles to the rise and fall of these competing parties or groupings? 3 / 4

Political parties are largely free to operate, though power has mostly been concentrated in the hands of the PL and the PN since the early 1980s. In 2013, LIBRE and the Anti-Corruption Party (PAC) participated in elections for the first time, winning a significant share of the vote and disrupting the dominance of the PL and the PN. PAC lost all but one of its seats in 2017, but LIBRE maintained its position as the second-largest party in the parliament.

B2. Is there a realistic opportunity for the opposition to increase its support or gain power through elections? 2 / 4

Opposition parties are competitive, and in 2017, opposition candidates took a significant portion of the vote in both the legislative and presidential elections. However, the many serious irregularities surrounding the TSE's administration of the 2017 presidential election prompted EU and OAS election monitors to question the validity of the vote count, and the opposition insisted that a PN-aligned TSE had denied the opposition candidate victory in the presidential race.

B3. Are the people's political choices free from domination by the military, foreign powers, religious hierarchies, economic oligarchies, or any other powerful group that is not democratically accountable? 1 / 4

Political and economic elites have traditionally exerted significant influence over political parties, limiting people's political choices. The military, after decades of ruling Honduras, remains politically powerful. President Hernández's appointments of military officials to civilian posts, many related to security, have underscored that influence. There were numerous reports of vote buying during the 2017 polling period.

B4. Do various segments of the population (including ethnic, religious, gender, LGBT, and other relevant groups) have full political rights and electoral opportunities? 2 / 4

All adult citizens may vote, and voting is compulsory. Ethnic minorities remain underrepresented in Honduras' political system and in the political sphere generally, though there have been modest efforts by the government to encourage their participation and representation. Nongovernmental organizations (NGOs) have also worked to improve minority representation in government. After being criticized for failing to do so in past elections, the TSE in 2017 printed voter information materials in indigenous and Afro-Honduran languages. However, no representatives of the Afro-Honduran (Garifuna) population were elected to Congress in 2017.

Women are also underrepresented in politics. The TSE has struggled to implement parity laws. In the 2017 elections, women won 27 of 128 congressional races and 23 of 298 mayoral posts. However, women's rights groups are becoming more visible in the political sphere.

C. FUNCTIONING OF GOVERNMENT: 5 / 12

C1. Do the freely elected head of government and national legislative representatives determine the policies of the government? 2 / 4

In 2014, the Hernández administration eliminated five cabinet-level ministries and created seven umbrella ministries in an effort to cut costs. Critics have argued that the restructuring concentrated power in too few hands. Two new executive decrees passed in March 2018 further consolidated power in the executive branch.

The opposition's ability to prevent the ruling party from achieving a legislative majority has forced political parties to form coalitions to pass legislation.

While the results of the 2017 presidential election were hotly disputed, stakeholders accepted the results of the year's legislative elections. The new government began its term in January.

C2. Are safeguards against official corruption strong and effective? 2 / 4

Corruption remains rampant in Honduras, but some safeguards have been implemented to address the issue. In December 2018, the mandate of the Special Commission for Purging and Transformation of the National Police was extended through January 2022, following its success in removing corrupt police officials. By the end of 2018, the commission's work had resulted in the removal of over 5,000 police officers for misconduct.

The MACCIH, which was established in 2016, has since helped facilitate the approval of new anticorruption legislation aimed at preventing illicit campaign donations. However, there are reports that political elites have taken efforts to undermine or interfere with its work. The head of the MACCIH, Juan Jiménez Mayor, resigned in February, citing hostility from the government and a lack of support from the OAS, which backs the panel. In May, the Supreme Court ruled that the public prosecutor's new anticorruption agency, the Fiscal Unit against Impunity and Corruption (UFECIC), which has worked closely with the MACCIH, was unconstitutional. Civil society activists assailed the decision as an attack on the anticorruption framework. However, the Public Prosecutor's Office responded to the ruling by stating that if the MACCIH was judged to be constitutional, then the UFECIC must also be constitutional, and the latter body continued its work.

In June, the MACCIH and the UFECIC announced charges against 38 government officials and politicians, who are accused of misusing public funds for the president's 2013 campaign, as well as opposition campaigns. The inquiry, known as the Pandora Case, has implicated high-ranking members of the ruling PN and opposition PL, a number of former government ministers, members of Congress, and the president's brother-in-law.

C3. Does the government operate with openness and transparency? 1 / 4

Government operations are generally opaque. Journalists and interest groups have difficulty obtaining information from the government. Secrecy laws passed in 2014 allow authorities to withhold information on security and national defense for up to 25 years. The laws cover information regarding the military police budget, which is funded by a security tax, as well as information related to the Supreme Court and the Foreign Affairs and International Cooperation Directorate.

CIVIL LIBERTIES: 26 / 60
D. FREEDOM OF EXPRESSION AND BELIEF: 9 / 16
D1. Are there free and independent media? 1 / 4

Authorities systematically violate the constitution's press freedom guarantees. Reporters and outlets covering sensitive topics or who are perceived as critical of authorities risk assaults, threats, blocked transmissions, and harassment. A 2017 reform to antiterrorism provisions in the Penal Code justified the jailing of journalists for inciting terrorism or hate. In September 2018, Congress voted to annul the law.

Threats and assaults of journalists remained common during the year. In February, reporter César Omar Silva of the Une TV channel was attacked during a live television broadcast. In August, radio host Sandra Maribel Sánchez reported that she received death threats after airing a segment critical of the government's health policies.

D2. Are individuals free to practice and express their religious faith or nonbelief in public and private? 4 / 4

Religious freedom is generally respected in Honduras.

D3. Is there academic freedom, and is the educational system free from extensive political indoctrination? 2 / 4

Academic freedom is undermined by criminal groups, who control all or parts of schools in some areas and subject staff to extortion schemes. Authorities sometimes move to suppress student demonstrations by arresting participants and dispersing the events, and violent clashes between police and student protesters sometimes occur. Student demonstrators at the National Autonomous University of Honduras (UNAH) in Tegucigalpa clashed with riot police in July and August 2018 as they occupied the campus to demand lower fuel costs and subsidized public transport. Police fired tear gas into the demonstration.

D4. Are individuals free to express their personal views on political or other sensitive topics without fear of surveillance or retribution? 2 / 4

Under the Special Law on Interception of Private Communications, passed in 2011, the government can intercept online and telephone messages. Violence, threats, and intimidation by state and nonstate actors curtails open and free private discussion among the general population.

E. ASSOCIATIONAL AND ORGANIZATIONAL RIGHTS: 4 / 12
E1. Is there freedom of assembly? 1 / 4

Freedom of assembly is constitutionally protected, but demonstrations are often met with a violent police response. In late 2017, following the elections, 23 protesters were killed in a police crackdown on demonstrations against the results, and hundreds were arrested. Election-related protests continued into January 2018, with police firing tear gas into protesters in Tegucigalpa and opening fire on a demonstration in the town of Saba, killing a man.

E2. Is there freedom for nongovernmental organizations, particularly those that are engaged in human rights- and governance-related work? 1 / 4

NGOs and their staff face significant threats, including harassment, surveillance, smear campaigns aimed at undermining their work, detention, and violence. Human rights defenders who work on environmental and land rights issues are particularly vulnerable to violence and harassment. In April 2018, human rights lawyer Carlos Hernández was shot and killed by unknown assailants at his office in Tela. Hernández was defending the mayor of Arizona, who had been charged with illegally occupying government property in protest of a hydroelectric project. The Inter-American Commission on Human Rights (IACHR) reported that between January 2014 and August 2018, at least 65 human rights defenders were murdered, and over 1,232 attacks against human rights defenders were documented between 2016 and 2017.

E3. Is there freedom for trade unions and similar professional or labor organizations? 2 / 4

Labor unions are well organized and can strike, though labor actions have resulted in clashes with security forces. The government does not always honor formal agreements entered with public-sector unions. Union leaders and labor activists in both the public and private sector face harassment, violence, and dismissal for their activities. A March 2018 report published by the Solidarity Center and the Network against Antiunion Violence found that between January 2015 and February 2018, 69 people were victimized by antiunion violence, which included threats, murders, and forced disappearances of union leaders.

F. RULE OF LAW: 5 / 16
F1. Is there an independent judiciary? 1 / 4

Political and business elites exert excessive influence over the judiciary, including the Supreme Court. Judicial appointments are made with little transparency. Judges have been removed from their posts for political reasons, and a number of legal professionals have been killed in recent years. Prosecutors and whistleblowers handling corruption cases are often subject to threats of violence.

In a controversial move in 2012, Congress voted to remove four of the five justices in the Supreme Court's constitutional chamber after they ruled a police reform law unconstitutional. In 2013, the legislature granted itself the power to remove from office the president, Supreme Court justices, legislators, and other officials. It also curtailed the power of the Supreme Court's constitutional chamber and revoked the right of citizens to challenge the constitutionality of laws. These moves laid the groundwork for the controversial 2015 constitutional change that allowed for the reelection of Juan Orlando Hernández in 2017.

F2. Does due process prevail in civil and criminal matters? 2 / 4

Due process is limited due to a compromised judiciary and a corrupt and often inept police force, in which many officers have engaged in criminal activities including drug trafficking and extortion. The government has increasingly utilized the armed forces to combat crime and violence. Arbitrary arrests and detentions are common, as is lengthy pretrial detention. In 2017, authorities established several new courts in an attempt to address lengthy trial delays. Authorities in the armed forces have dishonorably discharged members accused of rights violations before their trials have taken place.

In June 2018, Congress reelected Attorney General Óscar Chinchilla in a process that was widely criticized for alleged interference by the president and members of Congress, as well as a lack of transparency. Members of Congress who were under investigation for corruption were involved in the selection process, which, according to legal experts, created conflicts of interest.

In November, a court found seven of the eight suspects in the 2016 killing of indigenous rights activist Berta Cáceres guilty of murder. Among those convicted were two officials with a company constructing the hydroelectric dam Cáceres had opposed and former members of the military. Although rights activists viewed the convictions as a step forward in achieving justice for slain human rights defenders, they expressed concern that the masterminds of the crime had not been identified.

F3. Is there protection from the illegitimate use of physical force and freedom from war and insurgencies? 1 / 4

The number of homicides declined slightly in 2018 to 3,682, down from 3,864 homicides in 2017. However, violent crime and gang violence remain serious problems, and have prompted large-scale migration out of Honduras. Many parents opt to send their children towards the United States to avoid gang recruitment, and those who return to their neighborhoods are often targeted by gangs, and in some cases, killed for fleeing the community.

In response to widespread violence, the government has empowered the Military Police of Public Order (PMOP) and other security forces to combat security threats, and these units often employ excessive force when conducting security operations.

Prisons are overcrowded and underequipped, and prison violence remains rampant due in large part to the presence of gangs.

F4. Do laws, policies, and practices guarantee equal treatment of various segments of the population? 1 / 4

Violence and discrimination against LGBT (lesbian, gay, bisexual, and transgender) people and indigenous and Garifuna populations persist, and while antidiscrimination laws are on the books, in practice victims of such abuses have little recourse. In August 2018, the IACHR reported 177 murders of LGBT people in the previous five years, which resulted in 65 investigations and no convictions.

Honduras has among the highest femicide rates in the world, and few such murders are investigated. According to the UNAH, 380 women were murdered in 2018.

G. PERSONAL AUTONOMY AND INDIVIDUAL RIGHTS: 8 / 16

G1. Do individuals enjoy freedom of movement, including the ability to change their place of residence, employment, or education? 2 / 4

While authorities generally do not restrict free movement, ongoing violence and impunity have reduced personal autonomy for the country's residents. Those living in gang-controlled territories face extortion, and dangerous conditions limit free movement and options for education and employment. The Internal Displacement Monitoring Center estimated that there were 190,000 internally displaced people (IDPs) in Honduras as of the end of 2018, which was largely a result of gang activity, death threats, and extortion.

G2. Are individuals able to exercise the right to own property and establish private businesses without undue interference from state or nonstate actors? 2 / 4

Corruption, crime, and gang activity inhibits the ability to conduct business activities freely and dissuades entrepreneurs from establishing new businesses. Those who work in the transportation sector (taxi and bus drivers) are notable targets of gangs, but many are unable to flee for fear of retaliatory violence against themselves and their families.

G3. Do individuals enjoy personal social freedoms, including choice of marriage partner and size of family, protection from domestic violence, and control over appearance? 2 / 4

Same-sex marriage remains illegal in Honduras. In August 2018, Congress approved several articles of a bill that would ban same-sex couples from adopting children. The legislation awaited final passage at year's end. LGBT activists argued that the bill was unnecessary, since only married couples are allowed to adopt and same-sex marriage is illegal, and that the legislation was meant to stoke further hostility and discrimination against LGBT people.

Domestic violence remains widespread, and most such attacks go unpunished.

G4. Do individuals enjoy equality of opportunity and freedom from economic exploitation? 2 / 4

Lack of socioeconomic opportunities combined with high levels of crime and violence limit social mobility for most Hondurans, and exacerbate income inequality. High youth unemployment and low levels of education help to perpetuate the cycle of crime and violence.

Human trafficking is a significant issue in Honduras, which serves as a source country for women and children forced into prostitution; adults and children are also vulnerable to forced labor in the agriculture, mining, and other sectors, and as domestic servants.

Hungary

Population: 9,800,000
Capital: Budapest
Political Rights Rating: 3
Civil Liberties Rating: 3 ↓
Freedom Rating: 3.0
Freedom Status: Partly Free
Electoral Democracy: Yes

Status Change: Hungary's status declined from Free to Partly Free due to sustained attacks on the country's democratic institutions by Prime Minister Viktor Orbán's Fidesz party, which has used its parliamentary supermajority to impose restrictions on or assert control over the opposition, the media, religious groups, academia, NGOs, the courts, asylum seekers, and the private sector since 2010.

Overview: After taking power in 2010 elections, Prime Minister Viktor Orbán's Alliance of Young Democrats–Hungarian Civic Union (Fidesz) party pushed through constitutional and legal changes that have allowed it to consolidate control over the country's independent institutions. More recently, the Fidesz-led government has moved to institute policies that hamper the operations of opposition groups, journalists, universities, and nongovernmental organizations (NGOs) whose perspectives it finds unfavorable.

KEY DEVELOPMENTS IN 2018:

- Fidesz regained its two-thirds majority in April's parliamentary elections. The party's campaign was characterized by harsh antimigrant rhetoric and characterizations of Orbán as a defender of "traditional" Christian values in Europe. The opposition's ability to challenge Fidesz was significantly hampered by the ruling coalition's mobilization of state resources, media bias, and restrictions that affected opposition access to the advertising market.
- The State Audit Office (ÁSZ) issued fines against six opposition parties in January, which the parties had little opportunity to challenge. The treasury and tax authority suspended collection of the fines until after the elections.
- Constitutional amendments enacted during the year included provisions that make it the obligation of all state organs to defend Christian culture, and established new legal grounds for constraints on freedom of assembly.
- The government's continued refusal to sign an international agreement on the status of Central European University (CEU), a postgraduate institution with dual American-Hungarian accreditation, effectively forced the university out of Hungary.

POLITICAL RIGHTS: 27 / 40 (−1)

A. ELECTORAL PROCESS: 9 / 12

A1. Was the current head of government or other chief national authority elected through free and fair elections? 3 / 4

The National Assembly elects both the president and the prime minister, meaning the democratic legitimacy of these votes rests largely on the fairness of parliamentary elections. The president's duties are mainly ceremonial, but he or she may influence appointments and return legislation for further consideration before signing it into law. János Áder, a founding member of Fidesz, has been president since 2012, having won a second five-year term in 2017. Orbán has been prime minister since 2010, winning reelection in 2014 and 2018.

A2. Were the current national legislative representatives elected through free and fair elections? 3 / 4

Voters elect representatives every four years to a 199-seat, unicameral National Assembly under a mixed system of proportional and direct representation (106 from single-member districts and 93 from compensatory party lists). The coalition of Fidesz and its junior partner, the Christian Democratic People's Party (KDNP), won the April 2018 parliamentary elections with 49.3 percent of the vote, capturing exactly two-thirds (133) of the seats. The far-right Movement for a Better Hungary (Jobbik) took 26 seats, a coalition led by the center-left Hungarian Socialist Party (MSZP) won 20 seats, and smaller parties and individuals divided the remainder.

The report of a limited election observation mission from the Organization for Security and Co-operation in Europe (OSCE) said the elections were generally well administered, but it noted an "overlap between state and ruling party resources," and added that opaque campaign finance, media bias, and "intimidating and xenophobic rhetoric" also hampered voters' ability to make informed choices. While there was no evidence of electoral fraud that could have affected the elections' outcome, some irregularities were reported, and the OSCE found that rigid adherence to formal regulations by the National Election Commission (NVB) had in effect limited access to legal remedy.

A3. Are the electoral laws and framework fair, and are they implemented impartially by the relevant election management bodies? 3 / 4

Members of the NVB are nominated by the president and confirmed to nine-year terms by the parliament. There was no formal parliamentary debate or public consultation process to inform the selection of current NVB members, and many observers have raised concerns about the body's impartiality. The OSCE report on the 2018 elections noted that the NVB tended to rule in favor of the ruling party when confronted with questions about whether government advertising materials benefited the ruling coalition. The OSCE also indicated that citizens were not permitted to participate in election observation at polling places, and that "intimidating rhetoric by the government" discouraged public involvement in election-related activities. Combined with a lower level of opposition involvement, this resulted in numerous local election commissions operating without an opposition or nonpartisan presence for the 2018 polls.

After Fidesz took power in 2010, it used its parliamentary supermajority to redraw constituency boundaries in its own favor. Electoral bodies frequently reject referendums proposed by the opposition while approving government proposals of dubious constitutionality, including a controversial 2016 referendum on a European Union (EU) asylum quota plan.

In 2018, Prime Minister Orbán publicly criticized electoral law enforcement actions that disadvantaged the ruling coalition. These included a Supreme Court decision to invalidate votes received in irregular envelopes, as a decision to permit them likely would have resulted in an additional Fidesz seat in the parliament. The prime minister also publicly shamed the head of the electoral commission after it fined him for campaigning in kindergartens.

B. POLITICAL PLURALISM AND PARTICIPATION: 11 / 16 (−1)

B1. Do the people have the right to organize in different political parties or other competitive political groupings of their choice, and is the system free of undue obstacles to the rise and fall of these competing parties or groupings? 3 / 4

Political parties can organize legally, but they face some practical impediments in their efforts to garner popular support. Opposition parties are disadvantaged by the politicized distortion of the advertising market, including the market for the country's many billboards. Individual politicians face smear campaigns in progovernment media. Changes to the party registration and financing systems that took effect ahead of the 2014 parliamentary polls encouraged the registration of new parties, but the reforms were criticized as a means for Fidesz to divide the opposition. Similarly in 2018, the presence of a number of small, previously unknown parties on the parliamentary ballot prompted widespread suspicion. Several such parties had no website or visible campaign presence and were deemed "fake parties" by many observers, who suggested that their formation was encouraged by Fidesz to fragment the opposition vote and confuse voters.

Authorities have interfered with peaceful political activities by opposition figures. In December 2018, as a series of opposition rallies were taking place in Budapest, opposition lawmakers invoked their legal right to access public buildings in order to enter the headquarters of the public broadcaster, where they insisted that a list of the protesters' demands be read on the air. Security agents then forcibly removed two of the lawmakers, one of whom sustained minor injuries in the scuffle.

B2. Is there a realistic opportunity for the opposition to increase its support or gain power through elections? 2 / 4 (−1)

The Fidesz-led ruling coalition has dominated the political landscape since the 2010 elections. The opposition remains fragmented, and opposition parties increasingly contend with obstacles and restrictions that detract from their ability to gain power through elections.

These include unequal access to media and media smear campaigns, politicized audits, and a campaign environment skewed by the ruling coalition's mobilization of state resources.

While the 2018 parliamentary polls were generally well administered, the proliferation of obstacles faced by opposition parties and candidates diminished their ability to freely compete with Fidesz. The OSCE cited as particularly problematic the "pervasive overlap between state and ruling party resources," which often made extensive government advertising campaigns indistinguishable from Fidesz promotional materials. The ruling party also harnessed the public broadcaster to disseminate its message, with the OSCE's media monitoring mission describing "clear patterns of political bias" in its election-related programming.

A series of fines issued in January by the ÁSZ, which is led by a former Fidesz member, distracted opposition parties from their campaigns. The audit office fined six opposition parties for alleged financing violations, including Jobbik—now the largest opposition party—whose fine was equal to more than two-thirds of its annual state subsidy. The treasury and tax authority suspended the collection of the fines until after the elections, but the parties' ability to challenge the penalties was limited.

Score Change: The score declined from 3 to 2 because a variety of obstacles, including politicized audits, media bias, and the ruling party's abuse of state resources, hampered the ability of the opposition to rally support ahead of elections.

B3. Are the people's political choices free from domination by the military, foreign powers, religious hierarchies, economic oligarchies, or any other powerful group that is not democratically accountable? 3 / 4

People are largely able to participate in public affairs without encountering undue influence over their political choices. However, Fidesz has increasingly harnessed its members' political and economic power to unfairly sideline opposition groupings and prevent them from presenting a meaningful challenge to its dominant position.

B4. Do various segments of the population (including ethnic, religious, gender, LGBT, and other relevant groups) have full political rights and electoral opportunities? 3 / 4

Women are underrepresented in political life, and the share of women in the parliament remains low. Just 25 of 199 National Assembly members, or 12.56 percent, are women.

Hungary's constitution guarantees the right of ethnic minorities to form self-governing bodies, and all 13 recognized minorities have done so. Minorities can also register to vote for special minority lists—with a preferential vote threshold—in parliamentary elections, but they are then excluded from general party-list voting. One representative, a former Fidesz politician who had suspended his membership in the party, won a seat in 2018 as the elected representative of the German minority. The Romany minority has long been underrepresented in politics and government.

C. FUNCTIONING OF GOVERNMENT: 7 / 12

C1. Do the freely elected head of government and national legislative representatives determine the policies of the government? 3 / 4

Elected officials are generally able to draft and implement laws and policies without undue interference, though Fidesz continues to dominate governance through a parliamentary supermajority that it acquired in problematic elections. Prime Minister Orbán, the party's leader, exerts considerable influence over the legislature, meaning its ability to provide a check on executive power is limited.

C2. Are safeguards against official corruption strong and effective? 2 / 4

Corruption remains a problem in Hungary, and instances of high-level government corruption have not been properly investigated. For example, the prosecutor's office has been reluctant to investigate long-standing allegations that the government misused development funds provided by the EU. Influential business figures who fall out of favor with the government, such as Lajos Simicska, who once served as Fidesz party treasurer, have experienced financial and legal pressure. Transparency International's Hungarian chapter has reported that a number of companies with close ties to the government are supported primarily by public funds.

Fidesz has used legal and personnel changes to establish broad control over public institutions, including those with auditing and investigative tasks, such as the ÁSZ.

C3. Does the government operate with openness and transparency? 2 / 4

Hungary's Freedom of Information Act contains numerous exemptions, permits agencies to charge fees for the release of information, and is enforced inconsistently. In many cases, information is only made available as a result of litigation. Journalists have been banned from the parliament building at times. Major legislation is frequently rushed through to passage and enactment, leaving citizens, interest groups, and others little time to comment on it. In 2018, the government decided to take control of a significant portion of the budget of the Hungarian Academy of Sciences, and the institution was given less than an hour to comment on the development.

CIVIL LIBERTIES: 43 / 60 (−1)
D. FREEDOM OF EXPRESSION AND BELIEF: 10 / 16 (−1)
D1. Are there free and independent media? 2 / 4

The constitution protects freedom of the press, but complex and extensive media legislation enacted by Fidesz has created avenues for politicized media regulation, undermining this guarantee. While private, opposition-aligned media outlets exist, national, regional, and local media are increasingly dominated by progovernment outlets, which are frequently used to smear political opponents. The closure in 2016 of Hungary's largest independent daily, *Népszabadság*, represented a particularly serious blow to media diversity. In 2018, a number of independent, conservative-leaving outlets owned by Simicska, including the daily *Magyar Nemzet*, the weekly *Heti Válasz*, and the broadcast station Lánchíd Rádió, effectively ceased their operations after the year's elections, while his HírTV channel was taken over by government loyalists.

Late in the year, the owners of most progovernment media operations announced that they would donate their holdings to a new foundation, effectively creating a massive progovernment media conglomerate composed of almost 500 titles and outlets. The government exempted the transactions from the usual antitrust review, which would almost certainly have led to their suspension if conducted in accordance with the law.

Government advertising and sponsorships favor progovernment outlets, leaving independent and critical outlets in a financially precarious position.

D2. Are individuals free to practice and express their religious faith or nonbelief in public and private? 3 / 4 (−1)

The constitution guarantees religious freedom and provides for the separation of church and state, though these guarantees were weakened in the 2011 version of the constitution, whose preamble makes direct references to Christianity. Constitutional amendments enacted in 2018 reinforced those references, making it the obligation of all state organs to protect "Christian culture."

After the adoption of a 2011 law on churches, some 300 religious communities lost their status as incorporated churches—with which the state cooperates on community affairs, among other privileges—and were relegated to the new category of "religious organizations." The law made it the task of the parliament to determine which communities are recognized as churches, and many of the deregistered churches have not reacquired their previous status in the years since.

Government-led xenophobic campaigns in recent years have fueled anti-Muslim sentiment, which in turn has discouraged the open practice of Islam.

Score Change: The score declined from 4 to 3 because a number of churches have been unable to regain their previous status after it was revoked under a 2011 law, and because growing anti-Muslim sentiment has discouraged the open practice of Islam.

D3. Is there academic freedom, and is the educational system free from extensive political indoctrination? 2 / 4

The Fidesz-led government has accelerated efforts to bring schools and universities under its close supervision. A gradual overhaul of the public education system has raised concerns about excessive government influence on school curriculums, and legislation adopted in 2014 allows for government-appointed chancellors empowered to make financial decisions at public universities. Selective support by the government of certain academic institutions also threatens academic autonomy. In 2018, the government revoked accreditation from all gender studies programs, and senior officials—including Orbán, through a spokesperson—have questioned the rationale for this field of academic study.

The government's continued refusal to sign an international agreement on the status of CEU, a postgraduate institution with dual American-Hungarian accreditation that was founded by the Hungarian-born American financier and philanthropist George Soros, effectively forced the university out of Hungary at the end of 2018. Earlier in the year, CEU had closed its free nondegree program for asylum seekers and refugees as a consequence of new anti-immigration legislation.

Progovernment media outlets have published lists of activists, academics, programs, and institutions and labeled them as "Soros agents" or "mercenaries." The ideological attacks have targeted gender studies programs, but also broader research on inequality, or simply criticism of various government proposals. The effort has encouraged self-censorship. The government's decision to assume control of a large portion of funding for the Hungarian Academy of Sciences left the entity, the leading network of research institutions in the country, uncertain about its future.

D4. Are individuals free to express their personal views on political or other sensitive topics without fear of surveillance or retribution? 3 / 4

While freedom of expression is constitutionally protected, ongoing efforts to sideline voices and perspectives that authorities find unfavorable, including many found at the Hungarian Academy of Sciences, CEU, and various NGOs and media outlets, have discouraged open criticism of the government and other politically sensitive speech.

E. ASSOCIATIONAL AND ORGANIZATIONAL RIGHTS: 10 / 12
E1. Is there freedom of assembly? 4 / 4

The constitution provides for freedom of assembly, and the government generally respects this right in practice. Fidesz's electoral victory in 2018 prompted large crowds to turn out for peaceful antigovernment demonstrations.

Constitutional amendments approved in 2018 make it easier to restrict assemblies that are deemed to infringe on the right to private life; the changes were most likely prompted by demonstrations organized in front of the prime minister's home. The amendments replaced a 1989 measure that many saw as an outdated regulation. While the new language contained some improvements, it also included excessive restrictions, including bans on gatherings that interfere with traffic (as most protests in Budapest do) and those that take place on private property without permission, which would effectively prohibit, among other things, union demonstrations on company premises. Already under the new rules, the police banned an opposition demonstration against Turkish president Recep Tayyip Erdoğan's visit in October.

E2. Is there freedom for nongovernmental organizations, particularly those that are engaged in human rights- and governance-related work? 2 / 4

NGOs whose activities conflict with government priorities have come under pressure in recent years. Since taking power, the Fidesz government has instituted burdensome registration and reporting requirements for NGOs, and police illegally raided the offices of one group, the Ökotárs Foundation, in 2015.

In 2018, the parliament adopted a measure that the government had dubbed the "Stop Soros" law, which criminalized any assistance to "illegal migration" and carries a penalty of up to a year in prison. Activity that could be punished under the law includes working with NGOs that help asylum seekers, and preparing and distributing information leaflets that address migration or the needs of migrants. The Office of the UN High Commissioner for Human Rights condemned the law as "shameful and blatantly xenophobic," while the Council of Europe's Venice Commission concluded that it "infringes upon the right to freedom of association and expression and should be repealed." The European Commission said the measure violated EU law. The Hungarian law was complemented by subsequent legislation that introduced a 25 percent tax on "financial support for immigration."

E3. Is there freedom for trade unions and similar professional or labor organizations? 4 / 4

The government recognizes workers' rights to form associations and bargain collectively. However, there are limitations on what can be considered a lawful strike, and union membership is low. Trade unions are present in less than 30 percent of workplaces, and only 9 percent of workers belong to one.

F. RULE OF LAW: 10 / 16

F1. Is there an independent judiciary? 2 / 4

Judicial independence remains a matter of concern. All of the 11 judges appointed to the Constitutional Court between 2010 and 2014 were named by the Fidesz government, and it was only well after the government temporarily lost its two-thirds parliamentary majority that one opposition party was included in discussions over the selection of four new judges, in November 2016. Rulings in recent years have favored government interests.

The powerful National Judiciary Office (OBH) is headed by Tünde Handó, a close ally of Orbán who is married to the leader of Fidesz's delegation at the European Parliament; as OBH head she has the power to make senior judicial appointments and wields great authority over disciplinary proceedings and court finances. She has long been accused of using her position to install loyalist judges. In 2018, Handó came into conflict with the judicial self-governing body, the National Judicial Council (OBT), which after electing new members at the start of the year opened an investigation into her hiring practices; by March, a related lawsuit against her was proceeding. After the Fidesz victory in the April elections, a number of judges resigned from the OBT with little explanation, prompting speculation that they had been forced out. Judge Péter Szepesházi gave numerous media interviews in which he criticized Handó for intimidating judges with the threat of disciplinary procedures; in one case he remarked that the country's judges operated in "a general climate of fear" of repercussions for ruling against Fidesz interests; Szepesházi resigned in September.

In December, the parliament approved a measure allowing the establishment of a separate system of administrative courts that would be overseen by the justice minister, prompting concerns that it could be filled with judges sympathetic to the ruling party.

In September, the European Parliament narrowly adopted a resolution that marked the first step in triggering Article 7 proceedings against Hungary, with proponents citing attacks on the judiciary as one of the justifications. The proceedings could lead to EU sanctions for the violation of fundamental values related to democracy and human rights.

F2. Does due process prevail in civil and criminal matters? 3 / 4

Due process rights are enshrined in the constitution and are generally respected. However, Handó has faced criticism for using her power as OBH head to transfer certain cases to courts of her choice. There have been concerns about the quality of lawyers appointed for defendants who are unable or unwilling to retain legal counsel on their own. There have also been reports that police frequently interrogate or attempt to interrogate suspects without the presence of a lawyer.

F3. Is there protection from the illegitimate use of physical force and freedom from war and insurgencies? 3 / 4

Overcrowding, inadequate medical care, and poor sanitation in the country's prisons and detention centers remain problems. In 2017, the government revoked its cooperation agreement with the Hungarian Helsinki Committee, a human rights organization, effectively terminating the group's access to detention facilities.

F4. Do laws, policies, and practices guarantee equal treatment of various segments of the population? 2 / 4

The rights of refugees and asylum seekers are routinely violated in Hungary, where changes to asylum policy and the construction of barriers along the country's southern border in recent years have made it extremely difficult if not impossible for people to apply for asylum and receive protection. Only two asylum seekers are formally permitted to enter the country per day. Once allowed in, asylum seekers are frequently detained in poorly equipped transit zones, and few are recognized by Hungarian authorities as refugees. A 2018 judgment by the European Court of Human Rights (ECHR) compelled the government to change its policy of denying food to migrants in transit zones who were in the process of appealing denied asylum claims; the policy was apparently designed to encourage them to drop their claims and leave. The government continues to train special police units ("border hunters") with wide powers to remove migrants from the country. The European Commission in 2015 opened infringement procedures concerning Hungary's asylum and return policies, stating that they were in violation of minimum EU standards.

Members of the Romany population, Hungary's largest ethnic minority, face widespread discrimination, societal exclusion, and poverty. Romany students continue to be segregated or improperly placed in schools for children with mental disabilities, a practice that led the European Commission to begin an infringement procedure in 2016.

Women in Hungary are subject to employment discrimination and tend to be underrepresented in high-level business positions.

G. PERSONAL AUTONOMY AND INDIVIDUAL RIGHTS: 13 / 16

G1. Do individuals enjoy freedom of movement, including the ability to change their place of residence, employment, or education? 4 / 4

There are no significant restrictions on Hungarians' freedom of travel or the ability to change their place of residence, employment, and education.

G2. Are individuals able to exercise the right to own property and establish private businesses without undue interference from state or nonstate actors? 3 / 4

Individuals have the right to own property and establish private businesses. However, the recent difficulties of business owners who have fallen out of favor with the government illustrate the extent to which business success depends on government connections.

G3. Do individuals enjoy personal social freedoms, including choice of marriage partner and size of family, protection from domestic violence, and control over appearance? 3 / 4

The government generally does not restrict social freedoms, though the constitution enshrines the concept of marriage as a union between a man and a woman. Domestic violence and spousal rape are illegal, but the definition of rape hinges on the use of force or coercion, not on lack of consent. NGOs describe government responses to violence against women as inadequate. The right to life from conception is constitutionally protected, but access to abortion remained largely unrestricted in 2018.

G4. Do individuals enjoy equality of opportunity and freedom from economic exploitation? 3 / 4

Hungary is a transit point, source, and to a lesser extent, destination for trafficked persons, including women trafficked for prostitution. Prevention, coordination efforts, and processes to identify and support victims remain inadequate, while trafficking investigations and enforcement of relevant laws are unreliable.

In December 2018, Áder signed legislation derisively known as the "slave law," which increased the number of overtime hours employers can request from workers and allowed companies to wait up to three years to pay the workers for their extra labor, extended from one year under the previous rules. The measure prompted large antigovernment protests.

Iceland

Capital: Reykjavík
Population: 400,000
Political Rights Rating: 1
Civil Liberties Rating: 1
Freedom Rating: 1.0
Freedom Status: Free
Electoral Democracy: Yes

Overview: Iceland is a parliamentary democracy with a long history of upholding political rights and civil liberties. However, links between elected representatives and business interests remain a concern, as does the concentration of private media ownership. Reports of systematic exploitation of immigrant labor have escalated considerably.

KEY DEVELOPMENTS IN 2018:
- In November, a secret recording of six leading members of Parliament making misogynistic, anti-LGBT, and ableist remarks about their colleagues at a bar in Reykjavík caused an uproar. Four of the legislators involved petitioned the Reykjavík District Court to pursue charges against the woman who leaked the recording to the press for violating their privacy, but the court dismissed their claims in December.
- In February, the Reykjavík District Court lifted a controversial 2017 injunction filed against the newspaper *Stundin,* which had blocked the publication from using documents from Glitnir Bank in reporting on the financial dealings of former prime minister Bjarni Benediktsson. The decision again allowed the paper to use the Glitnir documents in its reporting.

POLITICAL RIGHTS: 37 / 40

A. ELECTORAL PROCESS: 12 / 12

A1. Was the current head of government or other chief national authority elected through free and fair elections? 4 / 4

The president serves as a largely ceremonial chief of state, is directly elected to a four-year term, and is not subject to term limits. President Gudni Thorlacius Jóhannesson was elected in 2016, taking 39.1 percent of the vote in a field of nine candidates. The Organization for Security and Co-Operation in Europe (OSCE) deployed an assessment mission ahead of the polls, and concluded that stakeholders had a high degree of confidence in Icelandic electoral processes. However, the OSCE reaffirmed past concerns about the possibility for early voting to begin before the candidate confirmation procedures closed. The OSCE declined to monitor the poll itself, and stakeholders accepted the results.

The prime minister is head of government. The leader of the ruling party or coalition usually becomes prime minister; thus the legitimacy of the prime minister rests primarily on the conduct of the parliamentary polls. The current prime minister, Katrín Jakobsdóttir of the Left-Green Movement (LGM), took office in November 2017, following parliamentary elections that were viewed as credible by international observers.

A2. Were the current national legislative representatives elected through free and fair elections? 4 / 4

The unicameral Parliament is elected for four-year terms. The October 2017 election was the third parliamentary election in four years, following the dissolution of the governing coalition in the wake of a scandal involving then prime minister Benediktsson.

An OSCE monitoring mission found the elections well administered and in line with international standards for democratic elections. The Independence Party (IP) took a plurality of seats, with 16, the second-place LGM took 11, and the Progressive Party (PP) finished third, taking 8 seats. A new coalition government comprised of those three parties was seated following several weeks of multiparty coalition talks.

A3. Are the electoral laws and framework fair, and are they implemented impartially by the relevant election management bodies? 4 / 4

The constitution, the election law of 2000, and related legislation establish a clear and detailed framework for conducting elections. Electoral laws are implemented impartially by a variety of national- and regional-level authorities. However, the division of responsibilities between the relevant bodies is not always well defined.

An extensive constitutional reform process, launched by popular initiative in 2009, led to the drafting of a new constitution that, among other things, would harmonize the number of votes per seat in all constituencies. The draft was approved by referendum in 2012, but the initiative has since stalled in the legislature.

B. POLITICAL PLURALISM AND PARTICIPATION: 15 / 16

B1. Do the people have the right to organize in different political parties or other competitive political groupings of their choice, and is the system free of undue obstacles to the rise and fall of these competing parties or groupings? 4 / 4

Political parties form and operate freely, and rise and fall according to political developments and the will of the public. In 2017, two new parties gained representation in the legislature: the Center Party (CP) and the People's Party.

B2. Is there a realistic opportunity for the opposition to increase its support or gain power through elections? 4 / 4

Opposition parties have the ability to gain power through free elections, as evidenced by the LGM's gains in 2017 and inclusion in the coalition government. However, the IP has only rarely lost its status as the largest party in Parliament, and is usually part of the ruling coalition.

B3. Are the people's political choices free from domination by the military, foreign powers, religious hierarchies, economic oligarchies, or any other powerful group that is not democratically accountable? 3 / 4

No military, foreign, or religious entities exert undemocratic influence over voters' choices. However, some politicians and parties are closely linked with various business sectors, resulting in avenues for well-coordinated business interests to exert influence over politics.

B4. Do various segments of the population (including ethnic, religious, gender, LGBT, and other relevant groups) have full political rights and electoral opportunities? 4 / 4

All Icelandic citizens of adult age may vote in local and national elections. Foreigners can vote in municipal elections if they have been residents for at least five years, or three years if they are citizens of Nordic countries. The interests of women and LGBT (lesbian, gay, bisexual, and transgender) people are well represented in politics. In Reykjavík´s May 2018 municipal elections, an unprecedented number of immigrants ran for office.

C. FUNCTIONING OF GOVERNMENT: 10 / 12

C1. Do the freely elected head of government and national legislative representatives determine the policies of the government? 4 / 4

The freely elected head of government and national legislative representatives determine the policies of the government.

C2. Are safeguards against official corruption strong and effective? 3 / 4

Corrupt behavior by public officials is often exposed by the media, and Iceland has robust anticorruption laws. However, officials implicated in corrupt or unsavory behavior often continue to serve in government. For example, while former prime minister Sigmundur Davíd Gunnlaugsson resigned in 2016 after the Panama Papers revealed that he and his wife held millions of dollars in offshore accounts, he went on to form a new party, the CP, and regained a seat in Parliament in 2017.

At the beginning of 2018, Prime Minister Jakobsdóttir commissioned a report to garner recommendations for improving public confidence in the government. The report's findings, released in September, called for legislation to facilitate access to information about public institutions and protection for whistleblowers in both the public and private sectors. A report published by the Council of Europe's Group of States against Corruption (GRECO) in April criticized Iceland for inadequate enforcement of rules regarding conflicts of interest for government officials, and urged the government to strengthen rules on accepting gifts from third parties.

C3. Does the government operate with openness and transparency? 3 / 4

Iceland's Information Act, passed in 2013 to strengthen existing legislation on transparency and freedom of information, has been criticized by press freedom advocates as having weak provisions. Public officials have sought to conceal information that may be embarrassing or implicate them in wrongdoing.

In November 2018, six leading members of Parliament from the PP and CP were secretly recorded making misogynistic, anti-LGBT, and ableist remarks about their colleagues at a bar in Reykjavík. An uproar ensued after the woman who recorded the conversation leaked it to the media. Four of the legislators involved petitioned the Reykjavík District Court to pursue charges against her for violating their privacy, but the court dismissed their claims in December.

CIVIL LIBERTIES: 57 / 60 (–1)
D. FREEDOM OF EXPRESSION AND BELIEF 15 / 16
D1. Are there free and independent media? 3 / 4

The constitution guarantees freedom of speech and of the press. The autonomous Icelandic National Broadcasting Service (RÚV) competes with private radio and television stations. Private media ownership is concentrated, with the media company 365 controlling most of the major private television and radio outlets, as well as the free newspaper *Frettabladid*, which enjoys the highest circulation in the print market.

In 2017, just prior to the elections, media broke the story that former prime minister Benediktsson had sold his shares in Glitnir Bank just hours before the financial crash of 2008. Soon afterward, in response to a request from Glitnir's bankruptcy estate, the Reykjavík district commissioner issued an injunction against the paper *Stundin* and the company Reykjavík Media barring use of documents from Glitnir's estate in media coverage. Press freedom advocates blasted the ruling, characterizing it as a move to put the interests of banks above journalists' duty to inform the public. In February 2018, the Reykjavík District Court lifted the injunction, again allowing the paper to use the Glitnir documents in its reporting. The case highlighted ongoing concerns about the growing use of legal mechanisms to hamstring reporting on issues relevant to the public interest.

D2. Are individuals free to practice and express their religious faith or nonbelief in public and private? 4 / 4

The constitution provides for freedom of religion, which is generally upheld in practice. About three-quarters of Icelanders belong to the Evangelical Lutheran Church. The state supports the church through a special tax, which citizens can choose to direct to the University of Iceland instead.

In January 2018, PP legislators proposed a bill that would ban circumcision of male children for nonmedical reasons. Opponents argued that the bill discriminates against practitioners of Judaism and Islam. In April, the Judicial Affairs and Education Committee decided not to refer the bill to the floor of Parliament for debate.

D3. Is there academic freedom, and is the educational system free from extensive political indoctrination? 4 / 4

Academic freedom is respected, and the education system is free of excessive political involvement.

D4. Are individuals free to express their personal views on political or other sensitive topics without fear of surveillance or retribution? 4 / 4

People in Iceland may freely discuss personal views on sensitive topics without fear or surveillance or retribution.

E. ASSOCIATIONAL AND ORGANIZATIONAL RIGHTS: 12 / 12
E1. Is there freedom of assembly? 4 / 4

Freedom of assembly is generally upheld.

E2. Is there freedom for nongovernmental organizations, particularly those that are engaged in human rights- and governance-related work? 4 / 4

Nongovernmental organizations (NGOs) may form, operate, and fundraise freely, and frequently inform policy discussions.

E3. Is there freedom for trade unions and similar professional or labor organizations? 4 / 4

The labor movement is robust, with more than 80 percent of all eligible workers belonging to unions. All unions have the right to strike, with the exception of the National Police Federation.

F. RULE OF LAW: 15 / 16
F1. Is there an independent judiciary? 4 / 4

The judiciary is generally independent. Judges are proposed by an Interior Ministry selection committee and formally appointed by the president, and are not subject to term limits.

F2. Does due process prevail in civil and criminal matters? 4 / 4

The law does not provide for trial by jury, but many trials and appeals use panels of several judges. Prison conditions generally meet international standards.

F3. Is there protection from the illegitimate use of physical force and freedom from war and insurgencies? 4 / 4

Police are generally responsive to incidents of violence. War and insurgencies are not a concern.

F4. Do laws, policies, and practices guarantee equal treatment of various segments of the population? 3 / 4

The constitution states that all people shall be treated equally before the law, regardless of sex, religion, ethnic origin, race, or other status. However, in 2017, the European Commission against Racism and Intolerance (ECRI) noted an apparent rise in racist discourse in Iceland in recent years.

The rate of refugee recognition in Iceland is very low compared to other northern European countries. In April 2018, the Directorate of Immigration ordered the deportation of a Nigerian asylum seeker who had arrived from Italy in 2017, as well as her infant son, who was born in Iceland. Critics argued that the deportation of the child would violate Icelandic law, which states that "a foreigner born in Iceland, who has since resided permanently and continuously in Iceland, cannot be denied entry to Iceland or expelled from Iceland." In June, the Foreign Affairs Appeals Committee reversed the deportation decision, allowing both the mother and son to remain in the country.

G. PERSONAL AUTONOMY AND INDIVIDUAL RIGHTS: 15 / 16 (-1)

G1. Do individuals enjoy freedom of movement, including the ability to change their place of residence, employment, or education? 4 / 4

Freedom of movement is constitutionally protected and respected in practice.

G2. Are individuals able to exercise the right to own property and establish private businesses without undue interference from state or nonstate actors? 4 / 4

There is generally no undue government interference in business or private property ownership.

G3. Do individuals enjoy personal social freedoms, including choice of marriage partner and size of family, protection from domestic violence, and control over appearance? 4 / 4

Parliament unanimously passed a law legalizing same-sex marriage in 2010, and a 2006 law established full and equal rights for same-sex couples in matters of adoption and assisted pregnancy. A comprehensive law on transgender issues adopted in 2012 aimed to simplify legal issues pertaining to gender reassignment surgery, to ensure full and equal rights for transgender people, and to guarantee relevant health care.

G4. Do individuals enjoy equality of opportunity and freedom from economic exploitation? 3 / 4 (-1)

Citizens generally enjoy fair access to economic opportunity. However, the systematic exploitation of migrant workers, including underpaying employees and denying overtime, has become a significant problem in recent years, especially in the tourism industry. Employers who exploit workers have largely acted with impunity due to an inadequate government response. Wage theft is not punishable by law. There are reports of forced labor, primarily involving migrants, in the construction and service industries, and of forced sex work in nightclubs.

While human trafficking was criminalized in 2009, the US State Department reported in 2018 that no one has been prosecuted or convicted of human trafficking in Iceland since 2010.

Score Change: The score declined from 4 to 3 because systematic exploitation of immigrant workers has emerged as a significant problem, and the legal framework and institutional capacity for addressing it is inadequate.

India

Population: 1,371,300,000
Capital: New Delhi
Political Rights Rating: 2
Civil Liberties Rating: 3
Freedom Rating: 2.5
Freedom Status: Free
Electoral Democracy: Yes

Overview: India maintains a robust electoral democracy with a competitive multiparty system at federal and state levels, though politics are beset by corruption. The constitution guarantees freedom of expression and the news media are vibrant. However, harassment and violence against journalists has increased under the administration of Prime Minister Narendra Modi and his right-leaning, Hindu nationalist Bharatiya Janata party (BJP), as have religiously motivated attacks against non-Hindus. India's minority groups—notably Muslims, scheduled castes (Dalits), and scheduled tribes (Adivasis)—enjoy legal equality and sometimes benefit from affirmative action programs. However, they remain economically and socially marginalized.

Note: The numerical ratings and status listed above do not reflect conditions in Indian-controlled Kashmir, which is examined in a separate report.

KEY DEVELOPMENTS IN 2018:
- The performance of the ruling BJP was mixed across several state elections held during the year, raising questions about whether it can maintain its dominance in upcoming national elections set for 2019.
- In July, the citizenship status of four million residents of Assam State was thrown in doubt after their names were excluded from a draft of the National Register of Citizens (NRC). Those affected, largely Bengali-speaking Muslims, must produce documentation that they or their ancestors came to the state before Bangladesh became independent in 1971. Accessing such documentation may not feasible for those living in poor communities wracked by illiteracy and displacement.
- In September, India's Supreme Court determined that a colonial-era law could no longer be interpreted to criminalize consensual homosexual acts.
- Violent attacks continued against minorities alleged to be involved in the mistreatment of cows.

POLITICAL RIGHTS: 35 / 40

A. ELECTORAL PROCESS: 12 / 12

A1. Was the current head of government or other chief national authority elected through free and fair elections? 4 / 4

Executive elections and selection procedures are generally regarded as free and fair. Executive power is vested in a prime minister, who is elected by members of the majority party in the Lok Sabha (House of the People), and a cabinet. Modi was sworn in as prime minister after the victory of the BJP and its NDA coalition in 2014 Lok Sabha elections. He succeeded Manmohan Singh of the Indian National Congress (known simply as Congress), who had been in office since 2004.

The president, who plays a largely symbolic role, is chosen for a five-year term by state and national lawmakers. Current president Ram Nath Kovind, a member of the lowest-caste Dalit community and a veteran BJP politician, was elected in 2017.

A2. Were the current national legislative representatives elected through free and fair elections? 4 / 4

Members of the lower house of Parliament, the 545-seat Lok Sabha, are directly elected in single-member constituencies for five-year terms, except for two appointed members representing Indians of European descent. The Lok Sabha determines the leadership and composition of the government.

The most recent Lok Sabha elections were held in 2014. The BJP won 282 seats and its NDA coalition won 336 seats, ensuring a stable majority for the new government. Voter turnout was 66 percent. Prime Minister Narendra Modi, a three-term chief minister from the western state of Gujarat, was sworn in as prime minister. The elections were broadly free and fair.

A3. Are the electoral laws and framework fair, and are they implemented impartially by the relevant election management bodies? 4 / 4

Elections for the central and state governments are overseen by the independent Election Commission of India. The head of the commission is appointed by the president and serves a fixed six-year term. The commission is generally respected and thought to function without undue political interference, although its impartiality and competence have been called into question, with critics saying it has selected election dates that favor the BJP. In 2018, officials with both BJP and Congress shared on social media the date of a regional election before the commission had announced it. The party officials said they had learned the dates from media reports, but the incident nevertheless prompting criticism of the commission, which pledged an investigation.

B. POLITICAL PLURALISM AND PARTICIPATION: 14 / 16

B1. Do the people have the right to organize in different political parties or other competitive political groupings of their choice, and is the system free of undue obstacles to the rise and fall of these competing parties or groupings? 4 / 4

Political life is vibrant. Citizens are generally able to form political parties and assert party membership or their own candidacies without interference. However, the opaque financing of political parties—notably through electoral bonds that allow donors to obscure their identities—remains a source of concern.

B2. Is there a realistic opportunity for the opposition to increase its support or gain power through elections? 4 / 4

India hosts a dynamic multiparty system. Alternation of power between parties is common at the central and state levels. In the 2014 Lok Sabha elections, the two main national parties won only about 50 percent of the vote combined. However, the translation of votes to seats put the BJP in the clear majority in the lower house, marking the first time a single party won a majority of seats in the Lok Sabha since 1984. February 2018 state assembly elections brought the BJP to power in three northeastern states. However, Congress posted strong performances in three key states in elections later in the year, casting doubt on the dominance of the BJP in the run-up to 2019 national elections.

B3. Are the people's political choices free from domination by the military, foreign powers, religious hierarchies, economic oligarchies, or any other powerful group that is not democratically accountable? 3 / 4

Political participation, while generally free, is hampered by insurgent violence in some areas. Indian society is heavily hierarchical, and conservative religious, caste, and gender norms can influence voting. Separately, in some areas political actors have harnessed polarizing topics, frequently involving religion, to inflame communal tensions with the goal of driving voters to support one party or another without giving full consideration to that party's positions.

B4. Do various segments of the population (including ethnic, religious, gender, LGBT, and other relevant groups) have full political rights and electoral opportunities? 3 / 4

Women, religious and ethnic minorities, and the poor vote in large numbers and have opportunities to gain political representation. Twenty-two Muslims were elected to the Lok Sabha in 2014. Quotas for the chamber ensure that 84 and 47 seats are reserved for the so-called scheduled castes (Dalits) and scheduled tribes (Adivasis), respectively. There are similar quotas for these historically disadvantaged groups in state assemblies and in local bodies, as well as quotas for women representatives. However, marginalized segments of the population face practical disadvantages in achieving true political representation.

C. FUNCTIONING OF GOVERNMENT: 9 / 12

C1. Do the freely elected head of government and national legislative representatives determine the policies of the government? 4 / 4

Elected leaders have the authority to govern in practice, but political corruption has a negative effect on government efficiency.

C2. Are safeguards against official corruption strong and effective? 2 / 4

Politicians and civil servants at all levels are regularly caught accepting bribes or engaging in other corrupt behavior. While large-scale scandals often come to light, a great deal of corruption is thought to go unnoticed and unpunished.

The Lokpal and Lokayuktas Act, which the president signed into law in 2014, creates independent government bodies tasked with receiving complaints of corruption against public servants or politicians, investigating claims, and pursuing convictions through the courts. Modi and members of his government have signaled support for the law, although implementation has been slow, and key oversight positions it mandates remain vacant.

C3. Does the government operate with openness and transparency? 3 / 4

The landmark 2005 Right to Information (RTI) Act is widely used to improve transparency and expose corrupt activities. Between 4 and 6 million requests are made under the act each year. Since the passage of the RTI Act, however, close to 80 right-to-information users and activists have been murdered, and hundreds have been assaulted or harassed, according to the National Campaign for People's Right to Information. Police stand accused of turning a blind eye to these attacks.

In 2015, the Lok Sabha adopted amendments to the 2014 Whistleblowers Protection Act. Opposition members criticized those changes, and subsequent ones, for undermining the act's effectiveness, which was already regarded as limited in scope.

CIVIL LIBERTIES: 40 / 60 (−2)

D. FREEDOM OF EXPRESSION AND BELIEF: 11 / 16 (−2)

D1. Are there free and independent media? 2 / 4 (−1)

The private media are vigorous and diverse, and investigations and scrutiny of politicians are common. Nevertheless, revelations of close relationships between politicians, business executives, and lobbyists, on one hand, and leading media personalities and owners of media outlets, on the other, have dented public confidence in the press. Authorities have used security, defamation, and hate speech laws, as well as contempt-of-court charges, to curb critical voices in the media. Hindu nationalist campaigns aimed at discouraging forms of expression deemed "antinational" have exacerbated self-censorship, and some media observers have suggested that media reporting has become less ambitious in recent years.

Journalists risk harassment, death threats, and physical violence in connection with their work. Such attacks are rarely punished and some have taken place with the complicity or active participation of police. The advocacy organization Reporters Without Borders (RSF) identified four incidents in which police attacked journalists in March 2018 alone; each of the incidents involved journalists attempting to cover protest actions. Deadly attacks against journalists are increasing. According to the Committee to Protect Journalists (CPJ), five journalists were killed in India in connection with their work during 2018, four of whom were murdered and one of whom was shot upon becoming caught in a firefight between Maoist militants and police. Four journalists had been killed in connection with their work in 2017, and two in 2016, according to CPJ.

Score Change: The score declined from 3 to 2 because journalists face increasing pressure, harassment, and physical violence.

D2. Are individuals free to practice and express their religious faith or nonbelief in public and private? 2 / 4 (−1)

While Hindus make up about 80 percent of the population, the Indian state is formally secular, and freedom of religion is constitutionally guaranteed. However, legislation in several Hindu-majority states criminalizes religious conversions that take place as a result of "force" or "allurement," which can be broadly interpreted to prosecute proselytizers. Some states require government permission for conversion.

A number of Hindu nationalist organizations and some local media outlets promote antiminority views, a practice that critics charge has been tolerated by the government of Prime Minister Modi. The year 2018 saw continued attacks against minorities in connection with the alleged slaughter or mishandling of cows, which are held to be sacred by Hindus. The media nonprofit IndiaSpend documented 31 cow-related violent incidents in 2018. Over 120 such attacks, including lynchings, have been reported since Modi came to power, and he and the BJP have faced criticism for failing to mount an adequate response.

Score Change: The score declined from 3 to 2 due to dozens of violent incidents over the past four years in which Hindu extremists have attacked others for the alleged mistreatment or slaughter of cows.

D3. Is there academic freedom, and is the educational system free from extensive political indoctrination? 3 / 4

Academic freedom is generally robust, though intimidation of professors, students, and institutions over political and religious issues has been increasing. The student wing of the Hindu nationalist organization Rashtriya Swayamsevak Sangh (RSS), from which the ruling BJP is widely regarded to have grown, has engaged in violent tactics on campuses across the country, including attacks on students and professors.

D4. Are individuals free to express their personal views on political or other sensitive topics without fear of surveillance or retribution? 4 / 4

Private discussion in India is generally open and free. However, a nationwide Central Monitoring System launched in 2013 is meant to enable authorities to intercept any digital communication in real time without judicial oversight. Colonial-era laws continue to be used to curb expression. In October 2018, three students were arrested for sedition after allegedly promoting "anti-India" slogans.

In 2017, the Supreme Court declared privacy to be a fundamental right protected by the Constitution. In September 2018, a court ruling on India's extensive national identification system, known as Aadhaar, imposed limits on its use. The decision notably voided a section that had allowed private entities to require people to prove their identity through Aadhaar.

E. ASSOCIATIONAL AND ORGANIZATIONAL RIGHTS: 10 / 12
E1. Is there freedom of assembly? 4 / 4

While there are some restrictions on freedoms of assembly and association—such as a provision of the criminal procedure code empowering authorities to restrict free assembly and impose curfews whenever "immediate prevention or speedy remedy" is required— peaceful protest events take place regularly. However, in recent years, central and state governments have frequently suspended mobile internet services to curb collective action by citizens.

E2. Is there freedom for nongovernmental organizations, particularly those that are engaged in human rights- and governance-related work? 3 / 4

A wide variety of nongovernmental organizations (NGOs) operate, but they continue to face threats, legal harassment, excessive police force, and occasionally lethal violence. Under certain circumstances, the Foreign Contributions Regulation Act (FCRA) permits the federal government to deny NGOs access to foreign funding, and authorities have been accused of abusing this power to target political opponents. Since 2011, the government has blocked more than 19,000 NGOs from receiving foreign financing under the FCRA's provisions.

In August 2018, a number of left-wing activists critical of Modi's administration saw their homes and offices raided by police on grounds that they were linked with banned Maoist groups. Rights groups denounced the crackdown as an unjustified attack on government critics. Later, in October, government financial crimes units conducted separate raids of offices of Greenpeace India and Amnesty International India, and froze their financial accounts. Amnesty International later reported that it was the target of an online smear campaign that some progovernment media outlets took part in.

E3. Is there freedom for trade unions and similar professional or labor organizations? 3 / 4

Although workers in the formal economy regularly exercise their rights to bargain collectively and strike, the Essential Services Maintenance Act has enabled the government to ban certain strikes.

F. RULE OF LAW: 9 / 16
F1. Is there an independent judiciary? 3 / 4

The judiciary is independent of the executive branch. However, the lower levels of the judiciary have been rife with corruption, and most citizens have great difficulty securing justice through the courts.

F2. Does due process prevail in civil and criminal matters? 2 / 4

Due process rights are not guaranteed. Citizens face substantial obstacles in the pursuit of justice, including demands for bribes and difficulty getting the police to file a First Information Report, which is necessary to trigger an investigation of an alleged crime. Corruption within the police force remains a problem. The justice system is severely backlogged and understaffed, leading to lengthy pretrial detention for suspects, many of whom remain in jail longer than the duration of any sentence they might receive if convicted.

F3. Is there protection from the illegitimate use of physical force and freedom from war and insurgencies? 2 / 4

Reports of torture, abuse, and rape by law enforcement and security officials persisted in 2018. A bill intended to prevent torture remains pending. Abuses against prisoners, particularly minorities and members of the lower castes, by prison staff are common. Official data released to the Indian parliament showed that approximately 1,680 deaths occurred in judicial or police custody between April 2017 and the end of February 2018.

Security forces battling regional insurgencies continue to be implicated in extrajudicial killings, rape, torture, arbitrary detention, kidnappings, and destruction of homes. While the criminal procedure code requires that the government approve the prosecution of security forces members, approval is rarely granted, leading to impunity. A number of security laws allow detention without charge or based on vaguely worded offenses.

The Maoist insurgency in the east-central hills region of India continues, although the annual number of casualties linked with it has decreased since its peak in 2010. Among other abuses, the rebels have allegedly imposed illegal taxes, seized food and places of shelter, and engaged in abduction and forced recruitment of children and adults. Local civilians and journalists who are perceived to be progovernment have been targeted. Tens of thousands of civilians have been displaced by the violence and live in government-run camps.

Separately, in India's seven northeastern states, more than 40 insurgent factions—seeking either greater autonomy or complete independence for their ethnic or tribal groups—continue to attack security forces and engage in intertribal violence. Such fighters have been implicated in bombings, killings, abductions, and rapes of civilians, and they operate extensive extortion networks.

F4. Do laws, policies, and practices guarantee equal treatment of various segments of the population? 2 / 4

The constitution bars discrimination based on caste, and laws set aside quotas in education and government jobs for historically underprivileged scheduled tribes, Dalits, and groups categorized by the government as "other backward classes." However, members of the lower castes and minorities face routine discrimination and violence, and the criminal justice system fails to provide equal protection to marginalized groups. Many Dalits are denied access to land, are abused by landlords and police, and work in miserable conditions.

In parts of the country, particularly in rural areas, informal community councils issue edicts concerning social customs. Their decisions sometimes result in violence or persecution aimed at those perceived to have transgressed social norms, especially women and members of the lower castes.

The citizenship status of millions of mostly Muslim residents in the state of Assam was thrown in doubt in 2018, after a draft of Assam's NRC released in July failed to include their names. Those affected, largely Bengali-speaking Muslims, must produce documentation that they or their ancestors came to the state before Bangladesh became independent in 1971. Accessing such documentation may not feasible for many poor communities wracked by illiteracy and displacement. While government officials have claimed that Assam's NRC was being updated to identify Bangladeshis living in India illegally, the government of Bangladesh has not accepted that this population is Bangladeshi, and is unlikely to accept them if India attempts to deport them. Separately, proposed changes to a key citizenship law that would expedite citizenship status for "persecuted minorities" in neighboring countries appear to involve the unequal treatment of religious groups.

In September 2018, the Supreme Court ruled that the use of Section 377 of the Indian Penal Code to ban homosexual intercourse was unconstitutional. However, discrimination continues against LGBT (lesbian, gay, bisexual, and transgender) individuals, including violence and harassment in some cases.

G. PERSONAL AUTONOMY AND INDIVIDUAL RIGHTS: 10 / 16

G1. Do individuals enjoy freedom of movement, including the ability to change their place of residence, employment, or education? 3 / 4

Article 19 of the constitution grants citizens the right to reside and settle in any part of the territory of India. However, freedom of movement is hampered in some parts of the country by insurgent violence or communal tensions.

G2. Are individuals able to exercise the right to own property and establish private businesses without undue interference from state or nonstate actors? 3 / 4

Property rights are somewhat tenuous for tribal groups and other marginalized communities, and members of these groups are often denied adequate resettlement opportunities and compensation when their lands are seized for development projects. While many states have laws to prevent transfers of tribal land to nontribal groups, the practice is reportedly widespread, particularly with respect to the mining and timber industries. Muslim personal laws and traditional Hindu practices discriminate against women in terms of property rights.

G3. Do individuals enjoy personal social freedoms, including choice of marriage partner and size of family, protection from domestic violence, and control over appearance? 2 / 4

Rape, harassment, and other transgressions against women are serious problems, and lower-caste and tribal women are especially vulnerable. Mass demonstrations after the fatal gang rape of a woman on a Delhi bus in 2012 prompted the government to enact significant legal reforms. However, egregious new rape cases have continued to prompt outrage. In what is widely seen as a positive development, the #MeToo movement rose to prominence in India in 2018. Women came forward to express their experiences with sexual harassment and assault, and to accuse high-profile entertainers, journalists, and political leaders of committing sexual harassment and assault; the movement notably prompted in the resignation of MJ Akbar, the minister of state for external affairs. Despite criminalization and hundreds of convictions each year, dowry demands continue. A 2006 law banned dowry-related harassment, widened the definition of domestic violence to include emotional or verbal abuse, and criminalized spousal sexual violence. However, reports indicate that enforcement is poor.

Muslim personal laws and traditional Hindu practices discriminate against women in terms of inheritance and adoption. The Muslim divorce custom of "triple talaq," by which a Muslim man can unilaterally divorce his wife by saying "talaq" three times, was ruled to be unconstitutional by the Supreme Court in 2017. After failing to pass legislation through Parliament to ban the custom, the government issued a temporary ordinance in September 2018 criminalizing the practice and mandating prison terms for perpetrators. The malign neglect of female children after birth remains a concern, as does the banned use of prenatal sex-determination tests to selectively abort female fetuses.

G4. Do individuals enjoy equality of opportunity and freedom from economic exploitation? 2 / 4

India's growing economy has created new avenues for economic opportunity, though serious inequalities also persist.

The constitution bans human trafficking, and bonded labor is illegal, but the practice is fairly common. Estimates of the number of affected workers range from 20 to 50 million. The government passed a controversial law in 2016 allowing children below the age of 14 to engage in "home-based work," as well as other occupations between the ages of 14 and 18. Children are not permitted to work in potentially hazardous industries, though the law is routinely flouted. There have been reports of complicity by law enforcement officials in human trafficking.

Indonesia

Population: 265,200,000
Capital: Jakarta
Political Rights Rating: 2
Civil Liberties Rating: 4
Freedom Rating: 3.0
Freedom Status: Partly Free
Electoral Democracy: Yes

Overview: Indonesia has made impressive democratic gains since the fall of an authoritarian regime in 1998, establishing significant pluralism in politics and the media and undergoing multiple, peaceful transfers of power between parties. However, the country continues to struggle with challenges including systemic corruption, discrimination and violence against some minority groups, separatist tensions in the Papua region, and the politicized use of defamation and blasphemy laws.

KEY DEVELOPMENTS IN 2018:

- In January, the Constitutional Court rejected a judicial review of the 2017 General Elections Law, which makes it more difficult for small or new parties to register presidential candidates by tying candidates' eligibility to their parties' past electoral success.
- Incumbent Joko Widodo ("Jokowi") of the Indonesian Democratic Party of Struggle (PDI-P), and former general Prabowo Subianto, head of the Great Indonesia Movement Party (Gerindra), announced their respective presidential candidates in August, setting up a rematch of the 2014 election. Each is backed by a larger coalition.
- In April, former House of Representatives (DPR) speaker and Golkar party chairman Setya Novanto was convicted of involvement in a $170 million corruption scandal surrounding procurements for a new identity card system, and was sentenced to 15 years in jail. He was one of the most senior officials ever to be convicted on corruption charges.
- National and local authorities and others continued to harass and threaten LGBT (lesbian gay, bisexual, and transgender) people and activists, driving the community further underground.

POLITICAL RIGHTS: 30 / 40

A. ELECTORAL PROCESS: 11 / 12

A1. Was the current head of government or other chief national authority elected through free and fair elections? 4 / 4

The president is directly elected and serves as both head of state and head of government. Presidents and vice presidents can serve up to two five-year terms. Jokowi, the PDI-P candidate, won the July 2014 presidential election with 53 percent of the vote, defeating former general Subianto. Limited voting irregularities and sporadic election-related violence were reported, but the contest was largely considered free and fair.

A2. Were the current national legislative representatives elected through free and fair elections? 4 / 4

The DPR, the main parliamentary chamber, consists of 560 members elected in 33 multimember districts. The 132-member House of Regional Representatives (DPD) is responsible for monitoring laws related to regional autonomy, and may also propose bills on the topic. All legislators serve five-year terms with no term limits.

The PDI-P, the party of former president Megawati Sukarnoputri, led the DPR elections in April 2014 with 19 percent of the vote and 109 seats. Golkar, the party of former authoritarian president Suharto, won 91 seats, followed by Prabowo's Gerindra party, with 73 seats. The Democratic Party (PD) of outgoing president Susilo Bambang Yudhoyono received 61 seats. Three Islamic parties—the National Mandate Party (PAN), the National Awakening Party (PKB), and the United Development Party (PPP)—increased their seats, taking 49, 47, and 39 seats, respectively. A fourth, the Prosperous Justice Party (PKS), fell to 40 seats. Partai NasDem and the People's Conscience Party (Hanura) won the remainder, with 35 and 16 seats, respectively.

The balloting was largely considered free and fair, though there were reports of irregularities in some regions, including political violence during the pre-election period in Aceh and voter-list inflation, ballot stuffing, and community bloc voting in Papua.

A3. Are the electoral laws and framework fair, and are they implemented impartially by the relevant election management bodies? 3 / 4

The legal framework for elections is largely democratic, and electoral authorities are mostly seen as impartial. However, some legal provisions are problematic. Under a 2012 law, the hereditary sultan of Yogyakarta is that region's unelected governor. The position is nonpartisan, and the sultan is subject to a verification process with minimum requirements—such as education—every five years. The prince of Paku Alaman serves as deputy governor of the region. Separately, a 2016 revision to the law governing local elections requires that the Election Oversight Agency (Bawaslu) and the General Elections Commission (KPU) conduct a binding consultation with the parliament and the government before issuing any new regulations or decisions. Activists expressed concern that the rules would reduce electoral authorities' independence.

In 2017, the DPR approved a new General Elections Law that requires parties or coalitions fielding 2019 presidential candidates to hold 20 percent of the seats in parliament or 25 percent of the national vote in 2014. The provision effectively bars new or smaller parties from fielding candidates in the presidential race. The same thresholds were used in the 2014 presidential election, but they pertained to the parliament elected just a few months earlier; the 2019 parliamentary and presidential votes will be held simultaneously. The Constitutional Court rejected a judicial review of the law in January 2018.

B. POLITICAL PLURALISM AND PARTICIPATION: 13 / 16

B1. Do the people have the right to organize in different political parties or other competitive political groupings of their choice, and is the system free of undue obstacles to the rise and fall of these competing parties or groupings? 4 / 4

The right to organize political parties is respected, and the system features competition among several major parties. However, recently the election laws have been amended to favor large parties by increasing eligibility requirements. Only 12 parties passed verification processes for the 2014 national elections, down from 48 in 1999. The 2017 General Elections Law requires new parties to undergo a "factual verification" process which involves confirming the accuracy of submitted documents on parties' management, membership, and operations.

The Constitutional Court's January 2018 ruling to uphold the General Elections Law's provisions tying presidential candidates' eligibility to their parties' past electoral success further limited the ability of small and new parties to register candidates. The candidates for the 2019 elections are the same candidates as in the 2014 elections— Jokowi and Prabowo.

Communist parties are banned, and those who disseminate communist symbols or promote communism can face punishment under laws carrying as many as 12 years' imprisonment.

B2. Is there a realistic opportunity for the opposition to increase its support or gain power through elections? 4 / 4

Indonesia has established a pattern of democratic power transfers between rival parties since 1999. The most recent such handover occurred in 2014, when Jokowi's PDI-P returned to power after losing the previous two presidential elections. The 2017 General Elections Law makes it more difficult for the opposition by tying presidential candidates' eligibility to their parties' past electoral success.

B3. Are the people's political choices free from domination by the military, foreign powers, religious hierarchies, economic oligarchies, or any other powerful group that is not democratically accountable? 3 / 4

While voters and candidates are generally free from undue interference, the military remains influential, with former commanders playing prominent roles in politics, and intimidation by nonstate actors—including Islamist radical groups—is a problem. Since the 2017 campaign for governor of Jakarta—in which incumbent Basuki Tjahaja Purnama ("Ahok"), a Christian, lost his bid for reelection after hard-line Islamist groups accused him of blasphemy—other campaigns have urged Muslims not to vote for *kafir*, or infidel, candidates—meaning non-Muslims.

B4. Do various segments of the population (including ethnic, religious, gender, LGBT, and other relevant groups) have full political rights and electoral opportunities? 2 / 4

Women enjoy equal political rights, but remain underrepresented in elected offices. Parties are subject to 30 percent gender quotas for steering committees and candidates. Women achieved 17 percent representation in the 2014–19 DPR.

Some local governments have discriminated against religious minorities by restricting access to identification cards, birth certificates, marriage licenses, and other bureaucratic necessities, limiting their political rights and electoral opportunities.

C. FUNCTIONING OF GOVERNMENT: 6 / 12

C1. Do the freely elected head of government and national legislative representatives determine the policies of the government? 3 / 4

Elected officials generally determine the policies of the government, though national authorities have faced difficulties in implementing their decisions due to resistance at the local level. Separately, observers have warned that the military is regaining influence over civilian governance and economic affairs.

In some areas the extent of corruption severely disrupts the functioning of government. In Malang, East Java, 41 of 45 local city council members were under investigation for graft in late 2018.

C2. Are safeguards against official corruption strong and effective? 1 / 4

Corruption remains endemic at all levels, including in national and local legislatures, civil service, judiciary, and police. Acrimony between rival agencies—particularly the Corruption Eradication Commission (KPK) and the national police—has hindered anticorruption efforts, and civilian investigators have no jurisdiction over the military. High-profile corruption suspects and defendants have often enjoyed impunity.

However, in April 2018, former DPR speaker and Golkar party chairman Setya Novanto was convicted of involvement in a $170 million corruption scandal surrounding procurements for a new identity card system, and was sentenced to 15 years in jail. Novanto was one of the most senior officials ever to be convicted on corruption charges.

C3. Does the government operate with openness and transparency? 2 / 4

Although civil society groups are able to comment on and influence pending policies or legislation, government transparency is limited by broad exemptions in the freedom of information law and obstacles such as a 2011 law that criminalizes the leaking of vaguely defined state secrets to the public.

CIVIL LIBERTIES: 32 / 60 (-2)
D. FREEDOM OF EXPRESSION AND BELIEF: 11 / 16 (-1)
D1. Are there free and independent media? 3 / 4

Indonesia hosts a vibrant and diverse media environment, though legal and regulatory restrictions hamper press freedom. The 2008 Law on Electronic Information and Transactions extended libel to online media, criminalizing the distribution or accessibility of information or documents that are "contrary to the moral norms of Indonesia," or involve gambling, blackmail, or defamation. Foreign journalists visiting Papua and West Papua continue to report bureaucratic obstacles and deportations.

Dozens of assaults, threats, arrests, and other forms of obstruction were directed against journalists during 2018, with perpetrators including politicians, police, and military officials. In June, journalist Muhammad Yusuf of the local news website *Kemajuan Rakyat* died in police custody, after being detained for weeks on charges of defamation and hate speech in connection with articles implicating a palm oil company in illegal land grabs. His family accused authorities of medical neglect.

D2. Are individuals free to practice and express their religious faith or nonbelief in public and private? 1 / 4

Indonesia officially recognizes Islam, Protestantism, Roman Catholicism, Hinduism, Buddhism, and Confucianism. Individuals may leave the "religion" section on their identity cards blank, but those who do—including adherents of unrecognized faiths—often face discrimination. Atheism is not accepted, and the criminal code contains provisions against blasphemy, penalizing those who "distort" or "misrepresent" recognized faiths.

National and local governments fail to protect religious minorities and exhibit bias in investigations and prosecutions. Building a new house of worship requires the signatures of 90 congregation members and 60 local residents of different faiths.

Violence and intimidation against Ahmadi and Shiite communities persists, and the central government continues to tolerate persecution of these groups.

Jokowi's choice of running mate in the 2019 presidential election prompted concerns about his commitment to religious freedom. His pick, Ma'ruf Amin, is an Islamic cleric known for controversial fatwas as chairman of the Majelis Ulama Indonesia (MUI), the Indonesian Ulama Council. Under his leadership, MUI issued fatwas against Shia Islam and Ahmadiyya, as well as the 2016 fatwa declaring that Ahok, the former governor of Jakarta, insulted the Quran, paving the way for Ahok's 2017 blasphemy conviction.

D3. Is there academic freedom, and is the educational system free from extensive political indoctrination? 3 / 4 (-1)

Threats to academic freedom have increased in recent years. Academics have been charged with defamation and removed from their posts for criticism of public officials. In 2018, there were at least two suits brought against academics who had served as expert witnesses in corruption cases. Additionally, in April, police delivered a summons for questioning to a scientist in connection with his research on tsunamis. The summons was issued after his findings were widely misrepresented on social media and by media outlets as a warning that a large tsunami would strike Indonesia, and began to be viewed as threatening to coastal real estate developments. Several other people who had attended the conference at which he presented the research were also reportedly contacted by police.

Hard-line groups are known to threaten discussions on LGBT matters, interfaith issues, and the 1965–66 anti-communist massacres.

Score Change: The score declined from 4 to 3 due to a gradual erosion in academic freedom, illustrated most recently by at least two lawsuits brought against academics serving as witnesses in court proceedings, and a police investigation targeting a researcher whose findings were misinterpreted in a manner that threatened economic development.

D4. Are individuals free to express their personal views on political or other sensitive topics without fear of surveillance or retribution? 4 / 4

Laws against blasphemy, defamation, and certain other forms of speech may sometimes inhibit the expression of personal views on sensitive topics, including on social media. In a 2018 blasphemy case in North Sumatra, an ethnic Chinese woman was sentenced in August to 18 months in prison after complaining that the call to prayer at a nearby mosque was too loud. In January, an 18-year-old student was found guilty of defaming the president on Facebook and sentenced to 18 months in jail.

E. ASSOCIATIONAL AND ORGANIZATIONAL RIGHTS: 7 / 12 (-1)

E1. Is there freedom of assembly? 2 / 4

Freedom of assembly is usually upheld, and peaceful protests are common. However, assemblies addressing sensitive political topics—such as the 1965–66 massacres or regional separatism—are regularly dispersed, with participants facing intimidation or violence from hard-line vigilantes or police.

E2. Is there freedom for nongovernmental organizations, particularly those that are engaged in human rights- and governance-related work? 2 / 4 (-1)

While nongovernmental organizations (NGOs) are active in Indonesia, they are subject to government monitoring and interference. A 2013 law requires all NGOs to register with the government and submit to regular reviews of their activities. It limits the types of activities NGOs can undertake and bars them from committing blasphemy or espousing ideas that conflict with the official Pancasila ideology, such as atheism and communism. The government is empowered to dissolve noncompliant organizations without judicial oversight.

Authorities and influential Muslim organizations have continued to intimidate and harass LGBT people and activists. In recent years, authorities have closed a transgender boarding school, raided a gym and sauna that also functioned as a health center for gay and bisexual men, and banned or attempted to ban foreign funding for LGBT groups. Nahdlatul Ulama, Indonesia's largest Muslim organization, has called for LGBT activism to be criminalized. The cumulative effect of this campaign has been to drive the LGBT activist community underground, and to hamper groups seeking to provide services to LGBT people.

Separately, in January 2018, an environmental activist was sentenced to 10 months in jail under an anticommunism law, after he displayed a hammer and sickle icon at a protest against a gold mining company in east Java.

Score Change: The score declined from 3 to 2 due to a multiyear crackdown on civil society groups and activists serving the LGBT community.

E3. Is there freedom for trade unions and similar professional or labor organizations? 3 / 4

Workers can join independent unions, bargain collectively, and with the exception of civil servants, stage strikes. Legal strikes can be unduly delayed by obligatory arbitration processes, and laws against antiunion discrimination and retaliation are not well enforced. As a result of a memorandum of understanding signed in January 2018, the military can assist police in dealing with strikes and demonstrations. The development sparked criticism from human rights and labor activists, who expressed concerns about military repression or intimidation of workers.

F. RULE OF LAW: 5 / 16
F1. Is there an independent judiciary? 2 / 4

The judiciary has demonstrated its independence in some cases, particularly in the Constitutional Court, but the court system remains plagued by corruption and other weaknesses. Judges occasionally rely on public opinion or religious rulings rather than a case's legal merits.

F2. Does due process prevail in civil and criminal matters? 1 / 4

Police reportedly engage in arbitrary arrests and detentions, particularly of protesters or activists suspected of separatism. Existing safeguards against coerced confessions are ineffective, and defendants are sometimes denied proper access to legal counsel, including in death penalty cases.

A number of districts and provinces have ordinances based on Sharia (Islamic law) that are unconstitutional and contradict Indonesia's international human rights commitments.

F3. Is there protection from the illegitimate use of physical force and freedom from war and insurgencies? 1 / 4

Security forces regularly go unpunished or receive lenient sentences for human rights violations. Military service members accused of crimes against civilians are tried in military courts, which lack impartiality and often impose light punishments. Deadly confrontations between security forces and separatists are common in Papua and West Papua. Amnesty International reported in July 2018 that 95 people had been unlawfully killed by Indonesian security forces in Papua between January 2010 and February 2018.

Torture by law enforcement agencies is not specifically criminalized. Prisons are over-crowded and corrupt, leading to riots, protests, and jailbreaks. Violence related to natural resource extraction remains a problem. In Aceh, regulations under Sharia permit provincial authorities to use caning as punishment for offenses related to gambling, alcohol consumption, and illicit sexual activity.

F4. Do laws, policies, and practices guarantee equal treatment of various segments of the population? 1 / 4

Some national laws and numerous local ordinances discriminate against women either explicitly or in effect.

LGBT people suffer from widespread discrimination, and authorities, including cabinet members, continue to target LGBT people with inflammatory and discriminatory rhetoric. LGBT people also risk attacks by hard-line Islamist groups, sometimes with support from local authorities. Recent years have seen a series of police raids of private gatherings of LGBT people, and subsequent mass arrests. A July 2018 report by advocacy group Human Rights Watch (HRW) said the continued crackdown hampered public health outreach to LGBT people at a time when the rate of HIV infections among men who have sex with men was increasing.

Ethnic Chinese, who make up approximately 1 percent of the population but reputedly hold much of the country's wealth, continue to face harassment.

Indonesia grants temporary protection to refugees and migrants, but is not party to the 1951 Refugee Convention and does not accept refugees for asylum and resettlement.

G. PERSONAL AUTONOMY AND INDIVIDUAL RIGHTS: 9 / 16

G1. Do individuals enjoy freedom of movement, including the ability to change their place of residence, employment, or education? 3 / 4

The freedoms to travel and change one's place of residence, employment, or higher education are generally respected. However, the ability to make such changes can be limited by the need for bribes.

G2. Are individuals able to exercise the right to own property and establish private businesses without undue interference from state or nonstate actors? 2 / 4

Private business activity is hampered by corruption. Property rights are threatened by state appropriation and licensing of communally owned land to companies. Ethnic Chinese in Yogyakarta face restrictions on private property ownership under a 1975 decree that contravenes national laws.

G3. Do individuals enjoy personal social freedoms, including choice of marriage partner and size of family, protection from domestic violence, and control over appearance? 2 / 4

Abortion is illegal except to save a woman's life or in instances of rape. Adults over 15 years of age must have corroboration and witnesses to bring rape charges.

Sharia-based ordinances in a number of districts impose restrictions on dress, public conduct, and sexual activity that are disproportionately enforced against women and LGBT people.

Marriages must be conducted under the supervision of a recognized religion, which can obstruct interfaith marriages. The minimum age for marriage, defined in the 1974 Marriage Law, is 16 for women and 19 for men; child marriage is relatively common for girls. In

December 2018, the Constitutional Court ruled the minimum age of 16 for women to marry was unconstitutional, though the parliament will have to pass legislation in order for the age to be legally increased.

G4. Do individuals enjoy equality of opportunity and freedom from economic exploitation? 2 / 4

National, provincial, and local authorities set standards for working conditions and compensation, but enforcement is inconsistent. Indonesian workers are trafficked abroad, including women in domestic service and men in the fishing industry. Traffickers are often able to avoid punishment by paying bribes.

Iran

Population: 81,600,000
Capital: Tehran
Political Rights Rating: 6
Civil Liberties Rating: 6
Freedom Rating: 6.0
Freedom Status: Not Free
Electoral Democracy: No

Overview: The Islamic Republic of Iran holds elections regularly, but they fall short of democratic standards due in part to the influence of the hard-line Guardian Council, an unelected body that disqualifies all candidates it deems insufficiently loyal to the clerical establishment. Ultimate power rests in the hands of the country's supreme leader, Ayatollah Ali Khamenei, and the unelected institutions under his control. These institutions, including the security forces and the judiciary, play a major role in the suppression of dissent and other restrictions on civil liberties.

KEY DEVELOPMENTS IN 2018:

- Approximately 4,900 people were reportedly detained in nationwide antigovernment protests over the worsening economy and corruption that erupted in late December 2017 and stretched into January; at least 21 people were killed in clashes with security forces during the demonstrations.
- In April, the government banned the popular messaging app Telegram, which was used by 40 million Iranians.
- In June, authorities arrested prominent human rights lawyer Nasrin Sotoudeh, who had defended several women detained for protesting the compulsory hijab (headscarf) earlier in the year. She was charged with "propaganda against the state" and "assembly and collusion." Her trial commenced in late December. At least seven attorneys were arrested and detained in 2018 in connection with their work
- In May, the United States withdrew from the 2015 nuclear deal and announced the reimposition of sanctions, which exacerbated Iran's economic problems and contributed to the collapse of the national currency.

POLITICAL RIGHTS: 7 / 40
A. ELECTORAL PROCESS: 3 / 12

A1. Was the current head of government or other chief national authority elected through free and fair elections? 1 / 4

The supreme leader, who has no fixed term, is the highest authority in the country. He is the commander in chief of the armed forces and appoints the head of the judiciary, the heads of state broadcast media, and the Expediency Council—a body tasked with mediating disputes between the Guardian Council and the parliament. He also appoints six of the members of the Guardian Council; the other six are jurists nominated by the head of the judiciary and confirmed by the parliament, all for six-year terms. The supreme leader is appointed by the Assembly of Experts, which also monitors his work. However, in practice his decisions appear to go unchallenged by the assembly, whose proceedings are kept confidential. The current supreme leader, Ali Khamenei, succeeded Islamic Republic founder Ruhollah Khomeini in 1989.

The president, the second-highest-ranking official in the Islamic Republic, appoints a cabinet that must be confirmed by the parliament. He is elected by popular vote for up to two consecutive four-year terms. In the 2017 presidential election, only six men were allowed to run out of some 1,600 candidates who had applied. All 137 women candidates were disqualified by the Guardian Council. President Rouhani's main challenger, hard-line cleric Ebrahim Raisi, was known for his role as a judge involved in Iran's mass executions of political opponents in the 1980s. In the run-up to the election, the authorities intensified a crackdown on the media, arresting several journalists and administrators of reformist channels on Telegram, the popular messaging app. However, Rouhani's victory, with 57 percent of the vote amid roughly 70 percent turnout, appeared to reflect the choice of the electorate among the available candidates.

A2. Were the current national legislative representatives elected through free and fair elections? 1 / 4

In 2016, elections were held for the both the unicameral 290-seat Islamic Consultative Assembly and the Assembly of Experts, a body of 86 clerics who are elected to eight-year terms by popular vote. Members of the Islamic Consultative Assembly are elected to four-year terms, with 285 members directly elected, and 5 seats reserved for Zoroastrians, Jews, Armenians, and Christians. Only 51 percent of candidates who had applied to run for seats in the parliament were approved by the Guardian Council, the lowest figure to date. Only 20 percent of candidates were approved to run for the Assembly of Experts, also a record low.

At the end of the process, relatively moderate Rouhani supporters held more than 40 percent of seats in the parliament, while independents—who included a number of reformists—and hard-liners each took about a third. The result was perceived as a victory for moderates and reformists, though the exact orientations and allegiances of individual lawmakers are often unclear. Moderates and reformists similarly made symbolic gains in the Assembly of Experts, but because so many had been disqualified, the supposedly moderate lists included conservative candidates. A majority of the new Assembly of Experts ultimately chose hard-line cleric Ahmad Jannati, head of the Guardian Council, as the body's chairman.

A3. Are the electoral laws and framework fair, and are they implemented impartially by the relevant election management bodies? 1 / 4

The electoral system in Iran does not meet international democratic standards. The Guardian Council, controlled by hard-line conservatives and ultimately by the supreme leader, vets all candidates for the parliament, the presidency, and the Assembly of Experts. The council typically rejects candidates who are not considered insiders or deemed fully loyal to the clerical establishment, as well as women seeking to run in the presidential election. As a result, Iranian voters are given a limited choice of candidates.

B. POLITICAL PLURALISM AND PARTICIPATION: 2 / 16

B1. Do the people have the right to organize in different political parties or other competitive political groupings of their choice, and is the system free of undue obstacles to the rise and fall of these competing parties or groupings? 0 / 4

Only political parties and factions loyal to the establishment and to the state ideology are permitted to operate. Reformist parties and politicians have come under increased state repression, especially since 2009.

B2. Is there a realistic opportunity for the opposition to increase its support or gain power through elections? 1 / 4

In 2015, two new reformist parties—Nedaye Iranian (Voice of Iranians) and Ettehad Mellat Iran (Iranian National Unity)—were established ahead of the 2016 parliamentary elections. However, most candidates from these and other reformist groups were disqualified by the Guardian Council ahead of the voting.

Top opposition figures remain subject to restrictions on their movement and access to the media. Mir Hossein Mousavi, Zahra Rahnavard, and Mehdi Karroubi—leaders of the reformist Green Movement, whose protests were violently suppressed following the disputed 2009 presidential election—have been under house arrest since February 2011. Reformist former president Mohammad Khatami continues to face a media ban that prohibits the press from mentioning him and publishing his photos. Former hard-line president Mahmoud Ahmadinejad, who fell out of favor for challenging Khamenei, was barred from running in the 2017 presidential election.

B3. Are the people's political choices free from domination by the military, foreign powers, religious hierarchies, economic oligarchies, or any other powerful group that is not democratically accountable? 0 / 4

The choices of both voters and politicians are heavily influenced and ultimately circumscribed by Iran's unelected state institutions and ruling clerical establishment.

B4. Do various segments of the population (including ethnic, religious, gender, LGBT, and other relevant groups) have full political rights and electoral opportunities? 1 / 4

Women remain significantly underrepresented in politics and government. In 2017, Rouhani appointed two women among his several vice presidents but failed to name any women as cabinet ministers. Rouhani's advisor on citizens' rights, Shahindokht Molaverdi, a champion of women's empowerment, resigned in November 2018. No women candidates have ever been allowed to run for president.

Despite the quota that sets aside five parliamentary seats for recognized non-Muslim minorities, ethnic and especially religious minorities are rarely awarded senior government posts, and their political representation remains weak.

C. FUNCTIONING OF GOVERNMENT: 2 / 12

C1. Do the freely elected head of government and national legislative representatives determine the policies of the government? 1 / 4

The elected president's powers are limited by the supreme leader and other unelected authorities. The powers of the elected parliament are similarly restricted by the supreme leader and the unelected Guardian Council, which must approve all bills before they can become law. The council often rejects bills it deems un-Islamic. Nevertheless, the parliament has been a platform for heated political debate and criticism of the government, and legislators have frequently challenged presidents and their policies.

C2. Are safeguards against official corruption strong and effective? 0 / 4

Corruption remains endemic at all levels of the bureaucracy, despite regular calls by authorities to tackle the problem. Powerful actors involved in the economy, including the Islamic Revolutionary Guard Corps (IRGC) and bonyads (endowed foundations), are above scrutiny, and restrictions on the media and civil society activists prevent them from serving as independent watchdogs to ensure transparency and accountability.

C3. Does the government operate with openness and transparency? 1 / 4

An access to information law was passed in 2009, and implementing regulations were finally adopted in 2015. In 2017, the Information and Communications Technology Ministry unveiled an online portal to facilitate information requests. However, the law grants broadly worded exemptions allowing the protection of information whose disclosure would conflict with state interests, cause financial loss, or harm public security, among other stipulations. In practice, the transparency of Iran's political system remains extremely limited, and powerful elements of the state and society remain unaccountable to the public.

CIVIL LIBERTIES: 11 / 60
D. FREEDOM OF EXPRESSION AND BELIEF: 3 / 16
D1. Are there free and independent media? 1 / 4

Freedom of expression and media independence are severely limited both online and offline. The state broadcasting company is tightly controlled by hard-liners and influenced by the security apparatus. News and analysis are heavily censored, while critics and opposition members are rarely, if ever, given a platform on state-controlled television, which remains a major source of information for many Iranians. State television has a record of airing confessions extracted from political prisoners under duress, and it routinely carries reports aimed at discrediting dissidents and opposition activists.

Newspapers and magazines face censorship and warnings from authorities about which topics to cover and how. Tens of thousands of foreign-based websites are filtered, including news sites and major social media services. Satellite dishes are banned, and Persian-language broadcasts from outside the country are regularly jammed. Authorities periodically raid private homes and confiscate satellite dishes. Iranian authorities have pressured journalists working for Persian-language media outside the country by summoning and threatening their families in Iran.

Independent journalists face potential arrest, prosecution, and imprisonment. In July and August 2018, at least six journalists from the news site *Majzooban-e-Noor* were sentenced to prison terms ranging from 7 to 26 years for their coverage of February protests by members of the Sufi Muslim order Nematollahi Gonabadi.

D2. Are individuals free to practice and express their religious faith or nonbelief in public and private? 0 / 4

Iran is home to a majority Shiite Muslim population and Sunni, Baha'i, Christian, and Zoroastrian minorities. The constitution recognizes only Zoroastrians, Jews, and certain Christian communities as religious minorities, and these small groups are relatively free to worship. However, conversion from Islam to another religion is illegal, as is proselytizing. The regime cracks down on Muslims who are deemed to be at variance with the state ideology and interpretation of Islam. Sunni Muslims complain that they have been prevented from building mosques in major cities.

In recent years, there has been increased pressure on the Nematollahi Gonabadi, including destruction of their places of worship and the jailing of some of their members. In February 2018, authorities detained 300 Gonabadi dervishes protesting the detention of their members in Tehran. The protest, which descended into violence, led to the deaths of five security officers. More than 200 of the protesters were subsequently convicted and sentenced to prison terms, and a bus driver was hanged in June following a murder conviction for killing three police officers during the protest. Amnesty International claimed that the only evidence used in the trial was a confession the accused made after being severely beaten by the police.

The government also subjects some non-Muslim minorities to repressive policies and discrimination. Baha'is are systematically persecuted, sentenced to prison, and banned from access to higher education. According to Human Rights Watch (HRW), there were at least 79 Baha'is imprisoned as of November. There is an ongoing crackdown on Christian converts; in the past several years, a number of informal house churches have been raided and their pastors or congregants detained.

D3. Is there academic freedom, and is the educational system free from extensive political indoctrination? 1 / 4

Academic freedom remains limited in Iran. Khamenei has warned that universities should not be turned into centers for political activities. Students have been prevented from continuing their studies for political reasons or because they belong to the Baha'i community. Foreign scholars visiting Iran are vulnerable to detention on trumped-up charges.

At least 150 university students were detained between December 2017 and January 2018 for attending antigovernment protests. Many of the students detained were from the University of Tehran, which was a site of mass demonstrations during the unrest. The Center for Human Rights in Iran reported that by August, at least 19 students had been sentenced to prison terms ranging from a few months to 12 years for their participation in the protests.

D4. Are individuals free to express their personal views on political or other sensitive topics without fear of surveillance or retribution? 1 / 4

Iran's vaguely defined restrictions on speech, harsh criminal penalties, and state monitoring of online communications are among several factors that deter citizens from engaging in open and free private discussion. Despite the risks and limitations, many do express dissent on social media, in some cases circumventing official blocks on certain platforms. In April 2018, the government banned Telegram, which was used by 40 million Iranians. Authorities claimed that the app spreads antigovernment propaganda and encourages unrest. However, many users were able to continue using the app by employing virtual private networks (VPNs).

E. ASSOCIATIONAL AND ORGANIZATIONAL RIGHTS: 1 / 12
E1. Is there freedom of assembly? 0 / 4

The constitution states that public demonstrations may be held if they are not "detrimental to the fundamental principles of Islam." In practice, only state-sanctioned demonstrations are typically permitted, while other gatherings have in recent years been closely monitored and forcibly dispersed by security personnel, who detain participants. Approximately 4,900 people were reportedly detained in the nationwide protests that erupted in late December 2017 and early January 2018 over the worsening economy and corruption, and at least 21 people were killed in clashes with security forces surrounding the demonstrations.

The authorities restricted access to social media platforms that were being used to spread information about the protests.

E2. Is there freedom for nongovernmental organizations, particularly those that are engaged in human rights– and governance-related work? 0 / 4

Nongovernmental organizations (NGOs) that have highlighted human rights violations have been suppressed. They include the Center for Human Rights Defenders, which remains closed with several of its members in jail, and the Mourning Mothers of Iran (Mothers of Laleh Park), which had been gathering in a Tehran park to bring attention to human rights abuses.

According to HRW, the IRGC had arrested at least 50 environmental activists by August 2018, in an unprecedented crackdown. At year's end, eight activists from the Persian Wildlife Heritage Foundation, who were arrested in January, remained in detention awaiting trial on espionage charges. The organization's managing director, Kavous Seyed-Emami, who had been arrested along with his colleagues, died in prison in February. The judiciary said Seyed-Emami's death was a suicide, but critics called for an independent investigation into the incident.

E3. Is there freedom for trade unions and similar professional or labor organizations? 1 / 4

Iran does not permit the creation of labor unions; only state-sponsored labor councils are allowed. Labor rights groups have come under pressure in recent years, with key leaders and activists sentenced to prison on national security charges. Workers who engage in strikes are vulnerable to dismissal and arrest.

F. RULE OF LAW: 3 / 16

F1. Is there an independent judiciary? 1 / 4

The judicial system is used as a tool to silence regime critics and opposition members. The head of the judiciary is appointed by the supreme leader for renewable five-year terms. Under the current head, Ayatollah Sadegh Larijani, human rights advocates and political activists have been subjected to unfair trials, and the security apparatus's influence over judges has reportedly grown.

F2. Does due process prevail in civil and criminal matters? 1 / 4

Activists are routinely arrested without warrants, held indefinitely without formal charges, and denied access to legal counsel or any contact with the outside world. Many are later convicted on vague security charges in trials that sometimes last only a few minutes.

Lawyers taking up sensitive political cases have been jailed and banned from practicing. A number of lawyers have been forced to leave the country to escape prosecution. In June 2018, authorities arrested prominent human rights lawyer Nasrin Sotoudeh, who had defended several women detained for protesting the compulsory hijab earlier in the year. Sotoudeh, who had been sentenced to five years in prison in absentia on another charge in 2016, was charged with "propaganda against the state" and "assembly and collusion." Her trial commenced in late December. At least seven attorneys were arrested and detained in 2018 in connection with their work.

Dual nationals and those with connections abroad have also faced arbitrary detention, trumped-up charges, and denial of due process rights in recent years.

F3. Is there protection from the illegitimate use of physical force and freedom from war and insurgencies? 0 / 4

Former detainees have reported being beaten during arrest and subjected to torture until they confess to crimes dictated by their interrogators.

Prisons are overcrowded, and prisoners often complain of poor detention conditions, including denial of medical care. Hunger strikes by political prisoners continued to be reported in 2018. In December, activist and political prisoner Vahid Sayadi Nasiri died after a 60-day hunger strike in protest of inhumane conditions at the Qom prison.

Iran has generally been second only to China in the number of executions it carries out each year. Convicts can be executed for offenses other than murder, such as drug trafficking and financial crimes, and for crimes they committed when they were less than 18 years old. According to the NGO Iran Human Rights, at least 273 people were executed in 2018, a significant decrease from the 507 executions reported by Amnesty International in 2017. The decrease was attributed to legislation enacted in 2017 that significantly increased the quantity of illegal drugs required for a drug-related crime to incur the death penalty, which prompted sentence reviews for thousands of death-row inmates.

The country faces a long-term threat from terrorist and insurgent groups that recruit from disadvantaged Kurdish, Arab, and Sunni Muslim minority populations. In September, gunmen attacked a military parade in Ahvaz, killing 29. Both the Islamic State (IS) and a separatist Arab group claimed responsibility for the attack. The government blamed Arab nationalists, which it claimed acted with the support of the United States and Arab nations. In the two months following the attacks, authorities arrested as many as 800 Arabs, and rights activists claim that 22 people were secretly executed during the crackdown.

F4. Do laws, policies, and practices guarantee equal treatment of various segments of the population? 1 / 4

Women do not receive equal treatment under the law and face widespread discrimination in practice. For example, a woman's testimony in court is given only half the weight of a man's, and the monetary compensation awarded to a female victim's family upon her death is half that owed to the family of a male victim. Women, unlike men, are unable to pass their nationality on to foreign-born husbands or their children.

Ethnic minorities complain of various forms of discrimination, including restrictions on the use of their languages. Some provinces with large minority populations remain underdeveloped. Activists campaigning for the rights of ethnic minorities and greater autonomy for minority regions have come under pressure from the authorities, and some have been jailed.

The penal code criminalizes all sexual relations outside of traditional marriage, and Iran is among the few countries where individuals can be put to death for consensual same-sex conduct. Members of the LGBT (lesbian, gay, bisexual, and transgender) community face harassment and discrimination, though the problem is underreported due to the criminalized and hidden nature of these groups in Iran.

G. PERSONAL AUTONOMY AND INDIVIDUAL RIGHTS: 4 / 16

G1. Do individuals enjoy freedom of movement, including the ability to change their place of residence, employment, or education? 1 / 4

Freedom of movement is restricted, particularly for women and perceived opponents of the regime. Women are banned from certain public places, such as sports stadiums, and can obtain a passport to travel abroad only with the permission of their fathers or husbands. Many journalists and human rights activists have also been barred from traveling abroad.

G2. Are individuals able to exercise the right to own property and establish private businesses without undue interference from state or nonstate actors? 1 / 4

Iranians have the legal right to own property and establish private businesses. However, powerful institutions like the IRGC play a dominant role in the economy, and bribery is said to be widespread in the business environment, including for registration and obtaining business licenses. Women are denied equal rights in inheritance matters.

G3. Do individuals enjoy personal social freedoms, including choice of marriage partner and size of family, protection from domestic violence, and control over appearance? 1 / 4

Social freedoms are restricted in Iran. Women are subject to obligatory rules on dress and personal appearance, and those who are deemed to have inadequately covered their hair and body face state harassment, fines, and arrest. In February 2018, police arrested 29 women for publicly removing their hijabs in protest of the law, and at least three received prison sentences after being convicted for their role in the demonstrations. Men are subject to less strict controls on personal appearance.

Police conduct raids on private gatherings that breach rules against drinking alcohol and mixing with unrelated members of the opposite sex. Those attending can be detained and fined or sentenced to corporal punishment in the form of lashes.

Women do not enjoy equal rights in divorce and child custody disputes.

G4. Do individuals enjoy equality of opportunity and freedom from economic exploitation? 1 / 4

The government provides no protection to women and children forced into sex trafficking, and both Iranians and migrant workers from countries like Afghanistan are subject to forced labor and debt bondage. The IRGC has allegedly used coercive tactics to recruit thousands of Afghan migrants living in Iran to fight in Syria. In 2017, HRW reported that children as young as 14 are among those recruited.

Iraq

Population: 40,200,000
Capital: Baghdad
Political Rights Rating: 5
Civil Liberties Rating: 6
Freedom Rating: 5.5
Freedom Status: Not Free
Electoral Democracy: No

Overview: Iraq holds regular, competitive elections, and the country's various partisan, religious, and ethnic groups enjoy some representation in the political system. However, democratic governance is impeded in practice by corruption and security threats. In the Kurdistan region, democratic institutions lack the strength to contain the influence of long-standing power brokers. Civil liberties are generally respected in Iraqi law, but the state has limited capacity to prevent and punish violations.

KEY DEVELOPMENTS IN 2018:

- Reconstruction of areas liberated from the Islamic State (IS) militant group's control continued throughout the year. However, nearly two million Iraqis remained internally displaced at the end of 2018, and the threat of terrorism persisted.

- National elections in May were generally viewed as credible and led to a peaceful transfer of power. Allegations of fraud and irregularities in the new electronic voting system prompted a recount that did not significantly change the results. Political gridlock caused long delays in the formation of the new government, which was headed by Prime Minister Adel Abdul Mahdi.
- In July, protests erupted in Basra over corruption and poor infrastructure, among other issues. Security forces responded by firing tear gas and live ammunition at protesters, killing over a dozen people, and scores more were arrested.
- In September, Kurdish regional prime minister Nechirvan Barzani's Kurdistan Democratic Party (KDP) won the most seats in Iraqi Kurdistan's parliamentary elections, despite the KDP's perceived vulnerabilities following its mishandling of a controversial 2017 independence referendum, which led to conflict with Baghdad and substantial territorial losses for the regional government. The September elections were tarnished by widespread allegations of fraud.

POLITICAL RIGHTS: 17 / 40 (+1)

A. ELECTORAL PROCESS: 8 / 12

A1. Was the current head of government or other chief national authority elected through free and fair elections? 2 / 4

After national elections, the Council of Representatives (CoR) chooses the largely ceremonial president, who in turn appoints a prime minister nominated by the largest bloc in the parliament. The prime minister, who holds most executive power and forms the government, serves up to two four-year terms. The national elections held in May 2018 were generally viewed as credible by international observers, despite low turnout and allegations of fraud, which was particularly prevalent in the Kurdish provinces and neighboring Kirkuk. In October, after a five-month delay, the new CoR chose Kurdish politician Barham Salih as president, and Adel Abdul Mahdi, a Shiite independent, was appointed as prime minister. Cabinet posts were still being filled at year's end amid ongoing interparty negotiations.

The Kurdistan Regional Government (KRG), composed of Iraq's northernmost provinces, is ostensibly led by a president with extensive executive powers. The draft Kurdish constitution requires presidential elections every four years and limits presidents to two terms. However, after eight years as president, Masoud Barzani of the KDP had his term extended by two years in a 2013 political agreement with another party, the Patriotic Union of Kurdistan (PUK). In 2015, Barzani unilaterally prolonged his term by another two years, which was met with condemnation by opposition leaders. Barzani remained in office until November 2017, finally resigning after he organized an unauthorized September referendum on Kurdish independence that prompted the Iraqi central government to reassert control over the region's international borders and all territory occupied by Kurdish forces since the IS offensive in 2014. After Barzani stepped down, the presidency remained vacant, and executive power was held by Prime Minister Nechirvan Barzani, his nephew. After the Kurdish parliamentary elections in September 2018, the KDP nominated Nechirvan Barzani to become president and Masrour Barzani—Masoud Barzani's son—to serve as prime minster. Talks on government formation were ongoing at year's end.

A2. Were the current national legislative representatives elected through free and fair elections? 3 / 4

The 329-member CoR is elected every four years from multimember open lists in each province. The May 2018 elections were generally viewed as credible by international observers, despite some allegations of fraud. Reported irregularities in the new electronic voting system prompted the CoR to pass a law mandating a recount. During the recount, a storage facility containing many ballots caught fire, further undermining public trust in the process. The completed recount did not significantly alter the results. The Sairoon alliance, led by Shiite cleric Moqtada al-Sadr, won the most seats with 54, followed by the Conquest coalition led by Hadi al-Amiri with 48, outgoing prime minister Haider al-Abadi's Victory alliance with 42, and the State of Law coalition headed by former prime minister Nouri al-Maliki with 25. The top four alliances were all led by Shiite parties, though they made varying efforts to reach across sectarian lines. Among the several Kurdish parties, the KDP won 25 seats and the PUK won 19. The remaining seats were divided among Sunni-led coalitions, smaller parties, and independents.

Provincial council elections originally scheduled for 2017 have been repeatedly delayed. As of late 2018, they were expected to be held in 2019. Kirkuk, the subject of a dispute between the KRG and the central government, has not held provincial council elections since 2005.

In the Kurdistan region, the 111-seat Kurdistan Parliament is elected through closed party-list proportional representation in a single district, with members serving four-year terms. The September 2018 elections, originally due in 2017, resulted in the governing KDP increasing its plurality to 45 seats. The PUK received 21 seats, Gorran took 12, and several smaller parties and minority representatives accounted for the remainder. The elections were plagued by fraud allegations and other irregularities, and Gorran and other smaller parties rejected the results.

A3. Are the electoral laws and framework fair, and are they implemented impartially by the relevant election management bodies? 3 / 4

The Independent High Electoral Commission (IHEC) is responsible for managing elections in Iraq. The IHEC generally enjoys the confidence of the international community and, according to some polls, the Iraqi public. It faced criticism in 2018 from opposition leaders and outgoing prime minister Haider al-Abadi over its handling of electronic voting challenges and the subsequent recount, but international organizations praised the body for its professionalism and impartiality. A national census has not been conducted since 1987, which has resulted in skewed parliamentary seat allocations.

The Kurdistan Independent High Electoral and Referendum Commission (IHERC) administers elections in the Kurdistan region. In addition to the 2018 legislative balloting, the IHERC conducted the 2017 independence referendum, in which 93 percent of voters favored independence, though the exercise—which was not monitored by international observers—was allegedly marred by intimidation and fraud.

B. POLITICAL PLURALISM AND PARTICIPATION: 8 / 16 (+1)

B1. Do the people have the right to organize in different political parties or other competitive political groupings of their choice, and is the system free of undue obstacles to the rise and fall of these competing parties or groupings? 3 / 4

The constitution guarantees the freedom to form and join political parties, with the exception of the pre-2003 dictatorship's Baath Party, which is banned. A 2016 law strengthened the ban, criminalizing Baathist protests and the promotion of Baathist ideas. The measure applies to any group that supports racism, terrorism, sectarianism, sectarian cleansing, and other ideas contrary to democracy or the peaceful transfer of power. Individual Iraqis' freedom to run for office is also limited by a vague "good conduct" requirement in the electoral law.

In practice, Iraqis can generally form parties and operate without government interference. Party membership and multiparty alliances shift frequently. The IHEC registered 205 parties for the 2018 elections, reflecting both a relatively open political environment and deep fragmentation.

B2. Is there a realistic opportunity for the opposition to increase its support or gain power through elections? 3 / 4 (+1)

Elections are competitive, but most parties are dominated by one sectarian or ethnic group, meaning large and established parties representing the Shiite majority tend to govern and minority groups can only gain power as part of a cross-sectarian party or bloc. A number of new parties that are more secular and national in orientation participated in the 2018 elections, but Shiite parties continued to play the leading role. The strong performance of the newly formed Conquest coalition, which finished second, raised some concerns due to its inclusion of members associated with the Popular Mobilization Forces (PMF)—state-sponsored militia groups that fought against IS and have been accused of war crimes and Iranian ties. The former ruling party, Dawa, was split between the State of Law and Victory coalitions led by former prime ministers al-Maliki and al-Abadi, respectively, which created an opening for other lists like Sairoon and Conquest to gain seats and influence government formation. The transfer of power to the new prime minister proceeded far more smoothly than in 2014, when al-Maliki stepped down only after intense domestic and international pressure.

In the Kurdistan region, the traditional dominance of the KDP and the PUK was for a time challenged by the rise of the reformist group Gorran, but the repeated postponement of presidential and legislative elections before 2018 allowed entrenched interests to remain in power. Although the damaging crisis that followed the 2017 independence referendum appeared to threaten the KDP's electoral prospects, it ultimately retained its leading position in the 2018 legislative elections, while the PUK replaced Gorran as the second-largest party in the Kurdish parliament.

Score Change: The score improved from 2 to 3 because the outgoing national government facilitated competitive elections, which led to changes in the political balance in the parliament and a peaceful transfer of power to a new prime minister.

B3. Are the people's political choices free from domination by the military, foreign powers, religious hierarchies, economic oligarchies, or any other powerful group that is not democratically accountable? 1 / 4

The ability of IS to suppress normal political activity has waned significantly since 2017, when government forces successfully drove the group out of the territory it formerly controlled.

However, Iraq's political system remains distorted by interference from foreign powers, most notably Iran, which physically and politically threatens Iraqi policymakers who challenge its interests. The PMF have strong links to Iran, and dozens of figures associated with these militias ran in the 2018 elections and won seats in the CoR.

B4. Do various segments of the population (including ethnic, religious, gender, LGBT, and other relevant groups) have full political rights and electoral opportunities? 1 / 4

Despite legal and constitutional measures designed to protect the political rights of various religious and ethnic groups, the dominant role of ethno-sectarian parties and the allocation of key offices according to informal religious or ethnic criteria reduce the likelihood that politicians will act in the interests of the whole population.

Sunni Arabs, the largest ethno-sectarian minority, are represented in the parliament but often argue that the Shiite majority excludes them from positions of real influence. While the presidency and premiership are reserved in practice for a Kurd and a Shiite, the position of parliament speaker goes to a Sunni; Muhammad al-Halbusi was named speaker in September 2018.

A system of reserved seats ensures a minimum representation in the CoR for some of Iraq's smaller religious and ethnic minorities. There are five seats reserved for Christians and one each for Fayli Kurds (added in 2018), Yazidis, Sabean Mandaeans, and Shabaks. The Kurdish parliament reserves five seats for Turkmen, five for Christians, and one for Armenians. The political rights of minorities have been severely impeded by widespread displacement from formerly IS-occupied areas. Although polling stations were set up at encampments for the country's nearly two million internally displaced people (IDPs), in May 2018 the parliament voted to annul the votes of IDPs due to fraud claims.

The CoR and the Kurdish parliament reserve 25 percent and 30 percent of their seats for women, respectively, though such formal representation has had little obvious effect on state policies toward women, who are typically excluded from political debates and leadership positions. LGBT (lesbian, gay, bisexual, and transgender) people are unable to enjoy equal political rights in practice due to harsh societal discrimination, and the main political parties do not advocate for the interests of LGBT people in their platforms.

C. FUNCTIONING OF GOVERNMENT: 2 / 12

C1. Do the freely elected head of government and national legislative representatives determine the policies of the government? 1 / 4

Several factors, including irregular Kurdish occupation of some areas and extensive Iranian influence, have hindered the ability of elected officials to independently set and implement laws and policies. The United States and its allies also exert some policy influence through their support for Iraqi security forces and other state institutions. Iraq's fragmented politics can lead to gridlock and dysfunction, as demonstrated by the protracted negotiations on government formation following the May 2018 elections.

In the KRG, Masoud Barzani effectively suspended the parliament in 2015 after the speaker and many members opposed his extended presidential mandate. Although the parliament reconvened ahead of the independence referendum in 2017, some parties boycotted the session, and the executive governed without a legislature for most of the year. Separately, Kurdish lawmakers boycotted the CoR for several weeks in late 2017 amid the referendum crisis. The Kurdish legislature that was elected in September 2018 has met, but tension was still high between the KDP and PUK, and a government had not yet formed as of December. The office of president has remained vacant since Masoud Barzani stepped down in November 2017. Some parties have called for the post to be permanently abolished.

C2. Are safeguards against official corruption strong and effective? 0 / 4

Corruption remains a major problem in Iraq. Political parties, which siphon funds from the ministries they control and take kickbacks for government contracts, resist anticorruption efforts, while whistle-blowers and investigators are subject to intimidation and violence. The judicial system, itself hampered by politicization and corruption, takes action on only a fraction of the cases investigated by the Integrity Commission, one of three governmental anticorruption bodies. In response to widespread anticorruption protests in July 2018, the government referred several senior officials suspected of fraud to the Integrity Commission, and claimed that over 5,000 cases of corruption were being investigated. As of December, it was unclear whether any investigations had been referred for prosecution. The KRG suffers from similar corruption problems.

C3. Does the government operate with openness and transparency? 1 / 4

A few policies that promote openness have been adopted, including rules requiring public officials to disclose their assets, but the government does not generally operate with transparency. The CoR debates the budget, and interest groups are often able to access draft legislation. However, security conditions make elected representatives, who usually live and work in a restricted part of the capital, relatively inaccessible to the public. The public procurement system is nontransparent and corrupt, with no legal recourse available for unsuccessful bidders. The oil and gas industry also lacks transparency, and the government has failed to make adequate progress in meeting its commitments to the Extractive Industries Transparency Initiative. The government has not yet passed a comprehensive law on access to information.

ADDITIONAL DISCRETIONARY POLITICAL RIGHTS QUESTION

Is the government or occupying power deliberately changing the ethnic composition of a country or territory so as to destroy a culture or tip the political balance in favor of another group? −1 / 0

IS's loss of territorial control in 2017 largely halted its campaign to alter religious demography, though many Shiite Muslims and religious minorities who were displaced by the group remain unable to return to their homes, for both security and economic reasons. Iraqi government forces' return in late 2017 to territories held by Kurdish militias since 2014 resulted in another round of demographic changes in those areas, with some Kurdish residents leaving and displaced Arabs returning. There have also been reports of Sunni Arabs being displaced from areas liberated from IS by Shiite militias. As of December 2018, approximately four million Iraqis displaced by the IS offensive in 2014 had since returned to their home regions, while another 1.9 million people remained internally displaced.

CIVIL LIBERTIES: 15 / 60
D. FREEDOM OF EXPRESSION AND BELIEF: 5 / 16
D1. Are there free and independent media? 1 / 4

The constitution allows limits on free expression to preserve "public order" and "morality." Iraq's media scene appears lively and diverse, but there are few politically independent news sources. Journalists who do not self-censor can face legal repercussions or violent retaliation.

No journalists were killed in connection with their work in 2018, compared with eight in 2017. However, multiple cases of harassment and intimidation of journalists were documented during the year. In July, at least four journalists covering protests in Basra were assaulted by security forces. Journalists reporting on corruption also faced harassment and arrest.

In the Kurdistan region, seven reporters were attacked by Kurdish security forces, and at least two were detained, while covering protests against austerity measures in March.

D2. Are individuals free to practice and express their religious faith or nonbelief in public and private? 1 / 4

The constitution guarantees freedom of belief, but in practice many Iraqis have been subjected to violence and displacement due to their religious identity, and places of worship have often been targets for terrorist attacks. Blasphemy laws remain on the books, although enforcement is rare. A religious conversion law passed in 2015 discriminates against non-Muslims by automatically designating the children of a parent who has converted to Islam as Muslim, even if the other parent is a non-Muslim. Restaurants serving alcohol and liquor stores have faced harassment and attack, further eroding religious freedom.

Most political leaders expressed support for religious pluralism after IS's defeat, and Sunnis living in liberated areas were largely able to practice their religion freely in 2018.

D3. Is there academic freedom, and is the educational system free from extensive political indoctrination? 1 / 4

Educators have long faced the threat of violence or other repercussions for teaching subjects or discussing topics that powerful state or nonstate actors find objectionable. The country's official curriculum is often augmented in the classroom by religious or sectarian viewpoints.

Political activism by university students can result in harassment or intimidation.

D4. Are individuals free to express their personal views on political or other sensitive topics without fear of surveillance or retribution? 2 / 4

Social media posts on controversial topics sometimes result in retribution. Political speech in the Kurdistan region can also prompt arbitrary detentions or other reprisals from government or partisan forces.

The Iraqi government is known to restrict internet access in response to political turmoil. In July 2018, the government reacted to protests in Basra by shutting down the internet in a number of regions for several days, followed by a targeted restriction of access to social media platforms including WhatsApp, Twitter, and Facebook. The move was intended to curb the protests and stanch online criticism of the government.

E. ASSOCIATIONAL AND ORGANIZATIONAL RIGHTS: 5 / 12 (-1)

E1. Is there freedom of assembly? 1 / 4 (-1)

The constitution guarantees freedom of assembly, but protesters are frequently at risk of violence or arrest. Security forces used curfews, tear gas, and live ammunition to suppress a series of protests against corruption and poor infrastructure in Basra that began in July 2018 and continued as of December. Scores of people were arrested or injured, and at least 15 were killed. Numerous protesters were also beaten and detained during economic protests in Kurdistan in March.

Score Change: The score declined from 2 to 1 due to the violent suppression of protests, particularly those focused on living conditions in the southern city of Basra.

E2. Is there freedom for nongovernmental organizations, particularly those that are engaged in human rights- and governance-related work? 2 / 4

Nongovernmental organizations (NGOs) enjoy societal support and a relatively hospitable regulatory environment, though they must register with the government and obtain approval from the commission responsible for suppressing Baathism to operate. In the Kurdistan region, NGOs must renew their registration annually.

Several NGO leaders were abused or assassinated in 2018, raising concerns about renewed threats to civil society. In September 2018, Suad al-Ali, the leader of Al-Wid al-Alaiami for Human Rights, was murdered in her car in Basra. Al-Ali had been involved in the protests in Basra and was an outspoken advocate for women's rights. As of December, the crime, along with the other attacks on prominent activists, remained unsolved.

E3. Is there freedom for trade unions and similar professional or labor organizations? 2 / 4

Labor laws allow for collective bargaining (even by nonunionized workers), protect the rights of subcontractors and migrant workers, and permit workers to strike, among other features. However, public-sector workers are not allowed to unionize, there is no legal prohibition against antiunion discrimination, and workers do not have access to legal remedies if fired for union activity. Some state officials and private employers discourage union activity with threats, demotions, and other deterrents.

F. RULE OF LAW: 1 / 16 (+1)

F1. Is there an independent judiciary? 0 / 4

The judiciary is influenced by corruption, political pressure, tribal forces, and religious interests. The lines between the executive, legislative, and judicial branches are frequently blurred, and executive interference in the judiciary is widespread. Due to distrust of or lack of access to the courts, many Iraqis have turned to tribal bodies to settle disputes, even those involving major crimes.

F2. Does due process prevail in civil and criminal matters? 0 / 4

Criminal proceedings in Iraq are deeply flawed. Arbitrary arrests, including arrests without a warrant, are common. Terrorism cases in particular have been prone to fundamental violations of due process, with human rights groups describing systematic denial of access to counsel and short, summary trials with little evidence that the defendants committed specific crimes other than association with IS. In 2018, some trials of suspected IS members that resulted in death sentences lasted as little as 20 minutes. Hundreds of foreign wives and children of suspected IS fighters have also been arbitrarily detained and labeled terrorists, part of what some analysts describe as a campaign of retribution against IS fighters and their families.

F3. Is there protection from the illegitimate use of physical force and freedom from war and insurgencies? 1 / 4 (+1)

The end of large-scale combat with IS significantly improved the security environment. Though the organization remained active as a clandestine terrorist group in 2018, it no longer controlled Iraqi territory or civilian populations, and its ability to operate was diminished.

The use of torture to obtain confessions is widespread, including in death penalty cases. In 2018, the government continued to expedite executions of those convicted of terrorism. Detainees are often held in harsh, overcrowded conditions, and forced disappearances, particularly of suspected IS fighters, have been reported.

Score Change: The score improved from 0 to 1 due to the cessation of heavy fighting between progovernment forces and the IS militant group, which was driven from its last strongholds in the country at the end of 2017.

F4. Do laws, policies, and practices guarantee equal treatment of various segments of the population? 0 / 4

Women face widespread societal bias and discriminatory treatment under laws on a number of topics. Sexual harassment in the workplace is prohibited, but it is reportedly rare for victims to pursue formal complaints.

Members of a given ethnic or religious group tend to suffer discrimination or persecution in areas where they represent a minority, leading many to seek safety in other neighborhoods or provinces. Same-sex sexual relations are not explicitly prohibited, but LGBT people risk violence if they are open about their identity. People of African descent suffer from high rates of extreme poverty and discrimination.

G. PERSONAL AUTONOMY AND INDIVIDUAL RIGHTS: 4 / 16

G1. Do individuals enjoy freedom of movement, including the ability to change their place of residence, employment, or education? 1 / 4

Almost two million Iraqis remained internally displaced at the end of 2018. Freedom of movement improved somewhat as areas formerly controlled by IS were brought back under government control. However, large-scale destruction of housing and infrastructure, the presence of sectarian or partisan militias, and the ongoing threat of violence made it difficult for many displaced people to return home.

The movement of women is limited by legal restrictions. Women require the consent of a male guardian to obtain a passport and the Civil Status Identification Document, which is needed to access employment, education, and a number of social services.

G2. Are individuals able to exercise the right to own property and establish private businesses without undue interference from state or non-state actors? 1 / 4

Iraqis are legally free to own property and establish businesses, but observance of property rights has been limited by corruption and conflict, most recently the conflict with IS. Business owners face demands for bribes, threats, and violent attempts to seize their enterprises. Contracts are difficult to enforce. Women are legally disadvantaged with respect to inheritance rights and may face pressure to yield their rights to male relatives.

G3. Do individuals enjoy personal social freedoms, including choice of marriage partner and size of family, protection from domestic violence, and control over appearance? 1 / 4

Forced and early marriages are common, especially in the context of displacement and poverty. Nearly one in four Iraqi women aged 20 to 24 were married by age 18, and marriage between 15 and 18 is legal with parental approval. Laws on marriage and divorce favor men over women. Domestic violence is criminalized but widespread and rarely prosecuted. Rapists can avoid prosecution if they marry their victims; spousal rape is not prohibited. The law also allows reduced sentences for those convicted of so-called honor killings, which are seldom punished in practice.

Both men and women face pressure to conform to conservative standards on personal appearance. A number of high-profile women associated with the beauty and fashion industries were murdered in 2018, including Tara Fares, a social media star who was shot dead in Baghdad in September. The assailants remained unknown at year's end, but the government blamed extremist groups for the murders.

G4. Do individuals enjoy equality of opportunity and freedom from economic exploitation? 1 / 4

After the military defeat of IS, many Yazidi women who had been forced into sex slavery remained missing. Exploitation of children, including through forced begging and the recruitment of child soldiers by some militias, is a chronic problem. Foreign migrant workers frequently work long hours for low pay, and they are vulnerable to forced labor. Human trafficking is also a problem, and IDPs are particularly vulnerable. Thus far, the government's efforts to enforce trafficking laws have been inadequate.

Ireland

Population: 4,900,000
Capital: Dublin
Political Rights Rating: 1
Civil Liberties Rating: 1
Freedom Rating: 1.0
Freedom Status: Free
Electoral Democracy: Yes

Overview: Ireland is a stable democracy in which political rights and civil liberties are re-spected and defended. There is some limited societal discrimination, especially against the traditionally nomadic Irish Travellers. Corruption scandals have plagued the police force, and domestic violence remains a problem.

KEY DEVELOPMENTS IN 2018:

- Legislation legalizing abortion took effect in December, following a May referen-dum in which voters chose decisively to abolish a constitutional amendment that banned abortion in nearly all cases.
- In October, Michael D. Higgins was reelected as president. Voters overwhelming supported removing references to blasphemy from the Irish Constitution in a con-current referendum.
- Both Prime Minister Leo Varadkar and President Higgins condemned discrimina-tory statements against Irish Travellers after a presidential candidate voiced such remarks during the campaign period.

POLITICAL RIGHTS: 39 / 40

A. ELECTORAL PROCESS: 12 / 12

A1. Was the current head of government or other chief national authority elected through free and fair elections? 4 / 4

The Taoiseach, or prime minister, is nominated by House of Representatives (Dàil Eireann) and formally appointed by the president. Thus, the legitimacy of the prime minister is largely dependent on the conduct of Dàil elections, which historically have free and fair. The Dàil elected Varadkar, of the Fine Gael party, as Taoiseach in June 2017, following the decision by Enda Kenny, also of Fine Gael, to step down after six years. The son of an Indian immigrant and openly gay, Varadkar is also Ireland's youngest-ever Taoiseach, elected when he was 38 years old.

The president is elected to up to two seven-year terms, and as chief of state has mostly ceremonial duties. Higgins was reelected in October 2018. Voting in presidential elections has historically been free and fair.

A2. Were the current national legislative representatives elected through free and fair elec-tions? 4 / 4

The 2016 Dàil elections saw no major irregularities or unequal campaigning opportu-nities. Fine Gael remained the largest party, but with far fewer seats than it had taken in the 2011 general election, while Fianna Fáil more than doubled its share of the vote. Fine Gael formed a minority government with the support of some independent lawmakers and through a confidence-and-supply arrangement with Fianna Fáil, which in December 2018 was extended until 2020. (Under such arrangements, an opposition party agrees to support a minority government in confidence votes and matters relating to the budget, but may oppose it on other matters.)

A3. Are the electoral laws and framework fair, and are they implemented impartially by the relevant election management bodies? 4 / 4

Ireland's electoral framework is strong and government bodies are able to put on credible polls. However, there is no electoral commission in Ireland, and the organization of elections has been criticized at times. Plans are in progress to create an electoral commission in 2019.

Ireland has frequent referendums, especially on European Union (EU) treaties. While there is no evidence of interference in Ireland's elections or referendums to date, Prime Minister Varadkar has emphasized the need to strengthen the country's data protection systems to safeguard against external or nondemocratic forces interfering with future polls.

B. POLITICAL PLURALISM AND PARTICIPATION: 16 / 16

B1. Do the people have the right to organize in different political parties or other competitive political groupings of their choice, and is the system free of undue obstacles to the rise and fall of these competing parties or groupings? 4 / 4

Political parties in Ireland are free to form and compete. The two main parties—Fianna Fáil and Fine Gael—do not differ widely in ideology; they represent the successors of opposing sides in the nation's 1922–23 civil war. Other key parties include the Labour Party, Sinn Féin, and the Green Party. A record number of independent lawmakers, 23, entered the Dàil in 2016.

B2. Is there a realistic opportunity for the opposition to increase its support or gain power through elections? 4 / 4

Opposition parties generally do not encounter restrictions or harassment that affects their ability to gain power through elections. Fianna Fáil dominated politics after Ireland became independent, holding power for 61 out of 79 years until 2011. Fine Gael is now the largest party in parliament.

B3. Are the people's political choices free from domination by the military, foreign powers, religious hierarchies, economic oligarchies, or any other powerful group that is not democratically accountable? 4 / 4

People's political choices are generally free from domination by military, foreign powers, religious hierarchies, and other powerful groups.

B4. Do various segments of the population (including ethnic, religious, gender, LGBT, and other relevant groups) have full political rights and electoral opportunities? 4 / 4

Ethnic and other minorities are free to participate in politics. Women are active in politics but are underrepresented; 22 percent of Dàil representatives are women.

The roughly 30,000 members of the Irish Traveller minority have little political representation, and efforts to include them in political processes are minimal.

C. FUNCTIONING OF GOVERNMENT: 11 / 12

C1. Do the freely elected head of government and national legislative representatives determine the policies of the government? 4 / 4

Elected officials freely determine government policy.

C2. Are safeguards against official corruption strong and effective? 3 / 4

Ireland has a recent history of problems with political corruption, but has introduced anticorruption legislation in recent years. The Corruption Offences Act seeks to consolidate and modernize anticorruption laws, and took effect in July 2018. It faced criticism, however, that it does not adequately address bribery. Ongoing scandals involving Ireland's police force (An Garda Síochána) have raised concerns about a lack of safeguards against corruption in that sector.

In October 2018, a scandal relating to alleged corruption in the awarding of broadband contracts by the state led to the resignation of Denis Naughten, the minister for communications, climate action and the environment. An independent audit in November found no evidence that the procurement process had been tainted.

C3. Does the government operate with openness and transparency? 4 / 4

The public has broad access to official information under the 2014 Freedom of Information Act, though partial exemptions remain for the police and some other agencies. A Transparency Code requires open records on the groups and individuals that advise public officials on policy.

The government has been criticized for failing to consult meaningfully with civil society groups and relevant stakeholders in the formulation of some policies, particularly regarding members of the Romany minority, Travellers, and persons with disabilities.

CIVIL LIBERTIES: 58 / 60 (+1)
D. FREEDOM OF EXPRESSION AND BELIEF: 16 / 16
D1. Are there free and independent media? 4 / 4

Irish media are free and independent, and present a variety of viewpoints. The state may censor material deemed indecent or obscene, but this provision is rarely invoked. President Higgins officially removed references to criminal blasphemy offences from the constitution in November, following an October 2018 referendum in which roughly 65 percent of voters approved eliminating the offense.

D2. Are individuals free to practice and express their religious faith or nonbelief in public and private? 4 / 4

Freedom of religion is constitutionally guaranteed. Although religious oaths are still required from senior public officials, there is no state religion, and adherents of other faiths face few impediments to religious expression. In recent years, Ireland has faced a notable decline in religiosity following a series of sexual abuse and other scandals involving the Roman Catholic Church and Catholic clergy.

D3. Is there academic freedom, and is the educational system free from extensive political indoctrination? 4 / 4

Academic freedom is respected. The Catholic Church operates approximately 90 percent of Ireland's schools and most schools include religious education, but parents may exempt their children from it. The constitution requires equal funding for schools run by different denominations.

D4. Are individuals free to express their personal views on political or other sensitive topics without fear of surveillance or retribution? 4 / 4

There are no significant impediments to open and free private discussion, including in personal online communications.

E. ASSOCIATIONAL AND ORGANIZATIONAL RIGHTS: 12 / 12

E1. Is there freedom of assembly? 4 / 4

The right to assemble freely is respected, and peaceful demonstrations are held each year.

E2. Is there freedom for nongovernmental organizations, particularly those that are engaged in human rights- and governance-related work? 4 / 4

Freedom of association is upheld, and nongovernmental organizations (NGOs) can operate freely.

E3. Is there freedom for trade unions and similar professional or labor organizations? 4 / 4

Labor unions operate without hindrance, and collective bargaining is legal and unrestricted.

F. RULE OF LAW: 14 / 16

F1. Is there an independent judiciary? 4 / 4

Ireland has a generally independent judiciary and a legal system based on common law. However, the government has not yet acted upon most of the recommendations issued in 2014 by the Council of Europe's anticorruption body, known as GRECO, regarding the establishment of a Judicial Council and improvements to judicial appointments procedures. In a July 2018 report, GRECO expressed concern about a provision in proposed legislation that would permit a judicial appointments commission to be comprised largely of lay members.

F2. Does due process prevail in civil and criminal matters? 4 / 4

Due process generally prevails in civil and criminal matters. However, the police force has been rocked by repeated scandals over the past years. The head of the Irish police resigned in 2017 in the wake of investigations of her handling of investigations of irregular use of breathalyzer tests, and questions about her approach toward whistleblowers. Separately, the 2017 final report of the Fennelly Commission that investigated allegations that some Garda stations had illegally taped telephone calls found evidence of unlawful recordings, but concluded that it was neither widespread nor systematic. The Garda have also been accused of routinely wiping penalty points from driving licenses of police members. A new head of the Irish police force was appointed in September 2018.

A series of official inquiries in recent years have detailed decades of past physical and emotional abuse—including forced labor as recently as 1996—against women and children in state institutions and by Catholic priests and nuns, as well as collusion to hide the abuse. In August 2018, Pope Francis visited Ireland and recognized the "outrage" over such abuse, including the scandal relating to the 2017 discovery of a mass grave of children and babies in a long-closed Catholic-church run care home in Tuam, County Galway.

F3. Is there protection from the illegitimate use of physical force and freedom from war and insurgencies? 3 / 4

Irish prisons and detention facilities are frequently dangerous, unsanitary, and overcrowded. The government has taken some steps to address a 2015 Council of Europe report that criticized the continued lack of toilet access in some cells.

Some politicians and communities have expressed concern about the impact of the United Kingdom's impending departure from the EU (known as Brexit) on aspects of the 1998 Good Friday peace agreement, which ended a period of sectarian conflict in Northern Ireland known as the Troubles; some such concerns relate to a perceived risk of unrest at the Northern Ireland border. However, the threat of violence in Ireland remained low in 2018.

F4. Do laws, policies, and practices guarantee equal treatment of various segments of the population? 3 / 4

The Irish Travellers face discrimination in housing and hiring. Peter Casey, who ran for president in 2018, was criticized after making anti-Traveller remarks on a podcast he appeared on as part of his campaign. Both Higgins and Varadkar shortly afterward publicly denounced anti-Traveller sentiment, and Varadkar affirmed that his government recognized the Traveller ethnicity.

There are concerns that people with disabilities are persistently institutionalized and have suffered a severe reduction of social benefits as a result of a years-long austerity drive that followed the 2008–09 global financial crisis.

Irish law prohibits discrimination based on sexual orientation, but some social stigma against LGBT (lesbian, gay, bisexual, and transgender) people persists. In 2015, the parliament passed legislation to curtail an exemption that allowed health and educational institutions run by religious entities to practice employment discrimination on religious grounds—for example, on the basis of sexual orientation.

The asylum application process is complex, and asylum seekers can be housed for lengthy periods in poor living conditions. The 2015 International Protection Law expedites asylum procedures, although it focuses on enabling deportations rather than properly identifying and processing asylum cases.

Discrimination in the workplace on the basis of gender is illegal, but gender inequality in wages persists.

G. PERSONAL AUTONOMY AND INDIVIDUAL RIGHTS: 16 / 16 (+1)

G1. Do individuals enjoy freedom of movement, including the ability to change their place of residence, employment, or education? 4 / 4

There are no restrictions on travel or the ability to change one's place of residence, employment, or education.

G2. Are individuals able to exercise the right to own property and establish private businesses without undue interference from state or nonstate actors? 4 / 4

Private businesses are free to operate, and property rights are generally respected.

G3. Do individuals enjoy personal social freedoms, including choice of marriage partner and size of family, protection from domestic violence, and control over appearance? 4 / 4 (+1)

Domestic and sexual violence against women is a serious problem, and access to support for victims is particularly difficult for marginalized and immigrant women.

In 2015, referendum voters approved the extension of marriage rights to same-sex couples, and the Marriage Act was passed to legalize same-sex marriage. Also in 2015, the Children and Family Relationships Act extended adoption rights to same-sex and cohabiting couples, and the Gender Recognition Act began allowing transgender individuals to obtain legal recognition without medical or state intervention, and—for married transgender people—without divorcing.

In a May 2018 referendum, over 66 percent of Irish voters chose to abolish a constitutional amendment that recognized the equal right to life of the mother and the unborn, and thus made almost all abortions illegal. The Health (Regulation of Termination of Pregnancy) Bill legalizing abortion was signed into law in December.

Score Change: The score improved from 3 to 4 due to the legalization of abortion.

G4. Do individuals enjoy equality of opportunity and freedom from economic exploitation? 4 / 4

People generally enjoy equality of opportunity. However, although the government works to combat human trafficking and protect victims, undocumented migrant workers remain at risk of trafficking and labor exploitation.

Israel

Population: 8,500,000
Capital: Jerusalem
Political Rights Rating: 2 ↓
Civil Liberties Rating: 3
Freedom Rating: 2.5
Freedom Status: Free
Electoral Democracy: Yes

Note: The numerical ratings and status listed above do not reflect conditions in the West Bank and the Gaza Strip, which are examined in separate reports. Although the international community generally considers East Jerusalem to be part of the occupied West Bank, it may be mentioned in this report when specific conditions there directly affect or overlap with conditions in Israel proper.

Overview: Israel is a multiparty democracy with strong and independent institutions that guarantee political rights and civil liberties for most of the population. Although the judiciary is active in protecting minority rights, the political leadership and many in society have discriminated against Arab and other minorities, resulting in systemic disparities in areas including political representation, criminal justice, and economic opportunity.

KEY DEVELOPMENTS IN 2018:

- A new law with constitutional weight, adopted by the Knesset (parliament) in July, declared that the right to exercise self-determination in the State of Israel belongs uniquely to the Jewish people. Among other provisions, the law symbolically downgraded Arabic from an official language to a language with "special status."
- Also in July, the Knesset approved a law barring civil society groups that criticize the actions of Israeli soldiers from entering schools or addressing students.
- In February and December, police recommended the indictment of Prime Minister Benjamin Netanyahu in three separate corruption cases, but the attorney general had yet to decide on the recommendations at year's end.
- The governing coalition broke down in December, triggering new elections that were scheduled for April 2019.

POLITICAL RIGHTS: 35 / 40 (−1)

A. ELECTORAL PROCESS: 12 / 12

A1. Was the current head of government or other chief national authority elected through free and fair elections? 4 / 4

A largely ceremonial president is elected by the Knesset for one seven-year term. In 2014, Reuven Rivlin of the right-leaning Likud party was elected to replace outgoing president Shimon Peres, receiving 63 votes in a runoff against Meir Sheetrit of the centrist Hatnuah party.

The prime minister is usually the leader of the largest faction in the Knesset. In 2014, in a bid to create more stable governing coalitions, the electoral threshold for parties to win representation was raised from 2 percent to 3.25 percent, and the no-confidence procedure was revised so that opponents hoping to oust a sitting government must simultaneously vote in a new one. The incumbent prime minister in 2018, Benjamin Netanyahu of the conservative party Likud, had been in office since 2009, most recently securing reelection after the 2015 parliamentary polls.

A2. Were the current national legislative representatives elected through free and fair elections? 4 / 4

Members of the 120-seat Knesset are elected by party-list proportional representation for four-year terms, and elections are typically free and fair. In the 2015 contest, Likud secured 30 seats, followed by the center-left Zionist Union with 24. The Joint List—a coalition of parties representing Arab citizens of Israel, who often identify as Palestinian—earned 13 seats; the centrist Yesh Atid (There Is a Future), 11; Kulanu, also centrist, 10; Habayit Hayehudi (Jewish Home), 8; the ultra-Orthodox parties Shas and United Torah Judaism, 7 and 6, respectively; the right-wing Yisrael Beiteinu, 6; and the left-wing Meretz party, 5.

The governing coalition led by Likud collapsed in December 2018, after Yisrael Beiteinu withdrew its support in November. Early elections were scheduled for April 2019.

A3. Are the electoral laws and framework fair, and are they implemented impartially by the relevant election management bodies? 4 / 4

The fairness and integrity of elections are guaranteed by the Central Elections Committee, composed of delegations representing the various political groups in the Knesset and chaired by a Supreme Court judge. Elections are generally conducted in a peaceful and orderly manner, and all parties usually accept the results.

B. POLITICAL PLURALISM AND PARTICIPATION: 13 / 16 (−1)

B1. Do the people have the right to organize in different political parties or other competitive political groupings of their choice, and is the system free of undue obstacles to the rise and fall of these competing parties or groupings? 3 / 4

Israel hosts a diverse and competitive multiparty system. However, parties or candidates that deny Israel's Jewish character, oppose democracy, or incite racism are prohibited. Under a 2016 law, the Knesset can remove any members who incite racism or support armed struggle against the state of Israel with a three-quarters majority vote; critics allege that the law is aimed at silencing Arab representatives.

B2. Is there a realistic opportunity for the opposition to increase its support or gain power through elections? 4 / 4

Israel has undergone multiple, peaceful rotations of power among rival political groups during its history. Opposition parties control several major cities, including Tel Aviv, and many Arab-majority towns are run by mayors from the Joint List parties.

B3. Are the people's political choices free from domination by the military, foreign powers, religious hierarchies, economic oligarchies, or any other powerful group that is not democratically accountable? 4 / 4

Israeli voters are generally free from coercion or undue influence from interest groups outside the political sphere. A 2017 law imposes funding restrictions on organizations that are not political parties but seek to influence elections. While it was aimed at limiting political interference by outside groups and wealthy donors, critics of the law said its provisions could affect civil society activism surrounding elections and infringe on freedoms of association and expression.

B4. Do various segments of the population (including ethnic, religious, gender, LGBT, and other relevant groups) have full political rights and electoral opportunities? 2 / 4 (−1)

Women generally enjoy full political rights in law and in practice, though they remain somewhat underrepresented in leadership positions and can encounter additional obstacles in parties and communities—both Jewish and Arab—that are associated with religious or cultural conservatism.

In July 2018, the Knesset adopted a new "basic law" known as the nation-state law, which introduced the principle that the right to exercise self-determination in the State of Israel belongs uniquely to the Jewish people, among other discriminatory provisions. The basic laws of Israel are considered equivalent to a constitution, and critics of the nation-state law said it created a framework for the erosion of non-Jewish citizens' political and civil rights.

Arab or Palestinian citizens of Israel already faced some discrimination in practice, both legally and informally. The Joint List's representation in the Knesset falls short of Arabs' roughly one-fifth share of Israel's population, though some vote or run as candidates for other parties. No Arab party has ever been formally included in a governing coalition, and Arabs generally do not serve in senior positions in government.

The roughly 600,000 Jewish settlers in the West Bank and East Jerusalem are Israeli citizens and can participate in Israeli elections. Arab residents of East Jerusalem have the option of obtaining Israeli citizenship, though most decline for political reasons. While these noncitizens are entitled to vote in municipal as well as Palestinian Authority (PA) elections, most have traditionally boycotted Israeli municipal balloting, and Israel has restricted PA election activity in the city. A Palestinian Jerusalem resident who is not a citizen cannot become mayor under current Israeli law. Israeli law strips noncitizens of their Jerusalem residency if they are away for extended periods, and a new law adopted in March 2018 empowers the interior minister to revoke such residency for those deemed to be involved in terrorism or treason-related offenses. Citizenship and residency status are denied to Palestinian residents of the West Bank or Gaza Strip who are married to Israeli citizens.

Courts can revoke the citizenship of any Israeli convicted of spying, treason, or aiding the enemy. It was reported during 2017 that the Interior Ministry had revoked the citizenship of dozens and possibly thousands of Bedouins in recent years, citing decades-old registration errors.

Jewish immigrants and their immediate families are granted Israeli citizenship and residence rights; other immigrants must apply for these rights.

Score Change: The score declined from 3 to 2 because the parliament adopted a law with constitutional status that explicitly discriminates against the non-Jewish citizen population.

C. FUNCTIONING OF GOVERNMENT: 10 / 12

C1. Do the freely elected head of government and national legislative representatives determine the policies of the government? 4 / 4

The government and parliament are free to set and implement policies and laws without undue interference from unelected entities. Military service plays an important role in both political and civilian life, with many top officers entering politics at the end of their careers, but elected civilian institutions remain in firm control of the military.

C2. Are safeguards against official corruption strong and effective? 3 / 4

High-level corruption investigations are relatively frequent, with senior officials implicated in several scandals and criminal cases in recent years. In February and December 2018, police recommended the indictment of Prime Minister Netanyahu on charges stemming from three investigations into alleged fraud, breach of trust, and bribery; they pertained to his acceptance of expensive gifts, an apparent attempt to collude with the owner of the newspaper *Yedioth Ahronoth* to secure positive coverage, and the granting of regulatory favors to telecommunications operator and media conglomerate Bezeq in return for positive coverage. At year's end the attorney general was considering whether to proceed with the recommended indictments. Separately in June, Netanyahu's wife was indicted on charges of aggravated fraud and breach of trust related to inflated spending at the prime minister's residences. In November, police recommended charges against Netanyahu's former personal attorney and other suspects for alleged bribery related to a contract to purchase naval vessels.

A law passed in 2017 limits the circumstances under which the police can file indictment recommendations when investigating elected officials and senior civil servants, and increases the penalties for leaking a police recommendation or other investigative materials. While the law does not apply to existing investigations, the parliamentary opposition accused the majority of trying to weaken law enforcement agencies to protect its political leadership.

C3. Does the government operate with openness and transparency? 3 / 4

Israel's laws, political practices, civil society groups, and independent media generally ensure a substantial level of governmental transparency. Recent corruption cases have illustrated persistent shortcomings, though they also suggest that the system is eventually able to expose wrongdoing. The Freedom of Information Law grants every citizen and resident of Israel the right to receive information from a public authority. However, the law includes blanket exemptions that allow officials to withhold information on the armed forces, intelligence services, the Atomic Energy Agency, and the prison system, potentially enabling the concealment of abuses.

CIVIL LIBERTIES: 43 / 60
D. FREEDOM OF EXPRESSION AND BELIEF: 12 / 16
D1. Are there free and independent media? 3 / 4

The Israeli media sector as a whole is vibrant and free to criticize government policy. While the scope of permissible reporting is generally broad, print articles on security matters are subject to a military censor. According to the results of a freedom of information request, in 2017 the military partially or fully redacted a total of 2,358 news items, or 21 percent of the articles submitted to it by media outlets for prior review. The Government Press Office has occasionally withheld press cards from journalists to restrict them from entering Israel, citing security considerations.

A 2017 law allows police and prosecutors to obtain court orders that require the blocking of websites found to publish criminal or offensive content. Freedom of expression advocates warned that the measure could lead to the suppression of legitimate speech.

Netanyahu's dual role as prime minister and communications minister between 2014 and 2017 raised questions about conflicts of interest involving the ministry's regulatory functions. He was forced to resign as communications minister in light of the police investigations into his alleged attempts to arrange favorable coverage from certain private media outlets. Ayoub Kara, his replacement, was considered a close ally.

D2. Are individuals free to practice and express their religious faith or nonbelief in public and private? 3 / 4

While Israel defines itself as a Jewish state, freedom of religion is largely respected. Christian, Muslim, and Baha'i communities have jurisdiction over their own members in matters of marriage, divorce, and burial. The Orthodox establishment governs personal status matters among Jews, drawing objections from many non-Orthodox and secular Israelis. Most ultra-Orthodox Jews, or Haredim, have been excused from compulsory military service under a decades-old exemption for those engaged in full-time Torah study. In July 2018 the Knesset gave initial approval to a draft law that would regulate the conscription of Haredim, setting gradually rising recruitment targets for each year. However, the governing coalition's lack of agreement on a final bill contributed to its collapse in December 2018 and the calling of early elections, meaning debate on the conscription issue would be postponed until the new Knesset convened in 2019.

Although the law protects the religious sites of non-Jewish minorities, they face discrimination in the allocation of state resources as well as persistent cases of vandalism, which usually go unsolved.

Citing security concerns, Israeli authorities have set varying limits on access to the Temple Mount/Haram al-Sharif in East Jerusalem in recent years, affecting worshippers across the broader area. However, in August 2018 the government lifted restrictions on Jewish lawmakers visiting the site that had been in place for nearly three years.

D3. Is there academic freedom, and is the educational system free from extensive political indoctrination? 3 / 4

Primary and secondary education is universal, though divided into multiple public school systems (state, state-religious, Haredi, and Arabic). School quality and resources are generally lower in mostly non-Jewish communities. In July 2018, the Knesset approved a law to ban groups that are in favor of legal actions abroad against Israeli soldiers, or that otherwise undermine state educational goals by criticizing the military, from entering Israeli schools or interacting with students.

Israel's universities have long been centers for dissent and are open to all students, though security-related restrictions on movement limit access for West Bank and Gaza residents in practice. Universities have come under pressure from right-leaning groups and politicians in recent years.

D4. Are individuals free to express their personal views on political or other sensitive topics without fear of surveillance or retribution? 3 / 4

While private discussion in Israel is generally open and free, there are some restrictions on political expression. For example, the 2011 Boycott Law exposes Israeli individuals and groups to civil lawsuits if they advocate an economic, cultural, or academic boycott of the state of Israel or West Bank settlements.

E. ASSOCIATIONAL AND ORGANIZATIONAL RIGHTS: 9 / 12
E1. Is there freedom of assembly? 3 / 4

Israel has an active civil society, and demonstrations are widely permitted and typically peaceful. However, some protest activities—such as desecration of the flag of Israel or a friendly country—can draw serious criminal penalties, and police have sometimes attempted to restrict peaceful demonstrations.

E2. Is there freedom for nongovernmental organizations, particularly those that are engaged in human rights- and governance-related work? 2 / 4

In recent years the environment for nongovernmental organizations (NGOs) has gradually deteriorated. A law that took effect in 2012 requires NGOs to submit financial reports four times a year on support received from foreign government sources. Under a 2016 law, NGOs that receive more than half of their funding from foreign governments must disclose this fact publicly and in any written or oral communications with elected officials. The measure mainly affected groups associated with the political left that oppose Israel's policies toward the Palestinians; foreign funding for right-leaning groups that support Jewish settlements in the West Bank, for example, more often comes from private sources.

A 2017 law bars access to the country for any foreign individuals or groups that publicly support a boycott of Israel or its West Bank settlements. The measure was criticized by civil society organizations as an obstacle to the activity of many pro-Palestinian and human rights groups. In May 2018, the authorities ordered the deportation of Human Rights Watch's regional director, Omar Shakir, for allegedly supporting the boycott of Israel. However, action on the order was suspended after being challenged in court, and the case remained unresolved at year's end. In a separate case, authorities sought to bar entry to a US student pursuing a graduate degree in Israel on the grounds that she had been involved with a proboycott organization in the past. The Supreme Court ruled in October that the 2017 law did not apply to the student, in part because it was meant to be preventive rather than punitive.

E3. Is there freedom for trade unions and similar professional or labor organizations? 4 / 4

Workers may join unions and have the right to strike and bargain collectively. Most of the workforce either belongs to Histadrut, the national labor federation, or is covered by its social programs and bargaining agreements.

F. RULE OF LAW: 11 / 16

F1. Is there an independent judiciary? 4 / 4

The judiciary is independent and regularly rules against the government. Over the years, the Supreme Court has played an increasingly central role in protecting minorities and overturning decisions by the government and the parliament when they threaten human rights. The Supreme Court hears direct petitions from both Israeli citizens and Palestinian residents of the West Bank and Gaza Strip, and the state generally adheres to court rulings.

F2. Does due process prevail in civil and criminal matters? 3 / 4

Although due process is largely guaranteed in ordinary cases, those suspected of security-related offenses are subject to special legal provisions. Individuals can be held in administrative detention without trial for renewable six-month terms. According to the human rights group B'Tselem, there were a total of 5,370 Palestinians from the occupied territories in Israeli Prison Service facilities at the end of 2018, including 494 in administrative detention. Under criminal law, individuals suspected of security offenses can be held for up to 96 hours without judicial review under certain circumstances, and be denied access to an attorney for up to 21 days.

According to Defense for Children International (DCI) Palestine, 203 Palestinian children (aged 12–17) from the occupied territories were being held in Israeli military detention as of December 2018. Although Israeli law prohibits the detention of children younger than

12, some are occasionally held. Most Palestinian child detainees are serving sentences—handed down by a special military court for minors created in 2009—for throwing stones or other projectiles at Israeli troops in the West Bank; acquittals on such charges are very rare, and the military courts have been criticized for a lack of due process protections. East Jerusalem Palestinian minors are tried in Israeli civilian juvenile courts.

F3. Is there protection from the illegitimate use of physical force and freedom from war and insurgencies? 2 / 4

Israeli border communities receive occasional rocket and artillery fire from Syria and the Gaza Strip. Israeli security forces and civilians also face the ongoing threat of small-scale terrorist attacks, most often involving stabbings or vehicular assaults.

The authorities adopted a series of measures in 2015 to crack down on violent protests. A law that expired in 2018 established a three-year minimum prison sentence for stone throwers and the suspension of social benefits for the parents of juvenile offenders. Another law increased the maximum penalties for such crimes, with sentences of up to 20 years in prison for adults in Israel who throw objects at a vehicle with intent to harm the occupants. New regulations also authorized police to fire small-caliber bullets at stone throwers if a third party's life is threatened, not just when the officer's own life is in danger. Human rights groups have sometimes accused police of using deadly force against stone throwers or perpetrators of stabbing and vehicular attacks when they did not pose a lethal threat.

The Supreme Court banned torture in a 1999 ruling, but said physical coercion might be permissible during interrogations in cases involving an imminent threat. Human rights organizations accuse the authorities of continuing to use some forms of physical abuse and other measures such as isolation, sleep deprivation, psychological threats and pressure, painful binding, and humiliation.

F4. Do laws, policies, and practices guarantee equal treatment of various segments of the population? 2 / 4

Arab or Palestinian citizens of Israel face de facto discrimination in education, social services, and access to housing and related permits. Aside from the Druze minority, they are exempted from military conscription, though they may volunteer. Those who do not serve are ineligible for the associated benefits, including scholarships and housing loans. The 2018 nation-state law downgraded Arabic from an official language of the country to a language with "special status," though another clause said the change would not "affect the status given to the Arabic language before this law came into force," suggesting that it would be a largely symbolic demotion.

The nation-state law also declares that the state "views the development of Jewish settlement as a national value, and shall act to encourage and promote its establishment and strengthening." The Jewish National Fund (JNF-KKL), which owns about 13 percent of the land in Israel, has effectively maintained a Jewish-only land-leasing policy thanks to a land-swap arrangement with the Israel Land Authority, which grants the JNF replacement property whenever an Arab bidder obtains a parcel of its land.

Many of Israel's roughly 230,000 Bedouin citizens live in towns and villages that are not recognized by the state. Those in unrecognized villages cannot claim social services, are in some cases off the electricity grid, and have no official land rights, and the government routinely demolishes their unlicensed structures.

Israelis of Ethiopian origin, numbering around 130,000, suffer from discrimination—including in the criminal justice system—and lag behind the general population economically despite government integration efforts. During 2018, members of the Ethiopian Israeli community criticized the government for raising obstacles to the immigration of family members still residing in Ethiopia.

Women are treated equally in criminal and civil courts and have achieved substantial parity within Israeli society, though economic and other forms of discrimination persist, particularly among Arab and religious Jewish communities. Arab women are far less likely to be employed than either Arab men or Jewish women.

Discrimination based on sexual orientation is illegal, though LGBT (lesbian, gay, bisexual, and transgender) people continue to face bias in some communities. Gay and transgender Israelis are permitted to serve openly in the military.

Individuals who enter the country irregularly, including asylum seekers, can be detained for up to a year without charges. Asylum applications, when fully processed, are nearly always rejected. In recent years the authorities have pressured thousands of African migrants and asylum seekers who entered the country irregularly—mostly from Eritrea and Sudan—to agree to be repatriated or deported to a third country, such as Rwanda or Uganda. There have been few new irregular entries since a barrier along the border with Egypt was completed in 2013, though there were still between 30,000 and 40,000 African asylum seekers in the country as of 2018.

G. PERSONAL AUTONOMY AND INDIVIDUAL RIGHTS: 11 / 16

G1. Do individuals enjoy freedom of movement, including the ability to change their place of residence, employment, or education? 3 / 4

Security measures can sometimes present obstacles to freedom of movement, though military checkpoints are restricted to the West Bank. Informal local rules that prevent driving on the Sabbath and Jewish holidays can also hamper free movement.

G2. Are individuals able to exercise the right to own property and establish private businesses without undue interference from state or nonstate actors? 3 / 4

Property rights within Israel are effectively protected, and business activity is generally free of undue interference. Businesses face a low risk of expropriation or criminal activity, and corruption is not a major obstacle for private investors. However, Israel's general commitment to property rights has been called into question given its handling of unrecognized Bedouin villages and its settlement policies in the West Bank.

G3. Do individuals enjoy personal social freedoms, including choice of marriage partner and size of family, protection from domestic violence, and control over appearance? 3 / 4

Personal social freedoms are generally guaranteed. However, since religious courts oversee personal status issues, women face some disadvantages in divorce and other matters. Many ultra-Orthodox Jewish communities attempt to enforce unofficial rules on gender separation and personal attire. Marriages between Jews and non-Jews are not recognized by the state unless conducted abroad, nor are marriages involving a Muslim woman and a non-Muslim man. Israel recognizes same-sex marriages conducted abroad. Nonbiological parents in same-sex partnerships are eligible for guardianship rights. A law adopted in July 2018 extended surrogacy rights to women without a male partner but not to men without a female partner, effectively excluding gay men.

G4. Do individuals enjoy equality of opportunity and freedom from economic exploitation? 2 / 4

Israel remains a destination for human-trafficking victims, and African migrants and asylum seekers residing in the country are especially vulnerable to forced labor and sex trafficking. The government works actively to combat trafficking and protect victims. Israel's roughly 88,000 legal foreign workers are formally protected from exploitation by employers, but these guarantees are poorly enforced. About 18,000 foreigners work in the country illegally. Histadrut has opened membership to foreign workers and called on employers to grant them equal rights. Discrimination against and exploitation of Palestinians from the occupied territories working in Israel remains commonplace.

Italy

Population: 60,600,000
Capital: Rome
Political Rights Rating: 1
Civil Liberties Rating: 1
Freedom Rating: 1.0
Freedom Status: Free
Electoral Democracy: Yes

Overview: Italy's parliamentary system features competitive multiparty elections. Civil liberties are generally respected, though the judicial system is undermined by long trial delays, and problems like organized crime and corruption persist. The election of a populist government in 2018 raised concerns about the rights of migrants, asylum seekers, and ethnic minorities.

KEY DEVELOPMENTS IN 2018:
- In March, a center-right coalition won parliamentary elections with 37 percent of the vote, followed by the populist Five Star Movement with nearly 33 percent and a center-left coalition with 23 percent. The lack of a clear majority for any grouping led to a period of negotiations on a new government.
- In June, a coalition government consisting of the Five Star Movement and the right-wing Northern League, known simply as the League, was sworn into office.
- Legislation adopted late in the year tightened rules and conditions for asylum seekers and expanded government authority to detain and deport irregular migrants.

POLITICAL RIGHTS: 36 / 40

A. ELECTORAL PROCESS: 12 / 12

A1. Was the current head of government or other chief national authority elected through free and fair elections? 4 / 4

Parliament and regional representatives elect the president, whose role is largely ceremonial but sometimes politically influential, for a seven-year term. The legitimacy of the presidential vote rests largely on the fairness of legislative elections. Sergio Mattarella, a former constitutional judge backed by the center-left Democratic Party, was elected president in 2015.

The president appoints the prime minister, who serves as head of government and is often, but not always, the leader of the largest party in the Chamber of Deputies, Italy's lower house. The prime minister proposes a Council of Ministers that requires confirmation by Parliament.

Giuseppe Conte, an independent law professor who was not a member of Parliament, became prime minister in June 2018 as part of the coalition agreement between the Five

Star Movement and the League. Five Star leader Luigi Di Maio and League leader Matteo Salvini became deputy prime ministers.

A2. Were the current national legislative representatives elected through free and fair elections? 4 / 4

The bicameral Parliament consists of the 630-member Chamber of Deputies and the 315-member Senate. Members of both houses are popularly elected for five-year terms, though the president can appoint five additional senators based on merit, and former presidents are also entitled to Senate seats.

The March 2018 elections were considered free and fair by international observers. The center-right coalition comprising Forward Italy (Forza Italia), the League, Brothers of Italy, and We with Italy–Union of the Center obtained 265 seats in the Chamber of Deputies and 137 in the Senate. The Five Star Movement took 227 seats in the chamber and 111 in the Senate, while the center-left coalition comprising the Democratic Party, the Popular Civic List, More Europe, and Italy Europe Together won 122 seats in the chamber and 60 in the Senate. After months of negotiations, the League and the Five Star Movement formed a coalition government with a combined 352 seats in the chamber and 170 in the Senate.

A3. Are the electoral laws and framework fair, and are they implemented impartially by the relevant election management bodies? 4 / 4

While Italy's electoral framework and campaign finance regulations are complex, the elections they enable have consistently been deemed fair and credible.

In early 2017, the Constitutional Court struck down part of a 2015 electoral reform that was designed to encourage majorities and avoid postelection deadlock by mandating a two-round system that awarded a supermajority of 340 seats in the lower house to a single party. The ruling left a system in which a 340-seat supermajority would be awarded to a party that won more than 40 percent of the vote in a single election round. However, in November of that year, Parliament adopted a new electoral law that introduced a mixed system in both houses, with 36 percent of seats allocated using the first-past-the-post method, and 64 percent using a proportional, party-list method. Unlike the 2015 measure, the new law encouraged coalition governments, as demonstrated by the 2018 election results.

B. POLITICAL PLURALISM AND PARTICIPATION: 14 / 16

B1. Do the people have the right to organize in different political parties or other competitive political groupings of their choice, and is the system free of undue obstacles to the rise and fall of these competing parties or groupings? 4 / 4

Political parties are generally able to form and operate freely, and the political landscape features a high level of pluralism and competition. Since the beginning of the 1990s, politics have been characterized by unstable coalitions and the frequent emergence of new parties. The most prominent recent example is the Five Star Movement, whose rise in the 2013 elections changed the Italian party landscape into a tripolar system. The League is an older party, but after a change in its leadership and political program, it rose from about 4 percent of the vote in 2013 to about 17 percent in the 2018 elections.

B2. Is there a realistic opportunity for the opposition to increase its support or gain power through elections? 4 / 4

Italy has a long record of frequent changes in the governing coalition, with multiple transfers of power between left and right since the early 1990s. The 2018 elections ended a period of leadership by the Democratic Party that began in 2013.

B3. Are the people's political choices free from domination by the military, foreign powers, religious hierarchies, economic oligarchies, or any other powerful group that is not democratically accountable? 3 / 4

The public is generally free to make political choices without undue interference. However, organized crime groups retain some ability to threaten and influence politicians, especially at the local level.

B4. Do various segments of the population (including ethnic, religious, gender, LGBT, and other relevant groups) have full political rights and electoral opportunities? 3 / 4

Electoral laws contain provisions designed to encourage political participation by linguistic minorities. Women enjoy equal political rights under the law, though their interests are not always well represented in practice. Issues of concern to ethnic minorities play only a marginal role in national and local political agendas, and some municipal policies aggravate the exclusion of Roma.

Legal changes enacted at the end of 2018 tightened restrictions on citizenship and naturalization, forcing many applicants to wait several years for their documentation to be reviewed and introducing an Italian language fluency requirement in some cases.

C. FUNCTIONING OF GOVERNMENT: 10 / 12

C1. Do the freely elected head of government and national legislative representatives determine the policies of the government? 4 / 4

Elected officials are able to craft and implement policy without improper interference from unelected entities. Prime Minister Conte took office in 2018 without having won a seat in Parliament. However, he was chosen as a compromise candidate by the League and the Five Star Movement, which together commanded a legislative majority and generally appeared to control government decision-making. His nomination was approved by the elected president.

C2. Are safeguards against official corruption strong and effective? 3 / 4

Corruption remains a serious problem despite long-term efforts to combat it, and ties between organized crime and public officials persist. A number of local and regional officeholders have been sentenced to prison on graft charges in recent years. A 2017 antimafia law was intended to make some anticorruption procedures more efficient; it also created a government department to oversee assets confiscated in anticorruption cases.

C3. Does the government operate with openness and transparency? 3 / 4

A 2013 legislative decree established greater transparency of information within public administration. The government regularly complies with public requests for information, though delayed responses have been reported.

CIVIL LIBERTIES: 53 / 60

D. FREEDOM OF EXPRESSION AND BELIEF: 15 / 16

D1. Are there free and independent media? 3 / 4

Freedom of the press is constitutionally guaranteed. Despite the rapid growth of the online news industry, traditional media still play a large role in news consumption. There are more than 100 daily newspapers, most of them locally or regionally based, as well as political party papers, free papers, and weekly publications. Concentration of ownership remains a major concern, but many viewpoints are available in the country's media overall. Internet access is generally unrestricted.

Threats against journalists remain a problem. Scores of journalists have received temporary or long-term police protection in response to credible death threats, mostly from organized crime or extremist groups.

D2. Are individuals free to practice and express their religious faith or nonbelief in public and private? 4 / 4

Religious freedom is constitutionally guaranteed and respected in practice. There is no official religion; while the Roman Catholic Church receives certain benefits under a treaty with the state, other groups have access to similar benefits through their own accords. Some local governments have raised obstacles to the construction and recognition of mosques.

D3. Is there academic freedom, and is the educational system free from extensive political indoctrination? 4 / 4

Academic freedom is generally respected.

D4. Are individuals free to express their personal views on political or other sensitive topics without fear of surveillance or retribution? 4 / 4

There are no major restrictions on people's ability to discuss controversial or sensitive topics in public without fear of surveillance or retribution.

E. ASSOCIATIONAL AND ORGANIZATIONAL RIGHTS: 12 / 12
E1. Is there freedom of assembly? 4 / 4

The freedom to assemble peacefully is guaranteed in the constitution and typically upheld in practice.

E2. Is there freedom for nongovernmental organizations, particularly those that are engaged in human rights- and governance-related work? 4 / 4

NGOs are generally free to organize and operate. However, the government has had tense relations with those involved in rescue operations in the Mediterranean Sea, where hundreds and sometimes thousands of migrants and refugees die each year as they attempt to reach Europe from North Africa. Five NGOs, including Doctors Without Borders (MSF), refused to sign a new code of conduct issued by the government in 2017, citing concerns about rules that would allow police to board their vessels and that could limit their ability to transfer migrants from their own vessels to other ships. The new government in 2018 moved to ban NGO rescue vessels from docking at Italian ports, and at least one crew faced a criminal investigation during the year.

E3. Is there freedom for trade unions and similar professional or labor organizations? 4 / 4

Trade unions are generally free to organize and operate. The constitution recognizes the right to strike but places restrictions on strikes by employees in essential sectors like transportation, sanitation, and health, as well as by some self-employed individuals, including lawyers, doctors, and truck drivers.

F. RULE OF LAW: 12 / 16
F1. Is there an independent judiciary? 3 / 4

The judiciary is generally independent, though judicial corruption remains a concern.

F2. Does due process prevail in civil and criminal matters? 3 / 4

Due process rights are largely upheld. However, judicial procedures are often characterized by lengthy delays; Italy has one of the lowest numbers of judges per capita in the European Union. The government has been criticized for denying detained migrants access to lawyers.

F3. Is there protection from the illegitimate use of physical force and freedom from war and insurgencies? 3 / 4

While the population is generally free from major threats to physical security, there have been reports of excessive use of force by police, particularly against people in the country illegally. Asylum seekers and undocumented migrants have been held in overcrowded and unhygienic conditions. .

A 2017 law criminalized torture, though rights groups criticized it for defining torture narrowly and mandating a relatively short statute of limitations, which they identified as problematic in light of the delays that plague the justice system.

F4. Do laws, policies, and practices guarantee equal treatment of various segments of the population? 3 / 4

The law prohibits discrimination based on gender, race, sexual orientation, and other categories, and these protections are generally enforced. However, members of the Romany minority have unequal access to housing, and many live in segregated settlements that lack adequate infrastructure. LGBT (lesbian, gay, bisexual, and transgender) people face societal discrimination and occasional acts of violence.

Migration to Italy by sea has decreased since 2017, due in part to Italian cooperation with and investments in the Libyan coast guard. While the authorities have provided immediate emergency services to arriving migrants, many of whom are asylum seekers, they have struggled to organize long-term services such as housing and timely processing of asylum applications.

In late 2018, Parliament approved legal changes that tightened conditions for granting asylum and humanitarian protection, extended possible detention and eased deportation for irregular migrants, and reduced access to decentralized housing and integration services for asylum seekers. Salvini, in his capacity as interior minister, also increased pressure on NGOs engaged in search-and-rescue operations in the Mediterranean and began barring ships carrying rescued migrants from Italian ports.

G. PERSONAL AUTONOMY AND INDIVIDUAL RIGHTS: 14 / 16

G1. Do individuals enjoy freedom of movement, including the ability to change their place of residence, employment, or education? 4 / 4

Individuals are generally free to travel and to change their place of residence, employment, and education.

G2. Are individuals able to exercise the right to own property and establish private businesses without undue interference from state or nonstate actors? 3 / 4

The legal and regulatory framework supports property rights and the operation of private businesses, but corruption and organized crime can hinder normal business activity, as can onerous bureaucratic obstacles. Delays in court proceedings often undermine enforcement of protections for property rights.

G3. Do individuals enjoy personal social freedoms, including choice of marriage partner and size of family, protection from domestic violence, and control over appearance? 4 / 4

The law protects individual freedom on personal status issues such as marriage and divorce. Same-sex civil unions with nearly all the benefits of marriage are permitted, and courts have begun to recognize second-parent adoption rights for same-sex couples. Domestic violence is a persistent problem, though public awareness of the issue is increasing due to advocacy campaigns.

G4. Do individuals enjoy equality of opportunity and freedom from economic exploitation? 3 / 4

The authorities generally enforce legal protections against exploitative working conditions. However, informally employed workers, including the many migrants and asylum seekers who have entered the country in recent years, are more vulnerable to abuses. The trafficking of women and girls for sexual exploitation also remains a concern, but the government actively works to identify and prosecute traffickers and funds services for victims.

Jamaica

Population: 2,700,000
Capital: Kingston
Political Rights Rating: 2
Civil Liberties Rating: 2 ↑
Freedom Rating: 2.0
Freedom Status: Free
Electoral Democracy: Yes

Overview: Jamaica's political system is democratic, and features competitive elections and orderly rotations of power. However, corruption remains a serious problem, and long-standing relationships between officials and organized crime figures are thought to persist. Violent crime remains a concern, as does harassment and violence against LGBT (lesbian, gay, bisexual, and transgender) people.

KEY DEVELOPMENTS IN 2018:

- States of emergency were in place for much of the year in two districts of the country —St. Catherine North and St. James—to address increasing levels of violent crime. While they were seen as contributing to a reduction in the rate of murders and shootings, violence remained a major problem.
- In December, an audit of the state petroleum refinery showed evidence of serious corruption and mismanagement. The government attempted to block a parliamentary examination of the audit, but eventually indicated that it would assent.
- A new anticorruption body, the Integrity Commission, was established in February, and began monitoring government activities.

POLITICAL RIGHTS: 34 / 40

A. ELECTORAL PROCESS: 12 / 12

A1. Was the current head of government or other chief national authority elected through free and fair elections? 4 / 4

The British monarch is the ceremonial head of state and is represented by a governor general. The prime minister is the head of government; the position is appointed after elections by the governor general, and usually goes to the leader of the majority party or coalition. The prime minister's legitimacy rests largely on the conduct of legislative elections, which in Jamaica are generally free and fair. Jamaica Labour Party (JLP) leader Andrew Holness became prime minister after the party's narrow win in the 2016 elections.

A2. Were the current national legislative representatives elected through free and fair elections? 4 / 4

Jamaica's bicameral Parliament consists of a 63-member House of Representatives, elected for five years, and a 21-member Senate, with 13 senators appointed on the advice of the prime minister and 8 on the advice of the opposition leader. Senators also serve five-year terms.

In 2016, the opposition JLP won 32 seats in the legislature, in a narrow victory over the incumbent People's National Party (PNP), which took 31. Monitors from the Organization of American States (OAS) deemed the elections competitive and credible, but recorded instances of election-related violence ahead of the polls, and expressed concern about voter apathy, which was manifested in a historically low voter turnout of 48 percent.

A3. Are the electoral laws and framework fair, and are they implemented impartially by the relevant election management bodies? 4 / 4

Electoral laws are generally fair, but the 2016 OAS mission suggested various improvements, including strengthening campaign finance rules and making it easier for citizens to vote in areas outside their assigned polling station.

B. POLITICAL PLURALISM AND PARTICIPATION: 13 / 16

B1. Do the people have the right to organize in different political parties or other competitive political groupings of their choice, and is the system free of undue obstacles to the rise and fall of these competing parties or groupings? 4 / 4

Political parties form and operate without restriction. Although various smaller parties are active, politics at the national level are dominated by the social democratic PNP, and the more conservative JLP.

B2. Is there a realistic opportunity for the opposition to increase its support or gain power through elections? 4 / 4

Opposition parties operate freely, and political power has alternated between the PNP and JLP.

B3. Are the people's political choices free from domination by the military, foreign powers, religious hierarchies, economic oligarchies, or any other powerful group that is not democratically accountable? 2 / 4

Powerful criminal gangs can influence voters who live in areas under their control. Such groups have used intimidation or other tactics to ensure high voter turnout for particular candidates or parties in exchange for political favors.

B4. Do various segments of the population (including ethnic, religious, gender, LGBT, and other relevant groups) have full political rights and electoral opportunities? 3 / 4

Women are underrepresented in politics. Of the 152 candidates contesting the 2016 elections, 26 candidates, or 17.1 percent, were women. Eleven women were elected to the House of Representatives, amounting to 17.5 percent of the body. The LGBT community experiences harassment and violence, and this impacts the ability of LGBT people to engage in political and electoral processes.

C. FUNCTIONING OF GOVERNMENT: 9 / 12

C1. Do the freely elected head of government and national legislative representatives determine the policies of the government? 4 / 4

The elected prime minister and national legislative representatives determine the policies of the government. However powerful criminal gangs, as well as corruption in politics, can affect democratic policymaking.

C2. Are safeguards against official corruption strong and effective? 3 / 4

Long-standing links between officials and organized crime figures persist. Government bodies continue to pursue corruption investigations, and cases frequently end in convictions. However, the public prosecutor has faced criticism in the media and from nongovernmental organizations (NGOs) for a reluctance to pursue some cases. Government whistleblowers are not well protected.

Recent years have seen new legal efforts to fight corruption. These include the approval of the Integrity Commission Act of 2017, which requires lawmakers and public officials to disclose their income, liabilities, and assets; streamlined anticorruption laws; and empowered a single commission to monitor for compliance. The new commission was duly established in February 2018, and has begun to monitor activities within its scope.

Legislation approved in 2018 mandated the establishment of an independent Major Organised Crime and Anti-Corruption Agency (MOCA), and funding was allocated for its operations in July. (MOCA had already existed, but was affiliated with the Jamaica Constabulary Force; the new body is autonomous.)

In 2016, allegations emerged that PNP leaders had siphoned off millions of dollars' worth of funds donated to the party in order to bolster their personal campaigns for that year's general elections. The PNP established an internal oversight body to safeguard against such occurrences in the future, but no other action was taken. More recently, Finance Minister Audley Shaw faced scrutiny in 2017 after media outlets reported that he had racked up a J$8 million (US$60,000) phone bill; he issued an apology and claimed to have paid back part of the charge, and the issue was apparently not pursued further.

C3. Does the government operate with openness and transparency? 2 / 4

An access to information law has been in effect since 2004, though it contains a number of exemptions. Legislative processes are often opaque.

In December 2018, the government proved reluctant to allow the Public Accounts Committee of Parliament (PAC), which is chaired by an opposition lawmaker, to discuss an audit of the state petroleum refinery (Petrojam) that showed evidence of serious corruption and mismanagement. The government relented and began calling for an examination of the audit by the PAC after facing criticism from the opposition and scrutiny in the media.

CIVIL LIBERTIES: 44 / 60 (+1)

D. FREEDOM OF EXPRESSION AND BELIEF: 15 / 16

D1. Are there free and independent media? 4 / 4

The constitutional right to free expression is generally respected. Most newspapers are privately owned, and express a variety of views. Broadcast media are largely state-owned but espouse similarly pluralistic points of view. Journalists occasionally face intimidation, especially in the run-up to elections.

In May 2018, Reporters Without Borders (RSF) expressed concern over a proposed data-protection bill it said failed to "adequately distinguish gathering 'data' for journalistic activities from gathering data for regular commercial purposes." The group said the bill, if it became law, could allow authorities to compel journalists investigated under its provisions to reveal their sources.

D2. Are individuals free to practice and express their religious faith or nonbelief in public and private? 4 / 4

Freedom of religion is constitutionally protected and generally respected in practice. While laws banning Obeah—an Afro-Caribbean shamanistic religion—remain on the books, they are not actively enforced.

D3. Is there academic freedom, and is the educational system free from extensive political indoctrination? 4 / 4

The government does not restrict academic freedom.

D4. Are individuals free to express their personal views on political or other sensitive topics without fear of surveillance or retribution? 3 / 4

Individuals are generally free to express their personal views on political or other sensitive topics. However, the presence of powerful criminal gangs in some urban neighborhoods can discourage people from talking openly about such groups' activities.

In 2017, the House of Representatives passed the National Identification and Registration Bill, which established groundwork for a National Identification System that requires the collection of people's personal information. Privacy advocates expressed concern about possible overreach; it had not yet been implemented at the end of 2018.

E. ASSOCIATIONAL AND ORGANIZATIONAL RIGHTS: 10 / 12 (+1)
E1. Is there freedom of assembly? 3 / 4

Freedom of assembly is provided for by the constitution and is largely respected in practice. Occasionally protests are marred by violence or otherwise unsafe conditions. In 2017, protests in St. Thomas Parish over poor roads saw some participants throwing stones and setting debris on fire. Responding police deployed pepper spray against at least one demonstrator.

E2. Is there freedom for nongovernmental organizations, particularly those that are engaged in human rights–and governance-related work? 4 / 4 (+1)

Jamaica has a robust and vibrant civil society with many active community groups. However, some struggle financially or have difficulty attracting volunteers, negatively impacting their levels of engagement. Others are funded by the central government, but for the most part act autonomously. NGOs are well represented in the education, health, and environment sectors, and many provide support for the most marginalized groups in society.

Score Change: The score improved from 3 to 4 because a variety of NGOs are able to conduct work without interference, including those focused on human rights and governance.

E3. Is there freedom for trade unions and similar professional or labor organizations? 3 / 4

Around 20 percent of the workforce is unionized, and antiunion discrimination is illegal. Labor unions are politically influential and have the right to strike. However, workers in essential services must undergo an arbitration process with the Ministry of Labor and Social

Security before they may legally strike, and the definition of the work constituting "essential services" is broad. There are reports of private employers laying off unionized workers and then later hiring them as contract workers.

The Industrial Disputes Tribunal (IDT) is empowered to reinstate workers whose dismissals are found to be unjustified, although cases before the IDT often take much longer to settle than the 21 days stipulated by the law.

F. RULE OF LAW: 8 / 16

F1. Is there an independent judiciary? 3 / 4

Judicial independence is guaranteed by the constitution, and while the judiciary is widely considered independent, corruption remains a problem in some lower courts.

F2. Does due process prevail in civil and criminal matters? 2 / 4

A large backlog of cases and a shortage of court staff at all levels continue to undermine the justice system. Trials are often delayed for many years and at times cases are dismissed due to systemic failures. In an effort to reduce the backlog, the government passed the 2017 Criminal Justice (Plea Negotiations and Agreements) Act, which increased avenues for the resolution of civil cases outside of trial.

F3. Is there protection from the illegitimate use of physical force and freedom from war and insurgencies? 2 / 4

Killings by police remain a serious problem in Jamaica. According to the Independent Commission of Investigations, 137 people were killed by security personnel in 2018, though that was down from 168 the previous year.

Gang and vigilante violence remains a common occurrence. Kingston's insular "garrison" communities remain the epicenter of most violence and serve as safe havens for criminal groups. Jamaica is a transit point for cocaine, and much of the island's violence is the result of warfare between drug-trafficking organizations. A range of initiatives to address the problem have been undertaken by successive governments, but crime and violence remain deeply entrenched.

States of emergency were in place for much of 2018 in two districts of the country—St. Catherine North and St. Jame—to deal with increasing levels of violent crime, and states of emergency were declared for shorter periods in several other areas, for similar reasons. They were seen as contributing to a reduction in rate of murders and shootings. Through early August, murders declined by 17 percent, shootings by 15 percent, and robberies by 9 percent over the same period in 2017.

F4. Do laws, policies, and practices guarantee equal treatment of various segments of the population? 1 / 4

Harassment of and violence against LGBT people remains a major concern and is frequently ignored by the police. Legislation against sodomy, which is punishable by 10 years in prison with hard labor, was challenged in court in 2014; however, the case was withdrawn that year after death threats were made against the claimant and his family. In 2016, a report published by J-Flag (Jamaica Forum of Lesbians, All-Sexuals and Gays) found that approximately 88 percent of survey respondents felt that male homosexuality was immoral; 83.7 percent felt the same for female homosexuality; and 83.5 percent felt bisexual relationships were immoral; these results represented an increase on a similar survey conducted in 2011. However, there have been modest steps forward. In 2014, the government added a provision to the Offences against the Person Act that criminalized the production, recording, or distribution of any audio or visual materials that promote violence against any category of persons, including LGBT individuals. The next year saw the first public pride event, and it has grown in size since then. Some high profile politicians have also spoken out publicly in support of J-Flag.

Women enjoy the same legal rights as men but suffer employment discrimination and tend to make less money than men for performing the same job.

Employment discrimination against Rastafarians has fallen in recent years, as Rastafarian dress and practices have gained greater societal acceptance.

G. PERSONAL AUTONOMY AND INDIVIDUAL RIGHTS: 11 / 16

G1. Do individuals enjoy freedom of movement, including the ability to change their place of residence, employment, or education? 3 / 4

Although there are constitutional guarantees of freedom of movement, political and communal violence frequently precludes the full enjoyment of this right, and states of emergency or curfews are sometimes imposed as a result of gang activity. There are no formal restrictions on people's ability to change their place of employment or education.

G2. Are individuals able to exercise the right to own property and establish private businesses without undue interference from state or non-state actors? 3 / 4

Jamaica has an active private sector and a powerful pro-business lobby. Individuals are free to establish businesses subject to legal requirements, which are not onerous. Recent reforms have included expediting the incorporation process, making electricity in Kingston more consistent, and easing the import process. However, corruption and crime can still hamper normal business activity. The World Bank's 2019 *Doing Business* report (published in October 2018) noted difficulties in registering property and enforcing contracts.

G3. Do individuals enjoy personal social freedoms, including choice of marriage partner and size of family, protection from domestic violence, and control over appearance? 2 / 4

Legal protections for women and girls are poorly enforced, and violence and discrimination remain widespread. There is not a blanket ban on spousal rape, nor are there laws against sexual harassment. Child abuse, including sexual abuse, is widespread.

G4. Do individuals enjoy equality of opportunity and freedom from economic exploitation? 3 / 4

Residents of neighborhoods where criminal groups are influential are at a heightened risk of becoming victims of human traffickers. Because of the poverty in certain communities and high-profile tourism industry, child sex tourism is present in some of Jamaica's resort areas, according to local NGOs.

Japan

Population: 126,500,000
Capital: Tokyo
Political Rights Rating: 1
Civil Liberties Rating: 1
Freedom Rating: 1.0
Freedom Status: Free
Electoral Democracy: Yes

Overview: Japan is a multiparty parliamentary democracy. The ruling Liberal Democratic Party (LDP) has governed almost continuously since 1955, with stints in opposition from 1993 to 1994 and 2009 to 2012. Political rights and civil liberties are generally well respected. Outstanding challenges include ethnic and gender-based discrimination and claims of improperly close relations between government and the business sector.

KEY DEVELOPMENTS IN 2018:

- In September, Prime Minister Shinzō Abe won reelection as president of the LDP, defeating intraparty rival Shigeru Ishiba and clearing the way to become the longest-serving prime minister in postwar Japanese history.
- Responding to workforce challenges presented by the country's aging population and low fertility rate, the parliament passed legislation in December with the aim of attracting hundreds of thousands of foreign workers over the next five years.
- A total of 15 executions were carried out in 2018, the largest annual number since 2008. Amnesty International noted that some of the convicts had yet to fully exhaust their appeals.

POLITICAL RIGHTS: 40 / 40

A. ELECTORAL PROCESS: 12 / 12

A1. Was the current head of government or other chief national authority elected through free and fair elections? 4 / 4

Japan is a parliamentary democracy. The prime minister is the head of government and is chosen by the freely elected parliament. The prime minister selects the cabinet, which can include a limited number of ministers who are not members of the parliament. Japan's emperor serves as head of state in a ceremonial capacity.

Shinzō Abe has been prime minister since 2012, having previously served for a year in 2006–2007. In September 2018, the ruling LDP held the first contested election for its party presidency in six years. Abe won 329 of the 405 votes from LDP lawmakers, while Shigeru Ishiba won 73. Abe also won 224 of the 405 points awarded by rank-and-file LDP members, while Ishiba took 181. The outcome all but ensured that Abe would remain prime minister until the next parliamentary elections, which are due by late 2021.

A2. Were the current national legislative representatives elected through free and fair elections? 4 / 4

The parliament, or Diet, has two chambers. The more powerful lower house, the House of Representatives, has 465 members elected to maximum four-year terms through a mixture of single-member districts and proportional representation. The upper house, the House of Councillors, has 242 members serving fixed six-year terms, with half elected every three years using a mixture of nationwide proportional representation and prefecture-based voting. The prime minister and his cabinet can dissolve the House of Representatives, but not the House of Councillors. The lower house can also pass a no-confidence resolution that forces the cabinet to either resign or dissolve the House of Representatives.

Legislative elections in Japan are free and fair. In 2017, Prime Minister Abe dissolved the lower house and called for snap elections, citing a need for a fresh mandate in light of an increasing threat posed by North Korea, which had fired ballistic missiles over northern Japan. The LDP won 281 lower house seats, and an allied party, Komeito, took 29. The opposition Constitutional Democratic Party of Japan (CDP) won 54, the Party of Hope secured 50, and smaller parties and independents captured the remainder.

A3. Are the electoral laws and framework fair, and are they implemented impartially by the relevant election management bodies? 4 / 4

Japan's electoral laws are generally fair and well enforced. Campaigning is heavily regulated, which typically benefits incumbents, although the rules are applied equally to all candidates. Malapportionment in favor of the rural districts from which the LDP draws significant support has been a persistent problem. In 2017, a new redistricting law designed to reduce the voting weight disparities between urban and rural districts took effect. Districts will be revised again in 2020 after the census is conducted.

B. POLITICAL PLURALISM AND PARTICIPATION: 16 / 16

B1. Do the people have the right to organize in different political parties or other competitive political groupings of their choice, and is the system free of undue obstacles to the rise and fall of these competing parties or groupings? 4 / 4

Parties generally do not face undue restrictions on registration or operation. In 2017, liberal and left-leaning lawmakers who broke away from the opposition Democratic Party (DP) formed the CDP, which became the leading opposition party after that year's lower house elections. The Party of Hope, led by Tokyo governor Yuriko Koike, also formed in 2017, after she left the LDP. In May 2018, the Party of Hope merged with the DP to form the center-right Democratic Party for the People (DPFP).

B2. Is there a realistic opportunity for the opposition to increase its support or gain power through elections? 4 / 4

While the LDP has governed for most of Japan's postwar history, there have been democratic transfers of power to and from alternative parties, most recently when the LDP returned to government in 2012. Opposition parties are represented in the parliament and govern at the subnational level. In September 2018, for example, opposition politician Denny Tamaki won the Okinawa gubernatorial election, pledging to block a government plan to relocate a US military base within Okinawa and instead push for it to be removed entirely.

B3. Are the people's political choices free from domination by the military, foreign powers, religious hierarchies, economic oligarchies, or any other powerful group that is not democratically accountable? 4 / 4

People's political choices are generally free from improper interference by powerful interests that are not democratically accountable.

B4. Do various segments of the population (including ethnic, religious, gender, LGBT, and other relevant groups) have full political rights and electoral opportunities? 4 / 4

Citizens enjoy equal rights to vote and run in elections regardless of gender, ethnicity, religion, sexual orientation, or gender identity. Women remain underrepresented in government. In May 2018, the Diet passed a nonbinding measure to promote gender-balanced assemblies, urging parties to nominate equal numbers of male and female candidates.

Around 600,000 ethnic Koreans—mainly the multigenerational descendants of forced laborers brought to Japan before 1945—hold special residency privileges but not Japanese citizenship, and are therefore ineligible to participate in national elections. Most but not all are South Korean nationals, and they have the option of applying for Japanese citizenship.

C. FUNCTIONING OF GOVERNMENT: 12 / 12

C1. Do the freely elected head of government and national legislative representatives determine the policies of the government? 4 / 4

Elected officials are free to govern without interference, though senior civil servants have some influence over policy.

C2. Are safeguards against official corruption strong and effective? 4 / 4

The prevalence of corruption in government is relatively low, and media coverage of political corruption scandals is widespread and vigorous. However, some government officials have close relations with business leaders, and retiring bureaucrats often quickly secure high-paying positions with companies that receive significant government contracts. In July 2018, Futoshi Sano, a top Ministry of Education bureaucrat, was arrested in a bribery scandal for allegedly steering government subsidies to the Tokyo Medical University in exchange for his son's admission.

C3. Does the government operate with openness and transparency? 4 / 4

The government generally operates with openness and transparency. Access to information legislation allows individuals to request information from government agencies, but in practice the law has not always been implemented effectively. In March 2018, the Finance Ministry admitted that it had falsified government documents related to a scandal in which public land was sold on favorable terms to a private school with ties to the prime minister's wife.

CIVIL LIBERTIES: 56 / 60
D. FREEDOM OF EXPRESSION AND BELIEF: 15 / 16
D1. Are there free and independent media? 3 / 4

Freedom of the press is guaranteed in the constitution, and Japan has a highly competitive media sector. However, press freedom advocates have expressed concern about the Act on the Protection of Specially Designated Secrets, which took effect in 2014 and allows journalists to be prosecuted for revealing state secrets, even if that information was unknowingly obtained. A 2017 report by the UN special rapporteur on freedom of expression noted concern about pressure on the media from the government, and recommended the repeal of Article 4 of the Broadcast Act, which gives the government the power to determine what information is "fair" and thus acceptable for public broadcast.

Under the traditional *kisha kurabu* (press club) system, institutions such as government ministries and corporate organizations have restricted the release of news to those journalists and media outlets with membership in their clubs. In recent years, however, online media and weekly newsmagazines have challenged the daily papers' dominance of political news with more aggressive reporting.

D2. Are individuals free to practice and express their religious faith or nonbelief in public and private? 4 / 4

Freedom of religion is guaranteed by the constitution, and there are no substantial barriers to religious expression or the expression of nonbelief.

D3. Is there academic freedom, and is the educational system free from extensive political indoctrination? 4 / 4

Academic freedom is constitutionally guaranteed and mostly respected in practice, but education and textbooks have long been a focus of public and political debate. While there is not a national curriculum or single official history text, the Ministry of Education's screening process has approved textbooks that downplay Japan's history of imperialism and war atrocities. In 2017, the UN special rapporteur on freedom of expression called on the government to reevaluate its influence on the textbook approval process.

D4. Are individuals free to express their personal views on political or other sensitive topics without fear of surveillance or retribution? 4 / 4

The government does not restrict private discussion. Some observers have expressed concern that antiterrorism and anticonspiracy legislation that went into effect in 2017 could permit undue surveillance.

E. ASSOCIATIONAL AND ORGANIZATIONAL RIGHTS: 12 / 12

E1. Is there freedom of assembly? 4 / 4

Freedom of assembly is protected under the constitution, and peaceful demonstrations take place frequently. In 2018, protests were held on topics including scandals in the Abe administration, the proposed relocation of the US base on Okinawa, and a new immigration bill announced late in the year. On the immigration issue, far-right opponents of an increase in foreign workers were met with counterprotesters opposed to racism.

E2. Is there freedom for nongovernmental organizations, particularly those that are engaged in human rights– and governance-related work? 4 / 4

Nongovernmental organizations are generally free from undue restrictions and remained diverse and active in 2018.

E3. Is there freedom for trade unions and similar professional or labor organizations? 4 / 4

Most workers have the legal right to organize, bargain collectively, and strike. However, public-sector workers are barred from striking, and some, such as firefighters and prison staff, cannot form unions. Labor unions are active and exert political influence through the Japanese Trade Union Confederation and other groupings.

F. RULE OF LAW: 15 / 16

F1. Is there an independent judiciary? 4 / 4

Japan's judiciary is independent. For serious criminal cases, a judicial panel composed of professional judges and *saiban-in* (lay judges), selected from the general public, render verdicts.

F2. Does due process prevail in civil and criminal matters? 4 / 4

Constitutional guarantees of due process are generally upheld. However, observers have argued that trials often favor the prosecution. There are reports that suspects have been detained on flimsy evidence, arrested multiple times for the same alleged crime, or subjected to lengthy interrogations that yield what amount to forced confessions. Police can detain suspects for up to 23 days without charge. Access to those in pretrial detention is sometimes limited.

New legislation adopted in 2017 added nearly 300 categories of conspiracy offenses to the criminal code in order to help unravel terrorist plots and organized crime networks. Critics of the changes raised concerns that they gave the government too much authority to restrict civil liberties.

F3. Is there protection from the illegitimate use of physical force and freedom from war and insurgencies? 4 / 4

People in Japan are generally protected from the illegitimate use of physical force and the threat of war and insurgencies. Violent crime rates are low. However, organized crime is fairly prominent, particularly in the construction and nightlife sectors; crime groups also run drug-trafficking and loansharking operations.

There are frequent reports of substandard medical care in prisons. Prisoners facing death sentences or accused of crimes that could carry the death penalty are held in solitary confinement, sometimes for years at a time. A total of 15 executions were carried out in 2018, the largest annual number since 2008. All but two of those executed were members of the Aum Shinrikyo cult convicted of involvement in 1995 terrorist attacks. Amnesty International noted that some of the convicts had yet to fully exhaust their appeals; death row inmates can request retrials even after the Supreme Court has confirmed their sentences.

F4. Do laws, policies, and practices guarantee equal treatment of various segments of the population? 3 / 4

Societal discrimination against Japan's estimated three million *burakumin*—descendants of feudal-era outcasts—and the indigenous Ainu minority is declining, but it can affect their access to housing and employment. Japan-born descendants of colonial subjects (particularly ethnic Koreans and Chinese) continue to suffer similar disadvantages. A 2016 hate speech law calls on the government to take steps to eliminate discriminatory speech against ethnic minorities, but it does not carry any penalties for perpetrators.

LGBT (lesbian, gay, bisexual, and transgender) people face social stigma and in some cases harassment; there is no national law barring discrimination based on sexual orientation or gender identity, though Tokyo passed a municipal antidiscrimination law in October 2018. In 2016, sexual harassment regulations for national public officials were modified to prohibit harassment on the basis of sexual orientation or gender identity. Employment discrimination and sexual harassment against women are common.

Very few asylum seekers are granted asylum in Japan. Only 42 people received asylum during 2018, while nearly 10,500 applied. Japan also accepts a small number of refugees for third-country resettlement.

G. PERSONAL AUTONOMY AND INDIVIDUAL RIGHTS: 14 / 16

G1. Do individuals enjoy freedom of movement, including the ability to change their place of residence, employment, or education? 4 / 4

There are few significant restrictions on internal or international travel, or on individuals' ability to change their place of residence, employment, and education.

G2.Are individuals able to exercise the right to own property and establish private businesses without undue interference from state or nonstate actors? 4 / 4

Property rights are generally respected. People are free to establish private businesses, although Japan's economy is heavily regulated.

G3. Do individuals enjoy personal social freedoms, including choice of marriage partner and size of family, protection from domestic violence, and control over appearance? 3 / 4

While personal social freedoms are mostly protected, there are some limitations. The country's system of family registration, *koseki*, recognizes people as members of a family unit and requires married couples to share a surname, which usually defaults to the husband's last name. This can create legal complications for women as well as children born out of wedlock or to divorced parents, among others. There is no legal recognition of same-sex marriage in Japan. Domestic violence is punishable by law, and protective orders and other services are available for victims, but such abuse often goes unreported.

G4. Do individuals enjoy equality of opportunity and freedom from economic exploitation? 3 / 4

Individuals generally enjoy equality of opportunity, and the legal framework provides safeguards against exploitative working conditions. However, long workdays are common in practice and have been criticized as harmful to workers' health. In June 2018, the parliament passed legislation to cap overtime work at 45 hours per month and 360 hours per year, but it allowed up to 100 hours of overtime in a month under some circumstances, and it removed all overtime rules for professional workers who earn more than three times the average salary in Japan.

Many workers are temporary or contract employees with substantially lower wages, fewer benefits, and less job security than regular employees. In December 2018, the parliament approved a measure allowing the government to issue up to 345,000 five-year visas for foreign workers in sectors facing labor shortages. Critics of the measure said it could perpetuate the exploitation of temporary foreign workers rather than opening the door to permanent immigration. Foreign workers enrolled in existing state-backed technical "internships" sometimes face exploitative conditions and forced labor.

Commercial sexual exploitation also remains a problem. Traffickers frequently bring foreign women into the country for forced sex work by arranging fraudulent marriages with Japanese men.

Jordan

Population: 10,200,000
Capital: Amman
Political Rights Rating: 5
Civil Liberties Rating: 5
Freedom Rating: 5.0
Freedom Status: Partly Free
Electoral Democracy: No

Overview: Jordan is a monarchy in which the king plays a dominant role in politics and governance. The parliament's lower house is elected, but the electoral system continues to put the opposition at a disadvantage despite recent reforms, and the chamber wields little power in practice. The media and civil society groups are hampered by restrictive laws and government pressure. The judicial system is not independent and often fails to ensure due process.

KEY DEVELOPMENTS IN 2018:

- Responding to mass protests over tax increases and hikes in commodity prices, Hani Mulki resigned as prime minister in June, and was replaced by former World Bank economist Omar al-Razzaz.
- In March, the government began conferring legal status upon refugees living in urban areas without permits, reducing their risk of arrest and offering them more employment and education opportunities.
- However, in January, authorities rescinded the eligibility for subsidized health care for refugees living outside of camps. According to the United Nations, more than 670,000 refugees from Syria resided in Jordan at year's end.

POLITICAL RIGHTS: 12 / 40

A. ELECTORAL PROCESS: 3/ 12

A1. Was the current head of government or other chief national authority elected through free and fair elections? 0 / 4

King Abdullah II holds broad executive powers. He appoints and dismisses the prime minister and cabinet and may dissolve the bicameral National Assembly at his discretion. Omar al-Razzaz, a former World Bank economist and minister of education, was appointed prime minister in June 2018, replacing Hani Mulki. Mulki resigned in the wake of mass protests over proposed tax increases and hikes in fuel and electricity prices. Constitutional amendments adopted in 2016 empowered the king to make a number of other appointments, including the crown prince and a regent, without a royal decree countersigned by the prime minister or other cabinet ministers.

A2. Were the current national legislative representatives elected through free and fair elections? 1 / 4

The king appoints the 65 members of the upper house of the parliament, the Senate. The lower house, the House of Representatives, is elected for four-year terms or until the parliament is dissolved. The 115 seats are filled through races in 23 multimember districts, with 15 seats reserved for the leading women candidates who failed to win district seats. Twelve of the district seats are reserved for religious and ethnic minorities.

In the September 2016 elections for the House of Representatives, the first held under a new electoral system, the opposition Islamic Action Front (IAF), the political arm of the Muslim Brotherhood, participated after boycotting the last two elections. It took 10 seats, and allied groups won several more. However, as in past polls, most seats went to independents—typically tribal figures and businesspeople—who were considered loyal to the monarchy. Vote buying and other forms of manipulation remained a problem.

Elections were held in 2017 for mayors, local and municipal councils, and 12 new governorate councils created under a 2015 decentralization law. However, 15 percent of the governorate council seats are appointed, and the councils have no legislative authority. A quarter of the seats in the Amman municipal council are also appointed by the government. As with the parliamentary elections, independent tribal candidates won the vast majority of seats, while the IAF and its allies won a plurality of the few seats captured by party-based candidates.

A3. Are the electoral laws and framework fair, and are they implemented impartially by the relevant election management bodies? 2 / 4

Elections are administered by the Independent Election Commission (IEC), which generally receives positive reviews from international monitors in terms of technical management, though irregularities continue to be reported. The 2016 reform to Jordan's election law introduced multiple-vote proportional representation for parliamentary elections, replacing a single nontransferable vote system that favored progovernment tribal elites over opposition-oriented political parties. The new law redrew district lines in an attempt to mitigate acute malapportionment that has long placed urban voters at a severe disadvantage. However, even after the changes, rural and tribal voters, the base of support for the regime, remain heavily overrepresented in the parliament. For example, 59,000 eligible voters in the district of Ma'an elect four members of parliament, whereas the first district of Zarqa, which is dominated by Palestinian-origin Jordanian citizens, has over 450,000 voters electing six parliament members.

The legal framework for elections is unstable, with major changes often introduced just a month or two before polling day, causing confusion that can hinder campaigning and voting.

B. POLITICAL PLURALISM AND PARTICIPATION: 6 / 16

B1. Do the people have the right to organize in different political parties or other competitive political groupings of their choice, and is the system free of undue obstacles to the rise and fall of these competing parties or groupings? 2 / 4

Political parties based on ethnicity, race, gender, or religion are banned in Jordan. Parties must receive approval from the Ministry of Political and Parliamentary Affairs. Authorities have reportedly intimidated individuals attempting to form political parties. The main opposition party, the IAF, is tolerated, although the offices of its parent organization, the Muslim Brotherhood, were forcibly shuttered in 2016 after the regime prevented it from holding internal elections. The previous year, the government licensed an offshoot group, the Muslim Brotherhood Society, and moved to invalidate the original organization's legal registration. The decision exacerbated preexisting divisions within the Muslim Brotherhood, which further weakened it politically.

The system favors tribally affiliated independents over political parties with specific ideologies and platforms, as does the patronage-based political culture. In the 2016 elections, only 215 of 1,252 candidates ran for specific parties, according to the IEC.

B2. Is there a realistic opportunity for the opposition to increase its support or gain power through elections? 1 / 4

The Islamist opposition holds only about 12 percent of the lower house, and the political system—including the overrepresentation of rural voters—limits the ability of any party-based opposition to make significant gains. Moreover, the constitutional authority of the monarchy means that no opposition force can win control of the executive branch by democratic means alone.

B3. Are the people's political choices free from domination by the military, foreign powers, religious hierarchies, economic oligarchies, or any other powerful group that is not democratically accountable? 1 / 4

While voters and candidates are generally free from overt threats or violence, they remain heavily influenced by tribal affiliations and the state-sponsored patronage networks that accompany them. Citizens' political participation is also constrained by the fact that many important positions are appointed rather than elected.

B4. Do various segments of the population (including ethnic, religious, gender, LGBT, and other relevant groups) have full political rights and electoral opportunities? 2 / 4

Women have equal political rights, and female candidates have won some seats beyond the legal quotas set for the parliament and subnational councils, but cultural prejudices remain an obstacle to women's full participation in practice. Five women won parliamentary seats outside the quota system in 2016, and four won governorate council off-quota seats beyond the reserved positions in 2017. Women performed better at the municipal and local levels, but none won mayoral posts.

Nine seats in the House of Representatives are reserved for Christians and three for Circassians and Chechens together. Christians are not permitted to contest nonreserved seats. Citizens of Palestinian origin, who tend to live in urban areas, make up a majority of the overall population but remain underrepresented in the political system.

C. FUNCTIONING OF GOVERNMENT: 3 / 12

C1. Do the freely elected head of government and national legislative representatives determine the policies of the government? 0 / 4

The king dominates policymaking and the legislative process. The appointed government submits all draft legislation to the House of Representatives, which may approve, reject, or amend bills, though they require approval from the appointed Senate and the king. Groups of 10 or more lawmakers can propose legislation, but the House must then refer it to the government before it can return to the chamber as a draft law. Among other royal prerogatives, the king unilaterally appoints the heads of the armed forces, the intelligence service, and the gendarmerie.

C2. Are safeguards against official corruption strong and effective? 2 / 4

The government has undertaken some efforts to combat widespread corruption, and the Integrity and Anticorruption Commission is tasked with investigating allegations. However, successful prosecutions—particularly of high-ranking officials—remain rare. Anticorruption efforts are undermined by a lack of genuinely independent enforcement institutions and restrictions on investigative journalism and civil society activism.

C3. Does the government operate with openness and transparency? 1 / 4

Laws governing access to government information are vague, lack procedural detail, and contain sweeping exceptions. Officials are not required to make public declarations of their income and assets. The National Assembly does not exercise effective or independent oversight of the government's budget proposals.

CIVIL LIBERTIES: 25 / 60
D. FREEDOM OF EXPRESSION AND BELIEF: 7 / 16
D1. Are there free and independent media? 1 / 4

Jordan's media laws are restrictive, vague, and arbitrarily enforced. Various statutes penalize defamation, criticism of the king or state institutions, harming Jordan's relations with foreign states, blasphemy, and any content considered to lack objectivity. Government gag orders and informal instructions to media outlets regarding news coverage are common. News websites face onerous registration requirements that, if not met, can serve as a justification for blocking. Journalists rarely face serious violence or significant jail time for their work, but they often practice self-censorship. In January 2018, authorities arrested journalists Shadi al-Zinati and Omar Sabra al-Mahrama of the news site Jfranews, over the publication of an article accusing the finance minister of tax evasion. They were released on bail after one day in custody.

D2. Are individuals free to practice and express their religious faith or nonbelief in public and private? 2 / 4

Islam is the state religion. The government monitors sermons at mosques for political, sectarian, or extremist content and has begun issuing recommended texts and themes. Muslim clerics require government authorization to preach or issue religious guidance. Many Christian groups are recognized as religious denominations or associations and can worship freely, though they cannot proselytize among Muslims. While converts from Islam are not prosecuted for apostasy, they face bureaucratic obstacles and harassment in practice. Unrecognized religious groups are allowed to practice their faiths but suffer from a number of disadvantages stemming from their lack of legal status. Atheists and agnostics are required to list a religious affiliation on government documents.

D3. Is there academic freedom, and is the educational system free from extensive political indoctrination? 2 / 4

Intelligence services reportedly monitor academic events and campus life, and administrators work with state officials to scrutinize scholarly material for politically sensitive content.

D4. Are individuals free to express their personal views on political or other sensitive topics without fear of surveillance or retribution? 2 / 4

Open discussion of topics such as politics, the monarchy, religious affairs, and security issues is inhibited by the threat of punishment under the various laws governing expression. The telecommunications law requires companies to enable the tracking of private communications upon the issuance of a court order, and authorities are allowed to order surveillance of people suspected of terrorism. Many Jordanians hold a long-standing belief that government agents routinely listen to their phone calls and monitor their online activities.

E. ASSOCIATIONAL AND ORGANIZATIONAL RIGHTS: 3 / 12

E1. Is there freedom of assembly? 1 / 4

Jordanian law limits free assembly. Authorities require prior notification for any demonstration or event and have broad discretion to disperse public gatherings. Sometimes, the Interior Ministry cancels planned public events without advance notice or explanation. Violations of the law on assembly can draw fines and jail time. Security forces have in the past engaged in violent confrontations with protesters.

E2. Is there freedom for nongovernmental organizations, particularly those that are engaged in human rights- and governance-related work? 1 / 4

While many local and international nongovernmental organizations (NGOs) are able to operate in the country, there are significant restrictions on civil society. The Ministry of Social Development has the authority to deny registration and requests for foreign funding, and can disband organizations it finds objectionable. The ministry has broad supervisory powers over NGO operations and activities, and board members must be vetted by state security officials. In practice, these regulations are applied in an opaque and arbitrary manner.

In June 2018, Nidal Mansour, the director of the press freedom organization Center for Defending Freedom of Journalists, was convicted on charges related to the organization's financial management and for not adhering to the group's stated goals and objectives. In November, an appeals court reversed the conviction and cleared Mansour of all charges.

E3. Is there freedom for trade unions and similar professional or labor organizations? 1 / 4

Workers have the right to form unions, but only in 17 designated industries, and the groups must obtain government approval and join the country's semiofficial union federation. The right to strike is limited by requirements for advance notice and mediation, and participants in an illegal strike are subject to dismissal.

F. RULE OF LAW: 7 / 16

F1. Is there an independent judiciary? 2 / 4

The judiciary's independence is limited. Under the 2016 constitutional amendments, the king unilaterally appoints the entire Constitutional Court and the chair of the Judicial Council, which nominates judges for the civil court system and is made up mostly of senior members of the judiciary. Judges of both the civil and the Sharia (Islamic law) courts—which handle personal status matters for Muslims—are formally appointed by royal decree.

F2. Does due process prevail in civil and criminal matters? 1 / 4

Police can hold suspects for up to six months without filing formal charges, and governors are empowered to impose administrative detention for up to one year. In practice, the authorities often ignore procedural safeguards against arbitrary arrest and detention, holding individuals incommunicado or beyond the legal time limits. Criminal defendants generally lack access to counsel before trial, impairing their ability to mount a defense. Despite a constitutional prohibition, courts allegedly accept confessions extracted under torture.

F3. Is there protection from the illegitimate use of physical force and freedom from war and insurgencies? 2 / 4

Torture and other mistreatment in custody remain common and rarely draw serious penalties. Prison conditions are generally poor, and inmates reportedly suffer from beatings and other abuse by guards.

Terrorist attacks continued to threaten security in 2018. In August, a bomb attack on a police car, carried out by perpetrators who adhered to the ideology of the Islamic State (IS) militant group, killed one officer and injured six others. The subsequent raid to capture the suspects in the attack led to the deaths of four security officers and three suspected militants, in addition to 20 civilian injuries.

F4. Do laws, policies, and practices guarantee equal treatment of various segments of the population? 2 / 4

Women face discrimination in law and in practice. For example, women's testimony is not equal to men's in Sharia courts, and certain social benefits favor men over women. Jordanians of Palestinian origin are often excluded from jobs in the public sector and security forces, which are dominated by East Bank tribes. Discrimination against LGBT (lesbian, gay, bisexual, and transgender) people is also prevalent and includes the threat of violence, though consensual same-sex sexual activity is not specifically prohibited by law. The authorities have denied registration to NGOs that support the rights of LGBT people.

According to the United Nations, there were over 760,000 registered refugees in Jordan as of December 2018, including more than 670,000 from Syria, though the government has reported that the true figure may be double that number. Jordan does not accept refugees and asylum seekers for settlement but typically allows those in the country to remain while UN agencies seek more permanent solutions. Most refugees lack access to work permits and instead work informally. In March, authorities started to provide refugees living outside of camps without permits legal status, which reduced their risk of arrest and offered more employment and education opportunities. However, in January, the government decided to rescind the eligibility for subsidized health care for refugees living outside of camps.

G. PERSONAL AUTONOMY AND INDIVIDUAL RIGHTS: 8 / 16

G1. Do individuals enjoy freedom of movement, including the ability to change their place of residence, employment, or education? 2 / 4

Jordanians generally enjoy freedom of domestic movement and international travel. Refugees, however, face impediments to their rights to travel and change employers, and there have been reports of employers confiscating the passports of foreign migrant workers. Women cannot pass citizenship to their children, making it difficult for people with noncitizen fathers to access jobs, education, and health care without a special identity card that is often difficult to obtain.

In October 2018, Syria and Jordan agreed to reopen a border crossing in Nassib that had been closed for three years. Before its closure, the crossing facilitated billions of dollars in trade between the two countries.

G2. Are individuals able to exercise the right to own property and establish private businesses without undue interference from state or nonstate actors? 2 / 4

The legal framework generally supports property rights for citizens, but women do not have equal access to property under Sharia-based inheritance rules. Private business activity is hampered by obstacles such as corruption and the abuse of political or other connections.

G3. Do individuals enjoy personal social freedoms, including choice of marriage partner and size of family, protection from domestic violence, and control over appearance? 2 / 4

Personal social freedoms are limited by the country's conservative culture and laws. The government does not recognize marriages between Muslim women and non-Muslim men. Matters such as marriage and divorce are handled by religious courts, which place women and converts from Islam at a disadvantage and restrict some interfaith marriages.

Modest legal improvements have been enacted in recent years. In 2017, the parliament adopted legislation to better regulate the processing of domestic violence complaints. Other laws enacted in 2017 abolished a penal code provision that allowed rapists to avoid punishment by marrying their victims. However, reduced sentences are still possible for those who murder a spouse caught committing adultery, and spousal rape is not a crime.

G4. Do individuals enjoy equality of opportunity and freedom from economic exploitation? 2 / 4

There are approximately 1.4 million migrant workers in Jordan, of whom about a million have no work permit, making them especially vulnerable to exploitation. Labor rights organizations have raised concerns about poor working conditions, forced labor, and sexual abuse in Qualifying Industrial Zones, where mostly female and foreign factory workers process goods for export. The legal minimum wage remains below the poverty level and excludes large classes of workers. Rules governing matters such as working hours and safety standards are not well enforced.

Kazakhstan

Population: 18,400,000
Capital: Astana
Political Rights Rating: 7
Civil Liberties Rating: 5
Freedom Rating: 6.0
Freedom Status: Not Free
Electoral Democracy: No

Overview: President Nursultan Nazarbayev has ruled Kazakhstan since 1991. Parliamentary and presidential elections are neither free nor fair, and all major parties exhibit political loyalty to the president. The authorities have consistently marginalized or imprisoned genuine opposition figures. The dominant media outlets are either in state hands or owned by government-friendly businessmen. Freedoms of speech and assembly remain restricted, and corruption is endemic.

KEY DEVELOPMENTS IN 2018:

- In July, Nazarbayev signed a decree making him chairman of the Security Council for life. The decree gave the Security Council significant constitutional powers, which could allow Nazarbayev to maintain power even if he vacates the presidency.
- In March, the government declared the opposition Democratic Choice of Kazakhstan (DVK) movement an "extremist" organization, and its supporters faced prosecution and imprisonment during the year.
- By August, 88 foreign television channels had seen their licenses revoked for failing to register with authorities under provisions of a new media law that took effect in January.
- The new media law also prohibited websites from allowing anonymous comments starting in April, further limiting free expression.

POLITICAL RIGHTS: 5 / 40

A. ELECTORAL PROCESS: 1 / 12

A1. Was the current head of government or other chief national authority elected through free and fair elections? 0 / 4

According to the constitution, the president, who holds most executive power, is directly elected for up to two five-year terms. However, President Nazarbayev's special status as Kazakhstan's "first president" exempts him from term limits. In July 2018, Nazarbayev signed a decree making him chairman of the Security Council for life. The decree gave the Security Council significant constitutional powers, which could allow Nazarbayev to maintain power even if he vacates the presidency.

Presidential elections are not credible. Nazarbayev was most recently reelected in 2015 with 97.7 percent of the vote. His opponents were Turgun Syzdykov of the government-friendly Communist People's Party of Kazakhstan, and Abelgazi Kusainov, who ran as an independent but belonged to the ruling Nur Otan party; both candidates were virtually unknown before the election. The Organization for Security and Co-operation in Europe (OSCE) noted several major flaws in the process, including a stifling media environment, lack of a genuine opposition candidate, reports of fraud, and opaque counting and tabulation procedures.

A2. Were the current national legislative representatives elected through free and fair elections? 0 / 4

The upper house of the bicameral Parliament is the 47-member Senate, with 32 members chosen by directly elected regional councils and 15 appointed by the president. The senators, who are officially nonpartisan, serve six-year terms, with half of the 32 elected members up for election every three years. The lower house (Mazhilis) has 107 deputies, with 98 elected by proportional representation on party slates and 9 appointed by the Assembly of the People of Kazakhstan, which ostensibly represents the country's various ethnic groups. Members serve five-year terms.

Legislative elections do not meet democratic standards. Irregularities including ballot box stuffing, group and proxy voting, and manipulation of voter lists have been reported, and the ruling party benefits from a blurred distinction between it and the state. In the 2016 Mazhilis elections, Nur Otan took 84 of the 98 directly elected seats. Two other parties that are generally loyal to the president, Ak Zhol and the Communist People's Party, each secured 7 seats. No genuine opposition party was able to win representation.

A3. Are the electoral laws and framework fair, and are they implemented impartially by the relevant election management bodies? 1 / 4

The legal framework is not sufficient to ensure free and fair elections, and the safeguards that do exist are not properly enforced. Electoral laws make it difficult for opposition parties to obtain parliamentary representation. Parties must clear a 7 percent vote threshold to enter the Mazhilis, and they are barred from forming electoral blocs, which prevents opposition groups from pooling votes and campaign resources. Presidential candidates must also pass a Kazakh language test with unclear evaluation criteria. Moreover, the Assembly of the People of Kazakhstan is appointed by the president at his discretion, giving the executive influence over the nine Mazhilis members chosen by the assembly.

Election laws introduced in 2017 imposed further restrictions on who can become a presidential candidate, requiring at least five years of experience in public service or elected positions and the submission of medical records. The latter rule raised the possibility that candidates could be arbitrarily disqualified for health reasons. The 2017 legal changes also banned self-nomination of presidential candidates, effectively excluding independents and requiring a nomination from a registered party or public association.

B. POLITICAL PLURALISM AND PARTICIPATION: 3 / 16

B1. Do the people have the right to organize in different political parties or other competitive political groupings of their choice, and is the system free of undue obstacles to the rise and fall of these competing parties or groupings? 1 / 4

The ability of political parties to organize is heavily restricted by the 2002 Law on Political Parties. To register, a party must have 40,000 documented members, and parties based on ethnic origin, religion, or gender are prohibited. The registration process is onerous, and officials have broad discretion to delay or deny party registration in practice.

Opposition parties have also been banned or marginalized through laws against "extremism" and trumped-up criminal charges against their leaders. In March 2018, the opposition movement DVK, allegedly funded by oligarch and fugitive Mukhtar Ablyazov (who lives abroad and is wanted for embezzlement by Kazakhstan, Russia, and Ukraine), was classified as an "extremist" organization by a court in Astana and banned. DVK members and supporters have been prosecuted and imprisoned for their activities. In 2018, the activist Aset Abishev was sentenced to four years in prison in November on charges of supporting the DVK.

B2. Is there a realistic opportunity for the opposition to increase its support or gain power through elections? 0 / 4

Kazakhstan has never experienced a peaceful transfer of power through elections. Nazarbayev has been the chief executive since before the country gained independence from the Soviet Union, and he holds a special constitutional status as "first president," entitling him to unlimited terms in office, legal immunity, and other privileges. Genuine opposition parties hold no seats in the legislature, and the governors of regions and major cities are presidential appointees, meaning the opposition has virtually no opportunity to present itself as a credible alternative to the ruling party.

B3. Are the people's political choices free from domination by the military, foreign powers, religious hierarchies, economic oligarchies, or any other powerful group that is not democratically accountable? 1 / 4

While voters and candidates are not subject to undue influence by the military or foreign powers, the political system is dominated a small group of elites surrounding the president and his family. The country's politics are shaped largely by competition among these elites for resources and positions, arbitrated by the president.

B4. Do various segments of the population (including ethnic, religious, gender, LGBT, and other relevant groups) have full political rights and electoral opportunities? 1 / 4

The legal ban on parties with an ethnic, religious, or gender focus—combined with the dominance of Nur Otan—limits the ability of women and minority groups to organize independently and advocate for their interests through the political system. The language test for presidential candidates also presents an obstacle for non-Kazakh minorities, as well as many Kazakhs. Women currently hold 27 percent of the seats in the Mazhilis and less than 11 percent of the seats in the Senate.

C. FUNCTIONING OF GOVERNMENT: 1 / 12

C1. Do the freely elected head of government and national legislative representatives determine the policies of the government? 0 / 4

Government policies are determined by the executive branch, which is not freely elected, irrespective of the constitutionally defined roles of the executive, judiciary, and legislature. Nazarbayev wields ultimate power with regard to policy and other decisions. Parliament does not serve as an effective check on the executive, and instead largely provides formal approval for the government's legislative initiatives.

However, changes to the constitution adopted by Parliament and the president in 2017 shifted some powers from the president to the Mazhilis. The amendments gave Parliament greater influence over the choice of prime minster and cabinet members, and authority to dismiss them. They also limited the president's ability to rule by decree.

C2. Are safeguards against official corruption strong and effective? 1 / 4

Corruption is widespread at all levels of government. Corruption cases are often prosecuted at the local and regional levels, but charges against high-ranking political and business elites are rare, typically emerging only after an individual has fallen out of favor with the leadership. Journalists, activists, and opposition figures are often prosecuted for supposed financial crimes.

The extent of corruption within the government was highlighted by a series of high-profile cases in 2018. Most notably, in March, former economy minister Kuandyk Bishimbayev was sentenced to 10 years in prison for bribery and embezzlement. Bishimbayev was convicted of accepting bribes worth $2 million while serving as chairman of the national holding company Bayterek. Analysts believe that Bishimbayev's prosecution may be the result of an internal power struggle between high-level government officials. In October, former Almaty mayor Viktor Khrapunov and his wife were convicted in absentia of money laundering, abuse of office, and embezzlement, among other charges, and sentenced to 17 years and 14 years in prison, respectively. The pair remained in Switzerland, where they had fled to in 2008, at the end of the year. Khrapunov has insisted that the trial was politically motivated.

C3. Does the government operate with openness and transparency? 0 / 4

The government and legislature offer little transparency on their decision-making processes, budgetary matters, and other operations. The media and civil society do not have a meaningful opportunity to provide independent commentary and input on pending laws and policies. A law on public access to government information was adopted in 2015, but it is poorly implemented in practice. Officials' asset and income declarations are not publicly available.

CIVIL LIBERTIES: 17 / 60
D. FREEDOM OF EXPRESSION AND BELIEF: 4 / 16

D1. Are there free and independent media? 0 / 4

Media independence is severely limited in Kazakhstan. While the constitution provides for freedom of the press, most of the media sector is controlled by the state or government-friendly owners, and the government has repeatedly harassed or shut down independent outlets. Libel is a criminal offense, and the criminal code prohibits insulting the president. Self-censorship is common. The authorities engage in periodic blocking of online news sources and social media platforms.

New legislation that came into force in January 2018 has further tightened the media environment. The law requires journalists to verify the accuracy of information prior to publication by consulting with the relevant government bodies or officials, obtaining consent for the publication of personal or otherwise confidential information, and acquiring accreditation as foreign journalists if they work for foreign outlets. The application of the law had a dramatic effect on broadcast media. As of August, 88 foreign television channels had their licenses revoked by the Ministry of Information and Communication for failing to comply with new registration requirements within six months of the law's implementation.

Independent media outlets continued to face legal and regulatory pressure throughout the year. In May, a judge handed down a one-year ban on the news site Ratel.kz for defying reregistration rules in its use of the Ratel.kz domain after the death of its owner, among other allegations. Prior to the ruling, in March, former finance minister Zeynulla Kakimzhanov lodged a criminal defamation suit against Ratel.kz and *Forbes Kazakhstan* for spreading false information related to their coverage of Kakimzhanov's connection to corruption cases. The offices of Ratel.kz and *Forbes Kazakhstan* were subsequently raided, equipment was confiscated, and journalists from both outlets were detained. In response, human rights defenders called on the government to drop the charges, arguing that the law was being used to harass and silence journalists.

D2. Are individuals free to practice and express their religious faith or nonbelief in public and private? 1 / 4

The constitution guarantees freedom of worship, and some religious communities practice without state interference. However, activities by unregistered religious groups are banned, and registered groups are subject to close government supervision. The government has broad authority to outlaw organizations it designates as "extremist."

The 2011 Law on Religious Activities and Religious Associations prohibited the distribution of religious literature outside places of worship, required the approval of all religious literature by the state, and prohibited unregistered missionary activity, among other provisions. In September 2018, amendments to the law that would impose stricter controls on religious freedom were passed by the Senate, and now await final passage by the Mazhilis. If they are approved, the amended law would further restrict attendance at religious services, prohibit religious teaching without state permission, and impose greater censorship on religious literature.

Local officials continue to harass groups defined as "nontraditional," including Protestant Christians, Jehovah's Witnesses, and Muslims who do not adhere to the government-approved version of Islam. In the first half of 2018, 79 administrative prosecutions were brought against individuals for practicing their faith. In April, a Karaganda court sentenced three alleged members of Tablighi Jamaat—an international Islamic organization banned in Kazakhstan—to three years in prison for their supposed involvement in the group.

D3. Is there academic freedom, and is the educational system free from extensive political indoctrination? 2 / 4

Academic freedom remains constrained by political sensitivities surrounding certain topics, including the president, his inner circle, and relations with Russia. Self-censorship on such topics is reportedly common among scholars and educators.

In April 2018, a new law was passed giving universities greater freedom to choose the content of their academic programs.

D4. Are individuals free to express their personal views on political or other sensitive topics without fear of surveillance or retribution? 1 / 4

Authorities are known to monitor social media, and users are regularly prosecuted on charges such as inciting social and ethnic hatred, insulting government officials, and promoting separatism or terrorism. The government's monitoring of individuals' online activities led to arrests and prosecutions in 2018. In March, for example, a woman was arrested and charged with funding an extremist organization for browsing the DVK website.

The media law that came into force in January 2018 now makes it impossible for internet users to leave anonymous comments online, further limiting free expression.

To ensure that Facebook Live videos posted by Mukhtar Ablyazov are not seen, in March the government began to throttle internet connections in the evening, which had the effect of slowing or blocking individuals' access to social media platforms including Facebook and Twitter.

E. ASSOCIATIONAL AND ORGANIZATIONAL RIGHTS: 1 / 12

E1. Is there freedom of assembly? 0 / 4

Despite constitutional guarantees, the government imposes tight restrictions on freedom of assembly. Any potential public gathering requires permission from the local government administration 10 days in advance. Permits are routinely denied for antigovernment protests, and police frequently break up unsanctioned gatherings. Organizers and participants, including individuals who call for unauthorized protests on social media, are subject to fines and jail terms.

In May 2018, authorities detained dozens of people protesting against torture and human rights abuses in Almaty, Astana, and other cities. Police also took preemptive action and detained participants and journalists ahead of further planned protests in June. The spate of demonstrations were in response to calls from Mukhtar Ablyazov on Facebook to protest against the "paranoid dictatorship."

E2. Is there freedom for nongovernmental organizations, particularly those that are engaged in human rights– and governance-related work? 1 / 4

Nongovernmental organizations (NGOs) continue to operate but face government harassment when they attempt to address politically sensitive issues. There are extensive legal restrictions on the formation and operation of NGOs, including onerous financial rules and harsh penalties for noncompliance. Organizations can incur fines and other punishments for vaguely defined offenses like interfering with government activities or engaging in work outside the scope of their charters.

Prominent civil society activists often face criminal prosecution and imprisonment in retaliation for their work. In July 2018, human rights activist Yelena Semyonova was placed under investigation for "intentionally spreading false information" after testifying at the European Parliament about prison conditions in Kazakhstan. Semyonova was later barred from travelling to France in October to meet with members of the Parliamentary Assembly of the Council of Europe (PACE) to further discuss the human rights situation in Kazakhstan's prisons.

E3. Is there freedom for trade unions and similar professional or labor organizations? 0 / 4

Workers have limited rights to form and join trade unions and participate in collective bargaining, but the government is closely affiliated with the largest union federation and major employers, and genuinely independent unions face repressive actions by the authorities. The major independent trade union body, the Confederation of Independent Trade Unions (KNPRK), was dissolved in 2017, and its key leaders were later sentenced to prison for protesting the group's termination.

F. RULE OF LAW: 4 / 16

F1. Is there an independent judiciary? 1 / 4

The judiciary is effectively subservient to the executive branch, with the president nominating or directly appointing judges based on the recommendation of the Supreme Judicial Council, which is itself appointed by the president. Judges are subject to political influence, and corruption is a problem throughout the judicial system.

F2. Does due process prevail in civil and criminal matters? 1 / 4

Police reportedly engage in arbitrary arrests and detentions, and violate detained suspects' right to assistance from a defense lawyer. Prosecutors, as opposed to judges, are empowered to authorize searches and seizures. Defendants are often held in pretrial detention for long periods. Politically motivated prosecutions and prison sentences against activists, journalists, and opposition figures are common.

F3. Is there protection from the illegitimate use of physical force and freedom from war and insurgencies? 1 / 4

Conditions in pretrial detention facilities and prisons are harsh. Police at times use excessive force during arrests, and torture is widely employed to obtain confessions, with numerous allegations of physical abuse and other mistreatment documented each year. In August 2018, for example, Kayrat Egimbayev died in the hospital after allegedly being tortured while incarcerated in a penal colony.

Terrorist violence remains rare, though a pair of attacks in 2016 killed some 35 people.

F4. Do laws, policies, and practices guarantee equal treatment of various segments of the population? 1 / 4

While the constitution guarantees equality before the law and prohibits discrimination based on gender, race, and other categories, major segments of society do face discrimination in practice. Traditional cultural biases limit economic and professional opportunities for women, and the law offers no protection against sexual harassment in the workplace. Members of the sizable Russian-speaking minority have complained of discrimination in employment and education.

The LGBT (lesbian, gay, bisexual, and transgender) community continues to face societal discrimination, harassment, and violence, despite the decriminalization of same-sex sexual activity in 1998. In August 2018, LGBT activist Zhanar Sekerbayeva was fined for "minor hooliganism" for taking part in a public photo shoot in Almaty to raise awareness of issues related to menstruation—a taboo topic in Kazakhstan.

G. PERSONAL AUTONOMY AND INDIVIDUAL RIGHTS: 8 / 16

G1. Do individuals enjoy freedom of movement, including the ability to change their place of residence, employment, or education? 2 / 4

Kazakhstani citizens can travel freely but must register their permanent residence with local authorities. New rules that went into effect in 2017 under the pretext of fighting terrorism require citizens to register even temporary residences lasting more than a month with local authorities or face fines. The change increases the ability of the authorities to monitor internal movement and migration, but critics also suggested that it would lead to corruption and create a black market for false registration documents.

G2. Are individuals able to exercise the right to own property and establish private businesses without undue interference from state or nonstate actors? 2 / 4

While the rights of entrepreneurship and private property are formally protected, they are limited in practice by bureaucratic hurdles and the undue influence of politically connected elites, who control large segments of the economy.

G3. Do individuals enjoy personal social freedoms, including choice of marriage partner and size of family, protection from domestic violence, and control over appearance? 2 / 4

There are no significant legal restrictions on personal social freedoms, but NGOs continue to report instances of early and forced marriage, particularly in rural areas. Domestic violence is a serious problem that often goes unpunished, as police are reluctant to intervene in what are regarded as internal family matters.

G4. Do individuals enjoy equality of opportunity and freedom from economic exploitation? 2 / 4

Migrant workers from neighboring countries often face poor working conditions and a lack of effective legal safeguards against exploitation. Both migrants and Kazakhstani workers from rural areas are vulnerable to trafficking for the purposes of forced labor and prostitution in large cities. The authorities reportedly make little effort to assist foreign victims of trafficking.

Kenya

Population: 51,000,000
Capital: Nairobi
Political Rights Rating: 4
Civil Liberties Rating: 4
Freedom Rating: 4.0
Freedom Status: Partly Free
Electoral Democracy: No

Overview: Kenya is a multiparty democracy that holds regular elections, but its political rights and civil liberties are seriously undermined by pervasive corruption and brutality by security forces. The country's media and civil society sectors are vibrant, even as journalists and human rights defenders remain vulnerable to restrictive laws and intimidation.

KEY DEVELOPMENTS IN 2018:

- In March, following months of unrest and a lengthy political standoff in the wake of the disputed 2017 presidential election, Raila Odinga met with President Uhuru Kenyatta, and a widely circulated photograph of the two men shaking hands stoked controversy and confusion. Odinga accepted the results of the election in the meeting and the two leaders pledged to work together, but few substantive details of their discussion were disclosed.

- The government stepped up anticorruption efforts during the year; a number of high-level officials, including the deputy chief justice of the Supreme Court, were arrested for graft in 2018.
- In January, authorities shut down four television stations after they defied a warning by the government to not broadcast a mock swearing-in ceremony for Raila Odinga. The government then ignored a court order to allow the stations back on the air for several days before ending the shutdown in February.
- In February, the government began deportation proceedings against opposition politician and Odinga supporter Miguna Miguna, despite the fact that he held dual Kenyan-Canadian citizenship. A March court order requiring the government to release Miguna from police custody at the Nairobi airport was defied, and his deportation was carried out. In December, the High Court ruled that Miguna was indeed a Kenyan citizen, and that his deportation was unlawful. The court ordered the government to issue Miguna a passport and allow his return to the country, and authorities indicated that they would comply.

POLITICAL RIGHTS: 19 / 40
A. ELECTORAL PROCESS: 6 / 12
A1. Was the current head of government or other chief national authority elected through free and fair elections? 1 / 4

The president and deputy president, who can serve up to two five-year terms, are directly elected by majority vote; they are also required to win 25 percent of the votes in at least half of Kenya's 47 counties.

President Kenyatta was reelected in October 2017 in a disputed election, the rerun of which was boycotted by the main opposition candidate, Raila Odinga, on account of a lack of electoral reforms. The first presidential election, held in August, was annulled the following month by the Supreme Court, which ruled that vote-counting procedures by the Independent Electoral and Boundaries Commission (IEBC) had been severely flawed, and that a rerun should be held. (The count had returned a solid victory by Kenyatta, which many analysts had predicted.) In the ruling's wake, the main opposition coalition, the National Super Alliance (NASA), threatened to boycott the rerun unless a number of reforms were implemented at the IEBC. Some of these reforms were not met, prompting a boycott of the rerun by Odinga, who urged his supporters not to participate in the poll. The final results showed that Kenyatta won the rerun with 98.3 percent of the vote. Turnout for the rerun was just 38.8 percent—much lower than turnout for the August polls, which reached nearly 80 percent. Odinga continued to harshly criticize the election process after the rerun, and Kenyatta began his final term facing a significant legitimacy crisis.

Violence and intimidation marred the presidential election period. Chris Msando, the IEBC member in charge of the vote-counting system, was murdered days ahead of the August vote, with his body showing signs of torture. In the weeks between the annulled election and the rerun, one IEBC commissioner fled Kenya for the US, prompting the IEBC chairman to assert that the body could not guarantee a free election given the atmosphere of intimidation. Police in Nairobi and Kisumu used excessive force in an attempt to quell sometimes violent opposition protests. Several dozen people were reportedly killed by police in the capital alone, according to Human Rights Watch (HRW).

A2. Were the current national legislative representatives elected through free and fair elections? 3 / 4

The bicameral Parliament consists of the 349-seat National Assembly and the 67-seat Senate. In the National Assembly, 290 members are directly elected from single-member constituencies. A further 47 special women representatives are elected from the counties, and political parties nominate 12 additional members according to the share of seats won. The Senate has 47 elected members representing the counties, 16 special women representatives nominated by political parties based on the share of seats won, and four nominated members representing youth and people with disabilities. Both houses have speakers who are ex-officio members.

Stakeholders broadly accepted the results of the 2017 parliamentary contests. Irregularities and violations were reported, but they were not systematic and did not harm or benefit any specific party.

A3. Are the electoral laws and framework fair, and are they implemented impartially by the relevant election management bodies? 2 / 4

The IEBC is mandated with conducting free and fair elections, and operates under a robust electoral framework. However, the IEBC faces frequent allegations of favoritism toward the incumbent Jubilee Coalition, and in 2017 its members experienced violence and intimidation severe enough to prompt its chairman to declare that he could not guarantee the integrity of the presidential rerun. After the annulment of the first presidential election, in 2017 the National Assembly approved controversial measures mandating that if a candidate withdraws from a rerun election, the other candidate would automatically win the poll. The amendments additionally limited the Supreme Court's power to annul election results. The measures took effect a few days after the rerun was held.

B. POLITICAL PLURALISM AND PARTICIPATION: 8 / 16

B1. Do the people have the right to organize in different political parties or other competitive political groupings of their choice, and is the system free of undue obstacles to the rise and fall of these competing parties or groupings? 2 / 4

Citizens are free to organize into political parties. Kenyan parties represent a range of ideological, regional, and ethnic interests, but are notoriously weak, and are often amalgamated into coalitions designed only to contest elections. Under the Political Parties Act, parties that receive at least 5 percent of the votes cast in a national election are eligible for public funds.

Opposition leaders sometimes face harassment and threats from authorities, and opposition rallies and demonstrations are frequently met with a violent police response. In January 2018, security forces used tear gas to disperse some opposition supporters who were attending a mock swearing-in event for Raila Odinga, but the authorities allowed the event to proceed without a major crackdown. On the day of the ceremony, the Interior Ministry declared Odinga's newly formed National Resistance Movement (NRM), an offshoot of the NASA, to be an illegal organization, leaving its members vulnerable to arrest.

In February, the government began deportation proceedings against opposition politician and Odinga supporter Miguna Miguna, despite the fact that he held dual Kenyan-Canadian citizenship. A March court order requiring the government to release Miguna from police custody at the Nairobi airport was ignored, and his deportation was carried out. In December, the High Court ruled that Miguna was indeed a Kenyan citizen, and that his deportation was unlawful. The court ordered the government to issue Miguna a passport and allow his return to the country, and authorities indicated that they would comply.

B2. Is there a realistic opportunity for the opposition to increase its support or gain power through elections? 2 / 4

Opposition parties and candidates are competitive in Kenyan elections, and the 2017 polls saw a high number of incumbents voted out of office. However, Odinga's decision to boycott the rerun election in protest of a lack of reforms at the IEBC left Kenyatta opponents without a viable candidate to vote for, effectively guaranteeing Kenyatta's reelection.

In March 2018, following months of unrest and a lengthy political standoff in the wake of the boycotted rerun election, Odinga met with President Kenyatta, and a widely circulated photograph of the two men shaking hands stoked controversy and confusion. Odinga accepted the results of the election in the meeting and the two leaders pledged to work together, but few substantive details of their discussion were disclosed. Several of Kenyatta's opponents in Parliament condemned "the handshake," claiming that it undermined Odinga's credibility and would further weaken and fragment the opposition.

Following the meeting, Kenyatta and Odinga formed the Building Bridges Initiative. Under the initiative, a 14-member task force convened in May, which was entrusted with gathering public opinion on the problems that plague Kenyan politics such as ethnic strife, corruption, and political dysfunction, and ultimately producing recommendations for reform. Although some analysts praised the initiative for its efforts to build consensus, a number of opposition politicians sharply criticized it, claiming that it was a waste of government resources and that members of the task force were insufficiently vetted.

B3. Are the people's political choices free from domination by the military, foreign powers, religious hierarchies, economic oligarchies, or any other powerful group that is not democratically accountable? 2 / 4

People's political choices are generally free from undue influence by powerful, democratically unaccountable actors. However, ethnicity remains the most salient organizing principle in Kenyan politics, and two ethnic groups—the Kikuyu and Kalenjin—have dominated the presidency since independence.

B4. Do various segments of the population (including ethnic, religious, gender, LGBT, and other relevant groups) have full political rights and electoral opportunities? 2 / 4

The 2010 constitution was intended to reduce the role of ethnicity in elections. Fiscal and political devolution, implemented in 2013, has served to generate more intraethnic competition at the county level. Nevertheless, the ongoing politicization of ethnicity at the national level hinders effective representation of different segments of Kenya's diverse population, limits voter choice, and impedes meaningful policy debates

The stipulation that all voters must possess a National Identity Card hinders historically marginalized groups from obtaining greater access to the political process, particularly the nearly seven million pastoralists from the upper Rift Valley and the North Eastern Province. There are significant implicit barriers to the participation of non-Christian and LGBT (lesbian, gay, bisexual, and transgender) people in national politics.

C. FUNCTIONING OF GOVERNMENT: 5 / 12

C1. Do the freely elected head of government and national legislative representatives determine the policies of the government? 2 / 4

The ability of elected officials to set and implement policy is undermined by corruption and other dysfunction. Although the 2010 constitution reduced the powers of the executive branch and improved the oversight role of Parliament, corruption limits the independence of the legislative branch, and in practice, Parliament is generally subordinate to the president.

C2. Are safeguards against official corruption strong and effective? 1 / 4

Corruption continues to plague national and county governments in Kenya, and state institutions tasked with combating corruption have been ineffective. The Ethics and Anti-Corruption Commission (EACC) lacks prosecutorial powers and has been largely unsuccessful in pursuing corruption cases. The EACC's weakness is compounded by shortcomings at the Office of the Director of Public Prosecutions (ODPP) and within the judiciary.

Despite these challenges, with the April 2018 appointment of Noordin Haji as the Director of Public Prosecutions (DPP), the ODPP stepped up anticorruption investigations, arresting and charging a number of high-profile officials with graft. In May, Richard Ndubai, the director of the National Youth Service, was arrested along with 40 other government employees, for allegedly stealing $78 million in public funds. The accused awaited trial at year's end. In August, Supreme Court Deputy Chief Justice Philomena Mwilu was arrested and charged with allegedly receiving bribes and failing to pay her taxes. It remains to be seen whether the revitalization of the ODPP will lead to an increase in corruption convictions of high-level officials.

C3. Does the government operate with openness and transparency? 2 / 4

Elaborate rules govern public finance in Kenya, but enforcement is often lacking. Parliament's Budget and Appropriations Committee effectively delegates the budget process to the Treasury, and the legislature has demonstrated limited willingness to ensure that the Treasury respects budget-making procedures. When budget information is made available, it is generally released long after the planning stages during which stakeholders could offer input.

Many of the central government's expenditures are not disclosed. In October 2018, the auditor general accused several counties of fraudulent use of funds. However, in recent years, counties have more frequently made budget documents accessible to the public. The 2016 Access to Information Law contains a broad exemption for national security matters.

CIVIL LIBERTIES: 29 / 60

D. FREEDOM OF EXPRESSION AND BELIEF: 10 / 16

D1. Are there free and independent media? 2 / 4

Kenya has one of the more vibrant media landscapes on the African continent, with journalists actively working to expose government corruption and other wrongdoing. However, several laws restrict press freedom, and the government and security forces harass journalists, leading to self-censorship in some cases. In January 2018, authorities shut down four television stations after they defied a warning by the government to not broadcast Raila Odinga's mock swearing-in ceremony. The government then ignored a court order to allow the stations back on the air for several days before ending the shutdown in February.

In May, President Kenyatta signed the controversial Computer Misuse and Cybercrimes Act 2018 into law. Vaguely worded provisions in the law criminalized abuse on social media and "publication of false information," which was made punishable with hefty fines and up to two years in prison. Rights activists condemned the legislation for undermining press freedom. However, in May, the High Court suspended the provisions that most concerned press freedom advocates.

D2. Are individuals free to practice and express their religious faith or nonbelief in public and private? 2 / 4

The government generally respects the constitutional guarantee of freedom of religion. However, counterterrorism operations against the Somalia-based Shabaab militant group have left Muslims exposed to state violence and intimidation. Shabaab militants have at times specifically targeted Christians in Kenya.

D3. Is there academic freedom, and is the educational system free from extensive political indoctrination? 3 / 4

Academic freedom in Kenya, though traditionally robust, is increasingly threatened by political interference, ethnic divisions, and violence.

Student union elections have led to allegations of fraud and violent protests. In addition, there is evidence that ethnic considerations have influenced university hiring, leaving the staff of some institutions with significant ethnic imbalances.

D4. Are individuals free to express their personal views on political or other sensitive topics without fear of surveillance or retribution? 3 / 4

The relatively unfettered freedom of private discussion in Kenya has suffered somewhat from state counterterrorism operations and intimidation by security forces and ethnically affiliated gangs. The government in recent years has used its broadly defined surveillance powers to monitor mobile phone and internet communications.

E. ASSOCIATIONAL AND ORGANIZATIONAL RIGHTS: 7 / 12
E1. Is there freedom of assembly? 2 / 4

The constitution guarantees the freedom of assembly. However, the law requires organizers of public meetings to notify local police in advance, and in practice police have regularly prohibited gatherings on security or other grounds, and violently dispersed assemblies that they had not explicitly banned.

E2. Is there freedom for nongovernmental organizations, particularly those that are engaged in human rights- and governance-related work? 2 / 4

Kenya has an active nongovernmental organization (NGO) sector, but civil society groups have faced growing obstacles in recent years, including repeated government attempts to deregister hundreds of NGOs for alleged financial violations. The attempts were seen in part as an effort to silence criticism of the government's human rights record. NGO leaders who criticized the government faced harassment and threats of arrest in 2018, as well.

At year's end, the government had still not implemented the Public Benefits Organizations (PBO) Act, which was passed in 2013 to improve the regulatory framework for NGOs and create more space for civil society.

E3. Is there freedom for trade unions and similar professional or labor organizations? 3 / 4

The 2010 constitution affirmed the rights of trade unions to establish their own agendas, bargain collectively, and strike. Unions are active in Kenya, with approximately 40 unions representing nearly two million workers. However, labor leaders sometimes experience intimidation, notably in the wake of strike actions. A number of strikes have taken place in the past several years, including those organized by medical workers and university staff.

F. RULE OF LAW: 5 / 16
F1. Is there an independent judiciary? 2 / 4

The judiciary is generally considered to be independent, but judicial procedures are inefficient. The government's refusal to comply with court orders to release Miguna Miguna and halt his deportation, and to end the shutdown of several television stations that aired Odinga's swearing-in ceremony, threatened judicial independence in 2018.

After the High Court annulled the first 2017 presidential election, members of the ruling Jubilee Coalition threatened and intimidated judges. In June 2018, President Kenyatta signed an appropriations bill that significantly reduced the budget for the judiciary to $143 million, compared to $173 million the previous year. Some critics claim that the budget cut was retaliation for the 2017 election annulment, and judges denounced the decision as an attack on the judiciary's independence.

F2. Does due process prevail in civil and criminal matters? 1 / 4

Constitutional guarantees of due process are poorly upheld. There remains a significant backlog of court cases. The police service is thoroughly undermined by corruption and criminality.

F3. Is there protection from the illegitimate use of physical force and freedom from war and insurgencies? 1 / 4

The Shabaab militant group continued to pose a security threat in 2018. Violence against suspects and detainees by security forces remains a serious concern, and abuses are rarely punished. Extrajudicial killings were also frequent during the year. According to the *Daily Nation,* the police killed 222 people in 2018, a slight decline from the 256 people killed in 2017. A report released by the Kenya National Human Rights Commission (KNCHR) in November 2018 implicated security forces in widespread rape and sexual abuse during the 2017 election period.

F4. Do laws, policies, and practices guarantee equal treatment of various segments of the population? 1 / 4

Consensual same-sex sexual activity is criminalized under the penal code, with a maximum penalty of 14 years in prison. Members of the LGBT community continue to face discrimination, abuse, and violent attacks. In 2016, a High Court judge in Mombasa upheld the use of forced anal examinations and testing for HIV and hepatitis B as a means of gathering supposed evidence of same-sex sexual activity. The UN special rapporteur on torture and other experts have condemned such practices. Reports of police abuses against refugees and asylum seekers continued.

G. PERSONAL AUTONOMY AND INDIVIDUAL RIGHTS: 7 / 16

G1. Do individuals enjoy freedom of movement, including the ability to change their place of residence, employment, or education? 2 / 4

While the constitution provides protections for freedom of movement and related rights, they are impeded in practice by security concerns and ethnic tensions that lead many residents to avoid certain parts of the country. Hundreds of people fled their homes in Narok South in September 2018 as a result of communal clashes that continued through the end of the year.

G2. Are individuals able to exercise the right to own property and establish private businesses without undue interference from state or nonstate actors? 1 / 4

Organized crime continues to threaten legitimate business activity in Kenya. Political corruption and ethnic favoritism also affect the business sector and exacerbate existing imbalances in wealth and access to economic opportunities, including public-sector jobs.

Forced evictions are prevalent in low-income areas, particularly in Nairobi. In July and August 2018, thousands of people were evicted from their homes in Nairobi, which were bulldozed to make room for a new railroad. The government did not provide those evicted with compensation or new housing. Authorities also forcibly evicted thousands of indigenous people from protected forest lands during the year.

G3. Do individuals enjoy personal social freedoms, including choice of marriage partner and size of family, protection from domestic violence, and control over appearance? 2 / 4

The constitution recognizes marriage as a union between two people of the opposite sex, but otherwise does not place explicit restrictions on social freedoms. Polygamy is legal, and approximately 10 percent of the married population are in polygamous marriages. Rape and domestic violence remain common and are rarely prosecuted.

G4. Do individuals enjoy equality of opportunity and freedom from economic exploitation? 2 / 4

Kenya remains an unequal society, with wealth generally concentrated in towns and cities. The arid and semiarid north and northeastern parts of the country have particularly high poverty rates.

Refugees and asylum seekers from neighboring countries, particularly children, have been vulnerable to sex trafficking and forced labor in Kenya, though Kenyan children are also subject to such abuses. Kenyan workers are recruited for employment abroad in sometimes exploitative conditions, particularly in the Middle East.

Kiribati

Population: 100,000
Capital: Tarawa
Political Rights Rating: 1
Civil Liberties Rating: 1
Freedom Rating: 1.0
Freedom Status: Free
Electoral Democracy: Yes

Overview: Kiribati is a multiparty democracy that holds regular elections and has experienced peaceful transfers of power between competing groups. Civil liberties are generally upheld, though outstanding problems include a ban on same-sex sexual activity, and some forms of gender discrimination.

KEY DEVELOPMENTS IN 2018:

- At least 80 people were killed in a ferry disaster in January, when the Butiraoi, an interisland ferry, sank while traveling to Tarawa from the atoll of Nonouti.
- The government faced criticism for declining to release its report on the disaster. In December pledged to do so, following the conclusion of a related police investigation.
- A deal was signed in May with the Asian Development Bank to provide high-speed internet to Kiribati via submarine cable.

POLITICAL RIGHTS: 37 / 40 (−1)

A. ELECTORAL PROCESS: 12 / 12

A1. Was the current head of government or other chief national authority elected through free and fair elections? 4 / 4

The president is elected through a nationwide popular vote and may serve up to three four-year terms. Three to four presidential candidates are nominated by the legislature from among its members, and cabinet members must also be members of the legislature. The president can be removed through a no-confidence vote, but this also triggers general elections.

Taneti Maamau of the Tobwaan Kiribati Party (TKP) was elected president in March 2016, taking 60 percent of the vote in a free and fair contest. His two opponents—Rimeta Beniamina and Tianeti Ioane, both of the Boutokan te Koaua Party (BTK)—received 39 percent and 1 percent, respectively. Incumbent president Anote Tong of the BTK was ineligible to run again, having reached his three-term limit.

A2. Were the current national legislative representatives elected through free and fair elections? 4 / 4

The unicameral House of Assembly (Maneaba ni Maungatabu) has 46 members, all but two of whom are elected through a two-round runoff system from 26 constituencies. An appointed member is selected by representatives of people originally from the island of Banaba (Ocean Island) who now live on Fiji's Rabi Island, having been displaced by phosphate mining during the 20th century. The attorney general holds a seat ex officio.

Free and fair parliamentary elections were held in December 2015, with a runoff round in January 2016. The BTK took 26 seats, while two parties that merged to form the TKP after the elections won 19.

A3. Are the electoral laws and framework fair, and are they implemented impartially by the relevant election management bodies? 4 / 4

The constitution and legal framework provide for democratic elections, and balloting is well administered in practice. Losing candidates and parties typically accept the final outcome of elections, and rarely raise accusations of malfeasance.

B. POLITICAL PLURALISM AND PARTICIPATION: 15 / 16 (−1)

B1. Do the people have the right to organize in different political parties or other competitive political groupings of their choice, and is the system free of undue obstacles to the rise and fall of these competing parties or groupings? 4 / 4

There are no constraints on the formation of or competition between political parties. The country's parties are relatively loose alliances that lack formal platforms and are subject to periodic mergers and reconfigurations. Geographic and ancestral ties continue to play an important role in political affiliation.

B2. Is there a realistic opportunity for the opposition to increase its support or gain power through elections? 4 / 4

Kiribati has a history of smooth and democratic transfers of power between government and opposition parties, with the most recent change in executive leadership occurring in 2016.

B3. Are the people's political choices free from domination by the military, foreign powers, religious hierarchies, economic oligarchies, or any other powerful group that is not democratically accountable? 4 / 4

There are no significant constraints on the choices of voters and candidates imposed by forces not democratically accountable.

B4. Do various segments of the population (including ethnic, religious, gender, LGBT, and other relevant groups) have full political rights and electoral opportunities? 3 / 4 (−1)

All citizens enjoy full political rights. However, women's political participation is somewhat inhibited in practice by traditional social norms. Only three women hold seats in the legislature.

Score Change: The score declined from 4 to 3 due to low political representation and participation of women.

C. FUNCTIONING OF GOVERNMENT: 10 / 12

C1. Do the freely elected head of government and national legislative representatives determine the policies of the government? 4 / 4

The president and cabinet are able to both form and implement their policy agenda without undue interference, while the legislature provides oversight and a check on executive authority.

C2. Are safeguards against official corruption strong and effective? 3 / 4

While there is virtually no large-scale corruption in Kiribati, petty graft and nepotism in public appointments remain problems.

C3. Does the government operate with openness and transparency? 3 / 4

Kiribati lacks comprehensive regulations on public asset disclosure for officials, access to government information, and other transparency matters. In 2017, a former president told lawmakers that he had been denied access to basic data on copra production despite multiple requests. However, later in 2017 the president signed a new law, the Kiribati Audit Act, which strengthened the autonomy of the country's Audit Office and established an independent board to oversee its work. (The office previously reported to the Finance Ministry.) The law also laid out enforcement mechanisms and broadened the scope of the Audit Office's mandate, allowing more thorough assessments of budgets, expenditures, and government performance.

Some 80 people were killed in a ferry disaster in January 2018, when the Butiraoi, an interisland ferry, sank while traveling to Tarawa from the atoll of Nonouti. The government faced criticism after it failed to release its report on the disaster, but in December said it would be made public after a police investigation into the accident was completed.

CIVIL LIBERTIES: 56 / 60 (+1)

D. FREEDOM OF EXPRESSION AND BELIEF: 16 / 16

D1. Are there free and independent media? 4 / 4 (+1)

While the market does not support a large and diverse media sector, there are no significant restrictions on the flow of news and information, which is often disseminated informally. A small number of private news outlets operate freely, and foreign radio services are available. A deal was signed in May with the Asian Development Bank to provide high-speed internet to Kiribati via submarine cable, potentially expanding access to media outlets.

Score Change: The score improved from 3 to 4 because while the market does not support a large and diverse media sector, there are no significant restrictions on the flow of news and information.

D2. Are individuals free to practice and express their religious faith or nonbelief in public and private? 4 / 4

The constitution guarantees freedom of religion. Religious organizations of a certain size are required to register with the government, but there are no penalties for failing to do so. On two islands in the southern part of the archipelago that have overwhelmingly Protestant populations, members of small religious minorities are discouraged from engaging in public worship or proselytizing, though only a few dozen people are believed to be affected.

D3. Is there academic freedom, and is the educational system free from extensive political indoctrination? 4 / 4

The school system is free of political indoctrination, and religious education by various denominations is available in public schools but not mandatory. There are no restrictions on academic freedom in the country, which hosts a campus of the Fiji-based University of the South Pacific as well as a teachers' college and technical training centers.

D4. Are individuals free to express their personal views on political or other sensitive topics without fear of surveillance or retribution? 4 / 4

The government does not impose constraints on freedom of speech or the expression of personal views.

E. ASSOCIATIONAL AND ORGANIZATIONAL RIGHTS: 12 / 12
E1. Is there freedom of assembly? 4 / 4

Freedom of assembly is constitutionally protected and generally upheld in practice.

E2. Is there freedom for nongovernmental organizations, particularly those that are engaged in human rights- and governance-related work? 4 / 4

There are no undue constraints on nongovernmental organizations. The Kiribati Association of Non-Governmental Organisations (KANGO) serves as an umbrella group for some 39 local NGOs, including church-based groups and health associations.

E3. Is there freedom for trade unions and similar professional or labor organizations? 4 / 4

Workers have the right to organize unions, strike, and bargain collectively. The Kiribati Trade Union Congress, an affiliate of the International Trade Union Confederation, claims some 3,000 members and includes unions and associations for nurses, teachers, fishermen, and seafarers.

F. RULE OF LAW: 15 / 16
F1. Is there an independent judiciary? 4 / 4

The judicial system is modeled on English common law, and the courts are independent in practice. The chief justice is appointed by the president on the advice of the cabinet and the Public Service Commission; other High Court judges are appointed by the president on the advice of the chief justice and the Public Service Commission. Judges cannot be removed unless a special tribunal and the legislature find evidence of misbehavior, or an inability to perform their functions.

F2. Does due process prevail in civil and criminal matters? 4 / 4

Due process guarantees are typically respected during arrests, initial detentions, and trials. Detainees have access to lawyers, and defendants are usually granted bail while awaiting trial.

F3. Is there protection from the illegitimate use of physical force and freedom from war and insurgencies? 4 / 4

Police brutality is uncommon, and procedures for punishing such abuse are effective. Prison conditions are not considered harsh or inhumane. Kiribati has no army, relying on Australia and New Zealand to provide defense assistance under bilateral agreements. The use of traditional communal justice systems, which can include corporal punishment, is increasingly rare.

F4. Do laws, policies, and practices guarantee equal treatment of various segments of the population? 3 / 4

Women face legal discrimination on some issues as well as societal bias that limits their access to employment in practice. Citizenship laws favor men over women; for example by allowing fathers but not mothers to confer citizenship on their children.

Same-sex sexual activity is a criminal offense, though the ban is rarely enforced; discrimination in employment based on sexual orientation is prohibited.

In September 2018, Kiribati launched its first national disability action plan. The plan, to run through 2021, aims to help Kiribati implement the UN Convention on the Rights of Persons with Disabilities, to which it became a signatory in 2013.

G. PERSONAL AUTONOMY AND INDIVIDUAL RIGHTS: 13 / 16

G1. Do individuals enjoy freedom of movement, including the ability to change their place of residence, employment, or education? 4 / 4

There are no significant constraints on freedom of movement, though in the past village councils have used banishment as a punishment for wrongdoing.

Kiribati is considered among the world's most environmentally vulnerable countries as a result of climate change and associated rising sea levels, which will affect coastal regions. The effects will likely have a detrimental impact on farming, fishing, and people's access to fresh water and could ultimately make the country uninhabitable. As a result, the government has begun to develop a relocation plan to help citizens "migrate with dignity."

G2. Are individuals able to exercise the right to own property and establish private businesses without undue interference from state or nonstate actors? 3 / 4

The government operates a system of land registration and generally upholds property rights. Land is owned on either an individual or a kinship basis, and inheritance laws pertaining to land favor sons over daughters. The World Bank has reported some bureaucratic obstacles to private business activity.

G3. Do individuals enjoy personal social freedoms, including choice of marriage partner and size of family, protection from domestic violence, and control over appearance? 3 / 4

Same-sex marriage is not permitted. Domestic violence is criminalized but remains a serious and widespread problem despite government efforts to combat it. Cultural norms deter formal complaints and police interventions.

G4. Do individuals enjoy equality of opportunity and freedom from economic exploitation? 3 / 4

There are few economic opportunities in Kiribati, with most citizens engaged in subsistence agriculture.

Although forced labor and other exploitative working conditions are uncommon, some local women and girls are vulnerable to commercial sexual exploitation, often involving the crews of visiting ships.

Kosovo

Population: 1,800,000
Capital: Priština
Political Rights Rating: 3
Civil Liberties Rating: 4
Freedom Rating: 3.5
Freedom Status: Partly Free
Electoral Democracy: Yes

Overview: Kosovo holds credible and relatively well-administered elections, but its institutions remain weak, and rampant corruption has given rise to deep public distrust in the government. Journalists face serious pressure, and risk being attacked in connection with their reporting. The rule of law is inhibited by executive interference in the judiciary.

KEY DEVELOPMENTS IN 2018:

- In January, Oliver Ivanović, a moderate Serb politician in northern Kosovo and leader of the Freedom, Democracy, Justice Party, was assassinated in North Mitrovica. Three suspects, including two police officers, were arrested in connection with the murder in November. Milan Radoičić, the vice president of the Serb List, was named as a suspect, but he fled to Serbia, where he remained at year's end.
- In March, the Assembly approved the border demarcation deal with Montenegro, which was one of the conditions for Kosovo citizens to enjoy visa-free travel in Europe's Schengen zone
- In August, state prosecutor Elez Blakaj resigned his post after receiving numerous threats while pursuing a case related to fraud in the pension system for veterans. Assembly deputy Shkumbin Demaliaj, who had been indicted in the pension case, was charged in September with publicly threatening Blakaj.

POLITICAL RIGHTS: 24 / 40
A. ELECTORAL PROCESS: 9 / 12
A1. Was the current head of government or other chief national authority elected through free and fair ? 3 / 4

Kosovo's prime minister, who serves as head of government, is indirectly elected for a five-year term by at least a two-thirds majority of the unicameral Assembly. Snap general elections were held in June 2017 following a vote of no confidence in the government. The elections were considered credible by international observers, although there were inaccuracies in the voter lists and intimidation in Serb enclaves against both voters and candidates. After no party won sufficient seats to form a government, the political deadlock ended after three months, when Ramush Haradinaj, a former guerilla fighter and leader of the Alliance for the Future of Kosovo (AAK), was elected prime minister by the Assembly.

The president, who serves as head of state, is elected to a five-year term by a two-thirds majority of the Assembly. President Hashim Thaçi was elected in 2016.

A2. Were the current national legislative representatives elected through free and fair elections? 3 / 4

Members of the 120-seat Assembly are directly elected by proportional representation to four-year terms. International observers assessed the snap elections held in June 2017 as credible, but noted that voter lists contained a number of inaccuracies, including deceased voters and voters being assigned polling stations relatively far from their homes.

A3. Are the electoral laws and framework fair, and are they implemented impartially by the relevant election management bodies? 3 / 4

The Central Election Commission (CEC), which administers elections, generally acts transparently and fairly. However, because elections must take place between 30 and 45 days after the dissolution of the parliament, the CEC struggled to meet important deadlines, send materials to voters living abroad, and adjudicate preelection complaints in a timely manner during the 2017 election period.

B. POLITICAL PLURALISM AND PARTICIPATION: 10 / 16

B1. Do the people have the right to organize in different political parties or other competitive political groupings of their choice, and is the system free of undue obstacles to the rise and fall of these competing parties or groupings? 3 / 4

A proliferation of parties compete in Kosovo. However, political parties sometimes face intimidation and harassment that can negatively impact their ability to operate. The Serb List has been accused of harassing rival parties and creating an environment where voters fear supporting any alternatives. In January 2018, Oliver Ivanović, a moderate Serb politician in northern Kosovo and leader of the Freedom, Democracy, Justice Party, was assassinated in North Mitrovica. Three suspects, including two police officers, were arrested in connection with the murder in November. Milan Radoičić, the vice president of the Serb List, was named as a suspect, but he fled to Serbia to escape prosecution, where he remained at year's end.

B2. Is there a realistic opportunity for the opposition to increase its support or gain power through elections? 3 / 4

Opposition parties have a reasonable chance of gaining power through elections. The ruling PANA coalition, which includes the three largest parties—the AAK, the Democratic Party of Kosovo (PDK), and the Social Democratic Initiative (NISMA)—lost 15 seats in the 2017 parliamentary elections. Vetëvendosje, a nationalist party, gained 16 seats. In March 2018, as a result of a rift within Vetëvendosje, 12 of its Assembly members left the party and ultimately joined the Social Democratic Party.

During the 2017 campaign in Serb areas, independent candidates and political parties other than Serb List experienced intimidation and violence.

B3. Are the people's political choices free from domination by the military, foreign powers, religious hierarchies, economic oligarchies, or any other powerful group that is not democratically accountable? 2 / 4

Serbia continues to exert influence on the platform of the Serb List, as well as the political choices of ethnic Serbs generally. Serbs in Kosovo who work for institutions funded by Serbia, including in education, social services, and health care, were reportedly pressured to attend a rally for Serbian president Aleksandar Vučić during his visit to the country in September 2018.

Several top political figures in Kosovo, including President Thaçi, have links to organized crime, which plays a powerful role in politics and influences the positions of key leaders.

B4. Do various segments of the population (including ethnic, religious, gender, LGBT, and other relevant groups) have full political rights and electoral opportunities? 2 / 4

While several political parties represent the Serb minority, the population is not fully integrated into the electoral process or Kosovo's institutions. Serb List members have halted their participation in government over political disputes. Three Serb List ministers, including the deputy prime minister, resigned in March 2018, reducing Serb representation in the government.

Seven minority groups are officially recognized and politically represented. Serbs are allocated 10 parliamentary seats, and 10 more are reserved for representatives from smaller minority groups.

Kosovo has the largest participation of women in its parliament among western Balkan countries, thanks to gender quotas enshrined in the constitution. However, women's interests are not consistently represented by the government. Many women in rural areas are disenfranchised through the practice of family voting, in which the male head of a household casts ballots for the entire family.

C. FUNCTIONING OF GOVERNMENT: 5 / 12

C1. Do the freely elected head of government and national legislative representatives determine the policies of the government? 2 / 4

The lengthy deadlock before the formation of a coalition government in 2017 highlighted the dysfunction and instability that troubles the political system.

Serbia still maintains influence in northern Kosovo, where Kosovar institutions do not have a strong presence. In recent years, the government has advanced the decentralization process, granting self-rule to Serb enclaves in the southern part of Kosovo, which weakened parallel structures run by the Serbian government in those areas. A 2015 agreement between Kosovo and Serbia laid the groundwork for the Community of Serb Municipalities, a body intended to promote the interests of Serbs, which includes a proposed legislature for the Serb community. The establishment of the community remains at an impasse, however; opposition parties, including Vetëvendosje, believe it threatens Kosovo's sovereignty.

Turkey reportedly pressured the Kosovo government to arrest and extradite six Turkish nationals who taught at local schools linked to the Gulenist movement in March 2018.

C2. Are safeguards against official corruption strong and effective? 1 / 4

Corruption remains a serious problem, and the institutional framework to combat it is weak. The mandates of Kosovo's four main anticorruption bodies overlap, and they have difficulty coordinating their efforts. Authorities have shown little commitment to prosecuting high-level corruption, and when top officials are prosecuted, convictions are rare. At the end of 2018, four government ministers who had been charged with corruption or conflict of interest remained in office, despite the charges against them.

C3. Does the government operate with openness and transparency? 2 / 4

Despite the passage of the Law on Access to Public Documents in 2010, which was intended to make government documents available upon request, in practice government institutions frequently deny requests for information with little or no justification. Courts are slow to respond to complaints from those denied government information due to persistent backlogs in the judicial system.

The government has made a number of key decisions with limited transparency and without consulting the Assembly.

CIVIL LIBERTIES: 30 / 60 (+2)

D. FREEDOM OF EXPRESSION AND BELIEF: 9 / 16

D1. Are there free and independent media? 2 / 4

The constitution guarantees press freedom and a variety of media outlets operate in Kosovo. However, the government and business interests exert undue influence on editorial lines, and journalists report frequent harassment and intimidation. The Association of Journalists of Kosovo reported that there were 16 attacks on journalists in 2018, two of which involved physical assaults. Such occurrences of intimidation and violence lead many journalists to practice self-censorship.

D2. Are individuals free to practice and express their religious faith or nonbelief in public and private? 2 / 4

The constitution guarantees religious freedom. However, the Law on Freedom of Religion prevents some religious communities from registering as legal entities, a designation that would allow them to more easily buy and rent property, access burial sites, establish bank accounts, and carry out other administrative activities. Tensions between Muslims and Orthodox Christians occasionally flare up. In May 2018, protesters blocked the road to a Serbian Orthodox church in Petrič, where 50 Serbs were visiting for a ceremony. One man was assaulted during the incident.

The government has reacted strongly to the threat of attacks by Islamic extremists and the radicalization of some Kosovar citizens. Bulk arrests and heavy-handed tactics by authorities have led some members of Kosovo's majority Muslim community to raise concerns about religious persecution. However, a leading imam was acquitted in March on charges of inciting terrorism, which were based on claims that his sermons had radicalized some individuals. In May, the Justice Ministry signed an agreement with an association that represents Kosovo's Muslim clerics, which was aimed at engaging imams in order to deradicalize extremists imprisoned on terrorism charges.

D3. Is there academic freedom, and is the educational system free from extensive political indoctrination? 2 / 4

Academic freedom has improved in recent years. However, the university system is subject to political influence, as evidenced by 2017 revelations of a spate of suspicious promotions at the University of Priština. In late 2017, the minister of education, science, and technology dismissed the board and acting director of the Kosovo Accreditation Agency (KAA), which accredits the country's universities. In February 2018, the European Quality Assurance Register for Higher Education ruled that the dismissals were improper and potentially compromised the independence of the KAA.

D4. Are individuals free to express their personal views on political or other sensitive topics without fear of surveillance or retribution? 3 / 4

Individuals are largely free to express their political views without fear of retribution. In recent years, space has opened for discussion on sensitive topics such as ethnic relations, Roma communities, and LGBT (lesbian, gay, bisexual, and transgender) matters, though some people are still uncomfortable discussing these issues.

E. ASSOCIATIONAL AND ORGANIZATIONAL RIGHTS: 8 / 12 (+2)

E1. Is there freedom of assembly? 3 / 4 (+1)

Freedom of assembly is generally respected, though demonstrations are occasionally restricted for security reasons. A number of demonstrations occurred in 2018 without incident, and there have been few instances of violence at protests in recent years.

Score Change: The score improved from 2 to 3 because demonstrations have been common and relatively free from violence in recent years.

E2. Is there freedom for nongovernmental organizations, particularly those that are engaged in human rights- and governance-related work? 3 / 4 (+1)

Nongovernmental organizations (NGOs) function freely, though the courts can ban groups that infringe on the constitutional order or encourage ethnic hatred. NGOs occasionally experience pressure to curtail criticism of the government. Despite this pressure, many NGOs continue to criticize the authorities, and NGOs have largely been able to engage in advocacy work without interference. Funding for NGOs remained an issue in 2018, as international sources of support have declined in recent years, and the financial support provided by the government is limited.

Score Change: The score improved from 2 to 3 because NGOs have been more free to operate and advocate for policy and other changes in recent years.

E3. Is there freedom for trade unions and similar professional or labor organizations? 2 / 4

The constitution protects the right to establish and join trade unions, but employers frequently do not respect collective bargaining rights. It is difficult to form a private-sector union because employers often intimidate workers to prevent them from organizing. As a result, few private-sector unions exist in Kosovo.

F. RULE OF LAW: 6 / 16

F1. Is there an independent judiciary? 1 / 4

Political interference in the judiciary, particularly from the executive branch, remains a problem. Widespread judicial corruption also negatively impacts the branch's independence. Resource constraints and a lack of qualified judges hinder the performance of the judiciary.

F2. Does due process prevail in civil and criminal matters? 1 / 4

Prosecutors and courts remain susceptible to political interference and corruption by powerful political and business elites, undermining due process. In August 2018, state prosecutor Elez Blakaj resigned his post after receiving numerous threats while pursuing a case related to fraud in the pension system for veterans. Assembly deputy Shkumbin Demaliaj, who had been indicted in the pension case, was charged in September with publicly threatening Blakaj.

Although the law states that defendants should not be detained before trial unless they are likely to flee or tamper with evidence, judges often order suspects detained without cause. Lengthy pretrial detentions are common due to judicial inefficiency and resource constraints.

F3. Is there protection from the illegitimate use of physical force and freedom from war and insurgencies? 2 / 4

Although the European Union (EU) brokered an agreement in 2015 between Kosovo and Serbia to disband the Serb Civilna Zastita (Civil Protection) security force in northern Kosovo, there have been reports that the force is still operating illegally. Prison conditions have improved in recent years, but violence and poor medical care remain problems. The police sometimes abuse detainees in custody.

A number of former Kosovo Liberation Army (KLA) members—including Prime Minister Haradinaj—have been accused of war crimes, yet hold high-level positions in the government. The government has attempted to stop the work of a war crimes court based in the Hague through efforts to repeal or renegotiate the 2015 law establishing its existence. Some former KLA members have been convicted by other courts.

F4. Do laws, policies, and practices guarantee equal treatment of various segments of the population? 2 / 4

Kosovo's Roma, Ashkali, and Gorani populations face discrimination in employment, education, and access to social services. Attacks on Serbs are common in Albanian areas, and perpetrators are rarely prosecuted. LGBT people face social pressure to hide their sexual orientation or gender identity and face obstacles in making legal changes on the latter. In October 2018, Priština hosted its second pride parade, which had the support of both the president and prime minister.

Women experience discrimination in employment, particularly in regard to hiring for high-level positions in government and the private sector.

G. PERSONAL AUTONOMY AND INDIVIDUAL RIGHTS: 7 / 16

G1. Do individuals enjoy freedom of movement, including the ability to change their place of residence, employment, or education? 2 / 4

Security concerns, particularly in Serb enclaves, can make travel difficult. The government refuses to accept travel documents issued by the Serbian government that show towns in Kosovo as the place of residence, which hinders travel for many Serbs.

In March 2018, the Assembly approved the border demarcation deal with Montenegro, which was one of the conditions for Kosovo citizens to enjoy visa-free travel in Europe's Schengen zone.

G2. Are individuals able to exercise the right to own property and establish private businesses without undue interference from state or nonstate actors? 1 / 4

The legal framework on property rights is poorly outlined, and those rights are inadequately enforced in practice. While the law states that inheritance must be split equally between male and female heirs, strong patriarchal attitudes lead to pressure on women to relinquish their rights to male family members. Property reclamation by displaced persons is hindered by threats of violence and resistance to accepting returnees from local communities.

G3. Do individuals enjoy personal social freedoms, including choice of marriage partner and size of family, protection from domestic violence, and control over appearance? 2 / 4

Domestic violence remains a problem despite the government's five-year strategy that was launched in 2017 to address the issue. Domestic violence is considered a civil matter unless the victim is physically harmed. When criminal cases are referred, prosecutions and convictions are rare. Rape is illegal, but spousal rape is not addressed by the law. Courts often give convicted rapists sentences that are lighter than the prescribed minimum.

G4. Do individuals enjoy equality of opportunity and freedom from economic exploitation? 2 / 4

Equal opportunity is inhibited by persistently high levels of unemployment. Kosovo is a source, transit point, and destination for human trafficking, and corruption within the government enables perpetrators. Children are at particular risk of exploitation by traffickers, who can force them to beg or engage in sex work.

Kuwait

Population: 4,200,000
Capital: Kuwait City
Political Rights Rating: 5
Civil Liberties Rating: 5
Freedom Rating: 5.0
Freedom Status: Partly Free
Electoral Democracy: No

Overview: Kuwait is a constitutional emirate ruled by the Sabah family. While the monarchy holds executive power and dominates most state institutions, the elected parliament plays an influential role, often challenging the government. Partly due to friction between lawmakers and the executive, government reshuffles and snap parliamentary elections have been frequent since 2011. State authorities have constrained freedoms of speech and assembly in recent years.

KEY DEVELOPMENTS IN 2018:

- In July, the Cassation Court confirmed prison sentences for a group of opposition figures, including current and former members of parliament, who had played a role in 2011 protests that included the storming of the parliament building. A Constitutional Court ruling in December removed the two sitting lawmakers from office as a result of their convictions.
- A Kuwaiti blogger was arrested in February for "insulting" the United Arab Emirates (UAE), and in October several Kuwaitis were arrested for "insulting" Saudi Arabia on social media.
- In April, Kuwait expelled the ambassador of the Philippines after his staff helped a number of Filipino domestic workers to escape from households where they said their employers had abused them.

POLITICAL RIGHTS: 13 / 40

A. ELECTORAL PROCESS: 2 / 12

A1. Was the current head of government or other chief national authority elected through free and fair elections? 0 / 4

The emir, the hereditary head of state, chooses the prime minister and appoints cabinet ministers on the prime minister's recommendation. At least one cabinet minister must be an elected member of parliament. The parliament can remove cabinet ministers through a vote of no confidence, and the emir can respond to a similar vote against the prime minister either by forming a new cabinet or by dissolving the parliament and holding elections.

The current emir, Sabah al-Ahmad al-Jaber al-Sabah, took office after the death of his half-brother in 2006. The current prime minister, Jaber al-Mubarak al-Hamad al-Sabah, has held his post since 2011. All prime ministers and most senior cabinet ministers have been members of the ruling family.

A2. Were the current national legislative representatives elected through free and fair elections? 1 / 4

The 50-member National Assembly (parliament) is elected by popular vote on a formally nonpartisan basis. The emir may appoint up to 15 cabinet ministers who were not elected members of the assembly, and these are considered additional ex-officio members, though no ministers can take part in confidence votes. The parliament in theory serves four-year terms. However, the emir and the Constitutional Court have the power to dissolve the assembly, which has occurred four times since 2011. Most dissolutions come in response to serious disputes between the appointed government and lawmakers, and the timing of elections is effectively determined by the executive for political reasons. Kuwaiti elections are relatively competitive, but they are not typically observed by independent, well-established monitoring organizations, and corruption and nepotism in campaigns remain a concern.

The most recent dissolution of parliament was in October 2016. In the ensuing November elections, opposition factions—including Islamist, nationalist, and liberal blocs—won 24 of the 50 seats. Approximately 70 percent of eligible voters turned out.

A3. Are the electoral laws and framework fair, and are they implemented impartially by the relevant election management bodies? 1 / 4

Elections are administered by the Interior Ministry rather than an independent institution, and the electoral system lacks transparency, as evidenced by an opaque voter registration process. The emir has used his extensive powers to implement changes to electoral laws in close proximity to elections. In 2012, he issued a decree two months ahead of elections that reduced the number of candidates elected in each district from four to one—a move that was allegedly designed to limit the opposition's ability to build effective coalitions in the parliament.

B. POLITICAL PLURALISM AND PARTICIPATION: 7 / 16

B1. Do the people have the right to organize in different political parties or other competitive political groupings of their choice, and is the system free of undue obstacles to the rise and fall of these competing parties or groupings? 2 / 4

Formal political parties are banned, and while parliamentary blocs are permitted, the prohibition on parties inhibits political organization and the sharing of resources among like-minded candidates.

Politicians have some space to criticize the government, but those who challenge the emir's authority or seek to increase the role of elected representatives have faced criminal charges. In July 2018 the Cassation Court ordered the imprisonment of a group of opposition figures, including two current and several former lawmakers, on long-contested charges related to the storming of the parliament building during 2011 protests calling for the resignation of the prime minister. The court imposed sentences ranging from two to three and a half years, and the two sitting lawmakers, both Islamists, were removed from office following a Constitutional Court ruling in December. One of the former National Assembly members sentenced, prominent opposition leader Musallam al-Barrack, had completed a two-year prison term in 2017 on separate charges of insulting the emir.

B2. Is there a realistic opportunity for the opposition to increase its support or gain power through elections? 2 / 4

The constitutional system does not allow democratic transfers of power at the executive level. Opposition blocs are able to gain representation in the parliament, as demonstrated by the results of the 2016 legislative elections. Only 20 members of the outgoing parliament were reelected, though the turnover was attributed in large part to the fact that many opposition candidates had boycotted the previous two elections, in 2012 and 2013, to protest the emir's unilateral introduction of the new electoral system.

B3. Are the people's political choices free from domination by the military, foreign powers, religious hierarchies, economic oligarchies, or any other powerful group that is not democratically accountable? 2 / 4

The hereditary emir and the ruling family frequently interfere in political processes, including through the harassment of political and media figures, and the government impedes the activities of opposition parliamentary blocs.

Since 2014, dozens of people, including journalists, activists, and clerics, have been stripped of citizenship for criticizing the government. However, the government has slowed its use of citizenship revocation as a form of political reprisal, and in 2017 it reinstated the citizenship of a number of people who had it revoked.

In the absence of political parties, major tribes hold their own informal and technically illegal primary elections to unite their members behind certain parliamentary candidates, who then typically use their public office to generate economic benefits for members of their tribe.

B4. Do various segments of the population (including ethnic, religious, gender, LGBT, and other relevant groups) have full political rights and electoral opportunities? 1 / 4

The electorate consists of men and women over 21 years of age who have been citizens for at least 20 years and who have a Kuwaiti father. Most members of state security agencies are barred from voting. About 70 percent of the country's residents are noncitizens; citizenship, normally transmitted by a Kuwaiti father, is extremely difficult to obtain for those without at least one Kuwaiti parent, and cannot be granted to non-Muslims. More than 100,000 residents, known as bidoon, are stateless.

The Shiite Muslim minority makes up about a third of the citizen population but is not well represented in the political system. Shiite candidates won six seats in the 2016 parliamentary elections, down from eight in the previous elections.

Women have had the right to vote and run for office since 2005, and there is one female member of parliament. Entrenched social attitudes hamper more active participation by women in the political process, and the interests of women are poorly represented in practice. Societal and legal discrimination against LGBT (lesbian, gay, bisexual, and transgender) people prevents them from playing any open role in political affairs.

C. FUNCTIONING OF GOVERNMENT: 4 / 12

C1. Do the freely elected head of government and national legislative representatives determine the policies of the government? 1 / 4

While some laws initiated by elected members of parliament are adopted and implemented, policymaking authority is concentrated in the hands of the hereditary emir and his appointed government. The emir has repeatedly used his power to dissolve the National Assembly when it imposes checks on the executive. He can also veto legislation and issue executive decrees when the assembly is not in session.

C2. Are safeguards against official corruption strong and effective? 1 / 4

Corruption is pervasive in Kuwait, and allegations of corruption lodged by lawmakers against government ministers have been at the heart of the country's recurring political crises. Members of the ruling elite regularly disregard parliamentary calls for accountability and often obstruct elected officials' efforts to investigate graft and abuse of power. The cabinet resigned in 2017 to halt parliamentarians' questioning of a key minister over alleged financial and administrative irregularities.

The government issued implementing regulations for the Anti-Corruption Authority (ACA) in 2015, allowing the new body to begin its work. It has referred some cases for prosecution, but in general its activities appear insufficient given the perceived scale of the problem.

C3.Does the government operate with openness and transparency? 2 / 4

Transparency in government spending is inadequate, and there are few mechanisms that encourage officials to disclose information about government operations. Kuwait does not have any legislation guaranteeing the right to access public information. The State Audit Bureau provides some oversight on revenue and expenditures, reporting to both the government and the National Assembly, though not necessarily to the public. In March 2018, the parliament approved legislation meant to regulate conflicts of interest among public officials.

CIVIL LIBERTIES: 23 / 60
D. FREEDOM OF EXPRESSION AND BELIEF: 6 / 16
D1. Are there free and independent media? 1 / 4

The authorities limit press freedom. Kuwaiti law provides penalties for the publication of material that insults Islam, criticizes the emir, discloses information considered secret or private, or calls for the regime's overthrow. Kuwaiti journalists also risk imprisonment under a restrictive 2016 cybercrimes law that criminalizes the dissemination online of information on similar topics. However, foreign media outlets operate relatively freely.

The government has instructed internet service providers (ISPs) to block certain websites for political or moral reasons. A 2014 telecommunications law created the Commission for Mass Communications and Information Technology, granting the regulator sweeping powers to monitor, block, and censor online material.

D2. Are individuals free to practice and express their religious faith or nonbelief in public and private? 2 / 4

Islam is the state religion, and blasphemy is a punishable offense. The government appoints Sunni imams and oversees their sermons. Shiite Muslims have their own religious institutions, including Sharia (Islamic law) courts, though the government does not permit training of Shiite clerics in the country. Non-Muslim religious minorities are generally permitted to practice their faiths in private; they are forbidden from proselytizing.

D3. Is there academic freedom, and is the educational system free from extensive political indoctrination? 2 / 4

Academic freedom is impeded by self-censorship on politically sensitive topics, as well as by broader legal restrictions on freedom of expression, including the prohibitions on "insulting" the emir and defaming Islam.

D4. Are individuals free to express their personal views on political or other sensitive topics without fear of surveillance or retribution? 1 / 4

Freedom of expression is curtailed by state surveillance and the criminalization of some forms of critical speech, especially if it touches on the emir or the rulers of friendly states. The cybercrimes law that took effect in 2016, for example, imposes prison sentences of up to 10 years as well as fines for online speech that criticizes the emir, judicial officials, religious figures, or foreign leaders.

Individuals are prosecuted in practice for their online comments. In February 2018, a court sentenced blogger Abdullah al-Saleh to five years' imprisonment in absentia for "insulting" the UAE; he had already received other prison sentences for separate commentary about neighboring states. In October, several Kuwaitis, including the head of a local think tank, were arrested for "insulting" Saudi Arabia on social media.

E. ASSOCIATIONAL AND ORGANIZATIONAL RIGHTS: 4 / 12
E1. Is there freedom of assembly? 1 / 4

Freedom of assembly is constrained in practice. Kuwaitis must notify officials of a public meeting or protest, and those who participate in unauthorized protests are subject to prison terms or, for noncitizens, deportation. Nevertheless, some peaceful protests have been allowed without a permit. Family members and other supporters of the opposition figures and activists accused of storming the parliament in 2011 held a series of protests on the defendants' behalf during 2018.

E2. Is there freedom for nongovernmental organizations, particularly those that are engaged in human rights- and governance-related work? 2 / 4

The government restricts the registration and licensing of nongovernmental organizations (NGOs), forcing many groups to operate without legal standing. Representatives of licensed NGOs must obtain government permission to attend foreign conferences, and critical groups may be subject to harassment. The government closed down the Kuwait chapter of Transparency International in 2015.

E3. Is there freedom for trade unions and similar professional or labor organizations? 1 / 4

Private-sector workers who are Kuwaiti citizens have the right to join labor unions and bargain collectively, and a limited right to strike, but labor laws allow for only one national union federation. Noncitizen migrant workers, who form most of the labor force, do not enjoy these rights and can face dismissal and deportation for engaging in union or strike activity. Civil servants and household workers are also denied such rights; most citizen workers are public employees and do not have the right to strike. Migrant workers have from time to time participated in risky illegal labor actions to protest nonpayment of wages and other abuses.

Labor uncertainty, particularly in light of low oil prices that threatened to cause widespread layoffs in 2016, has led to public tensions between workers and the state in recent years. Civil aviation workers organized a sit-in in July 2018 over demands for the payment of allowances.

F. RULE OF LAW: 7 / 16
F1. Is there an independent judiciary? 1 / 4

Kuwait lacks an independent judiciary. The emir has the final say in judicial appointments, which are proposed by a Supreme Judicial Council made up of senior judges as well as the attorney general and deputy justice minister, and the executive branch approves judicial promotions. Judges who are Kuwaiti citizens are appointed for life, while noncitizens receive contracts for up to three years, reflecting a wider tendency to keep noncitizens employed on precarious short-term contracts.

The courts frequently rule in favor of the government in cases related to politics. In rare instances the Constitutional Court has ruled against the emir, for example in 2012, when it declared his most recent call for elections to be unconstitutional, dissolving the new parliament and reinstating the previous one. However, this appeared to be politically convenient for the emir's government at the time, as the former parliament had a progovernment majority and the more recently elected one had reached a standoff with the executive.

F2. Does due process prevail in civil and criminal matters? 2 / 4

Arbitrary arrests and detentions, which are illegal under Kuwaiti law, still occur with some frequency. Authorities may detain suspects for four days without charge. State prosecutors have issued orders that favor government interests, such as a 2017 ban on the publication of information related to state security cases. Noncitizens arrested for minor offenses are subject to detention and deportation without due process or access to the courts.

F3. Is there protection from the illegitimate use of physical force and freedom from war and insurgencies? 2 / 4

Kuwait is generally free from armed conflict, despite a deadly terrorist bombing at a mosque in 2015, and has relatively low levels of criminal violence. However, while the constitution prohibits torture and other forms of cruel and unusual punishment, these protections are not always upheld. Detainees, especially bidoon, continue to experience torture and beatings while in custody. Overcrowding and unsanitary conditions are significant problems at prisons and deportation centers.

In 2017, the government carried out its first execution in four years, and a total of seven people were executed by hanging that year. The advocacy group Human Rights Watch has reported violations of due process in capital cases.

F4. Do laws, policies, and practices guarantee equal treatment of various segments of the population? 2 / 4

Despite some legal protections from bias and abuse, women remain underrepresented in the workforce and face unequal treatment in several areas of law and society. Women account for a majority of university students, but the government enforces gender segregation in educational institutions. LGBT people face societal discrimination, and the penal code prescribes prison sentences for sex between men and "imitating the opposite sex."

Officials consider the country's more than 100,000 bidoon to be illegal residents, and they lack the protections and benefits associated with citizenship. They often live in poor conditions and have difficulty accessing public services and obtaining formal employment. Noncitizen migrant workers are also excluded from the legal protections granted to citizens on a variety of topics.

G. PERSONAL AUTONOMY AND INDIVIDUAL RIGHTS: 6 / 16

G1. Do individuals enjoy freedom of movement, including the ability to change their place of residence, employment, or education? 2 / 4

For the most part, Kuwait does not place constraints on the movement of its citizens, but migrant workers often face de facto restrictions on freedom of travel and residence. The labor sponsorship system limits migrant workers' freedom to change jobs without permission from their existing employer, though a 2016 policy allows some categories of migrant workers to do so after three years.

G2. Are individuals able to exercise the right to own property and establish private businesses without undue interference from state or nonstate actors? 1 / 4

Kuwaiti law allows citizens and foreign nationals, but not bidoon, to own private property. Although the law permits the establishment of businesses, bureaucratic obstacles sometimes slow the process. Companies are legally prohibited from conducting business with citizens of Israel.

Sharia-based inheritance rules put women at a disadvantage, particularly those pertaining to Sunni families.

G3. Do individuals enjoy personal social freedoms, including choice of marriage partner and size of family, protection from domestic violence, and control over appearance? 2 / 4

Personal status laws favor men over women in matters of marriage, divorce, and child custody. For example, Sunni women must have the approval of a male guardian in order to marry, and they are only permitted to seek a divorce when deserted or subjected to domestic violence. Domestic abuse and spousal rape are not specifically prohibited by law, and rapists can avoid punishment if they marry their victims.

G4. Do individuals enjoy equality of opportunity and freedom from economic exploitation? 1 / 4

Foreign domestic servants and migrant workers are highly vulnerable to abuse and exploitation, often forced to live and work in poor or dangerous conditions for low pay. In 2015, the National Assembly passed legislation expanding the rights of domestic workers, including the right to paid leave and limits on working hours, but implementation remains problematic. In April 2018, Kuwait expelled the Philippine ambassador after videos surfaced that appeared to show embassy staff helping Filipino domestic workers escape their employers, who allegedly abused them. The two governments reached an agreement in May on new safeguards for Filipino workers in the country.

Kyrgyzstan

Population: 6,100,000
Capital: Bishkek
Political Rights Rating: 5
Civil Liberties Rating: 4 ↑
Freedom Rating: 4.5
Freedom Status: Partly Free
Electoral Democracy: No

Overview: After two revolutions that ousted authoritarian presidents in 2005 and 2010, Kyrgyzstan adopted a parliamentary form of government. Governing coalitions have proven unstable, however, and corruption remains pervasive. In recent years, the ruling Social Democratic Party of Kyrgyzstan (SDPK) has sought to consolidate power, using the justice system to suppress political opponents and civil society critics.

KEY DEVELOPMENTS IN 2018:

- A January power plant failure in Bishkek, which left much of the city's population without heat during record-low temperatures, sparked a corruption investigation into contracts dating to 2013 with a Chinese company to repair and modernize the plant. A number of current and former high-ranking officials closely aligned with former president Atambayev, including the mayor of Bishkek and former prime ministers Sapar Isakov and Jantoro Satybaldiyev, were arrested on corruption charges in connection with the contracts.
- In October, the Supreme Court ruled that immunity from prosecution for former presidents was unconstitutional, and in December, the SDPK-led parliament approved the first reading of legislation to strip all former presidents of immunity. The move could clear the way for the potential arrest and prosecution of former presi-

dent Almazbek Atambayev, who had feuded with President Jeenbekov throughout the year.

POLITICAL RIGHTS: 12 / 40

A. ELECTORAL PROCESS: 4 / 12

A1. Was the current head of government or other chief national authority elected through free and fair elections? 1 / 4

The directly elected president, who shares executive power with a prime minister, serves a single six-year term with no possibility of reelection. The 2017 presidential election was marked by inappropriate use of government resources to support Sooronbay Jeenbekov of the SDPK, who had served as prime minister under outgoing president Atambayev. There were also reports of voter intimidation, including pressure on public-sector employees. Jeenbekov defeated 10 other candidates, securing 54 percent of the vote amid 56 percent turnout. Omurbek Babanov of the Respublika party placed second with about 33 percent.

President Jeenbekov dismissed Prime Minister Sapar Isakov in April 2018, after Isakov's cabinet lost a no-confidence vote in the parliament, which was considered a move to purge several of Atambayev's closest allies in the government. The parliament approved SDPK member Mukhammedkaliy Abylgaziyev as prime minister the same month, who formed a coalition government with three other parties: Bir Bol, Respublika–Ata Jurt, and the Kyrgyzstan party.

A2. Were the current national legislative representatives elected through free and fair elections? 2 / 4

The unicameral parliament consists of 120 deputies elected by party list in a single national constituency to serve five-year terms. No single party is allowed to hold more than 65 seats. Observers from the Organization for Security and Co-operation in Europe (OSCE) found that the 2015 parliamentary elections were competitive and that the 14 registered parties offered voters a wide range of options. However, the monitoring group noted significant procedural problems, flaws in the rollout of a new biometric registration system, inadequate media coverage, and widespread allegations of vote buying. Civil society groups and media reports raised concerns that the SDPK had used state resources and pressure on public employees to enhance its position. Six parties cleared the 7 percent vote threshold to secure representation. The SDPK led the voting with 38 seats, followed by Respublika–Ata Jurt (28), the Kyrgyzstan party (18), Onuguu-Progress (13), Bir Bol (12), and Ata Meken (11).

A3. Are the electoral laws and framework fair, and are they implemented impartially by the relevant election management bodies? 1 / 4

The Central Commission for Elections and Referenda exhibited political bias during the 2017 presidential election, according to international observers. Amendments to the election law that were enacted ahead of the poll made it more difficult for nongovernmental organizations (NGOs) to field observers and appeal decisions by election officials.

In 2016, a referendum on constitutional amendments was conducted hastily, with little transparency or opportunities for public debate on the package of proposed changes, which ultimately won adoption. Administrative resources were reportedly used to support a "yes" vote, and state employees faced pressure to participate in the effort.

B. POLITICAL PLURALISM AND PARTICIPATION: 5 / 16

B1. Do the people have the right to organize in different political parties or other competitive political groupings of their choice, and is the system free of undue obstacles to the rise and fall of these competing parties or groupings? 2 / 4

Citizens have the freedom to organize political parties and groupings, especially at the local level. However, in addition to the 7 percent national threshold, parties must win at least 0.7 percent of the vote in each of the country's nine regional divisions to secure seats in the parliament, which discourages locally organized groups from participating in national politics.

Political parties are primarily vehicles for a handful of strong personalities, rather than mass organizations with clear ideologies and policy platforms. Although the 2015 elections featured several new parties, almost all were the result of splits or mergers among the factions in the previous parliament, meaning the actual roster of deputies changed very little.

B2. Is there a realistic opportunity for the opposition to increase its support or gain power through elections? 1 / 4

The 2010 constitutional reforms aimed to ensure political pluralism and prevent the reemergence of an authoritarian, superpresidential system. Since 2012, however, observers noted that the ruling party has consolidated power and used executive agencies to target political enemies. Opposition members and outside observers have accused the SDPK of attempting to improperly influence electoral and judicial outcomes. Constitutional amendments approved in 2016 included measures that made it more difficult to bring down a sitting government or withdraw from a coalition, effectively solidifying the position of the SDPK.

In recent years, opposition leaders have faced politically motivated criminal investigations and prosecutions. Presidential runner-up Omurbek Babanov, leader of the Respublika party, was accused in 2017 of "incitement to interethnic violence" based on remarks he made at a campaign rally with ethnic Uzbeks. Babanov fled the country and resigned as a member of parliament. In March 2018, authorities commenced another investigation against Babanov, for allegedly planning riots and attempting to seize power. Although investigators dropped the case in September, the criminal probe from 2017 remained open. Babanov continued to live in exile at the end of 2018.

B3. Are the people's political choices free from domination by the military, foreign powers, religious hierarchies, economic oligarchies, or any other powerful group that is not democratically accountable? 1 / 4

While largely free from military domination, Kyrgyzstani politics are subject to the influence of organized crime and economic oligarchies. Political affairs are generally controlled by a small group of elites who head competing patronage networks.

B4. Do various segments of the population (including ethnic, religious, gender, LGBT, and other relevant groups) have full political rights and electoral opportunities? 1 / 4

Ethnic minority groups face political marginalization. Politicians from the Kyrgyz majority have used ethnic Uzbeks as scapegoats on various issues in recent years, and minority populations remain underrepresented in elected offices, even in areas where they form a demographic majority.

Women enjoy equal political rights and have attained some notable leadership positions, but they are also underrepresented, having won 19 percent of the seats in the last parliamentary elections despite a 30 percent gender quota for party candidate lists.

C. FUNCTIONING OF GOVERNMENT: 4 / 12

C1. Do the freely elected head of government and national legislative representatives determine the policies of the government? 1 / 4

Unresolved constitutional ambiguities regarding the division of power among the president, the prime minister, and the parliament—combined with the need to form multiparty coalitions—have contributed to the instability of governments in recent years. The prime minister has been replaced nearly a dozen times since 2010.

C2. Are safeguards against official corruption strong and effective? 1 / 4

Corruption is pervasive in politics and government. Political elites use government resources to reward clients—including organized crime figures—and punish opponents. A new anticorruption office within the State Committee of National Security (GKNB) was formed in 2012, but it has primarily been used to target the administration's political enemies in the parliament and municipal governments.

A January 2018 power-plant failure in Bishkek, which left much of the city's population without heat during record-low temperatures, sparked a corruption investigation into contracts dating to 2013 with a Chinese company to repair and modernize the plant. A number of current and former high-ranking officials closely aligned with former president Atambayev, including the mayor of Bishkek and former prime ministers Sapar Isakov and Jantoro Satybaldiyev, were later arrested on corruption charges in connection with the contracts. Some analysts viewed the charges as an attempt by Jeenbekov to neutralize Atambayev, who has publicly criticized his successor. The suspects awaited trial at year's end.

C3. Does the government operate with openness and transparency? 2 / 4

Kyrgyzstan's laws on access to public information are considered relatively strong, but implementation is poor in practice. Similarly, although public officials are obliged to disclose information on their personal finances, powerful figures are rarely held accountable for noncompliance or investigated for unexplained wealth. Oversight of public contracts is inadequate; corruption scandals in recent years have often centered on procurement deals or sales of state assets.

ADDITIONAL DISCRETIONARY POLITICAL RIGHTS QUESTION

Is the government or occupying power deliberately changing the ethnic composition of a country or territory so as to destroy a culture or tip the political balance in favor of another group? −1 / 0

Southern Kyrgyzstan has yet to fully recover from the ethnic upheaval of 2010, which included numerous documented instances of government involvement or connivance in violence against ethnic Uzbeks in the region, with the aim of tipping the political and economic balance in favor of the Kyrgyz elite. Many Uzbek homes and businesses were destroyed or seized. While intimidation has continued and little has been done to reverse the outcomes of the violence, some steps have been taken to restore Uzbek-language media in the region, and fears of further unrest have eased over time.

CIVIL LIBERTIES: 26 / 60 (+1)

D. FREEDOM OF EXPRESSION AND BELIEF: 10 / 16

D1. Are there free and independent media? 2 / 4

The media landscape is relatively diverse but divided along ethnic lines, and prosecutions for inciting ethnic hatred have tended to focus on minority writers despite the prevalence of openly racist and anti-Semitic articles in Kyrgyz-language media. A 2014 law criminalized the publication of "false information relating to a crime or offense" in the media, which international monitors saw as a contradiction of the country's 2011 decriminalization of defamation. The law assigns penalties of up to three years in prison, or five years if the claim serves the interests of organized crime or is linked to the fabrication of evidence.

Journalists continued to risk arrest, prosecution, and civil suits for critical reporting in 2018. In February, freelance journalist Elnura Alkanova was arrested and charged with disclosing confidential information for 2017 articles she wrote about alleged corruption. In April, however, authorities dropped the charges against her. In May, former president Atambayev dropped libel charges he had filed against the online news outlet Zanoza and two journalists in 2017, which stemmed from articles that Atambayev claimed were insulting.

D2. Are individuals free to practice and express their religious faith or nonbelief in public and private? 2 / 4

All religious organizations must register with the authorities, a process that is often cumbersome and arbitrary. Groups outside the traditional Muslim and Orthodox Christian mainstream reportedly have difficulty obtaining registration, and the 2009 Law on Religion deems all unregistered groups illegal. Organizations such as the Jehovah's Witnesses often face police harassment. Nevertheless, some unregistered religious communities have been able to practice their faiths without state intervention, and the authorities have investigated and punished relatively rare acts of violence against religious figures or minorities. The government monitors and restricts Islamist groups that it regards as a threat to national security, particularly Hizb ut-Tahrir.

D3. Is there academic freedom, and is the educational system free from extensive political indoctrination? 3 / 4

The government does not formally restrict academic freedom, though teachers and students have reportedly faced pressure to participate in political campaigns and voting, including in the 2017 presidential election.

D4. Are individuals free to express their personal views on political or other sensitive topics without fear of surveillance or retribution? 3 / 4

Private discussion is generally free in the country, and prosecutions of individuals for the expression of personal views on social media are rare. However, state and local authorities regularly raid homes where they believe members of banned groups like Hizb ut-Tahrir or certain religious minorities, such as Jehovah's Witnesses, are meeting to discuss their beliefs.

E. ASSOCIATIONAL AND ORGANIZATIONAL RIGHTS: 5 / 12 (+1)
E1. Is there freedom of assembly? 1 / 4

A 2012 law allows peaceful assembly, and small protests and civil disobedience actions, such as blocking roads, take place regularly. Nevertheless, domestic and international watchdogs remain concerned about police violations of the right to demonstrate, including arrests and other forms of interference. Intimidation by counterprotesters has also emerged as a problem in recent years.

E2. Is there freedom for nongovernmental organizations, particularly those that are engaged in human rights– and governance-related work? 2 / 4 (+1)

NGOs participate actively in civic and political life, and public advisory councils were established in the parliament and most ministries in 2011, permitting improved monitoring and advocacy by NGOs. However, human rights workers who support ethnic Uzbek victims face threats, harassment, and physical attacks. Ultranationalists have harassed US and European NGOs as well as domestic counterparts that are perceived to be favored by foreign governments and donors.

The threats and harassment from both state and nonstate actors receded significantly in 2018, and no attacks from vigilante groups were reported during the year, allowing NGOs to operate more freely.

Score Change: The score improved from 1 to 2 due to decreased incidents of pressure from state and nonstate actors on nongovernmental organizations in 2018, which has allowed them to act with greater freedom.

E3. Is there freedom for trade unions and similar professional or labor organizations? 2 / 4

Kyrgyzstani law provides for the formation of trade unions, which are generally able to operate without obstruction. However, strikes are prohibited in many sectors. Legal enforcement of union rights is weak, and employers do not always respect collective-bargaining agreements.

F. RULE OF LAW: 4 / 16
F1. Is there an independent judiciary? 1 / 4

The judiciary is not independent and remains dominated by the executive branch. Corruption among judges is widespread.

In October 2018, the Supreme Court ruled that immunity from prosecution for former presidents was unconstitutional. Following the decision, in December, the SDPK-led parliament approved the first reading of legislation to strip all former presidents of immunity, which could clear the way for the potential arrest and prosecution of Atambayev.

F2. Does due process prevail in civil and criminal matters? 1 / 4

Defendants' rights, including the presumption of innocence, are not always respected, and evidence allegedly obtained through torture is regularly accepted in courts. Some observers expressed concern about a lack of due process in high-profile corruption cases against Atambayev's allies in 2018.

F3. Is there protection from the illegitimate use of physical force and freedom from war and insurgencies? 1 / 4

There are credible reports of torture during arrest and interrogation, in addition to physical abuse in prisons. Most such reports do not lead to investigations and convictions. Few perpetrators of the violence against the Uzbek community in southern Kyrgyzstan in 2010 have been brought to justice.

F4. Do laws, policies, and practices guarantee equal treatment of various segments of the population? 1 / 4

Legal bans on gender discrimination in the workplace are not effectively enforced. Traditional biases also put women at a disadvantage regarding education and access to services. Ethnic minorities—particularly Uzbeks, who make up nearly half of the population in Osh—continue to face discrimination on economic, security, and other matters. Uzbeks are often targeted for harassment, arrest, and mistreatment by law enforcement agencies based on dubious terrorism or extremism charges. Same-sex sexual activity is not illegal, but discrimination against and abuse of LGBT (lesbian, gay, bisexual, and transgender) people at the hands of police are pervasive. Ultranationalist groups have also engaged in intimidation of LGBT activists.

G. PERSONAL AUTONOMY AND INDIVIDUAL RIGHTS: 7 / 16

G1. Do individuals enjoy freedom of movement, including the ability to change their place of residence, employment, or education? 2 / 4

The government generally respects the right of unrestricted travel to and from Kyrgyzstan, though journalists and human rights activists sometimes face bans and other obstacles. Barriers to internal migration include a requirement that citizens obtain permits to work and settle in particular areas of the country.

G2. Are individuals able to exercise the right to own property and establish private businesses without undue interference from state or nonstate actors? 2 / 4

The misuse of personal connections, corruption, and organized crime impair private business activity. The ethnic violence of 2010 has affected property rights in the south, as many businesses, mainly owned by ethnic Uzbeks, were destroyed or seized.

G3. Do individuals enjoy personal social freedoms, including choice of marriage partner and size of family, protection from domestic violence, and control over appearance? 2 / 4

Cultural constraints and inaction by law enforcement officials discourage victims of domestic violence and rape from contacting the authorities. Legislation enacted in 2017 aimed to broaden the definition of domestic abuse and improve both victim assistance and responses from law enforcement bodies, but the law was weakly enforced in 2018.

The practice of bride abduction persists despite the strengthening of legal penalties in 2013, and few perpetrators are prosecuted. In May, a young woman, who was kidnapped twice by the same man in a case of bride abduction, was murdered by her abductor after police placed them in the same jail cell near Bishkek. In December, the perpetrator was sentenced to 20 years in prison, following widespread outrage over the brutal crime.

G4. Do individuals enjoy equality of opportunity and freedom from economic exploitation? 1 / 4

The government does not actively enforce workplace health and safety standards. Child labor is restricted by law but reportedly occurs, particularly in the agricultural sector. The trafficking of women and girls into forced prostitution abroad is a serious problem. Police have been accused of complicity in the trafficking and exploitation of victims. Kyrgyzstani men are especially vulnerable to trafficking for forced labor abroad.

Laos

Population: 7,000,000
Capital: Vientiane
Political Rights Rating: 7
Civil Liberties Rating: 6
Freedom Rating: 6.5
Freedom Status: Not Free
Electoral Democracy: No

Overview: Laos is a one-party state in which the ruling Lao People's Revolutionary Party (LPRP) dominates all aspects of politics and harshly restricts civil liberties. There is no organized opposition and no truly independent civil society. News coverage of the country is limited by the remoteness of some areas, repression of domestic media, and the opaque nature of the regime. Economic development has led to a rising tide of disputes over land and environmental issues. In recent years, a wide-ranging anticorruption campaign has had some positive impact.

KEY DEVELOPMENTS IN 2018:

- The government ramped up a wide-ranging anticorruption campaign, with at least 80 government officials, including some senior figures, coming under investigation.
- dam collapsed in southern Laos in July, unleashing some 5 billion cubic meters (176 trillion cubic feet) of water on low-lying villages and towns. Authorities sought to suppress coverage of the disaster, and local residents and aid agencies indicated that the government death toll of 43, issued in November, was far too low. The collapse also prompted questions about oversight of ongoing dam construction being undertaken by the government and foreign investors.
- A prominent Chinese businessperson was murdered in a home invasion in Vientiane in August, the latest in a series of violent attacks against Chinese nationals in Laos in recent years.
- In January, Zhao Wei, a China-born business tycoon who controls a casino complex in northern Laos, was identified by the US Treasury Department as being a kingpin of an allegedly massive illegal trade in wildlife, narcotics, and people. There was no apparent reaction to the US statement by Lao authorities.

POLITICAL RIGHTS: 2 / 40 (+1)

A. ELECTORAL PROCESS: 0 / 12

A1. Was the current head of government or other chief national authority elected through free and fair elections? 0 / 4

Laos is a one-party communist state and the ruling LPRP's 61-member Central Committee, under the leadership of the 11-member Politburo, makes all major decisions. The LPRP vets all candidates for election to the National Assembly, whose members elect the president and prime minister.

The LPRP selected new leaders through an opaque process at a party congress in 2016. After that year's tightly controlled National Assembly elections, lawmakers chose Bounnhang Vorachith to serve as president, and Thongloun Sisoulith to serve as prime minister.

A2. Were the current national legislative representatives elected through free and fair elections? 0 / 4

National Assembly elections are held every five years, but are not free or fair, and international observers are not permitted to monitor them. The LPRP won 144 of 149 seats in the 2016 legislative elections, with the remainder going to carefully vetted independents.

A3. Are the electoral laws and framework fair, and are they implemented impartially by the relevant election management bodies? 0 / 4

The electoral laws and framework are designed to ensure that the LPRP, the only legal party, dominates every election and controls the political system.

B. POLITICAL PLURALISM AND PARTICIPATION: 0 / 16

B1. Do the people have the right to organize in different political parties or other competitive political groupings of their choice, and is the system free of undue obstacles to the rise and fall of these competing parties or groupings? 0 / 4

The constitution makes the ruling LPRP the sole legal political party, and grants it a leading role at all levels of government.

B2. Is there a realistic opportunity for the opposition to increase its support or gain power through elections? 0 / 4

Although the LPRP is the only legal party, National Assembly candidates are not required to be members. However, all candidates must be approved by National Assembly–appointed committees. In practice, almost all lawmakers belong to the LPRP, and legislate alongside a handful of party-vetted independents.

B3. Are the people's political choices free from domination by the military, foreign powers, religious hierarchies, economic oligarchies, or any other powerful group that is not democratically accountable? 0 / 4

The authoritarian one-party system in Laos excludes the public from any genuine and autonomous political participation.

B4. Do various segments of the population (including ethnic, religious, gender, LGBT, and other relevant groups) have full political rights and electoral opportunities? 0 / 4

The right to vote and run for office are guaranteed in the constitution, but due to the one-party system, no portion of the population may exercise full political rights and electoral opportunities. Nominal representatives of ethnic minorities hold positions in the Politburo, Central Committee, and National Assembly, but they are limited in their ability to advocate for policies that benefit minorities. Women hold approximately 28 percent of the National Assembly seats, but their presence in the legislature similarly does not guarantee that the interests of women are represented in politics. At the local level, village-level leaders are responsible for many of the decisions affecting daily life, and nearly all village chiefs are men.

C. FUNCTIONING OF GOVERNMENT: 2 / 12 (+1)

C1. Do the freely elected head of government and national legislative representatives determine the policies of the government? 0 / 4

None of the country's nominally elected officials are chosen through free and fair contests, and major policy decisions are reserved for the LPRP. In recent years the government has more frequently passed laws, rather than decrees, to govern, though due to the choreographed nature of elections the representatives approving these bills cannot be said to be enacting the will of the electorate.

C2. Are safeguards against official corruption strong and effective? 1 / 4 (+1)

Corruption by government officials is widespread. Laws aimed at curbing graft are not well enforced, and government regulation of virtually every facet of life provides many opportunities for bribery and fraud.

However, Prime Minister Thongloun has initiated an anticorruption drive since taking office in 2016. After taking office, he empowered the State Audit Organization (SAO) to conduct financial and budget investigations. The office has since uncovered several instances of misappropriated state funds and unreported expenditures, and some LPRP officials have apparently returned money that they stole to the national treasury. Thongloun's efforts intensified in 2018, when investigations were launched against numerous officials across many provinces; Radio Free Asia reported in May that at least 80 government officials had been investigated for graft so far during the year, though the actual number is likely substantially higher. Several senior government officials were arrested and face graft charges as a result of the effort.

The prime minister also placed a ban on export timber in 2016, in an effort to crack down on illegal logging and the extensive deforestation of the country. In 2017, he restricted some mining and fruit plantation operations that were accused of causing environmental damage and being conduits for graft. Two provincial governors have been fired, one in late 2017 and one in February 2018, over alleged links to graft in the timber trade.

Score Change: The score improved from 0 to 1 because the government has pursued a relatively serious campaign against graft since 2016.

C3. Does the government operate with openness and transparency? 1 / 4

There are no access to information laws in Laos. However, the 2012 Law on Making Legislation increased legislative transparency by requiring bills proposed at the central and provincial levels to be published for comment for 60 days and, once passed, to be posted for 15 days before coming into force.

A 2014 asset declaration program has helped identify corrupt government officials. Meanwhile, the State Inspection Authority (SIA) reported that over 240,000 government officials and employees submitted asset declarations for review in 2017. Also in 2017, SAO reported that over $120 million of unapproved state spending was discovered in the 2015–16 budget. Thongloun repeatedly promised in 2018 to make government more transparent to the citizenry, although he has been unclear about how he will do so.

Authorities released little information about the July 2018 dam collapse, and what information was released was often contradictory.

CIVIL LIBERTIES: 12 / 60 (+1)
D. FREEDOM OF EXPRESSION AND BELIEF: 4 / 16
D1. Are there free and independent media? 0 / 4

Authorities use legal restrictions and intimidation tactics against state critics, and as a result, self-censorship is widespread. The state owns nearly all media, though some independent outlets, primarily entertainment magazines that steer clear of political commentary, have emerged in recent years. Coverage of a catastrophic July 2018 dam collapse was suppressed, and as a result the death toll from the incident remains unclear; observers have suggested that the government death toll of 43, issued in November, was far too low.

D2. Are individuals free to practice and express their religious faith or nonbelief in public and private? 2 / 4

Religious freedom is guaranteed in the constitution, but in practice is constrained, in part through the LPRP's control of clergy training and supervision of temples. There have been multiple cases in recent years of Christians being briefly detained or sentenced to jail for unauthorized religious activities, or pressured by authorities to renounce their faith. A ban on public proselytizing is generally enforced, and authorities make some efforts to monitor the importation of religious materials.

D3. Is there academic freedom, and is the educational system free from extensive political indoctrination? 1 / 4

University professors cannot teach or write about politically sensitive topics, though Laos has invited select foreign academics to teach courses in the country, and some young people go overseas for university education.

D4. Are individuals free to express their personal views on political or other sensitive topics without fear of surveillance or retribution? 1 / 4

Government surveillance of the population has been scaled back in recent years, but security agencies and LPRP-backed mass organizations continue to monitor for public dissent, which is punishable under a variety of laws. As a result, there is little space for open and free private discussion of sensitive issues. The government attempts to monitor social media usage for content and images that portray Laos negatively, and courts have handed down heavy sentences in response individuals' posting of such material.

Nevertheless, a Chinese railway construction project that has displaced citizens and prompted the government to take on debt, as well as the 2018 dam collapse, have been controversial enough to prompt some criticism of the government among ordinary people.

E. ASSOCIATIONAL AND ORGANIZATIONAL RIGHTS: 0 / 12
E1. Is there freedom of assembly? 0 / 4

Although protected in the constitution, the government severely restricts freedom of assembly. Protests are rare, and those deemed to be participating in unsanctioned gatherings can receive lengthy prison sentences. The government occasionally allows demonstrations that pose little threat to the LPRP.

In 2017, Laos's government arrested 14 villagers in Sekong Province protesting alleged land grabs, and since then reports have emerged that some have been subject to severe mistreatment in custody. Three of the protesters were released in June.

E2. Is there freedom for nongovernmental organizations, particularly those that are engaged in human rights- and governance-related work? 0 / 4

Alongside LPRP-affiliated mass organizations, there are some domestic nongovernmental welfare and professional groups, but they are prohibited from pursuing political agendas. Registration and regulatory mechanisms for NGOs are onerous and allow for arbitrary state interference. A new decree on associations, which came into force in 2017, mandates that NGOs secure government approval for their initiatives and funding, among other new restrictions. NGOs report that this law has made it more difficult for them to register and launch new initiatives.

The 2012 disappearance of prominent antipoverty activist Sombath Somphone remained unsolved in 2018.

E3. Is there freedom for trade unions and similar professional or labor organizations? 0 / 4

Most unions belong to the official Lao Federation of Trade Unions. Strikes are not expressly prohibited, but workers rarely stage walkouts. Collective bargaining is legally permitted, but rarely exercised by workers.

F. RULE OF LAW: 2 / 16
F1. Is there an independent judiciary? 0 / 4

The courts are wracked by corruption and subject to LPRP influence. Major decisions are often made secretly.

F2. Does due process prevail in civil and criminal matters? 0 / 4

Due process rights are outlined in the law, but these rights are routinely denied. Defendants are often presumed guilty, and long procedural delays in the judicial system are common. Appeals processes are often nonexistent or delayed, sometimes indefinitely. Searches without warrants occur and arbitrary arrests continue, particularly those arrested for drug use or activism. Villages are encouraged to settle noncriminal disputes in local mediation units, which are outside the formal judicial system.

In January, Zhao Wei, a China-born business tycoon who controls a casino complex in northern Laos, was identified by the US Treasury Department as being a kingpin of an allegedly massive illegal trade in wildlife, narcotics, and people. There was no apparent reaction to the US statement by Lao authorities.

F3. Is there protection from the illegitimate use of physical force and freedom from war and insurgencies? 1 / 4

Security forces often illegally detain suspects. Prison conditions are substandard, with reports of inadequate food and medical facilities. Torture of prisoners is occasionally reported, as with the group of fourteen villagers detained in 2017 for protesting land grabbing, many of whom were still being held in 2018. One of the detainees died in January 2018, and his relatives disputed official claims that he had committed suicide. Three others, including two minors, were released in June.

F4. Do laws, policies, and practices guarantee equal treatment of various segments of the population? 1 / 4

Equal rights are constitutionally guaranteed, but are not upheld in practice. Discrimination against members of ethnic minority tribes is common. The Hmong, who fielded a guerrilla army allied with US forces during the Vietnam War, are particularly distrusted by the government and face harsh treatment. Asylum for refugees is protected by law, but not always granted.

There have been multiple violent attacks, including murders, of Chinese nationals in Laos in recent years. A prominent Chinese businessperson was murdered in a home invasion in Vientiane in August 2018.

While same-sex sexual acts are legal and violence against LGBT (lesbian, gay, bisexual, and transgender) is rare, no legislation provides explicit protection against discrimination based on sexual preference or gender identity.

Gender-based discrimination and abuse are widespread. Discriminatory traditions and religious practices have contributed to women's limited access to education, employment opportunities, and worker benefits.

G. PERSONAL AUTONOMY AND INDIVIDUAL RIGHTS: 6 / 16 (+1)

G1. Do individuals enjoy freedom of movement, including the ability to change their place of residence, employment, or education? 2 / 4 (+1)

The dominance of the LPRP over most aspects of society can effectively restrict individuals' ability to choose their place of residence, employment, or education. Freedom of movement is sometimes restricted for ethnic Hmong. Security checkpoints in central Laos can hamper travel, though the military has in recent years reduced controls in the region.

Score Change: The score improved from 1 to 2 because the military has reduced controls on movement in the central part of the country.

G2. Are individuals able to exercise the right to own property and establish private businesses without undue interference from state or nonstate actors? 1 / 4

All land is owned by the state, though citizens have rights to use it. However, in recent years land rights have become an increasing source of public discontent. Construction began on a high-speed rail line from China through Laos at the end of 2016, resulting in the displacement of over 4,000 families, and many villagers remain uncertain of what kind of compensation they will receive.

Villagers who live on or near the sites of planned dams on the Mekong River are also increasingly caught up in land disputes. Apparent deficiencies revealed by the catastrophic dam collapse in southern Laos in July 2018, which killed dozens of people and left thousands homeless, have not prompted the government to reevaluate its dam-building projects. Observers have charged that the Laotian government has been developing dam projects with investors in the absence of appropriate oversight. Still, Laos has announced plans for a fourth dam on the Mekong River.

Foreign investors are subject to expropriation of joint ventures without due process in Laotian courts.

G3. Do individuals enjoy personal social freedoms, including choice of marriage partner and size of family, protection from domestic violence, and control over appearance? 2 / 4

Social freedoms can be restricted, especially for women and children. Marriage to foreign citizens requires approval by the government. In 2016, a survey supported by the United Nations and the World Health Organization (WHO) revealed that close to one third of women in Laos had experienced domestic violence. Abortion is illegal and only permitted when the mother's life is at risk. Underage marriage is permitted with parental permission.

G4. Do individuals enjoy equality of opportunity and freedom from economic exploitation? 1 / 4

Trafficking in persons, especially to Thailand, is common, and enforcement of antitrafficking measures is hindered by a lack of transparency and weak rule of law. The building of new roads through Laos in recent years has aided trafficking operations. There are no penalties for facilitating child prostitution.

Children as young as 12 years old may be legally employed in Laos. Inspections of workplaces, including those for industries considered hazardous, are required by law but do not take place regularly. Public workers are not always paid on time.

Latvia

Population: 1,900,000
Capital: Riga
Political Rights Rating: 2
Civil Liberties Rating: 2
Freedom Rating: 2.0
Freedom Status: Free
Electoral Democracy: Yes

Overview: Latvia developed into a democracy after regaining independence in 1991. Elections are regarded as free and fair, and freedoms of assembly and association are generally respected in practice. However, corruption remains a major problem affecting politics, the judiciary, and the wider criminal justice system. The country's ethnic Russians face discrimination.

KEY DEVELOPMENTS IN 2018:

- In October, Latvians voted for a new parliament (Saeima). About two-thirds of incumbent lawmakers failed to win reelection, while a number of newly founded right- and left-wing parties entered the chamber. The new, highly fragmented Saeima had yet to form a ruling coalition at year's end.
- Authorities passed two laws aimed at reducing or eliminating instruction in Russian and other minority languages at the country's public and private schools and universities.
- In June, anticorruption officers charged Latvia's longtime central bank governor with accepting a bribe, and he was suspended from the office.
- Continued economic growth has improved opportunity and reduced hardships associated with the 2009 financial crisis.

POLITICAL RIGHTS: 35 / 40

A. ELECTORAL PROCESS: 12 / 12

A1. Was the current head of government or other chief national authority elected through free and fair elections? 4 / 4

The Saeima elects the president, who may serve up to two four-year terms. The prime minister is nominated by the president and approved by the parliament. Both the 2016 parliamentary confirmation of the current prime minister, Māris Kučinskis of the Union of Greens and Farmers (ZZS), and the 2015 election of president Raimonds Vējonis, a former ZZS leader, took place according to legal requirements. Kučinskis stayed on as a caretaker prime minister after inconclusive October 2018 legislative elections, while coalition talks took place.

A2. Were the current national legislative representatives elected through free and fair elections? 4 / 4

The Latvian constitution provides for a unicameral, 100-seat Saeima, whose members are elected to four-year terms. The parliamentary elections in October 2018 were viewed as competitive and credible, and stakeholders accepted the results. An Organization for Security and Cooperation in Europe (OSCE) monitoring mission noted that some polling stations were too small to adequately accommodate the number of voters that turned out, and encouraged a number of relatively minor refinements to the electoral process.

The 2018 polls saw a significant loss by all three governing parties—the ZZS, the right-center Unity party, and the conservative National Alliance—which jointly took only 32 seats. The opposition Harmony party, which mainly defends the interests of Latvia's ethnic Russians, took 23 seats, one fewer than in the previous election. Newly founded movements took the remaining 45 mandates: the populist Who Owns the State? (KPV LV) and the right-wing New Conservative Party (JKP) each took 16 seats, and the liberal coalition Development/For! (LA/KP) took the remaining 13. Coalition talks were ongoing at year's end.

A3. Are the electoral laws and framework fair, and are they implemented impartially by the relevant election management bodies? 4 / 4

In general, the electoral framework is implemented fairly by the Central Election Commission (CEC) and regional and local election administrations.

The president has traditionally been elected through a closed vote, but in October 2018, the outgoing Saeima amended the constitution to make future balloting open.

B. POLITICAL PLURALISM AND PARTICIPATION: 14 / 16

B1. Do the people have the right to organize in different political parties or other competitive political groupings of their choice, and is the system free of undue obstacles to the rise and fall of these competing parties or groupings? 4 / 4

Latvia's political parties organize and compete freely. However, Latvian political candidates cannot run as independents, and those who belonged to communist or pro-Soviet organizations after 1991 may not hold public office. Parliamentary elections usually result in the entry of new political parties to the Saeima.

B2. Is there a realistic opportunity for the opposition to increase its support or gain power through elections? 4 / 4

Opposition parties compete freely and have a realistic chance of increasing their power through elections. However, Harmony and its predecessors, mostly supported by Latvia's Russian-speaking population, have never been invited to participate in forming a government.

B3. Are the people's political choices free from domination by the military, foreign powers, religious hierarchies, economic oligarchies, or any other powerful group that is not democratically accountable? 3 / 4

In the summer of 2017, the political scene was shaken by the so-called Oligarch Talks scandal—the release of transcripts of talks between politically influential businesspeople and their associates that took place from 2009–11. The conversations included discussions of efforts to replace the general prosecutor and other officials, and influence media outlets and strategic Latvian companies. In response, the Saeima created a special parliamentary commission to investigate the matter. However, it has been widely criticized as deliberately vague, and its investigation has been marred with controversy.

Authorities and other observers continue to express concern about the presence of disinformation and Russian propaganda in Latvian media, and other attempts by Russia to influence domestic politics.

B4. Do various segments of the population (including ethnic, religious, gender, LGBT, and other relevant groups) have full political rights and electoral opportunities? 3 / 4

Approximately 240,000 of Latvia's registered residents are stateless persons, most of whom are ethnic Russians. They may not vote, hold public office, work in government offices, or establish political parties. Children of non-citizens born after August 1991 can gain Latvian citizenship if they reside in Latvia permanently and have never acquired citizenship in another state. Lawmakers in September 2017 rejected legislation that would have granted citizenship to Latvian-born children of noncitizens automatically.

Women hold 31 percent of seats in the new Saeima that was elected in October 2018, up from 19 percent previously.

C. FUNCTIONING OF GOVERNMENT: 9 / 12

C1. Do the freely elected head of government and national legislative representatives determine the policies of the government? 3 / 4

While elections are held on time and elected representative duly seated, Latvian governments are fragmented and often short-lived. Although the government is generally capable of developing and implementing policies, certain business groups have tended to exploit the fragility of government coalitions to influence government decisions.

C2. Are safeguards against official corruption strong and effective? 3 / 4

In recent years, the Latvian government has taken efforts to fight corruption and money laundering. Latvia's admission to the Organisation for Economic Co-operation and Development (OECD) in 2016 has raised its international credibility. However, investigative and auditing bodies have seen only limited results in efforts to tame the corrupt behavior of politicians, due in part to institutions' inability to consolidate power within their own fields of competence.

However, in June 2018, anticorruption officers charged Ilmārs Rimšēvičs, Latvia's longtime central bank governor, with taking a bribe, and authorities suspended him from the office. Separately, at the end of the year, a corruption scandal related to public procurement in municipal transport shook Riga's local government and forced its deputy mayor to resign.

C3. Does the government operate with openness and transparency? 3 / 4

The legislative framework for ensuring openness and transparency of the government is extensive. However, there is a notable lack of transparency in functioning of state companies, and in public procurement processes.

CIVIL LIBERTIES: 52 / 60
D. FREEDOM OF EXPRESSION AND BELIEF: 14 / 16 (−1)
D1. Are there free and independent media? 3 / 4

While Latvian media outlets publicize a wide range of political views in both Latvian and Russian, government offices and courts sometimes interfere with media outlets' and reporters' work. The "Oligarch Talks" recordings released in 2017 revealed influence on Latvian media by politically powerful businesspeople.

Libel remains a criminal offense.

Authorities have occasionally restricted Russian radio and news websites, citing concerns about propaganda.

D2. Are individuals free to practice and express their religious faith or nonbelief in public and private? 4 / 4

Freedom of religion is generally respected. However, in the wake of the 2015 refugee crisis, social pressure on the country's roughly 1,000 Muslims has increased.

D3. Is there academic freedom, and is the educational system free from extensive political indoctrination? 3 / 4 (−1)

Recent years have seen lawmakers begin to place some limitations on academic instruction. In 2015, parliament adopted a law mandating that schools provide children a "moral education" that coincides with the values of the constitution, including traditional views of marriage and family life. A law that came into effect in January 2017 enabled the firing of teachers found to be "disloyal to the state."

Authorities in 2018 ramped up a drive to discourage or eliminate the use of minority languages in schools and universities, with the measures generally viewed as targeting Russian-language instruction. In March, the parliament passed amendments to the Education Law that would phase out the use of minority languages in public and private high schools, and significantly reduce their use in primary schools. In June, lawmakers approved a measure that prevented private and public higher education institutions from offering programs conducted in Russian and other minority languages, with an exception granted for philology. At the start of the year, approximately one-third of students at private colleges were enrolled in programs conducted in Russian.

Score Change: The score declined from 4 to 3 due to efforts by the government to restrict the use of Russian and other minority languages in schools and universities.

D4. Are individuals free to express their personal views on political or other sensitive topics without fear of surveillance or retribution? 4 / 4

Private discussion is generally open and free. The public display of Soviet and Nazi symbols is banned.

E. ASSOCIATIONAL AND ORGANIZATIONAL RIGHTS: 12 / 12

E1. Is there freedom of assembly? 4 / 4

Freedom of assembly is protected by law and generally respected in practice.

E2. Is there freedom for nongovernmental organizations, particularly those that are engaged in human rights- and governance-related work? 4 / 4

The government does not restrict the activities of nongovernmental organizations (NGOs). However, advocacy by NGOs is increasingly viewed as partisan activity.

E3. Is there freedom for trade unions and similar professional or labor organizations? 4 / 4

Workers may establish trade unions, strike, and engage in collective bargaining.

F. RULE OF LAW: 12 / 16

F1. Is there an independent judiciary? 3 / 4

While judicial independence is generally respected, inefficiency, politicization, and corruption within the judicial system persist. European Union (EU) polling has shown significant distrust of the courts among the general public and companies alike. In a 2016 survey conducted by European Network of Councils for the Judiciary, 30 percent of polled judges in Latvia agreed that individual judges accept bribes.

F2. Does due process prevail in civil and criminal matters? 3 / 4

The legal system is overburdened and hampered by corruption and inefficiency. By law, legal aid must be provided to people who cannot retain their own, but this is inconsistently enforced. Suspects are sometimes interrogated without the presence of a lawyer. Lengthy pretrial detention remains a concern.

F3. Is there protection from the illegitimate use of physical force and freedom from war and insurgencies? 3 / 4

Latvia has one of the highest prison population rates in the EU. Prisons continue to suffer from overcrowding, and abuses of detainees and prisoners by law enforcement agents has been reported.

The rate of intentional homicides in Latvia was among the highest in the EU, according to data from Eurostat, the EU's statistics agency, for 2016.

F4. Do laws, policies, and practices guarantee equal treatment of various segments of the population? 3 / 4

Latvia has no specific gender equality law. While there are some associated protections in the country's labor laws, women often face employment and wage discrimination. Members of the country's Roma minority face discrimination in schools and workplaces. Latvian laws do not offer specific protection against discrimination on the basis of sexual orientation (except in employment) or gender identity.

According to the International Convention on the Elimination of All Forms of Racial Discrimination, the country's strict language policies have set the stage for discrimination against minorities in the public and private spheres.

G. PERSONAL AUTONOMY AND INDIVIDUAL RIGHTS: 14 / 16 (+1)

G1. Do individuals enjoy freedom of movement, including the ability to change their place of residence, employment, or education? 4 / 4

Citizens and noncitizens may travel freely within the country and internationally.

G2. Are individuals able to exercise the right to own property and establish private businesses without undue interference from state or nonstate actors? 4 / 4

Years of reform efforts have created an environment in which people may freely establish businesses and own property, though corruption can impede business activities.

G3. Do individuals enjoy personal social freedoms, including choice of marriage partner and size of family, protection from domestic violence, and control over appearance? 3 / 4

Domestic violence is not frequently reported, and police do not always take meaningful action when it is. Same-sex marriage was banned in 2005, and Latvia is one of six remaining countries in the EU that does not recognize same-sex partnerships.

G4. Do individuals enjoy equality of opportunity and freedom from economic exploitation? 3 / 4 (+1)

Around 28 percent of Latvia's population was at risk of social exclusion or poverty in 2018, per Eurostat. The shadow economy is extensive, and informal workers are vulnerable to labor abuses and being drawn into criminal operations.

However, the Latvian economy has rebounded since the 2008–09 financial crisis, which inflicted severe economic hardship. Unemployment declined to 7.4 percent in 2018, from 17.3 percent in 2009, and a record high of 21.3 percent in 2010. GDP per capita reached 67 percent of the EU average in 2017, from 52 percent in 2009. A 2017 measure boosted the monthly minimum wage by €50 ($57), to €430 ($490), starting in 2018.

Score Change: The score improved from 2 to 3 because economic growth over the past several years has improved opportunity and reduced hardships associated with the 2008–09 financial crisis.

Lebanon

Population: 6,100,000
Capital: Beirut
Political Rights Rating: 5 ↑
Civil Liberties Rating: 4
Freedom Rating: 4.5
Freedom Status: Partly Free
Electoral Democracy: No

Overview: Lebanon's political system ensures representation for its many sectarian communities, but suppresses competition within each community and impedes the rise of cross-sectarian or secularist parties. It effectively elevates communities over individuals and communal leaders over state institutions. Residents enjoy some civil liberties and media pluralism, but the rule of law is undermined by political interference. The government struggles to provide services for and uphold the rights of the refugees who make up more than a quarter of Lebanon's population. Refugees from Syria face particularly serious discrimination and harassment.

KEY DEVELOPMENTS IN 2018:

- In May, citizens voted for new national representatives for the first time in nine years. The polls, despite some irregularities, were relatively free and fair.
- However, Lebanese leaders spent the subsequent seven months locked in negotiations over the cabinet's composition and their respective shares within it, and were unable to form a government by the end of the year.
- Although journalists were generally able to report freely on corruption, elections, political intrigue, and other issues, Lebanese authorities also detained, interrogated, and tried reporters for work seen as unfavorable to various Lebanese leaders, parties, and state institutions like the military.
- The Social Media Exchange (SMEX), a Lebanon-based digital rights group, recorded 38 legal cases initiated in response to information posted online, a sharp increase from previous years. Most involved criticism of politicians, security agencies, or the president.

POLITICAL RIGHTS: 14 / 40 (+3)

A. ELECTORAL PROCESS: 5 / 12 (+2)

A1. Was the current head of government or other chief national authority elected through free and fair elections? 1 / 4 (+1)

The president, who is elected to a six-year term by the parliament, appoints the prime minister after consulting with the parliament. The president and prime minister choose the cabinet, which holds most formal executive power. According to long-standing de facto agreements on sectarian power-sharing, the president must be a Maronite Christian, the prime minister must be a Sunni Muslim, and the speaker of the National Assembly must be a Shiite Muslim.

Recently, the presidency was vacant for two years due to a lack of political consensus on a successor to Michel Suleiman, whose term expired in 2014. In October 2016, lawmakers finally elected former military commander Michel Aoun as president, and Aoun nominated Saad Hariri as prime minister that November. The parliament approved Hariri's unity cabinet, which included representatives of most major factions, in December 2016. While these steps ended the long deadlock over Lebanon's executive leadership, they were carried out by a parliament whose electoral mandate had expired in 2013, critically undermining their democratic legitimacy.

Aoun named Hariri prime minister-designate shortly after the 2018 parliamentary elections. While the elections brought about the end of Lebanon's long executive leadership crisis, the new parliament's term opened with another round of political paralysis, as parties had yet to form a government by year's end.

Score Change: The score improved from 0 to 1 because the election of a new parliament in May enabled the designation of a prime minister with an electoral mandate.

A2. Were the current national legislative representatives elected through free and fair elections? 2 / 4 (+1)

Parliamentary elections were originally due in 2013, but disagreement over electoral reforms led the parliament to extend its own term until late 2014. Citing security concerns associated with the Syrian conflict, lawmakers in 2014 extended their mandate again, this time until June 2017. That month, the parliament adopted a new electoral law that among other things introduced proportional representation and preferential voting, and scheduled elections for May 2018. Lebanese citizens then duly voted, according to that schedule, for the 128-member National Assembly for the first time since 2009—ending the five-year period in which the incumbent legislature had operated with no electoral mandate.

The May 2018 election saw the Shiite militant group Hezbollah maintain its National Assembly seats, while its allies posted gains. Christian parties also gained seats, all mainly at the expense of Hariri and his Future Movement. Although the elections were conducted peacefully and were free and fair in many respects, vote buying was rampant and the electoral framework retained a number of fundamental structural flaws linked to the sectarian political system. Turnout was less than 50 percent, and was even lower in some Sunni areas of Beirut, reflecting an apparent lack of confidence in Hariri among many Sunni voters.

Score Change: The score improved from 1 to 2 because long-overdue parliamentary elections were held in 2018, ending a five-year period in which the incumbent legislature had operated with no electoral mandate.

A3. Are the electoral laws and framework fair, and are they implemented impartially by the relevant election management bodies? 2 / 4

Elections in Lebanon are overseen by the Interior Ministry rather than an independent electoral commission. Parliamentary seats are divided among major sects under a constitutional formula that does not reflect their current demographic weight. No official census has been conducted since the 1930s. The electoral framework is generally inclusive and supports pluralism, but it is the product of bargaining among established leaders and tends to entrench the existing sectarian and communalist political system.

The 2017 electoral law introduced proportional representation and preferential voting, and improved opportunities for diaspora voting. However, the districts were still drawn along communal lines, with most featuring a strong confessional majority. Meanwhile, the mechanisms for seat allocation favor incumbent parties. The 2017 law sharply raised registration fees for candidates as well as spending caps for campaigns, and allowed private organizations and foundations to promote coalitions and candidates, which increased advantages accorded to wealthier groups and individuals. As under past electoral laws, members of security services, and citizens who have been naturalized for less than 10 years, cannot participate in elections.

B. POLITICAL PLURALISM AND PARTICIPATION: 7 / 16

B1. Do the people have the right to organize in different political parties or other competitive political groupings of their choice, and is the system free of undue obstacles to the rise and fall of these competing parties or groupings? 3 / 4

Citizens are free to organize in different political groupings, and the system features a variety of competing parties in practice. While parties do rise and fall to some extent based on their performance and voters' preferences, most of Lebanon's political parties are vehicles for an established set of communal leaders who benefit from patronage networks, greater access to financing, and other advantages of incumbency.

B2. Is there a realistic opportunity for the opposition to increase its support or gain power through elections? 1 / 4

A handful of political parties have dominated Lebanese politics since 2005. Under the country's prevailing power-sharing system, none of them behave as opposition groups; consolidation of power among political elites also hampers intraparty competition. The incumbent parties collaborated to formulate the 2017 election law, which gave them advantages in the 2018 parliamentary elections and made it difficult for smaller parties and independents to compete.

B3. Are the people's political choices free from domination by the military, foreign powers, religious hierarchies, economic oligarchies, or any other powerful group that is not democratically accountable? 1 / 4

A variety of forces that are not democratically accountable—including entrenched patronage networks, religious institutions, armed nonstate actors such as Hezbollah, and competing foreign powers—use a combination of financial incentives and intimidation to exert influence on Lebanese voters and political figures. The 2018 elections saw a number of credible allegations of vote buying, as well as analyses pointing to the role of establishment parties' patronage networks in mobilizing or incentivizing voters.

B4. Do various segments of the population (including ethnic, religious, gender, LGBT, and other relevant groups) have full political rights and electoral opportunities? 2 / 4

Lebanon officially recognizes 18 religious communities, and the political system ensures that nearly all of these groups are represented, though not according to their actual shares of the population. Individuals who are not or do not wish to be affiliated with the recognized groups are effectively excluded. Moreover, the country's unusually large refugee population, including decades-old Palestinian communities, are not eligible to acquire citizenship and have no political rights.

Women have many of the same political rights as men, but they are marginalized in practice due to religious restrictions, institutionalized inequality, political culture, and societal discrimination. Only six women hold seats in the parliament elected in 2018. Neither the 2017 parliamentary electoral law nor informal understandings regarding power-sharing include rules to guarantee—let alone increase—women's participation in politics.

C. FUNCTIONING OF GOVERNMENT: 2 / 12 (+1)

C1. Do the freely elected head of government and national legislative representatives determine the policies of the government? 1 / 4 (+1)

When the government is able to develop policies, they tend to be the result of negotiation among the country's dominant political figures, regardless of formal titles and positions; meanwhile, the legislature generally facilitates these policies rather than serving as an independent institutional check on the government. The authority of the government is also limited in practice by the power of autonomous militant groups like Hezbollah and states with interests in Lebanon.

The elections of a president, parliament, parliament speaker, and prime minister since 2016 have eased the country's political deadlock, though lengthy negotiations on cabinet appointments were ongoing at the end of 2018.

Score Change: The score improved from 0 to 1 because the elections of a president, parliament, parliament speaker, and prime minister since 2016 have eased the country's political deadlock, though lengthy negotiations on cabinet appointments were ongoing at the end of 2018.

C2. Are safeguards against official corruption strong and effective? 0 / 4

Political and bureaucratic corruption is widespread, businesses routinely pay bribes and cultivate ties with politicians to win contracts or avoid unfavorable state actions, anticorruption laws are loosely enforced, and patronage networks generally operate unchecked. State expenditures remain irregular, with few mechanisms for effective oversight. Institutions such as the Central Inspection Bureau and Supreme Disciplinary Board remain woefully underfunded and understaffed.

C3. Does the government operate with openness and transparency? 1 / 4

While the National Assembly approved an access to information law in 2017, it is not fully implemented, and government documents remain difficult to obtain in practice. Officials often negotiate behind closed doors, outside of state institutions, and with little regard for formal procedures. There are few practical opportunities for civil society groups to influence pending policies or legislation, though they and the media are able to discuss proposals that have been made public.

CIVIL LIBERTIES: 31 / 60 (−1)
D. FREEDOM OF EXPRESSION AND BELIEF: 11 / 16 (−1)
D1. Are there free and independent media? 2 / 4 (−1)

Press freedom is constitutionally guaranteed but inconsistently upheld. While the country's media are among the most open and diverse in the region, nearly all outlets depend on the patronage of political parties, wealthy individuals, or foreign powers, and consequently practice some degree of self-censorship. Books, movies, plays, and other artistic works are subject to censorship, especially when the content involves politics, religion, sex, or Israel. It is a criminal offense to criticize or defame the president or Lebanese security forces. An audiovisual media law bans broadcasts that seek to harm the state, undermine foreign relations, or incite sectarian violence—with relevant provisions being broadly-worded. Authorities use such laws and rules to prosecute or—more often, harass and temporarily detain—journalists who disseminate criticism of politicians and government officials, or powerful nonstate actors.

Press freedom deteriorated in 2018, which saw intensifying legal and other harassment of journalists by state officials, and instances of intimidation by security forces. In January, a military tribunal sentenced in absentia Hanin Ghaddar, a Washington-based Lebanese journalist, to six months in prison, only to later, upon appeal, drop the charges and refer the case to a military prosecutor. In July, Beirut's Publication Court convicted five journalists of defamation-related charges and handed down fines ranging from 1 million to 10 million Lebanese pounds ($600 to $6,600). In November, Abdel Hafez al-Houlani, a correspondent for the Syrian pro-opposition news website Zaman al-Wasl, was detained without charge after publishing an article linking the miscarriages of a number of pregnant refugee women to polluted water, and which criticized refugee aid agencies; he was reportedly released after three weeks' detention, after paying a fine. Al-Houlani, who generally reported on refugees and their rights, had also been temporarily detained by the Defense Ministry in May in connection with his work. In December, Lebanese police raided the offices of Daraj, an independent online media website, and detained and interrogated its editor in chief for two hours before releasing him without charge. In December, Lebanese military personnel physically beat, harassed, and otherwise intimidated four journalists covering an antigovernment protest.

Score Change: The score declined from 3 to 2 due to an increase in legal and other harassment of journalists by state authorities.

D2. Are individuals free to practice and express their religious faith or nonbelief in public and private? 3 / 4

The constitution protects freedom of conscience, and the state does not typically interfere with the practice or expression of religious faith or nonbelief. While blasphemy is a criminal offense, enforcement varies and is generally lax. Individuals may face societal pressure to express faith or allegiance to a confessional community. Leaders and members of different communities discourage proselytizing by other groups.

D3. Is there academic freedom, and is the educational system free from extensive political indoctrination? 3 / 4

Academic freedom is generally unimpaired. Individuals are mostly free to select subjects for research and disseminate their findings. However, various laws and customary standards—including restrictions on defamation, blasphemy, and work or opinions related to Israel—deter open debate on certain issues. The state does not engage in extensive political indoctrination through education, though religious and other nonstate entities do seek to reinforce communal identities and perspectives.

D4. Are individuals free to express their personal views on political or other sensitive topics without fear of surveillance or retribution? 3 / 4

Private discussion and expression of personal views are largely uninhibited. Even so, the authorities monitor social media and other communications. Individuals sometimes face arrests, short detentions, or fines if they criticize the government, the military, foreign heads of state, or other powerful entities. SMEX, a Lebanon-based digital rights group, recorded 38 prosecutions launched in 2018 in response to information posted online, a sharp increase from previous years. Most instances involved criticism of politicians, security agencies, or the president. Nonstate actors and individuals who feel that they have been harmed by critical speech may seek retribution through defamation suits or, more rarely, violence and intimidation.

E. ASSOCIATIONAL AND ORGANIZATIONAL RIGHTS: 8 / 12

E1. Is there freedom of assembly? 3 / 4

The authorities generally respect the right to assemble, which is protected under the constitution, and demonstrators have been able to mount protests against government dysfunction and lack of services in recent years. While protests over a garbage crisis in 2015 led to mass arrests and police violence that caused hundreds of injuries, assemblies since then have been more peaceful.

A number of protests took place with little disruption in 2018, including against political paralysis, corruption, and controversies and irregularities related to the parliamentary elections. However, Lebanese military and security services personnel used excessive force against participants in a December protest in the capital, which was apparently inspired by France's "gilets jaunes" or yellow vests, antigovernment demonstrations.

E2. Is there freedom for nongovernmental organizations, particularly those that are engaged in human rights- and governance-related work? 3 / 4

Nongovernmental organizations (NGOs) tend to operate freely in Lebanon, though they must comply with the Law on Associations, which has not been thoroughly updated since

1909, and other applicable laws relating to labor, finance, and immigration. NGOs must also register with the Interior Ministry, which may oblige them to undergo an approval process and can investigate a group's founders, officers, and staff.

E3. Is there freedom for trade unions and similar professional or labor organizations? 2 / 4

Individuals may establish, join, and leave trade unions and other professional organizations. However, the Labor Ministry has broad authority over the formation of unions, union elections, and the administrative dissolution of unions. The state regulates collective bargaining and strikes, and many unions are linked to political parties and serve as tools of influence for political leaders. Public employees, agricultural workers, and household workers are not protected by the labor code and have no legal right to organize, though they have formed unrecognized representative organizations in practice.

F. RULE OF LAW: 5 / 16

F1. Is there an independent judiciary? 1 / 4

Lebanon's judiciary is not independent. Political leaders exercise significant influence over judicial appointments, jurisdiction, processes, and decisions, which are also affected by corruption and undue influence of other prominent people.

F2. Does due process prevail in civil and criminal matters? 1 / 4

Due process is subject to a number of impediments, including violations of defendants' right to counsel and extensive use of lengthy pretrial detention. Due process guarantees are particularly inadequate in the country's exceptional courts, including the military courts, whose judges do not require a background in law and are authorized to try civilians and juveniles in security-related cases. In practice, military courts have asserted jurisdiction over cases involving human rights activists and protesters in addition to those focused on alleged spies and militants.

The reach of military courts drew international attention in 2018, after a military tribunal convicted the US-based Lebanese journalist Ghaddar of defamation. She appealed, and following an international outcry from press freedom advocates the tribunal reversed the conviction, ruling that it did not have the authority to prosecute a civilian. The case was then handed to a military prosecutor, who could potentially refer it to a civilian court, though no further developments were clear by year's end.

F3. Is there protection from the illegitimate use of physical force and freedom from war and insurgencies? 2 / 4

Prisons and detention centers are badly overcrowded and poorly equipped, and the use of torture by law enforcement, military, and state security personnel remains a problem. Since 2017, torture has been an offense under the criminal code, and evidence extracted under torture has been barred from admission at trial. However, Lebanese legislators have not yet criminalized other forms of ill-treatment and confined the definition of torture to specific situations related to investigations and trials. And, even with respect to torture, prescribed penalties remain insufficient and subject to a statute of limitations.

The presence of a variety of armed militias and terrorist groups in 2018 continue to undermine security in Lebanon, and acts of targeted violence that can also endanger civilians occasionally take place. In January 2018, a member of the Islamist political and militant group Hamas was injured in a car bombing severe enough to destroy his vehicle.

F4. Do laws, policies, and practices guarantee equal treatment of various segments of the population? 1 / 4

The country's legal system is meant to protect members of recognized confessional communities against mistreatment by the state, but mutually hostile groups have engaged in discriminatory behavior toward one another in practice—and people who do not belong to a recognized community have difficulty obtaining official documents, government jobs, and other services.

Despite some legal protections, women are barred from certain types of employment and face discrimination in wages and social benefits. LGBT (lesbian, gay, bisexual, and transgender) people face both official and societal discrimination and harassment. In July 2018, an appeals court ruled that same-sex intercourse was not illegal, though a rarely enforced law banning "sexual intercourse against nature" remains on the books. And although NGOs may work to uphold the human rights of LGBT people, with social acceptance being more common in certain urban areas such as Beirut, authorities in May 2018 did detain the organizer of Beirut Pride and reportedly released him only after he signed a pledge to cancel the event, which he then upheld.

There were approximately 1.5 million Syrian refugees in Lebanon as of 2018, about a third of which were not registered with relevant UN agencies. Syrian refugees have faced arbitrary arrests and other forms of harassment and most live in poverty, partly due to limitations on refugees' employment options. In April, Human Rights Watch (HRW) reported that at least 13 Lebanese municipalities had evicted some 3,600 Syrian refugees from their homes from 2016 through the first quarter of 2018. In July, attackers burned Syrian refugees' tents and property at a camp near town of Al-Muhammara.

About 450,000 Palestinian refugees were registered in Lebanon as of 2014, but a 2017 survey conducted by the Lebanese government reported that only 175,000 remain in country. They also face longstanding restrictions on economic activity, contributing to widespread poverty, unemployment, and underemployment.

G. PERSONAL AUTONOMY AND INDIVIDUAL RIGHTS: 7 / 16

G1. Do individuals enjoy freedom of movement, including the ability to change their place of residence, employment, or education? 2 / 4

Citizens enjoy constitutional and legal rights to freedom of movement, though it is extremely difficult to transfer one's official place of residence for voting purposes. Other impediments to internal movement include de facto sectarian boundaries or militia checkpoints in some areas and curfews on Syrian refugees in many municipalities. Migrant workers can lose their legal residency if they are dismissed by or leave their registered employer. Restrictive social customs in some communities allow men to control female relatives' movements and employment outside the home.

G2. Are individuals able to exercise the right to own property and establish private businesses without undue interference from state or nonstate actors? 2 / 4

Lebanese law protects citizens' rights to own property and operate private businesses, but powerful groups and individuals sometimes engage in land-grabbing and other infringements without consequence, and business activity is impaired by bureaucratic obstacles and corruption.

Refugees, including longtime Palestinian residents, have few property rights. Women have weaker property rights than men under the religious codes that govern inheritance and other personal status issues in Lebanon, and they often face family pressure to transfer property to male relatives.

G3. Do individuals enjoy personal social freedoms, including choice of marriage partner and size of family, protection from domestic violence, and control over appearance? 2 / 4

Because the religious codes and courts of each confessional community determine personal status law in Lebanon, an individual's rights regarding marriage, divorce, and child custody depend on his or her affiliation, though women are typically at a disadvantage to men. Women cannot pass Lebanese citizenship to foreign husbands or children.

In 2017, the parliament repealed Article 522 of the penal code, which allowed rapists to evade criminal prosecution if they subsequently married their victims for a period of at least three years. However, the change did not affect a similar article related to sex with a minor, and spousal rape is still not a criminal offense.

G4. Do individuals enjoy equality of opportunity and freedom from economic exploitation? 1 / 4

Communal affiliation can either enhance or restrict an individual's economic opportunities in a given area, company, or public-sector entity, depending on which group is in a dominant position. Individuals must also contend with political patronage and clientelism, layered on top of communally enabled corruption, in the public and private sectors.

Refugees and migrant workers are especially vulnerable to exploitative working conditions and sex trafficking. The authorities do not effectively enforce laws against child labor, which is common among Syrian refugees, rural Lebanese, and segments of the urban poor.

Lesotho

Population: 2,300,000
Capital: Maseru
Political Rights Rating: 3
Civil Liberties Rating: 3
Freedom Rating: 3.0
Freedom Status: Partly Free
Electoral Democracy: Yes

Overview: Lesotho is a constitutional monarchy. In recent years, the army's involvement in the country's already fragile politics has resulted in political instability and a security crisis. Corruption remains a challenge. Customary practice and law restricts women's rights in areas such as property, inheritance, and marriage and divorce.

KEY DEVELOPMENTS IN 2018:

- In May, Lesotho's Constitutional Court declared criminal defamation unconstitutional, which was viewed by analysts as an important step forward for press freedom.
- In September, King Letsie III suspended Chief Justice Nthomeng Majara, on the recommendation of Prime Minister Thomas Thabane. The suspension was ostensibly based on a controversial rental transaction involving Majara and her alleged mismanagement of the court, but civil society groups argued that the move was politically motivated.
- Former deputy prime minister Mothetjoa Metsing of the Lesotho Congress for Democracy (LCD), who fled Lesotho for South Africa along with other opposition

politicians in 2017 and faced potential corruption charges, returned to the country in November. His return followed the signing of an agreement to participate in a governance reform process facilitated by the Southern African Development Community (SADC), which stated that he would not face any criminal charges while the reforms were ongoing. However, Metsing again fled for South Africa in December, after the Constitutional Court struck down the agreement, making him once more vulnerable to prosecution.

POLITICAL RIGHTS: 27 / 40

A. ELECTORAL PROCESS: 10 / 12

A1. Was the current head of government or other chief national authority elected through free and fair elections? 3 / 4

Lesotho is a constitutional monarchy. King Letsie III serves as the ceremonial head of state. The prime minister is head of government; the head of the majority party or coalition automatically becomes prime minister following elections, making the prime minister's legitimacy largely dependent on the conduct of the polls. Thomas Thabane became prime minister after his All Basotho Convention (ABC) won snap elections in 2017. Thabane, a fixture in the country's politics, had previously served as prime minister from 2012–14, but spent two years in exile in South Africa amid instability that followed a failed 2014 coup.

A2. Were the current national legislative representatives elected through free and fair elections? 4 / 4

The lower house of Parliament, the National Assembly, has 120 seats; 80 are filled through first-past-the-post constituency votes, and the remaining 40 through proportional representation. The Senate—the upper house of Parliament—consists of 22 principal chiefs who wield considerable authority in rural areas and whose membership is hereditary, along with 11 other members appointed by the king and acting on the advice of the Council of State. Members of both chambers serve five-year terms.

In 2017, the coalition government of Prime Minister Pakalitha Mosisili—head of the Democratic Congress (DC)—lost a no-confidence vote. The development triggered the third round of legislative elections held since 2012. Election observers declared the elections peaceful, generally well administered and competitive. However, some isolated instances of political violence were noted, as was a heavy security presence at many polling places, which electoral officials said intimidated some voters. Thabane's ABC won a plurality of seats and formed a coalition government.

A3. Are the electoral laws and framework fair, and are they implemented impartially by the relevant election management bodies? 3 / 4

Although the IEC faces capacity constraints, and the credibility of the voters' roll has been questioned in the past, it has been commended for its independence and its efforts to uphold electoral laws and oversee credible elections. In 2017, international election observer missions broadly commended the IEC's administration of the snap polls, but noted deficiencies they linked to the body's lack of capacity, including late disbursement of campaign funds to political parties.

B. POLITICAL PLURALISM AND PARTICIPATION: 11 / 16

B1. Do the people have the right to organize in different political parties or other competitive political groupings of their choice, and is the system free of undue obstacles to the rise and fall of these competing parties or groupings? 3 / 4

Political parties may form freely and are allocated funding by the IEC, and 27 parties contested the 2017 elections. However, politics have been unstable since a failed 2014 coup. In recent years, the country has seen politically motivated assassinations and assassination attempts, and political leaders operate within the country at some risk to their personal safety.

B2. Is there a realistic opportunity for the opposition to increase its support or gain power through elections? 3 / 4

Opposition parties have a realistic chance of gaining power through elections, and power has rotated frequently between DC- and ABC-led coalitions. However, political instability and associated violence and intimidation has at times prompted opposition leaders to flee the country. In 2017, a number of opposition politicians, including former deputy prime minister Mothetjoa Metsing of the LCD, fled for South Africa. Metsing claimed that he feared for his life, but the government said he fled to escape potential corruption charges and sought his extradition. In November 2018, Metsing returned to Lesotho after signing an agreement to participate in a governance reform process facilitated by the SADC, which stated that he would not face any criminal charges while the reforms were ongoing. However, Metsing again fled for South Africa in December, after the Constitutional Court struck down the agreement, once more making him vulnerable to prosecution.

B3. Are the people's political choices free from domination by the military, foreign powers, religious hierarchies, economic oligarchies, or any other powerful group that is not democratically accountable? 2 / 4

Recent political instability is largely related to politics becoming entangled in disputes among factions of the Lesotho Defence Force (LDF). Although the heavy military presence at voting stations during the 2017 elections was questioned, no instances of interference with voters were reported. Traditional chiefs wield some political influence over their rural subjects.

In 2018, Lesotho-based Chinese businessman Yan Xie caused controversy when he claimed that he has made large donations to most of the country's political parties. Critics argue that Yan's financial clout has given him considerable influence over the country's political elites, exemplified by his 2017 appointment as "head of special projects and the prime minister's special envoy and trade adviser on the China-Asia trade network."

B4. Do various segments of the population (including ethnic, religious, gender, LGBT, and other relevant groups) have full political rights and electoral opportunities? 3 / 4

The constitution guarantees political rights for all. However, societal norms discourage women from running for office, and women remain underrepresented in Parliament; following the 2017 elections, 23 percent of seats are held by women, down from 25 percent previously. The inaccessibility of some polling stations to persons living with disabilities was raised as a concern during the 2017 elections. LGBT (lesbian, gay, bisexual, and transgender) individuals generally face societal discrimination, and this discourages them from advocating for their rights in the political sphere.

C. FUNCTIONING OF GOVERNMENT: 6 / 12

C1. Do the freely elected head of government and national legislative representatives determine the policies of the government? 2 / 4

While elections are held without delays and representatives are duly seated, persistent political instability disrupts normal government operations.

C2. Are safeguards against official corruption strong and effective? 2 / 4

Official corruption and impunity remains a problem. The main anticorruption agency, the Directorate on Corruption and Economic Offences (DCEO), lacks full prosecutorial powers, and faces capacity and funding challenges. Despite its shortcomings, DCEO officers do work to fulfill the body's mandate. In 2018, it pursued several controversial cases that involved high-ranking government officials. In February, for example, the DCEO opened an investigation into Prime Minister Thabane over corruption allegations involving the powerful Gupta family's mining interests in Lesotho.

The Asset Forfeiture Unit, which was established in 2016 to recover property connected to corruption cases, had only four people on its staff as of June, hampering its effectiveness.

C3. Does the government operate with openness and transparency? 2 / 4

Lesotho has no access to information law, and responses to information requests are not guaranteed. The management of public finances is shrouded in secrecy. Government procurement decisions and tenders generally cannot be accessed online. Although high-level government and elected officials are required to disclose their assets and business interests, these declarations are not made public, and enforcement of the rules is limited by resource constraints.

CIVIL LIBERTIES: 36 / 60 (−1)

D. FREEDOM OF EXPRESSION AND BELIEF: 12 / 16

D1. Are there free and independent media? 2 / 4

Freedom of the press is only indirectly protected under constitutional guarantees of freedom of expression. Journalists are subject to threats and intimidation from both authorities and private citizens. Both state and private media stand accused of being openly biased. In August 2018, the management of a privately owned radio station, MoAfrika, was summoned to a hearing by Lesotho's Broadcasting Dispute Resolution Panel (BDRP) following government complaints about its critical reporting on state affairs. Also in August, Ts'epang Makakula, one of the station's reporters, was arrested while reporting on a strike by factory workers in the town of Maputsoe. The BDRP then fined the station in October over a program that was critical of the communications minister.

In May, the Constitutional Court declared criminal defamation laws unconstitutional, in a positive step for press freedom.

D2. Are individuals free to practice and express their religious faith or nonbelief in public and private? 4 / 4

The constitution provides legal protections for freedom of religion and prohibits religious discrimination, and religious freedom is generally upheld in practice.

D3. Is there academic freedom, and is the educational system free from extensive political indoctrination? 3 / 4

Academic freedom is generally respected in practice. However, in November 2018, the National University of Lesotho suspended student leader Thabang Rapapa for two years, for allegedly instigating riots that broke out in August over delays in the disbursement of student allowances. Rapapa denied instigating the unrest.

D4. Are individuals free to express their personal views on political or other sensitive topics without fear of surveillance or retribution? 3 / 4

The constitution provides legal protections for freedom of expression. However, political violence in recent years has discouraged some open political debate.

E. ASSOCIATIONAL AND ORGANIZATIONAL RIGHTS: 7 / 12

E1. Is there freedom of assembly? 2 / 4

Protests and demonstrations are permitted, but organizers must seek a permit seven days in advance. Demonstrations take place each year, but are sometimes broken up violently by police.

E2. Is there freedom for nongovernmental organizations, particularly those that are engaged in human rights- and governance-related work? 3 / 4

Nongovernmental organizations (NGOs) generally operate without restrictions. However, some civil society groups act cautiously when working on politically sensitive issues.

E3. Is there freedom for trade unions and similar professional or labor organizations? 2 / 4

While labor and union rights are constitutionally guaranteed, the union movement is weak and highly fragmented, and these challenges have undermined unions' ability to advance the rights of workers. The government has also been accused of undermining bodies like the National Advisory Committee on Labour (NACOLA), Wages Advisory Board, and Industrial Relations Council. Many employees in the textile sector—Lesotho's largest formal employer—face obstacles when attempting to join unions. In October 2018, authorities suspended the Lesotho Police Staff Association (LEPOSA) "for security purposes."

In August, police fired rubber bullets and tear gas into a protest organized by striking factory workers near Maseru.

F. RULE OF LAW: 8 / 16 (−1)

F1. Is there an independent judiciary? 2 / 4 (−1)

The constitution protects judicial independence, but the judiciary remains underresourced and some appointments have been criticized. The 2017 reappointment of Justice Kananelo Mosito as head of the Court of Appeal raised questions among many observers, as he had resigned earlier that year to avoid impeachment over allegations of tax evasion. In February 2018, the High Court nullified his appointment, but the decision was overturned in October by the Court of Appeal.

In September, King Letsie III suspended Chief Justice Nthomeng Majara, on the recommendation of Prime Minister Thabane. The suspension was ostensibly based on a controversial rental transaction involving Majara and her alleged mismanagement of the court, but civil society groups argued that the move was politically motivated. The suspension also defied two orders by the High Court issued in May, which had ruled that the government could not take any action against Majara.

F2. Does due process prevail in civil and criminal matters? 2 / 4

Courts uphold fair trial rights in most judiciary proceedings. However, the large backlog of cases often leads to trial delays and lengthy pretrial detention. The shortage of judicial officers has aggravated the situation, and by late 2018, the backlog numbered over 3,000 cases. In July, Amnesty International expressed concern about repeated delays in the trial of five soldiers implicated in the 2016 attempted murder of *Lesotho Times* editor Lloyd Mutungamiri. At year's end, the trial had still not commenced.

The Court of Appeal did not convene between April 2017 and November 2018 due to the litigation surrounding Mosito's appointment. Officials within the criminal justice system have also faced intimidation.

F3. Is there protection from the illegitimate use of physical force and freedom from war and insurgencies? 2 / 4

Following years of violence related to factional disputes in the army, in July 2018, the SADC appointed a facilitation team to work with the government on a reform process that includes comprehensive security-sector reform. The reforms are intended to end the upheavals and instability that has plagued the military for years, in addition to addressing the human rights violations committed by the LDF, including extrajudicial executions.

Although the constitution provides legal protections against torture, allegations of torture have been levelled against the police, LDF, and prison authorities. In April, some opposition parties petitioned the ombudsman to review allegations of torture and address impunity. Prison conditions are inadequate and detainees are subject to physical abuse.

F4. Do laws, policies, and practices guarantee equal treatment of various segments of the population? 2 / 4

Rights are restricted for some groups. Same-sex sexual relations between men is illegal, though this law is not enforced. LGBT individuals face societal discrimination, and discrimination on the basis of sexual orientation or gender identity is not prohibited by law. Schools often lack facilities for students with disabilities. Customary law and other traditional societal practices continue to discriminate against women and girls. For example, under customary law, women are considered minors under the guardianship of their fathers before marriage and their husbands after marriage.

G. PERSONAL AUTONOMY AND INDIVIDUAL RIGHTS: 9 / 16

G1. Do individuals enjoy freedom of movement, including the ability to change their place of residence, employment, or education? 3 / 4

The constitution protects freedom of movement, and this is generally upheld. In recent years, a high incidence of rape on a path near the Ha Lebona and Ha Koeshe villages has prompted some women to reduce travel in the area.

G2. Are individuals able to exercise the right to own property and establish private businesses without undue interference from state or nonstate actors? 2 / 4

The constitution protects property rights, though in practice the related laws are inconsistently upheld. Customary practice and law still restricts women's rights in areas such as property and inheritance, including chieftainships, which can only be inherited by men. Expropriation is provided for in the constitution but is unlikely, and subject to fair compensation. Government instability and the country's volatile politics hampers normal business activity.

G3. Do individuals enjoy personal social freedoms, including choice of marriage partner and size of family, protection from domestic violence, and control over appearance? 2 / 4

Traditional practices and harmful patriarchal attitudes negatively affect women. Violence against women is high, and there is no domestic violence law, despite government promises to enact one. Forced and child marriages remain an ongoing problem. Customary practices and law restrict women's rights in marriage and divorce.

G4. Do individuals enjoy equality of opportunity and freedom from economic exploitation? 2 / 4

Human trafficking also remains an ongoing challenge for Lesotho. The US State Department's 2018 *Trafficking in Persons Report* found Lesotho's legal framework for prosecuting human trafficking to be weak, without strong penalties to serve as a deterrent. Other identified problems include a lack of criminal convictions for trafficking, a large backlog of trafficking cases, and a failure to investigate officials implicated in trafficking. However, the government has improved its capacity to identify and provide support to potential victims of trafficking. Child labor and forced labor for both men and women, however, remains a problem.

Liberia

Population: 4,900,000
Capital: Monrovia
Political Rights Rating: 3
Civil Liberties Rating: 3
Freedom Rating: 3.0
Freedom Status: Partly Free
Electoral Democracy: Yes

Overview: Liberia has enjoyed more than a decade of peace and stability since the second civil war ended in 2003. During this time, the country has made considerable progress rebuilding government capacity, reestablishing the rule of law, and ensuring the political rights and civil liberties of citizens, and 2017 saw the first peaceful transfer of power between leaders since 1944. However, Liberia still faces serious issues with corruption, violence against women, and discrimination against LGBT people.

KEY DEVELOPMENTS IN 2018:

- The inauguration of George Weah in January marked the first peaceful transfer of power since 1944. Weah, of the opposition Coalition for Democratic Change (CDC), had defeated incumbent vice president Joseph Boakai of the Unity Party in the presidential election runoff in late 2017.
- A conflict between the legislative and judicial branches became apparent when the House of Representative passed a bill of impeachment against an associate justice of the Supreme Court, ignoring a writ of prohibition against the procedure from the same court.
- In September, Weah signed into law two important measures: the Land Rights Act, which aims to formalize communities' ownership of ancestral land; and the Local Government Act, which is intended to give more powers to local political subdivisions through decentralization.
- In September, the government said a shipment of Liberian bank notes worth L$16 billion (US$100 million) being imported to the country by the Liberian Central Bank had gone missing. Weeks later, the Central Bank of Liberia announced that no money was missing, and that it had accounted for the bills. Mass street protest by citizens demanding accountability were peaceful, but faced criticism from Weah.

POLITICAL RIGHTS: 27 / 40
A. ELECTORAL PROCESS: 8 / 12
A1. Was the current head of government or other chief national authority elected through free and fair elections? 3 / 4

Liberia's president is directly elected, and can serve up to two six-year terms. Since the end of the civil wars in 2003, Liberia has had three peaceful presidential elections. The most recent election, held in 2017, was commended by domestic and international observers who assessed it as generally peaceful and credible, while also noting difficulties including long queues at polling places and challenges related to voter identification.

A runoff between George Weah of the Coalition for Democratic Change (CDC) and incumbent vice president Joseph Boakai of the Unity Party, the top two finishers in the first round of the 2017 polling, was delayed when third-place finisher Charles Brumskine of the Liberty Party challenged the first-round results on grounds of fraud. The Supreme Court found that his fraud claim was not supported by evidence, and the run-off was held several weeks later than scheduled, in late December. Weah won the runoff with 61.5 percent of the vote, and Boakai conceded defeat. Observers noted procedural and administrative improvements in the run-off, compared to the first round. Weah's inauguration in 2018 marked the first peaceful transfer of power since 1944.

A2. Were the current national legislative representatives elected through free and fair elections? 3 / 4

Liberia has a bicameral legislature composed of a 30-member Senate and a 73-member House of Representatives; senators are elected to nine-year terms, and representatives to six-year terms. Legislative elections were held concurrently with the first round of the presidential election in October 2017. While there were some administrative problems, including complaints that registered voters could not be found on the voter rolls, observers said the elections were generally peaceful and well administered. There were minor incidents of violence between political party supporters during the campaigning period, but candidates were largely able to campaign freely.

A3. Are the electoral laws and framework fair, and are they implemented impartially by the relevant election management bodies? 2 / 4

The independence of Liberia's National Elections Commission (NEC) is mandated by law, and political parties expressed confidence in its impartiality during the 2017 election campaign. However, its capacity is limited, and it struggles to enforce electoral laws.

The 2017 elections were the first to apply the provisions of the 2014 National Code of Conduct Act, which laid out rules applying to government officials seeking to run for elected office, and included measures aimed at avoiding conflicts of interest. The NEC attempted to enforce the provisions of the Code of Conduct during the elections. However, the Supreme Court reversed the NEC's rulings in two instances where the NEC had disqualified high-profile candidates for failing to meet the Code of Conduct's eligibility requirements. Separately, the NEC failed to enforce a provision of the Election Law stipulating that parties must field candidates in at least half of all constituencies. Eleven political parties did not meet this requirement, but were permitted to run. The NEC additionally struggled to complete voter lists.

The NEC also struggled to conduct two major by-elections in 2018 to fill the seats vacated by President Weah, the former senator of Montserrado County, and Vice President Jewel Howard-Taylor, the former senator of Bong County. The polls were held long after the required constitutional time frame due to a lack of funding, which also hampered civic and voter education efforts. Turnout for both elections was reportedly very low.

B. POLITICAL PLURALISM AND PARTICIPATION: 12 / 16

B1. Do the people have the right to organize in different political parties or other competitive political groupings of their choice, and is the system free of undue obstacles to the rise and fall of these competing parties or groupings? 3 / 4

Political parties generally do not face undue legal or practical obstacles that prevent them from forming or operating. However, in the run-up to the 2017 elections, election monitors recorded allegations that the ruling party drew on public resources to fund political campaigns—notably by taking advantage of state-owned vehicles and facilities.

B2. Is there a realistic opportunity for the opposition to increase its support or gain power through elections? 3 / 4

Opposition parties hold support among the population and have a realistic chance of gaining power through elections. In the 2017 presidential election, Weah, of the opposition CDC, won the presidency over the incumbent party's candidate. Similarly, the Congress for Democratic Change, the largest party within the CDC coalition that backed Weah, won 21 seats in the legislature in the elections, and displaced the Unity Party as the party with the greatest representation.

In the 2018 senatorial by-election in Bong County, the main opposition parties rallied behind an independent candidate and successfully defeated the ruling party candidate to fill the seat left vacant by current vice president Jewel Howard Taylor. However, in the by-election in Montserrado County, a traditional stronghold of the ruling party, the opposition failed in their bid despite forming a loose coalition.

B3. Are the people's political choices free from domination by the military, foreign powers, religious hierarchies, economic oligarchies, or any other powerful group that is not democratically accountable? 3 / 4

Allegations of undue influence or pressure on voters by powerful groups not democratically accountable to the people are generally rare. However, in the run-up to the 2018 senatorial by-election in Bong County, Vice President Howard-Taylor implied that local civil servants who did not join the CDC would lose their jobs. After the election, a number of Bong County officials, including the labor and agricultural commissioners, were indeed replaced by CDC members, though some argued that Taylor had the authority to select her preferred appointees. There were several additional reports of purges of opposition members in the in the civil service in 2018, including at the finance, gender, foreign affairs, and state ministries.

Separately, a general wariness of the potential for election-related violence persists in Liberia, though the 2017 general elections and 2018 by-elections were generally peaceful

B4. Do various segments of the population (including ethnic, religious, gender, LGBT, and other relevant groups) have full political rights and electoral opportunities? 3 / 4

Members of Lebanese and Asian minority groups whose families have lived in Liberia for generations are denied citizenship, and cannot participate in political processes. While former Liberian president Ellen Johnson Sirleaf became the first elected female head of state in Africa in 2005, and Liberia's current vice president is a woman, women are poorly represented in national politics and hold few leadership positions in political parties. Just 3 seats in the 30-seat Senate and 9 in the 73-seat House of Representatives are held by women. Social stigma against LGBT (lesbian, gay, bisexual, and transgender) people discourages then from advocating for their rights in the context of Liberian politics.

C. FUNCTIONING OF GOVERNMENT: 7 / 12
C1. Do the freely elected head of government and national legislative representatives determine the policies of the government? 3 / 4

Once elected, government officials are duly installed in office, and elected legislators generally operate without interference. However, bribery and corruption can influence policy prioritization.

In September 2018, Weah signed the Local Government Act, which is intended to give more powers to local political subdivisions through decentralization.

C2. Are safeguards against official corruption strong and effective? 2 / 4

Many institutions are devoted to fighting corruption, but they lack the resources and capacity to function effectively, and corruption remains pervasive. In October 2018, President Weah submitted a bill to the legislature that would remove tenure security from all positions in the executive branch; the measure would effectively rescind tenure protections for those in a number bodies whose mandates include safeguarding against corruption, including the Liberia Anti-Corruption Commission (LACC), the Public Procurement and Concession Commission, the General Auditing Commission, and the Governance Commission, among others. The bill secured approval in the House, with the Senate expected to consider it in 2019. If it becomes law, the measure will allow the president to appoint and fire at his will employees at these agencies.

Furthermore, anticorruption bodies including the LACC and the Financial Intelligence Unit experienced severe budget cuts in 2018. The LACC was also initially excluded from the investigation into a major financial scandal involving the disappearance of about L\$16 billion (US\$100 million) brought into the country by the Central Bank of Liberia, and was only invited to the investigative committee after public outcries.

C3. Does the government operate with openness and transparency? 2 / 4

Liberia's Freedom of Information Act is rarely used, and government responsiveness to requests tends to be slow. Transparency guidelines for public procurement processes are not fully enforced. In 2018, many new public officials, including most in the executive branch, failed to declare their access as required by law; and the president only declared his assets six months after assuming office. However, the LACC, which collects asset declarations, is not obligated to disclose those submitted by members of the executive branch, and all efforts by civil society and media to gain access to Weah's declaration have failed.

CIVIL LIBERTIES: 35 / 60
D. FREEDOM OF EXPRESSION AND BELIEF: 11 / 16
D1. Are there free and independent media? 2 / 4

Liberia's constitution provides for freedom of speech and the press, but these rights are often restricted in practice. While the media express a range of views, Liberia has long been criticized for its onerous criminal and civil libel laws, which authorities have invoked to harass and intimidate journalists. In July 2018, the House passed a bill that would decriminalize libel, but the Senate had yet to approve it at year's end. Meanwhile, the government also moved to suspend the licenses of media outlets that had received them during the first six months of 2018 for a review process that was expected to take up to a year. Critics argued the move was aimed at newly established news outlets perceived critical of government. Investigative reporters frequently receive threats, including by members of the government who have vowed to launch lawsuits in response to legitimate journalistic inquiries into government spending and affairs. Weah has at times taken an adversarial stance toward media, including by making vague denunciations of "fake news" that purportedly threatened national stability.

D2. Are individuals free to practice and express their religious faith or nonbelief in public and private? 3 / 4

Religious freedom is protected in the constitution, and there is no official religion. However, about 86 percent of the population is Christian, and the Muslim minority reports discrimination. In 2015, a proposal to amend the constitution to establish Christianity as the official religion contributed to interreligious tensions. While then president Sirleaf shelved this proposal, some discussion of it reemerged during the 2017 campaign period. Since his election, George Weah has made efforts to reach out to the Muslim population.

D3. Is there academic freedom, and is the educational system free from extensive political indoctrination? 3 / 4

The government does not restrict academic freedom, though educational quality and infrastructure remain inadequate.

D4. Are individuals free to express their personal views on political or other sensitive topics without fear of surveillance or retribution? 3 / 4

People are generally free to engage in private discussion while in public spaces, but some topics are taboo, such as discussion of issues affecting LGBT people. The government is not known to illegally monitor online communications.

E. ASSOCIATIONAL AND ORGANIZATIONAL RIGHTS: 8 / 12

E1. Is there freedom of assembly? 3 / 4

Freedom of assembly is constitutionally guaranteed and largely respected. While there have been some instances of violence between political party supporters, people are largely able to gather and protest freely. A number of protests took place in 2018, including against sexual violence, corruption, and economic hardships. In October, Weah criticized demonstrations by citizens angry about the missing $L16 billion in bank notes, calling the protesters "rebellious" and implying that they threatened stability.

E2. Is there freedom for nongovernmental organizations, particularly those that are engaged in human rights– and governance-related work? 3 / 4

Numerous civil society groups, including human rights organizations, operate in the country. However, groups focused on LGBT issues tend to keep a low profile due to fears of retribution for their activism.

E3. Is there freedom for trade unions and similar professional or labor organizations? 2 / 4

Unions are free to form and mobilize, and are well organized. The rights of workers to strike, organize, and bargain collectively are recognized. However, the law does not protect workers from employer retaliation for legal strike activity. Labor disputes can turn violent, particularly at the country's various mines and rubber plantations.

F. RULE OF LAW: 7 / 16

F1. Is there an independent judiciary? 2 / 4

Constitutional provisions guarantee an independent judiciary. Although petty corruption and backlogs remain major impediments to justice, some rulings by the nation's highest court in recent years point to increased judicial independence and increased willingness to intervene to protect people's rights.

However, the August 2018 vote by the House of Representatives voted to impeach Associate Justice Kabineh Ja'neh exposed a conflict between the legislative and judicial branches and threatened the authority of the Supreme Court. Ja'neh was impeached on allegations of misconduct and abuse of office in connection with his rulings. The move came despite a stay order from the Supreme Court that was issued so it could examine Ja'neh's objection that irregularities in the House procedures against him had violated his right to due process.

F2. Does due process prevail in civil and criminal matters? 1 / 4

The right to due process under the law is guaranteed by the constitution but poorly upheld. Many people accused of crimes spend more time in pretrial detention than the length they would serve for a guilty sentence. Citizens of means may be able to bribe judges to rule in their favor. Reports of arbitrary arrest by law enforcement agents continue.

F3. Is there protection from the illegitimate use of physical force and freedom from war and insurgencies? 2 / 4

The security environment in Liberia has improved dramatically in the years since warfare ended in 2003. However, the police force is still viewed as corrupt, and lacks the financial support to be able to provide robust protection for Liberia's people. Prison conditions are very poor, and reports of abuse and threats against detainees and prisoners by law enforcement agents and prison guards continue.

F4. Do laws, policies, and practices guarantee equal treatment of various segments of the population? 2 / 4

Some minority ethnic groups continue to be stigmatized as outsiders, and the Muslim population experiences some discrimination. LGBT people face social stigma and the threat of violence. The penal code makes "voluntary sodomy" a misdemeanor offense that can carry up to a year in prison, and this provision can be invoked against LGBT people. In a 2017 presidential debate with 9 candidates, none supported same-sex marriage.

G. PERSONAL AUTONOMY AND INDIVIDUAL RIGHTS: 9 / 16

G1. Do individuals enjoy freedom of movement, including the ability to change their place of residence, employment, or education? 3 / 4

While some unofficial border checkpoints remain, at which border patrol agents sometimes attempt to extract bribes, people have enjoyed a gradual increase in the right to move about freely in the years since large-scale violence ended.

G2. Are individuals able to exercise the right to own property and establish private businesses without undue interference from state or nonstate actors? 2 / 4

Conflicts over land remain pervasive. Many of these conflicts originated in the civil wars and subsequent displacement and resettlement. Others are the result of opaque concession agreements granting foreign corporations access to lands for mining, or production of timber or palm oil. The Legislature in 2018 passed the Land Rights Act, which aims to formalize communities' ownership of ancestral land, with implementation expected in 2019. Customary law practices that prevail in large parts of the country disadvantage women in matters of land rights and inheritance.

G3. Do individuals enjoy personal social freedoms, including choice of marriage partner and size of family, protection from domestic violence, and control over appearance? 2 / 4

While men and women enjoy equal legal rights under civil law, gender disparities are common in customary law, which remains dominant in many parts of the country and disadvantages women in matters involving child custody and other matters. Violence against women and children, particularly rape, is a pervasive problem. In 2017, the Senate voted to make rape a bailable offense—a decision that sparked protests outside the Capitol building by women's rights activists.

G4. Do individuals enjoy equality of opportunity and freedom from economic exploitation? 2 / 4

Human trafficking for the purpose of forced labor and prostitution remains a problem, with most victims trafficked from rural areas to cities. Many trafficking victims are children, who can be found working in diamond mines, agricultural operations, or as domestic laborers, or engaged in forced begging or prostitution.

Libya

Population: 6,500,000
Capital: Tripoli
Political Rights Rating: 7
Civil Liberties Rating: 6
Freedom Rating: 6.5
Freedom Status: Not Free
Electoral Democracy: No

Overview: While a popular armed uprising in 2011 deposed longtime dictator Mu'ammar al-Qadhafi, Libya is now racked by internal divisions, and international efforts to bring rival administrations together in a unity government have failed. A proliferation of weapons and autonomous militias, flourishing criminal networks, and the presence of extremist groups have all undermined security in the country. The ongoing violence has displaced hundreds of thousands of people, and human rights conditions have steadily deteriorated.

KEY DEVELOPMENTS IN 2018:

- A number of consultative meetings were held as part of a UN Support Mission for Libya (UNSMIL) action plan. The plan aims to address the breakdown of the internationally brokered 2015 Libyan Political Agreement (LPA), which had been designed to unite rival governments and pave the way toward the approval of a new constitution and fresh elections. Efforts to organize elections faltered in 2018, and the United Nations at year's end was proposing elections for 2019.
- In the fall, the internationally recognized legislature approved a framework for a constitutional referendum, and submitted it to the electoral commission. However, there has been speculation that the new law and accompanying amendments will face legal challenges.
- Violence continued in various parts of the country. The Libyan National Army (LNA), a military alliance led by Khalifa Haftar, continued its siege of the eastern city of Derna, taking some degree of control of it by mid-year. In Tripoli, rival armed groups competing for resources and vital institutions fought from late August through late September, leaving over 100 people dead and nearly 600 injured, and displacing thousands.
- Food, fuel, water, electricity and medical supplies became increasingly difficult to obtain, and health care and public services have become less accessible.

POLITICAL RIGHTS: 1 / 40

A. ELECTORAL PROCESS: 0 / 12

A1. Was the current head of government or other chief national authority elected through free and fair elections? 0 / 4

Libya's current, internationally recognized executive leadership was appointed as part of the LPA, an internationally brokered accord sealed in late 2015. The agreement was intended to end the political gridlock and armed fighting that started in 2014 between the rival Tubruk-based House of Representatives (HoR), which enjoyed widespread international recognition, and the Tripoli-based General National Congress (GNC)—each of which had its own allied military coalitions. The appointment of a nine-member Presidency Council (PC) under the leadership of Prime Minister Fayez al-Serraj followed. The PC assumed office in Tripoli in 2016 and was tasked with forming a unity government, the Government of National Accord (GNA), to serve as an executive branch.

The LPA text granted a one-year mandate to the GNA upon its approval by the HoR, with a one-time extension if necessary. However, the HoR has never approved it.

A2. Were the current national legislative representatives elected through free and fair elections? 0 / 4

Under the LPA, the unicameral, 200-seat HoR was to remain in place as the interim legislature. The agreement also created the High Council of State (HCS), a secondary consultative body composed of a handful of members of the rival GNC. However, the HoR never formally approved the LPA's provisions or recognized the GNA.

Members of the HoR were elected over four years ago in polls marked by violence, and which saw the participation of only about 15 percent of the electorate. Its mandate formally expired in 2015, though it has ruled to extend it. HCS members were elected six years ago, as part of the 2012 GNC elections.

A3. Are the electoral laws and framework fair, and are they implemented impartially by the relevant election management bodies? 0 / 4

An August 2011 constitutional declaration, issued by an unelected National Transitional Council, serves as the governing document for the ongoing transitional period between the revolution and the adoption of a permanent constitution. Despite some legal developments, Libya lacks a functioning electoral framework in practice.

An electoral law was published in the aftermath of the 2011 revolution, and members of the High National Election Commission (HNEC) were appointed. In 2017, a Constitutional Drafting Assembly elected in 2014 voted to approve a draft constitution. In the fall of 2018, the HoR approved a law containing a framework for a constitutional referendum, along with several accompanying amendments to the 2011 constitutional declaration. It then submitted the former, the Referendum Law, to the HNEC, but there has been speculation that the new law and amendments will face legal challenges.

A number of consultative meetings were held in 2018 as part of an UNSMIL action plan, unveiled in 2017, to address the breakdown of the LPA. The plan included amending the agreement, convening a national conference with all political actors, and holding the constitutional referendum, to be followed by parliamentary and presidential elections. The UN at year's end was proposing elections for 2019.

Separately, in May, the Islamic State (IS) militant group attacked the HNEC headquarters, resulting in a least 12 deaths, most of them civilians.

B. POLITICAL PLURALISM AND PARTICIPATION: 1 / 16

B1. Do the people have the right to organize in different political parties or other competitive political groupings of their choice, and is the system free of undue obstacles to the rise and fall of these competing parties or groupings? 1 / 4

A range of political parties organized to participate in the 2012 GNC elections, but all candidates were required to run as independents in the 2014 HoR elections. Civilian politics have since been overshadowed by the activities of armed groups, who wield significant power and influence on the ground. While various political groups and coalitions exist, the chaotic legal and security environment does not allow for normal political competition.

B2. Is there a realistic opportunity for the opposition to increase its support or gain power through elections? 0 / 4

Libya remained divided between rival political and military factions throughout 2018, with little movement toward the organization of elections and thus no opportunity for a democratic rotation of power. United Nations–backed efforts to organize elections faltered in 2018, and the UN at year's end was proposing elections for 2019.

B3. Are the people's political choices free from domination by the military, foreign powers, religious hierarchies, economic oligarchies, or any other powerful group that is not democratically accountable? 0 / 4

Oil interests, foreign governments, smuggling syndicates, and armed groups wield significant influence over the political sphere. Citizens and civilian political figures are subject to violence and intimidation by various armed groups, which continued to engage in active fighting during 2018.

B4. Do various segments of the population (including ethnic, religious, gender, LGBT, and other relevant groups) have full political rights and electoral opportunities? 0 / 4

The ongoing political impasse and civil conflict prevented all segments of the population from exercising their basic political rights in 2018. Communities that lacked an affiliation with a powerful militia were especially marginalized.

C. FUNCTIONING OF GOVERNMENT: 0 / 12

C1. Do the freely elected head of government and national legislative representatives determine the policies of the government? 0 / 4

The limited authority of the internationally recognized government is dependent on powerful militia groups, which are often in conflict with one another. Militias have effective control over a number of critical government institutions and ministries.

The eastern part of Libya is largely controlled by Khalifa Haftar and his LNA. De facto authorities in the eastern part of the country have established a parallel central bank and state oil company.

C2. Are safeguards against official corruption strong and effective? 0 / 4

Corruption is pervasive among government officials, and opportunities for corruption and criminal activity abound in the absence of functioning fiscal, judicial, and other institutions.

C3. Does the government operate with openness and transparency? 0 / 4

There are no effective laws guaranteeing public access to government information, and none of the competing authorities engage in transparent budget-making and contracting practices.

CIVIL LIBERTIES: 8 / 60

D. FREEDOM OF EXPRESSION AND BELIEF: 4 / 16

D1. Are there free and independent media? 1 / 4

Most Libyan media outlets are highly partisan, producing content that favors one of the country's political and military factions. The civil conflict and related violence by criminal and extremist groups have made objective reporting dangerous. Many journalists and media outlets have censored themselves or ceased operations to avoid retribution for their work, and journalists continue to flee the country.

D2. Are individuals free to practice and express their religious faith or nonbelief in public and private? 1 / 4

Religious freedom is often violated in practice. Nearly all Libyans are Sunni Muslims, but Christians form a small minority. Christian and other minority communities have been targeted by armed groups, including IS. Salafi Muslim militants, whose beliefs reject the veneration of saints, have destroyed or vandalized Sufi Muslim shrines with impunity.

D3. Is there academic freedom, and is the educational system free from extensive political indoctrination? 1 / 4

There are no effective laws guaranteeing academic freedom. The armed conflict has damaged many university facilities and altered classroom dynamics; for example, professors can be subject to intimidation by students who are aligned with militias.

D4. Are individuals free to express their personal views on political or other sensitive topics without fear of surveillance or retribution? 1 / 4

Although the freedom of private discussion and personal expression improved dramatically after 2011, the ongoing hostilities have taken their toll, with many Libyans increasingly withdrawing from public life or avoiding criticism of powerful figures.

E. ASSOCIATIONAL AND ORGANIZATIONAL RIGHTS: 2 / 12

E1. Is there freedom of assembly? 1 / 4

A 2012 law on freedom of assembly is generally compatible with international human rights principles, but in practice the armed conflict and related disorder seriously deter peaceful assemblies in many areas.

However, demonstrations do take place. In August, a group of detained migrants forced their way out of the detention center where they were being held and marched toward the capital, demanding assistance from the United Nations and human rights organizations. In December, dozens of members of the ethnic Tuareg tribe protested against a US airstrike in southwestern Libya that reportedly targeted members of IS, but which protesters said had killed civilians.

E2. Is there freedom for nongovernmental organizations, particularly those that are engaged in human rights– and governance-related work? 1 / 4

The number of active nongovernmental organizations (NGOs) has declined in recent years due to armed conflict and the departure of international donors. Militias with varying political, tribal, and geographic affiliations have attacked civil society activists with impunity. Many NGO workers have fled abroad or ceased their activism in the wake of grave threats to themselves or their families.

E3. Is there freedom for trade unions and similar professional or labor organizations? 0 / 4

Some trade unions, previously outlawed, formed after 2011. However, normal collective-bargaining activity is impossible in the absence of basic security and a functioning legal system.

F. RULE OF LAW: 0 / 16

F1. Is there an independent judiciary? 0 / 4

The role of the judiciary remains unclear without a permanent constitution, and judges, lawyers, and prosecutors face frequent threats and attacks. The national judicial system has essentially collapsed, with courts unable to function in much of the country. In some cases, informal dispute-resolution mechanisms have filled the void.

F2. Does due process prevail in civil and criminal matters? 0 / 4

Since the 2011 revolution, the right of citizens to a fair trial and due process has been challenged by the continued interference of armed groups and inability to access lawyers and court documents. Militias and semiofficial security forces regularly engage in arbitrary arrests, detentions, and intimidation with impunity. Thousands of individuals remain in custody without any formal trial or sentencing.

In an August 2018 mass trial, the judiciary convicted 99 defendants, sentencing 45 to death and 54 to five years in prison. The defendants had been accused of playing various roles in what has become known as the Abu Saleem Highway Massacre, which took place in Tripoli during the 2011 revolution and saw alleged Qadhafi sympathizers and allied security forces kill 146 anti-Qadhafi protesters.

F3. Is there protection from the illegitimate use of physical force and freedom from war and insurgencies? 0 / 4

Libya's warring militias operate with little regard for the physical security of civilians. Various armed groups have carried out indiscriminate shelling of civilian areas, torture of detainees, summary executions, rape, and the destruction of property. Militias also engage in criminal activity, including extortion and other forms of predation on the civilian population.

In 2018, violence continued in various parts of the country. The LNA continued a two-years-old siege of the eastern city of Derna, and by mid-year appeared to have wrested some control of the city from the Derna Mujahedeen Shura Council, an alliance of anti-LNA Islamist groups. Civilians in the city faced shortages of vital supplies. Although IS was largely ousted from its stronghold in Sirte, on the central Mediterranean coast in 2016, it maintains a presence in the region and has continued to carry out attacks.

In Tripoli, rival armed groups competing for resources and vital institutions fought from late August through late September, leaving over 100 people dead and nearly 600 injured, including many children, according to the UN International Children's Emergency Fund (UNICEF). Hundreds of families were trapped as a result of the fighting and at least 5,000 families were displaced, according to the agency. The UN brokered a ceasefire deal, but tensions between armed groups continue.

F4. Do laws, policies, and practices guarantee equal treatment of various segments of the population? 0 / 4

Libyans from certain tribes and communities—often those perceived as pro-Qadhafi, including the Tawerghans—face discrimination, violence, and displacement. The Tebu and Tuareg minorities in the south also face discrimination. Migrant workers from sub-Saharan Africa have been subject to severe mistreatment, including detention in squalid facilities by both authorities and armed groups.

Women are not treated equally under the law and face practical restrictions on their ability to participate in the workforce. Widows and displaced women in particular are vulnerable to economic deprivation and other abuses.

Under Libya's penal code, sexual activity between members of the same sex is punishable by up to five years in prison. LGBT (lesbian, gay, bisexual, and transgender) people face severe discrimination and harassment, and have been targeted by militant groups.

G. PERSONAL AUTONOMY AND INDIVIDUAL RIGHTS: 2 / 16

G1. Do individuals enjoy freedom of movement, including the ability to change their place of residence, employment, or education? 0 / 4

The 2011 constitutional declaration guarantees freedom of movement, but government and militia checkpoints restrict travel within Libya, while poor security conditions more generally affect movement as well as access to education and employment. Airports in Benghazi, Tripoli, Sabha, and Misrata have been attacked and damaged, severely limiting access to air travel.

G2. Are individuals able to exercise the right to own property and establish private businesses without undue interference from state or nonstate actors? 1 / 4

While Libyans formally have the right to own property and can start businesses, legal protections are not upheld in practice. Businesses and homes have been damaged amid fighting or other unrest, or confiscated by militias, particularly in Libya's eastern regions. Ongoing unrest has severely disrupted ordinary commerce, allowing armed groups to dominate smuggling networks and informal markets.

G3. Do individuals enjoy personal social freedoms, including choice of marriage partner and size of family, protection from domestic violence, and control over appearance? 1 / 4

Laws and social customs based on Sharia (Islamic law) disadvantage women in personal status matters including marriage and divorce. Libyan women with foreign husbands do not enjoy full citizenship rights and cannot transfer Libyan citizenship to their children. There are no laws that specifically address or criminalize domestic violence, and most such violence goes unreported due to social stigma and the risk of reprisals. The law imposes penalties for extramarital sex and allows rapists to avoid punishment by marrying their victims. Rape and other sexual violence have become increasingly serious problems in the lawless environment created by the civil conflict.

G4. Do individuals enjoy equality of opportunity and freedom from economic exploitation? 0 / 4

There are few protections against exploitative labor practices. Forced labor, sexual exploitation, abuse in detention facilities, and starvation are widespread among migrants and refugees from sub-Saharan Africa, the Middle East, and South Asia, many of whom are beholden to human traffickers. The International Organization for Migration (IOM) said in the fall of 2018 it had identified 670,000 migrants in the country.

Libya lacks comprehensive laws criminalizing human trafficking, and the authorities have been either incapable of enforcing existing bans or complicit in trafficking activity. Traffickers have taken advantage of civil unrest to establish enterprises in which refugees and migrants are loaded into overcrowded boats that are then abandoned in the Mediterranean Sea, where passengers hope to be rescued and taken to Europe. The voyages often result in fatalities.

Liechtenstein

Population: 40,000
Capital: Vaduz
Political Rights Rating: 2
Civil Liberties Rating: 1
Freedom Rating: 1.5
Freedom Status: Free
Electoral Democracy: Yes

Overview: The Principality of Liechtenstein combines a powerful monarchy with a parliamentary system of government. The prince has an influential political role, which was enhanced by a constitutional referendum in 2003. Human rights and civil liberties are generally respected in the country.

KEY DEVELOPMENTS IN 2018:
- In response to recommendations by a Council of Europe anticorruption body, the government in July approved a modification of the law on party financing to increase transparency, though the legislation had yet to win final passage at year's end.
- In October, the Economic and Financial Affairs Council (ECOFIN) of the European Union (EU) removed Liechtenstein from its "grey list" of tax havens, finding that the country was fully compliant with all EU tax standards.

POLITICAL RIGHTS: 33 / 40

A. ELECTORAL PROCESS: 10 / 12

A1. Was the current head of government or other chief national authority elected through free and fair elections? 2 / 4

Liechtenstein has one of the most politically powerful hereditary monarchies in Europe. In a 2003 constitutional referendum, voters granted significantly more power to the prince. As head of state, the prince appoints the prime minister and cabinet on the recommendation of the parliament and has the authority to veto legislation and the outcome of public plebiscites, as well as to dismiss the government and dissolve the parliament.

Prince Hans-Adam II is the current head of state, but he delegated his governmental authority to his son, Hereditary Prince Alois, in 2004. Adrian Hasler has been prime minister since 2013, when his Progressive Citizens' Party (FBP) won legislative elections.

A2. Were the current national legislative representatives elected through free and fair elections? 4 / 4

The Landtag, the unicameral parliament, consists of 25 deputies chosen by proportional representation every four years. International observers considered the 2017 parliamentary elections to be credible. The ruling conservative FBP led the voting with nine seats, followed by its coalition partner, the center-right Patriotic Union (VU), with eight. The right-wing populist Independents (DU) and the center-left Free List (FL) won five and three seats, respectively.

A3. Are the electoral laws and framework fair, and are they implemented impartially by the relevant election management bodies? 4 / 4

The electoral framework provides a sound basis for democratic balloting. There are no formal provisions for election observation, but domestic and international observers are free to monitor the process. Voting is compulsory under the law, but the rule is not enforced.

B. POLITICAL PLURALISM AND PARTICIPATION: 13 / 16

B1. Do the people have the right to organize in different political parties or other competitive political groupings of their choice, and is the system free of undue obstacles to the rise and fall of these competing parties or groupings? 4 / 4

There are no limits on the establishment or participation of political parties. The 8 percent vote threshold for representation in the parliament is comparatively high, though the 2013 elections marked the first time that four parties had won seats.

B2. Is there a realistic opportunity for the opposition to increase its support or gain power through elections? 3 / 4

The unelected prince wields significant governmental authority, meaning the extent to which power can change hands through elections is limited. The FBP and VU have traditionally dominated the parliament, competing with each other and usually forming coalition governments. The FL has long served as a smaller opposition party, and DU has gained ground since entering the legislature with four seats in 2013, winning an additional seat in 2017. DU has campaigned on the theme that the political elite is out of touch and corrupt, and it makes occasional appeals to xenophobia.

B3. Are the people's political choices free from domination by the military, foreign powers, religious hierarchies, economic oligarchies, or any other powerful group that is not democratically accountable? 3 / 4

Although citizens' political choices are largely free from undue interference, the prince has the power to veto the outcome of national referendums and popular initiatives. He has occasionally threatened to use this power, thereby influencing the outcome of the votes. In a 2012 constitutional referendum, however, 76 percent of voters rejected a proposal to limit the prince's veto power.

Transparency of political financing remains a concern. In a compliance report published in May 2018, the Council of Europe's Group of States against Corruption (GRECO) noted that 12 out of its 20 earlier recommendations relating to corruption and party financing had been satisfactorily implemented, but that significant gaps remained. In response, the government in July approved a draft modification of the law on party financing that would increase transparency, in part by setting a cap on the size of anonymous donations. The bill was still under consideration by the parliament at year's end.

B4. Do various segments of the population (including ethnic, religious, gender, LGBT, and other relevant groups) have full political rights and electoral opportunities? 3 / 4

Women and minorities generally enjoy formal political equality, though some disparities persist in practice. The number of women in the parliament declined in 2017 from six to three, which led to calls for the introduction of a gender quota. In 2016, in a move that showed some government commitment to representing women's interests, Liechtenstein signed the Istanbul Convention on Preventing and Combating Violence against Women and Domestic Violence. However, in June 2018, representatives from nine nongovernmental organizations (NGOs) presented reports in which they accused the government of passivity regarding concrete measures to support gender equality.

Approximately one-third of the population consists of foreign nationals—mostly from neighboring countries—who do not have political rights. Under Liechtenstein's restrictive naturalization criteria, one must live in the country for 30 years, or marry a resident Liechtenstein citizen and live in the country for more than 10 years, to qualify for citizenship.

C. FUNCTIONING OF GOVERNMENT: 10 / 12

C1. Do the freely elected head of government and national legislative representatives determine the policies of the government? 2 / 4

Although elected executive and legislative officials set the policy agenda, the prince has significant governmental authority with no electoral mandate. He can dismiss the government and the parliament and veto legislation and referendums, and he plays a powerful role in the appointment of judges.

C2. Are safeguards against official corruption strong and effective? 4 / 4

Anticorruption laws are effectively implemented, and levels of corruption are reportedly low. The May 2018 GRECO compliance report applauded Liechtenstein for the recent implementation of reforms to the criminal code, including the addition of charges for bribery in the private sector and the expansion of the definition of "public officials" to include a wider range of personnel, including all assembly members and parliamentary employees.

C3. Does the government operate with openness and transparency? 4 / 4

Although there is no constitutional guarantee of access to information, laws are in place to provide for government transparency, and these are largely respected in practice.

The government has made efforts in recent years to increase transparency in the banking sector. In October 2018, ECOFIN removed Liechtenstein from its "grey list" of tax havens, finding that the country—though not an EU member—was fully compliant with all EU tax standards. The country's large financial industry has historically been criticized for enabling foreign clients to hide wealth from their respective governments and potentially aiding corruption or other criminal activity.

CIVIL LIBERTIES: 57 / 60

D. FREEDOM OF EXPRESSION AND BELIEF: 16 / 16

D1. Are there free and independent media? 4 / 4

The constitution guarantees freedom of the press, which is respected in practice. Liechtenstein has one private television station, one public radio station, and two main newspapers that are owned by the two major political parties. The local media sector lacks pluralism, but residents have access to foreign news outlets, including broadcasts from Germany, Austria, and Switzerland.

D2. Are individuals free to practice and express their religious faith or nonbelief in public and private? 4 / 4

Although the constitution establishes Roman Catholicism as the state religion, religious freedom is constitutionally guaranteed and protected in practice. Catholic or Protestant education is mandatory in all primary schools, but exemptions are routinely granted. Islamic religious classes have been offered in some primary schools since 2008. All religious groups have tax-exempt status.

D3. Is there academic freedom, and is the educational system free from extensive political indoctrination? 4 / 4

Academic freedom is largely respected, with no significant restrictions by state or nonstate actors.

D4. Are individuals free to express their personal views on political or other sensitive topics without fear of surveillance or retribution? 4 / 4

The law guarantees freedom of expression, but prohibits public insults directed against a race or ethnic group. There are no restrictions on internet access or online communication.

E. ASSOCIATIONAL AND ORGANIZATIONAL RIGHTS: 12 / 12
E1. Is there freedom of assembly? 4 / 4

The constitution guarantees freedom of assembly, and this right is respected in practice.

E2. Is there freedom for nongovernmental organizations, particularly those that are engaged in human rights- and governance-related work? 4 / 4

Domestic and international nongovernmental organizations (NGOs) are able to function freely. The government largely cooperates with NGOs and is receptive to their viewpoints.

E3. Is there freedom for trade unions and similar professional or labor organizations? 4 / 4

The law facilitates the formation of trade unions and collective bargaining, and workers enjoy freedom of association in practice. The principality has at least one trade union. While a 2008 legal change removed a ban on strikes for civil servants, the right to strike in general is not explicitly protected by law. Major labor disputes are rare in the country.

F. RULE OF LAW: 14 / 16
F1. Is there an independent judiciary? 3 / 4

The judiciary is generally independent and impartial, but the constitution gives the prince a powerful influence over the appointment of judges, meaning the process lacks a key element of democratic accountability. The appointments of ad hoc judges, who often serve for a short time, are not publicly announced.

F2. Does due process prevail in civil and criminal matters? 4 / 4

The constitution provides for the right to a fair trial, and the rights of defendants are usually respected. Most trials are public, and defendants are considered innocent until proven guilty. In a 2017 report, the Council of Europe's Committee for the Prevention of Torture expressed concerns about some aspects of police custody procedures, including the fact that police can deny the presence of a lawyer during initial questioning.

F3. Is there protection from the illegitimate use of physical force and freedom from war and insurgencies? 4 / 4

People in Liechtenstein are largely free from the illegitimate use of physical force. Violent crime is extremely rare. While the country's small prison facility can hold up to 16 men and four women in short-term detention, convicted offenders serve their sentences in neighboring Austria.

F4. Do laws, policies, and practices guarantee equal treatment of various segments of the population? 3 / 4

The legal framework prohibits discrimination on various grounds, though some short-comings remain. In a report published in May 2018, the European Commission against Racism and Intolerance (ECRI) reiterated the need for Liechtenstein to ratify Protocol 12 to the European Convention on Human Rights, which provides a general prohibition against discrimination. The commission highlighted the absence of a regulatory office to address hate speech in the media, and the need to endorse the Additional Protocol to the Convention on Cybercrime to combat online hate speech. In addition, ECRI called on Liechtenstein to ban the formation of racist groups.

Despite the presence of antidiscrimination laws, women, particularly Muslim women, and LGBT (lesbian, gay, bisexual, and transgender) people experience employment discrimination. LGBT individuals face social stigma, and according to a leading human rights group, often do not disclose their sexual orientation or gender identity out of fear of bias.

G. PERSONAL AUTONOMY AND INDIVIDUAL RIGHTS: 15 / 16

G1. Do individuals enjoy freedom of movement, including the ability to change their place of residence, employment, or education? 4 / 4

There are no significant restrictions on freedom of movement in Liechtenstein.

G2. Are individuals able to exercise the right to own property and establish private businesses without undue interference from state or nonstate actors? 4 / 4

The legal framework generally protects property rights and supports private business activity without undue restrictions. Nonresidents are not allowed to establish a business in Liechtenstein, but prospective business owners exploit loopholes to work around the law.

G3. Do individuals enjoy personal social freedoms, including choice of marriage partner and size of family, protection from domestic violence, and control over appearance? 3 / 4

Personal social freedoms are largely protected. Same-sex registered partnerships are legal, but the prince has expressed opposition to adoption rights for same-sex couples. While single LGBT people can adopt children, same-sex couples cannot.

Domestic violence and spousal rape are illegal in Liechtenstein, and authorities effectively prosecute offenders and protect victims. Abortion is criminalized unless the woman is at risk of death or serious harm to her health, or was under age 14 at the time of conception. A 2011 referendum to expand the conditions for legal abortion was defeated by voters.

G4. Do individuals enjoy equality of opportunity and freedom from economic exploitation? 4 / 4

Liechtenstein is largely free from economic exploitation and human trafficking. Despite the country's overall wealth and low unemployment rates, however, relative poverty persists among some communities. Immigrants in particular often struggle to achieve economic security and social mobility.

Lithuania

Population: 2,800,000
Capital: Vilnius
Political Rights Rating: 1
Civil Liberties Rating: 1
Freedom Rating: 1.0
Freedom Status: Free
Electoral Democracy: Yes

Overview: Lithuania is a democracy in which political rights and civil liberties are generally respected. However, corruption and income inequality are issues that often arouse public dissatisfaction with the government.

KEY DEVELOPMENTS IN 2018:

- In June, Parliament's Committee on National Security and Defense presented the findings of an investigation which concluded that a number of large corporations have advanced their interests by influencing the policy positions of members of parliament and other politicians through media pressure, bribes, and blackmail.
- August marked the beginning of a major corruption trial against the Labor Party, the Liberal Movement, three of the parties' current and former leaders, and the former vice president of investment management company MG Baltic. The trial was ongoing at year's end.
- In September, the Lithuanian Farmers and Greens Union (LVŽS) formed a new governing coalition with the newly formed Lithuanian Social Democratic Labor Party (LSDLP) and the Order and Justice (TT) party.

POLITICAL RIGHTS: 38 / 40
A. ELECTORAL PROCESS: 12 / 12

A1. Was the current head of government or other chief national authority elected through free and fair elections? 4 / 4

The president, who is chief of state and whose main competencies lie in foreign affairs, is directly elected to up to two five-year terms. The prime minister, who as a head of government is the central executive authority, is appointed by the president with the approval of Parliament.

The present prime minister, Saulius Skvernelis, was appointed after the parliamentary elections in October 2016 and began serving that December. The current president, Dalia Grybauskaitė, was elected to a second term of office in 2014. Both the appointment of the prime minister and election of the president took place in a free and fair manner.

A2. Were the current national legislative representatives elected through free and fair elections? 4 / 4

A unicameral, 141-seat Parliament (Seimas) consists of 71 members elected in single-mandate constituencies and 70 chosen by proportional representation, all for four-year terms. The most recent parliamentary elections took place in October 2016. The elections were somewhat unexpectedly won by the centrist LVŽS, which took 56 seats. The party formed a coalition government with the Lithuanian Social Democratic Party (LSDP), which received 17 seats. The main opposition Homeland Union–Lithuanian Christian Democrats (HU-LCD) gained 31 seats.

The elections were considered free and fair, though the election commission faced criticism for delays in announcing the official results—problems linked to issues with new electronic infrastructure for the polls. While relatively few irregularities were reported, there was one notable case of vote buying, to benefit the TT. The election commission subsequently stripped lawmaker Kęstas Komskis of the TT of his parliamentary mandate in connection with the events.

A3. Are the electoral laws and framework fair, and are they implemented impartially by the relevant election management bodies? 4 / 4

The legislative framework for conducting elections is clear and detailed. The boundaries of single-mandate districts of parliamentary elections were redrawn at the end of 2015 to comply with a ruling by the Constitutional Court. The Central Electoral Commission (VRK) has historically been known to operate and adjudicate election-related complaints in a fair manner.

In March 2018, VRK chairperson Laura Matjošaitytė survived a no-confidence vote initiated by the opposition in Parliament. Matjošaitytė had been accused of concealing the results of an investigation into alleged impropriety by Agrokoncernas, an agricultural company owned by LVŽS leader Ramūnas Karbauskis, which was accused of providing illegal support to the LVŽS between 2013 and 2016. A VRK working group that investigated the allegations produced a report with its conclusions in 2017, which was never publicized, but did not find that the law had been violated. Opposition parties alleged that Matjošaitytė was appointed in 2017 in exchange for blocking the report's release.

B. POLITICAL PLURALISM AND PARTICIPATION: 16 / 16

B1. Do the people have the right to organize in different political parties or other competitive political groupings of their choice, and is the system free of undue obstacles to the rise and fall of these competing parties or groupings? 4 / 4

Lithuania's political parties generally operate freely. Citizens of other European Union (EU) member states are eligible to become members of Lithuanian political parties but cannot found them.

In the fall of 2017, the LSDP party council voted to leave the governing coalition, but the LSDP members of parliament refused to comply with the decision and remained in the government. Eleven of those members subsequently left the LSDP and established a new party, the Lithuanian Social Democratic Labor Party (LSDLP), which joined a new governing coalition with the LVŽS and the TT in September 2018.

B2. Is there a realistic opportunity for the opposition to increase its support or gain power through elections? 4 / 4

Lithuanian politics are dynamic, and opposition parties usually come to power after every parliamentary election.

B3. Are the people's political choices free from domination by the military, foreign powers, religious hierarchies, economic oligarchies, or any other powerful group that is not democratically accountable? 4 / 4

Sporadic cases of vote buying during national elections have been observed, and clientelism can influence politics at the local levels. However, people are generally free to exercise their political choices without undue influence or interference.

The State Security Department (VSD) has issued numerous warnings about efforts by Russians to influence politics, including through its energy policies and by influencing the country's ethnic minorities.

B4. Do various segments of the population (including ethnic, religious, gender, LGBT, and other relevant groups) have full political rights and electoral opportunities? 4 / 4

Political rights of minorities are generally upheld. In the 2016 parliamentary elections, the Lithuanian Poles Electoral Action (LLRA), which represents the Polish minority, for the second consecutive time overcame the 5 percent electoral threshold for parties, and took seats in Parliament.

Women are underrepresented in politics, though they do hold senior political positions, including the presidency. In the 2016 parliamentary elections, women won 21 percent of the contested seats. Nongovernmental organizations (NGOs) working toward greater representation of women in politics and business, and combating violence against women, are active in the political sphere.

C. FUNCTIONING OF GOVERNMENT: 10 / 12

C1. Do the freely elected head of government and national legislative representatives determine the policies of the government? 4 / 4

Lithuania's freely elected lawmakers are seated according to schedule and can design and implement policies. However, bribery scandals that erupted in 2016 raised concerns about the influence of large businesses on politics. In June 2018, Parliament's Committee on National Security and Defense presented the findings of an investigation which concluded that a number of large corporations have advanced their interests by influencing the policy positions of members of parliament and other politicians through media pressure, bribes, and blackmail.

C2. Are safeguards against official corruption strong and effective? 3 / 4

Corruption remains an issue in Lithuania, and certain sectors, including health care and construction, are perceived as prone to corruption. While anticorruption bodies are active, there are sometimes considerable delays in the investigation of political corruption cases. In 2016, the leaders of three political parties were implicated in separate bribery scandals involving illicit deals with Lithuanian businesses. In August 2018, in response to two of the scandals, the corruption trial of the Labor Party, the Liberal Movement, three of the parties' current and former leaders, and the former vice president of investment management company MG Baltic, commenced, and was ongoing at year's end.

The protection of whistle-blowers and journalists who report on corruption cases is guaranteed, though at the local level it is less effective than nationally.

C3. Does the government operate with openness and transparency? 3 / 4

Lithuanian law grants the public the right to request information, and the government generally complies with information requests. However, the operations of state companies remain somewhat opaque, and prone to financial misconduct. Improvements to make public procurement fairer and more open to public scrutiny have been limited.

CIVIL LIBERTIES: 53 / 60

D. FREEDOM OF EXPRESSION AND BELIEF: 16 / 16

D1. Are there free and independent media? 4 / 4

The government generally respects freedoms of speech and the press. While the media market is vibrant, some owners of media outlets attempt to use their position to influence political processes. Local outlets are usually financially dependent on the local government.

D2. Are individuals free to practice and express their religious faith or nonbelief in public and private? 4 / 4

Freedom of religion is guaranteed by law and largely upheld in practice. However, nine so-called traditional religious communities enjoy certain government benefits, including annual subsidies that are not granted to other groups. Despite the presence of a Muslim community, Vilnius has been without a mosque since one was demolished by the Soviet government in the 1960s, and the planned construction of a new mosque remains stalled.

D3. Is there academic freedom, and is the educational system free from extensive political indoctrination? 4 / 4

Academic freedom is respected, and the educational system is generally free from political influence.

D4. Are individuals free to express their personal views on political or other sensitive topics without fear of surveillance or retribution? 4 / 4

Private discussion is generally robust and unrestricted. However, in the wake of increasing concerns about Russia's aggressive foreign policy, individuals who criticize the government's foreign policy stances can face pressure.

E. ASSOCIATIONAL AND ORGANIZATIONAL RIGHTS: 11 / 12
E1. Is there freedom of assembly? 4 / 4

Freedom of assembly is generally respected. In March 2018, thousands of people gathered in Vilnius to protest a failed vote in Parliament to impeach legislator Mindaugas Bastys, who was allegedly under the influence of Russian business interests.

E2. Is there freedom for nongovernmental organizations, particularly those that are engaged in human rights– and governance-related work? 4 / 4

Nongovernmental organizations may register without facing serious obstacles, and operate without restrictions.

E3. Is there freedom for trade unions and similar professional or labor organizations? 3 / 4

Workers may form and join trade unions and engage in collective bargaining, though there have been reports of employees being punished for attempting to organize. In 2017, a new Labor Code came into force, which among other things provided additional instruments to organize strikes.

F. RULE OF LAW: 12 / 16
F1. Is there an independent judiciary? 3 / 4

Businesspeople and politicians closely linked with business interests exert pressure on the judiciary, and according to the most recent results of an EU survey, only about half of the general public and representatives of the business sector believe that judicial independence is guaranteed. Nontransparent decisions by the courts also remain an issue.

F2. Does due process prevail in civil and criminal matters? 3 / 4

Defendants generally enjoy the presumption of innocence and freedom from arbitrary arrest and detention, but detained suspects are not always granted timely access to an attorney. Pretrial detention rates are high, even though the law states that pretrial detention should only be employed in exceptional circumstances. Lengthy pretrial detentions also remain common.

F3. Is there protection from the illegitimate use of physical force and freedom from war and insurgencies? 3 / 4

Police abuse of detainees is a lingering issue. Conditions at some prisons are substandard, interprisoner violence remains a problem, and physical abuse by correctional officers persists. Despite a reduction in homicides in recent years, Lithuania still has one of the highest homicide rates in the EU.

F4. Do laws, policies, and practices guarantee equal treatment of various segments of the population? 3 / 4

Public signs must be written only in Lithuanian, even in areas predominantly inhabited by minorities who speak different languages. The Romany population experiences widespread societal discrimination. Members of the LGBT (lesbian, gay, bisexual, and transgender) community face discrimination, and there have been several cases in the past in which public information about rights for LGBT people has been restricted.

Men and women enjoy the same legal rights, though women generally earn less than men per hour worked.

G. PERSONAL AUTONOMY AND INDIVIDUAL RIGHTS: 14 / 16

G1. Do individuals enjoy freedom of movement, including the ability to change their place of residence, employment, or education? 4 / 4

Lithuanian residents may travel freely within the country and internationally.

G2. Are individuals able to exercise the right to own property and establish private businesses without undue interference from state or nonstate actors? 4 / 4

Successive Lithuanian administrations have worked to maintain a well-regulated market economy, and economic freedoms are generally ensured.

G3. Do individuals enjoy personal social freedoms, including choice of marriage partner and size of family, protection from domestic violence, and control over appearance? 3 / 4

Domestic violence remains a problem, and cultural attitudes lead many Lithuanians to blame women for gender-based violence. A survey commissioned by the Seimas Equal Opportunities Ombudsperson's Office in 2017 found that more than half of respondents believed that women tend to provoke violent outbursts by men. Lithuania's constitution defines marriage as a union between a man and a woman, and same-sex partnership is not legally established. Legal regulations that would allow sex reassignment procedures are not in place.

G4. Do individuals enjoy equality of opportunity and freedom from economic exploitation? 3 / 4

Regional economic disparities remain acute. The minimum wage remains one of the lowest within the EU, and the share of the population at risk of poverty and social exclusion is around 30 percent.

Trafficking of adults and children for the purposes of forced labor or sex work occurs in Lithuania. The government actively works to prosecute traffickers, and provides aid to victims in conjunction with NGOs.

Luxembourg

Population: 600,000
Capital: Luxembourg
Political Rights Rating: 1
Civil Liberties Rating: 1
Freedom Rating: 1.0
Freedom Status: Free
Electoral Democracy: Yes

Overview: Luxembourg is a constitutional monarchy with a democratically elected government. Political rights and civil liberties are generally respected. Ongoing concerns include insufficient government transparency and inadequate safeguards against conflicts of interest.

KEY DEVELOPMENTS IN 2018:

- The center-right Christian Social People's Party (CSV) won the most seats for a single party in October general elections, but three rival parties—the Democratic Party (DP), the Luxembourg Socialist Workers' Party (LSAP), and the Greens (DG)—renewed their governing coalition.
- The new government took office in December. While Xavier Bettel of the DP remained prime minister, the DG and the LSAP both received deputy prime minister positions.
- The Constitutional Revision Committee completed its draft of a new constitution in June. Before being applied, the text would have to be approved by the parliament and by the public in a referendum. It had yet to win passage in the parliament at year's end.

POLITICAL RIGHTS: 38 / 40
A. ELECTORAL PROCESS: 12 / 12
A1. Was the current head of government or other chief national authority elected through free and fair elections? 4 / 4

The prime minister is the head of government and serves five-year terms. The leader of the majority coalition formed after parliamentary elections is appointed prime minister by the hereditary monarch, the grand duke, whose powers are largely ceremonial.

Incumbent prime minister Xavier Bettel was appointed to form a new government in October 2018 following that month's parliamentary elections. The new government, which took office in December, was based on the existing coalition of the DP, the LSAP, and the DG. The elections were generally viewed as credible.

A2. Were the current national legislative representatives elected through free and fair elections? 4 / 4

The unicameral legislature, the Chamber of Deputies, consists of 60 members elected to five-year terms by proportional representation. In the October 2018 elections, the DP led the ruling coalition parties with 12 seats, followed by the LSAP with 10 and the DG with 9. The main opposition party, the CSV, won 21 seats. The populist right-wing Alternative Democratic Reform Party (ADR) won 4 seats, while the Pirate Party and the Left each took 2. The elections were generally seen as free and fair, though the campaign was marked by some anti-Semitic vandalism of DP candidate posters.

A3. Are the electoral laws and framework fair, and are they implemented impartially by the relevant election management bodies? 4 / 4

The electoral laws and framework are considered fair, and they are generally implemented impartially. Voting is compulsory. In 2017, the government passed a law allowing postal ballots for all citizens.

A multiparty Constitutional Revision Committee completed its draft of a new constitution in June 2018. The charter, which did not include major changes to the political system, would take effect only after it had been approved by the parliament and by the public in a referendum. The parliament had yet to approve the draft at year's end.

B. POLITICAL PLURALISM AND PARTICIPATION: 16 / 16

B1. Do the people have the right to organize in different political parties or other competitive political groupings of their choice, and is the system free of undue obstacles to the rise and fall of these competing parties or groupings? 4 / 4

The political system is open to the establishment of new parties, which do not face undue obstacles in their formation or activities. Three parties have traditionally dominated politics: the CSV, historically aligned with the Catholic Church; the LSAP, a formerly radical but now center-left party representing the working class; and the DP, which favors free-market economic policies. Three smaller parties, the DG, the ADR, and the Left, have also won representation since at least the 1990s.

B2. Is there a realistic opportunity for the opposition to increase its support or gain power through elections? 4 / 4

The country has a record of peaceful transfers of power between rival parties. Both the DP and the DG were in the opposition before forming the governing coalition with the LSAP in 2013. The CSV, which had played a leading role in most governments since 1945, was forced into opposition in 2013 for the first time since 1979, and it remained out of government following the 2018 elections.

B3. Are the people's political choices free from domination by the military, foreign powers, religious hierarchies, economic oligarchies, or any other powerful group that is not democratically accountable? 4 / 4

Citizens are generally able to make political choices without undue interference from any democratically unaccountable groups.

B4. Do various segments of the population (including ethnic, religious, gender, LGBT, and other relevant groups) have full political rights and electoral opportunities? 4 / 4

Women engage actively in politics, and the government has taken measures to encourage greater participation. A 2016 law mandates that at least 40 percent of each party's electoral candidates be women; parties risk losing a portion of their public financing if they do not meet the quota. Twelve women won seats in the 2018 parliamentary elections. Citizens who belong to ethnic and other minorities, including LGBT (lesbian, gay, bisexual, and transgender) people, enjoy full political rights and are free to participate in practice. Bettel became the nation's first openly gay prime minister in 2013.

About 47 percent of the population consists of foreign nationals, most of whom are citizens of other European Union (EU) member states, with Portugal accounting for the largest single contingent. The law allows naturalization and dual nationality, and children automatically gain citizenship when a parent is naturalized. Foreign residents are entitled to vote in municipal elections.

C. FUNCTIONING OF GOVERNMENT: 10 / 12

C1. Do the freely elected head of government and national legislative representatives determine the policies of the government? 4 / 4

The prime minister, cabinet, and parliament are able to determine and implement the government's policies without improper interference from unelected entities.

C2. Are safeguards against official corruption strong and effective? 3 / 4

Corruption is not widespread in Luxembourg, and allegations of corruption are generally investigated and prosecuted. However, the Council of Europe's Group of States against

Corruption (GRECO) has criticized the government for failing to develop a comprehensive strategy to prevent corruption. In addition, rules on accepting gifts, lobbying, and mitigating conflicts of interest after government officials leave office are lacking.

C3. Does the government operate with openness and transparency? 3 / 4

While the legislative process and government operations are largely transparent, there is no comprehensive freedom of information law in place, and in practice the media and civil society groups often have difficulty obtaining official information. Cabinet members are obligated to disclose any shares in companies that they own, but there are no penalties for those who do not cooperate.

CIVIL LIBERTIES: 60 / 60
D. FREEDOM OF EXPRESSION AND BELIEF: 16 / 16
D1. Are there free and independent media? 4 / 4

Freedom of the press is guaranteed by the constitution and generally respected in practice. A single conglomerate, RTL, dominates broadcast radio and television, though numerous print, online, and foreign news sources are also available and present a broad range of views. Internet access is not restricted.

D2. Are individuals free to practice and express their religious faith or nonbelief in public and private? 4 / 4

Freedom of religion is largely respected in practice. The state has historically paid the salaries of clergy from a variety of Christian groups, but a 2016 law ended the practice for all clergy hired after that point. Under the law, the government continued to provide some funding to six major recognized religious communities, including the Muslim community, based on their size. Religious instruction in secondary and primary schools was phased out in 2016–17. In April 2018, the parliament adopted legislation that banned face coverings in schools, medical facilities, public buildings, public transport, and retirement homes. The law was widely understood to be aimed at Muslims, though the wearing of such garments is extremely rare in the country.

D3. Is there academic freedom, and is the educational system free from extensive political indoctrination? 4 / 4

Academic freedom is generally respected in practice.

D4. Are individuals free to express their personal views on political or other sensitive topics without fear of surveillance or retribution? 4 / 4

Freedom of expression is largely respected, and individuals can voice their political views without fear of retribution.

E. ASSOCIATIONAL AND ORGANIZATIONAL RIGHTS: 12 / 12
E1. Is there freedom of assembly? 4 / 4

Freedom of assembly is guaranteed by the constitution and generally respected in practice.

E2. Is there freedom for nongovernmental organizations, particularly those that are engaged in human rights- and governance-related work? 4 / 4

Nongovernmental organizations (NGOs) are largely free to operate without any undue restrictions.

E3. Is there freedom for trade unions and similar professional or labor organizations? 4 / 4

Workers are free to organize in trade unions and bargain collectively. The right to strike is guaranteed once conciliation procedures are formally exhausted. Employers are subject to penalties for antiunion discrimination.

F. RULE OF LAW: 16 / 16

F1. Is there an independent judiciary? 4 / 4

Judicial independence is generally upheld. Judges are appointed by the grand duke and cannot be removed arbitrarily. In June 2018, as part of an effort to further strengthen judicial independence, the minister of justice presented a bill that would establish a Supreme Council of Justice tasked with nominating judges for appointment by the grand duke. The council would consist of six magistrates, including three elected by their peers, and three nonmagistrates representing civil society, academia, and the legal profession. The bill, which had yet to be adopted at year's end, also included provisions meant to ensure prosecutorial independence and modernize the court system.

F2. Does due process prevail in civil and criminal matters? 4 / 4

Due process is largely upheld in civil and criminal matters. Defendants have the right to a fair and public trial, and this right is generally respected. Trials can be lengthy because many defendants are foreign nationals, and cases often involve other foreign individuals or institutions. Police typically observe safeguards against arbitrary arrest and detention.

F3. Is there protection from the illegitimate use of physical force and freedom from war and insurgencies? 4 / 4

There are no major threats to civilians' physical security. Prison conditions and protections against the illegitimate use of force are adequate, and violent crime is rare.

F4. Do laws, policies, and practices guarantee equal treatment of various segments of the population? 4 / 4

Discrimination on the basis of race, religion, disability, age, sex, gender identity, or sexual orientation is prohibited by law. The rights of LGBT (lesbian, gay, bisexual, and transgender) people are generally respected.

Women have benefited from reductions in the gender pay gap and an increase in their labor participation rate in recent years, though women still hold significantly fewer senior positions than men, for example on boards of directors.

G. PERSONAL AUTONOMY AND INDIVIDUAL RIGHTS: 16 / 16

G1. Do individuals enjoy freedom of movement, including the ability to change their place of residence, employment, or education? 4 / 4

Individuals generally enjoy freedom of movement, and there are no significant restrictions on their ability to change their place of residence, employment, or institution of higher education.

G2. Are individuals able to exercise the right to own property and establish private businesses without undue interference from state or nonstate actors? 4 / 4

The rights to own property and operate private businesses are legally protected and respected in practice.

G3. Do individuals enjoy personal social freedoms, including choice of marriage partner and size of family, protection from domestic violence, and control over appearance? 4 / 4

Individual freedom on issues such as marriage and divorce is generally guaranteed. Same-sex marriage has been legal since 2014, and same-sex couples have full adoption rights. Abortions are legal on request within the first trimester of pregnancy; later abortions require two doctors to determine that the pregnancy threatens the woman's life or health. The authorities generally uphold laws and practices meant to address rape and domestic violence.

G4. Do individuals enjoy equality of opportunity and freedom from economic exploitation? 4 / 4

The country's residents largely enjoy equality of opportunity, and the government enforces legal protections against exploitative working conditions. Occasional cases of forced labor in the construction and food-service industries have been reported, especially among migrant workers.

Macedonia

Population: 2,100,000
Capital: Skopje
Political Rights Rating: 4
Civil Liberties Rating: 3
Freedom Rating: 3.5
Freedom Status: Partly Free
Electoral Democracy: No

Overview: Macedonia is a parliamentary republic. A left-leaning government took power in 2017 after credible allegations of a massive, government-sponsored wiretapping and surveillance program emerged in 2015, prompting a crisis that paralyzed normal political activity. Macedonia continues to struggle with corruption, and while the media and civil society are active, journalists and activists face pressure and intimidation.

KEY DEVELOPMENTS IN 2018:
- In June, Skopje and Athens signed a comprehensive pact, the Prespa Agreement, to rename the country the Republic of North Macedonia, in exchange for Greek support for its European Union (EU) and NATO membership bids.
- A referendum held in September on the name change received the backing of more than 90 percent of voters, but the turnout was only 37 percent, below the 50 percent threshold required for the vote to be valid. Leaders in the Internal Macedonian Revolutionary Organization–Democratic Party for Macedonian Unity (VMRO–DPMNE), including President Gjorge Ivanov, had urged voters to boycott the vote, contributing to the low turnout. As a result, the parliament passed legislation in October to rename the country, potentially paving the way for EU and NATO accession.
- In May, former prime minister Nikola Gruevski was sentenced to two years in prison followng a corruption conviction stemming from the purchase of a $700,000 Mercedes in 2012. Gruevski then fled to Hungary in November with the assistance of Hungarian diplomats, and claimed political asylum there, which was reportedly granted by the Hungarian government.

POLITICAL RIGHTS: 22 / 40 (+1)

A. ELECTORAL PROCESS: 6 / 12

A1. Was the current head of government or other chief national authority elected through free and fair elections? 1 / 4

The president is elected to as many as two five-year terms through a direct popular vote. President Ivanov of the VMRO–DPMNE won a second term in the 2014 general elections, which were criticized by international observers for a number of shortcomings. The presidential portion was marked by relatively low turnout.

The unicameral Assembly elects the prime minister, who is head of government and holds most executive power. The formation of a new government was delayed for months after December 2016 elections, as Ivanov refused a request by the Social Democratic Union of Macedonia (SDSM) for a mandate to form a government after the VMRO–DMPNE, which had won a plurality of seats in the elections, was unable to cobble together enough support to form its own. VMRO–DMPNE deputies, meanwhile, filibustered a vote to install an SDSM-backed Assembly speaker, Talat Xhaferi, a member of the Democratic Union for Integration (DUI), an Albanian party.

In April 2017, after Xhaferi was finally elected, VMRO–DMPNE supporters stormed the Assembly and violently assaulted several opposition leaders, including Zaev and Radmila Šekerinska Jankovska, a former prime minister. In May, following mediation by the US State Department, the SDSM and their Albanian coalition partners were finally able to form a government, with Zaev as prime minister.

A2. Were the current national legislative representatives elected through free and fair elections? 2 / 4

Members of the 120-seat Assembly are elected by proportional representation to four-year terms. Parliamentary elections took place in 2016. An Organization for Security and Co-operation in Europe (OSCE) monitoring mission deemed the polls "competitive," but said issues with the media and voter rolls had "yet to be addressed in a sustainable manner," noted instances of voter intimidation, and concluded that the polls were marked by "a lack of public trust in institutions and the political establishment." The formation of the SDSM-led government in 2017 marked a democratic transfer of power between parties, and capped the period of political uncertainty that followed the 2016 polls.

A3. Are the electoral laws and framework fair, and are they implemented impartially by the relevant election management bodies? 3 / 4

Election laws are fairly robust, and the 2017 polls saw some minor improvements in the overall accessibility of election results and reporting by the State Election Commission. However, some ambiguities in election laws have yet to be addressed, including regulations governing the registration of candidates, and resolution mechanisms for election-related disputes. Additionally, observers have expressed concerns about inaccuracies in the electoral roll, which have not yet been adequately addressed.

In September 2018, the government held a controversial referendum to approve the Prespa Agreement signed with Greece in June to change the country's name to North Macedonia, which received the backing of more than 90 percent of voters. However, the turnout was only 37 percent, below the 50 percent required for the results to count. Leaders in the VMRO-DPMNE, including President Ivanov, had urged voters to boycott the vote, contributing to the low turnout. As a result, the parliament passed legislation in October to rename the country, potentially paving the way for EU and NATO accession. OSCE observers stated that the referendum "was administered impartially and fundamental freedoms were respected throughout the campaign." However, they noted that the content of the referendum was not adequately explained, and the election commission lacked transparency in carrying out the poll. Opposition parties also declined to organize a campaign against the referendum's passage, while the SDSM ran a robust campaign in its favor, making it difficult for the media to offer balanced coverage of the vote.

Analysts expressed concern about a social media disinformation campaign, which reportedly originated in Russia, urging Macedonians to boycott the vote.

B. POLITICAL PLURALISM AND PARTICIPATION: 10 / 16 (+1)

B1. Do the people have the right to organize in different political parties or other competitive political groupings of their choice, and is the system free of undue obstacles to the rise and fall of these competing parties or groupings? 3 / 4 (+1)

While the constitution protects the right to establish and join political parties, vast patronage networks hamper democratic competition. In 2017, the election of a SDSM-backed parliament speaker was immediately followed by violent attacks on the floor of the assembly by VMRO–DPMNE backers. Around 100 people were injured in the melee. Tensions between the parties decreased significantly in 2018, and there was no repeat of the previous year's violence in the Assembly, including during contentious constitutional reform debates.

Score Change: The score improved from 2 to 3 because there was no repetition of the previous year's partisan violence in the Assembly, and political forces were able to operate in a more peaceful environment.

B2. Is there a realistic opportunity for the opposition to increase its support or gain power through elections? 2 / 4

In 2017, power transferred from the right-nationalist VMRO–DPMNE—which had been in power since 2006—to the left-leaning SDSM, which had held power through much of the 1990s and early 2000s. The SDSM had boycotted the parliament on several occasions before taking power in 2017 over claims of electoral fraud, as well as issues related to allegations that the administration of former prime minister Gruevski had directed the secret service to operate a massive wiretapping and surveillance program.

B3. Are the people's political choices free from domination by the military, foreign powers, religious hierarchies, economic oligarchies, or any other powerful group that is not democratically accountable? 2 / 4

While voters are largely free to make political decisions, reports of intimidation and vote buying remain common. Patronage networks remain influential in Macedonia political life, and can influence political outcomes.

B4. Do various segments of the population (including ethnic, religious, gender, LGBT, and other relevant groups) have full political rights and electoral opportunities? 3 / 4

Ethnic Albanians make up about 25 percent of the population, and a political party representing Albanians has sat in each ruling coalition. Certain types of legislation must pass with a majority of legislators from both major ethnic groups in the Assembly. In March, the SDSM-led government passed a new language law extending the official use of Albanian to all state-level institutions, including the parliament. Macedonia's Roma community, however, remains politically marginalized.

Despite the introduction of parity laws, and joint initiatives on behalf of nongovernmental organizations (NGOs) and electoral authorities, societal attitudes discourage women from participating in politics. Some women are disenfranchised through the practice of family voting. Despite these challenges, the first female defense minister was appointed in 2017.

Small LGBT (lesbian, gay, bisexual, and transgender) advocacy groups are politically active, but LGBT people are poorly represented in politics—as reflected in Macedonia's lack of any law protecting against discrimination on grounds of sexual orientation or gender identity.

C. FUNCTIONING OF GOVERNMENT: 6 / 12

C1. Do the freely elected head of government and national legislative representatives determine the policies of the government? 2 / 4

For much of 2017, the parliament did not function effectively due to VMRO–DPMNE attempts to prevent the formation of an SDSM-led government, as well as the parliamentary melee in which Zoran Zaev and other SDSM lawmakers were injured. However, the formation of the new government in mid-2017 ushered in a return to more normal parliamentary activity, which continued in 2018.

The government dominates the legislative branch, and the parliament generally does not play an effective oversight role.

C2. Are safeguards against official corruption strong and effective? 2 / 4

Corruption remains a serious problem, and there has been widespread impunity for corrupt government officials, including members of parliament and the judiciary.

In May 2018, former prime minister Gruevski was sentenced to two years in prison following a corruption conviction stemming from the purchase of a $700,000 Mercedes in 2012. Gruevski fled to Hungary in November with the assistance of Hungarian diplomats, and claimed political asylum there, which was reportedly granted by the Hungarian government.

C3. Does the government operate with openness and transparency? 2 / 4

The law on open access to public information is inconsistently enforced. While the government has pledged to undertake reforms aimed at increasing government transparency, it has yet to register concrete progress.

CIVIL LIBERTIES: 37 / 60

D. FREEDOM OF EXPRESSION AND BELIEF: 11 / 16

D1. Are there free and independent media? 2 / 4

Macedonian journalists are subject to political pressure and harassment, and physical attacks continue to be reported, although the frequency of such attacks reportedly declined during the year. According to the Association of Journalists of Macedonia (AJM), 6 reporters were attacked between January and September 2018, down from 18 during the same period in 2017. In March, the Independent Trade Union of Journalists and Media Workers held a protest against Bekir Asani, a senior official in the DUI, who had allegedly threatened the head of the AJM, Naser Selmani, over a Facebook post by Selmani that criticized Asani's behavior during a traffic dispute.

Macedonia's media landscape is deeply polarized along political lines, and private media outlets are often tied to political or business interests that influence their content. Some critical and independent outlets operate and are found mainly online.

D2. Are individuals free to practice and express their religious faith or nonbelief in public and private? 3 / 4

The constitution guarantees freedom of religion. However, Islamophobia is present in the rhetoric of politicians and in public discourse, which is directed primarily at the ethnic Albanian community.

D3. Is there academic freedom, and is the educational system free from extensive political indoctrination? 3 / 4

Academic freedom is largely respected. However, corruption in universities is significant, and the large-scale emigration of young scholars has been detrimental to the country's research institutions. Many textbooks minimally cover the postindependence period, primarily because ethnic Macedonians and ethnic Albanians interpret the 2001 civil conflict differently.

D4. Are individuals free to express their personal views on political or other sensitive topics without fear of surveillance or retribution? 3 / 4

Allegations of widespread wiretapping and monitoring of private citizens, journalists, politicians, and religious leaders by the previous VMRO–DPMNE government helped bring about its ouster. The SDSM-led government has taken some steps to reform the security services, which were widely believed to have carried out the wiretapping and surveillance program under Gruevski's direction. In December 2018, the parliament passed a law that removed the secret police from overseeing surveillance, bringing it under greater civilian control. Analysts believe that this legislation will reduce potential abuse of surveillance powers. As a result of the change in government, private discussion has been less constrained.

E. ASSOCIATIONAL AND ORGANIZATIONAL RIGHTS: 8 / 12
E1. Is there freedom of assembly? 3 / 4

Constitutional guarantees of freedom of assembly are generally well respected. However, protests have sometimes given way to property damage, and are typically monitored by riot police. In June 2018, a protest in Skopje against the Prespa Agreement turned violent when the police fired tear gas and flash grenades into the crowd to disperse the demonstration.

E2. Is there freedom for nongovernmental organizations, particularly those that are engaged in human rights- and governance-related work? 3 / 4

The government has indicated support for civil society. However, groups that focus on human rights- and governance-related work, and particularly those that receive foreign funding, face pressure from the VMRO–DPMNE and its supporters. In 2017, several figures associated with the party announced the establishment of a movement aimed at scrutinizing NGOs funded by the Hungarian-born liberal philanthropist George Soros.

E3. Is there freedom for trade unions and similar professional or labor organizations? 2 / 4

Workers may organize and bargain collectively, though trade unions lack stable financing and skilled managers, and journalists have reportedly been fired for their union activities. The informal economy is large, leaving many workers vulnerable to abuses by employers.

F. RULE OF LAW: 8 / 16
F1. Is there an independent judiciary? 2 / 4

Concerns remain about the efficacy and independence of the judiciary. The EU has stressed judicial reforms as a key priority for the new government. In 2018, the government adopted a number of reforms aimed at enhancing judicial independence, including the strengthening of mechanisms to address misconduct by judges. However, analysts noted that not all of the judicial reforms promised by the government had been implemented at year's end.

F2. Does due process prevail in civil and criminal matters? 2 / 4

Due process rights remain compromised by corruption and patronage within the justice system, which has a low level of public confidence. In November 2018, authorities announced the commencement of a preliminary investigation into the wiretapping of 70 prosecutors in the Public Prosecution Office building, which began in 2016. Political interference in the work of prosecutors remains a problem, as well as the selective application of justice, although the government has carried out some reforms intended to improve the situation.

F3. Is there protection from the illegitimate use of physical force and freedom from war and insurgencies? 2 / 4

After the attack against SDSM lawmakers on the parliament floor in 2017, calm was later restored, and a number of police officers and interior ministry employees were disciplined for the slow response to the violence. In 2017, a VMRO–DPMNE supporter was sentenced to four years in prison for assaulting Šekerinska Jankovska, a former prime minister, during the melee.

There are occasional outbreaks of violence in Macedonia. In late 2017, a number of men were convicted of crimes connected to a deadly 2015 clash between police and gunmen in an Albanian neighborhood of Kumanovo. Considerable controversy surrounds the events; prosecutors said the men were terrorists bent on destabilizing the country, while the defendants and their supporters claimed that the men had acted in self-defense against a politically motivated police raid. In 2018, some critics continued to call for an international inquiry into the incident.

F4. Do laws, policies, and practices guarantee equal treatment of various segments of the population? 2 / 4

A 2010 antidiscrimination law does not prohibit discrimination on the basis of sexual orientation or gender identity, and anti-LGBT sentiment is widespread. Laws prohibit workplace sexual harassment, but sexual harassment against women is rarely reported, and remains a problem.

Albanians suffer from discrimination in employment and anti-Albanian sentiment has flared in recent years. Romany people face employment and other discrimination.

G. PERSONAL AUTONOMY AND INDIVIDUAL RIGHTS: 10 / 16

G1. Do individuals enjoy freedom of movement, including the ability to change their place of residence, employment, or education? 3 / 4

Travel and movement are generally unrestricted. Corruption can hamper people's ability to freely choose their place of employment or education.

G2. Are individuals able to exercise the right to own property and establish private businesses without undue interference from state or nonstate actors? 3 / 4

The right to own property and establish private businesses is generally respected, though corruption remains a barrier to free enterprise.

G3. Do individuals enjoy personal social freedoms, including choice of marriage partner and size of family, protection from domestic violence, and control over appearance? 2 / 4

Rape, including spousal rape, is illegal, as is domestic violence, which remains common; both are infrequently reported. The government and some NGOs provide services to victims of domestic violence.

A 2017 ruling by the Administrative Court allowed people to change their gender in the country's official registry.

G4. Do individuals enjoy equality of opportunity and freedom from economic exploitation? 2 / 4

Laws do not impose rigid barriers to social mobility, though rampant corruption can effectively hamper individuals from rising to higher income levels.

Human trafficking remains a problem. The government has taken some steps to better identify trafficking victims, notably at government-run transit centers that house migrants and refugees. However, government support to NGOs that aid trafficking victims has decreased.

Madagascar

Population: 26,300,000
Capital: Antananarivo
Political Rights Rating: 3
Civil Liberties Rating: 4
Freedom Rating: 3.5
Freedom Status: Partly Free
Electoral Democracy: Yes

Overview: An unelected administration governed Madagascar following a 2009 coup, but the country returned to electoral politics in 2013. Politics since have been unstable, and government corruption and a lack of accountability persist. Defamation and other laws restrict press freedom. Authorities frequently deny permits for demonstrations, and disperse many that take place. The government has struggled to manage lawlessness, particularly in the south. However, the courts have shown increasing independence, and in 2018 issued rulings that calmed an escalating political crisis.

KEY DEVELOPMENTS IN 2018:

- In April, the Malagasy legislature passed a new electoral law, parts of which opposition leaders said were unconstitutional and intended to make it difficult to challenge the incumbent in the upcoming presidential election. In a May decision that reflected its independence from the executive, the High Constitutional Court (HCC) struck down the sections in question.
- The electoral law controversy prompted mass demonstrations among opposition supporters, and two people were killed at one such protest in April when police fired on participants. The demonstrations continued after the HCC's decision to void the relevant parts of the law, with participants doubling down on calls for President Hery Rajaonarimampianina to resign.
- As the political crisis worsened, the HCC in late May ruled that the president must dissolve the government and appoint a consensus prime minister and unity government. In June, President Rajaonarimampianina appointed Christian Ntsay to serve as prime minister. The country's local representative of the International Labour Organisation (ILO), Ntsay was seen as a compromise candidate who could help resolve the crisis.

- The presidential election was held in two rounds in November and December. Provisional results showed that Andry Rajoelina had bested Marc Ravalomanana (both former presidents) in the runoff. While Ravalomanana alleged fraud, civil society and international observers assessed the polls as credible, and the HCC was expected to confirm the results in January 2019.

POLITICAL RIGHTS: 24 / 40
A. ELECTORAL PROCESS: 9 / 12
A1. Was the current head of government or other chief national authority elected through free and fair elections? 3 / 4

Madagascar is a semipresidential republic, with a president elected for a five-year term and a prime minister nominated by the National Assembly and appointed by the president. Rajaonarimampianina of the New Forces for Madagascar party (HVM) was elected president in 2013; neither Rajoelina nor Ravalomanana ran in the election under an internationally brokered agreement aimed at resolving an ongoing political crisis. In September 2018, Rajaonarimampianina resigned in order to stand in the next election. Rivo Rakotovao, president of the Senate, took over as acting president until the inauguration of the new elected president.

The first round of the 2018 election was held in November, and contested among 36 candidates. Rajoelina and Ravalomanana emerged as the top two candidates by a wide margin, though neither took more than the 50 percent necessary to avoid a runoff. The runoff took place in December, and provisional results released by the election commission at the end of the year showed that Rajoelina had bested Ravalomanana, with 55 percent of the vote. Ravalomanana alleged "massive fraud," and his supporters staged protests.

While a bitter rivalry between Rajoelina and Ravalomanana persists, campaigning in 2018 was relatively peaceful. Despite Ravalomanana's protests (and earlier allegations of fraud in the first round, by Rajaonarimampianina, who finished a distant third), civil society and international observers accepted the results of both election rounds. The High Constitutional Court (HCC) was expected to confirm the results in January 2019.

Christian Ntsay was appointed prime minister in June 2018, after the HCC ordered then president Rajaonarimampianina to dissolve his government and name a consensus prime minister in order to bring about a resolution to a worsening political crisis.

A2. Were the current national legislative representatives elected through free and fair elections? 3 / 4

The bicameral legislature consists of the 63-seat Senate, in which one-third of seats are appointed by the president; the remaining two-thirds are indirectly elected from an electoral college; senators serve five-year terms. Members of the 151-seat National Assembly are directly elected to five-year terms. The National Assembly elections, organized with the presidential election in 2013, were deemed competitive and credible by international observers, though irregularities with the voter rolls were noted. The With Andry Rajoelina (MAPAR) party won 49 of 151 National Assembly seats, and over 50 other parties and independent candidates took the remainder. The next elections are scheduled in 2019, as the term of office expires in February of that year.

The HVM won more than half the races in 2015 Senate elections. Though the electoral process was relatively free and fair, the opposition made accusations of fraud, and challenged the results. Ultimately, the HCC upheld the elections' results in early 2016.

A3. Are the electoral laws and framework fair, and are they implemented impartially by the relevant election management bodies? 3 / 4

The Independent National Electoral Commission (CENI) is subject to some influence by the executive, which controls member nomination and budget allocation processes. A new electoral code was adopted in April 2018, though provisions that would have prevented Rajoelina and Ravalomanana from running prompted mass demonstrations, and were ruled unconstitutional by the HCC in early May.

B. POLITICAL PLURALISM AND PARTICIPATION: 10 / 16

B1. Do the people have the right to organize in different political parties or other competitive political groupings of their choice, and is the system free of undue obstacles to the rise and fall of these competing parties or groupings? 3 / 4

Almost 200 registered political parties participated in recent elections. However, the political parties law is widely viewed as a flawed document that places undue burdens on individual candidates, effectively mandating a high cost for political candidacy. Political leaders frequently use religion, ethnicity, and caste as instruments to mobilize voters.

B2. Is there a realistic opportunity for the opposition to increase its support or gain power through elections? 3 / 4

Opposition parties have the opportunity to increase their support through elections, but most political parties lack the financial resources to engage in vibrant competition. The vast majority of candidates running in the 2018 presidential election were perceived as attempting to establish status, with the aim of winning cabinet or other positions in an administration headed by either Rajoelina or Ravalomanana.

The government habitually denies opposition parties permits to hold demonstrations, and opposition and independent political figures have experienced harassment in the form of frivolous legal cases.

B3. Are the people's political choices free from domination by the military, foreign powers, religious hierarchies, economic oligarchies, or any other powerful group that is not democratically accountable? 2 / 4

Economic networks compete for power through strategic support of political candidates. In turn, a narrow group of political elites maintain their status by supporting the interests of their private-sector patrons. As a result, lines between public and private expenditures are blurry, and democratic accountability is reduced.

The military also has some influence over politics. As the 2018 political crisis escalated in the spring, it threatened to intervene if leaders could not reach an agreement.

B4. Do various segments of the population (including ethnic, religious, gender, LGBT, and other relevant groups) have full political rights and electoral opportunities? 2 / 4

The constitution guarantees political and electoral rights for all citizens, but in practice, discrimination impedes the political representation of some groups. While there is a small, active LGBT community in the capital, LGBT people face social stigma that discourages political participation and open advocacy for LGBT rights. Cultural norms can restrict the political participation of women, who hold approximately 20 percent of Senate and National Assembly seats. Muslims are disproportionately affected by the nationality code, which can make it difficult for them to secure citizenship documents and thus voting rights. Ethnicity and caste are important political determinants, but generally do not affect political rights.

C. FUNCTIONING OF GOVERNMENT: 5 / 12

C1. Do the freely elected head of government and national legislative representatives determine the policies of the government? 2 / 4

Following a 2009 coup, the country returned to electoral politics in 2013. However, government instability since has been reflected in the frequent replacement of the prime minister, and frequent changes to the composition of the cabinet. In June 2018, in response to a HCC ruling intended to resolve an escalating political crisis, Rajaonarimampianina appointed Ntsay, the country's local representative of the ILO, to serve as prime minister. A consensus government was set up days later.

According to the constitution, the president determines policies, and Parliament writes laws and votes on them. However, in practice the National Assembly lacks the strength to act as an effective check on executive power. Additionally, economic elites have significant influence on the president and other elected officials.

C2. Are safeguards against official corruption strong and effective? 1 / 4

Corruption remains a serious problem in Madagascar, despite a series of recent reforms and anticorruption strategies aimed at addressing it. Investigations and prosecutions of corruption by the underfunded Independent Anticorruption Bureau (BIANCO) are infrequent, and rarely target high-level officials.

C3. Does the government operate with openness and transparency? 2 / 4

The constitution provides for the right to information, but no law defines a formal procedure for requesting government information. However, ministers and officials often hold press briefings, and laws, decrees, and high court decisions are posted on the internet.

There is little oversight of procurement processes. Asset declarations are required for most government officials, and while many complied with these laws, there are few practical consequences for those who refuse.

CIVIL LIBERTIES: 32 / 60
D. FREEDOM OF EXPRESSION AND BELIEF: 10 / 16
D1. Are there free and independent media? 2 / 4

The constitution provides for freedom of the press. However, this guarantee is undermined by criminal libel laws and other restrictions, as well as safety risks involved in the investigation of sensitive subjects such as cattle rustling and the illicit extraction and sale of natural resources. The government controls the issuance of broadcast licenses and can confiscate equipment or shut down stations if they are deemed to have violated the Communications Code.

In September 2018, the government banned the publication of the results of one pre-election poll. In October, a radio station was shut down in Morondava for allegedly issuing calls to revolt.

D2. Are individuals free to practice and express their religious faith or nonbelief in public and private? 2 / 4

Religious freedom is provided for in the constitution, though this right is upheld inconsistently. Religious leaders have noted that some workers were unable to practice their religion due to poor enforcement of labor laws. The government has restricted the Muslim community's access to education by threatening to close down Islamic schools. Several church facilities have been attacked by armed individuals, some apparently attempting robberies.

D3. Is there academic freedom, and is the educational system free from extensive political indoctrination? 3 / 4

Academic freedom is generally respected. However, a lack of resources and frequent strikes hamper normal operations of public universities.

D4. Are individuals free to express their personal views on political or other sensitive topics without fear of surveillance or retribution? 3 / 4

There were no official reports of the government monitoring online activity. However, a cybercrimes law prohibits online defamation, and has been used to prosecute social media users.

E. ASSOCIATIONAL AND ORGANIZATIONAL RIGHTS: 8 / 12

E1. Is there freedom of assembly? 2 / 4

The constitution guarantees freedom of assembly, but authorities routinely decline requests for protests and rallies in the name of public security. Political demonstrators risk violence from security forces. In April 2018, two people were killed and more than a dozen were injured when police fired upon a mass demonstration against proposed electoral laws that would have prevented Rajoelina and Ravalomanana from running in the year's presidential election. Days later, authorities announced that all political demonstrations were prohibited. Nevertheless, demonstrations took place later in the year, including among Ravalomanana's supporters, who disputed provisional results showing that Rajoelina had won the presidency.

E2. Is there freedom for nongovernmental organizations, particularly those that are engaged in human rights- and governance-related work? 3 / 4

Freedom of association is provided for in the constitution and is generally respected. A wide variety of nongovernmental organizations (NGOs) are active. Although no restrictions are placed on NGOs, the government is not always receptive to their opinions. Domestic human rights groups often lack the resources to operate independently. Groups focused on the environment or human rights face pressure from powerful interests.

E3. Is there freedom for trade unions and similar professional or labor organizations? 3 / 4

Workers have the right to join unions, engage in collective bargaining, and strike. However, more than 80 percent of workers are engaged in agriculture, fishing, and forestry at a subsistence level, and therefore have no access to unions.

F. RULE OF LAW: 7 / 16 (+1)

F1. Is there an independent judiciary? 2 / 4 (+1)

The executive influences judicial decisions through the reassignment of judges. Trial outcomes are frequently predetermined and the Malagasy people generally regard the judiciary as corrupt. Local tribunals in particular are seen as overburdened and corrupt.

However, in 2018, key HCC rulings reflected its independence from the executive. The court ruled in early May to strike down election laws that would have prevented key figures from competing against President Rajaonarimampianina in the year's presidential election. The court weeks later ruled that the president must dissolve the government and appoint a consensus prime minister and unity government that reflected the results of the 2013 election. The decision, meant to bring about a resolution to an escalating political crisis, was formally predicated on Rajaonarimampianina's failure to constitute a new court to adjudicate political disputes and allegations of high level misconduct.

Score Change: The score improved from 1 to 2 because the High Constitutional Court issued key rulings that reflected its independence from the executive.

F2. Does due process prevail in civil and criminal matters? 1 / 4

Due process rights are poorly upheld. A lack of training, resources, and personnel hampers the effectiveness of the criminal justice system. Case backlogs are lengthy, and, as of 2017, 55 percent of all prisoners were being detained before facing trial, according to an October 2018 report by the rights group Amnesty International. Many people held in pretrial detention do not have access to lawyers, and the successful assertion of due process rights is often tied to the ability of family and friends to intercede on behalf of the accused.

F3. Is there protection from the illegitimate use of physical force and freedom from war and insurgencies? 2 / 4

The police and military are unable to assert authority over the entire country, and areas in southern Madagascar are subjected to raids and violence by bandits and criminal groups. Security forces operate with little oversight or accountability for extrajudicial killings, particularly against cattle thieves, known as *dahalo*.

Detainees and prisoners suffer from harsh and sometimes life-threatening conditions due to overcrowding in detention facilities, and substandard hygiene and health care. People convicted of crimes can be sentenced to hard labor.

F4. Do laws, policies, and practices guarantee equal treatment of various segments of the population? 2 / 4

Legal provisions prohibit discrimination based on race, gender, disability, and social status, but these are upheld inconsistently. Traditional, cultural, social, and economic constraints can prevent women from having equal opportunities as men. Some ethnic groups face discrimination outside of their home regions. There are no legal protections against discrimination on the basis of sexual orientation or gender identity, and members of the LGBT (lesbian, gay, bisexual, and transgender) community face social stigma, particularly in rural areas, and experience employment discrimination and occasional acts of violence. Muslims have experienced employment and education discrimination.

G. PERSONAL AUTONOMY AND INDIVIDUAL RIGHTS: 7 / 16 (−1)

G1. Do individuals enjoy freedom of movement, including the ability to change their place of residence, employment, or education? 2 / 4 (−1)

Citizens are generally allowed to move freely within Madagascar, and may travel internationally. However, authorities have struggled to address bandit attacks in the south and even in the west, and travel in affected areas is dangerous.

Score Change: The score declined from 3 to 2 because authorities have struggled to address activity by bandits that has made travel dangerous in the south and parts of the west.

G2. Are individuals able to exercise the right to own property and establish private businesses without undue interference from state or nonstate actors? 2 / 4

Madagascar's legal structure provides protections for private property rights, though enforcement of these protections is inconsistent, in part because the vast majority of farmers do not hold the official rights to their land. There is a history of competition between the state-recognized property rights system and customary land use practices, as well as attempts by the state to permit mining, commercial agriculture, and other economic pursuits on land where ownership is disputed.

In recent years, Madagascar has made it easier to start a business by reducing the number of procedures to register a business, and simplifying the payment of registration fees.

G3. Do individuals enjoy personal social freedoms, including choice of marriage partner and size of family, protection from domestic violence, and control over appearance? 2 / 4

Women and children have limited social freedoms in Madagascar, especially in rural areas. Forced child marriage and domestic abuse are common. Although sexual harassment is illegal, the law is not enforced and harassment is common. Abortion is illegal in Madagascar. No law prohibits same-sex sexual relations.

G4. Do individuals enjoy equality of opportunity and freedom from economic exploitation? 1 / 4

Most people work in subsistence agriculture, making advancement in the local economy extremely challenging.

Government officials have been implicated in colluding with human trafficking offenders, and no effort has been made to investigate the allegations.

Malawi

Population: 19,100,000
Capital: Lilongwe
Political Rights Rating: 3
Civil Liberties Rating: 3
Freedom Rating: 3.0
Freedom Status: Partly Free
Electoral Democracy: Yes

Overview: Malawi holds regular elections and has undergone multiple transfers of power between political parties, though the changes were frequently a result of rifts among ruling elites rather than competition between distinct parties. Political rights and civil liberties are for the most part respected by the state. However, corruption is endemic, police brutality and arbitrary arrests are common, and discrimination and violence toward women, minority groups, and people with albinism remain problems.

KEY DEVELOPMENTS IN 2018:

- At year's end, the Access to Information Act, which was signed into law in 2017, had still not been implemented.
- The Political Parties Act, which bans politicians from using cash handouts and other incentives to garner votes, came into force in December.
- Former agriculture minister George Chaponda, who allegedly facilitated maize purchases from Zambia in 2016 at an inflated price, in a corruption scandal known as Maizegate, was acquitted on graft charges related to the purchases in May.
- In December, a court issued an injunction that prevented the parliament from debating the draconian NGO Act Amendment Bill, pending a judicial review of the legislation.

POLITICAL RIGHTS: 26 / 40

A. ELECTORAL PROCESS: 8 / 12

A1. Was the current head of government or other chief national authority elected through free and fair elections? 3 / 4

In Malawi, the president is directly elected for five-year terms and exercises considerable executive authority. Malawi's last general election was held in 2014. The polls were marred by logistical problems and postelection controversy surrounding allegations of vote rigging made by incumbent president Joyce Banda, but were largely regarded as credible by local and international observers. Peter Mutharika of the Democratic Progressive Party (DPP) was declared the winner, with 36 percent of the vote. Lazarus Chakwera of the Malawi Congress Party (MCP) placed second, with 28 percent.

A2. Were the current national legislative representatives elected through free and fair elections? 3 / 4

The unicameral National Assembly is comprised of 193 members elected by popular vote to five-year terms. The last legislative elections, held concurrently with the presidential election in 2014, were generally regarded as credible, despite a number of irregularities and logistical problems. In the parliamentary elections, the DPP won the most seats with 50.

A3. Are the electoral laws and framework fair, and are they implemented impartially by the relevant election management bodies? 2 / 4

Although it lacks resources and is often unprepared to carry out elections, the Malawi Electoral Commission (MEC) is generally viewed as impartial. Two biometric voter registration kits went missing in August 2018, which led to further questions about the MEC's competence. Civil society groups and opposition parties demanded an independent investigation into the loss of the equipment, but authorities had not complied with these demands at year's end.

International analysts have called for requiring political parties to disclose their sources of financing and to report on campaign spending.

B. POLITICAL PLURALISM AND PARTICIPATION: 12 / 16

B1. Do the people have the right to organize in different political parties or other competitive political groupings of their choice, and is the system free of undue obstacles to the rise and fall of these competing parties or groupings? 3 / 4

Malawi has four main political parties—the DPP, the MCP, the People's Party (PP), and the United Democratic Front (UDF)—all of which have held power at some point. The parties are loosely formed, with politicians frequently moving between parties or breaking away to form their own parties.

For the most part, people can organize in political parties without undue burden. However, the government has frequently held up the registration of new parties that present a threat to the incumbent. In July 2018, Vice President Saulos Chilima left the ruling DPP to form his own party, the United Transformation Movement (UTM). The party's registration was rejected on a technicality related to the party's name. In November, the High Court in Blantyre ruled that the party should be registered within seven days. The attorney general appealed the decision to the Supreme Court of Appeal, which upheld the ruling, and the UTM was subsequently registered.

B2. Is there a realistic opportunity for the opposition to increase its support or gain power through elections? 3 / 4

Political parties are generally able to campaign freely throughout the country. Opposition parties have demonstrated their ability to grow their support and gain power through elections. However, an opposition party has never defeated an elected incumbent party since the transition to democracy in 1994. Although President Mutharika defeated Joyce Banda of the PP in 2014, Banda only came to power in 2012 after the death of Mutharika's older brother, former president Bingu wa Muthariku, who was also a member of the DPP.

The playing field during election campaigns is often skewed toward the governing party. During the year, opposition parties accused the state-owned broadcaster, the Malawi Broadcasting Corporation (MBC), of bias toward the DPP in its coverage of the upcoming 2019 general elections. As a result, opposition parties have sought exposure from private broadcasters.

Opposition parties sometimes face violence and intimidation. In April 2018, DPP youths reportedly attacked MCP supporters during the campaign for a parliamentary by-election in Mulanje.

B3. Are the people's political choices free from domination by the military, foreign powers, religious hierarchies, economic oligarchies, or any other powerful group that is not democratically accountable? 3 / 4

Local traditional leaders can have an influence on voters' choices, especially in smaller villages. Some chiefs have publically endorsed the incumbent, which is likely to sway the opinion of their constituents. In December 2018, the government implemented a 100 percent increase in the financial honoraria chiefs receive for service to their communities. Some opposition leaders suggested that the move was intended to solidify chiefs' support for the DPP ahead of the 2019 polls.

To address vote buying, which has been frequently employed by political parties in past elections, in 2017 the parliament passed the Political Parties Act, which came into force in December 2018. The law bans politicians from using cash handouts and other incentives to garner votes.

B4. Do various segments of the population (including ethnic, religious, gender, LGBT, and other relevant groups) have full political rights and electoral opportunities? 3 / 4

All ethnic, religious, and gender groups have full political rights. However, women remain underrepresented in politics, and according to Afrobarometer, are less likely than men to become politically involved. In May 2018, the MEC announced that women would pay 25 percent less than men to register as a parliamentary candidate in the 2019 elections, in an effort to encourage more female candidates. While more women ran as candidates in the 2014 elections, only 32 were elected to the 193-seat National Assembly.

Political parties often appeal to ethnic, regional, and religious groups. The LGBT (lesbian, gay, bisexual, and transgender) community faces societal discrimination, and political parties do not advocate for LGBT rights in their platforms. In 2018, six people with albinism declared their intention to run for the parliament or local races in the 2019 elections, in an effort to advocate for their rights and highlight ongoing discrimination against the marginalized group.

C. FUNCTIONING OF GOVERNMENT: 6 / 12

C1. Do the freely elected head of government and national legislative representatives determine the policies of the government? 3 / 4

Executive and legislative representatives are generally able to determine the policies of government unhindered. However, patronage and clientelism are common, and wealthy business leaders often have great influence over policymaking, forging relationships with elected officials and extracting policy outcomes favorable to their business interests.

C2. Are safeguards against official corruption strong and effective? 1 / 4

Corruption is endemic in Malawi. Civil society leaders have accused the Anti-Corruption Bureau (ACB), which is responsible for investigating corruption, of being ineffective and compromised. A number of major corruption scandals have shaken Malawi in recent years, and high-level officials have generally acted with impunity. Former agriculture minister George Chaponda, who allegedly facilitated maize purchases from Zambia in 2016 at an inflated price, in a corruption scandal known as Maizegate, was acquitted on graft charges related to the purchases in May 2018.

A report by the ACB which was leaked in June contained allegations that President Mutharika received a kickback in 2016 from a $4 million contract with a firm to provide food to the police force. Mutharika vehemently denied the claims, while civil society leaders called for the president's resignation.

C3. Does the government operate with openness and transparency? 2 / 4

Malawi lacks budgetary transparency; the government still fails to make year-end budget audit reports available to the public.

At year's end, the Access to Information Act, which was signed into law in 2017, had still not come into effect. Civil society groups sharply criticized the government for its failure to implement the law.

Laws require high-level public officials to declare their assets and other financial interests while in public service. Mutharika declared his assets in 2015, but many legislators and other officials fail to do so. President Mutharika took no action against cabinet minister Grace Chiumia, who reportedly failed to declare her assets in 2017, despite an October 2018 letter from the director of public officers' declarations recommending that she be removed from office.

CIVIL LIBERTIES: 38 / 60 (+1)
D. FREEDOM OF EXPRESSION AND BELIEF: 14 / 16 (+1)
D1. Are there free and independent media? 3 / 4

Freedom of the press is legally guaranteed and generally respected in practice. However, news outlets have experienced intimidation. In June 2018, authorities shut down the headquarters of the Times Group media conglomerate, whose outlets have criticized the government. The government claimed that the closure was over a tax dispute, but the Times asserted that the shutdown, which lasted for several days, was due to its critical reporting.

Also in June, police officers assaulted two radio journalists with the Zodiak Broadcasting Station (ZBS), who were covering a police crackdown on street vendors in Mzuzu. A vaguely worded cybersecurity law passed in 2016 criminalizes the posting of "offensive" content online, which could place journalists at risk of prosecution. A law against insulting the leader of Malawi remains on the books, although it is rarely enforced.

D2. Are individuals free to practice and express their religious faith or nonbelief in public and private? 4 / 4

The constitution upholds freedom of religion, and this right is respected in practice.

D3. Is there academic freedom, and is the educational system free from extensive political indoctrination? 4 / 4 (+1)

Malawi's education system is largely free from political indoctrination. In recent years, there have been no significant constraints on academic freedom, and students and professors have been free to carry out research and political activities without interference.

Score Change: The score improved from 3 to 4 because there were no reported infringements on academic freedom in recent years, and professors and students are generally able to conduct research and campus advocacy without interference.

D4. Are individuals free to express their personal views on political or other sensitive topics without fear of surveillance or retribution? 3 / 4

Citizens are largely free to express their personal views on political and sensitive topics without fear of surveillance or retribution. However, many Malawians do not feel comfortable criticizing the government and engage in self-censorship.

Civil society leaders suspect that the government surveils private electronic communications. The Malawi Communications Regulatory Authority (MACRA) implemented the Consolidated ICT Regulatory Management System (CIRMS), also known as the "spy machine," in 2017. Although the government claims the system is for quality control, critics fear that it is used to monitor phone calls and text messages.

E. ASSOCIATIONAL AND ORGANIZATIONAL RIGHTS: 8 / 12

E1. Is there freedom of assembly? 3 / 4

Freedom of assembly is guaranteed in the constitution, but the government has sometimes limited this right. Two nationwide anticorruption protests, in April and September 2018, occurred without interference from security forces. However, in June, police used teargas and live ammunition to disperse the crowd at a meeting of MCP supporters in Blantyre.

E2. Is there freedom for nongovernmental organizations, particularly those that are engaged in human rights- and governance-related work? 2 / 4

Nongovernmental organizations (NGOs) have generally operated without interference from the government. However, the NGO Act Amendment Bill introduced in 2017 led to an outcry among civil society leaders for potentially placing serious restrictions on their activities. If the bill passes, an NGO board would approve NGOs' applications for funding from donors and require that the applications align with the policies of the government. NGOs would also be required to register with the NGO board, which would have the power to deregister them. In December 2018, a court issued an injunction that prevented the parliament from debating the bill, pending a judicial review of the legislation.

In January, the government increased annual fees for most local NGOs from approximately $68 to $340. An April ruling by the High Court in Blantyre halted the new fees, but the NGO Board reportedly defied the court order and continued to collect the higher fees throughout the year.

E3. Is there freedom for trade unions and similar professional or labor organizations? 3 / 4

The rights to organize labor unions and to strike are legally protected, but workers in essential services have limitations on their right to strike. Unions are active and collective bargaining is practiced, but retaliations against unions that are unregistered and strikers are not illegal.

F. RULE OF LAW: 9 / 16

F1. Is there an independent judiciary? 3 / 4

Judicial independence is generally respected. However, the appointments process for judges lacks transparency and undermines the legitimacy of the judiciary.

Although the judiciary asserted its independence with some rulings in 2018, including the decision that halted debate on the controversial NGO bill, the acquittal of Chaponda in the Maizegate case by the Zomba Magistrate Court, despite arguments from civil society leaders that there was ample evidence against him, raised concerns about the effects of political pressure on judicial decisions.

F2. Does due process prevail in civil and criminal matters? 2 / 4

Arbitrary arrests and detentions are common in Malawi. Defendants are legally entitled to legal representation, but in practice, they are frequently forced to represent themselves in court. Although the law requires that suspects be released or charged with a crime within 48 hours of arrest, these rights were often denied.

F3. Is there protection from the illegitimate use of physical force and freedom from war and insurgencies? 2 / 4

Police brutality and extrajudicial killings are not uncommon in Malawi. The police are poorly trained and often ineffective. As a result, vigilantism has increased in recent years.

Prison conditions are dire, characterized by overcrowding and extremely poor health conditions; many inmates die from AIDS and other diseases.

F4. Do laws, policies, and practices guarantee equal treatment of various segments of the population? 2 / 4

The constitution explicitly guarantees the rights of all humans. However, consensual sexual activity between same-sex couples remains illegal and punishable by up to 14 years in prison. LGBT persons are subject to arbitrary arrests and detainment from police in Malawi, and are sometimes physically assaulted while in detention.

Despite constitutional guarantees of equal protection, customary practices perpetuate discrimination against women in education, employment, business, and inheritance and property rights. Persons with albinism experience discrimination and have been attacked, abducted, killed, and mutilated.

G. PERSONAL AUTONOMY AND INDIVIDUAL RIGHTS: 7 / 16

G1. Do individuals enjoy freedom of movement, including the ability to change their place of residence, employment, or education? 2 / 4

The constitution establishes freedom of internal movement and foreign travel, which are generally respected in practice. However, government policy confines refugees to two camps, and the police frequently round up those found outside of the camps and return them.

G2. Are individuals able to exercise the right to own property and establish private businesses without undue interference from state or nonstate actors? 2 / 4

Property rights are inadequately protected in Malawi. Most land is held under customary land tenure and the process of creating titles that would allow legal ownership of land have moved slowly. Starting a business can be a cumbersome process, a problem worsened by corruption in several key government agencies.

G3. Do individuals enjoy personal social freedoms, including choice of marriage partner and size of family, protection from domestic violence, and control over appearance? 1 / 4

Domestic violence is common in Malawi, but victims rarely come forward and the police generally do not intervene in domestic violence cases. Child sexual abuse is prevalent. Around half of all girls are married before the age of 18, in violation of the law.

G4. Do individuals enjoy equality of opportunity and freedom from economic exploitation? 2 / 4

Revenues from large, state-run industries tend to benefit the political elite. Income inequality remains a problem and inhibits economic mobility.

The enforcement of labor laws is weak, and employees are often paid extremely low wages, despite minimum wage laws. Child labor is a persistent issue, particularly on tobacco estates.

Malaysia

Population: 32,500,000
Capital: Kuala Lumpur
Political Rights Rating: 4
Civil Liberties Rating: 4
Freedom Rating: 4.0
Freedom Status: Partly Free
Electoral Democracy: No

Overview: The same political coalition ruled Malaysia from independence in 1957 until 2018, maintaining power by manipulating electoral districts, appealing to ethnic nationalism, and suppressing criticism through restrictive speech laws and politicized prosecutions of opposition leaders. The coalition lost to an opposition alliance in the May 2018 general elections, and the new government began to deliver on its promises of reform, though the momentum for legislative changes appeared to ebb by year's end.

KEY DEVELOPMENTS IN 2018:

- The opposition Pakatan Harapan (PH) coalition defeated the governing Barisan Nasional (BN) coalition in May general elections, bringing an end to more than six decades of rule by the United Malays National Organisation (UMNO) and its allies. The new government was led by 93-year-old Mahathir Mohamad, who had served as prime minister from 1981 to 2003 but broke with UMNO and the BN in 2016 over a corruption scandal focused on incumbent prime minister Najib Razak.
- After losing office, Najib was arrested in July and subsequently charged with dozens of financial crimes, most of which were related to the misuse or embezzlement of billions of dollars from the state investment fund known as 1MDB. Najib's wife was arrested as part of the sprawling investigation in October, as was his former deputy prime minister.
- Veteran opposition leader Anwar Ibrahim, who had been jailed since 2015 on politically motivated sodomy charges, was pardoned and released in May after the change in government. He returned to Parliament by winning a by-election in October and was expected to eventually succeed Mahathir as prime minister.
- The PH government took some steps to fulfill its pledges of reform during the year. In August, the lower house of Parliament voted to repeal a repressive "fake news" law that had been adopted shortly before the elections, but the Senate blocked the repeal bill in September. Among other actions, the government secured the adoption of changes to a restrictive law on universities and placed a moratorium on executions in October, though it failed to abolish the death penalty or repeal the colonial-era Sedition Act by the end of the year.
- In November, the government backtracked on earlier promises to ratify the International Convention on the Elimination of All Forms of Racial Discrimination (ICERD). Opponents of the convention, who organized a large rally against it in December, argued that it would endanger constitutional and other privileges reserved for the country's ethnic Malay and Muslim majority.

POLITICAL RIGHTS: 21 / 40 (+3)

A. ELECTORAL PROCESS: 6 / 12

A1. Was the current head of government or other chief national authority elected through free and fair elections? 2 / 4

The prime minister is the head of government and chief executive. Though formally appointed by the monarch, the prime minister and cabinet must have the support of a majority in the lower house of Parliament. Najib Razak of UMNO, who had served as prime minister since the resignation of his predecessor in 2009, was replaced by Mahathir Mohamad of the Malaysian United Indigenous Party (PPBM)—part of the PH coalition—as a result of the May 2018 parliamentary elections.

The monarch, known as the Yang di-Pertuan Agong, is elected for five-year terms by and from among the hereditary rulers of 9 of Malaysia's 13 states. Sultan Muhammad V of Kelantan took office as the country's head of state in 2016. The role of the monarch is largely ceremonial.

A2. Were the current national legislative representatives elected through free and fair elections? 2 / 4

The upper house of the bicameral Parliament, the Senate or Dewan Negara, consists of 44 members appointed by the monarch on the advice of the prime minister and 26 members elected by the 13 state legislatures, serving three-year terms. The Senate has limited power to amend or block legislation passed by the lower house. The House of Representatives, or Dewan Rakyat, has 222 seats filled through direct elections in single-member constituencies.

In the May 2018 elections, the PH won 113 seats in the House of Representatives, followed by the BN with 79, the Malaysian Islamic Party (PAS) with 18, the Sabah Heritage Party (Warisan) with 8, the Homeland Solidarity Party with 1, and independents with 3. The PH victory came despite lopsided electoral conditions that gave the BN significant advantages, such as gerrymandered and seriously malapportioned voting districts, weak regulation of campaign spending, and legal constraints on media independence and expressions of dissent.

A3. Are the electoral laws and framework fair, and are they implemented impartially by the relevant election management bodies? 2 / 4

The Election Commission (EC), which administers elections and is responsible for voter rolls and the delineation of electoral boundaries, was considered subservient to the government under the BN. A new EC chairman was appointed in September 2018, and he pledged to reexamine the voter registry and electoral maps put in place by the previous commission, which were suspected of facilitating fraud and disenfranchisement.

B. POLITICAL PLURALISM AND PARTICIPATION: 9 / 16 (+2)

B1. Do the people have the right to organize in different political parties or other competitive political groupings of their choice, and is the system free of undue obstacles to the rise and fall of these competing parties or groupings? 2 / 4

The party system in Malaysia is diverse and competitive, but groups that challenged BN rule often faced obstacles such as unequal access to the media, restrictions on campaigning and freedom of assembly, and politicized prosecutions. The Registrar of Societies (ROS) oversees the registration of political parties and has been known to issue politicized decisions. In April 2018, shortly before the general elections, the ROS temporarily suspended the PPBM for allegedly failing to submit requested documents.

B2. Is there a realistic opportunity for the opposition to increase its support or gain power through elections? 3 / 4 (+1)

Although opposition parties had long governed in a number of Malaysia's states, the 2018 elections produced the country's first democratic transfer of power between rival political groups at the federal level since independence in 1957.

Shortly after the elections, Anwar Ibrahim, leader of the People's Justice Party (PKR)—part of the PH coalition—received a royal pardon. Anwar, a key opposition figure under BN rule, had been imprisoned since 2015 based on a politically motivated sodomy conviction. He won a seat in Parliament in an October 2018 by-election made possible by the resignation of another PKR member. Mahathir pledged to eventually step down and allow Anwar to succeed him as prime minister, though suspicions that he would not fulfill this promise were reportedly causing tensions within the PH at year's end, as Mahathir's PPBM courted defectors from UMNO to strengthen its political position.

The PH's election manifesto called for the leader of the opposition in Parliament to be given the status of a federal minister, but the new government backed away from that commitment.

Score Change: The score improved from 2 to 3 due to the Pakatan Harapan coalition's electoral victory in May, which demonstrated the ability of the opposition to win power at both the state and federal levels.

B3. Are the people's political choices free from domination by the military, foreign powers, religious hierarchies, economic oligarchies, or any other powerful group that is not democratically accountable? 2 / 4

The military is not active in politics, and foreign powers do not directly meddle in domestic political affairs, though the BN's increasingly close ties with China were a prominent issue in the 2018 election campaign.

During its decades in power, the BN built strong connections with Malaysia's business elites and used these relationships to influence electoral outcomes, including through favorable coverage by mainstream private media and greater access to financial resources. The BN administration was also suspected of using government-linked companies and investment vehicles for political purposes, and the PH government had yet to undertake a comprehensive reform of these entities at year's end.

B4. Do various segments of the population (including ethnic, religious, gender, LGBT, and other relevant groups) have full political rights and electoral opportunities? 2 / 4 (+1)

Suffrage in Malaysia is universal for adult citizens. However, social and legal restrictions limit political participation among some minority groups—including LGBT (lesbian, gay, bisexual, and transgender) people. Women's interests remain generally underrepresented in politics. In a positive change, the new government formed in 2018 included more women and minority representatives in more powerful positions, and it began consideration of increased autonomy for the East Malaysian states of Sabah and Sarawak, which are located on the island of Borneo and are home to distinct ethnic groups. A special cabinet committee focused on the autonomy issue held its first meeting in December.

UMNO and the PAS remained influential in opposition as defenders of long-standing policies that favor the ethnic Malay and Muslim majority. In November, the PH government backtracked on an earlier pledge to ratify the ICERD, and opponents of the convention held a large demonstration in December.

Score Change: The score improved from 1 to 2 because the new federal government represented a more diverse coalition of ethnic and religious interests than its predecessor.

C. FUNCTIONING OF GOVERNMENT: 6 / 12 (+1)

C1. Do the freely elected head of government and national legislative representatives determine the policies of the government? 2 / 4

While elected officials determine and implement government policy, the unfair electoral framework has historically weakened their legitimacy. Decision-making power has typically been concentrated in the hands of the prime minister and his close advisers, though the PH government showed some signs of broader consultation in 2018, and the budget for the prime minister's office was slashed by more than half.

C2. Are safeguards against official corruption strong and effective? 2 / 4 (+1)

High-level corruption was a critical weakness of the BN government, and Najib's efforts to avoid accountability for the 1MDB scandal had crippled the country's anticorruption mechanisms more generally. The Malaysian Anti-Corruption Commission (MACC) and other law enforcement institutions grew more active after the change in government, unleashing a raft of investigations against the former leadership. Najib himself was arrested in July, eventually facing dozens of counts of money laundering and other charges, most of them linked to 1MDB. His wife, Rosmah Mansor, was arrested in October and charged with money laundering and bribery, and his successor as UMNO leader, former deputy prime minister Ahmad Zahid Hamidi, was arrested the same month. Other former officials were also charged during the year.

Score Change: The score improved from 1 to 2 because anticorruption authorities under the new government were allowed to pursue charges against former officials, including the former prime minister, who had previously avoided accountability for alleged abuses.

C3. Does the government operate with openness and transparency? 2 / 4

The BN government had a poor record on transparency, and a lack of independent oversight regarding state-affiliated companies and investment funds has long created conditions conducive to corruption. The PH government pledged to operate with greater openness, but its initial performance was uneven. At the end of 2018 it had yet to make public the findings of the Institutional Reforms Committee, which was formed after the elections and produced more than 200 recommendations meant to improve government integrity and prevent corruption. The government was also still reviewing a possible freedom of information act and amendments to existing laws, such as the Official Secrets Act, that deter whistle-blowers and journalists from exposing information in the public interest.

CIVIL LIBERTIES: 31 / 60 (+4)

D. FREEDOM OF EXPRESSION AND BELIEF: 9 / 16 (+2)

D1. Are there free and independent media? 3 / 4 (+1)

Freedom of expression is constitutionally guaranteed but was limited in practice under the BN government. Prior to the 2018 elections, most private news publications and television stations were controlled by political parties or businesses allied with the BN, and state news outlets similarly reflected government views. The market began to change after the PH took power, with some BN-linked outlets suffering financially and others producing more neutral coverage, even as independent outlets benefited from a reduction in political pressure and harassment.

The PH government pledged to reform restrictive media laws, but its progress during the year was limited. The House of Representatives voted in August to repeal the Anti–Fake News Act, which the BN had hastily adopted in April, but the Senate—still controlled by the BN—blocked the repeal in September. The original law, which remained in place at year's end, prescribes large fines and up to six years in prison for the publication of wholly or partly false news. The PH also failed to act on its promise to repeal the Sedition Act, though it did oversee a change in enforcement, with authorities dropping cases against prominent critics of the former government, including a well-known political cartoonist.

The Malaysian Communication and Multimedia Commission (MCMC) monitors websites and can order the removal of material considered provocative or subversive. A 2012 amendment to the 1950 Evidence Act holds owners and editors of websites, providers of web-hosting services, and owners of computers or mobile devices accountable for information published through their services or property. While there were no major reforms to the legal framework for online media in 2018, the MCMC did end its blocking of a number of websites in May, including *Sarawak Report* and the blogging platform Medium.

Score Change: The score improved from 2 to 3 because mainstream media outlets generally became more politically neutral in their coverage following the change in government, authorities dropped sedition charges against some critics, and certain news sites were unblocked by regulators.

D2. Are individuals free to practice and express their religious faith or nonbelief in public and private? 1 / 4

While Malaysia is religiously diverse, legal provisions restrict religious freedom. Ethnic Malays are constitutionally defined as Muslim and are not entitled to renounce their faith. Practicing a version of Islam other than Sunni Islam is prohibited, and Shiites and other sects face discrimination. Some 50 people were arrested in Kelantan in August 2018 for allegedly practicing Shia Islam. Muslim children and civil servants are required to receive religious education using government-approved curriculums and instructors. The powerful Malaysian Islamic Development Department (JAKIM) played a central role in shaping and enforcing the practice of Islam in Malaysia under the BN government; the PH government began exploring reforms of the department during 2018.

Non-Muslims are not able to build houses of worship as easily as Muslims, and the state retains the right to demolish unregistered religious statues and houses of worship. In November 2018, a dispute over the relocation of a Hindu temple triggered rioting, with assailants allegedly linked to a property developer storming the temple and beating worshippers.

D3. Is there academic freedom, and is the educational system free from extensive political indoctrination? 2 / 4

There is some degree of academic freedom in Malaysia. Under the BN government, instructors and students who espoused antigovernment views or engaged in political activity were subject to disciplinary action under the Universities and University Colleges Act (UUCA) of 1971. Under the new government, in December 2018, Parliament amended the UUCA to allow students to engage in political activity on campus. In August, the government abolished two youth-oriented BN projects, the National Service Training Programme and the National Civics Bureau, that had been criticized for indoctrinating participants and wasting public funds. The government continues to control appointments of top officials at public universities; in 2018 the PH education minister replaced several university chairmen who had been installed by the BN.

D4. Are individuals free to express their personal views on political or other sensitive topics without fear of surveillance or retribution? 3 / 4 (+1)

The Sedition Act and other restrictive laws have been used to deter and punish individual expression on sensitive political and religious topics, including on social media. Under the PH in 2018, the authorities dropped sedition cases against prominent public figures who had criticized the BN government, and the Sedition Act was temporarily suspended in October as lawmakers prepared to amend or repeal it. The suspension was lifted in late November in response to the violence surrounding the Hindu temple dispute, and some new cases were opened during the year over alleged hate speech as well as defamation of senior officials. An UMNO-affiliated blogger was arrested in November for a Facebook post in which he attacked ethnic Indians. Nevertheless, the government's statements and initiatives during the year generally created a more open environment for public discussion of issues that had previously been considered off limits.

Score Change: The score improved from 2 to 3 because the new government's pledges to abolish the Sedition Act and other restrictions on expression, though still largely unfulfilled, encouraged more open discussion of previously sensitive political issues, including abuses of power under the previous government.

E. ASSOCIATIONAL AND ORGANIZATIONAL RIGHTS: 6 / 12

E1. Is there freedom of assembly? 2 / 4

Freedom of assembly can be limited on the grounds of maintaining security and public order. The law delineates 21 public places where assemblies cannot be held—including within 50 meters of houses of worship, schools, and hospitals—and prohibits persons under the age of 15 from attending any public assembly. Those who proceed with a banned protest are subject to penalties including high fines. Despite the legal restrictions, demonstrations are often held in practice. Police continued to enforce existing laws under the PH government, arresting and charging unauthorized protesters on multiple occasions during 2018, though authorities approved the large opposition-led protest against ratification of ICERD in December.

E2. Is there freedom for nongovernmental organizations, particularly those that are engaged in human rights- and governance-related work? 2 / 4

During the BN era, many nongovernmental organizations (NGOs) worked with opposition parties to campaign for electoral, anticorruption, and other reforms, and a wide array of civil society groups continue to operate in Malaysia. However, NGOs must be approved and registered by the government, which has refused or revoked registrations for political reasons in the past. Some international human rights organizations have been forbidden from forming local branches. Individual activists remained subject to police harassment and criminal charges after the 2018 change in government, and certain NGOs were affected by the authorities' efforts to freeze assets that could be linked to the 1MDB scandal.

E3. Is there freedom for trade unions and similar professional or labor organizations? 2 / 4

Most Malaysian workers can join trade unions, but the law contravenes international guidelines by restricting unions to representing workers in a single or similar trade. The director general of trade unions can refuse or withdraw registration arbitrarily. Collective-bargaining rights are limited, particularly in designated high-priority industries, as is the right to strike.

F. RULE OF LAW: 7 / 16 (+2)

F1. Is there an independent judiciary? 2 / 4 (+1)

Under the BN government, judicial independence was compromised by extensive executive influence. Arbitrary or politically motivated verdicts were common, as seen in the convictions of Anwar Ibrahim in 1999, 2000, and 2014 on charges of corruption and sodomy. In June 2018, Chief Justice Raus Sharif and Court of Appeal president Zulkefli Ahmad Makinudin resigned. Both had been controversially appointed in 2017 despite being over the mandatory retirement age and were seen as loyal to the BN administration. A new chief justice, Richard Malanjum, took office in July; he was considered more independent and was the first person from East Malaysia to serve in the post. Among other, similar personnel changes, Zaharah Ibrahim became the second woman to serve as chief judge of Malaya, the country's third-highest judicial office.

Score Change: The score improved from 1 to 2 due to the replacement of senior judicial officials who were seen as politically biased and dependent on the former government.

F2. Does due process prevail in civil and criminal matters? 2 / 4

A number of existing laws undermine due process guarantees, and they remained in place throughout 2018 despite PH plans to review them. The 2012 Security Offences (Special Measures) Act allows police to detain anyone for up to 28 days without judicial review for broadly defined "security offenses," and suspects may be held for 48 hours before being granted access to a lawyer. It was renewed for another five years in 2017. Also that year, lawmakers amended the Prevention of Crime Act—a law ostensibly aimed at combating organized crime—to revoke detainees' right to address the government-appointed Prevention of Crime Board, which is empowered to order the detention of individuals listed by the Home Ministry for renewable two-year terms without trial or legal representation. The 2015 Prevention of Terrorism Act together with the National Security Council (NSC) Act from the same year gives the NSC—led by the prime minister—wide powers of arrest, search, and seizure without a warrant in areas deemed as security risks and in the context of countering terrorism.

Malaysia's secular legal system is based on English common law. However, Muslims are subject to Sharia (Islamic law), the interpretation of which varies by state, and the constitution's Article 121 stipulates that all matters related to Islam should be heard in Sharia courts. This results in vastly different treatment of Muslims and non-Muslims in "moral" and family law cases.

F3. Is there protection from the illegitimate use of physical force and freedom from war and insurgencies? 2 / 4 (+1)

Torture and abuse in police custody remain problems, and prisons are often overcrowded and unsafe. A number of criminal offenses can be punished with caning, including immigration violations.

In October 2018, the PH government announced plans to abolish the death penalty, instituting an immediate moratorium on executions for the roughly 1,300 prisoners on death row. Most were convicted under the country's harsh laws on drug trafficking. The proposed legal changes were still pending at year's end.

Score Change: The score improved from 1 to 2 because the new government placed a moratorium on executions for the roughly 1,300 prisoners on death row, most of whom were convicted of drug offenses.

F4. Do laws, policies, and practices guarantee equal treatment of various segments of the population? 1 / 4

Although the constitution provides for equal treatment of all citizens, it grants a "special position" to ethnic Malays and other indigenous people, known collectively as *bumiputera*. The government maintains programs intended to boost the economic status of bumiputera, who receive preferential treatment in areas including property ownership, higher education, civil service jobs, business affairs, and government contracts.

Women are placed at a disadvantage by a number of laws, particularly Sharia-related provisions. They are legally barred from certain occupations and work schedules, and they suffer from de facto discrimination in employment.

LGBT Malaysians face widespread discrimination and harassment. Same-sex sexual relations are punishable by up to 20 years in prison under the penal code, though this is generally not enforced. Some states apply their own penalties to Muslims under Sharia statutes. In September 2018, a Sharia court in Terengganu subjected two women to caning as punishment for attempting to have same-sex relations. Transgender people can also be punished under state-level Sharia laws.

G. PERSONAL AUTONOMY AND INDIVIDUAL RIGHTS: 9 / 16

G1. Do individuals enjoy freedom of movement, including the ability to change their place of residence, employment, or education? 3 / 4

Citizens are generally free to travel within and outside of Malaysia, as well as to change residence and employment. However, professional opportunities and access to higher education are affected by regulations and practices that favor bumiputera and those with connections to political elites. Although the practice is illegal, employers of migrant workers commonly hold their passports, preventing them from leaving abusive situations.

G2. Are individuals able to exercise the right to own property and establish private businesses without undue interference from state or nonstate actors? 3 / 4

Malaysia has a vibrant private sector. Bribery, however, is common in the business world, and the close nexus between political and economic elites distorts normal business activity and fair competition. Some laws pertaining to property and business differentiate between bumiputera and non-bumiputera, and Sharia-based inheritance rules for Muslims often favor men over women.

G3. Do individuals enjoy personal social freedoms, including choice of marriage partner and size of family, protection from domestic violence, and control over appearance? 2 / 4

While some personal social freedoms are protected, Muslims face legal restrictions on marriage partners and other social choices. Social pressures may also regulate dress and appearance, especially among Malay women. Sharia courts often favor men in matters of divorce and child custody. The minimum age for marriage is generally 16 for girls and 18 for boys, but Sharia courts in some states allow younger people to marry. In October 2018, Mahathir called on all state governments to raise the minimum age to 18 for Muslims and non-Muslims of both genders.

G4. Do individuals enjoy equality of opportunity and freedom from economic exploitation? 1 / 4

Rural residents and foreign workers, especially those working illegally, are vulnerable to exploitative or abusive working conditions, including forced labor or debt bondage. Foreign workers make up over a fifth of the country's workforce; about two million are documented, and estimates of the undocumented range from one million to more than two million. The authorities' periodic crackdowns on illegal foreign workers can result in punishment rather than protection for victims of human trafficking.

There have been no convictions of Malaysians for involvement in a network of human trafficking camps along the Thai-Malaysian border since the sites were discovered in 2015. The camps included mass graves holding the bodies of dozens of victims, and corrupt Malaysian officials were thought to have been complicit in the operation.

Maldives

Population: 400,000
Capital: Malé
Political Rights Rating: 5
Civil Liberties Rating: 5
Freedom Rating: 5.0
Freedom Status: Partly Free
Electoral Democracy: No

Overview: Following decades of authoritarian rule under former president Maumoon Abdul Gayoom, the Maldives held its first multiparty presidential election in 2008. However, democratic gains have been reversed in recent years amid severe restrictions on opposition activities, the imprisonment of opposition figures, restrictions on freedoms of expression and assembly, politicization of the judiciary and other independent institutions, and increasing Islamist militancy. An opposition victory in the 2018 presidential election raised hopes for improved conditions.

KEY DEVELOPMENTS IN 2018:
- In February, the Supreme Court ordered the release of and new trials for nine opposition leaders and the reinstatement of 12 opposition lawmakers who had been removed from the parliament in 2017 after defecting from the ruling Progressive Party of Maldives (PPM). Facing a loss of control over the legislature, President Abdulla Yameen declared a state of emergency, during which security forces raided the Supreme Court and arrested the chief justice and another justice; the remaining justices then reversed the court's decision. Former president Gayoom, who had aligned himself with the opposition despite being Yameen's half-brother, was among many others arrested under the state of emergency, which ended in late March.
- The government continued to repress the opposition until the September presidential election, but Ibrahim Mohamed Solih, the candidate of an opposition alliance, soundly defeated Yameen and took office in November.
- Soon after assuming office, Solih created a commission to free political detainees, many of whom had been released by year's end. The Supreme Court, in a series of rulings in October, also reinstated the 12 opposition lawmakers whose defection from the PPM had helped trigger the crisis.

POLITICAL RIGHTS: 14 / 40
A. ELECTORAL PROCESS: 5 / 12

A1. Was the current head of government or other chief national authority elected through free and fair elections? 2 / 4

The president is directly elected for up to two five-year terms. The run-up to the September 2018 election was marred by the misuse of state resources on behalf of incumbent president Yameen, police interference with opposition campaign efforts, and various forms of manipulation by electoral officials. The Maldivian Democratic Party (MDP) and other opposition groups endorsed Solih, an MDP lawmaker, after former president Mohamed Nasheed was disqualified over a dubious 2015 terrorism conviction. Despite the impediments to his campaign, Solih won the election with over 58 percent of the vote amid high turnout, leaving Yameen with less than 42 percent.

A2. Were the current national legislative representatives elected through free and fair elections? 2 / 4

The unicameral People's Majlis is composed of 85 seats, with members elected from individual districts to serve five-year terms. Elections held in 2014 were largely transparent and competitive, though they also featured some Supreme Court interference, vote buying, and other problems. The PPM won 33 seats, while the MDP captured 26. The Jumhooree Party won 15 seats, the Maldives Development Alliance won 5, and independents took an additional 5. The Adhaalath Party won the remaining seat. Subsequent party-switching gave the PPM a majority.

In July 2017, after a number of defections from the PPM threatened its control over the legislature, the Supreme Court ruled that members of parliament who switch or are expelled from their parties should lose their seats; the constitution contained no such provision. The decision did not apply retroactively, but the PPM and the Elections Commission argued that 12 members who defected to the opposition earlier in the year had not been officially removed from the party registry until after the ruling, and their seats were formally vacated as court challenges continued.

The 12 lawmakers were reinstated under a Supreme Court ruling on February 1, 2018, but following the arrest of the chief justice and an associate justice under a state of emergency, the rump court reversed its ruling on February 18, suspending the members in question. They were finally reinstated again through a series of court rulings that followed the September presidential election.

A3. Are the electoral laws and framework fair, and are they implemented impartially by the relevant election management bodies? 1 / 4

The independence of the Elections Commission, whose members are appointed by the president with approval from the parliament, has been seriously compromised in recent years, with key decisions favoring the PPM. The commission played an important role in the removal of opposition lawmakers under then president Yameen. In the run-up to the 2018 presidential election, its officials were accused of tampering with the voter reregistration process and arbitrarily changing vote-counting procedures, among other controversial actions. In July, two months before the election, the parliament passed amendments to electoral laws that increased the monetary deposits presidential candidates had to submit to the Elections Commission. After the commission ultimately declared Solih the winner, four of its five members fled the country, citing intimidation by Yameen supporters.

B. POLITICAL PLURALISM AND PARTICIPATION: 6 / 16

B1. Do the people have the right to organize in different political parties or other competitive political groupings of their choice, and is the system free of undue obstacles to the rise and fall of these competing parties or groupings? 2 / 4

Political pluralism and participation deteriorated during Yameen's presidency as the authorities subjected opposition leaders and their supporters to judicial harassment. Restrictions on and dispersals of political rallies, raids on opposition offices, and arbitrary detentions and convictions of opposition politicians were common for most of 2018.

In July, former president Gayoom's breakaway faction of the PPM organized as the Maumoon Reform Movement, though it had yet to register as a separate political party at year's end. A week after the September presidential election, Gayoom and his son, lawmaker Faris Maumoon, were released on bail, having been arrested in February 2018 and July 2017, respectively, and charged with a variety of politically fraught offenses. Both men had convictions on some charges overturned in October, but others were still pending at year's end.

Former president Nasheed, the MDP leader who had been sentenced to 13 years' imprisonment on dubious terrorism charges in 2015 and had been living in exile since securing medical leave in 2016, returned home in November 2018. Later in the month, the Supreme Court canceled his 2015 conviction, ruling that he had been wrongfully charged. Among other such releases and reversed convictions for political figures in late 2018, the courts overturned a 2016 terrorism verdict against Adhaalath Party leader Sheikh Imran Abdulla and a 2017 bribery conviction against Jumhooree Party leader Gasim Ibrahim.

B2. Is there a realistic opportunity for the opposition to increase its support or gain power through elections? 2 / 4

Under Yameen, the government and the PPM used the politicized justice system and the security forces to cripple the opposition and maintain control of the legislature. Although Yameen and his allies attempted to subvert the 2018 presidential election, the opposition secured victory thanks to deep public dissatisfaction with his rule and a reported turnout of nearly 90 percent. Yameen initially conceded, then sought to have the election annulled due to alleged fraud and vote rigging, but the Supreme Court rejected his request in October. Solih duly took office in November. Also that month, Gasim Ibrahim was elected as the new speaker of parliament following the reinstatement of ousted members and the resignation of the incumbent PPM speaker.

B3. Are the people's political choices free from domination by the military, foreign powers, religious hierarchies, economic oligarchies, or any other powerful group that is not democratically accountable? 1 / 4

The Yameen government exerted improper influence over a number of state institutions to restrict the political choices of voters and politicians. In addition to using security forces, the Elections Commission, and the justice system to suppress dissent, Yameen's allies reportedly threatened public and private-sector employees with dismissal for participating in opposition protests or other political activities. Such workers were also forced to attend progovernment events. Vote buying remains a problem during elections, and allegations of bribery and corruption have surrounded instances of party switching in recent years.

B4. Do various segments of the population (including ethnic, religious, gender, LGBT, and other relevant groups) have full political rights and electoral opportunities? 1 / 4

The Maldivian constitution and legal framework require all citizens to be Muslims and all candidates for elected office to be followers of Sunni Islam, explicitly excluding religious minorities. Societal discrimination against women has limited their political participation; five women won seats in the parliament in 2014. LGBT (lesbian, gay, bisexual, and transgender) people are unable to openly take part in political affairs given the criminalization of same-sex sexual activity and the prevalence of societal bias. Foreign workers, who make up between a quarter and a third of the population, have no political rights.

C. FUNCTIONING OF GOVERNMENT: 3 / 12

C1. Do the freely elected head of government and national legislative representatives determine the policies of the government? 1 / 4

Elected officials generally determine and implement government policies, but the functioning of the parliament was seriously impaired from mid-2017 to late 2018 by then president Yameen's heavy-handed attempts to retain control in the face of defections to the opposition. In February 2018, acting under the state of emergency declared by Yameen, security forces shut down the parliament building and prevented a number of lawmakers from entering. With some opposition members in detention and many others boycotting parliamentary sessions, the legislature lacked the quorum required by the constitution for much of the year, but it nevertheless continued to adopt laws. The Supreme Court, without its two members who were arrested in February, ruled in April that the parliament could act without a quorum. The parliament began to return to more normal operations after the change in government, the reinstatement of ousted opposition members, and the election of a new speaker late in the year.

C2. Are safeguards against official corruption strong and effective? 1 / 4

Corruption remains endemic at all levels of government. The Anti-Corruption Commission is only moderately effective, often launching investigations and taking other actions in response to public complaints, but rarely holding powerful figures to account for abuses. Since 2016, whistle-blowers and journalists reporting on corruption have been either jailed or forced into exile in the face of political persecution.

C3. Does the government operate with openness and transparency? 1 / 4

Large state contracts for infrastructure and other projects are regularly awarded through opaque processes, in which bribery and kickbacks are widely believed to play a role. The president, cabinet ministers, and members of parliament are required by the constitution to submit annual asset declarations, but these are not made public, and the relevant agencies have even resisted disclosing how many officials comply with the rule.

In September 2018, the Organized Crime and Corruption Reporting Project (OCCRP) released an investigative report that provided further evidence implicating Yameen and others in a corrupt 2014–15 scheme to lease Maldivian islands and lagoons to developers without the required public tenders. A 2016 legal amendment allowed such leases without public tenders.

CIVIL LIBERTIES: 21 / 60

D. FREEDOM OF EXPRESSION AND BELIEF: 3 / 16

D1. Are there free and independent media? 1 / 4

The constitution guarantees freedom of expression so long as it is exercised in a manner that is "not contrary to any tenet of Islam," a vague condition that encourages self-censorship in the media. Regulatory bodies, especially the Maldives Broadcasting Commission (MBC), have displayed bias in favor of the government and restricted coverage of the opposition. A 2016 law imposed criminal penalties for defamation or any other expression that "threatens national security" or "contradicts social norms," and it was used to intimidate journalists and media outlets. The parliament repealed that law in November 2018.

During the 2018 presidential election period, state-run media outlets devoted most of their airtime to positive coverage of the ruling PPM. The authorities threatened media outlets that carried news on jailed opposition figures and fined those whose content criticized Yameen. Foreign journalists had difficulty securing visas in time for the election due to bureaucratic obstacles.

In August, a criminal court acquitted two men charged with the forced disappearance in 2014 of journalist Ahmed Rilwan, stating that the police and prosecution had conducted an incomplete investigation. The trial of alleged religious extremists charged with the 2017 murder of liberal blogger Yameen Rasheed remained at preliminary stages. In November, President Solih set up a commission to examine the Rilwan and Rasheed cases.

D2. Are individuals free to practice and express their religious faith or nonbelief in public and private? 0 / 4

Freedom of religion is severely restricted. Islam is the state religion, and all citizens are required to be Muslims. Imams must use government-approved sermons. Non-Muslim foreigners are allowed to observe their religions only in private. In recent years, growing religious extremism, stoked in part by the Yameen administration, has led to an increase in threatening rhetoric and physical attacks against those perceived to be insulting or rejecting Islam. Secularist writers and defenders of freedom of conscience have faced pressure from the authorities as well as death threats.

D3. Is there academic freedom, and is the educational system free from extensive political indoctrination? 1 / 4

Academic freedom has narrowed in recent years as the government stepped up monitoring and punishments for academics and teachers who espouse opposition political views or participate in protests. Islam is a compulsory subject in schools and is incorporated into all other subject areas. School and university curriculums have come under increased influence from hard-line religious leaders, resulting in some content that denigrates democracy and promotes jihadist narratives.

D4. Are individuals free to express their personal views on political or other sensitive topics without fear of surveillance or retribution? 1 / 4

It has become increasingly dangerous for individuals to express political and religious opinions freely, as demonstrated by the murder of Yameen Rasheed and police harassment of other social media activists. Although the new government that took power in November 2018 was expected to be more open to democracy and human rights, individuals who speak out on behalf of minority groups or basic freedoms are still at risk of attack from violent nonstate actors.

E. ASSOCIATIONAL AND ORGANIZATIONAL RIGHTS: 6 / 12
E1. Is there freedom of assembly? 2 / 4

Freedom of assembly has been subject to severe constraints in recent years. A 2016 law requires protest organizers to obtain police permission for their events and restricts demonstrations to certain designated areas. Assemblies were banned during the 2018 state of emergency. However, in the run-up to the September election, conditions improved due in part to the looming threat of targeted sanctions by the European Union, which adopted a framework for such penalties in July. The authorities granted the opposition somewhat greater leeway to campaign and hold rallies after consistently refusing permits in the past. In early September, the MDP was able to hold its first rally in the capital's central carnival area in three years. Separately, in August, an annual rally organized by the family of forcibly disappeared journalist Ahmed Rilwan was allowed to proceed uninterrupted for the first time since 2014.

E2. Is there freedom for nongovernmental organizations, particularly those that are engaged in human rights- and governance-related work? 2 / 4

Nongovernmental organizations (NGOs) continue to operate in a restrictive environment. They are required to obtain government approval before seeking domestic or foreign funding, and regulators have broad discretion to investigate and dissolve NGOs. The Human Rights Commission of Maldives is not independent in practice. In recent years, Maldivian human rights groups have increasingly become targets of surveillance, harassment, and threats of violence, including from extremist nonstate actors. A prominent human rights defender, Shahindha Ismail of the Maldivian Democracy Network, was questioned by the police and investigated for alleged blasphemy in April 2018.

E3. Is there freedom for trade unions and similar professional or labor organizations? 2 / 4

The constitution and labor laws allow workers to form trade unions, and a number of unions are active. However, collective bargaining is not protected, and strikes are prohibited in many sectors, including the crucial tourism industry.

F. RULE OF LAW: 5 / 16
F1. Is there an independent judiciary? 0 / 4

Judicial independence is seriously compromised. Many judges are unqualified, and the courts are widely considered vulnerable to corruption or political influence. The Supreme Court has repeatedly intervened in political affairs and apparently exceeded its constitutional authority, typically acting according to political interests.

In February 2018, acting under Yameen's state of emergency, the military raided the Supreme Court and arrested two of its justices, including the chief justice. This came days after the court unexpectedly ordered the release and retrial of nine opposition leaders who had been jailed on various charges, as well as the reinstatement of the 12 lawmakers who had abandoned the governing majority. The three justices remaining on the Supreme Court after the raid subsequently reversed those decisions.

In March, the parliament passed legislation—without a quorum—that allowed judges to be removed once their conviction is upheld by the Supreme Court, despite the constitution's requirement that judges be removed through a two-thirds vote in the parliament after a finding of gross misconduct or incompetence. In May and June, both of the detained Supreme Court justices received prison terms for "obstruction of justice" and other offenses, and their appeals were denied, leading to their formal removal. Yameen appointed replacements in June.

In November, after the change in government, the jailed former justices were released to house arrest, as were a former prosecutor general and a magistrate who had been arrested in 2016. Some of the former justices' charges or convictions were dismissed or overturned by year's end, but others appeared to remain pending.

F2. Does due process prevail in civil and criminal matters? 1 / 4

Police have regularly engaged in arbitrary arrests in recent years, often to disrupt opposition activities, protests, or the work of journalists. Due process rights are not well enforced in practice, and under Yameen, opposition figures were subjected to deeply flawed trials on politically motivated charges, according to human rights groups and international monitors.

F3. Is there protection from the illegitimate use of physical force and freedom from war and insurgencies? 2 / 4

The constitution and the Anti-Torture Act ban torture, but police brutality and the abuse of detainees and prison inmates remain problems. Flogging and other forms of corporal punishment are authorized for some crimes, and flogging sentences are issued in practice for offenses such as extramarital sex. Prisons are overcrowded, inmates reportedly lack proper access to medical care, and human rights groups have reported an increase in deaths in custody.

F4. Do laws, policies, and practices guarantee equal treatment of various segments of the population? 2 / 4

Gender-based discrimination in employment is prohibited by law, but women continue to face discrimination in practice. Girls and women from underprivileged backgrounds are disproportionately affected by Sharia (Islamic law) penalties for crimes like fornication and adultery.

Migrant workers in the country encounter disparate treatment by state authorities and have difficulty accessing justice.

Same-sex sexual acts are prohibited by law and can draw prison sentences and corporal punishment. As a result, LGBT people rarely report societal discrimination or abuse.

G. PERSONAL AUTONOMY AND INDIVIDUAL RIGHTS: 7 / 16

G1. Do individuals enjoy freedom of movement, including the ability to change their place of residence, employment, or education? 2 / 4

Freedom of movement is provided for by law, but there are some restrictions in practice. Authorities have imposed travel bans on members of opposition parties and other perceived government opponents. Migrant workers are also subject to constraints on their movement, including through retention of their passports by employers.

G2. Are individuals able to exercise the right to own property and establish private businesses without undue interference from state or nonstate actors? 2 / 4

Property rights are limited, with most land owned by the government and leased to private entities or commercial developers through what is often an opaque process. A number of islanders faced relocation for an airport development project during 2018.

G3. Do individuals enjoy personal social freedoms, including choice of marriage partner and size of family, protection from domestic violence, and control over appearance? 1 / 4

Personal social freedoms are restricted by Sharia-based laws and growing religious extremism in society. Among other rules on marriage and divorce, citizen women are barred from marrying non-Muslim foreigners, while citizen men can marry non-Muslim foreigners only if they are Christian or Jewish. Extramarital sex is criminalized, and there is a high legal threshold to prove rape allegations. Women face increasing pressure to dress more conservatively, in keeping with hard-line interpretations of Islam.

G4. Do individuals enjoy equality of opportunity and freedom from economic exploitation? 2 / 4

The legal framework provides some protections against worker exploitation, including rules on working hours and bans on forced labor. However, migrant workers are especially vulnerable to abuses such as debt bondage and withholding of wages. Women and children working in domestic service may also be subject to exploitative conditions.

Mali

Population: 17,300,000
Capital: Bamako
Political Rights Rating: 4 ↑
Civil Liberties Rating: 4
Freedom Rating: 4.0
Freedom Status: Partly Free
Electoral Democracy: No

Overview: Mali experienced a political transition away from authoritarian rule beginning in the early 1990s, and gradually built up its democratic institutions for about 20 years. However, the country displayed characteristics of state fragility along the way that eventually contributed to a 2012 military coup, and a rebellion in northern Mali that erupted the same year. Though constitutional rule was restored and a peace agreement signed in the north in 2015, the events have left an enduring situation of insecurity.

KEY DEVELOPMENTS IN 2018:

- President Ibrahim Boubacar Keïta won a second five-year term in the year's presidential election, and was sworn in in September. While insecurity in the central and northern regions led to the closure of some polling stations and disruptions at many others, voting took place peacefully in the south, where most of Mali's population is located. Insecurity notwithstanding, international observers characterized polling as generally well conducted.
- The opposition rejected the election as fraudulent, and filed a complaint with the Constitutional Court, which rejected it and certified Keïta's victory.
- Scores of people were killed and more were displaced in intercommunal violence in central Mali, particularly in Mopti Region. The violence has included attacks on schools and houses of worship.
- In June, mass graves containing the bodies of 25 militants were discovered in Mopti Region. The Defense Ministry issued a statement saying the Malian armed forces were implicated in "gross violations," and instructed military prosecutors to investigate the killings.

POLITICAL RIGHTS: 18 / 40 (+1)

A. ELECTORAL PROCESS: 6 / 12

A1. Was the current head of government or other chief national authority elected through free and fair elections? 2 / 4

The president, who appoints the prime minister, is elected by popular vote and may serve up to two five-year terms. In a two-round presidential election in 2018, Ibrahim Boubacar Keïta, the incumbent president known by his initials, IBK, took 67 percent of the vote; he defeated

Soumaïla Cissé, a former finance minister, who took 33 percent. International election observers said polling was relatively well conducted. However, a fragile security situation led to very low turnout in parts of northern and central Mali. Approximately 20 percent of polling stations were affected by violent disruptions nationwide, according to authorities, and 3 percent were closed entirely. Additionally, internet access was blocked ahead of the run-off vote, and authorities refused to answer journalists' questions about the disruption.

The political opposition, led by Cissé, rejected the election's results as fraudulent, and filed a complaint with the Constitutional Court, which rejected it and certified Keïta's victory. The opposition then boycotted President Keïta's inauguration in September, though Keïta has received international recognition as the election's winner. Soumeylou Boubèye Maïga was reappointed as prime minister and unveiled his government in September, which was largely unchanged from the previous one.

Despite the election's relative success, the political system remains fragile due to the security situation, and as the country continues to address the aftermath of the 2012 coup.

A2. Were the current national legislative representatives elected through free and fair elections? 2 / 4

Members of the 147-seat unicameral National Assembly serve five-year terms. Thirteen seats are reserved to represent Malians living abroad. IBK's Rally for Mali (RPM) party won 66 seats in legislative elections held in 2013, and its allies took an additional 49 seats. Cissé's Union for the Republic and Democracy (URD) won 17 seats, and the third-largest party, the Alliance for Democracy (ADEMA), won 16.

In October 2018, the Constitutional Court delayed the year's legislative elections, which had been set to take place over two rounds in October and November, agreeing with a petition arguing that some candidates had not been able to register due to a strike by judges. The court ruled that the elections would instead take place in June 2019, and extended lawmakers' mandates accordingly.

A3. Are the electoral laws and framework fair, and are they implemented impartially by the relevant election management bodies? 2 / 4

Electoral operations are divided among three administrative bodies in Mali—the Ministry of Territorial Administration, the Independent National Electoral Commission (CENI), and the General Office of Elections (DGE). The Constitutional Court also participates in the electoral process by validating election results and resolving disputes.

Electoral bodies have struggled to establish secure polling places in areas where armed groups operate. Voters have been disenfranchised due to delays in the distribution of electoral identity cards, and an outdated voter registry.

B. POLITICAL PLURALISM AND PARTICIPATION: 8 / 16 (+1)

B1. Do the people have the right to organize in different political parties or other competitive political groupings of their choice, and is the system free of undue obstacles to the rise and fall of these competing parties or groupings? 2 / 4

The creation and the functioning of political parties are determined by a legal framework known as the Political Parties Charter, which is generally considered fair. The Charter prohibits the creation of political parties on an "ethnic, religious, linguistic, regionalist, sexist, or professional basis."

There are more than 100 registered political parties in Mali, though fewer than 20 are active. Parties are relatively weak, and are usually based around support for a particular personality, and policy differences between parties are not always clear. Parties are often poorly funded, which hampers their ability to effectively organize and win voter support.

B2. Is there a realistic opportunity for the opposition to increase its support or gain power through elections? 2 / 4

Electoral competition is open to opposition forces. A 2014 law institutionalized specific privileges for opposition parties in the parliament, such as the ability to choose an official leader of the opposition. However, in 2016 the ruling majority passed, over the objections of opposition parties, amendments to the electoral code that favored establishment and majority parties by requiring candidates to make a significant financial campaign deposit, and to receive support from national councilors. Even so, more than 20 candidates were able to run in the 2018 presidential election.

B3. Are the people's political choices free from domination by the military, foreign powers, religious hierarchies, economic oligarchies, or any other powerful group that is not democratically accountable? 2 / 4 (+1)

Political choices remain the privilege of the Malian people, though these choices are occasionally influenced by the promise of patronage appointments or other benefits in exchange for political support.

Insecurity has restricted people's ability to vote in northern and central Mali, including during the 2018 presidential election. Approximately 20 percent of polling stations saw violent disruptions nationwide, and about 3 percent were closed due to security risks, according to authorities. A polling officer was shot and killed in Arkodia during the presidential runoff by armed men authorities described as "jihadists." Additionally, many of the roughly 500,000 people displaced within and outside Mali were unable to exercise their voting rights in 2018.

Nevertheless, it appeared that more polling stations in regions affected by ongoing insecurity remained opened during the 2018 presidential election, compared to the 2016 local polls. Polling generally took place peacefully in the south, where the vast majority of the population is concentrated. The rate of deadly violence against those involved in election administration was lower in 2018 than in 2016, when five military members transporting ballots were reportedly killed in an ambush near Douentza.

Score Change: The score improved from 1 to 2 because insecurity in the northern and central regions did not disrupt polling in 2018 as severely as in 2016.

B4. Do various segments of the population (including ethnic, religious, gender, LGBT, and other relevant groups) have full political rights and electoral opportunities? 2 / 4

No law limits the political rights of minorities, and no single ethnic group dominates the government or security forces. Tuareg pastoralist groups in the north have historically occupied a marginal position in national political life, but members from these groups hold at least 16 National Assembly seats.

Societal attitudes can discourage women from participating in political processes. Only about 14 percent of candidates in the 2013 legislative elections were women, and women occupy less than 10 percent of National Assembly seats. In the country's 2018 presidential election, Djeneba N'Diaye was the sole female candidate.

C. FUNCTIONING OF GOVERNMENT: 4 / 12

C1. Do the freely elected head of government and national legislative representatives determine the policies of the government? 2 / 4

The president was elected in 2018 polls that were generally credible but marred by violence in some areas. National Assembly members were freely elected in the 2013 polls, though at the end of 2018 remained seated beyond their constitutional mandate, with new polls scheduled for 2019. The prime minister is generally able to set national policy, and the parliament to enact new laws. However, the executive branch has exhibited influence on the other branches of government.

The volatile security situation in northern and central Mali limits government activity there.

C2. Are safeguards against official corruption strong and effective? 1 / 4

Corruption remains a problem in government, notably in public procurement. Bribery and embezzlement of public funds is common and impunity for corrupt officials is the norm. The Office of the Auditor General is an independent office responsible for analyzing public spending, but despite identifying sizable embezzlement cases, very few prosecutions have been made.

C3. Does the government operate with openness and transparency? 1 / 4

Government operations remain generally opaque. Mali does not have a comprehensive freedom of information regime, although numerous laws do provide for public access to some official documents and information. However, such laws are replete with extensive and vague exceptions, and journalists have faced obstacles when attempting to obtain information, particularly about the military.

CIVIL LIBERTIES: 26 / 60 (-1)
D. FREEDOM OF EXPRESSION AND BELIEF: 10 / 16 (-1)
D1. Are there free and independent media? 2 / 4

The media environment in Mali's capital, Bamako, and in the rest of the south is relatively open, though there are sporadic reports of censorship, self-censorship, and threats against journalists. Reporting on the situation in the north remains dangerous due to the presence of active militant groups. Defamation is a crime that can draw fines or prison time.

Elections in Mali are often accompanied by an uptick in press freedom violations. In June 2018, as campaigning was ramping up, a number of journalists were chased off by police as they attempted to cover a banned opposition demonstration. The following month, three journalists with France's TV Monde were arrested and interrogated upon their arrival at the Bamako airport, though were released without charge. In August, Bamako authorities unilaterally closed Radio Renouveau FM, citing allegations of inciting hatred, after the host of one of its programs alleged that Keïta and his allies had committed electoral fraud and had engaged in vote-buying. In closing the station, authorities bypassed the High Authority for Communication (HAC), Mali's media regulator, which is the only authority with power to issue legal rulings on media content.

D2. Are individuals free to practice and express their religious faith or nonbelief in public and private? 2 / 4 (-1)

Freedom of religion is constitutionally guaranteed in Mali, which is a secular state, and discrimination of the basis of religion is prohibited. The population is predominantly Sunni Muslim, and Sufism plays a role in the beliefs of most residents.

Armed extremist groups have terrorized northern and central Mali, and have attacked those who they perceive as failing to follow their strict interpretation of Islam. They have occasionally carried out targeted kidnappings of Christians and subjected them to sometimes violent harassment.

In 2018, serious violations of religious freedom accompanied increasing intercommunal violence in central Mali. Islamist armed groups have reportedly compelled civilians to attend lectures at mosques, at which they promote their interpretations of Islam and discourage residents from having contact with the government and UN and French peacekeeping forces. There were a number of reports of armed attacks on mosques, as well as detentions and murders committed within.

Score Change: The score declined from 3 to 2 because intercommunal violence in central Mali has brought about violations of religious freedom, including attacks on houses of worship.

D3. Is there academic freedom, and is the educational system free from extensive political indoctrination? 3 / 4

Academic freedom is upheld in areas with a consolidated government presence, but restricted in areas with a heavy militant presence.

D4. Are individuals free to express their personal views on political or other sensitive topics without fear of surveillance or retribution? 3 / 4

Private discussion is generally open and free in areas under government control, but is more restricted in areas with a militant presence or where intercommunal violence has flared. The government temporarily restricted social media use in 2017, in an apparent attempt to prevent activists from organizing protests against constitutional revisions. In 2018, internet access was again blocked ahead of the presidential run-off vote.

E. ASSOCIATIONAL AND ORGANIZATIONAL RIGHTS: 6 / 12
E1. Is there freedom of assembly? 2 / 4

The constitution guarantees freedom of assembly, but participants in public gatherings risk violence by state security forces. In December 2017, one person was killed and 15 were injured after the police opened fire on demonstrators in Konsiga who had blocked the city hall for a week in an attempt to force the mayor's resignation. In June 2018, 16 people were injured when police broke up a peaceful demonstration in Bamako organized by the opposition, which had been prohibited by the government.

E2. Is there freedom for nongovernmental organizations, particularly those that are engaged in human rights- and governance-related work? 2 / 4

Many nongovernmental organizations (NGOs) operate in Mali without state interference. However, large, established NGOs with ties to the political elite are influential, and can overshadow smaller and more innovative groups, particularly in the competition for funding. Ongoing insecurity in some parts of the country hampers NGO efforts to provide aid and services to returning refugees and others affected by instability.

E3. Is there freedom for trade unions and similar professional or labor organizations? 2 / 4

The constitution guarantees workers the right to form unions and to strike, with some limitations for essential services workers, and requirements involving compulsory arbitration. The government has broad discretionary power over the registration of unions and recognition of collective bargaining, and the authorities do not effectively enforce laws against antiunion discrimination.

F. RULE OF LAW: 6 / 16
F1. Is there an independent judiciary? 2 / 4

The judiciary is beholden to the executive, despite constitutional guarantees of judicial independence. Judges are appointed by the president, while the minister of justice supervises both law enforcement and judicial functions. Additionally, the overall efficiency of the judicial system remains low. Militant attacks against judicial personnel have prompted some judges to vacate their posts. In November 2017, Malian judge Soungalo Koné was kidnapped in central Mali by armed men who asked for the release of detained militants in exchange for his freedom. He had not been released by the end of 2018.

F2. Does due process prevail in civil and criminal matters? 2 / 4

Due process rights are inconsistently upheld, and a 2017 AfroBarometer survey reported that the police and justice system are perceived to be the least trustworthy institutions in the country. Detainees are not always charged within the 48-hour period set by law, and arbitrary arrests are common. Since a deadly 2015 hotel attack in Bamako, a national state of emergency has remained in force, and was extended in October 2018 for another year. The emergency designation gives security services greater authority to search homes without a warrant, detain suspects, and restrict protests.

The trial of Amadou Sanogo, the former army captain who staged a military coup in Mali in 2012, and more than a dozen codefendants began in late 2016 on charges related to the abduction and killing of 21 soldiers. The trial was quickly adjourned, and at the end of 2018 Sanogo remained in detention while awaiting the trial's reopening. Separately, in April, Al Hassan Ag Abdoul Aziz Ag Mohamed Ag Mahmoud, a former member of the militant Islamist group Ansar Dine, made his first appearance before the International Criminal Court (ICC) in The Hague. He is set to be tried for war crimes and crimes against humanity committed in Timbuktu between 2012 and 2013.

The Truth, Justice and Reconciliation Commission created in 2014 is responsible for investigating human rights violations committed since 1960, but its activities are restricted by the rise of terrorist activities and intercommunal tensions within Mali's borders.

F3. Is there protection from the illegitimate use of physical force and freedom from war and insurgencies? 1 / 4

Islamist militant groups not party to Mali's 2015 peace agreement continued to carry out acts of violence against civilians in the northern and central regions. Ongoing instability has contributed to the spread of organized crime, and accompanying violence and kidnappings. Scores were killed and many more were displaced in 2018 in incidents of intercommunal violence. The Fulani ethnic group are facing growing pressure over allegations of ties to al-Qaeda extremists. In one dire attack in June, more than 30 members of the Fulani community were killed in the Mopti town of Koumaga.

Malian armed forces have committed human rights violations, including extrajudicial killings, enforced disappearances, and torture. In April 2018, several Fulani civic associations accused the army of killing 14 Fulani civilians. Mali's army maintained that those killed were suspected militants. In June, mass graves containing the bodies of 25 militants were discovered in Mopti Region. The Defense Ministry issued a statement saying the Malian armed forces were implicated in "gross violations," and instructed military prosecutors to investigate. This was considered by some to be an encouraging sign that authorities were moving to address grave human rights abuses by the security forces.

Separately, in January, three dozen Malian soldiers from an elite unit were arrested for refusing to deploy in a conflict zone. The desertions were attributed to lack of necessary equipment and training.

Prisons are characterized by overcrowding, insufficient medical care, and a lack of proper food and sanitation. The government made some effort in 2017 to improve conditions by holding staff trainings and building a new prison with a capacity of about 2,500 prisoners.

F4. Do laws, policies, and practices guarantee equal treatment of various segments of the population? 1 / 4

Members of a northern caste known as black Tamasheqs face societal discrimination, including slavery-like treatment and hereditary servitude. Authorities sometimes deny them official documents or discriminate against them in housing, schooling, and police protection.

Same-sex sexual acts are legal, but LGBT (lesbian, gay, bisexual, and transgender) people face discrimination, including cases of violence from family members meant as a corrective punishment.

Although equal rights are provided for in the constitution, the law does not provide for the same legal status for women and men, and women are required by law to obey their husbands. Sexual harassment is not prohibited by law and is a common practice in schools and the workplace.

Conditions in northern Mali have left many refugees unable or unwilling to return, as continuing insecurity in the region complicates resettlement. According to the UNHCR, there were more than 137,000 Malian refugees in Burkina Faso, Mauritania, and Niger as of November 2018.

G. PERSONAL AUTONOMY AND INDIVIDUAL RIGHTS: 4 / 16

G1. Do individuals enjoy freedom of movement, including the ability to change their place of residence, employment, or education? 1 / 4

Freedom of movement and choice of residence remain affected by insecurity, especially in northern and central Mali. According to the United Nations, 827 schools were closed as of December 2018, including 62 percent of schools in the Mopti Region. Schools have been targeted in militant attacks.

G2. Are individuals able to exercise the right to own property and establish private businesses without undue interference from state or nonstate actors? 1 / 4

Citizens have the right to own property and conduct business activity, but these rights are not consistently respected and widespread corruption hampers normal business activities. It is generally necessary to pay bribes in order operate a business.

Traditional customs sometimes undermine the right of women to own property. The law discriminates against women in matters of marriage, divorce, and inheritance.

G3. Do individuals enjoy personal social freedoms, including choice of marriage partner and size of family, protection from domestic violence, and control over appearance? 1 / 4

Rape and domestic violence against women are widespread, and most such crimes go unreported. There are no specific laws prohibiting spousal rape or domestic violence. Female genital mutilation or cutting is legal and commonly practiced in the country. LBGT couples cannot adopt children in Mali.

G4. Do individuals enjoy equality of opportunity and freedom from economic exploitation? 1 / 4

Although trafficking in persons is a criminal offense, prosecutions are infrequent. Many judicial officials remain unaware of the antitrafficking law, and the police lack adequate resources to combat trafficking. Traditional forms of slavery and debt bondage persist, particularly in the north, with thousands of people estimated to be living in such conditions.

Although the government has taken steps to eliminate child labor, it is a significant concern, especially in the agricultural and artisanal gold-mining sectors. Armed groups also regularly recruited and use child soldiers.

Malta

Population: 500,000
Capital: Valletta
Political Rights Rating: 2 ↓
Civil Liberties Rating: 1
Freedom Rating: 1.5
Freedom Status: Free
Electoral Democracy: Yes

Overview: Malta is a parliamentary democracy with regular, competitive elections and periodic rotations of power. Civil liberties are widely respected. However, the political system makes it difficult for new or smaller groups to challenge the dominance of the two main parties, and recent revelations have underscored the threat of official corruption.

KEY DEVELOPMENTS IN 2018:

- The trial of the three men implicated in the 2017 murder of journalist Daphne Caruana Galizia was ongoing at year's end, but the masterminds of the suspected contract killing had not yet been apprehended.
- In July, a magisterial inquiry into corruption allegations against Michelle Muscat, the prime minister's wife, who had allegedly laundered money for the government of Azerbaijan, concluded by clearing both her and the prime minister of wrongdoing. Several other investigations into alleged corruption by high-level officials were ongoing at year's end.
- The government's close relationship with powerful economic interests continued to cause controversy throughout the year, notably with the September approval of a large-scale apartment and hotel construction project in Pembroke to be built by prominent developer and campaign donor the db Group, which had provoked fierce opposition from the local community due to environmental and noise concerns.
- In December, the Council of Europe's Venice Commission issued a report noting shortcomings in Malta's anticorruption framework and procedures for judicial appointments, as well as inadequate checks and balances to constrain the prime minister.

POLITICAL RIGHTS: 35 / 40 (−1)

A. ELECTORAL PROCESS: 12 / 12

A1. Was the current head of government or other chief national authority elected through free and fair elections? 4 / 4

The president, primarily a ceremonial head of state, is elected by the parliament for a single five-year term. The president nominates the prime minister, who is usually the leader of the majority party or coalition in the parliament. The prime minister serves five-year terms.

In June 2017, Prime Minister Joseph Muscat won a second term after his Labour Party was victorious in parliamentary snap elections that were considered credible.

A2. Were the current national legislative representatives elected through free and fair elections? 4 / 4

Members of Malta's unicameral legislature, the House of Representatives, are elected for five-year terms through a single-transferable-vote system in multimember districts. Snap elections were held in June 2017, about nine months ahead of schedule. The ruling Labour Party won 55 percent of the vote and 37 seats, leaving the opposition Nationalist Party and its allies with 30 seats.

A3. Are the electoral laws and framework fair, and are they implemented impartially by the relevant election management bodies? 4 / 4

The constitution and the electoral law provide for democratic elections, and balloting is generally free and fair in practice. Members of the Electoral Commission are appointed by the president following consultation between the government and the opposition, and both major parties have representatives on the panel. The electoral system has been criticized for electoral boundaries that favor the incumbent parties and a voting system that makes it difficult for smaller parties to win representation. In practice, a party must take 16–17 percent of the valid votes in one of the 13 electoral districts to enter the parliament.

B. POLITICAL PLURALISM AND PARTICIPATION: 14 / 16

B1. Do the people have the right to organize in different political parties or other competitive political groupings of their choice, and is the system free of undue obstacles to the rise and fall of these competing parties or groupings? 3 / 4

There are no significant restrictions on the formation of political parties, though the ruling party benefits from progovernment bias in the state media, and smaller parties have difficulty competing against the two established parties given the voting system and their superior access to private donations. The newly formed Democratic Party won two seats in the 2017 elections only by forging an alliance with the Nationalists and running candidates on their lists.

The 2015 Financing of Political Parties Act was adopted to improve the transparency of party fundraising, but critics have noted that compliance is overseen by the Electoral Commission, whose members are appointed by the two parties. The law caps individual donations, but imposes no overall cap on electoral spending, and parties are not obliged to identify donors who contribute less than €7,000 ($8,000). In 2017, the Nationalist Party was accused of using false invoices to conceal unreported donations, which led to an investigation by the Electoral Commission. In October 2018, the Constitutional Court upheld an appeal by the Nationalist Party to halt the investigation, ruling that the Electoral Commission cannot be both the investigator and the judge in party-finance cases. In response, the government announced that it would propose amendments to the law in order to comply with the court ruling.

B2. Is there a realistic opportunity for the opposition to increase its support or gain power through elections? 4 / 4

The Labour Party and its rival, the Nationalist Party, have regularly alternated in power since independence from Britain in 1964, establishing a strong pattern of peaceful democratic transfers after elections. The most recent change occurred in 2013.

B3. Are the people's political choices free from domination by the military, foreign powers, religious hierarchies, economic oligarchies, or any other powerful group that is not democratically accountable? 3 / 4

Voters are generally free from undue interference in their political choices, and no military, foreign, or religious entities exert undemocratic influence over the vote.

However, in recent years, observers have highlighted the influence of powerful economic interests that donate to political parties. According to the Labour Party's 2017 disclosures on the previous year's donations, several construction companies made seven-figure contributions. The Nationalist Party has also been accused of receiving large donations from private corporations in violation of the law. The Labour government has favored the construction and land-development industries in its policies, and the two sides have maintained a close relationship. In September 2018, a controversial large-scale apartment and hotel construction project in Pembroke to be built by prominent developer the db Group (which has been a donor to both major parties), was approved by a government board. The proposed project had provoked intense opposition from local residents, who argued that the environmental impact and noise from the construction would significantly reduce the quality of life.

B4. Do various segments of the population (including ethnic, religious, gender, LGBT, and other relevant groups) have full political rights and electoral opportunities? 4 / 4

Women and minority groups enjoy full political rights and electoral opportunities, though conservative societal norms have limited women's participation to some extent. Women hold 10 parliament seats, or about 15 percent of the total, in addition to the presidency.

C. FUNCTIONING OF GOVERNMENT: 9 / 12 (−1)

C1. Do the freely elected head of government and national legislative representatives determine the policies of the government? 4 / 4

Elected officials are largely free to make and implement laws and policies without improper obstacles from unelected groups. A report published by The Venice Commission of the Council of Europe in December 2018 found that disproportionate power is concentrated in the executive branch and that the current system features inadequate checks and balances to constrain the prime minister.

C2. Are safeguards against official corruption strong and effective? 2 / 4 (−1)

The Panama Papers have led to a series of corruption allegations against Maltese officials since 2016, and related investigations were ongoing throughout 2018. One of the most important cases involves a government minister and the prime minister's chief of staff, who set up trusts in New Zealand and secret accounts in Panama shortly after taking office in 2013. In July 2018, a magisterial inquiry into corruption allegations against Michelle Muscat, the prime minister's wife, who had allegedly laundered money for the government of Azerbaijan, concluded by clearing both her and the prime minister of wrongdoing.

Another ongoing inquiry involves claims of kickbacks to Muscat's chief of staff from a controversial program that issues Maltese passports to foreign investors. A key whistle-blower in these cases, former bank employee and Russian national Maria Efimova, fled the country in 2017, saying she feared for her life after journalist Daphne Caruana Galizia's murder.

In a report published in January, a mission from the European Parliament criticized the Maltese government for the small number of criminal investigations into money laundering surrounding the revelations in the Panama Papers, contributing to impunity among high-level officials accused of corruption.

Two posts on the Permanent Commission against Corruption, which had been empty since mid-2017, were finally filled in January 2018, allowing the body to resume its work. However, the commission lacks prosecutorial powers, severely limiting its effectiveness. Very few cases investigated by the commission have resulted in prosecutions.

Score Change: The score declined from 3 to 2 due the inefficacy of the country's anticorruption institutions in investigating the myriad corruption scandals that have emerged from the Panama Papers and other sources.

C3. Does the government operate with openness and transparency? 3 / 4

Malta has a freedom of information law and asset disclosure rules for public officials. However, the Swiss Leaks scandal in 2015 revealed that a number of politicians had apparently hidden assets in Swiss bank accounts, and investigations by tax authorities were still under way as of 2018. In May, the finance minister announced that the government would not be publishing a list of names of "politically exposed" people, including prominent government officials, who held Swiss bank accounts, arguing that the list's publication would be illegal. The decision contradicted a promise made by Prime Minister Muscat in 2015 to reveal the names.

Following the passage of legislation in 2017 calling for the appointment of a commissioner for standards in public life to monitor ethical standards among public officials, in November, the first commissioner was sworn in. However, the commissioner is only able to investigate matters from after October 30.

The government has been criticized in recent years for withholding important details on a series of large public contracts, which are often heavily redacted for public release. According to government statistics, nearly half of the requests for information received by government bodies under the Freedom of Information Act between 2015 and 2017 were rejected.

CIVIL LIBERTIES: 56 / 60
D. FREEDOM OF EXPRESSION AND BELIEF: 15 / 16
D1. Are there free and independent media? 3 / 4

The media are generally free and diverse. Residents have access to international news services as well as domestic outlets, though the opposition often complains that state-owned media favor the government.

Caruana Galizia's murder in a 2017 car bombing added a new level of physical danger to the work of journalists in Malta, particularly those investigating political corruption. The trial of the three suspects accused of the murder was ongoing at the end of 2018. In October, a mission led by Reporters without Borders (RSF) criticized the Maltese authorities for "not living up to their obligations to guarantee and safeguard freedom of expression and press freedom." The mission pointed to the slow pace of the trial against the suspects in Caruana Galizia's murder, as well as the failure of investigators to arrest the masterminds behind the crime, which is believed to be a contract killing.

In April, the parliament passed a new law decriminalizing libel. However, investigative journalists continued to face libel suits throughout 2018, including a lawsuit against Caruana Galizia that was not dropped posthumously, and a separate suit against her son, both filed by the prime minister.

D2. Are individuals free to practice and express their religious faith or nonbelief in public and private? 4 / 4

The constitution establishes Roman Catholicism as the state religion, but religious minorities are generally able to worship freely. A 2016 legal reform decriminalized the vilification of religion, or blasphemy, and instead expanded a provision banning incitement of hatred to include religious hatred.

D3. Is there academic freedom, and is the educational system free from extensive political indoctrination? 4 / 4

Scholarship and the education system are free from political control and indoctrination.

D4. Are individuals free to express their personal views on political or other sensitive topics without fear of surveillance or retribution? 4 / 4

There are no significant constraints on the expression of personal views among the general public, notwithstanding laws banning incitement of hatred on various grounds.

E. ASSOCIATIONAL AND ORGANIZATIONAL RIGHTS: 12 / 12
E1. Is there freedom of assembly? 4 / 4

The constitution provides for freedom of assembly, and the government generally respects this right in practice.

E2. Is there freedom for nongovernmental organizations, particularly those that are engaged in human rights- and governance-related work? 4 / 4

Nongovernmental organizations (NGOs), including those that investigate human rights issues, operate without state interference.

E3. Is there freedom for trade unions and similar professional or labor organizations? 4 / 4

The law recognizes the rights to form and join trade unions, engage in collective bargaining, and strike. The government enforces labor protections, and antiunion discrimination by employers is relatively uncommon.

F. RULE OF LAW: 15 / 16
F1. Is there an independent judiciary? 4 / 4

The judiciary is generally considered independent. The president appoints senior judges on the advice of the prime minister. A 2016 constitutional reform created a Judicial Appointments Committee (JAC) to make recommendations to the prime minister, except in the case of the chief justice, who chairs the committee. If the prime minister rejects the committee's recommendations, he is obliged to explain his reasons in writing and before the parliament. However, the Venice Commission's 2018 report noted some weaknesses in the justice system that undermine judicial independence, including the dual roles held by the attorney general as both an advisor to the government and a prosecutor. It also observed that despite the establishment of the JAC, the prime minister still maintains considerable power over judicial appointments, making the judiciary vulnerable to political interference.

F2. Does due process prevail in civil and criminal matters? 4 / 4

Police and prosecutors typically observe due process guarantees, including access to defense counsel and protections against arbitrary arrest. However, civil society activists have criticized the authorities for failing to bring the organizers of Caruana Galizia's murder to justice, as well as the small number of criminal investigations into the corruption scandals that have embroiled the country in recent years.

F3. Is there protection from the illegitimate use of physical force and freedom from war and insurgencies? 4 / 4

The authorities do not engage in torture or other ill-treatment of detainees. Rates of violent crime are comparatively low, though various forms of organized crime remain a problem, and a series of car bombings in recent years preceded the 2017 murder of Caruana Galizia.

F4. Do laws, policies, and practices guarantee equal treatment of various segments of the population? 3 / 4

Discrimination based on gender, race, sexual orientation, and other such categories is prohibited by law, and these rules are generally enforced, though some forms of societal discrimination—a gender pay gap, for example—persist in practice.

Malta largely complies with international and EU rules on refugees and asylum seekers; a legal amendment adopted in 2017 gave asylum seekers the right to appeal decisions on their claims. However, the country has been criticized for resisting acceptance of migrants rescued at sea, and advocates for migrants and refugees sometimes report police harassment and hostility from far-right groups.

G. PERSONAL AUTONOMY AND INDIVIDUAL RIGHTS: 14 / 16

G1. Do individuals enjoy freedom of movement, including the ability to change their place of residence, employment, or education? 4 / 4

Residents are largely free to move within the country and travel abroad, and to change their place of employment or education without undue interference.

G2. Are individuals able to exercise the right to own property and establish private businesses without undue interference from state or nonstate actors? 4 / 4

There are no significant restrictions on property rights, and the legal framework is generally supportive of private business activity.

G3. Do individuals enjoy personal social freedoms, including choice of marriage partner and size of family, protection from domestic violence, and control over appearance? 3 / 4

Divorce was legalized in 2011, and subsequent laws have allowed transgender people to express their gender identity on government documents, legalized same-sex marriage, and permitted adoption by same-sex couples.

Malta is the only EU country where abortion is strictly prohibited in all cases, even when the woman's life is in danger. Domestic violence remains a problem despite government efforts to combat it.

G4. Do individuals enjoy equality of opportunity and freedom from economic exploitation? 3 / 4

Residents generally enjoy fair access to economic opportunity and protections from labor exploitation, though migrant workers in particular are vulnerable to labor and sex trafficking or conditions that amount to forced labor.

Marshall Islands

Population: 60,000
Capital: Majuro
Political Rights Rating: 1
Civil Liberties Rating: 1
Freedom Rating: 1.0
Freedom Status: Free
Electoral Democracy: Yes

Overview: The Republic of the Marshall Islands is a stable democracy with regular, competitive elections, an independent judiciary, and a free press. Civil liberties are generally respected. Persistent problems include corruption, gender discrimination, and domestic violence.

KEY DEVELOPMENTS IN 2018:

- In March, a measure that would make the Marshall Islands the first country in the world to introduce cryptocurrency as legal tender became law, drawing international criticism due to the scheme's risks.
- In November, President Hilda Heine narrowly survived a confidence vote brought against her. Her opponents in the parliament claimed the vote was due to the controversial cryptocurrency plan, but Heine argued that it was because of her refusal to support plans to create a tax haven that would be governed independently.

POLITICAL RIGHTS: 38 / 40 (+1)

A. ELECTORAL PROCESS: 12 / 12

A1. Was the current head of government or other chief national authority elected through free and fair elections? 4 / 4

The president, who is elected by the unicameral legislature from among its members for four-year terms, nominates fellow lawmakers to serve as cabinet ministers, and they are formally appointed by the parliament speaker.

In January 2016, following legislative elections in November 2015, Casten Nemra was elected president by a narrow margin with support from the governing Aelon Kein Ad (AKA) party. However, he lost a confidence vote only two weeks later after shifts in party affiliation gave the opposition Kien Eo Am (KEA) party a majority. Hilda Heine was chosen to replace Nemra. In November 2018, Heine narrowly survived a confidence vote brought against her. Her opponents in the parliament claimed the vote was due to a controversial plan to introduce cryptocurrency as legal tender, but Heine argued that it was because of her refusal to support plans to create a tax haven that would be governed independently.

A2. Were the current national legislative representatives elected through free and fair elections? 4 / 4

The parliament, known as the Nitijela, consists of 33 members, with 19 directly elected in single-member districts and five in multimember districts with between two and five seats. Elections are officially nonpartisan, and lawmakers are free to form alliances and change party affiliations after taking office.

The 2015 elections featured significant turnover, with 14 of the 33 seats changing hands. The results were a blow to the government of incumbent president Chris Loeak, who saw about half of his cabinet members voted out of office. There were no reports of violence or complaints of fraud or irregularities. Voter turnout was lower than usual at 46 percent, though some observers suggested that the list of registered voters was inflated with deceased citizens, making the turnout figure artificially low.

A3. Are the electoral laws and framework fair, and are they implemented impartially by the relevant election management bodies? 4 / 4

The constitutional and legal framework provides for democratic elections, and it is implemented impartially.

B. POLITICAL PLURALISM AND PARTICIPATION: 16 / 16 (+1)

B1. Do the people have the right to organize in different political parties or other competitive political groupings of their choice, and is the system free of undue obstacles to the rise and fall of these competing parties or groupings? 4 / 4 (+1)

Despite the fact that parliamentary elections are technically nonpartisan, politicians can organize in party groupings that compete freely and do not encounter obstacles from state or nonstate actors. Parties tend to function as loose coalitions among lawmakers, and party switching is common.

Score Change: The score improved from 3 to 4 because although parliamentary elections are formally nonpartisan, politicians organize in party groupings that compete freely in practice.

B2. Is there a realistic opportunity for the opposition to increase its support or gain power through elections? 4 / 4

The country has an established record of democratic transfers of power between rival party groups. Some governments have been replaced as a result of elections, while others have been toppled by no-confidence votes like that which brought Heine to power in 2016.

B3. Are the people's political choices free from domination by the military, foreign powers, religious hierarchies, economic oligarchies, or any other powerful group that is not democratically accountable? 4 / 4

There are no significant undue constraints on the political choices of voters or candidates. Traditional chiefs play an influential but gradually waning role in politics.

The influence of China on lawmakers in the Marshall Islands was a source of controversy in 2018. President Heine claimed that the confidence vote against her was coordinated by Chinese business interests seeking to create an independently governed tax haven on an atoll in the Marshall Islands; Heine opposed the plan, arguing that it would enable widespread money laundering. She claimed that several of the legislators who initiated the confidence vote had ties to a Chinese businessman who had initially proposed the tax-haven plan.

B4. Do various segments of the population (including ethnic, religious, gender, LGBT, and other relevant groups) have full political rights and electoral opportunities? 4 / 4

Naturalized citizens were allowed to run as candidates in the 2015 elections after a court ruling found that a 1980 law requiring parliamentary candidates to have at least one Marshallese parent and traditional land rights was unconstitutional.

Women have full political rights, though traditional gender roles have limited their participation to some extent, and just three women won seats in the 2015 elections. Heine is the country's first female president and the first female leader of a Pacific island state.

C. FUNCTIONING OF GOVERNMENT: 10 / 12

C1. Do the freely elected head of government and national legislative representatives deter-mine the policies of the government? 4 / 4

There are no undue restrictions on the elected government's ability to form and implement laws and policies. A body of traditional leaders, the Council of Iroij, has an advisory role under the constitution. Its 12 members can offer joint opinions and request reconsideration of any bill affecting customary law, traditional practices, land tenure, and related matters.

The Republic of the Marshall Islands has close relations with the United States under a 1986 Compact of Free Association, which allows the US military to operate in the country in exchange for defense guarantees and development assistance. A component of the compact in force through 2023 calls for the United States to provide about $70 million in annual aid, including contributions to a trust fund for the country. US funds to the Marshall Islands for fiscal year 2018 were directed to the education, health, and infrastructure sectors.

C2. Are safeguards against official corruption strong and effective? 3 / 4

Corruption has been a chronic problem, though auditing bodies and the independent courts are somewhat effective in detecting abuses and holding officials accountable. High-ranking public officials, however, are rarely prosecuted for corruption. Corruption is most prevalent in foreign aid, government procurement, and transfers.

C3. Does the government operate with openness and transparency? 3 / 4

There is not a strong legal mechanism for obtaining access to government information, but documents can often be obtained through the courts. Auditors have repeatedly found invalid or poorly documented spending practices at government ministries, agencies, and state-owned enterprises. In November 2018, the government and the World Bank began a program aimed at strengthening public-procurement and budget-reporting processes, with the ultimate goal of enhancing transparency.

CIVIL LIBERTIES: 55 / 60
D. FREEDOM OF EXPRESSION AND BELIEF: 16 / 16
D1. Are there free and independent media? 4 / 4

The government generally respects the freedoms of speech and the press. A privately owned newspaper, the *Marshall Islands Journal*, publishes articles in English and Marshallese. Broadcast outlets include both government- and church-owned radio stations, and cable television offers a variety of international news and entertainment programs. Internet access is expanding, reaching nearly 40 percent of the population by 2018, but it remains limited due to poor infrastructure and high costs.

D2. Are individuals free to practice and express their religious faith or nonbelief in public and private? 4 / 4

Religious freedoms are respected in practice. Religious groups are not required to register with the government, but those that register as nonprofits are eligible for tax exemptions.

D3. Is there academic freedom, and is the educational system free from extensive political indoctrination? 4 / 4

There are no significant restrictions on academic freedom.

D4. Are individuals free to express their personal views on political or other sensitive topics without fear of surveillance or retribution? 4 / 4

Citizens are generally free to discuss their political opinions, and there are no reports of improper government surveillance.

E. ASSOCIATIONAL AND ORGANIZATIONAL RIGHTS: 11 / 12
E1. Is there freedom of assembly? 4 / 4

The government upholds constitutional guarantees of freedom of assembly. Protests in recent years have addressed issues including climate change, women's rights, and the legacy of US nuclear weapons tests in the country.

E2. Is there freedom for nongovernmental organizations, particularly those that are engaged in human rights– and governance-related work? 4 / 4

Civil society groups, many of which are sponsored by or affiliated with church organizations and provide social services, are able to operate freely.

E3. Is there freedom for trade unions and similar professional or labor organizations? 3 / 4

Constitutional and legal provisions that protect freedom of association also apply to trade unions. However, there are no laws regulating the right to strike, and few employers are large enough to support union activity among their workers.

F. RULE OF LAW: 15 / 16
F1. Is there an independent judiciary? 4 / 4

The constitution provides for an independent judiciary, and the judiciary generally operates without political interference. Judges are appointed by the cabinet on the recommendation of the Judicial Service Commission, and the legislature confirms the appointments. High Court and Supreme Court judges can only be removed by a two-thirds vote in the Nitijela, for clear failure or inability to perform their duties or for serious crimes or abuses.

F2. Does due process prevail in civil and criminal matters? 4 / 4

The authorities generally observe legal safeguards against arbitrary arrest and detention. The state provides lawyers for indigent defendants, and due process standards for trials are upheld.

F3. Is there protection from the illegitimate use of physical force and freedom from war and insurgencies? 4 / 4

Violent street crime and other such threats to physical security are relatively rare, though conditions in the country's few prison and jail facilities are sometimes overcrowded or otherwise below international standards.

F4. Do laws, policies, and practices guarantee equal treatment of various segments of the population? 3 / 4

Women generally enjoy equal treatment under the law, but there is no explicit ban on discrimination in employment, and women face disadvantages in the workplace in practice. While same-sex sexual activity was decriminalized in 2005, discrimination based on sexual orientation and gender identity is not prohibited by law.

G. PERSONAL AUTONOMY AND INDIVIDUAL RIGHTS: 13 / 16
G1. Do individuals enjoy freedom of movement, including the ability to change their place of residence, employment, or education? 4 / 4

Freedom of movement is generally respected. Marshallese citizens have the right to live and work in the United States and to travel there without a visa.

G2. Are individuals able to exercise the right to own property and establish private businesses without undue interference from state or nonstate actors? 3 / 4

Individuals have the rights to own property and establish private businesses, and these rights are largely observed in practice.

G3. Do individuals enjoy personal social freedoms, including choice of marriage partner and size of family, protection from domestic violence, and control over appearance? 3 / 4

Personal social freedoms are mostly upheld. However, the minimum age for marriage is 16 for women and 18 for men; about a quarter of women aged 20–24 were married by age 18. While domestic violence remains widespread, reporting of the problem has apparently increased in recent years due to improved processes for obtaining orders of protection.

G4. Do individuals enjoy equality of opportunity and freedom from economic exploitation? 3 / 4

The government enforces a minimum wage law, though it does not apply to the informal sector. Some local and East Asian women are subjected to forced prostitution in a trade that depends on visiting freight or fishing vessels. According to the US State Department's 2018 *Trafficking in Persons Report*, the government has increased law enforcement efforts against trafficking and provided more services for victims.

Mauritania

Population: 4,500,000
Capital: Nouakchott
Political Rights Rating: 6
Civil Liberties Rating: 5
Freedom Rating: 5.5
Freedom Status: Not Free
Electoral Democracy: No

Overview: The president came to power in 2008 through a military coup, and has since confirmed his position through flawed elections. Freer legislative elections were held in 2018, but the executive dominates the legislative branch. A variety of media outlets operate, but journalists risk arrest for reporting on sensitive topics and many self-censor. Black Mauritanians, the Haratin population, women, and LGBT (lesbian, gay, bisexual, and transgender) people face discrimination. The government has taken increased steps to implement laws that address the problem of institutionalized slavery and discrimination, but continues to arrest antislavery and antidiscrimination activists.

KEY DEVELOPMENTS IN 2018:
- Legislative and municipal elections held in September saw the participation of 98 political parties, including major opposition parties that had boycotted previous elections. The ruling Union for the Republic (UPR) retained a solid majority in the parliament.

- An opposition coalition claimed the elections were fraudulent, but the results were accepted by most stakeholders. African Union (AU) observers said polling was credible, some irregularities notwithstanding.
- In March, a court sentenced three people to 10 and 20 years in prison for practicing slavery. Meanwhile, it continued to refuse official accreditation for one of the country's most prominent antislavery organizations, and jailed several antislavery activists.
- In April, the parliament passed a new law that strengthens the existing punishment of the death penalty for certain forms of blasphemy.

POLITICAL RIGHTS: 11 / 40 (+2)

A. ELECTORAL PROCESS: 5 / 12 (+2)

A1. Was the current head of government or other chief national authority elected through free and fair elections? 1 / 4

The president is chief of state and is directly elected to up to two five-year terms by popular vote. Mohamed Ould Abdel Aziz, who first came to power through a military coup in 2008, won a second term in 2014 representing the UPR, taking 82 percent of the vote. Most opposition parties, including the main opposition coalition, the National Front for the Defense of Democracy (FNDU), boycotted the election, claiming that the process was flawed and biased. The antislavery activist Biram Dah Abeid ran as an independent and captured 9 percent of the vote. His allegations of electoral misconduct and fraud were dismissed by the authorities.

The prime minister is head of government and is appointed by the president. Mohamed Salem Ould Bechir of the UPR, a former energy minister, was appointed to the post in November 2018, after the year's parliamentary elections.

A2. Were the current national legislative representatives elected through free and fair elections? 2 / 4 (+1)

Constitutional reforms adopted through a 2017 referendum dissolved the Senate, leaving the 157-seat National Assembly as the country's legislative body. Members are directly elected to five-year terms in a mixed system of direct and plurality voting; four members are directly elected by the diaspora.

In September 2018, a new National Assembly was elected. Ninety-eight political parties participated in the polls, including parties of the opposition coalition the FNDU, which had boycotted previous elections. The ruling UPR took a majority, with 89 seats, and the Islamist party Tawassoul confirmed its position as the leading opposition party with 14 seats.

An opposition coalition called the elections fraudulent, but most Mauritanian politicians as well as AU observers deemed them credible. The AU observers said "imperfections" in the process did not appear to have affected the polls' credibility.

Abeid, the former presidential candidate who is also head of the antislavery group the Initiative for the Resurgence of the Abolitionist Movement in Mauritania (IRA Mauritania) won a seat in the new parliament, though he was being held in pretrial detention at the time of the election while authorities investigated claims that he had threatened a journalist. His arrest came weeks before the election, and was reportedly carried out in the absence of a warrant. IRA Mauritania denies the allegations against him. In late December, he was released after receiving a sentence shorter than the time he had already served.

The UPR posted a strong performance in concurrent municipal elections.

Score Change: The score improved from 1 to 2 due to the organization of legislative and municipal elections that were generally considered credible, and which featured the participation of many opposition parties.

A3. Are the electoral laws and framework fair, and are they implemented impartially by the relevant election management bodies? 2 / 4 (+1)

In April 2018, the government appointed a new Independent National Electoral Commission (CENI) following a series of dialogues with some opposition parties. However, the FNDU, which had boycotted the dialogue process, rejected the new commission and demanded its dissolution. In July, the government appointed a new president of the CENI who had once been a member of the FNDU. Despite the controversies over its composition during the first half of the year, the new electoral commission organized the year's elections, which were generally viewed as successful.

Score Change: The score improved from 1 to 2 due to the formation of a new electoral commission, which organized credible legislative and municipal elections.

B. POLITICAL PLURALISM AND PARTICIPATION: 2 / 16

B1. Do the people have the right to organize in different political parties or other competitive political groupings of their choice, and is the system free of undue obstacles to the rise and fall of these competing parties or groupings? 1 / 4

A number of obstacles prevent parties from successfully mobilizing their bases. Authorities often break up or otherwise prevent demonstrations organized by political parties. The ruling party is frequently successful in efforts to co-opt leaders of smaller parties with comparatively fewer resources. Authorities have denied registration to activist parties, including the Forces of Progress for Change, which opposes racial discrimination. The party's legal petition to gain recognition has been pending before the Supreme Court since 2015.

B2. Is there a realistic opportunity for the opposition to increase its support or gain power through elections? 1 / 4

Most opposition parties lack an institutional base, and many are formed by splinter factions of the ruling party that later rejoin it, sometimes as a result of active co-optation. In combination with advantages inherent in UPR's incumbency, it is very difficult for opposition groupings to increase their support through elections.

Most opposition parties boycotted both the 2013 parliamentary elections and the 2014 presidential election, citing a system dominated by the UPR, which since its creation in 2009 has won every election handily. Though opposition parties took part in the September 2018 elections, the ruling party remained dominant, winning a solid majority of legislative seats. Opposition parties fared somewhat better in the municipal and regional elections.

B3. Are the people's political choices free from domination by the military, foreign powers, religious hierarchies, economic oligarchies, or any other powerful group that is not democratically accountable? 0 / 4

The political choices of Mauritanians are greatly influenced by the military, which dominates the political system. Since 1978, Mauritania has either been under military rule or led by a military leader, with the exception of 18 months of civilian government between 2007 and 2008.

Traditional religious leaders exert influence on voters, often backing the ruling UPR and urging voters to support its initiatives.

B4. Do various segments of the population (including ethnic, religious, gender, LGBT, and other relevant groups) have full political rights and electoral opportunities? 0 / 4

The Bidhan ethnic group dominates the Mauritanian government, while black Mauritanians and the Haratin ethnic group are underrepresented in elected positions and in high-level government roles. Discrimination hinders the ability of these groups to gain power. Thousands of black Mauritanians who were forced out of their villages by the military in 1989 have been allowed to return, but face difficulties when trying to enroll in the census and register to vote.

Women participate in politics at lower levels than men, largely due to traditional cultural norms, and women's interests are poorly represented in national politics. Thirty-one seats in the National Assembly are held by women.

C. FUNCTIONING OF GOVERNMENT: 4 / 12

C1. Do the freely elected head of government and national legislative representatives determine the policies of the government? 1 / 4

The executive dominates the legislative branch: the president has the power to dissolve the National Assembly, but the legislature has no impeachment power over the president. The military remains a powerful force in the Mauritanian government, and still has a great deal of influence on policymaking.

C2. Are safeguards against official corruption strong and effective? 2 / 4

Although the government has adopted numerous anticorruption laws and in 2005 signed the African Union Convention on Preventing and Combating Corruption, corruption remains widespread and the laws are not effectively enforced. Public contracts are typically awarded in exchange for bribes or on the basis of patronage. Bribes are often necessary in order to ensure the completion of ordinary government processes like obtaining licenses and permits.

A report published in 2017 by Sherpa, a nongovernmental organization (NGO), documented multiple cases of corruption at the highest levels of the Aziz administration that have gone unpunished. Among other cases, the report alleges that the president's son used his influence to ensure that the French subsidiary of a Finnish company, Wärtsilä, received a contract to construct a power plant in exchange for a payment of over $11 million.

C3. Does the government operate with openness and transparency? 1 / 4

The government does not operate with transparency, particularly in granting mining and fishing licenses, land distribution, government contracts, and tax payments. The construction of a new airport in Nouakchott that opened in 2016 drew criticism—a company with no experience in airport construction won a contract to build the facility through an opaque procurement process.

CIVIL LIBERTIES: 21 / 60

D. FREEDOM OF EXPRESSION AND BELIEF: 9 / 16

D1. Are there free and independent media? 2 / 4

Mauritania has a vibrant media landscape, with several privately owned newspapers, television stations, and radio stations in operation. However, journalists who cover sensitive topics or scrutinize the political elite can face harassment and arrest. In March, a French-Moroccan journalist who was investigating the issue of slavery was arrested, held for three days, and expelled from Mauritania.

In 2014, a court in Nouadhibou sentenced Mohamed Cheikh Ould Mohamed M'Kheitir, an independent blogger, to death for apostasy in an expedited judicial process. Ould M'Kheitir had criticized the unequal social order in Mauritania and the prophet Muhammad. In November 2017, an appeals court in Nouadhibou reduced Ould M'Kheitir's death sentence to two years in prison, which he had already served. In May 2018, the government said that Ould M'Kheitir remained in custody under "administrative detention" for reasons of his own security; he was still in custody at the end of the year.

Criminal defamation laws remain on the books, and are sometimes enforced against journalists. In August, two journalists were arrested on charges of defamation after each had separately republished a third-party article that criticized a lawyer close to the government; they were held for over a week before being acquitted. Most journalists practice a degree of self-censorship when covering potentially contentious issues such as the military, corruption, and slavery.

D2. Are individuals free to practice and express their religious faith or nonbelief in public and private? 2 / 4

Mauritania is an Islamic republic. Non-Muslims cannot proselytize or become citizens, and those who convert from Islam to another religion lose their citizenship. In practice, however, non-Muslim communities are generally not targeted for persecution.

Apostasy is a crime punishable by death. To date, no one has been executed for the crime. However, in April, the parliament passed a new law that strengthens the existing death penalty punishment for certain blasphemy offenses. The new law removes the possibility of repentance as a way to avoid a death sentence for committing some forms of blasphemy.

D3. Is there academic freedom, and is the educational system free from extensive political indoctrination? 3 / 4

Academic freedom is largely respected. However, the increasing use of Arabic as the lingua franca at universities has hindered access to education for black Mauritanians, who mainly speak other languages. Student activists sometimes face pressure from university administrators, including threats of expulsion and intimidation.

D4. Are individuals free to express their personal views on political or other sensitive topics without fear of surveillance or retribution? 2 / 4

Individuals have faced reprisals for expressing views critical of the government on social media, including termination of employment from government agencies. In October 2017, Abdellahi Ould Mohamed Ould El Haimer was fired from his job at the National Rural Water Agency after writing a Facebook post critical of the prime minister. The director of the agency claimed he was fired for "gross misconduct." In January 2018, activist Abdallahi Salem Ould Yali was arrested in connection with a Facebook post in which he urged members of the marginalized Haratin community to resist racial discrimination. In October, he was charged with incitement to violence, and remained in pretrial detention at year's end.

In January the government adopted a new law that toughens sanctions for discrimination and racism, but penalties are very heavy: in April, at least two people received one-year prison sentences for insulting other Mauritanians by denigrating them as slaves on social media.

E. ASSOCIATIONAL AND ORGANIZATIONAL RIGHTS: 4 / 12
E1. Is there freedom of assembly? 1 / 4

While the constitution guarantees freedom of assembly, organizers are required to obtain consent from the government for large gatherings, which is often denied. In 2018, protests and demonstrations, including several organized by IRA Mauritania activists denouncing the arrests of their leader, were often violently broken up by authorities. In 2017, police had used tear gas to suppress a peaceful demonstration in Nouakchott convened to address youth unemployment, and arrested over two dozen participants.

E2. Is there freedom for nongovernmental organizations, particularly those that are engaged in human rights- and governance-related work? 1 / 4

NGOs, particularly antislavery organizations, frequently encounter intimidation, violence, and repression in carrying out their activities. The antislavery group IRA Mauritania has repeatedly been denied permission to register as an NGO. In 2018, Abeid, the leader of IRA Mauritania, spent five months in prison awaiting trial on charges of incitement to hatred and violence following a complaint by a journalist he allegedly threatened. In late December, he was released after receiving a sentence shorter than the time he had already served. In July, two other members of IRA Mauritania were released after spending two years in prison. Separately, in February, visiting representatives of Human Rights Watch (HRW) were denied permission to hold a press conference at a hotel in the capital.

E3. Is there freedom for trade unions and similar professional or labor organizations? 2 / 4

Workers have the legal right to unionize, but unions require approval from the public prosecutor to operate and often confront hostility from employers. Approximately 25 percent of Mauritanians are employed in the formal economy, but around 90 percent of workers in the industrial and commercial sectors are unionized. The right to collective bargaining is not always respected, and the government sometimes pressures union members to withdraw their membership. The right to strike is limited by notice requirements and other onerous regulations.

In July, police violently repressed a protest by striking dockworkers at the Nouakchott port.

F. RULE OF LAW: 4 / 16

F1. Is there an independent judiciary? 1 / 4

Mauritania's judiciary lacks independence. The president has the power to unilaterally appoint many key judges, including three of the six judges on the Constitutional Court and the chair of the Supreme Court. The courts are subject to political pressure from the executive branch. Instances of judges facing retaliatory measures for issuing rulings against the government have been reported.

F2. Does due process prevail in civil and criminal matters? 1 / 4

Due process rights are often not respected in practice. Suspects are frequently arrested without being informed of the charges against them. Lengthy pretrial detentions are common.

Arbitrary arrests of opposition politicians, journalists, and human rights activists occur with some frequency. In August 2017, Mohamed Ould Ghadda, a senator who opposed the 2017 referendum to abolish the Senate, was arrested on vague corruption charges. Ould Ghadda was released and placed under judicial control in September 2018, after spending a year in prison.

F3. Is there protection from the illegitimate use of physical force and freedom from war and insurgencies? 1 / 4

Torture and abuse at Mauritania's prisons and detention centers remained a problem in 2018, and perpetrators are rarely held accountable. Police frequently beat suspects following arrest. In July, Mohamed Ould Brahim died at a police station only five hours after his arrest by antidrug forces. The government claimed that he died of a heart attack, while family members and civil society representatives maintain that he died as result of police brutality.

Prisons are plagued by violence, are overcrowded, and lack basic sanitation. Food shortages are also common in prisons. Children are sometimes held with the adult prison population.

F4. Do laws, policies, and practices guarantee equal treatment of various segments of the population? 1 / 4

Same-sex sexual activity is illegal in Mauritania and punishable by death for men. LGBT individuals generally hide their sexual orientation or gender identity due to severe discrimination. Racial and ethnic discrimination remains a serious problem.

Sharia law as it is applied in Mauritania discriminates against women. The testimony of two women is equal to that of one man. Female victims of crime are entitled to only half the financial compensation that male victims receive.

There were reports of refugees being expelled and ultimately abandoned just across the border in Senegal.

G. PERSONAL AUTONOMY AND INDIVIDUAL RIGHTS: 4 / 16

G1. Do individuals enjoy freedom of movement, including the ability to change their place of residence, employment, or education? 1 / 4

While the Bidhan population is relatively free to make personal decisions about residence, employment, and education, the choices of black Mauritanians and the Haratin are often constrained by racial and caste-based discrimination. People lacking government identity cards are not allowed to travel in some regions, which disproportionately affects black Mauritanians.

In July 2018, authorities blocked five activists from traveling to Switzerland to participate in the UN Committee against Torture's periodic review of Mauritania.

G2. Are individuals able to exercise the right to own property and establish private businesses without undue interference from state or nonstate actors? 2 / 4

Though the law guarantees property rights, these rights are not always enforced in practice, as it can be difficult to get property disputes fairly adjudicated in court. Complex laws and an opaque bureaucracy present challenges to starting a business.

Many black Mauritanians who left their homes in the Senegal River Valley in the wake of the 1989 conflict have returned, but have been unable to regain ownership of their land. Local authorities reportedly allow the Bidhan to appropriate land used by the Haratin and black Mauritanians.

G3. Do individuals enjoy personal social freedoms, including choice of marriage partner and size of family, protection from domestic violence, and control over appearance? 1 / 4

According to UNICEF's 2016 *State of the World's Children* report, 37 percent of girls are married before the age of 18. In January 2017, the government sent the parliament a bill that would ban marriage for girls under 18. The bill failed in the National Assembly, largely due to pressure from religious leaders.

Female genital mutilation is illegal, but the law is rarely enforced and the practice is still common. Domestic violence and rape remained problems in 2018, victims rarely seek legal redress, and convictions for these crimes are rare. Laws banning adultery and morality offenses discourage victims of sexual assault from reporting it to police.

G4. Do individuals enjoy equality of opportunity and freedom from economic exploitation? 0 / 4

Despite amendments to the antislavery law passed in 2015 meant to address the problem more robustly, slavery and slavery-like practices continued in 2018, with many former slaves still reliant on their former owners due to racial discrimination, poverty, and other socioeconomic factors. The government cracks down on NGOs that push for greater enforcement of the law and rarely prosecutes perpetrators, but at the same time has shown an increased commitment to enforcing laws against slavery. In March, a court handed down 10- and 20-year prison sentences to three people for practicing slavery.

Trafficking in persons remains a problem in Mauritania in 2018. The government failed to prosecute a recruitment agency that allegedly recruited more than 200 women under false pretenses into forced prostitution and domestic slavery in Saudi Arabia in 2016.

Mauritius

Population: 1,300,000
Capital: Port Louis
Political Rights Rating: 1
Civil Liberties Rating: 2
Freedom Rating: 1.5
Freedom Status: Free
Electoral Democracy: Yes

Overview: Mauritius is home to an open, multiparty system that has allowed for the regular handover of power between parties through free and fair elections. However, the political leadership remains dominated by a few families, corruption is a problem, journalists occasionally face harassment and legal pressure, and LGBT (lesbian, gay, bisexual, and transgender) people face threats and discrimination.

KEY DEVELOPMENTS IN 2018:

- In March, Ameenah Gurib-Fakim, who was elected the country's first woman president in 2015, resigned after allegations emerged that she had made some $26,000 worth of personal purchases using a credit card issued to her by a nongovernmental organization (NGO).
- In July, the minister of gender equality and the deputy assembly speaker resigned after the findings of a commission of inquiry suggested that each had links to drug traffickers.
- In October, the parliament approved a broadly worded amendment to the Information and Communications Technologies Act (ICT) Act that made the online publication of material deemed false, harmful, or illegal punishable by up to 10 years in prison.
- In June, the annual Mauritius Pride March was cancelled after the organizer received death threats, and police indicated that they might not be able to protect participants from threatening groups of opponents that had gathered along the parade route.

POLITICAL RIGHTS: 37 / 40
A. ELECTORAL PROCESS: 12 / 12

A1. Was the current head of government or other chief national authority elected through free and fair elections? 4 / 4

The president, whose role is mostly ceremonial, is elected by the unicameral National Assembly to a five-year term. Ameenah Gurib-Fakim, elected the country's first woman president in 2015, resigned in March 2018 after being implicated in a financial scandal. Vice President Paramasivum Pillay Vyapoory became acting president, according to legal procedure.

Executive power resides with the prime minister, who is appointed by the president from the party or coalition with the most seats in the legislature. After the 2014 general elections, Anerood Jugnauth, leader of the Militant Socialist Movement (MSM), was appointed to the post for his sixth nonconsecutive term since 1982. He resigned in January 2017 and named his son, Pravind Jugnauth, as his replacement. The opposition decried the power handover as immoral, though it was approved by the president and considered legal under the constitution. The developments reflected the dynastic character of Mauritian politics.

A2. Were the current national legislative representatives elected through free and fair elections? 4 / 4

Of the National Assembly's 70 members, 62 are directly elected and up to 8 "best losers" are appointed from among unsuccessful candidates who gained the largest number of votes. The members of the National Assembly serve five-year terms.

The 2014 elections took place peacefully, and stakeholders accepted the results. Mauritius's two main political parties—former prime minister Navinchandra Ramgoolam's ruling Mauritian Labour Party (PTR) and former prime minister Paul Bérenger's Mauritian Militant Movement (MMM)—unexpectedly lost the elections to the Alliance Lepep coalition, made up of the MSM, the Mauritian Social Democratic Party (PMSD), and the Liberation Movement (ML). The 2014 election results were widely interpreted as a reaction to Ramgoolam's proposed constitutional reform to increase the power of the president. The Alliance Lepep won 47 of the 62 elected seats, while PTR-MMM alliance gained 13 of the elected seats. In 2016, the PMSD left the Alliance Lepep and joined the opposition.

A3. Are the electoral laws and framework fair, and are they implemented impartially by the relevant election management bodies? 4 / 4

The Electoral Supervisory Commission has impartially supervised the electoral process. There have been 10 general elections in Mauritius since the country became independent in 1968.

Long-running discussions on electoral reforms and party financing laws continued in 2018, but no changes had been approved by the parliament at year's end. There is no law on the financing of electoral campaigns.

B. POLITICAL PLURALISM AND PARTICIPATION: 15 / 16

B1. Do the people have the right to organize in different political parties or other competitive political groupings of their choice, and is the system free of undue obstacles to the rise and fall of these competing parties or groupings? 4 / 4

Political parties are generally free to form and operate. Forty-five parties competed in the 2014 elections.

B2. Is there a realistic opportunity for the opposition to increase its support or gain power through elections? 4 / 4

Since independence, political power has peacefully rotated among the three largest parties—the PTR, the MSM, and the MMM.

B3. Are the people's political choices free from domination by the military, foreign powers, religious hierarchies, economic oligarchies, or any other powerful group that is not democratically accountable? 4 / 4

Voters and candidates are generally able to express their political choices without pressure from actors not democratically accountable. However, money plays an important role in politics, and there is no law on the financing of electoral campaigns. There are some concerns about the influence of drug trafficking groups on the country's politics, potentially exercised in part through campaign donations.

B4. Do various segments of the population (including ethnic, religious, gender, LGBT, and other relevant groups) have full political rights and electoral opportunities? 3 / 4

The Hindu majority is viewed as maintaining most positions of political influence. Women hold a handful of cabinet seats and other high-level political positions, but are generally underrepresented in politics. Local elections require that one third of political parties' candidates in each district be women.

Discrimination against LGBT people can discourage their active political participation.

C. FUNCTIONING OF GOVERNMENT: 10 / 12

C1. Do the freely elected head of government and national legislative representatives determine the policies of the government? 4 / 4

Elected representatives are duly seated, and the government has generally been able to make policy without interference or major political disruptions. However, politics in Mauritius are dominated by a few families, with coordination among the head of the government, members of the National Assembly, and other relevant individuals. Only five different individuals have held the post of prime minister since independence in 1968.

In July 2018, the minister of gender equality and the deputy assembly speaker resigned after the findings of a commission of inquiry suggested that they had links to drug traffickers.

C2. Are safeguards against official corruption strong and effective? 3 / 4

The country's anticorruption framework is robust, but sometimes inconsistently upheld. In March 2018, Gurib-Fakim, who was elected the country's first woman president in 2015, resigned after allegations emerged in the media that she had made some $26,000 worth of personal purchases using a credit card issued to her by an NGO.

C3. Does the government operate with openness and transparency? 3 / 4

The government openly debates the country's budget in the National Assembly and publishes it and other legislation online and in the press. In recent years, the authorities have worked to implement other transparency initiatives, though the country still lacks a freedom of information act. In April 2018, the minister of technology, communication, and innovation launched the National Open Data Portal, through which the various cabinet ministries will release data. In December, lawmakers approved an asset declaration bill that applied to a wide range of public officials.

CIVIL LIBERTIES: 52 / 60
D. FREEDOM OF EXPRESSION AND BELIEF: 15 / 16
D1. Are there free and independent media? 3 / 4

The constitution guarantees freedom of expression. Several private daily and weekly publications report on the ruling and opposition parties, but the state-owned Mauritius Broadcasting Corporation's radio and television services generally reflect government viewpoints. A small number of private radio stations compete with the state-run media.

Journalists occasionally face legal pressure. One of the main newspapers, *L'Express*, has faced verbal attacks by authorities, who have also reduced advertising with the outlet, and its journalists have faced legal and other harassment.

D2. Are individuals free to practice and express their religious faith or nonbelief in public and private? 4 / 4

Religious freedom is generally upheld. The government grants subsidies to Hindu, Roman Catholic, Muslim, Anglican, Presbyterian, and Seventh-day Adventist communities, but not to smaller groups, though all religious groups may apply for tax-exempt status. Tensions between Muslim and Hindu communities continue to be reported.

D3. Is there academic freedom, and is the educational system free from extensive political indoctrination? 4 / 4

Academic freedom is generally upheld.

D4. Are individuals free to express their personal views on political or other sensitive topics without fear of surveillance or retribution? 4 / 4

Private discussion is generally unrestricted. However, in October, the parliament approved a broadly worded amendment to the ICT Act that made the online publication of material deemed false, harmful, or illegal punishable by up to 10 years in prison.

E. ASSOCIATIONAL AND ORGANIZATIONAL RIGHTS: 12 / 12
E1. Is there freedom of assembly? 4 / 4

Freedom of assembly is usually upheld. However, in June 2018, the 13th annual Mauritius Pride March was cancelled after police said they might not be able to protect participants from groups of opponents holding antigay signs, some of whom were reportedly armed, that had gathered along the parade route. The main organizer also received a series of death threats ahead of the planned event. Both Prime Minister Jugnauth and the Roman Catholic Church in Mauritius condemned the antigay protesters and regretted the march's cancellation. Later in June, a smaller pride event was held near the waterfront in Port Louis.

E2. Is there freedom for nongovernmental organizations, particularly those that are engaged in human rights– and governance-related work? 4 / 4

Civil society groups operate freely. However, many are reliant upon government funding that could compromise their independence.

E3. Is there freedom for trade unions and similar professional or labor organizations? 4 / 4

Unions regularly meet with government leaders, protest, and advocate for improved compensation and workers' rights. There are more than 300 unions in Mauritius.

F. RULE OF LAW: 13 / 16
F1. Is there an independent judiciary? 3 / 4

The generally independent judiciary administers a legal system that combines French and British traditions. However, judicial independence has been questioned in some cases involving politicians.

Mauritius has maintained the right of appeal to the Privy Council in London.

F2. Does due process prevail in civil and criminal matters? 4 / 4

Constitutional guarantees of due process are generally upheld. However, Mauritian criminal law allows for police to charge suspects provisionally, and then hold them for months until a formal charge is issued. Due to court backlogs, many of those being held in prison are in pretrial detention, and some detainees reportedly wait years before facing trial.

F3. Is there protection from the illegitimate use of physical force and freedom from war and insurgencies? 3 / 4

Mauritius is free from war and insurgencies. However, allegations of abuses by police continue. A measure establishing an Independent Police Complaints Commission (IPCC) was passed in 2016, and it became operational in April 2018. By October, the IPCC had received 303 complaints.

F4. Do laws, policies, and practices guarantee equal treatment of various segments of the population? 3 / 4

The Equal Opportunities Commission (EOC), set up by the 2008 Equal Opportunities Act, prohibits discrimination, promotes equality of opportunity in the public and private sectors, and investigates possible cases of discrimination. Though the law and the EOC do not allow for discrimination in the workforce, some citizens view economic leadership to be closed to ethnic minorities. Women generally earn less money than men for equal work.

LGBT people face discrimination and the risk of targeted violence. Laws that criminalize same-sex sexual activity remain on the books, but are rarely invoked. At least two small LGBT (lesbian, gay, bisexual, and transgender) groups are active in Mauritius, and seek to raise visibility of LGBT issues and counter homophobia.

G. PERSONAL AUTONOMY AND INDIVIDUAL RIGHTS: 12 / 16

G1. Do individuals enjoy freedom of movement, including the ability to change their place of residence, employment, or education? 4 / 4

Citizens are generally allowed to move freely within Mauritius but there are some restrictions on travel in the Chagos Islands, which are disputed between Mauritius and Great Britain. Mauritians are free to change their place of residence, employment, and education.

G2. Are individuals able to exercise the right to own property and establish private businesses without undue interference from state or nonstate actors? 3 / 4

Mauritius is considered among the most business-friendly countries in Africa. However, the Non-Citizen Property Restriction Act limits most noncitizens from owning or acquiring property. Corruption can hamper business activity.

G3. Do individuals enjoy personal social freedoms, including choice of marriage partner and size of family, protection from domestic violence, and control over appearance? 3 / 4

The government generally does not limit social freedoms, though same-sex unions are not recognized. Rape is against the law, but spousal rape is not specifically criminalized. Although Domestic violence is illegal but remains a significant concern.

G4. Do individuals enjoy equality of opportunity and freedom from economic exploitation? 2 / 4

Women and children are vulnerable to sex trafficking, and while the government has made some efforts to prosecute traffickers and provide services to victims, these efforts are generally inadequate.

The position of migrant workers in the manufacturing and construction sectors can be precarious. There have been reports of employers confiscating workers' passports, and of migrant workers becoming beholden to unscrupulous recruitment agents who charge huge fees for placement in a job.

Mexico

Population: 130,800,000
Capital: Mexico City
Political Rights Rating: 3
Civil Liberties Rating: 3
Freedom Rating: 3.0
Freedom Status: Partly Free
Electoral Democracy: Yes

Overview: Mexico has been an electoral democracy since 2000, and alternation in power between parties is routine at both the federal and state levels. However, the country suffers from severe rule-of-law deficits that limit full citizen enjoyment of political rights and civil liberties. Violence perpetrated by organized criminals, corruption among government officials, human rights abuses by both state and nonstate actors, and rampant impunity are among the most visible of Mexico's many governance challenges.

KEY DEVELOPMENTS IN 2018:

- General elections in July resulted in an overwhelming victory for left-wing candidate Andrés Manuel López Obrador, the runner-up in the previous two presidential elections. López Obrador's campaign focused on themes of corruption and social service provision; he attacked the establishment as a "mafia of power" while pledging central government austerity and a crackdown on graft to generate funds for increased welfare spending.
- The electoral coalition led by López Obrador's National Regeneration Movement (MORENA) also garnered majorities in both houses of the Mexican Congress. The results of the year's elections represented a stark repudiation of the outgoing administration of President Enrique Peña Nieto and the Institutional Revolutionary Party (PRI).
- Criminal violence rose for the fourth straight year, and included the murder of scores of candidates and campaign workers in the run-up to the July elections. The Committee to Protect Journalists (CPJ) reported that at least four journalists were murdered during the year as a result of their work.
- López Obrador released a plan to contain criminal violence in November. However, the strategy centered on creating a new security force, the National Guard, which was sharply criticized by rights advocates for deepening the militarization of public security.

- As one of his first acts as president, López Obrador decreed the creation of a truth commission to investigate the notorious mass disappearance of 43 students in Iguala, Guerrero, in 2014.

POLITICAL RIGHTS: 27 / 40 (+1)

A. ELECTORAL PROCESS: 9 / 12

A1. Was the current head of government or other chief national authority elected through free and fair elections? 3 / 4

The president is elected to a six-year term and cannot be reelected. López Obrador of the left-leaning MORENA party won the July poll with a commanding 53 percent of the vote. His closest rival, Ricardo Anaya—the candidate of the National Action Party (PAN) as well as of the Democratic Revolution Party (PRD) and Citizens' Movement (MC)—took 22 percent. The large margin of victory prevented a recurrence of the controversy that accompanied the 2006 elections, when López Obrador had prompted a political crisis by refusing to accept the narrow election victory of conservative Felipe Calderón. The results of the 2018 poll also represented a stark repudiation of the outgoing administration of President Peña Nieto and the PRI; the party's candidate, José Antonio Meade, took just 16 percent of the vote.

The election campaign was marked by violence and threats against candidates for state and local offices. Accusations of illicit campaign activities remained frequent at the state level, including during the 2018 gubernatorial election in Puebla, where the victory of PAN candidate Martha Érika Alonso—the wife of incumbent governor Rafael Moreno—was only confirmed in December, following a protracted process of recounts and appeals related to accusations of ballot manipulation. (Both Alonso and Moreno died in a helicopter crash later that month.)

A2. Were the current national legislative representatives elected through free and fair elections? 3 / 4

Senators are elected for six-year terms through a mix of direct voting and proportional representation, with at least two parties represented in each state's delegation. In the Chamber of Deputies, the lower house of the bicameral Congress, 300 members are elected through direct representation and 200 through proportional representation, each for three-year terms. Under 2013 electoral reforms, current members of Congress are no longer barred from reelection and candidates are permitted to run as independents. For legislators elected in 2018, elected senators will be eligible to serve up to two six-year terms, and deputies will be permitted to serve up to four three-year terms.

In the 2018 elections, MORENA achieved a 255-seat majority in the Chamber of Deputies, and with the support of its coalition allies, the Workers' Party (PT) and the Social Encounter Party (PES), held just over 300 seats. The PAN won 79 seats, while the PRI plummeted from winning 202 seats in the 2015 midterms to just 47 seats in 2018. Similarly, the MORENA-led coalition now commands a clear majority in the 128-member Senate with 70 seats, compared to 24 for the PAN and 15 for the PRI.

Accusations of illicit campaign activities are frequent at the state level, and violations including vote buying, ballot stealing, and misuse of public funds were reported in 2018. The year's campaign was also marked by threats and violence against legislative candidates. In one of many incidents reflecting the poor security environment for campaign activities, in June, Fernando Puron, a congressional candidate in Piedras Negras, was shot dead in broad daylight while posing for photographs with supporters.

A3. Are the electoral laws and framework fair, and are they implemented impartially by the relevant election management bodies? 3 / 4

Mexico's National Electoral Institute (INE) supervises elections and enforces political party laws, including strict regulations on campaign financing and the content of political advertising—although control is weaker in practice. While the 2018 elections were generally considered free and fair, the INE and the Federal Electoral Tribunal (TEPJF) struggled to comprehensively address problems including misuse of public funds, vote-buying, and ballot stealing, and to ensure transparent campaign finance.

An October referendum on whether to continue construction of a new airport near Mexico City and a subsequent set of referendums on infrastructure and social spending held in November were not supervised by INE, had few protections against fraud, and featured the participation of only a tiny proportion of Mexico's electorate.

B. POLITICAL PLURALISM AND PARTICIPATION: 13 / 16 (+1)

B1. Do the people have the right to organize in different political parties or other competitive political groupings of their choice, and is the system free of undue obstacles to the rise and fall of these competing parties or groupings? 4 / 4 (+1)

Mexico's multiparty system features few official restrictions on political organization and activity. Opposition parties are competitive in many states, and independent candidacies are becoming more common despite continued registration hurdles. In 2018, the electoral victory of López Obrador and his relatively new MORENA party reflected the political system's openness to pluralistic competition, and ended leftist fears that powerful actors would block the left's electoral path to power.

In addition to the national election results, MORENA candidates won five of the governor's races at stake, the chief of government's office in Mexico City, and large numbers of legislative seats and mayoral offices at the state and municipal levels. The PRI's failure to win any gubernatorial elections was another manifestation citizens' rejection of the Peña Nieto administration.

Score Change: The score improved from 3 to 4 because the electoral victory of Andrés Manuel López Obrador and his relatively new MORENA party demonstrated the political system's openness to pluralistic competition.

B2. Is there a realistic opportunity for the opposition to increase its support or gain power through elections? 4 / 4

Power has routinely changed hands at the national level since 2000. The dominant victory of López Obrador and MORENA in 2018 followed six years of government control by the PRI, which had ruled Mexico without interruption from 1929 to 2000, before losing consecutive presidential races to the right-leaning PAN in 2000 and 2006.

B3. Are the people's political choices free from domination by the military, foreign powers, religious hierarchies, economic oligarchies, or any other powerful group that is not democratically accountable? 2 / 4

Criminal groups, while increasingly fragmented, exert powerful influence on the country's politics through threats and violence against candidates, election officials, and campaign workers. At least 152 politicians were murdered between fall 2017 and election day in July 2018. Scores of politicians are believed to have withdrawn 2018 candidacies due to fears of violence.

Separately, in states and municipalities with lower levels of multiparty contestation, locally dominant political actors often govern in a highly opaque manner that limits political activity and citizen participation.

B4. Do various segments of the population (including ethnic, religious, gender, LGBT, and other relevant groups) have full political rights and electoral opportunities? 3 / 4

Mexico has a large indigenous population, and indigenous people and groups are free to participate in politics. There are some provisions for the integration of traditional community customs in electing leaders, and parties that serve indigenous communities often compete in states with large indigenous populations. However, in practice, indigenous people are underrepresented in political institutions.

The 2018 election confirmed the success of gender requirements for candidacies and party lists: female representatives increased their share of seats in the Chamber of Deputies to 48 percent and in the Senate to 49 percent.

C. FUNCTIONING OF GOVERNMENT: 5 / 12

C1. Do the freely elected head of government and national legislative representatives determine the policies of the government? 2 / 4

Organized crime and related violence have limited the effective governing authority of elected officials in some areas of the country. Members of organized crime groups have persisted in their attempts to infiltrate local governments in order to plunder municipal coffers and ensure their own impunity. The notorious mass disappearance of 43 students in Iguala, Guerrero in 2014 was linked to a deeply corrupt local government working in conjunction with a drug gang. In the most violent regions, the provision of public services has become more difficult, as public-sector employees face extortion and pressure to divert public funds.

C2. Are safeguards against official corruption strong and effective? 1 / 4

Official corruption remains a serious problem. The billions of dollars in illegal drug money that enter the country each year from the United States profoundly affect politics, as does rampant public contract fraud and other forms of siphoning off state funds. Attempts to prosecute officials for alleged involvement in corrupt or criminal activity have often failed due to the weakness of the cases brought by the state.

In September 2018, federal charges of campaign finance violations against top PRI official Alejandro Gutiérrez were dismissed, generating accusations of a cover-up. In September, former Veracruz governor Javier Duarte, who was accused of kleptocratic management of the state, pleaded guilty to graft charges in exchange for a nine-year prison term. However, many of his alleged cronies were released from custody, prompting allegations of prosecutorial incompetence and political protection. In another high-profile case, corruption charges against longtime teachers' union leader Elba Esther Gordillo were dismissed and she was released from house arrest in August, after a judge ruled that prosecutors had obtained her financial records without a warrant.

In a positive development, Tabasco ex-governor Andrés Granier received a nearly 11-year sentence in March following an embezzlement conviction. However, the corruption cases that advanced during the year focused on out-of-favor former PRI governors such as Granier and Duarte, and the implementation of a new National Anticorruption System (SNA) that took effect in 2017 has been slow.

C3. Does the government operate with openness and transparency? 2 / 4

Despite some limitations, several freedom of information laws passed since 2002 have successfully strengthened transparency at the federal level, though enforcement is uneven across states. In recent years the government has failed to release relevant information on some of the country's most controversial issues, including abuses by the security forces, the investigation into the missing 43 students, and, since 2017, the contracts with an Israeli company that provided spyware that was used against journalists and activists.

CIVIL LIBERTIES: 36 / 60
D. FREEDOM OF EXPRESSION AND BELIEF: 13 / 16
D1. Are there free and independent media? 2 / 4

The security environment for journalists remains highly problematic. Reporters probing police issues, drug trafficking, and official corruption face an increasingly high risk of physical harm. Reporters Without Borders (RSF) tallied dozens of attacks against the press in the months preceding the election, while the Committee to Protect Journalists (CPJ) said four journalists were killed in direct connection with their work in 2018. Self-censorship has increased, with many newspapers in violent areas avoiding publication of stories concerning organized crime. Press watchdog groups hailed the 2012 federalization of crimes against journalists as well as a 2015 law in Mexico City aimed at protecting journalists and human rights defenders, but they have decried the slow pace of the federal government's special prosecutor for crimes against freedom of expression since the office gained authority in 2013. Despite improvements in legal status, community radio stations continue to face occasional harassment from criminals and state authorities.

News coverage in many media outlets is affected by dependence on the government for advertising and subsidies. In 2017, the Supreme Court ordered Congress to pass statutes regulating the distribution of government advertising. Congress complied in April 2018, but media watchdogs criticized the new law, which will take effect in 2019, as failing to adequately ensure equity and transparency in the awarding of public advertising contracts.

Broadcast media are dominated by a corporate duopoly composed of Televisa and TV Azteca. A 2013 telecommunications law established a new telecommunications regulator and the Federal Economic Competition Commission. However, civil society groups have criticized the limited scope of the reforms and their effectiveness in promoting increased broadcast diversity.

Mexico has been at the forefront of citizen-led efforts to ensure internet access. The government amended Article 6 of the constitution in 2013 to make access to the internet a civil right. However, gangs have targeted bloggers and online journalists who report on organized crime, issuing threats and periodically murdering online writers.

D2. Are individuals free to practice and express their religious faith or nonbelief in public and private? 4 / 4

Religious freedom is protected by the constitution and is generally respected in practice, though religious minorities, particularly indigenous Evangelical communities in Chiapas, face occasional persecution by local authorities.

D3. Is there academic freedom, and is the educational system free from extensive political indoctrination? 4 / 4

The government does not restrict academic freedom, though university students and some academics are occasionally threatened for their political activism.

D4. Are individuals free to express their personal views on political or other sensitive topics without fear of surveillance or retribution? 3 / 4

While there are no formal impediments to free and open discussion, fear of criminal monitoring restricts citizens' willingness to converse publicly about crime in some areas of the country.

E. ASSOCIATIONAL AND ORGANIZATIONAL RIGHTS: 7 / 12
E1. Is there freedom of assembly? 3 / 4

Constitutional guarantees regarding free assembly and association are largely upheld, and protests are frequent. However, political and civic expression is restricted in some regions, and in recent years have resulted in violence against protesters which at times has been deadly.

E2. Is there freedom for nongovernmental organizations, particularly those that are engaged in human rights- and governance-related work? 2 / 4

Although highly active, nongovernmental organizations (NGOs) sometimes face violent resistance; in 2018 alone, 10 activists had been murdered by mid-September. Environmental activists and representatives of indigenous groups contesting large-scale infrastructure projects have been particularly vulnerable. In 2012, civil society pressure prompted the government to create a Protection Mechanism for Human Rights Defenders and Journalists. It has offered protection to hundreds of people, though rights groups say it is neglected by the government and tends to operate slowly.

Revelations emerged in 2017 that a number of civil society activists and journalists had been the victims of attempts to spy on their electronic communications, presumably by government agencies. The scandal has accelerated the already rapid decline of civil society trust in the government; there was no visible progress toward accountability for the spying in 2018.

E3. Is there freedom for trade unions and similar professional or labor organizations? 2 / 4

Trade unions, long a pillar of the PRI, have diminished significantly, and independent unions have faced interference from the government. Informal, nontransparent negotiations between employers and politically connected union leaders often result in "protection contracts" that govern employee rights but are never seen by workers. Several large unions are considered opaque and antagonistic to necessary policy reforms.

F. RULE OF LAW: 6 / 16
F1. Is there an independent judiciary? 2 / 4

Mexico's justice system is plagued by delays, unpredictability, and corruption, leading to impunity. A 2008 constitutional reform replaced the civil-inquisitorial trial system with an oral-adversarial one. Although implementation has slowly proceeded and some elements of due process have improved, human rights groups have raised concerns about the weak protections it affords to those suspected of involvement in organized crime. Implementation of the new system was technically completed in 2016, but deficient training and a lack of commitment to the initiative by authorities have produced poor prosecutorial results.

F2. Does due process prevail in civil and criminal matters? 1 / 4

Lower courts—and law enforcement in general—are undermined by widespread bribery and suffer from limited capacity. According to a government survey released in September 2018, more than 90 percent of crimes committed in 2017 went unreported, in large part because the underpaid police were viewed as either inept or in league with criminals. Even when investigations are conducted, only a handful of crimes end in convictions.

F3. Is there protection from the illegitimate use of physical force and freedom from war and insurgencies? 1 / 4

Abuses during criminal investigations are rife; in 2015, a UN special rapporteur released a report characterizing torture as "generalized" within Mexican police forces. In 2017, a comprehensive General Law on Torture took effect that attempts to modernize protection from torture. Rights advocates suggest it has contributed to mild progress in excluding torture-based confessions from prosecutions, but remain concerned about gaps in implementation.

Human rights advocates for years have expressed concern about a lack of accountability for rights abuses committed by members of the military, including torture, forced disappearances, and extrajudicial executions. Only a handful of soldiers have been convicted in civilian courts for abuses against civilians.

In 2017, the Congress passed a General Law on Disappearances intended to confront the problem of forced disappearance, which affects an unknown portion of the more than 36,000 Mexicans registered as disappeared in a national database. The 2014 disappearance of the 43 students in Iguala highlighted shortcomings on both torture and missing persons investigations. In 2016, international experts cast doubt on numerous crucial pieces of evidence backing the government's claims that the murdered Iguala students were incinerated at a dump, with the ashes thrown in a nearby river. In April 2018, the local office of the UN High Commission on Human Rights published a report alleging that dozens of key detainees in the Iguala case had been subjected to torture, potentially nullifying the evidentiary value of their statements. Subsequently, one of López Obrador's first acts as president was to decree the creation of a truth commission to investigate the incident.

Prisons are violent, and it is common for prisoners to continue criminal activity while incarcerated. The National Human Rights Commission (CNDH), long maligned due to its perceived passivity in the face of rampant rights abuses, began to regain some credibility following the appointment of a new director in 2014 and has since issued multiple reports implicating state security forces in grave human rights abuses.

The number of deaths attributed to organized crime has increased since 2014, and in 2018, homicides reached a record number; violence was particularly acute in Colima, Baja California, Guerrero, and Guanajuato. Gang murders continue to feature extreme brutality designed to maximize the psychological impact on civilians, authorities, and rival groups. As of the end of 2017, the Internal Displacement Monitoring Center estimated that there were more than 345,000 internally displaced people (IDPs) in Mexico, many of whom had fled cartel-related violence.

As in previous years, the government's primary response to insecurity was the deployment of various military units to violence hotspots. However, the high rate of violence in 2018 generated renewed pressure for strategic changes in state efforts to contain the carnage. During and after his campaign, López Obrador and his allies pledged a new tack on security issues, and a National Plan for Peace and Security released in November contained provisions for drug law reform and crime prevention programs. However, the strategy centered on creating a new security force, the National Guard, which was sharply criticized by rights advocates for deepening the militarization of public security. The National Guard proposal came despite a November Supreme Court ruling that the Internal Security Law, passed in 2017 to regulate the deployment of the military to fight crime, was unconstitutional.

In August and September 2018, officials in the incoming López Obrador administration also held a series of listening forums to receive feedback from victims about their needs and demands. Some of their suggestions, especially greater spending on programs for youth employment and other alternatives to criminality, were incorporated into the National Plan for Peace and Security and the 2019 budget.

F4. Do laws, policies, and practices guarantee equal treatment of various segments of the population? 2 / 4

Mexican law bans discrimination based on ethnic origin, gender, age, religion, and sexual orientation. Nevertheless, the large indigenous population has been subject to social and economic discrimination, and at least 70 percent of indigenous people live in poverty. Southern states with high concentrations of indigenous residents suffer from particularly deficient services. Indigenous groups have been harmed by criminal violence. In recent years, a series of communities in Guerrero and Michoacán have formed self-defense groups, some of which were subsequently legalized.

Mexican law has strong protections for LGBT (lesbian, gay, bisexual, and transgender) people, but they are not uniformly enforced. Transgender women in particular face discrimination and violence.

Rights groups frequently detail the persecution and criminal predation faced by migrants from Central America, many of whom move through Mexico to reach the United States. Despite government initiatives to improve protections, pressure from the United States to crack down on migration pathways generated ongoing accusations of abuses against migrants in 2018.

G. PERSONAL AUTONOMY AND INDIVIDUAL RIGHTS: 10 / 16

G1. Do individuals enjoy freedom of movement, including the ability to change their place of residence, employment, or education? 3 / 4

Citizens are generally free to change their place of residence, employment, or education. However, criminals have impeded freedom of movement by blocking major roads in several states in recent years, and ordinary citizens avoid roads in many rural areas after dark.

G2. Are individuals able to exercise the right to own property and establish private businesses without undue interference from state or nonstate actors? 2 / 4

Property rights in Mexico are protected by a modern legal framework, but the weakness of the judicial system, frequent solicitation of bribes by bureaucrats and officials, and the high incidence of criminal extortion harm security of property for many individuals and businesses. Large-scale development projects have been accompanied by corruption and rights-related controversy in recent years, exemplified in 2018 by the conflict over the construction of a new airport to serve Mexico City, which was plagued by accusations of land expropriation from local communities and corrupt contracting processes. The airport project appeared to be dead following the October referendum, though negotiations with the project's bondholders continued as of the end of 2018.

G3. Do individuals enjoy personal social freedoms, including choice of marriage partner and size of family, protection from domestic violence, and control over appearance? 3 / 4

Sexual abuse and domestic violence against women are common, and perpetrators are rarely punished. Implementation of a 2007 law designed to protect women from such crimes remains halting, particularly at the state level, and impunity is the norm for the killers of hundreds of women each year. State authorities can issue "gender alerts" that trigger greater scrutiny and an influx of resources to combat an epidemic of violence against women, but in October 2018 a European Union (EU) report described various problems inhibiting the effectiveness of the mechanism. Abortion has been a contentious issue in recent years, with many states reacting to Mexico City's 2007 liberalization of abortion laws by strengthening their own criminal bans on the procedure.

Mexico has taken significant steps toward equality for the LGBT population, courtesy of Supreme Court rulings in 2015 that struck down state laws defining the purpose of marriage as procreation. However, implementing the jurisprudence in all Mexican states will take time, as the court's rulings do not apply in blanket form.

G4. Do individuals enjoy equality of opportunity and freedom from economic exploitation? 2 / 4

Equality of opportunity is limited in Mexico, which has one of the highest rates of income inequality in the developed world. Migrant agricultural workers face brutally exploitative conditions in several northern states. In December the Supreme Court ruled that Mexico's millions of domestic workers—the vast majority of whom are women—must be incorporated into the formal sector and receive social security and health benefits.

Mexico is a major source, transit, and destination country for trafficking in persons, including women and children, many of whom are subject to forced labor and sexual exploitation. Organized criminal gangs are heavily involved in human trafficking in Mexico and into the United States. Government corruption is a significant concern as many officials are bribed by or aid traffickers.

Micronesia

Population: 100,000
Capital: Palikir
Political Rights Rating: 1
Civil Liberties Rating: 1
Freedom Rating: 1.0
Freedom Status: Free
Electoral Democracy: Yes

Overview: The Federated States of Micronesia (FSM) is a relatively stable democracy that holds regular, competitive elections. However, secessionist movements have sometimes unsettled the country's politics and threatened its unity. The judiciary is independent, and civil liberties are generally respected. Ongoing problems include underreporting of domestic violence and the exploitation of migrant workers.

KEY DEVELOPMENTS IN 2018:

- In September, the Philippines government banned all overseas Filipino workers from employment in Micronesia due to reports of abuse and maltreatment.
- In November, Congress passed a landmark law, which was signed by the president in December, prohibiting discrimination based on sexual orientation.
- A referendum scheduled for March 2019 on the independence of the state of Chuuk was postponed indefinitely by the Chuuk State Legislature in December.

POLITICAL RIGHTS: 37 / 40

A. ELECTORAL PROCESS: 12 / 12

A1. Was the current head of government or other chief national authority elected through free and fair elections? 4 / 4

The FSM president and vice president are indirectly elected for four-year terms by members of Congress from among the legislature's four at-large state representatives, known as senators. In 2015, Congress named Peter Christian, the senator representing the state of Pohnpei, as president and Yosiwo George, the senator for Kosrae, as vice president.

Each of the four states (Yap, Chuuk, Pohnpei, and Kosrae) also has its own elected governor.

A2. Were the current national legislative representatives elected through free and fair elections? 4 / 4

The 14-member Congress, Micronesia's unicameral legislature, consists of one senator elected by each state to serve four-year terms and 10 members elected for two-year terms in single-member districts that are allocated according to population. Each state also has its own elected legislature.

In 2017, the FSM held congressional elections for the 10 two-year seats. Eight of the incumbents were returned to office, and all candidates ran as independents. There were no reports of fraud or irregularities.

A3. Are the electoral laws and framework fair, and are they implemented impartially by the relevant election management bodies? 4 / 4

Elections in Micronesia, which are generally considered free and fair, are administered by a government agency headed by a national election director and one commissioner for each state. Constitutional amendments must be approved by three-quarters of voters in at least three of the four states.

B. POLITICAL PLURALISM AND PARTICIPATION: 15 / 16

B1. Do the people have the right to organize in different political parties or other competitive political groupings of their choice, and is the system free of undue obstacles to the rise and fall of these competing parties or groupings? 4 / 4

There are no formal political parties, but there are no restrictions on their formation. All candidates ran as independents in the 2015 general elections and the 2017 congressional elections.

B2. Is there a realistic opportunity for the opposition to increase its support or gain power through elections? 4 / 4

The country has an established record of democratic power transfers. Under an informal agreement, the presidency has typically rotated among the four states, but Congress has sometimes chosen to deviate from this pattern.

B3. Are the people's political choices free from domination by the military, foreign powers, religious hierarchies, economic oligarchies, or any other powerful group that is not democratically accountable? 4 / 4

Traditional leaders and institutions exercise significant influence in society, especially at the village level. However, neither these nor donor countries like the United States and China exert undue control over the political choices of voters or candidates.

B4. Do various segments of the population (including ethnic, religious, gender, LGBT, and other relevant groups) have full political rights and electoral opportunities? 3 / 4

Women and minority groups formally have full political rights, and they are free to participate in practice, though women's political engagement is limited to some extent by traditional biases. Two female candidates ran unsuccessfully in the 2017 congressional elections, and the FSM remained one of the few countries in the world with no women in its national legislature.

C. FUNCTIONING OF GOVERNMENT: 10 / 12

C1. Do the freely elected head of government and national legislative representatives determine the policies of the government? 4 / 4

Elected officials determine and implement policy and legislation at the federal level, though considerable authority is vested in the states and their elected governments. Some leading politicians from Chuuk, by far the most populous state, have advocated independence from the FSM in recent years, and during 2018, the issue remained a topic of public discussion under the guidance of the Chuuk Political Status Commission. Opponents of Chuuk's secession have argued that its separation from the FSM would be unconstitutional. In August, Robert Riley, the US ambassador to the FSM, warned against the state's independence, asserting that an independent Chuuk would lose US aid funds. In response to Riley's statements, critics accused the ambassador of meddling in the country's internal affairs. A referendum on independence for Chuuk was scheduled for March 2019, but in December, the Chuuk State Legislature decided to postpone the vote indefinitely, a move that was condemned by independence advocates.

The FSM relies on defense guarantees and economic assistance from the United States under a 1986 Compact of Free Association. Under the current terms of the compact, the United States will provide more than $130 million in annual aid through 2023, in addition to funding from applicable US federal programs. China has also become an increasingly important partner for trade and development aid in recent years, though its role does not amount to undue interference in FSM governance.

C2. Are safeguards against official corruption strong and effective? 3 / 4

Official corruption is a problem and a source of public discontent. Complaints about misuse of public resources are frequent, particularly from US authorities overseeing aid funds. Government entities responsible for combating corruption, including the attorney general's office and a public auditor, are independent and fairly effective, though some corrupt officials reportedly enjoy impunity.

C3. Does the government operate with openness and transparency? 3 / 4

Government operations and legislative processes are generally transparent, though there is no comprehensive law guaranteeing public access to government information. Limited technical capacity and the country's sprawling geography pose practical barriers to openness and accountability in the FSM. Officials are not legally obliged to submit asset disclosures.

CIVIL LIBERTIES: 55 / 60 (−1)
D. FREEDOM OF EXPRESSION AND BELIEF: 16 / 16
D1. Are there free and independent media? 4 / 4

The news media operate freely. Print outlets include government-published newsletters and several small, privately owned weekly and monthly newspapers. There are a number of radio stations, cable television is available, and satellite television is increasingly common. More than a third of the population has internet access.

D2. Are individuals free to practice and express their religious faith or nonbelief in public and private? 4 / 4

Religious freedom is generally respected, and religious groups are not required to register with the government. About 99 percent of the population is Christian. A small Ahmadi Muslim community has reported some instances of discrimination and vandalism.

D3. Is there academic freedom, and is the educational system free from extensive political indoctrination? 4 / 4

There were no reports of restrictions on academic freedom in 2018.

D4. Are individuals free to express their personal views on political or other sensitive topics without fear of surveillance or retribution? 4 / 4

The constitution guarantees freedom of expression, and there are no significant constraints on this right in practice. The government does not improperly monitor personal communications or social media activity.

E. ASSOCIATIONAL AND ORGANIZATIONAL RIGHTS: 11 / 12
E1. Is there freedom of assembly? 4 / 4

Freedom of assembly is protected by the constitution, and demonstrations typically proceed peacefully.

E2. Is there freedom for nongovernmental organizations, particularly those that are engaged in human rights- and governance-related work? 4 / 4

Citizens are free to organize in civic groups, and a number of students' and women's organizations are active.

E3. Is there freedom for trade unions and similar professional or labor organizations? 3 / 4

Union rights are generally respected, and there are no laws to prevent workers from forming unions, engaging in collective bargaining, or striking. However, such activities are not specifically protected or regulated by law, and few employers are large enough to support unionization in practice.

F. RULE OF LAW: 15 / 16
F1. Is there an independent judiciary? 4 / 4

The judiciary is independent. The chief justice, who administers the judicial system, and the associate justices of the Supreme Court are appointed by the president with the approval of a two-thirds majority in Congress. They are appointed for life terms and cannot be removed arbitrarily.

F2. Does due process prevail in civil and criminal matters? 4 / 4

The police respect legal safeguards against arbitrary arrest and detention, and defendants are generally provided with basic due process guarantees surrounding trials and appeals. However, a shortage of lawyers may sometimes impair detainees' access to counsel in practice.

F3. Is there protection from the illegitimate use of physical force and freedom from war and insurgencies? 4 / 4

There were no reports of physical abuse or inhumane treatment by police or prison officials in 2018. Criminal activity does not pose a major threat to physical security, though police have struggled to deal with illegal fishing.

F4. Do laws, policies, and practices guarantee equal treatment of various segments of the population? 3 / 4

The constitution gives citizens equal protection under the law and prohibits discrimination based on race, ancestry, national origin, gender, sexual orientation, language, or social status. In November 2018, Congress passed a landmark law prohibiting discrimination based on sexual orientation, which President Christian signed in December. However, the law did not mention gender identity, leaving transgender people vulnerable to continued discrimination. That vulnerability was demonstrated in November, when a senator from Yap introduced a bill in Congress that would ban transgender people from employment in the federal government. The bill had not been debated at year's end.

Women generally receive equal pay in formal employment, though they continue to suffer from a degree of societal discrimination.

G. PERSONAL AUTONOMY AND INDIVIDUAL RIGHTS: 13 / 16 (−1)

G1. Do individuals enjoy freedom of movement, including the ability to change their place of residence, employment, or education? 4 / 4

Freedom of movement is generally respected. Under the Compact of Free Association, Micronesians are free to travel to the United States without visas for residence, education, and employment. Many Micronesians have migrated to US Pacific states or territories such as Hawaii and Guam.

G2. Are individuals able to exercise the right to own property and establish private businesses without undue interference from state or nonstate actors? 3 / 4 (−1)

Property rights are protected by law, and individuals are able to operate private businesses; most such enterprises are small and family owned in practice. However, property and business rights are somewhat restricted for foreigners. Noncitizens are legally prohibited from owning land, and a number of regulations limit the kinds of businesses that they can own and operate.

Score Change: The score declined from 4 to 3 due to restrictions on noncitizens' ability to own property and operate businesses in certain sectors.

G3. Do individuals enjoy personal social freedoms, including choice of marriage partner and size of family, protection from domestic violence, and control over appearance? 3 / 4

Personal social freedoms are largely protected. However, there are no specific laws against spousal rape, and both rape and domestic violence are rarely prosecuted due to societal inhibitions against reporting such crimes.

G4. Do individuals enjoy equality of opportunity and freedom from economic exploitation? 3 / 4

Forced labor is prohibited, and the government effectively enforces basic standards for working conditions in the formal sector. Foreign migrant workers nevertheless remain vulnerable to exploitative labor practices, including on foreign fishing vessels in FSM waters, and some Micronesian women are reportedly trafficked for sexual exploitation. In

September 2018, the Philippines government banned all overseas Filipino workers from employment in Micronesia due to reports of abuse and maltreatment.

Moldova

Population: 3,500,000
Capital: Chişinău
Political Rights Rating: 3
Civil Liberties Rating: 4 ↓
Freedom Rating: 3.5
Freedom Status: Partly Free
Electoral Democracy: Yes

Note: The numerical ratings and status listed above do not reflect conditions in Transnistria, which is examined in a separate report.

Overview: Moldova has a competitive electoral environment, and the freedoms of assembly, speech, and religion are largely protected. Nonetheless, pervasive corruption in the government sector, links between major political parties and powerful economic interests, and deficiencies in the rule of law continue to hamper democratic governance.

KEY DEVELOPMENTS IN 2018:

- The Supreme Court of Justice invalidated the Chişinău mayoral runoff election in June after the results showed a victory by a reformist candidate. The ruling prompted protests and drew sharp criticism from the United States and the European Union (EU).
- The president in August signed a controversial "fiscal amnesty" measure under which individuals may declare and register assets without providing information about where they came from, if they pay a 3 percent tax on the assets in question. The provision was denounced by the opposition and prompted statements of concern from international financial institutions. ·
- An LGBT (lesbian, gay, bisexual, and transgender) demonstration in May received heavy police protection, but it was nonetheless disrupted by counterprotesters who tried to breach a police cordon.

POLITICAL RIGHTS: 24 / 40 (−2)

A. ELECTORAL PROCESS: 9 / 12 (−1)

A1. Was the current head of government or other chief national authority elected through free and fair elections? 4 / 4

A prime minister nominated by the president and confirmed by Parliament holds most executive authority. The current prime minister, Pavel Filip of the Democratic Party of Moldova (PDM), took office in January 2016 after his predecessor lost a confidence vote in October 2015.

In 2016, Moldova held its first direct presidential election since 1996, after shifting back from an indirect system. The president is elected by direct popular vote for up to two four-year terms. If no candidate receives more than 50 percent of the votes in the first round, the two leading candidates compete in a second round. Socialist Party (PSRM) candidate Igor Dodon defeated Maia Sandu of the Action and Solidarity Party in the 2016 runoff, 52 percent to 48 percent. This followed a first round in which nine candidates had competed. International observers concluded that the election was largely credible. However, state resources were occasionally misallocated, and transparency in campaign funding was lacking.

A2. Were the current national legislative representatives elected through free and fair elections? 3 / 4

Voters elect the 101-seat unicameral Parliament by proportional representation for four-year terms. Although observers praised the most recent parliamentary elections in 2014 as genuinely competitive and generally well administered, there were some significant deficiencies. The pro-Russian Patria Party was disqualified days before the vote on the grounds that it received campaign funds from abroad. The distribution of overseas polling places favored residents of EU countries over those living in Russia. Nevertheless, the Constitutional Court approved the election results, rejecting challenges by opposition parties. The PSRM took 25 seats, the Liberal Democratic Party of Moldova (PLDM) 23 seats, the Party of Communists of the Republic of Moldova (PCRM) 21, the PDM 19, and the Liberal Party (PL) 13. By the end of 2017, however, the ruling PDM had more than doubled its share of seats and become the largest party in Parliament through a series of defections from the PLDM and PCRM. The PSRM remained the largest opposition party.

A3. Are the electoral laws and framework fair, and are they implemented impartially by the relevant election management bodies? 2 / 4 (−1)

Elections have typically been administered professionally and impartially, despite a lack of resources. In 2018, however, the competitive and generally well-run Chişinău mayoral election was invalidated through a series of court decisions that prompted concerns about the politicized enforcement of electoral laws.

In the Chişinău contest, held in two rounds in May and June, Andrei Năstase, leader of the reformist Dignity and Truth (DA) party, defeated PSRM candidate Ion Ceban in the runoff. While the election's result was initially recognized by the stakeholders and by international observers, a court annulled the vote on the grounds that Năstase and Ceban had violated provisions of the electoral code by campaigning on social media after the end of the legal campaign period; the Supreme Court of Justice upheld the decision in late June. (Năstase claimed that he and Ceban had simply posted messages urging citizens to vote, and had not been actively campaigning; Ceban said that only Năstase had engaged in improper activity.)

The decision to invalidate an election over a minor violation raised suspicions that the rulings were politically motivated, and the affair prompted criticism from both the EU and the United States. The EU response emphasized that the Supreme Court's decision undermined trust in state institutions, while the United States called the election's invalidation "a threat to Moldovan democracy" and the final ruling "unusual and unwarranted"; both condemned the Supreme Court decision as nontransparent. As a result of the annulment, an acting mayor was set to serve until a new election could be held in 2019.

Parliamentary elections scheduled for February 2019 would be governed by a 2017 revision to electoral rules that replaced the previous proportional system with a mixed system featuring both single-member constituencies and seats allocated proportionally by party list. The Venice Commission of the Council of Europe had strongly urged against the switch to single-member constituencies, arguing that they could allow powerful local business interests to subvert the needs of constituents.

PDM-backed legislation signed by Dodon in December will permit a referendum on reducing the number of lawmakers in Parliament to be held on the same day as the 2019 parliamentary elections. The opposition criticized the plan as politicking meant to benefit the PDM.

Score Change: The score declined from 3 to 2 because the courts took the unusual step of invalidating an internationally recognized mayoral election in Chişinău based on minor campaign violations, raising suspicions that the decision was politically motivated.

B. POLITICAL PLURALISM AND PARTICIPATION: 11 / 16

B1. Do the people have the right to organize in different political parties or other competitive political groupings of their choice, and is the system free of undue obstacles to the rise and fall of these competing parties or groupings? 3 / 4

There are no legal restrictions on party formation in Moldova. In the 2014 parliamentary elections, 21 political parties participated, and five gained seats. However, business elites, aided by weak campaign finance laws, dominate party politics, and this effectively discourages the formation and rise of new parties while hampering the competitiveness of those that already exist.

Campaign finance laws also favor parties over independent candidates. For the 2014 legislative elections, the cap on private donations was doubled for political parties but remained the same for independent candidates. The ability of the Central Election Commission (CEC) to monitor the financing of campaigns is limited.

B2. Is there a realistic opportunity for the opposition to increase its support or gain power through elections? 3 / 4

Opposition parties have a strong presence in Parliament and other elected offices, and they are able to increase their support through elections. However, the ruling PDM has maintained power in recent years by enticing many elected opposition members to leave their parties. In some cases the defections have been accompanied by allegations of bribery and coercion.

B3. Are the people's political choices free from domination by the military, foreign powers, religious hierarchies, economic oligarchies, or any other powerful group that is not democratically accountable? 2 / 4

Economic oligarchies and business interests underpin political party structures in Moldova, harming political accountability. Wealthy businessmen with political interests, principally PDM chairman Vladimir Plahotniuc, are able to use their private assets to exercise undue influence over political affairs.

B4. Do various segments of the population (including ethnic, religious, gender, LGBT, and other relevant groups) have full political rights and electoral opportunities? 3 / 4

Women and minorities do not face legal barriers to political participation, though social obstacles prevent women from playing a more active role at all levels of Moldovan politics, and some minority groups remain underrepresented. The Gagauz, a Turkic minority concentrated in the country's south, enjoy regional autonomy, but their leaders allege that their interests are not well represented at the national level. Although the first two Romany women were elected to local councils in 2015, Roma in general face discrimination and suffer from low levels of political participation. LGBT people continue to organize and advocate for equal rights, but the harassment they encounter discourages political engagement.

C. FUNCTIONING OF GOVERNMENT: 4 / 12 (–1)

C1. Do the freely elected head of government and national legislative representatives determine the policies of the government? 2 / 4 (–1)

Unelected business elites hold sway over the government and government policies. Plahotniuc has an outsized influence on policymaking, even though he does not hold elected office and his party finished fourth in the 2014 elections. He was instrumental in building a governing coalition around the PDM and effectively sets the agenda for the government, announcing government plans at regular public briefings and presenting himself as a de facto leader.

The functioning of government has been complicated by clashes between the PDM-led cabinet and Parliament on the one hand and President Dodon on the other. Dodon has repeatedly refused to promulgate legislation or approve candidates put forward by Parliament for various posts, and lawmakers have secured a series of Constitutional Court rulings that temporarily suspend Dodon from office to overcome the obstruction. The suspensions grant the Parliament speaker temporary authority to sign the bills or approve the appointments in question. The constitution allows the president to return adopted bills to Parliament for reconsideration, but he must promulgate them if they are approved a second time.

Score Change: The score declined from 3 to 2 due to the increasingly open and prominent role of Democratic Party leader Vladimir Plahotniuc, a wealthy businessman who holds no elected office or government position, in determining and presenting government policies.

C2. Are safeguards against official corruption strong and effective? 1 / 4

Corruption remains a widespread problem at all levels of government, and existing anticorruption laws are inadequately enforced. Moldova is still reeling from a 2014 scandal involving the Central Bank, in which $1 billion was stolen. In 2016, former prime minister Vlad Filat was sentenced to nine years in prison in connection with the scandal, but there have been few other high-level prosecutions.

In July 2018, Parliament adopted a controversial "fiscal amnesty" measure that permits people to declare and register assets without providing information about where they came from, if they pay a 3 percent tax on the assets they reveal. The provision, signed by the president in August as part of a larger financial reform package, came under sharp criticism from the opposition, including Năstase, who said the amnesty was tantamount to legalizing fraud. The World Bank and International Monetary Fund (IMF) also expressed concern about the package, with the former saying it could "undermine the Moldovan government's commitment to fighting corruption."

C3. Does the government operate with openness and transparency? 1 / 4

The government does not operate with transparency. Most political activity takes place behind the scenes in negotiations between and within political parties. A number of laws have been passed in recent years to increase transparency in decision-making processes and require public officials to disclose their assets, but they have not been effectively enforced due to lack of political will.

CIVIL LIBERTIES: 34 / 60 (–1)

D. FREEDOM OF EXPRESSION AND BELIEF: 11 / 16 (–1)

D1. Are there free and independent media? 2 / 4

The media environment is dominated by outlets connected to political parties, particularly the PDM. More than 80 percent of domestic television stations are owned by people affiliated with political parties, and some 70 percent of the market is controlled by Plahotniuc. Reporters often experience political pressure from the government, such as denial of access to information, public institutions, and events, or public denunciations or threats of legal action by government officials. This contributes to self-censorship and the suppression of critical news coverage. Some independent journalists have reported suspicions of surveillance and claimed that opposition figures are reluctant to speak with them on the telephone due to fears of wiretaps.

D2. Are individuals free to practice and express their religious faith or nonbelief in public and private? 3 / 4

The constitution upholds religious freedom and establishes no religious authority in the state, though it provides special status to the Moldovan Orthodox Church. Religious minorities have reported discrimination by local officials and difficulties in establishing houses of worship.

D3. Is there academic freedom, and is the educational system free from extensive political indoctrination? 3 / 4

Academic freedom is generally respected. However, the Gagauz community has complained of exclusion from the mainstream higher education system, as most Gagauz are more fluent in Russian than Romanian, the official language in Moldova.

D4. Are individuals free to express their personal views on political or other sensitive topics without fear of surveillance or retribution? 3 / 4 (−1)

Individuals have generally been able to engage in discussions of a sensitive or political nature without fear of retribution. However, there are growing concerns that expressing criticism of the government or other powerful actors may result in loss of employment or damaged career prospects, particularly in the public sector. Suspicions of increased surveillance targeting journalists and civil society activists have also discouraged open political discussion among private citizens.

Score Change: The score declined from 4 to 3 due to growing concerns that individuals are subject to monitoring and retribution, including damaged career prospects, for criticism of the ruling party or other powerful actors.

E. ASSOCIATIONAL AND ORGANIZATIONAL RIGHTS: 8 / 12
E1. Is there freedom of assembly? 3 / 4

Freedom of assembly is guaranteed by the constitution and mostly upheld in practice. A series of protests condemning the annulment of the Chişinău mayoral elections in 2018 proceeded peacefully. However, an LGBT march that took place in May was disrupted by counterprotesters who attempted to break through a line of police officers protecting event participants. Police responded with tear gas. In 2017, a similar march had been cut short by police, who cited the potential for a violent confrontation with counterprotesters amassed along the route.

Also in 2017, protest leader and opposition politician Grigore Petrenco had received a four-and-a-half-year suspended prison sentence for "organizing mass disturbances" in 2015, a charge that the opposition claimed was politically motivated.

E2. Is there freedom for nongovernmental organizations, particularly those that are engaged in human rights- and governance-related work? 3 / 4

The nongovernmental organization (NGO) sector is vibrant. However, the government tends to ignore scrutiny of its initiatives by NGOs and has excluded them from policy drafting processes, while NGO leaders continue to report that the government unfairly brands them as political partisans. Human rights lawyers and activists have endured media smear campaigns and targeted criminal investigations and prosecutions. Civil society activists have voiced concerns about wiretapping and noted the increasing number of wiretap requests approved by Moldova's judges.

E3. Is there freedom for trade unions and similar professional or labor organizations? 2 / 4

Trade unions are permitted to operate in Moldova, and the government has passed regulations protecting the rights of workers. However, collective bargaining is not allowed in some sectors, and union membership is declining. The government often fails to enforce the right to collective bargaining when it is denied by employers. Antiunion discrimination is illegal, but workers have no effective legal recourse when they are fired for union activity.

F. RULE OF LAW: 6 / 16

F1. Is there an independent judiciary? 1 / 4

Moldova's judicial branch is susceptible to political pressures that hamper its independence, and judicial appointment processes lack transparency. Judges have been dismissed for their decisions. In a high-profile case, appellate judge Domnica Manole was dismissed in 2017 after her decision requiring the CEC to hold a referendum on constitutional amendments proposed by reform activists. Manole faced criminal charges for her ruling; her case opened in April 2018, and at year's end it was apparently ongoing. The Supreme Court of Justice's decision in June 2018 to annul the Chişinău mayoral election further contributed to perceptions that the judiciary is politically compromised. In December, the government named three judges considered to be aligned with the ruling party to the Constitutional Court. Their appointment came after two judges on the court had resigned before their mandates ended, without explanation; the third seat had been vacant.

F2. Does due process prevail in civil and criminal matters? 1 / 4

Due process is often lacking in the Moldovan justice system. Some prosecutions are politically motivated, especially those against human rights lawyers and opposition figures. Important cases have been held behind closed doors, despite legislation mandating audio and video recordings. Lengthy pretrial detention is common. There have been relatively few prosecutions in connection with the 2014 banking scandal, and the lost funds, equivalent to 13 percent of the country's gross domestic product (GDP), have not yet been recovered.

F3. Is there protection from the illegitimate use of physical force and freedom from war and insurgencies? 2 / 4

Prisoners and detainees have experienced maltreatment and torture. Prosecution for such offenses is rare, and very few of those convicted in torture cases receive prison sentences. The case of Andrei Braguţa, who in 2017 was jailed on a traffic violation and beaten to death by his cellmates, drew domestic and international attention to violence within the penitentiary system. Overcrowding and unsanitary conditions are also prevalent in the country's prisons.

F4. Do laws, policies, and practices guarantee equal treatment of various segments of the population? 2 / 4

Members of the Romany minority experience discrimination in housing, education, and employment, and have been targets of police violence.

While discrimination based on sexual orientation is not explicitly banned by the main article of the 2012 Law on Ensuring Equality, it is understood to be covered under a reference to discrimination on "any other similar grounds." Nevertheless, LGBT people face discrimination and harassment. The law prohibits discrimination in employment on the basis of sexual orientation, but not gender identity.

Despite legal protections and government programs meant to promote gender equality, women continue to face disadvantages in employment and compensation in practice.

G. PERSONAL AUTONOMY AND INDIVIDUAL RIGHTS: 9 / 16

G1. Do individuals enjoy freedom of movement, including the ability to change their place of residence, employment, or education? 3 / 4

The law protects freedom of internal movement and foreign travel, and the government generally respects these rights. There are no formal restrictions on the right to change one's place of employment or education, but bribery is not uncommon in educational institutions.

G2. Are individuals able to exercise the right to own property and establish private businesses without undue interference from state or nonstate actors? 2 / 4

Although Moldovan law guarantees property rights, they are undermined by a weak and corrupt judiciary. Widespread corruption and related advantages for politically connected businessmen also affect normal business activity and fair competition. Allies of powerful individuals have been accused of benefiting economically from selective enforcement of business regulations.

G3. Do individuals enjoy personal social freedoms, including choice of marriage partner and size of family, protection from domestic violence, and control over appearance? 2 / 4

Some personal social freedoms are protected, but domestic violence and sexual assault are common in Moldova. A joint report submitted by several Moldovan NGOs in 2016 found that more than 63 percent of women over the age of 15 have experienced at least one form of violence (physical, psychological, or sexual) in their lifetimes; the same report found that over 20 percent of men admitted to having had sex with a woman without her consent. Laws covering domestic violence are inadequately enforced, and abuse that does not result in significant injury is subject only to administrative penalties. Neither marriage nor civil unions for same-sex couples are recognized under the law.

G4. Do individuals enjoy equality of opportunity and freedom from economic exploitation? 2 / 4

Persistent poverty, extensive emigration, and a lack of job opportunities for trained and educated workers bedevil the Moldovan economy. Human trafficking remains a problem, although the authorities have accelerated efforts to prosecute traffickers. Despite legal protections, child labor remains a pervasive problem in the country. Regulations meant to prevent exploitative or unsafe working conditions remain inadequate.

Monaco

Population: 40,000
Capital: Monaco
Political Rights Rating: 3
Civil Liberties Rating: 1
Freedom Rating: 2.0
Freedom Status: Free
Electoral Democracy: Yes

Overview: The Principality of Monaco is a constitutional monarchy headed by Prince Albert II. The prince appoints the government, which is responsible only to him. Legislative power is exercised jointly by the prince and the freely elected parliament. Civil liberties are generally respected.

KEY DEVELOPMENTS IN 2018:

- Parliamentary elections in February resulted in a landslide victory for the new political movement Priorité Monaco. The movement's leader, Stéphane Valeri, became president of the National Council, Monaco's parliament.
- In June, former attorney general Jean-Pierre Dréno was charged in connection with the Rybolovlev corruption scandal, which revealed extensive malfeasance in Monaco's judicial system. While Dréno was later released, in November another nine suspects were identified, including the head and deputy head of the Monegasque judicial police.

POLITICAL RIGHTS: 26 / 40 (+1)

A. ELECTORAL PROCESS: 8 / 12 (+1)

A1. Was the current head of government or other chief national authority elected through free and fair elections? 0 / 4

The hereditary monarch holds extensive executive authority, including the exclusive right to change the government, and there are no constitutional provisions allowing citizens to alter this system. The current prince, Albert II, took the throne after his father's death in 2005. The head of government, known as the minister of state, is traditionally appointed by the monarch from a candidate list of three French nationals submitted by the French government. Serge Telle, the current minister of state, took office in 2016.

A2. Were the current national legislative representatives elected through free and fair elections? 4 / 4

The 24 members of the unicameral National Council are elected for five-year terms; the 16 candidates who receive the most votes are elected, and the remaining 8 seats are filled through list-based proportional representation. The February 2018 elections were evaluated as credible by international observers. The new political movement Priorité Monaco, led by veteran politician Stéphane Valeri and defectors from the more established Horizon Monaco, won 58 percent of the vote and 21 seats. Horizon Monaco itself took 26 percent and 2 seats, while the Union Monégasque took 16 percent and the remaining seat. After the elections, Valeri became president of the National Council, which is regarded as the most powerful elected office in Monaco.

A3. Are the electoral laws and framework fair, and are they implemented impartially by the relevant election management bodies? 4 / 4 (+1)

The legal framework provides an adequate basis for credible elections, and a number of recent changes have improved the conduct of elections, including the modification of campaign finance rules in 2017 and the broadening of suffrage rights for detainees in 2014. However, in a 2018 report, the Organization for Security and Co-operation in Europe (OSCE) argued that the campaign finance system could be further strengthened.

Municipal authorities, led by the mayor of Monaco, form an Electoral Committee that administer elections with support from the Interior Ministry, and observers view their conduct to be credible. However, technical meetings in preparation for elections are not open to the public, limiting the committee's transparency.

Score Change: The score improved from 3 to 4 because the legal framework governing the 2018 elections featured recent changes that increased its fairness and transparency, especially with respect to campaign finance regulations and suffrage rights for detainees.

B. POLITICAL PLURALISM AND PARTICIPATION: 10 / 16

B1. Do the people have the right to organize in different political parties or other competitive political groupings of their choice, and is the system free of undue obstacles to the rise and fall of these competing parties or groupings? 3 / 4

Political associations, groupings of people who hold similar political viewpoints, compete in Monaco, rather than traditional parties. There are no undue restrictions on the formation of new political associations. However, office seekers are prohibited from running as individual independent candidates; independents must instead form a list of at least 13 candidates to participate in elections.

B2. Is there a realistic opportunity for the opposition to increase its support or gain power through elections? 2 / 4

Opposition political associations are able to gain seats in the parliament. In 2018, the new political movement Priorité Monaco, also known as Primo!, won 21 seats, while Horizon Monaco fell from 20 seats to just 2. However, there are structural limits on the opposition's ability to secure executive power through elections, as the cabinet—appointed by the prince—is not responsible to the elected parliament.

B3. Are the people's political choices free from domination by the military, foreign powers, religious hierarchies, economic oligarchies, or any other powerful group that is not democratically accountable? 2 / 4

The fact that the head of government is a French national appointed from a list submitted by the French government, and that the powerful head of state is an unelected monarch, means that people's political participation is heavily circumscribed by democratically unaccountable forces. Nevertheless, voters' and candidates' choices with respect to parliamentary representation is largely free from domination by such entities.

B4. Do various segments of the population (including ethnic, religious, gender, LGBT, and other relevant groups) have full political rights and electoral opportunities? 3 / 4

Only about 9,000 of Monaco's residents are citizens, and noncitizens do not have the right to vote or run for office, though a number of legal routes to naturalization are available. Most noncitizen residents are nationals of neighboring France or Italy. Women and members of minority groups are free to participate in elections, both as voters and candidates, but women's interests are not always well represented in the political system, and only eight women were elected to the parliament in 2018.

C. FUNCTIONING OF GOVERNMENT: 8 / 12

C1. Do the freely elected head of government and national legislative representatives determine the policies of the government? 2 / 4

The hereditary prince has significant governing authority, including the exclusive power to initiate legislation, conduct foreign policy, and approve changes to the constitution. However, all legislation and the budget require parliamentary approval, and the parliament is generally free from interference by unelected groups.

C2. Are safeguards against official corruption strong and effective? 3 / 4

Despite recent improvements in the anticorruption legal framework, several loopholes remain. The parliament lacks a code of conduct on accepting gifts or potential conflicts of interest. High-level corruption is a problem, and officials sometimes act with impunity. In 2017, Director of Judicial Services Philippe Narmino resigned after it was revealed that wealthy Russian businessman Dmitriy Rybolovlev gave him gifts in exchange for pursuing fraud charges against an art dealer. The Rybolovlev case revealed extensive corruption in Monaco's judicial system. Former attorney general Jean-Pierre Dréno was charged in connection with the case in June 2018, though he was later released; nine additional suspects, including the head and deputy head of the judicial police, were identified in November.

C3. Does the government operate with openness and transparency? 3 / 4

The law generally provides for public access to government information, including draft laws and proposed legislation. However, a 2017 report by the Council of Europe's Group of States against Corruption (GRECO) highlighted insufficient mechanisms to ensure transparency in parliamentary work, including a lack of consultation with the public on proposed legislation and the confidentiality of committee meetings. There are no financial disclosure laws in place for lawmakers or officials appointed by the prince.

CIVIL LIBERTIES: 56 / 60 (−1)

D. FREEDOM OF EXPRESSION AND BELIEF: 16 / 16

D1. Are there free and independent media? 4 / 4

The constitution provides for freedom of expression, and press freedom is generally respected in practice. Monaco has a weekly government newspaper, an English-language monthly, and several online publications. In addition, there is one public television channel and one privately owned channel. French and Italian broadcast and print media are widely available, and internet access is not restricted.

D2. Are individuals free to practice and express their religious faith or nonbelief in public and private? 4 / 4

Roman Catholicism is the official state religion, but the constitution guarantees freedom of religion and public worship, and this is largely respected in practice. Jehovah's Witnesses have struggled to secure official recognition as a religious association, which confers the ability to own property and hire employees.

D3. Is there academic freedom, and is the educational system free from extensive political indoctrination? 4 / 4

There are no undue restrictions on academic freedom.

D4. Are individuals free to express their personal views on political or other sensitive topics without fear of surveillance or retribution? 4 / 4

People are generally free to express their personal views without fear of retribution. Insulting the ruling family is illegal and can result in prison sentences of up to five years, but the law is infrequently enforced.

E. ASSOCIATIONAL AND ORGANIZATIONAL RIGHTS: 12 / 12

E1. Is there freedom of assembly? 4 / 4

The constitution provides for freedom of assembly, which is generally respected in practice.

E2. Is there freedom for nongovernmental organizations, particularly those that are engaged in human rights- and governance-related work? 4 / 4

No significant restrictions are imposed on the formation or operation of nongovernmental organizations (NGOs).

E3. Is there freedom for trade unions and similar professional or labor organizations? 4 / 4

The law grants workers the right to establish unions and bargain collectively, and anti-union discrimination is prohibited. All workers except government employees have the right to strike. Unions and employers engage in collective bargaining in practice.

F. RULE OF LAW: 14 / 16 (−1)

F1. Is there an independent judiciary? 3 / 4

The constitution provides for an independent judiciary. The prince names five full members and two judicial assistants to the Supreme Court based on nominations by the National Council, government bodies, and the lower courts. The recruitment process for judges lacks transparency, which contributes to a perception that they may lack independence. The Judicial Service Commission is ostensibly responsible for ensuring the independence of the judiciary, but in practice it lacks enforcement power. The director of judicial services, who oversees the judicial and law enforcement systems, is responsible only to the prince. Approximately half of the judges in Monaco are Monegasque nationals, and the other half are French nationals.

F2. Does due process prevail in civil and criminal matters? 4 / 4

Due process rights are generally respected. Defendants are presumed innocent until proven guilty and are informed of the charges against them promptly. Defendants have access to attorneys and sufficient time to prepare a defense.

F3. Is there protection from the illegitimate use of physical force and freedom from war and insurgencies? 4 / 4

The population faces no major threats to physical security. Violent crime and excessive use of force by police are both rare in Monaco.

F4. Do laws, policies, and practices guarantee equal treatment of various segments of the population? 3 / 4 (−1)

Monaco lacks a law that broadly prohibits discrimination based on race or ethnicity, though insults and defamation on such grounds are illegal. In the absence of a comprehensive law, Article 14 of the European Convention on Human Rights is used to prevent and punish discrimination. The government established the Office of the High Commissioner for the Protection of Rights, Liberties, and for Mediation in 2013 to address discrimination. The government does not publish statistics on hate crimes.

The law prohibits discrimination based on gender, and women's rights are generally respected. However, the European Commission against Racism and Intolerance has noted that women do not enjoy the same rights to social benefits as their male counterparts, as men receive head of household status by default, and called for the establishment of a program guaranteeing the equal treatment of LGBT (lesbian, gay, bisexual, and transgender) people. An October 2018 decree allowed women civil servants residing in Monaco to serve as head of household for the purposes of social benefits, potentially affecting about 530 women. A similar change for private-sector workers, which would have a broader impact, required negotiations with France.

Score Change: The score declined from 4 to 3 because the country lacks comprehensive antidiscrimination legislation and has been slow to address legal gaps identified by international experts.

G. PERSONAL AUTONOMY AND INDIVIDUAL RIGHTS: 14 / 16

G1. Do individuals enjoy freedom of movement, including the ability to change their place of residence, employment, or education? 4 / 4

There are no significant restrictions on freedom of internal movement or foreign travel.

G2. Are individuals able to exercise the right to own property and establish private businesses without undue interference from state or nonstate actors? 3 / 4

Property rights are respected, and noncitizens holding a residence permit may purchase property and establish businesses. However, obtaining government approval to start a business is often a lengthy and complex process, and related costs can be prohibitively expensive.

G3. Do individuals enjoy personal social freedoms, including choice of marriage partner and size of family, protection from domestic violence, and control over appearance? 3 / 4

Personal social freedoms are generally respected. However, abortion is legal only under special circumstances, including rape and medical necessity. Monaco does not recognize same-sex marriages; a law allowing civil unions was under consideration at the end of 2018. Domestic violence is outlawed in Monaco, and there are few reported incidents. The government and NGOs provide a network of support services for victims of domestic violence.

G4. Do individuals enjoy equality of opportunity and freedom from economic exploitation? 4 / 4

Legal protections against labor exploitation are adequately enforced.

Mongolia

Population: 3,200,000
Capital: Ulaanbaatar
Political Rights Rating: 1
Civil Liberties Rating: 2
Freedom Rating: 1.5
Freedom Status: Free
Electoral Democracy: Yes

Overview: Following a peaceful revolution in 1990, Mongolia began holding multiparty elections and established itself as an electoral democracy. Political rights and civil liberties have been firmly institutionalized, though the two dominant parties continue to rely on patronage networks, and widespread corruption increasingly hampers further development.

KEY DEVELOPMENTS IN 2018:

- Prime Minister Ukhnaagiin Khürelsükh, who had formed a new government in 2017, survived a parliamentary no-confidence motion in late November that was initiated by a faction of his own Mongolian People's Party (MPP). The vote was prompted by a corruption scandal in which high-ranking officials were accused of siphoning off funds meant to support small businesses.
- Khürelsükh accused parliament speaker Miyeegombo Enkhbold, also of the MPP, of seeking to oust his government because its reform efforts were threatening the corrupt economic interests of Enkhbold and his allies. Enkhbold was under investigation during the year over claims that he had sold government jobs to raise funds for the 2016 parliamentary election campaign.

POLITICAL RIGHTS: 36 / 40

A. ELECTORAL PROCESS: 11 / 12

A1. Was the current head of government or other chief national authority elected through free and fair elections? 4 / 4

Under the 1992 constitution, the president is directly elected for up to two four-year terms. Khaltmaa Battulga of the Democratic Party (DP) was elected in 2017 following a campaign that offered little discussion of policy and was instead characterized by allegations of corruption levied by the candidates against one another. No candidate took a majority in the first round, and a runoff was necessary for the first time in Mongolia's democratic history.

In the first round of voting, some voters voiced their frustration with the choices offered by the main parties by selecting a none-of-the-above option. The number of blank ballots jumped to 8.2 percent in the second round of voting, in which Battulga took 50.6 percent, defeating Enkhbold of the MPP. An Organization for Security and Cooperation in Europe (OSCE) election monitoring mission assessed the polls as well run and credible, but noted a lack of analytical media coverage during the campaign.

The prime minister, who holds most executive power in Mongolia's semipresidential system, is nominated by the party or coalition with the most seats in the parliament and is approved by lawmakers with the agreement of the president. Amid factional infighting that followed the party's loss in the 2017 presidential election, the MPP-dominated parliament voted to remove the incumbent government and install Khürelsükh as prime minister.

A2. Were the current national legislative representatives elected through free and fair elections? 4 / 4

Members of the 76-seat parliament, the State Great Hural, are directly elected for four-year terms. In the 2016 elections, which were held under a new majoritarian, or first-past-the-post, system, the MPP won 65 seats. The formerly governing DP was reduced to just 9 seats, with an independent popular singer and a lone representative of the Mongolian People's Revolutionary Party claiming the remainder. The OSCE mission reported that polling took place in an orderly manner.

A3. Are the electoral laws and framework fair, and are they implemented impartially by the relevant election management bodies? 3 / 4

The electoral laws are generally fair, though they are often changed shortly before elections and tend to favor the two largest parties. In 2016, the OSCE criticized electoral reform processes that brought about the majoritarian parliamentary system as rushed and opaque, and noted that new districts were drawn inequitably. While the General Election Commission is often regarded with some suspicion as to possible political influence, it was found to have conducted the 2017 presidential election in an impartial manner.

B. POLITICAL PLURALISM AND PARTICIPATION: 16 / 16

B1. Do the people have the right to organize in different political parties or other competitive political groupings of their choice, and is the system free of undue obstacles to the rise and fall of these competing parties or groupings? 4 / 4

Mongolia features a multiparty system, though the 2016 electoral reforms encouraged a shift to two-party dominance. Political parties are built around patronage networks rather than political ideologies. Representatives of large business groups play an important role in funding and directing the two largest parties.

New political movements may form and operate freely, and smaller political parties have held legislative seats and remained viable. However, a perceived need for significant funding may dissuade some potential organizers of new political movements.

B2. Is there a realistic opportunity for the opposition to increase its support or gain power through elections? 4 / 4

There are no undue barriers preventing opposition parties from gaining power through elections. The MPP and DP have remained the two largest political forces in the country, regularly alternating in government and establishing a record of peaceful transfers of authority.

B3. Are the people's political choices free from domination by the military, foreign powers, religious hierarchies, economic oligarchies, or any other powerful group that is not democratically accountable? 4 / 4

Powerful business interests have some influence over candidates, whom they are able to support through a nontransparent party financing system. However, candidates and voters are generally free to make political choices without excessive outside influence, in part because corporate interests are balanced across various factions of the two main parties.

B4. Do various segments of the population (including ethnic, religious, gender, LGBT, and other relevant groups) have full political rights and electoral opportunities? 4 / 4

All adult citizens other than those who are incarcerated are entitled to full political rights, and these are generally observed in practice. However, despite quotas supporting gender diversity, women remain underrepresented in politics, holding about 17 percent of parliament seats and few senior government posts. LGBT (lesbian, gay, bisexual, and transgender) people also face some societal discrimination that hampers their ability to advocate for their rights in the political sphere, though such advocacy has been increasing.

C. FUNCTIONING OF GOVERNMENT: 9 / 12

C1. Do the freely elected head of government and national legislative representatives determine the policies of the government? 4 / 4

Freely elected representatives are duly seated and generally able to craft government policy without improper interference. However, corporations, aided by opaque party finance procedures, can influence policymaking.

C2. Are safeguards against official corruption strong and effective? 2 / 4

Corruption is endemic in Mongolia and is widely perceived to have grown worse in recent years, particularly with respect to state involvement in the mining sector. Anticorruption laws are vaguely written and infrequently enforced. Investigations into corruption allegations are often dropped by prosecutors before reaching definitive conclusions. The Independent Authority against Corruption has been criticized as ineffective in pursuing cases, most prominently one in which parliament speaker Enkhbold allegedly sought to sell state offices to bolster party finances in 2016.

In October 2018, evidence began to emerge in the media that leading political figures and state officials had siphoned off funds from a government program meant to support small and medium-sized enterprises. A faction of MPP lawmakers attempted to oust the government with a no-confidence vote in November in response to the scandal, but the government survived, and Prime Minister Khürelsükh denounced the vote as an attempt by Enkhbold and his allies to protect their own corrupt interests. An effort to remove Enkhbold as speaker was pending at year's end.

C3. Does the government operate with openness and transparency? 3 / 4

There are many laws and regulations designed to maintain government transparency and accountability. However, implementation and enforcement of these laws is inconsistent. The 2011 Law on Information Transparency and Right to Information contains exemptions allowing certain types of information to be withheld from the public. Authorities often invoke these exemptions, as well as the State Secrets Law, to limit disclosures.

CIVIL LIBERTIES: 49 / 60
D. FREEDOM OF EXPRESSION AND BELIEF: 14 / 16
D1. Are there free and independent media? 3 / 4

Press freedom is generally respected, and media outlets collectively present a wide range of views. However, coverage can be partisan, and the OSCE noted xenophobic rhetoric and unsupported allegations of corruption in the media during the 2017 election campaign. Ownership of media companies remains opaque and subject to much speculation. Many journalists practice self-censorship in order to avoid offending political or business interests and facing costly libel suits. Journalists can also be forced to pay administrative fines for publishing false and defamatory information under a broadly worded 2017 law.

D2. Are individuals free to practice and express their religious faith or nonbelief in public and private? 4 / 4

Individuals are free to practice their religion under the law and in practice, though religious groups are required to register with the government, and the ease of registration procedures varies by region and locality.

D3. Is there academic freedom, and is the educational system free from extensive political indoctrination? 4 / 4

Academic freedom is generally respected.

D4. Are individuals free to express their personal views on political or other sensitive topics without fear of surveillance or retribution? 3 / 4

There are few significant impediments to free and open private discussion. However, there were some reports of a tense environment in which voters felt dissuaded from criticizing political parties during the 2016 parliamentary election campaign. Fear of repercussions from powerful actors may continue to deter open expression for some.

E. ASSOCIATIONAL AND ORGANIZATIONAL RIGHTS: 11 / 12
E1. Is there freedom of assembly? 4 / 4

Freedom of assembly is upheld in practice. A number of protests took place without incident in 2018, including events to demand government action to reduce pollution, call for reforms to the mining industry, and press for accountability in the wake of corruption scandals.

E2. Is there freedom for nongovernmental organizations, particularly those that are engaged in human rights– and governance-related work? 4 / 4

Numerous environmental, human rights, and social welfare groups operate without restrictions, though most are very small. Individual activists sometimes report intimidation and harassment in the course of their work.

E3. Is there freedom for trade unions and similar professional or labor organizations? 3 / 4

Trade unions are independent and active, and the government generally respects their rights to bargain collectively and engage in legal strike actions. However, labor rights are restricted for certain groups, such as foreign and temporary workers, and there are some reports of employers unlawfully disrupting union activity. A number of public-sector unions held strikes during 2018 over salaries and other issues.

F. RULE OF LAW: 12 / 16
F1. Is there an independent judiciary? 3 / 4

Judges are appointed by the president on the recommendation of the Judicial General Council, whose five members in turn are nominated by the three tiers of courts, the bar association, and the Justice Ministry. Once appointed, judges are fairly independent, though corruption and political influence remain concerns.

F2. Does due process prevail in civil and criminal matters? 3 / 4

Due process rights are generally respected, but some cases of arbitrary arrest and detention have been reported, and the right to a fair trial can be undermined by intimidation or bribery.

F3. Is there protection from the illegitimate use of physical force and freedom from war and insurgencies? 3 / 4

While the population faces few major threats to physical security, there have been reports of police illegally using physical abuse to obtain confessions. Some prison and detention facilities feature insufficient nutrition, heat, and medical care.

In July 2018, an apparent extralegal attempt by Turkish agents to seize and repatriate a Turkish educator living in Mongolia was thwarted after supporters, including students and alumni of Turkish schools in the country, mobilized to prevent the abduction, with prominent politicians joining their calls for the defense of the rule of law and the rejection of foreign interference. Mongolian authorities prevented a Turkish plane from leaving the airport with the educator; after he was released, he sought asylum in Mongolia.

F4. Do laws, policies, and practices guarantee equal treatment of various segments of the population? 3 / 4

There are no formal barriers to equal treatment under the law. Discrimination based on gender, race, sexual orientation, gender identity, and other categories is prohibited. However, women and LGBT people continue to face societal discrimination and harassment, including in the workplace. Public events in support of equality for LGBT people grew in attendance and visibility in 2018, with an eight-day series of gatherings in August.

G. PERSONAL AUTONOMY AND INDIVIDUAL RIGHTS: 12 / 16

G1. Do individuals enjoy freedom of movement, including the ability to change their place of residence, employment, or education? 4 / 4

The government generally respects freedom of movement, including internal and foreign travel. Exit bans imposed on individuals involved in legal cases are overseen by the courts.

G2. Are individuals able to exercise the right to own property and establish private businesses without undue interference from state or nonstate actors? 3 / 4

People are generally free to own property and establish private businesses, though state-owned enterprises play a prominent role in some sectors. Corruption also hampers many private business activities. Officials have reportedly withheld operating licenses and other documentation from businesses until bribes are paid. There is a history of corruption and government interference in the mining industry.

G3. Do individuals enjoy personal social freedoms, including choice of marriage partner and size of family, protection from domestic violence, and control over appearance? 3 / 4

Individual rights on personal status issues such as marriage and divorce are protected by law. However, domestic violence remains a problem. The government has initiated programs to encourage better police responses to domestic violence complaints in recent years. A government survey conducted with the United Nations, published in June 2018, found that nearly a third of women said they had faced physical or sexual abuse from a partner, and just 10 percent of those who had suffered severe sexual violence by a nonpartner had reported the crimes to the authorities.

G4. Do individuals enjoy equality of opportunity and freedom from economic exploitation? 2 / 4

The government has struggled to cope with economic inequality, particularly as large numbers of rural Mongolians migrate to cities that lack sufficient housing and infrastructure. New housing continues to be constructed, but many existing residents have reportedly been left homeless by urban redevelopment projects.

Women, children, people living in poverty, and other vulnerable segments of the population are at some risk of becoming victims of traffickers and compelled to engage in sex work or forced labor or begging. Workers in the mining industry are subject to exploitative conditions, as are contract workers from China. The government has taken efforts to better prosecute trafficking cases, but corruption and a lack of will to address the issue impedes progress.

Montenegro

Population: 600,000
Capital: Podgorica
Political Rights Rating: 4 ↓
Civil Liberties Rating: 3
Freedom Rating: 3.5
Freedom Status: Partly Free
Electoral Democracy: Yes

Overview: While numerous political parties compete for power in Montenegro, the opposition is fragmented, and the governing Democratic Party of Socialists (DPS) has been in power since 1991. Corruption is a serious issue. Investigative journalists and journalists critical of the government face pressure.

KEY DEVELOPMENTS IN 2018:

- In April, Milo Đukanović of the DPS was elected president, cementing his control over the government. Đukanović has held either the presidency or the post of prime minister for most of the last two decades.
- The trial of 14 people, including two opposition leaders, on charges of plotting an attempted coup in 2016, was ongoing at year's end.
- The June firing of Andrijana Kadija, director of the public broadcaster Radio and Television of Montenegro (RTCG), was condemned by rights organizations as an attempt by the DPS to reassert control over the entity after it displayed greater objectivity and independence in 2017.

POLITICAL RIGHTS: 23 / 40 (–2)

A. ELECTORAL PROCESS: 8 / 12

A1. Was the current head of government or other chief national authority elected through free and fair elections? 3 / 4

The president is chief of state and is directly elected for up to two five-year terms. In April 2018, Milo Đukanović of the DPS, who has served as either prime minister or president for most of the last two decades, was elected president with 53.9 percent of the vote. Independent candidate Mladen Bojanić finished second with 33.4 percent. Bojanić announced his candidacy just one month before the election, while Đukanović began campaigning three weeks before polling. Đukanović refused to participate in public debates with the other candidates. While some irregularities such as misuse of public resources were reported, the Organization for Security and Co-operation in Europe (OSCE), which monitored the election, stated that the polling was generally credible and respected fundamental rights. However, the mission noted that Đukanović and the DPS enjoyed significant institutional advantages that reduced the competitiveness of the process.

The president nominates the prime minister, who requires legislative approval. Parliament confirmed Prime Minister Duško Marković of the DPS, an ally of Đukanović, in November 2016, following legislative elections.

A2. Were the current national legislative representatives elected through free and fair elections? 2 / 4

Members of the unicameral, 81-seat Parliament—the Skupština—are directly elected for four-year terms.

Đukanović's DPS posted the strongest performance in the 2016 polls, taking 36 seats—5 seats short of a governing majority—and formed a coalition government with several smaller parties. The main opposition Democratic Front (DF) took 18 seats. Alleging electoral fraud, the opposition rejected the results and initiated a boycott of Parliament. However, the majority of opposition members had returned to Parliament by 2018, with the exception of the Democratic Montenegro (DCG) party and United Reform Action (URA).

While OSCE election monitors assessed the 2016 polls as credible, numerous violations were reported. The nongovernmental organization (NGO) MANS accused the government of trading tax or debt relief for votes, estimating that the DPS could have effectively bought as many as six legislative seats through such efforts. The government also suspended some mobile messaging applications on election day, citing "illegal marketing" on the platforms.

Additionally, on election day, authorities arrested 20 people on charges of plotting a coup that allegedly involved plans to assassinate Đukanović. Đukanović accused the DF of plotting the alleged coup, but offered no evidence for his claims; the DF in turn accused Đukanović of manufacturing the events as a means of securing support for the DPS in the elections, and decreasing turnout. A number of people, including two opposition leaders, were charged in connection with the alleged coup, and the trial of 14 suspects was ongoing at the end of 2018.

A3. Are the electoral laws and framework fair, and are they implemented impartially by the relevant election management bodies? 3 / 4

The conduct of elections in Montenegro is facilitated by a comprehensive legal and administrative framework. In October 2018, Parliament voted to form a committee, comprised of seven members from the ruling coalition and seven from the opposition, which is tasked with formulating new legislation to reform the electoral laws. The committee was established to implement OSCE recommendations from the 2016 parliamentary elections and 2018 presidential election, as well as recommendations published by the European Commission in April. The OSCE recommendations from 2016 included harmonizing electoral legislation and permitting media access to meetings of the State Election Commission. Some opposition parties refused to participate in the reform process, which Đukanović said will lead to only minor changes, and demanded more comprehensive reform of the electoral framework.

B. POLITICAL PLURALISM AND PARTICIPATION: 9 / 16 (−1)

B1. Do the people have the right to organize in different political parties or other competitive political groupings of their choice, and is the system free of undue obstacles to the rise and fall of these competing parties or groupings? 2 / 4

Political parties are for the most part able to form and operate without direct interference. The new DCG gained eight seats in the 2016 elections, and according to polls its support is increasing. This party has worked to create strategic partnerships with government opponents in civil society, media, and the intelligentsia.

However, the DPS-led government has relentlessly worked to delegitimize political activity that deviates from its preferred policies, characterizing it as a threat to the state or public order. In November 2018, lawmaker Nebojša Medojević, one of the leaders of the DF, was arrested for refusing to testify in a corruption case, drawing widespread condemnation. Medojević spent two weeks in jail before the Constitutional Court ordered his release in December.

B2. Is there a realistic opportunity for the opposition to increase its support or gain power through elections? 2 / 4

The DPS has been in power since 1991, which provides it with significant structural advantages over opposition parties. Observers have noted that the line between DPS party structures and government institutions has blurred, further disadvantaging the opposition. While numerous political parties compete in elections, the opposition is fragmented and weak, and frequently boycotts political processes. The position of opposition parties weakened further in 2018, as they suffered defeats in both the April presidential election and May municipal elections.

B3. Are the people's political choices free from domination by the military, foreign powers, religious hierarchies, economic oligarchies, or any other powerful group that is not democratically accountable? 2 / 4 (-1)

While voters are generally free to express their political choices, extensive patronage systems and widespread corruption encourage loyalty to the ruling party, which has been in power for nearly three decades. Many members of the ruling party have alleged ties to organized crime, further cementing the DPS's grip on power. Both public-sector employers, and private-sector employers with links to the state, pressure employees to vote for the ruling coalition. Marginalized populations, such as the Roma, have been mobilized by the DPS through vote-buying schemes.

Score Change: The score declined from 3 to 2 because President Đukanović and his party have used an extensive network of patronage and corruption, including alleged links to organized crime, to maintain power for nearly three decades.

B4. Do various segments of the population (including ethnic, religious, gender, LGBT, and other relevant groups) have full political rights and electoral opportunities? 3 / 4

All citizens have full political rights and electoral opportunities. Small political parties representing minority interests participate in the political sphere, and minorities are represented in larger parties, though the Romany minority is underrepresented. In the 2016 elections, voter materials were provided in the Albanian language, but not Romany.

Women are underrepresented in political leadership positions and politics generally. The government has taken steps to increase women's participation, including through gender quotas on electoral lists, though implementation is uneven. Draginja Vuksanović, the first female presidential candidate in Montenegrin history, won 8 percent of the vote in the 2018 poll.

C. FUNCTIONING OF GOVERNMENT: 6 / 12 (-1)

C1. Do the freely elected head of government and national legislative representatives determine the policies of the government? 2 / 4 (-1)

Đukanović has wielded vast personalized power for decades, through his tenure as both prime minister and president, as well as during his time outside of government as chair of the DPS. He maintains extensive control over most public institutions. Although the constitution provides for a parliamentary system of government, Parliament passed a new law after Đukanović's April 2018 election that greatly expands presidential powers. The law allows the president to form councils, committees, and working groups. Critics claim that the changes could amount to a de facto move toward a semipresidential system of government.

Parliament remains weak and has limited capacity to exercise its oversight functions. The opposition boycott of Parliament further diminished the power of the legislative branch.

Score Change: The score declined from 3 to 2 due to President Đukanović's personalized concentration of power, and the passage of legislation that further expanded presidential powers at the expense of the parliamentary system of government provided for in the constitution.

C2. Are safeguards against official corruption strong and effective? 2 / 4

Corruption and cronyism remain widespread, though there have been modest efforts by authorities to address them, prompted in part by EU accession requirements. A new anticorruption agency began its work in 2016, but a European Commission report published in April 2018 criticized the body for its ineffectiveness and noted the continued prevalence of high-level corruption, despite some recent improvements. Senior officials implicated in corruption schemes rarely face prosecution. Civil society and independent media provide some accountability by reporting on official corruption and its effects.

C3. Does the government operate with openness and transparency? 2 / 4

The government publishes some information online, but citizens have few opportunities for meaningful participation in public consultations on legislation. Budget plans are not widely available, nor is information on government contracts.

CIVIL LIBERTIES: 42 / 60
D. FREEDOM OF EXPRESSION AND BELIEF: 11 / 16
D1. Are there free and independent media? 2 / 4

A variety of independent media operate in Montenegro, and media coverage tends to be partisan and combative. The government frequently denies opposition media outlets advertising contracts from publicly owned or controlled entities. Journalists self-censor to avoid threats, political pressure, costly defamation suits, or job loss. Reporters who cover corruption and organized crime risk violence. In May 2018, investigative journalist Olivera Lakić, who reports on crime and corruption among government elites, was shot in the leg outside her apartment. At year's end, the assailants had not yet been identified.

In June, Andrijana Kadija, the director of the public broadcaster RTCG, was fired for allegedly abusing her position and behaving unprofessionally. The move was condemned by rights organizations as an attempt by the DPS to reassert control over the broadcaster after it displayed greater objectivity and independence in 2017.

D2. Are individuals free to practice and express their religious faith or nonbelief in public and private? 3 / 4

The constitution guarantees freedom of religious belief. However, the canonically recognized Serbian Orthodox Church and a self-proclaimed Montenegrin Orthodox Church continue to clash over the ownership of church properties.

D3. Is there academic freedom, and is the educational system free from extensive political indoctrination? 3 / 4

Academic freedom is guaranteed by law and generally upheld. However, in 2017, the rector of the University of Montenegro, who was appointed in 2014 and enacted a series of reforms, was removed by the new government. The events prompted speculation that the move was a reflection of clashes between personalities in the DPS.

D4. Are individuals free to express their personal views on political or other sensitive topics without fear of surveillance or retribution? 3 / 4

People are generally free to engage in public discussions. The existence of extensive, DPS-linked patronage networks has fostered an environment where vocal opposition to the government or its policies is widely believed to jeopardize employment opportunities, both in the public and private sector.

E. ASSOCIATIONAL AND ORGANIZATIONAL RIGHTS: 9 / 12

E1. Is there freedom of assembly? 3 / 4

While citizens generally enjoy freedom of assembly, authorities in the past have attempted to limit protests organized by the DF, and violence at demonstrations erupts occasionally.

E2. Is there freedom for nongovernmental organizations, particularly those that are engaged in human rights- and governance-related work? 3 / 4

Although most NGOs operate without interference, those that investigate corruption or criticize the government face pressure. During his 2018 presidential campaign, Đukanović made a number of inflammatory statements directed at civil society, saying on a television appearance that some NGOs and members of the media are "unscrupulous fighters for power" willing to destroy the government in the pursuit of foreign donations. Civil society leaders condemned the remarks for creating a hostile environment for NGOs.

E3. Is there freedom for trade unions and similar professional or labor organizations? 3 / 4

There is freedom for trade unions, which remain relatively strong in the public sector. However, reports of intimidation of labor activists by employers continue.

F. RULE OF LAW: 10 / 16

F1. Is there an independent judiciary? 2 / 4

Efforts to bolster judicial independence continue, though the judiciary remains susceptible to pressure from the government, and judicial corruption remains a problem.

The trial of two DF members and several others on charges of plotting a 2016 coup, which was ongoing at year's end, has been denounced by the opposition as an attempt by the DPS to maintain its support base. The outcome of their cases will reflect the level of transparency, openness, and accountability in the judicial system.

F2. Does due process prevail in civil and criminal matters? 2 / 4

Constitutional guarantees of due process are inconsistently upheld. Legal proceedings are lengthy and often highly bureaucratic, particularly when involving business dealings. Police frequently hold suspects in extended pretrial detention while completing investigations. Courts are poorly funded and often overburdened.

F3. Is there protection from the illegitimate use of physical force and freedom from war and insurgencies? 3 / 4

Violent crime is not a significant problem, although violence connected to organized crime has risen in recent years. Prison conditions do not meet international standards for education or health care, and prison guards reportedly abuse inmates regularly and with impunity.

F4. Do laws, policies, and practices guarantee equal treatment of various segments of the population? 3 / 4

Romany, Ashkali, Egyptians, LGBT (lesbian, gay, bisexual, and transgender) people, and other minority groups face discrimination. Women in Montenegro are legally entitled to equal pay for equal work, but patriarchal attitudes often limit their salary levels, as well as their educational opportunities.

G. PERSONAL AUTONOMY AND INDIVIDUAL RIGHTS: 12 / 16

G1. Do individuals enjoy freedom of movement, including the ability to change their place of residence, employment, or education? 3 / 4

The freedom of movement and the right of citizens to choose their residence, employment, and institution of higher education, are generally respected in practice. However, many jobs are awarded through patronage, limiting access for those without connections.

G2. Are individuals able to exercise the right to own property and establish private businesses without undue interference from state or nonstate actors? 3 / 4

The state sector dominates much of Montenegro's economy, and related clientelism, as well as corruption, pose obstacles to normal business activity.

G3. Do individuals enjoy personal social freedoms, including choice of marriage partner and size of family, protection from domestic violence, and control over appearance? 3 / 4

Domestic violence remains a problem. In December 2018, the government passed a draft law that would legalize same-sex unions. Parliament will likely vote on the legislation in 2019.

G4. Do individuals enjoy equality of opportunity and freedom from economic exploitation? 3 / 4

Most workers employed in the private sector remain unprotected from exploitation and arbitrary decisions of their employers.

Trafficking in persons for the purposes of prostitution and forced labor remains a problem, although the government has increased its efforts to prosecute traffickers, according to the US State Department's 2018 *Trafficking in Persons Report*.

Morocco

Population: 35,200,000
Capital: Rabat
Political Rights Rating: 5
Civil Liberties Rating: 5
Freedom Rating: 5.0
Freedom Status: Partly Free
Electoral Democracy: No

Note: The numerical ratings and status listed above do not reflect conditions in Western Sahara, which is examined in a separate report.

Overview: Morocco holds regular multiparty elections for Parliament, and reforms in 2011 shifted some authority over government from the monarchy to the elected legislature. Nevertheless, King Mohammed VI maintains dominance through a combination of substantial formal powers and informal lines of influence in the state and society. Many civil liberties are constrained in practice.

KEY DEVELOPMENTS IN 2018:

- In June, four leaders of the Hirak Rif protest movement were sentenced to 20 years in prison for their role in 2017 demonstrations in the Rif region that roiled the country. The sentences spurred further mass protests, including a July demonstration in Rabat that attracted tens of thousands of protesters.
- The abduction, rape, and torture of 17-year-old Khadija Okkarou by at least 12 men over a two-month period, which was first reported in August, caused international outrage. The incident, as well as other highly publicized acts of violence against women, inspired a new movement called #Masaktach (I will not be silenced).
- In September, a new law went into effect that criminalized domestic violence and forced marriage, and imposed more stringent penalties on those convicted of rape. Although the law was considered a step forward, critics faulted the legislation for failing to outlaw marital rape, not providing a clear definition of domestic violence, and for not mandating the government to provide greater support for victims of gender-based violence
- In December, two Scandinavian women were murdered while hiking in the Atlas Mountains. The assailants posted a video of the murders on social media, and pledged allegiance to the Islamic State (IS), raising concerns about radicalization in Morocco.

POLITICAL RIGHTS: 14 / 40

A. ELECTORAL PROCESS: 5 / 12

A1. Was the current head of government or other chief national authority elected through free and fair elections? 1 / 4

Constitutional reforms in 2011 required the king to appoint the prime minister from the party that wins the most seats in parliamentary elections, but the reforms preserved nearly all of the king's existing powers. The monarch can disband the legislature, rule by decree, and dismiss or appoint cabinet members.

After the 2016 parliamentary elections, political disagreement over the composition of a new government consumed more than five months. In 2017, the king finally used his royal prerogative to appoint Saad Eddine Othmani, a former Party of Justice and Development (PJD) foreign minister, as prime minister, replacing Abdelilah Benkirane, also of the PJD. However, the PJD holds a weak position in a fragile coalition. In August, 2018, the left-wing Party of Progress and Socialism (PPS) threatened to withdraw from the government amid political infighting. Technocrats loyal to the palace obtained key economic portfolios when the government formed, and the PJD was similarly excluded from the "strategic ministries" of interior, foreign affairs, justice, and Islamic affairs.

The 2016 elections were considered credible by observers, but there were some instances of irregularities such as vote buying.

A2. Were the current national legislative representatives elected through free and fair elections? 2 / 4

The lower house of Parliament, the Chamber of Representatives, has 395 directly elected members who serve for five-year terms. Of these, 305 are elected from 92 multi-member constituencies. The remaining 90 are elected from a single nationwide constituency, with 60 seats reserved for women and 30 for people under the age of 40. Members of the 120-seat upper house, the Chamber of Counselors, are chosen by an electoral college—made up of professional, labor, and business organizations as well as local and regional officials—to serve six-year terms.

In the 2016 parliamentary elections, the PJD placed first with 125 seats in the Chamber of Representatives, followed by the royalist Party of Authenticity and Modernity (PAM) with 102. Both increased their share of seats compared with 2011. Istiqlal fell by 14 seats to 46; the National Rally of Independents (RNI) declined by 15 seats to 37; the Popular Movement (MP) dropped 5 seats to 27; and the Socialist Union of Popular Forces (USFP) fell by 19 seats to 20. The PPS won 12 seats, a decline of 6. Official turnout was 43 percent of registered voters, lower than the 45 percent in 2011 and representing only 23 percent of eligible voters. Authorities placed limits on some foreign observers, and instances of vote buying and other irregularities were reported, but the elections largely provided a genuine choice to voters.

A3. Are the electoral laws and framework fair, and are they implemented impartially by the relevant election management bodies? 2 / 4

The constitutional and legal framework allows for competitive legislative elections, but the transparency of the process is not guaranteed in practice. Elections are overseen by the Interior Ministry, with some participation by the Justice Ministry, rather than an independent electoral commission. Approximately three million Moroccans live abroad, and the electoral laws made it exceedingly difficult for voters outside of Morocco to cast their ballots in 2016.

B. POLITICAL PLURALISM AND PARTICIPATION: 6 / 16

B1. Do the people have the right to organize in different political parties or other competitive political groupings of their choice, and is the system free of undue obstacles to the rise and fall of these competing parties or groupings? 2 / 4

Morocco has a multiparty system, but the parties are generally unable to assert themselves relative to the power of the palace. Of the two largest parties, the PJD polls strongly in urban areas, while the PAM dominates rural areas. Smaller parties tend to be unstable and are sometimes built around the personalities of their leaders. Justice and Charity is an illegal Islamist movement that does not participate in elections. Nevertheless, it enjoys widespread support and authorities largely tolerate its other activities.

B2. Is there a realistic opportunity for the opposition to increase its support or gain power through elections? 2 / 4

Prior to 2011, the PJD was a vocal, official opposition party, and its entry into government shows that the system allows some rotation of power. However, this opportunity is permanently limited by the presence and influence of the monarchy, both formally and in practice. Although the PJD won a plurality of seats in the 2016 elections, it struggled to form a governing coalition, and its ability to exercise power has been undermined by the king's support for parties loyal to the palace.

B3. Are the people's political choices free from domination by the military, foreign powers, religious hierarchies, economic oligarchies, or any other powerful group that is not democratically accountable? 1 / 4

The constitution and informal practice give the king considerable influence over political affairs, including government formation after elections. The monarch and his associates also wield enormous private economic power that can be used to shape political outcomes more indirectly through patronage networks.

B4. Do various segments of the population (including ethnic, religious, gender, LGBT, and other relevant groups) have full political rights and electoral opportunities? 1 / 4

The political system features universal suffrage, but parties based on religious, ethnic, or regional identity are prohibited, and the concerns and interests of women and the Amazigh (Berber) population are not adequately addressed.

Some 40 percent of the population is Amazigh, and the vast majority of Moroccans have Amazigh roots. Prominent Amazigh elites enjoy access to the monarchy and also have their interests represented in Parliament, but the bulk of the indigenous population is politically marginalized. Unrest throughout 2017 and 2018 in Al-Hoceima, the surrounding Rif region, and other cities across the country stemmed in large part from the inequities experienced by Amazigh residents and their inability to find redress for their grievances through the political system.

A system of reserved seats for women is meant to encourage their participation in the electoral process at both the national and local level, partly offsetting traditional social pressures that deter such engagement. Women won a greater share of seats in Parliament in 2016, taking 21 percent of the House of Representatives, compared with 17 percent in 2011. Nevertheless, these women remain underrepresented in party and cabinet leadership positions.

C. FUNCTIONING OF GOVERNMENT: 3 / 12

C1. Do the freely elected head of government and national legislative representatives determine the policies of the government? 1 / 4

While elected officials are duly installed in government, their power to shape policy is sharply constrained by the king, who sets national and foreign policy and commands the armed forces and intelligence services. Royal commissions tend to wield more power than government ministers. The king's power over the government was on display in August 2018, when he dismissed the finance minister, Mohamed Boussaid of the RNI, and subsequently replaced him with Abdelkader Amara of the PJD. The decision came in the midst of a national boycott of major Moroccan brands that began in April, which was spurred by widespread anger over poor economic performance and substandard living conditions.

C2. Are safeguards against official corruption strong and effective? 1 / 4

Corruption is rife in state institutions and the economy. Despite the government's rhetoric about combating corruption, it has a mixed record on enforcement. The Central Authority for the Prevention of Corruption (ICPC) was strengthened under a 2015 law and renamed as the National Body for Integrity, Prevention, and the Fight against Corruption (INPLC). In December 2018, the king finally appointed the body's head after the post remained empty for three years.

The government initiated plans for a National Anticorruption Strategy in 2016, but delays in forming the National Anticorruption Commission to administer the strategy stretched to mid-2018, when the body held its first meeting.

C3. Does the government operate with openness and transparency? 1 / 4

Overall transparency is limited. The government publishes budget and financial information online. Public officials—including Parliament members, judges, and civil servants—are required to declare their assets. However, the monarchy itself, with its vast array of economic interests, is not subject to these rules. In February 2018, the government adopted a controversial access to information law, which civil society leaders faulted for provisions that criminalize "misuse" of government information or "distortion of content."

CIVIL LIBERTIES: 25 / 60

D. FREEDOM OF EXPRESSION AND BELIEF: 7 / 16

D1. Are there free and independent media? 1 / 4

The state dominates the broadcast media, but more affluent segments of the population have access to foreign satellite television channels. Although the independent press enjoys a significant degree of freedom when reporting on economic and social policies, the authorities use a number of financial and legal mechanisms to punish critical journalists, particularly those who focus on the king, his family, the status of Western Sahara, or Islam. The authorities also occasionally disrupt websites and internet platforms. Bloggers are harassed for posting content that offends the monarchy, although many online activists operate anonymously.

Human rights groups continued to criticize the government's efforts to suppress reporting in the restive Rif region. In June 2018, Hamid al-Mahdaoui of the online outlet Badil was sentenced to three years in prison for not reporting a wiretapped 2017 phone call to the authorities. Al-Mahdaoui received the call from an activist who told him that he intended to smuggle weapons into Morocco. Al-Mahdoui's legal defense protested that the wiretap was illegal, since the wiretap order was not executed until after the conversation in question. Separately, in 2017 al-Mahdaoui was sentenced to one year in prison for "inciting people to participate in an unauthorized protest," after he criticized the government's decision to ban a planned demonstration by the Hirak Rif protest movement.

D2. Are individuals free to practice and express their religious faith or nonbelief in public and private? 2 / 4

Nearly all Moroccans are Muslims, and the king, identified as "commander of the faithful" in the constitution, has ultimate authority over religious affairs. Imams are required to obtain state certification, and mosques are monitored by the authorities. The government operates a well-financed training program for imams and female religious counselors tasked with promoting a state-sanctioned version of "moderate Islam," which some critics charge is also intended to promote political quiescence. Despite deep societal prejudices, the small Jewish community is permitted to practice its faith. The Christian community, which numbers approximately 50,000, experiences discrimination and harassment, and Christian marriages are not legally recognized by the government.

D3. Is there academic freedom, and is the educational system free from extensive political indoctrination? 2 / 4

Universities generally provide a more open space for discussion, but professors practice self-censorship when dealing with sensitive topics like the Western Sahara, the monarchy, and Islam. Salafists, adherents of a fundamentalist form of Islam, are closely monitored in universities.

Violence between university student groups, often stoked by Morocco's political, ethnic, and sectarian schisms, is widespread, and inhibits the right to peaceful student activism. In May 2018, clashes between proindependence Sahrawi activists and a student group advocating for Amazigh rights at the University of Ibn Zohr, in Agadir, led to the death of a 24-year-old law student.

D4. Are individuals free to express their personal views on political or other sensitive topics without fear of surveillance or retribution? 2 / 4

There is some freedom of private discussion, but state surveillance of online activity and personal communications has been a growing concern, and the arrests of journalists, bloggers, and activists for critical speech serve as a deterrent to uninhibited debate among the broader population.

E. ASSOCIATIONAL AND ORGANIZATIONAL RIGHTS: 5 / 12

E1. Is there freedom of assembly? 1 / 4

Freedom of assembly is restricted. The authorities sometimes use excessive force and violence to disperse protests, and harass activists involved in organizing demonstrations that criticize the government.

The government has suppressed protests in the Rif region that erupted after the 2016 death of Al-Hoceima fish vendor Mouhcine Fikri, which was captured on video. His stock of swordfish had been confiscated by authorities because it was caught out of season; when he climbed into a garbage truck to retrieve it, the trash compactor was turned on—allegedly on orders from a police officer—and he was killed. The ensuing Hirak Rif protest movement against corruption and economic deprivation gained support from activists across Morocco.

The government reacted harshly to the movement, dispersing assemblies and arresting Hirak Rif leader Nasser Zefzafi and other protest leaders in 2017. In June 2018, Zefzafi and three other activists were sentenced to 20 years in prison for their role in the demonstrations, while an additional 50 activists were sentenced to between 1 and 15 years imprisonment on lesser charges. The convictions spurred further mass protests, including a July demonstration in Rabat that drew tens of thousands of protesters.

Authorities also cracked down on protests in the northeastern mining town of Jerada in March, which began in response to the deaths of two coal miners, who reportedly died as a result of dangerous working conditions in their mine. Police used excessive force in dispersing the protests, and arrested dozens of demonstrators.

E2. Is there freedom for nongovernmental organizations, particularly those that are engaged in human rights- and governance-related work? 2 / 4

Civil society organizations are quite active, but they are subject to legal harassment, travel restrictions, and other impediments to their work. The authorities routinely deny registration to nongovernmental organizations (NGOs) with links to Justice and Charity or that assert the rights of marginalized communities. The Moroccan Association for Human Rights (AMDH), one of Morocco's most prominent NGOs, is frequently targeted by the government. According to Human Rights Watch (HRW), 16 AMDH events were cancelled between January 2017 and July 2018 due to pressure on venue owners or security forces directly blocking access to event spaces. Amnesty International has been prohibited from carrying out research in Morocco since 2015.

E3. Is there freedom for trade unions and similar professional or labor organizations? 2 / 4

Workers are permitted to form and join independent trade unions, and the 2004 labor law prevents employers from punishing workers who do so, but there are undue legal and employer restrictions on collective bargaining and strikes. The authorities sometimes forcibly break up labor-related protests. Unions are often closely affiliated with political parties.

F. RULE OF LAW: 6 / 16

F1. Is there an independent judiciary? 1 / 4

The court system is not independent of the monarch, who chairs the Supreme Council of the Judiciary. In practice, the courts are regularly used to punish perceived opponents of the government, including dissenting Islamists, human rights and anticorruption activists, and critics of Moroccan rule in Western Sahara.

F2. Does due process prevail in civil and criminal matters? 2 / 4

Due process is not consistently upheld. Law enforcement officers often violate legal and procedural safeguards against arbitrary arrest and detention, and many convictions rely on confessions that may have been coerced. Pretrial detainees are reportedly held beyond a one-year limit in practice, and there are no provisions in the law allowing for pretrial detainees to challenge their detentions in court. Some suspects, particularly those accused of terrorism, are held in secret detention for days or weeks before formal charges are filed.

F3. Is there protection from the illegitimate use of physical force and freedom from war and insurgencies? 2 / 4

Cases of excessive force by police and torture in custody continue to occur. A number of the Jerada protesters detained during 2018 reported being beaten and injured during arrest, and a few detainees were subjected to prolonged solitary confinement while awaiting trial. Prisons often suffer from overcrowding.

Terrorism remains a threat to physical security in the country, though the authorities have had some success in preventing attacks. In December 2018, two Scandinavian women were murdered while hiking in the Atlas Mountains. The assailants posted a video of the murders on social media, and pledged allegiance to the Islamic State (IS). At year's end, 15 suspects had been charged in connection with the murders, which have raised concerns about radicalization within the country.

F4. Do laws, policies, and practices guarantee equal treatment of various segments of the population? 1 / 4

Constitutional reforms in 2011 granted official status to Tamazight languages, which have been promoted in schools along with Amazigh culture. Nevertheless, Amazigh and other communities that do not identify with the dominant Arab culture tend to face educational and economic disadvantages. Civil society groups that promote Amazigh rights have faced government interference.

Gender equality was also recognized in the 2011 constitution, but women continue to face significant discrimination at the societal level and are seriously underrepresented in the labor force. LGBT (lesbian, gay, bisexual, and transgender) people face harsh discrimination and occasional violence. Same-sex sexual relations can be punished with up to three years in prison. The government has granted temporary residency permits to refugees and migrants as part of an effort to regularize their status and provide them with basic services, which earned Morocco international praise in recent years. However, in 2018, authorities cracked down on refugees, asylum seekers, and migrants from sub-Saharan Africa. Beginning in July, security forces conducted a series of raids in which thousands of people were arrested, bused to a remote area near the Algerian border, and abandoned. The arrests were condemned by international rights groups for violating international law, as well as the basic human rights of those affected.

G. PERSONAL AUTONOMY AND INDIVIDUAL RIGHTS: 7 / 16

G1. Do individuals enjoy freedom of movement, including the ability to change their place of residence, employment, or education? 2 / 4

Moroccan law guarantees freedom of movement and the ability to change one's place of employment or education, but in practice poor economic conditions and corruption limit these rights. Widespread bribery, nepotism, and misconduct within the educational sector constrain merit-based advancement.

G2. Are individuals able to exercise the right to own property and establish private businesses without undue interference from state or nonstate actors? 2 / 4

Well over a third of the land is collectively owned by tribes and managed by the Interior Ministry, and in recent years it has been subject to private development without fair compensation to previous occupants. Moreover, under tribal rules of inheritance, women cannot hold the rights to occupy and use such lands, leaving them more vulnerable to displacement. Ordinary inheritance rules also put women at a disadvantage, generally granting them half the property of an equivalent male heir.

Private business activity is hampered in part by the dominant role of the king and his family. Among other assets, they have a majority stake in the National Investment Company (SNI), a massive conglomerate with businesses in virtually every economic sector, including mining, tourism, food, banking, construction, and energy.

G3. Do individuals enjoy personal social freedoms, including choice of marriage partner and size of family, protection from domestic violence, and control over appearance? 2 / 4

The 2004 family code granted women increased rights in the areas of marriage, divorce, and child custody, though a number of inequities and restrictions remain, and implementation of the code has been uneven. Domestic violence is rarely reported or punished due to social stigma. All extramarital sexual activity is illegal, which deters rape victims from bringing charges, among other repercussions.

In September 2018, a new law went into effect that criminalized domestic violence and forced marriage, and imposed more stringent penalties on those convicted of rape. Although the law was considered a step forward, critics faulted the legislation for failing to outlaw marital rape, not providing a clear definition of domestic violence, and for not mandating the government to provide greater support for victims of gender-based violence.

The abduction, rape, and torture of 17-year-old Khadija Okkarou by at least 12 men over a two-month period, which was first reported in August, highlighted the entrenched nature of gender-based violence and misogyny in Morocco, and caused international outrage. The incident, as well as other highly publicized acts of violence against women, inspired a new movement called #Masaktach (I will not be silenced). After the victim spoke out about her ordeal, 12 men were arrested for her abduction, and they awaited trial at year's end.

G4. Do individuals enjoy equality of opportunity and freedom from economic exploitation? 1 / 4

Poverty is widespread, and economic opportunities are scarce for a large portion of the population. The death of 20-year-old Hayat Belkacem in September 2018 typified the desperation felt by many young Moroccans with poor job prospects. Belkacem died after the navy opened fire on a boat full of migrants attempting to travel to Spain. Three other passengers were wounded. According to the Spanish Interior Ministry, over 10,000 Moroccan irregular migrants had arrived in Spain as of October, compared to 1,310 over the same period in 2016.

Child laborers, especially girls working as domestic helpers, are denied basic rights and are frequently abused by their employers. A new labor law to protect girls employed as household workers entered into force in October. It requires employers to use written contracts, sets a minimum working age of 18 (after a five-year phase-in period during which 16- and 17-year-olds are allowed to work), mandates a day off each week, and sets a minimum wage. The law's passage was met with skepticism from rights groups, who criticized the legislation for failing to provide support to reintegrate domestic workers into society, as well as permitting girls under 18 to work until 2023.

Separately, Parliament adopted a law in 2016 to criminalize human trafficking; existing measures had defined and banned only some forms of trafficking and left many victims unprotected.

Mozambique

Population: 30,500,000
Capital: Maputo
Political Rights Rating: 4
Civil Liberties Rating: 4
Freedom Rating: 4.0
Freedom Status: Partly Free
Electoral Democracy: No

Overview: The ruling party's unbroken incumbency before, and since the introduction of multiparty elections in 1994 has allowed it to establish significant control over state institutions. The opposition has disputed the results of recent elections, and its armed wing fought a low-level conflict against government forces that persisted until a truce was signed in December 2016. Mozambique also struggles with corruption, and journalists who report on it and other sensitive issues risk violent attacks.

KEY DEVELOPMENTS IN 2018:

- In May, the parliament overwhelmingly approved constitutional reforms that will allow the indirect election of provincial governors, district administrators, and mayors. The changes were viewed as beneficial to the main opposition party, and a step toward greater decentralization and political stability.
- In the fall, the National Election Commission (CNE) faced sharp criticism over its flawed stewardship of municipal polls in the Marromeu District.
- In March, Ericino de Salema, a journalist and government critic, was abducted and beaten by unidentified assailants.
- Islamic extremists continued to carry out attacks in the northern districts of Cabo Delgado. At least 10 people were killed in one of the bloodiest attacks, in September.

POLITICAL RIGHTS: 19 / 40 (−1)

A. ELECTORAL PROCESS: 5 / 12 (−1)

A1. Was the current head of government or other chief national authority elected through free and fair elections? 2 / 4

The president, who appoints the prime minister, is elected by popular vote for up to two five-year terms. President Filipe Nyusi of the Front for the Liberation of Mozambique (FRELIMO) won the presidential contest in 2014 with 57 percent of the vote. Voting was marred by reported incidents of ballot box stuffing, inaccuracies in the voting register, and irregularities in the tabulation process in some precincts. Despite these flaws, international observers asserted that the election was largely credible. Afonso Dhlakama, the Mozambique National Resistance (RENAMO) candidate and the party's leader, denounced the results as fraudulent and called for new elections.

A2. Were the current national legislative representatives elected through free and fair elections? 2 / 4

Members of the 250-seat unicameral Assembly of the Republic are elected to five-year terms. The 2014 legislative elections were held concurrently with the presidential election. Incidents of ballot-box stuffing, inaccuracies in the voting register, and irregularities in the tabulation process marred the polls. International observers, while acknowledging these flaws, determined that overall, the election was conducted credibly.

Despite the death in May 2018 of Dhlakama, RENAMO saw increased support in 2018 municipal elections, especially in northern Mozambique and in the industrial city of Matola.

A3. Are the electoral laws and framework fair, and are they implemented impartially by the relevant election management bodies? 1/ 4 (−1)

Elections are administered by the CNE. FRELIMO controls the process by which the CNE members are appointed, which critics contend affects the impartiality of the body. The CNE is supported by the Technical Secretariat for Electoral Administration (STAE), which handles the technical details of elections. STAE performs well generally, but is viewed with distrust by opposition parties.

In 2018, the CNE faced sharp criticism over its stewardship of municipal polls in the Marromeu District, where the elections were partially rerun due to irregularities. FRELIMO-affiliated members of the CNE reportedly implemented rerun-related decisions without the support of RENAMO- and other opposition-affiliated members, including changing the number of reported voters in Marromeu, a move they failed to explain. RENAMO later alleged a litany of violations in the Marromeu rerun and vote count and attempted a legal challenge of the results, but the courts declined to hear the case. The Catholic Justice and Peace Commission and several Mozambican observer missions criticized the rerun's conduct, while the US embassy in a December statement said it was "gravely concerned" that reports of irregularities in the Marromeu recount would "cast a shadow on the overall electoral contest."

Separately, in May 2018, the parliament overwhelmingly approved constitutional reforms that in coming years would allow the indirect election of provincial governors, district administrators, and mayors. The changes were viewed as beneficial to RENAMO and a step toward greater decentralization and political stability.

Score Change: The score declined from 2 to 1 due to the CNE's flawed stewardship of municipal elections in the Marromeu District.

B. POLITICAL PLURALISM AND PARTICIPATION: 9 / 16

B1. Do the people have the right to organize in different political parties or other competitive political groupings of their choice, and is the system free of undue obstacles to the rise and fall of these competing parties or groupings? 2 / 4

The right to form political parties is largely respected. A preponderance of parties compete, although most lack resources to campaign effectively and build a public following. Opposition leaders can face harassment and threats for speaking out against the government. Figures within FRELIMO perceived as acting in conflict with the aims of the party can encounter obstacles, including intraparty disciplinary measures.

B2. Is there a realistic opportunity for the opposition to increase its support or gain power through elections? 2 / 4

FRELIMO first took power in 1975, upon Mozambique's independence, and has remained in power since the 1992 agreement that ended the country's 1977–92 civil war and since the introduction of multiparty elections in 1994. However, opposition parties made major gains in the 2014 elections: FRELIMO lost 47 seats, while RENAMO gained 38 seats.

FRELIMO's use of public resources to fund campaign activities has provided it with an unfair electoral advantage. Separately, during the 2014 campaign period, opposition parties had difficulty entering some FRELIMO strongholds due to hostile local crowds.

In October 2018, during the campaign period for local elections, the MDM office in Bilene was burned down.

B3. Are the people's political choices free from domination by the military, foreign powers, religious hierarchies, economic oligarchies, or any other powerful group that is not democratically accountable? 2 / 4

Unelected elites in FRELIMO, including former president Armando Guebuza, retain great influence and play a large role in shaping the party's platform.

B4. Do various segments of the population (including ethnic, religious, gender, LGBT, and other relevant groups) have full political rights and electoral opportunities? 3 / 4

Ethnic minorities are generally able to participate fully in political life, and people from various ethnic groups hold high-level government positions. However, FRELIMO's support base lies in the extreme north and extreme south, and ethnic groups from other regions, such as the Ndau and Macua, are underrepresented.

Women participate robustly in politics, both as voters and candidates for office. Of the 250 members of parliament in 2018, 40 percent were women, one of the highest rates in the world. However, cultural factors still inhibit the participation of many women, and women are underrepresented in local government positions.

C. FUNCTIONING OF GOVERNMENT: 5 / 12

C1. Do the freely elected head of government and national legislative representatives determine the policies of the government? 2 / 4

Power remains generally centralized in the executive branch, which dominates the parliament and all other branches of government—though the 2018 constitutional reforms introduced some measures to reduce centralization. Foreign donors have significant influence on policymaking, specifically as it relates to economic policy and public-sector reform. Business elites connected to FRELIMO have a strong impact on government decisions, particularly on foreign investment in the oil, gas, and agriculture sectors.

C2. Are safeguards against official corruption strong and effective? 1 / 4

Corruption remains widespread at the highest levels of government. Patronage networks are deeply entrenched, with various groupings competing for state resources. The anticorruption legal framework is undermined by a variety of loopholes: for example, embezzlement is not included in the Anti-Corruption Law. A judiciary susceptible to pressure from the executive branch further complicates attempts to enforce anticorruption laws.

In October 2018 it was reported that Helena Taipo, the former minister of labor and current ambassador to Angola, was under investigation in connection with the misdirection of over $1 million from the National Institute of Social Security (INSS). In December, former finance minister Manuel Chang was arrested in South Africa following an accusation of financial crimes by the United States, which is seeking his extradition.

C3. Does the government operate with openness and transparency? 2 / 4

Despite the passage of a freedom of information law in 2014, it is difficult to attain government information in practice. In May 2017, two nongovernmental organizations (NGOs) released a report claiming that out of 49 government entities they contacted requesting information, only 18 percent responded within 21 days, as required by law.

CIVIL LIBERTIES: 32 / 60

D. FREEDOM OF EXPRESSION AND BELIEF: 9 / 16

D1. Are there free and independent media? 2 / 4

State-run outlets dominate Mozambique's media sector, and authorities often direct such outlets to provide coverage favorable to the government. However, a number of smaller independent outlets provide important coverage.

Journalists frequently experience government pressure, harassment, and intimidation, which encourages self-censorship. The government is known to retaliate against journalists who criticize it by cancelling public advertising contracts.

Journalists and political commentators appearing on television programs have been the targets of attacks and kidnappings in recent years. In March 2018, Ericino de Salema, a journalist and political commentator who regularly expressed criticisms of the government on the television talk show Pontas de Vista, was abducted and attacked before being left on the side of a road in Maputo.

In August 2018, authorities introduced a set of media licensing fees for domestic and foreign journalists and outlets, ranging from several hundred to several thousand dollars. The government postponed the measures, which were introduced in the absence of consultations with journalists' groups, in the wake of an outcry from rights activists and journalists.

D2. Are individuals free to practice and express their religious faith or nonbelief in public and private? 3 / 4

Religious freedom is generally respected, but government responses to attacks by armed Islamists have alarmed human rights activists. In 2017, a group of Muslim extremists attacked police stations in Cabo Delgado, a northern province, killing at least two police officers. The government responded to the attacks by sending troops to the region; several Muslim leaders were among the more than 300 people subsequently detained, and several mosques were closed.

In 2018, Islamic insurgents reportedly killed a local Islamic religious figure and burned a mosque in Cabo Delgado's Macomia District.

D3. Is there academic freedom, and is the educational system free from extensive political indoctrination? 2 / 4

There are no legal restrictions on academic freedom. However since 2015, when law professor Gilles Cistac was murdered after supporting RENAMO in a televised appearance, academics have been more hesitant to criticize the government and frequently practice self-censorship. Indoctrination at primary schools has been reported, particularly in Gaza, where some teachers have added FRELIMO propaganda to their curricula.

D4. Are individuals free to express their personal views on political or other sensitive topics without fear of surveillance or retribution? 2 / 4

Civil society groups claim that authorities monitor criticism of the government posted online. There have been reports of government intelligence agents monitoring the e-mails of opposition party members.

E. ASSOCIATIONAL AND ORGANIZATIONAL RIGHTS: 7 / 12
E1. Is there freedom of assembly? 2 / 4

Freedom of assembly is constitutionally guaranteed, but the right to assemble is subject to notification and timing restrictions. The government frequently disallows protests on the basis of errors in the organizers' official applications. In July 2018, one person was killed and two were injured when police responded with disproportionate violence to a protest against a mining company in Inhassunge District, whose activities had reportedly forced local residents to relocate.

E2. Is there freedom for nongovernmental organizations, particularly those that are engaged in human rights- and governance-related work? 3 / 4

Most NGOs operate without significant restrictions. However, rights defenders and members of groups perceived as critical of the government continue to report acts of intimidation.

At the end of 2018, the registration of the Mozambican Association for the Defense of Sexual Minorities (LAMBDA) had still not been approved by the government. LAMBDA first applied for registration in 2008, and has had no success in attaining government approval despite multiple resubmissions.

E3. Is there freedom for trade unions and similar professional or labor organizations? 2 / 4

Workers have the right to form unions, but a number of restrictions impede the right to strike and make the practice rare. Public-sector workers are not allowed to strike. In 2017, administrative and technical staff at Eduardo Mondlane University (UEM) organized a strike to protest the nonpayment of a bonus. The university declared the strike illegal, and riot police broke up the picket line using tear gas and rubber bullets.

F. RULE OF LAW: 7 / 16
F1. Is there an independent judiciary? 2 / 4

Judicial independence is hampered by the dominance of the executive branch. The attorney general is directly appointed by the president, with no legislative confirmation process. Pressure from FRELIMO's leadership often impedes investigations into corruption and fraud. Former president Guebuza and members of his administration have been credibly implicated in fraud and embezzlement scandals, but there have been no prosecutions. Observers claim that this judicial inaction results from the influence of FRELIMO's leadership.

F2. Does due process prevail in civil and criminal matters? 2 / 4

Although due process rights are constitutionally guaranteed, these rights are not always respected in practice. RENAMO leaders assert that the police arrest members of their party arbitrarily. Due to resource constraints and an understaffed judiciary, lengthy pretrial detentions are common.

F3. Is there protection from the illegitimate use of physical force and freedom from war and insurgencies? 1 / 4

The December 2016 truce to halt more than a year of fighting between RENAMO and FRELIMO held up throughout 2018, though tensions between the leaders of both parties remained high.

No one has been held accountable for a number of high profile, apparently politically motivated attacks that took place in late 2015 and 2016.

Residents of Cabo Delgado continue to suffer from violence committed by Islamist insurgents. In September, an attack in a village in Macomia District left at least 10 people dead. In November and December, attacks intensified in the northern districts of the province. Security forces deployed to fight the militants have been accused of kidnappings and other abuses.

F4. Do laws, policies, and practices guarantee equal treatment of various segments of the population? 2 / 4

Mozambican police reportedly discriminate against Zimbabwean, Somali, and Chinese immigrants. People with albinism continued to face discrimination, persecution, and violence. Government efforts to protect people with albinism have been inadequate.

Women experience discrimination in education and employment; on average, women are less educated and earn less than men. Sexual harassment in the workplace and at schools remains widespread.

G. PERSONAL AUTONOMY AND INDIVIDUAL RIGHTS: 9 / 16

G1. Do individuals enjoy freedom of movement, including the ability to change their place of residence, employment, or education? 3 / 4

Although Mozambicans face no formal restrictions on domestic or international travel, movement is hampered by the presence of checkpoints manned by corrupt police officials, who often harass and demand bribes from travelers.

G2. Are individuals able to exercise the right to own property and establish private businesses without undue interference from state or nonstate actors? 2 / 4

The law does not recognize private property outside urbanized areas; citizens instead obtain land use rights from the government. Many citizens are uninformed about the land law and fail to properly register their holdings. The government must approve all formal transfers of land use rights in an often opaque and protracted process. As a result, most land transactions occur on an extralegal market.

Under customary law, women usually cannot inherit property. The government does not frequently intervene to protect women's property rights when inheritance is denied.

G3. Do individuals enjoy personal social freedoms, including choice of marriage partner and size of family, protection from domestic violence, and control over appearance? 2 / 4

Domestic violence is pervasive in Mozambique and laws against it are infrequently enforced. According to the Ministry of Women and Social Action, at least 54 percent of women will endure some form of physical or sexual violence at some point in their lives. Early and forced marriages remain common in rural areas. The International Center for Research on Women reports that 56 percent of girls marry before reaching the age of 18.

G4. Do individuals enjoy equality of opportunity and freedom from economic exploitation? 2 / 4

Many women and girls from rural areas are at risk of becoming drawn into sex trafficking and domestic servitude. Government efforts to confront trafficking are inadequate, according to the US State Department's most recent *Trafficking in Persons Report*, but authorities have made increased efforts to investigate trafficking claims and prosecute traffickers.

Child labor is permitted for children between 15 and 17 years old with a government permit. However, children under 15 frequently labor in the agriculture, mining, and fishing sectors, where they often work long hours and do not attend school. According to an August 2017 report released by the Ministry of Labor, Employment, and Social Security, more than one million children between the ages of 7 and 17 are actively employed.

Myanmar

Population: 53,900,000
Capital: Nay Pyi Taw
Political Rights Rating: 5
Civil Liberties Rating: 5
Freedom Rating: 5.0
Freedom Status: Partly Free
Electoral Democracy: No

Overview: Myanmar's transition from military dictatorship to democracy has faltered under the leadership of the National League for Democracy (NLD), which came to power in relatively free elections in 2015 but has failed to uphold human rights or bring security to areas affected by armed conflict. The military retains significant influence over politics, and the country is under international pressure regarding a 2017 military operation that forced more than 700,000 members of the Rohingya minority, a mostly Muslim ethnic group, to flee to Bangladesh.

KEY DEVELOPMENTS IN 2018:

- More than 900,000 Rohingya refugees from Myanmar's Rakhine State remained in Bangladesh during the year, including the more than 700,000 who fled there since late August 2017. Civilians also continued to flee fighting between government forces and ethnic minority rebels in Shan and Kachin States.
- A panel of the International Criminal Court (ICC) ruled in September that the ICC had jurisdiction over prosecution of alleged crimes against the Rohingya. The ICC then began examining whether there was enough evidence to proceed to a full investigation.
- The UN Independent International Fact-Finding Mission on Myanmar briefed the UN Security Council in October, with the mission chair calling the Rohingya crisis "an ongoing genocide."
- In September, despite international pressure on their behalf, Reuters journalists Wa Lone and Kyaw Soe Oo were sentenced to seven years in prison on charges of violating the 1923 Official Secrets Act while reporting on a massacre in Rakhine State. The journalists were widely understood to have been entrapped by police and subjected to an unfair trial in reprisal for their work.

POLITICAL RIGHTS: 13 / 40

A. ELECTORAL PROCESS: 5 / 12

A1. Was the current head of government or other chief national authority elected through free and fair elections? 2 / 4

The legislature elects the president, who is chief of state and head of government. Military members of the legislature have the right to nominate one of the three presidential candidates, and the elected members of each chamber nominate the other two. The candidate with the largest number of votes in a combined parliamentary vote wins the presidency; the other two candidates become vice presidents, ensuring that a military nominee is always either president or vice president. Htin Kyaw, the NLD candidate, won the presidency in the 2016 election. He resigned in March 2018 and was replaced by Win Myint, one of NLD leader Aung San Suu Kyi's aides.

Aung San Suu Kyi holds the powerful position of state counselor, a post akin to that of a prime minister, which was created for her in 2016 through legislation designed to circumvent provisions in the 2008 military-drafted constitution that had barred her from running for president because members of her immediate family hold foreign citizenship.

The commander in chief of the armed forces holds broad powers, including control over security-related cabinet ministries, and is selected through an opaque process by the military-dominated National Defense and Security Council (NDSC).

A2. Were the current national legislative representatives elected through free and fair elections? 2 / 4

The bicameral Assembly of the Union consists of the 440-seat lower House of Representatives and the 224-seat upper House of Nationalities. Representatives serve five-year terms. A quarter of the seats in both houses are reserved for the military and filled through appointment by the commander in chief of the armed forces.

International electoral observers concluded that the 2015 legislative polls were generally credible and that the outcome reflected the will of the people, despite a campaign period marked by anti-Muslim rhetoric, the exclusion of Muslim candidates, and the disenfranchisement of hundreds of thousands of Rohingya. The NLD, with 57 percent of the overall popular vote in a first-past-the-post system, won 135 of the 168 elected seats in the upper house, 255 of 330 elected seats in the lower house, and 496 of 659 seats across 14 state and regional legislatures. The military-backed Union Solidarity and Development Party (USDP) placed second with 28 percent of the popular vote, 12 seats in the upper house, 30 in the lower house, and 76 in the states and regions. The remaining seats were captured by ethnic minority and other parties as well as independents.

The NLD did not perform as well in November 2018 by-elections, winning 7 out of 13 available seats in various national and subnational legislative chambers. Of those, the party lost 5 out of 6 in ethnic minority areas.

A3. Are the electoral laws and framework fair, and are they implemented impartially by the relevant election management bodies? 1 / 4

Various features of the electoral framework undermine the democratic nature of the country's elections. These include the military's role in presidential nominations and appointments to both chambers of parliament, as well as rigid citizenship laws and excessive residency requirements that prevent large numbers of people from voting or standing for office.

The Union Election Commission (UEC), which is responsible for electoral administration, is empowered to adjudicate complaints against itself. Its members are appointed by the president and confirmed by the legislature, which has only limited authority to reject nominees. Election monitors have expressed concern about the potential for early voting procedures to facilitate fraud.

B. POLITICAL PLURALISM AND PARTICIPATION: 8 / 16

B1. Do the people have the right to organize in different political parties or other competitive political groupings of their choice, and is the system free of undue obstacles to the rise and fall of these competing parties or groupings? 2 / 4

New political parties were generally allowed to register and compete in the 2015 elections, which featured fewer restrictions on party organization and voter mobilization than the 2010 vote. Only sporadic interference from government officials was reported. Ninety-one parties competed in the elections, and many of them convened meetings and large rallies throughout the country.

However, competition is skewed in part by the USDP's systematic support from the military, whose personnel and their families are eligible to vote, casting ballots in military barracks in some cases. Moreover, some legal provisions can be invoked to restrict parties' operations. The constitution contains a requirement that political parties be loyal to the state, which carries the potential for abuse. Laws allow for penalties, including deregistration, against political parties that accept support from foreign governments or religious bodies, or that are deemed to have abused religion for political purposes or disrespected the constitution.

B2. Is there a realistic opportunity for the opposition to increase its support or gain power through elections? 3 / 4

As evidenced by both the NLD's overwhelming parliamentary victory in 2015 and its losses in the 2018 by-elections, there is a realistic opportunity for the opposition to increase its support and gain power through competitive balloting. However, the military's constitutional prerogatives, as well as its close ties to the USDP, limit the degree to which any opposition force can secure control over the executive or the legislature through elections.

B3. Are the people's political choices free from domination by the military, foreign powers, religious hierarchies, economic oligarchies, or any other powerful group that is not democratically accountable? 2 / 4

The results of the 2015 elections and subsequent transition talks suggested that the military had a waning ability or determination to influence electoral outcomes. Nevertheless, the military retains considerable power over political affairs, particularly in conflict areas where it has a dominant presence, and in 2015 the USDP reportedly benefited from pressure on public employees and students to attend rallies and cast ballots for the party.

B4. Do various segments of the population (including ethnic, religious, gender, LGBT, and other relevant groups) have full political rights and electoral opportunities? 1 / 4

Minority groups face restrictions on their political rights and electoral opportunities. In particular, citizenship, residency, and party registration laws disadvantage ethnic and religious minorities, particularly the mainly Muslim Rohingya, the majority of whom were rendered stateless by the 1982 citizenship law. In 2015, under pressure from Buddhist nationalists, the president issued a decree revoking the temporary identification cards, or "white cards," that had allowed Rohingya to vote in previous elections. A Constitutional Tribunal ruling later in 2015 then found that voting by white-card holders was unconstitutional. Nearly all Rohingya were consequently left off the voter rolls for the 2015 elections. In addition, a sitting Rohingya lawmaker from the USDP was barred from running in the polls.

Other Muslims with citizenship documents were able to vote, but of more than 6,000 candidates on the final list, only about 28 were Muslim. No Muslim sits in the current parliament.

While ethnic parties generally fared poorly in the 2015 legislative elections, the Shan Nationalities League for Democracy (SNLD) and the Arakan National Party (ANP) performed well in their respective states. The SNLD won a lower house seat in the 2018 by-elections.

Women remain underrepresented in the government and civil service, due largely to societal biases that discourage their political participation. Notwithstanding the prominence of Aung San Suu Kyi, whose father led Myanmar's independence struggle, few women have achieved ministerial-level appointments.

C. FUNCTIONING OF GOVERNMENT: 4 / 12

C1. Do the freely elected head of government and national legislative representatives determine the policies of the government? 2 / 4

Although elected officials are able to set policy in some subject areas, the military is guaranteed control over the Defense, Home Affairs, and Border Affairs Ministries. The military also effectively controls at least six seats on the powerful 11-member NDSC. The 2008 constitution allows the military to dissolve the civilian government and parliament and rule directly if the president declares a state of emergency. Governance is contested in some areas between the armed forces and ethnic minority rebel groups.

C2. Are safeguards against official corruption strong and effective? 1 / 4

Corruption is rampant at both the national and local levels, and recent government initiatives aimed at curbing it have generally not produced meaningful results. For example, an Anti-Corruption Commission (ACC) established in 2014 has yet to establish a strong track record of investigations against high-ranking officials. In its most prominent cases to date, the ACC brought bribery charges against the chief of the Food and Drug Administration in April 2018 and a number of senior regional law enforcement officials in Yangon in September.

Privatization of state-owned companies and other economic reforms in recent years have allegedly benefited family members and associates of senior officials. The government has ignored tax evasion by the country's wealthiest companies and individuals.

C3. Does the government operate with openness and transparency? 1 / 4

The government does not operate with openness and transparency. A draft Right to Information Law was developed in 2016, and a new draft was released in December 2017, but the measure remained stalled in the parliament during 2018. Some information about the budget has been released in recent years, but it receives limited parliamentary scrutiny.

ADDITIONAL DISCRETIONARY POLITICAL RIGHTS QUESTION
Is the government or occupying power deliberately changing the ethnic composition of a country or territory so as to destroy a culture or tip the political balance in favor of another group? –4 / 0

The government has long used violence, displacement, and other tactics to alter the demographics of states with ethnic unrest or insurgencies. The Rohingya in Rakhine State have faced particularly harsh restrictions for decades, including limits on family size and the ability and right to marry, the denial of legal status and social services, and disenfranchisement and loss of citizenship. Human rights experts and the United Nations have labeled the abuses against the Rohingya as crimes against humanity and ethnic cleansing, and some analysts have argued that they constitute either genocide or a precursor to genocide.

Repression of the Rohingya escalated in 2017, after rebels from the Arakan Rohingya Salvation Army (ARSA) attacked multiple police posts with rudimentary weapons. The military launched a severe counteroffensive against Rohingya communities across the northern part of the state, leading to reports of torture, rape, indiscriminate killings, and the burning of villages, worsening already-dire humanitarian conditions and causing an outflow of more than 700,000 Rohingya refugees to Bangladesh. Those refugees joined another 200,000 who had crossed into Bangladesh to escape previous rounds of persecution before 2017. Aung San Suu Kyi has drawn sharp criticism from international observers for her reluctance to explicitly condemn state violence against Rohingya civilians. Attempts to organize a repatriation system that would allow refugees to return to Myanmar made little progress during 2018, as the government failed to address the conditions that had caused the Rohingya to flee.

The UN Independent International Fact-Finding Mission on Myanmar, chaired by former Indonesian attorney general Marzuki Darusman, released its full report in September 2018. Darusman briefed the UN Security Council in October, calling the situation in Myanmar "an ongoing genocide" in which Rohingya who remain in Rakhine State are "at grave risk." A panel of the ICC ruled in September that the court has jurisdiction over prosecution of the crime of deportation of the Rohingya, and later that month the ICC chief prosecutor launched a preliminary inquiry to establish whether there was enough evidence to proceed to a full investigation. Myanmar is not a signatory of the ICC's founding Rome Statute, but Bangladesh is; the ICC judges ruled that they had jurisdiction because the deportations occurred on the territory of Bangladesh.

CIVIL LIBERTIES: 17 / 60 (−1)

D. FREEDOM OF EXPRESSION AND BELIEF: 5 / 16 (−1)

D1. Are there free and independent media? 1 / 4 (−1)

Media freedoms have improved since the official end of government censorship and prepublication approval in 2012. However, existing laws allow authorities to deny licenses to outlets whose reporting is considered insulting to religion or a threat to national security, and the risk of prosecution under criminal defamation laws encourages self-censorship. While internet access has expanded in recent years, online activity is still subject to criminal punishment under several broadly worded legal provisions, particularly those in the Electronic Transactions Law. Journalists and social media users continued to face defamation and incitement cases during 2018.

Surveillance of journalists by the military-controlled Home Affairs Ministry remains a common practice, and reporters covering sensitive topics risk harassment, physical violence, and imprisonment. In the most prominent case of 2018, two Reuters journalists were sentenced in September to seven years in prison for violating the Official Secrets Act after a deeply flawed trial. The charges stemmed from an incident in late 2017 in which the reporters met with a police officer at his invitation at a restaurant in Yangon. When they got up to leave, the officer handed them supposedly secret documents, and they were quickly arrested in front of the restaurant before they could even look at the papers. The reporters, Wa Lone and Kyaw Soe Oo, were investigating a 2017 massacre of Rohingya at Inn Din village in Rakhine State, and the case against them was criticized internationally as an unjust reprisal for their work.

Score Change: The score declined from 2 to 1 due to increasing restrictions on the media's ability to cover sensitive topics including the military's actions in Rakhine State, as illustrated by the entrapment, conviction, and imprisonment of two journalists who had investigated atrocities by security forces.

D2. Are individuals free to practice and express their religious faith or nonbelief in public and private? 1 / 4

The constitution provides for freedom of religion. It distinguishes Buddhism as the majority religion, but also recognizes Christianity, Islam, Hinduism, and animism. The government occasionally interferes with religious assemblies and attempts to control the Buddhist clergy. Authorities discriminate against minority religious groups in practice, refusing to grant them permission to hold gatherings and restricting educational activities, proselytizing, and construction and repair of houses of worship.

Anti-Muslim hate speech and discrimination have been amplified by social media, and by some state institutions and mainstream news websites. Facebook, which had received criticism for allowing such hate speech on its platform, removed hundreds of Myanmar accounts during 2018, including many linked to the military. The officially illegal Buddha Dhamma Parahita Foundation, formerly known as Ma Ba Tha, agitates for the protection of Buddhist privileges, urges boycotts against Muslim-run businesses, and disseminates anti-Muslim propaganda. Reports have detailed systematic discrimination against Muslims in obtaining identity cards, as well as the creation of "Muslim-free" villages with the complicity of officials.

D3. Is there academic freedom, and is the educational system free from extensive political indoctrination? 1 / 4

Political activity on university campuses is generally restricted, and universities are not autonomous. Student unions are discouraged, have no formal registration mechanisms, and are viewed with suspicion by authorities.

In January 2018, 14 students at Mandalay's Yadanabon University were expelled for holding a campus protest calling for more education funding. More than 20 other students were reportedly expelled that month for taking part in similar protests at other schools. The Ministry of Education issued a directive in May that required students to get permission from the head of their university to hold events on campus, obliging them to submit names and biographies of speakers, titles of public talks, and the number of people expected to attend. After students file their application, the request must be submitted to the ministry's Higher Education Department for approval.

D4. Are individuals free to express their personal views on political or other sensitive topics without fear of surveillance or retribution? 2 / 4

Private discussion and personal expression are constrained by state surveillance and laws that inhibit online speech. Numerous defamation cases involving online commentary have been filed under Section 66(d) of the 2013 Telecommunications Law, which includes bans on online activity deemed to be threatening or defamatory.

Social media users and those quoted in the media have faced prosecution for expressing their views on particular topics, particularly when they entail criticism of the authorities. A former child soldier, Aung Ko Htwe, was sentenced to two years in prison for incitement in March 2018 due to a media interview in which he spoke about being abducted by the military at age 14 and claimed that he had faced abuse by officials during a previous trial for a 2007 murder that occurred while he was escaping from the military. In September, a social media user in Mon State was sentenced to a year in prison for allegedly defaming the state's chief minister.

E. ASSOCIATIONAL AND ORGANIZATIONAL RIGHTS: 6 / 12
E1. Is there freedom of assembly? 2 / 4

Under the Peaceful Assembly and Peaceful Procession Law as revised in 2016, unauthorized demonstrations are still punishable with up to six months in prison; a variety of other vaguely defined violations can draw lesser penalties. Protesters no longer have to ask permission for assemblies, but they do need to notify authorities 48 hours in advance, and local officials often treat this process as a request for permission in practice. Additional problematic amendments to the law were under consideration in 2018. Separately, a blanket ban on protests in 11 townships of central Yangon has been in place since November 2017, though it is selectively enforced.

Among other cases during the year, the authorities arrested 47 antiwar protesters across the country in May 2018, charging them with offenses such as disturbing the public, staging an unlawful protest, and criminal defamation. The peaceful demonstrations were held to protest the conduct of military operations in Kachin State.

E2. Is there freedom for nongovernmental organizations, particularly those that are engaged in human rights- and governance-related work? 2 / 4

The 2014 Association Registration Law features simple, voluntary registration procedures for local and international nongovernmental organizations (NGOs) and no restrictions or criminal punishments for noncompliance. Although the law was seen as a positive development, in 2015 the Home Affairs Ministry issued implementing regulations that required NGOs to obtain government approval prior to registration, drawing sharp criticism from civil society leaders.

E3. Is there freedom for trade unions and similar professional or labor organizations? 2 / 4

A ban on independent trade unions was lifted in 2011, and union activity has taken root in Myanmar. In recent years, factory workers have held strikes in Yangon with fewer repercussions and arrests than in the past. However, trade unionists continue to face retaliation for their efforts, and legal protections against abuse by employers are weak. In October 2018, a group of men armed with metal rods attacked striking garment workers in Yangon; six workers were hospitalized for head injuries.

F. RULE OF LAW: 1 / 16

F1. Is there an independent judiciary? 0 / 4

The judiciary is not independent. Judges are nominated by the president, and lawmakers can reject the choice only if it is clearly proven that the nominee does not meet the legal qualifications for the post. The courts generally adjudicate cases in accordance with the government's interests, particularly in major cases with political implications.

F2. Does due process prevail in civil and criminal matters? 1 / 4

Administrative detention laws allow individuals to be held without charge, trial, or access to legal counsel for up to five years if they are deemed a threat to state security or sovereignty. A 2017 assessment by the British-based NGO Justice Base found that the country performed poorly in nearly every measure of international fair trial standards.

In 2016, the parliament repealed the 1950 Emergency Provisions Act, which the former military government had invoked frequently to silence and imprison dissidents. The 1975 State Protection Act, which was used to hold then opposition leader Aung San Suu Kyi under house arrest during the period of military rule, was also repealed in 2016. Nevertheless, individuals who are considered political prisoners continue to be held in the country. According to the Assistance Association for Political Prisoners (Burma), as of December 2018 there were 35 serving sentences, 56 in pretrial detention, and 236 awaiting trial outside prison.

F3. Is there protection from the illegitimate use of physical force and freedom from war and insurgencies? 0 / 4

The NLD government's push for the creation of a more comprehensive peace mechanism remained hampered in 2018 by military offensives against various ethnic rebel groups, particularly in Shan and Kachin States, as well as by attacks from such groups against security forces and continued divisions among signatories and nonsignatories to a 2015 national cease-fire agreement. The NLD's own approach to dealing with ethnic minorities has also been faulted for inhibiting peace efforts.

Indiscriminate shelling, extrajudicial killings, forced disappearances, and other abuses by the military continue to be reported, while rebel groups engage in forced disappearances and forced recruitment. Areas in the north remain riddled with landmines planted by both rebels and the army. Authorities at times prevent aid groups from reaching populations affected by violence. Civilians continued to flee fighting in Shan and Kachin States in 2018, leaving more than 100,000 internally displaced by year's end. Episodes of fighting and displacement were also reported in Karen and Chin States.

Prisons in Myanmar are severely overcrowded, and conditions for inmates are sometimes life-threatening.

F4. Do laws, policies, and practices guarantee equal treatment of various segments of the population? 0 / 4

Some of the country's worst human rights abuses, commonly committed by government troops, are against ethnic and religious minorities. The government's failure to protect victims, conduct investigations, and punish perpetrators is well documented.

The 1982 Citizenship Law discriminates based on ethnicity. The law does not allow for anyone who entered the country or is descended from someone who entered the country after 1948 to become a full citizen. Naturalization of spouses is only allowed if the spouse holds a Foreigner's Registration Certificate from before the enactment of the 1982 law. Only those who are descended from ethnic groups deemed to be indigenous to the country prior to 1823 are considered full citizens who can run for public office. Full citizens cannot have their citizenship revoked unless they become a citizen of another country.

In addition to conflict-related violence, women are subject to discrimination in employment, against which there are no explicit legal protections. A number of laws create a hostile environment for LGBT (lesbian, gay, bisexual, and transgender) residents. Same-sex sexual conduct is criminalized under the penal code, and police subject LGBT people to harassment, extortion, and physical and sexual abuse.

G. PERSONAL AUTONOMY AND INDIVIDUAL RIGHTS: 5 / 16

G1. Do individuals enjoy freedom of movement, including the ability to change their place of residence, employment, or education? 2 / 4

Freedom of internal travel is generally respected outside of conflict zones for Myanmar citizens. This is not the case for Myanmar's large population of stateless residents, who have significant restrictions on their travel, particularly Rohingya in Rakhine State. Numerous exiled activists who returned to the country after the transition to partial civilian rule have experienced substantial delays and evasion from government authorities when attempting to renew visas and residency permits. Illegal toll collection by state and nonstate actors has been a problem in some areas. The parliament voted in 2016 to repeal a long-standing rule requiring overnight houseguests to be registered with local authorities; guests staying for more than a month must still be registered.

G2. Are individuals able to exercise the right to own property and establish private businesses without undue interference from state or nonstate actors? 1 / 4

Contentious disputes over land grabbing and business projects that violate human rights continued in 2018. Myanmar's property transfer laws prohibit transfers to or from a foreigner except in certain state-approved cases of inheritance, and require registration of foreign-owned property. Stateless residents, including the Rohingya, cannot legally buy or sell property or set up a business.

Instances of forced eviction and displacement, confiscation, lack of sufficient compensation, and direct violence against landholders by state security officials abound. Court cases are frequently brought against farmers for trespassing on land that was taken from them. In May 2018, for example, 33 farmers were found guilty of trespassing on land that was seized by a military-run economic entity in 1996 but never developed.

Amnesty International reported in March that the military was involved in a massive land grab in Rakhine State, building military infrastructure over razed Rohingya villages.

G3. Do individuals enjoy personal social freedoms, including choice of marriage partner and size of family, protection from domestic violence, and control over appearance? 1 / 4

Men and women formally enjoy equal rights on personal status issues, though there are restrictions on marriages of Buddhist women to non-Buddhist men. Laws that might protect women from domestic abuse and rape are weak and poorly enforced, and such violence is an acute and persistent problem. The army has a record of using rape as a weapon of war against ethnic minority women, and security personnel typically enjoy impunity for sexual violence.

G4. Do individuals enjoy equality of opportunity and freedom from economic exploitation? 1 / 4

Human trafficking, forced labor, child labor, and the recruitment of child soldiers all remain serious problems in Myanmar, and the government's efforts to address them are inadequate. Child soldiers are enlisted by the military and ethnic rebel groups, which also recruit civilians for forced labor. Various commercial and other interests continue to use forced labor despite a formal ban on the practice since 2000. Trafficking victims include women and girls subjected to forced sex work and domestic servitude. People displaced by conflict are especially vulnerable to exploitation.

Namibia

Population: 2,500,000
Capital: Windhoek
Political Rights Rating: 3 ↓
Civil Liberties Rating: 2
Freedom Rating: 2.5
Freedom Status: Free
Electoral Democracy: Yes

Overview: Namibia is a multiparty democracy, though the ruling party, SWAPO, has been in power since independence. Protections for civil liberties are generally robust. Minority ethnic groups accuse the government of favoring the majority Ovambo in allocating services. Nomadic San people suffer from poverty and marginalization. Other human rights concerns include the criminalization of same-sex sexual relations under colonial-era laws, and discrimination against women under customary law and other traditional practices.

KEY DEVELOPMENTS IN 2018:

- In May, two former SWAPO members of Parliament were among a group of defendants found guilty of defrauding the Social Security Commission. However, both men were sentenced to a fine of N$60,000 (US$4,400) or three years imprisonment, which allowed them to avoid jail time for their roles in the crime.

- In June, the Namibia Central Intelligence Service (NCIS) lost a court case to prevent the *Patriot* newspaper from reporting on allegedly corrupt land deals involving former intelligence officials.
- In October, Namibia held the long-awaited Second National Land Conference, which resulted in the passage of 40 resolutions, including a resolution that calls for allowing expropriation of agricultural land owned by foreigners with "just compensation," and another that allows expropriation of underused land owned by Namibians.

POLITICAL RIGHTS: 29 / 40 (−1)

A. ELECTORAL PROCESS: 10 / 12

A1. Was the current head of government or other chief national authority elected through free and fair elections? 4 / 4

The president is both chief of state and head of government, and is directly elected for up to two five-year terms. In the 2014 election, Hage Geingob defeated numerous rivals for the presidency, winning 87 percent of the vote. The polls were deemed competitive and credible by election observers, though some logistical glitches with electronic voting machines were reported.

A2. Were the current national legislative representatives elected through free and fair elections? 3 / 4

The National Council, the upper chamber of the bicameral Parliament, is comprised of 42 seats, with members appointed by regional councils for six-year terms. The lower house, the National Assembly, has 96 seats filled by popular election for five-year terms using party-list proportional representation.

The 2014 polls were seen as competitive and credible by election observers, though some logistical glitches with electronic voting machines were reported. SWAPO won 80 percent of the vote, giving it 77 National Assembly seats. The Democratic Turnhalle Alliance of Namibia (DTA) followed, winning 4.8 percent of the vote for 5 seats, and eight additional parties won the remaining seats. While voter intimidation was not reported, opposition parties had some difficulty achieving visibility due to the dominance of SWAPO, which some observers said was reinforced by provisions of the Third Constitutional Amendment.

A3. Are the electoral laws and framework fair, and are they implemented impartially by the relevant election management bodies? 3 / 4

The 2014 polls were the first held under the Third Constitutional Amendment, which increased the number of members in Namibia's bicameral legislature by 40 percent. SWAPO was criticized for rushing passage of the new law, which was seen to be in its favor given its dominant position in politics, in advance of the elections. However, the electoral framework is otherwise robust and well implemented.

B. POLITICAL PLURALISM AND PARTICIPATION: 11 / 16

B1. Do the people have the right to organize in different political parties or other competitive political groupings of their choice, and is the system free of undue obstacles to the rise and fall of these competing parties or groupings? 3 / 4

Political parties may form and operate freely. However, candidate registration fees can place an undue burden on smaller parties with limited resources. In 2015, ahead of regional elections, opposition parties claimed it would have cost them nearly N$300,000 (US$21,500) to run candidates in all of the country's 121 constituencies. Political parties represented in Parliament receive funding annually from the government based on the number of seats they hold, which disproportionately benefits SWAPO due to its dominant position in Parliament.

B2. Is there a realistic opportunity for the opposition to increase its support or gain power through elections? 2 / 4

Opposition parties may freely compete in elections and generally do not encounter intimidation or harassment during election campaigns. However, in practice the opposition is weak and fragmented, and does not pose any significant threat to SWAPO's political dominance. SWAPO's significant financial advantage over opposition parties further consolidates its control of the political system, making it difficult for rival parties to compete effectively in elections.

B3. Are the people's political choices free from domination by the military, foreign powers, religious hierarchies, economic oligarchies, or any other powerful group that is not democratically accountable? 3 / 4

People are generally able to express their political choices without any undue influence from actors that are not democratically accountable. However, the continued domination of SWAPO—an ideologically diverse "big tent" party whose energies are often consumed by intraparty disputes—limits voters' ability to directly express a preference for particular policies.

B4. Do various segments of the population (including ethnic, religious, gender, LGBT, and other relevant groups) have full political rights and electoral opportunities? 3 / 4

The constitution guarantees political rights for all, and the government makes efforts to uphold these rights. Namibia has made great strides in increasing women's representation in Parliament; women now hold 48 of 104 seats in the National Assembly, making it more likely that women's interests and voices are robustly represented in the political sphere. Nevertheless, societal attitudes can discourage women from running for political office.

Almost all of the country's ethnic groups are represented in Parliament and in senior political positions. However, members of the ethnic San have faced restrictions on their political rights due to widespread discrimination and marginalization. Members of the LGBT (lesbian, gay, bisexual, and transgender) community face societal discrimination that hampers their ability to openly advocate for their interests.

C. FUNCTIONING OF GOVERNMENT: 8 / 12 (–1)

C1. Do the freely elected head of government and national legislative representatives determine the policies of the government? 3 / 4

Namibia has a functioning system of democracy with a government and a national legislature that freely execute duties and determine policies. However, 2014 reforms increased executive power, including by permitting new president-appointed members of Parliament and limits on the National Council's power to review certain bills.

C2. Are safeguards against official corruption strong and effective? 3 / 4

Namibia has a sound legal framework for combating corruption. However, anticorruption laws are inconsistently enforced. The Anti-Corruption Commission (ACC) has moved slowly on cases involving high-profile public officials, and in 2017, its head was accused of ignoring recommendations by ACC staff for reforms that could have increased the commission's independence and effectiveness.

In March 2018, Minister of Education, Arts, and Culture Katrina Hanse-Himarwa was charged with corruption for allegedly providing government funds for housing to relatives during her time as governor of the Hardap Region. Hanse-Himarwa's trial began in October and was ongoing at year's end. In May, two former SWAPO members of Parliament were among a group of defendants found guilty of defrauding the Social Security Commission. However, both men were sentenced to a fine of N$60,000 (US$4,400) or three years imprisonment, which allowed them to avoid jail time for their roles in the crime.

C3. Does the government operate with openness and transparency? 2 / 4 (−1)

Namibia lacks access-to-information laws and does not have an institutional culture of transparency. Accessing information from many government agencies remains a challenge. There is not frequent disclosure of private interests by public representatives. A veil of secrecy exists over the extractive industry, military spending, State House upgrades, and state security infrastructure.

At times, the government has withheld relevant information that is potentially sensitive or controversial from the public, often on national security grounds. In September 2018, the prosecutor general informed the *Namibian* newspaper that records of the closed-door trial proceedings of an official from the NCIS, who killed himself during his trial in August, would remain secret unless the High Court ordered the information released. The government claimed that the trial of the official, who was accused of fraud and corruption, was held secretly due to national security concerns.

After delaying the release of a list of beneficiaries from a controversial land resettlement program, the Ministry of Land Reform finally produced the document in August, following threats by the ombudsman to sue the ministry for the information.

Score Change: The score declined from 3 to 2 because the continued absence of an access to information law reduces transparency, and government agencies are largely unresponsive to requests for information.

CIVIL LIBERTIES: 46 / 60 (−1)
D. FREEDOM OF EXPRESSION AND BELIEF: 14 / 16
D1. Are there free and independent media? 3 / 4

Namibia's constitution guarantees media freedom and freedom of expression. In practice, journalists face few legal restrictions and may generally work without risking their personal safety. While self-censorship is common in state media, private media remains critical of the government. State officials, including President Geingob, have frequently spoken harshly about the media, which, according to observers, is intended to intimidate journalists.

In June 2018, the NCIS lost a court case to prevent the *Patriot* newspaper from reporting on allegedly corrupt land deals involving former intelligence officials. The NCIS claimed that publishing the story would threaten national security, but rights activists viewed the High Court ruling as an important step forward for press freedom and transparency.

D2. Are individuals free to practice and express their religious faith or nonbelief in public and private? 4 / 4

Religious freedom is generally respected in practice.

D3. Is there academic freedom, and is the educational system free from extensive political indoctrination? 4 / 4

Academic freedom is guaranteed by law and generally respected in practice.

D4. Are individuals free to express their personal views on political or other sensitive topics without fear of surveillance or retribution? 3 / 4

Freedom of expression is guaranteed in law and generally observed in practice. Social media is increasingly used to express political dissent. The 2009 Communications Act allows the government to conduct surveillance on various forms of communication without a warrant. In early 2018, the *Namibian* published a series of articles stating that there was evidence of widespread surveillance of online and mobile communications by authorities, and that the government has purchased a significant trove of surveillance technology from abroad.

E. ASSOCIATIONAL AND ORGANIZATIONAL RIGHTS: 11 / 12 (−1)

E1. Is there freedom of assembly? 3 / 4 (−1)

Freedom of assembly is guaranteed in law and is usually observed in practice, but can be restricted during a national emergency. Authorities occasionally prevent peaceful protests from taking place, and have increasingly used violence to disperse demonstrators. In August 2018, student protesters in Windhoek, who had marched to the Higher Education Ministry to hand over a petition demanding government funding for tuition fees, were assaulted by police. The police claimed that the force applied was in response to demonstrators acting in a "disorderly" manner, which the student activists denied.

In July, police arrested several members of the Caprivi Concerned Group, which advocates for secession of the Zambezi Region, while they were attempting to hold a public meeting near Katima Mulilo. Six members of the group were subsequently charged with sedition and several other crimes, but the charges were quickly dropped.

Score Change: The score declined from 4 to 3 due to aggressive police responses to protests in 2018, including assaults on peaceful protesters.

E2. Is there freedom for nongovernmental organizations, particularly those that are engaged in human rights- and governance-related work? 4 / 4

Human rights groups generally operate without interference, though government leaders sometimes use public platforms to attack civil society.

E3. Is there freedom for trade unions and similar professional or labor organizations? 4 / 4

Constitutionally guaranteed union rights are respected and observed in practice, though essential public-sector workers do not have the right to strike. Collective bargaining is not widely practiced outside the mining, construction, agriculture, and public-service industries. Union membership has declined in recent years, with 25 percent of the labor force unionized.

F. RULE OF LAW: 11 / 16

F1. Is there an independent judiciary? 3 / 4

The constitution provides for an independent judiciary. In practice, the separation of powers is observed and judges are not frequently subject to undue influence. The establishment of the Office of the Judiciary separate from the Ministry of Justice in late 2015 affords the former administrative and financial independence. However, the judiciary is underresourced. Judges are appointed by the president upon the recommendation of the Judicial Service Commission, a body whose composition the president has some influence over.

F2. Does due process prevail in civil and criminal matters? 3 / 4

Namibia's constitution protects the rule of law and the right to a fair trial. However, equal access to justice is obstructed by many factors, including economic and geographic barriers, a shortage of public defenders, and delays and backlogs in the court system that can last up to a decade.

F3. Is there protection from the illegitimate use of physical force and freedom from war and insurgencies? 3 / 4

Namibia is free from war and insurgencies. However, police brutality is a problem, and several incidents of abuse of suspects in custody during the year concerned rights activists. In October 2018, the human rights group NamRights reported that a suspected poacher died from injuries allegedly sustained when he was beaten during a police interrogation. The police promised a full investigation into the man's death. Namibia currently lacks an antitorture law.

F4. Do laws, policies, and practices guarantee equal treatment of various segments of the population? 2 / 4

While the constitution guarantees the right to equality and prohibits discrimination, challenges remain. The indigenous San people face widespread societal discrimination and remain marginalized, and San languages are not taught in schools.

Same-sex sexual relations remain criminalized (though the prohibition is not enforced) and women face discrimination under customary law and traditional societal practices. However, discrimination against people living with albinism is reportedly decreasing due to government and NGO programs to educate the public about the condition, as well as support from the government for the albino population.

A government job-placement program for "struggle kids"—children born or raised in exile during the independence movement from South Africa—has drawn criticism for favoring SWAPO members and Ovambo speakers.

G. PERSONAL AUTONOMY AND INDIVIDUAL RIGHTS: 10 / 16

G1. Do individuals enjoy freedom of movement, including the ability to change their place of residence, employment, or education? 3 / 4

Freedom of movement is a constitutionally guaranteed right generally observed in practice. However, in 2017, the Helao Nafidi town council passed a resolution that placed restrictions on the free movement of Angolan and other non-Namibian traders.

G2. Are individuals able to exercise the right to own property and establish private businesses without undue interference from state or nonstate actors? 3 / 4

Private property rights are guaranteed in law and the constitution prohibits expropriation without compensation. There are no legal barriers to women's access to land. However, customary norms regarding inheritance procedures and property rights limit women. The Helao Nafidi town council restrictions implemented in 2017 mandate that non-Namibian traders may only engage in business three days a week.

Land rights remain a contentious issue, and a government land resettlement program faced intense public scrutiny and allegations that certain groups are favored. The long-awaited Second National Land Conference took place in October 2018. Forty resolutions were passed, including a resolution that allows expropriation of agricultural land owned by foreigners with "just compensation," and another that allows expropriation of underused land owned by Namibians. None of the resolutions passed are legally binding.

G3. Do individuals enjoy personal social freedoms, including choice of marriage partner and size of family, protection from domestic violence, and control over appearance? 2 / 4

Not all groups enjoy social freedoms. LGBT people face harassment, discrimination, and attacks. Same-sex marriages are not recognized and many churches have indicated their unwillingness to recognize or perform them, though the state ombudsman in 2016 expressed support for the legalization of same-sex marriage. Rates of gender-based violence are high. Forced and child marriages do occur. Approximately 7 percent of girls are married before they turn 18.

G4. Do individuals enjoy equality of opportunity and freedom from economic exploitation? 2 / 4

The constitution outlaws slavery or servitude. However, forced child labor is rife in the agricultural sector and in people's homes. Human trafficking is a challenge, and Namibia still lacks minimum standards required to confront it. In March 2018, President Geingob signed the Combating of Trafficking in Persons Act, but the law had not yet become operational at year's end.

Nauru

Population: 10,000
Capital: Yaren District
Political Rights Rating: 2
Civil Liberties Rating: 2
Freedom Rating: 2.0
Freedom Status: Free
Electoral Democracy: Yes

Overview: People in Nauru generally enjoy political rights and civil liberties, though the government has taken steps to sideline its political opponents, and corruption is a serious problem. Asylum seekers and refugees housed in Nauru under an agreement with Australia live in dire conditions, and the country has attracted sustained international criticism over the persistent reports of abuses against them.

KEY DEVELOPMENTS IN 2018:

- In October, the aid group Doctors Without Borders (MSF) left the country after being asked by Nauruan officials to stop providing care for asylum seekers and refugees. In the days afterward, MSF condemned conditions for asylum seekers and refugees in Nauru, and said officials had forced them out.
- Citing delays and the government's failure to comply with a directive to pay the defendants' legal fees, a Supreme Court justice in September granted a permanent stay on proceedings against the "Nauru 19," who had been charged with a variety of crimes, including rioting, in connection with a 2015 antigovernment protest. In his ruling, Justice Geoffrey Muecke sharply questioned the motivations of the government, suggesting it sought the defendants' conviction and imprisonment, and was "willing to expend whatever resources, including financial resources, as are required to achieve that aim."

- The government banned the Australian Broadcasting Corporation from entering the country ahead of the September Pacific Islands Forum to be held in Nauru, describing the outlet as an "activist media organization."

POLITICAL RIGHTS: 34 / 40 (−1)

A. ELECTORAL PROCESS: 12 / 12

A1. Was the current head of government or other chief national authority elected through free and fair elections? 4 / 4

Nauru is a parliamentary republic, and the parliament chooses the president and vice president from among its members.

The 2016 parliamentary elections, which were considered generally free, led to the reelection of President Baron Waqa and his government. Waqa moved to consolidate his control after the election by appointing seven new assistant ministers, after obtaining legislative approval of the 2016 Assistant Ministers Bill.

A2. Were the current national legislative representatives elected through free and fair elections? 4 / 4

The 19-member unicameral Parliament is popularly elected from eight constituencies for three-year terms. A Commonwealth election monitoring mission found the 2016 elections generally well conducted. The polls resulted in the reelection of all but one of the members of Parliament (MPs) who served in President Waqa's government, and the defeat of four suspended opposition legislators, permitting the Waqa-led government to return with an increased majority. (The opposition MPs had been suspended without pay in 2014 for what was deemed unruly behavior, and for making remarks to foreign media that were critical of the government.)

The opposition voiced some complaints that they did not receive equal airtime prior to the elections.

A3. Are the electoral laws and framework fair, and are they implemented impartially by the relevant election management bodies? 4 / 4

The electoral laws are generally fair and implemented impartially. The Nauru Electoral Commission is responsible for managing the entire election process. Voting is compulsory.

B. POLITICAL PLURALISM AND PARTICIPATION: 14 / 16 (−1)

B1. Do the people have the right to organize in different political parties or other competitive political groupings of their choice, and is the system free of undue obstacles to the rise and fall of these competing parties or groupings? 4 / 4

Although political parties are permitted, most candidates run as independents.

A contempt-of-court law enacted in May 2018 was criticized as being designed to intimidate opposition figures and others inclined to criticize the prosecution of the Nauru 19. The law makes criticism of witnesses, judicial officers, or legal representatives in a pending court matter illegal, as well as undermining judicial officials or the authority of courts. Violations of the law, which contains exemptions for government officials deemed to be acting in good faith or the interests of national security, are punishable by fines of up to $20,000 for individuals and $50,000 for corporations.

B2. Is there a realistic opportunity for the opposition to increase its support or gain power through elections? 3 / 4

Intense political rivalries created political instability prior to 2013. However, President Waqa's government served a full term from 2013–16, and was reelected in 2016. Opposition members claimed some measures implemented by Waqa's first administration, such as higher candidate fees and a requirement that public employees running for office must resign three months prior to an election, were made to discourage opposition candidates from running in the 2016 polls.

Five opposition MPs were suspended without pay in 2014 for what was deemed unruly behavior, and for making remarks to foreign media that were critical of the government. Four ran for reelection in the 2016 polls, though only one secured reelection. The fifth chose not to compete.

In September, Supreme Court justice Geoffrey Muecke, an Australian national, granted permanent stays on the proceedings against the Nauru 19 antigovernment protesters, agreeing with the defendants that the legal process had dragged on for too long and that the Nauru government had not complied with a court directive to meet some of their costs. The government plans to appeal Muecke's decision. Three members of the Nauru 19 who had already pleaded guilty remained in jail.

B3. Are the people's political choices free from domination by the military, foreign powers, religious hierarchies, economic oligarchies, or any other powerful group that is not democratically accountable? 4 / 4

People's political choices are generally free from domination by powerful interests that are not democratically accountable.

B4. Do various segments of the population (including ethnic, religious, gender, LGBT, and other relevant groups) have full political rights and electoral opportunities? 3 / 4 (−1)

The constitution provides for universal suffrage. However, widely held biases regarding the role of women in society have discouraged women's participation in politics and elections; few women ran in the 2016 elections, and just one woman sits in Parliament.

Score Change: The score declined from 4 to 3 due to the persistence of societal biases that discourage women's participation in politics and elections.

C. FUNCTIONING OF GOVERNMENT: 8 / 12

C1. Do the freely elected head of government and national legislative representatives determine the policies of the government? 3 / 4

The freely elected Parliament, led by the prime minister, sets and makes policy. However, Australia has had considerable influence over politics because its Nauru-based processing center for asylum seekers is critical to the Nauruan economy.

C2. Are safeguards against official corruption strong and effective? 3 / 4

Corruption remains a problem. Allegations of improper payments to senior government officials, including Waqa, by an Australian phosphate company emerged in 2016, and an investigation by Australian federal police remained ongoing in 2018. Legal proceedings related to the scandal also took place in Singapore in 2018, where a local company was fined for bribing a Nauruan MP.

In 2016, Australia's Westpac Bank announced it would no longer handle accounts for the Nauruan government, with media reports suggesting that the decision came in response to concerns about suspected financial mismanagement by the government, including money laundering and tax evasion.

C3. Does the government operate with openness and transparency? 2 / 4

Nauru lacks a law on access to public information, but the Government Information Office releases some budget figures. Government officials are not required to disclose financial information.

In July 2017, the Organization for Economic Co-operation and Development (OECD) upgraded Nauru's tax transparency rating, giving it a "largely compliant" rating. Earlier, in May, the government completed an audit of the 2013–14 government accounts. The audit capped a 15-year audit gap that officials blamed on an absence of qualified staff.

CIVIL LIBERTIES: 44 / 60 (–2)

D. FREEDOM OF EXPRESSION AND BELIEF: 13 / 16

D1. Are there free and independent media? 2 / 4

Freedom of expression is constitutionally guaranteed, but this right is not always respected in practice. Foreign journalists have a particularly difficult time operating in Nauru, as the government has implemented restrictions that appear to be aimed at deterring outside coverage of conditions for asylum seekers and refugees. Since 2014, foreign journalists have been subject to a visa application fee of roughly $6,000, up from approximately $150 previously.

There were reports of foreign journalists being denied visas to cover the 2016 elections. And after the 2016 polls, Justice Minister David Adeang attacked the foreign press, claiming that that the Australian and New Zealand media were misleading the public and not accurately reporting progress that Nauru has made towards strengthening democracy. Ahead of the 2018 Pacific Islands Forum, held in Nauru in September, the government banned the Australian Broadcasting Corporation from entering the country, describing it as an "activist media organization."

Separately, the 2016 Crimes Act introduced criminal charges for defamation, now punishable with up to three years in prison.

D2. Are individuals free to practice and express their religious faith or nonbelief in public and private? 4 / 4

The constitution provides for freedom of religion, which the government generally respects in practice.

D3. Is there academic freedom, and is the educational system free from extensive political indoctrination? 4 / 4

Academic freedom is generally respected.

D4. Are individuals free to express their personal views on political or other sensitive topics without fear of surveillance or retribution? 3 / 4

Asylum seekers are closely monitored.

Authorities are not known to illegally monitor private online communications. For three years, the government blocked Facebook, citing a need to protect users from obscene and pornographic content; the policy more likely represented another example of the government attempting to restrict coverage of the Australian processing center for asylum seekers. The ban was ultimately lifted in January 2018.

E. ASSOCIATIONAL AND ORGANIZATIONAL RIGHTS: 9 / 12

E1. Is there freedom of assembly? 3 / 4

The constitution upholds the right to assemble peacefully, but this right has not always been respected in practice. Demonstrations related to the treatment of asylum seekers housed at the Australian processing center are often repressed. Legal proceedings against the Nauru 19 group of antigovernment protesters continued into 2018, and while they were eventually stayed in September, three defendants who had pleaded guilty were serving sentences at year's end.

E2. Is there freedom for nongovernmental organizations, particularly those that are engaged in human rights- and governance-related work? 3 / 4

There are no legal restrictions on the formation of nongovernmental organizations (NGOs) in Nauru. There are several advocacy groups for women, as well as development-focused and religious organizations. However, authorities have interfered with the operations of activists seeking to improve the treatment of asylum seekers.

E3. Is there freedom for trade unions and similar professional or labor organizations? 3 / 4

There are no formal trade unions and only limited labor protection laws, partly because there is little large-scale private employment. The right to strike and collectively bargain are not protected by law.

F. RULE OF LAW: 10 / 16

F1. Is there an independent judiciary? 2 / 4

There have been concerns about undue influence on the judiciary by the government, which has been accused of dismissing judges for rulings officials found unfavorable. There have been concerns that government officials have pressured the judiciary in connection with the Nauru 19 case.

The Supreme Court is the highest authority on constitutional issues in Nauru. Appeals had previously been heard in the high court of Australia, but in March 2018, Nauruan Justice Minister Adeang announced that the country would sever links with Australia's justice system, citing both onerous costs associated with case proceedings in another country, and the need for Nauru to establish greater independence. However, some skeptics suggested that the development was a means of denying the Nauru 19 an avenue to appeal their cases. Nauru later completed the signing of memoranda with neighboring Pacific countries, including Papua New Guinea, Kiribati, Solomon Islands, and Vanuatu, which will provide justices for Nauru's new Court of Appeals. Appeals of Supreme Court Justice Muecke's decision to stay the proceedings against the Nauru 19 were expected to be heard at the new court in 2019.

F2. Does due process prevail in civil and criminal matters? 3 / 4

The constitution provides for due process rights and those rights are generally respected. However, in 2017, the government passed a law that distinguishes between public servants who testify in favor of the government or against it. Analysts said it appeared that those who miss work to testify against the government would be placed on leave without pay, and that the law appeared to represent an attempt to discourage civil servants from testifying in favor of the Nauru 19.

Legal proceedings against the so-called Nauru 19 were permanently stayed in September by Justice Muecke, who agreed with the defendants that the legal process had dragged on for too long and that the Nauru government had not complied with a court directive to meet some of the defendants' costs. He stated in his ruling that the "government of Nauru does not want these defendants to receive a fair trial" and that it sought to see them "convicted and imprisoned for a long time, and that the government of Nauru is willing to expend whatever resources, including financial resources, as are required to achieve that aim." Three members of the group who had pleaded guilty were unsuccessful in their appeal to overturn their sentences, and were serving jail sentences at year's end. The government has since withheld the passports of three of those among the Nauru 19.

F3. Is there protection from the illegitimate use of physical force and freedom from war and insurgencies? 3 / 4

Civilian authorities control the small police force. Nauru has no armed forces; Australia provides defense assistance under an informal agreement.

The Australian processing center for asylum seekers has received considerable international criticism for poor treatment of asylum seekers housed there. Few arrests have been made in connection with alleged abuses of its residents.

F4. Do laws, policies, and practices guarantee equal treatment of various segments of the population? 2 / 4

The constitution provides for equal treatment regardless of race, country of origin, ethnicity, politics, or gender, but those rights are not always protected in practice. There are few legal protections against discrimination, which is notably a problem for women in the workplace. In 2016, the government decriminalized homosexuality, which had previously been punishable by up to 14 years of hard labor.

Reports of widespread abuse of refugees and asylum seekers forcibly transferred to Nauru under its agreement with Australia continued in 2018. Crimes committed against asylum seekers outside the processing center where most are housed frequently go uninvestigated. The asylum seekers suffer from grossly inadequate housing; denial of health care for life-threatening conditions; and a high rate of self-harm attempts among residents who wait, at times for years, for their asylum applications to be processed.

G. PERSONAL AUTONOMY AND INDIVIDUAL RIGHTS: 12 / 16 (−2)

G1. Do individuals enjoy freedom of movement, including the ability to change their place of residence, employment, or education? 3 / 4 (−1)

Most people in Nauru are free to move around the island. However, while asylum seekers were granted freedom of movement across the island in 2015, there are limits on their ability to leave, including in order to accompany family members who receive emergency medical care in Australia, and they face significant difficulties in obtaining employment and education. Many asylum seekers still live in tents and converted storage containers at the Australian processing center, where they remain under heavy surveillance. In October, the aid group MSF was asked by Nauru officials to stop providing care for asylum seekers, and the group subsequently left the country. In the days afterward, MSF condemned conditions for the asylum seekers and refugees in Nauru, and said the organization had been forced out.

The government has withheld the passports of some political opponents in recent years, including at least three people associated with the Nauru 19, among them two former opposition lawmakers.

Score Change: The score declined from 4 to 3 due to the expulsion of aid workers serving asylum seekers, the withholding of passports from some opponents of the government, and limitations on the ability of asylum seekers and refugees to obtain employment or education.

G2. Are individuals able to exercise the right to own property and establish private businesses without undue interference from state or nonstate actors? 3 / 4 (−1)

The constitution protects the right to own property and people in Nauru are able to freely establish businesses. However, as of 2014, foreigners must pay approximately $4,500 a year for a business visa, up from $300.

In his ruling on the Nauru 19 case, Judge Muecke said that the government of Nauru maintained an unwritten "blacklist" under which the Nauru 19 were denied employment and the right to conduct business on the island.

Score Change: The score declined from 4 to 3 due to politically motivated restrictions on the business activities of government opponents.

G3. Do individuals enjoy personal social freedoms, including choice of marriage partner and size of family, protection from domestic violence, and control over appearance? 3 / 4

Domestic violence, which mostly affects women, remains a serious problem, and children are also vulnerable to violence. However, authorities have taken some efforts to address these problems, notably by approving the new protections within the 2017 Domestic Violence and Family Protection Bill, and the 2016 Child Protection and Welfare Act. Marital rape was also made a criminal offense in 2016. Same-sex marriage is not recognized by law. Abortion is only allowed when the mother's life is in danger, but not in cases of rape; the ban on abortion in cases of rape sparked controversy in 2016, with regard to the treatment of a pregnant asylum seeker who said she was raped at the Australian-run processing center.

G4. Do individuals enjoy equality of opportunity and freedom from economic exploitation? 3 / 4

With the exception of asylum seekers, individuals generally enjoy equal economic opportunities. However, economic opportunities are limited to sectors such as phosphate mining and the public sector. The Australian Broadcasting Corporation reported in 2018 that many family members of Nauruan politicians owned shares of the land where the Australian-run processing center is situated, and disproportionately benefit from their ability to collect high rents or secure high-paying jobs or other contracts at the center.

There are no health and safety laws to protect workers outside the public sector and issues have been raised in regards to dust exposure for phosphate miners. According to the US State Department, there have been no reports of human trafficking in Nauru in recent years.

Nepal

Population: 29,700,000
Capital: Kathmandu
Political Rights Rating: 3
Civil Liberties Rating: 4
Freedom Rating: 3.5
Freedom Status: Partly Free
Electoral Democracy: No

Overview: Since the end of a decade-long civil war in 2006, Nepal has held a series of competitive elections and adopted a permanent constitution. As politics have stabilized, pressure on journalists has decreased, and authorities have been somewhat more tolerant of peaceful assembly. However, political protests are still sometimes marred by violence, and corruption remains endemic in politics, government, and the judicial system. Other problems include gender-based violence, underage marriage, and bonded labor. Transitional justice bodies have struggled to fulfill their mandates.

KEY DEVELOPMENTS IN 2018:

- Khadga Prasad Sharma Oli was sworn in as prime minister in February, following national elections in late 2017 that were generally well conducted.
- In May, the Communist Party of Nepal–Maoist (UCPN–M) and the Communist Party of Nepal–Unified Marxist-Leninist (CPN–UML) officially merged into one party, the Nepal Communist Party (NCP).
- A new criminal code which came into effect in August included privacy provisions that press freedom advocates claimed could criminalize normal newsgathering activities.

POLITICAL RIGHTS: 25 / 40

A. ELECTORAL PROCESS: 10 / 12

A1. Was the current head of government or other chief national authority elected through free and fair elections? 3 / 4

The president is the head of state and is elected to up to two five-year terms by a parliamentary electoral college and state assemblies. The prime minister is elected by Parliament. Thus, the legitimacy of executive office holders is largely determined by the conduct of legislative and provincial elections.

Khadga Prasad Sharma Oli (widely known as KP Oli) was sworn in as prime minister in February 2018 after his party, the CPN–UML, won majorities in the elections for the upper house of Parliament, the House of Representatives, in late 2017, as well as the lower house, the National Assembly, in February. An election observation mission from the European Union (EU) declared the 2017 polls largely credible, despite incidents of violence at some campaign events.

The current president, Bidhya Devi Bhandari, was reelected in March.

A2. Were the current national legislative representatives elected through free and fair elections? 4 / 4

Members of the 275-seat House of Representatives are elected to five-year terms; 165 members are directly elected in single-seat constituencies, while 110 members are elected by proportional representation. The 56 members of the National Assembly are indirectly elected to six-year terms by an electoral college comprised of provincial and local leaders.

Local elections—the first since 1997—were held in several stages in 2017, and national and provincial elections were held late in 2017. The polls were generally well conducted and saw healthy turnout, and their results were accepted by the participating parties. However, the Rastriya Janata Party-Nepal (RJP-N), an umbrella group representing ethnic Madhesis, boycotted several rounds of local polls due to grievances related to provisions in the 2015 constitution.

While more peaceful than the 2013 election period, there were occasional incidents of election-related violence in 2017. Police killed three people during a CPN–UML campaign rally. There was sporadic violence in the lead-up to the national elections, in which one temporary police officer was killed. There was a significant uptick in violent incidents before elections held in the south; those clashes were related to interparty tensions and separatist opposition.

A3. Are the electoral laws and framework fair, and are they implemented impartially by the relevant election management bodies? 3 / 4

The legal framework for elections is largely sound and facilitates the conduct of credible polls. However, Parliament has yet to address the grievances that many have with the 2015 constitution, which are related to province demarcation, proportional representation based on population, and provisions in the citizenship law.

B. POLITICAL PLURALISM AND PARTICIPATION: 10 / 16

B1. Do the people have the right to organize in different political parties or other competitive political groupings of their choice, and is the system free of undue obstacles to the rise and fall of these competing parties or groupings? 3 / 4

Political parties are generally free to form and operate, though the risk of political violence represents an effective restriction on free political participation. Opposition figures sometimes face arrest. CK Raut, the leader of the Alliance for Independent Madhesh, which has advocated for secession from Nepal, was arrested in October 2018 on charges of disturbing law and order and voicing views against the state and nationality, over his remarks at a demonstration. Raut remained in custody at year's end, and his case was ongoing.

In May, the UCPN–M and the CPN-UML, which had formed an alliance to contest the 2017 parliamentary elections, officially merged into one party, the Nepal Communist Party (NCP).

B2. Is there a realistic opportunity for the opposition to increase its support or gain power through elections? 3 / 4

Opposition parties have a realistic chance of gaining power through elections. The CPN–UML won control of the government as an opposition party following the 2017 elections. Smaller opposition parties have difficulty gaining power at the national level, partly due to a 3 percent threshold parties must reach to win proportional-representation seats in the House of Representatives. However, smaller parties perform better at the local level.

B3. Are the people's political choices free from domination by the military, foreign powers, religious hierarchies, economic oligarchies, or any other powerful group that is not democratically accountable? 2 / 4

People's ability to freely exercise their political choices is limited by sporadic outbursts of political violence, as well as by heavy-handed security agents who at times have cracked down on political demonstrations. There were reports of vote buying during the 2017 campaign period.

B4. Do various segments of the population (including ethnic, religious, gender, LGBT, and other relevant groups) have full political rights and electoral opportunities? 2 / 4

Though the constitution has requirements for the participation of women and minorities in the legislature, discrimination continues to hinder the political involvement of these groups. A limited definition of citizenship has resulted in the disenfranchisement of stateless people. Bhandari is Nepal's first female president, but few women hold senior positions in politics.

C. FUNCTIONING OF GOVERNMENT: 5 / 12

C1. Do the freely elected head of government and national legislative representatives determine the policies of the government? 3 / 4

Nepal ratified a new constitution in 2015, which represented an important step in its democratic transition. Successful legislative elections were held in 2017, with new lawmakers seated in 2018. However, despite democratic improvements and political stabilization in recent years, representative rule has yet to be consolidated.

C2. Are safeguards against official corruption strong and effective? 1 / 4

Corruption is endemic in Nepali politics and government and often goes unpunished. Corruption by officials continued to obstruct the delivery of foreign aid that poured into the country after a devastating 2015 earthquake.

In 2017, the Commission for Investigation of Abuse of Authority filed charges against Chudamani Sharma, former director of the Inland Revenue Department at the Tax Settlement Commission, for alleged embezzlement and the improper granting of tax exemptions to large businesses. Additional charges of illegal wealth possession were filed against Sharma in January 2018. After a number of delays, the case against Sharma was ongoing at year's end.

C3. Does the government operate with openness and transparency? 1 / 4

The government generally operates with opacity. The Election Commission, as well as the Truth and Reconciliation Commission (TRC) and Commission of Investigation on Enforced Disappeared Persons (CIEDP) are among bodies that have been criticized for a lack of transparency. Mechanisms for utilizing the 2007 Right to Information Act are poorly defined, and the law is inconsistently enforced.

CIVIL LIBERTIES: 29 / 60 (–1)
D. FREEDOM OF EXPRESSION AND BELIEF: 9 / 16 (–1)
D1. Are there free and independent media? 2 / 4 (–1)

The 2015 constitution provides for freedom of expression and prohibits prior restraints on press freedom, though these rules can be suspended in a national emergency. The constitution also states that the prohibition against prior restraint does not forbid restraints placed on the press in the interest of national security.

A newly revised criminal code, which came into effect in August 2018, includes provisions that criminalize publicizing private information about a person without consent, photographing an individual without consent, and satire that is "disrespectful." Press freedom advocates argued that the new code could be used to prosecute journalists engaged in normal newsgathering activities.

High-level government officials have attempted to muzzle criticism in the media through pressure, intimidation, and legal maneuvers. In February, the chief justice of the Supreme Court issued an order to prevent the *Kantipur Daily* newspaper from publishing unflattering reports about him. In November, the minister of information and communications directed state media outlets to minimize reporting that criticized the government response to the murder of a 13-year-old girl.

Also in 2018, the Ministry of Information and Communications advised public institutions to "prioritize" state-run media outlets when selling advertisements, a move that some rights activists claimed was intended to financially hobble private media.

Score Change: The score declined from 3 to 2 due to growing restrictions on journalistic activity, including broadly written new criminal code provisions that impede newsgathering on privacy grounds, political interference with state broadcasters, and bias in the distribution of government advertising.

D2. Are individuals free to practice and express their religious faith or nonbelief in public and private? 2 / 4

Like the interim constitution before it, the 2015 constitution identifies Nepal as a secular state, signaling a break with the Hindu monarchy that was toppled as part of the resolution of the civil war in 2006 (it was formally abolished in 2008). Religious freedom is protected under the new constitution, and tolerance is broadly practiced, but members of some religious minorities occasionally report official harassment. Muslims in Nepal are a particularly impoverished group, occupying a marginalized space. Proselytizing is prohibited under a 2017 law, and some Christians have been prosecuted under the law.

D3. Is there academic freedom, and is the educational system free from extensive political indoctrination? 2 / 4

The government does not restrict academic freedom, and much scholarly activity takes place freely, including on political topics. Student unions affiliated with the country's major political parties sometimes clash violently, and the police occasionally use force to disperse demonstrations organized by student unions. Minorities, including Hindi- and Urdu-speaking Madhesi groups, have complained that Nepali is enforced as the language of education in government schools.

D4. Are individuals free to express their personal views on political or other sensitive topics without fear of surveillance or retribution? 3 / 4

The freedom to engage in private discussions on sensitive topics has expanded alongside Nepal's political stabilization. However, authorities have cracked down on some individuals who post content on social media that criticizes or insults the government. In August 2018, a man was arrested and detained for several weeks for posting an image on Facebook that superimposed the prime minister's head on the body of a monkey.

E. ASSOCIATIONAL AND ORGANIZATIONAL RIGHTS: 6 / 12

E1. Is there freedom of assembly? 2 / 4

Although the constitution guarantees freedom of assembly, security forces violently disperse some protests and demonstrations, particularly in the southern regions, where there is a large Madhesi population. In August 2018, a teenage boy was killed, and dozens more were injured, when security forces opened fire on a protest in Mahendranagar against the police response to the rape and murder of a 13-year-old girl. In July, dozens of people were injured when the police fired tear gas and used batons to disperse a protest in Kathmandu demanding improved health care.

E2. Is there freedom for nongovernmental organizations, particularly those that are engaged in human rights- and governance-related work? 2 / 4

Although the new constitution allows nongovernmental organizations (NGOs) to form and operate within the country, legal restrictions have made this difficult in practice. The District Administration Office (DAO), which is responsible for registering NGOs and associations, is often understaffed and lacks essential resources. Foreign NGOs must enter project-specific agreements with the Nepalese government. There is a widespread view that NGOs should not be overly political, which hinders some groups from engaging in certain forms of public advocacy.

E3. Is there freedom for trade unions and similar professional or labor organizations? 2 / 4

The 2015 constitution provides for the right to form trade unions. Labor laws protect the freedom to bargain collectively, and unions generally operate without state interference. Workers in a broad range of "essential" industries cannot stage strikes.

F. RULE OF LAW: 6 / 16

F1. Is there an independent judiciary? 2 / 4

The 2015 constitution provides for an independent judiciary. However, judicial independence is compromised by endemic corruption in most courts.

The state has generally ignored local court verdicts, Nepalese Supreme Court decisions, and National Human Rights Commission (NHRC) recommendations addressing crimes committed during the 1996–2006 civil war.

F2. Does due process prevail in civil and criminal matters? 1 / 4

Constitutional guarantees of due process are poorly upheld in practice. Reports of arbitrary arrests continue. Due to heavy case backlogs and a slow appeals process, suspects are frequently kept in pretrial detention for periods longer than the sentences they would face if tried and convicted. The government provides legal counsel to those who cannot afford their own, but only at a defendant's request. Therefore, those unaware of their right to a public defender often end up representing themselves.

F3. Is there protection from the illegitimate use of physical force and freedom from war and insurgencies? 2 / 4

Rights advocates continue to criticize Nepal for failing to punish abuses and war crimes committed during the 1996–2006 civil war. Moreover, there has been no institutional reform of the security forces, which stand accused of carrying out torture, murder, and forced disappearances during the conflict. Some alleged perpetrators of wartime abuses serve in government.

Due to a lack of will on the part of the security forces and political parties, neither the TRC nor the CIEDP, two key transitional justice bodies, have implemented reforms demanded by the United Nations and two Nepali Supreme Court rulings. The mandates of both bodies were extended by one year in February 2018. Although the TRC and CIEDP have received thousands of reports of human rights violations and enforced disappearances, no alleged perpetrators have been prosecuted.

F4. Do laws, policies, and practices guarantee equal treatment of various segments of the population? 1 / 4

The 2015 constitution enshrines rights for sexual minorities. The first passport on which the holder was permitted to select a third gender was issued in 2015. However, LGBT (lesbian, gay, bisexual, and transgender) people reportedly face harassment by the authorities and other citizens, particularly in rural areas.

The constitution frames the protection of fundamental human rights for Nepali citizens only. This potentially leaves equal rights of noncitizens, including migrants and people who cannot prove citizenship, unprotected.

Tibetans in Nepal face difficulty achieving formal refugee status due to Chinese pressure on the Nepalese government. Women rarely receive the same educational and employment opportunities as men.

G. PERSONAL AUTONOMY AND INDIVIDUAL RIGHTS: 8 / 16

G1. Do individuals enjoy freedom of movement, including the ability to change their place of residence, employment, or education? 3 / 4

Freedom of movement is generally respected in Nepal. There are legal limits on the rights of refugees to move freely, but restrictions are inconsistently enforced. Citizens generally enjoy choice of residence, though bribery is common in the housing market, as well as to gain admittance to universities.

In rural areas, women remain subject to *chaupadi,* a traditional practice in which menstruating women are separated from their families and communities in sheds. The practice was criminalized under a law that went into effect in August 2018, but enforcement is uneven.

G2. Are individuals able to exercise the right to own property and establish private businesses without undue interference from state or nonstate actors? 2 / 4

Although citizens have the right to own private businesses, starting a business in Nepal often requires bribes to a wide range of officials. Licensing and other red tape can be extremely onerous. Women face widespread discrimination when starting businesses, and customs and border police are notoriously corrupt in dealing with cross-border trade.

G3. Do individuals enjoy personal social freedoms, including choice of marriage partner and size of family, protection from domestic violence, and control over appearance? 2 / 4

Gender-based violence against women remains a major problem. The number of reported rapes nearly doubled from 2016 to 2017, which some analysts partly attribute to a greater willingness to report the crime. The August 2018 rape and murder of a 13-year-old girl highlighted the extent of the problem, and caused widespread outrage. The 2009 Domestic Violence Act provides for monetary compensation and psychological treatment for victims, but authorities generally do not prosecute domestic violence cases. Underage marriage of girls is widespread.

Foreign men married to Nepali women must wait at least 15 years to obtain naturalized citizenship, while foreign women married to Nepali men can immediately become citizens. Furthermore, children of foreign-born fathers and Nepali mothers must apply for naturalized citizenship, while children of foreign-born mothers and Nepali fathers are automatically granted citizenship.

G4. Do individuals enjoy equality of opportunity and freedom from economic exploitation? 1 / 4

Trafficking of children and women from Nepal for prostitution in India is common, and police rarely intervene. Bonded labor is illegal but remains a serious problem throughout Nepal. Child labor also remains a problem, and children can be found working in the brickmaking, service, and other industries, as well as engaged in forced begging and sex work.

The 2015 earthquake left millions of people homeless. Many of those affected lack opportunities for social mobility, as they struggle to recover from the disaster.

Netherlands

Population: 17,200,000
Capital: Amsterdam
Political Rights Rating: 1
Civil Liberties Rating: 1
Freedom Rating: 1.0
Freedom Status: Free
Electoral Democracy: Yes

Overview: The Netherlands is a parliamentary democracy with a strong record of safeguarding political rights and civil liberties. Nevertheless, wariness of immigration and Muslim minorities has grown in recent years, and polarization around cultural identity issues has increased. Harsh policies toward irregular migrants and asylum seekers have been a source of controversy.

KEY DEVELOPMENTS IN 2018:

- In a consultative referendum held in March, a plurality of voters rejected the controversial Intelligence and Security Services Act passed by the parliament in 2017, which gave the government sweeping powers to access telephone and internet records and stoked criticism that it could enable dragnet surveillance of private communications. Despite the referendum results, the law entered into force in May.
- Also in March, the national ombudsman issued a report which concluded that municipalities and security forces, citing public-safety concerns, sometimes restrict assembly rights by confining protesters to certain areas or prohibiting demonstrations if authorities fear violence or disorder.
- In June, the parliament passed a controversial law banning the burqa and niqab (facial veil) in public places including schools, hospitals, public transportation, and government buildings.

POLITICAL RIGHTS: 40 / 40

A. ELECTORAL PROCESS: 12 / 12

A1. Was the current head of government or other chief national authority elected through free and fair elections? 4 / 4

The Netherlands is a parliamentary constitutional monarchy. The role of the monarch is largely ceremonial. The prime minister is the head of government and is chosen by the parliament after elections. The incumbent prime minister, Mark Rutte, won a third term following parliamentary elections held in March 2017. He formed a coalition government consisting of his own right-wing People's Party for Freedom and Democracy (VVD) alongside the Christian Democratic Appeal (CDA), Democrats 66 (D66), and the Christian Union.

A2. Were the current national legislative representatives elected through free and fair elections? 4 / 4

The Netherlands has a bicameral parliament that consists of the 75-seat First Chamber, which is elected indirectly to four-year terms in a proportional vote by the members of the 12 provincial councils; and the 150-seat Second Chamber, which is elected to terms of four years by proportional representation. The latest parliamentary elections, for the Second Chamber in March 2017, were well administered, and all parties accepted the results. The parliament now has thirteen parties, the most since 1972. The far-right Party for Freedom (PVV), which is led by Geert Wilders and has drawn condemnation for its anti-Muslim and xenophobic rhetoric, won 20 seats, the second highest total. However, all other parties refused to form a coalition with the PVV, effectively shutting it out of government.

A3. Are the electoral laws and framework fair, and are they implemented impartially by the relevant election management bodies? 4 / 4

Elections are administered by the Electoral Council, which works impartially and professionally to carry out Dutch elections.

B. POLITICAL PLURALISM AND PARTICIPATION: 16 / 16

B1. Do the people have the right to organize in different political parties or other competitive political groupings of their choice, and is the system free of undue obstacles to the rise and fall of these competing parties or groupings? 4 / 4

Political parties operate freely and regularly rotate in and out of power. The Elections Law does not impose any undue restrictions on the creation of political parties and the registration of candidates for elections. In the 2017 parliamentary elections, the ruling VVD lost 8 seats, while its former coalition partner, the Labor Party, lost 29. Government funding extends to all parties that have participated in the most recent parliamentary elections and have gained at least one seat.

B2. Is there a realistic opportunity for the opposition to increase its support or gain power through elections? 4 / 4

Opposition parties have a realistic opportunity to increase support or gain power, as evidenced by the 2017 election results in which a number of opposition parties gained seats. The CDA, D66, and the Christian Union joined the governing coalition in 2017 after being in the opposition during the second Rutte cabinet.

B3. Are the people's political choices free from domination by the military, foreign powers, religious hierarchies, economic oligarchies, or any other powerful group that is not democratically accountable? 4 / 4

The people are free to make their own political choices without pressure from groups that are not democratically accountable.

B4. Do various segments of the population (including ethnic, religious, gender, LGBT, and other relevant groups) have full political rights and electoral opportunities? 4 / 4

Minority groups participate freely in the political process, and a number of political parties represent their interests. The DENK (THINK) party, which seeks to represent a broad spectrum of ethnic and religious minorities, as well as voters with migrant backgrounds, won three seats in the 2017 parliamentary elections. The DENK party also won seats in 13 municipalities during the March 2018 municipal elections, including in Amsterdam and Rotterdam. The party has been controversial and centrist parties have accused it of enflaming discontent among migrant communities. On the other hand, the far-right, anti-immigrant Forum for Democracy, whose leader Thierry Baudet has been accused of racism and sexism, won two seats in Amsterdam's assembly in the 2018 elections.

While most major parties addressed gender issues in their party manifestos, the PVV's does not mention women.

C. FUNCTIONING OF GOVERNMENT: 12 / 12

C1. Do the freely elected head of government and national legislative representatives determine the policies of the government? 4 / 4

Government policies reflect the choices of freely elected members of parliament. Following the 2017 parliamentary elections, it took a record 225 days for the governing coalition to form, manifesting the fragmentation in Dutch politics.

C2. Are safeguards against official corruption strong and effective? 4 / 4

The Netherlands has low levels of corruption and anticorruption mechanisms are generally effective.

In an evaluation report published in June 2018, the Council of Europe's Group of States against Corruption (GRECO) noted that the Dutch government had not made sufficient progress in establishing rules and procedures for the parliament to prevent conflicts of interest and regulate dealings with lobbyists and other third parties.

C3. Does the government operate with openness and transparency? 4 / 4

Laws are in place recognizing the right to request government information, and they are generally enforced, although critics contend that long delays in responding to requests for information are common. Additionally, these laws do not apply to legislative and judicial bodies. Legislation that would require government institutions to make documents available online rather than by request only has been stalled in the parliament since the Second Chamber passed the bill in 2016.

CIVIL LIBERTIES: 59 / 60
D. FREEDOM OF EXPRESSION AND BELIEF: 16 / 16
D1. Are there free and independent media? 4 / 4

A free and independent press thrives in the Netherlands. In June 2018, reports emerged that the phone records of journalist Jos van de Ven of the newspaper *Brabants Dagblad* had been seized, as part of a police investigation into a leak that enabled the reporter to reveal the names of candidates for mayor of the city of Den Bosch in 2017, which normally remain confidential. The revelation highlighted the importance of a new law that came into force in October, which strengthened protections for the confidentiality of journalists' sources.

D2. Are individuals free to practice and express their religious faith or nonbelief in public and private? 4 / 4

The constitution guarantees freedom of religion, which is generally respected in practice.

D3. Is there academic freedom, and is the educational system free from extensive political indoctrination? 4 / 4

Academic freedom is largely respected in the Netherlands.

D4. Are individuals free to express their personal views on political or other sensitive topics without fear of surveillance or retribution? 4 / 4

There are no restrictions on freedom of speech or expression, apart from the criminalization of hate speech. In May 2018, the government implemented the controversial 2017 Intelligence and Security Services Act, which gives intelligence agencies greater latitude in accessing telephone and internet records and stoked criticism that it could enable dragnet surveillance of private communications. The law came into force despite a March consultative referendum in which voters rejected the legislation.

The Netherlands has had lèse majesté laws, which forbid insulting the monarchy, in place since 1881. In April, the Second Chamber passed legislation that would reduce penalties for insulting the king and his family from up to five years in prison to a maximum of four months imprisonment. At year's end, the legislation awaited passage by the First Chamber.

E. ASSOCIATIONAL AND ORGANIZATIONAL RIGHTS: 12 / 12
E1. Is there freedom of assembly? 4 / 4

Freedom of assembly is constitutionally guaranteed and generally respected in practice. However, in March 2018 the national ombudsman issued a report which concluded that municipalities and security forces, citing public-safety concerns, sometimes restrict assembly rights by confining protesters to certain areas or prohibiting demonstrations if authorities fear violence or disorder. For example, members of a protest group called Kick Out Black

Pete, which demonstrates against an annual Christmas tradition in which people dress as a character known as Black Pete and wear blackface, claimed that in November, the mayors of eight cities either prevented protesters from standing near the events' locations or banned the demonstrations altogether. Most of the mayors feared violence between the anti–Black Pete protesters and counterdemonstrators, some of whom attacked protesters with eggs and bananas and shouted racist epithets.

E2. Is there freedom for nongovernmental organizations, particularly those that are engaged in human rights- and governance-related work? 4 / 4

Nongovernmental organizations (NGOs) operate freely and without interference from the government or nonstate actors.

E3. Is there freedom for trade unions and similar professional or labor organizations? 4 / 4

Workers' rights to organize, bargain collectively, and strike are protected.

F. RULE OF LAW: 15 / 16

F1. Is there an independent judiciary? 4 / 4

The judiciary is independent, and the rule of law generally prevails in civil and criminal matters.

F2. Does due process prevail in civil and criminal matters? 4 / 4

The right to a fair trial is legally guaranteed and respected in practice. Defendants have access to legal counsel, and counsel is provided for them if they cannot afford an attorney.

In December 2018, the newspaper *NRC Handelsblad* published a report contending that a legal provision in place since 2008, which allows the Public Prosecution Service to adjudicate certain cases involving low-level offenses without a judge, has led to thousands of wrongful convictions.

F3. Is there protection from the illegitimate use of physical force and freedom from war and insurgencies? 4 / 4

The police are under civilian control, and prison conditions mostly meet international standards. However, people suspected or convicted of terrorism may experience treatment that NGOs have considered inhumane, including constant surveillance and regular full-body searches.

F4. Do laws, policies, and practices guarantee equal treatment of various segments of the population? 3 / 4

The Netherlands has antidiscrimination laws and hate speech laws on the books. While Dutch society is known for its tolerance, rising anti-immigrant sentiment in recent years has been accompanied by more open expression of anti-Islamic views. Perceived discrimination against Muslims is higher in the Netherlands than in many other European countries. Muslims and immigrants experience harassment and intimidation.

Dutch asylum policies have long drawn criticism for being unduly harsh. Asylum seekers and irregular migrants often experience prolonged detentions in prison-like facilities before deportation.

According to the Netherlands Institute for Human Rights, a government body, 35 percent of the discrimination claims it received in 2017 were filed by pregnant women, who experience widespread discrimination in employment.

G. PERSONAL AUTONOMY AND INDIVIDUAL RIGHTS: 16 / 16

G1. Do individuals enjoy freedom of movement, including the ability to change their place of residence, employment, or education? 4 / 4

Residents generally enjoy freedom of movement and choice of residence, employment, and institution of higher education. A counterterrorism law passed in 2017 allows the government to restrict the movement of people suspected of terrorist links. Human rights advocates have complained that the law is vulnerable to abuse.

G2. Are individuals able to exercise the right to own property and establish private businesses without undue interference from state or non-state actors? 4 / 4

Property rights are legally protected and generally upheld in practice.

G3. Do individuals enjoy personal social freedoms, including choice of marriage partner and size of family, protection from domestic violence, and control over appearance? 4 / 4

Personal social freedoms are largely respected. However, in June 2018 the parliament passed a law banning the burqa and niqab in public places including schools, hospitals, public transportation, and government buildings. The passage of the law was applauded by far-right politicians such as Geert Wilders and condemned by critics as discriminatory.

Domestic violence is a persistent problem. According to the Ministry of Justice and Security, over 6 percent of Dutch women surveyed in 2017 experienced domestic violence in the previous five years.

Female genital mutilation, although illegal, still occurs in some immigrant communities. The Ministry of Health, Welfare, and Sport runs a project to prevent the practice.

G4. Do individuals enjoy equality of opportunity and freedom from economic exploitation? 4 / 4

While the Netherlands is a source, destination, and transit point for human trafficking, the government makes strong efforts to combat it, vigorously investigating and prosecuting suspected traffickers. However, a report published by the Council of Europe's Group of Experts on Action against Trafficking in Human Beings (GRETA) in October 2018 noted that the number of trafficking prosecutions and convictions has decreased in recent years.

Despite government efforts to combat the exploitation of migrant workers, particularly those from Poland, some employment agencies continue to deny migrant workers overtime pay, demand long work hours, and enable sexual harassment and abuse.

New Zealand

Population: 4,900,000
Capital: Wellington
Political Rights Rating: 1
Civil Liberties Rating: 1
Freedom Rating: 1.0
Freedom Status: Free
Electoral Democracy: Yes

Overview: New Zealand is a parliamentary democracy with a long record of free and fair elections and of guaranteeing political rights and civil liberties. Concerns include discrimination against the Māori and other minority populations, as well as reports of foreign influence in politics and the education sector.

KEY DEVELOPMENTS IN 2018:

- An increased annual intake quota of 1,000 refugees came into effect during the year, and the government has committed to further increases, with plans to resettle up to 1,500 refugees in 2020.
- In December, Parliament passed legislation aimed at reducing child poverty, a policy priority of the current government.
- Adding to concerns about foreign interference in the education sector, a prominent China studies professor at the University of Canterbury was subjected throughout the year to a campaign of intimidation that was seen as a response to her research on Beijing's overseas influence operations.

POLITICAL RIGHTS: 40 / 40
A. ELECTORAL PROCESS: 12 / 12
A1. Was the current head of government or other chief national authority elected through free and fair elections? 4 / 4

A governor general, appointed by Queen Elizabeth II on advice from the prime minister, represents the British monarch as New Zealand's ceremonial head of state. The prime minister, the head of government, is appointed by the governor general and is usually the leader of the majority party or coalition in the directly elected Parliament. Jacinda Ardern, leader of the Labour Party, became prime minister in 2017 following that year's legislative elections.

A2. Were the current national legislative representatives elected through free and fair elections? 4 / 4

The 120 members of Parliament's single chamber, the House of Representatives, serve three-year terms. The mixed electoral system combines voting in geographic districts with proportional representation. In the 2017 elections, no single party won the 61 seats required to form a government. Although the incumbent National Party led with 56 seats, the Labour Party, which won 46 seats, formed a coalition with two smaller parties: New Zealand First, a populist and anti-immigration party that claimed 9 seats, and the Green Party, which took 8 seats. Elections in New Zealand are generally well administered, and their results considered credible.

A3. Are the electoral laws and framework fair, and are they implemented impartially by the relevant election management bodies? 4 / 4

The legal framework supports democratic elections, and it is fairly implemented in practice. The independent New Zealand Electoral Commission administers elections and referendums, promotes compliance with electoral laws, and provides public education on electoral issues.

B. POLITICAL PLURALISM AND PARTICIPATION: 16 / 16
B1. Do the people have the right to organize in different political parties or other competitive political groupings of their choice, and is the system free of undue obstacles to the rise and fall of these competing parties or groupings? 4 / 4

New Zealanders are able to organize political parties without undue legal restrictions or other obstacles, and parties are free to operate and campaign for support.

B2. Is there a realistic opportunity for the opposition to increase its support or gain power through elections? 4 / 4

The political system features regular democratic transfers of power between rival parties after elections. Power has traditionally alternated between the center-left Labour Party and the center-right National Party. Currently, the National Party serves as a strong opposition force in Parliament.

B3. Are the people's political choices free from domination by the military, foreign powers, religious hierarchies, economic oligarchies, or any other powerful group that is not democratically accountable? 4 / 4

People are generally able to act on their political preferences without undue influence from powerful groups. However, several studies in recent years have claimed that some lawmakers and parties have accepted sizable political donations from Chinese businesspeople and other Chinese figures, raising the possibility that such donations might influence their positions.

B4. Do various segments of the population (including ethnic, religious, gender, LGBT, and other relevant groups) have full political rights and electoral opportunities? 4 / 4

Political rights and electoral opportunities are granted to all New Zealand citizens, and permanent residents have the right to vote. Seven of Parliament's constituency seats are reserved for representatives of the Māori population, though Māori may also vote or run in general electoral districts. In the 2017 elections, Golriz Ghahraman, from Iran, became the first refugee to win a seat in Parliament.

Women are relatively well represented in politics, and the government has taken steps to encourage their participation. Ardern is the third woman to serve as the country's prime minister.

In November 2018, the Supreme Court confirmed a lower court's finding that a 2010 law barring all prisoners serving sentences from voting was inconsistent with the country's Bill of Rights. Previous rules had allowed prisoners serving terms of less than three years to vote. The decision had no immediate effect, as it did not require Parliament to change the law. Restrictions on prisoners' voting rights particularly affect indigenous people, who make up a disproportionate share of inmates.

C. FUNCTIONING OF GOVERNMENT: 12 / 12

C1. Do the freely elected head of government and national legislative representatives determine the policies of the government? 4 / 4

The prime minister and cabinet ministers, with the support of a majority in the House of Representatives, determine and implement the government's policy agenda without improper interference from any unelected entity.

C2. Are safeguards against official corruption strong and effective? 4 / 4

Government corruption is not considered a significant problem in New Zealand, and cases of official malfeasance are routinely investigated and prosecuted.

Despite the country's strong anticorruption record, there is some concern about a "revolving door" between political or government posts and private-sector lobbying groups, which can entail conflicts of interest.

C3. Does the government operate with openness and transparency? 4 / 4

The government operates with a high level of transparency, and new legislation is openly discussed in Parliament and the media. Parliamentary records, government policies, and commissioned reports are published online and readily available as required by law. The government upholds transparency in budgetary procedures, and members of Parliament must submit annual financial disclosure statements.

CIVIL LIBERTIES: 58 / 60
D. FREEDOM OF EXPRESSION AND BELIEF: 16 / 16
D1. Are there free and independent media? 4 / 4

New Zealand has a free and robust independent media sector, including a Māori-language public network and radio station.

Events surrounding the murder of a British tourist in Auckland in December 2018 raised concerns about the effects of judicial suppression orders on media coverage. Intense media interest in naming the accused murderer was thwarted by a court order meant to protect the suspect's due process rights, although major overseas news aggregators including Google allowed the suspect's name to be published, leading Prime Minister Ardern to criticize the company's "lackadaisical" efforts to respect New Zealand law.

D2. Are individuals free to practice and express their religious faith or nonbelief in public and private? 4 / 4

Religious freedom is protected by law and generally respected in practice. Only religious organizations that wish to collect donations and receive tax benefits need to register with the government, and the process is not onerous.

D3. Is there academic freedom, and is the educational system free from extensive political indoctrination? 4 / 4

Academic freedom typically prevails at all levels of instruction. However, concerns persist regarding Chinese interference in New Zealand's higher education sector. Beginning in late 2017 and throughout 2018, a prominent China studies professor at the University of Canterbury in Christchurch, Anne-Marie Brady, was subjected to a campaign of intimidation, including threatening letters, damage to her car, and theft of materials related to her research, which has been critical of the Chinese Communist Party. Reports of Chinese government attempts to influence student groups and monitor Chinese students in New Zealand also emerged in 2017.

D4. Are individuals free to express their personal views on political or other sensitive topics without fear of surveillance or retribution? 4 / 4

New Zealanders are free to discuss personal views on sensitive topics. However, new intelligence and security legislation adopted in 2017 allows law enforcement agencies to access private communications under certain conditions in order to protect national security. Separately, state security officials warned the government in late 2017 that Beijing may have attempted to "unduly influence expatriate communities."

E. ASSOCIATIONAL AND ORGANIZATIONAL RIGHTS: 12 / 12
E1. Is there freedom of assembly? 4 / 4

The government generally respects freedom of assembly. Large protests on a variety of topics have proceeded without incident in recent years, though in July 2018 protesters demonstrating against the use of a chemical pesticide were prevented from crossing Auckland's Harbour Bridge by police on public safety grounds.

E2. Is there freedom for nongovernmental organizations, particularly those that are engaged in human rights- and governance-related work? 4 / 4

There are no significant restrictions on nongovernmental organizations' ability to form, operate, and solicit funds.

E3. Is there freedom for trade unions and similar professional or labor organizations? 4 / 4

Workers may freely organize and bargain collectively, and trade unions actively engage in political debates and campaigns. Workers also have the right to strike, with the exception of uniformed police personnel.

F. RULE OF LAW: 15 / 16
F1. Is there an independent judiciary? 4 / 4

The New Zealand judiciary is generally independent. Most judges are appointed by the governor general on the recommendation of the attorney general, who first consults with senior jurists.

F2. Does due process prevail in civil and criminal matters? 4 / 4

Law enforcement practices and court procedures provide for due process protections in civil and criminal matters. Defendants and detainees are presumed innocent until proven guilty and by law must immediately be notified of the charges against them.

Pretrial detention durations have increased in recent years, as authorities have tightened bail requirements and relaxed the time limit in which cases must be concluded.

F3. Is there protection from the illegitimate use of physical force and freedom from war and insurgencies? 4 / 4

Rates of violent crime are relatively low, and residents have legal recourse to seek redress for violations of their physical security. Prison conditions generally meet international standards, though some facilities are poorly equipped to house detainees with disabilities or mental health problems.

F4. Do laws, policies, and practices guarantee equal treatment of various segments of the population? 3 / 4

The 1993 Human Rights Act protects all people in New Zealand from discrimination on the basis of gender, religion, ethnicity, and sexual orientation, among other categories, and its provisions are generally respected in practice. However, Māori—who account for approximately 16 percent of the population—and Pacific Islanders experience some discrimination in schools, the workplace, and the health system. Indigenous people are also disproportionately represented in the penal system, accounting for just over half of the prison population as of December 2018. Recent campaigns to recruit more officers of Māori, Pacific Islander, and Asian descent aim to improve cultural and ethnic sensitivity within the police force, and to combat profiling and discrimination. According to the 2018 Child Poverty Monitor Technical Report, nearly 20 percent of children experienced food insecurity, and children of Māori and Pacific Islander descent are especially vulnerable. In December, Parliament adopted the Child Poverty Reduction Act, which requires the government to report on child poverty rates and produce plans to address the problem.

Women continue to face some disparities in employment, including a 9.4 percent gender pay gap and underrepresentation in leadership positions in both the public and private sectors. The government enforces strong legislation protecting the rights of LGBT (lesbian, gay, bisexual, and transgender) people.

In 2018, the government increased the number of refugees accepted annually for resettlement from 750 to 1,000. Prime Minister Ardern announced in September that the government will further increase its refugee intake to 1,500 in 2020. The New Zealand Human Rights Commission has raised concerns that refugees are not always given sufficient information to enable them to access important services such as interpreters, housing, and English language instruction. Separately, asylum seekers are sometimes detained alongside criminal inmates while their identity is being confirmed. As of June 2018, six asylum seekers were being detained in New Zealand prisons and subjected to general prison conditions.

G. PERSONAL AUTONOMY AND INDIVIDUAL RIGHTS: 15 / 16

G1. Do individuals enjoy freedom of movement, including the ability to change their place of residence, employment, or education? 4 / 4

The government respects freedom of movement, and neither state nor nonstate actors place undue restrictions on people's ability to change their place of residence, employment, or education.

G2. Are individuals able to exercise the right to own property and establish private businesses without undue interference from state or nonstate actors? 4 / 4

New Zealand's legal and regulatory frameworks are broadly supportive of private business activity and provide strong protections for property rights.

G3. Do individuals enjoy personal social freedoms, including choice of marriage partner and size of family, protection from domestic violence, and control over appearance? 4 / 4

Personal social freedoms are broadly protected, including on issues like marriage and divorce. Same-sex marriage was legalized in 2013, and same-sex couples may jointly adopt children. However, violence against women and children remains a critical problem in many communities. A 2016 government paper reported that one in three women has been a victim of sexual violence in her lifetime. Abortion is legal under certain conditions, such as when the mental or physical health of the woman is at risk. New Zealand's Law Commission recommended to the justice minister in October 2018 that the laws be amended to treat abortion as a health issue rather than a criminal matter, including by repealing criminal offenses related to abortion.

G4. Do individuals enjoy equality of opportunity and freedom from economic exploitation? 3 / 4

Residents generally have access to economic opportunities, but the Māori and Pacific Islander populations have disproportionately high rates of unemployment, affecting their economic and social mobility.

Migrant workers are vulnerable to exploitative conditions including forced labor in industries such as fishing, agriculture, construction, hospitality, and domestic service. The government has taken action to combat these abuses, though the US State Department reports that additional resources are needed to improve enforcement.

Nicaragua

Population: 6,300,000
Capital: Managua
Political Rights Rating: 6 ↓
Civil Liberties Rating: 5 ↓
Freedom Rating: 5.5
Freedom Status: Not Free
Electoral Democracy: No

Status Change: Nicaragua's status declined from Partly Free to Not Free due to authorities' brutal repression of an antigovernment protest movement, which has included the arrest and imprisonment of opposition figures, intimidation and attacks against religious leaders, and violence by state forces and allied armed groups that resulted in hundreds of deaths.

Overview: The election of Sandinista leader Daniel Ortega in 2006 began a period of democratic deterioration marked by the consolidation of all branches of government under his party's control, the limitation of fundamental freedoms, and unchecked corruption in government. In 2018, state forces, with the aid of informally allied armed groups, responded to a mass antigovernment movement with violence and repression. The rule of law collapsed as the government moved to put down the movement, with rights monitors reporting the deaths of over 300 people, extrajudicial detentions, disappearances, and torture.

KEY DEVELOPMENTS IN 2018:

- More than 300 people were killed and at least 2,000 were injured in a ferocious crackdown on an antigovernment protest movement that began in April, after authorities announced reforms to social security. The movement continued even after the proposed changes were canceled later that month. Human rights groups reported severe abuses amid an accompanying collapse in the rule of law, including arbitrary detentions, disappearances, and torture.
- Opposition figures were arrested during the year on trumped-up charges, including terrorism.
- A number of prominent media outlets and civil society organizations were closed, and saw their offices raided and property removed.
- A wave of illegal land occupations by progovernment groups accompanied the crisis.

POLITICAL RIGHTS: 10 / 40 (–2)

A. ELECTORAL PROCESS: 3 / 12

A1. Was the current head of government or other chief national authority elected through free and fair elections? 1 / 4

The constitution provides for a directly elected president, and elections are held every five years. Constitutional reforms in 2014 eliminated term limits and required the winner of the presidential ballot to secure a simple plurality of votes.

President Ortega was reelected in 2016 with over 72 percent of the vote in a severely flawed election that was preceded by the Supreme Court's move to expel the main opposition candidate, Eduardo Montealegre, from his Independent Liberal Party (PLI). The decision crippled the PLI, and Montealegre withdrew from the election. Ortega's closest competitor, Maximino Rodríguez of the Constitutionalist Liberal Party (PLC), received just 15 percent of the vote, with no other candidate reaching 5 percent. Ortega's wife, Rosario Murillo, ran as Ortega's vice presidential candidate.

Ortega's Sandinista National Liberation Front (FSLN) won 135 of 153 mayorships contested in 2017 municipal elections. There were reports ahead of the polls that the FSLN had ignored local primary surveys in order to put its preferred candidates up for election. Seven people were killed in postelection clashes between government and opposition supporters, according to the Nicaraguan Center of Human Rights (CENIDH).

A2. Were the current national legislative representatives elected through free and fair elections? 1 / 4

The constitution provides for a 92-member unicameral National Assembly. Two seats in the legislature are reserved for the previous president and the runner-up in the most recent presidential election. Legislative elections are held every five years.

In 2016 legislative elections, Ortega's FSLN increased its majority to 70 seats in the National Assembly, followed by the PLC with 13 seats. The PLI won just 2 seats, in contrast to the 26 seats it won in the 2011 election. Ortega refused to allow international election monitoring. Montealegre was expelled from the PLI a few months ahead of the polls, severely damaging the party's competitiveness.

Nicaragua's North Atlantic Autonomous Region (RAAN) and South Atlantic Autonomous Region (RAAS) have regional councils, for which elections were last held in 2014; the FSLN won the largest share of the vote in each, prompting protests by the majority-indigenous YATAMA party.

A3. Are the electoral laws and framework fair, and are they implemented impartially by the relevant election management bodies? 1 / 4

The Supreme Electoral Council (CSE) generally serves the interests of the FSLN. In 2016, it pushed 16 opposition members of the National Assembly from their seats in response to their failure to recognize the Supreme Court's move to expel Montealegre from the PLI; later that year it certified Ortega's reelection following a severely flawed electoral process. In 2017, CSE head Roberto Rivas was sanctioned by the United States because, among other offenses, he allegedly "perpetrated electoral fraud undermining Nicaragua's electoral institutions;" Rivas resigned in May 2018. The judiciary has interpreted Nicaragua's electoral laws in the FSLN's favor.

B. POLITICAL PLURALISM AND PARTICIPATION: 4 / 16 (-2)

B1. Do the people have the right to organize in different political parties or other competitive political groupings of their choice, and is the system free of undue obstacles to the rise and fall of these competing parties or groupings? 1 / 4

Political parties face legal and practical obstacles to formation and operations. Party leaders are easily co-opted or disqualified by Ortega-aligned institutions. Membership to the FSLN is often required in order to hold civil service positions, discouraging people from registering as members of other parties. Under 2014 constitutional reforms, legislators must follow the party vote or risk losing their seats.

B2. Is there a realistic opportunity for the opposition to increase its support or gain power through elections? 0 / 4 (-1)

Years of political repression under Ortega, including through politicized court rulings and other measures that prevented opposition figures from participating in politics, severely limited the ability of the opposition to gain power through elections, and very few opposition figures hold legislative seats or other government positions. In 2018, the ferocity of the crackdown on the year's protest movement reflected the president's determination to quash any challenge to his rule. Police and progovernment armed groups employed lethal force against peaceful protesters, and thousands of protest participants were arrested. Many of the protesters wore masks for fear of being persecuted if their identities were known, and by year's end numerous protest leaders had fled the country. A number of prominent opposition figures were arrested during the year on trumped-up charges of terrorism and involvement in organized crime. The CENIDH counted over 500 political prisoners being held in Nicaragua at year's end.

Score Change: The score declined from 1 to 0 due to severe repression of the political opposition, including through the arrest and imprisonment of opposition figures and violent attacks against peaceful opposition protesters.

B3. Are the people's political choices free from domination by the military, foreign powers, religious hierarchies, economic oligarchies, or any other powerful group that is not democratically accountable? 1 / 4

President Ortega has consolidated all branches of government and most public institutions, as well as the country's media, under his party's control, allowing him and the FSLN great influence over people's political choices.

Public-sector workers experienced pressure to keep away from the antigovernment protest movement in 2018. At least 300 health professionals were dismissed from public hospitals for providing assistance to protestors or for their alleged role in antigovernment demonstrations.

B4. Do various segments of the population (including ethnic, religious, gender, LGBT, and other relevant groups) have full political rights and electoral opportunities? 2 / 4 (−1)

Minority groups, especially the indigenous inhabitants of Nicaragua's eastern and Caribbean regions, are politically underrepresented across parties, and the government and FSLN largely ignore their grievances. The 2018 crackdown signaled Ortega's intolerance of activism that could be perceived as challenging his government, including by indigenous activists and other segments of the population seeking greater political rights. In October, two indigenous activists were removed from an airplane in Managua and questioned. One of them, Haydee Castillo, was imprisoned in the apparent absence of formal charges.

As per a new municipal electoral law approved in 2012, half of each party's candidates for mayoralties and council seats must be women. Women also hold 45 percent of National Assembly seats. In practice, successful political advocacy by women is generally restricted to initiatives that enjoy the support of the FSLN, which has not prioritized women's policy concerns.

Score Change: The score declined from 3 to 2 because Ortega's broad crackdown on dissent in 2018 left indigenous and other societal groups fewer opportunities to advocate for their interests.

C. FUNCTIONING OF GOVERNMENT: 3 / 12
C1. Do the freely elected head of government and national legislative representatives determine the policies of the government? 1 / 4

The FSLN dominates most public institutions, working closely with labor and private business in a tripartite alliance (COSEP) that is recognized in Article 98 of the constitution.

The manipulation of the 2016 election and the expulsion of 16 opposition politicians from the legislature prevented elected representatives from determining government policies.

Ortega has a wide degree of discretionary powers to set policy. The constitutional reforms of 2014 included provisions allowing the president to issue binding decrees and direct changes in tax policy without legislative approval.

C2. Are safeguards against official corruption strong and effective? 1 / 4

Because the justice system and other public bodies are generally subservient to Ortega and the FSLN, there is little chance that allegations of corruption against government officials will see a thorough investigation or prosecution. Corruption charges against high-ranking government officials are rare, while corruption cases against opposition figures are often criticized for being politically motivated.

Ortega's sons and daughters have been appointed to prominent positions such as ambassador and presidential adviser.

C3. Does the government operate with openness and transparency? 1 / 4

Government operations and policymaking are generally opaque. The 2007 Law on Access to Public Information requires public entities and private companies doing business with the state to disclose certain information. Government agencies at all levels generally ignore this law.

Ortega rarely holds press conferences. The Communications and Citizenry Council, which oversees the government's press relations, is directed by Vice President Rosario Murillo and has been accused of limiting access to information.

CIVIL LIBERTIES: 22 / 60 (–10)
D. FREEDOM OF EXPRESSION AND BELIEF: 8 / 16 (–3)
D1. Are there free and independent media? 1 / 4

The press has faced increased political and judicial harassment since 2007, when Ortega returned to power, with the administration engaging in systematic efforts to obstruct and discredit media critics. Journalists covering the 2018 crisis have been subject to threats, arrest, and physical attacks. Journalist Ángel Gahona was shot and killed in April, while covering a protest in Bluefields. The Special Monitoring Commission for Nicaragua (MESENI), a mission of the Inter-American Commission on Human Rights (IACHR), received complaints of police checkpoints being established near the homes of journalists and media employees. The IACHR has granted protectionary measures to several journalists in light of harassment and death threats.

As the 2018 protests continued, the Nicaraguan Institute of Telecommunications and Postal Services (Telcor), the state institution that acts as the media regulator, ordered television companies and mobile phone service providers to stop transmitting several independent news channels through their systems. In December, police raided and confiscated equipment from the facilities of the digital news platform Confidencial and the television program *Esta Semana*. News station 100% Noticias was closed by police the same month, and its director, Miguel Mora, was arrested on charges of fomenting hate and violence. Notably, the independent news outlet *La Prensa* continued to operate in 2018.

D2. Are individuals free to practice and express their religious faith or nonbelief in public and private? 3 / 4 (–1)

Religious freedom was generally respected prior to the 2018 crisis, though some Catholic and evangelical church leaders had reported retaliation by the government for criticism of the Ortega administration, including the confiscation or delay of imported goods and donations. In 2018, however, church officials were denounced and smeared by authorities for accompanying or defending antigovernment protestors. In July, Ortega responded to Roman Catholic clergy members' condemnation of police violence by accusing church leaders of backing a coup attempt. Managua's auxiliary bishop, Silvio José Báez, was repeatedly smeared by state media for his defense of the protesters, and was physically attacked by progovernment demonstrators on at least one occasion. Progovernment mobs also attacked churches where antigovernment protesters were sheltering.

Faith leaders have criticized attempts by the Ortega administration to co-opt religious belief for political ends. The government has required public employees to attend government-sponsored religious festivals, making them miss official Catholic Church events.

Score Change: The score declined from 4 to 3 due to denunciations of Roman Catholic bishops' involvement in the political crisis, and physical attacks against Catholic clergy and churches.

D3. Is there academic freedom, and is the educational system free from extensive political indoctrination? 2 / 4 (-1)

Prior to the 2018 crisis, academic freedoms were generally respected, although some academics refrained from open criticism of the government. In the public primary and secondary school system, there have been reports of students being required to attend progovernment rallies, and of pro-FSLN materials displayed in school buildings.

In 2018, universities were sites of protest and repression. In July, progovernment armed forces attacked the Autonomous University of Nicaragua in Managua (UNAN), in which dozens of young people had barricaded themselves inside as an act of protest; at least two people were killed in the ensuing fighting and parts of the campus were heavily damaged. Dozens of university professors, administrators, and students were arbitrarily dismissed from UNAN in the aftermath. In May, the University of Central America (UCA) was attacked by progovernment armed forces while it sheltered protestors who were fired on by Managua police and informally allied forces. Later, in August, it was forced to suspend classes after the government failed to transfer funds to the school. Separately, in September, a professor at the Polytechnic University of Nicaragua (UPOLI) with a history of involvement with civil society movements was arbitrarily detained and charged with directing a terrorist group from the university.

Score Change: The score declined from 4 to 3 due to the repression of students, professors, and universities perceived as having supported the antigovernment protest movement.

D4. Are individuals free to express their personal views on political or other sensitive topics without fear of surveillance or retribution? 2/ 4 (-1)

In past years, private discussion remained mostly free, although some prominent individuals self-censored for fear of retribution. In 2018, repression and intimidation by state and progovernment forces contributed to a generalized climate of fear and terror that restricted free expression.

Access to the internet remains unrestricted, though in March Vice President Murillo said the government would "review the use of social networks," raising concerns about the censorship of online activity. Nevertheless, many people still speak their minds freely on social networks.

Score Change: The score declined from 3 to 2 because large-scale, violent repression of opposition supporters contributed to increased self-censorship and fear of reprisals for expressing opposition to the government.

E. ASSOCIATIONAL AND ORGANIZATIONAL RIGHTS: 2 / 12 (–3)

E1. Is there freedom of assembly? 0 / 4 (–2)

Freedom of assembly deteriorated severely in 2018, when more than 300 people were killed and at least 2,000 were injured in a ferocious crackdown on an antigovernment protest movement that began in April, after authorities announced social security reforms. A majority of the abuses have been attributed to the national police and armed allied groups, which the Office of the UN High Commissioner for Human Rights (OHCHR) said in an August report operate with "total impunity." The OHCHR noted some instances of violence by antigovernment protesters, but said there was no evidence that such violence was preplanned or coordinated, and that police, with aid from allied forces, responded with lethal force to nonlethal threats. The office concluded that "the majority of protesters were peaceful."

As the movement continued, authorities moved to restrict demonstrations. In July, the government passed the Law against Money Laundering, the Financing of Terrorism, and the Proliferation of Weapons of Mass Destruction, which has vaguely worded provisions that expand the definition of terrorism. Those convicted under the law, which was widely viewed as tool to intimidate and prosecute antigovernment protesters, can receive sentences of up to 20 years. In September, the National Police issued a statement declaring unauthorized marches and demonstrations "illegal." The police have subsequently denied permits for public demonstrations, and have occupied public spaces to prevent protests.

In mid-2018, more than 1,900 people had been arrested for participating in protests, according to CENIDH. Amnesty International reported that some had been charged with terrorism, while hundreds more were being held without charge. IACHR reported in December that more than 500 people remained in detention in connection with actions taken during protests.

Score Change: The score declined from 2 to 0 due to the large-scale, violent repression of an antigovernment protest movement, in which more than 300 people were killed, the detention of hundreds of protesters, and restrictive measures implemented in an attempt to crush the movement.

E2. Is there freedom for nongovernmental organizations, particularly those that are engaged in human rights- and governance-related work? 0 / 4 (–1)

Groups critical of the government or which focus on issues like corruption have operated within an increasingly restrictive environment under the Ortega administration, which among other things has used registration laws to choke off their sources of funding. Since April 2018, human rights defenders and leaders of civil society organizations have experienced severe harassment, arbitrary detention, and arbitrary expulsion. In September, an arrest warrant was issued for Félix Maradiaga, the director of the Institute of Strategic Studies and Public Policies (IEEPP) in Managua on charges of involvement in organized crime and financing terrorism, allegedly by channeling funds from the institute to protesters. During the year, nine prominent opposition civil society organizations had their legal status revoked, their offices raided, and property removed. In December, the Ortega administration expelled from the country two international human rights missions—the Interdisciplinary Group of Independent Experts (GIEI) and MESENI.

Score Change: The score declined from 1 to 0 because the targeted persecution of rights groups, including legal harassment, arbitrary closure, and arbitrary expulsion, has left them unable to operate in Nicaragua.

E3. Is there freedom for trade unions and similar professional or labor organizations? 2 / 4

The FSLN controls many of the country's labor unions, and the legal rights of non-FSLN unions are not fully guaranteed in practice. Although the law recognizes the right to strike, approval from the Ministry of Labor is almost never granted. Employers sometimes form their own unions to avoid recognizing legitimate organizations. Employees have reportedly been dismissed for union activities, and citizens have no effective recourse when those in power violate labor laws.

F. RULE OF LAW: 4 / 16 (-2)
F1. Is there an independent judiciary? 1 / 4

The judiciary remains dominated by FSLN and PLC appointees, and the Supreme Court is a largely politicized body controlled by Sandinista judges.

F2. Does due process prevail in civil and criminal matters? 0 / 4 (-1)

Since protests erupted in April 2018, UN investigators and other human rights organizations have documented rampant violations of due process. These include widespread arbitrary arrests and detentions by police and allied progovernment forces, failure to produce search or arrest warrants, no discussion of detainees' rights, no public registry of detainees or their location, and individuals being held incommunicado during initial detention.

Reforms to the penal code and to judicial processes approved in 2017 increased the centralization of criminal justice procedures in ways damaging to due process rights. They include measures that allow "technical" judges to preside over many cases, instead of juries, as well as provisions that allow the transfer of certain kinds of cases from regional courts to the central public ministry.

Score Change: The score declined from 1 to 0 due to widespread systematic violations of basic due process protections.

F3. Is there protection from the illegitimate use of physical force and freedom from war and insurgencies? 1 / 4 (-1)

The 2018 antigovernment protest movement was met with violent repression by police and informally allied armed forces, resulting in the deaths of more than 300 people. In an August 2018 report on repression of the protest movement, the OHCHR detailed severe abuses including psychological and physical torture of detainees, including sexual violence, forced confessions, disappearances, and extrajudicial killings. Thousands of Nicaraguans fled the country in 2018, with more than 24,000 seeking asylum in Costa Rica alone.

Changes to the military code and national police passed in 2014 give the president power to deploy the army for internal security purposes and appoint the national police chief, and permitted the police to engage in political activity. The 2015 sovereign security law has been criticized for militarizing civilian agencies.

Nicaragua has generally been spared the high rates of crime and gang violence that plague its neighbors to the north.

Score Change: The score declined from 2 to 1 due to violent repression by police and informally allied armed forces of an antigovernment protest movement, and severe abuses committed against those detained for their participation in it.

F4. Do laws, policies, and practices guarantee equal treatment of various segments of the population? 2 / 4

The constitution and laws nominally recognize the rights of indigenous communities, but those rights have not been respected in practice. Approximately 5 percent of the population is indigenous and lives mostly in the RAAN and the RAAS.

The country's LGBT (lesbian, gay, bisexual, and transgender) population is subject to intermittent threats and discriminatory treatment.

G. PERSONAL AUTONOMY AND INDIVIDUAL RIGHTS: 8 / 16 (−2)

G1. Do individuals enjoy freedom of movement, including the ability to change their place of residence, employment, or education? 2 / 4 (−1)

Marches and blockades erected by protesters limited mobility throughout the country for several months in 2018. There was a de facto curfew for several months in 2018 because people feared encountering FSLN-aligned mobs (known as turbas) after dark.

Freedom of movement was generally respected prior to the crisis, though poor infrastructure limits movement in some majority-indigenous areas.

Score Change: The score declined from 3 to 2 because demonstrations and blockades, and a de facto curfew inspired by fears of violence, limited free movement during the year.

G2. Are individuals able to exercise the right to own property and establish private businesses without undue interference from state or nonstate actors? 2 / 4 (−1)

Property rights are protected on paper but can be tenuous in practice. Titles are often contested, and individuals with connections to the FSLN sometimes enjoy an advantage during property disputes. Individuals and communities in the construction zone for a planned interoceanic canal report intimidation by surveyors and anonymous actors. Conflict over land in the RAAN between Miskito residents and settlers continued in 2018.

There was a wave of illegal land occupations by progovernment groups during the 2018 crisis. By the end of July, as many as 4,000 hectares had been illegally occupied with government assistance. Owners of the land claimed that the government was aiding in the confiscations in order to intimidate its opponents, or to reward supporters with plots of land.

Score change: The score declined from 3 to 2 due to a wave of land grabs that accompanied the year's political crisis.

G3. Do individuals enjoy personal social freedoms, including choice of marriage partner and size of family, protection from domestic violence, and control over appearance? 2 / 4

Violence against women and children remains widespread and underreported, and few cases are ever prosecuted. The 2012 Comprehensive Law against Violence toward Women addresses both physical and structural forms of violence, and recognizes violence against women as a matter of public health and safety. The legislation codified femicide and establishes sentencing guidelines for physical and psychological abuses against women. However, 2017 reforms to the penal code narrowed the definition of femicide.

A 2013 reform to the law allows mediation between the victim and accuser, despite concerns from rights groups. The family code includes protections for pregnant minors and the elderly, establishes equal duties of mothers and fathers, and prohibits physical punishment of children. It defines marriage as a union between a man and a woman and, as such, deprives same-sex couples the right to adopt children or the ability to receive fertility treatment.

Abortion is illegal and punishable by imprisonment, even when performed to save the mother's life or in cases of rape or incest. The criminalization of abortion can cause women to seek out risky illegal abortions that can jeopardize their health.

G4. Do individuals enjoy equality of opportunity and freedom from economic exploitation? 2 / 4

Nicaragua is a source country for women and children forced into prostitution; adults and children are also vulnerable to forced labor, notably in the agriculture and mining sectors, and as domestic servants. While recognizing the government's "significant efforts" to tackle human trafficking, the 2018 US State Department's *Trafficking in Persons Report* said the country did not demonstrate increasing efforts over the previous year, and that the Atlantic coast continued to be disproportionately affected due to weaker institutions there.

Much of the economy is informal, and workers in these sectors lack legal protections associated with formal employment. The legal minimum wage is inadequate to cover the cost of basic goods.

Niger

Population: 20,600,000
Capital: Niamey
Political Rights Rating: 4
Civil Liberties Rating: 4
Freedom Rating: 4.0
Freedom Status: Partly Free
Electoral Democracy: No

Overview: The current regime in Niger was democratically elected in 2011 and reelected in 2016 in a polling process plagued by serious irregularities. The struggle to meet security challenges posed by active militant groups has served as an alibi for the government to restrict civil liberties. Security, transparency, economic prosperity, and gender equality are limited.

KEY DEVELOPMENTS IN 2018:

- In October, opposition parties sent delegates to the National Committee for Political Dialogue (CNDP), a framework for discussing issues related to the formation of the electoral commission and revision of the electoral code. While the move ended a nearly two-year-long opposition boycott of political dialogue with the government, the thaw was short-lived: they again suspended participation in November.
- In March, police responded violently to a protest by civil society organizations in response to increased taxes on housing and electricity. Dozens of activists were arrested, with some imprisoned for months. In April, a number of civil society leaders were arrested in connection with their involvement in the protest movement.
- The security situation in Niger remained fragile. Some jihadist attacks took place in Diffa and northern Tillabéri, while a reliance on nonstate armed groups for counterterrorism operations has inflamed intercommunal tensions around the Niger-Mali

border, leading to instances of violence. Increased attacks by jihadist groups on the Burkina Faso border have prompted concerns about the potential for a new jihadist hotspot in that area.

- In April, opposition leader Hama Amadou lost his appeal of a one-year prison sentence handed down in 2017 upon his conviction of involvement in a baby-trafficking operation. In June, Amadou, who lives in exile in France, was removed from his seat in the National Assembly.

POLITICAL RIGHTS: 20 / 40
A. ELECTORAL PROCESS: 6 / 12
A1. Was the current head of government or other chief national authority elected through free and fair elections? 2 / 4

The president is directly elected to up to two five-year terms. President Mahamadou Issoufou was reelected for a second term in 2016. The elections took place in a context of political tension, as Amadou, Issoufou's most significant challenger, was jailed during the entire electoral process, accused of involvement in a baby-trafficking scandal. The elections themselves were plagued with irregularities including vote buying, underage voting, and rigging of election results.

A2. Were the current national legislative representatives elected through free and fair elections? 2 / 4

There are 171 seats in the unicameral National Assembly, 158 of which are directly elected from 8 multimember constituencies; 8 which are reserved for minority representatives, who are elected directly from special single-seat constituencies; and 5 that are reserved for Nigeriens living abroad.

In the 2016 polls, Issoufou's Party for Democracy and Socialism (PNDS) won 75 seats in the 171-seat legislature, while Amadou's Nigerien Democratic Movement for an African Federation (MODEN/FA) won 25 seats, and former prime minister Seini Oumarou's National Movement for a Developing Society (MNSD) took 20 seats. Thirteen smaller parties divided the remaining seats. The elections took place as several opposition candidates were held in prison after being accused of involvement in a foiled coup attempt, or participation in unauthorized protests. The polls, held concurrently with the year's presidential election, were plagued by similar irregularities.

A3. Are the electoral laws and framework fair, and are they implemented impartially by the relevant election management bodies? 2 / 4

The electoral code offers a framework for fair elections. However, the opposition, pointing to reports of widespread irregularities in the 2016 polls, among other issues, has cast doubt over the impartiality and capacity of the Independent National Electoral Commission (CENI), which with the Constitutional Court approves the list of candidates and validates election results.

In 2017, the government and the opposition disagreed once again over the appointment of a new electoral commission to organize the 2021 presidential and legislative elections; the government unilaterally appointed the new electoral commission after the opposition boycotted the process. In October 2018, the opposition briefly returned to discussions related to the CENI and electoral reforms within the framework of the CNDP, but suspended participation again in November.

B. POLITICAL PLURALISM AND PARTICIPATION: 8 / 16

B1. Do the people have the right to organize in different political parties or other competitive political groupings of their choice, and is the system free of undue obstacles to the rise and fall of these competing parties or groupings? 2 / 4

By law, political parties may freely organize and conduct their activities. However, the PNDS-led government has employed a variety of tactics to interfere in the operation of opposition parties, including persecution of opposition leaders and the co-optation of key opposition figures. In 2017, opposition leader Hama Amadou, while in exile in France, was sentenced to one year in prison for alleged involvement in a baby-trafficking operation. He lost an appeal of the sentence in April 2018, and in June was removed from his seat in the National Assembly. Other members of the opposition have been temporarily arrested on charges of participation in unauthorized protests.

B2. Is there a realistic opportunity for the opposition to increase its support or gain power through elections? 2 / 4

In theory, the opposition can mobilize support and increase its membership. However, the opposition has suffered a lack of leadership, partly due to the absence of Amadou, who is in exile. Currently the opposition parties are divided into five different coalitions and face serious difficulties in challenging the overwhelming dominance of the ruling coalition. In addition, the government's continuous repression of members of the opposition and attempts to co-opt key leaders has further hindered the opposition's ability to mobilize its base and gain power through elections.

B3. Are the people's political choices free from domination by the military, foreign powers, religious hierarchies, economic oligarchies, or any other powerful group that is not democratically accountable? 2 / 4

Niger has experienced a number of military coups, the most recent in 2010, and the influence of the military still looms over the political sphere. The government claimed to have foiled another coup attempt in 2015, though it did not produce evidence. In December 2018, multiple military officers were arrested; though no formal charges have been issued, the timing and circumstances of the arrests appear similar to those of the alleged foiled coup attempt in 2015.

B4. Do various segments of the population (including ethnic, religious, gender, LGBT, and other relevant groups) have full political rights and electoral opportunities? 2 / 4

The law provides for equal opportunity for all Nigeriens to seek political office and participate in political processes. However, in practice women have been underrepresented both in elected and cabinet positions. A parity law calls for women to hold 10 percent of parliamentary seats and 25 percent of cabinet positions. While the law has improved women's representation, the quota has not been respected, nor does it guarantee that women may participate equally once elected or installed in cabinet positions.

While two ethnic groups, Hausa and Zarma (or Djerma), have dominated many government positions, ethnic minorities are increasingly visible in politics, particularly Tuareg and Arabs.

C. FUNCTIONING OF GOVERNMENT: 6 / 12

C1. Do the freely elected head of government and national legislative representatives determine the policies of the government? 2 / 4

Elected representatives were duly installed into office following the 2016 polls. However, the harassment of the opposition during the 2016 presidential and legislative election campaigns, as well as irregularities in the elections themselves, damage the government's legitimacy.

C2. Are safeguards against official corruption strong and effective? 2 / 4

There are a number of anticorruption authorities and programs. The High Authority for Combating Corruption and Related Crimes (HALCIA) is the official anticorruption body. The government operates an anticorruption hotline, and has established a program aiming to end corruption in the judiciary. In 2017, President Issoufou started a campaign calling for zero tolerance of corruption.

Despite these measures, corruption continues. No one in government has been held accountable for the so-called Uraniumgate scandal that emerged in 2017, which involved reports that a high ranking official had in 2011 illegally certified a $320 million uranium transaction, and that the national treasury never received the money. Corruption is thought to be particularly high in the country's taxation agencies. Bribes are sometimes required to gain access to public services.

C3. Does the government operate with openness and transparency? 2 / 4

Implementation and enforcement of the 2011 Charter on Access to Public Information and Administrative Documents has been uneven. Government information related to the mining, uranium, and oil sectors, and state-operated companies, is often not disclosed.

In 2017, Niger, a global leader in uranium production, withdrew from the Extractive Industries Transparency Initiative (EITI). The development came a month after EITI had suspended the country, citing its failure to meet standards for transparent licensing allocation and contract disclosure, lacking a comprehensive public license register, and other concerns.

CIVIL LIBERTIES: 29 / 60
D. FREEDOM OF EXPRESSION AND BELIEF: 11 / 16
D1. Are there free and independent media? 2 / 4

In 2010, Niger adopted a press law that eliminated prison terms for media offenses and reduced the threat of libel cases. However, journalists continue to face difficulties, including occasional police violence while covering protests, and detention or prosecution in response to critical or controversial reporting. In April 2018, Baba Alpha, a journalist with Bonferey TV, was expelled to Mali after spending a year in prison after being convicted of using forged identity documents, with which authorities said he had been able to acquire Nigerien citizenship. Alpha had long been a government critic, and rights groups expressed concern about his conviction and expulsion to Mali, a country in which he had never lived. Earlier, in February, over a dozen news outlets, including radio, television, and newspapers, suspended their programming for one day to protest repeated attempts by authorities to confiscate journalists' equipment, as well as a proposal for a wide-ranging tax audit that would ensnare many media outlets, and was denounced by media owners and others as an intimidation tactic.

D2. Are individuals free to practice and express their religious faith or nonbelief in public and private? 3 / 4

Freedom of religion is generally respected in this overwhelmingly Muslim country. However, citing security concerns, the government has attempted to impose strict control over certain religious activities, including preaching, sermons in mosques, religious education, and religious holidays. In 2017, police arrested Muslims in Zinder for attempting to celebrate the Muslim holiday Eid al-Fitr on a different day than decreed by state officials.

D3. Is there academic freedom, and is the educational system free from extensive political indoctrination? 3 / 4

Academic freedom is generally upheld, but universities are underfunded and poorly equipped. Frequent protests and strikes by students and faculty inhibit normal academic activities, and sometimes draw heavy-handed police responses. In April 2018, police responded violently to a student protest at the University of Niamey over the expulsion of five students who had allegedly assaulted a faculty member. Dozens of students were injured and university campuses were temporarily closed.

D4. Are individuals free to express their personal views on political or other sensitive topics without fear of surveillance or retribution? 3 / 4

Freedom of expression is generally upheld in Niger. However, the government has shown some intolerance of criticism, and has prosecuted people over remarks posted to social media platforms.

E. ASSOCIATIONAL AND ORGANIZATIONAL RIGHTS: 6 / 12

E1. Is there freedom of assembly? 2 / 4

Freedom of assembly is constitutionally guaranteed, but authorities do not always respect this right in practice, and police have at times used force to break up demonstrations. In 2017, the government announced the prohibition of public protests on "business days." In 2018, authorities refused to authorize several public protests, most of which were organized in opposition to a new Finance Law that had raised taxes on housing and electricity, or against the presence of foreign military forces in the country. In March, over two dozen activists were arrested on charges of participation in one such protest that went ahead without authorization. Authorities forcibly dispersed the gathering, and many of those arrested spent months in prison.

E2. Is there freedom for nongovernmental organizations, particularly those that are engaged in human rights- and governance-related work? 2 / 4

The government occasionally restricts the operations of nongovernmental organizations (NGOs), and a lack of security in certain regions also impedes their functioning. In April, the heads of several NGOs were arrested for their roles in organizing antigovernment protests against the new Finance Law. In October, authorities expelled a doctor from Doctors Without Borders (MSF) for announcing what they alleged was a "false" death toll from malaria.

E3. Is there freedom for trade unions and similar professional or labor organizations? 2 / 4

While the constitution and other laws guarantee workers the right to join unions and bargain for wages, a large portion of the workforce is employed informally and lacks access to formal union representation. The legal definition of "essential" workers not permitted to strike is broad, and the can invoke mandatory arbitration processes to settle strikes.

F. RULE OF LAW: 6 / 16

F1. Is there an independent judiciary? 1 / 4

The constitution provides for an independent judiciary, and courts have shown some level of independence, though the judicial system is subject to executive interference. Recent rulings against opposition leaders and civil society activists have decreased trust in the judiciary.

F2. Does due process prevail in civil and criminal matters? 2 / 4

Arbitrary arrests and imprisonments are frequent. Many people accused of crimes are held in pretrial detention for extended periods of time, sometimes in the same population as people convicted of crimes. In 2018, several military officers accused of plotting a coup against Issoufou's regime in late 2015 received between 5- and 15-year prison sentences, but only after they had spent over two years in pretrial detention.

States of emergency declared in several regions allow the army to engage in mass arrests and detain those suspected of links with terrorist organizations.

F3. Is there protection from the illegitimate use of physical force and freedom from war and insurgencies? 1 / 4

Insecurity continues to plague many parts of the country. Some jihadist attacks took place in Diffa and northern Tillabéri. A reliance on nonstate armed groups to conduct counterterrorism operations has inflamed intercommunal tensions near the Niger-Mali border, leading to instances of violence. Furthermore, increased attacks by jihadist groups on the Burkina Faso border have prompted concerns about the potential for a new jihadist hotspot in that area. The government has extended states of emergency in the regions of Diffa, Tillabéri, and Tahoua several times in response to ongoing attacks.

F4. Do laws, policies, and practices guarantee equal treatment of various segments of the population? 2 / 4

The rights of ethnic minority groups are protected by law. While two ethnic groups, Hausa and Zarma (or Djerma), have dominated economic positions, Tuareg and Arabs are increasingly represented. Same-sex sexual activity is not illegal in Niger, but same-sex relationships are highly stigmatized, and there is no protection against discrimination based on sexual orientation. Although the 2010 constitution prohibits gender discrimination, women suffer widespread discrimination in practice. The application of the law by customary courts often discriminates against women.

Niger has made efforts to welcome Malian and Nigerian refugees and other forcibly displaced populations.

G. PERSONAL AUTONOMY AND INDIVIDUAL RIGHTS: 6 / 16

G1. Do individuals enjoy freedom of movement, including the ability to change their place of residence, employment, or education? 2 / 4

The constitution guarantees freedom of movement, but in practice free movement is hampered by militant activity and bribery by security officials who guard checkpoints.

G2. Are individuals able to exercise the right to own property and establish private businesses without undue interference from state or nonstate actors? 2 / 4

A number of complications undermine legal guarantees of the right to own property. Few people hold formal ownership documents for their land, though customary law provides some protection. However, the enforcement of both state and customary law often gives way to tensions and confusion. Women have less access to land ownership than men due to inheritance practices and inferior status in property disputes.

G3. Do individuals enjoy personal social freedoms, including choice of marriage partner and size of family, protection from domestic violence, and control over appearance? 1 / 4

Family law gives women inferior status in divorce proceedings. Female genital mutilation was criminalized in 2003 and has declined, but it continues among a small percentage of the population. Penalties for rape are heavy, but societal attitudes and victims' fears of retribution discourage reporting, and when rape is reported it is often poorly investigated. Domestic violence is not explicitly criminalized, though women may lodge criminal allegations of battery against partners. Some cases have resulted in convictions, but reporting is similarly discouraged in practice.

G4. Do individuals enjoy equality of opportunity and freedom from economic exploitation? 1 / 4

Although slavery was criminalized in 2003 and banned in the 2010 constitution, it remains a problem in Niger. Estimates of the number of enslaved people vary widely, but is generally counted in the tens of thousands. Niger remains a source, transit point, and destination for human trafficking. Extreme poverty and food insecurity precludes upward socioeconomic mobility for many people.

Nigeria

Population: 195,900,000
Capital: Abuja
Political Rights Rating: 3
Civil Liberties Rating: 5
Freedom Rating: 4.0
Freedom Status: Partly Free
Electoral Democracy: No

Overview: Nigeria has made significant improvements in the competiveness and quality of national elections in recent years, though political corruption remains endemic, particularly in the petroleum industry that dominates the economy. Security challenges, including the ongoing insurgency by the Boko Haram militant group, as well as communal and sectarian violence in the restive Middle Belt region, threaten the human rights of millions of Nigerians. The response by the military and law enforcement agencies to the widespread insecurity often involves extrajudicial killings, torture, and other abuses. Civil liberties are also undermined by religious and ethnic bias, and discrimination against women and LGBT (lesbian, gay, bisexual, and transgender) people. The vibrant media landscape is impeded by criminal defamation laws, as well as the frequent harassment and arrests of journalists who cover politically sensitive topics.

KEY DEVELOPMENTS IN 2018:
- Internal divisions roiled the governing All Progressives Congress (APC) in 2018, leading to a wave of defections beginning in July, including three governors, more than 50 National Assembly members (including the speaker of the House), and other high-ranking officials. By the end of the year, the defections had significantly narrowed the APC's majorities in the National Assembly.
- Throughout the year, Nigeria's security forces confronted a protracted insurgency by the Boko Haram militant group in the northeast, as well as a worsening communal conflict in the Middle Belt region, which, according to the International Crisis Group, led to 1,949 deaths in 2018.

- In February, the National Assembly passed the Electoral Act Amendment Bill 2018, which would enhance the transparency of elections, but President Buhari sent it back to the legislature three times before vetoing it in December on the grounds that its passage would not allow the Independent National Electoral Commission (INEC) enough time to prepare for the February 2019 national elections.
- In October, soldiers responded to rock-throwing protesters from the Islamic Movement of Nigeria (IMN) in Abuja by opening fire and killing as many as 45 people. President Buhari declined to condemn the shootings and the military defended the actions of the soldiers.

POLITICAL RIGHTS: 25 / 40

A. ELECTORAL PROCESS: 9 / 12

A1. Was the current head of government or other chief national authority elected through free and fair elections? 3 / 4

The president is elected by popular vote for no more than two four-year terms. Local and international observer organizations assessed the 2015 presidential election as competitive and generally well conducted, with improvements in voter identification and reductions in election-related violence compared with 2011. However, hundreds of thousands of Nigerians were still prevented from voting, either because they were internally displaced by the Boko Haram insurgency or because they failed to receive their permanent voter cards in time. Muhammadu Buhari, the candidate of the APC, defeated incumbent president Goodluck Jonathan of the People's Democratic Party (PDP), 54 percent to 45 percent. Jonathan quickly conceded defeat, helping to ensure a peaceful and orderly transfer of power.

A2. Were the current national legislative representatives elected through free and fair elections? 3 / 4

Members of the bicameral National Assembly, consisting of the 109-seat Senate and the 360-seat House of Representatives, are elected for four-year terms. The 2015 elections, held concurrently with the presidential vote, were similarly considered credible by local and international observer organizations. In the House of Representatives, the APC took 212 seats, while the PDP won 140, and smaller parties captured the remaining 8. In the Senate, the APC won 60 seats, while the PDP secured 49.

A3. Are the electoral laws and framework fair, and are they implemented impartially by the relevant election management bodies? 3 / 4

The 2015 parliamentary and presidential elections were postponed by about six weeks, due mainly to security concerns, but the INEC was widely lauded for its professionalism and impartiality. In September 2018, a joint preelection assessment mission from the National Democratic Institute (NDI) and the International Republican Institute (IRI) praised the INEC for improvements in election administration, including increased efficiency of the biometric voter verification system. However, the mission noted a number of potential obstacles that could impinge on the integrity of the 2019 national elections, including delays in releasing funds for the INEC to carry out electoral preparations.

In May, President Buhari signed a constitutional amendment into law which lowered the minimum age for candidates to run for the National Assembly and the presidency. In February, the National Assembly passed the Electoral Act Amendment Bill 2018, which observers believe would enhance the transparency of the INEC and the electoral process as a whole. However, President Buhari refused to sign the bill, sending it back to the National

Assembly three times before vetoing it in December on the grounds that its passage could create legal confusion leading up to February 2019 national elections.

B. POLITICAL PLURALISM AND PARTICIPATION: 10 / 16

B1. Do the people have the right to organize in different political parties or other competitive political groupings of their choice, and is the system free of undue obstacles to the rise and fall of these competing parties or groupings? 3 / 4

Nigerians generally have the right to organize in different political parties, though this is occasionally hindered in practice. At the end of 2018, the number of political parties registered by the INEC reached 91, as the body registered 23 new parties. The constitutional amendment signed by Buhari in May allowed independent candidates to compete in federal and state elections for the first time.

However, lack of internal party democracy and high candidate nomination fees to participate in primaries make it difficult for many prospective candidates to compete for nominations in the major political parties.

B2. Is there a realistic opportunity for the opposition to increase its support or gain power through elections? 3 / 4

Nigeria's multiparty system provides an opportunity for opposition parties to gain power through elections, as demonstrated by the APC's sweeping victory in 2015, which marked the first democratic transfer of power between rival parties in the country's history. The vote appeared to reflect the ethnic and religious divisions in the country, with Buhari, a northern Muslim, winning primarily in the northern states, and Jonathan, a Christian from the southern Niger Delta region, gaining an overwhelming majority in the south. However, Buhari's ability to gain support from many non-northern and non-Muslim voters was a significant factor in his success.

Internal divisions roiled the APC in 2018, leading to a wave of defections beginning in July, including three governors, more than 50 National Assembly members (including the speaker of the House), and other high-ranking officials. Some of the defectors created a new faction, the Reformed All Progressives Congress (R-APC), while others joined the PDP. By the end of the year, the defections had significantly narrowed the APC's majorities in the National Assembly.

B3. Are the people's political choices free from domination by the military, foreign powers, religious hierarchies, economic oligarchies, or any other powerful group that is not democratically accountable? 2 / 4

Despite the improved elections and peaceful rotation of power, citizens' political choices remain impaired or undermined to some degree by vote buying and intimidation, the influence of powerful domestic and international economic interests, and the local domination of either the Nigerian military or illegal armed groups in certain regions of the country.

Powerful "godfathers," or wealthy political sponsors, often dispense patronage and use their considerable influence to cultivate support for the candidates they back, and in return, winning candidates use their political offices to further enrich their godfathers.

B4. Do various segments of the population (including ethnic, religious, gender, LGBT, and other relevant groups) have full political rights and electoral opportunities? 2 / 4

The legal framework generally provides for equal participation in political life by the country's various cultural, religious, and ethnic groups. However, politicians and parties still often rely on voters' ethnic loyalties, and the interests of a given group may be poorly addressed in areas where it forms a minority or when affiliated parties are not in power.

Women enjoy formal political equality, but restrictive societal norms limit their participation in practice. Women maintained 8 of 109 Senate seats in the 2015 elections, and their share of the 360 seats in the House of Representatives fell from 24 to 18. The criminalization of same-sex sexual activity and a ban on gay advocacy organizations deter LGBT people from openly running for office or working to advance their political interests.

C. FUNCTIONING OF GOVERNMENT: 6 / 12

C1. Do the freely elected head of government and national legislative representatives determine the policies of the government? 2 / 4

Elected officials generally make and implement policy in Nigeria, but their ability to do so is impaired by factors including corruption, partisan conflict, poor control over areas of the country where militant groups are active, and the president's undisclosed health problems. In August 2018, following the wave of defections from the APC to the PDP, security personnel from the State Security Service (SSS) temporarily blocked legislators from entering the National Assembly, in a move viewed by some critics as an act of intimidation against opposition lawmakers. Vice President Yemi Osinbajo, serving as acting president during the incident, condemned the actions of the SSS and fired its director general, Lawal Musa Daura.

Partisan gridlock and legislative dysfunction caused delays in passing the federal budget for the third straight year in 2018. The National Assembly passed the 2018 budget bill in May, and Buhari signed it in June, six months after it should have taken effect.

C2. Are safeguards against official corruption strong and effective? 2 / 4

Corruption remains pervasive, particularly in the oil and security sectors. The Buhari administration continued its efforts to reduce graft and improve transparency during 2018. A whistle-blower policy introduced in 2016, which rewards Nigerians who provide information on government corruption, had led to the recovery of 540 billion naira (US$1.5 billion) in stolen funds as of May, according to the minister of information and culture. The National Assembly passed the long-awaited Petroleum Industry Governance Bill—the first of several measures designed to increase transparency and reduce corruption in Nigeria's oil and gas industries—in March, but the president refused to sign it, citing the large budgetary allocations for a new oversight body, the Petroleum Regulatory Commission, which would be established under the bill.

The Economic and Financial Crimes Commission (EFCC) and the Independent Corrupt Practices Commission (ICPC) opened new investigations into several high-level current and former officials in 2018, and corruption convictions secured by the EFCC increased from 189 in 2017 to 312 in 2018. Notably, the former governors of Plateau State and Taraba State were sentenced to 14 years in prison after corruption convictions in May and June, respectively. However, the opposition PDP has accused the federal government of political bias in its anticorruption efforts. While institutional safeguards against corruption at the federal level have increased, the culture of corruption at the state and local level persists.

C3. Does the government operate with openness and transparency? 2 / 4

The 2011 Freedom of Information (FOI) Act guarantees the right to access public records, but nongovernmental organizations (NGOs) have criticized government agencies for routinely refusing to release information sought through the law. In March 2018, the Akure Division of the Appeal Court ruled that the FOI Act is applicable to state governments as well as the federal government.

CIVIL LIBERTIES: 25 / 60

D. FREEDOM OF EXPRESSION AND BELIEF: 9 / 16

D1. Are there free and independent media? 2 / 4

Freedoms of speech, expression, and the press are constitutionally guaranteed. However, these rights are limited by laws on sedition, criminal defamation, and publication of false news. Sharia (Islamic law) statutes in 12 northern states impose severe penalties for alleged press offenses. Government officials also restrict press freedom by publicly criticizing, harassing, and arresting journalists, especially when they cover corruption scandals, human rights violations, separatist and communal violence, or other politically sensitive topics. In August 2018, Samuel Ogundipe, a journalist for the online newspaper *Premium Times*, was arrested and charged with stealing a police document after publishing an article that provided details on the investigation of the security personnel who denied lawmakers access to the National Assembly in July. Ogundipe spent three days in police custody, where investigators allegedly pressured him to reveal the source of his information, which he refused to provide. Ogundipe's trial, which began in November, was ongoing at year's end. Journalists and media entities have also been attacked and intimidated by nonstate actors, including Boko Haram.

Internet service providers sometimes block websites, particularly those that advocate for Biafran independence, at the request of the Nigerian Communications Commission (NCC).

D2. Are individuals free to practice and express their religious faith or nonbelief in public and private? 1 / 4

Religious freedom is constitutionally and legally protected and is generally respected by the federal government in practice. Nevertheless, in some instances state and local governments have placed limits on religious activities and endorsed a dominant faith. In 2016, authorities in Kaduna State banned the IMN, the country's largest Shiite organization, after protesters blocked an army convoy in 2015 and soldiers killed hundreds of IMN members in response. IMN's leader, Ibrahim el-Zakzaky, who preaches nonviolence, was arrested in the aftermath of the incident and detained for over two years before being charged in May 2018 with culpable homicide and unlawful assembly. He awaited trial at year's end.

Nonstate actors have also attempted to limit religious freedom. Boko Haram has deliberately attacked Christians and moderate Muslims, and their respective houses of worship. Communal clashes between Muslims and Christians have broken out for decades in and around the states of Kaduna and Plateau, often killing hundreds of people and displacing thousands at a time.

D3. Is there academic freedom, and is the educational system free from extensive political indoctrination? 3 / 4

The federal government generally respects academic freedom. However, some state governments mandate religious instruction in elementary and secondary curriculums, and student admission and faculty hiring policies are subject to political interference. Boko Haram's assault on secular education has included the closure or destruction of primary, secondary, and tertiary institutions. In February 2018, Boko Haram abducted approximately 110 girls from a boarding school in Dapchi, Yobe State. Negotiations between the government and the militant group led to the release of 104 of the girls two weeks later. Five died in captivity, and one remained in the hands of Boko Haram at the end of the year. UNICEF estimated in April that Boko Haram had abducted over 1,000 children since 2013, and the insurgency had left some three million children in northern Nigeria without access to a school.

D4. Are individuals free to express their personal views on political or other sensitive topics without fear of surveillance or retribution? 3 / 4

Nigerians are generally free to engage in discussions on politics and other topics, though expression of critical views on political leaders or sensitive subjects like the military, religion, and ethnicity occasionally leads to arrests or violent reprisals. Although both houses of the National Assembly passed the Digital Rights and Freedom Bill by March 2018, the bill had not yet been submitted to President Buhari for his assent by the end of the year. The bill would expand freedom of expression online by regulating government surveillance of online activities and making internet shutdowns illegal, among other provisions.

E. ASSOCIATIONAL AND ORGANIZATIONAL RIGHTS: 7 / 12

E1. Is there freedom of assembly? 2 / 4

The right to peaceful assembly is constitutionally guaranteed. However, federal and state governments frequently ban public events perceived as threats to national security, including those that could incite political, ethnic, or religious tension. Rights groups have criticized federal and state governments for prohibiting or dispersing protests that are critical of authorities or associated with controversial groups like the IMN and the separatist group Indigenous People of Biafra (IPOB). In October 2018, soldiers responded to rock-throwing protesters from the IMN in Abuja, who were protesting the continued detention and charges against Ibrahim el-Zakzaky, by opening fire and killing as many as 45 people. In response to criticism of the shootings, the army's official Twitter account posted a video of US president Donald Trump arguing—in the context of US border security—that stones thrown at the military should be considered firearms. President Buhari declined to condemn the shootings and the military continued to defend the actions of its security forces through the end of the year.

E2. Is there freedom for nongovernmental organizations, particularly those that are engaged in human rights- and governance-related work? 2 / 4

Nigeria has a broad and vibrant civil society sector. Members of some organizations face intimidation and physical harm for speaking out against Boko Haram, or encounter obstacles when investigating alleged human rights abuses committed by the military against Boko Haram suspects. Groups operating in the restive Niger Delta region face similar impediments. In December 2018, the army responded to an Amnesty International report, on the alleged failure of the military to protect residents vulnerable to attacks in central Nigeria, by threatening to shut down the group's Nigeria office.

In early 2018, the National Assembly declined to pass a bill that would have imposed intrusive state regulations on NGOs' funding and operations, including requiring government approval to carry out projects.

E3. Is there freedom for trade unions and similar professional or labor organizations? 3 / 4

Under the constitution, workers have the right to form and join trade unions, engage in collective bargaining, and conduct strikes. Nevertheless, the government forbids strike action in a number of essential services, including public transportation and security.

F. RULE OF LAW: 4 / 16

F1. Is there an independent judiciary? 2 / 4

Judicial independence is constitutionally and legally enshrined. The judiciary has achieved some degree of independence and professionalism in practice, but political interference, corruption, and a lack of funding, equipment, and training remain important problems. In October 2018, the National Judicial Council, headed by the chief justice, dismissed two prominent judges accused of corruption by the EFCC. The council also announced in October that it was investigating 26 additional judges for misconduct.

F2. Does due process prevail in civil and criminal matters? 1 / 4

There have been numerous allegations of extortion and bribe taking within the police force. Federal and state authorities have been criticized for disregarding due process, with prolonged pretrial detention of suspects even after courts ordered their release on bail. Former national security adviser Sambo Dasuki, who was arrested in 2015 on corruption charges, remained imprisoned at the end of 2018 despite the rulings of four different courts that he be released on bail, including a July court order mandating his release. Dasuki's trial was ongoing at year's end.

In February, 205 suspected Boko Haram members, many of whom had been detained for years without charge, were convicted in mass trials for their involvement with the group. Human Rights Watch (HRW) criticized the trials for being "fraught with irregularities, including lack of interpreters, inadequate legal defense, lack of prosecutable evidence or witnesses, and nonparticipation of victims."

F3. Is there protection from the illegitimate use of physical force and freedom from war and insurgencies? 0 / 4

The military has been repeatedly criticized by local and international human rights groups for extrajudicial killings, torture, and other abuses, including during counterinsurgency efforts in the northeast and operations against separatist movements in the southeast.

Sectarian and communal clashes between herders and farmers in the Middle Belt region claimed the lives of 1,949 people in 2018, according to the International Crisis Group. Domestic and international rights groups, including Amnesty International, fault the government, particularly the military, for inadequate intervention to halt the bloodshed. The offensive against Boko Haram weakened the group in 2018, but it maintained its ability to wage asymmetric warfare, including the use of women and children in suicide attacks against civilian targets in the northeast. According to the Council on Foreign Relations (CFR), more than 800 people were killed in incidents involving Boko Haram in 2018, compared to more than 1,800 in 2017. In November, a breakaway faction of Boko Haram loyal to the Islamic State (IS) killed at least 44 soldiers in Metele, near the border with Niger.

Violent crime is a serious problem in certain areas of Nigeria, as is the trafficking of drugs and small arms. Abductions are common in the Niger Delta and the southeastern states of Abia, Imo, and Anambra. In 2018, banditry in Zamfara State led to hundreds of deaths, with conditions worsening to the point where Governor Abdulaziz Yari called on President Buhari to declare a state of emergency in December. Various vigilante groups are active in Nigeria, and a bill that would officially recognize the security role of a national organization, the Vigilante Group of Nigeria, was passed by the National Assembly in 2017, but President Buhari had not yet signed it at the end of 2018.

F4. Do laws, policies, and practices guarantee equal treatment of various segments of the population? 1 / 4

Despite constitutional safeguards against ethnic discrimination, many ethnic minorities experience bias by state governments and other societal groups in areas including employment, education, and housing.

Women are subject to widespread societal discrimination regarding matters such as education and employment. Many poor families choose to send sons to school while daughters become street vendors or domestic workers. Women also face significant legal disadvantages in states governed by Sharia statutes.

The government and society continue to discriminate against LGBT people. Same-sex sexual activity can be punished with prison terms under the penal code, and with death under Sharia statutes in some states. The 2014 Same Sex Marriage (Prohibition) Act outlaws LGBT advocacy organizations and activities as well as any public display of same-sex relationships. Dozens of people were arrested in connection with these laws during 2018, including 57 attendees of a birthday party in Lagos in August.

G. PERSONAL AUTONOMY AND INDIVIDUAL RIGHTS: 5 / 16

G1. Do individuals enjoy freedom of movement, including the ability to change their place of residence, employment, or education? 1 / 4

Freedoms of internal movement and foreign travel are legally guaranteed. However, security officials frequently impose dusk-to-dawn curfews and other movement restrictions in areas affected by communal violence or the Islamist insurgency. More than two million people remained displaced by the conflict in northeastern Nigeria at the end of 2018.

G2. Are individuals able to exercise the right to own property and establish private businesses without undue interference from state or nonstate actors? 2 / 4

Nigeria's poorly regulated property-rights system hinders citizens and private businesses from engaging in the efficient and legal purchase or sale of land and other types of property. Bribery is a common practice when starting a business and registering property. However, the climate for private enterprise in recent years has benefited from advancements in credit accessibility, ease of starting a business, ease of paying taxes, and property registration.

Women belonging to certain ethnic groups are often denied equal rights to inherit property due to customary laws and practices.

G3. Do individuals enjoy personal social freedoms, including choice of marriage partner and size of family, protection from domestic violence, and control over appearance? 1 / 4

Despite the existence of strict laws against rape, domestic violence, female genital mutilation, and child marriage, these offenses remain widespread, with low rates of reporting and prosecution. Women and girls in camps for displaced persons have reported sexual abuse by members of the military and other authorities. Boko Haram's attacks on women's rights have been particularly egregious, with victims often subjected to forced marriage and rape, among other acts.

Abortion is illegal unless the life of the mother is in danger. As a result, many women seek out dangerous illegal abortions. The Nigerian Institute of Medical Research estimates that 34,000 women per year die from unsafe abortions.

G4. Do individuals enjoy equality of opportunity and freedom from economic exploitation? 1 / 4

Nigerian organized crime groups are heavily involved in human trafficking. Boko Haram has subjected children to forced labor and sex slavery. Both Boko Haram and a civilian vigilante group that opposes the militants have forcibly recruited child soldiers, according to the US State Department. Meanwhile, several of Nigeria's states have not implemented the 2003 Child Rights Act, which protects children from sexual exploitation and other abuses. The National Agency for the Prohibition of Trafficking in Persons (NAPTIP) continues to rescue trafficking victims and prosecute some suspected traffickers, but its funding is reportedly inadequate, and there have been few prosecutions against labor traffickers.

North Korea

Population: 25,600,000
Capital: Pyongyang
Political Rights Rating: 7
Civil Liberties Rating: 7
Freedom Rating: 7.0
Freedom Status: Not Free
Electoral Democracy: No

Overview: North Korea is a one-party state led by a dynastic totalitarian dictatorship. Surveillance is pervasive, arbitrary arrests and detention are common, and punishments for political offenses are severe. The state maintains a system of camps for political prisoners where torture, forced labor, starvation, and other atrocities take place. While some social and economic changes have been observed in recent years, including a growth in small-scale private business activity, human rights violations are still widespread, grave, and systematic.

KEY DEVELOPMENTS IN 2018:
- After a year of tense exchanges with the United States over North Korea's nuclear program, Supreme Leader Kim Jong-un met with US President Donald Trump in June for an historic summit in Singapore. The summit produced a vague agreement in which the North Korean government committed to "work towards" denuclearization of the Korean peninsula, but did not prescribe any concrete actions to achieve that end.
- Kim also met with South Korean President Moon Jae-in three times in 2018, which led to a commitment from North Korea to close a missile-test facility, as well as an agreement from both sides to end military drills along the Military Demarcation Line. Nevertheless, North Korea had not yet taken significant steps to eliminate its nuclear program by the end of the year.
- Despite its diplomatic overtures, the government continued to rule with absolute authority throughout the year, tightly controlling access to information, suppressing all dissent, and heavily surveilling residents to maintain control over the population.

POLITICAL RIGHTS: 0 / 40

A. ELECTORAL PROCESS: 0 / 12

A1. Was the current head of government or other chief national authority elected through free and fair elections? 0 / 4

Kim Jong-un became the country's supreme leader after the death of his father, Kim Jong-il, in 2011. The elder Kim had led North Korea since the 1994 death of his own father, Kim Il-sung, to whom the office of president was permanently dedicated in a 1998 constitutional revision. In 2016, the Supreme People's Assembly established the State Affairs Commission as the country's top ruling organ and elected Kim Jong-un as chairman. Kim already held a variety of other titles, including first chairman of the National Defense Commission—previously the highest state body—and supreme commander of the Korean People's Army.

A2. Were the current national legislative representatives elected through free and fair elections? 0 / 4

The 687-seat Supreme People's Assembly, North Korea's unicameral legislature, is elected to five-year terms. All candidates are preselected by the Democratic Front for the Reunification of the Fatherland—a coalition dominated by the ruling Korean Workers' Party (KWP) with representation from a handful of subordinate parties and organizations. Each candidate then runs unopposed. All citizens aged 17 and older are eligible to vote, and voting rates are reported at close to 100 percent. In the last elections in 2014, the official voter turnout figure was 99.97 percent.

Elections were held in July 2015 for 28,452 provincial, city, and county people's assembly members. Voter turnout was again reported to be 99.97 percent, with all candidates preselected and running unopposed.

A3. Are the electoral laws and framework fair, and are they implemented impartially by the relevant election management bodies? 0 / 4

Although there is a clear framework for conducting elections, including official election monitors, the system's structure denies voters any choice and rules out any opposition to the incumbent leadership. The government uses the mandatory elections as an unofficial census, keeping track of whether and how people voted, and interprets any rejection of the preselected candidates as treason.

B. POLITICAL PLURALISM AND PARTICIPATION: 0 / 16

B1. Do the people have the right to organize in different political parties or other competitive political groupings of their choice, and is the system free of undue obstacles to the rise and fall of these competing parties or groupings? 0 / 4

North Korea is effectively a one-party state. Although a small number of minor parties and organizations legally exist, all are members of the KWP-led Democratic Front for the Reunification of the Fatherland.

B2. Is there a realistic opportunity for the opposition to increase its support or gain power through elections? 0 / 4

Any political dissent or opposition is prohibited and harshly punished. The country has been ruled by the KWP since its founding, and the party itself has always been controlled by the Kim family. Kim Jong-il was dubbed the "eternal general secretary" of the party after his death. At the KWP's tightly controlled seventh party congress in 2016, Kim Jong-un, previously the party's "first secretary," was elected to the newly created position of chairman.

B3. Are the people's political choices free from domination by the military, foreign powers, religious hierarchies, economic oligarchies, or any other powerful group that is not democratically accountable? 0 / 4

The general public has no opportunity for political participation, and even KWP elites operate under the threat of extreme penalties for perceived dissent or disloyalty. The party is subject to regular purges aimed at reinforcing the leader's personal authority, and the regime has executed senior officials who have fallen out of favor with Supreme Leader Kim.

B4. Do various segments of the population (including ethnic, religious, gender, LGBT, and other relevant groups) have full political rights and electoral opportunities? 0 / 4

North Korea is ethnically homogeneous, with only a small Chinese population and few non-Chinese foreign residents. Foreigners are not allowed to join the KWP or serve in the military or government. Religious groups are harshly suppressed and unable to organize politically. Women hold few leadership positions in the ruling party and about 16 percent of the seats in the Supreme People's Assembly; the system does not allow such representatives to independently address the interests of women. The government typically denies the existence of LGBT (lesbian, gay, bisexual, and transgender) people in North Korea.

C. FUNCTIONING OF GOVERNMENT: 0 / 12

C1. Do the freely elected head of government and national legislative representatives determine the policies of the government? 0 / 4

North Korea has no freely elected officials. Kim Jong-un and his inner circle determine the policies of the government, and the Supreme People's Assembly gathers for brief sessions once or twice a year to unanimously approve all decisions.

C2. Are safeguards against official corruption strong and effective? 0 / 4

Corruption is believed to be endemic at every level of the state and economy, and bribery is pervasive. There are no independent or impartial anticorruption mechanisms.

C3. Does the government operate with openness and transparency? 0 / 4

The government is neither transparent in its operations nor accountable to the public. Information about the functioning of state institutions is tightly controlled for both domestic and external audiences.

CIVIL LIBERTIES: 3 / 60

D. FREEDOM OF EXPRESSION AND BELIEF: 0 / 16

D1. Are there free and independent media? 0 / 4

All domestic media outlets are run by the state. Televisions and radios are permanently fixed to state channels, and all publications and broadcasts are subject to strict supervision and censorship. For example, television coverage of North Korea's summits with the United States and South Korea in 2018 was carefully edited and quickly pulled from circulation, which, according to some analysts, reflected the government's desire to avoid appearing too close to its long-standing adversaries.

In recent years, several foreign news agencies have established bureau offices in Pyongyang. However, access is still tightly controlled for these organizations, and the government has been known to expel media crews in retaliation for their work. Select foreign media are often invited into the country to cover key political events and holidays, although authorities strictly manage their visits.

Voice of America, Radio Free Asia, BBC, and several South Korean outlets broadcast shortwave and medium-wave Korean-language radio programming into North Korea. Campaigns to send information into the country via USB and SD cards are common, though North Koreans' consumption of either foreign radio broadcasts or these contraband devices is subject to severe punishment if detected by authorities.

D2. Are individuals free to practice and express their religious faith or nonbelief in public and private? 0 / 4

Although freedom of religion is guaranteed by the constitution, it does not exist in practice. State-sanctioned churches maintain a token presence in Pyongyang, but some North Koreans who live near the Chinese border are known to practice their faiths furtively. Intense state indoctrination and repression preclude free and open exercise of religion and North Koreans caught practicing a religious faith are arrested and face harsh punishments, including imprisonment in labor camps. Foreigners caught proselytizing also risk arrest and detention.

D3. Is there academic freedom, and is the educational system free from extensive political indoctrination? 0 / 4

There is no academic freedom. The state must approve all curriculums, including those of educational programs led by foreigners. Although some North Koreans are permitted to study abroad at both universities and short-term educational training programs, those granted such opportunities are subject to monitoring and reprisals for perceived disloyalty.

D4. Are individuals free to express their personal views on political or other sensitive topics without fear of surveillance or retribution? 0 / 4

Nearly all forms of private communication are monitored by a huge network of informants. Domestic mobile-phone service has been available since 2008, with around five million users nationally, though the phones are also hardwired to record and transmit calls and text messages back to state security agencies for surveillance purposes. Smartphone users do not have access to the global internet, but must connect through the state-run intranet. Domestic and international mobile services are kept strictly separate, and crackdowns on users of Chinese-origin phones have been reported. In September 2018, the government reportedly blocked access to Chinese mobile networks prior to South Korean President Moon Jae-in's visit to Pyongyang.

E. ASSOCIATIONAL AND ORGANIZATIONAL RIGHTS: 0 / 12

E1. Is there freedom of assembly? 0 / 4

Freedom of assembly is not recognized, and participants in any unauthorized gatherings are subject to severe punishment, including prison sentences.

E2. Is there freedom for nongovernmental organizations, particularly those that are engaged in human rights- and governance-related work? 0 / 4

There are no legal associations or organizations other than those created by the state and ruling party.

E3. Is there freedom for trade unions and similar professional or labor organizations? 0 / 4

Strikes, collective bargaining, and other organized labor activities are illegal and can draw severe punishment for participants, including prison sentences.

F. RULE OF LAW: 0 / 16

F1. Is there an independent judiciary? 0 / 4

North Korea's judiciary is subordinate to the political leadership in law and in practice. According to the constitution, the Central Court, the country's highest court, is accountable to the Supreme People's Assembly, and its duties include protecting "state power and the socialist system."

F2. Does due process prevail in civil and criminal matters? 0 / 4

The right to due process is not respected in practice. It is estimated that between 80,000 and 120,000 political prisoners are held in detention camps.

Detention of foreigners for allegedly breaking North Korean laws is a recurring problem. In May 2018, ahead of the first-ever US-North Korea summit in Singapore, authorities released three US citizens who had been detained for alleged espionage and hostile acts against the state. In August, the government released a South Korean national who had been captured after crossing the border into the North the previous month, but at the end of the year, six other South Koreans remained imprisoned in North Korea.

F3. Is there protection from the illegitimate use of physical force and freedom from war and insurgencies? 0 / 4

Documented North Korean human rights violations include widespread torture, public executions, forced labor by detainees, and death sentences for political offenses.

Ignoring international objections, the Chinese government continues to return refugees and defectors to North Korea, where they are subject to torture, harsh imprisonment, or execution.

North Korea's nuclear program threatens the security of the entire Korean peninsula. In June 2018, Supreme Leader Kim met with US President Donald Trump for an historic summit in Singapore, leading to a vague agreement in which the North Korean government committed to "work towards" denuclearization of the Korean peninsula without prescribing concrete actions to achieve that end. Kim Jong-un and President Moon also met for three summits during the year to discuss preventing war between North and South Korea. The third summit, held in Pyongyang in September, led to a commitment from North Korea to close a missile-test facility, as well as an agreement from both sides to end military drills along the Military Demarcation Line, among other provisions. Despite these promises and the agreement with the United States, North Korea had not yet taken significant steps to eliminate its nuclear program by the end of the year.

F4. Do laws, policies, and practices guarantee equal treatment of various segments of the population? 0 / 4

The most prevalent form of discrimination is based on perceived political and ideological nonconformity rather than ethnicity. All citizens are classified according to their family's level of loyalty and proximity to the leadership under a semihereditary caste-like system known as *songbun*.

Women have legal equality, but they face rigid discrimination in practice and are poorly represented in public employment and the military. Although they have fewer opportunities in the formal sector, women are economically active outside the socialist system, exposing them to arbitrary state restrictions.

The law does not prohibit same-sex sexual activity, but the government maintains that the practice does not exist in North Korea.

In 2017, authorities allowed the UN special rapporteur on the rights of persons with disabilities, Catalina Devandas-Aguilar, to tour the country. She noted that North Korea's Federation for the Protection of the Disabled promotes the creation of associations for people with disabilities, including deaf and blind people, but said "there is still a long way to go" to realize their rights. In March 2018, North Korea sent two athletes to compete in the Winter Paralympics in Pyeongchang, South Korea, marking the country's first participation in the event.

G. PERSONAL AUTONOMY AND INDIVIDUAL RIGHTS: 3 / 16

G1. Do individuals enjoy freedom of movement, including the ability to change their place of residence, employment, or education? 0 / 4

Residents have no freedom of movement, and forced internal resettlement is routine. Emigration is illegal. A person's *songbun* classification affects his or her place of residence as well as employment and educational opportunities, access to medical facilities, and even access to stores. All foreign travel—whether for work, trade, or educational opportunities—is strictly controlled by the government. Freedom of movement for foreigners in North Korea is also limited and subject to arbitrary constraints.

G2. Are individuals able to exercise the right to own property and establish private businesses without undue interference from state or nonstate actors? 1 / 4

The formal economy remains both centrally planned and grossly mismanaged. Business activity is also hobbled by a lack of infrastructure, a scarcity of energy and raw materials, an inability to borrow on world markets or from multilateral banks because of sanctions, lingering foreign debt, and ideological isolationism. However, expanding informal and government-approved private markets and service industries have provided many North Koreans with a growing field of activity that is relatively free from government control. Local officials have had some authority in the management of special economic zones and over small-scale experiments with market-oriented economic policies.

G3. Do individuals enjoy personal social freedoms, including choice of marriage partner and size of family, protection from domestic violence, and control over appearance? 1 / 4

Men and women have formal equality in personal status matters such as marriage and divorce. However, sexual and physical violence against women—in the home, in prisons and labor camps, and in other situations—is common, and victims have little legal recourse. There are no specific legal penalties for domestic violence. UN bodies have noted the use of forced abortions and infanticide against pregnant women who are forcibly repatriated from China.

G4. Do individuals enjoy equality of opportunity and freedom from economic exploitation? 1 / 4

Forced labor is common in prison camps, mass mobilization programs, and state-run contracting arrangements in which North Korean workers are sent abroad. There have been widespread reports of trafficked women and girls among the tens of thousands of North Koreans who have crossed into China. Due to changing economic conditions, prostitution has reportedly become common within North Korea in recent years.

Economic opportunity has been affected by escalating international sanctions in response to North Korea's weapons tests and threats of military aggression. New sanctions imposed during 2017 targeted a variety of civilian industries such as textiles and seafood, and tightened banking restrictions to limit North Korea's access to international financial institutions. Nevertheless, markets and quasi-private businesses have expanded over time. Agricultural reforms have allowed larger percentages of crop yields to be kept by households, presumably to either consume or sell in the markets.

Norway

Population: 5,300,000
Capital: Oslo
Political Rights Rating: 1
Civil Liberties Rating: 1
Freedom Rating: 1.0
Freedom Status: Free
Electoral Democracy: Yes

Overview: Norway is one of the most robust democracies in the world. Elections are free and fair, and power regularly rotates between parties. Civil liberties are respected, with independent media and civil society actors holding the government to account. Discrimination against Roma and other minorities remains a problem.

KEY DEVELOPMENTS IN 2018:

- In June, the parliament adopted legislation that prohibited face-covering garments, such as the niqab and burqa, in classrooms at all levels of education.
- In March, parliament speaker Olemic Thommessen resigned due to a scandal over mismanagement of a public construction project. In a separate scandal in August, Per Sandberg resigned as fisheries minister after violating security rules during private travel to Iran.
- Allegations involving sexual harassment by key party officials across the political spectrum developed throughout the year, resulting in a number of sanctions and resignations.

POLITICAL RIGHTS: 40 / 40
A. ELECTORAL PROCESS: 12 / 12

A1. Was the current head of government or other chief national authority elected through free and fair elections? 4 / 4

The constitutional monarch, currently King Harald V, appoints the prime minister, who is the leader of the majority party or coalition in the parliament. While the monarch is officially the head of state and commander in chief of the armed forces, his duties are largely ceremonial. The prime minister as of 2018, Conservative Party leader Erna Solberg, first took office in 2013 and received a new mandate following her center-right coalition's victory in the 2017 general elections.

A2. Were the current national legislative representatives elected through free and fair elections? 4 / 4

Norway's unicameral parliament, the Storting, has 169 members who are directly elected for four-year terms through a system of proportional representation in multimember districts.

An election monitoring mission from the Organization for Security and Co-operation in Europe (OSCE) concluded that the 2017 elections were well conducted, offering notable praise for the country's early voting mechanisms. However, the mission found that visually impaired voters experience some difficulties. The opposition Labour Party led the voting with 49 seats, followed by the ruling Conservatives with 45 seats, the right-wing populist Progress Party with 27, the Centre Party with 19, the Socialist Left Party with 11, the Christian Democratic Party and the Liberal Party with 8 each, and the Green Party and Red Party with 1 each. The Conservatives renewed their governing coalition with the Progress Party, and the Liberal Party joined the bloc in early 2018, though it still fell short of an outright majority. Talks on adding the Christian Democrats were under way at year's end.

A3. Are the electoral laws and framework fair, and are they implemented impartially by the relevant election management bodies? 4 / 4

Elections are regulated by the constitution and the Representation of the People Act of 2002. The National Electoral Committee, whose members are appointed by the king from all parliamentary parties, oversees the conduct of elections with the support of local-level committees. The 2017 OSCE election monitoring mission noted a high degree of public confidence in the country's electoral infrastructure.

B. POLITICAL PLURALISM AND PARTICIPATION: 16 / 16

B1. Do the people have the right to organize in different political parties or other competitive political groupings of their choice, and is the system free of undue obstacles to the rise and fall of these competing parties or groupings? 4 / 4

A range of political parties operate freely in Norway.

B2. Is there a realistic opportunity for the opposition to increase its support or gain power through elections? 4 / 4

Norway has a long history of democratic and peaceful transfers of power after elections. The center-left Labour Party on the one hand and center-right coalitions led by the Conservatives or the Christian Democrats on the other have typically rotated in and out of government.

B3. Are the people's political choices free from domination by the military, foreign powers, religious hierarchies, economic oligarchies, or any other powerful group that is not democratically accountable? 4 / 4

Citizens are generally free from undue interference in their political choices, and no military, foreign, or religious entities exert undemocratic pressure on voters. Public funding is the main source of party revenue, though the 2017 OSCE election monitoring mission noted a sharp increase in private contributions and conveyed concerns that this could allow wealthy donors to acquire undue influence over Norwegian politics.

B4. Do various segments of the population (including ethnic, religious, gender, LGBT, and other relevant groups) have full political rights and electoral opportunities? 4 / 4

Women and minority groups enjoy full political rights and electoral opportunities. Women are well represented in Norwegian politics: The posts of prime minister, foreign minister, and finance minister, among others, were held by women in 2018, and more than 40 percent of parliament members are women. The interests of minorities and LGBT (lesbian, gay, bisexual, and transgender) people are addressed in part through robust antidiscrimination laws and various protections for same-sex couples.

The indigenous Sami population, in addition to participating in the national political process, has its own legislature, the Sameting, which has worked to protect the group's language and cultural rights and to influence the national government's decisions about Sami land and resources. The national government has a deputy minister tasked specifically with handling Sami issues.

C. FUNCTIONING OF GOVERNMENT: 12 / 12

C1. Do the freely elected head of government and national legislative representatives determine the policies of the government? 4 / 4

The freely elected government and parliament are able to develop and implement policy without undue influence from actors who are not democratically accountable.

C2. Are safeguards against official corruption strong and effective? 4 / 4

Provisions of the penal code criminalizing corrupt activity are generally upheld. Official corruption is not viewed as a significant problem in Norway.

C3. Does the government operate with openness and transparency? 4 / 4

The government generally operates with transparency. Several audits of public grants and other government spending were conducted in 2017, with auditors turning up some evidence of inadequate management. Olemic Thommessen was forced to resign as president of the Storting in March 2018 due to significant mismanagement of a public construction project overseen by his office. The Office of the State Auditor General found that the parliament had disregarded standard procurement rules and other safeguards for major building projects, leading costs to balloon from an initially budgeted 70 million kroner ($8.6 million) to more than 2.3 billion kroner ($282 million).

In August, Per Sandberg resigned as fisheries minister after violating security rules during a private trip to Iran with his Iranian-born girlfriend. He failed to give the government prior notice of the trip and brought his official mobile phone to the country.

The 2006 Freedom of Information Act provides for access to government documents, though it contains exemptions for some information pertaining to national security and foreign policy. Investigative journalists have in the past complained that senior government officials use various tactics to avoid or delay inquiries that would expose negligence or wrongdoing.

CIVIL LIBERTIES: 60 / 60
D. FREEDOM OF EXPRESSION AND BELIEF: 16 / 16
D1. Are there free and independent media? 4 / 4

Freedom of the press is constitutionally guaranteed and generally respected in practice. Norwegians have access to news and commentary from a wide variety of independent outlets. In recent years the courts have grappled with legal questions related to the protection of journalists' sources in criminal cases. In 2017, the European Court of Human Rights (ECHR) ruled that the Norwegian government could not compel journalists to reveal their sources, even if the source had come forward independently. The ECHR case was filed by a journalist who was fined in 2012 for defying a legal order to discuss contacts with a source of information about problems at the Norwegian Oil Company.

D2. Are individuals free to practice and express their religious faith or nonbelief in public and private? 4 / 4

Freedom of religion is protected by the constitution and generally upheld in practice. However, religiously motivated hate crimes have been on the rise in recent years. According to a police report issued in March 2018, the number of hate crimes linked to religion in Oslo increased by 80 percent to 43 in 2017, from 24 in 2016. Muslims were the targets in most of the incidents.

D3. Is there academic freedom, and is the educational system free from extensive political indoctrination? 4 / 4

Academic freedom is generally respected.

D4. Are individuals free to express their personal views on political or other sensitive topics without fear of surveillance or retribution? 4 / 4

Private discussion in Norway is free and vibrant.

E. ASSOCIATIONAL AND ORGANIZATIONAL RIGHTS: 12 / 12
E1. Is there freedom of assembly? 4 / 4

The right to freedom of assembly is respected in most cases. There have been tensions in recent years over demonstrations by extremist groups and their potential threat to public security, with some critics calling for far-right marches to be prohibited. In 2017, police blocked one far-right demonstration in order to prevent clashes with left-wing opponents, but later allowed another such event to proceed.

E2. Is there freedom for nongovernmental organizations, particularly those that are engaged in human rights- and governance-related work? 4 / 4

Norwegian nongovernmental organizations (NGOs) are able to form and operate without undue restrictions.

E3. Is there freedom for trade unions and similar professional or labor organizations? 4 / 4

The right to strike is legally guaranteed—except for members of the military and senior civil servants—and is generally respected in practice. All workers have the right to engage in collective bargaining.

F. RULE OF LAW: 16 / 16

F1. Is there an independent judiciary? 4 / 4

The judiciary is generally considered independent, and the court system, headed by the Supreme Court, operates fairly at the local and national levels. The king appoints judges on the advice of the Judicial Appointments Board, which is composed of legal and judicial professionals as well as representatives of the public.

F2. Does due process prevail in civil and criminal matters? 4 / 4

Law enforcement agencies and the courts generally observe legal safeguards against arbitrary arrest and detention. Criminal defendants have access to counsel at the government's expense, and the principles of due process are typically respected during trial.

F3. Is there protection from the illegitimate use of physical force and freedom from war and insurgencies? 4 / 4

The police are under civilian control, and physical abuse by law enforcement authorities is rare. Prison conditions generally meet international standards.

F4. Do laws, policies, and practices guarantee equal treatment of various segments of the population? 4 / 4

The equality and antidiscrimination ombudsman is responsible for enforcing the country's Gender Equality Act, the Antidiscrimination Act, and other laws designed to protect the basic rights of women, minorities, and other groups at risk of mistreatment. These laws are generally upheld in practice. With regard to the Sami, the national government supports Sami-language instruction and media outlets in the relevant regions.

However, the Council of Europe has encouraged Norwegian authorities to address widespread discriminatory attitudes toward Romany communities, and to ensure that Roma have equal access to education and employment. In September 2018, the European Court of Human Rights found that the Norwegian Child Welfare Service had violated the rights of a Romany woman by denying her contact with a daughter who was removed from her care in 2011.

While the number of people seeking refuge in Norway has declined dramatically since 2016, concerns about the refoulement of refugees have persisted, notably with regard to Afghan nationals. In November 2017, the parliament approved legislation that would allow asylum seekers who came to Norway as minors, but were due to be deported following their 18th birthdays, to file new asylum applications. Many of those affected by the law had fled to Norway from Afghanistan. They were given a May 2018 deadline to refile their asylum claims.

The #MeToo movement has drawn attention to the problem of workplace sexual harassment in Norway since 2017. In addition to reported cases in academia and the arts, political parties on both the left and the right were coping with multiple complaints against their members and officials during 2018.

G. PERSONAL AUTONOMY AND INDIVIDUAL RIGHTS: 16 / 16

G1. Do individuals enjoy freedom of movement, including the ability to change their place of residence, employment, or education? 4 / 4

Freedom of movement in Norway is generally respected. People have the ability to change their place of residence, employment, and education.

G2. Are individuals able to exercise the right to own property and establish private businesses without undue interference from state or nonstate actors? 4 / 4

The rights to own property and operate private businesses are established in Norwegian law and upheld in practice.

G3. Do individuals enjoy personal social freedoms, including choice of marriage partner and size of family, protection from domestic violence, and control over appearance? 4 / 4

The government generally does not restrict personal social freedoms. The Gender Equality Act provides equal rights for men and women with respect to marriage, divorce, and other personal status matters.

Domestic violence is a problem, though the government has worked to uphold criminal penalties for offenders and provide services to victims.

In June 2018, the parliament passed a government-proposed law that bans face coverings, including the niqab and burqa, from teaching environments at all levels of education, effectively placing limits on individuals' choice of dress and personal appearance. The ban, which took force in August, did not apply outside classroom settings, for instance during recess or staff meetings.

G4. Do individuals enjoy equality of opportunity and freedom from economic exploitation? 4 / 4

The principle of equality of opportunity and legal protections against economic exploitation are generally upheld. The government has been active in combating labor and sex trafficking and works to provide services to victims, though the US State Department has recommended that Norwegian authorities increase training and dedicate resources for police, prosecutors, and others responsible for handling trafficking cases.

Oman

Population: 4,700,000
Capital: Muscat
Political Rights Rating: 6
Civil Liberties Rating: 5
Freedom Rating: 5.5
Freedom Status: Not Free
Electoral Democracy: No

Overview: Oman is a hereditary monarchy, and power is concentrated in the hands of Sultan Qaboos bin Said al-Said, who has ruled since 1970. The regime restricts virtually all political rights and civil liberties, imposing criminal penalties for criticism and dissent.

KEY DEVELOPMENTS IN 2018:

- In January, the government issued a new penal code that included tighter restrictions and harsher punishments affecting freedom of assembly, freedom of association, and other basic rights.
- Abdullah Habib, a well-known writer and activist who had been sentenced to prison in 2016 for a series of Facebook posts addressing political and human rights issues, was pardoned and released in June, but a number of other dissidents faced jail terms or arbitrary detentions during the year.

POLITICAL RIGHTS: 6 / 40

A. ELECTORAL PROCESS: 2 / 12

A1. Was the current head of government or other chief national authority elected through free and fair elections? 0 / 4

Sultan Qaboos bin Said has ruled Oman since seizing power from his father, Sultan Said bin Taimur, in 1970. The sultan, who issues laws by decree, also serves as prime minister; heads the ministries of defense, foreign affairs, and finance; and is the governor of Oman's central bank. Despite his age and uncertain health, plans for a successor to Sultan Qaboos and the transfer of political power in Oman remain secret.

A2. Were the current national legislative representatives elected through free and fair elections? 1 / 4

The 1996 basic law, promulgated by decree, created a bicameral body consisting of an appointed Council of State (Majlis al-Dawla) and a wholly elected Consultative Council (Majlis al-Shura). Citizens elect the Consultative Council for four-year terms, but the chamber has no legislative powers and can only recommend changes to new laws.

Consultative Council elections were held in October 2015, with 590 nonpartisan candidates competing for the council's 85 seats. Voter turnout was 57 percent. In November 2015, the sultan appointed the 85 members of the Council of State for a new four-year term.

Oman held its first-ever municipal council elections in 2012. In the most recent elections in 2016, voters chose among 731 nonpartisan candidates to fill 202 seats on the 11 councils, which correspond to Oman's 11 governorates. Turnout was about 49 percent.

A3. Are the electoral laws and framework fair, and are they implemented impartially by the relevant election management bodies? 1 / 4

The electoral framework allows all citizens over the age of 21 to vote, unless they are in the military or security forces. However, it applies only to the Consultative Council and municipal councils, which serve largely as advisory bodies. Elections are administered by the Interior Ministry rather than an independent commission.

B. POLITICAL PLURALISM AND PARTICIPATION: 2 / 16

B1. Do the people have the right to organize in different political parties or other competitive political groupings of their choice, and is the system free of undue obstacles to the rise and fall of these competing parties or groupings? 0 / 4

Political parties are not permitted, and the authorities do not tolerate other forms of organized political opposition. A 2014 law allows the revocation of citizenship for Omanis who join organizations deemed harmful to national interests.

B2. Is there a realistic opportunity for the opposition to increase its support or gain power through elections? 0 / 4

The sultan maintains a monopoly on political power. The structure of the system excludes the possibility of a change in government through elections.

B3. Are the people's political choices free from domination by the military, foreign powers, religious hierarchies, economic oligarchies, or any other powerful group that is not democratically accountable? 1 / 4

The nonpartisan nature of Oman's limited elections, the overwhelming dominance of the sultan in Omani society, and the authorities' suppression of dissent leave voters and candidates with little autonomy in their political choices.

B4. Do various segments of the population (including ethnic, religious, gender, LGBT, and other relevant groups) have full political rights and electoral opportunities? 1 / 4

Noncitizens, who make up about 44 percent of the population, have no political rights or electoral opportunities. Citizenship is generally transmitted from Omani fathers. Foreign residents must live legally in the country for 20 years to qualify for citizenship, or 15 and 10 years for foreign husbands and wives of Omani citizens, respectively, if they have a son. These and other conditions make naturalizations relatively rare.

Omani women can legally vote and run for office, but they have few practical opportunities to organize independently and advance their interests in the political system. Just one woman was elected to the Consultative Council in 2015, and seven women won seats on municipal councils in 2016, up from four in 2012. Fourteen women serve on the appointed Council of State.

C. FUNCTIONING OF GOVERNMENT: 2 / 12

C1. Do the freely elected head of government and national legislative representatives determine the policies of the government? 0 / 4

Government policy is set by the sultan and an inner circle of advisers and senior ministers. The Council of State and the Consultative Council are advisory bodies with no lawmaking powers.

C2. Are safeguards against official corruption strong and effective? 2 / 4

Oman's legal code does not provide an effective framework for the prevention, exposure, and impartial prosecution of corruption. However, government officials are required to declare their assets and sources of wealth, and several high-profile corruption cases involving government officials and executives from Oman's oil industry have resulted in convictions and prison terms in recent years.

C3. Does the government operate with openness and transparency? 0 / 4

The law does not provide freedom of information guarantees. Openness and transparency are limited in practice by the concentration of power and authority in a small inner circle around the sultan. The State Audit Institution monitors ministerial spending, conflicts of interest, and state-owned companies, but its findings are not released to the public, and it does not cover the sultan's court or the military.

CIVIL LIBERTIES: 17 / 60
D. FREEDOM OF EXPRESSION AND BELIEF: 5 / 16
D1. Are there free and independent media? 1 / 4

Freedom of expression is limited, and criticism of the sultan is prohibited. There are private media outlets in addition to those run by the state, but they typically accept government subsidies, practice self-censorship, and face punishment if they cross political redlines. The government has broad authority to close outlets, block websites, revoke licenses, and prosecute journalists for content violations.

In 2017, the authorities blocked the website of the independent online magazine *Mowaten* after it relocated to Britain to avoid government harassment in Oman; it remained blocked in 2018. Also in 2017, the Supreme Court issued a final ruling that permanently closed the newspaper *Al-Zaman*, whose publication was suspended in 2016 following an article that examined allegations of corruption among senior officials and interference in the judiciary.

The government's efforts to suppress critical news and commentary extends to books and social media. In January 2018, former media presenter Khaled al-Rashdi was sentenced to one year in prison and a fine for criticizing state institutions on social media. Authorities confiscated a number of books at an international book fair sponsored by the Culture Ministry in February and March. Abdullah Habib, a well-known writer and activist who had been sentenced to three years in prison in 2016 for a series of Facebook posts addressing political and human rights issues, was pardoned and released in June. Among other cases during the year, internet activist Yousif Sultan al-Arimi was arrested in April in response to his social media commentary and released later that month, and two online writers—Sultan al-Maktoumi and Salem al-Arimi—were arbitrarily detained in October ahead of a visit by the Israeli prime minister.

D2. Are individuals free to practice and express their religious faith or nonbelief in public and private? 2 / 4

Islam is the state religion. Non-Muslims have the right to worship, but they are banned from proselytizing. Religious organizations must register with the government. The Ministry of Awqaf (religious charitable bequests) and Religious Affairs distributes standardized texts for mosque sermons, and imams are expected to stay within the outlines of these texts.

D3. Is there academic freedom, and is the educational system free from extensive political indoctrination? 1 / 4

The government restricts academic freedom by preventing the publication of material on politically sensitive topics and placing controls on contacts between Omani universities and foreign institutions.

D4. Are individuals free to express their personal views on political or other sensitive topics without fear of surveillance or retribution? 1 / 4

The authorities reportedly monitor personal communications, and the growing number of arrests, interrogations, and jail terms related to criticism of the government on social media has encouraged self-censorship among ordinary citizens in recent years. A new penal code issued by the government in January 2018 increased the maximum penalties for slander of the sultan and blasphemy to 7 and 10 years in prison, respectively, from three years for both under the old code.

E. ASSOCIATIONAL AND ORGANIZATIONAL RIGHTS: 3 / 12
E1. Is there freedom of assembly? 0 / 4

A limited right to peaceful assembly is provided for in Oman's basic law. However, all public gatherings require official permission, and the government has the authority to prevent organized public meetings without any appeals process. The 2018 penal code prescribes prison terms and fines for individuals who initiate or participate in a gathering of more than 10 people that threatens security or public order, or who fail to comply with an official order to disperse. A series of protests against unemployment were reported in January, leading to the arrest of at least some participants.

E2. Is there freedom for nongovernmental organizations, particularly those that are engaged in human rights- and governance-related work? 1 / 4

The basic law allows the formation of nongovernmental organizations, but civic life remains limited in practice. The government has not permitted the establishment of independent human rights organizations and generally uses the registration and licensing process to block the formation of groups it sees as a threat to stability. Individual activists focused on issues including labor rights and internet freedom continued to risk arrest during 2018. The 2018 penal code includes vague clauses that allow prison terms for individuals who establish, operate, or finance an organization aimed at challenging the "political, economic, social, or security principles of the state" or promoting class conflict.

E3. Is there freedom for trade unions and similar professional or labor organizations? 2 / 4

Omani workers are legally able to organize unions, bargain collectively, and strike. However, there is only one authorized trade union federation, and neither government employees nor household workers are permitted to join unions. Strikes, which are banned in the oil and gas industry, are rare in practice, partly because disputes are often resolved through employer concessions or government mediation.

F. RULE OF LAW: 4 / 16
F1. Is there an independent judiciary? 0 / 4

The judiciary is not independent and remains subordinate to the sultan, who is empowered to appoint and remove senior judges. The sultan also chairs the Supreme Judicial Council, which nominates judges and oversees the judicial system, though a 2012 reform replaced the justice minister with the head of the Supreme Court as the council's deputy chair.

F2. Does due process prevail in civil and criminal matters? 1 / 4

Arbitrary arrest is formally prohibited, but suspects in vaguely defined security cases can be held for up to 30 days before being charged, and security forces do not always adhere to other rules on arrest and pretrial detention. Ordinary detainees are generally provided with access to legal representation.

Defendants in politically sensitive cases may face harsher treatment from the justice system. For example, prior to his trial in 2017, Mansour bin Nasser al-Mahrazi, a writer and researcher who was eventually sentenced to three years in prison for offenses including "insulting the sultan," spent at least two months in incommunicado detention, and the judge refused to hear defense witnesses.

F3. Is there protection from the illegitimate use of physical force and freedom from war and insurgencies? 2 / 4

Prisons are not accessible in practice to independent monitors, but former detainees have reported beatings and other abuse. Online activist Hassan al-Basham, who had been sentenced to three years in prison in 2016 for allegedly using the internet in ways that could be "prejudicial to religious values," died in custody in April 2018 after reportedly being denied medical care.

The country is generally free from armed conflict, and violent street crime is relatively rare.

F4. Do laws, policies, and practices guarantee equal treatment of various segments of the population? 1 / 4

The 1996 basic law banned discrimination on the basis of sex, religion, ethnicity, and social class, but noncitizens are not protected from discrimination in practice, while women face disparate treatment under personal status laws and de facto bias in employment and other matters. Same-sex sexual activity is punishable with up to three years in prison, and LGBT (lesbian, gay, bisexual, and transgender) people face societal discrimination.

There were reports during 2018 of arbitrary detentions targeting people from the Al-Shuhuh tribe, who are culturally distinct from most Omanis and form a majority in the exclave of Musandam on the Strait of Hormuz.

G. PERSONAL AUTONOMY AND INDIVIDUAL RIGHTS: 5 / 16

G1. Do individuals enjoy freedom of movement, including the ability to change their place of residence, employment, or education? 1 / 4

Most Omani citizens enjoy freedom of movement, but travel bans are often imposed on political dissidents. Foreign workers cannot leave the country without permission from their employer and risk deportation if they change employers without documentation releasing them from their previous contract.

G2. Are individuals able to exercise the right to own property and establish private businesses without undue interference from state or nonstate actors? 2 / 4

While the legal framework protects property rights, state-owned companies and the ruling family are dominant forces in the economy, limiting the role and autonomy of small and other private businesses. Women generally receive less property than men under inheritance laws.

G3. Do individuals enjoy personal social freedoms, including choice of marriage partner and size of family, protection from domestic violence, and control over appearance? 1 / 4

Omani citizens require permission from the Ministry of Interior to marry noncitizens from countries outside the Gulf Cooperation Council. Omani women who marry foreigners cannot transmit citizenship to their spouses or children. Omani law does not specifically address domestic violence and sexual harassment or criminalize spousal rape, while extramarital sex is criminalized. Women are at disadvantage under laws governing matters such as divorce and child custody. The 2018 penal code included a new provision that criminalized the wearing of women's clothing by men.

G4. Do individuals enjoy equality of opportunity and freedom from economic exploitation? 1 / 4

Oman's labor policies put migrant workers at a severe disadvantage and effectively encourage exploitation. Household workers, who are not covered by the labor law, are especially at risk of abuse by employers. The government has pursued an "Omanization" process to replace foreign workers with native Omanis. Among other tactics, temporary visa bans for foreign workers in various professions have been issued or extended since 2013. Despite a 2008 antitrafficking law and some recent efforts to step up enforcement, the authorities do not proactively identify or protect human trafficking victims.

Pakistan

Population: 200,600,000
Capital: Islamabad
Political Rights Rating: 5 ↓
Civil Liberties Rating: 5
Freedom Rating: 5.0
Freedom Status: Partly Free
Electoral Democracy: No

Note: The numerical ratings and status listed above do not reflect conditions in Pakistani-controlled Kashmir, which is examined in a separate report.

Overview: Pakistan holds regular elections under a competitive multiparty political system. However, the military exerts enormous influence over security and other policy issues, intimidates the media, and enjoys impunity for indiscriminate or extralegal use of force. The authorities impose selective restrictions on civil liberties, and Islamist militants carry out attacks on religious minorities and other perceived opponents.

KEY DEVELOPMENTS IN 2018:

- Imran Khan's Pakistan Tehreek-e-Insaf (PTI) emerged as the largest party in July's general elections, and Khan went on to become prime minister in August. The elections took place following serious manipulation of the campaign environment by elements of the military and judicial establishment that aimed to hamper the incumbent Pakistan Muslim League–Nawaz (PML-N) and increase Khan's chances of attaining a parliamentary majority.
- The preelection period was marked by corruption and other legal cases targeting the PML-N and its leader, former prime minister Nawaz Sharif, who had been banned from holding political office and was jailed at the time the polls took place. Pressure on and interference with the media also resulted in muted coverage of the PML-N's campaign.
- The media environment in general deteriorated during the year. Broadcasts by Geo TV and distribution of the newspaper *Dawn* were temporarily blocked in large parts of the country in the spring, apparently at the behest of the security services. Journalists reported an intimidation campaign by men who credibly presented themselves as security agents and sought to suppress or direct news coverage.
- State agencies mounted a sustained campaign to restrict the peaceful activities of the newly emerged Pashtun Tahafuz Movement (PTM), which campaigned against violence by both the state and Islamist militants in ethnic Pashtun areas.

POLITICAL RIGHTS: 17 / 40 (−2)

A. ELECTORAL PROCESS: 5 / 12 (−1)

A1. Was the current head of government or other chief national authority elected through free and fair elections? 1 / 4 (−1)

A prime minister responsible to the bicameral parliament holds most executive power under the constitution. The president, who plays a more symbolic role, is elected for up to two five-year terms by an electoral college comprising the two chambers of parliament and the provincial assemblies. PTI-nominated candidate Arif Alvi was elected president in September 2018 by the electoral college, which had been newly constituted after the general elections in July.

Imran Khan became prime minister in August 2018 after the PTI emerged from the general elections as the largest party. In the run-up to the polls, observers documented concerted efforts by elements of the country's military and judicial establishment to hamper the PML-N in order to increase the chances that Khan would attain a parliamentary majority. These included corruption, contempt-of-court, and terrorism charges against PML-N leaders and candidates, and their apparently politicized adjudication. PML-N leader Sharif, Khan's principal rival, had been forced to step down as prime minister as a result of a 2017 Supreme Court ruling that his failure to disclose certain assets left him in violation of a vague constitutional clause requiring parliament members to be "honest." Critics of the ruling noted that the court had accepted, without a trial, the findings of an ad hoc investigative panel that included military members, and many observers tied Sharif's ouster to his long-standing rivalry with the military over control of foreign policy and national security matters. Sharif was permanently banned from politics in April 2018, prosecuted on corruption charges and found guilty in July, and jailed for two months before his sentence was suspended. His ouster from the country's political arena left the PML-N with severely weakened leadership in the run-up to the 2018 polls.

Observers also noted pressure on and interference with the media, apparently at the behest of the security services, that resulted in muted coverage of the PML-N's campaign.

Score Change: The score declined from 2 to 1 due to apparent efforts by the military and judicial establishment to shape the outcome of the 2018 elections and ensure the installation of Imran Khan as the new prime minister.

A2. Were the current national legislative representatives elected through free and fair elections? 2 / 4

The parliament consists of a 342-member National Assembly and a 104-member Senate. Members of the National Assembly are elected for five years. Of the 342 seats, 272 are filled through direct elections in single-member districts, 60 are reserved for women, and 10 are reserved for non-Muslim minorities. The reserved seats are filled through a proportional representation system with closed party lists.

In the Senate, each provincial assembly chooses 23 members, National Assembly members representing the former Federally Administered Tribal Areas (FATA) elected 8, and 4 are chosen by the National Assembly to represent the Islamabad capital territory. Senators serve six-year terms, with half of the seats up for election every three years. The most recent Senate elections were held in March 2018—before the final adoption in May of a constitutional amendment providing for the FATA's absorption into Khyber Pakhtunkhwa (PKP) province.

International and domestic election observers, including the European Union Election Observation Mission, delivered a mixed verdict on the July 2018 National Assembly elections. Polling was orderly and generally took place according to the electoral law, though serious technical difficulties with the Result Transmission System resulted in delays in results reporting.

At the same time, the rush of judicial actions against PML-N leaders and restrictions on and interference with media coverage significantly disadvantaged the party, contributing to a spectacular rise in PTI representation in the National Assembly. The PTI received 32 percent of the vote and 149 seats, compared with just 35 seats previously. The PML-N received 24 percent of the vote and 82 seats, down from 157 seats previously. The Pakistan People's Party (PPP) received 13 percent of the vote and 54 seats, an increase of 12 from its previous representation. Another notable feature of the elections was the participation of parties and candidates linked to active Islamist militant groups. These included Tehreek-e-Labaik Pakistan (TLP) and Allah-o-Akbar Tehreek (AAT). The PTI formed a coalition government at the national level, with the support of the Muttahida Qaumi Movement (MQM), other minor parties, and independents. Voter turnout was 52 percent.

Provincial assembly elections were held concurrently with the 2018 National Assembly elections. In Punjab, the PML-N took the largest number of seats, but it fell short of a majority, and the PTI succeeded in forming a coalition government. The largest party in Baluchistan, the Baluchistan Awami Party, entered a coalition with the PTI in that province. The PPP again formed the provincial government in Sindh, as did the PTI in KPK. In keeping with the constitutional amendment providing for the FATA's absorption into KPK, elections to fill KPK provincial assembly seats for new constituencies in the former FATA were scheduled for 2019.

A3. Are the electoral laws and framework fair, and are they implemented impartially by the relevant election management bodies? 2 / 4

Elections are administered by the Election Commission of Pakistan (ECP), whose members are current or retired senior judges nominated through a consultative process that includes the government and the parliamentary opposition. The electoral laws are largely fair and impartially implemented, and candidates have extensive access to the courts in electoral disputes.

The 2018 election observer missions acknowledged that the formal electoral framework and its implementation complied with international standards. However, the ECP proved unable to counteract efforts by elements of the judicial and military establishment and their allies to manipulate the campaign environment. According to the Human Rights Commission of Pakistan, politically orchestrated judicial activism resulted in the disqualification of candidates, while the "censorship, intimidation, harassment, and abduction" of journalists who were critical of the security establishment or favored the PML-N or PPP ensured uneven access to the media.

Other, ongoing problems include lower rates of voter registration among women, a requirement that members of the Ahmadi religious minority register as non-Muslims despite considering themselves Muslims, and vague moral requirements for candidate nomination.

B. POLITICAL PLURALISM AND PARTICIPATION: 7 / 16 (−1)

B1. Do the people have the right to organize in different political parties or other competitive political groupings of their choice, and is the system free of undue obstacles to the rise and fall of these competing parties or groupings? 2 / 4 (−1)

Pakistan has had a thriving and competitive multiparty system. Several major parties and numerous smaller parties and independents are represented in the parliament and provincial legislatures. However, established parties maintain patronage networks and other advantages of incumbency that hamper competition in their respective provincial strongholds, and a party's electoral success is also influenced by the strength of its relationship with unelected arms of the state.

In 2018, preelection interference by the military and judicial establishment disrupted the operations of the PML-N. Such activity included politicized prosecutions and detentions of party leaders and candidates, as well as efforts to intimidate PML-N candidates into defecting to other parties or running as independents. The PML-N also accused members of the security forces of harassing, attacking, or detaining hundreds of its supporters.

Meanwhile, the MQM was greatly reduced as an electoral force in Karachi by a series of splits and defections, most of which seemed to have been similarly orchestrated by the security forces. The entry into electoral politics of the militant-linked Islamist parties TLP and AAT was interpreted as a military-endorsed move to erode support for the PML-N in Punjab.

Score Change: The score declined from 3 to 2 due to selective military and judicial pressure on the PML-N ahead of the elections, including the intimidation and prosecution of its candidates.

B2. Is there a realistic opportunity for the opposition to increase its support or gain power through elections? 3 / 4

Opposition parties are free to campaign and contest elections, and each of the last three national elections has resulted in an erstwhile opposition party taking power at the federal level. Opposition forces continue to hold power or significant shares of assembly seats at the provincial level. Most recent complaints of political repression have concerned alleged attempts by the military and reputedly allied groups like the PTI to weaken other parties.

B3. Are the people's political choices free from domination by the military, foreign powers, religious hierarchies, economic oligarchies, or any other powerful group that is not democratically accountable? 1 / 4

The manipulation of politics by religious extremists and the powerful military limits voters' ability to freely express their political preferences.

In 2018, the heavy presence of security agents at many polling stations was interpreted by observers including the Human Rights Commission of Pakistan as tantamount to voter intimidation. A number of candidates in the 2018 election campaign had links with extremist groups that had advocated or carried out acts of violence, further contributing to a sense of unease among many voters.

B4. Do various segments of the population (including ethnic, religious, gender, LGBT, and other relevant groups) have full political rights and electoral opportunities? 1 / 4

A joint electorate system allows members of non-Muslim minorities to participate in the general vote while also being represented by reserved seats in the national and provincial assemblies through the party-list system. However, the participation of non-Muslims in the political system continues to be marginal. Political parties nominate members to the legislative seats reserved for non-Muslim minorities, leaving non-Muslim voters with little say in the selection of their supposed representatives. Ahmadis, members of a heterodox Muslim sect, face political discrimination and are registered on a separate voter roll.

Political parties maintain women's wings that are active during elections, but women face practical restrictions on voting, especially in KPK and Baluchistan, where militant groups and traditional societal constraints are more prevalent. Women rarely achieve leadership positions in parties or the government. The interests of LGBT (lesbian, gay, bisexual, and transgender) people are generally not represented by elected officials.

C. FUNCTIONING OF GOVERNMENT: 5 / 12
C1. Do the freely elected head of government and national legislative representatives determine the policies of the government? 1 / 4

Formally, the elected prime minister and cabinet make policy in consultation with the parliament, which holds full legislative powers. However, there has been a long-running struggle between these civilian structures and the military establishment for control of national security policy. The military has asserted primacy on relations with India, Afghanistan, China, and the United States, as well as on counterterrorism policy within Pakistan. In the last two years of the PML-N government, it appeared that the civilian administration aspired to act independently of some military priorities, most notably through exploring détente with India. In May 2018, Sharif provoked a sharp reaction from the military when he suggested that anti-India militant groups were present in Pakistan and had effectively been permitted to cross the border to carry out a devastating 2008 terrorist attack in Mumbai. After the installation of the PTI government in August, the civilian administration seemed to align itself more closely with the priorities set by the military.

C2. Are safeguards against official corruption strong and effective? 1 / 4

There are numerous formal safeguards against official corruption, including a dedicated agency, the National Accountability Bureau (NAB). The military and judiciary have their own disciplinary systems. However, corruption is believed to remain endemic in practice, and the use of accountability mechanisms is often selective and politically driven.

Senior figures in the PML-N and PPP faced corruption investigations and prosecutions in 2018, and these played a key role in the transition to a PTI government. Former prime minister Sharif and his daughter were convicted in July for holding assets beyond their means; they were jailed and banned from politics, but subsequently released in September after the suspension of their sentences. Sharif's younger brother Shahbaz Sharif—the opposition leader in parliament and a former Punjab chief minister—was arrested in October for alleged corruption in a housing scheme, although this did not prevent him from being elected chair of the National Assembly's Public Accounts Committee in December. In addition, a travel ban was imposed on former president Asif Ali Zardari of the PPP in December, amid investigations into alleged corruption. A number of other senior figures in the PML-N and the PPP were charged with corruption during the year.

C3. Does the government operate with openness and transparency? 3 / 4

Accessing official information remains difficult, and existing provisions for obtaining public records are ineffective. At the federal level, a 2002 ordinance on access to information remains in force and is widely considered to be weaker than current international standards.

Think tanks, civil society organizations, and universities all contribute to lively debate on many aspects of public policy. However, debate on certain aspects of national security policy, such as the insurgency in Baluchistan, disappearances, and the military's alleged support for militant groups targeting Afghanistan and Indian-controlled Kashmir, has in effect remained taboo.

CIVIL LIBERTIES: 22 / 60 (−2)
D. FREEDOM OF EXPRESSION AND BELIEF: 6 / 16 (−1)
D1. Are there free and independent media? 1 / 4 (−1)

Pakistan has a relatively vibrant media sector that presents a range of news and opinions, but state agencies and the military seek to control media activity through legal and extralegal means. While coverage of corruption scandals and other politically sensitive topics was notably tolerated in 2017, there was a clampdown on coverage in 2018 as authorities sought to tighten their grip on the operations of investigative outlets. In March and April, Geo TV was blocked across much of the country; after the government asserted that it was not responsible for the ban, some observers suggested that the block had come at the behest of figures in the military. Authorities also targeted the newspaper *Dawn* in May after it published an interview with Nawaz Sharif; security agencies blocked the paper's distribution in some 20 cantonment areas. In September, the Lahore High Court placed *Dawn* journalist Cyril Almeida on the Exit Control List (ECL) and issued a warrant for his arrest in connection with a May interview he conducted with Sharif, though in October the court ordered his name removed from the ECL and the warrant withdrawn. Multiple media-related figures have reported a system of "press advice," whereby men claiming credibly to be from security agencies contact them to warn them against covering taboo subjects such as the PTM, or to dictate coverage on political issues; these figures have warned of consequences for defying the advice.

Access to certain areas is prohibited by the military, impeding coverage of issues there. In Baluchistan, local journalists are often caught between authorities who order them not to cover separatist rebel activity and rebel groups that threaten them for siding with the government.

Twenty-two journalists have been murdered in Pakistan over the last 10 years, according to the Committee to Protect Journalists, which noted in October 2018 that a recent decline in fatal violence against journalists "masks [a] decline in press freedom" characterized by the military's pervasive intimidation of journalists. The perpetrators of violence against the media typically enjoy impunity.

Score Change: The score declined from 2 to 1 due to authorities' increased interference with the media during the year, including reports of guidance on coverage and obstruction of certain outlets' distribution networks.

D2. Are individuals free to practice and express their religious faith or nonbelief in public and private? 1 / 4

Constitutional guarantees of religious freedom have not provided effective safeguards against discriminatory legislation, social prejudice, and sectarian violence. Hindus have complained of vulnerability to kidnapping and forced conversions, and some continue to migrate to India. Members of the Christian minority and others remain at risk of blasphemy accusations that can arise from trivial disputes and escalate to criminal prosecution and mob violence. This was illustrated by the latest development in the case of Aasia Bibi, a Christian woman sentenced to death for allegedly insulting the prophet Muhammad. In October 2018, after she had spent eight years on death row, the Supreme Court acquitted her. But in the wake of mass protests by Islamist activists, the government agreed to seek a review of the decision and to block her from leaving the country. At year's end, she remained in protective custody.

The most specific discriminatory legislation has been directed at members of the Ahmadi community, who are prohibited from calling themselves Muslims. The practical effects of this were exacerbated in March 2018, when the Islamabad High Court ruled that a declaration of religious faith was mandatory for those applying for government jobs, including positions in the armed forces, the judiciary, and the civil service, and in order to access key documents including passports. The same court in July ruled that citizens have a right to know the religion of key officials. The most prominent case of anti-Ahmadi discrimination in 2018 occurred when Prime Minister Khan appointed Atif Mian, an Ahmadi, as a member of the Economic Advisory Council in September. Following pressure from Islamist groups against the appointment of an Ahmadi to such a prestigious position, the government asked Mian to withdraw from the council.

D3. Is there academic freedom, and is the educational system free from extensive political indoctrination? 2 / 4

Pakistani authorities have a long history of using the education system to portray Hindus and other non-Muslims negatively and to rationalize enmity between Pakistan and India, among other ideological aims. Past attempts to modernize education and introduce tolerance into school textbooks have made little progress. Some space has opened for scholars to discuss sensitive issues involving the military in recent years.

D4. Are individuals free to express their personal views on political or other sensitive topics without fear of surveillance or retribution? 2 / 4

Pakistanis are free in practice to discuss many topics both online and off, but the 2016 Prevention of Electronic Crimes Act (PECB) gives the executive-controlled Pakistan Telecommunication Authority (PTA) unchecked powers to censor material on the internet, and law enforcement agencies have cracked down on allegedly blasphemous content in particular. In recent years, evidence has emerged of widespread state surveillance of social media and internet activity. In 2017, a Shiite man convicted of blasphemy became the first person to receive a death sentence for a social media posting. That same year, a Christian man was similarly sentenced to death for sharing allegedly blasphemous material on the messaging application WhatsApp.

Extralegal violence also serves as a deterrent to unfettered speech. In 2017, five bloggers who had criticized Islamist militant groups and the military were forcibly disappeared, allegedly by military intelligence personnel; all five had been released by March 2018. Also in 2017, a student at a university in KPK was shot and beaten to death by a mob after being accused of blasphemy.

E. ASSOCIATIONAL AND ORGANIZATIONAL RIGHTS: 6 / 12

E1. Is there freedom of assembly? 3 / 4

The constitution guarantees the right to assemble peacefully, though the government can harness legal provisions to arbitrarily ban gatherings or any activity designated a threat to public order. In 2018, the authorities arbitrarily and systematically prevented PTM supporters from holding rallies to protest the killing by police of a Karachi-based aspiring fashion model, Naqibullah Mehsud, in January. The authorities tried to block rallies in Lahore in April and in Karachi in May through mass arrests, by preventing PTM leaders from flying, and by restricting media coverage of the movement. In May, the Human Rights Commission of Pakistan expressed concern over reports that more than 150 PTM activists had been detained or disappeared in the run-up to the Karachi rally. Later, 19 leaders of the movement were named in a police complaint regarding antistate activities, in connection with their participation in a demonstration in Swabi in August, and at least one of them was put on the ECL. In contrast, when Islamist groups held violent demonstrations in Islamabad to protest the acquittal of Aasia Bibi, the authorities eventually dropped proceedings against those accused of participating in the violence, prompting widespread criticism.

E2. Is there freedom for nongovernmental organizations, particularly those that are engaged in human rights- and governance-related work? 1 / 4

The government has continued a crackdown on nongovernmental organizations (NGOs), enforcing rigid regulations and subjecting organizations to intrusive vetting by military intelligence. Officials can demand that civil society organizations obtain a "no-objection certificate" (NOC) before undertaking even the most innocuous activity. As part of the process of implementing its new centralized registration procedures for international

NGOs, the authorities in late 2017 refused applications from 18 such groups, including the well-known South Africa–based ActionAid, and demanded that they close down; in December 2018, the deadline expired for the groups to end their operations. The European Union and key democracies including Canada and Australia issued a joint statement to express concern about the NGOs' closure "without clear justification," while foreign diplomats claimed that 11 million Pakistanis would be affected by loss of access to services provided by the departing organizations.

E3. Is there freedom for trade unions and similar professional or labor organizations? 2 / 4

The rights of workers to organize and form trade unions are recognized in law, and the constitution grants unions the rights to collective bargaining and to strike. However, many categories of workers are excluded from these protections, which are not strongly enforced. Roughly 70 percent of the workforce is employed in the informal sector, where unionization and legal protections are minimal. The procedures that need to be followed for a strike to be legal are onerous. Strikes and labor protests are organized regularly, though they often lead to clashes with police and dismissals by employers.

F. RULE OF LAW: 4 / 16 (−1)

F1. Is there an independent judiciary? 1 / 4 (−1)

The judiciary is politicized and frequently issues rulings that are seen as aligned with the priorities of the military. During 2018, the judiciary was involved in multiple cases and judgments against former prime minister Sharif, his family, and his close political allies, in what amounted to a campaign of judicial activism to drive the PML-N from power. In one episode during the series of anti-Sharif cases, an Islamabad High Court judge was fired over his criticism of the Inter-Services Intelligence Directorate (ISI), Pakistan's top spy agency. The judge, in a July speech, had accused the ISI of issuing directives to the judiciary on their dealings with Sharif. The ISI in response lodged a complaint with the Supreme Judicial Council, which recommended the judge's removal. He was ultimately fired by President Alvi in October, marking only the second time in the nation's history that the Supreme Judicial Council had taken such action against a judge. Separately, the chief justice of the Supreme Court faced criticism in 2018 for drawing attention to economic issues and infrastructure projects in a manner viewed as damaging to the PML-N.

The broader court system is marred by endemic problems including corruption, intimidation, insecurity, a large backlog of cases, and low conviction rates for serious crimes.

Score Change: The score declined from 2 to 1 due to a lack of impartiality in the judiciary's handling of politically fraught cases against former prime minister Nawaz Sharif and his associates.

F2. Does due process prevail in civil and criminal matters? 1 / 4

Police have long been accused of biased or arbitrary handling of initial criminal complaints, and both the police and the prosecution service have been criticized for a chronic failure to prosecute terrorism cases. The government responded in 2015 by allowing for some civilians to be tried in military courts, despite concerns that they lack transparency and due process guarantees, such as access to a competent defense. In December 2018, the army stated that the military courts had ruled on 546 terrorism cases since 2015, and had issued 310 death sentences. At the end of the month, the government decided to extend the courts' operation for another two years, though passing the necessary legislation would require opposition support in the National Assembly.

The FATA were considered outside the jurisdiction of the Supreme Court and subject to the colonial-era Frontier Crimes Regulation (FCR) instead of the criminal code, effectively exempting them from most due process guarantees. However, the outgoing PML-N administration pushed through a constitutional amendment providing for the FATA's absorption into KPK, which was signed by the president in May 2018 and was viewed as a major step forward for the legal rights of FATA residents. The FCR was repealed as part of the change, but it was replaced by the FATA Interim Governance Regulation, which preserved a number of problematic FATA institutions. The Peshawar High Court ruled the interim regulation unconstitutional in October, and an appeal was pending at year's end.

F3. Is there protection from the illegitimate use of physical force and freedom from war and insurgencies? 1 / 4

A multiyear decline in terrorist violence continued in 2018, with a total of 697 people killed in terrorist incidents during the year, compared with 1,260 in 2017 and a peak of over 11,700 in 2009. The reduction is due in large part to the military's suppression of an Islamist insurgency in KPK and the former FATA, and the pacification of unrest in Karachi. Nevertheless, terrorist attacks continue. In July 2018 alone, 230 people were reported to have been killed in terrorist strikes, including a suicide attack on an election rally in Mastung District that killed 128 and another in Peshawar that killed senior Awami National Party leader Haroon Bilour and some 20 supporters. A separatist insurgency continued in Baluchistan, and Islamist militants were still able to stage high-profile attacks elsewhere in the country.

The military denies long-standing allegations that it supports militant groups targeting Afghanistan and Indian-controlled Kashmir. Seven people charged in connection with the devastating 2008 terrorist attack in Mumbai remained on trial in a Rawalpindi court during 2018, but the proceedings had been stalled for years, and little progress was reported.

Civilians also face the threat of extralegal violence by state actors, including enforced disappearances. The number of pending cases of people registered as missing by an official commission of inquiry on enforced disappearances, led by a retired judge, rose to 2,116 by the end of November. However, there was no sign of the commission's deliberations leading to any effective sanctions against the agencies undertaking the disappearances. Most victims were from KPK, the former FATA, or Baluchistan, and typically had been held incommunicado by security and intelligence agencies on suspicion of terrorism, rebellion, or espionage. Although the commission tracks cases, it has refrained from attributing responsibility.

F4. Do laws, policies, and practices guarantee equal treatment of various segments of the population? 1 / 4

Women face discrimination in employment despite legal protections, and they are placed at a disadvantage under personal status laws. Women are also subject to a number of harmful traditional practices and societal abuses, the perpetrators of which often enjoy impunity.

Other segments of the population that suffer legal or de facto discrimination and violence include ethnic and religious minorities, Afghan refugees, and LGBT people. The penal code prescribes prison terms for consensual sex "against the order of nature," deterring LGBT people from acknowledging their identity or reporting abuses. Members of the transgender and intersex community are authorized to register for official documents under a "third gender" classification recognized by the Supreme Court since 2009, and some transgender people were recognized in the 2017 census. However, transgender and intersex people continue to face targeted violence as well as discrimination in housing and employment.

G. PERSONAL AUTONOMY AND INDIVIDUAL RIGHTS: 6 / 16

G1. Do individuals enjoy freedom of movement, including the ability to change their place of residence, employment, or education? 2 / 4

There are some legal limitations on travel and the ability to change one's residence, employment, or institution of higher learning. The authorities routinely hinder internal movement in some parts of the country for security reasons. The main tool for restricting foreign travel is the ECL, which blocks named individuals from using official exit points from the country. It is meant to include those who pose a security threat and those facing court proceedings, though periodically it has been used as a means of controlling dissent.

G2. Are individuals able to exercise the right to own property and establish private businesses without undue interference from state or non-state actors? 2 / 4

In principle, Pakistan's constitution, legal system, and social and religious values all guarantee private property and free enterprise. In reality, however, organized crime, corruption, a weak regulatory environment, and the subversion of the legal system often render property rights precarious. Powerful and organized groups continue to engage in land grabbing, particularly in Karachi and Punjab.

Inheritance laws discriminate against women, and women are often denied their legal share of inherited property through social or familial pressure.

G3. Do individuals enjoy personal social freedoms, including choice of marriage partner and size of family, protection from domestic violence, and control over appearance? 1 / 4

In some parts of urban Pakistan, men and women enjoy personal social freedoms and have recourse to the law in case of infringements. However, traditional practices in much of the country subject individuals to social control over personal behavior and especially choice of marriage partner. "Honor killing," the murder of men or women accused of breaking social and especially sexual taboos, remains common. Most incidents go unreported. Successive attempts to abolish the practice, most recently in a 2016 law, have not been fully implemented.

G4. Do individuals enjoy equality of opportunity and freedom from economic exploitation? 1 / 4

Extreme forms of labor exploitation remain common. Bonded labor was formally abolished in 1992, and there have been long-standing efforts to enforce the ban and related laws against child labor. Gradual social change has also eroded the power of wealthy landowning families involved in such exploitation. Nevertheless, employers continue to use chronic indebtedness to restrict laborers' rights and hold actual earnings well below prescribed levels, particularly among sharecroppers and in the brick-kiln industry.

Palau

Population: 20,000
Capital: Ngerulmud
Political Rights Rating: 1
Civil Liberties Rating: 1
Freedom Rating: 1.0
Freedom Status: Free
Electoral Democracy: Yes

Overview: Palau's presidential system of government is maintained through regular democratic elections. The judiciary and the media are independent, and civil liberties are generally upheld. A Compact of Free Association with the United States provides defense guarantees and financial assistance. The government has sought to combat official corruption in recent years. Many in the country's large population of foreign workers remain vulnerable to exploitation.

KEY DEVELOPMENTS IN 2018:

- In October, the European Union (EU) said that Palau authorities had pledged to implement certain reforms, and that it had consequently removed the country from its list of tax havens.
- The administration of President Tommy Remengesau freely governed and implemented policy during the year, including several measures prioritizing environmental protection.

POLITICAL RIGHTS: 37 / 40

A. ELECTORAL PROCESS: 12 / 12

A1. Was the current head of government or other chief national authority elected through free and fair elections? 4 / 4

The president, who serves as both head of state and head of government, is directly elected for up to two consecutive four-year terms using a two-round system, with a runoff vote if no candidate wins an absolute majority in the first round. President Tommy Remengesau won reelection in November 2016, defeating his brother-in-law, Senator Surangel Whipps, with 51.3 percent of the vote.

A2. Were the current national legislative representatives elected through free and fair elections? 4 / 4

The bicameral National Congress consists of a 13-member Senate and a 16-member House of Delegates. The Senate is directly elected by block vote in one national constituency. Members of the House of Delegates are elected from single-member constituencies corresponding to the country's 16 states, which vary in population. All members of the National Congress are elected for four-year terms. In the November 2016 elections, held concurrently with the presidential vote, 13 incumbents were returned to the House and 8 to the Senate.

A3. Are the electoral laws and framework fair, and are they implemented impartially by the relevant election management bodies? 4 / 4

Electoral administration is widely considered to be fair and impartial. A review of the Senate's size and electoral system is undertaken every eight years by a Reapportionment Commission. In June 2016 the commission recommended that the Senate be maintained in its current form. In response to a citizen petition, the Supreme Court initially ruled that because the population had decreased, the number of senators should be reduced from 13 to 11, but the court restored the original plan after an appeal in October of that year.

B. POLITICAL PLURALISM AND PARTICIPATION: 15 / 16

B1. Do the people have the right to organize in different political parties or other competitive political groupings of their choice, and is the system free of undue obstacles to the rise and fall of these competing parties or groupings? 4 / 4

There are no laws restricting the formation of political parties, but in practice all candidates run and compete freely as independents. Politicians tend to organize in loose political alliances, often based on clan or family relationships.

B2. Is there a realistic opportunity for the opposition to increase its support or gain power through elections? 4 / 4

Although there are no political parties, lawmakers do organize into informal progovernment and opposition camps, and no single political force has control of the legislature. Power is transferred democratically between rival politicians. Remengesau returned to the presidency in 2013 by defeating the incumbent, Johnson Toribiong, in the 2012 election.

B3. Are the people's political choices free from domination by the military, foreign powers, religious hierarchies, economic oligarchies, or any other powerful group that is not democratically accountable? 4 / 4

Palau receives financial assistance from the United States under its Compact of Free Association, but the US government does not exert improper influence over the country's internal politics. While the political views of traditional chiefs are respected, they do not have authoritative control over the choices of voters.

B4. Do various segments of the population (including ethnic, religious, gender, LGBT, and other relevant groups) have full political rights and electoral opportunities? 3 / 4

Women generally have equal political rights in law and in practice. Some legislative seats at the state level are reserved for traditionally male chiefs, though chiefs in turn are customarily chosen by councils of female elders. In the last national elections, women won two seats in the House and two in the Senate.

About a third of the population consists of foreign nationals who do not have political rights in Palau. Citizenship must be inherited from at least one parent, as there are no provisions for naturalization.

C. FUNCTIONING OF GOVERNMENT: 10 / 12

C1. Do the freely elected head of government and national legislative representatives determine the policies of the government? 4 / 4

Palau's democratically elected government determines and implements policy without undue interference. Several policies prioritizing environmental protection were implemented in 2018.

Traditional chiefs formally play an advisory role regarding customary matters through the national Council of Chiefs. While they also exercise informal influence over government policy, this is widely seen as a positive check on potential mismanagement or abuse of power by elected officials.

The Compact of Free Association with the United States, in effect since Palau became independent in 1994, ensures self-government in the country but also provides for close military and economic relations with the United States, including US responsibility for Palau's defense. A scheduled 15-year review of the compact resulted in a 2010 bilateral agreement on development aid and other benefits to last until the next review in 2024, but legislation to implement that agreement remained stalled in the US Congress for several years, during which time Congress continued to appropriate basic aid funds on an annual basis. At the end of 2017, US President Donald Trump signed a defense bill that included implementing provisions for the compact review agreement. The two countries are working on installing new radar systems in Palau.

C2. Are safeguards against official corruption strong and effective? 3 / 4

High-ranking public officials have faced corruption charges in recent years, and several have been convicted. The government and lawmakers have deliberated on strategies to deal with corruption more effectively, and in April 2017 the finance minister issued a statement to reiterate the government's ethics rules and a whistle-blower protection policy. The Office of the Ombudsman has asked for a clearer legal mandate with greater independence, as it currently operates as part of the president's office under an executive order.

In October 2018, the European Union (EU) said that Palau authorities had pledged to implement certain reforms, and that it had consequently removed the country from its list of tax havens.

C3. Does the government operate with openness and transparency? 3 / 4

A 2014 Open Government Act provides for public access to official documents and hearings, and government officials are obliged to submit annual financial disclosures that are available to the public. However, authorities have sometimes resisted disclosing requested information, particularly at the subnational level.

CIVIL LIBERTIES: 55 / 60
D. FREEDOM OF EXPRESSION AND BELIEF: 16 / 16
D1. Are there free and independent media? 4 / 4

Freedom of the press is respected. There are several independent news outlets, including newspapers and broadcasters, but they often struggle financially. Regional and international news services are also available. Internet access has been hampered by high costs and lack of connectivity outside the main islands.

D2. Are individuals free to practice and express their religious faith or nonbelief in public and private? 4 / 4

Constitutional guarantees of religious freedom are upheld in practice. Although religious organizations are required to register as nonprofit organizations, the process is not onerous or restrictive. Foreign missionaries are also required to obtain a permit.

D3. Is there academic freedom, and is the educational system free from extensive political indoctrination? 4 / 4

There have been no reports of restrictions on academic freedom.

D4. Are individuals free to express their personal views on political or other sensitive topics without fear of surveillance or retribution? 4 / 4

There are no constraints on political discussion, and the government does not monitor personal communications.

E. ASSOCIATIONAL AND ORGANIZATIONAL RIGHTS: 11 / 12
E1. Is there freedom of assembly? 4 / 4

Freedom of assembly is protected by the constitution and respected in practice.

E2. Is there freedom for nongovernmental organizations, particularly those that are engaged in human rights- and governance-related work? 4 / 4

Nongovernmental organizations operate freely, with various groups focusing on issues such as environmental conservation, youth development, public health, and women's rights.

E3. Is there freedom for trade unions and similar professional or labor organizations? 3 / 4

Workers can freely organize unions and bargain collectively, but there are no laws specifically regulating trade unions or strikes or prohibiting antiunion discrimination. Union membership and activity are low in practice, as the private-sector economy consists mostly of small, family-run businesses.

F. RULE OF LAW: 15 / 16

F1. Is there an independent judiciary? 4 / 4

The judiciary has a reputation for a high degree of independence and integrity. The president appoints judges for life terms based on recommendations from an independent Judicial Nominating Commission, which is made up of three presidential appointees, three jurists named by their peers, and the chief justice.

F2. Does due process prevail in civil and criminal matters? 4 / 4

The authorities generally uphold legal safeguards against arbitrary arrest and detention, and trial proceedings ensure due process.

F3. Is there protection from the illegitimate use of physical force and freedom from war and insurgencies? 4 / 4

Law enforcement agencies maintain internal order, and instances of abuse or impunity are rare, though overcrowding in the country's limited detention facilities remains a problem.

F4. Do laws, policies, and practices guarantee equal treatment of various segments of the population? 3 / 4

The legal system prohibits discrimination based on gender, race, place of origin, and other categories. Sexual orientation and gender identity are not protected categories, but Palau repealed legal provisions that criminalized consensual same-sex sexual activity in 2014. Women generally enjoy equal treatment in practice.

Foreign nationals sometimes face discrimination regarding employment, education, and other matters. Growing tourism from China in particular has created jobs but also raised the cost of living, and some locals regard the presence of Chinese businesses and residents with hostility. (In 2018, the number of Chinese tourists in Palau declined after China's government in late 2017 instructed agencies to cease commercial flights and group tours to the country—likely a response to Palau's diplomatic relations with Taiwan.)

G. PERSONAL AUTONOMY AND INDIVIDUAL RIGHTS: 13 / 16

G1. Do individuals enjoy freedom of movement, including the ability to change their place of residence, employment, or education? 4 / 4

There are no significant restrictions on freedom of movement, including internal and international travel.

G2. Are individuals able to exercise the right to own property and establish private businesses without undue interference from state or nonstate actors? 3 / 4

The legal framework generally supports property rights and private businesses activity, and the government has undertaken reforms to improve conditions in recent years, though some bureaucratic obstacles and corruption-related impediments persist.

Noncitizens cannot purchase land, which is inherited matrilineally among Palauans.

G3. Do individuals enjoy personal social freedoms, including choice of marriage partner and size of family, protection from domestic violence, and control over appearance? 3 / 4

Personal social freedoms are largely respected, and women have equal rights regarding marriage, child custody, and other personal status matters. Rape, including spousal rape, and domestic violence are criminal offenses, though victims of domestic abuse are often unwilling to report it to police.

G4. Do individuals enjoy equality of opportunity and freedom from economic exploitation? 3 / 4

Residents generally have access to economic opportunity, and the law provides some protections against exploitative labor practices. However, enforcement of such safeguards is inadequate, and foreign workers remain vulnerable to sexual exploitation, forced labor, or otherwise abusive working conditions in sectors including domestic service and fisheries. The minimum wage law does not apply to foreign workers. Some officials have been accused of complicity in human trafficking.

Panama

Population: 4,200,000
Capital: Panama City
Political Rights Rating: 1↑
Civil Liberties Rating: 2
Freedom Rating: 1.5
Freedom Status: Free
Electoral Democracy: Yes

Overview: Panama's political institutions are democratic, with competitive elections and orderly rotations of power. Freedoms of expression and association are generally respected. However, corruption and impunity are serious challenges, affecting the justice system and the highest levels of government. Discrimination against racial minorities is common, and indigenous groups have struggled to uphold their legal rights with respect to land and development projects.

KEY DEVELOPMENTS IN 2018:
- Corruption remained a serious problem across state institutions, with multiple investigations opened and accusations made against officials during the year.
- Former president Ricardo Martinelli, who faced corruption and wiretapping charges in Panama, was extradited from the United States in June. His trial was set to begin in 2019.

POLITICAL RIGHTS: 36 / 40 (+1)

A. ELECTORAL PROCESS: 12 / 12

A1. Was the current head of government or other chief national authority elected through free and fair elections? 4 / 4

The president is elected by popular vote for a single five-year term. In 2014, incumbent vice president Juan Carlos Varela of the Panameñista Party (PP) won the presidency with 39 percent of the national vote. Former housing minister José Domingo Arias of Democratic Change (CD) won 31 percent, and former Panama City mayor Juan Carlos Navarro of the Democratic Revolutionary Party (PRD) won 28 percent, with four other candidates splitting the remaining votes. International observers considered the elections generally free and fair, though the Organization of American States and the International Republican Institute criticized executive interference in the electoral process, including through the misuse of public resources, and noted that campaign financing was poorly regulated.

A2. Were the current national legislative representatives elected through free and fair elections? 4 / 4

Members of the 71-seat unicameral legislature, the National Assembly, are elected for five-year terms. The 2014 elections were held concurrently with the presidential vote, drawing the same assessment from international monitors. The United for Change alliance—formed by the CD and the Nationalist Republican Liberal Movement (MOLIRENA)—won 32 seats, followed by the PRD with 25, the PP with 12, and the Popular Party with 1; an independent candidate also won a seat.

A3. Are the electoral laws and framework fair, and are they implemented impartially by the relevant election management bodies? 4 / 4

The country's electoral framework is generally fair and impartially implemented. The Electoral Tribunal of Panama (TE) is responsible for reviewing the electoral code after each election and submitting any reforms to the National Assembly. In 2017, the legislature adopted reforms proposed by the TE in 2016 that included tighter regulation of campaign donations, spending, and advertising. The 2019 elections will be held under the new rules, including a cap on public and private funding for presidential and National Assembly campaigns and reduced campaign periods for primary and general elections.

B. POLITICAL PLURALISM AND PARTICIPATION: 15 / 16

B1. Do the people have the right to organize in different political parties or other competitive political groupings of their choice, and is the system free of undue obstacles to the rise and fall of these competing parties or groupings? 4 / 4

Political parties are free to form and compete in Panama's multiparty system, and since the 2014 elections, candidates have also been able to register as independents. The electoral regulations adopted in 2017 reduced the number of signatures an independent needs to run for office. However, the 2019 presidential race had multiple independent contenders as of 2018, and the reforms stipulate that only the three with the most signatures will qualify. The main political parties formally registered their 2019 electoral coalitions in December 2018.

B2. Is there a realistic opportunity for the opposition to increase its support or gain power through elections? 4 / 4

Elections are competitive in practice, and orderly transfers of power between rival parties have been the norm since the end of de facto military rule in 1989.

B3. Are the people's political choices free from domination by the military, foreign powers, religious hierarchies, economic oligarchies, or any other powerful group that is not democratically accountable? 4 / 4

Voters and candidates are generally free from undue interference by groups outside the political system, though the threat that improper donations by drug traffickers and other powerful interests could influence the political process remains a concern, even after the campaign finance reforms introduced in 2017.

B4. Do various segments of the population (including ethnic, religious, gender, LGBT, and other relevant groups) have full political rights and electoral opportunities? 3 / 4

The law does not limit the political rights of any segment of the citizen population. Women are free to participate in politics, and women's advocacy organizations have campaigned to improve their representation in elected offices. The electoral code requires gender parity in internal party primary systems, but in practice this has not led to more women winning general elections. Less than 20 percent of National Assembly seats went to women in the 2014 elections.

The country's racial minorities and LGBT (lesbian, gay, bisexual, and transgender) community continue to face obstacles to the full exercise of their political rights, which are equal under the law. In 2017, activists created a new progressive party, Creemos, with a platform that included legalization of same-sex marriage, but it has failed to gain traction and was not expected to participate in the 2019 elections. The constitution establishes five indigenous territories—three at the provincial level and two at the municipal level—and these are duly represented in the system of constituencies for the National Assembly, but the interests of indigenous people, who make up about 11 percent of the population, remain inadequately addressed by the political system as a whole.

C. FUNCTIONING OF GOVERNMENT: 9 / 12 (+1)

C1. Do the freely elected head of government and national legislative representatives determine the policies of the government? 4 / 4

The elected government and legislature generally determine and implement laws and policies without interference, though evidence of official corruption has raised concerns about the possibility that unelected entities could unduly influence governance.

C2. Are safeguards against official corruption strong and effective? 2 / 4

Safeguards against official corruption are relatively weak and ineffective, due in part to irregular application of the laws and a lack of resources for the judicial system. Investigations have revealed extensive corruption in previous administrations. The current government has been criticized for inaction on this issue, though the president remains publicly supportive of anticorruption efforts. In 2018, the legislature continued to hold up several proposed reforms designed to strengthen protections against official malfeasance and money laundering; at least one measure approved by lawmakers during the year was vetoed by the president.

Two ministers from the administration of former president Martinelli were arrested in 2017 for alleged money laundering in connection with the Odebrecht case, a massive corruption scandal centered on a Brazilian construction firm that has affected much of Latin America. President Varela has admitted to receiving donations for his 2009 vice-presidential campaign from an individual with ties to Odebrecht, but said the funds were received legally and reported to the TE. Martinelli, who has faced multiple investigations himself, was arrested in the United States in 2017 and extradited to Panama in June 2018. He was set to be tried in 2019. Despite the scandal surrounding Odebrecht, the company continued to be awarded government contracts.

A number of officials from the current administration and members of the National Assembly have resigned after being implicated in corruption and other wrongdoing. The Public Ministry reported in October 2018 that over 1,100 people had been charged in high-profile cases since 2014, and the Special Anti-Corruption Prosecutor's Office reported that over 700 corruption cases, many related to financial crimes, were opened between January and April 2018. However, prosecutors have failed to secure convictions in many such cases.

C3. Does the government operate with openness and transparency? 3 / 4 (+1)

The law provides mechanisms for public access to government information, and while the government does not always operate with transparency in practice, the National Authority for Transparency and Access to Public Information (ANTAI) has reported increasing institutional compliance with a 2002 transparency law in recent years. In its monitoring report for December 2018, the authority found that 66 percent of the public entities evaluated were fully compliant. The government adopted a new open data policy through an executive decree in late 2017 and a resolution issued in January 2018, instructing public institutions to make data accessible to the public in clear, open, and machine-readable formats.

Score Change: The score improved from 2 to 3 because government agencies have gradually increased compliance with an existing transparency law, among other positive steps.

CIVIL LIBERTIES: 48 / 60
D. FREEDOM OF EXPRESSION AND BELIEF: 15 / 16
D1. Are there free and independent media? 3 / 4

News consumers have access to a wide variety of private media outlets that present a range of views, but the constitutional guarantee of freedom of the press is not consistently upheld. Libel is both a civil and a criminal offense, and cases are filed against journalists in practice. Independent, critical journalists and outlets reportedly face editorial pressure from the government, and some journalists have experienced harassment when covering stories and opinions unfavorable to the government.

D2. Are individuals free to practice and express their religious faith or nonbelief in public and private? 4 / 4

The constitution recognizes Roman Catholicism as the majority religion and requires general "respect for Christian morality and public order," but freedom of religion is otherwise guaranteed and broadly upheld in practice. Catholic religious instruction is offered but not mandatory in public schools.

D3. Is there academic freedom, and is the educational system free from extensive political indoctrination? 4 / 4

The government generally honors academic freedom, and the schools are free from political indoctrination.

D4. Are individuals free to express their personal views on political or other sensitive topics without fear of surveillance or retribution? 4 / 4

Private discussion is free and vibrant, and use of social media platforms for the expression of personal views, including views on political or social issues, is generally not restricted.

E. ASSOCIATIONAL AND ORGANIZATIONAL RIGHTS: 11 / 12
E1. Is there freedom of assembly? 4 / 4

Freedom of assembly is generally respected, and peaceful demonstrations are common, though protests that block roads and highways often result in arrests and altercations with police.

E2. Is there freedom for nongovernmental organizations, particularly those that are engaged in human rights- and governance-related work? 4 / 4

Nongovernmental organizations operate freely, but some activists—particularly those focused on environmental issues and indigenous rights—have complained of harassment and intimidation, including through lawsuits by private companies.

E3. Is there freedom for trade unions and similar professional or labor organizations? 3 / 4

The law generally protects workers' rights to unionize, bargain collectively, and engage in legal, peaceful strikes. However, enforcement of labor protections is inadequate, and labor-related protests frequently feature clashes with police. Public employees are allowed to form associations to engage in collective bargaining and strike activities, but their rights are not as robust as those of unions; legislation that would give public-sector workers the right to form unions was under consideration at the end of 2018.

F. RULE OF LAW: 10 / 16

F1. Is there an independent judiciary? 2 / 4

The country's judicial system is plagued by corruption and inefficiency. Public disagreements between the attorney general's office and judges over rulings that impeded major corruption cases in recent years have raised doubts about whether such cases would be heard impartially. The Varela administration was criticized during 2018 over allegations that the National Security Council had interfered with corruption investigations that should have been handled by law enforcement bodies and the judiciary.

F2. Does due process prevail in civil and criminal matters? 2 / 4

Due process is constitutionally guaranteed but inconsistently upheld in practice. The justice system features extensive use of lengthy pretrial detention, with pretrial detainees accounting for a majority of prison inmates. In 2017, the attorney general claimed that prosecutors working on corruption investigations had received threats and pressure from powerful elites. In July 2018, the attorney general's office reported that it had broken up a network of corrupt prosecutors in Azuero. Police and other security forces have also been implicated in criminal activity in recent years.

F3. Is there protection from the illegitimate use of physical force and freedom from war and insurgencies? 3 / 4

The country is free from major threats to physical security such as war and insurgencies. However, police have been accused of beatings and other forms of excessive force, including while dispersing protests. The prison system is marked by overcrowding, lack of security, and poor health conditions.

The illegal drug trade and related criminal violence remain problems, though the homicide rate is well below those of most countries in the region. The number of homicides rose slightly to 439 in 2018, from 412 in 2017, according to statistics from the attorney general's office.

F4. Do laws, policies, and practices guarantee equal treatment of various segments of the population? 3 / 4

Discrimination based on gender, race, and other such categories is prohibited by law, but sexual orientation and gender identity are not covered, and racial minorities—including indigenous people, Panamanians of African descent, and certain immigrant groups—face some discrimination in practice. Indigenous communities enjoy a significant degree of autonomy and self-government, but many live in poverty and lack equal access to basic services.

An influx of migrants and asylum seekers from Venezuela, Cuba, and other troubled countries in the region has stoked anti-immigrant sentiment in recent years. During 2017, the government took several steps to curb illegal immigration, tightening restrictions on the length and renewal of tourist visas for some countries and stepping up the deportation of migrants without documentation. In 2018, thousands of residence permits were canceled due to evidence that they were obtained fraudulently.

G. PERSONAL AUTONOMY AND INDIVIDUAL RIGHTS: 12 / 16

G1. Do individuals enjoy freedom of movement, including the ability to change their place of residence, employment, or education? 4 / 4

The government generally respects freedom of foreign travel and internal movement, including the freedom to change one's place of residence, employment, or education.

G2. Are individuals able to exercise the right to own property and establish private businesses without undue interference from state or nonstate actors? 3 / 4

Individuals can own private property and establish businesses freely under the law, but there are some practical impediments to defending property rights and operating businesses, including corruption and interference from organized crime.

Although indigenous groups have substantial land rights under the law, implementation has been problematic. Such groups have long protested the encroachment of illegal settlers on their lands, government delays in the formal demarcation of collective land, and large-scale development projects that proceed despite dissent within indigenous communities. During 2018, indigenous groups protested against the Ministry of Environment for delays in the issuance of their collective land titles.

G3. Do individuals enjoy personal social freedoms, including choice of marriage partner and size of family, protection from domestic violence, and control over appearance? 3 / 4

Personal social freedoms are largely unrestricted. However, domestic violence is a concern; according to official statistics, over 15,000 domestic violence cases were registered in 2018. Abortion is permitted in cases of rape or incest or to preserve the life or health of the woman, though there are significant procedural obstacles as well as potential penalties for abortions that do not meet the legal standard.

In a January 2018 advisory opinion, the Inter-American Court of Human Rights ruled that member states should recognize same-sex marriage, adding to existing pressure on Panama to legalize such unions.

G4. Do individuals enjoy equality of opportunity and freedom from economic exploitation? 2 / 4

Human trafficking for sexual exploitation and forced labor remains a serious problem despite some government efforts to combat it. Both Panamanian and migrant workers in certain sectors—including the agricultural sector, where many workers are indigenous people—are subject to exploitative working conditions. Enforcement of basic labor protections is weak in rural areas and among informal workers.

Papua New Guinea

Population: 8,500,000
Capital: Port Moresby
Political Rights Rating: 4 ↓
Civil Liberties Rating: 3
Freedom Rating: 3.5
Freedom Status: Partly Free
Electoral Democracy: Yes

Overview: Papua New Guinea is a democracy in which elections are held regularly, but the polls have often been marred by irregularities and violence. Party allegiances are unstable, and only two governments have survived for a full term since independence in 1975. However, since the turn of the century, a boom in mineral resources extraction has helped successive incumbent governments to consolidate control. The judiciary retains significant independence, and the media are mostly free to criticize the government. Corruption remains a serious problem.

KEY DEVELOPMENTS IN 2018:

- A nine-month state of emergency was declared in the Southern Highlands in June after an election-related court decision prompted riots.
- In August, police dropped their investigations into two corruption scandals that had implicated the prime minister and other senior officials.
- In October, the central government and the government of Bougainville agreed on the wording of a referendum set for 2019 that would allow voters on the island to choose between greater autonomy and independence.

POLITICAL RIGHTS: 23 / 40 (−2)

A. ELECTORAL PROCESS: 7 / 12 (−1)

A1. Was the current head of government or other chief national authority elected through free and fair elections? 3 / 4

The governor general represents the British monarch as head of state and formally appoints the prime minister, who is the head of government, following an election process in Parliament. A law provides that the largest political party emerging from a general election has the first right to nominate a prime minister. While the prime minister's legitimacy is partly rooted in the conduct of the legislative elections, the election of the prime minister by members of Parliament (MPs) is a highly competitive process. Following the victory of the People's National Congress Party (PNC) in the 2017 elections, Peter O'Neill was reelected as prime minister in a parliamentary vote of 60 to 46.

A2. Were the current national legislative representatives elected through free and fair elections? 2 / 4

Voters elect members of the unicameral, 111-member National Parliament for five-year terms. A limited preferential voting system allows voters to choose up to three preferred candidates on their ballots.

Serious flaws, including bribery and voter fraud, were reported in the 2017 elections. Some areas, notably the Highlands Region, experienced election-related violence that resulted in dozens of deaths, as well as severe property damage. Due to irregularities, election results in the Southern Highlands were released several months late and sparked renewed violence in the town of Mendi once made public. The electoral process was smoother in coastal areas, but even those regions were not completely free from irregularities and violence. Allegations of deliberate manipulation of voter rolls to favor the incumbent government were widespread, but most clear abuses were localized in the Highlands. Election observers expressed disappointment that past recommendations to clean up voter rolls had been disregarded.

The Parliament seats were ultimately divided among numerous small parties, with the PNC taking nearly a quarter of the total and the National Alliance placing a distant second. Independents made up the third-largest group.

A3. Are the electoral laws and framework fair, and are they implemented impartially by the relevant election management bodies? 2 / 4 (−1)

The electoral law, which requires voters to rank three candidates on a preferential ballot, is fair but complex to administer. The voter rolls are poorly maintained. At the local level, election management bodies are chronically lacking in independence, particularly in all parts of the Highlands. Irregularities do not necessarily benefit incumbents, more than half of whom usually lose their seats at elections. A 2018 Australian National University analysis found considerable evidence of local-level fraud and malpractice by electoral management bodies. Separately, in November, Electoral Commissioner Patilias Gamato was found guilty of contempt of court for failing to follow court orders to hold local government by-elections in six Highlands provinces.

Score Change: The score declined from 3 to 2 due to emerging evidence of blatant bias by local-level election management bodies at the 2017 polls and the conviction of the country's electoral commissioner for failing to hold local by-elections as ordered by the courts.

B. POLITICAL PLURALISM AND PARTICIPATION: 13 / 16

B1. Do the people have the right to organize in different political parties or other competitive political groupings of their choice, and is the system free of undue obstacles to the rise and fall of these competing parties or groupings? 4 / 4

Political parties are able to form and operate freely, but many candidates run as independents and join factions only after reaching Parliament. Electoral loyalties are driven by local and personal factors at the constituency level. MPs frequently switch affiliations and alliances. A law constraining freedom of movement between parties was ruled unconstitutional in 2010.

The law granting the largest party the first opportunity to form a government creates an incentive for parties to register with the Registrar of Political Parties, as does government funding for parties.

B2. Is there a realistic opportunity for the opposition to increase its support or gain power through elections? 4 / 4

The opposition has a reasonable chance of dislodging the government in elections or through a no-confidence vote on the floor of Parliament. Since independence in 1975, only two governments have served out a full five-year term: those led by Michael Somare in 2002–07 and Peter O'Neill in 2012–17. Immediately after the 2017 elections, the opposition benches were stronger than under the previous government. However, most MPs from the major opposition party, Pangu, later defected to join O'Neill's government, as did several other lawmakers.

The frequency of no-confidence votes has been diminished somewhat by a provision that grants an incoming prime minister an 18-month "grace period."

B3. Are the people's political choices free from domination by the military, foreign powers, religious hierarchies, economic oligarchies, or any other powerful group that is not democratically accountable? 2 / 4

Most citizens and candidates are generally free to make political choices without undue interference. However, some local leaders, politicians, and candidate agents control the balloting process, particularly in the Highlands, and complete the ballot papers in bulk—a form of "assisted voting." As a result, the affected citizens are effectively denied the right to vote.

B4. Do various segments of the population (including ethnic, religious, gender, LGBT, and other relevant groups) have full political rights and electoral opportunities? 3 / 4

Although all citizens have equal political rights under the law, women are underrepresented in elected offices. The 2017 elections featured the highest number of women candidates ever, but none won legislative seats, and there are currently no women in the 111-seat Parliament. LGBT (lesbian, gay, bisexual, and transgender) people face societal discrimination that impedes their ability to advocate for their interests in the political sphere.

A 2005 agreement ended a civil war in Bougainville and provided for an independence referendum to be held between 2015 and 2020. While the Autonomous Bougainville Government has been building its own civil service in preparation for the possibility of becoming an independent nation, and laying groundwork for a referendum, central authorities have expressed opposition to the island's possible secession. In October 2018, the two sides agreed on the wording of the question to be put to voters, allowing them to choose between greater autonomy and independence. However, the referendum, scheduled for 2019, would not be legally binding on Papua New Guinea's government.

C. FUNCTIONING OF GOVERNMENT: 3 / 12 (−1)

C1. Do the freely elected head of government and national legislative representatives determine the policies of the government? 2 / 4

The prime minister heads the government, but cabinet ministers often exert considerable control over their portfolios without necessarily being answerable to the cabinet. There are no powerful external forces that determine the policies of government, though logging and mining companies have been known to court influence. The government has only a limited ability to implement its policies across the country, as the state's presence in more remote areas is minimal.

C2. Are safeguards against official corruption strong and effective? 0 / 4 (−1)

Corruption is pervasive and remains the most important hindrance to development. Anticorruption institutions have been subject to political interference. Task Force Sweep was established in 2011 to root out corruption, and it carried out a variety of investigations against politicians, civil servants, and businessmen. However, when the unit turned its attention to millions of dollars' worth of fraudulent payments to local law firm Paraka Lawyers that were allegedly authorized by O'Neill, the prime minister responded by disbanding the task force; when courts ordered its resurrection, the government cut its funding. The police force formally dropped the Paraka case against the prime minister in August 2018.

Separately, O'Neill suspended Minister for Public Enterprise and State Investment William Duma and then defense minister Fabian Pok in 2017 over claims that they had profited from a multimillion-dollar land deal associated with plans to relocate the Port Moresby naval base. However, Duma and Pok were reelected to Parliament later in the year, and their United Resources Party became a key player in O'Neill's new coalition government. Pok assumed the powerful petroleum and energy portfolio, and Duma took his previous position. In August 2018, police dropped investigations into the naval base scandal.

Score Change: The score declined from 1 to 0 because law enforcement authorities have failed to pursue corruption allegations implicating the prime minister and other powerful politicians in recent years.

C3. Does the government operate with openness and transparency? 1 / 4

Government operations are generally opaque, and the government does not frequently release accurate information about public expenditures, procurement processes, or officials' assets. Papua New Guinea does not have an access to information law. The veracity of spending and revenue figures issued by the government during 2018 was questioned by at least one outside economist.

CIVIL LIBERTIES: 41 / 60 (+3)
D. FREEDOM OF EXPRESSION AND BELIEF: 14 / 16 (+1)
D1. Are there free and independent media? 3 / 4

Freedom of the press is generally respected. Local media provide independent coverage of the political opposition, as well as controversial issues such as alleged police abuse and official corruption. Politicians have been known to harass media professionals over negative stories, and journalists can also face physical attacks in the course of their work. In February 2018, a group of men working for the governor of Morobe assaulted a newspaper reporter over his reporting. Four assailants were arrested and paid a small fine. A journalist was fired from a state-owned television station in November over his coverage of the government, but was reinstated under public pressure.

D2. Are individuals free to practice and express their religious faith or nonbelief in public and private? 4 / 4 (+1)

Religious freedom is generally upheld. There have been reports of larger churches criticizing newer and smaller groups, and of anti-Muslim rhetoric that has accompanied the arrival of Muslim refugees, but no major infringements on religious liberty have been alleged in recent years.

Score Change: The score improved from 3 to 4 because there have been no reports of significant restrictions on religious freedom in recent years.

D3. Is there academic freedom, and is the educational system free from extensive political indoctrination? 3 / 4

Academic freedom is generally respected, though the police have at times violently suppressed student demonstrations on campus.

D4. Are individuals free to express their personal views on political or other sensitive topics without fear of surveillance or retribution? 4 / 4

There are no major constraints on the expression of personal views. However, a 2016 cybercrime law allows the prosecution of people who publish defamatory material or incite violence on social media, raising concerns that it could be misused to punish legitimate speech.

E. ASSOCIATIONAL AND ORGANIZATIONAL RIGHTS: 10 / 12 (+1)
E1. Is there freedom of assembly? 3 / 4

The constitution provides for freedom of assembly. However, marches and demonstrations require 14 days' notice and police approval, and authorities sometimes deny permits. Police have used force to suppress demonstrations by asylum seekers on Manus Island.

E2. Is there freedom for nongovernmental organizations, particularly those that are engaged in human rights- and governance-related work? 4 / 4 (+1)

A number of nongovernmental organizations operate in the country, including groups focused on human rights and environmental causes, as well as some that provide social services. Most are small and lack resources, but they are otherwise free of serious constraints on their activities.

Score Change: The score improved from 3 to 4 due to the lack of any significant state restrictions on NGOs or recent reports of interference with their work.

E3. Is there freedom for trade unions and similar professional or labor organizations? 3 / 4

Workers' rights to strike, organize, and engage in collective bargaining are largely respected. However, the government has frequently imposed arbitration in labor disputes to avert strikes, and protections against antiunion discrimination are unevenly enforced. Most workers are employed in the informal sector and lack access to union protections.

F. RULE OF LAW: 8 / 16 (+1)
F1. Is there an independent judiciary? 3 / 4 (+1)

While successive governments have exerted political pressure on the court system, the judiciary is generally independent. Judges are appointed by the largely apolitical Judicial and Legal Services Commission and cannot be removed arbitrarily. Laypeople sit on village courts to adjudicate minor offenses under customary and statutory law. In recent years, the higher courts have repeatedly demonstrated their impartiality by ruling against the government and its political interests.

Score Change: The score improved from 2 to 3 because the higher courts have displayed relative independence in recent years, striking down government initiatives and attempting to hold some officials accountable for malfeasance.

F2. Does due process prevail in civil and criminal matters? 1 / 4

Constitutional guarantees of due process are poorly upheld. Arbitrary detention is relatively common, and opportunities to challenge such abuses are limited in practice. A shortage of trained judicial personnel is a key cause of lengthy detentions and trial delays.

F3. Is there protection from the illegitimate use of physical force and freedom from war and insurgencies? 2 / 4

Law enforcement officials have been implicated in brutality and corruption. Prison conditions are poor, and the correctional service is understaffed. Prison breaks are common. Lack of economic opportunities exacerbates social unrest, frequently resulting in violent clashes, injuries, and deaths. An Australian police assistance program exists, but its officers lack powers of arrest and are restricted by a 2005 court ruling that removed immunities from prosecution under local law.

In June 2018, the government declared a nine-month state of emergency in the Southern Highlands after a court decision, which rejected a challenge to the 2017 election of the provincial governor, prompted a wave of violence by armed rioters. A separate court case challenging the same election was ongoing at year's end.

F4. Do laws, policies, and practices guarantee equal treatment of various segments of the population? 2 / 4

The constitution guarantees equality regardless of race, tribe, religion, sex, and other categories, but various forms of discrimination are common in practice. Same-sex sexual relations are a criminal offense that can draw up to 14 years in prison, though the relevant laws are rarely enforced. There is some discrimination against people of Chinese origin, which is mainly linked to resentment toward a growing Chinese business presence that is viewed as disadvantaging other groups. Women face legal discrimination in employment in addition to societal biases. Allegations of sorcery have been used to target women for violence.

Australia pays the Papua New Guinean government to accept asylum seekers who arrived in Australian waters by boat. Those who are not granted refugee status or do not agree to settle in Papua New Guinea are left in limbo, with Papua New Guinea's government claiming that these people are Australia's responsibility. Papua New Guinea's Supreme Court ruled in 2016 that Australia's Manus Island detention center was unconstitutional, and the facility officially closed in 2017, but hundreds of refugees and asylum seekers remain in other accommodation on the island amid reports of poor living conditions, violence, and health problems. The Australian government has been reluctant to allow refugees to enter Australia, but some have been sent to the United States as part of a deal between the US and Australian governments.

G. PERSONAL AUTONOMY AND INDIVIDUAL RIGHTS: 9 / 16

G1. Do individuals enjoy freedom of movement, including the ability to change their place of residence, employment, or education? 3 / 4

There are few constraints on freedom of movement for citizens. Movement remains restricted for those who were detained at the Australian-run detention center on Manus Island. In November 2018, dozens of asylum seekers and refugees were transferred from Port Moresby, where they had been receiving medical treatment, back to Manus Island as part of the preparations for an international summit in the capital.

G2. Are individuals able to exercise the right to own property and establish private businesses without undue interference from state or nonstate actors? 2 / 4

In Papua New Guinea, 97 percent of the land area is theoretically under customary tenure, but Special Agriculture and Business Leases (SABLs) have been used to facilitate land grabs by unscrupulous investors. In 2017, O'Neill claimed that all SABLs had been canceled, but Lands and Physical Planning Minister Justin Tkatchenko acknowledged in 2018 that most of the leases were still being contested in court. Women face disadvantages regarding property rights and inheritance, particularly under customary law.

G3. Do individuals enjoy personal social freedoms, including choice of marriage partner and size of family, protection from domestic violence, and control over appearance? 2 / 4

The law provides some protections for individual rights on personal status matters like marriage and divorce, but early or forced marriage remains a problem, and legislation meant to combat widespread family violence and aid victims is poorly enforced. About two-thirds of partnered women have experienced physical abuse, according to multiple studies. Abortion is illegal except when it is necessary to save the woman's life.

G4. Do individuals enjoy equality of opportunity and freedom from economic exploitation? 2 / 4

Legal safeguards against exploitative working conditions are weakly enforced, and frequent abuses in sectors including logging and mining have been reported. The government does not actively prosecute human traffickers, and efforts to identify victims are inadequate. The United States Department of Labor has assembled evidence of child labor in the coffee, cocoa, palm oil, and rubber sectors, as well as in commercial sexual exploitation. The US State Department describes bride-price payments as facilitating labor and sexual exploitation.

Paraguay

Population: 6,900,000
Capital: Asunción
Political Rights Rating: 3
Civil Liberties Rating: 3
Freedom Rating: 3.0
Freedom Status: Partly Free
Electoral Democracy: Yes

Overview: Paraguay's democracy is dominated by the conservative Colorado Party. Corruption is decreasing but remains widespread, while organized crime and environmental destruction damage the rights of rural and indigenous populations. Poverty and gender-based discrimination also limit the rights of women and children in particular.

KEY DEVELOPMENTS IN 2018:

- Mario Abdo Benítez of the Colorado Party was elected president in April by a close margin. The Colorado Party also secured a majority in the Chamber of Deputies, but no party won a majority in the Senate. Opposition parties alleged fraud, but international observers recognized the election as generally fair.
- Mass anticorruption demonstrations erupted in mid-2018, and a number of senators, deputies, and judicial officials, resigned and came under investigation in their wake. In September, the new government scrapped the so-called *autoblindaje* law, which had raised the number of legislative votes necessary to remove a lawmaker from their seat for corruption or other violations.
- The Abdo Benítez administration cut funding for the Grupo Lince, a rapid-reaction police force created in 2017 to tackle urban crime that had been criticized for heavy-handed tactics. However, the move was unpopular with much of the public, and authorities announced the restoration of its funding in September.
- While an advisory role is reserved in the Senate for former presidents, Cartes attempted to extend his political influence by running for a Senate seat with full voting rights, and the Supreme Court controversially approved his initiative. He won the seat, but in June the Senate blocked him from taking it. Cartes had previously prompted protests in 2017 when he attempted to introduce presidential reelection.

POLITICAL RIGHTS: 28 / 40 (+1)

A. ELECTORAL PROCESS: 10 / 12

A1. Was the current head of government or other chief national authority elected through free and fair elections? 3 / 4

The president is directly elected to no more than one five-year term. In 2017, a secretive, unconstitutional attempt by President Horacio Cartes and his allies to permit presidential reelection sparked major protests, and Cartes ultimately abandoned the initiative. The Colorado Party has held the presidency for most of the past 70 years. The election of left-wing President Fernando Lugo in 2008 broke the Colorado Party's dominance, but Lugo was removed from office in a legal, if highly controversial "express impeachment" in 2012.

The December 2017 primaries were characterized by significant political activity and spending by the major parties. However, 2018 election campaign was muted and featured fewer campaign events, with observers attributing the decreased activity to voters' frustration with corruption, and mistrust in political institutions. Mario Abdo Benítez of the Colorado Party won the presidency, taking a little over 46 percent of the vote. Efraín Alegre, the candidate of the opposition Alianza Ganar coalition, took 43 percent. While Alegre accused the electoral authority of fraud, observers including the European Union (EU) described the election as largely fair. The EU's media monitoring mission, however, noted that media outlets focused almost exclusively on the candidacies of Abdo Benítez and Alegre, and offered scant coverage to the eight other candidates in the race.

The elections were marred by reports of vote buying, and renewed claims that limitations were placed on the movement of indigenous voters in some areas ahead of the election, in apparent attempts to prevent them from voting or selling their votes.

A2. Were the current national legislative representatives elected through free and fair elections? 4 / 4

The bicameral Congress consists of an 80-member Chamber of Deputies and a 45-member Senate, all elected for five-year terms. The 2018 legislative elections resulted in a majority for the Colorado Party in the Chamber of Deputies, but no party won a majority in the Senate. While monitoring missions reported some irregularities, the parliamentary polls were considered generally competitive and credible.

A3. Are the electoral laws and framework fair, and are they implemented impartially by the relevant election management bodies? 3 / 4

The Superior Electoral Court of Justice (TSJE) regulates electoral processes. The government has yet to implement many recommendations the previous EU election observation mission issued in 2013, including initiatives to improve the independence of the TSJE to allow for a thorough examination of campaign financing, as well as to implement a mechanism for vote recounts, which are not currently possible. Following the 2018 elections, the EU again made a series of recommendations as to how Paraguay should improve the independence and professionalism of the TSJE. A planned constitutional reform in 2019, as well as changes to the electoral code under discussion at year's end, may address some of these issues.

The 2018 EU monitoring mission also noted local authorities' failure to consistently enforce decisions made by the TSJE.

B. POLITICAL PLURALISM AND PARTICIPATION: 12 / 16

B1. Do the people have the right to organize in different political parties or other competitive political groupings of their choice, and is the system free of undue obstacles to the rise and fall of these competing parties or groupings? 3 / 4

The system is open to the rise of different political parties, although the Colorado Party has been in power for most of the past 70 years. The national scene is dominated by the Colorado Party and opposition PLRA, though factions regularly depart and build different coalitions.

Several smaller parties emerged or increased their standing in the 2018 elections, including Patria Querida (PPQ), Hagamos (PPH), and Movimiento Cruzada Nacional (MCN), suggesting the grip of the two traditional parties is weakening somewhat.

B2. Is there a realistic opportunity for the opposition to increase its support or gain power through elections? 4 / 4

Despite the dominance of the Colorado Party, opposition parties have a realistic chance of gaining power through elections. Lugo was able to come to power in 2008 due to a split in the Colorado Party, while a liberal-left coalition, Alianza Ganar, came close to taking the presidency in 2018. In addition, rival factions within the Colorado Party serve as a kind of internal opposition. Abdo Benítez of the conservative Colorado Añetete faction defeated the preferred candidate of former president Horacio Cartes in the Colorado Party primary in late 2017, and his administration is already enacting shifts in some policy areas.

B3. Are the people's political choices free from domination by the military, foreign powers, religious hierarchies, economic oligarchies, or any other powerful group that is not democratically accountable? 3 / 4

Citizens are generally free from undue interference in their political choices. However, there is some concern over the growing influence of Brazilian landowners in eastern regions.

Media outlets are concentrated among a handful of families, including that of former president Cartes, granting these few owners a powerful platform from which they may attempt to define the political sphere. The constitution bars military personnel from politics.

B4. Do various segments of the population (including ethnic, religious, gender, LGBT, and other relevant groups) have full political rights and electoral opportunities? 2 / 4

No Afro-Paraguayans or indigenous people held legislative office in 2018, although an indigenous political movement gained strength. Women held only 20 out of 125 seats in Congress in 2018, and no regional governorship was held by a woman. A gender quota law mandating 50 percent female participation on party lists for all positions was approved by the Senate in September, but vetoed by the president at the end of year with the support of lawmakers, over "inconsistencies" they said could hamper its efficacy.

C. FUNCTIONING OF GOVERNMENT: 6 / 12 (+1)

C1. Do the freely elected head of government and national legislative representatives determine the policies of the government? 2 / 4

While elected officials determine government policy, the making and implementation of decisions is often influenced or hampered by organized crime and corruption.

In 2018, Cartes attempted to extend his political influence beyond his presidential term, but was thwarted by the Senate. The Supreme Court early in the year controversially ruled that Cartes could run for a Senate seat with full voting rights. Critics said that this contravened the constitution, which states that former presidents become senators for life, but lack voting rights and may only contribute to debates. Cartes won a Senate seat in the

April elections, but the Senate in June blocked his move to step down from the presidency early to take his seat; this precluded him from being sworn in, as the Constitution does not permit the president to simultaneously serve as a senator. Cartes then reluctantly withdrew his resignation.

C2. Are safeguards against official corruption strong and effective? 2 / 4 (+1)

Corruption is a serious problem, and anticorruption laws have been poorly implemented. Cases often languish for years in the courts without resolution, and many offenses go unpunished due to political influence in the judiciary.

However, mass anticorruption demonstrations erupted in mid-2018, and a number of senators, deputies, and judicial officials, including some aligned with the Abdo Benítez government and the Colorado Party, resigned and were investigated and prosecuted in their wake. The resignations were in part prompted by a somewhat firmer line against corruption from the Abdo Benítez government. Among other initiatives, in September, the government scrapped the so-called *autoblindaje* law, which had taken effect just weeks earlier, in July; the law had raised the number of legislative votes necessary to remove a congressperson from their seat for corruption or other violations two a two-thirds majority, up from the simple majority mandated by the Constitution.

Additionally, in September 2018, the Health Ministry announced that an apparently wide-reaching corruption scandal within the health service involving the irregular purchase of vast quantities of medicines had been uncovered, and was reported to prosecutors.

Score Change: The score improved from 1 to 2 because the government's efforts to investigate and prosecute a number of corrupt officials, and its move to scrap a law that had made it more difficult to remove corrupt lawmakers, reflected greater resolve to tackle corruption.

C3. Does the government operate with openness and transparency? 2 / 4

Government transparency, especially in public administration, is gradually improving, and the effective implementation of access to information laws has bolstered investigative journalism. Citizens are showing an increasing intolerance for corruption and opaque government. This was reflected in the anticorruption demonstrations of 2018, as well as the large-scale 2017 protests against a secretive, ultimately unsuccessful attempt by the Cartes government and allied sectors of opposition parties to change the constitution to allow presidential reelection.

CIVIL LIBERTIES: 37 / 60
D. FREEDOM OF EXPRESSION AND BELIEF: 12 / 16
D1. Are there free and independent media? 2 / 4

Constitutional freedoms of expression and the press are unevenly upheld in practice. Direct pressure against journalists, including threats by criminal groups and corrupt authorities, encourages self-censorship, and violent attacks against journalists take place occasionally.

In March 2018, a journalist who released a series of audio tapes incriminating Colorado Party congressmen in corruption cases faced aggressive questioning by prosecutors and was asked to reveal her sources, provoking expressions of concern from press freedom organizations.

D2. Are individuals free to practice and express their religious faith or nonbelief in public and private? 4 / 4

Paraguay is home to diverse religious groups that are generally able to worship freely.

D3. Is there academic freedom, and is the educational system free from extensive political indoctrination? 3 / 4

Although academia is generally independent, primary and secondary schools teach a pro-Colorado version of history. University politics are dominated by the Colorado Party and the PLRA, with student elections and professional advancement often dependent on party affiliation.

D4. Are individuals free to express their personal views on political or other sensitive topics without fear of surveillance or retribution? 3 / 4

Citizens can for the most part engage in free and open private discussion, though the presence of armed groups in some areas can serve as a deterrent.

E. ASSOCIATIONAL AND ORGANIZATIONAL RIGHTS: 8 / 12
E1. Is there freedom of assembly? 3 / 4

Demonstrations and protests are common, but are sometimes repressed or marred by violence.

Sustained anticorruption protests in 2018 proceeded without interference, and prompted the resignation of several notoriously corrupt legislators.

E2. Is there freedom for nongovernmental organizations, particularly those that are engaged in human rights- and governance-related work? 3 / 4

Paraguay has a strong culture of largely free nongovernmental organizations (NGOs) working in the field of human rights and governance. However, the government is generally unresponsive to the concerns of NGOs that scrutinize it.

E3. Is there freedom for trade unions and similar professional or labor organizations? 2 / 4

Registration procedures for trade unions are cumbersome and employees are often unprotected from employer retaliation. However, labor activism was nevertheless robust in 2018. In August, workers protested the creation of a new pensions regulatory body; the same month, workers occupied the water utility Essap, over the entity's delay in appointing a new president.

F. RULE OF LAW: 7 / 16
F1. Is there an independent judiciary? 2 / 4

The judiciary is nominally independent, but money laundering, drug trafficking and other criminal operations have been able to co-opt or otherwise assert control over local judicial authorities, particularly in regions adjacent to Brazil. Politicians commonly attempt to influence judges and prosecutors. The Supreme Court's 2018 ruling to permit Cartes to run for a Senate seat prompted some criticism.

F2. Does due process prevail in civil and criminal matters? 1 / 4

Constitutional guarantees of due process are poorly upheld, largely due to corruption that permeates the judicial system. Individuals with influence or access to money are frequently able to obtain favorable treatment in the justice system.

In July 2018, the Supreme Court acquitted 11 peasant farmers, *campesinos,* and directed the release of four still in prison who were accused of perpetrating a deadly 2012 clash between farmers and police in Curuguaty, in which 6 officers and 11 campesinos were killed. The original trial was beset with irregularities, and Amnesty International hailed the decision as a "victory for human rights." However, the deaths of campesinos at Curuguaty are yet to be investigated.

F3. Is there protection from the illegitimate use of physical force and freedom from war and insurgencies? 2 / 4

Paraguay is one of the region's safer countries. However, the Paraguayan People's Army (EPP), a guerilla group, is still active in the northeast. Gang warfare takes place along the Brazilian border. Illegal detention by police and torture during incarceration still occur. Overcrowding, unsanitary conditions, and mistreatment are serious problems in prisons.

The Abdo Benítez administration took steps to rein in the Grupo Lince, a rapid-reaction police force created in 2017 to tackle urban crime, but which has been criticized for heavy-handed arrests and inspections. For example, the administration drastically cut the group's funding, and mandated that agents wear identifying badges and keep their faces visible. The efforts were unpopular with much of the public, and reduced activity by the group was widely blamed for an apparent uptick in violent crime. In September, authorities announced the restoration of the group's funding.

F4. Do laws, policies, and practices guarantee equal treatment of various segments of the population? 2 / 4

Paraguay lacks legislation protecting against all forms of discrimination. While same-sex sexual activity is legal, members of the LGBT (lesbian, gay, bisexual, and transgender) community face endemic discrimination. Indigenous people similarly face discrimination and lack access to adequate health care. Rampant deforestation and forced evictions threaten the last indigenous Ayoreo groups in voluntary isolation and indigenous Guaraní settlements.

G. PERSONAL AUTONOMY AND INDIVIDUAL RIGHTS: 10 / 16

G1. Do individuals enjoy freedom of movement, including the ability to change their place of residence, employment, or education? 3 / 4

Freedoms of movement is generally respected, though the presence of armed or criminal groups can discourage travel in some areas.

G2. Are individuals able to exercise the right to own property and establish private businesses without undue interference from state or nonstate actors? 3 / 4

Although there are few formal restrictions on private business activity and property rights, land disputes, often linked to historic misappropriation of public land, remain a problem. Additionally, the EPP has threatened, kidnapped, and extorted ranchers in its areas of operations. Evictions of indigenous populations from their ancestral lands are commonplace. Separately, in 2018, Amnesty International warned of judicial persecution and threats of renewed violent eviction against campesino communities, notably at Guahory in eastern Paraguay.

G3. Do individuals enjoy personal social freedoms, including choice of marriage partner and size of family, protection from domestic violence, and control over appearance? 2 / 4

Women and children continue to suffer from high levels of domestic and sexual abuse. Abortion remains illegal, as do same-sex marriage and civil unions.

G4. Do individuals enjoy equality of opportunity and freedom from economic exploitation? 2 / 4

Government statistics for 2017 suggested that 4.4 percent of the population lives in extreme poverty, and 26.4 percent lives in poverty, although both figures have fallen slightly in recent years. Indigenous populations are particularly affected by poverty. Income inequality is a serious problem and social mobility is extremely limited. A 2016 Oxfam report said 70 percent of agricultural land is owned by just 1 percent of farms. In 2018, media reports called attention to forced labor in the cattle farming industry in the Chaco, and the UN Special Rapporteur on contemporary forms of slavery also highlighted the serious issue of forced labor in the region.

The ongoing illegal practice of *criadazgo*—or temporary adoption in which children, generally from poor families, work without pay for families of higher income—severely limits the freedom of roughly 47,000 children across the country.

Peru

Population: 32,200,000
Capital: Lima
Political Rights Rating: 2
Civil Liberties Rating: 3
Freedom Rating: 2.5
Freedom Status: Free
Electoral Democracy: Yes

Overview: Peru has established democratic political institutions and undergone multiple peaceful transfers of power, though recent, high-profile corruption scandals have eroded public trust in democratic institutions and hampered normal political operations. Indigenous groups suffer from discrimination and inadequate political representation.

KEY DEVELOPMENTS IN 2018:
- President Pedro Pablo Kuczynski resigned in March, just before an expected impeachment vote over corruption allegations against him.
- A standoff between the executive branch and the opposition-controlled Congress continued under Kuczynski's successor, Martín Vizcarra. However, Vizcarra appeared to gain the upper hand by earning overwhelming support for a set of anti-corruption reforms he put to a national referendum in December.
- Secretly recorded phone conversations revealed abuses of power at the highest levels of the Peruvian judiciary in July, prompting resignations and a wave of citizen demonstrations.
- Opposition leader Keiko Fujimori was arrested in October for allegedly accepting illegal political contributions from the Brazilian construction firm Odebrecht, becoming the latest high-profile figure implicated in a sweeping scandal with the firm at its center.

POLITICAL RIGHTS: 31 / 40

A. ELECTORAL PROCESS: 11 / 12

A1. Was the current head of government or other chief national authority elected through free and fair elections? 4 / 4

The president is chief of state and head of government. Presidents are directly elected to a five-year term and may serve nonconsecutive terms. The 2016 election was closely contested, with Kuczynski winning by a historically small margin of 0.2 percent over Keiko Fujimori. The elections took place peacefully, and stakeholders accepted the close result.

Kuczynski resigned in March 2018, as lawmakers prepared to hold an impeachment vote against him over corruption allegations. Vice president Martín Vizcarra was quickly sworn in to replace him, in accordance with legal procedures.

A2. Were the current national legislative representatives elected through free and fair elections? 4 / 4

Members of the 130-member unicameral Congress are elected for five-year terms. Congressional balloting employs an open-list, region-based system of proportional representation, with a 5 percent vote hurdle for a party to enter the legislature.

Legislative elections were held concurrently with presidential elections in 2016. Keiko Fujimori's Popular Force party captured 73 of the 130 seats, followed by the Broad Front with 20 seats and Kuczynski's Peruvians for Change with 18 seats. The elections were considered free and fair.

A3. Are the electoral laws and framework fair, and are they implemented impartially by the relevant election management bodies? 3 / 4

The National Board of Elections (JNE) has taken steps to improve transparency surrounding the electoral process, but insufficiently regulated campaign finance remains a serious issue.

B. POLITICAL PLURALISM AND PARTICIPATION: 13 / 16

B1. Do the people have the right to organize in different political parties or other competitive political groupings of their choice, and is the system free of undue obstacles to the rise and fall of these competing parties or groupings? 4 / 4

Peruvian parties, while competitive, are both highly fragmented and extremely personalized. Though there are limits on individual donations, there are no constraints on spending by political parties, offering an outsized advantage to parties able to secure abundant funds.

B2. Is there a realistic opportunity for the opposition to increase its support or gain power through elections? 4 / 4

Opposition political parties have a realistic chance of winning power through elections. The opposition Popular Force party has used its legislative majority as a strong counterweight to the executive.

B3. Are the people's political choices free from domination by the military, foreign powers, religious hierarchies, economic oligarchies, or any other powerful group that is not democratically accountable? 3 / 4

While voters and candidates are generally able to exercise their political choices without undue influence, businesses regularly seek to bribe or otherwise influence political candidates' positions.

B4. Do various segments of the population (including ethnic, religious, gender, LGBT, and other relevant groups) have full political rights and electoral opportunities? 2 / 4

The concerns of ethnic and cultural minorities, especially in remote mountain and Amazonian areas, remain inadequately addressed in politics. The 2011 Law of Prior Consultation, which guaranteed consultation with indigenous groups before mining and other development projects were undertaken, has fostered increased recognition of indigenous participation.

While the political participation of women has increased over recent years, women hold just 28 percent of seats in Congress and few leadership roles in local and regional governments.

C. FUNCTIONING OF GOVERNMENT: 7 / 12

C1. Do the freely elected head of government and national legislative representatives determine the policies of the government? 3 / 4

Elected leaders and representatives are the key agents in creating and implementing policy. However, businesses and special interest groups influence officials through bribes and other illicit payments. The last four presidents and opposition leader Keiko Fujimori have all been accused of accepting illegal funds.

Partisan polarization has disrupted normal government functions in recent years. The opposition Popular Force has used its legislative majority to censure or dismiss top-level ministers and to pursue impeachment votes against President Kuczynski in late 2017 and 2018. Kuczynski resigned in March 2018 in the wake of numerous corruption allegations. His replacement, Martín Vizcarra, continued to battle with the legislature, at one point threatening to initiate a procedure that could permit him to dissolve Congress and call new elections. Politics had stabilized somewhat by year's end, after Vizcarra's anticorruption initiatives were approved in a referendum.

C2. Are safeguards against official corruption strong and effective? 2 / 4

Government corruption remains a critical problem in Peru, though law enforcement authorities frequently investigate and prosecute corruption allegations. Recent years have seen scandals involving allegations of illicit deals between the Brazilian firm Odebrecht and a number of the country's most senior political figures.

President Kuczynski grappled with corruption allegations since taking office in 2016. In March 2018, he resigned after the emergence of videos that appeared to show officials in his administration attempting to exchange politically beneficial public contracts for lawmakers' support in the impending impeachment vote against him. Kuczynski was already facing allegations that his investment firm had improperly accepted payments from Odebrecht. Opposition leader Keiko Fujimori was arrested in October for allegedly taking unlawful campaign contributions from Odebrecht. And, in November, former president Alan García was prohibited from leaving the country for 18 months after reports surfaced suggesting that he had accepted kickbacks from Odebrecht in return for contracts to construct the Lima metro, and had been secretly paid $100,000 by the firm for a speech he gave in 2012. Former president Ollanta Humala continued to await a money-laundering trial in connection with allegations that he too had accepted illegal campaign funds from Odebrecht. In April, Peru's Supreme Court ordered that he be released from pretrial detention.

After taking office, President Vizcarra proposed four anticorruption reforms, which were put to a referendum in December 2018. Three of the measures—including a ban on consecutive reelection for lawmakers, limits on campaign contributions, and an overhaul of the judicial appointment process—were approved by more than 85 percent of voters. The fourth measure, to reinstitute a 50-member Senate, was rejected by a little over 90 percent of voters. The result was a triumph for Vizcarra, who had campaigned heavily for the three successful reforms, but advocated against the fourth due to a modification made by the opposition-controlled Congress that would have curtailed executive power.

A recent survey released in October by Datum International, a Peruvian market research company, found that 94 percent of respondents viewed corruption as being widespread in Peru, and 82 percent believe it had increased in the last five years.

C3. Does the government operate with openness and transparency? 2 / 4

Some government agencies have made progress on transparency, but much information related to defense and security policies remains classified under a 2012 law.

CIVIL LIBERTIES: 42 / 60
D. FREEDOM OF EXPRESSION AND BELIEF: 15 / 16
D1. Are there free and independent media? 3 / 4

Peru's dynamic press is mostly privately owned, and ownership is highly concentrated. Defamation is criminalized, and journalists are regularly convicted under such charges, though their sentences are usually suspended. Verbal and physical attacks against journalists are reported each year. In October 2018, Congresswoman Esther Saavedra physically attacked journalist Edgar Alarcón, who had reported that Saveedra's résumé misrepresented her educational background.

D2. Are individuals free to practice and express their religious faith or nonbelief in public and private? 4 / 4

The Peruvian constitution guarantees freedom of religion and belief, and these rights are generally respected.

D3. Is there academic freedom, and is the educational system free from extensive political indoctrination? 4 / 4

Academic freedom is unrestricted.

D4. Are individuals free to express their personal views on political or other sensitive topics without fear of surveillance or retribution? 4 / 4

People are generally free to engage in private discussion without fear of retribution or surveillance.

E. ASSOCIATIONAL AND ORGANIZATIONAL RIGHTS: 8 / 12
E1. Is there freedom of assembly? 3 / 4

The authorities generally recognize the constitutionally guaranteed right to peaceful assembly. In the past, local disputes and protests—notably those related to extractive industries, land rights, and resource allocation among marginalized populations—have resulted in instances of excessive use of force by security personnel. However, substantial efforts by the state ombudsman and the National Office of Dialogue and Sustainability (ONDS) have seemingly contributed to a reduction in protest-related violence.

E2. Is there freedom for nongovernmental organizations, particularly those that are engaged in human rights- and governance-related work? 3 / 4

Freedom of association is generally respected. However, efforts by environmental activists to discourage land development have been met with intimidation.

E3. Is there freedom for trade unions and similar professional or labor organizations? 2 / 4

Peruvian law recognizes the right of workers to organize and bargain collectively. Strikes are legal with advance notification to the Ministry of Labor, but few strikers abide by this regulation. Lengthy processes involved in registering a new union create a window in which labor leaders and activists can be easily dismissed from their jobs. Short-term contracts in many industries makes unionization difficult. Less than 10 percent of the formal workforce is unionized.

F. RULE OF LAW: 8 / 16

F1. Is there an independent judiciary? 2 / 4

The judiciary is perceived as one of the most corrupt institutions in the country. In July 2018, secretly recorded tapes revealed five judges trading reduced sentences or judicial appointments in exchange for bribes. All of the judges resigned or were suspended and the revelations prompted a wave of citizen demonstrations. In December, voters approved a reform that would replace the National Council of Judges, the body which selects and appoints judges, with a new National Board of Justice, whose members would be voted on by the public and restricted to one five-year term.

F2. Does due process prevail in civil and criminal matters? 2 / 4

Constitutional guarantees of due process are unevenly upheld. Lawyers provided to indigent defendants are often poorly trained, and translation services are rarely provided for defendants who do not speak Spanish. Impunity for violence against environmental activists who challenge land development remains a problem.

In October, Peru's Supreme Court ordered former authoritarian president Alberto Fujimori back to prison. In 2009, Fujimori was sentenced to 25 years' imprisonment for human rights abuses committed while in office, but Kuczynski had issued a controversial medical pardon for him in 2017.

F3. Is there protection from the illegitimate use of physical force and freedom from war and insurgencies? 2 / 4

According to the 2016–17 Latin American Public Opinion Project (LAPOP) survey, Peru has one of the highest crime victimization rates in the Americas, with over 30 percent of Peruvians reporting that they were victims of a crime in the last twelve months, though many of these were nonviolent offenses.

Conditions in Peruvian jails are extremely poor. As of November 2018, the prison population was more than double the country's capacity; 40 percent of detainees were in pretrial detention.

F4. Do laws, policies, and practices guarantee equal treatment of various segments of the population? 2 / 4

Discrimination against indigenous populations and Afro-Peruvians is pervasive. LGBT (lesbian, gay, bisexual, and transgender) people face discrimination, hostility, and violence.

In September 2018, Peru passed a sweeping new disability rights law acknowledging the equal legal rights of every individual, regardless of physical, mental, sensory, or intellectual disability. The law also established a new system through which people with disabilities may obtain support in dealing with legal and other important matters.

G. PERSONAL AUTONOMY AND INDIVIDUAL RIGHTS: 11 / 16

G1. Do individuals enjoy freedom of movement, including the ability to change their place of residence, employment, or education? 4 / 4

Peru does not place formal restrictions on movement, and movement around the country has become easier in recent years due to a decrease in protest actions that involve road blockages. People are able to freely change their place of employment or education.

G2. Are individuals able to exercise the right to own property and establish private businesses without undue interference from state or nonstate actors? 3 / 4

The rights to own property and establish business are mostly respected, though tensions persist between extractive industries and indigenous communities who oppose land development. The Prior Consultation Law is designed in part to better protect indigenous rights to land. Its implementation has resulted in positive outcomes for communities that have taken part in consultation processes—though prior consultation still does not always take place.

G3. Do individuals enjoy personal social freedoms, including choice of marriage partner and size of family, protection from domestic violence, and control over appearance? 2 / 4

Gender-based violence is widespread in Peru, with more than half of Peruvian women reporting instances of physical, sexual, or emotional abuse. Proposals to recognize civil unions for same-sex partners have been repeatedly introduced and rejected in Congress. Abortion is permitted only in instances where a woman's health is in danger.

G4. Do individuals enjoy equality of opportunity and freedom from economic exploitation? 2 / 4

Peruvian women and girls—especially from the indigenous community—fall victim to sex trafficking. Men, women, and children are subject to forced labor in mines and the informal economy. According to the US State Department's 2018 *Trafficking in Persons Report*, the Peruvian government has expanded its efforts to prosecute trafficking cases, but continues to fall short in assisting victims and preventing human trafficking.

Raúl Becerra, a former chief of the national police, was among 14 people arrested in November 2018 for allegedly operating a baby-trafficking ring that pressured low-income mothers into giving away their children, who were then likely sold for illegal adoption or organ trafficking. The group reportedly sought out pregnant women in part by purporting to offer abortions, which are illegal in most circumstances in Peru.

Philippines

Population: 107,000,000
Capital: Manila
Political Rights Rating: 3
Civil Liberties Rating: 3
Freedom Rating: 3.0
Freedom Status: Partly Free
Electoral Democracy: Yes

Overview: Although the Philippines transitioned from authoritarian rule in 1986, the rule of law and application of justice are haphazard and heavily favor ruling elites. Long-term violent insurgencies have continued for decades. Impunity remains the norm for crimes against activists and journalists, and President Rodrigo Duterte's war on drugs since 2016 has led to thousands of extrajudicial killings as well as vigilante justice.

KEY DEVELOPMENTS IN 2018:
- The government revoked the certificate of incorporation for the news site Rappler in January, for allegedly violating regulations that prohibit any foreign control over domestic media outlets. Rappler reporters were then banned in February from the

presidential palace and from all official presidential events. Editor-in-chief Maria Ressa was subsequently charged with tax evasion in November.
- The government filed a petition with a Manila court in February to declare 649 individuals, many of them prominent opponents of the government, members of the Communist Party of the Philippines (CPP), which would effectively designate them as terrorists.
- In May, the Supreme Court voted eight to six to grant a petition by the solicitor general to cancel the 2010 appointment of Chief Justice Maria Lourdes Sereno, a high-profile critic of Duterte, due to allegations that she had failed to disclose some of her assets. Sereno's ouster was condemned by the opposition as politically motivated.
- In July, President Duterte signed the Bangsamoro Organic Law to create an autonomous region in Mindanao, which was considered an important step toward peace in the restive region. Despite the gains, Congress voted in December to extend martial law and the suspension of habeas corpus in Mindanao for another year.

POLITICAL RIGHTS: 26 / 40 (−1)

A. ELECTORAL PROCESS: 9 / 12

A1. Was the current head of government or other chief national authority elected through free and fair elections? 3 / 4

The president is both head of state and head of government, and is directly elected to a single six-year term. Rodrigo Duterte of the Philippine Democratic Party–People's Power (PDP-Laban) won the 2016 presidential election with 39 percent of the vote, followed by Manuel Roxas II of the Liberal Party, with 23 percent. While they were marked by dozens of violent episodes, including a number of killings, there were fewer such incidents compared to previous election years. Other persistent problems included media bias and vote buying, offers for which affected nearly 20 percent of voters in 2016.

The vice president is directly elected on a separate ticket and may serve up to two successive six-year terms. Maria Leonor "Leni" Robredo won the closely contested vice presidency in 2016 with 35 percent of the vote.

A2. Were the current national legislative representatives elected through free and fair elections? 3 / 4

Elections for the bicameral Congress took place concurrently with the presidential vote and suffered from the same limitations. No single party won an outright majority in either house, but the PDP-Laban Party secured unprecedented majority alliances in both. The 24 members of the Senate are elected on a nationwide ballot and serve six-year terms, with half of the seats up for election every three years. The 297 members of the House of Representatives serve three-year terms, with 238 elected in single-member constituencies and the remainder elected through party-list voting.

Local elections originally scheduled for 2016 were held across the country in May 2018. Violence plagued the campaign period, leading to at least 33 deaths, including a former member of Congress who was shot dead while delivering a campaign speech.

A3. Are the electoral laws and framework fair, and are they implemented impartially by the relevant election management bodies? 3 / 4

The president appoints the Commission on Elections (Comelec), whose performance was generally praised in 2016. However, frequent litigation complicates the interpretation of electoral laws and makes the already complex framework even less accessible to the public.

B. POLITICAL PLURALISM AND PARTICIPATION: 10 / 16 (−1)

B1. Do the people have the right to organize in different political parties or other competitive political groupings of their choice, and is the system free of undue obstacles to the rise and fall of these competing parties or groupings? 3 / 4

The Philippines has a strong record of open competition among multiple parties, though candidates and political parties typically have weak ideological identities. Legislative coalitions are exceptionally fluid, and politicians often change party affiliation.

B2. Is there a realistic opportunity for the opposition to increase its support or gain power through elections? 2 / 4 (−1)

The Philippines has seen a regular rotation of power, but opposition politicians have faced increasing harassment and even arrest in recent years. In 2017, Senator Leila de Lima, one of the most outspoken critics of President Duterte's war on drugs, was arrested on charges viewed as politically motivated by the opposition, of accepting money from drug dealers; she remained in jail at the end of 2018, nearly two years after her arrest. In September 2018, another vocal critic of the president, Senator Antonio Trillanes, was arrested after Duterte voided the amnesty granted to him in 2010 for leading mutinies in 2003 and 2007, when he was an officer in the navy. The action revived rebellion and coup cases against Trillanes in the lower courts. Trillanes posted bail on the day of his arrest and awaited trial at year's end. In addition, the president's son and son-in-law filed libel charges against Trillanes in December, over accusations lodged by the senator that both men were involved in smuggling methamphetamine. Trillanes also posted bail on those charges.

Duterte has cracked down on the CPP and its armed wing, the New People's Army (NPA). In late 2017, Duterte signed a proclamation stating that both the CPP and the NPA are terrorist organizations. In February, the government filed a petition with a Manila court to declare 649 individuals CPP and NPA members, which would effectively designate them as terrorists. The names on the list include actual members of the CPP, as well as other critics of the president, the UN special rapporteur on the rights of indigenous peoples, and a former member of Congress. If the court approves the petition, those on the list could be closely monitored by the government. Human Rights Watch (HRW) called the list a "virtual hit list," since people officially accused of involvement with the NPA are often assassinated. The case was pending at year's end.

Score Change: The score declined from 3 to 2 due to the arrest of a second senator who has opposed President Duterte and a government attempt to have more than 600 people—including leftist critics of the administration—designated as members of the Communist Party and terrorists.

B3. Are the people's political choices free from domination by the military, foreign powers, religious hierarchies, economic oligarchies, or any other powerful group that is not democratically accountable? 2 / 4

Distribution of power is heavily affected by kinship networks. Political dynasties are prevalent at the provincial and municipal levels, with implications at the national level as politicians there often draw on a regional base of support. The nature of election-related funding contributes to the concentration of power: there are no limits on campaign contributions and a significant portion of political donations come from a relatively small number of donors.

The Roman Catholic Church has historically played a significant role in politics. The activities of armed rebel groups and martial law also continue to affect politics in the south of the country and on part of the main island of Luzon.

B4. Do various segments of the population (including ethnic, religious, gender, LGBT, and other relevant groups) have full political rights and electoral opportunities? 3 / 4

While women make up about a quarter of the legislature, political life is male-dominated and few women are elected without following in the footsteps of a male relative. Muslims and indigenous groups are not well represented; perceptions of relative socioeconomic deprivation and political disenfranchisement, along with resentment toward Christian settlements in traditionally Muslim areas, have played a central role in the Philippines' Muslim separatist movements.

In 2013, the Supreme Court ruled that the party-list portion of the electoral framework for the House of Representatives, traditionally meant to represent marginalized or underrepresented demographic groups, could also be open to other groups, including national political parties, provided that they do not stand in the single-member constituency contests. A number of party-list groups gained seats in 2016 not by representing national sectors or interests as intended, but through substantial support from kinship networks in single geographic regions.

C. FUNCTIONING OF GOVERNMENT: 7 / 12

C1. Do the freely elected head of government and national legislative representatives determine the policies of the government? 3 / 4

Elected government officials and legislative representatives determine state policies, but corruption and cronyism are rife, including in business. A few dozen families continue to hold a disproportionate share of political authority. Local "bosses" often control their respective areas, limiting accountability and committing abuses of power.

C2. Are safeguards against official corruption strong and effective? 2 / 4

A culture of impunity, stemming in part from backlogs in the judicial system, hampers the fight against government corruption. In a nod to his campaign promise, President Duterte has fired tens of officials due to corruption, including the interior minister in 2017. However, the anticorruption drive had led to few convictions by the end of 2018. In December, an anticorruption court acquitted former senator Ramon Revilla Jr. on plunder charges for allegedly embezzling over $4 million in government funds, although one of his aides was convicted. In November, former first lady and current member of Congress Imelda Marcos was found guilty of corruption for improperly moving $200 million into Swiss foundations as governor of Manila in the 1970s. She was sentenced to between 6 and 11 years in prison. Marcos posted bail and filed an appeal with the Supreme Court, which had not yet heard her case at year's end.

The country's official anticorruption agencies, the Office of the Ombudsman and the Presidential Anti-Graft Commission (PAGC), have mixed records. The PAGC lacks enforcement capabilities. The Ombudsman focuses on major cases against senior government officials and those involving large sums of money, and some cases languish for years in the special anticorruption court (Sandiganbayan).

C3. Does the government operate with openness and transparency? 2 / 4

Governmental transparency remains limited despite some positive initiatives. Local governments have been required to post procurement and budget data on their websites, and in 2012 the national government began participatory budgeting at various levels. Duterte issued an order establishing the country's first freedom of information directive in 2016, but it mandates public disclosure only in the executive branch and allows major exemptions.

CIVIL LIBERTIES: 35 / 60

D. FREEDOM OF EXPRESSION AND BELIEF: 14 / 16

D1. Are there free and independent media? 2 / 4

The constitution provides for freedoms of expression and the press. Private media are vibrant and outspoken, although content often lacks fact-based claims or substantive investigative reporting. The country's many state-owned television and radio stations cover controversial topics and criticize the government, but they too lack strict journalistic ethics. While the censorship board has broad powers to edit or ban content, government censorship is generally not a serious problem in practice.

However, the Philippines remains one of the most dangerous places in the world for journalists, and the president's hostile rhetoric toward members of the media continued to exacerbate an already perilous situation in 2018. According to the Philippine Center for Investigative Journalism, there were 85 recorded verbal and physical attacks on journalists in the first 22 months of Duterte's administration, through April 2018.

Other obstacles to press freedom include Executive Order 608, which established a National Security Clearance System to protect classified information, and the Human Security Act, which allows journalists to be wiretapped based on suspicion of involvement in terrorism. Libel is a criminal offense, and libel cases have been used frequently to quiet criticism of public officials.

In January, the government revoked the certificate of incorporation for the news site Rappler, which has been critical of Duterte's war on drugs, for violation of regulations that forbid foreign entities from exerting any control over domestic news outlets. Reporters for Rappler, accused by Duterte of being part of a "fake news outlet," were banned in February from the presidential palace and from all official presidential events. The outlet's editor-in-chief, Maria Ressa, was charged with tax evasion in November, which rights activists assailed as an attempt to further intimidate independent media; she posted bail the following month.

D2. Are individuals free to practice and express their religious faith or nonbelief in public and private? 4 / 4

Freedom of religion is guaranteed under the constitution and generally respected in practice.

D3. Is there academic freedom, and is the educational system free from extensive political indoctrination? 4 / 4

Academic freedom is generally respected.

D4. Are individuals free to express their personal views on political or other sensitive topics without fear of surveillance or retribution? 4 / 4

There are no significant impediments to free and open private discussion. The internet is widely available. Rights groups have expressed concern about threats against and censorship of anonymous online criticism and the criminalization of libelous posts, but this has yet to have a major impact on private discussion.

E. ASSOCIATIONAL AND ORGANIZATIONAL RIGHTS: 8 / 12

E1. Is there freedom of assembly? 3 / 4

Citizen activism and public discussion are robust, and demonstrations are common. However, permits are required for rallies, and police sometimes use violence to disperse antigovernment protests.

E2. Is there freedom for nongovernmental organizations, particularly those that are engaged in human rights- and governance-related work? 2 / 4

Assassination of civil society activists is a serious problem in the Philippines, and President Duterte's public threats against activists who oppose his policies have exacerbated an already dangerous atmosphere of impunity. The Ireland-based human rights group Front Line Defenders reported that 39 human rights defenders were killed in the Philippines in 2018. Despite the danger, the Philippines hosts many active human rights and social welfare groups.

E3. Is there freedom for trade unions and similar professional or labor organizations? 3 / 4

Trade unions are independent, though less than 10 percent of the labor force is unionized. Among them, collective bargaining is common, and strikes may be called as long as unions provide notice and obtain majority approval from their members. Violence against labor leaders has been part of the broader trend of extrajudicial killings over the past decade.

F. RULE OF LAW: 3 / 16

F1. Is there an independent judiciary? 1 / 4 (−1)

Judicial independence has deteriorated during President Duterte's administration. Chief Justice of the Supreme Court Maria Lourdes Sereno, a harsh critic of the president, was ousted in May 2018 when the court voted eight to six to grant a petition by the solicitor general to cancel her 2010 appointment, due to allegations that she had failed to disclose some of her assets. The decision was sharply criticized by the opposition as politically motivated and a brazen attack on the independence of the judiciary. Mereno argued that her removal was improper, because the only means of removing a Supreme Court Justice prescribed by the constitution is through congressional impeachment proceedings.

The efforts of the judiciary are stymied by inefficiency, low pay, intimidation, corruption, and high vacancy rates. Judges and lawyers often depend on local power holders for basic resources and salaries, which can lead to compromised verdicts.

Score Change: The score declined from 2 to 1 due to the removal of a Supreme Court chief justice who had clashed with the president through a court proceeding initiated by the government rather than a congressional impeachment as mandated by the constitution.

F2. Does due process prevail in civil and criminal matters? 0 / 4

Due process is seriously compromised. Arbitrary detention, disappearances, kidnappings, and abuse of suspects continue. The police and military have been implicated in corruption, extortion, and involvement in the illegal drug trade. In the drug war, the police have used watch lists to identify targets for extrajudicial execution. In December 2018, Congress voted to extend martial law and the suspension of habeas corpus, which was first approved in May 2017, for one year in the restive southern region of Mindanao.

F3. Is there protection from the illegitimate use of physical force and freedom from war and insurgencies? 1 / 4 (+1)

The police and military routinely torture detainees. Lack of effective witness protection has been a key obstacle to investigations against members of the security forces. President Duterte's war on drugs has led to widespread extrajudicial killing. Authorities stated in December 2018 that 5,000 people had been killed in the campaign, but human rights groups estimate as many as 20,000 deaths. The victims include civilians and children who were deliberately targeted. Convictions for extrajudicial killings and other such crimes are rare, and Duterte has appeared to encourage the actions. In February, the International Criminal Court

(ICC) announced that it would conduct a preliminary examination into the war on drugs. In response, President Duterte declared in March that the Philippines was withdrawing its ratification of the Rome Statute, effectively ending the country's participation in the ICC.

With drug users fearfully turning themselves in to police en masse, jails and prisons have become dangerously overcrowded, leading to the spread of disease and heightened violence. According to the Philippine Center for Investigative Journalism, the corrections system in the Philippines is now the most overcrowded in the world.

Conflict in Mindanao has caused severe hardship, more than 120,000 deaths, and the displacement of tens of thousands of people since it erupted in 1972. Both government and rebel forces have committed summary killings and other human rights abuses. In 2017, a group of Islamic State–linked foreign fighters and local militants attacked the city of Marawi; more than 1,200 people were killed in a five-month siege of the city. Heavy fighting subsided in 2018 due to the end of the siege.

In July, President Duterte signed the Bangsamoro Organic Law, creating a self-governing region, Bangsamoro, to replace and add territory to the current Autonomous Region in Muslim Mindanao. The law was the next crucial step outlined in a landmark 2014 peace treaty between the previous administration and the Moro Islamic Liberation Front (MILF), the country's largest rebel group. However, some militant groups that had broken away from MILF and were not included in the deal continued to carry out attacks even after the law was signed.

In August, President Duterte stated that he was ending peace talks with the Communist Party of the Philippines–New People's Army–National Democratic Front of the Philippines (CPP-NPA-NDFP), dashing hopes that the 50-year violent insurgency could see a peaceful end during his administration. Deadly clashes between the NPA and the Philippine army continue to occur regularly throughout the country, though the violence has declined in recent years.

Score Change: The score improved from 0 to 1 due to the end of heavy fighting between government forces and Islamist militants in the city of Marawi.

F4. Do laws, policies, and practices guarantee equal treatment of various segments of the population? 1 / 4

Equal treatment is severely limited. Indigenous rights are generally upheld, but land disputes and local development projects regularly cause friction and sometimes lead to violence. Indigenous people often live in conflict areas and are targeted by combatants for their perceived loyalties.

LGBT (lesbian, gay, bisexual, and transgender) people face bias in employment, education, and other services, as well as societal discrimination. In a landmark vote in 2017, the House of Representatives passed the Sexual Orientation and Gender Identity and Expression Equality (SOGIE) bill, which if passed by the Senate would formally protect the rights of the LGBT community against gender-based discrimination. However, the Senate failed to pass the bill in 2018, leaving its future in question.

G. PERSONAL AUTONOMY AND INDIVIDUAL RIGHTS: 10 / 16

G1. Do individuals enjoy freedom of movement, including the ability to change their place of residence, employment, or education? 3 / 4

Citizens enjoy freedom of travel and choice of residence, with the exception of the conflict zones. Martial law in Mindanao includes enabling the military to set up roadblocks and checkpoints. In June 2018, President Duterte announced a campaign against loitering, which led to the arrests of thousands of people in public places in Manila.

G2. Are individuals able to exercise the right to own property and establish private businesses without undue interference from state or nonstate actors? 2 / 4

Private business activity is often dependent on the support of local power brokers in the complex patronage system that extends throughout the country. Outside of conflict zones, individuals are generally able to exercise the right to own property and establish private businesses without undue interference from state or nonstate actors, notwithstanding the domination and corruption of the economic dynasties.

G3. Do individuals enjoy personal social freedoms, including choice of marriage partner and size of family, protection from domestic violence, and control over appearance? 3 / 4

Most individuals enjoy personal social freedoms. Divorce is illegal in the Philippines, though annulments are allowed under specified circumstances, and Muslims may divorce via Sharia (Islamic law) courts. Violence against women continues to be a significant problem, and while spousal rape is a crime, very few cases are prosecuted. President Duterte's public statements on women's rights have evoked misogyny.

G4. Do individuals enjoy equality of opportunity and freedom from economic exploitation? 2 / 4

Income inequality in the Philippines is increasing and there is an uneven urban-rural wealth distribution. Manila's metro area accounts for just 12.5 percent of the population but is responsible for 36.5 percent of national GDP.

The Philippines is a source country for human trafficking, with some Filipinos taken abroad and forced to work in the fishing, shipping, construction, or other industries, or forced to engage in sex work. The country's various insurgent groups have been accused of using child soldiers.

Poland

Population: 38,400,000
Capital: Warsaw
Political Rights Rating: 2 ↓
Civil Liberties Rating: 2
Freedom Rating: 2.0
Freedom Status: Free
Electoral Democracy: Yes

Overview: Poland's democratic institutions took root at the start of its transition from communist rule in 1989. Rapid economic growth and other societal changes have benefited some segments of the population more than others, contributing to a deep divide between liberal, pro-European parties and those purporting to defend national interests and "traditional" Polish Catholic values. Since taking power in late 2015, the populist, socially conservative Law and Justice (PiS) party has enacted numerous measures that increase political influence over state institutions—notably the judiciary—and threaten Polish democracy.

KEY DEVELOPMENTS IN 2018:

- Amendments to the electoral code endangered the independence of the National Electoral Commission (PKW), which manages elections and oversees party finances, by shifting responsibility for many of its nominations to PiS-controlled institutions. The reform underwent no public consultation, and was criticized by the PKW head and opposition lawmakers.
- A second reform that came into effect in 2018 gave authority to validate or reject election and referendum results to a new Supreme Court chamber that is vulnerable to politicization.
- In October, European Court of Justice (ECJ) ruled that Poland must suspend a law mandating a new, lower retirement age for Supreme Court justices, which had required 27 out of 73 judges to retire. President Andrzej Duda signed legislation reinstating the retired judges in December.
- In February 2018, parliament passed a law criminalizing claims of Polish complicity in crimes committed during the Holocaust, carrying a potential prison sentence of up to three years. The government walked back the law following an international outcry, making it a civil offense punishable by fines.

POLITICAL RIGHTS: 35 / 40 (−1)

A. ELECTORAL PROCESS: 11 / 12 (−1)

A1. Was the current head of government or other chief national authority elected through free and fair elections? 4 / 4

The president of Poland is directly elected for up to two five-year terms. The president's appointment of a prime minister must be confirmed by the Sejm, the lower house of parliament. While the prime minister holds most executive power under the constitution, the president is also meant to have influence, particularly over defense and foreign policy matters.

Andrzej Duda of PiS won the second round of Poland's May 2015 presidential election with 52 percent of the vote, defeating incumbent Bronisław Komorowski in a process that was held in accordance with democratic standards. Komorowski was supported by the centrist Civic Platform (PO), which at that time had led the government since 2007.

The current prime minister, Mateusz Morawiecki, was appointed and confirmed in December 2017 with the approval of the PiS majority in parliament, although he does not hold a seat in parliament or any other elected position. In practice, PiS party chairman Jarosław Kaczyński, who retains no formal state position other than being a member of parliament, has vast influence over the government.

A2. Were the current national legislative representatives elected through free and fair elections? 4 / 4

Members of the bicameral National Assembly are elected to four-year terms. The 460-seat Sejm is elected by proportional representation and holds most legislative authority. The 100 members of the Senate, the upper house, are elected in single-member constituencies. The Senate can delay and amend legislation, but has few other powers.

PiS won 37.5 percent of the vote in the October 2015 parliamentary elections, increasing its representation in the Sejm to 235 seats. This made it the first party in postcommunist Poland to win an outright parliamentary majority, allowing it to rule without coalition partners. PO came in second with slightly more than 24 percent of the vote and 138 seats. Third and fourth place both went to new parties: Kukiz'15, a right-wing, antiestablishment party led by former rock musician Paweł Kukiz, which took 42 seats; and the liberal probusiness party

Modern, which won 28. The agrarian Polish People's Party (PSL) won 5 percent of the vote and 16 seats. A representative of the ethnic German minority received the remaining seat.

In the Senate, PiS took 61 seats, PO 34, and PSL 1. International observers deemed the election competitive and credible.

A3. Are the electoral laws and framework fair, and are they implemented impartially by the relevant election management bodies? 3 / 4 (−1)

While Poland's electoral framework and its implementation have generally ensured free and fair elections, recent legal changes threaten to increase political control over election administration. Amendments to the electoral code signed by President Duda in January 2018 endangered the independence of the PKW, which manages elections and oversees party finances. Previously, all nine members of the PKW were nominated by courts. Under the amendments, seven members are chosen by parliament, and only two members are selected by courts. The largest parliamentary group is allowed to pick no more than three members, but PiS can exert influence over the member selected by the Constitutional Tribunal (TK), which is currently led by PiS-installed judges. The reform—which will require the replacement of current PKW members under the new nomination system after 2019 legislative elections—underwent no public consultation, and the PKW head and opposition figures in the Sejm warned ahead of its approval that it endangered the body's ability to oversee credible elections.

Additionally, a judicial reform that came into force in 2018 gave authority to validate or reject election and referendum results to a newly created chamber of the Supreme Court, the Chamber of Extraordinary Control and Public Affairs, whose members are appointed by the newly politicized National Council of the Judiciary. (Under a law that took effect in 2018, parliament appoints the majority of members to the National Council of the Judiciary.) The chamber's substantial power, along with its vulnerability to politicization, could further threaten the integrity of electoral oversight.

Score Change: The score declined from 4 to 3 due to the implementation of reforms that increase political control over the electoral commission, and establish a powerful new Supreme Court chamber that is vulnerable to politicization.

B. POLITICAL PLURALISM AND PARTICIPATION: 16 / 16

B1. Do the people have the right to organize in different political parties or other competitive political groupings of their choice, and is the system free of undue obstacles to the rise and fall of these competing parties or groupings? 4 / 4

Poland's political parties are able to organize and operate freely.

B2. Is there a realistic opportunity for the opposition to increase its support or gain power through elections? 4 / 4

There have been multiple rotations of power among rival parties since the transition from communist rule, and the PiS victory in the last national elections ended a lengthy period of rule by the PO, now the largest opposition party. However, opposition parties are currently weak and divided, and they face potential long-term obstacles that could impact their ability to gain power in parliament. Propaganda by PiS-controlled public media amplifies the ruling party's message, while attempting to discredit opposition voices. The changes to the electoral framework that took effect in 2018 could permit PiS to consolidate control over the electoral process, with negative consequences for the opposition.

B3. Are the people's political choices free from domination by the military, foreign powers, religious hierarchies, economic oligarchies, or any other powerful group that is not democratically accountable? 4 / 4

Voters and politicians are generally free from undue interference by outside groups, though there are some concerns that the personnel changes associated with the PiS government's assertion of control over various state institutions could be exploited to mobilize political support among public employees ahead of future local and national elections.

The Roman Catholic Church remains politically influential. The Church strongly supported legislation introducing a Sunday trading ban, which mandated the closure of supermarkets and other retail operations on many Sundays, and took effect in March 2018. Powerful priest Tadeusz Rydzyk, an ally of the PiS, uses his media outlets to support the government's message, and has received generous state grants for organizations under his control, as well as access to high-level decision-makers.

B4. Do various segments of the population (including ethnic, religious, gender, LGBT, and other relevant groups) have full political rights and electoral opportunities? 4 / 4

Women have equal political rights and hold senior positions in government, including about 28 percent of the seats in the Sejm. Both PO and PiS fielded female candidates for prime minister in the 2015 elections.

Ethnic, religious, and other minority groups enjoy full political rights and electoral opportunities. Electoral lists representing recognized national minorities are not subject to the minimum vote threshold for parliamentary representation.

C. FUNCTIONING OF GOVERNMENT: 8 / 12

C1. Do the freely elected head of government and national legislative representatives determine the policies of the government? 3 / 4

Freely elected officials generally determine and implement laws and policies without interference, but PiS chairman Kaczyński continues to play a dominant role in the government despite not holding any official executive position. PiS has also, throughout its time in power, sought to limit parliamentary scrutiny of legislation through various means, including by introducing legislation unexpectedly, sometimes in the middle of the night, giving legislators inadequate time for review, and limiting opportunities for the opposition to question or amend legislation.

C2. Are safeguards against official corruption strong and effective? 3 / 4

Cronyism, a problem under all previous Polish governments, appears widespread under PiS. The government has altered, lowered, or simply removed many criteria for staffing of public institutions, allowing for appointments based on party loyalty and personal connections.

The Supreme Audit Office (NIK), a state watchdog, has raised concerns about the mishandling or misuse of public funds. In June 2018, the NIK accused the Justice Ministry of illegally transferring $6.7 million from a fund intended for victims of crimes to the Central Anticorruption Bureau (CBA). The NIK also published research showing that in 2017, the government awarded bonuses to senior officials that were 12 times higher than those awarded under the previous administration. Public outrage over the bonuses led Kaczyński to order ministers to return the money in April 2018—though to a charity run by the Catholic Church, rather than back into the state coffers.

Although corruption remains a problem, the CBA robustly pursued several high-profile cases in 2018. Most notably, in November, the CBA arrested Marek Chrzanowski, the former head of the Financial Supervision Authority (KNF), and charged him with corruption for allegedly demanding that a bank owner hire a particular lawyer and pay him $10.5 million in exchange for "support" and "protection" for the bank. (Chrzanowski had stepped down just a week earlier after media outlets broke news of the allegations.) Some opposition members have linked the scandal to powerful Central Bank Governor Adam Glapiński, a close friend and ally of Prime Minister Morawiecki, and have called for his resignation. Glapiński denied the allegations.

Money from large state-owned companies is increasingly used to support the ruling party's initiatives, such as an advertising campaign in 2017 to promote the government's judicial reforms that was paid for with funds from state firms ostensibly intended for promoting Poland abroad.

C3. Does the government operate with openness and transparency? 2 / 4

The right to public information is guaranteed by the constitution and by the 2001 Act on Access to Public Information, but obtaining records and data from public institutions can be slow and difficult. The courts' ability to uphold transparency laws has been uneven. However, in June 2018, after a two-year legal battle, the Supreme Administrative Court ordered the Education Ministry to comply with a request from a nongovernmental organization (NGO) to reveal the names of experts hired to advise on the new school curriculum.

The government avoids consulting outside experts or civil society organizations on policy ideas, and tends to introduce and pass legislation rapidly, with little opportunity for debate or amendment. The PiS government is also openly hostile to critical or independent media outlets and engages almost exclusively with state-run and progovernment outlets. Reporters from *Gazeta Wyborcza*, the country's largest non-tabloid newspaper, have difficulty gaining access to officials. Nevertheless, reporting on government activities and corruption remains fairly robust.

CIVIL LIBERTIES: 49 / 60

D. FREEDOM OF EXPRESSION AND BELIEF: 14 / 16

D1. Are there free and independent media? 3 / 4

The constitution guarantees freedom of expression and forbids censorship. Libel remains a criminal offense, though a 2009 amendment to the criminal code eased penalties. In addition, Poland has a suite of "insult laws," for example against blasphemy (punishable by up to two years in prison) and insulting the president (up to three years). In February 2018, parliament passed a law criminalizing claims of Polish complicity in crimes committed during the Holocaust, carrying a potential prison sentence of up to three years. Following an international outcry, the government softened the law, making it a civil offense punishable by fine but not incarceration.

Poland's media is pluralistic and most outlets are privately owned. However, the public media and their governing bodies have been purged of dissenting voices since PiS came to power in 2015. TVP, the public television broadcaster, promotes the government's message on topics ranging from peaceful antigovernment protests, which it depicts as attempted coups, to critical NGOs, which are portrayed as agents of the opposition or foreign forces. In 2018, news broadcasts on public television were used to openly support the ruling party's local election campaign and to discredit opposition campaigns.

Since 2015, state-controlled companies have shifted their advertising to private media outlets that support the PiS government. More critical outlets have suffered a corresponding drop in advertising revenue, as well as a sharp decline in subscriptions from government ministries.

• Independent media outlets have faced regulatory pressure and investigations for their reporting. In January 2018, the National Broadcasting Council (KRRiT) withdrew the fine of nearly 1.5 million złoty ($415,000) it had issued against private television station TVN24 in 2017 for "promoting illegal activities and inciting violence" through its coverage of antigovernment protests. However, in a statement on the decision that could be perceived as a warning, KRRiT implored the media to behave responsibly, and urged journalists to self-regulate. Also in January, however, prosecutors opened an investigation into the news channel TVN24 over a documentary it had aired that included undercover reporting on the activities of Polish neo-Nazis. Government ministers and PiS-linked media suggested that some of the events depicted in the documentary were staged. In November, authorities briefly opened an investigation into the documentary's cameraperson for propagating fascism, and visited his home.

The PiS leadership continues to express its desire to pass a long-planned law to "deconcentrate" and "repolonize" private media by reducing foreign ownership, a move that would disproportionately affect the outlets that most vigorously seek to hold the current government to account. The government often blames the presence of German and other foreign owners in the Polish media market for negative coverage of its activities.

D2. Are individuals free to practice and express their religious faith or nonbelief in public and private? 4 / 4

The state generally respects freedom of religion. The PiS government is aligned with the Roman Catholic Church, which wields significant influence in the country. Some prominent clergy members have distanced themselves from the ruling party, especially on its strong opposition to the settlement of Muslim refugees in Poland. However, others endorse the government's nativist and socially conservative policies, particularly its ongoing efforts to further restrict access to abortion.

Religious groups are not required to register with the authorities but receive tax benefits if they do. Minority faiths are generally able to obtain registration in practice. There is a formal ban on state funding for church construction, but a church can obtain Culture Ministry funding in practice if, like the Temple of Divine Providence in Warsaw, it includes a museum.

D3. Is there academic freedom, and is the educational system free from extensive political indoctrination? 3 / 4

The ruling party has sought to discredit academics who challenge its preferred historical narrative, particularly in regard to the events of World War II. The new "Holocaust law," though it includes a clause exempting academic work, was widely regarded within the academic community as an attempt to discourage research into and discussion of World War II–era Polish crimes against Jews. In March 2018, two PiS senators issued a statement criticizing the Museum of the History of Polish Jews in Warsaw after it held events marking the 50th anniversary of antisemitic purges in Poland, accusing the museum of making false claims about antisemitism.

D4. Are individuals free to express their personal views on political or other sensitive topics without fear of surveillance or retribution? 4 / 4

People are free to engage in private discussions on political and other matters without fear of harassment or retribution.

E. ASSOCIATIONAL AND ORGANIZATIONAL RIGHTS: 10 / 12

E1. Is there freedom of assembly? 3 / 4

Freedom of assembly is generally respected in law and in practice, but in recent years, protesters have increasingly risked surveillance, intimidation, physical attack by counterprotesters, use of force by authorities, arrest, and prosecution for their activities. Public demonstrations are held with some regularity, though local authorities can limit demonstrations in their districts on grounds of maintaining public order. A new registration law favoring regularly scheduled gatherings has been criticized for allowing authorities to amplify some forms of public speech and suppress others. Authorities have declined to intervene in or prosecute instances in which far-right protesters have assaulted counterdemonstrators.

A new round of largescale "black protests" by women in March 2018 again prompted the government to back away from attempts to pass a citizens' initiative to further tighten abortion laws.

E2. Is there freedom for nongovernmental organizations, particularly those that are engaged in human rights- and governance-related work? 3 / 4

Although NGOs have generally operated without government interference in Poland, public media and top government officials have systematically undermined the credibility of civil society in recent years, accusing many groups of lacking financial transparency and pursuing an opposition-led political agenda. In 2017, a new law centralized distribution of public NGO funding, including money from the EU and non-EU countries like Norway, through a new body attached to the prime minister's office. Critics of the new funding mechanism warned that it could be used to muzzle criticism of PiS and to deny money to projects that do not match the ruling party's perspective and priorities. The NGO law was widely condemned by domestic and international NGOs, as well as by Poland's human rights ombudsman.

NGO leaders have also been subjected to investigations by the police and other authorities in recent years. In August 2018, Lyudmyla Kozlovska, the Ukrainian head of a Warsaw-based human rights NGO, was expelled from the Schengen Area at Poland's request and deported back to Ukraine. Poland's Internal Security Agency, in a statement about the expulsion, raised doubts about the organization's funding sources without providing further information. Kozlovska claims that she was targeted due to her claims that PiS's reform agenda violates the rule of law.

E3. Is there freedom for trade unions and similar professional or labor organizations? 4 / 4

Poland has a robust labor movement, though certain groups—including the self-employed, private contractors, and those in essential services—cannot join unions. Complicated legal procedures hinder workers' ability to strike.

F. RULE OF LAW: 11 / 16

F1. Is there an independent judiciary? 1 / 4

Since taking power in 2015, the PiS government has moved aggressively to assert control over the judiciary. One of its first steps was to pass legislation designed to curb the powers of the TK, and it subsequently refused to publish TK decisions that it considered invalid. By the end of 2016, after a lengthy dispute over the tribunal's membership and authority, the TK was dominated by progovernment judges. In 2017, three new judicial reforms were adopted. The first gave the justice minister the power to appoint and dismiss presidents and deputy presidents of courts, a power he subsequently used several times.

The second and third reforms came into force in 2018 undermined the independence of the judiciary even further. Under one new law, parliament now appoints the majority of members to the National Council of the Judiciary (KRS), which is responsible for nominating judges. Previously, judges made most nominations to the body. Of the 15 new members appointed in March, many had links to the ruling party.

In July, a new, lower retirement age for Supreme Court justices came into force, which required 27 out of 73 judges to retire unless they received presidential approval to continue. The head of the Supreme Court, Małgorzata Gersdorf, who was among the judges slated for retirement, refused to step down on the basis that Poland's constitution guaranteed that her six-year term could not be cut short. In October, the ECJ, following an infringement procedure initiated by the European Commission (EC), ordered Poland to suspend the retirement age mandate. Consequently, the Polish parliament passed legislation reinstating the retired judges, which was signed into law by President Duda in December. However, other troubling aspects of the recent reforms remain in place, including a measure that enlarged the Supreme Court to 120 judges and created two powerful new chambers, which will be filled with judges appointed by the newly politicized KRS and could further entrench PiS's dominance of the judiciary.

Also retained under recent reforms is a system of "extraordinary appeals" that allows cases up to twenty years old to be reopened, which could allow for retroactive, politically motivated proceedings. During 2018, there were also a number of disciplinary proceedings initiated against judges who questioned the politicization of the justice system.

The judicial reforms have raised concerns among EU member states about the independence of Poland's judiciary and its adherence to the EU's values. Article 7 proceedings over the rule of law in Poland, launched by the EU in 2017, received the backing of a large majority in the European Parliament in March 2018.

F2. Does due process prevail in civil and criminal matters? 3 / 4

Defendants generally enjoy due process protections, though the law allows for extended pretrial detention, which can be lengthy in practice, and there is a large backlog of cases. A law passed in 2016, which merges the offices of the justice minister and prosecutor general, has led to concerns about potential abuse and politicization of the justice system.

Law enforcement agencies have broad authority to monitor citizens' communications activity, including the ability to access metadata without a court order and monitor the movements of foreign citizens without prior court approval. Terrorism suspects can be held without charge for up to two weeks.

F3. Is there protection from the illegitimate use of physical force and freedom from war and insurgencies? 4 / 4

Civilians are largely free from extralegal violence, though some incidents of abuse by police have been alleged in the context of antigovernment demonstrations. Human rights groups have reported inadequate medical care in prison facilities.

F4. Do laws, policies, and practices guarantee equal treatment of various segments of the population? 3 / 4

Women and ethnic minorities generally enjoy equality before the law. Some groups, particularly the Roma, experience discrimination in employment and housing, racially motivated insults, and occasional physical attacks. Members of the LGBT (lesbian, gay, bisexual, transgender) community continue to face discrimination. Hate crimes, particularly against Muslims or people believed to be Muslim by their attackers, have risen significantly over the last few years. According to a 2018 survey of people who identify as Jewish, carried out and published by the EU Agency for Fundamental Rights, a large majority of respondents in Poland said antisemitism in public life was a significant, increasing problem.

Human rights NGOs have accused Poland of violating national and international law by turning away large numbers of asylum seekers at its border with Belarus. In August 2018, Poland deported a Chechen refugee to Russia, where he disappeared after being taken from his home in a raid by Russian security forces.

G. PERSONAL AUTONOMY AND INDIVIDUAL RIGHTS: 14 / 16

G1. Do individuals enjoy freedom of movement, including the ability to change their place of residence, employment, or education? 4 / 4

People in Poland typically enjoy freedom of travel and choice of residence, employment, and institution of higher education.

G2. Are individuals able to exercise the right to own property and establish private businesses without undue interference from state or nonstate actors? 4 / 4

Citizens have the right to own property and establish private businesses. However, onerous restrictions on the sale and ownership of agricultural land, ostensibly to protect small-scale farmers, limit property rights. State and religious institutions are not bound by the restrictions.

G3. Do individuals enjoy personal social freedoms, including choice of marriage partner and size of family, protection from domestic violence, and control over appearance? 3 / 4

Since PiS assumed power in 2015, the government has consistently pursued policies that undermine reproductive rights. Under Polish law, abortion is only permissible if a woman's health or life is in danger, if the pregnancy is the result of a criminal act such as rape, or if the fetus is severely damaged. A bill that would have removed most of these exceptions and imposed five-year prison terms for illegal abortions triggered mass protests and failed to pass in 2016. Another legislative effort in 2018 to tighten abortion laws prompted more protests, leading parliament to again back away. Nevertheless, senior PiS figures and the president have signaled that they will pursue laws that ban abortion in cases where the fetus has a congenital disorder.

Since 2017, emergency contraceptive pills have been available by prescription only, making Poland one of only two EU countries with this restriction, along with Hungary. In many rural areas, gynecologists are rare, limiting reliable and timely access to contraception and other reproductive health services.

Same-sex civil partnerships, marriage, and adoption are not permitted, and Poland's constitution defines marriage as between a man and a woman.

G4. Do individuals enjoy equality of opportunity and freedom from economic exploitation? 3 / 4

The law provides meaningful protections against abusive working conditions and child labor, especially in the formal sector. The authorities work to combat human trafficking, but women and children are still subjected to trafficking for sexual exploitation. Romany children are frequently engaged in forced begging, and foreign migrant workers are vulnerable to forced labor.

Portugal

Population: 10,300,000
Capital: Lisbon
Political Rights Rating: 1
Civil Liberties Rating: 1
Freedom Rating: 1.0
Freedom Status: Free
Electoral Democracy: Yes

Overview: Portugal is a stable parliamentary democracy with a multiparty political system and regular transfers of power between the two largest parties. Civil liberties are generally protected. Ongoing concerns include corruption, certain legal constraints on journalism, poor or abusive conditions for prisoners, and the persistent effects of racism and xenophobia. Prosecutors have pursued corruption cases against top officials in recent years.

KEY DEVELOPMENTS IN 2018:

- Although the country has achieved some progress regarding racial discrimination, minority groups continue to face disparities in access to education, employment, and housing, and there was a sharp increase in formal discrimination complaints during the year.
- In February, the parliament amended the criminal code to give journalists a protected status, increasing penalties for those who threaten, constrain, or defame members of the press.
- Former prime minister José Sócrates and numerous other high-profile defendants were awaiting possible trial at the end of the year after being charged with extensive corruption offenses in late 2017.

POLITICAL RIGHTS: 39 / 40
A. ELECTORAL PROCESS: 12 / 12

A1. Was the current head of government or other chief national authority elected through free and fair elections? 4 / 4

In Portugal's parliamentary system, the prime minister holds most executive power, though the directly elected president can delay legislation through a veto and dissolve the parliament to trigger early elections. The president serves up to two five-year terms. In the 2016 presidential election, a center-right candidate supported by the opposition Social Democratic Party (PSD) and its allies, Marcelo Rebelo de Sousa, won with 52 percent of the vote, easily defeating a leftist candidate backed by the ruling Socialist Party (PS), António Sampaio da Nóvoa, who took less than 23 percent.

Prime Minister António Costa of the PS took office in 2015 as the head of a new government consisting of the PS, the Left Bloc (BE), the Communist Party (PCP), and the Greens (PEV).

A2. Were the current national legislative representatives elected through free and fair elections? 4 / 4

The 230 members of the unicameral Assembly of the Republic are directly elected every four years using a system of proportional representation in 22 multimember constituencies. In the 2015 elections, the incumbent Portugal Ahead coalition, comprising the PSD and the Democratic Social Center–People's Party (CDS-PP), won 107 of the 230 seats. It remained the largest single force, but suffered losses compared with the 2011 elections, in which it took 132 seats. The PS, then in opposition, won 86 seats; the BE took 19; the Democratic Unity Coalition, composed of the PCP and PEV, took 17; and the Party for People, Animals, and Nature (PAN) captured 1.

A3. Are the electoral laws and framework fair, and are they implemented impartially by the relevant election management bodies? 4 / 4

Elections in Portugal are generally free and fair. The constitution was amended in 1997 to allow Portuguese citizens living abroad to vote in presidential and legislative elections, as well as in national referendums.

B. POLITICAL PLURALISM AND PARTICIPATION: 16 / 16

B1. Do the people have the right to organize in different political parties or other competitive political groupings of their choice, and is the system free of undue obstacles to the rise and fall of these competing parties or groupings? 4 / 4

Political parties operate freely. The main parties are the center-left PS, the center-right PSD, and the Christian democratic CDS-PP. There is no legal vote threshold for representation in the parliament, meaning smaller parties can win a seat with little more than 1 percent of the overall vote in practice.

B2. Is there a realistic opportunity for the opposition to increase its support or gain power through elections? 4 / 4

Portugal has established a strong pattern of peaceful power transfers through elections since it returned to democracy in the late 1970s. The PS and PSD have rotated in and out of government several times in recent decades, most recently in 2015.

B3. Are the people's political choices free from domination by the military, foreign powers, religious hierarchies, economic oligarchies, or any other powerful group that is not democratically accountable? 4 / 4

Both voters and politicians are free from undue interference by forces outside the political system.

B4. Do various segments of the population (including ethnic, religious, gender, LGBT, and other relevant groups) have full political rights and electoral opportunities? 4 / 4

Women and minority groups enjoy full political rights and can participate in the political process in practice. Women hold more than a third of the seats in the parliament. The autonomous regions of Azores and Madeira—two island groups in the Atlantic—have their own political structures with legislative and executive powers.

C. FUNCTIONING OF GOVERNMENT: 11 / 12

C1. Do the freely elected head of government and national legislative representatives determine the policies of the government? 4 / 4

Elected officials are free to determine and implement laws and policies without improper interference by unelected groups.

C2. Are safeguards against official corruption strong and effective? 3 / 4

The country has struggled in recent years with major corruption scandals involving high-ranking politicians, officials, and businesspeople, though many have been duly prosecuted.

Manuel Vicente, Angola's vice president from 2012 to 2017 and the previous head of the country's state oil company, was charged by Portuguese prosecutors in 2017 for allegedly bribing a Portuguese magistrate to suspend an investigation into his financial activities. The trial began in January 2018, but in May Portuguese authorities transferred the case to Angola.

Also in 2017, former prime minister José Sócrates was formally indicted on corruption charges as part of a wide-ranging investigation that began in 2013. The case overlapped with that of Ricardo Salgado, former head of the defunct Banco Espírito Santo (BES), who was accused of bribing Sócrates through middlemen to secure favorable decisions and commercial benefits. As of the end of 2018, a judge had yet to decide whether Sócrates and some two dozen other defendants would stand trial. Other high-profile corruption trials and investigations were ongoing during the year.

C3. Does the government operate with openness and transparency? 4 / 4

Portuguese law provides for public access to government information, and state agencies generally respect this right. A ministerial order was issued in September 2018 to allow citizens to access judicial proceedings electronically.

CIVIL LIBERTIES: 57 / 60 (−1)
D. FREEDOM OF EXPRESSION AND BELIEF: 16 / 16
D1. Are there free and independent media? 4 / 4

Freedom of the press is constitutionally guaranteed. Public broadcasting channels are poorly funded and face strong competition from commercial television outlets, which provide a wide range of information and viewpoints. Internet access is not restricted.

Portugal remains one of the few countries in Europe where defamation is still a criminal offense, and although prosecutions are uncommon, the European Court of Human Rights (ECtHR) has repeatedly ruled against Portuguese authorities for their handling of both civil and criminal defamation cases.

In February 2018, the parliament adopted changes to the criminal code that granted journalists a protected status, increasing the penalties for those who threaten, defame, or constrain them. Others with such status include judges, lawyers, witnesses, and security personnel.

D2. Are individuals free to practice and express their religious faith or nonbelief in public and private? 4 / 4

Portugal is overwhelmingly Roman Catholic, but the constitution guarantees freedom of religion and forbids religious discrimination. The Religious Freedom Act provides benefits for religions that have been established in the country for at least 30 years or recognized internationally for at least 60 years. However, other groups are free to register as religious corporations and receive benefits such as tax-exempt status, or to practice their faith without registering.

D3. Is there academic freedom, and is the educational system free from extensive political indoctrination? 4 / 4

Academic freedom is respected. Schools and universities operate without undue political or other interference.

D4. Are individuals free to express their personal views on political or other sensitive topics without fear of surveillance or retribution? 4 / 4

There are no significant restrictions on private discussion or the expression of personal views.

E. ASSOCIATIONAL AND ORGANIZATIONAL RIGHTS: 12 / 12

E1. Is there freedom of assembly? 4 / 4

Freedom of assembly is upheld by the authorities. Protests organized during 2018 addressed problems including racism, gentrification, and the rising cost of housing.

E2. Is there freedom for nongovernmental organizations, particularly those that are engaged in human rights- and governance-related work? 4 / 4

Freedom of association is respected. National and international nongovernmental organizations, including human rights groups, operate in the country without interference.

E3. Is there freedom for trade unions and similar professional or labor organizations? 4 / 4

Workers enjoy the right to organize, bargain collectively, and strike, though there are some limits on the right to strike in a wide range of sectors and industries that are deemed essential. In September 2018, taxi drivers' unions held nationwide strikes to protest what they said were insufficient new regulations covering online ride-hailing services such as Uber.

F. RULE OF LAW: 14 / 16 (−1)

F1. Is there an independent judiciary? 4 / 4

The judiciary is independent, but staff shortages and inefficiency have contributed to a considerable backlog of pending trials.

In February 2018, the Supreme Court suspended two judges after they were deemed persons of interest in an investigation of alleged corruption, tax fraud, and money laundering centered on the leadership of a major Lisbon soccer club.

F2. Does due process prevail in civil and criminal matters? 4 / 4

The authorities generally observe legal safeguards against arbitrary arrest and detention, though court backlogs result in lengthy pretrial detention for some defendants. Due process rights are guaranteed during trial.

F3. Is there protection from the illegitimate use of physical force and freedom from war and insurgencies? 3 / 4

Human rights groups and the Council of Europe have expressed concern over abuse of detainees and excessive use of force by police, particularly against members of racial and ethnic minorities. Overcrowding in prisons remains a problem, as do poor health and safety conditions. In 2017, prosecutors charged 18 police officers with physically abusing six men of African descent in 2015. As of late 2018, the trial was still in progress.

F4. Do laws, policies, and practices guarantee equal treatment of various segments of the population? 3 / 4 (−1)

Equal treatment under the law is guaranteed by the constitution. Various laws prohibit discrimination based on factors including sex, race, disability, gender identity, and sexual orientation. Nevertheless, some problems persist with respect to gender bias and discrimination against minorities, particularly Roma and people of African descent.

A report from the European Commission against Racism and Intolerance (ECRI) published in October 2018 found that living conditions in Romany communities are generally poor, with 25 percent of Romany residents lacking basic sanitation. Romany children also face segregation at school, and 90 percent leave school prematurely. Just over half of Romany men are employed. Although by some measures Portugal is considered a less discriminatory environment for people of African descent than other European Union countries, black residents are also susceptible to disparities in housing, education, and employment.

In 2017, Portugal ratified a European Convention on Human Rights (ECHR) protocol that bans all discrimination and strengthened protections against hate crimes by passing a new antidiscrimination law. However, the country's Commission for Equality and Against Racial Discrimination (CICDR) reported an increase of more than 90 percent in the number of complaints filed during 2018 compared with the previous year, and there were few convictions for discrimination-related crimes.

Score Change: The score declined from 4 to 3 due to persistent discrimination against Roma and people of African descent, including with respect to housing, education, and employment.

G. PERSONAL AUTONOMY AND INDIVIDUAL RIGHTS: 15 / 16

G1. Do individuals enjoy freedom of movement, including the ability to change their place of residence, employment, or education? 4 / 4

Freedom of movement and associated rights are protected by the constitution and laws, and the government respects these rights in practice.

G2. Are individuals able to exercise the right to own property and establish private businesses without undue interference from state or nonstate actors? 4 / 4

The government does not interfere with the rights to own property, establish private businesses, and engage in commercial activity.

G3. Do individuals enjoy personal social freedoms, including choice of marriage partner and size of family, protection from domestic violence, and control over appearance? 4 / 4

There are no major restrictions on personal social freedoms. Portugal legalized same-sex marriage in 2010 and extended adoption rights to same-sex couples in 2015. A new law that went into force in August 2018 eliminated the need for transgender people to obtain a medical certificate to formally change their gender or first name. Domestic violence remains a problem despite government efforts aimed at prevention, education, and victim protection.

G4. Do individuals enjoy equality of opportunity and freedom from economic exploitation? 3 / 4

The authorities generally enforce legal safeguards against exploitative working conditions. However, Portugal remains a destination and transit point for victims of human trafficking, particularly those from Eastern Europe, Asia, and West Africa. Although forced labor is prohibited by law, there have been some reports of the practice, especially in the agriculture, hospitality, and construction sectors, and in domestic service. Immigrant workers are especially vulnerable to economic exploitation.

Qatar

Population: 2,700,000
Capital: Doha
Political Rights Rating: 6
Civil Liberties Rating: 5
Freedom Rating: 5.5
Freedom Status: Not Free
Electoral Democracy: No

Overview: Qatar's hereditary emir holds all executive and legislative authority, and ultimately controls the judiciary as well. Political parties are not permitted, and the only elections are for an advisory municipal council. While Qatari citizens are among the wealthiest in the world, the vast majority of the population consists of noncitizens with no political rights, few civil liberties, and limited access to economic opportunity.

KEY DEVELOPMENTS IN 2018:

- The government promulgated modest reforms pertaining to permanent residency, migrant workers, and asylum that departed from the laws of Qatar's peers in the Gulf Cooperation Council (GCC), indicating that the leadership no longer felt constrained by the GCC consensus given the diplomatic and trade restrictions imposed on the country since mid-2017 by Bahrain, Egypt, Saudi Arabia, and the United Arab Emirates (UAE).
- Preparations for soccer's 2022 World Cup, which have highlighted concerns about corruption and labor rights in Qatar, continued to dominate the economic landscape, with major infrastructure projects accelerating as the event drew nearer.

POLITICAL RIGHTS: 7 / 40

A. ELECTORAL PROCESS: 2 / 12

A1. Was the current head of government or other chief national authority elected through free and fair elections? 0 / 4

The emir appoints the prime minister and cabinet, and selects an heir-apparent after consulting with the ruling family and other notables. In 2013, Sheikh Hamad bin Khalifa Al-Thani abdicated as emir, handing power to his fourth-born son, Sheikh Tamim bin Hamad al-Thani. Sheikh Abdullah bin Nasser al-Thani, a member of the ruling family, became prime minister as well as interior minister.

A2. Were the current national legislative representatives elected through free and fair elections? 1 / 4

The 2003 constitution stipulated that 30 of the 45 seats on the Advisory Council (Majlis al-Shura) should be filled through elections every four years, with the emir appointing the other 15 members. However, elections have been repeatedly postponed, so all members are still appointed. In November 2017, the emir renewed the membership of some members and appointed 28 new members. He said the first elections to the Advisory Council would be held in 2019.

Nonpartisan elections have been held since 1999 for the 29-member Central Municipal Council, a body designed to advise the minister for municipal affairs. Members serve four-year terms. In the 2015 elections, turnout rose substantially to 70 percent of registered voters, from 43 percent in 2011, but the actual number registered fell by 40 percent to a record low of 21,735, out of roughly 150,000 eligible voters.

A3. Are the electoral laws and framework fair, and are they implemented impartially by the relevant election management bodies? 1 / 4

Electoral laws currently in force cover only the Central Municipal Council elections, and the absence of a legal framework for Advisory Council elections has been a factor in their repeated postponement. Qatari citizens over the age of 18 are eligible to vote, except those in the military or working for the Interior Ministry.

B. POLITICAL PLURALISM AND PARTICIPATION: 2 / 16

B1. Do the people have the right to organize in different political parties or other competitive political groupings of their choice, and is the system free of undue obstacles to the rise and fall of these competing parties or groupings? 0 / 4

The government does not permit the existence of political parties or other political groupings. All candidates for the municipal council elections run as independents.

B2. Is there a realistic opportunity for the opposition to increase its support or gain power through elections? 0 / 4

The ruling family maintains a monopoly on political power, and the system excludes the possibility of a change in government through elections.

As part of the diplomatic clash between Qatar and Saudi Arabia, the UAE, Bahrain, and Egypt that began in June 2017, dissident members of the Qatari ruling family living abroad emerged to advocate political change in Qatar, though they did not appear to have any organized public support within the country.

B3. Are the people's political choices free from domination by the military, foreign powers, religious hierarchies, economic oligarchies, or any other powerful group that is not democratically accountable? 1 / 4

Public participation in the political arena is extremely limited. Voters and candidates who do take part in the municipal elections are often influenced by tribal and family ties.

B4. Do various segments of the population (including ethnic, religious, gender, LGBT, and other relevant groups) have full political rights and electoral opportunities? 1 / 4

Up to 90 percent of Qatar's population is composed of noncitizens, including expatriates and migrant workers, who have no political rights or electoral opportunities. Citizenship is inherited exclusively from a Qatari father; residents can apply for citizenship after 25 years in the country, but this is rarely granted.

Qatari women enjoy some political rights, though they have little opportunity to organize independently and advocate for their interests. In the 2015 municipal council elections, five of the 130 candidates were women, and two of them won seats, up from one in the previous council. Four women were among the new Advisory Council members appointed in 2017, becoming the first women to serve on the council.

C. FUNCTIONING OF GOVERNMENT: 3 / 12

C1. Do the freely elected head of government and national legislative representatives determine the policies of the government? 0 / 4

Decision-making authority is concentrated in the hands of the emir and his family, and there is no elected legislature to offset executive power.

C2. Are safeguards against official corruption strong and effective? 2 / 4

The authorities regularly punish lower-level public officials for bribery and embezzlement, but corruption remains a concern, and the country lacks genuinely independent anticorruption mechanisms that can hold senior officials and members of the ruling family publicly accountable for the allocation of state resources. Qatar has been accused of employing corrupt tactics in its successful bid to host soccer's 2022 World Cup, and allegations of bribery surrounding the 2010 decision continued to emerge during 2018.

C3. Does the government operate with openness and transparency? 1 / 4

Official information is tightly controlled, and critics complain of a lack of transparency in state procurement. Although the State Audit Bureau prepares budgets and accounts for government institutions, it does not share their full details with the public or the appointed Advisory Council. A 2016 law empowered the bureau to make some aspects of its findings public, but the security ministries remained exempt from its oversight.

CIVIL LIBERTIES: 18 / 60 (+1)
D. FREEDOM OF EXPRESSION AND BELIEF: 7 / 16
D1. Are there free and independent media? 1 / 4

Both print and broadcast media are influenced by leading families and subject to state censorship. The international television network Al-Jazeera is privately held, but the government has reportedly paid to support its operating costs since its inception in 1996. All journalists in Qatar practice a degree of self-censorship and face possible jail sentences for defamation and other press offenses. Access to the independent English-language website Doha News was blocked in late 2016 on the grounds that it did not have the required operating permit, and the blocking remained in place during 2018.

D2. Are individuals free to practice and express their religious faith or nonbelief in public and private? 2 / 4

Islam is the official religion, though the constitution explicitly provides for freedom of worship. The Ministry of Islamic Affairs oversees the construction of mosques, the hiring of imams, and guidance for sermons. Churches have been built for Qatar's growing Christian community, but non-Muslims are not allowed to proselytize or worship in public.

D3. Is there academic freedom, and is the educational system free from extensive political indoctrination? 2 / 4

The constitution guarantees academic freedom, but scholars often self-censor on politically sensitive topics. Foreign universities have established branches in Qatar under a program to strengthen the country's educational institutions.

D4. Are individuals free to express their personal views on political or other sensitive topics without fear of surveillance or retribution? 2 / 4

While residents enjoy some freedom of private discussion, security forces reportedly monitor personal communications, and noncitizens often self-censor to avoid jeopardizing their work and residency status. Social media users can face criminal penalties for posting politically sensitive content. After Saudi Arabia and its allies imposed their diplomatic boycott and trade sanctions on Qatar in June 2017, citizens and residents became more active in debating current affairs and regional developments, without apparent retribution.

E. ASSOCIATIONAL AND ORGANIZATIONAL RIGHTS: 2 / 12
E1. Is there freedom of assembly? 1 / 4
The constitutional right to freedom of assembly is limited by restrictive laws and does not apply to noncitizens. Organizers of public events must obtain a permit from the Interior Ministry, and protests are rare in practice.

E2. Is there freedom for nongovernmental organizations, particularly those that are engaged in human rights- and governance-related work? 0 / 4
All nongovernmental organizations need state permission to operate, and the government closely monitors their activities. There are no independent human rights organizations, though a government-appointed National Human Rights Committee investigates alleged abuses. Independent activists are subject to state harassment. In 2018, human rights lawyer Najeeb al-Nuaimi remained under a travel ban imposed by the attorney general in 2017.

E3. Is there freedom for trade unions and similar professional or labor organizations? 1 / 4
A 2005 labor law expanded worker protections, but the rights to form unions and to strike remain restricted. The only trade union allowed to operate is the General Union of Workers of Qatar, and the law prohibits union membership for noncitizens, government employees, and household workers. Foreign workers who engage in labor protests risk deportation.

F. RULE OF LAW: 5 / 16 (+1)
F1. Is there an independent judiciary? 1 / 4
Despite constitutional guarantees, the judiciary is not independent in practice. Many judges are foreign nationals serving under temporary contracts that are renewed annually. The Supreme Council of the Judiciary, composed of senior judges, administers the courts and plays a role in nominating judges for appointment by the emir.

F2. Does due process prevail in civil and criminal matters? 1 / 4
Certain laws allow lengthy detentions without charge or access to a lawyer for suspects in cases involving national security or terrorism. Even under normal criminal procedure, judges can extend pretrial detention for up to half of the maximum prison term allowed for the alleged crime. Many laws contain ill-defined offenses and other language that gives prosecutors and judges broad discretion to determine guilt. A 2014 law on cybercrimes has been criticized for the vague wording of offenses that carry prison sentences of up to three years, including online dissemination of "false news" or content that undermines "general order."

F3. Is there protection from the illegitimate use of physical force and freedom from war and insurgencies? 3 / 4 (+1)
Violent crime is rare in Qatar, and prison conditions reportedly meet international standards. Legal bans on torture and other mistreatment of detainees have generally been respected in recent years, though international experts have called for further legislative and other improvements. Corporal punishment in the form of flogging, which can be imposed on Muslim defendants for certain offenses under Sharia (Islamic law), is not commonly implemented in practice. The death penalty is permitted, including for crimes other than murder, but no executions have been carried out since 2003.

Score Change: The score improved from 2 to 3 because there have been few documented cases of torture, corporal punishment, or other illegitimate applications of physical force by the authorities in recent years.

F4. Do laws, policies, and practices guarantee equal treatment of various segments of the population? 0 / 4

Noncitizens reportedly face discrimination in the courts and from police. While the constitution bars gender-based discrimination, women do not receive equal treatment under a number of laws, and their testimony is worth less than that of men in certain types of cases. LGBT (lesbian, gay, bisexual, and transgender) people are subject to legal and societal discrimination; vague wording in the penal code can be interpreted to criminalize same-sex sexual activity, and Sharia prohibits any sexual acts outside of heterosexual marriage. Same-sex relationships must be hidden in practice.

In September 2018, the government issued a law to permit grants of asylum, making recipients eligible for various forms of state support. The law also provides some protection against refoulement. However, asylum seekers and recognized refugees would be barred from engaging in political activity in Qatar, and they would need government approval to change their place of residence.

G. PERSONAL AUTONOMY AND INDIVIDUAL RIGHTS: 4 / 16

G1. Do individuals enjoy freedom of movement, including the ability to change their place of residence, employment, or education? 1 / 4

Qataris face no major restrictions on freedom of movement within the country or on type or place of employment. Such freedoms, however, are not extended to noncitizens and foreign workers, who face a variety of constraints. A reform law that took effect in December 2016 eased foreign workers' ability to change employers at the end of a contract and leave the country without an employer's permission, but an amendment in early 2017 effectively meant that employers could still hamper workers' attempts to obtain exit visas. A new law issued in September 2018 prevented employers from banning most migrant laborers from leaving the country; it does not apply to certain categories of workers, including military and public-sector personnel and household workers.

As part of the diplomatic clash that began in June 2017, Saudi Arabia and its allies closed Qatar's only land border, closed their airspace to Qatari flights, expelled Qatari nationals, and banned their nationals from visiting Qatar.

In September 2018 the emir signed a law allowing permanent residency—though not citizenship—for the children and foreign spouses of Qatari women as well as for individuals who provide exceptional skills or services to the country. Up to 100 people per year could receive the designation, giving them access to state education and health benefits and greater rights to own property and run businesses in Qatar.

G2. Are individuals able to exercise the right to own property and establish private businesses without undue interference from state or nonstate actors? 1 / 4

Qataris are permitted to own property and start private businesses, although the process of obtaining necessary commercial permits can be cumbersome. With some exceptions, noncitizens are generally barred from owning property and require Qatari partners to own and operate businesses. Women do not have rights equal to those of men under inheritance laws.

G3. Do individuals enjoy personal social freedoms, including choice of marriage partner and size of family, protection from domestic violence, and control over appearance? 1 / 4

There are a number of legal constraints on marriage, and women are typically at a disadvantage to men under laws on personal status matters. Marriage contracts require the consent of the woman's male guardian, and citizens must obtain government permission to marry foreigners. The foreign wives of Qatari men can obtain citizenship, but foreign husbands of Qatari women are eligible only for residency. Domestic violence and spousal rape are not specifically criminalized. Extramarital sex is illegal.

G4. Do individuals enjoy equality of opportunity and freedom from economic exploitation? 1 / 4

Many foreign nationals face economic abuses including the withholding of salaries, contract manipulation, poor living conditions, and excessive working hours. However, fear of job loss and deportation often prevents them from asserting their limited rights. Female household workers are particularly vulnerable to abuse and exploitation. International organizations have drawn attention to the harsh working conditions of migrants building the infrastructure for the 2022 World Cup.

The government has undertaken reforms to mitigate some of these problems. In 2017, the emir ratified a new law that provided labor rights to household workers, guaranteeing a maximum 10-hour working day, one rest day a week, three weeks of annual leave, and an end-of-service payment, among other provisions, though it failed to set out enforcement mechanisms to ensure compliance. Its standards are also weaker than those in the main labor law.

Romania

Population: 19,500,000
Capital: Bucharest
Political Rights Rating: 2
Civil Liberties Rating: 2
Freedom Rating: 2.0
Freedom Status: Free
Electoral Democracy: Yes

Overview: Romania's multiparty system has ensured regular rotations of power through competitive elections. Civil liberties are generally respected, but they have come under growing pressure as entrenched political interests push back against civic and institutional efforts to combat systemic corruption. Discrimination against minorities and other vulnerable groups is a long-standing problem, as is control of key media outlets by businessmen with political interests.

KEY DEVELOPMENTS IN 2018:

- In January, Prime Minister Mihai Tudose resigned amid friction with the leadership of the ruling Social Democratic Party (PSD). He was replaced by Viorica Dăncilă, who became Romania's first woman prime minister.
- Laura Codruța Kövesi, head of the National Anticorruption Directorate (DNA), was forced out of office in July after the Constitutional Court upheld the justice minister's request for the president to dismiss her. The directorate, which had aggressively prosecuted corruption among leading PSD officials and others, was headed by an interim leader at year's end.

- Also in July, Parliament approved changes to the criminal code that were criticized for weakening safeguards against corruption. President Klaus Iohannis objected to the proposed changes, and the Constitutional Court ruled in October that many of the amendments were unconstitutional.
- Large anticorruption protests in August led to violent clashes between demonstrators and police, who were accused of using excessive force.

POLITICAL RIGHTS: 34 / 40 (−1)

A. ELECTORAL PROCESS 11 / 12

A1. Was the current head of government or other chief national authority elected through free and fair elections? 4 / 4

The president, who holds some significant powers in Romania's semipresidential system, is directly elected for up to two five-year terms. The president appoints the prime minister in consultation with the parliamentary majority, and the prime minister's government requires the confidence of Parliament. Both presidential and parliamentary elections since 1991 have been generally free and fair.

Klaus Iohannis, a centrist who had belonged to the National Liberal Party (PNL), was elected president in 2014, defeating Victor Ponta of the PSD, 54 percent to 46 percent, in a runoff vote. The PSD regained control of the prime minister's office after winning parliamentary elections in 2016. In January 2018, after six months in the post, Prime Minister Tudose lost the support of the party leadership and was replaced by Dăncilă.

A2. Were the current national legislative representatives elected through free and fair elections? 4 / 4

Members of the bicameral Parliament, consisting of a 136-seat Senate and a 330-seat Chamber of Deputies, are elected to four-year terms in a closed party-list proportional system. The PSD led the 2016 parliamentary elections with 67 Senate seats and 154 seats in the lower house. It formed a governing coalition with the Liberal-Democrat Alliance (ALDE), which took 9 and 20 seats in the Senate and lower house, respectively. The opposition PNL placed second with 30 and 69 seats; smaller parties and ethnic minority representatives divided the remainder. International election monitors assessed the polls positively, and stakeholders accepted the results.

A3. Are the electoral laws and framework fair, and are they implemented impartially by the relevant election management bodies? 3 / 4

The legal framework generally provides for fair and competitive elections. However, the 2016 parliamentary elections revealed some gaps in the electoral code of 2015, such as flawed procedures for vetting candidate eligibility, registering as an observer, and conducting ballot recounts.

Ahead of an October 2018 referendum to define marriage as a union between a man and a woman in the constitution, the government eased controls designed to detect fraud and extended voting across two days rather than one in a bid to boost turnout. The effort ultimately failed, with the turnout of about 20 percent falling well below the 30 percent threshold for the vote to be valid.

B. POLITICAL PLURALISM AND PARTICIPATION: 14 / 16

B1. Do the people have the right to organize in different political parties or other competitive political groupings of their choice, and is the system free of undue obstacles to the rise and fall of these competing parties or groupings? 4 / 4

Romania's multiparty system features active competition between rival blocs. Under the 2015 electoral law, the number of signatures needed to create a new party decreased from 25,000 to 3, leading to the registration of many new parties. However, critics have argued that the signature thresholds to register candidates for local and parliamentary elections still place new and smaller parties at a disadvantage.

Multiple new parties were formed during 2018. Former PSD prime minister Victor Ponta founded PRO România, and former technocratic prime minister Dacian Cioloş created the Liberty, Unity, and Solidarity Party (PLUS) at the end of the year. Cătălin Ivan, a PSD defector and member of the European Parliament, launched the Alternative for National Dignity (ADN).

Also during the year, political activists reported facing harassment and obstacles from local authorities while collecting signatures for an effort by the opposition Save Romania Union (USR) to enact a constitutional amendment that would ban convicted people from holding office.

B2. Is there a realistic opportunity for the opposition to increase its support or gain power through elections? 4 / 4

The country has established a record of peaceful transfers of power between rival parties, and no single force has been able to control both the executive and legislative branches since 2012. The PNL and other parliamentary opposition parties initiated votes of no confidence in the PSD government in June and December 2018, citing threats to the rule of law, but both efforts failed.

B3. Are the people's political choices free from domination by the military, foreign powers, religious hierarchies, economic oligarchies, or any other powerful group that is not democratically accountable? 3 / 4

People are generally free to make political choices without undue pressure from unaccountable actors. However, clientelism in local politics remains a problem. Watchdogs have also expressed concern over the increasing presence of disinformation and propaganda in the media, which could allow powerful interests to improperly influence public views.

B4. Do various segments of the population (including ethnic, religious, gender, LGBT, and other relevant groups) have full political rights and electoral opportunities? 3 / 4

Ethnic, religious, and other minority groups enjoy full political rights under the law. Romania's constitution grants one lower house seat to each national minority whose representative party or organization fails to win any seats under the normal rules, and 17 such seats were allotted to minority representatives following the 2016 elections. President Iohannis, an ethnic German and a Lutheran, is the country's first president from either minority group.

Roma, who make up over 3 percent of the population, are underrepresented in politics. While a number of women hold cabinet-level positions, including the prime minister as of 2018, women are underrepresented in the Chamber of Deputies, where they hold 21 percent of seats, and in regional assemblies, where they hold 17 percent of seats. None of the major political parties are led by a woman. Social discrimination against LGBT (lesbian, gay, bisexual, and transgender) people discourages political advocacy for their rights.

C. FUNCTIONING OF GOVERNMENT: 9 / 12 (−1)
C1. Do the freely elected head of government and national legislative representatives determine the policies of the government? 4 / 4

Elected officials are generally able to craft and implement government policy without outside interference. However, PSD leader Liviu Dragnea, who served as speaker of the lower house but could not become prime minister due to a criminal conviction, was accused of exerting undue influence over the government during 2018, having played a key role in the replacement of the prime minister in January.

C2. Are safeguards against official corruption strong and effective? 2 / 4 (−1)

High levels of corruption, bribery, and abuse of power remain a problem. The DNA has won international praise for fairly investigating corruption cases across the political spectrum and frequently securing convictions of powerful figures. Those receiving sentences during 2018 included the former head of Romania's integrity agency, agribusiness magnate Ioan Niculae, media mogul Sorin Ovidiu Vîntu, former cabinet ministers, the former chief prosecutor for organized crime cases, and a former mayor. In May and June, prosecutors requested a three-year jail sentence for Senate president Călin Popescu-Tăriceanu—the head of the PSD's junior coalition partner, ALDE—and a court sentenced Liviu Dragnea to three and a half years in prison in a second abuse of power case, though the decision was not final.

In July, after a protracted effort, the government secured the dismissal of DNA chief Laura Codruța Kövesi in what was seen as a blow to the directorate's independence. The justice minister initiated the move, and the president carried it out after the Constitutional Court ruled in May that he could not refuse to do so. The justice minister nominated Adina Florea to replace Kövesi, but she was rejected by the president and the Superior Council of Magistracy on grounds of insufficient political impartiality. An interim official was leading the DNA at year's end. In October, the justice minister initiated procedures to remove general prosecutor Augustin Lazăr, adding to the pressure on law enforcement bodies.

Separately in July, the president promulgated legal amendments adopted by Parliament in late 2017 that created a special prosecution unit for cases against magistrates, transferring the relevant cases away from the DNA, and Parliament adopted additional changes to the criminal code that would weaken the scope of and penalties for corruption offenses. President Iohannis referred the new amendments to the Constitutional Court, which ruled in October that many of them were unconstitutional. They had not taken effect at year's end.

Score Change: The score declined from 3 to 2 due to a series of efforts by the government to weaken anticorruption laws and mechanisms, including its successful bid to dismiss the head of the National Anticorruption Directorate.

C3. Does the government operate with openness and transparency? 3 / 4

Citizens have the legal right to obtain public information and can petition government agencies for it. Some new mechanisms implemented in recent years were designed to improve transparency. For example, in its first year of operation, between mid-2017 and September 2018, a software system managed by National Integrity Agency reportedly prevented 68 conflict-of-interest cases in public contracting. However, in May 2018 the government issued an emergency ordinance that made it more difficult to challenge the results of public tenders. This and other legislative measures were adopted during the year with little opportunity for public debate or consultation.

CIVIL LIBERTIES: 47 / 60 (−2)
D. FREEDOM OF EXPRESSION AND BELIEF: 13 / 16 (−1)
D1. Are there free and independent media? 3 / 4

Although the media environment is relatively free and pluralistic, key outlets remain controlled by businessmen with political interests, and their coverage is highly distorted by the priorities of the owners. Multiple journalists were allegedly targeted for physical abuse by police while covering antigovernment protests in August 2018.

D2. Are individuals free to practice and express their religious faith or nonbelief in public and private? 3 / 4

Religious freedom is generally respected. While the Romanian Orthodox Church remains dominant and politically powerful, the government formally recognizes 18 religions, each of which is eligible for proportional state support. Others can register as religious associations. Religious education is not mandatory in schools. There have been reports of discrimination and harassment against religious minorities. In July 2018 President Iohannis promulgated a law that criminalized the promotion of antisemitism.

D3. Is there academic freedom, and is the educational system free from extensive political indoctrination? 3 / 4 (−1)

The government generally does not restrict academic freedom, but the education system is weakened by widespread corruption and politically influenced appointments and financing. In 2018, the government was criticized for funding changes that appeared to reward underperforming universities for their political support while punishing successful universities known for challenging government education policies and fostering dissent.

Score Change: The score declined from 4 to 3 because independent public universities reported reductions in state funding that were apparently linked to their lack of political support for the ruling coalition.

D4. Are individuals free to express their personal views on political or other sensitive topics without fear of surveillance or retribution? 4 / 4

People are generally free to express their opinions without fear of retribution, though there were anecdotal reports during 2018 of official repercussions for individuals who displayed opposition to the ruling party.

E. ASSOCIATIONAL AND ORGANIZATIONAL RIGHTS: 10 / 12 (−1)
E1. Is there freedom of assembly? 3 / 4 (−1)

Romania's constitution guarantees freedom of assembly, and numerous peaceful public demonstrations were held during 2018. However, a large protest against government corruption in August was met with tear gas and police violence. Hundreds of people required medical attention in the wake of the clashes. In October, the High Court of Cassation and Justice banned spontaneous public gatherings under most circumstances, requiring assemblies to be declared in advance; the ruling contributed to further national protests that month.

Score Change: The score declined from 4 to 3 due to violent clashes between police and protesters and a court ruling that sharply limited spontaneous public gatherings.

E2. Is there freedom for nongovernmental organizations, particularly those that are engaged in human rights- and governance-related work? 4 / 4

Nongovernmental organizations (NGOs) operate without major formal restrictions. Nevertheless, many human rights and governance groups suffer from funding shortages and often face hostility and smears from politicians and other actors. In October 2018, Parliament approved legislation to combat money laundering that would impose onerous reporting obligations on NGOs. While that measure was under review and had not taken effect at year's end, executive ordinances adopted separately during the year made it more difficult for businesses to donate to NGOs.

E3. Is there freedom for trade unions and similar professional or labor organizations? 3 / 4

Workers have the right to form unions and a limited right to strike and bargain collectively, though laws against the violation of these rights are not well enforced. There are legal constraints on the ability of unions to participate in political activity, and the International Labour Organization has expressed concern about the level of government supervision of unions' finances.

F. RULE OF LAW: 12 / 16

F1. Is there an independent judiciary? 3 / 4

The judiciary is generally independent, but it faces increasing pressure from the executive and legislative branches. For example, in October 2018, having exhausted his options for challenging it, the president promulgated a law that encouraged mass departures from the judiciary by allowing magistrates to request early retirement and receive pensions greater than their working salaries.

F2. Does due process prevail in civil and criminal matters? 3 / 4

The law provides safeguards against arbitrary arrest and detention, and these are generally respected, but the right to a fair and timely trial is often undermined by institutional problems including corruption, political influence, staffing shortages, and inefficient resource allocation. Many government officials and lawmakers retain their positions despite criminal indictments or convictions by exploiting such weaknesses in the system. The Venice Commission has warned that recent changes to laws governing the justice system will "likely undermine" the independence of its officials. An executive ordinance issued in October 2018 increased the mandatory experience level for top prosecutorial positions from 8 to 15 years, potentially affecting current officeholders.

F3. Is there protection from the illegitimate use of physical force and freedom from war and insurgencies? 3 / 4

The population faces no major threats to physical security, but prisons and detention centers feature harsh conditions, and the abuse of detainees by police and fellow prisoners remains a problem.

F4. Do laws, policies, and practices guarantee equal treatment of various segments of the population? 3 / 4

The law provides broad protections against discrimination based on gender, race, ethnicity, sexual orientation, and other categories. However, people with disabilities, LGBT people, Roma, and HIV-positive children and adults face discrimination in education, employment, medical service provision, and other areas. The constitution guarantees women equal rights, but gender discrimination remains a problem in many aspects of life. In August 2018 the president signed a law that imposes fines for sexual and psychological harassment in public and private spaces.

G. PERSONAL AUTONOMY AND INDIVIDUAL RIGHTS: 12 / 16

G1. Do individuals enjoy freedom of movement, including the ability to change their place of residence, employment, or education? 4 / 4

Citizens face no significant restrictions on freedom of movement, whether for internal or external travel.

G2. Are individuals able to exercise the right to own property and establish private businesses without undue interference from state or nonstate actors? 2 / 3

Property rights are protected by law, but despite significant progress, the country has struggled to adjudicate restitution claims for property confiscated during the communist era. Bureaucratic barriers, corruption, and broader weaknesses in the rule of law hamper private business activity.

G3. Do individuals enjoy personal social freedoms, including choice of marriage partner and size of family, protection from domestic violence, and control over appearance? 3 / 4

While personal social freedoms are generally protected, domestic violence remains a serious problem, and laws meant to combat it are poorly enforced. Same-sex marriages are not permitted under Romanian law, but in July 2018 the Constitutional Court recognized the residency rights of same-sex couples married elsewhere provided that one member of the couple is a European Union citizen. A government-backed referendum meant to define marriage in the constitution as a union between a man and a woman failed in October due to low turnout.

G4. Do individuals enjoy equality of opportunity and freedom from economic exploitation? 3 / 4

The law provides basic protections against exploitative working conditions, though they are unevenly enforced, particularly in the large informal economy. Economic opportunity varies widely between urban and rural areas, and such disparities limit social mobility for some.

Human trafficking for the purpose of forced labor and prostitution remains a serious problem in Romania. Women and children from the Romany minority are especially vulnerable to forced begging.

Russia

Population: 147,300,000
Capital: Moscow
Political Rights Rating: 7
Civil Liberties Rating: 6
Freedom Rating: 6.5
Freedom Status: Not Free
Electoral Democracy: No

Overview: Power in Russia's authoritarian political system is concentrated in the hands of President Vladimir Putin. With loyalist security forces, a subservient judiciary, a controlled media environment, and a legislature consisting of a ruling party and pliable opposition factions, the Kremlin is able to manipulate elections and suppress genuine dissent. Rampant corruption facilitates shifting links among bureaucrats and organized crime groups.

KEY DEVELOPMENTS IN 2018:

- Vladimir Putin easily won a fourth term as president in a March election that excluded viable opposition candidates.

- In October, compelled by budget constraints, Putin signed deeply unpopular pension legislation that increased the retirement age for men from 60 to 65 and for women from 55 to 60. Thousands of people had participated in protests against the change, leading to hundreds of arrests across the country.
- The pro-Kremlin United Russia party generally dominated regional elections during the year, though it lost its hold on the governorship in four of the 22 regions at stake.
- The authorities blocked the popular messaging application Telegram in April. Also that month, journalist Maksim Borodin was found dead at his Yekaterinburg residence under suspicious circumstances, after investigating the deaths of Russian mercenaries fighting in Syria.

POLITICAL RIGHTS: 5 / 40
A. ELECTORAL PROCESS: 0 / 12
A1. Was the current head of government or other chief national authority elected through free and fair elections? 0 / 4

The 1993 constitution established a strong presidency with the power to dismiss and appoint, pending parliamentary confirmation, the prime minister. As with his past elections, President Putin's campaign for a new six-year term in 2018 benefited from advantages including preferential media treatment, numerous abuses of incumbency, and procedural irregularities during the vote count. His most potent rival, Aleksey Navalny, had been disqualified before the campaign began due to a politically motivated criminal conviction, creating what the Organization for Security and Co-operation in Europe (OSCE) called "a lack of genuine competition." The funding sources for Putin's campaign were notably opaque. He was ultimately credited with 77 percent of the vote, followed by the Communist Party's Pavel Grudinin with 12 percent, Vladimir Zhirinovsky of the ultranationalist Liberal Democratic Party of Russia (LDPR) with 6 percent, and five others—including token liberals—who divided the remainder.

The Kremlin's preferred candidates lost in four of the year's 22 gubernatorial elections, though the nominal opposition contenders who were permitted to participate were also approved by the federal leadership. In Vladimir and Khabarovsk, LDPR candidates ousted United Russia incumbents, and a Communist challenger defeated a United Russia incumbent in Khakasia. In Primorsky Kray, the results of a September runoff election were annulled due to blatant manipulation meant to prevent Communist challenger Andrey Ishchenko's victory over the incumbent, Andrey Tarasenko. Ishchenko was blocked from participating in the rerun election in December, and the Kremlin used the interim to elevate Oleg Kozhemyako as the new acting governor and United Russia candidate. Kozhemyako won with the help of increased federal spending and support from state-controlled media, defeating an LDPR opponent.

A2. Were the current national legislative representatives elected through free and fair elections? 0 / 4

The Federal Assembly consists of the 450-seat State Duma and an upper chamber, the 170-seat Federation Council. Half the members of the upper chamber are appointed by governors and half by regional legislatures, usually with strong federal input. Half of Duma members are elected by nationwide proportional representation and the other half in single-member districts, with all serving five-year terms.

In the 2016 Duma elections, United Russia won 343 seats, securing a supermajority that allows it to change the constitution without the support of other parties. The three main Kremlin-approved "opposition" parties—the Communists, LDPR, and A Just Russia—won the bulk of the remainder, taking 42, 39, and 23 seats, respectively. The Central Electoral Commission reported a turnout of 48 percent, the lowest in Russia's post-Soviet history. The OSCE and the election monitoring group Golos cited numerous violations, including ballot stuffing, pressure on voters, and illegal campaigning. Some opposition candidates were simply not permitted to register, so the outcome of many races was clear even before election day.

A3. Are the electoral laws and framework fair, and are they implemented impartially by the relevant election management bodies? 0 / 4

Russia's electoral system is designed to maintain the dominance of United Russia. The authorities make frequent changes in the laws and the timing of elections in order to ensure that their preferred candidates will have maximum advantage. Opposition candidates have little chance of success in appealing these decisions, or securing a level playing field.

Since 2011, only locally elected politicians have been eligible to serve in the Federation Council; the change was designed to benefit United Russia, as most local officeholders are party members. The current mixed electoral system for the Duma was adopted following the 2011 elections, when United Russia garnered just less than 50 percent of the vote under a system that used only nationwide proportional representation. This and other rule changes were considered to have contributed to United Russia's supermajority in 2016.

In April 2018, regional lawmakers in Sverdlovsk voted to abolish direct mayoral elections in the regional capital, Yekaterinburg, where a genuine opposition figure, Yevgeniy Royzman, was about to complete his term. The change, which followed a series of similar moves in other regions in recent years, reduced the number of regional capitals with direct mayoral elections to just eight out of 83.

B. POLITICAL PLURALISM AND PARTICIPATION: 3 / 16

B1. Do the people have the right to organize in different political parties or other competitive political groupings of their choice, and is the system free of undue obstacles to the rise and fall of these competing parties or groupings? 1 / 4

The multiparty system is carefully managed by the Kremlin, which tolerates only superficial competition with the dominant United Russia party. Legislation enacted in 2012 liberalized party registration rules, allowing the creation of hundreds of new parties. However, none posed a significant threat to the authorities, and many seemed designed to encourage division and confusion among the opposition. In August 2018, the Justice Ministry refused once again to register Navalny's political party. He had been attempting to register a party since 2012, but his applications were always delayed or rejected based on technicalities.

B2. Is there a realistic opportunity for the opposition to increase its support or gain power through elections? 0 / 4

Russia has never experienced a democratic transfer of power between rival groups. Putin, then the prime minister, initially received the presidency on an acting basis from the retiring Boris Yeltsin at the end of 1999. He served two four-year presidential terms from 2000 to 2008, then remained the de facto paramount leader while working as prime minister until he returned to the presidency in 2012, violating the spirit if not the letter of the constitution's two-term limit. A 2008 constitutional amendment extended presidential terms to six years, meaning Putin's current term will leave him in office until 2024.

Opposition politicians and activists are frequently targeted with fabricated criminal cases and other forms of administrative harassment that are apparently designed to prevent their participation in the political process. Navalny was jailed three separate times in 2018 alone, for stints ranging from 15 to 30 days, in connection with unauthorized demonstrations. Amnesty International declared him a prisoner of conscience, asserting that he had committed no crime.

B3. Are the people's political choices free from domination by the military, foreign powers, religious hierarchies, economic oligarchies, or any other powerful group that is not democratically accountable? 1 / 4

Russia's numerous security agencies work to maintain tight control over society and prevent any political challenges to the incumbent regime. The country's leadership is also closely intertwined with powerful economic oligarchs, who benefit from government patronage in exchange for political loyalty and various forms of service. The Russian Orthodox Church similarly works to support the status quo, receiving financial support and a privileged status in return.

B4. Do various segments of the population (including ethnic, religious, gender, LGBT, and other relevant groups) have full political rights and electoral opportunities? 1 / 4

The formation of parties based on ethnicity or religion is not permitted by law. In practice, many ethnic minority regions are carefully monitored and controlled by federal authorities. Most republics in the restive North Caucasus area and some autonomous districts in energy-rich western Siberia have opted out of direct gubernatorial elections; instead, their legislatures choose a governor from candidates proposed by the president.

Women are underrepresented in politics and government. They hold less than a fifth of seats in the State Duma and the Federation Council. Only 4 of 32 cabinet members are women.

C. FUNCTIONING OF GOVERNMENT: 2 / 12

C1. Do the freely elected head of government and national legislative representatives determine the policies of the government? 0 / 4

Russia's authoritarian president dominates the political system, along with powerful allies in the security services and in business. These groups effectively control the output of the parliament, which is not freely elected. The federal authorities have limited ability to impose policy decisions in Chechnya, where Chechen leader Ramzan Kadyrov has gained unchecked power in exchange for keeping the republic within the Russian Federation.

C2. Are safeguards against official corruption strong and effective? 1 / 4

Corruption in the government and the business world is pervasive, and a growing lack of accountability enables bureaucrats to engage in malfeasance with impunity. Many analysts have argued that the political system is essentially a kleptocracy, a regime whose defining characteristic is the plunder of public wealth by ruling elites.

Navalny's anticorruption organization has posted a series of videos exposing graft among Russia's leading figures. In August 2018, the group alleged in a video that National Guard head Viktor Zolotov had grown rich by embezzling millions of dollars through procurement contracts, prompting Zolotov to publicly challenge Navalny, then in prison, to a duel. After Navalny responded by proposing televised debates, Zolotov opted to sue him for defamation instead.

C3. Does the government operate with openness and transparency? 1 / 4

There is little transparency and accountability in the day-to-day workings of the government. Decisions are adopted behind closed doors by a small group of individuals whose identities are often unclear, and announced to the population after the fact.

In June 2018, as many citizens celebrated the opening of soccer's World Cup tournament in Russia, the government announced legislation to raise the retirement age and delay pension eligibility, allowing for essentially no public discussion. After authorities suppressed protests against the deeply unpopular changes and offered symbolic concessions, the final bill was adopted in September, and the president signed it in October.

CIVIL LIBERTIES: 15 / 60

D. FREEDOM OF EXPRESSION AND BELIEF: 3 / 16

D1. Are there free and independent media? 0 / 4

Although the constitution provides for freedom of speech, vague laws on extremism grant the authorities great discretion to crack down on any speech, organization, or activity that lacks official support. The government controls, directly or through state-owned companies and friendly business magnates, all of the national television networks and many radio and print outlets, as well as most of the media advertising market. A handful of independent outlets still operate, most of them online and some headquartered abroad.

Attacks, arrests, and threats against journalists are common. In April 2018, Maksim Borodin, an investigative correspondent for the independent news website *Novy Den*, died after falling from the balcony of his fifth-floor apartment in Yekaterinburg under suspicious circumstances. He had reported on the use of Russian private military contractors in Syria. In September, rights activist and website publisher Pyotr Verzilov was rushed to the hospital and received treatment in Germany after apparently being poisoned. *Novaya Gazeta* reporter Denis Korotkov received death threats in October, just before the paper published his article accusing Yevgeniy Prigozhen, a businessman closely connected to the Kremlin, of murder and other crimes.

BlogSochi editor Aleksandr Valov received a sentence of six years in prison and $10,000 in fines for extortion in December. He had written widely about corruption in and around Sochi. In June, a Russian court sentenced Ukrainian journalist Roman Sushchenko to 12 years in prison for alleged espionage; he had been jailed since 2016.

A Moscow court fined the magazine *New Times* approximately $330,000, the most ever for a Russian publication, in October for allegedly failing to submit funding declarations to regulators on time. Editor Yevgeniya Albats claimed that the penalty was retribution for her radio interview with Navalny on the liberal station Ekho Moskvy. Russian readers quickly donated the money to pay the fine.

D2. Are individuals free to practice and express their religious faith or nonbelief in public and private? 1 / 4

Freedom of religion is respected unevenly. A 1997 law on religion gives the state extensive control and makes it difficult for new or independent groups to operate. The Russian Orthodox Church has a privileged position, working closely with the government on foreign and domestic policy priorities.

Regional authorities continue to harass nontraditional groups, such as Jehovah's Witnesses and Mormons. Antiterrorism legislation approved in 2016 grants the authorities powers to repress religious groups that are deemed extremist. In 2017, the Supreme Court upheld the Justice Ministry's decision to ban the Jehovah's Witnesses as an extremist organization. There are an estimated 175,000 members of the group in Russia. More than 80 had been subjected to detention, house arrest, or restricted liberty as of December 2018, and several thousand had fled abroad. Many Muslims have also been detained in recent years for alleged membership in banned Islamist groups such as Hizb ut-Tahrir.

D3. Is there academic freedom, and is the educational system free from extensive political indoctrination? 1 / 4

The higher education system and the Academy of Sciences are hampered by bureaucratic interference, state-imposed international isolation, and increasing pressure to toe the Kremlin line on politically sensitive topics, though some academics continue to express dissenting views. In August 2018, the authorities restored the teaching license of the European University in St. Petersburg, having last rescinded it in March 2017. The decision had forced the independent institution, known for its high-quality instruction in the social sciences and humanities, to cancel classes for a full year and put its future in doubt. In June 2018, the state education regulator revoked the teaching license of the Moscow School of Social and Economic Sciences (Shaninka), another important private college, claiming that its courses and instructors did not meet quality standards.

Historians researching the Stalinist era have faced pressure from the regime. Sergey Koltyrin and Yuriy Dmitriyev, who have conducted research at a site in Karelia where many victims of Stalinist persecution are buried, both faced unrelated criminal charges during 2018 that appeared to be motivated by their work.

D4. Are individuals free to express their personal views on political or other sensitive topics without fear of surveillance or retribution? 1 / 4

Pervasive, hyperpatriotic propaganda and political repression—particularly since Russian forces' invasion of Ukraine in 2014—have had a cumulative impact on open and free private discussion, and the chilling effect is exacerbated by growing state efforts to control expression on the internet.

The government's surveillance capabilities have increased significantly in recent years, and while most citizens are not subject to regular state supervision, authorities are thought to monitor the activities and personal communications of activists, journalists, and opposition members, according to the human rights organization Agora.

The authorities have developed a number of strategies for managing online discussion. In April 2018, a Russian court banned the popular messaging application Telegram after it failed to grant the Federal Security Service (FSB) access to encrypted communications. In September, however, the Supreme Court issued new guidance that raised the evidentiary threshold for using extremism laws to prosecute internet users over their online activity. A number of high-profile cases and sharp numerical increases in prosecutions had led to criticism that the laws were being applied too broadly. Similarly, in December, Putin signed a law that imposed administrative rather than criminal penalties for first-time offenders in cases involving incitement to hatred.

E. ASSOCIATIONAL AND ORGANIZATIONAL RIGHTS: 3 / 12

E1. Is there freedom of assembly? 1 / 4

The government restricts freedom of assembly. Overwhelming police responses, the use of force, routine arrests, and harsh fines and prison sentences have discouraged unsanctioned protests, while pro-Kremlin groups are able to demonstrate freely. Despite the risks, thousands of people have turned out for a series of antigovernment demonstrations in recent years. In September 2018, police arbitrarily detained hundreds of people who came to the streets to protest the government's pension legislation.

E2. Is there freedom for nongovernmental organizations, particularly those that are engaged in human rights– and governance-related work? 0 / 4

The government continued its relentless campaign against nongovernmental organizations (NGOs) in 2018. Authorities impede NGO activities in part by requiring groups that receive foreign funding and are deemed to engage in political activity to register as "foreign agents." This designation, which is interpreted by much of the Russian public as denoting a foreign spying operation, mandates onerous registration requirements, obliges groups to tag their materials with a "foreign agent" label, and generally makes it extremely difficult for them to pursue their objectives. In 2017, authorities removed the "foreign agent" designation from a number of groups that had stopped accepting funding from abroad. As of the end of 2018, the Justice Ministry classified 73 groups as "foreign agents."

Separately, a total of 15 foreign NGOs have been deemed "undesirable organizations" on the grounds that they threaten national security. This designation gives authorities the power to issue a range of sanctions against the blacklisted groups and individuals who work with them.

Other forms of harassment and intimidation also hinder NGO activities. The head of the human rights organization Memorial's office in Chechnya, Oyub Titiyev, was detained for alleged possession of illegal drugs in January 2018. Shortly before his arrest, the head of the Chechen parliament had blamed US sanctions against Kadyrov on local human rights activists. Titiyev remained in pretrial detention at year's end. In October, Amnesty International researcher Oleg Kozlovsky was detained, beaten, and subjected to a mock execution by masked assailants as he tried to research protests against a recent border agreement between Chechnya and Ingushetia. The attackers sought information about his local contacts and threatened to kill his wife and children.

E3. Is there freedom for trade unions and similar professional or labor organizations? 2 / 4

While trade union rights are legally protected, they are limited in practice. Strikes and worker protests have occurred in prominent industries, such as automobile manufacturing, but antiunion discrimination and reprisals for strikes are not uncommon, and employers often ignore collective-bargaining rights. The largest labor federation works in close cooperation with the Kremlin, though independent unions are active in some industrial sectors and regions.

In January 2018, a St. Petersburg court liquidated the independent Interregional Trade Union Workers' Association, accusing it of improperly accepting funds from abroad. The group had about 4,000 members and first gained prominence for a series of strikes at a Ford plant in 2007 that served as a model for numerous subsequent strikes.

F. RULE OF LAW: 2 / 16

F1. Is there an independent judiciary? 1 / 4

The judiciary lacks independence from the executive branch, and career advancement is effectively tied to compliance with Kremlin preferences. The Presidential Personnel Commission and court chairmen control the appointment and reappointment of the country's judges, who tend to be promoted from inside the judicial system rather than gaining independent experience as lawyers.

F2. Does due process prevail in civil and criminal matters? 1 / 4

Safeguards against arbitrary arrest and other due process guarantees are regularly violated, particularly for individuals who oppose or are perceived as threatening the interests of the political leadership and its allies. Many Russians have consequently sought justice from international courts, but a 2015 law authorizes the Russian judiciary to overrule the decisions of such bodies, and it has since done so on a number of occasions. In November 2018, the European Court of Human Rights ordered Russia to pay financial damages to

Navalny for several arrests in 2012–14 that it found to have been politically motivated with the purpose of "suppressing political pluralism."

Memorial designated 195 people as political prisoners in Russia as of October 2018, up from 117 a year earlier. The list included human rights activists, journalists, Ukrainian citizens opposed to Russia's occupation of Crimea, and people imprisoned for their religious beliefs, among others.

F3. Is there protection from the illegitimate use of physical force and freedom from war and insurgencies? 0 / 4

Use of excessive force by police is widespread, and rights groups have reported that law enforcement agents who carry out such abuses have deliberately employed electric shocks, suffocation, and the stretching of a detainee's body so as to avoid leaving visible injuries. Prisons are overcrowded and unsanitary; inmates lack access to health care and are subject to abuse by guards. In August 2018, *Novaya Gazeta* posted videos of guards engaging in organized beatings of prisoners in Yaroslavl. The authorities arrested at least 12 guards at the prison after a public outcry, but the NGO Public Verdict reported systematic abuse at another prison in the region in December.

Parts of the country, especially the North Caucasus area, suffer from high levels of violence; victims include officials, Islamist insurgents, and civilians. In Chechnya, Kadyrov allegedly uses abductions, torture, extrajudicial killings, and other forms of violence to maintain control.

F4. Do laws, policies, and practices guarantee equal treatment of various segments of the population? 0 / 4

Immigrants and ethnic minorities—particularly those who appear to be from the Caucasus or Central Asia—face governmental and societal discrimination and harassment.

LGBT (lesbian, gay, bisexual, and transgender) people remain subject to considerable discrimination. Beginning in 2017, hundreds of men suspected of being gay were kidnapped and tortured by Chechen authorities, and some were killed. Many fled the republic and the country. An OSCE report released in December 2018 found serious human rights violations in Chechnya, including the crackdown on LGBT people, and called on Russia to conduct a full investigation. Separately, a 2013 federal law bans dissemination of information promoting "nontraditional sexual relationships," effectively making it illegal to talk about homosexuality in public. The ECHR ruled in 2017 that the law was discriminatory and violated freedom of expression, but it remains in place and has led to increased harassment and violence against LGBT people. In November 2018, the ECHR ruled that Russia had violated human rights by consistently prohibiting demonstrations by the LGBT community.

Despite some legal guarantees of gender equality, women continue to face various forms of discrimination. In July 2018, the State Duma rejected a bill first drafted in 2003 that would have expanded employment protections for women, in part by setting a definition for sexual harassment as unwanted sexual attention. The only existing law on the topic is a criminal code article that addresses the use of coercion to compel a person to perform sexual acts.

G. PERSONAL AUTONOMY AND INDIVIDUAL RIGHTS: 7 / 16

G1. Do individuals enjoy freedom of movement, including the ability to change their place of residence, employment, or education? 2 / 4

The government places some restrictions on freedoms of movement and residence. Adults must carry internal passports while traveling and to obtain many government services. Some regional authorities impose registration rules that limit the right of citizens to choose their place of residence, typically targeting ethnic minorities and migrants from the Caucasus and Central Asia. Most Russians are free to travel abroad, but more than four million employees tied to the military and security services were banned from foreign travel under rules issued during 2014.

G2. Are individuals able to exercise the right to own property and establish private businesses without undue interference from state or nonstate actors? 1 / 4

Power and property are intimately connected, with senior officials often using their government positions to amass vast property holdings. State takeovers of key industries and large tax penalties imposed on select companies after dubious legal proceedings have illustrated the precarious nature of property rights under Putin's rule, especially when political interests are involved. Private businesses more broadly are routinely targeted for extortion or expropriation by law enforcement officials and organized criminal groups.

G3. Do individuals enjoy personal social freedoms, including choice of marriage partner and size of family, protection from domestic violence, and control over appearance? 2 / 4

Domestic violence is a serious problem, but it receives little attention from the authorities. In 2017, Putin signed a law that decriminalized acts of domestic violence that do not result in permanent physical harm. Residents of certain regions, particularly in the North Caucasus, face tighter societal restrictions on personal appearance and relationships, and some so-called honor killings have been reported. In Chechnya, Kadyrov has spoken in favor of polygamy and sought to compel divorced couples to remarry.

G4. Do individuals enjoy equality of opportunity and freedom from economic exploitation? 2 / 4

Legal protections against labor exploitation are poorly enforced. Migrant workers are often exposed to unsafe or exploitative working conditions. At least 21 workers reportedly died in accidents at World Cup construction sites ahead of the 2018 tournament. Both Russians facing economic hardship and migrants to Russia from other countries are vulnerable to sex and labor trafficking.

Rwanda

Population: 12,600,000
Capital: Kigali
Political Rights Rating: 6
Civil Liberties Rating: 6
Freedom Rating: 6.0
Freedom Status: Not Free
Electoral Democracy: No

Overview: The Rwandan Patriotic Front (RPF), led by President Paul Kagame, has ruled the country since 1994, when it ousted forces responsible for that year's genocide and ended a civil war. While the regime has maintained stability and economic growth, it has also suppressed political dissent though pervasive surveillance, intimidation, and suspected assassinations.

KEY DEVELOPMENTS IN 2018:

- In September, two opposition candidates from the Democratic Green Party of Rwanda (DGPR) won seats in Rwanda's parliamentary elections for the first time, though President Kagame and the RPF maintained firm control of Parliament in an electoral process that did not adhere to democratic standards.
- Beginning in February, the government closed thousands of mostly Pentecostal churches and dozens of mosques as it strengthened its control over religious organizations.
- Pressure on opposition leaders eased slightly in 2018, as President Kagame ordered the release of 2010 presidential candidate Victoire Ingabire in September, along with over 2,000 other prisoners. In December, the high court acquitted 2017 opposition presidential candidate Diane Rwigara and her mother on charges that included forgery and inciting insurrection.

POLITICAL RIGHTS: 9 / 40 (+1)

A. ELECTORAL PROCESS: 2 / 12

A1. Was the current head of government or other chief national authority elected through free and fair elections? 0 / 4

Rwanda's 2003 constitution grants broad powers to the president, who has the authority to appoint the prime minister and dissolve the bicameral Parliament. Amendments passed in 2015 retained a two-term limit for the presidency and shortened the terms from seven to five years. The changes also explicitly stated, however, that the current president—Paul Kagame—was eligible for one additional seven-year term, after which he may run for two of the new five-year terms, which would extend Kagame's rule until 2034.

Kagame easily won the 2017 presidential election, taking 98.8 percent of the vote, according to official results. Frank Habineza of the DGPR and the independent Philippe Mpayimana split the remainder. The electoral process was marred by numerous irregularities, including political intimidation, unfair registration practices, and alleged fraud during the balloting itself.

The National Electoral Commission (NEC) blocked the candidacies of other would-be challengers, including independent and Kagame critic Diane Rwigara, who was barred from running on the grounds that some of the required signatures she had collected were invalid. She claimed that her followers were harassed and jailed as they attempted to gather signatures. The government also orchestrated a campaign of media smears and intimidation against Rwigara, and she was subsequently arrested along with her mother and sister.

Local authorities impeded the electoral campaigns of opposition presidential candidates, and some citizens were coerced into attending RPF rallies and voting for Kagame. Rwandans were also made to attend "solidarity" camps and listen to RPF propaganda, while local authorities tasked traditional leaders with persuading their communities to vote for Kagame. Access to the media and the content of electoral coverage were both skewed in favor of the RPF.

On election day, observers reported ballot stuffing, poll workers showing favoritism toward the ruling party, and denial of access to the vote-counting process, among other violations. Ballot secrecy was not always respected.

A2. Were the current national legislative representatives elected through free and fair elections? 1 / 4

The 26-seat Senate, the upper house, consists of 12 members elected by regional councils, 8 appointed by the president, 4 chosen by a forum of political parties, and 2 elected representatives of universities, all serving eight-year terms. The 80-seat Chamber of Deputies, the lower house, includes 53 directly elected members, 24 women chosen by local councils, 2 members from the National Youth Council, and 1 member from the Federation of Associations of the Disabled, all serving five-year terms.

The RPF dominated the Chamber of Deputies elections held in September 2018, capturing 40 of the 53 elected seats. The DGPR gained two seats, marking the first time a genuine opposition party has won representation in Parliament. Three other parties allied with the RPF—the Social Democratic Party, the Liberal Party, and the Social Party—won five, four, and two seats respectively. As with other elections in recent years, the government's repression of legitimate opposition parties and strict control of the media helped to ensure an overwhelming victory for the RPF.

A3. Are the electoral laws and framework fair, and are they implemented impartially by the relevant election management bodies? 1 / 4

The electoral laws are not impartially implemented by the NEC, whose members are proposed by the government and appointed by the RFP-dominated Senate. Elections in Rwanda routinely feature unfair barriers to registration, campaigning, poll monitoring, and media access for opposition parties and candidates, among other problems.

The 2015 constitutional amendments were adopted through a flawed petition and referendum process. Rights groups and news organizations cited reports that some signatures on the petition were not given voluntarily. The details of the amendments were not widely distributed or discussed ahead of the December 2015 referendum, in which 98 percent of voters signaled their approval, according to the NEC. The government limited the political activities of groups opposed to the amendments, and the referendum was not monitored by any independent international observer groups.

B. POLITICAL PLURALISM AND PARTICIPATION: 2 / 16 (+1)

B1. Do the people have the right to organize in different political parties or other competitive political groupings of their choice, and is the system free of undue obstacles to the rise and fall of these competing parties or groupings? 1 / 4 (+1)

The government-controlled Rwanda Governance Board (RGB) is responsible for registering political parties. In practice it can deny registration at its discretion without proper justification. The government has a long history of repressing its political opponents. For example, Diane Rwigara was arrested and imprisoned in 2017, along with her mother and sister, on charges that included forgery of signatures to support her candidacy, tax evasion, and inciting insurrection.

In 2018, however, repression of opposition figures eased slightly. In September, President Kagame ordered the release of 2,140 prisoners, including Victoire Ingabire, 2010 presidential candidate for the unregistered United Democratic Forces–Inkingi (FDU-Inkingi), who had been serving a 15-year prison sentence for engaging in terrorist activities. In October, a high court judge released Rwigara and her mother on bail, and they were subsequently acquitted in December. Some observers claimed that the moves signaled a potential democratic opening, although many analysts believe the prisoner releases were a strategic concession to ensure the appointment of Rwanda's foreign minister, Louise Mushikiwabo, as secretary-general of the International Organization of the Francophonie (OIF). Mushikiwabo's nomination had received pushback due to Rwanda's poor human rights record, but she was confirmed as head of the OIF in October. After Ingabire gave an interview in which she claimed not to have sought clemency while imprisoned, Kagame threatened to reimprison her and other recently released dissidents on the floor of Parliament in September.

The two seats won by the DGPR in the September parliamentary elections marked the first time a legitimate opposition party would be represented in Parliament, and therefore reflected a small yet consequential improvement in the ability of opposition parties to function effectively.

Score Change: The score improved from 0 to 1 because restrictions on opposition parties eased enough to enable the Democratic Green Party of Rwanda to win two seats in Parliament, the first time a genuine opposition party has won representation; also, repression of opposition leaders reduced slightly with the release of former presidential candidates Victoire Ingabire and Diane Rwigara from prison.

B2. Is there a realistic opportunity for the opposition to increase its support or gain power through elections? 0 / 4

The RPF has ruled Rwanda without interruption since 1994, banning and repressing any opposition group that could mount a serious challenge to its leadership. All registered parties currently belong to the National Consultative Forum for Political Organizations, which is meant to promote political consensus. Despite the two seats in Parliament won by the DGPR in 2018, the RPF maintains a firm hold on power. The DGPR remains vastly outnumbered, holds no other positions of authority, and is unlikely to increase its support to the point where it can seriously challenge the RPF in the near future.

B3. Are the people's political choices free from domination by the military, foreign powers, religious hierarchies, economic oligarchies, or any other powerful group that is not democratically accountable? 0 / 4

Both voters and candidates face significant intimidation aimed at controlling their political choices. Even Rwandans living outside the country have been threatened, attacked, forcibly disappeared, or killed, apparently in response to their public or suspected opposition to the regime.

B4. Do various segments of the population (including ethnic, religious, gender, LGBT, and other relevant groups) have full political rights and electoral opportunities? 1 / 4

Although the constitution calls on the president to ensure "representation of historically marginalized communities" in the Senate through his appointees, asserting one's ethnic identity in politics is banned, meaning the level of representation is unclear. The prohibition on discussion of ethnicity makes it nearly impossible for disadvantaged groups, including the indigenous Twa, to organize independently and advocate for their interests.

The 2003 constitution requires women to occupy at least 30 percent of the seats in each chamber of Parliament. They currently hold 10 of the 26 Senate seats and 49 of the 80 seats in the Chamber of Deputies, but women have little practical ability to engage in politics outside the RPF structure.

C. FUNCTIONING OF GOVERNMENT: 5 / 12

C1. Do the freely elected head of government and national legislative representatives determine the policies of the government? 1 / 4

Government policy is largely set and implemented by the executive, with the security and intelligence services playing a powerful role. Parliament generally lacks independence, merely endorsing presidential initiatives.

C2. Are safeguards against official corruption strong and effective? 2 / 4

The government takes some measures to limit corruption, including regular firings and prosecutions of low-level officials suspected of malfeasance. In August 2018, for example, President Kagame sacked at least two dozen civil servants in the Ministry of Health for fraud and mismanagement. According to the *EastAfrican,* there were 289 corruption convictions between June 2017 and June 2018, a significant increase from 121 convictions in 2016.

In June, Parliament passed revisions to the penal code which expanded the list of crimes considered corruption and increased penalties for those convicted. However, graft remains a problem, and few independent organizations or media outlets are able to investigate or report on corruption issues due to fear of government reprisals.

C3. Does the government operate with openness and transparency? 2 / 4

While a 2013 law provides for public access to government information, implementation has been weak. Data published on Sobanukirwa, a website created by the government to ease the process of requesting access to documents, suggest that only a small fraction of requests result in positive and timely responses.

CIVIL LIBERTIES: 14 / 60 (–1)
D. FREEDOM OF EXPRESSION AND BELIEF: 3 / 16 (–1)
D1. Are there free and independent media? 0 / 4

The government imposes legal restrictions and informal controls on freedom of the press, and most media outlets practice self-censorship. The few journalists in the country who engage in independent reporting are subject to criminal charges and intimidation. The penal code revisions passed in 2018 criminalized cartoons or writing that "humiliate" Rwandan leaders, but also decriminalized defamation, which the Rwanda Journalists Association (ARJ) considered an improvement to the highly restrictive legal framework.

Many Rwandan journalists have fled the country and work in exile. Due in part to this phenomenon, the government has increasingly blocked access to news services and websites based abroad. The BBC's Kinyarwanda-language service has been suspended in the country since 2014.

D2. Are individuals free to practice and express their religious faith or nonbelief in public and private? 2 / 4 (–1)

Religious freedom has historically been respected, but the government took steps to assert greater control over religious institutions in 2018. Beginning in February, authorities shut down more than 8,000 mostly Pentecostal churches and dozens of mosques for allegedly failing to adhere to building safety standards. President Kagame complained publicly in March that Rwanda has too many churches, while in the same month, six Pentecostal pastors who had criticized the closures were arrested for holding "illegal meetings with bad intentions" and detained briefly. Also in March, the government banned mosques in Kigali from broadcasting the call to prayer over loudspeakers.

In July, Parliament passed a new law that further regulates religious organizations. The law requires religious leaders to have a theology degree before establishing churches, mandates that religious organizations report grants to the Rwanda Governance Board, and only allows donations to faith-based groups to be deposited in Rwandan banks.

Jehovah's Witnesses face arrest for refusing to participate in security duties or oath-taking involving the national flag.

Score Change: The score declined from 3 to 2 due to the government's efforts to assert control over religious institutions, including the closure of thousands of churches and doz-

ens of mosques, and a new law passed by Parliament requiring religious leaders to have a theology degree before establishing churches, among other provisions.

D3. Is there academic freedom, and is the educational system free from extensive political indoctrination? 1 / 4

The government restricts academic freedom by enforcing official views on the genocide and other sensitive topics. Scholars and students are subject to suspension for "divisionism" and engage in self-censorship to avoid such penalties.

D4. Are individuals free to express their personal views on political or other sensitive topics without fear of surveillance or retribution? 0 / 4

The space for free private discussion is limited in part by indications that the government monitors personal communications. Social media are widely believed to be monitored, and the law allows for government hacking of telecommunications networks. The authorities reportedly use informants to infiltrate civil society, further discouraging citizens from expressing dissent.

E. ASSOCIATIONAL AND ORGANIZATIONAL RIGHTS: 2 / 12

E1. Is there freedom of assembly? 0 / 4

Although the constitution guarantees freedom of assembly, this right is limited in practice. Fear of arrest serves as a deterrent to protests, and gatherings are sometimes disrupted even when organizers obtain official authorization. In February 2018, police fired live ammunition into two crowds of Congolese refugees in Karongi town and Kiziba refugee camp protesting cuts in assistance, killing at least 11 and injuring at least 20. At the end of the year, there had not yet been an investigation into the police's use of force during the demonstrations, but 65 protesters were arrested and charged with holding an illegal demonstration and violence against the police, among other allegations. Most of the protesters awaited trial at year's end.

E2. Is there freedom for nongovernmental organizations, particularly those that are engaged in human rights- and governance-related work? 1 / 4

Registration and reporting requirements for both domestic and foreign nongovernmental organizations (NGOs) are onerous, and activities that the government defines as divisive are prohibited. Many organizations receive funds from the RGB, which challenges their independence. Several organizations have been banned in recent years, leading others to self-censor. The government has been accused of employing infiltration tactics against human rights organizations.

E3. Is there freedom for trade unions and similar professional or labor organizations? 1 / 4

The constitution provides for the rights to form trade unions, engage in collective bargaining, and strike, but free collective bargaining and strikes are limited by binding arbitration rules and rare in practice. Public workers and employees in broadly defined "essential services" are generally not allowed to strike. Enforcement of rules against antiunion discrimination is weak. The country's largest union confederation has close ties to the RPF, and the government allegedly interferes in union elections.

F. RULE OF LAW: 2 / 16

F1. Is there an independent judiciary? 0 / 4

The Rwandan judiciary lacks independence from the executive. Top judicial officials are appointed by the president and confirmed by the RPF-dominated Senate. Judges rarely rule against the government in politically sensitive cases.

F2. Does due process prevail in civil and criminal matters? 1 / 4

The police and military regularly engage in arbitrary arrests and detentions, targeting opposition figures and dissidents as well as homeless people, street vendors, and suspected petty criminals.

In 2017, Human Rights Watch (HRW) released a report detailing a system of secret unlawful detention at military facilities for suspected members of armed rebel groups or exiled opposition factions. Such detainees are allegedly denied basic due process rights, and many who are later brought to trial are convicted based on coerced confessions.

F3. Is there protection from the illegitimate use of physical force and freedom from war and insurgencies? 0 / 4

Both ordinary criminal suspects and political detainees are routinely subjected to torture and other ill-treatment in custody. Extrajudicial executions of suspected criminals by security personnel still occur with some frequency. In July 2018, the UN Subcommittee on Prevention of Torture cancelled its planned visit to Rwanda, citing lack of government cooperation.

F4. Do laws, policies, and practices guarantee equal treatment of various segments of the population? 1 / 4

Equal treatment for all citizens under the law is guaranteed, and there are legal protections against discrimination. However, the Tutsi minority group is often accused of receiving preferential treatment for high-ranking jobs and university scholarships under the pretext of an affirmative action program for "genocide survivors." Members of the Hutu majority often face unofficial discrimination when seeking public employment or scholarships. The indigenous Twa minority continues to suffer from de facto disadvantages in education, employment, and health care.

While women enjoy broad legal equality and have a significant presence in the economy as workers and business owners, gender-based discrimination persists in practice. Same-sex sexual activity is not criminalized in Rwanda, though social stigma still exists for LGBT (lesbian, gay, bisexual, and transgender) people. No laws specifically provide protection against discrimination based on sexual orientation or gender identity.

G. PERSONAL AUTONOMY AND INDIVIDUAL RIGHTS: 7 / 16

G1. Do individuals enjoy freedom of movement, including the ability to change their place of residence, employment, or education? 2 / 4

An easily attainable national identity card is required to move within the country. However, all government officials must receive approval from the president or prime minister's office before traveling for personal or professional reasons; some current and former security officials have been arrested for unauthorized travel. Members of opposition groups have also reported restrictions on foreign travel or reentry to Rwanda.

G2. Are individuals able to exercise the right to own property and establish private businesses without undue interference from state or nonstate actors? 2 / 4

While the government is generally supportive of economic growth through private business activity, it has been criticized for seizing land for infrastructure and development projects without proper compensation, and for imposing agricultural and land-consolidation policies without adequate input from farmers.

The law grants the same property and inheritance rights to men and women, though women are not always able to assert their rights in practice.

G3. Do individuals enjoy personal social freedoms, including choice of marriage partner and size of family, protection from domestic violence, and control over appearance? 2 / 4

The law generally grants equal rights to men and women regarding marriage and divorce, but informal marriages under customary law, including polygamous unions, lack such protections. The penalties for spousal rape are much lighter than for other forms of rape. Domestic violence remains widespread and seldom reported despite government programs to combat it.

Abortion is a criminal offense unless it is the result of rape, incest, or forced marriage, or the mother or child's life is endangered. Abortion convictions can lead to significant prison terms. The 2018 penal code revisions removed a requirement that a judge must approve all abortions, leaving the final decision in the hands of the patient and her doctor.

G4. Do individuals enjoy equality of opportunity and freedom from economic exploitation? 1 / 4

Regulations governing wage levels and conditions of work in the formal sector are poorly enforced. While Rwanda increased prosecutions for transnational trafficking in recent years, Rwandan children are trafficked internally for domestic service under abusive conditions, or for commercial sex work, and little effort is made to hold internal traffickers to account. Many children work informally in the agricultural sector. Young Congolese and Burundian refugees are vulnerable to sexual exploitation and coerced recruitment into armed groups linked to Rwandan security forces.

Samoa

Population: 200,000
Capital: Apia
Political Rights Rating: 2
Civil Liberties Rating: 2
Freedom Rating: 2.0
Freedom Status: Free
Electoral Democracy: Yes

Overview: Samoa has a democratic political system with regular elections, though the same political party has been in government for decades, and only traditional heads of families are eligible to run as candidates. The judiciary is independent, and civil liberties are generally respected.

KEY DEVELOPMENTS IN 2018:

- A new political party, Samoa First, registered in July to contest general elections scheduled for 2021.
- In September, Afamasaga Su'a Pou Onesemo, the head of Samoa's Ministry of Works, Transport, and Infrastructure, was dismissed by the Public Service Commission for mismanagement and breach of contract. He had been suspended earlier in the year after being implicated in a bribery scheme.

POLITICAL RIGHTS: 30 / 40

A. ELECTORAL PROCESS: 9 / 12

A1. Was the current head of government or other chief national authority elected through free and fair elections? 3 / 4

The parliament elects a ceremonial head of state every five years; there are no term limits. By custom rather than constitutional requirement, the position is given to one of the country's four paramount chiefs. In 2017, the parliament elected Tuimalealiifano Vaaletoa Sualauvi II as head of state.

The head of government is the prime minister, who requires the parliament's support. Prime Minister Tuilaepa of the Human Rights Protection Party (HRPP) has been in office since 1988, having been reelected most recently in 2016.

A2. Were the current national legislative representatives elected through free and fair elections? 3 / 4

The Legislative Assembly, or Fono, consists of 47 members elected in traditional village-based constituencies and 2 members elected by voters in "urban" constituencies—including citizens of mixed or non-Samoan heritage who lack village ties. Additional members can be added from among the unsuccessful candidates with the most votes in order to meet a minimum 10 percent quota of women members. Elections are held every five years.

In the 2016 parliamentary elections, the HRPP won 35 of the 50 seats; one seat was added to meet the gender quota. Independents took 13 seats and the opposition Tautua Samoa Party (TSP) held two. After the elections, 12 of the independents joined the HRPP, and the 13th joined the opposition.

A3. Are the electoral laws and framework fair, and are they implemented impartially by the relevant election management bodies? 3 / 4

The constitutional and legal framework for elections is largely democratic and fairly implemented. However, only citizens with *matai* status (chiefs or family heads) are allowed to stand as candidates. There are some 17,000 *matai*, but only about 10 percent are women. A 2015 amendment to the Electoral Act replaced two at-large parliament seats representing voters of non-Samoan heritage with two "urban" constituencies with defined boundaries, though they still overlapped with territorial constituencies and pertained to voters who either lacked or chose not to register according to traditional village ties.

B. POLITICAL PLURALISM AND PARTICIPATION: 12 / 16

B1. Do the people have the right to organize in different political parties or other competitive political groupings of their choice, and is the system free of undue obstacles to the rise and fall of these competing parties or groupings? 3 / 4

There are no major constraints on the formation and operation of political parties, but parties must win a minimum of eight seats to qualify for formal recognition within the legislature. The TSP, which fell from 13 seats to just three after the 2016 elections, lost this status, leading opposition members to criticize the rule for producing a "one-party state."

A new political party, Samoa First, registered in July 2018 to contest the general elections scheduled for 2021.

B2. Is there a realistic opportunity for the opposition to increase its support or gain power through elections? 3 / 4

There are no obvious obstacles that prevent the opposition from increasing its support and gaining power through elections. However, the ruling HRPP has been in power since

1988 and has developed an effective campaign machinery during its incumbency, raising concerns about whether its long say in power is due to the party's popularity or features of the electoral system that may put the opposition at a disadvantage.

B3. Are the people's political choices free from domination by the military, foreign powers, religious hierarchies, economic oligarchies, or any other powerful group that is not democratically accountable? 3 / 4

While voters and candidates are largely free from undue interference with their political choices, traditional village councils consisting of local leaders with *matai* titles exercise considerable influence through candidate endorsements. Those who use the electoral laws to challenge the councils' preferred candidates in court have sometimes faced customary penalties such as banishment.

B4. Do various segments of the population (including ethnic, religious, gender, LGBT, and other relevant groups) have full political rights and electoral opportunities? 3 / 4

Women and ethnic minorities have full voting rights, but the fact that candidates must be *matai* title holders means fewer women are eligible to run for office. The 2016 elections marked the first application of the gender quota ensuring that at least five seats in the parliament are held by women. If fewer than that number are elected in normal constituency contests, the unsuccessful women candidates with the most votes are awarded additional seats. One extra seat was consequently added to the 2016 parliament. Few women participate in village council meetings.

C. FUNCTIONING OF GOVERNMENT: 9 / 12

C1. Do the freely elected head of government and national legislative representatives determine the policies of the government? 3 / 4

The prime minister and cabinet determine and implement government policies without improper interference by outside groups. However, the weak opposition presence in the parliament undermines its role as a check on the executive, and the democratic credentials of the government are tarnished somewhat by restrictive features of the electoral system.

C2. Are safeguards against official corruption strong and effective? 3 / 4

Independent entities including the Office of the Ombudsman, the Public Service Commission, and law enforcement agencies pursue allegations of corruption by public officials. However, corruption remains a problem and a cause of public discontent, and the government has at times resisted calls for a stronger response. In September 2018, the chief executive of Samoa's Ministry of Works, Transport, and Infrastructure was dismissed by the Public Service Commission, which cited mismanagement and breach of contract; he had been suspended earlier in the year after being implicated in a bribery scheme.

C3. Does the government operate with openness and transparency? 3 / 4

The government generally operates with transparency, and received praise from the International Monetary Fund in 2017 for its efforts to make statistical data more accessible online. However, the effectiveness of the state auditing system remains the subject of public debate, and the country lacks a freedom of information law.

CIVIL LIBERTIES: 51 / 60 (+1)

D. FREEDOM OF EXPRESSION AND BELIEF: 14 / 16

D1. Are there free and independent media? 3 / 4

While freedom of the press is generally respected, politicians and other powerful actors have used libel or defamation suits to respond to remarks or stories about them. In December 2017, the parliament passed legislation that reintroduced criminal libel, which had been abolished in 2013.

There are several public and privately owned print and broadcast news outlets in operation, and internet access has expanded rapidly in recent years.

D2. Are individuals free to practice and express their religious faith or nonbelief in public and private? 3 / 4

Freedom of religion is guaranteed in Article 11 of the Constitution, and is mostly respected in practice. However, in June 2017, the parliament passed the Constitution Amendment Bill, which shifted references to Samoa being a Christian nation from the preamble of the Constitution to the body. As such, the text can potentially be used in legal action.

There is strong societal pressure at the village level—including from village councils—to participate in the activities of the main local church.

D3. Is there academic freedom, and is the educational system free from extensive political indoctrination? 4 / 4

There are no significant restrictions on academic freedom.

D4. Are individuals free to express their personal views on political or other sensitive topics without fear of surveillance or retribution? 4 / 4

There are no serious constraints on private discussion or the expression of personal views. However, in March, the prime minister threatened to ban Facebook in response to critical comments by anonymous users.

E. ASSOCIATIONAL AND ORGANIZATIONAL RIGHTS: 11 / 12 (+1)

E1. Is there freedom of assembly? 4 / 4

Freedom of assembly is protected by law and respected in practice. In March 2018, the Samoa Solidarity International Group (SSIG) submitted a request to the Ministry of Police for a license to peacefully march in the island of Savai'i, to raise awareness about land rights. In April, hundreds participated in the protest march without incident. SSIG held another protest march in December.

E2. Is there freedom for nongovernmental organizations, particularly those that are engaged in human rights- and governance-related work? 3 / 4

Nongovernmental organizations, including human rights groups, operate freely.

E3. Is there freedom for trade unions and similar professional or labor organizations? 4 / 4 (+1)

Workers have the right to form and join trade unions, bargain collectively, and strike. Multiple unions exist, representing both public- and private-sector employees. These are often called "associations"—such as the Samoa Ports Authority Staff Association, the Development Bank of Samoa Staff Association, the Samoa National Provident Fund Staff Association, and the Samoa Nurses Association. The Samoa Workers Congress (SWC) is an umbrella body for all the workers' unions. As of February 2018, it had seven affiliates, representing a total of 4,100 workers, an increase from 2016, when there were six affiliates and 3,000 workers represented.

Union members' rights are governed by the Constitution and the 2013 Labour and Employment Relations Act; the latter recognizes unions and employees' roles and rights, the rights to collective bargaining, and rights to maternity and paternity leave, and mandates the establishment of a National Tripartite Forum, which provides for workers benefits and consults on employment policies and conditions.

Samoa became a member of the International Labor Organization (ILO) in 2005 and had ratified all eight of the ILO's fundamental Conventions by 2008. Unions are still learning about how to best represent their members. Moreover, some cultural factors hinder the ability of workers and unions to pursue their rights.

Score Change: The score improved from 3 to 4 because the establishment of a robust legal framework for trade unions has strengthened worker rights and enabled unions' growth.

F. RULE OF LAW: 14 / 16

F1. Is there an independent judiciary? 4 / 4

The judiciary is independent. The head of state, on the recommendation of the prime minister, appoints the chief justice. Other Supreme Court judges are appointed by the Judicial Service Commission, which is chaired by the chief justice and includes the attorney general and a Justice Ministry appointee. Judges typically serve until they reach retirement age, and cannot be removed arbitrarily.

F2. Does due process prevail in civil and criminal matters? 3 / 4

The authorities generally observe due process safeguards against arbitrary arrest and detention, and the courts provide defendants with the conditions necessary for a fair trial. However, village councils settle many disputes, and their adherence to due process standards varies. They have the authority to impose penalties including fines and banishment, though council decisions can be appealed in the court system.

F3. Is there protection from the illegitimate use of physical force and freedom from war and insurgencies? 4 / 4

Violent crime rates are relatively low. Police officers are occasionally accused of physical abuse. Prisons are under resourced, resulting in poor conditions for prisoners including overcrowding, as well as occasional difficulties keeping facilities themselves secure. In early 2018, there was a spate of escapes from the Tafaigata national prison.

F4. Do laws, policies, and practices guarantee equal treatment of various segments of the population? 3 / 4

The constitution prohibits discrimination based on descent, sex, religion, and other categories. The Labour and Employment Relations Act also prohibits discrimination against employees on such grounds as ethnicity, race, color, sex, gender, religion, political opinion, sexual orientation, social origin, marital status, pregnancy, HIV status, and disability. However, these are enforced unevenly. In practice women face some discrimination in employment and other aspects of life, and same-sex sexual activity remains a criminal offense for men. Ethnic Chinese residents at times encounter societal bias and restrictions on the location of their businesses.

G. PERSONAL AUTONOMY AND INDIVIDUAL RIGHTS: 12 / 16

G1. Do individuals enjoy freedom of movement, including the ability to change their place of residence, employment, or education? 3 / 4

While there are few constraints on freedom of movement, village councils still occasionally banish individuals from their communities as a penalty for serious violations of their bylaws.

G2. Are individuals able to exercise the right to own property and establish private businesses without undue interference from state or nonstate actors? 3 / 4

Private business activity is encouraged, and property rights are generally protected, though roughly 80 percent of the country's land is communally owned, meaning it is overseen by *matai* title holders and other village leaders. The rest consists of freehold and state-owned land.

G3. Do individuals enjoy personal social freedoms, including choice of marriage partner and size of family, protection from domestic violence, and control over appearance? 3 / 4

While personal social freedoms are generally not restricted by law, domestic violence against women and children is a serious problem. The Crimes Act of 2013 made spousal rape a crime, and the Family Safety Act of 2013 empowers the police, public health officials, and educators to assist victims of domestic violence. Nevertheless, many victims do not report abuse due to strong social biases and fear of reprisal.

G4. Do individuals enjoy equality of opportunity and freedom from economic exploitation? 3 / 4

Individuals generally enjoy equality of opportunity and fair working conditions. However, most adults engage in subsistence agriculture, and local custom obliges residents to perform some labor on behalf of the community; those who fail to do so can be compelled.

San Marino

Population: 30,000
Capital: San Marino
Political Rights Rating: 1
Civil Liberties Rating: 1
Freedom Rating: 1.0
Freedom Status: Free
Electoral Democracy: Yes

Overview: San Marino is a parliamentary democracy in which political rights and civil liberties are generally upheld. Corruption is a problem, and while investigative journalists are active, heavy fines for defamation can encourage self-censorship. Women are underrepresented in politics.

KEY DEVELOPMENTS IN 2018:

- In June, a judge filed documents explaining the full reasoning behind sentences that had been imposed the previous year on 17 high-ranking officials convicted of money laundering and criminal association as part of the so-called Conto-Mazzini case. The filing allowed the appeals process to begin.
- In November, the Great and General Council—San Marino's parliament—approved a law allowing civil unions for same-sex couples.

POLITICAL RIGHTS: 38 / 40

A. ELECTORAL PROCESS: 12 / 12

A1. Was the current head of government or other chief national authority elected through free and fair elections? 4 / 4

Executive power rests with the 10-member State Congress (cabinet), which is accountable to the parliament and is headed by two captains regent. As the joint heads of state with largely ceremonial roles, the captains are elected every six months by members of the legislature from among its own members. Although there is no official prime minister, the secretary of state for foreign and political affairs is regarded as the head of government. Nicola Renzi was elected to the post in 2016.

A2. Were the current national legislative representatives elected through free and fair elections? 4 / 4

The 60 members of the unicameral Great and General Council are elected every five years. The 2016 elections were considered credible and free, and their results were accepted by stakeholders and the public. After two rounds of elections, the center-left Adesso.sm coalition finished first with 35 seats, unseating the ruling San Marino First coalition, which took 16 seats. The newly formed Democracy in Motion coalition took the remaining 9 seats.

A3. Are the electoral laws and framework fair, and are they implemented impartially by the relevant election management bodies? 4 / 4

The electoral laws provide a sound basis for the organization of free and fair elections. However, in 2016 the Council of Europe's Group of States against Corruption (GRECO) urged San Marino to adopt legislation on the financing of political parties, finding that the current funding rules are insufficiently transparent.

B. POLITICAL PLURALISM AND PARTICIPATION: 15 / 16

B1. Do the people have the right to organize in different political parties or other competitive political groupings of their choice, and is the system free of undue obstacles to the rise and fall of these competing parties or groupings? 4 / 4

Parties are free to form and operate in San Marino, and a great number of them contest elections. Since 2008, most parties have participated in larger electoral coalitions, as the electoral system awards a majority seat bonus to the coalition that obtains a plurality of votes.

B2. Is there a realistic opportunity for the opposition to increase its support or gain power through elections? 4 / 4

There are no restrictions preventing the opposition from increasing support through elections. Multiple opposition groups are represented in the Great and General Council.

B3. Are the people's political choices free from domination by the military, foreign powers, religious hierarchies, economic oligarchies, or any other powerful group that is not democratically accountable? 4 / 4

The political choices of voters and candidates are free from undue pressure by unaccountable groups.

B4. Do various segments of the population (including ethnic, religious, gender, LGBT, and other relevant groups) have full political rights and electoral opportunities? 3 / 4

While citizens generally enjoy full political rights, women are underrepresented in the Great and General Council, where they hold 23 percent of seats, and in politics generally. An assessment mission from the Organization for Co-operation and Security in Europe that was deployed ahead of the 2016 polls noted that gender quotas on candidate lists were undercut by the country's preferential voting system. Women are better represented in the country's Electoral Council and in polling administration.

About 19 percent of the population consists of noncitizens who do not have political rights in the country; most are Italian nationals. Under San Marino's strict naturalization criteria, individuals without a citizen spouse, parent, or grandparent generally must live in the country for over 30 years to be eligible for citizenship.

C. FUNCTIONING OF GOVERNMENT: 11 / 12

C1. Do the freely elected head of government and national legislative representatives determine the policies of the government? 4 / 4

The government and legislature are able to exercise their powers without improper interference from unelected entities.

C2. Are safeguards against official corruption strong and effective? 3 / 4

In response to scandals involving high-ranking officials, San Marino has launched a series of programs to combat corruption and money laundering. In a 2018 report, GRECO found that progress had been made in closing key gaps in the legal framework, but that further improvements were required, particularly regarding trading in influence and bribery in the private and judicial sectors.

In 2017, a large number of former officials were convicted for their involvement in bribery, corruption, money laundering, and vote buying in the so-called Conto-Mazzini case. Multiple former captains regent and ministers received prison sentences ranging from two to eight years. In June 2018, the judge issued documents laying out the full reasoning behind the sentences, which allowed the appeals process to formally begin.

C3. Does the government operate with openness and transparency? 4 / 4

Laws providing for the accessibility of government information are in place, and the government generally respected those laws. Public officials are not required to disclose their assets, though political candidates must report their income from the previous year as well as assets or investments.

CIVIL LIBERTIES: 57 / 60 (−2)

D. FREEDOM OF EXPRESSION AND BELIEF: 15 / 16

D1. Are there free and independent media? 3 / 4

Freedom of the press is generally upheld. Local media are pluralistic, and journalists investigate key issues including financial crimes. However, the risk of heavy fines or civil damages under San Marino's strict defamation laws can prompt self-censorship among journalists. News consumers also have access to Italian media, and internet access is not restricted.

D2. Are individuals free to practice and express their religious faith or nonbelief in public and private? 4 / 4

Religious freedom is broadly upheld in San Marino. Religious discrimination is prohibited by law. There is no state religion, although Roman Catholicism is dominant. Catholic religious instruction is offered in schools but is not mandatory.

D3. Is there academic freedom, and is the educational system free from extensive political indoctrination? 4 / 4

Academic freedom is generally respected.

D4. Are individuals free to express their personal views on political or other sensitive topics without fear of surveillance or retribution? 4 / 4

Freedom of expression is legally safeguarded, and people are generally free to discuss their views on politics and other sensitive topics, though the law prohibits hate speech based on various characteristics.

E. ASSOCIATIONAL AND ORGANIZATIONAL RIGHTS: 12 / 12
E1. Is there freedom of assembly? 4 / 4

Freedom of assembly is upheld in practice. Demonstrations on various topics routinely proceed without incident.

E2. Is there freedom for nongovernmental organizations, particularly those that are engaged in human rights- and governance-related work? 4 / 4

Nongovernmental organizations may operate without undue restrictions, and a number of human rights groups are active in the country.

E3. Is there freedom for trade unions and similar professional or labor organizations? 4 / 4

Workers are free to strike, organize in trade unions, and bargain collectively, unless they work in military occupations. Approximately half of the workforce is unionized. The law prohibits antiunion discrimination and provides avenues for recourse for workers penalized for union activity.

F. RULE OF LAW: 15 / 16 (−1)
F1. Is there an independent judiciary? 4 / 4

The judiciary is independent. Its affairs are managed by a Judicial Council made up of first-instance and appellate judges.

F2. Does due process prevail in civil and criminal matters? 4 / 4

Due process rights surrounding charges and trials are generally upheld in practice. The authorities respect legal safeguards against arbitrary arrest and detention.

F3. Is there protection from the illegitimate use of physical force and freedom from war and insurgencies? 4 / 4

The population does not face major threats to physical security. There is one prison in San Marino, and the inmate population is small, with no reports of serious mistreatment. Law enforcement officers generally operate with professionalism.

F4. Do laws, policies, and practices guarantee equal treatment of various segments of the population? 3 / 4 (−1)

The law criminalizes the dissemination of ideas related to racial or ethnic superiority; acts of violence or discrimination on various grounds, including sexual orientation and gender identity; and incitement to such acts. However, color and language are not covered by these criminal provisions, and San Marino lacks broader legislation—including civil laws—guaranteeing equality and freedom from employment or other discrimination for LGBT (lesbian, gay, bisexual, and transgender) people. A 2018 report from the European Commission against Racism and Intolerance (ECRI) reiterated concerns about the absence of a strong and comprehensive antidiscrimination framework in the country. The Office of the United Nations High Commissioner for Human Rights has also urged San Marino to strengthen its laws against discrimination, in particular gender discrimination. Women face societal prejudices that affect their access to employment and economic opportunity.

Score Change: The score declined from 4 to 3 because the country lacks comprehensive antidiscrimination legislation and has been slow to address legal gaps identified by international experts.

G. PERSONAL AUTONOMY AND INDIVIDUAL RIGHTS: 15 / 16 (−1)

G1. Do individuals enjoy freedom of movement, including the ability to change their place of residence, employment, or education? 4 / 4

There are no restrictions on freedom of movement, and San Marino residents may freely change their place of residence, employment, and education.

G2. Are individuals able to exercise the right to own property and establish private businesses without undue interference from state or nonstate actors? 4 / 4

The rights to own property and operate private businesses are upheld.

G3. Do individuals enjoy personal social freedoms, including choice of marriage partner and size of family, protection from domestic violence, and control over appearance? 3 / 4 (−1)

Personal social freedoms are generally safeguarded in San Marino. In November 2018, a law allowing civil unions for same-sex couples was adopted by the Great and General Council, and partners in such unions may adopt each other's children. However, same-sex marriage is not recognized, and same-sex couples do not have the right to adopt children together. Abortion is a criminal offense unless the woman's life is in danger, and reform advocates have met with fierce resistence from conservative Catholic groups in recent years. Reports of domestic violence, which is prohibted by law, are rare.

Score Change: The score declined from 4 to 3 due to the persistence of some restrictions on personal social freedoms, including the criminalization of abortion under nearly all circumstances.

G4. Do individuals enjoy equality of opportunity and freedom from economic exploitation? 4 / 4

The government generally upholds labor protections for workers and provides assistance to low-income individuals. The Council of Europe's commissioner for human rights in 2015 called on San Marino to continue with efforts to better protect foreign women employed as caregivers or household workers, and ECRI renewed this advice in 2018.

São Tomé and Príncipe

Population: 200,000
Capital: São Tomé
Political Rights Rating: 2
Civil Liberties Rating: 2
Freedom Rating: 2.0
Freedom Status: Free
Electoral Democracy: Yes

Overview: São Tomé and Príncipe holds regular, competitive national elections and has undergone multiple transfers of power between rival parties. Civil liberties are generally respected, but poverty and corruption have weakened some institutions and contributed to dysfunction in the justice system. Threats to judicial independence have been a growing concern in recent years.

KEY DEVELOPMENTS IN 2018:

- In the October parliamentary elections, the ruling Independent Democratic Action (ADI) party won the most seats, but failed to form a government. The Movement for the Liberation of São Tomé and Príncipe–Social Democratic Party (MLSTP-PSD) and a party coalition that includes the Democratic Convergence Party, the Union of Democrats for Citizenship and Development, and the Force for Democratic Change Movement (PCD-UDD-MDFM) successfully formed a government in October. Jorge Bom Jesus of the MLSTP-PSD was appointed prime minister.
- The creation of a new Constitutional Court with ultimate authority over election results, approved by the National Assembly in 2017, was a continued source of controversy in 2018. In January, the Supreme Court ruled that the new court was unconstitutional, but the government defied the ruling, and the National Assembly elected five judges to the Constitutional Court later in the month, in a vote that the opposition boycotted.
- The judicial crisis intensified further in May, when the National Assembly voted to dismiss three judges on the Supreme Court, including the court's president, after some legislators accused the judges of issuing a politicized ruling regarding the ownership of Rosema Brewery. In July, four judges were elected by the ADI to replace the ousted judges, as well as a fourth judge who had resigned in protest.
- At the end of December, the National Assembly, now controlled by the MLSTP-PSD and PCD-UDD-MDFM, voted to reinstate the four Supreme Court judges who had been dismissed or resigned, and to remove the five judges who had been elected to the Constitutional Court by the ADI-controlled National Assembly.

POLITICAL RIGHTS: 34 / 40
A. ELECTORAL PROCESS: 11 / 12
A1. Was the current head of government or other chief national authority elected through free and fair elections? 4 / 4

The president is directly elected for up to two consecutive five-year terms. The prime minister, who holds most day-to-day executive authority, is appointed by the president based on the results of legislative elections. Executive elections are typically considered free and fair.

In the July 2016 presidential election, Evaristo Carvalho, a former prime minister and member of the ruling ADI party, led the first round with just under 50 percent of the vote; he was initially credited with over 50 percent, but the National Electoral Commission (CEN) revised the total downward, citing late results from certain areas. Carvalho's leading opponent, incumbent president and independent Manuel Pinto da Costa, was credited with nearly 25 percent, but he boycotted the August runoff vote, alleging irregularities in the first round. Carvalho was consequently elected unopposed. Despite this dispute, African Union observers generally praised the conduct of the election.

In the October 2018 legislative elections, the ADI, the party of incumbent prime minister Patrice Trovoada, won the most seats, but failed to form a government. In November, President Carvalho invited the MLSTP-PSD, under the leadership of Jorge Bom Jesus, and the PCD-UDD-MDFM party coalition, to form a new government. Jesus was appointed prime minister later in November.

A2. Were the current national legislative representatives elected through free and fair elections? 4 / 4

Members of the unicameral, 55-seat National Assembly are elected by popular vote to four-year terms. In the October 2018 legislative elections, the ADI secured 25 seats, followed by the MLSTP-PSD with 23, the coalition PCD-UDD-MDFM with 5, and the Movement of Independent Citizens with 2. Following the elections, in a bid to secure an absolute majority, Trovoada requested that the Constitutional Court order a recount of ballots that had been ruled invalid, which the court agreed to. The opposition condemned the court's decision as biased in favor of the ADI, and demonstrations held outside the site of the recount were violently dispersed by security forces, who fired tear gas into the crowd. However, later in October, the Constitutional Court certified the initial election results, and the ADI did not gain any seats. Despite the controversy, international observers deemed the elections largely credible.

A3. Are the electoral laws and framework fair, and are they implemented impartially by the relevant election management bodies? 3 / 4

The electoral laws and framework are generally fair, but implementation suffers from lack of resources and staff. Municipal elections and elections in the autonomous region of Príncipe, which had been scheduled for 2017 but delayed due to funding shortages, were held concurrently with the parliamentary elections in October 2018.

In 2017, the ADI parliamentary majority adopted legislation that would have reorganized the composition of the CEN in a manner that the opposition claimed would allow the ADI to manipulate future elections. In March, however, the ADI government chose to maintain the CEN's structure, negating the legislation.

B. POLITICAL PLURALISM AND PARTICIPATION: 14 / 16

B1. Do the people have the right to organize in different political parties or other competitive political groupings of their choice, and is the system free of undue obstacles to the rise and fall of these competing parties or groupings? 4 / 4

The multiparty system features free and vigorous competition between the ADI, MLSTP-PSD, PCD-UDD-MDFM, and a variety of other parties.

B2. Is there a realistic opportunity for the opposition to increase its support or gain power through elections? 4 / 4

Manuel Pinto da Costa and the MLSTP-PSD ruled São Tomé and Príncipe as a one-party state from independence in 1975 until 1991. Since then there have been multiple democratic transfers of power between rival parties. Individual governments have tended to be short-lived, partly due to the country's system of proportional representation, which encourages coalition or minority governments.

B3. Are the people's political choices free from domination by the military, foreign powers, religious hierarchies, economic oligarchies, or any other powerful group that is not democratically accountable? 3 / 4

Voters and politicians are generally free from undue interference with their decisions. The practice of vote buying by political parties and candidates remains a problem, but was reportedly less prevalent during the 2018 elections. While the country experienced military coups in 1995 and 2003, normal civilian rule was swiftly restored in both cases.

B4. Do various segments of the population (including ethnic, religious, gender, LGBT, and other relevant groups) have full political rights and electoral opportunities? 3 / 4

Women and minority groups enjoy full political rights, though societal discrimination inhibits women's participation to some degree. Maria das Neves of the MLSTP-PSD, the country's first woman prime minister from 2002 to 2004, placed third in the 2016 presidential election. Women won 10 out of 55 seats in the 2018 parliamentary elections.

C. FUNCTIONING OF GOVERNMENT: 9 / 12

C1. Do the freely elected head of government and national legislative representatives determine the policies of the government? 4 / 4

The prime minster and cabinet determine the policies of the government, under the supervision of the National Assembly and the president. They are able to implement laws and policies without improper interference from unelected entities.

In June 2018, a former agriculture minister and a sergeant in the army were arrested for allegedly plotting to assassinate then prime minister Trovoada and kidnap President Carvalho as part of a coup plot, but the suspects were released for lack of evidence.

C2. Are safeguards against official corruption strong and effective? 2 / 4

Corruption is a major problem. Oversight mechanisms, the opposition, and the media have repeatedly uncovered evidence of official malfeasance, sometimes resulting in dismissals and other repercussions, but on the whole, anticorruption laws are poorly enforced.

C3. Does the government operate with openness and transparency? 3 / 4

The government generally does not restrict access to information about its operations. However, there is no specific law guaranteeing public access to government information. Officials rarely disclose their assets and income, although the new Jesus government announced in December 2018 that all ministers would declare their assets. In May, the Court of Auditors reported that 18 of 38 public institutions had failed to submit annual financial reports in the previous two years, as required by law.

CIVIL LIBERTIES: 49 / 60 (+1)

D. FREEDOM OF EXPRESSION AND BELIEF: 15 / 16

D1. Are there free and independent media? 3 / 4

Freedom of the press is constitutionally guaranteed and largely respected in practice. Public media convey opposition views and grant some access to opposition leaders, but only a handful of private media outlets are available, and a degree of self-censorship is reported at both public and private outlets. There are no restrictions on online media, though the sector is poorly developed. Less than a third of the population has internet access.

D2. Are individuals free to practice and express their religious faith or nonbelief in public and private? 4 / 4

The constitution provides for freedom of religion. Religious groups are required to register with the Justice Ministry and can face penalties for failure to do so, but the process is not reported to be biased or restrictive.

D3. Is there academic freedom, and is the educational system free from extensive political indoctrination? 4 / 4

The constitution prohibits political indoctrination in education, and academic freedom is generally respected in practice.

D4. Are individuals free to express their personal views on political or other sensitive topics without fear of surveillance or retribution? 4 / 4

There are no restrictions on individuals' freedom of expression, which is guaranteed by the constitution. The government is not known to engage in improper surveillance of personal communications or monitoring of online content.

E. ASSOCIATIONAL AND ORGANIZATIONAL RIGHTS: 11 / 12 (+1)

E1. Is there freedom of assembly? 4 / 4

The constitution protects freedom of assembly, which the government generally observes in practice. However, organizers are obliged to give authorities two days' notice before public gatherings. Following the October 2018 elections, the police banned demonstrations for 72 hours, drawing criticism from opposition parties and rights activists.

E2. Is there freedom for nongovernmental organizations, particularly those that are engaged in human rights and governance-related work? 4 / 4 (+1)

Nongovernmental organizations (NGOs), including organizations that focus on human rights and governance issues, are free to operate. The government has not placed any significant restrictions on NGOs in recent years, but a lack of funding limits their activities.

Score Change: The score improved from 3 to 4 because nongovernmental organizations are generally free to operate without restrictions.

E3. Is there freedom for trade unions and similar professional or labor organizations? 3 / 4

Workers have the legal rights to organize, strike, and bargain collectively, and these are mostly respected, though there are no provisions to regulate bargaining or punish antiunion practices by employers. Most union negotiations are conducted with the government, which remains the country's dominant formal-sector employer.

F. RULE OF LAW: 12 / 16

F1. Is there an independent judiciary? 3 / 4

The constitution provides for an independent judiciary, and the courts are relatively autonomous in practice, but they are susceptible to political influence and corruption. The system is also understaffed and underfunded.

Controversial legislation adopted and signed by the president in 2017, which mandated the creation of a separate Constitutional Court as called for in the constitution, continued to be a source of political conflict in 2018. The new court was granted ultimate authority over election results, and its members could be appointed by a simple parliamentary majority if an initial vote failed to reach a two-thirds majority. Opposition parties criticized the measure as undemocratic, noting that it had been promulgated while still under review by the Supreme Court, which had performed constitutional review functions in the absence of a separate tribunal. In January 2018, the Supreme Court ruled that the law was unconstitutional. However, the government defied the ruling, and the National Assembly elected five judges to the Constitutional Court later in the month, in a vote that the opposition boycotted.

The judicial crisis intensified further in May, when the National Assembly voted to dismiss three judges on the Supreme Court, including the court's president, after some legislators accused the judges of issuing a politicized ruling regarding the ownership of Rosema Brewery, one of the largest companies in the country. The opposition and legal scholars argued that the removal of the judges was unconstitutional and threatened the independence of the Supreme Court. In May, the National Assembly passed legislation allowing itself to elect new judges, to replace those dismissed. The judges initially elected, however, refused to fill the vacancies on the grounds that the removals were unconstitutional. In July, four other judges were elected by the ADI to replace the ousted judges, as well as a fourth judge who had resigned in protest, and were ultimately seated.

At the end of December, the National Assembly, now controlled by MLSTP-PSD and PCD-UDD-MDFM, voted to reinstate the four Supreme Court judges who had been dismissed or resigned in protest, and to remove the five judges who had been elected to the Constitutional Court by the ADI-controlled National Assembly.

F2. Does due process prevail in civil and criminal matters? 3 / 4

Law enforcement authorities generally observe legal safeguards against arbitrary arrest and detention as well as guarantees for a fair trial, but police corruption is a problem, and indigent defendants are sometimes denied access to a lawyer.

F3. Is there protection from the illegitimate use of physical force and freedom from war and insurgencies? 3 / 4

Police are sometimes accused of beating suspects during arrest. In October 2018, a young man was beaten to death while in the custody of police officers in the city of Trindade, drawing widespread condemnation. Prisons suffer from overcrowding and other harsh conditions. The country is relatively free of major violence or unrest.

F4. Do laws, policies, and practices guarantee equal treatment of various segments of the population? 3 / 4

Equal treatment is guaranteed by law, but a degree of societal discrimination against women persists, hampering their access to economic and educational opportunities. Although same-sex sexual activity is not criminalized, discrimination against LGBT (lesbian, gay, bisexual, and transgender) people is sometimes reported, and the law does not specifically address such bias.

G. PERSONAL AUTONOMY AND INDIVIDUAL RIGHTS: 11 / 16

G1. Do individuals enjoy freedom of movement, including the ability to change their place of residence, employment, or education? 4 / 4

The constitution establishes the freedom of internal movement, foreign travel, emigration, and repatriation. The government has generally respected these rights.

G2. Are individuals able to exercise the right to own property and establish private businesses without undue interference from state or nonstate actors? 3 / 4

The legal framework and government policies are generally supportive of property rights and private business activity, though bureaucratic obstacles and corruption pose challenges in practice.

G3. Do individuals enjoy personal social freedoms, including choice of marriage partner and size of family, protection from domestic violence, and control over appearance? 2 / 4

There are few formal restrictions on personal social freedoms. However, domestic violence is reportedly common and rarely prosecuted. The minimum age for marriage with parental consent is 14 for girls and 16 for boys, as opposed to 18 without parental consent for both. Roughly a third of girls marry before age 18.

G4. Do individuals enjoy equality of opportunity and freedom from economic exploitation? 2 / 4

Forced labor is prohibited and child labor is restricted by law. There are also basic legal protections against exploitative or dangerous working conditions. However, the government lacks the capacity to enforce these rules effectively, particularly in the informal agricultural sector.

The economy depends in large part on foreign aid, and the government has sought assistance from a variety of sources.

Saudi Arabia

Population: 33,400,000
Capital: Riyadh
Political Rights Rating: 7
Civil Liberties Rating: 7
Freedom Rating: 7.0
Freedom Status: Not Free
Electoral Democracy: No

Overview: Saudi Arabia's absolute monarchy restricts almost all political rights and civil liberties. No officials at the national level are elected. The regime relies on extensive surveillance, the criminalization of dissent, appeals to sectarianism and ethnicity, and public spending supported by oil revenues to maintain power. Women and religious minorities face extensive discrimination in law and in practice. Working conditions for the large expatriate labor force are often exploitative.

KEY DEVELOPMENTS IN 2018:

- A long-standing ban on women driving was lifted in June, but in the run-up to the change, the authorities arrested several activists who had campaigned for women's right to drive; the activists were accused of conspiring with foreign governments, and some were reportedly tortured in custody. The crackdown was widely interpreted as an indication that the leadership sought to discourage independent activism and did not want civil society to share credit for any reforms.

- In August, the Saudi government withdrew its ambassador to Canada, ended all new trade and investment activity with the country, and brought back Saudis who had been in Canada for education or medical treatment. The actions were triggered by a statement from the Canadian foreign minister calling for the release of Saudi human rights activists including Samar Badawi, the sister of detained liberal blogger Raif Badawi.

- In September, prosecutors formally requested the death penalty in the case of prominent dissident cleric Salman al-Awdah, who had been detained since 2017 and was known for his criticism of the government on religious grounds. Among other charges, he was accused of links to the Muslim Brotherhood, which is banned in the country.

- In October, the authorities admitted that Jamal Khashoggi, a well-known Saudi journalist who had gone into self-imposed exile in the United States to call for reform, had been killed by Saudi intelligence agents after traveling to the Saudi consulate in Istanbul to obtain documents related to his planned marriage to a

Turkish woman. His death became a lightning rod for international criticism of the leadership's lawlessness and harsh suppression of dissent.

POLITICAL RIGHTS: 1 / 40 (+1)

A. ELECTORAL PROCESS: 0 / 12

A1. Was the current head of government or other chief national authority elected through free and fair elections? 0 / 4

Saudi Arabia's king is chosen by his predecessor from among male descendants of the country's founder, though the choice must be approved by a council of senior princes. The king rules for life. King Salman bin Abdulaziz al-Saud appointed his son Mohammed bin Salman as crown prince in 2017, displacing the prince's older cousin, Mohammed bin Nayef, who was stripped of all official positions and put under house arrest. The cabinet, which is appointed by the king, passes legislation that becomes law once ratified by royal decree. King Salman also serves as prime minister, and Mohammed bin Salman serves as deputy prime minister and minister of defense.

A2. Were the current national legislative representatives elected through free and fair elections? 0 / 4

The king appoints the 150 members of the Majlis al-Shura (Consultative Council), who serve in an advisory capacity, for four-year terms. The council has no legislative authority.

Limited nonpartisan elections for advisory councils at the municipal level were introduced in 2005. In the 2015 elections, two-thirds of the seats on the 284 councils were open to voting, while the minister of municipal and rural affairs held responsibility for filling the remainder through appointment. Women were allowed to vote and run as candidates for the first time, and a small number won seats.

A3. Are the electoral laws and framework fair, and are they implemented impartially by the relevant election management bodies? 0 / 4

The electoral framework lacks constitutional protections, and the 2015 elections for municipal councils were subject to a number of onerous restrictions. The kingdom's rules on gender segregation were applied to campaigns, meaning no candidates could produce posters showing their faces or meet in person with voters of the opposite sex. Candidates were also barred from giving media interviews, leading many to campaign via social media. A number of candidates were disqualified for unclear reasons, though some were reinstated after appeals. Ultimately only a small fraction of the citizen population participated in the elections, reflecting doubts about the effectiveness of the advisory councils.

B. POLITICAL PLURALISM AND PARTICIPATION: 0 / 16

B1. Do the people have the right to organize in different political parties or other competitive political groupings of their choice, and is the system free of undue obstacles to the rise and fall of these competing parties or groupings? 0 / 4

Political parties are forbidden, and political dissent is effectively criminalized. Some of the country's most prominent political rights organizations and activists, including founding members of the banned Saudi Civil and Political Rights Association (ACPRA), have been arrested and sentenced to prison in recent years, and the crackdown persisted in 2018. Among those arrested during the year was ACPRA member Mohammed al-Bajadi. Many other political activists continued to serve lengthy prison sentences.

B2. Is there a realistic opportunity for the opposition to increase its support or gain power through elections? 0 / 4

The current leadership has given no indication that it plans to allow competitive elections for positions of executive or legislative authority in the future. Opposition movements are banned, and the government is increasingly intolerant even of moderate critics. The Muslim Brotherhood, a Sunni Islamist political organization, is believed to have the sympathy of a substantial minority of Saudis, but it remains banned and has been designated as a terrorist group by the Saudi government since 2014.

Other groups and individuals that criticize the regime or call for political reform—whether Sunni or Shiite, Islamist or secularist—are subject to arbitrary detention. Many of those arrested in the crackdown that began in September 2017 had questioned or declined to vocally support the government's campaign to isolate Qatar over its relations with the Muslim Brotherhood and Iran. These included prominent reformist clerics such as Salman al-Awdah and Awad al-Qarni; prosecutors said in September 2018 that they were seeking the death penalty for both men.

B3. Are the people's political choices free from domination by the military, foreign powers, religious hierarchies, economic oligarchies, or any other powerful group that is not democratically accountable? 0 / 4

The monarchy generally excludes the public from any meaningful political participation. In the absence of political parties, voters in Saudi Arabia's limited municipal elections are heavily influenced by tribal and religious leaders, many of whom benefit from close ties to the ruling establishment.

B4. Do various segments of the population (including ethnic, religious, gender, LGBT, and other relevant groups) have full political rights and electoral opportunities? 0 / 4

Although political rights are curtailed for all Saudi citizens, women, religious minorities, and LGBT (lesbian, gay, bisexual, and transgender) people face additional obstacles to participation given the kingdom's strict laws and customs on matters such as gender segregation and sexual activity, and its intolerance of religious groups that deviate from Wahhabism, a highly conservative and literalist interpretation of Sunni Islam. Some 30 women serve on the appointed Majlis al-Shura, and women secured about 1 percent of the seats in the 2015 municipal council elections. Shiites reportedly hold a small number of seats on the Majlis al-Shura and many seats on municipal councils in Shiite-majority areas. Women and religious minorities are mostly excluded from leadership positions in the government. A woman was appointed in February 2018 as deputy minister of labor and social development to promote women's employment opportunities.

Noncitizens, who make up roughly a third of the population in Saudi Arabia, have no political rights, and citizenship can only be directly transmitted by a citizen father whose marriage is recognized by the state.

C. FUNCTIONING OF GOVERNMENT: 1 / 12

C1. Do the freely elected head of government and national legislative representatives determine the policies of the government? 0 / 4

The kingdom's only elected officials serve on local advisory councils and have little or no influence over national laws and policies.

C2. Are safeguards against official corruption strong and effective? 1 / 4

Corruption remains a significant problem. Although the government generates massive revenue from the sale of oil, which it redistributes through social welfare programs and as patronage, little is known about state accounting or the various direct ways in which public wealth becomes a source of private privilege for the royal family and its clients.

Crown Prince Mohammed bin Salman heads an anticorruption committee, which in 2017 ordered the detention of more than 200 people, many of whom were coerced into turning over billions of dollars in assets to the state. The crown prince's campaign coincided with a crackdown on dissent and targeted potential rivals within the royal family, leading observers to suggest that it was part of a broader effort to consolidate Mohammed bin Salman's political and economic control.

Independent whistle-blowers and anticorruption advocates continue to face punishment. Salah al-Shehi, a columnist at *Al-Watan*, was arrested in January 2018 and sentenced in February to five years in prison after he suggested in a television appearance that there was corruption in the royal court.

C3. Does the government operate with openness and transparency? 0 / 4

The functioning of government is largely opaque. There is little transparency on whether or how state funds are disbursed, or on the internal decision-making process that allocates them, and there is no public mechanism for holding senior decision-makers accountable. The state's oil revenues make up the vast majority of its financial resources, but these are tightly controlled by the royal family, which uses the same income to support itself.

ADDITIONAL DISCRETIONARY POLITICAL RIGHTS QUESTION
Is the government or occupying power deliberately changing the ethnic composition of a country or territory so as to destroy a culture or tip the political balance in favor of another group? 0 / 0 (+1)

The government has long sought to suppress Shiite religious and cultural identity, associating it with Iran and regarding it as a threat to the regime's official Sunni and Wahhabi underpinnings. Systemic discrimination has stoked periodic protests in Shiite-majority areas, and the authorities have responded with harsh and often arbitrary security measures. In 2017, this included a decision to demolish a historic neighborhood in the largely Shiite town of Awamiya, which has long been a center for political unrest. The effort, which entailed the eviction of thousands of residents, prompted armed resistance and an extended siege. However, no similar incidents were reported in 2018.

Score Change: The score improved from −1 to 0 because there was no repetition of a 2017 incident in which the authorities physically destroyed a historic Shiite neighborhood as part of an effort to suppress dissent among the marginalized Shiite minority.

CIVIL LIBERTIES: 6 / 60 (−1)
D. FREEDOM OF EXPRESSION AND BELIEF: 2 / 16 (−1)
D1. Are there free and independent media? 0 / 4

The government controls domestic media content and dominates regional print and satellite-television coverage. Journalists can be imprisoned for a variety of vaguely defined crimes. A 2011 royal decree amended the press law to criminalize, among other things, any criticism of the country's grand mufti, the Council of Senior Religious Scholars, or government officials; violations can result in fines and forced closure of media outlets. All blogs and websites, or anyone posting news or commentary online, must have a license from the Ministry of Information or face fines and possible closure of the website.

In October 2018, Reporters Without Borders said that 15 journalists and bloggers or citizen journalists had been detained over the previous 12 months; the group estimated that between 25 and 30 were being held at the end of the year. Also in October, one of the country's most prominent journalists, Jamal Khashoggi, was murdered by Saudi agents inside the Saudi consulate in Istanbul. Khashoggi, who had been critical of the government under Mohammed bin Salman, had been working in the United States as a columnist at the *Washington Post*, but traveled to the consulate to obtain documents ahead of his planned marriage to a Turkish woman. Saudi officials denied for two weeks that he had died, and subsequently blamed rogue intelligence agents, but the evidence suggested that the crown prince had been involved.

During the two weeks between Khashoggi's death and the official admission that he had been killed, Saudi media blamed regional rival Qatar for supposedly fabricating his disappearance in order to harm Saudi Arabia's image. The state-controlled media have increasingly relied on defensive nationalist sentiment in response to criticism of human rights problems.

The country's first movie theater since the 1970s opened in April 2018, though films were still expected to be censored to some extent.

D2. Are individuals free to practice and express their religious faith or nonbelief in public and private? 0 / 4

The 1992 Basic Law declares that the Quran and the Sunna are the country's constitution. Islam is the official religion, and all Saudis are required by law to be Muslims. A 2014 royal decree punishes atheism with up to 20 years in prison. The government prohibits the public practice of any religion other than Islam and restricts the religious practices of the Shiite and Sufi Muslim minority sects. The construction of Shiite mosques is constrained through licensing rules and prohibited outside of Eastern Province, where most Shiites live. Although the government recognizes the right of non-Muslims to worship in private, it does not always respect this right in practice.

Online commentary that touches on religion can be harshly punished. Among other prominent cases, liberal blogger Raif Badawi, arrested in 2012, received a 10-year prison sentence for blasphemy in 2014 and remained behind bars in 2018.

D3. Is there academic freedom, and is the educational system free from extensive political indoctrination? 1 / 4

Academic freedom is restricted, and informers monitor classrooms for compliance with curriculum rules, including a ban on teaching secular philosophy and religions other than Islam. Despite changes to textbooks in recent years, intolerance in the classroom remains a significant problem, as some educators continue to espouse discriminatory and hateful views of non-Muslims and Muslim minority sects.

Academics face punishment for critical public analysis of government policies. Hatoon al-Fassi, a history professor and women's rights advocate, was arrested in June 2018, days after she had been quoted in the *New York Times* about her views on the crown prince's reforms. In October, well-known economist Essam al-Zamil, who had critiqued plans to privatize part of the state oil company, was charged with terrorism.

D4. Are individuals free to express their personal views on political or other sensitive topics without fear of surveillance or retribution? 1 / 4 (−1)

Saudis are able to engage in some degree of private discussion on political and other topics, including criticism of certain aspects of government performance, both online and offline. However, severe criminal penalties deter more direct criticism of the regime and free discussion on topics like religion or the royal family. Laws are often vaguely worded to allow the state considerable discretion to determine what constitutes illegal expression.

The climate for free expression deteriorated during 2018, as the arrests of women's rights activists and various others who had criticized government policies—as well as the assassination of Jamal Khashoggi—served as warnings to ordinary Saudis to avoid public dissent. Following Khashoggi's disappearance in October, law enforcement officials reminded citizens and residents that they could face five years in prison for spreading rumors or "fake news."

Surveillance is extensive inside Saudi Arabia, and even Saudis living abroad are vulnerable to spying. In October, the University of Toronto's Citizen Lab found surveillance software on the phone of Omar Abdulaziz, a Saudi dissident living in Canada who was in regular contact with Khashoggi before his assassination.

Score Change: The score declined from 2 to 1 because the detention of women's rights activists and other mild critics of the government, and the assassination of journalist Jamal Khashoggi in Turkey, further deterred open discussion among ordinary residents.

E. ASSOCIATIONAL AND ORGANIZATIONAL RIGHTS: 0 / 12

E1. Is there freedom of assembly? 0 / 4

Freedom of assembly is not respected, and the government has imposed harsh punishments—including the death penalty—on those who lead or participate in public protests. In one case in 2018, six Shiite activists were put on trial in a terrorism court for protest-related offenses. Five of the six faced possible death sentences, including Israa al-Ghomgham, a female activist.

E2. Is there freedom for nongovernmental organizations, particularly those that are engaged in human rights- and governance-related work? 0 / 4

Nongovernmental organizations must obtain a license from the government to operate. Until the adoption of a law on the topic in 2015, officials had approved licenses only for charitable groups; the authorities have expressed a desire to encourage the growth of civil society, but they continue to discourage independent work on human rights and governance issues. Reformist organizations have reportedly been denied licenses in practice, in some cases through arbitrary delays. Human rights activists and other civil society representatives face regular harassment and detention.

A number of prominent activists were serving lengthy prison sentences during 2018, and new arrests were also reported. In May, a month before women were allowed to drive for the first time, the authorities arrested several women who had campaigned for the change. They included activist Lujain al-Hathloul, blogger Eman al-Nafjan, and 70-year-old Aisha al-Manea. Several were accused of conspiring with foreign countries or terrorist groups. The arrests were seen as a signal that the government did not want activists to take any credit for its reform, and sought to discourage further independent activism on women's rights. In July, Samar Badawi—sister of detained blogger Raif Badawi—and Nassima al-Sadah, prominent campaigners against the kingdom's male guardianship laws, were also arrested. Saudi Arabia cut its diplomatic relations and restricted trade and travel with Canada in August after the Canadian foreign minister called for the release of the detained women's rights activists.

E3. Is there freedom for trade unions and similar professional or labor organizations? 0 / 4

No laws protect the rights to form independent labor unions, bargain collectively, or engage in strikes. Workers who engage in union activity are subject to dismissal or detention.

F. RULE OF LAW: 2 / 16

F1. Is there an independent judiciary? 1 / 4

The judiciary has very little independence in practice. Judges are appointed by the king and overseen by the Supreme Judicial Council, whose chairman is also the justice minister. A special commission of judicial experts issues opinions that serve as guidelines for judges on the interpretation of Sharia (Islamic law), which forms the basis of Saudi law. Judges have significant discretion in how they interpret Sharia and do not have to publish an explanation of their judgments.

F2. Does due process prevail in civil and criminal matters? 1 / 4

Defendants' rights are poorly protected by law. Detainees are often denied access to legal counsel during interrogation, and lengthy pretrial detention and detention without charge are common. Statistics on prisoners are lacking, and the number of political prisoners is therefore difficult to assess.

An antiterrorism law that took effect in 2014 includes lengthy prison sentences for criticizing the monarchy or the government. Among other provisions, it expanded the power of police to conduct raids targeting suspected antigovernment activity without judicial approval.

The hundreds of people arrested in the anticorruption crackdown in 2017 did not go to trial or pass through the judicial system, but were instead compelled to hand over assets to the government in return for being released. Supporters of the government claimed that the courts lacked the capacity to process the cases swiftly, and that taking the judicial route would have led to a years-long process.

F3. Is there protection from the illegitimate use of physical force and freedom from war and insurgencies? 0 / 4

Allegations of torture by police and prison officials are common, and access to prisoners by independent human rights and legal organizations is extremely limited. Physical abuse was allegedly used to force cooperation by detainees in the 2017 anticorruption campaign. Corporal punishment, most often lashing, is common in criminal sentencing. Capital punishment is applied to a wide range of crimes other than murder, including drug and protest-related offenses; juvenile offenders are not exempt from the penalty. According to the British human rights group Reprieve, Saudi authorities carried out close to 150 executions in 2018.

Terrorism remains a serious threat. Saudi Arabia has also faced cross-border attacks, including ballistic missile strikes, by the Houthis, the armed rebel group that controls much of Yemen and is fighting a Saudi-led military campaign to dislodge them. Most of the missiles have caused little damage, but they have been aimed at oil facilities and Riyadh airport, among other apparent targets.

F4. Do laws, policies, and practices guarantee equal treatment of various segments of the population? 0 / 4

The courts engage in routine discrimination against various groups, citing their interpretations of Sharia. A woman's testimony is generally given half the weight of a man's, and the testimony of anyone other than observant Sunni Muslims can be disregarded by judges.

Shiites, who make up 10 to 15 percent of the population, face socioeconomic disadvantages, discrimination in employment, and underrepresentation in government positions and the security forces.

Education and economic rights for Saudi women have improved somewhat in recent years, but women are still subject to extensive legal and societal discrimination, most notably through the guardianship system, in which every woman must rely on a close male relative to approve basic activities. For example, employers often require women to obtain their guardians' permission to work.

Same-sex sexual activity is generally understood to be prohibited under Sharia, and LGBT people, including transgender people, are at risk of harassment, discrimination, criminal punishment, and violence. In January 2018, several men were arrested after being seen in a video of what appeared to be a gay wedding, and in 2017 the police arrested nearly three dozen transgender women from Pakistan, at least one of whom died in custody.

G. PERSONAL AUTONOMY AND INDIVIDUAL RIGHTS: 2 / 16

G1. Do individuals enjoy freedom of movement, including the ability to change their place of residence, employment, or education? 0 / 4

The government punishes activists and critics by limiting their ability to travel outside the country, and reform advocates are routinely stripped of their passports.

Gender segregation restricts freedom of movement for both men and women, but male guardianship and other factors impose especially onerous constraints on women. The long-standing ban on women driving was formally lifted in June 2018. In January, women were able to attend sporting events in stadiums for the first time, and both men and women could visit the movie theaters that began opening in April.

Foreign workers cannot change jobs unless they have a no-objection letter from their existing employer, and some employers confiscate workers' passports to prevent them from leaving.

G2. Are individuals able to exercise the right to own property and establish private businesses without undue interference from state or nonstate actors? 1 / 4

While a great deal of business activity in the kingdom is dominated by or connected to members of the government, the ruling family, or other elite families, officials have given assurances that special industrial and commercial zones are free from interference by the royal family.

Women require permission from a male guardian to obtain business licenses. Women also face legal discrimination regarding property rights, with daughters typically receiving half the inheritance awarded to sons.

G3. Do individuals enjoy personal social freedoms, including choice of marriage partner and size of family, protection from domestic violence, and control over appearance? 0 / 4

The religious police enforce rules governing gender segregation and personal attire, but their authority has been sharply curtailed in both law and practice since 2016.

There are a number of official restrictions on marriage. For example, Muslim women may not marry non-Muslims, citizens typically require permission to marry noncitizens, and men are barred from marrying women from certain countries. All sexual activity outside of marriage is criminalized, and the death penalty can be applied in certain circumstances. Women face legal disadvantages in divorce and custody proceedings.

A 2013 law broadly defined and criminalized domestic abuse, prescribing fines and up to a year in prison for perpetrators. However, enforcement remains problematic, with some officials prioritizing privacy and family integrity over safety and justice for victims. Women's ability to leave abusive relationships is also severely limited by the guardianship system.

G4. Do individuals enjoy equality of opportunity and freedom from economic exploitation? 1 / 4

A number of amendments to the labor law that went into effect in 2015 granted broader rights and protections to workers in the private sector. However, the law does not apply to household workers, who are governed by separate regulations that provide fewer safeguards against exploitative working conditions.

Foreign workers—who make up more than half of the active labor force—enjoy only limited legal protections and remain vulnerable to trafficking and forced labor, primarily through employers' exploitation of the *kafala* visa-sponsorship system. In 2014, the Ministry of Labor ruled that expatriate workers who are not paid their salaries for more than three consecutive months are free to switch their work sponsors without approval. In practice, foreign workers are subject to periodic mass deportations for visa violations or criminal activity, though due process is often lacking in such cases. Government programs give preferential treatment to companies that hire certain percentages of Saudi citizens and penalize those that fail to meet such targets.

Senegal

Population: 16,300,000
Capital: Dakar
Political Rights Rating: 2
Civil Liberties Rating: 3 ↓
Freedom Rating: 2.5
Freedom Status: Free
Electoral Democracy: Yes

Overview: Senegal is one of Africa's most stable electoral democracies and has undergone two peaceful transfers of power between rival parties since 2000. However, politically motivated prosecutions of opposition leaders and changes to the electoral laws have reduced the competitiveness of the opposition in recent years. The country is known for its relatively independent media and free expression, though defamation laws continue to constrain press freedom. Other ongoing challenges include corruption in government, weak rule of law, and inadequate protections for the rights of women and LGBT (lesbian, gay, bisexual, and transgender) people.

KEY DEVELOPMENTS IN 2018:

- An electoral law passed in April requires all aspiring presidential candidates to obtain the signatures of 0.8 percent of the electorate from at least seven regions to appear on the ballot. The opposition condemned the legislation as an attempt to neutralize President Sall's competition for the 2019 presidential election.
- In March, one of President Sall's most prominent political opponents, former mayor of Dakar Khalifa Sall, was found guilty of embezzlement and sentenced to five years in prison. According to rights groups, the trial violated the defendant's due process rights.
- Throughout the year, the government cracked down on assembly rights by banning protests around tense political moments, refusing to authorize a number of demonstrations, and violently dispersing peaceful gatherings.

POLITICAL RIGHTS: 30 / 40 (-1)
A. ELECTORAL PROCESS: 10 / 12

A1. Was the current head of government or other chief national authority elected through free and fair elections? 4 / 4

The president is directly elected to a maximum of two consecutive terms; in 2016, the presidential term was reduced via referendum from seven years to five, effective after President Macky Sall's current term ends in 2019. In the 2012 presidential election, Abdoulaye Wade of the Senegalese Democratic Party (PDS) ran for a controversial third term in a campaign that was marred by violence and intimidation, but resulted in a peaceful transfer of power. Representing the Alliance for the Republic (APR), Sall—Wade's former prime minister and campaign director—won a runoff with 66 percent of the vote. International observers declared the election credible.

A2. Were the current national legislative representatives elected through free and fair elections? 3 / 4

Members of Senegal's 165-seat National Assembly are elected to five-year terms—105 are elected in single-member districts, and 60 by proportional representation. In the July 2017 parliamentary elections, the president's APR-led Benno Bokk Yakaar coalition won 125 seats, followed by Wade's PDS-led Winning Coalition–Wattu Senegaal with 19 seats. Khalifa Sall's Mankoo Taxawu Senegaal coalition took 7 seats, and 11 groups divided the remainder. International observers deemed the elections transparent despite some significant procedural errors and logistical challenges.

New biometric voting cards were only distributed to 70 percent of eligible voters before the elections. To address the problem, the president proposed and the Constitutional Council approved a plan to allow voters to use alternative forms of identification. Some voters were allegedly disenfranchised because of difficulties related to the identification measures, which were approved just four days before the elections.

A3. Are the electoral laws and framework fair, and are they implemented impartially by the relevant election management bodies? 3 / 4

The National Autonomous Electoral Commission (CENA) administers elections. Although the CENA is nominally independent, its members are appointed by the president. The opposition criticized the government for making important changes ahead of the 2017 legislative balloting, including the introduction of the new biometric voting system, without engaging in dialogue or building political consensus. The changes were approved in January 2017, only six months before the elections, which observers argued did not provide sufficient time for logistical information about the new electoral framework to be disseminated in a coordinated fashion.

A new electoral law passed in April 2018 requires all aspiring presidential candidates to obtain the signatures of 0.8 percent of the electorate from at least seven regions to appear on the ballot, and all groups presenting National Assembly lists to obtain signatures from 0.5 percent of voters in at least seven regions. The government asserted that the legislation was necessary to reduce the proliferation of parties that field candidates in elections. The opposition boycotted the vote, arguing that the bill disadvantaged prospective candidates and parties with limited means and was intended to make the 2019 presidential election less competitive.

B. POLITICAL PLURALISM AND PARTICIPATION: 12 / 16 (−1)

B1. Do the people have the right to organize in different political parties or other competitive political groupings of their choice, and is the system free of undue obstacles to the rise and fall of these competing parties or groupings? 3 / 4

Registration requirements for new political parties are not onerous and registered parties can organize and operate without government interference. Opposition candidates still face major financial inequities when competing with incumbents. There is no public financing for political parties, but the ruling group deploys a vast set of state resources to garner support, whereas opposition leaders are often forced to rely on personal wealth to finance party operations.

B2. Is there a realistic opportunity for the opposition to increase its support or gain power through elections? 3 / 4 (–1)

The opposition can increase its support or gain power through elections—the 2012 election marked the second victory by an opposition presidential candidate in 12 years. However, the 2018 electoral law was criticized by opposition leaders for making it more difficult for candidates to appear on the ballot, and was widely seen as a move to clear the field and ensure President Sall's reelection in 2019.

The prosecutions of some of President Sall's most prominent political opponents in recent years has reduced the competitiveness of the opposition. Dakar mayor Khalifa Sall, considered one of President Sall's foremost rivals and a prospective 2019 presidential candidate, was arrested in 2017 after the government alleged that $2.9 million in funding for his office was accounted for with false receipts. The mayor and his defense attorneys argued that such funds are commonly used as political financing and that Sall's prosecution was politically motivated. The National Assembly lifted Sall's parliamentary immunity, which he had acquired after being elected to the legislature earlier that year, in late 2017. In March 2018, Sall was found guilty, sentenced to five years in prison, and fined 5 million CFA francs ($8,900). Opposition lawmaker Barthélémy Dias was sentenced to six months in prison in April for "contempt of court, incitement to disturb public order, and discrediting a judicial decision" after sharply criticizing the verdict. Sall was removed from office as mayor of Dakar in August. At year's end, his eligibility to stand as a presidential candidate was contingent upon a Supreme Court decision on his conviction, which was expected in January 2019.

Score Change: The score declined from 4 to 3 because a new law electoral law makes it more difficult for opposition candidates to appear on the ballot, and the politicized prosecutions of prominent opponents of the president reduced the competitiveness of opposition parties.

B3. Are the people's political choices free from domination by the military, foreign powers, religious hierarchies, economic oligarchies, or any other powerful group that is not democratically accountable? 3 / 4

People's political choices are largely free from domination by groups that are not democratically accountable. Sufi Muslim marabouts exercise some influence on voters and politicians, particularly in regard to social issues such as homosexuality, marriage, and abortion rights.

B4. Do various segments of the population (including ethnic, religious, gender, LGBT, and other relevant groups) have full political rights and electoral opportunities? 3 / 4

For the first time in 2017, 15 of 165 parliamentary seats were reserved for the Senegalese diaspora. Thanks to a 2010 law requiring gender parity on candidate lists, women were elected to 70 of 165 seats in 2017. However, women's overall rate of participation in politics, such as voting and engaging in local political activities, is lower than men's. Citizens of all ethnicities and religions have political rights. Due to high levels of discrimination and social stigma, LGBT people have no meaningful political representation.

C. FUNCTIONING OF GOVERNMENT: 8 / 12

C1. Do the freely elected head of government and national legislative representatives determine the policies of the government? 3 / 4

President Sall, his cabinet, and national legislative representatives determine government policies. However, power is concentrated in the executive branch, and the National Assembly is limited in its ability to act as a check on the president. A study published in May 2018 on the National Assembly's oversight of public policies found that the executive branch blocked certain parliamentary inquiries on government concessions and did not always respond to parliamentary questions.

C2. Are safeguards against official corruption strong and effective? 2 / 4

Corruption remains a serious problem, and high-level officials often act with impunity. Anticorruption bodies enforce the law unevenly and are sometimes viewed as politically motivated. The corruption case against Khalifa Sall, for example, was seen by many observers as an effort to neutralize one of the president's most powerful opponents.

C3. Does the government operate with openness and transparency? 3 / 4

The government generally operates with openness, though there are reportedly problems with competition and transparency in the awarding of government contracts. The government frequently awards contracts without any formal tender process and does not always publicly release its contracts or bilateral agreements before they are signed.

A 2014 law requires confidential asset disclosures by the prime minister, cabinet members, top National Assembly officials, and the managers of large public funds; the president's asset disclosures are made public.

CIVIL LIBERTIES: 42 / 60 (−2)

D. FREEDOM OF EXPRESSION AND BELIEF: 13 / 16

D1. Are there free and independent media? 2 / 4

The constitution guarantees freedom of speech, but defamation laws are occasionally enforced against journalists. There are many well-known independent media entities, as well as state-controlled television, radio, and newspapers.

Several journalists who provided critical coverage of the government or gave a platform to critics of the regime were attacked or detained in 2018. In January, reporter Selle Mbaye was assaulted by a police officer while filming the Khalifa Sall trial and briefly detained. In April, Serigne Diagne, director of the news site Dakaractu, was arrested at the outlet's headquarters and detained along with three employees. The police had arrived to apprehend Barthélémy Dias, who was scheduled to make an appearance on one of Dakaractu's programs and had criticized the Khalifa Sall verdict earlier that day. The journalists were released after several hours.

Senegal's controversial 2017 press code increased punishments for defamation offenses, allows authorities to shut down press outlets without judicial approval, and enables the government to block internet content deemed "contrary to morality."

D2. Are individuals free to practice and express their religious faith or nonbelief in public and private? 4 / 4

There is no state religion, and freedom of worship is constitutionally protected and respected in practice. Muslims constitute 96 percent of the population.

D3. Is there academic freedom, and is the educational system free from extensive political indoctrination? 4 / 4

Academic freedom is guaranteed by the constitution and generally respected in practice.

D4. Are individuals free to express their personal views on political or other sensitive topics without fear of surveillance or retribution? 3 / 4

Private discussion is generally open and free. However, individuals have occasionally been arrested for social media posts deemed offensive by the government.

In November 2018, the National Assembly passed a bill on electronic communications, which included a vaguely worded provision that expanded the regulatory power of the government over social media companies. Rights activists expressed concern that the law could be used to shut down, tax, or surveil communications on popular social media platforms.

E. ASSOCIATIONAL AND ORGANIZATIONAL RIGHTS: 9 / 12 (–1)
E1. Is there freedom of assembly? 2 / 4 (–1)

The constitution guarantees freedom of assembly, but the Ministry of Interior must approve protests in advance. In 2018, the government cracked down on assembly rights by banning protests around tense political moments and violently dispersing some demonstrations. In April, for example, authorities banned protests in the center of Dakar ahead of the National Assembly vote on the contentious electoral reform law. Security forces then fired tear gas into the demonstration and arrested several protesters. Authorities also refused to authorize a number of demonstrations during the year, including a planned opposition protest in Dakar in March, which the police also dispersed with tear gas.

Score Change: The score declined from 3 to 2 due to authorities banning protests around tense political moments, refusing to authorize demonstrations, and employing excessive force against protesters.

E2. Is there freedom for nongovernmental organizations, particularly those that are engaged in human rights– and governance-related work? 4 / 4

Nongovernmental organizations (NGOs) generally operate without interference from state or nonstate actors.

E3. Is there freedom for trade unions and similar professional or labor organizations? 3 / 4

Formal-sector workers, with the exception of security employees, have rights to organize, bargain collectively, and strike, though the right to strike is impinged by legal provisions that ban pickets and sit-down strikes, among other activities. Trade unions must be authorized by the Ministry of the Interior, and unions lack legal recourse if registration is denied.

F. RULE OF LAW: 9 / 16 (–1)
F1. Is there an independent judiciary? 2 / 4

The judiciary is formally independent, but the president controls appointments to the Constitutional Council, the Court of Appeal, and the Council of State. Judges are prone to pressure from the government on matters involving high-level officials. Judge Ibrahima Dème, a well-known jurist who resigned from the Higher Council of the Judiciary in 2017, again resigned from the bench in protest in March 2018, citing the judiciary's lack of independence. Throughout 2018, the Senegalese Union of Magistrates called for reform of the Higher Council of the Judiciary, which recommends judicial appointments to the executive branch. The council is headed by the president and minister of justice, which critics argue compromises its independence.

F2. Does due process prevail in civil and criminal matters? 2 / 4 (–1)

The law guarantees fair public trials and defendants' rights, but arbitrary arrest and detention remains a concern. Though the government is obligated to supply attorneys to felony defendants who cannot afford them, this representation is inconsistent in practice. A number of people charged with terrorism were denied access to lawyers and detained for more than 48 hours before seeing a judge during 2018. Lengthy pretrial detention remains a problem as well.

Opposition leaders have also faced unfair trials in recent years. In June 2018, the Economic Community of West African States (ECOWAS) Court of Justice determined that Khalifa Sall's preventive detention was arbitrary. It also found that his rights to an attorney and the presumption of innocence had been infringed.

Score Change: The score declined from 3 to 2 because due process was undermined by the arbitrary detention and unfair trial against opposition politician Khalifa Sall and the lengthy preventive detentions of other accused people, particularly in terrorism cases.

F3. Is there protection from the illegitimate use of physical force and freedom from war and insurgencies? 3 / 4

Individuals are generally protected from the illegitimate use of physical force. However, Senegalese prisons are overcrowded, and human rights groups have documented incidents of excessive force and cruel treatment by prison authorities.

The low-level separatist conflict in the Casamance region was ongoing at year's end. After several years of reduced violence that followed a de facto cease-fire, separatists killed 14 people in an attack near the city of Ziguinchor in January 2018. Negotiations for a more permanent peace agreement had not yet begun at year's end.

F4. Do laws, policies, and practices guarantee equal treatment of various segments of the population? 2 / 4

The caste system is still prevalent among many of Senegal's ethnic groups. Individuals of lower castes are subject to discrimination in employment. Women face persistent inequities in employment, health care, and education.

Same-sex sexual activity remains criminalized. While these laws are rarely enforced, violence, threats, and mob attacks are common against LGBT people, who face discrimination in housing, employment, and health care.

G. PERSONAL AUTONOMY AND INDIVIDUAL RIGHTS: 11 / 16

G1. Do individuals enjoy freedom of movement, including the ability to change their place of residence, employment, or education? 3 / 4

Citizens generally enjoy freedom of movement and can change their residence, employment, and educational institution without serious restrictions, though the threat of land mines and rebel activity has hindered travel through parts of the Casamance region.

G2. Are individuals able to exercise the right to own property and establish private businesses without undue interference from state or nonstate actors? 3 / 4

The civil code facilitates ownership of private property, and property rights are generally respected. Commercial dispute resolution can be drawn out, and property title and land registration protocols are inconsistently applied, though the government has worked to ease property acquisition and registration. Traditional customs limit women's ability to purchase property, and local rules on inheritance make it difficult for women to become beneficiaries.

G3. Do individuals enjoy personal social freedoms, including choice of marriage partner and size of family, protection from domestic violence, and control over appearance? 3 / 4

Rates of female genital mutilation have declined due in part to campaigns to discourage the practice, but it remains a problem. The government launched a plan to reduce early marriage in 2016, given that almost one in three Senegalese girls marries before age 18. Husbands are legally regarded as heads of households. Rape and domestic abuse are common and rarely punished. The law allows abortion only to save a woman's life, and abortions for medical reasons are difficult to obtain in practice.

G4. Do individuals enjoy equality of opportunity and freedom from economic exploitation? 2 / 4

Child labor remains a problem, particularly in the informal economy, and laws restricting the practice are inadequately enforced. Forced begging by students at religious schools is common, and teachers suspected of abuse are rarely prosecuted.

Sex trafficking remains a concern, although according to the US State Department, the government has increased its efforts to prosecute perpetrators. However, it is difficult to discern the robustness if the law enforcement response, since the government does not publicize records on sex trafficking arrests and prosecutions.

Serbia

Population: 7,000,000
Capital: Belgrade
Political Rights Rating: 3
Civil Liberties Rating: 3 ↓
Freedom Rating: 3.0
Freedom Status: Partly Free
Electoral Democracy: Yes

Status Change: Serbia's status declined from Free to Partly Free due to deterioration in the conduct of elections, continued attempts by the government and allied media outlets to undermine independent journalists through legal harassment and smear campaigns, and President Aleksandar Vučić's de facto accumulation of executive powers that conflict with his constitutional role.

Overview: Serbia is a parliamentary democracy with competitive multiparty elections, but in recent years the ruling Serbian Progressive Party (SNS) has steadily eroded political rights and civil liberties, putting pressure on independent media, the political opposition, and civil society organizations. Despite these trends, the country has continued to move toward membership in the European Union (EU).

KEY DEVELOPMENTS IN 2018:

- Local elections held in Belgrade in March were marked by media bias and allegations of pressure on voters, misuse of public resources, and intimidation of independent observers, among other irregularities.
- Opposition figures continued to face harassment and violence, including a November attack on prominent politician Borko Stefanović, who was brutally beaten by seven men before a scheduled debate in Kruševac.
- The Stefanović assault led to antigovernment protests that continued through the end of the year, with participants focusing on alleged corruption and attacks on opposition figures and the media under President Vučić and the SNS.
- The Independent Journalists' Association of Serbia (NUNS) documented 102 incidents of pressure or violence against journalists in 2018, as independent media continued to endure smear campaigns, harassment, and physical threats.

POLITICAL RIGHTS: 24 / 40 (–4)

A. ELECTORAL PROCESS: 8 / 12 (–1)

A1. Was the current head of government or other chief national authority elected through free and fair elections? 3 / 4

The president is directly elected for up to two five-year terms. In April 2017, Vučić won election with 55 percent of the vote in a field of 11 candidates. The campaign was characterized by media bias and allegations of misuse of public resources and vote buying. Vučić remained prime minister throughout the election period, blurring the line between official and electoral activities.

The prime minister is elected by the parliament. Vučić named Ana Brnabić, then the minister for local government and public administration, to succeed him as prime minister following the 2017 presidential election, and she was subsequently confirmed in office by lawmakers.

A2. Were the current national legislative representatives elected through free and fair elections? 2 / 4 (–1)

The Serbian National Assembly is a unicameral, 250-seat legislature, with deputies elected to four-year terms under a system of proportional representation with closed party lists.

In the wake of the snap parliamentary elections held in 2016, leaders of several opposition parties accused the SNS of rigging the polls, including by tampering with ballot boxes. Election observers from the Organization for Security and Co-operation in Europe (OSCE) noted pressure on public-sector workers to vote for the ruling party. Private television outlets largely favored the SNS in their coverage.

While the SNS and its coalition partners won the largest portion of the vote, enabling Vučić to remain prime minister, they lost 27 seats, falling from 158 to 131. Foreign Minister Ivica Dačić's Socialist Party of Serbia (SPS) and its allies, running separately from the SNS-led list, took 29 seats. The far-right Serbian Radical Party (SRS) placed third with 22 seats, returning to the parliament after a four-year absence. The progressive Enough Is Enough movement and a coalition led by the Democratic Party (DS) each won 16 seats. The pro-EU Alliance for a Better Serbia bloc won 13 seats, as did the conservative and Euroskeptic Dveri–Democratic Party of Serbia. The remaining seats went to smaller parties representing ethnic minorities. The SNS also performed will

City council elections held in March 2018 in Belgrade were, according to domestic observers, marred by procedural errors and numerous irregularities. Some voters were pressured to vote for the SNS, while others were allegedly provided with completed ballots. Media coverage was largely biased in favor of the ruling party, and there were multiple reports of the misuse of administrative resources for campaigning. Some independent observers from the Center for Research, Transparency, and Accountability (CRTA) were threatened and expelled from polling stations before vote counting commenced.

Score Change: The score declined from 3 to 2 due to reports of numerous irregularities during the 2018 local elections in Belgrade, including voters being pressured to vote for the SNS and provided with premarked ballots, misuse of administrative resources for campaigning, and intimidation of domestic observers.

A3. Are the electoral laws and framework fair, and are they implemented impartially by the relevant election management bodies? 3 / 4

Electoral laws largely correspond to international standards, but aspects of the electoral process are poorly regulated, and implementation of existing rules is flawed in some respects. The Republic Electoral Commission's composition before the 2017 presidential election raised concerns about partisan influence. A parliamentary oversight committee meant to monitor the campaign was never established, and the media regulator did not proactively track and punish biased media coverage.

B. POLITICAL PLURALISM AND PARTICIPATION: 10 / 16 (−2)

B1. Do the people have the right to organize in different political parties or other competitive political groupings of their choice, and is the system free of undue obstacles to the rise and fall of these competing parties or groupings? 3 / 4

Political parties may be established freely and can typically operate without encountering formal restrictions. However, campaign finance regulations are weakly enforced and place no overall cap on the private funds raised and spent by parties and candidates. Following the 2017 presidential election, the OSCE reported that the Anti-Corruption Agency (ACA) had decreased the resources dedicated to proactively monitoring campaign funds and did not thoroughly investigate dubious donations. The SNS campaign enjoyed a considerable financial advantage over its rivals and reportedly benefited from the misuse of public resources, including support from state media and use of public buses to transport loyalists to rallies. The Balkan Investigative Reporting Network (BIRN) found that the SNS had orchestrated the use of thousands of proxy donors to bypass legal limits on individual donations and disguise the true source of funding.

B2. Is there a realistic opportunity for the opposition to increase its support or gain power through elections? 2 / 4 (−1)

There have been peaceful transfers of power between rival parties over the past two decades, and the political system remains competitive. However, the ruling party has used various tactics to unfairly reduce the opposition's electoral prospects. These include manipulating the timing of snap elections, exerting pressure on independent state institutions, and mobilizing public resources to support the SNS's campaigns.

The SNS has expanded its influence over the media through both state-owned enterprises and an array of private outlets that are dependent on government funding, and it has harnessed this influence to strengthen its political position and discredit its rivals, further reducing opposition parties' competitiveness. Opposition figures have also faced escalating harassment and violence in recent years. In November 2018, prominent politician Borko Stefanović of the Serbian Left party was severely beaten by seven men before a scheduled debate in the city of Kruševac. The attack on Stefanović, as well as the intimidation of other opposition leaders, was symptomatic of a broader campaign carried out by the ruling party to dehumanize the opposition.

Score Change: The score declined from 3 to 2 because increased harassment of and attacks on opposition figures, and the ruling party's use of state-owned and state-funded media to discredit the opposition, have significantly reduced the competitiveness of opposition parties.

B3. Are the people's political choices free from domination by the military, foreign powers, religious hierarchies, economic oligarchies, or any other powerful group that is not democratically accountable? 2 / 4 (−1)

Voters enjoy a significant degree of freedom to make political decisions without undue interference, though the ruling party and allied private businesses allegedly use patronage networks to influence political outcomes. Various incentives have also been used in recent years to convince hundreds of local elected officials to form alliances with the SNS or change their party affiliation after elections. Separately, Russia has been accused of attempting to influence Serbian politics through its state-owned media and an array of small pro-Russian parties, media outlets, and civil society groups in Serbia.

During the 2017 election, there were widespread reports of employees at state or state-affiliated entities facing pressure to support the SNS and to compel their friends and families to do the same. Allegations of bribery, usually with money or food, in exchange for SNS votes, were extensive during the 2018 local elections. Citizens were also reportedly intimidated by SNS operatives who knocked on doors and pressured them to vote.

Score Change: The score declined from 3 to 2 due to credible allegations that forces associated with the ruling party engaged in widespread vote buying and voter intimidation during local elections.

B4. Do various segments of the population (including ethnic, religious, gender, LGBT, and other relevant groups) have full political rights and electoral opportunities? 3 / 4

The country's 5 percent electoral threshold for parliamentary representation does not apply to parties representing ethnic minorities. Groups centered on the ethnic Albanian, Bosniak, Slovak, and Hungarian communities won a total of 10 seats in the 2016 legislative elections. Nevertheless, ethnic minorities have a relatively muted voice in Serbian politics in practice. No party representing the interests of the Romany minority ran in the 2016 elections.

Women enjoy equal political rights. According to electoral regulations, women must account for at least 33 percent of a party's candidate list, and women currently hold 34 percent of seats in the parliament. Ana Brnabić became Serbia's first woman and first gay prime minister in 2017, but critics argued that her appointment was a superficial bid to showcase the government's claims of openness toward the LGBT (lesbian, gay, bisexual, and transgender) community without systematic engagement on policy issues important to LGBT people.

C. FUNCTIONING OF GOVERNMENT: 6 / 12 (−1)

C1. Do the freely elected head of government and national legislative representatives determine the policies of the government? 2 / 4 (−1)

Vučić's move to the presidency in 2017 raised new concerns about the personalization of governance and politicization of state institutions. Vučić has remained the dominant figure in government despite the presidency's limited executive powers under the constitution.

Moreover, the executive largely controls the legislative process, and opposition lawmakers are sidelined through the disproportionate use of disciplinary measures, frequent use of accelerated legislative procedures, and late changes to the legislative agenda, among other tactics. The budget for 2019, among the most important pieces of legislation passed in 2018, was adopted in December without meaningful parliamentary debate, largely because the ruling party filled the allotted time by filing scores of insignificant amendments. The dominance of the executive branch over the legislature was also reflected in the findings of a CRTA report showing that between November 2017 and July 2018, 95 percent of the laws adopted were proposed by the government.

Score Change: The score declined from 3 to 2 due to the continued concentration of power in the hands of the president as well as the manipulation of legislative procedures to stifle debate and sideline opposition lawmakers.

C2. Are safeguards against official corruption strong and effective? 2 / 4

Although the number of arrests and prosecutions for corruption has risen in recent years, high-profile convictions are very rare. In October 2018, Finance Minister Siniša Mali, who has been accused of money laundering and other financial crimes, was ordered to pay a small fine, while the investigation against him was dropped by prosecutors, raising concerns about impunity for senior officials. The work of the ACA is undermined in part by the ambiguous division of responsibilities among other entities tasked with combating corruption.

Critics have credibly accused President Vučić and the SNS government of having ties to organized crime, and cronyism—in the form of jobs provided to allies of the president and the ruling party—is reportedly common.

C3. Does the government operate with openness and transparency? 2 / 4

The government has received sustained criticism for a lack of transparency in large-scale infrastructure projects and for secrecy surrounding public tenders. Details about the state-funded Belgrade Waterfront project, for example, which includes the construction of hotels and luxury apartments and has been beset by controversy since its announcement in 2012, have not been made available to the public.

Members of parliament do not have adequate opportunities to ask questions about government activities and legislation, and the vast majority of parliamentary questions go unanswered by the government.

Public officials are subject to asset disclosure rules overseen by the ACA, but penalties for violations are uncommon. While a 2004 freedom of information law empowers citizens and journalists to obtain information of public importance, authorities frequently obstruct requests in practice.

CIVIL LIBERTIES: 43 / 60 (−2)
D. FREEDOM OF EXPRESSION AND BELIEF: 12 / 16 (−1)
D1. Are there free and independent media? 2 / 4

Despite a constitution that guarantees freedom of the press and a penal code that does not treat libel as a criminal offense, media freedom is undermined by the threat of lawsuits or criminal charges against journalists for other offenses, lack of transparency in media ownership, editorial pressure from politicians and politically connected media owners, and high rates of self-censorship. The state and ruling party exercise influence over private media in part through advertising contracts and other indirect subsidies. While many outlets take a progovernment line or avoid criticism of the leadership, some continue to produce independent coverage.

A number of critical journalists and outlets faced smear campaigns, punitive tax inspections, and other forms of pressure in 2018. According to NUNS, there were 102 media freedom violations against journalists during the year. They included physical assaults, though most incidents involved aggressive rhetoric and other forms of pressure or intimidation. In December 2018, investigative reporter Milan Jovanović, who has reported extensively on corruption, was the victim of an arson attack in which unknown assailants threw a Molotov cocktail into his home.

D2. Are individuals free to practice and express their religious faith or nonbelief in public and private? 4 / 4

The constitution guarantees freedom of religion, which is generally respected in practice.

D3. Is there academic freedom, and is the educational system free from extensive political indoctrination? 3 / 4

Academic freedom has largely been upheld, though recent legal changes have raised concerns about political influence. The Law on Higher Education, adopted by the National Assembly in 2017, increased the presence of state-appointed members on the National Council for Higher Education and a national accreditation body; another education law, also adopted in 2017, gave the education minister centralized control over the appointment of school principals.

D4. Are individuals free to express their personal views on political or other sensitive topics without fear of surveillance or retribution? 3 / 4 (−1)

Private discussion is generally free and vibrant, but a pattern of retribution against high-profile critics of the government has contributed to an increasingly hostile environment for free expression and open debate. Throughout 2018, perceived government opponents including journalists, civil society leaders, and celebrities were targeted with sophisticated smear campaigns in progovernment media outlets as well as investigations and other retaliatory measures. In October, authorities began an investigation of a health charity run by actor Sergej Trifunović, who has openly criticized the government on social media and in public appearances. Analysts viewed the investigation, as well as the removal of Trifunović's play from a local theater festival in November, apparently at the request of an SNS official, as acts of retaliation.

Score Change: The score declined from 4 to 3 because open debate has been discouraged by retaliatory measures, including media smears and official investigations, against high-profile critics of government policies.

E. ASSOCIATIONAL AND ORGANIZATIONAL RIGHTS: 10 / 12
E1. Is there freedom of assembly? 4 / 4

Citizens generally enjoy freedom of assembly. However, in October 2018, the director of a symphony hall in the city of Niš denied the opposition Alliance for Serbia access to the venue for a political rally, allegedly at the direction of local officials, despite the alliance's claim that it reserved the space in advance; the rally was ultimately held on the street.

The assault on Stefanović in November prompted massive demonstrations against the SNS and President Vučić, which continued through the end of 2018. Demonstrators called on the government to cease attacks on the press and opposition figures, and voiced objections to corruption within the government and the SNS.

E2. Is there freedom for nongovernmental organizations, particularly those that are engaged in human rights– and governance-related work? 3 / 4

Foreign and domestic nongovernmental organizations (NGO) generally operate freely, but those that have taken openly critical stances toward the government or address sensitive or controversial topics have faced threats and harassment in recent years. Throughout 2018, Jelena Milić, director of the NGO the Center for Euro-Atlantic Studies, was the subject of a sustained smear campaign in the media in response to her support for war-crimes prosecutions and Serbian membership in the North Atlantic Treaty Organization (NATO).

E3. Is there freedom for trade unions and similar professional or labor organizations? 3 / 4

Workers may legally join unions, engage in collective bargaining, and strike, but the International Trade Union Confederation has reported that organizing efforts and strikes are often restricted in practice.

F. RULE OF LAW: 9 / 16

F1. Is there an independent judiciary? 2 / 4

The independence of the judiciary is compromised by political influence over judicial appointments, and many judges have reported facing external pressure regarding their rulings. Politicians regularly comment on judicial matters, including by discussing ongoing cases or investigations with the media.

F2. Does due process prevail in civil and criminal matters? 2 / 4

Due process guarantees are upheld in some cases, but corruption, lack of capacity, and political influence often undermine these protections. Among other problems, rules on the random assignment of cases to judges and prosecutors are not consistently observed, and mechanisms for obtaining restitution in civil matters are ineffective. High-profile, politically sensitive cases are especially vulnerable to interference. The failure of police and prosecutors to make any visible progress on the investigation of illegal 2016 demolitions in the Savamala district on Belgrade's waterfront was widely seen as an effort to protect politically powerful perpetrators.

F3. Is there protection from the illegitimate use of physical force and freedom from war and insurgencies? 3 / 4

The population is generally free from major threats to physical security, though some prison facilities suffer from overcrowding, abuse, and inadequate health care. Radical right-wing organizations and violent sports fans who target ethnic minorities and others also remain a concern.

F4. Do laws, policies, and practices guarantee equal treatment of various segments of the population? 2 / 4

Legal safeguards for socially vulnerable groups are poorly enforced. For example, women are legally entitled to equal pay for equal work, but this rule is not widely respected. The Romany minority is especially vulnerable to discrimination in employment, housing, and education. LGBT people continue to face hate speech, threats, and even physical violence, and perpetrators are rarely punished despite laws addressing hate crimes and discrimination. However, the government has made some gestures of support for the rights of LGBT people; Brnabić attended the annual pride parade in Belgrade in September 2018.

G. PERSONAL AUTONOMY AND INDIVIDUAL RIGHTS: 12 / 16 (−1)

G1. Do individuals enjoy freedom of movement, including the ability to change their place of residence, employment, or education? 4 / 4

There are no formal restrictions on freedom of movement. Serbians are free to change their place of employment and education, and have the right to travel. Citizens have been able to enter the Schengen area of the EU without a visa since 2010.

G2. Are individuals able to exercise the right to own property and establish private businesses without undue interference from state or nonstate actors? 3 / 4

In general, property rights are respected, but adjudication of disputes is slow, and problems such as illegal construction and fraud persist. Approximately 1.5 million buildings in Serbia are not registered. Romany residents are often subject to forced evictions, and those evicted are generally not offered alternative housing or access to legal remedies to challenge eviction notices.

G3. Do individuals enjoy personal social freedoms, including choice of marriage partner and size of family, protection from domestic violence, and control over appearance? 3 / 4

A new law aimed at preventing domestic violence took effect in 2017, but such violence remains a problem; Serbia has one of the highest rates of domestic violence in Europe. Early and forced marriage is reportedly more common among the Romany minority, with more than half of Romany girls marrying before the legal age of 18.

G4. Do individuals enjoy equality of opportunity and freedom from economic exploitation? 2 / 4 (−1)

Residents generally have access to economic opportunity, but factors such as weak macroeconomic growth and a relatively high rate of unemployment contribute to labor exploitation in some industries. Several reports in recent years have described worsening conditions in factories, particularly those that produce shoes and garments, including low wages, unpaid overtime, and hazardous work environments. Legal protections designed to prevent such abuses are not well enforced. According to the Ministry of Labor, Employment, Veterans Affairs, and Social Affairs, 24 people died in workplace accidents in the first seven months of 2018.

Score Change: The score declined from 3 to 2 because working conditions in factories have deteriorated in recent years, and legal protections designed to prevent exploitation are not well enforced.

Seychelles

Population: 100,000
Capital: Victoria
Political Rights Rating: 3
Civil Liberties Rating: 3
Freedom Rating: 3.0
Freedom Status: Partly Free
Electoral Democracy: Yes

Overview: A single party dominated politics starting from independence, and for years after multiparty politics were introduced in the 1990s. In 2016, an opposition coalition won a majority of seats in the National Assembly, reflecting increasing political pluralism in practice. However, government corruption remains a problem, as does lengthy pretrial detention. Migrant workers remain vulnerable to abuse.

Key Developments in 2018:

- In December, President Faure signed an amendment establishing a permanent chief electoral officer to oversee the Electoral Commission (EC) secretariat and its operations. Its provisions were intended to alleviate concerns about inefficiencies in the electoral system, and about the separation of powers between the EC secretariat and EC board.
- Authorities struggled during the year to address allegations of judicial misconduct through the relevant mechanisms.
- In November, Seychelles opened a domestic violence shelter, the only such facility in the country.
- In response to persistent reports of the exploitation of Bangladeshi workers, the government in October announced a six-month moratorium on the recruitment of Bangladeshi nationals to work in the country, as well as its intentions to work with officials in Bangladesh to address the issue. In November, a Bangladeshi man was sentenced to three years in prison in a human trafficking case in which four Bangladeshi nationals were defrauded and subjected to forced labor.

POLITICAL RIGHTS: 28 / 40
A. ELECTORAL PROCESS: 10 / 12
A1. Was the current head of government or other chief national authority elected through free and fair elections? 3 / 4

The president is chief of state and head of government, and is directly elected for up to two five-year terms. The president nominates cabinet ministers and a vice president, all of which require National Assembly approval.

President James Michel of Parti Lepep (PL) was narrowly reelected in 2015. International observers noted allegations of vote buying.

In October 2016, President Michel resigned. He gave no reason for his resignation, but it followed parliamentary elections in which the opposition coalition, Seychelles Democratic Alliance (LDS), took control of the legislature. Vice President Danny Faure became president, and is to complete Michel's five-year term.

A2. Were the current national legislative representatives elected through free and fair elections? 4 / 4

Members of the unicameral National Assembly are directly elected in 25 constituencies, while up to 10 additional seats are assigned by parties according to a proportional calculation of the vote.

The opposition coalition LDS won the majority of seats in the 2016 elections to the National Assembly, marking the first transfer of power between parties in the country's postindependence history. An African Union (AU) election monitoring mission generally praised the elections, but noted reports of attempted vote buying.

A3. Are the electoral laws and framework fair, and are they implemented impartially by the relevant election management bodies? 3 / 4

The EC has faced some criticism from opposition parties and others for enforcing its mandates inconsistently. The 2016 AU election monitoring mission recommended that the EC take steps to improve transparency, carefully scrutinize the voter rolls, and improve efforts to inform the public about voter registration processes and voting procedures.

A forum for discussion of electoral reforms was set up in 2017, and included representatives from political parties and election observer groups. In late 2017, the EC released recommendations for reform based on the forum's findings; these included allowing Seychellois citizens abroad to register to vote, cleaning up the voter rolls, reinforcing the integrity of balloting by placing serial numbers on ballots, and separating of the roles of the EC chairperson and the EC secretariat. In what was described as a move to address the separation-of-powers recommendation, in December 2018 President Faure approved an amendment to the Elections Act establishing a permanent chief electoral officer to oversee the EC secretariat and its operations. The establishment of a permanent chief electoral officer was also intended to alleviate concerns about the efficiency of the previous system, in which a chief electoral officer was appointed a few months before an election.

B. POLITICAL PLURALISM AND PARTICIPATION: 11 / 16

B1. Do the people have the right to organize in different political parties or other competitive political groupings of their choice, and is the system free of undue obstacles to the rise and fall of these competing parties or groupings? 3 / 4

There were no significant threats to or intimidation of political parties ahead of parliamentary elections in 2016. However, during the 2015 presidential election, several opposition parties claimed the government was engaged in systematic harassment and intimidation of candidates.

Legal challenges from the LDS blocked the registration of two parties, preventing their candidates from competing in the 2016 National Assembly elections. LDS (known locally as Linyon Demokratik Seselwa) successfully argued that the parties' names—the Lafors Sosyal Demokratik (LSD) and the Linyon Sanzman—were too similar to its name and would mislead voters.

In November 2018, the PL formally changed its name to United Seychelles, a moniker apparently referencing the Seychelles People's United Party that governed after independence. The party has changed its name on a number of past occasions.

B2. Is there a realistic opportunity for the opposition to increase its support or gain power through elections? 3 / 4

The 2016 National Assembly elections changed the political scene significantly, as the LDS, a new alliance of opposition parties, became the first political grouping to defeat the PL and gain a majority of legislative seats. The PL for the first time became the minority party. The developments reflected increasing political pluralism in Seychelles.

B3. Are the people's political choices free from domination by the military, foreign powers, religious hierarchies, economic oligarchies, or any other powerful group that is not democratically accountable? 3 / 4

The people's political choices are generally free from domination by powerful groups that are not democratically accountable. However, there have been reports of vote buying and voter intimidation by political parties.

B4. Do various segments of the population (including ethnic, religious, gender, LGBT, and other relevant groups) have full political rights and electoral opportunities? 2 / 4

The constitution mandates equal suffrage for adult citizens. Early voting procedures are designed to encourage the participation of some groups, including pregnant women, elderly people, and those with disabilities.

There are still no mechanisms that allow citizens living abroad to vote. Few women hold senior political office as a result of a number of factors, including longstanding traditional beliefs about the role of women, and lack of commitment on the part of political parties to nominate women for office. The PL is the only party that typically includes high numbers of women among its political candidates. Political life is dominated by people of European and South Asian origin.

C. FUNCTIONING OF GOVERNMENT: 7 / 12

C1. Do the freely elected head of government and national legislative representatives determine the policies of the government? 3 / 4

The head of government and national legislative representatives are generally able to determine the policies of the government, though widespread corruption can influence policymaking.

C2. Are safeguards against official corruption strong and effective? 2 / 4

Concerns over government corruption persist. In 2016, the National Assembly passed an anticorruption law that established the first independent anticorruption commission in the country, and strengthened the legal framework to fight corruption. By the end of 2018, the commission had recorded 117 cases of corruption., but few major investigations have followed. In December 2018, the commission's former complaints and communications manager was found guilty on three counts of corruption and sentenced by the Supreme Court to eight years imprisonment and a fine of 75,000 Seychelles rupees ($5,000).

C3. Does the government operate with openness and transparency? 2 / 4

Concerns about corruption often focus on a lack of transparency in the privatization and allocation of government-owned land, as well as in Seychelles' facilitation of international finance.

There are laws allowing public access to government information, but compliance is inconsistent. Some government officials are required to declare assets, but they do not always comply, and the declarations are not made public unless a legal challenge forces their release.

In July 2018, President Faure signed the Access to Information Act, which grants the right to obtain information about government authorities and public bodies, and mandated the establishment of an independent Information Commission to oversee the new law's implementation.

CIVIL LIBERTIES: 43 / 60

D. FREEDOM OF EXPRESSION AND BELIEF: 12 / 16

D1. Are there free and independent media? 2 / 4

There are two privately owned newspapers, five political party weeklies, and the online news of the Seychelles News Agency. The government owns the only television station and two radio stations; there is one independent radio station. The law prohibits political parties and religious organizations from operating radio stations.

Media workers practice a degree of self-censorship to keep from endangering their earnings from advertising. Newspaper reporting is generally politicized. Although Seychelles has strict defamation laws, they have not been used for years. There are few reports of abuses against journalists.

D2. Are individuals free to practice and express their religious faith or nonbelief in public and private? 4 / 4

Religious freedom is generally respected. The government grants larger religious groups programming time on state radio, subject in most cases to advance review and approval, but smaller religious groups do not have access to dedicated broadcast time. Non-Catholic students in public schools providing Catholic instruction have no access to alternative activities during those classes.

D3. Is there academic freedom, and is the educational system free from extensive political indoctrination? 3 / 4

Some activists have claimed that the government limits academic freedom by not allowing educators to reach senior positions in the academic bureaucracy without demonstrating at least nominal loyalty to the PL, which holds the presidency and dominated the parliament for years ahead of its defeat in the 2016 elections.

D4. Are individuals free to express their personal views on political or other sensitive topics without fear of surveillance or retribution? 3 / 4

As the government seeks above all to protect the country's image as a tourist paradise, many sensitive subjects are considered off limits. Individuals who criticize the government publicly or privately sometimes suffer reprisals, such as harassment by police or the loss of jobs or contracts.

E. ASSOCIATIONAL AND ORGANIZATIONAL RIGHTS: 9 / 12

E1. Is there freedom of assembly? 3 / 4

The government passed a revised law in 2015 on public assembly, which several observers credited with permitting a more open and free political environment. However, the law still contains some restrictive provisions, including the need to give five days' notice to the police for assemblies. It also empowers the head of the police to disperse assemblies on grounds of preserving public health, morality, and safety, and sets conditions on the timing and location of assemblies.

E2. Is there freedom for nongovernmental organizations, particularly those that are engaged in human rights– and governance-related work? 3 / 4

Human rights groups and other nongovernmental organizations (NGOs) operate without restriction. However, some groups lack the resources necessary to operate and advocate effectively.

E3. Is there freedom for trade unions and similar professional or labor organizations? 3 / 4

Unions are permitted, but only about 15 percent of the workforce is unionized, and collective bargaining is relatively rare. Workers have the right to strike, but only if all other arbitration procedures have been exhausted.

F. RULE OF LAW: 11 / 16

F1. Is there an independent judiciary? 2 / 4

Judges sometimes face interference in cases involving major commercial or political interests. Due to the low number of legal professionals in Seychelles, the country brings in expatriate judges to serve fixed-term contracts on the Supreme Court. The government controls the negotiations and renewal of expatriate contracts, potentially allowing officials to compromise the impartiality of the non-Seychellois magistrates. The judiciary also lacks budget independence from the executive, and can be subject to external influence. The Supreme Court remains a target of political threats and intimidation.

In 2018, Seychelles struggled to address separate allegations of misconduct lodged against two senior judges through the relevant mechanisms. One of the judges was eventually cleared of wrongdoing by an international tribunal, but the controversy prompted concern about judicial independence in Seychelles, and the durability of aspects of the justice system in its current form.

F2. Does due process prevail in civil and criminal matters? 3 / 4

While constitutional rights to due process are generally respected, prolonged pretrial detention is common. The courts introduced new systems in 2016 intended to expedite the processing of cases, but their effect has been limited.

In June 2018, the National Assembly voted unanimously to establish a new Human Rights Commission, and Faure signed the bill the following month. The new body, which has greater powers than the one it replaces, will be able to conduct investigations, initiate proceedings at the Constitutional Court, and assist complainants financially under certain circumstances.

F3. Is there protection from the illegitimate use of physical force and freedom from war and insurgencies? 3 / 4

Security forces have occasionally been accused of using excessive force, and impunity for such offenses remains a problem. Police corruption continues, particularly the solicitation of bribes. Prisons remain overcrowded.

F4. Do laws, policies, and practices guarantee equal treatment of various segments of the population? 3 / 4

Same-sex sexual activity between men was decriminalized in 2016, though societal discrimination against LGBT (lesbian, gay, bisexual, and transgender) activists remains a problem. Prejudice against foreign workers has been reported.

G. PERSONAL AUTONOMY AND INDIVIDUAL RIGHTS: 11 / 16

G1. Do individuals enjoy freedom of movement, including the ability to change their place of residence, employment, or education? 3 / 4

The government does not restrict domestic travel, but may deny passports for unspecified reasons based on "national interest."

G2. Are individuals able to exercise the right to own property and establish private businesses without undue interference from state or nonstate actors? 3 / 4

Individuals may generally exercise the right to own property and establish private business without undue interference from state or nonstate actors. An underdeveloped legal framework can hamper business activities, as can corruption.

G3. Do individuals enjoy personal social freedoms, including choice of marriage partner and size of family, protection from domestic violence, and control over appearance? 2 / 4

Inheritance laws do not discriminate against women, and the government does not impose explicit restrictions on personal social freedoms. However, domestic violence against women remains a problem. In November 2018, Seychelles opened a domestic violence shelter, the only such facility on the country.

G4. Do individuals enjoy equality of opportunity and freedom from economic exploitation? 3 / 4

Economic life is dominated by people of European and South Asian origin.

The government has made minimal progress in preventing or prosecuting instances of human trafficking and labor exploitation. Worker rights in the Seychelles International Trade Zone are different from the rest of the islands, and migrant laborers are vulnerable to abuse there. There were some reports of employers seizing migrant workers' passports upon arrival, a practice that is not currently illegal under Seychelles law.

In October 2018, in response to persistent reports of abuse of foreign workers from Bangladesh, authorities announced a six-month moratorium on the recruitment of Bangladeshi nationals to work in the country and said it would cooperate with Bangladeshi officials to address the issue. The following month, a Bangladeshi national was sentenced to three years in prison in a trafficking case in which he was found to have defrauded four other Bangladeshi nationals of large sums of money with promises of work, and then subjected them to forced labor.

Sierra Leone

Population: 7,700,000
Capital: Freetown
Political Rights Rating: 3
Civil Liberties Rating: 3
Freedom Rating: 3.0
Freedom Status: Partly Free
Electoral Democracy: Yes

Overview: In 2018, Sierra Leone held its fourth national elections since the end of the civil war in 2002. However, opposition parties have faced police violence and restrictions on assembly. Government corruption is pervasive, and the work of journalists is hampered by the threat of defamation charges. Other longstanding concerns include gender-based violence and female genital mutilation (FGM).

KEY DEVELOPMENTS IN 2018:

- In the presidential election, Julius Maada Bio of the Sierra Leone People's Party (SLPP) defeated Samura Kamara of the incumbent All People's Congress (APC) in the second round of voting in March. Despite some allegations of violence and intimidation during the campaign period, international observers determined that the election was credible.
- In July, the Anti-Corruption Commission (ACC) indicted two officials from the previous APC government for corruption: former vice president Victor Bockarie Foh and former minister of mines Minkailu Mansaray. A sweeping inquiry into corruption during the administration of former president Ernest Bai Koroma was slated to begin at the beginning of 2019. The APC claimed that the inquiry was politically motivated and condemned it as a "witch hunt."
- In January, restrictive new regulations which increase government oversight of nongovernmental organizations (NGOs) came into effect. Rights advocates

expressed deep concern that the regulations would severely undermine the independence of civil society and discourage NGOs from criticizing the government.

POLITICAL RIGHTS: 28 / 40

A. ELECTORAL PROCESS: 10 / 12

A1. Was the current head of government or other chief national authority elected through free and fair elections? 3 / 4

The president is elected directly by popular vote for up to two five-year terms. In the March 2018 presidential election, Julius Maada Bio of the SLPP defeated Samura Kamara of the incumbent APC in the second round of voting, marking the second peaceful transfer of power since the end of the civil war in 2002. Sixteen candidates competed in the first round, but none gained the required 55 percent of valid votes to win the election outright. A legal challenge to the first-round results by an APC member, who alleged irregularities, delayed the second round by four days, highlighting the authorities' inability to adjudicate disputes in a timely manner. Allegations of violence and voter intimidation marred the campaign period. Nevertheless, international observers determined that the election was credible, praising the National Election Commission (NEC) in particular for carrying out its duties effectively, despite budget constraints, logistical challenges, and pressure from the government, which disbursed election funds late and threatened to withhold resources on occasion.

A2. Were the current national legislative representatives elected through free and fair elections? 3 / 4

In the unicameral Parliament, 132 members are chosen by popular vote, and 14 seats are reserved for indirectly elected paramount chiefs. Parliamentary elections are held concurrently with the presidential election every five years. During the 2018 parliamentary elections, the APC retained its majority, winning 68 seats, while the SLPP increased its share to 49 seats, up from 42 in 2012. Two new parties, the Coalition for Change (C4C) and the National Grand Coalition (NGC), entered Parliament with 8 and 4 seats, respectively. Despite some procedural errors, international observers stated that the parliamentary elections were credible.

A3. Are the electoral laws and framework fair, and are they implemented impartially by the relevant election management bodies? 4 / 4

The electoral laws and framework are generally deemed to be fair, although restrictions which limit who can run for office, such as a requirement that candidates are citizens by birth, have drawn criticism from international observers. During the 2018 campaign period, the major political parties interpreted the citizenship provision to exclude people with dual citizenship from standing for office. Analysts believe this interpretation was meant to push the NGC's presidential candidate, Dr. Kandeh Kolleh Yumkella, out of the race. Yumkella ultimately continued his campaign and finished in third place. Many candidates also reportedly failed to secure nominations from their parties due to their dual citizenship. Additionally, only around 25 percent of Parliament members, many of whom hold dual citizenship, sought reelection in 2018.

The NEC, which administers elections, works impartially and independently.

B. POLITICAL PLURALISM AND PARTICIPATION: 11 / 16

B1. Do the people have the right to organize in different political parties or other competitive political groupings of their choice, and is the system free of undue obstacles to the rise and fall of these competing parties or groupings? 2 / 4

Although people have the right to organize in different political parties, opposition parties and leaders faced intimidation and harassment from the government and the APC when it held the presidency. The SLPP government also intimidated some opposition politicians after it took power in 2018. In July, for example, Mohamed Kamarainba Mansaray, the leader of the Alliance Democratic Party (ADP), was questioned by the police following a series of interviews in which he criticized President Bio's performance during his first hundred days in office.

The APC and SLPP are the main political parties, but 17 parties are officially registered. In 2017, several high-profile figures left the SLPP to form the NGC, which won four seats in Parliament during the 2018 elections.

B2. Is there a realistic opportunity for the opposition to increase its support or gain power through elections? 3 / 4

The SLPP, the main opposition party, won the presidency in 2018, despite the APC's continued use of public resources during the campaign. The APC won the previous two presidential elections, in 2007 and 2012. Both main parties gained seats in the 2018 parliamentary elections.

Despite government subsidies for candidate nomination fees, the costs to run for office, as well as a rule requiring people in public-sector posts to resign 12 months in advance of an election, remained a barrier to entry for many candidates.

B3. Are the people's political choices free from domination by the military, foreign powers, religious hierarchies, economic oligarchies, or any other powerful group that is not democratically accountable? 3 / 4

Sierra Leoneans generally enjoy freedom in their political choices, although traditional and religious leaders remain influential on the political choices of voters. Local elites from both major parties often control the selection of candidates for Parliament, limiting voters' choices.

B4. Do various segments of the population (including ethnic, religious, gender, LGBT, and other relevant groups) have full political rights and electoral opportunities? 3 / 4

Ethnic and religious minorities typically enjoy full political rights and electoral opportunities. Women's political participation remains a challenge, with only 18 of 146 parliament seats held by women in 2018, while 5 of 26 members of the president's cabinet are women.

Sierra Leoneans who are not of African descent must become naturalized citizens to be able to vote, and they are not allowed to run for elected office.

C. FUNCTIONING OF GOVERNMENT: 7 / 12

C1. Do the freely elected head of government and national legislative representatives determine the policies of the government? 3 / 4

The president and Parliament generally determine the policies of the government, although most power lies in the executive branch. China has become the largest investor in Sierra Leone, providing billions of dollars of aid and infrastructure financing since 2013. It cultivated a close relationship with the Koroma administration, which led civil society leaders to claim that China has an undue influence on policymaking. The SLPP maintained a cooler stance toward China throughout its 2018 election campaign, and in October, the new SLPP government cancelled a controversial $318 million deal with China to build a new airport near Freetown, signaling increased resistance to Chinese influence.

C2. Are safeguards against official corruption strong and effective? 1 / 4

Corruption remains a pervasive problem at every level of government. In recent years, the ACC has made some progress toward uncovering corruption among high-level officials, but it has a poor prosecutorial record, especially in trials involving former president Koroma's friends, family, and political allies.

The new administration of President Bio promised to take measures to tackle systemic corruption and hold corrupt officials from Koroma's presidency accountable. An incendiary government report published in June 2018 alleged widespread, systemic corruption in the former APC government. In July, the ACC indicted two officials from the previous government for corruption: former vice president Victor Bockarie Foh and former minister of mines Minkailu Mansaray. Their trial was ongoing at year's end, and a sweeping inquiry into Koroma-era corruption was slated to begin at the beginning of 2019. The APC claimed that the inquiry was politically motivated and condemned it as a "witch hunt."

C3. Does the government operate with openness and transparency? 3 / 4

Sierra Leone has an uneven record on transparency. The Right to Access Information Commission was created in 2013 to facilitate transparency and openness in government, but its effectiveness has been hampered by lack of funding and limited public outreach.

Sierra Leone continues to review and make public all mining and lease agreements, retaining its Extractive Industries Transparency Initiative (EITI) compliance designation. The latest review of its compliance began in September 2018.

CIVIL LIBERTIES: 37 / 60 (-1)
D. FREEDOM OF EXPRESSION AND BELIEF: 12 / 16
D1. Are there free and independent media? 2 / 4

Numerous independent newspapers circulate freely, and there are dozens of public and private radio and television outlets. However, public officials have employed the country's libel and sedition laws to target journalists, particularly those reporting on high-level corruption. In December 2018, President Bio promised that he would push for the repeal of the laws, which press freedom advocates viewed as an encouraging development.

Nevertheless, some journalists faced intimidation and even physical attacks during the year. In July, in the wake of protests against the removal of fuel subsidies, the police issued a statement warning the media against the publication of "misleading, disrespectful, and inciting" pronouncements, which was viewed as a threat by many journalists. Political party activists from both the APC and SLPP also attacked or threatened a number of journalists throughout the year, particularly around the election campaign.

D2. Are individuals free to practice and express their religious faith or nonbelief in public and private? 4 / 4

Freedom of religion is protected by the constitution and respected in practice.

D3. Is there academic freedom, and is the educational system free from extensive political indoctrination? 3 / 4

Academic freedom is generally upheld, but resource strains within the university system have led to strikes by professors. Student protests have also been violently dispersed by security forces in recent years.

D4. Are individuals free to express their personal views on political or other sensitive topics without fear of surveillance or retribution? 3 / 4

Private discussion remains largely open. Authorities reportedly monitor discussions on social media platforms, including WhatsApp, although few arrests have been made for online discussions or comments. On election day in 2018, the police briefly shut down the internet, preventing people from communicating about the polls and the results.

E. ASSOCIATIONAL AND ORGANIZATIONAL RIGHTS: 6 / 12 (-1)
E1. Is there freedom of assembly? 2 / 4

While freedom of assembly is constitutionally guaranteed, the police have repeatedly refused to grant permission to organizers planning protests, and violently cracked down on a number of peaceful demonstrations in recent years. In July 2018, authorities arrested the organizer of a protest against the removal of fuel subsidies for "organizing an unlawful demonstration."

E2. Is there freedom for nongovernmental organizations, particularly those that are engaged in human rights– and governance-related work? 2 / 4 (-1)

NGOs and civic groups generally operate freely. However, several laws and policy regulations enacted in 2009 subject civil society groups to significant government oversight and intervention. Stricter regulations were adopted in late 2017 and went into effect in January 2018. The new regulations include a requirement that NGOs renew their registration annually, as well as a provision requiring NGOS to sign an agreement with the ministry relevant to their work before they can commence operations. Additionally, all projects must be discussed with the relevant ministry and registered before they can commence. Some civil society groups were unaware of the regulations until February, a month after they came into force. Rights advocates expressed deep concern that the regulations would severely undermine the independence of civil society and discourage NGOs from criticizing the government.

Since the elections in March, the new SLPP government has indicated that it is open to reviewing and revising the policy in cooperation with NGOs.

Score Change: The score declined from 3 to 2 due to the implementation of a restrictive new policy regulating nongovernmental organizations, which threatened to undermine their independence and ability to speak out against the government.

E3. Is there freedom for trade unions and similar professional or labor organizations? 2 / 4

While workers have the right to join independent trade unions, there are no laws preventing discrimination against union members or prohibiting employers from interfering in the formation of unions.

F. RULE OF LAW: 9 / 16
F1. Is there an independent judiciary? 2 / 4

While the constitution provides for an independent judiciary, in practice the judiciary is prone to interference from the executive branch, particularly in corruption cases. A lack of clear procedures for appointing and dismissing judges makes these processes vulnerable to abuse. Corruption, poor salaries, and a lack of resources impede judicial effectiveness.

F2. Does due process prevail in civil and criminal matters? 2 / 4

Resource constraints and a shortage of lawyers hinder access to legal counsel. Although the constitution guarantees a fair trial, this right is sometimes limited in practice, largely due to corruption. The average defendant spends between three and five years in detention awaiting trial. In 2017, the judiciary developed new bail and sentencing guidelines to limit the amount of time prisoners spend in pretrial detention facilities.

F3. Is there protection from the illegitimate use of physical force and freedom from war and insurgencies? 3 / 4

Detention facilities are under strain, with occupancy levels at 233 percent of official capacity as of November 2018, according to the Institute for Criminal Policy Research at the University of London. Prisons and detention facilities fail to meet basic standards of health and hygiene, and infectious disease is prevalent.

Police are rarely held accountable for abuses and extrajudicial killings, which remain frequent. People can report abuse or ill treatment to the Police Complaints, Discipline, and Internal Investigations Department (CDIID) or the Independent Police Complaints Board (IPCB), although these agencies have limited capacity.

F4. Do laws, policies, and practices guarantee equal treatment of various segments of the population? 2 / 4

Members of the LGBT (lesbian, gay, bisexual, and transgender) community face discrimination in employment and access to health care, and are vulnerable to violence. Discrimination against LGBT people is not explicitly prohibited by the constitution. Women experience discrimination in employment, education, and access to credit. Employers frequently fire women who become pregnant during their first year on the job.

G. PERSONAL AUTONOMY AND INDIVIDUAL RIGHTS: 10 / 16

G1. Do individuals enjoy freedom of movement, including the ability to change their place of residence, employment, or education? 3 / 4

Sierra Leoneans generally enjoy freedom of movement. However, petty corruption is common and parents often must pay bribes to register their children in primary and secondary school. In August 2018, the government launched a program offering all children free education at primary and secondary schools, starting in September.

G2. Are individuals able to exercise the right to own property and establish private businesses without undue interference from state or nonstate actors? 3 / 4

Property rights are constitutionally guaranteed, but the laws do not effectively protect those rights. There is no land titling system. Outside of Freetown, land falls under customary law and its use is determined by chiefs. The government often fails to regulate the activities of international investors, exacerbating threats to property rights.

Laws passed in 2007 grant women the right to inherit property, but many women have little power to contest land issues within the customary legal system. In 2016, Sierra Leone reduced the cost of registering a new business.

G3. Do individuals enjoy personal social freedoms, including choice of marriage partner and size of family, protection from domestic violence, and control over appearance? 2 / 4

The law prohibits domestic violence, but gender-based violence remained a serious problem in 2018. Reports of rape and domestic violence rarely result in conviction, and the police unit responsible for investigating and prosecuting these crimes remains underfunded and understaffed. Women experience discrimination in marriage and divorce laws. Customary law guides many of these issues, and under such laws women are often considered equal to children and the property of their husbands.

FGM is not prohibited by law and the practice remains widespread. A challenge to a 2015 ban preventing "visibly pregnant" girls from attending school was filed in the Economic Community of West African States (ECOWAS) Community Court of Justice in May 2018. The case had not yet been heard at year's end, and the ban remained in place. Child marriage remains a problem, with almost half of all girls married before the age of 18.

G4. Do individuals enjoy equality of opportunity and freedom from economic exploitation? 2 / 4

Reports of economic exploitation of workers in the natural-resource sector are common. Barriers to access remain for individuals who wish to seek redress for economic exploitation.

Human trafficking remained a problem in 2018, and the government has made minimal efforts to combat it. According to the US State Department's 2018 *Trafficking in Persons Report,* authorities investigated 33 allegations of trafficking between April 2017 and March 2018, which resulted in 7 prosecutions and no convictions. Child labor is prevalent, despite laws limiting it.

Singapore

Population: 5,800,000
Capital: Singapore
Political Rights Rating: 4
Civil Liberties Rating: 4
Freedom Rating: 4.0
Freedom Status: Partly Free
Electoral Democracy: No

Overview: Singapore's parliamentary political system has been dominated by the ruling People's Action Party (PAP) and the family of current prime minister Lee Hsien Loong since 1959. The electoral and legal framework that the PAP has constructed allows for some political pluralism, but it constrains the growth of credible opposition parties and limits freedoms of expression, assembly, and association.

KEY DEVELOPMENTS IN 2018:

- In January, Parliament established a Select Committee on Deliberate Online Falsehoods. In March, after a local historian asserted in a submission to the committee that the PAP government had itself disseminated falsehoods by misrepresenting a past crackdown on alleged communist plots against the state, he was questioned for six hours in a public hearing led by the home affairs minister. The combative hearing and others like it raised concerns about freedom of expression and academic freedom.
- In April, the president signed the Public Order and Safety (Special Powers) Act, which granted the home affairs minister and police enhanced authority in the context of a "serious incident" such as a terrorist attack or mass protest. Officials would be permitted to potentially use lethal force and halt media coverage and online communications surrounding the incident in question.
- Two PAP-run town councils pressed lawsuits against three members of Parliament (MPs) from the opposition Workers' Party (WP) for alleged breaches of their fi-

duciary duties. The cases, which placed the defendants under significant financial pressure, began to be heard in October and were ongoing at year's end.

POLITICAL RIGHTS: 19 / 40

A. ELECTORAL PROCESS: 4 / 12

A1. Was the current head of government or other chief national authority elected through free and fair elections? 1 / 4

The government is led by a prime minister and cabinet formed by the party that controls the legislature. The current prime minster, Lee Hsien Loong, has been in power since 2004 and secured a new mandate after the 2015 parliamentary elections. While polling-day procedures are generally free of irregularities, numerous structural factors impede the development of viable electoral competition.

The president, whose role is largely ceremonial, is elected by popular vote for six-year terms, and a special committee is empowered to vet candidates. Under 2016 constitutional amendments on eligibility, none of Singapore's three main ethnic groupings (Malays, Chinese, and Indians or others) may be excluded from the presidency for more than five consecutive terms, and presidential candidates from the private sector, as opposed to senior officials with at least three years of service, must have experience leading a company with at least S\$500 million (US\$370 million) in shareholder equity. Only one candidate—Halimah Yacob, backed by the PAP—was declared eligible for the 2017 presidential election, making her the winner by default.

A2. Were the current national legislative representatives elected through free and fair elections? 2 / 4

The unicameral Parliament elected in 2015 includes 13 members from single-member constituencies and 76 members from Group Representation Constituencies (GRCs). The top-polling party in each GRC wins all of its three to six seats, which has historically bolstered the majority of the dominant PAP. As many as nine additional, nonpartisan members can be appointed to Parliament by the president, and another nine can come from a national compensatory list meant to ensure a minimum of opposition representation. Members serve five-year terms, with the exception of appointed members, who serve for two and a half years.

In the 2015 elections, the PAP secured nearly 70 percent of the popular vote and 83 of the 89 elected seats. The largest opposition group, the WP, retained the six elected seats it had won in 2011, but lost a seat it won in a 2013 by-election. Three compensatory seats were awarded to the opposition to achieve the minimum of nine.

A3. Are the electoral laws and framework fair, and are they implemented impartially by the relevant election management bodies? 1 / 4

Singapore lacks an independent election commission; the country's Elections Department is a government body attached to the Prime Minister's Office. The electoral framework suffers from a number of other features—including the GRC system and the onerous eligibility rules for presidential candidates—that favor the PAP-dominated political establishment. The PAP has also altered electoral boundaries to ensure an incumbent advantage. The new electoral districts for 2015 were announced just seven weeks before the elections.

B. POLITICAL PLURALISM AND PARTICIPATION: 8 / 16

B1. Do the people have the right to organize in different political parties or other competitive political groupings of their choice, and is the system free of undue obstacles to the rise and fall of these competing parties or groupings? 2 / 4

Singapore has a multiparty political system, and a total of nine parties contested the last parliamentary elections in 2015. However, a variety of factors have helped to ensure the PAP's dominant position, including an electoral framework that favors the incumbents, restrictions on political films and television programs, the threat of defamation suits, the PAP's vastly superior financial resources, and its influence over the mass media and the courts.

In October 2018, hearings began in lawsuits filed by two PAP-led town councils against a group of WP officials—including three current MPs—who were accused of mismanaging public finances while the councils were under WP control. The expenses associated with the cases forced the defendants to solicit donations for a legal defense fund. The proceedings were ongoing at year's end.

B2. Is there a realistic opportunity for the opposition to increase its support or gain power through elections? 2 / 4

The opposition has made some progress in mounting stronger election campaigns over the last decade. Opposition factions collectively put forward candidates for all 89 directly elected Parliament seats in 2015, a first since independence. However, the WP lost one seat compared with the outgoing Parliament, and the PAP managed to win a higher percentage of the popular vote than in 2011, indicating that the opposition is unlikely to secure a majority in the foreseeable future.

In July 2018, representatives of seven opposition parties met to consider the possibility of forming a coalition to contest the next general election, though the WP did not participate. Coalition discussions continued through the end of the year.

B3. Are the people's political choices free from domination by the military, foreign powers, religious hierarchies, economic oligarchies, or any other powerful group that is not democratically accountable? 2 / 4

The corporatist structure of the economy creates dense ties between business and political elites that have been criticized as oligarchic in nature. Many senior government officials formerly served as military officers, and the military has a close relationship with the PAP, but it does not directly engage in politics.

B4. Do various segments of the population (including ethnic, religious, gender, LGBT, and other relevant groups) have full political rights and electoral opportunities? 2 / 4

Ethnic and religious minority groups have full voting rights, but critics—including civil society organizations—have questioned whether the GRC system really achieves its stated aim of ensuring representation for minorities. Separately, the new rules for presidential candidacy have been criticized for excluding non-Malays from the 2017 election.

Women remain somewhat underrepresented in senior government and political positions, though women candidates won 21 of the 89 directly elected Parliament seats in 2015, and the president who took office in 2017 is a woman. A cabinet reshuffle in May 2018 increased the number of women ministers to three. LGBT (lesbian, gay, bisexual, and transgender) groups operate openly but do not have vocal representation in Parliament.

C. FUNCTIONING OF GOVERNMENT: 7 / 12

C1. Do the freely elected head of government and national legislative representatives determine the policies of the government? 2 / 4

Elected officials determine the policies of the government, but the PAP's political and institutional dominance ensures its victory at the polls, and the party leadership maintains discipline among its members. The constitution stipulates that lawmakers lose their seats if they resign or are expelled from the party for which they stood in elections.

C2. Are safeguards against official corruption strong and effective? 3 / 4

Singapore has been lauded for its lack of bribery and corruption. However, its corporatist economic structure entails close collaboration between the public and private sectors that may produce conflicts of interest. Lawmakers often serve on the boards of private companies, for example.

In a high-profile criminal prosecution initiated by the Corrupt Practices Investigation Bureau, the former general manager of a PAP-led town council went on trial in September 2018 for allegedly taking bribes. The trial was ongoing at year's end.

C3. Does the government operate with openness and transparency? 2 / 4

The government provides some transparency on its operations. The Singapore Public Sector Outcome Review is published every two years and provides extensive metrics on the functioning of the bureaucracy; regular audits of public-sector financial processes are also made accessible to the public. However, other data, including key information on the status of the national reserves, are not made publicly available, and there is no freedom of information law giving citizens the right to obtain government records.

CIVIL LIBERTIES: 32 / 60 (–1)
D. FREEDOM OF EXPRESSION AND BELIEF: 9 / 16 (–1)
D1. Are there free and independent media? 2 / 4

All domestic newspapers, radio stations, and television channels are owned by companies linked to the government. Editorials and news coverage generally support state policies, and self-censorship is common, though newspapers occasionally publish critical content. The government uses racial or religious tensions and the threat of terrorism to justify restrictions on freedom of speech. Media outlets, bloggers, and public figures have been subjected to harsh civil and criminal penalties for speech deemed to be seditious, defamatory, or injurious to religious sensitivities. Major online news sites must obtain licenses and respond to regulators' requests to remove prohibited content. However, foreign media and a growing array of online domestic outlets—including news sites and blogs—are widely consumed and offer alternative views, frequently publishing articles that are critical of the government or supportive of independent activism.

In November 2018, regulators blocked access to the independent news website *States Times Review* after it reported that Singapore institutions had been involved in a massive Malaysian corruption scandal; a successor site was blocked the following month. Also in November, another website, *The Online Citizen*, was placed under investigation for criminal defamation over a post alleging high-level corruption in the country.

D2. Are individuals free to practice and express their religious faith or nonbelief in public and private? 3 / 4

The constitution guarantees freedom of religion as long as its practice does not violate any other regulations, and most groups worship freely. However, religious actions perceived as threats to racial or religious harmony are not tolerated, and the Jehovah's Witnesses and the Unification Church are banned. Religious groups are required to register with the government under the 1966 Societies Act.

D3. Is there academic freedom, and is the educational system free from extensive political indoctrination? 1 / 4 (−1)

Public schools include a national education component that has been criticized for presenting a history of Singapore that focuses excessively on the role of the PAP. All public universities and political research institutions have direct government links that enable political influence and interference in hiring and firing; recent faculty turnover at two major universities has increased concerns about political pressure. Academics engage in political debate, though self-censorship on Singapore-related topics is common.

After Parliament established a Select Committee on Deliberate Online Falsehoods in January 2018, historian Thum Ping Tjin argued in a submission to the panel that the PAP government itself had disseminated falsehoods by misrepresenting a past crackdown on alleged communist plots against the state in order to justify mass detentions without trial for political reasons. Thum advocated legal reforms to strengthen freedom of speech, freedom of the press, and freedom of information. In March, he was called before the committee and subjected to nearly six hours of questioning led by the home affairs minister, who challenged Thum's academic credentials. The committee's activities were thought to have had a chilling effect on academic discussion of domestic political topics.

Score Change: The score declined from 2 to 1 due to lawmakers' public interrogation of a historian over his research as well as concerns about the role of political pressure in recent staff changes at local universities.

D4. Are individuals free to express their personal views on political or other sensitive topics without fear of surveillance or retribution? 3 / 4

Private discussion is generally open and free, though legal restrictions on topics that involve race and religion constrain dialogue. The threat of defamation suits and related charges are also deterrents to free speech, including on social media. Among other high-profile cases during 2018, activist Jolovan Wham and politician John Tan of the Singapore Democratic Party were convicted of contempt of court in October for Facebook posts in which they questioned the judiciary's independence. Their sentences were pending at year's end.

E. ASSOCIATIONAL AND ORGANIZATIONAL RIGHTS: 4 / 12
E1. Is there freedom of assembly? 2 / 4

Public assemblies are subject to extensive restrictions. Police permits are required for assemblies that occur outdoors; limited restrictions apply to indoor gatherings. Speakers' Corner at Hong Lim Park is the designated site for open assembly, though events there can likewise be restricted if they are deemed disruptive. Non-Singaporeans are generally prohibited from participating in or attending public assemblies that are considered political or sensitive. An amendment to the Public Order Act adopted in 2017 increased the authorities' discretion to ban public meetings and barred foreign nationals from organizing, funding, or even observing gatherings that could be used for a political purpose.

The Public Order and Safety (Special Powers) Act, passed by Parliament in March 2018 and signed by the president in April, granted the home affairs minister and police enhanced authority in the context of a "serious incident," which was vaguely defined to include scenarios ranging from terrorist attacks to peaceful protests. Officials would be permitted to potentially use lethal force and to halt newsgathering and online communications in the affected area. The special powers could even be invoked in advance of a likely or threatened incident.

E2. Is there freedom for nongovernmental organizations, particularly those that are engaged in human rights- and governance-related work? 1 / 4

The Societies Act requires most organizations of more than 10 people to register with the government; the government enjoys full discretion to register or dissolve such groups. Only registered parties and associations may participate in organized political activity. Despite these restrictions, a number of nongovernmental organizations engage in human rights and governance-related work, advocating policy improvements and addressing the interests of constituencies including migrant workers and women.

E3. Is there freedom for trade unions and similar professional or labor organizations? 1 / 4

Unions are granted some rights under the Trade Unions Act, though restrictions include a ban on government employees joining unions. Union members are prohibited from voting on collective agreements negotiated by union representatives and employers. Strikes must be approved by a majority of members, as opposed to the internationally accepted standard of at least 50 percent of the members who vote. Workers in essential services are required to give 14 days' notice to an employer before striking. In practice, many restrictions are not applied. Nearly all unions are affiliated with the National Trade Union Congress, which is openly allied with the PAP.

F. RULE OF LAW: 7 / 16

F1. Is there an independent judiciary? 1 / 4

The country's top judges are appointed by the president on the advice of the prime minister. The government's consistent success in court cases that have direct implications for its agenda has cast serious doubt on judicial independence. The problem is particularly evident in defamation cases and lawsuits against government opponents. However, the judiciary is perceived to act more professionally and impartially in business-related cases, which has helped to make the country an attractive venue for investment and commerce.

F2. Does due process prevail in civil and criminal matters? 2 / 4

Defendants in criminal cases enjoy most due process rights; political interference does not occur in a large majority of cases. However, the colonial-era Internal Security Act (ISA) allows warrantless searches and arrests to preserve national security. ISA detainees can be held without charge or trial for two-year periods that can be renewed indefinitely. In recent years it has primarily been used against suspected Islamist militants. The Criminal Law Act, which is mainly used against suspected members of organized crime groups, similarly allows warrantless arrest and preventive detention for renewable one-year periods. The Misuse of Drugs Act empowers authorities to commit suspected drug users, without trial, to rehabilitation centers for up to three years.

F3. Is there protection from the illegitimate use of physical force and freedom from war and insurgencies? 2 / 4

Singaporeans are largely protected against the illegitimate use of force and are not directly exposed to war or insurgencies. Prisons generally meet international standards. However, the penal code mandates corporal punishment in the form of caning, in addition to imprisonment, for about 30 offenses, and it can also be used as a disciplinary measure in prisons. Singapore continues to impose the death penalty for crimes including drug trafficking. Thirteen people were executed during 2018, up from eight in 2017 and four in 2016.

F4. Do laws, policies, and practices guarantee equal treatment of various segments of the population? 2 / 4

The law forbids ethnic discrimination, though in some instances minorities may face discrimination in private- or public-sector employment. Women enjoy the same legal rights as men on most issues, and many are well-educated professionals, but no laws protect against gender-based discrimination in employment.

The LGBT community faces significant legal obstacles. The penal code criminalizes consensual sex between adult men, setting a penalty of up to two years in prison. The law is not actively enforced, but the Court of Appeal upheld its constitutionality in 2014. The Pink Dot parade, held annually in support of equal rights for LGBT people since 2009, drew another large turnout in 2018, despite a ban on foreign funding and participation.

G. PERSONAL AUTONOMY AND INDIVIDUAL RIGHTS: 12 / 16

G1. Do individuals enjoy freedom of movement, including the ability to change their place of residence, employment, or education? 3 / 4

Citizens enjoy freedom of movement and the ability to change their place of employment. Policies aimed at fostering ethnic balance in subsidized public housing, in which a majority of Singaporeans live, entail some restrictions on place of residence, but these do not apply to open-market housing. There are practical limits on freedom of movement for foreign workers.

G2. Are individuals able to exercise the right to own property and establish private businesses without undue interference from state or nonstate actors? 3 / 4

Individuals face no extensive restrictions on property ownership, though public housing units are technically issued on 99-year leases rather than owned outright. While the state is heavily involved in the economy through its investment funds and other assets, private business activity is generally facilitated by a supportive legal framework.

G3. Do individuals enjoy personal social freedoms, including choice of marriage partner and size of family, protection from domestic violence, and control over appearance? 3 / 4

Men and women generally have equal rights on personal status matters such as marriage and divorce, though same-sex marriage and civil unions are not recognized. Social pressures deter some interreligious marriages and exert influence on personal appearance. The government has generally barred Muslim women from wearing headscarves in public-sector jobs that require a uniform, but the issue remains a subject of public debate and President Yacob herself wears a headscarf. Penal code reforms that would abolish spousal immunity for rape were under consideration at the end of 2018.

G4. Do individuals enjoy equality of opportunity and freedom from economic exploitation? 3 / 4

Singapore's inhabitants generally benefit from considerable economic opportunity, but some types of workers face disadvantages. The country's roughly 200,000 household workers are excluded from the Employment Act and are regularly exploited. Several high-profile trials of employers in recent years have drawn public attention to the physical abuse of such workers. Laws and regulations governing their working conditions have modestly improved formal protections over the past decade, but the guarantees remain inadequate. In October 2018, the Ministry of Manpower issued a new work-permit condition that banned employers from holding the paid wages and other money of foreign household workers for safekeeping. Existing laws such as the Foreign Worker Dormitories Act of 2015 are intended to ensure the food and shelter needs of foreign workers. However, illegal practices such as passport confiscation by employers remain common methods of coercion, and foreign workers are vulnerable to exploitation and debt bondage in the sex trade or industries including construction and manufacturing.

Slovakia

Population: 5,400,000
Capital: Bratislava
Political Rights Rating: 1
Civil Liberties Rating: 2 ↓
Freedom Rating: 1.5
Freedom Status: Free
Electoral Democracy: Yes

Overview: Slovakia's parliamentary system features regular multiparty elections and peaceful transfers of power between rival parties. While civil liberties are generally protected, democratic institutions are hampered by political corruption, entrenched discrimination against the Romany minority, and growing political hostility toward potential migrants and refugees.

KEY DEVELOPMENTS IN 2018:

- In February, investigative reporter Ján Kuciak and his fiancée were murdered at their home in southern Slovakia. It was the first time in Slovakia's modern history that a journalist was killed because of their work. Kuciak had been working on a report that uncovered alleged links between the Italian mafia and Prime Minister Robert Fico's office.
- The murder shocked the country and prompted the biggest demonstrations since the fall of communism. Tens of thousands of people took to the streets, demanding an independent investigation and the resignation of the prime minister, the interior minister, and the head of the police. The protesters also called for early elections.
- In March, an ultimatum from junior coalition partner Most–Híd led to Fico's resignation and a government reconstruction. President Andrej Kiska appointed Peter Pellegrini, a member of Fico's Direction–Social Democracy (Smer-SD) party, to head the new government. Fico stayed on as leader of Smer-SD's parliamentary caucus.
- Local elections in November resulted in serious defeats for Smer-SD in Slovakia's major cities, but the party remained the largest political force at year's end.

POLITICAL RIGHTS: 36 / 40

A. ELECTORAL PROCESS: 12 / 12

A1. Was the current head of government or other chief national authority elected through free and fair elections? 4 / 4

Slovakia is a parliamentary republic with government under the leadership of the prime minister. There is also a directly elected president with important but limited executive powers. President Andrej Kiska was elected in 2014; as an independent newcomer he gained 59 percent of the vote and defeated then prime minister Robert Fico in a run-off.

The president appoints the prime minister, who is usually the head of the majority party or coalition. In March 2018, an ultimatum from Smer-SD's junior coalition partner, Most–Híd, led to Fico's resignation, and President Kiska appointed Peter Pellegrini of Smer-SD party as prime minister. The coalition partners of the previous Fico government, the nationalist Slovak People's Party (SNS) and the center-right Most–Híd, continued to lend their support to the new cabinet.

A2. Were the current national legislative representatives elected through free and fair elections? 4 / 4

The 150 members of the unicameral parliament are directly elected to four-year terms in a single national constituency by proportional representation vote. The last elections took place in 2016. The ruling Smer-SD lost its outright majority and formed a coalition with two other parties, SNS and Most–Híd. The vote took place peacefully and its results were accepted by stakeholders and certified by the State Commission for Elections and the Control of Funding for Political Parties (State Commission).

A3. Are the electoral laws and framework fair, and are they implemented impartially by the relevant election management bodies? 4 / 4

The legal framework is generally fair, and 2014 legislation that addressed some gaps and inconsistencies in electoral laws was praised by a 2016 Organization for Co-operation and Security in Europe (OSCE) election monitoring mission. However, electoral legislation leaves ambiguous whether meetings of the State Commission—which is tasked with oversight of party funding, vote tabulation, and electoral preparations—should be open to the public. In 2016, OSCE monitors were permitted to attend meetings, but they called for explicit regulations allowing the attendance of citizen observers.

B. POLITICAL PLURALISM AND PARTICIPATION: 15 / 16

B1. Do the people have the right to organize in different political parties or other competitive political groupings of their choice, and is the system free of undue obstacles to the rise and fall of these competing parties or groupings? 4 / 4

Citizens can freely organize in political parties and movements. In 2016, 23 parties competed in the year's elections and 8 of them entered the parliament.

The constitution and other laws prohibit parties that threaten the democratic order. In July, the Special Prosecutor's Office pressed charges against Marián Kotleba, the leader of the extreme right People's Party–Our Slovakia (L'SNS), for demonstrating support for racist and Nazi ideology. Several of his fellow party members were also being prosecuted for similar crimes. The party faces the prospects of dissolution on the grounds that its activities violate the Constitution and are aimed at eliminating Slovakia's democratic regime. L'SNS had entered the parliament in 2016, after taking an unexpected 8 percent of the vote.

B2. Is there a realistic opportunity for the opposition to increase its support or gain power through elections? 4 / 4

There have been regular alterations of parties in government in the last two decades. In November 2018, opposition and independent candidates defeated incumbents supported by Smer-SD in most major cities in local elections.

B3. Are the people's political choices free from domination by the military, foreign powers, religious hierarchies, economic oligarchies, or any other powerful group that is not democratically accountable? 4 / 4

There are few direct limitations on the political choices of citizens in Slovakia.

B4. Do various segments of the population (including ethnic, religious, gender, LGBT, and other relevant groups) have full political rights and electoral opportunities? 3 / 4

Nearly all relevant political parties have expressed bias against LGBT (lesbian, gay, bisexual, and transgender) people, who are poorly represented in politics. The Romany minority is poorly represented, and there have been reports of vote-buying in Romany settlements in local and regional elections.

Women hold one-fifth of seats in the parliament, and are underrepresented in politics generally. The government has worked to implement action plans aimed at achieving gender equality, but no major changes have been achieved.

C. FUNCTIONING OF GOVERNMENT: 9 / 12

C1. Do the freely elected head of government and national legislative representatives determine the policies of the government? 4 / 4

Democratically elected politicians are the key agents for determining public policy.

C2. Are safeguards against official corruption strong and effective? 3 / 4

Corruption remains a long-standing problem, and few high-profile corruption cases have led to convictions. In a significant decision in November 2018, the Supreme Court sentenced former ministers Marián Janušek and Igor Štefanov to 11 and 9 years in prison, respectively, for deliberately bypassing legal guidelines for public procurement and favoring a group of contractors close to the political leadership. However, the number of corruption convictions has declined in the last two years, and an overwhelming majority of convictions result in suspended sentences. A Transparency International–commissioned public opinion poll published in November 2018 revealed that the number of Slovaks willing to report corruption had declined to its lowest level since the country became independent in 1993.

Despite improvements to the legislation protecting whistleblowers and the establishment of an anticorruption department in the office of the government, senior officials continue to be implicated in corruption. The investigation into the murder of Kuciak exposed links between a wealthy oligarch and high-ranking politicians and officials. In April 2018, the European Union's OLAF anticorruption agency opened investigation into the misuse of EU funds in the field of agriculture; the investigation was apparently prompted by Kuciak's reporting.

In 2018, a European Commission annual report singled out the fight against corruption as a sphere in which the country made no visible progress. It noted the "the lack of accountability in bodies tasked with fighting corruption" and the "only moderately effective whistle-blower protection."

C3. Does the government operate with openness and transparency? 2 / 4

The law obliges mandatory publication of all contracts in which a state or public institution is a party, but enforcement is inconsistent. Many business leaders believe that corruption was the main reason behind their failure in securing public tenders.

CIVIL LIBERTIES: 52 / 60 (−1)

D. FREEDOM OF EXPRESSION AND BELIEF: 14 / 16 (−1)

D1. Are there free and independent media? 2 / 4 (−1)

The February 2018 murder of Ján Kuciak, an investigative reporter who was working on corruption and tax fraud cases, represented the worst attack on media in recent Slovak history. Police confirmed that murder was linked to Kuciak's investigative work and charged three suspects in October; one of the suspects linked the murder to a controversial businessman with ties to politicians across the board. The businessman had been arrested in an unrelated case in mid-2018.

Shortly after the murder, then prime minister Robert Fico promised a swift and independent investigation. However, Fico himself had been criticized for contributing to the hateful atmosphere against journalists; he has verbally attacked the media throughout his career, and even after his resignation as prime minister in March. In November, after another round of verbal insults, over 500 Slovak journalists published a declaration condemning Fico's attacks.

Media ownership is concentrated in the hands of a few business groups and individuals. In addition, concerns over the independence of public broadcaster Radio and Television of Slovakia (RTVS) increased as dozens of its reporters were laid off or left in 2018, citing political pressures by newly appointed editors.

Score Change: The score declined from 3 to 2 due to signs of increased interference in the work of independent journalists, including the murder of an investigative reporter, verbal attacks against journalists by the leader of the largest party, and the departure of a significant number of senior staff from the public broadcaster amid political pressure from management.

D2. Are individuals free to practice and express their religious faith or nonbelief in public and private? 4 / 4

Religious freedom is guaranteed by the Constitution and generally upheld by state institutions. Registered churches and religious societies are eligible for tax exemptions and government subsidies.

D3. Is there academic freedom, and is the educational system free from extensive political indoctrination? 4 / 4

Academic freedom is guaranteed by the Constitution and upheld by authorities.

D4. Are individuals free to express their personal views on political or other sensitive topics without fear of surveillance or retribution? 4 / 4

People may discuss sensitive or political topics without fear of retribution or surveillance.

E. ASSOCIATIONAL AND ORGANIZATIONAL RIGHTS: 12 / 12
E1. Is there freedom of assembly? 4 / 4

Freedom of assembly is constitutionally guaranteed and upheld by state authorities, and peaceful demonstrations are common. A series of demonstrations sparked by the murder of Ján Kuciak and led to the eventual resignation of Prime Minister Fico. However, in November, the police interrogated protest organizers, citing an anonymous and highly dubious accusation that they had been plotting a coup. The investigation was later shelved, but critics accused the police of attempting to intimidate civic activists. Several international organizations protested the actions of the police.

E2. Is there freedom for nongovernmental organizations, particularly those that are engaged in human rights- and governance-related work? 4 / 4

Nongovernmental organizations (NGOs) are free to operate and criticize state authorities. However, in 2018, NGOs came under pressure from Fico who, following public demonstrations after the Kuciak murder, accused them of organizing antigovernment protests with the aim of "overthrowing" the legitimate government. Fico linked the organizers to George Soros, a Hungarian-American billionaire and philanthropist who has been scapegoated by nationalist and extremists politicians in several other countries, and argued that

NGOs needed to be under closer scrutiny. In October, the parliament adopted a law requiring NGOs to register with state authorities. Despite initial fears that the law would be similar to the restrictive "foreign agent" laws in Russia or Hungary, the adopted version does not contribute an additional burden to NGOs' activities.

E3. Is there freedom for trade unions and similar professional or labor organizations? 4 / 4

Trade unions in Slovakia are pluralistic and operate freely.

F. RULE OF LAW: 12 / 16

F1. Is there an independent judiciary? 3 / 4

The constitution provides for an independent judiciary. However, there is a widespread perception of a lack of transparency and an abundance of corruption in the functioning of the judicial system. Individual judicial panels occasionally release controversial decisions that critics suggest reflect corruption or intimidation within the judiciary.

In 2018, the parliament discussed reforming the appointment procedure to the Constitutional Court. Currently, the parliament selects twice as many candidates as the number of vacancies by a simple majority, and the president appoints candidates from this list. Earlier, President Kiska had refused to appoint the ruling party's candidates, resulting in a three-year-long vacancy on the court. The parliament failed to agree on any changes to the law by the end of 2018, raising the prospect of a deadlock at the Constitutional Court, where the terms of 9 out of 13 sitting judges expire in early 2019.

F2. Does due process prevail in civil and criminal matters? 3 / 4

Due process usually prevails in civil and criminal matters. However, there have been reports of warrantless detentions or detentions otherwise carried out without other appropriate authorization.

F3. Is there protection from the illegitimate use of physical force and freedom from war and insurgencies? 3 / 4

While Slovakia is free from war, insurgencies, and high rates of violent crime, police abuse of suspects is a persistent problem. Separately, in 2018, Slovak authorities were accused of complicity in the 2017 abduction of a Vietnamese citizen by Vietnamese security services. According to media reports, a Slovak airplane was used in the forced transfer of Trinh Xuan Thanh, a Vietnamese businessman who had sought asylum in Germany, back to Vietnam, where he was convicted of corruption and sentenced to life imprisonment. Slovak authorities admitted to irregularities but strongly denied witting involvement in the kidnapping.

F4. Do laws, policies, and practices guarantee equal treatment of various segments of the population? 3 / 4

The Romany population faces persistent employment and other kinds of discrimination. Romany children in primary schools are regularly segregated into all-Roma classes, and many are educated in schools meant to serve children with mental disabilities. The Interior Ministry in January 2018 proposed a new strategy aimed at strengthening police powers in Romany settlements, which was criticized by various NGOs concerned about ethnic profiling and further discrimination.

In a groundbreaking March 2018 ruling, the Košice Regional Court held that a municipality had discriminated against a job-seeking Romany woman when it preferred a less qualified non-Romany candidate. A separate court decision in July ruled that municipal authorities had violated antidiscrimination laws when relocating Romany tenants of a public housing to a segregated area.

Women enjoy the same legal rights as men but are underrepresented in senior-level business and government positions.

G. PERSONAL AUTONOMY AND INDIVIDUAL RIGHTS: 14 / 16

G1. Do individuals enjoy freedom of movement, including the ability to change their place of residence, employment, or education? 4 / 4

The government respects the freedom of movement and the right of citizens to freely change their place of residence, employment, and education.

G2. Are individuals able to exercise the right to own property and establish private businesses without undue interference from state or nonstate actors? 4 / 4

In general, the government does not arbitrarily interfere with citizens' rights to own property and to establish private businesses.

G3. Do individuals enjoy personal social freedoms, including choice of marriage partner and size of family, protection from domestic violence, and control over appearance? 3 / 4

Personal social freedoms, including choice of marriage partner and size of family, are guaranteed and upheld by the state authorities, but a 2014 constitutional amendment defines marriage as a "unique bond" between one man and one woman. LGBT partners do not have the right to conclude civil unions.

G4. Do individuals enjoy equality of opportunity and freedom from economic exploitation? 3 / 4

Severe marginalization of the Roma harms their opportunities for social mobility.

Human trafficking is a problem, and mainly involves the transport of men, women, and children to countries in Western and Central Europe, where they are engaged in forced labor, sex work, and begging. The government has recently increased antitrafficking efforts, including by more frequently investigating and prosecuting organizers. However, sentences are sometimes light, and victim identification and services are inadequate.

Slovenia

Population: 2,100,000
Capital: Ljubljana
Political Rights Rating: 1
Civil Liberties Rating: 1
Freedom Rating: 1.0
Freedom Status: Free
Electoral Democracy: Yes

Overview: Slovenia is a parliamentary republic with a freely elected government. Political rights and civil liberties are generally respected. Corruption remains an issue, though media are proactive in exposing it. The judiciary, while somewhat distrusted, has nevertheless established a record of independent rulings, and the rule of law is generally respected. Public discourse regarding migration and other issues has been increasingly rancorous.

KEY DEVELOPMENTS IN 2018:

- In June, parliamentary elections were held, resulting in the formation of a center-left minority government that took office in September. Local elections in all 212 municipalities were held in November and December. The year's polls were peaceful, and considered free and fair.
- In April, the Constitutional Court struck down a cap on damages claimed by the "Erased," people who were removed from official records in 1992.
- In January, lawmakers approved measures that distributed fees incurred by public information requests more evenly among the parties involved, lessening the financial burden on journalists and other information requesters.
- Harassment and threats against journalists increased. There were multiple reports of threatening mail being sent to journalists, including one item containing a white powdery substance (later found to be nontoxic); and of social media harassment including death threats. In August, a driver attempted to ram his vehicle into a television crew.

POLITICAL RIGHTS: 39 / 40

A. ELECTORAL PROCESS: 12 / 12

A1. Was the current head of government or other chief national authority elected through free and fair elections? 4 / 4

The prime minister is appointed by the National Assembly (Državni Zbor) and serves as the head of the executive branch. The president holds the mostly ceremonial position of chief of state, and is directly elected for up to two five-year terms.

Parliamentary elections were held in June 2018, and after extended negotiations, a minority center-left coalition government took office in September. Prime Minister Marjan Šarec—formerly a two-term mayor of Kamnik, and before that, a comedian—heads the new administration.

In November and December, two rounds of local elections were held in all 212 municipalities. While some mayoral results were appealed, and a few instances of recounts observed, the process was free and fair.

A2. Were the current national legislative representatives elected through free and fair elections? 4 / 4

The bicameral legislature is composed of the 40-seat Senate and the 90-seat National Assembly. Senators are indirectly elected to five-year terms by an electoral college. Of the 90 National Assembly members, 88 are directly elected by proportional representation vote. Two seats are reserved for Italian and Hungarian minorities, and are directly elected in special constituencies by a simple majority vote. National Assembly members serve four-year terms.

Monitors from the Organization for Security and Co-operation in Europe (OSCE) deemed the June 2018 National Assembly elections free and fair. The election took place a few weeks before the previous parliament was due to finish its term, because Prime Minister Miro Cerar had resigned in March after the Supreme Court ordered that a new referendum take place on an infrastructure project that was a major part of his development plan. Although the center-right Slovenian Democratic Party (SDS), led by former prime minister Janez Janša, won the most seats with 25, it was the second-place party List of Marjan Šarec (LMŠ) that was able to form a center-left minority government. Šarec's party took 13 seats; members of his coalition members include the Social Democrats (SD) and the Modern Center Party (SMC), which each took 10 seats, the Democratic Party of Pensioners of Slovenia

(DeSUS), which took 5 seats, and the Party of Alenka Bratušek (SAB) which also took 5 seats. The coalition is supported by the left-most party, Levica, which won 9 seats.

A3. Are the electoral laws and framework fair, and are they implemented impartially by the relevant election management bodies? 4 / 4

The National Election Commission is an independent and impartial body that supervises free and fair elections, and ensures electoral laws are properly implemented.

B. POLITICAL PLURALISM AND PARTICIPATION: 16 / 16

B1. Do the people have the right to organize in different political parties or other competitive political groupings of their choice, and is the system free of undue obstacles to the rise and fall of these competing parties or groupings? 4 / 4

The constitutional right to organize in different political parties is upheld in practice. Twenty-five parties participated in the 2018 parliamentary election, including several formed during the last election cycle. Local elections saw a flurry of parties and independent candidates running for municipal offices. Reaching just over 51 percent, turnout beat expectations and was the highest since 2006.

B2. Is there a realistic opportunity for the opposition to increase its support or gain power through elections? 4 / 4

Political power rotates between center-left and center-right parties. Past governments were comprised of parties from various parts of the political spectrum.

B3. Are the people's political choices free from domination by the military, foreign powers, religious hierarchies, economic oligarchies, or any other powerful group that is not democratically accountable? 4 / 4

People's political choices are free from domination by powerful groups that are not democratically accountable.

B4. Do various segments of the population (including ethnic, religious, gender, LGBT, and other relevant groups) have full political rights and electoral opportunities? 4 / 4

Citizens generally enjoy full political rights and electoral opportunities. In the National Assembly, one seat each is reserved for Hungarian and Italian minorities. Roma are given seats on 20 municipal councils, but are not represented in the legislature.

Women's political interests are relatively well represented. However, after the 2018 election, some 24 percent of members of the National Assembly are women, a decline from the last term. Men and women must each have at least 35 percent representation on party lists. Political parties that have failed to do so have had their lists rejected.

C. FUNCTIONING OF GOVERNMENT: 11 / 12

C1. Do the freely elected head of government and national legislative representatives determine the policies of the government? 4 / 4

Elected officials are free to set and implement government policy without undue interference.

C2. Are safeguards against official corruption strong and effective? 3 / 4

Corruption in Slovenia primarily takes the form of conflicts of interest involving contracts between government officials and private businesses. Despite a recent push in the National Assembly to address the problem, the issue persists. The Commission for the Prevention of Corruption (KPK) has been mired in controversy, including the fining of the KPK president in March 2018 for misuse of personal data. In July, the Constitutional Court overturned key aspects of a 2011 law on seizure of assets from criminal activities, a decision that caused some corruption cases against current and former public officials to be withdrawn.

Also in July, Zmago Jelinčič of SNS was appointed vice chair of a parliamentary foreign relations committee, in spite of a Council of Europe decision in June to ban him for life from the Council for corruption.

Media have been increasingly proactive in exposing corruption, bringing such practices into sharper public focus. For example, the media reported in March on overpayment of tenders issued by the government for a new railway segment and in January on irregularities in procurement in the health sector.

C3. Does the government operate with openness and transparency? 4 / 4

The government generally operates with openness and transparency. In January 2018, amendments to the Access to Public Information Act distributed the fees incurred by public information requests more evenly among the parties involved, thus lessening the financial burden on journalists and other information requesters.

The Information Commissioner reported in May that in 2017 the number of complaints against the state over access to public information had increased while the number of such complaints against municipalities had decreased.

CIVIL LIBERTIES: 55 / 60 (+1)
D. FREEDOM OF EXPRESSION AND BELIEF: 14 / 16
D1. Are there free and independent media? 3 / 4

Freedom of speech and freedom of the press are constitutionally guaranteed, but journalists can be legally compelled to reveal their sources. State-owned enterprises continue to hold a stake in several media outlets, leaving them vulnerable to government intervention. Public broadcaster Radiotelevizija Slovenija frequently faces pressure from political actors.

Defamation remains a criminal offense, and there have been several high-profile cases involving media in recent years, Two ongoing cases by journalists against the leader of the SDS, Janez Janša, were resolved in 2018 in the journalists' favor. In a separate criminal proceeding over the same issue, in November a three-month suspended sentence was handed down to Janša for defaming two journalists. The case is on appeal. In December, the two journalists received hate mail at their television station that included a white powdery substance, which later turned out to be nontoxic.

The number of journalists facing harassment and threats rose in 2018. Television crews have been attacked, including in one case in August in which a driver attempted to ram his vehicle into a film crew. Also in August, the editor of a daily newspaper stated that a call for his execution had been posted on social media; the case was turned over to the authorities but no charges were filed. Since the middle of autumn, participants in a grassroots campaign have criticized state-owned Telekom Slovenije's advertising with a right-wing outlet that has published incendiary and hateful content. After a long debate between free-speech and anti-hate-speech advocates, Prime Minister Šarec in November opined that while press freedom is a foundation of democracy, state-owned companies should consider whether advertising with media that publish hateful content is compatible with their mission. Telekom Slovenije continued to advertise with the outlet in question.

Journalists face a continuing threat to their livelihood, be it by cost-cutting across newsrooms or outright terminations. A February 2018 court ruling declared a series of individual terminations at the *Delo* daily newspaper over the years as a "mass termination," throwing the legality of terminations and compensation packages (widely criticized as meager) into doubt.

D2. Are individuals free to practice and express their religious faith or nonbelief in public and private? 3 / 4

The Slovenian constitution guarantees religious freedom and contains provisions that prohibit inciting religious intolerance or discrimination. After a decades-long struggle to build a mosque in Ljubljana, a groundbreaking ceremony was held in 2013, but its construction has been delayed. It was announced in July 2018 that funding to complete it would be provided by Qatar.

There are occasional instances of vandalism of religious buildings, and hate speech by high-profile figures.

D3. Is there academic freedom, and is the educational system free from extensive political indoctrination? 4 / 4

Academic freedom is generally respected.

D4. Are individuals free to express their personal views on political or other sensitive topics without fear of surveillance or retribution? 4 / 4

Individuals are generally free to express their personal beliefs without fear of reprisal. Defamation remains a criminal offense, though officials may no longer bring defamation cases through the state prosecutor, and instead must pursue such claims as private citizens.

Debates about polarizing issues such as migration, and the right to access abortion have become increasingly combative.

E. ASSOCIATIONAL AND ORGANIZATIONAL RIGHTS: 12 / 12

E1. Is there freedom of assembly? 4 / 4

The rights to peaceful assembly and association are guaranteed by the constitution and respected in practice. Assemblies must be registered with the authorities in advance, and in some instances permits are required.

E2. Is there freedom for nongovernmental organizations, particularly those that are engaged in human rights- and governance-related work? 4 / 4

Numerous nongovernmental organizations (NGOs) operate freely and play a role in policymaking.

In September 2018, the outgoing interior minister accused humanitarian NGOs of helping migrants enter the country illegally. The allegations were not proven, and one of the implicated NGOs has questioned motives behind the claims.

E3. Is there freedom for trade unions and similar professional or labor organizations? 4 / 4

Workers may establish and join trade unions, strike, and bargain collectively. The Association of Free Trade Unions of Slovenia controls the four trade union seats in the National Council.

F. RULE OF LAW: 15 / 16 (+1)

F1. Is there an independent judiciary? 4 / 4 (+1)

The Constitution provides for an independent judiciary. In 2018, higher-instance courts issued several important rulings that generally went against state overreach, including in terms of asset seizure and campaign finance. However, several surveys have shown that a significant portion of the general public still has a negative perception of the courts, despite a record of impartial judgements and improvements in efficiency.

Score Change: The score improved from 3 to 4 due to a record of impartial judgements by Slovenia's courts.

F2. Does due process prevail in civil and criminal matters? 4 / 4

The rule of law is respected in civil and criminal matters. Programs aimed at reducing court backlogs have seen some success in recent years.

F3. Is there protection from the illegitimate use of physical force and freedom from war and insurgencies? 4 / 4

People in Slovenia are generally free from threats of physical force. Prison conditions meet international standards, though overcrowding has been reported.

There were two notable cases in 2018 involving the formation of paramilitary groups that espoused antigovernment or antimigrant agendas. An indictment was filed against the leader of one such group in December.

F4. Do laws, policies, and practices guarantee equal treatment of various segments of the population? 3 / 4

In 2017, rights activists criticized the amendments to the Aliens Act as lacking appropriate guarantees against indirect *refoulement*, and the Human Rights Ombudsman filed a request asking the Constitutional Court to rule on the constitutionality of the amendments. The case remained pending at the end of 2018. Additionally, the Ombudsman during the year opened an investigation into claims the police were deporting migrants who had legally requested asylum. Combative public discourse about migration has prompted concerns about an increasing presence of racist rhetoric.

The "Erased" are a group of more than 25,000 non-Slovene citizens purged from official records in 1992. Their status was reinstated in 2010 and a compensation scheme started in 2014. In April 2018, the Constitutional Court struck down a provision capping the amount of damages, paving the way for a substantial increase in compensations for injustice suffered. In December, lawmakers passed a measure that imposed a cap on interest. Many cases relating to compensation remain pending in the courts.

Roma face widespread poverty and societal marginalization. While there are legal protections against discrimination based on sexual orientation, discrimination against LGBTQ people is common.

G. PERSONAL AUTONOMY AND INDIVIDUAL RIGHTS: 14 / 16

G1. Do individuals enjoy freedom of movement, including the ability to change their place of residence, employment, or education? 4 / 4

Citizens enjoy the right to change their residence, employment, and place of education.

G2. Are individuals able to exercise the right to own property and establish private businesses without undue interference from state or nonstate actors? 4 / 4

Individuals may exercise the right to own property and establish private business in practice. Expropriation is an extreme measure and is legally regulated. Relative transparency surrounding business endeavors helps to foster a free environment for business and property ownership.

G3. Do individuals enjoy personal social freedoms, including choice of marriage partner and size of family, protection from domestic violence, and control over appearance? 3 / 4

Individuals generally enjoy personal social freedoms. People entering same-sex partnerships enjoy most of the rights conferred by marriage, but cannot adopt children or undergo in-vitro fertilization procedures. Marriage is still legally defined as a union between a man and a woman. Although domestic violence is illegal, it remains a concern in practice, with up to 3,000 cases reported annually.

G4. Do individuals enjoy equality of opportunity and freedom from economic exploitation? 3 / 4

Men from other countries in Central and Eastern Europe can be found engaged in forced begging, and women and children are subject to forced prostitution. However, authorities actively prosecute suspected human traffickers and work to identify victims.

Solomon Islands

Population: 700,000
Capital: Honiara
Political Rights Rating: 2 ↑
Civil Liberties Rating: 2
Freedom Rating: 2.0
Freedom Status: Free
Electoral Democracy: Yes

Overview: Political rights and civil liberties are generally respected in the Solomon Islands. There are weaknesses in the rule of law, and corruption remains a serious concern, but recent governments have taken steps to address it. Violence against women is also a significant problem.

KEY DEVELOPMENTS IN 2018:

- In July, Parliament passed two measures, the Anti-Corruption Act and the Whistleblowers Protection Act, that were designed to strengthen institutional protections against corruption.
- Investigations by a special anticorruption task force led to a number of high-profile arrests during the year.
- Lawmaker Freda Tuki Soriocomua lost her seat in Parliament in October after being convicted of bribing voters.

POLITICAL RIGHTS: 30 / 40 (+2)
A. ELECTORAL PROCESS: 9 / 12
A1. Was the current head of government or other chief national authority elected through free and fair elections? 3 / 4

The prime minister, who serves as the head of government, is elected by Parliament. Irregularities are frequent in the run-up to prime ministerial elections, known as the "second election." Leading contenders usually separate into camps in Honiara's major hotels and bid for the support of other members of Parliament (MPs) with promises of cash or ministerial portfolios.

A boat used to transport legislators to and from a neighboring island (to prevent defections) ahead of the 2014 prime ministerial vote was fired upon by unknown assailants in an apparent effort to disrupt the second election. The MPs nevertheless were able to participate, and Manasseh Sogavare was chosen as prime minister.

In 2017, Sogavare was ousted in a no-confidence vote. However, the opposition failed to hold together to elect an alternative leader. Instead, a group of opposition members crossed the floor to join Sogavare in electing Rick Houenipwela ("Hou" for short), a former central bank governor and World Bank employee, as the country's new prime minister.

Parliament also selects a governor general to represent the British monarch as head of state for five-year terms. The governor general appoints members of the cabinet on the advice of the prime minister. In 2014, Frank Kabui won a second term as governor general.

A2. Were the current national legislative representatives elected through free and fair elections? 3 / 4

The 50 members of the National Parliament are directly elected in single-seat constituencies by a simple majority vote to serve four-year terms. The parliamentary elections in 2014 were considered a significant improvement over previous elections, though ongoing concerns about vote buying and other abuses were reported. Independent candidates dominated the voting, taking a record 32 seats. The Democratic Alliance Party won 7, followed by the United Democratic Party with 5, the People's Alliance Party with 3, and three smaller parties with 1 each. A Commonwealth observer mission concluded that "the election was credible and the results reflected the wishes of the people." The next elections were scheduled to be held in early 2019.

A3. Are the electoral laws and framework fair, and are they implemented impartially by the relevant election management bodies? 3 / 4

The legal framework generally provides for democratic elections. The electoral rolls have been improved since the introduction in late 2013 of a biometric voter registration system, which reduced the previous practice whereby many Honiara voters were registered twice, both in their urban residence and on their home islands. In November 2018, the Solomon Islands Electoral Commission said it had identified 60,000 instances of multiple registration; these were referred to the police.

B. POLITICAL PLURALISM AND PARTICIPATION: 14 / 16 (+1)

B1. Do the people have the right to organize in different political parties or other competitive political groupings of their choice, and is the system free of undue obstacles to the rise and fall of these competing parties or groupings? 4 / 4

There are no restrictions on the right to organize political parties, but in practice political alliances are driven more by personal ties and local allegiances than formal policy platforms or ideology, and party affiliations shift frequently, often as part of efforts to dislodge incumbent governments. The 2014 Political Parties Integrity Act was meant to encourage a stronger party system through more formalized registration mechanisms. Many formerly party-aligned legislators responded by standing as independents in that year's elections (including the prime minister), calculating that doing so left them with greater flexibility under the new law.

B2. Is there a realistic opportunity for the opposition to increase its support or gain power through elections? 4 / 4

Opposition parties and candidates may campaign freely, and power shifts frequently between rival groups. Since 1978, three governments have been ousted in opposition-led no-confidence votes, and prime ministers have resigned to fend off no-confidence challenges on two occasions. No incumbent prime minister has been able to win reelection, although both Sogavare and former prime minister Solomon Mamaloni were able to return to the prime minister's office after a period on the opposition benches.

B3. Are the people's political choices free from domination by the military, foreign powers, religious hierarchies, economic oligarchies, or any other powerful group that is not democratically accountable? 3 / 4 (+1)

People's political choices are generally unconstrained, though in some regions of the country church or tribal leaders exert strong influence. On the island of New Georgia, the Christian Fellowship Church secured reelection of its candidate, Job Dudley Tausinga, for decades, but schisms have since emerged on that island.

Score Change: The score improved from 2 to 3 because there have been few undemocratic constraints on the public's political choices in recent years.

B4. Do various segments of the population (including ethnic, religious, gender, LGBT, and other relevant groups) have full political rights and electoral opportunities? 3 / 4

Women and ethnic minorities enjoy full political rights under the law, but discrimination limits political opportunities for women in practice. Just one woman, Freda Tuki Soriocomua, won a seat in the 2014 elections. She lost her position in October 2018 after a court found that she had bribed voters. Another woman, Lanelle Tanangada, was elected in a May 2018 by-election, taking her husband's seat after he lost it in 2017, also for bribing voters in 2014. Many lawmakers have voiced support for increasing women's participation in the National Parliament, including through reserved seats for women.

C. FUNCTIONING OF GOVERNMENT: 7 / 12 (+1)

C1. Do the freely elected head of government and national legislative representatives determine the policies of the government? 3 / 4 (+1)

Solomon Islands governments have generally been able to determine national policy without outside interference, but the country's fractious politics hamper efficient policy-making. Prime ministers have struggled to sustain legislative majorities, and splits within the cabinet are frequent. Ministries are often run as ministers' personal fiefdoms, lacking accountability to the prime minister. The exigencies of political survival can lead prime ministers to lose focus on their policy agenda. However, since the establishment of Rick Hou's premiership in late 2017, the government has been able operate with relative stability, adopting long-sought anticorruption laws and other key legislation during 2018.

Score Change: The score improved from 2 to 3 because the current government has proven stable enough to adopt important legislation on corruption and other matters.

C2. Are safeguards against official corruption strong and effective? 3 / 4

Corruption and abuse of office are serious problems. The Sogavare government struggled to win support for anticorruption legislation in 2016 and 2017, largely due to resistance from within the cabinet. In July 2018, Hou's government secured passage of the Anti-Corruption Act, which establishes an independent anticorruption commission, and the Whistleblowers Protection Act. Some opposition MPs criticized the new laws as having been watered down, for example by allowing the use of local custom as a defense in corruption cases and by stipulating that the law cannot be applied retroactively.

Under both the Sogavare and Hou governments, a number of senior officials have been investigated or arrested in connection with corruption charges due to the efforts of Task

Force Janus, a joint anticorruption initiative by the police force and the Finance Ministry. Among other cases during 2018, MP Dickson Mua was arrested in October for allegedly misappropriating some SI$3 million (US$370,000) in shipping grants.

C3. Does the government operate with openness and transparency? 1 / 4

Successive governments in the Solomon Islands have not operated transparently. State dealings with foreign logging companies are not open to scrutiny. Efforts to improve accountability for funds spent by MPs in their constituencies have not been greatly successful. Transparency Solomon Islands reported in August 2018 that the government had been taking funds from the ministries to supply the Constituency Development Funds administered by MPs. There is no law stipulating a formal process by which members of the public may request official information.

CIVIL LIBERTIES: 49 / 60 (+5)
D. FREEDOM OF EXPRESSION AND BELIEF: 16 / 16 (+2)
D1. Are there free and independent media? 4 / 4 (+1)

Freedom of the press is usually respected. While politicians and elites sometimes use legal and extralegal means to intimidate journalists, such incidents have been relatively rare in recent years. There are several print newspapers. The government operates a national radio station, and subnational and private radio stations are also available. Subscription television services offer some local content in addition to foreign broadcasts. The adoption of the Whistleblowers Protection Act in 2018 was expected to facilitate journalistic efforts to report on political corruption.

Score Change: The score improved from 3 to 4 because intimidation and harassment of the media have been rare in recent years, and a new law protecting whistle-blowers strengthened the legal framework for reporting on corruption.

D2. Are individuals free to practice and express their religious faith or nonbelief in public and private? 4 / 4

Freedom of religion is generally respected. Registration requirements for religious groups are not onerous, and religious education is not mandatory.

D3. Is there academic freedom, and is the educational system free from extensive political indoctrination? 4 / 4

Academic freedom is generally respected.

D4. Are individuals free to express their personal views on political or other sensitive topics without fear of surveillance or retribution? 4 / 4 (+1)

While social taboos persist regarding the open discussion of some topics, including domestic violence, rape, and child abuse, individuals are generally free to express their views on politics and other sensitive matters.

Score Change: The score improved from 3 to 4 due to a lack of any significant constraints on or retribution for the expression of personal views.

E. ASSOCIATIONAL AND ORGANIZATIONAL RIGHTS: 10 / 12 (+1)
E1. Is there freedom of assembly? 3 / 4

The constitution guarantees freedom of assembly, and the government generally upholds this right. However, peaceful demonstrations can give way to civil unrest, particularly during contentious parliamentary debates, elections, or large-scale labor actions. Some smaller protests proceeded without incident during 2018.

E2. Is there freedom for nongovernmental organizations, particularly those that are engaged in human rights- and governance-related work? 4 / 4 (+1)

Nongovernmental organizations (NGOs) in the country operate informally in many cases, and the government is not always receptive to the viewpoints of governance-focused groups. Locally based NGOs often lack resources and reportedly grow dependent on the funds and priorities of international donors. Nevertheless, there are no major constraints on the activities of NGOs in the Solomon Islands.

Score change: The score improved from 3 to 4 due to the lack of any meaningful state restrictions on NGOs or recent reports of interference with their work.

E3. Is there freedom for trade unions and similar professional or labor organizations? 3 / 4

Workers are free to organize, and strikes are permitted with certain restrictions. Laws against antiunion discrimination by employers are reportedly ineffective. The country's main labor union, the Solomon Islands National Union of Workers, was disbanded by court order in late 2013 after lengthy litigation over an illegal strike by plantation workers. However, labor activists registered a new entity, the Workers Union of Solomon Islands (WUSI), in 2014. In 2018, a nurses' association won concessions by threatening to strike over working conditions, and authorities agreed to reduce a transportation tax increase after transport workers mounted a one-day strike.

F. RULE OF LAW: 11 / 16 (+2)

F1. Is there an independent judiciary? 4 / 4 (+1)

The judiciary has a reputation for independence, though a severe lack of resources has contributed to case backlogs. Judges are appointed by the governor general on the advice of an impartial Judicial and Legal Service Commission. The Court of Appeal is mainly reliant on foreign judges.

Score change: The score improved from 3 to 4 because although insufficient resources have hampered the effectiveness of the court system, there are no major impediments to judicial independence and impartiality.

F2. Does due process prevail in civil and criminal matters? 2 / 4

Deficiencies in due process are somewhat common, but they are mainly a result of limited resources and capacity constraints. Due to case backlogs, roughly half of the country's prison inmates are on remand awaiting trial.

F3. Is there protection from the illegitimate use of physical force and freedom from war and insurgencies? 3 / 4 (+1)

There are few major threats to physical security, though crime remains a problem in some areas. While the country has a history of internal conflict, the threat has subsided over the past two decades, thanks in large part to security aid from international partners. Rebuilding the police force was the major focus of the 2003–17 Australian-led Regional Assistance Mission to the Solomon Islands (RAMSI). The local police force was disarmed in 2003, and its paramilitary unit, the Police Field Force (which had participated in a 2000 coup) was disbanded. Nearly all of the police officers serving in the Royal Solomon Islands Police Force (RSIPF) have resigned, retired, or been dismissed since 2003, and an extensive training program has created a much more youthful force, with better representation of officers from across the country, and a better gender balance. In 2016, RAMSI undertook a limited rearmament of the police force. RAMSI concluded its mission in the Solomon Islands in 2017, but a residual Australian police advisory program continues, and Australia and New Zealand have extended RAMSI programs under bilateral auspices. The Solomon Islands police commissioner, Matthew Varley, is an Australian, as was his predecessor. Fifteen years after the wholesale restructuring of the RSIPF, there are now signs of significant improvements in the functioning of the police force.

Score Change: The score improved from 2 to 3 because 15 years of internationally supervised reforms to the police force have improved its performance and bolstered security in the country.

F4. Do laws, policies, and practices guarantee equal treatment of various segments of the population? 2 / 4

The constitution prohibits discrimination based on race, place of origin, sex, and some other categories, but the legal framework does not provide robust protections. De facto discrimination limits economic opportunities for women. Same-sex sexual activity can be punished with up to 14 years in prison. While cases are reportedly rare, the government has resisted international pressure to decriminalize such activity.

Discrimination based on regional differences also remains a factor. The Guadalcanal Plains Palm Oil Ltd. (GPPOL) operation on northern Guadalcanal, one of the country's biggest employers, avoids employing laborers from the nearby island of Malaita, even on a casual basis picking loose fruit, for fear of antagonizing local Guadalcanal communities.

G. PERSONAL AUTONOMY AND INDIVIDUAL RIGHTS: 12 / 16

G1. Do individuals enjoy freedom of movement, including the ability to change their place of residence, employment, or education? 3 / 4

Residents generally enjoy freedom of movement, but some impediments exist, particularly in parts of rural Guadalcanal where people from the island of Malaita were expelled during the unrest in 1999–2000. Hostility to Malaitan settlement also persists in parts of the Western Province.

G2. Are individuals able to exercise the right to own property and establish private businesses without undue interference from state or nonstate actors? 3 / 4

The legal and regulatory framework largely supports property ownership and private business activity. However, property rights are frequently contested. GPPOL has had its administrative buildings attacked on several occasions. Logging concessions have been disputed by local groups, as have tourism operations.

G3. Do individuals enjoy personal social freedoms, including choice of marriage partner and size of family, protection from domestic violence, and control over appearance? 3 / 4

Individual freedoms on personal status issues such as marriage and divorce are generally protected. However, the legal age of marriage is 15, and about a fifth of women are married by age 18. The 2014 Family Protection Act, which formally criminalized domestic violence and enabled victims to apply for protection orders, has been implemented, and police have received training on how to interact with victims and handle cases. Nevertheless, domestic violence and rape are serious and underreported problems, and there is a reluctance among many victims who do report offenses to take their cases to court.

G4. Do individuals enjoy equality of opportunity and freedom from economic exploitation? 3 / 4
Legal protections against exploitative working conditions are not consistently enforced, though authorities have made efforts to update and implement laws against human trafficking in recent years. Local and foreign women and children are vulnerable to sex trafficking and domestic servitude, including through forced marriages or "adoptions" to pay off debts. Migrant workers sometimes face forced labor in the mining, logging, and fishing industries.

Somalia

Population: 15,200,000
Capital: Mogadishu
Political Rights Rating: 7
Civil Liberties Rating: 7
Freedom Rating: 7.0
Freedom Status: Not Free
Electoral Democracy: No

Note: The numerical ratings and status listed above do not reflect conditions in Somaliland, which is examined in a separate report.

Overview: Somalia has struggled to reestablish a functioning state since the collapse of an authoritarian regime in 1991. The country's territory is divided among an internationally supported national government, the Shabaab militant group, a fledgling federalist system with states often at odds with the central government, and a separatist government in Somaliland. No direct national elections have been held to date, and political affairs are dominated by clan divisions. Amid ongoing insecurity, impunity for human rights abuses by both state and nonstate actors is the norm. However, citizens have experienced modest gains in civil liberties in recent years as the government and international troops have reclaimed territory from the Shabaab.

KEY DEVELOPMENTS IN 2018:

- Critics accused President Mohamed Abdullahi Mohamed, also known as "Farmajo," of seeking to centralize power following his support for a no-confidence motion against Parliament Speaker Mohamed Osman Jawari that ultimately led to Jawari's resignation in April, as well as the ouster in May of the chief justice of the Supreme Court. Both positions were filled by individuals close to the executive.
- In September, leaders from all five federal member states suspended ties with the federal government in Mogadishu, citing their disapproval with the government's efforts to influence internal state politics as well as its performance in a number of national policy areas.
- In December, Abdiasis Mohammed, or "Laftagareen," an ally of President Mohamed, won South West State's presidential election. His controversial victory

followed the arrest of his man challenger, former Shabaab leader Mukhtar Robow, who had built a large public following in the preceding months.

- Also in December, a group of parliamentarians filed a motion to impeach President Mohamed, but it was dropped after 14 parliamentarians whose names appeared on the document claimed never to have signed it.

POLITICAL RIGHTS: 1 / 40

A. ELECTORAL PROCESS: 0 / 12

A1. Was the current head of government or other chief national authority elected through free and fair elections? 0 / 4

Under the 2012 provisional constitution, the president is elected by a two-thirds vote in the Federal Parliament to serve a four-year term. In February 2017, legislators who were not freely elected themselves chose Mohamed, also known as "Farmajo," as president. He then nominated Hassan Ali Khayre as prime minister, who was confirmed by the parliament.

In December 2018, a group of parliamentarians filed a motion to impeach the president on grounds that he had signed secret bilateral agreements, and had unlawfully extradited criminals to other countries. The motion was dropped later in the month after 14 parliamentarians whose names appeared on the document claimed never to have signed it.

Also in December, Abdiasis Mohammed, or "Laftagareen," a former federal minister and ally of President Mohamed, won South West State's presidential election. His controversial victory followed the arrest by Ethiopian peacekeeping forces of his main challenger, former Shabaab leader Mukhtar Robow, who had built a large public following in the preceding months. (The Ethiopian troops were part of an African Union peacekeeping force supporting Somalia's federal government.)

A2. Were the current national legislative representatives elected through free and fair elections? 0 / 4

Limited indirect elections for the Federal Parliament were held between October 2016 and February 2017, with the goal of holding direct general elections in 2020 and 2021. Members of the 54-seat upper house were elected by state assemblies, while the lower house was elected under a system in which 135 clan elders chose 275 electoral colleges, each of which comprised 51 people and elected one lawmaker. Corruption reportedly played a major role in the elections and the operations of the legislature once constituted.

A3. Are the electoral laws and framework fair, and are they implemented impartially by the relevant election management bodies? 0 / 4

The electoral framework in use for the 2016–17 parliamentary elections did not provide for universal suffrage. The balloting was the result of an ad hoc process based on lengthy negotiations among the country's main clans.

In May 2018, the government lent rhetorical support and pledged $3 million toward a constitutional review process, to be completed by the end of 2019, in preparation for 2020–21 elections. However, little progress has been made in establishing the conditions for successful polls.

B. POLITICAL PLURALISM AND PARTICIPATION: 1 / 16

B1. Do the people have the right to organize in different political parties or other competitive political groupings of their choice, and is the system free of undue obstacles to the rise and fall of these competing parties or groupings? 1 / 4

Legislation signed in 2016 allowed the first formal registration of political parties since 1969. The National Independent Electoral Commission (NIEC) had registered more than 20 parties by August 2018.

B2. Is there a realistic opportunity for the opposition to increase its support or gain power through elections? 0 / 4

The lack of direct elections prevents any grouping from gaining power through democratic means. However, there was an orderly transfer of power in February 2017, and opportunities for individuals not selected for the presidency to remain engaged through the legislative process.

B3. Are the people's political choices free from domination by the military, foreign powers, religious hierarchies, economic oligarchies, or any other powerful group that is not democratically accountable? 0 / 4

Ordinary citizens are largely unable to participate in the political process as voters, and the indirect electoral process in 2016–17 was reportedly distorted by vote buying, intimidation, and violence.

B4. Do various segments of the population (including ethnic, religious, gender, LGBT, and other relevant groups) have full political rights and electoral opportunities? 0 / 4

The current political system is designed to ensure some representation for the country's many clans, but the prevailing "4.5" formula gives the four largest groups eight out of every nine positions, marginalizing all other clans. The system is also dominated by clan leaders, who do not necessarily represent the interests of their respective groups. Women's political participation is limited by cultural constraints and hostility from incumbent elites. Women constitute 24 percent of parliamentarians.

C. FUNCTIONING OF GOVERNMENT: 0 / 12

C1. Do the freely elected head of government and national legislative representatives determine the policies of the government? 0 / 4

The government, which is not democratically elected, has little practical ability to implement its laws and policies even in parts of the country it controls. Its basic operations remain heavily dependent on international bodies and donor governments.

In 2018, the executive sought to exert greater influence over the Parliament. In April, the executive backed the removal of Parliament Speaker Mohamed Osman Jawari through a no-confidence motion. Jawari resigned prior to the vote and was replaced by former defense minister Mohamed Mursal Abdirahman, an ally of President Mohamed.

In 2018, various Arab states sought to influence Somali leaders to gain their support amid the so-called Gulf Cooperation Council (GCC) crisis, which in 2017 saw Bahrain, Egypt, Saudi Arabia, and the United Arab Emirates (UAE) impose diplomatic and trade restrictions on Qatar. Reverberations from the crisis have contributed to state dysfunction by exacerbating existing factionalism among officials in Mogadishu, as well as tensions between Mohamed's administration and Somalia's federal states.

In September, leaders from all five federal states suspended ties with the government in Mogadishu, citing their disapproval of the government's efforts to influence internal state politics as well as its performance in a number of national policy areas.

C2. Are safeguards against official corruption strong and effective? 0 / 4

Corruption is rampant in Somalia and state agencies tasked with combating it do not function effectively. Impunity is the norm for public officials accused of malfeasance.

C3. Does the government operate with openness and transparency? 0 / 4

Government transparency is limited. Officials are not required to make public declarations of their income and assets, and oversight procedures for public contracts are not well enforced. There is no law guaranteeing public access to government information.

CIVIL LIBERTIES: 6 / 60

D. FREEDOM OF EXPRESSION AND BELIEF: 3 / 16

D1. Are there free and independent media? 1 / 4

While the provisional constitution calls for freedom of the press, journalists regularly face harassment, arbitrary detention and fines, and violence from both state and nonstate actors. For the fourth year, Somalia in 2018 topped the Committee to Protect Journalists' Global Impunity Index, with 25 unresolved cases of journalist murders. In July, SBS TV cameraman Abdirizak Kasim Iman was shot and killed after a dispute with a police officer at a security checkpoint in Mogadishu. At year's end, a police officer remained at large following a failed assassination attempt in December against Ahmed Sheikh Mohamed, the director of Radio Daljir in Bosaso. The attack came in retaliation for the station's critical coverage of Asad Osman Abdullahi, the former head of Puntland Security Forces and Puntland presidential candidate. (The attacker had reportedly shouted about the station's coverage of Abdullahi as he was firing shots.)

In September, intelligence services detained Radio Kulmiye journalist Mohamed Abdiwali Tohow without charge following a report on Shabaab operations in Galmudug that the Somali government deemed "false news." He was sentenced to a six-month prison term by a military court in October, but then immediately released. In November, the secretary general of the National Union of Somali Journalists released a statement criticizing the prime minister's office as one of "the most intolerant" to the media in Somalia's history; the statement referred to threats and intimidation against journalists by the prime minister's staff, and bribery of journalists and owners, among other violations.

D2. Are individuals free to practice and express their religious faith or nonbelief in public and private? 0 / 4

Nearly all Somalis are Sunni Muslims, though there is a very small Christian community. The provisional constitution recognizes Islam as the official religion, requires presidential candidates to be Muslims, and forbids the promotion of any other faith. However, it also includes clauses promoting religious freedom and forbidding discrimination on the basis of religion. In areas under its control, the Shabaab use violence to enforce their interpretation of Islam, including execution as a penalty for alleged apostasy.

D3. Is there academic freedom, and is the educational system free from extensive political indoctrination? 1 / 4

Despite limited funding and infrastructure and other challenges, there are functioning universities in major cities. Academics reportedly practice self-censorship on sensitive topics. Islamic instruction is required in all schools except those operated by non-Muslim minorities. Schools under Shabaab control integrate radical interpretations of Islam into the curriculum.

D4. Are individuals free to express their personal views on political or other sensitive topics without fear of surveillance or retribution? 1 / 4

Individuals enjoy some freedom of expression in more secure areas of the country, but criticism of powerful figures in the state and society can draw reprisals. Open debate is severely restricted in areas controlled or threatened by the Shabaab.

E. ASSOCIATIONAL AND ORGANIZATIONAL RIGHTS: 3 / 12 (+1)

E1. Is there freedom of assembly? 1 / 4

Although the provisional constitution guarantees freedom of assembly, security officials require approval for demonstrations and have used violence to suppress unauthorized protests. Nevertheless, citizens do assemble in urban centers. In August, mostly young protesters in Mogadishu called on authorities to make arrests for the murder of Mohamed Sheikh Ali, an entrepreneur known for his attempts to promote small business in the city. December saw protests in the capital against the legislative proposal to impeach President Mohamed.

Separately, the same month, a parliamentarian and a bystander were killed when security forces fired on a protest in Baidoa against the arrest by Ethiopian peacekeeping forces of Robow, a former Al-Shabaab leader who was running in South West State's presidential election.

E2. Is there freedom for nongovernmental organizations, particularly those that are engaged in human rights– and governance-related work? 1 / 4

Local civil society groups, international nongovernmental organizations (NGOs), and UN agencies have been able to conduct a wide range of activities in some parts of the country, but they face difficult and often dangerous working conditions. Regional authorities and security forces have reportedly harassed, extorted, obstructed, and attempted to control NGOs and aid groups, and the Shabaab generally do not allow such organizations to operate in their territory.

E3. Is there freedom for trade unions and similar professional or labor organizations? 1 / 4 (+1)

Independent labor unions are active in Somalia and have worked to expand their operations and capacity. However, constitutional and legal protections for union activity are not always respected. The Federation of Somali Trade Unions has reported threats, dismissals, attempts at co-optation, and other forms of repression and interference from both government officials and private employers.

Score Change: The score improved from 0 to 1 because trade unions are allowed to operate and enjoy some legal protections, albeit in a constrained environment.

F. RULE OF LAW: 0 / 16

F1. Is there an independent judiciary? 0 / 4

The judicial system in Somalia is fractured, understaffed, and rife with corruption. Its authority is not widely respected, with state officials ignoring court rulings and citizens often turning to Islamic or customary law as alternatives. In May 2018, President Mohamed fired Chief Justice Ibrahim Idle Suleyman, and replaced him with Bashe Yusuf Ahmed, who took office in June. While the move was described as part of a broader reform effort, critics accused the president of circumventing proper procedure in the removal and of attempting to centralize power by installing loyalists.

F2. Does due process prevail in civil and criminal matters? 0 / 4

Safeguards against arbitrary arrest and detention are not observed by the country's police, intelligence, and military services; their performances are undermined by corruption. Clan politics and other external factors often play a role in the outcome of court cases. Military courts routinely try civilians, including for terrorism-related offenses, and do not respect basic international standards for due process.

F3. Is there protection from the illegitimate use of physical force and freedom from war and insurgencies? 0 / 4

The ongoing civil conflict has seen numerous terrorist attacks on government, international, and civilian targets. Government security services, international troops, and various local militias have also been implicated in indiscriminate lethal violence and the use of excessive force against civilians. Authorities carry out executions ordered by military courts after flawed proceedings. Detainees are at risk of torture in custody, and perpetrators generally enjoy impunity.

F4. Do laws, policies, and practices guarantee equal treatment of various segments of the population? 0 / 4

While the provisional constitution and legal system offer some formal protections against discrimination based on sex, clan, and other categories, they have little force in practice. Women face widespread disadvantages in areas including housing, education, and employment, while members of marginalized clans suffer disproportionately from economic exclusion and violence.

LGBT (lesbian, gay, bisexual, and transgender) people generally do not make their identity public. Same-sex sexual activity can be punished with up to three years in prison under the penal code, and individuals accused of such conduct are subject to execution in Shabaab-controlled areas.

G. PERSONAL AUTONOMY AND INDIVIDUAL RIGHTS: 0 / 16 (−1)

G1. Do individuals enjoy freedom of movement, including the ability to change their place of residence, employment, or education? 0 / 4

Travel throughout Somalia is dangerous due the presence of extremist groups in many parts of the country. Travel is further hampered by the presence of checkpoints controlled by security forces, militants, and other armed groups that commonly extract arbitrary fees and bribes from travelers.

According to the UN High Commissioner for Refugees, approximately 2.6 million people were internally displaced in 2018; some 78 percent were forced to move due to conflict and insecurity.

G2. Are individuals able to exercise the right to own property and establish private businesses without undue interference from state or nonstate actors? 0 / 4 (−1)

The provisional constitution guarantees property rights, but securing ownership is complicated by a mixture of formal and informal or traditional systems governing land rights. Procedures for registering property and businesses are impeded by corruption and other barriers, and disputes can lead to intimidation and violence. Shabaab and militants associated with the Islamic State (IS) militant group manage elaborate corruption and taxation schemes, placing tremendous pressure on businessmen and inhibiting free operations. Women do not enjoy equal rights to inherit property and are often denied the assets to which they are legally entitled due to discriminatory cultural norms.

Score Change: The score declined from 1 to 0 due to taxation schemes by militant groups that have restricted businesses' ability to operate.

G3. Do individuals enjoy personal social freedoms, including choice of marriage partner and size of family, protection from domestic violence, and control over appearance? 0 / 4

Sexual violence remains a major problem, especially for displaced persons. Perpetrators include government troops and militia members. Female genital mutilation or cutting is extremely widespread in practice despite a formal ban. Early marriages are common. The Shabaab impose forced marriages with their fighters, and individuals can face strong societal pressure to marry or not marry within certain clans. In September 2018, Ahmed Mukhtar Salah was lynched and burned alive by a mob in Mogadishu after his nephew, an ethnic Bantu, married an ethnic Somali.

G4. Do individuals enjoy equality of opportunity and freedom from economic exploitation? 0 / 4

Child labor and trafficking in persons for the purposes of sexual exploitation or forced labor are common. Refugees and displaced persons are particularly vulnerable. Children are abducted or recruited to serve as fighters by the Shabaab and to a lesser extent by government and militia forces. A February report by Human Rights Watch (HRW) documented government abuses of children, included incommunicado detention and beatings, who had been arrested or captured in security sweeps of Shabaab camps.

South Africa

Capital: Pretoria
Population: 57,700,000
Political Rights Rating: 2
Civil Liberties Rating: 2
Freedom Rating: 2.0
Freedom Status: Free
Electoral Democracy: Yes

Overview: South Africa is a constitutional democracy. Since the end of apartheid in 1994, it has been regarded globally as a proponent of human rights and a leader on the African continent. However, in recent years, the ruling African National Congress (ANC) has been accused of undermining state institutions in order to protect corrupt officials and preserve its power as its support base began to wane. In 2018, a widely respected anticorruption commission began hearing testimony about high-level corruption allegations.

KEY DEVELOPMENTS IN 2018:

- In February, the ruling ANC forced President Jacob Zuma to resign, weeks after his preferred successor had been defeated for the position of ANC president at the party's 54th elective conference in 2017. Zuma faces a number of serious corruption charges, and attended related court proceedings during the year.
- Cyril Ramaphosa was elected to the presidency by parliament after Zuma stepped down, and is set to serve out the term of the current government, which ends in May 2019. The Independent Electoral Commission (IEC) announced that national elections would take place that month.
- In August, a special commission chaired by Deputy Chief Justice Raymond Zondo and tasked with investigating claims of state capture, corruption, and public-sector fraud began hearing testimony. The commission focused in large part on members

of the wealthy Gupta family, who are accused of wide-reaching graft facilitated by their close relationship with Zuma. By year's end, the Guptas had fled the country.
- In August, at least four people were killed, many more were injured, and shops were looted during xenophobic mob attacks in Soweto that targeted Somali shop owners.

POLITICAL RIGHTS: 33 / 40 (+1)

A. ELECTORAL PROCESS: 12 / 12

A1. Was the current head of government or other chief national authority elected through free and fair elections? 4 / 4

The National Assembly, the lower house of South Africa's bicameral Parliament, elects the president to serve concurrently with its five-year term, and can vote to replace him or her at any time. Presidents can serve a maximum of two terms. The most recent national elections, held in 2014, were declared free and fair by domestic and international observers. The ANC won with 62.2 percent of the national vote, and the party's president, Jacob Zuma, was elected to a second term as the nation's president.

Zuma survived four parliamentary no-confidence votes—the last one, in August 2017, being quite close—before ANC delegates elected Deputy President Cyril Ramaphosa to be the party's new leader at the 54th ANC party conference that December. Ramaphosa narrowly defeated former African Union Commission Chairperson Nkosazana Dlamini-Zuma, President Zuma's ex-wife. The defeat of Dlamini-Zuma, Zuma's preferred successor, made it difficult for Zuma to hold on to his position as president of the country, and in February 2018, the ANC's executive committee forced him to resign. Ramaphosa was then elected acting president by the National Assembly. The next presidential election will take place following general elections set for May 2019.

A2. Were the current national legislative representatives elected through free and fair elections? 4 / 4

The 400-seat National Assembly is elected by party-list proportional representation. The 90 members of the upper chamber, the National Council of Provinces, are selected by provincial legislatures. In the 2014 national elections, the ANC's 62.2 percent of the vote translated into 249 of 400 seats in the National Assembly, and clear majorities in eight of nine provinces. The Democratic Alliance (DA) remained the largest opposition party, winning 89 seats with 22.2 percent of the vote, up from 16.7 percent in the previous election, and maintained control over the Western Cape. The Economic Freedom Fighters (EFF), then a new party, won 25 seats; the Inkhatha Freedom Party (IFP) took 10 seats; and nine smaller parties shared the remainder. The elections were deemed free and fair by international observers.

A3. Are the electoral laws and framework fair, and are they implemented impartially by the relevant election management bodies? 4 / 4

The IEC is largely considered independent, and the electoral framework fair, though recent years have seen some questions raised concerning the integrity of the commission's leadership. The 2017 appointment of Sy Mamabolo to the position of chief electoral officer has given new hope that the IEC will be able to reinvigorate its perception of integrity. Mamabolo is well respected and has an excellent track record in his more than two decades of work with the IEC.

In 2018, deputy IEC chairman Terry Tselane, a former ANC anti-apartheid activist, revealed that after the ANC lost control of major metropolitan municipalities such as Johannesburg and Pretoria in 2016 municipal elections, party leaders had accused him of contributing to the ANC's electoral misfortunes. Tselane stepped down from the IEC in November, saying he had been asked to do so a few weeks ahead of schedule; sitting commissioner Janet Love replaced him as deputy chair, and the commission's three vacancies were filled shortly afterward. One of the seats went to former chief electoral officer Mosotho Moepya. His appointment prompted some controversy, as years earlier a public prosecutor had recommended disciplinary action against him in connection with a probe into the improper procurement of a lease for IEC headquarters.

The IEC has been working to comply with a 2016 Constitutional Court directive that it accurately record the addresses of all voters on the roll. In 2017, the IEC launched an online campaign to encourage South Africa's 26 million registered voters to check their details and update them accordingly. In 2018 it asked for, and was granted, the postponement of its implementation; it cited logistical difficulties and a need for more time to accurately capture the addresses of voters. The body expects to complete the process by November 2019.

B. POLITICAL PLURALISM AND PARTICIPATION: 13 / 16

B1. Do the people have the right to organize in different political parties or other competitive political groupings of their choice, and is the system free of undue obstacles to the rise and fall of these competing parties or groupings? 3 / 4

The ANC, which is part of a tripartite governing alliance with the Congress of South African Trade Unions (COSATU) and the South African Communist Party (SACP), has won every election since 1994. Nevertheless, the political environment is generally free from formal constraints, and opposition parties have gained significant ground in recent elections. Several new groupings have also recently emerged. The country's biggest union—the National Union of Metalworkers of South Africa, which represents mostly private-sector workers—is sponsoring the establishment of a socialist party. The former Democratic Alliance mayor of Cape Town, Patricia de Lille, has also formed her own party after her bitter resignation from the official opposition that governs the Western Cape Province and the city.

Independent candidates may not run for national office, though Mosiuoa Lekota, the leader of the small opposition Congress of the People (COPE), is sponsoring a law that would change this.

Nontransparent mechanisms for the funding of political parties have benefit the ANC, though reforms to party financing laws were being discussed in 2018.

Over two dozen political murders have taken place in KwaZulu-Natal Province since early 2016. In 2017, ANC deputy chairperson of Harry Gwala region, Khaya Thobela, died after being shot in his home. The same year, former ANC Youth League leader Sindiso Magaqa was shot and later died in the hospital.

B2. Is there a realistic opportunity for the opposition to increase its support or gain power through elections? 3 / 4

The ANC has won every election since 1994. It won the 2014 polls by a comfortable margin but with a smaller majority than in previous elections—a trend that has persisted for three consecutive elections. In the 2016 municipal elections, the ANC's support declined to its lowest level—53.9 percent—since it took power. The party also lost control of major municipalities, including Tshwane, the metropolitan area that includes Pretoria, the national capital. Opposition gains in local elections in South Africa are especially significant because of the taxation powers and autonomy afforded to municipalities, presenting opposition parties with an opportunity to demonstrate governance capacity.

B3. Are the people's political choices free from domination by the military, foreign powers, religious hierarchies, economic oligarchies, or any other powerful group that is not democratically accountable? 3 / 4

People's political choices in South Africa are largely free from domination from external actors, and the military is professional and generally stays out of politics. However, there is widespread corruption within the ANC, including vote buying from delegates to the party conference and bribes to influence political appointments. There have also been reports of individuals buying party membership cards in bulk in order to hold full control of specific branches of the party. A 2016 report on state capture, issued by a former public prosecutor, and other investigations revealed that the Gupta family's close relationship with Zuma enabled it to exercise influence over a wide range of political and economic activities.

Despite fears that Zuma, and the Guptas, would use vote-buying tactics to engineer the election of their favored candidate as party president at the December 2017 ANC congress, Ramaphosa—a figure perceived to be opposed to the Zuma faction—emerged victorious.

B4. Do various segments of the population (including ethnic, religious, gender, LGBT, and other relevant groups) have full political rights and electoral opportunities? 4 / 4

The constitution prohibits discrimination and provides full political rights for all adult citizens. Women are well represented in government, holding 42 percent of the seats in the National Assembly and two of nine provincial premierships. South Africa has one of the world's most liberal legal environments for LGBT (lesbian, gay, bisexual, and transgender) people. However, in practice discrimination and the threat of violence can discourage LGBT people from political participation.

C. FUNCTIONING OF GOVERNMENT: 8 / 12 (+1)

C1. Do the freely elected head of government and national legislative representatives determine the policies of the government? 3 / 4 (+1)

Pervasive corruption and apparent interference by nonelected actors has hampered the proper functioning of government, particularly during the Zuma administration, in which the Gupta family had great influence. However, Ramaphosa has promised to clean up corruption. In January 2018, he appointed a Judicial Commission of Inquiry into state capture, or external influence held over an administration—in this case that of the Gupta family over Zuma's. Ramaphosa also amended the terms of the state capture inquiry to pave the way for evidence gathered to be used in prosecutions. Significantly, the ANC supports the inquiry's work, even as its leaders stand to be exposed for culpability. The public nature of the inquiry and the participation of senior ministers and commercial banks in it have allowed the commission to establish credibility, and there are increasing signs that the South African public resents the dominance of unaccountable groups and supports the use of available mechanisms to eject state capturers.

Testimony offered at the state capture commission, as well as media reports, strongly suggest that the Gupta family held vast influence in government. For example, the group of brothers was reportedly able to convince top ANC leaders, including Zuma and some in his cabinet, to pressure South African banks to reopen bank accounts that had been shut due to suspicions of money laundering activities. The brothers also reportedly held influence over Zuma's cabinet selections, and board posts at state-owned companies. The Ramaphosa administration has removed figures linked to the Guptas from the boards of such companies, including the logistics firm Transnet, energy utility Eskom, and arms manufacturer Denel. At the end of 2018, the Gupta brothers were living in Dubai, having left South Africa to avoid prosecution.

Score Change: The score improved from 2 to 3 because the powerful Gupta family's influence on governance has been curtailed since government and media investigations revealed the extent of influence they had within the Jacob Zuma administration.

C2. Are safeguards against official corruption strong and effective? 2 / 4

Comprehensive anticorruption laws and several agencies tasked with combating corruption exist, but enforcement has been inadequate. However, in 2017, the Supreme Court of Appeal (SCA) upheld a 2016 High Court ruling to reinstate 783 corruption charges that had been brought against Zuma before he became president. Since he was removed from office, he has appeared in court on corruption charges.

The government's anticorruption stance in the past was predominantly rhetorical because the National Prosecuting Authority was hobbled by political interference by Zuma and his allies. However, Ramaphosa appointed highly regarded prosecutor Shamila Batohi as head of the National Prosecuting Authority (NPA) in December 2018; the appointment was preceded by a transparent interview process that was open to the media—the first of its kind. Given Ramaphosa's public undertaking to clean up the NPA, and Batohi's promise to professionalize it, there is hope for improvements in the institution's performance in prosecuting both petty corruption cases, as well as large-scale corruption cases likely to arise from the state capture commission of inquiry.

Ramaphosa in November also sacked Tom Moyane, the head of the South African Revenue Services (SARS), who presided over a corruption-riddled and mismanaged agency; his sacking followed a recommendation by retired judge Robert Nugent, who had been appointed by Ramaphosa to investigate the governance failures of what was once a world-class revenue collector. In addition to the axing of Moyane, Nugent recommended wide-ranging changes at SARS, including changing the governance structure and appointing more competent officials to run it.

C3. Does the government operate with openness and transparency? 3 / 4

Section 32(1) of the South African constitution states that everyone has the right to access "any information held by the state" and requires that private bodies release information necessary for the exercise and protection of rights. The 2000 Promotion of Access to Information Act created a framework for access to information procedures in both public and private entities. However, in practice the procedure of accessing information is laborious and bureaucratic.

State contracts worth hundreds of millions of rand were awarded to companies linked to the Gupta family without following proper procedures. A similar lack of transparency and competitive bidding has affected the awarding of other government contracts.

CIVIL LIBERTIES: 46 / 60
D. FREEDOM OF EXPRESSION AND BELIEF: 15 / 16
D1. Are there free and independent media? 3 / 4

Freedom of expression and the press are protected in the constitution and generally respected in practice. South Africa features a vibrant and often adversarial media landscape, including independent civic groups that help counter government efforts to encroach on freedom of expression. In 2017, the media played a crucial role in exposing the corruption linked to the Gupta family and the involvement of British public relations firm Bell Pottinger in stirring up racial tensions in the country.

However, journalists face harassment for critical reporting and occasional attack, and the government has exerted pressure on both state-run and independent outlets. In a high-profile incident in October 2018, the *Sunday Times* printed an apology for several stories printed in past years it said had been inaccurate, adding, "we committed mistakes and allowed ourselves to be manipulated by those with ulterior motives." The controversy involving one of the country's most prominent newspapers prompted talk by the ANC about dusting off its plan to establish a media appeals tribunal, which media practitioners have consistently criticized.

Journalists and rights groups have expressed concern that the misuse of surveillance laws, notably the 2002 Regulation of Interception of Communications and Provision of Communication-Related Information Act (RICA), can enable spying on reporters. In 2017, the amaBhungane Centre for Investigative Journalism launched a constitutional challenge to the act, which was ongoing at the end of 2018.

D2. Are individuals free to practice and express their religious faith or nonbelief in public and private? 4 / 4

Freedom of religion is constitutionally guaranteed and actively protected by the government. Religious leaders are largely free to engage in discussions of a political nature without fear of adverse consequences.

D3. Is there academic freedom, and is the educational system free from extensive political indoctrination? 4 / 4

Academic freedom in South Africa is constitutionally guaranteed and actively protected by the government.

D4. Are individuals free to express their personal views on political or other sensitive topics without fear of surveillance or retribution? 4 / 4

South Africans are generally free to engage in private conversations of a political nature without harassment. However, a 2016 report from the UN Human Rights Committee expressed concern about the government's use of surveillance and about RICA, the law governing surveillance. A legal challenge to RICA was ongoing at the end of 2018.

E. ASSOCIATIONAL AND ORGANIZATIONAL RIGHTS: 12 / 12
E1. Is there freedom of assembly? 4 / 4

Freedom of assembly is constitutionally guaranteed and generally respected, and South Africa has a vibrant protest culture. Demonstrators must notify police of events ahead of time, but are rarely prohibited from gathering; in November 2018, the Constitutional Court ruled that a failure to notify authorities of intent to protest could not be classified as a crime. Protests over the government's shortcomings in the provision of public services are common in South Africa, and sometimes turn violent. Police have faced accusations of provoking some protest violence.

E2. Is there freedom for nongovernmental organizations, particularly those that are engaged in human rights– and governance-related work? 4 / 4

South Africa hosts a vibrant civil society. Nongovernmental organizations (NGOs) can register and operate freely, and lawmakers regularly accept input from NGOs on pending legislation.

E3. Is there freedom for trade unions and similar professional or labor organizations? 4 / 4

South African workers are generally free to form, join, and participate in independent trade unions, and the country's labor laws offer unionized workers a litany of protections.

Contract workers and those in the informal sector enjoy fewer safeguards. Strike activity is very common, and unionized workers often secure above-inflation wage increases. Union rivalries, especially in mining, sometimes result in the use of violent tactics to recruit and retain members and to attack opponents.

F. RULE OF LAW: 9 / 16

F1. Is there an independent judiciary? 3 / 4

The constitution guarantees judicial independence, and courts operate with substantial autonomy. The Judicial Services Commission recommends to the president the appointment of Constitutional Court judges based on both merit and efforts to racially diversify the judiciary.

A number of recent court judgments held the executive and legislative branches to account in such a manner as to suggest that the judiciary commands significant independence. In 2017, the Constitutional Court ruled that the vote of no confidence for Zuma could be held by secret ballot, and left the decision on whether to use this method to the speaker of the national assembly, which they did. The SCA's ruling that same year allowing corruption charges against Zuma to be reinstated also demonstrated the independence of the judiciary.

F2. Does due process prevail in civil and criminal matters? 2 / 4

Prosecutorial independence in South Africa has been undermined in recent years; notably, the NPA experienced a string of politically motivated appointments and ousters. However, Ramaphosa appointed a new NPA head in 2018, who is seeking to reform the institution.

Shortages of judicial staff and financial resources undermine defendants' procedural rights, including the right to a timely trial and state-funded legal counsel. Many detainees wait months for their trials to begin, and some are held beyond the legal maximum of two years.

F3. Is there protection from the illegitimate use of physical force and freedom from war and insurgencies? 2 / 4

According to a Judicial Inspectorate for Correctional Services (JICS) 2017–18 annual report, there is severe overcrowding in some prisons—in part due to delays in holding trials. During this period, 82 unnatural deaths were reported in prisons, and there were 988 complaints of assault by prison officials on inmates.

Despite constitutional prohibitions, there are many reports of police torture and excessive force during arrest, interrogation, and detention. The Independent Police Investigative Directorate (IPID) is required by law to investigate allegations of police offenses or misconduct. In its annual report for the 2017–18 fiscal year, the IPID recorded 637 reported deaths either in police custody or as a result of police action, 105 reported rapes by police officers, 217 reports of torture, and 3,661 reports of assault. Overall, there was a 19 percent decrease in total reported incidents from the previous period.

Official statistics released in 2018 continue to show high levels of violent crimes in some parts of the country.

F4. Do laws, policies, and practices guarantee equal treatment of various segments of the population? 2 / 4

The constitution prohibits discrimination based on a range of categories, including race, sexual orientation, and culture. State bodies such as the South African Human Rights Commission (SAHRC) and the Office of the Public Protector are empowered to investigate and prosecute discrimination cases. Affirmative-action legislation has benefited previously disadvantaged racial groups in public and private employment as well as in education but racial imbalances in the workforce persist. White people, constituting a small minority, still own a majority of the country's business assets. The indigenous, nomadic Khoikhoi and Khomani San peoples suffer from social and legal discrimination.

The constitution guarantees equal rights for women, which are actively promoted by the Commission on Gender Equality. Nevertheless, women are subject to wage discrimination in the workplace and are not well represented in top management positions.

Xenophobic violence against immigrants from other African countries has broken out sporadically in recent years. In August 2018, at least four people were killed, many more were injured, and shops were looted during xenophobic mob attacks in Soweto that targeted Somali shop owners; the attacks were reportedly sparked by rumors circulating on social media that the storeowners were selling fake or expired goods, which were then picked up by the media. Political leadership on countering xenophobic violence has been lacking, and in some cases political leaders have blamed foreign nationals for their own failure to deliver on political promises. However, in May 2018, regional authorities provided protection to foreign merchants in KwaZulu-Natal after they were threatened by a business association.

There are frequent reports of physical attacks against LGBT people, including instances of so-called corrective rape, in which men rape lesbians, claiming that the action can change the victim's sexual orientation.

Services and accommodations for disabled people remain generally inadequate. In 2018, some 600,000 disabled children were not able to attend school, according to Human Rights Watch (HRW).

G. PERSONAL AUTONOMY AND INDIVIDUAL RIGHTS: 10 / 16

G1. Do individuals enjoy freedom of movement, including the ability to change their place of residence, employment, or education? 3 / 4

While there are no official restrictions on housing, employment, or freedom of movement for most South Africans, travel and some other personal freedoms are inhibited by the country's high crime rate. For many foreigners, the threat of xenophobic violence impedes freedom of movement as well. The legacy of apartheid continues to segregate the population and restrict nonwhite opportunity for employment and education.

G2. Are individuals able to exercise the right to own property and establish private businesses without undue interference from state or nonstate actors? 3 / 4

The state generally protects citizens from arbitrary deprivation of property. However, the vast majority of farmland remains in the hands of white South Africans, who make up some 9 percent of the population. Illegal squatting on white-owned farms is common, as are attacks on white farm owners.

At its 54th elective conference in December 2017, the ANC resolved there was a need to expropriate land without compensation for redistribution purposes, on the condition that such expropriation should not negatively affect the economy or compromise food security. Since then, there has been intense public debate about the best way to effect meaningful land reform to address apartheid-era inequalities in property ownership.

Despite constitutional protections, women suffer de facto discrimination with regard to inheritance and property rights, particularly in rural areas.

G3. Do individuals enjoy personal social freedoms, including choice of marriage partner and size of family, protection from domestic violence, and control over appearance? 2 / 4

Despite a robust legal framework criminalizing domestic violence and rape, both are grave problems. Only a small percentage of rapes are reported. According to the 2017–18

South Africa Police Service report, an average of 109.7 rapes were recorded each day. Sexual harassment is common, and reports of forced marriages persist.

Same-sex couples have the same adoption rights as heterosexual married couples, and same-sex marriage is legal.

G4. Do Individuals enjoy equality of opportunity and freedom from economic exploitation? 2 / 4

Inequality levels in South Africa are among the highest in the world. Only a small percentage of the population benefits from large state industries, and the economy is controlled by a relatively small number of people belonging to the political and business elite. The government, businesses, and the biggest labor federation agreed to institute a minimum wage, to go into effect at the start of 2019, that could benefit more than six million poor workers. High levels of unemployment persist.

South Africans predominantly from rural regions, as well as foreign migrants, are vulnerable to sex trafficking and forced labor. Organized criminal syndicates are responsible for the bulk of trafficking.

South Korea

Population: 51,800,000
Capital: Seoul
Political Rights Rating: 2
Civil Liberties Rating: 2
Freedom Rating: 2.0
Freedom Status: Free
Electoral Democracy: Yes

Overview: South Korea's democratic system features regular rotations of power and robust political pluralism, with the largest parties representing conservative and liberal views. Personal freedoms are generally respected, though the country struggles with minority rights and social integration. Legal bans on pro–North Korean activity have sometimes affected legitimate political expression, though since the start of inter-Korean rapprochement in early 2018, there has been greater pressure on those airing negative views of North Korea and inter-Korean engagement.

KEY DEVELOPMENTS IN 2018:

- The government of President Moon Jae-in pursued a peace and security dialogue with North Korea that began with talks on the North's participation in the February Winter Olympics in South Korea and soon led to meetings between Moon and North Korean leader Kim Jong-un in April, May, and September. The rapprochement was accompanied by government efforts to exclude or pressure specific journalists and activists who were seen as threats to Moon's foreign policy efforts.
- The ruling party performed well in June local elections, but numerous scandals within the Moon administration and a lack of economic progress contributed to social unrest and the resumption of large-scale weekend protests in the second half of the year.

- Also during the year, former presidents Park Geun-hye, who had been impeached and removed from office in 2017, and Lee Myung-bak were both sentenced to lengthy prison terms for corruption-related offenses.

POLITICAL RIGHTS: 33 / 40
A. ELECTORAL PROCESS: 11 / 12
A1. Was the current head of government or other chief national authority elected through free and fair elections? 4 / 4

The 1988 constitution vests executive power in a directly elected president, who is limited to a single five-year term. Executive elections in South Korea are largely free and fair. Moon Jae-in of the liberal Minjoo Party won a May 2017 snap presidential election following the impeachment of former president Park. He took 41 percent of the vote, followed by Hong Jun-pyo of the conservative Liberty Korea Party with 24 percent and Ahn Cheol-soo of the centrist People's Party with 21 percent. About 77 percent of registered voters turned out for the election.

In the June 2018 local elections, the Minjoo Party won 14 of 17 metropolitan mayoral and gubernatorial offices, with two of the others going to the Liberty Korea Party and one to an independent. Turnout for the local elections was 60.2 percent, marking the first time the voting rate had surpassed 60 percent for local elections since 1995.

A2. Were the current national legislative representatives elected through free and fair elections? 4 / 4

The unicameral National Assembly is composed of 300 members serving four-year terms, with 253 elected in single-member constituencies and 47 through national party lists. The contests are typically free of major irregularities. In the 2016 elections, the Minjoo Party won 123 seats, while the Saenuri Party (which later became the Liberty Korea Party) won 122. The People's Party took 38 seats, and minor parties and independents secured the remaining 17 seats.

A3. Are the electoral laws and framework fair, and are they implemented impartially by the relevant election management bodies? 3 / 4

Elections are managed by the National Election Commission, an independent nine-member body appointed for six-year terms. Three members are chosen by the president, three by the National Assembly, and three by the Supreme Court.

While elections are generally considered free and fair, National Assembly constituencies have historically been affected by malapportionment, giving outsized voting power to thinly populated rural areas. A revised map adopted for the 2016 elections mitigated the problem, in keeping with a 2014 Constitutional Court ruling, though the largest constituency population can still be twice the size of the smallest.

B. POLITICAL PLURALISM AND PARTICIPATION: 13 / 16
B1. Do the people have the right to organize in different political parties or other competitive political groupings of their choice, and is the system free of undue obstacles to the rise and fall of these competing parties or groupings? 3 / 4

Political pluralism is robust, with multiple parties competing for power, though party structures and coalitions are rather fluid. In addition to the two main parties—the liberal Minjoo Party and conservative Liberty Korea Party—several smaller groups are represented in the National Assembly, as are a handful of unaffiliated members. Only once has the

Constitutional Court legally dissolved a political party—the United Progressive Party in 2014—for violations of the National Security Law, which bans pro–North Korean activities.

B2. Is there a realistic opportunity for the opposition to increase its support or gain power through elections? 4 / 4

There have been multiple transfers of power between rival conservative and liberal parties since the early 1990s, and the orderly election and inauguration of President Moon in 2017 reinforced this democratic pattern.

B3. Are the people's political choices free from domination by the military, foreign powers, religious hierarchies, economic oligarchies, or any other powerful group that is not democratically accountable? 3 / 4

Family-controlled business empires known as *chaebol* dominate the country's economy and have amassed significant political influence, which generally enables them to protect their interests despite calls for reform. Corruption scandals involving bribery by the chaebol have affected almost all of South Korea's former presidents.

The National Intelligence Service (NIS) has been implicated in a series of scandals in recent years, including allegations that it sought to influence the 2012 presidential election and later conducted illegal surveillance targeting Park's opponents.

B4. Do various segments of the population (including ethnic, religious, gender, LGBT, and other relevant groups) have full political rights and electoral opportunities? 3 / 4

Although the country's few ethnic minority citizens enjoy full political rights under the law, they rarely win political representation. There were no lawmakers of non-Korean ethnicity in the National Assembly as of 2018. Residents who are not ethnic Koreans face extreme difficulties obtaining citizenship, which is based on parentage. North Korean defectors are eligible for citizenship.

Women also enjoy legal equality but remain underrepresented, with just 17 percent of the seats in the National Assembly. Conservative Christian groups have used their political influence to prevent legislators from adopting stronger laws that would protect LGBT (lesbian, gay, bisexual, and transgender) people from discrimination.

C. FUNCTIONING OF GOVERNMENT: 9 / 12

C1. Do the freely elected head of government and national legislative representatives determine the policies of the government? 4 / 4

Elected officials generally determine and implement state policy without undue interference from unelected entities and interests.

C2. Are safeguards against official corruption strong and effective? 3 / 4

Despite government anticorruption efforts, bribery, influence peddling, and extortion persist in politics, business, and everyday life. The Kim Young-ran Act, or Improper Solicitation and Graft Act, establishes stiff punishments for those convicted of accepting bribes. The law, which took effect in 2016, applies to government officials as well as their spouses, journalists, and educators.

Corruption scandals have affected the highest levels of government in recent years. Former president Park, who was impeached in late 2016 and removed from office in 2017, was convicted by a lower court in April 2018 on a number of charges, including bribery, revealing state secrets, and abuse of power; she was sentenced to 24 years in prison. In a parallel case in July, she received a sentence of eight years in prison for violation of election laws and illegal receipt of funds from a state agency. The next month, a Seoul appeals court upheld the first conviction but added another year to Park's sentence, for a total of 25 years in that case. A final appeal was pending in the Supreme Court at year's end. Separately in October, former president Lee Myung-bak was convicted of bribery and embezzlement, both while he was campaigning for the presidency and during his time in office (2008–13); he was sentenced to 15 years in prison.

Several people from Park's administration and its partners in the private sector have been convicted of related crimes. Lee Jae-young, heir to the Samsung conglomerate, was sentenced in 2017 to five years in prison for paying $7.8 million in bribes to secure Park's support for a business deal that strengthened his control over Samsung Electronics. In February 2018, Lee's sentence was reduced and suspended, and he was released from prison, after an appeals court lowered the estimate of the bribes to $3.3 million; he was awaiting a final ruling from the Supreme Court at year's end.

C3. Does the government operate with openness and transparency? 2 / 4

The investigations surrounding Park's impeachment illuminated extensive collusion between Park and her friend and main coconspirator, Choi Soon-sil, that also involved business conglomerates and the national pension fund, among other entities, affecting government decision-making on a variety of topics. Despite Moon's pledge to increase transparency and reduce corruption, his administration has had several similar problems.

In March 2018, former National Assembly member Kim Ki-sik was appointed as the new head of the Financial Supervisory Service (FSS), but he resigned 17 days later, in mid-April, after the National Election Commission ruled that a large political donation he made before the end of his National Assembly term violated the Public Official Election Act. Also in April, funding for a Korea-focused research center at a US university was abruptly cut by the Korean government after the center refused the government's demands to replace its leadership and adopt rules that would give the government direct influence over its operations. The funding was granted by the Korea Institute for International Economic Policy (KIEP), but the decision to withdraw funding was made at the board level of the National Research Council (NRC). The administration denied involvement, but evidence later showed that enormous pressure to make this decision had been placed on KIEP and NRC by presidential aides.

In August, President Moon dismissed Hwang Soo-kyeong, the commissioner of Statistics Korea, after the agency reported negative income and employment statistics and Hwang refused the president's request to change the statistical methodology. She was replaced by Kang Shin-wook, a former researcher at the Korea Institute for Health and Social Affairs who had proposed a redesign and reinterpretation of the controversial analysis to achieve more positive results.

CIVIL LIBERTIES: 50 / 60 (−1)
D. FREEDOM OF EXPRESSION AND BELIEF: 14 / 16
D1. Are there free and independent media? 3 / 4

The news media are generally free and competitive, reporting aggressively on government policies and allegations of official and corporate wrongdoing. However, a defamation law authorizes sentences of up to seven years in prison, encouraging a certain degree of self-censorship, and journalists at major news outlets often face political interference from managers or the government.

News coverage or commentary that is deemed to favor North Korea can be censored and lead to prosecution under the National Security Law, and access to North Korean media is banned. Nevertheless, under President Moon in 2018 there was pressure to keep media coverage of North Korea and the inter-Korean diplomatic process relatively positive. During the third summit between Moon and Kim Jong-un, held in Pyongyang in September, a Korean Voice of America (VOA) journalist was removed from an official messaging group, which was meant to update foreign media on summit events, after he reported stories about South Korean involvement in North Korea's evasion of sanctions on its coal exports.

In October, the Ministry of Unification (MOU) preemptively banned *Chosun Ilbo* newspaper reporter Kim Myeong-sung from covering high-level inter-Korean talks because of his status as a North Korean defector. MOU apparently decided that his presence could jeopardize the success of the talks and threatened to ban *Chosun Ilbo* from the press pool entirely if Kim was not replaced. South Korean and international press freedom and human rights groups condemned the decision.

D2. Are individuals free to practice and express their religious faith or nonbelief in public and private? 4 / 4

Freedom of religion is guaranteed by the constitution and generally respected in practice. However, the military conscription system makes no allowances for conscientious objection, and hundreds of men—nearly all of them Jehovah's Witnesses—are imprisoned at any given time for refusing military service. In June 2018, the Constitutional Court upheld the punishment of conscientious objectors, but it also ruled that failure to provide alternative forms of service was unconstitutional and required the government to rewrite the Military Service Act so as to introduce such options by the end of 2019. In November, the Supreme Court acquitted a man who refused military service due to religious beliefs, overturning a ruling made in 2004 and potentially setting a precedent for 227 similar cases pending in the Supreme Court and for more than 900 conscientious objectors currently on trial.

D3. Is there academic freedom, and is the educational system free from extensive political indoctrination? 3 / 4

Academic freedom is mostly unrestricted, though the National Security Law limits statements supporting the North Korean regime. The 2016 anticorruption law subjects teachers and administrators to the same tight restrictions as public officials. Certain portrayals of sensitive historical issues—such as imperial Japan's wartime sexual enslavement of Korean women, known as "comfort women"—can be subject to government censorship or prosecution under the country's defamation laws.

D4. Are individuals free to express their personal views on political or other sensitive topics without fear of surveillance or retribution? 4 / 4

Private discussion is typically free and open, and the government generally respects citizens' right to privacy. A 2016 antiterrorism law granted the NIS expanded authority to monitor private communications, and the measure's vague definition of "terrorism" raised concerns that it would enable the agency to track government critics, particularly online. The National Security Law restricts speech that is considered pro–North Korean. However, the law was not strictly enforced amid the inter-Korean diplomatic process during 2018; concerns about potential constraints on free expression shifted to those who opposed or could complicate rapprochement with the North, including North Korean defectors and human rights activists.

E. ASSOCIATIONAL AND ORGANIZATIONAL RIGHTS: 11 / 12
E1. Is there freedom of assembly? 4 / 4

The government generally respects freedom of assembly, which is protected under the constitution. However, several legal provisions conflict with this guarantee, sometimes creating tension between the police and protesters over the application of the law.

Beginning in May 2018, a series of mass protests were organized to demand a stronger government response to the phenomenon of illegal hidden cameras targeting women, especially in public restrooms, with the resulting images often posted online. In September, the first LGBT festival ever held in Incheon was met by a group of some 1,000 counterprotesters. Police arrested eight of the anti-LGBT demonstrators. In the second half of the year, large weekend protests took place in downtown Seoul, with tens of thousands of people gathering peacefully to air views on a range of issues, including support for Park Geun-hye's release, opposition to Moon's policy toward North Korea, and demands for stronger labor protections. In November, an estimated 160,000 workers led by the Korean Confederation of Trade Unions held a half-day strike across the country, accusing the government of taking steps to roll back policies that favored labor.

E2. Is there freedom for nongovernmental organizations, particularly those that are engaged in human rights- and governance-related work? 3 / 4

Human rights groups and other nongovernmental organizations (NGOs) are active and generally operate freely, though they have occasionally faced political pressure when they criticize the government or other powerful interests. Many South Korean NGOs rely on government grants, despite their independent agendas. In June 2018, the Moon administration cut funding for the planned Seoul office of the North Korea Human Rights Foundation, an organization envisioned in the 2016 North Korean Human Rights Act that had yet to be fully established by the MOU. The foundation was tasked in part with issuing funding to NGOs working on North Korean human rights issues. A number of such groups experienced difficulty in obtaining both public and corporate funding during the year. There were also reports that the government discouraged activists from engaging in speech or events that could jeopardize the diplomatic process.

E3. Is there freedom for trade unions and similar professional or labor organizations? 4 / 4

Workers have the right to form independent unions and engage in strikes and collective bargaining. The country's independent labor unions advocate for workers' interests in practice, organizing high-profile strikes and demonstrations that sometimes lead to arrests. However, labor unions in general have diminished in strength and popularity, especially as the employment of temporary workers increases. Some major employers reportedly engage in antiunion activity, though in a sign of the state's willingness to enforce workers' rights, prosecutors in September 2018 charged 32 executives from Samsung and its associated firms with illegally preventing employees from creating and participating in labor unions since 2013.

In September 2017, journalism unions organized strikes to protest attacks on editorial independence as well as unfair labor practices at the two main public broadcasters, and to call for the resignations of their chief executives. Two months after the strikes began, the union members at one broadcaster, Munhwa Broadcasting Corporation (MBC), ended their strike following the MBC president's dismissal. In January 2018, union members at the second network, Korean Broadcasting System (KBS), ended their strike after the KBS president was also terminated by the board of directors.

F. RULE OF LAW: 12 / 16 (−1)

F1. Is there an independent judiciary? 3 / 4 (−1)

The judiciary is generally considered to be independent. The chief justice and justices of the Supreme Court are appointed by the president with the consent of the National Assembly. The appointments are made based on recommendations from the chief justice, who is assisted by an expert advisory committee. The chief justice is also responsible for appointments to the lower courts, with the consent of the other Supreme Court justices. The president, the National Assembly, and the chief justice each nominate three members of the Constitutional Court.

In June 2018, investigations began into the Supreme Court's National Court Administration (NCA), which manages the judicial branch's daily operations and administrative tasks. The NCA and Yang Sung-tae, who served as chief justice from 2011 to 2017, were accused of influencing trials and suits in favor of the Park administration, paying off judges through a slush fund that drew resources from lower courts, and other related crimes. In September, prosecutors raided the office of a former presidential legal secretary, Kim Jong-il, who was suspected of serving as a liaison between the NCA and Park's office. The current Supreme Court chief justice, Kim Myeong-su, said in September that the NCA would be dissolved and a new council staffed by outside experts would be created.

Score Change: The score declined from 4 to 3 due to revelations indicating corruption centered on the Supreme Court and improper collusion between the former chief justice and the Park administration.

F2. Does due process prevail in civil and criminal matters? 3 / 4

Judges render verdicts in all cases. While there is no trial by jury, an advisory jury system has been in place since 2008, and judges largely respect juries' decisions. Ordinary legal proceedings are generally considered fair, but the courts have sometimes been accused of denying due process and impartiality to defendants in National Security Law cases.

F3. Is there protection from the illegitimate use of physical force and freedom from war and insurgencies? 3 / 4

Reports of abuse by guards in South Korea's prisons are infrequent, and prison conditions generally meet international standards. Violent crime is relatively rare, but the country is still technically at war with North Korea, resulting in a heavy military presence in some areas and the constant threat of renewed combat. Minor incidents of violence near the de facto border are not uncommon, although in September 2018, the two Koreas signed a military confidence-building agreement calling for measures to reduce the military buildup along the Demilitarized Zone (DMZ).

F4. Do laws, policies, and practices guarantee equal treatment of various segments of the population? 3 / 4

South Korea lacks a comprehensive antidiscrimination law. Members of the country's small population of ethnic minorities encounter legal and societal discrimination. Children of foreign-born residents suffer from systemic exclusion from the education and medical systems. There are about 30,000 North Korean defectors in South Korea. They can face months of detention and interrogations upon arrival, and some have reported abuse in custody and societal discrimination.

Women generally enjoy legal equality but face social and employment discrimination in practice. South Korea has the highest gender pay gap among Organisation for Economic Co-operation and Development (OECD) countries, at 37.2 percent in 2017, with women earning on average only 63 percent as much as their male counterparts. In November 2018, the Supreme Court upheld a lower court ruling that sentenced Park Gi-dong, former chief executive of Korea Gas Safety Corporation (KGS), to four years in prison for discriminatory recruiting practices, including falsifying interview scores to select men over women because he believed female employees would take maternity leave and thus impede work progress.

Sexual harassment of women in the workplace is common, and the #MeToo movement against such abuses has gained momentum. In January 2018, public prosecutor Seo Ji-hy-eon accused former senior Justice Ministry official Ahn Tae-geun of sexual harassment and abuse of power; she claimed that news of her case caused her to be transferred to a less prominent branch. Since then, there have been many prominent cases of accusations and apologies for sexual harassment in the workplace as well as the illegal placement of hidden cameras in public women's restrooms. In August, former presidential hopeful Ahn Hee-jung was acquitted of sexual assault by the Seoul Western District Court. His secretary had accused him of assault in March, but the court found that there was not enough evidence to prove she had been coerced.

Same-sex sexual relations are generally legal, and the law bars discrimination based on sexual orientation. However, there are no specific penalties for such discrimination, and transgender people are not protected as such. A "disgraceful conduct" provision of the Military Criminal Act is used to punish sexual acts between male soldiers.

G. PERSONAL AUTONOMY AND INDIVIDUAL RIGHTS: 13 / 16

G1. Do individuals enjoy freedom of movement, including the ability to change their place of residence, employment, or education? 4 / 4

Travel both within South Korea and abroad is unrestricted, except for travel to North Korea, which requires government approval. School is free for children between the ages of 6 and 15, but senior high schools charge modest tuition fees, and many families spend heavily on private academies to supplement public education. Individuals can change jobs freely, though the leading business conglomerates tend to focus their recruitment on graduates of specific universities.

G2. Are individuals able to exercise the right to own property and establish private businesses without undue interference from state or nonstate actors? 3 / 4

South Korea fully recognizes property rights and has a well-developed body of laws governing the establishment of commercial enterprises. However, the economy remains dominated by large family-owned conglomerates that have been accused of collusion with political figures.

The inter-Korean rapprochement process has led to pressure from President Moon on some of South Korea's chaebol, especially Samsung, to create investment plans for North Korea that can be offered as part of formal negotiations. Lee Jae-young, the Samsung vice chairman whose corruption case was still being adjudicated in 2018, was considered a key delegate to the inter-Korean summit in Pyongyang in September.

G3. Do individuals enjoy personal social freedoms, including choice of marriage partner and size of family, protection from domestic violence, and control over appearance? 3 / 4

Women generally have equal rights in divorce and custody matters. Marriage and other forms of legal partnership are not available to same-sex partners. Abortion is considered a crime punishable with imprisonment except in cases of rape, incest, threats to the mother's health, or designated disorders or diseases; all abortions after 24 weeks of pregnancy are prohibited. Domestic violence is common, despite laws in place to prevent such crimes.

G4. Do individuals enjoy equality of opportunity and freedom from economic exploitation? 3 / 4

Protections against exploitative working conditions are enforced by the authorities. Nevertheless, foreign migrant workers remain vulnerable to illegal debt bondage and forced labor, including forced prostitution. Korean women and foreign women recruited by international marriage brokers can also become sex-trafficking victims. Although the government actively prosecutes human trafficking cases, those convicted often receive light punishments.

South Sudan

Population: 13,000,000
Capital: Juba
Political Rights Rating: 7
Civil Liberties Rating: 7
Freedom Rating: 7.0
Freedom Status: Not Free
Electoral Democracy: No

Overview: South Sudan, which gained independence from Sudan in 2011, descended into civil war in 2013, when a rift between President Salva Kiir and the vice president he dismissed, Riek Machar, triggered fighting among their supporters and divided the country along ethnic lines. A peace agreement reached in 2018 further delayed overdue national elections, instituting an uneasy power-sharing arrangement among political elites who have presided over rampant corruption, economic collapse, and atrocities against civilians, journalists, and aid workers.

KEY DEVELOPMENTS IN 2018:

- Under pressure from the international community, President Kiir and rebel leader Riek Machar signed a peace deal in September to end the civil war. The agreement barely differed from a 2015 agreement that was repeatedly broken by both sides, and its implementation remained in doubt at year's end.
- Several smaller rebel factions refused to sign the peace deal, complaining that it failed to address governance issues that caused the war.
- The humanitarian crisis stemming from the war showed no signs of abating. According to the United Nations, approximately 4.3 million South Sudanese had fled abroad or were internally displaced as of late 2018. In September, the London School of Tropical Hygiene and Medicine estimated that 400,000 people had died as a direct or indirect result of the war.

POLITICAL RIGHTS: –2 / 40
A. ELECTORAL PROCESS: 1 / 12
A1. Was the current head of government or other chief national authority elected through free and fair elections? 0 / 4

Kiir was elected president of the semiautonomous region of Southern Sudan in 2010, and inherited the presidency of South Sudan at independence in 2011. A revised version of Southern Sudan's 2005 interim constitution, adopted at independence, gives sweeping powers to the chief executive. The president cannot be impeached and has the authority to fire state governors and dissolve the parliament and state assemblies. A permanent constitution was due to be passed by 2015, but a draft had yet to be published as of 2018.

Elections due in 2015 were postponed as a result of the civil war. A peace agreement reached that year extended Kiir's mandate until April 2018. In July 2018, the parliament voted to further extend Kiir's term to 2021, along with the mandates of his vice presidents, state legislators, and governors. The Revitalized Agreement on the Resolution of the Conflict in South Sudan (R-ARCSS), signed in September, reset the timetable once again, initiating an eight-month interim period after which a Revitalized Transitional Government of National Unity (RTGoNU) headed by Kiir would be formed and serve a three-year term. Riek Machar would be first vice president, alongside four additional vice presidents. The new government would include representatives from five political factions, with most members from the wing of the Sudan People's Liberation Movement (SPLM) that remained loyal to Kiir. As of end of the 2018, Kiir's incumbent government remained in place.

A2. Were the current national legislative representatives elected through free and fair elections? 0 / 4

South Sudan has not held elections for its bicameral National Legislature since 2010, and its original mandate expired in 2015; that year's peace agreement extended it to 2018. The R-ARCSS in September then extended the mandate until May 2022. The lower house, the Transitional National Legislative Assembly (TNLA), was expanded to 550 members, including 332 affiliated with Kiir's government, 128 from Machar's splinter faction of the SPLM, and the remainder from other groups. The upper house, the Council of States, was to be reformulated pending a review by a newly established body, the Independent Boundaries Commission. The IBC was tasked with deciding how many states South Sudan should have and where their borders should be; it had yet to begin its work at the end of 2018. The R-ARCSS established a power-sharing formula for state and local government posts, with Kiir loyalists receiving a 55 percent share.

A3. Are the electoral laws and framework fair, and are they implemented impartially by the relevant election management bodies? 1 / 4

The R-ARCSS called for a new, impartial National Elections Commission to be established by the end of the first year of the transition. It also mandated changes to the 2012 Electoral Act, to bring it in line with international standards. These steps were still pending as of late 2018.

B. POLITICAL PLURALISM AND PARTICIPATION: 1 / 16

B1. Do the people have the right to organize in different political parties or other competitive political groupings of their choice, and is the system free of undue obstacles to the rise and fall of these competing parties or groupings? 1 / 4

The SPLM dominates the political landscape, and most competition takes place within the movement, which splintered at the outbreak of the civil war. Kiir's hostility toward dissent within the SPLM contributed to the conflict.

The R-ARCSS granted non-SPLM parties 80 of the 550 seats in the TNLA, but they lack the resources to operate effectively and the experience to formulate policy and set party platforms.

The agreement tasked a National Constitutional Amendment Committee with reviewing the Political Parties Act of 2012 to ensure that it meets international best practices. The process was ongoing at year's end.

B2. Is there a realistic opportunity for the opposition to increase its support or gain power through elections? 0 / 4

If fully implemented, the R-ARCSS would eventually provide an opportunity for opposition groups to contest long-overdue elections. However, South Sudan's last elections, in 2010, featured violence and intimidation against opposition parties and SPLM members whose loyalty to Kiir was in doubt.

B3. Are the people's political choices free from domination by the military, foreign powers, religious hierarchies, economic oligarchies, or any other powerful group that is not democratically accountable? 0 / 4

The civil war has stifled ordinary politics and created a climate of fear. South Sudan's military, the Sudan People's Liberation Army (SPLA), exercises an overbearing influence on political affairs and public life, and the activities of various other armed groups tied to partisan and ethnic factions have made political participation by civilians all but impossible.

B4. Do various segments of the population (including ethnic, religious, gender, LGBT, and other relevant groups) have full political rights and electoral opportunities? 0 / 4

Under Kiir's leadership, the SPLM has sidelined citizens who are not members of the Dinka ethnic group. The exclusion of ethnic groups such as Machar's Nuer has gone far beyond the denial of political opportunities to include violent attacks, sexual exploitation, and the destruction of property.

In an attempt to address the chronic underrepresentation of women in political leadership positions, the R-ARCSS established a 35 percent quota for women in the planned RTGoNU.

C. FUNCTIONING OF GOVERNMENT: 0 / 12

C1. Do the freely elected head of government and national legislative representatives determine the policies of the government? 0 / 4

South Sudan's government and legislature, which lack electoral legitimacy, are unable to exercise control over the national territory.

A clique of Dinka leaders surround Kiir and exert undue influence on decision-making. The UN Security Council has accused the group of deliberately sabotaging peacemaking efforts and stirring up ethnic hatred.

Although Sudan and Uganda helped to broker the 2018 peace deal, they have supported opposing sides in the civil war, with Khartoum at times backing Machar and Kampala defending Kiir. Observers raised concerns that the two neighboring powers would continue to wield undue influence following the accord.

C2. Are safeguards against official corruption strong and effective? 0 / 4

Corruption is pervasive among political and military leaders. The state's resources, including its oil revenues, are concentrated among an elite associated with the president. Military commanders have gained enormous wealth through corrupt procurement deals. President Kiir has facilitated corruption by appointing officials who were previously accused of embezzlement. In 2017, the US Department of the Treasury froze the assets of three officials linked to Kiir, accusing them of orchestrating violence and "enriching themselves at the expense of the South Sudanese people."

C3. Does the government operate with openness and transparency? 0 / 4

Under the interim constitution, citizens have the right to access public information and records held by state entities. These rights are not respected in practice by the government, which is hostile to scrutiny and lacks the capacity to perform its functions.

ADDITIONAL DISCRETIONARY POLITICAL RIGHTS QUESTION
Is the government or occupying power deliberately changing the ethnic composition of a country or territory so as to destroy a culture or tip the political balance in favor of another group? −4 / 0

Both sides in the civil war have committed atrocities against civilians from rival ethnic groups, but government-aligned forces have been responsible for the worst attacks. In one case from 2018, UN officials found that troops loyal to Kiir had murdered more than 200 mainly Nuer civilians during an offensive in Unity State between April and May. In addition, more than 100 women and girls were reportedly raped or gang raped.

The United Nations and the African Union (AU) have documented numerous other incidents of murder, torture, rape, looting, displacement along ethnic lines, and forced starvation. Both organizations have accused Kiir's leadership of planning and coordinating such attacks. UN observers have noted the use of hate speech by senior officials, including Kiir himself.

In 2017, the UN Commission on Human Rights in South Sudan presented evidence of government attempts to reconfigure the population by flying in Dinka to take up residence in places that other ethnic groups have fled and steering humanitarian assistance in their direction.

CIVIL LIBERTIES: 4 / 60
D. FREEDOM OF EXPRESSION AND BELIEF: 2 / 16
D1. Are there free and independent media? 0 / 4

South Sudan's transitional constitution guarantees freedom of the press, but this right is not respected in practice. According to the Committee to Protect Journalists, at least six members of the media have been killed in the course of their work since 2015.

Kiir's government has threatened and detained journalists for reports it does not like or for conducting interviews with opposition officials. Defamation is prosecuted under criminal law, stifling free speech. The National Security Service (NSS) seizes pressruns of newspapers or temporarily closes media organizations that breach its arbitrary standards on what can be reported. In March 2018, the Media Regulatory Authority said it was suspending the UN-run Radio Miraya, claiming that it was in violation of its broadcasting license; the station, based in a UN compound, continued to operate.

D2. Are individuals free to practice and express their religious faith or nonbelief in public and private? 1 / 4

The interim constitution guarantees religious freedom, but houses of worship—used as places of refuge for civilians—have been attacked by gunmen seeking members of rival ethnic groups. An investigation by Radio Tamazuj in 2017 found that at least 40 church leaders had been killed since the civil war began. Places of worship have also been vulnerable to land grabs by corrupt officials. In June 2018, President Kiir acknowledged that Muslims had been targeted by these seizures and ordered property to be returned.

D3. Is there academic freedom, and is the educational system free from extensive political indoctrination? 1 / 4

There are no formal government restrictions on academic freedom. However, the education system was seriously disrupted by the civil war, with many schools closed or commandeered for military use. A report by the Assessment Capacities Project, a nongovernmental organization (NGO), estimated that by 2016, one-quarter of schools that had been open at any point since independence were nonfunctional.

D4. Are individuals free to express their personal views on political or other sensitive topics without fear of surveillance or retribution? 0 / 4

The NSS has extensive powers to conduct surveillance and monitor communications. According to the United Nations, agents have used these powers to intimidate and detain journalists, opposition activists, civil society representatives, non-Dinka citizens, and even members of faith-based organizations, forcing many to flee the country.

E. ASSOCIATIONAL AND ORGANIZATIONAL RIGHTS: 2 / 12

E1. Is there freedom of assembly? 1 / 4

South Sudan's commitment to freedom of assembly under the interim constitution is rarely put to the test in the current conditions of war, displacement, and hunger, as demonstrations seldom occur. Past protests have been met with excessive force by the authorities.

E2. Is there freedom for nongovernmental organizations, particularly those that are engaged in human rights- and governance-related work? 0 / 4

The government, including Kiir himself, has adopted a hostile stance toward NGOs. According to the United Nations, the NSS has infiltrated civil society organizations, fomenting an atmosphere of fear and distrust. A law passed in 2016 requires NGOs to get written permission from the authorities to conduct activities and hold a bank account in South Sudan, and at least 80 percent of staff must be South Sudanese.

Special hostility has been directed toward UN agencies, which Kiir has accused—without foundation—of siding with his rivals. Humanitarian operations have been consistently blocked, workers deliberately targeted, and food supplies looted. Since the war began, more than 100 aid workers have been killed. The government has also used fees and other bureaucratic barriers to complicate the acquisition of work permits for aid workers.

In September 2018, a group of 10 soldiers received prison sentences from a military court for their involvement in a 2016 attack on a hotel housing foreign aid workers. Several women were raped and a South Sudanese journalist was murdered during the assault.

E3. Is there freedom for trade unions and similar professional or labor organizations? 1 / 4

A new labor law signed at the end of 2017 took effect in 2018, providing for the rights to participate in trade unions, bargain collectively, and strike under certain conditions. However, the law was not effectively implemented, and legal protections for workers are poorly enforced in practice. The country's limited union activity has historically been concentrated in the public sector.

F. RULE OF LAW: 0 / 16

F1. Is there an independent judiciary? 0 / 4

Judicial independence exists in theory but not in practice. A Supreme Court judge who resigned in 2017 complained of continual interference from the executive. Earlier that year, South Sudan's judges went on a five-month strike to protest poor pay and working conditions, during which the president dismissed more than a dozen judges; he did not cite specific misconduct or a recommendation from the National Judicial Service Commission, as required by the interim constitution. Kiir had similarly removed a deputy chief justice of the Supreme Court in 2016 without citing a formal cause or recommendation.

F2. Does due process prevail in civil and criminal matters? 0 / 4

Unlawful arrests and detentions are routine in South Sudan, according to UN observers. Under the National Security Service Law, which became operational in 2015, the NSS has almost unlimited powers to detain and interrogate suspects. Dysfunction and lack of capacity in the justice system have led to cases of indefinite detention, often without charge.

Among other cases during 2018, scholar and activist Peter Biar Ajak, a frequent critic of the government, was arbitrarily detained in July; he remained in custody at year's end and was reportedly held incommunicado, without access to counsel. The president amnestied a number of political prisoners in August and more later in the year as part of the R-ARCSS, but others continued to be held, and new detentions were reported.

F3. Is there protection from the illegitimate use of physical force and freedom from war and insurgencies? 0 / 4

Physical mistreatment and abuse are widespread within the criminal justice system. According to a September 2018 report by Amnesty International, hundreds of people have been detained in Juba by the NSS and military intelligence and subjected to torture and other ill-treatment since the beginning of the civil war. In addition to numerous deaths in custody during this period, the authorities have carried out formal executions, including of people who were children when convicted. At least seven people were executed in 2018.

In September 2018, the London School of Tropical Hygiene and Medicine estimated that 400,000 people had died as a direct or indirect result of the civil conflict. There is near-total impunity for perpetrators of violence and sexual abuse in the context of the war. Recognizing the inability of South Sudan's judiciary to prosecute these offenses, both the 2015 and 2018 peace agreements mandated the establishment of a hybrid court, under the auspices of the AU, to take charge of the process. Soon after the 2018 deal was signed, the government's information minister dismissed the idea of a court, describing it as a Western tool for regime change.

F4. Do laws, policies, and practices guarantee equal treatment of various segments of the population? 0 / 4

The UN, the AU, and other international monitors have documented repeated, deliberate attacks by government forces against members of non-Dinka ethnic groups, most of them civilians. The perpetrators have not been brought to justice. The UN Commission on Human Rights in South Sudan has concluded that these activities amount to a campaign of ethnic cleansing by the government.

The interim constitution includes guarantees on gender equality, but women are routinely exposed to discriminatory customary practices and gender-based violence. While same-sex sexual conduct is not explicitly illegal in South Sudan, "carnal intercourse against the order of nature" is punishable by up to 10 years in prison. LGBT (lesbian, gay, bisexual, and transgender) people face widespread discrimination and social stigma, including harassment and abuse by security forces.

G. PERSONAL AUTONOMY AND INDIVIDUAL RIGHTS: 0 / 16

G1. Do individuals enjoy freedom of movement, including the ability to change their place of residence, employment, or education? 0 / 4

South Sudan's interim constitution enshrines the rights of free movement and residence, as well as the right to an education. In reality, the civil war, multiple local conflicts, and poor to nonexistent service delivery have made it impossible for many people to exercise these basic rights. An estimated 1.8 million people were internally displaced as of December 2018, and 2.5 million South Sudanese refugees were living in neighboring countries.

G2. Are individuals able to exercise the right to own property and establish private businesses without undue interference from state or nonstate actors? 0 / 4

Disputes over land use and ownership are frequent causes of armed conflict in South Sudan, and returning refugees from earlier wars have exacerbated the problem. Property rights are weak and not respected in practice. There have been multiple allegations of land grabbing and forced evictions in recent years. Customary practices often deny women their legal rights to property and inheritance.

G3. Do individuals enjoy personal social freedoms, including choice of marriage partner and size of family, protection from domestic violence, and control over appearance? 0 / 4

Rape and other forms of sexual violence have been used extensively as weapons of war against both men and women. Domestic violence is not addressed by the law. A 2017 study by International Rescue Committee found that 65 percent of the women and girls surveyed had experienced physical or sexual violence, with 33 percent suffering sexual violence by a nonpartner.

Customary law puts women at a disadvantage in matters of divorce and child custody. Forced and early marriages are common, with about half of girls marrying by age 18, and spousal rape is not a crime.

G4. Do individuals enjoy equality of opportunity and freedom from economic exploitation? 0 / 4

The collapse of the national economy has led to rampant inflation that puts the prices of essential goods out of reach for ordinary people.

Trafficking in persons for forced labor and sexual exploitation is widespread, with rural woman and girls, the internally displaced, and migrants from neighboring countries among the most vulnerable to mistreatment. The use of child soldiers is also a serious problem. UNICEF, the UN Children's Fund, estimated that some 19,000 children had been recruited by armed groups since 2013, and it verified more than 1,200 cases of recruitment in 2017 alone.

Spain

Population: 46,700,000
Capital: Madrid
Political Rights Rating: 1
Civil Liberties Rating: 1
Freedom Rating: 1.0
Freedom Status: Free
Electoral Democracy: Yes

Overview: Spain's parliamentary system features competitive multiparty elections and peaceful transfers of power between rival parties. The rule of law prevails, and civil liberties are generally respected. Although political corruption remains a concern, high-ranking politicians and other powerful figures have been successfully prosecuted. Restrictive legislation adopted in recent years poses a threat to otherwise robust freedoms of expression and assembly. A persistent separatist movement in Catalonia represents the leading challenge to the country's constitutional system and territorial integrity.

KEY DEVELOPMENTS IN 2018:

- In June, for the first time in Spanish history, a vote of no confidence was approved by the parliament, leading Prime Minister Mariano Rajoy of the conservative Popular Party (PP) to resign and Pedro Sánchez of the Spanish Socialist Workers' Party (PSOE) to replace him at the head of a new minority government. The move came after several PP members were convicted on corruption charges in May.
- Tensions stemming from the separatist movement in Catalonia remained during the year, though the new national government began discussions on the issue with newly elected regional leaders. Meanwhile, a number of separatist figures were awaiting trial on charges of rebellion and other offenses related to an independence referendum that was held in defiance of court orders in late 2017.
- In December, the new party Vox won seats in Andalusia's regional elections, marking the first time since Spain's transition to democracy that a far-right party had gained representation in a regional legislature.

POLITICAL RIGHTS: 39 / 40 (+1)
A. ELECTORAL PROCESS: 11 / 12 (+1)

A1. Was the current head of government or other chief national authority elected through free and fair elections? 4 / 4

Following legislative elections, the monarch selects a candidate for prime minister, generally the leader of the party or coalition with a majority in the lower house. The parliament then votes on the selected candidate.

Inconclusive elections in December 2015 and June 2016 led to months of fruitless coalition talks, wither neither the PP nor the PSOE able to assemble a majority. The impasse finally ended when the PSOE agreed to allow incumbent prime minister Rajoy to establish a minority government in late 2016.

In June 2018, after several PP members were convicted on corruption charges and the PP itself was ordered to pay a large fine, the PSOE won a motion of no confidence against the government, forcing Rajoy to resign and allowing Sánchez, the PSOE leader, to form his own minority government. The leftist party Unidos Podemos and the Catalan and Basque nationalist parties voted in support of the motion, while the center-right Ciudadanos and the PP voted against.

A2. Were the current national legislative representatives elected through free and fair elections? 4 / 4

The lower house of Spain's bicameral parliament, the Congress of Deputies, is composed of 350 members elected in multimember constituencies for each of Spain's provinces, with the exception of the North African enclaves of Ceuta and Melilla, each of which has one single-member constituency. The Senate has 266 members, 208 of whom are elected directly, and 58 of whom are chosen by regional legislatures. Members of both chambers serve four-year terms.

Spain's elections are generally considered free and fair. In the 2016 parliamentary elections, the PP emerged with 137 seats in the Chamber of Deputies, followed by the PSOE with 85, Unidos Podemos with 45, Ciudadanos with 32, and several smaller parties with the remainder. The PP and its allies also took 130 directly elected seats in the Senate, giving them an overall majority of 151 in the upper chamber; the PSOE placed second with a total of 63 seats.

Regional elections in Catalonia were held in December 2017 after Rajoy dissolved the regional government in October in the wake of the illegal referendum on independence. Ciudadanos, which strongly opposes Catalan independence, led the voting with 36 seats, but the three separatist parties won a combined 70 seats in the 135-seat legislature. In May 2018, the legislature chose Quim Torra, a separatist independent, to lead a new regional government, ending a seven-month period of direct rule from Madrid.

Andalusia held regional assembly elections in December 2018. The PSOE led with 33 of the 109 seats, but right-leaning parties—the PP , Ciudadanos, and the far-right Spanish nationalist party Vox—collectively won a majority and were expected to form a new regional government in 2019. The 12 seats secured by Vox marked the first time since Spain's transition to democracy following the death of dictator Francisco Franco in 1975 that a far-right party was represented in a regional legislature.

A3. Are the electoral laws and framework fair, and are they implemented impartially by the relevant election management bodies? 4 / 4 (+1)

Spain's constitution and electoral laws provide the legal framework for democratic elections, and they are generally implemented fairly.

The initiation and conduct of the October 2017 independence referendum in Catalonia featured a number of fundamental flaws. The exercise was prohibited by the courts on constitutional grounds, and the actions of both regional authorities and the central government contributed to a chaotic environment that did not allow for fair and transparent balloting. The situation stabilized significantly during 2018 with the formation of new regional and national governments, even if the underlying dispute and numerous criminal cases against Catalan officials remained unresolved.

Score Change: The score improved from 3 to 4 because there was no repetition of a 2017 constitutional crisis surrounding a flawed referendum on Catalan independence.

B. POLITICAL PLURALISM AND PARTICIPATION: 16 / 16

B1. Do the people have the right to organize in different political parties or other competitive political groupings of their choice, and is the system free of undue obstacles to the rise and fall of these competing parties or groupings? 4 / 4

Citizens are free to organize political parties, which are able to function without interference in practice. While the PP and the PSOE once dominated the political system, corruption scandals and persistent economic woes in recent years have aided the rise of new alternatives including Unidos Podemos and Ciudadanos.

B2. Is there a realistic opportunity for the opposition to increase its support or gain power through elections? 4 / 4

There have been multiple democratic transfers of power between rival parties since Spain returned to democracy in the late 1970s. The new PSOE government that took office in 2018 ended more than six years of PP rule.

B3. Are the people's political choices free from domination by the military, foreign powers, religious hierarchies, economic oligarchies, or any other powerful group that is not democratically accountable? 4 / 4

Voting and political affairs in general are largely free from undue interference by unelected or external forces.

B4. Do various segments of the population (including ethnic, religious, gender, LGBT, and other relevant groups) have full political rights and electoral opportunities? 4 / 4

Women and minority groups enjoy full political rights. Women are relatively well represented in politics, holding approximately 39 percent of the seats in the Chamber of Deputies and the Senate. In the PSOE government formed in 2018, women held 61 percent of the ministerial positions.

Spain's system of regional autonomy grants significant powers of self-governance to the country's traditional national minorities, including Catalans and Basques. The autonomy of Catalonia, suspended following the illegal referendum in 2017, was restored after the region held elections and installed new leadership in May 2018.

Some of the Catalan officials and activists who were charged with offenses such as rebellion, sedition, and misuse of public funds as a result of the referendum remained in pretrial detention during 2018, while others, including former Catalan president Carles Puigdemont, remained outside the country. Meanwhile, the new PSOE government in Madrid sought to ease tensions, in part by moving the incarcerated politicians to Catalan prisons and meeting for talks with the regional government. In December, however, Sánchez threatened to send security forces to Catalonia, accusing regional authorities of mismanaging large proindependence protests.

C. FUNCTIONING OF GOVERNMENT: 11 / 12

C1. Do the freely elected head of government and national legislative representatives determine the policies of the government? 4 / 4

Elected officials are generally free to make and implement laws and policies without undue interference.

C2. Are safeguards against official corruption strong and effective? 3 / 4

Concerns about official corruption often center on party financing. Though most party expenses are funded by the state, a 2007 law confirmed the right of political parties to use commercial bank loans as well. In 2012, Spain strengthened rules on political financing by restricting access to loans, increasing transparency, and establishing an audit framework. In 2015, new legislation prohibited banks from forgiving debt owed by political parties.

Although the courts have a solid record of investigating and prosecuting corruption cases, the system is often overburdened, and cases move slowly. Among other high-profile proceedings during the year, in May 2018, after 10 years of investigation, the courts handed down convictions for 29 of the 37 people indicted over their alleged involvement in the illegal financing of the PP from 1999 to 2005. The party itself was found to have benefited from the schemes and was ordered to pay a €240,000 ($280,000) fine.

C3. Does the government operate with openness and transparency? 4 / 4

Legal safeguards to ensure government transparency include asset-disclosure rules for public officials and laws governing conflicts of interest. The Transparency Act, which took effect in 2014, is meant to facilitate public access to government records, though freedom of information activists have reported onerous procedures and called for improvements to the law.

CIVIL LIBERTIES: 55 / 60 (−1)

D. FREEDOM OF EXPRESSION AND BELIEF: 14 / 16 (−1)

D1. Are there free and independent media? 3 / 4

Spain has a free press that covers a wide range of perspectives and actively investigates high-level corruption. However, consolidation of private ownership and political interference at public outlets pose threats to media independence.

In June 2018, the new PSOE government issued a decree that temporarily replaced the board of directors of the Spanish Radio and Television Corporation (RTVE) until a stalled law to select the board through a public contest could be implemented. The law was finalized in July, and in December a group of board candidates was presented for consideration by the parliament. Separately, at year's end the leaders of the regional public broadcasters in Catalonia were under investigation for allegedly using the outlets as a platform to promote the illegal 2017 independence referendum.

A controversial public safety law that took effect in 2015, nicknamed the "gag law" by its critics, established large fines for offenses including spreading images that could endanger police officers or protected facilities. Journalists continued to face penalties for alleged violations of the law while reporting on police actions during 2018. For example, in November photojournalist Juan Carlos Mohr was fined €2,000 ($2,300) for allegedly disobeying police orders while covering a 2017 protest.

D2. Are individuals free to practice and express their religious faith or nonbelief in public and private? 4 / 4

Religious freedom is guaranteed in the constitution and respected in practice. As the country's dominant religion, Roman Catholicism enjoys benefits not afforded to others, such as financing through the tax system. However, the religious organizations of Jews, Muslims, and Protestants also have certain privileges through agreements with the state, including tax exemptions and permission to station chaplains in hospitals and other institutions. Other groups that choose to register can obtain a legal identity and the right to own or rent property.

D3. Is there academic freedom, and is the educational system free from extensive political indoctrination? 4 / 4

The government does not restrict academic freedom in law or in practice.

D4. Are individuals free to express their personal views on political or other sensitive topics without fear of surveillance or retribution? 3 / 4 (−1)

Private discussion remains open and vibrant, but more aggressive enforcement of laws banning the glorification of terrorism has begun to threaten free speech, with dozens of people—including social media users and several performers—found guilty in recent years for what often amounts to satire, artistic expression, or political commentary. At least 119 people were convicted of speech-related "terrorism" offenses between 2011 and 2017, almost four times more than during the period from 2004 to 2011, when Basque Fatherland and Freedom (ETA), a separatist terrorist group, was still active. In 2017, the Supreme Court ruled that a person could violate the law even if there was no intention to "glorify" a terrorist group or "humiliate" its victims.

Individuals have also been prosecuted for insulting the monarchy and other state institutions. In March 2018, the European Court of Human Rights found that Spain had violated the free expression rights of two Catalan men who were convicted and fined for publicly burning a photograph of the king in 2007.

Score Change: The score declined from 4 to 3 due to a pattern in which a broadly worded antiterrorism law and other legal provisions have been used to prosecute individuals for their political expression.

E. ASSOCIATIONAL AND ORGANIZATIONAL RIGHTS: 11 / 12

E1. Is there freedom of assembly? 3 / 4

The constitution provides for freedom of assembly, and the authorities typically respect this right in practice. However, the public safety act that took effect in 2015 imposed a number of restrictions, including fines of up to €600,000 ($680,000) for participating in unauthorized protests near key buildings or infrastructure. Participants in protests on a variety of local concerns have faced smaller but still substantial fines under the law.

Separately, two prominent Catalan independence activists, Jordi Cuixart and Jordi Sànchez, were charged with sedition in 2017 for leading protests aimed at preventing police from halting the banned referendum. They were also charged with rebellion in March 2018, and at year's end they remained in pretrial detention.

E2. Is there freedom for nongovernmental organizations, particularly those that are engaged in human rights- and governance-related work? 4 / 4

Domestic and international nongovernmental organizations operate without significant government restrictions.

E3. Is there freedom for trade unions and similar professional or labor organizations? 4 / 4

With the exception of members of the military and national police, workers are free to organize in unions of their choice, engage in collective bargaining, and mount legal strikes.

F. RULE OF LAW: 15 / 16

F1. Is there an independent judiciary? 4 / 4

The constitution provides for an independent judiciary, and the courts operate autonomously in practice. However, the Council of Europe has criticized the fact that under current law, the 12 judges who sit on the 20-member General Council of the Judiciary—which oversees the courts and ensures their independence—are not directly elected by their peers, but appointed through a three-fifths vote in the parliament, as with the other eight members.

F2. Does due process prevail in civil and criminal matters? 4 / 4

The authorities generally observe legal safeguards against arbitrary arrest and detention, though judges can authorize special restrictions on communication and delayed arraignment for detainees held in connection with acts of terrorism. Defendants enjoy full due process rights during trial.

F3. Is there protection from the illegitimate use of physical force and freedom from war and insurgencies? 4 / 4

The population faces no major threats to physical security. The potential for terrorist attacks by radical Islamist groups remains a concern, though ETA announced in April 2018 that it had formally dissolved, having ended its armed activity several years earlier.

Prison conditions generally meet international standards, but short-term internment centers for irregular migrants suffer from overcrowding and other problems. The country's ombudsman and Human Rights Watch have argued that the facilities violate human rights protections.

F4. Do laws, policies, and practices guarantee equal treatment of various segments of the population? 3 / 4

Women, racial minorities, and LGBT (lesbian, gay, bisexual, and transgender) people enjoy legal protections against discrimination and other mistreatment, though a degree of societal bias persists. Women continue to face inequities in employment and compensation, while some minority groups—including Roma—remain economically marginalized and are allegedly subject to police profiling.

Spain is a major point of entry to Europe for irregular migrants and refugees. More than 57,000 people crossed the Mediterranean to reach Spain during 2018, setting a new record for sea arrivals and outpacing other European countries like Italy and Greece. Thousands of migrants and refugees also congregate at the land border between Morocco and the Spanish enclaves of Ceuta and Melilla. In 2017, the European Court of Human Rights found that Spain's practice of summarily expelling those who manage to cross the border fence is unlawful under the European Convention on Human Rights. Such expulsions were authorized by the public safety act that took effect in 2015, and they continued to occur during 2018.

G. PERSONAL AUTONOMY AND INDIVIDUAL RIGHTS: 15 / 16

G1. Do individuals enjoy freedom of movement, including the ability to change their place of residence, employment, or education? 4 / 4

There are no significant restrictions on individuals' freedom to travel within the country or abroad, or to change their place of residence, employment, or education.

G2. Are individuals able to exercise the right to own property and establish private businesses without undue interference from state or nonstate actors? 4 / 4

The legal framework supports property rights, and there are no major restrictions on private business activity.

G3. Do individuals enjoy personal social freedoms, including choice of marriage partner and size of family, protection from domestic violence, and control over appearance? 4 / 4

Personal social freedoms are generally respected. Same-sex marriage has been legal in Spain since 2005, and same-sex couples may adopt children.

There are legal protections against domestic abuse and rape, including spousal rape; while both remain problems in practice, the government and civil society groups work actively to combat them. In April 2018, five men were acquitted of rape and convicted on a lesser charge of sexual abuse in a high-profile 2016 case in Pamplona, leading to protests and calls for the law to be amended so that specific evidence of physical violence or intimidation accompanying a sexual assault would not be needed to secure a rape conviction.

G4. Do individuals enjoy equality of opportunity and freedom from economic exploitation? 3 / 4

Residents generally have access to economic opportunity and protection from exploitative working conditions. Despite strong antitrafficking efforts by law enforcement agencies, however, migrant workers remain vulnerable to debt bondage, forced labor, and sexual exploitation.

The level of income inequality in Spain is among the worst in the European Union. The unemployment rate is still high for the region, though it dropped to 14.45 percent—a 10-year low—by the end of 2018.

Sri Lanka

Population: 21,700,000
Capital: Colombo
Political Rights Rating: 3
Civil Liberties Rating: 4
Freedom Rating: 3.5
Freedom Status: Partly Free
Electoral Democracy: Yes

Overview: Sri Lanka has experienced improvements in political rights and civil liberties since the 2015 election of President Maithripala Sirisena. However, the government hàs been slow to implement transitional justice mechanisms needed to address the aftermath of a 26-year civil war between government forces and Tamil rebels, which ended in 2009. Sirisena's reputation as a democratic reformer was further tarnished by a constitutional crisis in 2018, in which he attempted to unilaterally replace the prime minister, dissolve Parliament, and hold snap elections. The moves were blocked by the parliamentary majority and the courts.

KEY DEVELOPMENTS IN 2018:

- After a delay of more than two years, local council elections finally took place in February. The Sri Lanka People's Front (SLPP), a new political group headed by former president Mahinda Rajapaksa, won over 44 percent of the vote.
- In March, anti-Muslim rioting in the Kandy district, which included the participation of Buddhist politicians and the police, led to the destruction of mosques and other property, as well as documented assaults on Muslims and at least two deaths.
- In October, President Sirisena sacked Prime Minister Rani Wickremesinghe and attempted to replace with him with Rajapaksa. Parliament repeatedly staged no-confidence votes against Rajapaksa, and he was unable to establish his authority as head of government, prompting Sirisena in November to order the dissolution of Parliament and call snap elections. His actions were widely considered unconstitutional.
- In December, the Court of Appeal ruled that Rajapaksa could not take office, and the Supreme Court ruled unanimously against the president's dissolution of Parliament. The decisions effectively rolled back the president's moves and restored Wickremesinghe to the premiership.

POLITICAL RIGHTS: 24 / 40
A. ELECTORAL PROCESS: 9 / 12 (+1)
A1. Was the current head of government or other chief national authority elected through free and fair elections? 3 / 4

The 1978 constitution vested strong executive powers in the president, but the approval of the 19th Amendment in 2015 curtailed those powers by reintroducing term limits—holding the president to a maximum of two five-year terms—and requiring the president to consult the prime minister on ministerial appointments, among other changes. The prime minister and cabinet must maintain the confidence of Parliament.

President Sirisena was elected in 2015, defeating Rajapaksa, the incumbent, with 51 percent of the vote. Both were members of the Sri Lanka Freedom Party (SLFP), but Sirisena ran as the candidate of an opposition alliance. Monitors from the Commonwealth

Observer Group noted government abuses of administrative resources, as well as preelection violence that mainly affected Sirisena supporters, but deemed the election generally credible. Sirisena appointed Wickremesinghe as prime minister that year.

A2. Were the current national legislative representatives elected through free and fair elections? 3 / 4

The 225-member unicameral Parliament is elected for six-year terms through a mixed proportional representation system. In the 2015 parliamentary elections, Wickremesinghe's United National Party (UNP) led a coalition, the National Front for Good Governance, to victory with 106 seats. The SLFP-led United People's Freedom Alliance (UPFA) took 95 seats, and the Tamil National Alliance (TNA), the largest party representing the ethnic minority, won 16 seats. Three smaller groups divided the remainder. While dozens of violent incidents, including murder, were reported prior to the elections, the polling itself was considered credible.

Local council elections originally scheduled for 2015 were finally held in February 2018 after a delay of more than two years, which the government blamed on a dispute over delimitation of voting districts. Provincial council elections scheduled for 2017 were also repeatedly postponed and had not yet been held at the end of 2018, which the government also attributed to delimitation issues.

A3. Are the electoral laws and framework fair, and are they implemented impartially by the relevant election management bodies? 3 / 4 (+1)

The Election Commission of Sri Lanka, which administers and oversees all elections in the country, has built a reputation for independence in recent years. A member of the three-person commission was at the forefront in petitioning the Supreme Court against the president's dissolution of Parliament in November 2018. The commissioner's stance was important, as the controversial attempt by President Sirisena to call early parliamentary elections—part of his effort to replace Prime Minister Wickremesinghe—would have needed the approval of all commission members.

In 2017, after changes to the legal framework for local elections were adopted, the government cited constituency delimitation issues to justify the postponement of the elections. But the chairperson of the election commission declared that he would authorize elections in areas that were not affected by the delimitation concerns, which forced the government to finally hold the elections in all constituencies in February 2018. Analysts attributed the repeated delays to the ruling party's fear that it would be defeated in the local polls.

Score Change: The score improved from 2 to 3 because the election commission showed independence by holding local council elections despite the government's efforts to continue postponing them, and by resisting the president's unconstitutional attempt to call early parliamentary elections.

B. POLITICAL PLURALISM AND PARTICIPATION: 10 / 16

B1. Do the people have the right to organize in different political parties or other competitive political groupings of their choice, and is the system free of undue obstacles to the rise and fall of these competing parties or groupings? 3 / 4

A range of political parties are able to operate freely and contest elections. The success of the SLPP, founded in 2016 and led by former president Rajapaksa, in the February local council elections demonstrated that new parties can form and operate without significant interference.

However, political debates between parties sometimes involve an element of violence and intimidation, which became apparent during the 2018 constitutional crisis. Among other incidents, Rajapaksa supporters attacked legislators opposed to his appointment as prime minister with chairs and chili powder to prevent them from holding a no-confidence vote in November.

B2. Is there a realistic opportunity for the opposition to increase its support or gain power through elections? 3 / 4

Opposition groupings are generally free to carry out peaceful political activities and are able to win power through elections. Most recently, the opposition SLPP won control of 231 out of 340 local councils in the February 2018 elections. However, opposition figures and supporters sometimes face harassment. Election observers noted that some opposition party members were attacked and intimidated in the Northern Province during the 2015 parliamentary election campaign.

B3. Are the people's political choices free from domination by the military, foreign powers, religious hierarchies, economic oligarchies, or any other powerful group that is not democratically accountable? 2 / 4

The military often inserts itself into political affairs. Members of the military openly backed then president Rajapaksa ahead of the 2015 election, and the armed forces recognized his appointment as prime minister in October 2018 despite protests that the move was unconstitutional. Vote buying and political bribery are also a concern. Monitors said the government offered gifts and handouts to voters ahead of the 2015 presidential election, and Rajapaksa's efforts to win lawmakers' support during the 2018 constitutional crisis reportedly included bribery, with dueling allegations that bribes were either offered or demanded.

B4. Do various segments of the population (including ethnic, religious, gender, LGBT, and other relevant groups) have full political rights and electoral opportunities? 2 / 4

A number of parties explicitly represent the interests of ethnic and religious minority groups, including several Tamil parties and the Sri Lankan Muslim Congress, the country's largest Muslim party. Tamil political parties and civilians faced less harassment and fewer hindrances in voting during 2015 presidential and parliamentary elections compared with the 2010 elections. However, systemic discrimination, including via language laws and naturalization procedures, negatively affects Tamils' political participation. The interests of women are not well represented in Sri Lankan politics, and women hold less than 6 percent of the seats in Parliament.

C. FUNCTIONING OF GOVERNMENT: 6 / 12 (−1)

C1. Do the freely elected head of government and national legislative representatives determine the policies of the government? 2 / 4 (−1)

President Sirisena's effort in October 2018 to remove Prime Minister Wickremesinghe and replace him with Rajapaksa, and his subsequent attempt in November to dissolve Parliament and hold snap elections, were widely considered unconstitutional executive infringements on parliamentary authority. The crisis also left Sri Lanka without a fully functioning government for almost two months as the two claimants to the premiership sought to assert their legitimacy.

Nevertheless, Parliament demonstrated its independence by energetically resisting Rajapaksa's appointment, passing no-confidence votes and making it impossible for him to form a government. After a series of favorable court rulings, Wickremesinghe was restored to office in December.

Score Change: The score declined from 3 to 2 due to the disruption to governance caused by the president's unconstitutional and ultimately unsuccessful attempts to replace the prime minister, dissolve Parliament, and hold snap elections.

C2. Are safeguards against official corruption strong and effective? 2 / 4

The Sirisena administration's efforts to fight corruption, including arrests and indictments, have led to few convictions. Corruption remains a problem in the judiciary, public procurement, and customs.

In May 2018, Parliament approved a new law that created special courts to deal specifically with corruption. The change was meant to accelerate cases that have been delayed for years, many from former president Rajapaksa's administration. In September, Gotabhaya Rajapaksa, a former defense minister and brother of the former president, was indicted in an anticorruption court for allegedly misusing public funds to build a memorial to his parents. He awaited trial at the end of the year, and it remained to be seen whether the new courts would yield more corruption convictions.

C3. Does the government operate with openness and transparency? 2 / 4

Individuals have used the 2017 Right to Information Act to access government records, but some large contracts with Chinese companies have lacked transparency. Notably, the government did not publish the details of a controversial lease agreement, signed in late 2017, that authorized a Chinese company to run the new Hambantota seaport for 99 years. In February 2018, the auditor general admitted that he could not provide precise figures on the size of the national debt due to the mismanagement of loan data.

ADDITIONAL DISCRETIONARY POLITICAL RIGHTS QUESTION

Is the government or occupying power deliberately changing the ethnic composition of a country or territory so as to destroy a culture or tip the political balance in favor of another group? –1 / 0

Following the end of the civil war in 2009, the military presence in the Tamil-populated areas of the north and east increased. The Rajapaksa administration encouraged settlement by ethnic Sinhalese civilians by providing land certificates, housing, and other infrastructure, with the aim of diluting local Tamil majorities in these areas. While such policies ended after Rajapaksa left office in 2015, and some land has been released from military control, displacement of Tamil civilians remains a concern.

CIVIL LIBERTIES: 32 / 60 (+1)

D. FREEDOM OF EXPRESSION AND BELIEF: 8 / 16

D1. Are there free and independent media? 2 / 4

Freedom of expression is guaranteed in the constitution, and respect for this right has dramatically improved since 2015.

However, challenges to press freedom persist, and senior government officials and lawmakers sometimes threaten journalists. In June and July 2018, two local reporters, who worked with the *New York Times* on a story that scrutinized the Rajapaksa government's dealings with Chinese companies to build the Hambantota port, were attacked on social media and maligned by members of Parliament at a press conference.

Impunity for past crimes against journalists is a problem. Several investigations into journalists' killings have been reopened in recent years, but none have resulted in convictions.

D2. Are individuals free to practice and express their religious faith or nonbelief in public and private? 2 / 4

The constitution gives special status to Buddhism, while religious minorities face discrimination and occasional violence. The construction of new mosques sometimes leads to protests.

In March 2018, anti-Muslim rioting in the Kandy district, which included the participation of SLPP politicians and the police, led to the destruction of mosques and other property, as well as documented assaults on Muslims and at least two deaths. Violence against Christians remained a problem during the year; according to the National Christian Evangelical Alliance of Sri Lanka (NCEASL), there were 67 attacks against Christians reported between January and September.

D3. Is there academic freedom, and is the educational system free from extensive political indoctrination? 2 / 4

Academic freedom is generally respected, but there are occasional reports of politicization at universities and a lack of tolerance for dissenting views among both professors and students, particularly for academics who study issues related to the Tamil minority.

D4. Are individuals free to express their personal views on political or other sensitive topics without fear of surveillance or retribution? 2 / 4

The civil war remains a sensitive topic. State officials' harassment of civil society activists working on human rights issues in the north and east has deterred open discussion of those topics among private citizens. The attempted appointment of Rajapaksa—who was credibly accused of war crimes during his presidency—as prime minister in October 2018 contributed to a climate of fear among Tamils that also impeded free expression.

In an effort to suppress anti-Muslim rioting that broke out in March, the government blocked social media platforms including Facebook, Viber, and WhatsApp nationwide for three days.

E. ASSOCIATIONAL AND ORGANIZATIONAL RIGHTS: 8 / 12
E1. Is there freedom of assembly? 2 / 4

Although demonstrations occur regularly, authorities sometimes restrict freedom of assembly. Police occasionally use tear gas and water cannons to disperse protesters. The army has continued to impose some restrictions on assembly in the north and east, particularly for planned memorial events concerning the final battles of the long-running civil war, in which thousands of civilians were killed alongside Tamil rebels and their leaders.

E2. Is there freedom for nongovernmental organizations, particularly those that are engaged in human rights– and governance-related work? 3 / 4

Nongovernmental organizations (NGOs) are generally free to operate without interference, but some NGOs and activists were subjected to harassment and violent attacks in 2018. In July, Srishobana Yogalimgam, who campaigns against enforced disappearances, was assaulted in the northern city of Jaffna. Also that month, antitorture activist Amitha Priyanthi of the NGO Janasansadaya was attacked by two unidentified men on motorcycles near her home in Beruwela.

E3. Is there freedom for trade unions and similar professional or labor organizations? 3 / 4

Most of Sri Lanka's trade unions are independent and legally allowed to engage in collective bargaining. Except for civil servants, most workers can strike, though the 1989 Essential Services Act allows the president to declare any strike illegal.

While more than 70 percent of the mainly Tamil workers on tea plantations are unionized, employers routinely violate their rights. Harassment of labor activists and official intolerance of union activities, particularly in export processing zones, is regularly reported.

F. RULE OF LAW: 8 / 16 (+1)

F1. Is there an independent judiciary? 3 / 4 (+1)

Political interference with and intimidation of the judiciary have abated somewhat under the Sirisena administration, and the courts asserted their independence during the 2018 constitutional crisis. A series of preliminary rulings culminated in December, when the Court of Appeal determined that Rajapaksa could not act as prime minister without a legal basis for his authority, and the Supreme Court struck down President Sirisena's attempt to dissolve Parliament and call snap elections. Despite this display of autonomy from the highest courts, corruption and politicization remain problems in the lower courts.

Score Change: The score improved from 2 to 3 because the Supreme Court and Court of Appeal demonstrated their independence by ruling against President Sirisena's moves to replace the prime minister and dissolve Parliament.

F2. Does due process prevail in civil and criminal matters? 2 / 4

Due process rights are undermined by the Prevention of Terrorism Act (PTA), under which suspects can be detained for up to 18 months without charge. The law has been used to hold perceived enemies of the government, and many detained under the PTA's provisions have been kept in custody for longer than the law allows.

In September 2018, the cabinet approved a draft counterterrorism bill to replace the PTA. It would increase the powers of the Human Rights Commission to act as a check on abuses by security forces and reduce the number of acts that can be considered terrorism, among other improvements. However, the bill still allows the detention of terrorism suspects for up to one year without charge, and civil society organizations expressed concerns that its positive provisions could get watered down in Parliament.

F3. Is there protection from the illegitimate use of physical force and freedom from war and insurgencies? 2 / 4

Police and security forces are known to engage in abusive practices, including extrajudicial executions, forced disappearances, custodial rape, and torture, all of which disproportionately affect Tamils. Due to backlogs and a lack of resources, independent commissions have been slow to investigate allegations of police and military misconduct.

Of the numerous transitional justice mechanisms outlined in a 2015 UN resolution that Sri Lankan authorities assented to in order to address human rights violations in the aftermath of the civil war, the government has so far only established an Office of Missing Persons, which was created in 2017 and tasked with setting up a database of missing persons, advocating for missing persons and their families, and recommending means of redress. A bill to create an Office of Reparations was passed by Parliament in October 2018, while a truth commission and a war crimes court have not yet been created as mandated by the resolution.

F4. Do laws, policies, and practices guarantee equal treatment of various segments of the population? 1 / 4

Tamils report systematic discrimination in areas including government employment, university education, and access to justice.

LGBT (lesbian, gay, bisexual, and transgender) people face societal discrimination, occasional instances of violence, and some official harassment. A rarely enforced article of the penal code prescribes up to 10 years in prison for same-sex sexual activity.

Women suffer from sexual harassment and employment discrimination, as well as discriminatory legal provisions. In January 2018, President Sirisena reversed his finance minister's decision to lift a long-standing ban on women buying alcohol, as well as new regulations that would have allowed women to work in bars without a permit.

G. PERSONAL AUTONOMY AND INDIVIDUAL RIGHTS: 8 / 16

G1. Do individuals enjoy freedom of movement, including the ability to change their place of residence, employment, or education? 2 / 4

Freedom of movement is restricted by security checkpoints, particularly in the north, but recent years have featured greater freedom of travel. Women with children less than five years old are not allowed to travel abroad for work. Access to education is impeded by corruption, with bribes often required to obtain primary school admission.

G2. Are individuals able to exercise the right to own property and establish private businesses without undue interference from state or nonstate actors? 2 / 4

Government appropriation of land in the north and east after the civil war for economic development projects or to establish "high security zones" prevented many displaced people from returning to their property. However, the Sirisena administration has released some military-held land for resettlement. Corruption sometimes hinders the effective enforcement of property rights. Some women face gender-based disadvantages regarding inheritance under the customary laws of their ethnic or religious group.

G3. Do individuals enjoy personal social freedoms, including choice of marriage partner and size of family, protection from domestic violence, and control over appearance? 2 / 4

Rape of women and children and domestic violence remain serious problems, and perpetrators often act with impunity. According to government statistics, out of 2,036 rapes reported in 2016, not one resulted in a conviction. Although women have equal rights under civil and criminal law, matters related to the family—including marriage, divorce, and child custody—are adjudicated under the customary laws of each ethnic or religious group, and the application of these laws sometimes results in discrimination against women.

G4. Do individuals enjoy equality of opportunity and freedom from economic exploitation? 2 / 4

Migrant workers are often exposed to exploitative labor conditions. Although the government has increased penalties for employing minors, thousands of children continue to work as household servants, and many face abuse. Women and children in certain communities are also vulnerable to forced sex work. In recent years, the government has made some attempts to address human trafficking, including by establishing a specialized police unit to assist victims and those who report trafficking.

St. Kitts and Nevis

Population: 50,000
Capital: Basseterre
Political Rights Rating: 1
Civil Liberties Rating: 1
Freedom Rating: 1.0
Freedom Status: Free
Electoral Democracy: Yes

Overview: St. Kitts and Nevis is one of the world's smallest parliamentary democracies. The country has a history of competitive and credible elections, and civil liberties are generally upheld. There are some concerns about government corruption and transparency, particularly regarding the Citizenship by Investment Program (CIP). Authorities in recent years have struggled to address a rising crime rate.

KEY DEVELOPMENTS IN 2018:

- In October, the government obtained authorization from its Eastern Caribbean allies for a deployment of troops from the Barbados-based Regional Security System to help cope with a high rate of violent crime.
- Also in October, a report by the Organisation for Economic Co-operation and Development (OECD) warned that the CIP and the related Residence by Investment Program, which offer citizenship and residency rights in exchange for large sums of money, create the potential for abuse. Nevertheless, the CIP was expanded during the year.
- In two positive steps for transparency and accountability, a Freedom of Information Act was adopted in May, and rules mandated by the 2013 Integrity in Public Life Act were finally implemented in July.

POLITICAL RIGHTS: 36 / 40
A. ELECTORAL PROCESS: 10 / 12
A1. Was the current head of government or other chief national authority elected through free and fair elections? 4 / 4

The prime minister, usually the leader of the largest party in the parliament, is head of government. Prime ministers are normally appointed after legislative elections by the governor general, who represents the British monarch as the largely ceremonial head of state.

After the 2015 elections, Timothy Harris of Team Unity—an umbrella organization of the People's Action Movement (PAM) and the People's Labour Party (PLP) in St. Kitts and the Concerned Citizens Movement (CCM) in Nevis—was appointed prime minister.

A2. Were the current national legislative representatives elected through free and fair elections? 3 / 4

There are 14 seats in the unicameral National Assembly—8 for representatives from Saint Kitts, 3 for those from Nevis, and 3 for senators appointed by the governor general (2 on the advice of the prime minister and 1 on the advice of the opposition leader); all serve five-year terms.

Team Unity won the 2015 parliamentary elections, taking 7 of the 11 directly elected seats and unseating the Labour Party (SKNLP), which had been in government for two decades. The vote took place peacefully and was considered credible, but a number of shortcomings were observed. Opposition candidates and others criticized a lack of campaign finance legislation, and a monitoring mission from the Organization of American States (OAS) noted that the difference between state resources and SKNLP financing was not always clear. Some observers also noted that the government enjoyed disproportionate access to state-owned media for campaign purposes.

Nevis has its own local legislature, with five elected and three appointed members. Elections in 2017 resulted in a win for the incumbent CCM, which took four elected seats, leaving the Nevis Reformation Party with 1.

A3. Are the electoral laws and framework fair, and are they implemented impartially by the relevant election management bodies? 3 / 4

Electoral laws are generally fair and usually implemented impartially by the Electoral Commission. However, the lead-up to the 2015 elections featured an eleventh-hour dispute over district delineations and concerns about the Electoral Commission's independence. The SKNLP government introduced new electoral boundaries just a month before the polls. The new map was ultimately thrown out four days before the elections by the Privy Council in London, the highest court of appeal for St. Kitts and Nevis, after the opposition challenged the changes. Separately, OAS observers expressed concern that an election calendar with key dates was not shared publicly. A delay in reporting the results of the polls prompted questions about the independence of the Electoral Commission. In 2017, the former supervisor of elections was arrested and charged with misconduct in connection with the delayed transmission of the 2015 results. His case remained unresolved in 2018.

B. POLITICAL PLURALISM AND PARTICIPATION: 16 / 16

B1. Do the people have the right to organize in different political parties or other competitive political groupings of their choice, and is the system free of undue obstacles to the rise and fall of these competing parties or groupings? 4 / 4

There are no major constraints on the right to organize in different political parties and to form new parties. For example, the PLP was established in 2013 by two former members of the SKNLP and is now part of the Team Unity government.

B2. Is there a realistic opportunity for the opposition to increase its support or gain power through elections? 4 / 4

Opposition candidates are able to campaign without restrictions or interference, and there are realistic opportunities for opposition parties to increase their support or gain power through elections. In 2015, the Team Unity coalition unseated the SKNLP, which had been in government since 1995.

B3. Are the people's political choices free from domination by the military, foreign powers, religious hierarchies, economic oligarchies, or any other powerful group that is not democratically accountable? 4 / 4

Candidates and voters are generally able to make political choices without undue interference. However, in 2015 the OAS raised concerns about the lack of transparency of party and campaign financing, which could enable improper forms of political influence.

B4. Do various segments of the population (including ethnic, religious, gender, LGBT, and other relevant groups) have full political rights and electoral opportunities? 4 / 4

All citizens are formally entitled to equal political rights and electoral opportunities. While women play an active role in political parties and as grassroots organizers, only one woman won a seat in the National Assembly in 2015. The only woman member of the Nevis Island Assembly was appointed. The LGBT (lesbian, gay, bisexual, and transgender) community is marginalized, affecting LGBT people's ability to engage fully in political processes.

C. FUNCTIONING OF GOVERNMENT: 10 / 12

C1. Do the freely elected head of government and national legislative representatives determine the policies of the government? 4 / 4

The elected prime minister, cabinet, and national legislative representatives are able to freely determine the policies of the government.

C2. Are safeguards against official corruption strong and effective? 3 / 4

St. Kitts and Nevis's anticorruption laws are for the most part implemented effectively. However, while the Integrity in Public Life Act, which established a code of conduct for public officials and financial disclosure guidelines, was adopted in 2013, its implementation rules were not issued until July 2018.

In recent years, concerns have been raised about the country's Citizenship by Investment and Residence by Investment Programs, which allow foreigners to gain citizenship or residency through an economic investment. In a 2017 report, the US State Department noted that despite government efforts to improve the CIP's safeguards, it was still characterized by "significant deficiencies in vetting candidates," which could facilitate money laundering or permit the presence of people who threaten national security. The government does not release the exact number of passports issued or the nationalities of the recipients. An October 2018 OECD report similarly highlighted potential problems associated with the CIP. Investigations into alleged fraud and misappropriation of funds linked to the programs were ongoing at year's end.

Despite these concerns, a new Sustainable Growth Fund became operational in April 2018, featuring a lower investment requirement than the existing options—US$150,000 for a single applicant and US$195,000 for a family of four.

C3. Does the government operate with openness and transparency? 3 / 4

The government generally operates with transparency, though it long lacked a freedom of information law. The Freedom of Information Act was finally passed in May 2018, but had not yet been implemented at year's end. The government said that departments must have appropriate record-management systems in place before requests could be made. The law provides exemptions protecting information related to national security, court proceedings, trade secrets, intellectual property rights, and international relations.

CIVIL LIBERTIES: 53 / 60
D. FREEDOM OF EXPRESSION AND BELIEF: 15 / 16
D1. Are there free and independent media? 3 / 4

Freedom of expression is constitutionally guaranteed, and the government generally respects press freedom in practice. However, the state owns the sole local television station, and the opposition faces some restrictions on access to it, particularly around elections. Defamation is a criminal offense that can potentially carry a prison sentence. Some journalists reportedly self-censor in order to avoid pressure from government officials.

D2. Are individuals free to practice and express their religious faith or nonbelief in public and private? 4 / 4

Freedom of religion is constitutionally protected and generally respected in practice. However, Rastafarians face barriers to employment and other disadvantages as a result of their beliefs.

D3. Is there academic freedom, and is the educational system free from extensive political indoctrination? 4 / 4

The government generally respects academic freedom.

D4. Are individuals free to express their personal views on political or other sensitive topics without fear of surveillance or retribution? 4 / 4

There are no significant constraints on individuals' ability to express their personal views regarding political or other sensitive topics.

E. ASSOCIATIONAL AND ORGANIZATIONAL RIGHTS: 12 / 12
E1. Is there freedom of assembly? 4 / 4

Freedom of assembly is constitutionally guaranteed and generally respected in practice. Demonstrations on various topics routinely proceed without incident.

E2. Is there freedom for nongovernmental organizations, particularly those that are engaged in human rights– and governance-related work? 4 / 4

Nongovernmental organizations generally operate without restrictions.

E3. Is there freedom for trade unions and similar professional or labor organizations? 4 / 4

While workers may legally form unions, employers are not bound to recognize them. A union can engage in collective bargaining only if more than 50 percent of the company's employees are members. Antiunion discrimination is prohibited, and the right to strike, while not protected by law, is generally respected in practice.

F. RULE OF LAW: 13 / 16
F1. Is there an independent judiciary? 4 / 4

The judiciary is largely independent. The highest court is the Eastern Caribbean Supreme Court, but under certain circumstances there is a right of appeal to the Trinidad-based Caribbean Court of Justice and the Privy Council in London.

F2. Does due process prevail in civil and criminal matters? 3 / 4

Defendants are guaranteed a range of due process rights, which are mostly respected in practice; legal provisions for a fair trial are generally observed. Arbitrary arrests are prohibited, and security forces generally operate professionally. However, extended pretrial detention is a problem, with some detainees remaining in custody for more than two years before facing trial or having their cases dismissed.

F3. Is there protection from the illegitimate use of physical force and freedom from war and insurgencies? 3 / 4

While the country is free of war and other such threats to physical security, the government in recent years has struggled to contain a high rate of violent crime, which is linked primarily to street gangs fighting for territory and control of the domestic drug trade. Prison conditions remain overcrowded.

A total of 23 homicides were recorded in 2018, the same number as in 2017, giving St. Kitts and Nevis one of the world's highest homicide rates on a per capita basis. In an effort to address the problem, the St. Kitts and Nevis Defence Force was given police powers for a period of six months in August 2018, and troops from the Barbados-based Regional Security System were deployed to the country in October.

F4. Do laws, policies, and practices guarantee equal treatment of various segments of the population? 3 / 4

The law protects individuals against discrimination on various grounds, including race, sex, and religion, and these provisions are generally upheld. However, sexual orientation and gender identity are not similarly protected, and societal discrimination against LGBT people is pervasive. Under colonial-era laws, same-sex sexual conduct between men is illegal and punishable with imprisonment of up to 10 years. No law specifically prohibits sexual harassment, which has been reported in workplaces.

G. PERSONAL AUTONOMY AND INDIVIDUAL RIGHTS: 13 / 16

G1. Do individuals enjoy freedom of movement, including the ability to change their place of residence, employment, or education? 4 / 4

There are no significant restrictions on freedom of movement in St. Kitts and Nevis, and individuals are able to change their place of residence, employment, and education.

G2. Are individuals able to exercise the right to own property and establish private businesses without undue interference from state or non-state actors? 3 / 4

The legal framework generally supports property rights and private business activity, though there have been complaints about timely compensation for land confiscated through eminent domain laws, and the country scores poorly on World Bank assessments of the business environment.

G3. Do individuals enjoy personal social freedoms, including choice of marriage partner and size of family, protection from domestic violence, and control over appearance? 3 / 4

There are few restrictions on individual freedoms pertaining to personal status issues such as marriage and divorce, but same-sex marriage is not recognized. While domestic violence is criminalized, it remains a widespread problem in practice, and spousal rape is not specifically prohibited by law.

G4. Do individuals enjoy equality of opportunity and freedom from economic exploitation? 3 / 4

The law provides safeguards against exploitative working conditions, though lack of resources reportedly affects enforcement. Entrenched poverty represents a serious barrier to socioeconomic mobility for many people. Youth unemployment is high, and residents often rely on remittances from relatives working abroad.

St. Lucia

Population: 200,000
Capital: Castries
Political Rights Rating: 1
Civil Liberties Rating: 1
Freedom Rating: 1.0
Freedom Status: Free
Electoral Democracy: Yes

Overview: St. Lucia is a parliamentary democracy that holds competitive elections and has long experienced peaceful transfers of power between rival parties. Persistent challenges include government corruption and inadequate transparency, police brutality and a perception of impunity for such abuses, and discrimination against LGBT (lesbian, gay, bisexual, and transgender) people.

KEY DEVELOPMENTS IN 2018:

- Although the International Monetary Fund reported in June that St Lucia's economic growth was expected to continue, youth unemployment remained a barrier to broader economic opportunity, with over 38 percent of young people failing to find work.
- In October, an Organisation for Economic Co-operation and Development (OECD) report warned that St. Lucia's Citizenship by Investment Program (CIP) and others like it, which offer passports to foreigners in exchange for large sums of money, carry the potential for misuse.

POLITICAL RIGHTS: 38 / 40

A. ELECTORAL PROCESS: 11 / 12

A1. Was the current head of government or other chief national authority elected through free and fair elections? 4 / 4

The prime minister, usually the leader of the majority party in Parliament, is appointed as head of government by the governor general, who represents the British monarch as the largely ceremonial head of state. Allen Chastanet of the United Workers Party (UWP) was chosen as prime minister following the 2016 legislative elections, which were generally free and fair.

A2. Were the current national legislative representatives elected through free and fair elections? 4 / 4

The bicameral Parliament consists of the 17-seat House of Assembly, whose members are directly elected to five-year terms, and the 11-seat Senate, whose members are appointed. The prime minister chooses 6 Senate members, the opposition leader selects 3, and 2 are chosen in consultation with civic and religious organizations.

The most recent elections to the House of Assembly took place in 2016. The polls were considered competitive and credible, and stakeholders accepted the results. The UWP secured 11 seats, defeating the governing Saint Lucia Labour Party (SLP), which took 6.

A3. Are the electoral laws and framework fair, and are they implemented impartially by the relevant election management bodies? 3 / 4

Electoral laws are generally fair and implemented impartially by the Electoral Commission. However, differences in the sizes of constituencies have resulted in unequal voting power among citizens. While the largest constituency (Gros Islet) has more than 20,000 registered voters, the smallest (Dennery South) has only 5,000.

B. POLITICAL PLURALISM AND PARTICIPATION: 16 / 16

B1. Do the people have the right to organize in different political parties or other competitive political groupings of their choice, and is the system free of undue obstacles to the rise and fall of these competing parties or groupings? 4 / 4

Political parties may organize and operate freely. A number of small parties function, though the UWP and SLP have dominated politics since the 1960s, aided in part by the "first past the post" electoral system. Campaigns are financed entirely through private funds, which can also disadvantage new and small parties.

B2. Is there a realistic opportunity for the opposition to increase its support or gain power through elections? 4 / 4

The country has a long record of democratic transfers of power, with the UWP and SLP regularly alternating in government.

B3. Are the people's political choices free from domination by the military, foreign powers, religious hierarchies, economic oligarchies, or any other powerful group that is not democratically accountable? 4 / 4

Voters and candidates are generally free to make political choices without undue influence. However, a lack of transparency surrounding party and campaign financing raises concerns about the potential for improper influence by unaccountable foreign and domestic interests. There are few legal controls on the source of funds or on spending by candidates and parties.

B4. Do various segments of the population (including ethnic, religious, gender, LGBT, and other relevant groups) have full political rights and electoral opportunities? 4 / 4

All citizens are formally entitled to equal political rights and electoral opportunities. Women are underrepresented in politics; there were seven female candidates out of a total of 39 in the 2016 elections, and two won seats in the House of Assembly. Three members of the Senate are women. However, women have a more significant presence as electoral officials and within party structures.

The LGBT community is marginalized, and this affects the ability of LGBT people to engage fully in political processes.

C. FUNCTIONING OF GOVERNMENT: 11 / 12

C1. Do the freely elected head of government and national legislative representatives determine the policies of the government? 4 / 4

The elected prime minister, cabinet, and Parliament are able to determine the policies of the government without improper interference from unelected entities.

C2. Are safeguards against official corruption strong and effective? 3 / 4

Several state institutions are responsible for combating corruption, including the parliamentary commissioner, the auditor general, and the Public Service Commission, but their effectiveness is limited somewhat by a lack of resources.

A series of high-level officials have faced corruption allegations in recent years. During 2018, the media aired new details about long-standing allegations against Prime Minister Chastanet and Guy Joseph—the current minister for economic development, housing, urban renewal, transport, and civil aviation—in which they were accused of reaching a corrupt agreement with a US businessman involving an airport redevelopment project during the last UWP government (2007–2011).

In October, an OECD report warned that the country's CIP and other such programs, which offer citizenship and residency rights to foreigners in exchange for large sums of money, carry the potential for misuse. Opposition lawmaker Kenny Anthony initiated a legal case arguing that one project linked to the CIP was unconstitutional.

C3. Does the government operate with openness and transparency? 4 / 4

The government generally operates with openness and transparency. Access to information is legally guaranteed, and government officials are required by law to declare their financial assets annually to the Integrity Commission. However, the commission lacks the enforcement powers necessary to ensure full compliance.

CIVIL LIBERTIES: 54 / 60 (+1)
D. FREEDOM OF EXPRESSION AND BELIEF: 15 / 16
D1. Are there free and independent media? 3 / 4

The constitution guarantees freedom of expression and communication, and press freedom is largely upheld in practice. A number of private and independent news outlets carry content on a broad spectrum of issues. Internet access is not restricted. Criminal libel laws remain on the books, with convictions potentially drawing heavy fines and a jail sentence of up to five years, though civil suits are more common. In 2017, opposition lawmaker Philip Pierre was awarded EC$40,000 (US$14,800) in damages in libel cases filed against journalist Guy Ellis, the Mayers Printing Company, and the Mirror Publishing Company in connection with a 2011 letter to the editor published in the *Mirror* that described Pierre as corrupt.

D2. Are individuals free to practice and express their religious faith or nonbelief in public and private? 4 / 4

Freedom of religion is protected under the constitution and other laws, and these safeguards are largely upheld in practice. However, Rastafarians face some disadvantages as a result of their beliefs, and Muslims have reported occasional harassment.

D3. Is there academic freedom, and is the educational system free from extensive political indoctrination? 4 / 4

Academic freedom is generally respected.

D4. Are individuals free to express their personal views on political or other sensitive topics without fear of surveillance or retribution? 4 / 4

There are no significant restrictions on individuals' ability to express their personal views on political or other sensitive topics.

E. ASSOCIATIONAL AND ORGANIZATIONAL RIGHTS: 12 / 12
E1. Is there freedom of assembly? 4 / 4

The government generally respects the constitutionally protected right to free assembly. A number of protests took place peacefully in 2018, including a large SLP-led event in September at which participants cited various grievances against the government.

E2. Is there freedom for nongovernmental organizations, particularly those that are engaged in human rights–and governance-related work? 4 / 4

Independent nongovernmental organizations are free to operate.

E3. Is there freedom for trade unions and similar professional or labor organizations? 4 / 4

Most workers have the right under the law to form and join independent unions, go on strike, and bargain collectively. Antiunion discrimination is prohibited.

F. RULE OF LAW: 13 / 16 (+1)

F1. Is there an independent judiciary? 4 / 4 (+1)

The judicial system is independent and includes a high court under the Eastern Caribbean Supreme Court. Judges are appointed through an impartial Judicial and Legal Services Commission and cannot be dismissed arbitrarily. St. Lucia announced in 2014 that it would adopt the Caribbean Court of Justice (CCJ) as its final court of appeal, replacing the London-based Privy Council. However, its accession to the CCJ had not yet been finalized at the end of 2018.

Score Change: The score improved from 3 to 4 due to further long-term consolidation of an independent judiciary and a lack of tangible political interference in recent years.

F2. Does due process prevail in civil and criminal matters? 3 / 4

Detainees and defendants are guaranteed a range of legal rights, which are mostly respected in practice. However, police corruption is a concern, and court backlogs contribute to lengthy pretrial detention. Defendants charged with serious crimes may spend several years awaiting trial behind bars.

F3. Is there protection from the illegitimate use of physical force and freedom from war and insurgencies? 3 / 4

The population is mostly free from pervasive threats to physical security, and the number of homicides declined in 2018, but violent crime rates remain relatively high on a per capita basis. Police brutality has been seen as a significant problem in St. Lucia in recent years, and there is a widespread perception that members of the Royal Saint Lucia Police Force (RSLPF) enjoy impunity for abusive behavior. In 2013, the United States cut aid to the RSLPF due to credible allegations of gross human rights violations related to 12 extrajudicial killings that took place in 2010 and 2011. The government responded by inviting an international investigation of the killings. Although the investigation was completed in 2014 and members of the RSLPF were seen as culpable, no legal action was taken by prosecutors. As a consequence, St. Lucia remained excluded from security assistance from the United States under the so-called Leahy law, which prohibits such assistance for countries where security forces have been found to engage in serious human rights abuses. In response to the 2014 investigation, the government did define a "use of force" policy for the RSLPF, and members received mandatory human rights training.

F4. Do laws, policies, and practices guarantee equal treatment of various segments of the population? 3 / 4

While discrimination on the basis of race, sex, religion, and other such grounds is generally prohibited, the law does not provide full protection to LGBT people. The labor code prohibits dismissal of employees based on sexual orientation. However, same-sex sexual relations can draw up to 10 years in prison, and LGBT people are subject to significant societal prejudice.

G. PERSONAL AUTONOMY AND INDIVIDUAL RIGHTS: 14 / 16

G1. Do individuals enjoy freedom of movement, including the ability to change their place of residence, employment, or education? 4 / 4

There are no serious impediments to freedom of movement in St. Lucia, and individuals are generally free to change their place of residence, employment, or education.

G2. Are individuals able to exercise the right to own property and establish private businesses without undue interference from state or non-state actors? 4 / 4

The legal and regulatory framework is supportive of property rights and private business activity. The government has actively encouraged both domestic and foreign investors to do business in the country. St. Lucia performs well in World Bank assessments of business conditions in comparison with its neighbors.

G3. Do individuals enjoy personal social freedoms, including choice of marriage partner and size of family, protection from domestic violence, and control over appearance? 3 / 4

The law largely guarantees individual rights with respect to personal status issues like marriage and divorce, but the civil code distinguishes between "legitimate" and "illegitimate" children, which can lead to discrimination against unmarried mothers and their children in civil and family law cases. Domestic violence is a serious concern and often goes unreported, as does sexual assault. The law only criminalizes spousal rape when a couple is separated or when a court has issued a protection order.

G4. Do individuals enjoy equality of opportunity and freedom from economic exploitation? 3 / 4

Safety rules and other protections against worker exploitation are typically upheld. The economy continued to grow in 2018, potentially expanding economic opportunity, but unemployment remained a problem, particularly for younger workers. Youth unemployment remained high at over 38 percent. Young people are also particularly vulnerable to commercial sexual exploitation. The government has made some efforts to combat human trafficking, but investigations and prosecutions are rare. The country's national action plan against human trafficking has not been fully implemented because of inadequate resources. In addition to local youth, immigrants from Caribbean countries and from South Asia are vulnerable to sex trafficking and forced labor.

St. Vincent and the Grenadines

Population: 100,000
Capital: Kingstown
Political Rights Rating: 1
Civil Liberties Rating: 1
Freedom Rating: 1.0
Freedom Status: Free
Electoral Democracy: Yes

Overview: St. Vincent and the Grenadines is a parliamentary democracy that holds regular elections, though aspects of the most recent legislative polls have been disputed in court by the opposition. While civil liberties are generally upheld, journalists face the possibility of criminal defamation charges, and same-sex sexual conduct remains illegal. Violent crime is a growing concern.

KEY DEVELOPMENTS IN 2018:

- In September, Prime Minister Ralph Gonsalves was forced to deny the existence of a police "Black Squad" supposedly tasked with intimidating government opponents. The issue was raised after the US government evacuated 23 Peace Corps volunteers in August, apparently in response to reported threats and attacks.
- The country recorded 34 murders during the year, a decrease from unusually high totals of 39 in 2017 and 40 in 2016.

POLITICAL RIGHTS: 36 / 40

A. ELECTORAL PROCESS: 11 / 12

A1. Was the current head of government or other chief national authority elected through free and fair elections? 4 / 4

The prime minister, usually the leader of the majority party in the parliament, is appointed by the governor general, who represents the British monarch as the largely ceremonial head of state. Ralph Gonsalves retained his position as prime minister following the victory of his incumbent Unity Labour Party (ULP) in the 2015 legislative elections, which were considered generally free and fair.

A2. Were the current national legislative representatives elected through free and fair elections? 4 / 4

The constitution provides for the direct election of 15 representatives to the unicameral House of Assembly. In addition, the governor general appoints six senators to the chamber: four selected on the advice of the prime minister and two on the advice of the opposition leader. All serve five-year terms.

The 2015 legislative elections resulted in a narrow victory by the social democratic ULP, which took eight seats in the House of Assembly; the opposition New Democratic Party (NDP) won the remaining seven elected seats. International and domestic observers deemed the polls generally competitive and credible. However, the Organization of American States (OAS) observer mission expressed concerns about partiality of the presiding officer at the final vote count in the constituency of Central Leeward. According to the OAS report, the returning officer there continually refused requests for information or access from representatives of the NDP, while responding to requests from representatives of the ULP. The NDP mounted several mass protests alleging electoral irregularities and initiated two legal complaints regarding the conduct of polling in Central Leeward and North Windward. In July 2017, the High Court ruled that the petitions should be allowed to proceed, and both cases were ongoing at the end of 2018.

A3. Are the electoral laws and framework fair, and are they implemented impartially by the relevant election management bodies? 3 / 4

Electoral laws are generally fair and impartially implemented. Efforts to update voter lists were initiated in 2013, and ahead of the 2015 elections the legislature passed an amendment to the election law that removed almost 24,000 names from the lists. The amendment had bipartisan support. The 2015 OAS election monitoring mission welcomed the change, but said that authorities should implement a continuous updating and cleansing process; this has not yet been done. It also called for better standardization of voting procedures across polling sites.

B. POLITICAL PLURALISM AND PARTICIPATION: 15 / 16

B1. Do the people have the right to organize in different political parties or other competitive political groupings of their choice, and is the system free of undue obstacles to the rise and fall of these competing parties or groupings? 4 / 4

Political parties can organize freely. While there are a number of smaller political parties in the country, since 1998 only the ULP and NDP have won seats in the parliament. The "first past the post" electoral system has contributed to this pattern, but there are also concerns that unregulated private campaign financing puts smaller parties at a disadvantage. The limited state funding that is available goes only to parties represented in the previous parliament.

B2. Is there a realistic opportunity for the opposition to increase its support or gain power through elections? 4 / 4

The country has experienced multiple peaceful transfers of power between rival parties after elections, including two since it gained full independence in 1979. The ULP has been in government since 2001, but it has had only a narrow majority over the opposition NDP since 2010.

B3. Are the people's political choices free from domination by the military, foreign powers, religious hierarchies, economic oligarchies, or any other powerful group that is not democratically accountable? 4 / 4

The political choices of candidates and voters are generally free from interference by extrapolitical forces. However, the OAS raised concerns in 2015 about the lack of transparency regarding party and campaign financing, which could enable undue influence by private actors.

B4. Do various segments of the population (including ethnic, religious, gender, LGBT, and other relevant groups) have full political rights and electoral opportunities? 3 / 4

All citizens are formally entitled to full political rights and electoral opportunities, but women remain significantly underrepresented in the legislature and in politics generally. No women were elected to the House of Assembly in 2015; three were appointed. In its report on the 2015 elections, the OAS noted that there was a "pervasive reluctance" on the part of potential women candidates to take part in harsh political campaigns.

The LGBT (lesbian, gay, bisexual, and transgender) community is marginalized, and this affects the ability of LGBT people to engage fully in political processes.

C. FUNCTIONING OF GOVERNMENT: 10 / 12

C1. Do the freely elected head of government and national legislative representatives determine the policies of the government? 4 / 4

The elected prime minister, cabinet, and House of Assembly members are able to determine the policies of the government without improper interference from unelected entities.

C2. Are safeguards against official corruption strong and effective? 3 / 4

Corruption-related offenses by public officials are prohibited by law, and the independent judiciary and media provide additional checks on graft. However, there is no specialized national anticorruption agency, and claims of petty corruption continue to be reported.

C3. Does the government operate with openness and transparency? 3 / 4

The government generally operates with openness and transparency. Nevertheless, freedom of information legislation that was passed in 2003 has yet to be fully implemented, and there is no active legislation requiring government officials to disclose assets, income, or gifts.

CIVIL LIBERTIES: 55 / 60 (+1)

D. FREEDOM OF EXPRESSION AND BELIEF: 15 / 16

D1. Are there free and independent media? 3 / 4

The constitution guarantees the freedoms of expression and communication, and these rights are usually upheld in practice. The state owns the main local broadcaster, but a number of private newspapers are available, and news consumers also have access to foreign media and online outlets.

Journalists remain subject to criminal and civil defamation laws, and the 2016 Cybercrime Act broadened the definition and scope of defamation to include online publications; violation of its often vaguely worded provisions can carry a fine of as much as EC$500,000 (US$185,000) and up to seven years' imprisonment.

D2. Are individuals free to practice and express their religious faith or nonbelief in public and private? 4 / 4

Freedom of religion is constitutionally protected and respected in practice.

D3. Is there academic freedom, and is the educational system free from extensive political indoctrination? 4 / 4

Academic freedom is generally upheld.

D4. Are individuals free to express their personal views on political or other sensitive topics without fear of surveillance or retribution? 4 / 4

There are no significant restrictions on individuals' ability to express their personal views on political or other sensitive topics.

E. ASSOCIATIONAL AND ORGANIZATIONAL RIGHTS: 12 / 12

E1. Is there freedom of assembly? 4 / 4

Freedom of assembly is constitutionally protected and generally upheld in practice. There were reports of police using excessive force to disperse peaceful protests during the 2015 election period, but similar incidents have not been reported in recent years.

E2. Is there freedom for nongovernmental organizations, particularly those that are engaged in human rights-and governance-related work? 4 / 4

Nongovernmental organizations operate freely. However, reported security threats including a physical attack on a volunteer apparently prompted the US Peace Corps to withdraw 23 people from the country in August 2018. Responding to allegations that a police-affiliated "Black Squad," supposedly tasked with intimidating government opponents, was responsible for the pressure on the Peace Corps, Prime Minister Gonsalves denied that such a group existed.

E3. Is there freedom for trade unions and similar professional or labor organizations? 4 / 4

The constitution protects the right to form or join trade unions and other such associations. Unions are permitted to strike and engage in collective bargaining. The law prohibits antiunion discrimination and dismissal for engaging in union activities. The right to collective bargaining is generally upheld, though public-sector unions have recently criticized the government for failing to respect the bargaining process.

F. RULE OF LAW: 14 / 16 (+1)

F1. Is there an independent judiciary? 4 / 4 (+1)

The judiciary generally operates independently. Judges are appointed through an impartial Judicial and Legal Services Commission and cannot be dismissed arbitrarily. The country is subject to the Eastern Caribbean Supreme Court and recognizes the original jurisdiction of the Caribbean Court of Justice, but the Privy Council in London remains the final court of appeal.

Score Change: The score improved from 3 to 4 due to further long-term consolidation of an independent judiciary and a lack of tangible political interference in recent years.

F2. Does due process prevail in civil and criminal matters? 3 / 4

Detainees and defendants are guaranteed a range of legal rights, which are mostly respected in practice. However, there is a significant case backlog, which leads to prolonged pretrial detention. According to the US State Department, about 20 people had been held in pretrial detention for longer than two years as of 2017, with many of the cases featuring delays in obtaining psychiatric evaluations of the defendant.

F3. Is there protection from the illegitimate use of physical force and freedom from war and insurgencies? 4 / 4

While the population is free from war and other acute threats to physical security, the homicide rate has reached unusually high levels in recent years, with 40 murders in 2016 and 39 in 2017; the number fell to 34 in 2018, though for the previous decade it had most often been in the 20s. Prison conditions have improved since the opening of a new correctional facility in 2012, but the old prison in Kingstown is still in use and features substandard conditions. The government has strongly denied allegations in recent years that a supposed extralegal unit affiliated with the police is used to intimidate its perceived opponents.

F4. Do laws, policies, and practices guarantee equal treatment of various segments of the population? 3 / 4

The constitution prohibits discrimination based on race, sex, religion, and other such categories, but sexual orientation and gender identity are not similarly protected. Same-sex sexual conduct is illegal and carries penalties of up to 10 years in prison. While the law is rarely enforced, societal discrimination against LGBT people persists. Women reportedly face sexual harassment in the workplace, which is not specifically addressed by law.

G. PERSONAL AUTONOMY AND INDIVIDUAL RIGHTS: 14 / 16

G1. Do individuals enjoy freedom of movement, including the ability to change their place of residence, employment, or education? 4 / 4

There are no significant restrictions on freedom of movement, and individuals are able to change their place of residence, employment, and education.

G2. Are individuals able to exercise the right to own property and establish private businesses without undue interference from state or non-state actors? 4 / 4

Individuals are free to own property and to establish and operate businesses. The government has actively encouraged both domestic and foreign investors to do business in the country, though the World Bank has reported some regulatory difficulties with respect to registering property, obtaining credit, and resolving insolvency.

G3. Do individuals enjoy personal social freedoms, including choice of marriage partner and size of family, protection from domestic violence, and control over appearance? 3 / 4

Individual rights with respect to personal status matters like marriage and divorce are generally protected by law, though same-sex marriage is not recognized. The Domestic Violence Act of 2015, which went into effect in 2016 and provides for protective orders, offers some tools and resources to victims of domestic violence. However, such violence remains a serious and widespread problem, as does sexual assault.

G4. Do individuals enjoy equality of opportunity and freedom from economic exploitation? 3 / 4

The law provides safety and other basic protections against labor exploitation, and these are typically upheld, though there are some reports of inadequate enforcement. The Prevention of Trafficking in Persons Act of 2011 criminalizes forced labor and sex trafficking, and the government has increased its efforts to investigate violations and improve prevention and victim protection, but it has yet to secure any trafficking convictions, according to the US State Department.

Sudan

Capital: Khartoum
Population: 41,700,000
Political Rights Rating: 7
Civil Liberties Rating: 7
Freedom Rating: 7.0
Freedom Status: Not Free
Electoral Democracy: No

Overview: Sudan's political system is dominated by an authoritarian president, Omar al-Bashir, and his National Congress Party (NCP), which rely on repression and inducements to maintain power. The regime violently represses regional, religious, and ethnic groups that do not share its narrow nationalist vision. Civil society encounters severe restrictions, religious rights are not respected, and the media is closely monitored.

KEY DEVELOPMENTS IN 2018:

- Economic hardship and rising commodity prices sparked nationwide protests at both the beginning and end of the year. In December, largely peaceful demonstrations demanding President al-Bashir's resignation were violently suppressed by the authorities; Amnesty International reported that at least 37 people were killed in the violence. Hundreds of demonstrators were also arrested and detained without charge during the two spates of protests.
- In August, the NCP chose President al-Bashir as its candidate for the 2020 presidential election, despite the two-term limit that would require him to step down at the end of his current term. In December, a constitutional amendment was introduced in the parliament to abolish term limits, which would clear the way for al-Bashir's candidacy if passed.
- In September, in response to the worsening economic conditions, President al-Bashir dissolved the national unity government formed in 2017. The new government he subsequently formed was dominated by the NCP.

POLITICAL RIGHTS: 3 / 40 (-1)

A. ELECTORAL PROCESS: 2 / 12

A1. Was the current head of government or other chief national authority elected through free and fair elections? 1 / 4

The 2005 constitution established term limits, allowing presidents to serve no more than two five-year terms. President al-Bashir was reelected in 2015 with 94 percent of the vote. The governments of the US, Britain, and Norway condemned the process for its "failure to create a free, fair, and conducive elections environment." During the run-up to the election, opposition leaders were detained and the government cracked down on the media. The main opposition parties boycotted the election, arguing that free and fair elections were not possible until a national dialogue on Sudan's political and constitutional future was held. A dialogue held after the election was also boycotted by most of the opposition, which claimed it was an insincere effort by the NCP to stay in power.

The dialogue resulted in the formation of a national unity government in 2017 that contained a small number of opposition representatives and established the new position of prime minister, a step intended to reduce the powers of the executive. Al-Bashir awarded the position to a close ally, Bakri Hassan Saleh, who already held the post of first vice president.

A2. Were the current national legislative representatives elected through free and fair elections? 1 / 4

The upper chamber of the bicameral National Legislature is the 54-member Council of States, whose members are indirectly elected by state legislatures. In the 426-seat National Assembly, the lower chamber, 213 members are directly elected, 128 seats are reserved for women elected by proportional representation, and 85 additional members are elected by proportional representation. Members in both chambers serve six-year terms. The opposition boycott of the 2015 parliamentary elections, which were held concurrently with the presidential election, enabled the NCP to win a large majority in the National Assembly, where it claimed 323 of 426 seats. Many of the remaining seats were taken by NCP-aligned parties. As with the presidential election, the parliamentary elections were not held in accordance with democratic standards.

A3. Are the electoral laws and framework fair, and are they implemented impartially by the relevant election management bodies? 0 / 4

The National Election Commission is not independent; its chairman is an NCP official. In November 2018, the National Assembly approved a new election law which reduced the National Assembly to 380 seats and decreased the number of seats in the body reserved for women from 128 to 30, among other provisions. Although the government acceded to 18 of 19 demands made by the opposition on the substance of the bill, 34 opposition legislators walked out of the National Assembly before the vote in protest, reflecting a deep distrust of the NCP regime and its commitment to establishing a fair electoral framework.

In August, the NCP chose al-Bashir as its candidate for the 2020 presidential election, despite the two-term limit that would require him to step down at the end of his current term. In December, a constitutional amendment was introduced in the parliament to abolish term limits, which would clear the way for al-Bashir to run for reelection in 2020.

B. POLITICAL PLURALISM AND PARTICIPATION: 3 / 16 (–1)

B1. Do the people have the right to organize in different political parties or other competitive political groupings of their choice, and is the system free of undue obstacles to the rise and fall of these competing parties or groupings? 1 / 4

Sudan has more than 100 political parties, but regulatory hurdles as well as harassment, intimidation, and detention of opposition figures prevent them from freely operating and competing. As antigovernment protests erupted across the country in December 2018 over the tripling of bread prices and worsening economic conditions, security officials cracked down on opposition parties, arresting and detaining the leader of the Sudanese Congress Party, Omar el-Digeir; and raiding an opposition gathering in Khartoum, which led to the arrests of nine members of three political parties.

B2. Is there a realistic opportunity for the opposition to increase its support or gain power through elections? 0 / 4 (–1)

The harassment, intimidation, and arrests of opposition figures hinder their parties' ability to gain power. Hundreds of opposition leaders and activists were arrested in January and February 2018 for demonstrating against rising fuel prices and the government's handling of an economic crisis. Many were detained without charge for several weeks before being released, including the head of the Sudanese Communist Party and a deputy from the National Umma Party (NUP). In April, the head of the NUP, Sadiq al-Mahdi, was charged with plotting to overthrow the government. Al-Mahdi returned to Sudan in December after nearly a year in self-imposed exile, but no further legal action had been taken against him at year's end.

Several other developments in 2018 significantly reduced the ability of opposition parties to challenge the NCP. In late April, the National Consensus Forces, a coalition of center-left and left-wing opposition parties, announced it would boycott the 2020 elections. The decision by the NCP to nominate al-Bashir for another presidential term could significantly reduce the prospects for a transfer of power in 2020. In September, as the economic crisis worsened, al-Bashir dissolved the national unity government, and the new government he formed was dominated by the NCP.

Score Change: The score declined from 1 to 0 because the dissolution of the national unity government, the decision by opposition parties to boycott the 2020 elections, the announcement by al-Bashir that he intends to seek an additional presidential term (in violation of the two-term limit), and the continued harassment and arrests of opposition leaders all reduced the ability of political parties to increase their support.

B3. Are the people's political choices free from domination by the military, foreign powers, religious hierarchies, economic oligarchies, or any other powerful group that is not democratically accountable? 1 / 4

Al-Bashir surrounds himself with a clique of unelected internal security and military officials, who influence decision-making. The NCP has a sizable Islamist wing, although its influence over policymaking has waned in recent years.

B4. Do various segments of the population (including ethnic, religious, gender, LGBT, and other relevant groups) have full political rights and electoral opportunities? 1 / 4

Sudan's political system heavily favors the ethnic groups, predominantly Arab and Muslim, with populations concentrated around Khartoum. Peripheral regions—notably Darfur, the Two Areas of South Kordofan and Blue Nile, and eastern Sudan—are marginalized. A total of 128 seats in the National Assembly are reserved for women, but the election law passed by the National Assembly in November 2018 reduced that number to 30.

C. FUNCTIONING OF GOVERNMENT: 1 / 12

C1. Do the freely elected head of government and national legislative representatives determine the policies of the government? 1 / 4

President al-Bashir dominates the government, despite attempts to dilute the powers of the presidency by reestablishing the post of prime minister. In September 2018, al-Bashir demonstrated his continued dominance by dissolving the national unity government and replacing the prime minister.

The military and intelligence services are powerful forces in the government and support al-Bashir, while many high-level officials are drawn from the security sector.

C2. Are safeguards against official corruption strong and effective? 0 / 4

Corruption is rampant among the NCP-linked elite and security agencies, and efforts to control the problem have been insufficient. Nevertheless, an anticorruption drive announced by the government in July 2018 led to the arrests of a number of high-profile government officials throughout the year. In September, the former head of the Political Security Department at the National Intelligence and Security Services (NISS) was sentenced to seven years in prison by a military court after his conviction on corruption charges. However, anticorruption efforts are undermined by a lack of clarity in conflict of interest laws regarding the rights of government officials to operate private companies while in office. Many high-level officials own stakes in private enterprises, contributing to widespread cronyism and facilitating the continued proliferation of patronage networks.

C3. Does the government operate with openness and transparency? 0 / 4

Sudan's government operates in an unaccountable manner. The bloated security institutions, which receive 78 percent of the national budget, are opaque and corrupt. Government ministries run large off-budget accounts and bodies intended to oversee public spending have been eroded.

ADDITIONAL DISCRETIONARY POLITICAL RIGHTS QUESTION:

Is the government or occupying power deliberately changing the ethnic composition of a country or territory so as to destroy a culture or tip the political balance in favor of another group? –3 / 0

The government stands accused of attempting to change the ethnic composition of Sudan through its response to an insurgency led by marginalized non-Arab ethnic groups in

Darfur. Tactics include the alleged use of chemical weapons against civilians as recently as 2016 and terror campaigns against civilians conducted by a paramilitary group, the Rapid Support Forces (RSF), under the authority of the NISS. Al-Bashir faces outstanding arrest warrants from the International Criminal Court (ICC) on charges of war crimes, crimes against humanity, and—controversially—genocide in Darfur. Accusations of ethnically targeted violence have also been leveled against the government for its handling of the wars in the Two Areas of South Kordofan and Blue Nile, where there has been repeated, indiscriminate aerial bombardment of civilians. Al-Bashir declared a unilateral cease-fire in all three areas in 2016, which—despite violations by both sides—remained in place as of the end of 2018.

CIVIL LIBERTIES: 4 / 60
D. FREEDOM OF EXPRESSION AND BELIEF: 2 / 16
D1. Are there free and independent media? 0 / 4

Sudan's media faces many obstacles due to government restrictions, censorship, and harassment of journalists by NISS agents. The media environment for journalists further deteriorated in 2018, as the government cracked down on coverage of unrest through censorship, intimidation, and arrests of journalists. In January, NISS agents seized the print runs for eight newspapers in response to their coverage of protests; the agency continued to seize entire print runs of newspaper editions without explanation throughout the year. In December, nine journalists demonstrating in Khartoum against government harassment of the media were arrested and briefly detained. In the same month, at least three reporters covering antigovernment demonstrations were assaulted by security agents.

Journalists are forbidden to publish stories about 15 so-called red line issues, including articles about the NISS and the army. In July, the NISS, after a five-year hiatus, returned to inspecting newspapers before publication and ordering the removal of articles that do not meet its approval.

D2. Are individuals free to practice and express their religious faith or nonbelief in public and private? 0 / 4

Freedom of religion is guaranteed under the 2005 interim constitution but is not respected in practice. Since the independence of South Sudan, the small Christian community in Sudan has faced persecution and several churches have been shuttered. In February 2018, the government razed an Evangelical Presbyterian church in Khartoum North without warning. People who convert to Christianity risk apostasy charges. In October, nine Christians in South Darfur State were detained by the NISS for five days and allegedly tortured before eight of them agreed to convert to Islam. A priest who refused to convert was arrested and charged with apostasy, and awaited trial at year's end.

D3. Is there academic freedom, and is the educational system free from extensive political indoctrination? 1 / 4

The government views students as a source of opposition and harshly responds to signs of restiveness on university campuses, often using NCP-affiliated students to attack and intimidate protesters. In January 2018, security forces used tear gas to disperse a protest at the University of Khartoum against the government's handling of the economy, and arrested three demonstrators.

D4. Are individuals free to express their personal views on political or other sensitive topics without fear of surveillance or retribution? 1 / 4

The NISS intimidates individuals who engage in private discussion of issues of a political nature, and reportedly monitors private communications without adequate oversight or authorization. Authorities have increasingly used defamation laws to prosecute social media users who criticize the government.

E. ASSOCIATIONAL AND ORGANIZATIONAL RIGHTS: 1 / 12

E1. Is there freedom of assembly? 0 / 4

The authorities have repeatedly used deadly force against protesters. Security forces violently cracked down on a series of demonstrations across the country in December 2018 over the poor economy, in which many protesters demanded al-Bashir's resignation. Authorities fired tear gas and live ammunition into demonstrations. According to Amnesty International, at least 37 protesters were killed in the violence in December. In the midst of the protests, the government also blocked access to social media platforms including Twitter, Facebook, Instagram, and WhatsApp, and shut down the internet on several telecommunications networks through the end of the year.

E2. Is there freedom for nongovernmental organizations, particularly those that are engaged in human rights- and governance-related work? 1 / 4

Nongovernmental organizations (NGOs), particularly those that work on human rights issues, face harassment and arrest. In May 2018, human rights activist Hisham Ali Mohamed Ali, who has advocated against torture and official corruption, was detained upon arrival at the Khartoum International Airport, after being deported from Saudi Arabia. Ali remained in detention without charge at the end of the year.

The government eased some restrictions on the movement of humanitarian workers in conflict zones. In September, the government agreed to a United Nations plan to deliver humanitarian assistance to rebel-held areas of South Kordofan and Blue Nile.

E3. Is there freedom for trade unions and similar professional or labor organizations? 0 / 4

Trade union rights are minimal, and there are no independent unions. The Sudan Workers' Trade Unions Federation has been coopted by the government, which also must approve all strikes. Workers who strike risk arrest. In June 2018, security forces briefly detained a group of teachers staging a sit-in to protest low salaries and the closure of 200 secondary schools in El Gezira State.

F. RULE OF LAW: 0 / 16

F1. Is there an independent judiciary? 0 / 4

The judiciary is not independent. Lower courts provide some due process safeguards, but the higher courts are subject to political control. Special security and military courts do not apply accepted legal standards.

F2. Does due process prevail in civil and criminal matters? 0 / 4

The 2010 National Security Act gives the NISS sweeping authority to seize property, conduct surveillance, search premises, and detain suspects for up to four and a half months without judicial review. The NISS has systematically detained and tortured government opponents, including Darfuri activists, students, and journalists. Hundreds of people arrested during demonstrations in January and February 2018 were held without charge and denied legal representation, before being released in April. Dozens of additional demonstrators were arrested and detained without charge in December, and most remained in custody at year's end. Under the Police Act of 2008, police officers are immune from prosecution.

F3. Is there protection from the illegitimate use of physical force and freedom from war and insurgencies? 0 / 4

Torture and abuse of prisoners is rampant, with political detainees from Darfur and the Two Areas subject to particularly harsh treatment. Human rights abuses by the government or government-backed forces like the RSF are endemic. A report released in April 2018 by the African Centre for Justice and Peace Studies (ACJPS) documented serious abuses against civilians in South Kordofan by security forces between January and March, including rape and several killings. In Darfur, dozens of civilians were killed and thousands displaced in an upsurge in fighting during the spring between government-aligned forces and rebels in Jebel Marra. Security officials are rarely held accountable for human rights violations.

The death penalty is applied to a range of offenses and has been used against members of the political and armed opposition, particularly in Darfur. Sudanese criminal law is based on Sharia (Islamic law) and allows punishments such as flogging and cross-amputation (removal of the right hand and left foot).

F4. Do laws, policies, and practices guarantee equal treatment of various segments of the population? 0 / 4

Sudan's many ethnic, regional, and religious groups face political, social, and economic marginalization. Same-sex sexual acts are illegal, though this prohibition does not appear to be strongly enforced. Official and societal discrimination against LGBT (lesbian, gay, bisexual, and transgender) individuals is widespread. Sudan passed legislation in 2014 to strengthen the rights of asylum seekers, but these rights are not respected in practice. Refugees, particularly from Eritrea, face ill treatment and deportation.

G. PERSONAL AUTONOMY AND INDIVIDUAL RIGHTS: 1 / 16

G1. Do individuals enjoy freedom of movement, including the ability to change their place of residence, employment, or education? 0 / 4

The government restricts freedom of movement in conflict-affected areas, particularly in Darfur, the Two Areas, and Kassala State in eastern Sudan, where states of emergency remained in place at year's end. Women are not allowed to travel or obtain state identification without the permission of a male guardian. Authorities also seized passports and imposed international travel bans on several opposition politicians and civil society leaders during the year.

G2. Are individuals able to exercise the right to own property and establish private businesses without undue interference from state or nonstate actors? 1 / 4

Sudanese citizens are allowed to buy land and set up businesses but encounter many obstacles in practice. Weak land rights have been a chronic driver of conflict in Sudan, exploited by corrupt government officials and unscrupulous investors to evict smallholders to make way for commercial development. In 2018, the authorities continued to use force in demolishing settlements they claimed were illegally built. In April, for example, several women and children were injured and seven people were arrested when police demolished large portions of a village in El Gezira State.

G3. Do individuals enjoy personal social freedoms, including choice of marriage partner and size of family, protection from domestic violence, and control over appearance? 0 / 4

Women face extensive discrimination. Islamic law denies women equal rights in marriage, inheritance, and divorce. Traditional and religious law restricts the property rights of women. Women convicted of adultery can face the death penalty. Violence against women is a major problem, particularly in conflict-affected regions, and few perpetrators are brought to justice. Police use criminal code provisions outlawing "indecent and immoral acts" to prohibit women from wearing clothing of which they disapprove.

G4. Do individuals enjoy equality of opportunity and freedom from economic exploitation? 0 / 4

Economic mismanagement by the government and the concentration of wealth in the hands of a military, religious, and business elite linked to the NCP have deprived ordinary Sudanese of economic opportunity and condemned them to poverty.

According to the US Department of State, Sudan has failed to take adequate steps to eliminate the trafficking of persons, but the government did increase the number of trafficking arrests and prosecutions between April 2017 and March 2018.

Suriname

Population: 600,000
Capital: Paramaribo
Political Rights Rating: 2
Civil Liberties Rating: 3 ↓
Freedom Rating: 2.5
Freedom Status: Free
Electoral Democracy: Yes

Overview: Suriname is a constitutional democracy that holds generally free and fair elections. However, corruption is a pervasive problem in government, and attacks on judicial independence and due process, underscored by the president's interference in his own murder trial, remain a concern. Women, indigenous peoples, and the Maroon population are politically underrepresented.

KEY DEVELOPMENTS IN 2018:

- In October, murder proceedings against President Dési Bouterse resumed. He is accused of involvement in the execution of 15 opponents of the then military government in 1982, when he was head of the army. A verdict is expected in 2019.
- Lawmakers failed to approve bylaws necessary for the implementation of a 2017 anticorruption law, which as a consequence has not yet taken effect.
- The Independent Electoral Bureau (OKB), the body that will organize the 2020 elections, stated in October that it planned to remove from the voter lists those who had not shown up at the polls in the last 10 years. The plan prompted criticism from observers who said it favored the ruling party.
- In October, the Paramaribo office of the opposition National Party of Suriname (NPS) was shot at while party delegates were in a meeting. The following month, a pride flag and a Progressive Workers and Farmers Union (PALU) flag were set on fire at PALU's offices.

POLITICAL RIGHTS: 34 / 40
A. ELECTORAL PROCESS: 12 / 12

A1. Was the current head of government or other chief national authority elected through free and fair elections? 4 / 4

The president is chief of state and head of government, and is elected to five-year terms by a two-thirds majority of the 51-seat National Assembly. If no such majority can be reached, a United People's Assembly—consisting of lawmakers from the national, regional, and local levels—convenes to choose the president by a simple majority. The president is not subject to term limits. In 2015, the freely elected National Assembly reelected President Dési Bouterse in accordance with the law.

A2. Were the current national legislative representatives elected through free and fair elections? 4 / 4

The 1987 constitution provides for a unicameral, 51-seat National Assembly. Representatives are elected for five-year terms via proportional representation. The last legislative elections in 2015 were considered competitive and credible. Bouterse's NDP took 26 seats, the V7 opposition coalition took 18, and smaller groupings took the remainder.

A3. Are the electoral laws and framework fair, and are they implemented impartially by the relevant election management bodies? 4 / 4

Electoral laws meet international standards of fairness. The president appoints the members of the election commission, the OKB, and has the power to fire them. In October 2018, the OKB announced that the approximately 30,000 to 40,000 voters who had not shown up at polling stations for the last 10 years would be removed from the voter lists. Some observers criticized the measure as favoring the NDP, which has many young and disciplined supporters.

B. POLITICAL PLURALISM AND PARTICIPATION: 14 / 16

B1. Do the people have the right to organize in different political parties or other competitive political groupings of their choice, and is the system free of undue obstacles to the rise and fall of these competing parties or groupings? 4 / 4

Suriname's many political parties, which often reflect the country's ethnic cleavages, may generally form and operate freely. However, politics are rancorous, and the governing parties often seek to protect their power by leveraging economic and other tools. When businessman Ramsoender Jhauw started an opposition party in 2014, his company lost important orders from the government, bringing the business close to bankruptcy.

Separately, in October 2018, the Paramaribo office of the opposition National Party of Suriname (NPS) was shot at while party delegates were in a meeting. The following month, a pride flag and a Progressive Workers and Farmers Union (PALU) flag were set on fire at PALU's offices.

B2. Is there a realistic opportunity for the opposition to increase its support or gain power through elections? 4 / 4

Opposition parties can gain power through elections. Most parties form coalitions to contest elections. In the 2015 elections, the V7, an opposition coalition, won 18 of 51 seats in the National Assembly. The NDP holds the most seats, with 26.

In late 2018, Bouterse's government proposed a measure that would ban party alliances. While the NDP would be subject to the measure, its effects would be felt more by the country's many small opposition parties, which would face limitations on their ability to create alliances among themselves ahead of elections.

B3. Are the people's political choices free from domination by the military, foreign powers, religious hierarchies, economic oligarchies, or any other powerful group that is not democratically accountable? 3 / 4

People's political choices are generally not subject to undue coercion. However, opposition political parties have raised concerns about campaign financing, which is unregulated and lacks transparency, and the resulting influence that special interest groups can have on parties and candidates.

B4. Do various segments of the population (including ethnic, religious, gender, LGBT, and other relevant groups) have full political rights and electoral opportunities? 3 / 4

Parties are often formed along ethnic lines, meaning most ethnic groups have political representation. However, the interests of indigenous communities are often overlooked. Women have historically played a limited role in politics, but have experienced gains in recent years—in 2015, 13 out of the 51 representatives elected to the National Assembly were women, compared to 6 women elected in 2010. The interests of Maroons, the descendants of escaped slaves, are poorly represented in politics, though there are Maroon representatives at various levels of government.

C. FUNCTIONING OF GOVERNMENT: 8 / 12

C1. Do the freely elected head of government and national legislative representatives determine the policies of the government? 4 / 4

Freely elected representatives are able to determine laws and government policies.

C2. Are safeguards against official corruption strong and effective? 2 / 4

Government corruption is pervasive. In 2017, the National Assembly adopted a new anticorruption law, updating past laws that were severely outdated. However, it has not yet come into effect.

C3. Does the government operate with openness and transparency? 2 / 4

The government often does not operate with transparency. Officials are not legally required to disclose information about their finances. Suriname does not have laws to facilitate access to public information, and access is limited in practice.

CIVIL LIBERTIES: 43 / 60 (−1)
D. FREEDOM OF EXPRESSION AND BELIEF: 14 / 16 (−1)

D1. Are there free and independent media? 3 / 4

The constitution guarantees press freedom, and the media sector is fairly diverse. Although some journalists engage in self-censorship in response to pressure and intimidation from authorities, the press frequently publishes stories critical of the government.

D2. Are individuals free to practice and express their religious faith or nonbelief in public and private? 4 / 4

The constitution guarantees freedom of religion, which is typically upheld in practice.

D3. Is there academic freedom, and is the educational system free from extensive political indoctrination? 4 / 4

Academic freedom is generally respected.

D4. Are individuals free to express their personal views on political or other sensitive topics without fear of surveillance or retribution? 3 / 4 (−1)

Freedom of expression is enshrined in the constitution, and there are no formal constraints on the expression of personal views among the general public. However, Suriname's rancorous political atmosphere, continued attacks on the media and other government critics by officials, and separate 2018 incidents at political party offices in which shots were fired and flags were burnt, have prompted some residents to exercise increased caution when discussing sensitive issues

Score Change: The score declined from 4 to 3 due to increasing concerns about retribution for private speech, amid a rancorous political environment.

E. ASSOCIATIONAL AND ORGANIZATIONAL RIGHTS: 11 / 12

E1. Is there freedom of assembly? 4 / 4

The constitution guarantees freedom of assembly, which is generally respected in practice. However, members of the antigovernment protest movement We Zijn Moe-Dig (We Are Tired/Courageous), which was founded in 2015, say President Bouterse has characterized them as traitors.

E2. Is there freedom for nongovernmental organizations, particularly those that are engaged in human rights- and governance-related work? 4 / 4

Nongovernmental organizations (NGOs) function freely in Suriname.

E3. Is there freedom for trade unions and similar professional or labor organizations? 3 / 4

Workers are free to join independent trade unions, which are actively involved in politics. Civil servants lack the legal right to strike. There have been isolated reports of private-sector employers denying collective bargaining rights to unions.

F. RULE OF LAW: 8 / 16

F1. Is there an independent judiciary? 2 / 4

The courts are financially dependent on executive agencies, and executive influence over the understaffed judiciary remains a matter of concern. After a military court declared an amnesty law unconstitutional in June 2016, Bouterse sought to prevent a trial against him from moving forward, but was ultimately unsuccessful.

F2. Does due process prevail in civil and criminal matters? 1 / 4

Due process is undermined by corruption, a shortage of judges, and a lack of resources and staff to support the judiciary. The public prosecutor's office often pursues cases selectively. Low wages in the police corps creates vulnerability for corruption. Payments are sometimes made to obtain favorable outcomes in criminal and civil proceedings. There is a backlog of cases involving non-Dutch speakers, as interpreters who have gone unpaid have refused to work additional cases.

Pretrial detention, even for small crimes, is common, and due to the overload of the judicial system, it often takes a long time before defendants can appear in court.

President Bouterse has accepted "political responsibility" for his involvement in the abduction and extrajudicial killing of 15 political opponents in 1982, but has sought to disrupt legal proceedings against him. When his efforts to prevent a murder trial against him failed, Bouterse fired the justice minister and in March 2017 replaced her with a close ally. In 2017, the public prosecutor demanded a 20-year prison sentence against Bouterse. The government subsequently adopted a resolution warning the prosecutor to be "careful," and asking him to voluntarily resign. Bouterse later withdrew the resolution in the face of public outrage, and the trial resumed in October 2018.

F3. Is there protection from the illegitimate use of physical force and freedom from war and insurgencies? 3 / 4

The use of excessive force by law enforcement officials is prohibited, but cases of police abuse have been reported. Temporary detention facilities are characterized by unhygienic conditions, understaffing, and overcrowding. Suriname lies on a major drug-trafficking route, giving way to some trafficking-related violence. Violent crimes such as burglary and armed robbery are common, and police resources are insufficient to address the problem.

F4. Do laws, policies, and practices guarantee equal treatment of various segments of the population? 2 / 4

The constitution prohibits discrimination based on race or ethnicity. Nevertheless, the Maroon and indigenous people in the hinterland face inequality in areas such as education and employment. Despite a verdict by the Inter-American Court of Human Rights made public in 2016, minority groups still are dispossessed of their lands.

Same-sex sexual relations are legal, though the age of consent differs from that of heterosexual couples. Despite legal protections adopted in 2015, members of the LGBT (lesbian, gay, bisexual, and transgender) community face societal discrimination, harassment, and abuse by police, and contend with occasional instances of intimidation such as the burning of a pride flag at PALU offices in 2018.

The constitution bars gender discrimination, but in practice, women experience disadvantages in access to employment and education.

G. PERSONAL AUTONOMY AND INDIVIDUAL RIGHTS: 10 / 16

G1. Do individuals enjoy freedom of movement, including the ability to change their place of residence, employment, or education? 3 / 4

The government generally upholds constitutional freedoms of internal movement and residence, though the lack of protections for indigenous and Maroon lands leave those communities vulnerable to displacement by unregulated logging and mining operations.

G2. Are individuals able to exercise the right to own property and establish private businesses without undue interference from state or nonstate actors? 2 / 4

Although Suriname's constitution guarantees property rights, they are sometimes inadequately protected. Corruption can hinder private business activity, especially regarding land policy, government contracts, and licensing. Women face inequality related to inheritance and property due to discriminatory local customs.

G3. Do individuals enjoy personal social freedoms, including choice of marriage partner and size of family, protection from domestic violence, and control over appearance? 3 / 4

Domestic violence remains a serious problem, and laws criminalizing it are not well-enforced. The October 2018 murder of 37-year-old Monaliza Maynard by her former partner in Paramaribo shocked Suriname and brought the subject to public attention. Hundreds of people participated in a protest march against domestic violence organized after the murder.

G4. Do individuals enjoy equality of opportunity and freedom from economic exploitation? 2 / 4

Despite efforts of the government, trafficking in persons remains a serious problem. Women and migrant workers are especially at risk of human trafficking, sexual exploitation, and forced labor in various industries. Construction and mining work often do not receive attention from labor inspectors. Venezuela's deteriorating economy has increased Venezuelan women's vulnerability to sex trafficking in Suriname. Corruption has facilitated the criminal activities of traffickers.

Sweden

Population: 10,200,000
Capital: Stockholm
Political Rights Rating: 1
Civil Liberties Rating: 1
Freedom Rating: 1.0
Freedom Status: Free
Electoral Democracy: Yes

Overview: Sweden is a parliamentary monarchy with free and fair elections and a strong multiparty system. Civil liberties and political rights are legally guaranteed and respected in practice, and the rule of law prevails.

KEY DEVELOPMENTS IN 2018:

- A general election was held in September in which neither the center-right nor the center-left bloc won a majority in the parliament. The populist, anti-immigrant party, Sweden Democrats, won 62 seats. Parties in both main blocs refused to form a coalition government with Sweden Democrats, and the impasse had not been resolved by year's end.
- In late September, Prime Minister Stefan Löfven of the Social Democratic Party (SAP) lost a vote of no confidence in the parliament, but pledged to continue as prime minister until a coalition government was formed. After lengthy negotiations, in December, the parliament rejected another attempt by Löfven to form a government
- In August, a court ordered a translation company to pay a Muslim woman $4,500, after finding that it discriminated against her during a 2016 job interview that abruptly ended when she declined to shake a male employee's hand for religious reasons.

POLITICAL RIGHTS: 40 / 40

A. ELECTORAL PROCESS: 12 / 12

A1. Was the current head of government or other chief national authority elected through free and fair elections? 4 / 4

The prime minister is the head of government and is appointed by the speaker of the freely elected parliament, or Riksdag, and confirmed by the body as a whole. Prime Minister Stefan Löfven of the SAP was appointed in 2014 following parliamentary elections, and formed a minority government with the Green Party. King Carl XVI Gustaf, crowned in 1973, is the ceremonial head of state.

A2. Were the current national legislative representatives elected through free and fair elections? 4 / 4

The unicameral Riksdag is comprised of 349 members who are elected every four years by proportional representation. A party must receive at least 4 percent of the vote nationwide or 12 percent in an electoral district to win representation. Swedish elections are broadly free and fair.

In the September 2018 parliamentary elections, neither main bloc won a majority, with the center-left bloc winning 144 seats and the center-right bloc winning 143 seats. The populist, anti-immigrant party, Sweden Democrats, won 62 seats, up from 49 previously. However, the party's gains fell short of the expectations of many analysts. Parties in both the center-right and center-left blocs refused to form a coalition government with the Sweden Democrats. In late September, Prime Minister Löfven lost a vote of no confidence in the parliament, but pledged to continue in his role until a coalition government was formed. After lengthy negotiations, in December, the parliament rejected another attempt by Löfven to form a government.

A report published in November by election monitors from the Organization for Security and Co-operation in Europe (OSCE) stated that although the integrity of the elections was not in doubt, the secrecy of the vote was sometimes compromised.

A3. Are the electoral laws and framework fair, and are they implemented impartially by the relevant election management bodies? 4 / 4

Elections are regulated by the Swedish Election Authority, which effectively upholds its mandates.

B. POLITICAL PLURALISM AND PARTICIPATION: 16 / 16

B1. Do the people have the right to organize in different political parties or other competitive political groupings of their choice, and is the system free of undue obstacles to the rise and fall of these competing parties or groupings? 4 / 4

Political parties may form and operate without restriction. Eight political parties gained representation in the Riksdag in 2018, with the SAP, the Moderates, and the Sweden Democrats holding the most seats.

B2. Is there a realistic opportunity for the opposition to increase its support or gain power through elections? 4 / 4

Sweden has a strong multiparty system with a robust opposition.

B3. Are the people's political choices free from domination by the military, foreign powers, religious hierarchies, economic oligarchies, or any other powerful group that is not democratically accountable? 4 / 4

People's political choices are generally free from domination by actors that are not democratically accountable.

B4. Do various segments of the population (including ethnic, religious, gender, LGBT, and other relevant groups) have full political rights and electoral opportunities? 4 / 4

The country's principal religious, ethnic, and immigrant groups are represented in the parliament, as are many women. Since 1993, the indigenous Sami community has elected its own legislature, which has significant powers over community education and culture, and serves as an advisory body to the government.

C. FUNCTIONING OF GOVERNMENT: 12 / 12

C1. Do the freely elected head of government and national legislative representatives determine the policies of the government? 4 / 4

Sweden's freely elected representatives develop and implement policy. The strong performance by the far-right Sweden Democrats in the 2018 parliamentary elections, and the refusal of both the center-right bloc and center-left bloc to work with the party, contributed to the failure to form a functioning government by the end of the year.

C2. Are safeguards against official corruption strong and effective? 4 / 4

Corruption is relatively low in Sweden. Anticorruption mechanisms are generally effective. The country's lively free press also works to expose corrupt officials. However, Sweden has faced some criticism for insufficient enforcement of foreign bribery laws.

C3. Does the government operate with openness and transparency? 4 / 4

The country has one of the most robust freedom of information statutes in the world, and state authorities generally respect the right of both citizens and noncitizens to access public information.

CIVIL LIBERTIES: 60 / 60
D. FREEDOM OF EXPRESSION AND BELIEF: 16 / 16

D1. Are there free and independent media? 4 / 4

Sweden's media are independent. Most newspapers and periodicals are privately owned, and the government subsidizes daily newspapers regardless of their political affiliation. Public broadcasters air weekly radio and television programs in several minority languages.

Threats and intimidation of journalists have increased in recent years, particularly against those who report on organized crime, religion, extremist groups, or other sensitive topics. In August 2018, a member of the Nordic Resistance Movement, a neo-Nazi party, was arrested for plotting to kill two journalists with Mittmedia, a large media group. In September, the suspect was convicted of illegally possessing firearms, but acquitted of the more serious charge of preparing to commit murder.

D2. Are individuals free to practice and express their religious faith or nonbelief in public and private? 4 / 4

Religious freedom is constitutionally guaranteed and generally respected. State authorities document religion-based hate crimes, investigate and prosecute cases, and provide adequate resources for victims. The police force includes a permanent unit trained to handle hate crimes.

In August 2018, a court ordered a translation company to pay a Muslim woman $4,500, after finding that it discriminated against her during a 2016 job interview that abruptly ended when she declined to shake a male employee's hand for religious reasons. The court ruled that the European Convention on Human Rights protected the woman's right to refuse a handshake on religious grounds.

Anti-Semitic attacks have occurred in recent years, including a Molotov cocktail attack on a synagogue in Gothenburg in late 2017. Three people were arrested in connection with the incident; in June, all three suspects were found guilty and sentenced to prison terms ranging from one to two years.

D3. Is there academic freedom, and is the educational system free from extensive political indoctrination? 4 / 4

Academic freedom is generally respected.

D4. Are individuals free to express their personal views on political or other sensitive topics without fear of surveillance or retribution? 4 / 4

Private discussion is open and vibrant.

E. ASSOCIATIONAL AND ORGANIZATIONAL RIGHTS: 12 / 12
E1. Is there freedom of assembly? 4 / 4

Freedom of assembly is generally respected in law and in practice. However, violence has occasionally erupted between far-right demonstrators and counterprotesters.

E2. Is there freedom for nongovernmental organizations, particularly those that are engaged in human rights– and governance-related work? 4 / 4

Nongovernmental organizations of all kinds function freely.

E3. Is there freedom for trade unions and similar professional or labor organizations? 4 / 4

The rights to strike and organize in labor unions are guaranteed. Trade union federations, which represent approximately 70 percent of the workforce, are strong and well organized.

F. RULE OF LAW: 16 / 16
F1. Is there an independent judiciary? 4 / 4

The judiciary is independent.

F2. Does due process prevail in civil and criminal matters? 4 / 4

The rule of law prevails in civil and criminal matters. Defendants are presumed innocent until proven guilty, and the state must provide legal counsel to people accused of criminal offenses.

F3. Is there protection from the illegitimate use of physical force and freedom from war and insurgencies? 4 / 4

Following a 2017 attack in which a man drove a truck through central Stockholm and into a department store, killing 5 people and wounding 10 others, the government introduced new antiterrorism measures. The law focused on tighter security in public places, greater information sharing between government agencies, and tighter controls on individuals deemed to pose a security threat.

In August 2018, groups of masked youths set fire to approximately 100 cars in western Sweden, mainly in Gothenburg, in what appeared to be coordinated attacks.

Conditions in prisons and temporary detention facilities are adequate, but concerns have been raised about excessive use of long detention periods. Changes to the law regarding detention have been proposed in the parliament. Swedish courts have jurisdiction to try suspects for genocide committed abroad.

F4. Do laws, policies, and practices guarantee equal treatment of various segments of the population? 4 / 4

The Swedish state works to ensure equal protection and rights for all members of the population. An equality ombudsman oversees efforts to prevent discrimination on the basis of gender, ethnicity, disability, and sexual orientation. However, the United Nations has called for the ombudsman's powers to be strengthened, and has noted problems with discrimination by police and correctional personnel.

In August 2018, a "cis-man-free" music festival was held in Gothenburg, which was advertised as an event open to women, transgender people, and nonbinary people. The festival was founded to create a safe space for women after a series of rapes at music festivals in 2017. In December, the ombudsman found the festival guilty of discrimination for its exclusionary advertising, though no penalties were assessed.

In 2017, in the wake of growing right-wing sentiment and increasing immigration from abroad, the Swedish government voted to place limits on parental leave benefits for immigrants. In 2016, the parliament passed a law that tightened restrictions on asylum seekers, which included limiting family reunification

G. PERSONAL AUTONOMY AND INDIVIDUAL RIGHTS: 16 / 16

G1. Do individuals enjoy freedom of movement, including the ability to change their place of residence, employment, or education? 4 / 4

Freedom of movement is legally guaranteed and generally respected in practice. However, asylum seekers may be assigned to a place of residence, and at times may be forced to change locations. Sweden continues to maintain checkpoints on its external borders that were instituted during the 2015 refugee crisis.

G2. Are individuals able to exercise the right to own property and establish private businesses without undue interference from state or nonstate actors? 4 / 4

The government respects the rights of individuals to own property and establish private businesses. A 2011 Supreme Court ruling granted Sami reindeer herders common-law rights to disputed lands.

G3. Do individuals enjoy personal social freedoms, including choice of marriage partner and size of family, protection from domestic violence, and control over appearance? 4 / 4

Same-sex couples are legally allowed to marry and adopt; lesbian couples have the same rights to artificial insemination and in-vitro fertilization as heterosexual couples. The Lutheran Church allows same-sex marriage ceremonies.

The United Nations has criticized Sweden for not doing enough to prevent domestic violence against women and children. Despite its status as a model for gender equality, Sweden suffers from persistently high levels of rape and sexual assault. To address the issue, the parliament passed a groundbreaking law in May 2018 which legally recognizes that sex without consent amounts to rape. The law distinguishes Sweden from most other European countries, which continue to legally define rape in terms of force, threats, and coercion.

G4. Do individuals enjoy equality of opportunity and freedom from economic exploitation? 4 / 4

People in Sweden generally enjoy equality of opportunity. Women earn the equivalent of 95.5 percent of men's wages when differences in age, sector, and experience are taken into account. However, unemployment is higher among immigrants than it is among people who were born in Sweden.

Sweden is a destination and, to a lesser extent, a transit point for women and children trafficked for the purpose of sexual exploitation, but the Swedish government is proactive in combatting the problem. The government has established municipal-level antitrafficking working groups and action plans. Nevertheless, the United Nations has pointed out that Sweden lacks robust methods to prevent individuals, especially unaccompanied immigrant children, from falling victim to human trafficking. According to the US State Department's 2018 *Trafficking in Persons Report,* Sweden does not sufficiently screen migrants to identify trafficking victims.

Switzerland

Population: 8,500,000
Capital: Bern
Political Rights Rating: 1
Civil Liberties Rating: 1
Freedom Rating: 1.0
Freedom Status: Free
Electoral Democracy: Yes

Overview: The political system of Switzerland is characterized by decentralization and direct democracy. The multilingual state is typically governed by a broad coalition that includes members from the four largest political parties represented in the parliament. The 26 cantons that make up the Swiss Confederation have considerable decision-making power, and the public is often asked to weigh in on policy matters through referendums. Civil liberties are generally respected in the country, though laws and policies adopted in recent years have reflected a growing wariness of immigration and minority groups of foreign origin, which sometimes face societal discrimination.

KEY DEVELOPMENTS IN 2018:

- A new data-retention law came into effect in March, forcing mobile phone and internet service providers to retain user data for six months.
- Also in March, referendum voters rejected a proposal to eliminate general broadcasting fees that finance the operations of the country's public broadcaster.
- In a November referendum, voters rejected the so-called self-determination initiative, which would have prioritized Swiss law over international law.

POLITICAL RIGHTS: 39 / 40

A. ELECTORAL PROCESS: 12 / 12

A1. Was the current head of government or other chief national authority elected through free and fair elections? 4 / 4

Executive power is exercised by the seven-member Federal Council (cabinet), with each member elected by the bicameral Federal Assembly to four-year terms. The Federal Council represents a consensus-based coalition among all of the large parties in the Federal Assembly. The presidency is largely ceremonial and rotates annually among the Federal Council's members. In December 2018, Ueli Maurer of the Swiss People's Party (SVP) was elected president by the Federal Assembly in accordance with the law.

A2. Were the current national legislative representatives elected through free and fair elections? 4 / 4

The constitution provides for a Federal Assembly with two directly elected chambers: the 46-member Council of States, in which each canton has two members and each half-canton has one, and the 200-member National Council, whose seats are apportioned among the cantons based on population. All lawmakers serve four-year terms. Switzerland's electoral process is vibrant and pluralistic, garnering high levels of confidence from the public.

The last elections were held in 2015. In the National Council, the right-wing SVP won 65 seats, up from the 54 it previously held. The Social Democratic Party (SP) won 43 seats, the Free Democratic Party of Switzerland (FDP) took 33 seats, the Christian Democratic People's Party (CVP) captured 27 seats, and the Green Party won 7 seats. In the Council of States, the FDP and the CVP won 13 seats each, the SP took 12, and three other parties split the remainder.

A3. Are the electoral laws and framework fair, and are they implemented impartially by the relevant election management bodies? 4 / 4

Switzerland's electoral process is robust and well implemented. Electoral laws are fair, and the Election Commission of Switzerland, which administers elections, is considered impartial.

B. POLITICAL PLURALISM AND PARTICIPATION: 15 / 16

B1. Do the people have the right to organize in different political parties or other competitive political groupings of their choice, and is the system free of undue obstacles to the rise and fall of these competing parties or groupings? 4 / 4

Political parties are free to form and operate, and a wide range of parties are active at the federal and regional levels. The political system is stable, but it remains open to new groups.

B2. Is there a realistic opportunity for the opposition to increase its support or gain power through elections? 4 / 4

While most parties govern together by common agreement in the country's consensus-based political system, they compete vigorously in elections and can gain or lose influence depending on their performance at the polls. The government also relies on referendums to decide on contentious policy issues. The Federal Council currently comprises two members each from the SVP, the SP, and the FDP, and one member from the CVP.

B3. Are the people's political choices free from domination by the military, foreign powers, religious hierarchies, economic oligarchies, or any other powerful group that is not democratically accountable? 4 / 4

The people's political choices are generally free from domination by democratically unaccountable entities. However, the Council of Europe's Group of States against Corruption (GRECO) has criticized Switzerland for failing to address the lack of transparency in party financing. Civil society leaders contend that the opaque campaign finance system allows wealthy interests to influence the platforms of the major political parties. In March 2018, referendum voters in the cantons of Fribourg and Schwyz approved measures for increased party-finance transparency. Activists are currently pushing for a transparency referendum at the federal level, though the government in August said the initiative was not necessary.

B4. Do various segments of the population (including ethnic, religious, gender, LGBT, and other relevant groups) have full political rights and electoral opportunities? 3 / 4

Restrictive citizenship laws and procedures tend to exclude many immigrants, as well as their children, from political participation. About a quarter of the population is made of up noncitizens, though more than a third of these are citizens of neighboring countries. In August 2018, a Muslim couple was denied Swiss citizenship due in part to their refusal to shake hands with members of the other sex during talks on their naturalization.

Women participate robustly in Swiss politics, both as voters and candidates for office. In the 2015 elections, 64 women were elected to the National Council.

C. FUNCTIONING OF GOVERNMENT: 12 / 12

C1. Do the freely elected head of government and national legislative representatives determine the policies of the government? 4 / 4

Switzerland's freely elected officials are able to determine and effectively implement national and local policy through a decentralized system of government.

The 26 cantons have significant control over economic and social policy, with the federal government's powers largely limited to foreign affairs and some economic matters. Referendums, which are used extensively, are mandatory for any amendments to the federal constitution, the joining of international organizations, or major changes to federal laws.

C2. Are safeguards against official corruption strong and effective? 4 / 4

Safeguards against corruption are generally effective. In 2018, evidence emerged that Pierre Maudet, head of the Geneva cantonal government, had accepted benefits from the crown prince of Abu Dhabi in 2015, prompting the Geneva public prosecutor to announce plans for an investigation in August. Maudet resigned in September.

Switzerland remains on a European Union (EU) "grey list" of countries that have been uncooperative in abolishing questionable tax policies and discouraging tax avoidance, though it took steps to increase cooperation and the automatic exchange of tax information during 2018.

C3. Does the government operate with openness and transparency? 4 / 4

The government is generally transparent in its operations. In June 2018, the National Council rejected restrictions on access to government procurement documents for the public and the media, which had been proposed by the Federal Council as part of an ongoing overhaul of federal procurement laws.

CIVIL LIBERTIES: 57 / 60

D. FREEDOM OF EXPRESSION AND BELIEF: 15 / 16

D1. Are there free and independent media? 4 / 4

Freedom of the press is generally respected in practice. Switzerland has an open media environment, though the state-owned, editorially independent Swiss Broadcasting Corporation (SRG/SSR) dominates the broadcast market. In a March 2018 referendum, a clear majority of Swiss citizens rejected an initiative to abolish the broadcasting fees that finance the SRG/SSR. Consolidation of newspaper ownership in the hands of large media conglomerates has forced the closure of some smaller newspapers in recent years.

D2. Are individuals free to practice and express their religious faith or nonbelief in public and private? 3 / 4

Freedom of religion is guaranteed by the constitution, and the penal code prohibits discrimination against any religion. However, Muslims face legal and de facto discrimination. The construction of new minarets and mosques is prohibited as the result of a 2009 referendum. A debate surrounding proposals for a federal ban on burqas continued in 2018 and is likely to be put to a vote in the coming years. In September 2018, St. Gallen became the second canton to pass its own burqa ban, after Ticino in 2016.

D3. Is there academic freedom, and is the educational system free from extensive political indoctrination? 4 / 4

Academic freedom is largely respected.

D4. Are individuals free to express their personal views on political or other sensitive topics without fear of surveillance or retribution? 4 / 4

Individuals are generally able to express their personal views on political issues without fear of retribution, though the law punishes public incitement to racial hatred or discrimination as well as denial of crimes against humanity.

While the Federal Intelligence Service was granted wider surveillance powers in 2017, allowing it to monitor internet usage, bug private property, and tap the phone lines of suspected terrorists, the number of surveillance measures overall has declined in recent years. However, a law that came into effect in March 2018 requires mobile phone and internet service providers to retain user data for six months to facilitate the work of law enforcement agencies. This includes data on which websites users visited.

Also in 2018, a debate took place surrounding potential surveillance tactics to uncover social security and insurance fraud. The National Council in March approved measures such as the use of drones or location tracking, and a citizen initiative to stop these practices through a referendum failed in November.

E. ASSOCIATIONAL AND ORGANIZATIONAL RIGHTS: 12 / 12
E1. Is there freedom of assembly? 4 / 4

Freedom of assembly is guaranteed by the constitution and generally respected.

E2. Is there freedom for nongovernmental organizations, particularly those that are engaged in human rights- and governance-related work? 4 / 4

Nongovernmental organizations are free to operate without undue restrictions.

E3. Is there freedom for trade unions and similar professional or labor organizations? 4 / 4

Workers are generally free to form trade unions and other professional organizations. The rights to engage in collective bargaining and strikes are respected.

F. RULE OF LAW: 15 / 16
F1. Is there an independent judiciary? 4 / 4

While the judiciary is largely independent in practice, judges are affiliated with political parties and are selected based on a system of proportional party, linguistic, and regional representation in the Federal Assembly. In May 2018, a group of civil society leaders formally launched an initiative to appoint federal judges by lot from a pool of qualified candidates and thus depoliticize the appointment procedure.

A so-called self-determination initiative was rejected by voters in a November referendum. The initiative would have given primacy to Swiss constitutional law over international law and thus cast doubt on Swiss participation in a range of international treaties, including the jurisdiction of the European Court of Human Rights. At the end of the year, Switzerland was negotiating a framework agreement with the EU, a contentious topic in the country, which is not an EU member state. Among other things, the agreement would clarify the jurisdiction of the European Court of Justice in Switzerland and the applicability of EU law.

F2. Does due process prevail in civil and criminal matters? 4 / 4

The authorities generally observe legal safeguards against arbitrary arrest and detention. The constitution's due process guarantees ensure fair trial proceedings.

F3. Is there protection from the illegitimate use of physical force and freedom from war and insurgencies? 4 / 4

Switzerland is free from war and other major threats to physical security. Occasional instances of excessive force by police have been documented, but such abuses are relatively rare. Conditions in prisons and detention centers generally meet international standards, and the Swiss government permits visits by independent observers.

F4. Do laws, policies, and practices guarantee equal treatment of various segments of the population? 3 / 4

Although the law prohibits discrimination on the basis of race, gender, or religion, anti-immigrant attitudes have grown in recent years. An immigration law passed in 2016 included measures meant to curb mass migration from the EU. It also required employers to give preference to Swiss citizens in hiring practices. Despite this law and the government's negotiations with the EU on the matter, the SVP proposed a referendum in 2017 calling for an end to free movement between Switzerland and the EU. No date for such a vote had been set as of 2018.

The rights of cultural, religious, and linguistic minorities are legally protected, but minority groups—especially those of African and Central European descent, as well as Roma—face societal discrimination. Roma continue to seek official recognition as a minority in Switzerland. A report by the Federal Commission against Racism published in April 2018 noted a strong increase in racial discrimination over the past 10 years.

While women generally enjoy equal rights, gender pay gaps and discrimination in the workplace persist. The rights of LGBT (lesbian, gay, bisexual, and transgender) people are generally respected. In December 2018, the parliament passed an amendment to the anti-discrimination law that extended its protections to cover sexual orientation, but a similar amendment on gender identity was ultimately rejected.

G. PERSONAL AUTONOMY AND INDIVIDUAL RIGHTS: 15 / 16

G1. Do individuals enjoy freedom of movement, including the ability to change their place of residence, employment, or education? 4 / 4

Freedom of movement is respected, and there are no undue limitations on the ability to change one's place of residence, employment, or education.

G2. Are individuals able to exercise the right to own property and establish private businesses without undue interference from state or nonstate actors? 4 / 4

The rights to own property and operate private businesses remain unrestricted.

G3. Do individuals enjoy personal social freedoms, including choice of marriage partner and size of family, protection from domestic violence, and control over appearance? 4 / 4

Personal social freedoms are protected for most people. In a 2005 referendum, voters approved same-sex civil unions. Recognized since 2007, these unions grant many of the legal benefits of marriage. Limited adoption rights for same-sex civil partners came into effect in January 2018. The legalization of same-sex marriage and full adoption rights for same-sex couples were under consideration by the parliament during the year.

G4. Do individuals enjoy equality of opportunity and freedom from economic exploitation? 3 / 4

Although the government complies with international standards for combating human trafficking, according to the US State Department's *Trafficking in Persons Report*, Switzerland remains a destination country for victims. Labor regulations are generally enforced, but there is no national minimum wage, and migrant workers are more vulnerable to exploitive labor practices and dangerous working conditions.

Syria

Population: 18,300,000
Capital: Damascus
Political Rights Rating: 7
Civil Liberties Rating: 7
Freedom Rating: 7.0
Freedom Status: Not Free
Electoral Democracy: No

Overview: Political rights and civil liberties in Syria are severely compromised by one of the world's most repressive regimes and by other belligerent forces in an ongoing civil war. The regime prohibits genuine political opposition and harshly suppresses freedoms of speech and assembly. Corruption, enforced disappearances, military trials, and torture are rampant in government-controlled areas. Residents of contested regions or territory held by nonstate actors are subject to additional abuses, including intense and indiscriminate combat, sieges and interruptions of humanitarian aid, and mass displacement.

KEY DEVELOPMENTS IN 2018:
- In January, the Turkish military and allied Syrian militias attacked the Afrin district in the northwest, which was controlled by Kurdish militias affiliated with the leftist Democratic Union Party (PYD). The Turkish-led forces had largely secured the district by March, though the operation displaced thousands of civilians.
- In April, the Syrian government enacted legislation that would allow it to designate areas for redevelopment and reconstruction by decree. The law enables state confiscation of property without compensation or appeal if residents or owners fail to meet certain conditions.
- Also in April, a suspected chemical weapons attack killed more than 40 people in the opposition-held Damascus suburb of Douma. The United States, Britain, and France responded with a series of punitive missile strikes against government targets linked to chemical weapons near Damascus and Homs.
- Between February and July, government forces and their foreign partners recaptured the Damascus suburbs of Eastern Ghouta and rebel-held parts of Daraa and Quneitra in the south, leading to large-scale displacements of civilians and fighters. The campaigns effectively eliminated the rebel presence in southwestern Syria.
- In December, after parallel progovernment and US-led offensives in the east had left Islamic State (IS) militants with only a tiny sliver of territory near the Iraqi border, US president Donald Trump declared that IS had been defeated in Syria and that US troops would soon withdraw from the country.

POLITICAL RIGHTS: −3 / 40

A. ELECTORAL PROCESS: 0 / 12

A1. Was the current head of government or other chief national authority elected through free and fair elections? 0 / 4

President Bashar al-Assad was elected for a third seven-year term in 2014 with what the government claimed was 88.7 percent of the vote. The balloting was conducted only in government-controlled areas amid war and severe repression. Major democratic states denounced the election as illegitimate.

A2. Were the current national legislative representatives elected through free and fair elections? 0 / 4

The most recent elections for the 250-seat People's Council were held in 2016, but only in government-controlled territory. Several opposition groups that were traditionally tolerated by the authorities boycotted the polls, and state workers reportedly faced pressure to vote. Members of the military were permitted to participate in the elections for the first time. The ruling Baath Party and its declared allies took 200 of the 250 seats; the remainder went to nominal independents.

A3. Are the electoral laws and framework fair, and are they implemented impartially by the relevant election management bodies? 0 / 4

There is no transparency or accountability surrounding the official electoral process. The executive authorities, acting through the military-security apparatus, effectively grant or withhold permission to participate in elections in government-held areas. Although some provisional local councils in rebel-held areas have organized rudimentary elections since 2011, ongoing attacks by progovernment forces and Islamist militants have largely made such processes untenable. Kurdish-held areas in the north have a provisional constitution that allows local elections, but the PYD exercises ultimate control.

B. POLITICAL PLURALISM AND PARTICIPATION: 0 / 16

B1. Do the people have the right to organize in different political parties or other competitive political groupings of their choice, and is the system free of undue obstacles to the rise and fall of these competing parties or groupings? 0 / 4

A 2011 decree allowed the registration of new political parties, but it also imposed significant obstacles to party formation and prohibited parties based on religion, regional affiliation, and other criteria. In practice, all legal political groups and independents are either part of, allied with, or heavily vetted by the regime.

The local councils active in some opposition areas are often sponsored or appointed by prominent families or armed groups. In Kurdish areas, decentralized governance theoretically allows for open political participation, but in practice political affairs are dominated by the most powerful group, the PYD, which engages in arbitrary detentions of its political opponents.

B2. Is there a realistic opportunity for the opposition to increase its support or gain power through elections? 0 / 4

The Baath Party has governed Syria without interruption since the 1960s, led by Assad or his late father for nearly all of that time. The 2011 decree and 2012 constitutional reforms formally relaxed rules regarding the participation of non-Baathist parties, but in practice the government maintains a powerful intelligence and security apparatus to monitor and punish opposition movements that could emerge as serious challengers to Assad's rule.

B3. Are the people's political choices free from domination by the military, foreign powers, religious hierarchies, economic oligarchies, or any other powerful group that is not democratically accountable? 0 / 4

In its territory, the regime's security and intelligence forces, militias, and business allies are a serious obstacle to the autonomy of voters and politicians. Foreign actors including

Russia, Iran, and the Lebanese Shiite militia Hezbollah also exert heavy influence over politics in regime-held areas due to their involvement in the war and material support for the government. In opposition areas, civilian politics are often subordinated to armed groups and external funders, while the PYD and its affiliated militias exercise control over the political choices of residents in Kurdish regions.

B4. Do various segments of the population (including ethnic, religious, gender, LGBT, and other relevant groups) have full political rights and electoral opportunities? 0 / 4

Although the government is often described as an Alawite regime and a protector of other religious minorities, it is not an authentic vehicle for these groups' political interests. Political access is a function not primarily of sect, but of proximity and loyalty to Assad and his associates. The political elite is not exclusively Alawite and includes members of the majority Sunni sect, which also makes up most of the rebel movement. Meanwhile, Alawites, Christians, and Druze outside Assad's inner circle are just as politically disenfranchised as the broader Sunni population.

The opposition's dwindling territory is divided among moderate, Islamist, and radical jihadist rebels, with varying implications for ethnic and religious minorities. The PYD nominally ensures representation for minorities, but it has been accused of mistreating non-Kurdish residents, particularly those suspected of IS sympathies.

Women have equal political rights; they hold 13 percent of the seats in the legislature, and some have been appointed to senior positions in recent years. However, women are typically excluded from political decision-making in practice and have little ability to organize independently given state repression and the presence of hostile armed groups. All leadership positions in Kurdish areas are reportedly shared between a man and a woman, and women are well represented in political life, though they have limited autonomy outside PYD-led structures.

C. FUNCTIONING OF GOVERNMENT: 0 / 12

C1. Do the freely elected head of government and national legislative representatives determine the policies of the government? 0 / 4

De facto authority in government-controlled Syria lies with the president—who is not freely elected—and his political, security, and business allies rather than in formal institutions such as the cabinet and parliament. Foreign powers like Iran and Russia also wield considerable influence over state policy, and both opposition forces and Kurdish-led fighters hold large swaths of territory with the help of countries including Turkey and the United States, respectively.

C2. Are safeguards against official corruption strong and effective? 0 / 4

Members and allies of the ruling family are said to own or control much of the Syrian economy. The civil war has created new opportunities for corruption among the government, loyalist armed forces, and the private sector. The regime has regularly distributed patronage in the form of public resources, and implemented policies to benefit favored industries and companies, to secure its support base. Government contracts and trade deals have also been awarded to allies like Iran, possibly as compensation for political and military aid. Even basic state services are extended or withheld based on a community's demonstrated political loyalty to the Assad regime, providing additional leverage for bribe-seeking officials. Similar manipulation has been alleged in the distribution of humanitarian aid.

Corruption is also widespread in rebel-held areas. Some rebel commanders, including from brigades nominally aligned with democratic powers and their allies, have been accused of looting, extortion, and theft. Local administrators and activists complain that little of the international aid reportedly given to opposition representatives abroad seems to reach them, raising suspicions of graft.

C3. Does the government operate with openness and transparency? 0 / 4

The government has long operated with minimal transparency and public accountability, and conditions have worsened during the civil war amid the rise of militias that are nominally loyal to the regime but largely autonomous and free to exploit the population in areas they control. Officials have broad discretion to withhold government information, and they are not obliged to make public disclosures of their assets. Independent civil society groups and media outlets are harshly suppressed and cannot influence or shed light on state policies.

ADDITIONAL DISCRETIONARY POLITICAL RIGHTS QUESTION
Is the government or occupying power deliberately changing the ethnic composition of a country or territory so as to destroy a culture or tip the political balance in favor of another group? −3 / 0

Sunni Arab civilians bear the brunt of attacks by the Alawite-led government and loyalist militias. The regime has forcibly transferred thousands of civilians from captured opposition areas after bombing and besieging them, and these tactics were used again during 2018 as government forces took control of areas including Eastern Ghouta, Daraa, and Quneitra between February and July. The land-seizure component of a new reconstruction law adopted in April raised concerns that it would be used to consolidate or advance politicized population changes. Sunni Islamist and jihadist groups often persecute religious minorities and Muslims they deem impious. Kurdish militias have been accused of displacing Arab and Turkmen communities in the context of their fight against IS, and the Turkish-led offensive in Afrin in early 2018 was reportedly followed by the seizure and destruction of Kurdish civilian property. In the face of these threats, civilians of all backgrounds have sought safety among their respective religious or ethnic groups, contributing to the demographic shifts wrought by the war.

CIVIL LIBERTIES: 3 / 60 (+1)
D. FREEDOM OF EXPRESSION AND BELIEF: 3 / 16 (+1)
D1. Are there free and independent media? 0 / 4

The constitution nominally guarantees freedom of speech and the press, but in practice freedom of expression is heavily restricted in government-held areas, and journalists or ordinary citizens who criticize the state face censorship, detention, torture, and death in custody. All media must obtain permission to operate from the Interior Ministry. Private media in government areas are generally owned by figures associated with the regime. Media freedom varies in territory held by other groups, but local outlets are typically under heavy pressure to support the dominant militant faction in the area. Journalists face physical danger throughout Syria, especially from regime forces and extremist groups. At least nine were killed in 2018, according to the Committee to Protect Journalists, bringing the death toll to 127 since the war began in 2011.

D2. Are individuals free to practice and express their religious faith or nonbelief in public and private? 2 / 4 (+1)

While the constitution mandates that the president be a Muslim, there is no state religion, and the regime has generally allowed different confessional groups to practice their faiths as long as their religious activities are not politically subversive. The government monitors mosques and controls the appointment of Muslim religious leaders. The growing dominance of extremist groups in opposition-held areas of western Syria has threatened freedom of worship for local residents and displaced people, though IS's continued military defeats in the east during 2018—which left it with only a tiny sliver of territory near the Iraqi border at year's end—further reduced its ability to persecute religious activity that does not conform to its version of Sunni Islam.

Score Change: The score improved from 1 to 2 because the ouster of the Islamic State militant group from nearly all of the territory it previously controlled sharply reduced its ability to impose its religious views on the population.

D3. Is there academic freedom, and is the educational system free from extensive political indoctrination? 0 / 4

Academic freedom is heavily restricted. University professors in government-held areas have been dismissed or imprisoned for expressing dissent, and some have been killed for supporting regime opponents. Combatants on all sides of the war have regularly attacked or commandeered schools. Groups including the PYD—and prior to its military defeats, IS—have set up education systems in their territories, but they are infused with political indoctrination.

D4. Are individuals free to express their personal views on political or other sensitive topics without fear of surveillance or retribution? 1 / 4

The government engages in heavy surveillance of private and online discussion and harshly punishes dissent in areas it controls. The environment is somewhat more open in areas where neither the government nor an extremist group has a dominant presence, though the PYD and some opposition factions have allegedly suppressed freedom of speech.

E. ASSOCIATIONAL AND ORGANIZATIONAL RIGHTS: 0 / 12
E1. Is there freedom of assembly? 0 / 4

Freedom of assembly is severely restricted across Syria. Opposition protests in government-held areas are usually met with gunfire, mass arrests, and torture of those detained. Jihadist groups, the PYD, and some rebel factions have also used force to quash civilian dissent and demonstrations.

E2. Is there freedom for nongovernmental organizations, particularly those that are engaged in human rights- and governance-related work? 0 / 4

The regime generally denies registration to nongovernmental organizations with reformist or human rights missions, and regularly conducts raids and searches to detain civic and political activists. A variety of new grassroots civil society networks emerged in many parts of Syria following the 2011 uprising, monitoring human rights abuses by all sides and attempting to provide humanitarian and other services in opposition areas. However, such activists face violence, intimidation, and detention by armed groups, and must operate secretly in many cases.

E3. Is there freedom for trade unions and similar professional or labor organizations? 0 / 4

Professional syndicates in state-held areas are controlled by the Baath Party, and all labor unions must belong to the General Federation of Trade Unions, a nominally independent grouping that the government uses to control union activity. The war's economic and political pressures have made functioning labor relations virtually impossible across the country.

F. RULE OF LAW: 0 / 16

F1. Is there an independent judiciary? 0 / 4

The constitution forbids government interference in the civil judiciary, but judges and prosecutors are essentially required to belong to the Baath Party and are in practice beholden to the political leadership.

F2. Does due process prevail in civil and criminal matters? 0 / 4

Military officers can try civilians in both conventional military courts and field courts, which lack due process guarantees. While civilians may appeal military court decisions with the military chamber of the Court of Cassation, military judges are neither independent nor impartial, as they are subordinate to the military command. Extremist groups have set up religious courts in their territories, imposing harsh punishments for perceived offenses by civilians under their interpretation of religious law. The general breakdown of state authority and the proliferation of militias in much of the country has led to arbitrary detentions, summary justice, and extrajudicial penalties by all sides in the civil war.

F3. Is there protection from the illegitimate use of physical force and freedom from war and insurgencies? 0 / 4

More than 500,000 people have been killed in the civil war since 2011, according to prevailing estimates. Both the regime and insurgent groups frequently engage in extreme violence against civilians, including indiscriminate bombardment, extrajudicial killings, and torture of detainees. However, abuses by the government are the largest in scale. Regime forces have detained and tortured tens of thousands of people since the uprising began, and many have died in custody, though detention conditions that amount to enforced disappearance mean the fate of most detainees is unknown. The government began issuing death notices and updating civil registries at a faster rate during 2018, disclosing deaths in custody that occurred years earlier in many cases.

Among other violations, the regime has been accused of repeatedly using chemical weapons on civilian targets. A suspected chemical weapons attack that killed more than 40 people in the opposition-held Damascus suburb of Douma in April 2018 prompted the United States, Britain, and France to carry out a series of missile strikes on targets associated with the government's chemical weapons capability near Damascus and Homs. The United States had launched a similar punitive strike a year earlier.

Although IS's control over territory in Syria was virtually eliminated by the end of 2018, the group continued to carry out deadly terrorist attacks.

F4. Do laws, policies, and practices guarantee equal treatment of various segments of the population? 0 / 4

Women are subject to legal and societal inequities, including gender-based disadvantages in social benefits and a severe gender gap in labor force participation. Official mechanisms meant to safeguard women's rights are reportedly not functional, and the general deterioration of law and order has left women exposed to a range of abuses, particularly at the hands of extremist groups that impose their own interpretations of religious law.

The Kurdish minority has faced decades of state discrimination, including restrictions on the Kurdish language and persecution of Kurdish activists, though conditions have improved dramatically in areas controlled by Kurdish militias since 2011.

Syrian law discriminates against LGBT (lesbian, gay, bisexual, and transgender) people. According to the 1949 penal code, "unnatural sexual intercourse" is punishable with up to three years in prison. Individuals suspected of same-sex sexual activity are at risk of execution in areas held by extremist groups.

G. PERSONAL AUTONOMY AND INDIVIDUAL RIGHTS: 0 / 16

G1. Do individuals enjoy freedom of movement, including the ability to change their place of residence, employment, or education? 0 / 4

Ongoing combat and the proliferation of regime and militia checkpoints have severely restricted freedom of movement. More than 6 million people remained internally displaced at the end of 2018. Another 5 million have sought refuge abroad. Although some Syrians returned to their home areas as fighting there subsided in 2018, the government's new offensives in Eastern Ghouta, Daraa, and Quneitra and the Turkish-led campaign in Afrin resulted in the displacement of hundreds of thousands of people.

The government and other forces have systematically blockaded regions controlled by their opponents. However, the number of people living under siege fell dramatically during 2018 as the government captured the last rebel strongholds in the southeast, according to the Syria Institute, a US-based think tank.

G2. Are individuals able to exercise the right to own property and establish private businesses without undue interference from state or non-state actors? 0 / 4

Property rights have been routinely disregarded throughout the civil war. Businesses are frequently required to bribe officials to continue operating and to complete bureaucratic procedures. Access to markets dominated by regime members or allies is restricted. Militias also extort businesses and confiscate private property to varying degrees.

In April 2018, the government enacted Law No. 10, which allows the state to designate areas for reconstruction and redevelopment by decree. Individuals would then be required to meet a number of criteria to prove ownership of affected property, and those who fail to do so could have their property seized without compensation or appeal. The context of the war, including mass displacement and widespread lack of proper documentation, and the already-poor quality of official recordkeeping in Syria make it likely that property rights will be violated under the law. Moreover, the measure does not provide any basis for compensating the vast number of people whose property has already been destroyed during the conflict.

Personal status laws based on Sharia (Islamic law) discriminate against women on inheritance matters, and societal practices further discourage land ownership by women.

G3. Do individuals enjoy personal social freedoms, including choice of marriage partner and size of family, protection from domestic violence, and control over appearance? 0 / 4

Perpetrators of "honor crimes" can receive reduced sentences under the penal code, and rapists can avoid punishment by marrying their victims. Women cannot pass citizenship on to their children. Personal status laws for Muslims put women at a disadvantage regarding marriage, divorce, and child custody. Church law governs personal status issues for Christians, in some cases barring divorce. Early and forced marriages are a problem, with displaced families in particular marrying off young daughters as a perceived safeguard against endemic sexual violence or due to economic pressure. Personal social freedoms for women are uneven in areas outside government control, ranging from onerous codes of dress and behavior in extremist-held areas to formal equality under the PYD in Kurdish areas.

G4. Do individuals enjoy equality of opportunity and freedom from economic exploitation? 0 / 4

Many armed groups engage in forced conscription or the use of child soldiers. Displaced people are especially vulnerable to labor exploitation and human trafficking, and there is little equality of opportunity even in relatively stable government-controlled areas, as access to employment and investment is often dependent on personal, political, or communal affiliations.

Taiwan

Population: 23,600,000
Capital: Taipei
Political Rights Rating: 1
Civil Liberties Rating: 1
Freedom Rating: 1.0
Freedom Status: Free
Electoral Democracy: Yes

Overview: Taiwan's vibrant and competitive democratic system has allowed three peaceful transfers of power between rival parties since 2000, and protections for civil liberties are generally robust. Ongoing concerns include Chinese efforts to influence policymaking, the media, and Taiwan's democratic infrastructure; foreign migrant workers' vulnerability to exploitation; and disputes over the rights of LGBT (lesbian, gay, bisexual, and transgender) people.

KEY DEVELOPMENTS IN 2018:

- During the run-up to November local elections, an alleged Chinese disinformation campaign on social media meant to discredit the governing Democratic Progressive Party (DPP), along with funding from Beijing for a number of candidates, raised concerns about the scope of Chinese influence on Taiwanese politics.
- The DPP, struggling with low approval ratings, suffered extensive losses in the elections, leading President Tsai Ing-wen to step down as party chair.
- After the Constitutional Court ruled in 2017 that civil code provisions barring same-sex marriage violated the constitution, voters rejected such unions in a November referendum, throwing the future of the landmark ruling into doubt.

POLITICAL RIGHTS: 37 / 40
A. ELECTORAL PROCESS: 12 / 12
A1. Was the current head of government or other chief national authority elected through free and fair elections? 4 / 4

The president, who is directly elected for up to two four-year terms, appoints the premier with the consent of the legislature. The Executive Yuan, or cabinet, is made up of ministers appointed by the president on the recommendation of the premier. In practice, the president holds most executive authority.

President Tsai of the DPP was elected in January 2016 with 56 percent of the vote, defeating two opponents. Direct elections for the president, held since 1996, have generally been considered credible.

The November 2018 local elections, in which thousands of offices were contested, including county magistrate and mayoral posts, were shaken up by allegations of extensive Chinese meddling. There was evidence that Beijing used social media platforms to spread anti-DPP propaganda, and as of October, the Ministry of Justice was investigating at least

33 opposition Kuomintang (KMT) candidates who allegedly received campaign funds from China. It was unclear whether Beijing's efforts affected the electoral outcome. The DPP's popularity had been waning for economic and policy reasons in the run-up to the elections, and it suffered significant losses, prompting President Tsai to resign as party chair.

A2. Were the current national legislative representatives elected through free and fair elections? 4 / 4

The unicameral Legislative Yuan has 113 members elected to four-year terms; 73 are directly elected in single-member constituencies, 34 are elected by proportional representation, and 6 are elected by indigenous voters in two multiseat constituencies. In the last legislative elections in January 2016, the DPP won 68 seats, leaving the KMT with 35, the New Power Party with 5, the People First Party with 3, and the Non-Partisan Solidarity Union and an independent candidate with 1 seat each. The elections were considered free and fair by international observers.

A3. Are the electoral laws and framework fair, and are they implemented impartially by the relevant election management bodies? 4 / 4

Elections in Taiwan are administered by the Central Election Commission (CEC). The law mandates that no political party may hold more than one-third of the seats on the CEC. Since 2007, instances of vote buying and other electoral irregularities have gradually waned thanks to tighter enforcement of anticorruption laws. In November 2018, the chairperson of the CEC resigned in the wake of criticism over long lines at polling stations and the fact that provisional results were posted on election day as some voters were still waiting to cast their ballots.

In January, the revised Referendum Act came into effect, lowering thresholds to permit citizen-initiated ballot measures and decreasing the voting age for referendums from 20 to 18 years. In October, the CEC announced that it was referring evidence to prosecutors regarding forged signatures on a KMT-led petition for a referendum on slowly reducing the output of thermal power plants. Despite the fact that 182,848 out of 497,243 signatures on the petition were ruled invalid, the CEC approved it, and referendum voters endorsed the proposed policy change in November.

B. POLITICAL PLURALISM AND PARTICIPATION: 15 / 16

B1. Do the people have the right to organize in different political parties or other competitive political groupings of their choice, and is the system free of undue obstacles to the rise and fall of these competing parties or groupings? 4 / 4

The multiparty political system features vigorous competition between the two major parties, the DPP and KMT. Smaller parties are also able to function without interference and have played a significant role in both presidential and legislative contests.

B2. Is there a realistic opportunity for the opposition to increase its support or gain power through elections? 4 / 4

There have been regular democratic transfers of power between rival parties in recent years. In the 2016 general elections, amid widespread dissatisfaction with the incumbent KMT administration, voters handed the opposition DPP a resounding victory. The KMT in turn took advantage of the DPP government's unpopularity to win a convincing victory in the November 2018 local elections.

B3. Are the people's political choices free from domination by the military, foreign powers, religious hierarchies, economic oligarchies, or any other powerful group that is not democratically accountable? 3 / 4

Major business owners with interests in China remain an influential force in Taiwanese politics, largely through their close relationship with the KMT and support for its China-friendly policies. The KMT, which governed Taiwan as an authoritarian, one-party state for decades until democratic reforms took hold in the 1980s and 90s, has typically enjoyed a considerable financial advantage over rivals like the DPP, which has traditionally favored greater independence from China. However, the KMT's advantage has been whittled away in recent years by DPP government investigations into allegations that the KMT improperly acquired public assets during its rule, which has led to many of its accounts being frozen.

In response to concerns about Chinese meddling in the 2018 local elections, the cabinet in December introduced draft legislation that would ban local media and internet service providers from carrying campaign advertisements funded by foreign sources.

B4. Do various segments of the population (including ethnic, religious, gender, LGBT, and other relevant groups) have full political rights and electoral opportunities? 4 / 4

Taiwan's constitution grants all citizens the right to vote. This guarantee applies regardless of gender, ethnicity, religion, sexual orientation, or gender identity. The 2016 elections increased women's overall political representation, with female candidates winning the presidency and a record 38 percent of seats in the Legislative Yuan.

Six seats in the Legislative Yuan are reserved for indigenous candidates elected by indigenous voters. An additional two indigenous candidates won seats in 2016 through normal party-list voting. Members of Taiwan's 16 indigenous tribes make up roughly 2 percent of the population.

C. FUNCTIONING OF GOVERNMENT: 10 / 12

C1. Do the freely elected head of government and national legislative representatives determine the policies of the government? 4 / 4

Elected officials in Taiwan are free to set and implement policy without undue interference from foreign or other unelected actors, though consideration of China plays a significant role in Taiwanese policymaking.

Escalating Chinese pressure continues to threaten Taiwan's sovereignty. Three countries severed diplomatic relations with Taiwan in 2018, largely as a result of financial incentives offered by the Chinese government. At the end of the year, Taiwan had diplomatic recognition from just 17 countries. In September, in a bid to curtail Chinese influence, the cabinet approved draft legislation that would restrict unauthorized investment by Chinese companies in Taiwan, clearing the way for a review by the parliament.

C2. Are safeguards against official corruption strong and effective? 3 / 4

Corruption is significantly less pervasive than in the past, but it remains a problem. Political and business interests are closely intertwined, leading to malfeasance in government procurement. The current DPP-led government has moved to reduce these practices, including through a proposed reform of the Government Procurement Act. Corruption cases proceeded against former lawmakers from both major parties in 2018. In September, former KMT legislator Lee Ching-hua was indicted for allegedly embezzling government funds during his time in office. In December, the 2006 corruption conviction of former DPP legislator Kao Jyh-peng was upheld by the Supreme Court; he was sentenced to four years and six months in prison.

C3. Does the government operate with openness and transparency? 3 / 4

The 2005 Freedom of Government Information Law enables public access to information held by government agencies, including financial audit reports and documents about administrative guidance. Civil society groups are typically able to comment on and influence pending policies and legislation. In recent years, the government has announced plans to create innovative digital spaces for civic exchange and public participation in policymaking, but implementation remains in its early stages.

Although the government generally operates with openness, policies and regulations related to business are sometimes changed without properly informing the public or the business community.

CIVIL LIBERTIES: 56 / 60
D. FREEDOM OF EXPRESSION AND BELIEF: 16 / 16
D1. Are there free and independent media? 4 / 4

The news media reflect a diversity of views and report aggressively on government policies, though many outlets display strong party affiliation in their coverage. Beijing continues to exert influence on Taiwanese media. Key media owners have significant business interests in China or rely on advertising by Chinese companies, leaving them vulnerable to pressure and prone to self-censorship on topics considered sensitive by Beijing. In recent years, Taiwanese regulators have resisted proposed mergers that would have concentrated important media companies in the hands of such owners, and the press has been able to report freely on elections.

The onslaught of disinformation surrounding the 2018 local elections led some top officials to suggest revising the National Security Act to counter "fake news," raising concerns that any resulting legislation could be misused to silence and punish critical voices in the media.

D2. Are individuals free to practice and express their religious faith or nonbelief in public and private? 4 / 4

Taiwanese of all faiths can worship freely. Religious organizations that choose to register with the government receive tax-exempt status.

D3. Is there academic freedom, and is the educational system free from extensive political indoctrination? 4 / 4

Educators in Taiwan can generally write and lecture without interference, and past practices—including prosecutions—aimed at restricting academics' political activism have been rare in recent years.

D4. Are individuals free to express their personal views on political or other sensitive topics without fear of surveillance or retribution? 4 / 4

Private discussion is open and free, and there were no reports of the government illegally monitoring online communication in 2018. The government does not restrict internet access.

E. ASSOCIATIONAL AND ORGANIZATIONAL RIGHTS: 11 / 12
E1. Is there freedom of assembly? 4 / 4

The 1988 Assembly and Parade Act enables authorities to prosecute protesters who fail to obtain a permit or follow orders to disperse, but freedom of assembly is largely respected in practice. In August 2018, rights monitors called for an investigation into the alleged use of excessive force by police during two protests against forced evictions in Taipei.

E2. Is there freedom for nongovernmental organizations, particularly those that are engaged in human rights- and governance-related work? 4 / 4

All civic organizations must register with the government, though registration is freely granted. Nongovernmental organizations typically operate without harassment.

E3. Is there freedom for trade unions and similar professional or labor organizations? 3 / 4

Trade unions are independent, and most workers enjoy freedom of association, though the government strictly regulates the right to strike. Among other barriers, teachers, workers in the defense industry, and government employees are prohibited from striking.

F. RULE OF LAW: 15 / 16

F1. Is there an independent judiciary? 4 / 4

Taiwan's judiciary is independent. Court rulings are generally free from political or other undue interference.

F2. Does due process prevail in civil and criminal matters? 4 / 4

Constitutional protections for due process and defendants' rights are generally upheld, and police largely respect safeguards against arbitrary detention. Although prosecutors and other law enforcement officials have at times engaged in abusive practices, particularly in prominent and politically charged cases, such violations have been less common in recent years.

F3. Is there protection from the illegitimate use of physical force and freedom from war and insurgencies? 4 / 4

Both criminal violence and excessive use of force by police are rare in Taiwan, and attorneys are allowed to monitor interrogations to prevent torture.

After a four-year death penalty moratorium, the government resumed executions in 2010. Condemned inmates, after being sedated, are shot from behind at close range. Family members of inmates awaiting the death penalty are typically not informed about scheduled execution dates. Nearly all death sentences are imposed for murder. In August 2018, an inmate was executed for the first time in two years; he had been convicted of killing his former wife and young daughter.

F4. Do laws, policies, and practices guarantee equal treatment of various segments of the population? 3 / 4

The constitution provides for the equality of all citizens before the law, although indigenous people continue to face social and economic discrimination, leading to high unemployment, lower wages, and barriers to education and social services. In 2016, President Tsai offered the government's first formal apology to indigenous people for centuries of injustice, while launching a commission to investigate historical mistreatment. The 2017 Indigenous Languages Development Act designated the languages spoken by 16 officially recognized indigenous tribes as national languages of Taiwan, and authorized their formal use in legislative and legal affairs.

The constitution guarantees women equal rights, though Taiwanese women continue to face discrimination in employment and compensation. Taiwanese law prohibits discrimination in employment based on sexual orientation, and violence against LGBT people is adequately addressed by police.

Taiwanese law does not allow for asylum or refugee status. A long-awaited draft bill to address the problem passed committee review in the legislature in 2016. However, no substantial progress toward passage was reported in 2018.

G. PERSONAL AUTONOMY AND INDIVIDUAL RIGHTS: 14 / 16

G1. Do individuals enjoy freedom of movement, including the ability to change their place of residence, employment, or education? 4 / 4

Taiwan's residents enjoy freedom of movement, and Taiwanese authorities have gradually eased restrictions on travel between Taiwan and China in recent years. However, the number of Chinese tourists visiting Taiwan has dropped since the DPP government took office in 2016, allegedly due to Chinese government pressure on tour operators.

G2. Are individuals able to exercise the right to own property and establish private businesses without undue interference from state or nonstate actors? 3 / 4

Although property rights are generally respected, urban renewal and industrial projects have been criticized for unfairly displacing residents. Housing advocates have called for legal amendments to clarify residency rights, including protections against forced eviction, and the establishment of an appeals system to review alleged violations.

For much of 2018, indigenous protesters camped out in Taipei's Peace Memorial Park to oppose a 2017 regulation that returned some state-owned land to indigenous people but did not apply to private property; advocates claim the omission denies indigenous groups much of their ancestral territory.

G3. Do individuals enjoy personal social freedoms, including choice of marriage partner and size of family, protection from domestic violence, and control over appearance? 4 / 4

The Constitutional Court ruled in 2017 that it was unconstitutional to ban same-sex marriage, but opponents of such unions organized a ballot measure on the topic, and referendum voters supported the civil code's existing ban in November 2018. It was unclear at year's end how lawmakers and the courts would resolve the conflict between the 2017 ruling and the referendum result.

Citizenship laws discriminate against people from mainland China, as spouses from mainland China married to Taiwanese nationals must wait six years before becoming eligible for citizenship, whereas spouses of other nationalities are only required to wait four years.

Rape and domestic violence remain serious problems. Although the law permits authorities to investigate complaints without victims pressing charges, cultural norms inhibit many women from reporting these crimes to the police. Recent reforms have improved protections for accusers and encouraged reporting of rape and sexual assault, which appears to have increased prosecution and conviction rates.

G4. Do individuals enjoy equality of opportunity and freedom from economic exploitation? 3 / 4

Over 600,000 foreign migrants work in Taiwan, with many employed as domestic workers and fishermen who are not covered by the Labor Standards Act, excluding them from minimum wage, overtime, and paid leave protections. As a result, foreign migrant workers are at substantial risk of exploitation, with widespread accounts of unpaid wages, poor working conditions, physical and sexual abuse, and extortion and fraud by recruitment and brokerage agencies. To address the problem, the legislature passed amendments to the

Employment Services Act in November 2018, requiring employment agencies to swiftly report abuses against migrant workers or face severe fines.

Legislation to impose stricter worker protections on fishing companies took effect in 2017. However, labor advocates report poor implementation, citing ongoing mistreatment and abuse of foreign fishermen on Taiwanese vessels. In October 2018, Taiwan's Fisheries Agency fined and suspended the license of a Taiwanese fishing vessel after an investigation uncovered physical abuse, withholding of wages, and long work hours, among other violations.

Tajikistan

Population: 9,100,000
Capital: Dushanbe
Political Rights Rating: 7
Civil Liberties Rating: 6
Freedom Rating: 6.5
Freedom Status: Not Free
Electoral Democracy: No

Overview: The authoritarian regime of President Emomali Rahmon, who has ruled since 1992, severely restricts political rights and civil liberties. The political opposition has been devastated by a sustained campaign of repression in recent years, and the government exerts tight control over religious expression and activity. Wealth and authority are increasingly concentrated in the hands of the president and his family.

KEY DEVELOPMENTS IN 2018:

- The detention and harassment of former members of the banned opposition Islamic Renaissance Party of Tajikistan (IRPT) and their families continued throughout the year.
- In July, the Islamic State (IS) militant group claimed responsibility for a terrorist attack in the country's southern Danghara District that killed four foreign cyclists and injured three others. The government accused the IRPT, without evidence, of involvement in the attack.
- In November, a prison uprising in Sughd Province reportedly resulted in the deaths of two guards and as many as 50 prisoners. IS claimed responsibility for that incident as well.
- As part of its ongoing crackdown on observant Muslims, the government in March published a detailed "guidebook" on recommended dress for women that officially excluded the hijab (headscarf) and other such garments.

POLITICAL RIGHTS: 0 / 40 (−1)

A. ELECTORAL PROCESS: 0 / 12

A1. Was the current head of government or other chief national authority elected through free and fair elections? 0 / 4

The powerful president is elected for up to two seven-year terms under current rules, but constitutional amendments ratified in 2016 removed presidential term limits specifically for Rahmon, who holds the official status of "leader of the nation." In the last presidential election in 2013, Rahmon won a fourth term with 83.6 percent of the vote, defeating five little-known challengers who did not represent genuine opposition parties; the opposition's favored candidate was disqualified. Observers from the Organization for Security and Cooperation in Europe (OSCE) found that the election lacked "genuine choice and meaningful pluralism" and featured biased media and voting irregularities.

A2. Were the current national legislative representatives elected through free and fair elections? 0 / 4

The bicameral Supreme Assembly is composed of an upper house, the National Assembly, and a lower house, the Assembly of Representatives. The National Assembly comprises 25 members chosen by local assemblies and 8 appointed by the president; former presidents are also entitled to a seat in the chamber. The 63-member Assembly of Representatives is elected by popular vote through a mixed system of 41 single-member constituencies and 22 proportional-representation seats. Members of each body serve five-year terms.

Ahead of the 2015 elections, the government carried out an extensive campaign of repression against the opposition through state media and the persecution of many candidates, particularly those of the IRPT, leading to the disenfranchisement of the country's most significant opposition force. The ruling People's Democratic Party (PDP) won 51 of the 63 lower-house seats, and four small, mostly progovernment parties divided the remainder. According to OSCE monitors, the elections were marred by serious violations and failed to meet democratic standards.

A3. Are the electoral laws and framework fair, and are they implemented impartially by the relevant election management bodies? 0 / 4

The Central Commission for Elections and Referenda is subservient to the government and enforces electoral laws in an inconsistent and nontransparent manner. Shortly before the 2015 parliamentary elections, the IRPT representative on the commission was arrested. Despite reforms prior to those elections, constituencies still vary considerably in population, undermining equal suffrage.

B. POLITICAL PLURALISM AND PARTICIPATION: 0 / 16

B1. Do the people have the right to organize in different political parties or other competitive political groupings of their choice, and is the system free of undue obstacles to the rise and fall of these competing parties or groupings? 0 / 4

The government consistently marginalizes independent or opposition parties, which have become completely excluded from the political process. In the second half of 2015, the Justice Ministry revoked the IRPT's legal registration based on a technicality, and the Supreme Court declared the party a terrorist organization, criminalizing membership in or expression of support for the group. The constitutional amendments passed in a 2016 referendum banned faith-based political parties, effectively preventing the IRPT from reforming.

The authorities continued to harass and arrest former members of the IRPT, the political movement Group 24, and their families during 2018, interfering even with the travel of small children separated from their exiled parents. In July, officials refused to allow a four-year-old boy suffering from cancer to seek life-saving treatment abroad, where his father—leading IRPT activist Ruhullo Tillozoda—had been living in exile since 2015; the boy's grandfather was exiled IRPT leader Muhiddin Kabiri. In August, the 10-year-old daughter of former Group 24 activist Shabnam Khudoydodova was pulled off an international flight in Dushanbe with her grandmother and uncle, preventing her from rejoining her mother. Both children and their families were eventually allowed to travel in August following intense international pressure.

B2. Is there a realistic opportunity for the opposition to increase its support or gain power through elections? 0 / 4

Tajikistan has no record of peaceful transfers of power between rival parties. Rahmon first became chief executive in 1992, during Tajikistan's 1992–97 civil war, and has held the presidency since the office's creation in 1994. Under the 2016 constitutional revisions, he is entitled to run for reelection indefinitely and to overrule cabinet decisions even after leaving office as president. The amendments also lowered the minimum age for presidents from 35 to 30 years, which would allow Rahmon's son to seek the post in 2020.

Years of unrelenting repression of independent political activity have left opposition parties unable to compete in elections. The administration exerts control over the electoral process through its near-absolute dominance of the media, an extremely high threshold for the number of signatures required to run for office, and the exclusion of citizens working abroad—who constitute between 20 and 45 percent of the electorate—from the nomination process for the presidency and parliament. Many IRPT members and their relatives were beaten, harassed, and imprisoned before the 2015 elections, with some reportedly tortured in custody.

B3. Are the people's political choices free from domination by the military, foreign powers, religious hierarchies, economic oligarchies, or any other powerful group that is not democratically accountable? 0 / 4

Political affairs in Tajikistan are controlled almost exclusively by Rahmon and his extended family, leaving citizens with few avenues to exercise meaningful political choices or participate in the political process. Presidential family members hold numerous public positions and control key sectors of the private economy.

B4. Do various segments of the population (including ethnic, religious, gender, LGBT, and other relevant groups) have full political rights and electoral opportunities? 0 / 4

No segment of the population enjoys full political rights or electoral opportunities in practice. The regime, which generally seeks to suppress any genuine dissent, does not permit women or minorities to organize independently to advance their political interests. Women remain underrepresented in the political system, both as voters and in elected positions.

C. FUNCTIONING OF GOVERNMENT: 0 / 12 (−1)

C1. Do the freely elected head of government and national legislative representatives determine the policies of the government? 0 / 4

The president, who is not freely elected, and his inner circle are virtually unopposed in determining and implementing policy. The PDP-controlled legislature does not offer a meaningful check on the executive's expansive constitutional authority. Officials from the president's native Kulob District are dominant within government. In 2017, Rahmon strengthened his family's grip on power by installing his son, Rustam Emomali, as Dushanbe's mayor.

C2. Are safeguards against official corruption strong and effective? 0 / 4

Patronage networks and regional affiliations are central to political life, corruption is pervasive, and laws designed to prevent it are routinely ignored. Major irregularities have been reported at the National Bank of Tajikistan and the country's largest industrial firm, the state-owned Tajik Aluminum Company (TALCO).

C3. Does the government operate with openness and transparency? 0 / 4 (−1)

Government decision-making and budgetary processes lack transparency, and public officials are not required to disclose financial information. Crackdowns on the media, the opposition, and civil society have further reduced independent scrutiny of state operations. In recent years the government has concluded extensive infrastructure and resource-extraction agreements with the Chinese government and Chinese companies, with little consultation or transparency on the terms of the deals or accountability for their implementation. The pattern has added to concerns about corruption and public debt, among other possible ramifications. Two new mining concessions involving Chinese companies were announced in April and June 2018.

Score Change: The score declined from 1 to 0 because harsher repression of independent journalists, opposition groups, and civil society in recent years has further eroded transparency and accountability for government activities, including major investment deals with foreign states and companies.

CIVIL LIBERTIES: 9 / 60 (−1)

D. FREEDOM OF EXPRESSION AND BELIEF: 2 / 16

D1. Are there free and independent media? 0 / 4

The government controls most printing presses, newsprint supplies, and broadcasting facilities, effectively denying independent media access to them. The state also uses regulatory and licensing mechanisms to shut out independent outlets and encourage self-censorship. Independent journalists face harassment and intimidation. Civil libel charges have been used to cripple outlets that criticize the government. Authorities routinely block critical websites, news portals, and entire social media platforms, and use periodic wholesale blackouts of internet and messaging services to suppress criticism.

In July 2018, veteran journalist Khayrullo Mirsaidov was sentenced to 12 years in prison on trumped-up charges of embezzlement, false reporting to police, and other offenses after he published an open letter to the authorities detailing an incident of local corruption. Having spent eight months in detention, he was freed in August when an appellate court—amid an international campaign on his behalf—reduced his sentence to fines and community service.

D2. Are individuals free to practice and express their religious faith or nonbelief in public and private? 0 / 4

The government imposes severe restrictions on religious freedom, in part by limiting religious activities to state-approved venues and registered organizations. In 2018, authorities continued to prosecute individuals for alleged membership in banned religious organizations, including Christian and Muslim groups. Minors are generally barred from attending religious services in mosques, as are women in most cases.

A 2017 law that discourages religious clothing is widely perceived as an effort to limit the wearing of hijabs, which along with an unofficial ban on beards for men continued to be arbitrarily enforced in 2018. The government in March published a detailed "guidebook" on recommended dress for women that officially excluded the hijab and other such garments in favor of "traditional" or "national" alternatives. In addition, the government pressured students to adhere to these dress codes and established roadblocks in some areas to search cars for women in hijabs and men with beards.

D3. Is there academic freedom, and is the educational system free from extensive political indoctrination? 1 / 4

The government exerts significant political pressure on universities and academic personnel. In recent years, international scholars have noted the self-exile of Tajikistani academics who faced harassment from security services, surveillance and self-censorship within institutions of higher education, scrutiny of scholars who cooperate with foreign colleagues, and the appointment of officials backed by the security services to senior academic posts. Opportunities to study abroad, especially for religious education, are tightly restricted. In April 2018, the government closed the office and cut the internet access of an association that provides technology services to dozens of academic institutions in the country.

D4. Are individuals free to express their personal views on political or other sensitive topics without fear of surveillance or retribution? 1 / 4

Restrictive laws and government surveillance serve as deterrents to open discussion of sensitive topics, including criticism of the country's leadership. A 2017 law allows authorities to monitor citizens' online behavior and prescribes fines and prison sentences for those who visit "undesirable websites," among other provisions. In August 2018, a Tajikistani man was sentenced to five and a half years in prison for insulting the president by reposting and "liking" critical videos on social media while living and working in Russia; he was arrested after returning to the country in June. Other users were reportedly convicted during the year for sharing content associated with banned groups, including the IRPT.

E. ASSOCIATIONAL AND ORGANIZATIONAL RIGHTS: 2 / 12
E1. Is there freedom of assembly? 0 / 4

The government strictly limits freedom of assembly. Local government approval is required to hold demonstrations, and officials often refuse to grant permission. Protests in the Gorno-Badakhshan region in November 2018 reportedly triggered localized internet blackouts. Authorities there had warned the previous month that participation in unauthorized gatherings would result in criminal charges.

E2. Is there freedom for nongovernmental organizations, particularly those that are engaged in human rights- and governance-related work? 1 / 4

Nongovernmental organizations (NGOs) must register with the Ministry of Justice and are vulnerable to closure for minor technical violations. NGOs must disclose funding from foreign sources to the Ministry of Justice. Foreign funds must be logged in a state registry before organizations can access them, and the government has oversight of operations supported by the funds. Under legislation that was adopted by the parliament in December 2018 and awaiting the president's signature at year's end, NGOs would be obliged to comply with more expansive and vaguely worded financial reporting requirements and to maintain their own websites.

E3. Is there freedom for trade unions and similar professional or labor organizations? 1 / 4

Citizens have the legal right to form and join trade unions and to bargain collectively, but these rights and the right to strike are undermined by general legal restrictions on freedoms of assembly and association. There are no laws against antiunion discrimination by employers, and the country's trade union federation is controlled by the government.

F. RULE OF LAW: 1 / 16 (−1)
F1. Is there an independent judiciary? 0 / 4 (−1)

The judiciary lacks independence. Many judges are poorly trained and inexperienced, and bribery is widespread. The 2016 constitutional amendments abolished the Council of

Justice, which was responsible for nominating judges and was directly controlled by the president, and transferred most nomination and oversight functions to the Supreme Court instead. However, judicial appointments and oversight have remained under executive control in practice. The courts' opaque and biased adjudication of numerous cases against opposition figures and other dissidents, particularly since 2015, has further demonstrated their subordination to the political leadership.

Score Change: The score declined from 1 to 0 because the judiciary's biased handling of politicized cases in recent years has demonstrated its subordination to the executive branch.

F2. Does due process prevail in civil and criminal matters? 0 / 4

Arbitrary arrests and detentions are common, as is corruption among law enforcement agencies. Defendants are often denied timely access to an attorney, and politically fraught trials are frequently closed to the public. Nearly all defendants are found guilty.

F3. Is there protection from the illegitimate use of physical force and freedom from war and insurgencies? 0 / 4

Civilians are subject to physical abuse by security forces and have no meaningful opportunity to seek justice for such violations. Detainees are reportedly beaten in custody to extract confessions. Overcrowding and disease contribute to often life-threatening conditions in prisons.

In November 2018, an uprising in a high-security prison in Sughd Province reportedly resulted in the deaths of two guards and as many as 50 prisoners. The incident led to investigations into prison conditions and the arrest of the warden on charges of negligence and abuse of power.

IS claimed responsibility for the prison riot, as well as for a July terrorist attack in Danghara District that killed four cyclists from Europe and the United States and injured three others. Despite a video of the alleged perpetrators swearing allegiance to IS, the government accused the IRPT, without evidence, of involvement in the attack on the cyclists.

F4. Do laws, policies, and practices guarantee equal treatment of various segments of the population? 1 / 4

Discrimination against ethnic minorities is not a major problem. However, women face bias and disparate treatment in the workplace, and discrimination or violence against LGBT (lesbian, gay, bisexual, and transgender) people is common. There is no legislation against discrimination based on sexual orientation or gender identity. LGBT people frequently face abuse by security forces.

G. PERSONAL AUTONOMY AND INDIVIDUAL RIGHTS: 4 / 16

G1. Do individuals enjoy freedom of movement, including the ability to change their place of residence, employment, or education? 1 / 4

Most citizens can travel within the country, but they must register their permanent residence with local authorities. Students interested in studying Islamic theology are forbidden from seeking education abroad. Some areas, particularly Gorno-Badakhshan, feature a heavier security presence that includes police checkpoints, which hamper travel and provide opportunities for extortion and other abuses.

G2. Are individuals able to exercise the right to own property and establish private businesses without undue interference from state or nonstate actors? 1 / 4

Corruption and regulatory dysfunction affect enterprises ranging from peasant farms to large companies. The president's extended family and others from his native Kulob District maintain extensive business interests in the country and dominate key sectors of the economy, impeding business activity by those without such political connections.

By law, all land belongs to the state, which allocates usage rights in a process plagued by corruption and inefficiency.

G3. Do individuals enjoy personal social freedoms, including choice of marriage partner and size of family, protection from domestic violence, and control over appearance? 1 / 4

Although forced marriage and polygamy are legally prohibited, marriages arranged by parents and religious marriages that allow polygamy are both common in practice. Unlike under civil law, women are placed at a disadvantage under Islamic legal standards for divorce. Domestic violence is widespread, but cases are underreported and seldom investigated adequately.

Reports indicate that women sometimes face societal pressure to wear headscarves. Meanwhile, in addition to restricting hijabs for women and beards for men, the government interferes more broadly in matters of personal appearance. The government guidebook issued in March 2018 outlined acceptable and unacceptable styles of dress for women in great detail, barring clothing that could be deemed immodest or "foreign" in origin, among other considerations.

G4. Do individuals enjoy equality of opportunity and freedom from economic exploitation? 1 / 4

The government has reportedly improved enforcement of laws against forced labor and especially child labor in the cotton harvest in recent years, though such practices have persisted to some extent. Safeguards against other forms of labor exploitation and hazardous working conditions are not well enforced. The scarcity of economic opportunity has compelled citizens to seek work abroad in large numbers, and these migrant workers are at risk of exploitation by human traffickers.

Tanzania

Population: 59,100,000
Capital: Dodoma
Political Rights Rating: 4
Civil Liberties Rating: 5 ↓
Freedom Rating: 4.5
Freedom Status: Partly Free
Electoral Democracy: No

Overview: Tanzania has held regular multiparty elections since its transition from a one-party state in the early 1990s, but the opposition remains relatively weak, and the ruling party, Chama Cha Mapinduzi (CCM), has retained power for over half a century. Since the election of President John Magufuli in 2015, the government has cracked down with growing severity on its critics in the political opposition, the press, and civil society.

KEY DEVELOPMENTS IN 2018:

- A campaign of repression against opposition parties continued during the year with harassment, arrests, and detentions of prominent political figures, including Freeman Mbowe, chairman of the opposition party Chama Cha Demokrasia na Maendeleo (Chadema). He remained in jail at year's end, awaiting trial for his alleged role in a February protest in which police shot and killed a university student with a stray bullet.
- In April, the government issued the Electronic and Postal Communications (Online Content) Regulations, which imposed prohibitive registration fees of $900 for bloggers and other online content producers and included vaguely worded rules on content that could be used to silence government critics.
- A draft bill to amend the Political Parties Act that was introduced in the parliament in October would prohibit parties from engaging in "activism," a provision that opposition leaders claim could criminalize many legitimate party activities.
- In October, the regional commissioner of Dar es Salaam called on the public to report people suspected of being gay and established a committee to identify and arrest gay people who are active on social media.

POLITICAL RIGHTS: 20 / 40 (−2)

A. ELECTORAL PROCESS: 7 / 12

A1. Was the current head of government or other chief national authority elected through free and fair elections? 3 / 4

The president is elected by direct popular vote for up to two five-year terms. In the 2015 presidential election, CCM's John Magufuli won with 58 percent of the vote, while Edward Lowassa of Chadema took 40 percent. Observers generally deemed the election credible but noted areas of concern. An observer mission from the European Union (EU) described "highly competitive, generally well-organized elections, but with insufficient efforts at transparency from the election administrations." The EU mission noted that CCM had drawn on state resources, such as public stadiums, to support its campaign, while restricting access for opposition parties.

The semiautonomous region of Zanzibar elects its own president, who serves no more than two five-year terms. International observers deemed the 2015 presidential election to be credible, but the Zanzibar Electoral Commission (ZEC) annulled the vote before official results were announced, claiming that the poll was not free and fair. The opposition Civic United Front (CUF) accused the ZEC of annulling the results to save the CCM's incumbent president Ali Mohamed Shein from defeat. A rerun of the election was held in March 2016, but the opposition boycotted, allowing Shein to win reelection with ease. The preelection period featured an increased military presence and reports of attacks on political party offices and journalists. CCM legislators voted in 2017 to change Zanzibar's constitution, eliminating a CCM-CUF power-sharing arrangement that had enabled years of stability.

A2. Were the current national legislative representatives elected through free and fair elections? 2 / 4

Legislative authority lies with a unicameral, 393-seat National Assembly (the Bunge) whose members serve five-year terms. There are 264 seats filled through direct elections in single-member constituencies, 113 are reserved for women elected by political parties, 10 are filled by presidential appointment, and 5 members are elected by the Zanzibar legislature. The attorney general holds an ex officio seat. International observers generally viewed the 2015 parliamentary elections as credible, despite some minor irregularities. The CCM won a total of 253 seats, Chadema took 70, the CUF won 42, and the Alliance for Change and Transparency (ACT-Wazalendo) and the National Convention for Construction and Reform (NCCR-Mageuzi) each won one.

By-elections held during 2018 for both parliament seats and local government offices were racked by violence and other alleged irregularities. The US embassy publicly criticized the August polls, citing "credible accounts of election violence and irregularities." The National Electoral Commission (NEC) denied the claims and called on the embassy to "prove all the allegations it made."

Members of Zanzibar's 85-seat House of Representatives serve five-year terms and are seated through a mix of direct elections and appointments. The opposition boycott of the Zanzibari rerun elections in 2016 left the CCM with full control of the regional legislature.

A3. Are the electoral laws and framework fair, and are they implemented impartially by the relevant election management bodies? 2 / 4

The NEC is responsible for overseeing elections nationally, while the ZEC conducts elections for Zanzibar's governing institutions.

The structures of the NEC and ZEC contribute to doubts about their independence. The NEC is appointed by the Tanzanian president, and the ZEC is appointed by the Zanzibari president, though the opposition nominates two of the seven ZEC members. The national president retains the authority to appoint regional and district commissioners—administrative officials who are directly answerable to him and who can be influential during elections. In June 2018, President Shein appointed seven new members to the ZEC. While some observers approved of Shein's choices, others accused the new members of being CCM partisans whose impartiality could be compromised during the 2020 elections.

B. POLITICAL PLURALISM AND PARTICIPATION: 7 / 16 (−2)

B1. Do the people have the right to organize in different political parties or other competitive political groupings of their choice, and is the system free of undue obstacles to the rise and fall of these competing parties or groupings? 1 / 4 (−1)

Tanzanians have the right to organize into political parties, but the ruling CCM enjoys considerable incumbency advantages. For example, the system of state funding for parties under the Political Parties Act of 2015 disproportionately benefits CCM.

Authorities have stepped up efforts to constrain opposition parties in recent years. In 2016, the government banned all political rallies and demonstrations outside election periods, sharply curtailing parties' ability to mobilize public support. Opposition parties have promised to defy the ban in 2019. If passed, a draft bill to amend the Political Parties Act that was introduced in October 2018 could further erode the opposition's rights. The bill would criminalize politicians holding rallies outside of their constituencies, except in election years. It would also allow the registrar of political parties to suspend public financing of parties for up to six months and would forbid parties from engaging in "activism," a broad rule that opposition leaders claim could be used to crack down on legitimate political activity.

The government arrested several high-profile opposition figures in 2018, continuing its campaign of repression. In October, ACT-Wazalendo party leader Zitto Kabwe was arrested for incitement after claiming that more than 100 people died in fighting between herders and the police in his home district, a figure that the government disputed. In February, Chadema lawmaker Joseph Mbilinyi (a popular musician also known as Sugu) was sentenced to five months in prison for criticizing the president at a public meeting.

As of August 2018, CCM had successfully coopted as many as 100 local and national opposition politicians since 2015, which opposition parties said was the result of bribery.

Former CUF leader Julius Mtatiro defected to CCM in August after being held and interrogated by the police for criticizing the president on social media.

Score Change: The score declined from 2 to 1 due to increased government repression of opposition parties, including through arrests, harassment, and violence, as well as the cooptation of opposition politicians, all of which has hindered these parties' ability to function.

B2. Is there a realistic opportunity for the opposition to increase its support or gain power through elections? 1 / 4 (−1)

The CCM has governed without interruption for more than 50 years. Tanzania's opposition, which performed better in the 2015 elections than it ever had before, still only won 29 percent of the National Assembly seats. The opposition faces significant interference, harassment, violence, and criminal prosecutions by the government and its allies. Political parties are regulated by a registrar whom the opposition criticizes for partisan bias. The draft amendments to the Political Parties Act introduced in October 2018 would shield the registrar from legal complaints, further reducing accountability for the office.

Opposition parties faced intensifying violence and intimidation throughout the year. In early 2018, two Chadema party officials were murdered with machetes. Chadema leaders allege that both murders were assassinations planned by CCM. In Zanzibar, the police raided the headquarters of CUF in February and arrested the head of the party's Zanzibar wing in September.

Opposition campaign activities for by-elections were also met with violence. In February, a student was killed by a stray bullet when police dispersed a Chadema campaign event in Dar es Salaam. Authorities blamed the death on Chadema's "illegal demonstration." On the by-election day in August, Chadema lawmaker Godbless Lema and a local candidate were attacked and seriously injured in Arusha. In July, Chadema requested that the NEC suspend by-elections in seven wards after the disqualification of 17 of its candidates. In September, Chadema announced that it was boycotting subsequent by-elections due to police intimidation and violence during the August elections.

Opposition leaders faced arrest for their legitimate campaign activities throughout the year. Chadema chairman Freeman Mbowe and member of parliament Esther Matiko were charged with holding an illegal protest and incitement for the February campaign event that led to a student's death, and both were arrested in November for failing to appear in court. Mbowe and Matiko remained in jail awaiting trial at the end of the year.

Score Change: The score declined from 2 to 1 because the targeted arrests, violence, and intimidation faced by prominent opposition leaders inhibited the competitiveness of their parties in by-elections.

B3. Are the people's political choices free from domination by the military, foreign powers, religious hierarchies, economic oligarchies, or any other powerful group that is not democratically accountable? 3 / 4

Tanzanian voters and politicians are mostly free of undue influence from groups that are not democratically accountable. However, party militias were responsible for some violence and intimidation ahead of the 2015 polls. The ruling party has also allegedly used vote buying and other material incentives to influence voters.

B4. Do various segments of the population (including ethnic, religious, gender, LGBT, and other relevant groups) have full political rights and electoral opportunities? 2 / 4

Members of cultural, ethnic, religious, and other minority groups ostensibly have full political rights, but parties formed explicitly on the basis of ethnicity or religion are prohibited. The government threatens religious organizations that comment on political issues. In response to Easter messages issued by the Evangelical Lutheran Church of Tanzania (ELCT) and the Tanzania Episcopal Conference in March 2018, which were critical of the government, authorities wrote a letter to both churches demanding that they withdraw their criticisms or face potential legal action.

The constitution requires that women make up 30 percent of representatives in the parliament. As of 2018, 37 percent of the seats were held by women. However, despite numerically strong female political representation, many of CCM's policies under President Magufuli have actively undermined women's rights, including the expulsion of pregnant girls from school.

C. FUNCTIONING OF GOVERNMENT: 6 / 12

C1. Do the freely elected head of government and national legislative representatives determine the policies of the government? 2 / 4

Magufuli has consolidated political power in the presidency since taking office, sidelining the legislature—in part by suppressing dissent within the ruling party—and exerting greater control over cabinet ministers through dismissals and reshuffles. The CCM government has also reasserted its role in managing the activities of legislators and threatening those who are frequently absent.

C2. Are safeguards against official corruption strong and effective? 2 / 4

Magufuli's anticorruption drive has had mixed results. In 2018, the government continued to crack down on foreign firms in extractive industries for alleged tax evasion and money laundering, as well as on complicit government officials. In October, at least two government officials were charged with corruption for their alleged involvement in a tax evasion scheme at Acacia Mining, the largest gold-mining company in Tanzania.

Overall, corruption remains a problem in the country, despite some progress in recent years. The Prevention and Combating of Corruption Bureau (PCCB) has been accused of focusing on low-level corruption and doing little to address graft committed by senior officials.

C3. Does the government operate with openness and transparency? 2 / 4

An access to information act was adopted in 2016, but critics noted that it gives precedence to any other law governing the handling of government information, and appeals of decisions on information requests are handled by a government minister rather than an independent body. The law also imposes prison terms on officials who improperly release information, but no clear penalties for those who improperly withhold information.

According to research published by the Media Institute of Southern Africa's Tanzania branch in March 2018, local and regional government offices are uneven in their level of responsiveness to requests for information. Live broadcasts of parliament sessions have been suspended since 2016. In 2017, Tanzania withdrew from the Open Government Partnership, a multilateral platform designed to improve transparency and openness among its member states.

CIVIL LIBERTIES: 25 / 60 (−5)

D. FREEDOM OF EXPRESSION AND BELIEF: 7 / 16

D1. Are there free and independent media? 1 / 4

The crackdown on media in Tanzania expanded in 2018, affecting traditional news sources as well as social and online media.

The 2016 Media Services Act grants the government broad authority over media content and the licensing of outlets and journalists. It also prescribes harsh penalties, including prison terms, for publication of defamatory, seditious, or other illegal content. In some cases news outlets have sought to preempt formal punishments with self-imposed sanctions. In January 2018, *Nipashe Jumapili*, a Sunday newspaper, suspended itself for three months over an article perceived as insulting to Rwandan president Paul Kagame. The government's three-year ban on the newspaper *Mseto*, initially handed down for its reporting on alleged corruption in Magufuli's 2015 campaign, was struck down by the East African Court of Justice in June, but by the end of the year, the government had refused to grant a license to the publication. In December, the High Court of Tanzania reversed a two-year ban imposed on *Mawio* in 2017, though it was unclear whether the government would respect the court's decision and issue the outlet a license.

The government intensified its crackdown on online content and social media in 2018. In April, authorities issued the Electronic and Postal Communications (Online Content) Regulations, which require bloggers and owners of online discussion platforms and streaming services to pay over $900 per year in registration fees. In response, many bloggers who were unable to pay the fees shut down their outlets.

Attacks on journalists contributed to an atmosphere of fear and repression for independent media. Freelance journalist Azory Gwanda, who was investigating extrajudicial killings, has been missing since November 2017. In April, reporter Finnigan wa Simbeye of the *Guardian* was beaten unconscious and found in a ditch.

D2. Are individuals free to practice and express their religious faith or nonbelief in public and private? 3 / 4

Freedom of religion is generally respected, and interfaith relations are largely peaceful, though periodic sectarian violence has occurred. Muslims are a minority in Tanzania as a whole, but 99 percent of Zanzibar's population practices Islam. Political tensions between mainland Tanzania and Zanzibar often play out along religious lines. The government occasionally raises the specter of interreligious conflict as an excuse to detain political rivals, contributing to a general sense that Muslims are sometimes unfairly treated by authorities.

D3. Is there academic freedom, and is the educational system free from extensive political indoctrination? 2 / 4

Tanzania's reputation as a bastion of academic freedom was tarnished by the passage of 2015 Statistics Act, which requires data released publicly to be first approved by the National Bureau of Statistics, making the body the de facto arbiter of the validity of any data produced by academics. In September 2018, the parliament passed amendments to the Statistics Act that prescribed fines, a minimum of three years in prison, or both for anyone who disputes official government figures. The amendments effectively criminalized any academic data that contradict official government statistics.

D4. Are individuals free to express their personal views on political or other sensitive topics without fear of surveillance or retribution? 1 / 4

CCM traditionally monitors the population through a neighborhood-level party cell structure, but it has turned its attention to social media in recent years, and constraints on individuals' freedom to discuss political topics online have grown. The fees imposed by the Electronic and Postal Communications (Online Content) Regulations led to the brief closure of *Jamii Forums*, a popular news site and social media platform, in June 2018. Social media users are liable for content that "causes annoyance" or "leads to public disorder," among other vague standards that are prone to misapplication by authorities who wish to quash online discourse. The regulations also require internet cafés to install surveillance cameras. Violations of the regulations can be punished with fines and jail terms. The ambiguous language of the new rules has led to confusion among users about which acts could constitute a violation.

Social media users in 2018 continued to face the risk of prosecution under the 2015 Cybercrimes Act and other laws for offenses such as insulting the president, and government officials threatened to prosecute users for supposedly spreading homosexuality through social media.

E. ASSOCIATIONAL AND ORGANIZATIONAL RIGHTS: 5 / 12 (−1)
E1. Is there freedom of assembly? 2 / 4

The constitution guarantees freedom of assembly, but the government can limit this right. All assemblies require police approval, and political demonstrations are at times actively discouraged. A ban on political rallies has been in place since mid-2016.

Authorities, including the president, sometimes threaten protesters with violence. In April 2018, police threatened to beat demonstrators planning to participate in US-based activist Mange Kimambi's antigovernment protests "like stray dogs." The protests failed to draw substantial crowds amid government threats and a heavy police presence. President Magufuli also threatened protesters in March, saying, "Let them demonstrate and they will see who I am."

E2. Is there freedom for nongovernmental organizations, particularly those that are engaged in human rights- and governance-related work? 1 / 4 (−1)

Tanzania has a diverse and active civil society sector, but current laws give the government broad authority to deregister nongovernmental organizations (NGOs), and officials repeatedly threatened to use that power against critical groups in 2018. Government pressure on civil society intensified throughout the year in the form of threats, investigations, detentions, and restrictive regulations.

In August, the passport of Aidan Eyakuze, the executive director of Twaweza, a prominent NGO that has criticized the government, was seized amid an investigation into his citizenship status. The government has also stated that NGOs should focus on service delivery and avoid advocacy work that could be viewed as political. In July, the deputy registrar of NGOs warned civil society groups against violating the law.

The government is overhauling NGO legislation, ostensibly to bring all NGOs under one law, to ensure that their services reach all parts of Tanzania, and to facilitate coordination. A new registration policy introduced in September as part of the overhaul required NGOs to reregister with the government and provide detailed financial records within 30 days, or risk suspension. Civil society leaders expressed concerns that the objective of the pending legislation and new registration requirements was to exert greater political control over the NGO sector.

NGO leaders continued to risk arrest for carrying out their activities in 2018. In November, authorities detained and interrogated two visiting international staff members of the Committee to Protect Journalists, allegedly for holding meetings with local journalists.

Score Change: The score declined from 2 to 1 due to increased threats against and investigations of NGOs, in addition to government directives related to NGO registration and finance that civil society leaders claim will impose greater constraints on their ability to function.

E3. Is there freedom for trade unions and similar professional or labor organizations? 2 / 4

Trade unions are nominally independent of the government and are coordinated by the Trade Union Congress of Tanzania and the Zanzibar Trade Union Congress. The Tanzania Federation of Cooperatives represents most of Tanzania's agricultural sector. The government has significant discretion to deny union registration, and many private employers engage in antiunion activities. Essential public-sector workers are barred from striking, and other workers are restricted by complex notification and mediation requirements. Strikes are infrequent on both the mainland and Zanzibar.

F. RULE OF LAW: 6 / 16 (−2)

F1. Is there an independent judiciary? 2 / 4

Tanzania's judiciary suffers from underfunding and corruption. Judges are political appointees, and the judiciary does not have an independent budget, which makes it vulnerable to political pressure. In January 2018, newly confirmed chief justice Ibrahim Hamis Juma issued a stern rebuke for those who wish to politicize the judiciary, but it remained to be seen whether judicial independence would be more respected during his tenure.

F2. Does due process prevail in civil and criminal matters? 2 / 4

Due process does not always prevail in civil and criminal matters. Policies and rules regarding arrest and pretrial detention are often ignored, and pretrial detention commonly lasts for years due to case backlogs and inadequate funding for prosecutors. Arbitrary arrests of opposition politicians, journalists, and civil society leaders occurred throughout 2018.

F3. Is there protection from the illegitimate use of physical force and freedom from war and insurgencies? 1 / 4 (−1)

The police were increasingly accused of extrajudicial killings in 2018. Ongoing clashes in the Kigoma region between the government and pastoralists has led to an unknown number of deaths. In October, opposition leader Zitto Kabwe estimated that 100 people were killed in the violence, a claim that led to his arrest.

Abuse and torture of suspects while in custody is common. In March, a young man in Mbeya died shortly after being released from police custody, where he was allegedly beaten; in April, the brother of a Chadema lawmaker was stabbed to death while detained.

Several high-profile abductions and disappearances occurred in 2018, including that of business magnate Mohammed Dewji, who was kidnapped in October and returned safely one week after his abduction; the crime remained unsolved at year's end. Kabwe estimated that, as of May, nearly 350 people had gone missing from the Coast region as part of a government crackdown against Islamist extremists.

Score Change: The score declined from 2 to 1 due to an increase in alleged extrajudicial killings by police, as well as an uptick in kidnappings.

F4. Do laws, policies, and practices guarantee equal treatment of various segments of the population? 1 / 4 (−1)

Women's rights are constitutionally guaranteed but not uniformly protected. Women face de facto discrimination in employment, including sexual harassment, which is rarely addressed through formal legal channels. Women's socioeconomic disadvantages are more pronounced in rural areas and in the informal economy.

Same-sex sexual relations are punishable by lengthy prison terms, and LGBT (lesbian, gay, bisexual, and transgender) people face discrimination and police abuse in practice, leading most to hide their identities. In October 2018, Paul Makonda, Dar es Salaam's regional commissioner, called on the public to report people suspected of being gay and established a committee to identify and arrest gay people who are active on social media, which led to an international outcry. The national government later issued a statement distancing itself from the plan. However, in November, 10 men were arrested at a gay wedding in Zanzibar for suspected same-sex sexual activity and were forced to undergo anal examinations.

As of July 2018, more than 340,000 refugees and asylum seekers, primarily from Burundi and the Democratic Republic of Congo, were in Tanzania, with most living in overcrowded, unhygienic, and unsafe camps. The Tanzanian government has pressured refugees to return to their countries, restricting economic activity in the camps in order to push occupants out. The Office of the UN High Commissioner for Refugees (UNHCR) has strongly advised against promoting the repatriation of refugees.

Score Change: The score declined from 2 to 1 due to a crackdown on LGBT people, including the formation of an antigay task force by the regional commissioner of Dar es Salaam that encouraged people to turn in those suspected of being gay for arrest and prosecution.

G. PERSONAL AUTONOMY AND INDIVIDUAL RIGHTS: 7 / 16 (−2)

G1. Do individuals enjoy freedom of movement, including the ability to change their place of residence, employment, or education? 2 / 4 (−1)

Residents enjoy some basic freedoms pertaining to travel and choice of residence, employment, and education, though corruption remains an obstacle. The government has wide discretion in enforcing laws that can limit movement, particularly in Zanzibar, where the approval of local government appointees is often required for changes in employment, personal banking, and residency. Separately, the authorities in recent years have arbitrarily arrested and deported a number of Kenyans, many of whom had been granted Tanzanian citizenship.

The government at times imposes travel restrictions on prominent individuals. In December 2018, officials prohibited hip-hop star Diamond Platnumz from performing outside Tanzania due to his public performance of a song that had been banned for its sexually explicit lyrics.

Score Change: The score declined from 3 to 2 because of undue government restrictions on movement, including arbitrary arrests and deportations of Kenyan nationals.

G2. Are individuals able to exercise the right to own property and establish private businesses without undue interference from state or nonstate actors? 2 / 4

Tanzanians have the right to establish private businesses but are often required to pay bribes to license and operate them. The state owns all land and leases it to individuals and private entities, leading to clashes over land rights between citizens and companies engaged in extractive industries.

G3. Do individuals enjoy personal social freedoms, including choice of marriage partner and size of family, protection from domestic violence, and control over appearance? 1 / 4 (−1)

Rape, domestic violence, and female genital mutilation (FGM) are common but rarely prosecuted. Laws and practices regarding marriage, divorce, and other personal status issues favor men over women, particularly in Zanzibar. The government has stalled implementation and pursued appeals of a 2016 High Court ruling that called for the minimum age of marriage to be raised to 18 for girls as well as boys. Tanzania's adolescent fertility rate is more than twice the global average.

The government restricts access to family planning services. In September 2018, a government directive suspended advertisements by family planning organizations. In October, the government closed down 10 clinics run by the NGO Marie Stopes that offered such services. At the same time, girls can be expelled from school for becoming pregnant, and in 2017 the government prohibited those who had given birth from returning to school. In 2018, local authorities arrested some pregnant students.

Score Change: The score declined from 2 to 1 due to government efforts to curb access to birth control, including the suspension of advertisements by family planning organizations and the closure of health facilities that offered family planning services.

G4. Do individuals enjoy equality of opportunity and freedom from economic exploitation? 2 / 4

Sexual and labor exploitation remain problems, especially for children living in poor rural areas who are drawn into domestic service, agricultural labor, mining, and other activities. Child labor in gold mines, where working conditions are often dangerous, is common.

Most Tanzanians do not benefit from the country's extensive natural-resource wealth. Tanzania has one of the highest levels of income inequality in the world, and the poverty rate remains high.

Thailand

Population: 66,200,000
Capital: Bangkok
Political Rights Rating: 7 ↓
Civil Liberties Rating: 5
Freedom Rating: 6.0
Freedom Status: Not Free
Electoral Democracy: No

Overview: Thailand is ruled by a military junta that conducted a coup in 2014, claiming that it would put an end to a political crisis that had gripped the country for almost a decade. As the military government imposes its rule, it has exercised unchecked powers granted by the constitution to restrict civil and political rights, and to suppress dissent.

KEY DEVELOPMENTS IN 2018:
- In February, national elections, already repeatedly delayed, were again postponed until February 2019 by Prime Minister Prayuth Chan-ocha. The government later announced in September that elections would take place between February and May 2019.
- More than 130 prodemocracy activists were charged with illegal assembly in 2018 for peacefully pressuring the government to lift restrictions on basic rights and hold long-promised elections.
- In September, the government partially lifted a ban on political parties, allowing parties to hold meetings, recruit members, and select candidates; and in December, the National Council for Peace and Order (NCPO) lifted its ban on campaigning.

- Also in September, three members of the newly established Future Forward Party, including its founder Thanathorn Juangroongruangkit, were charged with spreading false information about the military government, over the content of a speech critical of the NCPO which was posted on Facebook. If convicted, they face up to five years in prison.

POLITICAL RIGHTS: 5 / 40 (−1)

A. ELECTORAL PROCESS: 0 / 12

A1. Was the current head of government or other chief national authority elected through free and fair elections? 0 / 4

Thailand is a constitutional monarchy ruled by King Maha Vajiralongkorn, who serves as head of state. Although the monarchy has limited formal power, the king is highly influential in Thai politics, and has significant clout over the military. Thailand's current head of government, Prime Minister Prayuth Chan-ocha, staged a military coup against the democratically elected government in 2014. Prayuth, who was then the army chief, was subsequently designated prime minister in the absence of elections.

The "road map" of the NCPO—the military junta that seized power in 2014—for a return to civilian rule has been delayed several times. In February 2018, Prime Minister Prayuth announced that national elections, which had previously been scheduled for November, would be postponed until 2019.

A2. Were the current national legislative representatives elected through free and fair elections? 0 / 4

The 2014 interim constitution promulgated by the NCPO created a 220-seat National Legislative Assembly (NLA), which quickly installed the prime minister and cabinet. The 200-member National Reform Steering Assembly (NRSA), tasked with making recommendations for reforms to government and the political process, was convened in 2015. Members of both the NLA and the NRSA were chosen by the NCPO.

A3. Are the electoral laws and framework fair, and are they implemented impartially by the relevant election management bodies? 0 / 4

The NCPO-appointed Constitutional Drafting Committee (CDC) developed a draft constitution that was approved in a tightly controlled 2016 referendum. The new constitution, which will govern future elections, was designed to weaken political parties and elected officials while strengthening unelected institutions. In the mixed-member apportionment system introduced in the charter, there will be 350 constituency seats and 150 party-list seats in the House of Representatives, the lower house of the parliament. Citizens will cast only one vote, rather than two distinct votes, which counts for a candidate as well as for that candidate's party for the party-list seats. Experts anticipate that without separate votes for each type of seat, parties will have difficulty gaining a majority, leading to unstable coalition governments. All 250 seats in the Senate, or upper house, will be appointed for the first five-year term by the junta, and will include six seats reserved for senior military officials. The Senate will have influence over the selection of the prime minister. In September 2018, after several postponements, the NCPO enacted two laws mandating that general elections be held between February and May 2019.

B. POLITICAL PLURALISM AND PARTICIPATION: 3 / 16

B1. Do the people have the right to organize in different political parties or other competitive political groupings of their choice, and is the system free of undue obstacles to the rise and fall of these competing parties or groupings? 1 / 4

In 2014, the NCPO enacted measures banning the formation of new political parties and prohibiting existing parties from meeting or conducting political activities. A Political Party Act approved in 2017 introduced costly provisions that are difficult for small parties to adhere to; these include annual fees and a requirement that parties establish branches in different parts of the country. Later in 2017, the government passed an amendment to the Political Party Act allowing for the formation of new political parties—though new parties require approval by the NCPO before they can begin operations.

In September 2018, the NCPO lifted many of the restrictions on political parties, allowing parties to hold meetings, recruit members, select candidates, and hold forums with the public in preparation for the 2019 elections. In December, the NCPO lifted its ban on campaigning.

In July, Thailand requested the extradition of former prime minister Yingluck Shinawatra of the Pheu Thai Party (PTP) from the United Kingdom, where she is believed to be living in exile. At year's end, the British government had not yet responded to the request. Yingluck was convicted in absentia in 2017 and given a five-year prison sentence over her alleged mismanagement of a rice-subsidy scheme.

In September, four ministers from the NCPO government formed a new political party, the Palang Pracharat Party, which observers believe will support any attempt by Prime Minister Prayuth to remain in power past the 2019 elections.

B2. Is there a realistic opportunity for the opposition to increase its support or gain power through elections? 1 / 4

With the ban on the activities of political parties, including those opposed to military rule, partially lifted in September 2018, opposition parties are expected to take part in the 2019 general elections that are set to transfer some power to an elected government. However, the electoral laws forbid former prime minister Thaksin Shinawatra of the PTP from any involvement in the campaign, hampering the party's competitiveness. In September, three members of the newly established Future Forward Party, including its founder Thanathorn Juangroongruangkit, were charged with spreading false information about the military government in violation of the Computer-Related Crime Act, over the content of a speech critical of the NCPO which was posted on Facebook. If convicted, they face up to five years in prison. The charges raised concerns about the potential repression of viable opposition parties ahead of the 2019 elections.

B3. Are the people's political choices free from domination by the military, foreign powers, religious hierarchies, economic oligarchies, or any other powerful group that is not democratically accountable? 0 / 4

Thailand is currently ruled by an unelected junta aligned with the country's monarchy and economic elites. Citizens are excluded from meaningful political participation.

B4. Do various segments of the population (including ethnic, religious, gender, LGBT, and other relevant groups) have full political rights and electoral opportunities? 1 / 4

Since political rights are broadly denied to residents, women and members of minority groups are generally unable to choose their representatives or organize independently to assert their interests in the political sphere. Malay Muslims in southern Thailand remain politically marginalized, and their efforts to achieve greater autonomy have been largely unrecognized by the government. Women are underrepresented in government at all levels, composing less than 5 percent of the parliament, and few women are in leadership roles in political parties.

C. FUNCTIONING OF GOVERNMENT: 2 / 12 (-1)

C1. Do the freely elected head of government and national legislative representatives determine the policies of the government? 0 / 4

The policies of the Thai government are determined by the unelected prime minister and his appointed government, the NCPO. The new constitution does not annul any of the repressive laws and policies passed by the junta since 2014, including those that were granted by Article 44 of the interim charter. This provision gives the head of the NCPO unchecked powers, including the ability to override existing legislation and issue new laws at will.

C2. Are safeguards against official corruption strong and effective? 1 / 4 (-1)

The National Anti-Corruption Commission (NACC) receives a high number of complaints each year, and the NCPO has passed vague anticorruption laws. However, while coup leaders cited corruption as one justification for the overthrow of the previous government, the current regime has engaged in corruption, cronyism, and nepotism. Corrupt high-level officials have acted with impunity in recent years. Beginning in late 2017, Minister of Defense Prawit Wongsuwan (who also serves as deputy prime minister) became embroiled in a scandal over his possession of at least 25 luxury watches, which were not included in his asset declaration, with an estimated value of $1.5 million. Prime Minister Prayuth defended Prawit, claiming the watches were lent to him. In December 2018, the NACC absolved Prawit of any wrongdoing, concluding that he had borrowed the watches from "old school friends."

Score Change: The score declined from 2 to 1 due to the authorities' failure to address allegations of official corruption, including against high-level officials in the NCPO, who have acted with impunity in recent years.

C3. Does the government operate with openness and transparency? 1 / 4

The NCPO largely operates without openness and transparency. High-level decisions are generally made, and the drafting of legislation carried out, with near-total opacity and no public consultation.

CIVIL LIBERTIES: 25 / 60
D. FREEDOM OF EXPRESSION AND BELIEF: 6 / 16
D1. Are there free and independent media? 1 / 4

Since taking power in 2014, the NCPO has systematically used censorship, intimidation, and legal action to suppress independent media. Journalists have been detained without charge and questioned by the NCPO in military camps, in an intimidation tactic known as an "attitude adjustment." Journalists and media outlets risk penalties for violating an NCPO ban on material that "maliciously" criticizes the government or is deemed divisive. Peace TV, a news channel frequently critical of the government, was suspended twice by the National Broadcasting and Telecommunications Commission (NBTC), in February and May 2018, for broadcasting "provocative" content. The second suspension lasted for 30 days. In September, Voice TV suspended two popular commentators on its Wake Up News program, after allegedly being pressured by the NBTC. The commentators had been accused of political bias against the NCPO.

In 2017, over the objections of a coalition of media organizations, the government passed a law mandating the creation of a regulatory media council with members appointed by the military government.

D2. Are individuals free to practice and express their religious faith or nonbelief in public and private? 3 / 4

There is no state religion, and religious freedom is respected in the majority of the country. Religious organizations operate freely, and there is no systemic or institutional discrimination based on religion. However, some restrictions exist. Speech considered insulting to Buddhism is prohibited by law. A long-running civil conflict in the south, which pits ethnic Malay Muslims against ethnic Thai Buddhists, continues to undermine citizens' ability to practice their religions.

D3. Is there academic freedom, and is the educational system free from extensive political indoctrination? 1 / 4

Academic freedom is constrained under the NCPO. University discussions and seminars on topics regarded as politically sensitive are subject to monitoring or outright cancellation by government authorities. In December 2018, a court dismissed illegal public assembly charges against five people, including the prominent academic Chayan Vaddhanaphuti. The charges stemmed from the 2017 International Conference on Thai Studies at Chiang Mai University, at which the defendants allegedly unfurled a banner stating that "an academic conference is not a military barracks," in response to the presence of security forces at the event.

Academics working on sensitive topics are subjected to oppressive tactics including summonses for questioning, home visits by security officials, surveillance of their activities, and arbitrary detention for the purpose of questioning. Some academics have fled into exile.

Since the 2014 coup, the junta has also bolstered its efforts to foster student support for government ideas, including through curriculum development.

D4. Are individuals free to express their personal views on political or other sensitive topics without fear of surveillance or retribution? 1 / 4

Security forces have enforced stringent surveillance on people viewed as critical of the NCPO, including surveillance of online activities.

The number of lèse-majesté cases has increased sharply under the NCPO. Cases have been used to target activists, scholars, students, journalists, and politicians. In addition to authorities' monitoring of social media sites for lèse-majesté violations, this type of social surveillance has also been undertaken by citizens who, either with the backing of the government or on their own initiative, scan online postings and report them to authorities.

Under the draconian Computer-Related Crime Act, social media users continued to face arrest for sharing posts critical of the government in 2018. In June, authorities issued an arrest warrant for Watana Ebbage, an activist based in London, for her Facebook posts on corruption in the military. After the issuance of Ebbage's arrest warrant, 29 Facebook users were arrested for sharing her posts.

E. ASSOCIATIONAL AND ORGANIZATIONAL RIGHTS: 4 / 12

E1. Is there freedom of assembly? 1 / 4

Prohibitions on political gatherings of five or more people continued to be enforced in 2018. What constitutes a political gathering is at the discretion of the authorities. Those who engage in symbolic actions or public protests advocating for democracy and human rights risk a spectrum of consequences, including fines, arrest, and being subject to political reeducation. In 2018, more than 130 prodemocracy activists were charged with illegal assembly for peacefully pressuring the government to lift restrictions on basic rights and hold elections as promised.

E2. Is there freedom for nongovernmental organizations, particularly those that are engaged in human rights- and governance-related work? 1 / 4

Thailand has a vibrant civil society, but groups focused on defending human rights or freedom of expression face restrictions, with the NCPO often insisting that such activities violate laws concerning political gatherings, or create "public disturbances." When such activities are allowed to move forward, authorities have cautioned organizers against opposing NCPO policies ahead of time, and heavily monitor the events. In 2018, authorities increased the number of sedition charges filed, and a number of nongovernmental organization (NGO) leaders were targeted. In September, four members of the Organization for Thai Federation, which advocates for abolishing the monarchy, were arrested and charged with sedition for selling and wearing t-shirts that supposedly supported republicanism.

In November, the Office of the Judiciary filed defamation lawsuits against the leaders of the Doi Suthep Forest Reclamation Network, an activist group which, beginning in April, had staged a number of environmental protests over the construction of a luxury housing project for judges on forested land near the city of Chiang Mai. In May, the government agreed to leave the buildings unoccupied and eventually restore the land. However, the lawsuits were filed after banners appeared in Chiang Mai in November criticizing the housing development.

E3. Is there freedom for trade unions and similar professional or labor organizations? 2 / 4

Thai trade unions are independent and have the right to collectively bargain. However, civil servants and temporary workers do not have the right to form unions, and less than 2 percent of the total workforce is unionized. Antiunion discrimination in the private sector is common, and legal protections for union members are weak and poorly enforced.

F. RULE OF LAW: 5 / 16

F1. Is there an independent judiciary? 1 / 4

Although the new constitution grants independence to the judiciary, in practice, Thailand's courts are politicized, and corruption in the judicial branch is common. The highly politicized Constitutional Court, which has been accused of favoring the military, has sweeping powers, including the ability to dissolve political parties, overthrow elected officials, and veto legislation. In March 2018, the government enacted a law that made criticism of the Constitutional Court with "rude, sarcastic, or threatening words" a criminal offense, further shielding the body from accountability.

F2. Does due process prevail in civil and criminal matters? 1 / 4

Restrictions implemented by the NCPO severely undermine due process rights. Orders issued in 2015 permit the detention of individuals without charge for up to seven days, and expanded the authority of military officers in the area of law enforcement, permitting them to arrest, detain, and investigate crimes related to the monarchy and national security.

Cases related to land and natural resources, particularly those deemed by the junta to be vital to the country's economic development, are susceptible to political interference.

F3. Is there protection from the illegitimate use of physical force and freedom from war and insurgencies? 1 / 4

While most of the country is free from terrorism or insurgencies, a combination of martial law and emergency rule has been in effect for over a decade in the four southernmost provinces, where Malay Muslims form a majority and a separatist insurgency has been ongoing since the 1940s. Civilians are regularly targeted in shootings, bombings, and arson attacks, and insurgents have focused on schools and teachers as symbols of the Thai state. Counterinsurgency operations have involved the indiscriminate detention of thousands of suspected militants and sympathizers, and there are long-standing and credible reports of torture and other human rights violations, including extrajudicial killings, by both government forces and insurgents. The police and military often operate with impunity, which is exacerbated by the absence of any law that explicitly prohibits torture.

Land and environmental activists risk serious and even deadly violence; the environmental rights group Global Witness has described Thailand as among the most dangerous countries in Asia for such activists to operate. Perpetrators of attacks against them generally enjoy impunity.

F4. Do laws, policies, and practices guarantee equal treatment of various segments of the population? 2 / 4

In Thailand's north, so-called hill tribes are not fully integrated into society. Many lack formal citizenship, which renders them ineligible to vote, own land, attend state schools, or receive protection under labor laws. Thailand is known for its tolerance of LGBT (lesbian, gay, bisexual, and transgender) people, though societal acceptance is higher for tourists and expatriates than for nationals, and unequal treatment and stigmatization remain challenges. Women face discrimination in employment, a problem which was highlighted by the decision of the Royal Police Cadet Academy in September 2018 to ban female cadets.

Thailand has not ratified the UN convention on refugees, who risk detention as unauthorized migrants and often lack access to asylum procedures. Authorities conducted a number of raids in 2018 that led to the detentions of hundreds of refugees and asylum seekers from Vietnam, Cambodia, and Pakistan.

G. PERSONAL AUTONOMY AND INDIVIDUAL RIGHTS: 10 / 16

G1. Do individuals enjoy freedom of movement, including the ability to change their place of residence, employment, or education? 3 / 4

Thai citizens generally have freedom of travel and choice of residence. However, travel may be restricted in areas affected by civil conflict, and the junta has at times imposed travel bans on its critics.

G2. Are individuals able to exercise the right to own property and establish private businesses without undue interference from state or nonstate actors? 2 / 4

The rights to property and to establish businesses are protected by law, though in practice business activity is affected by some bureaucratic delays, and at times by the influence of security forces and organized crime. The NCPO's policies to restore national forests through replanting programs and new restrictions on poaching, as well as plans to create special economic zones, have led to eviction orders for many communities.

G3. Do individuals enjoy personal social freedoms, including choice of marriage partner and size of family, protection from domestic violence, and control over appearance? 3 / 4

While women have the same legal rights as men, they are vulnerable to domestic abuse and rape, and victims rarely report attacks to authorities, who frequently discourage women from pursuing criminal charges against perpetrators.

In December 2018, the NCPO announced that it would support a bill which would make Thailand the first country in Asia to legalize same-sex unions.

G4. Do individuals enjoy equality of opportunity and freedom from economic exploitation? 2 / 4

Exploitation and trafficking of migrant workers (estimated between four and five million) and refugees from Myanmar, Cambodia, and Laos are serious and ongoing problems, as are child and sweatshop labor. Sex trafficking remains a problem in which some state officials are complicit. However, the government has made some efforts to prosecute and seize the assets of those suspected of involvement in human trafficking, including police officers and local officials.

In 2017, the NCPO passed a law imposing heavy fines on employers that hire migrant workers residing in Thailand illegally, as well as lengthy prison terms on irregular migrant workers themselves, causing a mass exodus of both registered and unregistered migrant workers. In March 2018, after sustained international criticism, the government passed revisions to the law which reduced fines on employers and removed prison sentences as a punishment for irregular migrants.

Timor-Leste

Population: 1,200,000
Capital: Dili
Political Rights Rating: 2
Civil Liberties Rating: 3
Freedom Rating: 2.5
Freedom Status: Free
Electoral Democracy: Yes

Overview: Timor-Leste has held competitive elections and undergone peaceful transfers of power, but its democratic institutions remain fragile, and disputes among the major personalities from the independence struggle dominate political affairs. Judicial independence and due process are undermined by serious capacity deficits and political influence.

KEY DEVELOPMENTS IN 2018:
- Parliament was dissolved in January and parliamentary elections were held for the second time in ten months in May. The Change for Progress Alliance (AMP), a coalition of sitting opposition parties, won an outright majority, and took power from the minority government led by the Revolutionary Front for an Independent East Timor (Fretilin).
- The elections were generally peaceful and orderly, despite a few violent incidents during the campaign period.
- After some debate, the new government approved a budget in September. The previous government had been dissolved in part due to its inability to approve a budget.
- A district court's May ruling involving the release of a Chinese fishing fleet caught in Timorese waters with a cargo of thousands of endangered sharks prompted criticism of the Timorese judiciary.

POLITICAL RIGHTS: 32 / 40

A. ELECTORAL PROCESS: 11 / 12

A1. Was the current head of government or other chief national authority elected through free and fair elections? 4 / 4

The directly elected president is a largely symbolic figure, with formal powers limited to the right to veto legislation and make certain appointments. The president may serve up to two five-year terms. Francisco Guterres, known as Lú-Olo, was elected president in 2017, following a campaign period a European Union (EU) observer mission praised for its generally peaceful conduct. The mission assessed the election itself as having been well administered.

The leader of the majority party or coalition in Parliament becomes prime minister, and serves as head of government. In June 2018, former independence fighter and former president José Maria Vasconcelos, popularly known as Taur Matan Ruak, was sworn in as prime minister.

A2. Were the current national legislative representatives elected through free and fair elections? 4 / 4

Members of the 65-seat, unicameral Parliament are directly elected and serve five-year terms. Because the minority government that was seated after the 2017 election could not pass a budget, the president dissolved parliament in January 2018 and called new elections, which were held in May. The sitting opposition parties—the National Congress for the Reconstruction of Timor-Leste (CNRT), the Kmanek Haburas Unidade Nasional Timor Oan (KHUNTO), and the People's Liberation Party (PLP)—came together as the AMP and won an outright majority of 34 seats. Fretilin won 23 seats, the Democratic Party (PD) won 5 seats, and the Democratic Development Front (FDD) won 3 seats.

An EU observer mission called the elections "transparent, well-managed and credible;" and they were generally peaceful and orderly, despite a few violent incidents during the campaign period.

A3. Are the electoral laws and framework fair, and are they implemented impartially by the relevant election management bodies? 3 / 4

The 2017 and 2018 EU election observation missions generally praised the National Election Commission (CNE) for its oversight of the years' polls, but expressed concern that changes to the election laws in 2017 somewhat reduced the body's supervisory responsibilities. Provisions governing elections are found across a number of pieces of legislation, and observers have called for legal mandates governing elections to be harmonized into a more coherent framework.

B. POLITICAL PLURALISM AND PARTICIPATION: 14 / 16

B1. Do the people have the right to organize in different political parties or other competitive political groupings of their choice, and is the system free of undue obstacles to the rise and fall of these competing parties or groupings? 4 / 4

Some campaign finance regulations favor larger parties, such as a lack of caps on spending, and a system in which government campaign subsidies are awarded after elections, according to the number of votes a party won.

Nevertheless, political parties are generally free to form and operate. Two new parties, the youth-aligned KHUNTO, and the PLP, concentrated enough support ahead of the 2017 elections to win 13 legislative seats between them that year. They later joined the AMP coalition in the 2018 elections, which won with an outright majority in parliament.

B2. Is there a realistic opportunity for the opposition to increase its support or gain power through elections? 4 / 4

The national elections in 2018 marked the third time since independence that governing power transferred between parties. The formation of a new majority AMP government comprised of the opposition parties from the 2017 elections includes the CNRT and two new parties, the PLP and KHUNTO.

While some smaller parties hold seats in parliament, parties associated with the independence movement continue to dominate politics, with the 2017 government led by Fretilin and the 2018 government led by a coalition which includes the CNRT.

B3. Are the people's political choices free from domination by the military, foreign powers, religious hierarchies, economic oligarchies, or any other powerful group that is not democratically accountable? 3 / 4

Politics are dominated by independence-movement figures who have formed political parties. However, some younger candidates have begun to emerge and win representation.

B4. Do various segments of the population (including ethnic, religious, gender, LGBT, and other relevant groups) have full political rights and electoral opportunities? 3 / 4

Ethnic minorities are generally well represented in politics. Due to parity laws, Timor-Leste has the highest percentage of women in Parliament in the Asia-Pacific region. However, women have overwhelmingly expressed the opinion that there would be few if any women candidates on party lists in the absence of parity laws, and that in practice women politicians have difficulty participating meaningfully in political processes. Since 2017, the Election Management Bodies have collected gender-disaggregated data, which showed that women's voter turnout in the 2018 elections was 48.6 percent.

C. FUNCTIONING OF GOVERNMENT: 7 / 12

C1. Do the freely elected head of government and national legislative representatives determine the policies of the government? 3 / 4

In 2017 and 2018, the government held competitive and peaceful elections without the supervision of a UN mission that had been deployed to help restore security following a 2006 political crisis. A new minority government was formed after the legislative elections in 2017, but due to inability to pass a budget was dissolved by the president in January 2018. The new government elected in May's early polls debated and approved a budget in September.

C2. Are safeguards against official corruption strong and effective? 2 / 4

Anticorruption bodies lack enough funding to operate effectively. The independent Anti-Corruption Commission (CAC) has no powers of arrest or prosecution and must rely on the prosecutor general, with input from police and the courts, to follow up on corruption investigations.

C3. Does the government operate with openness and transparency? 2 / 4

While the state has attempted to make budgets more accessible, procurement processes remain largely opaque. Requests for public information are not always granted, and at times require applicants to undertake inconvenient travel. Information is often issued in Portuguese, which may not be accessible to those who speak local languages.

CIVIL LIBERTIES: 38 / 60 (+1)

D. FREEDOM OF EXPRESSION AND BELIEF: 14 / 16 (+1)

D1. Are there free and independent media? 3 / 4

Media freedom is protected in the constitution. In practice, domestic media outlets are vulnerable to political pressure due to their reliance on government financial support in a small media market with limited nongovernmental sources of paid advertising. Journalists are often treated with suspicion, particularly by government officials, and practice self-censorship. However, in recent years, the country's journalists have been more willing to produce articles critical of the government.

D2. Are individuals free to practice and express their religious faith or nonbelief in public and private? 3 / 4

Freedom of religion is protected in the constitution, and Timor-Leste is a secular state. Approximately 97 percent of the population is Roman Catholic. Protestant groups have reported some cases of discrimination and harassment.

D3. Is there academic freedom, and is the educational system free from extensive political indoctrination? 4 / 4

Academic freedom is generally respected.

D4. Are individuals free to express their personal views on political or other sensitive topics without fear of surveillance or retribution? 4 / 4 (+1)

There are few constraints on open and free private discussion, and citizens are free to discuss political and social issues. Topics related to the 2006 unrest, in which armed clashes between the police and mobilized civilian groups resulted in numerous deaths and the displacement of some 150,000 people, remain sensitive.

Score Change: The score improved from 3 to 4 because citizens are largely free to discuss political topics without fear of surveillance or retribution.

E. ASSOCIATIONAL AND ORGANIZATIONAL RIGHTS: 8 / 12

E1. Is there freedom of assembly? 3 / 4

Freedom of assembly is constitutionally guaranteed, and while it is generally respected in practice, some laws can be invoked to restrict peaceful gatherings. Demonstrations deemed to be "questioning constitutional order," or disparaging the reputations of the head of state and other government officials, are prohibited. Demonstrations must be authorized in advance, and laws restrict how close they can be to government buildings and critical infrastructure.

E2. Is there freedom for nongovernmental organizations, particularly those that are engaged in human rights– and governance-related work? 3 / 4

Nongovernmental organizations (NGOs) can generally operate without interference, although the state actively monitors and regulates their work. Few NGOs operate outside of the capital.

E3. Is there freedom for trade unions and similar professional or labor organizations? 2 / 4

Workers, other than police and military personnel, are permitted to form and join labor unions and bargain collectively, though a 2011 law requires written notification of demands and allows for five days for a response from employers in advance of striking. If employers do not respond or if an agreement is not reached within 20 days, then five days' notice is required for a strike. In practice, few workers are unionized due to high levels of unemployment and informal economic activity.

F. RULE OF LAW: 7 / 16

F1. Is there an independent judiciary? 1 / 4

There is still reported political interference in the justice system, and for a period between 2014 and 2017, the work of the judiciary was disrupted by government mandates regarding the permissibility of foreign judges and legal workers. After independence, the judicial system depended on contracted foreign judges and lawyers. In 2014, however, the government terminated contracts and visas of foreigners working in judicial, prosecutorial, and anticorruption institutions. As a result, legal proceedings in some courts were delayed or forced to restart with new personnel, and the Legal and Judicial Training Centre was closed. Later, a 2017 law explicitly permitting foreign judges allowed training courses for Timorese judges to recommence after a three-year closure.

A 2018 ruling involving a Chinese fishing fleet caught in 2017 in Timorese waters with a cargo of thousands of endangered sharks prompted criticism of the Timorese judiciary. In May, the fleet's crew was released by a district court on a relatively low $100,000 bail payment, and allowed to keep their boats and cargo, which news outlets estimated to be worth up to $1 million. The court later stated that the fleet had not broken any laws, despite the protected status of the sharks.

F2. Does due process prevail in civil and criminal matters? 1 / 4

Due process rights are often restricted or denied, owing in part to a dearth of resources and personnel. The training of new magistrates following the 2014 dismissals of foreign judges has been slow, resulting in significant case backlogs, although this is improving as the Legal and Judicial Training Centre has reopened with a class of trainee judges completing training in 2018. According to the US State Department, the police force operates without a clear legal definition of its mandates, and civilian complaints to police are often met with repeated requests that the complaint be submitted in writing.

Alternative methods of dispute resolution and customary law are widely used, though they lack enforcement mechanisms and have other significant shortcomings, including unequal treatment of women. Nine of thirteen municipalities have no fixed courts and rely on mobile services. The use of Portuguese for court administration poses an obstacle, and a shortage of Portuguese interpreters often forces the adjournment of trials.

F3. Is there protection from the illegitimate use of physical force and freedom from war and insurgencies? 3 / 4

Police officers and soldiers are regularly accused of excessive force and abuse of power, though the courts have had some success in prosecuting them. Public perception of the police has improved in recent years, as have general feelings of security.

F4. Do laws, policies, and practices guarantee equal treatment of various segments of the population? 2 / 4

While hate crimes based on sexual orientation are considered an aggravating circumstance in the penal code, other protections against discrimination for LGBT (lesbian, gay, bisexual, and transgender) people are lacking. Issues like sexual orientation and gender identity receive little public attention, though a small number of LGBT advocacy organizations have been active in recent years.

Equal rights for women are constitutionally guaranteed, but discrimination and gender inequality persist in practice and in customary law.

G. PERSONAL AUTONOMY AND INDIVIDUAL RIGHTS: 9 / 16

G1. Do individuals enjoy freedom of movement, including the ability to change their place of residence, employment, or education? 3 / 4

Citizens generally enjoy unrestricted travel, though travel by land to the enclave of Oecusse is hampered by visa requirements and Indonesian and Timorese checkpoints. Individuals enjoy free choice of residence and employment, but unemployment rates are high, and most of the population still relies on subsistence farming.

G2. Are individuals able to exercise the right to own property and establish private businesses without undue interference from state or nonstate actors? 2 / 4

Timorese have the right to establish businesses, and the legal framework for doing so is fairly straightforward. However, practical aspects of establishing and operating a business are complicated by inefficiencies that make it difficult to gain appropriate permits and enforce contracts, as well as a difficulties in obtaining credit.

Property rights are complicated by past conflicts and the unclear status of communal or customary land rights. There is no formal mechanism to address competing claims. A national land law designed to establish formal tenure and to help resolve disputes through arbitration was enacted in 2017, but still requires several implementing regulations.

G3. Do individuals enjoy personal social freedoms, including choice of marriage partner and size of family, protection from domestic violence, and control over appearance? 2 / 4

Gender-based and domestic violence remain widespread. Civil society groups have criticized the courts' use of prison sentences for only the most severe and injurious domestic violence cases. Many victims are reluctant to seek justice.

Timor-Leste has a teenage pregnancy rate of 24 percent. An estimated 19 percent of teenage girls are married by age 18.

G4. Do individuals enjoy equality of opportunity and freedom from economic exploitation? 2 / 4

Timor-Leste is both a source and destination country for human trafficking. Timorese from rural areas are vulnerable to human trafficking for sexual exploitation and domestic servitude, and children are sometimes placed in bonded labor. The government has increased its efforts to prosecute offenders, including by promulgating a 2017 Law on Preventing and Combating Human Trafficking. However, no trafficking offenders have been convicted in the past five years.

Togo

Population: 8,000,000
Capital: Lomé
Political Rights Rating: 5 ↓
Civil Liberties Rating: 4
Freedom Rating: 4.5
Freedom Status: Partly Free
Electoral Democracy: No

Overview: While regular multiparty elections haven taken place since 1992, Togo's politics have been controlled since 1963 by the late Gnassingbé Eyadéma and his son, current president Faure Gnassingbé. Advantages including security services dominated by the president's ethnic group and malapportioned election districts have helped Gnassingbé and his party retain power. Opposition calls for constitutional and electoral reforms have been harshly repressed.

KEY DEVELOPMENTS IN 2018:

- Demonstrations in favor of a return to a two-term limit for the presidency continued during the year despite the use of lethal force by the authorities.
- Presidents from neighboring countries mediated discussions on the matter between the government and the opposition; a significant point of contention was whether the restoration of term limits would be retroactive. With the impasse unresolved, a referendum on constitutional amendments set for July was postponed first to December and then to 2019.
- Legislative elections, also delayed from July, proceeded in December amid an opposition boycott. Seats lost by the ruling party and the boycotting opposition groups were picked up by minor government-allied parties and independent candidates.

POLITICAL RIGHTS: 15 / 40 (−3)

A. ELECTORAL PROCESS: 4 / 12 (−2)

A1. Was the current head of government or other chief national authority elected through free and fair elections? 2 / 4

The president, who serves as head of state, is elected to a five-year term. The president appoints the prime minister, who serves as head of government. Presidential term limits were eliminated in 2002.

Faure Gnassingbé—who was initially installed as president by the military after the death of his father, Gnassingbé Eyadéma, in 2005—secured a third term in the 2015 election, in which he took 59 percent of the vote. The election was considered largely free and fair by African Union observers, but the opposition criticized numerous aspects of the electoral process, including a new electronic vote-tabulation system and bias on the electoral commission. The vote was postponed by 10 days to accommodate voter list revisions called for by the Economic Community of West African States (ECOWAS). Opposition leaders declined to dispute the results at the Constitutional Court, saying the court was tilted in favor of Gnassingbé.

A2. Were the current national legislative representatives elected through free and fair elections? 1 / 4 (−1)

Members of the 91-seat unicameral National Assembly are elected every five years through proportional representation in multimember districts. The most recent elections, originally scheduled for July 2018, were held in December. The main opposition parties led a 14-party boycott, citing a number of unmet demands regarding constitutional and electoral reform.

Gnassingbé's Union for the Republic (UNIR) won 59 of the 91 seats, down from 62 in 2013. A party that led the opposition before aligning itself with the government in 2010, the Union of Forces for Change (UFC), won 7 seats, up from 3 in 2013. Independents took 18 seats, and smaller parties captured the remainder. Observers from the African Union and ECOWAS said the elections had been held "properly" in a "calm environment," though opposition protests had been violently suppressed in the weeks before the balloting. Voter turnout, at 59 percent, was down from previous elections, and ranged from 95 percent in the UNIR-dominated far north to approximately 20 percent in the opposition-leaning capital in the south.

The constitution states that local territories should administer themselves through elected councils, but local elections have not been held since 1986. Postponements continued during 2018, and at year's end the local voting was planned for 2019.

Score Change: The score declined from 2 to 1 because the December legislative elections proceeded without long-overdue reforms amid intimidation, an opposition boycott, and low turnout.

A3. Are the electoral laws and framework fair, and are they implemented impartially by the relevant election management bodies? 1 / 4 (−1)

Elections are organized and supervised by the Independent National Electoral Commission (CENI), whose membership by law should be balanced between the ruling party and the opposition. In 2015, the opposition criticized delays in appointing the CENI vice president—a post to be held by the opposition—until the eve of the presidential election. In 2018, the CENI was dominated by progovernment members—with the government-aligned UFC claiming opposition seats—throughout the voter registration and election planning period, contributing to the eventual boycott by opposition parties. The Constitutional Court, which is responsible for verifying election results, is also considered to be stacked with close allies of the president.

District malapportionment has repeatedly resulted in outsized legislative majorities for the UNIR. The government in 2018 refused opposition demands to add districts to the underrepresented capital.

In 2017, the president's constitutional reform commission, which included no opposition members, proposed a two-term presidential limit that was not retroactive, which meant that Gnassingbé would be able to run again. After the proposal was defeated in the legislature, the government announced plans to hold a referendum in 2018, but this was delayed through the end of the year.

Score Change: The score declined from 2 to 1 because the electoral commission was under the control of government allies, in violation of the law, through most of the 2018 electoral process, and long-standing legislative malapportionment went unaddressed.

B. POLITICAL PLURALISM AND PARTICIPATION: 6 / 16 (−1)

B1. Do the people have the right to organize in different political parties or other competitive political groupings of their choice, and is the system free of undue obstacles to the rise and fall of these competing parties or groupings? 2 / 4

There is a multiparty political system, and opposition parties are generally free to form and operate. Candidates can also run as independents. However, the dominance of the UNIR—which controls government at all levels and can confer benefits on party members that are not available to outsiders—undermines the visibility and competitiveness of other parties. Opposition members are sometimes arrested in connection with peaceful political activities.

In 2017 and 2018, antigovernment protests organized by opposition parties were suppressed with deadly force, and a number of opposition supporters were arrested and tortured for their participation in the demonstrations.

B2. Is there a realistic opportunity for the opposition to increase its support or gain power through elections? 1 / 4

Gnassingbé's family has controlled Togo's powerful presidency since the 1960s. He and the UNIR have retained power thanks in large part to the structure of the electoral system, including district malapportionment in legislative elections and the single-round plurality vote in presidential elections, and their de facto control over institutions such as the CENI and the Constitutional Court. Among other reforms, the opposition has called for a return to the two-round presidential vote, which prevailed before a constitutional amendment in 2002.

B3. Are the people's political choices free from domination by the military, foreign powers, religious hierarchies, economic oligarchies, or any other powerful group that is not democratically accountable? 1 / 4 (−1)

The government is dominated by members of Gnassingbé's Kabyé ethnic group, who also make up the vast majority of security personnel. In 2005, the military installed Gnassingbé as president, in violation of the constitution. Since 2017, increased activity by the opposition has been met with increased use of force by the security apparatus. Hundreds of activists have been arrested, and many tortured, including the secretary general of the opposition Pan-African National Party (PNP). The party's leader remained in hiding in 2018. In the weeks before the December elections, security forces repeatedly used live ammunition against opposition protesters, killing several people.

While security forces defend the regime through intimidation, the UNIR has been accused of relying on patronage and financial incentives, including the distribution of benefits to buy votes at election time.

Score Change: The score declined from 2 to 1 because the Gnassingbé family used its informal patronage networks and personalized control over state institutions to extend its rule despite mounting pressure for reform.

B4. Do various segments of the population (including ethnic, religious, gender, LGBT, and other relevant groups) have full political rights and electoral opportunities? 2 / 4

The Éwé, Togo's largest ethnic group, have historically been excluded from positions of influence; they are prominent within the opposition. Since 2010, the community has been politically split, as the Éwé-dominated UFC reached a power-sharing agreement with the government while the majority remained loyal to opposition forces. Women are underrepresented in government and face some societal pressure that discourages their active and independent political participation, despite rules requiring equal representation on candidate lists.

C. FUNCTIONING OF GOVERNMENT: 5 / 12

C1. Do the freely elected head of government and national legislative representatives determine the policies of the government? 2 / 4

The president holds most policymaking power, and the National Assembly, which is controlled by the ruling party, does not serve as an effective check on executive authority. A pattern of flawed elections has undermined the legitimacy of both the executive and the legislature.

C2. Are safeguards against official corruption strong and effective? 1 / 4

Corruption is a serious and long-standing problem. The government continues to adopt legislation that is ostensibly designed to reduce corruption, such as a law passed by the National Assembly in April 2018 on money laundering and the funding of terrorism, but these have not been followed by effective enforcement or convictions of high-ranking officials. The majority of members of the High Authority for the Prevention and Fight against Corruption and Related Offenses (HAPLUCIA) are presidential appointees, raising concerns about the body's independence.

C3. Does the government operate with openness and transparency? 2 / 4

A 2016 freedom of information law guarantees the right to access government information, though some information is exempted, and the government does not always respond to requests. Most public officials are not required to disclose their assets. There is a lack of transparency regarding state tenders. In April 2018, French billionaire Vincent Bolloré was indicted in France for allegedly helping Gnassingbé win the 2010 presidential election in exchange for contracts to operate container ports in Lomé.

CIVIL LIBERTIES: 28 / 60 (−1)
D. FREEDOM OF EXPRESSION AND BELIEF: 9 / 16
D1. Are there free and independent media? 2 / 4

Freedom of the press is guaranteed by law but inconsistently upheld in practice. Numerous independent media outlets offer a variety of viewpoints, but a history of impunity for those who commit crimes against journalists, as well as restrictive press laws, encourage self-censorship. There is no mechanism to appeal decisions made by the High Authority for Audiovisual and Communication (HAAC), which can suspend outlets for the violation of broadly worded regulations. In 2017, the HAAC imposed a one-month suspension on a newspaper for publishing an article on political violence with photographs of victims and a list of alleged perpetrators.

Police have engaged in violence and other acts of intimidation to discourage press coverage of opposition protests that began in 2017. Authorities have also temporarily disrupted mobile phone and internet service during protests, hampering efforts to report on them.

D2. Are individuals free to practice and express their religious faith or nonbelief in public and private? 3 / 4

Religious freedom is constitutionally protected and generally respected. Islam and Catholic and Protestant Christianity are recognized by the state as religions; other groups must register as religious associations to receive similar benefits. The registration process has been subject to long delays and a large backlog in recent years.

D3. Is there academic freedom, and is the educational system free from extensive political indoctrination? 2 / 4

University figures are able to engage in political discussions. However, government security forces have repeatedly cracked down on student protests. In 2017, authorities arrested numerous students at the University of Lomé in connection with demonstrations at which participants demanded better facilities. Some of the students reported being beaten by security forces as they moved to quell the protests.

D4. Are individuals free to express their personal views on political or other sensitive topics without fear of surveillance or retribution? 2 / 4

Citizens are able to speak openly in private discussion, but they may be arrested on incitement or other charges for speaking critically of the government to journalists or human rights organizations.

In December 2018, the National Assembly adopted a new cybersecurity law that criminalizes publication of false information and breaches of public morality, among other problematic provisions that could affect online freedom of expression. The law also granted police greater authority to conduct electronic surveillance.

E. ASSOCIATIONAL AND ORGANIZATIONAL RIGHTS: 6 / 12

E1. Is there freedom of assembly? 1 / 4

While the constitution provides for freedom of assembly, a number of laws allow for its restriction, and police have periodically used deadly violence to disperse assemblies in practice. A 2011 legal reform retained problematic rules on prior notification for demonstrations and limits on their timing. A 2015 revision of the criminal code penalized participation in and organization of protests that had not gone through the necessary administrative procedures.

Protests that began in 2017 attracted hundreds of thousands of participants and continued during 2018, with protesters demanding the restoration of the presidential term limits and the two-round presidential election system. Authorities moved to suppress the demonstrations through temporary bans and other administrative restrictions, including a ban on all street protests during the December 2018 electoral period. Police used disproportionate force on a number of occasions, resulting in multiple deaths, arrests, and cases of torture in 2017 and 2018.

E2. Is there freedom for nongovernmental organizations, particularly those that are engaged in human rights- and governance-related work? 2 / 4

Nongovernmental organizations are subject to registration rules that have sometimes been enforced arbitrarily to suppress activism on sensitive topics such as torture and the rights of LGBT (lesbian, gay, bisexual, and transgender) people. Several civil society activists have been arrested and detained for their roles in the protest movement that began in 2017. In August 2018, youth activist Folly Satchivi, whose organization supported reinstating presidential term limits, was arrested while preparing to hold a press conference; he remained in pretrial detention at year's end. Another activist, Assiba Johnson, was arrested in April and sentenced in December to 18 months in prison (with 6 months suspended) over the publication of a report on the suppression of the protests.

E3. Is there freedom for trade unions and similar professional or labor organizations? 3 / 4

The government generally protects workers' rights to form and join labor unions outside the export-processing zone, where unions have fewer legal protections.

F. RULE OF LAW: 6 / 16 (−1)

F1. Is there an independent judiciary? 2 / 4

The constitution provides for an independent judiciary, but in practice it is heavily influenced by the presidency. The Constitutional Court in particular, appointed by the president and the UNIR-controlled National Assembly, is believed to be partial to the ruling party, which contributed to the opposition's decisions not to appeal the 2015 presidential election results or participate in the 2018 legislative elections in the absence of reforms. Judges on other courts are appointed by the executive based on the recommendations of a judicial council, which in turn is dominated by senior judges.

F2. Does due process prevail in civil and criminal matters? 1 / 4 (−1)

Executive influence and judicial corruption limit constitutional rights to a fair trial. Dozens of people arrested for participating in the antigovernment protest movement since 2017 have been charged, tried, and convicted in hasty proceedings, often without access to counsel. In December 2018, a group of 34 such detainees were subjected to an unannounced trial at which many lacked legal representation, and more than half received custodial sentences of up to five years.

Corruption and inefficiency are widespread among the police, and there are also reports of arbitrary arrest. The new cybersecurity law passed in December contains vague terrorism and treason provisions with hefty prison sentences, and grants additional powers to the police without adequate judicial control.

Score Change: The score declined from 2 to 1 due to a pattern in which antigovernment protesters and activists have been detained and tried without basic due process guarantees, including access to defense counsel.

F3. Is there protection from the illegitimate use of physical force and freedom from war and insurgencies? 2 / 4

Prisons suffer from overcrowding and inadequate food and medical care, sometimes resulting in deaths among inmates from preventable or curable diseases. The government periodically releases prisoners to address overcrowding, but the process by which individuals are chosen for release is not transparent.

The 2015 penal code criminalizes torture. However, its definition of torture does not conform to that in the UN Convention against Torture, and instances of torture by security forces continue to be reported, including against participants in recent antigovernment demonstrations.

F4. Do laws, policies, and practices guarantee equal treatment of various segments of the population? 1 / 4

Although women and men are ostensibly equal under the law, women continue to experience discrimination, and their opportunities for employment and education are limited. Official and societal discrimination has persisted against people with disabilities, certain regional and ethnic groups, and LGBT people, for whom antidiscrimination laws do not apply. Same-sex sexual activity is a criminal offense, and while the law is rarely enforced, LGBT people face police harassment.

G. PERSONAL AUTONOMY AND INDIVIDUAL RIGHTS: 7 / 16

G1. Do individuals enjoy freedom of movement, including the ability to change their place of residence, employment, or education? 2 / 4

The law provides for freedom of internal movement and foreign travel, but these rights are sometimes restricted by the authorities in practice. Domestic travel can involve arbitrary traffic stops at which police collect bribes.

G2. Are individuals able to exercise the right to own property and establish private businesses without undue interference from state or nonstate actors? 2 / 4

The country has made improvements in the ease of starting a business, but problems remain with regard to property rights. It is difficult to register property, and there is a widespread perception that judges can be bribed in cases involving land disputes. Women and men do not have equal inheritance rights under traditional or customary law, which is observed mainly in rural areas.

G3. Do individuals enjoy personal social freedoms, including choice of marriage partner and size of family, protection from domestic violence, and control over appearance? 1 / 4

Customary law puts women at a disadvantage regarding matters such as widowhood, divorce, and child custody. Polygamy is widely practiced and recognized under formal law. Child marriage remains a problem in some regions. Rape is illegal but rarely reported and, if reported, often ignored by authorities. Domestic violence, which is widespread, is not specifically addressed by the law. UN data indicate that about 5 percent of women and girls aged 15 to 49 have undergone genital mutilation or cutting, which is illegal and less prevalent among younger girls.

G4. Do individuals enjoy equality of opportunity and freedom from economic exploitation? 2 / 4

Protections against exploitative labor conditions, including rules on working hours, are poorly enforced, and much of the workforce is informally employed. Child labor is common in the agricultural sector and in certain urban trades; some children are subjected to forced labor. According to the US State Department, the government has made efforts to address human trafficking for forced labor and sexual exploitation, including by identifying more trafficking victims, but its prosecutions of perpetrators and public-awareness programs have faltered.

Tonga

Population: 100,000
Capital: Nuku'alofa
Political Rights Rating: 2
Civil Liberties Rating: 2
Freedom Rating: 2.0
Freedom Status: Free
Electoral Democracy: Yes

Overview: Tonga's constitutional monarchy has featured a prime minister backed by a mostly elected parliament since 2010. However, the king retains important powers, including the authority to veto legislation, dissolve the parliament, and appoint judicial officials. While civil liberties are generally protected, ongoing problems include political pressure on the state broadcaster and land laws that discriminate against women.

KEY DEVELOPMENTS IN 2018:

- 'Akilisi Pōhiva was formally reappointed as prime minister in January, after his parliamentary supporters won snap elections in November 2017 and voted him back into office that December. The snap elections followed a controversial dissolution of the parliament by the king.
- Former prime minister Lord Tu'ivakanō was charged in March with perjury, bribery, and money laundering in a scandal over the sale of passports.

POLITICAL RIGHTS: 30 / 40

A. ELECTORAL PROCESS: 9 / 12

A1. Was the current head of government or other chief national authority elected through free and fair elections? 3 / 4

The king is no longer the chief executive authority, but he retains significant powers, including the ability to veto legislation and dissolve the parliament. The current monarch, King Tupou VI, came to the throne in 2012 and is known to hold more conservative views than his late brother and predecessor, George Tupou V.

The prime minister, who chooses the cabinet, is formally appointed by the king on the recommendation of the parliament. Prime Minister Pōhiva first took office in 2014 after that year's elections. The king dissolved the parliament in 2017 after consulting with the speaker at the time, Lord Tu'ivakanō, who accused the prime minister of seeking to further reduce the monarch's constitutional authority. However, after snap elections later that year resulted in a victory for Pōhiva's supporters, the lawmakers returned him to the premiership, with the king formalizing the appointment in January 2018. There was continuing pressure from opponents during the year to impeach the prime minister on the grounds of poor performance and lack of transparency.

A2. Were the current national legislative representatives elected through free and fair elections? 3 / 4

The unicameral Fale Alea, or Legislative Assembly, consists of 17 members who are directly elected by commoners, nine noble members elected by their peers, and up to four additional members whom the prime minister may appoint to the cabinet from outside the parliament and who hold their seats ex officio. The speaker is appointed from among the noble members on the recommendation of the assembly.

In the 2017 snap elections, Pōhiva and his supporters in the loosely affiliated Democratic Party of the Friendly Islands won 14 of the 17 popularly elected seats, a sizeable gain from their previous share.

A3. Are the electoral laws and framework fair, and are they implemented impartially by the relevant election management bodies? 3 / 4

The Electoral Commission administers elections competently and fairly, though the framework for parliamentary elections falls short of universal suffrage due to the reservation of nine seats for the nobility.

B. POLITICAL PLURALISM AND PARTICIPATION: 14 / 16

B1. Do the people have the right to organize in different political parties or other competitive political groupings of their choice, and is the system free of undue obstacles to the rise and fall of these competing parties or groupings? 4 / 4

A formal party system has yet to develop, and all candidates technically run as independents in their single-member constituencies. Nevertheless, there are no major restrictions on political competition, and in practice politicians have begun to form loose partisan affiliations such as Pōhiva's Democratic Party of the Friendly Islands.

B2. Is there a realistic opportunity for the opposition to increase its support or gain power through elections? 4 / 4

Rival coalitions led by Pōhiva's popularly elected allies and more conservative noble politicians have alternated in government in recent years. Before Pōhiva took office in 2014, Lord Tu'ivakanō was the prime minister.

B3. Are the people's political choices free from domination by the military, foreign powers, religious hierarchies, economic oligarchies, or any other powerful group that is not democratically accountable? 3 / 4

The monarchy, the nobility, and the country's churches exert considerable political influence, but this has not prevented majority support for prodemocracy candidates in recent elections.

B4. Do various segments of the population (including ethnic, religious, gender, LGBT, and other relevant groups) have full political rights and electoral opportunities? 3 / 4

Women have the same formal political rights as men, and 15 women ran for seats in the 2017 parliamentary elections, but only two won office—an increase from zero in the previous legislature. Cultural biases tend to discourage women's political participation, and women cannot inherit noble titles, meaning the noble seats in the parliament are effectively reserved for men. Participation by ethnic minorities is subject to similar obstacles, though the population is mostly homogeneous, and many members of the small Chinese minority have been able to obtain citizenship and its associated political rights.

C. FUNCTIONING OF GOVERNMENT: 7 / 12

C1. Do the freely elected head of government and national legislative representatives determine the policies of the government? 3 / 4

The elected prime minister and his cabinet largely control the formulation and implementation of government policy, but the king continues to rely on a privy council—whose members he appoints himself—for advice regarding the use of his constitutional powers.

C2. Are safeguards against official corruption strong and effective? 2 / 4

Corruption and abuse of office are serious problems. While public officials and leaders of state-owned companies are sometimes held to account for bribery and other malfeasance, anticorruption mechanisms are generally weak and lacking in resources. An ombudsman was appointed in late 2016, but the post of anticorruption commissioner has been vacant since its creation in 2007. In March 2018, Lord Tuʻivakanō was charged with money laundering, perjury, and bribery in a scandal over the sale of passports. His case remained pending at year's end.

C3. Does the government operate with openness and transparency? 2 / 4

Tonga does not have a law to guarantee public access to government information, which can be difficult to obtain in practice, and officials are not legally obliged to disclose their assets and income. The government has at times resisted public scrutiny of pending policies or auditor general's reports. Nevertheless, the parliament generally operates openly, and the media and civil society are typically able to monitor its proceedings and comment on legislation.

CIVIL LIBERTIES: 49 / 60 (+4)

D. FREEDOM OF EXPRESSION AND BELIEF: 14 / 16 (+2)

D1. Are there free and independent media? 2 / 4

The constitution guarantees freedom of the press, and a variety of news outlets operate independently, including online. However, politicians have a history of exerting pressure on the media in response to critical coverage. Pōhiva has repeatedly complained about reporting by the state-run Tonga Broadcasting Commission (TBC), accusing the radio and television outlet of becoming "an enemy of government" in 2017. A series of leadership changes at TBC followed later that year, raising widespread concerns among press freedom advocates.

D2. Are individuals free to practice and express their religious faith or nonbelief in public and private? 4 / 4

Constitutional protections for religious freedom are generally upheld in practice. Religious groups are not required to register, but those that do receive various benefits. There are some restrictions on commercial activity on Sundays in keeping with a constitutional recognition of the Christian sabbath. The TBC's policy guidelines bar broadcasts of preaching outside the "mainstream Christian tradition," though this has reportedly not been strictly enforced.

D3. Is there academic freedom, and is the educational system free from extensive political indoctrination? 4 / 4 (+1)

Academic freedom is generally unrestricted. While there have been reports of self-censorship to avoid friction with the government in the past, no incidents of political interference have been reported in recent years. Tonga hosts one of the regional campuses of the University of the South Pacific as well as the late Tongan scholar Futa Helu's 'Atenisi Institute, which offers tertiary courses. In October 2018, Christ's University, which is owned by the Tokaikolo Church and opened in 2015, became Tonga's first locally owned university to be registered and accredited.

Score Change: The score improved from 3 to 4 because there have been no recent reports of improper state interference with education.

D4. Are individuals free to express their personal views on political or other sensitive topics without fear of surveillance or retribution? 4 / 4 (+1)

There are no major constraints on Tongans' ability to discuss politics and other topics in person or on social media. The government is not known to monitor personal communications.

Score Change: The score improved from 3 to 4 because there have been no reports of significant constraints on the expression of personal views in recent years.

E. ASSOCIATIONAL AND ORGANIZATIONAL RIGHTS: 10 / 12 (+1)

E1. Is there freedom of assembly? 4 / 4 (+1)

The constitution protects freedom of assembly, and demonstrations, though rare, generally remain peaceful. Political protests in 2006 degenerated into violent riots, prompting the government to declare a state of emergency that lasted until early 2011. However, there have been no similar incidents in the years since.

Score Change: The score improved from 3 to 4 due to the lack of any protest-related violence or state restrictions on assembly over the past several years.

E2. Is there freedom for nongovernmental organizations, particularly those that are engaged in human rights– and governance-related work? 3 / 4

Nongovernmental organizations have not reported harassment or other restrictions by the authorities. A number of different laws govern the registration processes for civil society groups, but they are not considered onerous.

E3. Is there freedom for trade unions and similar professional or labor organizations? 3 / 4

Workers have the legal right to organize in trade unions, but implementing regulations have never been issued, meaning the country's various de facto unions generally operate as associations. Tonga joined the International Labour Organization in 2016, though it has yet to ratify the organization's conventions on labor standards.

F. RULE OF LAW: 12 / 16

F1. Is there an independent judiciary? 3 / 4

The king retains authority over judicial appointments and dismissals. The Judicial Appointments and Discipline Panel, a committee of the privy council, provides advice on appointments, including for the lord chancellor, who has responsibility for administering the courts. The king in privy council has final jurisdiction over cases in the land court relating to hereditary estates and titles.

The judiciary is regarded as largely independent, but the prime minister has accused the royally appointed attorney general of interfering with judicial rulings, and has pressed for reforms that would bring the attorney general into the orbit of the elected government. Broader judicial reforms that would have increased the cabinet's influence over judicial appointments were adopted by the parliament in 2014, but the king never gave his assent.

F2. Does due process prevail in civil and criminal matters? 3 / 4

Due process provisions and safeguards against arbitrary arrest and detention are typically respected by the authorities. However, there is no mechanism to guarantee access to counsel for indigent defendants.

The police commissioner, Stephen Caldwell, is a New Zealander. The Police Act of 2010 gives control over the appointment of the police commissioner to the king's privy council, which has raised tensions with elected officials. Successive ministers of police, as well as Prime Minister Pōhiva, have sought to obtain control over the appointment.

F3. Is there protection from the illegitimate use of physical force and freedom from war and insurgencies? 3 / 4

Prison conditions are generally adequate, police brutality is rare, and crime rates remain relatively low. A number of police officers accused of misconduct have been investigated, dismissed, or convicted of crimes in recent years. However, rising public concern has focused on problems including the country's role as a transit point for drug trafficking, drug-related petty crime, and organized crime affecting the Chinese community.

F4. Do laws, policies, and practices guarantee equal treatment of various segments of the population? 3 / 4

The constitution includes a general provision for equality before the law, and this is upheld in many respects. However, women still face some forms of discrimination, including in land and inheritance laws and with regard to employment in practice. Same-sex sexual activity is criminalized, but the ban is not actively enforced, and in recent years local LGBT (lesbian, gay, bisexual, and transgender) groups have worked to raise awareness of their cause and lobbied the government to adopt legal reforms.

Continued bias and instances of crime against members of the Chinese minority have been reported, though nothing approaching the scale of the 2006 riots—which targeted Chinese-owned businesses—has occurred since the state of emergency was lifted in 2011.

G. PERSONAL AUTONOMY AND INDIVIDUAL RIGHTS: 13 / 16 (+1)

G1. Do individuals enjoy freedom of movement, including the ability to change their place of residence, employment, or education? 4 / 4

There are no significant constraints on freedom of movement or the ability to change one's place of residence or employment.

G2. Are individuals able to exercise the right to own property and establish private businesses without undue interference from state or nonstate actors? 3 / 4

The legal framework generally supports private business activity. However, individuals cannot own or sell land outright, as all land is technically the property of the king. Land rights, once granted by nobles or directly by the crown through an allotment system, can only be leased or inherited, and while women can obtain leases, they are not eligible to receive or inherit land allotments.

G3. Do individuals enjoy personal social freedoms, including choice of marriage partner and size of family, protection from domestic violence, and control over appearance? 3 / 4

Personal social freedoms are typically respected. However, domestic violence remains a problem despite state and civil society efforts to prevent it, and girls as young as 15—the legal minimum age for marriage with parental permission—are sometimes compelled by their parents to marry.

G4. Do individuals enjoy equality of opportunity and freedom from economic exploitation? 3 / 4 (+1)

The population generally has access to economic opportunities and protection from abusive working conditions, though enforcement of labor laws is affected by resource limitations, and some employers have violated workers' rights. While there is no law specifically regulating child labor, any such work typically entails informal participation in family agriculture and fishing.

Score Change: The score improved from 2 to 3 because although some employers have imposed exploitative conditions on their workers, acute forms abuse are not believed to be widespread.

Trinidad and Tobago

Population: 1,400,000
Capital: Port of Spain
Political Rights Rating: 2
Civil Liberties Rating: 2
Freedom Rating: 2.0
Freedom Status: Free
Electoral Democracy: Yes

Overview: The Republic of Trinidad and Tobago is a parliamentary democracy with vibrant media and civil society sectors. However, organized crime contributes to high levels of violence, and corruption among public officials remains a challenge. Other security concerns center on local adherents of Islamist militant groups. There is discrimination against the LGBT (lesbian, gay, bisexual, and transgender) community, though a 2018 court ruling effectively decriminalized same-sex sexual conduct.

KEY DEVELOPMENTS IN 2018:
- Parliament elected the country's first woman president, Paula-Mae Weekes, in January.
- In February, security forces arrested several people suspected of planning a terrorist attack on that month's Carnival festivities.
- The High Court ruled in April that sections of the Sexual Offences Act, which prohibited "buggery" and "serious indecency," were unconstitutional. In September the court changed the law to decriminalize same-sex sexual conduct between

consenting adults. The government said it would appeal the judgment to the Privy Council in London.

POLITICAL RIGHTS: 33 / 40

A. ELECTORAL PROCESS: 11 / 12

A1. Was the current head of government or other chief national authority elected through free and fair elections? 4 / 4

The president, the largely ceremonial head of state, is elected to a five-year term by a majority of the combined houses of Parliament. Paula-Mae Weekes, an independent former judge, was elected unopposed in January 2018 and took office in March.

The prime minister, who serves as head of government and is typically the leader of the majority party in Parliament, is appointed by the president. Keith Rowley became prime minister in 2015, after parliamentary elections resulted in a victory for his party, the center-right People's National Movement (PNM).

A2. Were the current national legislative representatives elected through free and fair elections? 4 / 4

Parliament consists of the directly elected, 41-member House of Representatives and the 31-member Senate, with members of both houses serving five-year terms. Of the 31 senators, 16 are appointed on the advice of the prime minister, 6 are appointed on the advice of the opposition leader, and 9 are appointed at the president's discretion based on merit.

In the 2015 parliamentary elections, the center-left People's Partnership (PP) coalition led by then prime minister Kamla Persad-Bissessar took 18 lower house seats and was defeated by Keith Rowley's PNM, which won 23. Election observers expressed confidence in the overall conduct of the balloting.

The semiautonomous island of Tobago has its own House of Assembly, with 12 members elected directly, 3 appointed on the advice of the chief secretary (the island's head of government), and 1 appointed on the advice of the minority leader. Elections took place in 2017, with the PNM taking 10 of the 12 elected seats and the Progressive Democratic Patriots taking the remainder.

A3. Are the electoral laws and framework fair, and are they implemented impartially by the relevant election management bodies? 3 / 4

Electoral laws are largely fair. The Elections and Boundaries Commission (EBC) is in charge of organizing elections, and it is generally trusted by the public to fulfill its mandate impartially.

After the 2015 elections, observation missions from the Caribbean Community (CARICOM) and the Commonwealth recommended that officials take steps to strengthen the transparency and accountability of campaign funding processes, and ensure that adequate training is provided for polling officials.

B. POLITICAL PLURALISM AND PARTICIPATION: 13 / 16

B1. Do the people have the right to organize in different political parties or other competitive political groupings of their choice, and is the system free of undue obstacles to the rise and fall of these competing parties or groupings? 3 / 4

Trinidad and Tobago has a number of political parties. While the PNM dominated the political landscape in the decades following independence, it has weakened somewhat in the last two decades, allowing greater competition. The national political arena is now largely divided between the PNM and the PP, a coalition that includes the United National Congress

(UNC) and the Congress of the People. Factors including the country's first-past-the-post voting system have made it difficult for less established parties to gain seats in Parliament.

B2. Is there a realistic opportunity for the opposition to increase its support or gain power through elections? 4 / 4

The country has built a record of peaceful transfers of power between rival parties, with multiple changes in government through elections since the 1980s.

B3. Are the people's political choices free from domination by the military, foreign powers, religious hierarchies, economic oligarchies, or any other powerful group that is not democratically accountable? 3 / 4

People's political choices are generally free from external pressure. However, observers have raised concerns about lack of transparency in campaign financing, which may enable improper influence and disadvantage opposition parties.

B4. Do various segments of the population (including ethnic, religious, gender, LGBT, and other relevant groups) have full political rights and electoral opportunities? 3 / 4

All ethnic groups enjoy full political rights, and political parties are technically multiethnic, though the PNM is favored by Afro-Trinidadians and the UNC is affiliated with Indo-Trinidadians.

Women's political participation has increased somewhat in recent years, but they remain generally underrepresented. In 2018, Weekes became the first woman to be elected president. Discrimination against LGBT people is widespread, affecting their ability to fully engage in political and electoral processes.

C. FUNCTIONING OF GOVERNMENT: 9 / 12

C1. Do the freely elected head of government and national legislative representatives determine the policies of the government? 4 / 4

The country's freely elected executive and legislative officeholders generally determine and implement government policies without undue interference.

C2. Are safeguards against official corruption strong and effective? 2 / 4

Corruption remains a pervasive problem, especially within the police force and among immigration officers. The government has sought to manage corruption through several pieces of legislation, but the laws are poorly enforced. During 2018, Prime Minister Rowley was accused of benefiting financially from the state-owned Petrotrin oil refinery, while Chief Justice Ivor Archie faced allegations that he had placed undue pressure on the Housing Development Corporation over the granting of a number of housing units. Both cases were unresolved at year's end.

C3. Does the government operate with openness and transparency? 3 / 4

Public officials are required to disclose their assets, income, and liabilities, but penalties against those who fail to comply are limited. The Integrity Commission, which is tasked with overseeing these financial disclosures, has been criticized for its lack of effectiveness.

The public has the right to access government documents by law, although numerous public institutions are exempt. Furthermore, there is no enforcement of a provision that requires the government to respond to information requests within 30 days. A 2015 law regulating public procurements has not been fully implemented.

CIVIL LIBERTIES: 49 / 60 (+1)

D. FREEDOM OF EXPRESSION AND BELIEF: 16 / 16 (+1)

D1. Are there free and independent media? 4 / 4

Freedom of the press is constitutionally guaranteed and generally upheld in practice. Media outlets are privately owned and vigorously pluralistic. However, those regarded as most favorable to the government receive the bulk of state advertising. Under the 2013 Defamation and Libel Act, "malicious defamatory libel known to be false" is punishable by up to two years in prison as well as a fine, but prosecutions are uncommon.

D2. Are individuals free to practice and express their religious faith or nonbelief in public and private? 4 / 4 (+1)

The constitution guarantees freedom of religion, and the government generally honors this provision. The requirements for registration of a religious organization, which confers tax benefits and other privileges, are not considered onerous. Some restrictions are placed on foreign missionaries; up to 35 per registered religious group are allowed in the country at one time, and they cannot stay longer than three consecutive years.

Score Change: The score improved from 3 to 4 because religious freedom has generally been upheld in recent years, with major Christian, Hindu, and Muslim groups emphasizing interfaith tolerance and cooperation.

D3. Is there academic freedom, and is the educational system free from extensive political indoctrination? 4 / 4

Academic freedom is generally upheld.

D4. Are individuals free to express their personal views on political or other sensitive topics without fear of surveillance or retribution? 4 / 4

Individuals are free to express their opinions in private conversations, and the government is not known to monitor online communications.

E. ASSOCIATIONAL AND ORGANIZATIONAL RIGHTS: 11 / 12

E1. Is there freedom of assembly? 4 / 4

The constitution provides for freedom of assembly, and the government generally respects this right.

E2. Is there freedom for nongovernmental organizations, particularly those that are engaged in human rights–and governance-related work? 4 / 4

Civil society is robust, with a range of domestic and international interest groups operating freely.

E3. Is there freedom for trade unions and similar professional or labor organizations? 3 / 4

Labor unions are well organized and politically active, though union membership has declined in recent years. Strikes are legal and occur frequently. The law contains a provision allowing the labor minister to petition the courts to end any strike deemed detrimental to national interests. Walkouts by workers considered essential, including hospital staff, firefighters, and telecommunication workers, are punishable by up to three years in prison and fines. The government threatened to impose criminal penalties in September 2018 prior to a series of strikes in protest against the planned closure of the Petrotrin refinery.

F. RULE OF LAW: 9 / 16

F1. Is there an independent judiciary? 3 / 4

The judicial branch is generally independent, but it is subject to some political pressure and corruption. Beginning in 2017, Chief Justice Ivor Archie was accused of placing undue pressure on the Housing Development Corporation regarding the granting of housing units. The *Trinidad Express* had also alleged that criminal elements had compromising information on him. In response, the Law Association of Trinidad and Tobago (LATT) created a special committee to investigate his conduct. Archie then sued LATT to prevent the committee from being established, but he lost on final appeal to the London-based Privy Council in August 2018. The underlying matter remained unresolved at year's end.

F2. Does due process prevail in civil and criminal matters? 2 / 4

Due process rights are provided for in the constitution, but they are not always upheld. Rising crime rates and institutional weakness have produced a severe backlog in the court system. Over 60 percent of the prison population is made up of pretrial detainees or remand prisoners. Defendants must wait many years for their cases to come to trial. Corruption in the police force, which is often linked to the illegal drugs trade, is endemic, and inefficiencies have resulted in the dismissal of some criminal cases. Intimidation of witnesses and jurors has been reported by judicial officials.

F3. Is there protection from the illegitimate use of physical force and freedom from war and insurgencies? 2 / 4

The government has struggled in recent years to address criminal violence, which is mostly linked to organized crime and drug trafficking. There were a reported 517 murders in 2018, exceeding the figure for 2017 and approaching a record high set in 2008. The United Nations ranks Trinidad and Tobago just below the 10 countries with the world's highest murder rates per capita. In 2017, the Organized Crime Intelligence Unit was established "to pursue, target, dismantle, disrupt and prosecute" organized criminal groups and networks. But the police have been criticized for excessive use of force, and many abuses by the authorities go unpunished.

Dozens of Trinidadian citizens have reportedly sought to join the Islamic State (IS) militant group in recent years. Trinidadian security forces, supported by US military personnel, raided multiple locations in February 2018 and arrested several individuals suspected of planning a terrorist attack on that month's Carnival celebration. The government also shared concerns that energy companies in the country might be targeted by local Islamist militants.

F4. Do laws, policies, and practices guarantee equal treatment of various segments of the population? 2 / 4

Despite legal protections against discrimination on various grounds, racial disparities persist, with Indo-Trinidadians accounting for a disproportionate share of the country's economic elite. Women continue to face discrimination in employment and compensation.

Human rights groups have criticized the government's unwillingness to address discrimination and violence against the LGBT community. However, in April 2018, the High Court ruled that sections of the Sexual Offences Act, which prohibited "buggery" and "serious indecency," were unconstitutional. In September the court changed the law to decriminalize same-sex sexual conduct between consenting adults. The government said it would appeal the judgment to the London-based Privy Council. Separately, Trinidad celebrated its first LGBT Pride festival in July.

Immigration law does not adequately protect refugees, and cases of asylum seekers being forcibly returned to their country of origin continue to be reported.

G. PERSONAL AUTONOMY AND INDIVIDUAL RIGHTS: 13 / 16

G1. Do individuals enjoy freedom of movement, including the ability to change their place of residence, employment, or education? 4 / 4

There are no significant constraints on freedom of movement or people's ability to change their place of residence, employment, or education.

G2. Are individuals able to exercise the right to own property and establish private businesses without undue interference from state or non-state actors? 3 / 4

While the government actively supports both domestic and foreign investment in the country, factors including corruption and weak state institutions can make it more difficult to start and operate businesses. There are particular problems associated with registering property and enforcing contracts.

G3. Do individuals enjoy personal social freedoms, including choice of marriage partner and size of family, protection from domestic violence, and control over appearance? 3 / 4

Most individual rights with respect to personal status issues like marriage and divorce are protected by law. The 2017 Marriage Act raised the legal marriage age to 18, officially making child marriage illegal.

Rape, including spousal rape, is illegal, and domestic violence is addressed by a specific law. However, enforcement of these provisions remains inadequate, with many perpetrators reportedly avoiding punishment.

Abortion is illegal in most cases, and there is reportedly little public awareness of legal exemptions for abortions to save a woman's life or preserve her physical or mental health. A woman can be imprisoned for up to four years for obtaining an illegal abortion.

G4. Do individuals enjoy equality of opportunity and freedom from economic exploitation? 3 / 4

The law provides basic protections against exploitative working conditions, though these do not apply or are poorly enforced for informal and household workers in particular. While the government has stepped up efforts to combat trafficking in persons, convictions have been lacking, and funding for victim services has been cut. Venezuelan women are especially vulnerable to sex trafficking in the country.

Tunisia

Population: 11,600,000
Capital: Tunis
Political Rights Rating: 2
Civil Liberties Rating: 3
Freedom Rating: 2.5
Freedom Status: Free
Electoral Democracy: Yes

Overview: After ousting a longtime autocrat from power in 2011, Tunisia began a democratic transition. Citizens enjoy unprecedented political rights and civil liberties, but the country's current political status is mixed. The influence of endemic corruption, economic challenges, security threats, and continued unresolved issues related to gender equality and transitional justice remain obstacles to full democratic consolidation.

KEY DEVELOPMENTS IN 2018:

- Large-scale protests broke out across the country in January over austerity measures passed by the government. More than 900 demonstrators were arrested, and the police reportedly beat many of those detained and denied some detainees access to a lawyer.
- In March, the parliament voted against extending the mandate of the Truth and Dignity Commission past the end of the year, which drew criticism from rights activists for weakening transitional justice. The commission was established in 2014 to investigate political, economic, and social crimes committed since 1956.
- Long-delayed municipal elections, the first since the 2011 uprising, were held in May. Independent candidates won 32 percent of seats, while the Ennahda Party won 29 percent, and the Nidaa Tounes party, which leads the governing coalition, won only 21 percent.
- In July, the government passed a law meant to strengthen the anticorruption legal framework, which requires the president, government ministers, and high-level public officials, among others, to publicly declare their assets.

POLITICAL RIGHTS: 31 / 40 (+1)

A. ELECTORAL PROCESS: 11 / 12 (+1)

A1. Was the current head of government or other chief national authority elected through free and fair elections? 4 / 4

The 2014 constitution lays out a semipresidential system in which a popularly elected president serves as head of state and exercises circumscribed powers, while the majority party in the parliament selects a prime minister, who serves as head of government, following parliamentary elections. The president is directly elected for up to two five-year terms. International and local observers concluded that the 2014 presidential election was generally competitive and credible, despite widespread claims of vote buying on behalf of the major candidates. President Beji Caid Essebsi of the secular Nidaa Tounes party defeated incumbent president Moncef Marzouki of the Islamist Ennahda Party in the second round of voting, 56 percent to 44 percent. In 2016, President Essebsi appointed Prime Minister Youssef Chahed after former prime minister Habib Essid was ousted in a vote of no confidence.

A2. Were the current national legislative representatives elected through free and fair elections? 4 / 4

Tunisia's 2014 constitution established a unicameral legislative body, the Assembly of the Representatives of the People (ARP), which consists of 217 representatives serving five-year terms, with members elected on party lists in 33 multimember constituencies. International and national observers declared the 2014 legislative elections generally competitive and credible, despite reports of vote buying and campaign finance violations. The Nidaa Tounes party won a plurality of votes with 86 seats, enabling the party to name a prime minister and lead a coalition government. The Ennahda Party, which had previously dominated the parliament, followed with 69 seats.

A3. Are the electoral laws and framework fair, and are they implemented impartially by the relevant election management bodies? 3 / 4 (+1)

The Independent High Authority for Elections (ISIE), a neutral nine-member commission, is tasked with supervising parliamentary and presidential elections. Since its inception in 2011, the ISIE's political independence and conduct of elections had been well regarded by Tunisian and international observers. However, the 2017 resignation of former ISIE president Chafik Sarsar raised doubts about the body's impartiality and independence. Sarsar claimed that he had faced political pressure and publicly questioned the ISIE's independence.

In May 2018, long-delayed municipal elections were held in 350 municipalities for 7,212 available council seats, and were widely considered credible. Prior to the elections, unelected local councils had been in place since the 2011 revolution.

Score Change: The score improved from 2 to 3 because municipal elections were held across the country after a long delay.

B. POLITICAL PLURALISM AND PARTICIPATION: 14 / 16

B1. Do the people have the right to organize in different political parties or other competitive political groupings of their choice, and is the system free of undue obstacles to the rise and fall of these competing parties or groupings? 4 / 4

Tunisia's numerous political parties represent a wide range of ideologies and political philosophies, and are generally free to form and operate. The 2018 municipal elections saw robust competition between political parties and independent candidates within electoral processes deemed generally free and credible by observers.

Campaign finance laws intended to prevent money from determining political outcomes are complex and often unclear, on occasion forcing parties to bend, if not break, the rules in order to campaign effectively; this contributes to tensions between parties. The US-based International Republican Institute (IRI), in an assessment of the 2014 elections, found that ambiguous campaign financing laws helped facilitate vote buying "with little chance of penalty."

B2. Is there a realistic opportunity for the opposition to increase its support or gain power through elections? 4 / 4

Opposition parties participate competitively in political processes. Nidaa Tounes won a plurality in the parliament in the 2014 legislative elections, displacing Ennahda, which had held the largest share of seats previously. During the 2018 municipal elections, independent candidates outperformed the major parties, winning 32 percent of seats, while Ennahda won nearly 29 percent, followed by Nidaa Tounes with 21 percent.

B3. Are the people's political choices free from domination by the military, foreign powers, religious hierarchies, economic oligarchies, or any other powerful group that is not democratically accountable? 3 / 4

While electoral outcomes are the result of transparent balloting, domestic economic oligarchies have a high degree of influence over policymaking, particularly on economic issues. In 2017, the parliament passed a controversial "administrative reconciliation" bill that granted amnesty to Ben Ali–era civil servants who are implicated in corrupt activity, but are deemed to have not personally benefitted from it. The bill was met with resistance by civil society, with activists claiming that it would undermine other justice processes. Analysts suggested that the bill was designed to reward powerful individuals linked with the Ben Ali regime who had supported Nidaa Tounes, and would have been negatively affected by the ongoing judicial and reconciliation processes.

Meanwhile, geopolitical competition between Gulf states has had reverberations in Tunisia, frequently coming in the form of financial and other support to political parties. For example, the United Arab Emirates (UAE) controversially gifted two armored cars to Essebsi in the run-up to Tunisia's 2014 elections, and has reportedly pressured the party to crack down on Ennahda. Ennahda, in turn, is thought to receive support from Qatar.

B4. Do various segments of the population (including ethnic, religious, gender, LGBT, and other relevant groups) have full political rights and electoral opportunities? 3 / 4

Nongovernmental organizations (NGOs) and international organizations continue working to increase the political participation of marginalized groups. In 2017, the parliament passed a law requiring an equal number of men and women at the top of candidate lists, as well as at least one candidate with a disability and three people under the age of 35 on each list. For the 2018 municipal elections, 50 percent of candidates were under the age of 35 and nearly half were women. Women ultimately won 48 percent of the seats.

Despite these positive developments, some segments of the population lack full political rights. Only Muslims may run for president. Additionally, societal discrimination and laws criminalizing homosexuality preclude many LGBT (lesbian, gay, bisexual, and transgender) people from active political participation, and political parties fail to address issues of relevance to LGBT people.

C. FUNCTIONING OF GOVERNMENT: 6 / 12

C1. Do the freely elected head of government and national legislative representatives determine the policies of the government? 3 / 4

The 2011 removal from power of Ben Ali and his close relatives and associates, who had used their positions to create private monopolies in several sectors, represented an important step in combating corruption and eliminating conflicts of interest. However, Essebsi has manipulated the national budget in such a way that the legislative branch is deeply underfunded, leaving it with little ability or resources to craft legislation on its own in 2018. As a result, lawmaking is largely a function of the executive.

Nidaa Tounes's losses in the 2018 municipal elections contributed to extensive discord within the party and led to speculation that Prime Minister Chahed could be removed from office. In September, as Chahed's relationship with President Essebsi and the president's son, who was appointed head of Nidaa Tounes in 2016, continued to deteriorate, Chahed was suspended from the party, creating uncertainty about the stability of the governing coalition.

C2. Are safeguards against official corruption strong and effective? 1 / 4

Corruption is endemic in Tunisia, and corrupt high-level officials often act with impunity. In 2017, Prime Minister Chahed launched a well-publicized war on corruption, frequently using powers granted under a state of emergency in force since late 2015 to detain those accused. The campaign has come under criticism for focusing in large part on emerging elites, while leaving corrupt figures associated with the Ben Ali regime largely untouched.

In July 2018, the parliament approved a new law designed to strengthen the anticorruption legal framework, which requires the president, government ministers, and high-level public officials, among others, to publicly declare their assets. Penalties for violating the law include hefty fines and prison terms of up to five years. The law, which went into effect in October, required 350,000 people to submit their asset declarations by year's end.

C3. Does the government operate with openness and transparency? 2 / 4

In 2016, the ARP adopted a freedom of information law, though it was criticized by watchdog groups for its security-related exemptions. Cabinet ministries often refuse requests for information.

Members of the governing coalition frequently craft policy behind closed doors, without input from other parties. The law passed in 2018 requiring public officials to declare their assets was a step forward in demanding transparency and accountability from the government, but it remains to be seen how effectively the legislation will be implemented.

CIVIL LIBERTIES: 38 / 60 (-2)
D. FREEDOM OF EXPRESSION AND BELIEF: 12 / 16
D1. Are there free and independent media? 2 / 4

The constitution guarantees freedom of opinion, thought, expression, information, and publication, subject to some restrictions. While independent media outlets exist in Tunisia, journalists continued to face pressure and intimidation from government officials in connection with their work in 2018. Journalists who cover the security forces are particularly vulnerable to harassment and arrest. In June, blogger and recently elected member of parliament Yassine Ayari was sentenced to three months in prison for "undermining the morale of the army," over a 2017 Facebook post critical of the military and the president. In November, Ayari had a separate sentence, over another 2017 Facebook post that mocked the appointment of a military commander, extended from 16 days to three months. At year's end, Ayari had not yet served prison time for the offenses.

In January, Minister of the Interior Lotfi Brahem admitted in a parliamentary hearing that journalists were being monitored, and stated that the ministry would prosecute anyone who "undermined the morale of security forces." The police had come under criticism earlier in the month for cracking down on protests.

Lawmakers also advanced legislation that would tighten defamation laws during the year. In March, 16 legislators from Nidaa Tounes introduced a bill that would make online defamation a criminal offense. Following an October suicide attack in Tunis, lawmakers pushed to expedite the consideration of a bill introduced in 2017, which would criminalize "denigration" of the security forces. Both bills remained under consideration at year's end.

D2. Are individuals free to practice and express their religious faith or nonbelief in public and private? 3 / 4

The constitution calls for freedom of belief and conscience for all religions, as well as for the nonreligious, and bans campaigns against apostasy and incitement to hatred and violence on religious grounds. However, blasphemy remains illegal and police may invoke it as a pretext for arrests. Islam is enshrined as the only religion of the state. Islamic education remains a required component of the curriculum in public schools.

During Ramadan, in May and June 2018, non-Muslims protested in Tunis over the closure of cafes and restaurants. While it is not illegal to eat during daylight hours of Ramadan, many restaurants close because the majority of the population participates in the observance. Converts to Christianity often experience harassment and discrimination.

D3. Is there academic freedom, and is the educational system free from extensive political indoctrination? 3 / 4

Article 33 of the constitution explicitly protects academic freedom, which continues to improve in practice. However, ingrained practices of self-censorship on the part of academics remain in some instances. Students have reported being unable to pursue dissertation research on topics including sexuality, gender identity, and critiques of Islam's role in violent extremism.

D4. Are individuals free to express their personal views on political or other sensitive topics without fear of surveillance or retribution? 4 / 4

Private discussion is generally open and free, though there is some reluctance to broach some topics, including criticism of the military. Homosexuality remains illegal, and the prohibition discourages open discussion of issues affecting LGBT (lesbian, gay, bisexual, and transgender) people.

E. ASSOCIATIONAL AND ORGANIZATIONAL RIGHTS: 7 / 12 (−2)

E1. Is there freedom of assembly? 2 / 4 (−1)

The constitution guarantees the rights to assembly and peaceful demonstration. Public demonstrations on political, social, and economic issues regularly take place. However, a controversial counterterrorism law adopted in 2015, and successive states of emergency issued in response to a 2015 terrorist attack, have imposed significant constraints on public demonstrations. The latest state of emergency, which was renewed in October 2018 and again in December, allows security forces to ban strikes, meetings, and large gatherings considered likely to incite disorder. Although the government claims that the continued state of emergency is due to security concerns, analysts argue that it remains in place largely as a political tool to suppress dissent.

Security forces also cracked down on demonstrations during the year. In January, more than 900 demonstrators were arrested during protests across the country over the passage of a budget law that included austerity measures, and the police reportedly beat many of those detained and denied some detainees access to a lawyer. The police also arrested dozens of activists who distributed leaflets that contained criticism of the government. Many of the protests were peaceful, but some demonstrators set fire to public buildings and committed acts of vandalism. Also in January, police forcefully dispersed a demonstration in Tunis planned by the Association of Free Thinkers, who demanded gender equality, freedom of conscience, and ending the criminalization of consensual same-sex relations and the use and possession of cannabis.

Score Change: The score declined from 3 to 2 because assembly rights were threatened by the mass arrests and mistreatment of protesters by security forces, and the extension of a state of emergency for what appears to be political rather than security reasons.

E2. Is there freedom for nongovernmental organizations, particularly those that are engaged in human rights- and governance-related work? 2 / 4 (−1)

Tens of thousands of new NGOs began operating after the revolution, and such groups continued to organize conferences, trainings, educational programs, and other gatherings throughout the country during 2018.

However, in July, the parliament passed a controversial new law establishing the National Registry of Institutions, and requiring all NGOs, as well as businesses, to register with the new body. Critics argue that including NGOs among the institutions that must register is meant to increase the monitoring and oversight of civil society by the government. Registration applications can be denied at the discretion of the Council of the National Registry. The law also requires NGOs to provide data on staff, assets, decisions to merge or dissolve, and operations. Failure to register may result in a year of imprisonment and a fine of $4,000.

In a statement issued before the law's passage, 24 leading NGOs argued that the legislation was not only unconstitutional, but would "lead to an aversion to civic work."

Score Change: The score declined from 3 to 2 due to the passage of a law that limits the freedom of nongovernmental organizations by requiring them to register with the National Registry of Institutions and provide extensive data on their operations, among other provisions.

E3. Is there freedom for trade unions and similar professional or labor organizations? 3 / 4

The constitution guarantees the right to form labor unions and to strike. Although the General Tunisian Labor Union (UGTT) is the predominant union, additional independent unions exist as well. The Tunisian economy has seen large-scale strike actions across all sectors since the revolution, with participants demanding labor reform, better wages, and improved workplace conditions. Unions have reported that some employers have taken actions to discourage union activities, including dismissing union activists.

F. RULE OF LAW: 9 / 16
F1. Is there an independent judiciary? 2 / 4

While the constitution calls for a robust and independent judiciary, judicial reform has proceeded slowly since the 2011 revolution, with numerous Ben Ali–era judges remaining on the bench and successive governments regularly attempting to manipulate the courts. Legislation adopted in 2016 established the Supreme Judicial Council, a body charged with ensuring the independence of the judiciary and appointing Constitutional Court judges. Council members were elected in 2016 by thousands of legal professionals. However, at the end of 2018, the Constitutional Court, which is intended to evaluate the constitutionality of decrees and laws, had not yet been established, nor its members formally appointed.

F2. Does due process prevail in civil and criminal matters? 2 / 4

In 2014, Tunisia established a Truth and Dignity Commission to examine political, economic, and social crimes committed since 1956. It has since registered tens of thousands of complaints and testimonies. In March 2018, the parliament voted against extending the commission's mandate for one year, a decision that drew criticism from rights activists for weakening transitional justice. In May, the commission's first public trial began, concerning the 1991 forced disappearance of Kamel Matmati, an Islamist political activist, although in October, the trial was postponed until 2019. The commission also transferred a number of cases to specialized courts that deal with human rights violations before winding down its activities in December.

The state of emergency in place since 2015 and renewed through the end of 2018 gives police broad license to arrest and detain people on security- or terrorism-related charges, and arbitrary arrests continued to take place during the year. Civilians are frequently tried in military courts, particularly on charges of defaming the army. Notably, Ayari's June conviction took place in a military court.

F3. Is there protection from the illegitimate use of physical force and freedom from war and insurgencies? 3 / 4

Tunisia has not experienced a major terrorist attack since 2015, although a suicide bomber in Tunis injured nine people in October 2018. Reports of the use of excessive force and torture by security agents continued in 2018. Critics of draft legislation introduced in 2017, entitled "Rejection of Assaults against the Armed Forces," say it would grant security officials the right to use excessive force without risking repercussions. If passed, the bill, which remained under consideration by the parliament at year's end, would allow security officials to use lethal force at protests to defend public order and property.

F4. Do laws, policies, and practices guarantee equal treatment of various segments of the population? 2 / 4

The constitution prohibits all forms of discrimination and calls for the state to create a culture of diversity. However, LGBT people continue to face legal discrimination. Homosexuality remains illegal, and the penal code calls for a three-year prison sentence for "sodomy."

Although the 2014 constitution guarantees gender equality, women experience discrimination in employment, and sexual harassment in public spaces remains prevalent.

Tunisia has no asylum law, leaving the United Nations as the sole entity processing claims of refugee status in the country. Irregular migrants and asylum seekers are often housed in informal detention centers, where they suffer from substandard living conditions. Delays in the issuance of residency permits make it impossible for many to work legally, forcing them to take informal jobs with no labor protections.

G. PERSONAL AUTONOMY AND INDIVIDUAL RIGHTS: 10 / 16

G1. Do individuals enjoy freedom of movement, including the ability to change their place of residence, employment, or education? 3 / 4

Freedom of movement has improved substantially since 2011. The constitution guarantees freedom of movement within the country, as well as the freedom to travel abroad. Women do not require the permission of a male relative to travel. In 2017, lawmakers approved measures that require authorities to go through more rigorous processes in order to issue travel bans or restrict passports. However, authorities still have broad license under the state of emergency to restrict individuals' movement without initiating formal charges, and thousands have been affected by such orders.

G2. Are individuals able to exercise the right to own property and establish private businesses without undue interference from state or nonstate actors? 2 / 4

The protection of property rights and establishment of new businesses continues to be an area of concern, closely linked to high levels of corruption as well as a large backlog of property disputes. The investment code passed in 2016 has yet to lead to substantial improvements.

The cabinet approved a bill in November 2018 that would establish equal inheritance rights for men and women. Currently, women are granted half the share of inheritance that men receive. The Ennahda Party expressed opposition to the bill, and it had not yet been passed by the parliament at year's end.

G3. Do individuals enjoy personal social freedoms, including choice of marriage partner and size of family, protection from domestic violence, and control over appearance? 3 / 4

Tunisia has long been praised for relatively progressive social policies, especially in the areas of family law and women's rights. However, women experience high rates of domestic abuse. In 2017, lawmakers approved a Law on Eliminating Violence against Women, which addressed domestic violence and also included language intended to protect women from harassment in public, and from economic discrimination. However, the law is not consistent with the penal code—which, for example, does not criminalize spousal rape. Critics of the law have faulted a provision allowing accusers to drop charges, noting that women who experience domestic abuse may be susceptible to pressure from abusers and others to withdraw allegations. At a conference in November 2018 that brought together government officials,

NGO representatives, and survivors of domestic violence, participants noted that implementation of the law has been limited by a shortage of trained agents to handle complaints, pressure on women from some agents to avoid taking their abusive husbands to court, and a number of logistical barriers to reporting abuse.

Public displays of affection can lead to charges of violating public morality laws, and jail time. In 2017, the Justice Ministry repealed a decree that had banned Tunisian women from marrying non-Muslim men.

G4. Do individuals enjoy equality of opportunity and freedom from economic exploitation? 2 / 4

Tunisian women and children are subject to sex trafficking and forced domestic work in both Tunisia and abroad. Refugees and other migrants are also susceptible to exploitation by traffickers. Cases of exploitation in the agriculture and textile sectors are prevalent; women often work long hours with no contracts, benefits, or legal recourse. The protests in early 2018 called attention to the lack of economic opportunity for average Tunisians due to high inflation, high unemployment, and a lack of meaningful reform to address such issues.

Turkey

Population: 81,300,000
Capital: Ankara
Political Rights Rating: 5
Civil Liberties Rating: 6
Freedom Rating: 5.5
Freedom Status: Not Free
Electoral Democracy: No

Overview: President Recep Tayyip Erdoğan's Justice and Development Party (AKP) has been the ruling party in Turkey since 2002. After initially passing some liberalizing reforms, the AKP government showed growing contempt for political rights and civil liberties, and its authoritarian nature has been fully consolidated since a 2016 coup attempt triggered a more dramatic crackdown on perceived opponents of the leadership. Constitutional changes adopted in 2017 concentrated power in the hands of the president, and worsening electoral conditions have made it increasingly difficult for opposition parties to challenge Erdoğan's control.

KEY DEVELOPMENTS IN 2018:

- In June, Erdoğan won a snap presidential election, and the AKP secured control of the parliament in alliance with the Nationalist Movement Party (MHP). The elections were contested on a deeply uneven playing field marked by media bias in favor of the AKP and intimidation, harassment, and attacks aimed at opposition candidates.
- Constitutional changes approved in 2017 took force upon Erdoğan's reelection, introducing a new presidential system of government that vastly expanded executive powers and eliminated the post of prime minister. The president can now rule by decree and appoint various officials and judges who are ostensibly meant to play an independent oversight role, eradicating key checks on executive power.

- Opposition leaders continued to face arrest and prosecution throughout the year. In September, Selahattin Demirtaş, the 2018 presidential candidate of the pro-Kurdish Peoples' Democratic Party (HDP), was convicted on terrorism charges and sentenced to four years and eight months in prison; he was awaiting trial on additional charges. Eren Erdem, a former Republican People's Party (CHP) lawmaker, was arrested in June and awaited trial at the end of the year for supposedly supporting a terrorist organization and exposing a government witness, among other charges.
- The erosion of civil liberties continued apace during the year, with frequent arrests and convictions of journalists and social media users who were critical of the government, as well as tight restrictions on assembly and union rights.

POLITICAL RIGHTS: 15 / 40 (−1)

A. ELECTORAL PROCESS: 5 / 12 (−1)

A1. Was the current head of government or other chief national authority elected through free and fair elections? 2 / 4

The president is directly elected for up to two five-year terms, but is eligible to run for a third term if the parliament calls for early elections during the president's second term. If no candidate wins an absolute majority of votes, a second round of voting between the top two candidates takes place. President Erdoğan of the AKP has retained a dominant role in government since moving from the post of prime minister to the presidency in 2014. A constitutional referendum passed in 2017 instituted a new presidential system of government, expanding presidential powers and eliminating the role of prime minister, effective after the snap presidential vote in June 2018.

The presidential election was originally scheduled for November 2019, but in April 2018, Erdoğan called for an earlier vote, claiming that it was essential to move Turkey to the new presidential system as soon as possible. Observers with the Organization for Security and Co-operation in Europe (OSCE) criticized the electoral process for favoring the ruling party, though voters were generally free to express their choice at the ballot box. Media coverage, particularly in state-run outlets, was tilted toward the AKP, and the campaign took place under a state of emergency that was first declared after the 2016 coup attempt, which limited campaign activities. Some opposition candidates were attacked during campaign events, especially those from the HDP. Demirtaş, the HDP presidential candidate, was forced to campaign from prison, where he had been awaiting trial on terrorism charges since his arrest in 2016. Erdoğan received 52 percent of the vote, while Muharrem İnce of the CHP finished second with 30 percent.

Many elected executive officials at the municipal level have been replaced with government appointees since the 2016 coup attempt. Most were removed under emergency powers that allowed appointed provincial authorities to take control of cities and towns whose elected leaders were suspected of supporting terrorism—a broadly defined term that is now commonly applied to Kurdish politicians, often from the HDP and its affiliates. The mayors of 94 out of 102 Kurdish-majority municipalities had been replaced with government-appointed "trustees" by October 2018. However, some mayors from other opposition parties have been removed as well. In 2017, for instance, the government took control of an Istanbul municipality held by the CHP, citing corruption allegations.

A2. Were the current national legislative representatives elected through free and fair elections? 2 / 4 (−1)

The 2017 constitutional referendum enlarged the unicameral parliament, the Grand National Assembly, from 550 seats to 600 seats, and increased term lengths from four to five years; these changes took effect with the June 2018 general elections. Members are elected by proportional representation.

According to the OSCE, the 2018 elections were marred by a number of flaws, including misuse of state resources by the ruling party to gain an electoral advantage, as well as intimidation of and attacks on the HDP and other opposition parties. Media coverage of the campaign, particularly in state-run outlets, definitively favored the AKP. Reports of irregularities such as proxy voting were more prevalent in the south and southeast. The People's Alliance, which formed in February and included the AKP and the far-right MHP, won a total of 344 seats with 53 percent of the vote, while the CHP won 146 seats with 22 percent. The HDP won 11 percent and 67 seats, and the İyi (Good) Party entered parliament for the first time with 10 percent of the vote and 43 seats.

In April, two HDP members of parliament were removed from office due to criminal convictions for "insulting a public employee" and membership in a terrorist organization, respectively, bringing to 11 the total number of HDP deputies ousted as a result of criminal convictions or absenteeism caused by imprisonment.

Score Change: The score declined from 3 to 2 because the parliamentary elections were contested on a deeply uneven playing field characterized by media coverage that favored the ruling party, intimidation of and attacks on opposition candidates, and the misuse of state resources to benefit the ruling party and its allies.

A3. Are the electoral laws and framework fair, and are they implemented impartially by the relevant election management bodies? 1 / 4

Judges on the Supreme Electoral Council (YSK) oversee voting procedures. In 2016, the parliament passed a judicial reform bill that allowed AKP-dominated judicial bodies to replace most YSK judges. In the 2017 constitutional referendum, the new degree of AKP control apparently contributed to a series of YSK decisions that favored the "yes" campaign. For example, late on the day of the vote, the YSK, according to an OSCE report, instructed electoral boards to accept as valid an unknown number of ballots that were improperly stamped by ballot box committees or had no committee control stamp at all.

Additional changes to the electoral framework passed by the parliament in March 2018, just three months before the general elections, further threatened the integrity of Turkish polls and appeared to favor the AKP. Under the new law, unstamped ballot papers can be counted, government officials are allowed to run polling stations, and security forces can monitor the voting process.

B. POLITICAL PLURALISM AND PARTICIPATION: 7 / 16

B1. Do the people have the right to organize in different political parties or other competitive political groupings of their choice, and is the system free of undue obstacles to the rise and fall of these competing parties or groupings? 2 / 4

Turkey has a competitive multiparty system, with five parties represented in the parliament. However, the rise of new parties is inhibited by the 10 percent vote threshold for parliamentary representation—an unusually high bar by global standards. The 2018 electoral law permits the formation of alliances to contest elections, allowing parties that would not meet the threshold alone to secure seats through an alliance. Parties can be disbanded for endorsing policies that are not in agreement with constitutional parameters, and this rule has been applied in the past to Islamist and Kurdish-oriented parties.

After a cease-fire with the militant Kurdistan Workers' Party (PKK) collapsed in 2015, the government accused the HDP of being a proxy for the group, which is designated as a terrorist organization. A 2016 constitutional amendment facilitated the removal of parliamentary immunity, and many of the HDP's leaders have since been jailed on terrorism charges. In September 2018, Demirtaş, the HDP's presidential candidate, was sentenced to four years and eight months in prison for a 2013 speech praising the PKK in the context of peace negotiations. At the end of the year, he awaited trial on additional terrorism charges that could lead to a prison sentence of up to 142 years. In November, the European Court of Human Rights (ECHR) ordered Demirtaş's immediate release, finding that his arrest was politically motivated and his nearly two-year pretrial detention was unreasonable. Despite the ECHR ruling, a Turkish court subsequently denied Demirtaş's petition for release.

B2. Is there a realistic opportunity for the opposition to increase its support or gain power through elections? 1 / 4

Since coming to power in 2002, the ruling AKP has asserted partisan control over the YSK, the judiciary, the police, and the media. The party has aggressively used such institutional tools to weaken or co-opt political rivals in recent years, severely limiting the capacity of the opposition to build support among voters and gain power through elections. In 2018, the AKP utilized the provision in the 2018 electoral law that allows for interparty alliances by joining forces with the MHP. The move allowed the AKP to form a majority coalition in the new parliament, since it won just 295 seats and 42 percent of the vote on its own, a seven-point decline from its performance in the previous parliamentary elections in 2015.

In addition to the prosecution of HDP politicians on terrorism charges, the government has used law enforcement agencies to attack the country's largest opposition party, the CHP. Former CHP member of parliament Eren Erdem was arrested in June 2018 and awaited trial at year's end for allegedly exposing a government witness and aiding a terrorist organization, among other charges.

B3. Are the people's political choices free from domination by the military, foreign powers, religious hierarchies, economic oligarchies, or any other powerful group that is not democratically accountable? 3 / 4

The civilian leadership in recent years has asserted its control over the military, which has a history of intervening in political affairs. This greater control was a factor behind the failure of the 2016 coup attempt, and the government has since purged thousands of military personnel suspected of disloyalty. However, the AKP's institutional dominance threatens to make the state itself an extension of the party that can be used to change political outcomes.

B4. Do various segments of the population (including ethnic, religious, gender, LGBT, and other relevant groups) have full political rights and electoral opportunities? 1 / 4

Critics charge that the AKP has a religious agenda favoring Sunni Muslims, evidenced by the expansion of the Directorate of Religious Affairs and the use of this institution for political patronage and to deliver government-friendly sermons in mosques. Secular residents are alienated by the government's expansion of religious schools and use of religious rhetoric, among other actions. The non-Sunni Alevi minority as well as non-Muslim religious communities have long faced political discrimination. While religious and ethnic minorities hold some seats in the parliament, particularly with the opposition CHP and HDP, the government's crackdown on opposition parties has seriously harmed political rights and electoral opportunities for Kurdish and other minorities.

Women remain underrepresented in politics and in leadership positions in government, though they won a slightly larger share of seats—104, or about 17 percent—in the 2018 parliamentary elections. The AKP uses rhetoric and pursues policies that often do not serve the interests of women, but the platforms and practices of some other major parties, notably the HDP, support expanded rights for both women and minorities.

C. FUNCTIONING OF GOVERNMENT: 3 / 12

C1. Do the freely elected head of government and national legislative representatives determine the policies of the government? 2 / 4

The new presidential system instituted in June 2018 vastly expanded the executive's already substantial authority. With the elimination of the prime minister's post, President Erdoğan now controls all executive functions, and he can rule by decree, appoint judges and other officials who are ostensibly meant to play an independent oversight role, and order investigations into any civil servant, among other powers. Erdoğan and his inner circle make all meaningful political decisions, and the capacity of the parliament to provide a check on his rule is, in practice, seriously limited.

The state of emergency, which gave the president the authority to suspend civil liberties and issue decrees without oversight from the Constitutional Court, was formally lifted in July 2018 after two years in effect. However, analysts argued that the change would do little to curb the continued consolidation and abuse of executive power.

C2. Are safeguards against official corruption strong and effective? 1 / 4

Corruption—including money laundering, bribery, and collusion in the allocation of government contracts—remains a major problem, even at the highest levels of government. Enforcement of anticorruption laws is inconsistent, and Turkey's anticorruption agencies are generally ineffective, contributing to a culture of impunity. The purge carried out since the 2016 coup attempt has greatly increased opportunities for corruption, given the mass expropriation of targeted businesses and nongovernmental organizations (NGOs). Billions of dollars in seized assets are managed by government-appointed trustees, further augmenting the intimate ties between the government and friendly businesses.

In May 2018, Turkish banker Mehmet Hakan Atilla was found guilty in a US court of helping Iran to avoid US sanctions. During the trial, Turkish-Iranian businessman Reza Zarrab testified that senior Turkish officials had accepted bribes as part of the scheme, and that Erdoğan himself approved some of the bribes during his tenure as prime minister.

C3. Does the government operate with openness and transparency? 0 / 4

The political and legal environment created by the government's purge and state of emergency has made ordinary democratic oversight efforts all but impossible. In 2016, the Council of Europe criticized the state of emergency for bestowing "almost unlimited discretionary powers" on the government. Although Turkey has an access to information law on the books, in practice the government lacks transparency and arbitrarily withholds information on the activities of state officials and institutions. External monitors like civil society groups and independent journalists are subject to arrest and prosecution if they attempt to expose government wrongdoing. For example, at the end of 2018, investigative journalist Pelin Ünker remained on trial for defamation after publishing two stories in 2017 on the "Paradise Papers," a trove of leaked documents indicating that former prime minister Binali Yıldırım and his son owned companies in Malta to evade taxes.

CIVIL LIBERTIES: 16 / 60
D. FREEDOM OF EXPRESSION AND BELIEF: 5 / 16
D1. Are there free and independent media? 1 / 4

The mainstream media, especially television broadcasters, reflect government positions and routinely carry identical headlines. Although some independent newspapers and websites continue to operate, they face tremendous political pressure and are routinely targeted for prosecution. More than 150 media outlets were closed in the months after the attempted coup in 2016.

According to the Committee to Protect Journalists, a total of 68 journalists remained behind bars as of December 2018, making Turkey the world's worst jailer of journalists for the third year in a row. The government's efforts to suppress critical journalism can extend beyond its borders. In October, a Turkish court requested that Interpol issue "red notices" for Can Dündar and İlhan Tanir, two prominent journalists now living abroad who were standing trial in absentia on espionage charges. Dündar and Tanir were previously tried along with 14 other journalists from the newspaper *Cumhuriyet*, but their cases were separated from that trial when the court reached its guilty verdict in April. The 14 journalists were convicted of aiding terrorist organizations for allegedly supporting the movement led by exiled Islamic preacher Fethullah Gülen—which the government blames for the 2016 coup attempt—and the PKK, and received prison sentences of between three and seven years.

The government continued to block scores of news sites and other online information sources in 2018, most notably Wikipedia, which had been subject to a nationwide ban since April 2017.

D2. Are individuals free to practice and express their religious faith or nonbelief in public and private? 2 / 4

While the constitution guarantees freedom of religion, the public sphere is increasingly dominated by Sunni Islam. Alevi places of worship are not recognized as such by the government, meaning they cannot access the subsidies available to Sunni mosques. The number of religious schools that promote Sunni Islam has increased under the AKP, and Turkish public education includes compulsory religious education courses that adherents of non-Muslim faiths are generally exempted from but Alevis and nonbelievers have difficulty opting out of. Three non-Muslim religious groups—Jews, Orthodox Christians, and Armenian Christians—are officially recognized. However, disputes over property and prohibitions on training of clergy remain problems for these communities, and the rights of unrecognized religious minorities are more limited.

D3. Is there academic freedom, and is the educational system free from extensive political indoctrination? 1 / 4

Academic freedom, never well respected in Turkey, was weakened further by the postcoup purge. Schools affiliated with the Gülen movement have been closed, and thousands of academics have been summarily dismissed for perceived leftist, Gülenist, or PKK sympathies. Academics and students continued to be prosecuted for expressing critical views of the government or for peaceful political action in 2018. For example, at the end of the year, four students from Middle East Technical University still faced charges of "insulting the president" after holding up a satirical banner at their graduation ceremony in July.

Also in July 2018, Erdoğan issued a decree that gives him the power to appoint rectors at both public and private universities, a move that could further threaten academic freedom. The government and university administrations now routinely intervene to prevent academics from researching sensitive topics, and political pressure has encouraged self-censorship among many scholars.

D4. Are individuals free to express their personal views on political or other sensitive topics without fear of surveillance or retribution? 1 / 4

Many Turkish citizens continue to voice their opinions openly with friends and relations, but more exercise caution about what they post online or say in public. While not every utterance that is critical of the government will be punished, the arbitrariness of prosecutions, which often result in pretrial detention and carry the risk of lengthy prison terms, is increasingly creating an atmosphere of self-censorship. In January and February 2018, hundreds of people, including doctors, construction workers, and high school students, were detained for social media posts criticizing a Turkish military offensive in the Afrin district of Syria.

E. ASSOCIATIONAL AND ORGANIZATIONAL RIGHTS: 3 / 12

E1. Is there freedom of assembly? 1 / 4

Although freedom of assembly is theoretically guaranteed in Turkish law, authorities have routinely disallowed gatherings by government critics on security grounds in recent years, while progovernment rallies are allowed to proceed. Restrictions have been imposed on May Day celebrations by leftist and labor groups, LGBT (lesbian, gay, bisexual, and transgender) events, protests by purge victims, and opposition party meetings. Police use force to break up unsanctioned protests. In August 2018, a weekly commemoration in Istanbul held by Saturday Mothers, a group that has protested forced disappearances since 1995, was broken up by police after authorities announced that the demonstrations would be banned; many participants, including elderly people, were arrested.

E2. Is there freedom for nongovernmental organizations, particularly those that are engaged in human rights- and governance-related work? 1 / 4

The government has cracked down on NGOs since the coup attempt, summarily shutting down at least 1,500 foundations and associations and seizing their assets. The targeted groups worked on issues including torture, domestic violence, and aid to refugees and internally displaced persons (IDPs). NGO leaders also face routine harassment, arrests, and prosecutions for carrying out their activities. Osman Kavala, perhaps Turkey's most prominent civil society leader and philanthropist, remained in pretrial detention at the end of 2018, having been arrested in 2017 based on vague allegations that he supported the 2016 coup attempt. No formal charges against him have been made public.

E3. Is there freedom for trade unions and similar professional or labor organizations? 1 / 4

Union activity, including the right to strike, is limited by law and in practice; antiunion activities by employers are common, and legal protections are poorly enforced. A system of representation threshold requirements make it difficult for unions to secure collective-bargaining rights. Trade unions and professional organizations have suffered from mass arrests and dismissals associated with the state of emergency and the general breakdown in freedoms of expression, assembly, and association. In September 2018, authorities broke up a strike that was organized to protest unsafe working conditions on the site of a new airport under construction in Istanbul. Most of the 500 strikers detained were ultimately released, but 61 people awaited trial for their role in the strike at the end of the year.

F. RULE OF LAW: 3 / 16 (+1)

F1. Is there an independent judiciary? 1 / 4

Judges still occasionally rule against the government, but the appointment of thousands of new, loyalist judges in recent years, the potential professional costs of ruling against the executive in a major case, and the effects of the ongoing purge have all severely weakened judicial independence in Turkey. More than 4,000 judges were removed in the coup's aftermath. The establishment of the new presidential system in June 2018 also increased executive control over the judiciary. Under the new structure, members of the Board of Judges and Prosecutors (HSK), a powerful body that oversees judicial appointments and disciplinary measures, are now appointed by the parliament and the president, rather than by members of the judiciary itself.

F2. Does due process prevail in civil and criminal matters? 0 / 4

A long-term erosion of due process guarantees accelerated under the state of emergency, and severe violations continued even after it was lifted in July 2018. Antiterrorism charges brought since the coup attempt often rely on the weakest of circumstantial evidence, secret testimony, or an ever-expanding web of guilt by association. A decree issued in 2017 apparently removed requirements that defendants hear all the evidence brought against them and have a defense attorney present during trial. In many cases, lawyers defending those accused of terrorism offenses have been arrested themselves. Lengthy pretrial detention has become routine. Authorities can detain individuals for up to 24 hours without access to a lawyer, though police have reportedly breached this limit in practice.

F3. Is there protection from the illegitimate use of physical force and freedom from war and insurgencies? 1 / 4 (+1)

Torture has become increasingly common, according to human rights organizations, and an emergency decree issued in 2017 appears to grant legal immunity to any individuals, including civilians, who take action against terrorists or others associated with the 2016 coup attempt.

The threat of terrorism decreased in 2018 with the weakening of the Islamic State (IS) militant group in neighboring Syria and Iraq; no large-scale terrorist attacks were reported during the year. The intensity of the conflict between security forces and the PKK, which has killed more than 4,000 people since 2015, also decreased in 2018, but more than 300 people were killed in fighting within Turkey's borders during the year.

Score Change: The score improved from 0 to 1 because there were fewer clashes between security forces and the PKK during the year, and the threat of terrorism decreased with the weakening of IS in neighboring countries.

F4. Do laws, policies, and practices guarantee equal treatment of various segments of the population? 1 / 4

Although Turkish law guarantees equal treatment, women as well as ethnic and religious minority groups suffer varying degrees of discrimination. For example, Alevis and non-Muslims reportedly face discrimination in employment, particularly in senior public-sector positions, and gender inequality in the workplace is common.

The conflict with the PKK has been used to justify discriminatory measures against Kurds, including the prohibition of Kurdish festivals for security reasons and the reversal of Kurdish municipal officials' efforts to promote Kurdish language and culture. Many Kurdish-language schools and cultural organizations have been shut down by the government since 2015.

As of December 2018, Turkey had accepted more than 3.6 million Syrian refugees. While the government attempts to provide them with basic services, a large minority of refugee children lack access to education, and few adults are able to obtain formal employment. The economic crisis that gripped Turkey in 2018 has fueled resentment toward refugees. Reports emerged during the year that some asylum seekers at the border with Syria were being given the choice of either waiving their asylum rights and returning to Syria, or facing lengthy detentions in Turkey, which rights groups argued was a violation of the principle of *nonrefoulement* under international law.

Same-sex sexual activity is legally permitted, but LGBT people are subject to widespread discrimination, police harassment, and occasional violence. There is no legislation to protect people from discrimination based on sexual orientation or gender identity.

G. PERSONAL AUTONOMY AND INDIVIDUAL RIGHTS: 5 / 16 (−1)

G1. Do individuals enjoy freedom of movement, including the ability to change their place of residence, employment, or education? 1 / 4

The conflict with the PKK has resulted in the forced relocation of hundreds of thousands of people, and there is evidence that the government is using curfews and cuts to utilities to push residents out of some areas.

More than 125,000 public-sector workers have been fired in the purges that followed the 2016 coup attempt, and those who are suspended or dismissed have no effective avenue for appeal. Moreover, many are not able to find new employment in the private sector due to an atmosphere of guilt by association, and they frequently have their passports confiscated.

G2. Are individuals able to exercise the right to own property and establish private businesses without undue interference from state or nonstate actors? 1 / 4

Private property rights are legally enshrined, but since 2013 many critics of the government have been subjected to intrusive tax and regulatory inspections. In the aftermath of the 2016 coup attempt, the assets of companies, NGOs, foundations, individuals, media outlets, and other entities deemed to be associated with terrorist groups have been confiscated. According to research published by the news site *European Interest* in June 2018, $11 billion in private business assets, ranging from corner stores to large conglomerates, have been seized.

G3. Do individuals enjoy personal social freedoms, including choice of marriage partner and size of family, protection from domestic violence, and control over appearance? 2 / 4

The government has shown increasing disinterest in protecting vulnerable individuals from forced marriage and domestic violence. Child marriages, often performed at unofficial religious ceremonies, are widespread, and Syrian refugees appear to be particularly vulnerable to the practice. Despite legal safeguards, rates of domestic violence remain high; police are often reluctant to intervene in domestic disputes, and shelter space is both extremely limited and often geographically inaccessible.

G4. Do individuals enjoy equality of opportunity and freedom from economic exploitation? 1 / 4 (−1)

The weakness of labor unions and the government's increasing willingness to take action against organized labor have undermined equality of opportunity, protection from economic exploitation, and workplace safety. Workplace accidents have become more frequent in recent years, and laborers have little recourse if injured. According to a report published by the Laborers Health and Occupational Safety Assembly, an advocacy group, at least 1,923 people died in workplace accidents in 2018. Refugee communities have provided a ready source of cheap, exploitable labor, including child labor, resulting in significant abuses.

Turkmenistan

Population: 5,900,000
Capital: Ashgabat
Political Rights Rating: 7
Civil Liberties Rating: 7
Freedom Rating: 7.0
Freedom Status: Not Free
Electoral Democracy: No

Overview: Turkmenistan is a repressive authoritarian state where political rights and civil liberties are almost completely denied in practice. Elections are tightly controlled, ensuring nearly unanimous victories for the president and his supporters. The economy is dominated by the state, corruption is systemic, religious groups are persecuted, and political dissent is not tolerated.

KEY DEVELOPMENTS IN 2018:

- In March, parties and candidates that support President Gurbanguly Berdimuhame-dov won all the seats in parliamentary elections. The president's son, Serdar Ber-dimuhamedov, was reelected to his seat, and his high-profile presence in the media fed speculation that he was being primed to succeed his father.
- The authorities stepped up measures during the year to curtail freedom of movement by barring people, especially young men, from leaving the country while also trying to force Turkmen citizens abroad to return home.
- The economic situation in the country continued to decline. Inflation was estimated to be as high as 294 percent in June, basic goods such as sugar and eggs were scarce, and the final remnants of a program providing free public utilities were eliminated.

POLITICAL RIGHTS: 0 / 40
A. ELECTORAL PROCESS: 0 / 12

A1. Was the current head of government or other chief national authority elected through free and fair elections? 0 / 4

The president is directly elected for an unlimited number of seven-year terms, extended from five years under a 2016 constitutional revision. Berdimuhamedov, the incumbent, was reelected for a third term in 2017 with 97.69 percent of the vote amid turnout of more than 97 percent, according to official results. His eight token opponents were either nominees of state-backed parties or members of the ruling Democratic Party of Turkmenistan (DPT) who ran as independents. The Organization for Security and Co-operation in Europe (OSCE) criticized the election process for failing to present voters with a genuine choice and noted that it took place in a strictly controlled political and media environment.

A2. Were the current national legislative representatives elected through free and fair elections? 0 / 4

The unicameral Mejlis is composed of 125 members elected from individual districts to serve five-year terms. Parliamentary elections are tightly controlled by the state and feature no genuine competition from opposition candidates.

In the March 2018 elections, the DPT won 55 seats, the Party of Industrialists and Entrepreneurs and the Agrarian Party each took 11, and candidates nominated by groups of citizens secured 48. Voter turnout was reported to be approximately 92 percent. As with the 2017 presidential election, the OSCE found that the Mejlis balloting "lacked important prerequisites of a genuinely democratic electoral process." The observers said that while there was a semblance of pluralism, in reality all parties and candidates supported the president, and the absence of media diversity interfered with citizens' ability to make a free and educated choice.

A3. Are the electoral laws and framework fair, and are they implemented impartially by the relevant election management bodies? 0 / 4

The legal framework for elections is neither fair nor impartially implemented. The Central Election Commission (ÇEC) is appointed by the president and operates with little transparency. The law allows virtually no opportunity for independent fund-raising or campaigning. In the 2017 presidential and 2018 parliamentary elections, the CEC organized and funded all campaign activities, according to international monitors.

The constitution and electoral code were amended in 2016 to remove the upper age limit of 70 for presidential candidates, extend the presidential term from five to seven years, and eliminate the right of public associations to nominate presidential candidates.

B. POLITICAL PLURALISM AND PARTICIPATION: 0 / 16

B1. Do the people have the right to organize in different political parties or other competitive political groupings of their choice, and is the system free of undue obstacles to the rise and fall of these competing parties or groupings? 0 / 4

The party system is dominated by the ruling DPT and controlled by the executive branch. The 2012 law on political parties specified the legal basis for citizens to form independent parties, but barred parties formed on professional, regional, or religious lines, and those created by government officials. Nevertheless, Berdimuhamedov subsequently announced plans to form two new groups—the Party of Entrepreneurs and Industrialists and the Agrarian Party. Both were then openly organized by sitting members of the DPT and formally registered in 2012 and 2014, respectively. The Agrarian Party won its first parliamentary seats in 2018.

B2. Is there a realistic opportunity for the opposition to increase its support or gain power through elections? 0 / 4

Turkmenistan has never experienced a peaceful transfer of power between rival parties through elections. Berdimuhamedov had served in the government of his late predecessor, Saparmurat Niyazov, who in turn had ruled the country since before its independence from the Soviet Union. The Soviet-era Communist Party became the DPT in 1991 and remains in power to date. All genuine opposition groups operate either illegally or in exile.

B3. Are the people's political choices free from domination by the military, foreign powers, religious hierarchies, economic oligarchies, or any other powerful group that is not democratically accountable? 0 / 4

The authoritarian political system offers voters no meaningful alternatives to the ruling party. At an informal level, politics within the regime are thought to be influenced by regional patronage networks, or "clans," that control different parts of the state and economy.

B4. Do various segments of the population (including ethnic, religious, gender, LGBT, and other relevant groups) have full political rights and electoral opportunities? 0 / 4

Members of the ethnic Turkmen majority and the president's tribal subdivision in particular are favored for leadership positions. While women and ethnic or religious minorities formally have full political rights, no segment of the country's population enjoys the practical ability to engage in independent political activity. About a quarter of candidates elected to the Mejlis in 2018 were women.

C. FUNCTIONING OF GOVERNMENT: 0 / 12

C1. Do the freely elected head of government and national legislative representatives determine the policies of the government? 0 / 4

The president, who is not freely elected, has ultimate decision-making authority. The executive branch determines laws and policies with no meaningful input or oversight from the rubber-stamp legislature. The People's Council—a body that includes elected Mejlis members and well as a variety of unelected officials and community leaders—was revived in 2018 after being abolished in 2008. The renewed council, headed and convened by the president, held its first session in September. It replaced a less powerful Council of Elders and is formally considered the country's top representative body, surpassing the role of the much smaller Mejlis. However, it meets infrequently and mainly endorses the president's decrees and policies.

C2. Are safeguards against official corruption strong and effective? 0 / 4

There are no independent institutions tasked with combating corruption, which is widespread in Turkmenistan. Crackdowns on corruption are typically selective and related to conflicts within the ruling elite. Anticorruption bodies have also allegedly been used to extort revenue from wealthy officials and businessmen.

Checks on nepotism and conflicts of interest are also lacking; the president's son, Serdar Berdimuhamedov, was reelected as a deputy to the Mejlis in 2018 and has held a number of government positions, including deputy foreign minister as of that year. Serdar's increasing visibility in the media and high-profile meetings with foreign dignitaries have fueled speculation that he is being primed to succeed his father.

C3. Does the government operate with openness and transparency? 0 / 4

Decisions on monetary policy, large-scale contracts with foreign companies, and the allocation of state profits from hydrocarbon exports are largely opaque and ultimately controlled by the president, without effective legal limits or independent oversight. Government officials and state-owned companies are not required to disclose their basic financial information to the public.

CIVIL LIBERTIES: 2 / 60 (–2)

D. FREEDOM OF EXPRESSION AND BELIEF: 0 / 16 (–1)

D1. Are there free and independent media? 0 / 4

Press freedom is severely restricted in Turkmenistan. The state controls nearly all broadcast and print media, and the state-run internet service provider blocks websites that carry independent news coverage or opposition-oriented content. Some citizens are able to access foreign satellite broadcasts, but in 2018 the government intensified efforts to remove receivers from houses in the countryside, following efforts in previous years to remove the dishes in major towns and cities. The heads of public institutions have also been told to order their employees not to watch foreign television.

Independent journalists, particularly those who work with Radio Free Europe/Radio Liberty (RFE/RL), are subject to harassment, detention, physical abuse, and prosecution on trumped-up charges. In May 2018, security officials apprehended and threatened RFE/RL journalist Soltan Achilova in Ashgabat; she was physically assaulted by two unidentified assailants in June.

D2. Are individuals free to practice and express their religious faith or nonbelief in public and private? 0 / 4

Legal restrictions, state monitoring and harassment, and the risk of penalties including fines and imprisonment have virtually extinguished the ability of individuals to freely practice religion. A 2016 law on religion maintained existing bans on religious activity outside state control, imposed a higher membership threshold for the registration of religious groups, and required all registered groups to reapply for registration. Senior Muslim clerics are appointed by the government, and Muslims who do not follow the officially approved interpretation of Islam are subject to persecution, including lengthy prison terms. Members of unregistered religious minority groups continue to face raids, beatings, and other forms of harassment. In 2018, at least 10 conscientious objectors, all Jehovah's Witnesses, were imprisoned for refusing to comply with compulsory military service.

D3. Is there academic freedom, and is the educational system free from extensive political indoctrination? 0 / 4

The government places significant restrictions on academic freedom, limiting research on politically sensitive topics and imposing onerous obstacles to the recognition of degrees from foreign institutions.

D4. Are individuals free to express their personal views on political or other sensitive topics without fear of surveillance or retribution? 0 / 4 (-1)

Private discussion and the expression of personal views are highly restricted due to intrusive supervision by state security services, including physical surveillance, monitoring of telephone and electronic communications, and the use of informers. In recent years the government has employed increasingly sophisticated methods to monitor the population. Authorities have reportedly used special software to eavesdrop on voice over internet protocol (VoIP) calls, operate computer cameras remotely, and record keystrokes. Social media users who post critical comments about the government are subject to intimidation and imprisonment, and blocking of social media sites and virtual private networks (VPNs) has expanded. There have also been reports that the government monitors the online contacts and posts of its citizens abroad.

Score Change: The score declined from 1 to 0 because the government has gradually enhanced its sprawling surveillance system for mobile and online communications, and it arrests users in connection with their online activity.

E. ASSOCIATIONAL AND ORGANIZATIONAL RIGHTS: 0 / 12

E1. Is there freedom of assembly? 0 / 4

The constitution guarantees freedom of assembly, and the 2015 Law on Assemblies defines the right of individuals and groups to hold peaceful gatherings with prior authorization. However, the law grants officials broad discretion to block assemblies, and in practice the authorities do not allow antigovernment demonstrations.

E2. Is there freedom for nongovernmental organizations, particularly those that are engaged in human rights- and governance-related work? 0 / 4

Onerous registration and regulatory requirements effectively prevent most independent nongovernmental organizations (NGOs) from operating legally or receiving foreign funding, and activities by unregistered groups can draw fines, detention, and other penalties. Individual activists face intimidation and harassment, as do the family members of human rights activists working in exile.

One of the president's sisters controls the National Red Crescent Society of Turkmenistan and has been accused of using the organization for personal enrichment.

E3. Is there freedom for trade unions and similar professional or labor organizations? 0 / 4

Workers have a legal right to join trade unions, but there are no protections against antiunion discrimination, and strikes are prohibited. The government-controlled Association of Trade Unions of Turkmenistan is the only union organization permitted to operate.

F. RULE OF LAW: 0 / 16
F1. Is there an independent judiciary? 0 / 4

The judicial system is subservient to the president, who appoints and dismisses judges unilaterally. In practice, the courts are commonly used to punish dissent and remove potential threats to the president's political dominance.

F2. Does due process prevail in civil and criminal matters? 0 / 4

Arbitrary arrests and detentions are common, particularly for dissidents, members of unapproved religious groups, activists, and journalists who work with foreign organizations. The authorities frequently deny defendants' basic rights of due process, including public trials and access to defense attorneys.

F3. Is there protection from the illegitimate use of physical force and freedom from war and insurgencies? 0 / 4

Prison conditions are extremely harsh, and security forces routinely use torture to extract confessions or punish inmates, which can result in deaths in custody. In June 2018, RFE/RL's Radio Azatlyk reported that an employee of the Ministry of National Security who was being held on charges of illegal currency conversion had been tortured to death. The lack of transparency surrounding many detentions amounts to enforced disappearance.

F4. Do laws, policies, and practices guarantee equal treatment of various segments of the population? 0 / 4

Employment and educational opportunities for ethnic minorities are limited by the government's promotion of Turkmen national identity, and activists who advocate for minority rights have faced persecution. Traditional social and religious norms help to restrict women's access to education and economic opportunity; there are no legal protections against sexual harassment in the workplace. The law does not protect LGBT (lesbian, gay, bisexual, and transgender) people from discrimination, and sexual activity between men can be punished with up to two years in prison.

G. PERSONAL AUTONOMY AND INDIVIDUAL RIGHTS: 2 / 16 (−1)
G1. Do individuals enjoy freedom of movement, including the ability to change their place of residence, employment, or education? 0 / 4 (−1)

Freedom of movement is restricted, with more than 30,000 individuals reportedly barred from traveling abroad as of 2018. Internal passports and a system of residency permits also obstruct travel within the country. There were numerous reports during the year of citizens living abroad who were tricked or pressured into returning to Turkmenistan and then found themselves in legal jeopardy, meaning they could be prevented from leaving the country again or face prison time. For example, Omriuzak Omarkulyev, a student living in Turkey, returned to Turkmenistan in February 2018 at the government's invitation and was then barred from leaving the country and sentenced to 20 years in prison. In other cases, students living abroad have found that their Turkmen bank cards no longer work. There have also been reports that young men in general are being blocked from leaving the country by border police at airports. The tensions are driven in part by an upsurge in attempted emigration linked to the dire economic situation in the country.

Score Change: The score declined from 1 to 0 because the government intensified efforts to prevent people from emigrating and in some cases pressured those already living abroad to return to Turkmenistan.

G2. Are individuals able to exercise the right to own property and establish private businesses without undue interference from state or nonstate actors? 1 / 4

The constitution establishes the right to property ownership, but the deeply flawed judiciary provides little protection to businesses and individuals, and the president's relatives monopolize key sectors of the economy that are not directly state controlled. Arbitrary evictions and confiscation of property are common.

G3. Do individuals enjoy personal social freedoms, including choice of marriage partner and size of family, protection from domestic violence, and control over appearance? 1 / 4

Domestic violence is reportedly common, but few victims file complaints with the authorities, and the government has not made significant efforts to monitor, prevent, or combat the problem. Reporting and prosecution of rape are similarly limited. While polygamy has long been illegal, it apparently persists in practice; a new law adopted in 2018 was meant to reinforce the ban.

G4. Do individuals enjoy equality of opportunity and freedom from economic exploitation? 0 / 4

The government forces thousands of students, public employees, and other citizens to participate in the annual cotton harvest with little or no pay. Impoverished residents of rural areas are especially vulnerable to trafficking abroad for forced labor or sexual exploitation, and the government does little to address the problem.

The state's mismanagement of a weak economy, including soaring inflation, has inhibited opportunity and imposed hardship on the population. Persistently low oil and gas prices have driven down vital export revenues in recent years, leading to reports of unpaid wages and shortages of basic goods. To raise funds, the government has at times increased various fees, cut subsidies, and pressured officials, businesspeople, and ordinary workers to make "voluntary" contributions. In September 2018, President Berdimuhamedov issued a decree to end what little remained of a program that provided free public utilities.

Score Change: The score declined from 2 to 1 due to the high rate of workplace accidents and deaths, which has increased in recent years.

Tuvalu

Population: 10,000
Capital: Funafuti
Political Rights Rating: 1
Civil Liberties Rating: 1
Freedom Rating: 1.0
Freedom Status: Free
Electoral Democracy: Yes

Overview: Tuvalu is a parliamentary democracy that holds regular, competitive elections. Civil liberties are generally upheld. Ongoing problems include a lack of antidiscrimination laws to protect women and LGBT (lesbian, gay, bisexual, and transgender) people.

KEY DEVELOPMENTS IN 2018:
- A move to add two seats to Parliament reserved for women was considered as part of a constitutional review process set to conclude in 2019.
- Former prime minister Apisai Ielemia died in November.

POLITICAL RIGHTS: 37 / 40

A. ELECTORAL PROCESS: 12 / 12

A1. Was the current head of government or other chief national authority elected through free and fair elections? 4 / 4

A governor general represents the British monarch as ceremonial head of state. The prime minister, chosen by Parliament, leads the government. Enele Sopoaga, who became prime minister after his predecessor was ousted in a no-confidence vote in 2013, secured a new term after the 2015 parliamentary elections, holding together his alliance of independent lawmakers.

A2. Were the current national legislative representatives elected through free and fair elections? 4 / 4

The unicameral, 15-member Parliament is directly elected through contests in eight geographical constituencies, all but one of which have two members each. In the 2015 elections, all candidates ran as independents, and 12 of the incumbents returned to office. Each of the main inhabited islands in Tuvalu is also governed by an elected local council.

A3. Are the electoral laws and framework fair, and are they implemented impartially by the relevant election management bodies? 4 / 4

Tuvalu's legal framework provides for democratic elections, and the laws are fairly and impartially implemented. An appointed secretary to the government is responsible for the supervision of elections and maintenance of voter rolls. Local polling officers are authorized to adjudicate election-related disputes in their districts, and there is a mechanism through which appeals may be filed.

B. POLITICAL PLURALISM AND PARTICIPATION: 15 / 16

B1. Do the people have the right to organize in different political parties or other competitive political groupings of their choice, and is the system free of undue obstacles to the rise and fall of these competing parties or groupings? 4 / 4

There are no formal political parties, though no law bars their formation. Candidates typically run as independents and form loose, frequently shifting alliances once in office.

B2. Is there a realistic opportunity for the opposition to increase its support or gain power through elections? 4 / 4

Tuvalu has an established pattern of democratic transfers of power. Individual prime ministers and governments have seldom lasted a full term in office in recent decades, with intense political rivalries often prompting no-confidence votes in Parliament.

B3. Are the people's political choices free from domination by the military, foreign powers, religious hierarchies, economic oligarchies, or any other powerful group that is not democratically accountable? 4 / 4

Traditional elders and the main Protestant church play an influential role in society, but they do not exercise undue control over the political choices of voters and candidates.

B4. Do various segments of the population (including ethnic, religious, gender, LGBT, and other relevant groups) have full political rights and electoral opportunities? 3 / 4

All Tuvaluans aged 18 and over who are present in the country on polling day but not imprisoned are eligible to vote. While women formally have full political rights, in practice their participation is somewhat inhibited by traditional biases. Three women ran for seats in the 2015 parliamentary elections, and one of them won office. A move to add two reserved seats for women is being considered as part of a constitutional review process scheduled to take place through mid-2019.

C. FUNCTIONING OF GOVERNMENT: 10 / 12

C1. Do the freely elected head of government and national legislative representatives determine the policies of the government? 4 / 4

Tuvalu's elected officials are able to develop and implement government policies and legislation without improper interference from any unelected entity.

C2. Are safeguards against official corruption strong and effective? 3 / 4

Corruption is not a severe problem in Tuvalu, and the country's independent auditing and law enforcement bodies are generally effective in combating graft, though there have been some corruption scandals in recent years. Former prime minister Ielemia was convicted in 2016 of receiving over $15,000 from Japanese and Taiwanese sources while in office and depositing the money in a personal bank account. The conviction was overturned by a higher court a few weeks later, but the fact that Ielemia had begun to serve a prison term led to his disputed removal from Parliament. Ielemia, who had been pursuing an appeal in the courts in 2017, died in November 2018.

C3. Does the government operate with openness and transparency? 3 / 4

Government operations and legislative processes are generally transparent, though there is no freedom of information law to guarantee and regulate public access to official records. While officials are legally obliged to disclose their assets and income, the rules are not consistently enforced, according to the US State Department.

An April 2018 report by the International Monetary Fund (IMF) found that Tuvalu had made progress in improving public financial management.

CIVIL LIBERTIES: 56 / 60 (−1)

D. FREEDOM OF EXPRESSION AND BELIEF: 16 / 16

D1. Are there free and independent media? 4 / 4

The constitution provides for freedom of the press, and there are no reported restrictions on this right, though the small media market does not support independent domestic news outlets. The government operates a radio station and a national newspaper. Many residents use satellite dishes to access foreign programming. Internet penetration has grown in recent years, though access is largely limited to the main island.

D2. Are individuals free to practice and express their religious faith or nonbelief in public and private? 4 / 4

The constitution and laws provide for freedom of religion, and this right is generally respected in practice. A Protestant church, the Congregational Christian Church of Tuvalu, has official status under the law, and about 97 percent of the population belongs. Traditional leaders are empowered to regulate local religious activities, and on smaller islands they sometimes discourage minority groups from proselytizing or holding public events.

D3. Is there academic freedom, and is the educational system free from extensive political indoctrination? 4 / 4

Academic freedom is generally respected.

D4. Are individuals free to express their personal views on political or other sensitive topics without fear of surveillance or retribution? 4 / 4

There are no significant restrictions on freedom of expression. The government does not improperly monitor personal communications or social media activity.

E. ASSOCIATIONAL AND ORGANIZATIONAL RIGHTS: 12 / 12

E1. Is there freedom of assembly? 4 / 4

The constitution provides for freedom of assembly, and the government typically upholds this right in practice.

E2. Is there freedom for nongovernmental organizations, particularly those that are engaged in human rights– and governance-related work? 4 / 4

Freedom of association is respected. Nongovernmental organizations operate without interference, providing a variety of health, education, and other services.

E3. Is there freedom for trade unions and similar professional or labor organizations? 4 / 4

Workers in the private sector have the right to organize unions, bargain collectively, and strike. Public-sector employees can join professional associations and engage in collective bargaining, but they are not permitted to strike. Most labor disputes are resolved through negotiations in practice. The only registered union represents seafarers.

F. RULE OF LAW: 15 / 16

F1. Is there an independent judiciary? 4 / 4

The judiciary is independent. The chief justice is appointed by the head of state on the advice of the cabinet, and other judges are appointed in the same manner after consultation with the chief justice. Judges cannot be removed arbitrarily.

F2. Does due process prevail in civil and criminal matters? 4 / 4

The authorities generally uphold due process during arrests, detentions, and trials. A public defense lawyer is available to detainees and defendants. However, the limited capacity of the legal system can lead to delays in court proceedings and access to counsel.

F3. Is there protection from the illegitimate use of physical force and freedom from war and insurgencies? 4 / 4

There were no reports of physical abuse by police or in the prison system during the year. Criminal activity does not pose a major threat to physical security.

F4. Do laws, policies, and practices guarantee equal treatment of various segments of the population? 3 / 4

While women generally enjoy equality before the law, traditional customs and social norms can limit women's role in society, and there are no specific legal protections against gender discrimination in employment.

Sexual activity between men can be punished with imprisonment, though the law is not actively enforced. Discrimination based on sexual orientation or gender identity is not specifically banned.

G. PERSONAL AUTONOMY AND INDIVIDUAL RIGHTS: 13 / 16 (−1)

G1. Do individuals enjoy freedom of movement, including the ability to change their place of residence, employment, or education? 4 / 4

Tuvaluans are free to travel within the country and abroad, and to relocate for purposes including employment and education.

G2. Are individuals able to exercise the right to own property and establish private businesses without undue interference from state or nonstate actors? 3 / 4 (−1)

The legal framework and government policies are generally supportive of property rights and private business activity. However, laws and practices surrounding land ownership and inheritance favor men over women.

Score Change: The score declined from 4 to 3 due to laws and practices surrounding land ownership and inheritance that favor men over women.

G3. Do individuals enjoy personal social freedoms, including choice of marriage partner and size of family, protection from domestic violence, and control over appearance? 3 / 4

Although personal social freedoms are generally respected, domestic violence often goes unreported because it is viewed as a private matter. There are no specific laws against spousal rape.

G4. Do individuals enjoy equality of opportunity and freedom from economic exploitation? 3 / 4

Forced labor is prohibited, and the government mandates basic protections against exploitative or dangerous working conditions, though enforcement is not proactive or consistent. Most of the labor force works in the informal sector or in small-scale fishing and agriculture.

Uganda

Population: 44,100,000
Capital: Kampala
Political Rights Rating: 6
Civil Liberties Rating: 5 ↓
Freedom Rating: 5.5
Freedom Status: Not Free
Electoral Democracy: No

Status Change: Uganda's status declined from Partly Free to Not Free due to attempts by long-ruling president Yoweri Museveni's government to restrict free expression, including through surveillance of electronic communications and a regressive tax on social media use.

Overview: While Uganda holds regular elections, their credibility has deteriorated over time, and the country has been ruled by the same party and president since 1986. The ruling party, the National Resistance Movement (NRM), retains power through the manipulation of state resources, intimidation by security forces, and politicized prosecutions of opposition leaders. Uganda's civil society and media sectors remain vibrant, despite suffering sporadic legal and extralegal harassment and state violence.

KEY DEVELOPMENTS IN 2018:
- In July, the government implemented a controversial social media tax, requiring users on a number of popular social media platforms including Facebook, Twitter, and WhatsApp to pay a daily fee of $0.05, which is prohibitively expensive for many users.
- A July Constitutional Court ruling, which upheld a 2017 amendment removing the presidential age limit of 75, potentially cleared the way for President Museveni to remain in office for life.
- In August, security forces arrested opposition Parliament members Robert Kyagulanyi (better known as Bobi Wine) and Kassiano Wadri during a campaign event for Wadri in Arua, after opposition supporters threw stones at President Museveni's motorcade. Security forces also shot at Wine's car, killing his driver. Wine, Wadri, and 32 additional defendants in the case awaited trial on treason charges at year's end.
- Also in August, security forces shot and killed at least six demonstrators across the country protesting the arrests of Wine and Wadri. Several journalists covering the demonstrations were beaten or arrested by authorities and had their equipment damaged or confiscated.

POLITICAL RIGHTS: 11 / 40
A. ELECTORAL PROCESS: 3 / 12
A1. Was the current head of government or other chief national authority elected through free and fair elections? 1 / 4

The president is directly elected to five-year terms. In the 2016 presidential contest, President Museveni won with 60.6 percent of the vote, according to official results. Kizza Besigye of the opposition Forum for Democratic Change (FDC) placed second, with 35.6 percent. According to international and regional observers, the 2016 elections were undermined by problems including the misuse of state resources and flawed administration by the Electoral Commission (EC).

In 2017, Parliament passed and President Museveni signed into law a constitutional amendment bill that removed the presidential age limit of 75, allowing the president to seek reelection in 2021. The amendment faced strong opposition by the public, opposition parties, and members of civil society, who argued that it could allow Museveni to become president for life.

A2. Were the current national legislative representatives elected through free and fair elections? 1 / 4

The 2016 legislative elections were held concurrently with the presidential vote. A total of 426 members of Parliament were chosen, including 289 elected in single-member districts, 112 elected to reserved seats for women, and 25 chosen to represent special interest groups (the military, youth, people with disabilities, and trade unions). Members serve terms of five years. The ruling party, the NRM, won an absolute majority with 293 seats. According to international and regional observers, the elections were undermined by problems including the misuse of state resources and flawed administration by the EC.

A3. Are the electoral laws and framework fair, and are they implemented impartially by the relevant election management bodies? 1 / 4

Independent observers, civil society, and opposition leaders have long critiqued and called for substantive reforms to Ugandan electoral laws. On election day in 2016, the EC experienced significant technical and logistical challenges, causing some citizens to wait for hours to cast their votes. The EC extended the voting time for polling stations that opened late, with voting in some areas continuing for an extra day even as counting was well under way. This fueled existing mistrust of the EC and raised suspicions of malfeasance.

Following the flawed 2016 elections, the Supreme Court ordered the attorney general to implement electoral reforms within two years and update the court on the progress of the changes. The deadline passed in March 2018 with no meaningful reforms advanced, and at year's end, no election-reform legislation had been passed.

In July, the EC suspended the Citizens Coalition of Electoral Democracy in Uganda (CCEDU), a prominent nongovernmental organization (NGO), from election observation and voter education activities. The EC claimed that the group is partisan and undermines the integrity of elections. However, after representatives from the CCEDU met with the EC in October, both sides indicated that they had reached an agreement to allow the group to resume its work.

B. POLITICAL PLURALISM AND PARTICIPATION: 5 / 16

B1. Do the people have the right to organize in different political parties or other competitive political groupings of their choice, and is the system free of undue obstacles to the rise and fall of these competing parties or groupings? 1 / 4

Opposition groups are hindered by restrictive party registration requirements and candidate eligibility rules, the use of government resources to support NRM candidates, a lack of access to state media coverage, state violence and harassment, and paramilitary groups that intimidate voters and government opponents.

In September 2018 some members of the largest opposition party, the Forum for Democratic Change (FDC), broke away to form a new party, the New Formation, which some observers argued will ultimately further fragment and weaken the position of the opposition.

B2. Is there a realistic opportunity for the opposition to increase its support or gain power through elections? 1 / 4

The ruling party dominates at all levels of government. However, there are numerous independents (although a number of them support the NRM) and several dozen opposition lawmakers in Parliament.

Presidential and parliamentary election campaigns are characterized by violence, intimidation, and harassment toward opposition parties. Opposition candidates are sometimes arrested on trumped-up charges of treason and other capital offenses. In August 2018, independent candidate Kassiano Wadri was arrested while campaigning for a parliamentary by-election in Arua, following the obstruction of President Museveni's motorcade (Museveni was campaigning on behalf of the NRM candidate) by opposition supporters, who threw stones at the vehicles. Security forces also shot at the car of opposition Parliament member Bobi Wine, who was campaigning for Wadri, killing Wine's driver. Wine, who is considered one of Museveni's most prominent opponents, was arrested along with Wadri, and both were allegedly tortured while in police custody. Wine, Wadri, and 32 additional defendants in the case awaited trial on treason charges at year's end. Despite the intense crackdown, opposition candidates managed to win five parliamentary by-elections in 2018.

B3. Are the people's political choices free from domination by the military, foreign powers, religious hierarchies, economic oligarchies, or any other powerful group that is not democratically accountable? 1 / 4

The military is closely aligned with Museveni and the NRM and holds 10 seats in Parliament. During the 2016 election period, the military and police services worked to dissuade any protests against the results, mounting a visible armed security presence with heavy deployments in and around the capital.

B4. Do various segments of the population (including ethnic, religious, gender, LGBT, and other relevant groups) have full political rights and electoral opportunities? 2 / 4

No group is systematically excluded from the electoral process. However, the dominant position and coercive tactics of the NRM impede free political participation and advocacy of interests by Uganda's various ethnic groups, including those affiliated with traditional kingdoms as well as smaller indigenous groups. An assessment of women's participation in the 2016 elections by the Women's Democracy Group, a coalition of Ugandan civil society organizations, noted a widespread perception that because a certain number of legislative seats are reserved for women, "they should not contest for direct positions so as to reduce on the competition for male contestants." Due to severe legal and societal discrimination, the interests of lesbian, gay, bisexual, and transgender (LGBT) people are not represented in politics.

C. FUNCTIONING OF GOVERNMENT: 3 / 12

C1. Do the freely elected head of government and national legislative representatives determine the policies of the government? 1 / 4

Power is concentrated in the hands of the NRM leadership, the security forces, and especially the president, who retains office through deeply flawed electoral processes. Lawmakers have little practical ability to influence legislation and government policies. The executive has pushed through legislation through inducement, harassment, and intimidation of the legislative branch. For example, in 2017, several opposition lawmakers were assaulted and forcibly removed from Parliament by plainclothes military officers during the reading of the constitutional amendment bill that removed the presidential age limit.

C2. Are safeguards against official corruption strong and effective? 1 / 4

Despite high-profile scandals, investigations, intense media attention, and laws and institutions designed to combat corruption, malfeasance continues and top government officials are rarely prosecuted for such offenses.

C3. Does the government operate with openness and transparency? 1 / 4

Many government departments deny requests for information under the country's Access to Information Act. Other laws related to national security and confidentiality also impede open access to information in practice. Public procurement procedures are generally opaque.

CIVIL LIBERTIES: 25 / 60 (–1)
D. FREEDOM OF EXPRESSION AND BELIEF: 10 / 16 (–1)
D1. Are there free and independent media? 2 / 4

Independent journalists face arrest, harassment, intimidation, and assault. In February 2018, journalist Charles Etukuri of the newspaper *New Vision* was abducted by security forces after the publication of an article connecting the Internal Security Organization (ISO) to the death of a Finnish businessman. Etukuri was held for six days before a court ordered his release. In July and August, while covering the campaigns for the parliamentary by-election in Arua and subsequent protests against the arrests of Wine and Wadri, several journalists were beaten or arrested by authorities and had their equipment damaged or confiscated.

Independent media outlets also risked suspension in 2018. In November, authorities shut down Unity FM, a radio station based in Lira, after it covered protests against the police's handling of the murder of a local child. Six staff at the station were arrested and briefly detained. The station reopened in December.

Despite these restrictions, independent journalists and media outlets are frequently critical of the government. There have been some improvements over the years in the legal protection of journalists, with leading journalists successfully turning to the courts to ensure that constitutional guarantees of freedom of expression are upheld. While spurious legal cases against journalists have continued, they rarely lead to convictions.

A directive issued by the Uganda Communications Commission (UCC) in March required "all online data communication service providers, including online publishers, online news platforms, online radio and television operators" to receive permission from the UCC to operate. Observers noted that the directive could further limit online speech.

D2. Are individuals free to practice and express their religious faith or nonbelief in public and private? 3 / 4

There is no state religion, and freedom of worship is both constitutionally protected and generally respected in practice. However, the government has barred religious leaders from engaging in political debates and restricted religious groups whose members allegedly pose security risks. A series of Muslim clerics have been murdered in recent years, and the investigations into the crimes had not yet led to any convictions at year's end.

D3. Is there academic freedom, and is the educational system free from extensive political indoctrination? 3 / 4

Academic freedom has been undermined by alleged surveillance of university lectures by security officials, and by the need for professors to obtain permission to hold public meetings at universities. In December 2018, 45 staff members at Makerere University in Kampala were dismissed for indiscipline, but critics argued that the dismissals were meant to silence critics of the government within the university.

D4. Are individuals free to express their personal views on political or other sensitive topics without fear of surveillance or retribution? 2 / 4 (–1)

Although private speech is relatively unrestrained and Ugandans openly criticize the government on social media, online communications are subject to government surveillance. In 2017, the government-appointed Uganda Media Centre announced that it had inaugurated a new unit that would scan social media websites for posts that are critical of the government, prompting concern from rights advocates

In July 2018, the government implemented a controversial social media tax, requiring users on a number of popular social media platforms including Facebook, Twitter, and WhatsApp, to pay a daily fee of $0.05, which is prohibitively expensive for many users. Critics assailed the tax as an attack on freedom of expression and an attempt to limit the exchange of criticism of the government and mobilization of the opposition online. According to the Uganda Communications Commission (UCC), the tax led to a decline in the number of social media users in the months following its introduction.

In November, President Museveni instructed the Uganda Revenue Authority (URA) to monitor all phone calls within the country, claiming that the government was losing significant tax revenue due to the underreporting of calls by telecommunications companies.

Score Change: The score declined from 3 to 2 due to increased surveillance by the government, including a directive by President Museveni instructing the Uganda Revenue Authority to monitor all phone calls for tax purposes; and efforts to curb criticism of the government on social media through the institution of a social media tax that is prohibitively expensive for many users.

E. ASSOCIATIONAL AND ORGANIZATIONAL RIGHTS: 4 / 12

E1. Is there freedom of assembly? 1 / 4

Freedom of assembly is restricted by the 2013 Public Order Management Act (POMA), which requires groups to register with local police in writing three days before any gathering, public or private, to discuss political issues. The police have authority to deny approval for such meetings if they are not deemed to be in the "public interest," and to use force to disperse assemblies judged unlawful.

In August 2018, security forces shot and killed at least six demonstrators in Kampala and other cities who were protesting the arrest and alleged torture of Bobi Wine and other opposition politicians.

E2. Is there freedom for nongovernmental organizations, particularly those that are engaged in human rights– and governance-related work? 1 / 4

Civil society in Uganda is active, and several NGOs address politically sensitive issues. However, their activities are vulnerable to various legal restrictions, burdensome registration requirements, and occasional threats.

Several NGOs that work on human rights issues have reported break-ins of their offices and burglaries in recent years, and the police have failed to adequately investigate the incidents.

E3. Is there freedom for trade unions and similar professional or labor organizations? 2 / 4

Workers' rights to organize, bargain collectively, and strike are recognized by law, except for workers providing essential government services. However, legal protections can go unenforced.

F. RULE OF LAW: 4 / 16

F1. Is there an independent judiciary? 1 / 4

Executive and military influence undermines judicial independence, as does systemic corruption. A July 2018 ruling by the Constitutional Court, which upheld the amendment that removed the presidential age limit of 75 and cleared the way for President Museveni to potentially remain in office for life, underscored the judiciary's lack of partiality. However, the court struck down a provision in the amendment that extended the terms of the president and Parliament by two years.

F2. Does due process prevail in civil and criminal matters? 1 / 4

Prolonged pretrial detention, inadequate resources, corruption, and poor judicial administration impede access to justice. Even amidst these challenges, however, due process prevails in criminal and civil matters in many instances.

F3. Is there protection from the illegitimate use of physical force and freedom from war and insurgencies? 1 / 4

Rape, extrajudicial violence, and torture and abuse of suspects and detainees by security forces are persistent problems, with few examples of prosecution of the perpetrators. The alleged torture of Bobi Wine and other opposition politicians in August 2018 led to widespread protests against police brutality. The government said it would investigate Wine's allegations of torture, but no charges had been filed at year's end.

The prison system is operating at more than twice its intended capacity, with pretrial detainees constituting much of the prison population.

F4. Do laws, policies, and practices guarantee equal treatment of various segments of the population? 1 / 4

The LGBT community continues to face overt hostility from the government and much of society. Homosexuality remains effectively criminalized under a colonial provision banning "carnal knowledge" among people of the same sex. Men and transgender women accused of consensual same-sex conduct may be forced to undergo an anal exam that Human Rights Watch (HRW) says could amount to torture.

Over a million refugees live in Uganda, and the government has been praised for its progressive asylum policies. However, it struggles to fund basic services for some refugee populations.

G. PERSONAL AUTONOMY AND INDIVIDUAL RIGHTS: 7 / 16

G1. Do individuals enjoy freedom of movement, including the ability to change their place of residence, employment, or education? 3 / 4 (+1)

Freedom of movement in Uganda is largely unrestricted, including for refugees, most of whom live outside of camps and have been able to move more freely in recent years. However, bribery is common in many facets of life, such as interacting with traffic police, gaining admittance to some institutions of higher education, and obtaining government jobs. Serious impediments to changing residence, employment, and education are largely financial.

Score Change: The score improved from 2 to 3 because individuals generally enjoy freedom of movement, including refugees, who have been able to move more freely in recent years.

G2. Are individuals able to exercise the right to own property and establish private businesses without undue interference from state or nonstate actors? 2 / 4

Customary land tenure is widespread in the north, and land disputes—some of them violent—are common, particularly when private development projects are at stake. Forced evictions sometimes occur in northern Uganda. In June 2018, 200 people from Apaa sought protection at the Office of the UN High Commissioner for Human Rights (OHCHR) after security forces allegedly burned their homes down. Residents returned home after a month, but forced evictions in the area have reportedly continued.

The law gives women the right to inherit land, but local customs sometimes trump legal provisions in practice.

G3. Do individuals enjoy personal social freedoms, including choice of marriage partner and size of family, protection from domestic violence, and control over appearance? 1 / 4

Domestic violence is widespread and underreported, and underage marriages are common in some communities. According to a UNICEF report published in August 2018, one in three women between the ages of 18 and 24 were victims of sexual violence as children, and more than 60 percent of young adults experienced physical abuse as children. In November, courts across the country began holding special sessions to address a backlog of thousands of rape and domestic violence cases.

G4. Do individuals enjoy equality of opportunity and freedom from economic exploitation? 1 / 4 (-1)

Poor enforcement of labor laws contributes to unsafe or exploitative conditions for some workers, including extremely low pay. Child labor in agriculture, domestic service, and a variety of other industries is a significant problem; more than two million children are estimated to be employed, and the issue is most prevalent in rural areas. Sexual exploitation of minors is an ongoing problem, as well.

Score Change: The score declined from 2 to 1 due to continued weak state oversight of employment conditions in the private sector and the ongoing prevalence of child labor.

Ukraine

Population: 42,300,000
Capital: Kyiv
Political Rights Rating: 3
Civil Liberties Rating: 4 ↓
Freedom Rating: 3.5
Freedom Status: Partly Free
Electoral Democracy: Yes

Note: The numerical ratings and status listed above do not reflect conditions in Crimea, which is examined in a separate report. *Freedom in the World* country reports assess the level of political rights and civil liberties in a given geographical area, regardless of whether they are affected by the state, nonstate actors, or foreign powers. Disputed territories are sometimes assessed separately if they meet certain criteria, including boundaries that are sufficiently stable to allow year-on-year comparisons. For more information, see the report methodology and FAQ.

Overview: Ukraine has enacted a number of positive reforms since the protest-driven ouster of President Viktor Yanukovych in 2014. However, corruption remains endemic, and initiatives to combat it are only partially implemented. Attacks against journalists, civil society activists, and members of minority groups are frequent and often go unpunished. Russia occupies the autonomous Ukrainian region of Crimea, which it invaded in the aftermath of Yanukovych's ouster, and its military supports armed separatists in the eastern Donbas area, where skirmishes continue to endanger civilians.

KEY DEVELOPMENTS IN 2018:

- Rights groups documented more than 50 attacks on activists and human rights defenders in the first nine months of the year. There were also a number of severe assaults by nationalist groups against the Romany minority. Investigations into these incidents generally took place only after significant pressure from civil society.
- Lawmakers and President Petro Poroshenko approved legislation to establish a long-awaited anticorruption court. However, domestic and international observers expressed concerns about the selection process for the 39 judges who would sit on the court.
- Intermittent fighting continued in Donbas. The United Nations reported that over 3,000 civilians have been killed since the outbreak of the conflict in 2014.
- In November, martial law was imposed in 10 Ukrainian regions for 30 days after Russian forces captured 24 Ukrainian sailors near Crimea. Provisions of the martial law decree allowed restrictions on free speech and assembly, but these were not invoked in practice.

POLITICAL RIGHTS: 26 / 40

A. ELECTORAL PROCESS: 9 / 12

A1. Was the current head of government or other chief national authority elected through free and fair elections? 4 / 4

The president is directly elected for a maximum of two five-year terms. After Viktor Yanukovych fled the country in February 2014, a snap presidential election was held that May. Petro Poroshenko won 54.7 percent of the overall vote and majorities in regions across the country. International observers deemed the vote competitive and credible, although polling could not take place in Crimea and separatist-held parts of Donbas.

A2. Were the current national legislative representatives elected through free and fair elections? 3 / 4

The 450 members of the unicameral Supreme Council, or Verkhovna Rada, are elected to five-year terms through a mixed system in which half of the members are chosen by closed-list proportional representation and the other half in single-member districts. Early parliamentary elections held in October 2014 were generally deemed competitive and credible, but voting was again impossible in Crimea and separatist-held parts of Donbas. Consequently, the elections filled only 423 of the 450 seats. The Petro Poroshenko Bloc won 133 seats, former prime minister Arseniy Yatsenyuk's People's Front took 81, Self-Reliance 33, the Opposition Bloc 29, the Radical Party 22, and Fatherland 19. Several smaller parties and 96 independents divided the remainder.

A3. Are the electoral laws and framework fair, and are they implemented impartially by the relevant election management bodies? 2 / 4

The current mixed electoral system for the parliament has been criticized as prone to manipulation and vote-buying.

Election monitors have expressed concern about courts' varying interpretations of electoral laws when faced with complaints regarding candidate registration and other topics, as well as about long delays in the adjudication of election-related cases. New electoral laws have sometimes been adopted in haste shortly before voting.

In September 2018, the parliament replaced more than a dozen members of the Central Election Commission whose mandates had long since expired. The new members were nominated by parties according to their parliamentary representation, but one seat on the 17-member panel, designated for the Opposition Bloc, remained vacant.

B. POLITICAL PLURALISM AND PARTICIPATION: 11 / 16

B1. Do the people have the right to organize in different political parties or other competitive political groupings of their choice, and is the system free of undue obstacles to the rise and fall of these competing parties or groupings? 3 / 4

With the exception of a 2015 ban on the Communist Party, there are no formal barriers to the creation and operation of political parties. A number of new political parties have appeared in recent years. A law that came into force in 2016 provides parliamentary parties with state funding, but the provision effectively favors established parties over newcomers.

B2. Is there a realistic opportunity for the opposition to increase its support or gain power through elections? 3 / 4

Opposition groups are represented in the parliament, and their political activities are generally not impeded by administrative restrictions or legal harassment. Newer grassroots parties have difficulty competing with more established parties that enjoy the support and financial backing of politically connected business magnates, known as oligarchs.

B3. Are the people's political choices free from domination by the military, foreign powers, religious hierarchies, economic oligarchies, or any other powerful group that is not democratically accountable? 2 / 4

Russia has been able to maintain influence over the course of Ukrainian political life through its occupation of Crimea, military support for separatists in the east, and imposition of economic sanctions on the rest of the country. Russian leverage within Ukrainian politics has declined since Yanukovych's ouster, though Moscow retains influence in some eastern and southern regions where the Opposition Bloc, a successor to Yanukovych's Party of Regions, performed well in the 2015 municipal elections. People living in occupied parts of Donbas are heavily exposed to Russian propaganda and other forms of control.

Ukraine's oligarchs exert significant influence over politics through their financial support for various political parties.

B4. Do various segments of the population (including ethnic, religious, gender, LGBT, and other relevant groups) have full political rights and electoral opportunities? 3 / 4

Women and members of minority groups are able to participate in political life in Ukraine. However, their voting and representation have been hindered by factors including the conflict in the east, illiteracy and lack of identity documents for many Roma, and rules against running as an independent for many local, district, and regional offices. Internally displaced persons (IDPs), of which there are over 1.5 million, face legal and practical barriers to voting. The Law on Local Elections mandates a 30 percent quota for women on party lists, but it is not effectively enforced. Societal discrimination against LGBT (lesbian, gay, bisexual, and transgender) people affects their ability to engage in political and electoral processes.

C. FUNCTIONING OF GOVERNMENT: 6 / 12

C1. Do the freely elected head of government and national legislative representatives determine the policies of the government? 3 / 4

Elected officials have demonstrated a capacity to craft and implement various reforms, though the process is ongoing and many initiatives stall due to opposition from powerful business groups and other special interests. Aside from the Donbas conflict, the main obstacle to effective governance in Ukraine is corruption.

C2. Are safeguards against official corruption strong and effective? 1 / 4

Corruption remains a serious problem, and there is little political will to fight it despite strong pressure from civil society. Anticorruption agencies have repeatedly been ensnared in politically fraught conflicts with other state entities and elected officials. While lawmakers and Poroshenko approved legislation in 2018 to create a long-awaited anticorruption court, at year's end the selection of judges was still under way.

C3. Does the government operate with openness and transparency? 2 / 4

Ukraine has made some progress in advancing transparency, for example by requiring that banks publish the identity of their owners, and by passing a 2016 law obliging politicians and bureaucrats to file electronic declarations of their assets. However, it is possible to bypass some regulations, in part because underdeveloped institutions are not fully capable of identifying and punishing violators.

A robust freedom of information law approved in 2011 is not well enforced.

CIVIL LIBERTIES: 34 / 60 (-2)

D. FREEDOM OF EXPRESSION AND BELIEF: 11 / 16

D1. Are there free and independent media? 2 / 4

The constitution guarantees freedoms of speech and expression, and libel is not a criminal offense. The media landscape features considerable pluralism and open criticism of the government. However, business magnates with varying political interests own and influence many outlets, using them as tools to advance their agendas. Poroshenko owns the television network Fifth Channel and has rebuffed press freedom groups' demands that he honor his earlier promise to sell it.

Authorities in 2018 renewed existing measures that bar a number of Russian news outlets from Ukrainian distribution networks and prohibit their journalists from entering the country. The year also featured growing pressure to limit publications in languages other than Ukrainian. The *Kyiv Post*, an English-language newspaper, warned that it and other outlets could be forced to close under a proposed bill that would require media outlets to produce Ukrainian versions of all reports and other materials. In September, the regional council in Lviv approved a measure banning the public use of Russian-language "culture products," including books and films.

Journalists continue to face the threat of violence and intimidation. The independent Institute of Mass Information registered 201 media freedom violations from January to November 2018. Of these incidents, 28 involved beatings or attacks, and 27 involved threats and intimidation.

Ukraine's courts and law enforcement agents sometimes fail to protect the rights of journalists. In September, a court granted a request by the prosecutor general's office to obtain information from a journalist's phone, including text conversations and location data, for a 17-month period. Earlier, in March, journalists and media experts accused the police of interfering in the work of the media and violating journalists' rights during aggressive removals of antigovernment protesters outside of the Rada. In February, journalists condemned police for performing an intrusive search of women journalists seeking to cover a court hearing at which Poroshenko was to appear via a video link.

The media environment in separatist-occupied parts of Donbas is marked by severe violations of press freedom, including censorship by the de facto authorities.

D2. Are individuals free to practice and express their religious faith or nonbelief in public and private? 3 / 4

The constitution and a 1991 law define religious rights in Ukraine, and these are generally respected. However, smaller religious groups continue to report some discrimination. Vandalism of Jewish structures and cemeteries continues, and in 2017 attackers reportedly threw an explosive device at Jewish pilgrims in Uman, though suspects were later arrested. Russian-backed forces in the Donbas regions of Donetsk and Luhansk have reportedly detained some religious leaders. In February 2018, separatist officials in Luhansk adopted a measure that banned religious groups not associated with "traditional" religions, which apparently included Protestants and Jehovah's Witnesses.

In October 2018, Ukrainian Orthodox clerics received permission from religious authorities in Istanbul, the historical seat of the Eastern Orthodox Church, to create their own "autocephalous" church and remove it from the canonical jurisdiction of the Russian Orthodox Church. A new Orthodox Church of Ukraine was formed in December to unite existing factions, and its autonomy was expected to be formalized in 2019. The Kremlin and church leaders in Moscow strongly objected to the move, and Ukrainian officials said they anticipated provocations, including disputes over church property. There were reports of Ukrainian intelligence agents searching Russian Orthodox churches and priests' homes, and of clergy seen as loyal to Moscow being summoned for questioning. However, the dispute did not meaningfully inhibit most individuals from practicing the faith of their choice.

D3. Is there academic freedom, and is the educational system free from extensive political indoctrination? 3 / 4

A 2014 law dramatically reduced the government's control over education and allowed universities much greater freedom in designing their own programs and managing their own finances.

A law adopted in 2017 was designed to align the country's education system with those in the European Union (EU), but it drew criticism for provisions that mandate the use of Ukrainian as the primary language of instruction in most publicly funded secondary schools by 2020, affecting numerous schools that currently teach in minority languages.

D4. Are individuals free to express their personal views on political or other sensitive topics without fear of surveillance or retribution? 3 / 4

Ukrainians generally enjoy open and free private discussion, although the polarizing effects of the conflict have weighed on political expression, and intimidation dampens free speech in the separatist-held areas.

E. ASSOCIATIONAL AND ORGANIZATIONAL RIGHTS: 7 / 12 (−2)

E1. Is there freedom of assembly? 2 / 4 (−1)

The constitution guarantees the right to peaceful assembly but requires organizers to give the authorities advance notice of demonstrations. Ukraine lacks a law governing the conduct of demonstrations and specifically providing for freedom of assembly.

Threats and violence by nonstate actors regularly prevent certain groups from holding events, particularly those advocating equal rights for women and LGBT people. In 2018, a few high-profile LGBT rights assemblies and events proceeded in Kyiv, Odesa, and Kryvyi Rih without serious violence, following significant international pressure on the government to allow them. However, many more were canceled or stopped due to threats or violence. In May, a major LGBT event in Kyiv was canceled just before it was to open, after far-right agitators arrived at the scene and threatened to attack participants while police stood by. In November, right-wing militants attacked participants in a transgender rights rally in Kyiv with smoke bombs and pepper spray. There were also reports of counterprotesters, allegedly with the aid of police officers, snatching away feminist banners carried by participants in a Kyiv march on International Women's Day. Police repeatedly insisted that they could not provide security for such events, despite adequate time for preparation.

Score Change: The score declined from 3 to 2 because right-wing extremists have increasingly used threats and violence to prevent or disrupt public discussions, meetings, and demonstrations.

E2. Is there freedom for nongovernmental organizations, particularly those that are engaged in human rights- and governance-related work? 2 / 4 (−1)

Numerous civic groups with a variety of social, political, cultural, and economic agendas emerged or were reinvigorated following the departure of Yanukovych in 2014, and many are able to influence decision-making at various levels of government.

However, in recent years NGOs have faced growing restrictions and threats of violence. In March 2017, Poroshenko signed a law that increased monitoring of NGOs focused on corruption by requiring their leaders, staff, and contractors to submit asset and income declarations. In 2018, attempts to nullify or relax the measure failed, and civil society activists began filing their declarations. Populist lawmakers then used the information to smear the groups as working to harm Ukraine on behalf of malicious "foreign agents." A so-called foreign agent bill that would impose onerous registration and other requirements on "agents acting under the influence of an aggressor state" was introduced in September. The bill, which enjoyed Poroshenko's support, effectively targeted Russian-backed groups, but it nevertheless raised concerns that civil society organizations with foreign grants could be affected.

Violence against civil society activists increased in 2018, with more than 50 attacks on activists and human rights defenders recorded in the first nine months of the year. Those under threat included anticorruption campaigners and defenders of the rights of LGBT people. In November, Kateryna Handzyuk, an anticorruption activist who monitored police activities in Kherson, died from injuries sustained when an attacker poured sulfuric acid on her months earlier. Mykola Bychko, a young environmental activist in Kharkiv who had organized campaigns against corruption and the pollution of local reservoirs by a waste treatment plant, was found hanging in a forest on the outskirts of his village in June. Bychko's death was considered suspicious by his friends and family and by other activists, but police refused to fully investigate the case and closed the probe at the end of the year.

Attacks on public events hosted by NGOs have contributed to an expectation among the groups that announcing plans for such events will result in threats of violence. The prosecutor general suggested in September that civil society activists brought attacks on themselves by criticizing the authorities.

Score Change: The score declined from 3 to 2 due to a wave of physical attacks on civil society activists and the authorities' failure to mount effective investigations and prosecutions in response.

E3. Is there freedom for trade unions and similar professional or labor organizations? 3 / 4

Trade unions function in the country, but strikes and worker protests are infrequent, as the largest trade union, stemming from the Soviet-era labor federation, lacks independence from the government and employers in practice. Factory owners are still able to pressure their workers to vote according to the owners' preferences. Some trade unions have limited or no access to oligarch-owned industrial enterprises in eastern Ukraine.

F. RULE OF LAW: 6 / 16

F1. Is there an independent judiciary? 1 / 4

Ukraine has long suffered from corrupt and politicized courts, and recent reform initiatives aimed at addressing the issue have stalled or fallen short of expectations. A competitive selection process for new Supreme Court judges was initiated in 2016, but it has since come under heavy criticism from civil society and other observers for a perceived lack of transparency and proper consultation, and for failing to weed out flawed candidates. The process will continue into 2019.

Poroshenko signed legislation in June 2018 to create a long-awaited anticorruption court. Following criticism from the International Monetary Fund (IMF) and the United States, the law was soon amended so that existing corruption cases would fall under its purview. Thirty-nine judges still had to be selected to serve on the new body. As with the Supreme Court appointments, concerns remain that provisions meant to ensure fair competition and screening of judges will not be followed.

In March, Ukraine's Public Integrity Council (PIC)—a body composed of civil society representatives that is tasked with advising the High Qualification Commission of Judges (HQCJ) about the ethics and integrity of judicial candidates—announced that it would withdraw from a wide-ranging judicial review process. The PIC said the HQCJ was ignoring its findings and that it had been "used to legitimize the needed result in the eyes of society and the international community."

F2. Does due process prevail in civil and criminal matters? 2 / 4

Although due process guarantees exist, in practice individuals with financial resources and political influence can escape prosecution for wrongdoing.

The government has made little progress in meeting domestic and international demands to investigate and prosecute crimes committed during the last months of the Yanukovych administration in late 2013 and early 2014, which included the shooting of protesters. The authorities have also failed to mount effective investigations into high-profile killings such as the murder of journalist Pavel Sheremet with a car bomb in central Kyiv in 2016.

F3. Is there protection from the illegitimate use of physical force and freedom from war and insurgencies? 1 / 4

Intermittent combat between Russian-backed separatist forces and the Ukrainian military continued in Donbas in 2018 and frequently endangered civilians. More than 10,000 people have been killed since the conflict began in April 2014, including more than 3,000 civilians, according to the Office of the UN High Commissioner for Human Rights

(OHCHR). The OHCHR has condemned a lack of institutional mechanisms to prevent and punish enforced disappearances, which have been reported during the conflict, particularly in its early years.

Outside of Donbas, there have been a number of high-profile assassinations and assassination attempts in recent years, some of which appeared to target political figures.

F4. Do laws, policies, and practices guarantee equal treatment of various segments of the population? 2 / 4

A 2012 law introduced a nonexclusive list of grounds on which discrimination is prohibited. Gender discrimination is explicitly banned under the constitution. However, these protections are inconsistently enforced, and the Romany minority and LGBT people experience significant discrimination in practice. Roma and LGBT people and groups generally only receive police protection or justice for attacks against them when there is intense pressure from civil society. Rights groups have reported that employers openly discriminate on the basis of gender and age.

Ukrainian nationalist groups actively targeted Roma in 2018. In one particularly severe attack in June, a 24-year-old man was killed and several people were injured, including a pregnant woman and a child, when masked men believed to be associated with a neo-Nazi group attacked a Romany settlement in Lviv. Authorities rarely open investigations into such violence, even when the perpetrators publicly claim responsibility on social media, the attacks are recorded by journalists, or police officers observe the incident. It was reported in June that one extremist organization involved in a number of attacks had received a grant from the Ministry of Youth and Sport.

G. PERSONAL AUTONOMY AND INDIVIDUAL RIGHTS: 10 / 16

G1. Do individuals enjoy freedom of movement, including the ability to change their place of residence, employment, or education? 3 / 4

While freedom of movement is generally not restricted in areas under government control, the ongoing conflict with Russian-backed separatists in the east has displaced many residents from their homes and hampered freedom of movement in those regions.

G2. Are individuals able to exercise the right to own property and establish private businesses without undue interference from state or nonstate actors? 2 / 4

The government has taken steps to scale back regulation of private businesses in recent years. However, the business environment is negatively affected by widespread corruption, and the parliament has repeatedly extended a moratorium on the sale of agricultural land.

In separatist-controlled areas, the de facto authorities have reportedly "nationalized" many enterprises and exert heavy control over business activities.

G3. Do individuals enjoy personal social freedoms, including choice of marriage partner and size of family, protection from domestic violence, and control over appearance? 3 / 4

The government generally does not restrict social freedoms, though same-sex marriages are not recognized in Ukraine. Domestic violence is widespread, and police responses to the few victims who report such abuse are inadequate.

G4. Do individuals enjoy equality of opportunity and freedom from economic exploitation? 2 / 4

The trafficking of women domestically and abroad for the purpose of prostitution continues. IDPs are especially vulnerable to exploitation for sex trafficking and forced labor.

Reports indicate that separatist commanders in the east have recruited children as soldiers and informants.

Labor laws establish a minimum wage that meets the poverty level, as well as a 40-hour work week and workplace safety standards. However, workers at times go unpaid, with wage arrears being a more acute problem in Donbas, and penalties for workplace safety violations are lenient.

United Arab Emirates

Population: 9,500,000
Capital: Abu Dhabi
Political Rights Rating: 7
Civil Liberties Rating: 6
Freedom Rating: 6.5
Freedom Status: Not Free
Electoral Democracy: No

Overview: The United Arab Emirates (UAE) is a federation of seven emirates led in practice by Abu Dhabi, the largest by area and richest in natural resources. Limited elections are held for a federal advisory body, but political parties are banned, and all executive, legislative, and judicial authority ultimately rests with the seven hereditary rulers. The civil liberties of both citizens and noncitizens, who make up an overwhelming majority of the population, are subject to significant restrictions.

KEY DEVELOPMENTS IN 2018:

- The UAE continued its hawkish approach to regional affairs with its participation in the war in Yemen and the partial blockade of Qatar, working closely with Saudi Arabia in both cases. Bilateral ties were further strengthened in June at the first meeting of the Saudi-Emirati Coordination Council.
- Also in June, state media published rare images of Sheikh Khalifa bin Zayed bin Sultan al-Nahyan, ruler of Abu Dhabi and president of the UAE, who had seldom appeared in public since suffering a serious stroke in 2014. Further appearances were reported in August and later in the year. There were no immediate indications that the president's reemergence would affect the position of his younger half-brother, de facto ruler Sheikh Mohammed bin Zayed bin Sultan al-Nahyan, or lead to any change in policy.
- The detention of a British doctoral student on espionage charges in May and his sentencing to life imprisonment in November marked a significant escalation in the authorities' assault on academic freedom. Amid diplomatic pressure on his behalf, the researcher was pardoned and released several days later.

POLITICAL RIGHTS: 5 / 40

A. ELECTORAL PROCESS: 1 / 12

A1. Was the current head of government or other chief national authority elected through free and fair elections? 0 / 4

The Federal Supreme Council, comprising the dynastic rulers of the seven emirates, is the country's highest executive body. It selects a president and vice president from among its members, and the president appoints a prime minister and cabinet. The emirate of Abu Dhabi has controlled the federation's presidency since its inception in 1971; the current president, Sheikh Khalifa bin Zayed bin Sultan al-Nahyan, succeeded his father in 2004. In 2006, Sheikh Mohammed bin Rashid al-Maktoum succeeded his late brother as ruler of the emirate of Dubai and as vice president and prime minister of the UAE.

A2. Were the current national legislative representatives elected through free and fair elections? 1 / 4

The unelected Federal Supreme Council is also the country's highest legislative authority, but it is advised by the 40-seat Federal National Council (FNC), which can review proposed laws and question government ministers.

Since 2006, half of the FNC's members have been elected for four-year terms by an electoral college chosen by the rulers of each emirate, while the government directly appoints the other half. The size of the electoral college has expanded over time; in 2015, it grew to more than 224,000 members, some 34 times larger than in 2006, though this still represented less than half of the voting-age citizen population. Voter turnout in the 2015 elections remained low, at 35 percent of those eligible.

There are no elected legislative bodies in the individual emirates.

A3. Are the electoral laws and framework fair, and are they implemented impartially by the relevant election management bodies? 0 / 4

The UAE's electoral framework applies only to the advisory FNC, and it lacks universal suffrage. While the electoral college has expanded, and overseas voting was permitted for the first time in 2015, there is no accountability for the procedures by which the rulers of each emirate draw up the lists of eligible voters. The geographical allocation of FNC seats results in significant overrepresentation for the smaller emirates.

B. POLITICAL PLURALISM AND PARTICIPATION: 2 / 16

B1. Do the people have the right to organize in different political parties or other competitive political groupings of their choice, and is the system free of undue obstacles to the rise and fall of these competing parties or groupings? 0 / 4

Political parties are banned, and all electoral candidates run as independents.

Since 2011, the UAE has aggressively cracked down on opposition activists, particularly if they are suspected of belonging to the Association for Reform and Guidance (Al-Islah), a group formed in 1974 to advocate for democratic reform. The government has accused members of Al-Islah of being foreign agents of the Muslim Brotherhood intent on overthrowing the regime, and designated the Muslim Brotherhood as a terrorist organization in 2014. Qatar's support for the Muslim Brotherhood has been a factor in efforts by the UAE, Saudi Arabia, and their regional allies to isolate that country since 2017. Dozens of activists, civil society leaders, academics, and students remained imprisoned during 2018 as part of the broader crackdown.

B2. Is there a realistic opportunity for the opposition to increase its support or gain power through elections? 0 / 4

The political system grants the emirates' hereditary rulers a monopoly on power and excludes the possibility of a change in government through elections.

B3. Are the people's political choices free from domination by the military, foreign powers, religious hierarchies, economic oligarchies, or any other powerful group that is not democratically accountable? 1 / 4

The political choices available to eligible voters are severely limited in practice, and the alignments of both voters and candidates are heavily influenced by tribal networks.

B4. Do various segments of the population (including ethnic, religious, gender, LGBT, and other relevant groups) have full political rights and electoral opportunities? 1 / 4

Approximately 90 percent of the population of the UAE consists of noncitizens who lack political rights and electoral opportunities, including thousands of stateless residents. There is no clear process for obtaining citizenship without Emirati parentage or marriage to an Emirati man; children of Emirati mothers and foreign fathers must apply for naturalization.

Women make up about 48 percent of the FNC electoral college, and 78 women ran as candidates in the 2015 elections. Only one woman was elected, and another eight were appointed by the government; one of them was named as speaker and president of the body, marking the first time that the position had been held by a woman. In practice, ordinary women have little opportunity to organize independently and advance their interests through the political system.

C. FUNCTIONING OF GOVERNMENT: 2 / 12

C1. Do the freely elected head of government and national legislative representatives determine the policies of the government? 0 / 4

Government policies are determined by the dynastic rulers of the seven emirates. The FNC performs only advisory functions and has struggled to arrange hearings with government ministers. In practice, policymaking authority has coalesced around the crown prince of Abu Dhabi, Mohammed bin Zayed al-Nahyan, since the titular UAE president suffered a stroke in 2014. The president, Khalifa bin Zayed al-Nahyan, began appearing more often in state media in June 2018, though there was no obvious change to the crown prince's de facto leadership.

C2. Are safeguards against official corruption strong and effective? 2 / 4

The UAE is considered one of the least corrupt countries in the Middle East, and the government has taken steps to increase efficiency and streamline bureaucracy. Nevertheless, there are no genuinely independent anticorruption mechanisms, and senior members of the ruling families are able to shield themselves and their associates from public scrutiny.

The collapse of the Abraaj Group private equity firm beginning in February 2018, several months after institutional investors questioned its alleged mismanagement of funds, highlighted regulatory and oversight weaknesses in the financial sector in Dubai that could also have implications for the strength of the country's safeguards against public-sector malfeasance.

C3. Does the government operate with openness and transparency? 0 / 4

The government generally lacks transparency, and despite legal provisions for access to public information, it remains difficult in practice. The State Audit Institution does not release public information about its reports, and its remit is limited to federal entities and state-owned companies, whereas most spending takes place in the individual emirates; the institution can conduct audits of an emirate's entities if asked by its ruler.

CIVIL LIBERTIES: 12 / 60

D. FREEDOM OF EXPRESSION AND BELIEF: 3 / 16

D1. Are there free and independent media? 0 / 4

The 1980 Publications and Publishing Law, considered one of the most restrictive press laws in the Arab world, regulates all aspects of the media and prohibits criticism of the government. Journalists commonly practice self-censorship, and outlets frequently publish government statements without criticism or comment. Media operate with more freedom in certain "free zones"—areas in which foreign media outlets can produce news content intended for foreign audiences—but the zones remain subject to UAE media laws and have additional regulatory codes and authorities.

Emirati-owned and UAE-based media outlets have participated actively in a government-backed media campaign against Qatar that began in May 2017. In June 2017, the attorney general issued a statement warning that anyone who showed sympathy or favoritism toward Qatar in any medium could be punished with three to 15 years in prison and a fine of at least 500,000 dirhams ($136,000) under the penal code and a highly restrictive 2012 cybercrime law.

A number of well-known commentators have been jailed in recent years for criticizing the authorities, expressing support for dissidents or human rights, or calling for political reform. In May 2018, leading human rights activist Ahmed Mansoor was sentenced to 10 years in prison for using social media to "publish false information that damages the country's reputation." He had been in detention since his arrest in March 2017.

D2. Are individuals free to practice and express their religious faith or nonbelief in public and private? 1 / 4

Islam is the official religion, and the majority of citizens are Sunni Muslims. The General Authority of Islamic Affairs and Endowments provides regular guidance to Muslim preachers; it and a Dubai counterpart appoint the country's Sunni imams. Shiite clergy have their own council to manage religious affairs. There have been some allegations of noncitizen Shiite Muslims facing discrimination or deportation in recent years. Christian, Hindu, and Sikh places of worship have been built on plots of land donated by ruling family members. Blasphemy is a criminal offense, as is proselytizing to Muslims by non-Muslim groups.

D3. Is there academic freedom, and is the educational system free from extensive political indoctrination? 1 / 4

The Ministry of Education censors textbooks and curriculums in both public and private schools. Islamic education is required in public schools and for Muslims in private schools. Several foreign universities have opened satellite campuses in the UAE, although faculty members are generally careful to avoid criticizing the government. At least 10 faculty members from New York University (NYU) have been denied entry to teach or conduct research at NYU's Abu Dhabi campus. Students, staff, and support personnel have also been denied entry. The UAE authorities have placed scholars and students who have criticized aspects of government policy on a unified Gulf Cooperation Council (GCC) security blacklist, barring them from the wider region.

In May 2018, a British doctoral student, Matthew Hedges, was arrested at Dubai International Airport after completing a research trip to the country. He was held in solitary confinement in Abu Dhabi for five months and ordered to stand trial on espionage charges. Hedges was convicted on November 21, after a trial that lasted five minutes, and sentenced to life imprisonment. Under international pressure, he was then pardoned by the UAE president five days later and promptly deported.

D4. Are individuals free to express their personal views on political or other sensitive topics without fear of surveillance or retribution? 1 / 4

A number of laws adopted in recent years give authorities broad discretion to punish individuals' speech on sensitive topics. The 2012 cybercrime law, which amended and replaced one passed in 2006, introduced lengthy prison terms for vaguely worded offenses such as damaging "the reputation or the stature of the state or any of its institutions." A 2014 counterterrorism law prescribes punishments including the death penalty for offenses like "undermining national security" and possession of material that opposes or denigrates Islam. A 2015 law against hate speech and discrimination contained loosely worded definitions and criminalized a wide range of free speech activities. These and other criminal laws have been actively enforced, including against ordinary social media users.

E. ASSOCIATIONAL AND ORGANIZATIONAL RIGHTS: 2 / 12

E1. Is there freedom of assembly? 1 / 4

The government places restrictions on freedom of assembly. Public meetings require government permits, and unauthorized political or labor protests are subject to dispersal by police.

E2. Is there freedom for nongovernmental organizations, particularly those that are engaged in human rights- and governance-related work? 0 / 4

Nongovernmental organizations must register with the Ministry of Social Affairs and can receive subsidies from the government, though they are subject to many restrictions. International human rights groups have been denied entry to the UAE. Local human rights activists are at serious risk of detention, prosecution, and mistreatment in custody.

E3. Is there freedom for trade unions and similar professional or labor organizations? 1 / 4

Workers—most of whom are foreign—do not have the right to form unions, bargain collectively, or strike. They can seek collective redress for grievances through state mediation or the courts, and the government sometimes arranges concessions and settlements. Workers occasionally protest against unpaid wages and poor working and living conditions, but such demonstrations are typically dispersed by security personnel, and noncitizens who participate risk deportation. Professional associations require government licenses and are closely monitored by the authorities.

F. RULE OF LAW: 3 / 16

F1. Is there an independent judiciary? 0 / 4

The judiciary is not independent, with court rulings subject to review by the political leadership. Judges are appointed by executive decree, and the judiciary as an institution is managed largely by executive officials. Many judges are foreigners working on short-term contracts.

F2. Does due process prevail in civil and criminal matters? 1 / 4

Detainees are often denied adequate access to legal counsel during interrogations, and lengthy detention without charge is not uncommon. Judges are empowered to extend such detention indefinitely. The mass trial of 94 political dissidents in 2013 was widely criticized for systematic violations of international due process standards, though serious violations have also been observed in other cases.

F3. Is there protection from the illegitimate use of physical force and freedom from war and insurgencies? 1 / 4

Authorities have been criticized by international human rights organizations for failure to investigate allegations of torture and mistreatment in custody. In 2016, the UN special rapporteur on torture found credible evidence that a group of Libyan nationals charged with—and later acquitted of—terrorism offenses had been tortured in UAE custody. Other detainees regularly report abuse by the authorities. Economist Nasser bin Ghaith, a high-profile detainee who had been sentenced to 10 years in prison in 2017 for social media posts that were deemed "insulting" to the UAE, engaged in a series of hunger strikes during 2018 to protest poor prison conditions.

Sharia (Islamic law) courts sometimes impose flogging sentences for offenses including drug use, prostitution, and extramarital sex.

F4. Do laws, policies, and practices guarantee equal treatment of various segments of the population? 1 / 4

Discrimination against noncitizens and foreign workers is common, and they are at risk of deportation for relatively minor offenses. Women face legal and societal discrimination on a variety of issues, including employment. Same-sex sexual relations can draw harsh criminal penalties, and LGBT (lesbian, gay, bisexual, and transgender) people are subject to widespread social stigma.

G. PERSONAL AUTONOMY AND INDIVIDUAL RIGHTS: 4 / 16

G1. Do individuals enjoy freedom of movement, including the ability to change their place of residence, employment, or education? 1 / 4

Emiratis face no apparent restrictions on freedom of movement within the UAE or on their type or place of employment, although under the country's *kafala* system, migrant workers' legal status is tied to their employers' sponsorship, meaning they can be punished or deported for leaving employment without meeting certain criteria. Stateless residents' freedom of movement is limited by their lack of travel documents; under a government program, many stateless people have received passports from the Comoros that ease travel and other activities but do not confer full citizenship. Societal norms sometimes restrict a woman's ability to travel without the consent of her husband or father. Qatari nationals have been barred from the UAE since 2017.

G2. Are individuals able to exercise the right to own property and establish private businesses without undue interference from state or nonstate actors? 1 / 4

The UAE has enacted reforms in recent years to ease procedures for establishing and operating businesses. However, the government and ruling families exercise considerable influence over the economy and are involved in many of the country's major economic and commercial initiatives.

Women generally receive smaller inheritances than men under Sharia, and women are excluded from state benefits aimed at supporting home ownership.

G3. Do individuals enjoy personal social freedoms, including choice of marriage partner and size of family, protection from domestic violence, and control over appearance? 1 / 4

Muslim women are forbidden to marry non-Muslims, while Muslim men may marry Christian or Jewish women. Women are generally at a distinct disadvantage under laws governing marriage and divorce. All sexual relations outside legal marriage are criminal offenses, which deters victims from reporting rape. No laws protect against spousal rape, and men are permitted to physically discipline their wives.

G4. Do individuals enjoy equality of opportunity and freedom from economic exploitation? 1 / 4

Foreign workers are often exploited and subjected to harsh working conditions, physical abuse, and withholding of passports with little to no access to legal recourse. A series of ministerial decrees issued in 2015 aimed to give migrant workers more flexibility to terminate employment under certain conditions. Foreign household workers were not covered by those decrees or by labor laws in general, leaving them especially vulnerable. A law adopted in 2017 guaranteed such household workers basic protections and benefits including sick leave and daily rest periods, though they were inferior to those in the national labor law, and household workers would still be unable to leave their employers without a breach of contract.

A competitive rivalry between Abu Dhabi and Dubai for eye-catching development projects masks deeper sensitivities in relations between these two emirates and the five less affluent emirates in the northeast. Economic disparities also persist among UAE citizens across the seven emirates and between citizens and the noncitizen majority.

United Kingdom

Population: 66,400,000
Capital: London
Political Rights Rating: 1
Civil Liberties Rating: 1
Freedom Rating: 1.0
Freedom Status: Free
Electoral Democracy: Yes

Overview: The United Kingdom (UK)—comprised of England, Scotland, Northern Ireland, and Wales—is a stable democracy that regularly holds free elections and is home to a vibrant media sector. While the government enforces robust protections for political rights and civil liberties, recent years have seen concerns about increased government surveillance of residents, as well as rising Islamophobia and anti-immigrant sentiment. In a 2016 referendum, UK voters narrowly voted to leave the European Union (EU), through a process known colloquially as "Brexit," which will have political and economic reverberations both domestically and across Europe in the coming years.

KEY DEVELOPMENTS IN 2018:

- In April, Home Secretary Amber Rudd resigned in the wake of the Windrush scandal, in which thousands of people who arrived in the UK from Commonwealth countries between 1948 and 1971 had been declared illegal immigrants in recent years; many were denied health coverage and housing, and threatened with deportation. At least 83 people may have been wrongfully deported.
- Also in April, a High Court ruling stated that the 2016 Investigatory Powers Act (IPA), which grants the government sweeping powers to access internet and phone records, did not comply with EU law due to inadequate oversight and provisions that allow authorities to obtain personal data outside of criminal investigations.
- At year's end, Northern Ireland had still failed to form a functioning government, nearly two years after elections to the Northern Ireland Assembly in March 2017.

- Reported hate crimes against immigrants and Muslims continued to rise in 2018, with some observers linking the increase to anti-immigrant rhetoric surrounding the contentious 2016 EU referendum campaign and a series of terrorist attacks in 2017.

POLITICAL RIGHTS: 39 / 40 (–1)

A. ELECTORAL PROCESS: 12 / 12

A1. Was the current head of government or other chief national authority elected through free and fair elections? 4 / 4

Executive power rests with the prime minister and cabinet, who must have the support of the House of Commons. The leader of the majority party or coalition usually becomes prime minister, and appoints the cabinet. Theresa May of the Conservative Party stayed on as prime minister following free and fair elections held in June 2017.

A2. Were the current national legislative representatives elected through free and fair elections? 4 / 4

The UK has a bicameral Parliament. The lower chamber, the House of Commons, has 650 members directly elected to serve five-year terms. Members of the upper chamber, the House of Lords, are appointed by the monarch, and the number of members, who do not have to stand for election, varies with time. As of 2018, there were 780 eligible lords. The body largely plays an oversight role in reviewing legislation passed by the House of Commons

While a general election was not due until 2020, Parliament in April 2017 voted to approve a call for snap elections by Prime Minister May, who sought to strengthen her position to negotiate the UK's exit from the EU.

The Organization for Security and Co-operation in Europe (OSCE) sent a limited mission to observe the elections, and in its final report offered relatively minor recommendations without questioning the integrity of the polls' results. The Conservative Party won 42 percent of the vote, which amounted to a loss of 13 seats, and resulted in a hung parliament. The Labour Party did better than expected, gaining 30 seats, with 40 percent of the vote. The Scottish National Party (SNP) lost 21 seats but still represented the third largest party in Parliament. The Liberal Democrats gained 4 seats, taking their share to 12 seats, and the conservative Northern Irish Democratic Unionist Party (DUP) increased its share of seats from 8 to 10. The Conservatives and the DUP forged an alliance whereby the DUP agreed to support May's minority government on key matters including Brexit and national security legislation.

A3. Are the electoral laws and framework fair, and are they implemented impartially by the relevant election management bodies? 4 / 4

The UK's electoral framework is robust and well implemented, though the limited OSCE mission that observed the 2017 snap polls urged lawmakers to consider reforms that could boost transparency surrounding campaign financing, as well as an annual cap on how much a single individual could donate to a party or candidate. As of 2018, no such limits are in place for donors.

The Conservative government has moved towards requiring voters to produce identification in order to vote. In May 2018, a pilot scheme was launched in five boroughs during local elections, and resulted in a small number of people being turned away at the polls. Further trials are planned for local elections in 2019, but a court case filed in December challenging their validity could derail the project. The Electoral Commission backs voter identification measures to prevent electoral fraud through impersonation, though some advocacy groups as well as the Labour Party maintain that it will discourage political participation among marginalized groups. Voter identification requirements already exist for elections that take place in Northern Ireland.

In September, the High Court ruled that the Electoral Commission had misinterpreted EU referendum laws, making it possible for the Vote Leave campaign to overspend during the 2016 Brexit referendum campaign.

Further evidence of Russian interference in the Brexit referendum emerged in 2018. In October, Twitter revealed that Russian trolls sent thousands of tweets encouraging people to vote leave around referendum day.

B. POLITICAL PLURALISM AND PARTICIPATION: 16 / 16

B1. Do the people have the right to organize in different political parties or other competitive political groupings of their choice, and is the system free of undue obstacles to the rise and fall of these competing parties or groupings? 4 / 4

Parties do not face undue restrictions on registration or operation. The Conservative Party and the Labour Party have dominated British politics for decades, though other parties regularly win seats in Parliament.

B2. Is there a realistic opportunity for the opposition to increase its support or gain power through elections? 4 / 4

Opposition parties operate freely, and have a realistic opportunity to increase their support and gain power through elections. The SNP supplanted the Liberal Democrats as the third-largest party in Parliament in the 2015 elections, a position it maintained after the 2017 elections.

B3. Are the people's political choices free from domination by the military, foreign powers, religious hierarchies, economic oligarchies, or any other powerful group that is not democratically accountable? 4 / 4

People's political choices are free from domination by powerful groups that are not democratically accountable, including the military, foreign powers, religious hierarchies, and economic oligarchies.

B4. Do various segments of the population (including ethnic, religious, gender, LGBT, and other relevant groups) have full political rights and electoral opportunities? 4 / 4

Under Britain's system of "devolution," the UK Parliament has granted different degrees of legislative power to the Northern Ireland Assembly, the Welsh Assembly, and the Scottish Parliament, augmenting the political representation of regional populations.

Women, LGBT (lesbian, gay, bisexual, and transgender) people, and members of racial or ethnic minority groups have been able to gain a political voice through their participation in the mainstream political parties. However, a government report released in February 2018 found that one in five staff working in Parliament had experienced sexual harassment in the prior 12 months. The report was published after numerous allegations of sexual harassment of women in Parliament by other lawmakers surfaced in late 2017, at least two of which prompted formal investigations.

C. FUNCTIONING OF GOVERNMENT: 11 / 12 (−1)

C1. Do the freely elected head of government and national legislative representatives determine the policies of the government? 3 / 4 (−1)

Britain's freely elected officials can make and implement national policy without significant influence from actors who are not democratically accountable.

Elections to the Northern Ireland Assembly took place in March 2017, but legislators had failed to form a functioning government by the end of 2018, breaking the record of 589 days previously held by Belgium for the longest time without a government. The initial source of the impasse involved corruption allegations in the renewable-energy sector, but longstanding disagreements on a number of issues between the two largest parties, the unionist Sinn Féin and the nationalist DUP, stymied negotiations to break the deadlock.

Score Change: The score declined from 4 to 3 due to the continued failure of Northern Ireland lawmakers to form a functioning regional government after elections held in March 2017.

C2. Are safeguards against official corruption strong and effective? 4 / 4

Large-scale corruption is not pervasive in domestic political and governance structures, and anticorruption bodies are generally effective. However, the UK is increasingly coming under scrutiny for the ways in which its banking and financial sectors, property market, and offshore services in overseas territories enable money laundering and facilitate corruption globally.

C3. Does the government operate with openness and transparency? 4 / 4

Members of Parliament are required to disclose assets and sources of income, and this information is made available to the public. The country's Freedom of Information Law is reasonably well implemented, and journalists have been able to access information under its provisions about topics of interest to the public. However, there are growing calls to extend the law's reach to private companies contracted by government departments and agencies.

CIVIL LIBERTIES: 54 / 60
D. FREEDOM OF EXPRESSION AND BELIEF: 14 / 16
D1. Are there free and independent media? 4 / 4

Press freedom is legally protected. The media are lively and competitive, and espouse viewpoints spanning the political spectrum. The state-owned British Broadcasting Corporation (BBC) is editorially independent and competitive with its counterparts in the commercial market.

In March 2018, the culture secretary announced that the controversial Section 40 of the Crime and Courts Act would not be implemented, and ultimately would be repealed. Section 40 stipulates that, in media-related court cases, publishers who are not members of a recognized self-regulator can be ordered to pay their opponents' legal costs, even if they win. At year's end, the section had not yet been repealed.

D2. Are individuals free to practice and express their religious faith or nonbelief in public and private? 4 / 4

Freedom of religion is protected in law and practice. A 2006 law bans incitement to religious hatred, with a maximum penalty of seven years in prison. Nevertheless, minority groups, particularly Muslims, continue to report discrimination, harassment, and occasional assaults. In October 2018, the Home Office released statistics that showed a 40 percent increase in the number of reported religious hate crimes in England and Wales for the coverage period between April 2017 and March 2018, compared to the same period in 2016–17. The Home Office partly attributed the rise to improved reporting mechanisms, but added that there was a spike in reports of religious hate crimes after a string of terrorist attacks in London and Manchester in 2017.

D3. Is there academic freedom, and is the educational system free from extensive political indoctrination? 3 / 4

Academic freedom is generally respected. However, the Counter-Terrorism and Security Act of 2015 requires schools and universities to work to prevent students from being drawn into terrorism by reporting any students suspected of extremism to a local government body, and vetting the remarks of visiting speakers, among other obligations. The program has raised concerns that open debate and academic inquiry is being stifled.

D4. Are individuals free to express their personal views on political or other sensitive topics without fear of surveillance or retribution? 3 / 4

Concerns about the effects of mass surveillance on free and open private discussion persisted in 2018. The 2016 IPA, known by critics as the "snoopers' charter," requires communications companies to store metadata on customers' activity for 12 months and, in some cases, allows this information to be accessed by police and other security officials without a warrant.

In April 2018, a High Court ruling stated that the government had until November to revise the IPA, as it did not comply with EU law due to inadequate oversight and provisions that allow authorities to access phone and internet records outside of criminal investigations. In September, the European Court of Human Rights declared in a landmark ruling that the UK's surveillance program violates the "right to respect for private and family life/communications" and lacks safeguards. In response to the High Court ruling, new regulations came into force in October, which allow authorities to only access communications data while investigating serious crimes, and require the approval of an independent commission to obtain such data.

E. ASSOCIATIONAL AND ORGANIZATIONAL RIGHTS: 12 / 12
E1. Is there freedom of assembly? 4 / 4

Freedom of assembly is generally respected.

E2. Is there freedom for nongovernmental organizations, particularly those that are engaged in human rights– and governance-related work? 4 / 4

Civic and nongovernmental organizations (NGOs) generally operate freely. However, groups identified as terrorist organizations can be banned, and there are concerns that the relevant legal provisions are broad enough that they could allow the ban or prohibition of legitimate associations and activism. In recent years, disclosures of surveillance of NGOs have drawn criticism.

A lobbying law adopted in 2014 concerning third-party campaigning was heavily criticized by NGOs for limiting the amount of money they can spend during election years.

E3. Is there freedom for trade unions and similar professional or labor organizations? 4 / 4

Workers have the right to organize trade unions, which have traditionally played a central role in the Labour Party. The rights to bargain collectively and strike are also respected.

F. RULE OF LAW: 14 / 16
F1. Is there an independent judiciary? 4 / 4

The judiciary is generally independent, and governmental authorities comply with judicial decisions. A new Supreme Court began functioning in 2009, improving the separation of powers by moving the highest court out of the House of Lords.

F2. Does due process prevail in civil and criminal matters? 4 / 4

While due process generally prevails in civil and criminal matters, rights groups and some figures within the judiciary have criticized severe cuts in legal aid under reforms that took effect in 2013, which left many vulnerable people without access to formal legal counsel. The cuts notably affected those with immigration-related cases, and parties to cases heard in family courts.

The 2015 Counter-Terrorism and Security Act has been criticized for giving excessive powers to police, including the authority to seize travel documents of individuals attempting to leave the country if they are suspected of planning to engage in terrorist-related activities abroad, and to forcibly relocate terrorism suspects within the country up to 200 miles away from their homes. In September 2018, the House of Commons approved the controversial Counter-Terrorism and Border Security Bill, which would make viewing terrorist content online punishable by up to 15 years in prison, and would allow law enforcement agencies to keep fingerprints and DNA of terrorism suspects for up to five years, even if no charges are ultimately filed. A final vote to approve the bill was expected in early 2019.

F3. Is there protection from the illegitimate use of physical force and freedom from war and insurgencies? 3 / 4

Following a string of deadly attacks in 2017, there was only one significant terrorist incident in 2018, in which a man hit and injured three people with a car at Westminster in August. However, the threat of terrorism remains a significant concern.

While prisons generally adhere to international guidelines, the problems of overcrowding, violence, self-harm, and drugs in prisons remain significant, and were noted by the chief inspector of prisons for England and Wales in his 2017–18 annual report.

In Northern Ireland, attacks by paramilitary groups have increased significantly in recent years. According to police statistics, violent attacks by such organizations increased by 60 percent between 2013 and 2017.

F4. Do laws, policies, and practices guarantee equal treatment of various segments of the population? 3 / 4

The contentious 2016 EU referendum campaign, which featured anti-immigrant rhetoric, as well as a series of terrorist attacks in 2017, seemed to contribute to increased hostility towards foreigners. In October 2018, the Home Office said there had been over 94,000 recorded hate crimes in England and Wales between April 2017 and March 2018, a 17 percent increase over the same period in 2016–17.

Immigrants and their descendants receive equal treatment under the law but frequently face living standards below the national average. Immigration laws that took effect in 2016 require landlords to check the immigration status of their tenants, oblige banks to perform background checks before opening an account, and make it a criminal offense for migrants to obtain jobs without appropriate paperwork.

In 2018, the Windrush scandal roiled British politics and spurred further debate about the treatment of immigrants and minorities. Thousands of people who arrived in the UK from Commonwealth countries (mainly in the Caribbean) between 1948 and 1971 had, in recent years, been declared illegal immigrants. Many were denied health coverage and housing, and threatened with deportation. Some were detained and denied legal counsel, and at least 83 people may have been wrongfully deported. In April, Home Secretary Amber Rudd resigned in the wake of the scandal. Responding to the outcry, the government introduced a scheme in May to grant citizenship to members of the "Windrush generation."

Asylum seekers and migrants can be detained indefinitely, and there have been persistent reports of poor conditions and abuse in immigration detention centers. The government has continued to hold children in immigration detention centers.

The authorities actively enforce a 2010 law barring discrimination on the basis of factors including sexual orientation and gender reassignment. While women receive equal treatment under the law, in practice gender discrimination persists in the workplace and elsewhere in society.

G. PERSONAL AUTONOMY AND INDIVIDUAL RIGHTS: 14 / 16

G1. Do individuals enjoy freedom of movement, including the ability to change their place of residence, employment, or education? 4 / 4

Citizens generally enjoy freedom of travel and choice of residence, employment, and institution of higher education.

As Brexit negotiations continued in 2018, the possibility that a "hard border" between Northern Ireland and the Republic of Ireland would again be imposed contributed to concerns that the movement of goods and people across the border would be curtailed, and that the tensions that fueled the decades-long conflict in Northern Ireland could resurface with the potential re-establishment of border checkpoints.

G2. Are individuals able to exercise the right to own property and establish private businesses without undue interference from state or nonstate actors? 4 / 4

Individuals may freely exercise the right to own property and establish private businesses.

G3. Do individuals enjoy personal social freedoms, including choice of marriage partner and size of family, protection from domestic violence, and control over appearance? 3 / 4

The government generally does not place explicit restrictions on personal social freedoms. However, in Northern Ireland, abortion is allowed only to protect the life or the long-term health of the mother, meaning most women seeking legal abortions must travel outside the region. In June 2018, the Supreme Court stated that Northern Ireland's abortion law was incompatible with the European Convention on Human Rights, but dismissed an effort to reverse it.

Same-sex marriage became legal in 2013 in England, Scotland, and Wales, but the Northern Ireland Assembly has blocked a similar change in Northern Ireland. The DUP, whose support allows Prime Minister May's minority government to survive, has consistently used its power to veto or obstruct legislation on marriage equality, even as polling has shown widespread support for same-sex marriage in Northern Ireland.

G4. Do individuals enjoy equality of opportunity and freedom from economic exploitation? 3 / 4

A 2016 report by a government commission expressed concern about the social and economic isolation of many members of ethnic and religious minorities, and of the poor. According to the Office for National Statistics, income inequality increased in 2018, a trend that was partly the result of a cut in government benefits. The 2015 Modern Slavery Act increased punishments for human traffickers and provides greater protections for victims. However, its implementation has been weak. Children and migrant workers are among those most vulnerable to forced labor and sex trafficking.

United States

Population: 328,000,000
Capital: Washington, DC
Political Rights Rating: 2
Civil Liberties Rating: 1
Freedom Rating: 1.5
Freedom Status: Free
Electoral Democracy: Yes

Overview: The United States is arguably the world's oldest existing democracy. Its people benefit from a vibrant political system, a strong rule-of-law tradition, robust freedoms of expression and religious belief, and a wide array of other civil liberties. However, in recent years its democratic institutions have suffered erosion, as reflected in partisan manipulation of the electoral process, bias and dysfunction in the criminal justice system, flawed new policies on immigration and asylum seekers, and growing disparities in wealth, economic opportunity, and political influence.

KEY DEVELOPMENTS IN 2018:

- The opposition Democratic Party took control of the lower house of Congress in November elections, which also featured contests for one-third of the Senate and numerous state-level offices. Turnout was the highest for midterm elections since 1914, and spending was the highest ever for US midterm elections.
- Among numerous other judicial appointments, President Donald Trump secured his second appointment to the Supreme Court in October, when the Senate narrowly approved Judge Brett Kavanaugh to succeed retiring justice Anthony Kennedy after a tempestuous hearing process in which Kavanaugh was accused of past sexual abuse.
- The administration took several steps aimed at tightening control over immigration that ran afoul of due process standards and both US and international law. They included an attempt to block asylum applications for those who cross the border outside official ports of entry, though that and other policies were being contested in the courts at year's end.
- The investigation into Russian interference in the 2016 presidential election made significant progress during the year, resulting in criminal charges against multiple Russian nationals and guilty pleas from several Americans associated with Trump's campaign.

POLITICAL RIGHTS: 33 / 40

A. ELECTORAL PROCESS: 10 / 12

A1. Was the current head of government or other chief national authority elected through free and fair elections? 3 / 4

The United States is a presidential republic, with the president serving as both head of state and head of government. Cabinet secretaries and other key officials are nominated by the president and confirmed by the Senate, the upper house of the bicameral Congress. Presidential elections are decided by an Electoral College, with electors apportioned to each state based on the size of its congressional representation. In most cases, all of the electors in a particular state cast their ballots for the candidate who won the statewide popular vote, regardless of the margin. Two states, Maine and Nebraska, have chosen to divide their electoral votes between the candidates based on their popular-vote performance in each congressional district. The Electoral College makes it possible for a candidate to win the presidency while losing the national popular vote, an outcome that took place in the presidential elections of 2000 and 2016. In 2016, Trump won the Electoral College vote, 304 to 227, while finishing nearly three million votes behind Democratic Party nominee Hillary Clinton in the popular ballot.

Unlike previous presidential elections, the 2016 contest featured a significant amount of interference from a foreign power. The US intelligence community has concluded that the Russian leadership carried out a broad campaign to undermine public faith in the democratic process, denigrate Clinton, and aid Trump's election chances. It included hacking of multiple targets, such as both major political parties and some electoral boards, as well as exploitation of leading social media platforms to spread divisive and misleading messages among US voters. Two 2018 reports commissioned by a Senate committee reinforced the intelligence findings, describing a massive Russian disinformation campaign designed to enhance the Trump candidacy and depress voting and other political engagement by Democratic-leaning constituencies.

Throughout 2017 and 2018, the Justice Department investigated the possibility that the Trump campaign had conspired or coordinated with the Russian government. The probe was overseen by Federal Bureau of Investigation (FBI) director James Comey until Trump fired him in May 2017. It was then taken up by Robert Mueller, the special counsel appointed by Deputy Attorney General Rod Rosenstein; Attorney General Jeff Sessions had recused himself from the matter due to his own involvement in the Trump campaign. Immediately after the November 2018 elections, Trump forced Sessions to resign, replacing him on an interim basis with Matthew Whitaker, the attorney general's chief of staff. The move raised concerns about fresh attempts to interfere with the probe, as Whitaker had criticized it before his appointment. Whitaker declined to recuse himself, but Rosenstein reportedly continued to oversee the investigation. The Senate was expected to consider Trump's nominee for a new attorney general in early 2019.

The White House repeatedly denounced the investigation as a baseless and politicized "witch hunt" during 2018, though the special counsel's team obtained indictments against more than two dozen Russian nationals for their alleged role in the 2016 interference, as well as guilty pleas from several Trump campaign associates for crimes such as attempting to obstruct justice and lying to the FBI—often to hide their contacts with Russians. Trump's former personal attorney, Michael Cohen, pleaded guilty to lying to Congress about a Moscow real-estate project that Trump's company pursued well into 2016, and in a parallel case, Cohen pleaded guilty to campaign finance violations related to payments he had arranged to silence two women who claimed to have had affairs with Trump years earlier. He told the court that he had arranged the payments at Trump's direction in late 2016 in order to protect his presidential candidacy.

A2. Were the current national legislative representatives elected through free and fair elections? 4 / 4

The Senate consists of 100 members—two from each of the 50 states regardless of population—serving six-year terms, with one-third coming up for election every two years. The lower chamber, the House of Representatives, consists of 435 members serving two-year terms. All national legislators are elected directly by voters in the districts or states that they represent.

The capital district, Puerto Rico, and four overseas US territories are each represented by an elected delegate in the House who can perform most legislative functions but cannot participate in floor votes.

Congressional elections are generally free and competitive, though partisan gerrymandering of House districts is a growing concern. In the 2018 midterm elections, the Republican Party retained control of the Senate with 53 seats, a gain of one. Democrats were left with 45 Senate seats, and there are two independent senators who generally vote with the Democrats. In the House, the Democrats gained 41 seats, winning a solid majority of 235 and reducing the Republicans to 199. Turnout exceeded 49 percent of the voter-eligible population, the highest percentage for midterm elections since 1914.

The quality of the voting and counting processes varied, as elections are administered by a patchwork of state and local authorities, but evidence of deliberate fraud was rare. One House race in North Carolina remained unresolved at year's end, as the ostensible winner, a Republican, allegedly benefited from a fraud scheme involving absentee ballots.

In response to the problems with security and foreign interference in the 2016 elections, a number of measures were taken to safeguard the integrity of the process in 2018. With some assistance from the Homeland Security Department, states attempted to upgrade voting equipment and monitor their systems for potential hacking. Social media companies, which had been criticized for failing to prevent foreign actors from using their platforms to fraudulently influence the political process, made an effort to delete fake accounts and otherwise thwart disinformation campaigns. However, many analysts argued that election security provisions remained inadequate, and foreign influence efforts reportedly continued during the election period.

A3. Are the electoral laws and framework fair, and are they implemented impartially by the relevant election management bodies? 3 / 4

Critics have argued that the Electoral College system for presidential elections is undemocratic, as it violates the principle that each citizen's vote should carry equal weight. Similar complaints have been made regarding the Senate, which grants each state two seats regardless of population. Defenders of these systems argue that they are fundamental to the United States' federal structure, in which the states enjoy a substantial degree of autonomy, and that they ensure due political attention to all parts of the country's territory.

While state borders are permanent, the borders of House districts are redrawn regularly—typically after each decennial census. In a practice known as gerrymandering, House districts, and those for state legislatures, are often crafted to maximize the advantage of the party in power in a given state. The redistricting system varies by state, but in most cases it is overseen by elected officials, and observers have expressed alarm at the growing strategic and technical sophistication of partisan efforts to capture state legislatures, control redistricting processes, and apply the latest data analysis to redraw maps. In 2018, the Supreme Court heard some cases on district maps but again declined to rule on the constitutionality of partisan gerrymandering. Meanwhile, voters in five states approved ballot measures that will place the redistricting process under the control of nonpartisan entities.

The midterm elections drew fresh attention to the fact that voting in many states is administered by elected, partisan officials who may be running for office themselves. The top election official in Georgia, Republican secretary of state Brian Kemp, made a successful run for governor, while Kansas secretary of state Kris Kobach, also a Republican, was defeated in his gubernatorial bid.

In January 2018, Trump disbanded the Presidential Advisory Commission on Electoral Integrity, of which Kobach had been the vice chair and de facto leader. The commission was established by executive order in May 2017, with a mandate to study and report on the registration and voting processes used in federal elections—particularly those that could lead to improper or fraudulent voting. The commission, which was not tasked with examining issues such as foreign interference or gerrymandering, was widely seen as an effort to follow up on Trump's unsubstantiated assertion that between three and five million votes were cast illegally in the 2016 elections, costing him the popular vote. The panel failed to produce any credible evidence of widespread fraud and was criticized for withholding information from its Democratic members.

B. POLITICAL PLURALISM AND PARTICIPATION: 14 / 16

B1. Do the people have the right to organize in different political parties or other competitive political groupings of their choice, and is the system free of undue obstacles to the rise and fall of these competing parties or groupings? 4 / 4

The intensely competitive US political environment is dominated by two major parties, the right-leaning Republicans and the left-leaning Democrats. The country's "first past the post" or majoritarian electoral system discourages the emergence of additional parties, as do a number of specific legal and other hurdles. However, the two parties' primary elections allow for a broad array of views and candidates to enter the political system. The 2018 midterm elections featured participation by ideologically diverse candidates across the country.

A number of independent or third-party candidates have influenced presidential races or won statewide office, and small parties—such as the Libertarian Party and the Green Party—have also modestly affected state and local politics in recent years.

B2. Is there a realistic opportunity for the opposition to increase its support or gain power through elections? 4 / 4

Power changes hands regularly at the federal level, and while certain states and localities are seen as strongholds of one party or the other, even they are subject to stiff competition and power transfers over time. After the 2018 elections, the Democrats held 23 state governorships, while Republicans were reduced to 27; Republicans retained control over a larger majority of state legislatures, though the Democrats made gains.

In an unusual development, outgoing Republican-led legislatures in Michigan and Wisconsin attempted to strip powers from executive offices that had just been captured by Democrats in the midterm elections. The efforts largely failed in Michigan, due in part to vetoes by the outgoing Republican governor, but the relevant measures were adopted in Wisconsin, where Democrats were set to become governor and attorney general. The Republican-controlled legislature in North Carolina had pioneered such moves after a Democrat won the governorship in 2016, leading to court battles that were ongoing in 2018.

B3. Are the people's political choices free from domination by the military, foreign powers, religious hierarchies, economic oligarchies, or any other powerful group that is not democratically accountable? 3 / 4

The influence of traditional party leadership bodies has steadily declined in recent decades, while various interest groups have come to play a potent role in the nominating process for president and members of Congress. This is partly because the expense and length of political campaigns places a premium on candidates' ability to raise large amounts of funds from major donors, especially at the early stages of a race. While there have been a number of attempts to restrict the role of money in political campaigning, most have been thwarted or watered down as a result of political opposition, lobbying by interest groups, and court decisions that protect political donations as a form of free speech.

Estimates for the cost of the 2018 elections easily surpassed $3.9 billion, making them the most expensive midterms ever, and the final total was expected to exceed $5 billion. As in other recent elections, much of the spending was routed through special "political action committees," or PACs, and other vehicles designed to minimize restrictions on donor anonymity and on the size and sources of contributions. Small donations made up an increasingly important share of candidates' fundraising, but a few extremely wealthy contributors played an outsized role in overall spending, with the top 10 individual donors accounting for more than $400 million.

Concerns about undue influence have also focused on lobbyists and other figures working for foreign governments who associate themselves with political campaigns. The Mueller investigation uncovered a number of cases of undisclosed consultant work for foreign powers and led to increased enforcement of the Foreign Agents Registration Act (FARA). Former Trump campaign chairman Paul Manafort and former Trump national security adviser Michael Flynn, who also worked with the campaign, are among those who have admitted to FARA-related violations since the probe began. Manafort had represented the interests of former Ukrainian president Viktor Yanukovych as well as Russian figures with ties to President Vladimir Putin prior to 2016, while Flynn worked on behalf of the Turkish government during 2016. Separately, one of Trump's personal lawyers, Rudolph Giuliani, continued to work as a consultant for various foreign interests in 2018 even as he represented the president in the Mueller inquiry.

B4. Do various segments of the population (including ethnic, religious, gender, LGBT, and other relevant groups) have full political rights and electoral opportunities? 3 / 4

A number of important laws are designed to ensure the political rights of racial and ethnic minorities. However, in 2013 the Supreme Court invalidated portions of the Voting Rights Act of 1965, a measure adopted to deal with racial discrimination in voting procedures. As a result, certain states that previously had to submit legal changes for preclearance by federal authorities were able to adopt election laws without prior review. A number of states, including some that were never subject to the preclearance rule, have rolled back innovations like early voting that contributed to higher rates of minority participation, or altered polling locations in ways that could disproportionately harm minority voters. Some have also enacted laws requiring voters to present specific forms of identification that may be cumbersome or costly to obtain—a provision that disproportionately affects minorities, elderly people, and those with disabilities.

Various state election-management policies in 2018 were criticized for having a disparate impact on minority voters. Under Kemp in Georgia, for example, the registrations of some 53,000 voters—most of them black—were stalled due to applicant information that did not exactly match government records, and hundreds of thousands of other voters had been purged from the rolls for failing to vote in recent elections. However, some states took steps to remove barriers that disproportionately affected minorities. Voters in Florida approved a constitutional change that restored suffrage rights to felons who had completed their prison terms, probation, or parole and were not convicted of murder or sex offenses, benefiting up to 1.4 million people.

The 2018 elections also demonstrated increased participation by women and minority candidates. The new Congress was set to include the first Native American women members, the first Muslim women, and record numbers of black, Hispanic, Asian American and Pacific Islander, and women lawmakers.

In a possible threat to the political rights of immigrant communities and their native-born relatives and neighbors, the Commerce Department announced in March that it would add a question on citizenship status to the 2020 census, despite expert warnings that the change would deter participation by many households. An undercount would have a range of negative effects, including a distortion of congressional reapportionment and of the allocation of government resources. Lawsuits aimed at blocking the added question were ongoing at year's end. Separately, the president said in October that he was considering an executive order to end "birthright citizenship," the right to automatic citizenship for all those born in the United States, but this would likely require a constitutional amendment.

C. FUNCTIONING OF GOVERNMENT: 9 / 12

C1. Do the freely elected head of government and national legislative representatives determine the policies of the government? 3 / 4

Hampered by partisan infighting and polarization, Congress has struggled in recent years to perform its various duties, particularly drafting and passing the government's annual appropriations bills. Instead it has frequently relied on short-term, stopgap spending measures to maintain government operations. After two brief shutdowns in early 2018, lawmakers made some progress, adopting five of the 12 appropriations bills using normal procedures. However, lack of agreement on the final seven in late December led to a partial government shutdown that was ongoing at year's end. President Trump refused to sign a stopgap bill unless it included sufficient funding to build a wall along the border with Mexico, his signature 2016 campaign promise.

The executive branch also continued to experience some dysfunction during the year. The Trump administration has been unusually slow in filling vacant positions across the higher levels of government departments and agencies, making it difficult for them to operate as intended by law. More than 250 of about 700 key posts requiring Senate confirmation remained without a nominee at year's end. The problem was exacerbated by an unusually high number of departures by senior officials. Those who announced their resignations or were dismissed by the president in 2018 alone included the secretary of state, secretary of defense, national security adviser, attorney general, UN ambassador, White House counsel, and White House chief of staff.

C2. Are safeguards against official corruption strong and effective? 3 / 4

The United States benefits from a number of strong safeguards against official corruption, including a largely independent law enforcement system, a free and vigorous press, and an active civil society sector. A variety of regulations and oversight institutions within government are designed to curb conflicts of interest and prevent other situations that could lead to malfeasance.

Since 2017, the Trump administration has presented a number of new challenges to existing norms of government ethics and probity. Anticorruption watchdogs criticized President Trump for shifting management of his real-estate development empire to his children rather than divesting ownership or establishing a stronger structural barrier between himself and his businesses. This lack of separation raised concerns that the president was using his office for personal enrichment, or that his official decisions were influenced by his private business interests; lawsuits that were ongoing in 2018 focused on a constitutional rule that forbids officeholders from receiving compensation, or "emoluments," from foreign governments, which Trump was accused of doing through his businesses. The president, his staff, and special interest groups of foreign and domestic origin all frequently visited and held events at Trump-branded properties in the United States during his first two years in office, generating publicity and income. Trump's decision to appoint his daughter and son-in-law as presidential advisers prompted similar concerns about their own business interests, as well as accusations of nepotism.

The Trump administration also notably undercut conflict-of-interest restrictions for White House and executive branch appointees. Although the president issued an executive order in 2017 that limited appointees' ability to shift to lobbying work after leaving government, the same order eased restrictions on lobbyists moving into government, and the administration initially resisted efforts to disclose waivers allowing appointees to skirt the rules that remained. In practice, many Trump nominees received such waivers. Journalistic and congressional investigations have routinely found conflicts of interest and other ethical violations among nominees and appointees, and key officials including the administrator of the Environmental Protection Agency (EPA) and the secretary of the interior stepped down amid ethics scandals during 2018.

C3. Does the government operate with openness and transparency? 3 / 4

The United States was the first country to adopt a Freedom of Information Act (FOIA) over 50 years ago, and the law is actively used by journalists, civil society groups, researchers, and members of the public. Government agencies' performance in responding to FOIA requests has been problematic in recent years, and a 2016 reform law was designed to ease disclosures. However, the Associated Press reported in March 2018 that responsiveness had declined during the 2017 fiscal year, which ended in September 2017, with applicants receiving either no records or redacted materials in response to 78 percent of requests.

The executive branch includes a substantial number of auditing and investigative agencies that are independent of political influence; such bodies are often spurred to action by the investigative work of journalists. Several inspector general posts across government remained vacant during 2018, though the offices continued to function under acting leaders.

Since assuming office, President Trump and members of his administration have frequently made statements that were either misleading or untrue, and typically failed to correct the record when such statements were challenged by the press and others. The *Washington Post* calculated that Trump himself had averaged more than 15 erroneous claims per day during 2018, for a total of more than 7,600 since he took office. The administration has also been criticized for operating with greater opacity than its immediate predecessors, for example by making policy and other decisions without meaningful input from relevant agencies and their career civil servants, removing information on certain issues—such as climate change—from government websites, and denying public access to logs of White House visitors. In a break with presidential tradition, Trump continued to refrain from releasing his personal tax records.

CIVIL LIBERTIES: 53 / 60
D. FREEDOM OF EXPRESSION AND BELIEF: 16 / 16
D1. Are there free and independent media? 4 / 4

The United States has a free, diverse, and constitutionally protected press. The media environment retains a high degree of pluralism, with newspapers, newsmagazines, traditional broadcasters, cable television networks, and news websites competing for readers and audiences. Internet access is widespread and unrestricted. While many larger outlets· have prospered, independent local sources of news have struggled to keep up with technology-driven changes in news consumption and advertising, contributing to significant ownership consolidation in some sectors. News coverage has also grown more polarized, with certain outlets and their star commentators providing a consistently right- or left-leaning perspective. The cable network Fox News in particular has grown unusually close to the Trump administration, with several prominent on-air personalities and executives migrating to government jobs since 2017, and key hosts openly endorsing Republican candidates or participating in campaign rallies ahead of the 2018 elections. Separately, major tabloid publisher American Media Inc. confirmed that it had participated in the scheme to suppress news of Trump's alleged extramarital affairs ahead of the 2016 election.

Since the 2016 presidential campaign, Trump has been harshly critical of the mainstream media, routinely using inflammatory language to accuse them of bias and mendacity. He has maintained a drumbeat of attacks on individual journalists and established outlets, describing them as—among other things—"fake news" and the "enemy of the American people." As of 2018 he had not followed through on past threats to strengthen libel laws or review certain outlets' broadcast licenses.

Despite increased hostility from political figures and their supporters on social media, the mainstream media—including national television networks and major newspapers—have devoted considerable resources to independent coverage of national politics. Outlets like the *New York Times*, the *Washington Post*, and CNN have conducted investigations into the business affairs of Trump and his associates, closely examined alleged contacts between the Trump presidential campaign and the Russian government, and regularly assessed the accuracy of the administration's claims.

A growing number of Americans look to social media and other online sources for political news, increasing their exposure to disinformation and propagandistic content of both foreign and domestic origin. The larger platforms have struggled to control false or hateful material without harming freedom of expression or their own business interests. During 2018, a series of major social media and streaming services decided to ban content from far-right conspiracy theorist Alex Jones and his InfoWars website, citing policies that prohibited hate speech and abusive behavior. Facebook and Twitter announced the deletion of hundreds of accounts linked to Russia and Iran that had apparently been used for fraudulent public manipulation efforts.

Serious cases of violence against journalists in the United States are unusual. In June 2018, however, five employees of the *Capital Gazette* in Annapolis, Maryland, were shot and killed by a man with a personal grudge against the newspaper. The gunman was in pretrial detention at year's end.

D2. Are individuals free to practice and express their religious faith or nonbelief in public and private? 4 / 4

The United States has a long tradition of religious freedom. The constitution protects the free exercise of religion while barring any official endorsement of a religious faith, and there are no direct government subsidies to houses of worship. The debate over the role of religion in public life is ongoing, however, and religious groups often mobilize to influence political discussions on the diverse issues in which they take an interest. The Supreme Court regularly adjudicates difficult cases involving the relationship between religion and the state.

Hate crimes and assaults based on religion are generally prosecuted vigorously by law enforcement authorities. FBI statistics have shown sharp increases in hate crimes linked to religious bias in recent years, with the bulk of incidents directed against Jews and Muslims. In an October 2018 attack, a man shot and killed 11 worshippers at a synagogue in Pittsburgh, Pennsylvania. The assailant, who was arrested, had a history of posting white supremacist and antisemitic messages on social media.

D3. Is there academic freedom, and is the educational system free from extensive political indoctrination? 4 / 4

The academic sphere has long featured a high level of intellectual freedom. While it remains quite robust by global standards, this liberty has come under some pressure in recent years. University students at a number of campuses have obstructed guest speakers whose views they find objectionable by shouting them down or holding strident and at times violent protests. In the most highly publicized cases, students and nonstudent activists have physically prevented presentations by controversial speakers, especially those known for their views on race, gender, immigration, and other sensitive issues. University faculty have also reported instances of harassment—including on social media—related to curriculum content, textbooks, or statements that some students strongly disagreed with. As a consequence, some professors have allegedly engaged in self-censorship. Separately, the American Association of University Professors has complained that the politicization of climate change and other scientific topics is contributing to a more hostile environment for those working in related fields, including instances of harassment.

D4. Are individuals free to express their personal views on political or other sensitive topics without fear of surveillance or retribution? 4 / 4

Americans generally enjoy open and free private discussion, including on the internet, though a number of threats to this freedom have gained prominence in recent years. Civil libertarians, many lawmakers, and other observers have pointed to the real and potential effects of National Security Agency (NSA) collection of communications data and other forms of intelligence-related monitoring on the rights of US citizens. A related debate about the need for and dangers of government restrictions on encryption technology remains unresolved. However, ongoing concerns about state surveillance have been partly displaced by new attention on foreign hacking, the sale or theft of personal data, and user intimidation on social media.

E. ASSOCIATIONAL AND ORGANIZATIONAL RIGHTS: 11 / 12 (+1)
E1. Is there freedom of assembly? 4 / 4 (+1)

In general, officials respect the constitutional right to public assembly. Demonstrations against government policies are frequently held in Washington, New York, and other major cities. In response to acts of violence committed in the course of some past demonstrations, local authorities often place restrictions on the location or duration of large protests. In August 2018, the National Park Service proposed charging fees and imposing other new rules for protests in Washington, DC. The plan was criticized by civil liberties groups and remained under consideration at year's end.

Protest activity was robust during 2018, with the Crowd Counting Consortium reporting over 1,700 events with up to 4.6 million participants in June alone. Large demonstrations were organized on topics including women's rights, immigration, and mass shootings at schools. The sorts of violent incidents that marred protests in 2016 and 2017, most notably the clashes between white supremacist marchers and counterprotesters in Virginia in 2017, were largely absent in 2018.

Score Change: The score improved from 3 to 4 because protests and demonstrations during 2018 featured less violence and fewer restrictions from the authorities than in the previous two years.

E2. Is there freedom for nongovernmental organizations, particularly those that are engaged in human rights– and governance-related work? 4 / 4

US laws and practices give wide freedom to nongovernmental organizations and activists to pursue their civic or policy agendas. Organizations committed to the protection of civil liberties, immigrants' rights, equality for women and minority groups, and freedom of speech have become more active since Trump's election, mounting campaigns and filing lawsuits to block actions by the administration that they considered harmful. A number of privately supported projects have also been established in recent years to address deficiencies in the electoral and criminal justice systems.

E3. Is there freedom for trade unions and similar professional or labor organizations? 3 / 4

Federal law guarantees trade unions the right to organize and engage in collective bargaining. The right to strike is also guaranteed, though many public employees are prohibited from striking. Over the years, the strength of organized labor has declined, and just 6.4 percent of the private-sector workforce belonged to unions in 2018. While public-sector unions have higher rates of membership, with 33.9 percent, they have come under pressure from officials concerned about the cost of compensation and pensions to states and municipalities. The overall unionization rate in the United States is 10.5 percent. The country's labor code and decisions by the National Labor Relations Board (NLRB) during Republican presidencies have been regarded as impediments to organizing efforts. Union organizing is also hampered by resistance from private employers.

In June 2018, public-sector unions were dealt a major setback when the Supreme Court, by a 5–4 majority, ruled that government employees cannot be required to contribute to unions that represent them in collective bargaining. The decision was expected to lead to further losses of union revenue and membership. Organized labor did score a modest victory when referendum voters in Missouri overturned a 2017 law that would have similarly allowed private-sector workers who benefit from union bargaining to opt out of paying union dues or fees. That left 27 states with such "right-to-work" legislation in place. The year also featured teachers' strikes over low pay and education funding in several states, with most winning modest concessions from state governments.

F. RULE OF LAW: 11 / 16 (−1)

F1. Is there an independent judiciary? 3 / 4

The American judiciary is largely independent. The courts have regularly demonstrated their autonomy during the Trump presidency by blocking or limiting executive actions. However, Trump has responded in some cases by verbally attacking the judges and courts responsible and accusing them of political bias. In November 2018, the president excoriated a federal judge at the Ninth Circuit Court of Appeals over an unfavorable ruling on asylum policy, and persisted in his public remarks despite a rare rebuke from Chief Justice John Roberts. Trump has also used his pardon power in a politicized fashion, overturning the convictions of several individuals whose cases were championed by conservatives, and has publicly discussed pardoning himself or other individuals caught up in the Mueller investigation.

Judicial appointments under Trump have raised further questions about politicization. Republican leaders in the Senate had stalled many federal judicial nominations in the final years of Barack Obama's presidency, resulting in an unusually large number of vacancies at the beginning of 2017. The most prominent was a seat on the Supreme Court that the Senate had held open during 2016 by refusing to hold hearings on Obama's nominee. In 2017, the Senate confirmed Trump's nominee for the position, Neil Gorsuch, but only after the Republican leadership changed Senate rules that had required a supermajority to end debate on Supreme Court nominations, allowing the confirmation to proceed with a simple-majority vote. By the end of 2018, Trump had filled 83 vacancies on federal appellate and district courts as well, a record for the modern era; this meant that one in six sitting federal appeals court judges were Trump appointees.

The president filled a second vacancy on the Supreme Court that was created by Justice Kennedy's retirement in July 2018. Trump's nominee, federal appellate court judge Brett Kavanaugh, faced a bitter confirmation battle after a woman came forward to accuse him of having sexually abused her while both were in high school. Kavanaugh denied that and subsequent allegations and was confirmed in October, with just one Senate Democrat joining Republicans to vote in his favor. During the confirmation hearings, the judge angrily denounced the campaign against him as a "political hit" orchestrated by "left-wing opposition groups," fueling doubts about his future impartiality on the bench.

In many states, judges are chosen through either partisan or nonpartisan elections, and a rise in campaign fundraising for such elections over the last two decades has increased the threat of bias and favoritism in state courts. In addition, executive and legislative officials in a few states have attempted to increase their control over state supreme courts, including through impeachments and constitutional changes.

F2. Does due process prevail in civil and criminal matters? 3 / 4

While the United States has a strong rule-of-law tradition, the criminal justice system has been criticized for a number of chronic weaknesses. Media reports and analyses in recent years have drawn new attention to the extensive use of plea bargaining in criminal cases, with prosecutors employing the threat of harsh sentences to avoid trial and effectively reducing the role of the judiciary; deficiencies in the parole system; long-standing funding shortages for public defenders, who represent low-income criminal defendants; and the practice of imposing court fees or fines for minor offenses as a means of raising local budget revenues, which can lead to jail terms for those who are unable to pay.

These problems and evolving enforcement and sentencing policies have contributed to major increases in incarceration over time. The population of sentenced state and federal prisoners soared from about 200,000 in 1970 to some 1.5 million as of 2016. The incarceration rate based on such counts rose from around 100 per 100,000 people in 1970 to a peak of more than 500 in the 2000s, then slipped to 450 as of 2016. There are also hundreds of thousands of pretrial detainees behind bars. Black and Hispanic inmates account for a majority of the prison population, despite representing around a third of the US population combined. Researchers and criminal justice professionals have reached a broad consensus that this level of incarceration is not needed to preserve public safety. Civil liberties organizations and other groups have also argued that prison sentences are often excessive and that too many people are incarcerated for minor drug offenses.

In December 2018, under pressure from a bipartisan coalition advocating for reforms to curb mass incarceration, Congress passed and the president signed a law that eased federal mandatory-minimum sentencing rules, among other modest changes. A majority of states have also passed laws in recent years to reduce sentences for certain crimes, decriminalize minor drug offenses, and combat recidivism.

F3. Is there protection from the illegitimate use of physical force and freedom from war and insurgencies? 3 / 4

Mass shootings remained a concern during 2018, though the overall US homicide rate, 5.3 per 100,000 inhabitants as of 2017, is relatively low by regional and historical standards, and crime rates generally have been in decline since the 1990s. Among the year's deadliest shootings were a rampage at a California bar that killed 13 people in November and two high school attacks that killed 10 people in Santa Fe, Texas, in May, and 17 people in Parkland, Florida, in February. In October, a Florida man was arrested for allegedly sending pipe bombs through the mail to a group of prominent critics of President Trump. None of the devices detonated.

The increased policy focus on the criminal justice system in recent years has coincided with a series of widely publicized incidents in which police actions led to the deaths of suspects, many of whom belonged to racial and ethnic minorities. When officers involved in fatal shootings have been brought to trial, the cases have typically ended in acquittals or sentences on reduced charges. In 2018, however, former police officers in Dallas and Chicago were convicted of murder for the killing of black men while on duty. The Trump administration has pulled back from previous Justice Department policies aimed at imposing reforms on troubled local police departments through court-approved agreements. Then attorney general Sessions argued that federal interventions in local crime-fighting efforts could harm police morale and safety.

Use of the death penalty has declined significantly in recent years. There were 25 executions across eight states in 2018—up from 23 in 2017 but down from a peak of 98 in 1999. The death penalty has been formally abolished by 20 states; in another 17 states where it remains on the books, executions have not been carried out for the past five years or more. In 2018, the Supreme Court of Washington State found that the death penalty violated the state constitution. The most recent federal execution was in 2003. Of particular importance in this downward trend have been the exoneration of some death-row inmates based on new DNA testing, states' inability to obtain chemicals used in lethal injections due to objections from producers, and legal challenges to the constitutionality of the prevailing methods of lethal injection. The US Supreme Court has effectively ruled out the death penalty for crimes other than murder and in cases where the perpetrator is a juvenile or mentally disabled, among other restrictions.

F4. Do laws, policies, and practices guarantee equal treatment of various segments of the population? 2 / 4 (−1)

An array of policies and programs are designed to protect the rights of individuals against discrimination based on race, ethnicity, gender, and other categories, including in the workplace. Women and some minority groups continue to suffer from disparities in various social indicators and overall economic standing. For example, although women constitute almost half of the US workforce and are well represented in many professions, the average compensation for female workers is roughly 80 percent of that for male workers, a gap that has remained relatively constant over the past several decades. Women also face other employment obstacles. A popular social media campaign that began in late 2017, dubbed the #MeToo movement, encouraged victims of sexual harassment and assault in the workplace—mainly women—to speak out about their experiences. The phenomenon has led to the sudden downfall of many powerful men in the worlds of politics, business, news, and entertainment, but it also underscored the scale of the problem in American society.

Federal antidiscrimination legislation does not explicitly include LGBT (lesbian, gay, bisexual, and transgender) people as a protected class, though many states have enacted such protections, and recent administrations have attempted to expand LGBT rights through administrative orders. For instance, the government bans discrimination based on sexual orientation or gender identity in federal employment and among federal contractors. The Trump administration reversed a 2016 guidance document that had directed schools to allow transgender students to use bathrooms and other facilities matching their gender identity, and has argued that existing legal protections against sex discrimination do not cover sexual orientation or gender identity, as some courts and government agencies have claimed. In 2017, Trump announced a ban on transgender people serving in the military, but it had not taken effect as of late 2018 due to challenges in federal court.

The Trump administration has made a series of decisions and proposals meant to reduce the number of asylum seekers, refugees, and undocumented immigrants entering and residing in the country, usually citing exaggerated security concerns as justification. The moves have in many cases been hasty, uncoordinated, and underfunded, leading to implementation problems as well as conflicts with existing laws, constitutional protections, and international human rights standards.

Beginning soon after his inauguration in January 2017, the president issued a series of three executive orders barring travel from a group of Muslim-majority countries on security grounds, twice revising the original order in response to lawsuits claiming that the bans were blatantly discriminatory. In June 2018, the Supreme Court upheld the third version, which banned most entries by citizens of Iran, Syria, Yemen, Libya, Somalia, and one non-Muslim country, North Korea. These orders, combined with other administration changes, helped to sharply reduce the number of refugees admitted to the United States for resettlement. The cap for the 2018 fiscal year was set at 45,000, the lowest since the resettlement program began in 1980, but fewer than 22,500 were admitted in practice. The cap for fiscal 2019 was set at 30,000. These reductions were accompanied by precipitous drops in both the number and percentage of admitted refugees who are Muslim; admissions of Middle Eastern Christian refugees also declined dramatically, even as the proportion of accepted refugees who are European rapidly increased.

The administration has sought to deter the growing number of Central Americans, often families with children, arriving at the southern border and applying for asylum in the United States. In 2018, US authorities pursued a "zero tolerance" policy of criminally prosecuting all adults who crossed the border irregularly, even if they were seeking asylum as permitted under US and international law. As a result, thousands of children were separated from their detained adult family members in a haphazard manner; after a public outcry and legal challenges, the president issued an order in June calling for such families to be kept together. Abrupt mass releases were later reported as family detention and shelter systems were overwhelmed. Meanwhile, children traveling alone were held in federal custody in record numbers and for longer periods, due in large part to a June policy requiring everyone in the household of a potential sponsor—usually a relative already in the United States—to be fingerprinted before a child was released to them. The policy was eased in December, by which time there were more than 14,000 children in government shelters. Separately, in June, the attorney general issued a ruling that asylum claims based on domestic violence or gang violence by nonstate actors should generally be considered invalid; a federal judge struck down the ruling in December. In November, a federal court blocked an administration attempt to automatically reject asylum bids by people who cross the border irregularly rather than applying at an official port of entry. Other government practices—including the "zero tolerance" prosecution policy and restrictions on the number of asylum seekers allowed to be processed at official entry points each day, known as "metering"—had already contributed to large backlogs of would-be applicants gathered in poor living conditions on the Mexican side of the border. In late December, the administration announced a plan to force asylum seekers to wait in Mexico until they received a ruling on their cases.

The administration has attempted to ramp up arrests and deportations of both undocumented immigrants, regardless of whether they had committed crimes, and legal immigrants or refugees who committed crimes in the United States, even if they had long since completed their sentences. The previous practice had been to focus deportation efforts on the most dangerous criminal aliens with the weakest ties to American communities. The new enforcement drive added to an existing backlog of cases in immigration courts; there were more than 800,000 pending cases as of November 2018, a 49 percent increase since Trump took office. The number of people in immigration detention was at record levels in 2018, with more than 40,000 people in custody at any given time. In August, a federal judge rejected an administration effort to end the Deferred Action for Childhood Arrivals (DACA) program, which prevents the deportation of undocumented immigrants who were brought to the United States as children.

Score Change: The score declined from 3 to 2 due to government policies and actions that improperly restricted the legal rights of asylum seekers, signs of discrimination in the acceptance of refugees for resettlement, and excessively harsh or haphazard immigration enforcement policies that resulted in the separation of children from adult family members, among other problematic outcomes.

G. PERSONAL AUTONOMY AND INDIVIDUAL RIGHTS: 15 / 16

G1. Do individuals enjoy freedom of movement, including the ability to change their place of residence, employment, or education? 4 / 4

There are no significant restrictions on freedom of movement within the United States, and residents are generally free to travel abroad without undue obstacles.

G2. Are individuals able to exercise the right to own property and establish private businesses without undue interference from state or nonstate actors? 4 / 4

Property rights are widely respected in the United States. The legal and political environments are supportive of entrepreneurial activity and business ownership, which have contributed to the relatively successful integration of immigrants into American society.

G3. Do individuals enjoy personal social freedoms, including choice of marriage partner and size of family, protection from domestic violence, and control over appearance? 4 / 4

Men and women generally enjoy equal rights in divorce and custody proceedings, and there are no undue restrictions on choice of marriage partner, particularly after a 2015 Supreme Court ruling that all states must allow same-sex marriage. The practice had already become legal in most states through court decisions, legislative action, or referendums. In recent years, a growing number of states have passed laws to eliminate exemptions that allow marriages of people under age 18 in certain circumstances. Rape and domestic violence remain serious problems, and the applicable laws vary somewhat by state, though spousal rape is a crime nationwide. Numerous government and nongovernmental programs are designed to combat such violence and assist victims. In the past several years, a series of new state laws have reduced women's access to abortion without overtly breaching prior Supreme Court decisions on the issue, and some have survived judicial scrutiny, adding to state-by-state variation in access.

G4. Do individuals enjoy equality of opportunity and freedom from economic exploitation? 3 / 4

The "American dream"—the notion of a fair society in which hard work will bring economic and social advancement, regardless of the circumstances of one's birth—is a core part of the country's identity, and voters tend to favor government policies that enhance equality of opportunity. In recent decades, however, studies have shown a widening inequality in wealth and a narrowing of access to upward mobility. One key aspect of inequality is the growing economic gap between Americans with university degrees and those with a high school degree or less; the number of well-compensated jobs for the less-educated has fallen over time as manufacturing and other positions are lost to automation and foreign competition, and successive governments have failed to improve access to education and training in response. Many states and municipalities have enacted substantial hikes in the minimum wage, and this trend continued in 2018, but workers face a variety of obstacles to stable and remunerative employment, including inadequate public transportation, high costs of living in economically dynamic regions, and a preference among many companies for fragmented and unpredictable shift work. Inequality remained a major problem even as the national unemployment rate fell below 4 percent during the year, reaching its lowest levels in decades.

Uruguay

Population: 3,500,000
Capital: Montevideo
Political Rights Rating: 1
Civil Liberties Rating: 1
Freedom Rating: 1.0
Freedom Status: Free
Electoral Democracy: Yes

Overview: Uruguay has a historically strong democratic governance structure and a positive record of upholding political rights and civil liberties while also working toward social inclusion. Although all citizens enjoy legal equality, there are still disparities in treatment and political representation for women, transgender people, Uruguayans of African descent, and the indigenous population.

KEY DEVELOPMENTS IN 2018:

- Courts ruled that former vice president Raúl Sendic should be prosecuted on charges of embezzlement and abuse of office during his time as head of the state oil group.
- On several occasions early in the year, farmers and other workers staged antigovernment protests at which they demanded government assistance for their industries, including cuts in fuel and electricity prices, and modifications to trade agreements and monetary policy.
- Lawmakers approved a bill allowing transgender people to change relevant information on their identification documents. The law also allows minors to have gender reassignment hormone therapy without parental or guardian permission, and set aside funds meant to ensure that transgender people have access to education and health care, and to provide pensions for transgender people who were persecuted by the country's 1973–85 military dictatorship.

POLITICAL RIGHTS: 40 / 40
A. ELECTORAL PROCESS: 12 / 12
A1. Was the current head of government or other chief national authority elected through free and fair elections? 4 / 4

The president is directly elected to a five-year term, and may hold nonconsecutive terms. The most recent general elections were held in 2014. The Tabaré Vázquez–Raúl Sendic ticket of the Frente Amplio captured the presidency and vice-presidency after a run-off. The elections took place peacefully and stakeholders accepted their results.

Sendic resigned in 2017 amid a probe into his alleged misuse of a corporate credit card while head of a state-run oil company. Lucia Topolansky, a senator, assumed the vice presidency under constitutional procedures, and became the first woman to hold the post.

A2. Were the current national legislative representatives elected through free and fair elections? 4 / 4

The bicameral General Assembly consists of the 99-member Chamber of Representatives and the 30-member Senate, with all members directly elected for five-year terms. In the 2014 elections, the Frente Amplio retained a majority in the parliament, winning 50 seats in the Chamber of Representatives and 15 seats in the Senate. The elections took place peacefully, and stakeholders accepted their results.

A3. Are the electoral laws and framework fair, and are they implemented impartially by the relevant election management bodies? 4 / 4

Uruguay's Electoral Court serves as the highest authority on elections and supervises the National Electoral Office, which oversees voter registration and has one office in each of the country's regional departments. Electoral laws are generally fair, and the Electoral Court, whose nine members are elected by both houses of Parliament with a two-thirds majority, is generally viewed as impartial. Voting is compulsory.

B. POLITICAL PLURALISM AND PARTICIPATION: 16 / 16

B1. Do the people have the right to organize in different political parties or other competitive political groupings of their choice, and is the system free of undue obstacles to the rise and fall of these competing parties or groupings? 4 / 4

Uruguay's multiparty system is open and competitive. The major political groupings are the Colorado Party, the National Party (also known as Blanco), the Independent Party, and the Frente Amplio coalition, which is currently in power.

B2. Is there a realistic opportunity for the opposition to increase its support or gain power through elections? 4 / 4

Opposition parties are regularly competitive in the national elections.

B3. Are the people's political choices free from domination by the military, foreign powers, religious hierarchies, economic oligarchies, or any other powerful group that is not democratically accountable? 4 / 4

People's political choices are generally free from undue influence from undemocratic actors.

B4. Do various segments of the population (including ethnic, religious, gender, LGBT, and other relevant groups) have full political rights and electoral opportunities? 4 / 4

The Afro-Uruguayan minority, comprising approximately 8 percent of the population, is significantly underrepresented in government and professional jobs. Indigenous peoples are also severely underrepresented, although there is a currently a grassroots campaign that aims to gain formal government recognition of the indigenous Charrúa people.

Representation of women in national, regional, and local government is low, though women hold about 20 percent of seats in the legislature and a number of mayorships. A gender quota system was implemented for the first time in the 2014 national elections to increase the participation of women as candidates.

C. FUNCTIONING OF GOVERNMENT: 12 / 12

C1. Do the freely elected head of government and national legislative representatives determine the policies of the government? 4 / 4

The head of government and national legislature determine the policies of the government without undue interference.

C2. Are safeguards against official corruption strong and effective? 4 / 4

The level of corruption in Uruguay is relatively low by regional standards.

In May 2018, a judge ruled that former vice president Sendic should be prosecuted on charges of embezzlement and abuse of office during his time as head of the state oil group, and an appeals court confirmed the ruling in December.

C3. Does the government operate with openness and transparency? 4 / 4

Government institutions have established a robust record of accountability to the electorate. Enforcement of the Transparency Law, which prohibits a range of offenses related to abuse of office, is relatively strong at the national level.

CIVIL LIBERTIES: 58 / 60
D. FREEDOM OF EXPRESSION AND BELIEF: 16 / 16
D1. Are there free and independent media? 4 / 4

Constitutional guarantees regarding free expression are generally respected. The press is privately owned; the broadcast sector includes both commercial and public outlets. There are numerous daily and weekly newspapers, some of which are connected to political parties. A study of media in Uruguay released in December 2017 by a coalition of international and local researchers found that ownership of outlets was heavily concentrated among three main media groups.

Despite the relatively open media environment, there have been some reports of intimidation against journalists.

D2. Are individuals free to practice and express their religious faith or nonbelief in public and private? 4 / 4

Freedom of religion is legally protected and broadly respected.

D3. Is there academic freedom, and is the educational system free from extensive political indoctrination? 4 / 4

Academic freedom is upheld.

D4. Are individuals free to express their personal views on political or other sensitive topics without fear of surveillance or retribution? 4 / 4

Private discussion is generally open and robust. However, the government operates an electronic surveillance system, and the circumstances under which it may be deployed are opaque.

E. ASSOCIATIONAL AND ORGANIZATIONAL RIGHTS: 12 / 12
E1. Is there freedom of assembly? 4 / 4

Freedom of assembly is protected by law, and the government generally respects this right in practice. Protests are frequent. On several occasions in early 2018, farmers, accompanied by some workers from other sectors, staged antigovernment protests at which participants demanded government assistance for their industries, including cuts in fuel and electricity prices, and modifications to trade agreements and monetary policy.

E2. Is there freedom for nongovernmental organizations, particularly those that are engaged in human rights- and governance-related work? 4 / 4

A wide array of community organizations and national and international human rights groups are active in civic life, and do not face government interference.

E3. Is there freedom for trade unions and similar professional or labor organizations? 4 / 4

Workers are free to exercise the right to join unions, bargain collectively, and hold strikes. Unions are well organized and politically powerful.

F. RULE OF LAW: 15 / 16

F1. Is there an independent judiciary? 4 / 4

Uruguay's judiciary is generally independent.

F2. Does due process prevail in civil and criminal matters? 3 / 4

The courts in Uruguay remain severely backlogged. However, new criminal procedures have reduced pretrial detention.

Efforts to seek justice for human rights violations committed under the military regime that ended in 1985 have been slow and inconsistent. The government created a special prosecutor's office to investigate unresolved cases; however, there has not been movement on any cases and victim groups are not optimistic. Many have pulled out of collaborating directly with the government's Working Group on Truth and Justice due to their lack of faith in the proceedings. Human rights investigators have reported receiving death threats.

F3. Is there protection from the illegitimate use of physical force and freedom from war and insurgencies? 4 / 4

Prisons are over capacity, and conditions in many facilities are inadequate. A prison riot in June 2018 highlighted these poor conditions. In response, President Vázquez days later submitted a bill to Congress that proposed major changes to the country's prison system, including decentralized management, a formal complaints procedure, and rehabilitation-focused programs.

F4. Do laws, policies, and practices guarantee equal treatment of various segments of the population? 4 / 4

Transgender people have historically been discriminated against in Uruguay. However, in October 2018 lawmakers approved, and the executive promulgated, a law allowing transgender people to change relevant information on their identification documents. The law also allows minors to have gender reassignment hormone therapy without parental or guardian permission, and set aside funds to help ensure that transgender people have access to education and health care, and to provide a pension for transgender people who were persecuted by the country's 1973–85 military dictatorship.

The Afro-Uruguayan minority continues to face economic and social inequalities. A 2013 affirmative action law included incentives to increase their graduation rates and an 8 percent quota in government employment. The law has seen some success in raising the enrollment rate of Afro-Uruguayans, but other mandates have not been fully implemented. The government has initiated additional programs aimed at seeing it realized, and also celebrated the first Afro-descendent month in July 2018, which recognized the cultural contributions of Afro-Uruguayans in the country.

The Senate in 2018 was discussing a bill that would provide greater protection against discrimination for people with disabilities, and enact a quota for hiring disabled people.

Women enjoy equal rights under the law but face discriminatory traditional attitudes and practices, including a persistent wage gap.

G. PERSONAL AUTONOMY AND INDIVIDUAL RIGHTS: 15 / 16

G1. Do individuals enjoy freedom of movement, including the ability to change their place of residence, employment, or education? 4 / 4

Freedom of movement is protected, and individuals are free to change their residence, employment, and institution of higher education without interference.

G2. Are individuals able to exercise the right to own property and establish private businesses without undue interference from state or nonstate actors? 4 / 4

The right to own property and establish private business is respected.

G3. Do individuals enjoy personal social freedoms, including choice of marriage partner and size of family, protection from domestic violence, and control over appearance? 4 / 4

Violence against women remains a serious concern, but authorities are making efforts to combat gender-based violence. The Parliament in 2017 voted to make femicide a special circumstance that can increase sentences, and has begun confiscating guns from policemen who have been convicted of domestic violence.

The parliament voted overwhelmingly to legalize same-sex marriage in 2013. Abortion for any reason during the first trimester has been legal since 2012. However, many women, especially in rural areas, lack access to legal abortions. Stigma connected to the procedure continues to impede full access for women.

G4. Do individuals enjoy equality of opportunity and freedom from economic exploitation? 3 / 4

Individuals generally enjoy equality of opportunity. However, according to reports, the government is not doing enough to combat transnational trafficking, and laws do not prohibit internal trafficking.

Uzbekistan

Population: 32,900,000
Capital: Tashkent
Political Rights Rating: 7
Civil Liberties Rating: 6 ↑
Freedom Rating: 6.5
Freedom Status: Not Free
Electoral Democracy: No

Overview: While ongoing reforms under a new president, Shavkat Mirziyoyev, have led to improvements on some issues, Uzbekistan remains a consolidated authoritarian regime. No genuine opposition parties operate legally. The legislature and judiciary effectively serve as instruments of the executive branch, which initiates reforms by decree, and the media remains tightly controlled by the state. Reports of torture and other ill-treatment remain common, although highly publicized cases of abuse have led to dismissals and prosecutions for some officials. Despite some high-profile releases, the government still holds numerous prisoners on political or religious grounds.

KEY DEVELOPMENTS IN 2018:

- Throughout the year, authorities continued to release prisoners of conscience who had been jailed under former president Islam Karimov, including human rights activist Fakhriddin Tillayev, who was freed in May after serving four years in prison.
- Also in May, journalists Bobomurod Abdullayev and Hayot Nasriddinov were released from prison, marking the first time in two decades that no journalists were imprisoned. However, self-censorship among journalists remains common.
- In August and September, eight religious bloggers were arrested and jailed for up to 15 days after criticizing the implementation of a nationwide school dress code that effectively banned hijabs in schools.
- Following President Mirziyoyev's pledge to reform the notorious National Security Service (SNB), the head of the agency was dismissed in January, and five senior SNB officials were convicted on torture charges in June and received lengthy prison sentences.

POLITICAL RIGHTS: 1 / 40

A. ELECTORAL PROCESS: 0 / 12

A1. Was the current head of government or other chief national authority elected through free and fair elections? 0 / 4

The president, who holds most executive power, is directly elected for up to two five-year terms. Longtime prime minister Shavkat Mirziyoyev was named acting president through an irregular parliamentary process in 2016, after Karimov, who had held the presidency since Uzbekistan's independence from the Soviet Union in 1991, suffered a stroke and died. The constitution called for the Senate chairman to serve as acting president, but the chairman declined the post. Mirziyoyev won a special presidential election at the end of 2016, taking a reported 88.6 percent of the vote and defeating nominal challengers whose parties in some cases openly campaigned for the incumbent. Election monitors from the Organization for Security and Co-operation in Europe (OSCE) concluded that "the dominant position of state actors and limits on fundamental freedoms undermine political pluralism and led to a campaign devoid of genuine competition."

A2. Were the current national legislative representatives elected through free and fair elections? 0 / 4

Uzbekistan has a bicameral legislature. The lower house is comprised of 150 seats, with 135 members directly elected in single-member constituencies and 15 representing the Ecological Movement of Uzbekistan, which holds separate indirect elections. The 100-member upper house, or Senate, has 84 members elected by regional councils and 16 appointed by the president. All members of the parliament serve five-year terms.

The 2014 lower house elections offered voters no meaningful choice, as all participating parties supported the government; observers from the OSCE reported that the elections "lacked genuine competition and debate." Karimov's Movement of Entrepreneurs and Businesspeople–Liberal Democratic Party (UzLiDeP) won the most votes and took 52 seats, while three loyalist parties split the remainder. Local human rights activists alleged serious disparities between reported turnout, which the government claimed was more than 88 percent, and the number of actual votes cast.

A3. Are the electoral laws and framework fair, and are they implemented impartially by the relevant election management bodies? 0 / 4

The electoral laws and framework are implemented in ways that offer no opportunities for independent political actors or parties to participate in elections at any level. Election management bodies are closely controlled by the government and have not been reformed since Karimov's death, though Mirziyoyev has indicated that he plans to implement electoral reforms at the local and regional level, including the introduction of direct elections for local and regional executives. In 2017, he signed legislation allowing the election of 11 district councils within Tashkent, in addition to the existing council for the city as a whole; Tashkent has the status of a region, and districts in the country's other regions already had elected councils.

B. POLITICAL PLURALISM AND PARTICIPATION: 0 / 16

B1. Do the people have the right to organize in different political parties or other competitive political groupings of their choice, and is the system free of undue obstacles to the rise and fall of these competing parties or groupings? 0 / 4

Only four political parties are registered—UzLiDep, the People's Democratic Party (PDPU), the Adolat (Justice) Social Democratic Party, and the Milliy Tiklanish (National Revival) Democratic Party. They indulge in mild criticism of one another and occasionally of government ministers, but all are effectively progovernment.

B2. Is there a realistic opportunity for the opposition to increase its support or gain power through elections? 0 / 4

No genuine opposition parties operate legally. Unregistered opposition groups function primarily in exile. Domestic supporters or family members of exiled opposition figures have been persecuted, and they are barred from participating in elections.

B3. Are the people's political choices free from domination by the military, foreign powers, religious hierarchies, economic oligarchies, or any other powerful group that is not democratically accountable? 0 / 4

Regional alliances of political elites hold the levers of government at all levels, creating economic oligarchies and patronage networks that stifle political competition. There is some intra-elite competition, but without the patronage of the established networks, political and economic advancement is all but impossible.

B4. Do various segments of the population (including ethnic, religious, gender, LGBT, and other relevant groups) have full political rights and electoral opportunities? 0 / 4

No registered party represents the specific interests of ethnic or religious minority groups, and no other parties or actors have the opportunity to achieve political representation. Women formally enjoy equal political rights, but they are unable to organize independently to advance their political interests in practice, and they remain underrepresented in leadership positions. Women hold 16 percent of the seats in the parliament's lower house and 17 percent of the seats in the Senate. No women ran for president in 2016.

C. FUNCTIONING OF GOVERNMENT: 1 / 12

C1. Do the freely elected head of government and national legislative representatives determine the policies of the government? 0 / 4

The country's leadership is not freely elected, and the legislature serves as a rubber stamp for the executive branch.

C2. Are safeguards against official corruption strong and effective? 0 / 4

Corruption is pervasive. Graft and bribery among low- and mid-level officials are common and at times conducted overtly and without subterfuge. In 2018, President Mirziyoyev spearheaded a crackdown on the notoriously corrupt security sector. In February, former prosecutor general Rashid Kadirov was arrested on corruption charges, which led to the arrests of dozens of security officials in connection with Kadirov's case. Kadirov awaited trial at the end of the year. Analysts contend that the purge is largely intended to neutralize security officials from the Karimov era.

Media discussion of corrupt practices has cautiously expanded since Karimov's death, but in some cases the journalists and commentators involved—rather than the corrupt officials—have come under pressure.

C3. Does the government operate with openness and transparency? 1 / 4

Government operations remain mostly opaque, but one of Mirziyoyev's first acts as president in late 2016 was the creation of new online mechanisms that offered citizens the opportunity to file complaints, report problems, and request services. The initial program was overwhelmingly popular and was quickly expanded to all ministries and local government offices, requiring local officials to interact with citizens and demonstrate responsiveness. The innovations contributed to a cultural change in governance, though they frequently encountered resistance at the local level.

CIVIL LIBERTIES: 8 / 60 (+2)
D. FREEDOM OF EXPRESSION AND BELIEF: 2 / 16 (+1)
D1. Are there free and independent media? 0 / 4

Despite constitutional guarantees, press freedom remains severely restricted. The state controls major media outlets and related facilities, and independent outlets were mostly shuttered or blocked under Karimov. Several foreign reporters were granted press passes in 2017 and 2018, but the presence of independent international outlets remained very limited. Domestic media, including news websites and live television programs, now cautiously discuss social problems and criticize local officials, reflecting a slight reduction in media repression since Mirziyoyev took power. However, even privately-owned media outlets often avoided openly criticizing Mirziyoyev and the government throughout the year.

Under Mirziyoyev, a number of journalists have been released from prison. In May 2018, journalists Bobomurod Abdullayev and Hayot Nasriddinov were released from custody after being charged in 2017 with "conspiracy to overthrow the constitutional regime." According to the Committee to Protect Journalists (CPJ), their release marked the first time in two decades that no journalists were in prison.

Despite the government's stated commitment to openness, access to popular social media sites like YouTube and Facebook was intermittently shut down at the end of the year without explanation.

D2. Are individuals free to practice and express their religious faith or nonbelief in public and private? 0 / 4

The government permits the existence of approved Muslim, Jewish, and Christian denominations but treats unregistered religious activity as a criminal offense. Suspected members of banned Muslim organizations and their relatives have faced arrest, interrogation, and torture. Arrested believers are frequently accused of founding previously unknown religious organizations, a charge that carries high penalties. In most cases, little evidence of the existence of such organizations is presented at the closed trials. In 2017, Mirziyoyev announced that some 16,000 individuals had been removed from a blacklist of roughly 17,000 people who had been suspected or previously convicted of religious extremism, and had been kept under close surveillance or on probation.

In 2018, however, many Islamic activists, bloggers, and clerics expressed disappointment with perceived setbacks in the movement toward greater religious tolerance. In September, Fazliddin Parpiyev, an imam in Tashkent, was fired after posting a video on Facebook appealing directly to the president to expand religious rights, including easing the ban on hijabs and beards. In December, Parpiyev fled the country after being threatened with prosecution for continuing to criticize restrictive religious policies on social media. Following their criticism of the August 2018 nationwide school dress code that effectively forbade girls from attending school wearing hijabs, eight religious bloggers were arrested and jailed for up to 15 days in August and September.

D3. Is there academic freedom, and is the educational system free from extensive political indoctrination? 1 / 4 (+1)

The government has long limited academic freedom, in part by controlling contacts between universities or scholars and foreign entities. Universities in Uzbekistan expanded their cooperation with foreign counterparts in 2018, notably with the November announcement that a new online university would be created in cooperation with an array of foreign academic institutions. In August, the government registered the American Councils for International Education, an academic exchange organization based in the US.

Presidential monographs that glorify former president Karimov are no longer required reading at universities.

Score Change: The score improved from 0 to 1 due to universities' increased autonomy, and new avenues for academic cooperation with foreign universities and academic institutions.

D4. Are individuals free to express their personal views on political or other sensitive topics without fear of surveillance or retribution? 1 / 4

The freedom of private discussion has long been limited by *mahalla* committees, traditional neighborhood organizations that the government has transformed into an official system for public surveillance and control. The government also engages in extensive surveillance of electronic communications. However, through its various reforms since 2016, the Mirziyoyev administration has signaled a greater tolerance for public criticism, modestly improving the climate for expression of personal views on sensitive topics.

E. ASSOCIATIONAL AND ORGANIZATIONAL RIGHTS: 1 / 12
E1. Is there freedom of assembly? 0 / 4

Despite constitutional provisions for freedom of assembly, authorities severely restrict this right in practice, breaking up virtually all unsanctioned gatherings and detaining participants.

E2. Is there freedom for nongovernmental organizations, particularly those that are engaged in human rights– and governance-related work? 1 / 4

Unregistered nongovernmental organizations (NGOs) face severe repression and harassment, though significant breaks with past policy continued in 2018, including Amnesty International's first official visit to the country in 14 years in May. A large international conference on human rights initiated by President Mirziyoyev was held in Samarkand in November, and included delegations from multiple international rights monitors. The conference demonstrated the government's newfound willingness to listen to the perspectives of NGOs, although some international participants noted the lack of participation by domestic NGOs.

Also in November, several international human rights groups released a combined statement calling on the Uzbek government to cease "harassing" local activists, noting that some NGO leaders, like Agzam Turgunov, whose 2017 release from prison raised hopes about the opening of civic space, continued to experience intimidation and near-constant surveillance from local authorities.

Authorities released prisoners of conscience who had been jailed under former president Karimov throughout the year, including human rights activist Fakhriddin Tillayev, who was released in May after serving over four years in prison following his conviction on politically motivated human-trafficking charges.

E3. Is there freedom for trade unions and similar professional or labor organizations? 0 / 4

The Federation of Trade Unions is controlled by the state, and no genuinely independent union structures exist. Organized strikes are extremely rare.

F. RULE OF LAW: 1 / 16 (+1)

F1. Is there an independent judiciary? 0 / 4

The judiciary is subservient to the president. In 2017, however, a number of judicial reforms were enacted through constitutional and legislative amendments, establishing specific terms in office for judges and creating a Supreme Judicial Council to oversee appointments and disciplinary action, among other changes. The council, whose chairperson is approved by the Senate on the president's recommendation, replaced a commission that was directly subordinate to the president.

In September 2018, the Supreme Court launched an interactive website that allows residents to access legal services, provides records of court rulings, and enables users to stream videos of trials. Pamela Spratlen, the US ambassador to Uzbekistan, praised the reforms for increasing transparency and fostering judicial independence.

F2. Does due process prevail in civil and criminal matters? 0 / 4

Due process guarantees remain extremely weak. Law enforcement authorities have routinely justified the arrest of suspected religious extremists or political opponents by planting contraband, filing dubious charges of financial wrongdoing, or inventing witness testimony. The Lawyers' Chamber, a regulatory body with compulsory membership, serves as a vehicle for state control over the legal profession. The judicial reforms adopted in 2017 gave judges rather than prosecutors the authority to approve certain investigative steps, such as exhumations and some forms of surveillance.

F3. Is there protection from the illegitimate use of physical force and freedom from war and insurgencies? 1 / 4 (+1)

A 2016 law on police prohibits torture, and a 2017 presidential decree that bars courts from using evidence obtained through torture took effect in March 2018. Despite the reforms, reports of physical abuse against detainees remained common during the year. However, abuse accusations in 2018 more frequently appeared in news reports or were circulated on social media, which increasingly resulted in consequences for perpetrators. In July, a video shared widely on social media, showing police in the Kattakurgan district of Samarkand forcing a woman in custody to strip as they verbally abused and threatened her, led to a sustained public outcry. In response, one of the police officers responsible for the incident was convicted on torture charges in November and sentenced to six years in prison.

President Mirziyoyev has promised to reform the notorious SNB, which has been accused of widespread abuses. In January, he removed SNB head Rustam Inoyatov, who led the agency for 23 years and presided over torture and other atrocities. In June, Rustam Azimov, the former SNB chief for the Bukhara region, was sentenced to 14 years in prison for torture and abuse of power; four other high-level SNB officials also received lengthy prison sentences after being convicted on the same charges.

Prisons suffer from severe overcrowding and shortages of food and medicine. As with detained suspects, prison inmates—particularly those sentenced for their religious beliefs—are often subjected to torture and other ill-treatment.

Score Change: The score improved from 0 to 1 due to increased reporting and public discussion of human rights abuses committed by security personnel, some of whom were removed from office or prosecuted for their transgressions.

F4. Do laws, policies, and practices guarantee equal treatment of various segments of the population? 0 / 4

Although racial and ethnic discrimination are prohibited by law, the belief that senior positions in government and business are reserved for ethnic Uzbeks is widespread. Women's educational and professional prospects are limited by discriminatory cultural and religious norms. Women are also barred from certain jobs under the labor code.

Sex between men is punishable with up to three years in prison. The law does not protect LGBT (lesbian, gay, bisexual, and transgender) people from discrimination, and social taboos deter the discussion of LGBT issues.

G. PERSONAL AUTONOMY AND INDIVIDUAL RIGHTS: 4 / 16

G1. Do individuals enjoy freedom of movement, including the ability to change their place of residence, employment, or education? 1 / 4

Permission is required to move to a new city, and bribes are commonly paid to obtain the necessary documents. Bribes are also frequently required to gain entrance to and advance in exclusive universities. The government took steps to ease travel within the country and to neighboring states in 2017, removing police checkpoints at internal borders, resuming direct flights to Tajikistan, and opening border crossings as part of an agreement with Kyrgyzstan. Exit visas were still required for foreign travel during the year, but in August 2018, the Mirziyoyev administration announced plans to abolish them beginning in January 2019.

G2. Are individuals able to exercise the right to own property and establish private businesses without undue interference from state or nonstate actors? 1 / 4

Widespread corruption and extensive state control over the economy limit private business opportunities and make property rights tenuous in practice.

G3. Do individuals enjoy personal social freedoms, including choice of marriage partner and size of family, protection from domestic violence, and control over appearance? 1 / 4

Victims of domestic violence are discouraged from pressing charges against perpetrators, who rarely face prosecution. Rape is also seldom reported or prosecuted, and spousal rape is not explicitly criminalized. Extralegal child marriage is reportedly practiced in some areas.

G4. Do individuals enjoy equality of opportunity and freedom from economic exploitation? 1 / 4

Economic exploitation remains a serious problem, as does the trafficking of women abroad for prostitution. A 2009 law imposed stronger penalties for child labor, and in 2012,

Mirziyoyev, then the prime minister, pledged to end the practice completely. In 2017, the president issued a decree to formally ban forced agricultural labor by students, health workers, and teachers. During the subsequent cotton harvests, the government increased incentives for voluntary labor and granted access to international observers. In November 2018, the International Labor Organization (ILO) noted that for the year's harvest, 93 percent of cotton workers were voluntarily employed, while child labor was not an issue. Nevertheless, local officials still faced pressure to meet government quotas, and reports of adult forced labor and abuse of workers persisted.

However, some local officials who employed forced labor were prosecuted and fined during the year. In October, President Mirziyoyev dismissed Deputy Prime Minister Zoyyir Mirzayev after photos of cotton farmers being forced to stand in cold irrigation ditches as punishment for a poor harvest were widely condemned on social media. Mirzayev was present during the incident, and reportedly insulted the farmers as they stood in the knee-deep water.

Vanuatu

Population: 300,000
Capital: Port Vila
Political Rights Rating: 2
Civil Liberties Rating: 2
Freedom Rating: 2.0
Freedom Status: Free
Electoral Democracy: Yes

Overview: Vanuatu conducts democratic elections but suffers from a pattern of unstable coalition governments that do not complete their terms. Although political corruption is a problem, the largely independent judiciary has been able to hold elected officials accountable in high-profile cases. Other persistent problems include domestic violence and societal discrimination against women.

KEY DEVELOPMENTS IN 2018:

- In April, reports in the Australian press that China was planning to build a military base on the island of Espiritu Santo were strenuously denied by the Vanuatu government.
- Deputy Prime Minister Joe Natuman was given a two-year suspended prison sentence in March for interfering with a police inquiry in 2014; he was ejected from Parliament in May.
- The government shelved its ambitious constitutional reform program in June after failing to reach consensus with the opposition, but at year's end it was reportedly planning to submit political reforms for a referendum in 2019.
- Prime Minister Charlot Salwai and his supporters defeated a parliamentary no-confidence motion in December.

POLITICAL RIGHTS: 33 / 40
A. ELECTORAL PROCESS: 10 / 12
A1. Was the current head of government or other chief national authority elected through free and fair elections? 3 / 4

The prime minister, who holds most executive authority and appoints his own cabinet, is chosen by Parliament from among its members. Prime ministerial elections and votes of no confidence often feature improprieties, as rival coalitions seek to entice members to shift allegiances with offers of cash or ministerial portfolios. Charlot Salwai of the Reunification of Movements for Change (RMC) party was elected to the post in 2016 and formed a governing coalition consisting of 11 of the 17 parties and more than two-thirds of the members in Parliament.

The largely ceremonial president is elected to serve a five-year term by an electoral college consisting of Parliament and the heads of the country's provincial councils. A two-thirds majority is required, and multiple rounds of voting can be held to reach this threshold. In 2017, Presbyterian pastor Tallis Obed Moses was elected to replace President Baldwin Lonsdale, who had died in office.

A2. Were the current national legislative representatives elected through free and fair elections? 4 / 4

The 52-seat unicameral Parliament is directly elected for four-year terms in 18 constituencies ranging from one to seven members in size. The last elections were held in early 2016 after the president dissolved Parliament, citing the conviction of 14 sitting lawmakers on corruption charges and the remaining members' inability to form a new governing majority. Eight independents and 17 parties won seats. The largest groups were the Vanua'aku Pati, the Union of Moderate Parties, and the Graon mo Jastis Pati (Land and Justice Party), each with six seats, though the totals fluctuated after the initial count due to party switching and by-elections.

A3. Are the electoral laws and framework fair, and are they implemented impartially by the relevant election management bodies? 3 / 4

The electoral framework is generally fair, and elections are administered without bias, but international observers have noted problems including an inaccurate voter roll and understaffing of election management bodies. Moreover, the use of the single-nontransferable-vote system, particularly in larger multimember constituencies, is believed to weaken political parties and encourage fragmentation. It is also especially unfair at by-elections, when voters may be filling only one vacant seat in a multiseat district.

B. POLITICAL PLURALISM AND PARTICIPATION: 15 / 16

B1. Do the people have the right to organize in different political parties or other competitive political groupings of their choice, and is the system free of undue obstacles to the rise and fall of these competing parties or groupings? 4 / 4

Numerous political parties operate without restrictions in Vanuatu. A total of 29 parties and dozens of independents contested the 2016 elections. Politicians frequently switch allegiances. In June 2018, the government withdrew proposed constitutional reforms that were meant in part to address party switching and political instability, having failed to reach consensus with the parliamentary opposition. At year's end, however, the government was reportedly planning to put several reform proposals to a referendum in 2019.

B2. Is there a realistic opportunity for the opposition to increase its support or gain power through elections? 4 / 4

The country has a record of frequent democratic transfers of power between rival parties.

B3. Are the people's political choices free from domination by the military, foreign powers, religious hierarchies, economic oligarchies, or any other powerful group that is not democratically accountable? 4 / 4

There are no major undue constraints on the choices of voters or candidates from outside the political system. Traditional chiefs—represented by the National Council of Chiefs, a consultative body for customary and language matters—exert some influence, but they do not control electoral decisions.

B4. Do various segments of the population (including ethnic, religious, gender, LGBT, and other relevant groups) have full political rights and electoral opportunities? 3 / 4

Ethnic minorities enjoy equal political rights. Political groupings have traditionally been divided in part along linguistic lines, with an Anglophone majority and a Francophone minority. However, Prime Minister Salwai is from the Francophone community and leads a coalition of mostly Anglophone parties.

Women's political participation is impaired by customary biases, and they are badly underrepresented in elected offices. No women were elected to Parliament in 2016. Some seats are reserved for women at the municipal level, and women's rights groups have lobbied for a quota at the national level as well.

C. FUNCTIONING OF GOVERNMENT: 8 / 12

C1. Do the freely elected head of government and national legislative representatives determine the policies of the government? 3 / 4

The elected prime minister and cabinet are able to determine and implement government policies without improper interference, and the legislature serves as a check on executive power. However, party fragmentation and frequent no-confidence votes have long disrupted governance. No government since 1995 has completed a full four-year term.

The Salwai government defeated a no-confidence motion at the end of 2017, by which time it was already the longest-serving government since 2008, but the governing coalition remained fractious in 2018. In December, another no-confidence motion against Salwai— launched on the grounds that he had unlawfully made a government appointment earlier in the year without the necessary budget allocation—was defeated.

C2. Are safeguards against official corruption strong and effective? 2 / 4

Abuse of office and corruption are serious problems, but prosecutors, the ombudsman, and other independent institutions are sometimes effective in combating them. The most dramatic corruption scandal in recent years occurred in 2015, when then deputy prime minister Moana Carcasses was convicted of bribing fellow lawmakers to help bring down the previous government. One of those found guilty, Parliament speaker Marcellino Pipite, attempted to pardon himself and 13 others while serving as acting head of state during an overseas trip by President Lonsdale, but the president revoked the pardons after his return. The 14 lawmakers in question, including Carcasses, were all released on parole in 2017, but they will remain barred from public office until 2025.

It was reported in August 2018 that the government's former principal aid negotiator, Victor Rory, had been charged with multiple counts of theft and money laundering as part of a larger scandal over stolen European development funds. His trial was pending at year's end.

C3. Does the government operate with openness and transparency? 3 / 4

The government largely operates with transparency. Parliament sessions are streamed live on the internet, and elected officials are required to submit financial disclosure reports that can be investigated by the ombudsman's office, but the documents are not made public.

A new freedom of information law that was adopted in 2016 took effect in early 2017, and the government issued an order on implementation later in the year. The law was widely welcomed as a positive step, though observers remained concerned about the establishment of fees and other potential obstacles to timely fulfillment of information requests.

There is growing concern about opaque government borrowing from China to fund infrastructure and other projects. In April 2018, the Australian media reported that Beijing was planning to build a military base on the island of Espiritu Santo, prompting firm denials from the Vanuatu government.

CIVIL LIBERTIES: 49 / 60 (+1)

D. FREEDOM OF EXPRESSION AND BELIEF: 15 / 16

D1. Are there free and independent media? 3 / 4

The government generally respects freedom of the press, though elected officials have sometimes been accused of threatening journalists for critical reporting. Publicly and privately owned newspapers publish in English and French. There are a small number of private broadcasters, but the state-owned broadcaster has a dominant position in the sector. Foreign news services are also available, and about a quarter of the population has access to the internet.

D2. Are individuals free to practice and express their religious faith or nonbelief in public and private? 4 / 4

The constitution's preamble states that the republic is founded on "Christian principles," but there is no official religion, and adherents of other faiths can worship freely. Authorities do not enforce a legal registration requirement for religious groups.

D3. Is there academic freedom, and is the educational system free from extensive political indoctrination? 4 / 4

There are no constraints on academic freedom.

D4. Are individuals free to express their personal views on political or other sensitive topics without fear of surveillance or retribution? 4 / 4

The government does not monitor personal communications, and individuals are able to discuss politics and other matters without interference.

E. ASSOCIATIONAL AND ORGANIZATIONAL RIGHTS: 11 / 12

E1. Is there freedom of assembly? 4 / 4

The law provides for freedom of assembly, and the government typically upholds this right in practice. Public demonstrations generally proceed without incident.

E2. Is there freedom for nongovernmental organizations, particularly those that are engaged in human rights– and governance-related work? 4 / 4

There are no significant constraints on the formation and operations of nongovernmental organizations (NGOs), which are not required to register with authorities. In 2017, the government intervened to bring about the reestablishment of the Vanuatu Association of Non-Government Organisations (VANGO), which had not held an annual meeting since 2014. A new board of directors was elected that year. The government explained that the independent association could help individual NGOs to improve their work and provide important services to the public.

E3. Is there freedom for trade unions and similar professional or labor organizations? 3 / 4

Workers can join unions, bargain collectively, and strike. The right to strike is somewhat impaired by notification rules and the government's ability to bar such actions in essential services; violations can draw criminal penalties. The umbrella Vanuatu Council of Trade Unions is an affiliate of the International Trade Union Confederation. Union leaders have raised concerns about antiunion pressure on seasonal workers who travel to New Zealand, including from recruiting agents within Vanuatu.

Among other labor actions during 2018, teachers' and airport workers' unions withdrew strike notices issued in May and July, respectively, after reaching agreements with their employers.

F. RULE OF LAW: 12 / 16 (+1)
F1. Is there an independent judiciary? 4 / 4 (+1)

The judiciary is largely independent, but a lack of resources hinders the hiring and retention of qualified judges and prosecutors. The president appoints the chief justice after consulting with the prime minister and the opposition leader. Other judges are appointed by the president on the advice of the Judicial Service Commission; judges cannot be removed arbitrarily. Tribal chiefs and island courts empowered to hear customary law cases adjudicate local disputes.

Vanuatu's courts have demonstrated impartiality in recent years through their adjudication of cases involving senior political figures. In March 2018, Deputy Prime Minister Joe Natuman received a two-year suspended prison sentence after he pleaded guilty to interfering with a police inquiry when he was prime minister in 2014. Natuman resigned as deputy prime minister in May, and the speaker ejected him from Parliament, declaring his seat vacant. After Natuman challenged that move, the Court of Appeal confirmed his ouster in July. A by-election was held in September to fill the seat.

Score Change: The score improved from 3 to 4 because the judiciary has continued to demonstrate considerable independence in handling cases against powerful politicians.

F2. Does due process prevail in civil and criminal matters? 2 / 4

Due process rights are guaranteed by law. However, police do not always uphold legal safeguards against arbitrary arrest and detention. Long periods of pretrial detention are not uncommon, largely due to case backlogs in the courts.

F3. Is there protection from the illegitimate use of physical force and freedom from war and insurgencies? 3 / 4

The police paramilitary unit, the Vanuatu Mobile Force (VMF), has a reputation for heavy-handed treatment of citizens. Civilian authorities have not been effective in punishing and preventing cases of police brutality. Deputy Prime Minister Natuman's conviction in March 2018 was for interfering with an investigation regarding high-ranking officers charged with mutiny. In his defense, Natuman claimed he was seeking to bring unity to the troubled police force.

Prisons have suffered from overcrowding, violence, poor living conditions, and lax management that contributes to frequent escapes. A new correctional facility funded by New Zealand's government opened in 2017, but escapes from the site were reported later in the year.

F4. Do laws, policies, and practices guarantee equal treatment of various segments of the population? 3 / 4

Women are guaranteed legal equality, but in practice they continue to face societal discrimination that affects their access to employment and economic opportunity. LGBT (lesbian, gay, bisexual, and transgender) people are not protected by antidiscrimination laws. The rapid expansion of Chinese-owned businesses has sometimes fueled resentment toward Chinese residents. Certain occupations are reserved for ni-Vanuatu as part of a policy to boost employment for the native population.

G. PERSONAL AUTONOMY AND INDIVIDUAL RIGHTS: 11 / 16

G1. Do individuals enjoy freedom of movement, including the ability to change their place of residence, employment, or education? 4 / 4

The constitution protects freedom of movement, which is also respected in practice.

G2. Are individuals able to exercise the right to own property and establish private businesses without undue interference from state or nonstate actors? 3 / 4

The legal framework is generally supportive of property rights and private business activity. However, irregularities surrounding land deals, and corruption in the Lands Ministry, are persistent problems. Legislation adopted in 2017 was designed to strengthen oversight for the leasing of customary land.

G3. Do individuals enjoy personal social freedoms, including choice of marriage partner and size of family, protection from domestic violence, and control over appearance? 2 / 4

Domestic violence is widespread. Social stigma and fear of reprisal inhibits reporting, particularly in more remote rural areas, and police and courts rarely intervene or impose strong penalties. Government and civil society efforts to combat the problem are inadequately funded. Spousal rape is not specifically criminalized. Women pursuing civil cases related to personal status matters face difficulties paying the required court fees. Only fathers can automatically pass citizenship to their children at birth.

G4. Do individuals enjoy equality of opportunity and freedom from economic exploitation? 2 / 4

Poverty is extensive, and more than three-quarters of the population rely on subsistence agriculture. The government does not properly enforce health and safety standards, leaving employees in construction, logging, and other industries exposed to hazardous working conditions. Children often perform agricultural work at the family level, and laws on child labor do not meet international standards.

Venezuela

Population: 31,800,000
Capital: Caracas
Political Rights Rating: 7 ↓
Civil Liberties Rating: 6 ↓
Freedom Rating: 6.5
Freedom Status: Not Free
Electoral Democracy: No

Overview: Venezuela's democratic institutions have deteriorated since 1999, but conditions have grown sharply worse in recent years due to the continued concentration of power in the executive, and harsher crackdowns on the opposition. Following a strong performance by the opposition in 2015 legislative elections, the powers of the National Assembly were curtailed by a politicized judiciary, and in 2017 the body was supplanted by a new National Constituent Assembly that serves the executive's interests. Government corruption is pervasive, and law enforcement has proven unable to halt violent crime. The authorities have closed off virtually all channels for political dissent, restricting civil liberties and prosecuting perceived opponents without regard for due process. The country's severe economic crisis has left millions struggling to meet basic needs, and driven mass emigration.

KEY DEVELOPMENTS IN 2018:

- President Nicolás Maduro was reelected in May, in a poll that failed to meet minimum international standards and was widely condemned as illegitimate. The election was held on an accelerated schedule designed to advantage Maduro, most prominent opposition parties and candidates were banned from participating, and record-low turnout reflected widespread dissatisfaction with the process.
- Authorities increasingly required citizens to use a special identity card to access social services and subsidized food. The Maduro administration urged voters to display these cards at special booths near polling stations, prompting a widespread perception that authorities were using the cards to monitor voting patterns.
- Venezuelans suffered from a worsening humanitarian and financial crisis characterized by acute food and medicine shortages, historically high hyperinflation, and rampant crime. The United Nations in November announced that over 3 million Venezuelans have fled the country due to the crisis.
- The Maduro administration continued its brazen crackdown on the political opposition, employing frequent arrests, torture, and temporary disappearances to quash dissent.

POLITICAL RIGHTS: 3 / 40 (-5)

A. ELECTORAL PROCESS: 0 / 12 (-2)

A1. Was the current head of government or other chief national authority elected through free and fair elections? 0 / 4 (-2)

The president serves six-year terms. Since 2009, neither the president nor other elected officials have been subject to term limits.

Incumbent president Nicolás Maduro won the 2018 snap presidential election with 67.9 percent of the vote, defeating Henri Falcón of the Progressive Advance party, who took 20.9 percent, and independent candidate Javier Bertucci, who took 10.8 percent. The election saw record-low turnout, with only 46 percent of voters participating, a sharp decline from the nearly 80 percent who participated in the last presidential election in 2013.

The poll was initially planned for December, but was moved up to April and then ultimately to May by the National Constituent Assembly, the progovernment body that in 2017 controversially supplanted the opposition-controlled National Assembly elected two years before. The decision to hold the poll early was widely criticized as a move to benefit Maduro by leaving a crippled and divided opposition little time to coalesce around a unity candidate, and by holding it before increasingly dire economic conditions became even worse. Leading opposition figures, including Leopoldo López and Henrique Capriles, were barred from competing. Maduro sought to intimidate voters by insisting that they present the so-called Fatherland ID card—the special identity card required to receive subsidized food and other services—at government-run booths near polling places. This drove a perception that those who did not vote could see aid revoked.

By most international accounts, the election lacked even a veneer of competitiveness. The Organization of American States (OAS) called it a "farce," while the Lima Group—comprised of mostly Latin American governments seeking address the crisis in Venezuela—deemed it illegitimate. The European Union said it did not comply with "minimum international standards for a credible process."

Score Change: The score declined from 2 to 0 because prominent opposition political parties and candidates were banned from participating in the presidential election, which was marked by voter intimidation and was held on an accelerated schedule designed to advantage the incumbent.

A2. Were the current national legislative representatives elected through free and fair elections? 0 / 4

The unicameral, 167-seat National Assembly is popularly elected for five-year terms, using a mix of majoritarian and proportional-representation voting. Three seats are reserved for indigenous representatives. In the 2015 elections, the opposition Democratic Unity Roundtable (MUD) coalition won 109 seats, while the United Socialist Party of Venezuela (PSUV) took 55. Subsequent government challenges against certain opposition victories—and notably the decision by the Supreme Tribunal of Justice (TSJ) to block the swearing-in of four representatives, three of whom were members of the opposition—deprived the MUD of a two-thirds majority.

The TSJ repeatedly nullified legislation passed by the National Assembly during 2016, and in 2017 the Maduro administration effectively replaced it with the National Constituent Assembly, a new body elected through an undemocratic process and comprised entirely of regime loyalists. Elections to the new assembly did not give voters the option to reject its establishment, were widely derided as unconstitutional, and were dismissed by the opposition, which boycotted the vote. Throughout 2018, the National Constituent Assembly functioned as a legislative body, solidifying its de facto replacement of the legitimate National Assembly. It is reportedly drafting a new constitution.

A3. Are the electoral laws and framework fair, and are they implemented impartially by the relevant election management bodies? 0 / 4

Venezuela's electoral system is heavily influenced by political manipulation and institutional interference in favor of the ruling party. The National Electoral Council (CNE) consists of five members, four of whom are openly aligned with the PSUV. The CNE rarely finds the ruling party has violated any rules, leading to a system in which the opposition is heavily regulated, while the government is unconstrained. After the National Constituent Assembly was created in 2017, it assumed the National Assembly's constitutional role of selecting and confirming members of the CNE. In addition, the National Constituent Assembly has taken over certain CNE functions, including setting election dates—a move that prompted significant controversy in 2018.

Recent elections, including the 2018 presidential election, have been characterized by disqualifications of prominent opposition candidates, government abuse of public resources, uneven access to the state-dominated media, the diminished presence of international observers, and intimidation of state employees.

B. POLITICAL PLURALISM AND PARTICIPATION: 3 / 16 (-3)

B1. Do the people have the right to organize in different political parties or other competitive political groupings of their choice, and is the system free of undue obstacles to the rise and fall of these competing parties or groupings? 0 / 4 (-1)

Opposition leaders are harassed, attacked, imprisoned, and otherwise impeded from participating in political processes or leading political parties in peaceful activities. Leopoldo López, founder of two opposition parties, remains under house arrest after spending more than three years in prison on spurious charges. Intelligence officials raided his home in March 2018 after the *New York Times* published an article based on dozens of interviews he had secretly given to one of its journalists.

Dozens of other political leaders have been subjected to harassment or arrest, and an apparent assassination attempt against President Maduro in August prompted a major crackdown. Opposition lawmaker Juan Requesens and Caracas councilman Fernando Albán were among those arrested for alleged involvement in the incident. After more than two days in which Requesens' whereabouts were unknown, videos surfaced in which he appeared to have been physically abused and likely tortured by state officials. Alban was arrested in October upon returning from an advocacy trip to the United Nations in New York. He was held by intelligence services for several days until his death was reported by officials as a suicide. Many opposition leaders and several foreign governments believe he was tortured and murdered by state officials; the United Nations has called for an investigation into his death. A number of other opposition figures have fled the country.

In 2018, the government increasingly adopted what human rights groups termed a "revolving door" approach to repress critics, employing more frequent detentions but for shorter periods of time. In many cases, detained individuals disappear for multiple days before any information is provided about their whereabouts. The effect has been to broaden the government's campaign to stifle protest and dissent while roughly maintaining the total number of political prisoners at a given time. A May report published by the OAS detailed the widespread use of torture to persecute government opponents. There have been over 12,800 arbitrary detentions since 2014 and there were 288 political prisoners at the end of 2018.

Score Change: The score declined from 1 to 0 due to sustained state-sanctioned violence and attacks against opposition leaders, including arbitrary arrests, forced disappearances, and torture.

B2. Is there a realistic opportunity for the opposition to increase its support or gain power through elections? 0 / 4 (-1)

While discontent with the Maduro administration continues to grow, the government has cut off virtually all avenues for political change. After pushing through the de facto replacement of the National Assembly with the National Constituent Assembly in 2017, Maduro went further in 2018 by ensuring that no publicly known opposition figure would be able to challenge him in the 2018 election. Opposition parties that had boycotted the 2017 municipal elections due to the unjust conditions were banned by the National Constituent Assembly from competing under their names in the presidential election, prompting the opposition MUD coalition to declare a boycott of the process. Opposition parties also boycotted the December 2018 municipal elections, in which, as a sign of widespread dissatisfaction, only 27 percent of voters participated.

Both Lopez and Henrique Capriles, a prominent opposition figure and former governor of Miranda State, are banned from holding public office.

Score change: The score declined from 1 to 0 because major opposition political parties and candidates were denied the ability to compete in presidential elections.

B3. Are the people's political choices free from domination by the military, foreign powers, religious hierarchies, economic oligarchies, or any other powerful group that is not democratically accountable? 1 / 4

State-affiliated *colectivos* routinely commit acts of violence against civilians with impunity, particularly at antigovernment protests, and carry out government efforts to intimidate voters.

The government's 2017 deployment of the Fatherland ID card—which is necessary to access subsidized food, subsidized oil medical procedures, and other services—has enabled authorities to institutionalize a form of political discrimination. In the lead-up to the 2018 presidential election, the government directed aid recipients to display their identification cards at government-run booths near polling stations. This fueled a widespread perception that those who failed to vote would see food aid withdrawn. Moreover, the government has also effectively bought votes by offering prizes of food to ID holders who vote. There were additionally reports of state employees being pressured to send photographs of themselves voting to their managers. The Reuters news agency, in a 2018 story on the Fatherland ID card, reported on the existence of a Justice Ministry list of state employees who had failed to vote.

B4. Do various segments of the population (including ethnic, religious, gender, LGBT, and other relevant groups) have full political rights and electoral opportunities? 2 / 4 (−1)

While several women hold senior positions in government, the general underrepresentation of women in politics contributes to a lack of policy discussions about issues that primarily affect women, such as gender-based violence. Discrimination against LGBT (lesbian, gay, bisexual, and transgender) Venezuelans impacts their ability to fully engage in political and electoral processes. The government has professed support for the rights of indigenous people, but in practice they too lack meaningful political representation. Three indigenous legislators were prevented from taking office after their victories in 2015 elections to the National Assembly in order to deny the opposition a two-thirds majority. Some indigenous leaders have been impeded from running for office and others have been targeted by government stigmatization campaigns.

The de facto replacement of the National Assembly with the progovernment National Constituent Assembly in 2017 effectively erased constitutional protections designed to ensure political representation for indigenous and other groups. Members of these groups now have little opportunity to advance any interests that fall outside of the body's agenda.

Score Change: The score declined from 3 to 2 because authorities' drive to quash dissent has left women, indigenous populations, and LGBT people with fewer opportunities to advocate for their interests.

C. FUNCTIONING OF GOVERNMENT: 0 / 12

C1. Do the freely elected head of government and national legislative representatives determine the policies of the government? 0 / 4

Venezuela does not function as a representative democracy. The opposition-controlled legislature has had no practical ability to carry out its constitutional mandate since the 2015 elections, and since August 2017 has been supplanted by a body packed with regime loyalists who were elected under undemocratic conditions. While the National Assembly was never formally dissolved, the new National Constituent Assembly granted itself sweeping legislative powers, essentially leaving the old assembly with no functional role.

Military officials, many of them in active service, occupy a number of top positions in government ministries and state-level administrations, and the armed forces perform routine government duties, blurring the lines between civilian and military functions. The unpopular Maduro administration relies heavily on support from the military to maintain power. In 2018, a growing number of military officers were arrested, as the administration became increasingly concerned about divisions within the ranks.

C2. Are safeguards against official corruption strong and effective? 0 / 4

Corruption is rampant in Venezuela. The government's economic policies—particularly its currency and price controls—have greatly increased opportunities for black-market activity and collusion between public officials and organized crime networks, while exacerbating the effects of the economic crisis for poor and middle-class Venezuelans. The scale of Venezuelan corruption is exemplified by Alejandro Andrade, former head of Venezuela's treasury, who was sentenced by a US court to 10 years in prison after pleading guilty to taking over $1 billion in bribes, in exchange for helping a network of elites purchase dollars at fixed exchange rates and resell them on the black market for a massive markup.

C3. Does the government operate with openness and transparency? 0 / 4

There is little transparency regarding government spending. The government has consistently failed to publish vital economic data, including monthly inflation statistics. In 2017, President Maduro fired the health minister after the ministry published data confirming a dramatic rise in maternal and infant mortality.

CIVIL LIBERTIES: 16 / 60 (−2)
D. FREEDOM OF EXPRESSION AND BELIEF: 7 / 16 (−1)
D1. Are there free and independent media? 1 / 4

Venezuela's independent journalists operate within a highly restrictive regulatory and legal environment, and risk arrest and physical violence in connection with their work. Most independent newspapers have shut down or moved to a digital format.

The Maduro government maintains a state communications infrastructure, bolstered by a broad legal framework, which is used to propagate its political and ideological program. Critical media face various forms of harassment. A series of private news outlets have changed ownership under financial pressure in recent years, and their coverage subsequently grew more favorable to the authorities.

In November 2017, the National Constituent Assembly passed a hate-speech law mandating fines and up to 20 years' imprisonment for anyone who disseminates information deemed "intolerant" via traditional or social media. In September 2018, two men were arrested by military counterintelligence officers under the law for posting a video that compared President Maduro to a donkey. They were held for several weeks before being "freed with restrictions."

Obstruction, intimidation, physical attacks, confiscations of equipment, and detentions and arrests of media workers continued in 2018. Venezuela's Press and Society Institute (IPYS) reported that there were 25 arbitrary detentions of journalists in the first nine months of 2018, and that two journalists had been prohibited from leaving the country as punishment for their reporting. A German freelance writer was detained in a military detention facility in mid-November on charges of spying and "violating security zones," and remained there at year's end, though authorities have not provided any evidence to support the charges.

In September, the National Telecommunications Commission (CONATEL) ordered internet service providers in Venezuela not to allow an investigative journalism website,

Armando.info, to publish a report about Alex Saab, a Colombian businessman responsible for importing staple foods for the government food-distribution program.

D2. Are individuals free to practice and express their religious faith or nonbelief in public and private? 3 / 4

Constitutional guarantees of religious freedom are generally respected, though tensions between the government and the Roman Catholic Church remain high. Government relations with the small Jewish community have also been strained at times.

D3. Is there academic freedom, and is the educational system free from extensive political indoctrination? 2 / 4

Academic freedom came under mounting pressure during Chávez's tenure, and a school curriculum developed by his government emphasizes socialist concepts. More recently, budget cuts and other funding problems have undermined universities' autonomy and prompted an exodus of academics from the country.

The OAS and Venezuelan civil society organizations have noted growing government efforts to stifle political speech by university students. In late 2017, the Inter-American Commission on Human Rights (CIDH), an OAS body, released a report expressing concern over the detention of more than 300 university students involved in a 2017 protest movement calling for political reforms. The report added that 21 students had been murdered amid the movement, and that 92 demonstrations called by university students or lecturers have been repressed.

D4. Are individuals free to express their personal views on political or other sensitive topics without fear of surveillance or retribution? 1 / 4 (−1)

Authorities' monitoring of citizens' behavior via their use of the Fatherland ID card and through scrutiny of content posted on social media platforms has created a climate of fear. Social media users have been subject to arrest in response to comments posted online, with at least 17 individuals detained since 2014 for opinions expressed on Twitter alone. In May 2018, Pedro Jaimes Criollo, a private citizen, was detained for tweeting information about the flight route of an aircraft carrying President Maduro. The incident was considered by many human rights groups to be a forced disappearance, given that after he was detained his whereabouts were unknown for more than a month. He was reportedly tortured while in custody.

The government has also employed the Fatherland ID system to monitor citizens' activities. With guidance from Chinese company ZTE, authorities have reportedly developed a sophisticated monitoring system that not only allows them to withhold food aid and other services from political opponents, but also enables them to gather vast troves of data on individuals' voting patterns, medical history, and other activity. Authorities have strongly encouraged citizens to sign up for the card.

Score Change: The score declined from 2 to 1 due to arrests of social media users for online comments, and the Maduro administration's use of the Fatherland ID card to monitor citizens' activities.

E. ASSOCIATIONAL AND ORGANIZATIONAL RIGHTS: 2 / 12
E1. Is there freedom of assembly? 0 / 4

Freedom of assembly is guaranteed in the constitution, but is not protected in practice. Widespread antigovernment protests in 2017 gave way to violent clashes with security forces, leading more than 1,900 injuries and 136 deaths, at least 102 of whom were apparently killed directly by security forces or state-affiliated *colectivos*.

There were fewer mass protests in 2018, likely due in part to the government's brutal crackdown on demonstrations the previous year. Most focused on discontent with the country's economic and social conditions, rather than the political situation. A growing number of professionals in the health sector, as well as transportation workers and grocery store owners, protested food and medicine shortages and criticized government policies. A peaceful march by 400 doctors and nurses in August was broken up by police.

E2. Is there freedom for nongovernmental organizations, particularly those that are engaged in human rights- and governance-related work? 1 / 4

Activists and nongovernmental organizations (NGOs) are routinely harassed, threatened, and subject to legal and administrative sanctions for their work. Dozens of civil society activists have been physically attacked in recent years. In 2017 and 2018, the government has focused mainly on attempting to delegitimize these organizations by accusing them of conspiring with foreign governments.

E3. Is there freedom for trade unions and similar professional or labor organizations? 1 / 4

Workers are legally entitled to form unions, bargain collectively, and strike, with some restrictions on public-sector workers' ability to strike. Control of unions has shifted from traditional opposition-allied labor leaders to new workers' organizations that are often aligned with the government. The competition has contributed to a substantial increase in labor violence as well as confusion and delays during industry-wide collective bargaining.

Public-sector unions, including in the oil industry, took to the streets in 2018 to express anger over low wages and poor working conditions, and to oppose government reforms that failed to stem hyperinflation.

F. RULE OF LAW: 1 / 16

F1. Is there an independent judiciary? 0 / 4

Politicization of the judicial branch increased dramatically under Chávez and has progressed further under Maduro. High courts generally do not rule against the government. In late 2015, the outgoing PSUV-controlled legislature stacked the TSJ with its own appointees before the opposition-controlled National Assembly took office. The progovernment National Constituent Assembly has since installed over a dozen regime loyalists on the TSJ, solidifying the judiciary's alignment with the executive branch. In opposition to these developments, a group of former "justices-in-exile" has been working internationally to bring largely symbolic charges against Maduro and other government officials.

F2. Does due process prevail in civil and criminal matters? 0 / 4

Opponents of the government and ruling party are routinely detained and prosecuted without regard for due process. In recent years, the Bolivarian National Intelligence Service (SEBIN) has increasingly carried out policing functions and arrested opposition politicians and journalists without informing the Public Ministry or presenting official charges. The military has also assumed roles previously reserved for civilian law enforcement institutions, and foreign governments allege that the military has adopted a permissive attitude toward drug trafficking. According to Venezuelan human rights groups, at least 800 civilians have been tried in military court proceedings since 2017.

In 2017, the National Constituent Assembly dismissed prosecutor general Luisa Ortega, who has been critical of Maduro. She then fled the country, saying she feared for her life.

F3. Is there protection from the illegitimate use of physical force and freedom from war and insurgencies? 0 / 4

Venezuela's violent crime rates rank among the highest in the world. A 2018 report by *Insight Crime* cited a homicide rate of 89 per 100,000 people—which would make Venezuela the most dangerous country in Latin America—and called the country a "mafia state" due to the degree of infiltration by organized crime into state institutions. Venezuela also ranked last of all 142 countries surveyed in Gallup's latest Global Law and Order report, with only 17 percent of Venezuelan respondents saying they feel safe walking at night and just 24 percent expressing confidence in the police.

The police and military have been prone to corruption, torture, and extrajudicial killings. Prison conditions in Venezuela remain among the worst in the Americas. *Pranes*, or gang leaders who operate from prisons, are able to coordinate criminal networks throughout Venezuela.

F4. Do laws, policies, and practices guarantee equal treatment of various segments of the population? 1 / 4

The rights of indigenous people, who make up about 2 percent of the population, are upheld by the constitution but poorly protected by local authorities. Although discrimination based on sexual orientation is barred, LGBT Venezuelans face widespread intolerance and are occasionally subjected to violence.

Despite legal protections, women suffer from violence and discrimination in practice, including earning lower salaries than men doing similar work.

Segments of the population that were already disadvantaged or marginalized appear to have suffered disproportionately from Venezuela's economic and health crises. Maternal mortality has increased in recent years. People living with HIV/AIDS—most of whom are gay men and transgender people—have suffered due to the government's decision to stop subsidizing antiretroviral drugs.

G. PERSONAL AUTONOMY AND INDIVIDUAL RIGHTS: 6 / 16 (–1)

G1. Do individuals enjoy freedom of movement, including the ability to change their place of residence, employment, or education? 2 / 4

The country's currency controls and other economic policies, combined with an enormous decline in the number of flights to and from Venezuela, and periodic border closures, have made it extremely difficult for Venezuelans to travel abroad. Venezuelans of all social classes nevertheless fled the country in massive numbers in 2018, even as neighboring countries imposed more rigorous passport and visa controls in an effort to slow the influx.

G2. Are individuals able to exercise the right to own property and establish private businesses without undue interference from state or nonstate actors? 1 / 4

Property rights have been affected by years of price controls, nationalizations, overregulation, and corruption. Accusations of mismanagement, underinvestment, graft, and politicized hiring practices within state-owned enterprises are common.

G3. Do individuals enjoy personal social freedoms, including choice of marriage partner and size of family, protection from domestic violence, and control over appearance? 3 / 4

The government generally does not restrict social freedoms. A 2007 law was designed to combat violence against women, but domestic violence and rape remain common and are rarely punished in practice.

G4. Do individuals enjoy equality of opportunity and freedom from economic exploitation? 0 / 4 (-1)

Venezuelan women and children are increasingly vulnerable to sex trafficking within Venezuela and in neighboring countries, as well as in Europe, with the problem exacerbated by worsening economic conditions. Migrants to Venezuela have also been subjected to forced labor and sex trafficking. The government has reportedly done little to combat human trafficking.

With job opportunities growing scarce and wages not keeping up with hyperinflation, more citizens have turned to jobs in the informal economy, where they are more exposed to dangerous or exploitative working conditions. Meanwhile, the United Nations estimated in December 2018 that roughly 5,500 Venezuelans were leaving the country each day due to a lack of employment opportunities, food shortages, and violence.

Score Change: The score declined from 1 to 0 due to the severe economic crisis, which has prompted mass emigration, and increases in sex trafficking and sexual exploitation, trafficking of children, forced child labor, and dangerous working conditions.

Vietnam

Population: 94,700,000
Capital: Hanoi
Political Rights Rating: 7
Civil Liberties Rating: 5
Freedom Rating: 6.0
Freedom Status: Not Free
Electoral Democracy: No

Overview: Vietnam is a one-party state, dominated for decades by the ruling Communist Party of Vietnam (CPV). Although some independent candidates are technically allowed to run in legislative elections, most are banned in practice. Freedom of expression, religious freedom, and civil society activism are tightly restricted. The authorities have increasingly cracked down on citizens' use of social media and the internet.

KEY DEVELOPMENTS IN 2018:

- Arrests, criminal convictions, and physical assaults against journalists, bloggers, and human rights activists continued during the year. Human rights groups reported that there were 244 prisoners of conscience in the country as of December.
- In June, the legislature passed a new cybersecurity law, set to come into force in 2019, that was expected to boost censorship of online content, force major companies like Google and Facebook to store information on Vietnamese users within Vietnam, and compel technology companies to share information about users with the Vietnamese government.
- Also in June, massive anti-China protests were sparked by an ongoing dispute over territory in the South China Sea, the possibility that Hanoi would create special economic zones with long-term leases to Chinese investors, and broader Vietnamese concerns about China's growing regional dominance.

POLITICAL RIGHTS: 3 / 40

A. ELECTORAL PROCESS: 0 / 12

A1. Was the current head of government or other chief national authority elected through free and fair elections? 0 / 4

The president is elected by the National Assembly for a five-year term, and is responsible for appointing the prime minister, who is confirmed by the legislature. However, all selections for top executive posts are predetermined in practice by the CPV's Politburo and Central Committee.

In 2016, nominees for president and prime minister were chosen at the CPV's 12th Party Congress in January, which also featured the reelection of Nguyễn Phú Trọng as the party's general secretary. In April of that year, the National Assembly formally confirmed Trần Đại Quang as president and Nguyễn Xuân Phúc as prime minister.

President Trần Đại Quang died in September 2018, and the National Assembly confirmed Nguyễn Phú Trọng as his replacement in October; Trọng retained the post of party general secretary.

A2. Were the current national legislative representatives elected through free and fair elections? 0 / 4

Elections to the National Assembly are tightly controlled by the CPV, which took 473 of the body's 500 seats in the 2016 balloting. Candidates who were technically independent but vetted by the CPV took 21 seats. More than 100 independent candidates, including many young civil society activists, were barred from running in the elections. Voter turnout of over 99 percent was recorded by the government, but there were reports that authorities stuffed ballot boxes in order to inflate this figure.

A3. Are the electoral laws and framework fair, and are they implemented impartially by the relevant election management bodies? 0 / 4

The electoral laws and framework ensure that the CPV, the only legally recognized party, dominates every election. The party controls all electoral bodies and vets all candidates, resulting in the disqualification of those who are genuinely independent.

B. POLITICAL PLURALISM AND PARTICIPATION: 1 / 16

B1. Do the people have the right to organize in different political parties or other competitive political groupings of their choice, and is the system free of undue obstacles to the rise and fall of these competing parties or groupings? 0 / 4

The CPV enjoys a monopoly on political power, and no other parties are allowed to operate legally. Splits between factions within the party exist, but in general they are not openly aired. Members of illegal opposition parties are subject to arrest and imprisonment. Several alleged members of banned political organizations received lengthy prison sentences during 2018.

B2. Is there a realistic opportunity for the opposition to increase its support or gain power through elections? 0 / 4

The structure of the one-party system precludes any democratic transfer of power. The Vietnam Fatherland Front (VFF), responsible for vetting all candidates for the National Assembly, is ostensibly an alliance of organizations representing the people, but in practice it acts as an arm of the CPV. The body banned numerous reform-minded independent candidates from running in the 2016 elections.

B3. Are the people's political choices free from domination by the military, foreign powers, religious hierarchies, economic oligarchies, or any other powerful group that is not democratically accountable? 0 / 4

The overarching dominance of the CPV effectively excludes the public from any genuine and autonomous political participation.

B4. Do various segments of the population (including ethnic, religious, gender, LGBT, and other relevant groups) have full political rights and electoral opportunities? 1 / 4

Although ethnic minorities are nominally represented within the CPV, they are rarely allowed to rise to senior positions, and the CPV leadership's dominance prevents effective advocacy on issues affecting minority populations. While Vietnam has enacted policies and strategies aimed at boosting women's political participation, in practice the interests of women are poorly represented in government, and societal biases discourage women from running for office.

C. FUNCTIONING OF GOVERNMENT: 2 / 12

C1. Do the freely elected head of government and national legislative representatives determine the policies of the government? 0 / 4

The CPV leadership, which is not freely elected or accountable to the public, determines government policy and the legislative agenda.

C2. Are safeguards against official corruption strong and effective? 1 / 4

CPV and government leaders have acknowledged growing public discontent with corruption, and there has been an increase in corruption-related arrests and prosecutions against senior officials in recent years. Notably, a former senior Politburo member who had managed the state oil and gas firm PetroVietnam was arrested on corruption charges in late 2017 and sentenced in January 2018 to 13 years in prison. He was tried on other charges in March and sentenced to an additional 18 years. Also in January, another former high-level PetroVietnam official—whom Vietnamese authorities allegedly had abducted in Germany in 2017—was sentenced to life in prison on corruption-related charges. In June, the government arrested four more current and former PetroVietnam subsidiary executives amid allegations of embezzlement. Many additional former senior managers at state firms, including banks, have been arrested and charged with financial malfeasance.

Despite the crackdown, enforcement of anticorruption laws is generally selective and often linked to political rivalries, and those who attempt to independently expose corruption continue to face censorship and arrest.

C3. Does the government operate with openness and transparency? 1 / 4

The CPV leadership operates with considerable opacity. The National Assembly passed an access to information law in 2016, but its provisions are relatively weak. It bars disclosure of information on "politics, defense, national security, foreign relations, economics, technology, or any other areas regulated by the law." Information can also be withheld if it could harm state interests or the well-being of the nation. The government has attempted in recent years to introduce more e-government services to slightly improve transparency.

CIVIL LIBERTIES: 17 / 60

D. FREEDOM OF EXPRESSION AND BELIEF: 4 / 16

D1. Are there free and independent media? 1 / 4

Although the constitution recognizes freedom of the press, journalists and bloggers are constrained by numerous repressive laws and decrees. Those who dare to report or comment independently on controversial issues also risk intimidation and physical attack.

The criminal code prohibits speech that is critical of the government, while a 2006 decree prescribes fines for any publication that denies revolutionary achievements, spreads "harmful" information, or exhibits "reactionary ideology." Decree 72, issued in 2013, gave the state sweeping new powers to restrict speech on blogs and social media. Websites considered reactionary are blocked, and internet service providers face fines and closure for violating censorship rules. The state controls all print and broadcast media.

In June 2018 the National Assembly approved a restrictive cybersecurity law that will, among other provisions, force companies like Facebook and Google to store information about Vietnamese users in Vietnam, making it potentially more accessible to state authorities. The law, which was set to come into force in January 2019, could also lead technology companies to censor content and otherwise cooperate with state investigations.

New arrests, beatings, criminal convictions, and cases of mistreatment in custody involving journalists and bloggers continued to be reported throughout 2018. In July, authorities detained an independent journalist who often worked for US media outlets; he was still being held in pretrial detention at the end of the year. In August, authorities beat a jailed videographer affiliated with Radio Free Asia, possibly to compel him to testify against an environmental activist who was then on trial. Also in August, a well-known blogger and activist, Phạm Đoan Trang, who had been detained multiple times during the year, was one of at least three people who were singled out for beatings after a police raid on a dissident singer's concert. In October, under intense foreign pressure, Hanoi released prominent blogger Nguyễn Ngọc Như Quỳnh, known as "Mother Mushroom," from prison, where she was serving a 10-year term. She went into exile, and said the next month that the Vietnamese government has a concerted strategy of pushing bloggers and other online writers to go into exile. As of December, the Committee to Protect Journalists reported that 11 journalists were behind bars in Vietnam as a result of their work.

D2. Are individuals free to practice and express their religious faith or nonbelief in public and private? 1 / 4

Religious freedoms remain restricted. All religious groups and most individual clergy members are required to join a party-controlled supervisory body and obtain permission for most activities. A 2016 Law on Belief and Religion, which has been gradually rolled out, reinforced registration requirements, will allow extensive state interference in religious groups' internal affairs, and gives authorities broad discretion to penalize unsanctioned religious activity. Members of unregistered Christian, Hoa Hao, Cao Dai, and other religious groups also face regular arrests and harassment from local and provincial authorities, and dozens of people are believed to be behind bars in connection with their religious beliefs.

D3. Is there academic freedom, and is the educational system free from extensive political indoctrination? 1 / 4

Academic freedom is limited. University professors must refrain from criticizing government policies and adhere to party views when teaching or writing on political topics. There have been reports that university students who participated in human rights advocacy have been prevented from graduating.

D4. Are individuals free to express their personal views on political or other sensitive topics without fear of surveillance or retribution? 1 / 4

Although citizens enjoy more freedom in private discussions than in the past, authorities continue to attack and imprison those who openly criticize the state, including on social media. The government engages in surveillance of private online activity.

E. ASSOCIATIONAL AND ORGANIZATIONAL RIGHTS: 1 / 12

E1. Is there freedom of assembly? 1 / 4

Freedom of assembly is tightly restricted. Organizations must apply for official permission to assemble, and security forces routinely use excessive force to disperse unauthorized demonstrations. After nationwide anti-China protests in June 2018, during which dozens of participants were assaulted and arrested, the courts convicted well over a hundred people of disrupting public order, and many were sentenced to prison terms. The protests were driven in part by opposition to a draft law allowing long-term leases of land in special economic zones that critics said would be dominated by Chinese companies. The legislation in question was postponed and still pending at year's end.

E2. Is there freedom for nongovernmental organizations, particularly those that are engaged in human rights– and governance-related work? 0 / 4

A small but active community of nongovernmental organizations (NGOs) promotes environmental conservation, land rights, women's development, and public health. However, human rights organizations are generally banned, and those who engage in any advocacy that the authorities perceive as hostile or unwanted risk arrest and imprisonment.

Criminal prosecutions and violence against activists persisted in 2018. Among other incidents during the year, in June and July unknown assailants repeatedly attacked the home of a prominent labor activist. In August, a farmer and activist who had joined the June anti-China protests died after reportedly being beaten by police. Separately that month, environmental activist and blogger Lê Đình Lượng was sentenced to 20 years in prison after a five-hour trial on charges of attempting to overthrow the government and cause social disorder.

Foreign human rights activists also face restrictions. In September, for example, authorities detained and deported the secretary general of the International Federation for Human Rights after she arrived in the country to attend a World Economic Forum event.

E3. Is there freedom for trade unions and similar professional or labor organizations? 0 / 4

The Vietnam General Conference of Labor (VGCL) is Vietnam's only legal labor federation and is controlled by the CPV. The right to strike is limited by tight legal restrictions. In recent years the government has permitted hundreds of independent "labor associations" without formal union status to represent workers at individual firms and in some service industries. However, independent labor activists remain subject to harassment, travel restrictions, and heavy prison sentences.

F. RULE OF LAW: 4 / 16

F1. Is there an independent judiciary? 1 / 4

Vietnam's judiciary is subservient to the CPV, which controls the courts at all levels. This control is especially evident in politically sensitive criminal prosecutions, with judges sometimes displaying greater impartiality in civil cases.

F2. Does due process prevail in civil and criminal matters? 1 / 4

Constitutional guarantees of due process are generally not upheld. Defendants have a legal right to counsel, but lawyers are scarce, and many are reluctant to take on cases involving human rights or other sensitive topics for fear of state harassment and retribution.

Defense lawyers do not have the right to call witnesses and often report insufficient time to meet with their clients. In national security cases, police can detain suspects for up to 20 months without access to counsel.

Amendments to the penal code approved in 2017 included a provision under which defense lawyers can be held criminally liable for failing to report certain kinds of crimes committed by their own clients. The new code took effect in January 2018.

The combination of vaguely defined offenses and politicized courts has resulted in the imprisonment of large numbers of people for peacefully exercising their rights. A coalition of international and Vietnamese civil society groups reported that there were 244 prisoners of conscience in Vietnam at the end of 2018, including bloggers, lawyers, labor or land rights activists, political dissidents, and religious believers.

F3. Is there protection from the illegitimate use of physical force and freedom from war and insurgencies? 1 / 4

There is little protection from the illegitimate use of force by state authorities, and police are known to abuse suspects and prisoners, sometimes resulting in death or serious injury. Prison conditions are poor.

The new penal code reduced the number of crimes that can draw the death penalty, though it can still be applied for crimes other than murder, including drug trafficking and corruption. Authorities carried out at least 85 executions during 2018, making Vietnam one of the world's most prolific users of the death penalty.

F4. Do laws, policies, and practices guarantee equal treatment of various segments of the population? 1 / 4

Ethnic minorities face discrimination in Vietnamese society, and some local officials restrict their access to schooling and jobs. Minorities generally have little input on development projects that affect their livelihoods and communities. Members of ethnic and religious minorities also face monitoring and harassment by authorities seeking to suppress dissent and suspected links to exile groups. The government has reportedly exerted pressure, via family members, on minorities who flee to neighboring countries; those who return are subject to mistreatment by authorities.

Men and women receive similar treatment in the legal system. Women generally have equal access to education, and economic opportunities for women have grown, though they continue to face discrimination in wages and promotions.

The law does not prohibit discrimination based on sexual orientation or gender identity, and societal discrimination remains a problem. Nevertheless, annual LGBT (lesbian, gay, bisexual, and transgender) pride events were held across the country for a seventh year in 2018.

G. PERSONAL AUTONOMY AND INDIVIDUAL RIGHTS: 8 / 16

G1. Do individuals enjoy freedom of movement, including the ability to change their place of residence, employment, or education? 2 / 4

Although freedom of movement is protected by law, residency rules limit access to' services for those who migrate within the country without permission, and authorities have restricted the movement of political dissidents and ethnic minorities on other grounds. Vietnamese citizens who are repatriated after attempting to seek asylum abroad can face harassment or imprisonment under the penal code.

G2. Are individuals able to exercise the right to own property and establish private businesses without undue interference from state or nonstate actors? 1 / 4

All land is owned by the state, which grants land-use rights and leases to farmers, developers, and others. Land tenure has become one of the most contentious issues in the country. The seizure of land for economic development projects is often accompanied by violence, accusations of corruption, and prosecutions of those who protest the confiscations.

G3. Do individuals enjoy personal social freedoms, including choice of marriage partner and size of family, protection from domestic violence, and control over appearance? 3 / 4

The government generally does not place explicit restrictions on personal social freedoms. Men and women have equal rights pertaining to matters such as marriage and divorce under the law. In 2015, Vietnam repealed a legal ban on same-sex marriage, but the government still does not officially recognize such unions. A revised civil code passed in 2015 recognized transgender people's right to legally change their gender identity, but only after undergoing sex reassignment surgery.

Domestic violence against women remains common, and the law calls for the state to initiate criminal as opposed to civil procedures only when the victim is seriously injured.

Societal preferences for male children have contributed to a significant imbalance in the sex ratio at birth.

G4. Do individuals enjoy equality of opportunity and freedom from economic exploitation? 2 / 4

Human trafficking remains a problem in Vietnam. The US State Department's 2018 *Trafficking in Persons Report* noted that while the Vietnamese government was working to provide guidance to local authorities on implementation of an antitrafficking plan, a lack of coordination between agencies, insufficient statistics, and inadequate funding were significant obstacles in the fight against trafficking. Vietnamese women seeking work abroad are subject to sex trafficking in nearby countries, and internationally brokered marriages sometimes lead to domestic servitude and forced prostitution. Male migrant workers are also vulnerable to forced labor abroad in a variety of industries. Within the country, enforcement of legal safeguards against exploitative working conditions, child labor, and workplace hazards remains poor.

Yemen

Population: 28,900,000
Capital: Sanaa
Political Rights Rating: 7
Civil Liberties Rating: 6
Freedom Rating: 6.5
Freedom Status: Not Free
Electoral Democracy: No

Overview: Yemen has been devastated by a civil war that began in 2015, when foreign powers led by Saudi Arabia intervened to support the government of President Abd Rabbu Mansur Hadi against the Houthi rebel movement—rooted in the Zaidi Shiite community, which forms a large minority in Yemen—and allied forces linked to former president Ali Abdullah Saleh. The civilian population has suffered from direct violence by both sides, as well as from hunger and disease caused by the interruption of trade and aid. Elections are long over-due, normal political activity has halted, and key state institutions have ceased to function.

KEY DEVELOPMENTS IN 2018:

- In September, UN-brokered peace talks in Geneva planned between the Hadi government and Houthi rebels broke down after the Houthi delegation failed to show.
- In December, both sides signed a cease-fire to halt the fighting in the strategic port city of Hodeidah. However, almost immediately after the deal took effect, fighting broke out in the city, violating the cease-fire. By year's end, the skirmishes had dissipated and the cease-fire remained in place.
- Yemen's humanitarian crisis resulting from the war worsened significantly in 2018, with the United Nations reporting in December that 20 million people in the country were hungry.
- Throughout the year, journalists and human rights defenders continued to face violent attacks from all parties in the conflict.

POLITICAL RIGHTS: 1 / 40

A. ELECTORAL PROCESS: 0 / 12

A1. Was the current head of government or other chief national authority elected through free and fair elections? 0 / 4

Under the existing constitution, the president is elected for seven-year terms. In 2011, under sustained pressure from the United States, the United Nations, and the Gulf Cooperation Council, longtime president Saleh signed a Saudi-brokered agreement that transferred his powers to then vice president Hadi in exchange for immunity from prosecution for his role in a violent crackdown on antigovernment protests. In 2012, Yemeni voters confirmed Hadi, who ran unopposed, as interim president with a two-year term. In 2014, the multiparty National Dialogue Conference (NDC), a months-long initiative in which more than 500 delegates aimed to reach agreement on Yemen's political future, concluded with a plan to transform the country into a federated state of six regions. The NDC also extended Hadi's term for one year so that the proposed reforms could be finalized in a new constitution.

However, the constitutional drafting process and election schedule were thrown into disarray by the Houthis, an armed rebel movement rooted in the Zaidi Shiite population of northwestern Yemen. Houthi forces took over large swaths of the country, eventually occupying Sanaa in September 2014. The Houthis subsequently refused to evacuate the capital as part of a tentative power-sharing agreement, leading Hadi and his cabinet to flee into exile in early 2015. Meanwhile, the Houthis assumed control of state institutions. Hadi retained international recognition as president but had no clear mandate and little control over the country.

A2. Were the current national legislative representatives elected through free and fair elections? 0 / 4

Under the existing constitution, the president selects the 111 members of the largely advisory upper house of Parliament, the Majlis al-Shura (Consultative Council). The 301 members of the lower house, the House of Representatives, are elected to serve six-year terms. The original six-year mandate of the last Parliament expired in 2009, and elections were put off again in 2011 amid the popular uprising against Saleh. In January 2014, the NDC declared that parliamentary elections would occur within nine months of a referendum on the new constitution being drawn up. The constitutional drafting committee completed its work in January 2015, but due to the outbreak of the civil war and the Saudi-led intervention in March of that year, no vote has yet taken place. The incumbent Parliament was disbanded after the Houthis seized control of the capital.

A3. Are the electoral laws and framework fair, and are they implemented impartially by the relevant election management bodies? 0 / 4

Presidential and legislative elections are now many years overdue, and no side in the civil war has been able to assert enough territorial control to implement any electoral framework.

B. POLITICAL PLURALISM AND PARTICIPATION: 1 / 16

B1. Do the people have the right to organize in different political parties or other competitive political groupings of their choice, and is the system free of undue obstacles to the rise and fall of these competing parties or groupings? 1 / 4

The Houthis have harshly suppressed political dissent in areas under their control since 2015. Reham al-Badr, a prominent and outspoken opponent of the Houthi forces and advocate for the return of the Hadi government, was killed by a Houthi sniper in February 2018 while distributing food aid in the city of Taiz. Political groups, including members of the al-Islah Party, an offshoot of the Muslim Brotherhood in Yemen, have been targeted for arrest and detention, as well as enforced disappearances, by security forces associated with the United Arab Emirates (UAE), which is part of the coalition fighting on behalf of the Hadi government.

B2. Is there a realistic opportunity for the opposition to increase its support or gain power through elections? 0 / 4

Parliamentary elections have not been held in Yemen since 2003 and have been on hold since 2009. The most recent presidential election, in 2012, featured only one candidate. No date has been set for future elections, and peaceful political opposition has been suppressed in the context of the civil war.

B3. Are the people's political choices free from domination by the military, foreign powers, religious hierarchies, economic oligarchies, or any other powerful group that is not democratically accountable? 0 / 4

Ordinary political activity is impeded by the presence of multiple armed groups throughout Yemen, including Houthi-led rebel forces, Sunni extremist groups, southern separatists, foreign troops from the Saudi-led coalition, Hadi government troops, and local or partisan militias.

B4. Do various segments of the population (including ethnic, religious, gender, LGBT, and other relevant groups) have full political rights and electoral opportunities? 0 / 4

All segments of the population lack political rights under current conditions in Yemen. Thirty percent of the NDC's delegates were women, and its final agreement called for similar representation in all branches of government under a new constitution, but the draft constitution has been on hold since the outbreak of war. Only one woman won a seat in the last parliamentary elections. A caste-like minority group with East African origins, known as the Akhdam or Muhamasheen, accounts for as much as 10 percent of the population but has long been marginalized in politics and in society. The group had one representative at the NDC.

C. FUNCTIONING OF GOVERNMENT: 0 / 12

C1. Do the freely elected head of government and national legislative representatives determine the policies of the government? 0 / 4

Yemen has no functioning central government, and any state institutions that continue to operate are controlled by unelected officials and armed groups. The Hadi government is largely dependent on its foreign patrons, particularly Saudi Arabia and the UAE.

C2. Are safeguards against official corruption strong and effective? 0 / 4

Government transparency and accountability were minimal even before the outbreak of war in 2015, as a network of corruption and patronage established under Saleh remained entrenched in public institutions, and formal anticorruption mechanisms were largely ineffective. The disruption to legal commerce caused by the civil war has increased the role of the black market and created further opportunities for graft. Food aid is often stolen and sold on the black market by officials on all sides of the conflict, including Houthis and armed forces linked to the Saudi military coalition, exacerbating a food-security crisis that has left millions at risk of malnutrition.

C3. Does the government operate with openness and transparency? 0 / 4

The only truly national institution that had continued to function during the civil war, the central bank, has been split between a government-backed version in Aden and a rebel-backed version in Sanaa since 2016, causing politicized disruptions to public-sector salaries and further reducing the transparency of state finances.

CIVIL LIBERTIES: 10 / 60 (−2)
D. FREEDOM OF EXPRESSION AND BELIEF: 3 / 16 (−2)
D1. Are there free and independent media? 0 / 4 (−1)

The state has historically controlled most terrestrial television and radio, though there have been several privately owned radio stations. Since the outbreak of the war, the belligerents have either taken over or enforced self-censorship at any surviving media outlets in the country. Houthi-backed authorities reportedly block certain news websites, online messaging and social media platforms, and satellite broadcasts. The Saudi-led coalition and Hadi government forces have also harassed and arrested reporters.

The war has made Yemen increasingly dangerous for journalists, who endure violent attacks, airstrikes, and enforced disappearances from all sides in the conflict. In April 2018, photographer Abdullah al-Qadry of the private outlet Belqees TV was killed in a missile attack while covering skirmishes in the province of Bayda; three other journalists were injured. Belqees TV accused Houthi forces of carrying out the attack. A Saudi airstrike hit the Al-Maraweah Radio Broadcasting Center in Hodeida in September, killing three employees and a civilian. In June, Anwar al-Rakan, a journalist who had previously worked for the government newspaper *Al-Gomhouria*, died two days after his release from a year-long detention by Houthi forces, where he was reportedly tortured. Al-Rakan was detained after Houthi authorities found his press card for the Yemeni Journalists Syndicate.

Score Change: The score declined from 1 to 0 because the country has grown increasingly dangerous for journalists, who have endured violent attacks, airstrikes, and enforced disappearances since the civil war began in 2015.

D2. Are individuals free to practice and express their religious faith or nonbelief in public and private? 1 / 4 (−1)

Islam is the official religion, and the constitution declares Sharia (Islamic law) to be the source of all legislation. Yemen has few non-Muslim religious minorities; their rights have traditionally been respected in practice, though conversion from Islam and proselytizing to Muslims is prohibited. The civil war has inflamed sectarian tensions between the Shiite Houthis and Sunni militant groups. Members of Yemen's Baha'i community in the north have reported increased persecution by Houthi-controlled rebel forces, which they see as a sign of growing Iranian influence. Baha'i members have increasingly faced spurious criminal charges, including 24 people who were arrested by Houthi forces in September 2018 and charged with apostasy and espionage. Legal proceedings in the case were ongoing at year's end.

Attacks on clerics have increased since the war's outbreak. In the two years leading up to August, up to 27 clerics were killed in the Aden area. Many of the clerics killed were members of an Islamist group favored by Saudi Arabia but viewed as an extremist organization by the UAE. No suspects had been identified in the murders at year's end.

Both Houthi and Saudi forces have destroyed many religious sites and mosques across the country during their military campaigns.

Score Change: The score declined from 2 to 1 due to attacks on clerics and religious sites in the context of the civil war as well as growing persecution of the Baha'i minority by Houthi forces in the north.

D3. Is there academic freedom, and is the educational system free from extensive political indoctrination? 1 / 4

Strong politicization of campus life, including tensions between supporters of Saleh's General People's Congress (GPC) party and the opposition al-Islah party, historically infringed on academic freedom at universities. Since 2015, Houthi forces have detained scholars as part of their crackdown on dissent. The civil war has also led to damage to school facilities across the country, suspension of classes and other activities at schools and universities, and deaths of children caught in either errant or deliberate military attacks on schools. Millions of students no longer attend school due to the war.

D4. Are individuals free to express their personal views on political or other sensitive topics without fear of surveillance or retribution? 1 / 4

Freedom of private discussion is severely limited as a result of intimidation by armed groups and unchecked surveillance by the Houthi authorities.

E. ASSOCIATIONAL AND ORGANIZATIONAL RIGHTS: 3 / 12
E1. Is there freedom of assembly? 1 / 4

Yemenis have historically enjoyed some freedom of assembly, with periodic restrictions and sometimes deadly interventions by the government. Demonstrations against both the Hadi government and Houthi authorities occurred in 2018. In October, Houthi officials arrested dozens of people protesting over declining living standards and high commodity prices in Sanaa, and Houthi supporters reportedly attacked a number of demonstrators at the event.

E2. Is there freedom for nongovernmental organizations, particularly those that are engaged in human rights- and governance-related work? 1 / 4

A number of nongovernmental organizations (NGOs) work in the country, but their ability to function is restricted by interference from armed groups in practice. Houthi forces have closed or raided NGO offices and detained activists, and both sides in the civil war have blocked or seized humanitarian aid. Human rights defenders risk arrest and detention by both Saudi and Houthi forces. In June 2018, Radhya al-Mutawakel and Abdulrasheed al-Faqih, of the NGO Mwatana for Human Rights, which has provided information about human rights abuses committed by all sides in the conflict, were arrested and briefly detained by Saudi forces at the Sayun Airport, en route to an event in Norway.

E3. Is there freedom for trade unions and similar professional or labor organizations? 1 / 4

The law acknowledges the right of workers to form and join trade unions, but in practice these organizations have had little freedom to operate. Virtually all unions belong to a single labor federation, and the government is empowered to veto collective bargaining agreements. Normal union activity has been disrupted by the civil war and the related breakdown of the economy.

F. RULE OF LAW: 2 / 16

F1. Is there an independent judiciary? 1 / 4

The judiciary, though nominally independent, is susceptible to interference from various political factions. Authorities have a poor record of enforcing judicial rulings, particularly those issued against prominent tribal or political leaders. Lacking an effective court system, citizens often resort to tribal forms of justice and customary law, practices that have increased as the influence of the state has continued to deteriorate.

F2. Does due process prevail in civil and criminal matters? 0 / 4

Arbitrary detention is common, with hundreds of cases documented in recent years. Many amount to enforced disappearances, with no available information about the victims' status or location. Detainees are often held at unofficial detention sites. As with other state institutions, security and intelligence agencies like the Political Security Organization (PSO) have been split into parallel Houthi- and Hadi-controlled structures, with each operating in territory controlled by its side in the civil war. In areas that lie within the UAE's sphere of influence in southern Yemen, Emirati special forces have been accused of operating a network of secret prisons and detention centers where torture is said to be rife.

F3. Is there protection from the illegitimate use of physical force and freedom from war and insurgencies? 0 / 4

The civil war has resulted in widespread violence across the country. Coalition air strikes have failed to distinguish between military and civilian targets, and artillery fire from Houthi forces has been similarly indiscriminate. A Saudi airstrike in August 2018, which hit a school bus in Saada and killed 40 children, led to international outrage and calls for accountability for civilian casualties in the conflict. A number of other armed factions, including foreign military units and extremist groups like Al-Qaeda in the Arabian Peninsula (AQAP), operate in the country with impunity for any abuses. According to the Armed Conflict Location & Event Data Project, as of November, more than 57,000 people had been killed in the conflict since the beginning of 2016.

UN-brokered peace talks in Geneva quickly broke down in September when the Houthi delegation failed to show, which the Houthi rebels and the UN special envoy for Yemen blamed on logistical difficulties. The Hadi government sharply criticized both the Houthis and the special envoy for the breakdown. In December, both sides signed a cease-fire to halt the fighting in the strategic port city of Hodeidah. However, almost immediately after the deal took effect, fighting broke out in the city, in violation of the cease-fire. By year's end, the skirmishes had dissipated and the cease-fire remained tenuously in place.

F4. Do laws, policies, and practices guarantee equal treatment of various segments of the population? 1 / 4

Despite the growing sectarian rift between the Sunni Muslim majority and the large Zaidi Shiite minority, Yemen is relatively homogeneous in terms of language and ethnicity. However, the Muhamasheen face severe social discrimination and poverty. Women also continue to face discrimination in many aspects of life, and their testimony in court is equivalent to half that of a man. Same-sex sexual activity is illegal, with possible penalties including lashes, imprisonment, and death. Due to the severe threats they face, few LGBT (lesbian, gay, bisexual, and transgender) Yemenis reveal their identity.

Migrants and refugees fleeing war and poverty in the Horn of Africa continue to arrive in Yemen. More than 280,000 refugees and asylum seekers remained in Yemen as of November 2018, according to UN data. Many of those entering were seeking work in the Gulf states but faced harsh conditions, violence, and barriers to further travel once in Yemen.

G. PERSONAL AUTONOMY AND INDIVIDUAL RIGHTS: 2 / 16

G1. Do individuals enjoy freedom of movement, including the ability to change their place of residence, employment, or education? 0 / 4

More than 2 million people were internally displaced in Yemen as of December 2018, according to the Office of the UN High Commissioner for Refugees. Movement within the country is impaired by combat, damage to infrastructure, and checkpoints at which a variety of armed groups engage in harassment and extortion.

Even in peacetime, a woman must obtain permission from her husband or father to receive a passport and travel abroad.

G2. Are individuals able to exercise the right to own property and establish private businesses without undue interference from state or nonstate actors? 1 / 4

Property rights and business activity have been severely disrupted by the civil war and unchecked corruption, as well as the retreat of state authorities from large areas of Yemen and the division of the country into Houthi- and Hadi-controlled spheres of influence. Women do not have equal rights in inheritance matters.

G3. Do individuals enjoy personal social freedoms, including choice of marriage partner and size of family, protection from domestic violence, and control over appearance? 1 / 4

Women face disadvantages in divorce and custody proceedings, and require a male guardian's permission to marry. Child marriage is a widespread problem. There are some restrictions on marriage to foreigners; a woman can confer citizenship on a child from a foreign-born spouse if the child is born in Yemen. The penal code allows lenient sentences for those convicted of "honor crimes"—assaults or killings of women by family members for alleged immoral behavior. Although female genital mutilation is banned in state medical facilities, it is still prevalent in some areas. Extremist groups have attempted to impose crude versions of Sharia in territory under their control, harshly punishing alleged violations related to sexual activity, personal appearance, and other matters.

G4. Do individuals enjoy equality of opportunity and freedom from economic exploitation? 0 / 4

The war has increased the risk of human trafficking, and after 2015 the government was no longer able to pursue antitrafficking efforts it had previously begun. Migrants, refugees, and the internally displaced are especially vulnerable to exploitation. Border controls and naval blockades imposed by the Saudi-led coalition have contributed to shortages of food, medicine, fuel, and other essential imports, leaving the public more exposed to famine and disease as well as coercion and deprivation by armed groups and black-market traders. In December 2018, the United Nations reported that 20 million people were hungry in Yemen. An ongoing cholera outbreak, which killed more than 2,200 people in 2017, continued through 2018, resulting in 372 deaths as of November, according to the World Health Organization.

Zambia

Population: 17,700,000
Capital: Lusaka
Political Rights Rating: 4
Civil Liberties Rating: 4
Freedom Rating: 4.0
Freedom Status: Partly Free
Electoral Democracy: No

Overview: The government regularly invokes the law to restrict freedom of expression and ban peaceful demonstrations and meetings, while the opposition faces onerous legal and practical obstacles in their operations.

KEY DEVELOPMENTS IN 2018:
- Opposition leaders continued to face harassment and arrest throughout the year. Notably, United Party for National Development (UPND) leader Hakainde Hichilema was summoned by the police for questioning in November, after being accused of inciting riots in the Copperbelt Province over his claim during a radio interview that a state-run timber company would be sold to Chinese nationals.
- Social media users risked arrest and prosecution for posts critical of the government in 2018. In January, a doctor was sentenced to seven years in prison for defaming the president on Facebook.
- In December, the Constitutional Court ruled that President Lungu could seek a third term in the 2021 presidential election, despite the constitutionally mandated two-term limit.

POLITICAL RIGHTS: 22 / 40
A. ELECTORAL PROCESS: 6 / 12
A1. Was the current head of government or other chief national authority elected through free and fair elections? 2 / 4

The president is elected to up to two five-year terms. In 2016, Edgar Lungu of the Patriotic Front (PF) was narrowly reelected with 50.35 percent of the vote, defeating Hakainde Hichilema of the UPND, who took 47.67 percent. The 2016 polls were marred by election-related violence between PF and UPND supporters, restrictions on opposition-aligned media, misuse of public resources by the ruling PF, and the use of the Public Order Act to restrict opposition rallies. While expressing serious concern over these issues, international election monitors deemed the results of the election credible.

A2. Were the current national legislative representatives elected through free and fair elections? 2 / 4

The unicameral National Assembly is comprised of 156 elected members, with 8 members appointed by the president, and 3 seats allocated for the vice president, the speaker, and the first deputy speaker. The 2016 legislative polls were held concurrently with the presidential election and were marred by the same issues, though as with the presidential election, international monitors found the polls generally credible. The PF won the majority of seats, followed by the UPND. In 2018, the PF added to its majority by winning two seats previously held by the UPND in hotly contested legislative by-elections in June and November.

A number of Lungu's cabinet members ran for legislative seats in 2016, and drew legal complaints over their failure to vacate their cabinet offices when the parliament was dissolved before the polls. (Election monitors and other critics said that by remaining in office during the campaign period, the ministers had improperly retained access to government resources.) The Constitutional Court in 2016 ordered them to vacate their offices and surrender back pay for the three months they were deemed to have been illegally in office. The court order had been ignored through the end of 2018.

A3. Are the electoral laws and framework fair, and are they implemented impartially by the relevant election management bodies? 2 / 4

Some elements of a new electoral law passed in 2016 were not fully applied during that year's presidential and legislative polls, in part because stakeholders did not have enough time to thoroughly review the law's provisions, and due to discrepancies between its contents and elements of the constitution.

The Electoral Commission of Zambia (ECZ) is responsible for managing the election process, but lacks capacity. The US-based Carter Center, which was among groups that monitored the 2016 polls, criticized the ECZ for "ineffective" management of vote tabulation and verification.

B. POLITICAL PLURALISM AND PARTICIPATION: 10 / 16

B1. Do the people have the right to organize in different political parties or other competitive political groupings of their choice, and is the system free of undue obstacles to the rise and fall of these competing parties or groupings? 2 / 4

Political parties are registered under the Societies Act and do not regularly face onerous registration requirements; independent candidates may also run for office.

The major political parties are the PF and the UPND, but the opposition UPND faces harassment and significant obstacles in accessing media coverage. Supporters of the ruling party sometimes disrupt private television and radio broadcasts, and even attack the stations when opposition politicians are scheduled to make appearances. In January 2018, National Democratic Congress (NDC) leader Chishimba Kambwili was forced to cancel a television appearance when reports surfaced that PF supporters intended to attack the studio during his interview.

Repression and arrests of opposition figures continued in 2018, as well, hindering their parties' ability to organize and function effectively. In April, New Labour Party leader Fresher Siwale was arrested and charged with defamation for accusing President Lungu of identity theft and claiming that Edgar Lungu is not his real name. He awaited trial at the end of the year.

B2. Is there a realistic opportunity for the opposition to increase its support or gain power through elections? 2 / 4

Despite intense pressure on the private media, and the use of the Public Order Act to restrict opposition events, the opposition UPND almost doubled its representation in parliament in the 2016 elections, while the PF lost several seats. However, political violence and government restrictions on opposition activities ahead of the elections created an environment in which voters were less able to freely elect representatives to determine government policies.

Opposition leaders also face harassment and arrest on trumped-up charges, and the sidelining of such key figures can seriously hamper the ability of opposition parties to gain power in elections. Threats of arrest and violence continued for UPND leader Hakainde Hichilema, Zambia's most prominent opposition figure, in 2018. In November, Hichilema was summoned by the police for questioning after he was accused of inciting riots in the Copperbelt Province. Hichilema had appeared on a local radio show and claimed that state-owned timber company ZAFFICO would be sold to Chinese nationals, which, according to Copperbelt Province Minister Japhen Mwakalombe, caused the riots. Analysts assert that the accusations could be used as a pretext by authorities to disqualify Hichilema from challenging Lungu in the 2021 presidential election.

B3. Are the people's political choices free from domination by the military, foreign powers, religious hierarchies, economic oligarchies, or any other powerful group that is not democratically accountable? 3 / 4

The people's political choices are for the most part free from domination by groups that are not democratically accountable. However, public-sector employers at times have made employment conditional on support for the ruling party. In July 2018, seven civil society groups released a joint statement declaring that they had evidence of widespread vote buying by the ruling party ahead of local elections held that month.

B4. Do various segments of the population (including ethnic, religious, gender, LGBT, and other relevant groups) have full political rights and electoral opportunities? 3 / 4

Suffrage in Zambia is universal for adult citizens. Women have equal political rights according to the constitution, but only occupy 31 of 156 seats in parliament, and few hold key positions in government. A requirement that elected officials be educated at least through high school in effect precludes many women from declaring political candidacies.

Presidents since independence have failed to honor the 1964 Barotseland Agreement, which promised the Western Province, which is home to the Lozi ethnic group, limited local self-governance. Several people accused of leading a separatist movement there remained in prison for treason at the end of 2018.

C. FUNCTIONING OF GOVERNMENT: 6 / 12

C1. Do the freely elected head of government and national legislative representatives determine the policies of the government? 2 / 4

The executive exhibits excessive dominance over the legislature. Nearly half of the PF's legislators hold positions in the cabinet, and the ruling party is able to push legislation through the National Assembly with little resistance from the opposition.

In 2017, the National Assembly approved an emergency decree following a string of arson attacks, which President Lungu blamed on the opposition. The three-month state of emergency further expanded presidential authority, allowing for the imposition of curfews, the prohibition of public gatherings, and detention of suspects without a warrant, among other powers. The vote was held in the absence of the 48 opposition lawmakers who were suspended over their decision to boycott Lungu's annual address.

C2. Are safeguards against official corruption strong and effective? 2 / 4

Corruption in government is widespread, and impunity is common. Prosecutions and court decisions on corruption cases, when they do occur, are often thought to reflect political motivations. The scope of corruption was shown with the September 2018 decision by the United Kingdom, Ireland, Finland, and Sweden to withdraw aid to Zambia amid allegations that $4.7 million in donor funds had been embezzled by government ministries. Lungu subsequently dismissed the minister of community development and social welfare and a senior Education Ministry official for their alleged roles in the scandal, but at the end of the year, no charges had been filed.

Limited funding and enforcement restricts the efficacy of institutional safeguards against corruption, and PF leaders and the government sometimes undermine the work of anticorruption bodies. The Financial Intelligence Centre (FIC), a government anticorruption watchdog, came under pressure over the June publication of its 2017 *Money Laundering/ Terrorist Financing Trends Report*, which found that corruption cost the government 4.5 billion kwacha (US$447 million) in 2017. In response to the report's publication, the PF's deputy media director called for the dissolution of the FIC and the arrest of the body's director.

C3. Does the government operate with openness and transparency? 2 / 4

Zambia continues to struggle with government accountability. There is no access to information law, and while the Anti-Corruption Act requires some public officeholders to make financial declarations, it is only loosely enforced.

However, government ministers in recent years have made more unprompted statements to the parliament, and according to the Extractive Industries Transparency Initiative (EITI), transparency in the mining sector has improved.

CIVIL LIBERTIES: 32 / 60 (–1)
D. FREEDOM OF EXPRESSION AND BELIEF: 9 / 16 (–1)
D1. Are there free and independent media? 1 / 4

Freedom of the press is constitutionally guaranteed, but restricted in practice. Outlets perceived as aligned with the opposition are subject to arbitrary closure by authorities, journalists risk frivolous lawsuits, arrest, and harassment by the government and political party supporters, and self-censorship remains common. Public media report along progovernment lines and neglect coverage of the opposition, though some private outlets carry sharp criticism of the government.

In December 2018, Derrick Sinjela, editor-in-chief of *Rainbow Newspaper*, was handed an 18-month prison sentence for contempt of court by the Supreme Court, after publishing an article that alleged corruption in the high court. The Committee to Protect Journalists (CPJ) called the sentence "disproportional" and claimed that it "sends a very grave message that journalists, and Zambians in general, cannot criticize the judiciary without risking their liberty."

D2. Are individuals free to practice and express their religious faith or nonbelief in public and private? 3 / 4

Constitutional protections for religious freedom are generally respected. However, the government has been criticized for engaging in activities that blur the separation of church and state, including backing a National Day of Prayer, Fasting, Repentance, and Reconciliation, and building an interdenominational church.

D3. Is there academic freedom, and is the educational system free from extensive political indoctrination? 3 / 4

The government generally does not restrict academic freedom. However, authorities have placed pressure on student unions in response to protests, and student demonstrators risk violent dispersal by the police and arrest. In October 2018, after protests over delayed meal allowances devolved into rioting at the University of Zambia, a student died when the police fired tear gas into her dorm room, while others were forced to jump out of their dorm windows.

In the aftermath of the riots, University of Zambia lecturer Austin Mbozi was arrested and charged with promoting tribal hate after he published an article which partially blamed President Lungu for the student's death.

D4. Are individuals free to express their personal views on political or other sensitive topics without fear of surveillance or retribution? 2 / 4 (−1)

Private discussion is generally free in Zambia, though the government appears to monitor and periodically restricts access to opposition websites. In 2018, internet users increasingly faced legal penalties for online speech viewed as critical of the government. In January, for example, a Mongu court sentenced a doctor to seven years in prison for insulting the president on Facebook in 2017.

In August, the cabinet approved the vaguely worded draft Cyber Security and Cybercrime Bill. The bill, which had not yet been passed by the National Assembly at year's end, would create a new body, the Zambia National Cyber Security Agency, which rights activists claim could be used to monitor and punish social media users and limit freedom of expression.

Despite public opposition, in August the government passed a statutory order imposing a tax on phone calls through online platforms such as WhatsApp and Skype.

Score Change: The score declined from 3 to 2 because social media users increasingly faced legal penalties in retaliation for remarks critical of the government.

E. ASSOCIATIONAL AND ORGANIZATIONAL RIGHTS: 7 / 12
E1. Is there freedom of assembly? 2 / 4

Freedom of assembly is guaranteed under the constitution, but is not consistently respected by the government. Peaceful protests against the government and political meetings are frequently restricted under the Public Order Act. Police must receive advance notice before all demonstrations. In 2018, police continued to deny permission for rallies, political meetings, and other demonstrations even after organizers had met legal requirements to host them.

In September, anticorruption protesters in Lusaka were attacked by suspected PF supporters, who threw rocks at the demonstrators. Although several of the assailants were detained by police, it was unclear whether they were criminally charged for the assaults. In December, six anticorruption demonstrators were acquitted of unlawful assembly charges for a protest held in front of parliament in 2017.

E2. Is there freedom for nongovernmental organizations, particularly those that are engaged in human rights- and governance-related work? 2 / 4

Nongovernmental organizations (NGOs) operate in a restrictive environment. NGOs are required to register every five years under the 2009 NGO Act. In October 2018, the police disrupted a gathering in Ndola held by the Centre for Trade Policy and Development to discuss the 2019 national budget, and arrested several of the group's leaders and a pastor for holding a meeting without a police permit.

Despite the constraints on civil society, the justice minister conceded in November that the controversial Cyber Security and Cybercrime Bill had not yet passed due to the opposition of rights activists.

E3. Is there freedom for trade unions and similar professional or labor organizations? 3 / 4

The law provides for the right to join unions, strike, and bargain collectively. Historically, Zambia's trade unions were among Africa's strongest, but the leading bodies, including the Zambia Congress of Trade Unions (ZCTU), have faced marginalization under PF rule.

F. RULE OF LAW: 8 / 16

F1. Is there an independent judiciary? 2 / 4

Judicial independence is guaranteed by law, but in practice the judiciary is subject to political pressure, including by Lungu, who in November 2018 warned that chaos would erupt if the Constitutional Court attempted to block his bid to run for a third term in 2021. In December, the court, comprised entirely of Lungu appointees, ruled unanimously that the president is eligible to run in 2021 without violating the two-term limit, because his first term only lasted one year and six months due to the death of former president Michael Sata in 2014.

F2. Does due process prevail in civil and criminal matters? 2 / 4

Pretrial detainees are sometimes held for years under harsh conditions, and many of the accused lack access to legal aid, owing to limited resources. In rural areas, customary courts of variable quality and consistency—whose decisions often conflict with the constitution and national law—decide many civil matters. Zambia's courts lack qualified personnel and resources, and significant trial delays are common. Bail is frequently denied to detainees.

F3. Is there protection from the illegitimate use of physical force and freedom from war and insurgencies? 2 / 4

Allegations of police brutality are widespread, and security forces generally operate with impunity. Conditions in pretrial detention facilities and prisons are poor, and reports of forced labor, abuse of inmates by authorities, and deplorable health conditions continue.

F4. Do laws, policies, and practices guarantee equal treatment of various segments of the population? 2 / 4

Consensual sexual activity between members of the same sex is illegal and punishable by between 15 years and life in prison, and the law is actively enforced. Women are constitutionally guaranteed the same rights as men, but in practice discrimination and sexual harassment of women are prevalent.

Refugees are protected under local and international law and as of December 2018, nearly 50,000 refugees resided in Zambia. However, there were issues with refugees' access to education, conditions in detention centers, and gender-based violence, among others.

In August, the Zambian government denied Zimbabwean opposition leader Tendai Biti asylum, deporting him back to Zimbabwe where he faced arrest on spurious charges, despite a court order staying his deportation pending a scheduled hearing. The United Nations High Commissioner for Refugees (UNHCR) called for an investigation to establish whether Zambia had breached international refugee law with the deportation.

Resentment over China's increasing economic influence in Zambia has fueled anti-Chinese discrimination and a spate of xenophobic attacks on Chinese businesses.

G. PERSONAL AUTONOMY AND INDIVIDUAL RIGHTS: 8 / 16

G1. Do individuals enjoy freedom of movement, including the ability to change their place of residence, employment, or education? 3 / 4

The government generally respects the constitutionally protected right to free internal movement and foreign travel. However, internal movement is often impeded by petty corruption, such as police demands for bribes at roadblocks.

G2. Are individuals able to exercise the right to own property and establish private businesses without undue interference from state or nonstate actors? 2 / 4

Most agricultural land is administered according to customary law. However, the president retains ultimate authority over all land, and can intercede to block or compel its sale or transfer. Women frequently experience discrimination in matters involving property and inheritance rights. The process of meeting requirements for starting and operating businesses can be opaque and time-consuming.

G3. Do individuals enjoy personal social freedoms, including choice of marriage partner and size of family, protection from domestic violence, and control over appearance? 2 / 4

Societal discrimination, low literacy levels, and violence remain serious obstacles to women's rights. Domestic abuse is common, and traditional norms inhibit many women from reporting assaults. Rape is widespread and punishable by up to life in prison with hard labor, but the law is not frequently enforced.

The rate of child marriage has decreased significantly in recent years, due in large part to the enactment of a 2016 national action plan to eliminate early marriage, which has had an effect on local and customary laws that permitted the practice.

G4. Do individuals enjoy equality of opportunity and freedom from economic exploitation? 1 / 4

Labor exploitation, child labor, and human trafficking remain prevalent despite laws meant to prevent them. Although Zambia significantly scaled back antitrafficking efforts in 2017, there were a number of arrests and prosecutions for trafficking in 2018. In April, three Congolese nationals and a Zambian were sentenced to 25 years in prison by the Mongu High Court for trafficking children.

Zimbabwe

Population: 14,000,000
Capital: Harare
Political Rights Rating: 5 ↑
Civil Liberties Rating: 5
Freedom Rating: 5.0
Freedom Status: Partly Free
Electoral Democracy: No

Status Change: Zimbabwe's status improved from Not Free to Partly Free because the 2018 presidential election, though deeply flawed, granted a degree of legitimacy to the rule of President Emmerson Mnangagwa, who had taken power after the military forced his predecessor's resignation in 2017.

Overview: Robert Mugabe and his Zimbabwe African National Union–Patriotic Front (ZA-NU-PF) dominated Zimbabwean politics since independence in 1980, in part by carrying out severe and often violent crackdowns against the political opposition, critical media, and other dissenters. However, as the ZANU-PF fragmented, Mugabe was removed from power in 2017 through a military intervention, and Emmerson Mnangagwa, the former vice president, was installed as president. The 2018 presidential election, while deeply flawed, restored elected executive power in the country. Endemic corruption, weak rule of law, and poor protections for workers and land rights remain among Zimbabwe's critical challenges.

KEY DEVELOPMENTS IN 2018:

- Mnangagwa narrowly won the presidential election, which was held in late July alongside parliamentary polls. International and local observers said the campaign and polling were peaceful and relatively well organized, but that a variety of factor tilted the elections in favor of the ruling ZANU-PF. Mnangagwa's victory nevertheless offered a degree of legitimacy to his presidency.
- As Zimbabweans waited for the Zimbabwe Electoral Commission (ZEC) to announce election results, the opposition Movement for Democratic Change Alliance (MDC Alliance) declared that its candidate had won the presidency, and antigovernment protests erupted in the capital. Six people were killed when security forces fired on demonstrators, and a number of opposition figures faced prosecution in the aftermath of the unrest. A commission of inquiry convened by Mnangagwa found that the security forces had used excessive force against protesters, but blamed the opposition for inciting the violence.
- A series of developments in the controversial prosecution of opposition leader Tendai Biti suggested strong executive influence and corruption in the justice system. Mnangagwa publicly stated that Biti was released from custody on his orders, while the publication of a text message sent by a senior prosecutor revealed apparent links between state prosecutors and the president's office, as well as an apparent chain of command that guided judicial rulings.
- Despite both its fragmentation and an uneven playing field, the results of the year's elections revealed that the main opposition MDC had increased its voter base.

POLITICAL RIGHTS: 12 / 40 (+2)

A. ELECTORAL PROCESS: 3 / 12 (+1)

A1. Was the current head of government or other chief national authority elected through free and fair elections? 1 / 4 (+1)

The president is directly elected, and limited to two five-year terms under the 2013 constitution, which also devolved some previously presidential powers to the parliament and the provinces. After 37 years in power, Mugabe was forced to resign as the result of a 2017 coup. The ZANU-PF then selected Mnangagwa as Mugabe's successor, and he was inaugurated as the new president of Zimbabwe. Mnangagwa soon announced that a presidential election would be held in 2018 as planned, and would be "free and fair."

The election, alongside parliamentary and local polls, was held in late July 2018. Twenty-three candidates ran for the presidency; Mnangagwa won, taking 50.8 percent of the vote. The MDC Alliance candidate, Nelson Chamisa, took 44.3 percent, and Thokozani Khupe of Movement for Democratic Change-Tsvangirai (MDC-T) took 9 percent.

International and local oversight groups (the former of which received accreditation for the first time since 2002) noted that campaign activities generally proceeded without interference and that the polls were peaceful and relatively well organized, but raised concerns about the overall conduct and integrity of the elections. The Southern African Development Community (SADC) observer mission noted challenges including difficulty by parties in accessing voter rolls, progovernment bias by the state broadcaster and state-owned newspapers, contested postal voting, the ZEC's lack of a cohesive election communication strategy that engaged stakeholders, and the denial of the diaspora's right to vote. A European Union (EU) mission noted similar bureaucratic challenges and problems with state media, as well as numerous reports of assisted voting, and of "inducements, intimidation and coercion against prospective voters to try to ensure a vote in favour of the ruling party," including threats of violence.

ZEC vote-tallying irregularities and delays led to tensions after the elections. The MDC Alliance leadership moved to declare victory in the presidential election before the official results were released, accused the ZANU-PF of attempting to rig the vote, and criticized the ZEC's delay in releasing the results. Opposition protests then erupted in Harare, and the army was deployed to disperse them. Six people were killed and more were injured when soldiers fired on the demonstrators.

The ZEC declared Mnangagwa the winner of the presidential election a few days later. Mnangagwa moved to constitute a commission of inquiry to investigate the circumstances that triggered the military deployment against the protesters. The commission's report, released in December, said the six deaths had resulted from the "disproportionate" use of force against civilians by soldiers and police, but recommended that they be disciplined "internally," and blamed the MDC Alliance for inciting the violence.

Score Change: The score improved from 0 to 1 because a presidential election was held and campaigning for it took place peacefully, though it was marred by numerous flaws and an outbreak of postelection violence.

A2. Were the current national legislative representatives elected through free and fair elections? 1 / 4

Zimbabwe has a bicameral legislature. In the lower chamber, the 270-seat National Assembly, 210 members are elected through a first-past-the-post system with one member per constituency, and 60 women are elected by proportional representation. The 80-seat Senate includes 6 members from each of Zimbabwe's 10 provinces who are elected through proportional representation. Eighteen traditional leaders and 2 lawmakers representing people with disabilities are appointed. Members in both houses serve five-year terms.

The ZANU-PF won 180 of the 270 National Assembly seats in the 2018 parliamentary elections, down from the 197 they won in 2013. The MDC Alliance won 87 National Assembly seats, and the MDC-T won one seat on proportional representation; together the MDC factions held 88 seats, up from 70 in 2013. The now independent but former ZANU-PF member Temba Mliswa won in Norton Constituency, a seat he first won through a 2016 by-election. The National Patriotic Front, a splinter from ZANU-PF, won a seat in Kwekwe. In the Senate, ZANU-PF secured 34 elected seats, MDC Alliance took 25, and MDC-T took a single seat.

The bureaucratic irregularities and media bias affecting the presidential election equally marred the parliamentary elections. Traditional leaders intimidated rural voters and acted in partisan ways, despite a constitutional ban on their participation in partisan politics.

A3. Are the electoral laws and framework fair, and are they implemented impartially by the relevant election management bodies? 1 / 4

The ZEC is responsible for election management and oversight, but its independence from the ZANU-PF has long been questioned. The body faced criticism from international election monitors for aspects of its management of the 2018 polls, including of its stewardship of the vote count; monitors also noted a general lack of transparency in ZEC operations including in its procurement processes, the body's lack of a communications strategy, and the irregular arrangement of the ballots, which appeared to favor certain candidates. Political parties and civil society had difficulty accessing the voter rolls, affecting roll audit and verification processes, contrary to the Electoral Act.

The introduction of biometric voter registration since 2017 has been rocky, and on polling day in July 2018, there was no biometric voter authentication. Separately, there was a noticeable decline in voter registration in Harare and Bulawayo, possibly due in part to fewer registration kits having been allocated there.

In May, weeks ahead of the elections, the Constitutional Court ruled that Zimbabweans abroad must return to Zimbabwe in order to register to vote if they were to participate in the polls. The ruling effectively contravened constitutional provisions guaranteeing every citizen the right to vote.

B. POLITICAL PLURALISM AND PARTICIPATION: 6 / 16

B1. Do the people have the right to organize in different political parties or other competitive political groupings of their choice, and is the system free of undue obstacles to the rise and fall of these competing parties or groupings? 2 / 4

Political parties may generally form without interference. More than 100 political parties expressed interest in contesting the 2018 elections, many of which formed in the months before the polls took place. However, state newspapers and broadcasting institutions tend not to cover opposition candidates, limiting parties' reach.

While authorities have suppressed opposition gatherings in the past, in 2018 opposition parties were able to hold most meetings with limited disruption. However, MDC Alliance supporters and leaders were arrested and prosecuted for the postelection violence that erupted in early August. Police, operating with a warrant, also raided and searched MDC Alliance headquarters.

Earlier, in June, a grenade exploded at a ZANU-PF rally at White City Stadium in Bulawayo. Two presidential security aides were killed and several others suffered shrapnel injuries.

Groups such as Mthwakazi Liberation Front (MLF) have been blocked from conducting memorial meetings for victims of Gukurahundi massacres of the 1980s. The MLF is regarded by the government as a secessionist political party, and its leaders have faced persecution.

B2. Is there a realistic opportunity for the opposition to increase its support or gain power through elections? 2 / 4

The main opposition MDC was generally able to hold preelection campaign events without interference in 2018, and despite both its fragmentation and factors that amounted to an uneven playing field, it managed to increase its voter base in the polls. The MDC Alliance presidential candidate gained almost a million more votes in 2018 than the MDC's candidate had in the last presidential election. In the National Assembly, MDC representation slightly increased from 70 seats in 2013, to 88 in 2018.

B3. Are the people's political choices free from domination by the military, foreign powers, religious hierarchies, economic oligarchies, or any other powerful group that is not democratically accountable? 1 / 4

The military continues to play a critical role in influencing political choices in Zimbabwe. The military were deployed in rural areas in lead-up to Mugabe's 2017 removal, and these soldiers participated in electoral preparations. The military leadership has issued statements denying meddling in politics, despite the secondment of senior military officials to the ZANU-PF secretariat.

Traditional leaders have intimidated villagers and issued political statements contrary to the Constitution and court orders. After Mugabe's removal, the president of the Chief's Council, Fortune Charumbira, publicly supported Mnangagwa's 2018 candidacy. The High Court in May ruled that any statements Charumbira made of a political nature should be retracted, but the order was not enforced.

B4. Do various segments of the population (including ethnic, religious, gender, LGBT, and other relevant groups) have full political rights and electoral opportunities? 1 / 4

Zimbabwe's ethnic Shona majority dominates ZANU-PF and the MDC-T, and in the past, members of the Ndebele minority have complained of political marginalization by both parties.

The 2018 elections saw a slight decline in the numbers of women elected outside proportional representation. Women now make up 34 percent of parliament, a decline from their 35 percent following the elections in 2013. The proportional representation quota expires in 2023, raising concerns about whether progress in women's representation will be sustained. Four of 23 presidential candidates in 2018, or 17 percent, were women.

LGBT (lesbian, gay, bisexual, and transgender) advocacy groups exist, but discrimination against LGBT people is severe and deters their ability to advocate for their rights in the political sphere. When asked about Zimbabwe's constitutional ban on same-sex marriage in a 2018 interview, Mnangagwa said that the people "who want it are the people who should canvass for it, but it's not my duty to campaign for this," adding that it was his duty to obey the constitution.

C. FUNCTIONING OF GOVERNMENT: 3 / 12 (+1)

C1. Do the freely elected head of government and national legislative representatives determine the policies of the government? 1 / 4 (+1)

Mnangagwa was made president by the ruling party in 2017 in the absence of elections. The 2018 presidential election, though deeply flawed, granted a degree of legitimacy to Mnangagwa's rule. MDC lawmakers staged a walkout during the official reopening of Parliament in September, but they subsequently attended and participated in normal parliamentary business.

While the cabinet appointed in 2018 includes a number of new faces, including technocrats in finance, mining, and commerce, the military and intelligence agencies retain a central role in government decision making.

Score Change: The score improved from 0 to 1 because representative rule was restored by the 2018 presidential election.

C2. Are safeguards against official corruption strong and effective? 1 / 4

Corruption is endemic, and the Zimbabwe Anti-Corruption Commission (ZACC) has little independent investigative or enforcement capacity. Reports by the country's auditor general revealing large-scale corruption in government have not been acted upon.

In May 2018, Mnangagwa announced the formation of a new anticorruption unit that would operate under the control of the Office of the President and Cabinet. The move prompted questions about the constitutionality and legality of a body that housed prosecutors under the president's direct control; its creation also seemed to reduce the competencies of the ZACC. The ZACC continued to operate in the wake of the announcement, with its deputy chair saying in December that 400 cases had come under investigation during the year.

Separately, in November, reports emerged that two magistrates with Mnangagwa's new anticorruption unit had received death threats in connection with their work.

C3. Does the government operate with openness and transparency? 1 / 4

Government processes are generally opaque. While the constitution protects the right to access information, a number of restrictive laws make it very difficult for the media and citizens to obtain public information from the government.

CIVIL LIBERTIES: 19 / 60 (−1)
D. FREEDOM OF EXPRESSION AND BELIEF: 8 / 16
D1. Are there free and independent media? 1 / 4

The constitution protects freedoms of the media and expression, but restrictive laws undermine these guarantees in practice. These include the Public Order and Security Act (POSA) and the Criminal Law (Codification and Reform) Act (CLCRA), which severely limit what journalists may publish and mandate harsh penalties—including long prison sentences—for violators. The country's repressive media laws contribute to significant self-censorship and have been characterized by representatives of the Media Institute for Southern Africa (MISA) as the biggest threat to independent journalism in the country.

The state-controlled Zimbabwe Broadcasting Corporation (ZBC) dominates broadcast media, and in a country where many people rely on the radio for information, media diversity is limited by authorities' sustained refusal to grant licenses to community radio stations. Commercial radio licenses have generally gone to state-controlled companies or individuals with close links to ZANU-PF. The government also controls the two main daily newspapers, though there are several independent print outlets. State media favors the ZANU-PF, and this prompted complaints from election observers who assessed the 2018 campaign and polling.

Journalists sometimes face interference by state officials when trying to cover government affairs. MISA said it received reports that a number of journalists were injured in the August 2018 antigovernment protests, both at the hands of security forces who attacked the crowd, and upon being struck by rocks that were hurled by demonstrators.

D2. Are individuals free to practice and express their religious faith or nonbelief in public and private? 3 / 4

Freedom of religion is generally respected in Zimbabwe. However, congregations perceived to be critical of the government have faced harassment.

D3. Is there academic freedom, and is the educational system free from extensive political indoctrination? 2 / 4

The Ministry of Higher Education supervises education policy at universities, and Mnangagwa as president, serves as the chancellor of all eight state-run universities. The government has the authority to discipline students and faculty at state-run universities.

Students still face violent responses to protest on campuses, though the number of such cases has declined in recent years. In February 2018, National University of Science and Technology (NUST) students protested over an extended strike by lecturers, and riot police used excessive force to quell the protests. In April, Great Zimbabwe University's Mashava campus students protested against poor food, unsafe drinking water, and increased tuition at the institution; riot police responded with tear gas, and three students were arrested and charged with violence before being released on bail.

D4. Are individuals free to express their personal views on political or other sensitive topics without fear of surveillance or retribution? 2 / 4

Zimbabweans enjoy some freedom and openness in private discussion, but official monitoring of public gatherings, prosecution of offenses like insulting or undermining the president, and the threat of political violence serve as deterrents to unfettered speech. Individuals have been arrested for circulating materials on social media and WhatsApp groups, prompting self-censorship online.

E. ASSOCIATIONAL AND ORGANIZATIONAL RIGHTS: 4 / 12

E1. Is there freedom of assembly? 1 / 4

Freedom of assembly and association are guaranteed in the constitution, but poorly upheld in practice. Authorities have long used a section of POSA requiring police approval for demonstrations and permitting civil and criminal penalties for violations to inhibit free assembly. However, in October 2018, the Constitutional Court struck down this provision. Rights advocates praised the move, but noted authorities' aggressive past use of POSA to prevent free assembly, and called on authorities to respect the court's decision.

Postelection antigovernment protests that erupted in August 2018 were violently put down by security forces, who killed six people when they fired on demonstrators. Authorities filed trumped-up charged against opposition figures in the aftermath, and the MDC said authorities abducted some protest leaders as part of an intimidation campaign meant to stamp out the movement.

E2. Is there freedom for nongovernmental organizations, particularly those that are engaged in human rights- and governance-related work? 2 / 4

Nongovernmental organizations (NGOs) are active, but remain subject to legal restrictions under the POSA, the CLCRA, and the Private Voluntary Organisations Act, despite rights for them laid out in the constitution.

E3. Is there freedom for trade unions and similar professional or labor organizations? 1 / 4

Due to unemployment and heightened informal employment that have accompanied Zimbabwe's economic crisis, trade unions are grossly underfunded. The Labour Act allows the government to veto collective bargaining agreements it deems harmful to the economy. Strikes are allowed except in "essential" industries.

In response to a nationwide nurses' strike in April 2018, Vice President Constantino Chiwenga summarily dismissed all nurses and ordered the recruitment of new nurses to cover the gaps. The Zimbabwe Nurses Association (ZINA) challenged the order in court, saying the vice president lacked the authority to issue such an order, and additionally claimed that members had been threatened when they had attempted to negotiate with the government. Authorities reversed the order later in April, and nurses returned to work.

F. RULE OF LAW: 2 / 16 (−1)

F1. Is there an independent judiciary? 1 / 4 (−1)

Over the years, pressure from the executive has substantially eroded the independence of the judiciary, and its credibility has been undermined by its overt bias toward the ruling party. In a key 2017 decision widely viewed as unconstitutional, a High Court judge upheld the military intervention that resulted in Mugabe's ouster.

In 2018, court decisions and other developments continued to suggest the strong influence of the executive and the ZANU-PF over the judiciary. Among them was a July decision by the Supreme Court to uphold a ZANU-PF appeal of an earlier ruling in favor of teachers who complained about the ZANU-PF's use of school facilities, and policies that teachers and students attend ZANU-PF rallies.

Separately, in August 2018, Mnangagwa noted on Twitter than a detained opposition leader, Tendai Biti—a former finance minister and the vice chair of the MDC Alliance—had been released "following my intervention," reflecting the extent to which the judicial system is subject to direct executive interference. Biti has been arrested at the border with Zambia, where he had unsuccessfully attempted to seek asylum, and was charged with inciting violence and violating electoral laws by announcing unofficial election results. Despite his release, charges against Biti were not dropped. Later in the year, the exposure of a text message from a senior prosecutor regarding Biti's case suggested corruption within the judiciary. According to Biti's lawyer and news reports, the prosecutor had attempted to send a text message to another prosecutor in Mnangagwa's newly established anticorruption unit. In it, he disparaged the presiding judge's decision to allow the Biti proceedings to be live-streamed, and added that she had not received permission to make such a decision from the chief justice. However, the message was sent in error to the wrong person, leading to its exposure.

Score Change: The score declined from 2 to 1 because a series of court rulings and other developments have demonstrated increased influence of the executive and ZANU-PF over the judiciary.

F2. Does due process prevail in civil and criminal matters? 0 / 4

Due process protections contained within the constitution are not enforced. Security forces frequently ignore basic rights regarding detention, searches, and seizures, and accused persons are often held and interrogated for hours without legal counsel and without being notified of the reason for their arrest. The December 2018 controversy surrounding the Biti case revealed apparent links between state prosecutors and the president's office.

F3. Is there protection from the illegitimate use of physical force and freedom from war and insurgencies? 0 / 4

Security forces backed by the ZANU-PF have long engaged in acts of violence, including against opposition supporters, for which they enjoy impunity. Police brutality is common.

Despite some improvements in recent years, prison conditions are harsh and sometimes life-threatening. Overcrowding, poor sanitation, and food shortages have contributed to the spread of HIV/AIDS, tuberculosis, and other illnesses among inmates.

F4. Do laws, policies, and practices guarantee equal treatment of various segments of the population? 1 / 4

While discrimination on the basis of a broad range of characteristics is prohibited under the 2013 constitution, discrimination on the basis of sexual orientation or gender identity is not expressly prohibited. Same-sex marriages are prohibited by the constitution. Sex between men is a criminal offense and can be punished with a fine and up to a year in prison. The country's land and indigenization policies have been criticized for discriminating against the white Zimbabwean minority.

G. PERSONAL AUTONOMY AND INDIVIDUAL RIGHTS: 5 / 16

G1. Do individuals enjoy freedom of movement, including the ability to change their place of residence, employment, or education? 2 / 4

In 2017, the new Mnangagwa administration directed that police roadblocks to be reduced, and it stripped police of the right to impose spot fines. The early months of 2018 were characterized by fewer roadblocks, but roadblocks and harassment of motorists increased following the elections. Separately, because certain laws have yet to be aligned with the 2013 Constitution, authorities continue to deny dual citizenship and passports to people who can constitutionally claim them.

G2. Are individuals able to exercise the right to own property and establish private businesses without undue interference from state or nonstate actors? 1 / 4

Land rights in Zimbabwe are poorly protected, and in rural areas, the nationalization of land has left both commercial farmers and smallholders with limited security of tenure. Controversies persist over efforts to enact new land reforms. Mnangagwa has stated that his administration will not reverse Mugabe's land reforms, but his administration has also indicated that the interests of remaining white farmers will be protected. A Land Commission mandated with auditing farm ownership and use finally began work in October 2018.

G3. Do individuals enjoy personal social freedoms, including choice of marriage partner and size of family, protection from domestic violence, and control over appearance? 1 / 4

Women enjoy extensive legal protections, but societal discrimination remains high and domestic abuse is a problem. Sexual abuse is widespread, especially against girls. Child marriages are illegal but factors such as poverty, religion, and lack of strong enforcement mechanisms have prolonged the practice. The Termination of Pregnancy Act makes abortion illegal except in very limited circumstances.

G4. Do individuals enjoy equality of opportunity and freedom from economic exploitation? 1 / 4

Due to the prevailing economic crisis, many workers are not adequately compensated, and some have gone for months without pay. A 2018 assessment by the International Trade Union Confederation (ITUC) Global Rights Index categorized Zimbabwe as one of the worst countries to work in. The report said that just 15 percent of workers had formal contracts, leaving the majority of workers vulnerable to exploitation and abuse. Authorities have cracked down on street vending since 2017, and in 2018 threatened to send the army to disperse vendors who attempted to return to their jobs.

The Zimbabwean government has continued efforts to combat human trafficking, though it remains a serious problem. Men, women, and children can be found engaged in forced labor in the agricultural sector, forced begging, and forced domestic work. Women and girls remain particularly vulnerable to sex trafficking.

Territory Reports

Abkhazia

Population: 240,000
Political Rights Rating: 4
Civil Liberties Rating: 5
Freedom Rating: 4.5
Freedom Status: Partly Free

Overview: Abkhazia, a breakaway region of Georgia, has maintained de facto independence since the end of a civil conflict in 1993. The government is financially dependent on Russia, which has a military presence in Abkhazia and is one of a handful of states that recognizes the territory's independence. The tumultuous political environment features significant opposition and civil society activity. Ongoing problems include a flawed criminal justice system, discrimination against ethnic Georgians, and a lack of economic opportunity.

KEY DEVELOPMENTS IN 2018:

- In January, a parliamentary commission declined to make any legal assessment of President Raul Khajimba's controversial December 2017 decision to pardon a Georgian guerrilla leader as part of a prisoner exchange involving Georgia and the breakaway Georgian territory of South Ossetia. Opposition critics of the pardon said it was illegal and called for Khajimba's resignation. The parliamentary commission referred the matter to the Constitutional Court, which had yet to rule on it at year's end.
- In May, the Syrian government recognized the independence of Abkhazia and South Ossetia. Tbilisi responded by breaking off diplomatic relations with Damascus.
- In August, the Bloc of Opposition Forces, the Union of Civic and Political Organizations, and the veterans' party Amtsakhara joined together to create the National Movement for the Protection of Statehood, accusing Khajimba and his government of jeopardizing Abkhazia's de facto sovereignty and calling for his resignation.
- Gennadiy Gagulia, who had been appointed as prime minister in April, was killed in a car crash in September. Valeriy Bganba was appointed to replace him.

POLITICAL RIGHTS: 18 / 40

A. ELECTORAL PROCESS: 6 / 12

A1. Was the current head of government or other chief national authority elected through free and fair elections? 3 / 4

Abkhazia's 1999 constitution established a presidential system, in which the president and vice president are elected for five-year terms. The prime minister and cabinet are appointed by and accountable to the president.

A snap presidential election was held in 2014 after incumbent Aleksandr Ankvab resigned amid protests. While most established election monitors do not assess Abkhazia's elections, informal observations indicated that the balloting was largely peaceful and transparent. In a field of four candidates, Raul Khajimba won with 51 percent of the vote, followed by former security head Aslan Bzhania with 36 percent.

A2. Were the current national legislative representatives elected through free and fair elections? 2 / 4

The parliament, or People's Assembly, comprises 35 members elected for five-year terms from single-seat constituencies. The 2017 parliamentary elections were marred by some instances of intimidation, with violent attacks on two candidates. The voting was voided and rescheduled in one district due to ballot irregularities. Independent deputies dominated the new legislature, and many were oriented toward the opposition. However, about 20 of the 35 lawmakers were considered supporters of the president, as was the new speaker, Valeriy Kvarchia.

A3. Are the electoral laws and framework fair, and are they implemented impartially by the relevant election management bodies? 1 / 4

The legal framework does not support fully democratic elections. Eight members of the Central Election Commission are chosen by the parliament, and seven are appointed by the president. Although the 2017 elections were quite competitive, all elections are predicated on the exclusion of ethnic Georgians.

B. POLITICAL PLURALISM AND PARTICIPATION: 8 / 16

B1. Do the people have the right to organize in different political parties or other competitive political groupings of their choice, and is the system free of undue obstacles to the rise and fall of these competing parties or groupings? 2 / 4

A large number of parties and social organizations participate in Abkhazia's fractious political system, and these movements generally enjoy freedom of association. Organizations representing veterans of the 1992–93 war with Georgia are particularly influential.

However, corruption within parties hampers their democratic functions, and a 2009 law forbids the formation of parties catering to the interests of any particular ethnic, religious, racial, or professional group. Parties are relatively weak as electoral vehicles and as forces within the parliament, with most candidates campaigning and serving as independents. In the 2017 parliamentary elections, 112 of 137 candidates ran as independents.

B2. Is there a realistic opportunity for the opposition to increase its support or gain power through elections? 3 / 4

Although independent candidates are not able to draw on the sort of support or infrastructure typically associated with membership in an established political party, those running against incumbents have enjoyed some success. For example, while no candidates for the opposition groups Amtsakhara or United Abkhazia were elected in 2017, most incumbent legislators—including government ministers—lost their seats. In addition, despite initial fears that the Central Election Commission would refuse to register his candidacy, ousted president Aleksandr Ankvab returned to politics and gained a seat in the parliament.

B3. Are the people's political choices free from domination by the military, foreign powers, religious hierarchies, economic oligarchies, or any other powerful group that is not democratically accountable? 2 / 4

While the people's choices influence domestic politics, the functioning of Abkhazia's political institutions is almost entirely dependent on economic and political support from Moscow.

B4. Do various segments of the population (including ethnic, religious, gender, LGBT, and other relevant groups) have full political rights and electoral opportunities? 1 / 4

Under the constitution, only a person of Abkhaz nationality who is a citizen of Abkhazia can be elected to the presidency. Ethnic Abkhaz dominate the political sphere; of the

35 members of the territory's parliament, 31 have Abkhaz surnames, three are Armenians, and one is part Georgian. The Armenian and Russian communities traditionally have an informal agreement whereby parties nominate ethnic minority candidates in districts where they predominate. The ethnic Georgian population is routinely excluded from elections and political representation. In 2017, authorities argued that the majority of Gali's residents were Georgian citizens and therefore not permitted to vote.

A handful of cabinet-level positions are held by women, and there is one female member of the parliament. Societal norms discourage women from running for office.

C. FUNCTIONING OF GOVERNMENT: 4 / 12

C1. Do the freely elected head of government and national legislative representatives determine the policies of the government? 1 / 4

While Abkhazia's president sets the tone for most domestic policy, the overall ability of elected authorities to determine and implement policies is limited by the economic and political influence of Moscow. The Russian government supplies most of the state budget, though its contributions have started to decline.

Several thousand Russian troops are permanently stationed in the territory. However, there has been significant pushback against a 2014 Russian-Abkhaz treaty, with critics arguing that some of its provisions threaten Abkhazia's autonomy. In one sign of Russian dominance in the security sector, Vasiliy Lunev, a career Russian military officer and former defense minister of South Ossetia, was appointed as chief of the general staff of the Abkhazian armed forces, succeeding another career Russian officer, Anatoliy Khrulyov.

In addition to foreign influence, Abkhazia's government is affected by a pattern of political instability. With the September 2018 appointment of Valeriy Bganba as prime minister, the administration had gone through five confirmed premiers in just four years.

C2. Are safeguards against official corruption strong and effective? 1 / 4

Corruption is believed to be extensive and is tolerated by the government, despite promises to combat it. In recent years, Russian officials have voiced concern at the large-scale embezzlement of funds provided by Moscow.

C3. Does the government operate with openness and transparency? 2 / 4

Legal amendments from 2015 allow citizens to request information about any government decisions not classified as state secrets, and to receive a response within a month. Nevertheless, the territory's political culture is nontransparent, and social stigmas prevent citizens from requesting information. Government officials are not required to provide declarations of income. In July 2018, a local civic anticorruption initiative proposed a bill to the parliament that would require all public officials to prove the legality and origin of their property and that of their close relatives. The parliament had yet to take up the bill at year's end.

CIVIL LIBERTIES: 23 / 60
D. FREEDOM OF EXPRESSION AND BELIEF: 8 / 16
D1. Are there free and independent media? 2 / 4

Broadcast media are largely controlled by the government, which operates the Abkhaz State Television and Radio Company (AGTRK). Abkhaz journalists have criticized AGTRK for failing to air material that could be perceived as unflattering to the government. Two state-owned newspapers compete with privately owned papers. The internet and social media have become increasingly popular sources of information. Major Russian television stations broadcast into Abkhazia, and residents of the Gali district have access to Georgian channels. Local outlets have difficulty competing with Russian media.

Some legal restrictions apply to both traditional and online media, including criminal libel statutes. In September 2018, a court sided with lawmaker and former interior minister Raul Lolua in his defamation suit against the editor of *Nuzhnaya Gazeta*, Izida Chania, after she criticized him in a number of articles, including an entry in her Radio Free Europe/ Radio Liberty (RFE/RL) blog. The Supreme Court began considering Chania's appeal in December, and it rejected an attempt by the plaintiff to prevent a journalist with RFE/RL from covering the trial on the grounds that it was not an accredited news outlet in Abkhazia.

D2. Are individuals free to practice and express their religious faith or nonbelief in public and private? 2 / 4

Orthodox Christianity is the dominant religion in Abkhazia, but the Georgian Orthodox Church faces discrimination and restrictions. Most practicing Christians adhere to one of the branches of the Abkhazian Orthodox Church.

Muslims are allowed to practice freely, though some community leaders have been attacked in the past. There are no widely reported restrictions on the minority who identify with Abkhazia's traditional pre-Christian religion. Jehovah's Witnesses are banned by a 1995 decree.

D3. Is there academic freedom, and is the educational system free from extensive political indoctrination? 1 / 4

The education system is affected by the separatist government's political priorities. Schools providing instruction in Russian and Armenian generally operate without interference. However, Georgian-language schools in Gali have been undergoing reorganization since 2015 with the aim of replacing Georgian with Russian.

Universities in the capital have recently become more lenient about the enrollment of Gali Georgians without Abkhaz passports. Nevertheless, bureaucratic complications still arise with respect to obtaining a diploma, and some argue that requiring aspiring university students to take Abkhaz-language proficiency exams as part of their graduation from secondary school disadvantages ethnic minorities.

D4. Are individuals free to express their personal views on political or other sensitive topics without fear of surveillance or retribution? 3 / 4

Social media have become vibrant platforms for discussion on political and other topics. However, there is some self-censorship on sensitive subjects, especially those relating to Georgians in Abkhazia and relations with Tbilisi.

In July 2018, the parliament approved a draft law in the first reading that would prescribe up to 15 years' imprisonment for vaguely defined "actions against the sovereignty of Abkhazia." Observers expressed concerns that the bill, if it were to win final passage and be enacted into law, could have negative repercussions for freedom of speech.

E. ASSOCIATIONAL AND ORGANIZATIONAL RIGHTS: 6 / 12
E1. Is there freedom of assembly? 3 / 4

Freedom of assembly is largely respected, and opposition and civil society groups regularly mount protests. Although violent confrontations between police and protesters have occurred in the past, demonstrations demanding Khajimba's resignation were held without incident outside government buildings during 2018.

E2. Is there freedom for nongovernmental organizations, particularly those that are engaged in human rights- and governance-related work? 2 / 4

Civil society organizations, particularly groups representing Abkhazia's war veterans, exert influence on government policies. Several hundred nongovernmental organizations (NGOs) are registered, though only a fraction of these are active. Many groups struggle to secure sustainable funding, in part because partnerships with foreign or international NGOs are complicated by Abkhazia's disputed status. NGOs that receive funding from governments or entities that do not recognize Abkhazia's independence face criticism from local journalists and authorities.

In March 2018, the parliament elected Asida Shakryl as Abkhazia's commissioner for human rights, or ombudsperson. The institution had been created by a 2016 law, but it had lacked funding to operate. The commissioner's office formally opened in November 2018.

E3. Is there freedom for trade unions and similar professional or labor organizations? 1 / 4

Trade unions exist, but unions and labor activists have struggled to effectively defend the rights of workers. In recent years the territory's federation of independent trade unions has clashed with the government over distribution of social insurance funds. In November 2018, trade union leaders threatened to organize mass protests in 2019 if officials did not meet their demands.

F. RULE OF LAW: 4 / 16

F1. Is there an independent judiciary? 1 / 4

Nepotism and corruption, often based on clan and ethnic ties, reportedly have a significant impact on Abkhazia's judiciary. Implementation of judicial decisions remains inconsistent.

The president's December 2017 pardon of Giorgi Lukava, a Georgian guerrilla leader who fought against the separatist authorities and had been serving a 20-year prison sentence imposed in 2013, raised questions about respect for judicial rulings and judicial independence. Critics said the pardon was illegal, as Khajimba made the decision unilaterally without the approval of the pardons commission. In January 2018, a parliamentary commission examining the matter declined to make any legal assessment and referred it instead to the Constitutional Court. The court had yet to issue a ruling at year's end, partly because disputes between the president and the parliamentary opposition had led to vacancies on the tribunal.

F2. Does due process prevail in civil and criminal matters? 1 / 4

The criminal justice system is undermined by limited defendant access to qualified legal counsel, violations of due process, and lengthy pretrial detentions.

F3. Is there protection from the illegitimate use of physical force and freedom from war and insurgencies? 1 / 4

Isolated acts of criminal and political violence occur in Abkhazia, and many observers have indicated that crime is increasing. Among other reported incidents, at least two Russian businessmen and the captain of a Turkish ship were kidnapped and later released under unclear circumstances during 2018.

Although there is a long-standing moratorium on use of the death penalty, capital punishment remains a feature of the law. In July 2018, the parliament gave initial approval to legislation that would impose the death penalty for distribution of illegal drugs. It had yet to win final approval at year's end.

F4. Do laws, policies, and practices guarantee equal treatment of various segments of the population? 1 / 4

Ethnic Georgian residents of the Gali region continue to face discrimination, including police harassment and unequal access to documentation, education, and public services. In 2017, Sukhumi began issuing residence permits to Gali Georgians for five-year renewable terms. Permit holders may retain Georgian citizenship, reside in Gali, and cross the border into Georgia proper. The separatist authorities stated that they would grant Abkhazian citizenship to any Georgian willing to "rediscover their Abkhaz ethnic heritage." Local officials warned Gali Georgians against attempting to hold both passports amid complaints of bureaucratic hurdles in obtaining the residency permits.

LGBT (lesbian, gay, bisexual, and transgender) people do not enjoy comprehensive legal protections.

G. PERSONAL AUTONOMY AND INDIVIDUAL RIGHTS: 5 / 16

G1. Do individuals enjoy freedom of movement, including the ability to change their place of residence, employment, or education? 1 / 4

Freedom of movement is limited by the ongoing dispute over Abkhazia's status. Travel permits remain expensive and burdensome to obtain. About 90 percent of Abkhazia's residents hold Russian passports, as Abkhaz travel documents are not internationally recognized.

In 2017, separatist authorities closed two pedestrian crossing points over the Inguri River into territory controlled by the Georgian government, leaving just two such crossings. The move made it more difficult for residents of border villages to obtain services and engage in economic activity on the other side of the de facto boundary.

The September 2018 death of Prime Minister Gennadiy Gagulia in a car crash drew attention to the territory's exceptionally poor record on road safety, which stems in part from corruption and impunity for violations.

G2. Are individuals able to exercise the right to own property and establish private businesses without undue interference from state or nonstate actors? 1 / 4

Criminal activity hampers the operations of local businesses. The constitution forbids foreigners, including Russians, from buying real estate in Abkhazia, a rule that has broad support in Abkhazian society. Uncertainty persists regarding property rights for ethnic Georgians in Gali, whose residency permits do not allow them to officially own or inherit property. The legal status of properties whose owners were expelled from Abkhazia during the 1990s is also unclear, as displaced people cannot return to claim them.

G3. Do individuals enjoy personal social freedoms, including choice of marriage partner and size of family, protection from domestic violence, and control over appearance? 2 / 4

Personal freedoms are somewhat inhibited by conservative social mores and societal disapproval of certain identities and behavior, including "nontraditional" sexual orientations and gender nonconformity. A 2016 law banned abortions in all circumstances apart from prior fetal death.

NGOs have expressed concern about so-called honor killings of young women accused of moral transgressions. Domestic violence and rape are serious problems, and victims lack access to effective remedies for such abuse. There is no specific law to address domestic violence.

G4. Do individuals enjoy equality of opportunity and freedom from economic exploitation? 1 / 4

Equality of opportunity is limited by Abkhazia's international isolation, as well as by corruption and criminality. In 2018, Russian and other foreign businessmen complained that criminal activity and arbitrary expropriations severely impaired their ability to work and invest in the territory.

In 2017, Abkhazia introduced a new labor code that makes employment contracts compulsory and prescribes fines for employers who violate workers' rights. However, observers reported that not all workers were aware of their new rights, and implementation of the code was incomplete.

NGOs have expressed concern about human trafficking in Abkhazia.

Crimea

Population: 2,300,000
Political Rights Rating: 7
Civil Liberties Rating: 6
Freedom Rating: 6.5
Freedom Status: Not Free

Overview: In early 2014, Russian forces invaded the autonomous Ukrainian region of Crimea and quickly annexed it to the Russian Federation through a referendum that was widely condemned for violating international law. The occupation government severely limits political and civil rights, has silenced independent media, and employs antiterrorism and other laws against political dissidents. Many Ukrainians have been deported from or otherwise compelled to leave Crimea. Members of the indigenous Crimean Tatar minority, many of whom vocally oppose the Russian occupation, have faced particularly acute repression by the authorities.

KEY DEVELOPMENTS IN 2018:

- Throughout the year, opposition figures and activists opposed to the Russian occupation continued to face harassment, arrest, and imprisonment for their peaceful activities, and Russian authorities routinely violated due process rights in pursuing cases against dissidents.
- In May, Russian officials opened the Kerch Bridge, which connects mainland Russia to Crimea. The bridge was sharply criticized by the international community for further consolidating Russian control over the peninsula.
- In November, Russian forces attacked and seized three Ukrainian naval vessels in the Black Sea near Crimea, further inflaming tensions; 24 Ukrainian military personnel who were detained during the attack remained in custody at the end of the year.
- In December, four Crimean Tatars received lengthy prison sentences for their alleged involvement with the Islamist group Hizb ut-Tahrir, which is designated as a terrorist organization in Russia but not in Ukraine.

POLITICAL RIGHTS: −2 / 40 (−1)

A. ELECTORAL PROCESS: 0 / 12

A1. Was the current head of government or other chief national authority elected through free and fair elections? 0 / 4

Under the administrative system established by Russia, the Crimean Peninsula is divided into the Republic of Crimea and the federal city of Sevastopol, a port of roughly 380,000 residents. Sevastopol's political institutions largely mirror those of Crimea proper. The head of the Republic of Crimea is elected by its legislature, the State Council of Crimea, for up to two consecutive five-year terms. Lawmakers choose the leader based on a list of nominees prepared by the Russian president. In October 2014, the legislature unanimously elected Sergey Aksyonov as the head of the republic in a process that did not conform to democratic standards. Aksyonov has led Crimea since February 2014, when a group of armed men forced legislators to elect him prime minister at gunpoint.

In March 2018, Crimea residents who accepted Russian citizenship voted in the Russian presidential election, which observers concluded was not genuinely competitive. Residents are not permitted to participate in some Ukrainian elections. However, they are able to participate in the presidential vote scheduled for March 2019, and the party-list portion of the October 2019 parliamentary elections, if they register ahead of time in mainland Ukraine.

A2. Were the current national legislative representatives elected through free and fair elections? 0 / 4

The State Council consists of 75 members elected to five-year terms. Two-thirds of the members are elected by party list and one-third in single-member districts. Legislative elections under the Russian-organized Crimean constitution were held in September 2014 in an environment that was neither fair nor competitive. All of the parties allowed to participate supported the annexation, pro-Ukraine parties were excluded, and the Crimean Tatar minority boycotted the voting. The ruling party in Russia, United Russia, took 70 seats, and the ultranationalist Liberal Democratic Party of Russia (LDPR) secured the remaining 5 seats.

A3. Are the electoral laws and framework fair, and are they implemented impartially by the relevant election management bodies? 0 / 4

The Russian occupation authorities have tailored the electoral system to ensure maximum control by Moscow. Legislators electing the chief executive are limited to candidates chosen by the Russian president. In the legislative elections, legitimate opposition forces are denied registration before the voting begins, leaving voters with the choice of either abstaining or endorsing pro-Russian candidates.

B. POLITICAL PLURALISM AND PARTICIPATION: 0 / 16

B1. Do the people have the right to organize in different political parties or other competitive political groupings of their choice, and is the system free of undue obstacles to the rise and fall of these competing parties or groupings? 0 / 4

Ukrainian political parties are banned, allowing Russia's ruling party and other Kremlin-approved factions to dominate the political system. Russia's Federal Security Service (FSB), the local police, and pro-Russian "self-defense" units use intimidation and harassment to suppress any political mobilization against the current government or Russia's annexation of Crimea.

B2. Is there a realistic opportunity for the opposition to increase its support or gain power through elections? 0 / 4

Because Ukrainian political parties are not allowed to compete in elections and Russia tightly controls the political and electoral systems, there is no opportunity for a genuine political opposition to form, compete, or take power in Crimea.

As in Russia, the authorities in the territory consistently crack down on opposition political activity. Crimean Tatars have continued to voice dissent and openly oppose the Russian occupation, but they risk harassment, arrest, and imprisonment for their actions. Other opposition figures also experience intimidation and police surveillance. For example, Dmitriy Kisiyev, a supporter of the Russian opposition leader Aleksey Navalny, had his apartment searched by the police in February 2018. Civil society groups reported that as of December, approximately 70 Ukrainians—including Crimean Tatars and ethnic Ukrainians—were imprisoned on the peninsula or in Russia for their political activities.

B3. Are the people's political choices free from domination by the military, foreign powers, religious hierarchies, economic oligarchies, or any other powerful group that is not democratically accountable? 0 / 4

Sergey Aksyonov, the chief executive, was originally installed by Russian security forces, and subsequent elections have been carefully controlled by the Russian government, which pressures citizens to vote. Among other abuses, during the 2016 Russian parliamentary elections, public- and private-sector workers were threatened with dismissal from their jobs if they failed to vote. During the March 2018 Russian presidential election, Crimean Tatar public employees were threatened with termination if they did not vote.

B4. Do various segments of the population (including ethnic, religious, gender, LGBT, and other relevant groups) have full political rights and electoral opportunities? 0 / 4

Russia's occupation authorities deny full political rights to all Crimea residents, but Crimean Tatars and ethnic Ukrainians are regarded with particular suspicion and face greater persecution than their ethnic Russian counterparts. The headquarters of the Mejlis, the Crimean Tatars' representative body, was closed by the authorities in 2014. The Mejlis's incumbent chairman, Refat Chubarov, and Crimean Tatar leader Mustafa Dzhemilev have been banned from the territory since then. The Mejlis was officially banned by Crimea's Supreme Court in 2016. In 2017, the International Court of Justice ordered Russia to "refrain from maintaining or imposing limitations on the ability of the Crimean Tatar community to conserve its representative institutions, including the Mejlis." The prohibition on Ukrainian political parties leaves ethnic Ukrainians with no meaningful representation.

Women formally have equal political rights, but they remain underrepresented in leadership positions in practice, and government officials demonstrate little interest in or understanding of gender-equality issues. Women hold about one-fifth of the seats in the State Council.

C. FUNCTIONING OF GOVERNMENT: 0 / 12

C1. Do the freely elected head of government and national legislative representatives determine the policies of the government? 0 / 4

All major policy decisions are made in Moscow and executed by Russian president Vladimir Putin's representatives in Crimea or the local authorities, who were not freely elected and are beholden to the Kremlin.

C2. Are safeguards against official corruption strong and effective? 0 / 4

Corruption is widespread in Crimea and occurs at the highest levels of government, as exemplified by the October 2018 arrest of Deputy Prime Minister Vitaliy Nakhlupin for bribery. Generally, efforts to investigate and prosecute corruption are inadequate. Some elements of the Russian-backed leadership, including Aksyonov, reputedly have ties to organized crime. In recent years, the FSB has arrested a number of Crimean officials as part of an ostensible campaign against graft; many of the arrests were related to allegations that local authorities embezzled Russian funds meant to support the occupation. However, some have also been linked to infighting between Crimean and Russian officials over control of the peninsula's assets.

C3. Does the government operate with openness and transparency? 0 / 4

With strict controls on the media and few other means of holding officials accountable, residents struggle to obtain information about the functioning of their government. Budget processes are nontransparent, and input from civil society, which is itself subject to tight restrictions, is limited.

ADDITIONAL DISCRETIONARY POLITICAL RIGHTS QUESTION

Is the government or occupying power deliberately changing the ethnic composition of a country or territory so as to destroy a culture or tip the political balance in favor of another group? −2 / 0 (−1)

Since the occupation began, the Russian government has taken decisive steps to solidify ethnic Russian domination of the peninsula and marginalize the Ukrainian and Crimean Tatar communities. The elimination of the Ukrainian language from school curriculums and the closure of most Ukrainian Orthodox churches since 2014 are indicative of this attempt to Russify the population.

Russian and local pro-Russian officials' policies and actions in Crimea have led to an influx of hundreds of thousands of people from Russia, including Russian troops, civilian personnel, and their families. People displaced by fighting and deprivation in eastern Ukraine—home to many ethnic Russians—have also come to Crimea. Ukrainian citizens from Crimea have been drafted into compulsory military service in the Russian armed forces, in contravention of international law. As of November 2018, approximately 12,000 Crimeans had been drafted into the Russian military.

Meanwhile, political persecution has led to an outflow of ethnic Ukrainians and Crimean Tatars. Russia instituted a policy of mass Russian naturalization for all residents of Crimea in 2014, in violation of international law. Once the policy was enacted, Crimeans had only 18 days to opt out of Russian citizenship. Ukrainian citizens, many of them long-term residents with immediate family on the peninsula, have been deported from Crimea since the beginning of the occupation, often for opting out of Russian citizenship.

Score Change: The score declined from −1 to −2 due to the continued influx of new residents from Russia to support the occupation, and the flight or forced removal of Ukrainians and Crimean Tatars from the peninsula amid political persecution.

CIVIL LIBERTIES: 10 / 60

D. FREEDOM OF EXPRESSION AND BELIEF: 3 / 16

D1. Are there free and independent media? 0 / 4

Media freedom is severely curtailed in Crimea. In addition to other restrictive Russian laws, a provision of the penal code prescribes up to five years in prison for public calls for action against Russia's territorial integrity, which has been interpreted to ban statements against the annexation, including in the media. Journalists in Crimea risk harassment, arrest, and imprisonment for carrying out their work. In March 2018, Crimean Tatar citizen journalist Nariman Memedeminov was arrested over YouTube videos he posted in 2013. As of December, he remained in a detention facility in Crimea.

A 2015 reregistration process overseen by the Russian media and telecommunications regulator Roskomnadzor effectively reduced the number of media outlets in Crimea by more than 90 percent. The occupation authorities have cut the territory off from access to Ukrainian television, and Crimea's internet service providers must operate under Russia's draconian media laws. Independent and pro-Ukraine media outlets no longer function openly on the peninsula, and Russian authorities have taken steps to prevent Ukrainian news sources from reaching Crimea. Russian officials blocked a number of Ukrainian news websites in 2018. A human rights group has concluded that Russian authorities also scramble the signals of Ukrainian radio stations in Crimea by transmitting Russian radio programming on the same frequencies.

D2. Are individuals free to practice and express their religious faith or nonbelief in public and private? 1 / 4

The occupation authorities forced religious organizations to reregister under new rules, sharply reducing the number of registered groups. All 22 Jehovah's Witnesses congregations were deregistered after the Russian Supreme Court ruled in 2017 that the group had violated laws against extremism. Mosques associated with the Crimean Tatars have been denied permission to register, and Muslims have faced legal discrimination. As of 2018, more than two dozen Crimeans had been charged with terrorism offenses for alleged involvement in Hizb ut-Tahrir. In December, four of them received sentences ranging from 9 to 17 years in prison.

The Ukrainian Orthodox Church–Kyiv Patriarchate (UOC-KP) did not reregister under Russian law after the occupation and faces pressure from occupation authorities, who have confiscated some of the church's property. Before the occupation, the UOC-KP had 52 parishes in Crimea, but as of October 2018 only 8 parishes remained. At least three UOC-KP churches have been appropriated by Russian authorities.

D3. Is there academic freedom, and is the educational system free from extensive political indoctrination? 1 / 4

Schools must use the Russian state curriculum. Instruction in the Ukrainian language has been almost completely eliminated. In a 2017 ruling, the International Court of Justice ordered Russia to ensure the availability of education in Ukrainian, but it does not appear that the authorities complied with this order in 2018. Access to education in the Crimean Tatar language has been more stable, declining only slightly since 2014.

D4. Are individuals free to express their personal views on political or other sensitive topics without fear of surveillance or retribution? 1 / 4

The FSB reportedly encourages residents to inform on individuals who express opposition to the annexation, and a climate of fear and intimidation seriously inhibits private discussion of political matters. Social media comments are reportedly monitored by authorities. The FSB frequently opens criminal cases against those who criticize the occupation and the oppression of Crimean Tatars. In July 2018, Ukrainian activist Volodymyr Balukh, who was arrested in 2016 on dubious weapons and explosives possession charges after he raised the Ukrainian flag on his property, was sentenced to five years in prison. A court overturned his initial 2017 conviction, but another court convicted him of the same charges in January, in addition to new charges that he attacked the warden of the prison where he was held.

E. ASSOCIATIONAL AND ORGANIZATIONAL RIGHTS: 1 / 12

E1. Is there freedom of assembly? 0 / 4

Freedom of assembly is severely restricted. Public events cannot proceed without permission from the authorities, and the Crimean government lists only 366 locations where they can be held. Permission to hold demonstrations is frequently denied, and when protests do proceed, participants are often arrested. In June 2018, for example, the organizers of a protest against local government policies toward businesses were detained by authorities.

E2. Is there freedom for nongovernmental organizations, particularly those that are engaged in human rights– and governance-related work? 0 / 4

The de facto authorities, including the FSB, repress all independent political and civic organizations. Nongovernmental organizations (NGOs) are subject to harsh Russian laws that enable state interference and obstruct foreign funding. NGO leaders are regularly harassed and arrested for their activities. In May 2018, Server Mustafayev and Edem Smailov, leaders of the human rights group Crimean Solidarity, were arrested and charged with involvement in Hizb ut-Tahrir. In December, Mustafayev was transferred to a psychiatric hospital, where he remained at the end of the year.

E3. Is there freedom for trade unions and similar professional or labor organizations? 1 / 4

Trade union rights are formally protected under Russian law but limited in practice. As in both Ukraine and Russia, employers are often able to engage in antiunion discrimination and violate collective-bargaining rights. Pro-Russian authorities have threatened to nationalize property owned by labor unions in Crimea.

F. RULE OF LAW: 0 / 16

F1. Is there an independent judiciary? 0 / 4

Under Moscow's rule, Crimea is subject to the Russian judicial system, which lacks independence and is effectively dominated by the executive branch. Opponents of Crimea's annexation argue that the judiciary is politicized and aggressively punishes dissidents in politically motivated cases. Russian laws bar dual citizenship for public officials, and Crimean judges were required to obtain Russian citizenship in order to return to their positions after the annexation.

F2. Does due process prevail in civil and criminal matters? 0 / 4

Russian authorities have replaced Ukrainian law with the laws of the Russian Federation, often using measures that were ostensibly adopted to fight terrorism, extremism, and separatism to target regime opponents. Arbitrary arrests and detentions, harsh interrogation tactics, falsification of evidence, pressure to waive legal counsel, and unfair trials are common. Many detainees and prisoners have been transferred from occupied Crimea to Russia in violation of international law. For example, Ukrainian film director Oleg Sentsov and left-wing activist Oleksandr Kolchenko, who both actively opposed Russia's annexation of Crimea, have been detained in Russia since shortly after their arrest in Crimea in 2014; they received lengthy prison sentences in 2015 after being convicted on extremism charges.

F3. Is there protection from the illegitimate use of physical force and freedom from war and insurgencies? 0 / 4

The Russian occupation authorities commonly engage in torture of detainees and other abuses. Victims of torture generally have no legal recourse, allowing security forces to act with impunity. Detention centers are often overcrowded and unhygienic.

The ongoing tensions between Russia and Ukraine threaten Crimea's security. In November 2018, Russian forces attacked and seized three Ukrainian naval vessels in the Black Sea near Crimea as they attempted to enter the Sea of Azov through the Kerch Strait. Russia then took the 24 Ukrainian military personnel on board into custody, where they remained at the end of the year. In defiance of international law on prisoners of war, Russia opened a criminal case against the sailors for unlawfully crossing into Russian waters. In May, Russia had opened the Kerch Bridge, which connects mainland Russia to Crimea. The opening of the bridge drew widespread international condemnation, as it bolstered Moscow's control over the peninsula and made it easier for Russian forces to block shipping to and from eastern Ukraine through the Kerch Strait.

F4. Do laws, policies, and practices guarantee equal treatment of various segments of the population? 0 / 4

In addition to official discrimination and harassment against ethnic Ukrainians and Crimean Tatars, women face de facto discrimination in the workplace, and the legal situation for LGBT (lesbian, gay, bisexual, and transgender) people has grown worse under the Russian occupation. After 2014, Crimea became subject to Russia's 2013 law banning dissemination of information that promotes "nontraditional sexual relationships," which tightly restricts the activities of LGBT people and organizations.

G. PERSONAL AUTONOMY AND INDIVIDUAL RIGHTS: 6 / 16

G1. Do individuals enjoy freedom of movement, including the ability to change their place of residence, employment, or education? 1 / 4

The occupation authorities have sought to compel Crimea's residents to accept Russian citizenship and surrender their Ukrainian passports. Those who fail to do so face the threat of dismissal from employment, loss of property rights, inability to travel to mainland Ukraine and elsewhere, and eventual deportation as foreigners.

G2. Are individuals able to exercise the right to own property and establish private businesses without undue interference from state or nonstate actors? 1 / 4

Property rights are poorly protected, and the Russian annexation has resulted in a redistribution of assets in favor of Russian and pro-Russian entities. After the occupation, the properties of many Ukrainian companies were seized by Russian authorities. In May 2018, a court in The Hague ordered Russia to pay $159 million to Ukrainian companies that had their property confiscated. The properties of Crimean Tatars who returned in the 1990s—after a Soviet-era mass deportation—and built houses without permits are also vulnerable to seizure by Russian authorities.

G3. Do individuals enjoy personal social freedoms, including choice of marriage partner and size of family, protection from domestic violence, and control over appearance? 2 / 4

Domestic violence remains a serious problem in Crimea, and Russian laws do not offer strong protections. In 2017, Putin signed legislation that partly decriminalized domestic abuse in Russia, prescribing only small fines and short administrative detention for acts that do not cause serious injuries. Russian law does not recognize same-sex marriage or civil unions.

G4. Do individuals enjoy equality of opportunity and freedom from economic exploitation? 2 / 4

Economic opportunity has been limited since the occupation due to international sanctions, restrictions on trade via mainland Ukraine, and reliance on trade with Russia. Pollution problems in Crimea worsened in September 2018, when sulfur dioxide emitted from a chemical factory led to the evacuation of over 4,000 children in the town of Armyansk, near the de facto border with mainland Ukraine. Residents' access to goods and services remains constrained, and vital industries like tourism and agriculture have stagnated.

As in both Ukraine and Russia, migrant workers, women, and children are vulnerable to trafficking for the purposes of forced labor or sexual exploitation.

Gaza Strip

Population: 1,837,000
Political Rights Rating: 7
Civil Liberties Rating: 6
Freedom Rating: 6.5
Freedom Status: Not Free

Note: The numerical ratings and status listed above do not reflect conditions in Israel or the West Bank, which are examined in separate reports. Prior to its 2011 edition, *Freedom in the World* featured one report for Israeli-occupied portions of the West Bank and Gaza Strip and another for Palestinian-administered portions.

Overview: The political rights and civil liberties of Gaza Strip residents are severely constrained. Israel's de facto blockade of the territory, along with its periodic military incursions and rule of law violations, has imposed serious hardship on the civilian population, as has Egypt's tight control over the southern border. The Islamist political and militant group Hamas gained control of Gaza in 2007, following its victory in the preceding year's legislative elections and a subsequent conflict with Fatah, the ruling party in the West Bank. The unresolved schism between Hamas and the Fatah-led Palestinian Authority (PA) has contributed to legal confusion and repeated postponement of elections, which have not been held in Gaza since 2006.

KEY DEVELOPMENTS IN 2018:

- More than 180 Palestinians were killed and thousands more were injured, in many cases by live ammunition from Israeli forces, during a series of demonstrations near the de facto border with Israel—known as the Great March of Return—that began in March and continued throughout the year.
- Following an Egyptian-brokered deal in 2017, reconciliation talks between Hamas and the Fatah-led PA stalled during 2018, obstructing any progress toward a functioning national unity government and new elections.
- Gaza's economy was on the verge of collapse at the end of the year due to the ongoing Israeli-imposed blockade, recent declines in overall donor support, and a reduction in budgetary transfers from the PA.
- A botched operation by Israeli forces in Gaza in November led to a brief flare-up in hostilities, with Israel carrying out air strikes and Palestinian militants launching rockets toward Israel. A cease-fire halted the fighting after two days.

POLITICAL RIGHTS: 3 / 40
A. ELECTORAL PROCESS: 0 / 12
A1. Was the current head of government or other chief national authority elected through free and fair elections? 0 / 4

The PA has not held a presidential election since 2005, when the Fatah faction's Mahmoud Abbas won with 62 percent of the vote. Following its win in 2006 legislative elections and a violent rift with Fatah and the West Bank–based PA in 2007, Hamas seized control of the Gaza Strip. Abbas's four-year electoral mandate expired in 2009, though he continued to govern in the West Bank as of 2018.

Under PA laws, the prime minister is nominated by the president and requires the support of the PLC. Hamas leader Ismail Haniya was nominated and sworn in as prime minister following the 2006 elections, and again in 2007 as part of a short-lived unity government, but he was dismissed by President Abbas after the Fatah-Hamas conflict that year. Hamas did not recognize this move. Despite repeated attempts to form new PA unity governments with Fatah, Hamas officials have exercised de facto executive authority in the Gaza Strip since then. The de facto head of government as of 2018, Yahya Sinwar, was chosen in a closed election by Hamas members in February 2017.

In October 2017, Hamas and Fatah signed a reconciliation agreement brokered by Egypt, but implementation remained stalled in 2018, with the PA demanding full political and security control in Gaza. No schedule for a Palestinian presidential election had been set at year's end.

A2. Were the current national legislative representatives elected through free and fair elections? 0 / 4

The PA has not held elections for the 132-seat PLC since 2006, when Hamas won 74 seats and Fatah took 45. The subsequent Fatah-Hamas schism and Israel's detention of many lawmakers left the full PLC unable to function, and the body's electoral mandate expired in 2010. Nonetheless, a Hamas-led rump legislature continued to operate in the Gaza Strip. In December 2018, President Abbas ordered the formal dissolution of the PLC, backed by a Supreme Constitutional Court ruling that also called for legislative elections within six months. Hamas rejected the decision.

The PA held municipal council elections in the West Bank in 2017, but Hamas refused to participate, and no voting was held in Gaza. The Gaza Strip was also excluded from the last municipal elections in 2012.

A3. Are the electoral laws and framework fair, and are they implemented impartially by the relevant election management bodies? 0 / 4

No open elections for any office have been held in Gaza since 2006. Decisions about the conduct of elections are highly politicized. For example, Hamas refused to participate in the 2017 PA municipal elections, which had been postponed from the previous year amid disputes between Hamas and Fatah over candidate lists. Following a 2016 PA court ruling to exclude the Gaza Strip from the elections, ostensibly due to concerns about judicial oversight, no agreement could be reached on how to arrange balloting in Gaza.

B. POLITICAL PLURALISM AND PARTICIPATION: 2 / 16

B1. Do the people have the right to organize in different political parties or other competitive political groupings of their choice, and is the system free of undue obstacles to the rise and fall of these competing parties or groupings? 1 / 4

Since 2007, Gaza has functioned as a de facto one-party state under Hamas rule, although smaller parties—including Islamic Jihad, the Popular Front for the Liberation of Palestine (PFLP), the Democratic Front for the Liberation of Palestine (DFLP), and a faction of Fatah not supported by President Abbas—are tolerated to varying degrees. Some of these groups have their own media outlets and hold rallies and gatherings. However, those affiliated with President Abbas and his supporters in Fatah are subject to persecution. An apparent assassination attempt was made against PA prime minister Rami Hamdallah during his visit to Gaza in March 2018; Hamas and the PA blamed each other for the incident.

B2. Is there a realistic opportunity for the opposition to increase its support or gain power through elections? 0 / 4

The indefinite postponement of elections in Gaza has prevented any opportunities for a change in the political status quo. Implementation of the 2017 reconciliation agreement, which would have eventually led to elections, faltered in part over the issue of control over Gaza's internal security, with Hamas seeking to retain its independent armed wing and a dominant security position in the territory.

B3. Are the people's political choices free from domination by the military, foreign powers, religious hierarchies, economic oligarchies, or any other powerful group that is not democratically accountable? 0 / 4

Israel's ongoing blockade of Gaza continued to hamper the development of normal civilian political competition, partly by providing a pretext for most political factions to maintain armed wings, seek patronage from foreign powers with their own political agendas, and neglect basic governance concerns.

During 2017, the West Bank–based PA reduced payments for electricity supplies and salaries for government employees in the Gaza Strip as part of an effort to increase political pressure on Hamas. The PA continued to cut funding in 2018, with aggregate PA transfers to the territory declining by an average of $30 million per month from 2017.

B4. Do various segments of the population (including ethnic, religious, gender, LGBT, and other relevant groups) have full political rights and electoral opportunities? 1 / 4

Hamas makes little effort to address the rights of marginalized groups within Gazan society. Women enjoy formal political equality under PA laws, and some women won seats in the PLC in 2006. However, women are mostly excluded from leadership positions in Hamas and absent from public political events in practice. Gazan women do actively participate in civil society gatherings that touch on political issues. There were no meaningful openings in the repressive environment for LGBT (lesbian, gay, bisexual, and transgender) people in Gaza during 2018.

C. FUNCTIONING OF GOVERNMENT: 1 / 12

C1. Do the freely elected head of government and national legislative representatives determine the policies of the government? 0 / 4

The expiration of the presidential and parliamentary terms has left Gaza's authorities with no electoral mandate. In 2018, Hamas continued to govern Gaza unilaterally, assigning responsibilities to its own officials as the reconciliation deal with Fatah remained unfulfilled.

The ability of Palestinian officials to make and implement policy in Gaza is severely circumscribed by Israeli and Egyptian border controls, Israeli military actions, and the ongoing schism with the PA in the West Bank. Israel maintains a heavy security presence around Gaza's land and sea perimeters, using live fire to keep anyone from entering buffer zones near these boundaries, which further reduces local control over the territory.

C2. Are safeguards against official corruption strong and effective? 1 / 4

Hamas has been accused of corruption in public service delivery and aid distribution, which is crucial to daily life in Gaza given that about 80 percent of the population depends on international assistance due to the blockade. In its 2017 annual report, the Coalition for Accountability and Integrity (AMAN) reported some civil society initiatives in Gaza that are meant to promote accountability, but it also highlighted continued challenges, including misuse of public funds and problems with corruption at the border crossings. No new anticorruption safeguards were announced when PA officials deployed to the border crossings in November 2017 as part of the reconciliation deal.

C3. Does the government operate with openness and transparency? 0 / 4

The Hamas-controlled government has no effective or independent mechanisms for ensuring transparency in its funding, procurements, or operations. Minor improvements in transparency were noted in AMAN's 2017 report, including civil society–organized discussions about consumer protection and the improvement of information dissemination on some government websites. However, political decision-making and the operations of Hamas's armed wing remain largely out of public view.

CIVIL LIBERTIES: 8 / 60 (−1)
D. FREEDOM OF EXPRESSION AND BELIEF: 4 / 16
D1. Are there free and independent media? 0 / 4

The media are not free in Gaza. West Bank–based newspapers have been permitted in the territory since 2014, and a number of political factions have their own media outlets. However, Gazan journalists and bloggers continue to face repression, usually at the hands of the Hamas government's internal security apparatus. In a 2018 report, Human Rights Watch detailed the arrest, interrogation, and in some cases beating and torture of journalists in Gaza.

The Palestinian Center for Development and Media Freedoms (MADA) documented 41 violations of press freedom by Palestinian authorities in the Gaza Strip during 2018, including numerous short detentions and interrogations as well as some physical attacks. Major Israeli violations were also reported, most notably shooting deaths and injuries of journalists covering the Great March of Return protests near the border fence. Journalists Yassir Murtaja and Ahmed Abu Hussein were killed by Israeli forces during the protests in April, despite the fact that they were wearing vests and helmets identifying them as members of the press. During the brief outbreak of fighting between Gaza-based militants and Israeli forces in November 2018, Israeli air strikes targeted and destroyed the headquarters of Al-Aqsa TV, which is affiliated with Hamas; workers had evacuated the building shortly before the attack.

D2. Are individuals free to practice and express their religious faith or nonbelief in public and private? 1 / 4

Freedom of religion is restricted. The PA Basic Law declares Islam to be the official religion of Palestine and states that "respect and sanctity of all other heavenly religions (Judaism and Christianity) shall be maintained." Blasphemy is a criminal offense. Hamas authorities have enforced conservative Sunni Islamic practices and attempted to exert political control over mosques. However, they have not enforced prayers in schools or compelled women to wear hijab in Gaza's main urban areas to the extent that they did in the early years of Hamas control.

D3. Is there academic freedom, and is the educational system free from extensive political indoctrination? 1 / 4

Primary and secondary schools in the Gaza Strip are run by Hamas, the UN Relief and Works Agency (UNRWA), or private entities. In the Hamas-run Islamic University, people are separated by gender, and women are obliged to cover their hair. Hamas intervenes in the schools under its control to uphold its views on Islamic identity and morality. It does not intervene extensively in private universities, but Hamas-led police have violently suppressed student demonstrations, including at least two in March 2018 at Al-Azhar University, which is overseen by the PA's Ministry of Higher Education in Ramallah. Some Gazan academics are believed to practice self-censorship. Israeli and Egyptian restrictions on trade and travel limit access to educational materials and academic exchanges.

D4. Are individuals free to express their personal views on political or other sensitive topics without fear of surveillance or retribution? 2 / 4

Intimidation by Hamas militants and other armed groups has some effect on open and free private discussion in Gaza, and the authorities monitor social media for critical content. A 2018 Human Rights Watch report documented a number of incidents of Hamas intimidation, detention, and abuse of individuals in response to their social media activity or attendance at political events, most notably those perceived to be supportive of Fatah or opposed to the Hamas government. For example, individuals have been detained and questioned about social media posts that were critical of the Hamas leadership and its handling of the electricity crisis.

E. ASSOCIATIONAL AND ORGANIZATIONAL RIGHTS: 2 / 12 (−1)
E1. Is there freedom of assembly? 0 / 4 (−1)

Hamas significantly restricts freedom of assembly, with security forces violently dispersing unapproved public gatherings. However, Hamas authorities actively encouraged the so-called Great March of Return, which began in March 2018 as a weekly demonstration to demand the return of Palestinian refugees to what is now Israel. Some of the participants engaged in violent acts, and Israeli forces positioned along the de facto border regularly fired on demonstrators with live ammunition, ostensibly to prevent any breaches of the fence, resulting in scores of fatalities. According to the UN Office for the Coordination of Humanitarian Affairs (OCHA), more than 180 Palestinians had been killed during the demonstrations in Gaza by year's end, and more than 25,000 had been injured, including those affected by tear gas.

Score Change: The score declined from 1 to 0 because over 180 people were killed and thousands more were injured during a series of demonstrations at the Israeli border that prompted a heavy-handed response by Israeli forces, including live fire.

E2. Is there freedom for nongovernmental organizations, particularly those that are engaged in human rights- and governance-related work? 1 / 4

There is a broad range of Palestinian nongovernmental organizations (NGOs) and civic groups, and Hamas operates a large social-services network. However, Hamas has restricted the activities of aid organizations that do not submit to its regulations, and many civic associations have been shut down for political reasons since the 2007 PA split. Aid and reconstruction efforts by NGOs after the 2014 conflict with Israel have been held up in part by disagreements over international and PA access to the territory and control over border crossings. A 2017 Human Rights Watch report detailed tighter Israeli restrictions on access to Gaza for human rights researchers and NGO staff in recent years.

E3. Is there freedom for trade unions and similar professional or labor organizations? 1 / 4

The Fatah-aligned Palestinian General Federation of Trade Unions, the largest union body in the territories, has seen its operations curtailed in Gaza. It still negotiates with employers to resolve labor disputes, but workers have little leverage due to the dire economic situation, extremely high unemployment, and the dysfunctional court system, which impedes enforcement of labor protections.

Hamas sometimes intervenes in labor union elections or in the activities of professional associations that are linked to Fatah, but no major interventions of this kind were reported in 2018. Hamas has established its own, parallel professional associations to compete with existing organizations that are more strongly affiliated with Fatah and rival groups. The civil servants' union for the Hamas-controlled public sector occasionally holds rallies and strikes.

F. RULE OF LAW: 0 / 16

F1. Is there an independent judiciary? 0 / 4

Hamas maintains an ad hoc judicial system that is separate from the PA structures head-quartered in the West Bank, which do not operate in the territory. The system is subject to political control, and Palestinian judges lack proper training and experience. There are also reportedly long delays in hearing cases related to a range of issues, including land disputes and personal status matters.

F2. Does due process prevail in civil and criminal matters? 0 / 4

Hamas security forces and militants regularly carry out arbitrary arrests and detentions. The court system overseen by Hamas generally fails to ensure due process, and in some cases civilians are subject to trial by special military courts.

There were 298 Palestinian security detainees and prisoners from Gaza in Israeli prisons as of December 2018, according to the Israeli human rights organization B'Tselem, which has noted that transporting prisoners outside of occupied territory is a breach of international law. Israel's military courts, which handle the cases of such detainees, lack the full due process guarantees of civilian courts.

F3. Is there protection from the illegitimate use of physical force and freedom from war and insurgencies? 0 / 4

Hamas-led authorities have applied the death penalty without due process or adequate opportunity for appeals, and without the legally required approval from the PA president. A total of 13 death sentences were issued during 2018, down slightly from 16 the previous year, and no new executions were carried out.

B'Tselem reported that Israeli forces killed a total of 255 Palestinians in Gaza during 2018, the most in a single year since the open warfare of 2014. Many of the casualties were civilian protesters near the border fence, but other deaths resulted from Israeli air strikes and exchanges of fire with Gaza-based militants. Intense hostilities occurred over the course of about two days in November, after a botched undercover operation by Israeli troops in the southern Gaza Strip triggered a gun battle that killed one Israeli and seven militants. Seven other Palestinians were killed as Israeli warplanes bombed the territory and Hamas launched hundreds of rockets toward Israel; a cease-fire eventually ended the episode.

F4. Do laws, policies, and practices guarantee equal treatment of various segments of the population? 0 / 4

The legal system operating in Gaza offers few protections against harassment and discrimination for women and other vulnerable groups, including LGBT people. Laws dating to the British Mandate era authorize up to 10 years in prison for sexual acts between men.

G. PERSONAL AUTONOMY AND INDIVIDUAL RIGHTS: 2 / 16

G1. Do individuals enjoy freedom of movement, including the ability to change their place of residence, employment, or education? 0 / 4

Freedom of movement for Gaza residents is severely limited, and conditions have continued to worsen in recent years. Both Israel and Egypt exercise tight control over border areas, and Hamas imposes its own restrictions. Israel often denies Gaza residents permits to travel outside of the territory on security grounds, permitting only certain medical patients and other individuals to leave. University students have difficulty acquiring the necessary permits to leave the territory to study abroad. Hamas allowed PA officials to deploy to Gaza's border crossings in 2017, but this did not lead to any practical changes in freedom of movement for Gazans. Corruption and the use of bribes at crossing points is common.

Beginning in May 2018, Egypt partially reduced its restrictions on the Rafah crossing, but it was still extremely difficult for individuals to receive the Hamas government clearance to travel and to be processed by Egyptian authorities, and the number of crossings each month remained low by historical standards.

G2. Are individuals able to exercise the right to own property and establish private businesses without undue interference from state or nonstate actors? 1 / 4

While Gaza residents are able to own property and engage in business activity, their rights have been seriously undermined by the effects of periodic conflicts between Hamas and Israel, among other factors. Only a fraction of the homes damaged or destroyed during the 2014 conflict had been reconstructed by the end of 2018, and nearly 20,000 people remained displaced during the year. Impediments to private enterprise in Gaza include persistent Israeli bans on imports of many raw materials.

G3. Do individuals enjoy personal social freedoms, including choice of marriage partner and size of family, protection from domestic violence, and control over appearance? 1 / 4

Palestinian laws and societal norms, derived in part from Sharia (Islamic law), put women at a disadvantage in matters such as marriage and divorce. Rape and domestic violence remain underreported and frequently go unpunished, as authorities are allegedly reluctant to pursue such cases. So-called honor killings reportedly continue to occur, though information on the situation in Gaza is limited. The Hamas authorities have enforced restrictions on personal attire and behavior that they deem immoral, though enforcement has relaxed in recent years.

G4. Do individuals enjoy equality of opportunity and freedom from economic exploitation? 0 / 4

PA officials have little ability to enforce legal protections against exploitative labor conditions in Gaza, and most private-sector wage earners receive less than the legal minimum, which is itself lower than the poverty threshold.

The blockade of the Gaza Strip's land borders and coastline has greatly reduced economic opportunity in the territory. Approximately 54 percent of Gaza's labor force was unemployed as of mid-2018, one of the highest unemployment rates in the world. Israel's intermittent restrictions on the entry of construction materials have hampered the economy. Israeli forces also prevent farming near the border fence and limit Gazan fishermen's access to coastal waters. Hamas has imposed price controls that may further dampen economic activity.

Inconsistent access to fuel imports and electricity due to Israeli, PA, and Egyptian policies hinders all forms of development in the territory, including domestic desalination that could improve access to clean water. In October 2018, Israel lifted some restrictions on fuel transfers, and Qatar began financing fuel and other aid to improve electricity generation and overall economic conditions.

Hong Kong

Population: 7,400,000
Political Rights Rating: 5
Civil Liberties Rating: 2
Freedom Rating: 3.5
Freedom Status: Partly Free

Overview: The people of Hong Kong, a special administrative region of China, have traditionally enjoyed substantial civil liberties and the rule of law under their local constitution, the Basic Law. However, the chief executive and half of the Legislative Council are chosen through indirect electoral systems that favor pro-Beijing interests, and the territory's freedoms and autonomy have come under threat in recent years due to growing political and economic pressure from the mainland.

KEY DEVELOPMENTS IN 2018:

- In September, the government officially banned the proindependence Hong Kong National Party (HKNP), marking the first blanket prohibition of a political party in Hong Kong since the territory's handover from Britain to China in 1997.
- In October, the government refused a visa renewal for a veteran foreign journalist, effectively expelling him from Hong Kong. The move was widely understood as a reprisal for the journalist's role in hosting an event that featured HKNP leader Andy Chan.
- Following the 2017 removal of democratically elected prodemocracy and localist Legislative Council (Legco) members from their posts on the grounds that they had improperly altered their oaths of office, the government in November 2018 further moved to invalidate the nomination of one of those individuals—Lau Siu-lai—to stand in a by-election to fill a vacant seat, citing her previous support for self-determination for Hong Kong.

POLITICAL RIGHTS: 15 / 40
A. ELECTORAL PROCESS: 2 / 12
A1. Was the current head of government or other chief national authority elected through free and fair elections? 0 / 4

The chief executive, who serves a five-year term, is chosen by a 1,200-member election committee. Some 200,000 "functional constituency" voters—representatives of elite business and social sectors, many with close Beijing ties—elect 900 of the committee's members, and the remaining 300 consist of Legco members, Hong Kong delegates to China's National People's Congress (NPC), religious representatives, and Hong Kong members of the Chinese People's Political Consultative Conference (CPPCC), a Chinese government advisory body.

In 2017, Carrie Lam, a former deputy to outgoing chief executive Leung Chun-ying and Beijing's favored candidate, was chosen as Hong Kong's fourth—and first female—chief executive, with 777 election committee votes. Her main opponent, former financial secretary John Tsang, received just 365 votes despite drawing far more support than Lam in public opinion polls. As in the past, the selection process featured reports of heavy lobbying by central government representatives.

A2. Were the current national legislative representatives elected through free and fair elections? 1 / 4

Of the Legco's 70 seats, 30 are elected by functional constituency voters, 35 are chosen through direct elections in five geographical constituencies, and the remaining five are directly elected after nominations by Hong Kong's 18 district councils from among their own members. Members serve four-year terms.

In the September 2016 elections, a growing movement emphasizing localism and self-determination emerged to compete with existing pro-Beijing and prodemocracy camps. Candidates from this movement, which grew out of the 2014 Umbrella Movement, captured six seats. Other prodemocracy parties took 23 seats, while pro-Beijing parties won 40; an independent took the remaining seat.

Authorities have responded to the new opposition dynamic by tightening qualification rules, forcing out some lawmakers, and making it increasingly difficult for localist and prodemocracy candidates to win office. In October 2016, after several localist and prodemocracy Legco members altered their oaths of office as a form of protest, the oaths of two newly elected localists—*Sixtus Baggio Leung* Chung-hang and *Yau Wai-ching*—were rejected. The NPC in Beijing issued an unusual Basic Law interpretation that November, requiring oaths to be taken "sincerely and solemnly," and the High Court then affirmed the two representatives' disqualifications. In August 2017, Hong Kong's Court of Final Appeal upheld the decision.

In July 2017, a court granted the government's request to remove four other Legco members who made political statements during their 2016 swearing-in ceremonies—localist-affiliated Nathan Law Kwun-chung and Lau Siu-lai, along with the prodemocracy politicians Edward Yiu Chung-yim and Leung Kwok-hung—even though their oaths had been accepted by the Legco at the time. In September 2017, Lau and Leung indicated their intent to appeal the decision, meaning by-elections to fill their seats would be postponed. By-elections for the remaining four seats left vacant by oath-related disqualifications were held in March 2018, and prodemocracy candidates recaptured only two of these seats.

In May 2018, Lau withdrew her appeal, citing the financial and psychological toll of the lengthy proceedings. In October, Lau submitted her nomination to run in a November by-election to fill the now-vacated seat. However, later that month the Electoral Affairs Commission (EAC) invalidated her nomination, citing her past advocacy in favor of self-determination for Hong Kong. A candidate aligned with the pro-Beijing establishment ultimately won the seat. Meanwhile, Leung's appeal of his disqualification was scheduled for an April 2019 hearing.

A3. Are the electoral laws and framework fair, and are they implemented impartially by the relevant election management bodies? 1 / 4

Universal suffrage, meaning direct elections, is the "ultimate aim" under the Basic Law, but only incremental changes to the electoral system have been permitted to date. Moreover, the system, which already favored pro-Beijing interests and prevented direct elections for many offices, has grown more hostile to dissenting views in recent years. Ahead of the 2016 Legco elections, the EAC required all candidates to attest in writing to their belief that Hong Kong is unquestionably a part of China, based on certain Basic Law provisions. The EAC invalidated the nominations of six localist candidates for failure to comply, preventing them from running. The NPC's 2016 Basic Law interpretation concerning "sincerity" and "solemnity" in oath-taking bolstered the EAC's authority to block future candidates on similar grounds.

In December 2018, Legco member Eddie Chu, who had announced his candidacy for a local village representative position, was disqualified by the local returning officer due to Chu's past support for "democratic self-determination," marking the first time that a village-level candidate had been disqualified from running in an election due to his or her political stance.

B. POLITICAL PLURALISM AND PARTICIPATION: 7 / 16

B1. Do the people have the right to organize in different political parties or other competitive political groupings of their choice, and is the system free of undue obstacles to the rise and fall of these competing parties or groupings? 2 / 4

Hong Kong residents' political choices are limited by the semidemocratic electoral system, which ensures the dominance of pro-Beijing parties and candidates. Some 18 political parties are currently represented in the Legco. The largest pro-Beijing party is the Democratic Alliance for the Betterment and Progress of Hong Kong. The main parties in the prodemocracy camp are the Civic Party and the Democratic Party, and key localist groupings include Youngspiration and Civic Passion. The Chinese Communist Party (CCP) is not formally registered in Hong Kong but exercises considerable influence.

In 2016, the Hong Kong Companies Registry refused to register the new HKNP on the grounds that its proindependence platform constituted illegal activity. In September 2018, Hong Kong's secretary for security announced that the HKNP was officially banned, citing party statements likely to "cause violence and public disorder" and invoking interests of national security, public safety, and public order. The move, based on a law previously used to combat organized crime, marked the first blanket prohibition of a political party in Hong Kong since the territory's 1997 handover from Britain to China. An October appeal of the decision by HKNP leaders was set to be heard by the Executive Council, effectively the chief executive's cabinet, in January 2019.

B2. Is there a realistic opportunity for the opposition to increase its support or gain power through elections? 1 / 4

Prodemocracy legislators have historically enjoyed substantial minority representation alongside their pro-Beijing counterparts. However, the EAC's disqualification of some localist candidates for the 2016 Legco elections, the subsequent ouster of six other prodemocracy candidates who won seats—including two who were not associated with the localist movement—and the October 2018 invalidation of Lau Siu-lai's by-election nomination demonstrate the limits of Beijing's tolerance for movements that threaten its influence. The subjective nature of the NPC's "sincere" and "solemn" standard for oath-taking raises substantial concern that further disqualifications will prevent opposition forces from regaining their former share of seats in the Legco and continue to erode their position.

B3. Are the people's political choices free from domination by the military, foreign powers, religious hierarchies, economic oligarchies, or any other powerful group that is not democratically accountable? 1 / 4

The CCP leadership in Beijing exerts a powerful influence on politics in Hong Kong through a variety of channels, including the NPC's ability to issue interpretations of the Basic Law, the cooptation of Hong Kong business leaders through their mainland assets and membership in the NPC or CPPCC, and lobbying or harassment of election committee members and other political figures to ensure favorable electoral outcomes.

B4. Do various segments of the population (including ethnic, religious, gender, LGBT, and other relevant groups) have full political rights and electoral opportunities? 3 / 4

While there are no formal restrictions preventing women or ethnic minorities from voting or running for office, their participation is somewhat limited in practice, with just 12 women and no ethnic minority candidates elected to the Legco in 2016. Hong Kong's first and only openly gay Legco member, initially elected in 2012, was reelected in 2016.

C. FUNCTIONING OF GOVERNMENT: 6 / 12

C1. Do the freely elected head of government and national legislative representatives determine the policies of the government? 1 / 4

Directly elected officials have little ability to set and implement government policies under the territory's political system, and mainland authorities are highly influential. The Basic Law restricts the Legco's lawmaking powers, prohibiting legislators from introducing bills that would affect Hong Kong's public spending, governmental operations, or political structure.

As a result of the 2017 removal of some prodemocracy lawmakers and the outcome of 2018 by-elections, the prodemocracy camp lost an important legislative veto power that requires control over a majority of geographical constituency seats. However, it would still be able to block Basic Law amendments, which require a two-thirds majority of all Legco members.

C2. Are safeguards against official corruption strong and effective? 3 / 4

Hong Kong is regarded as having generally low corruption rates, and some high-ranking officials have been successfully prosecuted for graft-related offenses in the past. However, residents perceive the government to be lagging in the fight against corruption. The Independent Commission Against Corruption (ICAC) was criticized for failing to appoint a permanent head of operations after the last official in that post was dismissed in 2016, in the middle of an investigation into then chief executive Leung. Ricky Yau Shu-chun, who had been serving as acting head of operations, was finally confirmed in office in August 2018.

C3. Does the government operate with openness and transparency? 2 / 4

Hong Kong has no freedom of information law. Although an administrative code—the Code of Access to Information—is intended to ensure open access to government records, it includes broad exemptions, and official adherence is inconsistent, prompting local journalists and watchdog groups to urge the government to give freedom of information requirements the force of law. The Law Reform Commission has been studying the subject since 2013. In December 2018, a subcommittee issued a consultation paper asking for public input on the issue of access to government information.

Consultations between Hong Kong officials and the Beijing government, represented by a Liaison Office in the territory, are largely opaque, leaving the extent of Beijing's influence on the local government's decisions unclear to the public.

CIVIL LIBERTIES: 44 / 60

D. FREEDOM OF EXPRESSION AND BELIEF: 12 / 16

D1. Are there free and independent media? 2 / 4

The Basic Law protects press freedom. Residents have access to a variety of print, broadcast, and digital news sources, and foreign media generally operate without interference. The mainland's internet censorship regime does not apply in Hong Kong.

However, in recent years the Hong Kong and Chinese governments, alongside businesses with close Beijing ties, have increased political and economic pressure on media independence, resulting in self-censorship among journalists. Some local news outlets have been acquired by mainland businesses or carried dubious "confessions" by mainland political detainees. The detention of five Hong Kong booksellers by mainland authorities in late 2015 has had a chilling effect on the territory's previously freewheeling book-publishing business.

In October 2018, the Hong Kong government refused an employment visa renewal for Victor Mallet, a veteran journalist for the *Financial Times* and vice president of Hong Kong's Foreign Correspondents' Club (FCC). While no official reason was given, it is widely believed that the expulsion was a reprisal for an August FCC event at which Mallet chaired a talk with HKNP leader Andy Chan. The visa denial, which was roundly condemned by rights monitors, was described as the first expulsion of a foreign journalist since the 1997 handover of Hong Kong from Britain to China. Journalists have also faced physical assaults in the course of or in retaliation for their work.

D2. Are individuals free to practice and express their religious faith or nonbelief in public and private? 4 / 4

Religious freedom is generally respected in Hong Kong. Adherents of the Falun Gong spiritual movement, which is persecuted in mainland China, are free to practice in public. However, they have complained of counterdemonstrations and harassment by members of the Hong Kong Youth Care Association (HKYCA), which has ties to the CCP.

D3. Is there academic freedom, and is the educational system free from extensive political indoctrination? 2 / 4

University professors can generally write and lecture freely, and political debate on campuses is lively. However, a series of incidents in recent years have stoked concerns about growing interference by the Hong Kong government and mainland authorities with Hong Kong's colleges and universities. In September 2018, for example, the new pro-Beijing president and vice chancellor of the University of Hong Kong responded to on-campus proindependence activities by warning that senior management of the university was opposed to independence and that the school should not be "a platform for political advocacy." He further stated that the staff and students were expected to obey the Basic Law and be mindful of the consequences of their actions and their responsibilities.

Government-led revisions of history curriculums and textbooks, and attempts to instill Chinese patriotism over the past decade, have stirred accusations of a pro-Beijing agenda in primary and secondary education, but such efforts typically face resistance from educators and the public.

D4. Are individuals free to express their personal views on political or other sensitive topics without fear of surveillance or retribution? 4 / 4

Private discussion is open and free, though mainland security agencies are suspected of monitoring the communications of prodemocracy activists.

E. ASSOCIATIONAL AND ORGANIZATIONAL RIGHTS: 8 / 12
E1. Is there freedom of assembly? 2 / 4

The Basic Law guarantees freedom of assembly. The Public Order Ordinance requires organizers to give police seven days' notice before protests and to obtain official assent, which is rarely denied. However, developments surrounding the 2014 Umbrella Movement protests have raised concerns that the government is growing less tolerant of political demonstrations, particularly by groups calling for greater democracy, self-determination, or independence for Hong Kong. Increased use of baton charges, pepper spray, and arrests by police as they attempted to break up that year's protest camps drew criticism, and the encampments also faced assaults by counterdemonstrators, many of whom were later found to have links with criminal gangs.

While most of the hundreds of protesters arrested in 2014 were quickly released, dozens were officially charged with unlawful assembly and related offenses. In 2016, student leaders Joshua Wong, Nathan Law Kwun-chung, and Alex Chow were found guilty of charges including "taking part in an unlawful assembly" and "inciting others to take part in an unlawful assembly" and sentenced to penalties ranging from community service to a suspended three-week jail term.

In 2017, following a rare government appeal seeking harsher punishments, the three received sentences of six to eight months in jail, with the Court of Appeal instructing lower courts to give greater weight to the need for deterrence when considering similar cases in the future. The Court of Appeal also imposed five-year bans from public office on the defendants. Although the Court of Final Appeal eventually overturned the jail sentences for Wong, Law, and Chow in February 2018, it nonetheless upheld the Court of Appeal's sentencing guidance for future cases of unlawful assembly.

Also in 2017, in a case related to a separate 2014 protest, the Court of Appeal similarly increased the penalties against 13 defendants from community service to between eight and 13 months in jail following an appeal by prosecutors. In September 2018, the Court of Final Appeal reduced those sentences to time already served and ordered the defendants released.

An annual vigil marking the 1989 Tiananmen Square massacre in June 2018 drew over 100,000 participants and proceeded without major incident, as did a July demonstration on the anniversary of Hong Kong's handover to China, with about 50,000 participants.

E2. Is there freedom for nongovernmental organizations, particularly those that are engaged in human rights- and governance-related work? 4 / 4

Hong Kong hosts a vibrant and largely unfettered nongovernmental organization (NGO) sector, including a number of groups that focus on human rights in mainland China.

E3. Is there freedom for trade unions and similar professional or labor organizations? 2 / 4

Trade unions are independent, but collective-bargaining rights are not recognized, and protections against antiunion discrimination are weak.

F. RULE OF LAW: 11 / 16

F1. Is there an independent judiciary? 2 / 4

The judiciary is largely independent, but the NPC reserves the right to make final interpretations of the Basic Law, limiting the independence of the Court of Final Appeal. The NPC's 2016 interpretation regarding oaths of office was unusual in a number of respects, particularly the fact that it was issued without a request from the Hong Kong government and before the local courts had ruled on the matter in question. It was therefore seen as a blow to the autonomy of the territory's legal system. Critics also noted that the interpretation introduced subjective concepts like "sincerity" and "solemnity" that could lead to politicized enforcement.

F2. Does due process prevail in civil and criminal matters? 3 / 4

The courts generally adjudicate civil and criminal matters fairly and efficiently. The Court of Appeal's 2017 decisions—in response to unusual government requests—to reconsider and substantially increase penalties handed down to protesters raised serious concerns about political motivation and due process protections, despite the Court of Final Appeal's more lenient 2018 rulings in those cases.

In another questionable case, police filed charges in 2017 against nine organizers of the 2014 protest movement, including the three regarded as its founders: academics Benny Tai Yiu-ting and Chan Kin-man, and Baptist minister Chu Yiu-ming. The charges, which carried penalties of up to seven years in prison, came immediately after Lam was elected as chief executive, leading observers to speculate that the case had been delayed to avoid harming her candidacy. Defense lawyers challenged the constitutionality of the charges, which included claims that the defendants had "incited others to incite public nuisance," meaning they were twice removed from the core offense. Their trial ended in December 2018, with a ruling expected in April 2019.

F3. Is there protection from the illegitimate use of physical force and freedom from war and insurgencies? 3 / 4

Police are forbidden by law to employ torture, disappearance, and other forms of abuse. They generally respect this ban in practice, and complaints of abuse are investigated.

However, the 2015 disappearances of five Hong Kong booksellers into police custody on the mainland continue to cast doubt on the local government's capacity to protect residents from abuses by Chinese authorities. One of the five, Lee Bo, was allegedly seized extralegally in Hong Kong and smuggled across the border to the mainland. He and three others were eventually released, but they reportedly faced surveillance and harassment; the fifth, Swedish citizen Gui Minhai, remained in some form of detention on the mainland in 2018. Meanwhile, Chinese billionaire Xiao Jianhua, who in 2017 was apparently abducted by Chinese officials from a Hong Kong hotel and escorted across the border to the mainland, remained in custody and was awaiting trial in 2018.

In 2017, Hong Kong and mainland officials reached agreement on an improved reciprocal notification system for detentions of their respective residents, pledging to inform each other within seven working days when a resident is arrested, detained, or prosecuted on minor charges, or when residents suffer unnatural deaths. Notification periods of 14 days and 30 days would apply to more serious criminal cases and cases involving terrorism or national security, respectively.

F4. Do laws, policies, and practices guarantee equal treatment of various segments of the population? 3 / 4

Citizens are generally treated equally under the law, though South Asian minorities face language barriers and de facto discrimination in education and employment. Women are also subject to some employment discrimination in practice. Antidiscrimination laws do not specifically protect LGBT (lesbian, gay, bisexual, and transgender) people.

Over 7,000 asylum seekers were thought to be in Hong Kong as of 2018, mostly from South or Southeast Asia. While the government does not accept refugees for settlement, it does offer protection from refoulement, and those deemed eligible can be referred to UN officials for third-country resettlement. As of July 2018, up to 3,000 individuals still had not had their cases screened by the Hong Kong government. Some applicants reportedly wait as long as 10 years for resolution of their cases, and only a tiny percentage of claims are approved. Asylum seekers are not permitted to work and receive small cash allowances.

G. PERSONAL AUTONOMY AND INDIVIDUAL RIGHTS: 13 / 16

G1. Do individuals enjoy freedom of movement, including the ability to change their place of residence, employment, or education? 3 / 4

Hong Kong residents generally enjoy freedom of movement, though authorities periodically deny entry to visiting political activists and Falun Gong practitioners, raising suspicions of Beijing-imposed restrictions. Some Hong Kong activists and politicians have also faced difficulty traveling to the mainland.

G2. Are individuals able to exercise the right to own property and establish private businesses without undue interference from state or nonstate actors? 3 / 4

While property rights are largely respected, collusion among powerful business entities with political connections is perceived as an impediment to fair competition.

G3. Do individuals enjoy personal social freedoms, including choice of marriage partner and size of family, protection from domestic violence, and control over appearance? 4 / 4

Hong Kong residents are legally protected from rape and domestic abuse, and police generally respond appropriately to reports of such crimes. Men and women enjoy equal rights in personal status matters such as marriage and divorce.

G4. Do individuals enjoy equality of opportunity and freedom from economic exploitation? 3 / 4

While most Hong Kong residents enjoy equality of opportunity and freedom from economic exploitation, certain vulnerable and marginalized communities face substantial risks of exploitation and abuse. For instance, Hong Kong's roughly 380,000 foreign household workers are vulnerable to a wide range of exploitative practices. Since they may face deportation if dismissed, many are reluctant to bring complaints against employers. While Chief Executive Lam vowed to increase government support for household workers' rights in an October 2018 speech, activists are concerned over a lack of specificity on steps for implementation. In addition, Hong Kong's more than 7,000 asylum seekers have virtually no means of legal economic subsistence, which further increases their vulnerability to exploitation and abuse.

Indian Kashmir

Population: 12,500,000
Political Rights Rating: 4
Civil Liberties Rating: 4
Freedom Rating: 4.0
Freedom Status: Partly Free
Electoral Democracy: No

Overview: Control of Kashmir has been divided between India and Pakistan since 1948, and Indian-administered Kashmir enjoys substantial autonomy under Article 370 of India's constitution. However, separatist and jihadist militants continue to wage a protracted insurgency against the government. Competitive elections are held, but they are often marred by violence. Indian security forces are frequently accused of human rights violations, but few are punished. Civil liberties are curtailed during times of unrest.

KEY DEVELOPMENTS IN 2018:

- In June, the state's governing coalition broke down, leading to the imposition of Governor's rule for six months, followed by the imposition of President's rule in December.
- The security situation remained precarious; at least 451 people were killed in terrorist violence in 2018, compared to 358 such deaths in 2017.

- In June, a prominent Kashmiri journalist, Shujaat Bukhari, was assassinated by unknown assailants in Srinagar—the first such murder in the region in nearly a decade.
- Municipal elections were held in October for the first time in 13 years, though polls were marred by opposition party boycotts and threats of violence, and turnout was low. Panchayat (local council) elections in November and December saw higher turnout in some constituencies.

POLITICAL RIGHTS: 22 / 40

A. ELECTORAL PROCESS: 9 / 12

A1. Was the current head of government or other chief national authority elected through free and fair elections? 3 / 4

Ordinarily, a chief minister—typically the head of the largest party in the lower house—is entrusted with executive power. The process for selecting the executive is an internal party matter. However, the withdrawal of the Bharatiya Janata Party (BJP) from the governing coalition in June 2018 prompted the resignation of the chief minister, Mehbooba Mufti, and the six-month imposition of rule by State Governor Narinder Nath Vohra. The state governor is appointed by the president of India, under the advice of the central government.

After Governor's rule expired, the state in December came under President's rule, placing the central government in charge of state affairs. The transfers took place according to the law. As of the end of the year, it had not been decided whether state assembly elections, slated for 2019, would be called early.

A2. Were the current national legislative representatives elected through free and fair elections? 3 / 4

Elections for national parliamentary seats and the state assembly in 2014 were broadly free and fair, with reduced levels of voter intimidation, harassment, and violence compared to past elections. However, in the April 2014 national elections, turnout was less than 40 percent in all districts in the Kashmir Valley due in part to threats of violence. State assembly elections held in November and December 2014 were marked by higher turnout.

Municipal elections were held in October for the first time in 13 years, though polls were marred by opposition party boycotts and threats of violence, and turnout was low. Panchayat (local council) elections in November and December saw high turnout in some constituencies.

A3. Are the electoral laws and framework fair, and are they implemented impartially by the relevant election management bodies? 3 / 4

The legal framework governing elections is broadly perceived as fair. Elections are overseen by the Election Commission of India, a respected and largely independent body. However, intimidation of election workers and electoral authorities by militant groups can interfere with the orderly implementation of electoral laws and regulations.

B. POLITICAL PLURALISM AND PARTICIPATION: 9 / 16

B1. Do the people have the right to organize in different political parties or other competitive political groupings of their choice, and is the system free of undue obstacles to the rise and fall of these competing parties or groupings? 2 / 4

The state permits a competitive multiparty system. While new political parties must register with the Electoral Commission, parties may generally form freely, and there are mechanisms by which independent candidates may stand for office. However, normal party politics are often disrupted by militant violence, intimidation, and separatist boycotts.

B2. Is there a realistic opportunity for the opposition to increase its support or gain power through elections? 3 / 4

For more than a decade, state-level power has rotated between the two largest Kashmiri parties: the People's Democratic Party (PDP) and the Jammu and Kashmir National Conference (JKNC). The Hindu nationalist BJP has made significant electoral inroads in recent years.

B3. Are the people's political choices free from domination by the military, foreign powers, religious hierarchies, economic oligarchies, or any other powerful group that is not democratically accountable? 2 / 4

Militant violence, intimidation, and separatist boycotts negatively affect the ability of people in many areas to assert their right to participate in political processes.

B4. Do various segments of the population (including ethnic, religious, gender, LGBT, and other relevant groups) have full political rights and electoral opportunities? 2 / 4

The state constitution allows all permanent residents over 18 the right to vote in state assembly elections. However, refugees from Pakistan are not entitled to permanent residency rights and may not vote in state elections. They may vote in parliamentary elections.

While Kashmir's chief minister in the first half of 2018 was a woman, women are generally underrepresented in politics.

C. FUNCTIONING OF GOVERNMENT: 4 / 12

C1. Do the freely elected head of government and national legislative representatives determine the policies of the government? 2 / 4

India has never held a referendum on allowing Kashmiri self-determination, as called for in a 1948 UN resolution. However, Jammu and Kashmir enjoys substantial autonomy under Article 370 of India's constitution. All laws passed by the Indian parliament, except those related to defense, foreign affairs, and financial matters, require the assent of the Kashmiri legislature to come into force in the state.

C2. Are safeguards against official corruption strong and effective? 1 / 4

Corruption in Jammu and Kashmir is widespread, and while the government has taken some steps to combat it, these have yet to bring about lasting improvements. A 2011 law established an anticorruption commission with far-reaching investigatory powers. The commission has processed more than a thousand complaints since the first commissioners were appointed in 2013 and has filed a handful of bribery charges against public officials. However, few corruption cases result in convictions. A survey conducted by the Indian think tank CMS in 2017 found that 84 percent of respondents believed corruption in the state to be increasing.

C3. Does the government operate with openness and transparency? 1 / 4

The state administration generally operates with opacity. In January 2018, the PDP-led government faced renewed allegations of making large numbers of illegal appointments based on nepotism.

CIVIL LIBERTIES: 27 / 60

D. FREEDOM OF EXPRESSION AND BELIEF: 9 / 16

D1. Are there free and independent media? 2 / 4

Print media thrive in Jammu and Kashmir, and online media have proliferated, providing new platforms for public discussion. However, threats of government reprisals, including the detention of journalists under the Public Safety Act, continue to intimidate media workers.

In June, a prominent Kashmiri journalist, Shujaat Bukhari, was assassinated by unknown assailants in Srinagar—the first such murder in the region in nearly a decade. The August arrest and detention of another journalist, Aasif Sultan—who was still being held at the end of the year—has raised further concerns about press freedoms.

D2. Are individuals free to practice and express their religious faith or nonbelief in public and private? 2 / 4

Freedom of worship is generally respected by the authorities. However, communal violence between Muslims and Hindus periodically flares up, and many have been injured and killed as a result. The alleged rape and murder of an eight-year-old Muslim girl by a group of Hindu men in January inflamed religious tensions in 2018, leading to sometimes-violent protests and clashes.

Separately, a ban against Muharram processions, which take place during a Shia period of mourning at the Islamic New Year, has been upheld for decades.

D3. Is there academic freedom, and is the educational system free from extensive political indoctrination? 2 / 4

Academic freedom is often circumscribed. Authorities monitor the research produced at Kashmiri universities, and a combination of proactive and self-censorship discourages students and professors from pursuing sensitive topics of inquiry. Colleges and universities were closed for over half of 2016 owing to unrest; further closures took place in 2017 and 2018.

D4. Are individuals free to express their personal views on political or other sensitive topics without fear of surveillance or retribution? 3 / 4

While private discussion is robust, fear of reprisals by government or militant forces can serve as a deterrent to uninhibited speech. The government frequently suspends access to mobile internet services, particularly in the southern districts of the Kashmir Valley, citing security concerns.

E. ASSOCIATIONAL AND ORGANIZATIONAL RIGHTS: 5 / 12

E1. Is there freedom of assembly? 1 / 4

Freedom of assembly is frequently restricted during times of unrest. Requests for permits for public gatherings submitted by the separatist All Parties Hurriyat Conference (APHC) are often denied. Separatist leaders are frequently arrested prior to planned demonstrations. Curfews were repeatedly imposed in parts of the state in 2018 in response to unrest and militant violence.

E2. Is there freedom for nongovernmental organizations, particularly those that are engaged in human rights– and governance-related work? 2 / 4

Although local and national civil rights groups are permitted to operate, they are sometimes harassed by security forces. The separatist APHC is technically allowed to function, but its leaders are frequently subjected to short-term detention.

E3. Is there freedom for trade unions and similar professional or labor organizations? 2 / 4

Although workers have the right to form unions and engage in collective bargaining under Indian law, union rights are inconsistently upheld.

F. RULE OF LAW: 5 / 16

F1. Is there an independent judiciary? 1 / 4

Courts are politicized, and act as an extension of Indian executive and military authority. The government and security forces frequently disregard court orders.

F2. Does due process prevail in civil and criminal matters? 2 / 4

The courts in Jammu and Kashmir, already facing large backlogs of cases, are further hampered by intermittent lawyers' strikes.

Broadly written legislation, such as the unpopular Armed Forces Special Powers Act (AFSPA) and the Disturbed Areas Act, allow security forces to search homes and arrest suspects without a warrant, shoot suspects on sight, and destroy buildings believed to house militants or arms. Under the AFSPA, prosecutions of security personnel cannot proceed without the approval of the central government, which is rarely granted. The state's Public Security Act allows detention without charge or trial for up to two years, though 2012 amendments barred the detention of minors under the law.

F3. Is there protection from the illegitimate use of physical force and freedom from war and insurgencies? 1 / 4

After several years of relative stability, security in the state deteriorated sharply after the 2016 killing of Burhan Muzaffar Wani, a popular separatist militant leader. The situation remained volatile in 2018, when at least 451 civilians, security personnel, and militants were reportedly killed in militant-related violence. Indian authorities in May announced that troops would respect a ceasefire over the month of Ramadan, but it collapsed after a rise in terror-related incidents.

Indian security personnel have continued to carry out arbitrary arrests and detentions, torture, forced disappearances, and custodial killings of suspected militants and their alleged civilian sympathizers, and generally enjoy impunity. In June, the Office of the UN High Commissioner for Human Rights (OHCHR) released a report highlighting human rights violations in the Kashmir region since 2016; the report condemned excessive and extrajudicial violence committed by Indian security forces, including the 2016 use of pellet guns against civilian protesters.

Militant groups based in Pakistan have killed pro-India politicians, public employees, suspected informers, members of rival factions, soldiers, and civilians. The militants also engage in kidnapping, extortion, and other forms of intimidation in Jammu and Kashmir. The OHCHR report also detailed severe rights violations committed by active militant groups.

Women continue to be subjected to harassment, intimidation, and violent attacks, including rape and murder, at the hands of both the security forces and militant groups

F4. Do laws, policies, and practices guarantee equal treatment of various segments of the population? 1 / 4

A pattern of violence targeting Pandits, or Kashmiri Hindus, has forced several hundred thousand Hindus to flee their homes in the region over the years, and many continue to reside in refugee camps. Other religious and ethnic minorities, such as Sikhs and Gurjars, have been targeted in the past, but such reports have recently become less frequent in recent years.

Women face some societal discrimination.

G. PERSONAL AUTONOMY AND INDIVIDUAL RIGHTS: 8 / 16

G1. Do individuals enjoy freedom of movement, including the ability to change their place of residence, employment, or education? 2 / 4

Freedom of movement is curtailed by both state and federal authorities. Curfews were imposed in parts of the state in 2018 in response to unrest and militant violence.

While the Indian government has loosened restrictions on the travel of foreigners to some areas within Jammu and Kashmir, internal movement is disrupted by roadblocks, checkpoints, and periodic protest-related shutdowns or curfews. Kashmiri residents face delays of up to two years to obtain and renew passports due to heightened levels of scrutiny.

G2. Are individuals able to exercise the right to own property and establish private businesses without undue interference from state or nonstate actors? 2 / 4

Property rights are undermined by displacement and military activity related to the conflict, and the regulatory environment constrains the establishment and operation of new businesses. While Jammu and Kashmir permanent residents can exercise property rights, outsiders are prohibited from acquiring property in the state.

G3. Do individuals enjoy personal social freedoms, including choice of marriage partner and size of family, protection from domestic violence, and control over appearance? 2 / 4

Many women face domestic violence and other forms of abuse.

G4. Do individuals enjoy equality of opportunity and freedom from economic exploitation? 2 / 4

Affirmative action in areas such as employment exists for members of several marginalized social groups. Child labor is reportedly prevalent in the region, but the government has taken few steps to combat it.

Nagorno-Karabakh

Population: 147,000
Political Rights Rating: 5
Civil Liberties Rating: 5
Freedom Rating: 5.0
Freedom Status: Partly Free

Overview: The Republic of Nagorno-Karabakh, also known as Artsakh, has enjoyed de facto independence from Azerbaijan since a 1994 cease-fire agreement ended roughly two years of open warfare, though its independence is not recognized by any UN member states. The territory's population is mostly ethnic Armenian, and given its geographical and diplomatic isolation, it is dependent on close political, economic, and military ties with Armenia. The tense security situation, with regular cease-fire violations and an ongoing threat of war, has had a negative effect on political rights and civil liberties and provided authorities with a pretext to consolidate their own power.

KEY DEVELOPMENTS IN 2018:

- Inspired by protests in neighboring Armenia that led to the resignation of Serzh Sargsyan as that country's prime minister, dozens of Nagorno-Karabakh residents rallied in the streets in early June after officers of the National Security Service assaulted a group of local civilians. The turmoil was resolved in part through the intervention of Armenia's new prime minister, Nikol Pashinyan, who called for dialogue and an end to the protests.

- State Minister Arayik Harutyunyan and a number of senior security officials resigned in response to the demonstrations, and President Bako Sahakyan promised not to seek reelection in 2020. At year's end Harutyunyan was reportedly preparing a bid to succeed him as president.

POLITICAL RIGHTS: 12 / 40

A. ELECTORAL PROCESS: 4 / 12

A1. Was the current head of government or other chief national authority elected through free and fair elections? 1 / 4

Under the constitutional system in place at the beginning of 2017, the president was directly elected for up to two five-year terms and appointed the prime minister. President Sahakyan, the incumbent since 2007, was reelected in 2012 with 66.7 percent of the vote. His main opponent, former deputy defense minister Vitaly Balasanyan, received 32.5 percent. Balasanyan alleged that administrative resources were misused to aid Sahakyan during the campaign.

In accordance with changes to the constitution that were approved in a February 2017 referendum, the parliament elected a transitional president who would hold office until the expiration of the current parliament's term, so that the presidential and parliamentary terms would be concurrent after 2020. Sahakyan, whose second term was coming to an end, was elected as transitional president in July 2017 with 28 votes in the 33-seat chamber, far more than the two-thirds majority required to win in the first round.

Under the new constitution, the president is both head of state and head of government, with full authority to appoint and dismiss cabinet members. After Sahakyan was inaugurated in September 2017, the office of prime minister was abolished.

A2. Were the current national legislative representatives elected through free and fair elections? 2 / 4

Of the unicameral National Assembly's 33 members, 11 are elected through single-mandate constituencies and 22 by party list. The most recent parliamentary elections were held in 2015. Seven parties participated, and five passed the threshold to gain seats. The Free Motherland (Azat Hayrenik) party maintained its dominant position in the legislature, winning 15 seats. The Armenian Revolutionary Federation (ARF)–Dashnaktsutyun and the Democratic Party of Artsakh (AZhK), both part of Free Motherland's ruling coalition, won seven and six seats, respectively. Two opposition parties gained representation: Movement 88 took three seats, while National Revival captured one. An independent candidate won the remaining seat.

Invited foreign observers reported that the elections were an improvement over the 2010 vote, which was marred by the absence of opposition candidates and the use of state resources to support progovernment candidates. However, some political parties still reported minor intimidation during the campaign process.

A3. Are the electoral laws and framework fair, and are they implemented impartially by the relevant election management bodies? 1 / 4

Amendments passed in 2014 led to some improvements to the electoral code. Among other changes, the number of parliamentary seats under the proportional system increased, and the vote threshold for representation decreased to 5 percent for political parties and 7 percent for electoral coalitions, allowing for broader political participation.

However, the constitutional referendum of February 2017 was criticized by opposition groups as a means to consolidate the power of the governing parties and extend the tenure of President Sahakyan beyond the constitutional limit of two five-year terms. With his indirect election as transitional president in July 2017, Sahakyan effectively gained greater authority without a direct mandate from voters. Supporters of the constitutional changes argued that a stronger presidency was necessary in light of Nagorno-Karabakh's security situation.

The election commission reported that 87.6 percent of referendum participants endorsed the changes, with turnout at 76.5 percent. Opposition groups and some civil society activists complained that state resources were used to promote the referendum, and observers noted suspicious results in some areas, with one of the 11 districts reporting 99 or 100 percent figures for both turnout and "yes" votes in most of its polling locations.

B. POLITICAL PLURALISM AND PARTICIPATION: 5 / 16

B1. Do the people have the right to organize in different political parties or other competitive political groupings of their choice, and is the system free of undue obstacles to the rise and fall of these competing parties or groupings? 2 / 4

There are few formal restrictions on the freedom to form and join political parties, but the political landscape is constrained in practice. Given the territory's contested status, open dissent and vigorous competition are still regarded as signs of disloyalty or even as a security risk. The incumbent leadership also allegedly uses patronage to maintain a network of political supporters who can be deployed to disrupt opposition activities, including through verbal and physical harassment.

The successful protest movement in Armenia in 2018 inspired greater grassroots activism in Nagorno-Karabakh, but this had yet to coalesce into a more conventional political movement capable of challenging the incumbent leadership in the next elections. Meanwhile, the changes in Armenia and Nagorno-Karabakh helped the radical Armenian opposition group Sasna Tsrer to overcome a years-long informal ban on open political activities in Nagorno-Karabakh; in November the group established an office in the territory.

B2. Is there a realistic opportunity for the opposition to increase its support or gain power through elections? 1 / 4

The leading political parties tend to form broad coalitions and co-opt potential rivals, leaving little room for genuine opposition. In the 2015 parliamentary elections, opposition parties won just four seats, though this represented an improvement. President Sahakyan appointed Balasanyan, his challenger in the 2012 election, as secretary of Nagorno-Karabakh's security council in 2016. In another example of co-optation, the president named his 2007 opponent, Masis Mayilyan, as foreign minister in 2017. Sahakyan's easy election as transitional president that year, with 28 votes from the 32 lawmakers present, illustrated the extent of political cohesion even regarding a de facto breach of term limits.

Armenia's so-called Velvet Revolution in 2018 considerably weakened this cohesion and apparently quashed Sahakyan's prospects for extending his rule after 2020. However, he retained some popularity as well as control over a strong coercive apparatus, meaning any organized opposition movement would still face daunting obstacles.

B3. Are the people's political choices free from domination by the military, foreign powers, religious hierarchies, economic oligarchies, or any other powerful group that is not democratically accountable? 1 / 4

Politics in Nagorno-Karabakh are heavily influenced by the threat of military aggression from Azerbaijan, which in turn increases the territory's political and military dependence on Armenia.

B4. Do various segments of the population (including ethnic, religious, gender, LGBT, and other relevant groups) have full political rights and electoral opportunities? 1 / 4

The population is almost entirely ethnic Armenian as a result of wartime displacement, and the constitution mandates a policy of preserving the Armenian character of the territory, partly by granting citizenship to ethnic Armenians who choose to reside there.

Formally, women have equal political rights, but social constraints and a prevailing sense of militarization in local life limit their participation in practice, and they are poorly represented in leadership positions. While the 2014 electoral code requires parties to ensure a minimum of 22 percent female representation on candidate lists, only five women hold seats in the parliament.

C. FUNCTIONING OF GOVERNMENT: 3 / 12

C1. Do the freely elected head of government and national legislative representatives determine the policies of the government? 1 / 4

The ability of locally elected officials to set and implement government policies is limited in practice by security threats along the cease-fire line, warnings from Baku, and the dominant role played by the Armenian government and other regional actors. The constitution calls for close cooperation with Armenia on political, economic, and military policy.

C2. Are safeguards against official corruption strong and effective? 1 / 4

Nagorno-Karabakh continues to suffer from significant corruption, particularly in the construction and infrastructure-development sectors. Officials practice favoritism in filling civil service positions.

C3. Does the government operate with openness and transparency? 1 / 4

A freedom of information law was adopted in 2004, but the government operates with little transparency in practice. Key decisions are negotiated by political actors, with few meaningful opportunities for public input.

CIVIL LIBERTIES: 19 / 60 (+1)

D. FREEDOM OF EXPRESSION AND BELIEF: 6 / 16

D1. Are there free and independent media? 1 / 4

The government controls most of Nagorno-Karabakh's media outlets, and the public television and radio stations have no local competition. Most journalists practice self-censorship, particularly on subjects related to the peace process. The internet penetration rate is low and has been slow to expand. Mobile internet service remains unaffordable for most residents.

Nevertheless, social media platforms are increasingly used by the public and by government officials for the dissemination and discussion of news. Some of the communications tactics that were employed successfully by the opposition in Armenia during 2018 have been adopted in Nagorno-Karabakh, where local opposition and protest groups are attempting to reach the public through social media. Young opposition leaders are also well connected with independent media outlets in Armenia, which are able to convey their views to news consumers in Nagorno-Karabakh.

D2. Are individuals free to practice and express their religious faith or nonbelief in public and private? 1 / 4

The constitution guarantees religious freedom but allows for restrictions in the name of security, public order, and other state interests. The charter also recognizes the Armenian Apostolic Church as the "national church" of the Armenian people. The religious freedom of other groups is limited in practice. A 2009 law banned religious activity by unregistered groups and proselytism by minority faiths, and made it more difficult for minority groups to register.

D3. Is there academic freedom, and is the educational system free from extensive political indoctrination? 1 / 4

Schools and universities are subject to political influence and pressure to avoid dissenting views on sensitive topics, particularly those related to the territory's status and security. Educators engage in a degree of self-censorship on such issues.

D4. Are individuals free to express their personal views on political or other sensitive topics without fear of surveillance or retribution? 3 / 4

Private discussion is generally open and free, though expression of dissent may be inhibited somewhat by the prevailing nationalist sentiment in politics and society.

E. ASSOCIATIONAL AND ORGANIZATIONAL RIGHTS: 4 / 12 (+1)
E1. Is there freedom of assembly? 2 / 4 (+1)

Protests are relatively rare in practice, and the authorities have blocked gatherings and demonstrations that they deem to be threats to public order. However, the environment improved during 2018 as local activists, inspired by events in Armenia, expanded the public space for political demonstrations, particularly through the protests in June that led the state minister and key security officials to resign and Sahakyan to forgo a reelection bid in 2020. Those protests were prompted by an incident in which officers of the National Security Service assaulted a group of local civilians. Authorities were apparently reluctant to suppress the demonstrations in light of the new political order in Yerevan.

Score Change: The score improved from 1 to 2 because authorities did not take harsh measures to obstruct an increase in grassroots political activity, including public demonstrations, in the wake of the protest movement and change in government in Armenia.

E2. Is there freedom for nongovernmental organizations, particularly those that are engaged in human rights– and governance-related work? 1 / 4

Freedom of association is limited. The few nongovernmental organizations that are active in the territory suffer from poor funding and competition from government-organized groups.

E3. Is there freedom for trade unions and similar professional or labor organizations? 1 / 4

Trade unions are allowed to organize, but in practice they are weak and relatively inactive, with little practical ability to assert workers' interests. There is political and social pressure to avoid major labor disputes that might harm national solidarity.

F. RULE OF LAW: 4 / 16
F1. Is there an independent judiciary? 1 / 4

The judiciary is not independent in practice. The courts are influenced by the executive branch as well as by powerful political, economic, and criminal groups.

F2. Does due process prevail in civil and criminal matters? 1 / 4

The constitution guarantees basic due process rights, but police and the courts do not always uphold them in practice. The human rights ombudsman received 14 complaints regarding the right to a fair trial during 2018, up from 12 the previous year and 5 in 2016. Outspoken political dissidents are subject to harassment by the authorities.

F3. Is there protection from the illegitimate use of physical force and freedom from war and insurgencies? 1 / 4

The security of the population is affected by regular incidents of violence along the cease-fire line. Soldiers as well as civilians on both sides are killed or injured each year, and casualties continued to be reported during 2018.

F4. Do laws, policies, and practices guarantee equal treatment of various segments of the population? 1 / 4

The constitution guarantees equal rights for women and bans discrimination based on gender, ethnicity, religion, and other categories. However, women are underrepresented in the public and private sectors and remain exposed to discrimination in practice. Only men are subject to military conscription. To preserve the Armenian character of the territory, state policies promote Armenian language and culture and encourage ethnic Armenians to migrate to Nagorno-Karabakh, partly through housing and other subsidies.

G. PERSONAL AUTONOMY AND INDIVIDUAL RIGHTS: 5 / 16

G1. Do individuals enjoy freedom of movement, including the ability to change their place of residence, employment, or education? 1 / 4

Freedom of movement within Nagorno-Karabakh and travel around the territory are hindered by its ambiguous legal and diplomatic status, the instability of the cease-fire, and the presence of land mines, which continue to cause deaths and injuries.

G2. Are individuals able to exercise the right to own property and establish private businesses without undue interference from state or nonstate actors? 1 / 4

Most major economic activity is tightly controlled by the government or a small group of powerful elites with political connections. The property rights of displaced Azerbaijanis have yet to be adequately addressed.

G3. Do individuals enjoy personal social freedoms, including choice of marriage partner and size of family, protection from domestic violence, and control over appearance? 2 / 4

Men and women have equal legal rights with respect to marriage and divorce, though the constitution defines marriage as a union between a man and a woman, precluding same-sex marriage. The government offers material incentives to encourage couples to have children, with the goal of repopulating the territory. Domestic violence is common and not effectively prosecuted.

G4. Do individuals enjoy equality of opportunity and freedom from economic exploitation? 1 / 4

Employment opportunities remain scarce and are mostly confined to the state sector or state-subsidized businesses.

Northern Cyprus

Population: 350,000
Political Rights Rating: 2
Civil Liberties Rating: 2
Freedom Rating: 2.0
Freedom Status: Free

Overview: The Turkish Republic of Northern Cyprus (TRNC) is a self-declared state recognized only by Turkey. It has a democratic, multiparty political system, and civil liberties are generally upheld. Ongoing concerns include undue political and economic influence from Turkey, corruption, discrimination against minority communities, and human trafficking.

KEY DEVELOPMENTS IN 2018:

- In January, Turkish president Recep Tayyip Erdoğan incited an attack on *Afrika* newspaper in which hundreds of demonstrators pelted the building with stones and other objects. Thousands of Turkish Cypriots responded with a march against interference from Ankara and in support of freedom of expression. Several people involved in the newspaper attack were later tried and convicted.
- Also in January, six parties won seats in parliamentary elections, with no single party taking a majority. Four parties then formed a broad coalition government that excluded two right-wing groups.
- Two new crossing points along the UN buffer zone between the TRNC and the Republic of Cyprus opened in November as a confidence-building measure ahead of the anticipated renewal of UN-sponsored reunification talks.

POLITICAL RIGHTS: 31 / 40
A. ELECTORAL PROCESS: 11 / 12
A1. Was the current head of government or other chief national authority elected through free and fair elections? 4 / 4

The president, who serves as head of state and represents the TRNC internationally, is popularly elected to five-year terms. In 2015, Mustafa Akıncı—backed by the social democratic Communal Democracy Party (TDP)—prevailed in a runoff election with just over 60 percent of the vote, defeating incumbent Derviş Eroğlu, who was supported by the right-wing National Unity Party (UBP).

The president appoints the prime minister and cabinet members, who must have the support of a legislative majority. Following the January 2018 parliamentary elections and the formation of a multiparty coalition, Tufan Erhürman of the center-left Republican Turkish Party (CTP)—which seeks reconciliation with the Greek Cypriots and European Union membership—became prime minister. He replaced Hüseyin Özgürgün of the UBP, which had pursued policies that were seen as more closely aligned with the government in Ankara.

A2. Were the current national legislative representatives elected through free and fair elections? 4 / 4

For elections to the 50-seat Assembly of the Republic, the TRNC employs a mixed voting system, with the proportional representation component setting a 5 percent vote threshold for parties to win seats. Members serve five-year terms. The UBP led the January 2018 parliamentary elections with 21 seats. However, it was left in opposition after the

CTP, with 12 seats, formed a coalition with the centrist-reformist People's Party (HP), with 9 seats, and the TDP and the center-right Democratic Party (DP), with three seats each. The coalition also excluded the Rebirth Party (YDP), a right-wing group formed primarily by Turkish settlers that won two seats.

A3. Are the electoral laws and framework fair, and are they implemented impartially by the relevant election management bodies? 3 / 4

The Supreme Election Committee is an independent body composed of judges, and elections in the TRNC are generally considered free and fair. In 2018, a complex new election law came into effect that allowed voters to choose a single party, individual candidates from multiple parties, or a combination of the two; voters were also able to choose candidates across more than one multimember constituency. The law made it more complicated to vote for individual candidates and therefore encouraged party voting.

B. POLITICAL PLURALISM AND PARTICIPATION: 13 / 16

B1. Do the people have the right to organize in different political parties or other competitive political groupings of their choice, and is the system free of undue obstacles to the rise and fall of these competing parties or groupings? 4 / 4

Turkish Cypriots are free to organize in political parties, and several parties compete in practice. Six parties were represented in the legislature as of 2018, including two—HP and YDP—that had entered the chamber for the first time after the January elections. Under a 2015 law, parties that receive at least 3 percent of the vote may obtain state funding.

B2. Is there a realistic opportunity for the opposition to increase its support or gain power through elections? 4 / 4

There have been multiple democratic transfers of power between rival parties in both the presidency and the premiership over the past two decades, with Akıncı ousting the incumbent president in the 2015 election. The ideologically diverse parties that formed a governing coalition in 2018 ousted a right-wing government led by the UBP.

B3. Are the people's political choices free from domination by the military, foreign powers, religious hierarchies, economic oligarchies, or any other powerful group that is not democratically accountable? 3 / 4

Although Turkey continues to exercise considerable influence over the TRNC, it has little direct control over voters, many of whom have recently supported candidates and parties that display independence from Ankara. Ahead of the 2018 elections, the CTP, HP, and TDP had campaigned on promises to reform a patronage-based political system associated with the UBP, in which the distribution of jobs and favors has depended in part on maintaining a smooth flow of economic support from Turkey.

B4. Do various segments of the population (including ethnic, religious, gender, LGBT, and other relevant groups) have full political rights and electoral opportunities? 2 / 4

All adult citizens may vote, but minority rights remain a concern. The few hundred Maronite and Greek Cypriots living in the TRNC are issued special identity cards and are unable to vote in TRNC elections. In 2018, discussions continued regarding the promised reopening of Maronite villages to resettlement and the potential expansion of Maronite political rights in the north, but no concrete actions were taken.

Women have full political rights, and a 2015 law requires 30 percent of a party's parliamentary candidate list to consist of women. However, women's political participation is limited in practice, particularly in leadership positions. In the 2018 elections, women won nine seats out of 50, an improvement from four in the previous legislature. Two of the 11 ministers in the new government were women.

C. FUNCTIONING OF GOVERNMENT: 7 / 12

C1. Do the freely elected head of government and national legislative representatives determine the policies of the government? 3 / 4

While elected officials generally develop and implement policies and legislation without direct interference from Ankara, the TRNC remains diplomatically, militarily, and financially dependent on Turkey, and this dependence sometimes allows the Turkish government to influence policymaking.

C2. Are safeguards against official corruption strong and effective? 2 / 4

Corruption, cronyism in the distribution of civil service jobs, and nepotism are serious impediments to good governance, and the media have exposed a number of scandals in recent years. An October 2018 report based on the methodology of the Corruption Perceptions Index compiled by Transparency International found that 89 percent of businesspeople in Northern Cyprus believe bribery and corruption are problems there.

C3. Does the government operate with openness and transparency? 2 / 4

Although there is a law providing for access to information, there has been very little progress in making government records available to the public in practice. Information is not always kept in an accessible form, and officials reportedly withhold data on sensitive topics such as the naturalization of Turkish settlers as TRNC citizens. Officials must periodically disclose their personal assets, but the disclosures are not made public.

CIVIL LIBERTIES: 50 / 60

D. FREEDOM OF EXPRESSION AND BELIEF: 15 / 16

D1. Are there free and independent media? 4 / 4

Freedom of the press is guaranteed by law, and TRNC authorities generally respect it in practice. The media often carry sharp criticism of both the TRNC and Turkish governments. However, journalists sometimes face obstruction or threats in the course of their work.

In January 2018, a statement by the Turkish president incited a violent attack on the offices of the newspaper *Afrika* after it published an article that compared Turkey's invasion of northern Syria with its 1974 occupation of Northern Cyprus. About 500 Turkish nationalists surrounded the building and pelted it with stones and other objects. In response to the attack, an estimated 5,000 Turkish Cypriots held a march against interference from Ankara and in support of freedom of expression. Several of the individuals responsible for the violence were later prosecuted and sentenced to as much as six months in jail. Separately, *Afrika*'s editor and a colleague were on trial at year's end for allegedly insulting Erdoğan with a political cartoon published in 2017.

D2. Are individuals free to practice and express their religious faith or nonbelief in public and private? 3 / 4

The TRNC is a secular state and legally guarantees freedom of worship, which is mostly respected in practice. However, authorities continue to impose restrictions on access to churches and otherwise interfere with church services. Christians and non-Sunni Muslims have complained that the government favors Sunni Islam in its policies on religious education and places of worship. The government's Religious Affairs Department staffs Sunni mosques with imams.

D3. Is there academic freedom, and is the educational system free from extensive political indoctrination? 4 / 4

Academic freedom is generally respected. While large numbers of teachers and professors have been fired or jailed for political reasons in Turkey since 2016, no similar purges had occurred in the TRNC as of 2018.

D4. Are individuals free to express their personal views on political or other sensitive topics without fear of surveillance or retribution? 4 / 4

There are no significant restrictions on freedom of private discussion, and individuals generally do not face repercussions for expressing their political views on social media.

E. ASSOCIATIONAL AND ORGANIZATIONAL RIGHTS: 11 / 12
E1. Is there freedom of assembly? 4 / 4

Freedom of assembly is guaranteed by the constitution and generally upheld in practice.

E2. Is there freedom for nongovernmental organizations, particularly those that are engaged in human rights- and governance-related work? 4 / 4

Numerous nongovernmental organizations are registered in the TRNC, and they typically operate without restrictions. Many such groups have worked with Greek Cypriot partners to advance reunification efforts.

E3. Is there freedom for trade unions and similar professional or labor organizations? 3 / 4

Workers may form independent unions, bargain collectively, and strike, and collective bargaining is reportedly common in the public sector. However, the government can limit strikes in ill-defined essential services, and employers are reportedly able to obstruct unionization in the private sector without legal repercussions.

F. RULE OF LAW: 13 / 16
F1. Is there an independent judiciary? 4 / 4

The judiciary is independent, and courts have often ruled against the government in recent years. The system is overseen by the Supreme Council of Judicature, which is headed by the president of the Supreme Court and includes that court's seven judges as well as one member each appointed by the president, the legislature, the attorney general, and the bar association. The council is responsible for judicial appointments, promotions, assignments, and disciplinary measures.

F2. Does due process prevail in civil and criminal matters? 3 / 4

Although due process rights are typically respected, police have been accused of violating protections against arbitrary detention and coerced confessions in some cases, for example by improperly denying suspects access to a lawyer.

There were no large-scale purges of security forces or other public employees in connection with the 2016 coup attempt in Turkey as of 2018, but due process has been a concern in the few cases that have been reported. For example, a small number of Turkish Cypriot civilians were arrested in 2017 for alleged involvement with the organization of US-based Islamic preacher Fethullah Gülen, which is considered a terrorist organization in Turkey, and dozens of police officers were screened or investigated for any such links.

F3. Is there protection from the illegitimate use of physical force and freedom from war and insurgencies? 3 / 4

The population is generally free from threats to physical security, but police have been accused of abusing detainees, and prisons feature overcrowding and other harsh conditions. In 2018 there were some reports of beatings in police custody as well as one disputed death of a detainee that police said was a suicide.

F4. Do laws, policies, and practices guarantee equal treatment of various segments of the population? 3 / 4

Women enjoy legal equality, but in practice they encounter some discrimination in employment, education, housing, and other areas.

The tiny Greek and Maronite minorities live in enclaves and suffer from social and economic disadvantages. The small Kurdish minority reportedly suffers from discrimination in employment. Both groups have complained of surveillance by TRNC authorities.

LGBT (lesbian, gay, bisexual, and transgender) people reportedly face social stigmatization, though same-sex sexual activity was decriminalized in 2014, and discrimination based on sexual orientation or gender identity is prohibited by law.

The TRNC lacks legal protections for asylum seekers, raising concerns about possible refoulement. In July 2018, a group of 45 Turkish nationals suspected of belonging to the Gülen movement were arrested by the TRNC police as they allegedly attempted to travel to Greece, having first fled from Turkey to Northern Cyprus. Among them were 17 children. The group was subsequently returned to Turkey.

G. PERSONAL AUTONOMY AND INDIVIDUAL RIGHTS: 11 / 16

G1. Do individuals enjoy freedom of movement, including the ability to change their place of residence, employment, or education? 3 / 4

Movement within the TRNC territory is generally unrestricted. However, travel abroad is complicated by the TRNC's lack of international recognition. The only direct flights from the TRNC are to Turkey. Most governments do not accept TRNC travel documents, so many Turkish Cypriots carry Republic of Cyprus passports, for which they are eligible. Movement across the UN buffer zone dividing the island has improved since 2004 due to a growing number of border crossings. In November 2018, two new crossing points opened at Deryneia and Lefka-Aplici.

G2. Are individuals able to exercise the right to own property and establish private businesses without undue interference from state or nonstate actors? 3 / 4

The authorities recognize the rights to own property and establish businesses. In practice these rights are somewhat limited, as authorities have in various ways attempted to prevent the sale of historically Turkish Cypriot properties to foreigners. The TRNC formed the Immovable Property Commission (IPC) in 2006 to resolve claims by Greek Cypriots who owned property in the north before the island's 1974 division. In 2010, the European Court of Human Rights recognized the commission as an "accessible and effective" mechanism. However, its work has been seriously impaired in recent years by a lack of funding from the government and Ankara.

G3. Do individuals enjoy personal social freedoms, including choice of marriage partner and size of family, protection from domestic violence, and control over appearance? 3 / 4

Personal social freedoms are generally respected, though women's organizations have criticized the government for failing to adequately address the problems of rape and domestic violence. According to a 2017 poll, one in three women have experienced violence in the home.

G4. Do individuals enjoy equality of opportunity and freedom from economic exploitation? 2 / 4

While TRNC citizens generally have access to economic opportunity and protections from abusive working conditions, noncitizens often experience exploitation and lack mechanisms for appeal. Human trafficking and forced prostitution are serious problems, despite a nominal legal ban on prostitution. The TRNC does not have adequate antitrafficking legislation and does not fund antitrafficking efforts. Observers also report that some authorities are complicit in trafficking.

Pakistani Kashmir

Population: 5,800,000
Political Rights Rating: 6
Civil Liberties Rating: 5
Freedom Rating: 5.5
Freedom Status: Not Free

Overview: Pakistani Kashmir is administered as two territories: Azad Jammu and Kashmir (AJK) and Gilgit-Baltistan (GB). Each has an elected assembly and government with limited autonomy, but they lack the parliamentary representation and other rights of Pakistani provinces, and Pakistani federal institutions have predominant influence over security, the courts, and most important policy matters. Politics within the two territories are carefully managed to promote the idea of Kashmir's eventual accession to Pakistan. Freedoms of expression and association, and any political activity deemed contrary to Pakistan's policy on Kashmir, are restricted.

KEY DEVELOPMENTS IN 2018:

- Firing and shelling across the Line of Control (LoC), in violation of a 2003 ceasefire agreement, continued during the year. According to the Pakistani military, Indian forces caused the deaths of 55 civilians and injuries to more than 300 others in AJK between January and early December.
- In May, the Pakistani government issued the Government of Gilgit-Baltistan Order 2018, which incorporated some but not all of the recommendations of a Pakistani parliamentary committee that had proposed greater integration for GB without granting formal provincial status. The order provoked protests and a legal challenge from those demanding full constitutional rights for the territory.

POLITICAL RIGHTS: 9 / 40

A. ELECTORAL PROCESS: 4 / 12

A1. Was the current head of government or other chief national authority elected through free and fair elections? 1 / 4

Both AJK and GB have locally elected executive leaders. However, the Pakistani government also controls—directly and indirectly—key executive functions, and it is not accountable to voters in the two territories.

Under AJK's 1974 interim constitution, a president elected by the Legislative Assembly serves as head of state, while the elected prime minister is the chief executive. After the 2016 elections, the new assembly elected the local leader of Pakistan's then ruling Pakistan Muslim League–Nawaz (PML-N), Raja Farooq Haider, as prime minister, and Masood Khan, formerly a senior Pakistani diplomat, as president.

An AJK Council is based in Pakistan's capital, Islamabad, consisting of both Kashmiri and Pakistani officials and chaired by the Pakistani prime minister. The council holds a number of executive, legislative, and judicial powers, such as control over the appointment of superior judges and the chief election commissioner.

In May 2018, the Pakistani government adopted the Government of Gilgit-Baltistan Order 2018 to replace GB's previous basic law, the 2009 Gilgit-Baltistan Empowerment and Self-Governance Order (GBESGO). Under the new order, which took effect in June, executive functions are shared between a Pakistani-appointed governor and a chief minister chosen by the GB Assembly (GBA), which was formerly called the GB Legislative Assembly. The governor signs legislation and has significant power over judicial appointments; his decisions cannot be overruled by the GBA. The 2018 order also grants extensive authority to the prime minister of Pakistan, including exclusive executive and legislative powers on a long list of specified topics.

Hafiz Hafeezur Rehman of the PML-N became chief minister of GB after the territory's 2015 elections and is scheduled to remain in office until 2020. However, after the July 2018 victory of the Pakistan Tehreek-e-Insaf (PTI) party in the Pakistani general elections, the GB governor resigned, and the new Pakistani government replaced him with the local president of the PTI, Raja Maqpoon, in September.

A2. Were the current national legislative representatives elected through free and fair elections? 2 / 4

Neither AJK nor GB is represented in the Pakistani Parliament.

Of the AJK Legislative Assembly's 49 seats, 41 are filled through direct elections: 29 with constituencies based in the territory and 12 representing Kashmiri "refugees" throughout Pakistan. Another eight are reserved seats: five for women and one each for representatives of overseas Kashmiris, technocrats, and religious leaders. In the 2016 elections, the PML-N won with 31 seats. The local branch of the Pakistan People's Party (PPP) won three seats, as did the Muslim Conference, and the PTI secured two. The remaining two seats were won by the Jammu Kashmir Peoples Party and an independent. The election process was largely peaceful, though both the PPP and the local PTI leader complained of preelection manipulation, including the use of federal development funds to boost support for the PML-N.

The 33-member GBA is composed of 24 directly elected members, six seats reserved for women, and three seats reserved for technocrats; the reserved seats are filled through a vote by the elected members. The GBA's legislative authority is limited to certain subjects, and even discussion of some topics—foreign affairs, defense, internal security, and judicial conduct—is prohibited by the 2018 order. However, the order does allow the GBA to exercise legislative powers that were previously allocated to the Gilgit-Baltistan Council (GBC). The council, which now has an advisory role, is headed by the Pakistani prime minister and vice-chaired by the GB governor, and includes six members chosen by the GBA and six Pakistani ministers or Parliament members chosen by the Pakistani prime minister. The GB chief minister also has a seat.

Elections to the assembly were held in 2015. In keeping with the well-established pattern of victory by the party in power in Islamabad, the PML-N took 15 of the 24 directly elected seats. No other party won more than two seats, including the previously governing PPP.

A3. Are the electoral laws and framework fair, and are they implemented impartially by the relevant election management bodies? 1 / 4

The electoral framework in both territories facilitates indirect control by the Pakistani authorities. For example, the AJK Council appoints the chief election commissioner, and the electoral system for the AJK Legislative Assembly disproportionately favors nonresident refugees over AJK residents. The nonresident elections are more vulnerable to manipulation by federal Pakistani authorities, and the party in office at the federal level tends to win these seats. Candidates in the AJK elections must formally endorse "the ideology of Pakistan" and Kashmir's accession to Pakistan.

Elections in GB are governed by Pakistani election law and a code of conduct drawn up by the local election commission. The first clause of the code of conduct dictates that parties and candidates must refrain from any action or speech which could be deemed contrary to the ideology of Pakistan or the country's security. This vague provision can be used to exclude candidates associated with nationalist parties or those disapproved of by the Pakistani authorities.

B. POLITICAL PLURALISM AND PARTICIPATION: 4 / 16

B1. Do the people have the right to organize in different political parties or other competitive political groupings of their choice, and is the system free of undue obstacles to the rise and fall of these competing parties or groupings? 1 / 4

Politics are dominated in both AJK and GB by local branches of the main Pakistani parties and some local parties, such as AJK's Muslim Conference, that are closely allied with the Pakistani establishment. Small nationalist parties that are opposed to union with Pakistan are actively marginalized or barred outright from the political process. Activists accused of opposition to Pakistani rule have been subject to surveillance, harassment, and sometimes imprisonment. The interim constitution of AJK bans political parties that do not endorse the territory's eventual accession to Pakistan, and similar rules prevail in GB.

There were no high-profile cases in which GB political activists were jailed during 2018. However, those previously jailed remained in detention, including Baba Jan, a leader of the left-wing Awami Workers Party who is serving a life sentence for his participation in protests.

B2. Is there a realistic opportunity for the opposition to increase its support or gain power through elections? 1 / 4

There is ample precedent for transfers of power between the major parties, though these are typically dictated by parallel changes at the federal level in Pakistan. The PML-N Pakistani government's decision to replace the GB governor in early 2015 was criticized as a bid to ensure the party's victory in the GB legislative elections, and federal authorities were similarly accused of working to manipulate the 2016 AJK Legislative Assembly elections in favor of the PML-N.

B3. Are the people's political choices free from domination by the military, foreign powers, religious hierarchies, economic oligarchies, or any other powerful group that is not democratically accountable? 1 / 4

Because voters in GB and AJK cannot participate in Pakistani elections, Pakistani federal officials and entities are not democratically accountable to them. Security agencies operating in both territories are federal institutions. They work to block and suppress any parties or politicians that adopt positions deemed to conflict with Pakistani interests.

B4. Do various segments of the population (including ethnic, religious, gender, LGBT, and other relevant groups) have full political rights and electoral opportunities? 1 / 4

Men and women have the right to vote in both territories. Although there is no bar on women contesting general seats, prevailing norms mean that women rarely exercise this right. Instead, general seats tend to be filled by men. The seats reserved for women are filled proportionally from party lists based on the general vote, meaning the parties themselves determine who will represent women's interests.

C. FUNCTIONING OF GOVERNMENT: 3 / 12

C1. Do the freely elected head of government and national legislative representatives determine the policies of the government? 1 / 4

The powers of the elected chief executives in AJK and GB are limited by the fact that the Pakistani prime minister, the Pakistani minister for Kashmir Affairs and Gilgit-Baltistan, and through them the federal civil service, exercise effective control over government operations in both territories. As in Pakistan, federal military and intelligence agencies also play a powerful role in governance and policymaking.

The territories lack any meaningful fiscal autonomy, as federal taxes are imposed on both, and they receive a share of the resulting funds from the federal government. The territories' local representatives are excluded from the Pakistani bodies that negotiate interprovincial resource allocation.

There has been a sustained debate within GB on the idea of enhancing the territory's status in the Pakistani constitution by designating it a provisional province, granting its legislators powers on par with those delegated to Pakistan's four existing provinces, and giving GB representation in the federal Parliament. Proponents have claimed that this would reduce any legal concerns hampering Chinese investment as part of the China-Pakistan Economic Corridor (CPEC) infrastructure project and grant GB residents the constitutional rights as those enjoyed by Pakistani citizens. However, figures associated with the struggle against Indian control of Kashmir have criticized the GB proposal as a weakening of the commitment to full Kashmiri accession to Pakistan.

A Pakistani parliamentary committee, headed by Sartaj Aziz, reviewed the constitutional status of GB in 2017 and recommended granting GB integration with Pakistan that stopped short of de jure provincial status. The report was formally submitted to the Pakistani prime minister in January 2018 for consideration by the cabinet. This eventually led to the Pakistani government adopting the Government of Gilgit-Baltistan Order 2018 in May. The order was criticized for failing to grant the provisional provincial status that many GB politicians had demanded. It took effect in June, was challenged in the courts and suspended by GB's highest judicial body later that month, then restored by Pakistan's Supreme Court in August.

C2. Are safeguards against official corruption strong and effective? 1 / 4

Both territories have formal safeguards against official corruption, and GB is within the jurisdiction of Pakistan's National Accountability Bureau, which has an office in Gilgit. However, as in Pakistan, corruption is believed to remain endemic, with enforcement actions subject to political influence.

C3. Does the government operate with openness and transparency? 1 / 4

Transparency and access to government information are limited in practice. The AJK government has made a gesture toward transparency by posting basic information about its departments online.

ADDITIONAL DISCRETIONARY POLITICAL RIGHTS QUESTION
Is the government or occupying power deliberately changing the ethnic composition of a country or territory so as to destroy a culture or tip the political balance in favor of another group? −2 / 0

The Sunni Muslim share of the population in GB—historically a Shiite-majority region—has increased significantly in the decades since a pre-1947 rule was abolished to allow immigration from different parts of Pakistan. State agencies are suspected of deliberately encouraging this migration to engineer a demographic change. Under the 2009 GBESGO, settlers were given formal citizenship rights in GB; critics of a clause in the Government of Gilgit-Baltistan Order 2018 have argued that it appears to extend GB citizenship rights to all Pakistani citizens, further encouraging settlement. The pre-1947 restrictions on acquiring residency and citizenship are still in place in AJK.

CIVIL LIBERTIES: 19 / 60
D. FREEDOM OF EXPRESSION AND BELIEF: 6 / 16
D1. Are there free and independent media? 1 / 4

AJK and GB are subject to laws that curb freedom of expression, particularly related to the political status of the regions. Media houses need permission from the AJK Council and the federal Ministry of Kashmir Affairs and Gilgit-Baltistan to operate. A wide range of media are present and active. However, coverage of news and politics does not diverge from official Pakistani narratives, including that India's hold over the Kashmir Valley is illegitimate and all Kashmiris aspire to Pakistan accession. This compliance is achieved through a mixture of censorship, self-censorship, and harassment. A number of outlets have faced closure by authorities in recent years.

D2. Are individuals free to practice and express their religious faith or nonbelief in public and private? 1 / 4

Both territories have a predominantly Muslim population, and there is no official or social tolerance of nonbelief. Tools used to compel expressions of belief and conformity with official interpretations of religious doctrine include laws criminalizing blasphemy, rules requiring observance of Ramadan, and an obligation to denounce the heterodox Ahmadi sect to obtain a Pakistani passport. Although there is a history of Sunni-Shiite sectarian violence in GB, there were no major outbreaks in 2018.

D3. Is there academic freedom, and is the educational system free from extensive political indoctrination? 2 / 4

Each territory is home to a growing education system, and education is much valued as a path to migration and employment. However, in academia there are acute sensitivities around the issue of constitutional status and no tolerance of debate or materials questioning Pakistan's claims over Kashmir. Student union activity has long been subject to state monitoring for signs of nationalist political views. Local languages and scripts are not taught in government schools. A series of bombing and arson attacks on schools in the Darel Valley and nearby areas during the summer of 2018 were attributed to Islamist militants who oppose secular and girls' education.

D4. Are individuals free to express their personal views on political or other sensitive topics without fear of surveillance or retribution? 2 / 4

Federal intelligence agencies maintain a prominent and intrusive presence in both territories. Discussion of heterodox political or religious views consequently carries significant risks. The authorities have increased their monitoring of social media and sporadically punish expression of anti-Pakistan or separatist opinions.

E. ASSOCIATIONAL AND ORGANIZATIONAL RIGHTS: 4 / 12

E1. Is there freedom of assembly? 1 / 4

The authorities' observance of freedom of assembly is highly discretionary. Protests that do not directly challenge Pakistani control or the territories' constitutional status tend to be tolerated. Local business interests in Gilgit continued their tradition of activism by protesting in May 2018 against the latest changes in taxation procedures. Earlier that month, police employed tear gas to disrupt protests against the Government of Gilgit-Baltistan Order 2018. In AJK there is official encouragement of demonstrations to condemn Indian atrocities on the other side of the LoC. However, protests and other activities by local nationalist groups are harshly punished. In March 2018, authorities used a ban and police violence to suppress a demonstration by the independence-oriented Jammu and Kashmir Liberation Front (JKLF) against cease-fire violations along the LoC.

E2. Is there freedom for nongovernmental organizations, particularly those that are engaged in human rights- and governance-related work? 1 / 4

Humanitarian nongovernmental organizations (NGOs) are subject to strict registration requirements and thus operate at the pleasure of the authorities. NGOs working on political or human rights issues face more intrusive government scrutiny and, in some cases, harassment.

E3. Is there freedom for trade unions and similar professional or labor organizations? 2 / 4

AJK is subject to labor laws similar to those in Pakistan. However, unions and professional organizations are frequently barred. Labor laws and union activities are poorly developed in GB.

F. RULE OF LAW: 3 / 16

F1. Is there an independent judiciary? 1 / 4

Both territories have nominally independent judiciaries, but the Pakistani federal government plays a powerful role in judicial appointments. On politically sensitive issues, the AJK and GB courts are not considered to operate with independence from the executive in Pakistan.

The president of AJK, in consultation with the AJK Council, appoints the chief justice of the territory's Supreme Court. Other judges of the superior courts are appointed by the AJK president on the advice of the council, after consultation with the chief justice. The chief judge and other judges of GB's Supreme Appellate Court are appointed for three-year terms by the prime minister of Pakistan on the recommendation of the governor.

F2. Does due process prevail in civil and criminal matters? 1 / 4

The civilian court system in both territories features basic due process guarantees, including defense lawyers and a right to appeal, but arbitrary arrests and other violations are not uncommon, particularly in security-related cases. Pakistan's Anti-Terrorism Act (ATA), which is often used to suppress dissent, includes vaguely defined offenses, allows extended detention without trial, and applies to juveniles, among other problematic features. Since 2015, the Pakistani government has allowed civilians facing charges of terrorism or sectarian violence to be tried in military courts, which have fewer due process protections and can impose the death penalty.

F3. Is there protection from the illegitimate use of physical force and freedom from war and insurgencies? 1 / 4

Torture and deaths in custody at the hands of security forces have been reported, especially for independence supporters and other activists. Separately, extremist groups devoted largely to attacks on Indian-administered Jammu and Kashmir operate from AJK and GB and have links with similar factions based in Pakistan and Afghanistan. A 2003 cease-fire agreement between the Indian and Pakistani armies is supposed to protect AJK from attacks across the LoC. However, intermittent firing and shelling continued throughout 2018. The Pakistani military reported in early December that 55 civilians had been killed and more than 300 had been injured in cease-fire violations during the year.

F4. Do laws, policies, and practices guarantee equal treatment of various segments of the population? 0 / 4

As in Pakistan, women in the territories face economic discrimination, disadvantages under personal status laws, and abusive customary practices, the perpetrators of which often enjoy impunity. LGBT (lesbian, gay, bisexual, and transgender) people, ethnic minorities, and non-Sunni religious groups also suffer from discrimination, and Afghan refugees have encountered increased harassment and pressure to return to Afghanistan since 2015. Pakistani authorities have been reluctant to offer citizenship to migrants displaced from Indian-administered Jammu and Kashmir. Periodically these refugees have been subjected to abuse and arbitrary arrest for demanding greater rights.

G. PERSONAL AUTONOMY AND INDIVIDUAL RIGHTS: 6 / 16

G1. Do individuals enjoy freedom of movement, including the ability to change their place of residence, employment, or education? 2 / 4

The people of AJK and GB have Pakistani national identity cards and passports. They are internationally recognized as Pakistani nationals. However, there are reports of passports being denied or not renewed for citizens suspected of questioning Pakistani control over the region. The territories' heavy military presence and the threat of shelling and other violence along the LoC restricts internal movement for civilians.

G2. Are individuals able to exercise the right to own property and establish private businesses without undue interference from state or nonstate actors? 2 / 4

AJK's pre-1947 state subject law, which bars outsiders from seeking permanent residency, allows only legal residents to own property. In GB, residents have raised concerns about possible displacement by CPEC development projects, and at least some forcible evictions have been reported to date. Procedures for establishing private enterprises in the territories are onerous in practice.

G3. Do individuals enjoy personal social freedoms, including choice of marriage partner and size of family, protection from domestic violence, and control over appearance? 1 / 4

In both territories, the legal framework criminalizes domestic violence and so-called honor killing, but harmful traditional practices related to sex, marriage, and personal behavior often prevail amid weak enforcement of formal protections, especially in more conservative areas. Informal justice mechanisms operating at the village level are the first point of recourse for many incidents involving sexual or domestic violence against women, and their judgments can inflict further harm on victims.

G4. Do individuals enjoy equality of opportunity and freedom from economic exploitation? 1 / 4

Both territories, but particularly GB, have historically been less economically developed than Pakistan, and their population has depended on labor migration to supplement incomes. The lack of local control over extractive industries prompts periodic complaints that residents are being deprived of the benefits of natural resources. There are divergent views in GB regarding the extent to which local people stand to gain from economic activity generated by the centrally managed CPEC.

Somaliland

Population: 4,500,000
Political Rights Rating: 4
Civil Liberties Rating: 5
Freedom Rating: 4.5
Freedom Status: Partly Free

Overview: Elections in Somaliland—whose self-declared independence from Somalia is not internationally recognized—have been relatively free and fair, but years-long delays have meant that elected officials at all levels serve well beyond their original mandates. Journalists face pressure from authorities. Minor clans are subject to political and economic marginalization, and violence against women remains a serious problem.

KEY DEVELOPMENTS IN 2018:

- Tensions between Somaliland and neighboring Puntland escalated after Somaliland's forces took the strategically important town of Tukaraq in January, in the disputed Sool region. Ensuing clashes during the year killed dozens of troops on both sides and left thousands of people displaced.
- Throughout the year, authorities arrested journalists, activists, writers, and entertainers for controversial social media posts, threatening freedom of expression online.
- In November, the National Election Commission (NEC) announced that long-delayed House of Representatives elections, last held in 2005 and most recently scheduled for March 2019, would again be delayed, with plans to hold them by November 2019.

POLITICAL RIGHTS: 19 / 40
A. ELECTORAL PROCESS: 5 / 12
A1. Was the current head of government or other chief national authority elected through free and fair elections? 3 / 4

The president is directly elected for a maximum of two five-year terms and appoints the cabinet. In November 2017, after two years of delay, Somaliland held its third presidential election. Muse Bihi Abdi of the Peace, Unity, and Development Party (Kulmiye) won the contest with 55 percent of the vote, followed by Abdurahman Mohamed Abdullahi of the Wadani party with 40 percent, and Faisal Ali Warabe of the For Justice and Development (UCID) party with 4 percent.

Despite some irregularities, including unstamped ballot papers, underage voting, and tabulation delays, international observers concluded that the process was credible and that the problems did not significantly affect the final result.

A2. Were the current national legislative representatives elected through free and fair elections? 0 / 4

Members of the 82-seat lower legislative chamber, the House of Representatives, are directly elected for five-year terms, while members of the 82-seat upper chamber, the Guurti, are clan elders indirectly elected for six-year terms. The last lower house elections were held in 2005, and new elections due in 2010 have been repeatedly postponed. The NEC announced in November 2018 that the elections, most recently scheduled for March 2019, would again be delayed, with plans to hold them by November 2019. Local council elections, last held in 2012, will be held concurrently with the lower house polls.

Members of the Guurti were chosen for an initial term in 1997, but due to a lack of legal clarity on how elections are to be held, their mandates have been repeatedly extended. In practice, seats have been passed to family members when a member dies or retires.

A3. Are the electoral laws and framework fair, and are they implemented impartially by the relevant election management bodies? 2 / 4

The legal and administrative framework for elections is largely fair, but ambiguities in some laws as well as technical and logistical challenges have led to chronic election delays. The NEC is generally considered impartial, but the opposition Wadani party accused it of bias in the aftermath of the 2017 presidential vote.

B. POLITICAL PLURALISM AND PARTICIPATION: 10 / 16

B1. Do the people have the right to organize in different political parties or other competitive political groupings of their choice, and is the system free of undue obstacles to the rise and fall of these competing parties or groupings? 3 / 4

The constitution allows for a maximum of three officially recognized political parties. The three groups that receive the most votes in local council elections are declared eligible to contest national elections, and compete freely in practice. The system is meant to encourage alliances across clan divisions, but clan and party affiliation remain closely aligned.

B2. Is there a realistic opportunity for the opposition to increase its support or gain power through elections? 3 / 4

The political system allows democratic transfers of power between rival parties, with the most recent handover at the presidential level in 2010. Opposition parties hold positions in the legislature and in subnational governments, though election delays have impaired their ability to challenge incumbents.

B3. Are the people's political choices free from domination by the military, foreign powers, religious hierarchies, economic oligarchies, or any other powerful group that is not democratically accountable? 2 / 4

Clan elders play an influential role in politics, both directly with their kinsmen and through the currently unelected Guurti, which has the authority to extend officials' terms in office and approve election dates.

B4. Do various segments of the population (including ethnic, religious, gender, LGBT, and other relevant groups) have full political rights and electoral opportunities? 2 / 4

Women and various clans formally enjoy equal political rights. However, larger clans tend to dominate political offices and leadership positions. Cultural barriers also limit women's political participation. In June 2018, the cabinet approved legislation that would impose a 20 percent quota for women and minority clans in the legislature and local councils, which would come into effect for the 2019 elections. However, the quota remained stalled in the parliament at year's end. The constitution requires that candidates for national office be Muslim.

C. FUNCTIONING OF GOVERNMENT: 4 / 12

C1. Do the freely elected head of government and national legislative representatives determine the policies of the government? 1 / 4

The 2017 election improved the democratic legitimacy of the president in determining government policy, and decisions made by the national authorities are implemented in most of Somaliland's claimed territory. However, clan leaders in the border regions maintain a separatist administration known as Khatumo State, over which Somaliland does not exercise full control.

C2. Are safeguards against official corruption strong and effective? 1 / 4

Somaliland has few institutional safeguards against corruption and nepotism. Former president Ahmed Mohamed Mohamoud "Silanyo" took some measures to combat corruption, but the anticorruption commission he created in 2010 has been largely ineffective in recent years, and prosecutions of officials for malfeasance are rare. In August 2018, the parliamentary Public Accounts Committee (PAC) released a report detailing widespread misuse of government funds by high-ranking officials, particularly during the Silanyo administration. The committee's request for the attorney general to investigate officials and entities named in the report was ignored. The chairman of the PAC, Nasir Ali Shire, was also removed from his chairmanship in August by the speaker of the parliament, after Shire exposed the undervaluing of public land sold to Dahabshiil, a money transfer company. Observers viewed Shire's removal as an attempt to undermine the PAC's anticorruption work and protect Dahabshiil.

C3. Does the government operate with openness and transparency? 2 / 4

The government operates with relative transparency in many respects, but it is more opaque regarding contracts for major projects. Journalists and civil society activists who attempt to scrutinize government activities often face harassment.

CIVIL LIBERTIES: 24 / 60 (−1)

D. FREEDOM OF EXPRESSION AND BELIEF: 6 / 16 (−1)

D1. Are there free and independent media? 1 / 4

A variety of print, television, and online news outlets operate, but many have political affiliations, and the state-run broadcaster has a monopoly in the radio sector. The penal code criminalizes defamation and other vaguely defined press offenses, such as circulation of "false, exaggerated, or tendentious news." The government has restricted the registration of new newspapers.

In June 2018, journalist Mohamed Adan Dirir, who was sentenced to 18 months in prison for publishing false news in 2017, was released by presidential pardon. In July, authorities lifted a 2014 ban on Haatuf Media Group for publishing false news and defaming government officials.

Despite these positive steps, the government continued to target journalists for covering controversial topics. Between December 2017 and December 2018, 28 journalists were arrested, although only 10 were prosecuted, and all those detained were ultimately released. The government targeted media outlets for covering the border dispute between Somaliland and Puntland. In May, authorities arrested and briefly detained Abdirahman Kayse Mohamed of Bulsho TV and Mohamed Ahmed Jama of SBS TV for reporting on the conflict.

SBS TV was subsequently suspended, along with SOMNews TV, on the grounds that they were involved in "political campaigns" and a "propaganda war." SOMNews was ultimately reinstated in June, while SBS TV remained suspended at year's end.

D2. Are individuals free to practice and express their religious faith or nonbelief in public and private? 2 / 4

Islam is the state religion. The constitution allows for freedom of belief, but prohibits conversion from Islam and proselytizing by members of other faiths. Places of worship must obtain government permission to operate, though there is no mechanism to register religious organizations.

D3. Is there academic freedom, and is the educational system free from extensive political indoctrination? 2 / 4

Teachers and professors are often able to pursue academic activities of a political and quasi-political nature without fear of intimidation. While funds allocated for public schools are uneven across the regions, they are generally free from overt political manipulation.

D4. Are individuals free to express their personal views on political or other sensitive topics without fear of surveillance or retribution? 1 / 4 (−1)

While individuals can express themselves with relative freedom on political matters, remarks on sensitive social and cultural issues are increasingly subject to censure and retribution. A spate of arrests and convictions during the year for controversial social media posts has contributed to greater self-censorship online among residents. In April 2018, writer Mohamed Kayse Mohamoud was sentenced to 18 months in prison for "offending the honor of the president," over a Facebook post that allegedly undermined President Bihi's role as "a national president." The president pardoned Mohamoud in June, leading to his release. Also in April, poet Nacima Abwaan Qorane was sentenced to three years in prison for defaming the government, over a Facebook post that called for unity with Somalia and referred to Somaliland as a "region." Following an international outcry, Qorane was released by presidential pardon in May.

Score Change: The score declined from 2 to 1 due to a spate of arrests and prosecutions for social media posts on controversial topics, which has discouraged other users from expressing their views online.

E. ASSOCIATIONAL AND ORGANIZATIONAL RIGHTS: 5 / 12

E1. Is there freedom of assembly? 1 / 4

The constitution allows for freedom of assembly, but organized public demonstrations are infrequent, and the authorities have sometimes employed violence to disperse protests. In May 2018, 57 protesters in Las Anod, in the disputed Sool region, were arrested for destabilizing security. The demonstrators were advocating for Somaliland to rejoin the federal government of Somalia.

E2. Is there freedom for nongovernmental organizations, particularly those that are engaged in human rights- and governance-related work? 2 / 4

Local and international nongovernmental organizations often operate without serious interference, but such groups can face harassment for their work.

E3. Is there freedom for trade unions and similar professional or labor organizations? 2 / 4

The constitution does not explicitly protect the right to strike, though it does permit collective bargaining. The right to belong to a union is generally respected.

F. RULE OF LAW: 7 / 16

F1. Is there an independent judiciary? 2 / 4

Although some progress has been made in reforming the judicial system in recent years, the judiciary lacks independence, sufficient funding, and proper training. Judges are often selected on the basis of clan or political affiliation and are subject to interference from the government.

F2. Does due process prevail in civil and criminal matters? 2 / 4

Due process is observed unevenly. Poverty and political factors play a role in how cases are charged and investigated, and whether there is adequate and timely representation for the defendant. Both customary law and Sharia (Islamic law) are used alongside civil law, which complicates adherence to statutory procedure. In practice, police often engage in arbitrary arrests and hold detainees without charge for extended periods. Lawyers are frequently denied access to detained clients. Long delays in court cases are common. According to the Somaliland Human Rights Centre (HRC), of the nearly 5,600 criminal cases brought to court as of November 2018, over half were still pending at the end of the year.

F3. Is there protection from the illegitimate use of physical force and freedom from war and insurgencies? 1 / 4

Somaliland's police and security forces have been accused of using excessive force. Conditions for detainees at police stations are harsh and overcrowded. In the contested border areas of Sool and Sanaag, Somaliland's security forces clashed with Puntland government forces throughout the year, killing dozens of troops on both sides and leaving thousands displaced. The fighting intensified after January 2018, when Somaliland forces took control of Tukaraq, a strategically important town in Sool only 56 miles from Puntland's capital. Tensions remained high at year's end, and inflammatory rhetoric from both sides threatened to escalate the conflict further.

F4. Do laws, policies, and practices guarantee equal treatment of various segments of the population? 2 / 4

Members of smaller clans face discrimination, limited access to public services, and prejudice in the justice system. Clan connections play a critical role in securing employment. Women also suffer from inequality, including in the Sharia and customary legal systems. Homosexuality is a criminal offense, and LGBT (lesbian, gay, bisexual, and transgender) people generally do not acknowledge their sexual orientation or gender identity publicly.

G. PERSONAL AUTONOMY AND INDIVIDUAL RIGHTS: 6 / 16

G1. Do individuals enjoy freedom of movement, including the ability to change their place of residence, employment, or education? 2 / 4

Freedom of movement is respected to some extent, but traffic between Somaliland and Puntland is restricted, and the Somaliland government limits travel to and from Somalia's federal capital, Mogadishu. Individuals' ability to relocate within the territory is impaired by clan divisions.

G2. Are individuals able to exercise the right to own property and establish private businesses without undue interference from state or nonstate actors? 2 / 4

Individuals are able to own property and operate private businesses without undue interference from the government. However, land disputes are common, as tenure is often complicated by lack of documentation and inconsistencies among different legal systems and state authorities.

G3. Do individuals enjoy personal social freedoms, including choice of marriage partner and size of family, protection from domestic violence, and control over appearance? 1 / 4

Personal social freedoms are constrained by a number of factors. Marriages between members of major and minor clans are stigmatized. The practice of female genital mutilation (FGM) is common. In February 2018, the Ministry of Religious Affairs released a religious edict banning one common type of FGM, but human rights groups criticized the edict for not fully prohibiting the practice.

Domestic violence remains a serious problem, and rape is rarely reported to authorities due to social pressures against such complaints. In April, the parliament passed the Sexual Offenses Bill, which criminalized many forms of gender-based violence, including rape. Under the legislation, rape is punishable with a prison sentence of up to 25 years. The bill's passage was considered a major step forward for women's rights. Although the president signed the bill into law in August, a number of clerics expressed strong opposition to the legislation, and it was subsequently sent to the Ministry of Religious Affairs for review. The review continued through the end of the year, delaying the law's implementation and leaving its future uncertain.

G4. Do individuals enjoy equality of opportunity and freedom from economic exploitation? 1 / 4

The informal sector, including traditional pastoral activities, accounts for much of the economy, and many households rely on remittances from relatives working in other countries. Trafficking in persons for forced labor or sexual exploitation abroad is a serious problem. Refugees from neighboring countries, including Yemen and Ethiopia, and internally displaced people, are also vulnerable to exploitation.

South Ossetia

Population: 53,500
Political Rights Rating: 7
Civil Liberties Rating: 6
Freedom Rating: 6.5
Freedom Status: Not Free

Overview: Large parts of South Ossetia, a breakaway territory of Georgia, enjoyed de facto independence after a civil conflict ended in 1992. A 2008 war that drew in Russian forces resulted in the expulsion of the remaining Georgian government presence and of many ethnic Georgian civilians. Only Russia and a handful of other states have since recognized South Ossetia's independence. The territory remains almost entirely dependent on Russia, and Moscow exerts a decisive influence over its politics and governance. Local media and civil society are largely controlled or monitored by the authorities, and the judiciary is subject to political influence and manipulation.

KEY DEVELOPMENTS IN 2018:

- Several political parties were prevented from registering, or complained of new bureaucratic hurdles to reregistration, in advance of 2019 legislative elections. Ruling party members made statements discouraging the formation and activity of opposition parties.
- Harassment of the territory's few independent journalists continued. In February, security services searched the office of Irina Kelekhsayeva after she published an article detailing strained relations between President Anatoly Bibilov and a Russian investor, and her editors at the Ir online newspaper later asked her to resign. In November, journalist and civil society activist Tamara Mearakishvili said she faced another round of criminal charges, but that she had not yet been informed of the exact allegations.
- In February, South Ossetian authorities detained three Georgian citizens on charges of "genocide" allegedly committed against South Ossetian civilians during the 2008 war. One of them, Archil Tatunashvili, died in custody shortly after his arrest, prompting international condemnation. The other two were released shortly afterward.
- A May report by the International Crisis Group (ICG), a Brussels-based think tank, described a quiet increase in informal trade between South Ossetia and Georgia—offering new economic opportunities, but also opportunities for corruption.

POLITICAL RIGHTS: 2 / 40

A. ELECTORAL PROCESS: 2 / 12

A1. Was the current head of government or other chief national authority elected through free and fair elections? 0 / 4

Although South Ossetia holds elections regularly, they are severely restricted at all stages of the process, and are not monitored by independent observers or recognized by the international community. In the most recent presidential election, in April 2017, former military leader Anatoly Bibilov was elected to a five-year term with 58 percent of the vote; he defeated the incumbent, Leonid Tibilov, who took 30 percent, and State Security Committee (KGB) official Alan Gagloyev, who took 11 percent.

Political analysts said that the conduct of the 2017 election was an improvement on the 2011 poll, the results of which had been disputed. Nevertheless, political debate and competition only occurred within a narrow field of candidates allowed by Russia and pro-Russian authorities.

A2. Were the current national legislative representatives elected through free and fair elections? 1 / 4

Current members of South Ossetia's unicameral 34-member parliament were elected through a proportional voting system. Legislative elections are not internationally recognized, and the extent of Russian influence in the territory's politics precludes truly competitive contests.

Nevertheless, parliamentary elections held in 2014 were considered an improvement from previous ones. Unlike in 2009, in which only three parties were able to participate, candidates from nine parties succeeded in registering in 2014. The opposition United Ossetia, led by Bibilov, won 20 seats, followed by the Unity of the People party with 6 seats. Smaller parties captured the remainder. The next parliamentary elections are scheduled for June 2019.

A3. Are the electoral laws and framework fair, and are they implemented impartially by the relevant election management bodies? 1 / 4

According to electoral laws, candidates must have permanently resided in South Ossetia for 10 years. Former president Eduard Kokoity, the only candidate who openly opposed annexation of South Ossetia by Russia, was barred from running in the 2017 presidential election due to his failure to meet the residency requirement. The Supreme Court rejected Kokoity's appeal, in which he claimed that the evidence put forth by the Central Election Commission (CEC) was falsified.

Authorities reportedly continue to restrict voting rights of remaining ethnic Georgian residents of South Ossetia. Russian political influence continues to call into question the independence of the CEC.

In a referendum held alongside the 2017 presidential election, over 80 percent of voters approved adding "The State of Alania" to the territory's name. The move was viewed as a precursor to potential constitutional changes to allow union with North Ossetia–Alania, which is a federal subject of Russia.

In 2017, President Bibilov declared that the 2019 legislative elections would be conducted by a mixed proportional and majoritarian system, instead of the fully proportional system that is currently in place. The decision was made without public input.

B. POLITICAL PLURALISM AND PARTICIPATION: 2 / 16

B1. Do the people have the right to organize in different political parties or other competitive political groupings of their choice, and is the system free of undue obstacles to the rise and fall of these competing parties or groupings? 1 / 4

Moscow exerts a decisive influence over politics and governance, in effect placing significant restrictions on the ability of political parties outside of a narrow political spectrum to operate freely.

A number of new political parties were able to register in the past few years, including the ruling United Ossetia, which has governed the territory since winning the most seats in the 2014 elections. However, figures from United Ossetia—which controls the de facto Ministry of Justice which in turn which oversees the party registration processes—have more recently indicated their intention to reduce the number of political parties ahead of the 2019 parliamentary elections. In March 2018, parliament speaker Pyotr Gassiev stated that the territory's 15 registered parties were excessive, and in July, Bibilov warned against the formation of opposition parties.

Attempts to register two new political parties (Towers, and the Alanian Union) failed in 2018, while the head of the opposition New Ossetia party has complained of new bureaucratic hurdles in reregistering existing parties before elections. The efforts appear to amount to an attempt to ensure that the 2019 vote favors United Ossetia.

B2. Is there a realistic opportunity for the opposition to increase its support or gain power through elections? 1 / 4

In the 2017 presidential election, Bibilov, the opposition candidate, challenged and defeated the incumbent. However, the success or failure of the territory's opposition politicians is largely determined by Moscow. South Ossetian government sources implied that banned presidential candidate Kokoity was not in Moscow's favor.

B3. Are the people's political choices free from domination by the military, foreign powers, religious hierarchies, economic oligarchies, or any other powerful group that is not democratically accountable? 0 / 4

The functioning of South Ossetia's institutions are almost entirely dependent on economic and political support from Moscow. There are few avenues for people to meaningfully participate in political processes if they wish to advocate for interests that fall outside of the narrow political spectrum defined by Russia and the territory's Russian-aligned authorities.

B4. Do various segments of the population (including ethnic, religious, gender, LGBT, and other relevant groups) have full political rights and electoral opportunities? 0 / 4

While the South Ossetian government includes several women ministers, the interests of women and minority groups are not represented politically. Most ethnic Georgian residents have either declined or have been denied the ability to participate in elections.

C. FUNCTIONING OF GOVERNMENT: 0 / 12

C1. Do the freely elected head of government and national legislative representatives determine the policies of the government? 0 / 4

The ability of elected officials to determine and implement policy is heavily influenced by the Russian government. A sweeping 2015 treaty on alliance and integration between Russia and South Ossetia closely integrates the territory's defense, security, and customs mechanisms with those of Russia, charging Moscow with protection of South Ossetia's borders; it is binding for 25 years with the possibility of extension. Russian aid comprises almost the entirety of South Ossetia's budget. Media reports detailing the increasingly important role of South Ossetia as a conduit for funds from Russia to the breakaway territories of eastern Ukraine continue to surface; details of the reports reflect the ability of Russian authorities to shape South Ossetia's financial and business regulations and infrastructure to serve their own purposes.

According to private emails leaked in 2016 that were apparently tied to senior Kremlin adviser Vladislav Surkov, Moscow mandated 13 working groups to review legislation drafted by the authorities in Tskhinvali, South Ossetia's de facto capital, and had a timetable for the bills' approval by the territory's legislature. Some of Bibilov's ministerial appointments reflect a long trend in the territory to nominate Russian citizens to key roles, including the territory's security services.

Like his predecessor, President Bibilov has spoken repeatedly of formally uniting the territory with Russia's North Ossetia–Alania, or joining the Russian Federation as a separate region.

C2. Are safeguards against official corruption strong and effective? 0 / 4

Official corruption is widespread in South Ossetia, and there is little to no systematic attempt to fight it.

C3. Does the government operate with openness and transparency? 0 / 4

Due in part to the significant level of Russian influence on domestic politics and decision-making, South Ossetia's government does not operate with transparency. Officials have not identified a lack of transparency as a policy priority.

ADDITIONAL DISCRETIONARY POLITICAL RIGHTS QUESTION:

Is the government or occupying power deliberately changing the ethnic composition of a country or territory so as to destroy a culture or tip the political balance in favor of another group? -2 / 0

During the 2008 war, Ossetian forces seized or razed property in previously Georgian-controlled villages, and large numbers of ethnic Georgians fled the fighting. Authorities in South Ossetia have since barred ethnic Georgians from returning to the territory unless they renounce their Georgian citizenship and accept Russian passports. Of approximately

20,000 ethnic Georgians displaced from their homes in South Ossetia, most have not been able to return. However, conditions for local residents have largely stabilized since the war, particularly due to the absence of open conflict across the administrative line separating the territory from Georgia.

CIVIL LIBERTIES: 8 / 60
D. FREEDOM OF EXPRESSION AND BELIEF: 3 / 16
D1. Are there free and independent media? 0 / 4

Local media, including the newspapers *Yuzhnaya Osetiya* and *Respublika* and online portals Res and Ir, and are almost entirely controlled by the authorities. Self-censorship is pervasive, and defamation charges are often employed against critical media. An increasing number of residents rely on online outlets for news and other information, and foreign media, including broadcasts from Russia and Georgia, remain accessible. The local version of Russian news portal *Sputnik*, accessible in both Russian and Ossetian, is increasingly popular.

Harassment of the territory's few critical and independent journalists continued throughout 2018. In February, security services searched the offices of Irina Kelekhsayeva after she published an article detailing the strained relations between Bibilov and a Russian investor. Kelekhsayeva's editors at Ir then asked her to resign, allegedly under pressure from the authorities.

The authorities continued to press charges against Tamara Mearakishvili, a journalist and civil society activist who works with international media outlets including Radio Free Europe/Radio Liberty (RFE/RL). While a district court dismissed three previous criminal accusations against Mearakishvili (concerning illegal acquisition of documents and defamation), she stated that authorities continued to harass her, and staged a hunger strike in July in protest. A fourth criminal case was opened against her in November 2018; at the time she said she had not been informed of the details of the charge.

D2. Are individuals free to practice and express their religious faith or nonbelief in public and private? 1 / 4

While the majority of the population is Orthodox Christian, there is a sizeable Muslim community. Followers of Russian Orthodoxy and Ossetian neopaganism also inhabit the territory. Some property of the Georgian Orthodox Church is controlled by the South Ossetian Orthodox Church (called the Eparchy).

The Eparchy has come under increasing pressure from Bibilov and others to merge with the Russian Orthodox Church. In April 2018, South Ossetian border guards confiscated the South Ossetian passport of the Eparchy's Bishop Ambrosi as he attempted to enter the territory from Russia, and refused him entry. Ambrosi had opposed the merger with the Russian Orthodox Church.

In 2017, South Ossetia's de facto Supreme Court outlawed Jehovah's Witnesses as an "extremist" organization; the group had been banned in Russia earlier that year.

D3. Is there academic freedom, and is the educational system free from extensive political indoctrination? 1 / 4

The government exerts strong influence over the education system. In 2017, the ministry of education began to phase out Georgian-language education, and this process continued throughout 2018. Teachers with no knowledge of Georgian have been dispatched to the Georgian-majority Leningor Region, one of whom attempted to prevent students and staff from speaking Georgian among themselves.

D4. Are individuals free to express their personal views on political or other sensitive topics without fear of surveillance or retribution? 1 / 4

Private discussion is constrained by the sensitivity of certain topics, particularly the territory's geopolitical standing. Speaking of the property rights and expulsion of the Georgian population is assumed to attract unwanted attention.

E. ASSOCIATIONAL AND ORGANIZATIONAL RIGHTS: 1 / 12

E1. Is there freedom of assembly? 1 / 4

Residents occasionally demonstrate against environmental degradation, the sluggish pace of postwar reconstruction, and more rarely, overtly political grievances. However, freedom of assembly is strictly limited. Participants in unsanctioned gatherings risk being charged with crimes, and authorities have responded to demonstrations by closing roads and deploying security forces to patrol.

E2. Is there freedom for nongovernmental organizations, particularly those that are engaged in human rights- and governance-related work? 0 / 4

Nongovernmental organizations (NGOs) that operate in the territory are subject to government influence and by extension, influence from Russia. Legislative amendments in 2014 increased the oversight capacity of local authorities over NGO activity, subjecting organizations receiving foreign funding to broader and more frequent reporting requirements and branding them "foreign agents;" it is unclear whether, or how, the provision applies to the numerous NGOs that draw funding from Russia. NGOs engaged in conflict resolution and reconciliation are smeared by the authorities and progovernment media as agents of Tbilisi or western intelligence services. In 2018 the South Ossetian state news agency reported that many NGOs had disbanded.

E3. Is there freedom for trade unions and similar professional or labor organizations? 0 / 4

Trade unions in South Ossetia largely defer to the policies of the separatist government. Conflict with Georgia has left trade unions weak and geographically divided.

F. RULE OF LAW: 1 / 16

F1. Is there an independent judiciary? 0 / 4

South Ossetia's judiciary is not independent. The justice system is manipulated to punish perceived opponents of the separatist leadership, as reflected, among other cases, by those against journalist Mearakishvili.

F2. Does due process prevail in civil and criminal matters? 0 / 4

South Ossetia uses a modified version of the Russian criminal code. Government allies reportedly continue to violate the law with relative impunity. Russian prosecutors have attempted to curb malfeasance by local officials, but the Russian court system itself remains deeply flawed.

Justice structures are undermined by a lack of qualified lawyers. In one high-profile case in 2017, a colonel arrested amid a professed anticorruption campaign by Bibilov was allegedly refused access to his lawyer and told by the local KGB that they were in charge and that there was no legal recourse. He remained in prison at the end of 2018.

F3. Is there protection from the illegitimate use of physical force and freedom from war and insurgencies? 0 / 4

Victims of human rights violations committed during the 2008 conflict have few avenues for legal recourse. Physical abuse and poor conditions are reportedly common in prisons and detention centers.

In February 2018, South Ossetian authorities detained three Georgian citizens on charges of "genocide" allegedly committed against South Ossetian civilians during the 2008 war. One of them, Archil Tatunashvili, died in custody shortly after his arrest, with South Ossetian officials claiming that he had suffered a heart attack while attempting to attack a police officer. His death prompted a rash of statements from democratic governments and European international organizations that ranged from grave concern to outrage and condemnation. South Ossetian officials for a time refused to return his body to his family in Georgia, though eventually relented; the two men detained with Tatunashvili were released shortly after his death.

F4. Do laws, policies, and practices guarantee equal treatment of various segments of the population? 1 / 4

Discrimination against ethnic Georgians continues. Reports of arbitrary discrimination and detention of ethnic Georgians continue to arise. There are no initiatives to support the rights of LGBT (lesbian, gay, bisexual, and transgender) people in this very conservative society.

G. PERSONAL AUTONOMY AND INDIVIDUAL RIGHTS: 3 / 16

G1. Do individuals enjoy freedom of movement, including the ability to change their place of residence, employment, or education? 1 / 4

Restrictions on freedom of movement between South Ossetia and Georgia were tightened in 2018, though travel to Russia remains largely unimpeded. As in past years, dozens of Georgian citizens were detained by border guards near the line of contact with Tbilisi-controlled territory and released after paying a fine. In November, the territory's parliament passed a new law increasing the fines for illegal border crossing by nearly four times. Several South Ossetian officials stated in 2018 that they aimed to finally close the one remaining border checkpoint with Georgia, prompting deepening concern among the territory's ethnic Georgians. In late December, authorities announced that a special pass issued by a security committee would be required necessary to cross the border from Georgia.

G2. Are individuals able to exercise the right to own property and establish private businesses without undue interference from state or nonstate actors? 0 / 4

The territory's political and military situation has negatively affected protections for property rights, particularly for residents close to the administrative border. The separatist authorities have consistently refused to countenance the return of ethnic Georgians expelled from their homes before or during the 2008 war.

Small businesses risk being seized or subjected to predatory behavior by larger, more powerful corporations.

G3. Do individuals enjoy personal social freedoms, including choice of marriage partner and size of family, protection from domestic violence, and control over appearance? 2 / 4

While no laws officially regulate individuals' public appearance, statements by public officials reflect intolerance for behavior that deviates from the territory's conservative norms. No laws or government programs specifically protect victims of domestic violence.

G4. Do individuals enjoy equality of opportunity and freedom from economic exploitation? 0 / 4

Although Bibilov promised an investment program and a rise in social spending in late 2018, there remains very little economic opportunity in South Ossetia. Populations living along the administrative border with Georgia face additional economic uncertainty due to divisions created by shifting and uncertain borders.

However, a 2018 report by the International Crisis Group (ICG), a Brussels-based think tank, described a quiet increase in informal trade between South Ossetia and Georgia, some of which has offered greater economic opportunity to displaced and other disadvantaged people. ICG attributed the trade, which is facilitated by the single road link between South Ossetia and Georgia, to increased demand for food and consumer goods in South Ossetia amid economic struggles in Russia. The report noted that the informal nature of the exchanges has also created avenues for corruption.

Tibet

Population: 3,370,000 [Note: This figure covers only the Tibet Autonomous Region.]
Political Rights Rating: 7
Civil Liberties Rating: 7
Freedom Rating: 7.0
Freedom Status: Not Free

Note: This report assesses the Tibet Autonomous Region and areas of eastern Tibet that are incorporated into neighboring Chinese provinces.

Overview: Tibet is ruled by the Chinese Communist Party (CCP) government based in Beijing, with local decision-making power concentrated in the hands of Chinese party officials. Residents of both Chinese and Tibetan ethnicity are denied fundamental rights, but the authorities are especially rigorous in suppressing any signs of dissent among Tibetans, including manifestations of uniquely Tibetan religious belief and cultural identity. State policies encourage migration from other parts of China, reducing the ethnic Tibetan share of the population.

KEY DEVELOPMENTS IN 2018:
- In March, the CCP announced significant structural reforms that placed the party's United Front Work Department more explicitly in charge of policy areas like religious affairs and ethnic minorities, including in Tibet.
- Businessman Tashi Wangchuk was sentenced to five years in prison in May on charges of inciting separatism; he had given an interview to the *New York Times* in 2015 about his efforts to use the Chinese legal system to challenge the lack of Tibetan-language education. The case illustrated the heavy penalties imposed on Tibetans who seek to preserve their culture.
- Chinese officials continued to consolidate control over Larung Gar, a major center for Tibetan Buddhist learning located in Sichuan Province, during the year. They have expanded CCP cadres' management of the center and increased the political education components of the curriculum in the wake of large-scale demolitions and evictions of monks and nuns that began in 2016.

- Amid tighter restrictions on passports for Tibetans, significantly fewer Tibetan pilgrims were able to travel to India to hear teachings of the Dalai Lama in 2018 compared with previous years.

POLITICAL RIGHTS: –2 / 40

A. ELECTORAL PROCESS: 0 / 12

A1. Was the current head of government or other chief national authority elected through free and fair elections? 0 / 4

The Chinese government rules Tibet through administration of the TAR and 12 Tibetan autonomous prefectures or counties in the nearby provinces of Sichuan, Qinghai, Gansu, and Yunnan. Under the Chinese constitution, autonomous areas have the right to formulate their own regulations and implement national legislation in accordance with local conditions. In practice, however, decision-making authority is concentrated in the hands of unelected ethnic (Han) Chinese officials of the CCP, which has a monopoly on political power. In 2016, Wu Yingjie replaced Chen Quanguo as TAR party secretary.

The few ethnic Tibetans who occupy senior executive positions serve mostly as figureheads or echo official doctrine. Che Dalha, one of two ethnic Tibetan members of the CCP's 205-member Central Committee, has served as chairman (governor) of the TAR since January 2017. The chairman is formally elected by the regional people's congress, but in practice such decisions are predetermined by the CCP leadership.

A2. Were the current national legislative representatives elected through free and fair elections? 0 / 4

The regional people's congress of the TAR, which is formally elected by lower-level people's congresses, chooses delegates to China's 3,000-member National People's Congress (NPC) every five years, but in practice all candidates are vetted by the CCP. The current TAR people's congress held its first session in January 2018, and the current NPC was seated in March 2018.

A3. Are the electoral laws and framework fair, and are they implemented impartially by the relevant election management bodies? 0 / 4

As in the rest of China, direct elections are only permitted at the lowest administrative levels. Tight political controls and aggressive state interference ensure that competitive races with independent candidates are even rarer in Tibet than in other parts of the country. Regulations published in 2014 placed significant restrictions on candidates for village elections, excluding those who have attended religious teachings abroad, have communicated with overseas Tibetans, or have relatives studying at monasteries outside China.

B. POLITICAL PLURALISM AND PARTICIPATION: 0 / 16

B1. Do the people have the right to organize in different political parties or other competitive political groupings of their choice, and is the system free of undue obstacles to the rise and fall of these competing parties or groupings? 0 / 4

All organized political activity outside the CCP is illegal and harshly punished, as is any evidence of loyalty to or communication with the Tibetan government in exile, based in Dharamsala, India.

The exile government includes an elected parliament serving five-year terms, a Supreme Justice Commission that adjudicates civil disputes, and a directly elected prime minister, also serving five-year terms. Votes are collected from the Tibetan diaspora around the world. The unelected Dalai Lama, the Tibetan spiritual leader who also traditionally served as head of state, renounced his political role in 2011. Lobsang Sangay was elected prime minister in the same year, replacing a two-term incumbent and becoming the exile government's top political official; he was reelected in April 2016.

B2. Is there a realistic opportunity for the opposition to increase its support or gain power through elections? 0 / 4

As in the rest of China, the one-party system rigorously suppresses the development of any organized political opposition. Tibet has never experienced a peaceful and democratic transfer of power between rival groups.

B3. Are the people's political choices free from domination by the military, foreign powers, religious hierarchies, economic oligarchies, or any other powerful group that is not democratically accountable? 0 / 4

The authoritarian CCP is not accountable to voters and denies the public any meaningful influence or participation in political affairs.

B4. Do various segments of the population (including ethnic, religious, gender, LGBT, and other relevant groups) have full political rights and electoral opportunities? 0 / 4

Political opportunities for ethnic Tibetans within Tibet remain limited by the dominance of ethnic Chinese officials at all levels of the CCP. The ethnic Tibetan population's objections to party policies are actively suppressed.

Women are well represented in many public-sector jobs and CCP posts within the TAR, though most high-level officials are men, and women are unable to organize independently to advance their political interests.

C. FUNCTIONING OF GOVERNMENT: 1 / 12

C1. Do the freely elected head of government and national legislative representatives determine the policies of the government? 0 / 4

Unelected CCP officials determine and implement government policies in Tibet. In March 2018, the CCP Central Committee announced significant structural reforms that reduced the already limited separation between the party and state governance, placing CCP entities—like the United Front Work Department—more explicitly in charge of policy areas including religious affairs and ethnic minorities, which are especially relevant for Tibet.

C2. Are safeguards against official corruption strong and effective? 1 / 4

As in the rest of China, corruption is believed to be extensive, though little information is available on the scale of the problem. There have been moves in recent years to curb graft among the region's officials as part of Chinese president Xi Jinping's nationwide anticorruption campaign. However, many prosecutions are believed to be politically selective or amount to reprisals for perceived political and religious disloyalty.

C3. Does the government operate with openness and transparency? 0 / 4

Governance is opaque in all of China, but even more so in Tibet. A study by the Chinese Academy of Social Sciences published in 2017 ranked cities and counties nationwide by their level of government transparency; Lhasa scored lowest among the cities, and the TAR's Nang County was the lowest among the counties under examination.

ADDITIONAL DISCRETIONARY POLITICAL RIGHTS QUESTION

Is the government or occupying power deliberately changing the ethnic composition of a country or territory so as to destroy a culture or tip the political balance in favor of another group? –3 / 0

The Chinese government's economic development programs in Tibet have strongly encouraged ethnic Chinese migration to the region, disproportionately benefited ethnic Chinese residents, and exacerbated the marginalization of ethnic Tibetans, who have also been displaced by mass resettlement campaigns within Tibet. Ethnic Tibetans account for some 90 percent of the permanently registered population of the TAR, but many ethnic Chinese migrants have moved to the region without changing permanent residency. In recent years, officials have announced major new urbanization projects that risk further diluting the region's Tibetan population; one such plan aims to increase the "permanent urban population" of Tibet by approximately 30 percent by 2020, with many new settlers likely to be ethnic Chinese.

CIVIL LIBERTIES: 3 / 60

D. FREEDOM OF EXPRESSION AND BELIEF: 0 / 16

D1. Are there free and independent media? 0 / 4

Chinese authorities tightly restrict all news media in Tibet. Individuals who use the internet, social media, or other means to share politically sensitive news content or commentary face arrest and heavy criminal penalties. Tibetan cultural expression, which the authorities associate with separatism, is subject to especially harsh restrictions; those incarcerated in recent years have included scores of Tibetan writers, intellectuals, and musicians.

Deliberate internet blackouts are common in Tibet, including in areas where public demonstrations have occurred. International broadcasts are jammed, and personal communication devices are periodically confiscated and searched. The online censorship and monitoring systems in place across China are applied even more stringently in the TAR, while censorship of Tibet-related keywords on WeChat has become more sophisticated. Heavy censorship of the news media and online communications was imposed in February 2018 to suppress news and information about a fire at Jokhang Temple in Lhasa, a UN Educational, Scientific, and Cultural Organization (UNESCO) World Heritage site, fueling concerns that the damage was more serious than officially claimed.

Access to the TAR is highly restricted for foreign journalists, who are also regularly prevented from entering Tibetan areas of Sichuan and other provinces, though no permission is technically required to travel there. Tibetans who communicate with foreign media without permission risk arrest and prosecution. Businessman Tashi Wangchuk was sentenced to five years in prison in May 2018 on charges of inciting separatism, having given an interview to the *New York Times* in 2015 about his efforts to use the Chinese legal system to challenge the lack of Tibetan-language education; his appeal was denied in August.

D2. Are individuals free to practice and express their religious faith or nonbelief in public and private? 0 / 4

Freedom of religion is harshly restricted in Tibet, in large part because the authorities interpret reverence for the Dalai Lama and adherence to the region's unique form of Buddhism as a threat to CCP rule. New regulations on religious affairs came into effect in February 2018, reiterating many existing restrictions while strengthening controls on places of worship, travel for religious purposes, and children's religious education, including in Tibetan areas.

Religious Affairs Bureaus control who can study in monasteries and nunneries. Officials enforce a minimum age requirement of 18 for those who wish to become monks or nuns, although some institutions continue to accept younger children without registration. Monks and nuns are required to sign a declaration rejecting Tibetan independence, expressing loyalty to the government, and denouncing the Dalai Lama. Since 2012, the CCP has set up committees of government officials within monasteries to manage their daily operations and enforce party indoctrination campaigns. Police posts are increasingly common even in smaller monasteries.

Ideological education campaigns reach most monasteries and nunneries in the region. In 2018, the effort included obligatory study of the "spirit" of the October 2017 19th Party Congress. Such campaigns typically force participants to recognize the CCP claim that China "liberated" Tibet and to denounce the Dalai Lama. They have been extended to the lay population in recent years, with students, civil servants, and farmers required to participate in discussions, singing sessions, and propaganda film screenings. Possession of Dalai Lama–related materials—especially in the TAR—can lead to official harassment, arrest, and punishment, including restrictions on commercial activity and loss of welfare benefits.

The Chinese government has asserted its intention to select the successor of the current Dalai Lama, who turned 83 in July 2018, and promoted its own appointee to serve as the Panchen Lama, a religious figure who plays an important role in identifying the reincarnation of a Dalai Lama according to traditional Tibetan Buddhist rituals. The location of the Panchen Lama who was originally recognized by the current Dalai Lama remains unknown, as he was abducted by Chinese officials in 1995, when he was six years old.

Chinese officials continued in 2018 to consolidate control over Larung Gar, a major center for Tibetan Buddhist learning located in Sichuan Province. Since June 2016, the center's size has been reduced dramatically through mass demolitions of buildings and evictions of monks and nuns. In 2017, CCP cadres were appointed to take over management of Larung Gar at every level. According to a January 2018 report by Human Rights Watch, real-name registration has been imposed on visitors, and 40 percent of the curriculum is now dedicated to political and nonreligious study. A similar campaign has affected Yachen Gar, another Tibetan Buddhist religious community in Sichuan Province.

D3. Is there academic freedom, and is the educational system free from extensive political indoctrination? 0 / 4

University professors cannot lecture on certain topics, and many must attend political indoctrination sessions. The government restricts course materials to prevent circulation of unofficial versions of Tibetan history and has reduced use of Tibetan as the language of instruction in schools in recent years. In 2018, students in Lhasa were reportedly required to sign a commitment to avoid religious activities during the summer break.

D4. Are individuals free to express their personal views on political or other sensitive topics without fear of surveillance or retribution? 0 / 4

Freedom of private discussion is severely limited by factors including the authorities' monitoring of electronic communications, the heavy security presence, and regular ideological campaigns in Tibetan areas.

Tibetans continue to be detained or sentenced to prison for actions like verbally expressing support for the Dalai Lama and freedom for Tibet, sharing images of the Dalai Lama or the Tibetan flag on social media, or sending information abroad about recent self-immolation protests. As they implement the 2017 Cybersecurity Law, authorities have held meetings with managers of WeChat groups in Tibetan areas, warning them to ensure that discussions in their groups remain "appropriate," while informing residents at monasteries of the risks of sharing illicit information. In January 2018, former political prisoner Tsegon Gyal was sentenced to three years in prison for a post on WeChat in which he criticized the Chinese government for failing to genuinely promote its proclaimed policy of "ethnic unity." In April, two Tibetan monks in Qinghai Province were reportedly detained after they admitted to posting politically sensitive images and articles on WeChat.

E. ASSOCIATIONAL AND ORGANIZATIONAL RIGHTS: 0 / 12

E1. Is there freedom of assembly? 0 / 4

Chinese authorities severely restrict freedom of assembly as part of the government's intensified "stability maintenance" policies in Tibet. Control and surveillance of public gatherings extends beyond major towns to villages and rural areas. Even nonviolent protesters are often violently dispersed and harshly punished. Nevertheless, Tibetans continue to seek ways to express dissatisfaction with government policies; several individuals held solo protests in public places during 2018, briefly calling for the return of the Dalai Lama and freedom in Tibet before being seized by police. As in the rest of China, authorities have occasionally responded to environmental protests with minor concessions, such as temporary suspension of mining operations.

At least three Tibetans set themselves on fire to protest Chinese rule during 2018, though self-immolations have declined in recent years, due in part to state-imposed deterrents. Officials respond to self-immolation incidents with information blackouts, a heightened security presence, increased surveillance, and large-scale arrests of those associated with the self-immolators. Engaging in self-immolation and organizing, assisting, or gathering crowds related to such acts are considered criminal offenses, including intentional homicide in some cases. In addition to mass arrests, the government employs collective-punishment tactics—for both self-immolations and other forms of protest—that include financial penalties on protesters' families, cancellation of public benefits for their households, and termination of state-funded projects in their communities.

E2. Is there freedom for nongovernmental organizations, particularly those that are engaged in human rights- and governance-related work? 0 / 4

Nongovernmental organizations, including those focused only on apolitical issues like development and public health, operate under highly restrictive agreements and periodically face closure. A July 2018 Human Rights Watch report documented the effects of a February TAR police notice and earlier regulations that banned a wide range of social and community engagement, including initiatives to promote the Tibetan language and to protect the environment, as well as traditional forms of mediation.

E3. Is there freedom for trade unions and similar professional or labor organizations? 0 / 4

As in the rest of China, independent trade unions are illegal. The only legal union organization is the government-controlled All-China Federation of Trade Unions, which has long been criticized for failing to properly defend workers' rights. Labor activism in Tibet is riskier and therefore much more rare than in other parts of China. According to the China Labour Bulletin, no strikes took place in the TAR during 2018, compared with about 1,700 strikes elsewhere in the country.

F. RULE OF LAW: 0 / 16

F1. Is there an independent judiciary? 0 / 4

The CCP controls the judicial system, and courts consequently lack independence. Courts at all levels are supervised by party political-legal committees that influence the appointment of judges, court operations, and verdicts and sentences. Given the political sensitivity of Tibetan areas, the scope for autonomous judicial decision-making is even more limited than elsewhere in China.

F2. Does due process prevail in civil and criminal matters? 0 / 4

Defendants lack access to meaningful legal representation. Trials are closed if state security interests are invoked, and sometimes even when no political crime is listed. Chinese lawyers who offer to defend Tibetan suspects have been harassed, disbarred, or blocked from attending relevant hearings. Security forces routinely engage in arbitrary detention, and detainees' families are often left uninformed as to their whereabouts or well-being.

F3. Is there protection from the illegitimate use of physical force and freedom from war and insurgencies? 0 / 4

Detained suspects and prisoners are subject to torture and other forms of abuse. Tibetan prisoners of conscience have died in custody under circumstances indicating torture, and others have been released in poor health, allegedly to avoid deaths in custody. According to a partial database maintained by the US Congressional-Executive Commission on China, there were still hundreds of Tibetan political prisoners behind bars as of late 2018.

F4. Do laws, policies, and practices guarantee equal treatment of various segments of the population? 0 / 4

Ethnic Tibetans face a range of socioeconomic disadvantages and discriminatory treatment by employers, law enforcement agencies, and other official bodies. The dominant role of the Chinese language in education and employment limits opportunities for many Tibetans; Tibetans receive preferential treatment in university admission examinations, but this is often not enough to secure entrance.

As in the rest of China, gender bias against women remains widespread, despite laws barring workplace discrimination. LGBT (lesbian, gay, bisexual, and transgender) people suffer from discrimination, though same-sex sexual activity is not criminalized. Social pressures discourage discussion of LGBT issues.

G. PERSONAL AUTONOMY AND INDIVIDUAL RIGHTS: 3 / 16

G1. Do individuals enjoy freedom of movement, including the ability to change their place of residence, employment, or education? 0 / 4

Obstacles including troop deployments, checkpoints, roadblocks, required bureaucratic approvals, and passport restrictions impede freedom of movement within and beyond Tibetan areas, particularly for travel to and from the TAR. Increased security efforts and Nepalese government cooperation have made it difficult for Tibetans to cross the border into Nepal. Obtaining a passport for foreign travel is extremely difficult for Tibetans. It was reported in March 2018 that at least 60 Tibetan pilgrims from Sichuan Province who had traveled to Nepal and India to visit religious sites were detained upon returning to the country. In December, many fewer pilgrims were able to travel to India to hear teachings by the Dalai Lama than in previous years, due in part to government campaigns to revoke Tibetans' passports.

Authorities continue to restrict access to the TAR for human rights researchers, as well as for some tourists. Foreigners are often denied entry surrounding politically sensitive dates. During other periods, tourists must travel in groups and obtain official permission to visit the TAR, and even then, last-minute travel bans are periodically imposed.

G2. Are individuals able to exercise the right to own property and establish private businesses without undue interference from state or nonstate actors? 1 / 4

The economy is dominated by state-owned enterprises and private businesses with informal ties to officials. Tibetans reportedly find it more difficult than ethnic Chinese residents to obtain permits and loans to open businesses.

Since 2003, the authorities have intensified efforts to resettle rural and nomadic Tibetans—forcibly or with incentives—into permanent-housing areas that often have little economic infrastructure. As in the rest of China, land expropriation for development projects is regularly carried out with little consultation and inadequate compensation.

G3. Do individuals enjoy personal social freedoms, including choice of marriage partner and size of family, protection from domestic violence, and control over appearance? 1 / 4

China's restrictive family-planning policies are formally more lenient for Tibetans and other ethnic minorities. Officials limit urban Tibetans to two children and encourage rural Tibetans to stop at three. As a result, the TAR is one of the few areas of China without a skewed sex ratio. Nevertheless, the authorities continue to regulate reproduction, and related abuses are occasionally reported. State policies actively encourage interethnic marriages with financial and other incentives, and couples must designate a single ethnicity for their children. Separately, Tibetan women are vulnerable to human trafficking schemes that result in forced marriage.

G4. Do individuals enjoy equality of opportunity and freedom from economic exploitation? 1 / 4

Exploitative employment practices are pervasive in many industries, as is the case across China, though ethnic Tibetans reportedly face additional disadvantages in hiring and compensation. Human trafficking that targets Tibetan women can lead to prostitution or exploitative employment in domestic service and other sectors elsewhere in China.

Transnistria

Population: 476,000
Political Rights Rating: 6
Civil Liberties Rating: 6
Freedom Rating: 6.0
Freedom Status: Not Free

Overview: Transnistria is a breakaway region of Moldova in which ethnic Russians and Ukrainians together outnumber ethnic Moldovans. The territory has enjoyed de facto independence since a brief military conflict in 1992, though it is internationally recognized as a part of Moldova. Its government and economy are heavily dependent on subsidies from Russia, which maintains a military presence and peacekeeping mission in the territory. Political competition is limited, and the dominant party is aligned with powerful local business interests. Impartiality and pluralism of opinion in media is very limited, and authorities closely control civil society activity.

KEY DEVELOPMENTS IN 2018:

- A restrictive new law on nongovernmental organizations (NGOs) took effect in May. It mandated more detailed reporting by NGOs, including on foreign funding, and prohibited foreign-backed NGOs from engaging in a broad scope of actions deemed "political activities."
- In November, lawmaker and Communist Party leader Oleg Horzhan was sentenced to four-and-a-half years in prison. He had been arrested and stripped of his parlia-

mentary immunity earlier in the year on charges including organizing an unauthorized demonstration.

- A number of agreements reached within the 5+2 negotiation framework were implemented during the year. These included the introduction of a new, neutral license plate that allows Transnistrian residents to drive into Moldova, the recognition in Moldova of Transnistrian educational documents, and permission for those on the right bank to access their farmland on the left bank, in Dubăsari.

POLITICAL RIGHTS: 10 / 40

A. ELECTORAL PROCESS: 3 / 12

A1. Was the current head of government or other chief national authority elected through free and fair elections? 1 / 4

The president is elected to up to two five-year terms. Parliament speaker Vadim Krasnoselsky, an independent closely associated with the Obnovleniye (Renewal) Party, defeated incumbent Yevgeniy Shevchuk in the 2016 presidential election, following a campaign characterized by corruption allegations traded between the two. Shevchuk was defeated even as his campaign draw significantly on public resources, including the state media, which heavily favored him and sought to portray Krasnoselsky as a crony of Sheriff Enterprises, the powerful business conglomerate that dominates the economy and backs the Renewal Party; Krasnoselsky had previously served as the company's security chief. Given Transnistria's political status, established election monitors did not send missions to oversee the contest.

Constitutional amendments approved in 2011 created a relatively weak post of prime minister. The president appoints the prime minister, who is approved by the parliament. Krasnoselsky tapped Alexander Martynov to serve as prime minister in late 2016.

A2. Were the current national legislative representatives elected through free and fair elections? 1 / 4

Members of the 43-seat, unicameral Supreme Council are elected to five-year terms. Renewal won a landslide victory in 2015 elections, due in large part to poor economic conditions and dissatisfaction with then president Shevchuk's government. A small group of Shevchuk's allies and supporters demonstrated against the results of the elections, claiming vote manipulation. As Transnistria is not internationally recognized, no established election monitor sent a mission to observe the election's conduct.

The winners of 2017 by-elections for seats left vacant by resignations were considered allies of Sheriff Enterprises. Several candidates were reportedly impeded from registration, including one who was favored to win his district.

A3. Are the electoral laws and framework fair, and are they implemented impartially by the relevant election management bodies? 1 / 4

Actors from various political camps have alleged that the Electoral Commission is subject to political pressure. In 2015, ahead of that year's elections, authorities unsuccessfully tried to evict the Electoral Commission from its offices, in what was viewed as an attempt to interfere with its operations.

In 2018, the Tiraspol-based Institute for Political Studies and Regional Development hosted discussions about transitioning from a majoritarian electoral system to a mixed one; proponents of a change argued that current system has resulted in the concentration of power among oligarchic interests. However, the debate did not appear to have been taken up in the parliament.

B. POLITICAL PLURALISM AND PARTICIPATION: 5 / 16

B1. Do the people have the right to organize in different political parties or other competitive political groupings of their choice, and is the system free of undue obstacles to the rise and fall of these competing parties or groupings? 1 / 4

Transnistria's entire political establishment, including nominal opposition parties and civil society organizations, supports the separatist system and Russia's role as patron. In the 2015 Supreme Council elections, Renewal won overwhelmingly with 35 of 43 seats; Proryv (Breakthrough) and the Communist Party each won 1 seat. Several independent deputies gained seats, but they are affiliated with Renewal. With the 2016 election of Krasnoselsky as president, the political establishment is now controlled by Renewal.

In past years, the Communist Party has been able to hold some events and speak out against the government in a limited way. However, in 2018, authorities jailed the party's leader, lawmaker Oleg Horzhan. In June, Horzhan was stripped of parliamentary immunity and arrested for organizing illegal demonstrations, criticizing an official, and interfering with law enforcement agents, and in November was sentenced to four-and-a-half years in prison. Horzhan's arrest reportedly came after he had organized his own rally in the wake of a ban on an annual May 1 Labor Day demonstration.

B2. Is there a realistic opportunity for the opposition to increase its support or gain power through elections? 2 / 4

The Renewal Party has long dominated the legislature. In recent years, opposition candidates have occasionally faced difficulties registering to compete in elections.

While the main candidates in the 2016 election to the country's powerful presidency were independents, the post effectively rotated between power bases when Shevchuk was defeated by Krasnoselsky.

A number of corruption cases were initiated against Shevchuk in 2017, and he has since fled the territory.

B3. Are the people's political choices free from domination by the military, foreign powers, religious hierarchies, economic oligarchies, or any other powerful group that is not democratically accountable? 1 / 4

The Transnistrian political establishment is dominated by the monopolistic conglomerate Sheriff Enterprises. Additionally, the influence of Russia is undergirded by the presence of 1,500 Russian troops, who are stationed to guard a Soviet-era ammunition depot and uphold a 1992 cease-fire between Transnistria and Moldova. The Moldovan government periodically calls for Russia to withdraw its forces.

B4. Do various segments of the population (including ethnic, religious, gender, LGBT, and other relevant groups) have full political rights and electoral opportunities? 1 / 4

Few women are included in the political elite (for example, there are only 3 women in the 43-seat Supreme Soviet). However, women are able to exercise some political rights and participate in campaigns.

While Transnistria has three official languages—Russian, Ukrainian, and Moldovan—Russian is used in governmental affairs. Authorities do not allow voting in Moldovan elections to take place in Transnistrian-controlled territory, but residents with Russian citizenship had access to polling stations during Russia's tightly controlled 2018 presidential election.

C. FUNCTIONING OF GOVERNMENT: 2 / 12

C1. Do the freely elected head of government and national legislative representatives determine the policies of the government? 1 / 4

Elected representatives are promptly inaugurated following elections. Sheriff Enterprises exerts a strong influence on government policies, which are also closely monitored by the Russian political establishment.

C2. Are safeguards against official corruption strong and effective? 0 / 4

Transnistrian politics have long been built on nepotism and favoritism. In 2017, several prosecutions for abuse of power were initiated against Shevchuk; beyond this, there are few visible safeguards against official corruption.

C3. Does the government operate with openness and transparency? 1 / 4

Although the authorities publish information on websites and are interviewed on television about their policies, many governmental discussions are not open to the media, and governmental openness and transparency are limited.

CIVIL LIBERTIES: 14 / 60

D. FREEDOM OF EXPRESSION AND BELIEF: 5 / 16

D1. Are there free and independent media? 0 / 4

Authorities closely monitor and control the public media, and Sheriff dominates private broadcasting, leading to widespread self-censorship. There are few independent print outlets and they have limited circulation. Critical reporting draws harassment by the government, which also uses bureaucratic obstruction and the withholding of information to inhibit independent media.

In 2016, the parliament passed legislation giving itself greater authority over state media outlets, including the power to appoint editorial staff. The legislation also enabled officials to limit media access to their activities and bar the use of recording devices. Transnistrian authorities deny Moldovan media outlets access to Transnistria.

D2. Are individuals free to practice and express their religious faith or nonbelief in public and private? 2 / 4

Most of the population is Christian Orthodox, and authorities have denied registration to several smaller religious groups, which at times face harassment by police and Orthodox opponents. A 2016 law imposed restrictions or penalties related to unauthorized distribution of religious literature, preaching in public spaces, and organized religious activities in residential buildings. Members of the Muslim community report a reluctance to practice their faith openly due to past intimidation by authorities. In 2018, a well-known imam fled the territory after being placed on a wanted list by the Committee for State Security.

D3. Is there academic freedom, and is the educational system free from extensive political indoctrination? 1 / 4

Academics and students may take part in international forums, but participation in events sponsored in Moldova is discouraged by concerns about retribution from Transnistrian authorities. Academic analysis of topics such as the 1992 conflict, the role of the Russian Federation and peacekeeping forces, and Transnistrian statehood are subject to censorship.

The eight Latin-script schools in Transnistria governed by the Moldovan constitutional authorities continue to face pressure from local authorities.

D4. Are individuals free to express their personal views on political or other sensitive topics without fear of surveillance or retribution? 2 / 4

While people do share their opinions in private settings, including on sensitive developments, legal restrictions on certain kinds of speech discourages free discussion. The Penal Code contains penalties for the public expression of disrespect for the Russian peacekeeping mission. Expression is also inhibited somewhat in public spaces by concerns about surveillance or retribution for voicing dissent.

E. ASSOCIATIONAL AND ORGANIZATIONAL RIGHTS: 2 / 12

E1. Is there freedom of assembly? 1 / 4

Authorities limit freedom of assembly through measures such as rejection on administrative grounds of applications for permits to hold meetings and protests. Reportedly, only two protests actions have received formal permission in the past five years, both in 2015. Participants in unsanctioned actions have faced administrative penalties or have been detained.

In 2018, authorities reportedly banned an annual May Day demonstration, prompting Communist Party leader Horzhan to attempt to organize a separate rally in June—efforts that led to his arrest and prison sentence. A number of participants in the June event were also reportedly arrested. Authorities reportedly banned an annual commemoration of the 1917 Bolshevik Revolution several days after Horzhan's sentencing.

E2. Is there freedom for nongovernmental organizations, particularly those that are engaged in human rights– and governance-related work? 1 / 4

Nongovernmental and civic work remains a challenge. Organizations working on human rights or which are perceived as threatening authorities face harassment. The local Coordination Council of Technical Aid must approve governance-related work. An NGO law that took effect in May 2018 mandated more detailed reporting by NGOs, including on foreign funding, and prohibited foreign-backed NGOs from engaging in a broad scope of actions deemed to be "political activities."

E3. Is there freedom for trade unions and similar professional or labor organizations? 0 / 4

Trade unions in Transnistria are unreformed since the Soviet era, and they are not independent. Local and regional authorities manipulate trade unions for political gain.

F. RULE OF LAW: 2 / 16

F1. Is there an independent judiciary? 0 / 4

The judiciary serves the interests of the authorities. The European Court of Human Rights (ECHR) has asserted that Russia is responsible for all decisions of Transnistrian courts, and that the courts do not meet minimum standards of fairness.

F2. Does due process prevail in civil and criminal matters? 0 / 4

Justice is applied arbitrarily and to serve the interests of those in power. Police continued to engage in arbitrary arrests and illegal detentions in 2018, according to the US State Department.

F3. Is there protection from the illegitimate use of physical force and freedom from war and insurgencies? 1 / 4

Transnistrian authorities adopted an Action Plan in 2015 to end torture in custody, but the practice is still reported, and prison conditions remain poor. Police mistreatment of suspects is common and there are few if any avenues for victims to gain recourse.

F4. Do laws, policies, and practices guarantee equal treatment of various segments of the population? 1 / 4

The Transnistrian constitution guarantees rights and freedoms of persons and citizens "without distinction as to sex, race, nationality, language, religion, social origin," and others, but these are not uniformly upheld. The Moldovan-speaking minority faces discrimination and harassment. Same-sex activity is illegal in Transnistria, and the LGBT (lesbian, gay, bisexual, and transgender) community has been forced underground as a result of widespread government and societal discrimination.

G. PERSONAL AUTONOMY AND INDIVIDUAL RIGHTS: 5 / 16

G1. Do individuals enjoy freedom of movement, including the ability to change their place of residence, employment, or education? 2 / 4

Approximately 300,000 people in Transnistria hold Moldovan citizenship and can travel freely to European Union (EU) countries. Cars with local license plates cannot cross the border to Moldova, but since October 2018, residents of Transnistria may obtain neutral license plates that allow them to drive on international roads. The agreement was reached as part of the 5+2 negotiation framework, comprised of the Organization for Security and Cooperation in Europe (OSCE), with Russia and Ukraine acting as mediators; also as part of the 5+2 framework, Moldovan authorities began recognizing Transnistrian educational documents in 2018. Earlier, in 2017, a key bridge between Transnistria and Moldova was opened, facilitating the easier movement of people and goods.

G2. Are individuals able to exercise the right to own property and establish private businesses without undue interference from state or nonstate actors? 1 / 4

Private property is only allowed for housing in Transnistrian region; other property rights, including land ownership, remain restricted. Procedures for establishing a private business are hampered by bureaucratic impediments. Since August 2018, residents on the right bank may access their farm land in Dubăsari region for an established period of 20 years.

G3. Do individuals enjoy personal social freedoms, including choice of marriage partner and size of family, protection from domestic violence, and control over appearance? 1 / 4

Same-sex marriage is not permitted. Many women are pressured to have large families. Domestic violence is a growing concern, with no law criminalizing it. However, the problem has become more public, including through television reports. Dedicated services, including psychological aid, a hotline for victims, and shelters are operated by civil society organizations supported by international donor organizations.

G4. Do individuals enjoy equality of opportunity and freedom from economic exploitation? 1 / 4

Economic opportunity remains very limited. Sheriff Enterprises dominates the economy. Despite increased international aid to ensure better opportunities for women, many still fall victim to traffickers who subject them to forced labor or sex work.

West Bank

Population: 2,798,000 [Note: This figure represents the Palestinian population only.]
Political Rights Rating: 7
Civil Liberties Rating: 5
Freedom Rating: 6.0
Freedom Status: Not Free

Note: The numerical ratings and status listed above do not reflect conditions in Israel or the Gaza Strip, which are examined in separate reports. This report includes conditions in East Jerusalem, which the international community generally considers to be part of the occupied West Bank. Prior to its 2011 edition, *Freedom in the World* featured one report for Israeli-occupied portions of the West Bank and Gaza Strip and another for Palestinian-administered portions.

Overview: The West Bank is under Israeli military occupation, which entails onerous physical barriers and constraints on movement, demolition of homes and other physical infrastructure, restrictions on political and civil liberties, and expanding Jewish settlements. Jewish settlers in the West Bank are Israeli citizens and enjoy the same rights and liberties as other Israelis. The West Bank's Palestinian residents, excluding those living in East Jerusalem, fall under the partial jurisdiction of the Palestinian Authority (PA), which is operating with an expired presidential mandate and has no functioning legislature. The PA governs in an authoritarian manner, engaging in acts of repression against journalists and human rights activists who present critical views on its rule. While a small number of East Jerusalem Palestinians have Israeli citizenship, most have a special residency status that provides them with a restricted set of rights compared with those of Israeli citizens.

KEY DEVELOPMENTS IN 2018:

- The Israeli Knesset (parliament) passed a law in July that limited Palestinians' direct access to the Supreme Court regarding administrative petitions against settlement construction, among other matters. Separately, an Israeli District Court ruling in August retroactively gave authorization to a previously unrecognized settlement outpost, establishing a possible precedent for Israeli grants of legal status to additional outposts, though all of the West Bank settlements are generally considered to be in violation of international law.
- New details on the PA's detention and harassment of individuals based on their political expression and social media posts emerged during the year, demonstrating that practices involving surveillance and retribution were not limited to prominent activists.
- In March, the Knesset passed a law allowing the interior minister to revoke the residency status of any Jerusalem residents deemed to be a threat to public safety or security or to the state of Israel, and to subsequently deport them.
- Jerusalem municipal elections were held in October, but turnout among East Jerusalem Palestinians was low. One Palestinian list dropped out in advance of the vote due to pressure from Israeli authorities and segments of the Palestinian public.

POLITICAL RIGHTS: 4 / 40 (−1)
A. ELECTORAL PROCESS: 1 / 12 (−1)

A1. Was the current head of government or other chief national authority elected through free and fair elections? 0 / 4

The PA has not held a presidential election since 2005. The four-year term of Mahmoud Abbas, who won that year with 62 percent of the vote, expired in 2009, but he has continued to rule with the support of the Palestine Liberation Organization (PLO), led by his party, Fatah. The primary obstacle to new Palestinian elections is the ongoing rift between the West Bank–based PA government and the de facto Hamas government in the Gaza Strip. Hamas, an Islamist political movement and militant group, seized control of Gaza in 2007. It had won 2006 legislative elections and formed a short-lived unity government with Fatah, but a brief armed struggle between the two left each in control of a separate territory.

Under PA laws, the prime minister is nominated by the president and requires the support of the Palestinian Legislative Council (PLC). However, the PLC elected in 2006 was unable to function due to the break with Hamas and Israel's detention of many lawmakers. Abbas has since appointed prime ministers and cabinets without legislative approval. The prime minister as of 2018, Rami Hamdallah, was first appointed in 2014.

A 2014 agreement between Hamas and Fatah representatives to form a unity government did not result in power sharing in practice. In 2017, the two sides recommitted to a reconciliation deal brokered by Egypt, but there was little progress on implementation. Talks foundered again in 2018 over the PA's demands for full political and security control in Gaza.

A2. Were the current national legislative representatives elected through free and fair elections? 0 / 4

Palestinians in the West Bank do not have a functioning legislative body. Elections for the 132-seat PLC have not been held since 2006, when Hamas won 74 seats and Fatah took 45. The 2007 schism between Fatah and Hamas left the postelection government and the PLC itself unable to function. The legislature's electoral mandate expired in 2010. Moreover, Israeli forces have repeatedly detained elected PLC members since 2006. In December 2018, President Abbas ordered the formal dissolution of the PLC, backed by a Supreme Constitutional Court ruling that also called for legislative elections within six months. Hamas rejected the decision.

Local council elections were held in the West Bank in 2017, after being postponed in 2016; however, they did not feature meaningful political competition, as key opposition groups declined to participate. Just 145 municipalities—fewer than half of the West Bank's total—had competitive races. Some two-thirds of those council seats went to independents, while Fatah captured nearly 28 percent and smaller groups divided the remainder. In 181 municipalities, a single candidate list ran unopposed and won automatically; Fatah won 75 percent of the seats in those locations.

Israeli municipal elections were held in Jerusalem in October 2018. It was reported that a disproportionately small number of polling locations were available in East Jerusalem, where Palestinian residents without Israeli citizenship are permitted to participate but most have traditionally boycotted. Palestinian mayoral candidate Aziz Abu Sarah and his list Al-Quds Lana dropped out in late September after he was told by Israeli authorities that his residency status was under review and after facing pressure from Palestinians opposed to his campaign. Another Palestinian list, Al-Quds Baladi, remained in the elections but did not win any council seats.

A3. Are the electoral laws and framework fair, and are they implemented impartially by the relevant election management bodies? 1 / 4 (−1)

The PA's laws provide a credible framework for elections, but presidential and legislative elections have not been held since 2005 and 2006, respectively. The Palestinian Central Elections Commission oversees elections in the West Bank and Gaza. The body's nine commissioners are appointed by the president, although the law requires them to be experienced and politically impartial judges, academics, or lawyers. Local elections that were set to be held in 2016 were postponed until 2017 while the judiciary heard a set of complaints, but the delay was seen by many as politically motivated.

Israel's Central Elections Committee oversees Knesset elections, in which Israeli citizens in the West Bank may participate, and its Interior Ministry manages municipal elections, including in Jerusalem. Such elections are generally conducted in a peaceful and orderly manner, with results accepted by all parties, though Palestinian residents of the West Bank are formally or effectively excluded.

Score Change: The score declined from 2 to 1 because Palestinian presidential and legislative elections have been delayed for over a decade, precluding the application of electoral laws by the appropriate authorities.

B. POLITICAL PLURALISM AND PARTICIPATION: 4 / 16

B1. Do the people have the right to organize in different political parties or other competitive political groupings of their choice, and is the system free of undue obstacles to the rise and fall of these competing parties or groupings? 1 / 4

In addition to Fatah, a number of small Palestinian parties operate relatively freely in the West Bank. However, the PA deals harshly with supporters of a breakaway Fatah faction led by exiled politician Mohammed Dahlan, and Abbas and his government have repeatedly taken administrative and bureaucratic actions to marginalize potential political rivals within Fatah. Israel detains and arrests political activists if they are perceived as threatening Israeli security.

The PA and Israeli forces in the West Bank have sought to suppress Hamas, periodically engaging in mass arrests and closures of affiliated institutions. Following a March 2018 bomb attack on Prime Minister Hamdallah's convoy as he visited Gaza, PA forces summoned and arrested a number of Hamas supporters in the West Bank. Another wave of arrests targeting Hamas supporters was reported in September.

East Jerusalem Palestinians can form party lists to run in municipal elections, as they did in 2018, but doing so may lead to increased scrutiny by Israeli authorities and pressure from Palestinians opposed to participation in Israeli elections.

B2. Is there a realistic opportunity for the opposition to increase its support or gain power through elections? 0 / 4

The prolonged and indefinite postponement of presidential and PLC elections has prevented any rotation of power in the West Bank, and the PA leadership has been accused of avoiding any contest that could lead to a Hamas victory. Moreover, the boycott of the 2017 local elections by Hamas and other major opposition groups left them largely unrepresented in West Bank local councils.

B3. Are the people's political choices free from domination by the military, foreign powers, religious hierarchies, economic oligarchies, or any other powerful group that is not democratically accountable? 1 / 4

In addition to its detentions and harassment of political figures from Hamas and some other factions, Israel's restrictions on freedom of movement—including checkpoints, roadblocks, and permit restrictions, as well as the continuous barrier it has constructed along the West Bank side of the pre-1967 border—can impede Palestinian political organizing and activity.

Foreign government donors sometimes exert influence over the PA to promote or marginalize certain politicians or political factions.

B4. Do various segments of the population (including ethnic, religious, gender, LGBT, and other relevant groups) have full political rights and electoral opportunities? 2 / 4

Women and religious or ethnic minorities enjoy formal political equality under PA laws, and both women and Christians have held PLC seats and cabinet positions. However, they tend to be underrepresented in such posts, and their particular interests are not necessarily addressed by the political system. About a fifth of the council seats in the 2017 municipal elections went to women.

Palestinian residents of East Jerusalem have the option to apply for Israeli citizenship, though most decline for political reasons. Similarly, while noncitizen residents can vote in Israeli municipal elections in Jerusalem, most have traditionally boycotted; noncitizens cannot vote in Knesset elections. A Palestinian Jerusalem resident who is not a citizen cannot become mayor under current Israeli law. Israeli law strips noncitizens of their Jerusalem residency if they are away for extended periods of time, and a new law adopted in March 2018 empowers the Israeli interior minister to revoke such residency for those deemed to be involved in terrorism or treason-related offenses. East Jerusalem Palestinians are entitled to vote in PA elections, but Israel has refused to allow PA elections in the city.

There are roughly 400,000 Jewish settlers in the West Bank excluding East Jerusalem, and approximately 200,000 Jewish settlers in East Jerusalem, all of whom are Israeli citizens with full political rights in Israel.

C. FUNCTIONING OF GOVERNMENT: 2 / 12

C1. Do the freely elected head of government and national legislative representatives determine the policies of the government? 0 / 4

The PA lacks an elected executive and legislature. Because the legislature has not functioned since 2007, new laws are introduced via presidential decree. The ability of the PA president and ministries to implement policy decisions is limited in practice by direct Israeli military control over much of the West Bank, including the movement and travel of PA officials, staff, and related personnel. The PA has virtually no ability to extend services to the relatively small share of Palestinians living in so-called Area C, the more than 60 percent of West Bank territory that is under exclusive Israeli control. Israel periodically withholds the transfer of tax revenues to the PA, which affects salary payments and policy implementation.

C2. Are safeguards against official corruption strong and effective? 1 / 4

Official corruption remains a major problem. In a set of representative polls conducted in March and June–July 2018 by the Palestinian Center for Policy and Survey Research, 78 to 80 percent of West Bank residents described PA institutions as corrupt. The PA's Anti-Corruption Commission is responsible for implementing an anticorruption strategy it developed for 2015–2018. In a report released in March 2018, the Coalition for Accountability and Integrity (AMAN) found some improvements in public-sector management, despite persistent challenges such as ensuring the rule of law, combating nepotism and favoritism, promoting information transparency, and safeguarding a strong and fair judiciary.

Israeli movement and access restrictions foster opportunities for bribery and corruption in the West Bank.

C3. Does the government operate with openness and transparency? 1 / 4

In 2017, Prime Minister Hamdallah released a five-year National Policy Agenda that emphasized improved efficiency, transparency, and accountability in government and promised a number of economic and social development initiatives. However, absent regular elections, incentives to improve transparency and accountability remain low. The PA is generally not tolerant of journalists, activists, and others who attempt to scrutinize its policies or internal operations.

The operations of Israeli military authorities in the West Bank are relatively opaque, and the Israeli military and civil administrations are not accountable to Palestinians.

ADDITIONAL DISCRETIONARY POLITICAL RIGHTS QUESTION

Is the government or occupying power deliberately changing the ethnic composition of a country or territory so as to destroy a culture or tip the political balance in favor of another group? −3 / 0

The growth of Jewish settlements, seizures of Palestinian land, and the demolition of Palestinian homes in the West Bank continued in 2018. The UN Office for the Coordination of Humanitarian Affairs (OCHA) reported that Israeli authorities seized or demolished 461 Palestinian homes or structures in the West Bank and East Jerusalem in 2018, citing the lack of building permits, which are very difficult for Palestinians to obtain. Implementation of a military order issued in April that would have facilitated accelerated demolitions of "new" structures in Area C was postponed in June pending a ruling by Israel's Supreme Court.

Construction starts in Jewish settlements increased in 2018 compared with the previous year, according to the nongovernmental organization (NGO) Americans for Peace Now and data from the Israeli Central Bureau of Statistics.

In July, the Knesset passed a law limiting Palestinians' direct access to the Supreme Court for administrative petitions, effectively increasing the hurdles faced by petitioners against West Bank settlement construction. In August, the Jerusalem District Court ruled in favor of the legalization of a previously unauthorized settler outpost, raising the possibility that the same legal mechanism could be used to retroactively grant legal status to more such outposts. A 2017 Israeli law authorized the retroactive, formal seizure of private Palestinian land, with compensation, where settlements had been built illegally, though its implementation remained suspended in 2018 pending a review by the Supreme Court. In July, it was revealed that over 99 percent of state lands in the West Bank are allocated to Israelis and Israeli settlements.

CIVIL LIBERTIES: 21 / 60 (−2)
D. FREEDOM OF EXPRESSION AND BELIEF: 7 / 16 (−1)
D1. Are there free and independent media? 1 / 4

The news media are generally not free in the West Bank. Under a 1995 PA press law, journalists may be fined and jailed, and newspapers closed, for publishing "secret information" on PA security forces or news that might harm national unity or incite violence. In 2017, President Abbas issued the Electronic Crimes Law, prescribing heavy fines and lengthy prison terms for a range of vaguely defined offenses, including the publication or dissemination of material that is critical of the state, disturbs public order or national unity, or harms family and religious values. Leaks of information by whistle-blowers or journalists can also draw fines or imprisonment under the law, as can use of online circumvention tools to access blocked websites.

Journalists and bloggers who criticize the PA have faced arbitrary arrests, threats, and physical abuse. Reporters are also subject to administrative detention and assault by Israeli forces. An October 2018 report by Human Rights Watch documented regular detention and occasional abuse of journalists and activists in the West Bank. The Palestinian Center for Development and Media Freedoms (MADA) reported 88 violations of media freedom by Palestinian authorities in the West Bank in 2018, a decline from the previous year. Most involved interrogations, arrests and detentions, and physical assaults of journalists. Israeli authorities were responsible for 455 violations in the Palestinian territories (including Gaza), according to the group, up from 376 in 2017. The majority of incidents involved physical attacks on or injuries of journalists, often as they covered Israeli military actions or clashes with Palestinian protesters.

D2. Are individuals free to practice and express their religious faith or nonbelief in public and private? 2 / 4

The PA Basic Law declares Islam to be the official religion of Palestine and states that "respect and sanctity of all other heavenly religions (Judaism and Christianity) shall be maintained." Blasphemy is a criminal offense. The 2017 Electronic Crimes Law criminalizes expression aimed at harming moral and religious values without defining those values, allowing for arbitrary enforcement.

Security-related restrictions on movement, and vandalism or physical assaults against worshippers or places of worship, affect Jewish, Muslim, and Christian residents of the West Bank to varying degrees. The Israeli authorities regularly prevent Palestinian Muslims in the West Bank from reaching Jerusalem to pray, and generally restrict access for young adult males to the Temple Mount/Haram al-Sharif compound on Fridays.

D3. Is there academic freedom, and is the educational system free from extensive political indoctrination? 2 / 4

The PA has administrative authority over Palestinian education. Some academic self-censorship has been reported. Israeli movement restrictions limit access to schools and academic institutions; schools have sometimes been damaged during military incursions, and student travel has been curtailed. According to the Association for Civil Rights in Israel, East Jerusalem's schools are underfunded compared with schools in West Jerusalem.

Political activism is common on university campuses, and student council elections generally proceed freely—an Islamist bloc sympathetic to Hamas has performed strongly in several of the past Birzeit University student council elections, for example. However, students affiliated with the bloc have been detained.

D4. Are individuals free to express their personal views on political or other sensitive topics without fear of surveillance or retribution? 2 / 4 (−1)

Residents have some freedom to engage in open private discussion, though Israeli and PA security forces are known to monitor online activity and arrest individuals for alleged incitement or criticism of Palestinian authorities, respectively. The adoption and enforcement of the Electronic Crimes Law in 2017 increased concerns about the freedom of personal expression online.

Human rights organizations have accused the PA of monitoring social media posts and detaining individuals for harsh questioning related to their comments. New details on the PA's detention and harassment of individuals based on their online activity were reported in 2018, and evidence emerged that the PA has engaged in extensive electronic surveillance of lawyers, activists, political figures, and others, which could have a deterrent effect on expression more broadly.

Score Change: The score declined from 3 to 2 due to further reports that the PA has en-gaged in electronic surveillance, social media monitoring, and retribution for expressions of dissent.

E. ASSOCIATIONAL AND ORGANIZATIONAL RIGHTS: 5 / 12

E1. Is there freedom of assembly? 1 / 4

The PA requires permits for demonstrations, and those held to protest against PA poli-cies are generally dispersed. In June 2018, PA police forcibly broke up a protest in Ramallah that was organized in opposition to PA policies in Gaza, beating participants, using tear gas and stun grenades, and breaking journalists' cameras.

Israel's Military Order 101 requires a permit for all "political" demonstrations of more than 10 people. Israeli authorities frequently restrict and disperse demonstrations, some of which become violent, and certain protest areas are designated as closed military zones. Protesters are at risk of injury by tear-gas canisters, rubber-coated bullets, or live ammuni-tion, and clashes between demonstrators and Israeli troops periodically result in fatalities.

E2. Is there freedom for nongovernmental organizations, particularly those that are engaged in human rights- and governance-related work? 2 / 4

A broad range of NGOs operate in the West Bank. However, Israeli restrictions on movement can impede civil society activity, human rights NGOs reportedly face harassment and threats from settlers and right-wing Israeli groups, Hamas-affiliated groups have been periodically shut down by Israeli or PA officials, and activists who criticize the PA leader-ship can face harassment and abuse by security services. In 2017, the Knesset approved a law that bars entry for any foreign groups that publicly support a boycott of Israel or its West Bank settlements. Because Israel controls all entry points into the West Bank, this could affect Palestinian organizations' access to Israel and foreign organizations' access to both Israel and the West Bank.

E3. Is there freedom for trade unions and similar professional or labor organizations? 2 / 4

Workers may establish unions without government authorization, but labor protections in general are poorly enforced. Palestinian workers seeking to strike must submit to arbi-tration by the PA Labor Ministry, and various other rules make it difficult to mount a legal strike. Palestinian workers in Jerusalem are subject to Israeli labor law.

F. RULE OF LAW: 4 / 16 (−1)

F1. Is there an independent judiciary? 2 / 4

Palestinians in the West Bank are subject to the jurisdiction of both the Palestinian judiciary and the Israeli military court system, neither of which is fully independent. The PA courts are administered by the High Judicial Council, which consists of Supreme Court judges, the heads of appellate courts, the attorney general, and the deputy justice minister. Enforcement of judicial decisions is impeded by PA noncompliance as well as lack of Pal-estinian jurisdiction in Area C, where the Israeli military exerts exclusive control.

The Israeli civilian courts, which have jurisdiction over Israeli settlers in the West Bank, are independent.

F2. Does due process prevail in civil and criminal matters? 1 / 4 (−1)

The opaque distinction between criminal and security-related offenses, the regular use of detention without trial by Palestinian and Israeli security forces, and the use of martial law and a military court system that applies exclusively to Palestinians in the West Bank all violate the due process rights of Palestinians. Jewish settlers are tried in Israeli civilian courts, which generally provide due process protections.

Human rights groups regularly document allegations of arbitrary detention by PA security forces. Palestinians are also regularly detained without charges for extended periods by Israeli authorities. The Israeli military frequently conducts home raids without a warrant. Conviction rates in Israeli military courts are high, and most convictions are based on confessions. The widespread use of pretrial detention encourages defendants to enter plea deals rather than remain in custody. According to the Israeli human rights group B'Tselem, there were 5,072 Palestinian security detainees and prisoners from the West Bank being held in Israeli prisons at the end of December 2018.

A reported 203 Palestinian children (aged 12–17) from the occupied territories were being held in Israeli prisons as security detainees and prisoners at the end of December 2018. Although Israeli law prohibits the detention of children younger than 12, some are occasionally held. Minors are often detained for throwing stones or other projectiles at Israeli troops. They are usually interrogated without a lawyer or parental guardian present and tried by a special military court for minors. Acquittals are very rare, and the courts have been criticized for a lack of due process protections. Ahed Tamimi, a Palestinian girl who was arrested in December 2017 at age 16 for slapping an Israeli soldier, was sentenced to eight months in prison in March and released in July after completing the term with time served. Her high-profile case drew attention to the treatment of minors in the Israeli military court system. East Jerusalem Palestinian minors are tried in Israeli civilian juvenile courts.

The Israeli law passed in July 2018 that limits Palestinians' direct access to the Supreme Court for administrative petitions, including those related to settlement planning and construction, requires such petitions to be heard first by the Jerusalem District Court. This is expected to slow down hearings that challenge unauthorized settlements in the West Bank and potentially introduce new costs for Palestinian complainants.

Score Change: The score declined from 2 to 1 due to the prevalence of arbitrary detentions by the PA, general due process concerns in the Israeli military court system, and Israel's adoption of a new law that impedes West Bank Palestinians' ability to bring land rights cases before the Israeli Supreme Court.

F3. Is there protection from the illegitimate use of physical force and freedom from war and insurgencies? 0 / 4

Penal codes applicable in the West Bank permit capital punishment, but no executions have been carried out since 2005. In June 2018, the State of Palestine became a signatory to the International Covenant on Civil and Political Rights, which severely restricts the use of capital punishment.

Physical abuse of detainees by PA authorities in the West Bank has been documented by human rights organizations. Individual testimonies also attest to the use of excessive violence by the Israeli military. In one example in 2018, Israeli forces' physical assaults and use of a stun grenade at close range resulted in the hospitalization of multiple members of a single family in Hebron in September.

Israeli soldiers accused of excessive force or abuse of Palestinian civilians are subject to Israeli military law, though convictions, which are rare, typically result in light sentences. Jewish settlers who attack Palestinian individuals, property, and agricultural resources generally enjoy impunity.

Israeli security personnel and civilians face small-scale terrorist attacks in the West Bank. B'Tselem reported that seven Israeli civilians and five security personnel were killed in the West Bank by Palestinians during 2018. Meanwhile, 34 Palestinians were killed by Israeli security forces, and four others were killed by settlers.

F4. Do laws, policies, and practices guarantee equal treatment of various segments of the population? 1 / 4

The legal arrangements operative in the West Bank are fundamentally discriminatory in that Israelis and Palestinians who reside or commit crimes in the same location are subject to different courts and laws.

Palestinian women are underrepresented in most professions and encounter discrimination in employment, though they have equal access to universities. Women are legally excluded from what are deemed dangerous occupations.

Although LGBT (lesbian, gay, bisexual, and transgender) people in the West Bank do not face prosecution for same-sex sexual activity, they have been subject to harassment and abuse by PA authorities and members of society.

G. PERSONAL AUTONOMY AND INDIVIDUAL RIGHTS: 5 / 16

G1. Do individuals enjoy freedom of movement, including the ability to change their place of residence, employment, or education? 1 / 4

Israeli checkpoints, travel permits, and other restrictions continue to seriously constrain freedom of movement, stunt trade, and limit Palestinian access to jobs, hospitals, and schools.

The Israeli separation barrier, 85 percent of which lies in West Bank territory and which was declared illegal in 2004 by the International Court of Justice, divides Palestinian communities and causes general hardship and disruption of services.

East Jerusalem Palestinians are vulnerable to revocation of their residency status if they leave the city for extended periods of time, affecting their freedom to travel. The Israeli law adopted in March 2018, which allows the interior minister to revoke the residency status of any Jerusalem residents deemed to be a threat to public safety, security, or the state of Israel, further exposes East Jerusalem Palestinians to displacement.

G2. Are individuals able to exercise the right to own property and establish private businesses without undue interference from state or nonstate actors? 1 / 4

While Palestinians are able to own property and engage in business activity, their rights are seriously undermined by Israel's movement and access restrictions and the expansion of Israeli settlements, which is encouraged by the Israeli government and private groups. Israeli authorities employ a variety of methods to prevent Palestinians from developing their privately owned land, particularly in Area C, for example by declaring nature reserves or denying permit requests. Palestinian property is also illegally damaged by Israeli settlers.

G3. Do individuals enjoy personal social freedoms, including choice of marriage partner and size of family, protection from domestic violence, and control over appearance? 2 / 4

Palestinian laws and societal norms, derived in part from Sharia (Islamic law), put women at a disadvantage in matters such as marriage and divorce. For Christians, personal status issues are governed by ecclesiastical courts. Rape and domestic abuse remain underreported and frequently go unpunished, as authorities are allegedly reluctant to pursue such cases. So-called honor killings continue to be reported; a March 2018 law amended a provision in the penal code that had been used to grant leniency to the perpetrators of honor killings, prohibiting its use in cases of serious crimes against women and children.

G4. Do individuals enjoy equality of opportunity and freedom from economic exploitation? 1 / 4

In 2017, the PA signed international protocols dealing with human trafficking, child trafficking, and child prostitution. However, child labor is still prevalent in the occupied territories. Many West Bank Palestinians, mostly male, work in Israel and the settlements, where the PA has no jurisdiction. While these workers are covered by Israeli labor laws, the International Labour Organization (ILO) reported in May 2018 that consistent application of these laws remains a concern. The Palestinians' work permits usually tie them to a single employer, creating a relationship of dependency, according to the ILO. Nonetheless, some laborers have achieved collective bargaining agreements with their Israeli employers. Tens of thousands of Palestinians work without permits, making them vulnerable to greater exploitation. Many Palestinians lose considerable income to "brokers" who are needed to connect Palestinian workers to jobs. Israel has revoked permits for those who share last names with individuals whom Israel considers to be security threats, even if they are not related.

Unemployment rates in the Palestinian territories are high compared with the rest of the Middle East and global averages. The excess supply of workers creates conditions in which labor exploitation is more likely.

Western Sahara

Population: 600,000
Capital: Laâyoune
Political Rights Rating: 7
Civil Liberties Rating: 7
Freedom Rating: 7.0
Freedom Status: Not Free
Electoral Democracy: No

Overview: Morocco has claimed authority over Western Sahara since 1975, but the United Nations does not recognize Morocco's control, calling Western Sahara a "non-self-governing territory." Morocco controls the most populous area along the Atlantic coastline, more than three-quarters of the territory. While the United Nations brokered a cease-fire in 1991, a long-promised referendum on the territory's status has yet to be held. The Moroccan-controlled area, which Morocco calls the "Southern Provinces," is represented in the Moroccan parliament. However, civil liberties are severely restricted, particularly as they relate to independence activism.

KEY DEVELOPMENTS IN 2018:

- In December, the first UN-brokered talks between the Polisario Front nationalist movement and the Moroccan government in six years took place. Although the negotiations did not lead to a settlement of the dispute, both sides agreed to continue talks in 2019.
- In June, a vocal critic of the Polisario Front, who was imprisoned for his outspoken criticism, was found dead at the Dheiba prison, apparently from hanging. The Polisario stated that the death was a suicide, but the man's family claimed it was an assassination and staged a sit-in close to the home of Polisario leader Ibrahim Ghali.

- In July, Rabat and the European Union (EU) signed a deal allowing European boats to use Moroccan fishing waters, which controversially included waters off the coast of Western Sahara that are not internationally recognized as Moroccan territory.
- In September, two journalists with the independent news site Smara News, Mohamed Salem Mayara and Mohamed El Joumayi, were sentenced to two years in prison after being convicted by a Moroccan court of spurious charges related to accusations that they threw stones and blocked a street.

POLITICAL RIGHTS: –3 / 40

A. ELECTORAL PROCESS: 0 / 12

A1. Was the current head of government or other chief national authority elected through free and fair elections? 0 / 4

Morocco controls more than three-quarters of Western Sahara and Moroccan authorities allow no pro-independence candidates to run for office. The Polisario Front, which is based in Tindouf, Algeria and leads a nationalist movement comprised of members of the Sahrawi ethnic group, controls the less-populated interior of the territory. The constitution of the government-in-exile states that the leader of the Polisario Front is the territory's president, but it does not hold regular elections within the territory.

A2. Were the current national legislative representatives elected through free and fair elections? 0 / 4

In the Moroccan-controlled portion of the territory, voters elect 13 representatives to the Moroccan parliament. The representatives who serve in the parliament in Rabat cannot contest the status of the region. The parliament members from Western Sahara are predominantly from the Justice and Development Party (PJD). Turnout in municipal and parliamentary elections in Western Sahara is difficult to ascertain, but reports are that it is chronically low.

The Sahrawi Arab Democratic Republic (SADR), the breakaway government, has a 51-member legislature called the Sahrawi National Council (SNC), which is indirectly elected by the General Popular Congress of the Polisario Front. Most voting occurs in refugee camps in Algeria. The Polisario Front organizes the elections and does not allow any political parties to compete.

A3. Are the electoral laws and framework fair, and are they implemented impartially by the relevant election management bodies? 0 / 4

The electoral framework is not fair, given the constraints on representation in the Moroccan-controlled territory, the prohibition of any candidate who challenges Moroccan control of the territory to run for the parliament, and Moroccan control of the media.

B. POLITICAL PLURALISM AND PARTICIPATION: 0 / 16

B1. Do the people have the right to organize in different political parties or other competitive political groupings of their choice, and is the system free of undue obstacles to the rise and fall of these competing parties or groupings? 0 / 4

The Polisario Front, which controls the government-in-exile and the eastern portion of the territory, does not allow other political parties to compete. In recent years, the Polisario has cracked down on political dissent, imprisoning a number of opponents of the regime. In June 2018, a vocal critic of the Polisario, who was imprisoned for his outspoken criticism, was found dead at the Dheibya prison, apparently from hanging. The Polisario stated that the death was a suicide, but the man's family claimed it was an assassination and staged a sit-in close to the home of Polisario leader Ibrahim Ghali.

In the Moroccan-controlled areas, the Polisario Front is banned, and pro-independence parties are not allowed to form.

B2. Is there a realistic opportunity for the opposition to increase its support or gain power through elections? 0 / 4

Since political parties that advocate for Sahrawi independence or autonomy cannot function in Moroccan-controlled areas, the most salient opposition elements cannot gain power through elections. No credible opposition exists in the eastern territory controlled by the Polisario Front due to the ban on other political parties.

B3. Are the people's political choices free from domination by the military, foreign powers, religious hierarchies, economic oligarchies, or any other powerful group that is not democratically accountable? 0 / 4

People's political choices in the Moroccan-controlled parts of the territory are dominated by the Moroccan government. The government-in-exile in Tindouf is ostensibly autonomous, but it works closely with Algerian authorities. As a "non-self-governing territory," the people in the region are unable to elect an independent government.

B4. Do various segments of the population (including ethnic, religious, gender, LGBT, and other relevant groups) have full political rights and electoral opportunities? 0 / 4

Due to the territory's lack of sovereignty, no segment of the population has full political rights or electoral opportunities. However, women play a significant role in politics. Many women are leaders in the independence movement and organize the refugee camps in Algeria.

C. FUNCTIONING OF GOVERNMENT: 0 / 12

C1. Do the freely elected head of government and national legislative representatives determine the policies of the government? 0 / 4

Western Sahara, which has not yet achieved self-determination, has no freely elected leaders. Thirteen representatives from the "Southern Provinces" serve in the 395-member parliament in Rabat. However, the Moroccan parliament is dominated by the monarchy, which determines government policies toward Western Sahara. The Polisario Front governs portions of the territory in its control.

In July 2018, Rabat and the EU signed a deal allowing European boats to use Moroccan fishing waters, which controversially included waters off the coast of Western Sahara that are not internationally recognized as Moroccan territory. In response, the Polisario Front claimed that the EU had sanctioned Moroccan occupation of the territory. The Polisario has long accused Morocco of exploiting Western Sahara's natural resources.

C2. Are safeguards against official corruption strong and effective? 0 / 4

Corruption among both Moroccan authorities and the Polisario Front is widespread and investigations are rare. Corruption occurs primarily to facilitate the exploitation of natural resources—phosphates, hydrocarbons, and fisheries—by Moroccan and international interests. In Tindouf, official corruption among members of the Polisario is similarly widespread and endemic.

C3. Does the government operate with openness and transparency? 0 / 4

Moroccan laws on access to information apply to Western Sahara. Information about Western Sahara is nearly nonexistent, which severely limits transparency. The Moroccan government publishes budget and financial information online, and public officials—including parliament members, judges, and civil servants—are required to declare their assets. However, nongovernmental organizations (NGOs) assert that many officials do not hand over this information, and the law provides no penalties for noncompliance.

ADDITIONAL DISCRETIONARY POLITICAL RIGHTS QUESTION:
Is the government or occupying power deliberately changing the ethnic composition of a country or territory so as to destroy a culture or tip the political balance in favor of another group? −3 / 0

Before and since the establishment of the UN Mission for the Referendum in Western Sahara (MINURSO) in 1991, Rabat has endeavored to tip the population's balance in Morocco's favor. Morocco also works to prevent a referendum that would determine the territory's final status. By some counts, Moroccans now outnumber Sahrawis in Western Sahara. Morocco constructed a sand berm to divide territory under its control from Sahrawi-controlled territory.

CIVIL LIBERTIES: 7 / 60
D. FREEDOM OF EXPRESSION AND BELIEF: 3 / 16
D1. Are there free and independent media? 0 / 4

Some pro-Sahrawi media outlets do operate, such as the all-volunteer Equipe Media group, but they face regular harassment by Moroccan authorities, who ensure that reporting does not dispute Morocco's sovereignty over Western Sahara. Morocco's 2016 Press Code criminalizes challenging the "territorial integrity" of the kingdom, which potentially criminalizes independent journalism that focuses on the dispute in Western Sahara. Print outlets found to violate this provision risk suspension, while news sites face potential blocking. Journalists accused of challenging Morocco's territorial integrity could face prison sentences of between six months and two years. Reporting by Moroccan journalists working in the territory is also sharply constrained.

In September 2018, two journalists with the independent news site Smara News, Mohamed Salem Mayara and Mohamed El Joumayi, were sentenced to two years in prison after being convicted by a Moroccan court of spurious charges related to accusations that they threw stones and blocked a street. The charges were filed after the reporters published photographs in March of a police officer with his gun drawn in Smara. Following the publication of the photographs, the police arrested Mayara and El Joumayi, and allegedly beat them while in custody.

International media are carefully vetted and scrutinized during their visits to the Moroccan-controlled territory; reporters visiting Tindouf reportedly enjoy greater freedom of movement and inquiry, but it is difficult to substantiate such claims.

In Sahrawi-controlled territory, press freedoms are also limited, with television and radio coverage reflecting the ideology and viewpoints of the Polisario. Some exiled groups provide coverage from outside Western Sahara. Internet access is limited throughout the territory.

D2. Are individuals free to practice and express their religious faith or nonbelief in public and private? 2 / 4

Moroccan authorities generally do not interfere with religious practices, though as in Morocco proper, mosques are monitored by authorities. Moroccan law prohibits any efforts to convert a Muslim to another faith. It is illegal to publicly criticize Islam.

D3. Is there academic freedom, and is the educational system free from extensive political indoctrination? 0 / 4

Educators must practice self-censorship around the status of Western Sahara, as Moroccan law criminalizes debate that calls this into question. Other sensitive topics include the monarchy and Islam. The University of Tifariti was established in 2013 as the first university in Polisario-controlled territory.

D4. Are individuals free to express their personal views on political or other sensitive topics without fear of surveillance or retribution? 1 / 4

As in Morocco proper, there is concern about state surveillance of online activity and personal communications, and people do not feel free to speak privately about the status of Western Sahara and other sensitive topics. Freedom of expression is sharply constrained in Polisario-controlled areas as well.

E. ASSOCIATIONAL AND ORGANIZATIONAL RIGHTS: 0 / 12

E1. Is there freedom of assembly? 0 / 4

Demonstrations and protests are broken up regularly, particularly on sensitive issues such as self-determination and Sahrawi prisoners held by Morocco. Protesters are frequently arrested and beaten. In June 2018, police assaulted at least seven activists at a protest in Laâyoune during a visit by the UN envoy for Western Sahara.

E2. Is there freedom for nongovernmental organizations, particularly those that are engaged in human rights- and governance-related work? 0 / 4

NGOs that advocate for independence or question Islam as the state religion are denied official registration by the Moroccan government. Organizations that meet the government's criteria are frequently denied registration as well. Foreign NGO representatives observing the human rights situation of Moroccan-controlled areas of Western Sahara have sometimes been expelled in recent years.

E3. Is there freedom for trade unions and similar professional or labor organizations? 0 / 4

Moroccan unions have a presence in Western Sahara, but they are largely inactive. Government restrictions limit the right to strike. Most people in unions work for the Moroccan government. The Polisario Front has a trade union called the Sahrawi Trade Union (UGTSA-RIO), which is also inactive; there is little economic activity in the refugee camps in Tindouf, and there is no functioning labor market in the territory controlled by the Polisario.

F. RULE OF LAW: 0 / 16

F1. Is there an independent judiciary? 0 / 4

Courts in Western Sahara are controlled by Morocco and their rulings reflect Rabat's interests. Executive interference and corruption significantly impede judicial independence.

F2. Does due process prevail in civil and criminal matters? 0 / 4

Due process rights are not respected. In 2017, a Rabat court of appeals handed 23 Sahrawis prison sentences ranging from two years to life for the 2010 deaths of 11 Moroccan security personnel during an uprising at the Gdeim Izik protest camp. Evidence at the trial included confessions allegedly obtained by torture. The court did not investigate these allegations.

Pro-independence advocates and other civil society leaders are often arbitrarily arrested, particularly in the aftermath of demonstrations. International human rights groups view many Sahrawis in Moroccan prisons, including human rights activists and pro-independence advocates, as political prisoners.

F3. Is there protection from the illegitimate use of physical force and freedom from war and insurgencies? 0 / 4

Tensions remain between the Moroccan military and the Polisario Front, with periodic mobilization of forces. A military standoff began in 2016 when the Polisario accused Morocco of breaking the terms of the cease-fire by attempting to build a road in the UN buffer zone. The standoff ended in 2017 when Morocco withdrew its troops.

In December 2018, the first UN-brokered talks between the Polisario and the Moroccan government in six years took place. Although the negotiations did not lead to a settlement of the dispute, both sides agreed to continue talks in 2019. Morocco has offered autonomy to Western Sahara, but the Polisario demands an independence referendum.

Torture and degrading treatment by Moroccan authorities continues to be a problem, especially against pro-independence advocates.

F4. Do laws, policies, and practices guarantee equal treatment of various segments of the population? 0 / 4

Sahrawis experience discrimination in access to education and employment. According to Sahrawi activists, Moroccan settlers are favored by employers in the phosphate mining industry, which is one of the predominant sources of jobs.

Although women play leadership roles at the Sahrawi camps in Algeria, cultural norms often dictate that women stay at home and manage the household. Moroccan law prohibits same-sex sexual acts.

G. PERSONAL AUTONOMY AND INDIVIDUAL RIGHTS: 4 / 16

G1. Do individuals enjoy freedom of movement, including the ability to change their place of residence, employment, or education? 1 / 4

Morocco and the Polisario Front both restrict free movement in Western Sahara. The sand berm, constructed by Morocco in the 1980s, is 1,700 miles long. The wall is surrounded on both sides by land mines, and constitutes what may be the longest continuous land mine field in the world.

G2. Are individuals able to exercise the right to own property and establish private businesses without undue interference from state or nonstate actors? 1 / 4

The territory's occupied status leaves property rights insecure. No credible free market exists within the territory. The SADR government routinely signs contracts with firms for the exploration of oil and gas, although these cannot be implemented given the territory's status.

G3. Do individuals enjoy personal social freedoms, including choice of marriage partner and size of family, protection from domestic violence, and control over appearance? 2 / 4

In the Polisario-controlled territory and in Tindouf, women have a relatively higher social status than in Morocco. However, social freedoms are curtailed. Moroccan law criminalizes both adultery and premarital sex. Spousal rape is not considered a crime.

G4. Do individuals enjoy equality of opportunity and freedom from economic exploitation? 0 / 4

Economic opportunity is inhibited by the territory's undetermined status. The economic activity generated by companies that exploit the country's natural resources generally does not benefit the Sahrawi population. Sex trafficking, often affecting young girls, takes place in coastal fishing villages.

Freedom in the World 2019
Methodology

INTRODUCTION

Freedom in the World is an annual global report on political rights and civil liberties, composed of numerical ratings and descriptive texts for each country and a select group of territories. The 2019 edition covers developments in 195 countries and 14 territories from January 1, 2018, through December 31, 2018.

The report's methodology is derived in large measure from the Universal Declaration of Human Rights, adopted by the UN General Assembly in 1948. *Freedom in the World* is based on the premise that these standards apply to all countries and territories, irrespective of geographical location, ethnic or religious composition, or level of economic development. *Freedom in the World* operates from the assumption that freedom for all people is best achieved in liberal democratic societies.

Freedom in the World assesses the real-world rights and freedoms enjoyed by individuals, rather than governments or government performance per se. Political rights and civil liberties can be affected by both state and nonstate actors, including insurgents and other armed groups.

Freedom in the World does not believe that legal guarantees of rights are sufficient for on-the-ground fulfillment of those rights. While both laws and actual practices are factored into scoring decisions, greater emphasis is placed on implementation.

Territories are selected for assessment in *Freedom in the World* based on the following criteria: whether the area is governed separately from the rest of the relevant country or countries, either de jure or de facto; whether conditions on the ground for political rights and civil liberties are significantly different from those in the rest of the relevant country or countries, meaning a separate assessment is likely to yield different ratings; whether the territory is the subject of enduring popular or diplomatic pressure for autonomy, independence, or incorporation into another country; whether the territory's boundaries are sufficiently stable to allow an assessment of conditions for the year under review, and whether they can be expected to remain stable in future years so that year-on-year comparisons are possible; and whether the territory is large and/or politically significant. Freedom House typically takes no position on territorial or separatist disputes as such, focusing instead on the level of political rights and civil liberties in a given geographical area.

HISTORY OF *FREEDOM IN THE WORLD*

Freedom House's first year-end reviews of freedom began in the 1950s as the *Balance Sheet of Freedom*. This modest report provided assessments of political trends and their implications for individual freedom. In 1972, Freedom House launched a new, more comprehensive annual study called *The Comparative Study of Freedom*. Raymond Gastil, a Harvard-trained specialist in regional studies from the University of Washington in Seattle, developed the methodology, which assigned political rights and civil liberties ratings to 151 countries and 45 territories and categorized them as Free, Partly Free, or Not Free. The findings appeared each year in Freedom House's bimonthly journal *Freedom at Issue* (later titled *Freedom Review*). *Freedom in the World* first appeared in book form in 1978 and included short narratives for each country and territory rated in the study, as well as a series of essays by leading scholars on related issues. *Freedom in the World* continued to be produced by Gastil until 1989, when a larger team of in-house analysts was established. In the mid-1990s, the expansion of the country and territory narratives necessitated the hiring of outside analysts—a group of regional experts from the academic, media, and human rights communities—and the project has continued to grow in size and scope in the years since.

A number of modest updates have been made to the methodology over time to adapt to evolving ideas about political rights and civil liberties. These changes are introduced incrementally in order to ensure the comparability of the ratings from year to year.

METHODODLOGY REVIEW, 2016–2017

In 2016–2017, Freedom House engaged a team of external experts to assist the staff in a thorough review of the *Freedom in the World* methodology. This represented the first such review since 2002. Approximately 20 experts with global, regional, and issue-based expertise participated in the exercise.

Following the review, the methodology's basic structure and most methodology questions remained the same. The review therefore does not affect the integrity of the *Freedom in the World* time-series data. Notable improvements include greater precision in the definition of each indicator, additional guidance on the handling of various real-world situations, and further detail on the interplay of new technological developments and fundamental freedoms. The review also led to the important step of including gender-related guidance questions under all relevant indicators.

One structural change that affected a very small number of countries was the elimination of Additional Discretionary Political Rights Question A. This indicator had awarded points to traditional monarchies that had no political parties or significant electoral processes but provided for some form of consultation with the public. Such consultation will now be addressed elsewhere in the methodology.

The revised methodology questions, appended below, were first used for the 2018 edition of *Freedom in the World*.

RESEARCH AND RATINGS REVIEW PROCESS

Freedom in the World is produced each year by a team of in-house and external analysts and expert advisers from the academic, think tank, and human rights communities. The 2019 edition involved more than 100 analysts and more than 30 advisers. The analysts, who prepare the draft reports and scores, use a broad range of sources, including news articles, academic analyses, reports from nongovernmental organizations, individual professional contacts, and on-the-ground research. The analysts score countries and territories based on the conditions and events within their borders during the coverage period. The analysts' proposed scores are discussed and defended at a series of review meetings, organized by region and attended by Freedom House staff and a panel of expert advisers. The final scores represent the consensus of the analysts, advisers, and staff. Although an element of subjectivity is unavoidable in such an enterprise, the ratings process emphasizes methodological consistency, intellectual rigor, and balanced and unbiased judgments.

SCORING PROCESS

Freedom in the World uses a three-tiered system consisting of **scores**, **ratings**, and **status**. The complete list of the questions used in the scoring process, and the tables for converting scores to ratings and ratings to status, appear at the end of this essay.

Scores – A country or territory is awarded 0 to 4 points for each of 10 political rights indicators and 15 civil liberties indicators, which take the form of questions; a score of 0 represents the smallest degree of freedom and 4 the greatest degree of freedom. The political rights questions are grouped into three subcategories: Electoral Process (3 questions), Political Pluralism and Participation (4), and Functioning of Government (3). The civil liberties questions are grouped into four subcategories: Freedom of Expression and Belief (4 questions), Associational and Organizational Rights (3), Rule of Law (4), and Personal Autonomy and Individual Rights (4). The political rights section also contains an additional discretionary question. For the discretionary question, a score of 1 to 4 may be subtracted, as applicable (the worse the situation, the more points may be subtracted). The highest overall score that can be awarded for political rights is 40 (or a score of 4 for each of the 10 questions). The highest overall score that can be awarded for civil liberties is 60 (or a score of 4 for each of the 15 questions). The scores from the previous edition are used as a benchmark for the current year under review. A score is typically changed only if there has been a real-world development during the year that warrants a decline or improvement (e.g., a crackdown on the media, the country's first free and fair elections), though gradual changes in conditions—in the absence of a signal event—are occasionally registered in the scores.

Political Rights and Civil Liberties Ratings – A country or territory is assigned two ratings—one for political rights and one for civil liberties—based on its total scores for the political rights and civil liberties questions. Each rating of 1 to 7, with 1 representing the greatest degree of freedom and 7 the smallest degree of freedom, corresponds to a specific range of total scores (see tables 1 and 2).

Free, Partly Free, Not Free Status – The average of a country or territory's political rights and civil liberties ratings is called the Freedom Rating, and it is this figure that determines the status of Free (1.0 to 2.5), Partly Free (3.0 to 5.0), or Not Free (5.5 to 7.0) (see table 3).

Electoral Democracy – *Freedom in the World* assigns the designation "electoral democracy" to countries that have met certain minimum standards for political rights and civil liberties; territories are not included in the list of electoral democracies. According to the methodology, an electoral democracy designation requires a score of 7 or better in the Electoral Process subcategory, an overall political rights score of 20 or better, *and* an overall civil liberties score of 30 or better. (The civil liberties threshold was added as part of the 2016–17 methodology review.) Freedom House's "electoral democracy" designation should not be equated with "liberal democracy," a term that implies a more robust observance of democratic ideals and a wider array of civil liberties. In *Freedom in the World*, most Free countries could be considered liberal democracies, while some Partly Free countries might qualify as electoral, but not liberal, democracies.

RATINGS AND STATUS CHARACTERISTICS
Political Rights

1 – Countries and territories with a rating of 1 enjoy a wide range of political rights, including free and fair elections. Candidates who are elected actually rule, political parties are competitive, the opposition plays an important role and enjoys real power, and the interests of minority groups are well represented in politics and government.

2 – Countries and territories with a rating of 2 have slightly weaker political rights than those with a rating of 1 because of such factors as political corruption, limits on the functioning of political parties and opposition groups, and flawed electoral processes.

3, 4, 5 – Countries and territories with a rating of 3, 4, or 5 either moderately protect almost all political rights or strongly protect some political rights while neglecting others. The same factors that undermine freedom in countries with a rating of 2 may also weaken political rights in those with a rating of 3, 4, or 5, but to a greater extent at each successive rating.

6 – Countries and territories with a rating of 6 have very restricted political rights. They are ruled by authoritarian regimes, often with leaders or parties that originally took power by force and have been in office for decades. They may hold tightly controlled elections and grant a few political rights, such as some representation or autonomy for minority groups.

7 – Countries and territories with a rating of 7 have few or no political rights because of severe government oppression, sometimes in combination with civil war. While some are draconian police states, others may lack an authoritative and functioning central government and suffer from extreme violence or rule by regional warlords.

Civil Liberties

1 – Countries and territories with a rating of 1 enjoy a wide range of civil liberties, including freedoms of expression, assembly, association, education, and religion. They have an established and generally fair legal system that ensures the rule of law (including an independent judiciary), allow free economic activity, and tend to strive for equality of opportunity for everyone, including women and minority groups.

2 – Countries and territories with a rating of 2 have slightly weaker civil liberties than those with a rating of 1 because of such factors as limits on media independence, restrictions on trade union activities, and discrimination against minority groups and women.

3, 4, 5 – Countries and territories with a rating of 3, 4, or 5 either moderately protect almost all civil liberties or strongly protect some civil liberties while neglecting others. The same factors that undermine freedom in countries with a rating of 2 may also weaken civil liberties in those with a rating of 3, 4, or 5, but to a greater extent at each successive rating.

6 – Countries and territories with a rating of 6 have very restricted civil liberties. They strongly limit the rights of expression and association and frequently hold political prisoners. They may allow a few civil liberties, such as some religious and social freedoms, some highly restricted private business activity, and some open and free private discussion.

7 – Countries and territories with a rating of 7 have few or no civil liberties. Their governments or powerful nonstate actors allow virtually no freedom of expression or association, do not protect the rights of detainees and prisoners, and often control most economic activity.

The gap between a country or territory's political rights and civil liberties ratings is rarely more than two points. Politically oppressive states typically do not allow a well-developed civil society, for example, and it is difficult, if not impossible, to maintain political freedoms in the absence of civil liberties like press freedom and the rule of law.

Because the designations of Free, Partly Free, and Not Free each cover a broad swath of the available scores, countries or territories within any one category, especially those at either end of the range, can have quite different human rights situations. For example, those at the lowest end of the Free category (2 in political rights and 3 in civil liberties, or 3 in political rights and 2 in civil liberties) differ from those at the upper end of the Free group (1 for both political rights and civil liberties). Also, a designation of Free does not mean that a country or territory enjoys perfect freedom or lacks serious problems, only that it enjoys comparatively more freedom than those rated Partly Free or Not Free (and some others rated Free).

FREEDOM IN THE WORLD 2019
Methodology Questions

The bulleted subquestions are intended to provide guidance to the analysts regarding what issues are meant to be considered in scoring each checklist question. The analysts do not need to consider every subquestion during the scoring process, as the relevance of each varies from one place to another.

POLITICAL RIGHTS (0–40 POINTS)

A. ELECTORAL PROCESS (0–12 points)

A1. Was the current head of government or other chief national authority elected through free and fair elections? (Note: Heads of government chosen through various electoral frameworks, including direct elections for president, indirect elections for prime minister by parliament, and the electoral college system for electing presidents, are covered under this question. In cases of indirect elections for the head of government, the elections for the legislature or other body that chose the head of government, as well as the selection process for the head of government itself, should be taken into consideration. In systems where executive authority is formally divided between a head of state and a head of government, greater weight should be given to elections for the official with the most executive authority.)

- Did independent, established, and reputable national and/or international election monitoring organizations judge the most recent election for head of government to have met democratic standards?
- Was the most recent election for head of government called in a timely manner, without undue, politically motivated delays or an accelerated schedule that unfairly limited campaign opportunities for some candidates?
- Was the registration of voters and candidates conducted in an accurate, timely, transparent, and nondiscriminatory manner?
- Were women allowed to register and run as candidates?
- Could all candidates make speeches, hold public meetings, and enjoy fair or proportionate media access throughout the campaign, free of intimidation?

- Did voting take place by secret ballot?
- Were voters able to vote for the candidate or party of their choice without undue pressure or intimidation?
- Was the vote count transparent and timely, and were the official results reported honestly to the public?
- Could election monitors from independent groups and representing parties/candidates watch the counting of votes to ensure its honesty?
- Did voters have equal access to polling places and opportunities to cast ballots?
- Has the most recently elected head of government been removed from office through violent, irregular, unconstitutional, or otherwise undemocratic means? (Note: Although a bloodless coup may ultimately lead to a positive outcome—particularly if it removes a head of government who was not freely and fairly elected—the new leader has not been freely and fairly elected and cannot be treated as such.)
- Has the head of government's electorally mandated term expired or been extended without new elections?
- In cases where elections for regional, provincial, or state governors and/or other subnational executive officials differ significantly in conduct from national elections, does the conduct of the subnational elections reflect an opening toward improved political rights in the country, or, alternatively, a worsening of political rights?

A2. Were the current national legislative representatives elected through free and fair elections?

- Did independent, established, and reputable domestic and/or international election monitoring organizations judge the most recent national legislative elections to have met democratic standards?
- Were the most recent legislative elections called in a timely manner, without undue, politically motivated delays or an accelerated schedule that unfairly limited campaign opportunities for some parties or candidates?
- Was the registration of voters and candidates conducted in an accurate, timely, transparent, and nondiscriminatory manner?
- Were women allowed to register and run as candidates?
- Could all candidates make speeches, hold public meetings, and enjoy fair or proportionate media access throughout the campaign, free of intimidation?
- Did voting take place by secret ballot?
- Were voters able to vote for the candidate or party of their choice without undue pressure or intimidation?
- Was the vote count transparent and timely, and were the official results reported honestly to the public?
- Could election monitors from independent groups and representing parties/candidates watch the counting of votes to ensure its honesty?
- Have members of the most recently elected national legislature been removed from office through violent, irregular, unconstitutional, or otherwise undemocratic means? (Note: Although a bloodless coup may ultimately lead to a positive outcome—particularly if it removes a legislature that was not freely and fairly elected—an appointed postcoup legislative body has not been freely and fairly elected and cannot be treated as such.)
- Has the legislature's electorally mandated term expired or been extended without new elections?

- In cases where elections for subnational councils/parliaments differ significantly in conduct from national elections, does the conduct of the subnational elections reflect an opening toward improved political rights in the country, or, alternatively, a worsening of political rights?

A3. Are the electoral laws and framework fair, and are they implemented impartially by the relevant election management bodies?

- Is there a clear, detailed, and fair legislative framework for conducting elections? (Note: Changes to electoral laws should not be made immediately preceding an election if these changes infringe on the ability of voters, candidates, or parties to fulfill their roles in the election.)
- Does the composition of election commissions ensure their independence?
- Are election commissions or other election authorities free from government or other pressure and interference?
- Do adult citizens enjoy universal and equal suffrage?
- Is the drawing of election districts conducted in a fair and nonpartisan manner, as opposed to malapportionment or gerrymandering for personal or partisan advantage?
- Has the selection of a system for choosing legislative representatives (such as proportional versus majoritarian) been improperly manipulated to advance certain political interests or to influence the electoral results?
- Are procedures for changing the electoral framework at the constitutional level, including referendums, carried out fairly and transparently, with adequate opportunity for public debate and discussion?

B. POLITICAL PLURALISM AND PARTICIPATION (0–16 points)

B1. Do the people have the right to organize in different political parties or other competitive political groupings of their choice, and is the system free of undue obstacles to the rise and fall of these competing parties or groupings?

- Do political parties encounter undue legal or practical obstacles in their efforts to form and operate, including onerous registration requirements, excessively large membership requirements, etc.?
- Do parties face discriminatory or onerous restrictions in holding meetings or rallies, accessing the media, or engaging in other peaceful activities?
- Are laws and regulations governing party financing fair and equitably enforced? Do they impose excessive obstacles to political and campaign activity, or give an effective advantage to certain parties?
- Are party members or leaders intimidated, harassed, arrested, imprisoned, or subjected to violent attacks as a result of their peaceful political activities?
- In systems dominated by political parties, can independent candidates register and operate freely?

B2. Is there a realistic opportunity for the opposition to increase its support or gain power through elections?

- Are various legal/administrative restrictions selectively applied to opposition parties to prevent them from increasing their support base or successfully competing in elections?
- Are there genuine opposition forces in positions of authority, such as in the national legislature or in subnational governments?
- Does intimidation, harassment, arrest, imprisonment, or violent attack as a result of peaceful political activities affect the ability of opposition party members or leaders to increase their support or gain power through elections?

- Is there a significant opposition vote?
- Did major opposition parties choose to boycott the most recent elections rather than participate in a flawed process?

B3. Are the people's political choices free from domination by the military, foreign powers, religious hierarchies, economic oligarchies, or any other powerful group that is not democratically accountable?

- Do such groups offer bribes or other incentives to voters in order to influence their political choices?
- Do such groups offer bribes or other incentives to political figures and/or parties in order to influence their political choices?
- Do such groups intimidate, harass, or attack voters and/or political figures in order to influence their political choices?
- Do major private or public-sector employers directly or indirectly control the political choices of their workers?

B4. Do various segments of the population (including ethnic, religious, gender, LGBT, and other relevant groups) have full political rights and electoral opportunities?

- Do national political parties of various ideological persuasions address issues of specific concern to minority or other relevant groups?
- When other parties fail to address the interests of certain groups, are political parties that are focused on those groups—provided they espouse peaceful, democratic values—legally permitted and de facto allowed to operate?
- Does the government inhibit the participation of certain groups in national or subnational political life through laws and/or practical obstacles—for example, by limiting access to voter registration or failing to publish public documents in certain languages?
- Are the interests of women represented in political parties—for example, through party manifestos that address gender issues, gender equality policies within parties, and mechanisms to ensure women's full and equal participation in internal party elections and decision-making?
- Are there unusually excessive or discriminatory barriers to acquiring citizenship that effectively deny political rights to a majority or large portion of the native-born or legal permanent population, or is citizenship revoked to produce a similar result?

C. FUNCTIONING OF GOVERNMENT (0–12 points)

C1. Do the freely elected head of government and national legislative representatives determine the policies of the government? (Note: Because the score for question C1 is partly dependent on the presence of a freely elected head of government and national legislative representatives, under most circumstances it will not exceed the average of the scores for questions A1 and A2.)

- Are the candidates who were elected freely and fairly duly installed in office, and were they able to form a functioning government within a reasonable period of time?
- Do other appointed or non–freely elected state actors interfere with or prevent freely elected representatives from adopting and implementing legislation and making meaningful policy decisions?
- Do nonstate actors, including criminal gangs and insurgent groups, interfere with or prevent elected representatives from adopting and implementing legislation and making meaningful policy decisions?

- Do the armed forces or other security services control or enjoy a preponderant influence over government policy and activities, including in countries that are nominally under civilian control?
- Do foreign governments control or enjoy a preponderant influence over government policy and activities by means including the presence of foreign military troops and the use of significant economic threats or sanctions? (Note: If a treaty was signed and ratified by a freely elected government, adherence to that treaty is typically not considered an improper external influence on policymaking, even if it limits a government's options in practice.)
- Is the freely elected government able to implement its decisions across the entire territory without interference from nonstate actors?
- Does the executive exhibit excessive dominance over the legislature?
- Has partisan polarization or obstructionism seriously impaired basic executive or legislative functions, such as approving a budget or filling important vacancies?

C2. Are safeguards against official corruption strong and effective?

- Has the government implemented effective anticorruption laws or programs to prevent, detect, and punish corruption among public officials, including conflicts of interest?
- Is the government free from excessive bureaucratic regulations, registration requirements, or other controls that increase opportunities for corruption?
- Are there independent and effective auditing and investigative bodies that function without impediment or political pressure or influence?
- Are allegations of corruption involving government officials thoroughly investigated and prosecuted without prejudice or political bias?
- Are allegations of corruption given extensive and substantive airing in the media?
- Do whistleblowers, anticorruption activists, investigators, and journalists enjoy legal protections that allow them to freely and safely report abuses?

C3. Does the government operate with openness and transparency?

- Do citizens have the legal right and practical ability to obtain information about state operations and the means to petition government agencies for it?
- Does the government publish information online, in machine-readable formats, for free, and is this information accessible by default?
- Are civil society groups, interest groups, journalists, and other citizens given a fair and meaningful opportunity to comment on and influence pending policies or legislation?
- Are elected representatives accessible to their constituents?
- Is the budget-making process subject to meaningful legislative review and public scrutiny?
- Does the state ensure transparency and effective competition in the awarding of government contracts?
- Are the asset declarations of government officials open to public and media scrutiny and verification?

ADDITIONAL DISCRETIONARY POLITICAL RIGHTS QUESTION

Q. Is the government or occupying power deliberately changing the ethnic composition of a country or territory so as to destroy a culture or tip the political balance in favor of another group? (−4 to 0 points)
- Is the government providing economic or other incentives to certain people in order to change the ethnic composition of a region or regions?
- Is the government forcibly moving people in or out of certain areas in order to change the ethnic composition of those regions?
- Is the government arresting, imprisoning, or killing members of certain ethnic groups in order change the ethnic composition of a region or regions?

CIVIL LIBERTIES (0–60 POINTS)

D. **FREEDOM OF EXPRESSION AND BELIEF (0–16 points)**
D1. **Are there free and independent media?** (Note: "Media" refers to all relevant sources of news and commentary—including formal print, broadcast, and online news outlets, as well as social media and communication applications when they are used to gather or disseminate news and commentary for the general public. The question also applies to artistic works in any medium.)
- Are the media directly or indirectly censored?
- Is self-censorship common among journalists (the term includes professional journalists, bloggers, and citizen journalists), especially when reporting on sensitive issues, including politics, social controversies, corruption, or the activities of powerful individuals?
- Are journalists subject to pressure or surveillance aimed at identifying their sources?
- Are libel, blasphemy, security, or other restrictive laws used to punish journalists who scrutinize government officials and policies or other powerful entities through either onerous fines or imprisonment?
- Is it a crime to insult the honor and dignity of the president and/or other government officials? How broad is the range of such prohibitions, and how vigorously are they enforced?
- If media outlets are dependent on the government for their financial survival, does the government condition funding on the outlets' cooperation in promoting official points of view and/or denying access to opposition parties and civic critics? Do powerful private actors engage in similar practices?
- Do the owners of private media exert improper editorial control over journalists or publishers, skewing news coverage to suit their personal business or political interests?
- Is media coverage excessively partisan, with the majority of outlets consistently favoring either side of the political spectrum?
- Does the government attempt to influence media content and access through means including politically motivated awarding or suspension of broadcast frequencies and newspaper registrations, unfair control and influence over printing facilities and distribution networks, blackouts of internet or mobile service, selective distribution of advertising, onerous operating requirements, prohibitive tariffs, and bribery?

- Are journalists threatened, harassed online, arrested, imprisoned, beaten, or killed by government or nonstate actors for their legitimate journalistic activities, and if such cases occur, are they investigated and prosecuted fairly and expeditiously?
- Do women journalists encounter gender-specific obstacles to carrying out their work, including threats of sexual violence or strict gender segregation?
- Are works of literature, art, music, or other forms of cultural expression censored or banned for political purposes?

D2. Are individuals free to practice and express their religious faith or nonbelief in public and private?

- Are registration requirements employed to impede the free functioning of religious institutions?
- Are members of religious groups, including minority faiths and movements, harassed, fined, arrested, or beaten by the authorities for engaging in their religious practices?
- Is state monitoring of peaceful religious activity so indiscriminate, pervasive, or intrusive that it amounts to harassment or intimidation?
- Are religious practice and expression impeded by violence or harassment by nonstate actors?
- Does the government appoint or otherwise influence the appointment of religious leaders?
- Does the government control or restrict the production and distribution of religious writings or materials?
- Is the construction of religious buildings banned or restricted?
- Does the government place undue restrictions on religious education? Does the government require religious education?
- Are individuals free to eschew religious beliefs and practices in general?

D3. Is there academic freedom, and is the educational system free from extensive political indoctrination?

- Are teachers and professors at both public and private institutions free to pursue academic activities of a political and quasi-political nature without fear of physical violence or intimidation by state or nonstate actors?
- Does the government pressure, strongly influence, or control the content of school curriculums for political purposes?
- Is the allocation of funding for public educational institutions free from political manipulation?
- Are student associations that address issues of a political nature allowed to function freely?
- Does the government, including through school administration or other officials, pressure students and/or teachers to support certain political figures or agendas, including by requiring them to attend political rallies or vote for certain candidates? Conversely, does the government, including through school administration or other officials, discourage or forbid students and/or teachers from supporting certain candidates and parties?

D4. Are individuals free to express their personal views on political or other sensitive topics without fear of surveillance or retribution?

- Are people able to engage in private discussions, particularly of a political nature, in public, semipublic, or private places—including restaurants, public transportation, and their homes, in person or on the telephone—without fear of harassment or detention by the authorities or nonstate actors?

- Do users of personal online communications—including direct messages, voice or video applications, or social media accounts with a limited audience—face legal penalties, harassment, or violence from the government or powerful nonstate actors in retaliation for critical remarks?
- Does the government employ people or groups to engage in public surveillance and to report alleged antigovernment conversations to the authorities?

E. ASSOCIATIONAL AND ORGANIZATIONAL RIGHTS (0–12 points)

E1. Is there freedom of assembly?

- Are peaceful protests, particularly those of a political nature, banned or severely restricted?
- Are the legal requirements to obtain permission to hold peaceful demonstrations particularly cumbersome or time-consuming?
- Are participants in peaceful demonstrations intimidated, arrested, or assaulted?
- Are peaceful protesters detained by police in order to prevent them from engaging in such actions?
- Are organizers blocked from using online media to plan or carry out a protest, for example through DDoS attacks or wholesale blackouts of internet or mobile services?
- Are similar restrictions and obstacles used to impede other public events, such as conferences, panel discussions, and town hall–style meetings?
- Are public petitions, in which citizens gather signatures to support a particular policy or initiative, banned or severely restricted?

E2. Is there freedom for nongovernmental organizations, particularly those that are engaged in human rights– and governance-related work? (Note: This includes civic organizations, interest groups, foundations, think tanks, gender rights groups, etc.)

- Are registration and other legal requirements for nongovernmental organizations particularly onerous or intended to prevent them from functioning freely?
- Are laws related to the financing of nongovernmental organizations unduly complicated and cumbersome, or are there obstacles to citizens raising money for charitable causes or civic activism?
- Are donors and funders of nongovernmental organizations free from government pressure?
- Are members of nongovernmental organizations intimidated, arrested, imprisoned, or assaulted because of their work?

E3. Is there freedom for trade unions and similar professional or labor organizations?

- Are trade unions allowed to be established and to operate without government interference?
- Are workers pressured by the government or employers to join or not to join certain trade unions, and do they face harassment, violence, or dismissal from their jobs if they fail to comply?
- Are workers permitted to engage in strikes, and do participants in peaceful strikes face reprisals? (Note: This question may not apply to workers in narrowly defined essential government services or public safety jobs.)
- Are unions able to bargain collectively with employers and negotiate agreements that are honored in practice?

- For states with primarily agricultural economies that do not necessarily support the formation of trade unions, does the government allow for the establishment of agricultural workers' organizations or their equivalents? Is there legislation expressly forbidding the formation of trade unions?
- Are professional organizations, including business associations, allowed to operate freely and without government interference?

F. RULE OF LAW (0–16 points)

F1. Is there an independent judiciary?

- Is the judiciary subject to interference from the executive branch of government or from other political, economic, or religious influences?
- Are judges appointed and dismissed in a fair and unbiased manner?
- Do judges rule fairly and impartially, or do they commonly render verdicts that favor the government or particular interests, whether in return for bribes or for other reasons?
- Do executive, legislative, and other governmental authorities comply with judicial decisions, and are these decisions effectively enforced?
- Do powerful private entities comply with judicial decisions, and are decisions that run counter to the interests of powerful actors effectively enforced?

F2. Does due process prevail in civil and criminal matters?

- Are defendants' rights, including the presumption of innocence until proven guilty, protected?
- Do detainees have access to independent, competent legal counsel regardless of their financial means?
- Are defendants given a fair, public, and timely hearing by a competent, independent, and impartial tribunal?
- Is access to the court system in general dependent on an individual's financial means?
- Are prosecutors independent of political control and influence?
- Are prosecutors independent of powerful private interests, whether legal or illegal?
- Do law enforcement and other security officials operate professionally, independently, and accountably?
- Do law enforcement officials make arbitrary arrests and detentions without warrants, or fabricate or plant evidence on suspects?
- Do law enforcement and other security officials fail to uphold due process because of influence by nonstate actors, including organized crime, powerful commercial interests, or other groups?

F3. Is there protection from the illegitimate use of physical force and freedom from war and insurgencies?

- Do law enforcement officials beat detainees during arrest or use excessive force or torture to extract confessions?
- Are conditions in pretrial detention facilities and prisons humane and respectful of the human dignity of inmates?
- Do citizens have the means of effective petition and redress when they suffer physical abuse by state authorities?
- Is violent crime common, either in particular areas or among the general population?
- Is the population subjected to physical harm, forced removal, or other acts of violence or terror due to civil conflict or war?

F4. Do laws, policies, and practices guarantee equal treatment of various segments of the population?

- Are members of various distinct groups—including ethnic, religious, gender, LGBT, and other relevant groups—able to effectively exercise their human rights with full equality before the law?
- Is violence against such groups considered a crime, is it widespread, and are perpetrators brought to justice?
- Do members of such groups face legal and/or de facto discrimination in areas including employment, education, and housing because of their identification with a particular group?
- Do noncitizens—including migrant workers and noncitizen immigrants—enjoy basic internationally recognized human rights, including the right not to be subjected to torture or other forms of ill-treatment, the right to due process of law, and the freedoms of association, expression, and religion?
- Do the country's laws provide for the granting of asylum or refugee status in accordance with the 1951 UN Convention Relating to the Status of Refugees, its 1967 Protocol, and other regional treaties regarding refugees? Has the government established a system for providing protection to refugees, including against *refoulement* (the return of persons to a country where there is reason to believe they would face persecution)?

G. PERSONAL AUTONOMY AND INDIVIDUAL RIGHTS (0–16 points)

G1. Do individuals enjoy freedom of movement, including the ability to change their place of residence, employment, or education?

- Are there restrictions on foreign travel, including an exit visa system, which may be enforced selectively?
- Is permission required from the authorities or nonstate actors to move within the country?
- Do state or nonstate actors control or constrain a person's ability to change their type and place of employment?
- Are bribes or other inducements needed to obtain the necessary documents to travel, change one's place of residence or employment, enter institutions of higher education, or advance in school?
- Is freedom of movement impaired by general threats to physical safety, such as armed conflict?
- Do women enjoy the same freedom of movement as men?

G2. Are individuals able to exercise the right to own property and establish private businesses without undue interference from state or nonstate actors?

- Are people legally allowed to purchase and sell land and other property, and can they do so in practice without undue interference from the government or nonstate actors?
- Do women face discrimination in property and inheritance rights?
- Are individuals protected from arbitrary expropriation, and do they receive adequate and timely compensation when property is seized?
- Are people legally allowed to establish and operate private businesses with a reasonable minimum of registration, licensing, and other requirements?
- Are bribes or other inducements needed to obtain the necessary legal documents to operate private businesses?
- Do private/nonstate actors, including criminal groups, seriously impede private business activities through such measures as extortion?

G3. Do individuals enjoy personal social freedoms, including choice of marriage partner and size of family, protection from domestic violence, and control over appearance?

- Are personalized forms of violence—including domestic violence, female genital mutilation/cutting, sexual abuse, and rape—widespread, and are perpetrators brought to justice?
- Does the government directly or indirectly control choice of marriage partner or other personal relationships through means such as bans on interfaith marriages, failure to enforce laws against child marriage or dowry payments, restrictions on same-sex relationships, or criminalization of extramarital sex?
- Do individuals enjoy equal rights in divorce proceedings and child custody matters?
- Do citizenship or residency rules undermine family integrity through excessively high or discriminatory barriers for foreign spouses or transmission of citizenship to children?
- Does the government determine the number of children that a couple may have, including by denying access to or imposing birth control, or by criminalizing or imposing abortion?
- Does the government restrict individuals' choice of dress, appearance, or gender expression?
- Do private institutions or individuals, including religious groups or family members, unduly infringe on the personal social freedoms of individuals, including choice of marriage partner, family size, dress, gender expression, etc.?

G4. Do individuals enjoy equality of opportunity and freedom from economic exploitation?

- Do state or private employers exploit their workers through practices including unfairly withholding wages, permitting or forcing employees to work under unacceptably dangerous conditions, or adult slave labor and child labor?
- Does tight government control over the economy, including through state ownership or the setting of prices and production quotas, inhibit individuals' economic opportunity?
- Do the revenues from large state industries, including the energy sector, benefit the general population or only a privileged few?
- Do private interests exert undue influence on the economy—through monopolistic practices, concentration of ownership, cartels, or illegal blacklists—that impedes economic opportunity for the general population?
- Do laws, policies, or persistent socioeconomic conditions effectively impose rigid barriers to social mobility, generally preventing individuals from rising to higher income levels over the course of their lives?
- Is the trafficking of persons for labor, sexual exploitation, forced begging, etc., widespread, and is the government taking adequate steps to address the problem?

KEY TO SCORES, PR AND CL RATINGS, STATUS			
Table 1		Table 2	
Political Rights (PR)		Civil Liberties (CL)	
Total Scores	PR Rating	Total Scores	CL Rating
36–40	1	53–60	1
30–35	2	44–52	2
24–29	3	35–43	3
18–23	4	26–34	4
12–17	5	17–25	5
6–11	6	8–16	6
0–5*	7	0–7	7

TABLE 3	
Combined Average of the PR and CL Ratings (Freedom Rating)	Freedom Status
1.0 to 2.5	Free
3.0 to 5.0	Partly Free
5.5 to 7.0	Not Free

* It is possible for a country or territory's total political rights score to be less than zero (between –1 and –4) if it receives mostly or all zeros for each of the 10 political rights questions *and* it receives a sufficiently negative score for the political rights discretionary question. In such a case, it would still receive a final political rights rating of 7.

Tables and Ratings

Country	PR	CL	Freedom Status
Afghanistan	5	6	Not Free
Albania*	3	3	Partly Free
Algeria	6	5	Not Free
Andorra*	1	1	Free
Angola	6	5 ▲	Not Free
Antigua and Barbuda*	2	2	Free
Argentina*	2	2	Free
Armenia	4 ▲	4	Partly Free
Australia*	1	1	Free
Austria*	1	1	Free
Azerbaijan	7	6	Not Free
Bahamas*	1	1	Free
Bahrain	7	6	Not Free
Bangladesh	5 ▼	5 ▼	Partly Free
Barbados*	1	1	Free
Belarus	7 ▼	6	Not Free
Belgium*	1	1	Free
Belize*	1	2	Free
Benin*	2	2	Free
Bhutan*	3	4	Partly Free
Bolivia*	3	3	Partly Free
Bosnia and Herzegovina	4	4	Partly Free
Botswana*	3	2	Free
Brazil*	2	2	Free
Brunei	6	5	Not Free
Bulgaria*	2	2	Free
Burkina Faso*	4	3	Partly Free
Burundi	7	6	Not Free
Cambodia	6	5	Not Free
Cameroon	6	6	Not Free

Country	PR	CL	Freedom Status
Canada*	1	1	Free
Cape Verde*	1	1	Free
Central African Republic	7	7	Not Free
Chad	7	6	Not Free
Chile*	1	1	Free
China	7	6	Not Free
Colombia*	3	3	Partly Free
Comoros	4 ▼	4	Partly Free
Congo (Brazzaville)	7	5	Not Free
Congo (Kinshasa)	7	6	Not Free
Costa Rica*	1	1	Free
Côte d'Ivoire	4	4	Partly Free
Croatia*	1	2	Free
Cuba	7	6	Not Free
Cyprus*	1	1	Free
Czech Republic*	1	1	Free
Denmark*	1	1	Free
Djibouti	6	5	Not Free
Dominica*	1	1	Free
Dominican Republic*	3	3	Partly Free
Ecuador*	3	3	Partly Free
Egypt	6	6	Not Free
El Salvador*	2	3	Free
Equatorial Guinea	7	7	Not Free
Eritrea	7	7	Not Free
Estonia*	1	1	Free
Eswatini	7	6	Not Free
Ethiopia	6 ▲	6	Not Free
Fiji*	3	3	Partly Free
Finland*	1	1	Free
France*	1	2	Free
Gabon	7	5	Not Free
Georgia*	3	3	Partly Free
Germany*	1	1	Free
Ghana*	1	2	Free
Greece*	1 ▲	2	Free
Grenada*	1	2	Free

Country	PR	CL	Freedom Status
Guatemala*	4	4	Partly Free
Guinea	5	4 ▲	Partly Free
Guinea-Bissau	5	4 ▲	Partly Free
Guyana*	2	3	Free
Haiti	5	5	Partly Free
Honduras	4	4	Partly Free
Hungary*	3	3 ▼	Partly Free ▼
Iceland*	1	1	Free
India*	2	3	Free
Indonesia*	2	4	Partly Free
Iran	6	6	Not Free
Iraq	5	6	Not Free
Ireland*	1	1	Free
Israel*	2 ▼	3	Free
Italy*	1	1	Free
Jamaica*	2	2 ▲	Free
Japan*	1	1	Free
Jordan	5	5	Partly Free
Kazakhstan	7	5	Not Free
Kenya	4	4	Partly Free
Kiribati*	1	1	Free
Kosovo*	3	4	Partly Free
Kuwait	5	5	Partly Free
Kyrgyzstan	5	4 ▲	Partly Free
Laos	7	6	Not Free
Latvia*	2	2	Free
Lebanon	5 ▲	4	Partly Free
Lesotho*	3	3	Partly Free
Liberia*	3	3	Partly Free
Libya	7	6	Not Free
Liechtenstein*	2	1	Free
Lithuania*	1	1	Free
Luxembourg*	1	1	Free
Macedonia	4	3	Partly Free
Madagascar*	3	4	Partly Free
Malawi*	3	3	Partly Free
Malaysia	4	4	Partly Free

Country	PR	CL	Freedom Status
Maldives	5	5	Partly Free
Mali	4 ▲	4	Partly Free
Malta*	2 ▼	1	Free
Marshall Islands*	1	1	Free
Mauritania	6	5	Not Free
Mauritius*	1	2	Free
Mexico*	3	3	Partly Free
Micronesia*	1	1	Free
Moldova*	3	4 ▼	Partly Free
Monaco*	3	1	Free
Mongolia*	1	2	Free
Montenegro*	4 ▼	3	Partly Free
Morocco	5	5	Partly Free
Mozambique	4	4	Partly Free
Myanmar	5	5	Partly Free
Namibia*	3 ▼	2	Free
Nauru*	2	2	Free
Nepal	3	4	Partly Free
Netherlands*	1	1	Free
New Zealand*	1	1	Free
Nicaragua	6 ▼	5 ▼	Not Free ▼
Niger	4	4	Partly Free
Nigeria	3	5	Partly Free
North Korea	7	7	Not Free
Norway*	1	1	Free
Oman	6	5	Not Free
Pakistan	5 ▼	5	Partly Free
Palau*	1	1	Free
Panama*	1 ▲	2	Free
Papua New Guinea*	4 ▼	3	Partly Free
Paraguay*	3	3	Partly Free
Peru*	2	3	Free
Philippines*	3	3	Partly Free
Poland*	2 ▼	2	Free
Portugal*	1	1	Free
Qatar	6	5	Not Free
Romania*	2	2	Free

Country	PR	CL	Freedom Status
Russia	7	6	Not Free
Rwanda	6	6	Not Free
Samoa*	2	2	Free
San Marino*	1	1	Free
São Tomé and Príncipe*	2	2	Free
Saudi Arabia	7	7	Not Free
Senegal*	2	3 ▼	Free
Serbia*	3	3 ▼	Partly Free ▼
Seychelles*	3	3	Partly Free
Sierra Leone*	3	3	Partly Free
Singapore	4	4	Partly Free
Slovakia*	1	2 ▼	Free
Slovenia*	1	1	Free
Solomon Islands*	2 ▲	2	Free
Somalia	7	7	Not Free
South Africa*	2	2	Free
South Korea*	2	2	Free
South Sudan	7	7	Not Free
Spain*	1	1	Free
Sri Lanka*	3	4	Partly Free
St. Kitts and Nevis*	1	1	Free
St. Lucia*	1	1	Free
St. Vincent and the Grenadines*	1	1	Free
Sudan	7	7	Not Free
Suriname*	2	3 ▼	Free
Sweden*	1	1	Free
Switzerland*	1	1	Free
Syria	7	7	Not Free
Taiwan*	1	1	Free
Tajikistan	7	6	Not Free
Tanzania	4	5 ▼	Partly Free
Thailand	7 ▼	5	Not Free
The Gambia	4	5	Partly Free
Timor-Leste*	2	3	Free
Togo	5 ▼	4	Partly Free
Tonga*	2	2	Free
Trinidad and Tobago*	2	2	Free

Country	PR	CL	Freedom Status
Tunisia*	2	3	Free
Turkey	5	6	Not Free
Turkmenistan	7	7	Not Free
Tuvalu*	1	1	Free
Uganda	6	5 ▼	Not Free ▼
Ukraine*	3	4 ▼	Partly Free
United Arab Emirates	7	6	Not Free
United Kingdom*	1	1	Free
United States*	2	1	Free
Uruguay*	1	1	Free
Uzbekistan	7	6 ▲	Not Free
Vanuatu*	2	2	Free
Venezuela	7 ▼	6 ▼	Not Free
Vietnam	7	5	Not Free
Yemen	7	6	Not Free
Zambia	4	4	Partly Free
Zimbabwe	5 ▲	5	Partly Free ▲

PR and CL stand for political rights and civil liberties, respectively; 1 represents the most free and 7 the least free rating.

▲ ▼ up or down indicates an improvement or decline in ratings or status since the last survey.

* indicates a country's status as an electoral democracy.

NOTE: The ratings reflect global events from January 1, 2018, through December 31, 2018.

Territories

Territory	PR	CL	Freedom Status
Abkhazia	4	5	Partly Free
Crimea	7	6	Not Free
Gaza Strip	7	6	Not Free
Hong Kong	5	2	Partly Free
Indian Kashmir	4	4	Partly Free
Nagorno-Karabakh	5	5	Partly Free
Northern Cyprus	2	2	Free
Pakistani Kashmir	6	5	Not Free
Somaliland	4	5	Partly Free
South Ossetia	7	6	Not Free
Tibet	7	7	Not Free
Transnistria	6	6	Not Free
West Bank	7	5	Not Free
Western Sahara	7	7	Not Free

PR and CL stand for political rights and civil liberties, respectively; 1 represents the most free and 7 the least free rating.

▲ ▼ up or down indicates an improvement or decline in ratings or status since the last survey.

NOTE: The ratings reflect global events from January 1, 2018, through December 31, 2018.

Freedom Ratings—Countries

FREE	Mongolia	Seychelles	Angola
1.0	Panama	Sierra Leone	Brunei
Andorra	Slovakia		Cambodia
Australia	United States	**3.5**	Djibouti
Austria		Bhutan	Iraq
Bahamas	**2.0**	Burkina Faso	Mauritania
Barbados	Antigua and Barbuda	Kosovo	Nicaragua
Belgium	Argentina	Macedonia	Oman
Canada	Benin	Madagascar	Qatar
Cape Verde	Brazil	Moldova	Turkey
Chile	Bulgaria	Montenegro	Uganda
Costa Rica	Jamaica	Nepal	
Cyprus	Latvia	Papua New Guinea	**6.0**
Czech Republic	Monaco	Sri Lanka	Cameroon
Denmark	Nauru	Ukraine	Congo (Brazzaville)
Dominica	Poland		Egypt
Estonia	Romania	**4.0**	Ethiopia
Finland	Samoa	Armenia	Gabon
Germany	São Tomé and Príncipe	Bosnia and Herzegovina	Iran
Iceland	Solomon Islands	Comoros	Kazakhstan
Ireland	South Africa	Côte d'Ivoire	Rwanda
Italy	South Korea	Guatemala	Thailand
Japan	Tonga	Honduras	Vietnam
Kiribati	Trinidad and Tobago	Kenya	
Lithuania	Vanuatu	Malaysia	**6.5**
Luxembourg		Mali	Azerbaijan
Marshall Islands	**2.5**	Mozambique	Bahrain
Micronesia	Botswana	Niger	Belarus
Netherlands	El Salvador	Nigeria	Burundi
New Zealand	Guyana	Singapore	Chad
Norway	India	Zambia	China
Palau	Israel		Congo (Kinshasa)
Portugal	Namibia	**4.5**	Cuba
San Marino	Peru	Guinea	Laos
Slovenia	Senegal	Guinea-Bissau	Libya
Spain	Suriname	Kyrgyzstan	Russia
St. Kitts and Nevis	Timor-Leste	Lebanon	Swaziland
St. Lucia	Tunisia	Tanzania	Tajikistan
St. Vincent and the		The Gambia	United Arab Emirates
Grenadines	**PARTLY FREE**	Togo	Uzbekistan
Sweden	**3.0**		Venezuela
Switzerland	Albania	**5.0**	Yemen
Taiwan	Bolivia	Bangladesh	
Tuvalu	Colombia	Haiti	**7.0**
United Kingdom	Dominican Republic	Jordan	Central African Republic
Uruguay	Ecuador	Kuwait	Equatorial Guinea
	Fiji	Maldives	Eritrea
1.5	Georgia	Morocco	North Korea
Belize	Hungary	Myanmar	Saudi Arabia
Croatia	Indonesia	Pakistan	Somalia
France	Lesotho	Zimbabwe	South Sudan
Ghana	Liberia		Sudan
Greece	Malawi	**NOT FREE**	Syria
Grenada	Mexico	**5.5**	Turkmenistan
Liechtenstein	Paraguay	Afghanistan	
Malta	Philippines	Algeria	
Mauritius	Serbia		

Freedom Ratings – Territories

FREE
2.0
Northern Cyprus

PARTLY FREE
3.5
Hong Kong

4.0
Indian Kashmir

4.5
Abkhazia
Somaliland

5.0
Nagorno-Karabakh

NOT FREE
5.5
Pakistani Kashmir

6.0
Transnistria
West Bank

6.5
Crimea
Gaza Strip
South Ossetia

7.0
Tibet
Western Sahara

Electoral Democracies (114)

Albania	Italy
Andorra	Jamaica
Antigua and Barbuda	Japan
Argentina	Kiribati
Australia	Kosovo
Austria	Latvia
Bahamas	Lesotho
Barbados	Liberia
Belgium	Liechtenstein
Belize	Lithuania
Benin	Luxembourg
Bhutan	Madagascar
Bolivia	Malawi
Botswana	Malta
Brazil	Marshall Islands
Bulgaria	Mauritius
Burkina Faso	Mexico
Canada	Micronesia
Cape Verde	Moldova
Chile	Monaco
Colombia	Mongolia
Costa Rica	Montenegro
Croatia	Namibia
Cyprus	Nauru
Czech Republic	Netherlands
Denmark	New Zealand
Dominica	Norway
Dominican Republic	Palau
Ecuador	Panama
El Salvador	Papua New Guinea
Estonia	Paraguay
Fiji	Peru
Finland	Philippines
France	Poland
Georgia	Portugal
Germany	Romania
Ghana	Samoa
Greece	San Marino
Grenada	Sao Tome and Principe
Guatemala	Senegal
Guyana	Serbia
Hungary	Seychelles
Iceland	Sierra Leone
India	Slovakia
Indonesia	Slovenia
Ireland	Solomon Islands
Israel	South Africa

South Korea
Spain
Sri Lanka
St. Kitts and Nevis
St. Lucia
St. Vincent and the Grenadines
Suriname
Sweden
Switzerland
Taiwan

Timor-Leste
Tonga
Trinidad and Tobago
Tunisia
Tuvalu
Ukraine
United Kingdom
United States
Uruguay
Vanuatu

Survey Team

RESEARCH AND EDITORIAL TEAM

Christopher Brandt, Editor
Isabel Linzer, Research Associate
Shannon O'Toole, Managing Editor
Sarah Repucci, Senior Director for Research and Analysis
Tyler Roylance, Staff Editor
Nate Schenkkan, Director of Special Research
Amy Slipowitz, Research Coordinator
Mai Truong, Research Director for Management and Strategy
Caitlin Watson, Program Officer & Research and Advocacy Fellow, Latin America

ANALYSTS

Aalaa Abuzaakouk is a Middle East and North Africa (MENA) analyst and manages a leadership program for MENA undergraduate students at Georgetown University.

Elen Aghekyan is an independent researcher focusing on democracy and history in the Caucasus.

Celia Alexander is an independent researcher specializing in security policy, with a particular focus on the Middle East.

Ignacio Arana is a postdoctoral fellow at the Institute for Politics and Strategy at Carnegie Mellon University.

Bojan Baća is an Ernst Mach Postdoctoral Fellow at the Center for Southeast European Studies, University of Graz, and research associate at the Global Digital Citizenship Lab, York University.

Angelita Baeyens is director of the international advocacy and litigation program at Robert F. Kennedy Human Rights and an adjunct professor of law at Georgetown University.

Ian Bateson is a journalist and Fulbright Scholar.

Bruno Binetti is a non-resident fellow at the Inter-American Dialogue.

Aljaž Pengov Bitenc is a Slovenian journalist, blogger, and podcaster. He is the editor-in-chief of Ljubljana-based Radio KAOS and regularly appears as a political commentator and analyst.

Gustavo Bonifaz Moreno is a senior researcher at Edelman Intelligence London and holds a PhD in Political Science from the London School of Economics and Political Science.

Victoria Bucătaru is the executive director of the Foreign Policy Association of Moldova.

Brett Carter is an assistant professor of international relations at the University of Southern California.

Sarah Cook is a senior research analyst at Freedom House and director of its China Media Bulletin.

Jack Corbett is a professor of politics at the University of Southampton.

Neil DeVotta is a professor of politics and international affairs at Wake Forest University.

Julian Dierkes teaches public policy and global affairs at the University of British Columbia.

Rose Dlougatch is a research assistant at Macquarie University.

Richard Downie is a senior associate with the Africa program at the Center for Strategic and International Studies.

Howard Eissenstat is an associate professor of Middle East history at St. Lawrence University and a non-resident senior fellow at the Project on Middle East Democracy.

Daniel Eizenga is a postdoctoral fellow with the Centre FrancoPaix de la Chaire Raoul-Dandurand at the Université du Québec à Montréal.

Anthony Elghossain is a lawyer and writer based in Beirut, Lebanon.

Golnaz Esfandiari is a senior correspondent with Radio Free Europe/Radio Liberty.

Jon Fraenkel is a professor of comparative politics in the School of History, Philosophy, Political Science and International Relations at Victoria University of Wellington, New Zealand.

Dustin Gilbreath is the deputy research director of CRRC-Georgia and communications manager at Transparify.

Frederick Golooba-Mutebi is a Rwanda- and Uganda-based independent researcher and newspaper columnist. He is also a research associate at the Overseas Development Institute.

Alyssa Maraj Grahame is a visiting assistant professor of government at Bowdoin College.

Liutauras Gudžinskas is an associate professor of comparative politics at the Institute of International Relations and Political Science of Vilnius University and editor-in-chief of the *Baltic Journal of Political Science.*

Ted A. Henken is an associate professor of sociology and Latin American studies at Baruch College, City University of New York.

Hannah Hills is an associate at The Governance Group.

Jonathan Hulland is a senior program officer with the American Jewish World Service.

Niklas Hultin is an assistant professor of global affairs at George Mason University.

Harry Hummel is a policy advisor based in the Netherlands.

Iati Iati is a senior lecturer in the politics and international relations program and the Centre for Strategic Studies at Victoria University of Wellington.

Rico Isaacs is a reader in politics at Oxford Brookes University.

Faysal Itani is a senior fellow at the Atlantic Council and an adjunct professor of Middle East politics at George Washington University.

Kristen Kao is a postdoctoral research fellow with the Program on Governance and Local Development at the University of Gothenburg, Sweden.

Valery Kavaleuski is affiliated with the Belarusian Institute of America.

Catherine Lena Kelly is an advisor in the research, evaluation, and learning division at the American Bar Association-Rule of Law Initiative. The views expressed in the report are her personal views and not those of ABA ROLI.

Nicholas Kerr is an assistant professor of political science at the University of Florida.

Jane Kinninmont is an analyst of Middle East politics and economies, based in London, and advises The Elders on conflict and peacebuilding.

Marko Kmezić is an assistant professor at the Centre for Southeast European Studies at the University of Graz, Austria.

Nirabh Koirala is a quantitative research assistant at the RAND Corporation.

Zsolt Körtvélyesi is an independent consultant specializing in Central and Eastern Europe.

Niklas Kossow is a PhD candidate at the Hertie School of Governance in Berlin.

Joshua Kurlantzick is a senior fellow for Southeast Asia at the Council on Foreign Relations.

Kelsey Lilley is a policy analyst for Yorktown Solutions.

Lone Lindholt is CEO of Lindholt Consult, operating globally in the field of human rights, law, and development.

Rafael A. Mangual is a fellow and deputy director of legal policy at the Manhattan Institute for Policy Research.

Philip Martin is a PhD candidate in the Department of Political Science at the Massachusetts Institute of Technology.

David McGrane is an associate professor of political studies at St. Thomas More College and the University of Saskatchewan.

Mpumelelo Mkhabela is a fellow at the Centre for the Study of Governance Innovation at the University of Pretoria.

Mushfiq Mohamed is a lawyer working with the Maldivian Democracy Network and a former public prosecutor in the Maldives.

Aurelien Mondon is a senior lecturer at the University of Bath.

Jasmin Mujanovic is an adjunct assistant professor of political science at Elon University.

Joachim Nahem is managing partner at The Governance Group.

Gareth Nellis is an assistant professor of political science at the University of California, San Diego.

Justus Nyang'aya is the executive director of LEAD Africa and an expert on governance, leadership, and social accountability.

Ibrahim Al-bakri Nyei is a PhD candidate in politics and international studies at the School of Oriental and African Studies, University of London. He is a columnist and commentator on political developments in Sub-Saharan Africa.

Robert Orttung is a research professor of international affairs at the George Washington University Elliott School of International Affairs.

Ana Pastor is a Spanish political analyst and journalist working for the human rights project Bridge Figures.

Robert Pekkanen is a professor at the Jackson School of International Studies at the University of Washington.

Nicole Phillips is a human rights and rule of law consultant and adjunct professor at the University of California Hastings College of Law.

Juvence F. Ramasy is a lecturer at the University of Toamasina, Madagascar.

Tyson Roberts is a lecturer in political science and international relations at the University of Southern California.

Marek Rybář is an associate professor of political science at Masaryk University Brno, Czech Republic.

Mitchell A. Seligson is the Centennial Professor of Political Science at Vanderbilt University.

Michael Semple is a professor at the Senator George Mitchell Institute for Global Peace, Security and Justice, Queen's University Belfast.

Debbie Sharnak is a lecturer at Harvard University.

Elton Skendaj is the Muir Associate Professor of Peace Studies at Manchester University in Indiana.

Olga Skrypnyk is head of the board of the Crimean Human Rights Group in Ukraine.

Nathan Stormont is an independent researcher.

Rachel Sweet is a postdoctoral scholar at Harvard University.

Farha Tahir is a program officer at the National Endowment for Democracy.

Jenny Town is a research analyst at the Henry L. Stimson Center and the managing editor of 38 North.

Noah Tucker is an associate for the Central Asia program at George Washington University and senior editor for RFE/RL's Uzbek service Ozodlik.

Romy Vasquez Morales is the president of Saranik y Asociados and a former ambassador of Panama to Canada.

Wouter Veenendaal is an assistant professor at the Institute of Political Science, Leiden University.

David Vivar is the academic coordinator for FLACSO-Honduras and a professor at the National Autonomous University of Honduras.

Gregory White is the Mary Huggins Gamble Professor and chair of Government at Smith College. He is a co-editor of the *Journal of North African Studies*.

ACADEMIC ADVISERS

Pashtoon Atif is studying for a master of public policy at the Blavatnik School of Government, University of Oxford.

Florian Bieber is a professor of Southeast European history and politics at the University of Graz, Austria.

Steve Coll is dean of the Graduate School of Journalism at Columbia University and a staff writer at the *New Yorker*.

Sumit Ganguly is a Distinguished Professor of Political Science and holds the Tagore Chair in Indian Cultures and Civilizations at Indiana University, Bloomington.

Ames C. Grawert is senior counsel at the John L. Neu Justice Council in the Justice Program at the Brennan Center for Justice at New York University School of Law.

Lane Greene is an editor and columnist at the *Economist*.

Steven Heydemann is the Janet W. Ketcham Chair in Middle East Studies and a professor of government at Smith College.

Jan Kubik is a professor of Slavonic and East European studies at University College London and a professor in the Department of Political Science at Rutgers University.

Melissa Labonte is interim dean of the Graduate School of Arts and Sciences and an associate professor of political science at Fordham University.

Adrienne LeBas is an associate professor of government at the School of Public Affairs of American University in Washington, DC.

Peter M. Lewis is a professor at Johns Hopkins University's School of Advanced International Studies.

Adam Luedtke is an assistant professor of political science at City University of New York, Queensborough Community College.

Peter Mandaville is a professor of international affairs in the Schar School of Policy and Government at George Mason University.

Richard R. Marcus is a professor and director of The Global Studies Institute and the international studies program at California State University, Long Beach.

Martha Minow is a professor at Harvard University. She was assisted by Gavin Duffy Gideon, a Harvard Law School student.

Alexander Motyl is a professor of political science at Rutgers University-Newark.

Alina Mungiu-Pippidi is chair of democracy studies at the Hertie School of Governance in Berlin.

Godfrey Musila is an adjunct professor at the Africa Center for Strategic Studies and a consultant based in Washington, DC.

Andrew J. Nathan is Class of 1919 Professor of Political Science at Columbia University.

Kuniaki Nemoto is an associate professor of political science at Musashi University, Tokyo, specializing in elections, parties and party systems, and legislative politics in Asia-Pacific democracies.

Susan L. Ostermann is an assistant professor of global affairs at the University of Notre Dame.

Bruce Pannier is a senior correspondent focusing on events in Central Asia at Radio Free Europe/Radio Liberty.

Scott Radnitz is an associate professor of international studies at the University of Washington.

Mausi Segun is the Africa director at Human Rights Watch.

Samer Shehata is the Colin and Patricia Molina de Mackey Associate Professor of Middle East Studies at the University of Oklahoma.

Scott Taylor is a professor and director of the African Studies Program at Georgetown University.

Bridget Welsh is an associate professor at John Cabot University.

Susanna D. Wing is an associate professor of political science at Haverford College.

METHODOLOGY REVIEWERS

In 2016–17, Freedom House engaged a team of external experts to assist the staff in a thorough review of the *Freedom in the World* methodology. This represented the first such review since 2002. The following experts with global, regional, and issue-based expertise participated in the exercise.

Dodi Ambardi is the executive director of the Indonesian Survey Institute (LSI).

David Armstrong is the Canada Research Chair in Political Methodology, an associate professor of political science, and an associate professor of statistics (by courtesy) at the University of Western Ontario.

Kojo Pumpuni Asante is a senior research fellow at the Ghana Center for Democratic Development.

Johanna Birnir is an associate professor of government and politics at the University of Maryland.

Andras Bozoki is a professor of political science at Central European University.

Alex Cooley is the Claire Tow Professor of Political Science at Barnard College, the director of Columbia University's Harriman Institute, and the coeditor of *Ranking the World: Grading States as a Tool of Global Governance.*

Larry Diamond is a senior fellow at the Hoover Institution, Stanford University, and founding coeditor of the *Journal of Democracy.*

Boniface Dulani is a senior lecturer and the social science faculty postgraduate coordinator at the University of Malawi, Chancellor College.

Laza Kekic is an independent consultant, and both the former regional director for Europe and the director for country forecasting services at the Economist Intelligence Unit (EIU).

Adrienne LeBas is an associate professor of government at American University's School of Public Affairs.

Juan Pablo Luna is a professor of political science at Pontificia Universidad Católica de Chile.

Marc Lynch is a professor of political science and international affairs at George Washington University.

Alicia Phillips Mandaville is the vice president of global development at InterAction, and previously served as chief strategy officer at the Millennium Challenge Corporation.

Peter Mandaville is a professor of international affairs at the Schar School of Policy and Government at George Mason University and a nonresident senior fellow at the Brookings Institution.

Winnie Mitullah is director of the Institute for Development Studies at the University of Nairobi; and core partner director at Afrobarometer.

Joachim Nahem is managing director of the Governance Group, and is affiliated with the Norwegian Institute of International Affairs.

Sameena Nazir is a strategic program advisor at Networks of Change.

Melina Ramirez is a researcher at the Mexican Institute for Competitiveness (IMCO).

Niranjan Sahoo is a senior fellow with the Governance and Politics Initiative at the Observer Research Foundation (ORF), India.

Saloua Zerhouni is an associate professor at the Faculty of Juridical, Economic and Social Sciences-souissi, at Mohammed V University in Rabat, Morocco.

Ethan Zuckerman is the director of the Center for Civic Media at the Massachusetts Institute of Technology (MIT).

Selected Sources for
Freedom in the World 2019

PUBLICATIONS/BROADCASTS/BLOGS

ABC Color [Paraguay], www.abc.com.py

Africa Energy Intelligence, www.africaintelligence
.com

African Elections Database, http://africanelections
.tripod.com

Aftenposten [Norway], www.aftenposten.no

Agence France-Presse (AFP), www.afp.com

Al-Arab al-Yawm [Jordan]: www.alarabalyawm.net

Al-Arabiya, www.alarabiya.net

Al-Akhbar [Lebanon], www.al-akhbar.com

Al-Dustour [Egypt], www.addustour.com

Al-Jazeera America, www.america.aljazeera.com

allAfrica.com, www.allafrica.com

Al-Masry al-Youm [Egypt], www.almasryalyoum
.com

Al-Ray Al-'am [Kuwait], www.alraialaam.com

Al-Quds al-Arabi, www.alquds.co.uk

Al-Thawra [Yemen], www.althawranews.net

Annual Review of Population Law (Harvard Law
School), www.hsph.harvard.edu/population

Arab News [Saudi Arabia], www.arabnews.com

Asharq Alawsat, www.asharqalawsat.com

Asia Times, www.atimes.com

Associated Press (AP), www.ap.org

Awareness Times [Sierra Leone], www.news.sl

Balkan Insight, www.balkaninsight.com

The Baltic Times, www.baltictimes.com

Bangkok Post, www.bangkokpost.com

British Broadcasting Corporation (BBC), www.bbc
.co.uk

BruDirect.com [Brunei], www.brudirect.com

Cameroon Tribune, www.cameroon-tribune.cm

Central News Agency [Taiwan], http://focustaiwan
.tw

China Post, www.chinapost.com.tw

CIA World Factbook, www.cia.gov/cia/publications
/factbook

Copenhagen Post [Denmark], www.cphpost.dk

Corriere della Sera [Italy], www.corriere.it

Czech News Agency, www.ceskenoviny.cz/news

Daily Excelsior [Indian Kashmir], www.daily
excelsior.com

Daily Star [Lebanon], www.dailystar.com.lb

Danas [Serbia], www.danas.rs/danasrs
/naslovna.1.html

Dani [Bosnia-Herzegovina], www.bhdani.com

Dawn [Pakistan], www.dawn.com

Der Spiegel [Germany], www.spiegel.de

Der Standard [Austria], www.derstandard.at

Deutsche Welle [Germany], www.dwelle.de

East Africa Standard [Kenya], www.eastandard.net

The Economist, www.economist.com

Ekho Moskvy [Russia], http://echo.msk.ru

El Mercurio [Chile], www.elmercurio.cl

El Pais [Uruguay], www.elpais.com.uy

El Tiempo [Colombia], www.eltiempo.com

El Universal [Venezuela], www.eluniversal.com

FBI Hate Crime Statistics, https://www.fbi.gov
/about-us/investigate/civilrights/hate_crimes

Federated States of Micronesia Information
Services, www.fsmpio.fm

Fiji Times Online, www.fijitimes.com

Financial Times, www.ft.com

Foreign Policy, www.foreignpolicy.com

France 24, www.france24.com

Global News Wire, www.lexis-nexis.com

The Guardian [Nigeria], www.ngrguardiannews
.com

The Guardian [United Kingdom], www.guardian
.co.uk

Gulf Daily News [Bahrain], www.gulf-daily-news
.com

Haaretz [Israel], www.haaretz.com

Harakah Daily [Malaysia], http://bm.harakahdaily
.net

Haveeru Daily [Maldives], www.haveeru.com.mv

Hindustan Times [India], www.hindustantimes.com

Hurriyet [Turkey], www.hurriyetdailynews.com

Iceland Review, www.icelandreview.com

The Independent [United Kingdom], www
.independent.co.uk

Indian Express, www.indian-express.com

Inter Press Service, www.ips.org

IRIN news, www.irinnews.org

Irish Independent, http://www.independent.ie

Irish Times, http://www.irishtimes.com

Islands Business Magazine, www.islandsbusiness
.com
Izvestia, www.izvestia.ru
Jadaliyya, www.jadaliyya.com
Jakarta Post, www.thejakartapost.com
Jamaica Gleaner, www.jamaica-gleaner.com
Jeune Afrique [France], www.jeuneafrique.com
Jordan Times, www.jordantimes.com
Journal of Democracy, www.journalofdemocracy
.org
Jyllands-Posten [Denmark], www.jp.dk
Kashmir Times [Indian Kashmir], www.
kashmirtimes.com
Kommersant [Russia], www.kommersant.ru
Kompas [Indonesia], www.kompas.com
Korea Times [South Korea], http://times.hankooki
.com
Kuensel [Bhutan], www.kuenselonline.com
Kyiv Post, www.kyivpost.com
L'Informazione di San Marino, www.libertas.sm
La Nación [Argentina], www.lanacion.com.ar
La Presse de Tunisie [Tunisia], www.lapresse.tn
La Repubblica [Italy], www.repubblica.it
La Tercera [Chile], www.latercera.com
Latin American Regional Reports, www.latinnews
.com
Le Faso [Burkina Faso], www.lefaso.net
Le Messager [Cameroon], quotidienlemessager.net
Le Monde [France], www.lemonde.fr
Le Quotidien [Senegal], www.lequotidien.sn
Le Temps [Switzerland], www.letemps.ch
Le Togolais [Togo], www.letogolais.com
The Local [Sweden], www.thelocal.se
L'Orient-Le Jour [Lebanon], www.lorientlejour.com
Mail & Guardian [South Africa], www.mg.co.za
Mada Masr, www.madamasr.com
Malaysiakini [Malaysia], www.malaysiakini.com
Manila Times, www.manilatimes.net
Marianas Variety [Micronesia], www.mvariety.com
Matangi Tonga Magazine, www.matangitonga.to
The Messenger [Georgia], www.messenger.com.ge
Middle East Report, www.merip.org
Maldives Independent, www.minivannews.com
Mongolia Focus, http://blogs.ubc.ca/mongolia
Moscow Times, www.themoscowtimes.com
Munhwa Ilbo [South Korea], www.munhwa.com
Nacional [Croatia], www.nacional.hr
The Namibian, www.namibian.com.na
The Nation [Thailand], www.nationmultimedia.com
The National [Papua New Guinea], www.the
national.com.pg
New Dawn [Liberia], www.thenewdawnliberia.com
New York Times, www.nytimes.com
New Zealand Herald, www.nzherald.co.nz

North Korea Economy Watch, www.nkeconwatch
.com
Nyasa Times [Malawi], www.nyasatimes.com
O Globo [Brazil], www.oglobo.globo.com
Oman Arabic Daily, www.omandaily.com
Outlook [India], www.outlookindia.com
Pacific Islands Report, http://pidp.eastwestcenter
.org/pireport
Página/12 [Argentina], www.pagina12.com.ar
Papua New Guinea Post-Courier, www.postcourier
.com.pg
Philippine Daily Inquirer, www.inquirer.net
Phnom Penh Post, www.phnompenhpost.com
Politics.hu [Hungary], www.politics.hu
Politika [Serbia], www.politika.rs
Prague Post, www.praguepost.com
Radio Free Europe-Radio Liberty, www.rferl.org
Radio Okapi [Congo-Kinshasa], www.radioOkapi
.net
Republika [Indonesia], www.republika.co.id
Rodong Sinmun [North Korea], www.rodong.rep.kp
African Arguments, africanarguments.org
Sahel Blog, http://sahelblog.wordpress.com
Semana [Colombia], www.semana.com
Slobodna Bosna [Bosnia-Herzegovina], www
.slobodna-bosna.ba
SME [Slovakia], www.sme.sk
Somaliland Times, www.somalilandtimes.net
South China Morning Post [Hong Kong], www
.scmp:com
Straits Times [Singapore], www.straitstimes.asia1
.com.sg
Syria Comment, www.joshualandis.com
Taipei Times, www.taipeitimes.com
Tamilnet.com, www.tamilnet.com
The Telegraph [United Kingdom], www.telegraph
.co.uk
Tico Times [Costa Rica], www.ticotimes.net
Times of Central Asia, www.times.kg
Trinidad Express, www.trinidadexpress.com
Union Patriótica de Cuba (UNPACU), www.unpacu
.org/acerca-de/sobre-unpacu
U.S. State Department Reports on Human Rights
Practices, www.state.gov/g/drl/rls/hrrpt
U.S. State Department Reports on Human
Trafficking, www.state.gov/g/tip
U.S. State Department International Religious
Freedom Reports, www.state.gov/g/drl/irf
Voice of America, www.voa.gov
Wall Street Journal, www.wsj.com
Washington Post, www.washingtonpost.com
Xinhua News, www.xinhuanet.com
Yemen Times, www.yementimes.com
Zambia Reports, zambiareports.com

ORGANIZATIONS

Afghan Independent Human Rights Commission, www.aihrc.org.af

Afrobarometer, www.afrobarometer.org

Alternative ASEAN Network on Burma, www.altsean.org

American Bar Association Rule of Law Initiative, www.abanet.org/rol

American Civil Liberties Union, www.aclu.org

Amnesty International, www.amnesty.org

Anti-Slavery International, www.antislavery.org

Arabic Network for Human Rights Information (ANHRI), www.anhri.net

Asian Center for Human Rights [India], www.achrweb.org

Assistance Association for Political Prisoners [Burma], www.aappb.org

Balkan Human Rights Web, www.greekhelsinki.gr

Belarusian Institute for Strategic Studies, www.belinstitute.eu

Brookings Institution, www.brookings.edu

B'Tselem [Palestine], www.btselem.org

Cairo Institute for Human Rights, www.cihrs.org

Carnegie Endowment for International Peace, www.carnegieendowment.org

Center for Strategic and International Studies, www.csis.org

Chatham House [United Kingdom], www.chathamhouse.org

Committee for the Prevention of Torture, www.cpt.coe.int

Committee to Protect Journalists, www.cpj.org

Council on Foreign Relations, www.cfr.org/index.html

Ditshwanelo – Botswana Centre for Human Rights, www.ditshwanelo.org.bw

Electoral Institute of Southern Africa, www.eisa.org.za

European Roma Rights Center, www.errc.org

Extractive Industries Transparency Initiative, www.eiti.org

Globe International [Mongolia], www.globeinter.org.mn/old/en/index.php

Hong Kong Human Rights Monitor, www.hkhrm.org.hk

Human Rights Commission of Pakistan, www.hrcp-web.org

Human Rights Watch, www.hrw.org

Index on Censorship, www.indexoncensorship.org

Indonesian Survey Institute, www.lsi.or.id

Institute for Democracy in Eastern Europe, www.idee.org

Institute for War and Peace Reporting, www.iwpr.net

Inter-American Press Association, www.sipiapa.com

Internal Displacement Monitoring Center, www.internal-displacement.org

International Campaign for Tibet, www.savetibet.org

International Centre for Not-for-Profit Law: *NGO Law Monitor*, www.icnl.org

International Crisis Group, www.crisisgroup.org

International Foundation for Electoral Systems, www.ifes.org

International Freedom of Expression Exchange, www.ifex.org

International Labour Organization, www.ilo.org

International Lesbian and Gay Association, www.ilga.org

International Monetary Fund, www.imf.org

International Organization for Migration, www.iom.int

Kashmir Study Group, www.kashmirstudygroup.net

Korea Development Institute, www.kdi.re.kr

MADA-Palestinian Center for Development and Media Freedoms, www.madacenter.org/index.php?lang=1

Media Institute of Southern Africa, www.misa.org

Migrant Assistance Programme Thailand, www.mapfoundationcm.org/eng

National Democratic Institute for International Affairs, www.ndi.org

National Human Rights Commission of Korea, www.humanrights.go.kr

National Peace Council of Sri Lanka, www.peace-srilanka.org

National Society for Human Rights [Namibia], www.nshr.org.na

Nicaragua Network, www.nicanet.org

Odhikar [Bangladesh], www.odhikar.org

Population Reference Bureau, www.prb.org

Reporters Sans Frontières, www.rsf.org

South African Human Rights Commission, www.sahrc.org.za

South Asia Terrorism Portal [India], www.satp.org

Transparency International, www.transparency.org

Truth and Reconciliation Commission of Liberia, www.trcofliberia.org

United Nations High Commissioner for Refugees, www.unhcr.org

United Nations Office for the Coordination of Humanitarian Affairs (OCHA), http://unocha.org

World Bank, www.worldbank.org

Freedom House

Freedom House supports global freedom through comprehensive analysis, dedicated advocacy, and concrete assistance for democratic activists around the world.

Founded in 1941, Freedom House has long been a vigorous proponent of the right of all individuals to be free. Eleanor Roosevelt and Wendell Willkie served as Freedom House's first honorary co-chairpersons.